"Il s'est dérangé."
"He is deranged."

The Frenchman and the Englishman are NOT saying the same thing in the above sentences.

One is describing how someone went to a great deal of trouble to do something, the other is claiming that somebody has gone completely out of his mind.

TREACHEROUS LOOK-ALIKES
are among the bilingual pitfalls that most often trap the translator. An extensive listing of such commonly used but tricky words is just one of the features that makes this dictionary so invaluable to the reader.

If you want to pronounce French correctly, know precisely what a word means and exactly how to use it, have rapid, easy reference to an extensive French and English vocabulary, KETTRIDGE is the *only* bilingual French and English dictionary for you.

Other SIGNET Reference Books
of Special Interest

KETTRIDGE'S
FRENCH-ENGLISH
ENGLISH-FRENCH
DICTIONARY

Edited by
Stanley and Eleanor Hochman

A Signet Reference Book
Published by The New American Library

SIGNET TRADEMARK REG. U.S. PAT. OFF. AND FOREIGN COUNTRIES
REGISTERED TRADEMARK—MARCA REGISTRADA
HECHO EN CHICAGO, U.S.A.

SIGNET REFERENCE BOOKS are published by
The New American Library, Inc.,
1301 Avenue of the Americas, New York, New York 10019

First Printing, November, 1968

PRINTED IN THE UNITED STATES OF AMERICA

CONTENTS

KEY TO INTERNATIONAL PHONETIC
TRANSCRIPTION

VOWELS

a   papa, femme, roi (papa, fam, rwa)

ɑ   passer, bâiller, bas, (pɑse, bɑje, bɑ)

ɑ̃   rampant, encan, temps (rɑ̃pɑ̃, ɑ̃kɑ̃, tɑ̃)

e   récréer, fée, chez (rekree, fe, ʃe)

ə   de, que, recevoir (də, kə, rəsəvwaːr)

ɛ   frais, près, rets, bel (frɛ, prɛ, rɛ, bɛl)

ɛ̃   bien, bain, vin, oint (bjɛ̃, bɛ̃, vɛ̃, wɛ̃)

i   civilité, nihiliste, y (sivilite, niilist, i)

o   gros, tôt, peau, aux (gro, to, po, o)

ɔ   colonne, opossum (kɔlɔn, ɔpɔsœm)

ɔ̃   componction, mont (kɔ̃pɔ̃ksjɔ̃, mɔ̃)

œ   œuf, cueillir, seul (œf, kœjiːr, sœl)

œ̃   un, parfum, défunt (œ̃, parfœ̃, defœ̃)

ø   bleu, creux, vœu (blø, krø, vø)

u   trou, goût, courroux (tru, gu, kuru)

y   vu, une, murmurer (vy, yn, myrmyre)

ː indicates that the sound represented by the preceding symbol is long; thus:

aː   car, bail, soir (kaːr, baːj, swaːr)

ɑː   passe, âme, paille (pɑːs, ɑːm, pɑːj)

ɑ̃ː   ambre, antre, centre (ɑ̃ːbr, ɑ̃ːtr, sɑ̃ːtr)

ɛː   faire, ère, guerre (fɛːr, ɛːr, gɛːr)

ɛ̃ː   sainte, linge, peintre (sɛ̃ːt, lɛ̃ːʒ, pɛ̃ːtr)

iː   fille, lyre, abîme (fiːj, liːr, abiːm)

oː   dôme, rose, haute (doːm, roːz, oːt)

ɔː   fort, bord, corps (fɔːr, bɔːr, kɔːr)

ɔ̃ː   fondre, pompe, onze (fɔ̃ːdr, pɔ̃ːp, ɔ̃ːz)

œː   œil, deuil, beurre (œːj, dœːj, bœːr)

œ̃ː   humble, défunte (œ̃ːbl, defœ̃ːt)

øː   creuse, aqueuse (krøːz, akøːz)

uː   tour, cours, bourre (tuːr, kuːr, buːr)

yː   murmure, usure (myrmyːr, yzyːr)

CONSONANTS

g   gangue, gué, exil (gɑ̃ːg, ge, egzil)

j   fiancé fouille, ayant (fjɑ̃se, fuːj, ɛjɑ̃)

ɲ   cognac, baigner (kɔɲak, bɛɲe)

ʃ   chat, chiche, hache (ʃa, ʃiʃ, aʃ)

ʒ   je, juge, géologie (ʒə, ʒyːʒ, ʒeɔlɔʒi)

ɥ   cuir, huile, fruit (kɥiːr, ɥil, frɥi)

vi

The following consonants have their usual values:

b	bonbon, bimbelot (bɔ̃bɔ̃, bɛ̃blo)	n	nonne, inanition (nɔn, inanisjɔ̃)
d	dedans, demande (dədɑ̃, dəmɑ̃ːd)	p	papier, obscur (papje, ɔpskyːr)
f	fifre, graphique (fifr, grafik)	r	rare, bizarrerie (raːr, bizarri)
h	=h aspirated about as in English (chiefly French interjections)	s	si, ceci, stoïcisme (si, səsi, stɔisism)
k	kaki, caquet, extra (kaki, kakɛ, ɛkstra)	t	quantité, théâtre (kɑ̃tite, teaːtr)
l	lilas, parallèle (lila, paralɛl)	v	vive, verve, wagon (viːv, vɛrv, vagɔ̃)
m	momie, minimum (momi, minimɔm)	w	ouest, gloire, allouer (wɛst, glwaːr, alwe)
		z	zigzag, magasin (zigzag, magazɛ̃)

The sounds of the symbols to be learned can only be acquired by hearing them spoken, just as colors must be seen to be appreciated.

NOTE

The author considers himself fortunate in having at his disposal the International Phonetic System, and if the reader will take the trouble to learn it, he will, the author feels sure, hold himself equally blessed.

Gone forever for all practical purposes are the fantastic "imitated" pronunciations. Every language has certain sounds which are peculiar to itself and have no equivalents in another. For this reason, imitated pronunciations, although capable of transcribing French into French phonetically, English into English, and so on, are inherently incapable of transliterating one language into another, and are responsible in large measure for many people's bad pronunciation of foreign languages.

Pronunciation of French is very difficult for the foreigner. Exceptions to rule, silent letters, and other peculiarities abound. Therefore, every time he refers to a word in the French vocabulary, the English reader is advised to compare, and correct if necessary, his notion of how it should be pronounced.

ARRANGEMENT

As far as is reasonably possible, set or inseparable word groups are entered under the first word of the group.

ABBREVIATIONS USED IN THIS DICTIONARY

†

ADVERBS

Most French adverbs of manner are formed by adding **-ment** to the feminine singular of the adjective, corresponding to the English suffix -ly (-le being changed into -ly, -ic into -ically, and -y into -ily); thus,

naturel (natyrɛl)	**correct** (kɔrɛkt)	**relatif** (rəlatif)
naturelle (rɛl)	**correcte** (rɛkt)	**relative** (tiːv)
naturellement (rɛlmɑ̃)	**correctement** (təmɑ̃)*	**relativement** (tivmɑ̃‡)
natural; naturally	correct; correctly	relative; relatively

So also with adjectives ending in **e** of identical form in both genders; as,

énergique (enɛrʒik); **énergiquement** (ʒikmɑ̃), energetic; energetically.
admirable (admirabl); **admirablement** (bləmɑ̃*), admirable; admirably.
ordinaire (ɔrdinɛːr); **ordinairement** (nɛrmɑ̃‡), ordinary; ordinarily.

Adjectives whose masculine form ends in **-ai** (as **vrai**), **-é** (as **modéré**), **-i** (as **hardi**), and **-u** (as **absolu**), add the suffix **-ment** to the masculine form; thus,

modéré (mɔdere)	**modérée** (re)	**modérément** (remɑ̃)
	moderate;	moderately

In order to economize space (most adverbs of manner being long words), French and English adverbs ending regularly as above, and with no appreciable change of meaning, are not given in the dictionary. Instead, the adjectives are marked † (e.g, **naturel, le**†, **modéré**†, e), in reference hereto. Adverbs not formed according to these rules, particularly those presenting peculiarity or difficulty, are given in the ordinary way.

* Note:—When two pronounced consonants immediately precede the ending **-ement**, the **e** of **ement** is pronounced (ə). Otherwise it is silent.

‡ Note that the vowel sound is short here, rəlatiːv, tivmɑ̃; ɔrdinɛːr, nɛrmɑ̃.

It may be observed that most ordinary English adverbs of manner for which no French form ending in **-ment** exists can be translated by *d'une manière*, plus the corresponding feminine adjective, as **satisfactorily**, *d'une manière satisfaisante*.

The swing dash (~) signifies repetition in the singular of a leading vocabulary word (word printed in **times roman type**). Followed by *s* (~*s*), it signifies the like repetition in the plural.

The paragraph (¶) also signifies repetition of a leading vocabulary word, but indicates the commencement of a different part of speech. This symbol is used to make the point of transition conspicuous.

An initial letter followed by a period signifies repetition of a translation.

[Brackets] enclose words, or parts of words, which can be used or omitted at will.

SUBJECT INDICATIONS

Avn.	Aviation	*Mach.*	Machinery; Machine
Agric.	Agriculture	*Math.*	Mathematics
Anat.	Anatomy	*Meas.*	Measurement; Measure
Arch.	Architecture		
Arith.	Arithmetic	*Mech.*	Mechanics
Artil.	Artillery	*Med.*	Medicine; Medical
Astr.	Astronomy	*Metall.*	Metallurgy
Bil.	Billiards	*Meteor.*	Meteorology
Biol.	Biology	*Mil.*	Military
Bkkpg.	Bookkeeping	*Min.*	Mining
Boat.	Boating	*Miner.*	Mineralogy
Bookb.	Bookbinding	*Mol.*	Mollusc
Bot.	Botany	*Motor.*	Motoring; Motor car
Box.	Boxing	*Mus.*	Music
Build.	Building	*Myth.*	Mythology
Carp.	Carpentry	*Nat. Hist.*	Natural History
Chem.	Chemistry	*Naut.*	Nautical
Com.	Commerce	*Nav.*	Navy; Naval
Conch.	Conchology, Shell-fish, Shells	*Need.*	Needlework
		Opt.	Optics
Cook.	Cookery	*Path.*	Pathology
Crust.	Crustacea(n)	*Phar.*	Pharmacy
Cust.	Customs	*Philos.*	Philosophy
Danc.	Dancing	*Phot.*	Photography
Eccl.	Ecclesiastical	*Phys.*	Physics
Elec.	Electricity; Electric	*Phys. Geog.*	Physical Geography
Emb.	Embroidery	*Poet.*	Poetry; Poetic
Engin.	Engineering	*Pol.*	Politics
Fenc.	Fencing	*Post*	Post Office; Postal
Fin.	Finance	*Pros.*	Prosody
Fish.	Fishing	*Radio*	Wireless
Foot.	Football	*Relig.*	Religion
Geog.	Geography	*Rhet.*	Rhetoric
Geol.	Geology	*Rly.*	Railway(s)
Geom.	Geometry	*Sch.*	School
Gram.	Grammar	*Ship.*	Shipping
Gym.	Gymnastics	*Shipbldg.*	Shipbuilding
Her.	Heraldry	*Stk Ex.*	Stock Exchange
Hist.	History; Historical	*Surg.*	Surgery
Horol.	Horology, Clocks & Watches	*Surv.*	Surveying
		Swim.	Swimming
Hort.	Horticulture	*Teleg.*	Telegraphy
Hunt.	Hunting	*Teleph.*	Telephony
Hyd.	Hydraulics	*Ten.*	Tennis
Inc. Tax	Income Tax	*Theat.*	Theater; Theatrical
Insce.	Insurance	*Theol.*	Theology
Join.	Joinery	*Typ.*	Typography; Printing
Jump.	Jumping		
Knit.	Knitting	*Univ.*	University
Lit.	Liturgy	*Vet.*	Veterinary
Log.	Logic	*Zool.*	Zoology

a	adjective
abb	abbreviation
abs	absolutely, i.e, (verb) used without its object
ad	adverb or adverbial phrase (see also †ADVERBS, page viii)
a.f	adjective feminine only, i.e, not masculine also
a.m	adjective masculine only, i.e, not feminine also
art	article
att	attributively, i.e, (noun) used as adjective
aux	auxiliary (verb)
c	conjunction or conjunctive phrase
Cf.	Compare
col	collectively, collective noun
comps	compounds; in combination
e.g	for example
Eng.	England; English
&	and, et (The sign & is used in the dictionary only to save space)
etc.	et cetera
f	feminine. In the French-English section, f = noun feminine
fig.	figuratively
f.pl.	feminine plural. In the French-English section, $f.pl$ = noun feminine plural
Fr.	France; French
f.s	feminine singular. In the French-English section, $f.s$ = noun feminine singular
i	interjection
i.e	that is to say
imp	impersonal
inv	invariable
ir	irregular (verb)
lit.	literally
m	masculine. In the French-English section, m = noun masculine
m,f	masculine & feminine (noun)
m.pl	masculine plural. In the French-English section, $m.pl$ = noun masculine plural
m.s	masculine singular. In the French-English section, $m.s$ = noun masculine singular
n	noun. In the French-English section, n = noun masculine & feminine (of persons)
neg.	negative; (used) negatively
oft.	often
opp.	opposed to
p.a	participial adjective
pers.	person(s)
pl	plural
pn	pronoun
p.p	participle past
p.pr	participle present
pr	preposition or prepositional phrase
s	singular
v.i	verb intransitive
v.i. & t	verb intransitive & verb transitive
v.pr.	verb pronominal
v.t	verb transitive
v.t. & i	verb transitive & verb intransitive

FRENCH-ENGLISH
DICTIONARY

FRENCH-ENGLISH DICTIONARY

A

a *see* **avoir.**

à (a) (à le *is contracted into* **au,** à les *into* **aux**) *pr,* to; at; in; within; into; on; by; with; for; of; after; from; under; according to; between; till, until; and. *When coupled with noun, often rendered in English by noun used attributively, as, canne à sucre,* sugar cane. *un homme ~ craindre,* a man to be feared or to fear. *~ prendre après les repas,* to be taken after meals. *~ ne pas confondre avec . . .,* not to be confused with *. . . de 2 ~ 3 fois par jour,* 2 or 3 times a day.

abaissement (abɛsmɑ̃) *m,* lowering; sinking; fall; humiliation. **abaisser** (se) *v.t,* to lower, let down; humble, abase. **s'~,** to subside; sink; humble oneself.

abandon (abɑ̃dɔ̃) *m,* abandonment, dereliction, desertion; unconstraint. *à l'~,* in confusion, at random, anyhow; derelict. **abandonnement** (dɔnmɑ̃) *m,* profligacy. **abandonner** (ne) *v.t,* to abandon, leave, desert, forsake; give up, relinquish, surrender; concede. **s'~ à,** to give way to, indulge in.

abaque (abak) *m,* abacus; diagram.

abasourdir (abazurdi:r) *v.t,* to dumbfound, stun.

abâtardir (s') (abɑtardi:r) *v.pr,* to degenerate.

abat-jour (abaʒu:r) *m,* shade, lampshade. **abats** (ba) *m.pl.* Same as *abattis.* **abat-son** (abasɔ̃) *m,* louvers. **abattage** (bata:ʒ) *m,* felling; slaughtering. **abattant** (tɑ̃) *m,* flap. **abattement** (tmɑ̃) *m,* prostration, depression, dejection, despondency; deductions (*for dependents, Inc. Tax*). **abatteur** (tœ:r) *m,* feller; slaughterman. **abattis** (ti) *m,* demolitions; fell; kill; giblets. **abattoir** (twa:r) *m,* slaughterhouse, abattoir. **abattre** (tr) *v.t.ir,* to knock down; bring down; cut down; lay; fell; slaughter, kill; mine; deject. **s'~,** to fall down; become depressed; subside. **abattu, e** (ty) *a,* depressed, low-spirited, downcast.

abat-vent (abavɑ̃) *m,* windshield. **abat-voix** (abavwa) *m,* sounding board.

abbaye (abɛi) *f,* abbey. **abbé** (be) *m,* abbot; priest. **abbesse** (bɛs) *f,* abbess.

abcès (apsɛ) *m,* abscess, gathering. *~ aux gencives,* gumboil.

abdication (abdikasjɔ̃) *f,* abdication. **abdiquer** (ke) *v.t. & abs,* to abdicate; surrender, waive.

abdomen (abdɔmɛn) *m,* abdomen.

abeille (abɛ:j) *f,* bee. *~ ouvrière,* worker b.

aberration (abɛrasjɔ̃) *f,* aberration.

abêtir (abɛti:r) *v.t,* to make dull.

abhorrer (abɔre) *v.t,* to abhor, loathe, detest.

abîme (abi:m) *m,* abyss, gulf, chasm. **abîmer** (bime) *v.t,* to swallow up; ruin, spoil. **s'~,** to bury (*or* immerse) oneself, welter; get spoiled.

abject, e (abʒɛkt) *a,* abject, mean. **abjection** (sjɔ̃) *f,* abjectness, etc.

abjurer (abʒyre) *v.t,* to abjure, forswear, renounce.

ablatif (ablatif) *m,* ablative [case].

abnégation (abnegasjɔ̃) *f,* abnegation, self-denial.

aboiement (abwamɑ̃) *m,* bark[ing], bay[ing]. **aux abois** (bwa), at bay; hard pressed, at one's wit's end.

abolir (abɔli:r) *v.t,* to abolish. **abolition** (lisjɔ̃) *f,* abolition; repeal.

abominable† (abɔminabl) *a,* abominable, nefarious. **abomination** (sjɔ̃) *f,* abomination. **abominer** (ne) *v.t,* to abominate.

abondance (abɔ̃dɑ̃:s) *f,* abundance, plenty, galore; fullness. *parler d'~,* to speak extempore. **abondant, e** (dɑ̃, ɑ̃:t) *a,* abundant, plentiful, plenteous. profuse.

abondamment (damã) *ad*, abundantly, etc. **abonder** (de) *v.i*, to abound. ~ *dans le sens de*, to quite agree with, chime in with.

abonné, e (abɔne) *n*, subscriber; commuter; consumer (*gas, elec.*). **abonnement** (nmã) *m*, subscription, season ticket; commutation ticket. **abonner** (ne) *v.t*, to subscribe for. s'~, to subscribe.

abonnir (abɔniːr) *v.t*, to improve.

abord (abɔːr) *m*, landing; approach, access. [*tout*] *d'*~, *au premier* ~, *de prime* ~, at first, first of all, to begin with. **abordable** (bɔrdabl) *a*, accessible, approachable. **abordage** (daːʒ) *m*, landing; collision, fouling. **aborder** (de) *v.i. & t*, to land; approach; broach; board; collide with, foul.

aborigène (abɔriʒɛːn) *a. & m*, aboriginal; (*m.pl.*) aborigines.

abortif, ive (abɔrtif, iːv) *a*, abortive (*of premature birth*).

aboucher (abuʃe) *v.t*, to bring together; join up.

aboutir (abutiːr) *v.i*, to end, lead; eventuate, materialize; come to a head, culminate.

aboutissement (abutismã) *m*, result, issue, outcome, effect.

aboyer (abwaje) *v.i*, to bark, bay; be in full cry; cry out. **aboyeur** (jœːr) *m*, barker (*circus, etc.*).

abrégé (abreʒe) *m*, abridgement, epitome, abstract, summary. *en* ~, shortly, briefly; abbreviated. **abréger** (ʒe) *v.t*, to abridge, epitomize; abbreviate.

abreuver (abrœve) *v.t*, to water; season; soak, steep, drench; prime (*pump*). s'~, to drink, soak, fill oneself, wallow, bathe. **abreuvoir** (vwaːr) *m*, watering place, horse pond, drinking trough.

abréviation (abrevjasjɔ̃) *f*, abbreviation; contraction.

abri (abri) *m*, shelter, cover, dugout; cab (*locomotive*). *à l'* ~ *de*, under cover of, sheltered from. ~ *blindé*, bombshelter.

abricot (abriko) *m*, apricot. **abricotier** (kɔtje) *m*, apricot tree.

abriter (abrite) *v.t*, to shelter, shield, screen.

abrivent (abrivã) *m*, shelter, hut; matting; screen.

abrogation (abrɔgasjɔ̃) *f*, abrogation, repeal. **abroger** (ʒe) *v.t*, to abrogate.

abrupt, e (abrypt) *a*, abrupt, sheer.

abruti, e (abryti) *p.a*, brutish, besotted, sottish. ¶ *m*, beast (*pers.*). **abrutir** (tiːr) *v.t*, to brutalize, besot. **abrutissement** (tismã) *m*, brutishness.

absence (apsãːs) *f*, absence. ~ [*d'esprit*], absence of mind. **absent, e** (sã, ãːt) *a*, absent, away [from home], out, not at home. ~ *par congé*, away on holiday. ¶ *m*, absentee. **s'absenter** (sãte) *v.pr*, to absent oneself, keep away.

abside (apsid) *f*, apse.

absinthe (apsɛ̃ːt) *f*, wormwood; absinth.

absolu†, e (apsɔly) *a*, absolute; hard & fast; positive; peremptory.

absolution (apsɔlysjɔ̃) *f*, absolution; acquittal.

absorbant, e (apsɔrbã, ãːt) *a*, absorbent, bibulous; absorbing, engrossing. **absorber** (be) *v.t. & abs*, to absorb, drink in, imbibe; engross. **absorption** (psjɔ̃) *f*, absorption.

absoudre (apsudr) *v.t.ir*, to absolve.

abstème (apstɛːm) *a*, abstemious. ¶ *n*, abstainer. **s'abstenir** (stəniːr) *v.pr*, to abstain, refrain, forbear. **abstention** (stãsjɔ̃) *f*, abstention. **abstinence** (stinãːs) *f*, abstinence, temperance.

abstraction (apstraksjɔ̃) *f*, abstraction. ~ *faite de*, apart from, setting aside. **abstraire** (strɛːr) *v.t.ir*, to abstract. **abstrait, e** (strɛ, ɛːt) *a*, abstract. **l'abstrait**, *m*, the abstract (opp. *concrete*).

abstrus, e (apstry, yːz) *a*, abstruse, recondite.

absurde† (apsyrd) *a*, absurd, preposterous. **l'absurde**, *m*, the absurd, an absurdity. **absurdité** (dite) *f*, absurdity, nonsense.

abus (aby) *m*, abuse, misuse; breach. **abuser** (ze) *v.t*, to deceive, delude, mislead, misguide. ~ *de*, to abuse, misuse, trespass on. s'~, to delude oneself. **abu-**

sif, ivet† (zif, iːv) *a*, abusive, improper.

abysse (abis) *m*, abyss.

Abyssinie (l') (abisini) *f*, Abyssinia. **abyssinien, ne** (njē, ɛn) *a*. & A~, *n*, ou **abyssin, e** (sē, in) *a*. & A~, *n*, Abyssinian.

acabit (akabi) *m*, stamp, sort, nature, kidney.

acacia (akasja)*m*, acacia.

académicien, ne (akademisjē, ɛn) *n*, academician. **académie** (mi) *f*, academy, college; academy figure. **académique** (mik) *a*, academic(al).

acagnarder (akaɲarde) *v.t*, to make lazy.

acajou (akaʒu) *m*, mahogany. ~ *des Antilles*, Spanish mahogany.

acare (akaːr) *m*, mite, tick.

acariâtre (akarjɑːtr) *a*, peevish, sour[-tempered].

accablant (akablɑ̃) *a*, crushing; overwhelming.

accablement (akabləmɑ̃) *m*, despondency, dejection; prostration; great pressure (*of business*). **accabler** (ble) *v.t*, to overwhelm, crush, overcome.

accalmie (akalmi) *f*, lull.

accaparer (akapare) *v.t*, to corner, buy up, monopolize. **accapareur, euse** (rœːr, øːz) *n*, monopolist.

accéder à (aksede), to accede to, consent to; reach.

accélérateur (akseleratœːr) *m*, accelerator. **accélérer** (re) *v.t*, to accelerate, quicken.

accent (aksɑ̃) *m*, accent; stress; tone; pronunciation; (*pl.*) strains. **accentuer** (tɥe) *v.t*, to accent, accentuate, emphasize, stress.

acceptable (aksɛptabl) *a*, acceptable. **acceptation** (sjɔ̃) *f*, acceptance. **accepter** (te) *v.t. & abs*, to accept, undertake. **accepteur** (tœːr) *m*, acceptor. **acception** (psjɔ̃) *f*, respect; acceptation (*of a word*).

accès (aksɛ) *m*, access, approach; fit, attack, flush. **accessible** (sɛsibl) *a*, accessible, approachable.

accession (aksɛsjɔ̃) *f*, accession, consent.

accessoiret† (aksɛswaːr) *a*, accessory. ¶ *m*, accessory, adjunct;

(*pl.*) fittings, furniture; properties (*Theat.*).

accident (aksidɑ̃) *m*, accident; smash; unevenness; hazard (*Golf*); accidental (*Mus.*). **accidenté, e** (te) *a*, hilly, broken; checkered, eventful. **accidentel, le†** (tɛl) *a*, accidental, casual.

acclamation (aklamasjɔ̃) *f*, acclamation, cheering. **acclamer** (me) *v.t*, to acclaim, hail, cheer.

acclimatation (aklimatasjɔ̃) *f*, acclimatization. *jardin d'~*, zoo. **acclimater** (te) *v.t*, to acclimatize.

accointance (akwɛ̃tɑ̃ːs) *f. oft. pl*, intimacy; dealings.

accolade (akɔlad) *f*, embrace, hug; brace, bracket (*Typ.*). **accoler** (le) *v.t*, to brace, bracket.

accommodation (akɔmɔdasjɔ̃) *f*, accommodation. **accommodement** (dmɑ̃) *m*, compromise, arrangement, settlement, terms. **accommoder** (de) *v.t*, to suit; please; reconcile; adapt; prepare (*food*); arrange, settle. *s'~ à*, to adapt oneself to. *s'~ de*, to put up with.

accompagnateur, trice (akɔ̃paɲatœːr, tris) *n*, accompan[y]-ist. **accompagnement** (ɲmɑ̃) *m*, accompaniment; concomitant. **accompagner** (ɲe) *v.t*, to accompany, attend, escort.

accompli, e (akɔ̃pli) *a*, accomplished, thorough. **accomplir** (pliːr) *v.t*, to accomplish, achieve, perform, carry out. **accomplissement** (plismɑ̃) *m*, accomplishment, etc.

accord (akɔːr) *m*, accord, agreement; harmony, concord; consent; chord (*Mus.*); tune; (*pl.*) betrothal. *d'~*, agreed, granted; in tune. *d'un commun ~*, with one accord. **accordage** (kɔrdaːʒ) *m*, tuning. **accordailles** (daːj) *f.pl*, betrothal. **accordéon** (deɔ̃) *m*, accordion. **accorder** (de) *v.t*, to accord, grant, bestow, allow, afford; spare; reconcile; tune; attune. *s'~*, to agree; accord; tune [up]. **accordeur** (dœːr) *m*, tuner.

accort, e (akɔːr, ɔrt) *a*, amiable, pleasing.

accaster (akɔste) *v.t*, to accost; come alongside.

accotement (akɔtmɑ̃) *m*, side path, greensward, verge. **accoter** (te) *v.t*, to hold up; lean, rest. **accotoir** (twa:r) *m*, rest, arm.

accouchement (akuʃmɑ̃) *m*, confinement, lying-in, childbirth. **accoucher** (ʃe) *v.i*, to be confined, give birth, deliver, bring forth; speak out. **accoucheur** (ʃœ:r) *m*, maternity doctor. **accoucheuse** (jø:z) *f*, midwife.

accouder (s') (akude) *v.pr*, to rest (*or* lean) on one's elbow(s). **accoudoir** (dwa:r) *m*, arm; rail.

accouple (akupl) *f*, leash. **accoupler** (ple) *v.t*, to couple, connect, yoke; pair, mate.

accourcie (akursi) *f*, shortcut. **accourcir** (si:r) *v.t*, to shorten.

accourir (akuri:r) *v.i.ir*, to run [up], rush.

accoutrement (akutrəmɑ̃) *m*, trappings, garb, rig. **accoutrer** (tre) *v.t*, to rig out.

accoutumance (akutymɑ̃:s) *f*, habit, use. **accoutumer** (me) *v.t*, to accustom, inure.

accréditer (akredite) *v.t*, to accredit, open a credit for. **s'~**, to gain credence.

accroc (akro) *m*, rent, tear; snag, hitch; stain.

accroche-coeur (akrɔʃkœ:r) *m*, lovelock, kiss-curl. **accrocher** (ʃe) *v.t*, to hook; grapple; hang [up]; run against; catch. **s'~**, to hang on.

accroire (akrwa:r) *v.t: faire ~ à*, to cause to believe. *en faire ~ à*, to impose [up]on. *s'en faire ~*, to be conceited.

accroître (akrwa:tr) *v.t. & i. ir*, to increase, grow, accrue. **accroissement** (krwasmɑ̃) *m*, increase, etc.

accroupir (s') (akrupi:r) *v.pr*, to squat, crouch, cower.

accueil (akœ:j) *m*, reception, welcome; honor (*bill*). **accueillir** (kœji:r) *v.t.ir*, to receive, welcome, greet; entertain; honor, meet (*bill*).

accul (akyl) *m*, cove, creek; lair. **acculer** (akyle) *v.t*, to [drive into a] corner. **s'~**, to stand at bay; jib. *s'~ contre*, to set one's back against.

accumulateur (akymylatœ:r) *m*, accumulator, [storage] battery. **accumulation** (sjɔ̃) *f*, accumulation. **accumuler** (le) *v.t. & abs. & s'~*, to accumulate; gather.

accusateur, trice (akyzatœ:r, tris) *n*, accuser. ¶ *a*, accusing. **accusatif** (tif) *m*, accusative [case]. **accusation** (sjɔ̃) *f*, accusation, charge; indictment. **accusé, e** (ze) *n*, accused, prisoner at the bar. **accusé de réception**, *m*, acknowledgment. **accuser** (ze) *v.t*, to accuse, charge; indict; impeach; blame; show, betray; bring out; complain of (*medically*). *~ réception de*, to acknowledge receipt of. **s'~ de**, to avow, acknowledge, confess. *s'~ soi-même*, to plead guilty.

acerbe (aserb) *a*, sour, sharp, harsh.

acéré, e (asere) *a*, steeled, sharp, keen, cutting. **acérer** (re) *v.t*, to steel.

acétique (asetik) *a*, acetic.

achalandage (aʃalɑ̃da:ʒ) *m*, bringing custom; custom, connection, patronage. **achalandé, e** (de) *p.a*, patronized. **achalander** (de) *v.t*, to bring custom; commercialize. **s'~**, to get custom.

acharné, e (aʃarne) *a*, rabid, furious, fierce, desperate, relentless, ruthless; obstinate, bitter, inveterate, confirmed; intense, eager; fleshed. **acharnement** (nəmɑ̃) *m*, rabidness, etc. **acharner** (ne) *v.t*, to set on, set against; flesh. **s'~**, to attack furiously; be set, be bent, be insatiable, be inveterate.

achat (aʃa) *m*, purchase, buying.

acheminement (aʃminmɑ̃) *m*, way; progress; forwarding; routing; step. **acheminer** (ne) *v.t*, to direct; expedite; forward, dispatch, route. **s'~**, to proceed.

acheter (aʃte) *v.t*, to buy, purchase. **acheteur, euse** (tœ:r, ø:z) *n*, buyer, purchaser.

achevé, e (aʃve) *a*, accomplished, perfect, thorough, out & out, arrant. **achèvement** (ʃɛvmɑ̃) *m*, finishing, completion. **achever** (ʃve) *v.t*, to finish, perfect, end. *achevez donc!* out with it!

achopper (aʃɔpe) *v.i.* & s'~, to stumble.

achromatique (akrɔmatik) *a*, achromatic.

acide (asid) *a*, acid, sour, sharp, tart. ¶ *m*, acid. **acidité** (dite) *f*, acidity, etc. **aciduler** (dyle) *v.t*, to acidulate.

acier (asje) *m*, steel. **aciérer** (sjere) *v.t*, to steel, caseharden. **aciérie** (ri) *f*, steel works.

acné (akne) *f*, acne.

acolyte (akolit) *m*, acolyte.

acompte (akɔ̃:t) *m*, installment; cover, margin. ~ *de dividende*, interim dividend. ~ *de préférence*, option money (*on a property*). ─

aconit (akɔnit) *m*, aconite, monk's-hood, wolfsbane.

acoquinant, e (akɔkinɑ̃, ɑ̃:t) *a*, enticing. **s'acoquiner à, auprès** (ne), to get fond of, become attached to.

Açores (les) (asɔ:r) *f.pl*, the Azores.

à-coup (aku) *m*, jerk, shock.

acoustique (akustik) *a*, acoustic. ¶ *f*, acoustics.

acquéreur (akerœ:r) *m*, purchaser, buyer. **acquérir** (ri:r) *v.t.ir*, to acquire, get, win, purchase; (*abs.*) to improve. s'~, to accrue.

acquêts (akɛ) *m.pl*, acquisition; windfall.

acquiescement (akjɛsmɑ̃) *m*, acquiescence. **acquiescer (se)** *v.i*, to acquiesce.

acquis, e (aki, i:z) *p.a*, acquired; earned; devoted; vested (*rights*). ¶ *m. s. & pl*, acquirements, attainments, experience. **acquisition** (kizisjɔ̃) *f*, acquisition, purchase; haul.

acquit (aki) *m*, receipt, discharge. [*pour*] ~, received [with thanks], paid. *à l'*~ *de*, on behalf of, on account of. **acquit-à-caution** (kitakosjɔ̃) *m*, bond note, transhipment bond. **acquitté, e** (te) *a*, duty-paid (*Cust.*).*à* **l'acquitté**, *ad*, duty paid, ex bond. **acquittement** (tmɑ̃) *m*, discharge, acquittal. **acquitter** (te) *v.t*, to acquit, discharge; receipt (*bill*). s'~, to acquit oneself, perform; be quits, catch up (*games*).

âcre (ɑ:kr) *a*, acrid, tart, sour, sharp, pungent. **âcreté** (ɑkrəte) *f*, acridity, etc.

acrimonie (akrimɔni) *f*, acrimony. **acrimonieux, euse** (njø, ø:z) *a*, acrimonious.

acrobate (akrɔbat) *n*, acrobat, tumbler. **acrobatie** (si) *f*, acrobatics; stunt. **acrobatique** (tik) *a*, acrobatic.

acrostiche (akrɔstiʃ) *m.* & *a*, acrostic.

acte (akt) *m*, act, action; deed, indenture, instrument, document, agreement, contract; bond; certificate; licence; (*pl.*) transactions (*of a society*). ~ *d'accusation*, indictment. ~ *de dernière volonté*, last will & testament. ~ *de naissance, de mariage, de décès*, certificate of birth, of marriage, of death. ~ *dommageable*, tort (*law*). ~ *sous seing privé* (sɛ̃), simple contract. [*pièce en un*] ~, one-act play. **acteur, trice** (tœ:r, tris) *n*, actor, actress, player. ~ *à transformations*, quick-change artist.

actif, ive (aktif, i:v) *a*, active, brisk; busy. ¶ *m*, active voice; assets.

action (aksjɔ̃) *f*, action, act, deed; effect, agency; share, (*pl.*) stock. ~s *au porteur*, bearer shares, b. stock. ~[*s*] *de grâce*, thanksgiving. ~s *de priorité*, ~s *privilégiées*, preference shares, preferred stock. ~s *nominatives*, registered shares, r. stock. ~s *gratuites*, bonus shares. ~s [*entièrement*] *libérées*, fully paid shares. ~s *non libérées*, partly paid shares. *par* ~s, joint-stock (*att.*). **actionnaire** (ɔnɛ:r) *n*, shareholder, stockholder.

actionner (aksjɔne) *v.t*, to drive, actuate, run, work; bring an action against, sue.

activement (aktivmɑ̃) *ad*, actively, briskly. **activer** (ve) *v.t*, to quicken, urge, press, rouse, stir up, speed up, hurry. **activité** (vite) *f*, activity, briskness. *en* ~ [*de service*], on active service. *en pleine* ~, in full operation, in full swing.

actuaire (aktɥɛ:r) *m*, actuary.

actualité (aktɥalite) *f*, actuality, present state; (*pl.*) passing (*or* current) events, questions of the hour; news (*movies*). **~s de la mode**, present-day fashions. **actuel, le** (tɥɛl) *a*, present, for the time being. **actuellement** (lmɑ̃) *ad*, now, at present.

acuité (akɥite) *f*, sharpness, acuteness, keenness; shrillness.

adage (ada:ʒ) *m*, adage, saying, saw. **~ de droit**, legal maxim.

adapter (adapte) *v.t*, to adapt, fit, suit. **adapteur** (tœ:r) *m*, adapter (*Phot.*).

addition (adisjɔ̃) *f*, addition, cast, tot; bill (*at restaurant*). **additionnel, le** (ɔnɛl) *a*, additional. **additionner** (ne) *v.t*, to add [up], cast, tot up.

adénoïde (adenɔid) *a*, adenoid.

adepte (adɛpt) *n*, adept.

adhérence (aderɑ̃:s) *f*, adherence, adhesion. **adhérent, e** (rɑ̃, ɑ̃:t) *n*, adherent, supporter, member. **adhérer** (re) *v.i*, to adhere, cohere, stick. **adhésion** (zjɔ̃) *f*, adhesion, adhesiveness; membership.

adieu (adjø) *i. & m*, good-bye, farewell, adieu; parting.

adipeux, euse (adipø, ø:z) *a*, adipose, fatty.

adjacent, e (adʒasɑ̃, ɑ̃:t) *a*, adjacent, adjoining.

adjectif (adʒɛktif) *a.m*, adjectival. ¶ *m*, adjective. **~ attribut**, predicative a. **~ épithète**, attributive a. **~ verbal**, participial a. (*present*). **adjectivement** (tivmɑ̃) *ad*, adjectivally, attributively.

adjoindre (adʒwɛ̃:dr) *v.t.ir*, to join, associate. **adjoint, e** (ʒwɛ̃, ɛ̃:t) *a. & n*, assistant.

adjudant (adʒydɑ̃) *m*, sergeant major. **~ major**, adjutant.

adjudicataire (adʒydikatɛ:r) *n*, purchaser; contractor. **adjudication** (sjɔ̃) *f*, adjudication; award of contract; auction. **adjuger** (ʒe) *v.t*, to adjudge, adjudicate; award; award the contract for; knock down.

adjurer (adʒyre) *v.t*, to adjure, beseech.

admettre (admɛtr) *v.t.ir*, to admit, allow, grant; pass (*at exam*).

administrateur, trice (administratœ:r, tris) *n*, director; administrator, trix. **~ délégué, ~ directeur**, managing director. **administration** (sjɔ̃) *f*, administration, management, direction; board, directorate; authorities. **~ publique**, civil service. **administrer** (tre) *v.t*, to administer, manage, direct.

admirable† (admirabl) *a*, admirable, wonderful, capital. **admirateur, trice** (tœ:r, tris) *n*, admirer. **admiration** (sjɔ̃) *f*, admiration, wonder. **admirer** (re) *v.t*, to admire, wonder at.

admis (admi) *a*, admitted; accepted; conventional.

admissible (admisibl) *a*, admissible. **admission** (sjɔ̃) *f*, admission, admittance; intake; entrance.

admonester (admɔnɛste) *v.t*, to admonish, reprimand. **admonestation** (tasjɔ̃) *f*, **admonition** (nisjɔ̃) *f*, admonition, etc.

adolescence (adɔlɛsɑ̃:s) *f*, adolescence, youth. **adolescent, e** (sɑ̃, ɑ̃:t) *a*, adolescent. ¶ *n*, adolescent, youth, girl.

adonner (s') (adɔne) *v. pr*, to give (*or* apply) oneself, addict oneself, take.

adopter (adɔpte) *v.t*, to adopt, carry, pass, confirm. **adoptif, ive** (tif, i:v) *a*, adoptive, adopted. **adoption** (sjɔ̃) *f*, adoption, etc.

adorable (adɔrabl) *a*, adorable, charming, lovely, delightful. **adorateur, trice** (tœ:r, tris) *n*, adorer, worshiper, votary. **adoration** (sjɔ̃) *f*, adoration, worship. **adorer** (re) *v.t*, to adore, worship.

adosser (adose) *v.t*, to back, lean. **s'~**, to lean one's back against.

adoucir (adusi:r) *v.t*, to sweeten; soften; smooth, temper, subdue, allay, alleviate, soothe, ease, appease, assuage, mollify, qualify.

adresse (adrɛs) *f*, address, direction; skill, dexterity, craft, deftness; shrewdness; handiness; clever move. **adresser (se)** *v.t*, to address, direct, send. **s'~ à**, to address, apply to; inquire of; cater for.

Adriatique (adriatik) *a.* & *f*, Adriatic.

adroit, e† (adrwa, at) *a*, adroit, dext[e]rous, deft, handy, skillful, clever, neat; shrewd.

adulateur, trice (adylatœ:r, tris) *a*, adulatory. **adulation** (sjɔ̃) *f*, adulation. **aduler** (le) *v.t*, to adulate.

adulte (adylt) *a.* & *n*, adult, grown-up.

adultère (adyltɛ:r) *n*, adulterer, ess; (*m.*) adultery. ¶ *a*, adulterous.

advenir (advəni:r) *v.i.ir*, to happen, occur, befall, come to pass. *advienne que pourra*, come what may, whate'er betide.

adverbe (advɛrb) *m*, adverb. ~ *de quantité*, a. of number. **adverbial, e†** (bjal) *a*, adverbial.

adversaire (advɛrsɛ:r) *m*, adversary, opponent, foe. **adverse** (vɛrs) *a*, adverse, opposing. **adversité** (site) *f*, adversity, misfortune.

aérage (aera:ʒ) *m*, **aération** (rasjɔ̃) *f*, ventilation, airing; draft; aeration. **aérer** (re) *v.t*, to ventilate, air; aerate.

aérien, ne (aerjẽ, ɛn) *a*, aerial, airy, air (*att.*); overhead.

aérodrome (aerɔdro:m) *m*, airport, aviation ground.

aérodynamique (aerɔdinamik) *a*, aerodynamic; streamlined. ¶ *f*, aerodynamics. **aérodynamisme** (mism) *m*, streamlining.

aérogare (aerɔga:r) *f*, air terminal.

aérolithe (aerɔlit) *m*, aerolite, meteorite.

aéronaute (aerɔno:t) *n*, aeronaut. **aéronautique** (notik) *a*, aeronautic(al), air (*att.*). ¶ *f*, aeronautics.

aéronef (aerɔnɛf) *m*, aircraft.

aéroplane (aerɔplan) *m*, [air]-plane.

aéroport (aerɔpɔ:r) *m*, airport.

aérostat (aerɔsta) *m*, lighter than air machine; balloon. **aérostation** (sjɔ̃) *f*, lighter than air aviation *or* branch (*army*); ballooning. **aérostier** (tje) *m*, balloonist.

affabilité (afabilite) *f*, affability. **affable** (bl) *a*, affable.

affadir (afadi:r) *v.t*, to sicken; make insipid, flatten. **affadissement** (dismã) *m*, loss of flavor; nauseousness.

affaiblir (afɛbli:r) *v.t*, to weaken, enfeeble; reduce (*Phot.*).

affaire (afɛ:r) *f*, affair, matter, case, thing, job, proposition, business, piece of business, concern; transaction, dealing, bargain; lawsuit; re (*law*); engagement (*Mil.*). ~*s par correspondance*, mail order business. ~ *roulante*, going concern. *ce malade est hors d'*~, this patient is out of danger. *son* ~ *est faite*, he's done for. **affairé, e** (fɛre) *a*, busy. ¶ *n*, busy man, woman.

affaissement (afɛsmã) *m*, subsidence, sinking; collapse. **affaisser (se)** *v.t*, to cause to subside; weigh down. **s'**~, to subside, sink, collapse.

affamé, e (afame) *a*, famished, hungry, starving, craving. ¶ *n*, starveling. **affamer** (me) *v.t*, to famish, starve.

affecté, e (afɛkte) *a*, affected; prim. **affecter** (te) *v.t*, to assign, design, charge, apply, set aside; aspire to; assume; affect; move. **affectation** (tasjɔ̃) *f*, assignment (*Mil.*); affectation; appropriation. **affection** (afɛksjɔ̃) *f*, affection, liking; complaint (*Med.*). **affectionné, e** (ɔne) *a*, **affectueux, euse†** (tɥø, ø:z) *a*, affectionate, fond, loving. **affectionner** (ɔne) *v.t*, to be fond of, like.

affermer (afɛrme) *v.t*, to lease, let out, farm [out], rent.

affermir (afɛrmi:r) *v.t*, to strengthen.

affété, e (afete) *a*, affected, mincing. **afféterie** (tri) *f*, affectation.

affiche (afiʃ) *f*, poster, bill, placard; sign. ~ *lumineuse*, electric sign. **afficher** (ʃe) *v.t*, to post, bill, placard, stick (*bills*); proclaim, advertise, show up. **s'**~, to show off. **afficheur** (ʃœ:r) *m*, billposter, billsticker.

affilé, e (afile) *a*, sharp (*tongue*). **d'affilée**, *ad*, at a stretch. **affiler** (le) *v.t*, to sharpen (*tools*).

affilier (afilje) *v.t*, to affiliate.

affiloir (afilwa:r) *m*, steel; strop.

affinage (afin:aʒ) *m*, refining.

affiner (ne) *v.t*, to refine. **affinerie** (nri) *f*, refinery. **affineur** (nœːr) *m*, refiner.

affinité (afinite) *f*, affinity.

affiquets (afikɛ) *m.pl*, getup, finery.

affirmatif, ive† (afirmatif, iːv) *a. & f*, affirmative. **affirmation** (sjɔ̃) *f*, affirmation. **affirmer** (me) *v.t*, to affirm, assert, aver, vouch.

affixe (afiks) *m*, affix.

affleurement (aflœrmɑ̃) *m*, leveling; outcrop (*Geol.*). **affleurer** (re) *v.t*, to level, flush; (*v.i.*) to crop out.

affliction (afliksjɔ̃) *f*, affliction. **affliger** (ʒe) *v.t*, to afflict, distress, grieve; mortify; curse.

affluence (aflyɑ̃ːs) *f*, affluence; crowd; flow, flood; concourse. **affluent** (ɑ̃) *m*, tributary, affluent, feeder. **affluer** (e) *v.i*, to flow; run; abound, flock.

affolement (afɔlmɑ̃) *m*, panic; distraction. **affoler** (afɔle) *v.t*, to infatuate; madden; distract.

affouiller (afuje) *v.t*, to undermine, wash away.

affourché, e (afurʃe) *a*, astride, astraddle.

affranchi, e (afrɑ̃ʃi) *n*, emancipated slave. **affranchir** (ʃiːr) *v.t*, to [set] free, liberate; relieve; prepay, stamp (*Post*). **affranchissement** (ʃismɑ̃) *m*, emancipation, enfranchisement; prepayment.

affres (afr) *f.pl*, pangs, throes.

affrètement (afretmɑ̃) *m*, freighting, chartering. **affréter** (frete) *v.t*, to charter. **affréteur** (tœːr) *m*, charterer.

affreux, euse† (afrø, øːz) *a*, frightful, fearful, ghastly.

affriander (afriɑ̃de) & **affrioler** (ɔle) *v.t*, to allure, tempt; make attractive.

affront (afrɔ̃) *m*, affront; slight, cut.

affronter (afrɔ̃te) *v.t*, to front, confront, face, brave.

affubler (afyble) *v.t*, to dress up.

affût (afy) *m*, hiding place; stand; [gun] carriage. *à l'~*, on the watch, on the lookout.

affûter (afyte) *v.t*, to sharpen, grind.

afghan, e (afgɑ̃, an) *a. & A~, n*, Afghan.

afin de (afɛ̃) *pr*, in order to, so as to, to. **afin que**, *c*, in order that, so that, that.

africain, e (afrikɛ̃, ɛn) *a. & A~, n*, African. **l'Afrique** (frik) *f*, Africa.

agacer (agase) *v.t*, to set on edge, irritate, annoy; provoke, excite. **agacement** (smɑ̃) *m*, setting on edge, etc. **agacerie** (sri) *f*, provocation.

agate (agat) *f*, agate.

âge (ɑːʒ) *m*, age. *l'~ de raison*, years of discretion. *l'~ ingrat*, the awkward age. *l'~ viril*, man's estate. *quel ~ a-t-il?* how old is he? *il n'est pas en ~*, he is not of (*or* is under) age. **âgé, e** (aʒe) *a*, aged, old. *~ de*, of age, old.

agence (aʒɑ̃ːs) *f*, agency, bureau. *~ d'information*, news agency, press a. *~ de renseignements*, mercantile office, m. agency. *~ immobilière*, real estate agency.

agencé, e (aʒɑ̃se) *p.p*, dressed, got up. **agencement** (smɑ̃) *m*, arrangement; fittings & fixtures. **agencer** (se) *v.t*, to arrange, fit [up].

agenda (aʒɛ̃da) *m*, diary; agenda; memorandum book.

agenouiller [(s')] (aʒnuje) *v.pr*, to kneel [down]. **agenouilloir** (jwaːr) *m*, hassock.

agent (aʒɑ̃) *m*, agent; broker; officer; medium. *~ comptable*, accountant. *~ de change*, stockbroker (*nominated by the government*). *~ de la douane*, customs officer. *~ de liaison*, liaison officer. *~ [de police]*, policeman. *~ de police des côtes à terre*, coastguard. *~ de recouvrements*, debt collector, dun. *~ du service sanitaire*, health officer. *~ en douane*, customs agent. *~ maritime*, shipping agent. *~s s'abstenir*, no agents.

aggloméré (aglomere) *m*, briquet[te]. **agglomérer** (re) *v.t*, to agglomerate.

agglutiner (aglytine) *v.t*, to agglutinate.

aggraver (agrave) *v.t,* to aggravate; increase.

agile† (aʒil)*a,* agíle, nimble, lithe, active. **agilité** (lite) *f,* agility, etc.

agio (aʒjo) *m,* exchange [premium], agio; discount charges.

agiotage (ʒjɔta:ʒ) *m,* gambling, jobbery, rigging; exchange business. **agioter** (te) *v.i,* to speculate, gamble. **agioteur** (tœ:r) *m,* speculator, gambler.

agir (aʒi:r) *v.i,* to act, operate, work, do; proceed (*law*). **s'~,** *v.imp,* to be the matter, be in question. **agissant, e** (ʒisɑ̃, ɑ̃:t) *a,* active. **agissements** (smɑ̃) *m. pl,* goings-on, doings (*underhand*).

agitateur (aʒitatœ:r) *m,* agitator (*Pol.*); stirrer (*rod*). **agiter** (te) *v.t,* to agitate, perturb, shake, stir; wag; wave; debate, discuss, *nuit agitée,* restless night. *mer agitée,* rough sea. **agitation** (tasjɔ̃) *f,* agitation; unrest.

agneau (aɲo) *m,* lamb. **~femelle,** ewe lamb. **agneler** (nəle) *v.i,* to lamb, yean. **agnelet** (lɛ) *m,* lambkin.

agonie (agɔni) *f,* [death] agony, death struggle. *à l'~,* dying. **agonir** (ni:r) *v.t,* to load (*with abuse*). **agonisant, e** (nizɑ̃, ɑ̃:t) *a,* dying. **agoniser** (ze) *v.i,* to be dying.

agrafe (agraf) *f,* hook, clasp, fastener, snap, staple, cramp. **~ & porte,** hook & eye. **agrafer** (fe) *v.t,* to hook, etc; do up (*dress*); grab, nab.

agraire (agrɛ:r) *a,* agrarian, land (*att.*).

agrandir (agrɑ̃di:r) *v.t,* to enlarge. **agrandisseur** (disœ:r) *m,* enlarger (*Phot.*).

agréable† (agreabl) *a. & m,* agreeable, pleasant, nice, congenial; acceptable, palatable.

agréé (agree) *m,* lawyer (at *tribunal de commerce*). **agréer** (gree) *v.t,* to accept, approve, agree; (*v.i*) to please, suit. *agréez, monsieur, mes salutations empressées,* yours faithfully.

agrégation (agregasjɔ̃) *f,* admission; aggregation. **agréger** (ʒə) *v.t,* to admit (*as member*).

agrément (agremɑ̃) *m,* consent, approval; agreeableness, pleasantness, amenity; pleasure, charm; trimming (*dress*). **agrémenter** (te) *v.t,* to adorn, ornament, trim.

agrès (agrɛ) *m.pl,* tackle, gear, rigging.

agresseur (agrɛsœ:r) *m,* aggressor. **agressif, ive** (sif, i:v) *a,* aggressive. **agression** (sjɔ̃) *f,* aggression.

agreste (agrɛst) *a,* rustic; uncouth.

agricole (agrikɔl) *a,* agricultural. **agriculteur** (kyltœ:r) *m,* agricultur[al]ist, farmer. **agriculture** (ty:r) *f,* agriculture, farming, husbandry.

agriffer (s') (agrife) *v.pr,* to claw, cling, lay hold.

agripper (agripe) *v.t,* to lay hold of, clutch, grab, grip.

agronome (agrɔnɔm) *m,* agronomist. **agronomie** (mi) *f,* agronomy, husbandry.

aguerrir (agɛri:r) *v.t,* to harden to war; inure, season.

aguets (être aux) (agɛ), to be on the watch *or* lookout.

aheurtement (aœrtəmɑ̃) *m,* obsession. **s'aheurter** (te) *v.pr.,* to cling, be obsessed, be bent.

ahurir (ayri:r) *v.t,* to flurry, fluster, bewilder, daze.

aide (ɛ:d) *f,* aid, help, assistance. *à l'~!* help! ¶ *n,* assistant, helper, mate. *~ de camp, m,* aide-decamp. **aider** (ɛde) *v.t,* to aid, help, assist. **s'~ de,** to make use of.

aide-mémoire (ɛdmemwa:r) *m,* handbook, manual; aide-mémoire (*diplomatic*).

aïe (a:j) *i,* oh! O dear! (*of pain*).

aïeul, e (ajœl) *n,* grandfather, -mother. **aïeux** (ajø) *m.pl,* forefathers.

aigle (ɛgl) *m,* eagle (*male bird*); genius, mastermind; (*f.*) eagle (*hen bird & standard*). **aiglon, ne** (glɔ̃, ɔn) *n,* eaglet.

aigre† (ɛ:gr) *a,* sour, tart; bitter; sharp; churlish; shrill. ¶ *m,* sourness, etc; chill (*in the air*). **~-doux, ce** (ɛgrədu, us) *a,* bitter-sweet, sub-acid. **aigrefin** (fɛ̃) *m,* sharper; haddock. **aigrelet, te**

(lε, εt) *a*, sourish, tart. **aigret, te** (grε, εt) *a*, sourish, tartish.

aigrette (εgrεt) *f*, aigrette, egret, plume. **aigretté, e** (te), *a*, tufted, crested.

aigreur (εgrœːr) *f*, sourness, acerbity. **aigrir** (griːr) *v.t*, to sour, embitter.

aigu, ë (egy) *a*, acute, sharp, pointed; shrill. ¶ *m*, upper register (*Mus.*).

aigue-marine (εgmarin) *f*, aquamarine.

aiguière (εgjεːr) *f*, ewer.

aiguillade (egɥijad) *f*, goad.

aiguille (egɥiːj) *f*, needle; hand, pointer; switch (*Rly.*) ~ *à coudre*, sewing needle. ~ *à passer*, bodkin. ~ *à repriser*, darning needle. ~ *à tricoter*, knitting n., k. pin. ~ *de glace*, icicle. **aiguillée** (gɥije) *f*, needleful. **aiguiller** (egɥije) *v.t*, to shunt; switch (*Rly.*).

aiguillon (egɥijɔ̃) *m*, goad; sting; prickle; spur, stimulus, incentive. **aiguillonner** (jone) *v.t*, to goad, spur on, stimulate.

aiguiser (egɥize) *v.t*, to sharpen, grind, whet; stimulate.

ail (aːj) *m*, garlic. *gousse d'~*, garlic clove.

aile (εl) *f*, wing; aisle; flange; blade, vane; fender. **ailé, e** (le) *a*, winged. **aileron** (lrɔ̃) *m*, pinion; fin; paddle board; aileron.

ailleurs (ajœːr) *ad*, elsewhere, somewhere else. *par ~*, incidentally. *d'~*, *ad*, besides, moreover.

aimable† (εmabl) *a*, amiable, pleasant; kind; lovable. **aimant, e** (mã, ãːt) *a*, loving, affectionate.

aimant (εmã) *m*, magnet. **aimanter** (te) *v.t*, to magnetize.

aimer (εme) *v.t. & abs*, to love; be fond of; like.

aine (εn) *f*, groin (*Anat.*).

ainé, e (ene) *a. & n*, elder; eldest; senior. **ainesse** (nεs) *f*, seniority.

ainsi (ɛ̃si) *ad*, so, thus. ~ *soit-il*, so be it. ~ *que*, *c*, [just] as; as also.

air (εːr) *m*, air; look, likeness; manner; way; mien; aria; tune, song. *en l'~*, in the air, airy (*schemes*); idle (*tales*); groundless (*fears*); empty (*threats*). *de plein ~*, out-

door (*as games*). *en plein ~*, in the open air, alfresco.

airain (εrɛ̃) (*Poet.*) *m*, bronze, brass.

aire (εːr) *f*, area, floor; eyrie; threshing floor. ~ *de vent*, point of the compass.

aisance (εzãːs) *f*, ease; freedom; affluence, sufficiency, competence. **aise** (εːz) *a*, glad, pleased. ¶ *f*, ease, comfort; joy, pleasure; (*pl.*) creature comforts. **aisé, e** (ze) *a*, easy; comfortable; well-off, affluent. **aisément** (mã) *ad*, easily; comfortably; readily.

aisselle (εsεl) *f*, armpit.

ajonc (aʒɔ̃) *m*, furze, gorse, whin.

ajouré, e (aʒure) *a*, perforated; pierced; open-work (*att.*).

ajourner (aʒurne) *v.t*, to adjourn, postpone, put off; subpoena; defer (*draft*).

ajouté (aʒute) *m*, rider, addition. **ajouter** (te) *v.t*, to add; implement.

ajustage (aʒystaːʒ) *m*, fitting, setting up. **ajustement** (təmã) *m*, adjustment; arrangement, settlement. **ajuster** (te) *v.t*, to adjust, fit [up]; lay out; deck out, array; set straight; aim at (*with gun*). *s'~*, to tidy oneself up. **ajusteur** (tœːr) *m*, fitter, artificer.

ajutage (aʒytaːʒ) *m*, nozzle, jet.

alambic (alãbik) *m*, still. **alambiquer** (ke) *v.t*, to puzzle; spin out, wiredraw (*fig.*).

alanguir (alɑ̃giːr) *v.t*, to make languid.

alarmant, e (alarmã, ãːt) *a*, alarming. **alarme** (larm) *f*, alarm. **alarmer** (me) *v.t*, to alarm; startle.

albâtre (albɑːtr) *m*, alabaster.

alcali (alkali) *m*, alkali. **alcalin, e** (lɛ̃, in) *a*, alkaline.

alchimie (alʃimi) *f*, alchemy. **alchimiste** (mist) *m*, alchemist.

alcool (alkɔl) *m*, alcohol, spirit[s]. ~ *ammoniac aromatique*, sal volatile. ~ *dénaturé*, ~ *à brûler*, methylated spirit. **alcoolique** (kɔlik) *a. & n*, alcoholic.

alcôve (alkoːv) *f*, alcove, recess. ~ *de dortoir*, cubicle.

alcyonien (alsjɔnjɛ̃) *a.m*, halcyon.

aléa (alea) *m*, chance. **aléatoire**

(twa:r) *a*, uncertain, contingent, aleatory.

alène (alɛ:n) *f*, awl.

alentour (alɑ̃tu:r) *ad*, around, round about. *d'~*, surrounding. *~s*, *m.pl*, surroundings.

alerte (alɛrt) *a*, alert, wide-awake. ¶ *i*, up! look out! ¶ *f*, alarm, alert.

aléser (aleze) *v.t*, to ream, broach, bore [out]. **alésage** (za:ʒ) *m*, reaming, etc; bore. **alésoir** (zwa:r) *m*, reamer, broach.

alevin (alvɛ̃) *m*, fry, young fish.

Alexandrie (alɛksɑ̃dri) *f*, Alexandria. **alexandrin, e** (drɛ̃, in) *a*, Alexandrian; Alexandrine.

alfa (alfa) *m*, alfa [grass], esparto [grass].

algarade (algarad) *f*, storm of abuse, blowing up.

algèbre (alʒɛbr) *m*, algebra; Greek (*fig.*).

Alger (alʒe) *m*, Algiers. **l'Algérie** (ʒeri) *f*, Algeria. **algérien, ne** (rjɛ̃, ɛn) *a*. & A~, *n*, Algerian.

algue (alg) *f*, seaweed, alga.

alibi (alibi) *m*, alibi.

aliboron (alibɔrɔ̃) *m: un maître ~*, an ass, a blockhead.

aliéné, e (aljene) *n*, mental patient, lunatic. **aliénation d'esprit,** *~ mentale* (nasjɔ̃), insanity, lunacy, madness. **aliéner** (ne) *v.t*, to alienate, estrange; derange, unhinge (*mind*); transfer (*property*).

aligner (aliɲe) *v.t*, to align, range; finish off (*phrases*). **alignement** (ɲmɑ̃) *m*, alignment, etc; building line.

aliment (alimɑ̃) *m*, food; nutriment; fuel (*fig.*); (*pl.*) sustenance; (*pl.*) cud. **alimentaire** (tɛ:r) *a*, alimentary, feeding, feed, food (*att.*). **alimentation** (tasjɔ̃) *f*, feeding; feed. **alimenter** (te) *v.t*, to feed, supply.

alinéa (alinea) *m*, [fresh] paragraph, new par[agraph]; subsection.

alité, e (alite) *a*, laid up, bedridden. **aliter** (te) *v.t*, to keep in bed.

alizé (alize) *a*, trade (*wind*).

allaiter (alɛte) *v.t*, to suckle, nurse.

allant, e (alɑ̃, ɑ̃:t) *a*, active. ¶ *m*,

activity; go; initiative. *~s & venants*, passersby, comers & goers.

allécher (aleʃe) *v.t*, to allure, entice.

allée (ale) *f*, walk, lane, path; drive; passage. *~ en berceau*, covered walk. *~s & venues*, coming & going, running about.

allégation (alegasjɔ̃) *f*, allegation.

allège (alɛ:ʒ) *f*, lighter, barge, craft. **alléger** (leʒe) *v.t*, to lighten; thin; alleviate. **allégement** (lɛʒmɑ̃) *m*, lightening, etc.

allégorie (allegɔri) *f*, allegory. **allégorique†** (rik) *a*, allegoric(al).

allègre (allɛ:gr) *a*, lively, cheerful, brisk. **allégresse** (allegrɛs) *f*, joy[fulness], cheerfulness.

alléguer (alege) *v.t*, to allege, adduce; plead, urge; quote, cite.

Alléluia (alleluija) *m*, hallelujah.

Allemagne (l') (almaɲ) *f*, Germany. **allemand, e** (mɑ̃, ɑ̃:d) *a*. & A~, *n*, German. **l'allemand, e** *m*, German (*language*).

aller (ale) *m*, going, outward journey. *~ & retour*, roundtrip ticket. *l'~ & le venir*, the come-&-go. *~ à la dérive*, to drift. ¶ *v.i.ir*, to go; run; be (*well, ill, etc.*); get; do; fare; fit, suit. *~ à bicyclette*, to cycle. *~ à cheval*, to ride. *~ en auto*, *~ en voiture*, to drive. *s'en ~*, to go [away], be off.

alliage (alja:ʒ) *m*, alloy. **alliance** (jɑ̃:s) *f*, alliance, union; match; intermarriage; wedding ring. *cousin, par ~*, cousin by marriage. **allié, e** (je) *n*, ally; relation [by marriage]. **allier** (je) *v.t*, to ally, unite; match; alloy. *s'~*, to unite; marry; intermarry.

alligator (aligato:r) *m*, alligator.

allô (alo) (*Teleph.*) *i*, hello!

allocation (allɔkasjɔ̃) *f*, allocation, allowance.

allocution (allɔkysjɔ̃) *f*, speech, address.

allonge (alɔ̃:ʒ) *f*, lengthening piece; rider (*to bill of exchange*). **allonger** (lɔ̃ʒe) *v.t*, to lengthen, elongate; eke out; stretch [out]; deal (*blow*).

allouer (alwe) *v.t*, to allocate, allow, grant.

allumage (alymaːʒ) *m*, lighting, ignition. **allumer** (me) *v.t*, to light, ignite; kindle; fire; stir up. ~ *la lumière*, ~ *l'électricité*, to switch (*or* turn) on the light. **allumette** (mɛt) *f*, match. ~ *bougie*, wax vesta. ~*s de sûreté*, safety matches. ~*s en carnet*, book matches. **allumeur** (mœːr) *m*, lighter.

allure (alyːr) *f*, walk, gait, pace; demeanor, carriage; trim; way.

allusion (allyzjɔ̃) *f*, allusion; hint, innuendo.

almanach (almana; *in liaison*, -nak) *m*, almanac.

aloès (alɔɛs) *m*, aloe. [*suc d'*] ~, aloes.

aloi (alwa) *m*, standard, quality; legal tender. *de bon* ~, genuine.

alors (alɔːr) *ad*, then. ~ *que*, *a*, when.

alouette (alwɛt) *f*, lark. ~ *des champs*, skylark.

alourdir (alurdiːr) *v.t*, to make heavy.

aloyau (alwajo) *m*, sirloin (*beef*).

alpaga (alpaga) *m*, alpaca.

Alpes (les) (alp) *f.pl*, the Alps. **alpestre** (pɛstr) *a*, Alpine.

alpha (alfa) *m*, alpha. **alphabet** (bɛ) *m*, alphabet; A B C, primer. **alphabétique†** (betik) *a*, alphabetical.

alpin, e (alpɛ̃, in) *a*, Alpine. **l'alpinisme** (pinism) *m*, mountaineering. **alpiniste** (nist) *n*, Alpinist, mountaineer.

Alsace (l') (alzas) *f*, Alsace. **alsacien, ne** (sjɛ̃, ɛn) *a*. & A~, *n*, Alsatian.

altérant, e (alterɑ̃, ɑ̃ːt) *a*, thirst-creating.

altération (alterasjɔ̃) *f*, alteration, change; adulteration; faltering voice; heavy thirst.

altercation (altɛrkasjɔ̃) *f*, altercation.

altérer (altere) *v.t*, to change; debase, adulterate; garble; weather (*Geol.*); make thirsty. *altéré de sang*, bloodthirsty.

alternatif, ive† (altɛrnatif, iːv) *a*, alternative; alternate; alternating. ¶ *f*, alternative; option. **alterner** (ne) *v.i*. & *t*, to alternate.

altesse (altɛs) *f*, highness (*title*).

altier, ère (altje, ɛːr) *a*, haughty, lofty, lordly.

altitude (altityd) *f*, altitude, height, elevation.

alto (alto) *m*, alto; tenor violin, viola; alto saxhorn.

altruiste (altryist) *n*, altruist. ¶ *a*, altruistic.

aluminium (alyminjɔm) *m*, aluminum.

alun (alœ̃) *m*, alum.

alvéole (alveɔl) *m*, cell; socket (*tooth*).

amabilité (amabilite) *f*, amiability, kindness.

amadou (amadu) *m*, tinder, touchwood. **amadouer** (dwe) *v.t*, to coax, wheedle, cajole.

amaigrir (amegriːr) *v.t*, to [make] thin, emaciate.

amalgame (amalgam) *m*, amalgam; mixture. **amalgamer** (me) *v.t*, to amalgamate.

amande (amɑ̃ːd) *f*, almond. **amandier** (mɑ̃dje) *m*, almond [tree].

amant (amɑ̃) *m*, paramour; lover.

amariner (amarine) *v.t*, to make a sailor of; man (*prize ship*).

amarre (amaːr) *f*, [mooring] rope, fast, line; hawser. **amarrer** (mare) *v.t*, to make fast, moor; lash, seize; berth; belay.

amas (amɑ) *m*, heap, pile, mass, collection; drift (*snow*); hoard. **amasser (se)** *v.t*, to amass, heap [up], pile up, lay up, hoard.

amateur (amatœːr) *m*, lover (*devotee*); amateur; fancier. *il est* [*grand*] ~ *de* . . ., he is [very] fond of . . . (*e.g, art, collecting, gardening*); . . . is his hobby.

amazone (amazoːn) *f*, Amazon; horsewoman. [*habit d'*]~, riding habit. **l'A~**, *m*, **le fleuve des A~s**, the Amazon (*river*).

ambages (ɑ̃baːʒ) *f.pl*, circumlocution. *sans* ~, candidly.

ambassade (ɑ̃basad) *f*, embassy; errand. **ambassadeur, drice** (dœːr, dris) *n*, ambassador, dress; messenger. *l'~ de France*, the French ambassador.

ambiance (ɑ̃bjɑ̃ːs) *f*, environment. **ambiant, e** (ɑ̃, ɑ̃ːt) *a*, surrounding, ambient.

ambigu†, ë (ɑ̃bigy) *a*, ambiguous.

¶ *m*, mixture. **ambiguïté** (gɥite) *f*, ambiguity.

ambitieux, euse† (ăbisjø, ø:z) *a*, ambitious. **ambition** (sjɔ̃) *f*, ambition. **ambitionner** (ɔne) *v.t*, to be eager for, aspire to.

ambre (ɑ̃:br) *m*, amber. ~ *gris*, ambergris.

ambroisie (ăbrwazi) *f*, ambrosia.

ambulance (ăbylɑ̃:s) *f*, ambulance. **ambulant, e** (lă, ɑ̃:t) *a*, itinerant, strolling; traveling.

âme (ɑ:m) *f*, soul, mind, spirit, ghost, life, heart; mainstay; soundpost; core; web; bore (*gun*); motto. *dans l'~*, at heart. ~ *damnée*, [mere] tool (*pers.*).

améliorer (ameljɔre) *v.t*, & *s'~*, to ameliorate, better, improve, mend; appreciate.

aménager (amenaʒe) *v.t*, to lay out, fit; harness (*waterfall*); reclaim (*submerged land*). **aménagement** (ʒmɑ̃) *m*, layout; accommodation, appointments.

amende (amɑ̃:d) *f*, fine. ~ *honorable*, apology.

amender (amɑ̃de) *v.t*, to amend; improve.

amène (amɛ:n) *a*, pleasing, agreeable.

amener (amne) *v.t*, to bring, lead; lead up to; haul down; strike (*colors*). *amené de loin*, far-fetched. *s'~*, to arrive, turn up.

aménité (amenite) *f*, amenity, graciousness.

amenuiser (amənɥize) *v.t*, to thin.

amer, ère† (amɛ:r) *a*, bitter; briny. ¶ *m*, bitter, bitterness; (*pl.*) bitters; gall; sea mark, landmark (*Naut.*).

américain, e (amerikɛ̃, ɛn) *a*. & A~, *n*, American. **l'Amérique** (rik) *f*, America.

amerrir (ameri:r) *v.i*, to alight [on the water] (*seaplane*).

amertume (amɛrtym) *f*, bitterness.

ameublement (amœbləmɑ̃) *m*, [suite of] furniture.

ameuter (amøte) *v.t*, to train in a pack (*dogs*); stir up (*mob*). *s'~*, to assemble.

ami, e (ami) *a*, friendly; kindly. ¶ *n*, friend; lover. ~ *de cœur*, bosom friend. *amis & parents*,

kith & kin; *petite ~e*, mistress.

amiable† (mjabl) *a*, **amical, e†** (mikal) *a*, amicable, friendly, kind. *amiable compositeur*, arbitrator (*law*). *à l'amiable*, amicably; by private treaty (*sale*).

amidon (amidɔ̃) *m*, starch. **amidonner** (dɔne) *v.t*, to starch.

amincir (amɛ̃si:r) *v.t*, to thin.

amiral (amiral) *m*, admiral; flagship. ~ *commandant d'escadre*, admiral of the fleet.

amirauté (rote) *f*, admiralty; admiralship.

amitié (amitje) *f*, friendship, kindness, love, liking; (*pl.*) kind regards.

ammoniaque (amɔnjak) *f*, ammonia.

amnistie (amnisti) *f*, amnesty, oblivion.

amodier (amɔdje) *v.t*, to farm out.

amoindrir (amwɛ̃dri:r) *v.t*, to lessen, decrease.

amollir (amɔli:r) *v.t*, to soften, mollify; enervate.

amonceler (amɔ̃sle) *v.t*, to heap [up], pile up, drift.

amont (amɔ̃) *m*, headwaters; upper part. *en ~*, *ad*, upstream, up. *en ~ de*, *pr*, above, up.

amorçage (amɔrsa:ʒ) *m*, priming; starting (*Elec.*); baiting (*fish*). **amorce** (amɔrs) *f*, bait; allurement; [percussion] cap; priming; beginning, start. **amorcer** (se) *v.t*, to bait, lure, etc; energize (*Elec.*).

amorphe (amɔrf) *a*, amorphous.

amortir (amɔrti:r) *v.t*, to deaden, damp; redeem, amortize, sink, pay off; write off, depreciate. **amortisseur** (tisœ:r) *m*, shock absorber (*motor*); damper (*Radio*).

amour (amu:r) *m*, love; passion; idol; (*pl.*) love affairs, amours. ~ *intéressé*, cupboard love. *mal d'~*, lovesickness. *pour l'~ de*, for the sake (*or* love) of. **amouracher** (muraʃe) *v.t*, to enamor. **amoureux, euse†** (rø, ø:z) *a*, in love, enamored; loving, amorous; tender, soft. ¶ *n*, lover, sweetheart. **amour-propre** (amurprɔpr) *m*, self-respect, pride; self-esteem.

amovible (amɔvibl) *a*, removable, detachable.

ampère (ɑ̃pɛːr) *m*, ampere.

amphibie (ɑ̃fibi) *a*, amphibious. ¶ *m*, amphibian.

amphithéâtre (ɑ̃fiteɑːtr) *m*, amphitheater.

ample† (ɑ̃ːpl) *a*, ample, full; wide. **ampleur** (ɑ̃plœːr) *f*, ampleness, etc. **ampliation** (pliasjɔ̃) *f*, duplicate, office copy. *pour ~*, [certified] a true copy. **amplificateur** (fikatœːr) *m*, enlarger (*Phot.*); amplifier (*Radio*). **amplifier** (fje) *v.t*, to amplify. **amplitude** (tyd) *f*, amplitude.

ampoule (ɑ̃pul) *f*, phial; blister; bulb (*elec. lamp, thermometer*). **ampoulé, e** (le) *a*, inflated, bombastic, high-flown.

amputer (ɑ̃pyte) *v.t*, to amputate, cut off.

amulette (amylɛt) *f*, amulet, charm.

amure (amyːr) *f*, tack (*sail*).

amuser (amyze) *v.t*, to amuse, entertain; beguile, fool, trifle with. *s'~*, to amuse (*or* enjoy) oneself; dally, loiter. **amusement** (zmɑ̃) *m*, amusement, etc. **amusette** (zɛt) *f*, plaything.

amygdale (amigdal) *f*, tonsil. **amygdalite** (lit) *f*, tonsillitis.

an (ɑ̃) *m*, year. *il a 10 ~s*, he is 10 years old. *le jour de l'~*, New Year's day.

anachorète (anakɔrɛt) *m*, anchoret, anchorite.

anachronisme (anakrɔnism) *m*, anachronism.

analogie (analɔʒi) *f*, analogy. **analogue** (lɔg) *a*, analogous, like.

analyse (analiːz) *f*, analysis. *~ grammaticale*, parsing. **analyser** (lize) *v.t*, to analyze; parse. **analyste** (list) *m*, analyst. **analytique†** (tik) *a*, analytic(al).

ananas (anana) *m*, pineapple.

anarchie (anarʃi) *f*, anarchy. **anarchique†** (ʃik) *a*, anarchic(al). **anarchiste** (ʃist) *n. & a*, anarchist.

anatomie (anatɔmi) *f*, anatomy. **anatomique†** (mik) *a*, anatomical.

ancestral, e (ɑ̃sɛstral) *a*, ancestral. **ancêtre** (sɛːtr) *m*, ancestor.

anche (ɑ̃ːʃ) *f*, reed (*Mus.*).

anchois (ɑ̃ʃwa) *m*, anchovy.

ancien, ne (ɑ̃sjɛ̃, ɛn) *a*, ancient, old; of long standing; former; bygone; quondam; late, ex-; senior. *ancien combattant*, ex-service man. ¶ *m*, ancient; elder (*Eccl.*). **anciennement** (ɛnmɑ̃) *ad*, anciently, of old, formerly. **ancienneté** (nte) *f*, ancientness, antiquity; seniority. *de toute ~*, from time immemorial.

ancolie (ɑ̃kɔli) *f*, columbine (*Bot.*)

ancrage (ɑ̃kraːʒ) *m*, anchorage; anchoring.

ancre (ɑ̃ːkr) *f*, anchor. *~ à jet*, kedge [a.]. *~ de veille* (*Naut.*) & *~ de salut* (fig.), sheet anchor. **ancrer** (ɑ̃kre) (*Build.*) *v.t*, to anchor, fix.

andain (ɑ̃dɛ̃) *m*, swath, wind row.

andouille (ɑ̃duːj) *f*, chiterlings; fool, boob.

andouiller (ɑ̃duje) *m*, tine, antler.

âne (ɑːn) *m*, ass, jackass, donkey; dunce, dolt.

anéantir (aneɑ̃tiːr) *v.t*, to annihilate, crush; prostrate. *s'~*, to humble oneself.

anecdote (anɛgdɔt) *f*, anecdote.

anémie (anemi) *f*, anemia. **anémique** (mik) *a*, anemic.

ânerie (ɑnri) *f*, gross stupidity.

anéroïde (aneroid) *a*, aneroid.

ânesse (ɑnɛs) *f*, [she] ass, jenny.

anesthésie (anɛstezi) *f*, anesthesia. *~ à la reine*, twilight sleep. **anesthésique** (zik) *a. & m*, anesthetic.

anfractueux, euse (ɑ̃fraktɥø, øːz) *a*, winding; craggy.

ange (ɑ̃ːʒ) *m*, angel. *~ déchu*, fallen a. *être aux ~s*, to be in raptures. **angélique†** (aʒelik) *a*, angelic(al)). ¶ *f*, angelica. **Angélus** (lyːs) *m*, angelus [bell].

angine (ɑ̃ʒin) *f*, angina, quinsy. *~ de poitrine*, angina pectoris.

anglais, e (ɑ̃glɛ, ɛːz) *a*, English; British; imperial. A~, *n*, Englishman, -woman, Briton. *l'anglais, m*, English (*language*).

angle (ɑ̃ːgl) *m*, angle, corner.

Angleterre (l') (ɑ̃glətɛːr) *f*, England. **anglicisme** (glisism) *m*, Anglicism. **anglomanie** (glɔmani) *f*, Anglomania. **les îles Anglo-Normandes**, the Channel Islands.

anglophile (fil) *a. & n*, Anglophile, pro-British. **anglophobe** (fɔb) *a. & n*, Anglophobe, anti-British. **anglo-saxon, ne** (saksɔ̃, ɔn) *a. & A~-S~, n*, Anglo-Saxon.

angoisse (ɑ̃gwas) *f*, anguish, pang. **angoisser** (se) *v.t*, to distress, pain. *poire d'~*, choke pear.

angora (ɑ̃gɔra) *m*, Persian [cat].

anguillade (ɑ̃gijad) *f*, lash, cut.

anguille (ɑ̃gi:j) *f*, eel. *~ de mer*, conger [eel]. *quelque ~ sous roche (fig.)*, something in the wind.

angulaire (ɑ̃gylɛ:r) *a*, angular, corner (*att.*). *pierre ~*, cornerstone.

anicroche (anikrɔʃ) *f*, hitch, snag.

ânier, ère (ɑnje, ɛ:r) *n*, donkey driver.

animal, e (animal) *a*, animal. ¶ *m*, animal, dumb animal, beast, brute; creature.

animateur, trice (animatœ:r, tris) *n*, animator, moving spirit. **animation** (sjɔ̃) *f*, animation, liveliness, bustle, life. **animé, e** (me) *a*, animate; animated, lively, buoyant, spirited, brisk, bustling, agog, astir; instinct. **animer** (me) *v.t*, to animate, quicken, brighten, enliven, inspirit; actuate, impel.

animosité (animozite) *f*, animosity, animus, spite.

anis (ani) *m*, anise. *[graine d']~*, aniseed.

ankylose (ɑ̃kilo:z) *f*, anchylosis; cramp. **ankyloser** (lose) *v.t*, to stiffen.

annales (anal) *f.pl*, annals.

anneau (ano) *m*, ring; coil (*snake*); ringlet; link.

année (ane) *f*, year, twelvemonth. *~ à millésime*, vintage year.

annexe (anɛks) *f*, annex; dependency (*country*); schedule; enclosure; tender (*boat*). *lettre ~*, covering letter. **annexer** (kse) *v.t*, to annex, attach. **annexion** (ksjɔ̃) *f*, annexation.

annihiler (aniile) *v.t*, to annihilate; annul.

anniversaire (anivɛrsɛ:r) *a & m*, anniversary. *l'~ de ma naissance*, my birthday.

annonce (anɔ̃:s) *f*, announcement,

advertisement; bans. *~-article, f*, puff paragraph. *~ de fantaisie, ~ courante*, display advertisement. *petite annonce*, classified ad. **annoncer** (nɔ̃se) *v.t*, to announce, advertise, proclaim, herald; give out; betoken, foreshadow; inform; state; show in, usher in; preach; foretell. **annonceur** (sœ:r) *m*, advertiser; announcer. **l'Annonciation** (sjasjɔ̃) *f*, the Annunciation, Lady-day.

annoter (anɔte) *v.t*, to annotate.

annuaire (anɥɛ:r) *m*, annual, year book, directory (*telephone*); list (*Army, Navy, etc.*). **annuel, le** (nɥɛl) *a*, annual, yearly. **annuité** (nɥite) *f*, annuity.

annulaire (anylɛ:r) *a*, annular. *[doigt] ~, m*, ring finger, third f.

annulation (anylasjɔ̃) *f*, annulment; cancellation.

annuler (anyle) *v.t*, to annul, nullify, quash, cancel; contra.

anoblir (anɔbli:r) *v.t*, to ennoble.

anode (anɔd) *f*, anode.

anodin, e (anɔdɛ̃, in) *a*, anodyne, soothing; harmless, mild, tame. ¶ *m*, anodyne.

anomal, e (anɔmal) *a*, anomalous. **anomalie** (li) *f*, anomaly.

ânon (ɑnɔ̃) *m*, young ass, foal. **ânonner** (nɔne) *v.i*, to falter, hem & haw.

anonyme (anɔnim) *a*, anonymous; unnamed.

anormal, e (anɔrmal) *a*, abnormal.

anse (ɑ̃:s) *f*, handle; bow; cove. *faire le pot à deux ~s*, to set one's arms akimbo.

anspect (ɑ̃spɛk) *m*, handspike.

antagonisme (ɑ̃tagɔnism) *m*, antagonism. **antagoniste** (nist) *m*, antagonist, opponent.

antan (ɑ̃tɑ̃) *m*, yesteryear.

antarctique (ɑ̃tar[k]tik) *a*, antarctic.

antécédent, e (ɑ̃tesedɑ̃, ɑ̃:t) *a. & m*, antecedent.

antédiluvien, ne (ɑ̃tedilyvjɛ̃, ɛn) *a*, antediluvian.

antenne (ɑ̃tɛn) *f*, antenna, feeler; horn; aerial (*Radio*); branch line (*Rly.*). *~ d'appartement*, indoor aerial.

antérieur, e† (ɑ̃terjœ:r) *a*, anterior, prior, previous. **antériorité** (rjorite) *f*, priority.

anthère (ătɛːr) *f*, anther.

anthologie (ătɔlɔʒi) *f*, anthology.

anthracite (ătrasit) *m*, anthracite.

anthrax (ătraks) *m*, carbuncle. (*Med.*)

anthropophage (ătrɔpɔfaːʒ) *a*. & *m*, cannibal.

anti-aérien, ne (ătiaerjɛ̃, ɛn) *a*, antiaircraft.

antialcoolique (ătialkɔɔlik) *a*, teetotal.

antichambre (ătiʃãːbr) *f*, antechamber, anteroom. *faire~chez*, to dance attendance on.

antichar (ătiʃaːr) *m*, antitank weapon.

anticipation (ătisipasjɔ̃) *f*, anticipation, advance. **anticiper** (pe) *v.t*, to anticipate, forestall. ~ *sur*, to encroach on.

antidater (ătidate) *v.t*, to antedate.

antidérapant, e (ătiderapã, ã:t) *a*, nonskid.

antidote (ătidɔt) *m*, antidote.

antienne (ătjɛn) *f*, anthem.

Antilles (les) (ătiːj) *f.pl*, the West Indies, the Antilles. *la mer des ~*, the Caribbean sea.

antilope (ătilɔp) *f*, antelope.

antimoine (ătimwan) *m*, antimony.

antipathie (ătipati) *f*, antipathy, dislike. **antipathique** (tik) *a*, antipathetic.

antipatriotique (ɑtipatriɔtik) *a*, unpatriotic.

antipodes (ătipɔd) *m.pl*, antipodes.

antiquailles (ătikɑːj) *f.pl*, worthless antiques. **antiquaire** (kɛːr) *n*, antiquary, -rian. **antique** (tik) *a*, ancient; antique. ¶ *m*, antique (*style*); (*f*.) antique (*relic*). **antiquité** (kite) *f*, antiquity.

antiseptique (ătisɛptik) *a*. & *m*, antiseptic; preservative (*for perishable foodstuffs*).

antithèse (ătitɛːz) *f*, antithesis.

antre (ɑ̃ːtr) *m*, cave, den, lair.

anus (anyːs) *m*, anus.

Anvers (ɑ̃vɛːr, -vɛrs) *m*, Antwerp. **anversois, e** (vɛrswa, aːz) *a*, of Antwerp.

anxiété (ăksjete) *f*, anxiety. **anxieux, euse** (ksjø, øːz) *a*, anxious.

aorte (aɔrt) *f*, aorta.

août (u) *m*, August.

apache (apaʃ) *m*, Apache, desperado; hooligan, rough.

apaiser (apɛze) *v.t*, to appease, allay, assuage, quiet, quell, quench. *s'~*, to abate.

aparté (aparte) *m*, aside, stage whisper.

apathie (apati) *f*, apathy, **apathique** (tik) *a*, apathetic, lackadaisical.

apatride (apatrid) *m*, stateless person.

apercevoir (apɛrsəvwaːr) *v.t*, to perceive, see, espy. *s'~*, to perceive, find. **aperçu** (sy) *m*, outline, summary; rough estimate; insight.

apéritif (aperitif) *m*, appetizer.

aphorisme (afɔrism) *m*, aphorism.

apiculture (apikyltyːr) *f*, beekeeping.

apitoyer (apitwaje) *v.t*, to move to pity.

aplanir (aplaniːr) *v.t*, to level; smooth.

aplatir (aplatiːr) *v.t*, to flat[ten]; squash; smooth; plane. **aplatissement** (tismã) *m*, flatt[en]ing; flatness.

aplomb (aplɔ̃) *m*, perpendicularity, plumb; self-possession. **d'~**, plumb, upright.

Apocalypse (apɔkalips) *f*, Revelation, Apocalypse.

apogée (apɔʒe) *m*, apogee; height; zenith, acme, high watermark (*fig.*).

apologétique (apɔlɔʒetik) *a*, apologetic. **apologie** (ʒi) *f*, apology, justification.

apoplectique (apɔplɛktik) *a*. & *m*, apoplectic. **apoplexie** (ksi) *f*, apoplexy.

apostasie (apostazi) *f*, apostasy, defection. **apostat** (ta) *m*. & *att*, apostate.

aposter (apɔste) *v.t*, to station, post, set.

apostille (apɔstiːj) *f*, marginal note, side note; recommendation. **apostiller** (tije) *v.t*, to make a note on.

apostolat (apɔstɔla) *m*, apostolate, apostleship. **apostolique**† (lik) *a*, apostolic(al).

apostrophe (apɔstrɔf) *f*, apostrophe; reproach. **apostropher** (fe) *v.t*, to apostrophize; upbraid.

apothéose (apɔteoːz) *f*, apotheosis.

apôtre (apoːtr) *m*, apostle. *bon* ~, hypocrite.

apparaître (aparɛːtr) *v.i.ir*, to appear.

apparat (apara) *m*, state, show, pomp.

appareil (aparɛːj) *m*, array; apparatus, appliance, plant, gear, tackle, rig; attachment (*to machine*); dressing (*on wound*); camera. ~ *à douche d'air*, hair drier. ~ *à sous*, coin machine. **appareillage** (jaːʒ) *m*, installation; equipment; preparation; accessories; matching (*colors, etc.*); getting under weigh (*Naut.*). **appareiller** (rɛje) *v.t. & i*, to match, pair, mate; fit; get under weigh. **appareilleur** (jœːr) *m*, fitter.

apparemment (aparamɑ̃) *ad*, apparently. **apparence** (rɑ̃ːs) *f*, appearance, look; guise; likelihood. **apparent, e** (rɑ̃, ɑ̃ːt) *a*, apparent, seeming.

apparenté, e (aparɑ̃te) *a*, related, akin, connected. **apparenter** (te) *v.t*, to connect, ally. **s'**~, to marry (*à* = into); blend.

apparier (aparje) *v.t*, to match, pair.

appariteur (aparitœːr) *m*, usher; beadle.

apparition (aparisjɔ̃) *f*, appearance, advent; apparition.

appartement (apartəmɑ̃) *m*, [suite of] rooms, apartment.

appartenir (apartəniːr) *v.i.ir*, to belong, [ap]pertain, concern. **s'**~, to be one's own master *or* mistress.

appas (apɑ) *m.pl*, attractions, charms. **appât** (pɑ) *m*, bait, allurement, lure, draw. **appâter** (te) *v.t*, to bait; allure; cram (*poultry*).

appauvrir (apovriːr) *v.t*, to impoverish, beggar; thin (*wine*).

appeau (apo) *m*, bird call.

appel (apɛl) *m*, call, calling [up]; appeal; invitation; muster; challenge. ~ *de fonds*, call. ~[*nominal*], roll call, muster, call over. **appelant** (plɑ̃) *m*, decoy bird. **appeler** (ple) *v.t. & i*, to call; term; appeal; invite; challenge. **s'**~, to be called. *je m'appelle Adam*, my name is Adam.

appendice (apɛ̃dis) *m*, appendage, appendix. **appendicite** (sit) *f*, appendicitis.

appendre (apɑ̃ːdr) *v.t*, to hang up.

appentis (apɑ̃ti) *m*, lean-to, penthouse; outhouse.

appesantir (apəzɑ̃tiːr) *v.t*, to make heavy, dull, weigh down.

appéter (appete) *v.t*, to crave for, long for.

appétissant, e (apetisɑ̃, ɑ̃ːt) *a*, appetizing, tempting. **appétit** (ti) *m*, appetite; desire, lust.

applaudir (aplodiːr) *v.t. & i*, to applaud, cheer. ~ *à*, to commend. **s'**~ *de*, to congratulate oneself on. **applaudissement** (dismɑ̃) *m. oft. pl*, applause, cheer, plaudit.

application (aplikasjɔ̃) *f*, application; infliction; diligence. [*dentelle d'*]~, appliqué lace. **applique** (plik) *f*, appliqué [work] (*metal*); sconce, bracket. **appliqué, e** (ke) *p.a*, applied; close; studious. **appliquer** (ke) *v.t*, to apply, put, lay on; give charge; inflict.

appoint (apwɛ̃) *m*, addition; small coin, [small] change, odd money; help. **appointements** (tmɑ̃) *m.pl*, salary. **appointer** (te) *v.t*, to put on a salary basis (*in p.p*, salaried); point; sew up, stitch together.

appontement (apɔ̃tmɑ̃) *m*, wharf.

apport (apɔːr) *m*, bringing; transfer, assignment; capital brought in; assets transferred *or* taken over; contribution; collection (*of goods by Rly. Co.*); drift (*Geol.*). *valeurs d'*~, vendor's assets. **apporter** (pɔrte) *v.t*, to bring, fetch; transfer, assign; give; waft. *apporte!* fetch it! (*to dog*). **apporteur** (tœːr) *m*, vendor.

apposer (apoze) *v.t*, to affix, put, append, set. **apposition** (zisjɔ̃) *f*,

affixture, etc; apposition. *en ~*
(*Gram.*), in apposition; attributively.

appréciable (apresjabl) *a*, appreciable; measurable. **appréciation** (sjɔ̃) *f*, valuation, estimate;
appreciation. **apprécier** (sje) *v.t*,
to value; estimate; esteem.

appréhender (apreɑ̃de) *v.t*, to
apprehend; arrest. **appréhension**
(sjɔ̃) *f*, apprehension; arrest.

apprendre (aprɑ̃:dr) *v.t. & abs.
ir*, to learn, hear, understand;
teach; inform, tell. *mal appris*,
ill-bred.

apprenti, e (aprɑ̃ti) *n*, apprentice; learner; novice, tyro. **apprentissage** (sa:ʒ) *m*, apprenticeship; articles. *mettre en ~*, to
apprentice.

apprêt (aprɛ) *m*, dressing; affectation; (*pl.*) preparations. **apprêté, e** (te) *a*, affected. **apprêter**
(te) *v.t*, to prepare; dress prime.

apprivoiser (aprivwaze) *v.t*, to
tame. **s' ~**, to grow tame; become
sociable.

approbation (aprɔbasjɔ̃) *f*, approbation, approval, confirmation.

approchant, e (aprɔʃɑ̃, ɑ̃:t) *a*,
approximating, like. **approche**
(prɔʃ) *f*, approach. **approcher** (ʃe)
v.t. & i, to approach, draw near;
resemble, border on.

approfondi, e (aprɔfɔ̃di) *p.a*,
thorough, exhaustive. **approfondir** (di:r) *v.t*, to deepen; dive into.

approprier (aprɔprie) *v.t*, to
adapt, suit. **s'~**, to appropriate.

approuver (apruve) *v.t*, to approve, countenance, confirm,
pass.

approvisionner (aprɔvizjɔne)
v.t, to supply, store, stock, provision. **s' ~ de**, to lay in [a stock
of]. **approvisionnement** (nmɑ̃) *m*,
supplying, etc; supply, etc.

approximatif, ive† (aprɔksi-
matif, i:v) *a*, approximate, rough.
approximation (sjɔ̃) *f*, approximation.

appui (apɥi) *m*, support, rest; fulcrum; stress (*Gram.*); windowsill.
à hauteur d'~, elbow-high,
breast-high. **~-main**, *m*, maul-
stick. **appuyer** (pɥije) *v.t. & i*, to
support; back; second; hold up;

lean, rest; bear; press; lay stress.
s'~, to rest, lean; rely, depend.

âpre† (ɑ:pr) *a*, rough, harsh;
sharp; ruthless; greedy, grasping.

après (aprɛ) *pr*, after. *ap. J.-C.*,
A.D. *¶ ad*, after[wards]. **~ que**,
c, after, when. **d'~**, *pr*, according
to, after, from. **~ coup**, *ad*, too
late, after the event, a day after
the fair. **~-demain**, *ad. & m*, the
day after tomorrow. **d'~-guerre**,
a, postwar. **~-midi**, *m*, afternoon. *de l'~-midi*, post meridiem, p.m.

âpreté (aprəte) *f*, roughness, etc,
as *âpre*; asperity.

à-propos (aprɔpo) *m*, aptness;
opportuneness.

apte (apt) *a*, fit[ted], competent,
qualified; apt. **aptitude** (tityd)
f, aptitude, aptness, etc; faculty,
flair.

apurer (apyre) *v.t*, to agree, reconcile; wipe off (*debt, etc.*);
audit; get discharged, get can-
celed.

aquafortiste (akwafɔrtist) *m*,
etcher.

aquaplane (akwaplan) *m*, surf-
board.

aquarelle (akwarɛl) *f*, water-
color.

aquarium (akwarjɔm) *m*, aquarium.

aquatique (akwatik) *a*, aquatic,
water (*att.*).

aqueduc (akdyk) *m*, aqueduct.

aqueux, euse (akø, ø:z) *a*, aqueous, watery.

à quia (kɥia), nonplussed.

aquilin (akilɛ̃) *a.m*, aquiline,
hook[ed], Roman (*nose*).

ara (ara) *m*, macaw, ara.

arabe (arab) *a*, Arab; Arabian;
Arabic. *¶ m*, Arabic (*language*).
A~, *n*, Arab[ian] (*pers.*). **arabes-
que** (bɛsk) *f*, arabesque, **l'Arabie**
(bi) *f*, Arabia. **Arabique** (bik) *a*,
Arabian (*gulf*).

arable (arabl) *a*, arable, tillable.

arachide (araʃid) *f*, groundnut,
peanut, monkey nut.

araignée (arɛɲe) *f*, spider.

aratoire (aratwa:r) *a*, agricultural, farming.

arbitrage (arbitra:ʒ) *m*, arbitration; arbitrament; arbitrage.

arbitraire† (trɛːr) *a*, arbitrary; high-handed. **arbitre** (tr) m, arbitrator, arbiter; referee, umpire. ~ *de lignes*, linesman (*Ten.*). **arbitrer** (tre) *v.t*, to arbitrate; arrange; referee, umpire.

arborer (arbɔre) *v.t*, to raise, hoist, set up; flaunt.

arbre (arbr) *m*, tree; shaft, axle, spindle, mandrel, -il, arbor. ~ *de haute futaie*, timber tree. ~ *de plein vent*, standard. ~ *en espalier*, wall tree. ~ *moteur*, ~ *de couche*, driving shaft. ~ *toujours vert*, evergreen. **arbrisseau** (briso) *m*, shrub.

arbuste (arbyst) *m*, bush.

arc (ark) *m*, bow; arc; arch. **arcade** (kad) *f*, archway; arch; (*pl.*) arcade.

arc-boutant (arkbutɑ̃) *m*, [flying] buttress; raking shore; strut, spur, brace. **arc-bouter** (te) *v.t*, to buttress.

arceau (arso) *m*, arch; hoop; cradle (*Surg.*).

arc-en-ciel (arkɑ̃sjɛl) *m*, rainbow.

archaïque (arkaik) *a*, archaic.

archange (arkɑ̃ːʒ) *m*, archangel.

arche (arʃ) *f*, arch; ark. *l'~ d'alliance*, the Ark of the Covenant. *l'~ de Noé* (nɔe), Noah's ark.

archéologie (arkeɔlɔʒi) *f*, archaeology. **archéologique** (ʒik) *a*, archaeologic(al). **archéologue** (lɔg) *m*, archaeologist.

archer (arʃe) *m*, archer, bowman. **archet** (ʃɛ) *m*, bow, fiddlestick.

archevêché (arʃəveʃe) *m*, archbishopric; palace. **archevêque** (vɛːk) *m*, archbishop.

archidiacre (arʃidjakr) *m*, archdeacon.

archipel (arʃipɛl) *m*, archipelago.

architecte (arʃitɛkt) *m*, architect. **architectural, e** (tyral) *a*, architectural. **architecture** (tyːr) *f*, architecture.

archives (arʃiːv) *f.pl*, archives, records.

arçon (arsɔ̃) *m*, saddle bow; bow.

arctique (arktik) *a*, arctic.

ardent, e (ardɑ̃, ɑ̃ːt) *a*, burning, hot, fiery, raging, blazing, live; ardent, keen, fervent, fervid;

eager, earnest, spirited; passionate. **ardemment** (damɑ̃) *ad*, ardently, etc. **ardeur** (dœːr) *f*, ardor, heat, etc; zest. ~ *d'estomac*, heartburn.

ardoise (ardwaːz) *f*, slate. **ardoisé, e** (dwaze) *a*, s.-colored. **ardoisière** (zjɛːr) *f*, s. quarry.

ardu, e (ardy) *a*, steep; arduous, hard, uphill.

are (aːr) *m*, are = 100 square meters *or* 119.60 sq. yards.

arène (arɛn) *f*, arena, lists, ring; cockpit; sand (*Poet.*).

arête (arɛt) *f*, [fish]bone; ridge, edge, arris; arête; groin, hip (*Arch.*); awn, beard (*Bot.*). ~ *vive*, sharp edge.

argent (arʒɑ̃) *m*, silver; money, cash. ~ *comptant*, ready money, spot cash. ~ *doré*, silver-gilt. *un* ~ *fou*, a mint of money. ~ *liquide*, ready money. ~ *mignon*, small savings (*to spend on pleasure*). ~ *sec*, hard cash. ~ *sur table*, cash down. **argenter** (te) *v.t*, to silver[-plate], [electro]-plate. **argenterie** (tri) *f*, silver, [s.] plate. **argentin, e** (tɛ̃, in) *a*, argentine, silvery, silvern. ¶ *a.* & A~, *n*, Argentine (*Geog.*). l'**Argentine**, *f*, the Argentine.

argile (arʒil) *f*, clay. ~ *réfractaire*, fire clay. **argileux, euse** (lø, øːz) *a*, clayey, argillaceous.

argot (argo) *m*, slang.

arguer (argɥe) *v.t*, to infer, deduce. **argument** (gymɑ̃) *m*, argument; synopsis. **argumenter** (te) *v.i*, to argue.

argutie (argysi) *f*, quibble, cavil, hairsplitting.

aria (arja) *m*, bother, ado, to-do.

aride (arid) *a*, arid, dry, barren. **aridité** (dite) *f*, aridity, etc.

aristocrate (aristɔkrat) *n*, aristocrat. ¶ *att.* & **aristocratique†** (tik) *a*, aristocratic(al). **aristocratie** (si) *f*, aristocracy.

arithméticien, ne (aritmetisjɛ̃, ɛn) *n*, arithmetician. **arithmétique†** (tik) *a*, arithmetical. ¶ *f*, arithmetic.

arlequin (arləkɛ̃) *m*, harlequin; turncoat (*pers.*); scraps, leavings, leftovers, orts, hash. **arlequinade** (kinad) *f*, harlequinade.

armateur (armatœːr) *m*, [ship]-

owner, [registered] manager (*ship's*).

armature (armaty:r) *f*, trussing; bracing; fastening, strap; reinforcement; armor, sheathing, plating; gear (*pump*); armature (*Phys.*); key signature (*Mus.*); framework (*fig.*).

arme (arm) *f*, arm, weapon; (*pl.*) arms (*Mil.*); branch of the service; [coat of] arms, [armorial] bearings. ~ *à feu*, firearm. ~ [*à feu*] *portative*, small arm. ~ *blanche*, side arm; cold steel. *sans* ~*s*, unarmed. *faire* (ou *tirer*) *des* ~*s*, to fence.

armée (arme) *f*, army, force[s]; host. *A*~ *du Salut*, Salvation Army.

armeline (armɔlin) *f*, ermine (*fur*).

armement (armɔmɑ̃) *m*, arming; armament; fitting out, equipment; manning; shipping; shipowners.

Arménie (**l'**) (armeni) *f*, Armenia. **arménien, ne** (njɛ̃, ɛn) *a*. & *A*~, *n*, Armenian.

armer (arme) *v.t*, to arm; fit out, equip; man; commission (*ship*); truss, brace; reinforce, armor, sheathe; set (*Phot. shutter*); cock (*gun*), sign (*clef*); dub (*knight*); (*v.i.*) to arm.

armoire (armwa:r) *f*, cupboard, cabinet, wardrobe. ~ *à pharmacie*, medicine cabinet. ~ *vitrée*, display cabinet, china cabinet.

armoiries (armwari) *f.pl*, [coat of] arms, [armorial] bearings. **armorial, e** (mɔrjal) *a*. & *m*, armorial. **armorier** (rje) *v.t*, to [em]blazon.

armure (army:r) *f*, armor, sheathing; armature (*Phys.*). ~ *complète*, suit of armor. **armurier** (myrje) *m*, gunsmith; armorer.

arnica (arnika) *f*, arnica.

aromatique (arɔmatik) *a*, aromatic. **arôme** (ro:m) *m*, aroma.

arpège (arpɛ:ʒ) *m*, arpeggio.

arpent (arpɑ̃) *m*, acre.

arpentage (arpɑ̃ta:ʒ) *m*, land measuring, surveying. **arpenter** (te) *v.t*, to measure, survey; pace, tramp. **arpenteur** (tœr:r) *m*, [land] surveyor.

arquer (arke) *v.t*. & *i*. & *s'*~, to arch, curve, bend.

arrache-clou (araʃklu) *m*, nail extractor. **d'arrache-pied**, *ad*, without intermission; on end, at a stretch. **arracher** (ʃe) *v.t*, to pluck, pull, tear, draw; drag; uproot, dig up; extract; wring; snatch; squeeze, extort, screw out. **arracheur, euse** (ʃœ:r, ø:z) *n*, drawer, puller; (*f.*) grubber.

arraisonner (arɛzɔne) *v.t*, to visit. (*Cust.*).

arrangeant, e (arɑ̃ʒɑ̃, ɑ̃:t) *a*, accommodating, obliging. **arrangement** (ʒmɑ̃) *m*, arrangement; settlement. **arranger** (ʒe) *v.t*, to arrange; settle. **s'**~, to agree, come to terms; settle down; get on, manage. *arrangez-vous!* do the best you can! do as you like!

arrenter (arɑ̃te) *v.t*, to lease.

arrérager (areraʒe) *v.i*, to get (*or* fall) into arrear[s]. **arrérages** (ra:ʒ) *m.pl*, interest (*on Government stocks or the like*); rent, pension, or the like, accrued & due.

arrestation (arɛstasjɔ̃) *f*, arrest, custody. **arrêt** (rɛ) *m*, stoppage, stop; arrest; seizure, detention; standstill; catch; tackle (*Foot.*); judgment, sentence; decree. ~ *en cours de route*, break of journey. ~ *facultatif*, cars stop here if required. ~ *fixe*, all cars stop here. *aux* ~*s*, under arrest (*Mil.*); kept in (*Sch.*). **arrêté, e** (te) *p.a*, decided, settled, preconcerted. ¶ *m*, order, decree; making up, closing, ruling off, rest (*Bkkpg.*). **arrêter** (te) *v.t*. & *i*, to stop; arrest; seize, detain; fix; retain, engage; conclude; make up, close, rule off (*Bkkpg.*); fasten off (*Need.*); agree upon; decide on; (*v.t*. & *abs.*) point, set (*dog*). **s'**~, to stop, stay, call; draw up (*carriage*).

arrhes (a:r) *f.pl*, deposit, earnest [money].

arrière (arjɛ:r) *m*, back [part]; back (*Foot.*); rear; tail; stern. **en** ~, behind; behind-hand; back, at the back, in the rear; astern; with one's back to the engine.

Note: arrière in *comps* is pronounced arjɛr, thus, ~*-bouche* (arjɛrbuʃ) *f*, fauces. ~*-garde*, *f*, rear guard. *arrière-grand-mère*, *f*, *arrière-grand-père*, *m*, greatgrandmother, -father. ~*-main*, *m*, backhand (*Ten.*). ~*-neveu*, *m*, ~*-nièce*, *f*, grandnephew, -niece. ~*-pensée*, *f*, ulterior motive, mental reservation. ~*-petite-fille*, *f*, great-granddaughter. ~*-petit-fils*, *m*, g.-grandson. ~*-petits-enfants*, *m.pl*, g.-grandchildren. ~*-plan*, *m*, background. ~*-point*, *m*, backstitch (*Need.*). ~*-port*, *m*, inner harbor. **arriéré, e** (rjere) *a*, overdue, in arrear[s]; outstanding, owing; behindhand; backward (*child*); old-fashioned. ¶ *m*, arrears. **arriérer** (re) *v.t*, to put off, defer, hold over. **s'~**, to fall behind; get into arrears.

arrimer (arime) *v.t*, to stow, trim. **arrimeur** (mœːr) *m*, stower, trimmer; stevedore.

arrivage (arivaːʒ) *m*, arrival. **arrivée** (ve) *f*, arrival, coming; finish[ing] (*sport*), [winning] post; home (*running*); inlet. à l'~ & d'~, incoming; at the finish, finishing. **arriver** (ve) *v.i*, to arrive, come; get; finish; happen, come about, c. to pass, occur, befall; be due (*train*); succeed. ~ *à égalité*, to tie (*sport*). *arrive que pourra*, come what may, whate'er betide. **arriviste** (arivist) *m. f*, pusher, social climber.

arrogamment (arɔgamɑ̃) *ad*, arrogantly. **arrogance** (gɑ̃ːs) *f*, arrogance, assumption. **arrogant, e** (gɑ̃, ɑ̃ːt) *a*, arrogant, overbearing. **s'arroger** (ɔʒe) *v.pr*, to arrogate [to oneself], assume.

arroi (arwa) *m*, plight, pickle.

arrondir (arɔ̃diːr) *v.t*, to round [off]. **arrondissement** (dismɑ̃) *m*, rounding; ward, district.

arroser (aroze) *v.t*, to water, [be]sprinkle, bedew, wet; baste; stand treat. *ça s'arrose*, that calls for a drink. **arrosoir** (zwaːr) *m*, watering can.

arsenal (arsənal) *m*, arsenal. ~ *maritime*, naval dockyard.

art (aːr) *m*, art, skill; artfulness,

artifice. ~*s d'agrément*, accomplishments.

artère (artɛːr) *f*, artery; thoroughfare; feeder (*Elec.*). **artériel, le** (terjɛl) *a*, arterial.

artésien, ne (artezjɛ̃, ɛn) *a*, Artesian.

arthrite (artrit) *f*, arthritis.

artichaut (artiʃo) *m*, artichoke; spikes.

article (artikl) *m*, article, subject, matter; section, clause, item, entry; requisite, material, commodity, (*pl.*) wares. ~ *à côté*, side line. ~ *de fond*, leading article, leader. ~[*s*] *de Paris*, artistic novelties, fancy goods. ~*s dépareillés*, oddments.

articulation (artikylasjɔ̃) *f*, articulation, joint; deployment; knuckle; utterance. **articuler** (le) *v.t. & i. & s'~*, to articulate, joint, link; utter.

artifice (artifis) *m*, artifice, artfulness, craft; contrivance; art. ~*s de théâtre*, stage effects. **artificiel, le†** (sjɛl) *a*, artificial. **artificier** (sje) *m*, pyrotechnist. **artificieux, euse†** (sjø, øːz) *a*, artful, cunning, crafty.

artillerie (artijri) *f*, artillery, ordnance; gunnery. ~ *de place*, garrison artillery. **artilleur** (jœːr) *m*, artilleryman, gunner.

artimon (artimɔ̃) *m*, mizzen mast; m. sail.

artisan, e (artizɑ̃, an) *n*, artisan; craftsman; operative; (*fig.*) author, originator, artificer, architect. ~ *en bois*, woodworker.

artison (artizɔ̃) *m*, wood worm; clothes moth. **artisonné, e** (zɔne) *a*, worm-eaten; moth-eaten.

artiste (artist) *n*, artist; artiste, performer. **artiste† & artistique** (tik) *a*, artistic.

aryen, ne (arjɛ̃, ɛn) *a*, Aryan.

as (ɑːs) *m*, ace. ~ *de l'aviation*, flying ace. ~ *de pique*, ace of spades (*Cards*); rump, parson's nose (*fowl*).

asbeste (azbɛst) *m*, asbestos.

ascendance (asɑ̃dɑ̃ːs) *f*, ancestry.

ascendant, e (asɑ̃dɑ̃, ɑ̃ːt) *a*, ascending, upward. ¶ *m*, ascendant, -ent; ascendancy, -ency; (*pl.*) ancestry. **ascenseur** (sœːr) *m*, elevator. **ascension** (sjɔ̃) *f*, ascent, climb, rising, ascension. l'A~, Ascension day. **ascensionniste** (ɔnist) *n*, climber, mountaineer.

ascète (asɛt) *n. &* **ascétique** (setik) *a*, ascetic.

asiatique (azjatik) *a. &* A~, *n*, Asiatic. l'Asie (zi) *f*, Asia. *l'~ Mineure*, Asia Minor.

asile (azil) *m*, asylum, shelter; home; haven, sanctuary. *~ d'aliénés*, mental institution.

aspect (aspɛ) *m*, aspect, sight, appearance, look, bearing; complexion.

asperge (aspɛrʒ) *f*, asparagus.

asperger (aspɛrʒe) *v.t*, to [be]sprinkle, asperse.

aspérité (asperite) *f*, asperity, roughness.

aspersion (aspɛrsjɔ̃) *f*, aspersion, sprinkling.

asphalte (asfalt) *m*, asphalt.

asphyxie (asfiksi) *f*, asphyxia, suffocation, gassing. **asphyxier** (sje) *v.t*, to asphyxiate, etc.

aspic (aspik) *m*, asp; slanderer, backbiter; aspic.

aspirail (aspiraːj) *m*, air hole, vent, flue.

aspirant, e (aspirɑ̃, ɑ̃ːt) *n*, aspirant, suitor; candidate. *~* [*de marine*], midshipman. **aspirateur** [*de poussières*] (ratœːr) *m*, vacuum cleaner. **aspiration** (sjɔ̃) *f*, aspiration; inspiration; yearning. **aspirer** (re) *v.t*, to inspire, inhale, exhaust, suck, draw; aspirate; (*v.i.*) to aspire.

aspirine (aspirin) *f*, aspirin.

assagir (asaʒiːr) *v.t*, to make wiser; sober; steady.

assaillant (asajɑ̃) *m*, assailant. **assaillir** (jiːr) *v.t.ir*, to assail, assault.

assainir (aseniːr) *v.t*, to cleanse, sanitate.

assaisonnement (asɛzɔnmɑ̃) *m*, seasoning, flavoring; dressing (*salad*); condiment, relish. **assaisonner** (ne) *v.t*, to season, etc. leaven (*fig.*).

assassin, e (asasɛ̃, in) *n*, assassin, murderer, ess. *à l'~!* murder! ¶ *a*, bewitching, killing (*looks, eyes*). **assassinat** (sina) *m*, assassination, murder. **assassiner** (ne)

v.t, to assassinate, murder, kill; tire to death, bore, plague.

assaut (aso) *m*, assault, storming, onset, onslaught; match, bout. *~ d'armes*, assault of (*or* at) arms, fencing match. *~ de démonstration*, sparring match.

assèchement (asɛʃmɑ̃) *m*, drainage; drying. **assécher** (seʃe) *v.t. & i*, to drain, dry.

assemblage (asɑ̃blaːʒ) *m*, assemblage, congregation; joint (*in wood, metal, etc.*). **assemblée** (ble) *f*, meeting, assembly, conclave, congregation; meet (*Hunt.*). **assembler** (ble), *v.t*, to assemble, collect, gather, summon; join. s'~, to meet, assemble, congregate, flock.

assener (asəne) *v.t*, to strike, deal (*blow*).

assentiment (asɑ̃timɑ̃) *m*, assent.

asseoir (aswaːr) *v.t.ir*, to seat, set, bed, base, fix, secure, establish; pitch (*camp, tent*). s'~, to sit [down].

assermenter (asɛrmɑ̃te) *v.t*, to swear in.

assertion (asɛrsjɔ̃) *f*, assertion.

asservir (asɛrviːr) *v.t*, to enslave.

assez (ase) *ad*, enough, rather, pretty, fairly.

assidu, e (asidy) *a*, assiduous, sedulous, industrious; regular. **assiduité** (dɥite) *f*, assiduity, etc. **assidûment** (dymɑ̃), *ad*, assiduously, etc.

assiégeant (asjeʒɑ̃) *m*, besieger. **assiéger** (ʒe) *v.t*, to besiege, beleaguer, beset, crowd round, throng; dun.

assiette (asjɛt) *f*, plate; seat, seating, bed, base, foundation; basis; set, firmness, steadiness, stability, security; trim (*ship*). **assiettée** (te) *f*, plateful.

assignation (asiɲasjɔ̃) *f*, assignation; assignment; charge; summons; writ; subpoena. **assigner** (ɲe) *v.t*, to assign; charge; summon; cite; subpoena.

assimiler (asimile) *v.t*, to assimilate, liken, compare.

assis (asi) *p.a*, seated, sitting; established.

assise (asiːz) *f*, bed, foundation;

course (*Build.*); (*pl.*) assize[s]
(*law*).

assistance (asistɑ̃ːs) *f*, assistance, aid, help; attendance, audience. ~ *judiciaire*, legal aid. ~ *privée*, private charity. ~ *publique*, public assistance *or* relief. ~ *sociale*, social welfare work. **assistant, e** (tɑ̃, ɑ̃ːt) *n*, assistant; bystander, onlooker. **assister** (te) *v.t*, to assist, aid, help. ~ *à*, to attend, be present at, witness.

association (asɔsjasjɔ̃) *f*, association; society; g[u]ild; partnership. **associé, e** (sje) *n*, associate, member, partner. **associer** (sje) *v.t*, to associate; take into partnership.

assoiffé (aswafe) *a*, thirsty.

assolement (asɔlmɑ̃) *m*, rotation (*crops*).

assombrir (asɔ̃briːr) *v.t*, to darken, gloom, cloud.

assommant, e (asɔmɑ̃, ɑ̃ːt) *a*, killing, oppressive, overwhelming, tiresome, wearisome, boring. **assommer** (me) *v.t*, to knock down, fell, strike dead; beat, thrash, nearly kill; overwhelm, weary to death, bore. **assommoir** (mwaːr) *m*, bludgeon, life preserver, lethal weapon; pole-axe; deadfall; dram shop.

assomption (asɔ̃psjɔ̃) *f*, Assumption (*Eccl.*).

assortiment (asɔrtimɑ̃) *m*, assortment; set; blend; match. **assortir** (tiːr) *v.t. & i*, to assort, supply; stock; blend; match; suit. **assortissant, e** (tisɑ̃, ɑ̃ːt) *a*, suitable, becoming.

assoupir (asupiːr) *v.t*, to make drowsy, send to sleep, lull, deaden; hush up. s'~, to doze; die down. **assoupissant, e** (pisɑ̃, ɑ̃ːt) *a*, dull, humdrum. **assoupissement** (pismɑ̃) *m*, drowsiness; lethargy.

assouplir (asupliːr) *v.t*, to make supple; make tractable; soften.

assourdir (asurdiːr) *v.t*, to deafen, muffle; tone down.

assouvir (asuviːr) *v.t*, to satiate, glut.

assujettir (asyʒɛtiːr) *v.t*, to subject, subdue; bind, tie down; fix, fasten.

assumer (asyme) *v.t*, to assume.

assurance (asyrɑ̃ːs) *f*, assurance; confidence; security, pledge; insurance. ~ *contre les accidents du travail*, workmen's compensation i. ~ *maritime*, marine i., sea i. ~*s sociales*, social security. ~ *sur la vie*, life i. **assuré†, e** (re) *a*, assured, sure, safe; confident, bold. *mal* ~, insecure, unsafe. ¶ (*pers.*) *n*, insured, assured. **assurer** (re) *v.t*, to assure, ensure, insure, secure, guarantee; make fast, steady, set, strengthen; affirm; confirm. s'~, to make sure; trust; insure (*Insce.*). **assureur** (rœːr) *m*, insurer, underwriter.

Assyrie (l') (asiri) *f*, Assyria. **assyrien, ne** (rjɛ̃, ɛn) *a. & A~, n*, Assyrian.

aster (astɛːr) *m*, aster.

astérisque (asterisk) *m*, asterisk, star.

astéroïde (asterɔid) *m*, asteroid.

asthmatique (asmatik) *a. & n*, asthmatic. **asthme** (asm) *m*, asthma.

asticot (astiko) *m*, gentle, maggot.

asticoter (astikɔte) *v.t*, to tease.

astigmate (astigmat) *a*, astigmatic.

astiquer (astike) *v.t*, to polish.

astre (astr) *m*, star, luminary.

astreindre (astrɛ̃ːdr) *v.t.ir*, to bind, tie down, compel. **astreinte** (trɛ̃ːt) *f*, penalty.

astringent, e (astrɛ̃ʒɑ̃, ɑ̃ːt) *a. & m*, astringent.

astrologie (astrɔlɔʒi) *f*, astrology. **astrologue** (lɔg) *m*, astrologer.

astronome (astrɔnɔm) *m*, astronomer. **astronomie** (mi) *f*, astronomy. **astronomique†** (mik) *a*, astronomic(al).

astuce (astys) *f*, astuteness, artfulness, craftiness, guile. **astucieux, euse†** (sjø, ɸːz) *a*, astute, etc.

atelier (atəlje) *m*, [work]shop, mill, house, workroom, studio; staff; students.

atermoiement (atɛrmwamɑ̃) *m*, delay, procrastination, evasion. **atermoyer** (je) *v.i*, to procrastinate.

athée (ate) *m*, atheist. ¶ *a*, atheistic. **athéisme** (teism) *m*, atheism.

Athènes (atɛn) *f*, Athens. **athénien, ne** (tenjɛ̃, ɛn) *a.* & A~, *n*, Athenian.

athlète (atlɛt) *m*, athlete. **athlétique** (letik) *a*, athletic. **athlétisme** (letism) *m*, athletics.

atlantique (atlɑ̃tik) *a*, Atlantic. l'[océan] A~, *m*, the A. [ocean].

atlas (atlɑːs) *m*, atlas; [book of] plates.

atmosphère (atmɔsfɛːr) *f*, atmosphere; medium (*ether*). **atmosphérique** (ferik) *a*, atmospheric(al), air (*att.*).

atome (atoːm) *m*, atom; mote. **atomique** (tɔmik) *a*, atomic(al).

atone (atoːne) *a*, atonic, toneless, lackluster, dull; unstressed (*Gram.*).

atours (atuːr) *m.pl*, finery.

atout (atu) *m*, trump [card], trumps.

âtre (ɑːtr) *m*, hearth, fireplace.

atroce† (atrɔs) *a*, atrocious, heinous, outrageous; excruciating. **atrocité** (site) *f*, atrocity, etc.

atrophie (atrɔfi) *f*, atrophy, wasting away.

attabler (s') (atable) *v.pr*, to sit down [to table].

attachant, e (ataʃɑ̃, ɑ̃ːt) *a*, interesting; engaging, winning. **attache** (taʃ) *f*, tie, fastening, leash, binder, bond, band, clip, paper fastener; attachment. **attaché** (ʃe) *m*, attaché. **attachement** (ʃmɑ̃) *m*, attachment; fondness; devotion. **attacher** (ʃe) *v.t*, to attach, tie, fasten, bind; rivet (*attention*). s'~, to fasten, devote oneself, cling, stick.

attaque (atak) *f*, attack, onset, onslaught, raid; fit, stroke, seizure, **attaquer** (ke) *v.t*, to attack, set on, assault; spur on; impugn. ~ en justice, to bring an action against. s'~à, to attack; tackle, grapple with.

attardé (atarde) *a*, belated; backward, old-fashioned.

attarder (s') (atarde) *v.pr*, to loiter, linger.

atteindre (atɛ̃ːdr) *v.t.ir*, to reach, attain; strike; hit; overtake, catch [up]; affect. **atteinte** (tɛ̃ːt) *f*, reach, etc.; blow, stroke, cut; reflection, slur.

attelage (atlaːʒ) *m*, harnessing;

coupling; team. **atteler** (tle) *v.t*, to harness, yoke, attach, couple.

attelle (atɛl) *f*, splint; (*pl*.) hames.

attenant, e [à] (atnɑ̃, ɑ̃ːt) *a*, adjoining.

attendant (en) (atɑ̃dɑ̃) *ad*, meanwhile, in the mean time. ¶ *pr*, pending. **en attendant que**, *c*, till, until. **attendre** (tɑ̃ːdr) *v.t.* & *i*, to wait for, wait, stay, expect, await, bide, look forward to. s'~ à, to expect, look for; rely on.

attendrir (atɑ̃driːr) *v.t*, to soften, move, melt, affect.

attendu (atɑ̃dy) *pr*, considering. ~ **que**, *c*, seeing that, whereas.

attentat (atɑ̃ta) *m*, (criminal) attempt, assault, outrage. **attentatoire** (twaːr) *a*, prejudicial.

attente (atɑːt) *f*, waiting, expectation.

attenter à (atɑ̃te), to make an attempt on.

attentif, ive† (atɑ̃tif, iːv) *a*, attentive, careful, mindful. **attention** (sjɔ̃) *f*, attention; notice; care[fulness]; heed; kindness. *faire* ~, to pay attention, mind.

atténuer (atenɥe) *v.t*, to attenuate, weaken; minimize; extenuate.

atterrer (atɛre) *v.t*, to overwhelm, dumbfound.

atterrir (atɛriːr) *v.i*, to land, alight.

attestation (atɛstasjɔ̃) *f*, attestation; certificate, testimonial. **attester** (te) *v.t*, to attest, testify, vouch, certify, witness.

attiédir (atjediːr) *v.t*, to cool; warm; make lukewarm.

attifer (atife) *v.t*, to dress up.

attique (atik) *a*, Attic.

attirail (atiraːj) *m*, appliances, apparatus, implements, habiliment; string; baggage, paraphernalia; show, pomp.

attirance (atirɑːs) *f*, attraction. **attirer** (re) *v.t*, to attract, draw; lure; win. s'~, to incur, win.

attiser (atize) *v.t*, to stir, poke; fan (*fig.*).

attitré, e (atitre) *a*, accredited, recognized; by appointment.

attitude (atityd) *f*, attitude, posture.

attouchement (atuʃmɑ̃) *m*, touching, contact.

attractif, ive (atraktif, i:v) *a*, attractive (*Phys.*). **attraction** (ksjɔ̃) *f*, attraction; draw; loadstone; (*pl.*) varieties (*Theat.*); (*pl.*) cabaret [show].

attrait (atrɛ) *m*, attraction; draw; appeal; inclination, bent; (*pl.*) charms.

attrape (atrap) *f*, trap, catch, hoax. **~nigaud**, *m*, booby trap. **attraper** (pe) *v.t*, to [en]trap, [en]snare, catch, take in, hoax; draw (*in lottery*); hit; hit off. **s'~**, to get caught.

attrayant, e (atrɛjɑ̃, ɑ̃:t) *a*, attractive, engaging, winning.

attribuer (atribɥe) *v.t*, to attribute, ascribe; predicate; father; allot. **attribuable** (abl) *a*, attributable, etc. **attribut** (by) *m*, attribute; predicate. **attributaire** (tɛ:r) *n*, allottee. **attribution** (sjɔ̃) *f*, attribution; allotment. *les ~s*, powers, duties.

attrister (atriste) *v.t*, to sadden.

attrition (atrisjɔ̃) *f*, attrition, abrasion.

attroupement (atrupmɑ̃), *m*, unlawful assembly; mob; riot.

aubade (obad) *f*, aubade; catcalling.

aubaine (obɛn) *f*, windfall, godsend.

aube (o:b) *f*, dawn; alb; blade, vane, paddle, float.

aubépine (obepin) *f*, hawthorn.

auberge (obɛrʒ) *f*, inn; hostel. **aubergiste** (ʒist) *n*, innkeeper, landlord, -lady.

aubergine (obɛrʒin) *f*, eggplant.

aubier (obje) *m*, sapwood.

aucun, e (okœ̃, yn) *a. & pn*, any; anyone; (*neg.*) no, none; no one. **aucunement** (kynmɑ̃) *ad*, in any way; (*neg.*) not at all, by no means, nowise.

audace (odas) *f*, audacity, boldness, daring. *payer d'~*, to face the music. **audacieux, euse†** (sjø, ø:z) *a*, audacious, etc.

au-delà, au-dessous *see* delà, dessous.

au-devant (odvɑ̃) *ad*, forward, ahead. *aller ~ de*, to go to meet.

audience (odjɑ̃:s) *f*, audience, hearing; court. **audience, trice** (ditœ:r, tris) *n*, hearer, listener, auditor; prosecutor. **audition**

(sjɔ̃) *f*, hearing, audition; concert; recital. **auditoire** (twa:r) *m*, audience; auditorium; congregation.

auge (o:ʒ) *f*, **auget** (oʒɛ) *m*, trough, bucket. **augée** (oʒe) *f*, troughful, bucketful.

augmenter (ɔgmɑ̃te) *v.t. & i*, to increase, augment, enlarge, enhance; supplement. **augmentation** (tasjɔ̃) *f*, increase; raise (*in salary*).

augure (ogy:r) *m*, augury, omen; prophet, augur. **augurer** (gyre) *v.t*, to augur, make.

auguste (ogyst) *a*, august.

aujourd'hui (oʒurdɥi) *ad. & m*, today. *d'~ en huit, en quinze*, a week from today, fortnight.

aumône & l'aumône (omo:n) *f*, alms, charity. **aumônier** (monje) *m*, chaplain.

aune (o:n) *m*, alder.

auparavant (oparavɑ̃), *ad*, before[hand].

auprès (oprɛ) *ad*, near, close [by], [near] at hand. **~ de**, *pr*, near, close to *or* by, by; [attached] to; with; in.

auquel *see* lequel.

auréole (oreɔl) *f*, aureole, halo; halation (*Phot.*).

auriculaire (ɔrikylɛ:r) *a*, auricular, ear (*att.*). [**doigt**] **~**, *m*, little (*or* fourth) finger.

aurifère (ɔrifɛ:r) *a*, auriferous, gold (*att.*).

aurore (ɔrɔ:r) *f*, dawn, daybreak, morn; aurora. **~ boréale**, aurora borealis, northern lights.

ausculter (ɔskylte) *v.t*, to sound (*Med.*).

auspice (ospis) *m*, auspice, omen.

aussi (osi) *ad*, also, too, likewise; so; as. ¶ *c*, therefore, consequently, so. **~ bien**, besides, moreover. **~ bien que**, *c*, as well as. **aussitôt** (to) *ad*, directly, at once. **~ dit, ~ fait**, no sooner said than done. **~ que**, *c*, as soon as.

austère† (ostɛ:r) *a*, austere, stern. **austérité** (terite) *f*, austerity, etc.

austral (ostral) *a*, austral, southern. **l'Australasie** (lazi) *f*, Australasia. **l'Australie** (li),

Australia. **australien, ne** (ljɛ̃, ɛn) *a.* & A~, *n,* Australian.

autan (otɑ̃) (*Poet.*) *m,* storm, blast.

autant (otɑ̃), *ad,* as (*or* so) much, as many, as far, as well, as good, as often. ~ *que,* as much as, as far as. **d'~ que,** *c,* especially as.

autel (otɛl) *m,* altar.

auteur (otœːr) *m,* author; writer; composer; originator; founder (*race*); progenitor; perpetrator (*crime*); party at fault (*accident*); inventor; designer; informant; doer. *les* ~*s de nos jours,* our progenitors. ~ *dramatique,* playwright.

authentique† (otɑ̃tik) *a,* authentic, genuine. **authenticité** (site) *f,* authenticity, etc.

auto (otɔ, oto) *préfixe,* auto, self-, *e.g, papier* ~*-vireur,* self-toning paper (*Phot.*).

auto (ɔto, oto)*f,* auto, car.

autobiographie (otɔbiɔgrafi) *f,* autobiography.

autobus (otɔbyːs) *m,* bus.

autocar (otɔkaːr) *m,* bus.

autochenille (otɔʃniːj) *f,* caterpillar tractor.

autocrate, trice (otɔkrat, tris) *n,* autocrat. **autocratie** (si) *f,* autocracy. **autocratique** (tik) *a,* autocratic(al).

autodidacte (otɔdidakt) *a,* self-taught.

autogène (otɔʒɛːn) *a,* autogenous.

autographe (otɔgraf) *m.* & *a,* autograph.

automate (otɔmat) *m,* automaton. **automatique†** (tik) *a,* automatic(al), self-acting.

automnal, e (otɔmnal) *a,* autumnal. **automne** (tɔn) *m,* autumn, fall.

automobile (o- *ou* ɔtɔmɔbil) *a,* self-propelling, motor (*att.*). ¶ *f,* automobile. **automobilisme** (lism) *m,* motoring. **automobiliste** (list) *n,* motorist.

autonome (otɔnɔm) *a,* autonomous, self-governing. **autonomie** (mi) *f,* autonomy, self-government.

autopsie (otɔpsi) *f,* postmortem, autopsy.

autorisation (otɔrizasjɔ̃) *f,* authorization, leave; warrant. **autoriser** (ze) *v.t,* to authorize, empower, allow. **autoritaire** (tɛːr) *a,* authoritative. **autorité** (te) *f,* authority; power. *faire* ~, to be regarded as an authority.

autoroute (otorut) *f,* express highway.

autour (otuːr) *m,* goshawk.

autour (otuːr) *ad.* & **autour de,** *pr,* round, around, about.

autre (oːtr) *a* & *pn,* other; another; next (*world*); else. *un* ~ *soi-même,* one's second self. ~ *part,* elsewhere. *à d'*~*s!* nonsense! **autrefois** (otrəfwa) *ad,* formerly; once [upon a time]. **d'~,** of old, of yore; bygone. **autrement** (otrəmɑ̃) *ad,* otherwise; differently; [or] else.

Autriche (l') (otriʃ) *f,* Austria. **autrichien, ne** (ʃjɛ̃, ɛn) *a.* & A~, *n,* Austrian.

autruche (otryʃ) *f,* ostrich.

autrui (otrɥi) *pn,* others, other people.

auvent (ovɑ̃) *m,* penthouse; weatherboard; porch roof; hood.

auxiliaire (oksiljɛːr) *a.* & *m;* auxiliary.

avachi, e (avaʃi) *a,* flabby, baggy; out of shape.

aval (aval) *m,* lower part; tail; guarantee, backing; endorsement. **en** ~, *ad,* downstream, down. **en** ~ **de,** *pr,* down, below.

avalanche (avalɑ̃ːʃ) *f,* avalanche; shower (*fig.*).

avaler (avale) *v.t,* to swallow, devour; stomach; lower; (*v.i.*) to go downstream.

avaliser (avalize) *v.t,* to guarantee, back.

avaloire (avalwaːr) *f,* gullet, throat.

avance (avɑ̃ːs) *f,* advance, start; lead; projection; fast (*on clock*). **à l'~, d'~, en** ~, **par** ~, *ad,* in advance, beforehand. **avancé, e** (vɑ̃se) *p.a,* advance[d]; projecting; late (*hour, etc.*); high (*meat*). **avancer** (se) *v.t,* to advance, put forward, push, hasten; help; promote, further; put on (*clock*); (*v.i.*) to advance; project, jut out; gain (*of clock*). **avance-**

ment (smɑ̃) *m,* advancement; feed (*Mach.*).

avanie (avani) *f,* affront, insult.

avant (avɑ̃) *pr,* before; till, until. *av. J.C., B.C. avant terme,* premature(ly) (*childbirth*). ~ [que] **de,** *pr,* ~ **que,** *c,* before. ¶ *ad,* forward, before, far, deep[ly]. *de l'*~ *à l'arrière,* fore & aft (*Naut.*). **en** ~, *ad,* forward, on, onward[s], ahead, before. *en* ~! forward! go ahead! on! *en* ~, *marche!* quick march! ¶ *m,* front, forepart; fore; head, bow (*Naut.*); steerage; forward (*Foot.*). ~ [*du*] *centre,* center forward. ~*-bras, m,* forearm. ~*-coureur, m,* forerunner, harbinger, herald; (*att.*) premonitory. ~*-dernier, ère, a. & n,* last but one. ~*-garde, f,* van[guard]. ~*-goût, m,* foretaste, earnest. *d'*~*-guerre, a,* prewar. ~*-hier, ad. & m,* the day before yesterday. ~*-hier soir,* the night before last. ~*-main, m,* forehand (*Ten.*). ~*-port, m,* outer harbor. ~*-poste, m,* outpost. ~*-première, f,* dress rehearsal; private view (*art*). ~*-projet, m,* rough draft. ~*-propos, m,* foreword, preface. ~*-scène, f,* proscenium; stage box. ~*-toit, m,* eaves. *l'*~*-veille, f,* two days before.

avantage (avɑ̃taːʒ) *m,* advantage, benefit; odds; leverage; upper hand, pull. ~ [*de jeu*], [ad]vantage [game] (*Ten.*). **avantager** (taʒe) *v.t,* to benefit, favor, endow. **avantageux, euse†** (ʒø, øːz) *a,* advantageous, good, beneficial.

avare† (avaːr) *a,* avaricious; miserly, sparing, chary. ¶ *n,* miser, screw. **avarice** (varis) *f,* avarice. **avaricieux, euse** (sjø, øːz) *a,* avaricious.

avarie (avari) *f,* damage; average (*Marine Law*). **avarier** (rje) *v.t,* to damage. *s'*~, to deteriorate, go bad (*meat, etc.*).

avec (avɛk) *pr,* with. *d'*~, from.

aveline (avlin) *f,* filbert, cob[nut]. **avelinier** (nje) *m,* filbert [tree].

avenant (avnɑ̃) *m,* endorsement (*Insce.*). *à l'*~ **de,** *pr,* in keeping with.

avenant, e (avnɑ̃, ɑ̃ːt) *a,* prepossessing, comely.

avènement (avɛnmɑ̃) *m,* accession; advent, coming (*of Christ*).

avenir (avniːr) *m,* future, prospect, outlook; promise. *à l'*~, *ad,* in future, hereafter; henceforth.

avent (l') (avɑ̃) *m,* advent (*Eccl.*).

aventure (avɑ̃tyːr) *f,* [ad]venture. *dire la bonne* ~, to tell fortunes. *à l'*~, *ad,* haphazard, at random. *d'*~, *par* ~, by chance, perchance. **aventurer** (tyre) *v.t,* to [ad]venture. **aventureux, euse** (rø, øːz) *a,* [ad]venturous. **aventurier, ère** (rje, ɛːr) *n,* adventurer, ess.

avenue (avny) *f,* avenue; drive.

avéré, e (avere) *p.a,* established, proved. **avérer** (avere) *v.t,* to establish; authenticate.

avers (avɛːr) *m,* obverse (*coin*).

averse (avɛrs) *f,* shower.

aversion (avɛrsjɔ̃) *f,* aversion, dislike.

avertir (avɛrtiːr) *v.t,* to notify, [fore]warn, caution. **avertissement** (tismɑ̃) *m,* notification; warning; demand note (*taxes*). **avertisseur** (sœːr) *m,* call boy; alarm; hooter; horn. ~ *d'incendie,* fire alarm.

aveu (avø) *m,* avowal, admission, confession; consent.

aveugle (avœːgl) *a,* blind. ¶ *n,* blind man, woman. *les* ~*s, m.pl,* the blind. **aveuglement** (gləmɑ̃) *m,* blindness (*fig.*). **aveuglément** (glemɑ̃) *ad,* blindly. **aveugler** (gle) *v.t,* to blind; stop (*leak*). *à l'aveuglette* (glɛt), blindly.

aviateur, trice (avjatœr, tris) *a,* flying, flight (*att.*). ¶ *n,* aviator, flier. **aviation** (sjɔ̃) *f,* aviation, flying.

avide† (avid) *a,* greedy, grasping, eager, athirst, avid. **avidité** (dite) *f,* avidity, greed[iness].

avilir (aviliːr) *v.t,* to degrade, debase; depreciate.

aviné, e (avine) *a,* intoxicated; smelling of drink; tipsy (*walk*).

avion (avjɔ̃) *m,* airplane. ~ *à réaction,* jet. *par* ~, by airmail.

aviron (avirɔ̃) *m,* oar. ~ *de*

couple, scull. ~ *de pointe*, single oar (opp. *scull*). *l'*~, rowing.

avis (avi) *m*, opinion; mind; [way of] thinking; judgment; advice; notice, intimation. **avisé, e** (ze) *a*, prudent, circumspect, canny. **aviser** (ze) *v.t*, to advise, notify, warn; espy. *s'*~ *de*, to bethink oneself of, dare to. **aviso** (zo) *m*, dispatch boat.

aviver (avive) *v.t*, to revive, brighten; sharpen (*tool*).

avocasserie (avɔkasri) *f*, pettifoggery. **avocat** (ka) *m*, counsel, lawyer; advocate. ~ *général*, attorney general. **avocate** (kat) *f*, woman barrister.

avoine (avwan) *f*, oats.

avoir (avwaːr) *m*, possessions, property, holding(s); credit[or], Cr (*Bkkpg.*). *tout son* ~, one's all. ¶ *v.t.ir*, to have; hold; keep; get; be; measure; have on; be the matter with, ail. *en* ~, to have some *or* any. *il y a*, there is, there are; it is; ago; for. *il y en a*, there is (are) some. *il n'y en a plus*, there is none left.

avoisinant, e (avwazinɑ̃, ɑ̃ːt) *a*, neighboring, bordering on. **avoisiner** (ne) *v.t*, to border on.

avortement (avɔrtəmɑ̃) *m*, abortion; miscarriage (*fig.*). **avorter** (te) *v.i*, to abort; miscarry. **avorton** (tɔ̃) *m*, abortion (*creature*).

avoué, e (avwe) *p.a*, acknowledged; ostensible. ¶ *m*, lawyer. **avouer** (we) *v.t*, to avow, confess; acknowledge, own. *s'*~ *coupable*, to plead guilty.

avril (avril) *m*, April. *donner un poisson d'* ~ *à*, to make an April fool of.

axe (aks) *m*, axis; spindle; axle. ~ *de manivelle*, crankshaft.

axiome (aksjoːm) *m*, axiom.

ayant cause (ɛjɑ̃) *m*, assign. **ayant droit**, *m*, party [entitled].

azalée (azale) *f*, azalea.

azotate (azɔtat) *m*, nitrate. **azote** (zɔt) *m*, nitrogen. **azoteux, euse** (tø, øːz) *a*, nitrous. **azotique** (tik) *a*, nitric.

azur (azyːr) *m*, azure. **azuré, e** (zyre) *a*, azure.

azyme (azim) *a*, unleavened.

B

babeurre (babœːr) *m*, buttermilk; churn dash[er].

babil (babi) *m*, chatter, tattle, prattle, babble. **babillard, e** (bijaːr, ard) *n*, chatterbox. **babiller** (je) *v.i*, to chatter, etc.

babine (babin) *f*, lip, chap, chop.

babiole (babjɔl) *f*, toy, plaything; trifle, bauble, gewgaw.

bâbord (babɔːr) *m*, port [side] (*Naut.*).

babouches (babuʃ) *f.pl*, mules (*slippers*).

babouin (babwɛ̃) *m*, baboon. *petit* ~, *petite babouine* (win), young monkey (*child*).

babylonien, ne (babilɔnjɛ̃, ɛn) *a*, Babylonian.

bac (bak) *m*, ferry[boat]; vat, trough. ~ *d'éléments*, cell jar (*Elec.*). ~ *transbordeur*, train ferry.

baccalauréat (bakalɔrea) *m*, bachelor's degree.

bacchanal (bakanal) *m*, row; orgy. **bacchanales** (nal) *f.pl*, Bacchanalia.

bâche (baːʃ) *f*, sheet; cloth; tilt; tank; forcing frame. ~ *goudronnée*, tarpaulin.

bachelier, ère (baʃəlje, ɛːr) *n*, bachelor (*science*).

bachique (baʃik) *a*, Bacchic; drinking (*song*).

bachot (baʃo) *m*, wherry; punt; bachelor's degree.

bacille (basil) *m*, bacillus.

bâcler (bɑkle) *v.t*, to bar, bolt; scamp.

bactéries (bakteri) *f.pl*, bacteria.

badaud, e (bado, oːd) *n*, saunterer, idler, gaper.

badigeon (badiʒɔ̃) *m*, distemper (*paint*).

badin, e (badɛ̃, in) *a*, playful, jocose. ¶ *n*, wag. **badine** (din) *f*, switch, cane; (*pl.*) tongs. **badiner** (ne) *v.i*, to jest, poke fun, banter, play, toy; flutter.

bafouer (bafwe) *v.t*, to scoff at.

bafouiller (bafuje) *v.t*, to stammer; talk foolishness.

bâfrer (bɑfre) *v.i*, to guzzle, gormandize.

bagage (bagaːʒ) *m. oft. pl*, luggage, baggage.

bagarre (baga:r) *f*, fray, brawl, broil, scuffle.

bagatelle (bagatɛl) *f*, trifle, bagatelle.

bagne (baɲ) *m*, convict prison.

bagnole (baɲɔl) *f*, cart; automobile.

bagou (bagu) *m*, gift of gab.

bague (bag) *f*, ring; collar; bush (*Mach.*).

baguenauder (bagnode) *v.i*, to trifle, fiddle, peddle, fool about.

baguer (bage) *v.t*, to tack, baste (*Need.*).

bagues sauves (bag so:v), safe & sound, without a scratch.

baguette (bagɛt) *f*, rod, stick, wand; loaf of bread; ramrod; bead (*Arch., etc.*). ~s *à jour*, open clocks *or* clox (*stockings*). ~ *divinatoire* (divinatwa:r), dowsing rod, divining rod.

bahut (bay) *m*, chest, trunk.

bai, e (bɛ) *a. & m*, bay (*horse*).

baie (bɛ) *f*, bay (*Geog.*); berry (*Bot.*); opening (*in wall*). ~ *de porte*, doorway.

baignade (bɛɲad) *f*, bathing; dip; bathing place. **baigner** (ɲe) *v.t. & i. se* ~, to bathe, dip; wash; steep; suffuse; welter. **baigneur, euse** (ɲœ:r, ø:z) *n*, bather; bathman, bath attendant. **baignoire** (ɲwa:r) *f*, bath (*tub*); box (*Theat.*).

bail (ba:j) *m*, lease.

bâiller (baje) *v.i*, to yawn, gape; be ajar.

bailleur, eresse (bajœ:r, jrɛs) *n*, lessor. *bailleur de fonds*, money lender; silent partner.

bâillon (baj5) *m*, gag. **bâillonner** (jɔne) *v.t*, to gag.

bain (bɛ̃) *m*, bath; (*pl. & s.*) bathing; (*pl.*) watering place, spa. ~ *de développement*, ~ *révélateur*, developing bath (*Phot.*). ~ -*douche*, shower bath. ~ *de siège*, sitz b., hip b. ~ *de soleil*, sunbath. ~s *de soleil*, sunbathing. ~ *de virage-fixage*, fixing & toning bath (*Phot.*). ~-*marie* (mari) *m*, water bath; double saucepan; boiler (*in range*). ~ *mixte*, mixed bathing.

baïonnette (bajɔnɛt) *f*, bayonet.

baisemain (bɛzmɛ̃) *m*, kissing [of] hands. **baiser** (ze) *m*, kiss.

¶ *v.t*, to kiss. *Note:* (*slang*) to have sexual intercourse. I kissed my sister, is in French *j'ai embrassé ma sœur.* **baisoter** (zɔte) *v.t*, to smother with kisses, kiss & cuddle.

baisse (bɛs) *f*, fall, drop. **baisser** (se) *v.t. & i*, to lower, let down, put down; drop; cast down; fall; sink. se ~, to stoop, bend. **baissier** (sje) (*Stk Ex.*) *m*, bear, short.

baisure (bɛzy:r) *f*, kissing crust.

bajoue (baʒu) *f*, chop, chap.

bal (bal) *m*, ball, dance; d. hall. ~ *costumé*, ~ *travesti*, fancy dress ball. ~ *masqué*, masked ball. ~ *par souscription*, subscription dance.

balader (balade) *v.i*, to stroll; take a walk. **baladeur** (dœ:r) *m*, stroller, saunterer; selector rod (*auto*). **baladeuse** (dø:z) *f*, trailer; handcart; portable lamp.

baladin, e (baladɛ̃, in) *n*, mountebank, clown; buffoon.

balafre (balafr) *f*, gash, slash; scar. **balafrer** (fre) *v.t*, to gash, etc.

balai (balɛ) *m*, broom; brush; windshield wiper. ~ *d'âtre*, hearth brush. ~ *de bouleau*, birch broom, besom. ~ *de tapis*, carpet broom. ~ *garde-robe*, lavatory brush. ~ *mécanique pour tapis*, carpet sweeper.

balance (balɑ̃:s) *f*, balance; poise; scale; [pair of] scales; suspense. ~ *de vérification*, ~ *d'ordre*, trial balance (*Bkkpg.*). **balancer** (lɑ̃se) *v.t. & i*, to balance, poise, weigh, offset; swing, sway, rock; hold in suspense, be in suspense, waver, halt; dismiss, fire; throw away. se ~, to swing, sway, rock; seesaw; hover. **balancement** (smɑ̃) *m*, balancing. **balancier** (sje) *m*, balancing pole (*tight rope*); beam, bob (*Mach.*); fly press; balance wheel (*Horol.*); pendulum (*Horol.*); scale maker. ~ *monétaire*, coining press. **balançoire** (swa:r) *f*, seesaw; swing (*child's*); twaddle.

balayage (balɛja:ʒ) *m*, sweeping. **balayer** (je) *v.t*, to sweep [out, up]; scavenge. **balayette** (jɛt) *f*, whisk [brush, broom], flick. **balayeur, euse** (jœ:r, ø:z) *n*, sweeper, scavenger. **balayeuse,** f, street sweeper (*Mach.*). ~ *mécanique pour tapis,* carpet sweeper. **balayures** (jyːr) f.pl, sweepings.

balbutier (balbysje) v.t. & i, to stammer, mumble.

balcon (balkɔ̃) m, balcony. [*premier*] ~, dress circle.

baldaquin (baldakɛ̃) m, canopy; tester.

baleine (balɛn) f, whale; whalebone; steel (*corset*); rib (*umbrella*). **baleineau** (no) m, whale calf. **baleinier** (nje) m, whaler (*ship*). **baleinière** (njɛːr) f, whaleboat.

balise (baliːz) f, beacon; sea mark; tow path. **baliser** (lize) v.t, to beacon; buoy.

baliverne (balivɛrn) f. *oft. pl,* twaddle.

Balkans (les) (balkɑ̃) m.pl, the Balkans. **balkanique** (kanik) a, Balkan.

ballade (balad) f, ballad (*poem*).

ballant, e (balɑ̃, ɑ̃ːt) a, swinging, dangling.

ballast (balast) m, ballast (*road, Rly*).

balle (bal) f, ball; bullet, shot; bale; pack; husk, chaff; glume; fore! (*Golf*). ~ *à la volée,* trap ball. ~ *au but,* ~ *mise,* hit.

ballerine (balrin) f, ballet girl. **ballet** (lɛ) m, ballet (*Theat.*).

ballon (balɔ̃) m, balloon; ball; flask, bulb (*Chem.*). ~ *au panier,* basketball. ~ *d'enfant,* toy balloon, ~ *d'essai,* pilot balloon; feeler (*fig.*). ~ *de boxe,* punching bag. ~ [*de football*], [foot]ball. **ballonné, e** (lone) p.a, distended; ballooned (*dress*). **ballonner** (ne) v.t, to distend (*stomach*).

ballot (balo) m, bale; pack; pack (*Mil.*). **ballotter** (lɔte) v.t. & i, to toss, shake, rattle; bob; send from pillar to post; bandy [about].

balnéaire (balneɛːr) a, bathing, watering (*place*), seaside (*resort*).

balourd, e (baluːr, urd) n, lumpish person, hulking fellow. **balourdise** (lurdiːz) f, stupidity; blunder.

balsamier (balzamje) m, balsam [tree]. **balsamine** (min) f, garden

balsam (*plant*). **balsamique** (mik) a, balsamic; balmy.

Baltique (la) [mer] (baltik), the Baltic sea [sea].

balustrade (balystrad) f, balustrade; railing. **balustre** (tr) m, baluster, banister; railing.

bambin, e (bɑ̃bɛ̃, in) n, kid, youngster.

bamboche (bɑ̃bɔʃ) f, spree.

bambou (bɑ̃bu) m, bamboo.

ban (bɑ̃) m, ban. ~*s de mariage,* banns. *mettre aux* ~*s,* to outlaw, banish.

banal, e (banal) a, banal, common[place], trite, hackneyed, humdrum. **banaliser** (lize) v.t, to vulgarize.

banane (banan) f, banana. **bananier** (nje) m, banana [plant, tree].

banc (bɑ̃) m, bench, form, seat, settle; box (*jury*); bank, bed, reef; shoal (*sand, fish*); school (*fish*); floe (*ice*). ~ *à coulisses,* sliding seat (*rowboat*). ~ [*d'église*], pew, ~ *des prévenus,* dock. *sur les* ~*s,* at school (*fig.*).

bancal, e (bɑ̃kal) a, bandy[-legged]; rickety.

bandage (bɑ̃daːʒ) m, bandage; tire; stretching. ~ [*herniaire*] (ɛrnjɛːr), truss. **bande** (bɑ̃ːd) f, band, strip, slip, tape, belt, strap, bandage; streak; wrapper; heel, list (*Naut.*); cushion (*Bil.*); blurb; troop, company, pack, gang, crew, party, set; ring; flock, flight. ~ *molletière,* puttee. ~ *noire,* terrorist band. ~ *sonore,* sound track. **bandeau** (bɑ̃do) m, headband, bandeau; bandage (*over eyes*); veil (*fig.*), **bander** (de) v.t, to bandage, bind, tie up; stretch, tense, bend, key up; brace; tire (*wheels*). ~ [*les yeux à, de*], to blindfold; hoodwink.

banderole (bɑ̃drɔl) f, bande-rol[e], streamer.

bandit (bɑ̃di) m, bandit, robber; ruffian.

bandoulière (bɑ̃duljɛːr) f, bandolier, shoulder strap. *en* ~, slung [over shoulder].

banlieue (bɑ̃ljø) f, suburbs, outskirts. *de* ~, suburban.

banne (ban) f, sheet; tilt; awning; blind (*shop*); hamper.

bannière (banjɛːr) *f*, banner.

bannir (baniːr) *v.t*, to banish; expel.

banque ((bãːk) *f*, bank; banking.

banqueroute (bãkrut) *f*, bankruptcy. *faire* ~, to go bankrupt. **banqueroutier, ère** (tje, ɛːr) *n*, bankrupt.

banquet (bãkɛ) *m*, banquet.

banquette (bãkɛt) *f*, bench, seat; bunker (*golf*).

banquier (bãkje) *m*, banker; broker. ~ *en valeurs*, stockbroker. ¶ *a*, banking.

banquise (bãkiːz) *f*, ice floe.

banquiste (bãkist) *m*, humbug, charlatan.

baptême (batɛːm) *m*, baptism, christening. ~ *du tropique*, ~ *de la ligne*, crossing the line ducking. **baptiser** (tize) *v.t*, to baptize, christen; bless (*bell, etc.*); nickname, dub; water, dilute. **baptismal, e** (tismal) *a*, baptismal. **baptistère** (tɛːr) *m*, baptistry.

baquet (bakɛ) *m*, bucket, tub, trough. ~-*baignoire*, *m*, bathtub.

bar (baːr) *m*, bar (*drinking*); bass (*fish*).

baragouin (baragwɛ̃) *m*, gibberish, jargon, lingo. **baragouiner** (gwine) *v.i. & t*, to gibber; jabber.

baraque (barak) *f*, hut; booth; hovel.

baraterie (baratri) *f*, barratry.

baratte (barat) *f*, churn. **baratter** (te) *v.t*, to churn.

Barbade (la) (barbad), Barbado[e]s.

barbare (barbaːr) *a*, barbaric; barbarian; barbarous. ¶ *m*, barbarian. **barbarie** (bari) *f*, barbarism; barbarity. **barbarisme** (rism) *m*, barbarism (*Gram.*).

barbe (barb) *f*, beard; shaving; shave; barb (*feather*); awn; whiskers (*cat*); wattle; (*pl.*) burr; mold (*fungi*). *B-~-Bleue*, *m*, Bluebeard. ~ *de bouc*, goatee. *se faire faire la* ~, to get shaved. **barbelé, e** (bəle) *a*, barbed, spiked. **barbiche** (biʃ) *f*, goatee. **barbier** (bje) *m*, barber. **barbifier** (fje) *v.t*, to shave. **barbon** (bɔ̃) *m*, [old] fog[e]ly.

barboter (barbɔte) *v.i*, to dabble, paddle, splash about; flounder; wade; mumble. **barbotage** (taːʒ) *m*, dabbling, etc; mash (*for cattle*). **barboteur** (tœːr) *m*, paddler; mudlark; muddler, flounderer; duck (*tame*). **barboteuse** (tøːz) *f*, rompers.

barbouiller (barbuje) *v.t*, to daub, [be]smear; blur; scribble; bungle; mumble.

barbu, e (barby) *a*, bearded. ¶ *f*, brill.

Barcelone (barsəlɔn) *f*, Barcelona.

bardane (bardan) *f*, burdock, bur[r].

barde (bard) *m*, bard, poet; (*f.*) packsaddle; slice of bacon.

bardot (bardo) *m*, hinny.

barème (barɛm) *m*, ready reckoner; scale; graph.

barguigner (bargiɲe) *v.t*, to shilly-shally, haggle.

baril (bari) *m*, barrel, cask. **barillet** (rijɛ) m, keg; cylinder, barrel, drum.

bariolage (barjɔlaːʒ) *m*, medley, motley. **bariolé (le)** *p.a*, motley, particolored, pied.

baromètre (barɔmɛtr) *m*, barometer, glass. **barométrique** (metrik) *a*, barometric(al).

baron, ne (barɔ̃, ɔn) *n*, baron, ess.

baroque (barɔk) *a*, odd, queer, quaint.

barque (bark) *f*, boat, smack, bark.

barrage (bɑraːʒ) *m*, barrier; dam; weir; barrage; closing (*street*); paying off (*tie*). **barre** (baːr) *f*, bar, rod, rail; stroke; stripe; cross (*on letter t*); helm, tiller, wheel (*Naut.*). ~ *à sphères*, barbell. ~ *d'eau*, [tidal] bore. ~ *de flot*, tidal wave. ~ *de plage*, surf. ~ *fixe*, horizontal bar. [*jeu de*] ~*s*, prisoner's base. **barreau** (bɑro) *m*, bar (*lit. & law*); rung. **barrer** (re) *v.t*, to bar, rail; fence off; close; dam; cross out, strike out, blue-pencil. **barrette** (rɛt) *f*, (small) bar; bar brooch; biretta; cardinal's cap. **barreur** (rœːr) *m*, man at the wheel; helmsman; coxswain.

barricade (barikad) *f*, barricade.

barricader (de) *v.t*, to barricade.

barrière (barjɛːr) *f*, barrier, fence; bar; gate; toll gate; starting post; lists (*Hist.*).

barrique (barik) *f*, cask, hogshead.

barrir (bariːr) *v.i*, to trumpet (*elephant*).

baryton (baritɔ̃) *m*, baritone; b. saxhorn.

bas, se (bɑ, ɑːs) *a*, low, lower, nether, down; shallow; cloudy; mean, vile, base, degrading; vulgar; cheap. *bas âge*, infancy. *avoir la vue basse*, to be shortsighted. **bas,** *ad*, low, low down, down; off. ¶ *m*, bottom, foot; lower notes (*Mus.*); stocking; (*pl.*) hose. à ~, *ad*, down [with] . . . ! *bas les mains!* hands off! **en ~,** *ad*, at the bottom; below; down; downward; downstairs.

basalte (bazalt) *m*, basalt.

basane (bazan) *f*, sheepskin, roan, basan, basil. **basané, e** (ne) *a*, tanned, tawny, swarthy, sunburnt.

bas-bleu (bɑblø) *m*, bluestocking.

bas-côté (bɑkote) *m*, aisle.

bascule (baskyl) *f*, balanced lever; rocker; seesaw. [*balance à*] ~, weighing machine, scale[s]. ~ *romaine*, platform scales. **basculer** (le) *v.i*, to seesaw, swing, rock, tip [up], tilt. *faire ~*, to dip (*auto headlights*).

base (bɑːz) *f*, base, bottom, foot; basis, groundwork. *jeter les ~s*, to lay foundations.

bas-fond (bɑfɔ̃) *m*, lowland, flat, bottom; shallows (*Naut.*). ~*s de la société*, underworld.

basilic (bazilik) *m*, [sweet] basil; basilisk.

basilique (bazilik) *f*, basilica.

basique (bazik) *a*, basic, basal.

basque (bask) *f*, skirt, tail.

bas-relief (barəljɛf) *m*, low relief, bas-relief.

basse (bɑːs) *f*, bass [voice, singer, string, tuba]; cello; reef, flat (*Naut.*)

basse-cour (bɑskuːr) *f*, farmyard, barnyard, poultry yard, stable yard.

bassement (bɑsmɑ̃) *ad*, meanly, basely. **bassesse** (sɛs) *f*, meanness, etc; humbleness (*birth*).

basset (bɑsɛ) *m*, basset. ~ *allemand*, dachshund.

bassin (bɑsɛ̃) *m*, basin, bowl, pan; scale (*pan*); [collection] plate; ornamental lake; dock; pelvis. ~ *à flot*, wet dock. ~ *à sec*, dry dock. ~ [*de garde-robe*], ~ *pour malade*, = de lit, bedpan. **bassine** (sin) *f*, pan, copper. **bassinet** (nɛ) *m*, buttercup. **bassinoire** (nwaːr) *f*, warming pan.

basson (bɑsɔ̃) *m*, bassoon.

bastonnade (bastɔnad) *f*, cudgeling.

bas-ventre (bɑvɑ̃ːtr) *m*, lower part of the abdomen.

bât (bɑ) *m*, packsaddle.

bataclan (bataklɑ̃) *m*, traps, hamper.

bataille (bataːj) *f*, battle, fight, fray. **batailler** (taje) *v.i*, to battle, fight; struggle; wrangle. **batailleur, euse** (jœːr, øːz) *a*, combative, pugnacious. **bataillon** (tajɔ̃) *m*, battalion, host; heap. ~ *de travailleurs*, labor battalion.

bâtard, e (bɑtaːr, ard) *a. & n*, bastard, mongrel; loaf of bread. **bâtardise** (tardiːz) *f*, bastardy.

bateau (bato) *m*, boat, ship, vessel; smack. ~ *à rames*, row[ing] boat. ~ *à roues*, paddle b. ~ *à vapeur*, steamboat. ~ *à voiles*, sailing b. ~*-citerne*, tanker. ~ *d'habitation*, houseboat. ~ *de passage*, ferryboat. ~ *de promenade*, row[ing] b. (*pleasure*). ~ *de sauvetage*, lifeboat. ~*-feu*, lightship. ~ *omnibus*, ~*-mouche*, water [omni]bus. ~*-porte*, *m*, caisson (*dock*). **batelage** (tlaːʒ) *m*, lighterage; knock-about tricks. **batelée** (tle) *f*, boatload. **bateleur** (tlœːr) *m*, knock-about comedian. **batelier** (təlje) *m*, bargeman, bargee, lighterman. **batellerie** (tɛlri) *f*, inland navigation; small craft.

bâti (bɑti) *m*, tacking, basting (*Need.*); frame[work], casing. ~ [*d'assise*], bed plate. ~ *de forge*, smith's hearth.

batifoler (batifɔle) *v.i*, to romp, frolic, skylark; dally (*amorously*).

bâtiment (batimɑ̃) m, building; house; vessel, ship. ~ *de guerre*, man-of-war. **bâtir** (tiːr) v.t, & abs, to build; tack, baste (*Need.*). **bâtisse** (tis) f, masonry.

batiste (batist) f, cambric, batiste.

bâton (batɔ̃) m, stick; cudgel; singlestick; staff; truncheon; baton; pole; perch; support (*fig.*). ~ *d'or*, wallflower. ~ *de rouge* [*pour les lèvres*], lipstick. *à* ~*s rompus*, by fits & starts, desultorily. **bâtonner** (tɔne) v.t, to beat; cudgel. **bâtonnet** (nɛ) m, [tip]cat; chopstick.

battage (bataːʒ) m, beating; threshing; churning. **battant** (tɑ̃) m, clapper (*bell*); leaf (*door*). ~ *neuf*, brand-new. *pluie battante*, pelting rain. **batte** (bat) f, beater. ~ *à beurre*, churn dash[er]. **battement** (tmɑ̃) m, beating, beat, etc, as *battre*. **batterie** (tri) f, fight, scuffle; battery; beat[ing]; set, utensils; percussion instruments; (*s. & pl.*) plan(s), tactics. ~ *de tambour*, roll of the drum. **batteur** (tœːr) m, beater; whisk. ~ *de pavé*, lounger, loafer. ~ *en grange*, thresher (*pers.*). **batteuse** (tøːz) f, threshing machine. **battoir** (twaːr) m, beater; battledore. **battre** (tr) v.t. & i. ir, to beat, strike, batter; scour (*country*); thrash; thresh; churn; hammer; ram; coin, mint; raise (*money*); fly (*national flag*); shell (*Mil.*); clap (*hands*); shuffle (*cards*); bang; flap; jar; throb, pulsate; pant; tick (*clock*). ~ *contre-vapeur*, to reverse steam. *se* ~, to fight. *se* ~ *les flancs*, to lash its tail. **battu, e** (ty) p.a, beaten. ¶ f, drive, battue, beat (*Hunt.*); tramp (*of horse*).

bau (bo) m, beam (*ship's timber*).

baudet (bodɛ) m, donkey.

baudrier (bodrie) m, cross belt.

baudruche (bodryʃ) f, goldbeater's skin.

baume (boːm) m, balsam, balm. **baumier** (bomje) m, balsam [tree].

bavarder (bavarde) v.i, to prate, blab; gossip.

bavarois, e (bavarwa, aːz) a. & B~, n, Bavarian.

bave (baːv) f, drivel; slobber; slime. **baver** (bave) v.i, to drivel; slobber. **bavette** (vɛt) f, bavoir (vwaːr) m, bib, feeder. **bavure** (vyːr) f, smear; burr; seam.

Bavière (la) (bavjɛːr), Bavaria.

bayer aux corneilles (bɛje), to stargaze, gape [at the moon].

bayette (bɛjɛt) f, baize.

bazar (bazaːr) m, bazaar, arcade (*of shops*); (*cheap*) stores.

béant, e (beɑ̃, ɑ̃ːt) a, gaping, yawning, open.

béat, e† (bea, at) a, sanctimonious; blissful; smug, self-satisfied. ¶ n, saint. **béatifier** (tifje) v.t, to beatify. **béatitude** (tyd) f, beatitude, blessedness, bliss.

beau, bel, belle (bo, bɛl) a, beautiful, fine, handsome, fair, pretty, comely, lovely, good, nice; graceful; fashionable, smart; bright; palmy (*days*). *le beau monde*, fashionable society. *avoir beau dire*, to speak in vain. *bel esprit*, [man of] wit; witling. *bel & bien*, ad, fairly; plainly. *à la belle étoile*, in the open [air]. **beau**, m, beautiful; beau, Adonis. *au* ~, *au* ~ *fixe*, at fair, at set fair (*barometer*). *faire le* ~, to beg (*dog*). **beaucoup** (ku) ad. & m, a great (*or* good) deal, a good (*or* great) many, very much; much, many, greatly. *de* ~, by far. **beau-fils**, m, stepson. **beau-frère**, m, brother-in-law. **beau-père**, m, father-in-law; stepfather.

beaupré (bopre) m, bowsprit.

beauté (bote) f, beauty, fairness, loveliness, comeliness; belle.

beaux-arts (bozaːr) m.pl, fine arts, art.

bébé (bebe) m, baby; [baby] doll. ~ *dormeur*, sleeping doll.

bec (bɛk) m, beak, bill; nose, nozzle, snout; jaw; spout; mouthpiece; mouth; lip, tip; burner, jet; nib; point; cutwater.

bécarre (bekaːr) (*Mus.*) m. & a, natural, cancel.

bécasse (bekas) f, woodcock. **bécasseau** (so) m, sandpiper. **bécassine** (sin) f, snipe.

bec-de-lièvre (bɛkdəljɛ:vr) *m*, harelip.

bêche (bɛʃ) *f*, spade. **bêcher** (ʃe) *v.t*, to dig, spade.

becqueter (bɛkte) *v.t*, to peck, pick. **se ~**, to bill.

bedeau (bədo) *m*, beadle; verger.

beffroi (bɛfrwa) *m*, belfry; gantry.

bégayer (begɛje) *v.i. & t*, to stutter, stammer, lisp, falter. **bégaiement** (gɛmɑ̃) *m*, stuttering, etc.

bègue (bɛ:g) *n*, stutterer, stammerer.

bégueule (begœl) *f*, prude. ¶ *a*, prudish, squeamish, straitlaced. **bégueulerie** (lri) *f*, prudery, etc.

beignet (bɛɲɛ) *m*, fritter (*Cook.*).

bêlement (bɛlmɑ̃) *m*, bleat[ing], baa[ing]. **bêler** (le) *v.i*, to bleat, baa.

belette (bəlɛt) *f*, weasel.

belge (bɛlʒ) *a. & B~*, *n*, Belgian. **la Belgique** (ʒik), Belgium.

bélier (belje) *m*, ram, tup; battering ram.

belladone (bɛladɔn) *f*, belladonna, deadly nightshade.

bellâtre (bɛlɑ:tr) *a*, dandified, foppish.

belle (bɛl) *f*, beauty; deciding game, rubber. *la B~ au bois dormant*, the Sleeping Beauty. *la B~ & la Bête*, Beauty & the Beast. **~-de-jour**, *f*, convolvulus. **~-fille**, *f*, stepdaughter; daughter-in-law. **bellement** (lmɑ̃) *ad*, softly, gently. **belle-mère**, *f*, stepmother; mother-in-law. **belles-lettres**, *f.pl*, polite letters *or* literature. **belle-sœur**, *f*, sister-in-law.

belligérant, e (bɛliʒerɑ̃, ɑ̃:t) *a. & n*, belligerent. **belliqueux, euse** (bɛlikø, ø:z) *a*, warlike, bellicose.

bellot, te (bɛlo, ɔt) *a*, pretty; dapper.

belvédère (bɛlvedɛ:r) *m*, belvedere, lookout.

bémol (bemɔl) *m. & att*, flat (*Mus.*).

bénédicité (benedisite) *m*, grace, blessing (*before meals*). **bénédiction** (ksjɔ̃) *f*, consecration, blessing; benediction. *que c'est une ~*, with a vengeance, & no mistake.

bénéfice (benefis) *m*, advantage,

benefit; profit; living, benefice (*Eccl.*). **bénéficiaire** (sjeːr) *a*, [showing a] profit; in credit. ¶ *n*, beneficiary, payee. **bénéficier** (sje) *v.i*, to [make a] profit, benefit.

benêt (bənɛ) *a.m*, silly, simple, foolish. ¶ *m*, booby, simpleton, noodle.

bénévole† (benevɔl) *a*, kind; voluntary.

Bengale (le) (bɛ̃gal), Bengal. **bengali** (li) *a.inv. & (bird) m. & B~* (*pers.*) *m*, Bengali.

béni, e (beni) *p.p*, blessed, blest. **bénin, igne†** (nɛ̃, iɲ) *a*, benign, benignant, kind; mild. **bénir** (niːr) *v.t*, to consecrate; bless; thank. **bénit, e** (ni, ite) *p.p*, consecrated, holy (*bread, water*). **bénitier** (tje) *m*, holy-water basin, stoup.

benjoin (bɛ̃ʒwɛ̃) *m*, benzoin, benjamin.

benne (bɛn) *f*, hamper, basket; bucket, kibble, tub (*Min.*).

benzine (bɛzin) *f*, benzine.

benzol (bɛzɔl) *m*, benzol, benzene.

béquille (bekiːj) *f*, crutch; crutch handle; crutch key; spud (*Agric.*).

bercail (bɛrkaːj) *m*, fold (*Relig.*).

berceau (bɛrso) *m*, cradle; cot; arbor, bower. **bercelonnette** (səlɔnɛt) *f*, bassinet, cot. **bercer (se)** *v.t*, to rock, dandle; lull; bring up; cherish. **berceuse** (sø:z) *f*, rocker (*pers.*); rocking chair; lullaby.

béret [basque] (berɛ) *m*, beret.

bergamote (bɛrgamɔt) *f*, bergamot (*orange, pear*). **bergamotier** (tje) *m*, bergamot [tree] (*orange*).

berge (bɛrʒ) *f*, bank (*river, road*).

berger (bɛrʒe) *m*, shepherd; swain. **bergère** (ʒɛ:r) *f*, shepherdess, nymph; easy chair. **bergerie** (ʒəri) *f*, [sheep]fold, pen. **bergeronnette** (rɔnɛt) *f*, wagtail.

Bermudes (les) (bɛrmyd) *f.pl*, the Bermudas.

bernacle (bɛrnakl) *f*, barnacle (*Crust.*). **bernard-l'ermite** (narlɛrmit) *m*, hermit crab.

berne (bɛrn) *f*, banter. *en ~*, at half-mast (*flag*). **berner** (ne) *v.t*, to make fun of; chaff.

bernique (bɛrnik) *i*, nothing doing!

béryl (beril) *m*, beryl.

besace (bəzas) *f*, scrip, wallet (*beggar's*). réduit à la ~, reduced to beggary.

besicles (bəzikl) *f.pl*, eyeglasses.

besogne (bəzɔɲ) *f*, [piece of] work, task, job. ~ *alimentaire*, potboiler. **besogneux, euse** (ɲø, ø:z) *a*, needy, impecunious. **besoin** (zwɛ̃) *m*, need; requirement; pinch; [referee in] case of need (*Com.*).

bestial, e† (bɛstjal) *a*, bestial; beastly; hoggish. **bestiaux** (tjo) *m.pl*, cattle. **bêta** (bɛta) *m*, blockhead, fool. **bétail** (beta:j) *m*, cattle. **bête** (bɛ:t) *f*, beast, animal; creature; fool. ~ à bon Dieu, ladybird. ~ noire, pet aversion. ~ fauves, deer; wild beasts (*big felines*). chercher la petite ~, to look for trouble. ¶ †, *a*, stupid, foolish, silly. **bêtise** (beti:z) *f*, stupidity; nonsense.

béton (betɔ̃) *m*, concrete. ~ armé, reinforced concrete.

bette (bɛt) *f*, beet. **betterave** (tra:v) *f*, beetroot, beet. ~ à sucre, sugar beet. ~ fourragère, mangel[-wurzel].

beugler (bøgle) *v.i. & t*, to bellow, low, moo; bawl.

beurre (bœ:r) *m*, butter. ~ d'anchois, anchovy paste. un oeil au ~ noir, a black eye. **beurrée** (bœre) *f*, slice of bread & butter. **beurrer** (re) *v.t*, to butter. **beurrier** (rje) *m*, butter dish.

bévue (bevy) *f*, blunder; howler.

biais (bjɛ) *m*, slant; skew; bias; bent; dodge, shift. **biaiser** (ze) *v.i*, to slant; dodge, shuffle, shift.

bibelot (biblo) *m*, curio, knick-knack.

biberon, ne (bibrɔ̃, ɔn) *n*, tippler; (*m.*) feeding bottle.

Bible (bibl) *f*, Bible. **bibliographie** (bliɔgrafi) *f*, bibliography. **bibliophile** (fil) *m*, bibliophile, book-lover. **bibliothécaire** (tekɛ:r) *n*, librarian. **bibliothèque** (tɛk) *f*, library; bookcase; bookstall. ~ circulante, circulating library. ~ de prêt, lending l. ~ où les livres se consultent sur place & ~ d'ouvrages à consulter, reference li-

brary. **biblique** (blik) *a*, biblical; Bible (*Society*). **biblorhapte** (blɔrapt) *m*, binder.

biceps (bisɛps) *m*, biceps.

biche (biʃ) *f*, hind (*deer*).

bichon, ne (biʃɔ̃, ɔn) *n*, Maltese [dog, bitch], lap dog. **bichonner** (ʃɔne) *v.t*, to curl; titivate.

bicoque (bikɔk) *f*, shanty.

bicycle (bisikl) *m*, bicycle. **bicyclette** (klɛt) *f*, [safety] bicycle, cycle. ~ de course, racer. **bicycliste** (klist) *n*, [bi]cyclist.

bidet (bidɛ) *m*, nag, cob; bidet.

bidon (bidɔ̃) *m*, canteen, water bottle (*Mil.*); drum (*gasoline, etc.*), can.

bief (bjɛf) *m*, race[way] (*mill*); pond (*canal*).

bielle (bjɛl) *f*, [connecting] rod; strut, brace.

bien (bjɛ̃) *ad*, well; right; proper; nicely; all right; clearly; fully, thoroughly; much; very; far; fast; fain; indeed; duly; really, quite. ~ de, much, many. ~ que, c, [al]though. ¶ *m*, good; weal; blessing; endowment; mercy; (*oft. pl.*) possessions, property, chattel, estate, substance. ~s mal acquis, ill-gotten gains. ~s [transmissibles par voie de succession], hereditament.

bien-aimé, e ou **bienaimé, e** (bjɛ̃nɛme) *a. & n*, [well-]beloved, darling.

bien-dire (bjɛ̃di:r) *m*, fine speaking. **bien-disant, e** (dizã, ã:t) *a*, well-spoken, fair-spoken.

bien-être (bjɛ̃nɛ:tr) *m*, well-being; welfare.

bienfaisance (bjɛ̃fəzã:s) *f*, beneficence; benevolence; bounteousness; charity, donations. **bienfaisant, e** (zã, ã:t) *a*, beneficent, etc. **bienfait** (fɛ) *m*, kindness, benefaction, benefit; boon; mercy. **bienfaiteur, trice** (tœ:r, tris) *n*, benefactor, tress.

bienheureux, euse (bjɛ̃nœrø, ø:z) *a*, blessed; blissful.

biennal, e (bjɛnal) *a*, biennial.

bienséant, e (bjɛ̃seã, ã:t) *a*, proper, becoming, decorous.

biens-fonds (bjɛ̃fɔ̃) *m.pl*, real estate.

bientôt (bjɛ̃to) *ad*, soon, shortly.

bienveillant, e (bjɛ̃vɛjɑ̃, ɑ̃ːt) *a*, kind[ly], friendly.

bienvenue (bjɛ̃vny) *f*, welcome; footing.

bière (bjɛːr) *f*, beer; coffin. ~ *au tonneau*, ~ *à la pompe*, draught beer. ~ *blonde*, pale ale. ~ *brune*, dark ale.

biffer (bife) *v.t*, to strike out, cross out, delete, rule out, cancel.

bifteck (biftɛk) *m*, [beef]steak.

bifurcation (bifyrkasjɔ̃) *f*, bifurcation, fork; junction.

bigame (bigam) *a*, bigamous. ¶ *n*, bigamist. **bigamie** (mi) *f*, bigamy.

bigarade (bigarad) *f*, Seville orange.

bigarré, e (bigare) *p.a*, variegated, particolored, pied, motley. **bigarrer** (re) *v.t*, to variegate, medley; [inter]lard.

bigorneau (bigɔrno) *m*, [peri]winkle (*Crust.*).

bigot, e (bigo, ɔt) *a*, bigoted. ¶ *n*, bigot. **bigoterie** (gɔtri) *f*, bigotry.

bigoudi (bigudi) *m*, hair curler.

bijou (biʒu) *m*, jewel, gem; darling. **bijouterie** (tri) *f*, jewelry. **bijoutier, ère** (tje, ɛːr) *n*, jeweler.

bilan (bilɑ̃) *m*, balance sheet; statement of affairs. *déposer son* ~, to file a petition in bankruptcy.

bilboquet (bilbɔkɛ) *m*, cup & ball.

bile (bil) *f*, bile. **bilieux, euse** (ljø, øːz) *a*, bilious.

billard (bijaːr) *m*, billiards. [*salle de*] ~, billiard room.

bille (biːj) *f*, ball; billiard ball; marble (*games*); sawlog; bar.

billet (bijɛ) *m*, note, bill; ticket. ~ *à ordre*, note of hand, promissory note. ~ *à prix réduit*, cheap ticket. ~ *d'aller & retour*, round-trip ticket. ~ *de banque*, bank note. ~ *de complaisance*, accommodation note. ~ *de faire-part*, wedding or funeral announcement. ~ *de faveur*, free pass, complimentary ticket. ~ *de quai*, platform ticket. ~ *de logement*, billet (*Mil.*). ~ *doux*, love letter. ~ *garde-place*, ~ *de location de place*, reserved seat ticket. ~ *global*, through ticket

(*sea-land-sea*). ~ *perdant*, blank (*lottery*).

billevesée (bilvəze) *f*, nonsense.

billion (biljɔ̃) *m*, billion.

billon (bijɔ̃) *m*, ridge (*Agric.*); copper &/or nickel [coin].

billot (bijo) *m*, [chopping] block.

bimbelot (bɛ̃blo) *m*, fancy article. **bimbeloterie** (blɔtri) *f*, fancy goods.

bimensuel, le (bimɑ̃sɥɛl) *a*, semimonthly, twice monthly. **bimestriel, le** (mɛstriɛl) *a*, bimonthly, [in] alternate months.

biner (bine) *v.t*, to hoe. **binette** (nɛt) *f*, hoe.

binocle (binɔkl) *m*, eyeglasses.

biographe (biɔgraf) *m*, biographer. **biographie** (fi) *f*, biography.

biologie (biɔlɔʒi) *f*, biology. **biologiste** (ʒist) or **biologue** (lɔg) *m*, biologist.

bipède (bipɛd) *a*, biped[al]. ¶ *m*, biped.

biplan (biplɑ̃) *m*, biplane.

bique (bik) *f*, nanny [goat].

birman, e (birmɑ̃, an) *a*. & **B~**, *n*, Burmese. **la Birmanie** (mani), Burma.

bis, e (bi, iːz) *a*, brownish gray; brown (*bread*).

bis (bis) *ad*, bis, repeat (*Mus.*); encore. ¶ *m*, encore. ¶ *a*, ᴬ, ½ (*house number*).

bisaïeul, e (bizajœl) *n*, great-grandfather, -mother.

bisannuel, le (bizanɥɛl) *a*, biennial.

bisbille (bizbiːj) *f*, squabble. *en* ~, at loggerheads.

biscornu, e (biskɔrny) *a*, misshapen; queer, odd.

biscotte (biskɔt) *f*, rusk. **biscuit** (kɥi) *m*, biscuit; zwieback. ~ *de Savoie*, sponge cake.

bise (biːz) *f*, north wind.

biseau (bizo) *m*, bevel. **biseauter** (te) *v.t*, to bevel.

bismuth (bismyt) *m*, bismuth.

bison (bizɔ̃) *m*, bison.

bissac (bisak) *m*, wallet, bag.

bissection (bisɛksjɔ̃) *f*, bisection.

bisser (bise) *v.t*, to encore.

bissextile (bisɛkstil) *a*, leap (*year*).

bistourner (bisturne) *v.t*, to twist, wrench.

bitume (bitym) *m*, bitumen, pitch, asphalt. **bitumineux, euse** (minø, ø:z) *a*, bituminous; tarry.

bivalve (bivalv) *a. & m*, bivalve.

bivouac (bivwak) *m*, bivouac. **bivouaquer** (ke) *v.i*, to bivouac, camp out.

bizarre† (biza:r) *a*, odd, queer, peculiar, freakish, outlandish. **bizarrerie** (zarri) *f*, oddness, etc.

blackbouler (blakbule) *v.t*, to blackball.

blafard, e (blafa:r, ard) *a*, pale, pallid, wan; lurid.

blague (blag) *f*, [tobacco] pouch; gammon, bunkum, rubbish, humbug, blarney, chaff; bounce, brag. *sans* ~, you don't say. **blaguer** (blage) *v.i*, to joke; rib. **blagueur** (gœ:r) *m*, joker; humbug.

blaireau (blɛro) *m*, badger; shaving brush.

blâme (bla:m) *m*, blame, reprimand. **blâmer** (blame) *v.t*, to blame.

blanc, che (blɑ̃, ɑ̃:ʃ) *a*, white; hoary; blank, clean; fair (*skin*). *le mont Blanc*, Mont Blanc. ~ *de lessive*, fresh from the wash. ¶ *m*, white (*color, man, etc.*); blank; margin (*book page*), chalk (*Bil.*); breast (*fowl*). ~ *de baleine*, spermaceti. ~ *de céruse*, white lead. ~ *de champignon*, mushroom spawn. ~ *de chaux*, whitewash. ~ *de craie*, whiting. ~ *de grand fond*, front margin. ~ *de petit fond*, back margin, (*pl. col.*) gutter. ~ *de pied*, bottom margin. ~ *de terre à pipe*, pipe clay. ~ *de tête*, top margin. *nuit blanche*, sleepless night.

blanc-bec (blɑ̃bɛk) *m*, callow youth.

blanchaille (blɑ̃ʃɑ:j) *f*, fry; whitebait.

blanchâtre (blɑ̃ʃɑ:tr) *a*, whitish. **blanche** (blɑ̃:ʃ) *f*, white (*woman, ball*); minim (*Mus.*). **blancheur** (blɑ̃ʃœ:r) *f*, whiteness. **blanchir** (ʃi:r) *v.t. & i*, to whiten; blanch; bleach; whitewash; wash; wash for; launder; clean up; scald. ~ *à la chaux*, to whitewash. **blanchisserie** (ʃisri) *f*, laundry. **blanchisseuse** (sø:z) *f*, washerwoman. ~ *[de fin]*, [fine] laundress.

blanc-manger (blɑ̃mɑ̃ʒe) *m*, blancmange.

blanc-seing (blɑ̃sɛ̃) *m*, blank signature.

blaser (blɑze) *v.t*, to blunt, surfeit, pall on.

blason (blazɔ̃) *m*, coat of arms, armorial bearings; blazon[ry], heraldry. **blasonner** (zɔne) *v.t*, to [em]blazon; malign.

blasphémateur, trice (blasfematœ:r, tris) *n*, blasphemer. **blasphématoire** (twa:r) *a*, blasphemous. **blasphème** (fɛ:m) *m*, blasphemy; profanity. **blasphémer** (feme) *v.i. & t*, to blaspheme, curse.

blatte (blat) *f*, cockroach, black beetle.

blé (ble) *m*, wheat. [*champ de*] ~, wheatfield. ~ *à moudre*, grist. ~ *de Turquie*, Indian corn, maize. ~ *noir*, buckwheat.

blême (blɛ:m) *a*, pale, pallid, wan, ghastly. **blêmir** (blemi:r) *v.i*, to [turn] pale.

bléser (bleze) *v.i*, to lisp.

blesser (blɛse) *v.t*, to wound, hurt, injure, gall; grate upon (*ear*); shock, offend; pinch (*shoes*). ~ *à mort*, to injure fatally. ~ *quelqu'un au cœur*, to hurt someone's feelings. **blessure** (sy:r) *f*, wound, etc.

blet, te (blɛ, blɛt) *a*, overripe, soft.

bleu, e (blø) *a*, blue; underdone (*meat*); ¶ *m*, blue; blue mark (*bruise*); blueprint; recruit (*Mil.*). ~ *de ciel*, ~ *céleste*, sky blue. ~ *marine*, navy b. *conte* ~, fairy tale. **bleuâtre** (ɑ:tr) *a*, bluish. **bleuet** (ɛ) *m*, cornflower. **bleuir** (i:r) *v.t. & i*, to blue.

blindage (blɛ̃da:ʒ) *m*, armorplating; armor; sheeting.

bloc (blɔk) *m*, block, lump; coalition (*Pol.*); guardroom. ~ *journalier*, block calendar.

blocage (blɔka:ʒ) *m*, rubble-[work]; clamping, as *bloquer*. **blocaille** (kɑ:j) *f*, rubble[stone], ballast.

bloc-film (blɔkfilm) *m*, film pack.

blockhaus (blɔko:s) *m*, blockhouse; conning tower.

bloc-mémorandum (blɔkmemɔrɑ̃dɔm) *m*, scribbling block. **bloc-notes** (nɔt) *m*. ou

bloc de correspondance, [*writing*] pad. **bloc-sténo** (steno) *m*, shorthand notebook.

blocus (blɔky:s) *m*, blocade.

blond, e (blɔ̃, ɔ̃:d) *a*, fair, flaxen, blond, e; light. ¶ *n*, fair-haired person, blond, e. ¶ *m*, blond, e, flaxen (*color*). ~ *ardent*, auburn. ~ *cendré*, ash blonde. ~ *doré*, golden (*hair*). ~ *hasardé*, reddish (*hair*). ~ *platine*, platinum blonde. ~ *roux*, sandy (*hair*).

bloquer (blɔke) *v.t*, to clamp, lock; tie up; lump; blockade, block.

blottir (se) (blɔti:r) *v.pr*, to squat, crouch, couch, cower; lie hid; cuddle up, nestle, snuggle, nuzzle, huddle.

blouse (blu:z) *f*, smock; blouse. ~ [-*paletot*], *f*, overalls. **blouser** (bluze) *v.t*, to take in, dupe.

bluette (blyɛt) *f*, literary trifle. **bluter** (blyte) *v.t*, to bolt, sift.

boa (bɔa) *m*, boa (*wrap*). ~ *constrictor* (kɔ̃striktɔ:r), boa constrictor.

bobine (bɔbin) *f*, bobbin, drum, reel, spool; coil (*Elec.*). **bobiner** (ne) *v.t*, to wind, coil.

bobo (bɔbo) *m*, slight injury; bump.

bocage (bɔka:ʒ) *m*, grove. **bocager, ère** (kaʒe, ɛːr) *a*, sylvan, wood (*nymph*).

bocal (bɔkal) *m*, bottle, jar; globe, fishbowl.

bocard (bɔka:r) *m*, stamp [*mill*]. **bocarder** (karde) *v.t*, to mill, stamp (*ore*).

bock (bɔk) *m*, glass (*for, or of, beer*).

bœuf (bœf) *m*, ox, bullock; beef. ~ *salé*, corned beef.

bohème (bɔɛːm) *n. & a*, Bohemian (*n. & a.*), free & easy. **la** ~, Bohemia (*fig.*). **bohémien, ne** (emjɛ̃, ɛn) *n*, gypsy.

boire (bwa:r) *v.t. & i. ir*, to drink; absorb; imbibe; swallow, pocket (*insult*); drown. ~ *un coup*, to have a drink.

bois (bwɑ) *m*, wood; park; horns, antlers, head (*stag*); stock (*rifle, plane*); stuff (*one is made of*); (*pl.*) wood[-wind] (*Mus.*). ~ *à brûler*, ~ *de chauffage*, firewood. ~ *contreplaqué*, plywood. ~ [*de*

charpente], timber, lumber. ~ *de lit*, bedstead. ~ *de placage*, veneer. ~ *de rose*, tulip wood. ~*de satin*, satin w. ~ *plaqué triplé*, 3-ply w. **boisage** (za:ʒ) *m*, timbering. **boisement** (zmɑ̃) *m*, afforestation. **boiser** (ze) *v.t*, to timber; wainscot; afforest. **boiserie** (zri) *f*, woodwork; wainscoting.

boisseau (bwaso) *m*, bushel.

boisson (bwasɔ̃) *f*, drink, beverage, liquor.

boîte (bwa:t) *f*, box, case, chest, caddy, canister, can. ~ [*à conserves*], [*preserving*] can. ~ *à musique*, music box. ~ *de nuit*, nightclub. ~ *de vitesses*, gear box. *mettre en* ~, to pull somebody's leg.

boiter (bwate) *v.i*, to limp, halt, hobble. **boiterie** (tri) *f*, lameness. **boiteux, euse** (tø, ø:z) *a*, lame; halting; rickety.

boîtier (bwatje) *m*, box with divisions; case (*watch*).

bol (bɔl) *m*, bowl, basin; bolus. ~ *rince-doigts*, finger bowl.

Bolivie (la) (bɔlivi), Bolivia. **bolivien, ne** (vjɛ̃, ɛn) *a. & B~**, *n*, Bolivian.

Bologne (bɔlɔɲ) *f*, Bologna.

bombance (bɔ̃bɑ̃:s) *f*, feasting, junketing.

bombardement (bɔ̃bardəmɑ̃) *m*, bombardment; shelling; bombing. **bombarder** (de) *v.t*, to bombard. ~ *quelqu'un à une place*, to pitchfork someone into an office. **bombe** (bɔ̃:b) *f*, bomb; ball (*signal*); bombshell (*fig.*).

bomber (bɔ̃be) *v.t. & i. & se* ~, to bulge, swell, camber, belly; bend.

bon, ne (bɔ̃, ɔn) *a*, good; sound; kind; nice; fine; boon (*companion*); palatable; fit; right; proper; safe; fast (*color*). **bon**, *comps:* ~ *enfant*, good-natured. [*à*] *marché, a*, cheap. *à* ~ *marché, ad*, cheap[ly]. ~ *sens* (sɑ̃), [*common*] sense, [*right*] senses. **bonne**, *comps:* **la** ~ *année*, a happy New Year. ~ *bouche*, tidbit. ~ *femme*, simple good-natured woman. ~ *fin*, meeting (*engagement, bills*); protection (*bills*). ~ *maman*, grandmama, granny. **bon**, stet

(*Typ.*). **bon à tirer,** [for] press (*Typ.*). ¶ *m,* good; cream (*of story*); order, note; license; voucher; bond; draft; scrip; profit. (*un*) ~ **à rien,** *m. & a,* (a) good-for-nothing, (a) ne'er-do-well. ~ *d'ouverture,* inspection order (*Cust.*). ~ *de bord,* mate's receipt.

bonasse (bɔnas) *a,* good-hearted; easy-going; simple-minded.

bonbon (bɔ̃bɔ̃) *m,* candy; (*pl.*) confectionery. ~*s de chocolat,* chocolates. **bonbonnière** (bɔ̃bjɛːr) *f,* confectionery box, chocolate box; sweet bowl; pretty little place (*house*).

bond (bɔ̃) *m,* bound, bounce, spring; rebound; spurt.

bonde (bɔ̃ːd) *f,* bung[hole]; bung, plug. **bonder** (bɔ̃de) *v.t,* to fill to the bung, cram.

bondir (bɔ̃diːr) *v.i,* to bound, etc, as *bond.*

bondon (bɔ̃dɔ̃) *m,* bung; bondon. **bondonner** (dɔne) *v.t,* to bung.

bonheur (bɔnœːr) *m,* happiness, welfare; [good] luck; blessing. *le* ~ *du célibat,* single blessedness.

bonhomie (bɔnɔmi) *f,* good nature, geniality; credulity. **bonhomme** (nɔm) *m,* simple good-natured man. *le* ~ *Noël,* Santa Claus.

bonification (bɔnifikasjɔ̃) *f,* improvement; allowance. **bonifier** (fje) *v.t,* to improve; allow, credit.

boniment (bɔnimɑ̃) *m,* patter (*showman's*); claptrap.

bonjour (bɔ̃ʒuːr) *m,* good morning, good afternoon, good day.

bonne (bɔn) *f,* [maid]servant, servant[girl]; waitress. ~ *à tout faire,* general servant, maid-of-all-work. [*d'enfant*], nurse[maid].

bonnement (bɔnmɑ̃) *m,* candidly, plainly.

bonnet (bɔnɛ) *m,* cap, hat. ~ *de police,* forage cap. ~ *magique,* wishing cap. *gros* ~, bigwig.

bonneterie (bɔntri) *f,* hosiery.

bonneteur (bɔntœːr) *m,* card-sharper.

bonnetier (bɔntje) *m,* hosier.

bonsoir (bɔ̃swaːr) *m,* good evening, good night.

bonté (bɔ̃te) *f,* goodness, kindness.

bookmaker (bukmɛkɛːr) *m,* bookmaker. ~ *marron,* welsher.

borax (bɔraks) *m,* borax.

bord (bɔːr) *m,* edge, border, brink, verge, fringe, rim, margin; brim; flap; edging, binding, hem; bank, side, shore, coast, strand; board, side (*ship*); tack (*Naut.*); ship. *à* ~, on board, aboard. *à grands* ~*s,* broad-brimmed (*hat*). *à pleins* ~*s,* brimful. *par-dessus* ~, overboard.

bordé (bɔrde) *m,* braid; gimp; planking; plating (*ship*).

bordeaux (bɔrdo) *m,* Bordeaux, claret.

bordée (bɔrde) *f,* broadside; volley (*fig.*); board, tack (*ship*); watch (*Naut.*).

border (bɔrde) *v.t,* to border, edge, hem, bind; flange; tuck in (*bed*); line; plate (*ship*); ship (*oars*); run along, fringe; curb.

bordereau (bɔrdəro) *m,* memorandum, list, schedule, statement, slip, note, contract [note].

bordier (bɔrdje) *a.m. & m,* lop-sided (*boat*).

bordure (bɔrdyːr) *f,* border, edge, edging, binding, hem, skirt, rim; curb; front (*sea, river*). ~ *de fleurs vivaces,* herbaceous border.

bore (bɔːr) *m,* boron (*Chem.*).

boréal, e (bɔreal) *a,* boreal, north[ern].

borgne (bɔrɲ) *a. & n,* one-eyed (person); blind; dark, dingy; frowsy; low, of ill fame.

borique (bɔrik) *a,* boric, boracic.

borne (bɔrn) *f,* bound[ary], landmark, post; spur; terminal (*Elec.*). ~ *kilométrique,* milestone. ~ *postale,* pillar box. **borner** (ne) *v.t,* to bound, confine, mark out; restrict; stint.

bornoyer (bɔrnwaje) *v.t,* to squint over (*an alignment*).

Bosphore (le) (bɔsfɔːr), the Bosphorus.

bosquet (bɔskɛ) *m,* grove, spinney, thicket, shrubbery.

bosse (bɔs) *f,* hunch, hump; bump; dent, dint, bruise; mound; painter (*boat*). **bosseler** (sle) *v.t,* to [em]boss; dent, dint, bruise, batter. **bossoir** (swa;r) *m*, davit; cathead. **bossu, e** (sy) *a*, hunchbacked, humpbacked. ¶ *n*, hunchback, humpback. **bossuer** (sɥe) *v.t*, to dent, dint, bruise, batter.

bot (bo) *a.m*, club (*foot*).

botanique (bɔtanik) *a*, botanic(al). ¶ *f*, botany. **botaniste** (nist) *m*, botanist.

botte (bɔt) *f*, bundle, bunch; truss; coil; clump; thrust, lunge, pass; [high] boot. ~*s à genouillère*, jackboots. ~*s à l'écuyère*, riding boots. ~*s à revers*, top boots. ~*s cuissardes* (kɥisard) thigh boots; waders. ~*s montant aux genoux*, Wellingtons. **botteler** (tle) *v.t*, to bundle, bunch; truss (*hay*). **botter** (te) *v.t*, to boot, fit, put boots on. **bottier** (tje) *m*, bootmaker. **bottine** (tin) *f*, [half] boot. ~*s d'escalade*, climbing boots.

bottin (bɔtɛ̃) *m*, directory; who's who.

bouc (buk) *m*, he-goat, billy g. ~ *émissaire*, scapegoat.

boucan (bukɑ̃) *m*, noise, racket, etc.

boucanier (bukanje) *m*, buccaneer.

boucaut (buko) *m*, cask, hogshead.

bouche (buʃ) *f*, mouth; muzzle (*gun*); nozzle; hydrant, plug, flue; living. ~ *à feu*, piece of ordnance. ~ *béante*, ~ *bée*, openmouthed. ~ *close*! not a word! mum['s the word]! **bouchée** (ʃe) *f*, mouthful, bite; patty, pasty. **boucher** (ʃe) *v.t*, to stop, obstruct; shut; close; plug, seal; bung; stopper, cork. *se* ~ *le nez*, to hold one's nose. *bouché à l'émeri*, stoppered (*bottle*). **boucher** (buʃe) *m*, butcher. **boucherie** (ʃri) *f*, butcher's shop; butchery; slaughter.

bouche-trou (buʃtru) *m*, stopgap.

bouchon (buʃɔ̃) *m*, stopper, cork; plug, cap, bung; wisp; bundle; tavern; float. *goût de* ~, corky taste. **bouchonner** (ʃɔne) *v.t*, to bundle up; rub down (*horse*).

boucle (bukl) *f*, buckle, ring, shackle; loop; sweep; eye, bight;

curl, lock, ringlet; handle. ~ *d'amarrage*, ringbolt. **boucler** (kle) *v.t, & i*, to buckle; ring (*bull, etc.*); curl; loop; bulge; lock up; put away; balance (*budget*). ~ *la boucle*, to loop the loop. **bouclier** (klie) *m*, shield, buckler.

bouddhique (budik) *a*, buddhist. **bouddhiste** (dist) *m*, buddhist.

bouder (bude) *v.i*, to sulk; shirk.

boudin (budɛ̃) *m*, blood-sausage; corkscrew curl; saddlebag; flange. ~ *d'air*, inner tube.

boue (bu) *f*, mud, dirt, mire; slime, sludge, swarf.

bouée (bue) *f*, buoy. ~ *de sauvetage*, life b.

boueux, euse (buø, ø;z) *a*, muddy, dirty, miry, mud (*spring*). ¶ *m*, scavenger.

bouffe (buf) *a*, comic.

bouffée (bufe) *f*, puff, breath, fume, whiff, gust; fit. **bouffer** (fe) *v.i*, to puff, swell; rise; bulge. **bouffi, e** (fi) *a*, puffy, swollen, bloated; turgid, bombastic. **bouffir** (fi;r) *v.t*, to swell, bloat.

bouffon, ne (bufɔ̃, ɔn) *a*, comic(al), clownish, farcical. ¶ *m*, buffoon, jester, clown; laughingstock, butt. **bouffonnerie** (fɔnri) *f*, buffoonery, foolery.

bouge (bu;ʒ) *m*, hole, hovel, den; bulge; bilge (*cask*).

bougeoir (buʒwa;r) *m*, candlestick.

bouger (buʒe) *v.i*, to budge, move, stir.

bougie (buʒi) *f*, candle. ~ *d'allumage*, spark plug. *une lampe de 60* ~*s*, a 60 candlepower lamp.

bougonner (bugɔne) *v.i*, to grumble, grouse.

bougran (bugrɑ̃) *m*, buckram.

bougre (bu;gr) *m*, fellow, guy.

bouillant, e (brijɑ̃, ɑ̃;t) *a*, boiling; fiery; hotheaded. **bouillie** (ji) *f*, pap; porridge, gruel; pulp; mush. **bouillir** (ji;r) *v.i.ir*, to boil. *faire* ~, to boil, *v.t*, ~ *à demi*, to parboil. **bouilloire** (jwa;r) *f*, kettle. ~ *à sifflet*, singing k. **bouillon** (jɔ̃) *m*, bubble; gush, spirt, spurt; broth, soup, bouillon, cup of broth, tea (*beef, etc.*); slops (*liquid diet*); restaurant; blow[hole]; puff, returns (*newspaper*).

bouillonner (jɔne) *v.i*, to bubble, boil, seethe. **bouillotte** (jɔt) *f*, kettle; foot warmer. ~ *à eau chaude*, hot-water bottle.

boujaron (buʒarɔ̃) *m*, tot (*of rum, etc.*).

boulanger, ère (bulɑ̃ʒe, ɛːr) *n*, baker. **boulangerie** (ʒri) *f*, baking; bakery.

boule (bul) *f*, ball; bowling ball. ~ *d'eau chaude*, hot-water bottle. ~ *de neige*, snowball; guelder rose. [*jeu de*] ~s, [game of] bowls.

Boule (bul) *m*, buhl[work].

bouleau (bulo) *m*, birch [tree]. ~ *blanc*, silver birch. [*verge de*] ~, birch [rod].

bouledogue (buldɔg) *m*, bulldog.

bouler (bule) *v.t*, to send rolling; swell; blunder.

boulet (bulɛ) *m*, cannon ball; ball. **boulette** (lɛt) *f*, pellet.

boulevard (bulvaːr) *m*, boulevard, avenue; bulwark (*fig.*).

bouleverser (bulvɛrse) *v.t*, to convulse, wreck, upset, overthrow.

boulier (bulje) *m*, ball frame, abacus; scoring board, string (*Bil.*).

boulin (bulɛ̃) *m*, pigeonhole (*in dovecot*); putlog.

boulingrin (bulɛ̃grɛ̃) *m*, lawn, grass plot.

boulon (bulɔ̃) *m*, bolt, pin. **boulonner** (lɔne) *v.t*, to bolt.

boulot, te (bulo, ɔt) *a*, dumpy, squat, squab[by], stumpy. ¶ *m*, work.

bouquet (bukɛ) *m*, bouquet, nosegay, posy, bunch, cluster, tuft; clump; aroma; crowning piece; climax; prawn. **bouquetière** (ktjɛːr) *f*, flower girl.

bouquetin (buktɛ̃) *m*, ibex.

bouquin (bukɛ̃) *m*, old he-goat; buck hare; buck rabbit; [old] book (*of little value*). **bouquineur** (kinœːr) *m*, book hunter; lover of old books. **bouquiniste** (nist) *m*, secondhand bookseller.

bourbe (burb) *f*, mud. **bourbeux, euse**, (bø, ø:z) *a*, muddy. **bourbier** (bje) *m*, slough, quag[mire]; scrape, fix.

bourde (burd) *f*, fib; blunder.

débiter des ~s, to fib. *donneur* (*ou conteur*) *de* ~s, fibber.

bourdon (burdɔ̃) *m*, pilgrim's staff; bumblebee; great bell; drone (*Mus.*); drone [bee]; out[, see copy] (*Typ.*). **bourdonner** (dɔne) *v.i. & t*, to hum, buzz, drone, boom, din, sing (*in ears*).

bourg (buːr) *m*, market town, borough. **bourgade** (burgad) *f*, small town, straggling village.

bourgeois, e (burʒwa, aːz) *a*, middle-class; homely, plain (*cooking, etc.*); private (*house*). *en bourgeois*, in plain clothes, in mufti. ¶ *n*, middle-class man, woman. **bourgeoisie** (ʒwazi) *f*, middle class[es]; bourgeoisie.

bourgeon (burʒɔ̃) *m*, bud; shoot; pimple. **bourgeonner** (ʒɔne) *v.i*, to bud, etc.

bourgogne *ou* vin de B~(burgɔɲ) *m*, burgundy.

bourlinguer (burlɛ̃ge) *v.i*, to wallow; strain (*Naut.*); rough it.

bourrade (burad) *f*, blow, thump.

bourrasque (burask) *f*, squall; gust; tantrum.

bourre (buːr) *f*, hair, flock, waste, down, fluff, floss; padding, stuffing, wad.

bourreau (buro) *m*, executioner, headsman, hangman; tyrant; tormentor. ~ *d'argent*, spendthrift. ~ *des cœurs*, lady-killer. **bourreler** (rle) *v.t*, (*of conscience*) to torment, prick, sting. *avoir une conscience bourrelée de remords*, to be conscience-stricken.

bourrelet (burlɛ) *m*, cushion; pad; flange. **bourrelier** (rəlje) *m*, harness maker.

bourrer (bure) *v.t*, to stuff, pad; cram, choke; tamp, ram, pack; snap at; belabor; thrash.

bourriche (buriʃ) *f*, basket, frail.

bourrique (burik) *f*, she-ass; donkey.

bourru, e (bury) *a*, surly, churlish, crusty, grumpy, gruff; rough; downy. ¶ *m*, churl, bear, curmudgeon.

bourse (burs) *f*, purse, bag, pouch; scholarship; exhibition; stock exchange, market, house; session, business day, working day. (*stock market*). ~ *à pasteur*, shepherd's-purse (*Bot.*). ~

[*des valeurs*], stock exchange. ~ *de marchandises*, ~ *de commerce*, produce exchange, commercial sale rooms. **boursicoter** (sikɔte) *v.i*, to dabble on the stock exchange. **boursier, ère** (sje, ɛːr) *n*, scholarship holder; speculator.

boursouflé, e (bursufle) *p.a*, inflated, turgid, bombastic. **boursoufler** (fle) *v.t.* & se ~, to swell, puff, bloat.

bousculade (buskylad) *f*, scrimmage, hustle, rush. **bousculer** (le) *v.t*, to upset; push about, jostle, hustle; ride out (*polo*).

bouse (buːz) *f*, dung (*cattle*).

bousillage (buzijaːʒ) *m*, cob, daub, mud; bungle, botch.

boussole (busɔl) *f*, [magnetic] compass, dial; (*fig.*) head, wits; guide. ~ *marine*, mariner's compass. *perdre la* ~, to go mad.

bout (bu) *m*, end; finish; extremity; tip; cap; bottom; bit, stump; ferrule; button. [*petit*] ~ *d'homme*, midget, chit, manikin. ~ *de lettre*, line or two. ~ *de rôle*, small part (*Theat.*). *au* ~ *de son rouleau*, at the end of one's rope. *faire un* ~ *de toilette*, to tidy oneself up. ~ *de vergue*, yardarm. ~ *du sein*, nipple, teat. *à* ~ *portant*, point-blank.

boutade (butad) *f*, whim, crotchet, fancy, fit; sally (*wit*). *par* ~s, in fits & starts.

boute-en-train (butɑ̃trɛ̃) *m*, life [& soul] (*of the party*).

boutefeu (butfø) (*fig.*) *m*, firebrand, mischief-maker.

bouteille (butɛːj) *f*, bottle, flask, jar. ~ *thermos*, thermos. ~ *à gaz*, gas cylinder.

boutique (butik) *f*, shop, stall, booth, stand; stock (*in shop*); shady concern; concern. **boutiquier, ère** (kje, ɛːr) *n*, shopkeeper, tradesman, -woman.

boutoir (butwaːr) *m*, snout (*boar*).

bouton (butɔ̃) *m*, bud; pimple; button; stud (*collar*); knob, handle. ~ *à pression*, snap fastener. ~ *d'or*, buttercup. ~s *de manchettes*, cuff links. ~ *de manivelle*, crank pin. ~ *de sonnette*, bell push. ~ *du sein*, nipple, teat.

boutonner (tɔne) *v.t*, button [up]; (*v.i.*) to bud; break out in pimples. se ~, to button oneself up. **boutonnière** (njɛːr) *f*, buttonhole; cut, gash.

bouture (butyːr) *f*, slip, cutting (*Hort.*).

bouverie (buvri) *f*, cattle pen, ox stall. **bouvier, ère** (vje, ɛːr) *n*, cowherd, herdsman. **bouvillon** (vijɔ̃) *m*, steer.

bouvreuil (buvrœːj) *m*, bullfinch.

bovin, e (bɔvɛ̃, in) *a*, bovine, neat, cattle (*att.*).

box (bɔks) *m*, box stall (*horse*).

boxe (bɔks) *f*, boxing. ~ *à poings nus*, bare-fist boxing, knuckle fighting. ~ *contre son ombre*, shadowboxing. **boxer** (kse) *v.i.* & *t*, to box, spar. **boxeur** (ksœːr) *m*, boxer. ~ *professionnel*, prizefighter.

boyau (bwajo) *m*, gut; hose (*pipe*); tubular [tire] (*bicycle*); passageway. ~ *de tranchée*, communication trench.

bracelet (braslɛ) *m*, bracelet, wristlet, strap, bangle. ~-*montre*, wristwatch.

braconner (brakɔne) *v.i*, to poach. **braconnier** (nje) *m*, poacher.

braguette (bragɛt) *f*, fly (*trousers*).

brahmane (braman) *m*, brahmin.

brai (brɛ) *m*, pitch, tar.

brailler (brɑje) *v.i*, to bawl, squall.

braiment (brɛmɑ̃) *m*, bray[ing]. **braire** (brɛːr) *v.i.ir*, to bray.

braise (brɛːz) *f*, embers; breeze, cinders. **braiser** (brɛze) *v.t*, to braise. **braisière** (zjɛːr) *f*, stewpan.

bramer (brame) *v.i*, to bell, troat.

brancard (brɑ̃kaːr) *m*, stretcher; shaft; wheelbarrow. **brancardier** (kardje) *m*, stretcher-bearer.

branchage (brɑ̃ʃaːʒ) *m*, branches; horns. **branche** (brɑ̃ːʃ) *f*, branch; leg (*compass, tripod*); prong, tooth, tine; shank; stick. ~ *de tranchée*, communication trench. ~ *gourmande*, sucker (*Hort.*). **branchement** (brɑ̃ʃmɑ̃) *m*, branch[ing]; branch pipe;

branch, tap (*Elec.*); lead (*Elec. service*); turnout (*Rly.*). **brancher** (ʃe) *v.t*, to branch; connect, plug in; (*v.i.*) to perch. **branchette** (ʃɛt) *f*, twig. **branchies** (ʃi) *f.pl*, gills (*fish*).

brande (brɑ̃:d) *f*, heather; heath, moor[land].

brandiller (brɑ̃dije) *v.t*, to swing, dangle.

brandir (brɑ̃di:r) *v.t*, to brandish, flourish.

brandon (brɑ̃dɔ̃) *m*, [fire]brand; spark (*from conflagration*).

branlant, e (brɑ̃lɑ̃, ɑ̃:t) *a*, shaky, loose, rocking. **branle** (brɑ̃:l) *m*, swing[ing]; jangle; impulse, impetus; (*fig.*) dance, running, lead, example. **en ~-bas** (brɑ̃lbɑ), astir, agog. **branler** (brɑ̃le) *v.t. & i*, to swing, shake, wag[gle], be loose, dance, bob.

braque (brak) *m*, hound; madcap. **braquer** (ke) *v.t*, to aim (*gun*); point (*telescope*); fix (*eyes*).

bras (brɑ) *m*, arm; flipper; (*pl.*) hands (*workmen*); handle (*oar, etc.*); brace (*Naut.*); (*pl.*) jaws (*of death*). **en ~ de chemise**, in shirt sleeves. **~ de mer**, arm of sea, sound. **~ dessus, ~ dessous**, arm in arm. **à [force de] ~**, [by] hand[-power], manual.

braser (brɑze) *v.t*, to braze, hardsolder.

brasero (brɑzero) *m*, brazier; fire basket. **brasier** (zje) *m*, bright fire; inferno. **brasiller** (zije) *v.t*, to broil; (*v.i.*) to sparkle.

brassage (brɑsa:ʒ) *m*, brewing; stirring.

brassard (brɑsa:r) *m*, armlet, brassard, badge, band.

brasse (brɑs) *f*, fathom (Fr. *brasse marine* = 1 meter 62; Eng. *fathom* = 6 feet); stroke (*distance covered at one swimming movement*); breaststroke. **brassée** (brɑse) *f*, armful; stroke (*one swimming movement*).

brasser (brɑse) *v.t*, to brew, mash; stir; dispatch; brace (*Naut.*). **brasserie** (sri) *f*, brewery, restaurant. **brasseur** (sœ:r) *m*, brewer. **~ d'affaires**, man with many irons in the fire; shady financier.

brassiage (brɑsja:ʒ) *m*, fathoming, sounding.

brassière (brɑsjɛ:r) *f*, vest (*baby's*); shoulder strap; (*pl.*) leading strings. **~ de sauvetage**, life jacket, cork j.

brasure (brɑzy:r) *f*, brazing; braze (*joint*).

bravache (bravaʃ) *m*, blusterer, swaggerer, bully, hector. **bravade** (vad) *f*, bravado, bluster. **brave** (brɑ:v) *a*, brave, gallant, bold, stout; honest, good, worthy. **¶ m**, brave man. **mon ~**, my good man. **bravement** (bravmɑ̃) *ad*, bravely, etc; ably. **braver** (ve) *v.t*, to brave, face; dare, defy. **bravo** (vo) *ad*, bravo! hurrah, -ray! well done! hear! hear! **¶ m**, cheer. **bravoure** (vu:r) *f*, bravery, gallantry.

brayer (brɛje) *m*, truss (*Surg.*).

break (brɛk) *m*, break, brake, waggonette.

brebis (brəbi) *f*, ewe, sheep. **~ galeuse**, plague, nuisance (*pers.*); black sheep (*fig.*).

brèche (brɛʃ) *f*, breach, gap; nick.

bredouille (brədu:j) *a*, empty-handed. **bredouiller** (duje) *v.i*, to stammer, mumble.

bref, ève (brɛf, ɛ:v) *a*, brief; curt. [*syllabe*] **brève**, *f*, short [syllable]. **bref**, *ad*, briefly, in short, in fine.

breloque (brəlɔk) *f*, charm (*seal, etc.*).

brème (brɛm) *f*, bream (*fish*).

Brême (brɛ:m) *f*, Bremen.

Brésil (le) (brezil), Brazil. **brésilien, ne** (ljẽ, ɛn) *a. & B~, n*, Brazilian.

Bretagne (la) (brətaɲ), Brittany.

bretelle (brətɛl) *f*, brace, suspender, sling; (*pl.*) suspenders, (*men's*); shoulder straps (*women's*).

breuil (brœ:j) *m*, covert (*game*).

breuvage (brœva:ʒ) *m*, beverage, drink; draught.

brevet (brəvɛ) *m*, diploma, certificate; patent, license. indentures (*apprenticeship*). **breveter** (vte) *v.t*, to patent; license.

bréviaire (brevjɛ:r) *m*, breviary; favorite author (*book*).

bribes (brib) *f.pl*, scraps, leavings; odds & ends; excerpts; snatches.

bric, *ad : de* ~ *& de broc* (brik, brɔk), here a little & there a little. **bric-à-brac** (kabrak) *m*, bric-à-brac.

brick (brik) *m*, brig (*Naut.*).

bricole (brikɔl) *f*, breast strap; (*pl.*) odd jobs.

bride (brid) *f*, bridle; rein[s]; curb, check; clamp, cramp; flange; treble (*crochet*). *à toute* ~, *à* ~ *abattue*, at full speed. **brider** (de) *v.t. & i*, to bridle; check, curb; bind; pinch, be tight; clamp. *des yeux bridés*, slit (*or* almond) eyes.

bridge (bridʒ) *m*, bridge (*cards*). ~ *aux enchères*, auction b. ~ *plafond*, ~ *contrat*, contract b.

brièvement (briɛvmɑ̃) *ad*, briefly, shortly. **brièveté** (vte) *f*, brevity.

brigade (brigad) *f*, brigade; party, posse, gang. **brigadier** (dje) *m*, colonel commandant; bombardier; corporal (*cavalry*); sergeant (*police*); bowman (*boat*).

brigand (brigɑ̃) *m*, brigand, highwayman, robber; scamp. **brigandage** (da:ʒ) *m*, brigandage, highway robbery.

brigue (brig) *f*, intrigue; faction. **briguer** (ge) *v.i. & t*, to intrigue; intrigue for; canvass, court, aspire to.

brillamment (brijamɑ̃) *ad*, brilliantly, brightly. **brillant, e** (jɑ̃, ɑ̃:t) *a*, brilliant, bright, shining; glittering, glistering; splendid; glossy (*phot. paper*). ¶ *m*, brilliant (*diamond*). **brillantine** (jãtin) *f*, brilliantine. **briller** (je) *v.i*, to shine, brighten; glitter, glisten; glow.

brimade (brimad) *f*, practical joke (*on newcomer*).

brimbale (brɛ̃bal) *f*, pump handle. **brimbaler** (le) *v.i*, to dangle; wobble.

brimborion (brɛ̃bɔrjɔ̃) *m*, knick-knack, bauble.

brin (brɛ̃) *m*, blade; slip; sprig; shoot; strand (*rope*); joint (*fishing rod*); bit. ~ *d'osier*, withe, withy. *un beau* ~ *d'homme, de*

fille, a fine youth, girl. **brindille** (di:j) *f*, sprig, twig.

brioche (briɔʃ) *f*, brioche; blunder.

brique (brik) *f*, brick; bar (*soap, etc.*).

briquet (brikɛ) *m*, lighter (*gasoline, etc.*); tinder box, [flint &] steel.

briquetage (brikta:ʒ) *m*, brickwork. **briqueterie** (ktri) *f*, brickfield. **briquetier** (ktje) *m*, brickmaker. **briquette** (kɛt) *f*, briquet[te].

bris (bri) *m*, breaking; wreck-[age]. **brisant** (zɑ̃) *m*, reef; breakwater; breaker (*wave*); (*pl.*) broken water.

brise (bri:z) *f*, breeze (*wind*).

brise-bise (brizbi:z) *m*, draft protector; short curtain, brisebise. **brisées** (ze) *f.pl*, footsteps (*fig.*). **brise-jet** (brizʒɛ) *m*, antisplash tap nozzle. **brise-lames** (lam) *m*, breakwater. **brisement** (zmɑ̃) *m*, breaking, etc, as *briser*. ~ *de cœur*, contrition (*Theol.*); heartbreak. **briser** (ze) *v.t. & i*, to break, smash, shatter, shiver, dash; exhaust. se ~, to break; come apart (*be detachable*), fold [up]. **brise-tout** (ztu) *m*, destructive person. **briseur** (zœ:r) *m*, breaker (*pers.*). **brisure** (zy:r) *f*, break; wristband; neckband.

britannique (britanik) *a*, British, Britannic. *les îles B~s*, the British Isles.

broc (bro) *m*, jug, pitcher. ~ *de toilette*, water jug, ewer.

brocanter (brokɑ̃te) *v.i*, to deal in works of art, curios, bargains, used goods.

brocard (broka:r) *m*, gibe, lampoon.

brocart (broka:r) *m*, brocade.

brochant sur le tout (broʃɑ̃), to cap all. **broche** (brɔʃ) *f*, spit, broach; knitting needle; spindle, arbor; spike; pin, pintle; drift-[pin]; brooch; (*pl.*) tusks (*wild boar*). **brochée** (ʃe) *f*, spitful. **brocher** (ʃe) *v.t*, to brocade; stitch, sew (*books*); drift (*rivets*); scamp (*work*). *un livre broché*, a paperback book. **brochet** (ʃɛ) *m*, pike, jack (*fish*). **brochette** (ʃɛt) *f*, skewer. **brochure** (ʃy:r) *f,* interwoven pattern (*fabrics*); stitching, sewing; pamphlet, booklet, brochure; paperback binding.

brocoli (brɔkɔli) *m,* broccoli.

brodequin (brɔdkɛ̃) *m,* lace boot; buskin; sock (*comedy*).

broder (brɔde) *v.t,* to embroider. **broderie** (dri) *f,* embroidery. ~ *à fils couchés,* couching. ~-*application,* appliqué (*or* applied) work. **brodeur, euse** (dœːr, øːz) *n,* embroiderer, ess.

brome (broːm) *m,* bromine. **bromure** (brɔmyːr) *m,* bromide.

broncher (brɔ̃ʃe) *v.i,* to stumble, trip; flinch, falter.

bronches (brɔ̃ʃ) *f.pl,* bronchia. **bronchite** (brɔ̃ʃit) *f,* bronchitis.

bronze (brɔ̃ːz) *m,* bronze. ~ [*industriel*] gun metal. **bronzer** (brɔ̃ze) *v.t,* to bronze; (*fig.*) steel, [case]harden; tan.

broquette (brɔkɛt) *f,* tack(s).

brosse (brɔs) *f,* brush. ~ *à barbe,* shaving b. ~ *à cheveux,* ~ *à tête,* hairbrush. ~ *à cirer,* shoe b. ~ *à dents,* toothbrush. ~ *à habits,* clothes b. ~ *à laver,* scrubbing b. ~ *à miettes* [*pour la table*], crumb b. ~ *rude, douce,* hard, soft, b. *cheveux en* ~, crew cut. **brossée** (se) *f,* brushing; beating, drubbing. **brosser** (se) *v.t,* to brush; scrub (*floor*); thrash, drub. *se* ~ *la tête, les dents,* to brush one's hair, teeth. **brosserie** (sri) *f,* brush making; b. works. **brossier, ère** (sje, ɛːr) *n,* brush maker.

brou (bru) *m,* husk (*walnut, almond*); juice (*of walnut husk*).

brouette (bruɛt) *f,* [wheel]barrow.

brouhaha (bruaa) *m,* hubbub, din, pother.

brouillamini (brujamini) *m,* disorder, muddle.

brouillard (brujaːr) *m,* fog, mist, haze; rough book. **brouillasse** (jas) *f,* [Scotch] mist. **brouille** (bruːj) *f,* discord, misunderstanding. **brouiller** (bruje) *v.t,* to jumble, muddle, blur, embroil; shuffle (*cards*); scramble (*eggs*). *se* ~, to break up (*weather*); fall out; get confused,

be at loggerheads. **brouillon, ne** (jɔ̃, ɔn) *n,* muddler; (*m.*) [rough] draft; rough copy; scratch pad.

brouir (bruiːr) *v.t,* to wither, blast, blight. **brouissure** (isyːr) *f,* blight.

broussailles (brusɑːj) *f.pl,* brushwood, undergrowth, scrub. *en* ~, unkempt. **brousse** (brus) *f,* bush (*scrub*).

broussin (brusɛ̃) *m,* gnarl (*on tree*).

brout (bru) *m,* browse. **brouter** (te) *v.t. & abs,* to browse (on), nibble; chatter (*tool*).

broutilles (brutiːj) *f.pl,* twigs; trifles.

broyer (brwaje) *v.t,* to crush, grind, mill.

bruant (bryɑ̃) *m,* bunting (*bird*).

brucelles (brysɛl) *f.pl,* tweezers.

brugnon (brynɔ̃) *m,* nectarine.

bruine (brɥin) *f,* drizzle, mizzle. **bruiner** (ne) *v.imp,* to drizzle, mizzle.

bruire (brɥiːr) *v.i.ir,* to murmur, rustle, sough. **bruissement** (ismɑ̃) *m,* murmur, etc.

bruit (brɥi) *m,* noise, row, racket, din, clatter, ado, fuss; rumor, report, news. ~ *de pas,* tramp.

brûlant, e (brylɑ̃, ɑ̃ːt) *a,* burning, hot, scorching, broiling; afire. **brûle-gueule** (bryl) *m,* short tobacco pipe. **brûle-parfum,** *m,* incense burner. *à brûle-pourpoint* (purpwɛ̃) *ad,* point-blank, to one's face. **brûlé** (le) *m,* burning (*smell, taste*). **brûler** (le) *v.t. & i,* to burn, scorch, parch, sear; singe; nip; roast; mull (*wine*). *je me suis brûlé le bras,* I have burnt my arm. *se* ~ *la cervelle,* to blow one's brains out. **brûleur** (lœːr) *m,* burner. **brûlure** (lyːr) *f,* burn; scald.

brume (brym) *f,* fog, mist, haze. **brumeux, euse** (mø, øːz) *a,* foggy; wintry.

brun, e (brœ̃, yn) *a,* brown; dark, dusky. ¶ *m,* brown; (*f.*) dusk, gloaming. **brunâtre** (brynɑːtr) *a,* brownish. **brunet** (nɛ) *m,* dark man, dark boy. **brunette** (nɛt) *f,* brunette. **brunir** (niːr) *v.t,* to brown; tan; burnish. **brunissage** (nisaːʒ) *m,* burnishing.

brusque† (brysk) *a*, blunt, bluff, brusque, offhand, curt, abrupt, gruff. **brusquer** (ke) *v.t*, to treat abruptly; precipitate, rush. ~ *l'aventure*, to chance it. **brusquerie** (kəri) *f*, bluntness, etc.

brut, e (bryt) *a*, raw, crude; uncut (*gem*); unmanufactured; unpolished; unsweetened (*wine*); rough; gross (*Com.*); inorganic; brute (*beast, force*). **brutal, e†** (tal) *a*, brutal; brutish, coarse, rough. ¶ *m*, brute, bully. **brutaliser** (lise) *v.t*, to maltreat; bully. **brutalité** (te) *f*, brutality, etc. **brute** (bryt) *f*, brute.

Bruxelles (brysɛl) *f*, Brussels.

bruyant, e (bryjɑ̃, ɑ̃:t) *a*, noisy, boisterous, rollicking, clamorous, loud, blatant; hoydenish. **bruyamment** (jamɑ̃) *ad*, noisily.

bruyère (bryjɛ:r) *f*, heather; heath, moor; brier, briar (*pipe wood*).

buanderie (byɑ̃dri) *f*, washhouse, laundry. **buandier, ère** (dje, ɛ:r) *n*, bleacher.

buccin (byksɛ̃) *m*, whelk (*Mol.*).

bûche (by:ʃ) *f*, log, billet, chump; Swiss roll; blockhead. ~ *de Noël*, yule log. **bûcher** (byʃe) *m*, woodshed; pile, stack (*firewood*); pyre; stake (*for burning alive*). ¶ *v.t. & i*, to rough-hew, dress, trim; swot. **bûcheron** (ʃrɔ̃) *m*, woodman, lumberman. **bûchette** (ʃɛt) *f*, stick. **bûcheur, euse** (ʃœ:r, ø:z) *n*, plodder, brain worker.

bucolique (bykɔlik) *a. & f*, bucolic.

budget (bydʒɛ) *m*, budget; estimates (*parliamentary*).

buée (bye) *f*, steam, moisture; fumes.

buffet (byfɛ) *m*, cupboard; sideboard, buffet; refreshment bar *or* room; running buffet.

buffle (byfl) *m*, buffalo. [*peau de*] ~, buff [leather].

bugle (bygl) *m*, flügel horn; (*f.*) bugle (*Bot.*).

buire (bɥi:r) *f*, beaker, flagon, jug.

buis (bɥi) *m*, box [tree]; boxwood.

buisson (bɥisɔ̃) *m*, bush. **buis-** sonneux, euse (sɔnø, ø:z) *a*, bushy. faire l'école buissonnière (njɛ:r), to play hooky.

bulbe (bylb) *f*, bulb (*Bot.*); (*m.*) bulb (*Anat.*). **bulbeux, euse** (bø, ø:z) *a*, bulbous.

bulgare (bylga:r) *a. & B~, n*, Bulgarian. **la Bulgarie** (gari), Bulgaria.

bulle (byl) *f*, bubble; blister; bleb; bull (*Pope's*).

bulletin (byltɛ̃) *m*, paper, note, bulletin, letter; ticket; voucher; form; list; report. ~ *de la cote*, stock exchange daily official list. ~ *de vote*, ballot. ~ *météorologique*, weather forecast.

buraliste (byralist) *n, in France*, keeper of a state-owned tobacco shop (*bureau de tabac*), where also postage stamps are sold, & licenses, such as for bicycles, are issued. *Also*, clerk, tax collector. **bureau** (ro) *m*, writing table; table, desk; bureau; office; counting house; agency; exchange; committee, executive. ~ *américain*, ~ *à rideau*, rolltop desk. ~ [*central téléphonique*], [telephone] exchange. ~ *d'esprit*, coterie of wits. ~ [*de location*], box office. ~ *de garantie*, government assay office. ~ *de placement*, employment agency, registry office. ~ *de police*, police station. ~ *de poste*, post office. ~ *de scrutin*, polling station. ~ *de tabac*, tobacconist's shop. ~ *des objets trouvés*, lost property office. ~ *des rebuts*, dead letter office. ~ *ministre*, pedestal desk, kneehole d. ~ *municipal de placement gratuit*, labor exchange. *à* ~[*x*] *ouvert*[*s*], on demand, on presentation. ~ *restant*, to be called for. *sur le* ~, (*matter*) under consideration. *le deuxième* ~, Intelligence Dept. (*Mil.*). **bureaucrate** (krat) *m*, bureaucrat. **bureaucratie** (si) *f*, bureaucracy.

burette (byrɛt) *f*, bottle (*oil, vinegar*); cruet (*Eccl.*). ~ [*à huile*], oil can.

burin (byrɛ̃) *m*, graver; chisel. ~ [*à froid*], cold chisel. **buriner** (rine) *v.t*, to engrave; chisel, chip.

burlesque (byrlɛsk), *a. & m*, burlesque, farcical; comic(al).

buse (byːz) *f*, buzzard; air pipe; nozzle; blockhead.

buste (byst) *m*, bust.

but (by; *in liaison*, byt) *m*, butt, mark; target; goal; winning post; aim, object, end, intention, purpose, point. ~ *de transformation*, converted goal. *de* ~ *en blanc*, point-blank, bluntly. ~ *à* ~, even (*games*).

butée (byte) *f*, abutment (*bridge*); shore (*prop*); thrust (*Mech.*); stop. **buter** (te) *v.i. & t*, to butt; stumble; shore. *se* ~ *à* (*fig.*), to be bent on; be up against.

butin (bytɛ̃) *m*, booty, spoil, loot, plunder. **butiner** (tine) *v.i. & t*, to pillage, plunder, loot.

butoir (bytwaːr) *m*, stop; stop blocks; buffer.

butor (bytɔːr) *m*, bittern; dolt.

butte (byt) *f*, mound, knoll, hillock; butts (*behind target*). **butter** (te) *v.t*, to ridge; earth, hill.

buvable (byvabl) *a*, drinkable; acceptable. **buvard** (vaːr) *m*, blotter, blotting pad *or* case. **buvette** (vɛt) *f*, refreshment bar *or* room; pump room (*spa*). **buveur, euse** (vœːr, øːz) *n*, drinker. ~ *d'eau*, teetotaller. **buvoter** (vɔte) *v.i*, to sip; tipple.

C

ça (sa) *pn*. Contraction of *cela*.

çà (sa) *ad*: ~ & *là*, here & there, hither & thither, this way & that. *ah! çà, i*, now then! come now!

cabale (kabal) *f*, cabal; caucus. **cabaler** (le) *v.i*, to plot, intrigue.

cabane (kaban) *f*, cabin, hut; kennel; hutch. ~ *de bois*, log cabin, 1. hut. **cabanon** (nɔ̃) *m*, padded cell.

cabaret (kabarɛ) *m*, wine shop *or* cellar; tavern, public house; restaurant; set *or* service (*china, liqueur, etc.*). **cabaretier, ère** (bartje, ɛːr) *n*, innkeeper; publican.

cabas (kabɑ) *m*, frail; shopping basket.

cabestan (kabɛstɑ̃) *m*, capstan; winch.

cabillaud (kabijo) *m*, cod[fish].

cabine (kabin) *f*, cabin; box; cage, car; telephone booth.

cabinet (kabinɛ) *m*, room, closet; chambers; den; practice (*professional*); cabinet (*ministerial*); collection (*curiosities*). ~*s* ou ~ [*d'aisances*], toilet. ~ *de consultation*, consulting room, surgery. ~ *de débarras*, lumber room. ~ *de lecture*, reading room, newsroom; lending library. ~ *de toilette*, dressing room, toilet. ~ *de travail*, study. ~ *de verdure*, arbor, bower. ~ *noir*, darkroom (*Phot.*). *vie de* ~, indoor life.

câble (kɑːbl) *m*, rope, cable, line, wire, cord. **câbler** (kɑble) *v.t*, to cable (*Teleg.*).

caboche (kabɔʃ) *f*, pate, noddle, head; hobnail. **cabochon** (ʃɔ̃) *m*, cabochon; brass nail.

cabosser (kabɔse) *v.t*, to dent, batter.

cabotage (kabɔtaːʒ) *m*, coasting; coasting trade, home trade. **caboter** (te) *v.i*, to coast. **caboteur** (tœːr) *m*, coaster.

cabotin, e (kabɔtɛ̃, in) *n*, strolling player; ham actor; theatrical person (*affected*).

cabrer (se) (kabre) *v.pr*, to rear; jib (*fig.*), take offense. **cabri** (kabri) *m*, kid (*goat*). **cabriole** (ɔl) *f*, leap, caper. **cabrioler** (le) *v.i*, to caper. **cabriolet** (lɛ) *m*, gig, cabriolet; handcuffs (*of cord*).

cacahuète (kakawɛt) *f*, peanut.

cacao (kakao) *m*, cacao, cocoa. **cacaoyer** (ɔje) *ou* **cacaotier** (ɔtje) *m*, cacao [tree].

cacatoès (kakatɔɛs) *m*, cockatoo, parakeet.

cachalot (kaʃalo) *m*, sperm whale, cachalot.

cache (kaʃ) *f*, hiding place; mask (*Phot.*). ~**-ampoule**, *m*, bulb shade (*Elec.*). ~**-cache**, *m*, hide-&-seek. ~**-corset**, *m*, camisole, underbodice.

cachemire (kaʃmiːr) *m*, cashmere.

cache-nez (kaʃne) *m*, muffler, comforter, scarf. **cache-pot** (po) *m*, jardinière (*pot*). **cache-poussière** (pusjɛːr) *m*, dust coat. **cacher** (ʃe) *v.t*, to hide, conceal, secrete; mask. ~ *son jeu*, to be underhanded. **cachet** (ʃɛ) *m*, seal, signet; cachet; ticket, voucher; stamp (*fig.*); fee, salary. **cacheter** (ʃte) *v.t*, to seal, do up. **cachette** (ʃɛt) *f*, hiding place. **en ~**, secretly, stealthily, covertly, on the sly. **cachot** (ʃo) *m*, dungeon, cell. **cachotter** (ʃote) *v.t*, to make a mystery of. **cachottier, ère** (tje, ɛːr) *n*, slyboots; (*att.*) secretive.

cachou (kaʃu) *m*, cachou.

cacochyme (kakoʃim) *a*, sensitive [to illness]; queer.

cacophonie (kakofoni) *f*, cacophony.

cactus (kaktyːs) *m*, cactus.

cadastre (kadastr) *m*, cadastral survey; valuation list (*basis for taxes*). **cadastrer** (tre) *v.t*, to survey [& value]; enter (*in valuation list*).

cadavéreux, euse (kadaverø, øːz) *a*, cadaverous, corpselike. **cadavre** (dɑːvr) *m*, corpse; carcass; skeleton.

cadeau (kado) *m*, present, gift.

cadenas (kadnɑ) *m*, padlock. **cadenasser** (dnase) *v.t*, to padlock; fasten.

cadence (kadɑ̃ːs) *f*, cadence, rhythm, time, step; tune (*fig.*). *aller en ~*, to keep time.

cadet, te (kadɛ, ɛt) *a. & n*, younger (brother, sister); cadet, junior, minor; caddie (*golf*); least (*fig.*).

Cadix (kadiks) *m*, Cadiz.

cadran (kadrɑ̃) *m*, dial [plate], face [plate]. *~ [solaire]*, [sun] dial.

cadre (kɑːdr) *m*, frame, framework; frame aerial; limits, scheme, scope, compass. **cadrer** (kadre) *v.i*, to square, agree, tally, suit, fit, match. .

caduc, uque (kadyk) *a*, broken, decrepit, declining, frail; lapsed, statute barred. **caducité** (dysite) *f*, dilapidated state; decrepitude, senile decay; lapsing, nullity.

cafard, e (kafaːr, ard) *n*, canter, hypocrite; tell-tale, sneak; (*m.*) cockroach, black beetle; desert madness. *avoir le ~*, to have the blues.

café (kafe) *m*, coffee; café. *~ complet*, coffee, roll & butter. **caféier** (feje) *m*, coffee tree; c.

planter. **cafetier, ère** (ftje, ɛːr) *n*, café keeper, caterer; (*f.*) coffeepot.

cage (kaːʒ) *f*, cage; case; housing; shaft (*lift*). *~ à poulets*, chicken coop. *~ d'escalier*, staircase, stairway.

cagnard, e (kaɲaːr, ard) *a*, lazy, slothful. ¶ *n*, lazybones. **cagnardise** (ɲardiːz) *f*, laziness, sloth.

cagneux, euse (kaɲø, øːz) *a*, knock-kneed; crooked (*legs*).

cagnotte (kaɲot) (*cards*) *f*, pool, kitty, pot.

cagot, e (kago, ot) *n*, hypocrite; (*att.*) sanctimonious.

cagoule (kagul) *f*, (monk's) hooded cloak; penitent's hood.

cahier (kaje) *m*, notebook. *~ de dessin*, sketch book. *~ des charges*, specification.

cahin-caha (kaɛ̃kaa) *ad*, so so, middling. *aller ~*, to jog on.

cahot (kao) *m*, jolt, bump; vicissitude. **cahoter** (ote) *v.t. & i*, to jolt, bump; toss about.

cahute (kayt) *f*, hovel; hut.

caille (kɑːj) *f*, quail.

caillé (kɑje) *m*, **caillebotte** (kajbot) *f*, curd[s]. **cailler** (kɑje) *v.t. & se ~*, to curd[le]; clot.

cailletage (kɑjtaːʒ) *m*, gossip. **caillette** (jɛt) *f*, gossip (*pers.*).

caillot (kajo) *m*, clot.

caillou (kaju) *m*, pebble; flint; stone; boulder (*Geol.*). **caillouteux, euse** (tø, øːz) *a*, pebbly; stony, flinty. **cailloutis** (ti) *m*, pebblestone, roadstones.

Caire (le) (kɛːr), Cairo.

caisse (kɛs) *f*, case, box; tub (*for shrub*); body (*vehicle*); drum; cash; cash box, cash register, till; coffer, chest; cashier's office *or* desk *or* counter, pay office; bank, treasury, fund, association. *en ~*, in (*or* on) hand, in the till. *~ à eau*, tank. *~ à médicaments*, medicine chest. *~ claire*, snare drum. *~ d'amortissement*, sinking fund. *~ de dépôts*, safe deposit (*institution*). *~ de retraites pour la vieillesse*, old-age pension fund. *~ doublée de ferblanc*, tin-lined case. *~ enregistreuse*, *~ contrôleuse*, cash register. *~ d'épargne*, savings bank.

caissier, ère (kɛsje, ɛːr) *n*, cashier; teller (*bank*). **~-comptable**, cashier & bookkeeper. **~ des titres**, securities clerk.

caisson (kɛsɔ̃) *m*, caisson, pontoon; bin, bunker, box, locker.

cajoler (kaʒɔle) *v.t*, to cajole, wheedle, coax. **cajolerie** (lri) *f*, cajolery, etc.

cal (kal) *m*, callosity, callus.

calaison (kalɛzɔ̃) *f*, load draught (*ship*.)

calamité (kalamite) *f*, calamity. **calamiteux, euse** (tø, øːz) *a*, calamitous.

calandre (kalɑ̃ːdr) *f*, calender; mangle; weevil. **calandrer** (lɑ̃dre) *v.t*, to calender; mangle.

calcaire (kalkɛːr) *m*, limestone. ¶ *a*, calcareous, lime[stone] (*att.*)

calciner (kalsine) *v.t*, to calcine, burn.

calcium (kalsjɔm) *m*, calcium.

calcul (kalkyl) *m*, calculation, reckoning; arithmetic; sum; calculus, stone (*Med.*). **calculer** (le) *v.t. & abs*, to calculate, reckon.

cale (kal) *f*, hold (*of ship*); wedge, key, scotch. **~** [*de construction*], stocks, slip[s] (*Shipbldg.*). **~ de halage**, slipway. **~ sèche, ~ de radoub**, dry dock.

calebasse (kalbas) *f*, calabash, gourd.

caleçon (kalsɔ̃) *m*, pants, drawers. **~ de bain**, swimming trunks.

calembour (kalɑ̃buːr) *m*, pun. **faire des ~s**, to pun. **faiseur de ~s**, punster.

calembredaine (kalɑ̃brədɛn) *f*. *oft. pl*, nonsense, foolery.

calendes (kalɑ̃ːd) *f.pl*, calends. **~ grecques** (*fig.*), doomsday. **calendrier** (lɑ̃drie) *m*, calendar.

calepin (kalpɛ̃) *m*, notebook; working drawing.

caler (kale) *v.t. & i*, to wedge, key; scotch; draw (*so much water—ship*); strike (*sail*); stall (*motor*). **~** [*la voile*], to give in, knuckle down, k. under, sing small. **être calé en**, to be well up in (*subject*).

calfater (kalfate) *v.t*, to calk.

calfeutrer (kalføtre) *v.t*, to list (*door*). **se ~**, to make oneself cosy, shut oneself in.

calibre (kalibr) *m*, caliber, bore; standing (*fig.*); gauge; template, pattern, shape; calliper[s]. **calibrer** (bre) *v.t*, to gauge, calliper, calibrate.

calice (kalis) *m*, chalice, communion cup, cup; calyx.

calicot (kaliko) *m*, calico.

calife (kalif) *m*, caliph.

Californie (la) (kalifɔrni), California. **californien, ne** (njɛ̃, ɛn) *a. & C~*, *n*, Californian.

califourchon (à) (kalifurʃɔ̃) *ad*, astride, astraddle.

câlin, e (kɑlɛ̃, in) *a*, caressing, wheedling. ¶ *n*, pet, darling; wheedler. **câliner** (line) *v.t*, to fondle, pet, cuddle; wheedle. **câlinerie** (nri) *f*, fondling; wheedling.

calleux, euse (kalø, øːz) *a*, callous, horny.

calligraphie (kaligrafi) *f*, calligraphy, penmanship.

callosité (kalozite) *f*, callosity.

calmant (kalmɑ̃) *m*, sedative, soother.

calmar (kalmaːr) *m*, calamary, squid.

calme (kalm) *a*, calm, quiet, still; composed, collected, cool. ¶ *m*, calm, calmness. **~ plat**, dead calm. **calmer** (me) *v.t. & i. & se ~**, to calm; soothe, salve; subside, abate.

calomnie (kalɔmni) *f*, calumny, slander. **calomnier** (nje) *v.t*, to calumniate, slander. **calomnieux, euse** (njø, øːz) *a*, calumnious, slanderous.

calorie (kalɔri) *f*, calorie. **calorifère** (rifɛːr) *m*, heater. **~ à feu continu**, slow-combustion stove. **calorique** (rik) (*Phys.*), *m*, caloric, heat.

calot (kalo) *m*, forage cap. **calotte** (lɔt) *f*, skull cap; cap; calotte; canopy (*heaven*); cuff (*blow*). **calotter** (te) *v.t*, to cuff.

calque (kalk) *m*, tracing; copy (*fig.*). **calquer** (ke) *v.t*, to trace; copy.

calus (kalyːs) *m*, callus, callosity.

Calvaire (kalvɛːr) *m*, Calvary (*place*). **calvaire**, (*representation*); cross (*fig.*).

calvitie (kalvisi) *f*, baldness.

camarade (kamarad) *n*, comrade, fellow, mate, chum, companion. ~ d'atelier, fellow work-man. ~ d'école, schoolfellow, schoolmate. ~ de bord, ship-mate. ~ de bouteille, boon com-panion. ~ de collège, fellow student. ~ de jeu, playfellow, playmate. ~ de lit, ~ de cham-brée, bedfellow, roommate. ~ de malheur, fellow sufferer. ~ de plat, messmate. ~ de pro-motion, class mate. camaraderie (dri) f, comradeship, fellowship, friendship.

camard, e (kama;r, ard) a, snub-nosed. la camarde, [grim] death (fig.).

cambouis (kãbwi) m, cart grease.

cambrer (kãbre) v.t. & se ~, to camber, arch, bend, curve.

cambriolage (kãbriɔlaːʒ) m, housebreaking, burglary. **cam-brioler** (le) v.t, to burgle. **cam-brioleur** (lœːr) m, burglar, cracksman. ~ chat, cat burglar.

cambrure (kãbryːr) f, camber. ~-support, f, arch support (for foot in shoe).

cambuse (kãbyːz) f, steward's room (ship). **cambusier** (byzje) m, steward's mate; storekeeper (Naut.).

came (kam) f, cam, wiper, lifter.

camée (kame) m, cameo.

caméléon (kameleɔ̃) m, chame-leon; trimmer, time server.

camélia (kamelja) m, camellia.

camelot (kamlo) m, hawker, street vender (as newsboy), hand-bill distributor. **camelote** (lɔt) f, rubbish, trash.

camion (kamjɔ̃) m, wagon, truck; ~-citerne, m, tank truck. **ca-mionnage** (ɔnaːʒ) m, cartage. **camionnette** (nɛt) f, light truck, **camionneur** (nœr) m, truck driver, carter, carman; van horse, vanner.

camisole (kamizɔl) f, vest (wom-an's). ~ de force, straitjacket.

camomille (kamɔmiːj) f, camo-mile.

camouflage (kamuflaːʒ) m, camouflage. **camoufler** (fle) v.t, to disguise, camouflage.

camouflet (kamuflɛ) m, snub.

camp (kã) m, camp, field; side. ~ de concentration (civil), ~ de prisonniers (Mil.), internment

camp. ~ volant, flying column; flying visit.

campagnard, e (kãpaɲaːr, ard) n, countryman, -woman. **cam-pagne** (paɲ) f, country, country-side, fields; field (Mil.); cam-paign; run; cruise (Nav.).

campagnol (kãpaɲɔl) m, vole.

campanile (kãpanil) m, campa-nile, bell tower.

campanule (kãpanyl) f, campa-nula, bell [flower]. ~ à grandes fleurs, Canterbury Bell.

campêche (kãpɛʃ) m, logwood.

campement (kãpmã) m, en-campment; camping [out]. **cam-per** (pe) v.i. & t, to [en]camp; lodge, ensconce; put, clap, stick. ~ là, to leave in the lurch.

camphre (kã;fr) m, camphor. **camphrer** (kãfre) v.t, to cam-phorate.

campos (kãpo) m, holiday.

camus, e (kamy, y;z) a, flat-nosed, snub-nosed; pug-nosed.

Canada (le) (kanada), Canada. **canadien, ne** (djɛ̃, ɛn) a. & C~, n, Canadian; sheepskin jacket.

canaille (kanaːj) f, rabble, mob, riffraff, ragtag [& bobtail]; black-guard, scoundrel, rascal.

canal (kanal) m, canal, channel, duct, pipe, passage, race[way], ditch, sluice[way]. ~ de dériva-tion, leat. ~ maritime, ship canal. **canalisation** (lizasjɔ̃) f, canalization, piping, pipeline; mains. **canaliser** (ze) v.t, to canalize, pipe; (fig.) concen-trate, focus, centralize.

canapé (kanape) m, sofa, couch, lounge. ~-divan, m, chesterfield. ~-lit, sofa bed.

canard (kanaːr) m, duck, drake; canard, hoax; rag (worthless newspaper). bâtiment ~, pitch-ing ship. **canarder** (narde) v.t, to snipe (Mil.); pepper (with shot); (v.i.) to pitch (ship). **canardière** (djeːr) f, duck pond; decoy (place); fowling piece.

canari (kanari) m, canary (bird). les [îles] Canaries, f.pl, the Ca-nary Islands, the Canaries.

cancan (kãkã) m, cancan (dance); tattle, scandal, back-biting.

cancer (kɑ̃sɛːr) m, cancer (Med.),

le ~, crab (*Astr.*). **cancéreux, euse** (serǿ, ǿːz) *a*, cancerous.

cancre (kɑ̃ːkr) *m*, crab (*Crust.*); dunce, duffer.

cancrelat (kɑ̃krəla) *m*, cockroach.

candélabre (kɑ̃delaːbr) *m*, candelabrum; multi-light fixture.

candeur (kɑ̃dœːr) *f*, guilelessness, ingenuousness.

candidat, e (kɑ̃dida, at) *n*, candidate; examinee. ~ *à la députation*, parliamentary candidate. **candidature** (tyːr) *f*, candidature.

candide† (kɑ̃did) *a*, guileless, ingenuous.

candir (se) (kɑ̃diːr) *v.pr*, to candy. *fruits candis* (di), crystalized fruits. [**sucre**] **candi** (di), *m*, [sugar] candy.

cane (kan) *f*, duck (*female*). **caner** (ne) *v.i*, to run away, show the white feather. **caneton** (ntɔ̃) duckling (*male*). **canette** (nɛt) *f*, duckling (*female*); [spring-stoppered] bottle (*for, or of, beer*); bobbin.

canevas (kanvɑ) *m*, canvas; sketch; groundwork, outline, skeleton.

caniche (kaniʃ) *n. & a*, poodle.

canicule (kanikyl) *f*, dog days.

canif (kanif) *m*, penknife.

canin, e (kanɛ̃, in) *a*, canine, dog (*att.*).

caniveau (kanivo) *m*, gutter, gully, kennel [stone]; conduit.

canne (kan) *f*, cane; stick; walking stick; singlestick. ~ *à épée*, sword stick. ~ *à lancer*, casting rod (*Fish.*). ~ *à mouche*, fly rod (*Fish.*). ~ *à pêche*, fishing rod. ~ *à sucre*, sugarcane. ~ *plombée*, loaded stick. ~*-siège*, sportsman's seat, stick s.

canneberge (kanbɛrʒ) *f*, cranberry.

canneler (kanle) *v.t*, to channel, flute, groove, corrugate, rifle.

cannelle (kanɛl) *f*, cinnamon; butt cock.

cannelure (kanlyːr) *f*, channel-[ling], etc. as *canneler*.

canner (kane) *v.t*, to cane (*chairs*).

cannibale (kanibal) *m*, cannibal,

man-eater; savage (*fierce man*).

canoë (kanɔe) *m*, canoe.

canon (kanɔ̃) *m*, gun, cannon; cañon, canyon; barrel, pipe, tube; canon (*rule—Eccl.*). ~ *d'amarrage*, bollard. ~ *de campagne à tir rapide*, quick-firing field gun. *droit* ~, canon law. **canonicat** (nɔnika) *m*, canonicate, canonry; sinecure. **canoniser** (ze) *v.t*, to canonize. **canonnade** (nad) *f*, cannonade. **canonnage** (naːʒ) *m*, gunnery. **canonner** (ne) *v.t*, to cannonade, bombard, shell. **canonnier** (nje) *m*, gunner. **canonnière** (njeːr) *f*, gunboat; pop gun (*toy*).

canot (kano) *m*, boat; dinghy; cutter. ~ *à rames*, rowboat. ~ *de sauvetage*, lifeboat. **canotage** (nɔtaːʒ) *m*, boating, rowing. **canoter** (te) *v.i*, to boat, row. **canotier** (tje) *m*, rower, oarsman; boatman, waterman; boat keeper. [*chapeau*] ~, boater.

cantate (kɑ̃tat) *f*, cantata. **cantatrice** (tris) *f*, professional singer (*woman*), vocalist.

cantharide (kɑ̃tarid) *f*, Spanish fly.

cantine (kɑ̃tin) *f*, canteen. **cantinier, ère** (nje, ɛːr) *n*, canteen keeper.

cantique (kɑ̃tik) *m*, canticle, song, hymn.

canton (kɑ̃tɔ̃) *m*, canton, district. **cantonade** (tɔnad) *f*, wings (*Theat.*). **cantonnement** (nmɑ̃) *m*, cantonment, quarters; billets. ~ *de pêche*, stretch of fishing. **cantonner** (ne) *v.t. & i*, to canton, quarter, billet. *se* ~ *dans*, to withdraw to; keep oneself to. **cantonnier** (nje) *m*, roadman, road mender.

canule (kanyl) *f*, nozzle; butt cock.

caoutchouc (kautʃu) *m*, rubber, elastic; [rubber] tire; waterproof, mackintosh; galosh, golosh, overshoe. ~ *durci*, vulcanite. **caoutchouter** (ʃute) *v.t*, to rubber[ize], waterproof; rubber-tire.

cap (kap) *m*, cape, headland, foreland; head. ~ *à pic*, bluff. *le* ~ *de Bonne-Espérance*, the Cape of Good Hope. *le* ~ *Vert*, Cape Verde.

capable (kapabl) *a*, capable; able, fit; efficient, qualified. **capacité** (site) *f*, capacity, capability, etc.

caparaçonner (kaparasɔne) *v.t*, to caparison.

cape (kap) *f*, hooded cape; hood; bowler [hat]. *rire sous* ~, to laugh up one's sleeve, chuckle. **capeline** (plin) *f*, hood.

capharnaüm (kafarnaɔm) *m*, jumble shop.

capillaire (kapillɛ:r) *a*, capillary. ¶ *m*, maidenhair [fern].

capilotade (kapilɔtad) *f*, hash; pulp.

capitaine (kapitɛn) *m*, captain; master, skipper. ~ *au long cours*, deep-sea captain, master of foreign-going vessel. ~ *d'armement*, marine superintendent. ~ *d'entraînement*, coach. ~ *de corvette*, lieutenant commander (*Nav.*). ~ *de frégate, commander* (*Nav.*). ~ *de port*, harbor master. ~ *de vaisseau*, captain (*Nav.*). ~ *marchand*, captain of merchant ship, master mariner.

capital, e (kapital) *a*, capital, principal, main, essential; deadly (*sins*). ¶ *m. oft. pl*, principal, capital, capital sum; capital stock; money; assets. ~*-actions*, *m*, share capital. ~ *de roulement*, working capital. ~ *engagé*, trading capital. *le* ~ *& le travail*, Capital & Labor. ¶ *f*, capital (*town, letter*); metropolis. **capitaliser** (lize) *v.t*, to capitalize. **capitaliste** (list) *n*, capitalist.

capitan (kapitɑ̃) *m*, blusterer.

capitation (kapitasjɔ̃) *f*, poll tax.

capiteux, euse (kapitø, ø:z) *a*, heady.

capitonner (kapitɔne) *v.t*, to upholster; quilt.

capituler (kapityle) *v.i*, to capitulate; compromise (*with conscience*).

capon, ne (kapɔ̃, ɔn) *n*, coward; sneak (*Sch.*).

caporal (kapɔral) *m*, corporal; caporal (*tobacco*).

capot (kapo) *m*, bonnet, hood, cover. *être* ~, to be defeated. *faire* ~, to capsize. **capote** (pɔt) *f*, greatcoat, overcoat (*Mil.*);

hood, bonnet, cowl. **capoter** (te) *v.i*, to capsize, overturn.

câpre (kɑ:pr) *f*, caper (*Bot.*).

caprice (kapris) *m*, caprice, whim, freak; [passing] fancy; vagary. **capricieux, euse,†** (sjø, ø:z) *a*, capricious; temperamental; wayward.

capsule (kapsyl) *f*, capsule; seal (*bottle*); [percussion] cap.

capter (kapte) *v.t*, to catch, collect, save, recover; obtain by undue influence. *vouloir* ~, to make a bid for.

captieux, euse (kapsjø, ø:z) *a*, captious.

captif, ive (kaptif, i:v) *a. & n*, captive. **captiver** (tive) *v.t*, to captivate. **captivité** (vite) *f*, captivity, bondage. **capture** (ty:r) *f*, capture. **capturer** (tyre) *v.t*, to capture, take; catch.

capuce (kapys) *m*, **capuchon** (ʃɔ̃) *m*, hood, cowl.

capucin, e (kapysɛ̃, in) *n*, Capuchin friar, nun; (*f.*) nasturtium. **capucinade** (sinad) *f*, dull discourse.

caque (kak) *f*, barrel, keg. **caquer** (ke) *v.t*, to cure (*herrings*); barrel.

caquet (kakɛ) *m*, cackle; chatter. **caqueter** (kte) *v.i*, to cackle.

car (ka:r) *c*, for, because. ¶ *m*, bus.

carabin (karabɛ̃) *m*, medical student; saw-bones. **carabine** (bin) *f*, carbine, rifle. **carabiné, e** (ne) *a*, strong, stiff.

caracole (karakɔl) *f*, caracole.

caractère (karaktɛ:r) *m*, character; characteristic, property, nature; complexion; authority; temper; type, (*pl.*) print. *écrire en* ~*s d'imprimerie*, to write in block letters. **caractériser** (terize) *v.t*, to characterize. **caractéristique** (ristik) *a*, characteristic. ¶ *f*, characteristic, feature.

carafe (karaf) *f*, water bottle, jug, decanter. **carafon** (fɔ̃) *m*, [small] decanter.

carambolage (karɑ̃bɔla:ʒ) *m*, cannon (*Bil.*).

caramel (karamɛl) *m*, caramel.

carapace (karapas) *f*, carapace, shell.

carat (kara) *m*, carat; carat

goods. *sot à vingt-quatre (ou à trente-six)* ~*s*, champion idiot, out & out fool.

caravane (karavan) *f*, caravan. **caravansérail** (vãsera:j) *m*, caravanserai.

carbonate (karbɔnat) *m*, carbonate. **carbone** (bɔn) *m*, carbon. **carbonifère** (nifɛ:r) *a*, carboniferous, coal[-bearing]. **carbonique** (nik) *a*, carbonic. **carboniser** (ze) *v.t*, to carbonize, char. **carbonnade** (nad) *f*, grill[ed meat]. *à la* ~, grilled.

carburant (karbyrã) *m*, motor fuel.

carburateur (karbyratœ:r) *m*, carburetor. **carbure** (by:r) *m*, carbide.

carcan (karkã) *m*, carcan (*Hist.*); yoke.

carcasse (karkas) *f*, carcass, carcase, body, skeleton, shell, frame[work]; shape (*hat, etc.*).

cardiaque (kardjak) *a*, cardiac. ¶ *n*, heart case (*pers.*).

cardinal (kardinal) *a*, cardinal. ¶ *m*, cardinal (*Eccl.*).

carême (karɛ:m) *m*, lent.

carence (karã:s) *f*, assets nil; insolvency.

carène (karɛn) *f*, bottom (*of ship*). **caréner** (rene) *v.t*, to careen.

caresse (karɛs) *f*, caress, endearment; blandishment. **caresser** (se) *v.t*, to caress; fondle; stroke; pat; cherish; flatter; indulge.

cargaison (kargɛzɔ̃) *f*, cargo, lading.

cargo (kargo) *m*, cargo boat.

cari (kari) *m*, curry.

caricature (karikaty:r) *f*, caricature; cartoon; sight. **caricaturer** (tyre) *v.t*, to caricature. **caricaturiste** (rist) *n*, caricaturist, cartoonist.

carie (kari) *f*, caries, decay; rot. **carier** (rje) *v.t, & se* ~, to rot, decay.

carillon (karijɔ̃) *m*, chime[s]; carillon; peal; racket, row. **carillonner** (jone) *v.i. & t*, to chime, ring a peal; clatter; noise abroad. **carillonneur** (nœ:r) *m*, [bell] ringer.

carlin (karlɛ̃) *m*, pug [dog].

carlingue (karlɛ̃:g) *f*, ke[e]lson (*Naut.*); cockpit (*Avn.*).

carme (karm) *m*, Carmelite [friar]. **carmélite** (melit) *f*, Carmelite [nun].

carmin (karmɛ̃) *m*, carmine.

carnage (karna:ʒ) *m*, carnage, slaughter, bloodshed. **carnassier, ère** (nasje, ɛ:r) *a*, carnivorous. ¶ *m*, carnivore; (*f.*) game bag.

carnaval (karnaval) *m*, carnival.

carné, e (karne) *a*, flesh-colored; meaty (*food*); meat (*diet*).

carneau (karno) *m*, flue.

carnet (karnɛ) *m*, notebook, memorandum book; book. ~ *de bal*, dance program. ~ *de chèques*, checkbook. ~ *de compte,* ~ *de banque*, [bank] pass book. ~*-répertoire*, address book.

carnier (karnje) *m*, game bag.

carnivore (nivɔ:r) *a*, carnivorous. ~*s, m.pl*, carnivora.

caroncule (karɔ̃kyl) *f*, wattle (*turkey*).

carotte (karɔt) *f*, carrot; bore core; plug, twist (*tobacco*); trick. *des cheveux* ~, carroty hair, ginger hair.

caroube (karub) *f*, carob [bean], locust [bean].

Carpathes (les) (karpat) *m.pl*, the Carpathians.

carpe (karp) *f*, carp (*fish*). *m*, wrist.

carpette (karpɛt) *f*, bordered [& seamless] carpet; rug.

carquois (karkwa) *m*, quiver (*for arrows*).

carré, e (kare) *a*, square. ¶ *m*, square; bed, patch (*Hort.*); landing, floor. ~ *des officiers*, ward room; mess room. ~ *long*, rectangle, oblong. **carreau** (ro) *m*, tile; floor; squab, cushion; hassock; diamonds (*cards*); pane, square. **carrefour** (karfu:r) *m*, crossroads; intersection (*in city*). *de* ~, street (*musician*); gutter (*language*). **carrelage** (rla:ʒ) *m*, tile floor[ing]. ~ *en briques*, brick paving. **carrelet** (rlɛ) *m*, square ruler; square file; plaice. **carrément** (remã) *ad*, square[ly], outright, flat[ly], straightforwardly. **carrer** (re) *v.t*, to square. **se** ~, to strut, swagger; settle oneself.

carrier (kɑrje) *m*, quarryman. **carrière** (ɛ:r) *f*, career, course, scope, play, vent, head; walk of life; quarry, pit.

carriole (karjɔl) *f*, light cart.

carrosse (karos) *m*, coach. **carrosserie** (sri) *f*, coachbuilding; (*car*) body; bodywork. **carrossier** (sje) *m*, coachbuilder; motor body builder; coach horse.

carrousel (karuzɛl) *m*, tournament; merry-go-round, whirligig.

carrure (kary:r) *f*, breadth of shoulders.

cartable (kartabl) *m*, satchel (*Sch.*).

carte (kart) *f*, card; ticket; map, chart. ~s à jouer, playing cards. ~ blanche, free hand, full discretionary power. ~ céleste, star map, map of the heavens. ~ d'abonnement, season ticket. ~ d'adresse, address card, business c. ~ d'État-major, ordnance [survey] map. ~ de résultats, scoring card (golf). ~ [de visite], [visiting] card. ~ des vins, wine list. ~ du jour, bill of fare, menu. ~ en courbes de niveau, contour map. ~ postale illustrée, picture postcard.

cartel (kartɛl) *m*, challenge; cartel; coalition.

carter (kartɛ:r) *m*, gear case.

cartilage (kartila:ʒ) *m*, cartilage, gristle.

cartographe (kartɔgraf) *m*, cartographer, map producer.

cartomancien, ne (kartɔmɑ̃sjɛ̃, ɛn) *n*, fortuneteller (by cards).

carton (kartɔ̃) *m*, cardboard, pasteboard, millboard; [cardboard] box or case, carton; mount (Phot.); cartoon; off-cut (Bookb.); cancel (Bookb.). ~ à chapeau, hat box. ~ de débarquement, landing ticket. ~ de dessins, portfolio of drawings. ~ de modiste, bandbox. ~-paille, *m*, strawboard. ~-pâte, *m*, papier-mâché. **cartonné, e** (tɔne) *p.a*, in boards (book). **cartonnier** (nje) *m*, cardboard [box] maker; file case.

cartouche (kartuʃ) *f*, cartridge, round [of ammunition]; case (firework); (*m.*) cartouche. ~ à balle, ball cartridge. ~ à blanc, blank c. **cartoucherie** (ʃri) *f*, cartridge factory. **cartouchière** (ʃjɛ:r) *f*, cartridge pouch.

carvi (karvi) *m*, caraway.

cas (kɑ) *m*, case, event, circumstance, instance; matter; cause (law). ~-limite, borderline case.

casanier, ère (kazanje, ɛ:r) *a*. & *n*, stay-at-home.

casaque (kazak) *f*, jumper (woman's). tourner ~, to sell out (Pol.).

cascade (kaskad) *f*, cascade, waterfall, fall[s]; prank, spree; gag (actor's). **cascatelle** (tɛl) *f*, cascade.

case (kɑ:z) *f*, compartment, division, pigeon hole; square (chessboard); frame, space (on printed form); locker; bin; native hut, cabin.

casemate (kazmat) *f*, casemate.

caser (kɑze) *v.t*, to put away; find a situation for, settle.

caserne (kazɛrn) *f*, barrack[s]. **caserner** (ne) *v.t*, to barrack.

casier (kɑzje) *m*, cabinet, nest of drawers, [set of] pigeon holes; bin; rack. ~ judiciaire, police records.

casino (kazino) *m*, casino.

Caspienne (la mer) (kaspjɛn), the Caspian sea.

casque (kask) *m*, helmet; headphones, earphones. ~ blindé, crash helmet. ~ de soleil, sun helmet. ~ en moelle, pith helmet. ~ respiratoire, smoke helmet, gas mask (fire). **casquette** (kɛt) *f*, (man's or boy's) [peak] cap.

cassant, e (kɑsɑ̃, ɑ̃:t) *a*, brittle, crisp, short, hard; blunt, curt. **cassation** (sasjɔ̃) *f*, cassation, quashing, reduction to the ranks. **casse** (kɑ:s) *f*, breakage, breakages; cassia; case (Typ.); ladle, scoop. ¶ (kas) comps: ~-cou, *m*, breakneck [place]; death trap; dare-devil; roughrider; (i.) look out! mind! ~-croûte, *m*, snack; s. bar. ~-noisettes, *m*, nutcrackers; nuthatch. ~-noix, *m*, nutcrackers; nutcracker (bird). ~-pierres, *m*, stone breaker (Mach.). ~-tête, *m*, club, life preserver; puzzle, teaser. **casser** (kɑse) *v.t. & i*, to break, crack, snap; shatter; quash, set aside (*law*); cashier; reduce to the ranks. ~ *aux gages*, to pay off. *se ~ la tête*, to break one's head; puzzle (*or* rack) one's brains.

casserole (kasrɔl) *f*, saucepan, stewpan. ~ [*en terre cuite*], casserole.

cassette (kasɛt) *f*, casket; case; money box; privy purse.

casseur (kasœːr) *m*, breaker. ~ *d'assiettes*, brawler.

cassier (kasje) *m*, cassia tree.

cassine (kasin) *f*, country cottage.

cassis (kɑsis) *m*, black currant(s); b. c. bush; b. c. cordial; water bar (*across road*).

cassonade (kasɔnad) *f*, moist sugar, brown s.

cassure (kɑsyːr) *f*, break, crack, fracture.

castagnette (kastaɲɛt), *f*, castanet.

caste (kast) *f*, caste.

castor (kastɔːr) *m*, beaver. ~ *du Canada*, musquash (*fur*).

castration (kastrasjɔ̃) *f*, castration; gelding.

casuel, le (kazɥɛl) *a*, casual; case (*ending—Gram.*). ¶ *m*, casual profits; perquisites.

casuistique (kazɥistik) *f*, casuistry.

cataclysme (kataklism) *m*, cataclysm, disaster.

catacombe (katakɔ̃b) *f*, catacomb.

catafalque (katafalk) *m*, catafalque.

catalogue (katalɔg) *m*, catalog, list. ~ *par ordre de matières*, subject catalog. ~ *raisonné*, descriptive c. **cataloguer** (ge) *v.t*, to catalog, list.

cataplasme (kataplasm) *m*, poultice.

catapulte (katapylt) *f*, catapult (*Hist. & Avn.*).

cataracte (katarakt) *f*, cataract (*falls & Med.*); (*pl.*) sluice gates (*of heaven*).

catarrhe (kataːr) *m*, catarrh.

catastrophe (katastrɔf) *f*, catastrophe.

catéchiser (kateʃize) *v.t*, to catechize; reason with, try to persuade. **catéchisme** (ʃism) *m*, catechism.

catégorie (kategɔri) *f*, category,

class; predicament (*Log.*). **catégorique**† (rik) *a*, categorical; flat (*refusal*).

cathédrale (katedral) *f*, cathedral, minster.

cathode (katɔd) *f*, cathode.

catholicisme (katɔlisism) *m*, catholicism, Roman Catholicism. **catholique** (lik) *a*, catholic, Roman Catholic; orthodox. ¶ *n*, catholic, Roman Catholic.

catimini (en) (katimini) *ad*, stealthily, on the sly.

Caucase (le) (kokɑːz), the Caucasus. **caucasien, ne** (kazʃɛ̃, ɛn) *a*. & **C~**, *n*, Caucasian.

cauchemar (koʃmaːr) *m*, nightmare, incubus; bugbear.

caudataire (kodatɛːr) *m*, train bearer; toady, toadeater, lickspittle.

cause (koːz) *f*, cause, occasion, ground[s]; case, action (*law*); brief (*law*); consideration (*equivalent, law*). ~ *célèbre*, famous case. *à ~ de*, on account of, because of, for; for the sake of, through. *en tout état de ~*, in any case. *& pour ~*, & for good reasons, & very properly. *sans ~*, briefless (*lawyer*). **causer** (koze) *v.t*, to cause, occasion.

causer (koze) *v.i*, to talk, converse, chat; talk of; not void (*a dance*). *assez causé!* that'll do! **causerie** (zri) *f*, talk, chat, chit-chat; causerie. **causette** (zɛt) *f*, little chat. **causeur, euse** (zœːr, øːz) *n*, talker, conversation[al]ist; (*f.*) settee.

caustique (kostik) *a*, caustic, biting, cutting. ¶ *m*, caustic (*Phar.*).

cauteleux, euse (kotlø, øːz) *a*, cunning, crafty.

cautère (kotɛːr) *m*, cautery. **cautériser** (terize) *v.t*, to cauterize, sear.

caution (kosjɔ̃) *f*, surety, security, guarantee, -ty, guarantor, indemnity, bail. *se rendre ~ pour*, to go bail for. *sujet à ~*, unreliable. **cautionnement** (ɔnmɑ̃) *m*, security, indemnity, deposit, bail, surety (*or* indemnity) bond, qualification (*in shares*). **cautionner** (ne) *v.t*, to become security for, guarantee, bail; give security for, answer for.

cavalcade (kavalkad) *f*, cavalcade; pageant; ride.

cavalerie (kavalri) *f*, cavalry; horse (*troop*); stable (*horses*). **cavalier, ère†** (lje, ɛ:r) *a*, offhand, cavalier; free & easy; riding (*track*); bridle (*path*). ¶ *m*, horseman, rider, equestrian; trooper; gentleman, man; cavalier, escort; partner (*at dance*); knight (*chess*); [wire] staple. ¶ *f*, horsewoman, rider, equestrian.

cave (ka:v) *a*, hollow, sunk[en]. ¶ *f*, cellar, vault; pool (*cards*). ~ à liqueurs, liqueur case or set; tantalus. ~ forte, strong room. **caveau** (kavo) *m*, [small] cellar; vault (*family grave*). **caver** (ve) *v.t*, to hollow, scoop out, [under]mine, wear away or hollow; put up (*money at cards*). **caverne** (vɛrn) *f*, cavern, cave; den. **caverneux, euse** (nø, ø:z) *a*, cavernous, hollow.

caviar (kavja:r) *m*, caviar[e].

cavité (kavite) *f*, cavity, hollow.

cawcher, ère (kauʃe, ɛ:r) *a*, kosher.

ce, cet, cette, *pl*. **ces** (sə, sɛt, sɛt, se) *a*, this; that; such [a]; (*pl.*) these; those; such. *cette rue-ci & non cette rue-là*, this street & not that street. *ce soir*, this evening, tonight. *cette nuit*, last night.

ce (sə), **c' ou ç'** *as in* c'est, ç'a été, *pn*, it; this, that; he, she; they; those. *c'est-à-dire* (*abb*. c.-à-d.) that is to say, i.e., viz. *ce que*, what, that which.

ceci (səsi) *pn*, this.

cécité (sesite) *f*, blindness. ~ des neiges, snow b. ~ pour les couleurs, color b.

cédant, e (sedɑ̃, ɑ̃:t) *n*, transferor, assignor. **céder** (de) *v.t. & i. & abs*, to cede, yield, give up; give in, surrender, cave in; assign, transfer; dispose of, give way. [le] ~ à, to yield [the palm] to, be second to.

cédille (sedi:j) *f*, cedilla.

cédrat (sedra) *m*, citron.

cèdre (sɛ:dr) *m*, cedar. ~ du Liban (libɑ̃), c. of Lebanon.

cédule (sedyl) *f*, schedule (*Inc. Tax*).

ceindre (sɛ̃:dr) *v.t.ir*, to surround, [en]compass, [en]circle, gird[le], belt, wreathe. **ceinture** (sɛ̃ty:r), *f*, belt, girdle, sash, waistband; waist, middle; waist lock (*wrestling*); enclosure. ~ cartouchière, cartridge belt. ~ de sauvetage, life b. ~ porte-jarretelles, suspender b. ~ ventrière (vɑ̃triɛ:r), abdominal b. **ceinturer** (tyre) *v.t*, to grasp round the body. **ceinturon** (r5) *m*, belt (*sword, etc.*).

cela (səla) *pn*, that; it; so. *c'est* ~, that is it; that's right, just so.

célèbre (selɛbr) *a*, celebrated, famous, noted. **célébrer** (lebre) *v.t*, to celebrate; solemnize, hold (*funeral*); sing (*praises of*). **célébrité** (brite) *f*, celebrity.

celer (səle) *v.t*, to conceal, hide.

céleri (selri) *m*, celery.

célérité (selerite) *f*, celerity, swiftness, dispatch.

céleste (selɛst) *a*, celestial, heavenly; of the heavens (*map*), star (*map*); sky (*blue*).

célibat (seliba) *m*, celibacy, single life. **célibataire** (tɛ:r) *n*, bachelor, celibate, single man, woman.

cellérier (sɛlerje) *m*, cellarer. **cellier** (lje) *m*, storeroom (*wines*).

cellulaire (sɛlylɛ:r) *a*, cellular. voiture ~, police van. **cellule** (lyl) *f*, cell. **celluloïd** (lɔid) *m*, celluloid. **cellulose** (lo:z) *f*, cellulose.

Celte (sɛlt) *n*, Celt, Kelt. **celtique** (tik) *a. & m.* (*language*), Celtic, Keltic.

celui, celle, *pl*. **ceux, celles** (səlɥi, sɛl, sø, sɛl) *pn*, he, she, those; the one. *celui-ci, celle-ci*, this one, this, the latter. *celui-là, celle-là*, that one, that, the former.

cémenter (semɑ̃te) *v.t*, to cement (*metal*); caseharden.

cendre (sɑ̃:dr) *f. oft. pl*, ash[es]; dust; embers. **cendré, e** (sɑ̃dre) *a*, ash[-colored], ashen, ashy; gray (*brain matter*). ¶ *f*, cinders (*track*). **cendrier** (drie) *m*, ash pan; ash tray. ~ sur pied, smokers' stand.

Cendrillon (sɑ̃drijɔ̃) *f*, Cinderella.

Cène (sɛːn) *f*, Last Supper; Lord's supper.

cenelle (sənɛl) *f*, haw; holly berry.

cénotaphe (senɔtaf) *m*, cenotaph.

censé, e (sɑ̃se) *a*, deemed, reputed, supposed. **censément** (mɑ̃) *ad*, supposedly, virtually. **censeur** (sœːr) *m*, censor; critic; auditor; vice principal (*college*); examiner (*plays*). **censure** (sy:r) *f*, censorship; [vote of] censure; [board of] censors. **censurer** (syre) *v.t*, to censure, criticize, find fault with, reprehend.

cent (sɑ̃) *a. & m*, hundred. **centaine** (tɛn) *f*, hundred [or so], about a hundred.

centaure (sɑ̃toːr) *m*, centaur.

centenaire (sɑ̃tnɛːr) *n*, centenarian; (*m*.) centenary.

centième (sɑ̃tjɛm) *a. & m*, hundredth.

centigrade (sɑ̃tigrad) *a*, centigrade. Water freezes 0° Cent. = 32 Fahr. Water boils 100° C. = 212 F. *To convert :*—F. = ⅘ C. + 32 [thus, 100 C. × 9 = 900 ÷ 5 = 180 + 32 = 212 F.]. C. = ⅝ (F. − 32) [thus, 212 F. − 32 = 180 × 5 = 900 ÷ 9 = 100 C.].

centigramme (sɑ̃tigram) *m*, centigram = ¹⁄₁₀₀ gram *or* 0.154 grain.

centilitre (sɑ̃tilitr) *m*, centiliter = ¹⁄₁₀₀ liter *or* 0.070 gill.

centime (sɑ̃tim) *m*, centime = ¹⁄₁₀₀ of franc.

centimètre (sɑ̃timɛtr) *m*, centimeter = ¹⁄₁₀₀ meter *or* 0.3937 inch; tape measure (divided into cms, 1½ meters long). ~ *carré*, square centimeter = 0.15500 sq. inch. ~ *cube*, cubic centimeter = 0.0610 cub. inch.

central, e (sɑ̃tral) *a*, central. ¶ *m*, telephone exchange. **centraliser** (lize) *v.t*, to centralize. **centre** (sɑːtr) *m*, center, middle; hub (*fig.*). ~ *de table*, table center. ~ *de villégiature*, holiday resort. **centrer** (sɑ̃tre) *v.t*, to center. **centrifuge** (trify:ʒ) *a*, centrifugal. **centripète** (pɛt) *a*, centripetal.

centuple (sɑ̃typl) *m*, centuple, hundredfold.

cep (sɛp) *m*, stock (*vine*); (*pl.*) stocks (*Hist.*). **cépée** (sepe) *f*, head of shoots (*willow, etc.*).

cependant (səpɑ̃dɑ̃) *ad*, in the mean time, meantime, meanwhile. ¶ *c*, yet, still, nevertheless, though.

céramique (seramik) *f*, ceramics.

cerceau (sɛrso) *m*, hoop; cradle (*Surg.*).

cercle (sɛrkl) *m*, circle; ring, hoop, band; club (*of people*). ~ *des fées*, fairy ring. *en* ~*s*, in the wood (*wine*). **cercler** (kle) *v.t*, to hoop (*casks*).

cercueil (sɛrkœːj) *m*, coffin, shell.

céréale (sereal) *a.f. & f*, cereal.

cérébral, e (serebral) *a*, cerebral, brain (*att.*).

cérémonial (seremɔnjal) *m*, ceremonial. **cérémonie** (ni) *f*, ceremony, circumstance, fuss, ado, to-do. **cérémonieux, euse†** (njø, ø:z) *a*, ceremonious, formal.

cerf (sɛːr & sɛrf) *m*, stag, hart, deer.

cerfeuil (sɛrfœːj) *m*, chervil.

cerf-volant (sɛrvɔlɑ̃) *m*, stag beetle; kite (*paper*).

cerisaie (sərize) *f*, cherry orchard. **cerise** (ri:z) *f*, cherry. ¶ *a. & m*, cherry-red; cerise. **cerisier** (rizje) *m*, cherry [tree].

cerne (sɛrn) *m*, ring (*tree, eyes, moon*), circle. **cerner** (ne) *v.t*, to surround, [en]circle, [en]compass, ring, hem in; invest (*Mil.*); shell (*nuts*); dig round (*tree*). *les yeux cernés*, rings under the eyes.

certain, e (sɛrtɛ̃, ɛn) *a*, certain; sure; stated; some. *le certain*, fixed (*rate of*) exchange. **certainement** (tɛnmɑ̃) *ad*, certainly, of course, by all means. **certes** (sɛrt) *ad*, most certainly, indeed.

certificat (sɛrtifika) *m*, certificate, scrip; testimonial, character. ~ *d'action(s)*, stock certificate. **certifier** (fje) *v.t*, to certify; witness.

certitude (sɛrtityd) *f*, certainty.

céruse (sery:z) *f*, ceruse, white lead.

cerveau (sɛrvo) *m*, brain; brains,

intellect, mind, head. ~ *brûlé*, madcap, hothead. ~ *creux*, dreamer. **cervelle** (vɛl) *f*, brain[s], mind, head; pith (*palm tree*); (*s. & pl. Cook.*) brains. *rompre la ~ à quelqu'un*, to drive someone crazy.

Cervin (le mont) (sɛrvɛ̃), the Matterhorn.

cessation (sɛsasjɔ̃) *f*, cessation, discontinuance; suspension. **sans cesse** (sɛs), without cease, unceasingly. **cesser** (se) *v.i. & t*, to cease, leave off, break off, stop. *faire ~*, to put a stop to.

cessible (sɛsibl) *a*, transferable. **cession** (sjɔ̃) *f*, transfer, assignment. **cessionnaire** (ɔnɛ:r) *n*, transferee.

Ceylan (selɑ̃) *m*, Ceylon.

chablis (ʃabli) *m*, windfall (*tree*); Chablis (*wine*).

chabot (ʃabo) *m*, chub (*fish*).

chacal (ʃakal) *m*, jackal.

chacun, e (ʃakœ̃, yn) *pn*, each, each one, every one. ¶ *m*, everybody, everyone, every one.

chafouin, e (ʃafwɛ̃, in) *a. & n*, sorry (fellow), poor (creature).

chagrin, e (ʃagrɛ̃, in) *a*, sorrowful, glum, moody, grieved, vexed, fretful. ¶ *m*, grief, sorrow, vexation, fret[fulness], chagrin; shagreen. ~ *d'amour*, disappointment in love. **chagriner** (grine) *v.t*, to grieve, afflict; vex. *se ~*, to grieve, fret, repine.

chah (ʃa) *m*, shah.

chahut (ʃay) *m*, uproar; prank.

chaîne (ʃɛ:n) *f*, chain; range (*hills*); (*pl.*) fetters, bonds; warp. ~ *de mailles*, chain of stitches, casting off (*Knit.*). *faire une ~ de mailles*, to cast off. *travail à la ~*, assembly-line work. **chaînette** (ʃɛnɛt) *f*, chain (*small*). **chaînon** (nɔ̃) *m*, link. ~ *manquant*, missing link.

chair (ʃɛ:r) *f*. sometimes *pl*, flesh; meat; pulp (*of fruit*). ~ *à pâté*, mincemeat. ~*s baveuses*, proud flesh. ~ *de poule*, gooseflesh (*fig.*). *cela fait venir la ~ de poule*, it makes one's flesh creep.

chaire (ʃɛ:r) *f*, pulpit; desk; throne (*bishop's*); chair, professorship; mastership; see.

chaise (ʃɛ:z) *f*, chair, seat; stall

(*choir*); hanger (*Mach.*). ~ *à porteurs*, sedan [chair]. ~ *de pont*, deck chair. ~ *paillée*, rush-seat chair. ~ [*percée*], [night] commode.

chaland (ʃalɑ̃) *m*, barge, lighter, scow.

chaland, e (ʃalɑ̃, ɑ̃:d) *n*, customer, patron.

châle (ʃɑ:l) *m*, shawl, wrap.

chalet (ʃalɛ) *m*, chalet, cottage. ~ *de nécessité*, public convenience.

chaleur (ʃalœ:r) *f*, heat, warmth, glow. **chaleureux, euse†** (lœrø, ø:z) *a*, warm (*fig.*), cordial.

chaloupe (ʃalup) *f*, launch, longboat. ~ *canonnière*, gunboat.

chalumeau (ʃalymo) *m*, blowpipe; reed; drinking straw; [shepherd's] pipe.

chalut (ʃaly) *m*, trawl [net]. **chalutier** (tje) *m*, trawler.

chamade (ʃamad) *f*, parley, chamade.

chamailler (se) (ʃamɑje) *v.pr*, to bicker, wrangle, squabble, brawl.

chamarrer (ʃamare) *v.t*, to bedizen, bedeck; lard (*fig.*).

chambranle (ʃɑ̃brɑ̃:l) *m*, frame (*door, window*).

chambre (ʃɑ̃:br) *f*, room, chamber, apartment, lodging; cabin (*ship's*); house; committee; court. ~ *à air*, inner tube (*tire*). ~ [*à coucher*], [bed]room. ~ *à deux lits*, double[-bedded] room. ~ *à un lit*, single r. ~ *d'ami*, guest room, spare [bed]room. ~ *d'enfants*, nursery. ~ *d'explosion*, combustion chamber (*motor*). ~ *de chauffe*, stokehole; boiler room. ~ *de compensation*, clearing house. ~ *de* [*mise à*] *mort*, death chamber. *C~ des communes, des pairs*, House of Commons, of Lords. *C~ des députés*, Chamber of Deputies. ~ *des valeurs*, strong room (*ship*). ~*s en enfilade*, suite of rooms. ~ *sur le derrière*, ~ *sur la cour*, back room. ~ *sur le devant*, ~ *sur la rue*, front r. ~ *syndicale des agents de change*, stock exchange committee. ~ **noire**, darkroom (*Phot.*); camera obscura. **chambrée** (ʃɑ̃bre) *f*, roomful; house (*audience*); barrack room. **chambrer** (bre) *v.t*, to confine, closet; chamber, hollow out; take the chill off (*wine*).

chameau (ʃamo) *m*, camel. **chamelier** (məlje) *m*, c. driver. **chamelle** (mɛl) *f*, she camel.

chamois (ʃamwa) *m*, chamois. [*peau de*] ~, wash leather, chamois [leather].

champ (ʃɑ̃) *m*, field, ground; scope, range; edge. ~s *communs*, common [land]. ~ *d'aviation*, airfield. ~ *de courses*, racecourse. ~ *de manœuvres*, drill ground, parade g. ~ *de massacre*, shambles. ~ *de tir*, rifle range, shooting r. ~ *du repos*, churchyard, God's Acre.

champagne *ou* **vin de C**~ (ʃɑ̃paɲ) *m*, champagne. ~ *frappé* [*de glace*], iced c.

champêtre (ʃɑ̃pɛːtr) *a*, rural, country (*att.*), rustic, sylvan.

champignon (ʃɑ̃piɲɔ̃) *m*, mushroom, wigstand. ~ [*vénéneux*], fungus, toadstool. **champignonnière** (ɲɔnjɛːr) *f*, mushroom bed.

champion (ʃɑ̃pjɔ̃) *m*, champion. **championnat** (ɔna) *m*, championship.

chance (ʃɑ̃ːs) *f*, chance; luck.

chanceler (ʃɑ̃sle) *v.i*, to totter, reel, stagger; waver, falter.

chancelier (ʃɑ̃səlje) *m*, chancellor. **chancelière** (ljɛːr) *f*, foot muff. **chancellerie** (sɛlri) *f*, chancellery.

chanceux, euse (ʃɑ̃sø, øːz) *a*, lucky; hazardous.

chancre (ʃɑ̃ːkr) *m*, canker; ulcer.

chandail (ʃɑ̃daːj) *m*, sweater (*dress*).

chandelier (ʃɑ̃dəlje) *m*, chandler; candlestick. **chandelle** (dɛl) *f*, candle; prop, post, shore; lob (*Ten.*).

chanfrein (ʃɑ̃frɛ̃) *m*, chamfer; forehead (*horse*).

change (ʃɑ̃ːʒ) *m*, exchange (*Fin.*). bureau de ~, foreign exchange office. **changeant, e** (ʃɑ̃ʒɑ̃, ɑ̃ːt) *a*, changeable, variable; fitful; fickle; shot (*fabrics*). **changement** (ʒmɑ̃) *m*, change, alteration; turn (*tide*); shift (*wind*);

amendment (*to document*). ~ *à vue*, transformation scene. ~ *de décor*[*ation*], scene shifting. ~ *de marche*, reversing; r. gear. ~ *de vitesse*, gear shift. ~ [*de voie*], switch points (*Rly.*).

changer (ʒe) *v.t. & abs. & i*, to change, alter; turn; exchange; shift; amend. ~ *d'avis, de linge*, to change one's mind, one's linen. ~ *de pas*, to change step. **changeur** (ʒœːr) *m*, money changer.

chanoine (ʃanwan) *m*, canon (*Eccl.*).

chanson (ʃɑ̃sɔ̃) *f*, song, ballad, ditty; lay; story. ~ [*de bord*], [sea] chanty. ~ *de circonstance*, topical song. ~ *de route*, marching song. ~s, [~s]! nonsense! humbug! fiddlesticks! **chansonner** (sɔne) *v.t*, to lampoon. **chansonnette** (nɛt) *f*, ditty; comic song. **chansonnier, ère** (nje, ɛːr) *n*, song writer; (*m.*) song book; small revue-theater.

chant (ʃɑ̃) *m*, singing, song, lay, chant; melody; canto; warbling, crowing, chirp. ~ *d'allégresse*, carol. ~ *du coq*, cockcrow[ing]. ~ *du cygne*, swan song. ~ *funèbre*, ~ *de mort*, dirge, lament. de ~, edgeways, edgewise, on edge.

chantage (ʃɑ̃taːʒ) *m*, blackmail.

chantant, e (ʃɑ̃tɑ̃, ɑ̃ːt) *a*, musical, tuneful; singsong.

chanteau (ʃɑ̃to) *m*, [c]hunk, cutting (*snip of cloth*).

chanter (ʃɑ̃te) *v.i. & t*, to sing, chant, play the air; warble, crow, chirp; talk [about], say, cry. ~ *toujours la même antienne*, to be always harping on the same string. ~ *victoire sur*, to crow over. *faire* ~ *quelqu'un*, to blackmail someone. *si ça vous chante*, if that suits you. **chanterelle** (trɛl) *f*, highest string; call bird. **chanteur, euse** (tœːr, øːz) *n*, singer, vocalist; songster, songstress; (*att.*) song (*bird*).

chantier (ʃɑ̃tje) *m*, yard; floor (*foundry*); shipyard; dockyard; dunnage; gantry; scantling (*for cask*). *sur le* ~, work in hand.

chantonner (ʃɑ̃tɔne) *v.i*, to hum (*tune*).

chantourner (ʃɑ̃turne) *v.t*, to jig-saw.

chantre (ʃɑ̃ːtr) *m*, cantor; Bard.

chanvre (ʃɑ̃ːvr) *m*, hemp.

chaos (kao) *m*, chaos. **chaotique** (ɔtik) *a*, chaotic.

chape (ʃap) *f*, cope; chape; cover; cap, lid; shell; strap; bearings; coating, covering.

chapeau (ʃapo) *m*, hat, bonnet; cap, cover, hood. ~ *à cornes*, cocked hat. ~ *claque*, crush h., opera h. ~ *haut de forme*, ~ *de soie*, high hat, silk h. ~ *melon*, bowler [h.]. ~ *rabattu*, slouch h. ~ *souple*, felt h.

chapechute (ʃapʃyt) *f*, godsend, windfall.

chapelain (ʃaplɛ̃) *m*, chaplain.

chapelet (ʃaplɛ) *m*, rosary; [string of] beads; string, rope.

chapelier (ʃapəlje) *m*, hatter. [**malle**] **chapelière** (ɛːr) *f*, Saratoga [trunk].

chapelle (ʃapɛl) *f*, chapel; meeting house; [church] plate; coterie, set. ~ *ardente*, mortuary chapel. ~ *de la Vierge*, Lady chapel. ~ *sépulcrale*, mortuary chapel.

chapellerie (ʃapɛlri) *f*, hat trade; h. shop.

chapelure (ʃaplyːr) *f*, grated bread crumbs.

chaperon (ʃaprɔ̃) *m*, chaperon; coping. **chaperonner** (prɔne) *v.t*, to chaperon; cope (*wall*).

chapiteau (ʃapito) *m*, capital (*Arch.*); head, cap, top.

chapitre (ʃapitr) *m*, chapter (*book, canons*); head[ing]; item; subject, matter, point. **chapitrer** (tre) *v.t*, to lecture, reprimand.

chapon (ʃapɔ̃) *m*, capon.

chaque (ʃak) *a*, each, every; either.

char (ʃaːr) *m*, chariot; wagon. ~ *à bancs*, charabanc (*horse*). ~ *d'assaut*, tank (*Mil.*). ~ [*de deuil*], ~ *funèbre*, hearse.

charade (ʃarad) *f*, charade; conundrum.

charançon (ʃarɑ̃sɔ̃) *m*, weevil.

charbon [ʃarbɔ̃] *m*, coal[s]; charcoal; carbon; embers; carbuncle (*Med.*); anthrax; blight (*Agric.*). ~ *à dessin*, charcoal [pencil]. en ~, burnt to a cinder (*meat*). *faire du* ~, to coal. *sur des* ~*s* [*ardents*], on tenterhooks. **charbonnage** (bonaːʒ) *m*, coal mining; (*pl.*) coal mines. **charbonner** (ne) *v.t*, to black (*face, etc.*). se ~, *v.pr. ou* ~, *v.i*, to char, carbonize; (*v.i.*) to smoke (*lamp*). **charbonnerie** (nri) *f*, coal yard. **charbonnier** (nje) *m*, charcoal burner; coal merchant; coalman; coal cellar; collier (*ship*).

charcuter (ʃarkyte) *v.t*, to hack, mangle (*in carving*). **charcuterie** (tri) *f*, pork butchery; [dressed] pork, pig meat. **charcutier, ère** (tje, ɛːr) *n*, pork butcher.

chardon (ʃardɔ̃) *m*, thistle; spikes. ~ *à bonnetier*, ~ *à foulon*, teasel. **chardonneret** (dɔnrɛ) *m*, goldfinch.

charge (ʃarʒ) *f*, load, burden; charge, encumbrance, onus; expense; stress; pressure; head [of water]; loading; shipment; cargo; trust, care, custody; cure (*of souls*); duty, office; practice; membership, seat; instructions, directions; caricature; overacting; impersonation (*Theat.*); joke. ~ *à la cueillette*, general cargo. *à* [*la*] ~ *de*, on condition that, provided that. *à la* ~ *de*, chargeable to, payable by, at the expense of; dependent on. *en* ~, live (*Elec.*); load (*water line*); [now] loading (*ship*). **chargé, e** (ʒe) *a*, loaded; full; live (*shell*); furred (*tongue*); overcast, heavy (*weather*); insured (*Post*). **chargé d'affaires**, *m*, chargé d'affaires. **chargement** (ʒəmɑ̃) *m*, loading, lading; charging, filling; shipping, shipment; cargo; consignment; insurance (*Post*); registered package. ~ *en plein jour*, daylight loading (*Phot.*). **charger** (ʒe) *v.t*, to load, lade, burden; charge, fill; stress; inflate (*account*); clog, saddle; lie heavy on; ship; instruct, order, direct; entrust; overact; overdo; overdraw; overcharge; caricature; [in]criminate; insure (*Post*). se ~ *de*, to undertake, take charge of, attend to. **chargeur** (ʒœːr) *m*, charger; loader; shipper; stoker (*Mach.*).

chariot (ʃarjo) *m*, truck, wagon,

wain, trolley, car; go-cart; carriage, carrier.

charitable† (ʃaritabl) *a*, charitable, benevolent. **charité** (te) *f*, charity; alms; dole.

charivari (ʃarivari) *m*, charivari, hubbub.

charlatan (ʃarlatɑ̃) *m*, charlatan, quack. **charlatanerie** (tanri) *f*, quackery.

charmant, e (ʃarmɑ̃, ɑ̃:t) *a*, charming, fascinating, delightful. **charme** (ʃarm) *m*, charm, spell; attraction; allurement; hornbeam, yoke elm. *sous le* ~, spellbound. **charmer** (me) *v.t*, to charm, delight, bewitch; beguile, while away. **charmeur, euse** (mœ:r, ø:z) *n*, charmer. **charmille** (mi:j) *f*, hedge *or* bower (*of hornbeam*).

charnel, le† (ʃarnɛl) *a*, carnal, sensual. **charnier** (nje) *m*, charnel house, ossuary.

charnière (ʃarnjɛ:r) *f*, hinge. *à* ~, *à* ~*s*, hinged.

charnu, e (ʃarny) *a*, fleshy, brawny. **charnure** (ny:r) *f*, flesh (*of pers.*). **charogne** (ʃarɔɲ) *f*, carrion.

charpente (ʃarpɑ̃:t) *f*, frame[work]. ~ [*en bois*], timber work. ~ *en fer*, ironwork. ~ *métallique*, iron & steel constructional work. **charpenter** (pɑ̃te) *v.t*, to carpenter, frame, put together. *bien charpenté*, well-knit, well-built, of sturdy build. **charpenterie** (tri) *f*, carpentry; (*ship's*) timber yard. **charpentier** (tje) *m*, carpenter. ~ *de vaisseau*, shipwright. ~ *en fer*, ironworker.

charpie (ʃarpi) *f*, lint; shreds.

charretée (ʃarte) *f*, cartload. **charretier, ère** (tje, ɛ:r) *n*, carter. **charrette** (rɛt) *f*, cart. ~ *anglaise*, dogcart, trap. **charrier** (rje) *v.t*, to cart, carry, convey; drift. **charroi** (rwa) *m*, cartage. **charroyer** (rwaje) *v.t*, to cart. **charron** (rɔ̃) *m*, wheelwright.

charrue (ʃary) *f*, plow. ~ *multiple*, gang p.

charte (ʃart) *f*, charter; deed (*ancient*). ~*partie*, *f*, charter [party]. ~ *de grain*, grain charter.

chartreuse (ʃartrø:z) *f*, Carthusian monastery; lone cottage;

chartreuse (*liqueur*). **chartreux** (trø) *m*, Carthusian [monk].

chas (ʃa) *m*, eye (*needle, etc.*).

chasse (ʃas) *f*, chase, hunt, hunting; shooting; shoot; pursuit; kill (*of game*); play, clearance (*Mech.*); set (*of saw teeth*); (*pl.*) squares (*bookbinding*). ~ *à courre* (ku:r), hunt[ing] (*riding to hounds*). ~ *à la grosse bête*, big-game hunting. ~ *au cerf à l'affût*, deer stalking. ~ *au lévrier*, coursing. ~ *aux oiseaux*, fowling. ~ *d'air*, blast (*or* rush) of air. ~ [*d'eau*], flush. ~ *gardée*, ~ *réservée*, [game] preserves.

châsse (ʃɑ:s) *f*, reliquary, shrine; frame (*spectacles*); scales (*lancet*).

chassé (ʃase) *m*, chassé (*Danc.*).

chasse-mouches (ʃasmuʃ) *m*, fly whisk; fly net. **chasse-neige** (nɛ:ʒ) *m*, snow squall; snowplow.

chasser (ʃase) *v.t. & abs. & i*, to drive, drive away *or* out *or* off *or* in; expel; chase; chevy, chivy; hound out; hunt; shoot; course; pursue; dismiss; dispel; drift; drag (*anchor*); chassé (*Danc.*). ~ *à l'affût*, to stalk. **chasseur, euse** (sœ:r, ø:z) *n*, hunter, huntress, huntsman; -catcher (*butterflies, etc.*); messenger, commissionaire, page[boy]; chaser (*Nav.*). fighter (*Avn.*).

chassieux, euse (ʃasjø, ø:z) *a*, gummy (*eyes*), blear-eyed.

châssis (ʃasi) *m*, frame; sash; chassis (*motor*); panel (*radio*); chase (*Typ.*); flat (*Theat.*); stretcher (*for painter's canvas*). ~ *à fiches*, casement, French sash.

chaste† (ʃast) *a*, chaste. **chasteté** (təte) *f*, chastity.

chasuble (ʃazybl) *f*, chasuble.

chat (ʃa) *m*, **chatte** (ʃat) *f*, cat, tom [cat], he-cat, she-cat, puss, pussy [cat]; (*m.*) tag (*game*). *le Chat botté*, Puss in Boots. *cambrioleur* ~, cat burglar. ~ *d'Espagne*, tortoise-shell cat. ~ *de Siam*, Siamese c. ~ *de gouttières*, stray c. ~ *persan*, ~ *angora*, Persian c.

châtaigne (ʃatɛɲ) *f*, [sweet]

chestnut. **châtaignier** (nje) *m*, chestnut [tree]. **châtain, e** (tɛ̃, ɛn) *a*, [chestnut-]brown (*hair*).

château (ʃɑto) *m*, castle; palace; manor [house], [country] seat, mansion, hall. ~ *d'eau*, water tower. ~ *de cartes*, house of cards. ~*x en Espagne*, castles in the air *or* in Spain. **châtelain** (tlɛ̃) *m*, lord of the manor, squire. **châtelaine** (tlɛn) *f*, lady of the manor; chatelaine, key chain.

chat-huant (ʃaɥɑ̃) *m*, tawny owl, brown o.

châtier (ʃɑtje) *v.t*, to chastise, castigate; chasten. **châtiment** (timɑ̃) *m*, chastisement, etc.

chatoiement (ʃatwamɑ̃) *m*, shimmer; sheen; play of light.

chaton (ʃatɔ̃) *m*, kitten; bezel; setting (*jewel*).

chatouiller (ʃatuje) *v.t*, to tickle; touch up. **chatouilleux, euse** (tujø, øːz) *a*, ticklish; touchy, sensitive.

chatoyant, e (ʃatwajɑ̃, ɑ̃ːt) *a*, iridescent; shot (*fabrics*). **chatoyer** (je) *v.i*, to shimmer; sparkle.

châtrer (ʃɑtre) *v.t*, to castrate, geld; prune, thin.

chattemite (ʃatmit) *f*, unctuous hypocrite, Chadband.

chatteries (ʃatri) *f.pl*, blandishments; delicacies, dainties.

chaud, e† (ʃo, oːd) *a*, hot, warm. *à chaud*, [while] hot. *pleurer à chaudes larmes*, to cry bitterly. *avoir chaud*, to be warm (*of pers.*).

chaudière (ʃodjɛːr) *f*, boiler; copper. **chaudron** (drɔ̃) *m*, caldron, pot. [**petite**] **chaudronnerie** (drɔnri) *f*, coppersmith's [& brazier's] trade. [**grosse**] **chaudronnerie**, boiler-making *or* works. **chaudronnier** (nje) *m*, coppersmith, brazier; boiler maker. ~ *ambulant*, tinker.

chauffage (ʃofaːʒ) *m*, heating, warming; stoking, firing. ~ *central*, central heating. **chauffard** (faːr) *m*, reckless driver, etc. **chauffe** (ʃoːf) *f*, fire chamber; stoking, firing; heat, melt; heating. ~-**bain** (ʃof) *m*, water heater. ~-**lit**, *m*, warming pan. ~-**pieds**,

m, foot warmer. ~-**plats**, *m*, chafing dish. **chauffer** (ʃofe) *v.t*, to heat, warm; air (*linen*); stoke, fire, fuel; push on with; urge on; cram (*exam*); (*v.i*.) to heat, get hot; run hot; get up steam. *se* ~, to warm oneself, bask. *se* ~ *les pieds*, to warm one's feet. **chaufferette** (frɛt) *f*, foot warmer. **chaufferie** (fri) *f*, chafery; stokehole; boiler room. **chauffeur** (fœːr) *m*, stoker, fireman; driver (*auto*), chauffeur. ~-*mécanicien*, engineman. **chauffeuse** (føːz) *f*, woman driver, fireside chair.

chaufour (ʃofuːr) *m*, lime kiln. **chaufournier** (furnje) *m*, lime burner.

chauler (ʃole) *v.t*, to lime.

chaume (ʃoːm) *m*, culm (*Bot*.); stubble; s. field; thatch; cottage (*fig*.). *couvrir en* ~, to thatch. **chaumière** (ʃomjɛːr) *f*, [thatched] cottage.

chaussée (ʃose) *f*, bank; causeway, road[way].

chausse-pied (ʃospje) *m*, shoehorn. **chausser** (se) *v.t*, to put on (*shoes, stockings*); shoe, boot, make shoes for; suit, fit (*of footwear*); hill, earth up. *se* ~ *d'une opinion*, to get an opinion into one's head. **chaussettes** (sɛt) *f.pl*, socks, half-hose. **chausson** (sɔ̃) *m*, slipper (*list*); shoe; bootee; bed sock; savate; turnover (*Cook*.). **chaussure** (syːr) *f*, footwear; shoe. ~ [*montante*], boot. ~*s de marche, de ski*, walking, ski, boots. ~*s vernies*, patent leather shoes; dress shoes.

chauve (ʃoːv) *a*, bald. ¶ *m*, baldhead (*pers*.). ~-**souris** (ʃovsuri) *f*, bat.

chauvinisme (ʃovinism) *m*, chauvinism, jingoism.

chaux (ʃo) *f*, lime. ~ *vive*, quicklime.

chavirer (ʃavire) *v.i*, to capsize, overturn, upset; fail. [**faire**] ~, *v.t*, to capsize, etc; tip, dump, shoot.

chef (ʃɛf) *m*, head, chief; chieftain; commander, commanding officer; general (*Mil*.); leader; principal; master; superior; superintendent; manager; foreman; head, heading; authority; right. ~ *d'accusation*, count of indictment. ~ *d'atelier*, shop foreman. ~ *d'attaque*, leader (*violin, chorus*). ~ *d'émeute*, ringleader. ~ *d'équipe*, foreman. ~ *d'orchestre*, conductor. ~ *de bataillon*, major. ~ [*de cuisine*], head cook, chef. ~ *de file*, leader; file leader; fugleman; leading ship. ~ *de gare*, station master. ~ *de maison*, householder. ~ *de musique*, bandmaster (*Mil.*). ~ *de nage*, stroke (*oarsman*). ~ *de pièce*, gun captain. ~ *de salle*, headwaiter. ~ *de théâtre*, musical director. ~ *du jury*, foreman of the jury. ~ *du service des ateliers*, works manager. ~ *éclaireur*, scout master. *de ce* ~, under this head[ing], hereunder.

chef-d'œuvre (ʃɛdœːvr) *m*, masterpiece; mess.

chef-lieu (ʃɛfljø) *m*, capital (*department, county*), county seat; headquarters, seat.

cheik (ʃɛk) *m*, sheikh.

chelem (ʃlɛm) *m*, slam (*cards*).

chemin (ʃəmɛ̃) *m*, way, road, lane, path, track; headway. ~ *d'escalier*, stair carpet. ~ *de fer*, railway, railroad. ~ *de halage*, tow[ing] path. ~ *des écoliers*, longest way round, roundabout way. ~ *de la croix*, stations of the Cross. ~ *de traverse*, crossroad. ~ *faisant*, on the way. *faire son* ~, to make one's way. *il n'y va pas par quatre* ~*s*, he doesn't beat about the bush.

chemineau (ʃəmino) *m*, tramp, hobo.

cheminée (ʃəmine) *f*, chimney, smoke stack, shaft, funnel; fireplace, chimney piece, mantelpiece; chimney pot; vent; chute, shoot.

cheminer (ʃəmine) *v.i*, to tramp, walk; trudge; move along, proceed; meander, creep.

cheminot (ʃəmino) *m*, railwayman.

chemise (ʃəmiːz) *f*, shirt (*man's*); chemise (*woman's*); jacket (*water, steam*); cover, lining, case, wrapper. ~ *de nuit*, nightshirt (*man's*); n. dress, n. gown (*wo-*

man's). ~ *de soirée*, dress shirt. ~ *de ville*, tunic s. ~ [*pour dossier*], folder. **chemiserie** (mizri) *f*, shirt making, hosiery. **chemisier, ère** (zje, ɛːr) *n*, shirtmaker, hosier.

chenal (ʃənal) *m*, channel, race, course; fairway; gutter.

chenapan (ʃnapɑ̃) *m*, scamp, rogue.

chêne (ʃɛn) *m*, oak. ~-liège, *m*, cork tree.

chéneau (ʃeno) *m*, gutter (*eaves*).

chenet (ʃənɛ) *m*, [fire]dog, andiron.

chènevis (ʃɛnvi) *m*, hemp seed.

chenil (ʃəni) *m*, kennel (*hounds*); hovel.

chenille (ʃəniːj) *f*, caterpillar; track.

chenu, e (ʃəny) *a*, snow-capped; snow-clad; bare at the top (*trees*).

chèque (ʃɛk) *m*, check. ~ *sans provision*, worthless c.

cher, ère† (ʃɛːr) *a*, dear, high [-priced], expensive, costly; precious, scarce (*time*). *ma chère*, my dear. *mon cher*, my dear fellow. **cher**, *ad*, dearly; much.

chercher (ʃɛrʃe) *v.t*, to look for, try to find, search for, hunt for, seek; beg; pick (*quarrel*). *aller* ~, to go for, [go &] fetch, go to look for. *venir* ~, to come for, come & fetch, come to look for. **chercheur, euse** (ʃœːr, ø:z) *n*, seeker, searcher, inquirer, investigator, research worker. ~ *d'aventures*, adventurer. ~ *d'or*, gold digger. ¶ *att*, inquiring (*mind*, *etc.*).

chère (ʃɛːr) *f*, living, fare, cheer. *faire bonne* ~, to fare (*feed*) well. *faire maigre* ~, to fare badly.

chérir (ʃeriːr) *v.t*, to cherish, hold dear; cling to, hug (*as error*). *mon chéri, ma chérie*, my love, my darling, dearest.

cherté (ʃɛrte) *f*, dearness, costliness.

chérubin (ʃerybɛ̃) *m*, cherub.

chester (ʃɛstɛːr) *m*, in France, Cheddar *or* Cheshire cheese.

chétif, ive† (ʃetif, iːv) *a*, mean, miserable, sorry, paltry, puny, stunted, sickly, wretched.

cheval (ʃəval) *m*, horse. ~ *à bascule*, rocking h. ~ *côtier*, ~

de renfort, trace h. ~ *d'attelage*, carriage h. ~ *de bât*, packhorse, drudge. ~ *de bataille*, war horse, charger; pet argument. *chevaux de bois*, merry-go-round. ~ *de charrette*, cart h. ~ *de chasse*, hunter. ~ *de course*, racehorse. ~ *de louage*, hack. ~ *de race*, ~ *pur sang*, thoroughbred [horse]. ~ *de retour*, old offender, jail bird. ~ *de volée*, leader (*horse*). ~ [*vapeur*], horse power (Fr. h.p. = 75 kilogrammeters per second; Eng. h.p. = 550 foot pounds per sec.). *une* [*automobile de*] *10 chevaux*, a 10 horse [power] car. *à* ~, on horseback. **chevalement** (lmã) *m*, trestle shore; [pit-]head-frame; derrick. **chevaler** (le) *v.t*, to shore. **chevaleresque** (lrɛsk) *a*, chivalrous, knightly. **chevalerie** (lri) *f*, knighthood, chivalry. ~ *errante*, knight errantry. **chevalet** (lɛ) *m*, horse, trestle; easel; rest (*Bil.*, *etc.*); bridge (*violin, etc.*). **chevalier** (lje) *m*, knight, chevalier. ~ *d'industrie*, adventurer, swindler. **chevalière** (ljɛːr) *f*, signet ring. **chevalin, e** (lɛ̃, in) *a*, equine, horsy; horse (*species*). **chevauchée** (voʃe) *f*, ride. **chevaucher** (ʃe) *v.i. & t*, to ride; straddle; span; overlap.

chevelu, e (ʃəvly) *a*, long-haired; hairy; bearded. **chevelure** (vlyːr) *f*, [head of] hair, locks; scalp (*trophy*); coma (*Bot. & comet*); foliage.

chevet (ʃəvɛ) *m*, bolster, pillow; bedhead; bedside.

cheveu (ʃəvø) *m*, (*a single human*) hair. *les* ~*x*, the hair. ~*x en brosse*, crewcut.

cheville (ʃəviːj) *f*, pin, peg; tree-nail; bolt; pintle; spike; expletive (*in verse*). ~ [*du pied*], ankle. ~ *ouvrière*, king bolt, center pin; mainspring (*fig.*), master mind, prime mover. **cheviller** (vije) *v.t. & i*, to pin, peg, bolt; pad (*verses*).

chèvre (ʃɛːvr) *f*, goat (*in general*); she-goat, nanny [goat]; gin (*Mech.*); sawhorse; jack. ~ *de carrossier*, carriage jack. ~ [*verticale*], derrick [crane]. **chevreau** (ʃəvro) *m*, kid; kid [leather]. **chèvrefeuille** (ʃɛvrəfœːj) *m*,

honeysuckle, woodbine. **chevrette** (ʃəvrɛt) *f*, kid; she-goat; roe-doe; shrimp, prawn; trivet. **chevreuil** (vrœːj) *m*, roebuck; venison. **chevrier, ère** (vrie, ɛːr) *n*, goatherd. **chevron** (vrɔ̃) *m*, rafter; chevron; stripe (*long Mil. service*). **chevroter** (vrɔte) *v.i*, to bleat (*goat & fig.*); quaver, shake; kid. **chevrotin** (tɛ̃) *m*, fawn; musk deer; kid [leather]. **chevrotine** (tin) *f*, buckshot.

chez (ʃe) *pr*, at; at (*or* to) (*or* in) the house, etc, of; care of, c/o; of, stocked by; with; among, in. ~ *moi*, ~ *lui*, ~ *vous*, at home. *mon* ~-*moi*, my home. ~ *soi*, [at] home. *un* ~-*soi*, a home of one's own.

chiasse (ʃjas) *f*, speck (*fly*); cast (*worm*); scum, dross (*metal*).

chic (ʃik) *a*, stylish, chic, natty, smart, swell. ¶ *m*, stylishness.

chicane (ʃikan) *f*, chicanery, quibble, pettifoggery, cavil, shuffle; baffle [plate]. **chicaner** (kane) *v.i*, to chicane; (*v.t.*) to cavil at, carp at; dispute every inch of (*ground*); hug (*wind, Naut.*). **chicanerie** (nri) *f*, chicanery, etc.

chiche† (ʃiʃ) *a*, stingy, mean, niggardly, chary, sparing.

chicorée (ʃikɔre) *f*, chicory.

chicot (ʃiko) *m*, stump, snag. **chicoter** (kɔte) *v.i*, to wrangle (*about trifles*).

chien, ne (ʃjɛ̃, ɛn) *n*, dog, bitch, hound; (*m.*) hammer, cock (*of gun*); dog, pawl, catch. ~ *couchant*, setter. *faire le* ~ *couchant*, to toady, cringe. ~ *courant*, ~ *de chasse*, hound. ~ *d'arrêt*, pointer. ~ *de berger*, sheep dog. ~ *de garde*, ~ *d'attache*, watch d. ~ *de luxe*, fancy d. ~ *de mer*, dog fish. ~ *de Saint-Bernard*, St. Bernard dog. ~ *de salon*, lap d. ~-*loup*, Alsatian. ~ *savant*, performing dog. *entre chien & loup*, at dusk.

chiendent (ʃjɛ̃dã) *m*, couch [grass].

chiffe (ʃif) *f*, rag. **chiffon** (fɔ̃) *m*, bit of stuff (*old or new*); rag, clout; scrap; fallal; chiffon; (*pl.*) dress, finery. **chiffonner** (fɔne) *v.t*, to [c]rumple; ruffle, annoy, vex, bother; (*v.i.*) to do needlework, use one's needle. **chiffonnier, ère** (nje, ɛːr) *n,* rag picker *or* merchant, rag [& bone] man; (*m.*) chiffonier.

chiffre (ʃifr) *m,* figure, number, numeral, cipher; amount; monogram; colophon. **un** [*seul*] **~,** a digit (*0-9*). **en ~s connus,** in plain figures. **~ d'affaires,** turnover. **~-indice,** index number. **mot en chiffré** (fre) word in cipher. **chiffrer** (fre) *v.i,* to reckon, cipher; figure, appear; (*v.t.*) to number, figure, cipher. **se ~,** to figure out, work out, amount.

chignon (ʃiɲɔ̃) *m,* chignon.

Chili (le) (ʃili), Chile, **-li. chilien, ne** (ljẽ, ɛn) *a.* & **C~,** *n,* Chilean.

chimère (ʃimɛːr) *f,* chimera. **chimérique** (merik) *a,* chimerical; visionary, fanciful.

chimie (ʃimi) *f,* chemistry. **chimique**† (mik) *a,* chemical; actinic (*rays*). **chimiste** (mist) *n,* chemist (*scientist*).

chimpanzé (ʃɛ̃pɑ̃ze) *m,* chimpanzee.

Chine (la) (ʃin), China. **chinois, e** (nwa, aːz) *a.* & **C~** (*pers.*), *n,* Chinese. **le chinois,** Chinese (*language*). **chinoiserie** (nwazri) *f,* Chinese curio; (*pl.*) red tape, complicated formalities.

chiper (ʃipe) *v.t,* to swipe, filch, pilfer.

chipie (ʃipi) *f,* ill-natured woman. **chipoter** (pɔte) *v.i,* to nibble; haggle.

chique (ʃik) *f,* quid, chew (*of tobacco*).

chiquenaude (ʃiknoːd) *f,* fillip, flip, flick; snap of fingers.

chiquer (ʃike) *v.t.* & *i,* to chew (*tobacco*).

chirographaire (kirɔgrafɛːr) *a,* unsecured (*creditors, debts*); simple, naked (*debentures*).

chiromancie (kirɔmɑ̃si) *f,* palmistry, chiromancy. **chiromancien, ne** (sjẽ, ɛn) *n,* palmist, chiromancer.

chirurgical, e (ʃiryrʒikal) *a,* surgical. **chirurgie** (ʒi) *f,* surgery. **chirurgien** (ʒjẽ) *m,* surgeon.

chiure (ʃjyːr) *f,* flyspeck.

chlorate (klɔrat) *m,* chlorate. **chlore** (klɔːr) *m,* chlorine. **chlo-**

rhydrique (klɔridrik) *a,* hydrochloric, muriatic (*acid*). **chloroforme** (rɔfɔrm) *m,* chloroform. **chloroformer** (me) *v.t,* to chloroform. **chlorure** (ryːr) *m,* chloride. **~ de chaux,** c. of lime.

choc (ʃɔk) *m,* shock, impact, brunt, onset, onslaught, clash; clink (*glasses*).

chocolat (ʃɔkɔla) *m,* chocolate. **~ au lait,** c. with milk; milk c. **~s fourrés à la crème,** c. creams. **~ lacté,** milk c. **chocolatier, ère** (latje ɛːr) *n,* c. manufacturer; c. seller; (*f.*) c. pot.

chœur (kœːr) *m,* choir, quire; chorus; chancel. *faire ~ au refrain,* to join in the chorus.

choir (ʃwaːr) *v.i.ir,* to fall.

choisi, e (ʃwazi) *a,* select, choice. **choisir** (ziːr) *v.t,* to choose, select, pick. **choix** (ʃwa) *m,* choice, selection; pick; option; quality. *au ~,* all at the same price.

choléra (kɔlera) *m,* cholera.

chômage (ʃomaːʒ) *m,* closing, idleness, standing [idle], shutting down, unemployment; demurrage (*Rly.*); lying up (*ship*). **~ du dimanche,** Sunday closing. **chômer** (me) *v.i,* to close, lie idle; lie fallow; shut down, stop work, be out [of work]; be short; (*v.t.*) to keep (*une fête = a saint's day*). **chômeur, euse** (mœːr, øːz) *n,* unemployed person. *les chômeurs,* the unemployed.

chope (ʃɔp) *f,* glass (*for, or of, beer*). **chopine** (pin) *f,* pint (about ½ liter). **chopiner** (ne) *v.i,* to tipple.

chopper (ʃɔpe) *v.i,* to stumble; blunder.

choquant, e (ʃɔkɑ̃, ɑ̃ːt) *a,* shocking; offensive. **choquer** (ke) *v.t,* to shock, strike, clash with; clink, chink; offend.

choral, e (kɔral) *a,* choral. [*société*] *chorale, f,* choral society. **chorégraphie** (kɔregrafi) *f,* choreography.

choriste (kɔrist) *n,* chorister; chorus singer (*opera*). **faire chorus** (ryːs), to [repeat in] chorus.

chose (ʃoːz) *f,* thing; matter; fact; chattel; property; compliment. *la ~ publique,* the common weal, the public welfare. **~ qui va sans**

dire, matter of course. *où en sont les ~s?* how do things stand?

chott (ʃɔt) *m*, salt lake (*N. Africa*).

chou (ʃu) *m*, cabbage. *~ de Bruxelles*, Brussels sprouts. *~ de Milan* (milɑ̃), savoy. *~-fleur*, *m*, cauliflower. *~ frisé*, kale. *~ marin*, sea kale. *~-navet*, rutabaga. *~-rave*, *m*, kohlrabi. **chou-[chou]**, *m*, darling, ducky, honey. *le chouchou*, the pet.

choucas (ʃukɑ) *m*, jackdaw.

choucroute (ʃukrut) *f*, sauerkraut.

chouette (ʃwɛt) *f*, owl.

choyer (ʃwaje) *v.t*, to pamper, pet, coddle; cherish.

chrétien, ne (kretjɛ̃, ɛn) *a. & n*, Christian. **chrétiennement** (ɛnmɑ̃) *ad*, christianly. **chrétienté** (ête) *f*, Christendom. **le Christ** (krist), Christ. **christ**, *m*, crucifix. **christianiser** (tjanize) *v.t*, to christianize. **christianisme** (nism) *m*, Christianity.

chromate (krɔmat) *m*, chromate.

chromatique (krɔmatik) *a*, chromatic.

chrome (kro:m) *m*, chromium, chrome. **chromé e** (krome) *a*, chrome (*steel, leather*); chromium (*steel*); chromium-plated.

chronique (krɔnik) *a*, chronic. ¶ *f*, chronicle; gossip; intelligence, notes (*in newspaper*). **chroniqueur** (kœ:r) *m*, chronicler; reporter (*news*).

chronographe (krɔnɔgraf) *m*, chronograph; stop-watch.

chronologie (krɔnɔlɔʒi) *f*, chronology. **chronologique†** (ʒik) *a*, chronological.

chronométrage (krɔnɔmetra:ʒ) *m*, timing (*race*). **chronomètre** (mɛtr) *m*, chronometer. **chronométrer** (metre) *v.i*, to time. **chronométreur** (trœ:r) *m*, timekeeper (*Sport*).

chrysalide (krizalid) *f*, chrysalis, pupa.

chrysanthème (krizɑ̃tɛ:m) *m*, chrysanthemum.

chuchoter (ʃyʃote) *v.i. & t*, to whisper. **chuchoterie** (tri) *f*, whispering. **chuchoteur, euse** (tœ:r, ø:z) *n*, whisperer.

chuinter (ʃɥête) *v.i*, to hoot (*owl*).

chut (ʃyt, ʃt) *i*, hush!

chute (ʃyt) *f*, fall, drop; downfall, collapse, smash, crash; failure (*of a play*); spray (*flowers, Need.*). *~ [d'eau]*, [water]fall, falls. *la ~ des reins*, the small of the back. *la ~ du jour*, the close of day, nightfall, eventide.

chuter (ʃyte) *v.t*, to hiss (an actor).

Chypre (ʃipr) *f*, Cyprus.

ci (si) *ad*, here. *~-après*, hereinafter, further on, below. *~-contre*, opposite. *~-dessous*, below, undermentioned, hereunder. *~-dessus*, above[-mentioned]. *~-devant*, formerly, late. *~-gît*, here lies (*grave*). *~-inclus, e & ci-joint, e*, enclosed, herewith, subjoined. ¶ *pn*, this.

cible (sibl) *f*, target; butt (*fig.*).

ciboire (sibwa:r) *m*, ciborium, pyx.

ciboule (sibul) *f*, spring onion. **ciboulette** (lɛt) *f*, chive.

cicatrice (sikatris) *f*, scar, mark. **cicatriser** (ze) *v.t. & se ~*, to scar; mark; heal, skin over.

cicerone (siseron) *m*, cicerone, guide.

cidre (si:dr) *m*, cider.

ciel (sjɛl) *m*, heaven, heavens, sky; air; climate, clime; tester, canopy; roof. *à ~ ouvert*, in the open air; open-cast, daylight (*Min.*).

cierge (sjɛrʒ) (*Eccl.*) *m*, [wax] candle, taper.

cigale (sigal) *f*, cicada, grasshopper.

cigare (siga:r) *m*, cigar. *~ de la Havane*, Havana c. **cigarette** (garɛt) *f*, cigarette.

cigogne (sigɔɲ) *f*, stork.

ciguë (sigy) *f*, *hemlock*.

cil (sil) *m*, eyelash; hair (*Bot.*). **ciller** (sije) *v.i*, to blink; move an eyelid.

cime (sim) *f*, top, summit, peak.

ciment (simɑ̃) *m*, cement. **cimenter** (te) *v.t*, to cement.

cimeterre (simtɛ:r) *m*, scimitar.

cimetière (simtjɛ:r) *m*, cemetery, burial ground, graveyard, churchyard.

cimier (simje) *m*, crest; haunch (*venison*); buttock (*beef*).

cinabre (sina:br) *m*, cinnabar.

cinématographe (sinematɔgraf), **cinéma**, *abb*, *m*, movie theater; movies.

cinéraire (sinerɛ:r) *a*, cinerary. ¶ *f*, cineraria (*Bot.*).

cinétique (sinetik) *a*, kinetic.

cingalais, e (sɛ̃galɛ, ɛ:z) *a*. & C~, *n*, Cingalese.

cinglé (sɛ̃gle) *a*, nutty, crazy, etc.

cingler (sɛ̃gle) *v.t*, to lash, cut, whip; shingle (*Metall.*); to sail, scud.

cinq (sɛ̃[:]k; *before a consonant*, sɛ̃) *a*. & *m*, five; fifth; cinq[ue]. **cinquantaine** (sɛ̃kɑ̃tɛn) *f*, fifty [or so]; golden wedding. **cinquante** (kɑ̃:t) *a*. & *m*, fifty. **cinquantenaire** (kɑ̃tnɛ:r) *m*, fiftieth anniversary. **cinquantième** (tjɛm) *a*. & *n*, fiftieth. **cinquième†** (kjɛm) *a*. & *n*, fifth.

cintre (sɛ̃:tr) *m*, arch, curve; center (*for arch*); clothes hanger. **cintrer** (sɛ̃tre) *v.t*, to arch, bend, curve.

cipaye (sipa:j) *m*, sepoy.

cirage (sira:ʒ) *m*, waxing; polishing; shoe polish.

circoncire (sirkɔ̃si:r) *v.t.ir*, to circumcise.

circonférence (sirkɔ̃ferɑ̃:s) *f*, circumference, girth.

circonflexe (sirkɔ̃flɛks) *a*. & *m*, circumflex.

circonlocution (sirkɔ̃lɔkysjɔ̃) *f*, circumlocution.

circonscription (sirkɔ̃skripsjɔ̃) *f*, circumscription; area. ~ *électorale*, constituency. **circonscrire** (skri:r) *v.t.ir*, to circumscribe; locate.

circonspect, e (sirkɔ̃spɛ[k], ɛkt) *a*, circumspect, cautious, wary, guarded.

circonstance (sirkɔ̃stɑ̃:s) *f*, circumstance, occasion; nonce. **circonstancié, e** (stɑ̃sje) *p.a*, circumstantial, detailed (*account*). **circonstancier** (sje) *v.t*, to detail.

circonvenir (sirkɔ̃vni:r) *v.t.ir*, to circumvent, outwit, overreach.

circonvoisin, e (sirkɔ̃vwazɛ̃, in) *a*, surrounding.

circuit (sirkɥi) *m*, circuit, round. ~ *de paroles*, circumlocution.

circulaire† (sirkylɛ:r) *a*. & *f*, circular. **circulant, e** (lɑ̃, ɑ̃:t) *a*, circulating, floating. **circulation** (lasjɔ̃) *f*, circulation, running, traveling, working; traffic; currency; turnover, sales. **circuler** (le) *v.i*, to circulate, run, travel. **circulez!** move on! pass along!

cire (si:r) *f*, wax. ~ *à cacheter*, sealing wax. **ciré** (sire) *m*, oilskin. **cirer** (re) *v.t*, to wax; polish (*shoes*). **cireur** (rœ:r) *m*, bootblack. **cireuse** (rø:z) *f*, floor polisher (*Mach.*). **cirier** (rje) *m*, wax chandler.

ciron (sirɔ̃) *m*, mite (*insect*).

cirque (sirk) *m*, circus; corrie.

cirrhose (siro:z) *f*, cirrhosis.

cirrus (sir[r]y:s) *m*, cirrus (*Meteor.*).

cisailler (sizɑje) *v.t*, to shear, clip. **cisailles** (zɑ:j) *f.pl*, shears, shearing machine. **ciseau** (zo) *m*, chisel. ~ *à déballer*, case opener. ~ *à froid*, cold chisel. ~x, *pl*, [pair of] scissors; shears, clippers. **ciseler** (zle) *v.t*, to chisel; chase. **ciselet** (zlɛ) *m*, graver. **ciselure** (zly:r) *f*, chiseling; chasing.

citadelle (sitadɛl) *f*, citadel; stronghold.

citadin, e (sitadɛ̃, in) *n*, townsman, citizen.

citation (sitasjɔ̃) *f*, citation, quotation; summons, subpoena. ~ *à l'ordre de l'armée*, mention in dispatches.

cité (site) *f*, city.

citer (site) *v.t*, to cite, quote; mention; instance; summon; summons; subpoena.

citérieur, e (siterjœ:r) *a*, hither (*Geog.*).

citerne (sitɛrn) *f*, tank, cistern.

cithare (sita:r) *f*, zither.

citoyen, ne (sitwajɛ̃, ɛn) *n*, citizen.

citrique (sitrik) *a*, citric. **citron** (trɔ̃) *m*, lemon; citron. ~ *pressé*, lemon squash. **citronnade** (trɔnad) *f*, lemonade. **citronnier** (nje) *m*, lemon tree; citron tree.

citrouille (situru:j) *f*, pumpkin.

cive[tte] (siv[ɛt]) *f*, chive.

civet de lièvre (sivε) *m*, jugged hare.

civette (sivεt) *f*, civet [cat].

civière (sivjε:r) *f*, handbarrow; stretcher, litter; bier.

civil, e† (sivil) *a*, civil; calendar (*month*, *year*). ¶ *m*, civilian; noncombatant. **en ~**, in plain clothes, in mufti. **civilisateur, trice** (lizatœ:r, tris) *a*, civilizing. **civilisation** (sjɔ̃) *f*, civilization. **civiliser** (ze) *v.t*, to civilize. **civilité** (te) *f*, civility; (*pl.*) compliments.

civique (sivik) *a*, civic.

clabauder (klabode) *v.i*, to babble (*of hound*); backbite.

claie (klε) *f*, hurdle; fence. *passer à la ~*, to screen.

clair, e† (klε:r) *a*, clear; bright; light; thin; plain, explicit. *sabre au clair*, with drawn sword. *tirer au clair*, *v.t*, to clear up. **clair, ad**, clearly, plainly; thinly. ¶ *m*, light; plain language (*Teleg.*). **~ de lune**, moonlight. **clairet** (klεrε) *a.m*, pale (*wine*, *precious stone*).

claire-voie (klεrvwa) *f*, grating. *à ~*, openwork, lattice (*att.*).

clairière (klεrjε:r) *f*, glade; clearing; lane.

clair-obscur (klεrɔpsky:r) *m*, chiaroscuro, light & shade.

clairon (klεrɔ̃) *m*, bugle; bugler; clarion. **claironner** (rɔne) *v.t*, to noise abroad.

clairsemé, e (klεrsəme) *a*, thinly sown; sparse; few & far between.

clairvoyance (klεrvwajɑ̃:s) *f*, clear-sightedness, shrewdness.

clameur (klamœ:r) *f*, clamor, outcry.

clampin (klɑ̃pɛ̃) *m*, slowcoach.

clan (klɑ̃) *m*, clan, set.

clandestin, e† (klɑ̃dεstɛ̃, in) *a*, clandestine, underhand.

clapet (klapε) *m*, clack [valve], flap.

clapier (klapje) *m*, rabbit burrow, r. hutch.

clapoter (klapɔte) *v.i*, to plash, swash. **clapoteux, euse** (tø, ø:z) *a*, choppy (*water*).

clapper (klape) *v.i*, to smack (*tongue*).

claque (klak) *f*, slap, smack;

claque (*Theat.*). ¶ *m*, crush hat, opera hat.

claquedent (klakdɑ̃) *m*, starveling; brothel; gambling den.

claquemurer (klakmyre) *v.t*, to coop up, immure, closet.

claquer (klake) *v.i. & t*, to clap, clatter, slap, snap, crack, chatter, slam; die; go to pièces. **claquet** (kε) *m*, **claquette** (kεt) *f*, **claquoir** (kwa:r) *m*, clapper. **claquettes**, *f.pl*, step dance, tap d.

clarifier (klarifje) *v.t*, to clarify, fine.

clarine (klarin) *f*, cowbell.

clarinette (klarinεt) *f*, clarinet.

clarté (klarte) *f*, clearness; brightness; light.

classe (klɑ:s) *f*, class, order; rate; grade (*at school*); school; contingent (*of recruiting year*). **~ moyenne**, middle class[es]. [*salle de*] **~**, classroom. **classement** (klɑsmɑ̃) *m*, classing, classification; rating; filing; order, position (*running, etc.*). **classer (se)** *v.t*, to class, classify; sort, grade; file (*letters, etc.*); position; marshal. **classeur** (sœ:r) *m*, file; filing cabinet; stationery rack. **classification** (klasifikasjɔ̃) *f*, classification. **classique†** (sik) *a*, classic; classical; class, school (*att.*); educational; standard. ¶ *m*, classic.

claudication (klodikasjɔ̃) *f*, lameness.

clause (klo:z) *f*, clause, term, provision, stipulation.

claustral, e (klostral) *a*, claustral, cloistral.

claveau (klavo) *m*, arch-stone, voussoir; sheep pox.

clavecin (klavsɛ̃) *m*, harpsichord.

clavelée (klavle) *f*, sheep pox.

clavette (klavεt) *f*, key, cotter, pin. **~ d'essieu**, axle pin, linch-pin. **~ fendue**, split pin.

clavicule (klavikyl) *f*, collar bone.

clavier (klavje) *m*, keyboard; manual; (*musical*) compass, range.

clayonnage (klεjɔna:ʒ) *m*, wattling; mat[tress].

clef, sometimes clé (kle) *f*, key; clue (*puzzle*); wrench; plug, spigot; clef. **~ à marteau**, screw hammer; adjustable wrench. ~ *anglaise*, monkey wrench. ~ *d'ut*, C (*or* tenor) (*or* alto) clef. ~ *de fa*, F (*or* bass) c. ~ *de sol*, G (*or* treble) c. ~ *de voûte*, keystone. *sous* ~, locked up, under lock & key.

clématite (klematit) *f*, clematis.

clémence (klemɑ̃:s) *f*, clemency, mercy, leniency; mildness. **clément, e** (mɑ̃, ɑ̃:t) *a*, clement, etc.

cleptomane (klɛptoman) *n*, kleptomaniac. **cleptomanie** (ni) *f*, kleptomania.

clerc (klɛ:r) *m*, clerk (*Relig.*, *law*). **clergé** (klɛrʒe) *m*, clergy; priesthood. **clérical, e** (klerikal) *a. & m*, clerical.

cliché (kliʃe) *m*, plate (*Typ.*); negative (*Phot.*); stock phrase, hackneyed p., tag. ~ *au trait*, linecut, line engraving. ~ *simili*, ~ *tramé*, half-tone engraving. **clicher** (ʃe) *v.t*, to stereotype.

client, e (kliɑ̃, ɑ̃:t) *n*, client, customer; patient. **clientèle** (ɑ̃tɛl) *f*, clientele, public, connection, custom; goodwill, practice.

cligner (kliɲe) *v.i*, to wink; blink; wince. **clignoter** (ɲɔte) *v.i*, to blink, twinkle; twitch.

climat (klima) *m*, climate. **climatérique** (materik) *a*, climacteric (*Med.*); climatic. **climatique** (tik) *a*, climatic. **climatiser** (tize) *v.t*, to air-condition.

clin d'œil (klɛ̃dœj) *m*, wink; twinkling of an eye, trice.

clinicien (klinisjɛ̃) *m*, clinician. **clinique** (nik) *a*, clinical. ¶ *f*, clinic; nursing home; surgery (*room*).

clinquant (klɛ̃kɑ̃) *m*, tinsel; foil; showiness.

clique (klik) *f*, clique, set, gang; drums & bugles (*Mil. band*).

cliquet (klikɛ) *m*, pawl, click, catch. ~ [*à canon*], engineer's ratchet brace. ~ [*simple*], ratchet. **cliqueter** (kte) *v.i*, to click, clank, clash, rattle, jingle. **cliquetis** (kti) *m*, click[ing], *etc*. **cliquettes** (kɛt) *f.pl*, bones, castanets.

clisser (klise) *v.t*, to wicker (*bottles*).

clivage (kliva:ʒ) *m*, cleavage (*Miner.*).

cloaque (klɔak) *m*, cesspool; sink (*fig.*).

clochard (klɔʃa:r) *m*, tramp, hobo.

cloche (klɔʃ) *f*, bell; bell glass; bell jar; dish cover; cloche. ~ *à fromage*, cheese cover. ~ *à plongeur*, diving bell.

clochement (klɔʃmɑ̃) *m*, hobble, limp.

cloche-pied (à) (klɔʃpje) *ad*, on one leg. *sauter à* ~, to hop.

clocher (klɔʃe) *m*, belfry. ~ [*pointu*], steeple. *de* ~ (*fig.*), parish (*att.*), parochial.

clocher (klɔʃe) *v.i*, to hobble, limp, halt, be lame. *il y a quelque chose qui cloche*, something's wrong.

clocheton (klɔʃtɔ̃) *m*, bell turret.

clochette (klɔʃɛt) *f*, hand bell; bell [flower]. ~ *d'hiver*, snowdrop.

cloison (klwazɔ̃) *f*, partition; bulkhead; septum. [*émail*] **cloisonné** (zɔne) *m*, cloisonné [enamel]. **cloisonner** (ne) *v.t*, to partition [off].

cloître (klwɑ:tr) *m*, cloister. **cloîtrer** (wɑtre) *v.t*, to cloister, immure.

clopin-clopant (klɔpɛ̃klɔpɑ̃) *ad*, hobbling along. **clopiner** (pine) *v.i*, to hobble.

cloporte (klɔpɔrt) *m*, wood louse.

cloque (klɔk) *f*, blister; rust (*Agric.*).

clore (klɔ:r) *v.t. & i. ir*, to close, shut; enclose; conclude. **clos** (klo) *m*, enclosure. **clôture** (kloty:r) *f*, enclosure, fence, fencing; screen (*choir*); closure; closing. ~ *à claire voie*, paling.

clou (klu) *m*, nail; boil (*Med.*). *les* ~s, studded crossing (*pedestrian*). ~ *à crochet*, tenterhook. ~ *à dessin*, drawing pin. ~ *à deux pointes*, [wire] staple. ~ *de girofle*, clove. ~ *de la fête*, chief attraction, star turn. ~ *de Paris*, French nail, wire n. ~ *découpé*, cut n. **clouer** (klue) *v.t*, to nail [up, down]; pin; tie. ~ *la bouche à quelqu'un*, to shut someone up (*silence*). **clouter** (te) *v.t*, to stud. *passage clouté*, studded crossing (*pedestrian crossing*).

clouterie (tri) *f*, nailmaking; n. works. **cloutier** (tje) *m*, nail-maker.

clovisse (klɔvis) *f*, cockle (*Mol.*).

clown (klun) *m*, clown. **clownerie** (nri) *f*, clownery.

club (klyb) *m*, club. ~ *de golf*, golf club (*people & stick*).

coaguler (koagyle) *v.t*, to coagulate.

coaliser (se) (koalize) *v.pr*, to combine. **coalition** (sjɔ̃) *f*, coalition; combine, ring.

coaltar (kɔlta:r) *m*, coal tar.

coasser (koase) *v.i*, to croak (*frog*).

cobalt (kɔbalt) *m*, cobalt.

cobaye (kɔba:j) *m*, guinea pig.

cobra (kɔbra) *m*, cobra.

cocaïne (kɔkain) *f*, cocaine.

cocarde (kɔkard) *f*, cockade, rosette.

cocasse (kɔkas) *a*, droll, comical.

coccinelle (kɔksinɛl) *f*, ladybird.

coche (kɔʃ) *f*, sow; notch, score. ¶ *m*, stagecoach.

cochenille (kɔʃni:j) *f*, cochineal.

cocher (kɔʃe) *m*, coachman, driver. ~ *de fiacre*, cabman.

cocher (kɔʃe) *v.t*, to notch, score.

cochet (kɔʃɛ) *m*, cockerel.

cochon (kɔʃɔ̃) *m*, hog, pig, porker, swine; dirty pig (*man*). ~ *d'Inde*, guinea pig. ~ *de lait*, sucking pig. **cochonnée** (ʃone) *f*, farrow, litter. **cochonner** (ne) *v.i*, to farrow, pig. **cochonnerie** (nri) *f*, filthiness, obscenity.

coco (kɔko) *m*, coco[nut].

coco (kɔko) *m*, **cocotte** (kɔt) *f*, darling.

cocon (kɔkɔ̃) *m*, cocoon.

cocorico (kɔkɔriko) *m*, cock-a-doodle-doo.

cocotier (kɔkɔtje) *m*, coco[nut] palm.

code (kɔd) *m*, code; statute book; law; canons (*taste*). ~ *de la route*, highway code, road code, code of the road. *mettre en* ~, to dim (*auto lights*). Cf. *phare-code*.

codétenteur, trice (kodetɑ̃tœ:r, tris) *n*, joint holder.

codex [pharmaceutique] (kɔdɛks) *m*, pharmacopoeia.

codicille (kɔdisil) *m*, codicil.

codifier (kɔdifje) *v.t*, to codify.

codirecteur, trice (kodirɛktœ:r, tris) *n*, joint manager, ess.

coefficient (koefisjɑ̃) *m*, coefficient.

cœur (kœ:r) *m*, heart; courage; feelings; core; height (*of summer*); depth (*of winter*); hearts (*cards*).

coffre (kɔfr) *m*, chest, box, trunk, bin, locker, coffer; case. ~-**fort** (frəfɔ:r) *m*, safe. **coffrer** (fre) *v.t*, to lock up (*pers.*). **coffret** (frɛ) *m*, casket, box, chest. ~ *à monnaie*, cash box. ~ *de pharmacie*, medicine chest.

cogérant, e (kɔʒerɑ̃, ɑ̃:t) *n*, joint manager, ess.

cognac (kɔɲak) *m*, cognac, brandy.

cognassier (kɔɲasje) *m*, quince [tree].

cognée de bûcheron (kɔɲe) *f*, felling axe. **cogner** (ɲe) *v.t. & i*, to drive in; knock, bump, thump.

cohabiter (koabite) *v.i*, to cohabit.

cohérence (kɔerɑ̃:s) *f*, coherence. **cohérent, e** (rɑ̃, ɑ̃:t) *a*, coherent, connected; cohesive. **cohésion** (zjɔ̃) *f*, cohesion.

cohorte (kɔɔrt) *f*, cohort.

cohue (kɔy) *f*, crowd, crush.

coi, te (kwa, at) *a*, still, quiet.

coiffe (kwaf) *f*, headdress; cap; lining (*hat*). **coiffer** (fe) *v.t*, to hat; cap; fit, suit (*hat*); dress (*or do*) [the hair of]. *se* ~ *de* (*fig.*), to be infatuated with. **coiffeur, euse** (fœ:r, ø:z) *n*, hairdresser. ¶ *f*, dressing table. ~ *psyché*, cheval d. t. **coiffure** (fy:r) *f*, headdress, headgear; style of hairdressing. ~ *à la Ninon* (ninɔ̃), ~ *à la Jeanne d'Arc* (ʒandark), bob[bed hair]. ~ *de cotillon*, paper hat (*Danc.*).

coin (kwɛ̃) *m*, corner, angle; wedge, key, quoin; die; stamp; mark; plot, patch (*land*). ~ *du feu*, fireside, chimney corner. **coincer** (kwɛ̃se) *v.t*, to wedge, key; jam.

coïncidence (kɔɛ̃sidɑ̃:s) *f*, coincidence. **coïncider** (de) *v.i*, to coincide.

coing (kwɛ̃) *m*, quince (*fruit*).

coïntéressé, e (kɔɛ̃terɛse) *n*, co-adventurer.

coke (kɔk) *m*, coke.

col (kɔl) *m*, collar; neck (*bottle*); pass, col, saddle. ~ *rabattu*, double collar, turndown c. (*attached*). ~ *souple*, soft c. ~ *tenant*, c. attached (*to shirt*). ~ *transformable*, two-way c. *faux* ~, [shirt] collar (*detached*). *faux* ~ *cassé*, wing c. *faux* ~ *montant*, *faux* ~ *droit*, high c., stand-up c. *faux* ~ *rabattu*, double c., turn-down c.

coléoptère (kɔleɔptɛ:r) *a*, coleopterous. ¶ *m*, coleopter[an], beetle.

colère (kɔlɛ:r) *f*, anger, rage, passion, temper, fume. ~ *bleue*, towering rage. **colère & colérique** (lerik) *a*, quick-tempered, hasty, peppery, choleric.

colibri (kɔlibri) *m*, humming bird.

colifichet (kɔlifiʃɛ) *m*, knick-knack; (*pl.*) frippery.

colimaçon (kɔlimasɔ̃) *m*, snail. *en* ~, spiral.

colin-maillard (kɔlɛ̃maja:r) *m*, blindman's buff.

colique (kɔlik) *f*, colic, gripes.

colis (kɔli) *m*, parcel, package; article [of luggage]. ~ *à livrer par exprès*, express parcel (*Post.*). ~*-avion*, air p. ~ *contre remboursement*, cash on delivery p. *par* ~ *postal*, by parcel post.

collaborateur, trice (kɔlabɔratœ:r, tris) *n*, collaborator, contributor. **collaborer** (re) *v.i*, to collaborate. ~ *à*, to contribute to, write for (*journal*).

collage (kɔla:ʒ) *m*, sticking, pasting; gluing; sizing; hanging (*paper*); fining (*wine*). **collant, e** (lɑ̃, ɑ̃:t) *a*, sticky; tacky; tight, close-fitting.

collatéral, e (kɔlateral) *a*, collateral, side (*att.*).

collation (kɔlasjɔ̃) *f*, collation; light meal, snack. **collationner** (ɔne) *v.t*, to collate, compare, read over; repeat; (*v.i.*) to have a snack.

colle (kɔl) *f*, glue, paste; oral test (*exams*); detention (*Sch.*); difficult question. ~ [*de poisson*], isinglass; fish glue. ~ *forte*, glue.

collecte (kɔlɛkt) *f*, collection

(*money*); collect. **collecteur** (tœ:r) *m*, collector; main (*drain*). ~ *d'impôts*, tax collector. **collectif, ive†** (tif, i:v) *a*, collective, joint. **collection** (sjɔ̃) *f*, collection; file (*newspapers*). **collectionner** (ɔne) *v.t*, to collect. **collectionneur, euse** (nœ:r, ø:z) *n*, collector.

collège (kɔlɛ:ʒ) *m*, college, school. ~ *électoral*, electoral college. **collégial, e** (leʒjal) *a*, collegiate. **collégien, ne** (ʒjɛ̃, ɛn) *n*, collegian; schoolboy, -girl.

collègue (kɔlɛg) *m*, colleague.

coller (kɔle) *v.t*, to stick; paste; glue; size; hang (*paper*); fine (*wine*); fix, fasten; cushion (*Bil.*); to fail (*exam*); (*v.i.*) to fit tightly, cling. *se* ~, to stick, cling, cleave.

collerette (kɔlrɛt) *f*, collaret[te]; flange.

collet (kɔlɛ) *m*, collar; collet; neck; scrag (*mutton*); scruff of the neck; flange. ~ *monté* (*fig.*), straitlaced; prim. **colleter** (lte) *v.t*, to collar, grapple with.

colleur (kɔlœ:r) *m*, paperhanger; billposter, billsticker; examiner (*Sch.*).

collier (kɔlje) *m*, necklace; collar; strap; ring. ~ *de misère*, drudgery.

colline (kɔlin) *f*, hill.

collision (kɔlizjɔ̃) *f*, collision, clash.

collocation (kɔlɔkasjɔ̃) *f*, settling the list of creditors; dividend (*to creditors*). *bordereau de* ~, list of creditors.

colloque (kɔlɔk) *m*, colloquy, conversation.

colloquer (kɔlɔke) *v.t*, to collocate; foist.

collusion (kɔlysjɔ̃) *f*, collusion.

colombe (kɔlɔ̃:b) *f*, dove.

Colombie (la) (kɔlɔ̃bi), Columbia.

colombier (kɔlɔ̃bje) *m*, dovecote.

colon (kɔlɔ̃) *m*, colonist, settler.

colonel (kɔlɔnɛl) *m*, colonel.

colonial, e (kɔlɔnjal) *a*, colonial. **colonie** (ni) *f*, colony, settlement. *la* ~ *du Cap*, Cape Colony. **coloniser** (nize) *v.t*, to colonize.

colonnade (kɔlɔnad) *f*, colonnade. **colonne** (lɔn) *f*, column, pillar; post.

colophane (kɔlɔfan) *f*, resin (*violin*).

colorer (kɔlɔre) *v.t*, to color; stain (*glass*). **colorier** (rje) *v.t*, to color. **coloris** (ri) *m*, color[ing], hue.

colossal, e† (kɔlɔsal) *a*, colossal. **colosse** (lɔs) *m*, colossus; giant.

colporter (kɔlpɔrte) *v.t*, to hawk, peddle. **colporteur** (tœːr) *m*, peddler.

coltineur (kɔltinœːr) *m*, porter (*dock*); heaver (*coal*).

colza (kɔlza) *m*, colza.

coma (kɔma) *m*, coma (*Med.*). **comateux, euse** (tø, øːz) *a*, comatose.

combat (kɔ̃ba) *m*, combat, fight, battle, action; war (*elements*); contest, bout, match. ~ *de boxe*, boxing match. ~ *de boxe professionnel*, prize fight[ing]. ~ *de près*, infighting (*Box.*). **combativité** (tivite) *f*, combativeness. **combattant** (tɑ̃) *m*, combatant, fighter. *ancien* ~, veteran. **combattre** (tr) *v.t. & i. ir*, to fight; oppose; combat; contend with; strive; vie.

combe (kɔ̃ːb) *f*, coomb, combe, dale.

combien (kɔ̃bjɛ̃) *ad*, how much; how many; how far; how. ~ *de fois?* how many times? how often? ~ *de temps?* how long?

combinaison (kɔ̃binɛzɔ̃) *f*, combination; plan, contrivance, scheme; lady's slip; overalls. **combiner** (ne) *v.t*, to combine; contrive, devise.

comble (kɔ̃ːbl) *a*, full, crowded. ¶ *m*, heaping; top, height, highest pitch; acme, summit, sum; last straw; roof. ~ *brisé*, mansard roof. **combler** (kɔ̃ble) *v.t*, to heap, shower, fill, load, overwhelm; make up, make good.

combustible (kɔ̃bystibl) *a*, combustible; fuel (*att.*). ¶ *m*, fuel, firing. **combustion** (tjɔ̃) *f*, combustion; burning; conflagration, fire (*fig.*).

Côme (le lac de) (koːm), Lake Como.

comédie (kɔmedi) *f*, comedy; theatricals; players; sham. **comé-**

dien, ne (djɛ̃, ɛn) *n*, comedian, actor, tress, player.

comestible (kɔmɛstibl) *a*, edible. ~*s*, *m.pl*, eatables, provisions.

comète (kɔmɛt) *f*, comet; headband (*Bookb.*).

comice agricole (kɔmis) *m*, agricultural show, cattle show.

comique† (kɔmik) *a*, comic; comical; funny, ludicrous. ¶ *m*, comedy; c. writer; comic actor; funny part, joke. ~ *de la troupe* (*fig.*), funny man.

comité (kɔmite) *m*, committee.

commandant (kɔmɑ̃dɑ̃) *m*, commander, commanding officer; commandant; major (*Mil.*); commodore (*Naut.*); squadron leader (*Avn.*). **commande** (mɑ̃ːd) *f*, order; indent; driving; drive; driving gear; control. *de* ~, [arranged] to order; feigned. *sur* ~, (*made*) to order, commissioned. **commandement** (mɑ̃dmɑ̃) *m*, command, order; commandment; behest; word of command. **commander** (de) *v.t. & i*, to command, order, bespeak; govern; demand; drive (*Mach.*).

commanditaire (kɔmɑ̃ditɛːr) *m*, silent partner. **commandite** (dit) *f*, limited liability; finance, interest. **commandité** (te) *m*, acting partner. **commanditer** (te) *m*, acting partner. **commanditer** (te) *v.t*, to finance, take an interest in.

comme (kɔm) *ad*, as, like, such as; how. ~ *ci*, ~ *ça*, so so, middling. ¶ *c*, as, since.

commémorer (kɔmemɔre) *v.t*, to commemorate.

commençant, e (kɔmɑ̃sɑ̃, ɑ̃ːt) *n*, beginner, tyro, learner. **commencement** (smɑ̃) *m*, beginning, start, commencement, inception, outset. **commencer** (se) *v.t. & i*, to begin, commence, start.

commensal, e (kɔmɑ̃sal) *n*, messmate, fellow boarder.

comment (kɔmɑ̃) *ad*, how; what! why!

commentaire (kɔmɑ̃tɛːr) *m*, commentary; comment. **commenter** (te) *v.t*, ou ~ *sur*, to comment on.

commérage (kɔmeraːʒ) *m*, gossip, tittle-tattle.

commerçant, e (kɔmɛrsɑ̃, ɑ̃:t) *a*, commercial, trading, business (*att.*). ¶ *n*, trader, merchant. **commerce** (mɛrs) *m*, commerce, trade, trading, business; traders; intercourse, dealings. ~ *de détail*, retail trade. *d'un* ~ *agréable*, easy to get on with. **commercer** (mɛrse) *v.i*, to trade, deal; hold intercourse. **commercial, e†** (sjal) *a*, commercial, business, trade, trading (*att.*); produce (*market*).

commère (kɔmɛ:r) *f*, fellow sponsor; gossip; busybody; shrewd woman; leading lady (*revue*).

commettant (kɔmɛtɑ̃) *m*, principal (*law*); (*pl.*) constituents (*Pol.*). **commettre** (mɛtr) *v.t.ir*, to commit; perpetrate; appoint; entrust; compromise. **commis** (mi) *m*, clerk. ~ *aux vivres*, ship's steward. ~ *d'entreprise*, clerk of [the] works. ~ *de magasin*, shop assistant. ~ *voyageur*, traveling salesman. **commissaire** (sɛ:r) *m*, commissioner; officer (*emigration*); steward (*fête, race meeting, etc.*); purser (*ship*); paymaster (*navy*); superintendent (*police*). ~ *des* (*ou aux*) *comptes*, auditor. ~ *priseur*, auctioneer. **commissariat** (sarja) *m*, the status *or* office (rooms) of a *commissaire*; thus, ~ *de police*, central police station. ~ *des comptes*, auditorship.

commission (kɔmisjɔ̃) *f*, commission; errand; committee. **commissionnaire** (ɔnɛ:r) *m*, agent, commission agent, factor; messenger; porter. ~ *chargeur*, shipping agent. ~ *de transport[s]*, forwarding a. ~ *en douane*, customs a. **commissionner** (ne) *v.t*, to commission.

commode (kɔmɔd) *f*, [chest of] drawers. ¶ *a*, convenient, handy; commodious, pleasant; easy, easy-going. **commodément** (demɑ̃) *ad*, conveniently. **commodité** (dite) *f*, convenience; commodiousness; (*pl.*) toilet.

commotion (kɔmosjɔ̃) *f*, commotion, upheaval; shock; shell shock. ~ *au cerveau*, concussion of the brain.

commuer (kɔmɥe) *v.t*, to commute.

commun, e (kɔmœ̃, yn) *a*, common; usual; general; ordinary; commonplace; vulgar; average. *peu* ~, uncommon. ¶ *m*, generality, run. *en, hors du,* ~, in, out of, the, common. **communal, e** (mynal) *a*, communal; parish (*att.*). ¶ *m*, common [land]. **communauté** (note) *f*, community; commonwealth; sisterhood. *la C*~ *d'Australie*, the Commonwealth of Australia. **commune** (myn) *f*, commune, parish (*civil*). **communément** (nemɑ̃) *ad*, commonly, generally.

communiant, e (kɔmynjɑ̃, ɑ̃:t) *n*, communicant.

communicatif, ive (kɔmynikatif, i:v) *a*, communicative. **communication** (sjɔ̃) *f*, communication; touch; intercourse; interchange; discovery; access (*of, to, documents*); call (*Teleph.*).

communier (kɔmynje) *v.i. & t*, to communicate (*Eccl.*). **communion** (njɔ̃) *f*, communion; sacrament; fellowship; persuasion, faith, denomination.

communiqué (kɔmynike) *m*, official statement (*to press*); communiqué. **communiquer** (ke) *v.t. & i*, to communicate; impart, convey; produce (*documents*).

communisme (kɔmynism) *m*, communism. **communiste** (nist) *n*, communist.

commutateur (kɔmytatœ:r) *m*, switch; commutator. **commutation** (sjɔ̃) *f*, commutation.

compacité (kɔ̃pasite) *f*, compactness, closeness. **compact, e** (pakt) *a*, compact, dense; concise, compendious.

compagne (kɔ̃paɲ) *f*, companion; mate; partner (*wife*). ~ *de voyage*, fellow passenger, f. traveler. **compagnie** (ɲi) *f*, company; companionship; bevy; covey. *de bonne* ~, well-bred, gentlemanly, ladylike. *de mauvaise* ~, ill-bred, ungentlemanly, unladylike. *& Cie* (e kɔ̃paɲi), & Co. **compagnon** (ɲɔ̃) *m*, companion; mate; journeyman. ~ *de malheur*, fellow sufferer. ~ *de voy-*

age, fellow passenger, f. traveler.

comparable (kɔparabl) *a*, comparable. **comparaison** (rɛzɔ̃) *f*, comparison; simile.

comparaitre (kɔparɛːtr) *v.i.ir*, to appear (*law*).

comparatif, ive† (kɔparatif, iːv) *a*, comparative. ¶ *m*, comparative (*Gram.*). **comparé, e** (re) *p.a*, comparative (*sciences*). **comparer** (re) *v.t*, to compare, liken.

comparse (kɔpars) *n*, supernumerary (*Theat.*); (*m.*) cipher (*pers.*).

compartiment (kɔpartimɑ̃) *m*, compartment.

comparution (kɔparysjɔ̃) *f*, appearance (*law*).

compas (kɔpɑ) *m*, [pair of] compasses; compass. **compassé** (se) *a*, formal, stiff; regular. **compasser** (se) *v.t*, to measure.

compassion (kɔpasjɔ̃) *f*, compassion. **compatible** (tibl) *a*, compatible, consistent. **compatir** (tiːr) *v.i*, to sympathize, bear. **compatissant, e** (usɑ̃, ɑ̃ːt) *a*, compassionate.

compatriote (kɔpatriɔt) *n*, compatriot, [fellow] countryman, -woman.

compendieusement (kɔpɑ̃djøzmɑ̃) *ad*, briefly. compendium (pɛ̃djɔm) *m*, compendium.

compensateur, trice (kɔpɑ̃satœːr, tris) *a*, compensating; countervailing (*duty*). **compensation** (sjɔ̃) *f*, compensation; set off, offset; quid pro quo; making up (*Stk Ex.*); clearing (*banking*). **compenser** (se) *v.t*, to compensate, offset; make up; clear. ~ *les dépens*, to order each party to pay its own costs.

compère (kɔpɛːr) *m*, fellow sponsor; fellow; crony; confederate; leading man (*revue*); compère. ~**-loriot**, *m*, sty (*eye*).

compétence (kɔpetɑ̃ːs) *f*, competence; jurisdiction; province. **compétent, e** (tɑ̃, ɑ̃ːt) *a*, competent.

compétiteur, trice (kɔpetitœːr, tris) *n*, competitor. **compétition** (sjɔ̃) *f*, competition.

compiler (kɔpile) *v.t. & abs*, to compile.

complainte (kɔplɛ̃ːt) *f*, ballad, lay.

complaire à (kɔplɛːr) *v.ir*, to gratify, humor. se **complaire**, to take pleasure, [take] delight, fancy oneself, pat oneself on the back. **complaisamment** (plɛzamɑ̃) *ad*, complacently; obligingly. **complaisance** (zɑ̃ːs) *f*, complaisance; deference; kindness; willingness; complacence, -cy; accommodation (*Fin.*). **complaisant, e** (zɑ̃, ɑ̃ːt) *a*, obliging, willing; complaisant, accommodating, compliant; complacent. ¶ *n*, time server.

complément (kɔplemɑ̃) *m*, complement. ~ *de poids*, make-weight. **complémentaire** (tɛːr) *a*, complementary, fuller.

complet, ète (kɔplɛ, ɛt) *a*, complete, total, whole, full; unabridged; utter; wholemeal (*bread*). *wagon complet*, *charge complète*, truckload. *complet*, houseful (*Theat.*). ¶ *m*, complement; suit [of clothes] (*man's*). *au* ~, complete, full. **complètement** (plɛtmɑ̃) *ad*, completely; quite; thoroughly. ¶ *m*, completion. **compléter** (plete) *v.t*, to complete.

complexe (kɔplɛks) *a*, complex; many-sided; compound. ¶ *m*, complex. ~ *d'infériorité*, inferiority c.

complexion (kɔplɛksjɔ̃) *f*, constitution; disposition.

complexité (kɔplɛksite) *f*, complexity.

complication (kɔplikasjɔ̃) *f*, complication; intricacy.

complice (kɔplis) *a*, accessory, privy, a party (*de* = to). ¶ *n*, accomplice, confederate. ~ *en adultère*, co-respondent. **complicité** (site) *f*, complicity.

complies (kɔpli) *f.pl*, complin[e] (*Eccl.*).

compliment (kɔplimɑ̃) *m*, compliment, congratulation; (*pl.*) kind regards. **complimenter** (te) *v.t*, to compliment. **complimenteur, euse** (tœːr, øːz) *a*, overcivil. ¶ *n*, flatterer.

compliquer (kɔ̃plike) *v.t*, to complicate.

complot (kɔ̃plo) *m*, plot. **comploter** (plote) *v.t*, to plot.

componction (kɔ̃pɔ̃ksjɔ̃) *f*, compunction.

comporter (kɔ̃pɔrte) *v.t*, to admit of; call for, require. **se ~**, to behave.

composant, e (kɔ̃pozɑ̃, ɑ̃:t) *a. & m*, component, constituent. **composé, e** (ze) *a*, compound, composite; composed, demure. **bien composée**, select (*company of people*). ¶ *m*, compound. **composer** (ze) *v.t. & i*, to compose; compound; settle; set (*Typ.*); dial (*Teleph.*). **se ~**, to be composed, consist. **compositeur, trice** (pozitœ:r, tris) *n*, composer; compositor, [type] setter. **composition** (sjɔ̃) *f*, composition; settlement; [type] setting; essay; examination (*Sch.*); paper (*Sch.*). **composteur** (pɔstœ:r) *m*, composing stick; office printing outfit.

compote (kɔ̃pɔt) *f*, compote, stewed fruit. **~ de pommes**, stewed apples. **en ~**, overdone (*meat*); to a jelly (*face injury*). **compotier** (tje) *m*, fruit bowl.

compréhensif, ive (kɔ̃preɑ̃sif, i:v) *a*, comprehensive. **compréhension** (sjɔ̃) *f*, comprehension, understanding. **comprendre** (prɑ̃:dr) *v.t.ir*, to comprehend, understand, make out; comprise, include, cover. *y compris*, including. *non compris*, not including, exclusive of.

compresse (kɔ̃prɛ:s) *f*, compress (*Med.*). **compresseur** (prɛsœ:r) *m*, compressor. **compression** (sjɔ̃) *f*, compression; repression; cut (*in expenditure*). **comprimer** (prime) *v.t*, to compress; repress; restrain.

comprimé (kɔ̃prime) *m*, pill, tablet.

compromettre (kɔ̃prɔmɛtr) *v.t. & i. ir*, to compromise; impair. **se ~**, to compromise (*or commit*) oneself. **compromis** (mi) *m*, compromise; bond.

comptabilité (kɔ̃tabilite) *f*, bookkeeping; accountancy; accounts. **comptable** (bl) *a*, accountable, responsible; book (*entry, value*); accounting *or* bookkeeping (*machine*). ¶ *n*, accountant, bookkeeper. **comptant** (tɑ̃) *m*, cash, prompt (*or* spot) cash, ready money. [*au*] **~**, in (*or* for) cash, cash down. **compte** (kɔ̃:t) *m*, counting, count, reckoning; account. **~-gouttes** (kɔ̃tgut) *m*, dropper. **~-pas**, *m*, pedometer. **~ rendu**, report; review. **~ rond**, round figures, r. numbers; even money. **à ~**, on account. *tout ~ fait*, all told. *se rendre ~ de*, to realize. **compter** (kɔ̃te) *v.t. & i*, to count, reckon, number; rely, depend, calculate; intend, mean. **compteur** (tœ:r) *m*, meter, counter; taximeter, clock; computer. **~ de bicyclette**, cyclometer. **~ de sport**, stopwatch, recorder. **~ de tours**, speed (*or* revolution) counter. **~ de vitesse**, speedometer. **comptoir** (twa:r) *m*, counter; bar; branch, agency; office.

compulser (kɔ̃pylse) *v.t*, to go through, examine.

comte (kɔ̃:t) *m*, count (*title*). **comté** (kɔ̃te) *m*, county, shire. **comtesse** (tɛs) *f*, countess.

concasser (kɔ̃kase) *v.t*, to pound, break, crush.

concave (kɔ̃ka:v) *a*, concave. **concavité** (kavite) *f*, concavity.

concéder (kɔ̃sede) *v.t*, to concede, grant.

concentration (kɔ̃sɑ̃trasjɔ̃) *f*, concentration. **concentrer** (tre) *v.t*, to concentrate; center (*fig.*); repress. **concentrique** (trik) *a*, concentric.

conception (kɔ̃sɛpsjɔ̃) *f*, conception.

concernant (kɔ̃sɛrnɑ̃) *pr*, concerning. **concerner** (ne) *v.t*, to concern, affect.

concert (kɔ̃sɛ:r) *m*, concert; chorus (*fig.*). **concertant, e** (sɛrtɑ̃, ɑ̃:t) *n*, concert performer. **concerter** (te) *v.t*, to concert, plan. **concerto** (sɛrto) *m*, concerto.

concession (kɔ̃sɛsjɔ̃) *f*, concession, grant, claim, license. **concessionnaire** (ɔnɛ:r) *n*, concession[n]aire, grantor, claimholder.

concevable (kɔ̃s[ə]vabl) *a*, conceivable. **concevoir** (səvwa:r) *v.t. & abs*, to conceive; entertain; understand; word, couch.

concierge (kɔ̃sjɛrʒ) *n*, doorkeeper, [hall] porter, caretaker, housekeeper; keeper (*prison*).

concile (kɔ̃sil) *m*, council (*Eccl.*).

concilier (kɔ̃silje) *v.t*, to conciliate, reconcile; win.

concis, e (kɔ̃si, i:z) *a*, concise, terse, crisp, brief. **concision** (sizjɔ̃) *f*, conciseness, brevity.

concitoyen, ne (kɔ̃sitwajɛ̃, ɛn) *n*, fellow citizen.

concluant, e (kɔ̃klyɑ̃, ɑ̃:t) *a*, conclusive. **conclure** (kly:r) *v.t. & i. ir*, to conclude, end; clinch; infer. **conclusion** (klyzjɔ̃) *f*, conclusion, inference; (*pl.*) pleas (*law*).

concombre (kɔ̃kɔ̃:br) *m*, cucumber.

concordance (kɔ̃kɔrdɑ̃:s) *f*, agreement, reconciliation; concordance; concord. **concordat** (da) *m*, composition; concordat. **concorde** (kɔrd) *f*, concord, harmony. **concorder** (de) *v.i*, to agree, tally.

concourir (kɔ̃kuri:r) *v.i.ir*, to concur; compete; rank. **concours** (ku:r) *m*, concurrence; assistance, help; concourse; confluence; competition, contest; meeting; show; [competitive] examination; equality. ~ *orthographique*, spelling bee.

concret, ète (kɔ̃krɛ, ɛt) *a*, concrete. *le concret*, the concrete (opp. *abstract*).

conçu, *p.p*, concevoir.

concubine (kɔ̃kybin) *f*, concubine.

concupiscence (kɔ̃kypisɑ̃:s) *f*, concupiscence.

concurrence (kɔ̃kyrɑ̃:s) *f*, competition; equality [of rank]. *à ~ de*, amounting to. *jusqu'à ~ de*, up to, not exceeding. **concurrent**, e (rɑ̃, ɑ̃:t) *a*, concurrent. ¶ *n*, competitor.

concussion (kɔ̃kysjɔ̃) *f*, misappropriation.

condamnation (kɔ̃dɑnasjɔ̃) *f*, condemnation; sentence; judgment; conviction. **condamné**, e (ne) *n*, convict. ~ *à mort*, condemned man, woman. **condam-**

ner (ne) *v.t*, to condemn; doom; convict; sentence; mulct; give up (*patient*); block up (*door*); board up (*window*); batten down (*Naut.*).

condensateur (kɔ̃dɑsatœ:r) *m*, condenser (*Phys., Elec., Opt.*). **condensation** (sjɔ̃) *f*, condensation. **condenser** (dɑse) *v.t*, to condense; boil down. **condenseur** (sœ:r) *m*, condenser (*steam*).

condescendance (kɔ̃dɛsɑ̃dɑ̃:s) *f*, condescension. **condescendre** (dr) *v.i*, to condescend; comply.

condiment (kɔ̃dimɑ̃) *m*, condiment.

condisciple (kɔ̃disipl) *m*, fellow student, schoolfellow.

condition (kɔ̃disjɔ̃) *f*, condition; (*pl.*) terms; position. ~*provisionnelle*, proviso. *à ~*, on approval. *en ~*, in (*domestic*) service. **conditionnel**, le† (ɔnɛl) *a*, conditional. **conditionner**(ne) *v.t*, to condition; make up.

condoléance (kɔ̃dɔleɑ̃:s) *f*, condolence.

conducteur, trice (kɔ̃dyktœ:r, tris) *n*, conductor, tress; driver; drover; guard (*Rly.*). ~ *des travaux*, foreman of job, factory foreman (*Build.*). ~ *principal*, main, lead (*Elec.*). **conduire** (dɥi:r) *v.t. & abs. ir*, to conduct, lead, guide, show; direct, manage, run; drive; steer; take, carry, convey; conduce. se ~, to behave. **conduit** (dɥi) *m*, pipe, conduit, duct. **conduite** (dɥit) *f*, conduct, behavior; bearing; management; lead; care; driving; pipe. ~ [*maîtresse*], main.

cône (ko:n) *m*, cone; taper.

confection (kɔ̃fɛksjɔ̃) *f*, making up; ready-made clothes, *or* business; outfitting. **confectionner** (ɔne) *v.t*, to make up; concoct. **confectionneur, euse** (nœ:r, ø:z) *n*, clothier, outfitter.

confédération (kɔ̃federasjɔ̃) *f*, confederation, confederacy. se **confédérer** (re) *v.pr*, to confederate.

conférence (kɔ̃ferɑ̃:s) *f*, conference; lecture; debating society. **conférencier, ère** (rɑ̃sje, ɛ:r) *n*, lecturer. **conférer** (re) *v.i. & t*, to confer; bestow; compare.

confesse (kɔ̃fɛs) *f*, confession
(*to priest*). confesser (se) *v.t*,
to confess, own. se ~, to confess
[one's sins]. confesseur (sœːr)
m, confessor. confession (sjɔ̃) *f*,
confession. confessionnal (ɔnal)
m, confessional [box]. confessionnel, le (nɛl) *a*, confessional;
denominational.

confiance (kɔ̃fjɑ̃ːs) *f*, confidence,
trust, faith, reliance, dependence.
confiant, e (ɑ̃, ɑ̃ːt) *a*, confident,
sanguine, hopeful; confiding.
confidemment (fidamɑ̃) *ad*, con-
fidentially. confidence (dɑ̃ːs) *f*,
confidence, secrecy. confident, e
(dɑ̃, ɑ̃ːt) *n*, confidant, e. confidentiel, le† (sjɛl) *a*, confidential.
confier (fje) *v.t*, to entrust, confide; trust, commit; vest. se ~,
to confide, rely.

configuration (kɔ̃figyrasjɔ̃) *f*,
configuration, lie, lay.

confiner (kɔ̃fine) *v.i*, to border;
(*v.t.*) to confine. confins (fɛ̃)
m.pl, confines; ends.

confire (kɔ̃fiːr) *v.t.ir*, to preserve;
pickle.

confirmer (kɔ̃firme) *v.t*, to confirm.

confiscation (kɔ̃fiskasjɔ̃) *f*, confiscation.

confiserie (kɔ̃fizri) *f*, confectionery; confectioner's shop.
confiseur, euse (zœːr, ϕːz) *n*,
confectioner.

confisquer (kɔ̃fiske) *v.t*, to confiscate; impound.

confiture (kɔ̃fityːr) *f*. *oft*. *pl*,
preserve, jam. ~ *d'oranges*,
[orange] marmalade.

conflagration (kɔ̃flagrasjɔ̃) *f*,
conflagration.

conflit (kɔ̃fli) *m*, conflict, clash,
strife.

confluent (kɔ̃flyɑ̃) *m*, confluence, meeting. confluer (flye) *v.i*,
to join, meet.

confondre (kɔ̃fɔ̃ːdr) *v.t*, to confound; mingle; blend; confuse;
mistake; discomfit; overwhelm.

conformation (kɔ̃fɔrmasjɔ̃) *f*,
conformation. conforme (fɔrm)
a, conformable; according; in
harmony; agreeable. *pour copie*
~, [certified] a true copy. con-
formé, e (me) *p.a*, (*well, ill*)
formed. conformément (mɑ̃) *ad*,

conformably, according. conformer (me) *v.t. & se* ~, to conform. conformité (mite) *f*, con-
formity, compliance.

confort (kɔ̃fɔːr) *m*, comfort(s).
confortable† (fɔrtabl) *a*, comfortable, snug.

confraternité (kɔ̃fratɛrnite) *f*,
confraternity, brotherhood. confrère (frɛːr) *m*, colleague, con-
frere, brother; contemporary.
confrérie (freri) *f*, brotherhood,
sisterhood; confraternity.

confronter (kɔ̃frɔ̃te) *v.t*, to confront; compare.

confus, e (kɔ̃fy, yːz) *a*, confused;
jumbled; indiscriminate; embarrassed. confusément (fyzemɑ̃)
ad, confusedly; dimly. confusion
(zjɔ̃) *f*, confusion; embarrassment.

congé (kɔ̃ʒe) *m*, leave; vacation;
furlough; dismissal, discharge;
notice [to quit]; permission;
clearance (*ship*); cart note
(*Cust.*); fillet (*Arch.*). congédier
(dje) *v.t*, to dismiss, discharge;
pay off.

congélation (kɔ̃ʒelasjɔ̃) *f*, con-
gelation, freezing; frostbite. congeler (ʒle) *v.t. & se* ~, to congeal, freeze.

congénital, e (kɔ̃ʒenital) *a*, congenital.

congestion (kɔ̃ʒɛstjɔ̃) *f*, congestion. ~ *cérébrale, pulmonaire,
sanguine*, c. of the brain, of the
lungs, of the blood. congestionner (ɔne) *v.t*, to congest (*Med.*).

conglomérat (kɔ̃glɔmera) *m*,
conglomerate.

congratulation (kɔ̃gratylasjɔ̃)
f, congratulation. congratuler
(le) *v.t*, to congratulate.

congre (kɔ̃ːgr) *m*, conger [eel].

congrégation (kɔ̃gregasjɔ̃) *f*,
congregation (*Eccl.*).

congrès (kɔ̃grɛ) *m*, congress.
congressiste (sist) *n*, member of
the (*or* a) congress.

congru, e (kɔ̃gry) *a*, congruous,
fitting. *à la portion congrue*, on
short pay, on a meager income.
congrûment (grymɑ̃) *ad*, congru-
ously.

conifère (kɔnifɛːr) *a*, coniferous.
¶ *m*, conifer.

conique (kɔnik) *a,* conic(al); taper[ing].

conjectural, e† (kɔ̃ʒɛktyral) *a,* conjectural. **conjecture** (ty:r) *f,* conjecture, surmise, guess. **conjecturer** (tyre) *v.t,* to conjecture.

conjoindre (kɔ̃ʒwɛ̃:dr) *v.t.ir,* to [con]join, unite. **conjoint, e†** (ʒwɛ̃, ɛ̃:t) *a,* [con]joint. ¶ *n,* party to a (*or* the) marriage (*law*). **conjonction** (ʒɔ̃ksjɔ̃) *f,* conjunction, union. **conjoncture** (ʒɔ̃kty:r) *f,* conjuncture.

conjugaison (kɔ̃ʒygɛzɔ̃) *f,* conjugation.

conjugal, e† (kɔ̃ʒygal) *a,* conjugal, connubial, matrimonial, marriage (*tie*), married (*life*).

conjuguer (kɔ̃ʒyge) *v.t,* to conjugate. *machines conjuguées,* twin engines.

conjuration (kɔ̃ʒyrasjɔ̃) *f,* conspiracy; conjuration. **conjuré** (re) *m,* conspirator. **conjurer** (re) *v.t. & i,* to conspire; conjure.

connaissance (kɔnɛsɑ̃:s) *f,* knowledge; ken; acquaintance; consciousness, senses; cognizance; (*pl.*) learning, attainments, acquirements. *avoir sa ~,* to be conscious (*awake*). *en ~ de cause,* advisedly. *figure de ~,* familiar face. *prendre ~ de,* to take note of. *sans ~,* unconscious, insensible, senseless.

connaissement (kɔnɛsmɑ̃) *m,* bill of lading.

connaisseur, euse (kɔnɛsœ:r, ø:z) *n,* connoisseur, judge. **connaître** (nɛ:tr) *v.t. & abs. ir,* to know, be acquainted with; be aware of; take cognizance of. *se ~ à* (ou *en*), to be a [good] judge of. *se faire ~ ,* to introduce oneself, make oneself known; become known.

connexe (kɔnɛks) *a,* connected, allied, like. & *~s,* & the like. **connexion** (ksjɔ̃), **connexité** (ksite) *f,* connection.

connivence (kɔnivɑ̃:s) *f,* connivance. *être de ~ pour,* to connive at.

connu (le) (kɔny), the known.

conque (kɔ̃:k) *f,* conch.

conquis, *p.p,* **conquérir.**

conquérant, e (kɔ̃kerɑ̃, ɑ̃:t) *n,* conqueror, ess. **conquérir** (ri:r) *v.t.ir,* to conquer. **conquête** (kɛ:t) *f,* conquest.

consacrer (kɔ̃sakre) *v.t,* to consecrate, hallow; dedicate; devote; appropriate, set apart; sanction. *consacré* (à la mémoire de), sacred. *terme consacré,* accepted term.

consanguinité (kɔ̃sɑ̃ginite) *f,* consanguinity, blood relationship.

conscience (kɔ̃sjɑ̃:s) *f,* conscience; conscientiousness; consciousness. *se faire ~ de,* to be reluctant to. **consciencieux, euse†** (ɑ̃sjø, ø:z) *a,* conscientious. **conscient, e** (sjɑ̃, ɑ̃:t), *a,* conscious (*aware*); sentient (*being*).

conscription (kɔ̃skripsjɔ̃) *f,* conscription. **conscrit** (skri) *m,* conscript, draftee; tyro; freshman (*Sch.*).

consécration (kɔ̃sekrasjɔ̃) *f,* consecration; dedication; sanction.

consécutif, ive† (kɔ̃sekytif, i:v) *a,* consecutive.

conseil (kɔ̃sɛ:j) *m,* advice, counsel; board; council; court; counsel (*pers. law*). *~ de prud'hommes,* conciliation board. *C~ des ministres, C~ de Cabinet,* cabinet council. *~ d'administration,* board [of directors]. *~ de guerre,* council of war; court martial. **conseiller** (sɛje) *v.t,* to advise, counsel. **conseiller, ère** (je, ɛ:r) *n,* adviser, councilor. **conseilleur, euse** (jœ:r, ø:z) *n,* officious adviser.

consentement (kɔ̃sɑ̃tmɑ̃) *m,* consent; assent. **consentir** (ti:r) *v.i.ir,* to consent, agree.

conséquemment (kɔ̃sekamɑ̃) *ad,* consequently, accordingly. *~ à,* consistently with. **conséquence** (kɑ̃:s) *f,* consequence; outcome, sequel; inference. **conséquent, e** (kɑ̃, ɑ̃:t) *a,* consistent, rational; consequent. *par conséquent,* consequently, accordingly, therefore.

conservateur, trice (kɔ̃sɛrvatœ:r, tris) *n,* conservator, keeper; warden; ranger; curator, trix; conservative (*Pol.*); registrar (*mortgages*). **conservation** (sjɔ̃) *f,* preservation; care; registry. *~*

par le froid, cold storage. **con-servatoire** (twa:r) *m*, school, academy (*music, etc.*); museum. **conserve** (sɛrv) *f*, preserve; (*pl.*) canned food; (*pl.*) dark glasses; consort (*Naut.*). ~*s au vinaigre*, pickles. **conserver** (ve) *v.t. & abs*, to preserve; pickle; conserve, keep. ~ *la composition*, to keep the type standing.

considérable† (kɔ̃siderabl) *a*, considerable; eminent; large. **con-sidérant** (rɑ̃) *m*, preamble. **con-sidération** (rasjɔ̃) *f*, considera-tion; regard. **considérer** (re) *v.t*, to consider; esteem; regard, deem.

consignataire (kɔ̃siɲatɛ:r) *m*, trustee; consignee. **consignateur** (tœ:r) *m*, consignor. **consigna-tion** (sjɔ̃) *f*, deposit; consign-ment. **consigne** (siɲ) *f*, orders (*to sentry*); confinement to bar-racks; checkroom, baggage room. **consigner** (ɲe) *v.t*, to deposit; consign; record, chronicle; con-fine [to barracks]. ~ *à la porte*, to refuse admittance.

consistance (kɔ̃sistɑ̃:s) *f*, con-sistence, -cy; stability; credit; standing. **consistant, e** (tɑ̃, ɑ̃:t) *a*, firm, set. **consister** (te) *v.i*, to consist. **consistoire** (twa:r) *m*, consistory.

consolateur, trice (kɔ̃sɔlatœ:r, tris) *n*, consoler, comforter. **con-solation** (sjɔ̃) *f*, consolation, comfort, solace, cheer. **console** (sɔl) *f*, bracket; console; console table. **consoler** (le) *v.t*, to con-sole.

consolider (kɔ̃sɔlide) *v.t*, to con-solidate, strengthen; unify, fund (*debt*); exercise, take up (*op-tion*). **consolidation** (dasjɔ̃) *f*, consolidation.

consommateur (kɔ̃sɔmatœ:r) *m*, consumer; customer (*at café*). **consommation** (sjɔ̃) *f*, consump-tion, use; drink; consummation. **consommé, e** (me) *a*, consum-mate. ¶ *m*, stock (*Cook.*); clear soup. **consommer** (me) *v.t*, to consume; use; drink, spend (*money in café*); consummate. **consomption** (sɔ̃psjɔ̃) *f*, consump-tion (*destruction & Med.*).

consonance (kɔ̃sɔnɑ̃:s) *f*, con-sonance. **consonant, e** (nɑ̃, ɑ̃:t)

a, consonant. **consonne** (sɔn) *f*, consonant.

consorts (kɔ̃sɔ:r) *m.pl*, confed-erates. **consortium** (sɔrsjɔm) *m*, syndicate, consortium.

conspirateur, trice (kɔ̃spira-tœ:r, tris) *n*, conspirator, plot-ter. **conspiration** (sjɔ̃) *f*, con-spiracy, plot. **conspirer** (re) *v.i. & t*, to conspire, plot; tend.

conspuer (kɔ̃spɥe) *v.t*, to con-spue; hoot, boo, barrack. *con-spuez-le!* down with him!

constamment (kɔ̃stamɑ̃) *ad*, constantly. **constance** (stɑ̃:s) *f*, constancy; steadfastness; persist-ence, perseverance; patience. *avec* ~, steadfastly. **constant, e** (stɑ̃, ɑ̃:t) *a*, constant; steadfast; enduring; obvious. ¶ *f*, constant.

constater (kɔ̃state) *v.t*, to ascer-tain; verify, prove, establish; de-clare; attest; evidence; record; note; show; mention; be of opinion. **constatation** (tasjɔ̃) *f*, ascertainment, etc.

constellation (kɔ̃stɛllasjɔ̃) *f*, constellation; galaxy (*fig.*). **con-stellé, e** (stɛlle) *a*, constellated; studded.

consternation (kɔ̃stɛrnasjɔ̃) *f*, consternation, dismay. **consterner** (ne) *v.t*, to dismay, stagger.

constipation (kɔ̃stipasjɔ̃) *f*, con-stipation, costiveness. **constiper** (pe) *v.t*, to constipate, bind.

constituant, e (kɔ̃stitɥɑ̃, ɑ̃:t) *a*, constituent, component. **con-stituer** (tɥe) *v.t*, to constitute; form, incorporate; settle; in-struct; brief; appoint. *se* ~ *pri-sonnier*, to give oneself up [to the police]. **constitution** (tysjɔ̃) *f*, constitution; composition. ~ *de dot*, marriage settlement. **con-stitutionnel, le**† (ɔnɛl) *a*, con-stitutional; temperamental.

constructeur (kɔ̃stryktœ:r) *m*, builder, maker, constructor. **con-struction** (sjɔ̃) *f*, construction; building; making; build; engi-neering; erection; structure. **con-struire** (strɥi:r) *v.t.ir*, to con-struct; build, erect; make; con-strue.

consul (kɔ̃syl) *m*, consul. *le C~ britannique*, the British c. *le* ~ *de France*, the French c. **consu-**

laire (lɛːr) *a*, consular. **consulat** (la) *m*, consulate; consulship.

consultant, e (kɔ̃syltɑ̃, ɑ̃ːt) *a*, consulting. **consultation** (tasjɔ̃) *f*, consultation; opinion (*legal*), advice. **consulter** (te) *v.t. & i*, to consult; refer to.

consumer (kɔ̃syme) *v.t*, to consume; waste, spend.

contact (kɔ̃takt) *m*, contact; touch; connection (*Elec.*).

contagieux, euse (kɔ̃taʒjø, øːz) *a*, contagious, infectious, catching. **contagion** (ʒjɔ̃) *f*, contagion; contagiousness.

contamination (kɔ̃taminasjɔ̃) *f*, contamination. **contaminer** (ne) *v.t*, to contaminate.

conte (kɔ̃ːt) *m*, story; tale, yarn; short story; fable. ~ *de bonne femme*, ~ *de vieille*, ~ *à dormir debout*, nonsense. ~ *de fées*, ~ *bleu*, fairy tale. ~ *rimé*, nursery rhyme. ~*s en l'air*, cock-&-bull story, moonshine.

contemplatif, ive (kɔ̃tɑ̃platif, iːv) *a*, contemplative. **contemplation** (sjɔ̃) *f*, contemplation; gazing. **contempler** (ple) *v.t*, to contemplate, view; gaze on; meditate upon.

contemporain, e (kɔ̃tɑ̃pɔrɛ̃, ɛn) *a*, contemporaneous, contemporary. ¶ *n*, contemporary.

contempteur, trice (kɔ̃tɑ̃ptœːr, tris) *n*, scorner.

contenance (kɔ̃tnɑ̃ːs) *f*, capacity, content; countenance, demeanor, bearing. **contenant** (tnɑ̃) *m*, container. **contenir** (tniːr) *v.t.ir*, to contain; hold; accommodate; comprise; restrain, control.

content, e (kɔ̃tɑ̃, ɑ̃ːt) *a*, content; contentedly; satisfied; pleased; glad. ¶ *m*, fill; heart's content. **contentement** (tɑ̃tmɑ̃) *m*, content[ment]; satisfaction. **contenter** (te) *v.t*, to content, satisfy, gratify.

contentieux, euse (kɔ̃tɑ̃sjø, øːz) *a*, contentious, law (*att.*). ¶ *m*, law department or office; contentious business. **contention** (sjɔ̃) *f*, application, intentness.

contenu (kɔ̃tny) *m*, contents.

conter (kɔ̃te) *v.t*, to tell, relate.

contestable (kɔ̃tɛstabl) *a*, questionable, debatable, moot. **contestation** (sjɔ̃) *f*, dispute, contestation. **sans conteste** (tɛst), indisputably. **contester** (te) *v.t. & abs*, to contest, challenge, question, dispute.

conteur, euse (kɔ̃tœːr, øːz) *n*, narrator; storyteller.

contexte (kɔ̃tɛkst) *m*, context. **contexture** (kɔ̃tɛkstyːr) *f*, [con]texture.

contigu, ë (kɔ̃tigy) *a*, contiguous, adjoining. **contiguïté** (gɥite) *f*, contiguity.

continence (kɔ̃tinɑ̃ːs) *f*, continence. **continent, e** (nɑ̃, ɑ̃ːt) *a*, continent; modest.

continent (kɔ̃tinɑ̃) *m*, continent, mainland. *le c*~, the Continent (*Europe*). **continental, e** (tal) *a*, continental.

contingence (kɔ̃tɛ̃ʒɑ̃ːs) *f*, contingency. **contingent, e** (ʒɑ̃, ɑ̃ːt) *a*, contingent. ¶ *m*, contingent, share; quota. **contingentement** (ʒɑ̃tmɑ̃) *m*, curtailment. **contingenter** (te) *v.t*, to fix quotas for.

continu, e (kɔ̃tiny) *a*, continuous; direct (*Elec. current*). **continuation** (nɥasjɔ̃) *f*, continuation; continuance. **continuel, le†** (nɥɛl) *a*, continual, unceasing. **continuer** (nɥe) *v.t. & i*, to continue; carry on; go on; proceed; keep on. **continuité** (nɥite) *f*, continuity; ceaselessness. **continûment** (nymɑ̃) *ad*, continuously.

contondant, e (kɔ̃tɔ̃dɑ̃, ɑ̃ːt) *a*, blunt (*instrument*).

contorsion (kɔ̃tɔrsjɔ̃) *f*, contortion; twist.

contour (kɔ̃tuːr) *m*, contour, outline. ~ *de hanches, de poitrine*, hip, bust, measurement. **contourner** (turne) *v.t*, to contort, twist; encircle.

contractant, e (kɔ̃traktɑ̃, ɑ̃ːt) *a*, contracting. ¶ *n*, contractant. **contracter** (te) *v.t. & abs*, to contract; enter into; take out, effect (*Insce. policy*). **contraction** (sjɔ̃) *f*, contraction, shrinkage. **contractuel, le** (tɥɛl) *a*, contractual.

contradiction (kɔ̃tradiksjɔ̃) *f*, contradiction; discrepancy. **contradictoire** (twaːr) *a*, contradictory; conflicting; after trial;

check, control (*att.*), joint. *examen* ~, cross-examination.

contraindre (kɔ̃trɛːdr) *v.t.ir*, to constrain, compel, force, coerce, drive; restrain. ~ *par saisie de biens*, to distrain upon (*pers.*). **contrainte** (trɛ̃ːt) *f*, constraint, compulsion.

contraire (kɔ̃trɛːr) *a*, contrary, converse, opposed; unfavorable. ¶ *m*, contrary, reverse, converse, opposite. *au* ~, on the contrary. **contrairement** (trɛrmɑ̃) *ad*, contrarily, contrary, counter.

contralto (kɔ̃tralto) *m*, contralto.

contrariant, e (kɔ̃trarjɑ̃, ɑ̃ːt) *a*, trying, provoking. **contrarier** (rje) *v.t. & abs*, to thwart, interfere with, impede, cross; vex. **contrariété** (rjete) *f*, contrariety; annoyance, nuisance.

contraste (kɔ̃trast) *m*, contrast. **contraster** (te) *v.i. & t*, to contrast.

contrat (kɔ̃tra) *m*, contract; agreement; deed, indenture; articles; letter; bond. *dresser un* ~, to draw up a deed.

contravention (kɔ̃travɑ̃sjɔ̃) *f*, contravention; breach, infringement; offense. *dresser une* ~ *à*, to summons (*legal*).

contre (kɔ̃ːtr) *pr. & ad*, against; contrary to; to (*as* 3 *to* 1); by, close to; versus. ~ *nature*, unnatural.

contre-allée (kɔ̃trale) *f*, side walk.

contre-amiral (kɔ̃tramiral) *m*, rear admiral.

contre-attaque (kɔ̃tratak) *f*, counterattack.

contre-avions (kɔtravjɔ̃) *a*, antiaircraft.

contrebalancer (kɔ̃trəbalɑ̃se) *v.t*, to counterbalance, counterpoise.

contrebande (kɔ̃trəbɑ̃ːd) *f*, smuggling, contraband. *de* ~ (*fig.*), counterfeit. **contrebandier, ère** (bɑ̃dje, ɛːr) *n*, smuggler.

contrebas (en) (kɔ̃trəba) *ad*, below, lower down; downwards.

contrebasse (kɔ̃trəbɑːs) *f*, double bass, contrabass.

contrecarrer (kɔ̃trəkɑre) *v.t*, to thwart, cross; counteract.

contrecœur (à) (kɔ̃trəkœːr) *ad*, reluctantly.

contrecoup (kɔ̃trəku) *m*, rebound; recoil; reaction.

contredire (kɔ̃trədiːr) *v.t. & abs. ir*, to contradict, gainsay. *se*~, to contradict oneself; conflict. *sans* **contredit** (di), unquestionably.

contrée (kɔ̃tre) *f*, country, region.

contre-écrou (kɔ̃trekru) *m*, locknut.

contre-expertise (kɔ̃trɛkspɛrtiːz) *f*, countervaluation.

contrefaçon (kɔ̃trəfasɔ̃) *f*, counterfeit; forgery; infringement; piracy; imitation. ~ *littéraire*, ~ *de librairie*, infringement of copyright. **contrefacteur** (faktœːr) *m*, counterfeiter, etc. **contrefaire** (fɛːr) *v.t.ir*, to counterfeit; mimic, take off; pretend to be; disguise; deform. **contrefaiseur, euse** (fəzœːr, øːz) *n*, mimic.

contre-fiche (kɔ̃trəfiʃ) *f*, strut, brace; raking shore.

contre-fil (à) (kɔ̃trəfil) *ad*, against the grain.

contrefort (kɔ̃trəfɔːr) *m*, buttress; spur.

contre-haut (en) (kɔ̃trəo) *ad*, above, higher up; upwards.

contre-jour (kɔ̃trəʒuːr) *m*, unfavorable light; backlighting. *à* ~, against the light; with one's back to the light.

contremaître (kɔ̃trəmɛːtr) *m*, foreman; first mate (*Naut.*).

contremander (kɔ̃trəmɑ̃de) *v.t*, to countermand; call off.

contremarque (kɔ̃trəmark) *f*, countermark; pass-out check (*Theat.*).

contrepartie (kɔ̃trəparti) *f*, counterpart; contra; contrary [opinion]; other side *or* party; another dealer; running stock (*against one's client*).

contrepasser (kɔ̃trəpase) *v.t*, to write back, reverse, contra; endorse back.

contre-pédaler (kɔ̃trəpedale) *v.i*, to back-pedal.

contre-petterie (kɔ̃trəpɛtri) *f*, Spoonerism.

contre-pied (kɔ̃trəpje) *m*, opposite (*course, view*).

contreplaqué (kɔ̃trəplake) *m*, plywood. ~ *en trois*, three-ply [wood].

contrepoids (kɔ̃trəpwa) *m*, counterweight, counterpoise, counterbalance, balance weight.

contre-poil (à) (kɔ̃trəpwal), the wrong way.

contrepoint (kɔ̃trəpwɛ̃) *m*, counterpoint.

contre-pointe (kɔ̃trəpwɛ̃:t) *f*, loose headstock, tailstock.

contrepoison (kɔ̃trəpwazɔ̃) *m*, antidote.

contre-porte (kɔ̃trəpɔrt) *f*, screen door.

contreseing (kɔ̃trəsɛ̃) *m*, counter signature.

contresens (kɔ̃trəsɑ̃:s) *m*, misconstruction; mistranslation; misinterpretation; bull; wrong way *or* sense.

contresigner (kɔtrəsiɲe) *v.t*, to countersign.

contretemps (kɔ̃trətɑ̃) *m*, mishap, unfortunate occurrence, awkward incident, hitch. *à* ~, inopportunely.

contre-torpilleur (kɔ̃trətɔrpijœ:r) *m*, [torpedo-boat] destroyer.

contrevenir à (kɔ̃trəvəni:r) *v.ir*, to contravene, infringe, transgress.

contrevent (kɔ̃trəvɑ̃) *m*, outside shutter.

contrevérité (kɔ̃trəverite) *f*, untruth.

contribuable (kɔ̃tribɥabl) *n*, taxpayer. ¶ *a*, taxable. **contribuer** (bɥe) *v.i*, to contribute; conduce. **contribution** (bysjɔ̃) *f*, contribution; tax; excise.

contrister (kɔ̃triste) *v.t*, to sadden, grieve.

contrit, e (kɔ̃tri, it) *a*, contrite. **contrition** (sjɔ̃) *f*, contrition.

contrôle (kɔ̃tro:l) *m*, control; supervision; roster; hallmark; inspection; check; ticket office; box office. ~ *de présence*, timekeeping. **contrôler** (trole) *v.t*, to control; inspect; supervise; check; hallmark. **contrôleur** (lœ:r) *m*, controller, comptroller; supervisor; examiner; ticket collector; inspector; checker; timekeeper; telltale (*Mach.*). ~ *des tours*, lap scorer.

contrordre (kɔ̃trɔrdr) *m*, counter instructions.

controuvé, e (kɔ̃truve) *p.p*, fabricated, invented.

controverse (kɔ̃trɔvɛrs) *f*, controversy. **controversé, e** (se) *p.p*, debated.

contumace (kɔ̃tymas) *f*, contumacy.

contus, e (kɔ̃ty, y:z) *a*, bruised. **contusion** (tyzjɔ̃) *f*, bruise, contusion. **contusionner** (ɔne) *v.t*, to bruise, contuse.

convaincant, e (kɔ̃vɛ̃kɑ̃, ɑ̃:t) *a*, convincing, cogent. **convaincre** (vɛ̃:kr) *v.t.ir*, to convince; convict.

convalescence (kɔ̃valɛsɑ̃:s) *f*, convalescence. **convalescent, e** (sɑ̃, ɑ̃:t) *a. & n*, convalescent.

convenable† (kɔ̃vnabl) *a*, proper, fit, [be]fitting, becoming, decorous; suitable, convenient; expedient. **convenance** (vnɑ̃:s) *f*, propriety, fitness, congruity; harmony; convenience; expedience, -cy. **convenir** (vni:r) *v.i.ir*, to agree; own; suit; befit; be expedient; become, do. *mot convenu*, code word. *rédiger en langage convenu*, to code. **convention** (vɑ̃sjɔ̃) *f*, covenant; agreement, contract; convention. *de* ~ & **conventionnel, le** (ɔnɛl) *a*, conventional.

converger (kɔ̃vɛrʒe) *v.i*, to converge.

convers, e (kɔ̃vɛ:r, ɛrs) *a*, lay (*brother, sister*). **converse,** *a.f. & f*, converse. conversation, talk; call (*Teleph.*).

conversation (kɔ̃vɛrsasjɔ̃) *f*, **converser** (se) *v.i*, to converse, talk, commune; wheel (*Mil.*). **conversion** (sjɔ̃) *f*, conversion; change. **convertible** (tibl) *a*, convertible. **converti, e** (ti) *n*, convert. **convertir** (ti:r) *v.t*, to convert, change, turn. *se* ~, to become converted (*Relig.*). **convertissable** (tisabl) *a*, convertible (*Fin.*). **convertissement** (smɑ̃) *m*, conversion (*Fin.*). **convertisseur** (sœ:r) *m*, converter.

convexe (kɔ̃vɛks) *a*, convex. **convexité** (ite) *f*, convexity.

conviction ((kɔ̃viksjɔ̃) *f*, conviction.

convié, e (kɔ̃vje) *n*, guest. **convier** (vje) *v.t*, to invite; (*fig.*), urge. **convive** (vi:v) *n*, guest; table companion.

convocation (kɔ̃vɔkasjɔ̃) *f*, convocation, calling; notice [of meeting]; calling-up (*Mil.*).

convoi (kɔ̃vwa) *m*, convoy; train (*Rly.*); funeral [procession].

convoiter (kɔ̃vwate) *v.t*, to covet, lust after. **convoiteux, euse** (tø, (ø:z) *a*, covetous. **convoitise** ti;z) *f*, covetousness; lust.

convoler (kɔ̃vɔle) *v.i. & abs*, to marry again. ~ *en secondes, en troisièmes, noces*, to marry a second, a third, time.

convoquer (kɔ̃vɔke) *v.t*, to convoke, call, summon, convene; call together.

convoyer (kɔ̃vwaje) *v.t*, to convoy; escort.

convulsif, ive† (kɔ̃vylsif, i;v) *a*, convulsive. **convulsion** (sjɔ̃) *f*, convulsion; upheaval.

coopératif, ive (kɔɔperatif, i;v) *a*, cooperative. [*société*] *coopérative*, cooperative society. **coopération** (sjɔ̃) *f*, cooperation. **coopérer** (re) *v.i*, to cooperate.

coordonner (kɔɔrdɔne) *v.t*, to coordinate.

copain (kɔpɛ) *m*, buddy, pal.

copeau (kɔpo) *m*, shaving; chip.

Copenhague (kɔpɛnag) *f*, Copenhagen.

copie (kɔpi) *f*, copy; paper (*Sch.*). **copier** (pje) *v.t. & abs*, to copy; transcribe; imitate.

copieux, euse† (kɔpjø, ø:z) *a*, copious, full; hearty (*meal*).

copiste (kɔpist) *n*, copyist.

copropriétaire (kɔprɔprietɛ:r) *n*, joint owner.

copulation (kɔpylasjɔ̃) *f*, copulation.

coq (kɔk) *m*, cock, rooster; weathercock; bantam (*Box.*); cook (*ship's*). ~-*à-l'âne*, *m*, cock-&-bull story. ~ *d'Inde*, turkeycock. ~ *de bruyère*, heathcock, blackcock, moor cock. ~ *de combat*, game c. ~ *du village*,

cock of the walk. [~] *faisan*, cock pheasant.

coque (kɔk) *f*, shell; hull (*ship*); husk; pod; cocoon; cockle (*Mol.*); loop (*of ribbon, hair*).

coquelicot (kɔkliko) *m*, poppy.

coqueluche (kɔklyʃ) *f*, whooping cough; darling.

coquemar (kɔkma:r) *m*, kettle, pot.

coquerico (kɔkəriko) *m*, cock-a-doodle-doo.

coquet, te† (kɔkɛ, ɛt) *a*, coquettish, skittish; stylish, smart, natty, trim. ¶ *n*, flirt, coquette. **coqueter** (kte) *v.i*, to coquet, flirt.

coquetier (kɔktje) *m*, egg cup; egg merchant.

coquetterie (kɔkɛtri) *f*, coquetry; as *coquet, te*.

coquillage (kɔkija:ʒ) *m*, shellfish; shell, conch. **coquille** (ki:j) *f*, shell; bush (*Mach.*); misprint, literal [error]; demy (*paper*).

coquin, e (kɔkɛ, in) *n*, rogue, rascal, knave, scamp; (*f.*) hussy, jade, minx. **coquinerie** (kinri) *f*, knavery, roguery, rascality.

cor (kɔ:r) *m*, horn (*Mus.*); corn (*on foot*); antler, tine. ~ *d'harmonie*, French horn. *à* ~ *& à cri*, clamorously.

corail (kɔra:j) *m*, coral. **corailleur** (rajœ:r) *m*, coral fisher. **banc corallifère** (ralifɛ:r), coral reef.

Coran (kɔrɑ̃) *m*, Koran.

corbeau (kɔrbo) *m*, raven; crow; corbel.

corbeille (kɔrbɛ:j) *f*, basket; dress circle (*Theat.*). ~ *à papiers*, wastepaper b. ~ [*de mariage*], (bridegroom's) wedding presents.

corbillard (kɔrbija:r) *m*, hearse.

cordage (kɔrda:ʒ) *m*, rope; (pl.) cordage. **corde** (kɔrd) *f*, rope, cord, line; band; thread; string; halter (*hanging*); chord. *les* ~*s*, the strings (*orchestra*). *à*~*s*, string[ed] (*Mus.*). ~ *à boyau*, catgut. ~ *à linge*, clothes line. ~ *à piano*, piano wire. ~ *à sauter*, skipping rope. ~ *sensible*, sensitive spot. **cordeau** (do) *m*, line, string; chalk-line (*cord*); fuse. **cordelette** (dəlɛt) *f*, cord, string. **cordelière** (ljɛ:r) *f*, girdle. **corder** (de) *v.t*, to twist; cord, rope. **corderie** (dri) *f*, rope works; r. making.

cordial, e† (kɔrdjal) *a*, cordial, hearty. ¶ *m*, cordial. **cordialité** (lite) *f*, cordiality, etc.

cordier (kɔrdje) *m*, rope maker; drifter (*boat*). **cordon** (dɔ̃) *m*, strand, twist; string; cord; lace (*shoe*); pull (*bell*); border; milled edge; row; cordon, ribbon. **cordonner** (dɔne) *v.t*, to twist, twine. **cordonnerie** (nri) *f*, shoemaker's shop; boot & shoe trade. **cordonnet** (nɛ) *m*, braid, cord, twist; milled edge; overcast (*Emb.*). **cordonnier, ère** (nje, ɛːr) *n*, boot & shoe repairer, shoemaker.

Corée (la) (kɔre), Korea. **coréen, ne** (reɛ̃, ɛn) *a.* & C~, *n*, Korean.

coriace (kɔrjas) *a*, leathery, tough.

corindon (kɔrɛ̃dɔ̃) *m*, corundum.

Corinthe (kɔrɛ̃ːt) *f*, Corinth. **corinthien, ne** (rɛ̃tjɛ̃, ɛn) *a.* & C~, *n*, Corinthian.

cormoran (kɔmɔrɑ̃) *m*, cormorant.

cornac (kɔrnak) *m*, mahout; keeper; guide.

cornaline (kɔrnalin) *f*, carnelian.

corne (kɔrn) *f*, horn; dog['s] ear; gaff (*spar*). ~ *d'abondance*, horn of plenty, cornucopia. ~ *de cerf*, deerhorn. **corné, e** (ne) *a*, horny.

corneille (kɔrnɛːj) *f*, crow; rook. *bayer aux ~s*, to rubberneck.

cornemuse (kɔrnəmyːz) *f*, bagpipe[s].

corner (kɔrne) *v.i*, to sound a horn; hoot (*auto*); speak in ear trumpet; din; ring (*ears*); (*v.t*.) to trumpet, din; dog ear, turn down. **cornet** (nɛ) *m*, horn; cornet (*cone*). ~ [*à dés*], dice box. ~ *à pistons*, cornet (*Mus.*). ~ [*acoustique*], ear trumpet. ~ [*avertisseur*], horn (*auto*).

corniche (kɔrniʃ) *f*, cornice; ledge.

cornichon (kɔrniʃɔ̃) *m*, gherkin.

cornier, ère (kɔrnje, ɛːr) *a*, angle (*att.*). ¶ *f*, angle iron.

Cornouailles (la) (kɔrnwɑːj), Cornwall.

cornu, e (kɔrny) *a*, horned; absurd. ¶ *f*, retort, still.

corollaire (kɔrɔlɛːr) *m*, corollary.

coron (kɔrɔ̃) *m*, (*coal*) miner's dwelling; mining village.

corporation (kɔrpɔrasjɔ̃) *f*, corporation, guild. **corporel, le†** (rɛl) *a*, corporeal; corporal, bodily. **corps** (kɔːr) *m*, body; substance; corps, brigade; bodice; barrel, cylinder; hull (*ship*). ~ *6, 8 ou ~ de 6, de 8, points*, 6, 8, point [size] (*Typ.*). ~ *à ~*, hand to hand (*fight*); clinch (*Box.*). ~ *composé*, compound (*Chem.*). ~ *de garde*, guardhouse, guardroom. ~ *de logis*, ~ *de bâtiment*, main [portion of] building. ~ *de métier*, guild. ~ *électoral*, electorate, country. ~ *& biens*, crew & cargo, life & property. ~ [*mort*], [dead] body, corpse. ~ *mort*, dolphin, moorings (*Naut.*). *à ~ perdu*, recklessly. ~ *simple*, element (*Chem.*). *prendre ~*, to take shape.

corpulence (kɔrpylɑ̃ːs) *f*, stoutness, corpulence, -ency, portliness, burliness. **corpulent, e** (lɑ̃, ɑ̃ːt) *a*, corpulent.

corpuscule (kɔrpyskyl) *m*, corpuscle.

correct, e† (kɔrɛkt) *a*, correct. **correcteur, trice** (tœːr, tris) *n*, corrector. ~ *d'imprimerie*, proofreader. **correctif** (tif) *m*, corrective. **correction** (sjɔ̃) *f*, correction; correctness; propriety; punishment. ~ *des épreuves*, proofreading. **correctionnel, le†** (ɔnɛl) *a*, correctional.

corrélatif, ive (kɔrelatif, iːv) *a*, correlative.

correspondance (kɔrɛspɔ̃dɑ̃ːs) *f*, correspondence; letters; connection, transfer point, interchange. **correspondant, e** (dɑ̃, ɑ̃ːt) *a*, corresponding. ¶ *n*, correspondent; friend acting for parents (*to pupil*). **correspondre** (pɔ̃ːdr) *v.i*, to correspond; tally; communicate.

corridor (kɔridɔːr) *m*, corridor, passage.

corrigé (kɔriʒe) *m*, fair copy (*Sch.*); pony (*book*). **corriger** (ʒe) *v.t*, to correct; compensate for; chastise.

corroborer (kɔrɔbɔre) *v.t*, to corroborate.

corroder (kɔrɔde) *v.t*, to corrode.

corroi (kɔrwa) *m*, currying (*leather*); puddle (*clay*).

corrompre (kɔrɔ̃:pr) *v.t*, to corrupt, taint, spoil; bribe.

corrosif, ive (kɔrozif, i:v) *a. & m*, corrosive. **corrosion** (zjɔ̃) *f*, corrosion.

corroyer (kɔrwaje) *v.t*, to curry (*leather*); puddle, pug; weld; trim, dress.

corruptible (kɔryptibl) *a*, corruptible. **corruption** (sjɔ̃) *f*, corruption; bribery.

corsage (kɔrsa:ʒ) *m*, bust; bodice, corsage.

corsaire (kɔrsɛ:r) *m*, corsair, privateer; shark (*Fin.*).

Corse (la) (kɔrs), Corsica. **corse**, *a. & C~, n*, Corsican.

corsé, e (kɔrse) *p.a*, full-bodied (*wine*); strong, forcible (*language*). **corser** (se) *v.t*, to fortify, strengthen. **se~**, to become serious.

corset (kɔrsɛ) *m*, corset, stays. **corseter** (səte) *v.t*, to corset. **corsetier, ère** (tje, ɛ:r) *n*, corset maker.

cortège (kɔrtɛ:ʒ) *m*, retinue, train; procession; pageant.

corvée (kɔrve) *f*, statute (*or* forced) labor, corvée; fatigue (*Mil.*); drudgery.

cosmétique (kɔsmetik) *a. & m*, cosmetic.

cosmique (kɔsmik) *a*, cosmic.

cosmopolite (kɔsmɔpɔlit) *m. & a*, cosmopolite; cosmopolitan.

cosse (kɔs) *f*, pod, cod, shell, husk, hull; thimble, eye[let] (*Naut.*).

cossu, e (kɔsy) *a*, well off; rich.

cosser (kɔse) *v.i*, to butt (*rams*).

costume (kɔstym) *m*, costume, dress, garb; suit; frock. *~ marin*, sailor suit. **costumer** (me) *v.t*, to dress (*in fancy dress*). **costumier, ère** (mje, ɛ:r) *n*, theatrical & fancy costumer; wardrobe keeper (*Theat.*).

cote (kɔt) *f*, quota, share, contribution; assessment, rating; quotation(s), price(s), rates, mark(s), marking, call, list; due dating, (*bill*); character, class (*ship*); odds, betting; reading (*survey*). *~ d'amour*, favoritism, backstairs influence. *~ de la bourse*, stock exchange daily official list. *~ des changes*, [foreign] exchange rates. *~ mal taillée*, rough & ready settlement, compromise.

côte (ko:t) *f*, rib; slope; hill; [sea]coast, shore, seaboard. *à ~s*, ribbed, corded. *~ à ~*, side by side, alongside. *de la ~ de*, descended from. *faire ~*, to run ashore. *la C~ d'Azur*, the Riviera. *la C~ d'Ivoire*, the Ivory Coast. *la C~ de l'Or*, the Gold Coast.

côté (kote) *m*, side; way, direction; [broad]side (*Naut.*); beam ends (*Naut.*). *~ du vent*, weather side. *~ faible*, weak spot (*fig. of pers.*). *~ sous le vent*, lee [side]. *à ~*, *ad*, near, to one side. *à ~ de*, *pr*, by the side of; next to; next door to; beside. **de~**, *ad*, sideways; sidelong; aside, apart, on one side, by. **de l'autre ~**, on the other side *or* hand; over the way.

coteau (kɔto) *m*, hill, hillside, slope.

côtelé, e (kotle) *a*, ribbed, corduroy.

côtelette (kɔtlɛt) *f*, chop, cutlet. *~ de filet*, loin chop.

coter (kɔte) *v.t*, to letter; number; mark; page; assess, rate; quote; class; rank. *croquis coté*, dimensioned sketch.

coterie (kɔtri) *f*, set, clique, circle.

cothurne (kɔtyrn) *m*, buskin, cothurnus.

côtier, ère (kotje, ɛ:r) *a*, coast[ing]; inshore. [*bateau*] *côtier*, coaster. [*cheval*] *côtier*, trace horse.

cotillon (kɔtijɔ̃) *m*, petticoat; cotillion.

cotisation (kɔtizasjɔ̃) *f*, quota, share, contribution; subscription; fee; assessment. **cotiser** (ze) *v.t*, to assess. **se ~**, to club together; subscribe.

coton (kɔtɔ̃) *m*, cotton; c. wool; down, fluff. *~ hydrophile, m*, absorbent cotton. *~-poudre, m*, guncotton. **cotonnade** (tɔnad) *f*, cotton [cloth, goods]. **cotonneux, euse** (nø, ø:z) *a*, cottony; downy; fluffy; woolly. **cotonnier, ère** (nje, ɛ:r) *a*, cotton (*att.*). ¶ *m*, cotton plant.

côtoyer (kotwaje) *v.t. & abs*, to run along, hug (*shore*); skirt; coast; border upon.

cotre (kɔtr) *m*, cutter (*boat*). ∼ *de la douane*, revenue cutter.

cotret (kɔtrɛ) *m*, fagot, stick.

cotte (kɔt) *f*, petticoat; overalls. ∼ *de mailles*, coat of mail.

cou (ku) *m*, neck.

couard, e (kua:r, ard) *a*, coward[ly]. ¶ *n*, coward. **couardise** (kuardi:z) *f*, cowardice.

couchant (kuʃɑ̃) *m*, setting; west; wane, decline. **couche** (kuʃ) *f*, bed, couch; hotbed; layer; stratum; seam; sheet; coat[ing]; course; lap[ping]; diaper; ring (*in tree*); (*pl.*) confinement, lying-in, childbed; delivery, birth. **coucher** (kuʃe) *m*, going to bed; setting (*sun, etc.*); night's lodging, board; bed[ding]. ∼ *de soleil*, sunset. *au* ∼ *du soleil*, at sunset, at sundown. ¶ *v.t*, to lay; lay down; put to bed; lay low; beat down, slope. ∼ *en joue*, to aim (at). ∼ *par écrit*, to commit to (*or* put in) (*or* set down in) writing. ¶ *v.i*, to lie, lie down; spend the night, sleep. *se* ∼, to lie down, go to bed; couch; set, go down (*sun, moon*). **couchette** (ʃɛt) *f*, crib, cot; berth, bunk, couchette.

couci-couça (kusikusa), **couci-couci**, *ad*, so so, middling.

coucou (kuku) *m*, cuckoo; cowslip. [*pendule à*] ∼, cuckoo clock.

coude (kud) *m*, elbow; bend; crank. *jouer des* ∼*s*, to elbow one's way. **coudées franches** (kude) *f.pl*, elbowroom (*fig.*); scope.

cou-de-pied (kudpje) *m*, instep.

couder (kude) *v.t*, to bend, crank. **coudoyer** (dwaje) *v.t*, to elbow, jostle; run up against; come very near to.

coudre (kudr) *v.t. & abs. ir*, to sew; s. up; s. on; stitch; piece, tack (*fig.*).

coudrier (kudrie) *m*, hazel (*bush*).

couenne (kwan) *f*, rind (*bacon*); crackling (*pork*); mole (*Med.*).

couguar (kugwa:r) *m*, cougar, puma.

coulage (kula:ʒ) *m*, running; pouring, casting; leakage. **coulant, e** (lɑ̃, ɑ̃:t) *a*, flowing, easy, liquid, running, loose; accommodating. ¶ *m*, runner (*Hort. & Mech.*); slide. **coulé** (le) *m*, slur (*Mus.*); follow [shot] (*Bil.*); casting. **coulée** (le) *f*, running; flow; cast[ing]; tapping; run (*animal track*); running hand. **couler** (le) *v.t*, to pour, tap, cast; strain; sink, slide; slur (*Mus.*); (*v.i.*) to flow, run; trickle; gutter; leak; glide, slide, slip. ∼ *ou* ∼ *à fond ou* ∼ *à pic ou* ∼ *bas*, to sink, founder, go down. *faire* ∼, to spill, shed; slip, turn on water. *se* ∼, to slide, slip.

couleur (kulœ:r) *f*, color; coloring; paint; dye; complexion; suit (*cards*); (*pl.*) colors (*flag*). *sous* ∼ *de*, under color of (*fig.*).

couleuvre (kulœ:vr) *f*, snake; bitter pill (*fig.*). ∼ *à collier*, common snake.

coulis (kuli) *m*, grout[ing].

coulisse (kulis) *f*, slide; slideway; heading, hem (*for tape*); link (*Mach.*); link motion; side scene (*Theat.*); (*pl.*) slips, wings (*Theat.*); coulisse (*unofficial or free market on Paris Bourse*). *dans la* ∼, behind the scenes. *à* ∼, sliding. *regard en* ∼, side-long glance. **coulissier** (sje) *m*, coulissier (*broker on Paris coulisse market*).

couloir (kulwa:r) *m*, passage, corridor; lobby.

couloire (kulwa:r) *f*, strainer.

coup (ku) *m*, blow; stroke; hit; chop; coup; knock; thrust; poke; cut, slash; nip; prick; dig; whack; slap; stab; shock; clap, peal; flap; rap; wave, sweep; touch; shot; report; rush; beat; blast; gust; move (*chess, etc.*); knack; glass, drink; time, moment; try, go; pitch (*angler's*). ∼ *au but*, hit. ∼ *d'air*, rush of air; chill (*Med.*). ∼ *d'amende*, penalty stroke (*golf*). ∼ *d'assommoir*, knock-down blow (*fig.*). ~ *d'envoi*, kick-off (*Foot.*). ~ *d'épaule*, lift. ~ *d'épingle*, pin prick. ~ *d'éponge* (*fig.*), clean slate. ~ *d'essai*, first attempt, trial shot. ~s *d'essai*, practice (*Ten.*). ~ *d'œil*, glance, twinkling; look; judgment; view. ~ *d'ongle*, scratch. à ~s de, with (*blows from*). ~ *de balai*, sweep. ~ *de bec*, peck. ~ *de brosse*, brush. ~ *de chapeau*, salute, bow. ~ *de chiffon*, wipe, rub with a cloth. à ~s *de ciseaux*, with scissors & paste (*fig.*). ~ *de collier*, tug. ~ *de corne*, butt. ~ *de coude*, nudge. ~ *de dents*, bite. *traduire à ~s de dictionnaire*, to translate by looking up every other word in the dictionary. ~ *de feu*, shot. ~ *de filet*, cast; haul; catch. ~ *de fleuret*, pass (*Fenc.*). ~ *de force*, feat of strength. ~ *de foudre*, thunderbolt. ~ *de fouet*, lash; fillip. ~ *de froid*, cold snap; chill (*Med.*). ~ *de grâce*, finishing stroke, quietus. ~ *de griffe*, scratch. à ~s *de hache*, in a rough & ready fashion. ~ *de hasard*, fluke. ~ *de l'étrier*, stirrup cup. ~ *de lumière*, burst of light. ~ [*de lunette*], sight. ~ *de main*, surprise attack; swift bold stroke (*action*), lightning move; helping hand. ~ *de marteau*, knock (*at the door*). ~ *de massue*, stunning blow. *un* ~ *de mer*, a great wave, a heavy sea. ~ *de patte*, dig (*fig.*). ~ [*de pied*], kick. ~ *de poing*, punch; fisticuffs; knuckle-duster. ~ *de sang*, [apoplectic] stroke. ~ *de sifflet*, [blast of a] whistle. ~ *de soleil*, sunstroke. ~ *de sonnette*, ring [of a bell]. ~ *de téléphone*, ring [of the telephone]. ~ *de tête*, butt; rash act. ~ *de théâtre*, stage trick; sensation[al event]. ~ *de tonnerre*, thunderclap, peal of t. ~ *de vent*, squall, gust of wind; flurry; blast; gale. ~ *déloyal*, foul (*Box.*). ~s & *blessures*, assault & battery. ~ *manqué*, miss, failure. ~ *monté*, put-up job. ~ *sur* ~, one after another. à ~ *sûr*, assuredly, for a certainty.

coupable (kupabl) *a*, guilty, culpable; sinful. ¶ *n*, culprit, offender.

coupage (kupa:ʒ) *m*, blending (*wines*). **coupant, e** (pã, ã:t) *a*, cutting, sharp; edge[d]. ¶ *m*, [cutting] edge. **coupe** (kup) *f*, cutting; cutting out (*clothes*); cut; division; section; length (*piece of a stuff*); overarm stroke (*swim.*); cup, chalice, goblet, glass; bowl, dish; cup (*sport*); plate (*turf*). **coupé** (pe) *m*, brougham; coupé. **coupe-cigares**, *m*, cigar cutter. **coupe-circuit**, *m*, cut-out (*Elec.*). **coupe-gorge**, *m*, cutthroat place. **coupe-jarret**, *m*, cutthroat (*pers.*). **coupe-verre à molette**, *m*, wheel glass cutter. **coupé-lit**, *m*, sleeping compartment (*Rly.*). **coupelle** (pɛl) *f*, cupel. **coupeller** (le) *v.t*, to cupel. **coupe-papier**, *m*, paper knife. **couper** (pe) *v.t. & abs*, to cut; c. off; c. down; c. in (*on road, etc.*); c. out; chop off; intersect, cross; slice (*ball*); blend (*wines*); dilute, water; interrupt; switch off. *se* ~, to cut oneself; cut; contradict oneself; intersect. *se faire* ~ *les cheveux*, to have one's hair cut. **couperet** (prɛ) *m*, cleaver, chopper; knife.

couperose (kupro:z) *f*, copperas, vitriol; acne; blotched face.

coupeur, euse (kupœ:r, ø:z) *n*, cutter. ~ *de bourses*, pickpocket.

couple (kupl) *f*, couple, two; brace; yoke; leash. ¶ *m*, couple (*pers.*); pair; cell (*Elec.*); timber (*ship*). ~ [*moteur*], torque, couple. **coupler** (ple) *v.t*, to couple, connect. **couplet** (plɛ) *m*, verse; strap hinge.

coupole (kupɔl) *f*, cupola, dome.

coupon (kupɔ̃) *m*, remnant; short length; coupon; half (*Rly. ticket*), **coupure** (py:r) *f*, cut; clipping (*newspaper*); denomination.

cour (ku:r) *f*, court; [court]yard; courtship, suit. ~ *de cassation*, supreme court of appeal. ~ *de l'église*, churchyard. *faire la* ~ à, to court, woo, make love to.

courage (kura:ʒ) *m*, courage, fortitude, spirit, pluck, nerve. ~ *arrosé*, Dutch courage. ¶ *i*, courage! cheer up! **courageux, euse†** (razø, ø:z) *a*, courageous, game.

couramment (kuramã) *ad,* fluently; usually, commonly. **courant, e** (rã, ã:t)) *a,* current; running; instant, present; run (*measurement*). ¶ *m,* current; stream; tide; course; current (*or* present) month. ~ *alternatif,* alternating current (*Elec.*). ~ *continu,* direct c. ~ *d'affaires,* turnover. ~ *d'air,* draft; blast. ~ *de jusant,* ebb tide. ~ *de palan,* tackle fall. *fin* ~, at end of the month. ¶ *f,* diarrhea.

courbatu, e (kurbaty) *a,* tired out; stiff in the joints. **courbature** (ty:r) *f,* stiffness, tiredness.

courbe (kurb) *a,* curve[d]. ¶ *f,* curve, bend, sweep. ~ *de niveau,* contour line. **courber** (be) *v.t.* & *i.* & *se* ~, to bend, curve, bow. **courbette** (bɛt) *f,* curvet. *faire des* ~*s,* to curvet; bow & scrape. *faire une* ~, to duck. **courbure** (by:r) *f,* curvature, bend.

coureur, euse (kurœ:r, ø:z) *n,* runner; racer; wanderer, rover; gadabout; frequenter; rake. ~ *cycliste,* racing cyclist. ~ *de bals,* dancing man. ~ *de spectacles,* playgoer. ~ *de vitesse,* sprinter.

courge (kurʒ) *f,* pumpkin; gourd. ~ *à la moelle,* vegetable marrow.

courir (kuri:r) *v.i.* & *t. ir,* to run; go; run about; hurry; slip (*or* pass) away; race; sail; circulate, go round; be in fashion; be rife; accrue; tramp up & down; run after; pursue; frequent; hunt; course; hunt after; incur; go through; travel. *le bruit court que . . .,* it is reported that . . ., there is a rumor abroad that . . .

courlis (kurli), **courlieu** (ljø) *m,* curlew.

couronne (kurɔn) *f,* crown; wreath; coronet; corona; circlet; ring; tonsure. ~ [*mortuaire*], wreath (*funeral*). **couronnement** (nmã) *m,* coronation; crowning; crowning piece; coping; taffrail. **couronner** (ne) *v.t,* to crown; wreathe; cap; cope; award a prize to; reward; surround.

courrier (kurje) *m,* mail, post, letters; courier, messenger; news, intelligence; mail coach. **courriériste** (rjerist) *m,* par writer.

courroie (kurwa) *f,* belt, band;

strap. ~*s* [*de transmission*], belting.

courroucer (kuruse) *v.t,* to incense, anger. **courroux** (ru) *m,* wrath, anger, ire, rage.

cours (ku:r) *m,* course; flow; run; stream; way; class (*Sch.*); currency; tender (*legal*); price, rate, quotation; avenue. ~ *authentique & officiel,* stock exchange daily official list. ~ *d'eau,* stream, watercourse. ~ *de danse,* dancing class, school of dancing. *en* ~, current; present; instant; in progress.

course (kurs) *f,* run; race; (*pl.*) running, racing; outing, trip; errand; way; course; career; fare; stroke, travel; privateering. *de* ~, racing (*as cycle, ski*); race (*as horse*); speed (*skates*). *en* ~, out [on business]. *à pied,* foot race. ~ *d'obstacles,* steeplechase; obstacle race. ~ *de barrage,* runoff (*from dead heat*). ~ *de chars,* chariot race. ~ *de côte,* hill climb. ~ *de demifond,* middle-distance race. ~ *de fond,* long-distance r.; distance swim. ~ *de haies,* hurdle race. ~*s de lévriers,* greyhound racing, dog r., dogs. ~ *de* (ou *à*) *relais,* relay r. ~ *de taureaux,* bullfight. ~ *en sacs,* sack race. ~ *nulle,* ~ *à égalité,* dead heat. ~ *par équipes,* team race. ~ *sur piste,* track r. ~ *sur route,* road race. ~*s sur route,* road racing. **coursier** (sje) *m,* charger (*horse*), steed, courser.

court, e (ku:r, urt) *a,* short; limited. *à courtes vues,* short-sighted (*fig.*). *à court de,* short of; out of stock of. **court,** *ad,* short.

court (kɔrt *ou* ku:r) *m,* court (*Ten.*).

courtage (kurta:ʒ) *m,* broking; brokerage; commission.

courtaud, e (kurto, o:d) *n,* thickset (*or* dumpy) person. **courtauder** (tode) *v.t,* to crop the tail of.

court-circuit (kursirkɥi) *m,* short [circuit].

courte-botte (kurtəbɔt) *m,* shrimp (*pers.*).

courtement (kurtəmã) *ad,* shortly.

courtepointe (kurtəpwɛ̃:t) *f*, [down] quilt.

courtier, ère (kurtje, ɛ:r) *n*, broker.

courtisan (kurtizɑ̃, an) *a*, flattering, obsequious. ¶ *m*, courtier. ¶ *f*, courtesan. **courtiser** (ze) *v.t*, to court; woo; fawn on. **courtois, e†** (twa, a:z) *a*, courteous; courtly, urbane. **courtoisie** (twazi) *f*, courtesy, etc.

couseur, euse (kuzœ:r, ø:z) *n*, sewer (*Need.*).

cousin, e (kuzɛ̃, in) *n*, cousin; friend. ~ *germain, e*, first cousin. ~ *issu(e) de germain*, second c. ¶ *m*, gnat, midge. **cousiner** [**ensemble**] (zine) *v.i*, to get on well [together].

coussin (kusɛ̃) *m*, cushion; hassock; bolster; pillow; pad. **coussinet** (sinɛ) *m*, [small] cushion; pad; bearing, brass, bush; [screwing] die; [rail] chair (*Rly.*).

coût (ku) *m*, cost.

couteau (kuto) *m*, knife; cutter; knife edge. ~ *à découper*, carving knife, [meat] carver. ~ *à dessert*, cheese knife. ~ *à virole*, ~ *à cran d'arrêt*, clasp k., jackknife. **à** ~, eating (*apples, etc.*). *à* ~*x tirés*, at daggers drawn (*fig.*). *le* ~ *à la gorge*, a pistol [held] at one's head (*fig.*). **coutelas** (tlɑ) *m*, big kitchen knife. **coutelier, ère** (təlje, ɛ:r) *n*, cutler. **coutellerie** (tɛlri) *f*, cutlery; c. works *or* shop.

coûter (kute) *v.i*, to cost; (*abs.*) to cost money. *coûte que coûte*, at all costs. **coûteusement** (tøzmɑ̃) *ad*, expensively. **coûteux, euse** (tø, ø:z) *a*, costly, expensive.

coutil (kuti) *m*, [canvas] tick[ing]; drill; duck.

coutume (kutym) *f*, custom, usage, habit, practice, wont. *de* ~, usual. **coutumier, ère** (mje, ɛ:r) *a*, accustomed, in the habit; customary; common, unwritten (*law*). ~ *du fait*, in the habit of doing so.

couture (kuty:r) *f*, seam; sewing; needlework; scar; pock, pit. ~ [*à la main*], plain sewing. *battre à plate* ~, to beat hollow (*or* soundly). **couturer** (tyre)

v.t, to scar, seam (*with wounds*); pock, pit. **couturier** (rje) *m*, costum[i]er, mantlemaker. **couturière** (rjɛ:r) *f*, dressmaker; seamstress, needlewoman.

couvain (kuvɛ̃) *m*, nest of (*insects'*) eggs. **couvaison** (vɛzɔ̃) *f*, brooding time, sitting t. **couvée** (ve) *f*, brood, hatch, clutch; progeny.

couvent (kuvɑ̃) *m*, convent, monastery, nunnery; convent school.

couver (kuve) *v.t*, to sit on (*eggs*); hatch; incubate; (*abs.*) to brood, sit; mother (*fig.*); (*v.i.*) to smolder; brew. ~ *des yeux*, to gaze at; gloat over. *mettre* ~, to set (*hen*).

couvercle (kuvɛrkl) *m*, cover, lid, cap, head.

couvert, e (kuvɛ:r, ɛrt) *p.a*, covered; clad; overgrown; wooded; shady; overcast. ¶*covert.* ¶ *m*, table [things]; knife, fork, & spoon; spoon & fork; cover; shady retreat. *le* ~, shelter, lodging. *mettre, ôter, le* ~, to lay, clear, the table. *à* ~, under cover, sheltered; covered; packed (*consignment*). ¶ *f*, blanket; glaze (*on pottery*). **couverture** (vɛrty:r) *f*, covering; cover; margin; roofing; blanket; counterpane; rug (*traveling*); cloth (*horse*).

couveuse (kuvø:z) *f*, brood hen, sitting hen; incubator. **couvi** (vi) *a.m*, addle[d].

couvre-chef (kuvrəʃɛf) *m*, headgear. **couvre-engrenages** (vrɑ̃grəna:ʒ) *m*, gearcase. **couvre-feu** (vrə) *m*, lights out (*Mil.*); curfew. **couvre-joint**, *m*, welt, butt strap. **couvre-lit**, *m*, bedspread. **couvre-livre**, *m*, jacket, dust cover (*book*). **couvre-pied**, *m*, down quilt. **couvre-théière**, *m*, tea cosy. **couvreur** (vrœ:r) *m*, slater; tiler; thatcher. **couvrir** (vri:r) *v.t.ir*, to cover; roof; load (*with praise, abuse*); drown (*sounds*). **se** ~, to cover oneself, wrap up; put one's hat on; become overcast.

crabe (krab) *m*, crab (*Crust.*).

crac (krak) *m*, crack, snap; (*i.*) before you could say Jack Robinson.

crachat (kraʃa) *m*, spit[tle], star

(*decoration*). **crachement** (ʃmã) *m*, spitting. **cracher** (ʃe) *v.i*, to spit; spit out; splutter; splash (*tap*); spout. *tout craché*, to a tee. **crachoir** (ʃwaːr) *m*, spittoon.

crack (krak) *m*, crack (*racehorse*).

Cracovie (krakɔvi) *f*, Krakow.

craie (krɛ) *f*, chalk.

craindre (krɛ̃ːdr) *v.t. & abs. ir*, to fear, be afraid of, dread; cannot stand. *craint l'humidité, la chaleur*, to be kept dry, cool *or* in a dry, cool, place. **crainte** (krɛ̃ːt) *f*, fear, dread, awe. **craintif, ive†** (krɛ̃tif, iːv) *a*, timid, timorous, fearful, afraid.

cramoisi, e (kramwazi) *a. & m*, crimson.

crampe (krãːp) *f*, cramp (*Med.*); staple. **crampon** (krãpɔ̃) *m*, cramp [iron], clamp, holdfast; fastener, catch; staple; [dog] spike; crampon, stud; bore (*pers.*). **cramponner** (pɔne) *v.t*, to cramp, clamp, fasten; pester. *se* ~, to cling, fasten.

cran (krã) *m*, notch, nick; peg (*fig.*); pluck, mettle. ~ *d'arrêt*, safety catch.

crâne (kraːn) *m*, skull, cranium. ¶ †, *a*, plucky, jaunty. **crâner** (krane) *v.i*, to swagger; brazen it out.

crapaud (krapo) *m*, toad; low easy chair; baby grand; firecracker; flaw. *laid comme un* ~, [as] ugly as sin. **crapaudière** (djɛːr) *f*, toad hole. **crapaudine** (din) *f*, toadstone; strainer, grating; plug hole; center casting.

crapoussin, e (krapusɛ̃, in) *n*, shrimp (*pers.*).

crapule (krapyl) *f*, debauchery; debauchee. **crapuleux, euse†** (lø, øːz) *a*, debauched, lewd; filthy.

craque (krak) *f*, fib, cram.

craquelin (kraklɛ̃) *m*, cracknel.

craquelure (kraklyːr) *f*, crack(s) (*in enamel, etc.*). **craquer** (ke) *v.i*, to crack, crackle, crunch, creak. **craqueter** (kte) *v.i*, to crackle.

crasse (kras) *a.f*, crass. ¶ *f*, dirt, filth, grime, squalor; scum, dross, slag, clinker; scale; gutter (*fig.*); sordidness. **crasseux, euse** (sø,

øːz) *a*, dirty, filthy, grimy, grubby, unwashed, foul, squalid.

cratère (kratɛːr) *m*, crater.

cravache (kravaʃ) *f*, riding whip, horsewhip, crop. **cravacher** (ʃe) *v.t*, to flog; horsewhip.

cravan (kravã) *m*, barnacle (*on ship*).

cravate (kravat) *f*, [neck]tie; bow & tassels (*of color staff*). ~ *de soirée*, dress bow.

crayeux, euse (krɛjø, øːz) *a*, chalky. **crayon** (jɔ̃) *m*, pencil; sketch, outline. ~ *à mine de plomb*, lead pencil. ~ *pastel*, crayon. **crayonner** (jɔne) *v.t*, to pencil; sketch, outline.

créance (kreãːs) *f*, credence, belief, trust; credit; [book] debt; indebtedness; claim. **créancier, ère** (ãsje, ɛːr) *n*, creditor. ~ *hypothécaire*, mortgagee.

créateur, trice (kreatœːr, tris) *n*, creator, tress, maker; founder, foundress; (*att.*) creative. **création** (sjɔ̃) *f*, creation; founding. **créature** (tyːr) *f*, creature.

crécelle (kresɛl) *f*, rattle (*toy, etc.*).

crécerelle (kresrɛl) *f*, kestrel.

crèche (krɛːʃ) *f*, crib, manger; day nursery, crèche.

crédence (kredãːs) *f*, sideboard; credence [table].

crédibilité (kredibilite) *f*, credibility. **crédit** (di) *m*, credit; trust; influence; repute; creditor; bank; (*pl.*) supplies (*parliamentary*). *au comptant ou à* ~, cash or terms (*sales*). ~ *municipal*, mortgage loan office & pawnshop. **créditer** (te) *v.t*, to credit. **créditeur** (tœːr) *m. & att*, creditor.

credo (kredo) *m*, creed, credo; gospel (*fig.*). **crédule** (kredyl) *a*, credulous, gullible. **crédulité** (lite) *f*, credulity.

créer (kree) *v.t. & abs*, to create; make; establish; found; make out, write out (*check*).

crémaillère (kremajɛːr) *f*, pothook; rack (*toothed*). *pendre la* ~, to give a housewarming.

crémation (kremasjɔ̃) *f*, cremation.

crème (krɛm) *f*, cream; custard. ~ *chocolatée*, chocolate cream.

~ *glacée*, ice cream, cream ice. **crémerie** (mri) *f*, dairy; creamery; tea shop. **crémeux, euse** (kremø, ø:z) *a*, creamy. **crémier, ère** (mje, ε:r) *n*, dairyman, -woman; (*m.*) cream jug.

Crémone (kremɔn) *f*, Cremona. c~, *f*, espagnolette.

créneau (kreno) *m*, battlement; loophole. **créneler** (nle) *v.t*, to crenellate, castellate, battlement, embattle; tooth, ratchet; mill (*coin*).

créole (kreɔl) *n. & a*, creole.

créosote (kreɔzɔt) *f*, creosote.

crêpe (krɛ:p) *m*, crape, crêpe; (*f.*) pancake. **crêper** (krɛpe) *v.t*, to crimp, crisp, frizz[le].

crépi (krepi) *m*, roughcast (*Build.*).

crépine (krepin) *f*, fringe; strainer, rose.

crépins (krepɛ̃) *m.pl*, grindery.

crépir (krepi:r) *v.t*, to roughcast; grain (*leather*).

crépiter (krepite) *v.i*, to crackle; patter (*rain*); crepitate.

crépu, e (krepy) *a*, woolly, fuzzy (*hair*).

crépuscule (krepyskyl) *m*, twilight, gloaming; decline.

crescendo (krɛsɛ̃do) *ad. & m*, crescendo.

cresson (krəsɔ̃) *m*, cress, watercress. **cressonnière** (sɔnjɛ:r) *f*, watercress bed.

Crésus (krezy:s) *m*, Croesus.

Crète (la) (krɛ:t), Crete.

crête (krɛ:t) *f*, comb; crest; ridge. ~*-de-coq*, cockscomb (*Bot.*). **crêté, e** (krɛte), *a*, crested.

crétin, e (kretɛ̃, in) *n*, cretin; idiot; dunce.

cretonne (krətɔn) *f*, cretonne.

creuser (krøze) *v.t. & abs*, to dig; hollow; excavate; scoop; sink; deepen. se ~, to grow hollow; rise (*sea*). ~ *la tête*, to rack one's brains. **creusage** (za:ʒ), **creusement** (zmɑ̃) *m*, digging.

creuset (krøzɛ) *m*, crucible, [melting] pot.

creux, euse (krø, ø:z) *a*, hollow; deep; sunken; shallow, empty. ¶ *m*, hollow, cavity; hole; pit; trough (*wave*); space; hollowness; mold.

crevaison (krəvɛzɔ̃) *f*, death

(*animals*); bursting; puncture (*tire*).

crevasse (krəvas) *f*, crevice, chink, crack, fissure, rift, crevasse; chap (*skin*). **crevasser** (se) *v.t*, to crack; chap.

crève-cœur (krɛvkœ:r) *m*, keen disappointment, wrench (*fig.*).

crever (krəve) *v.i. & t*, to burst; break; crack; split; puncture; put out (*eyes*); die. à crevés (ve), slashed, slit (*dress*).

crevette (krəvɛt) *f*: ~ [*grise*], shrimp. ~ [*rose*], prawn.

cri (kri) *m*, cry, shout; scream; shriek, screech; squeal; halloo; chirp; outcry; opinion. ~ *de guerre*, war cry; slogan (*Pol.*). **criailler** (ɑje) *v.i*, to squeal; scold, nag. **criant, e** (ɑ̃, ɑ̃:t) *a*, crying, glaring. **criard, e** (a:r, ard) *a*, squealing, squalling, screaming, clamorous; blatant; pressing (*debts*).

crible (kribl) *m*, sieve, riddle, screen. **cribler** (ble) *v.t*, to sift, riddle, screen; honeycomb. **criblure** (bly:r) *f*, siftings, screenings.

cric (kri) *m*, [lifting] jack. ~ *crac!* (krikkrak) crack! snap!

cricri (krikri) *m*, chirp; cricket (*insect*).

criée (krie) *f*, auction. **crier** (e) *v.i. & t*, to cry, shout; scream; shriek, screech; call out, clamor, protest; halloo; chirp; creak; keep telling. **crieur, euse** (œ:r, ø:z) *n*, crier; hawker. ~ *de journaux*, newsboy.

crime (krim) *m*, crime; felony; offense; sin. ~ *d'État*, treason. ~ *de faux*, forgery. ~ *passionnel* (pasjonɛl), love tragedy.

Crimée (la) (krime), the Crimea.

criminel, le† (kriminɛl) *a*, criminal; felonious; guilty. ¶ *n*, criminal; felon.

crin (krɛ̃) *m*, [horse]hair; (*vegetable*) fiber; (*pl.*) mane [& tail]. à *tous* ~*s*, out & out.

crincrin (krɛ̃krɛ̃) *m*, (*bad*) fiddle.

crinière (krinjɛ:r) *f*, mane; horsetail plume; abundant crop (*hair*).

crique (krik) *f*, creek, inlet (*sea*).

criquet (krikɛ) *m*, locust; cricket.

crise (kri:z) *f*, crisis; shortage,

slump; attack, fit. ~ *du logement,* housing problem.
crispation (krispasjɔ̃) *f,* shrivel-
ing; twitching; (*pl.*) fidgets.
crisper (pe) *v.t,* to clench. **se ~,**
to shrivel [up].
crisser (krise) *v.t. & i,* grate;
squeak (*brakes*).
cristal (kristal) *m,* crystal; [crys-
tal] glass. ~ *taillé,* cut [crystal]
glass. *cristaux de soude,* [wash-
ing] soda. **cristallerie** (lri) *f,*
crystal glass[ware] making *or*
works. **cristallin, e** (lɛ̃, in) *a,*
crystalline. ¶ *m,* crystalline lens
(*eye*). **cristalliser** (lize) *v.t. & i.
& se ~,* to crystallize. **cristallomancie** (talɔmɑ̃si) *f,* crystal
gazing.
critère (kritɛ:r), **criterium** (ter-
jɔm) *m,* criterion, standard;
eliminating test, preliminary trial.
critiquable (kritikabl) *a,* criticizable, open to criticism, ex-
ceptionable. **critique** (tik) *a,*
critical, censorious; crucial; ticklish. ¶ *m,* critic; reviewer. ¶ *f,*
criticism, critique; review; critics
(*pers.*); censure, stricture. **critiquer** (ke) *v.t,* to criticize, censure.
croasser (krɔase) *v.i,* to caw,
croak.
croc (kro) *m,* hook; boat hook;
fang; tusk (*walrus, etc.*). **en ~,**
curled, turned up (*moustache*).
¶ (krɔk) *i,* [s]crunch! **~-en-
jambe** (krɔkɑ̃ʒɑ̃:b) *m,* trip [up];
leg lock; dirty trick. **croche**
(krɔʃ) *a,* crooked. ¶ *f,* quaver
(*Mus.*). **crochet** (ʃɛ) *m,* hook;
crook; crank tool; tenterhook;
crochet (*Need.*); c. hook; picklock, skeleton key; sudden turn,
swerve; detour; fang; [square]
bracket; hook (*Box.*). ~ *à la
fourche,* hairpin crochet. ~ *de
suspension,* hanger, hook. *aux
~s de,* at the expense of. **crocheter** (ʃte) *v.t,* to pick, force
the lock of. **crochu, e** (ʃy) *a,*
hooked, crooked.
crocodile (krɔkɔdil) *m,* crocodile.
croire (krwa:r) *v.t. & abs. ir,* to
believe; trust; think; take for.
croisade (krwazad) *f,* crusade.
croisé, e (ze) *p.a,* crossed; cross;

double-breasted (*coat*). ¶ *m,*
crusader; twill. ¶ *f,* crossing;
casement [window]. **croisement**
(zmɑ̃) *m,* crossing; cross; crossbreeding; frog (*Rly.*). **croiser** (ze)
v.t, to cross; fold; pass; thwart;
twill; (*v.i.*) to lap over; cruise.
se ~, to intersect; fold (*one's
arms*). **croiseur** (zœ:r) *m,* cruiser. ~ *cuirassé de combat,* battle
c. **croisière** (zjɛ:r) *f,* cruise;
cruising ground; cruising fleet.
croisillon (zijɔ̃) *m,* cross [piece];
arm (*of cross*); bar (*window*).
croissance (krwasɑ̃:s) *f,* growth.
croissant, e (sɑ̃, ɑ̃:t) *a,* growing, increasing. ¶ *m,* crescent;
billhook; pruning hook; horseshoe roll. **croître** (krwa:tr) *v.i.
ir,* to grow; increase; rise; draw
out (*days*); wax (*moon*).
croix (krwa) *f,* cross; rood; dagger, obelisk (*Typ.*). ~ *de Malte,*
Maltese cross. *la C~ Rouge,*
the Red Cross.
croquant, e (krɔkɑ̃, ɑ̃:t) *a,*
crisp.
croque-mitaine (krɔkmitɛn)
m, bog[e]y [man]; bugbear.
croque-mort, *m,* undertaker's
man.
croquer (krɔke) *v.i. & t,* to [s]-
crunch; munch; gobble up;
sketch; croquet. **croquet** (kɛ)
m, croquet (*game*). **croquette**
(kɛt) *f,* croquette (*Cook.*). **croquis** (ki) *m,* sketch.
crosse (krɔs) *f,* crosier, crook;
butt (*rifle*); crosshead (*piston*);
crutch (*or* hook) stick; stick
(*hockey*); club (*golf*); crosse
(*lacrosse*). *la ~ canadienne,* lacrosse. **crossée** (se) *f,* drive
(*golf*). **crosser** (se) *v.t,* to strike
(*ball*); spurn.
crotte (krɔt) *f,* (*street*) mud, dirt;
gutter (*fig.*); dung, droppings.
crotté, e (te) *p.a,* muddy, dirty.
crotter (te) *v.t,* to dirty, bespatter. **crottin** (tɛ̃) *m,* dung (*horse*).
crouler (krule) *v.i,* to collapse;
sink; crumble.
croup (krup) *m,* croup (*Med.*).
croupe (krup) *f,* croup[e], crupper, rump; ridge (*hill*); hip
(*roof*). **croupier** (pje) *m,* croupier (*gaming*). **croupière** (pjɛ:r)
f, crupper (*harness*); sternfast.

croupion (pjɔ̃) *m*, rump; parson's nose (*fowl*). **croupir** (pi;r) *v.i*, to wallow; stagnate. **crouopissant, e** (pisɑ̃, ɑ̃;t) *a*, stagnant.

croustillant, e (krustijɑ̃, ɑ̃;t) *a*, crisp, crusty, short. **croustille** (ti;j) *f*, (*bit of*) crust (*bread*). **croustilleux, euse** (tijø, ø;z) *a*, spicy, smutty. **croûte** (krut) *f*, crust; rind (*cheese*); scab; daub. *casser la ~*, to have a snack. **croûton** (tɔ̃) *m*, crust[y] end; sippet; [old] fogy.

croyable (krwajabl) *a*, credible, believable; trustworthy. **croyance** (jɑ̃;s) *f*, belief; credit; creed; faith; persuasion. **croyant, e** (jɑ̃, ɑ̃;t) *a*, believing. ¶ *n*, believer; (*pl.*) the faithful.

cru, *p.p*, **croire**.

crû, *p.p*, **croître**.

cru (kry) *m*, growth; vintage; invention.

cru, e (kry) *a*, raw, crude; garish, indigestible; hard (*water*); blunt; free, broad. **à cru,** next the skin; bareback[ed] (*riding*).

cruauté (kryote) *f*, cruelty.

cruche (kryʃ) *f*, pitcher, jug; dolt, dunce.

crucifiement (krysifimɑ̃) *m*, crucifixion. **crucifier** (fje) *v.t*, to crucify. **crucifix** (fi) *m*, crucifix. **crucifixion** (fiksjɔ̃) *f*, crucifixion.

crudité (krydite) *f*, rawness; raw food; crudity, crudeness; hardness (*water*); belching.

crue (kry) *f*, rising, flood, spate, freshet; advance (*glacier*).

cruel, le† (kryɛl) *a*, cruel; grievous; sore; bitter.

crûment (krymɑ̃) *ad*, crudely, bluntly.

crustacé, e (krystase) *a. & m*, crustacean.

crypte (kript) *f*, crypt; follicle.

cubage (kyba;ʒ) *m*, cubic content; measurement; yardage.

cubain, e (kybɛ̃, ɛn) *a. & C~*, *n*, Cuban.

cube (kyb) *m*, cube. ¶ *a*, cubic, cube (*root*). **cuber** (be) *v.t*, to cube; measure, gauge.

cubilot (kybilo) *m*, cupola [furnace].

cubique (kybik) *a*, cubic(al); cube (*root*). **cubisme** (bism) *m*, cubism. **cubiste** (bist) *n*, cubist.

cueillette (kœjɛt) *f*, gathering, picking; crop. **cueilleur, euse** (jœ;r, ø;z) *n*, picker. **cueillir** (ji;r) *v.t.ir*, to gather, pick, cull, pluck; snatch (*kiss*); buttonhole (*pers.*).

cuiller *ou* **cuillère** (kɥijɛ;r) *f*, spoon; ladle; scoop; spoon [bait]. *~ à café, ~ à moka*, coffee spoon. *~ à dessert, ~ à entremets*, dessert s. *~ à potage*, soup ladle. *~ à ragoût*, gravy spoon. *~ à soupe*, tablespoon. *~ à thé*, teaspoon. **cuillerée** (jre) *f*, spoonful. *~ à bouche*, tablespoonful.

cuir (kɥi;r) *m*, leather; hide, skin; strop; incorrect liaison (*in speaking*). *~ chevelu*, scalp (*Anat.*). *~ de porc*, pigskin. *~ de vache*, cowhide. *~ verni*, patent leather.

cuirasse (kɥiras) *f*, cuirass; armor [plating]; sheathing; saddle (*lathe*). **cuirassé, e** (se) *a*, armored, ironclad; (*fig.*) steeled; [case]hardened; proof. [*navire*] *cuirassé*, battleship, ironclad. **cuirassier** (sje) *m*, cuirassier.

cuire (kɥi;r) *v.t. & i. ir*, to cook; roast; bake; burn, fire (*bricks*); boil; ripen; smart. **cuisant, e** (kɥizɑ̃, ɑ̃;t) *a*, smarting, burning; biting (*cold*); bitter. **cuisine** (zin) *f*, kitchen; galley, caboose; cookery, cooking; food; machination. **cuisiner** (ne) *v.i*, to cook; (*v.t.*) to cook; (*fig.*) concoct, fudge; pump (*pers.*). **cuisinier, ère** (nje, ɛ;r) *n*, cook. ¶ *m*, cookery book. ¶ *f*, kitchener; cooker, cooking range; Dutch oven.

cuisse (kɥis) *f*, thigh; leg (*fowl*).

cuisson (kɥisɔ̃) *f*, cooking; baking; burning, firing; smarting.

cuissot (kɥiso) *m*, haunch (*venison*).

cuistre (kɥistr) *m*, self-conceited pedant; ill-mannered man.

cuit (kɥi) *a*, cooked; baked; done. *trop ~*, overdone. *~ à point*, done to a turn. **cuite** (kɥit) *f*, baking. *prendre une ~*, to get drunk.

cuivre (kɥi;vr) *m*, copper; copperplate; copper bit (*soldering*). *~ [jaune]*, brass. *~ [rouge]*, copper. *les ~s*, the brass (*Mus.*).

cuivré, e (kɥivre) *a*, copper-colored; metallic (*voice*); brassy; lurid. **cuivrer** (vre) *v.t*, to copper.

cul (ky) *m*, backside; tail (*cart*). **culasse** (las) *f*, breech (*gun*). *se chargeant par la* ~, breech-loading. **culbutant** (kylbytɑ̃) *m*, tumbler (*pigeon*). **culbute** (byt) *f*, somersault; tumble; fall. **culbuter** (te) *v.i. & t*, to tumble, topple over; tip, tilt, dump, shoot; overthrow; rout. **cul-de-jatte** (kydʒat) *m*, legless cripple. **cul-de-lampe** (kydlɑ̃:p) *m*, cul-de-lampe; tailpiece (*Typ.*). **cul-de-sac** (kydsak) *m*, blind alley, dead end. **culée** (kyle) *f*, abutment (*bridge*).

culinaire (kylinɛ:r) *a*, culinary.

culminant, e (kylminɑ̃, ɑ̃:t) *a*, culminating. **culminer** (ne) *v.i*, to culminate (*Astr.*).

culot (kylo) *m*, container (*lamp*); base; cap; plug; youngest; nerve. *avoir du* ~, to have a lot of nerve. **culotte** (lɔt) *f*, breeches; knee b—s; knickerbockers; knickers; rump (*beef*). ~ *courte*, shorts, trunks. ~ *de cheval*, riding breeches. ~ *de peau*, buckskins. ~ *pour le golf*, plus-fours. **culotté, e** (te) *p.p*, trousered. **culotter** (te) *v.t*, to put trousers on; season (*pipe*).

culpabilité (kylpabilite) *f*, culpability, guilt.

culte (kylt) *m*, worship; cult; creed. *le* ~ *des scientistes chrétiens*, Christian science.

cultivateur, trice (kyltivatœ:r, tris) *n*, cultivator, grower, agricultur[al]ist, farmer, husbandman. **cultiver** (ve) *v.t*, to cultivate, grow; raise; farm; till. **culture** (ty:r) *f*, culture, cultivation, farming; (*pl.*) land [under cultivation]. ~ *maraîchère*, market gardening.

cumul (kymyl) *m*, plurality (*of offices*). **cumulatif, ive** (latif, i:v) *a*, cumulative. **cumulus** (ly:s) *m*, cumulus.

cunéiforme (kyneifɔrm) *a*, cuneiform.

cupide (kypid) *a*, covetous, grasping.

Cupidon (kypidɔ̃) *m*, Cupid.

curable (kyrabl) *a*, curable.

curage (kyra:ʒ) *m*, cleansing; flushing.

curatelle (kyratɛl) *f*, guardianship, trusteeship. **curateur, trice** (tœ:r, tris) *n*, guardian, trustee; administrator, trix.

curatif, ive (kyratif, i:v) *a. & m*, curative. **cure** (ky:r) *f*, cure; vicarship, rectorship; vicarage, rectory. **curé** (kyre) *m*, parish priest; vicar, rector.

cure-dent (kyrdɑ̃) *m*, toothpick.

curée (kyre) *f*, quarry (*given to hounds*); scramble.

curer (kyre) *v.t*, to cleanse, clean; flush; pick (*teeth*). **curette** (rɛt) *f*, scraper, cleaner. **cureur** (rœ:r) *m*, cleaner; sewerman.

curieux, euse† (kyrjø, ø:z) *a*, curious; interested; odd; quaint; inquisitive, prying. ¶ *n*, curious (*or* inquisitive) person; sightseer; onlooker; bystander; (*m.*) curious part *or* thing; collector (*art, books*). **curiosité** (ozite) *f*, curiosity; quaintness; curio; (*pl.*) sights (*of a city*).

curseur (kyrsœ:r) *m*, runner, slide[r] (*Mech.*). **cursif, ive** (sif, i:v) *a*, cursive, running.

curviligne (kyrviliɲ) *a*, curvilinear.

cutané, e (kytane) *a*, cutaneous, skin (*att.*). **cuticule** (tikyl) *f*, cuticle.

cuve (ky:v) *f*, vat. ~*-matière*, mash tun. **cuvée** (kyve) *f*, vatful; vintage. **cuveler** (vle) *v.t*, to tub, case (*Min.*).

cuver (kyve) *v.i*, to ferment (*wine*). ~ *son vin*, to sleep off a drunk. **cuvette** (vɛt) *f*, washbasin; basin; dish; tray; bowl; cup, cistern (*barometer*). **cuvier** (vje) *m*, washtub.

cyanure (sjany:r) *m*, cyanide.

cyclamen (siklamɛn) *m*, cyclamen.

cycle (sikl) *m*, cycle; cycle trade. **cyclisme** (klism) *m*, cycling. **cycliste** (klist) *n*, cyclist.

cyclone (siklon) *m*, cyclone.

cygne (siɲ) *m*, swan.

cylinder (silɛ̃:dr) *m*, cylinder; roller; roll; barrel, drum. ~ *compresseur à vapeur*, steamroller. **cylindrer** (lẽdre) *v.t*, to roll; mangle; calender; round. **cylindrique** (drik) *a*, cylindrical; parallel (*drill shank*).

cymbales (sẽbal) *f.pl*, cymbals.

cynique† (sinik) *a*, cynic, cynical. ¶ *m*, cynic. **cynisme** (nism) *m*, cynicism.

cyprès (siprɛ) *m*, cypress.

cytise (siti:z) *m*, laburnum.

D

dactylographe (daktilɔgraf) *n*, typist. **dactylographie** (fi) *f*, typewriting, typing.

dada (dada) *m*, gee-gee; hobby horse; pet subject, fad.

dadais (dadɛ) *m*, booby, ninny.

dague (dag) *f*, dagger, dirk.

dahlia (dalja) *m*, dahlia.

daigner (dɛɲe) *v.i*, to deign to, be pleased to, vouchsafe.

daim (dẽ) *m*, [fallow] deer, buck. [*peau de*] ~, buckskin, doeskin. **daine** (dɛn) *f*, doe.

dais (dɛ) *m*, canopy; hood (*car*).

dallage (dala:ʒ) *m*, flagging, pavement. **dalle** (dal) *f*, flag-[stone]; slab. **daller** (le) *v.t*, to pave, flag.

dalmate (dalmat) *a*, Dalmatian. **la Dalmatie** (si), Dalmatia.

dalot (dalo) *m*, scupper.

daltonisme (daltənism) *m*, color-blindness.

damas (damɑ) *m*, damask; damson. **D~**, *m*, Damascus. **damasquiner** (maskine) *v.t*, to damascene.

dame (dam) *f*, lady; dame; partner (*dance*); queen (*cards, chess*); king (*checkers*); beetle, rammer. *la* ~, Mrs. (*law*). *les* ~*s*, checkers (*game*). ~ *d'onze heures*, star of Bethlehem. ~ *de compagnie*, lady companion. ~ [*de nage*], rowlock. ~-*jeanne* (ʒɑ:n), *f*, demijohn. ¶ *i*, why! indeed! well! **damer** (me) *v.t*, to crown (*checkers*); queen (*chess*); tamp, ram. **damier** (mje) *m*, checkerboard.

damnable† (dɑnabl) *a*, damnable. **damnation** (sjɔ̃) *f*, damnation. **damné, e** (ne) *a. & n*,

damned. **damner** (ne) *v.t*, to damn.

damoiseau (damwazo) *m*, galant.

dandiner (se) (dɑ̃dine) *v.pr*, to waddle.

dandy (dɑ̃di) *m*, dandy.

Danemark (le) (danmark), Denmark.

danger (dɑ̃ʒe) *m*, danger, jeopardy; fear. **dangereux, euse**† (ʒrø, ø:z) *a*, dangerous.

danois, e (danwa, a:z) *a. &* (*language*) *m*, Danish. **D~** (*pers.*) *n*, Dane.

dans (dɑ̃) *pr*, in; into; within; during; among; about; out of; with; hence. ~ *les présentes*, herein (*law*). ~ *œuvre*, inside, in the clear (*Meas.*).

dansant, e (dɑ̃sɑ̃, ɑ̃:t) *a*, dancing; dance (*tea*). **danse** (dɑ̃:s) *f*, dance; dancing. ~ *de Saint-Guy* (gi), St. Vitus's dance. *D~ macabre*, Dance of Death, Dance Macabre. **danser** (dɑ̃se) *v.i. & t*, to dance. **danseur, euse** (sœ:r, ø:z) *n*, dancer; partner; ballet dancer. ~ *mondain, e*, ballroom dancer.

dard (da:r) *m*, dart; sting (*insect's*); pistil; dace (*fish*). **darder** (darde) *v.t*, to dart, hurl, fling, shoot; spear.

dare-dare (darda:r) *ad*, posthaste.

dartre (dartr) *f*, dartre, skin disease.

date (dat) *f*, date (*time*). *de longue* ~, of long standing. **dater** (te) *v.t*, to date. *à* ~ *de*, from, on & after.

datif (datif) *m*, dative [case].

datte (dat) *f*, date (*fruit*). **dattier** (tje) *m*, date palm.

dauber (dobe) *v.t*, to drub, thump; jeer at. ~ *sur*, to jeer at.

dauphin (dofẽ) *m*, dolphin (*Zool.*).

davantage (davɑ̃ta:ʒ) *ad*, more, further; longer.

davier (davje) *m*, forceps (*dentist's*); davit (*Naut.*).

de (də), **d'** (d) (**de le** *is contracted into* **du**, **de les** *into* **des**) *pr*, of; from; by; for; in; on; some; any; than; between; with; to. *When coupled with Fr. noun,* *often rendered in Eng. by noun used attributively, as, mine de charbon,* coal mine.

dé (de) *m,* thimble; die (*gaming & Mach.*); bearing (*Mach.*); tee (*golf*).

débâcle (debɑːkl) *f,* breaking up (*ice*); crash, collapse; landslide (*Pol.*). **débâcler** (bɑkle) *v.t,* to clear; (*v.i.*) to break up.

déballage (debalaːʒ) *m,* unpacking; show (*of wares*). **déballer** (le) *v.t,* to unpack.

débandade (debɑ̃dad) *f,* stampede, rout. *à la ~,* helter-skelter; anyhow. **débander** (de) *v.t,* to relax, unbend; unbandage; to disband (*Mil.*). se ~, to break ranks in disorder.

débaptiser (debatize) *v.t,* to change the name of, rename.

débarbouiller (debarbuje) *v.t,* to wash (*someone's*) face; extricate.

débarcadère (debarkadɛːr) *m,* landing [place *or* stage], wharf; platform (*Rly.*).

débarder (debarde) *v.t,* to unload. **débardeur** (dœːr) *m,* docker; longshoreman.

débarquer (debarke) *v.t. & i,* to land, disembark; detrain; discharge; get rid of; alight. **débarquement** (kəmɑ̃) *m,* landing, *etc. au ~,* ex ship, ex steamer (*sales*).

débarras (debarɑ) *m,* riddance; lumber room; storeroom. **débarrasser** (rase) *v.t,* to clear, rid, extricate, disburden, relieve. se ~ de, to get rid of, scrap.

débat (deba) *m,* discussion; debate; (*pl.*) proceedings; (*pl.*) trial, hearing; dispute. **débattre** (tr) *v.t.ir,* to debate, discuss, argue; arrange. se ~, to struggle; flounder; wriggle.

débauche (deboːʃ) *f,* debauch[ery]; carousal; riot (*fig.*); treat. ~ *de boisson,* drunken bout. **débauché, e** (boʃe) *n,* debauchee, rake. **débaucher** (ʃe) *v.t,* to debauch, corrupt; induce to strike; seduce from duty; lead astray; reduce the staff.

débile† (debil) *a,* weakly; weak; feeble. **débilité** (lite) *f,* debility;

weakness. **débiliter** (te) *v.t,* to debilitate, enfeeble.

débit (debi) *m,* sale (*retail*); market, demand; (*government*) license to sell; (*licensed*) shop; flow, discharge, yield, output, capacity, feed; delivery (*pump, speech*); cutting up, chopping; debit [side], debtor [side]. ~ *de tabac,* license to sell tobacco; tobacconist's shop. **débitant, e** (tɑ̃, ɑ̃ːt) *n,* dealer, retailer. ~ *de spiritueux,* licensed victualler. ~ *de tabac,* tobacconist. **débiter** (te) *v.t,* to retail, sell; discharge; yield; deliver, utter; spread (*news*); spin (*yarns*); cut up; saw; chop (*firewood*); debit. **débiteur, euse** (tœːr, øːz) *n,* utterer (*lies*); -monger (*news, scandal*); (*f.*) (*also* **débitrice**) (*In Fr. stores*) girl who conducts customers to cash desk to see that they pay. **débiteur, trice** (tœːr, tris) *n. & att,* debtor, debit (*att.*). ~ *hypothécaire,* mortgagor.

déblai (deblɛ) *m,* cut[ting], excavation; (*s. & pl.*) waste, rubbish, spoil.

déblatérer contre (deblatere), to abuse.

déblayer (deblɛje) *v.t,* to clear, c. out, c. away.

déboire (debwaːr) *m,* (*nasty*) aftertaste; disappointment.

déboiser (debwaze) *v.t,* to deforest.

déboîtement (debwatmɑ̃) *m,* dislocation (*limb*). **déboîter** (te) *v.t,* to dislocate; disjoint.

débonder (debɔ̃de) *v.t,* to unstop; open the sluice gates of; open, relax (*Med.*). [se] ~, to burst forth, break out, escape.

débonnaire† (debɔnɛːr) *a,* meek; easy-going; accommodating.

débordement (debɔrdəmɑ̃) *m,* overflow; outburst; excess, licentiousness. **déborder** (de) *v.i,* to overflow, brim over, run over; slop [over]; break out; (*v.t.*) to overlap; outflank; untuck; trim the edges of; unship (*oars*).

débotter (debɔte) *v.t,* to take (*someone's*) boots off. se ~, to take one's boots off. **au débotté** (te), immediately upon arrival.

débouché (debuʃe) *m*, opening, outlet, issue; waterway; prospects; market sale. **déboucher** (ʃe) *v.t*, to open, unstop, uncork; (*v.i.*) to open, emerge, debouch; lead into.

déboucler (debukle) *v.t*, to unbuckle; uncurl.

débouler [**dans**] (debule) *v.i*, to tumble down (*as stairs*).

déboulonner (debulɔne) *v.t*, to unrivet; debunk.

débourber (deburbe) *v.t*, to clean out, cleanse; extricate.

débourrer (debure) *v.t*, to ream (*pipe*); unstop; break in (*horse*).

débours (debuːr) & **déboursé** (burse) *m, both mostly pl*, disbursement, out of pocket expense, outlay. **débourser** (se) *v.t*, to disburse, lay out, spend.

debout (dəbu) *ad*, on end, erect; standing; up; head (*wind*). **mourir ~**, to die in harness.

débouter (debute) *v.t*, to nonsuit, dismiss (*law*).

déboutonner (debutɔne) *v.t*, to unbutton. **se ~** (*fig.*), to open out, speak one's mind.

débraillé, e (debraje) (*fig.*) *a*, dissolute. **se débrailler** (je) *v.pr*, to unbutton oneself (*unbecomingly*).

débrayer (debrɛje) (*Mech.*) *v.t*, to throw out of gear, disconnect.

débrider (debride) *v.t*, to unbridle. **sans ~**, without stopping.

débris (debri) *m.pl*, remains, debris, litter; scrap; wreck[age].

débrouiller (debruje) *v.t*, to unravel, disentangle, clear up. **se ~**, to extricate oneself; manage.

débucher (debyʃe) *v.i*, to break cover.

débusquer (debyske) *v.t*, to dislodge, drive out; oust.

début (deby) *m*, beginning, opening, outset, outbreak, start; first appearance; f. work; coming out (*in society*). **débutant, e** (tɑ̃, ɑ̃ːt) *n*, beginner; **débutant, e. débuter** (te) *v.i*, to begin, start, make one's first appearance; lead (*cards*).

deçà (dəsa) *ad*, on this side. **~, delà** ou **~ & delà**, here & there, to & fro. **en ~ de**, *pr*, on this side of.

décacheter (dekaʃte) *v.t*, to unseal, open.

décade (dekad) *f*, ten days; decad[e] (*books*).

décadence (dekadɑ̃ːs) *f*, decadence, decline, decay. **décadent, e** (dɑ̃, ɑ̃ːt) *a*, decadent.

décagone (dekagɔn) *m*, decagon.

décaisser (dekɛse) *v.t*, to unpack; withdraw (*money*).

décalage (dekalaːʒ) (*fig.*) *m*, setback.

décalcomanie (dekalkɔmani) *f*, transfer (*for china & as toy*); decal.

décaler (dekale) *v.t*, to unwedge; set forward, set back.

décalitre (dekalitr) *m*, decaliter = 10 liters *or* 2.200 gallons.

décalque (dekalk) *m*, transfer (*Emb.*).

décamètre (dekamɛːtr) *m*, decameter = 10 meters *or* 10.936 yards. **~ d'arpenteur**, measuring tape.

décamper (dekɑ̃pe) *v.i*, to decamp, make off.

décanat (dekana) *m*, deanery (*office*).

décanter (dekɑ̃te) *v.t*, to decant.

décaper (dekape) *v.t*, to scour.

décapiter (dekapite) *v.t*, to behead, decapitate.

décéder (desede) *v.i*, to decease.

déceler (desle) *v.t*, to reveal, betray.

décembre (desɑ̃ːbr) *m*, December.

décemment (desamɑ̃) *ad*, decently. **décence** (sɑ̃ːs) *f*, decency, propriety.

décennal, e (desɛnal) *a*, decennial.

décent, e (desɑ̃, ɑ̃ːt) *a*, decent; proper.

décentraliser (desɑ̃tralize) *v.t*, to decentralize.

déception (desɛpsjɔ̃) *f*, disappointment.

décerner (desɛrne) *v.t*, to award.

décès (desɛ) *m*, death, decease, demise.

décevant, e (desvɑ̃, ɑ̃ːt) *a*, deceptive, misleading. **décevoir** (s[ə]vwaːr) *v.t*, to deceive; disappoint.

déchaîner (deʃɛne) *v.t*, to unchain, let loose. se ~, break loose; break out.

déchanter (deʃɑ̃te) *v.i,* to sing small, change one's tone.

décharge (deʃarʒ) *f,* discharge; unloading; outflow; outfall; volley; release; relief; composition (*to creditors*); waste heap. **décharger** (ʒe) *v.t. & abs,* to discharge; unload; empty; relieve, disburden, ease; deal (*blow*); come off (*ink*). **déchargeur** (ʒœːr) *m,* stevedore; lightning rod.

décharné, e (deʃarne) *p.a,* emaciated, gaunt, skinny, scraggy.

déchausser (deʃose) *v.t,* to take off (*someone's*) shoes; [lay] bare; dislodge.

déchéance (deʃeɑ̃ːs) *f,* [down] fall; loss, forfeiture; lapse, expiration.

déchet (deʃɛ) *m. oft. pl,* waste, loss; scrap, refuse.

déchiffrer (deʃifre) *v.t. & abs,* to decipher, decode, make out, read (*or* play) at sight.

déchiqueter (deʃikte) *v.t,* to slash; jag; shred.

déchirant, e (deʃirɑ̃, ɑ̃ːt) *a,* heartrending, harrowing. **déchirer** (re) *v.t,* to tear, rend, rip, lacerate; tear up; break up; harrow; split (*ears with noise*). **déchirure** (ryːr) *f,* tear, rent, rip.

déchoir (deʃwaːr) *v.i.ir,* to fall, decline. ~ *de,* to forfeit.

décibel (desibɛl) *m,* decibel (*Phys.*).

décidé, e (deside) *a,* decided; settled, determined. **décidément** (mɑ̃) *ad,* decidedly; definitely. **décider** (de) *v.t. & abs,* to decide, settle, resolve, determine; induce, persuade, prevail upon. se ~, to decide, make up one's mind.

décidu, e (desidy) *a,* deciduous.

décigramme (desigram) *m,* decigram = ⅒ gram *or* 1.543 grains.

décilitre (desilitr) *m,* deciliter = ⅒ liter *or* 0.176 pint.

décimal, e (desimal) *a. & f,* decimal.

décime (desim) *m,* 10 centimes; 10% surtax. **décimer** (me) *v.t,* to decimate.

décimètre (desimɛtr) *m,* decimeter = ⅒ meter *or* 3.937 inch-

es; decimeter rule. *double* ~, 2-decimeter rule. ~ *carré,* square d. = 15.500 sq. ins. ~ *cube,* cubic d. = 61.024 cub. ins.

décisif, ive† (desizif, iːv) *a,* decisive; critical; positive. **décision** (zjɔ̃) *f,* decision; conclusion; resolution; ruling, award.

déclamateur (deklamatœːr) *m,* stump orator, spouter. **déclamation** (sjɔ̃) *f,* declamation, elocution; delivery; rant. **déclamer** (me) *v.t. & abs. & i,* to declaim; recite; spout, rant.

déclaration (deklarasjɔ̃) *f,* declaration; statement; return; proclamation; finding (*jury*). ~ *sous serment,* affidavit. **déclarer** (re) *v.t,* to declare, state, report; proclaim; certify; disclose; find (*juries*). se ~, to declare oneself; show itself; break out.

déclassé, e (deklase) *n,* [social] outcast. **déclasser** (se) *v.t,* to degrade; transfer from one class to another.

déclencher (deklɑ̃ʃe) *v.t,* to trip, release; disengage (*Mech.*); launch (*attack*). **déclencheur** (ʃœːr) *m,* [shutter] release (*Phot.*).

déclic (deklik) *m,* trigger, catch, trip, release.

déclin (deklɛ̃) *m,* decline, wane. **déclinaison** (klinɛzɔ̃) *f,* declination; declension (*Gram.*). **décliner** (ne) *v.i. & t,* to decline; wane; give, state (*name, etc.*).

déclive (dekliːv) *a,* sloping. **déclivité** (klivite) *f,* declivity, slope.

décocher (dekoʃe) *v.t,* to let off, let fly.

décoction (dekoksjɔ̃) *f,* decoction.

décoiffer (dekwafe) *v.t,* to take off the hat of; uncork, crack (*a bottle*); disarrange (*hair*).

décoller (dekole) *v.t,* to unstick; (*v.i.*) to go away; take off (*Avn.*). se ~, to come unstuck, part.

décolleté, e (dekolte) *a,* low-necked; free, licentious. ¶ *m,* low-necked dress; court shoes.

décolorer (dekolore) *v.t,* to discolor.

décombres (dekɔ̃ːbr) *m.pl,* demolitions, rubbish.

décommander (dekɔmɑ̃de) *v.t*, to countermand, cancel; call off; ask not to come.

décomposer (dekɔpoze) *v.t*, to decompose; distort.

décompte (dekɔ̃:t) *m*, deduction; working out; table, sheet. *éprouver du ~ dans*, to be disappointed in. **décompter** (kɔ̃te) *v.t. & abs*, to deduct; work out; suffer disappointment.

déconcerter (dekɔ̃sɛrte) *v.t*, to disconcert; upset.

déconfire (dekɔ̃fi:r) *v.t.ir*, to nonplus. **déconfiture** (fity:r) *f*, insolvency.

déconseiller (dekɔ̃sɛje) *v.t*, to dissuade.

déconsidérer (dekɔ̃sidere) *v.t*, to discredit.

décontenancer (dekɔ̃tnɑ̃se) *v.t*, to abash.

déconvenue (dekɔ̃vny) *f*, discomfiture.

décor (dekɔ:r) *m*, decoration; set (*Theat.*); (*pl.*) scenery; (*pl.*) regalia (*freemasons'*). **décorateur** (kɔratœ:r) *m*, decorator; scene painter, stage designer. **décoratif, ive** (tif, i:v) *a*, decorative. **décoration** (sjɔ̃) *f*, decoration; order, medal; scenery. **décorer** (re) *v.t*, to decorate; dignify.

décortiquer (dekɔrtike) *v.t*, to bark; peel.

décorum (dekɔrɔm) *m*, decorum; etiquette.

découcher (dekuʃe) *v.i*, to sleep out.

découdre (dekudr) *v.t.ir*, to unstitch; rip.

découler (dekule) *v.i*, to trickle, run down; proceed, issue.

découper (dekupe) *v.t. & abs*, to carve (*meat*); cut up; cut out; fretsaw; punch [out]. *se ~*, to stand out. **découpeur, euse** (pœ:r, ø:z) *n*, carver (*pers.*).

découpler (dekuple) *v.t*, to slip, uncouple.

découpoir (dekupwa:r) *m*, [hollow] punch. **découpure** (py:r) *f*, cutting out; fretwork.

découragement (dekuraʒmɑ̃) *m*, discouragement, despondency. **décourager** (ʒe) *v.t*, to discourage, dishearten, depress, dispirit;

daunt; deter. *se ~*, to lose heart, despond.

décousu, e (dekuzy) (*fig.*) *a*, loose, disconnected, disjointed, rambling, desultory. ¶ *m*, looseness.

découvert, e (dekuvɛ:r, ɛrt) *a*, uncovered, bare, open, unprotected. *à découvert, ad*, uncovered, open; unpacked; unsecured (*loan*); overdrawn. **découvert**, *m*, overdraft; bear account, bears (*Stk Ex.*). **découverte**, *f*, discovery; find; detection; disclosure. *aller à la ~*, to scout. **découvrir** (vri:r) *v.t.ir*, to uncover, bare, open; discover, detect; descry, espy; find; f. out. *se ~*, to expose oneself; take one's hat off; come to light.

décrasser (dekrase) *v.t*, to cleanse, clean, scour.

décréditer (dekredite) *v.t*, to discredit.

décrépit, e (dekrepi, it) *a*, decrepit. **décrépitude** (tyd) *f*, decrepitude, senile decay.

décret (dekrɛ) *m*, decree, fiat, ordinance, order, enactment. **décréter** (krete) *v.t*, to decree, enact, ordain.

décri (dekri) *m*, disrepute. **décrier** (krie) *v.t*, to decry, run down.

décrire (dekri:r) *v.t. & abs. ir*, to describe.

décrocher (dekrɔʃe) *v.t*, to unhook; take down.

décroître (dekrwɑ:tr) *v.i.ir*, to decrease, shorten, dwindle, wane.

décrotter (dekrɔte) *v.t*, to clean, brush, scrape. **décrotteur** (tœ:r) *m*, bootblack (*pers.*). **décrottoir** (twa:r) *m*, scraper [mat].

décrue (dekry) *f*, fall (*river*); retreat (*glacier*). **déçu, p.p**, **décevoir**.

décuple (dekypl) *a. & m*, tenfold. **décupler** (ple) *v.t. & i*, to increase tenfold.

dédaigner (dedɛɲe) *v.t*, to disdain, scorn, despise. **dédaigneux, euse**† (ɲø, ɲø:z) *a*, disdainful, scornful, supercilious. **dédain** (dɛ̃) *m*, disdain, disregard, scorn.

dédale (dedal) *m*, maze, labyrinth.

dedans (dədɑ̃) *ad*, inside, in. *de*

~, from within. (*rire*) en ~, ad, inwardly. en ~ de, *pr*, within. ¶ *m*, inside, interior.

dédicace (dedikas) *f*, dedication; inscription. **dédier** (dje) *v.t*, to dedicate; devote; inscribe.

dédire (dedi:r) *v.t.ir*, to gainsay. se ~ de, to retract, unsay. **dédit** (di) *m*, retractation; penalty, forfeit.

dédommagement (dedɔmaʒmɑ̃) *m*, indemnity, compensation, damages. **dédommager** (ʒe) *v.t*, to compensate, recoup, indemnify.

dédoubler (deduble) *v.t*, to divide into two; duplicate (*train*); unline. ~ *les rangs*, to form single file.

déductif, ive (dedyktif, i:v) *a*, deductive, inferential. **déduction** (ksjɔ̃) *f*, deduction; allowance, relief; inference. **déduire** (dɥi:r) *v.t.ir*, to deduct; deduce, infer.

déesse (deɛs) *f*, goddess.

défaillance (defajɑ̃:s) *f*, swoon, fainting [fit]; lapse; failing; default; eclipse. **défaillant, e** (jɑ̃, ɑ̃:t) *a*, failing; drooping; defaulting. ¶ *n*, defaulter. **défaillir** (ji:r) *v.i.ir*, to faint; fail; flinch; falter.

défaire (defɛ:r) *v.t.ir*, to undo; take off; defeat, rout. se ~, to come undone. se ~ de, to get rid of; unload (*stocks*); make away with. **défait, e** (fɛ, ɛt) *a*, undone; defeated; drawn (*look*). **défaite**, *f*, defeat; shuffle, evasion.

défalcation (defalkasjɔ̃) *f*, deduction. **défalquer** (ke) *v.t*, to deduct.

défaut (defo) *m*, defect, fault, flaw, blemish; default; failure; want, lack, deficiency.

défaveur (defavœ:r) *f*, disfavor. **défavorable**† (vɔrabl) *a*, unfavorable, inauspicious.

défectif, ive (defɛktif, i:v) *a*, defective. **défection** (sjɔ̃) *f*, defection. **défectueux, euse**† (tɥø, ø:z) *a*, defective, faulty, deficient. **défectuosité** (tɥozite) *f*, defect, fault, flaw.

défendable (defɑ̃dabl) *a*, defensible. **défendeur, eresse** (dœ:r, drɛs) *n*, defendant; respondent (*law*). **défendre** (fɑ̃:dr) *v.t*, to defend; protect, shield; forbid, prohibit. se ~, to defend oneself; deny; excuse oneself. **défense** (fɑ̃:s) *f*, defense; (*pl.*) plea; protection; prohibition; tusk; fender (*Naut.*). ~ *d'afficher*, post no bills. ~ *d'entrer* [*sans autorisation*], no admittance [except on business], private. ~ *d'entrer sous peine d'amende*, trespassers will be prosecuted. ~ *de circuler sur l'herbe*, [please] keep off the grass. ~ *de fumer*, no smoking. ~ *de passer*, no thoroughfare. ~ *de toucher*, [please] do not touch. ~ *expresse* (ou *absolue*) *de fumer*, smoking strictly prohibited. **défenseur** (fɑ̃sœ:r) *m*, defender; advocate; counsel for the defense. **défensif, ive** (sif, i:v) *a. & f*, defensive.

déféquer (defeke) *v.t. & i*, to defecate.

déférence (deferɑ̃:s) *f*, deference, respect. **déférent, e** (rɑ̃, ɑ̃:t) *a*, deferential. **déférer** (re) *v.t*, to confer, bestow; refer (*to court*); hand over (*to justice*); administer (*oath*); (*v.i.*) to defer (*submit*).

déferler (defɛrle) *v.t*, to unfurl; (*v.i.*) to break (*waves*).

déferrer (defere) *v.t*, to unshoe (*horse*); disconcert.

défi (defi) *m*, challenge; defiance. **défiance** (fjɑ̃:s) *f*, distrust, mistrust. ~ *de soi-même*, diffidence. **défiant, e** (ɑ̃, ɑ̃:t) *a*, distrustful, mistrustful; wary.

déficit (defisi) *m*, deficit, deficiency, short[age], minus quantity. **déficitaire** (tɛ:r) *a*, debit (*att.*), showing a loss, adverse; short.

défier (defje) *v.t*, to challenge; brave; dare; defy, baffle. se ~ de, to distrust, mistrust; beware of.

défigurer (defigyre) *v.t*, to disfigure; deface; distort.

défilé (defile) *m*, defile; march past; procession; parade. **défiler** (le) *v.t*, to unthread; (*v.i.*) to defile; file off; march past. se ~ (*fig.*), to make off.

défini, e (defini) *p.a*, definite; finite (*mood, Gram.*). **définir** (ni:r) *v.t*, to define; describe; determine; decide. **définissable**

(nisabl) *a*, definable. **définitif, ive†** (tif, i:v) *a*, definitive; absolute (*decree*); final; ultimate; standard (*edition*). **en définitive,** *ad*, finally, in short. **définition** (sjɔ̃) *f*, definition; decision.

déflation (deflasjɔ̃) *f*, deflation (*Fin.*).

défléchir (defleʃi:r) *v.t*, to deflect.

défleurir (deflœri:r) *v.i*, to shed its blossoms; (*v.t.*) to deflower, strip of flowers. **défloraison** (flɔrɛzɔ̃) *f*, defloration (*stripping*). **défloration** (rasjɔ̃) *f*, defloration (*ravishment*). **déflorer** (re) *v.t*, to deflower (*strip of flowers* or *ravish*); take the freshness off (*news*).

défoncer (defɔ̃se) *v.t*, to stave [in]; break up.

déformer (defɔrme) *v.t*, to deform; distort; strain (*Mech.*).

défourner (defurne) *v.t*, to take out of the oven.

défraîchi, e (defrɛʃi) *p.a*, shopworn. **défraîchir** (ʃi:r) *v.t. & se ~*, to fade.

défrayer (defrɛje) *v.t*, to defray; entertain; keep up (*conversation*).

défricher (defriʃe) *v.t*, to clear, grub, reclaim.

défriser (defrize) *v.t*, to uncurl; disconcert.

défroncer (defrɔ̃se) *v.t*, to iron out; smooth.

défroque (defrɔk) *f*, cast-off clothing. **défroquer** (ke) *v.t*, to unfrock.

défunt, e (defœ̃, œ̃:t) *a. & n*, deceased, defunct, departed, late (*a.*).

dégagé, e (degaʒe) *a*, free, easy, unconstrained; perky. **dégagement** (ʒmɑ̃) *m*, redemption; clearing; disengagement, evolution; exit. **dégager** (ʒe) *v.t*, to redeem; make out (*meaning*); relieve; extricate; free, disengage, give off, evolve, emit; clear; set off (*figure*).

dégaine (degɛ:n) *f*, awkwardness. **dégainer** (gɛne) *v.t. & abs*, to unsheathe, draw.

déganter (se) (degɑ̃te) *v.pr*, to take off one's gloves.

dégarnir (degarni:r) *v.t*, to strip, dismantle.

dégât (degɑ) *m. oft. pl*, damage, havoc.

dégauchir (degoʃi:r) *v.t*, to true, straighten.

dégel (deʒɛl) *m*, thaw. **dégeler** (ʒle) *v.t. & i. & se ~*, to thaw.

dégénérer (deʒenere) *v.i*, to degenerate. **dégénérescence** (rɛsɑ̃:s) & **dégénération** (rasjɔ̃) *f*, degeneration, degeneracy.

dégingandé, e (deʒɛ̃gɑ̃de) *a*, ungainly, gawky.

dégoiser (degwaze) *v.t*, to spout (*abuse*).

dégommer (degɔme) *v.t*, to ungum; oust.

dégonfler (degɔ̃fle) *v.t*, to deflate; relieve. **se ~**, to collapse; back down.

dégorger (degɔrʒe) *v.t*, to disgorge; unstop. **[se] ~**, to discharge; overflow.

dégouliner (deguline) *v.i*, to trickle, drip.

dégourdi, e (degurdi) *p.a*, wideawake, alive. **dégourdir** (di:r) *v.t*, to revive. **faire ~**, to take the chill off (*water*).

dégoût (degu) *m*, want of appetite; distaste, dislike, disrelish; disgust, loathing, aversion; disappointment. **dégoûtant, e** (tɑ̃, ɑ̃:t) *a*, disgusting, loathsome; disheartening. **dégoûter** (te) *v.t*, to make one sick of; disgust. **faire le dégoûté**, to be fastidious, be squeamish.

dégoutter (degute) *v.i. & abs*, to drip, trickle, dribble.

dégradateur (degradatœ:r) *m*, vignetter (*Phot.*). **dégradation** (sjɔ̃) *f*, degradation; defacement; dilapidation. **dégrader** (de) *v.t*, to degrade; deface; dilapidate; damage; shade [off], vignette.

dégrafer (degrafe) *v.t*, to unhook, unfasten.

dégraisser (degrɛse) *v.t*, to take off the grease (*or* fat) from; skim; scour.

dégras (degrɑ) *m*, dubbin[g].

degré (dəgre) *m*, degree; step, stair; grade; stage; pitch; extent.

dégrèvement (degrɛvmɑ̃) *m*, relief, reduction, cut (*taxes*). **dégrever** (grəve) *v.t*, to relieve;

cancel; disencumber (*from mortgage*).

dégringolade (degrēgɔlad) *f*, tumble; collapse, slump. **dégringoler** (le) *v.t*, to rush down. ~ *dans*, to tumble (*or* fall) down *or* into.

dégriser (degrize) *v.t*, to sober; disillusion.

dégrossir (degrosiːr) *v.t*, to rough down; rough-hew; sketch out; break in.

déguenillé, e (degnije) *a*, tattered, ragged.

déguerpir (degɛrpiːr) *v.i*, to move out; pack off.

déguisement (degizmɑ̃) *m*, disguise; fancy dress. **déguiser** (ze) *v.t*, to disguise; conceal; change (*name*). se ~, to disguise oneself, masquerade.

dégustateur (degystatœːr) *m*, taster. **dégustation** (sjɔ̃) *f*, tasting. **déguster** (te) *v.t*, to taste, sample.

déhanchement (deɑ̃ʃmɑ̃) *m*, waddle.

déharnacher (dearnaʃe) *v.t*, to unharness.

dehors (dəɔːr) *ad*, out; outside; out of doors; in the offing. ¶ ~*!* out! (*Box., etc.*). *de* ~, from without. *en* ~, *ad*, outside, outward; frank. *en* ~ *de*, *pr*, outside, without. ¶ *m*, outside, exterior; (*pl.*) outworks (*Mil.*); (*pl.*) grounds (*of mansion*); (*pl.*) appearances.

déifier (deifje) *v.t*, to deify. **déité** (te) *f*, deity.

déjà (deʒa) *ad*, already; before.

déjection (deʒɛksjɔ̃) *f*, evacuation (*bowels*).

déjeter (deʒte) *v.t. & se* ~, to warp (*wood*); buckle.

déjeuner (deʒœne) *v.i*, to breakfast; lunch. ¶ *m*, breakfast set, b. service. *petit* ~, breakfast.

déjouer (deʒwe) *v.t*, to baffle, thwart, frustrate, foil, outwit, outmaneuver.

déjucher (deʒyʃe) (*fig.*) *v.i*, to come down; (*v.t.*) to bring down.

delà (dəla) *pr*, beyond. *au*-~, beyond; more. *au*-~ *de*, beyond; more. [*plus*] *en* ~, farther [off]. *par*-~, beyond. *l'au*-~, *m*, the beyond (*future life*).

délabré, e (delabre) *p.a*, dilapidated; brokendown; tumbledown; ramshackle, gimcrack. **délabrement** (brəmɑ̃) *m*, dilapidation; wreck. **délabrer** (bre) *v.t*, to dilapidate, shatter.

délacer (delase) *v.t*, to unlace.

délai (delɛ) *m*, time, extension [of time]; delay. ~ *de congé*, [term of] notice.

délaissement (delɛsmɑ̃) *m*, abandonment, desertion; destitution. **délaisser** (se) *v.t*, to forsake; abandon, desert; jilt.

délassement (delɑsmɑ̃) *m*, relaxation, recreation. **délasser** (se) *v.t. & abs*, to refresh, relax.

délateur, trice (delatœːr, tris) *n*, informer.

délaver (delave) *v.t*, to soak; dilute.

délayer (delɛje) *v.t*, to add water to, thin; spin out.

deleatur (deleatyːr) *m*, delete (*sign, Typ.*).

délecter (delɛkte) *v.t. & se* ~, to delight.

délégation (delegasjɔ̃) *f*, delegation, deputation. **délégué, e** (ge) *n*, delegate; deputy. **déléguer** (ge) *v.t*, to delegate, depute.

délester (delɛste) *v.t*, to unballast; relieve.

délétère (deletɛːr) *a*, deleterious.

délibération (deliberasjɔ̃) *f*, deliberation, consideration, proceedings; transaction, business; decision, resolution. **délibéré†, e** (re) *a*, deliberate. **délibérer** (re) *v.i*, to deliberate, consult; (*v.t.*) to decide, resolve on. ~ *sur*, to consider, transact (*business at meeting*).

délicat, e† (delika, at) *a*, delicate; nice; refined; dainty, fastidious, squeamish; tender; ticklish, tricky. **délicatesse** (tɛs) *f*, delicacy.

délice (delis) *m*, delight, pleasure, luxury. ~*s*, *f.pl*, delight(s), pleasure(s), delectation. **délicieux, euse†** (sjø, øːz) *a*, delicious; delightful; charming.

délictueux (deliktyø) *a*, unlawful, illegal, felonious.

délié, e (delje) *a*, thin, slender, slim; glib. ¶ *m*, thin stroke, up stroke. **délier** (lje) *v.t*, to untie; loose[n]; release.

délimiter (delimite) *v.t*, to delimit.

délinéation (delineasjɔ̃) *f*, delineation.

délinquant, e (delɛ̃kɑ̃, ɑ̃:t) *n*, delinquent, offender.

déliquescence (delikɥesɑ̃:s) *f*, deliquescence; corruption (*fig.*).

délirant, e (delirɑ̃, ɑ̃:t) *a*, delirious; frenzied. **délire** (li:r) *m*, delirium; frenzy. **délirer** (lire) *v.i*, to be delirious.

délit (deli) *m*, offense, misdemeanor. *en flagrant* ~, in the act.

délivrance (delivrɑ̃:s) *f*, deliverance; rescue; release; delivery; issue. **délivrer** (vre) *v.t*, to deliver; rescue; release; hand [over]; issue (*tickets*).

déloger (delɔʒe) *v.i*, to [re]move; (*v.t.*) to turn out; dislodge.

déloyal, e† (delwajal) *a*, disloyal; unfair; dishonest. **déloyauté** (jote) *f*, disloyalty.

delta (dɛlta) *m*, delta.

déluge (dely:ʒ) *m*, deluge, flood; [down]pour.

déluré, e (delyre) *a*, wide-awake; knowing.

démagogue (demagɔg) *m*, demagogue.

démailler (demɑje) *v.t*, to undo (*knitting*). se ~, to run (*stocking*).

demain (dəmɛ̃) *ad. & m*, tomorrow. ~ *matin*, tomorrow morning.

démancher (demɑ̃ʃe) *v.t*, to unhandle; dislocate.

demande (dəmɑ̃:d) *f*, request, desire; application; inquiry; demand; call; indent; claim; bid; instance; suit; proposal (*marriage*); question. ~ *d'emploi*, situation wanted. **demander** (mɑ̃de) *v.t*, to ask, a. for; request; charge; inquire; apply for; claim; want; bid [for]; beg; sue for. ~ *par voie d'annonces*, to advertise for. *on demande un . . .*, wanted a . . . se ~, to ask onself, wonder. **demandeur, euse** (dœ:r, ø:z) *n*, petitioner; applicant. **demandeur, eresse** (dœ:r, drɛs) *n*, plaintiff.

démangeaison (demɑ̃ʒɛzɔ̃) *f*, itch[ing]; urge; longing. **déman-**

-ger (ʒe) *v.i*, to itch; long. *le bras me démange*, my arm itches. *la langue lui démange*, he is itching (*or* longing) to speak.

démanteler (demɑ̃tle) *v.t*, to dismantle.

démantibuler (demɑ̃tibyle) *v.t*, to break to pieces.

démarcation (demarkasjɔ̃) *f*, demarcation.

démarche (demarʃ) *f*, gait, walk, bearing; step, measure. **démarcheur** (ʃœ:r) *m*, canvasser, runner, share pusher.

démarier (demarje) *v.t*, to unmarry; thin (*plants*).

démarrage (demara:ʒ) *m*, unmooring; starting. **démarrer** (re) *v.t*, to unmoor; (*v.i.*) to leave her moorings; cast off; start; stir. **démarreur** (œ:r) *m*, starter (*auto*).

démasquer (demaske) *v.t*, to unmask; uncover; show up.

démâter (demɑte) *v.t*, to dismast.

démêlé (demɛle) *m*, contention. **démêler** (le) *v.t*, to disentangle, unravel; comb out; quarrel about. *se ~ de*, to get out of. **démêloir** (lwa:r) *m*, rake comb.

démembrer (demɑ̃bre) *v.t*, to dismember.

déménagement (demenaʒmɑ̃) *m*, removal, moving. **déménager** (ʒe) *v.t. & abs*, to remove, move [out] (*house*); (*v.i.*) to be off; go off one's head. **déménageur** (ʒœ:r) *m*, removal contractor, [furniture] remover.

démence (demɑ̃:s) *f*, insanity, madness, dementia.

démener (se) (demne) *v.pr*, to throw oneself about; strive hard.

dément, e (demɑ̃, ɑ̃:t) *a. & n*, crazy, mad (person).

démenti (demɑ̃ti) *m*, denial, contradiction, lie; failure, disappointment. **démentir** (ti:r) *v.t.ir*, to give the lie to; contradict; belie.

démérite (demerit) *m*, demerit, unworthiness. **démériter** (te) *v.i. & abs*, to deserve censure, offend.

démesuré†, e (dem[ə]zyre) *a*, inordinate; enormous, huge.

démettre (demɛtr) *v.t.ir*, to dislocate, put out of joint. se ~ de, to resign, retire.

demeurant (au) (dəmœrɑ̃), after all, in other respects. **demeure** (mœːr) *f*, residence, dwelling, abode; delay. *à* ~, fixed, stationary, set. *en* ~, in arrears. **demeurer** (mœre) *v.i*, to reside, live, dwell; stay, remain, stop; lie.

demi, e (dəmi) *a*, half. **demi**, *ad*, half. ¶ *m*, half; halfback (*Foot.*). *à* ~, *ad*, half, by halves.

demi (dəmi) *comps*: ~**-bas**, *m.pl*, half-hose. ~**-cercle**, *m*, semicircle. ~**-dieu**, *m*, demigod. ~**-finale**, *f*, semi-final. ~**-frère**, *m*, half-brother, stepbrother. ~**-gros**, *m*, small wholesale trade. *une* ~**-heure**, half an hour. ~**-jour**, *m*, half-light, twilight. ~**-lune**, *f*, crescent (*of buildings*). ~**-mot**, *m*, hint. ~**-pensionnaire**, *n*, day boarder. ~**-place**, *f*, half fare, half price. ~**-relief**, *m*, mezzo-relievo. ~**-sœur**, *f*, half-sister, stepsister. *en* ~**-solde**, on half pay (*Mil.*). ~**-ton**, *m*, semitone. *à* ~**-voix**, in an undertone.

demie (dəmi) *f*, (a) half; half-hour; half past. *une heure &* ~, an hour & a half; half-past one.

démission (demisjɔ̃) *f*, resignation. **démissionner** (ɔne) *v.i*, to resign.

démobiliser (demɔbilize) *v.t*, to demobilize.

démocrate (demɔkrat) *m*, mezzocrat. **démocratie** (si) *f*, democracy. **démocratique** (tik) *a*, democratic.

démodé, e (demɔde) *a*, old-fashioned; out of date.

demoiselle (dəmwazɛl) *f*, young lady; girl; single woman, maiden [lady], spinster; miss; damsel; dragon fly; beetle, rammer; rowlock. ~ *de compagnie*, lady companion.

démolir (demɔliːr) *v.t*, to demolish, break up; explode (*fig.*). **démolisseur** (lisœːr) *m*, breaker (*house, ship*); iconoclast. **démolition** (sjɔ̃) *f*, demolition; (*pl.*) demolitions.

démon (demɔ̃) *m*, demon, devil, fiend; demon, genius; imp. ~ *familier*, familiar [spirit].

démonétiser (demɔnetize) *v.t*, to demonetize, call in; discredit.

démoniaque (demɔnjak) *a*, demoniac(al). ¶ *n*, demoniac.

démonstrateur (demɔ̃stratœːr) *m*, demonstrator. **démonstratif, ive** (tif, iːv) *a*, conclusive; demonstrative. **démonstration** (sjɔ̃) *f*, demonstration; proof. ~ *par l'absurde*, reduction to absurdity, reductio ad absurdum.

démontable (demɔ̃tabl) *a*, sectional. **démonter** (te) *v.t*, to dismount; unhorse, throw; take to pieces; upset, nonplus.

démontrer (demɔ̃tre) *v.t*, to demonstrate, prove; show.

démoraliser (demɔralize) *v.t*, to demoralize.

démordre (demɔrdr) *v.i*, to let go; desist.

démunir (se) de (demyniːr), to part with.

démuseler (demyzle) *v.t*, to unmuzzle.

dénaturer (denatyre) *v.t*, to denature; pervert, render unnatural; distort; misrepresent.

dénégation (denegasjɔ̃) *f*, denial; disclaimer.

déni (deni) *m*, denial; refusal.

déniaiser (denjɛze) *v.t*, to sharpen (*wits*).

dénicher (deniʃe) *v.t*, to take out of the nest; ferret out; (*v.i.*) to fly [away]. **dénicheur** (ʃœːr) *m*, birds'-nester; hunter (*curios*).

denier (dənje) *m*: ~ *à Dieu*, earnest money; key money. *le* ~ *de la veuve*, the widow's mite. *le* ~ *de Saint-Pierre*, Peter's pence. ~**s**, *pl*, money, funds.

dénier (denje) *v.t*, to deny; disclaim.

dénigrer (denigre) *v.t*, to disparage, run down, detract from.

dénombrement (denɔ̃brəmɑ̃) *m*, count; census.

dénominateur (denɔminatœːr) *m*, denominator. **dénommer** (me) *v.t*, to name, denominate.

dénoncer (denɔ̃se) *v.t*, to proclaim, declare; denounce; inform against. **dénonciation** (sjasjɔ̃) *f*, denunciation; information.

dénoter (denɔte) *v.t*, to denote, betoken.

dénouement (denumɑ̃) *m*, upshot; ending. **dénouer** (nwe) *v.t,* to untie, undo; loosen; unravel.

denrée (dãre) *f, oft. pl,* commodity, produce. ~ *alimentaire,* foodstuff.

dense (dã:s) *a,* dense, close; thick. **densité** (dãsite) *f,* density.

dent (dã) *f,* tooth; prong; cog; tusk; serration; [jagged] peak. ~*s de dessous, de dessus, de devant, du fond, de lait, de sagesse,* lower, upper, front, back, milk, wisdom, teeth. **dentaire** (tɛ:r) *a,* dental (*Anat.*). **dental, e** (tal) *a,* dental (*Anat. & phonetics*). ¶ *f,* dental (*phonetics*). **denté, e** (te) *a,* toothed, cogged; dentate. ~ *en scie,* serrate. **denteler** (tle) *v.t,* to indent, notch, jag, serrate. **dentelle** (tɛl) *f,* lace; laced paper; tracery. ~ *à l'aiguille,* needle-made lace. ~ *au point à l'aiguille,* needle-point l. ~ *aux fuseaux,* pillow l. **dentelure** (tly:r) *f,* indentation, serration. **dentier** (tje) *m,* set of (*artificial*) teeth, denture, [dental] plate. **dentifrice** (tifris) *m,* toothpaste; tooth powder. **dentiste** (tist) *m,* dentist; (*att.*) dental (*surgeon*). **dentition** (sjɔ̃) *f,* dentition, teething. **denture** (ty:r) *f,* set of (*natural*) teeth; teeth (*cogs*). ~ *artificielle,* denture, [dental] plate.

dénuder (denyde) *v.t,* to denude, bare, strip.

dénué, e (denɥe) *a,* devoid, destitute. **dénuement** (nymã) *m,* destitution, penury. **se dénuer de** (nɥe), to part with.

dépannage (depana:ʒ) *m,* auto repairs. **dépanner** (ne) *v.t,* to repair; help.

dépaqueter (depakte) *v.t,* to unpack.

dépareillé, e (depareje) *a,* odd (*pair or set*). **dépareiller** (je) *v.t,* to break (*a set*).

déparer (depare) *v.t,* to strip; spoil, mar; pick out the best.

déparler (deparle) *v.i, with neg,* to stop talking.

départ (depa:r) *m,* departure, sailing; start; parting (*Chem.*). *faire le* ~ *entre, de,* to discriminate between. ~ *arrêté,* standing start. ~ *lancé,* flying start. ~ *usines,* ex works, ex mill (*sales*).

départager (departaʒe) *v.t,* to decide between. ~ *les voix,* to give the casting vote.

département (departəmã) *m,* department; county; province, line. **départemental, e** (tal) *a,* departmental.

départir (departi:r) *v.t.ir,* to divide; part (*metals*); distribute, dispense, endow. **se** ~, to desist, swerve (*fig.*).

dépasser (depase) *v.t,* to go beyond, go over, exceed, be above, top; turn (*a certain age*); pass, leave behind, overshoot, overreach; be longer; project beyond.

dépaver (depave) *v.t,* to unpave.

dépaysé, e (depeize) *p.a,* lost; among strangers; out of one's element. **dépayser** (ze) *v.t,* to remove from usual surroundings.

dépecer (depəse) *v.t,* to cut up; break up.

dépêche (depɛ:ʃ) *f,* dispatch; message; telegram. **dépêcher** (peʃe) *v.t,* to dispatch. **se** ~, to make haste, be quick, hurry up; look sharp.

dépeindre (depɛ̃:dr) *v.t.ir,* to depict, portray, delineate, picture.

dépenaillé, e (depnaje) *a,* in rags; ill-dressed.

dépendance (depãdã:s) *f,* dependence; subjection; dependency; outbuilding, outhouse; annex[e]. **dépendant, e** (dã, ã:t) *a,* dependent. **dépendre** (pã:dr) *v.i,* to depend, belong; be a dependency (*de* = of); to take down, to unhang.

dépens (depã) *m.pl,* expense; [law] costs. **dépense** (pã:s) *f,* expense, charge, cost, expenditure; efflux; steward's room. ~ *de bouche,* living expenses. **dépenser** (pãse) *v.t,* to spend, expend. **dépensier, ère** (sje, ɛ:r) *a,* extravagant, thriftless. ¶ *n,* spendthrift; bursar.

déperdition (depɛrdisjɔ̃) *f,* waste, loss.

dépérir (deperi:r) *v.i,* to dwindle, pine away, wither, decay.

dépêtrer (depɛtre) *v.t,* to extricate.

dépeupler (depœple) *v.t,* to depopulate; unstock.

dépiler (depile) v.t, to depilate, pluck; unhair.

dépiquer (depike) v.t, to unquilt; transplant; thresh (*grain*); cheer up.

dépister (depiste) v.t, to track down, run to earth; throw off the scent, foil.

dépit (depi) m, spite, spleen, despite. **dépiter** (te) v.t, to vex; spite.

déplacé, e (deplase) a, out of place, ill-timed; uncalled for. **déplacement** (smã) m, displacement, removal, shift[ing]; traveling. **déplacer** (se) v.t, to displace; [re]move, shift.

déplaire (deplɛ:r) v.i.ir, to be displeasing, offend. ~ **à**, to displease. **se ~**, to be unhappy; not to thrive. **déplaisant, e** (plɛzã, ã:t) a, unpleasing, unpleasant. **déplaisir** (zi:r) m, displeasure.

déplanter (deplãte) v.t, to take up. **déplantoir** (twa:r) m, trowel (*Hort.*).

dépliant (depliã) m, folder. **déplier** (plie) v.t, to unfold.

déplisser (deplise) v.t, to unpleat, iron out.

déploiement (deplwamã) m, unfolding; deployment.

déplorable† (deplɔrabl) a, deplorable. **déplorer** (re) v.t, to deplore, bewail.

déployer (deplwaje) v.t, to unfold; unfurl; deploy; spread [out]; expand; display.

déplumer (deplyme) v.t, to pluck, deplume. **se ~**, to molt. **déplus**, p.p, **déplaire**.

dépolir (depɔli:r) v.t, to take the surface off. *verre dépoli*, ground glass, frosted glass.

déportements (depɔrtəmã) m.pl, misconduct.

déporter (deporte) v.t, to deport; transport (*convict*). **se ~**, to withdraw claims (*law*).

déposant, e (depozã, ã:t) n, deponent; depositor, customer (*bank*). **dépose** (po:z) f, taking up; t. down; t. off. **déposer** (poze) v.t, to lay down; l. aside; deposit, place, lodge, hand in; file, lay; depose; register (*trade mark*); prefer; take up, t. down, t. off. **se ~**, to settle. **dépositaire** (pozi-

tɛ:r) n, depositary; trustee; storer (*furniture warehouseman*). **déposition** (sjɔ̃) f, deposition; evidence.

déposséder (deposede) v.t, to dispossess, oust.

dépôt (depo) m, deposit; deposition; trust; handing in; filing; depot, store[house], warehouse, repository, depository; shed; yard; cells (*prison*); sediment. *en ~*, on sale [or return]; in bond.

dépoter (depɔte) v.t, to plant out; decant.

dépouille (depu:j) f, slough (*serpent, worm*); skin (*wild beast*); spoil; remains (*mortal*). **dépouiller** (puje) v.t, to skin; cast (*skin*); strip, divest, despoil; go through; analyze; count (*votes*). **se ~**, to slough, cast its skin; shed its leaves.

dépourvoir (depurvwa:r) v.t.ir, to deprive. **dépourvu, e** (vy) p.a, destitute, bereft, devoid. **au dépourvu**, ad, unawares, napping.

dépravation (depravasjɔ̃) f, depravation; depravity. **dépraver** (ve) v.t, to deprave, vitiate.

dépréciation (depresjasjɔ̃) f, depreciation. **déprécier** (sje) v.t, to depreciate, underrate, undervalue, disparage.

déprédation (depredasjɔ̃) f, depredation.

déprendre (se) (deprã:dr) v.pr. ir, to break away, part.

dépression (depresjɔ̃) f, depression. ~ **nerveuse**, nervous breakdown. **déprimer** (prime) v.t, to depress; dispirit.

depuis (dəpɥi) pr. & ad, since, for, from. ~ **quand?** how long? since when? ~ **que**, c, since.

députation (depytasjɔ̃) f, deputation; membership (*parliament*). **député** (te) m, deputy; congressman; delegate. **députer** (te) v.t, to depute.

déraciné, e (derasine) (*pers.*) n, fish out of water. **déraciner** (ne) v.t, to uproot, eradicate.

déraidir (se) (derɛdi:r) (*fig.*) v.pr, to unbend, thaw.

dérailler (derɑje) v.i, to derail; go astray (*fig.*).

déraison (derɛzɔ̃) f, unreason-

[ableness]. **déraisonnable†** (zɔnabl) *a*, unreasonable, preposterous. **déraisonner** (ne) *v.i*, to talk nonsense.

dérangement (derãʒmã) *m*, derangement; disturbance; fault. **déranger** (ʒe) *v.t*, to disarrange; disturb; upset; trouble; put out of order; derange, unsettle.

déraper (derape) *v.t. & i*, to trip (*anchor*); skid; side-slip.

déréglé, e (deregle) *a*, out of order; lawless. **dérèglement** (rɛgləmã) *m*, disordered state; irregularity; derangement; profligacy. **dérégler** (regle) *v.t*, to put out of order; derange; disorder.

dérider (deride) *v.t*, to smooth, unwrinkle; cheer up.

dérision (derizjɔ̃) *f*, derision. **dérisoire** (zwaːr) *a*, derisory, laughable.

dérivation (derivasjɔ̃) *f*, derivation; deflection; loop [line]; flume; shunt (*Elec.*). **dérive** (riːv) *f*, leeway; drift; breakaway. en ~, à la ~, adrift. **dérivé** (ve) *m*, derivative. **dériver** (ve) *v.t*, to divert; shunt (*Elec.*); unrivet; (*v.i.*) to be derived; spring, originate; drift, drive (*Naut.*).

dernier, ère (dɛrnje, ɛːr) *a*, last; hindmost; latter; late; latest; final; closing; junior (*partner*); highest; utmost; extreme; dire; lowest, worst. *dernier cri*, latest [thing out]. *dernier jugement*, crack of doom. *dernières galeries*, gallery (*Theat.*) *dernière main*, finishing touches. **dernièrement** (njɛrmã) *ad*, lately, latterly, not long ago.

dérobé, e (derɔbe) *a*, secret, hidden, concealed; spare (*time*). à la dérobée, *ad*, by stealth, on the sly. **dérober** (be) *v.t*, to steal, rob; snatch; conceal, hide. *se ~ à*, to shirk. *se ~ de*, to steal away from. *se ~ sous*, to give way under.

déroger (derɔʒe) *v.i*, to derogate.

dérouiller (deruje) *v.t*, to rub off the rust from; brush up (*fig.*).

dérouler (derule) *v.t*, to unroll; unwind; unfold.

déroute (derut) *f*, rout; ruin. *mettre en ~*, to rout. **dérouter**

(te) *v.t*, to lead astray; baffle, nonplus.

derrière (dɛrjɛːr) *pr. & ad*, behind; aft; astern. ¶ *m*, back; rear; hinder part; tail (*cart*).

derviche (dɛrviʃ) *ou* **dervis** (vi) *m*, dervish.

des *see* de.

dès (dɛ) *pr*, from; since. ~ à présent, from now onward. ~ lors, ever since then; consequently. ~ que, *c*, as soon as.

désabonner (se) (dezabɔne) *v.pr*, to discontinue one's subscription *or* season ticket.

désabuser (dezabyze) *v.t*, to disabuse, undeceive.

désaccord (dezakɔːr) *m*, disagreement; discord (*Mus.*). **désaccorder** (kɔrde) *v.t*, to put out of tune. *se ~*, to break their engagement (*marriage*).

désaccoupler (dezakuple) *v.t*, to uncouple.

désaccoutumer (dezakutyme) *v.t*, to break of the habit.

désaffection (dezafɛksjɔ̃) *f*, disaffection.

désagréable† (dezagreabl) *a*, disagreeable, unpleasant. ~ au goût, distasteful; unpalatable.

désagréger (dezagreʒe) *v.t*, to disintegrate, weather.

désagrément (dezagremã) *m*, source of annoyance; unpleasantness; vexation.

désajuster (dezaʒyste) *v.t*, to derange; disarrange.

désaltérer (dezaltere) *v.t*, to quench (*someone's*) thirst.

désamorcer (dezamɔrse) *v.t*, to unprime.

désappointement (dezapwɛ̃tmã) *m*, disappointment. **désappointer** (te) *v.t*, to disappoint.

désapprendre (dezaprãːdr) *v.t. & abs. ir*, to forget; unlearn.

désapprobation (dezaprɔbasjɔ̃) *f*, disapprobation, disapproval. **désapprouver** (pruve) *v.t*, to disapprove [of], frown [up]on.

désarçonner (dezarsɔne) *v.t*, to unseat, unhorse; throw; silence; floor.

désarmement (dezarməmã) *m*, disarmament; laying up (*ship*). **désarmer** (me) *v.t. & i*, to disarm, unarm; uncock (*gun*); lay up.

désarroi (dezarwa) *m*, disarray, disorder.

désassembler (dezasãble) *v.t*, to take to pieces, disconnect, disjoint.

désastre (dezastr) *m*, disaster. **désastreux, euse** (trø, ø:z), *a*, disastrous.

désavantage (dezavãta:ʒ) *m*, disadvantage, drawback. **désavantager** (taʒe) *v.t*, to place at a disadvantage, handicap. **désavantageux, euse†** (ʒø, ø:z) *a*, disadvantageous.

désaveu (dezavø) *m*, disavowal, denial, disclaimer. **désavouer** (vwe) *v.t*, to disavow; disown; disclaim; disapprove.

desceller (desɛle) *v.t*, to unseal.

descendance (desãdã:s) *f*, descent, lineage; descendants. **descendant, e** (dã, ã:t) *a*, descending, downward; down (*train, etc*.); outgoing (*tide*). ¶ *n*, descendant; (*pl*.) progeny. **descendre** (sã:dr) *v.i. & t*, to descend, go down; alight, dismount, get down; stay, stop, put up (*at hotel*); lower; drop; fall; sink; make a descent. ~ [*à terre*], to land. ~ *en vol plané*, to plane down. **descente** (sã:t) *f*, descent; fall; lowering; slope, incline; downpipe; raid; run (*of depositors on bank*). ~ *de bain*, bath mat. ~ *de justice*, domiciliary visit. ~ *de lit*, bedside rug.

description (dɛskripsjɔ̃) *f*, description; inventory.

désemparer (dezãpare) *v.t*, to disable (*ship*); quit, leave. *sans* ~, on the spot, there & then; without intermission, continuous(ly).

désemplir (dezãpli:r) *v.t*, to partly empty; (*v.i.*) to empty. *ne pas* ~, to be always full.

désenchanter (dezãʃãte) *v.t*, to disenchant; disillusion.

désencombrer (dezãkɔ̃bre) *v.t*, to disencumber, clear.

désenfiler (dezãfile) *v.t*, to unthread.

désenfler (dezãfle) *v.t*, to deflate; (*v.i.*) to go down (*swelling*).

désenivrer (dezãnivre) *v.t*, to sober. *il ne désenivre point*, he is never sober.

désennuyer (dezãnɥije) *v.t*, to divert, amuse.

désenrhumer (dezãryme) *v.t*, to cure of a cold. **désenrouer** (rwe) *v.t*, to cure of hoarseness.

déséquilibré, e (dezekilibre) *a*, unbalanced.

désert, e (dezɛ:r, ɛrt) *a*, desert; deserted, empty, desolate. ¶ *m*, desert, wilderness. **déserter** (zɛrte) *v.t. & abs*, to desert, forsake. ~ *de*, to leave. **déserteur** (tœ:r) *m*, deserter. **désertion** (sjɔ̃) *f*, desertion. **désertique** (tik) *a*, desert.

désespérance (dezɛsperã:s) *f*, despair. **désespérant, e** (rã, ã:t) *a*, heartbreaking. **désespéré†, e** (re) *a*, desperate, hopeless. ¶ *n*, desperate man, woman, madman. **désespérer** (re) *v.i. & abs*, to despair; (*v.t.*) to drive to despair. **désespoir** (pwa:r) *m*, despair; desperation.

déshabillé (dɛzabije) *m*, undress, dishabille; wrap; true colors (*fig.*). **déshabiller** (je) *v.t*, to undress, disrobe; strip; lay bare (*fig.*).

déshabituer (dezabitɥe) *v.t*, to break of the habit.

déshérence (dezerã:s) *f*, escheat. **déshériter** (dezerite) *v.t*, to disinherit.

déshonnête† (dezɔnɛ:t) *a*, indecent, immodest.

déshonneur (dezɔnœ:r) *m*, dishonor, disgrace. **déshonorant, e** (nɔrã, ã:t) *a*, dishonorable, discreditable. **déshonorer** (re) *v.t*, to dishonor, disgrace.

desiderata (deziderata) *m.pl*, desiderata, wants.

désigner (deziɲe) *v.t*, to designate; indicate, point out; describe; nominate; appoint. **désignation** (ɲasjɔ̃) *f*, designation.

désillusionner (dezilyzjɔne) *v.t*, to disillusion, undeceive.

désincorporer (dezɛ̃kɔrpore) *v.t*, to disincorporate, disembody.

désinence (dezinã:s) *f*, ending (*word*).

désinfectant (dezẽfɛktã) *m*, disinfectant. **désinfecter** (te) *v.t*, to disinfect, deodorize. **désinfection** (sjõ) *f*, disinfection.

désintéressé, e (dezĕterɛse) *a*, not implicated; disinterested, candid; unselfish. **désintéressement** (smã) *m*, disinterestedness; unselfishness. **désintéresser** (se) *v.t*, to buy out, satisfy, pay off. *se ~ de*, to take no further interest in.

désinviter (dezẽvite) *v.t*, to ask not to come.

désinvolte (dezẽvɔlt) *a*, easy. **désinvolture** (ty:r) *f*, unconstraint; free & easy manner.

désir (dezi:r) *m*, desire, wish. **désirable** (zirabl) *a*, desirable. **désirer** (re) *v.t. & abs*, to desire, want, be desirous of, wish, w. for. **désireux, euse** (rø, ø:z) *a*, desirous, wishful, anxious.

désistement (dezistəmã) *m*, waiver (*law*); withdrawal. se **désister** de (te), to waive; withdraw from; stand down from (*candidacy*).

désobéir (dezobei:r) *v.i. & abs*, to disobey. *~ à*, to disobey (*v.t.*). **désobéissance** (isã:s) *f*, disobedience. **désobéissant, e** (sã, ã:t) *a*, disobedient.

désobligeance (dezɔbliʒã:s) *f*, disobligingness, unkindness. **désobligeant, e** (ʒã, ã:t) *a*, disobliging, unkind, ungracious. **désobliger** (ʒe) *v.t*, to disoblige.

désobstruer (dezɔpstrye) *v.t*, to clear.

désoccupé, e (dezɔkype) *a*, unoccupied.

désœuvré, e (dezøvre) *a*, idle, at a loose end. ¶ *n*, idler. **désœuvrement** (vrəmã) *m*, idleness.

désolation (dezɔlasjõ) *f*, desolation. **désolé, e** (le) *p.a*, desolate; disconsolate, forlorn, distressed, extremely sorry. **désoler** (le) *v.t*, to desolate, distress, grieve.

désopilant, e (dezɔpilã, ã:t) *a*, highly amusing.

désordonné, e (dezɔrdɔne) *a*, untidy; disorderly; inordinate. **désordre** (dr) *m*, disorder; disorderliness. *~s*, riots.

désorganiser (dezɔrganize) *v.t*, to disorganize.

désorienter (dezɔrjãte) *v.t*, to disconcert, bewilder.

désormais (dezɔrmɛ) *ad*, henceforth; hereafter.

désosser (dezose) *v.t*, to bone.

despote (dɛspɔt) *m*, despot. **despotique**† (tik) *a*, despotic. **despotisme** (tism) *m*, despotism.

dessaler (dɛsale) *v.t*, to unsalt; soak (*meat*); sharpen wits.

dessécher (deseʃe) *v.t*, to desiccate; dry up, drain; wither, parch. **dessèchement** (sɛʃmã) *m*, desiccation, etc.

dessein (dɛsẽ) *m*, design, plan, project; purpose. *à ~*, on purpose, designedly.

desseller (desɛle) *v.t*, to unsaddle.

desserrer (desɛre) *v.t*, to loosen, slack[en]; open.

dessert (desɛ:r) *m*, dessert (*dessert, cheese, fruit*).

desserte (desɛrt) *f*, duties. **desservir** (vi:r) *v.t.ir*, to serve; minister to (*Eccl.*). *~ [la table]*, to clear the table.

dessiccation (dɛsikasjõ) *f*, desiccation.

dessiller (desije) *v.t*, to open (*eyes*) (*fig.*).

dessin (desẽ) *m*, drawing, sketching; design, pattern; sketch; cartoon; plan. *~ à carreaux*, check [pattern]. *~ à main levée*, freehand drawing. *~ au trait*, outline d. *~ industriel*, mechanical d. *~ ombré*, shaded d. **dessinateur, trice** (sinatœ:r, tris) *n*, sketcher, drawer; draftsman; cartoonist; designer. *~ de jardins*, landscape gardener. **dessiner** (sine) *v.t*, to draw, sketch; design; show; outline. se *~*, to stand out; show up; loom; take shape.

dessoûler (desule) *v.t*, to sober. *il ne dessoule jamais*, he is never sober.

dessous (dəsu) *ad. & pr*, under; under it, them; underneath; beneath, below. *au~* (otsu) *ad*, under[neath], below. *au~ de*, *pr*, below, under, beneath. *en ~*, *ad*, underneath; underhand; stealthily; sly. *là-~*, *ad*, under there, under that, underneath.

par-~, pr. & ad, under[neath], beneath. ¶ *m,* under part, underside, bottom; face (*card*); wrong side (*fabric*); worst of it (*fig.*); (*pl.*) underclothing, underwear (*women's*). ~ *de plat,* table mat.

dessus (dəsy) *ad,* over, above; on, upon, [up]on it, them. *au-~* (otsy) *ad,* above [it], over it; upwards. *au-~ de, pr,* above, over; beyond. *en ~, ad,* on [the] top. *là-~, ad,* on that, thereon; thereupon. *par-~, pr. & ad,* over; into. *par-~ bord,* overboard. ¶ *m,* upper part; top; back (*hand*); treble (*Mus.*), soprano; right side (*fabric*); upper hand, mastery, whip hand; best of it. ~ *de coussin,* cushion cover. ~ *de fourneau,* top of grate. ~ *de plateau,* tray cloth. ~ *de lit,* bedspread. ~ *du panier,* pick of the basket.

destin (dɛstɛ̃) *m,* destiny, fate, lot, doom. **destinataire** (tinatɛ:r) *n,* consignee; receiver, recipient; addressee. *aux risques & périls du ~,* at owner's risk. **destination** (sjɔ̃) *f,* destination; purpose. *à ~ de,* [bound] for. **destinée** (ne) *f,* destiny, lot. **destiner** (ne) *v.t,* to destine, design, intend, mean; allot, assign; fate, doom. **destitué, e** (dɛstitɥe) *p.a,* devoid, lacking. **destituer** (tɥe) *v.t,* to dismiss, remove, displace. **destitution** (tysjɔ̃) *f,* dismissal; removal.

destructeur, trice (dɛstryktœ:r, tris) *a,* destructive. ¶ *n,* destroyer. **destructif, ive** (tif, i:v) *a,* destructive. **destruction** (sjɔ̃) *f,* destruction.

désuet, te (desɥɛ, ɛt) *a,* obsolete. **désuétude** (sɥetyd) *f,* disuse.

désunion (dezynjɔ̃) *f,* disunion. **désunir** (ni:r) *v.t,* to disunite.

détachement (detaʃmɑ̃) *m,* detachment; detail (*men*). **détacher** (ʃe) *v.t,* to detach, untie, undo, unfasten; take off, t. down; detail (*Mil.*). se ~, to come away; break off; b. away; stand out. **détail** (deta:j) *m,* detail, particular; retail. **détaillant, e** (tajɑ̃, ɑ̃:t) *n,* retailer. **détailler** (je) *v.t,* to cut up; retail, peddle; detail.

détaler (detale) *v.i,* to make off, scamper away.

détaxer (detakse) *v.t,* to return (*or* remit) the duties (*or* charges) on; untax.

détecteur (detɛktœ:r) *m,* detector (*radio*). **détective** (ti:v) *m,* detective.

déteindre (detɛ̃:dr) *v.t. & i. ir,* to fade. ~ *sur,* to come off on (*dye*); influence.

dételer (detle) *v.t. & abs,* to unharness; unyoke; ease off, stop.

détendre (detɑ̃:dr) *v.t, & abs. & se ~,* to unbend, slack[en], relax, expand; take down.

détenir (detni:r) *v.t.ir,* to hold; detain.

détente (detɑ̃:t) *f,* relaxation; expansion; trigger.

détenteur, trice (detɑ̃tœ:r, tris) *n,* holder (*pers.*). **détention** (sjɔ̃) *f,* holding; detention, detainment. **détenu, e** (tny) *n,* prisoner.

détérioration (deterjɔrasjɔ̃) *f,* deterioration, impairment, damage, dilapidation. se **détériorer** (re) *v.pr,* to deteriorate.

détermination (detɛrminasjɔ̃) *f,* determination; resolution; resolve. **déterminé, e** (ne) *a,* determinate, definite; determined, resolute; keen; specific. **déterminer** (ne) *v.t,* to determine; fix; decide (upon); resolve; bring about. se ~, to resolve, make up one's mind.

déterrer (detɛre) *v.t,* to unearth, dug up; disinter, exhume.

détestable (detɛstabl) *a,* detestable. **détester** (te) *v.t,* to detest, hate.

détonation (detɔnasjɔ̃) *f,* detonation, report. **détoner** (ne) *v.i,* to detonate.

détonner (detɔne) *v.i,* to be (*or* sing) (*or* play) out of tune; sing flat; jar; be out of keeping; be out of one's element.

détordre (detɔrdr) *v.t,* to untwist. **détors, e** (tɔ:r, ɔrs) *a,* untwisted. **détortiller** (tɔrtije) *v.t,* to untwist; disentangle.

détour (detu:r) *m,* winding; turn[ing]; detour; dodge. *sans ~,* straightforwardly. **détourné, e** (turne) *a,* by (*road*); roundabout, circuitous, devious. **dé-**

tourner (ne) *v.t*, to divert, deflect, distract, turn aside, avert; deter; twist; dissuade; make away with, misappropriate, misapply, embezzle, peculate; abduct. **détournement** (nəmɑ̃) *m*, diversion, etc.

détracteur (detraktœːr) *m*, detractor.

détraquer (detrake) *v.t*, to derange.

détrempe (detrɑ̃ːp) *f*, distemper (*paint*); softening (*steel*). **peindre à la ~**, to distemper. **détremper** (trɑ̃pe) *v.t*, to soak, sodden, dilute; soften.

détresse (detrɛs) *f*, distress; straits.

détriment (detrimɑ̃) *m*, detriment, prejudice.

détritus (detrityːs) *m*, detritus; litter, rubbish.

détroit (detrwa) *m*, strait, straits, sound. *le ~ de Gibraltar, du Pas de Calais*, the Straits of Gibraltar, of Dover.

détromper (detrɔ̃pe) *v.t*, to undeceive.

détrôner (detrone) *v.t*, to dethrone.

détrousser (detruse) *v.t*, to rob. **détrousseur** (sœːr) *m*, footpad.

détruire (detrɥiːr) *v.t. & abs. ir*, to demolish; destroy; ruin.

dette (dɛt) *f*, debt; indebtedness. **~** [*active*], assets. **~** [*passive*], liabilities.

deuil (dœːj) *m*, mourning; bereavement; mourners. *conduire le ~*, to be chief mourner. **~ de veuve**, widow's weeds.

Deutéronome (døterɔnɔm) *m*, Deuteronomy.

deux (dø; *in liaison* døz) *a*, two; second; a (*word, line*); a few (*steps*). *tous les ~ jours*, every other day. **~ jumeaux, elles**, twins. ¶*m*, two; deuce (*cards, dice*). **deuxième**† (døzjɛm) *a. & n*, second. **~ de change**, *f*, second of exchange.

deux-points (døpwɛ̃) *m*, colon.

dévaler (devale) *v.i. & t*, to go down.

dévaliser (devalize) *v.t*, to rifle, strip, rob.

dévaluation (devalɥasjɔ̃) *f*, devaluation.

devancer (dəvɑ̃se) *v.t*, to get the start of; precede; forestall; outstrip, outdo, outrival. **devancier, ère** (sje, ɛːr) *n*, predecessor.

devant (dəvɑ̃) *ad*, before, in front, ahead. ¶*pr*, before, in front of, ahead of. *aller au~ de*, to go to meet; anticipate. *par~*, *ad. & pr*, in front, before, in the presence of. ¶*m*, front; fore; frontage; (*pl.*) foreground.

devanture (d[ə]vɑ̃tyːr) *f*, front (*store, etc.*); window (*store*).

dévastateur, trice (devastatœːr, tris) *n*, devastator. **dévastation** (sjɔ̃) *f*, devastation. **dévaster** (te) *v.t*, to devastate.

déveine (devɛn) *f*, bad luck.

développateur (devlɔpatœːr) *m*, developer (*proper*) (*Phot.*). **développement** (pmɑ̃) *m*, opening out; spread; growth; development; evolution (*Geom.*); gear (*bicycle*). **développer** (pe) *v.t*, to open out; unwrap; develop.

devenir (dəvniːr) *v.i.ir*, to become; grow; wax; go; get.

dévergondage (devɛrgɔ̃daːʒ) *m*, licentiousness; extravagance (*fig.*). **dévergondé, e** (de) *a. & n*, licentious, shameless, profligate (person).

déverrouiller (devɛruje) *v.t*, to unbolt.

devers (dəvɛːr) *par~*, *pr*, by, before.

dévers, e (devɛːr, ɛrs) *a*, out of plumb, out of true. ¶*m*, cant. **déverser** (vɛrse) *v.t*, to warp; incline; discharge; pour. **déversoir** (swaːr) *m*, weir.

dévêtir (se) (devɛtiːr) *v.pr.ir*, to strip, undress; leave off some of one's (*warm*) clothes.

déviation (devjasjɔ̃) *f*, deviation; deflection. **~ de la colonne vertébrale**, curvature of the spine.

dévider (devide) *v.t*, to wind, reel; unwind. **dévidoir** (dwaːr) *m*, reel, spool.

dévier (devje) *v.i*, to deviate, swerve; curve (*spine*); (*v.t.*) to deflect, curve.

devin, ineresse (dəvɛ̃, vinrɛs) *n*, diviner, soothsayer. **deviner** (vine) *v.t, & abs*, to divine;

guess. **devinette** (nɛt) *f*, riddle, conundrum.

devis (dəvi) *m*, chat, talk; estimate; specification; manifest (*stowage*).

dévisager (devizaʒe) *v.t*, to stare at.

devise (dəvi:z) *f*, device; motto. ~ [*étrangère*], [foreign] currency, [f.] bill, [f.] exchange. ~ *publicitaire*, slogan.

deviser (dəvize) *v.i*, to chat.

dévisser (devise) *v.t*, to unscrew.

dévoiement (devwamɑ̃) *m*, looseness (*bowels*).

dévoiler (devwale) *v.t*, to unveil; reveal, disclose.

devoir (dəvwa:r) *m*, duty; exercise; (*pl.*) homework; (*pl.*) respects. ¶ *v.t. & abs. ir*, to owe. *Followed by infinitive*: should, ought; must, have to; am to.

dévolu, e (devɔly) *a*, devolved, vested.

dévorant, e (devɔrɑ̃, ɑ̃:t) *a*, ravenous; consuming; wasting; devouring. **dévorer** (re) *v.t*, to devour, lap up; swallow; stifle.

dévot, e† (devo, ɔt) *a*, devout, devotional; religious; sanctimonious. ¶ *n*, devout person; devotee. **dévotion** (vosjɔ̃) *f*, devotion, devoutness.

dévouement (devumɑ̃) *m*, devotion, self-sacrifice. **dévouer** (vwe) *v.t*, to dedicate; devote.

dévoyer (se) (devwaje) *v.pr.* (*Conjugated like envoyer, except Future* je dévoierai), to go astray (*fig.*).

dextérité (dɛksterite) *f*, dexterity, skill.

dextrine (dɛkstrin) *f*, dextrin.

diabète (djabɛt) *m*, diabetes.

diable (djɑ:bl) *m*, devil, deuce; dolly, truck. ¶ *i*, the devil! the deuce! the dickens! **diablerie** (djɑbləri) *f*, devilry, devilment. **diablesse** (blɛs) *f*, she-devil. **diablotin** (blɔtɛ̃) *m*, little devil, imp. **diabolique†** (bolik) *a*, diabolic(al), devilish, fiendish.

diacre (djakr) *m*, deacon.

diacritique (djakritik) *a*, diacritical.

diadème (djadɛm) *m*, diadem.

diagnostic (djagnɔstik) *m*, diag-

nosis. **diagnostiquer** (ke) *v.t*, to diagnose.

diagonal, e† (djagɔnal) *a. & f*, diagonal.

diagramme (djagram) *m*, diagram, chart.

dialecte (djalɛkt) *m*, dialect.

dialectique (djalɛktik) *f*, dialectics.

dialogue (djalɔg) *m*, dialogue. **dialoguer** (ge) *v.i*, to converse; write in dialogue.

diamant (djamɑ̃) *m*, diamond.

diamétral, e† (djametral) *a*, diametric. **diamètre** (mɛtr) *m*, diameter.

diane (djan) *f*, reveille (*Mil.*).

diantre (djɑ̃:tr) *m*, the deuce.

diapason (djapazɔ̃) *m*, diapason, pitch; compass, range. ~ *à bouche*, pitch pipe. ~ *à branches*, tuning fork. ~ *normal*, concert pitch.

diaphane (djafan) *a*, diaphanous.

diaphragme (djafragm) *m*, diaphragm; stop.

diaprer (djapre) *v.t*, to diaper, variegate. *étoffe diaprée*, diaper.

diarrhée (djare) *f*, diarrhea.

diatonique (djatɔnik) *a*, diatonic.

diatribe (djatrib) *f*, diatribe.

dictateur (diktatœ:r) *m*, dictator. **dictatorial, e** (tɔrjal) *a*, dictatorial. **dictature** (ty:r) *f*, dictatorship.

dictée (dikte) *f*, dictation. **dicter** (te) *v.t. & abs*, to dictate. **diction** (sjɔ̃) *f*, diction, delivery. **dictionnaire** (ɔnɛ:r) *m*, dictionary. ~ *géographique*, gazetteer. **dicton** (tɔ̃) *m*, saying, dictum; saw, byword.

didactique (didaktik) *a*, didactic.

dièse (djɛ:z) *m*, sharp (*Mus.*).

diète (djɛt) *f*, diet. ~ *absolue*, starvation d. **mettre à la** ~, *v.t*, **faire** ~, *v.i*, to diet.

Dieu (djø) *m*, God; goodness! **d~**, god.

diffamation (difamasjɔ̃) *f*, defamation, libel, slander. **diffamatoire** (twa:r) & **diffamant, e** (mɑ̃, ɑ̃:t) *a*, defamatory, etc. **diffamer** (me) *v.t*, to defame, malign.

différemment (diferamã) *ad*, differently. **différence** (rã:s) *f*, difference; odds. **différencier** (rãsje) *v.t*, to differentiate. **différend** (rã) *m*, difference, dispute. **différent, e** (rã, ã:t) *a*, different, various. **différentiel, le** (rãsjɛl) *a. & m*, differential. **différer** (re) *v.t. & abs*, to defer, delay, put off, postpone, hold over, tarry; (*v.i.*) to differ; be at variance.

difficile (difisil) *a*, difficult, hard; fastidious; trying. **difficilement** (lmã) *ad*, with difficulty. **difficulté** (kylte) *f*, difficulty; tiff. **difficultueux, euse** (tчø, ø:z) *a*, troublesome; fussy.

difforme (diform) *a*, deformed, misshapen, unshapely. **difformité** (mite) *f*, deformity.

diffus, e (dify, y:z) *a*, diffused; diffuse; long-winded, wordy. **diffuser** (fyze) *v.t*, to diffuse; broadcast. **diffusion** (zjõ) *f*, diffusion; broadcasting; long-windedness, wordiness.

digérer (diʒere) *v.t. & abs*, to digest; brook, stomach. *je ne digère pas la viande*, meat does not agree with me. **digestible** (ʒɛstibl) *a*, digestible. **digestif, ive** (tif, i:v) *a. & m*, digestive. **digestion** (tjõ) *f*, digestion. **digital, e** (diʒital) *a*, digital, finger (*att.*). ¶ *f*, foxglove; digitalis (*Phar.*).

digne (diɲ) *a*, worthy; deserving; dignified. **dignement** (ɲmã) *ad*, worthily, with dignity; adequately. **dignitaire** (ɲitɛ:r) *m*, dignitary. **dignité** (te) *f*, dignity; rank.

digression (digrɛsjõ) *f*, digression.

digue (dig) *f*, dike, dam; sea wall; barrier (*fig.*).

dilapider (dilapide) *v.t*, to squander; misappropriate.

dilater (dilate) *v.t*, to dilate; expand; swell.

dilemme (dilɛm) *m*, dilemma.

dilettante (dilɛttã:t) *m*, dilettante, amateur.

diligemment (diliʒamã) *ad*, diligently. **diligence** (ʒã:s) *f*, diligence; industry; despatch; proceedings, suit (*law*); stage

coach. **diligent, e** (ʒã, ã:t), *a*, diligent; industrious; expeditious.

diluer (dilЧe) *v.t*, to dilute; water (*stock, Fin.*).

diluvien, ne (dilyvjɛ̃, ɛn) *a*, diluvial; torrential (*rain*).

dimanche (dimã:ʃ) *m*, Sunday, sabbath. ~ *des Rameaux*, Palm Sunday.

dime (di:m) *f*, tithe.

dimension (dimãsjõ) *f*, dimension, size, measurement.

diminuer (diminЧe) *v.t. & i*, to diminish, decrease, reduce, abate, lower; taper; get thin. *aller en diminuant*, to taper. *entièrement diminué*, fully fashioned (*stocking*). **diminutif, ive** (nytif, i:v) *a*, diminutive (*Gram.*). ¶ *m*, diminutive (*Gram.*); miniature. **diminution** (sjõ) *f*, diminution, etc., as *diminuer*.

dinanderie (dinã:dri) *f*, brasswares; kitchen utensils. **dinandier** (dje) *m*, brazier.

dinatoire (dinatwa:r) *a*, substantial (*lunch*).

dinde (dɛ:d) *f*, turkey [hen]; goose (*fig.*). **dindon** (dɛ̃dõ) *m*, turkey [cock]; goose (*fig.*); dupe. **dindonneau** (dɔno) *m*, turkey poult.

diner (dine) *m*, dinner. ¶ *v.i*, to dine. **dinette** (nɛt) *f*, little dinner; doll's dinner party. **dîneur, euse** (nœ:r, ø:z) *n*, diner.

diocésain, e (djosezɛ̃, ɛn) *a*, diocesan. **diocèse** (sɛ:z) *m*, diocese.

dioptrie (diɔptri) *f*, diopter.

diphtérie (difteri) *f*, diphtheria.

diphtongue (diftõ:g) *f*, diphthong.

diplomate (diplomat) *m*, diplomat[ist]; (*att.*) diplomatic. **diplomatie** (si) *f*, diplomacy. **diplomatique** (tik) *a*, diplomatic. **diplôme** (plo:m) *m*, diploma, certificate. **diplômé, e** (plome) *a. & n*, certified (teacher, etc.).

dire (di:r) *m*, saying, assertion; allegation. ¶ *v.t.ir*, to say; tell; speak; bid (*adieu, etc.*); mean. ~ *son fait à quelqu'un*, to give someone a piece of one's mind. *dites donc!* look here!

direct, e (dirɛkt) *a*, direct; straight; through (*Rly.*); flat (*contradiction*). *un direct du* *droit, du gauche,* a straight right, left (*Box.*). **directement** (təmɑ̃) *ad,* directly, direct; straight; due; through.

directeur, trice (dirɛktœːr, tris) *n,* manager, ess; principal, headmaster, headmistress; editor; director; warden; leader. [*arbitre*] *directeur de combat,* referee (*Box.*). *directeur de conscience,* spiritual director. *directeur général des postes, télégraphes & téléphones,* postmaster general. **direction** (sjɔ̃) *f,* direction; strike (*lode*); way; management; manager's office; guidance; lead[ership]; mastership; steering. **Directoire** (twaːr) *m,* Directory; Directoire. **dirigeable** (riʒabl) *a,* dirigible. ¶ *m,* airship, dirigible. **diriger** (ʒe) *v.t,* to direct; manage; steer; train (*gun*). se ~, to make, steer (*vers =* for).

discernement (disɛrnəmɑ̃) *m,* discrimination; discernment. **discerner** (ne) *v.t,* to discern; distinguish; discriminate.

disciple (disipl) *m,* disciple, follower. **disciplinaire** (plinɛːr) *a,* disciplinary. ¶ *m,* disciplinarian. **discipline** (plin) *f,* discipline. **discipliner** (ne) *v.t,* to discipline.

discontinuer (diskɔ̃tinɥe) *v.t,* to discontinue.

disconvenance (diskɔ̃vnɑ̃ːs) *f,* dissimilarity, disparity. **disconvenir** (vniːr) *v.i.ir,* to deny. ~ *de,* to gainsay.

discordance (diskɔrdɑ̃ːs) *f,* discordance, disagreement; lack of harmony, difference. **discorde** (kɔrd) *f,* discord, strife, contention.

discourir (diskuriːr) *v.i. & abs. ir,* to discourse, descant. **discours** (kuːr) *m,* talk; discourse, speech, oration, address. ~ *d'apparat,* set speech.

discourtois, e (diskurtwa, aːz) *a,* discourteous. **discourtoisie** (twazi) *f,* discourtesy.

discrédit (diskredi) *m,* discredit, disrepute. **discréditer** (te) *v.t,* to discredit.

discret, ète† (diskrɛ, ɛt) *a,* discreet; unobtrusive; unpretentious; discrete. **discrétion** (kres-

jɔ̃) *f,* discretion; secrecy. *à* ~, as much as you want.

discrimination (diskriminasjɔ̃) *f,* discrimination.

disculper (diskylpe) *v.t,* to exculpate.

discursif, ive (diskyrsif, iːv) *a,* discursive. **discussion** (kysjɔ̃) *f,* discussion; debate; question, dispute. **discutable** (tabl) *a,* debatable, arguable, moot. **discuter** (te) *v.t. & abs. & v.i,* to discuss, debate, argue; controvert; auction off to pay debts.

disert, e (dizeːr, ɛrt) *a,* fluent.

disette (dizɛt) *f,* dearth, scarcity. ~ *d'argent,* penury. ~ *d'eau,* drought.

diseur, euse (dizœːr, øːz) *n,* talker. ~ *de bonne aventure,* fortune teller. ~ *de bons mots,* wit. ~ *de chansonnettes,* entertainer, humorist (*at concert*).

disgrâce (disgrɑːs) *f,* disgrace, disfavor; misfortune. **disgracier** (grasje) *v.t,* to dismiss from favor, disgrace. **disgracieux, euse** (sjø, øːz) *a,* uncouth, ungraceful.

disjoindre (disʒwɛ̃ːdr) *v.t.ir,* to disjoin.

disjoncteur (dizʒɔ̃ktœːr) *m,* switch, circuit-breaker.

disloquer (dislɔke) *v.t,* to dislocate, put out of joint; dismember; break up; dislodge. **dislocation** (kasjɔ̃) *f,* dislocation; breakaway.

dispache (dispaʃ) *f,* average adjustment (*Insce.*).

disparaître (disparɛːtr) *v.i.ir,* to disappear, vanish.

disparate (disparat) *a,* disparate, ill-assorted. ¶ *f,* incongruity. **disparité** (rite) *f,* disparity.

disparition (disparisjɔ̃) *f,* disappearance. **les disparus** (ry) *m.pl,* the missing (*soldiers*).

dispendieux, euse (dispɑ̃djø, øːz) *a,* expensive, costly.

dispensaire (dispɑ̃sɛːr) *m,* dispensary. **dispensateur, trice** (satœːr, tris) *n,* dispenser. **dispense** (pɑ̃ːs) *f,* dispensation; exemption. ~ *de bans,* marriage license. **dispenser** (pɑ̃se) *v.t,* to dispense, exempt, excuse, spare.

disperser (dispɛrse) *v.t,* to disperse, scatter. *ordre dispersé*, extended order (*Mil.*). **dispersion** (sjɔ̃) *f*, dispersion, dispersal.

disponibilité (disponibilite) *f*, availability; (*pl.*) available funds, liquid assets. **en ~**, unattached (*Mil.*). **disponible** (bl) *a*, available, spare, disposable; liquid; on hand; unattached; in print.

dispos, e (dispo, o:z) *a*, fit, well, hearty; good (*humor*). **disposer** (poze) *v.t*, to dispose; arrange; lay out; incline; provide; draw (*bill*). **dispositif** (pozitif) *m*, purview (*law*); device, arrangement, contrivance, gear. **~ à 3 vitesses**, 3-speed gear. **~ de fortune, ~ de circonstance**, makeshift. **~s de mines**, preparatory work (*Min.*). **disposition** (sjɔ̃) *f*, disposition, ordering, arrangement; lie; layout; tendency; tone; frame of mind; state; humor; aptitude, flair; disposal; provision (*of a law*); dispensation (*of Providence*); draft (*Fin.*).

disproportion (disprɔpɔrsjɔ̃) *f*, disproportion. **disproportionné, e** (ɔne) *a*, disproportionate.

disputailler (dispytaje) *v.i*, to wrangle, bicker. **dispute** (pyt) *f*, dispute; contest; contention. **disputer** (te) *v.i. & t*, to dispute; contend; vie; contest. **se ~**, to wrangle.

disqualifier (diskalifje) *v.t*, to disqualify (*sport*).

disque (disk) *m*, disk, disc; discus; wheel. **~ de phonographe**, phonograph record.

dissection (disɛksjɔ̃) *f*, dissection.

dissemblable (disɑ̃blabl) *a*, dissimilar. **dissemblance** (blɑ̃:s) *f*, dissimilarity.

disséminer (disemine) *v.t*, to disseminate; scatter.

dissension (disɑ̃sjɔ̃) *f*, dissension.

dissentiment (disɑ̃timɑ̃) *m*, dissent, disagreement.

disséquer (diseke) *v.t*, to dissect.

dissertation (disɛrtasjɔ̃) *f*, dissertation, disquisition, essay.

dissidence (disidɑ̃:s) *f*, dissidence, dissent. **dissident, e** (dɑ̃, ɑ̃:t) *a*, dissentient; dissenting. ¶ *n*, dissentient; dissenter.

dissimilaire (disimilɛ:r) *a*, dissimilar.

dissimulé, e (disimyle) *a*, secretive. **dissimuler** (le) *v.t. & abs*, to dissimulate; dissemble; conceal.

dissipateur, trice (disipatœ:r, tris) *n. & a*, spendthrift. **dissipation** (sjɔ̃) *f*, dissipation; extravagance. **dissiper** (pe) *v.t*, to dissipate; dispel; disperse, scatter; fritter away.

dissocier (disɔsje) *v.t*, to dissociate.

dissolu, e (disɔly) *a*, dissolute, profligate. **dissolution** (sjɔ̃) *f*, dissolution; solution; dissoluteness. **dissolvant, e** (vɑ̃, ɑ̃:t) *a. & m*, [dis]solvent.

dissonance (disɔnɑ̃:s) *f*, dissonance; discord. **dissonant, e** (nɑ̃, ɑ̃:t) *a*, dissonant, discordant.

dissoudre (disudr) *v.t.ir*, to dissolve.

dissuader (disɥade) *v.t*, to dissuade.

dissyllabe (disilab) *m*, disyllable.

dissymétrique (disimetrik) *a*, unsymmetrical.

distance (distɑ̃:s) *f*, distance; range; way [off]. *garder ses ~s* (*fig.*), to keep one's distance. **distancer** (tɑ̃se) *v.t*, to [out]distance. **distant, e** (tɑ̃, ɑ̃:t) *a*, distant; aloof.

distendre (distɑ̃:dr) *v.t*, to distend.

distillateur (distilatœ:r) *m*, distiller. **distillation** (sjɔ̃) *f*, distillation; distillate. **distiller** (le) *v.t*, to distil; exude. **distillerie** (lri) *f*, distillery.

distinct, e† (distɛ̃:kt) *a*, distinct; clear, plain. **distinctif, ive** (tɛktif, i:v) *a*, distinctive. **distinction** (sjɔ̃) *f*, distinction. **distingué, e** (tɛ̃ge) *a*, distinguished; refined; gentlemanly; ladylike. **distinguer** (ge) *v.t*, to distinguish; discriminate; make out; single out.

distique (distik) *m*, distich; couplet.

distorsion (distɔrsjɔ̃) *f*, distortion.

distraction (distraksjɔ̃) *f*, distraction; absence of mind; appropriation; severance; amusement, hobby. **distraire** (trɛ:r) *v.t.ir*, to distract; appropriate; set aside; take away, t. off; amuse. **distrait, e†** (trɛ, ɛt) *a*, absentminded; listless, vacant.

distribuer (distribɥe) *v.t*, to distribute, give out; deal out; issue; deliver (*letters*); arrange; cast (*actors' parts*). **distributeur, trice** (bytœ:r, tris) *n*, distributor; gasoline pump. *distributeur automatique*, automatic [delivery] machine, slot machine. **distribution** (sjɔ̃) *f*, distribution; issue; allotment; delivery (*post*); valve gear; arrangement, layout. ~ *de prix*, prize giving; speech day. ~ *des aumônes*, almsgiving. ~ [*des rôles*], cast[ing] (*Theat.*). ~ *par coulisse*, link motion.

district (distrikt) *m*, district, field.

dito (dito) (*abb.* dᵒ) *ad*, ditto, do.

diva (diva) *f*, prima donna, diva.

divagation (divagasjɔ̃) *f*, digression; wandering, rambling. **divaguer** (ge) *v.i*, to digress.

divan (divɑ̃) *m*, divan; settee.

divergence (divɛrʒɑ̃:s) *f*, divergence. **divergent, e** (ʒɑ̃, ɑ̃:t) *a*, divergent. **diverger** (ʒe) *v.i*, to diverge.

divers, e† (divɛ:r, ɛrs) *a*, different, diverse; sundry, miscellaneous; various, many. **diversifier** (vɛrsifje) *v.t*, to diversify, vary. **diversion** (sjɔ̃) *f*, diversion. **diversité** (site) *f*, diversity, variety, difference. **divertir** (ti:r) *v.t*, to divert; amuse, entertain. *se* ~ *aux dépens de*, to make fun of, make merry over. **divertissement** (tismɑ̃) *m*, diversion; amusement, entertainment; divertissement.

divette (divɛt) *f*, variety actress.

dividende (dividɑ̃:d) *m*, dividend.

divin, e† (divɛ̃, in) *a*, divine; godlike. **divination** (vinasjɔ̃) *f*, divination. **diviniser** (nize) *v.t*, to deify. **divinité** (te) *f*, divinity, godhead; deity.

diviser (divize) *v.t*, to divide; part. **diviseur** (zœ:r) *m*, divisor.

division (zjɔ̃) *f*, division; department; hyphen (*end of line*).

divorce (divɔrs) *m*, divorce. **divorcer** (se) *v.i*, to be divorced. ~ *d'avec*, to divorce.

divulguer (divylge) *v.t*, to divulge, blab.

dix (*in liaison,* diz; *before consonant or* 'h,' di) *a*, ten. ¶ (dis) *m*, ten; 10th. **~-huit** (dizɥit; *bef. cons. or* 'h,' ɥi) *a. & m*, eighteen; 18th. **~-huitième** (tjɛm) *a. & n*, eighteenth. **dixième†** (dizjɛm) *a. & n*, tenth. **dix-neuf** (diznœf; *in liaison,* nœv; *bef. cons. or* 'h,' nœ) *a. & m*, nineteen; 19th. **dix-neuvième** (vjɛm) *a. & n*, nineteenth. **dix-sept** (dissɛt; *bef. cons. or* 'h,' sɛ) *a. & m*, seventeen; 17th. **dix-septième** (tjɛm) *a. & n*, seventeenth.

dizain (dizɛ̃) *m*, ten-line stanza. **dizaine** (zɛn) *f*, ten [or so], about ten; ten; decade.

do (do) (*Mus.*) *m*, C.

docile† (dosil) *a*, docile, amenable, ductile. **docilité** (lite) *f*, docility.

dock (dɔk) *m*, dock; dock warehouse, warehouse, store. ~ *frigorifique*, cold store. **docker** (kɛ:r) *m*, docker.

docte† (dɔkt) *a*, learned. **docteur** (tœ:r) *m*, doctor. **doctoral, e†** (toral) *a*, doctoral; pompous; grandiloquent. **doctorat** (ra) *m*, doctorate.

doctrinaire (doktrinɛ:r) *m. & a*, doctrinaire. **doctrine** (trin) *f*, doctrine, tenet.

document (dɔkymɑ̃) *m*, document. **documentaire** (tɛ:r) *a*, documentary. **documenter** (te) *v.t*, to document.

dodeliner (dɔdline) *v.t*, to rock, dandle. ~ *de*, to wag (*head*).

dodo (dɔdo) *m*, bye-bye; cot.

dodu, e (dɔdy) *a*, plump, rotund.

dogmatique† (dogmatik) *a*, dogmatic. **dogmatiser** (ze) *v.i*, to dogmatize. **dogme** (dɔgm) *m*, dogma; tenet.

dogue (dɔg) *m*, big yard dog; bear (*fig., pers.*).

doigt (dwa) *m*, finger; digit; thimbleful, nip (*liquor*). ~ [*de pied*], toe. *à deux* ~*s de*, within an ace of. **doigté** (dwate) *m*, fingering (*Mus.*); diplomacy, tact. **doigter** (te) *v.i. & t*, to finger (*Mus.*). **doigtier** (tje) *m*, fingerstall.

doit (dwa) *m*, debit [side], debtor [side].

dol (dɔl) *m*, wilful misrepresentation.

doléance (dɔleã:s) *f*, complaint, grievance. **dolent, e** (lã, ã:t) *a*, doleful; painful; out of sorts.

dollar (dɔla:r) *m*, dollar.

domaine (dɔmɛn) *m*, domain, demesne, estate; property; land; province.

dôme (do:m) *m*, dome, canopy.

domesticité (dɔmɛstisite) *f*, service; [staff of] servants, household; domesticity. **domestique** (tik) *a*, domestic, home. ¶ *n*, servant, domestic; man[servant]; maid[servant]. **domestiquer** (ke) *v.t*, to domesticate.

domicile (dɔmisil) *m*, residence, abode, house, premises, domicile. *franco à* ~, free delivery. **domicilier** (lje) *v.t*, to domicile.

dominant, e (dɔminã, ã:t) *a*, dominant, ruling; prevailing. ¶ *f*, dominant (*Mus.*). **dominateur, trice** (natœ:r, tris) *n*, ruler; (*att.*) ruling; domineering. **domination** (sjɔ̃) *f*, domination; dominion; rule, sway. ~ *de la lie du peuple*, mob law. **dominer** (ne) *v.i. & t*, to dominate; overlook; tower above; rule; domineer.

dominicain, e (dɔminikɛ̃, ɛn) *n*, Dominican.

dominical, e (dɔminikal) *a*, dominical; Sunday (*rest*); Lord's (*prayer*).

domino (dɔmino) *m*, domino.

dommage (dɔma:ʒ) *m*, damage, injury, loss; pity (*regret*). ~*s-intérêts*, damages (*law*).

dompter (dɔ̃te) *v.t*, to tame; break in; subdue. **dompteur, euse** (tœ:r, ø:z) *n*, tamer.

don (dɔ̃) *m*, bestowal; gift; present; donation; dower; knack. **donataire** (dɔnatɛ:r) *n*, donee. **donateur, trice** (tœ:r, tris) *n*, donor. **donation** (sjɔ̃) *f*, donation, gift.

donc (dɔ̃; *in liaison or emphatically*, dɔ̃:k) *c*, therefore, then, hence, so; to be sure.

dondon (dɔ̃dɔ̃) *f*, bouncing girl; plump woman.

donjon (dɔ̃ʒɔ̃) *m*, keep (*castle*).

donnant, e (dɔnã, ã:t) *a*, generous. **donnant donnant**, *ad*, give & take, tit for tat. **donne** (dɔn) *f*, deal (*cards*). **donnée** (ne) *f*, datum; fundamental idea, motif. **donner** (ne) *v.t*, to give, bestow; impart, afford; tender; make; let; yield, give up; show; teach (*someone a lesson*); set (*task*); perform (*play*); deal (*cards*); (*v.i.*) to strike, hit; fall; run; sag. ~ *sur*, to face, front, look on, give on, overlook (*street, etc.*). **donneur, euse** (nœ:r, ø:z) *n*, giver; donor; dealer (*cards*). ~ *d'ordre*, principal.

Don Quichotte (dɔ̃kiʃɔt) *m*, Quixote, champion (*of lost causes*).

dont (dɔ̃) *pn*, whose; of whom; of *or* from *or* by whom *or* which; whereof; as per.

donzelle (dɔ̃zɛl) *f*, wench.

dorade (dɔrad) *f*, dorado, dolphin; goldfish. **doré, e** (re) *a*, gilt, gilded; golden. ~ *sur tranche*, gilt-edged. **dorée**, *f*, [John] dory.

dorénavant (dɔrenavã) *ad*, henceforth.

dorer (dɔre) *v.t*, to gild; block (*Bookb.*); glaze (*pastry*). **doreur, euse** (rœ:r, ø:z) *n*, gilder; blocker.

dorique (dɔrik) *a. & m*, Doric.

dorloter (dɔrlɔte) *v.t*, to coddle; pamper.

dormant, e (dɔrmã, ã:t) *a*, sleeping, dormant, still, standing, stagnant. ¶ *m*, casing, frame. **dormeur, euse** (mœ:r, ø:z) *n*, sleeper. ¶ *f*, lounge chair; stud earring; sleeping suit. **dormir** (mi:r) *v.i.ir*, to sleep, be asleep; lie dormant. **dormitif** (mitif) *m*, sleeping draft.

dorsal, e (dɔrsal) *a*, dorsal.

dortoir (dɔrtwa:r) *m*, dormitory.

dorure (dɔry:r) *f*, gilding; blocking (*Bookb.*); gilt; glazing (*pastry*).

dos (do) *m*, back; back, spine (*book*); bridge (*nose*). *en* ~ *d'âne*, hogbacked.

dose (do:z) *f*, dose, measure.

doser (doze) *v.t*, to proportion, measure out, dose.

dossier (dosje) *m*, back; bundle (*papers*); dossier; brief (*law*); record.

dot (dɔt) *f*, dowry, dower, [marriage] portion. **dotal,** e (tal) *a*, dowral, dotal. **dotation** (sjɔ̃) *f*, endowment. **doter** (te) *v.t*, to dower, portion; endow.

douairière (dwɛrjɛːr) *f*, dowager.

douane (dwan) *f*, customs; custom house. **douanier,** ère (nje, ɛːr) *a*, customs (*att*.). ¶ *m*, customs officer.

doublage (dublaːʒ) *m*, doubling; lining; sheathing (*ship*). **double** (bl) *a*, double; twofold; dual; double-dealing. ~ *croche,* *f*, semiquaver. ~ *emploi, m,* duplication. *à* ~ *face,* double-faced. ~ *fond, m,* false bottom. ¶ *ad*, double; in duplicate. ¶ *m*, double; duplicate, counterpart. ~ *messieurs, dames, mixte,* men's, women's, mixed, doubles (*Ten.*). **doublement** (bləmɑ̃) *ad*, doubly. ¶ *m*, doubling. **doubler** (ble) *v.t*, to double; understudy; overtake; line; sheathe; weather (*cape*); dub (*movies*); (*v.i.*) to double. *non doublé, e,* unlined. *doublé or,* rolled gold. **doublure** (blyːr) *f*, lining; understudy.

douceâtre (dusɑːtr) *a*, sweetish. **doucement** (smɑ̃) *ad*, gently; softly; sweetly; slowly; gingerly; quietly; peacefully; smoothly, easily; so-so; pretty well. **douceureux, euse** (srø, øːz) *a*, mawkish, sickly; mealy-mouthed, smooth-tongued. **douceur** (sœːr) *f*, sweetness; softness; gentleness; mildness; meekness; pleasure; (*pl.*) dainties, sweets; soft nothings.

douche (duʃ) *f*, shower (*bath*); douche. **doucher** (ʃe) *v.t*, to shower; douche.

doucine (dusin) *f*, ogee.

douer (dwe) *v.t*, to endow, endue, gift.

douille (duːj) *f*, socket, holder; case (*cartridge*).

douillet, te† (dujɛ, ɛt) *a*, soft, downy; cosy.

douleur (dulœːr) *f*, pain, ache;

throe; sorrow, grief, woe. **douloureux, euse†** (lurø, øːz) *a*, painful; sore; mournful, grievous, sad.

doute (dut) *m*, doubt, misgiving. **douter** (te) *v.i. & abs*, to doubt, question. ~ *de,* to doubt, question (*v.t.*). *se* ~ *de,* to suspect. **douteux, euse†** (tø, øːz) *a*, doubtful, dubious, questionable.

douve (duːv) *f*, stave (*cask*); ditch (*Agric.*); moat (*castle*); water jump (*turf*); water hazard (*golf*).

Douvres (duːvr) *m*, Dover.

doux, ouce (du, us) *a*, sweet; soft; dulcet; gentle; mild; meek; quiet (*horse*); smooth; easy; pleasant; fresh (*water*). **le doux,** the sweet (*opp.* the bitter).

douzaine (duzɛn) *f*, dozen. **douze** (duːz) *a. & m*, twelve; 12th. **douzième†** (duzjɛm) *a. & n*, twelfth.

doyen, ne (dwajɛ̃, ɛn) *n*, dean; doyen; senior. **doyenné** (jɛne) *m*, deanery.

drachme (drakm) *f*, drachma.

dragage (dragaːʒ) *m*, dredging; dragging; sweeping (*for mines*).

dragée (draʒe) *f*, sugar almond; pill; birdshot.

drageon (draʒɔ̃) *m*, sucker (*Bot., Hort.*).

dragon (dragɔ̃) *m*, dragon; dragoon; termagant, virago.

drague (drag) *f*, dredge[r]; drag; d. net; grains, draff. **draguer** (ge) *v.t*, to dredge, drag, sweep. **dragueur** (gœːr) *m*, dredger (*pers. & boat*). ~ *de mines,* mine sweeper.

drain (drɛ̃) *m*, drain; d. pipe. **drainage** (drɛnaːʒ) *m*, drainage; drain (*demand*). **drainer** (ne) *v.t*, to drain.

dramatique† (dramatik) *a*, dramatic; operatic. **dramatiser** (ze) *v.t*, to dramatize. **dramatiste** (tist) *m*, **dramaturge** (tyrʒ) *n*, dramatist, playwright, dramaturge. **drame** (dram) *m*, drama; tragedy, sensational affair. ~ *pleureur,* sob-stuff.

drap (dra) *m*, cloth; sheet; pickle (*fig.*). ~ *mortuaire,* pall. ~ *vert,* green baize. **drapeau** (po) *m*, flag, colors. **draper** (pe) *v.t*, to drape;

pillory (*fig.*). **draperie** (pri) *f*, drapery; cloth trade; bunting. **drapier** (pje) *m*, draper, clothier, cloth merchant; cloth manufacturer.

drastique (drastik) *a*, drastic.

drawback (drobak) *m*, drawback (*Cust.*).

drêche (drɛːʃ) *f*, grains, draff.

drelin-drelin (drəlɛ̃) tinkle! tinkle!

drenne (drɛn) *f*, missel thrush.

Dresde (drɛzd) *f*, Dresden.

dresser (drɛse) *v.t*, to erect, raise, set up, rear; prick up (*ears*); pitch (*tent*); set (*trap*); draw up, make out, prepare; make (*bed*, etc.); lay (*table*); trim; dish up; true, straighten, dress, face; train; drill; break in. **dresseur** (sœːr) *m*, trainer (*animals*). **dressoir** (swaːr) *m*, sideboard.

drille (driːj) *m*, fellow. ¶ *f*, drill, brace; (*pl.*) rags (*for paper-making*).

drisse (dris) *f*, halyard.

drogman (drɔgmɑ̃) *m*, dragoman.

drogue (drɔg) *f*, drug; nostrum; trash; worthless person. **droguer** (ge) *v.t*, to physic; drug; (*v.i.*) to wait, cool one's heels. **droguerie** (gri) *f*, druggist's business; drugstore.

droguet (drɔgɛ) *m*, drugget.

droguiste (drɔgist) *m*, druggist (*wholesale*); drysalter.

droit, e (drwa, at) *a*, straight; upright, erect, plumb; straightforward, honest; right, right-hand[ed]; single-breasted. **droit**, *ad*, straight; s. on; due (*south, etc.*) **droit**, *m*, right; due, duty, fee; law; reason. ~*s d'adaptation au cinématographe*, film rights. ~ *d'aînesse*, ~ *du sang*, birthright. ~ *d'auteur*, copyright; royalty. ~ *de cité*, citizenship. ~*s de reproduction dans les journaux & périodiques*, serial rights. ~ *de rétention*, lien. ~*s de succession*, inheritance taxes. ~ *de vendre*, license to sell. *de* ~, de jure. **droite**, *f*, right hand, r. side; right. *à* ~, on (*or* to) the right. **droitement** (tmɑ̃) *ad*, uprightly, righteously. **droitier, ère** (tje, ɛːr) *n*, right-handed per-

son *or* player. **droiture** (tyːr) *f*, uprightness, straightforwardness, rectitude.

drolatique (drɔlatik) *a*, comic, humorous. **drôle†** (droːl) *a*, funny, humorous, droll; queer, odd. *un* ~ *de corps*, a queer fellow, an oddity. ¶ *m*, funny (*queer*) man; rascal. **drôlerie** (drôlri) *f*, drollery, fun. **drôlesse** (lɛs) *f*, hussy.

dromadaire (drɔmadɛːr) *m*, dromedary.

drome (drɔm) *f*, raft.

dru, e (dry) *a*, thick; sturdy. **dru**, *ad*, thick[ly].

druide (drɥid) *m*, Druid.

dryade (driad) *f*, dryad.

dû, due (dy) *p.p. & p.a*, due; owing; forward (*carriage*); proper. ¶ *m*, due (*right*).

duc (dyk) *m*, duke. **ducal, e** (kal) *a*, ducal. **duché** (ʃe) *m*, duchy; dukedom. **duchesse** (ʃɛs) *f*, duchess.

ductile (dyktil) *a*, ductile.

duègne (dɥɛɲ) *f*, duenna.

duel (dɥel) *m*, duel. **duelliste** (list) *m*, duellist.

dûment (dymɑ̃) *ad*, duly, properly.

dune (dyn) *f*, dune, sand hill, down.

dunette (dynɛt) *f*, poop; poop deck.

Dunkerque (dœ̃kɛrk) *m*, Dunkirk.

duo (dyo) *m*, duet.

duodécimal, e (dyɔdesimal) *a*, duodecimal.

dupe (dyp) *f*, dupe, gull. **duper** (pe) *v.t*, to dupe, gull, take in, fool. **duperie** (pri) *f*, dupery, trickery, take-in. **dupeur, euse** (pœːr, øːz) *n*, trick[st]er.

duplicata (dyplikata) *m*, duplicate.

duplicité (dyplisite) *f*, duplicity; double dealing.

duquel see **lequel**.

dur, e (dyːr) *a*, hard; tough; hardened, inured; dire; harsh; hard-boiled (*egg*).

durable (dyrabl) *a*, durable, lasting, abiding.

durant (dyrɑ̃) *pr*, during, for.

durcir (dyrsiːr) *v.t. & i. & se* ~,

to harden. **durcissement** (sismã) *m*, hardening.

dure (dy:r) *f*, bare ground.

durée (dyre) *f*, duration, length, life.

durement (dyrmã) *ad*, hard; harshly.

durer (dyre) *v.i. & abs*, to last; hang heavy (*time*); hold out, stand; live.

dureté (dyrte) *f*, hardness; toughness; harshness. ~ *d'oreille*, hardness of hearing.

durillon (dyrijõ) *m*, callus, hard skin.

duvet (dyvɛ) *m*, down; nap. **duveté**, e (vte) *a*, downy, fluffy.

dynamique (dinamik) *a*, dynamic. ¶ *f*, dynamics.

dynamite (dinamit) *f*, dynamite.

dynamo (dinamo) *f*, dynamo. ~-**électrique** (mɔ) *a*, dynamo-electric.

dynastie (dinasti) *f*, dynasty.

dysenterie (disãtri) *f*, dysentery.

dyspepsie (dispɛpsi) *f*, dyspepsia.

E

eau (o) *f*, water; rain. ~ *bénite de cour*, fair promises, empty words. ~ *de boudin* (odbudɛ̃), thin air, smoke (*fig*.). ~ *de cale*, bilge water. ~~*-de-vie* (odvi), brandy. ~ *dentifrice*, mouthwash. ~~*-forte*, aqua fortis; etching. ~ *minérale* [*artificielle*], mineral [water]. ~ *minérale* [*naturelle*], mineral w.; table w. *de la plus belle* ~, of the finest water (*gem*); of the deepest dye (*fig*.). *être en* ~, to be in a sweat. *faire* ~, to make water, leak. *faire de l'*~, to [take in] water.

eaux (o) *f.pl*, waters; water; fountains; watering place, spa; tide; wake (*ship*). *marcher dans les* ~ *de*, to follow in the wake of (*Naut. & fig*.). ~ *à marée*, tidal water. ~ *d'égout*, slops. ~~*vannes*, waste water; sewage [water]. ~ *vives*, spring tide.

ébahir (ebai:r) *v.t*, to dumbfound, amaze.

ébarber (ebarbe) *v.t*, to take the burr off; trim (*edges*); wipe (*joint*).

ébattre (s') (ebatr) *v.pr.ir*. ou **prendre ses ébats** (eba), to frolic, gambol; hop about.

ébaubi, e (ebobi) *a*, dumbfounded.

ébauche (ebo:ʃ) *f*, [rough] sketch, draft, outline. **ébaucher** (boʃe) *v.t*, to sketch [out], draft; rough out; rough down.

ébène (ebɛn) *f*, ebony. **ébénier** (benje) *m*, ebony [tree]. **ébéniste** (nist) *m*, cabinetmaker. **ébénisterie** (tri) *f*, cabinetmaking; cabinetwork.

éblouir (eblui:r) *v.t. & abs*, to dazzle, glare.

ébonite (ebɔnit) *f*, ebonite, vulcanite.

éborgner (ebɔrɲe) *v.t*, to blind in one eye; disbud; shut out view from.

ébouillanter (ebujãte) *v.t*, to plunge into boiling water; scald.

éboulement (ebulmã) *m*, falling in, caving in; fall, slip. **ébouler** (le) *v.i*, to fall in, cave in, slip. **éboulis** (li) *m*, fall (*earth*).

ébourgeonner (eburʒɔne) *v.t*, to disbud.

ébouriffer (eburife) *v.t*, to dishevel, ruffle, tousle; stagger.

ébouter (ebute) *v.t*, to cut off the end of.

ébrancher (ebrãʃe) *v.t*, to lop.

ébranlement (ebrãlmã) *m*, shaking; shock, concussion; tottering; jangle. **ébranler** (le) *v.t*, to shake; jangle. s'~, to shake, totter; move off.

ébraser (ebraze) *v.t*, to splay.

ébrécher (ebreʃe) *v.t*, to chip, jag; break (*jaw*); make a hole in (*fortune*).

ébriété (ebriete) *f*, drunkenness.

ébrouer (s') (ebrue) *v.pr*, to sneeze (*animals*); snort.

ébruiter (ebrɥite) *v.t*, to noise abroad.

ébullition (ebylisjõ) *f*, boiling, ebullition; turmoil; whirl.

écacher (ekaʃe) *v.t*, to crush; flatten.

écaille (eka:j) *f*, scale; flake; chip; shell. ~ [*de tortue*], tortoise shell. **écailler** (kaje) *v.t*, to scale; open (*oysters*). s'~, to

scale, flake; peel [off]. **écailler,
ère** (je, ε:r) *n*, oysterman,
-woman. **écailleux, euse** (jø, ø:z)
a, scaly, flaky.

écale (ekal) *f*, shell; pod. **écaler**
(le) *v.t*, to shell.

écarbouiller (ekarbuje) *v.t*, to
crush, squash.

écarlate (ekarlat) *f. & a*, scarlet.

écarquiller (ekarkije) *v.t*, to
open wide (*eyes*). ~ *les yeux*, to
stare.

écart (eka:r) *m*, variation, difference; error; digression; flight;
straddling; strain (*Vet.*). *faire
un* ~, to side-step; (*horse*) shy.
à l'~, aside, on one side; aloof.
à l' ~ *de*, at some distance from.
écarté, e (karte) *p.a*, out-of-the-
way, remote, secluded, lonely.
écarté, *m*, écarté (*cards*).

écarteler (ekartəle) *v.t*, to quarter.

écartement (ekartəmã) *m*,
spreading; distance apart; d. between; gauge (*Rly.*). ~ *des essieux*, wheelbase. **écarter** (te) *v.t*,
to separate, spread, open; turn
(*or* push) aside *or* out of the
way; avert, ward off; divert; discard (*cards*). **s'**~, to stand aside;
deviate; wander, stray, swerve.

Ecclésiaste (l') (εklezjast) *m*,
Ecclesiastes. **ecclésiastique†** (tik)
a, ecclesiastical, clerical. ¶ *m*,
ecclesiastic, clergyman, cleric.
l'E~, Ecclesiasticus.

écervelé, e (esεrvəle) *a*, giddy,
hare-brained. ¶ *n*, madcap.

échafaud (eʃafo) *m*, scaffold,
stage. **échafaudage** (da:ʒ) *m*,
scaffolding; structure, fabric
(*fig.*). **échafauder** (de) *v.i*, to
erect a scaffold; (*v.t.*) to build
up (*fig.*).

échalas (eʃalɑ) *m*, pole (*hop,
etc.*); prop, stick. **échalasser**
(se) *v.t*, to pole, prop.

échalier (eʃalje) *m*, stile; hurdle
fence.

échalote (eʃalɔt) *f*, shallot, escha-
lot.

échancrer (eʃãkre) *v.t*, to cut
away (*neck of garment*); notch,
indent. *col très échancré*, very
low neck. **échancrure** (kry:r) *f*,
(*neck*) opening; notch; indentation.

échange (eʃã:ʒ) *m*, exchange,
barter; interchange. *quelques*
~*s*, practice (*Ten.*). **échanger**
(ʃãʒe) *v.t*, to exchange; barter.

échanson (eʃãsɔ̃) *m*, cupbearer.

échantillon (eʃãtijɔ̃) *m*, sample; dimension, size, section; pattern (*of stuff, etc.*), specimen,
taste. **échantillonner** (jɔne) *v.t*,
to sample, cut off a pattern from;
gauge; tram (*tapestry work*).

échappatoire (eʃapatwa:r) *f*,
loophole; evasion. **échappé, e**
(pe) *n*, runaway. ~ *de prison*,
escaped prisoner. **échappée** (pe)
f, prank; snatch; spell; turning
space; headroom. ~ [*de vue*],
vista; glimpse, peep. **échappement** (pmã) *m*, exhaust, release
(*steam*); escape, leak (*gas, etc.*);
escapement (*Horol.*); turning
space, headroom. **échapper** (pe)
v.i. & abs, to escape, run away;
slip; (*v.t.*) to escape. *l'*~ *belle*,
to have a narrow escape. **s'**~, to
escape; leak; fly off; vanish; forget oneself.

écharde (eʃard) *f*, splinter,
prickle.

écharpe (eʃarp) *f*, scarf; stole;
sash; sling. *en* ~, scarfwise;
aslant; in a sling. **écharper** (pe)
v.t, to cut to pieces, hack; lynch.

échasse (eʃa:s) *f*, stilt; pole (*scaffold*). **échassier** (ʃasje) *m*, wader
(*bird*).

échauder (eʃode) *v.t*, to scald.
s'~, (*fig.*), to burn one's fingers.

échauffé, e (eʃofe) *n*, hothead
(*pers.*). **échauffement** (fmã)
m, heating; overheating. **échauffer** (fe) *v.t*, to heat; overheat;
warm; parboil (*fig.*); excite.
s'~, to get warm *or* heated *or*
overheated *or* excited. **échauffourée** (fure) *f*, affray, brush.

échéance (eʃeã:s) *f*, due date;
date [payable]; maturity; tenor,
term, currency; expiration. **le
cas échéant** (ʃeã), in that case,
should it so happen.

échec (eʃek) *m*, check, failure,
repulse; (*pl.*) chess; chessmen.
¶ *i*, check! ~ *& mat*, checkmate.
faire quelqu'un ~ *& mat*, to
checkmate someone.

échelle (eʃεl) *f*, ladder; scale.
~ *à coulisse*, extension ladder.

~ *de sauvetage,* fire escape. ~ *double,* [pair of] steps. ~ *mobile,* sliding scale. ~s *du Levant,* Levantine ports. *faire la courte* ~, to give a helping hand. **échelon** (ʃlɔ̃) *m,* rung, round; step, stepping stone (*fig.*); echelon (*Mil.*). **échelonner** (ʃlɔne) *v.t,* to spread; echelon.

écheniller (eʃnije) *v.t,* to clear of caterpillars.

écheveau (eʃvo) *m,* skein, hank.

échevelé, e (eʃəvle) *a,* disheveled (*hair*).

échine (eʃin) *f,* spine, backbone; chine. **échinée** (ne) *f,* chine (*Cook.*). **échiner** (ne) *v.t,* to break (*someone's*) back; belabor. *s'*~, to break one's back; slave.

échiquier (eʃikje) *m,* chessboard; intricacies.

écho (eko) *m,* echo; (*pl.*) news items (*in paper*). *faire* ~, to echo (*v.i.*). *se faire l'* ~ *de,* to echo (*v.t.*).

échoir (eʃwa:r) *v.i.ir,* to fall, devolve; fall due, mature; expire. *intérêts à* ~, accruing interest.

échoppe (eʃɔp) *f,* stall, booth.

échouer (eʃwe) *v.i. & t. & s'*~, to strand, ground, beach; fail; miscarry, fall through. *échoué à sec,* high & dry (*Naut.*).

échu, e (eʃy) *p.a,* due, outstanding, owing; matured.

éclabousser (eklabuse) *v.t,* to splash, [be]spatter. **éclaboussure** (sy:r) *f,* splash, spatter.

éclair (klɛ:r) *m,* flash [of light]; [flash of] lightning; flash; glint, gleam. ~ *au chocolat,* chocolate éclair. ~[s] *de chaleur,* heat lightning, summer l. ~ *diffus,* ~ *en nappes,* sheet l. ~ *ramifié,* forked l. **éclairage** (klɛra:ʒ) *m,* lighting, illumination; light. ~ *par projection,* flood lighting. **éclairant, e** (rɑ̃, ɑ̃:t) *a,* lighting.

éclaircie (eklɛrsi) *f,* break, opening, rift; bright interval (*Meteor.*); clearing, glade; thinning out. **éclaircir** (si:r) *v.t,* to clear, c. up; brighten; thin, t. out; elucidate, enlighten.

éclairé, e (eklɛre) *p.p,* enlightened. **éclairer** (re) *v.t. & abs,* to light [up], lighten, illuminate, illumine; throw light upon; clear up; enlighten; reconnoiter (*Mil.*); (*v.i.*) to shine; (*v.imp.*) to lighten (*emit lightning*). **éclaireur** (rœ:r) *m,* scout; boy scout. **éclaireuse** (rø:z) *f,* girl scout.

éclanche (eklɑ̃:ʃ) *f,* shoulder of mutton.

éclat (ekla) *m,* splinter; chip; fragment; burst, roar, shout; peal, clap; noise, scandal; shake (*timber*); brilliancy, radiancy, brightness; flash; glare; glamour. **éclatant, e** (tɑ̃, ɑ̃:t) *a,* bright, brilliant, shining; piercing, shrill; splendid; striking, glaring, signal. **éclatement** (tmɑ̃) *m,* bursting, explosion. **éclater** (te) *v.i,* to burst, explode, blow up; fly, split; splinter; break out; burst out; shine, flash.

éclectique (eklɛktik) *a,* eclectic. **éclectisme** (tism) *m,* eclecticism.

éclipse (eklips) *f,* eclipse. **éclipser** (se) *v.t,* to eclipse; outshine, overshadow. *s'*~, to become eclipsed; vanish. **écliptique** (tik) *a. & f,* ecliptic.

éclisse (eklis) *f,* split-wood; splint (*Surg.*); fish[plate] (*Rly.*). **éclisser** (se) *v.t,* to fish[plate].

éclopé, e (eklɔpe) *a,* footsore, lame, crippled.

éclore (eklɔ:r) *v.i.ir,* to hatch; open (*flower*); come to light. **éclosion** (klozjɔ̃) *f,* hatching; opening.

écluse (ekly:z) *f,* (*canal*) lock; lock gate; floodgate (*fig.*). **éclusée** (klyze) *f,* (*lock*) feed; locking, lockage. **écluser** (ze) *v.t,* to lock; shut off. **éclusier, ère** (zje, ɛ:r) *n,* lock keeper.

écœurer (ekœre) *v.t,* to sicken, nauseate.

école (ekɔl) *f,* school; college; drill, training; blunder. ~ *d'anormaux,* school for defective children. ~ *de peloton,* squad drill. ~ *maternelle,* nursery school. ~ *normale,* normal school, training college (*teachers*). ~ *pratique,* technical school. ~ *professionnelle,* training center (*trade*). **écolier, ère** (lje, ɛ:r) *n,* schoolboy, -girl, pupil, scholar; tyro.

éconduire (ekɔ̃dɥi:r) *v.t.ir,* to show out; put off (*with excuse*).

économat (ekɔnɔma) *m*, stewardship, bursarship; bursar's office;
store. **économe** (nɔm) *a*, economical, thrifty, sparing. ¶ *n*,
steward; bursar; housekeeper.
économie (mi) *f*, economy, thrift,
saving; management; arrange-
ment. ~ *de bouts de chandelle*,
cheeseparing. ~ *domestique*,
domestic economy, housekeeping. ~ *politique*, political economy. ~ *rurale*, husbandry. **économique**† (mik) *a*, economical;
economic. **économiser** (ze) *v.t.*
& *abs*, to economize, save. **économiste** (mist) *m*, economist.

écope (ekɔp) *f*, scoop, bailer.
écoper (pe) *v.t*, to bail (*or* bale)
[out]; (*v.i.*) to catch it (*suffer*).

écoperche (ekɔpɛrʃ) *f*, scaffold
pole.

écorce (ekɔrs) *f*, bark; peel, rind,
skin; crust (*earth's*); surface
(*fig.*). **écorcer** (se) *v.t*, to bark;
peel.

écorcher (ekɔrʃe) *v.t*, to flay,
skin; abrade, graze, scrape, gall,
chafe; grate on (*ears*); fleece
(*fig.*). **écorcheur, euse** (ʃœːr, øːz)
n, shark, extortioner; (*m.*)
knacker. **écorchure** (ʃyːr) *f*,
abrasion, gall, graze, scrape.

écorner (ekɔrne) *v.t*, to break off
a horn *or* corner; chip; dogear;
curtail.

écornifler (ekɔrnifle) *v.t*, to
cadge; sponge on.

écornure (ekɔrnyːr) *f*, chip.

écossais, e (ekɔsɛ, ɛːz) *a*,
Scotch, Scottish. **É~**, *n*, Scotch-
man, -woman, Scot. **l'Écosse**
(kɔs) *f*, Scotland, North Britain.

écosser (ekɔse) *v.t*, to shell, hull.

écot (eko) *m*, share; score; reckoning; lopped tree; stick, fagot.

écoulement (ekulmã) *m*, flow,
outflow; drainage; discharge;
gleet; passing; placing; sale.
écouler (le) *v.t*, to place, sell.
s'~, to flow out *or* away, run off;
disperse; pass (*or* slip) away,
elapse; sell.

écourter (ekurte) to cut short;
crop, dock; curtail.

écoute (ekut) *f*, sheet (*Naut.*);
listening post. **aux écoutes**, on
the watch *or* lookout. **écouter**
(te) *v.t.* & *abs*, to listen to, listen,

hearken; listen in; hear. ~ *aux
portes*, to eavesdrop. *s'~ trop*, to
coddle oneself. **écouteur, euse**
(tœːr, øːz) *n*, listener. ~ *aux
portes*, eavesdropper. ¶ *m*, receiver, earpiece (*Teleph.*). **écouteux** (tø) *a.m*, skittish (*horse*).

écoutille (ekutiːj) *f*, hatch[way].

écouvillon (ekuvijɔ̃) *m*, mop;
sponge (*gun*); swab (*Med.*).

écrabouiller (ekrabuje) *v.t*, to
crush, squash.

écran (ekrɑ̃) *m*, screen; filter
(*Phot.*); shade. ~ *à pied*, fire
screen. ~ *fumigène* (fymiʒɛn),
smoke screen.

écrasé, e (ekraze) *p.a*, squat.
écraser (ze) *v.t*, to crush; squash;
run over; overwhelm. *s'~*, to collapse, crumple up, crash.

écrémer (ekreme) *v.t*, to cream,
skim.

écrevisse (ekrəvis) *f*, crayfish,
crawfish (*river*).

écrier (s') (ekrie) *v.pr*, to exclaim, cry; c. out.

écrin (ekrɛ̃) *m*, case, jewel case,
casket. ~ *manucure*, manicure
set.

écrire (ekriːr) *v.t.* & *abs. ir*, to
write; spell. ~ *à la machine*, to
type. **écrit** (kri) *m*, writing; document. **écrit, e** (kri, it) *p.p*, written; w. on; statute (*law*). **écriteau** (to) *m*, bill, notice; n. board.
écriture (tyːr) *f*, writing; handwriting. ~ *à la machine*, typewriting, typing. ~ *de pattes de
mouche*, crabbed handwriting.
l'Écriture [*sainte*] ou *les* [*saintes*]
Écritures, [Holy] Scripture, the
Scriptures, Holy Writ. **écrivailler**
(vɑje) ou **écrivasser** (vase) *v.i*, to
scribble (*of author*). **écrivailleur,
euse** (vɑjœːr, øːz) ou **écrivassier,
ère** (vasje, ɛːr) *n*, scribbler, hack,
penny-a-liner. **écrivain** (vɛ̃) *m*,
writer, author.

écrou (ekru) *m*, nut; entry (*in
prison register*). ~ *à huit pans*,
octagonal nut. ~ *à oreilles*, ~
papillon, wing n. ~ *à six pans*,
hexagonal n. **écrouer** (krue) *v.t*,
to enter (*in prison register*).

écroulement (ekrulmã) *m*, collapse. **s'écrouler** (le) *v.pr*, to collapse, give way.

écru, e (ekry) *a*, raw; unbleached;

écu (eky) *m*, shield; escutcheon; (*pl.*) money.

écueil (ekœ:j) *m*, reef, rock, shelf; pitfall; cause of downfall.

écuelle (ekyɛl) *f*, bowl; porringer. **écuellée** (le) *f*, bowlful.

éculer (ekyle) *v.t*, to wear down (*shoe*) at heel.

écume (ekym) *f*, foam; froth; lather; scum, dross, skimmings. ~ **de mer**, [sea] wrack; meerschaum. **écumer** (me) *v.i*, to foam, froth; (*v.t.*) to skim [off], scum; scour, rove (*seas*); pick up (*news*). **écumeux, euse** (mø, ø:z) *a*, foamy, frothy. **écumoire** (mwa:r) *f*, skimmer.

écurer (ekyre) *v.t*, to scour, cleanse, clean out.

écureuil (ekyrœ:j) *m*, squirrel.

écurie (ekyri) *f*, stable, (*pl.*) mews; stud (*racing*).

écusson (ekys5) *m*, [e]scutcheon, shield, hatchment.

écuyer, ère (ekɥije, ɛ:r) *n*, riding master; horseman, -woman; rider; equestrian; equerry; [e]squire (*Hist.*).

eczéma (egzema) *m*, eczema.

édelweiss (edɛlvajs *ou* -vɛs) *m*, edelweiss.

éden (eden) *m*, Eden (*fig.*). *l'É~*, [the Garden of] Eden.

édenté, e (edɑ̃te) *a*, toothless.

édicter (edikte) *v.t*, to decree, enact.

édicule (edikyl) *m*, kiosk, shelter; public convenience.

édification (edifikasj5) *f*, erection; edification. **édifice** (fis) *m*, edifice, building, structure. **édifier** (fje) *v.t*, to erect, build; b. up; edify; enlighten.

édile (edil) *m*, magistrate; aedile (*Hist.*). **édilité** (lite) *f*, magistrature.

Edimbourg (edɛ̃bu:r) *m*, Edinburgh.

édit (edi) *m*, edict.

éditer (edite) *v.t*, to publish; edit. **éditeur, trice** (tœ:r, tris) *n*, publisher; editor, tress. **édition** (sj5) *f*, edition; publishing. ~ **à tirage restreint**, limited edition.

édredon (edrəd5) *m*, eiderdown.

éducateur, trice (edykatœ:r, tris) *n*, educator. **éducation** (sj5) *f*, education; training; up-

bringing; rearing; nurture. *sans* ~, ill-bred. **éduquer** (ke) *v.t*, to bring up; train.

éfaufiler (efofile) *v.t*, to unravel.

effacé, e (efase) *p.a*, unobtrusive. **effacer** (se) *v.t*, to efface, obliterate, delete; erase, rub out, blot out, wipe out, expunge; outshine. s'~, to wear away; keep in the background; stand aside. **effaçure** (sy:r) *f*, obliteration, deletion; erasure.

effarement (efarmɑ̃) *m*, fright. **effarer** (re) *v.t*, to scare, frighten. **effaroucher** (ruʃe) *v.t*, to startle, frighten away. s'~, to take fright.

effectif, ive† (efɛktif, i:v) *a*, effective; real; actual; in cash, in coin; paid up (*capital*). ¶ *m*, effective, strength, complement, force (*men*). **effectuer** (tɥe) *v.t*, to effect, carry out, make, execute.

efféminé, e (efemine) *a*, effeminate, womanish, unmanly, ladylike. ¶ *m*, effeminate [man]. **efféminer** (ne) *v.t*, to [make] effeminate.

effervescence (efɛrvɛsɑ̃:s) *f*, effervescence, -ency; ferment (*fig.*), unrest. **effervescent, e** (sɑ̃, ɑ̃:t) *a*, effervescent.

effet (efɛ) *m*, effect; action; purpose, avail; impression; screw, break, spin (*on ball*); negotiable instrument; bill [of exchange], bill or note, draft; (*pl.*) effects, goods, belongings, things; securities, stock[s & shares]. ~ *à payer*, *à recevoir*, bill payable, receivable. *à* ~, intended for effect. *en* ~, in fact, indeed.

efficace† (efikas) *a*, efficacious; effectual; efficient; able; adequate. **efficacité** (site) *f*, efficacy; efficiency.

effigie (efiʒi) *f*, effigy.

effilé, e (efile) *a*, slender; slim; tapering, streamlined. ¶ *m*, fringe. **effiler** (le) *v.t*, to unravel. s'**effilocher** (lɔʃe) *v.pr*, to fray. **effilure** (ly:r) *f*, ravelings.

efflanqué, e (eflɑ̃ke) *p.a*, emaciated; lank[y].

effleurer (eflœre) *v.t*, to touch, t. on; graze; glance, skim; scratch.

effleurir (eflœri:r) *v.i. & s'~*, to

effloresce. efflorescence (εflɔrε-sɑ̃:s) *f*, efflorescence.

effluve (efly:v) *m*, effluvium.

effondrement (efɔ̃drəmɑ̃) *m*, fall; subsidence; collapse, downfall; slump. **effondrer** (dre) *v.t*, to break open, stave in. **s'~**, to fall in, cave in; collapse, slump. **effondrilles** (dri:j) *f.pl*, grounds, sediment.

efforcer (s') (efɔrse) *v.pr. & abs*, to endeavor, strive, do one's utmost. **effort** (fɔ:r) *m*, effort, exertion, endeavor; force; stress (*Mech.*); strain. **~ de traction**, pull.

effraction (efraksjɔ̃) *f*, housebreaking.

effraie (efrε) *f*, barn owl, screech owl.

effranger (efrɑ̃ʒe) *v.t*, to fray.

effrayant, e (efrεjɑ̃, ɑ̃:t) *a*, dreadful, frightful. **effrayer** (je) *v.t*, to frighten, scare.

effréné, e (efrene) *a*, unbridled, unrestrained; frantic.

effriter (efrite) *v.t*, to exhaust. **s'~**, to crumble.

effroi (efrwɑ) *m*, fright, terror.

effronté, e (efrɔ̃te) *a*, shameless, brazen, impudent, barefaced. **effrontément** (mɑ̃) *ad*, shamelessly. **effronterie** (tri) *f*, effrontery.

effroyable† (efrwajabl) *a*, frightful; awful.

effusion (εfyzjɔ̃) *f*, effusion, outpouring; shedding; overflowing; effusiveness. **~ de sang**, bloodshed.

égal, e (egal) *a*, equal; even, level; equable; alike; [all] the same, all one. ¶ *n*, equal (*of pers.*). *à l'égal de*, like. **également** (lmɑ̃) *ad*, equally, alike. **égaler** (le) *v.t*, to equalize, make equal; equal; match. **égaliser** (lize) *v.t*, to equalize; level. **égalité** (te) *f*, equality; evens (*betting*); evenness; smoothness. **~ à rien**, love all (*Ten.*). **~ de points**, tie (*sport*). **~ de voix**, tie (*voting*). *à ~*, deuce (*40 all*) (*Ten.*).

égard (ega:r) *m*, regard, consideration, respect; sake. *à l'~ de*, with regard (*or* respect) (*or* reference) to. *en ~ à*, considering.

égaré, e (egare) *a*, lost, stray[ed]; erring; wild (*eyes*). **égarer** (re)

v.t, to mislead, misguide, lead astray; bewilder; mislay. **s'~**, to go astray, lose one's way; miscarry.

égayer (egεje) *v.t*, to enliven, cheer [up], exhilarate. **s'~**, to make merry.

Égée (la mer) (eʒe), the Aegean sea.

égide (eʒid) *f*, aegis, wing.

églantier (eglɑ̃tje) *m*, wild (*or* dog) rose (*bush*). **~ odorant**, sweetbriar. **églantine** (tin) *f*, wild (*or* dog) rose (*flower*). **~ odorante**, sweetbriar, eglantine.

église (egli:z) *f*, church. *l'É~ anglicane* (ɑ̃glikan), the Church of England. *l'É~ d'État*, the established Church. **~ de monastère**, **~ abbatiale** (abasjal), minster.

égoïsme (egɔism) *m*, egoism, selfishness. **égoïste†** (ist) *a*, egoistic(al), selfish. ¶ *n*, egoist.

égorger (egɔrʒe) *v.t*, to cut the throat of; butcher, slaughter; ruin.

égosiller (s') (egozije) *v.pr*, to shout (*or* sing) oneself hoarse.

égotisme (egɔtism) *m*, egotism. **égotiste** (tist) *a*, egotistic(al). ¶ *n*, egotist.

égout (egu) *m*, drainage (*surplus water*); drip[pings]; sewer, drain. **égoutier** (tje) *m*, sewerman. **égoutter** (te) *v.t. & i. & s'~*, to drain; drip. **égouttoir** (twa:r) *m*, drainer, draining rack; plate rack. **égoutture** (ty:r) *f*, drainings; drippings.

égratigner (egratiɲe) *v.t*, to scratch. **égratignure** (ɲy:r) *f*, scratch.

égrener (egrəne) *v.t*, to pick off; shell; gin (*cotton*); tell (*beads*). **s'~**, to seed.

égrillard, e (egrija:r, ard) *a*, ribald.

Égypte (l') (eʒipt) *f*, Egypt. **égyptien, ne** (sjɛ̃, εn) *a. & É~*, *n*, Egyptian. **égyptologie** (tɔlɔʒi) *f*, Egyptology. **égyptologue** (lɔg) *m*, Egyptologist.

eh (e) *i*, [h]eh! **~ bien!** now then! well!

éhonté, e (eɔ̃te) *a*, shameless, barefaced.

eider (edε:r) *m*, eider [duck].

éjaculation (eʒakylasjɔ̃) *f*, ejaculation (*fluid*); fervent prayer. **éjaculer** (le) *v.t.* & *i*, to ejaculate (*fluid*).

éjecteur (eʒɛktœːr) *m*, ejector.

élaborer (elabɔre) *v.t*, to elaborate; work out, evolve.

élagage (elagaːʒ) *m*, lopping; pruning; prunings. **élaguer** (ge) *v.t*, to lop; prune.

élan (elɑ̃) *m*, bound, spring; dash, dart, rush, run[-up] (*Jump.*); [out]burst; impetus, momentum; flight; glow; elk, moose, eland. *avec ~*, running (*jump, dive*). *sans ~*, standing (*j., d.*). **élancé, e** (se) *a*, slender, slim. **élancements** (smɑ̃) *m.pl*, shooting pains, twinges; yearning (*soul*). **élancer** (se) *v.i*, to throb, shoot. *s'~*, to bound, spring, leap, dash, dart.

élargir (elarʒiːr) *v.t*, to enlarge; broaden; widen; let out; extend; release (*prisoner*).

élasticité (elastisite) *f*, elasticity, spring[iness], resilience. **élastique** (tik) *a*, elastic, spring[y], resilient; bouyant. ¶ *m*, elastic.

Elbe (l'île d') (ɛlb) *f*, the Island of Elba. **l'Elbe**, *m*, the Elbe (*river*).

eldorado (ɛldɔrado) *m*, El Dorado.

électeur, trice (elɛktœːr, tris) *n*, elector, constituent. **élection** (sjɔ̃) *f*, election, polling. *~ de remplacement*, by-election. **électorat** (tɔra) *m*, franchise.

électricien (elɛktrisjɛ̃) *m*, electrician. **électricité** (site) *f*, electricity. **électrification** (fikasjɔ̃) *f*, electrification. **électrifier** (fje) *v.t*, to electrify. **électrique** (trik) *a*, electric(al). **électriser** (ze) *v.t*, to electrify, electrize; thrill. **électro-aimant** (trɔɛmɑ̃) *m*, electromagnet. **électrocuter** (kyte) *v.t*, to electrocute. **électrode** (trɔd) *f*, electrode. **électrolyse** (liːz) *f*, electrolysis. **électron** (trɔ̃) *m*, electron. **électrotype** (tip) *m*, electrotype.

élégamment (elegamɑ̃) *ad*, elegantly, stylishly. **élégance** (gɑ̃ːs) *f*, elegance, stylishness. **élégant, e** (gɑ̃, ɑ̃ːt) *a*, elegant, stylish,

fashionable. ¶ *n*, man, woman, of fashion.

élégie (eleʒi) *f*, elegy.

élément (elemɑ̃) *m*, element; (*pl.*) rudiments (*of a science, an art*); unit; cell (*Phys.*). **élémentaire** (tɛːr) *a*, elementary.

éléphant (elefɑ̃) *m*, elephant.

élevage (elvaːʒ) *m*, breeding, rearing, stock farming. **élévateur** (elevatœːr) *m*, elevator. **élévation** (sjɔ̃) *f*, elevation; raising; rise; eminence; height; loftiness; altitude. **élévatoire** (twaːr) *m*, elevator (*Surg.*). **élève** (elɛːv) *n*, pupil, student; rearing (*animal reared*). *~ de l'école navale*, naval cadet. ¶ *f*, breeding, rearing (*act*). **élevé, e** (elve) *p.a*, high; lofty; bred, brought up. **élever** (ve) *v.t*, to elevate, raise, lift; erect; bring up, rear, breed. *s'~*, to rise; arise. *s'~ à*, to reach, amount to. **éleveur** (lvœːr) *m*, grazier; breeder.

elfe (ɛlf) *m*, elf, brownie.

élider (elide) *v.t*, to elide.

éligible (eliʒibl) *a*, eligible.

élimer (elime) *v.t*, to wear threadbare.

éliminatoire (eliminatwaːr) *a*. & *f*, eliminating *or* trial (*heat*). **éliminer** (ne) *v.t*, to eliminate; weed out.

élingue (elɛ̃ːg) *f*, sling.

élire (eliːr) *v.t.ir*, to elect; return.

élision (elizjɔ̃) *f*, elision.

élite (elit) *f*, elite.

élixir (eliksiːr) *m*, elixir.

elle (ɛl) *pn*, she; her; it; herself. *~-même*, herself; itself. *~s, pl*, they; them. *~-mêmes*, themselves.

ellipse (elips) *f*, ellipse; ellipsis. **elliptique**† (tik) *a*, elliptic(al).

élocution (elɔkysjɔ̃) *f*, elocution.

éloge (elɔːʒ) *m*, eulogy, praise, encomium. **élogieux, euse**† (lɔʒjøø, øːz) *a*, eulogistic.

éloigné, e (elwaɲe) *p.a*, distant, outlying, far [off *or* away], remote. **éloignement** (ɲmɑ̃) *m*, removal; estrangement; distance, remoteness; dislike. **éloigner** (ɲe) *v.t*, to remove; keep away; defer; estrange; disincline. *s'~*, to withdraw, go away; differ; swerve.

éloquemment (elɔkamɑ̃) *ad*, eloquently. **éloquence** (kɑ̃:s) *f*, eloquence, oratory. **éloquent, e** (kɑ̃, ɑ̃:t) *a*, eloquent.

Elseneur (ɛlsənœ:r) *f*, Elsinore.

élu, e (ely) *n*, elected member. *les élus*, the elect (*Relig.*).

élucider (elyside) *v.t*, to elucidate.

élucubration (elykybrasjɔ̃) *f*, lucubration.

éluder (elyde) *v.t*, to elude, evade, shirk.

élyme (elim) *m*, lyme-grass.

élysée & (*Myth.*) É~ (elize) *m*, Elysium. *l'É~*, the Élysée (*Paris*). **élyséen, ne** (zeɛ̃, ɛn) *a*, Elysian.

émacié, e (emasje) *a*, emaciated.

émail (ema:j) *m*, enamel; e. ware; glaze. **émaillage** (maja:ʒ) *m*, enameling. **émailler** (je) *v.t*, to enamel; glaze; stud; intersperse.

émanation (emanasjɔ̃) *f*, emanation, efflux, effluence.

émanciper (emɑ̃sipe) *v.t*, to emancipate. *s'~*, to overstep the mark (*fig.*), forget oneself.

émaner (emane) *v.i*, to emanate, issue.

émarger (emarʒe) *v.t*, to sign [in the margin]; draw (*salary*); trim the margins of.

émasculer (emaskyle) *v.t*, to emasculate.

emballage (ɑ̃bala:ʒ) *m*, packing; spurt, burst (*speed*). **emballement** (lmɑ̃) *m*, bolting (*horse*); racing (*Mach.*); boom (*Stk Ex.*); excitement. **emballer** (le) *v.t*, to pack [up], wrap [up]; pack off, bundle off; carry away (*fig.*). *s'~*, to bolt; race; be carried away. **emballeur** (lœ:r) *m*, packer.

embarcadère (ɑ̃barkadɛ:r) *m*, landing [place *or* stage]; wharf; platform (*Rly.*). **embarcation** (sjɔ̃) *f*, craft, boat, launch.

embardée (ɑ̃barde) *f*, lurch, [sudden] swerve; yaw. *faire une ~*, to yaw; swerve; catch a crab (*boating*).

embargo (ɑ̃bargo) *m*, embargo.

embarquement (ɑ̃barkəmɑ̃) *m*, embarkation; shipment; entrainment. **embarquer** (ke) *v.t*. & *s'~*, to embark; ship; entrain;

(*v.i.*) to ship water, ship a sea. *s'~ clandestinement*, to stow away.

embarras (ɑ̃bara) *m*, obstruction, block, jam; traffic jam; encumbrance; inconvenience; superfluity; airs (*affectation*); perplexity, fix, quandary, embarrassment; straits; difficulty, scrape. *~ de la langue*, impediment of speech, i. in one's s. *faire des ~*, to be fussy. **embarrassant, e** (sɑ̃, ɑ̃:t) *a*, cumbersome; awkward, embarrassing. **embarrasser** (se) *v.t*, to obstruct, block [up]; [en]cumber, hamper; be in the way of; entangle; embarrass, perplex, nonplus.

embâter (ɑ̃bate) *v.t*, to saddle.

emboucher (ɑ̃boʃe) *v.t*, to engage, take on (*workmen*). **embauchoir** (ʃwa:r) *m*, shoe tree.

embaumer (ɑ̃bome) *v.t*, to embalm; perfume, scent.

embéguiner (ɑ̃begine) *v.t*, to muffle up; infatuate.

embellie (ɑ̃bɛli) *f*, lull. **embellir** (li:r) *v.t*, to embellish, beautify; improve; (*v.i.*) to grow more beautiful.

emberlificoter (ɑ̃bɛrlifikɔte) *v.t*, to entangle.

embesogné, e (ɑ̃bəzɔɲe) *a*, very busy.

embêtant, e (ɑ̃bɛtɑ̃) *a*, annoying, boring.

embêter (ɑ̃bɛte) *v.t*, to annoy; bore.

emblée (d') (ɑ̃ble) *ad*, at the very outset, right away, straight off.

emblématique (ɑ̃blematik) *a*, emblematic(al). **emblème** (blɛ:m) *m*, emblem; attribute.

embob[el]iner (ɑ̃bɔb[l]ine) *v.t*, to wheedle, coax.

emboîter (ɑ̃bwate) *v.t*, to fit in[to], box, nest, house; socket.

embolie (ɑ̃bɔli) *f*, embolism.

embonpoint (ɑ̃bɔ̃pwɛ̃) *m*, stoutness, plumpness, flesh.

emboucher (ɑ̃buʃe) *v.t*, to put to one's mouth; blow. *mal embouché*, foul-mouthed. **embouchoir** (ʃwa:r) *m*, mouthpiece; shoe tree. **embouchure** (ʃy:r) *f*, mouthpiece; mouth.

embouer (ăbwe) *v.t*, to muddy.

embourber (ăburbe) *v.t*, to bog, mire; involve. **s'~**, to stick in the mud.

embourgeoiser (s') (ăburʒwaze) *v.pr*, to marry into (*or* mix with) the middle classes.

embout (ăbu) *m*, ferrule; capping.

embouteiller (ăbutɛje) *v.t*, to bottle; b. up; block (*traffic*).

embouter (ăbute) *v.t*, to ferrule, tip.

emboutir (ăbuti;r) *v.t*, to shape, stamp, press; ferrule.

embranchement (ăbrɑ̃ʃmɑ̃) *m*, branching [off]; junction (*Rly.*). **~ particulier**, private siding (*Rly.*). **embrancher** (ʃe) *v.t*, to branch off.

embrasement (ăbrazmɑ̃) *m*, conflagration, burning; illumination. **embraser** (ze) *v.t*, to [set on] fire; illuminate (*festively*).

embrassade (ăbrasad) *f*, embrace, hug. **embrasse** (bras) *f*, curtain holder. **embrassement** (smɑ̃) *m*, embrace. **embrasser** (se) *v.t*, to embrace, hug; kiss (Cf. *baiser*); take in; take up; espouse. *je vous embrasse* [*de tout cœur*], [with] [best] love (*letter*).

embrasure (ăbrazy;r) *f*, recess; embrasure.

embrayer (ăbrɛje) *v.t*, to engage (*Mach.*), throw into gear. **embrayage** (ja;ʒ) *m*, engaging; clutch.

embrever (ăbrəve) *v.t*, to joggle.

embrigader (ăbrigade) *v.t*, to brigade; enroll.

embrocation (ăbrɔkasjɔ̃) *f*, embrocation.

embrocher (ăbrɔʃe) *v.t*, to spit; run through, impale.

embrouillamini (ăbrujamini) *m*, confusion. **embrouiller** (je) *v.t*, to ravel, tangle; embroil, muddle, confuse.

embroussaillé, e (ăbrusaje) *a*, brushy; bushy; matted.

embrumer (ăbryme) *v.t*, to fog, shroud, darken. **embrun** (brɛ̃) *m*, spray, spindrift.

embryon (ăbriɔ̃) *m*, embryo. **embryonnaire** (ɔnɛ;r) *a*, embryonic.

embûche (ăbyʃ) *f*, trap. **embus-**

cade (byskad) *f*, ambush, ambuscade. *se tenir en ~*, to lie in wait. **embusqué** (ke) *m*, shirker. **embusquer** (ke) *v.t*, to place in ambush. **s'~**, to ambush, lie in wait; shirk.

émeraude (emro;d) *f*, emerald.

émerger (emɛrʒe) *v.i*, to emerge; loom; peep.

émeri (emri) *m*, emery.

émerillon (emrijɔ̃) *m*, merlin (*bird*); swivel. **émerillonné, e** (jone) *a*, bright, sparkling.

émérite (emerit) *a*, experienced; confirmed; emeritus.

émerveiller (emɛrvɛje) *v.t*, to astonish. **s'~**, to marvel.

émétique (emetik) *a. & m*, emetic.

émetteur (emetœ;r) *m*, issuer; (*att.*) transmitting (*Teleg.*). **émettre** (tr) *v.t.ir*, to emit, utter; express; issue.

émeute (emø;t) *f*, riot, disturbance, outbreak. **émeutier** (møtje) *m*, rioter.

émietter (emjɛte) *v.t. & s'~*, to crumble.

émigrant, e (emigrɑ̃, ɑ̃;t) *n*, emigrant. **émigration** (grasjɔ̃) *f*, emigration. **émigré, e** (gre) *n*, refugee; émigré (*Hist.*). **émigrer** (gre) *v.i*, to emigrate; migrate.

émincé, e (emɛ̃se) *p.p*, cut into thin slices. ¶ *m*, hash.

éminemment (eminamɑ̃) *ad*, eminently, highly. **éminence** (nɑ̃;s) *f*, eminence; height; ball (*thumb*). *Son E~*, *f*, His Eminence (*cardinal*). **éminent, e** (nɑ̃, ɑ̃;t) *a*, eminent; distinguished; prominent. **éminentissime** (nɑ̃tisim) *a*, most eminent.

émir (emi;r) *m*, emir; ameer, amir.

émissaire (emisɛ;r) *m*, emissary. **émission** (sjɔ̃) *f*, emission; issue; uttering; broadcasting, transmission.

emmagasiner (ămagazine) *v.t*, to store, s. up; warehouse.

emmailloter (ămajɔte) *v.t*, to swathe; bandage.

emmancher (ămɑ̃ʃe) *v.t*, to handle; fix; set about. **emmanchure** (ʃy;r) *f*, armhole.

emmêler (ămɛle) *v.t,* to [en]-tangle; muddle.

emménagement (ămenaʒmã) *m,* moving in (*house*); accommodation, appointments (*ship*). **emménager** (ʒe) *v.t,* to install, settle; move into; (*v.i.*) to move in.

emmener (ămne) *v.t,* to take away.

emmiellé, e (ămjɛle) *a,* honeyed.

emmitoufler (ămitufle) *v.t,* to muffle up.

emmortaiser (ămɔrtɛze) *v.t,* to mortise.

émoi (emwa) *m,* emotion, agitation, flutter.

émollient, e (emɔljã, ã:t) *a. & m,* emollient.

émoluments (emɔlymã) *m.pl,* emoluments.

émonder (emõde) *v.t,* to prune. **émondes** (mɔ:d) *f.pl,* prunings.

émotion (emosjõ) *f,* emotion; thrill; excitement.

émoucher (emuʃe) *v.t,* to drive away the flies from.

émouchet (emuʃɛ) *m,* kestrel. **émouchette** (emuʃɛt) *f,* fly net. **émouchoir** (ʃwa:r) *m,* fly whisk.

émoulu, e (emuly) *a: frais ~ de,* fresh from (*college*); well up in (*subject*).

émousser (emuse) *v.t,* to blunt, dull; remove the moss from.

émoustiller (emustije) *v.t,* to exhilarate.

émouvant (emuvã) *a,* moving, touching, thrilling.

émouvoir (emuvwa:r) *v.t.ir,* to move; stir [up], rouse.

empailler (ăpaje) *v.t,* to cover (*or* pack) (*or* stuff) with straw; stuff (*dead animal*). **empailleur, euse** (jœ:r, ø:z) *n,* chair caner, taxidermist.

empanacher (ăpanaʃe) *v.t,* to plume; adorn.

empaqueter (ăpakte) *v.t,* to pack [up]. **s'~,** to wrap [oneself] up.

emparer (s') de (ăpare) *v.pr,* to seize, take possession of; monopolize, engross.

empâter (ăpate) *v.t,* to paste; make sticky; fatten, force-feed (*poultry*); impaste.

empattement (ăpatmã) *m,*

footing (*Build.*); wheelbase; serif.

empaumer (ăpome) *v.t,* to strike (*ball*); manipulate (*pers.*).

empêché, e (ăpeʃe) *p.p,* puzzled, at a loss. **empêchement** (ʃmã) *m,* hindrance, impediment, obstacle, bar; prevention. **empêcher** (ʃe) *v.t,* to prevent, hinder, impede; keep from; preclude. **s'~,** to forbear, refrain, help.

empeigne (ăpɛɲ) *f,* vamp, upper (*shoe*).

empereur (ăprœ:r) *m,* emperor.

empesé, e (ăpəze) *a,* starchy, stiff. **empeser** (ze) *v.t,* to starch.

empester (ăpɛste) *v.t,* to infect; corrupt; (*abs.*) to stink.

empêtrer (ăpetre) *v.t,* to entangle, hamper; embarrass; involve.

emphase (ăfa:s) *f,* bombast, pomposity, fustian; magniloquence; emphasis. **emphatique†** (fatik) *a,* bombastic, pompous; magniloquent; emphatic.

empiècement (ăpjɛsmã) *m,* yoke (*dress*).

empierrer (ăpjɛre) *v.t,* to pave (*road*).

empiètement (ăpjɛtmã) *m,* encroachment, trespass. **empiéter sur** (pjete), to encroach on; trespass on (*fig.*).

empiffrer (ăpifre) *v.t,* to stuff, gorge.

empiler (ăpile) *v.t,* to pile [up]; stack; herd together.

empire (ăpi:r) *m,* dominion, sway, hold; mastery; rule; empire. ~ sur soi-même, self-control.

empirer (ăpire) *v.t,* to make worse; (*v.i.*) to grow worse.

empirique (ăpirik) *a,* empiric-(al), rule-of-thumb. ¶ *m,* empiric[ist]. **empiriquement** (kmã) *ad,* empirically, by rule of thumb. **empirisme** (rism) *m,* empiricism.

emplacement (ăplasmã) *m,* site, position, location.

emplâtre (ăpla:tr) *m,* plaster (*Phar.*); futile person. ~ adhésif, adhesive plaster.

emplette (ăplɛt) *f,* purchase, shopping; bargain.

emplir (ăpli;r) *v.t.* & *s'~*, to fill; (*v.i.*) to be swamped (*boat*).

emploi (ăplwa) *m*, employment; job; use; entry (*Bkkpg.*); part, line (*of actor*). **employé, e** (je) *n*, employee; clerk. *~ d'administration*, civil servant. *~ du gaz*, gas man. **employer** (je) *v.t*, to employ; use. *s'~*, to occupy (*or* exert) (*or* busy) oneself. **employeur, euse** (jœ;r, ø;z) *n*, employer.

emplumé, e (ăplyme) *p.a*, feathered. **emplumer** (me) *v.t*, to feather; tar & feather.

empocher (ăpɔʃe) *v.t*, to pocket.

empoignant, e (ăpwaɲă, ă;t) *a*, thrilling, poignant. **empoigner** (ɲe) *v.t*, to grasp; grip; clutch; grab; take to task, abuse; thrill.

empois (ăpwa) *m*, starch [paste].

empoisonnement (ăpwazɔnmă) *m*, poisoning. **empoisonner** (ne) *v.t*, to poison; infect; corrupt; (*abs.*) to be poisonous; stink. **empoisonneur, euse** (nœ;r, ø;z) *n*, poisoner; bad cook.

empoissonner (ăpwasɔne) *v.t*, to stock (*pond*) with fish.

emporté, e (ăpɔrte) *a*, hasty, quick-tempered, fiery, passionate. **emportement** (təmă) *m*, transport (*fig.*); outburst, fit of anger.

emporte-pièce (ăpɔrtəpjɛs) *m*, [hollow] punch. *à l'~* (*fig.*), trenchant.

emporter (ăpɔrte) *v.t*, to carry (*or* take) (*or* sweep) (*or* wash) away (*or* off) (*or* out); (*Mil.*) carry (*place*). **l'~** *sur*, to surpass, outdo; overrule; prevail over, preponderate over. **s'~**, to get angry, fire up; bolt (*horse*).

empoté, e (ăpɔte) *a*, clumsy. **empoter** (te) *v.t*, to pot.

empourprer (ăpurpre) *v.t*, to purple; crimson.

empreindre (ăprɛ̃;dr) *v.t.ir*, to imprint, impress, stamp. **empreinte** (prɛ̃;t) *f*, impress[ion], [im]print; stamp (*fig.*); mold (*Typ.*). *~ de pas*, *~ du pied*, footprint. *~ digitale*, fingerprint. *~ du doigt*, fingermark.

empressé, e (ăprɛse) *a*, eager, zealous; attentive. **empressement** (smă) *m*, eagerness, alacrity, readiness. **s'empresser** (se) *v.pr*, to hasten; be eager. *~ auprès de*, to dance attendance on.

emprise (ăpri;z) *f*, hold, ascendancy.

emprisonnement (ăprizɔnmă) *m*, imprisonment. *~ cellulaire*, separate cell system. **emprisonner** (ne) *v.t*, to imprison, confine.

emprunt (ăprœ̃) *m*, borrowing, loan; [making] use. *~ de la Défense nationale*, war loan. *d'~* (*fig.*), artificial, sham, assumed. **emprunté, e** (te) *p.a*, borrowed; assumed (*name*); awkward. **emprunter** (te) *v.t*, to borrow; assume (*name*); use, make use of. **emprunteur, euse** (tœ;r, ø;z) *n*, borrower.

empuantir (ăpɥăti;r) *v.t*, to infect.

empyrée (ăpire) *m*, empyrean.

ému, *p.p*, **émouvoir**.

émulation (emylasjɔ̃) *f*, emulation. **émule** (myl) *n*, emulator, rival.

émulsion (emylsjɔ̃) *f*, emulsion.

en (ă) *pr*, in; into; within; on; to; at; with; in the; in a; like [a]; as [a]; by; while; of; under. *~ voiture!* all aboard!

en (ă) *pn. & ad*, of it, its, of them, their, of him, of her; about it, about them, etc.; for (*or* by) (*or* with) (*or* from) it *or* them, etc.; some, any.

enamourer(s') (ănamure) *v.pr*, to fall in love.

encadrer (ăkadre) *v.t*, to frame; surround; incorporate; officer.

encager (ăkaʒe) *v.t*, to [en]cage.

encaisse (ăkɛs) *f*, cash [in hand]. *~ métallique*, cash & bullion in hand. **encaisser** (se) *v.t*, to [en]case; cash, collect; put in the cash box; embank (*river, road*).

encan (ăkă) *m*, auction.

encanailler (s') (ăkanaje) *v.i*, to contract low habits.

encaquer (ăkake) *v.t*, to barrel. *encaqués comme des harengs*, packed like sardines (*people*).

encart (ăka;r) *m*, insert (*Bookb.*). **encarter** (karte) *v.t*, to inset (*Bookb.*); insert (*Bookb.*).

en-cas (ăkɑ) *m*, something (*ready to eat*) in case of need; umbrella-sunshade.

encastrer (ākastre) *v.t*, to house; embed.

encaustique (ākostik) *a. & f*, encaustic. ~ *pour meubles*, furniture polish. **encaustiquer** (ke) *v.t*, to polish (*furniture*).

encaver (ākave) *v.t*, to cellar.

enceindre (āsɛ̃:dr) *v.t.ir*, to enclose, gird, surround. **enceinte** (sɛ̃:t) *a.f*, pregnant, with child, expectant. ¶ *f*, enclosure; precinct; ring (*Box*.); fencing; wall; hall. ~ *du pesage*, paddock (*turf*).

encens (āsā) *m*, incense. ~ *mâle*, frankincense. **encenser** (se) *v.t*, to [in]cense, burn i. to; flatter. **encensoir** (swa:r) *m*, censer.

encercler (āsɛrkle) *v.t*, to hoop; encircle.

enchaînement (āʃɛnmā) (*fig.*) *m*, chain, series, train. **enchaîner** (ne) *v.t*, to chain [up]; enchain, fetter, manacle; bind; link; enslave; enthrall.

enchantement (āʃātmā) *m*, enchantment, magic, spell; glamour, witchery; delight. **enchanter** (te) *v.t*, to enchant, bewitch; delight, enrapture. **enchanteur, eresse** (tœ:r, trɛ:s) *n*, enchanter, tress; (*att*.) enchanting, bewitching.

enchâsser (āʃase) *v.t*, to set, mount; enshrine; incorporate. **enchâssure** (sy:r) *f*, setting.

enchère (āʃɛ:r) *f*, bid[ding]; auction, sale. **enchérir** (ʃeri:r) *v.t*, to raise the price of; (*v.i.*) to rise in price; bid. ~ *sur*, to outbid; outdo. **enchérisseur** (risœ:r) *m*, bidder.

enchevêtrer (s') (āʃvetre) *v.pr*, to get [en]tangled (*or* confused).

enchifrènement (āʃifrɛnmā) *m*, cold in the head, snuffles.

enclave (ākla:v) *f*, land-locked property (*law*); enclave (*international*); recess (*Build*.). **enclaver** (klave) *v.t*, to enclose, shut in, fit in.

enclin, e (āklɛ̃, in) *a*, inclined, prone, minded, given.

enclore (āklɔ:r) *v.t.ir*, to enclose, fence in. **enclos** (klo) *m*, enclosure; paddock.

enclouer (āklue) *v.t*, to spike (*gun*). **enclouure** (kluy:r) (*fig.*) *f*, rub.

enclume (āklym) *f*, anvil.

encoche (ākɔʃ) *f*, notch, nick, slot. ~*s*, thumb index (*books*). **encocher** (ʃe) *v.t*, to notch.

encoignure (ākɔɲy:r) *f*, corner; corner cupboard.

encollage (ākɔla:ʒ) *m*, sizing; size (*glue*). **encoller** (le) *v.t*, to size.

encolure (ākɔly:r) *f*, neck; neck measurement, [neck] size; look (*fig.*).

encombrant, e (ākɔ̃brā, ā:t) *a*, bulky; cumbersome, in the way; embarrassing. **sans encombre** (kɔ̃:br), without hindrance. **encombrement** (kɔ̃brəmā) *m*, block, congestion, [over]crowding; glut[ting]; litter; space occupied, floor space; measurement (*Ship*.). **encombrer** (bre) *v.t*, to block, congest, overcrowd; glut, overstock; encumber, litter.

encontre (à l'~ de) (ākɔ̃:tr), in opposition to. *aller à l'~ de*, to run counter to.

encorbellement (ākɔrbɛlmā) *m*, cantilever.

encore (ākɔ:r) *ad*, still; yet; again; also; moreover; too; more; else. ~ *un, une*, one more, another. ~ *un coup*, once again, once more. ~ *un peu*, a little more *or* longer. ~ *que, c*, although.

encourager (ākuraʒe) *v.t*, to encourage, hearten, foster; promote; countenance, abet; halloo (*dogs*).

encourir (ākuri:r) *v.t.ir*, to incur, run.

encrasser (ākrase) *v.t*, to foul, dirty, grime; clog.

encre (ā:kr) *f*, ink. ~ *à marquer le linge*, marking i. ~ *de Chine*, Indian i. ~ *stylographique* (stilɔgrafik), fountain pen i. **encrer** (ākre) *v.t*, to ink. **encrier** (krie) *m*, inkstand, inkpot. ~ *d'écolier*, inkwell.

encroûté, e (ākrute) (*fig.*) *a*, crusted, fogyish.

encuver (ākyve) *v.t*, to vat; put in the tub.

encyclique (āsiklik) *a. & f*, encyclic(al).

encyclopédie (ãsikləpedi) *f*, [en]-cyclopedia.

endémique (ãdemik) *a*, endemic.

endenter (ãdãte) *v.t*, to tooth, cog.

endetté, e (ãdɛte) *p.a*, in debt. **endetter** (te) *v.t*, to involve in debt. **s'~,** to run into d.

endêvé, e (ãdɛve) *a*, exasperated. **endêver** (ve) *v.i*, to be furious.

endiablé, e (ãdjable) *a*, (*as if*) possessed; wild, frenzied. **endiabler** (ble) *v.i*, to be furious.

endiguer (ãdige) *v.t*, to dike; dam.

endimancher (s') (ãdimãʃe) *v.pr*, to put on one's Sunday best.

endive (ãdiːv) *f*, chicory; endive.

endoctriner (ãdɔktrine) *v.t*, to indoctrinate; coach.

endolorir (ãdɔlɔriːr) *v.t*, to make ache.

endommager (ãdmaʒe) *v.t*, to damage, injure.

endormant, e (ãdɔrmã, ã:t) *a*, soporific; wearisome. **endormeur** (mœ:r) *m*, bore. **endormi, e** (mi) *p.a*, asleep; sleepy; drowsy. ¶ *n*, sleepyhead. **endormir** (miːr) *v.t.ir*, to send to sleep; lull. **s'~,** to fall asleep, go to sleep.

endos[sement] (ãdo[smã]) *m*, endorsement. **endosser** (se) *v.t*, to put on, don; take on, shoulder; endorse. **endosseur** (sœ:r) *m*, endorser.

endroit (ãdrwa) *m*, place, spot, part; right side, face (*fabric*). **à l'~ de,** towards, regarding.

enduire (ãdɥiːr) *v.t.ir*, to smear; coat; render. **enduit** (dɥi) *m*, coat[ing]; rendering.

endurance (ãdyrã:s) *f*, endurance. **endurant, e** (rã, ã:t) *a*, patient. *rendre ~,* to harden. **endurcir** (si:r) *v.t. & s'~,* to harden. **endurcissement** (sismã) *m*, hardness, callousness, obduracy. **endurer** (re) *v.t*, to endure.

énergétique (enɛrʒetik) *f*, energetics (*Phys.*). **énergie** (ʒi) *f*, energy, power; emphasis; efficacy (*remedy*); backbone. **énergique†** (ʒik) *a*, energetic, powerful, strong; forcible, emphatic; strenuous.

énergumène (enɛrgymɛn) *m.f*, fanatic; ranter.

enerver (enɛrve) *v.t*, to enervate; exasperate.

enfance (ãfã:s) *f*, childhood; infancy; second childhood, dotage; A B C (*of an art*). **enfant** (fã) *n*, child; infant; boy; girl; fellow, lad. *~ de chœur,* choir boy, chorister. *~s perdus,* forlorn hope (*Mil.*). *~ prodige,* infant prodigy. *~ prodigue,* prodigal son. *~ trouvé,* foundling; stowaway. **enfantement** (tmã) *m*, birth (*fig.*). **enfanter** (te) *v.t*, to give birth to (*fig.*). **enfantillage** (tija:ʒ) *m*, childishness, **enfantin, e** (tɛ̃, in) *a*, infantile; childish; infant (*class*); nursery (*language*).

enfariner (ãfarine) *v.t*, to [cover with] flour.

enfer (ãfɛːr) *m*, hell, inferno. *les ~s,* the nether regions, the underworld, Hades. *d'~,* infernal; blazing (*fire*).

enfermer (ãfɛrme) *v.t*, to shut up; lock up; enclose; impound; contain.

enferrer (ãfɛre) *v.t*, to run through (*with sword*). **s'~,** to become involved. *s'~ soi-même,* to give oneself away.

enfieller (ãfjɛle) *v.t*, to embitter, sour.

enfilade (ãfilad) *f*, suite; series; string; row; enfilade. **enfiler** (le) *v.t*, to thread; string; run (*or* go) through; go along; enfilade, rake; draw in (*person to reckless gaming*).

enfin (ãfɛ̃) *ad*, at last, lastly, after all; in short, in fine; in fact; come now!

enflammer (ãflame) *v.t*, to [set on] fire, ignite; inflame. **s'~,** to catch (*or* take) fire, ignite, fire up.

enfler (ãfle) *v.t. & i. & s'~,* to swell, inflate. **enflure** (fly:r) *f*, swelling, etc.

enfoncer (ãfõse) *v.t*, to drive [in]; sink, bury, immerse; break open, stave in; b. up; stave in; (*v.i. & abs.*) to sink. **enfoncement** (smã) *m*, driving [in]; hollow, depression; recess; background.

enfonçure (sy:r) *f*, hole; bottom (*cask*).

enfouir (ãfwi:r) *v.t*, to bury, hide.

enfourcher (ãfurʃe) *v.t*, to bestride; ride to death (*fig.*).

enfourner (ãfurne) *v.t*, to put in the oven.

enfreindre (ãfrɛ̃:dr) *v.t.ir*, to infringe, break.

enfuir (s') (ãfɥi:r) *v.pr*, to flee; escape; run away; elope; leak; fly; vanish.

enfumer (ãfyme) *v.t*, to smoke; s. out.

engageant, e (ãgaʒã, ã:t) *a*, engaging, winning; inviting. **engagement** (ʒmã) *m*, engagement; booking; entry (*sporting event*); enlistment; signing on; commitment; liability, undertaking; pledging, pledge, pawning, hypothecation. **engager** (ʒe) *v.t*, to engage; book; enter; enlist; sign [on]; betroth; bind; plight; pledge, pawn; mortgage, hypothecate; invite, urge, induce; foul (*ropes*). **engagé**, *p.p*, on her beam ends; waterlogged (*boat*). **s'engager**, to undertake, covenant; enlist; enter; foul.

engainer (ãgɛne) *v.t*, to sheathe, case.

engeance (ãʒã:s) *f*, brood, lot (*of despicable people*).

engelure (ãʒly:r) *f*, chilblain.

engendrer (ãʒãdre) *v.t*, to beget; sire; engender; breed; generate.

engerber (ãʒɛrbe) *v.t*, to sheaf, bind.

engin (ãʒɛ̃) *m*, appliance, contrivance, gear, tackle; engine (*of war*); missile.

englober (ãglɔbe) *v.t*, to include, embody.

engloutir (ãgluti:r) *v.t*, to swallow; s. up; bolt (*food*); engulf, swamp.

engluer (ãglye) *v.t*, to [bird] lime; ensnare; take in.

engorger (ãgɔrʒe) *v.t*, to choke [up], stop up.

engouer (s') (ãgue) *v.pr*, to become infatuated.

engouffrer (ãgufre) *v.t*, to engulf, swallow up.

engourdir (ãgurdi:r) *v.t*, to [be] numb, dull.

engrais (ãgrɛ) *m*, fattening food; manure. ~ *chimique*, fertilizer. **engraisser (se)** *v.t*, to fatten; manure.

engranger (ãgrãʒe) *v.t*, to garner, get in.

engraver (ãgrave) *v.t*, to strand; (*v.i.*) to ground (*boat*).

engrenage (ãgrəna:ʒ) *m*, gear-[ing]; meshes, toils (*fig.*). **engrener** (ne) *v.t*, to [throw into] gear, mesh, engage; set going.

engrumeler (ãgrymle) *v.t*, to clot, curdle.

enguirlander (ãgirlãde) *v.t*, to garland, wreathe; wheedle.

enhardir (ãardi:r) *v.t*, to embolden.

énigmatique† (enigmatik) *a*, enigmatic(al). **énigme** (nigm) *f*, riddle, conundrum, puzzle, enigma.

enivrer (ãnivre) *v.t*. to intoxicate, inebriate; elate.

enjambée (ãʒãbe) *f*; stride. **enjamber** (be) *v.t. & abs*, to stride [over or along]; (*v.i.*) to encroach, project.

enjeu (ãʒø) *m*, stake (*wager*).

enjoindre (ãʒwɛ̃:dr) *v.t.ir*, to enjoin.

enjôler (ãʒole) *v.t*, to wheedle, inveigle, bamboozle.

enjoliver (ãʒɔlive) *v.t*, to embellish; set off.

enjoué, e (ãʒwe) *a*, playful, jocular, vivacious. **enjouement** (ʒumã) *m*, playfulness.

enlacer (ãlase) *v.t*, to [en]lace; entwine; clasp, fold.

enlaidir (ãlɛdi:r) *v.t*, to make ugly; disfigure.

enlevage (ãlva:ʒ) *m*, spurt (*rowing*). **enlever** (lve) *v.t*, to lift, raise; carry (*or* take) (*or* clear) (*or* sweep) away (*or* off); remove, collect; kidnap; abduct; rape; buy up; take up (*shares*); snap up (*bargain*). *être enlevé par la mer* ou *par les lames*, to be washed overboard. *se faire* ~ *par*, to elope with. **enlèvement** (lɛvmã) *m*, lifting, etc.; elopement.

enliser (s') (ãlize) *v.pr*, to sink [into the sand *or* mud].

enluminer (ãlymine) *v.t*, to color, illuminate (*MS.*); flush, redden. **enluminure** (ny;r) *f*, coloring; illumination; high color.

ennemi, e (ɛnmi) *n*, enemy, foe. ¶ *a*, enemy, inimical, hostile; averse; clashing.

ennoblir (ãnobli;r) *v.t*, to ennoble, uplift, dignify.

ennui (ãɥi) *m*, wearisomeness, tedium, boredom; bother, nuisance; worry, trouble. **ennuyer** (nɥije) *v.t*, to weary, tire, bore; annoy, worry. **ennuyeux, euse†** (jø, ø;z) *a*, tiresome, tedious, irksome; prosy.

énoncé (enõse) *m*, statement. **énoncer** (se) *v.t*, to state, enunciate, express, specify. **énonciation** (sjasjõ) *f*, stating, enunciation.

enorgueillir (ãnorgœji;r) *v.t*, to make proud, elate. s'~, to pride oneself.

énorme (enorm) *a*, enormous, huge, mountainous, tremendous; outrageous. **énormément** (memã) *ad*, enormously. **énormité** (mite) *f*, enormousness; enormity.

enquérir (s') (ãkeri;r) *v.pr.ir*, to inquire, ask. **enquête** (kɛ;t) *f*, inquiry, investigation; inquest.

enraciner (ãrasine) *v.t. & s'~*, to take root.

enragé, e (ãraʒe) *p.a*, mad; rabid; enraged, infuriated; raging; wild. ¶ *m*, madman, fiend (*fig.*). **enrageant, e** (ʒã, ã;t) *a*, maddening. **enrager** (ʒe) *v.i*, to fume. *faire ~*, to madden, infuriate.

enrayer (ãrɛje) *v.t*, to drag, skid, lock (*wheel*); spoke (*wheel*); brake; stop, check (*fig.*).

enrégimenter (ãreʒimãte) (*fig.*) *v.t*, to enroll.

enregistrer (ãrəʒistre) *v.t*, to register; file; score; record; book; chronicle. **enregistrement** (trəmã) *m*, registration; registry.

enrhumer (ãryme) *v.t*, to give (*someone*) a cold. s'~, to catch [a] cold.

enrichi, e (ãriʃi) *n*, one who has become rich. **enrichir** (ʃi;r) *v.t*, to enrich. s'~, to make money.

enrober (ãrobe) *v.t*, to encase.

enrôler (ãrole) *v.t*, to enroll, enlist.

enrouer (ãrwe) *v.t*, to make hoarse *or* husky.

enrouler (ãrule) *v.t*, to wind, coil, wrap, roll [up].

ensablement (ãsabləmã) *m*, sandbank. **ensabler** (ble) *v.t*, to sand [up]; run aground.

ensacher (ãsaʃe) *v.t*, to bag, sack.

ensanglanter (ãsãglãte) *v.t*, to stain with blood.

enseigne (ãsɛɲ) *f*, sign; sign [board]; ensign. *à bonnes ~s*, on sure grounds; on good security. *à telles ~s que*, in proof of which. *~ de vaisseau*, *m*, ensign (*Nav.*).

enseignement (ãsɛɲmã) *m*, teaching, tuition, training, education; (*pl.*) teachings, lessons. **enseigner** (ɲe) *v.t*, to show; tell of; teach, teach how.

ensellé, e (ãsɛle) *a*, saddlebacked.

ensemble (ãsã;bl) *ad*, together. ¶ *m*, whole; aggregate; general effect; unity, harmony. *~ deux pièces*, two-piece set, two-piece ensemble (*coat & skirt*).

ensemencer (ãsmãse) *v.t*, to sow (*land*).

enserrer (ãsere) *v.t*, to encompass, enclose; tie up (*fig.*); put under glass (*Hort.*).

ensevelir (ãsəvli;r) *v.t*, to bury, entomb; plunge; shroud.

ensoleillé, e (ãsolɛje) *a*, sunny; sunlit. **ensoleiller** (je) *v.t*, to sun; light up, brighten.

ensommeillé, e (ãsomɛje) *a*, sleepy, drowsy.

ensorceler (ãsorsəle) *v.t*, to bewitch.

ensuite (ãsɥit) *ad*, afterwards, then, next. **s'ensuivre** (sɥi;vr) *v.pr.ir*, to follow, ensue.

entablement (ãtabləmã) *m*, entablature.

entacher (ãtaʃe) *v.t*, to taint; vitiate.

entaille (ãta;j) *f*, notch, nick, groove, slot; gash, hack. **entailler** (taje) *v.t*, to notch.

entame (ãtam) *f*, first cut, outside [cut]. **entamer** (me) *v.t*, to cut [into] (*slightly*); injure; penetrate; break into, broach; shake (*one's faith*); fathom; begin, open, initiate.

entasser (ãtɑse) *v.t*, to heap up, pile up, stack, huddle.

ente (ã:t) (*Hort.*) *f*, graft; stock.

entendement (ãtãdmã) *m*, understanding; intelligence. **entendre** (tã:dr) *v.t. & abs*, to hear; listen to; understand; mean; require. *laisser* ~, to hint. ~ *à*, to consent to. **s'~**, to understand; u. each other; come to an understanding; get on; be subject to. **entendu, e** (tãdy) *a*, capable, businesslike; versed; arranged; conceived. *bien entendu*, clearly understood; of course. *entendu!* agreed! okay! **entente** (tã:t) *f*, understanding. *mot, phrase, à double* ~, word, phrase, with a double meaning, double entendre.

enter (ãte) *v.t*, to [en]graft.

entérique (ãterik) *a*, enteric.

enterrement (ãtɛrmã) *m*, burial, interment; funeral. **enterrer** (re) *v.t*, to bury, inter; sink (*money, a fortune, en* = in); outlive.

en-tête (ãtɛ:t) *m*, head[ing] (*letter, bill, ledger*).

entêté, e (ãtete) *p.a*, obstinate, headstrong, stubborn. **entêtement** (tmã) *m*, obstinacy. **entêter** (te) *v.t. & abs*, to make giddy; go to the head; infatuate. **s'~**, to be obstinate.

enthousiasme (ãtuzjasm) *m*, enthusiasm; rapture. **enthousiasmer** (me) *v.t*, to enrapture, carry away. **s'~**, to go into raptures. **enthousiaste** (ast) *a*, enthusiastic, ¶ *n*, enthusiast.

enticher (ãtiʃe) *v.t*, to taint; infatuate.

entier, ère (ãtje, ɛ:r) *a*, entire, whole; full; the same, as it was; headstrong, self-willed. ¶ *m*, entirety. [*nombre*] ~, whole number, integer. *en* ~, entirely, in full, right through. **entièrement** (tjɛrmã) *ad*, entirely, wholly; fully; quite; clean (*shaven*).

entité (ãtite) *f*, entity.

entoiler (ãtwale) *v.t*, to mount [on calico *or* linen]; bind in cloth.

entomologie (ãtɔmɔlɔ3i) *f*, entomology. **entomologiste** (3ist) *m*, entomologist.

entonner (ãtɔne) *v.t. & abs*, to intone, intonate; strike up (*tune*); barrel.

entonnoir (ãtɔnwa:r) *m*, funnel; hollow; shell hole; mine crater.

entorse (ãtɔrs) *f*, sprain, strain, twist, wrench. **entortiller** (tije) *v.t*, to twist, [en]twine, wind, wrap; get round (*someone*).

entour (ãtu:r) *m*: *à l'~*, around, round about. ~**s**, *pl*, environs, outskirts, purlieus; associates; aspects. **entourage** (tura:3) *m*, setting, surroundings; environment, associates. **entourer** (re) *v.t*, to surround, beset, hedge.

en-tout-cas (ãtukɑ) *m*, umbrella-sunshade.

entracte (ãtrakt) *m*, interval, entr'acte; interlude.

entraide (ãtrɛ:d) *f*, helpfulness to each other. **s'entraider** (trede) *v.pr*, to help one another.

entrailles (ãtrɑ:j) *f.pl*, entrails, bowels, inwards; compassion, heart.

entr'aimer (s') (ãtrɛme) *v.pr*, to love one another.

entrain (ãtrɛ̃) *m*, liveliness, spirit, go, gusto. **entraînant, e** (trenã, ã:t) *a*, inspiriting, stirring. **entraînement** (nmã) *m*, impulse; force; enthusiasm; training (*sport*); sparring; coaching; pacemaking; feed (*Mach.*). **entraîner** (ne) *v.t*, to carry (*or* draw) (*or* wash) away *or* along; drift; involve, entail; lead; train; coach; pace. *s'~ à la boxe*, to spar. **entraîneur** (nœ:r) *m*, trainer; coach; pacemaker.

entrait (ãtrɛ) *m*, tie beam; tie rod.

entrant, e (ãtrã, ã:t) *a*, ingoing; insinuating.

entrave (ãtra:v) *f*, fetter, shackle, trammel, clog, obstacle; hobble. **entraver** (trave) *v.t*, to fetter; impede, hinder, hamper.

entre (ã:tr) *pr*, between; in, into; among[st]; of. ~ *deux*, *ad*, in between; middling. ~ *deux âges*, middle-aged. ~ *deux eaux*, under water.

entrebâillé, e (ãtrəbaje) *a*,

half-open, ajar. **entrebâilleur de fenêtre** (jœːr) *m*, casement stay.

entrechat (ãtrəʃa) *m*, entrechat; caper.

entrechoquer (ãtrəʃɔke) *v.t*, to strike against each other. **s'~**, to clash, collide.

entrecôte (ãtrəkoːt) *f*, rib steak.

entrecouper (ãtrəkupe) *v.t*, to intersect; break.

entrecroiser (s') (ãtrəkrwaze) *v.pr*, to intersect; criss-cross.

entre-déchirer (s') (ãtrədeʃire) *v.pr*, to tear one another to pieces.

entre-deux (ãtrədø) *m*, space [between]; parting; trough (*sea*).

entrée (ãtre) *f*, entrance, entry; ingress; admittance, admission; [admission] ticket; way in; access; entrée; beginning; mouth; inlet; gate. ~ *dans le monde*, birth; coming out (*in society*). *les ~s de faveur*, the free list (*Theat.*). ~ *de serrure*, keyhole. ~ *en douane*, clearance (*or* entry) inwards. ~ *en séance*, opening of the sitting. [*droit d'*]~, import duty.

entrefaite (ãtrəfɛt) *f: sur ces ~s*, in the midst of all this.

entrefilet (ãtrəfile) *m*, [short] paragraph (*newspaper*).

entregent (ãtrəʒã) *m*, tact; gumption.

entrelacer (ãtrəlase) *v.t*, to interlace, intertwine, interweave.

entrelardé, e (ãtrəlarde) *p.a*, streaky (*meat*). **entrelarder** (de) *v.t*, to lard; interlard.

entre-ligne (ãtrəliɲ) *m*, interlineation.

entremêler (ãtrəmɛle) *v.t*, to [inter]mix, intermingle; intersperse.

entremets (ãtrəmɛ) *m*, side dish; dessert (*dinner course*).

entremetteur, euse (ãtrəmɛtœːr, øːz) *n*, go-between. **s'entremettre** (tr) *v.pr.ir*, to intervene. **entremise** (miːz) *f*, intervention; agency, medium.

entrepont (ãtrəpɔ̃) *m*, betweendecks.

entreposer (ãtrəpoze) *v.t*, to warehouse, store; bond. **entreposeur** (zœːr) *m*, warehouse keeper; bonded storekeeper. **en-**

trepositaire (ziteːr) *n*, bonder. **entrepôt** (po) *m*, warehouse, store; emporium, mart. ~ *frigorifique*, cold storage. ~ [*légal*], ~ *de douane*, bond[ed warehouse]. *en* ~ ou *à l'* ~ ou *en E.*, in bond[ed warehouse].

entreprenant, e (ãtrəprənã, ãːt) *a*, enterprising, pushing. **entreprendre** (prãːdr) *v.t.ir*, to undertake; contract for; tackle (*pers.*). ~ *sur*, to encroach on. **entrepreneur** (prənœːr) *m*, contractor. ~ *de monuments funéraires*, ~ *de pompes funèbres*, undertaker. ~ *de transports*, ~ *de roulage*, haulage contractor, carrier. **entreprise** (priːz) *f*, undertaking; enterprise; concern; business; contract; encroachment.

entrer (ãtre) *v.i*, to enter; come in; go in; walk in; march in; step in; get in; go; come. ~ *en déchargement*, to break bulk (*Ship.*). *X. entre* [*en scène*], enter X. (*Theat.*). ¶ *v.t*, to introduce. ~ *en fraude*, to smuggle in.

entresol (ãtrəsɔl) *m*, mezzanine [floor].

entre-temps (ãtrətã) *ad*, meanwhile. ¶ *m*, interval.

entretenir (ãtrətniːr) *v.t.ir*, to maintain; keep in repair; keep up; support, keep; speak to, report to. **s'~**, to last; hold together; converse. *s'~ la main*, to keep one's hand in. **entretien** (tjɛ̃) *m*, maintenance; upkeep; support; keep; clothes, dress; talk; interview.

entretoile (ãtrətwal) *f*, lace insertion.

entretoise (ãtrətwaːz) *f*, brace, strut, cross-piece; stay-bolt.

entrevoir (ãtrəvwaːr) *v.t.ir*, to catch a glimpse of; see indistinctly; sense. **s'~**, to see each other, meet. **entrevue** (vy) *f*, interview.

entrouvrir (ãtruvriːr) *v.t.ir*, to half-open.

énumérer (enymere) *v.t*, to enumerate, rehearse; recite.

envahir (ãvaiːr) *v.t*, to invade, break into; overrun; flood; overgrow; encroach on, trench on. **envahissement** (ismã) *m*, invasion;

inrush; encroachment. **envahisseur** (sœːr) m, invader.

envaser (s') (ãvaze) v.pr, to silt up; sink in the mud.

enveloppe (ãvlɔp) f, envelope; wrapper; cover[ing]; jacket[ing]; sheath[ing]; lagging; casing; exterior (fig.). ~ à panneau, ~ à fenêtre, window envelope. ~ affranchie pour la réponse, stamped addressed e. **envelopper** (vlɔpe) v.t, to envelop; wrap [up]; enfold; [en]shroud; cover; case; jacket; lag; involve.

envenimer (ãvnime) v.t, to poison; envenom, embitter.

envergure (ãvɛrgyːr) f, spread, span; wing spread, w. span; stretch; expanse; breadth.

envers (ãvɛːr) m, wrong side, back, reverse; seamy side. à l'~, inside out; topsy-turvy. ¶ pr, towards, to. ~ & contre tous, through thick & thin.

envi (à l') (ãvi), in emulation, vying.

envie (ãvi) f, envy; wish, desire, mind, longing, fancy; birthmark; agnail, hang-nail. **envier** (vje) v.t, to envy, begrudge. **envieux, euse** (vjø, øːz) a, envious.

environ (ãvirɔ̃) ad, about, thereabouts. ~s, m.pl, environs, outskirts, purlieus, neighborhood. **environner** (rɔne) v.t, to environ, surround; beset.

envisager (ãvizaʒe) v.t, to look in the face; look on; envisage; contemplate, view.

envoi (ãvwa) m, sending, forwarding, dispatch; sending in, s. out; remittance; consignment; parcel, package; article (Post). ~ contre remboursement, cash on delivery.

envol (ãvɔl) m, flight; taking off (Avn.). **envolée** (le) f, flight (fig.). **s'envoler** (le) v.pr, to fly [away]; take off (Avn.).

envoûter (ãvute) v.t, to bewitch.

envoyé, e (ãvwaje) n, envoy; messenger. ~ spécial, special correspondent. **envoyer** (je) v.t, to send, forward, dispatch; send in, s. out; remit; tender. **envoyeur, euse** (jœːr, øːz) n, sender.

éolien, ne (eɔljɛ̃, ɛn) a, Aeolian, wind (att.).

épagneul, e (epaɲœl) n, spaniel.

épais, e (epɛ, ɛːs) a, thick, dense. ~ de, thick (Meas.). **épais,** ad, thick[ly]. ¶ m, thickness. **épaisseur** (pɛsœːr) f, thickness; ply; thick; density. **épaissir** (siːr) v.t, to thicken. ~, v.i. & s'~, to thicken; get stout.

épanchement (epãʃmã) m, effusion, outpouring. ~ de synovie (sinɔvi), water on the knee. **épancher** (ʃe) v.t, to pour out; vent; open (heart). s'~, to overflow.

épandre (epãːdr) v.t, to spread; shed.

épanoui (epanwi) a, in full bloom; beaming, cheerful, etc. **épanouir** (epanwiːr) v.t. & s'~, to open, expand; brighten.

épargne (eparɲ) f, saving, economy, thrift. La petite ~, the small investor. **épargner** (ɲe) v.t, to save [up], lay by, economize, husband; spare, grudge, stint.

éparpiller (eparpije) v.t, to scatter; fritter away. **épars, e** (paːr, ars) a, scattered, straggling.

épatant (epatã) a, fine, wonderful, terrific.

épaté, e (epate) p.a, amazed; with crippled foot; flat (nose). **épater** (te) v.t, to astonish.

épaulard (epolaːr) m, grampus, orc.

épaule (epoːl) f, shoulder. **épaulée** (pole) f, push with the shoulder. **épaulement** (lmã) m, shoulder (Carp.). **épauler** (le) v.t, to splay; shoulder; bring (rifle) to the shoulder; back up. **épaulette** (lɛt) f, yoke (dress); shoulder strap; epaulet[te].

épave (epaːv) a, stray[ed]. ¶ f, stray; derelict, wreck; (pl.) wreckage; jetsam; flotsam; lagan; remnant.

épée (epe) f, sword. ~ de chevet, fallback; ruling passion.

épeler (eple) v.t, to spell. **épellation** (pɛlasjɔ̃) f, spelling.

éperdu†, e (epɛrdy) a, distracted; desperate.

éperlan (epɛrlã) m, smelt (fish).

éperon (eprɔ̃) m, spur; buttress; ram (battleship). **éperonner** (prɔne) v.t, to spur; s. on.

épervier (epɛrvje) *m*, sparrow hawk; sweep net, cast net.

éphélide (efelid) *f*, freckle.

éphémère (efemɛːr) *a*, ephemeral, mushroom. ¶ *m*, ephemera, -ron, Mayfly. **éphéméride** (merid) *f*, ephemeris; block calendar.

épi (epi) *m*, ear (*grain*); cob (*corn*); spike (*flower*); spray (*jewels*).

épice (epis) *f*, spice. **épicé, e** (se) *a*, spicy. **épicer** (se) *v.t*, to spice. **épicerie** (sri) *f*, grocery; grocer's shop; spices. **épicier, ère** (sje, ɛːr) *n*, grocer.

épicurien, ne (epikyrjɛ̃, ɛn) *a*. & *m*, epicurean.

épidémie (epidemi) *f*, epidemic, outbreak (*disease*). **épidémique** (mik) *a*, epidemic.

épiderme (epidɛrm) *m*, epidermis. *avoir l'~ sensible*, to be thin-skinned (*fig.*).

épier (epje) *v.t*, to spy [on], watch.

épieu (epjø) *m*, boar spear.

épiglotte (epiglɔt) *f*, epiglottis.

épigramme (epigram) *f*, epigram; skit.

épigraphe (epigraf) *f*, epigraph, quotation, motto (*prefixed to book or chapter*).

épilepsie (epilɛpsi) *f*, epilepsy. **épileptique** (tik) *a*. & *n*, epileptic.

épiler (epile) *v.t*, to depilate, pluck [out hairs].

épilogue (epilɔg) *m*, epilogue. **épiloguer** (ge) *v.i*, to find fault. **épilogueur, euse** (gœːr, ∅ːz) *n*, faultfinder.

épinard (*Bot.*) *m*. & *~s* (*Cook.*) *pl*. (epinaːr), spinach. *~s en branches*, leaf s.

épine (epin) *f*, thorn [bush]; thorn; spine (*Bot.*). *~ blanche*, hawthorn, whitethorn. *~ noire*, blackthorn. *~ dorsale*, spine, backbone. **épineux, euse** (nø, ∅ːz) *a*, thorny, spiny, prickly; knotty. **épine-vinette** (vinɛt) *f*, barberry, berberry.

épingle (epɛ̃ːgl) *f*, pin. *~ à friser*, hair curler. *~ à linge*, clothespin. *~ de sûreté*, *~ de nourrice*, *~ anglaise*, safety pin. *~s*, pin money. **épingler** (pɛ̃gle) *v.t*, to pin.

épinoche (epinɔʃ) *f*, stickleback.

Épiphanie (epifani) *f*, Epiphany.

épique (epik) *a*, epic.

épiscopal, e (episkɔpal) *a*, episcopal. **épiscopat** (pa) *m*, episcopate; episcopacy.

épisode (epizɔd) *m*, episode.

épisser (epise) *v.t*, to splice (*rope*). **épissoir** (swaːr) *m*, marline spike, marlinspike. **épissure** (syːr) *f*, splice.

épistolaire (epistɔlɛːr) *a*, epistolary. **épistolier, ère** (lje, ɛːr) *n*, letter writer (*pers.*).

épitaphe (epitaf) *f*, epitaph.

épithète (epitɛt) *f*, epithet.

épitomé (epitome) *m*, epitome.

épître (epiːtr) *f*, epistle; letter.

éploré, e (eplɔre) *a*, tearful, in tears, weeping.

éplucher (eplyʃe) *v.t*, to prepare, clean; peel, pare; preen, prink; sift (*fig.*), scan. *s'~*, to plume (*or* preen) (*or* prink) its feathers. **épluchures** (ʃyːr) *f.pl*, parings, peelings.

épointer (epwɛ̃te) *v.t*, to break the point of; point (*sharpen*).

éponge (epɔ̃ːʒ) *f*, sponge. **éponger** (pɔ̃ʒe) *v.t*, to sponge; mop; mop up; dab; blot.

épontille (epɔ̃tiːj) *f*, stanchion (*ship*).

épopée (epɔpe) *f*, epic, epopee, epos.

époque (epɔk) *f*, epoch; era, age; time, date, period.

époumoner (epumone) *v.t*, to puff.

épouse (epuːz) *f*, wife, spouse, consort. **épouser** (puze) *v.t*, to marry, wed; espouse. *~ [la forme de]*, to correspond (*or* conform) in shape to; adapt itself to, fit.

épousseter (epuste) *v.t*, to dust; rub down.

épouvantable† (epuvɑ̃tabl) *a*, frightful, fearful, dreadful. **épouvantail** (taːj) *m*, scarecrow; bugbear. **épouvante** (vɑ̃ːt) *f*, terror, fright. **épouvanter** (vɑ̃te) *v.t*, to terrify, frighten, scare.

époux (epu) *m*, husband, spouse, consort; (*pl.*) husband & wife, [married] couple.

épreindre (eprɛ̃ːdr) *v.t.ir*, to press [out], squeeze [out].

éprendre (s') (eprɑ̃ːdr) *v.pr.ir*, to be smitten, be enamored, be taken, fall in love. **épris** (epri) *a*, smitten; in love.

épreuve (eprœːv) *f*, test[ing]; trial; ordeal; proof (*Typ*.); heat (*sport*); event (*sport*). ~ *d'imprimerie*, printer's proof. ~ *en placard*, galley proof. [~] *finale*, final [heat]. ~ *négative*, negative (*Phot.*). ~ *nulle*, dead heat. ~ [*positive*], print, positive (*Phot.*). *à l'*~ *de*, proof against. *à l'*~ *du feu, des intempéries, des maladresses*, fireproof, weather-p., fool-p. *à toute* ~, unflinching; trusty. **éprouver** (pruve) *v.t*, to test, prove, try; experience, meet with, sustain, undergo; suffer; feel. **éprouvette** (vɛt) *f*, test glass; t. tube; t. piece; probe (*Surg.*).

épuisé, e (epɥize) *p.a*, exhausted, spent; effete; out of print. **épuiser** (ze) *v.t*, to exhaust; drain; empty. **épuisette** (zɛt) *f*, landing net; scoop, bailer.

épuration (epyrasjɔ̃) *f*, purification; refining. **épure** (pyːr) *f*, working drawing; diagram. **épurer** (pyre) *v.t*, to purify; refine; weed out.

équarrir (ekariːr) *v.t*, to square; quarter, cut up (*dead animal*). **équateur** (ekwatœːr) *m*, equator. *l'É*~ (*Geog.*), Ecuador. **équation** (ekwasjɔ̃) *f*, equation. **équatorial, e** (ekwatɔrjal) *a*, equatorial. ¶ *m*, equatorial [telescope].

équerre (ekɛːr) *f*, square (*instrument & at right angles*).

équestre (ekɛstr) *a*, equestrian. **équilibre** (ekilibr) *m*, equilibrium; [equi]poise; balance; b. of power (*Pol.*). **équilibrer** (bre) *v.t*, to equilibrate, poise, balance, counterbalance.

équinoxe (ekinɔks) *m*, equinox. **équinoxial, e** (ksjal) *a*, equinoctial.

équipage (ekipaːʒ) *m*, crew (*ship*); outfit, rig; set; train; equipage, turnout; plight. ~ *de chasse*, hunt. **équipe** (kip) *f*, train (*of boats*); shift, gang, corps, squad; crew (*boat*); team, side (*sport*). **équipée** (pe) *f*, escapade, lark. **équipement** (pmɑ̃) *m*, equipment; outfit. **équiper** (pe) *v.t*, to equip, fit out, rig [out].

équitable† (ekitabl) *a*, equitable, fair, just.

équitation (ekitasjɔ̃) *f*, riding, horsemanship.

équité (ekite) *f*, equity, fairness.

équivalent, e (ekivalɑ̃, ɑ̃ːt) *a*. & *m*, equivalent. **équivaloir** (lwaːr) *v.i.ir*, to be equivalent; be tantamount.

équivoque (ekivɔk) *a*, equivocal; ambiguous, dubious, questionable. ¶ *f*, equivocation, ambiguity, prevarication. **équivoquer** (ke) *v.i*, to equivocate, prevaricate.

érable (erabl) *m*, maple. ~ *madré*, bird's-eye maple.

éradication (eradikasjɔ̃) *f*, eradication.

érafler (erafle) *v.t*, to scratch, graze. **éraflure** (flyːr) *f*, scratch.

éraillé, e (eraje) *p.a*, frayed; husky, hoarse; bloodshot. **érailler** (je) *v.t*, to fray.

ère (ɛːr) *f*, era, epoch.

Érèbe (l') (erɛb) *m*, Erebus.

érection (erɛksjɔ̃) *f*, erection; raising.

éreinter (erɛ̃te) *v.t*, to break the back of; tire out; lash (*fig.*), slate, pull to pieces.

ergot (ɛrgo) *m*, spur (*bird*); snug, lug; pin; ergot (*Bot. & Med.*). **ergoté, e** (gɔte) *a*, spurred (*bird*). **ergoter** (te) *v.i*, to cavil, quibble.

Érié (le lac) (erje), Lake Erie.

ériger (eriʒe) *v.t*, to erect, put up; raise, set up.

ermitage (ɛrmitaːʒ) *m*, hermitage. **ermite** (mit) *m*, hermit.

éroder (erɔde) *v.t*, to erode. **érosion** (zjɔ̃) *f*, erosion.

érotique (erɔtik) *a*, erotic; amatory.

errant, e (ɛrɑ̃, ɑ̃ːt) *a*, wandering; roving; stray; errant. **erratique** (ratik) *a*, erratic (*Geol., Med., etc.*).

erratum (ɛratɔm) *m*, erratum. **erre** (ɛːr) *f*, [head]way (*Naut.*); (*pl.*) track, spoor; (*pl.*) footsteps (*fig.*). **errements** (ɛrmɑ̃) *m.pl*, ways, methods. **errer** (ɛre) *v.i*, to wander, roam, rove, stroll, stray; err. **erreur** (rœːr) *f*, error, mistake; fallacy. ~ *de calcul*, miscalculation. ~ *de nom*, misnomer. ~ *de* (ou *sur la*) *personne*, mistaken identity. ~ *typographique*, misprint. **erroné, e** (rɔne) *a*, erroneous, wrong, mistaken.

éructation (eryktasjɔ̃) *f*, eructation, belch[ing]. **éructer** (te) *v.i*, to eruct, belch.

érudit, e (erydi, it) *a*, erudite, scholarly, learned. ¶ *m*, scholar, learned man. **érudition** (disjɔ̃) *f*, erudition, learning, scholarship.

éruption (erypsjɔ̃) *f*, eruption; rash.

ès (ɛs) *pr*, of; in.

escabeau (ɛskabo) *m*. & **escabelle** (bɛl) *f*, stool.

escadre (ɛska:dr) *f*, squadron (*Nav.*). **escadrille** (kadri:j) *f*, flotilla (*Nav.*); squadron (*air*). **escadron** (drɔ̃) *m*, squadron (*cavalry*).

escalade (ɛskalad) *f*, scaling. **escalader** (de) *v.t*, to scale, climb [over].

escale (ɛskal) *f*, call (*Ship.*); port of call. *faire* ~, to call.

escalier (ɛskalje) *m*, stair[s], staircase. ~ *d'honneur*, grand staircase. ~ *roulant*, escalator. ~ *tournant*, spiral (*or* winding) stairs.

escalope (ɛskalɔp) *f*, cutlet.

escamotage (ɛskamɔta:ʒ) *m*, juggling, conjuring. **escamoter** (te) *v.t*, to conjure away, spirit away; filch; (*abs.*) to juggle, conjure. **escamoteur** (tœ:r) *m*, juggler, conjuror, -er; pickpocket.

escampette (ɛskɑ̃pɛt) *f: prendre la poudre d'*~, to bolt, skedaddle. **escapade** (kapad) *f*, escapade, prank, lark.

escarbille (ɛskarbi:j) *f*, [coal] cinder.

escarbot (ɛskarbo) *m*, dung beetle.

escargot (ɛskargo) *m*, (*edible*) snail.

escarmouche (ɛskarmuʃ) *f*, skirmish. **escarmoucher** (ʃe) *v.i*, to skirmish.

escarpe (ɛskarp) *f*, [e]scarp. ¶ *m*, cutthroat, desperado. **escarpé, e** (pe) *a*, precipitous, steep, bluff.

escarpement (pəmɑ̃) *m*, steepness; escarpment; slope.

escarpin (ɛskarpɛ̃) *m*, pump (*dress shoe*).

escarpolette (ɛskarpɔlɛt) *f*, swing (*child's*).

escarre (ɛska:r) *f*, scab (*Med.*).

Escaut (l') (ɛsko) *m*, the Scheldt.

escient (ɛsjɑ̃) *m*, knowledge. *à bon* ~, knowingly, wittingly.

esclaffer (s') (ɛsklafe) *v.pr*, to burst out laughing.

esclandre (ɛsklɑ̃:dr) *m*, scandal, scene.

esclavage (ɛsklava:ʒ) *m*, slavery, bondage, thraldom. **esclave** (kla:v) *n*, slave, thrall.

escobarder (ɛskɔbarde) *v.i*, to shuffle.

escogriffe (ɛskɔgrif) *m*, gawk, lout.

escompte (ɛskɔ̃:t) *m*, discount; discounting. **escompter** (kɔ̃te) *v.t*, to discount; cash (*a check for someone*); anticipate; bank on.

escorte (ɛskɔrt) *f*, escort; convoy. **escorter** (te) *v.t*, to escort; convoy.

escouade (ɛskwad) *f*, squad, gang.

escrime (ɛskrim) *f*, fencing, swordsmanship. **s'escrimer** (me) *v.pr*, to try hard.

escroc (ɛskro) *m*, swindler, sharper, crook. **escroquer** (krɔke) *v.t.* & *abs*, to swindle, swindle out of.

espace (ɛspɑs) *m*, space; room; (*f.*) space (*Typ.*). **espacer** (se) *v.t*, to space.

espadon (ɛspadɔ̃) *m*, swordfish.

espadrille (ɛspadri:j) *f*, canvas shoe with hempen sole.

Espagne (l') (ɛspaɲ) *f*, Spain. **espagnol, e** (ɲɔl) *a*. & (*language*) *m*, Spanish. **E~**, *n*, Spaniard. **espagnolette** (lɛt) *f*, espagnolette.

espalier (ɛspalje) *m*, espalier.

espar (ɛspa:r) *m*, spar (*Naut.*); handspike (*Mil.*).

espèce (ɛspɛs) *f*, kind, sort, species; case in point (*law*); (*pl.*) cash, coin, specie. *l'*~ *animale*, the brute creation. *l'*~ *humaine*, mankind. ~*s sonnantes*, hard cash.

espérance (ɛsperɑ̃:s) *f*, hope,

expectation; (*pl.*) promise. **espérer** (re) *v.t. & abs*, to hope for, expect; trust; hope.

espiègle (ɛspjɛgl) *a*, roguish, mischievous, impish, elfish; arch. ¶ *n*, rogue (*playfully*). **espièglerie** (gləri) *f*, roguishness, mischief, prank.

espion, ne (ɛspjõ, ɔn) *n*, spy. **espionnage** (ɔna:ʒ) *m*, espionage, spying. **espionner** (ne) *v.t. & abs*, to spy upon, watch; spy.

esplanade (ɛsplanad) *f*, esplanade, parade.

espoir (ɛspwa:r) *m*, hope, expectation.

esprit (ɛspri) *m*, spirit; ghost; mind; nous; feeling; sense; head; wit; temper. *l'~ de caste*, class consciousness. *~ de corps*, esprit de corps; team spirit. *~ fort*, free thinker. *le Saint-Esprit ou l'Esprit-Saint*, the Holy Ghost, the Holy Spirit.

esquif (ɛskif) *m*, skiff.

esquille (ɛski:j) *f*, splinter (*of bone*).

esquisse (ɛskis) *f*, sketch; outline. **esquisser** (se) *v.t*, to sketch.

esquive (ɛski:v) *f*, slip (*Box.*), dodging. **esquiver** (kive) *v.t*, to avoid, evade; dodge, slip. *s'~*, to slip away.

essai (ɛsɛ) *m*, test[ing], trial; attempt; assay[ing]; essay.

essaim (ɛsɛ̃) *m*, swarm (*bees*). **essaimer** (ɛseme) *v.i*, to swarm; branch out (*fig.*).

essanger (ɛsɑ̃ʒe) *v.t*, to soak (*dirty linen*).

essarter (ɛsarte) *v.t*, to clear; grub up.

essayage (ɛsɛja:ʒ) *m*, testing; fitting; trying on.

essayer (ɛsɛje) *v.t*, to try, essay, endeavor, attempt; try on (*clothes*); test, essay. *s'~ à*, to try one's hand (*or* skill) at. **essayeur, euse** (jœ:r, ø:z) *n*, essayer; fitter (*clothes*). **essayiste** (jist) *n*, essayist.

esse (ɛs) *f*, S; S hook; linchpin.

essence (ɛsɑ̃:s) *f*, essence; spirit; gasoline; kind *or* species (*of tree or wood*). *~ de bergamote*, bergamot oil. *~ de roses*, otto of roses, attar [of roses]. **essentiel,**

let† (sɑ̃sjɛl) *a*, essential, material. ¶ *m*, essential, main point.

esseulé, e (ɛsœle) *p.p*, lone[some].

essieu (ɛsjø) *m*, axle, axletree.

essor (ɛsɔ:r) *m*, flight, soaring, wing; play; scope; progress, strides.

essorer (ɛsɔre) *v.t*, to dry; wring (*washing*). **essoreuse** (rø:z) *f*, wringer.

essoriller (ɛsɔrije) *v.t*, to crop.

essoufler (ɛsufle) *v.t*, to blow, wind.

essuie-glace (ɛsɥi) *m*, windshield wiper. **essuie-main**, *m*, [hand] towel. **essuie-plume**, *m*, penwiper. **essuie-verres**, *m*, glass cloth. **essuyer** (sɥije) *v.t*, to wipe [up], dry; mop up; endure, go through; experience, meet with.

est (ɛst) *m*, east.

estacade (ɛstakad) *f*, wing dam; jetty; boom (*harbor*); coal stage.

estafette (ɛstafɛt) *f*, courier; dispatch rider.

estafilade (ɛstafilad) *f*, gash; rent.

estame (ɛstam) *f*, worsted (*fabric*).

estaminet (ɛstaminɛ) *m*, small café & bar.

estampe (ɛstɑ̃:p) *f*, print, engraving; swage. **estamper** (tɑ̃pe) *v.t*, to stamp; emboss; swage; dropforge; rub (*inscription*).

estampille (ɛstɑ̃pi:j) *f*, stamp; trademark. **estampiller** (pije) *v.t*, to stamp; mark.

esthétique (ɛstetik) *a*, aesthetic.

estimation (ɛstimasjõ) *f*, estimate, valuation; dead reckoning (*Naut.*). **estime** (tim) *f*, esteem, estimation; dead reckoning (*Naut.*). **estimer** (me) *v.t*, to estimate; value; esteem; deem; reckon.

estival, e (ɛstival) *a*, summer (*att.*). **estiver** (ve) *v.t*, to summer (*cattle*).

estoc (ɛstɔk) *m*, point (*sword*); stock (*tree*). **estocade** (kad) *f*, thrust (*Fenc.*). **estocader** (de) *v.t*, to thrust.

estomac (ɛstɔma) *m*, stomach; pluck. **estomaquer** (make) *v.t*, to take (*someone's*) breath away; offend.

estompe (ɛstõ:p) *f*, stump (*art*).

estomper (tõpe) *v.t*, to stump; tone down (*fig.*).

Estonie (l') (ɛstɔni) *f*, Estonia.

estouffade (ɛstufad) *f*, steaming (*Cook.*).

estrade (ɛstrad) *f*, platform, stage; dais.

estragon (ɛstragɔ̃) *m*, tarragon.

estropié, e (ɛstrɔpje) *n*, cripple. **estropier** (pje) *v.t*, to cripple, lame; maim; murder (*language*).

estuaire (ɛstyɛːr) *m*, estuary, firth.

esturgeon (ɛstyrʒɔ̃) *m*, sturgeon.

et (e) *c.* (*abb. &*), and, &. ~ . . . ~ . . ., both . . . and . . . ~ *ainsi de suite*, and so on; and so forth. ~ *patati*, ~ *patata* (patati, ta), and so on, and so forth.

étable (etabl) *f*, (*cattle*) shed, house; sty. **établer** (ble) *v.t*, to stable, stall; sty.

établi (etabli) *m*, [work] bench, stand. **établir** (bliːr) *v.t*, to establish; set up; set (*a sail*); lay down; settle; draw [up], make out; strike (*balance*); prove; substantiate. **établissement** (blismã) *m*, establishment, etc; institution; capital expenditure.

étage (etaːʒ) *m*, floor, stor[e]y; stage, level; step; tier; rank, degree; measures (*Geol.*). **étager** (taʒe) *v.t*, to range; terrace; spread. **étagère** (ʒɛːr) *f*, [set of] shelves; whatnot; dresser. ~ *de cheminée*, mantelpiece.

étai (etɛ) *m*, shore, prop, post; stay.

étain (etɛ̃) *m*, tin; pewter. *feuille d'*~, tinfoil.

étal (etal) *m*, butcher's shop. **étalage** (laːʒ) *m*, (*shop*) window [show]; window dressing; show; display; stall. **étalagiste** (laʒist) *n*, frontsman; stall holder; window dresser.

étale (etal) *a.inv*, slack (*water*) (*Naut.*).

étaler (etale) *v.t*, to expose for sale; show; show off, flaunt, air; display; lay out; spread [out]; stem (*the tide*). s'~, to sprawl.

étalon (etalɔ̃) *m*, stallion, stud horse; standard (*of values*). **étalonner** (lɔne) *v.t*, to stamp (*weights, etc.*); rate; standardize.

étambot (etãbo) *m*, sternpost (*ship*).

étamer (etame) *v.t*, to tin; silver (*mirror*).

étamine (etamin) *f*, bolting cloth; filter cloth; stamen (*Bot.*) ~ *à pavillon*, bunting.

étamper (etãpe) *v.t*, to stamp, press; swage; drop-forge.

étanche (etãːʃ) *a*, tight; water tight; impervious. **étanche** (tãʃe) *v.t*, to staunch, stop; make watertight; dry; quench, slake.

étançon (etãsɔ̃) *m*, shore; stanchion. **étançonner** (sɔne) *v.t*, to shore [up].

étang (etã) *m*, pond, pool.

étape (etap) *f*, stage, stopping place.

état (eta) *m*, state; condition; frame (*of mind*); plight; repair; order; fettle, trim; status; position, posture; profession, occupation; statement, account, return, list; state (*stage of en graved or etched plate*). en [bon] ~ *de navigabilité*, seaworthy; airworthy. ~ *de siège*, state of siege. ~ *des malades*, sick list. **État,** *m*, State government; *les* ~*s-Unis* [*d'Amérique*], the United States [of America]. **éta tisme** (tism) *m*, State socialism, nationalism. **État-major** (maʒɔːr) *m*, staff (*Mil.*); [staff] headquarters; senior officers, executive.

étau (eto) *m*, vise (*tool*). ~*-limeur* (limœːr), shaping machine.

étayer (etɛje) *v.t*, to shore [up]; prop, support.

et cætera (etsetera) *phrase & m.* (*abb.* etc.), et cetera, etc.

été (ete) *m*, summer; prime [of life]. ¶ *p.p*, être.

éteignoir (etɛɲwaːr) *m*, extinguisher (*light*); damper, wet blanket (*fig.*, *pers.*). **éteindre** (tɛ̃dr) *v.t.ir*, to extinguish, put out; silence (*enemy's fire*); slake, slack; quench; pay off; soften. ~ *la lumière*, ~ *l'électricité*, to switch off (*or* turn off) the light. s'~, to go out (*light*); pass away; die [out]. **éteint, e** (tɛ̃, ɛ̃t) *p.a*, extinct; out; dull.

étendage (etãdaːʒ) *m*, hanging out (*washing*); spreading; clothes-lines; lying at full length. **étan-**

dard (da:r) *m*, standard, flag, colors. **étendoir** (dwa:r) *m*, clothesline; drying yard. **étendre** (tã:dr) *v.t*, to spread, extend; expand; widen; stretch [out]; reach [out]; lay [out]; hang out; dilute. **s'~**, to extend; spread; stretch; reach; expatiate, enlarge. **étendu, e** (tãdy) *a*, extensive, wide, far-reaching; outspread; outstretched. **étendue** (dy) *f*, extent; area; compass; stretch, expanse, sweep, tract; reach; range; scope; length.

éternel, le† (etɛrnɛl) *a*, eternal, everlasting; never-ending. **éterniser** (nize) *v.t*, to eternalize; protract. **s'~**, to last (*or* stay) forever. **éternité** (te) *f*, eternity.

éternuement (etɛrnymã) *m*, sneezing; sneeze. **éternuer** (nɥe) *v.i*, to sneeze.

étêter (etɛte) *v.t*, to top, poll; take the head off.

éteule (etœl) *f*, stubble.

éther (etɛ:r) *m*, ether. **éthéré, e** (tere) *a*, ethereal.

Éthiopie (l') (etjɔpi) *f*, Ethiopia. **éthiopien, ne** (pjɛ̃, ɛn) *a. & É~, n*, Ethiopian.

éthique (etik) *a*, ethical. ¶ *f*, ethics.

ethnographie (ɛtnɔgrafi) *f*, ethnography. **ethnologie** (lɔʒi) *f*, ethnology. **ethnologique** (ʒik) *a*, ethnologic(al). **ethnologue** (lɔg) *m*, ethnologist.

éthyle (etil) *m*, ethyl.

étiage (etja:ʒ) *m*, low water; low-water mark (*river*).

étinceler (etɛ̃sle) *v.i*, to sparkle, glitter, glisten, flash. **étincelle** (sɛl) *f*, spark; sparkle, flash.

étioler (etjɔle) *v.t*, to etiolate, blanch. **s'~**, to droop, wilt.

étique (etik) *a*, emaciated, skinny.

étiqueter (etikte) *v.t*, to label; ticket. **étiquette** (kɛt) *f*, label; tally; ticket; etiquette. **~ volante**, tie-on label, tag label.

étirer (etire) *v.t*, to stretch, draw [out].

étoffe (etɔf) *f*, stuff; fabric; material; grit (*fig.*); establishment charges (*printer's*). **~ à carreaux**, **~ en damier**, check [material]. **étoffé, e** (fe) *p.a*, stuffed; stocky. **étoffer** (fe) *v.t*, to use

sufficient material in; stuff; fill out.

étoile (etwal) *f*, star; asterisk. **~ de mer**, starfish. **~ du matin**, **~ matinière** (matinjɛ:r), morning star. **~ tombante**, **~ filante**, shooting s., falling s. *à la belle ~*, in the open. **étoilé, e** (le) *a*, starry; starli[gh]t; starred.

étole (etɔl) *f*, stole.

étonnant, e (etɔnã, ã:t) *a*, astonishing, amazing, surprising; wonderful. **étonnamment** (namã) *ad*, astonishingly. **étonnement** (nmã) *m*, astonishment. **étonner** (ne) *v.t*, to astonish, amaze, surprise. **s'~**, to be astonished, wonder, marvel.

étouffant, e (etufã, ã:t) *a*, stifling, sultry; stuffy.

étouffée (etufe) *f*, steaming (*Cook.*).

étouffer (etufe) *v.t. & i*, to choke, stifle; smother; quell; hush up. **étouffoir** (fwa:r) *m*, charcoal extinguisher; damper (*piano*).

étoupe (etup) *f*, tow, junk, oakum. **étouper** (pe) *v.t*, to caulk.

étoupille (etupi:j) *f*, friction tube; fuse.

étourderie (eturdəri) *f*, thoughtlessness. **étourdi, e** (di) *a*, thoughtless, heedless; flighty. ¶ *m*, scatterbrain. **à l'étourdie** & **étourdiment** (dimã) *ad*, thoughtlessly. **étourdir** (di:r) *v.t*, to stun; deafen; din; make dizzy; daze; deaden. **s'~**, to forget (*or* drown) one's troubles. **étourdissement** (dismã) *m*, dizziness, giddiness; stupefaction.

étourneau (eturno) *m*, starling (*bird*); foolish youth.

étrange† (etrã:ʒ) *a*, strange, odd, queer; quaint. **étranger, ère** (trãʒe, ɛ:r) *a*, foreign; strange; unfamiliar; extraneous; alien, irrelevant. ¶ *n*, foreigner, alien; stranger. ¶ *m*, foreign parts. **à l'~**, *ad*, abroad. **de l'~**, from abroad. **étrangeté** (ʒte) *f*, strangeness, oddness; quaintness.

étranglement (etrãgləmã) *m*, strangulation. **étrangler** (gle) *v.t*, to strangle, throttle, choke; narrow; squeeze; strangulate; (*v.i.*) to choke.

étrave (etra:v) *f*, stem (*ship*).

être (ε:tr) *m*, being; creature;
thing; reality; stock (*tree*); (*pl.*)
ins & outs (*of a house*). ¶ *v.i.ir*,
to be; belong; come; have. *y* ~,
to get it, understand.

étrécir (etresi:r) *v.t.* & *i.* & *s'*~,
to narrow, shrink, contract.

étreindre (etrɛ̃:dr) *v.t.ir*, to
clasp, hug, grip; wring; bind.
étreinte (trɛ̃:t) *f*, grip, grasp;
hug, embrace.

étrenne (etrɛn) *f*, first use; (*pl.*)
New Year's gift, handsel; Christmas present. (*In Fr. presents
are given on or about Jan. 1*).
étrenner (trɛne) *v.t*, to be the
first customer of; use (*or wear*)
for the first time; handsel.

étrésillon (etrezijɔ̃) *m*, strut,
brace; flying shore.

étrier (etrie) *m*, stirrup; U bolt;
strap.

étrille (etri:j) *f*, currycomb.
étriller (trije) *v.t*, to curry; drub;
fleece.

étriper (etripe) *v.t*, to gut.

étriqué, e (etrike) *a*, scant[y],
narrow; cramped. **étriquer** (ke)
v.t, to skimp.

étrivière (etrivjɛ:r) *f*, stirrup
leather; (*pl.*) thrashing.

étroit, e† (etrwa, at) *a*, narrow;
limited; close; tight; strict. **étroitesse** (tɛs) *f*, narrowness, etc.

étude (etyd) *f*, study; preparation (*Sch.*); survey; (*lawyer's*)
office; practice. **étudiant, e** (djɑ̃,
ɑ̃:t) *n*, student. **étudier** (dje) *v.i.*
& *t*, to study; read; survey. **s'**~,
to try hard, be careful.

étui (etɥi) *m*, case, box; cover.

étuve (ety:v) *f*, drying stove;
oven (*fig.*). ~ *humide*, steam
room (*bath*). ~ *sèche*, hot room,
sweating r. (*bath*). **étuvée** (tyve)
f, steaming (*Cook.*). **étuver** (ve)
v.t, to stove; stew; foment
(*Med.*).

étymologie (etimɔlɔʒi) *f*, etymology. **étymologique†** (ʒik) *a*,
etymologic(al).

eucalyptus (økalipty:s) *m*, eucalyptus.

Eucharistie (økaristi) *f*, Eucharist, holy communion.

eugénie (øʒeni) *f*, eugenics.
eugénique (nik) *a*, eugenic.

euh (ø) *i*, hem! hum! h'm!

eunuque (ønyk) *m*, eunuch.

euphémique (øfemik) *a*, euphemistic. **euphémisme** (mism) *m*,
euphemism.

euphonie (øfɔni) *f*, euphony.
euphonique (nik) *a*, euphonic,
euphonious.

Euphrate (l') (øfrat) *m*, the
Euphrates.

Europe (l') (ørɔp) *f*, Europe.
européen, ne (peɛ̃, ɛn) *a.* & **E~**,
n, European.

eux (ø) *pn.m.pl*. See *lui*.

évacuer (evakɥe) *v.t* & *abs*, to
evacuate, void, clear out.

évader (s') (evade) *v.pr*, to escape, get away.

évaluation (evalɥasjɔ̃) *f*, valuation, estimate; casting off (*Typ.*).
évaluer (lɥe) *v.t*, to value, estimate; cast off.

évanescent, e (evanɛsɑ̃, ɑ̃:t) *a*,
evanescent.

évangélique† (evɑ̃ʒelik) *a*, evan-
gelic(al). **évangéliste** (list) *m*,
evangelist. **évangile** & **É~** (ʒil)
m, gospel.

évanouir (s') (evanwi:r) *v.pr*, to
faint, swoon; vanish, fade away.

évaporation (evapɔrasjɔ̃) *f*,
evaporation. **évaporé, e** (re) *n*,
feather-brained creature. **évaporer** (re) *v.t*, to evaporate; vent.
s'~, to evaporate.

évaser (evase) *v.t*, to flare, bellmouth.

évasif, ive† (evazif, i:v) *a*,
evasive. **évasion** (zjɔ̃) *f*, escape,
flight.

évêché (eveʃe) *m*, bishopric; see;
bishop's house.

éveil (evɛ:j) *m*, alert, guard;
warning; awakening (*fig.*). **éveillé,
e** (veje) *a*, wide-awake; perky.
éveiller (je) *v.t*, to wake [up].
s'~, to awaken (*fig.*).

événement (evɛnmɑ̃) *m*, event,
occurrence, incident; emergency;
outcome, issue.

évent (evɑ̃) *m*, [open] air; vent;
air hole; flaw; flatness (*liquor*).
éventail (ta:j) *m*, fan. **éventaire**
(tɛ:r) *m*, peddler's tray; pavement display (*shop*). **éventé, e**
(te) *p.a*, stale, flat, dead; giddy,
flighty. **éventer** (te) *v.t*, to fan;
air; turn over; flatten; fill (*sail*);
open; get wind of; let out.

éventrer (evãtre) *v.t*, to rip open, r. up; disembowel, eviscerate.

éventualité (evãtɥalite) *f*, eventuality, contingency. **éventuel, le†** (tɥɛl) *a*, contingent.

évêque (evɛːk) *m*, bishop.

évertuer (s') (evɛrtɥe) *v.pr*, to exert oneself, strive.

éviction (eviksjɔ̃) *f*, eviction.

évidence (evidãːs) *f*, evidence. **en ~**, in e., conspicuous. **évident, e** (dã, ãːt) *a*, evident, obvious, plain. **évidemment** (damã) *ad*, evidently.

évider (evide) *v.t*, to hollow out; cut away; groove, flute.

évier (evje) *m*, sink (*kitchen*).

évincer (evẽse) *v.t*, to evict; oust, turn out.

évitable (evitabl) *a*, avoidable. **évitage** (taː ʒ) *m*, ou **évitée** (te) *f*, sea room; swinging. **évitement** (tmã) *m*, ou *voie d'~* (*Rly.*), passing place, turnout, shunting loop. **éviter** (te) *v.t*, to avoid, shun; eschew; evade, dodge, steer clear of; help; (*v.i. & abs.*) to swing (*Naut.*). *~ de la tête*, to duck.

évocation (evɔkasjɔ̃) *f*, evocation, calling up, raising.

évoluer (evɔlɥe) *v.i*, to perform evolutions, maneuver, evolve. **évolution** (lysjɔ̃) *f*, evolution.

évoquer (evɔke) *v.t*, to evoke, conjure up.

ex- (ɛks) *pr*, ex-; ex; late.

exacerber (ɛgzasɛrbe) *v.t*, to exacerbate.

exact, e† (ɛgzakt) *a*, exact, accurate, correct; punctual. **exaction** (ksjɔ̃) *f*, exaction. **exactitude** (tityd) *f*, exactness, exactitude, accuracy; punctuality.

exagération (ɛgzaʒerasjɔ̃) *f*, exaggeration. **exagérer** (re) *v.t. & abs*, to exaggerate; overstate; overdo.

exalter (ɛgzalte) *v.t*, to exalt; extol; excite.

examen (ɛgzamẽ) *m*, examination; scrutiny. **examinateur, trice** (minatœːr, tris) *n*, examiner. **examiner** (ne) *v.t*, to examine; overhaul; look into.

exaspérer (ɛgzaspere) *v.t*, to exasperate; aggravate (*Med.*).

exaucer (ɛgzose) *v.t*, to hear (*prayer*), grant.

excavateur (ɛkskavatœːr) *m*, excavator, digger, shovel, navvy. **excavation** (sjɔ̃) *f*, excavation; pothole.

excédent, e (ɛksedã, ãːt) *a*, surplus (*att.*); overbearing. ¶ *m*, surplus, excess. *~ de bagages*, excess luggage. **excéder** (de) *v.t*, to exceed; weary, tire.

excellemment (ɛksɛlamã) *ad*, excellently. **excellence** (lãːs) *f*, excellence; choiceness. *par ~*, preeminently. *Son E~*, *f*, His Excellency. **excellent, e** (lã, ãːt) *a*, excellent. **exceller** (le) *v.i*, to excel.

excentricité (ɛksãtrisite) *f*, eccentricity; throw; remoteness. **excentrique** (trik) *a*, eccentric; outlying. ¶ (*Mech.*) *m*, eccentric, cam.

excepté (ɛksɛpte) *pr*, except[ing], save, but, barring. **excepter** (te) *v.t*, to except. **exception** (sjɔ̃) *f*, exception; plea (*law*). *~ péremptoire*, demurrer. **exceptionnel, le†** (ɔnɛl) *a*, exceptional.

excès (ɛksɛ) *m*, excess; abuse; violence. **excessif, ive†** (sɛsif, iːv) *a*, excessive; fulsome; undue.

excitant (ɛksitã) *m*, stimulant. **excitation** (tasjɔ̃) *f*, excitation; incitement; excitement. **exciter** (te) *v.t*, to excite; incite; stir up; urge; rouse; stimulate, fan.

exclamation (ɛksklamasjɔ̃) *f*, exclamation; ejaculation. **s'exclamer** (me) *v.pr*, to exclaim against.

exclure (ɛksklyːr) *v.t.ir*, to exclude; shut out, debar. **exclusif, ive†** (klyzif, iːv) *a*, exclusive; sole. **exclusion** (zjɔ̃) *f*, exclusion. **exclusivité** (zivite) *f*, exclusive (*or* sole) right(s).

excommunier (ɛkskɔmynje) *v.t*, to excommunicate.

excrément (ɛkskremã) *m*, excrement; scum (*fig.*).

excroissance (ɛkskrwasãːs) *f*, excrescence.

excursion (ɛkskyrsjɔ̃) *f*, excursion, trip, tour, outing. *~ à pied*, walking tour, hike. *~ accompagnée*, conducted tour. **excursionniste** (ɔnist) *n*, excursionist.

excuse (ɛksky:s) *f*, excuse; (*pl.*) apology. **excuser** (kyze) *v.t*, to excuse.

exeat (ɛgzeat) *m*, exeat; dismissal.

exécrable† (ɛgzekrabl) *a*, execrable. **exécrer** (kre) *v.t*, to execrate.

exécutable (ɛgzekytabl) *a*, workable, practicable. **exécutant, e** (tã, ã:t) *n*, performer (*Mus.*). **exécuter** (te) *v.t*, to execute; carry out; perform; fulfil; enforce; expel; buy in against, sell out against (*Stk Ex.*); distrain upon, sell up. **s'~**, to pay up; yield. **exécuteur (trice) testamentaire**, executor, trix. **exécution** (sjɔ̃) *f*, execution, etc. **exécutoire** (twa:r) *a*, executory; enforceable.

exemplaire (ɛgzãplɛ:r) *a*, exemplary. ¶ *m*, copy, specimen. **~ du souffleur**, prompt book. **exemple** (zã:pl) *m*, example; lead; illustration; instance; copy.

exempt, e (ɛgzã, ã:t) *a*, exempt, free. **exempter** (zãte) *v.t*, to exempt, free; excuse. **s'~ de**, to abstain from, get out of. **exemption** (zãpsjɔ̃) *f*, exemption; immunity; freedom.

exercer (ɛgzɛrse) *v.t*, to exercise; train; drill; practice; ply (*trade*); exert; wield (*power*); try (*patience*); inspect (*excise*). **exercice** (sis) *m*, exercise; drill[ing]; practice; office; tenure (*of office*); inspection; trading; [financial] year, [accounting] period. **~ de doigté**, five-finger exercise. **~s de tir**, musketry (*Mil.*).

exfolier (s') (ɛksfɔlje) *v.pr*, to exfoliate.

exhalaison (ɛgzalɛzɔ̃) *f*, exhalation (*mist*). **exhalation** (lasjɔ̃) *f*, exhalation (*act*). **exhaler** (le) *v.t*, to exhale; vent; reek with, reek of.

exhausser (ɛgzose) *v.t*, to raise.

exhiber (ɛgzibe) *v.t*, to exhibit, produce, show. **exhibition** (bisjɔ̃) *f*, exhibition.

exhorter (ɛgzɔrte) *v.t*, to exhort, urge.

exhumer (ɛgzyme) *v.t*, to exhume, disinter; rake up.

exigeant, e (ɛgziʒã, ã:t) *a*, particular, exacting, hard to please. **exigence** (ʒã:s) *f*, unreasonableness; requirement; exigence, -cy. **exiger** (ʒe) *v.t*, to exact, require, demand; call for. **exigibilité** (ʒibilite) *f*, [re]payability; demand; current liability. **exigible** (bl) *a*, [re]payable; claimable, exigible.

exigu, ë (ɛgzigy) *a*, exiguous, scanty, jejune, small, diminutive. **exiguité** (gɥite) *f*, exiguity.

exil (ɛgzil) *m*, exile. **exilé, e** (le) *n*, exile. **exiler** (le) *v.t*, to exile.

existence (ɛgzistã:s) *f*, existence; life; stock (*Com.*). **exister** (te) *v.i*, to exist, be; be extant.

ex-libris (ɛkslibri:s) *m*, bookplate, ex-libris.

exode (ɛgzɔd) *m*, exodus, flight. **l'E~**, Exodus (*Bible*).

exonérer (ɛgzɔnere) *v.t*, to exonerate, exempt.

exorbitamment (ɛgzɔrbitamã) *ad*, exorbitantly. **exorbitant, e** (tã, ã:t) *a*, exorbitant, extravagant.

exorciser (ɛgzɔrsize) *v.t*, to exorcise.

exorde (ɛgzɔrd) *m*, exordium; beginning.

exotique (ɛgzɔtik) *a*, exotic; foreign.

expansif, ive (ɛkspãsif, i:v) *a*, expansive; effusive. **expansion** (sjɔ̃) *f*, expansion.

expatrier (ɛkspatrie) *v.t*, to expatriate.

expectant, e (ɛkspɛktã, ã:t) *a*, expectant; wait-&-see. **expectative** (tati:v) *f*, expectation, expectancy.

expectorer (ɛkspɛktɔre) *v.t. & abs*, to expectorate.

expédient, e (ɛkspedjã, ã:t) *a*, expedient. ¶ *m*, expedient, resource, shift.

expédier (ɛkspedje) *v.t*, to expedite; dispose of; bolt (*food*); dispatch, send, forward, ship; copy & authenticate (*law*). **~ [en douane]** to clear (*a ship*) [outwards]. **expéditeur, trice** (ditœ:r, tris) *n*, sender; (*m.*) shipper; consignor; forwarding agent. **expéditif, ive** (tif, i:v) *a*, expeditious. **expédition** (sjɔ̃) *f*, expedition; disposal; dispatch, sending, forwarding; shipment, consignment; transit; adventure; clearance [outwards]; copy; (*pl.*) [ship's clearance] papers. **expéditionnaire** (ɔnɛːr) *a*, expeditionary. ¶ *m*, sender; dispatch clerk; shipping clerk; copying clerk.

expérience (ɛksperjɑ̃ːs) *f*, experiment; experience. **expérimental**, e† (rimɑ̃tal) *a*, experimental. **expérimenter** (te) *v.t*, to try; (*abs.*) to experiment.

expert, e (ɛkspɛːr, ɛrt) *a*, expert, skilled. ¶ *m*, expert; surveyor. **~-comptable**, professional accountant. **expertise** (pɛrtiːz) *f*, survey; examination; report. **expertiser** (tize) *v.t*, to survey.

expier (ɛkspje) *v.t*, to expiate, atone for.

expiration (ɛkspirasjɔ̃) *f*, expiration; expiry. **expirer** (re) *v.t. & i*, to expire.

explétif, ive (ɛkspletif, iːv) *a*, expletive.

explicatif, ive (ɛksplikatif, iːv) *a*, explanatory. **explication** (sjɔ̃) *f*, explanation; construction, rendering. **explicite†** (sit) *a*, explicit. **expliquer** (ke) *v.t*, to explain; account for; construe, render.

exploit (ɛksplwa) *m*, exploit, achievement, feat; writ. **exploitable** (tabl) *a*, workable; payable. **exploitant** (tɑ̃) *m*, operator, owner or [his] agent (*mine, etc.*). **exploitation** (tasjɔ̃) *f*, work-[ing], operation; mining; exploitation; workings; farming; trading. **~ agricole**, farm. **exploiter** (te) *v.t*, to work, run, operate; farm; mine; exploit. **exploiteur, euse** (tœːr, øːz) *n*, exploiter.

explorateur, trice (ɛksplɔratœːr, tris) *n*, explorer. **explorer** (re) *v.t*, to explore.

exploser (ɛksploze) *v.i*, to explode. **explosif** (zif) *m*, explosive. **explosion** (zjɔ̃) *f*, explosion; [out]burst.

exportateur (ɛkspɔrtatœːr) *m*, exporter. **exportation** (sjɔ̃) *f*, export[ation]. **exporter** (te) *v.t*, to export.

exposant, e (ɛkspozɑ̃, ɑ̃ːt) *n*, exhibitor; petitioner (*law*); (*m.*)

exponent, index (*Math.*). **exposé** (ze) *m*, statement; account. **exposer** (ze) *v.t. & abs*, to expose; show, display, exhibit; open; expound; explain; state. **exposition** (zisjɔ̃) *f*, exposition; exposure; exhibition, show; aspect, frontage (*of house*).

exprès, esse (ɛksprɛ, ɛs) *a*, express. **exprès**, on purpose, purposely. ¶ *m*, express messenger. [**train**] **express** (prɛs) *m*, express [train]. *bateau express*, fast boat. **expressément** (prɛsemɑ̃) *ad*, expressly.

expressif, ive (ɛksprɛsif, iːv) *a*, expressive. **expression** (sjɔ̃) *f*, expression; phrase. **exprimer** (prime) *v.t*, to express; squeeze out; voice.

exproprier (ɛksprɔprie) *v.t*, to expropriate.

expulser (ɛkspylse) *v.t*, to expel, drive out, eject.

expurger (ɛkspyrʒe) *v.t*, to expurgate, bowdlerize.

exquis, e (ɛkski, iːz) *a*, exquisite. ¶ *m*, exquisiteness. **exquisément** (kizemɑ̃) *ad*, exquisitely.

exsuder (ɛksyde) *v.i*, to exude.

extase (ɛkstɑːz) *f*, ecstasy; trance. **s'extasier** (tɑzje) *v.pr*, to go into ecstasies. **extatique** (tatik) *a*, ecstatic, rapturous.

extenseur (ɛkstɑ̃sœːr) *m*, extensor (*muscle*); chest expander; trouser stretcher. **extension** (sjɔ̃) *f*, extension. *par ~*, in a wider sense.

exténuer (ɛkstenɥe) *v.t*, to tire out, wear out.

extérieur, e† (ɛksterjœːr) *a*, exterior, external, outer, outside; outward; foreign. ¶ *m*, exterior, outside; foreign countries, abroad.

exterminer (ɛkstɛrmine) *v.t*, to exterminate.

externat (ɛkstɛrna) *m*, day school. **externe** (tɛrn) *a*, external, exterior. *pour l'usage ~*, for outward application, not to be taken (*Med.*). ¶ *n*, day scholar; nonresident assistant to hospital surgeon.

exterritorialité (ɛkstɛritɔrjalite) *f*, extraterritoriality.

extincteur [d'incendie] (ɛkstēktœ;r) *m*, [fire] extinguisher.

extinction (sjɔ̃) *f*, extinction; slaking; quenching; paying off; loss (*of voice*). ~ *des feux*, lights out (*Mil.*).

extirper (ɛkstirpe) *v.t*, to extirpate, eradicate.

extorquer (ɛkstɔrke) *v.t*, to extort, wring. **extorsion** (sjɔ̃) *f*, extortion.

extra (ɛkstra) *ad.* & *m*, extra.

extraction (ɛkstraksjɔ̃) *f*, extraction; winning (*Min.*); quarrying; birth, parentage.

extrader (ɛkstrade) *v.t*, to extradite. **extradition** (disjɔ̃) *f*, extradition.

extraire (ɛkstrɛ;r) *v.t.ir*, to extract, take out; excerpt; get, win; quarry. **extrait** (trɛ) *m*, extract; excerpt. ~*s d'auteurs*, extracts (*or* selections) from [the writings *or* works of] authors. ~ *de naissance*, birth certificate. ~ *mortuaire*, death c.

extraordinaire† (ɛkstraɔrdinɛ;r) *a.* & *m*, extraordinary; special; unusual.

extravagance (ɛkstravagɑ̃;s) *f*, extravagance; exorbitance; folly. **extravagant, e** (gɑ̃, ɑ̃;t) *a*, extravagant, wild. **extravaguer** (ge) *v.i*, to rave.

extrême (ɛkstrɛ;m) *a.* & *m*, extreme (*a.* & *m.*); utmost; drastic; dire. ~*-onction*, *f*, extreme unction. *l'E~-Orient*, *m*, the Far East. **extrêmement** (trɛmmɑ̃) *ad*, extremely; exceedingly; intensely. **extrémiste** (tremist) *n*, extremist. **extrémité** (te) *f*, extremity; end; tip.

extrinsèque (ɛkstrɛ̃sɛk) *a*, extrinsic.

exubérance (ɛgzyberɑ̃;s) *f*, exuberance; luxuriance. **exubérant, e** (rɑ̃, ɑ̃;t) *a*, exuberant; luxuriant.

exulter (ɛgzylte) *v.i*, to exult.

F

fa (fa) *m*, F (*Mus.*).

fable (fa;bl) *f*, fable; story; byword, laughing stock. **fablier** (fablie) *m*, fabulist; book of fables.

fabricant (fabrikɑ̃) *m*, manufacturer, maker. **fabricateur, trice** (katœ;r, tris) *n*, fabricator; forger. ~ *de fausse monnaie*, counterfeiter. **fabrication** (sjɔ̃) *f*, manufacture; make; work; fabrication. **fabrique** (brik) *f*, [manu]factory, works, mill; fabric (*edifice*); vestry, church council; invention (*fig.*). **fabriquer** (ke) *v.t*, to manufacture, make; fabricate, invent, trump up.

fabuleux, euse† (fabylø, ø;z) *a*, fabulous, fabled. **fabuliste** (list) *m*, fabulist.

façade (fasad) *f*, front, frontage, façade, frontispiece (*Arch.*).

face (fas) *f*, face; front; frontage (*extent of front*); side (*record*); obverse, head (*coin*); aspect. ~ *à*, facing. en ~, in the face; to one's face. en ~ *de*, *pr*, opposite, facing. *faire* ~ *à*, to face; keep pace with; front; meet.

face-à-main (fasamɛ̃) *m*, lorgnette.

facétie (fasesi) *f*, joke, jest. **facétieux, euse** (sjø, ø;z) *a*, facetious, waggish, jocular.

facette (fasɛt) *f*, facet. **facetter** (te) *v.t*, to facet.

fâché, e (faʃe) *p.a*, angry; sorry. **fâcher** (ʃe) *v.t*, to make angry, anger; grieve, pain. se ~, to get (*or* be) angry. **fâcherie** (ʃri) *f*, bad feeling; tiff. **fâcheux, euse**† (ʃø, ø;z) *a*, unfortunate, tiresome, troublesome; sad. ¶ *m*, unfortunate part; bore, nuisance (*pers.*).

facial, e (fasjal) *a*, facial; face (*att.*). **facies** (sje;s) *m*, facies; cast of features.

facile† (fasil) *a*, easy; facile; ready; fluent. **facilité** (lite) *f*, easiness, ease; facility; fluency; aptitude. **faciliter** (te) *v.t*, to facilitate.

façon (fasɔ̃) *f*, make; workmanship; making; labor; manner, fashion, way, wise, style, pattern; (*pl.*) manners; (*pl.*) ceremony, fuss. *de* ~ *à*, so as to. *de toute* ~, in any case. *en aucune* ~, by no means. *de* ~ *que*, so that. *faire des* ~*s*, to stand on ceremony.

faconde (fakɔ:d) *f*, flow of language.

façonné, e (fasɔne) *p.a*, figured (*textiles*). **façonner** (ne) *v.t*, to make; shape, fashion, form, mold; dress. **façonnier, ère** (nje, ɛ:r) *a*, [over-]ceremonious, fussy.

fac-similé (faksimile) *m*, facsimile.

factage (fakta:ʒ) *m*, parcels delivery; porterage. **facteur** (tœ:r) *m*, maker (*instruments*); postman; porter (*Rly.*); salesman; agent; factor, element. ~ *des télégraphes*, telegraph messenger, t. boy.

factice (faktis) *a*, imitation (*att.*), artificial; factitious; forced; meretricious.

factieux, euse (faksjø, ø:z), *a*, factious.

faction (faksjɔ̃) *f*, sentry duty, guard; faction. **factionnaire** (ɔnɛ:r) *m*, sentry.

factorerie (faktɔrri) *f*, [foreign *or* colonial] agency.

factotum (faktɔtɔm) *m*, factotum, man Friday.

factrice (faktris) *f*, postwoman.

factum (faktɔm) *m*, diatribe; statement of claim (*law*).

facture (fakty:r) *f*, invoice, bill; note; treatment (*music, art*); workmanship. ~ *fictive*, pro forma invoice. ~ *générale*, statement [of account]. **facturer** (tyre) *v.t*, to invoice.

facultatif, ive† (fakyltatif, i:v) *a*, optional. **faculté** (te) *f*, faculty; option; right; power; leave; liberty; property; branch [of study]; (*pl.*) means; (*pl.*) cargo, goods (*marine Insce.*).

fadaise[s] (fadɛ:z) *f.[pl.]*, twaddle, flummery, rubbish, stuff & nonsense.

fadasse (fadas) *a*, sickly, insipid. **fade†** (fad) *a*, insipid, tasteless, flat; mawkish; namby-pamby. **fadeur** (dœ:r) *f*, insipidity.

fagot (fago) *m*, fagot; bundle. **fagoter** (gɔte) *v.t*, to fagot, bundle; dress like a swell.

faiblard, e (fɛbla:r, ard) *a*, weakly. ¶ *n*, weakling. **faible†** (bl) *a*, weak; feeble; low; faint; shallow; slight; thin; light; small; scant[y]; slack; bare. ¶ *m*,

weak point; weakness, partiality, sneaking fondness; foible; failing. *les* ~*s*, the weak. **faiblesse** (blɛs) *f*, weakness; swoon. **faiblir** (bli:r) *v.i*, to weaken; slacken; give way; flag, fail.

faïence (fajɑ̃:s) *f*, earthenware, pottery, crockery, china. **faïencerie** (jɑ̃sri) *f*, pottery [works]; earthenware. **faïencier, ère** (sje, ɛ:r) *n*, earthenware; manufacturer *or* dealer.

faille (fa:j) *f*, faille (*fabric*); fault (*Geol.*). **failli** (faji) *m*, bankrupt, insolvent. **faillibilité** (bilite) *f*, fallibility. **faillible** (bl) *a*, fallible. **faillir** (ji:r) *v.i.ir*, to fail; to nearly . . .; to err. **faillite** (jit) *f*, failure; bankruptcy; insolvency.

faim (fɛ̃) *f*, hunger; starvation. *avoir* ~, *grand-*~, to be hungry, very hungry.

faîne (fɛ:n) *f*, beechnut; (*pl.*) beechmast.

fainéant, e (feneɑ̃, ɑ̃:t) *a*, idle, do-nothing. ¶ *n*, idler, lazybones, loafer. **fainéanter** (ɑ̃te) *v.i*, to idle, loaf. **fainéantise** (ti:z) *f*, idleness, etc.

faire (fɛ:r) *m*, technique (*art, etc.*). ¶ *v.t. & i. ir*, to make; do; create; form; perform; effect; write; play; commit; go; run; be; matter; have; get; keep; mind; get ready; lay; put; offer; o. up; give; take; take in (*provisions, etc.*); deal (*cards*); cut (*teeth*); make up (*face, the cash*); make out (*pretend*); wage (*war*); pay; ejaculate, say; charge; quote; accustom; call; turn. *cela fait mon affaire*, that suits me. *faites attention*, be careful. ~ *savoir*, to inform. *se* ~, to be done; be made; happen, take place; be; be getting; become; grow; make oneself; get; gain; turn. *ne vous en faites pas*, don't worry. **fairepart** (fɛrpa:r) *m*, announcement of betrothal, wedding, birth, death. **faisable** (fəzabl) *a*, feasible, practicable.

faisan, e (fɛzɑ̃, an) *n*, pheasant. **faisandé, e** (zɑ̃de) *a*, high, gamy; tainted. **faisandeau** (zɑ̃do) *m*, young pheasant. **se faisander** (de) *v. pr*, to get high. **faisan-**

derie (dri) *f*, pheasantry.

faisceau (fɛso) *m*, bunch, bundle, cluster, sheaf, nest; beam (*Opt.*); pencil (*Opt.*); pile, stack (*arms*); (*pl.*) fasces (*Hist.*).

faiseur, euse (fəzœːr, øːz) *n*, maker; doer; -monger; bluffer.

fait (fɛ; *in liaison*, fɛt) *m*, act, deed; feat; fact; point; occurrence, happening. ~s divers, news items. ~s & dits, sayings & doings. ~s & gestes, doings, exploits. *dans* (ou *par*) *le* ~ ou *en* ~, as a matter of fact. *de* ~, de facto, actual.

faite, e (fɛ, ɛt) *p.p. & p.a*: ~ *de boue & de crachat*, jerry-built. ~ *par tailleur*, tailormade. *un homme fait*, a full-grown man.

faîtage (fɛtaːʒ) *m*, roofing; ridge pole; ridge capping. **faîte** (fɛːt) *m*, top, apex, summit, zenith. **faîtière** (fɛtjɛːr) *a.f*, ridge (*att.*). ¶ *f*, ridge tile; ridge pole (*tent*).

fait-tout (fɛtu) *m*, stewpan.

faix (fɛ) *m*, burden, load, weight, incubus.

fakir (fakiːr) *m*, fakir.

falaise (falɛːz) *f*, cliff (*on seashore*).

falbalas (falbala) *m.pl*, furbelows.

fallacieux, euse† (falasjø, øːz) *a*, fallacious, misleading.

falloir (falwaːr) *v.imp.ir*, to be necessary, must, should, ought, shall, to have to, shall (*or will*) have to; to want; to require; to take. *s'en* ~, to be wanting; be far, fall short.

falot (falo) *m*, lantern.

falot, e (falo, ɔt) *a*, funny little (*pers.*).

falourde (falurd) *f*, bundle of firewood logs.

falsifier (falsifje) *v.t*, to adulterate; debase; falsify, tamper with; forge.

famé, e (fame) *a*, -famed.

famélique (famelik) *a*, starveling.

fameux, euse† (famø, øːz) *a*, famous; notorious; capital, first-rate, rare, champion (*att.*).

familial, e (familjal) *a*, family (*att.*). **familiariser** (ljarize) *v.t*, to familiarize, accustom. **famil-**

iarité (te) *f*, familiarity; intimacy; (*pl.*) liberties. **familier, ère** (lje, ɛːr) *a*, familiar; intimate; habitual; colloquial; household (*gods*). ¶ *m*, familiar.

famille (miːj) *f*, family; people. *en* ~, at home.

famine (famin) *f*, famine, starvation.

fanage (fanaːʒ) *m*, tedding; fallen leaves.

fanal (fanal) *m*, light, lamp.

fanatique (fanatik) *a*, fanatic(al); obsessed. ¶ *n*, fanatic; devotee. **fanatiser** (ze) *v.t*, to fanaticize. **fanatisme** (tism) *m*, fanaticism.

fanchon (fɑ̃ʃɔ̃) *f*, kerchief.

fane (fan) *f*, fallen leaf; top (*turnip, etc.*).

faner (fane) *v.t*, to ted, toss (*hay*); fade. **faneur, euse** (nœːr, øːz) (*pers.*) *n. &* (*Mach.*) *f*, haymaker, tedder.

fanfare (fɑ̃faːr) *f*, flourish of trumpets, fanfare; brass band. **fanfaron, ne** (farɔ̃, ɔn) *a*, blustering, swaggering, hectoring, bragging. **fanfaronnade** (rɔnad) *& fanfaronnerie* (nri) *f*, bluster, swagger, brag.

fanfreluches (fɑ̃frəlyʃ) *f.pl*, fallals, frills & furbelows.

fange (fɑ̃ːʒ) *f*, mire, mud, filth, muck; gutter (*fig.*). **fangeux, euse** (fɑ̃ʒø, øːz) *a*, miry.

fanion (fanjɔ̃) *m*, flag, banner. (*Mil.*) pennon.

fanon (fanɔ̃) *m*, dewlap; whalebone; fetlock; (*Eccl.*) maniple.

fantaisie (fɑ̃tɛzi) *f*, fancy, notion, whim; fantasy; fantasia. [*objet de*] ~, fancy [article]. **fantaisiste** (zist) *a*, fantastic, whimsical. **fantasmagorie** (tasmagori) *f*, phantasmagoria; fabrication. **fantasque** (task) *a*, whimsical, odd; temperamental.

fantassin (fɑ̃tasɛ̃) *m*, infantryman. ~ *de la flotte*, marine.

fantastique (fɑ̃tastik) *a. & m*, fantastic, fanciful; weird, eerie, uncanny.

fantoche (fɑ̃tɔʃ) *m*, puppet (*pers.*).

fantomatique (fɑ̃tomatik) *a*, ghostly, unearthly. **fantôme** (toːm) *m*, phantom, ghost.

faon (fɑ̃) *m*, fawn. **faonner** (fane) *v.i*, to fawn (*of deer*).

faquin (fakɛ̃) *m*, scurvy fellow, cad. **faquinerie** (kinri) *f*, scurvy trick.

faroud, e (faro, oːd) *n*, fop, dandy.

farce (fars) *f*, stuffing, forcemeat; farce; foolery; joke; practical joke; antic. *faire ses ~s*, to sow one's wild oats. **farceur, euse** (sœːr, øːz) *n*, joker, humorist; practical joker; comedian. **farcir** (siːr) *v.t*, to stuff; cram.

fard (faːr) *m*, paint, grease p., make-up; disguise, guile.

fardage (fardaːʒ) *m*, dunnage; top hamper; hamper.

fardeau (fardo) *m*, burden, load, weight, onus.

farder (farde) *v.t*, to paint, make up (*face*); gloss, varnish (*fig.*); dunnage (*ship*); (*v.i.*) to weigh [heavy]; sink. se ~, to make up.

fardier (fardje) *m*, trolley.

farfadet (farfadɛ) *m*, goblin, sprite.

farfouiller (farfuje) *v.i*, to rummage [about], fumble.

faribole[s] (faribɔl) *f.[pl.]*, twaddle.

farinacé, e (farinase) *a*, farinaceous. **farine** (rin) *f*, flour, meal, farina. ~ *de lin*, linseed meal. ~ *de riz*, ground rice. ~ *lactée*, malted milk. **farineux, euse** (nø, øːz) *a*, floury, mealy; farinaceous. **farinier, ère** (nje, ɛːr) *n*, flour dealer; miller.

farouch[e] (faruʃ) *m*, crimson clover.

farouche (faruʃ) *a*, wild, savage, fierce; grim; surly; unapproachable, shy, coy.

farrago (farago) *m*, mixture (*fodder*); farrago; hotchpotch.

fascicule (fasikyl) *m*, fascicle; number, part, instalment (*publication*).

fascinateur, trice (fasinatœːr, tris) *a*, fascinating. **fascination** (sjɔ̃) *f*, fascination; witchery.

fascine (fasin) *f*, fascine; fagot.

fasciner (fasine) *v.t*, to fascinate.

fascisme (fasism) *m*, fascism. **fasciste** (sist) *m*, fascist.

faste (fast) *m*. *no pl*, pomp, pageantry; show, ostentation; (*m.pl.*) fasti; annals.

fastidieux, euse† (fastidjø, øːz) *a*, tedious, wearisome, irksome, dull.

fastueux, euse† (fastɥø, øːz) *a*, given to display; ostentatious, showy, gaudy.

fat (fat) *a.m*, foppish. ¶ *m*, fop, coxcomb, jackanapes.

fatal, e† (fatal) *a*, fatal; fateful; latest, final. **fatalisme** (lism) *m*, fatalism. **fataliste** (list) *n*, fatalist. **fatalité** (te) *f*, fate, fatality; mischance.

fatidique (fatidik) *a*, fatidical, prophetic.

fatigant, e (fatigɑ̃, ɑ̃ːt) *a*, fatiguing, tiring; tiresome; tedious. **fatigue** (tig) *f*, fatigue, tiredness, fag; stress, [over]strain. *de ~*, working (*clothes*). **fatiguer** (ge) *v.t*, to fatigue, tire; stress, [over]strain, task, wear out; (*v.i.*) to labor (*ship*).

fatras (fatrɑ) *m*, jumble, medley. **fatrasser** (trase) *v.i*, to potter.

fatuité (fatɥite) *f*, self-conceit.

fauber[t] (fobɛːr) *m*, swab (*Naut.*).

faubourg (fobuːr) *m*, suburb; quarter (*town*). **faubourien, ne** (burjɛ̃, ɛn) *a.* & *n*, working-class suburban (dweller).

faucard (fokaːr) *m*, river weeding shear.

fauchage (foʃaːʒ) *m*, mowing. **faucher** (ʃe) *v.t*, to mow; m. down. **fauchet** (ʃɛ) *m*, hay rake. **faucheur** (ʃœːr) *m*, mower (*pers.*). ~ *ou* **faucheux** (ʃø) *m*, daddy longlegs. **faucheuse** (ʃøːz) *f*, mower (*Mach.*). **faucille** (siːj) *f*, sickle, reaping hook.

faucon (fokɔ̃) *m*, falcon, hawk. ~ *pèlerin*, peregrine [falcon]. **fauconnerie** (kɔnri) *f*, falconry; hawking. **fauconnier** (nje) *m*, falconer. **fauconnière** (jɛːr) *f*, saddle bag.

faufiler (fofile) *v.t*, to tack, baste (*Need.*); slip in, insinuate. **faufilure** (lyːr) *f*, tacking, basting.

faune (foːn) *m*, faun; (*f.*) fauna.

faussaire (fosɛːr) *n*, forger. **faussement** (smɑ̃) *ad*, falsely; wrongfully. **fausser** (se) *v.t*, to bend; buckle; warp; strain; upset; derange; foul; falsify, pervert. **fausset** (sɛ) *m*, falsetto (*voice*); spigot, vent peg. **fausseté** (ste) *f*, falseness, falsity; falsehood, untruth.

faute (foːt) *f*, fault; mistake, error; blame; foul (*Foot.*); want, lack. ~ *d'orthographe*, misspelling. ~ *d'impression*, printer's error, misprint. ~ *de copiste*, ~ *de plume*, clerical error. ~ *de*, failing, in default of, for want of. *sans* ~, without fail.

fauteuil (fotœːj) *m*, armchair, easy chair; chair; seat; orchestra seat (*Theat.*). ~ *à bascule*, rocking chair. ~ [*de la présidence*], chair (*at meeting*).

fautif, ive (fotif, iːv) *a*, faulty, at fault, offending.

fauve (foːv) *a*, fawn[-colored], fallow; fulvous; tawny; buff; lurid (*light*). ¶ *m*, fawn; buff (*color*); (*pl.*) deer; wild beasts (*big felines*).

fauvette (fovɛt) *f*, warbler (*bird*). ~ *à tête noire*, blackcap. ~ *des haies*, hedge sparrow.

faux (fo) *f*, scythe; falx.

faux, fausse (fo, oːs) *a*, false; wrong; untrue; base, counterfeit; forged; spurious; bogus; unjust (*weight*); improper (*navigation*); blank, blind (*window*); attempted (*suicide*). **faux**, *comps*: ~ *bourdon*, drone [bee]. ~ *brillant*, imitation [stone], paste; tinsel (*fig.*). ~ *col*, see col. ~ *coup de queue*, miscue. ~ *ébénier*, laburnum. ~ *frais*, incidental expenses; untaxed costs (*law*). ~*fuyant*, *m*, evasion, shift. ~*monnayeur*, *m*, counterfeiter. ~ *nom*, alias. ~ *numéro* [*d'appel*], wrong number (*Teleph.*). ~*pont*, *m*, orlop [deck]. ~ *témoignage*, false evidence, perjury. **fausse**, *comps*: ~ *boîte*, dummy [box]. ~ *couche*, miscarriage. ~ *déclaration*, misstatement, misrepresentation. ~ *équerre*, bevel [square]. ~ *honte*, false shame; bashfulness. ~ *manche*, sleeve protector. **faux**, *ad*, falsely, wrongly; out of tune. *à* ~, wrongly, unjustly. ¶ *m*, forgery. *le* ~, the false.

faveur (favœːr) *f*, favor; boon;

goodwill. **favorable**† (vɔrabl) *a*, favorable. **favori, ite** (ri, it) *a*, & *n*, favorite; pet; minion; (*m.pl.*) [side] whiskers. **favoriser** (ze) *v.t*, to favor, befriend; foster, promote. **favoritisme** (tism) *m*, favoritism.

fébrile† (febril) *a*, febrile, feverish.

fécond, e (fekɔ̃, ɔ̃ːd) *a*, fruitful, fecund, fertile, prolific; life-giving; bountiful. **féconder** (kɔ̃de) *v.t*, to fertilize, fecundate, impregnate; milt; fructify. **fécondité** (dite) *f*, fecundity, fertility, fruitfulness.

fécule (fekyl) *f*, starch, farina. **féculent, e** (lɑ̃, ɑ̃ːt) *a*, starchy (*food*).

fédéral, e (federal) *a*, federal. **fédération** (sjɔ̃) *f*, federation, union. **fédérer** (re) *v.t*, to federate.

fée (fe) *f*, fairy, pixy, -xie. **féerie** (feri) *f*, fairyhood; Fairyland; fairy scene. **féerique** (ferik) *a*, fairylike.

feindre (fɛ̃ːdr) *v.t. & abs. ir*, to feign, pretend, sham; feint. **feint, e** (fɛ̃, ɛ̃ːt) *p.a*, feigned, sham; false, blind (*door, etc.*). ¶ feint, pretence, sham.

fêler (fɛle) *v.t*, to crack.

félicitation (felisitasjɔ̃) *f*, congratulation. **félicité** (te) *f*, happiness, felicity. **féliciter** (te) *v.t*, to congratulate.

félidés (felide) *m.pl*, Felidae. **félin, e** (lɛ̃, in) *a. & m*, feline, cat (*att.*).

félon, ne (felɔ̃, ɔn) *a*, disloyal. **félonie** (lɔni) *f*, disloyalty.

fêlure (fɛlyːr) *f*, crack, split.

femelle (fəmɛl) *f. & a*, female, she; hen; cow (*elephant, etc.*). **féminin, e** (feminɛ̃, in) *a*, feminine; womanish (*voice*); female. ¶ *m*, feminine (*Gram.*). **féminiser** (nize) *v.t*, to feminize. **féminisme** (nism) *m*, feminism. **féministe** (nist) *a. & n*, feminist.

femme (fam) *f*, woman; female; wife. ~*caoutchouc*, ~*serpent*, *f*, contortionist. ~ *de chambre*, lady's maid; housemaid; chambermaid; stewardess (*ship*). ~ *de journée*, cleaning woman. ~ *de ménage*, cleaning woman.

femmelette (mlɛt) *f*, silly little woman; effeminate [man].

fémur (femy:r) *m*, femur.

fenaison (fənɛzɔ̃) *f*, haymaking.

fendant (fɑ̃dɑ̃) *m*, swaggerer.

fendiller (fɑ̃dije) *v.t*, to crack, fissure. **fendre** (fɑ̃:dr) *v.t*, to split, cleave; rend; rive; crack; slot, nick, slit; break (*heart*). ~ *un cheveu en quatre*, to split hairs. **fendu, e** (fɑ̃dy) *a*, split, cleft. *bien fendu*, longlegged (man).

fenêtrage (fənɛtra:ʒ) *m*, windows (*col.*). **fenêtre** (nɛ:tr) *f*, window. ~ *à guillotine*, sash w. ~ *à tabatière*, skylight. ~ *en saillie*, bay window. ~ [*ordinaire*], casement [window].

fenil (fəni) *m*, hayloft.

fenouil (fənu:j) *m*, fennel; f. seed.

fente (fɑ̃:t) *f*, crack, cleft, split, slit; fissure, crevice, cranny; slot; nick.

féodal, e (feodal) *a*, feudal. **féodalité** (lite) *f*, feudalism, feudality.

fer (fɛ:r) *m*, iron; bar; section; shoe; bit; head (*lance, etc.*); tag (*laces*); sword, weapon; (*pl.*) irons, chains, shackles; fetters, manacles; obstetrical forceps. ~ *à friser*, curling irons. ~ *à repasser*, [flat] iron. ~ *à souder*, soldering iron, soldering bit. ~[*s*] *cavalier*[*s*], horseshoe bars, h. iron, h. sections. ~ *de* (ou *à*) *cheval*, horseshoe. ~ *de fonte*, cast iron. ~ *de lance*, spear head. ~*s dorés*, gilt tooling (*Bookb.*). ~ *en barre*[*s*], bar iron. ~ *en lame*, sheet i. ~ [*forgé*], wrought i.

fer-blanc (fɛrblɑ̃) *m*, tin [plate], tinned [sheet] iron. **ferblanterie** (blɑ̃tri) *f*, tin plate working *or* trade; tinware. **ferblantier** (tje) *m*, tinsmith.

férir (feri:r) *v.t*: *sans coup ~*, without striking a blow.

ferler (fɛrle) *v.t*, to furl (*sail*).

fermage (fɛrma:ʒ) *m*, rent (*farm, land*); tenant farming.

fermant, e (fɛrmɑ̃, ɑ̃:t) *a*, lockup; closing.

ferme† (fɛrm) *a*, firm, solid, steady, steadfast, staunch. ¶ *ad*,

firmly, firm, fast, hard. ¶ *i*, steady! ¶ *f*, lease; farm; farmhouse; homestead; truss, girder (*Build.*); set piece (*Theat.*).

ferment (fɛrmɑ̃) *m*, ferment; leaven. **fermentation** (tasjɔ̃) *f*, fermentation; ferment (*fig.*). **fermenter** (te) *v.i*, to ferment; to [be at] work (*fig.*).

fermer (fɛrme) *v.t. & i*, to shut, s. up, s. down, close, c. up, c. down; do up; turn off, shut off; switch off; stop up; enclose. ~ [*à clef*] *v.t. & i*, to lock [up]. ~ *la marche*, to bring up the rear.

fermeté (fɛrməte) *f*, firmness, steadfastness, steadiness, strength.

fermeture (fɛrməty:r) *f*, shutting; closing; fastening; fastener. ~ *éclair*, zipper.

fermier, ère (fɛrmje, ɛ:r) *n*, farmer; tenant (*farm*); lessee; tenant farmer; (*att.*) leasing.

fermoir (fɛrmwa:r) *m*, clasp, fastener, snap; double-beveled chisel.

féroce (ferɔs) *a*, ferocious, fierce, savage, wild. **férocité** (site) *f*, ferocity.

ferrage (fɛra:ʒ) *m*, shoeing; tiring; tagging. **ferraille** (rɑ:j) *f*, old iron, scrap iron. **ferrailler** (rɑje) *v.i*, to slash about. **ferrailleur** (jœr) *m*, dealer in old iron; sword rattler. **ferré, e** (re)‑*p.a*, ironshod; shod; hobnailed; versed, conversant. ~ *à glace*, roughshod, frost-nailed. **ferrement** (fɛrmɑ̃) *m*, ironwork; shoeing; putting in irons. **ferrer** (re) *v.t*, to iron, bind (*with any metal*); shoe; tire; tag; strike (*fish*). **ferret** (rɛ) *m*, tag (*lace*). **ferreux** (rø) *a.m*, ferrous. **ferronnerie** (rɔnri) *f*, ironworks; iron warehouse; ironmongery. **ferronnier, ère** (nje, ɛ:r) *n*, iron worker; ironmonger. **ferrugineux, euse** (ryʒinø, ø:z) *a*, ferruginous, **ferrure** (ry:r) *f*, ironwork; binding; shoeing; fitting, mounting.

fertile (fɛrtil) *a*, fertile, fruitful; prolific; fat (*land*). **fertiliser** (lize) *v.t*, to fertilize. **fertilité** (te) *f*, fertility.

féru, e (fery) *a*, struck; smitten (*love*).

férule (feryl) *f*, ferula (*Bot.*);

bondage; cane (*Sch.*); lash (*fig.*).

fervent, e (fɛrvã, ã:t) *a*, fervent, earnest. ¶ *n*, enthusiast, devotee. **ferveur** (vœ:r) *f*, fervor, earnestness.

fesse (fɛs) *f*, buttock. **fessée (se)** *f*, spanking. **fesse-mathieu** (matjø) *m*, miser. **fesser (se)** *v.t*, to spank; birch.

festin (fɛstɛ̃) *m*, feast, banquet. **festiner** (tine) *v.t. & abs*, to feast. **festival** (val) *m*, musical festival.

feston (fɛstɔ̃) *m*, festoon; scallop (*edging*). **festonner** (tɔne) *v.t*, to festoon; scallop. ¶ *v.i*, to reel about (*drunk*).

festoyer (fɛstwaje) *v.t. & i*, to feast.

fête (fɛ:t) *f*, feast, festivity; festival; fête; holiday; saint's day; birthday; entertainment, treat. *la ~ de* [*l'anniversaire de*] *l'Armistice*, Armistice Day. *la Fête-Dieu*, Corpus Christi. *~ foraine*, fête (*at a fair*). *~ légale*, legal holiday. **fêter** (fɛte) *v.t*, to keep [as a holiday], celebrate; fête, entertain.

fétiche (fetiʃ) *m*, fetish; mascot (*as on car*); charm. **fétichisme** (ʃism) *m*, fetishism.

fétide (fetid) *a*, fetid, foul. **fétidité** (dite) *f*, fetidness, foulness.

fétu (fety) *m*, straw; (*fig.*) straw, rush, rap, fig, pin.

feu (fø) *m*, fire; flame; flare; flash; light; lamp; firing (*Mil.*); heat (*fig.*); home, hearth. *~ à éclipses*, intermittent light (*Naut.*). *~ concentré*, group firing (*Mil.*). *~ d'artifice*, firework. *~ de bengale*, Bengal light. *~ de bivouac*, campfire. *~ de cheminée*, chimney on fire. *~x de circulation*, traffic lights, stop & go lights. *~ de joie*, bonfire. *~ de paille* (*fig.*), flash in the pan. *~ de peloton*, volley firing (*Mil.*). *~ follet*, ignis fatuus, will-o'-the-wisp. *~ roulant*, running fire. *~! fire!* (*Mil.*). *au ~!* (*house, etc, on*) fire! *faire long ~*, to hang fire. *ni ~ ni lieu*, neither house nor home.

feu, e (fø) *a*, late, the late (*deceased*).

feuillage (fœja:ʒ) *m*, foliage,

leafage, leaves. **feuillaison** (jɛzɔ̃) *f*, leafing, foliation. **feuillard** (ja:r) *m*, hoop wood. *~ de fer*, hoop iron, strap iron, strip iron. **feuille** (fœ:j) *f*, sheet; leaf; slip; list; roll (*pay*); [news]paper; blade; flake; foil. *~ d'appel*, muster roll. *~ de chou*, rag (*worthless newspaper*). *~ de garde*, endpaper. *~s de placage*, veneer. *~ de présence*, time sheet, attendance s. *~ de rose*, rose leaf (*petal*). *~ de route*, waybill. *~ de tirée*, proof (*Typ.*). *~ de transfert*, transfer deed, [deed of] transfer. *~ de vigne*, fig leaf (*art*). *~ mobile*, looseleaf (*book*). *~ volante*, loose sheet (*paper*). **feuillé, e** (fœje) *a*, leafy, foliate. ¶ *f*, greenwood, trees. **feuillet** (jɛ) *m*, leaf (*book*); thin sheet, t. plate; lamina. **feuilleter** (fœjte) *v.t*, to run through, thumb (*book*); roll out (*pastry*); flake. **feuilleton** (tɔ̃) *m*, serial [story]. **feuillu, e** (jy) *a*, leafy. **feuillure** (jy:r) *f*, rabbet, rebate; fillister.

feutre (fø:tr) *m*, felt. *~ mou*, *~ souple*, soft felt (*hat*). *~ velours*, velours. **feutrer** (føtre) *v.t*, to felt, pad. *à pas feutrés*, stealthily.

fève (fɛ:v) *f*, bean. *~ de marais*, broad bean. **féverole** (fɛvrɔl) *f*, horse bean.

février (fevrie) *m*, February.

fez (fɛ:z) *m*, fez.

fi (fi) *i*, ugh! fie! *~ donc!* for shame! *faire ~ de*, to pooh-pooh.

fiacre (fjakr) *m*, cab, four-wheeler.

fiançailles (fjãsa:j) *f.pl*, engagement, betrothal. **fiancé, e** (se) *n*, fiancé, e, betrothed. **fiancer (se)** *v.t*, to betroth, engage, affiance.

fiasco (fjasko) *m*, fiasco, failure, breakdown.

fibre (fibr) *f*, fiber; string (*fig.*). *~ de coco*, coir. **fibreux, euse** (brø, ø:z) *a*, fibrous, stringy. **fibrille** (bril) *f*, fibril.

ficelé, e (fisle) *p.a*, dressed (*badly*). **ficeler** (sle) *v.t*, to [tie with] string, tie up. **ficelle** (sɛl) *f*, string, twine; packthread; dodge, trick, game.

fiche (fiʃ) *f*, hinge; peg, pin, stake; plug, key; slip (*paper*);

card (*loose index*); ticket; ~ *de consolation*, booby prize; some slight consolation. **ficher** (ʃe) *v.t*, to drive in, stick. **se ~ de**, to laugh at; not to care about. **fichier** (ʃje) *m*, card index; c. i. cabinet.

fichtre (fiʃtr) *i*, good gracious! **fichu** (fiʃy) *m*, neckerchief, fichu. ¶ *a*, done for.

fictif, ive† (fiktif, i:v) *a*, fictitious, sham. **fiction** (sjɔ̃) *f*, fiction, figment.

fidéicommis (fideikɔmi) *m*, trust (*law*).

fidèle† (fidɛl) *a*, faithful; loyal; true; reliable, trustworthy; fast; retentive. **les ~s**, *m.pl*, the faithful. **fidélité** (delite) *f*, fidelity, faithfulness; truthfulness; reliability; retentiveness.

fidibus (fidiby:s) *m*, spill, pipe light.

fiduciaire (fidysjɛ:r) *a*, fiduciary.

fief (fjɛf) *m*, fief, feud, fee (*Hist.*); preserve (*fig.*). **fieffé, e** (fe) *a*, arrant, downright, unmitigated, egregious, regular, outright, rank, out & out, of the deepest dye.

fiel (fjɛl) *m*, gall; rancor. **fielleux, euse** (ljø, ø:z) *a*, rancorous.

fiente (fjɑ̃:t) *f*, dung, droppings.

fier (fje) *v.t*, to entrust. **se ~**, to trust, rely.

fier, ère† (fjɛ:r) *a*, proud, haughty; lofty; stately; lordly; rare, fine; arrant. **fier-à-bras** (fjɛrabra) *m*, swaggerer. **fierté** (fjɛrte) *f*, pride; boldness (*touch*).

fièvre (fjɛ:vr) *f*, fever; heat (*fig.*). ~ *aphteuse* (aftø:z), foot-&-mouth disease. ~ *des foins*, hay fever. ~ *paludéenne*, malaria, marsh fever; ague. **fiévreux, euse**† (evrø, ø:z) *a*, feverish. ¶ *n*, fever case (*pers.*).

fifre (fifr) *m*, fife; fifer.

figé, e (fiʒe) *a*, frozen (*fig.*); set. **figer** (ʒe) *v.t. & se ~*, to congeal, coagulate, set.

fignoler (fiɲɔle) *v.t. & abs*, to overelaborate.

figue (fig) *f*, fig. ~ *de Barbarie*, prickly pear. **figuier** (gje) *m*, fig tree.

figurant, e (figyrɑ̃, ɑ̃:t) *n*, supernumerary; one who takes no prominent part. **figuratif, ive**† (ratif, i:v) *a*, figurative; pictorial (*plan, map*); picture (*writing*). **figure** (gy:r) *f*, figure; form, shape; face (*of pers.*), countenance; show[ing]; (*pl.*) court cards. ~ *de cire*, waxwork. ~ *de mots*, ~ *de rhétorique*, figure of speech. ~ *de proue*, figurehead (*ship*). ~ *en lame de couteau*, hatchet face. **figuré, e** (gyre) *p.a*, pictorial (*plan, map*); figure (*dance, stone*); figurative (*sense*). ¶ *m*, figurative sense. **figurément** (mɑ̃) *ad*, figuratively (*sense*). **figurer** (re) *v.t*, to figure, represent, picture, show; (*v.i.*) to appear, figure, show. **se ~**, to imagine, fancy, picture to oneself. **figurine** (rin) *f*, figurine, statuette.

fil (fil) *m*, thread; yarn; wire; filament; string (*pearls, etc.*); [cutting] edge; grain (*wood, etc.*); flaw. ~ *à plomb*, plumb line. ~ *carcasse des fleuristes*, flower wire. ~ *de fer barbelé*, barb[ed] wire. ~*s de la Vierge*, gossamer. ~ [*de lin*], linen [thread]. ~ *souple*, flex[ible wire] (*Elec.*). **filage** (la:ʒ) *m*, spinning; pouring (*oil on waves*). **filament** (lamɑ̃) *m*, filament; thread. **filandres** (lɑ̃:dr) *f.pl*, gossamer; strings. **filandreux, euse** (lɑ̃drø, ø:z) *a*, stringy; long-drawn; diffuse. **filant, e** (lɑ̃, ɑ̃:t) *a*, ropy (*liquid*); falling, shooting (*star*). **filasse** (las) *f*, tow (*flax, hemp*).

filateur, trice (filatœ:r, tris) *n*, spinner (*pers.*); (*m.*) spinner (*owner*). **filature** (ty:r) *f*, cotton mill; spinning; shadowing (*a pers.*).

file (fil) *f*, file, line.

filé (file) *m*, thread. **filer** (le) *v.t*, to spin; draw (*into wire*); pay out (*cable*); pour (*oil on waves*); shadow (*a pers.*); handle (*fig.*); (*v.i.*) to run; be off; make off; file off; flare (*lamp*). ~ *à l'anglaise*, to take French leave. ~ *doux*, to obey without a word.

filet (filɛ) *m*, thread; string; filament; fillet; undercut; loin (*mutton*); worm (*screw*); trickle, stream; dash (*admixture*); rule (*Typ.*); net; netting. ~ *à bagage*, luggage rack (*Rly.*). ~ *à provisions*, string bag, net b. ~*s de sole*, filleted sole. **filetage** (lta:ʒ) *m*, screw cutting. **fileter** (lte) *v.t*, to thread, screw. **fileur, euse** (lœːr, øːz) *n*, spinner, net maker.

filial, e† (filjal) *a*, filial. [société] **filiale**, *f*, subsidiary [company]. **filiation** (sjɔ̃) *f*, filiation; relationship.

filière (filjɛːr) *f*, draw plate; die [plate]; screw plate; [screw] stock; wire gauge; purlin; regular channel[s] (*fig.*). ~ *garnie*, stock & dies.

filigrane (filigran) *m*, filigree [work]; watermark (*paper*).

fille (fiːj) *f*, girl; maid; maiden; daughter; whore (*familiar*). ~ *de ferme*, dairy maid, milkmaid. ~ *de service*, maidservant, housemaid. **fillette** (fijɛt) *f*, little girl. **filleul, e** (fijœl) *n*, godchild, godson, god-daughter; protégé.

film (film) *m*, film; movie.

filon (filɔ̃) *m*, lode; mine (*fig.*).

filoselle (filozɛl) *f*, floss silk.

filou (filu) *m*, pickpocket; sharper; swindler. **filouter** (te) *v.t*, to rob, filch; cheat. **filouterie** (tri) *f*, robbery; swindle.

fils (fis) *m*, son; junior. ~ *de ses œuvres*, self-made man. ~ *de son père*, chip off the old block.

filtrage (filtraːʒ) *m*. & **filtration** (trasjɔ̃) *f*, filtration, straining; percolation. **filtre** (tr) *m*, filter; percolator (*coffee*). **filtrer** (tre) *v.t*. & *i*, to filter, strain; percolate, leach.

fin (fɛ̃) *f*, end, close, finish, last; finis; object, aim, purpose. ~ *d'alerte*, all clear (*Mil.*).

fin (fɛ̃) *m*, fine metal; fine linen. *or à tant de grammes de* ~, gold so many grams fine.

fin, e (fɛ̃, in) *a*, fine; delicate; choice; slender; small; keen, sharp; subtle; smart. *fin fond*, farthest end, very depths. *fin matois*, artful dodger. *le fin mot*, the last word; the long & the short of it, the upshot. *fine à l'eau*, brandy & soda. *fine champagne*, liqueur brandy. *fines herbes*, savory herbs.

final, e† (final) *a*, final; last; ultimate. ¶ *f*, final (*sport*). **final[e]**, *m*, finale (*Mus.*). **finalité** (lite) *f*, finality.

finance (finãːs) *f*, finance; (*pl.*) finances, cash, money. **financer** (nãse) *v.i*, to find money, finance. **financier, ère†** (sje, ɛːr) *a*, financial. ¶ *m*, financier.

finasser (finase) *v.i*, to finesse. **finasserie** (sri) *f*, trickery; cunning; (*pl.*) wiles. **finassier, ère** (sje, ɛːr) *n*, trickster.

finaud, e (fino, oːd) *a*, sly, wily. ¶ *n*, artful dodger, slyboots. **finauderie** (odri) *f*, sly dodge.

finement (finmã) *ad*, finely; shrewdly. **finesse** (nɛs) *f*, fineness.

fini, e (fini) *a*, finished; over; consummate; finite (*being*). ¶ *m*, finish; (the) finite. **finir** (niːr) *v.t*. & *abs*. & *i*, to finish, end. ~ *de parler*, to finish (*or* leave off) speaking. *en* ~, to finish.

Finlande (la) (fɛ̃lãːd) *f*, Finland. **finnois, e** (finwa, aːz) & **finlandais, e** (fɛ̃lãdɛ, ɛːz) *a*, Finnish. **Finnois, e** & **Finlandais, e**, *n*, Finn, Finlander. *le finnois*, Finnish (*language*).

fiole (fjɔl) *f*, flask, phial.

floriture (fjɔrityːr) *f*, grace [note]; flourish.

firmament (firmamã) *m*, firmament.

fisc (fisk) *m*, Treasury; taxes. **fiscal, e** (kal) *a*, fiscal (*att.*). **fiscalité** (lite) *f*, fiscal system; piling up of taxation; methods of [tax] collection.

fissure (fisyːr) *f*, fissure, crack, cleft; hiatus.

fistule (fistyl) *f*, fistula.

fixage (fiksaːʒ) *m*. & **fixation** (asjɔ̃) *f*, fixing, fixation; fastening. **fixatif** (tif) *m*, fixing [solution] (*Phot.*). **fixe†** (fiks) *a*, fixed, fast, stationary; intent; set. ¶ *i*, eyes front! ¶ *m*, fixed salary. ~-*cravate*, *m*, tie clip. **fixer** (kse) *v.t*, to fix, fasten, secure; set; settle; rivet (*fig.*). ~ *dans la mémoire*, to commit to memory, memorize. **fixité** (ksite) *f*, fixity, steadiness.

flaccidité (flaksidite) *f*, flaccidity, flabbiness.

flacon (flakɔ̃) *m*, bottle, flask,

flagon. ~ à couvercle vissé, screw-capped bottle. ~ à odeur, scent b., smelling b.

flageller (flaʒɛle) v.t, to scourge, flagellate.

flageoler (flaʒɔle) v.i, to tremble, shake. **flageolet** (lɛ) m, flageolet (Mus. & bean).

flagorner (flagɔrne) v.t, to fawn [up]on, toady to. **flagornerie** (nəri) f, toadyism, soft soap. **flagorneur, euse** (nœːr, øːz) n, toady.

flagrant, e (flagrɑ̃, ɑ̃ːt) a, flagrant, glaring. **en flagrant délit**, in the [very] act, redhanded.

flair (flɛːr) m, scent, smell, nose; acumen; keenness. **flairer** (flɛre) v.t. & abs, to scent, smell, scent out, nose [out].

flamand, e (flamɑ̃, ɑ̃ːd) a. & (language) m, Flemish. **F~,** n, Fleming (pers.).

flamant (flamɑ̃) m, flamingo.

flambant, e (flɑ̃bɑ̃, ɑ̃ːt) a, flaming, blazing; smart. **tout flambant neuf, toute flambante neuve,** brand new. **flambeau** (bo) m, torch; candlestick. **flambé, e** (be) p.p, lost, gone; done for. **flambée** (be) f, blaze. **flamber** (be) v.i, to flame, blaze, flare; (v.t.) to flame (needle, Surg.); singe. **flamberge** (bɛrʒ) f, sword (jocularly). **flamboyer** (bwaje) v.i, to blaze; flame, flare, flash.

flamme (flɑːm) f, flame; blaze, flare, light; passion; pennant, pendant, pennon, streamer. ~ **de bengale,** Bengal light. **flammèche** (flamɛʃ) f, spark, flake (ignited matter).

flan (flɑ̃) m, flan; blank (metal); mold (Typ.).

flanc (flɑ̃) m, side, flank; womb.

flancher (flɑ̃ʃe) v.i, to flinch; give in; break down (auto).

Flandre (la) (flɑ̃ːdr), Flanders.

flandrin (flɑ̃drɛ̃) m, lanky fellow.

flanelle (flanɛl) f, flannel. ~ **de coton,** flannelette.

flâner (flɑne) & **flânocher** (nɔʃe) v.i, to saunter; stroll; lounge, loaf. **flânerie** (nri) f, sauntering. **flâneur, euse** (nœːr, øːz) n, saunterer.

flanquer (flɑ̃ke) v.t, to flank; fling, throw, chuck; land (blow). ~ **à odeur.**

flaque (flak) f, puddle; pool, plash. **une flaquée d'eau** (ke) some water (thrown).

flasque (flask) a, flabby, limp, flaccid. ¶ f, cheek, side.

flatter (flate) v.t. & abs, to flatter; stroke; pat; humor; please. **flatterie** (tri) f, flattery. **flatteur, euse** (tœːr, øːz) n, flatterer. ¶ a, flattering.

flatulence (flatylɑ̃ːs) f, flatulence, -cy. **flatuosité** (tɥozite) f, flatus, wind.

fléau (fleo) m, flail; scourge, plague, bane, curse; beam (scale); bar.

flèche (flɛʃ) f, arrow, shaft; spire; jib, boom (crane); beam (plow); trail (gun carriage); flitch (bacon); sag, dip. ~ **littorale,** spit (Phys. Geog.). **fléchette** (fleʃɛt) f, dart.

fléchir (fleʃiːr) v.t. & i, to bend, bow, flex; sag; move; flag, yield; give way; relent. **fléchisseur** (ʃisœːr) a.m. & m, flexor.

flegmatique (flɛgmatik) a, phlegmatic; stolid. **flegme** (flɛgm) m, coolness, phlegm (fig.), stolidity.

flet (flɛ) m, flounder (fish). **flétan** (fletɑ̃) m, halibut.

flétrir (fletriːr) v.t, to fade, wither, wilt, blight; brand. **flétrissure** (trisyːr) f, fading, withering; blight; stigma.

fleur (flœːr) f, flower; blossom; bloom; pick; prime, heyday, blush, flush. ~ **de la Passion,** passion flower. ~**s des bois,** ~**s des champs,** ~**s des prés,** wild flowers. **la** ~ **des pois,** the pick of the bunch. **à** ~ **de,** level (or even) (or flush) with. **fleurer** (flœre) v.i, to smell.

fleuret (flœrɛ) m, foil (Fenc.); drill.

fleurette (flœrɛt) f, floweret. **conter** ~, to make love. **fleuri, e** (ri) a, in bloom; flowery; florid. **fleurir** (riːr) v.i, to flower, blossom, bloom; flourish; (v.t.) to deck with flowers. **fleuriste** (rist) n, florist; (att.) floral, flower. **fleuron** (rɔ̃) m, flower work; flower; floret; colophon.

fleuve (flœːv) m, river.

flexible (flɛksibl) *a,* flexible, pliant, pliable. **flexion** (ksjɔ̃) *f,* flection; deflection; inflection, ending (*Gram.*)

flibustier (flibystje) *m,* filibuster, freebooter; swindler.

flic (flik) *m,* cop.

flic flac (flikflak), crack, smack.

flirt (flœrt) *m,* flirtation. **flirter** (te) *v.i,* to flirt.

floc (flɔk) *m,* thud; slash.

flocon (flɔkɔ̃) *m,* flock, tuft; flake. **floconneux, euse** (kɔnø, ø:z) *a,* fleecy; flaky.

flonflon (flɔ̃flɔ̃) *m,* blare.

floraison (flɔrɛzɔ̃) *f,* flowering, blossoming, blooming. **floral, e** (ral) *a,* floral, flower (*att.*).

flore (flɔ:r) *f,* flora.

florence (flɔrɑ̃:s) *m,* sarsenet; [silkworm] gut.

florès (flɔrɛ:s): *faire ~,* to make a stir.

Floride (la) (flɔrid), Florida.

florissant, e (flɔrisɑ̃, ɑ̃:t) *a,* flourishing, thriving.

flot (flo) *m. oft. pl,* wave, billow; surge; rush; stream, flood; flood tide. *~ de la marée,* tidal wave. *à ~,* afloat. *à ~s,* in torrents. **flottage** (flɔta:ʒ) *m,* floating (*lumber*), rafting. **flottant, e** (tɑ̃, ɑ̃:t) *a,* floating; flowing, waving; baggy; wavering; evasive, elusive. **flotte** (flɔt) *f,* fleet; float; floater. **flottement** (tmɑ̃) *m,* swaying; wavering. **flotter** (te) *v.i,* to float; waft; wave; hang; waver, fluctuate. **flotteur** (tœ:r) *m,* raftsman; float; floater; ball. **flotille** (ti:j) *f,* flotilla.

flou, e (flu) *a,* fuzzy; woolly; hazy, blurry. **flou,** *ad,* fuzzily. ¶ *m,* fuzziness.

flouer (flue) *v.t,* to swindle.

fluctuation (flyktɥasjɔ̃) *f,* fluctuation.

fluet, te (flyɛ, ɛt) *a,* slender, thin.

fluide (flɥid) *a,* fluid, flowing. ¶ *m,* fluid (*imponderable*). **fluidité** (dite) *f,* fluidity.

fluor (flyɔ:r) *m,* fluorine. **fluorescent, e** (ɔrɛsɑ̃, ɑ̃:t) *a,* fluorescent.

flûte (flyt) *f,* flute; flute [glass]; baton (*bread*). *~ de Pan,* Pan's pipes. **flûté, e** (te) *a,* fluty. **flûter**

(te) *v.i,* to flute, pipe. **flûtiste** (tist) *n,* flutist.

fluvial, e (flyvjal) *a,* fluvial, river (*att.*). **fluviatile** (atil) *a,* fluviatile.

flux (fly) *m,* flux; flow; flood; flush (*cards*). **fluxion** (ksjɔ̃) *f,* swelling (*face*).

foc (fɔk) *m,* jib (*sail*).

focal, e (fɔkal) *a,* focal.

fœtus (fety:s) *m,* fetus.

foi (fwa) *f,* faith; troth; belief; reliance, trust; witness. *ajouter ~ à,* to credit, believe in. *ma ~ non! O* dear no!

foie (fwa) *m,* liver (*Anat.*).

foin (fwɛ̃) *m. oft. pl,* hay.

foire (fwa:r) *f,* fair, market.

fois (fwa) *f,* time. *à la ~,* at a time; at the same t., both; together.

foison (fwazɔ̃) *f,* plenty. *à ~,* galore. **foisonner** (zɔne) *v.i,* to abound, be plentiful; swarm; increase.

fol, folle, *see* fou.

folatre (fola:tr) *a,* playful, skittish, sportive, wanton. **folâtrer** (lɑtre) *v.i,* to play about, romp, frolic.

foliacé, e (fɔljase) *a,* foliaceous. **foliation** (sjɔ̃) *f,* foliation; leafing.

folichon, ne (fɔliʃɔ̃, ɔn) *a,* wanton, unchaste.

folie (fɔli) *f,* madness; folly; foolishness; mania, passion, hobby. *à la ~,* to distraction.

folio (fɔljo) *m,* folio. **foliole** (ɔl) *f,* leaflet (*Bot.*). **folioter** (ɔte) *v.t,* to folio.

folk-lore (fɔlklɔ:r) *m,* folklore.

follement (fɔlmɑ̃) *ad,* madly; foolishly. **follet, te** (lɛ, ɛt) *a,* frolicsome; downy, fluffy (*hair*). [esprit] **follet,** *m,* sprite, [hob]goblin, puck. **follette,** *f,* playful creature.

folliculaire (fɔlikylɛ:r) *m,* scribbler, hack (*writer*). **follicule** (kyl) *m,* follicle; leaflet.

fomentation (fɔmɑ̃tasjɔ̃) *f,* fomentation (*Med. & fig.*). **fomenter** (te) *v.t,* to foment.

foncé, e (fɔ̃se) *a,* dark, deep (*color*). **foncer** (se) *v.t,* to bottom (*cask, etc.*); sink (*well, etc.*); (*v.i.*) to rush; charge.

foncier, ère (fɔ̃sje, ɛːr) *a*, land-ed, land, ground, property (*att.*); deep-seated, fundamental. **fon-cièrement** (ɛrmɑ̃) *ad*, thoroughly.

fonction (fɔ̃ksjɔ̃) *f. oft. pl*, function, duty, office. *faire ~ de*, to act as. **fonctionnaire** (ɔnɛːr) *n*, official, officer, functionary. ~ *public, ique*, civil servant. **fonc-tionnarisme** (narism) *m*, official-dom; officialism. **fonctionnel, le** (nɛl) *a*, functional. **fonctionner** (ne) *v.i*, to function, run, work, act.

fond (fɔ̃) *m*, bottom; ground; substratum; crown (*hat*); depth; floor; back; head; groundwork; background; seat (*trousers, chair*); heart; substance; main issue (*law*); undertone; under-current; staying power, stamina. ~ *de cale*, bilge (*ship*). *à ~*, thoroughly; home. *au ~*, after all, in reality. *de ~ en comble*, from top to bottom. *faire ~ sur*, to rely on.

fondamental, e† (fɔ̃damɑ̃tal) *a*, fundamental, basic; founda-tion (*stone*).

fondant, e (fɔ̃dɑ̃, ɑ̃ːt) *a*, melt-ing (*ice*); that melts in the mouth, luscious, juicy. ¶ *m*, flux; fondant.

fondateur, trice (fɔ̃datœːr, tris) *n*, founder, foundress; promoter. **fondation** (sjɔ̃) *f*, foundation; bed; establishment.

fondé de pouvoir(s) (fɔ̃de) *m*, attorney; proxy; duly authorized representative.

fondement (fɔ̃dmɑ̃) *m. oft. pl*, foundation, ground, base, basis; fundament. **fonder** (de) *v.t*, to found; base, ground. *se ~*, to take one's stand; be based.

fonderie (fɔ̃dri) *f*, foundry; [smelting] works; founding. **fon-deur** (dœːr) *m*, founder.

fondre (fɔ̃:dr) *v.t*, to melt, dis-solve; smelt; fuse; cast, found; merge; blend; (*v.i.*) to melt, dis-solve, fuse; blow, go (*fuse*). ~ *sur*, to fall [up]on, pounce on, swoop down on.

fondrière (fɔ̃driɛːr) *f*, pit, hol-low, hole (*in road*); quagmire, morass.

fonds (fɔ̃) *m. oft. pl*, fund; funds; money, cash; capital; stock; se-curity. ~ *d'amortissement*, sink-ing fund. ~ [*de commerce*], goodwill, business. ~ *de pré-voyance*, contingency fund. ~ *de roulement*, working capital. ~ [*de terre*], estate, [piece of] land. *à ~ perdu*, with capital sunk (*as in an annuity*).

fongueux, euse (fɔ̃gø, øːz) *a*, fungous. **fongus** (gyːs) *m*, fun-gus.

fontaine (fɔ̃tɛn) *f*, fountain, spring, well; cistern (*house*). ~ *de Jouvence*, fountain of youth. **fontainier** (nje) *m*, maker of (*or* dealer in) domestic water ap-pliances (*cisterns, filters, etc.*); plumber; turncock; well sinker.

fonte (fɔ̃ːt) *f*, melting; smelting; casting, founding; melt; font (*Typ.*); holster. ~ *d'acier*, cast steel. ~ [*de fer*], [cast] iron. ~ [*en gueuses*], ~ *en saumons*, pig [iron].

fonts (fɔ̃) *m.pl*, font (*Eccl.*).

football (futbɔl) *m*, football (*game*). [~] *rugby*, Rugby [f.].

for (fɔːr) *m*: ~ *intérieur*, con-science.

forage (fɔraː ʒ) *m*, boring, drill-ing.

forain, e (fɔrɛ̃, ɛn) *a*, nonresi-dent; traveling, itinerant. ¶ *m*, [traveling] showman. [*mar-chand*] *forain*, market trader.

forban (fɔrbɑ̃) *m*, [sea] rover; pirate; shark (*fig.*).

forçage (fɔrsaː ʒ) *m*, forcing (*Hort.*); overweight (*coin*).

forçat (fɔrsa) *m*, convict.

force (fɔrs) *f*, force; power; strength; potency; might; press (*of sail*); many, plenty of; (*pl.*) shears. ~ *d'âme*, fortitude. ~ *d'inertie*, inertia. ~ *de bras*, hand power. ~ *de cheval*, ~ *en che-vaux*, horsepower. ~ *de l'âge*, prime of life. ~ *de levier*, lever-age. ~ *des choses*, force of cir-cumstances. ~ *du pouls*, pulse rate. ~ *du sang*, call of the blood (*fig.*). ~ *majeure*, force majeure, cause beyond control. *à ~ de*, by dint of. *à toute ~*, at all costs.

forcé, e (fɔrse) *p.a*, forced, com-pulsory; farfetched; strained.

forcément (mã) *ad*, perforce, necessarily.

forcené, e (fɔrsəne) *n*, madman; fury.

forceps (fɔrsɛps) *m*, obstetrical forceps.

forcer (fɔrse) *v.t*, to force; wrench open; compel; make; drive; obtrude; strain; constrain; overcome; overwork; crowd; run down (*Hunt.*). **forcerie** (səri) *f*, forcing bed (*Hort.*).

forclore (fɔrklɔːr) *v.t.ir*, to debar by time (*law*). **forclusion** (klyzjɔ̃) *f*, debarment by time.

forer (fɔre) *v.t*, to bore, drill.

forestier, ère (fɔrɛstje, ɛːr) *a*, forest (*att.*). ¶ *m*, forester.

foret (fɔrɛ) *m*, drill; bit. ~ *hélicoïdal*, twist drill.

forêt (fɔrɛ) *f*, forest; shock (*hair*). *la F~-Noire*, the Black Forest.

foreur (fɔrœːr) *m*, driller (*pers.*). **foreuse** (røːz) *f*, boring machine, drilling m.

forfaire à (fɔrfɛːr) *v.ir*, to fail in (*duty*); forfeit (*honor*). **forfait** (fɛ) *m*, crime; contract; fixed price, agreed sum. *à ~ ou* **forfaitaire** (tɛːr) *a*, on contract, contractual, at an agreed price; through (*rate*); standard (*charge*). **forfaiture** (tyːr) *f*, breach of trust.

forfanterie (fɔrfãtri) *f*, boasting, bragging.

forge (fɔrʒ) *f*, forge; smithy; blacksmith's shop; ironworks. **forger** (ʒe) *v.t*, to forge; fabricate; coin (*word*). *se ~*, to conjure up. **forgeron** (ʒərɔ̃) *m*, [black]smith. **forgeur, euse** (ʒœːr, øːz), *n*, fabricator, inventor (*stories, lies*); (*m.*) forgeman.

formaliser (se) (fɔrmalize) *v.pr*, to take exception, t. offense, t. amiss. **formaliste** (list) *a*, formal, precise. **formalité** (te) *f*, formality.

format (fɔrma) *m*, size (*book*), format. **formation** (sjɔ̃) *f*, formation; structure. **forme** (fɔrm) *f*, form, shape; block (*hat*); last (*shoe*); (*pl.*) manners; form (*Typ.*). *rester en ~*, to keep fit, keep in form. **formel, le†** (mɛl) *a*, formal; express; strict; flat.

former (me) *v.t*, to form, shape, fashion; frame; make; train. ~ *les faisceaux*, to stack arms (*Mil.*). ~ *une liste de jurés*, ~ *un tableau*, to impanel a jury.

formidable† (fɔrmidabl) *a*, formidable.

Formose (fɔrmoːz) *f*, Formosa.

formulaire (fɔrmylɛːr) *m*, formulary. **formule** (myl) *f*, formula; form; prescription (*Med.*). **formuler** (le) *v.t*, to draw up; write out; formulate.

fornication (fɔrnikasjɔ̃) *f*, fornication.

fort, e (fɔːr, ɔrt) *a*, strong; powerful; heavy; stout; stiff; fortified; steep; large; great, big; high; good; bad; full; loud; well up; overweight (*coin*); hard (*solder*). ~ *se faire fort* (*fort* is inv.), to undertake. **fort**, *ad*, hard; loud[ly]; very. ~ *avant dans la nuit*, far into the night. ¶ *m* (the) strong (*pers.*); market porter; strongest part; thick[est]; height; depth; strong point, forte; lair; fort, stronghold. *au plus ~ du combat*, in the thick of the fight. **forte** (fɔrte) *ad*, forte (*Mus.*). **fortement** (təmã) *ad*, strongly; highly; hard.

forteresse (fɔrtərɛs) *f*, fortress, stronghold.

fortification (fɔrtifikasjɔ̃) *f*, fortification. **fortifier** (fje) *v.t*, to strengthen, brace, invigorate; fortify.

fortin (fɔrtɛ̃) *m*, small fort.

fortuit, e† (fɔrtɥi, it) *a*, fortuitous, chance, casual, accidental.

fortune (fɔrtyn) *f*, fortune; luck, chance. ~ *de mer*, perils of the sea. *dîner à la ~ du pot*, to take pot luck. *de ~*, makeshift; chance (*att.*). **fortuné, e** (ne) *a*, fortunate, lucky; well-to-do, moneyed.

forum (fɔrɔm) *m*, forum.

forure (fɔryːr) *f*, bore, hole; pipe (*key*).

fosse (foːs) *f*, pit, hole; den; grave; deep (*ocean*); fosse. ~ [*d'aisances*], cesspool. ~ *septique*, septic tank.

fossé (fose) *m*, ditch, trench; moat; rift (*fig.*). *sauter le ~*, to take the plunge (*fig.*). **fossette** (fɔsɛt) *f*, dimple.

fossile (fɔsil) *a. & m*, fossil.

fossoyeur (foswajœːr) *m*, gravedigger.

fou, fol, folle (fu, fɔl) *a*, mad, insane; wild, frantic; foolish; passionately fond; uncontrollable; tremendous. ~ *à lier*, raving mad, stark m. *folle de son corps*, wanton (*woman*). **fou, folle,** *n*, madman, -woman, lunatic; (*m.*) fool; jester (*court*); bishop (*chess*).

fouailler (fwaje) *v.t*, to whip; castigate (*fig.*).

foucade (fukad) *f*, fit; start.

foudre (fudr) *f*, lightning; thunder, [thunder]bolt; (*m.*) thunderbolt (*fig. & Myth.*); tun. **foudroyer** (drwaje) *v.t*, to strike with lightning, blast; (*in. p.p.*) thunderstruck; crush.

fouet (fwɛ) *m*, whip; whipcord; whisk (*egg*); tip (*wing*). le ~, a flogging. **fouetter** (te) *v.t. & i*, to whip, flog, lash; beat; whisk; stir (*the blood*).

fougère (fuʒɛːr) *f*, fern. ~ [*à l'aigle*], bracken, brake. ~ *arborescente*, tree fern.

fougue (fug) *f*, fire (*fig.*), spirit, mettle. **fougueux, euse†** (gø, øːz) *a*, fiery, spirited, mettlesome.

fouille (fuːj) *f*, excavation, cut, trench, pit. **fouille-au-pot** (fujopo) *m*, cook's boy. **fouiller** (fuje) *v.t. & abs. & i*, to excavate; dig; mine; burrow in[to]; burrow; nuzzle; root; rummage, ransack; search, dive, peer into; fumble, grope; pry. **fouilleur** (jœːr) *m*, searcher. **fouillis** (ji) *m*, jumble, muddle, litter.

fouine (fwin) *f*, beech marten (*Zool.*); pitchfork; fish spear, grains. **fouiner** (ne) *v.i*, to slink away; nose about.

foulage (fulaːʒ) *m*, fulling; pressing (*grapes*); impression (*Typ.*).

foulard (fulaːr) *m*, foulard.

foule (ful) *f*, crowd, throng; mob.

fouler (fule) *v.t*, to press; full, mill (*cloth*); give an impression (*Typ.*); tread [on], trample [on]; harass, sprain, wrench; gall. ~

aux pieds, to tread underfoot; ride roughshod over. **foulon** (lɔ̃) *m*, fuller.

foulque (fulk) *f*, coot.

foulure (fulyːr) *f*, sprain, wrench.

four (fuːr) *m*, oven; kiln; furnace; failure, fiasco. ~ *crématoire* (krematwaːr), crematorium.

fourbe (furb) *a*, knavish. ¶ *m*, knave, cheat. ¶ *f. & fourberie* (bəri) *f*, knavery, cheating.

fourbir (furbiːr) *v.t*, to furbish, rub up.

fourbu, e (furby) *a*, foundered (*Vet.*); tired out.

fourche (furʃ) *f*, fork; pitchfork. **fourcher** (ʃe) *v.i*, to fork; branch off. **fourchette** (ʃɛt) *f*, fork (*table*); trencherman; frog (*horse*); wishbone. **fourchon** (ʃɔ̃) *m*, prong; fork (*tree*). **fourchu, e** (ʃy) *a*, forked; cleft; cloven.

fourgon (furgɔ̃) *m*, wagon; truck; van; poker, rake. ~ *de déménagements*, moving van. ~ *des bagages*, baggage car. **fourgonner** (gɔne) *v.i*, to poke [about].

fourmi (furmi) *f*, ant, emmet; (*pl.*) pins & needles (*fig.*). **fourmilier** (milje) *m*, anteater. **fourmilière** (ljeːr) *f*, ant's nest. **fourmi-lion** (ljɔ̃) *m*, ant lion. **fourmiller** (mije) *v.t*, to swarm; teem; abound; tingle.

fournaise (furnɛːz) *f*, furnace, inferno. **fourneau** (no) *m*, stove; furnace; bowl (*pipe*). ~ *à gaz, à pétrole*, gas, oil, stove. *haut* ~, blast furnace. *philanthropique*, soup kitchen. **fournée** (ne) *f*, batch.

fourni, e (furni) *p.a*, stocked; thick, bushy.

fournier, ère (furnje, ɛːr) *n*, baker (*for public*). **fournil** (ni) *m*, bakehouse.

fourniment (furnimɑ̃) *f*, equipment (*soldier's*). **fournir** (niːr) *v.t. & abs*, to furnish, supply, provide; afford; adduce; give; find; lodge, deposit; produce; follow (*cards*); (*v.i.*) to provide, contribute. ~ *la carrière*, to stay the course. ~ [*à*] *la couleur demandée*, to follow suit. **fournissement** (nismɑ̃) *m*, contribution. **fournisseur, euse** (sœːr, ø;z) *n*, supplier; dealer; contractor; tradesman. ~ *de l'armée*, army contractor. ~ *de navires*, ship chandler. marine store dealer. **fourniture** (ty:r) *f*, supply, store; requisite; (*pl.*) stationery; material; supplying; trimmings (*tailor's*); seasoning (*for salad, i.e, savory herbs*).

fourrage (fura:ʒ) *m*, fodder, provender, forage; fur lining. **fourrager** (raʒe) *v.i. & t*, to forage; rummage; ravage. **fourrageur** (ʒœ:r) *m*, forager.

fourré (fure) *m*, thicket, brake; cover (*game*); jungle. **fourré, e** (re) *p.a*, fur-lined; stuffed (*Cook.*); wooded; jungly.

fourreau (furo) *m*, scabbard, sheath; case; cover; sleeve, cylinder.

fourrer (fure) *v.t*, to thrust, poke, shove; stuff, cram; line [with fur]. **fourre-tout** (rtu) *m*, holdall. **fourreur, euse** (rœ:r, ø:z) *n*, furrier.

fourrier (furje) *m*, quartermaster; harbinger.

fourrière (furjɛ:r) *f*, pound (*dogs, etc.*). *mettre à la* ~, to impound.

fourrure (fury:r) *f*, fur, skin; welt, strap.

fourvoyer (furvwaje) *v.t*, to lead astray; mislead.

fox-terrier (fɔkstɛrje) *m*, fox terrier.

fox-trot (fɔkstrɔt) *m*, fox trot.

foyer (fwaje) *m*, hearth; furnace; fire box; stoker (*mechanical*); fireside; home; seat; hotbed; focus. ~ *d'étudiants*, hospice. ~ *des artistes*, greenroom. ~ [*du public*], foyer (*Theat.*). [*pierre de*] ~, hearthstone.

frac (frak) *m*, dress coat.

fracas (fraka) *m*, crash; roar; din, row, noise, bluster. **fracasser** (kase) *v.t*, to smash, shatter, shiver.

fraction (fraksjɔ̃) *f*, fraction; group (politics); breaking (*holy bread*). ~ *périodique*, recurring (*or* circulating) decimal. **fractionnaire** (ɔnɛ:r) *a*, fractional. **fractionner** (ne) *v.t*, to split.

fracture (frakty:r) *f*, fracture,

breaking. **fracturer** (tyre) *v.t*, to fracture, break.

fragile (fraʒil) *a*, fragile; brittle; frail; [on parcels] with care. **fragilité** (lite) *f*, fragility, etc.

fragment (fragmɑ̃) *m*, fragment, piece, scrap; snatch. **fragmentaire** (tɛ:r) *a*, fragmentary. **fragmenter** (te) *v.t*, to break [up].

frai (frɛ) *m*, spawning; spawn.

fraîchement (frɛʃmɑ̃) *ad*, in the cool; coolly; freshly, newly, lately. **fraîcheur** (ʃœ:r) *f*, freshness; cool[ness]; chill; bloom (*fig.*). **fraîchir** (ʃi:r) *v.i*, to freshen. **frais, aîche** (frɛ, ɛ:ʃ) *a*, fresh; cool; chilly; new (*bread, etc.*); recent; new-laid; wet (*paint, ink, fish*). *frais & gaillard, frais & dispos*, hale & hearty, fit & fresh. **frais, aîche** (*with p.p.*) *ad*, fresh[ly], newly, *e.g, des roses fraîches cueillies*, fresh[ly] gathered roses. **frais**, *m*, cool. *au* ~ *ou à la fraîche*, in the cool.

frais (frɛ) *m.pl*, expenses; expense; charges; cost; costs (*law*); efforts, pains. ~ *d'école*, ~ *scolaires*, tuition fees. ~ *de constitution*, preliminary expenses (*company*). ~ *de contentieux*, legal charges. ~ *divers*, general (*or* sundry) expenses. ~ *généraux*, standing (*or* establishment) (*or* overhead) expenses (*or* charges).

fraise (frɛ:z) *f*, strawberry; countersink [bit]; [milling] cutter; ruff (*Hist., dress*). ~ *des bois*, wild strawberry. **fraiser** (frɛze) *v.t*, to crimp; countersink; mill. **fraisier** (zje) *m*, strawberry plant.

fraisil (frɛzi) *m*, breeze (*cinders*).

framboise (frɑ̃bwa:z) *f*, raspberry. **framboisier** (bwazje) *m*, raspberry bush.

franc (frɑ̃) *m*, franc = 100 centimes. ~*s-or*, ~*s-argent*, ~*s-papier*, gold, silver, paper, francs.

franc, anche (frɑ̃, ɑ̃:ʃ) *a*, free; frank, candid, outspoken; open, open-hearted; aboveboard; clear (*complete, of days*); clean (*break, jump*); downright, out & out, regular, arrant; volunteer (*corps*); ungrafted (*tree*). franc arbitre, free will. franc (*anche*) de port ou franc le port (*inv.*), carriage free; post free. **franc,** *ad*, frankly, candidly.

français, e (frãsε, ε:z) *a*, French. **F~,** *n*, Frenchman, -woman. les Français, the French. le français, French (*language*).

franc-bord (frãbɔːr) *m*, free-board (*ship*); open space.

France (la) (frã:s), France.

Francfort (frãkfɔːr) *m*, Frankfort.

franchement (frãʃmã) *ad*, frankly, candidly, openly; down-right; heartily; boldly.

franchir (frãʃiːr) *v.t*, to jump over, leap o., pass o., get o.; pass through; clear; pass; cross; overstep; shoot (*rapids*); bridge; span; turn (*a certain age*); make (*hoop, croquet*).

franchise (frãʃiːz) *f*, exemption; franking (*Post*); frankness, outspokenness; plain dealing; freedom; immunity (*diplomatic*). ~ de poids, ~ de bagages, weight allowed free, free allowance of luggage.

francisation (frãsizasjɔ̃) *f*, Frenchification; registration (*ship*).

franciscain (frãsiskε̃) *m*, Franciscan, gray friar.

franciser (frãsize) *v.t*, to Frenchify, gallicize.

franc-maçon (frãmasɔ̃) *m*, free-mason. **franc-maçonnerie** (sɔnri) *f*, freemasonry.

franco (frãko) *ad*, free, f. of charge. ~ [à] bord, free on board. ~ à quai, free at wharf, ex wharf. ~ de port, carriage paid; post p. ~ wagon, ~ gare, free on rail, f. on truck.

francophile (frãkɔfil) *a. & n*, Francophile. **francophobe** (fɔb) *a. & n*, Francophobe.

franc-tireur (frãtirœːr) *m*, sniper; free-lance.

frange (frã:ʒ) *f*, fringe. **franger** (frãʒe) *v.t*, to fringe.

franquette (à la bonne) frãkεt), simply, without ceremony.

frappant, e (frapã, ã:t) *a*, strik-ing. **frappe** (frap) *f*, stamp; minting; set of matrices (*Typ.*).

Force de ~, striking force. **frapper** (pe) *v.t. & abs. & v.i*, to strike; hit; smite; tap; knock; slap; stamp; mint; impose, levy; be secured on. ~ [de glace], to ice. ~ de nullité, to render void.

frasque (frask) *f*, escapade.

frater (fratε:r) *m*, lay brother. **fraternel, le†** (tεrnεl) *a*, frater-nal, brotherly. **fraterniser** (nize) *v.i*, to fraternize. **fraternité** (te) *f*, fraternity, brotherhood. **fratri-cide** (trisid) *m*, fratricide; (*att.*) fratricidal.

fraude (froːd) *f*, fraud; smug-gling. la ~ fiscale, evasion of tax. **frauder** (frode) *v.t*, to de-fraud, cheat; evade [payment of]. **fraudeur, euse** (dœːr, øːz) *n*, defrauder; smuggler. ~ des droits du fisc, tax dodger. **frau-duleux, euse†** (dylø, øːz) *a*, fraudulent.

frayer (frεje) *v.t. & i*, to open up, clear, blaze; rub; spawn; rub shoulders, associate. se ~, to force (*a passage*); fight (*or* grope) (*one's way*).

frayeur (frεjœːr) *f*, fright, fear, dread.

fredaine (frədεn) *f*, prank.

fredonner (frədɔne) *v.i. & t*, to hum (*tune*).

frégate (fregat) *f*, frigate.

frein (frε̃) *m*, brake; curb, check (*fig.*); frenum (*Anat.*). ~ à ruban, ~ à bandé, band brake. ~ à vide, vacuum b. ~ sur jantes, rim b. ~ sur les quatre roues, four-wheel b. ~ sur moyeux, hub b. ~ sur pneu, spoon b. **freiner** (frεne) *v.i*, ou serrer les freins, to [put on (*or* apply) the] brake.

frelater (frəlate) *v.t*, to adul-terate, doctor.

frêle (frεːl) *a*, frail; weak.

frelon (frəlɔ̃) *m*, hornet.

freluche (frəlyʃ) *f*, tassel; tuft. **freluquet** (kε) *m*, whippersnap-per, puppy (*man*); coxcomb.

frémir (fremiːr) *v.i*, to rustle, murmur; simmer; vibrate, quiver, shudder. **frémissement** (fremis-mã) *m*, quivering, shivering, shuddering, etc.

frêne (frε:n) *m*, ash [tree, timber].

frénésie (frenezi) *f*, frenzy. **fré-nétique†** (tik) *a*, frantic, frenzied.

fréquemment (frekamã) *ad,* frequently, repeatedly, often. **fréquence** (kã:s) *f,* frequency; prevalence. **fréquent, e** (kã, ã:t) *a,* frequent; rapid (*pulse, etc.*). **fréquentation** (kãtasjõ) *f,* frequentation; (*pl.*) companionship. **fréquenté, e** (te) *p.p,* crowded. **fréquenter** (te) *v.i,* to frequent; resort to; associate with.

frère (frɛ:r) *m,* brother; (*pl.*) brethren (*Eccl.*); friar; sister [ship]. ~ *de lait,* foster brother. **frérot** (frero) *m,* [dear] little brother.

fresaie (frəzɛ) *f,* barn owl, screech owl.

fresque (frɛsk) *f,* fresco.

fressure (frɛsy:r) *f,* innards (*butchery*).

fret (frɛ) *m,* freight. *prendre à* ~, to charter. **fréter** (frete) *v.t,* to freight; charter. **fréteur** (tœ:r) *m,* [ship]owner.

frétiller (fretije) *v.i,* to frisk; wriggle; fidget; itch. ~ *de la queue,* to wag its tail (*dog*).

fretin (frətẽ) *m,* fry (*fish*); small fry (*pers.*); rubbish.

frette (frɛt) *f,* hoop, collar, band, ring, ferrule; fret (*Arch., Her.*). **fretter** (te) *v.t,* to hoop, bind.

freux (frø) *m,* rook (*bird*).

friable (friabl) *a,* friable, crumbly.

friand, e (friã, ã:d) *a,* dainty. ~ *de,* fond of. **friandise** (ãdi:z) *f,* dainty, delicacy, sweet.

Fribourg (fribu:r) *m,* Fribourg, Freiburg (*Switzerland*). **F~-en-Brisgau** (brizgo) *m,* Freiburg (*Baden*).

fricassée (frikase) *f,* fricassee. **fricasser** (se) *v.t,* to fricassee; fritter away. **fricasseur, euse** (sœ:r, ø:z) *n,* bad cook; squanderer.

friche (friʃ) *f,* waste land, fallow [land]. *en* ~, fallow; undeveloped.

fricot (friko) *m,* stew. **fricoter** (kɔte) *v.i,* to stew; cook badly; (*v.t.*) to squander. **fricoteur, euse** (tœ:r, ø:z) *n,* jobber; shirker.

friction (friksjõ) *f,* friction; rubbing; dry shampoo, scalp massage. **frictionner** (ɔne) *v.t,* to rub, chafe.

frigidité (friʒidite) *f,* frigidity, coldness. **frigorifier** (gɔrifje) *v.t,* to refrigerate, freeze (*meat, etc.*). **frigorifique** (fik) *a,* refrigerating, freezing, cold (*att.*). ¶ *m,* cold store.

frileux, euse (frilø, ø:z) *a,* chilly (*pers.*).

frimas (frimɑ) *m,* icy mist, rime.

frime (frim) *f,* sham, pretense.

frimousse (frimus) *f,* phiz, little face.

fringale (frẽgal) *f,* hunger; craving. *avoir la* ~, to be famishing.

fringant, e (frẽgã, ã:t) *a,* frisky, lively; smart. **fringuer** (ge) *v.i,* to frisk, skip about.

friper (fripe) *v.t,* to [c]rumple, crease. **friperie** (pri) *f,* cast-off clothes; second-hand furniture; frippery, trumpery; secondhand dealer's shop. **fripier, ère** (pje, ɛ:r) *n,* secondhand dealer.

fripon, ne (fripõ, ɔn) *n,* knave, rogue, rascal; hussy, minx; thief. ¶ *a,* knavish, roguish, rascally. **friponner** (pɔne) *v.t. & abs,* to cheat out of; steal from; cheat. **friponnerie** (nri) *f,* knavery, roguery, rascality.

friquet (frikɛ) *m,* tree sparrow.

frire (fri:r) *v.t. & i. ir,* to fry.

frise (fri:z) *f,* frieze. **la F~,** Friesland.

friser (frize) *v.t. & i,* to curl, frizzle, frizz, crimp; graze; border on. **frison** (zõ) *m,* curl.

frison, ne (frizõ, ɔn) *a. & F~, n,* Frisian.

frisotter (frizɔte) *v.t,* to frizz[le].

frisquet (friskɛ) *a.m. & a.f,* chilly.

frisquette (friskɛt) *f,* frisket (*Typ.*).

frisson (frisõ) *m,* shiver, shudder, quiver; thrill. **frissonner** (sɔne) *v.i,* to shiver, etc.

frisure (frizy:r) *f,* curling; curliness; (*pl.*) curls.

friture (frity:r) *f,* frying; crackling (*Teleph.*); fry; frying oil, frying fat; fried fish.

frivole (frivɔl) *a,* frivolous, flighty; trivial, fiddling, trumpery, flimsy, frothy. **frivolité** (lite) *f,* frivolity, trifle; tatting.

froc (frɔk) *m,* cowl; frock (*monk's*); monkery, monkhood.

froid, e† (frwa, ad) *a,* cold; frigid; cool, chill[y]. **à froid,** *ad,* cold, when cold; in cold blood. ¶ *m,* cold; c. weather; frost (*degrees of*); coldness; chill[iness]; coolness. **froideur** (dœːr) *f,* coldness, chilliness; coolness; frigidity. **froidure** (dyːr) *f,* coldness, cold.

froisser (frwase) *v.t,* to bruise; crush; [c]rumple; offend, hurt, wound.

frôler (frole) *v.t,* to graze, brush [against]; come very near to (*fig.*).

fromage (frɔmaːʒ) *m,* cheese; soft job, a snap. ~ *à la crème,* double-cream cheese. ~ *blanc,* cream cheese. ~ *de porc,* brawn. **fromager, ère** (maʒe, ɛːr) *n,* cheese maker; cheesemonger; (*att.*) cheese. **fromagerie** (ʒri) *f,* cheese dairy.

froment (frɔmɑ̃) *m,* wheat.

fronce (frɔ̃ːs) *f,* gather; pucker. ~*s smock* (smɔk), smocking. **froncer** (frɔ̃se) *v.t,* to wrinkle; purse, pucker (lips); gather (*Need.*). ~ *le[s] sourcil[s],* to frown, knit one's brows.

frondaison (frɔ̃dɛzɔ̃) *f,* foliation, leafing; foliage.

fronde (frɔ̃ːd) *f,* sling; catapult (*boy's*); frond (*Bot.*); obstruction (*fig.*). **fronder** (frɔ̃de) *v.i,* to catapult; obstruct; (*v.t.*) to find fault with. **frondeur** (dœːr) *m,* slinger; faultfinder; critic. ~, **euse** (øːz) *att,* fault-finding.

front (frɔ̃) *m,* front; front [line] (*Mil.*); forehead; brow; face; head; impudence, cheek. **de ~,** abreast; frontal; front.

frontière (frɔ̃tjɛːr) *f. & att,* frontier, border.

frontispice (frɔ̃tispis) *m,* frontispiece (*book*); title page. **fronton** (tɔ̃) *m,* fronton, pediment.

frottage (frɔtaːʒ) *m,* polishing (*floors*). **frottée** (te) *f,* drubbing, thrashing. **frottement** (tmɑ̃) *m,* rubbing; friction; contact, intercourse. **frotter** (te) *v.t. & i,* to rub; polish; scumble; drub, pommel; box (*ears*); strike (*match*). **se ~ à** (*fig.*), to rub shoulders with. **se ~ les mains,** to rub one's hands. **frotteur** (tœːr) *m,* floor polisher (*pers.*).

frottis (ti) *m,* scumble; rubbing (*copy*). **frottoir** (twaːr) *m,* rubber, polisher.

frou-frou (frufru) *m,* rustling, swish.

frousse (frus) *f,* fear, funk.

fructifier (fryktifje) *v.i,* to fructify. **fructueux, euse†** (tɥø, øːz) *a,* fruitful (*fig. & Poet.*), profitable.

frugal, e† (frygal) *a,* frugal. **frugalité** (lite) *f,* frugality.

fruit (frɥi) *m,* fruit; profit; benefit; batter (*Build.*). ~ *tombé,* windfall. **fruiterie** (tri) *f,* fruit shop; f. trade. **fruitier, ère** (tje, ɛːr) *n,* fruiterer, greengrocer; (*att.*) fruit.

frusques (frysk) *f.pl,* clothes.

frusquin (fryskɛ̃) *m,* worldly goods.

fruste (fryst) *a,* defaced, worn.

frustrer (frystre) *v.t,* to deprive; defraud; frustrate, balk.

fuchsia (fyksja) *m,* fuchsia.

fugace (fygas) *a,* fleeting; unretentive (*memory*). **fugitif, ive** (ʒitif, iːv) *a,* fugitive, fleeting, transitory, short-lived. ¶ *n,* fugitive, runaway.

fugue (fyg) *f,* fugue (*Mus.*); flight, bolt; elopement.

fuir (fɥiːr) *v.i.ir,* to flee, fly, flit, run away; escape; recede; vanish; leak; (*v.t.ir.*) to flee [from], run away from; shun; eschew. **fuite** (fɥit) *f,* flight; escape; leak[age].

fulguration (fylgyrasjɔ̃) *f,* heat (*or* summer) lightning.

fulmicoton (fylmikɔtɔ̃) *m,* guncotton.

fulminer (fylmine) *v.i. & t,* to fulminate, thunder, storm.

fumage (fymaːʒ) *m,* smoking (*meat, fish*); manuring. **fume-cigarette,** *m,* cigarette holder. **fumée** (me) *f. oft. pl,* smoke; fume; steam, vapor; reek; phantom, vanity; (*pl.*) dung. **fumer** (me) *v.i. & t,* to smoke; cure; steam; reek; fume; manure. *cheminée qui fume,* smoky chimney. **fumerie** (mri) *f,* opium den. **fumet** (mɛ) *m,* smell; bouquet; scent. **fumeur, euse** (mœːr, øːz) *n,* smoker. **fumeux, euse** (mø øːz) *a,* smoky; heady; hazy. **fumier** (mje) *m,* litter (*straw &*

dung), dung, manure; muck; dunghill.

fumigation (fymigasjɔ̃) *f*, fumigation.

fumiste (fymist) *m*, heating engineer; practical joker. **fumisterie** (tri) *f*, heating engineering; practical joke. **fumivore** (vɔːr) *a*, smoke-consuming. ¶ *m*, s. consumer, s. preventer. **fumoir** (mwaːr) *m*, smoke house; smoking room.

fumure (fymyːr) *f*, manuring; manure.

funambule (fynãbyl) *n*, funambulist; rope walker. **funambulesque** (lɛsk) *a*, funambulatory; fantastic.

funèbre (fynɛːbr) *a*, funeral; funereal; dead (*march*); illomened (*birds*). **funérailles** (nerɑːj) *f.pl*, funeral. **funéraire** (rɛːr) *a*, funeral.

funeste (fynɛst) *a*, deadly, baneful, baleful, fatal.

funiculaire (fynikylɛːr) *a. & m*, funicular, cable railway.

fur (fyːr) *m*: au ~ & à mesure, in proportion. au ~ & à mesure des besoins, as [& when] required. au ~ & à mesure que, as [& when].

furet (fyrɛ) *m*, ferret. **fureter** (rte) *v.i. & t*, to ferret, f. about, pry. **fureteur, euse** (rtœːr, øːz) *n*, ferreter, rummager; collector, hunter; nosybody.

fureur (fyrœːr) *f*, fury, rage, wrath; passion; distraction; craze; frenzy; furore. **furibond, e** (ribɔ̃, ɔ̃ːd) *a*, madman; fury. **furie** (ri) *f*, fury. F~, Fury (*Myth.*). **furieux, euse†** (rjø, øːz) *a*, furious, raging, mad, raving; tremendous. ¶ *n*, madman, -woman.

furoncle (fyrɔ̃ːkl) *m*, boil (*Med.*).

furtif, ive† (fyrtif, iːv) *a*, furtive, stealthy, sly.

fusain (fyzɛ̃) *m*, spindle tree; charcoal [pencil]; c. drawing.

fuseau (fyzo) *m*, spindle (*spinning*); pintle.

fusée (fyze) *f*, rocket, fuse; fusee (*Horol.*); (*axle*) journal; [out]-burst (*fig.*). ~ *volante*, sky rocket.

fuselage (fyzlaːʒ) *m*, fuselage.

fuselé, e (zle) *a*, spindle-shaped; tapering; streamlined.

fusible (fyzibl) *a*, fusible.

fusil (fyzi) *m*, gun, rifle; steel (*sharpener*). ~ *à air comprimé*, ~ *à vent*, air gun. ~ *à deux coups*, double-barrelled g. ~ *mitrailleur*, machine g. ~ *pour le tir à plomb*, shotgun. ~ *se chargeant par la culasse*, breech-loader. **fusilier** (zilje) *m*; ~ *marin*, marine. ~ *mitrailleur*, machine gunner. **fusillade** (zijad) *f*, fusillade. **fusiller** (je) *v.t*, to shoot (*spy, deserter*); bombard (*fig.*).

fusion (fyzjɔ̃) *f*, fusion, melting, smelting. **fusionner** (ɔne) *v.t. & i*, to amalgamate, merge.

fustiger (fystiʒe) *v.t*, to flog; rebuke.

fût (fy) *m*, stock (*rifle, plane*); handle; shank; shaft (*of column*); post; cask; drum.

futaie (fytɛ) *f*, timber-tree forest.

futaille (fytaːj) *f*, cask, barrel.

futaine (fytɛn) *f*, fustian.

futé, e (fyte) *a*, crafty; sly; sharp.

futile (fytil) *a*, futile, nugatory; trifling, idle. **futilité** (lite) *f*, futility; (*pl.*) trifles; (*pl.*) trash (*worthless contents of book*).

futur, e (fytyːr) *a*, future. ¶ *n*, intended (*husband, wife*). ¶ *m*, future; futurity. ~ *antérieur*, future perfect (*Gram.*). ~ [*simple*], future [tense].

fuyant, e (fɥijã, ãːt) *a*, receding, retreating; vanishing (*perspective*); shifty. **fuyard, e** (jaːr, ard) *n*, fugitive, runaway.

G

gabare (gabaːr) *f*, lighter, barge; dragnet.

gabarit (gabari) *m*, gauge, templet; mold (*ship*).

gabegie (gabʒi) *f*, mismanagement & dishonesty.

gabier (gabje) *m*, top[s]man (*Naut.*).

gâche (gɑːʃ) *f*, staple (*lock, wall*). **gâcher** (gɑʃe) *v.t*, to temper (*mortar*); spoil, botch, mess up. **gâchis** (ʃi) *m*, (*wet*) mortar; slush, sludge; mess.

gâchette (gaʃɛt) f, trigger; catch; pawl (*Mech.*).

gadoue (gadu) f, night soil, sewage.

gaffe (gaf) f, boat hook; gaff (*Fish.*); blunder, howler. **gaffer** (fe) v.t, to hook, gaff; (v.i.) to blunder.

gage (ga:ʒ) m, pledge, pawn, security, gage; hostage; forfeit (*at play*); token, proof; (*pl.*) wages, pay; forfeits (*game*). à ~s, paid, hired. **gager** (gaʒe) v.t, to pay; bet. **gageure** (ʒy:r) f, wager. **gagiste** (ʒist) m, employee.

gagnage (gaɲa:ʒ) m, pasturage.

gagnant, e (gaɲɑ̃, ɑ̃:t) n, winner; (*att.*) winning. **gagne-pain** (ɲpɛ̃) m, livelihood; breadwinner. **gagne-petit** (ɲpəti) m, knife grinder; one who earns (*or* makes) very little. **gagner** (ɲe) v.t. & abs. & i, to gain; be the gainer; get; make; earn; win; gain over; reach, get to; overtake; spread. ~ à être connu, to improve on acquaintance. se ~, to be catching (*disease*).

gai, e† (ge) a, gay, merry; lively; blithe; bright, cheerful. **gai, i,** merrily!

gaieté (gete) f, gaiety; cheerfulness; liveliness; merriment, mirth, glee. de ~ de cœur, out of sheer wantonness. **gaillard, e**† (gaja:r, ard) a, jolly, merry; hearty; free, ribald. ¶ m, fellow, fine f., jolly f. ¶ f, strapping gay wench. **gaillardise** (jardi:z) f, gaiety, jollity; broad humor.

gailletin (gajtɛ̃) m. ou **gaillette** (jɛt) f, cobbles, nuts (*coal*).

gain (gɛ̃) m, gain, profit, lucre; earnings; winning; winnings. ~ de cause, decision in one's favor; right, justification. en ~, in pocket, to the good.

gaine (gɛ:n) f, sheath, case; girdle; pedestal.

gala (gala) m, gala.

galamment (galamɑ̃) ad, courteously, gallantly; skillfully. **galant, e** (lɑ̃, ɑ̃:t) a, gallant (*to women*); amatory; stylish. ga-lant homme, gentleman. ¶ m, gallant; spark; philanderer; lover; slippery gentleman. **galanterie** (lɑ̃tri) f, politeness, gal-

lantry (*to women*); love affair.

galbe (galb) m, contour, outline.

gale (gal) f, itch; mange; scab.

galée (gale) f, composing galley.

galène (galɛn) f, galena.

galère (galɛ:r) f, galley (*Hist.*).

galerie (galri) f, gallery; arcade; level, drive, drift, road[way] (*Min.*); (pl, *Theat.*) balcony. ~ à écho, whispering gallery. ~ à flanc de coteau, adit. faire ~, to sit out.

galérien (galerjɛ̃) m, galley slave.

galerne (galɛrn) f, northwester (*wind*).

galet (galɛ) m, pebble; (*pl. or s.*) shingle; roller, wheel, runner; castor, caster.

galetas (galtɑ) m, garret, attic.

galette (galɛt) f, ship biscuit, hardtack.

galeux, euse (galø, ø:z) a, itchy; scabby; mangy; scurfy.

galhauban (galobɑ̃) m, backstay (*Naut.*).

galimafrée (galimafre) f, hash, hotchpotch.

galimatias (galimatja) m, balderdash, gibberish.

galion (galjɔ̃) m, galleon (*Hist.*).

galle (gal) f, gall [nut].

Galles (le pays de) (gal), Wales. la Galles du Nord, du Sud, North, South, Wales.

gallican, e (galikɑ̃, an) a. & n, Gallican. **gallicisme** (sism) m, gallicism.

gallois, e (galwa, a:z) a, Welsh. G~, n, Welshman, -woman. le gallois, Welsh (*language*).

gallophobe (galɔfɔb) a. & n, Gallophobe, anti-French.

galoche (galɔʃ) f, rubber, overshoe.

galon (galɔ) m, braid, galloon; gimp; stripe (*N.C.O.'s, & Navy*); band (*officer's*). **galonner** (lɔne) v.t, to braid, lace.

galop (galo) m, gallop; galop (*dance*); hot haste; scolding. **galoper** (lɔpe) v.i, to gallop; run, career. **galopin** (pɛ̃) m, urchin.

galuchat (galyʃa) m, shagreen.

galvanique (galvanik) a, galvanic. **galvaniser** (ze) v.t, to galvanize. **galvanisme** (nism) m, galvanism.

galvauder (galvode) v.t, to misuse; botch; (v.i.) to loiter. **se ~**, to sully one's name.

gambade (gãbad) f, gambol, frisk; (pl.) antics, capers. **gambader** (de) v.i, to gambol, etc.

Gambie (la) (gãbi), Gambia.

gambiller (gãbije) v.i, to skip about.

gambit (gãbi) m, gambit (chess).

gamelle (gamɛl) f, mess kit; mess (Nav.).

gamin, e (gamɛ̃, in) n, urchin; youngster; (f.) hoyden, romp. **~ des rues**, street child, s. arab. ¶ a, saucy. **gaminer** (mine) v.i, to play about. **gaminerie** (nri) f, child's prank; [tom]foolery.

gamme (gam) f, scale; gamut; range; tone, tune (fig.).

ganache (ganaʃ) f, lower jaw (horse); duffer, fogey.

Gand (gã) m, Ghent.

Gange (le) (gã:ʒ), the Ganges.

ganglion (gãgliɔ̃) m, ganglion.

gangrène (gãgrɛn) f, gangrene. **gangrener** (grəne) v.t, to gangrene; corrupt, canker.

gangue (gã:g) f, gangue, matrix.

ganse (gã:s) f, cord (braided); gimp; loop.

gant (gã) m, glove; gauntlet (fig.); (pl.) credit. **~s de peau glacée**, glacé kid gloves. **~s de Suède**, suède g—s. **gantelée** (tle) f, foxglove. **gantelet** (tlɛ) m, gauntlet. **ganter** (te) v.t, to glove. **se ~**, to put on one's gloves. **ganterie** (tri) f, glove trade. **gantier, ère** (tje, ɛ:r) n, glover.

garage (gara:ʒ) m, shunting (Rly.); garage, parking (motor); shed (cycle); docking (boat); hangar (Avn.).

garance (garã:s) f, madder.

garant, e (garã, ã:t) n, guarantor, surety (pers.); (m.) authority; warrant; [tackle] fall (Naut.). **garantie** (rãti) f, guarantee, guaranty, warranty; security, indemnity; safeguard; underwriting (Fin.). **garantir** (ti:r) v.t, to guarantee; warrant; secure; keep, protect, shield; vouch for; underwrite (Fin.).

garcette (garsɛt) f, gasket; rope end.

garçon (garsɔ̃) m, boy, lad; son; [young] man; fellow, chap; bach-elor, single man. **~ d'écurie**, stableboy. **~ d'honneur**, best man. **~ de bureau**, messenger, commissionaire. **~ de cabine**, steward. **~ [de café]**, waiter. **~ de course**, errand boy. **~ manqué**, tomboy, hoyden, romp. **garçonne** (sɔn) f, bachelor girl. **garçonnet** (sɔnɛ) m, little boy. **garçonnier, ère** (nje, ɛ:r) a, (of girl) mannish, masculine; fond of men's society. ¶ f, bachelor flat.

garde (gard) f, guardianship; guard; keeping, charge, [safe] custody; watch; heed, care; protection; notice; hilt; covering card; endpaper. **~ blanche**, flyleaf. **~ descendante**, old guard (Mil.). **~ montante**, new guard.

garde (gard) m, guard (pers.); keeper; watchman; watcher (Cust.); warder; ranger. **~-barrière**, n, gatekeeper (level crossing). **~-cendre**, m, fender (fireplace). **~ champêtre**, m, rural policeman. **~-chasse**, m, gamekeeper. **~-corps**, m, rail (ship). **~-côte**, m, coastguard ship. **~-crotte**, **~-boue**, m, fender (auto). **~-fou**, m, handrail, railing. **~-frein**, m, brakesman. **~-malades**, n, [sick] nurse. **~-manger**, m, pantry, larder. **~-meuble**, m, depository, furniture warehouse. **~-robe**, f, wardrobe; privy. **~-vue**, m, eyeshade.

gardénia (gardenja) m, gardenia.

garder (garde) v.t, to keep; retain; harbor; tend, look after, mind; guard, protect. **se ~ de**, to take care not to; beware of; refrain from. **garderie** (dəri) f, day nursery. **gardeur, euse** (dœ:r, ø:z) n, keeper, -herd (cow, swine). **gardien, ne** (djɛ̃, ɛn) n, guardian; keeper; caretaker, custodian, attendant, warder, dress. **~ de but**, goal keeper. **~ de la paix**, policeman.

gardon (gardɔ̃) m, roach (fish).

gare (ga:r) i, look out! take care! mind. ¶ f, station (Rly.). **~ d'embranchement**, ~ de bifurcation, junction. **~ d'évitement**, sidings. **~ maritime**, harbor station. **en ~**, ~ **restante**, [at railway station,] to be called for.

garenne (garɛn) *f*, [rabbit] warren.

garer (gare) *v.t*, to shunt, switch (*train*); garage (*car*). **se ~,** to shunt; pull to one side; get out of the way, take cover.

gargariser (se) (gargarize) *v.pr. & abs*, to gargle; gloat on. **gargarisme** (rism) *m*, gargle.

gargote (gargɔt) *f*, beanery.

gargouille (gargu:j) *f*, gargoyle; waterspout (*rain*). **gargouiller** (guje) *v.i*, to gurgle; rumble (*bowels*).

gargousse (gargus) *f*, cartridge (*cannon*).

garnement (garnəmã) *m*. ou *mauvais ~,* scapegrace, scamp.

garni (garni) *m*, furnished room. ¶ *a*, furnished, trimmed.

garnir (garni:r) *v.t. & abs*, to furnish; stock; fill; line; stuff; trim; garnish; decorate. **garnison** (nizɔ̃) *f*, garrison. **garniture** (ty:r) *f*, fittings; furniture; trimmings; packing, lagging, gasket; lining; garnish; seasoning (*of salad, i.e, (savory herbs*); set. **~ de foyer,** fire irons. **~ de table,** luncheon set.

garrot (garo) *m*, withers; tourniquet; garrote. **garrotter** (rɔte) *v.t*, to pinion; strangle.

gars (gɑ) *m*, lad, boy.

gascon, ne (gaskɔ̃, ɔn) *n*, braggart, Gascon. **gasconnade** (kɔnad) *f*, boasting, gasconade.

gaspiller (gaspije) *v.t*, to waste, squander.

gastéropode (gasterɔpɔd) *m*, gastropod. **gastrique** (trik) *a*, gastric. **gastrite** (trit) *f*, gastritis. **gastronome** (trɔnɔm) *m*, gastronome. **gastronomie** (mi) *f*, gastronomy. **gastronomique** (mik) *a*, gastronomic(al).

gâté, e (gate) *p.a*, spoiled; damaged, rotten.

gâteau (gato) *m*, cake; comb (*honey*); spoils. **~ au madère,** tipsy cake.

gâte-métier(gatmetje)*m*,[price] cutter; rat. **gâter** (te) *v.t*, to spoil, mar; soil; corrupt; taint; indulge, pamper. **gâterie** (tri) *f*, overindulgence (*to pers.*), spoiling.

gauche (go:ʃ) *a*, left; crooked; awkward, clumsy; tactless. ¶ *f*, left. ¶ **le [poing] gauche,** the left (*Box.*) **gauchement** (goʃmã) *ad*, awkwardly, clumsily. **gaucher, ère** (ʃe, ɛ:r) *a*, left-handed. ¶ *n*, left-hander (*pers. or player*). **gaucherie** (ʃri) *f*, awkwardness. **gauchir** (ʃi:r) *v.i. & t*, to turn aside; shuffle; buckle, bend; warp, wind.

gaudriole (godfiɔl) *f*, broad joke.

gaufre (go:fr) *f*, comb (*honey*); waffle; wafer. **gaufrer** (gofre) *v.t*, to goffer, crimp; emboss; figure; tool (*Bookb.*). **gaufrette** (fret) *f*, wafer [biscuit] (*flat*).

gaule (go:l) *f*, pole; fishing rod; switch (*stick*).

gaulois, e (golwa, a:z) *a*, Gallic; joyous, broad, free. **G~,** *n*, Gaul. **gauloiserie** (lwazri) *f*, broadness; broad humor.

gausser (se) de (gose), to poke fun at.

gavage (gava:ʒ) *m*, cramming; forcible feeding.

gave (ga:v) *m*, mountain torrent. **gaver** (gave) *v.t*, to cram (*poultry, pupil for exam*); feed forcibly; stuff.

gavotte (gavɔt) *f*, gavotte.

gaz (gɑ:z) *m*, gas; flatus, wind. **~ lacrymogène** (lakrimɔʒɛn), tear gas. **~ moutarde,** mustard g.

gaze (gɑ:z) *f*, gauze.

gazéifier (gazeifje) *v.t*, to gasify; aerate.

gazelle (gazɛl) *f*, gazelle.

gazer (gɑze) *v.t*, to cover with gauze; veil, tone down; gas (*war*).

gazette (gazɛt) *f*, gazette; newsmonger, gossip.

gazeux, euse (gazø, ø:z) *a*, gaseous; gassy; aerated; effervescing. **gazier** (zje) *m*, gas worker; gas fitter. **gazogène** (zɔʒɛn) *m*, gazogene, seltzogene; [gas] producer. **gazomètre** (mɛtr) *m*, gasometer.

gazon (gazɔ̃) *m*, grass; turf, sod; lawn, [green]sward. **gazonner** (zɔne) *v.t*, to turf.

gazouiller (gazuje) *v.i*, to warble, chirp, twitter; purl, babble; prattle.

geai (ʒe) *m*, jay (*bird*).

géant, e (ʒeã, ã:t) *n*, giant, ess; (*att.*) giant.

géhenne (ʒeɛn) f, Gehenna, hell.
geignard, e (ʒeɲaːr, ard) a, whining, fretful. **geindre** (ʒɛ̃ːdr) v.i.ir, to whine, fret.
gel (ʒɛl) m, frost, freezing.
gélatine (ʒelatin) f, gelatin[e]. **gélatineux, euse** (nø, øːz) a, gelatinous.
gelé, e (ʒəle) a, frozen; frostbitten. **gelée** (le) f, frost; jelly. ~ *blanche,* hoar frost, white f. ~ *noire,* ~ *à glace,* black f. **geler** (le) v.t. & i. & imp. & se ~, to freeze.
gémir (ʒemiːr) v.i, to groan, moan; complain. **gémissement** (mismã) m, groan[ing].
gemme (ʒɛm) f, gem; bud; (att.) gem (stone); rock (salt).
gênant, e (ʒɛnã, ãːt) a, in the way; awkward; troublesome.
gencive (ʒãsiːv) f, gum (Anat.).
gendarme (ʒãdarm) m, gendarme, policeman; Amazon; martinet; spark; flaw; red herring. **se gendarmer** (me) v.pr, to be up in arms, fire up.
gendre (ʒãːdr) m, son-in-law.
gêne (ʒɛn) f, discomfort; inconvenience; constraint; want; straits, straitened circumstances. *sans* ~, indifferent (to other people's convenience), unconcerned, cool; unconventional, free & easy.
généalogie (ʒenealɔʒi) f, genealogy; pedigree. **généalogique** (ʒik) a, genealogical, family (tree).
gêner (ʒɛne) v.t, to hinder, hamper, cramp; pinch (shoes, etc.); interfere with; inconvenience.
général, e† (ʒeneral) a, general; common; prevailing. le ~, the general (fig.). ~ *de corps d'armée,* lieutenant general. ~ *de division,* major general. ~ *en chef,* (full) general. ¶ f, general's wife; dress rehearsal; alarm call. **généralat** (la) m, generalship. **généraliser** (lize) v.t. & abs, to generalize. se ~, to become general. **généralissime** (sim) m, generalissimo, commander-in-chief. **généralité** (te) f, generality.
générateur, trice (ʒeneratœːr, tris) a, generating. ¶ m, genera-

tor. **génération** (sjɔ̃) f, generation.
généreux, euse† (ʒenerø, øːz) a, generous, bounteous, bountiful.
générique (ʒenerik) a, generic.
générosité (ʒenerozite) f, generosity, bounteousness; (pl.) acts of generosity.
Gênes (ʒɛːn) f, Genoa.
genèse (ʒənɛiz) f, genesis. la G~, Genesis (Bible).
genet (ʒənɛ) m, jennet (horse).
genêt (ʒənɛ) m, broom (Bot.). ~ *épineux,* furze, gorse, whin.
genette (ʒənɛt) f, genet (civet).
gêneur (ʒɛnœːr) m, nuisance (pers.).
Genève (ʒənɛːv) f, Geneva.
genévrier (ʒənevrie) m, juniper (genus).
génial, e (ʒenjal) a, [full] of genius. **génie** (ni) m, genius; spirit; Muse; bent; engineering.
genièvre (ʒənjɛːvr) m, juniper tree, berry; gin.
génisse (ʒenis) f, heifer.
génital, e (ʒenital) a, genital.
génitif (ʒenitif) m, genitive [case].
génois, e (ʒenwa, aːz) a. & G~, n, Genoese.
genou (ʒənu) m, knee; (pl.) lap. *à* ~*x,* on one's knees, kneeling.
genouillère (jɛːr) f, kneepad; knuckle [joint] (Mech.).
genre (ʒãːr) m, kind; sort; line; type; description; genus; manner, way; style; fashion; genre (real-life picture); gender (Gram.). le ~ *humain,* mankind.
gens (ʒã) m.pl. & f.pl, people, folk, men; servants, les ~ *du commun,* m.pl, [the] common people. **gent** (ʒã) f, tribe, race, folk.
gentiane (ʒãsjan) f, gentian.
gentil (ʒãti) m. & a.m, gentile.
gentil, le (ʒãti, iːj) a, nice, pretty, sweet; kind, good. ~ *à croquer,* perfectly sweet (pers.). **gentilhomme** (tijɔm) m, nobleman; gentleman. ~ *campagnard,* gentleman farmer. **gentilhommerie** (mri) f, gentility; gentlemanliness. **gentilhommière** (mjɛːr) f, country seat.

gentilité (ʒɑ̃tilite) f, pagandom; paganism.

gentillâtre (ʒɑ̃tijɑːtr) m, obscure gentleman.

gentillesse (ʒɑ̃tijɛs) f, prettiness; gracefulness; (*pl.*) pretty speeches; (*pl.*) pretty tricks; nasty trick. **gentillet, te** (jɛ, ɛt) a, rather nice. **gentiment** (mɑ̃) ad, nicely, prettily.

gentleman (dʒɛntləman) m, gentleman; (*att.*) gentlemanly.

génuflexion (ʒenyflɛksjɔ̃) f, genuflexion.

géodésie (ʒeɔdezi) f, geodesy. **géognosie** (ɔgnozi) f, geognosy. **géographe** (graf) m, geographer. **géographie** (fi) f, geography. **géographique†** (fik) a, geographic(al).

geôle (ʒoːl) f, jail; jailer's lodge. **geôlier, ère** (ʒolje, ɛːr) n, jailer; wardress.

géologie (ʒeɔlɔʒi) f, geology. ~ *sur le terrain*, field g. **géologique** (ʒik) a, geologic(al). **géologue** (lɔg) m, geologist.

géométral, e† (ʒeɔmetral) a, flat, plane. **géomètre** (mɛtr) m, geometer, geometrician; surveyor. ~ *du cadastre*, ordnance surveyor. **géométrie** (metri) f, geometry. **géométrique†** (trik) a, geometric(al); mathematical (*precise*).

Georgie (la) (ʒɔrʒi), Georgia (*U.S.A.*).

Géorgie (la) (ʒeɔrʒi), Georgia (*Asia*).

gérance (ʒerɑ̃ːs) f, management; board of directors.

géranium (ʒeranjɔm) m, geranium.

gérant, e (ʒerɑ̃, ɑ̃ːt) n, manager, ess; (*att.*) managing.

gerbe (ʒɛrb) f, sheaf; shower; spray (*flowers*). ~ *d'eau*, spray of water; splash. **gerber** (be) v.t, to bind, sheaf, pile.

gerboise (ʒɛrbwaːs) f, jerboa.

gerce (ʒɛrs) f, crack; clothes moth. **gercer** (se) v.t, to chap; crack. **gerçure** (syːr) f, chap; crack; shake (*timber*).

gérer (ʒere) v.t, to manage. *mal* ~, to mismanage.

germain, e (ʒɛrmɛ̃, ɛn) a, germane, own, full (*brother, sister*). Cf. *cousin*.

germe (ʒɛrm) m, germ; eye (*potato*); tread (*egg*); sprout; bud (*fig.*); seed (*fig.*). **germer** (me) v.i, to germinate; shoot, sprout; spring up, germ. **germination** (minasjɔ̃) f, germination.

gérondif (ʒerɔ̃dif) m, gerund.

géronte (ʒerɔ̃ːt) m, old man (*in comedy*); old fool.

gésier (ʒezje) m, gizzard.

gésir (ʒeziːr) v.i.ir, to lie (*sick, dead*).

gesse (ʒɛs) f, vetch, pea.

gestation (ʒɛstasjɔ̃) f, gestation.

geste (ʒɛst) m, gesture; motion, movement; action; wave, flourish, lift (*of the hand*); (*f.*) epic. **gesticuler** (tikyle) v.i, to gesticulate.

gestion (ʒɛstjɔ̃) f, management, administration; care.

geyser (ʒezeːr) m, geyser.

ghetto (gɛto) m, ghetto.

gibecière (ʒipsjɛːr) f, game bag, pouch; satchel, knapsack. **giberne** (bɛrn) f, pouch (*cartridge*); knapsack.

gibet (ʒibɛ) m, gibbet, gallows.

gibier (ʒibje) m, game (*Hunt.*). ~ *à poil*, ground g. ~ *de potence*, gallows bird.

giboulée (ʒibule) f, shower; hailstorm.

giboyer (ʒibwaje) v.i, to go shooting. **giboyeux, euse** (jø, øːz) a, full of game, gamy.

gicler (ʒikle) v.i, to spirt, squirt, splash. **gicleur** (klœːr) m, jet; nozzle.

gifle (ʒifl) f, slap, smack. **gifler** (fle) v.t, to slap, smack.

gigantesque (ʒigɑ̃tɛsk) a, gigantic.

gigot (ʒigo) m, leg (*of lamb, etc.*). **gigoter** (gɔte) v.t, to kick about.

gigue (ʒig) f, jig (*Mus., dance*).

gilet (ʒilɛ) m, waistcoat, vest; cardigan; woolly coat.

Gille (ʒil) m, clown, fool.

gingembre (ʒɛ̃ʒɑ̃ːbr) m, ginger.

girafe (ʒiraf) f, giraffe.

girandole (ʒirɑ̃dɔl) f, girandole; epergne.

giration (ʒirasjɔ̃) f, gyration. **giratoire** (twaːr) a, gyratory; traffic circle.

girofle (ʒirɔfl) m, clove (*spice*).

grioflée (fle) *f*, stock (*Bot.*). ~ *jaune*, wallflower. **giroflier** (flie) *m*, clove tree.

giron (ʒirɔ̃) *m*, lap (*of pers.*); bosom, pale (*of the church*); tread (*of stair step*).

girouette (ʒirwɛt) *f*, vane, weathercock (*lit. & fig.*).

gisant, e (ʒizɑ̃, ɑ̃:t) *a*, lying. ¶ *n*, recumbent figure (*statue*). **gisement** (zmɑ̃) *m*, lie, bearing (*Naut.*); bed, seam, deposit, stratum (*Geol.*).

gitane (ʒitan) *m, f*, gypsy.

gîte (ʒit) *m*, home, shelter, lodging; form (*hare*); bed, seam, deposit (*Geol.*); leg of beef.

givre (ʒi:vr) *m*, hoarfrost rime.

glabre (glɑ:br) *a*, glabrous, hairless; cleanshaven.

glace (glas) *f*. *sometimes pl. in sense of ice*, ice; ice cream. (*pl.*) frost, chill (*fig., of age*); glass; [looking] glass, mirror; icing (*sugar*); flaw. ~[*s*] *flottante*[*s*], ice floe. **glacé, e** (se) *p.a*, frozen; icy; chill; iced; stony (*look*); glacé. **glacer** (se) *v.t*, to freeze, chill; ice; glaze; gloss; scumble. **se ~**, to freeze; glaze. **glaciaire** (sjɛ:r) (*Geol.*) *a*, glacial, glacier, ice (*att.*). **glacial, e** (sjal) *a*, glacial, icy; frozen; frosty; frigid. **glacier** (sje) *m*, ice-cream vender; confectioner; glacier. **glacière** (sjɛ:r) *f*, ice house; freezer, ice-box. **glacis** (si) *m*, slope; glacis; glaze; scumble. **glaçon** (sɔ̃) *m*, floe; piece of ice; icicle.

gladiateur (gladjatœ:r) *m*, gladiator.

glaïeul (glajœl) *m*, gladiolus.

glaire (glɛ:r) *f*, glair, white of egg.

glaise (glɛ:z) *f*, clay; pug, puddle. **glaiser** (glɛze) *v.t*, to clay, pug, puddle. **glaisière** (zjɛ:r) *f*, clay pit.

glaive (glɛ:v) (*Poet.*) *m*, sword, brand.

glanage (glana:ʒ) *m*, gleaning.

gland (glɑ̃) *m*, acorn; (*pl.*) tassel.

glande (glɑ̃:d) *f*, gland; tumor. *des ~ au cou*, swollen glands.

glandée (glɑ̃de) *f*, acorn crop.

glane (glan) *f*, gleaning; rope (*of onions, etc.*). **glaner** (ne) *v.t. &*

abs, to glean. **glaneur, euse** (nœ:r, ø:z) *n*, gleaner. **glanure** (ny:r) *f*, gleanings.

glapir (glapi:r) *v.i*, to yelp, yap, bark.

glas (glɑ) *m*, knell, passing bell.

glauque (glo:k) *a*, glaucous.

glèbe (glɛ:b) *f*, glebe, soil.

glène (glɛ:n) *f*, socket (*bone*); coil (*rope*).

glissade (glisad) *f*, slide, sliding, slip; glissade. **glissant, e** (sɑ̃, ɑ̃:t) *a*, slippery. **glissé** (se) *m*, glide (*Danc.*). **glissement** (smɑ̃) *m*, sliding, slide, slip[ping]; slump; glide; gliding. **glisser** (se) *v.i. & t*, to slide; skid; slip; glide; slur. **glisseur, euse** (sœ:r, ø:z) *n*, slider (*pers.*). ¶ *m*, hydroplane, speed boat; glider (*Avn.*). ~ *de course*, racing boat. ~ *de croisière*, fast cruiser (*speedboat*). **glissière** (sjɛ:r) *f*, slide, guide (*Mach.*). **glissoire** (swa:r) *f*, slide (*track on ice*).

global, e† (glɔbal) *a*, total, inclusive, aggregate (*sum*); grand, sum (*total*). **globe** (glɔb) *m*, globe; ball; orb. **globulaire** (bylɛ:r) & **globuleux, euse** (lø, ø:z) *a*, globular. **globule** (byl) *m*, globule.

gloire (glwa:r) *f*, glory; fame; pride; boast. *se faire ~ de*, to glory in, pride oneself on. **glorieux, euse**† (glɔrjø, ø:z) *a*, glorious; proud; conceited. **glorifier** (rifje) *v.t*, to glorify, praise. *se ~ de*, to glory in, boast of. **gloriole** (rjɔl) *f*, vainglory, vanity; kudos.

glose (glo:z) *f*, gloss, commentary; criticism. **gloser [sur]** (gloze) *v.t. & i*, to find fault with. **glossaire** (glɔsɛ:r) *m*, glossary. **glossateur** (satœ:r) *m*, commentator.

glotte (glɔt) *f*, glottis.

glouglou (gluglu) *m*, gurgle, bubbling. **glouglouter** (te) *v.i*, to gobble (*of turkey*).

glousser (gluse) *v.i*, to cluck; chuckle; giggle; titter.

glouton, ne† (glutɔ̃, ɔn) *a*, gluttonous. ¶ *n*, glutton. **gloutonnerie** (tɔnri) *f*, gluttony.

glu (gly) *f*, birdlime; glue (*marine*). **gluant, e** (ɑ̃, ɑ̃:t) *a*, gluey, sticky. **gluau** (o) *m*, (*bird*) lime twig.

glucose (glykoːz) *f*, glucose.
glume (glym) *f*, glume; chaff.
gluten (glytɛn) *f*, gluten. **gluti-neux, euse** (tinø, ø͂ːz) *a*, glutinous.
glycérine (gliserin) *f*, glycerin[e].
glycine (glisin) *f*, wistaria.
gnangnan (nɑ͂nɑ͂) *n. & a*, lack-adaisical (person).
gneiss (gnɛs) *m*, gneiss.
gnome (gnoːm) *m*, gnome.
gnostique (gnɔstik) *m*, gnostic.
go (**tout de**) (go) *ad*, straight off, there & then.
gobelet (gɔblɛ) *m*, goblet; tumbler. *joueur des ~s*, shell game swindler.
gobelin (gɔblɛ͂) *m*, [hob]goblin, imp.
gobe-mouches (gɔbmuʃ) *m*, fly-catcher (*bird*); flytrap (*plant*); simpleton, gaper. **gober** (be) *v.t*, to bolt, gulp down; swallow (*fig.*).
goberger (**se**) (gɔbɛrʒe) *v.pr*, to do oneself well.
godailler (gɔdaje) *v.i*, to carouse.
godelureau (gɔdlyro) *m*, country bumpkin.
goder (gɔde) *v.i*, to pucker; bag (*trousers*). **godet** (dɛ) *m*, cup; noggin; bucket (*elevator*); saucer (*artist's*); pucker, ruck.
godiche (gɔdiʃ) *a. & n*, awkward (person), hobbledehoy.
godille (gɔdiːj) *f*, scull (*stern oar*). **godiller** (dije) *v.t*, to scull.
goéland (gɔelɑ͂) *m*, sea gull.
goélette (gɔelɛt) *f*, schooner.
goémon (gɔemɔ͂) *m*, seaweed, wrack.
gogo (gɔgo) *m*, simpleton, gull. *à ~*, in plenty; in clover.
goguenarder (gɔgnarde) *v.i*, to banter, crack jokes; jeer; sneer.
goguette (**être en**) (gɔgɛt), to be jolly (*in drink*).
goinfre (gwɛ͂ːfr) *m*, guzzler. **goinfrer** (gwɛ͂fre) *v.i*, to guzzle, gorge.
goitre (gwaːtr) *m*, goiter, wen.
golf (gɔlf) *m*, golf; golf course, golf links. *~ miniature*, *~ réduit*, miniature golf.
golfe (gɔlf) *m*, gulf, bay, bight. *~ Arabique*, Arabian Gulf. *~ de Gascogne* (gaskɔɲ). Bay of Biscay. *~ Persique* (pɛrsik), Persian Gulf.

gommage (gɔmaːʒ) *m*, gumming. **gomme** (gɔm) *f*, gum. *~ [à effacer]*, eraser. *~ à mâcher*, chewing gum. *~ arabique*, g. arabic. *~ [élastique]*, [india]rubber. **gommer** (me) *v.t*, to gum; erase. **gommeux, euse** (mø, ø͂ːz) *a*, gummy. **gommier** (mje) *m*, gum tree.
gold (gɔ͂) *m*, (*gate*) hook. *~ & penture*, hook & hinge.
gondole (gɔ͂dɔl) *f*, gondola.
gondoler (gɔ͂dɔle) *v.i*, to swell; warp.
gondolier (gɔ͂dɔlje) *m*, gondolier.
gonfler (gɔ͂fle) *v.t. & i. & se ~*, to swell, inflate, pump up (*tire*). **gonfleur** (flœːr) *m*, pump (*air*).
gong (gɔ͂g) *m*, gong.
gord (gɔːr) *m*, weir (*Fish.*).
goret (gɔrɛ) *m*, piglet, porker; pig (*child*).
gorge (gɔrʒ) *f*, throat, gullet; bosom, bust; neck; mouth (*of tunnel*); gorge; groove; tumbler (*lock*). **gorgée** (ʒe) *f*, mouthful, gulp. **gorger** (ʒe) *v.t*, to gorge, cram, load.
gorille (gɔriːj) *m*, gorilla.
gosier (gozje) *m*, throat, gullet.
gosse (gɔs) *m, f*, kid, brat, youngster, etc.
gothique (gɔtik) *a*, Gothic; old-fashioned.
goton (gɔtɔ͂) *f*, slut.
gouache (gwaʃ) *f*, gouache (*art*).
gouailler (gwaje) *v.t. & i*, to chaff, banter.
goudron (gudrɔ͂) *m*, tar. **goudronner** (drɔne) *v.t*, to tar, spray with tar. *toile goudronnée*, tarpaulin.
gouffre (gufr) *m*, gulf, abyss, chasm; whirlpool.
gouge (guːʒ) *f*, gouge (*tool*).
goujat (guʒa) *m*, cad, blackguard. **goujaterie** (tri) *f*, dirty trick.
goujon (guʒɔ͂) *m*, gudgeon (*fish & Mech.*); dowel, joggle, stud. **goujonner** (ʒɔne) *v.t*, to dowel; joggle, stud.
goule (gul) *f*, ghoul.
goulée (gule) *f*, mouthful, gulp. **goulet** (lɛ) *m*, narrows, gut (*Naut.*). **goulot** (lo) *m*, neck (*bottle*). **goulotte** (lɔt) *f*, spout.

goulu, e (ly) *a,* greedy. **goulû-ment** (lymã) *ad,* greedily.

goupille (gupi:j) *f,* pin; bolt. ~ *fendue,* split pin; cotter. **goupillon** (pijɔ̃) *m,* holy-water sprinkler; bottle brush.

gourbi (gurbi) *m,* hut; hovel; dugout.

gourd, e (gu:r, urd) *a,* numb.

gourde (gurd) *f,* gourd; flask; fool.

gourdin (gurdɛ̃) *m,* cudgel.

gourmade (gurmad) *f,* punch, blow.

gourmand, e (gurmã, ã:d) *a,* gourmand; greedy. ~ *de,* very fond of. ¶ *n,* gourmand; glutton. **gourmander** (mãde) *v.t,* to scold, chide; lard (*Cook.*). **gourmandise** (di:z) *f,* gluttony.

gourme (gurm) *f,* strangles (*Vet.*); wild oats (*fig.*).

gourmé, e (gurme) *p.a,* stiff, formal. **gourmer** (me) *v.t,* to curb (*horse*); punch, pommel.

gourmet (gurmɛ) *m,* gourmet, epicure; connoisseur, judge.

gourmette (gurmɛt) *f,* curb (*harness*). *lacher la gourmette à,* to give a free rein to (*horse, pers.*).

gousse (gus) *f,* pod, shell. ~ *d'ail,* clove of garlic. ~ *de plomb,* net sinker, n. weight.

gousset (gusɛ) *m,* pocket (*vest*); fob; gusset.

goût (gu) *m,* taste; relish; flavor; tang; liking, fondness; style. **goûter** (te) *m,* afternoon snack. ¶ *v.t,* to taste; try; relish; like.

goutte (gut) *f,* drop; drip; dram; sip; spot, splash; gout (*Med.*). **gouttelette** (tlɛt) *f,* tiny drop. **goutteux, euse** (tø, ø:z) *a,* gouty. **gouttière** (tjɛ:r) *f,* roof gutter; (*pl.*) caves.

gouvernail (guvɛrna:j) *m,* rudder; helm (*fig.*).

gouvernante (guvɛrnã:t) *f,* governess; housekeeper. **gouvernants** (nã) *m.pl,* government in power. **gouverne** (vɛrn) *f,* guidance; steering. **gouvernment** (nəmã) *m,* government; management; care. **gouverner** (ne) *v.t. & abs,* to steer (*Naut.*); govern, rule; look after. **gouverneur** (nœ:r) *m,* governor.

goyave (gɔja:v) *f,* guava. **goyavier** (javje) *m,* guava [tree].

grabat (graba) *m,* pallet, mean bed. **grabataire** (tɛ:r) *a. & n,* bedridden (person).

grabuge (graby:ʒ) *m,* row, brawl.

grâce (grɑ:s) *f,* grace; gracefulness; favor; mercy; pardon; thanks; (*pl.*) grace (*after meal*). *les* [*trois*] *G~s,* the Graces. *de* ~, *ad,* pray, please, for goodness' sake. **gracier** (grasje) *v.t,* to pardon, reprieve. **gracieusement** (sjøzmã) *ad,* graciously; gratuitously, free. **gracieuseté** (zte) *f,* graciousness; kindness; gratuity. **gracieux, euse** (søj, ø:z) *a,* graceful, pleasing; gracious. *à titre* ~, free of charge.

gracile (grasil) *a,* slender, slim. **gracilité** (lite) *f,* slenderness.

gradation (gradasjɔ̃) *f,* gradation. ~ [*ascendante*], climax (*Rhet.*). ~ *descendante,* anticlimax. **grade** (grad) *m,* grade; rank; rating; degree (*Univ.*). *prendre ses* ~*s,* to graduate. **gradé** (de) *m,* noncommissioned officer. ~*s & soldats,* rank & file. **gradin** (dɛ̃) *m,* tier; step; stope (*Min.*). **gradué, e** (dɥe) *n,* graduate (*Univ.*). **graduel, le†** (dɥɛl) *a,* gradual. **graduer** (dɥe) *v.t,* to graduate; grade.

graillon (grajɔ̃) *m,* burning (*smell, taste, of burned meat, fat*). **graillonner** (jɔne) *v.i,* to catch fire (*Cook.*); hawk (*with throat*).

grain (grɛ̃) *m,* grain; seed; berry; bean; bead; speck; dash; spice; modicum; squall (*Naut.*). ~ *de beauté,* beauty spot; mole (*on skin*). ~ *de grêle,* hailstone. ~ *de plomb,* pellet. ~ *de raisin,* grape.

graine (grɛ:n) *f,* seed; silkworms' eggs. ~ *d'anis,* aniseed. ~ *de lin,* linseed. ~ *des canaris,* canary seed. **grainier, ère** (nje, ɛ:r) *n,* seedsman.

graissage (grɛsa:ʒ) *m,* greasing, lubrication, oiling. **graisse** (grɛ:s) *f,* fat; grease; blubber; ropiness (*wine*). ~ *de rognon,* suet. ~ *de rôti,* dripping. **graisser** (grɛse) *v.t,* to grease, lubricate. ~ [*à l'huile*], to oil. **graisseur** (sœ:r)

m, greaser; oiler; lubricator.
graisseux, euse (sø, ø:z) *a*, greasy, oily; fatty; messy.

gramen (gramɛn) *m*, lawn grass. **une graminée** (mine) a grass (*plant*).

grammaire (grammɛ:r) *f*, grammar. *contre la* ~, ungrammatical. **grammairien, ne** (mɛrjɛ̃, ɛn) *n*, grammarian. **grammatical, e**† (matikal) *a*, grammatical.

gramme (gram) *m*, gram = 15.432 grains.

gramophone (gramɔfɔn) *m*, phonograph.

grand, e (grɑ̃, ɑ̃:d) *a*, great, large; big; noble; major (*prophet, etc.*); high; tall; grown-up; long; broad; wide; open (*air*); deep (*mourning*); full (*dress, orchestra*); high-class (*wine*); loud; heavy (*rain*); grand; main; trunk (*line*); general (*public*); much, many. **grand,** *comps:* ~ *canot*, launch, pinnace. ~ *chemin*, highway, main road. ~ *danois*, great Dane (*dog*). *un* ~ *homme manqué*, a might-have-been. *un homme* ~, a tall man. *au* ~ *jour*, in broad daylight; publicly. ~ *jour* [*de la publicité*], limelight. ~ *livre*, ledger; register (*share, stock*). ~ *magasin* [*de nouveautés*], big stores, department store. *le* ~ *monde*, [high] society, high life, the upper crust. *le* ~ *nettoyage*, the spring cleaning. ~ *rabbin*, chief rabbi. **grande,** *comps:* ~*s eaux*, spate, freshet; fountains. *à* ~*s journées*, by forced marches. ~ *largeur*, double width (*cloth*). ~ *marée*, spring tide. ~ *multiplication*, high gear. ~ *pêche*, deep-sea fishing (*whale & cod*). ~ *pédale*, loud pedal. ~ *personne*, grown-up. *à* [*la*] ~ *pluie*, at much rain (*barometer*). ~ *tenue & ~ toilette*, full dress. ~*s vacances*, summer holidays.

grand (grɑ̃) *m*, great man; adult, grown-up. (*the*) great; (*pl.*) (*the*) great ones (*of the earth*). ~ *de l'eau*, high-water mark. ~*s & petits*, old & young. *en* ~, on a large scale; life-size.

grand-chose (grɑ̃ʃo:z) *pn.* usually with *neg*, much.

grand-crosse (grɑ̃krɔs) *f*, driver (*golf club*).

Grande-Bretagne (la) (grɑ̃dbrətaɲ), [Great] Britain.

grandelet, te (grɑ̃dlɛ, ɛt) *a*, growing (*big*); rather tall. **grandement** (dmɑ̃) *ad*, grandly; nobly; greatly; altogether; ample, amply. **grandeur** (dœ:r) *f*, size; magnitude; height; greatness; mightiness; nobility; grandeur. ~ *naturelle*, life-size. *Votre G*~, your Grace; your Lordship.

grand-fer (grɑ̃fɛ:r) *m*, driving iron (*golf*).

grandiloquence (grɑ̃dilɔka:s) *f*, grandiloquence. **grandiloquent, e** (kɑ̃, ɑ̃:t) *a*, grandiloquent.

grandiose (grɑ̃djo:z) *a*, grandiose, imposing.

grandir (grɑ̃di:r) *v.i*, to grow taller; grow up; grow; (*v.t.*) to make taller *or* bigger; magnify. **grandissime** (disim) *a*, very great.

grand-maman (grɑ̃mamɑ̃) *f*, grandmamma, granny. **grand-mère** (grɑ̃mɛ:r) *f*, grandmother.

grand-messe (grɑ̃mɛs) *f*, high mass.

grand-oncle (grɑ̃tɔ̃:kl) *m*, great-uncle.

grand-père (grɑ̃pɛ:r) *m*, grandfather.

grand-route (grɑ̃rut) *ou* **grande route** (ɑ̃:d) *f*, highway, main road.

grand-tante (grɑ̃tɑ̃:t) *f*, great-aunt.

grand-voile (grɑ̃vwa:l) *f*, mainsail.

grange (grɑ̃:ʒ) *f*, barn.

granit (grani[t]) *m*, granite.

granule (granyl) *m*, granule. **granuler** (le) *v.t*, to granulate.

graphique† (grafik) *a*, graphic. ¶ *m*, diagram, chart, graph.

graphite (grafit) *m*, graphite, plumbago, black lead.

grappe (grap) *f*, bunch, cluster. **grappiller** (pije) *v.i.& t*, to glean (*grapes*); pick up, scrape up.

grappin (grapɛ̃) *m*, grapnel; creeper (*well*).

gras, se (grɑ, ɑ:s) *a*, fat; fatty; oily; oil (*varnish*); ropy (*wine*); plump (*chicken*); fatted (*calf*); greasy; thick; rich (*food, etc.*); meat (*diet, day, etc.*); full-face, bold-faced (*type*); smutty, ribald, broad (*story*). **gras**, *m*, fat. ~ **de la jambe**, calf. ~ **du bras**, fleshy part of the arm. **grassement** (grasmã) *ad*, (*to live*) on the fat of the land; handsomely. **grasset, te** (sɛ, ɛt) *a*, fattish. **grasseyer** (sɛje) *v.i*, to burr (*speaking*). **grassouillet, te** (sujɛ, ɛt) *a*, plump; chubby.

gratification (gratifikasjɔ̃) *f*, bonus, gratuity. **gratifier** (fje) *v.t*, to bestow, confer.

gratin (gratɛ̃) *m*, brown crust (*in pot*); gratin. **le ~**, the 400. **gratiner** (tine) *v.t*, to gratinate (*Cook.*).

gratis (gratis) *ad*, gratis, free.

gratitude (gratityd) *f*, gratitude.

gratte (grat) *f*, scrapings (*savings*); pickings, graft. **gratte-ciel**, *m*, skyscraper. **gratte-cul**, *m*, hip (*Bot.*). **gratte-miettes**, *m*, crumb scoop. **gratte-papier**, *m*, penpusher. **gratter** (te) *v.t*, to scrape; scratch; s. out, erase. **grattoir** (twa:r) *m*, knife eraser; scraper.

gratuit, e† (gratɥi, it) *a*, gratuitous, free; unpaid (*no salary*); wanton (*insult*). **gratuité** (te) *f*, gratuitousness.

grave (gra:v) *a*, grave; solemn; serious; weighty; severe; grievous; deep (*sound*); heavy. ¶ *m*, lower register (*Mus.*).

graveleux, euse (gravlø, ø:z) *a*, gravelly, gritty; smutty, ribald. **gravelle** (vɛl) *f*, gravel (*Med.*). **gravelure** (vly:r) *f*, smuttiness, ribaldry.

gravement (gravmã) *ad*, gravely; seriously; rather slowly (*Mus.*).

graver (grave) *v.t*, to engrave; grave; cut; inscribe; impress (*on memory*). ~ **à l'eau-forte**, to etch. ~ **en relief**, to emboss. **graveur** (vœ:r) *m*, engraver.

gravier (gravje) *m*, gravel, grit.

gravir (gravi:r) *v.i. & t*, to climb, clamber.

gravitation (gravitasjɔ̃) *f*, gravitation. **gravité** (te) *f*, gravity; weight (*fig.*); depth (*sound*). **graviter** (te) *v.i*, to gravitate.

gravure (gravy:r) *f*, engraving; cut; print; illustration. ~ **à l'eauforte**, etching. ~ **à la manière**

noire, mezzotint. ~ *au trait*, line engaving. ~ *dans le texte*, illustration in text. ~ *de mode*, fashion plate. ~ *en creux*, die sinking. ~ *hors texte*, illustration outside text. ~ *sur bois*, wood engraving; woodcut.

gré (gre) *m*, will; free will; wish; pleasure; liking; taste. *au ~ de*, according to; at the mercy of. *bon ~, mal ~*, willynilly. *de ~ ou de force*, by fair means or foul. *de ~ à ~*, by negotiation; by private treaty.

grèbe (grɛb) *m*, grebe.

grec, ecque (grɛk) *a*, Greek, Grecian. **G~**, *n*, Greek (*pers.*). *le grec*, Greek (*language*). **la Grèce** (grɛ:s), Greece. **grecque**, *f*, Greek fret (*Arch.*).

gredin, e (grədɛ̃, in) *n*, villain, scoundrel, miscreant. **gredinerie** (dinri) *f*, villainy.

gréement (gremã) (*Naut.*) *m*, rigging; gear. **gréer** (gree) *v.t*, to rig.

greffe (grɛf) *m*, registry (*legal*); (*f.*) graft (*Hort. & Surg.*), scion; grafting. **greffer** (fe) *v.t*, to graft. **greffier** (fje) *m*, clerk (*of court*); registrar. **greffon** (fɔ̃) *m*, graft, scion.

grégaire (grege:r) *a*, gregarious, herd (*att.*).

grège (grɛ:ʒ) *a*, raw (*silk*).

grégorien, ne (gregɔrjɛ̃, ɛn) *a*, Gregorian.

grêle (grɛ:l) *a*, slender, thin (*legs*, *voice*); small (*intestine*). ¶ *f*, hail, shower (*fig.*). **grêlé, e** (grɛle) *p.a*, pockmarked, pitted; most unfortunate. **grêler** (le) *v.imp*, to hail; (*v.t.*) to damage by hail.

grelin (grəlɛ̃) *m*, hawser.

grêlon (grɛlɔ̃) *m*, (*big*) hailstone.

grelot (grəlo) *m*, bell (*spherical with ball inside*). **grelotter** (lɔte) *v.i*, to shiver (*cold*).

grenade (grənad) *f*, pomegranate; grenade. **G~,** *f*, Granada (Spain). **la G~**, Grenada (*W. Indies*). **grenadier** (dje) *m*, pomegranate [tree]; grenadier; virago. **grenadille** (di:j) *f*, granadilla (*Bot.*). **grenadin** (dɛ̃) *m*, grenadine (*Cook.*). **grenadine** (din) *f*, grenadine (*cordial, fabric*).

grenaille (grəna:j) *f*, tailings (*grain*); shot.

grenat (grəna) *m*, garnet. ~ ~ *cabochon*, carbuncle.

greneler (grənle) *v.t*, to grain (*leather*). **grené** (ne) *m*, stipple (*art*). **grener** (ne) *v.i*, to seed; (*v.t.*) to granulate; grain. **grènetis** (grɛnti) *m*, milling (*on coin*). **grenier** (grənje) *m*, granary; loft; garner; garret; attic. *en* ~, in bulk.

grenouille (grənu:j) *f*, frog; money box; funds (*club, society*). **grenouillère** (nujɛ:r) *f*, froggery; swamp.

grenu, e (grəny) *a*, grainy, seedy; grained. ¶ *m*, graining (*on leather*).

grès (grɛ) *m*, sandstone; grit; stoneware. ~ *meulier* (mœlje), millstone grit.

grésil (grezi) *m*, (*tiny hard pellets of*) hail. **grésiller** (je) *v.imp*, to hail; (*v.t.*) to shrivel [up].

gresserie (grɛsri) *f*, sandstone quarry; sandstone (*work*); stoneware.

grève (grɛ:v) *f*, beach, shore, (*Poet.*) strand; strike. ~ *patronale*, lockout. ~ *perlée*, slowdown. ~ *sur le tas*, sitdown strike. ~ *surprise*, lightning s. *se mettre en* ~, *faire* ~, to [go on] strike.

grever (grəve) *v.t*, to burden, weight, encumber, saddle. [put] on, [put] upon.

gréviste (grevist) *n*, striker; (*att.*) strike.

grianneau (griano) *m*, young grouse.

gribouiller (gribuje) *v.t. & abs*, to scrawl; daub.

grief (griɛf) *m*, grievance; complaint. **grièvement** (ɛvmɑ̃) *ad*, seriously (*injured*).

griffe (grif) *f*, claw, talon; clutch; clip; grip; jaw; dog; tendril; facsimile signature; autograph stamp; stamp. **griffer** (fe) *v.t*, to claw, scratch; blaze (*tree*). **griffon** (fɔ̃) *m*, griffin, griffon. **griffonner** (fɔne) *v.t. & abs*, to scrawl; scribble. **griffure** (fy:r) *f*, scratch.

grignon (griɲɔ̃) *m*, crust[y] end (*bread*).

grignoter (griɲɔte) *v.t. & abs*,

to nibble; get a few pickings (*profit*).

grigou (grigu) *m*, miser, screw, hunks.

gril (gri) *m*, gridiron; grill; grating. *sur le* ~, on tenterhooks (*fig.*). **grillade** (grijad) *f*, grilling; broiling; grill (*meat*). **grillage** (ja:ʒ) *m*, roasting (*ore*); grating; [wire] netting; grillage. **grille** (gri:j) *f*, grating; grill[e], grid; screen; wire guard; grate; railing[s]. ~*-pain* (grijpɛ̃) *m*, toaster. **griller** (grije) *v.t. & i*, to grill; broil; toast; roast; scorch; burn; long, itch; grate, rail in.

grillon (grijɔ̃) *m*, cricket (*insect*).

grimace (grimas) *f*, grimace, wry face, grin; sham. **grimacer** (se) *v.i*, to grimace, make faces, grin; pucker, crease. **grimacier, ère** (sje, ɛ:r) *a*, grinning; mincing; sham.

grime (grim) *m*, dotard (*of comedy*). *se* **grimer** (me) *v.pr*, to make up (*Theat.*).

grimoire (grimwa:r) *m*, gibberish; scrawl.

grimper (grɛ̃pe) *v.i*, to climb, clamber; creep.

grincer (grɛ̃se) *v.i*, to grind, grate, creak. ~ *des* (ou *les*) *dents*, to grind (*or* gnash) one's teeth.

grincheux, euse (grɛ̃ʃø, ø:z) *a*, churlish, crabbed.

gringalet (grɛ̃galɛ) *m*, shrimp (*pers.*).

grippe (grip) *f*, influenza; dislike. **gripper** (pe) *v.t*, to snatch (*steal*); (*v.i.*) to seize (*Mach.*). *être grippé, e*, to have influenza. *se* ~, to pucker. **grippe-sou**, *m*, money grubber.

gris, e (gri, i:z) *a*, gray; brown (*paper*); grizzly; dull; tipsy, fuddled. ¶ *m*, gray. **grisaille** (grizɑ:j) *f*, grisaille. **grisailler** (zaje) *v.t*, to [paint] gray. **grisatre** (zɑ:tr) *a*, grayish. **griser** (ze) *v.t*, to fuddle, muddle, intoxicate. **grisette** (zɛt) *f*, grisette (*girl*); white-throat (*bird*).

grisoller (grizɔle) *v.i*, to carol (*lark*).

grison, ne (grizɔ̃, ɔn) *a*, grayish, grizzled (*hair*). ¶ *m*, graybeard;

donkey. **grisonner** (zɔne) *v.i*, to
gray.

grisou (grizu) *m*, firedamp.

grive (gri:v) *f*, thrush. ~ *chanteuse*, song t., throstle.

grivois, e (grivwa, a:z) *a*, broad,
ribald.

Groenland (le) (grɔēlɑ̃[:d]),
Greenland.

grog (grɔg) *m*, grog.

grogner (grɔɲe) *v.i*, to grunt;
grumble. **grognon** (ɲɔ̃) *m*, grum-
bler.

groin (grwɛ̃) *m*, snout (*pig*).

grommeler (grɔmle) *v.i*, to
grumble at, g. about.

gronder (grɔ̃de) *v.i*, to growl,
snarl; roar; rumble, mutter, peal;
howl (*wind*); grumble; (*v.t.*) to
scold.

groom (grum) *m*, groom; page
boy.

gros, se (gro, o:s) *a*, big; large;
great; broad; stout; loud; strong;
hearty; pregnant; fraught; swollen; coarse; gross; thick; deep;
high; heavy; structural (*repairs*).
gros, *comps*: ~ *bonnet*, bigwig.
~ *boulet*, heavy weight (*throwing*). ~ *galet*, boulder. ~ *morceau*, lump. ~ *mots*, bad language, foul words. ~ *murs*, main
walls. ~ *œuvre*, main structure
(*of a building*). ~ *plan*, close-up
(*Phot.*). ~ *poisson*, heavy fish.
grosse, *comps*: ~ *caisse*, bass
drum, big drum. ~ *pièce*, heavy
casting, heavy fish, etc. **gros**, *ad*,
a great deal, much. ¶ *m*, bulk,
body, mass; main part; large
(*coal*). **en ~**, *ad*, roughly,
broadly. [**commerce de** (*ou* **en**)]
~, wholesale [trade].

gros-bec (grobɛk) *m*, hawfinch,
grosbeak.

groseille (grozɛ:j) *f*, currant (*red,
white*). ~ *verte*, ~ *à maquereau*,
gooseberry. **groseillier** (zɛje) *m*,
currant bush. ~ *à maquereau*,
gooseberry bush.

grosse (gro:s) *f*, large hand, text
hand (*writing*); engrossment
(*law*); gross (*144*). **grossesse**
(grosɛs) *f*, pregnancy. **grosseur**
(sœ:r) *f*, size; swelling. ~ *de
ceinture, de poitrine*, waist, chest,
measurement.

grossier, ère† (grosje, ɛ:r) *a*,

coarse; rough; gross; rude; rank,
crass; glaring; unmannerly, boorish; ribald. **grossièreté** (ɛrte) *f*,
coarseness, etc.

grossir (grosi:r) *v.t. & i*, to make
bigger, enlarge; magnify; swell,
inflate; exaggerate.

grossiste (grosist) *m*, wholesaler.

grosso-modo (grosomɔdo) *ad*,
roughly.

grossoyer (groswaje) *v.t*, to engross (*law*).

grotesque† (grotɛsk) *a*, grotesque.
¶ *m*, grotesque[ness]; clown; (*f.*)
grotesque (*art*).

grotte (grɔt) *f*, grotto.

grouiller (gruje) *v.i*, to swarm,
be alive (*with vermin*); seethe;
move.

groupe (grup) *m*, group, batch,
knot, cluster; company; party;
unit (*Mil.*). **groupement** (pmɑ̃)
m, grouping; pool (*Fin.*). **grouper** (pe) *v.t*, to group.

grouse (gru:z) *f*, grouse (bird).

gruau (gryo) *m*, meal; groats;
gruel. ~ *d'avoine*, oatmeal.

grue (gry) *f*, crane (*bird & hoist*);
whore.

gruger (gryʒe) *v.t*, to bleed (*fig.*).

grume (grym) *f*, bark (*left on
felled tree*). **en** ~, in the log.

grumeau (grymo) *m*, clot, curd.
se grumeler (mle) *v.pr*, to clot,
curdle.

gruyère (gryjɛ:r) *m*, gruyère
[cheese].

guano (gwano) *m*, guano.

gué (ge) *m*, ford. **gréable** (abl) *a*,
fordable. **guéer** (gee) *v.t*, to ford
(*river*); water (*horse*); rinse
(*linen*).

guelte (gɛlt) *f*, commission (*on
sales*).

guenille (gəni:j) *f*, rag, tatter.

guenon (gɔnɔ̃) & **guenuche** (nyʃ)
f, she-monkey; fright (*woman*).

guêpe (gɛ:p) *f*, wasp. **guêpier**
(gɛpje) *m*, wasps' nest; hornets'
nest (*fig.*); bee eater.

guère (ne . . .) (ne . . . gɛ:r) *ad*,
hardly, h. any; barely; not much;
not many; but little; only; hardly
ever.

guéret (gerɛ) *m*, plowed land;
fallow land; (*poet.*) field.

guéridon (geridɔ̃) *m*, occasional
table; coffee t., cocktail t.

guérilla (gerilla) *f*, guerrilla.

guérir (geri:r) *v.t. & abs. & i. & se ~*, to cure; heal; recover; get better. guérison (riz5) *f*, cure, healing, recovery. guérisseur, euse (sœ:r, ø:z) *n*, healer; quack doctor, medicine man.

guérite (gerit) *f*, sentry box; signal box; lookout; hooded wicker chair.

Guernesey (gɛrnəzɛ) *f*, Guernsey.

guerre (gɛ:r) *f*, war, warfare; strife; feud. *~ d'usure*, war of attrition. *~ de mouvement*, open warfare. *~ de plume*, paper warfare. *~ sociale*, class war. *de bonne ~* (*fig.*), fair [play]. guerrier, ère (gɛrje, ɛ:r) *a*, warlike, martial, war (*att.*). ¶ *n*, warrior. guerroyer (rwaje) *v.i*, to [wage] war.

guet (gɛ) *m*, watch. ~-apens (gɛtapɑ̃) *m*, ambush; trap; trick.

guêtre (gɛ:tr) *f*, gaiter. *~s de ville*, spats.

guetter (gɛte) *v.t*, to watch. guetteur (tœ:r) *m*, lookout [man].

gueule (gœl) *f*, mouth; muzzle. ~-*de-loup*, antirrhinum, snapdragon.

gueuler (gœle) *v.i*, to yell, bawl, etc.

gueules (gœl) *m*, gules (*Her.*).

gueuse (gø:z) *f*, pig (*iron*); heavy weight.

gueuser (gøze) *v.i*, to beg. gueuserie (zri) *f*, beggary. gueux, euse (gø, ø:z) *n*, beggar; rascal. ¶ *a*, beggarly.

gui (gi) *m*, mistletoe.

guichet (giʃe) *m*, wicket [gate]; shutter; counter (*cashier's*). *~* [*de distribution des billets*], ticket office; ticket window. *à ~ ouvert*, on demand. guichetier (ʃtje) *m*, turnkey.

guide (gid) *m*, guide; conductor; guide [book]; (*f.*) [driving] rein. ~-*âne*, *m*, manual, handbook. guider (de) *v.t*, to guide, conduct; steer. guiderope (rɔp) *m*, guide rope, trail r. (*Avn.*). guidon (dɔ) *m*, pennant; handlebar (*cycle*); foresight (*gun*). *~ de renvoi*, reference [mark].

guigne (giɲ) *f*, black cherry; bad luck.

guigner (giɲe) *v.t. & abs*, to peep at; peep; have an eye to.

guignier (giɲje) *m*, black cherry [tree].

guignol (giɲɔl) *m*, Punch & Judy [show]; puppet.

guignon (giɲ5) *m*, bad luck.

guillaume (gijo:m) *m*, rabbet plane.

guillemeter (gijməte) *v.t*, to put in quotes. guillemets (mɛ) *m.pl*, quotation marks, (*in Fr. printed thus* « »; *written thus* « » *or thus* " ").

guilleret, te (gijrɛ, ɛt) *a*, lively, gay; broad (*story*).

guilleri (gijri) *m*, chirp[ing] (*sparrow*).

guillochis (gijoʃi) *m*, guilloche; engine turning; checkering.

guillotine (gijɔtin) *f*, guillotine. *fenêtre à ~*, sash window. guillotiner (ne) *v.t*, to guillotine.

guimauve (gimo:v) *f*, marshmallow (*Bot.*).

guimbarde (gɛbard) *f*, covered wagon; rattletrap (*vehicle*); Jew's harp.

guimpe (gɛ:p) *f*, wimple; blouse front.

guindé, e (gɛde) *p.a*, strained, stiff; stilted. guinder (de) *v.t*, to hoist; strain, force (*fig.*).

guinée (gine) *f*, guinea (21/-). la G~, Guinea (*Geog.*).

guingan (gɛgɑ̃) *m*, gingham (*fabric*).

guingois (gɛgwa) *m*, crookedness, wryness. *de ~*, awry, askew.

guinguette (gɛgɛt) *f*, tavern with gardens & dance hall.

guipure (gipy:r) *f*, guipure.

guirlande (girlɑ̃:d) *f*, garland, wreath.

guise (gi:z) *f*, way. *en ~ de*, by way of.

guitare (gita:r) *f*, guitar; repetition, (*same*) old story. *~ hawaïenne*, ukulele.

Gulf-Stream (gylfstri:m) *m*, Gulf Stream.

gustation (gystasj5) *f*, tasting.

gutta-percha (gytapɛrka) *f*, gutta-percha.

guttural, e (gytyral) *a. & f,* guttural.

Guyane (la) (gчijan) Guiana.

gymnase (ʒimnɑːz) *m,* gymnasium. **gymnasiarque** (nazjark) & **gymnaste** (nast) *m,* gymnast. **gymnastique** (tik) *a,* gymnastic. ¶ *f,* gymnastics, drill (*Swedish*); gymnastic (*of mind, etc.*). **gymnique** (nik) *f,* gymnastics.

gymnote (ʒimnɔt) *m,* electric eel.

gynécologie (ʒinekɔlɔʒi) *f,* gynecology.

gypse (ʒips) *m,* gypsum; plaster of Paris. **gypseux, euse** (sø, øːz) *a,* gypseous.

gyroscope (ʒirɔskɔp) *m,* gyroscope.

H

The sign ' *denotes that the* **h** *is aspirate in the French sense, i.e, no liaison or elision.*

habile† (abil) *a,* able, clever, skillful, cunning, skilled. **habileté** (lte) *f,* ability, skill.

habilité (abilite) *f,* competency (*law*). **habiliter** (te) *v.t,* to enable, capacitate.

habillement (abijmɑ̃) *m,* clothing; dress, raiment, habiliments. **habiller** (je) *v.t,* to dress, clothe; suit; abuse. **habilleuse** (jøːz) *f,* dresser (*Theat.*). **habit** (bi) *m.* mostly *pl,* clothes, suit; garb; habit; (*men's evening*) dress; vestment. ~ *d'arlequin,* motley. ~*s de tous les jours,* everyday clothes. ~ *de soirée,* dress coat; (*pl.*) dress [suit], dress clothes.

habitable (abitabl) *a,* [in]habitable.

habitacle (abitakl) *m,* abode; binnacle.

habitant, e (abitɑ̃, ɑ̃ːt) *n,* inhabitant, dweller; occupier; resident, occupant, inmate; denizen. **habitat** (ta) *m,* habitat. **habitation** (sjɔ̃) *f,* habitation, dwelling, residence, abode, house. **habiter** (te) *v.t,* to inhabit, occupy, live in, l. at; (*v.i.*) to live, dwell.

habitude (abityd) *f,* habit; use; practice; wont. **habitué, e** (tчe) *n,* frequenter. **habituel, le**† (tчɛl)

a, habitual, usual, wonted. **habituer** (tчe) *v.t,* to habituate, accustom, inure.

'hâblerie (ɑbləri) *f,* brag. **'hâbleur, euse** (blœːr, øːz) *n,* braggart.

'hache (aʃ) *f,* axe. ~ *à main,* hatchet. ~ *coupe-gazon,* edging knife. ~ *d'armes,* battle-axe, pole-axe. **'hacher** (ʃe) *v.t,* to chop [up]; hack; cut to pieces; hash, mince; hatch (*engrave*). **'hachis** (ʃi) *m,* hash, mince. **'hachoir** (ʃwaːr) *m,* mincer; chopping board.

'hagard, e (agaːr, ard) *a,* haggard, wild; drawn (*face*).

'haie (ɛ) *f,* hedge[row]; hurdle; line, row (*people*); beam (*plow*). ~ *vive,* quickset hedge.

'haillon (ɑjɔ̃) *m,* rag, tatter.

'haine (ɛːn) *f,* hatred; odium; dudgeon. **'haineux, euse** (ɛnø, øːz) *a,* full of hatred. **'haïr** (aiːr) *v.t,* to hate, loathe.

'haire (ɛːr) *f,* hair shirt.

'haïssable (aisabl) *a,* hateful.

Haïti (aiti) *f,* Haiti.

'halage ([h]alaːʒ) *m,* towing.

'halbran (albrɑ̃) *m,* young, wild duck.

'hâle (ɑːl) *m,* [heat of the] sun, sunburn. **'hâlé, e** (ɑle) *p.a,* sunburned, tanned, weather-beaten.

haleine (alɛn) *f,* breath, wind; training (*fig.*); suspense. *de longue ~,* (*work, etc.*) of time, requiring long persistent effort.

'haler ([h]ale) *v.t,* to tow, haul, pull, heave; set on (*dog*).

'hâler (ɑle) *v.t,* to burn, tan. *se ~,* to get sunburned.

'haletant, e (altɑ̃, ɑ̃ːt) *a,* panting; breathless. **'haleter** (te) *v.i,* to pant, gasp [for breath].

'hall ([h]ɔl) *m,* hall; lounge (*hotel*).

'halle (al) *f,* [covered] market; shed (*goods*).

'hallebarde (albard) *f,* halberd (*Hist.*).

'hallier (alje) *m,* covert (*game*).

hallucination (alysinasjɔ̃) *f,* hallucination.

'halo (alo) *m,* halo (*Astr., Anat.*); halation (*Phot.*).

'halot (alo) *m,* rabbit hole.

'halte (alt) *f*, halt, stop. ¶ ([h]alt) & ~-là *i*, halt! stop!

haltère (altɛːr) *m*, dumbbell.

'hamac (amak) *m*, hammock.

'Hambourg (ãbuːr) *m*, Hamburg.

'hameau (amo) *m*, hamlet.

'hameçon (amsɔ̃) *m*, [fish] hook; bait (*fig.*).

'hampe (ãːp) *f*, staff, shaft, handle; scape (*Bot.*).

'hanche (ãːʃ) *f*, hip; haunch.

'handicap (ãdikap) *m*, handicap (*sport*). 'handicaper (pe) *v.t*, to handicap. 'handicapeur (pœːr) *m*, handicapper.

'hangar (ãgaːr) *m*, shed, outhouse. ~ [*d'aviation*], hangar.

'hanneton (antɔ̃) *m*, cockchafer; scatterbrain.

'Hanovre (anɔːvr) *m*, Hanover (*town*). le H~, Hanover (*province*).

'hanter (ãte) *v.t*, to frequent, haunt; keep (*bad company*). 'hantise (tiːz) *f*, haunting; obsession.

'happe (ap) *f*, cramp [iron]; cramp, clamp. 'happer (pe) *v.t*, to snap up; catch.

'haquet (akɛ) *m*, dray.

'harangue (arãːg) *f*, harangue, speech. 'haranguer (rãge) *v.t. & i*, to harangue.

'haras (ara) *m*, stud farm; stud.

'harasse (aras) *f*, crate.

'harasser (arase) *v.t*, to tire out, weary.

'harceler (arsəle) *v.t*, to harass, harry, bait; worry, pepper; heckle.

'harde (ard) *f*, herd (*deer*); leash (*set of dogs*). 'harder (de) *v.t*, to leash.

'hardes (ard) *f.pl*, clothes (*worn*).

'hardi†, e (ardi) *a*, bold, daring; hardy; rash; forward, pert. 'hardiesse (djɛs) *f*, boldness, daring, hardihood; forwardness, pertness; liberty.

'harem (arɛm) *m*, harem.

'hareng (arã) *m*, herring. ~ bouffi, bloater. ~ salé & fumé, kipper. ~ saur (sɔːr), red herring. 'harengaison (gɛzɔ̃) *f*, herring season; h. fishery. 'harengère (ʒɛːr) *f*, fishwife. 'harenguier (gje) *m*, herring boat.

'hargneux, euse (arɲø, øːz) *a*, surly, peevish, ill-tempered, nagging, snappy, fractious; snarling.

'haricot (ariko) *m*, kidney bean, haricot. ~ d'Espagne, scarlet runner, runner bean. ~s secs, beans (*dried*). ~s verts, stringbeans.

'haridelle (aridɛl) *f*, jade (*horse*).

harmonica (armɔnika) *m*, harmonica; musical glasses. ~ à bouche, mouth organ. harmonie (ni) *f*, harmony; (*in*) keeping; band. harmonieux, euse† (njø, øːz) *a*, harmonious, tuneful. harmonique† (nik) *a*. & *m*, harmonic. harmoniser (ze) *v.t*, to harmonize; attune. s'~, to harmonize, tone. harmonium (njɔm) *m*, harmonium.

'harnachement (arnaʃmã) *m*, harnessing; harness; trappings, rig. 'harnacher (ʃe) *v.t*, to harness; rig out. 'harnais (nɛ) *m*, harness; gear, tackle. blanchir sous le harnois (nwa), to grow old in the service.

'haro (aro) *m*, hue & cry; outcry.

harpagon (arpagɔ̃) *m*, miser, skinflint.

'harpe (arp) *f*, harp; toothing (*Build.*).

'harpie (arpi) *f*, harpy; hellcat.

'harpiste (arpist) *n*, harpist.

'harpon (arpɔ̃) *m*, harpoon. 'harponner (pɔne) *v.t*, to harpoon.

'hart (aːr) *f*, withe, withy; halter; hanging.

'hasard (azaːr) *m*, chance, luck, risk, venture; hazard. au ~, at random. 'hasarder (zarde) *v.t*, to hazard, risk, venture. 'hasardeux, euse† (dø, øːz) *a*, venturesome; hazardous, risky.

'hase ([h]aːz) *f*, doe hare.

'hâte (ɑːt) *f*, haste, hurry. 'hâter (ɑte) *v.t*, to hasten, hurry; quicken; expedite; force (*Hort.*). se ~, to make haste, hurry. 'hâtif, ive† (tif, iːv) *a*, hasty, hurried; cursory; forward, early (*fruit, etc.*). 'hâtiveau (vo) *m*, early pear, apple, pea, etc.

'hauban (obã) *m*, shroud (*Naut.*); guy, stay.

'hausse (oːs) *f*, raise; flashboard;

wedge (*to pack up to level*); elevator (*in shoe*); backsight (*gun*); leaf (*rifle*). **'haussement d'épaules** (osmɑ̃) *m*, shrug[ging] [of the shoulders]. **'hausser** (se) *v.t*, to raise, lift; shrug; (*v.i.*) to raise. **'haussier** (sje) *m*, bull (*Stk Ex.*).

'haussière (osjɛːr) *f*, hawser.

'haut, e (o, oːt) *a*, high; tall; lofty; upper; top; up; high-class; loud; deep; remote (*antiquity*); big. *le haut commerce*, [the] big traders, the merchant class. *haut enseignement*, higher education. *haut fait* [*d'armes*], feat of arms. *de hauts faits*, doughty deeds. *haut fourneau*, blast furnace. *haute mer*, high seas, open sea. *haute taille*, tallness (*pers.*). **'haut,** *ad*, high; h. up; loudly, aloud. ~ *les mains!* hands up! ¶ *m*, top, head; higher notes (*Mus.*); perch (*fig.*). ~ *de casse*, upper case (*Typ.*). ~ *du pavé*, wall (*side of pavement*). de ~, high, in height. des ~s & des bas or du ~ & du bas, ups & downs. en ~, [up] above; aloft; upstairs.

'hautain, e (otɛ̃, ɛn) *a*, haughty, lordly; lofty, proud.

'hautbois (obwɑ) *m*, oboe, hautboy. **'hautboïste** (bɔist) *m*, oboist.

'hautement (otmɑ̃) *ad*, boldly, openly. **'hauteur** (tœːr) *f*, height; elevation; tallness (*steeple, etc.*); loftiness; altitude; level; hill; depth; haughtiness. *être à la ~ de*, to be equal to. ~ *de marche*, rise (*of step*). ~ [*musicale*], pitch (*of a sound*).

'haut-fond (ofɔ̃) *m*, shoal.

'haut-le-cœur (olkœːr) *m*, heave, retch, nausea.

'haut-le-corps (olkɔːr) *m*, start, jump.

'haut-parleur (oparlœːr) *m*, loudspeaker.

'havane (avan) *m*, Havana (*cigar*). ¶ *a*, brown, tan (*boots*). la H~, Havana (*Geog.*).

'hâve (ɑːv) *a*, wan, emaciated.

'havre (ɑːvr) *m*, haven. le H~, Havre (*Geog.*).

'havresac (ɑvrəsak) *m*, knapsack.

Hawaï (avai) *m*, Hawaii. ha-

waïen, ne (iɛ̃, ɛn) *a*. & H~, *n*, Hawaiian.

'Haye (la) (ɛ), the Hague.

'hé (e) *i*, hi! hoy! hey! hallo[a]! ~ *là-bas!* hallo[a] there!

hebdomadaire (ɛbdɔmadɛːr) *a*, weekly.

héberger (ebɛrʒe) *v.t*, to harbor; lodge, entertain, put up.

hébéter (ebete) *v.t*, to dull; stupefy, daze.

hébraïque (ebraik) *a*, Hebraic, Hebrew. **l'hébreu** (brø) *m*, Hebrew (*language*); Greek (*jargon*).

hécatombe (ekatɔ̃ːb) *f*, hecatomb.

hectare (ɛktaːr) *m*, hectare = 100 ares *or* 2.4711 acres.

hectique (ɛktik) *a*, hectic (*fever*).

hectogramme (ɛktɔgram) *m*, hectogram = 100 grams *or* 3.527 ozs avoirdupois. **hectolitre** (litr) *m*, hectoliter = 100 liters *or* 2.75 imperial bushels *or* 22.01 imperial gallons. **hectomètre** (mɛtr) *m*, hectometer = 100 meters *or* 109.36 yards.

hégémonie (eʒemɔni) *f*, hegemony.

'hein ([h]ɛ̃) *i*, ey! what [do you say]?

hélas (elɑːs) *i*, alas!

'héler ([h]ele) *v.t*, to hail, call; speak (*ship*).

hélianthe (eljɑ̃ːt) *m*, helianthus.

hélice (elis) *f*, helix, spiral; screw, propeller; spinner (*Fish.*). en ~ & **hélicoïdal, e** (kɔidal) *a*, spiral, helical, twist (*drill*). **hélicoptère** (kɔptɛːr) *m*, helicopter.

héliotrope (eljɔtrɔp) *m*, heliotrope; cherry-pie; bloodstone.

hélium (eljɔm) *m*, helium.

hélix (eliks) *m*, helix (*ear*).

hellénisme (ɛlenism) *m*, Hellenism.

hémisphère (emisfɛːr) *m*, hemisphere.

hémorragie (emɔraʒi) *f*, hemorrhage. **hémorroïdes** (rɔid) *f.pl*, hemorrhoids, piles.

'henné (ɛnne) *m*, henna.

'hennir ([h]ɛniːr) *v.i*, to neigh, whinny.

'hep (hɛp) *i*, fore! (*golf*).

héraldique (eraldik) *a*, heraldic. ¶ *f*, heraldry. **'héraut** (ro) *m*, herald (*Hist.*).

herbacé, e (ɛrbase) *a,* herbaceous. **herbage** (ba:ȝ) *m,* grass, pasture (*uncut*); herbage; green vegetables, green stuff, greens. **herbe** (ɛrb) *f,* herb; plant; grass; weed; wort (*Bot.*). l'~, grass court (*Ten.*). ~*s fines,* sweet herbs. l'~ *longue,* the rough (*golf*). ~ *menue,* fine grass. ~*s menues,* fine herbs (*fine in texture, as savory herbs*). ~ *potagère,* pot herb. **en** ~, green; unripe; budding (*fig.*); in embryo (*fig.*). **herbette** (bɛt) (*poet.*) *f,* [green]sward. **herbeux, euse** (bø, ø:z) *a,* grassy. **herbier** (bje) *m,* herbal, herbarium. **herbivore** (bivɔ:r) *a. & m,* herbivorous (animal). **herboriser** (bɔrize) *v.i,* to botanize, herborize. **herboriste** (rist) *n,* herbalist. **herbu, e** (by) *a,* grassy.

hercule (ɛrkyl) *m,* Hercules, strong man. **herculéen, ne** (leɛ̃, ɛn) *a,* Herculean.

'hère (ɛ:r) *m,* wretch, wight; young stag.

héréditaire† (eredite:r) *a,* hereditary. **hérédité** (te) *f,* heirship, inheritance (*right*); heredity.

hérésie (erezi) *f,* heresy. **hérétique** (tik) *a,* heretical. ¶ *n,* heretic.

'hérissé, e (erise) *p.a,* bristly; prickly; on end (*hair*); bristling, beset. **'hérisser (se)** *v.i. & se ~,* to bristle [up], stand on end; (*v.t.*) to bristle, erect; stud. **'hérisson** (sɔ̃) *m,* hedgehog; (*sea*) urchin; clod crusher; sprocket wheel.

héritage (erita:ȝ) *m,* inheritance; heritage. **hériter** (te) *v.i. & t,* to inherit. **héritier, ère** (tje, ɛ:r) *n,* heir, heiress.

hermaphrodite (ɛrmafrɔdit) *m,* hermaphrodite.

hermétique† (ɛrmetik) *a,* hermetic.

hermine (ɛrmin) *f,* ermine, stoat. **herminette** (ɛrminɛt) *f,* adze.

hernie (ɛrni) *f,* hernia, rupture.

héroï-comique (erɔikɔmik) *a,* heroicomic, mock-heroic. **héroïne** (in) *f,* heroine. **héroïque†** (ik) *a,* heroic. **héroïsme** (ism) *m,* heroism.

'héron (erɔ̃) *m,* heron. **'héronnière** (rɔnjɛ:r) *f,* heronry.

'héros (ero) *m,* hero.

herpès (ɛrpɛs) *m,* herpes.

'herse (ɛrs) *f,* harrow; portcullis. **'herser (se)** *v.t,* to harrow

hésitation (ezitasjɔ̃) *f,* hesitation. **hésiter** (te) *v.i,* to hesitate, waver; falter.

hétaïre (etai:r) *f,* hetaera, courtesan.

hétéroclite (eterɔklit) *a,* freak[ish], odd, queer; heteroclite. **hétérodoxe** (dɔks) *a,* heterodox, unorthodox. **hétérodoxie** (ksi) *f,* heterodoxy. **hétérogène** (ȝɛn) *a,* heterogeneous; mixed.

'hêtre (ɛ:tr) *m,* beech [tree, wood]. ~ *rouge,* copper beech.

heure (œ:r) *f. oft. pl,* hour; time; moment; present; o'clock. l' ~ *du coucher,* bedtime. ~ *du lieu,* local time. l' ~ *du repas,* meal t. ~*s de bureau,* ~*s d'ouverture,* business hours. ~ *de pointe,* ~*s d'affluence,* peak h—s, rush h—s. ~*s supplémentaires,* overtime. *à la bonne* ~, well & good, all right. *de bonne* ~, ad, early, betimes, in good time.

heureux, euse† (œrø, ø:z) *a,* happy; pleased; fortunate; prosperous; blissful; blessed; successful; lucky; safe (*arrival*).

'heurt (œ:r) *m,* shock, knock, bump. **'heurté, e** (œrte) *a,* contrasty. **'heurter** (te) *v.t. & i,* to run (against); knock; shock. **'heurtoir** (twa:r) *m,* stop blocks (*Rly.*); buffer.

hexagone (ɛgzagɔn) *m,* hexagon. ¶ *a,* hexagonal. **hexamètre** (mɛtr) *m,* hexameter.

hiatus (jaty:s) *m,* hiatus (*Gram.*).

hiberner (ibɛrne) *v.t,* to hibernate.

'hibou (ibu) *m,* owl; recluse; unsociable person.

'hic (ik) *m,* rub (*difficulty*).

'hideur (idœ:r) *f,* hideousness. **'hideux, euse†** (dø, ø:z) *a,* hideous.

'hie (i) *f,* beetle, rammer; pile driver.

hiemal, e (jemal) *a,* winter (*att.*).

hier (iɛ:r) *ad,* yesterday. ~ [*au*] *soir,* last night.

'hiérarchie (jerarʃi) f, hierarchy.

hiéroglyphe (jerɔglif) m, hieroglyph.

hilare (ila:r) a, hilarious, laughing. hilarité (larite) f, hilarity, merriment, laughter.

hindou, e (ɛ̃du) a. & H~, n, Hindu, -doo. l'hindoustani (stani) m, Hindustani.

hippique (ippik) a, horse (show, etc.), equine. hippocampe (ippɔkɑ̃:p) m, hippocampus, sea horse. hippodrome (dro:m) m, hippodrome, circus. hippopotame (pɔtam) m, hippopotamus.

hirondelle (irɔ̃dɛl) f, swallow. ~ de fenêtre, [house] martin. ~ de rivage, sand martin.

hirsute (irsyt) a, hirsute, shaggy; rough; boorish.

'hisser ([h]ise) v.t, to hoist; raise.

histoire (istwa:r) f, history; story, tale, yarn; fib; (pl.) fuss. le plus beau de l'~, the best of the story. historié, e (tɔrje) p.a, historiated, illuminated, ornamental. historien (rjɛ̃) m, historian. historier (rje) v.t, to ornament. historiette (rjet) f, anecdote. historique† (rik) a, historical; historic. ¶ m, history, account. ~ du régiment, regimental records.

histrion (istriɔ̃) m, histrion.

hiver (ivɛ:r) m, winter. hivernage (verna:ʒ) m, wintering. hivernal, e (nal) a, winter (att.), wintry. hiverner (ne) v.i. & t, to winter.

'ho (ho) i, hi! ~, du navire! ship ahoy!

'hobereau (ɔbro) m, hobby (bird); petty country gentleman.

'hoche (ɔʃ) f, notch, nick (on tally).

'hochement (ɔʃmɑ̃) m, shake; toss (head). 'hochepot (ʃpo) m, hodgepodge. 'hochequeue (kø) m, wagtail. 'hocher (ʃe) v.t. & i, to shake; toss; notch, nick. 'hochet (ʃe) m, rattle, coral; bauble, plaything.

'hockey (ɔkɛ) m, hockey. ~ sur glace, ice h.

hoir (wa:r) m, heir. hoirie (wari) f, inheritance.

'holà ([h]ɔla) i, hallo[a]! Hallo! enough!

'hollandais, e (ɔlɑ̃dɛ, ɛ:z) a, Dutch. 'H~, n, Dutchman, -woman. le h~, Dutch (language). la Hollande (lɑ̃:d), Holland.

holocauste (ɔlɔko:st) m, holocaust, burnt offering; sacrifice.

'hom ([h]ɔm) i, hum! humph!

'homard (ɔma:r) m, lobster.

homélie (ɔmeli) f, homily.

homéopathe (ɔmeɔpat) m, homoeopath[ist]. homéopathie (ti) f, homoeopathy. homéopathique (tik) a, homoeopathic.

homérique (ɔmerik) a, Homeric.

homicide (ɔmisid) a, homicidal. ¶ n, homicide (pers.); (m.) homicide (act). ~ excusable, justifiable h. ~ involontaire, manslaughter. ~ volontaire, willful murder.

hommage (ɔma:ʒ) m, homage; (pl.) respects, compliments; token, tribute.

hommasse (ɔmas) a, mannish, masculine (woman). homme (ɔm) m, man; (pl.) mankind. ~ à bonnes fortunes, lady-killer. ~ à femmes, ~ galant, ladies' (or lady's) man. ~ à projets, schemer. ~ à tout faire, man of all work, jack of all trades, handyman. ~ calé, man of substance; well-informed man. ~ -caoutchouc, ~-serpent, contortionist. ~ d'affaires, business man; business agent; steward. ~ d'État, statesman. ~ d'exécution, man of deeds. ~ dans les affaires, business man. ~ de barre, helmsman, steersman. ~ de couleur, mulatto. ~ de foyer, family man. l'~ de la rue, the man in the street. ~ de lettres, man of letters, literary m. ~ de métier, craftsman. ~ de mer, seaman, seafaring man. ~ de paille, strawman. ~ de peine, [common] laborer. ~ de science, scientist. ~ l'~ intérieur, the inner man. ~-orchestre, one-man band. ~-sandwich, sandwich man. ~ sans aveu, vagrant, outcast.

homogène (ɔmɔʒɛ:n) a, homogeneous.

homologuer (ɔmɔlɔge) *v.t*, to ratify; prove (*will*); accept (*a sport record*).

homonyme (ɔmɔnim) *m*, homonym, namesake.

ʼhongre (5:gr) *a.m*, gelded. ¶ *m*, gelding. **ʼhongrer** (5gre) *v.t*, to geld.

ʼHongrie (la) (5gri) Hungary. **ʼhongrois, e** (grwa, a:z) *a.* & ʼH~, *n*, Hungarian. *le hongrois*, Hungarian (*language*).

honnête† (ɔnɛ:t) *a*, honest, honorable, upright; respectable, straight, decent; well-bred, civil, courteous; fair, reasonable. **honnêteté** (nɛtte) *f*, honesty; decency, propriety; courtesy; fairness, reasonableness; recompense.

honneur (ɔnœ:r) *m*, honor; mettle; justice (*as to a meal*); credit; pleasure (*e.g, of seeing you*). *jouer pour l'~*, to play for love. *faire ~ à* (*Com.*), to honor, meet.

ʼhonnir (ɔni:r) *v.t*, to disgrace.

ʼhonorable† (ɔnɔrabl) *a*, honorable; reputable; respectable. **honoraire** (rɛ:r) *a*, honorary. **~s**, *m.pl*, fee[s], honorarium. **honorariat** (rarja) *m*, honorary membership. **honorer** (re) *v.t*, to honor; respect; favor; grace; dignify; do credit to. **honorifique** (rifik), *a*, honorary.

ʼhonte (5:t) *f*, shame, disgrace; reproach, scandal. *avoir ~*, to be ashamed. **ʼhonteux, euse** (5tø, ø:z) *a*, ashamed; bashful, shamefaced; sheepish; shameful, disgraceful, inglorious; uncomplaining (*poor*).

hôpital (ɔpital) *m*, hospital. *~ de contagieux*, isolation h.

ʼhoquet (ɔkɛ) *m*, hiccup; gasp.

horaire (ɔrɛ:r) *m*, timetable.

ʼhorde (ɔrd) *f*, horde.

ʼhorion (ɔrjɔ̃) *m*, thump, whack.

horizon (ɔrizɔ̃) *m*, horizon. **horizontal, e** (tal) *a*, horizontal. **horizontalement** (lmɑ̃) *ad*, horizontally; across (*crossword clues*).

horloge (ɔrlɔ:ʒ) *f*, clock (*big*). *~ à carillon*, chiming c., musical c. *~ à sonnerie*, striking c. *~ de la mort*, deathwatch [beetle]. *~ de parquet*, grandfather's clock.

horloger (ɔʒe) *m*, clockmaker, watchmaker. **horlogerie** (ʒri) *f*, horology; clock & watch making; clocks & watches.

hormis (ɔrmi) *pr*, except, but, save.

horoscope (ɔrɔskɔp) *m*, horoscope, nativity; fortune.

horreur (ɔrrœ:r) *f*, horror, fright; object. **horrible†** (ɔrribl) *a*, horrible, frightful; horrid. **horripiler** (ɔrripile) *v.t*, to exasperate.

ʼhors (ɔ:r) & ~ **de**, *pr*, out; out of; without; outside; over; beyond; beside; except; save. ~ *bord, a.* & *ad*, outboard. ~ *concours*, not competing [for prize]. ~ *courant*, dead (*wire*). ~ *-d'œuvre, m*, addition (*to a building*); hors-d'œuvre (*Cook.*); extra, digression. *hors d'œuvre, att*, (*part*) added (*to a building*); outside (*Meas.*); unmounted (*stone*); extra, digressive. ~ *de combat*, out of action; disabled. ~ *des limites*, out of bounds. ~ *ligne*, out of the common, exceptional. ~ *texte*, outside text (*plate, illustration, map, etc.*). **~-*texte, m*, plate [outside text]. ~ *tout*, over all (*Meas.*).

hortensia (ɔrtɑ̃sja) *m*, hydrangea.

horticole (ɔrtikɔl) *a*, horticultural. **horticulteur** (kyltœ:r) *m*, horticulturist. **horticulture** (ty:r) *f*, horticulture, gardening.

hosanna (ɔzanna) *m*, hosanna; hurrah.

hospice (ɔspis) *m*, asylum, home; almshouse; hostel; hospice. **hospitalier, ère** (talje, ɛ:r) *a*, hospitable; hospital (*att.*). ¶ *f*, sister of mercy, s. of charity. **hospitalisé, a** (lize) *n*, inmate; inpatient. **hospitalité** (te) *f*, hospitality.

hostie (ɔsti) *f*, host (*Eccl.*).

hostile† (ɔstil) *a*, hostile, unfriendly, inimical. **hostilité** (lite) *f*, hostility.

hôte, esse (o:t, otɛs) *n*, host, hostess; guest, visitor; inmate; denizen.

hôtel [*pour voyageurs*] (ɔtɛl) *m*, hotel. ~ [*particulier*], mansion; town house. ~ *de la Monnaie*, ~ *des Monnaies*, mint. ~ *de* *ville*, town hall. ~ *des postes*, general post office. ~ *des ventes*, auction rooms. ~*-Dieu*, hospital. ~ *garni*, rooming house. ~ *meublé*, furnished apartments. **hôtelier, ère** (tǝlje, ɛːr) *n*, hotelkeeper. **hôtellerie** (tɛlri) *f*, fashionable restaurant; (*archaic*) hostelry.

houblon (ublɔ̃) *m*, hop [plant]; hops. **houblonner** (blɔne) *v.t*, to hop (*beer*). **houblonnière** (njɛːr) *f*, hop field.

houe (u) *f*, hoe. **houer** (ue) *v.t*, to hoe.

houille (uːj) *f*, coal. ~ *blanche*, water power. **houiller, ère** (uje, ɛːr) *a*, coal (*att.*), carboniferous. ¶ *f*, coal mine. **houilleur** (jœːr) *m*, coal miner.

houle (ul) *f*, swell, surge. ~ *de fond*, ground swell. ~ *longue*, roller.

houlette (ulɛt) *f*, shepherd's crook; trowel (*Hort.*).

houleux, euse (ulø, øːz) *a*, swelling (*sea*); surging tumultuous.

houper (upe) *v.t*, to halloo, hollo (*Hunt.*).

houppe (up) & **houpette** (pɛt) *f*, tuft, tassel; (*powder*) puff.

hourder (urde) *v.t*, to roughcast; pug.

hourra (hurra) *m*, hurrah, hurray.

hourvari (urvari) *m*, hullabaloo.

houspiller (uspije) *v.t*, to maul; mob; taunt, abuse.

housse (us) *f*, horse cloth; hammer cloth; dust sheet; furniture cover. **housser** (se) *v.t*, to dust; put loose cover(s) on (*furniture*). **houssine** (sin) *f*, switch. **houssiner** (ne) *v.t*, to switch. **houssoir** (swaːr) *m*, whisk, flick; feather duster.

houx (u) *m*, holly.

hoyau (wajo) *m*, mattock.

hublot (yblo) *m*, scuttle, port [hole].

huche (yʃ) *f*, trough, bin.

hue (hy) *i*, gee up! **huée** (ɥe) *f*, whoop; hoot[ing]. **huer** (ɥe) *v.t*, to whoop, halloo; hoot, boo, barrack.

huette (ɥɛt) *f*, wood owl, tawny owl.

huguenote (ygnɔt) *f*, pipkin, casserole.

huilage (ɥilaːʒ) *m*, oiling. **huile** (ɥil) *f*, oil. ~ *à mécanisme*, machine o. ~ *d'éclairage*, lamp o. ~ *de coude*, elbow grease (*fig.*). ~ *de foie de morue*, cod-liver oil. ~ *de table*, ~ *comestible*, salad o. **huiler** (le) *v.t*, to oil. **huilerie** (lri), *f*, oil mill; oil shop. **huileux, euse** (lø, øːz) *a*, oily. **huilier** (lje) *m*, cruet; oil can.

huis clos (à) (ɥi), in camera. **huissier** (sje) *m*, usher; bailiff.

huit (ɥit; *before a consonant*, ɥi) *a. & m*, eight; eighth. ~ [*jours*] ou **huitaine [de jours]** (tɛn) *f*, week (e.g, *Friday to Friday*). **huitième**† (tjɛm) *a. & n*, eighth.

huître (ɥitr) *f*, oyster; booby, fool. ~*s du pays*, natives. ~ *perlière* (pɛrljɛːr), pearl oyster.

hulotte (ylɔt) *f*, wood owl, tawny owl.

humain, e† (ymɛ̃, ɛn) *a*, human; humane. **humaniser** (manize) *v.t*, to humanize. **humanitaire** (tɛːr) *a. & m*, humanitarian. **humanité** (te) *f*, humanity (all senses).

humble† (œ̃ːbl) *a*, humble, lowly.

humecter (ymɛkte) *v.t*, to moisten, damp, wet.

humer (yme) *v.t*, to suck in; sip; inhale.

humérus (ymeryːs) *m*, humerus.

humeur (ymœːr) *f*, humor, mood; temper; ill-humor, [ill-] temper, petulance.

humide† (ymid) *a*, damp, moist, humid; watery, wet. **humidifier** (difje) *v.t*, to damp. **humidité** (te) *f*, damp[ness].

humilier (ymilje) *v.t*, to humiliate, humble. **humilité** (lite) *f*, humility, lowliness.

humoriste (ymɔrist) *m*, humorist. ¶ ~ & **humoristique** (tik) *a*, humorous. **humour** (muːr) *m*, humor.

humus (ymyːs) *m*, humus, mold.

hune (yn)*f*, top (*Naut.*). **hunier** (nje) *m*, topsail.

huppe (yp) *f*, hoopoe; crest. **huppé, e** (pe) *a*, crested, tufted;

smart (*moving in high society*); clever.

'hure (yːr) *f*, head (*boar, etc.*); jowl (*fish*); brawn.

'hurler (yrle) *v.i*, to howl, yell.

hurluberlu (yrlybɛrly) *m*, harum-scarum.

'hutte (yt) *f*, hut, shanty.

hyacinthe (jasɛ̃ːt) *f*, hyacinth, jacinth.

hybride (ibrid) *a. & m*, hybrid.

hydrate (idrat) *m*, hydrate.

hydraulique (idrolik) *a*, hydraulic, water (*att.*). ¶ *f*, hydraulics.

hydravion (idravjɔ̃) *m*, seaplane. ~ *à coque*, flying boat.

hydre (iːdr) *f*, hydra.

hydrocarbure (idrɔkarbyːr) *m*, hydrocarbon. **hydrogène** (ʒɛn) *m. & att*, hydrogen. **hydrophile** (fil) *a*, absorbent (*cotton wool*). **hydrophobie** (fɔbi) *f*, hydrophobia, rabies. **hydropique** (pik) *a*, dropsical. **hydropisie** (pizi) *f*, dropsy. **hydroscope** (skɔp) *m*, water-diviner, dowser. **hydroscopie** (pi) *f*, water-divining, dowsing. **hydrothérapie** (terapi) *f*, hydropathy. **hydrothérapique** (pik) *a*, hydropathic.

hyène (jɛn) *f*, hyena.

hygiène (iʒjɛn) *f*, hygiene, hygienics, health, sanitation. **hygiénique**† (ʒjenik) *a*, hygienic, healthy, sanitary; toilet (*paper*).

hymen (imɛn) *ou* **hyménée** (mene) *m*, hymen; wedlock. **hyménoptères** (nɔptɛːr) *m.pl*, hymenoptera.

hymne (imn) *m*, hymn, song, anthem (*national*). ¶ *f*, hymn (*in church*).

hyperbole (ipɛrbɔl) *f*, hyperbole; hyperbola.

hypnotiser (ipnɔtize) *v.t*, to hypnotize. **hypnotisme** (tism) *m*, hypnotism.

hypocondriaque (ipɔkɔ̃driak) *a. & n*, hypochondriac. **hypocrisie** (krizi) *f*, hypocrisy, cant. **hypocrite**† (krit) *a*, hypocritical. ¶ *n*, hypocrite. **hypodermique** (dɛrmik) *a*, hypodermic. **hypothèque** (tɛk) *f*, mortgage. **hypothéquer** (ke) *v.t*, to mortgage. **hypothèse** (tɛːz) *f*, hypothesis. **hypothétique**† (tetik) *a*, hypothetic(al).

hystérie (isteri) *f*, hysteria. **hystérique** (rik) *a*, hysteric(al).

I

iambe (jãːb) *m. &* **ïambique** (jãbik) *a*, iambic.

ibis (ibis) *m*, ibis.

iceberg (isbɛrg) *m*, iceberg.

ichtyologie (iktjɔlɔʒi) *f*, ichthyology.

ici (isi) *ad*, here; this; now. ~-*bas*, here below. ~ *X.*, X. speaking (*Teleph.*). *d'*~ *là*, between now & then.

icône (ikoːn) *f*, icon. **iconoclaste** (kɔnɔklast) *m*, iconoclast.

ictère (iktɛːr) *m*, jaundice.

idéal, e† (ideal) *a. & m*, ideal. **idéaliste** (list) *n*, idealist. **idée** (de) *f*, idea, notion; thought; mind; impression; view. ~ *directrice*, guiding principle.

idem (idɛm) *ad*, idem, ditto.

identifier (idãtifje) *v.t*, to identify. **identique**† (tik) *a*, identical. **identité** (te) *f*, identity, sameness.

idiome (idjoːm) *m*, language, dialect.

idiosyncrasie (idjosēkrazi) *f*, idiosyncrasy.

idiot, e (idjo, ɔt) *a*, idiotic. ¶ *n*, idiot; imbecile, natural. **idiotie** (jɔsi) *f*, idiocy.

idiotisme (idjɔtism) *m*, idiom, locution.

idolâtre (idɔlɑːtr) *a*, idolatrous. ¶ *n*, idolater, tress. **idolâtrer** (latre) *v.t*, to idolize. **idolâtrique** (tri) *f*, idolatry. **idolâtrique** (trik) *a*, idolatrous. **idole** (dɔl) *f*, idol.

idylle (idil) *f*, idyll; romance (*love*).

if (if) *m*, yew [tree].

igname (iɲam) *f*, yam.

ignare (iɲaːr) *a*, ignorant. ¶ *n*, ignoramus.

igné, e (igne) *a*, igneous. **ignifuge** (nify:ʒ) *a*, fireproof. **ignifuger** (fyʒe) *v.t*, to fireproof. **ignition** (nisjɔ̃) *f*, ignition.

ignoble† (iɲɔbl) *a*, ignoble, base; filthy.

ignominie (iɲɔmini) *f*, ignominy. **ignominieux, euse**† (njø, ∅ːz) *a*, ignominious, inglorious.

ignorance (iɲɔrɑ̃ːs) *f*, ignorance; blunder. **ignorant, e** (rã, ã;t) *a,* ignorant; unacquainted. ¶ *n,* ignoramus, dunce. **ignoré, e** (re) *p.a,* unknown. **ignorer** (re) *v.t. & abs,* to be ignorant (*or* unaware) of, not to know.

iguane (igwan) *m,* iguana.

il (il) *pn,* he; it; she (*of ship*); there; (*pl.*) they.

ile (i;l) *f,* island, isle. *les îles Britanniques, les îles du Vent, etc.* See under *britannique, vent, etc.*

illégal, e† (illegal) *a,* illegal, unlawful. **illégitime†** (ʒitim) *a,* illegitimate; unlawful; spurious. **illégitimité** (mite) *f,* illegitimacy.

illettré, e (illɛtre) *a. & n,* illiterate.

illicite† (illisit) *a,* illicit, unlawful.

illico (illiko) *ad,* directly, at once.

illimité, e (illimite) *a,* unlimited, unbounded, boundless; indefinite (*leave*).

illisible† (illizibl) *a,* illegible; unreadable.

illogique (illɔʒik) *a,* illogical. **illogisme** (ʒism) *m,* illogicality.

illumination (illyminasjɔ̃) *f,* illumination; inspiration. ~ *par projection,* floodlighting. **illuminer** (ne) *v.t,* to illuminate; light up.

illusion (illyzjɔ̃) *f,* illusion; phantasm; delusion. ~ *d'optique,* optical illusion. **illusionner** (illyzjone) *v.t,* to fool, trick, deceive. **illusoire** (zwa;r) *a,* illusory, illusive.

illustration (illystrasjɔ̃) *f,* luster (*fig.*); celebrity (*pers.*); illustration. **illustre** (tr) *a,* illustrious. **illustrer** (tre) *v.t,* to make illustrious; illustrate. **illustrissime** (trisim) *a,* most illustrious.

ilot (ilo) *m,* islet; island, block (*houses*).

ilote (ilɔt) *m,* helot. **ilotisme** (tism) *m,* helotry.

image (ima;ʒ) *f,* image; reflection; picture; likeness; idea; (*pl.*) imagery. **imagé, e** (maʒe) *p.a,* picturesque, ornate. **imaginaire** (ʒinɛ;r) *a,* imaginary, fancied, fictive. **imagination** (nasjɔ̃) *f,* imagination, fancy. **imaginer** (ne) *v.t,*

to imagine; fancy; devise, invent. **s'~,** to imagine, think.

imbécile† (ɛ̃besil) *a,* silly, stupid, imbecile, fatuous. ¶ *n,* fool. **imbécillité** (silite) *f,* stupidity, fatuity.

imberbe (ɛ̃bɛrb) *a,* beardless; raw, callow.

imbiber (ɛ̃bibe) *v.t,* to soak, imbue, wet. **s'~ (de),** to imbibe, sink in.

imbriquer (ɛ̃brike) *v.t,* to imbricate, overlap.

imbrisable (ɛ̃brizabl) *a,* unbreakable.

imbroglio (ɛ̃brɔljo) *m,* imbroglio.

imbu, e (ɛ̃by) *a,* imbued.

imbuvable (ɛ̃byvabl) *a,* undrinkable.

imitateur, trice (imitatœ;r, tris) *n,* imitator, mimic. ¶ *a,* imitative, mimic. **imitation** (sjɔ̃) *f,* imitation. **imiter** (te) *v.t,* to imitate; mimic; resemble, be like.

immaculé, e (immakyle) *a,* immaculate.

immanent, e (immanã, ã;t) *a,* immanent.

immangeable (imm- *ou* ɛ̃mãʒabl) *a,* uneatable.

immanquable† (imm- *ou* ɛ̃mãkabl) *a,* sure [to happen]; unmistakable.

immatériel, le† (immaterjɛl) *a,* immaterial.

immatriculer (immatrikyle) *v.t,* to register, enter, enroll.

immédiat, e† (immedja, at) *a,* immediate; proximate; direct.

immémorial, e (immemɔrjal) *a,* immemorial.

immense (immã;s) *a,* immense, huge, vast; boundless. **immensément** (mãsemã) *ad,* immensely. **immensité** (site) *f,* immensity; vastness; infinitude. **immensurable** (syrabl) *a,* immeasurable.

immerger (immɛrʒe) *v.t,* to immerse, plunge, dip.

immérité, e (immerite) *a,* unmerited, undeserved, unearned.

immersion (immɛrsjɔ̃) *f,* immersion.

immeuble (immœbl) *m.* oft. *pl,* real estate, realty; premises.

immigration (immigrasjɔ̃) *f,* immigration.

imminence (immĭnã:s) *f,* imminence. **imminent, e** (nã, ã:t) *a,* imminent, impending.

immiscer (s') (immise) *v.pr,* to meddle, interfere. **immixtion** (mikstjɔ̃) *f,* interference.

immobile (immɔbil) *a,* immobile, set, unmovable, motionless, still; unmoved. **immobilier, ère** (lje, ɛ:r) *a,* real (*estate—law*); property (*market*); estate (*agency*); building (*society*). **immobilisations** (lizasjɔ̃) *f.pl,* capital expenditure. **immobiliser** (ze) *v.t,* to immobilize; lock up, tie up; capitalize.

immodéré†, e (immɔdere) *a,* immoderate; excessive; unrestrained.

immodeste† (immɔdɛst) *a,* immodest.

immolation (immɔlasjɔ̃) *f,* immolation, sacrifice; holocaust. **immoler** (le) *v.t,* to immolate, sacrifice; slay.

immonde (immɔ̃:d) *a,* unclean, foul. **immondice** (mɔ̃dis) *f, oft. pl,* dirt, refuse, rubbish, litter.

immoral, e (immɔral) *a,* immoral. **immoralité** (lite) *f,* immorality.

immortaliser (immɔrtalize) *v.t,* to immortalize. **immortalité** (te) *f,* immortality. **immortel, le†** (tɛl) *a,* immortal; everlasting, undying. **¶** *m,* immortal.

immuable† (immyabl) *a,* immutable, unchangeable; hard-&-fast.

immunité (immynite) *f,* immunity.

impair, e (ɛ̃pɛ:r) *a,* uneven, odd (*number*). **¶** *m,* blunder.

impalpable (ɛ̃palpabl) *a,* impalpable.

impardonnable (ɛ̃pardɔnabl) *a,* unpardonable, unforgivable.

imparfait, e† (ɛ̃parfɛ, ɛt) *a,* unfinished; imperfect. **¶***m,* imperfect [tense].

imparité (ɛ̃parite) *f,* unevenness, oddness.

impartial, e† (ɛ̃parsjal) *a,* impartial, unbiased.

impartir (ɛ̃parti:r) *v.t,* to impart, bestow.

impasse (ɛ̃pɑ:s) *f,* blind alley, dead end; deadlock, cleft stick.

impassible (ɛ̃pasibl) *a,* impassible; impassive.

impatiemment (ɛ̃pasjamã) *ad,* impatiently. **impatience** (sjã:s) *f,* impatience; (*pl.*) fidgets. **impatient, e** (ã, ã:t) *a,* impatient; agog. **impatientant, e** (ãtã, ã:t) *a,* provoking, tiresome. **impatienter** (te) *v.t,* to put out of patience, provoke. **s'~,** to grow impatient.

impatroniser (s') (ɛ̃patrɔnize) *v.pr,* to become master (*in a household*).

impayable (ɛ̃pɛjabl) *a,* impayable; invaluable, priceless; highly amusing. **impayé, e** (je) *a,* unpaid; dishonored (*bill*).

impeccable (ɛ̃pɛkabl) *a,* impeccable; infallible.

impedimenta (ɛ̃pedimɛta) *m. pl,* impedimenta.

impénétrable† (ɛ̃penetrabl) *a,* impenetrable; impervious; inscrutable.

impénitence (ɛ̃penitã:s) *f,* impenitence; obduracy. **impénitent, e** (tã, ã:t) *a,* impenitent; obdurate.

impératif, ive† (ɛ̃peratif, i:v) *a. & m,* imperative.

impératrice (ɛ̃peratris) *f,* empress.

imperceptible† (ɛ̃pɛrsɛptibl) *a,* imperceptible. **~** [*à l'ouïe*], inaudible.

imperfection (ɛ̃pɛrfɛksjɔ̃) *f,* imperfection; incompletion.

impérial, e (ɛ̃perjal) *a,* imperial. **¶** *f,* imperial (*beard*); top, upper deck, outside (*bus*). **impérialiste** (list) *m,* imperialist; (*att.*) imperialistic.

impérieux, euse† (ɛ̃perjø, ø:z) *a,* imperious.

impérissable (ɛ̃perisabl) *a,* imperishable, undying.

impéritie (ɛ̃perisi) *f,* incapacity.

imperméabiliser (ɛ̃pɛrmeabilize) *v.t,* to [water]proof. **imperméable** (bl) *a,* impermeable, impervious, -proof; -tight (*air, etc.*); waterproof. **¶** *m,* waterproof, raincoat.

impersonnel, le† (ɛ̃pɛrsɔnɛl) *a,* impersonal.

impertinemment (ɛ̃pɛrtinamã) *ad,* impertinently, pertly. **imper-**

tinence (nã:s) *f*, [piece of] impertinence, pertness. **impertinent, e** (nã, ã:t) *a*, impertinent, pert; irrelevant (*law*).

imperturbable† (ɛ̃pɛrtyrbabl) *a*, imperturbable, unruffled.

impétrant, e (ɛ̃petrã, ã:t) *n*, grantee.

impétueux, euse† (ɛ̃petɥ̃ø, ø:z) *a*, impetuous; hot-headed; gusty (*wind*). **impétuosité** (tɥozite) *f*, impetuosity.

impie (ɛ̃pi) *a*, impious, ungodly, godless; unholy. **impiété** (pjete) *f*, impiety.

impitoyable† (ɛ̃pitwajabl) *a*, pitiless, merciless, ruthless, relentless.

implacable† (ɛ̃plakabl) *a*, implacable.

implanter (ɛ̃plɑ̃te) *v.t*, to implant.

implicite† (ɛ̃plisit) *a*, implicit; implied. **impliquer** (ke) *v.t*, to implicate; involve; imply.

implorer (ɛ̃plɔre) *v.t*, to implore, beseech, crave.

impoli†, **e** (ɛ̃pɔli) *a*, impolite. **impolitesse** (tɛs) *f*, impoliteness, rudeness.

impolitique (ɛ̃pɔlitik) *a*, impolitic.

impondérable (ɛ̃põderabl) *a*. & *m*, imponderable.

impopulaire (ɛ̃pɔpylɛ:r) *a*, unpopular.

importance (ɛ̃pɔrtɑ̃:s) *f*, importance, moment; extent, magnitude. **d'~**, *ad*, soundly. **important, e** (tã, ã:t) *a*, important. *faire l'~*, to give oneself airs. ¶ *m*, main thing.

importateur (ɛ̃pɔrtatœ:r) *m*, importer. **importation** (sjõ) *f*, import[ation]. **importer** (te) *v.t*, to import; (*v.i.*) to matter, signify. *n'importe*, no matter. *n'importe où*, anywhere.

importun, e (ɛ̃pɔrtœ̃, yn) *a*, importunate, tiresome, troublesome. ¶ *n*, intruder; nuisance. **importuner** (tyne) *v.t*, to importune, worry, molest, pester. **importunité** (nite) *f*, importunity, molestation.

imposable (ɛ̃pozabl) *a*, taxable, assessable, dutiable. **imposé, e** (ze) *n*, taxpayer. **imposer** (ze)

v.t. & abs, to impose; enforce; lay [on]; thrust; tax, rate, assess; [over]awe. *en ~ à*, to impose [up]on, deceive. **imposition** (zisjõ) *f*, imposition; tax; assessment.

impossibilité (ɛ̃pɔsibilite) *f*, impossibility. **impossible** (bl) *a*, impossible. *l'~*, *m*, impossibilities; one's [very] utmost.

imposte (ɛ̃pɔst) *f*, impost (*Arch*.).

imposteur (ɛ̃pɔstœ:r) *m*, impostor, humbug. **imposture** (ty:r) *f*, imposture, imposition.

impôt (ɛ̃po) *m*, tax; duty; taxes; taxation. *~ du timbre*, stamp duty. *~ foncier*, land tax, property tax. *~ général* (*ou global*) *sur le revenu*, surtax. *~ sur le revenu* ou *~[s] cédulaire[s]* (sedylɛ:r), income tax.

impotent, e (ɛ̃pɔtã, ã:t) *a*, helpless, crippled. ¶ *n*, cripple.

impraticable† (ɛ̃pratikabl) *a*, impracticable; impassable.

imprécation (ɛ̃prekasjõ) *f*, imprecation, curse.

imprécis, e (ɛ̃presi, i:z) *a*, vague. **imprécision** (sizjõ) *f*, vagueness.

imprégner (ɛ̃preɲe) *v.t*, to impregnate.

imprenable (ɛ̃prənabl) *a*, impregnable.

impresario (ɛ̃prezarjo) *m*, impresario.

impression (ɛ̃prɛsjõ) *f*, impression; impress; printing, machining, striking off (*Typ*.); print; issue; priming (*paint*); sensation. **impressionnant, e** (ɔnã, ã:t) *a*, impressive. **impressionner** (ne) *v.t*, to impress, affect. **impressionnisme** (nism) *m*, impressionism.

imprévisible (ɛ̃previzibl) *a*, unforeseeable; unpredictable.

imprévoyance (ɛ̃prevwajã:s) *f*, shortsightedness, improvidence. **imprévu, e** (vy) *a. & m*, unforeseen; unexpected; contingency (*n.*).

imprimé (ɛ̃prime) *m*, printed book, form; p. paper; (*pl.*) p. matter, literature; handbill, leaflet. **imprimer** (me) *v.t*, to imprint; impress; print; prime (*paint*); impart. **imprimerie** (mri) *f*, printing (*art*); p. plant;

p. works, p. office. **imprimeur** (mœ:r) m, printer.

improbable (ɛ̃prɔbabl) a, improbable.

improbation (ɛ̃prɔbasjɔ̃) f, disapproval.

improbe (ɛ̃prɔb) a, dishonest.

improductif, ive (ɛ̃prɔdyktif, i:v) a, unproductive.

impromptu (ɛ̃prɔ̃[p]ty) ad, a. inv. & m, impromptu; extempore; offhand.

impropre† (ɛ̃prɔpr) a, wrong; inappropriate; unsuitable; unfit.

improuver (ɛ̃pruve) v.t, to disapprove [of].

improvisateur, trice (ɛ̃prɔvizatœ:r, tris) n, improvisator. **improviser** (ze) v.t. & abs, to improvise, extemporize; vamp (Mus.). à l'improviste (vist) ad, unexpectedly, unawares.

imprudemment (ɛ̃prydamɑ̃) ad, imprudently. **imprudence** (dɑ̃:s) f, imprudence. **imprudent, e** (dɑ̃, ɑ̃:t) a, imprudent, incautious.

impubliable (ɛ̃pybliabl) a, unprintable.

impudence (ɛ̃pydɑ̃:s) f, shamelessness; impudence. **impudent, e** (dɑ̃, ɑ̃:t) a. & n, shameless, etc, (person). **impudemment** (damɑ̃) ad, impudently, etc.

impudeur (ɛ̃pydœ:r) f, immodesty; indecency. **impudicité** (disite) f, impudicity, lewdness. **impudique†** (dik) a, unchaste, lewd.

impuissance (ɛ̃pɥisɑ̃:s) f, powerlessness; inability; impotence, -cy. **impuissant, e** (sɑ̃, ɑ̃:t) a, powerless; impotent.

impulsif, ive (ɛ̃pylsif, i:v) a, impulsive. **impulsion** (sjɔ̃) f, impulse; impetus; impulsion; spur (of the moment).

impunément (ɛ̃pynemɑ̃) ad, with impunity. **impuni, e** (ni) a, unpunished, scot-free. **impunité** (te) f, impunity.

impur, e† (ɛ̃py:r) a, impure; unclean. **impureté** (pyrte) f, impurity.

imputer (ɛ̃pyte) v.t, to impute, ascribe; charge.

inabordable (inabɔrdabl) a, inaccessible.

inacceptable (inaksɛptabl) a, unacceptable.

inaccessible (inaksɛsibl) a, inaccessible.

inaccordable (inakɔrdabl) a, irreconcilable; inadmissible.

inaccoutumé, e (inakutyme) a, unaccustomed; unusual.

inachevé, e (inaʃve) a, unfinished.

inactif, ive (inaktif, i:v) a, inactive; dull, flat. **inaction** (sjɔ̃) f, inaction, drift. **inactivité** (tivite) f, inactivity, dullness.

inadmissible (inadmisibl) a, inadmissible.

inadvertance (inadvɛrtɑ̃:s) f, inadvertence, oversight.

inaliénable (inaljenabl) a, inalienable.

inaltérable (inalterabl) a, unalterable.

inamical, e (inamikal) a, unfriendly.

inamovible (inamɔvibl) a, irremovable.

inanimé, e (inanime) a, inanimate, lifeless.

inanité (inanite) f, inanity, futility.

inanition (inanisjɔ̃) f, inanition, starvation.

inaperçu, e (inapɛrsy) a, unseen, unnoticed.

inappétence (inapetɑ̃:s) f, loss of appetite.

inapplicable (inaplikabl) a, inapplicable. **inappliqué, e** (ke) a, inattentive; unapplied.

inappréciable (inapresjabl) a, inappreciable; inestimable, priceless.

inapte (inapt) a, inapt, unfit.

inarticulé, e (inartikyle) a, inarticulate.

inattaquable (inatakabl) a, unassailable.

inattendu, e (inatɑ̃dy) a, unexpected.

inattention (inatɑ̃sjɔ̃) f, inattention.

inaugurer (inogyre) v.t, to inaugurate; unveil, open; usher in (fig.).

incalculable (ɛ̃kalkylabl) a, incalculable.

incandescence (ɛ̃kɑ̃dɛsɑ̃:s) f, incandescence, glow, white heat.

incandescent, e (sɑ̃, ɑ̃:t) *a*, incandescent, glowing, white-hot.

incantation (ɛ̃kɑ̃tasjɔ̃) *f*, incantation.

incapable (ɛ̃kapabl) *a*, incapable; unfit; unable, unequal; incompetent; inefficient. **les ~s,** *m.pl*, the unemployable. **incapacité** (site) *f*, incapacity, etc; disablement, disability.

incarcérer (ɛ̃karsere) *v.t*, to incarcerate.

incarnadin, e (ɛ̃karnadɛ̃, in) *a*, incarnadine. **incarnat, e** (na, at) *a*, rosy, pink, roseate. **incarnation** (sjɔ̃) *f*, incarnation, embodiment. **incarné, e** (ne) *p.a*, incarnate; ingrowing (*nail*).

incartade (ɛ̃kartad) *f*, prank, indiscretion, lapse; outburst, tirade.

incassable (ɛ̃kɑsabl) *a*, unbreakable.

incendiare (ɛ̃sɑ̃djɛːr) *a. & n*, incendiary. **incendie** (di) *m*, [outbreak of] fire. ~ *volontaire*, arson, incendiarism. **incendié, e** (dje) *n*, sufferer by a fire. **incendier** (dje) *v.t*, to [set on] fire, set f. to.

incertain, e (ɛ̃sɛrtɛ̃, ɛn) *a*, uncertain, unsettled. **incertitude** (tityd) *f*, uncertainty; suspense.

incessamment (ɛ̃sɛsamɑ̃) *ad*, incessantly; forthwith. **incessant, e** (sɑ̃, ɑ̃:t) *a*, incessant, unceasing, ceaseless.

incessible (ɛ̃sɛsibl) *a*, inalienable; not transferable.

inceste (ɛ̃sɛst) *m*, incest. **incestueux, euse†** (tɥø, ø:z) *a*, incestuous.

incidemment (ɛ̃sidamɑ̃) *ad*, incidentally. **incident, e** (dɑ̃, ɑ̃:t) *a*, incidental; incident (*ray*). ¶ *m*, incident; point of law; difficulty.

incinérateur (ɛ̃sineratœːr) *m*, incinerator, destructor. **incinérer** (re) *v.t*, to incinerate; cremate.

incirconcis, e (ɛ̃sirkɔ̃si, i:z) *a*, uncircumcised.

inciser (ɛ̃size) *v.t*, to incise, cut; lance. **incisif, ive** (zif, i:v) *a*, incisive. [dent.] **incisive** *f*, incisor. **incision** (zjɔ̃) *f*, incision; lancing.

incitation (ɛ̃sitasjɔ̃) *f*, incitement. **inciter** (te) *v.t*, to incite, instigate.

incivil, e† (ɛ̃sivil) *a*, uncivil. **incivilité** (lite) *f*, incivility.

inclément, e (ɛ̃klemɑ̃, ɑ̃:t) *a*, inclement.

inclinaison (ɛ̃wlinɛzɔ̃) *f*, inclination; gradient; slope; slant; cant; tilt; dip; pitch; rake. **inclination** (nasjɔ̃) *f*, inclination; leaning, bent; bow, nod; attachment, love, sweetheart. **incliner** (ne) *v.t. & i. & s'~,* to incline; lean; slope, slant; cant; tilt; dip; pitch; rake; bow [down]; nod; bank (*Avn.*).

inclure (ɛ̃kly:r) *v.t.ir*, to enclose. **inclusivement** (klyzivmɑ̃) *ad*, inclusively; inclusive (*dates*).

incognito (ɛ̃kɔɲito *ou* ɛ̃kɔgnito) *ad. & m*, incognito.

incohérence (ɛ̃kɔerɑ̃:s) *f*, incoherence. **incohérent, e** (rɑ̃, ɑ̃:t) *a*, incoherent; rambling.

incolore (ɛ̃kɔlɔːr) *a*, colorless.

incomber (ɛ̃kɔ̃be) *v.i*, to be incumbent, devolve, rest.

incombustible (ɛ̃kɔ̃bystibl) *a*, incombustible, fireproof.

incommensurable (ɛ̃kɔmɑ̃syrabl) *a*, incommensurable.

incommode (ɛ̃kɔmɔd) *a*, inconvenient; uncomfortable; tiresome. **incommodé, e** (de) *p.a*, poorly (*health*); crippled, disabled; embarrassed. **incommodément** (demɑ̃) *ad*, uncomfortably. **incommoder** (de) *v.t*, to inconvenience, incommode. **incommodité** (dite) *f*, inconvenience; nuisance (*law*); (*ship in*) difficulties (*navigation*).

incomparable† (ɛ̃kɔ̃parabl) *a*, incomparable.

incompatible (ɛ̃kɔ̃patibl) *a*, incompatible.

incompétent, e (ɛ̃kɔ̃petɑ̃, ɑ̃:t) *a*, incompetent.

incomplet, ète† (ɛ̃kɔ̃plɛ, ɛt) *a*, incomplete.

incompréhensible (ɛ̃kɔ̃preɑ̃sibl) *a*, incomprehensible.

incompris, e (ɛ̃kɔ̃pri, i:z) *a*, misunderstood; unappreciated.

inconcevable (ɛ̃kɔ̃svabl) *a*, inconceivable.

inconciliable (ɛ̃kɔ̃siljabl) *a*, irreconcilable.

inconduite (ɛ̃kɔ̃dɥit) *f*, misconduct, misbehavior.

incongru, e (ɛ̃kɔ̃gry) *a*, incongruous; uncouth. **incongruité** (gryite) f, incongruity; malapropism; impropriety.

inconnu, e (ɛ̃kɔny) a, unknown. ¶ n, unknown person; stranger; nobody . l'~, m, the unknown. [**quantité**] **inconnue**, f, unknown [quantity].

inconsciemment (ɛ̃kɔ̃sjamɑ̃) ad, unconsciously. **inconscience** (sjɑ̃:s) f, unconsciousness. **inconscient, e** (ɑ̃, ɑ̃:t) a, unconscious; irresponsible.

inconséquent, e (ɛ̃kɔ̃sekɑ̃, ɑ̃:t) a, inconsistent; inconsequent[ial]; flighty.

inconsidéré†, e (ɛ̃kɔ̃sidere) a, inconsiderate; thoughtless.

inconsistant, e (ɛ̃kɔ̃sistɑ̃, ɑ̃:t) a, inconsistent.

inconsolable† (ɛ̃kɔ̃sɔlabl) a, inconsolable. **inconsolé, e** (le) a, unconsoled, forlorn.

inconstant, e (ɛ̃kɔ̃stɑ̃, ɑ̃:t) a, inconstant; changeable; fickle.

inconstitutionnel, le† (ɛ̃kɔ̃stitysjɔnɛl) a, unconstitutional.

incontestable† (ɛ̃kɔ̃tɛstabl) a, undeniable. **incontesté, e** (te) a, undisputed.

incontinent, e (ɛ̃kɔ̃tinɑ̃, ɑ̃:t) a, incontinent, unchaste.

inconvenance (ɛ̃kɔ̃vnɑ̃:s) f, impropriety. **inconvenant, e** (vnɑ̃, ɑ̃:t) a, unbecoming, unseemly, indecorous.

inconvénient (ɛ̃kɔ̃venjɑ̃) m, inconvenience; drawback.

incorporer (ɛ̃kɔrpɔre) v.t, to incorporate; blend.

incorrect, e (ɛ̃kɔrɛkt) a, incorrect; inaccurate; unbusinesslike. **incorrectement** (təmɑ̃) ad, incorrectly, etc; ungrammatically. **incorrection** (ksjɔ̃) f, incorrectness, etc.

incorrigible† (ɛ̃kɔriʒibl) a, incorrigible, irreclaimable, hopeless.

incorruptible (ɛ̃kɔryptibl) a, incorruptible.

incrédibilité (ɛ̃kredibilite) f, incredibility. **incrédule** (dyl) a, incredulous. ¶ n, unbeliever. **incrédulité** (lite) f, incredulity; unbelief.

incréé, e (ɛ̃kree) a, uncreated.

incriminer (ɛ̃krimine) v.t, to incriminate; challenge.

incroyable† (ɛ̃krwajabl) a, incredible.

incrustation (ɛ̃krystasjɔ̃) f, incrustation; inlay, inlaid work; scale. **incruster** (te) v.t, to incrust; inlay; scale.

incubation (ɛ̃kybasjɔ̃) f, incubation.

inculpé, e (ɛ̃kylpe) n, accused. **inculper** (pe) v.t, to inculpate, charge.

inculquer (ɛ̃kylke) v.t, to inculcate, instill.

inculte (ɛ̃kylt) a, uncultivated, waste; wild; unkempt; uncultured, untutored.

incurable† (ɛ̃kyrabl) a. & n, incurable.

incurie (ɛ̃kyri) f, carelessness.

incursion (ɛ̃kyrsjɔ̃) f, incursion, raid, inroad, foray.

inde (ɛ̃:d) m. ou bleu d'~, indigo blue. l'I~, f, India.

indébrouillable (ɛ̃debrujabl) a, inextricable.

indécemment (ɛ̃desamɑ̃) ad, indecently. **indécence** (sɑ̃:s) f, indecency. **indécent, e** (sɑ̃, ɑ̃:t) a, indecent.

indéchiffrable (ɛ̃deʃifrabl) a, undecipherable; illegible; unintelligible.

indécis, e (ɛ̃desi, i:z) a, undecided; unsettled; drawn (battle, game). **indécision** (sisjɔ̃) f, indecision.

indécrottable (ɛ̃dekrɔtabl) a, uncleanable; incorrigible.

indéfendable (ɛ̃defɑ̃dabl) a, indefensible.

indéfini†, e (ɛ̃defini) a, indefinite; undefined. **indéfinissable** (sabl) a, indefinable; unaccountable; nondescript.

indélébile (ɛ̃delebil) a, indelible.

indélicat, e† (ɛ̃delika, at) a, indelicate; tactless; unscrupulous, sharp. **indélicatesse** (tɛs) f, indelicacy.

indémaillable (ɛ̃demajabl) a, (stocking) runproof.

indemne (ɛ̃demn) a, unscathed, scatheless, unhurt, scot-free. **indemniser** (nize) v.t, to indemnify, compensate. **indemnité** (te) f, indemnity, compensation; claim, loss (*Insce.*); allowance, remuneration, bonus. ~ *de chômage*, unemployment benefit. ~ *de vie chère*, cost-of-living bonus.

indéniable (ɛ̃denjabl) *a*, undeniable.

indépendamment (ɛ̃depɑ̃damɑ̃) *ad*, independently. ~ *de*, irrespective of. **indépendance** (dɑ̃ːs) *f*, independence. **indépendant, e** (dɑ̃, ɑ̃ːt) *a*, independent; free; self-contained.

indéracinable (ɛ̃derasinabl) *a*, ineradicable.

indescriptible (ɛ̃dɛskriptibl) *a*, indescribable.

indésirable (ɛ̃dezirabl) *a*, undesirable; objectionable. ¶ *n*, undesirable.

indestructible (ɛ̃dɛstryktibl) *a*, indestructible.

indéterminé, e (ɛ̃detɛrmine) *a*, undetermined; indeterminate.

indévot, e (ɛ̃devo, ɔt) *a*, irreligious.

index (ɛ̃dɛks) *m*, index; pointer; first finger, forefinger; blacklist. ~ [*expurgatoire*] (ɛkspyrgatwaːr), index [*expurgatorius*].

indicateur, trice (ɛ̃dikatœːr, tris) *n*, informer; (*m.*) timetable, time book; guide [book] (*Rly.*, *street, post*); indicator, gauge. ~ *universel des P.T.T.* (= *Postes, Télégraphes & Téléphones*), post office guide. **indicatif, ive** (tif, iːv) *a*, indicative. [**mode**] **indicatif**, *m*, i. [mood]. **indication** (sjɔ̃) *f*. *oft. pl*, indication; clue; information; particular; instruction, stage directions. ~ *de nom & de lieu de résidence de l'imprimeur*, printer's imprint. ~ *de nom* (ou *de firme*) *de l'éditeur*, publisher's imprint. **indice** (dis) *m*, indication; sign; index; figure; number. ~ *du coût de la vie*, cost-of-living figure. **indicible** (sible) *a*, unspeakable, unutterable.

indien, ne (ɛ̃djɛ̃, ɛn) *a. & I~*, *n*, Indian. ¶ *f*, print[ed cotton fabric].

indifféremment (ɛ̃diferamɑ̃) *ad*, indifferently; indiscriminately. **indifférence** (rɑ̃ːs) *f*, indifference; unconcern. **indifférent, e** (rɑ̃, ɑ̃ːt) *a*, indifferent; unconcerned.

indigène (ɛ̃diʒɛːn) *a*, native, indigenous. ¶ *n*, native.

indigent, e (ɛ̃diʒɑ̃, ɑ̃ːt) *a. & n*, indigent, poor, pauper (*n.*). ~ *de passage*, casual.

indigeste (ɛ̃diʒɛst) *a*, indigestible; undigested (*fig.*); crude. **indigestion** (tjɔ̃) *f*, indigestion.

indignation (ɛ̃diɲasjɔ̃) *f*, indignation. **indigne**† (diɲ) *a*, unworthy; undeserving; disqualified (*law*); outrageous. **indigné, e** (ɲe) *p.a*, indignant. **indigner** (ɲe) *v.t*, to exasperate. **indignité** (ʃite) *f*, unworthiness; indignity; outrage.

indigo (ɛ̃digo) *m*, indigo. **indigotier** (gɔtje) *m*, indigo plant.

indiquer (ɛ̃dike) *v.t*, to indicate, show, point out; mark; mention, state.

indirect, e† (ɛ̃dirɛkt) *a*, indirect; consequential (*damages*); crooked (*fig.*).

indiscipliné, e (ɛ̃disipline) *a*, unruly.

indiscret, ète† (ɛ̃diskrɛ, ɛt) *a*, indiscreet; forward; prying. **indiscrétion** (kresjɔ̃) *f*, indiscretion.

indiscutable† (ɛ̃diskytabl) *a*, indisputable.

indispensable† (ɛ̃dispɑ̃sabl) *a*, indispensable.

indisponible (ɛ̃dispɔnibl) *a*, inalienable; unavailable; not available.

indisposé, e (ɛ̃dispoze) *a*, indisposed, unwell, poorly, out of sorts. **indisposer** (ze) *v.t*, to upset; set against. **indisposition** (zisjɔ̃) *f*, indisposition.

indissoluble† (ɛ̃disɔlybl) *a*, indissoluble.

indistinct, e (ɛ̃distɛ̃ːkt) *a*, indistinct. **indistinctement** (tɛ̃ktamɑ̃) *ad*, indistinctly; indiscriminately.

individu (ɛ̃dividy) *m*, individual; fellow. *son ~*, oneself, number one. **individualité** (dɥalite) *f*, individuality. **individuel, le**† (dɥɛl) *a*, individual; several (*law*).

indivis, e (ɛ̃divi, iːz) *a*, undivided; joint. **par indivis** *ou* **indivisément** (vizemɑ̃) *ad*, jointly. **indivisible**† (zibl) *a*, indivisible.

Indochine (l') (ɛ̃doʃin) *f*, Indo-

China (*Cambodia, Laos, Vietnam*).

indocile (ɛ̃dɔsil) *a*, intractable.

indolemment (ɛ̃dɔlamɑ̃) *ad*, indolently; lazily. **indolence** (lɑ̃:s) *f*, indolence, sloth; apathy, indifference. **indolent, e** (lɑ̃, ɑ̃:t) *a*, indolent, slothful; apathetic, indifferent, lackadaisical; painless.

indomptable (ɛ̃dɔ̃tabl) *a*, untamable; indomitable; uncontrollable. **indompté, e** (te) *a*, untamed; unconquered; unsubdued.

indu, e (ɛ̃dy) *a*, untimely (*hour*).

indubitable† (ɛ̃dybitabl) *a*, indubitable, undoubted.

induction (ɛ̃dyksjɔ̃) *f*, induction; inference. **induire** (dɥi:r) *v.t.ir*, to lead; infer; induce. ~ **en erreur**, to mislead. **induit** (dɥi) *m*, armature (*dynamo*).

indulgence (ɛ̃dylʒɑ̃:s) *f*, indulgence; forbearance, leniency. **indulgent, e** (ʒɑ̃, ɑ̃:t) *a*, indulgent, lenient.

indûment (ɛ̃dymɑ̃) *ad*, unduly.

industrialiser (ɛ̃dystrialize) *v.t*, to industrialize. **industrialisme** (lism) *m*, industrialism. **industrie** (tri) *f*, ingenuity; industry; manufacture, trade. **~-clef**, key industry. ~ **d'art**, handicraft. **industriel, le†** (ɛl) *a*, industrial; manufacturing. ¶ *m*, manufacturer; millowner; industrialist. **industrieux, euse†** (ø, ø:z) *a*, industrious, busy.

inébranlable† (inebrɑ̃labl) *a*, unshakable; immovable; unyielding; steadfast.

inédit, e (inedi, it) *a*, unpublished (*book*); unusual.

ineffable (inefabl) *a*, ineffable, unutterable.

ineffaçable (inefasabl) *a*, ineffaceable.

inefficace† (inefikas) *a*, inefficacious; ineffectual; ineffective, nugatory.

inégal, e† (inegal) *a*, unequal; uneven. **inégalité** (lite) *f*, inequality; unevenness.

inélégant, e (inelegɑ̃, ɑ̃:t) *a*, inelegant.

inéligible (ineliʒibl) *a*, ineligible.

inemployable (inɑ̃plwajabl) *a*, unusable (*tool, etc.*). **inemployé,**

e (je) *a*, unemployed (*resources, etc.*).

inénarrable (inenarabl) *a*, indescribable.

inepte† (inɛpt) *a*, inept, inane, silly. **ineptie** (si) *f*, ineptitude.

inépuisable† (inepɥizabl) *a*, inexhaustible.

inerte (inɛrt) *a*, inert, sluggish. **inertie** (si) *f*, inertia; listlessness.

inespéré†, e (inɛspere) *a*, unhoped for, unexpected.

inestimable (inɛstimabl) *a*, inestimable, priceless.

inévitable† (inevitabl) *a*, inevitable; unavoidable.

inexact, e† (inɛgzakt) *a*, inexact, inaccurate, incorrect; unpunctual. **inexactitude** (tityd) *f*, inexactitude.

inexcusable (inɛkskyzabl) *a*, inexcusable.

inexécutable (inɛgzekytabl) *a*, unworkable; inexecutable. **inexécution** (sjɔ̃) *f*, nonperformance.

inexercé, e (inɛgzɛrse) *a*, unskilled.

inexigible (inɛgziʒibl) *a*, not due, undue.

inexistant, e (inɛgzistɑ̃, ɑ̃:t) *a*, nonexistent. **inexistence** (tɑ̃:s) *f*, nonexistence.

inexorable† (inɛgzɔrabl) *a*, inexorable.

inexpérience (inɛksperjɑ̃:s) *f*, inexperience. **inexpérimenté, e** (rimɑ̃te) *a*, inexperienced, unskilled.

inexplicable (inɛksplikabl) *a*, inexplicable. **inexpliqué, e** (ke) *a*, unexplained.

inexploré, e (inɛksplɔre) *a*, unexplored.

inexprimable (inɛksprimabl) *a*, inexpressible.

inexpugnable (inɛkspygnabl) *a*, impregnable.

in extenso (inɛkstɛ̃so) *ad*, in extenso, in full.

inextinguible (inɛkstɛ̃gɥibl) *a*, inextinguishable; unquenchable; irrepressible, uncontrollable.

inextricable (inɛkstrikabl) *a*, inextricable.

infaillible† (ɛ̃fajibl) *a*, infallible; unerring.

infamant, e (ɛ̃famɑ̃, ɑ̃:t) *a*, defamatory; opprobrious; infa-

mous (*law*). **infâme** (fɑːm) *a*,
infamous, foul. **infamie** (fami)
f, infamy.

infanterie (ɛ̃fɑ̃tri) *f*, infantry.

infanticide (ɛ̃fɑ̃tisid) (*act*) *m*.
& (*pers.*) *n*, infanticide. **infantile** (til) *a*, infant[ile] (*Med.*).

infatigable† (ɛ̃fatigabl) *a*, indefatigable, tireless.

infatuation (ɛ̃fatɥasjɔ̃) *f*, infatuation. **s'infatuer** (tɥe) *v.pr*,
to become infatuated.

infécond, e (ɛ̃fekɔ̃, ɔ̃ːd) *a*, barren.

infect, e (ɛ̃fɛkt) *a*, stinking, foul.
infecter (te) *v.t*, to infect, taint;
(*v.i.*) to stink. **infectieux, euse**
(sjø, ø̃ːz) *a*, infectious (*Med.*).
infection (sjɔ̃) *f*, infection;
stench.

inférence (ɛ̃ferɑ̃ːs) *f*, inference.
inférer (re) *v.t*, to infer.

inférieur, e (ɛ̃ferjœːr) *a*, lower,
bottom, under, nether; inferior,
less. ¶ *m*, inferior (*pers.*). **infériorité** (rjɔrite) *f*, inferiority.

infernal, e (ɛ̃fɛrnal) *a*, infernal,
hellish.

infertile (ɛ̃fɛrtil) *a*, infertile,
barren.

infester (ɛ̃fɛste) *v.t*, to infest,
overrun.

infidèle† (ɛ̃fidɛl) *a*, unfaithful;
faithless; inaccurate; dishonest;
infidel. ¶ *n*, unfaithful person;
infidel. **infidélité** (delite) *f*, in-
fidelity; unfaithfulness; dishonesty; breach of trust.

infiltrer (s') (ɛ̃filtre) *v.pr*, to
infiltrate, percolate.

infime (ɛ̃fim) *a*, lowest; insignificant; tiny.

infini, e (ɛ̃fini) *a*, infinite. **l'infini**, *m*, the infinite; infinity
(*Math., Phot.*). **à l'infini**, *ad*, *ad*
infinitum. **infiniment** (mɑ̃) *ad*,
infinitely. **infinité** (te) *f*, infinity,
infinitude. *une ~ de*, no end of.
infinitésimal, e (tezimal) *a*, infinitesimal. [**mode**] **infinitif** (tif)
m, infinitive [mood].

infirme (ɛ̃firm) *a*, infirm, invalid. ¶ *n*, invalid. **infirmer** (me)
v.t, to invalidate; quash; weaken.
infirmerie (məri) *f*, infirmary,
sick room (*Sch., etc.*). **infirmier,
ère** (mje, ɛːr) *n*, hospital attendant, h. orderly, h. nurse, male n.,

sick n. *infirmière en chef*, head
nurse, matron. **infirmité** (mite)
f, infirmity; frailty, weakness.

inflammable (ɛ̃flamabl) *a*, inflammable. **inflammation** (sjɔ̃)
f, ignition; inflammation.

inflation (ɛ̃flasjɔ̃) *f*, inflation
(*Fin.*).

infléchir (ɛ̃fleʃiːr) *v.t*, to inflect,
bend. **inflexible**† (flɛksibl) *a*, inflexible. **inflexion** (ksjɔ̃) *f*, inflection.

infliger (ɛ̃fliʒe) *v.t*, to inflict.

influence (ɛ̃flyɑ̃ːs) *f*, influence,
sway. **influencer** (ɑ̃se) *v.t*, to influence, sway. **influent, e** (ɑ̃, ɑ̃ːt)
a, influential. **influer sur** (e), to
influence.

in-folio (ɛ̃fɔljo) *a.m.* & *m*, folio
(*book*).

informateur, trice (ɛ̃fɔrma-
tœːr, tris) *n*, informant. **information** (sjɔ̃) *f. mostly pl*, inquiry;
(*pl.*) newscast (*radio*).

informe (ɛ̃fɔrm) *a*, shapeless,
formless; informal (*law*).

informé (ɛ̃fɔrme) *m*, inquiry
(*law*). **informer** (me) *v.t*, to inform, acquaint. *s' ~*, to inquire.

infortune (ɛ̃fɔrtyn) *f*, misfortune; adversity; mischance. **infortuné, e** (ne) *a.* & *n*, unfortunate.

infraction (ɛ̃fraksjɔ̃) *f*, infraction, infringement; breach; offense.

infranchissable (ɛ̃frɑ̃ʃisabl) *a*,
impassable; insuperable.

infréquenté, e (ɛ̃frekɑ̃te) *a*,
unfrequented.

infructueux, euse† (ɛ̃fryktɥø-
ø̃ːz) *a*, fruitless (fig.).

infus, e (ɛ̃fy, yːz) *a*, inborn, innate. **infuser** (fyze) *v.t*, infuse;
instill. [s']*~*, to draw (*tea*). **infusible** (zibl) *a*, infusible. **infusion** (zjɔ̃) *f*, infusion; tea. **in-
fusoires** (zwaːr) *m.pl*, infusoria.

ingambe (ɛ̃gɑ̃ːb) *a*, nimble.

ingénier (s') (ɛ̃ʒenje) *v.pr*, to
try, contrive.

ingénieur (ɛ̃ʒenjœːr) *m*, engineer. *~-conseil*, consulting e.

ingénieux, euse† (ɛ̃ʒenjø, ø̃ːz)
a, ingenious. **ingéniosité** (jozite)
f, ingenuity.

ingénu†, **e** (ɛ̃ʒeny) *a*, ingenuous, artless; unsophisticated. ¶

f, ingénue (*Theat.*). **ingénuité** (nцite) f, ingenuousness, etc.

ingérer (s') (ẽӡere) *v.pr*, to interfere, meddle.

ingouvernable (ẽguvɛrnabl) a, ungovernable; uncontrollable.

ingrat, e (ẽgra, at) a, ungrateful; thankless; unpromising; unpleasing. **ingratitude** (tityd) f, ingratitude.

ingrédient (ẽgredjã) m, ingredient, constituent.

inguérissable (ẽgerisabl) a, incurable; inconsolable.

inhabile† (inabil) a, incapable.

inhabitable (inabitabl) a, uninhabitable. **inhabité, e** (te) a, uninhabited, untenanted.

inhabitué (inabitye) a, unaccustomed.

inhaler (inale) *v.t*, to inhale.

inharmonieux, euse (inarmɔnjø, ø:z) a, inharmonious; unmusical.

inhérent, e (inerã, ã:t) a, inherent.

inhospitalier, ère (inɔspitalje, ɛ:r) a, inhospitable.

inhumain, e† (inymẽ, ɛn) a, inhuman. **inhumanité** (manite) f, inhumanity.

inhumer (inyme) *v.t*, to inter, bury.

inimaginable (inimaӡinabl) a, unimaginable.

inimitable (inimitabl) a, inimitable.

inimitié (inimitje) f, enmity, ill feeling.

ininflammable (inẽflamabl) a, uninflammable.

inintelligent, e (inẽtɛliӡã, ã:t) a, unintelligent. **inintelligible†** (ӡibl) a, unintelligible.

ininterrompu, u (inẽtɛrɔpy) a, uninterrupted, unbroken.

inique† (inik) a, iniquitous, nefarious, unrighteous. **iniquité** (kite) f, iniquity, sin.

initial, e (inisjal) a, initial; opening. ¶ f, initial [letter]. **initiation** (sjɔ̃) f, initiation. **initiative** (ti;v) f, initiative; push, drive. **initié, e** (sje) n, initiate. **initier** (sje) *v.t*, to initiate.

injecté, e (ẽӡɛkte) a, bloodshot; flushed; impregnated (*wood*). **injecter** (te) *v.t*, to inject. **injecteur**

(tœ;r) m, injector. **injection** (ksjɔ̃) f, injection.

injonction (ẽӡɔ̃ksjɔ̃) f, injunction.

injure (ẽӡy:r) f, injury, wrong; insult; (*pl.*) abuse; (*s. or pl.*) ravages. **injurier** (ӡyrje) *v.t*, to abuse, insult, revile. **injurieux, euse†** (rjø, ø;z) a, abusive, insulting, offensive, opprobrious, injurious.

injuste† (ẽӡyst) a. & m, unjust; unrighteous; unfair; inequitable; wrong. **injustice** (tis) f, injustice; unrighteousness; unfairness; wrong. **injustifiable** (tifjabl) a, unjustifiable.

inné, e (inne) a, innate, inborn, inbred. **innéité** (ite) f, innateness.

innocemment (inɔsamã) ad, innocently. **innocent, e** (sã, ã;t) a, innocent; guiltless, not guilty; sinless, blameless; guileless, artless; harmless. ¶ n, innocent; simpleton. **innocence** (sã;s) f, innocence, etc. **innocenter** (sãte) *v.t*, to find not guilty.

innocuité (innɔkцite) f, harmlessness.

innombrable (innɔ̃brabl) a, innumerable, numberless, countless, untold.

innomé, e (innɔme) a, unnamed. **innommable** (mabl) a, unnamable.

innovation (innɔvasjɔ̃) f, innovation, [new] departure.

inobservance (inɔpsɛrvã;s) & **inobservation** (vasjɔ̃) f, inobservance, disregard. **inobservé, e** (ve) a, not complied with (*rules*).

inoccupé, e (inɔkype) a, unoccupied, idle; vacant.

inoculation (inɔkylasjɔ̃) f, inoculation. **inoculer** (le) *v.t*, to inoculate.

inodore (inɔdɔ;r) a, odorless.

inoffensif, ive (inɔfãsif, i;v) a, innocuous; innoxious; inoffensive; harmless.

inondation (inɔ̃dasjɔ̃) f, inundation, flood. **inonder** (de) *v.t*, to inundate, flood, deluge.

inopérant, e (inɔperã, ã;t) a, inoperative.

inopiné†, e (inɔpine) a, unexpected, sudden.

inopportun, e (inɔpɔrtœ̃, yn) *a*, inopportune.

inorganique (inɔrganik) *a*, inorganic.

inoubliable (inubliabl) *a*, unforgettable.

inouï, e (inwi) *a*, unheard of.

inoxydable (inɔksidabl) *a*, stainless, rustless.

inquiet, ète (ɛ̃kjɛ, ɛt) *a*, uneasy; troubled; restless, fidgety. **inquiéter** (jete) *v.t*, to make uneasy; disquiet; disturb; trouble; molest. **inquiétude** (tyd) *f*, uneasiness, disquiet[ude]; restlessness.

inquisiteur, trice (ɛ̃kizitœːr, tris) *a*, inquisitive. **inquisition** (sjɔ̃) *f*, inquisition.

insaisissable (ɛ̃sɛzisabl) *a*, not distrainable; difficult to catch, elusive; imperceptible.

insalubre (ɛ̃salybr) *a*, unhealthy; insanitary.

insanité (ɛ̃sanite) *f*, insanity (*folly*), nonsense.

insatiable† (ɛ̃sasjabl) *a*, insatiable.

insciemment (ɛ̃sjamɑ̃) *ad*, unknowingly.

inscription (ɛ̃skripsjɔ̃) *f*, inscription; writing; epitaph; registration, registry; entry; matriculation; quotation (*in Stk Ex. list*). ~ *de* (ou *en*) *faux*, pleading of forgery. *prendre des* (*ses*) ~*s*, to matriculate. **inscrire** (skriːr) *v.t.ir*, to inscribe; register; enter; write; quote. *s'inscrire en faux*, to plead forgery (*law*); deny the truth (*contre* = of). *s'~*, to register.

inscrutable (ɛ̃skrytabl) *a*, inscrutable.

insecte (ɛ̃sɛkt) *m*, insect. **insecticide** (tisid) *a. & m*, insecticide. **insectivore** (vɔːr) *a*, insectivorous. ~*s*, *m.pl*, insectivora.

insécurité (ɛ̃sekyrite) *f*, insecurity.

insensé, e (ɛ̃sɑ̃se) *a*, insensate, mad; senseless. ¶ *n*, madman, -woman. **insensible†** (sibl) *a*, insensible; unfeeling, callous.

inséparable† (ɛ̃separabl) *a*, inseparable. ~*s*, *n.pl*, inseparables (*pers.*); love birds.

insérer (ɛ̃sere) *v.t*, to insert, put

in. **insertion** (sɛrsjɔ̃) *f*, insertion.

insidieux, euse† (ɛ̃sidjø, øːz) *a*, insidious.

insigne (ɛ̃siɲ) *a*, signal, conspicuous; distinguished; arrant, rank, notorious. ¶ *m*, badge; (*pl.*) insignia. ~*s de la royauté*, regalia.

insignifiant, e (ɛ̃siɲifjɑ̃, ɑ̃ːt) *a*, insignificant, trifling, trivial, vacuous.

insinuation (ɛ̃sinɥasjɔ̃) *f*, insinuation; innuendo. **insinuer** (nɥe) *v.t*, to insinuate; hint at; introduce.

insipide (ɛ̃sipid) *a*, insipid; tasteless, vapid.

insistance (ɛ̃sistɑ̃ːs) *f*, insistence. **insister** (te) *v.i*, to insist.

insociable (ɛ̃sɔsjabl) *a*, unsociable.

insolation (ɛ̃sɔlasjɔ̃) *f*, insolation; sun bathing; sunstroke.

insolemment (ɛ̃sɔlamɑ̃) *ad*, insolently. **insolence** (lɑ̃ːs) *f*, insolence. **insolent, e** (lɑ̃, ɑ̃ːt) *a*, insolent; overbearing; extraordinary.

insolite (ɛ̃sɔlit) *a*, unusual, unwonted.

insoluble (ɛ̃sɔlybl) *a*, insoluble.

insolvabilité (ɛ̃sɔlvabilite) *f*, insolvency. **insolvable** (bl) *a*, insolvent.

insomnie (ɛ̃sɔmni) *f. oft. pl*, insomnia, sleeplessness.

insondable (ɛ̃sɔ̃dabl) *a*, unfathomable, fathomless.

insonore (ɛ̃sɔnɔːr) *a*, soundproof.

insouciant, e (ɛ̃susjɑ̃, ɑ̃ːt) *a*, careless, unconcerned; jaunty. **insoucieux, euse** (sjø, øːz) *a*, heedless, regardless.

insoumis, e (ɛ̃sumi, iːz) *a*, unsubdued. ¶ *m*, absentee (*Mil.*).

insoutenable (ɛ̃sutnabl) *a*, untenable, indefensible; insufferable.

inspecter (ɛ̃spɛkte) *v.t*, to inspect, examine. **inspecteur, trice** (tœːr, tris) *n*, inspector; examiner; floorwalker. ~ *du travail*, factory inspector. **inspection** (ksjɔ̃) *f*, inspection, examination; inspectorship.

inspiration (ɛ̃spirasjɔ̃) *f*, inspiration. **inspirer** (re) *v.t*, to inspire (*air* & *fig.*); prompt.

instabilité (ēstabilite) *f*, instability. **instable** (bl) *a*, unstable, unsteady.

installation (ēstalasjɔ̄) *f*, installation; induction (*Eccl.*). **installer** (le) *v.t*, to install; induct; settle.

instamment (ēstamɑ̄) *ad*, earnestly; urgently. **instance** (stɑ̄:s) *f*, (*pl.*) entreaties; (*law*) instance. **instant, e** (stɑ̄, ɑ̄:t) *a*, urgent, instant. ¶ *m*, instant, moment. *à l'~*, a moment ago; at once. **instantané†, e** (stɑ̄tane) *a*, instantaneous. ¶ *m*, snapshot.

instar de (à l') (ēsta:r) *pr*, like, as in.

instigation (ēstigasjɔ̄) *f*, instigation.

instiller (ēstille) *v.t*, to instill (*liquid*).

instinct (ēstē) *m*, instinct. **instinctif, ive†** (stɛktif, i:v) *a*, instinctive.

instituer (ēstitɥe) *v.t*, to institute; appoint. **institut** (ty) *m*, institute, institution. **instituteur, trice** (tœ:r, tris) *n*, teacher; governess. **institution** (sjɔ̄) *f*, institution; school; hostel.

instructeur (ēstryktœ:r) *m*, instructor; drill sergeant. **instructif, ive** (tif, i:v) *a*, instructive. **instruction** (sjɔ̄) *f*, instruction; education; schooling; tuition; training; lesson; pleading (*law*). *~ par écrit*, pleadings (*law*). *sans ~*, uneducated. **instruire** (strɥi:r) *v.t.ir*, to instruct; teach; educate; train; inform; plead (*law*). *s'~*, to learn.

instrument (ēstrymɑ̄) *m*, instrument; implement; tool. **instrumental, e** (tal) *a*, instrumental. **instrumentiste** (tist) *n*, instrumentalist.

insu de (à l') (ēsy) *pr*, unknown to. *à mon insu*, without my knowledge.

insubmersible (ēsybmɛrsibl) *a*, unsinkable.

insubordonné, e (ēsybɔrdɔne) *a*, insubordinate.

insuccès (ēsyksɛ) *m*, failure, miscarriage.

insuffisamment (ēsyfizamɑ̄)

ad, insufficiently. **insuffisance** (zɑ̄:s) *f*, insufficiency, shortage. *~ d'imposition*, underassessment. **insuffisant, e** (zɑ̄, ɑ̄:t) *a*, insufficient, inadequate; incompetent.

insulaire (ēsylɛ:r) *a*, insular. ¶ *n*, islander.

Insulinde (ēsylē:d) *f*, Indian Archipelago.

insulte (ēsylt) *f*, insult. **insulter** (te) *v.t*, to insult. *~ à*, to jeer at; be an insult to.

insupportable† (ēsypɔrtabl) *a*, insupportable; unbearable; insufferable.

insurgé, e (ēsyrʒe) *a.* & *n*, insurgent. **s'insurger** (ʒe) *v.pr*, to revolt.

insurmontable (ēsyrmɔ̄tabl) *a*, insurmountable, insuperable.

insurrection (ēsyrɛksjɔ̄) *f*, insurrection.

intact, e (ētakt) *a*, intact; whole; unblemished.

intaille (ētɑ:j) *f*, intaglio.

intangible (ētɑ̃ʒibl) *a*, intangible.

intarissable† (ētarisabl) *a*, unfailing, perennial, inexhaustible.

intégral, e† (ētegral) *a*, integral, whole, entire, [in] full; unexpurgated. **l'intégralité** (lite) *f*, the whole, the entirety.

intègre (ētɛgr) *a*, upright; honest. **intégrité** (tegrite) *f*, integrity.

intellect (ētɛlɛkt) *m*, intellect. **intellectuel, le†** (tɥɛl) *a.* & *m*, intellectual; brain, *att*.

intelligemment (ētɛliʒamɑ̄) *ad*, intelligently. **intelligence** (ʒɑ̄:s) *f*, intelligence, intellect; understanding; knowledge; (*on good*) terms; (*pl.*) correspondence; (*pl.*) dealings. **intelligent, e** (ʒɑ̄, ɑ̄:t) *a*, intelligent. **intelligible†** (ʒibl) *a*, intelligible; audible.

intempérance (ētɑ̄perɑ̄:s) *f*, intemperance; insobriety; excess. **intempérant, e** (rɑ̄, ɑ̄:t) *a*, intemperate. **intempérie** (ri) *f. usually pl*, [inclemency of the] weather.

intempestif, ive† (ētɑ̄pɛstif, i:v) *a*, unseasonable, untimely, ill-timed.

intenable (ētnabl) *a*, untenable.

intendance (ɛ̃tɑ̃dɑ̃:s) *f,* stewardship. ~ *militaire,* commissariat. **intendant** (dɑ̃) *m,* steward, bailiff.

intense (ɛ̃tɑ̃:s) *a,* intense; strenuous. **intensif, ive**† (tɑ̃sif, i:v) *a,* intensive. **intensifier** (fje) *v.t,* to intensify. **intensité** (te) *f,* intensity; strength; depth (*color*). ~ *lumineuse en bougies,* candle-power.

intenter (ɛ̃tɑ̃te) *v.t,* to enter, bring, institute (*action at law*).

intention (ɛ̃tɑ̃sjɔ̃) *f,* intention; intent, purpose; meaning; will. *à l'~ de,* for [the sake of]. **intentionné, e** (ɔne) *a,* -intentioned, -meaning, -disposed. **intentionnel, le**† (nɛl) *a,* intentional.

inter (l') (ɛ̃tɛ:r) *abb,* trunks (*Teleph.*).

intercaler (ɛ̃tɛrkale) *v.t,* to intercalate.

intercéder (ɛ̃tɛrsede) *v.i,* to intercede.

intercepter(ɛ̃tɛrsɛpte) *v.t,* to intercept.

intercesseur (ɛ̃tɛrsɛsœ:r) *m,* intercessor. **intercession** (sjɔ̃) *f,* intercession.

interchangeable (ɛ̃tɛrʃɑ̃ʒabl) *a,* interchangeable.

interdiction (ɛ̃tɛrdiksjɔ̃) *f,* interdiction; prohibition; ban; deprivation (*rights*). **interdire** (di:r) *v.t.ir,* to interdict, prohibit; forbid; ban; taboo; inhibit; deprive (*Eccl.*); disconcert, nonplus. **interdit** (di) *m,* person under judicial interdiction; interdict (*Eccl.*). *sens ~,* no thoroughfare.

intéressé, e (ɛ̃terɛse) *n,* interested party. *¶ a,* selfish. **intéresser** (se) *v.t,* to interest; concern. **intérêt** (rɛ) *m,* interest; stake.

interférence (ɛ̃tɛrferɑ̃:s) *f,* interference (*Phys.*).

interfolier (ɛ̃tɛrfɔlje) *v.t,* to interleave.

intérieur, e† (ɛ̃terjœ:r) *a,* interior; internal; inner; inward; inside; inland; home, domestic. *¶ m,* interior, inside; home; home life, private life.

intérim (ɛ̃terim) *m,* interim. *faire l'~,* to deputize. **intérimaire** (mɛ:r) *a,* interim; acting.

interjection (ɛ̃tɛrʒɛksjɔ̃) *f,* interjection; ejaculation; lodging (*appeal*). **interjeter** (ʒəte) *v.t,* to lodge (*appeal*).

interligne (ɛ̃tɛrliɲ) *m,* space between lines; space (*Mus.*); (*f.*) lead (*Typ.*). **interligner** (ɲe) *v.t,* to lead. **interlinéaire** (lineɛ:r) *a,* interlinear.

interlocuteur, trice (ɛ̃tɛrlɔkytœ:r, tris) *n,* interlocutor.

interlope (ɛ̃tɛrlɔp) *a,* dubious, suspect.

interloquer (ɛ̃tɛrlɔke) *v.t,* to take aback.

interlude (ɛ̃tɛrlyd) *m,* interlude (*Mus., etc.*); voluntary (*organ*).

intermède (ɛ̃tɛrmɛd) *m,* intermezzo; interlude. **intermédiaire** (medjɛ:r) *a,* intermediate. *¶ m,* intermission; intermediary, middleman, go-between; instrumentality, medium.

interminable (ɛ̃tɛrminabl) *a,* interminable.

intermittent, e (ɛ̃tɛrmitɑ̃, ɑ̃:t) *a,* intermittent.

internat (ɛ̃tɛrna) *m,* boarding school; boarding-in, living-in; internship.

international, e (ɛ̃tɛrnasjɔnal) *a,* international; foreign (*postal system*). *¶ f,* international (*association*); internationale (*hymn*). **internationaliste** (list) *n. & a,* internationalist.

interne (ɛ̃tɛrn) *a,* internal; inward. [*élève*] ~, *n,* boarder. *¶ m,* intern. **interné, e** (ne) *n,* internee; inmate (*asylum*). **interner** (ne) *v.t,* to intern (*war, etc.*); place under restraint (*lunatic*).

interpeller (ɛ̃tɛrpɛlle) *v.t,* to interpellate.

interpoler (ɛ̃tɛrpole) *v.t,* to interpolate.

interposer (ɛ̃tɛrpoze) *v.t,* to interpose. *s'~,* to interpose, mediate.

interprétation (ɛ̃tɛrpretasjɔ̃) *f,* interpretation; construction; rendering. **interprète** (prɛt) *n,* interpreter; exponent. **interpréter** (prete) *v.t,* to interpret; render.

interrègne (ɛ̃tɛrrɛɲ) *m,* interregnum.

interrogateur, trice (ɛ̃tɛrɔgatœ:r, tris) *n,* interrogator, ques-

tioner; examiner. **interrogatif,**
ivet (tif, iːv) *a*, interrogative.
interrogation (sjɔ̃) *f*, interrogation; question, query. **interroga-**
toire (twaːr) *m*, interrogatory.
interroger (ʒe) *v.t*, to interrogate.
interrompre (ɛtɛrɔ̃ːpr) *v.t*, to
interrupt, break, stop. **interrup-**
teur, trice (ryptœːr, tris) *n*, in-
terrupter; (*m.*) switch; circuit
breaker. **interruption** (sjɔ̃) *f*, interruption, break.
intersection (ɛtɛrsɛksjɔ̃) *f*, intersection.
interstice (ɛtɛrstis) *m*, interstice.
interurbain, e (ɛtɛryrbɛ̃, ɛn) *a*,
interurban; trunk (*Teleph.*). Cf.
inter (*l'*).
intervalle (ɛtɛrval) *m*, interval;
space; gap; interlude.
intervenant (ɛtɛrvənɑ̃) *m*, acceptor for honor (*Com.*). **in-**
tervenir (vəniːr) *v.i.ir*, to intervene, interfere; happen. **inter-**
vention (vɑ̃sjɔ̃) *f*, intervention.
interversion (ɛtɛrvɛrsjɔ̃) *f*, inversion. **intervertir** (tiːr) *v.t*, to
invert.
interview (ɛtɛrvju) *f*, interview
(*for news*). **interviewer** (vjuve)
v.t, to interview.
intestat (ɛtɛsta) *a.inv*, intestate.
intestin, e (ɛtɛstɛ̃, in) *a*, intestine; internal. ¶ *m*, intestine,
bowel, gut. **intestinal, e** (tinal)
a, intestinal.
intime† (ɛtim) *a*, intimate; in-
[ner]most; inward; close, near;
private. ¶ *m*, intimate. **intimer**
(me) *v.t*, to notify.
intimider (ɛtimide) *v.t*, to intimidate, cow, overawe.
intimité (ɛtimite) *f*, intimacy,
closeness.
intitulé (ɛtityle) *m*, title, name;
premises (*deed*). **intituler** (le)
v.t, to entitle, call, name.
intolérable† (ɛtɔlerabl) *a*, intolerable, insufferable. **intolérance**
(rɑ̃ːs) *f*, intolerance. **intolérant,**
e (rɑ̃, ɑ̃ːt) *a*, intolerant.
intonation (ɛtɔnasjɔ̃) *f*, intonation.
intoxication (ɛtɔksikasjɔ̃) *f*,
poisoning. **intoxiquer** (ke) *v.t*,
to poison.

intraduisible (ɛtradɥizibl) *a*,
untranslatable.
intraitable (ɛtrɛtabl) *a*, intractable; unreasonable.
intransigeant, e (ɛtrɑ̃ziʒɑ̃,
ɑ̃ːt) *a*, intransigent, uncompromising. ¶ *n*, intransigent, die-
hard.
intransitif, ivet† (ɛtrɑ̃zitif,
iːv) *a*, intransitive.
intrépide† (ɛtrepid) *a*, intrepid,
fearless, dauntless. **intrépidité**
(dite) *f*, intrepidity, etc.
intrigant, e (ɛtrigɑ̃, ɑ̃ːt) *a*, intriguing, designing. ¶ *n*, intriguer, schemer, wirepuller. **in-**
trigue (trig) *f*, intrigue; plot. **in-**
triguer (ge) *v.t*, to rouse the interest (*or* curiosity) of, intrigue,
puzzle; (*v.i.*) to intrigue, plot,
scheme, pull the wires.
intrinsèque† (ɛtrɛ̃sɛk) *a*, intrinsic.
introducteur, trice (ɛtrɔdyk-
tœːr, tris) *n*, introducer. **intro-**
duction (ksjɔ̃) *f*, introduction;
opening (*law case*). **introduire**
(dɥiːr) *v.t.ir*, to introduce; show
in, usher in. **s'~**, to get in, gain
admittance; intrude.
introït (ɛtrɔit) *m*, introit.
introniser (ɛtrɔnize) *v.t*, to enthrone.
introspection (ɛtrɔspɛksjɔ̃) *f*,
introspection.
introuvable (ɛtruvabl) *a*, undiscoverable; peerless.
intrus, e (ɛtry, yːz) *n*, intruder,
interloper; trespasser. (*law*). **in-**
trusion (tryzjɔ̃) *f*, intrusion; trespass.
intuitif, ive (ɛtɥitif, iːv) *a*,
intuitive. **intuition** (sjɔ̃) *f*, intuition.
inusable (inyzable) *a*, hard-wear-
ing; for hard wear. **inusité, e**
(zite) *a*, uncustomary; obsolete.
inutile† (inytil) *a*, useless; unprofitable; unnecessary, needless.
inutilisable (lizabl) *a*, unusable;
unserviceable. **inutilisé, e** (ze)
a. & p.p, unutilized. **inutilité** (te)
f, uselessness; (*pl.*) useless
things.
invalide† (ɛvalid) *a*, invalid; invalided. ¶ *m*, old *or* disabled
soldier; pensioner. **invalider** (de)
v.t, to invalidate; unseat. **invali-**

dité (dite) f, invalidity; disablement, disability.

invariable† (ɛ̃varjabl) a, invariable, unchangeable.

invasion (ɛ̃vazjɔ̃) f, invasion; inrush; influx.

invective (ɛ̃vɛktiːv) f, invective. **invectiver** (tive) v.i, to inveigh, rail.

invendable (ɛ̃vɑ̃dabl) a, unsalable. **invendu, e** (dy) a, unsold.

inventaire (ɛ̃vɑ̃tɛːr) m, inventory; list; stock-taking; valuation; accounts, balance sheet & schedules. **inventer** (te) v.t, to invent; devise; trump up. **inventeur, trice** (tœːr, tris) n, inventor; discoverer; finder; author (fig.). **inventif, ive** (tif, iːv) a, inventive. **invention** (sjɔ̃) f, invention. **inventorier** (tɔrje) v.t, to inventory, list; take stock of; value.

inversable (ɛ̃vɛrsabl) a, uncapsizable (boat); unspillable (ink bottle).

inverse† (ɛ̃vɛrs) a, inverse; reciprocal; reverse; contrary; contra. ¶ m, inverse; reverse; reciprocal. **inverser** (se) v.t, to reverse. **inversion** (sjɔ̃) f, inversion; reversal.

invertébré, e (ɛ̃vɛrtebre) a. & m, invertebrate.

invertir (ɛ̃vɛrtiːr) v.t, to invert; reverse.

investigation (ɛ̃vɛstigasjɔ̃) f, investigation.

investir (ɛ̃vɛstiːr) v.t, to invest (all Eng. senses); vest; dignify; blockade. **investissement** (tismɑ̃) m, investment (Mil.). **investiture** (tyːr) f, investiture.

invétéré, e (ɛ̃vetere) p.a, inveterate, ingrained. **s'invétérer** (re) v.pr, to become inveterate.

invincible† (ɛ̃vɛ̃sibl) a, invincible; insurmountable.

inviolable† (ɛ̃vjɔlabl) a, inviolable. **inviolé, e** (le) a, inviolate.

invisible† (ɛ̃vizibl) a, invisible; never to be seen. devenir ~, to vanish.

invitation (ɛ̃vitasjɔ̃) f, invitation. **invite** (vit) f, call (cards). **invité, e** (te) n, guest. **inviter** (te) v.t, to invite, ask; court; request; tempt; call for (trumps).

invocation (ɛ̃vɔkasjɔ̃) f, invocation.

involontaire† (ɛ̃vɔlɔ̃tɛːr) a, involuntary; unintentional.

invoquer (ɛ̃vɔke) v.t, to invoke, call upon.

invraisemblable† (ɛ̃vrɛsɑ̃blabl) a, unlikely; improbable. **invraisemblablement** (blɑmɑ̃) ad, unlikely, improbably. **invraisemblance** (blɑ̃ːs) f, unlikelihood, improbability.

invulnérable (ɛ̃vylnerabl) a, invulnerable.

iode (jɔd) m, iodine.

ion (iɔ̃) m, ion.

ionien, ne (iɔnjɛ̃, ɛn), **ionique** (nik) a, Ionian, Ionic.

iota (jɔta) m, iota, jot, tittle, whit.

irascible (irasibl) a, irascible, testy.

iridium (iridjɔm) m, iridium.

iris (iris) m, iris; rainbow. ~ des marais, yellow iris, flag. **irisation** (zasjɔ̃) f, iridescence. **irisé, e** (ze) a, iridescent.

irlandais, e (irlɑ̃dɛ, ɛːz) a, Irish. **I~**, n, Irishman, -woman. **l'Irlandais**, m, Irish (language). **l'Irlande** (lɑ̃ːd) f, Ireland. mer d'Irlande, Irish Sea.

ironie (irɔni) f, irony. **ironique**† (nik) a, ironic(al).

irrachetable (iraʃtabl) a, irredeemable (Fin.).

irradiation (irradjasjɔ̃) f, irradiation.

irraisonnable (irrɛzɔnabl) a, irrational, unreasoning. **irrationnel, le** (irrasjɔnɛl) a, irrational.

irréalisable (irealizabl) a, unrealizable.

irréconciliable (irrekɔ̃siljabl) a, irreconcilable.

irrécouvrable (irrekuvrabl) a, irrecoverable.

irrécupérable (irrekypɛrabl) a, unrecoverable; irretrievable.

irrécusable (irrekyzabl) a, unimpeachable, unexceptionable.

irrédentisme (irredɑ̃tism) m, irredentism.

irréductible (irredyktibl) a, irreducible; indomitable (will).

irréel, le (irreɛl) a, unreal.

irréfléchi, e (irrefleʃi) a, unconsidered. **irréflexion** (flɛksjɔ̃) f, thoughtlessness.

irréfutable† (irrefytabl) *a*, irrefutable. **irréfuté, e** (te) *a*, unrefuted.

irrégularité (irregylarite) *f*, irregularity. **irrégulier, ère**† (lje, ɛːr) *a*, irregular; erratic.

irréligieux, euse† (irreliʒjø, øːz) *a*, irreligious.

irrémédiable† (irremedjabl) *a*, irremediable.

irremplaçable (irrɑ̃plasabl) *a*, irreplaceable.

irréparable† (irreparabl) *a*, irreparable, irretrievable.

irréprochable† (irreprɔʃabl) *a*, irreproachable.

irrésistible† (irrezistibl) *a*, irresistible.

irrésolu, e (irrezɔly) *a*, irresolute.

irrespectueux, euse† (irrɛspɛktɥø, øːz) *a*, disrespectful.

irrespirable (irrɛspirabl) *a*, unbreathable.

irresponsable (irrɛspɔ̃sabl) *a*, irresponsible.

irrétrécissable (irretresisabl) *a*, unshrinkable.

irrévérencieux, euse (irreverɑsjø, øːz) *a*, disrespectful. **irrévérent, e** (rɑ̃, ɑ̃ːt) *a*, irreverent.

irrévocable† (irrevɔkabl), *a*, irrevocable.

irrigateur (irrigatœːr) *m*, irrigator; garden hose, etc. **irrigation** (sjɔ̃) *f*, irrigation. **irriguer** (ge) *v.t*, to irrigate.

irritable (irritabl) *a*, irritable, testy. **irritation** (sjɔ̃) *f*, irritation. **irriter** (te) *v.t*, to irritate; anger; excite. **s'~**, to grow angry; fret, chafe.

irruption (irrypsjɔ̃) *f*, irruption, inroad, inrush.

Islam (islam) *m*, Islam.

islandais, e (islɑ̃dɛ, ɛːz) *a*. & (*language*) *m*, Icelandic. **I~**, *n*, Icelander. **l'Islande** (lɑ̃ːd) *f*, Iceland.

isolateur (izɔlatœːr) *m*, insulator. **isolé, e** (le) *a*, isolated; detached; unattached (*Mil.*); lonely; alone; aloof. **isolement** (lmɑ̃) *m*, isolation; loneliness; insulation. **isolément** (lemɑ̃) *ad*, separately; singly. **isoler** (le) *v.t*, to isolate; insulate. **isoloir** (lwar) *m*, insulator; voting booth.

isoloir (lwar) *m*, insulator; voting booth.

israélite (iz- *ou* israelit) *n*, Israelite, Jew. ¶ *a*, Jewish.

issu, e (isy) *a*, descended, born, sprung. **issue** (sy) *f*, issue; end; solution; egress, exit, way out; outlet; outcome, upshot; (*pl.*) offal, garbage; by-products. **à l'~ de**, *ad*, at the end of, on leaving.

isthme (ism) *m*, isthmus.

Italie (l') (itali) *f*, Italy. **italien, ne** (ljɛ̃, ɛn) *a*, & **I~**, *n*, Italian. **l'italien**, Italian (*language*).

italique (italik) *a*, italic. ¶ *m*, italics.

item (itɛm) *ad*, item, likewise; ditto.

itinéraire (itinerɛːr) *m*, itinerary, route.

ivoire (ivwaːr) *m*, ivory.

ivraie (ivrɛ) *f*, cockle, darnel; tares (*fig.*).

ivre (iːvr) *a*, drunk[en], intoxicated, inebriate[d], tipsy. **~ à pleurer**, maudlin. **~ mort**, dead drunk. **ivresse** (ivrɛs) *f*, drunkenness, intoxication; frenzy, rapture. **ivrogne** (vrɔɲ) *a*, drunken. ¶ *m*, drunkard, toper, inebriate, sot. **ivrognerie** (ɲri) *f*. drunkenness. **ivrognesse** (ɲɛs) *f*, drunkard, inebriate, sot.

J

jabot (ʒabo) *m*, crop (*bird*); frill. **jaboter** (bɔte) & **jacasser** (kase) *v.i*, to jabber, chatter.

jachère (ʒaʃɛːr) *f*, fallow [land]. **jachérer** (ʃere) *v.t*, to fallow.

jacinthe (ʒasɛ̃ːt) *f*, hyacinth (*Bot.*); jacinth (*Miner.*). **~ des bois**, wild hyacinth, bluebell.

jacobée (ʒakɔbe) *f*, ragwort.

jacobin (ʒakɔbɛ̃) *m*, jacobin.

jactance (ʒaktɑ̃ːs) *f*, boasting, brag.

jade (ʒad) *m*, jade (*Miner.*).

jadis (ʒɑdis) *ad*, formerly, once. **au temps ~**, in the olden time.

jaguar (ʒagwaːr) *m*, jaguar.

jaillir (ʒajiːr) *v.i*, to gush, spout, spurt, squirt, jet; fly; splash; spring; well; flash.

jais (ʒɛ) *m*, jet (*lignite*).

jalon (ʒalɔ̃) *m*, peg, stake, picket; range pole; landmark (*fig.*). **jalonner** (lɔne) *v.t*, to peg, stake [out]; dot. **jalonneur** (nœːr) *m*, marker (*Mil.*).

jalouser (ʒaluze) *v.t*, to be jealous of. **jalousie** (zi) *f*, jealousy; Venetian blind; jalousie. **jaloux, ouse†** (lu, uːz) *a*, jealous; anxious.

Jamaïque (la) (ʒamaik), Jamaica.

jamais (ʒamɛ) *ad*, ever; never. *à* ~ *ou pour* ~, forever. *ne* . . . ~, never, ne'er (*Poet.*).

jambage (ʒɑ̃baːʒ) *m*, pier (*Build.*); jamb; down stroke; pothook. **jambe** (ʒɑ̃ːb) *f*, leg; shank. ~ *de force*, strut. ~ *deça*, ~ *delà*, astride, astraddle. **jambière** (ʒɑ̃bjɛːr) *f*, legging; shin guard. **jambon** (bɔ̃) *m*, ham (*hog, boar*).

jante (ʒɑ̃ːt) *f*, felloe, felly; rim. **jantille** (ʒɑ̃tiːj) *f*, paddle [board] (*waterwheel*).

janvier (ʒɑ̃vje) *m*, January.

Japon (ʒapɔ̃) *m*, Japanese porcelain; J. paper. *le* ~, Japan (*Geog.*). **japonais, e** (pɔnɛ, ɛːz) *a. & J*~ (*pers.*) *n*, Japanese. *le japonais*, Japanese (*language*). **japonerie** (nri) *f*, Japanese curio, etc.

japper (ʒape) *v.i*, to yap, yelp.

jaquette (ʒakɛt) *f*, morning coat, tail c. (*man's*); short coat (*woman's*).

jard (ʒaːr) *m*, river gravel.

jardin (ʒardɛ̃) *m*, garden. ~ *de rocaille*, ~ *alpestre*, rock g. ~ *anglais*, landscape g. ~ *d'enfants*, kindergarten. ~ *de fenêtre*, window box. ~ *de l'église*, churchyard. ~ *des plantes*, botanical gardens. ~ *maraîcher*, market garden. ~ *potager*, kitchen garden. **jardinage** (dinaːʒ) *m*, gardening; garden plots. **jardiner** (ne) *v.i*, to garden. **jardinet** (nɛ) *m*, small garden. **jardinier, ère** (nje, ɛːr) *n*, gardener; (*f.*) flower stand, jardinière.

jargon (ʒargɔ̃) *m*, jargon; lingo; slang, cant; jargoon (*Miner.*). **jargonner** (ɡɔne) *v.i. & t*, to jabber.

jarre (ʒaːr) *f*, jar (*pot*).

jarret (ʒarɛ) *m*, bend of the knee; ham (*in man*); hock, hough (*horse*); knuckle (*veal*); shin (*beef*). **jarretelles** (rtɛl) *f.pl*, [sock and stocking] suspenders. **jarretière** (rtjɛːr) *f*, garter; gunsling.

jars (ʒaːr) *m*, gander.

jas (ʒɑ) *m*, stock (*anchor*).

jaser (ʒɑze) *v.i*, to chatter; blab. **jaserie** (zri) *f*, chatter. **jaseur, euse** (zœːr, øːz) *n*, chatterer.

jasmin (ʒasmɛ̃) *m*, jasmine.

jaspe (ʒasp) *m*, jasper. ~ *sanguin*, bloodstone. **jasper** (pe) *v.t*, to marble; mottle. **jaspure** (pyːr) *f*, marbling.

jatte (ʒat) *f*, bowl.

jauge (ʒoːʒ) *f*, gauge; gauging rod; register[ed tonnage] (*ship*). **jauger** (ʒoʒe) *v.t*, to gauge; measure (*ship*); size up (*pers.*).

jaunâtre (ʒonɑːtr) *a*, yellowish; sallow. **jaune** (ʒoːn) *a*, yellow; sallow; [light] brown (*boots*). *la mer Jaune*, the Yellow Sea. ¶ *m*, yellow; yolk (*egg*); strikebreaker; (*pl.*) yellow races. **jaunir** (ʒoniːr) *v.t. & i*, to yellow. **jaunisse** (nis) *f*, jaundice.

Java (ʒava) *m*, Java. **javanais, e** (nɛ, ɛːz) *a. & J*~, *n*, Javan[ese].

javelle (ʒavɛl) *f*, swath; chlorinated water,.

javelot (ʒavlo) *m*, javelin.

je, j' (ʒə, ʒ) *pn*, I.

jérémiade (ʒeremjad) *f*, jeremiad.

jersey (ʒɛrzɛ) *m*, stockinet; jersey. **J**~, *f*, Jersey (*Geog.*). **jersiais, e** (zje, ɛːz) *a*, Jersey (*cattle*).

Jérusalem (ʒeryzalɛm) *f*, Jerusalem.

jésuite (ʒezɥit) *m*, Jesuit. **jésuitique** (tik) *a*, Jesuitical.

Jésus (ʒezy) *m*, Jesus. **Jésus-Christ** (kri) *m*, Jesus Christ.

jet (ʒɛ) *m*, throw[ing]; cast[ing]; toss[ing]; fling; pouring (*metal*); catch (*fish*); folds (*drapery*); flash (*light*); spurt; burst; jet; stream; nozzle, spout; shoot, sprout; attempt, go. ~ *[à la mer]*, jettison. **jeté** (ʒəte) *m*, over (*Knit.*). ~ *de lit*, bedspread, overlay. **jetée** (te) *f*, jetty, pier. ~ *promenade*, pier (*seaside*). **jeter** (te) *v.t. & abs*, to throw;

cast; dash; fling; hurl; toss; pitch; splash; put; lay (*foundations*); shed (*light*); heave (*sigh*); utter (*cry*); run, discharge (*of abscess*); sprout; strike (*root*); pour, run (*metal*). ~ [*à la mer*], to jettison. se ~, to throw oneself; jump; fall, run. **jeton** (tõ), *m*, counter; tally; token. ~s **de présence**, directors' fees; fees.

jeu (ʒø) *m*, play; game; sport; pastime; gaming; gambling; speculation; execution; acting, trick; play (*Mech.*); slack; clearance; lash; stroke (*piston, etc.*); blowing [out] (*fuse*); set, assortment; stop (*organ*); pack (*cards*); hand (*cards*); stake[s]. ~ *d'adresse*, game of skill. ~ *d'anneaux*, ship quoits, ring quoits. ~ *d'esprit*, witticism. ~ *de baquet*, tipping (*or* tilting) the bucket. ~ *de boules*, [game of] bowls. ~ *de chat*, touch [last], tag. ~ *de fléchettes*, darts. ~ *de jambes*, foot work (*sport*). ~ [*bizarre*] *de la nature*, freak [of nature]. ~ *de la scie*, cat's-cradle. ~*x de main*, horseplay, rough & tumble. ~ *de mots*, play on words, pun. ~ *de patience*, jigsaw puzzle. ~ *de paume*, real tennis (*ancient game*). ~*x de physionomie*, play of features. ~*x de salon*, ~*x de société*, parlor games, indoor games. ~ *de scène*, stage trick. ~ *de tennis*, game of tennis; t. court. ~ *de volant*, badminton. ~ *du cochonnet*, [game of] bowls. ~*x innocents*, parlor games, forfeits. ~, *manche*, & *partie*, game-set-match (*Ten.*). ~ *muet*, dumb show. *pas du* (ou *de*) ~, not fair.

jeudi (ʒødi) *m*, Thursday.

jeun (à) (ʒœ̃) *ad*, fasting; on an empty stomach.

jeune (ʒœn) *a*, young; youthful; juvenile; rising (*generation*); younger; minor. ~ *personne*, *f*, young lady; young person, juvenile. [le] ~, junior, the younger. ¶ *n*, young person.

jeûne (ʒø:n) *m*, fast[ing]; abstinence. **jeûner** (ne) *v.i*, to fast.

jeunement (ʒœnmɑ̃) *ad*, youthfully. **jeunesse** (nɛs) *f*, youth;

childhood; youthfulness; boyhood; girlhood; girl. **jeunet, te** (nɛ, ɛt) *a*, [very] young.

jiu-jitsu (ʒyʒitsy) *m*, ju-jutsu, ju-jitsu, judo.

joaillerie (ʒwajri) *f*, jewelry. **joaillier, ère** (je, ɛːr) *n*, jeweler.

jobard, e (ʒobaːr, ard) *n*, simpleton, fool.

jockey (ʒokɛ) *m*, jockey (*turf*).

jocko (ʒoko) *m*, orangutan.

jocrisse (ʒokris) *m*, simpleton.

joie (ʒwa) *f*, joy[fulness], glee; mirth, merriment; pleasure; gaiety.

joignant, e [à] (ʒwaɲɑ̃, ɑ̃ːt) *a*, adjoining. **joindre** (ʒwɛːdr) *v.t. & i. ir. & se* ~, to join; unite; fold (*hands*); combine; adjoin; attach; add; meet. **joint** (ʒwɛ̃) *n*, joint, join. **jointif, ive** (tif, iːv) *a*, close. **jointoyer** (twaje) *v.t*, to point (*masonry*). **jointure** (tyːr) *f*, juncture; joint; knuckle.

joli, e (ʒoli) *a*, pretty; good-looking; nice; fine. **joliment** (mɑ̃) *ad*, prettily; very well.

jonc (ʒõ) *m*, rush; bulrush; cane; hoop ring. **joncher** (ʃe) *v.t*, to strew, litter.

jonction (ʒõksjõ) *f*, junction, meeting.

jongler (ʒõgle) *v.i*, to juggle. **jonglerie** (gləri) *f*, juggling; juggle, trick. **jongleur** (glœːr) *m*, juggler; trickster.

jonque (ʒõːk) *f*, junk (*Chinese*).

jonquille (ʒõkiːj) *f*, jonquil.

jouailler (ʒuaje) *v.i*, to play [for] low [stakes]; play a little (*music*).

joubarbe (ʒubarb) *f*, houseleek.

joue (ʒu) *f*, cheek; jowl; flange. *mettre* (ou *coucher*) *en* ~, to [take] aim at.

jouée (ʒwe) *f*, reveal (*Arch.*).

jouer (ʒwe) *v.i. & t. & abs*, to play; sport; toy; move (*chess, etc.*); gamble; be on the gamble; speculate; operate; work; perform; act (*Theat.*); trifle; trick; fool; stake; back (*horse*); feign; look like; blow [out] (*fuse*). ~ *sur le*(*s*) *mot*(*s*), to play on words, pun. *a qui à* ~? whose move is it? *se* ~ *de*, to make light of. **jouet** (ʒwɛ) *m*, toy; plaything; sport; butt. **joueur,**

euse (ʒwœːr, øːz), n, player; performer; gambler; speculator; operator; (good, bad) loser; (att.) fond of play. ~ un de plus, odd player (golf).

joufflu, e (ʒufly) a, chubby.

joug (ʒu[g]) m, yoke.

jouir de (ʒwiːr) to enjoy; e. the company of; avail oneself of the services of; use; have. **jouissance** (ʒwisãːs) f, enjoyment; pleasure, delight; use; possession; tenure; fruition; due date of coupon, interest payable (date).

joujou (ʒuʒu) m, plaything, toy.

jour (ʒuːr) m, day; daytime; [day]-light; opening, gap; day, surface, grass (Min.); (pl.) openwork (Need.). le ~ de l'an, New Year's Day. son ~ [de réception], her at-home day. le ~ des Cendres, Ash Wednesday. le ~ des morts, All Souls' Day. le ~ des propitiations, the day of atonement. ~ du terme, quarter day. ~ férié (ferje), [public] holiday; holy day. ~ gras, meat day (Eccl.). les ~s gras, Shrovetide. ~ maigre, fast day. à ~, open; openwork[ed]; through; up to date. à ce ~, to date. au ~ le ~, from day to day; from hand to mouth.

Jourdain (le) (ʒurdẽ), the Jordan.

journal (ʒurnal) m, journal; diary; log [book]; book; register; [news]paper; gazette. ~ parlé, weather & news (radio). **journalier, ère** (lje, ɛːr) a, daily; inconstant; fickle. ¶ m, day laborer. **journalisme** (lism) m, journalism; press. **journaliste** (list) m, journalist, reporter, columnist.

journée (ʒurne) f, day; daytime; day's work; day's pay. ~ de chemin, day's journey. **journellement** (nɛlmã) ad, daily.

joute (ʒut) f, joust; tilt[ing]; contest; fight. ~ sur l'eau, water tournament. **jouter** (te) v.i, to joust.

jouvenceau, elle (ʒuvãso, ɛl) n, youth, damsel.

jovial, e† (ʒɔvjal) a, jovial, merry, jolly.

joyau (ʒwajo) m, jewel.

joyeux, euse† (ʒwajø, øːz) a, joyful, joyous, jolly, genial, convivial, merry, jocund.

jubilaire (ʒybilɛːr) a, jubilee, holy (year). **jubilation** (lasjɔ̃) f, jubilation, jollification, jollity. **jubilé** (le) m, jubilee.

jucher (ʒyʃe) v.i. & se ~, to roost, perch. **juchoir** (ʃwaːr) m, roost, perch.

judaïque† (ʒydaik) a, Judaic. **Judas** (ʒyda) m, Judas (traitor). **j~**, spyhole, peephole, judas; window mirror.

judiciaire† (ʒydisjɛːr) a, judicial; legal.

judicieux, euse† (ʒydisjø, øːz) a, judicious, discerning.

juge (ʒyːʒ) m, judge; justice; magistrate; umpire. les Juges, Judges (Bible). ~ d'instruction, examining magistrate. **jugement** (ʒyʒmã) m, judgment; trial; estimation; discernment; sentence; decree. **juger** (ʒe) v.t. & abs, to judge; try (case); pass judgment; think, deem.

jugulaire (ʒygylɛːr) f, chin strap. [veine] ~, f, jugular [vein]. **juguler** (le) v.t, to strangle.

juif, ive (ʒɥif, iːv) n, Jew, Jewess. Juif errant, Wandering Jew. ¶ a, Jewish.

juillet (ʒɥijɛ) m, July.

juin (ʒɥẽ) m, June.

juiverie (ʒɥivri) f, ghetto.

jujube (ʒyʒyb) m, jujube. **jujubier** (bje) m, jujube [shrub].

julep (ʒylɛp) m, julep.

jumeau, elle (ʒymo, ɛl) a, twin; semidetached. ¶ n, twin; (f.) binocular [glass], glass[es]; upright, standard, housing. ~[s] de théâtre, opera glass[es]. **jumeler** (mle) v.t, to pair.

jument (ʒymã) f, mare.

jungle (ʒɔ̃ːgl) f, jungle.

jupe (ʒyp) f, skirt. ~-culotte, divided s. **jupier, ère** (pje, ɛːr) n, skirt maker. **jupon** (pɔ̃) m, petticoat.

juré, e (ʒyre) a, sworn. ¶ m, juryman, juror. **jurer** (re) v.t. & abs, to swear; s. by; blaspheme; vow; (v.i.) to clash, jar. **jureur** (rœːr) m, swearer.

juridiction (ʒyridiksjɔ̃) f, jurisdiction; province, line. **juridique†** (dik) a, juridical, law (att.). **ju**-

risconsulte (riskõsylt) *m*, jurist.
jurisprudence (prydã;s) *f*, jurisprudence, law. **juriste** (rist) *m*, jurist.

juron (ʒyrõ) *m*, (*profane*) oath.

jury (ʒyri) *m*, jury; selection committee. ~ *d'admission*, hanging committee (*art*). ~ *d'examen*, board of examiners.

jus (ʒy) *m*, juice; gravy; blurb. ~ *de réglisse*, licorice.

jusant (ʒyzã) *m*, ebb.

jusque & *poet.* **jusques** (ʒysk) *pr*, to; as (*or* so) far as; till, until; even; up to. *jusqu'à ce que*, till, until. *jusqu'à concurrence de*, up to, not exceeding. *jusqu'à quand?* till when? how long? *jusqu'ici*, so far, thus far; till now, hitherto. *jusqu'où?* how far? *jusque-là*, so far; till then.

juste (ʒyst) *a*, just; right; fair; legitimate; correct; accurate; exact; proper; true; condign; upright; righteous; tight (*fit*). ~ *milieu*, happy medium, golden mean. *à ~ titre*, fairly, rightly. **le ~**, the right. **les ~s**, *m.pl*, the just, the righteous. ¶ *ad*, just; right; barely. **justement** (təmã) *ad*, justly; exactly; just. **justesse** (tɛs) *f*, accuracy; correctness. **justice** (tis) *f*, justice; equity; right; rights; righteousness; justness, fairness; judicature; court of law; law; law officers. **justiciable** (sijabl) *a*, under the jurisdiction; amenable. **justicier** (sje) *m*, justiciary. **justifiable** (fjabl) *a*, justifiable, warrantable. **justificatif, ive** (fikatif, i;v) *a*, justificative; voucher (*att.*). **justifier** (fje) *v.t*, to justify; warrant; vindicate; prove.

jute (ʒyt) *m*, jute.

juter (ʒyte) *v.i*, to be juicy. **juteux, euse** (tø, ø;z) *a*, juicy.

juvénile (ʒyvenil) *a*, juvenile, youthful.

juxtaposer (ʒykstapoze) *v.t*, to juxtapose.

K

kaki (kaki) *a*, khaki.

kaléidoscope (kaleidɔskɔp) *m*, kaleidoscope.

kangourou (kãguru) *m*, kangaroo.

kaolin (kaɔlɛ̃) *m*, kaolin, china clay.

Kénia (le) (kenja), Kenya.

képi (kepi) *m*, cap (*peaked*).

kermesse (kɛrmɛs) *f*, kermis, fête, fair.

khédive (kedi;v) *m*, Khedive.

kilogramme (kilɔgram) *m*, kilogram = 1000 grams *or* 2.2046 (about 2⅕) lbs.

kilomètre (kilɔmɛtr) *m*, kilometer = 1000 meters *or* 0.62137 (about ⅝) mile. **Kilometrique** (metrik) *a*, kilometric(al).

kimono (kimɔno) *m*, kimono.

kiosque (kjɔsk) *m*, kiosk; stall; bookstall; conning tower (*submarine*). ~ *à musique*, bandstand. ~ *de jardin*, summer house.

krach (krak) *m*, crash, smash (*Fin.*).

kyrielle (kirjɛl) *f*, string, rigmarole.

kyste (kist) *m*, cyst (*Med.*).

L

la (la) *m*, A (*Mus.*). *donner le* ~ (*fig.*), to set the fashion.

là (la) *ad*, there; then; that. ~*-bas*, [over] yonder, over there. ~*-dedans*, in there; within. ~*-dehors*, outside, without. ~*-dessous*, under there, underneath. ~*-dessus*, on that, thereon; thereupon. ~*-haut*, up there. *de ~*, away, off; out of there; from then. *par ~*, that way; through there, thereby. ¶ *i*, there [now]! *oh ~ ~!* wow!

labeur (labœ;r) *m*, labor, toil; book work (*Typ.*).

labial, e (labjal) *a.* & *f*, labial.

laboratoire (labɔratwa;r) *m*, laboratory.

laborieux, euse† (labɔrjø, ø;z) *a*, laborious, hard-working; working (*class*); arduous, toilsome, hard; labored.

labour (labu;r) *m*, plowing, tillage. **labourable** (burabl) *a*, arable, plow (*land*). **labourage** (ra;ʒ) *m*, plowing, tillage. **labourer** (re) *v.t. & abs*, to plow, till;

plow up; drag (*anchor*); graze (*sea bottom*). **laboureur** (rœːr) *m*, plowman.

labyrinthe (labirɛ̃ːt) *m*, labyrinth, maze.

lac (lak) *m*, lake, mere. *Note.—* For named lakes, see under proper name, e.g, *le lac Léman,* under *Léman.* ~ *de cirque,* tarn. ~ *salé,* salt lake.

lacer (lase) *v.t,* to lace [up].

lacérer (lasere) *v.t,* to lacerate, tear.

lacet (lasɛ) *m,* lace (*shoe, etc.*); winding (*road*); nosing (*of locomotive*); snare, noose; (*pl.*) toils.

lâche† (lɑːʃ) *a,* loose; slack; lax; faint-hearted, cowardly, unmanly, dastardly, mean. **lâcher** (lɑʃe) *v.t,* to loose[n]; slacken; let out; relax; let fly; release; liberate; let go; let down; jilt; drop; [let] slip; blurt out; open, turn on (*tap*); utter; fire (*shot*). ~ *pied,* to give way. ~ *prise,* to let go. **lâcheté** (ʃte) *f,* cowardice; meanness.

lacis (lasi) *m,* network; plexus.

laconique† (lakɔnik) *a,* laconic.

lacrymal, e (lakrimal) *a,* lachrymal, tear (*att.*).

lacs (lɑ) *m,* toils (*fig.*). ~ *d'amour,* love knot, true-love[r's] knot.

lacté, e (lakte) *a,* lacteal; milk (*att.*); milky.

lacune (lakyn) *f,* lacuna; gap; hiatus; blank.

lacustre (lakystr) *a,* lacustrine, lake (*att.*).

lad (lad) *m,* stable boy (*turf*).

ladre (lɑːdr) *n,* miser, niggard, skinflint. ¶ *a,* stingy, mean, niggardly. **ladrerie** (lɑdrəri) *f,* stinginess.

lagune (lagyn) *f,* lagoon.

lai (lɛ) *a.m,* lay (*brother*). ¶ *m,* lay (*poem*).

laïc see **laïque.**

laîche (lɛʃ) *f,* sedge.

laid, e (lɛ, ɛd) *a,* ugly, plain, ill-favored, unsightly; naughty. **laideron** (drɔ̃) *m,* plain girl. **laideur** (dœːr) *f,* ugliness.

laie (lɛ) *f,* wild sow.

lainage (lɛnaːʒ) *m,* woolen goods, woolens; teaseling. **laine** (lɛn) *f,* wool. ~ *peignée,* worsted. **lainer** (lɛne) *v.t,* to teasel. **lainerie** (nri) *f,* woolen mill; w. trade; wool shop. **laineux, euse** (nø, øːz) *a,* woolly. **lainier, ère** (nje, ɛːr) *a,* wool (*trade, etc.*) ¶ *m,* woolen manufacturer.

laïque (laik) *a. & m,* laic, lay-(man); undenominational.

laisse (lɛs) *f,* leash, slip; sea ware; watermark (*tidal*).

laissé-pour-compte (lɛse) *m,* returned or rejected article.

laissées (lɛse) *f.pl,* droppings, dung.

laisser (lɛse) *v.t,* to leave; let; allow; let have. ~ *aller* & ~ *échapper,* to let go. ~ *courre* (kuːr), to slip (*hounds*). ~ *tomber,* to drop; let fall. *laissez donc!* leave off! **laisser-aller,** *m,* unconstraint; carelessness. **laisser-faire,** *m,* noninterference, drift. **laissez-passer,** *m,* pass.

lait (lɛ) *m,* milk. ~ *condensé,* ~ *concentré,* ~ *conservé,* condensed m. ~ *de beurre,* buttermilk. ~ *de chaux,* whitewash. **laitage** (taːʒ) *m,* milk food. **laitance** (tɑ̃ːs) *ou* **laite** (lɛt) *f,* soft roe, milt. **laité, e** (te) *a,* soft-roed. **laiterie** (tri) *f,* dairy. **laiteux, euse** (tø, øːz) *a,* milky.

laitier (lɛtje) *m,* slag, scoria[e].

laitier, ère (lɛtje, ɛːr) *m,* milkman, milkmaid, dairyman. ¶ *f,* milker (*cow*).

laiton (lɛtɔ̃) *m,* brass.

laitue (lɛty) *f,* lettuce. ~ *pommée,* cabbage l. ~ *romaine,* Romaine lettuce.

laize (lɛːz) *f,* width (*of cloth*).

lama (lama) *m,* lama (*pers.*); llama (*Zool.*).

lamaneur (lamanœːr) *m,* branch pilot.

lamantin (lamɑ̃tɛ̃) *m,* manatee, sea cow.

lambeau (lɑ̃bo) *m,* rag, tatter; shred; remnant.

lambin, e (lɑ̃bɛ̃, in) *n,* dawdler, slowcoach; (*att.*) dawdling, slow, dilatory, leisurely. **lambiner** (bine) *v.i,* to dawdle, lag.

lambourde (lɑ̃burd) *f,* joist; wall-plate.

lambris (lɑ̃bri) *m,* wainscot, paneling. ~ *d'appui,* dado. ~

dorés, gilded apartments. **lambrisser** (se) *v.t*, to wainscot; panel; line.

lame (lam) *f*, [thin] sheet; plate; lamina; flake; blade; cutter; lath, slat (*blind*); spangle; wave, sea, billow; swordsman. **lamé, e** (lame) *a.* & *m*, lamé. **lamelle** (mɛl) *f*, lamina, flake.

lamentable† (lamɑ̃tabl) *a*, lamentable, deplorable, pitiful, pitiable; woeful. **lamentation** (sjɔ̃) *f*, lament[ation], wail[ing]. **se lamenter** (te) *v.pr*, to lament, wail. **se ~ sur**, to bewail, deplore.

laminer (lamine) *v.t*, to roll (*metal*); laminate. **laminoir** (nwa:r) *m*, rolling mill.

lampadaire (lɑ̃padɛ:r) *m*, lamp standard.

lampas (lɑ̃pɑ) *m*, lampas (*silk & Vet.*).

lampe (lɑ̃:p) *f*, lamp; radio tube. **~ à alcool**, spirit lamp. **~ à pied**, floor l. **~ de poche**, **~ électrique**, flashlight. **~ de travail**, reading lamp. **~-éclair**, *f*, flashbulb.

lamper (lɑ̃pe) *v.t*, to toss off, swill, swig.

lampion (lɑ̃pjɔ̃) *m*, fairy light, f. lamp. **~ en papier**, paper lantern. **lampiste** (pist) *m*, lampman. **lampisterie** (təri) *f*, lamp room.

lamproie (lɑ̃prwa) *f*, lamprey.

lampyre (lɑ̃pi:r) *m*, glowworm.

lance (lɑ̃:s) *f*, spear; lance; [hose] branch. **~-flamme**, *m*, flamethrower. **lancement** (lɑ̃smɑ̃) *m*, throwing; launch[ing]; floating, promotion. **~ du javelot, du disque, du gros boulet, du marteau**, throwing the javelin, the discus, the heavy weight, the hammer. **~ du poids**, putting the shot. **lancer** (se) *m*, release (*pigeons*); starting (*Hunt.*) ¶ *v.t*, to throw; cast; put (*the shot*); fling; hurl; shy; drop (*bombs*); dart; shoot; fire; toss; pitch; let off; ejaculate; initiate; launch; catapult (*airplane*); float; promote; issue; set (*dog on, fashion*); deliver (*ball, Ten.*); fly (*kite*); start (*stag, game*). **lancette** (sɛt) *f*, lancet. **lanciers** (sje) *m.pl*, lancers (*Danc.*). **lancinant, e** (sinɑ̃, ɑ̃:t) *a*, shooting (*pain*).

landau (lɑ̃do) *m*, landau. **~** [*pour enfant*], baby carriage, perambulator. **~ pliant**, folding carriage. **landaulet** (lɛ) *m*, landaulet.

lande (lɑ̃:d) *f*, heath, moor[land]) links.

langage (lɑ̃ga:ʒ) *m*, language, speech, parlance. **~ de poissarde, ~ des halles**, abusive language.

lange (lɑ̃:ʒ) *m*, diaper; (*pl, lit. & fig.*) swaddling clothes.

langoureux, euse† (lɑ̃guɾø, ø:z) *a*, languorous.

langouste (lɑ̃gust) *f*, spiny lobster, (*sea*) crayfish.

langue (lɑ̃:g) *f*, tongue; language, speech. **~ verte**, slang. **~ vulgaire**, vernacular. **languette** (lɑ̃gɛt) *f*, tongue; pointer, feather (*as on a board—Carp., & Mach.*); strip; cleat.

langueur (lɑ̃gœ:r) *f*, languor; listlessness; languishment. **languir** (gi:r) *v.i*, to languish, pine [away]; mope; long, weary; droop, flag, drag. **languissant, e** (gisɑ̃, ɑ̃:t) *a*, languishing; languid; lackadaisical; flat, dull.

lanière (lanjɛ:r) *f*, thong, lash; strip; lace (*leather*).

lanterne (lɑ̃tɛrn) *f*, lantern; lamp; (*pl.*) nonsense. **~ sourde**, dark l. **~-tempête**, hurricane lamp. **~ vénitienne**, paper lantern. **lanterner** (ne) *v.i*, to shilly-shally; trifle; (*v.t.*) to humbug. **lanternier** (nje) *m*, lantern maker; lamplighter; shilly-shallier.

lapalissade (lapalisad) *f*, truism.

laper (lape) *v.i.* & *t*, to lap [up], lick up.

lapereau (lapro) *m*, young rabbit.

lapidaire (lapidɛ:r) *a.* & *m*, lapidary. **lapider** (de) *v.t*, to stone; throw stones at; pelt; set on (*someone*).

lapin, e (lapɛ̃, in) *n*, [buck, doe] rabbit, coney. **~ bélier**, lop-ear[ed r.]. **~ domestique, ~ de clapier, ~ de choux**, tame r. **~ de garenne**, wild r. **lapinière** (pinjɛ:r) *f*, rabbitry.

lapis[-lazuli] (lapis[lazyli]) *m*, lapis lazuli.

lapon, one (lapɔ̃, ɔn) *a.* & **L~,**

n, Lapp, Laplander (*n.*). **la Laponie** (pɔni), Lapland.

laps de temps (laps) *m*, lapse of time. **lapsus** (sy:s) *m*, lapsus, lapse, slip.

laquais (lakɛ) *m*, lackey, flunkey, menial.

laque (lak) *f*, lac; lake (*paint*). ~ *en écailles*, shellac. ¶ *m*, lacquer, l. work; japan. **laquer** (ke) *v.t*, to lacquer, japan, enamel.

larbin (larbɛ̃) *m*, flunkey.

larcin (larsɛ̃) *m*, larceny; crib, plagiarism.

lard (la:r) *m*, bacon; fat; blubber. **larder** (larde) *v.t*, to lard (*Cook.*); [inter]lard; load; pierce. **lardon** (dɔ̃) *m*, lardoon, gibe.

lares (la:r) *m.pl*, home. [**dieux**] ~, Lares.

large† (larʒ) *a*, broad; wide; large; loose; extensive; sweeping; free; liberal. ¶ *m*, room, space; open sea; offing. *au* ~, in the offing; out at sea; well off. *au* ~*!* keep off! *de* ~, wide, broad (*Meas.*). **largesse** (ʒɛs) *f*, liberality; bounty, largess[e]. **largeur** (ʒœ:r) *f*, breadth; width; beam (*ship*); gauge (*Rly. track*).

larguer (large) *v.t*, to let go, cast off, slip.

larix (lariks) *m*, larch [tree].

larme (larm) *f*, tear; drop (*of drink*). **larmier** (mje) *m*, drip-[stone]. **larmoiement** (mwamɑ̃) *m*, watering of the eyes. **larmoyant, e** (jɑ̃, ɑ̃:t) *a*, weeping; in tears; tearful; maudlin. **larmoyer** (je) *v.i*, to water; weep, shed tears.

larron (larɔ̃) *m*, thief.

larve (larv) *f*, larva, grub.

laryngite (larɛ̃ʒit) *f*, laryngitis. **larynx** (rɛ̃:ks) *m*, larynx.

las, asse (lɑ, ɑ:s) *a*, tired, weary.

lascif, ive† (lasif, i:v) *a*, lascivious, wanton.

lasser (lɑse) *v.t*, to tire; weary.

lasso (laso) *m*, lasso.

latent, e (latɑ̃, ɑ̃:t) *a*, latent, hidden.

latéral, e† (lateral) *a*, lateral, side (*att.*).

latex (latɛks) *m*, latex.

latin, e (latɛ̃, in) *a. & m*, Latin. ~ *de cuisine*, dog Latin.

latitude (latityd) *f*, latitude; scope.

latte (lat) *f*, lath. **latter** (te) *v.t*, to lath. **lattis** (ti) *m*, lathing.

laudanum (lodanɔm) *m*, laudanum.

laudatif, ive (lodatif, i:v) *a*, laudatory.

lauréat (lɔrea) *a.m*, laureate. ¶ *m*, prizeman; prize winner. **laurier** (rje) *m*, laurel, bay; (*pl, fig.*) laurels. ~*-rose*, *m*, oleander.

lavable (lavabl) *a*, washable. **lavabo** (bo) *m*, washstand; bath-room. **lavage** (va:ʒ) *m*, washing, w. out.

lavallière (lavaljɛ:r) *f*, Lavallière [neck]tie.

lavande (lavɑ̃:d) *f*, lavender.

lavasse (lavas) *f*, slops.

lave (la:v) *f*, lava.

lavement (lavmɑ̃) *m*, enema; washing (*hands, feet*).

laver (lave) *v.t*, to wash; w. out; scrub. ~ *la vaisselle*, to wash the dishes. **laverie** (vri) *f*, washhouse. **lavette** (vɛt) *f*, dish mop; dish cloth. **laveur, euse** (vœ:r, ø:z) *ŋ*, washer. *laveuse de linge*, washer-woman. *laveuse mécanique*, washing machine. **lavis** (vi) *m*, wash (*art*); wash drawing. **lavoir** (vwa:r) *m*, washhouse, scullery; washer (*Mach.*).

lawn-tennis (lɔntɛnis) *m*, lawn tennis.

laxatif, ive (laksatif, i:v) *a. & m*, laxative, aperient, opening (medicine).

layetier (lɛjtje) *m*, box maker. ~ *emballeur*, packing-case maker. **layette** (jɛt) *f*, baby linen, layette.

lazaret (lazarɛ) *m*, lazaret[to].

lazzi (lazi) *m*, buffoonery.

le, l'; la, l'; les (lə, l; la, l; le) *art*, the; a, an (*weight, etc.*). Often untranslated, as in *le paradis*, paradise. *l'enfer*, hell. *le Japon*, Japan. *la nature*, nature. *l'histoire*, history. *la France*, France. *les enfers*, Hades.

le, l'; la, l'; les (lə, l; la, l; le) *pn*, him; her; it; them; he; she; they; so.

lé (le) *m*, width(*of cloth*).

leader (lidœ:r) (*pers.*) *m*, leader (*political*).

lèche (lɛʃ) *f*, thin slice. **lèchefrite**

(frit) *f*, dripping pan. **lécher**
(leʃe) *v.t*, to lick; overelaborate.
~ *les vitrines*, to go window-
shopping.

leçon (ləsɔ̃) *f*, lesson; lecture; reading (*text*); story. ~ *de choses*,
object lesson.

lecteur, trice (lɛktœːr, tris) *n*,
reader. **lecture** (ty:r) *f*, reading;
perusal.

ledit, ladite, lesdits, lesdites
(lədi, ladit, ledi, ledit) *a*, the said
(*law*).

légal, e† (legal) *a*, legal; statutory;
lawful. **légaliser** (lize) *v.t*, to le-
galize.

légat (lega) *m*, legate. **légataire**
(tɛ:r) *n*, legatee. ~ *particulier*,
specific l. ~ *universel*, residuary l.
légation (sjɔ̃) *f*, legation.

lège (lɛ:ʒ) *a*, light (*Naut.*).

légendaire (leʒɑ̃dɛːr) *a*, legend-
ary, fabled. **légende** (ʒɑ̃:d) *f*, legend; characteristics, reference
note, explanatory note, signs &
symbols (*on map*).

léger, ère† (leʒe, ɛːr) *a*, light;
flighty, frivolous; fast; slight;
mild; weak (*tea, etc.*). ~ *à la
course*, fleet of foot. *à la légère*,
lightly, scantily; without due consideration. **légèreté** (ʒɛrte) *f*,
lightness; levity.

légion (leʒjɔ̃) *f*, legion. *ils s'appellent* ~, their name is legion.

législateur, trice (leʒislatœːr,
tris) *n*, legislator, lawgiver. **légis-
latif, ive** (tif, iːv) *a*, legislative;
parliamentary (*election*). **législation** (sjɔ̃) *f*, legislation. **législature** (ty:r) *f*, legislature. **légiste**
(ʒist) *m*, legist, lawyer. **légitime†**
(ʒitim) *a*, legitimate; lawful;
rightful. ~ *défense*, self-defense.
légitimer (me) *v.t*, to legitimatize;
legitimate; justify. **légitimité**
(mite) *f*, legitimacy, lawfulness.

legs (lɛg *ou* lɛ) *m*, legacy, bequest.
léguer (lege) *v.t*, to bequeath,
will, devise, leave.

légume (legym) *m*, vegetable. ~*s
légumes*, bigshots. **légumier** (mje)
m, vegetable dish. **légumineux,
euse** (minø, øːz) *a*, leguminous.
¶ *f*, legume[n], pulse.

leitmotiv (laitmɔtif) *m*, leitmotiv,
-if.

Léman (**le lac**) (lemɑ̃), the Lake
of Geneva, Lake Leman.

lendemain (lɑ̃dmɛ̃) *m*, next day,
day after, morrow; future. *sans*
~, short-lived.

Léningrad (leningrad) *m*, Leningrad.

lent, e† (lɑ̃, ɑ̃:t) *a*, slow; dilatory;
lingering; low (*fever, speed*). ¶ *f*,
nit. **lenteur** (lɑ̃tœːr) *f*, slowness.

lenticulaire (lɑ̃tikylɛːr) *a*, lenticular. **lentille** (tiːj) *f*, lentil;
lens; freckle; bob, ball. ~ *d'eau*,
~ *de marais*, duckweed.

lentisque (lɑ̃tisk) *m*, lentisk,
mastic [tree].

léonin, e (leɔnɛ̃, in) *a*, leonine;
one-sided.

léopard (leɔpaːr) *m*, leopard.

lépas (lepɑs) *m*, limpet.

lépidoptères (lepidɔptɛːr) *m.pl*,
Lepidoptera.

lèpre (lɛpr) *f*, leprosy. **lépreux,
euse** (leprø, øːz) *a*, leprous. ¶ *n*,
leper. **léproserie** (prozri) *f*, leper
hospital.

**lequel, laquelle, lesquels,
lesquelles** (ləkɛl, lakɛl, lekɛl)
pn, who; whom; which.

lèse-majesté (lɛzmaʒɛste) *f*,
[high] treason; lese-majesty. **léser** (leze) *v.t*, to injure; wrong.

lésiner (lezine) *v.i*, to be stingy,
haggle. **lésinerie** (nri) *f*, stinginess, meanness.

lésion (lezjɔ̃) *f*, lesion, injury, hurt.

lessive (lɛsiːv) *f*, washing; wash;
lye; detergent. **lessiver** (sive) *v.t*,
to wash; scrub, swill; leach. **les-
siveuse** (vøːz) *f*, wash boiler.

lest (lɛst) *m*, ballast.

leste† (lɛst) *a*, nimble; smart; flippant; free, indecorous.

lester (lɛste) *v.t*, to ballast. *se* ~
l'estomac, to line one's stomach.

léthargie (letarʒi) *f*, lethargy.
léthargique (ʒik) *a*, lethargic.
Léthé (lete) *m*, Lethe.

léthifère (letifɛːr) *a*, deadly,
lethal.

letton, one (letɔ̃, ɔn) *a.* & **L~,** *n*,
Lett; Latvian. **la Lettonie** (tɔni),
Latvia.

lettrage (lɛtraʒ) *m*, lettering.
lettre (tr) *f*, letter; note. ~
avion, airmail letter. ~ *close*
(*fig.*), sealed book. ~ *d'un autre
œil*, wrong font. ~ *de change*,

bill of exchange. ~ *de crédit*, ~ *de créance*, letter of credit. ~*s de créance*, credentials. ~ *de* [*faire*] *part*, notice announcing a birth, marriage, or death. ~*s de naturalisation*, naturalization papers. ~[*s*] *de service*, commission (*officer's*). ~ *de voiture*, consignment note. ~ *missive*, letter missive. ~ *moulée*, block letter. ~ *recommandée*, registered letter. *en toutes* ~, in full, fully. **lettré, e** (tre) *a. & n*, lettered, literate, well-read (*person*). **lettrine** (trin) *f*, drop letter (*Typ.*); catchword (*at head of dictionary page*).

leur (lœːr) *a*, their. **le** ~, **la**, ~ **les** ~**s**, *pn*, theirs.

leurre (lœːr) *m*, lure; catch (*fig.*). **leurrer** (lœre) *v.t*, to lure. **se** ~, to delude oneself.

levain (ləvɛ̃) *m*, leaven, yeast, barm. *sans* ~, unleavened.

levant (ləvɑ̃) *a.m*, rising (*sun*). ¶ *m*, east. *du* ~ *au couchant*, from east to west. **L**~, *m*, Levant.

levantin, e (tɛ̃, in) *a. & L*~, *n*, Levantine.

levé [**de plans**] (ləve) *m*, survey-[ing]. **levée** (ve) *f*, raising; lifting; lift; levy, removal; close (*sitting*); collection (*letters*); clearing (*letter box*); trick (*cards*); embankment; causeway. **lever** (ve) *m*, rising, getting up (*from bed*); rise (*sun*). ~ [*de plans*], survey[ing]. ~ *de rideau*, curtain raiser. ¶ *v.t*, to lift; hoist; raise; take up; remove; cut off; levy; clear (*letter box*); close (*sitting*); break up (*camp*); weigh (*anchor*); plot (*plan*); (*v.i.*) to rise; shoot (*plant*). *faire* ~, to raise, leaven (*dough*). **se**~, *v.pr.* & *abs*, to rise, get up; stand up.

léviathan (levjatɑ̃) *m*, leviathan.

levier (ləvje) *m*, lever; handspike.

lévite (levit) *m*, Levite; priest; satellite. **le Lévitique** (tik), Leviticus.

levraut (ləvro) *m*, leveret, young hare.

lèvre (lɛːvr) *f*, lip.

levrette (ləvrɛt) *f*, greyhound [bitch]. **lévrier** (levrie) *m*, greyhound. ~ *de la mer*), ocean greyhound (*fig.*). ~ *russe*, borzoi.

levure (ləvyːr) *f*, yeast, barm.

lexicographe (lɛksikɔgraf) *m*, lexicographer. **lexique** (sik) *m*, lexicon.

Leyde (lɛd) *f*, Leyden.

lézard (lezaːr) *m*, lizard.

lézarde (lezard) *f*, crack, crevice, chink. **lézarder** (de) *v.i*, to sun oneself. *v.t*, to crack, split (*plaster*). **se** ~, to crack, split.

liais (ljɛ) *m*, kind of Portland stone.

liaison (ljɛzɔ̃) *f*, connection; bond; liaison; slur (*Mus.*); tie (*Mus.*); thickening (*Cook.*). **liaisonner** (zɔne) *v.t*, to bond (*masonry*).

liane (ljan) *f*, liana, liane.

liant, e (ljɑ̃, ɑ̃ːt) *a*, pliant; sociable, responsive. ¶ *m*, pliancy.

liard (ljaːr) *m*, farthing (*fig.*), rap. **liarder** (arde) *v.i*, to haggle.

lias (ljɑ) *m*, lias (*Geol.*). **liasique** (azik) *a*, liassic.

liasse (ljas) *f*, bundle; file.

libation (libasjɔ̃) *f*, libation; drinking.

libelle (libɛl) *m*, libel.

libellé (libɛlle) *m*, drawing [up]; wording; particulars. **libeller** (le) *v.t*, to draw [up]; make; word.

libelliste (libɛllist) *m*, libeler.

libellule (libɛlyl) *f*, dragonfly.

libéral, e† (liberal) *a*, liberal, open-handed; learned (*profession*, in France such as médicin, avocat, notaire, not in the pay of the State, or under its control). ¶ *m*, liberal. **libéralisme** (lism) *m*, liberalism. **libéralité** (te) *f*, liberality.

libérateur, trice (liberatœːr, tris) *n*, liberator, deliverer. **libération** (sjɔ̃) *f*, liberation; discharge; release; paying up. **libérer** (re) *v.t*, to liberate. **liberté** (bɛrte) *f*, liberty, freedom. ~ [*de langage*], ~ *de parole*, outspokenness. ~ *de parler*, free-[dom of] speech.

libertin, e (libɛrtɛ̃, in) *a*, libertine, rakish; wayward. ¶ *m*, libertine, rake. **libertinage** (tinaːჳ) *m*, licentiousness; waywardness.

librairè (librɛːr) *m*, bookseller. ~-*éditeur*, b. & publisher. **librairie** (brɛri) *f*, book trade; bookstore; publishing house.

libre† (libr) *a*, free; at liberty, disengaged; available; vacant; spare; open; welcome; clear (*way*); unstamped (*paper*). ~ *arbitre*, *m*, free will. ~-*échange*, *m*, f. trade. ~-*échangiste* (eʃɑ̃ʒist) *m*, f. trader. ~ *parole*, f. speech. ~ *penseur*, freethinker. ~-*service*, self-service.

librettiste (librɛtist) *m*, librettist.

lice (lis) *f*, lists, arena; bitch hound; warp.

licence (lisɑ̃:s) *f*, license; licentiate's degree; leave; licentiousness. **licencié, e** (sɑ̃sje) *n*, licentiate, bachelor (*laws*, *arts*). **licencier** (sje) *v.t*, to disband (*troops*); dismiss, discharge. **licencieux, euse**† (sjø, ø:z) *a*, licentious, ribald.

lichen (likɛn) *m*, lichen.

licite† (lisit) *a*, licit, lawful.

licorne (likɔrn) *f*, unicorn.

licou (liku) *or poet.*, *before vowel*, **licol** (kɔl) *m*, halter (*harness*).

licteur (liktœːr) *m*, lictor.

lie (li) *f*, lees, dregs; offscourings, scum. **faire chère lie**, to live well.

lié, e (lje) *p.a*, bound, tied; intimate, thick.

liège (ljɛ:ʒ) *m*, cork.

lien (ljɛ̃) *m*, bond; tie; link; binder; strap. **lier** (lje) *v.t*, to bind; tie [up]; join; link; knit; connect; enter into; tie (*Mus.*); slur (*Mus.*); thicken (*sauce*).

lierre (ljɛ:r) *m*, ivy. ~ *terrestre*, ground i.

lieu (ljø) *m*, place; stead; ground[s]; occasion; (*s. & pl.*) spot; (*pl.*) premises. ~*x* [*d'aisance*] ou *petit* ~, watercloset, privy, latrine, john. ~*x communs*, commonplaces (*Rhet. & platitudes*). ~*x de pêche*, where to fish. *au* ~ *de*, instead of, in lieu of. *au* ~ *que*, whereas. *avoir* ~, to take place.

lieue (ljø) *f*, league (= 4 kilometers); mile(s) (*long way*). *d'une* ~, a mile off.

lieur (ljœːr) (*pers.*) *m. & lieuse* (ø:z) (*Mach.*) *f*, binder (*sheaf*).

lieutenant (ljøtnɑ̃) *m*, lieutenant; mate (*ship*). ~-*colonel*, lieutenant colonel. ~ *de vaisseau*, [naval] lieutenant.

lièvre (ljɛ:vr) *m*, hare.

ligament (ligamɑ̃) *m*, ligament. **ligature** (tyːr) *f*, ligature.

lige (liːʒ) *a. & vassal* ~, *m*, liege.

ligne (liɲ) *f*, line; rank. ~ *d'autobus*, bus route. ~ *de but*, *de touche*, goal, touch, l. (*Foot.*). ~ *de départ*, starting l.; scratch l. ~ *de faîte*, watershed. ~ *de flottaison* (flɔtɛzɔ̃), water line (*ship*). ~ *de fond*, *de côté*, *de service*, *médiane de service*, base, side, service, center service, l. (*Ten.*). ~ *supplémentaire*, ledger l. (*Mus.*).

lignée (liɲe) *f*, issue, line, stock.

ligneux, euse (liɲø, ø:z) *a*, ligneous, woody. **lignite** (ɲit) *m*, lignite.

ligoter (ligɔte) *v.t*, to bind, lash.

ligue (lig) *f*, league. **liguer** (ge) *v.t*, to l.

lilas (lilɑ) *m. & att*, lilac.

lilliputien, ne (lilipysjɛ̃, ɛn) *a*, Lilliputian.

limace (limas) *f*, slug (*Mol.*); Archimedean screw. **limaçon** (sɔ̃) *m*, snail (*Mol.*). *en* ~, spiral, winding.

limaille (limaːj) *f*, filings, dust.

limande (limɑ̃:d) *f*, dab (*fish*).

limbe (lɛ̃:b) *m*, limb (*Math.*); (*pl.*) limbo.

lime (lim) *f*, file (*tool*). **limer** (me) *v.t*, to file; polish (*fig.*).

limier (limje) *m*, bloodhound; sleuth-hound.

liminaire (liminɛ:r) *a*, prefatory.

limitation (limitasjɔ̃) *f*, limitation. ~*des naissances*, birth control. **limite** (mit) *f*, limit; bound[ary]. ~ *des neiges éternelles*, snow line. **limiter** (te) *v.t*, to limit; bound; restrict. **limitrophe** (trɔf) *a*, bordering.

limon (limɔ̃) *m*, mud, slime, ooze, silt; clay (*fig.*); string (*stairs*); shaft, thill (*cart*); lime (*citrus*). **limonade** (mɔnad) *f*, lemonade. ~ *gazeuse*, carbonated lemonade. ~ *non gazeuse*, still lemonade. **limonadier, ère** (dje, ɛ:r) *n*, light refreshment caterer, café keeper. **limoneux, euse** (nø, ø:z) *a*, muddy, slimy. **limonier** (nje) *m*, lime [tree] (*citrus*).

limousine (limuzin) *f*, limousine.

limpide (lɛ̃pid) *a*, limpid, clear, pellucid.

limure (limy:r) *f*, filing; filings.
lin (lẽ) *m*, flax; linen.
linceul (lẽsœl *ou* œ:j) *m*, shroud, winding sheet.
linéaire (linεε:r) *a*, linear; lineal.
linéament (neamã) *m*, lineament, feature; outline.
linge (lẽ:ʒ) *m*, linen; cloth. ~ *à thé*, tea cloth. ~ *de table*, table linen. **linger, ère** (lẽʒe, ε:r) *n*, lingerie maker; fancy draper; (*f*.) wardrobe keeper. **lingerie** (ʒri) *f*, fancy drapery, lingerie; linen room.
lingot (lẽgo) *m*, ingot; slug (*bullet & Typ*.).
lingual, e (lẽgwal) *a. & f*, lingual. **linguiste** (gɥist) *m*, linguist. **linguistique** (tik) *f*, linguistics.
linière (linjε:r) *a.f*, linen (*industry*). ¶ *f*, flax field.
liniment (linimã) *m*, liniment.
linoléum (linɔleɔm) *m*, linoleum. ~ *imprimé*, printed linoleum, oil-cloth. ~ *incrusté*, inlaid linoleum.
linon (linɔ̃) *m*, linon; lawn.
linot (lino) *m*, *ou* **linotte** (nɔt) *f*, linnet.
linotype (linɔtip) *a. & f*, linotype.
linteau (lẽto) *m*, lintel, transom.
lion (ljɔ̃) *m*, lion. ~ *marin*, sea l. **lionceau** (so) *m*, l. cub, l. whelp. **lionne** (ɔn) *f*, lioness; fury.
lippe (lip) *f*, thick underlip. *faire la* ~, to pout. **lippu, e** (py) *a*, thick-lipped.
liquéfaction (likefaksjɔ̃) *f*, liquefaction. **liquéfier** (fje) *v.t*, to liquefy. **liqueur** (kœ:r) *f*, liquor, drink; solution (*Chem*.). ~ *d'ammoniaque*, liquid ammonia, hartshorn. ~ [*de dessert*], liqueur. ~ *de ménage*, homemade wine. ~*s fortes*, strong drink. ~*s fraîches*, nonalcoholic drinks. ~ [*spiritueuse*], spirit.
liquidateur (likidatœ:r) *m*, liquidator. **liquidation** (sjɔ̃) *f*, liquidation, winding up; closing; settlement, account (*Stk Ex*.); [liquidation] sale, closing-down sale, selling off.
liquide (likid) *a*, liquid; wet (*goods*). *argent* ~, ready cash. ¶ *m*, liquid; fluid; liquor (*alcoholic*); (*f*.) liquid (*Gram*.).
liquider (likide) *v.t*, to liquidate;

wind up; close; settle; pay off; sell off.
liquoreux, euse (likɔrø, ø:z) *a*, sweet (*wine*). **liquoriste** (rist) *n*, wine & spirit merchant.
lire (li:r) *v.t. & abs. ir*, to read; hear from.
lis (lis) *m*, lily. ~ *tigré*, tiger lily.
Lisbonne (lizbɔn) *f*, Lisbon.
liseré (lizere) *m*, piping (*braid*); border.
liseron (lizrɔ̃) *ou* **liset** (ze) *m*, bindweed.
liseur, euse (lizœ:r, ø:z) *m*, reader. ~ *de pensées*, mind r. ¶ *f*, reading stand; bed jacket. **lisible†** (zibl) *a*, legible; readable (*interesting*).
lisière (lizjε:r) *f*, selvedge, list; leading-strings; border, edge, skirt.
lisse (lis) *a*, smooth; sleek; plain; flush. ¶ *f*, warp; rail (*ship*). **lisser** (se) *v.t*, to smooth. **lissoir** (swa:r) *m*, smoother.
liste (list) *f*, list, roll; panel (*jury*). ~ *des admis*, pass list (*exams*). ~ *électorale*, register of voters.
lit (li) *m*, bed; bedstead; layer; marriage; set (*of tide, etc*.). ~ *à colonnes*, four-poster. ~ *de douleur*, sick bed. *être exposé sur un* ~ *de parade*, to lie in state.
litanie (litani) *f*, rigmarole; (*pl*.) litany.
liteau (lito) *m*, stripe (*on cloth*); runner (*for shelf*); haunt (*wolves'*).
litée (lite) *f*, group (*collection of animals in the same den or lair*).
literie (litri) *f*, bedding.
litharge (litarʒ) *f*, litharge.
lithine (litin) *f*, lithia. **lithium** (tiɔm) *m*, lithium.
lithographe (litɔgraf) *m*, lithographer. **lithographie** (fi) *f*, lithography; lithograph. **lithographier** (fje) *v.t*, to lithograph. **lithographique** (fik) *a*, lithographic.
litière (litjε:r) *f*, litter (*straw & dung; also palanquin*).
litige (liti:ʒ) *m*, litigation; dispute. **litigieux, euse** (tiʒjø, ø:z) *a*, litigious; contentious.
litorne (litɔrn) *f*, fieldfare.
litre (litr) *m*, liter. = 1.75980

(about 1¾) pints; liter measure; liter bottle.

littéraire† (literɛːr) *a*, literary.

littéral, e† (literal) *a*, literal.

littérateur (literatœːr) *m*, literary man. **littérature** (tyːr) *f*, literature; learning; empty talk.

littoral, e (litɔral) *a*, littoral. ¶ *m*, littoral, seaboard.

Lit[h]uanie (la) (lityani), Lithuania.

liturgie (lityrʒi) *f*, liturgy.

liure (ljyːr) *f*, cart rope.

livide (livid) *a*, livid, ghastly.

Livourne (livurn) *f*, Leghorn.

livrable (livrabl) *a*, deliverable. ¶ (*Com.*) *m*, forward, terminal, [for] shipment; futures, options. **livraison** (vrɛzɔ̃) *f*, delivery; part, number (*publication*).

livre (liːvr) *f*, pound = ½ kilogram; franc. *Note.*—The word *livre* (meaning a present-day French franc) is still sometimes used, but almost exclusively in literature. ~ [*sterling*], pound [sterling]. *la* ~, sterling, the £.

livre (liːvr) *m*, book; journal; register; diary; day book. *grand* ~, ledger. ~ *à feuille[t]s mobiles*, looseleaf book. ~ *à succès*, ~ *à grand tirage*, bestseller. ~*s d'agrément*, light reading. ~ *d'exemples*, copybook. ~ *d'images*, picture b. ~ *d'office*, ~ *d'église*, ~ *de prières*, prayer b. ~ *de bord* & ~ *de loch*, log [b.]. ~ *de chevet*, favorite b. ~ *de lecture*, reader. ~ *de signatures*, autograph book. ~ *feint*, dummy book (*for bookshelf*). ~ *généalogique*, stud b.; herd b. ~ *de poche*, paperback book. *à* ~ *ouvert*, at sight. *faire un* ~, to make book (*betting*).

livrée (livre) *f*, livery; servants; badge.

livrer (livre) *v.t*, to deliver; d. up; surrender; consign; commit; confide; join, give (*battle*). ~ *par erreur*, to misdeliver.

livret (livrɛ) *m*, book (*small register*); handbook; libretto. ~ *militaire*, service record.

livreur, euse (livrœːr ∅ːz) *n*, delivery man or boy or girl.

lobe (lɔb) *m*, lobe.

lobélie (lɔbeli) *f*, lobelia.

local, e† (lɔkal) *a*, local. ¶ *m*. oft. *pl*, premises. **localiser** (lize) *v.t*, to place; localize. **localité** (te) *f*, locality, place. **locataire** (tɛːr) *n*, tenant, occupier; leaseholder; lodger; renter; hirer. **locatif, ive** (tif, iːv) *a*, tenant's (*repairs*); rental, letting (*value*). **location** (sjɔ̃) *f*, letting, renting, hire; reservation, booking; tenancy.

loch (lɔk) *m*, log (*float—ship's*).

loche (lɔʃ) *f*, loach (*fish*); slug (*Mol.*).

lock-out (lɔkaut) *m*, lockout.

locomobile (lɔkɔmɔbil) *f*, agricultural engine, traction e. **locomoteur, trice** (tœːr, tris) *a*, locomotive. **locomotion** (sjɔ̃) *f*, locomotion. **locomotive** (tiːv) *f*, locomotive, [railway] engine.

locuste (lɔkyst) *f*, locust; shrimp, prawn.

locution (lɔkysjɔ̃) *f*, phrase.

lof (lɔf) *m*, windward side (*ship*); luff. **lofer** (fe) *v.t*, to luff.

logarithme (lɔgaritm) *m*, logarithm.

loge (lɔːʒ) *f*, lodge (*porter's, freemasons'*); loggia; box (*Theat.*); dressing room (*actor's*); cage (*menagerie*); loculus. **logeable** (lɔʒabl) *a*, tenantable, [in]habitable. **logement** (ʒmɑ̃) *m*, lodging, housing, billeting; accommodation, quarters. **loger** (ʒe) *v.i. & t*, to lodge, live; stay; accommodate; house; billet; stable. **logeur, euse** (ʒœːr, ∅ːz) *n*, landlord, -lady, lodging-house keeper.

logicien (lɔʒisjɛ̃) *m*, logician. **logique**† (ʒik) *a*, logical. ¶ *f*, logic.

logis (lɔʒi) *m*, house, home.

loi (lwa) *f*, law; enactment; statute; act; standard (*of coin*). *hors la* ~, outlaw.

loin (lwɛ̃) *ad*, far, f. away, f. off; f. back; afar; afield; a long way. ~ *de compte*, out of one's reckoning, wide of the mark. **lointain, e** (tɛ̃, ɛn) *a*, remote, far off, distant. ¶ *m*, distance.

loir (lwaːr) *m*, dormouse.

loisible (lwazibl) *a*, permissible. **loisir** (ziːr) *m. oft. pl*, leisure, [spare] time. *à* ~, *ad*, at leisure.

lombaire (lɔ̃bɛːr) *a*, lumbar.

Lombardie (la) (lɔ̃bardi), Lombardy.

lombes (lɔ̃:b) *m.pl*, loins.

londonien, ne (lɔ̃dɔnjɛ̃, ɛn) *a*, London. **L~, n,** Londoner. **Londres** (lɔ̃:dr) *m*, London.

long, ongue (lɔ̃, ɔ̃:g) *a*, long; lengthy; slow, dilatory. *long échange,* rally (*Ten.*). *à la longue,* in the long run, in the end. ¶ *m,* length. *au ~,* at length, at large. *au ~ & au large,* far & wide. *de ~,* long (*Meas.*). *de ~ en large,* to & fro, up & down. *en ~,* lengthways. *le ~ de,* along; alongside. [*syllabe*] *longue, f,* long [syllable].

longanimité (lɔ̃ganimite) *f,* long-suffering, forbearance.

long-courrier (lɔ̃kurje) *m,* ocean-going ship. **long cours, m,** deep-sea navigation; ocean (*or* foreign) voyage.

longe (lɔ̃:ʒ) *f,* lead rope (*attached to halter*); leading rein; tether; loin (*veal*).

longer (lɔ̃ʒe) *v.t,* to run along, skirt.

longévité (lɔ̃ʒevite) *f,* longevity.

longitude (lɔ̃ʒityd) *f,* longitude. **longitudinal, e**† (dinal) *a,* longitudinal.

longtemps (lɔ̃tɑ̃) *ad,* long; a long while. **longuement** (lɔ̃gmɑ̃) *ad,* long; lengthily. **longuet, te** (gɛ, ɛt) *a,* longish. **longueur** (gœ:r) *f,* length; lengthiness; delay. *en ~,* lengthways; slowly. **longue-vue** (lɔ̃gvy) *f,* telescope, spyglass.

lopin (lɔpɛ̃) *m,* patch, plot (*of ground*), allotment.

loquace (lɔkwas) *a,* loquacious, talkative, garrulous. **loquacité** (site) *f,* loquacity.

logue (lɔk) *f,* rag, tatter.

loquet (lɔkɛ) *m,* latch (*door*). **loqueteau** (kto) *m,* catch (*window*).

loqueteux, euse (lɔktø, ø:z) *a. & n,* ragged (person).

lord (lɔ:r) *m,* lord (*Eng.*).

lorgner (lɔrɲe) *v.t,* to quiz; eye; ogle, leer at. **lorgnette[s] de spectacle** (ɲɛt) *f.* [*pl.*], opera glass[es]. **lorgnon** (ɲɔ̃) *m,* eyeglasses, pince-nez.

loriot (lɔrjo) *m,* [golden] oriole.

lors (lɔ:r) *ad,* then. *~ de,* at the time of. *~ même que,* even though. **lorsque** (lɔrskə) *c,* when.

losange (lɔzɑ̃:ʒ) (*Geom.*) *m,* lozenge, rhomb[us], diamond.

lot (lo) *m,* lot; portion; prize (*lottery*). *gros ~,* jackpot. **loterie** (lɔtri) *f,* lottery; sweepstake[s]; raffle, draw; gamble.

lotion (lɔsjɔ̃) *f,* lotion; washing.

lotir (lɔti:r) *v.t,* to allot, parcel out. *bien loti,* lucky. **lotissement** (tismɑ̃) *m,* allotment; development (*land*).

loto (lɔto) *m,* lotto (*game*).

lotus (lɔty:s) *ou* **lotos** (tos) *m,* lotus.

louable (lwabl) *a,* laudable, praiseworthy; deserving of praise.

louage (lwa:ʒ) *m,* letting, renting, hiring; hire.

louange (lwɑ̃:ʒ) *f,* praise; commendation. **louanger** (ɑ̃ʒe) *v.t,* to laud [to the skies].

louche (luʃ) *a,* cross-eyed, squint-[ing]; cloudy; shady, suspicious. ¶ *f,* soup ladle. **loucher** (ʃe) *v.i,* to squint.

louer (lwe) *v.t,* to let [out], rent, hire; reserve, book; praise, laud. *à ~,* to [be] let; for hire. *se ~ de,* to be pleased with. **loueur (euse) de chaises** (lwœ:r, ø:z), chair attendant.

lougre (lu:gr) *m,* lugger (*Naut.*).

louis (lwi) *m,* louis (*old gold coin* = 20 *present-day francs*).

Louisiane (lwizjan) *f,* Louisiana.

loulou (lulu) *m,* Pomeranian [dog], pom.

loup (lu) *m,* wolf; waster. **loup-cervier** (sɛrvje) *m,* [common] lynx (*N. Europe*). *~ de mer* (*pers.*), hard-bitten sailor, old salt, [jack] tar.

loupe (lup) *f,* wen (*Med.*); bur[r] (*on tree*); lens, [magnifying] glass. **louper** (pe) *v.i,* to slack; (*v.t.*) to botch.

loup-garou (lugaru) *m,* werewolf; bugbear; bear (*pers.*).

lourd, e† (lu:r, urd) *a,* heavy; weighty; dull; sluggish; close (*weather*). **lourdaud, e** (lurdo, o:d) *n,* lubber, lout, bumpkin, dolt, fathead, oaf. **lourdeur** (dœːr) *f*, heaviness.

loustic (lustik) *m*, wag, funny man.

loutre (lutr) *f*, otter.

louve (luːv) *f*, [she-]wolf; lewis. **louveteau** (luvto) *m*, wolf cub (*Zool. & scouting*).

louvoyer (luvwaje) *v.i*, to tack [about].

lover (love) *v.t*, to coil (*rope*).

loyal, e† (lwajal) *a*, honest, straight[forward]; fair; true, loyal. **loyalisme** (lism) *m*, loyalty, allegiance (*to sovereign*); loyalism. **loyaliste** (list) *a. & n*, loyalist. **loyauté** (jote) *f*, honesty, etc.

loyer (lwaje) *m*, rent; hire; price; wages.

lubie (lybi) *f*, whim, crotchet, vagary, fad, kink.

lubricité (lybrisite) *f*, lubricity, lewdness. **lubrifier** (fje) *v.t*, to lubricate, grease. **lubrique** (brik) *a*, lewd, wanton.

lucarne (lykarn) *f*, dormer [window].

lucide (lysid) *a*, lucid, clear. **lucidité** (dite) *f*, lucidity.

luciole (lysjɔl) *f*, firefly; glowworm.

Lucques (lyk) *f*, Lucca.

lucratif, ive (lykratif, iːv) *a*, lucrative. **lucre** (lykr) *m*, lucre, pelf, gain.

luette (lɥɛt) *f*, uvula.

lueur (lɥœːr) *f*, glimmer; gleam; glimpse; spark.

luge (lyːʒ) *f*, luge. **luger** (lyʒe) *v.i*, to luge.

lugubre† (lygyːbr) *a*, lugubrious, doleful, gloomy.

lui, leur (lɥi, lœːr) *pn*, [to] him, her, it, them; at him, etc.

lui, eux (lɥi, ø) *pn.m*, he, it, they; him, it, them. *lui-même, eux-mêmes*, himself, itself, themselves.

luire (lɥiːr) *v.i.ir*, to shine, gleam. **luisant, e** (lɥizɑ̃, ɑ̃ːt) *a*, shining, gleaming; bright; glossy. ¶ *m*, shine, gloss, sheen.

lumbago (lɔ̃bago) *m*, lumbago.

lumière (lymjɛːr) *f*, light; luminary (*pers.*); [port] hole; oil hole; spout hole; hole; vent; mouth; throat; (*pl.*) understanding, insight; (*pl.*) enlightenment. ~ **éclair**, flash (*Phot.*). ~ **magnésique** (maɲezik), magnesium light. **lumignon** (miɲɔ̃) *m*, snuff (*wick*); candle end; dim light. **luminaire** (nɛːr) *m*, luminary; light; lights; lights. **lumineux, euse**† (nø, øːz) *a*, luminous; bright.

lunaire (lynɛːr) *a*, lunar. ¶ *f*, honesty (*Bot.*).

lunatique (lynatik) *a. & n*, whimsical (person).

lundi (lœ̃di) *m*, Monday.

lune (lyn) *f*, moon. ~ **de miel**, honeymoon; threshold (*fig.*). *clair de* ~, moonlight.

lunetier (lyntje) *m*, spectacle maker, optician. **lunette** (nɛt) *f*, (*pl.*) spectacles, glasses, goggles; wishing bone, merrythought; rim (*watch*). ~ [*d'approche*], [refracting] telescope. ~ **de repère**, finder. ~*s en écaille*, horn-rimmed spectacles.

lupin (lypɛ̃) *m*, lupin[e] (*Bot.*).

lupus (lypyːs) *m*, lupus.

lurette (lyrɛt) *f*: *il y a belle* ~ *que*, it is ages since.

luron (lyrɔ̃) *m*, jolly sturdy fellow. **luronne** (rɔn) *f*, jovial stout-hearted woman.

lusin (lyzɛ̃) *m*, marline.

lustre (lystr) *m*, luster; gloss; foil (*fig.*); chandelier. **lustrer** (tre) *v.t*, to luster; gloss; glaze.

lut (lyt) *m*, lute (*cement*). **luter** (te) *v.t*, to lute.

luth (lyt) *m*, lute (*Mus.*). **lutherie** (tri) *f*, musical instrument making.

luthérien, ne (lyterjɛ̃, ɛn) *a. & n*, Lutheran.

luthier (lytje) *m*, musical instrument maker.

lutin, e (lytɛ̃, in) *a*, roguish, impish. ¶ *m*, [hob]goblin, sprite, elf, imp. **lutiner** (tine) *v.t. & i*, to plague, tease.

lutrin (lytrɛ̃) *m*, lectern, reading desk.

lutte (lyt) *f*, wrestling; struggle; fight, contest, tussle, fray. ~ *à la corde*, tug of war. ~ *libre*, no holds barred. **lutter** (te) *v.i*, to wrestle; struggle, fight, contend; vie. **lutteur** (tœːr) *m*, wrestler.

luxation (lyksasjõ) *f*, dislocation (*Surg.*).
luxe (lyks) *m*, luxury; sumptuousness; profusion.
Luxembourg (lyksãbu:r) *m*, Luxemburg.
luxer (lykse) *v.t*, to dislocate.
luxueux, euse (lyksɥø, ø:z) *a*, luxurious. **luxure** (ksy:r) *f*, lust. **luxuriant, e** (ksyrjã, ã:t) *a*, luxuriant, lush, rank. **luxurieux, euse** (rjø, ø:z) *a*, lustful, lewd.
luzerne (lyzɛrn) *f*, alfalfa.
lycée (lise) *m*, secondary school. **lycéen, ne** (seẽ, ɛn) *n*, student (*at a lycée*), schoolboy, -girl.
lymphe (lẽ:f) *f*, lymph; sap.
lyncher (lẽʃe) *v.t*, to lynch.
lynx (lẽ:ks) *m*, lynx.
Lyon (ljõ) *m*, Lyons.
lyre (li:r) *f*, lyre. **& toute la ~,** & all the rest of it. **lyrique** (lirik) *a*, lyric; lyrical; opera (*house*). ¶ *m*, lyric poet. **lyrisme** (rism) *m*, lyricism.

M

ma *see* **mon**.
macabre (makɑ:br) *a*, macabre; grim, gruesome, ghastly.
macadam (makadam) *m*, macadam. **macadamiser** (mize) *v.t*, to macadamize.
macaque (makak) *m*, macaco, macaque.
macareux (makarø) *m*, puffin.
macaron (makarõ) *m*, macaroon.
macaroni (makarɔni) *m*, macaroni.
macédoine (masedwan) *f*, macédoine, salad (*fruit*); medley.
macérer (masere) *v.t*, to macerate.
mâchefer (mɑʃfɛ:r) *m*, clinker.
mâcher (mɑʃe) *v.t*, to chew; masticate; champ (*bit*). **ne pas le ~,** not to mince matters. **mâcheur, euse** (ʃœ:r, ø:z) *n*, chewer.
machiavélique (makjavelik) *a*, Machiavellian.
machin (maʃẽ) *m*, thing, gadget; what's-his-name.
machinal, e† (maʃinal) *a*, mechanical (*fig.*). **machination** (sjõ) *f*, machination. **machine** (ʃin) *f*,

machine; (*pl.*) machinery; engine; gadget. **~ à coudre,** sewing machine. **~ à écrire,** typewriter. **~ à vapeur,** steam engine. **~ -outil,** *f*, machine tool. **~ routière,** traction engine. **machiner** (ne) *v.t*, to scheme, plot. **machinerie** (nri) *f*, machinery; engine room, e. house. **machinisme** (nism) *m*, mechanization. **machiniste** (nist) *m*, scene shifter; engineer; bus driver.
mâchoire (mɑʃwa:r) *f*, jaw.
mâchonner (mɑʃɔne) *v.t*, to chew; mumble.
mâchurer (mɑʃyre) *v.t*, to black, smudge.
macis (masi) *m*, mace (*spice*).
macle (makl) *f*, twin (*crystal*).
maçon (masõ) *m*, mason; bricklayer. **maçonnage** (sɔnaːʒ) *m*, masonry; brickwork. **maçonner** (ne) *v.t*, to mason; brick up. **maçonnerie** (nri) *f*, masonry; stonework; brickwork. **maçonnique** (nik) *a*, masonic.
macule (makyl) *f*, spot, stain; sun spot, macula. **maculer** (le) *v.t. & i*, to stain; offset (*Typ.*).
madame, *oft.* **M~** (madam) *f*, madam; Mrs.; mistress; lady.
madeleine (madlɛn) *f*, sponge cake.
mademoiselle, *oft.* **M~** (madmwazɛl) *f*, Miss; lady; waitress!
Madère (madɛ:r) *f*, Madeira.
madone (madɔn) *f*, madonna.
madras (madra[:s]) *m*, madras (*fabric*).
madré, e (mɑdre) *a*, speckled, spotted; bird's-eye (*maple*); crafty, deep.
madrépore (madrepɔ:r) *m*, madrepore.
madrier (madrie) *m*, plank.
madrigal (madrigal) *m*, madrigal.
mafflu, e (mafly) *a*, heavycheeked.
magasin (magazẽ) *m*, shop; store[s]; warehouse; magazine. **~ à prix unique,** one-price shop; five and ten. **~ à succursales multiples,** chain store. **~ général,** bonded warehouse. **en ~,** in stock. **magasinage** (zinaːʒ) *m*, warehousing, storage. **magasinier** (nje) *m*, storekeeper, ware-

houseman. **magazine** (zin) *m*, magazine (*periodical*).

mages (ma:ʒ) *m.pl*, Magi.

magicien, ne (maʒisjɛ̃, ɛn) *n*, magician; wizard; sorcerer. **magie** (ʒi) *f*, magic, wizardry; witchery. ~ *noire*, black magic, b. art. **magique** (ʒik) *a*, magic(al).

magister (maʒistɛːr) *m*, pedagogue. **magistère** (tɛːr) *m*, dictatorship. **magistral, e†** (tral) *a*, magisterial; masterly; masterful. **magistrat** (tra) *m*, magistrate; judge. **magistrature** (tyːr) *f*, magistracy. ~ *assise*, bench. ~ *debout*, body of public prosecutors.

magnanerie (maɲanri) *f*, silkworm nursery; s. breeding.

magnanime† (maɲanim) *a*, magnanimous. **magnanimité** (mite) *f*, magnanimity.

magnat (magna) *m*, magnate (*Fin.*, *etc.*).

magnésie (maɲezi) *f*, magnesia. **magnésium** (zjɔm) *m*, magnesium.

magnétique (maɲetik) *a*, magnetic; mesmeric. **magnétisation** (zasjɔ̃) *f*, magnetization (*Phys.*). **magnétiser** (ze) *v.t*, to mesmerize, magnetize (*fig.*). **magnétiseur** (zœːr) *m*, mesmerizer. **magnétisme** (tism) *m*, magnetism (*Phys. & fig.*); magnetics; mesmerism. **magnéto** (to) *f*, magneto. ~-**électrique**, *a*, magneto-electric.

magnificat (magnifikat) *m*, magnificat.

magnificence (maɲifisɑ̃ːs) *f*, magnificence; grandeur; (*pl.*) lavishness; (*pl.*) fine things. **magnifier** (fje) *v.t*, to magnify (*the Lord*). **magnifique†** (fik) *a*, magnificent, splendid, grand, fine; munificent.

magnolia (magnɔlja) *m*, magnolia.

magot (mago) *m*, magot (*ape & Chinese figure*); Barbary ape; fright (*pers.*); hoard.

mahométan, e (maɔmetɑ̃, an) *n, & att*, Mohammedan, Moslem, Muslim. **mahométisme** (tism) *m*, Mohammedanism.

mai (mɛ) *m*, May (*month*); maypole.

maigre (mɛːgr) *a*, lean; meager; scanty; thin; skinny; straggling (*beard*); poor; spare; meatless (*meal*); fast (*day*); vegetable (*soup*). ¶ *m*, lean. **maigrelet, te** (mɛgrəlɛ, ɛt) *a*, thinnish, slight. **maigrement** (grəmɑ̃) *ad*, meagerly, scantily. **maigreur** (grœːr) *f*, leanness. **maigrir** (griːr) *v.i*, to grow thin; (*v.t.*) to [make] thin.

maille (maːj) *f*, stitch (*Knit., crochet, etc.*); mesh; speckle; bud; (*pl.*) mail (*armor*). ~ *échappée*, ~ *perdue*, run (*stocking*); dropped stitch (*Knit.*). ~ *glissée*, slip stitch (*Knit.*).

maillechort (majʃɔːr) *m*, German silver.

maillet (majɛ) *m*, mallet. **mailloche** (jɔʃ) *f*, mallet, maul.

maillon (majɔ̃) *m*, link (*chain*); shackle.

maillot (majo) *m*, swaddling clothes (*baby*); tights, *or* any close-fitting woven garment, as (*bathing, swimming*) costume, suit, dress; (*football*) jersey; (*running*) zephyr.

main (mɛ̃) *f*, hand; hand[writing]; handle (*drawer*); scoop; tendril; quire (*in Fr. 25 sheets*); trick (*cards*); lead (*cards*); deal (*cards*). ~ *courante*, handrail. ~-*d'œuvre*, workmanship; labor. ~-*forte*, assistance (to police).

mainmise (mɛ̃miːz) *f*, hold (*influence*).

mainmorte (mɛ̃mɔrt) *f*, mortmain. *biens de* ~, property in mortmain.

maint, e (mɛ̃, ɛ̃ːt) *a*, many a, many.

maintenant (mɛ̃tnɑ̃) *ad*, now. **maintenir** (tniːr) *v.t.ir*, to maintain, keep; uphold. *se* ~, to keep; hold one's own. **maintien** (tjɛ̃) *m*, maintenance, keeping; deportment, bearing.

maïolique (majɔlik) *f*, majolica.

maire (mɛːr) *m*, mayor. **mairie** (mɛri) *f*, mayoralty; town hall, town clerk's office, registry [office].

mais (mɛ) c. & ad, but; why. ~ non! why no! not at all! ¶ m, but, objection.

maïs (mais) m, maize, Indian corn.

maison (mɛzɔ̃) f, house; home; household; firm; friary; convent. ~ d'aliénés, mental institution. ~ d'arrêt, prison, jail; lockup; guardhouse. ~ d'éducation, educational establishment. ~ d'habitation, dwelling house. ~ de commerce, business house, firm. ~ de correction, reformatory. ~ de jeu, gaming house. ~ de plaisance, weekend cottage. ~ de rapport, revenue-earning house. ~ de retraite, home for the aged. ~ de santé, nursing home. ~ de ville, town hall. ~ des étudiants, hostel. ~ isolée, detached house. ~ jumelle, semi-detached house. ~ pour fournitures (de sports, etc.), outfitter. à la ~, [at] home, indoors. **maisonnée** (zɔne) f, household, family. **maisonnette** (nɛt) f, bungalow.

maistrance (mɛstrɑ̃ːs) f, petty officers (Nav.). **maître** (mɛːtr) m, master; teacher; Mr. (courtesy title of lawyers); petty officer. ~-autel, high altar. ~ chanteur, blackmailer. ~-coq (ship's). ~ d'armes, fencing master. ~ [d'équipage], boatswain; master of the hounds. ~ d'hôtel, [house] steward; headwaiter; superintendent (restaurant). ~ de chapelle, choirmaster. ~ de conférences, lecturer. ~ de forges, ironmaster. ~ de timonerie, quartermaster (Naut.). ~ des cérémonies, Master of the Ceremonies. ~ drain, main drain. ~ homme, masterful man. ~ Jacques, Jack of all work or trades. ~ sot, champion idiot. **maîtresse** (mɛtrɛs) f, mistress; paramour. ~ de piano, piano teacher. ~ femme, masterful woman. ~ poutre, main beam. **maîtrise** (triːz) f, mastery; control; choir. **maîtriser** (trize) v.t, to [over]master; overpower; subdue; control.

majesté (maʒɛste) f, majesty; stateliness. Sa M~, His (or Her)

Majesty. **majestueux, euse†** (tɥø, øːz) a, majestic; stately.

majeur, e (maʒœːr) a, major; greater. être ~, to come of [full] age (law). le lac Majeur, Lago Maggiore.

majolique (maʒɔlik) f, majolica.

major (maʒɔːr) (Mil.) m, adjutant; medical officer. état-~, staff. **majoration** (ʒɔrasjɔ̃) f, increase (price); overvaluation; overcharge. **majordome** (dɔm), majordomo; comptroller of the Royal Household. **majorer** (re) v.t, to increase (price); overvalue; overcharge for or in. **majorité** (rite) f, majority.

Majorque (maʒɔrk) f, Majorca.

majuscule (maʒyskyl) a. & f, capital (letter).

mal (mal) m, evil; ill; wrong; harm; hurt; mischief; difficulty; damage; pain; ache; sore; ailment; trouble; disease; illness, sickness. j'ai ~ au doigt, I have a sore finger. ~ aux yeux, ~ d'yeux, eye trouble, sore eyes. ~ blanc, gathering sore. ~ d'enfant, labor [pains]. ~ de cœur, sickness, qualms. ~ de dents, ~ aux dents, toothache. ~ de gorge, sore throat. ~ de mer, seasickness. avoir le ~ de mer, to be seasick. ~ de tête, headache. ~ du pays, homesickness. ¶ ad, ill; badly; evil; wrong; amiss. ~ famé, e, ill-famed. ~ gérer, to mismanage. ~ réussir, to fail, turn out badly. mal venu, e, stunted; ill-advised. de ~ en pis, from bad to worse. ~ ¶ a. inv, bad.

malachite (malakit) f, malachite.

malade (malad) a, ill, sick, unwell; diseased; bad, sore; in a bad way. ¶ n, sick person; invalid; patient. ~ du dehors, out-patient. ~ interné, e, in-patient. faire le ~ ou simuler la maladie, to malinger. **maladie** (di) f, illness, sickness, complaint, disease, disorder; obsession. ~ de langueur, decline. ~ [des chiens], distemper. ~ du sommeil, sleeping sickness. ~ professionnelle, industrial disease. **maladif, ive** (dif, iːv) a, sickly; morbid.

maladresse (maladrɛs) *f*, awkwardness, clumsiness. **maladroit**, e† (drwa, at) *a*. & *n*, awkward, clumsy (person), maladroit.

malais, e (malɛ, ɛːz) *a*. & **M~**, *n*, Malay[an].

malaise (malɛːz) *m*, indisposition; uneasiness; straits. **malaisé**, e (lɛze) *a*, difficult; not easy; awkward. **malaisément** (mã) *ad*, with difficulty.

Malaisie (la) (malɛzi), Malaysia.

malandrin (malãdrɛ̃) *m*, bandit.

malappris, e (malapri, iːz) *a*. & *n*, ill-bred (person).

malaria (malarja) *f*, malaria.

malart (malaːr) *m*, mallard.

malavisé, e (malavize) *a*, ill-advised; unwise.

malaxer (malakse) *v.t*, to mix; work up (*butter*).

malbâti, e (malbati) *a*. & *n*, misshapen (person).

malchance (malʃãːs) *f*, ill luck; mischance. **malchanceux, euse** (ʃãsø, øːz) *a*. & *n*, unlucky (person).

maldonne (maldɔn) *f*, misdeal (*cards*).

mâle (mɑːl) *m*. & *a*, male; he; cock; buck; bull; dog; man (*child*); masculine; manly, virile.

malédiction (malediksjɔ̃) *f*, malediction, curse.

maléfice (malefis) *m*, [evil] spell.

malencontreux, euse† (malãkɔ̃trø, øːz) *a*, untoward, unlucky, unfortunate.

mal-en-point (malãpwɛ̃) *ad*, in a bad way, in a sorry plight.

malentendu (malãtãdy) *m*, misunderstanding, misapprehension, misconception.

malfaçon (malfasɔ̃) *f*, bad workmanship.

malfaisant, e (malfəzã, ãːt) *a*, malicious; injurious. **malfaiteur** (fɛtœːr) *m*, malefactor, evildoer. ~ *public*, public menace (*pers*.).

malfamé, e (malfame) *a*, ill-famed.

malformation (malfɔrmasjɔ̃) *f*, malformation.

malgracieux, euse (malgrasjø, øːz) *a*, ungracious, rude.

malgré (malgre) *pr*, in spite of, notwithstanding. ~ *tout*, for all that.

malhabile† (malabil) *a*, unskillful; tactless.

malheur (malœːr) *m*, misfortune; ill luck; unhappiness; evil days; woe. **malheureux, euse**† (lœrø, øːz) *a*, unlucky; unfortunate; unhappy, miserable; woeful; sad; wretched; pitiful. ¶ *n*, unfortunate [person]; wretch.

malhonnête† (malɔnɛːt) *a*, dishonest; rude, ill-mannered, unmannerly. **malhonnêteté** (nɛtte) *f*, dishonesty; rudeness.

malice (malis) *f*, malice, spite; artfulness; roguishness; practical joke. **malicieux, euse**† (sjø, øːz) *a*, malicious, spiteful; roguish, arch.

malignité (maliɲite) *f*, malignity; maliciousness; mischievousness (*playful*). **malin, igne**† (lɛ̃, iɲ) *a*. & *n*, malicious; malignant; evil (*spirit*); mischievous, wicked, roguish; artful (person). *le malin* [*esprit*], the Evil One.

maline (malin) *f*, spring tide.

malines (malin) *f*, Mechlin [lace].

malingre (malɛ̃ːgr) *a*, sickly, puny.

malintentionné, e (malɛ̃tãsjone) *a*. & *n*, evil-disposed (person).

malitorne (malitɔrn) *m*, lout.

mal-jugé (malʒyʒe) *m*, miscarriage of justice.

malle (mal) *f*, trunk; mail (*post*); mail steamer; m. boat; m. packet. ~*-armoire*, wardrobe trunk. ~ *de paquebot*, ~ *de cabine*, cabin t. ~[-*poste*], mail [coach] (*stage*).

malléable (malleabl) *a*, malleable.

malléole (malleɔl) *f*, ankle [bone].

malletier (maltje) *m*, trunk & bag manufacturer. **mallette** (lɛt) *f*, suitcase; attaché c. ~ *garnie*, dressing c., fitted c.

malmener (malməne) *v.t*, to abuse; maul, handle roughly.

malotru, e (malɔtry) *n*, ill-bred person.

malpeigné (malpɛɲe) *m*, unkempt fellow.

malpropre† (malprɔpr) *a*, dirty;

indecent. **malpropreté** (prəte) *f*, dirtiness, etc.

malsain, e (malsɛ̃, ɛn) *a*, unhealthy; noisome; unwholesome; insanitary, unsanitary.

malséant, e (malseɑ̃, ɑ̃ːt) *a*, unbecoming, unseemly.

malsonnant, e (malsɔnɑ̃, ɑ̃ːt) *a*, offensive (*words*).

malt (malt) *m*, malt.

maltais, e (maltɛ, ɛːz) *a.* & M~, *n*, Maltese. **Malte** (malt) *f*, Malta.

malterie (maltəri) *f*, malting, malt house.

maltôte (maltoːt) *f*, extortion (*taxes*).

maltraiter (maltrɛte) *v.t*, to maltreat, ill-treat, ill-use, misuse; wrong.

malveillance (malvɛjɑ̃ːs) *f*, malevolence, ill will, spite. **malveillant, e** (jɑ̃, ɑ̃ːt) *a.* & *n*, malevolent, ill-disposed (person).

malvenu, e (malvəny) *a*, stunted; ill-advised.

malversation (malvɛrsasjɔ̃) *f*, malpractice, embezzlement, peculation.

mamamouchi (mamamuʃi) *m*, panjandrum.

maman (ma- *ou* mɑ̃mɑ̃) *f*, mama.

mamelle (mamɛl) *f*, breast; udder. **mamelon** (mlɔ̃) *m*, nipple, teat; hummock, mamelon, pap.

mamel[o]uk (mamluk) *m*, Mameluke (*Hist.*); henchman, myrmidon.

mamillaire (mamillɛːr) *a*, mamillary.

mammifère (mamifɛːr) *m*, mammal, (*pl.*) mammalia.

mammouth (mamut) *m*, mammoth.

mamours (mamuːr) *m.pl*, caresses, billing & cooing.

manant (manɑ̃) *m*, boor, churl.

manche (mɑ̃ːʃ) *m*, handle, helve, haft; stick (*umbrella*); neck (*violin*); knuckle [bone] (*mutton*). ~ *à balai*, broomstick. ¶ *f*, sleeve; hose (*pipe*); channel; game, hand (*cards*); set (*Ten.*). ~ *à air*, ~ *à vent*, ventilator (*ship*). ~ *de chemise*, shirt sleeve. la M~, the [English] Channel. **manchette** (mɑ̃ʃɛt) *f*, cuff (*dress*); ruffle; headline (*news*). **man-**

chon (ʃɔ̃) *m*, muff (*ladies'*); coupling (*Mach.*); sleeve; socket; bush[ing]; mantle (*gas*). ~ *d'embrayage*, clutch.

manchot, e (mɑ̃ʃo, ɔt) *a.* & *n*, one-handed *or* one-armed (person); (*m.*) penguin.

mandant (mɑ̃dɑ̃) *m*, principal, mandator.

mandarin (mɑ̃darɛ̃) *m*, mandarin. **mandarine** (rin) *f*, mandarin[e] [orange], tangerine [orange].

mandat (mɑ̃da) *m*, mandate; order; instructions; trust; procuration, power [of attorney], proxy; order [to pay], money order, withdrawal notice; writ, warrant (*law*). ~[-*poste*], money order, postal o. **mandataire** (tɛːr) *m*, mandatary, -ory; agent; attorney; proxy. **mandater** (te) *v.t*, to authorize [the payment of]; commission.

mandement (mɑ̃dmɑ̃) *m*, charge, pastoral letter. **mander** (de) *v.t*, to tell; inform.

mandibule (mɑ̃dibyl) *f*, mandible; jaw.

mandoline (mɑ̃dɔlin) *f*, mandolin.

mandragore (mɑ̃dragɔːr) *f*, mandrake.

mandrill (mɑ̃dril) *m*, mandrill (*Zool.*).

mandrin (mɑ̃drɛ̃) *m*, mandrel, -il; spindle; arbor; chuck (*lathe*); drift[pin].

manège (manɛːʒ) *m*, training (*horses*); horsemanship, riding; r. school; horse gear; trick. ~ *de chevaux de bois*, merry-go-round.

mânes (mɑːn) *m.pl*, manes, shades.

manette (manɛt) *f*, handle, lever.

manganèse (mɑ̃ganɛːz) *m*, manganese.

mangeable (mɑ̃ʒabl) *a*, eatable. **mangeaille** (ʒɑːj) *f*, food, feed. **mangeoire** (ʒwaːr) *f*, manger, crib. **manger** (ʒe) *v.t.* & *abs*, to eat; feed; have one's meals, mess; eat up; devour; squander; clip (*one's words*). ¶ *m*, food. **mangetout** (mɑ̃ʒtu) *m*, spendthrift; skinless pea *or* bean. **mangeur, euse** (ʒœːr, øːz) *n*, eater, feeder. **man-**

geure (ʒy:r) *f*, bite (*place bitten by worm, mouse*).

manglier (māglie) *m*, mangrove.

mangouste (māgust) *f*, mongoose.

mangue (mā:g) *f*, mango. **manguier** (māgje) *m*, mango [tree].

maniable (manjabl) *a*, supple; manageable; handy.

maniaque (manjak) *a*, maniac(al). ¶ *n*, maniac; faddist, crank. **manie** (ni) *f*, mania; craze; fad.

maniement (manimā) *m*, feeling; handling; management, conduct, care. ~ *des* (ou *d'*)*armes*, manual [exercise], rifle drill. **manier** (nje) *v.t*, to feel; handle; wield; work; ply; manage, conduct. *au* ~, by the feel.

manière (manjɛ:r) *f*, manner, way, wise; sort, kind; mannerism; style; (*pl.*) manners (*bearing*). *par* ~ *d'acquit*, perfunctorily. ~ *noire*, mezzotint. **maniéré, e** (jere) *a*, affected, finical; mannered (*style, etc.*). **maniérisme** (rism) *m*, mannerism.

manieur (manjœ:r) *m*, one who knows how to handle (*money, men*).

manifestant, e (manifɛstā, ā:t) *n*, demonstrator (*Pol., etc.*). **manifestation** (tasjɔ̃) *f*, manifestation; demonstration. **manifeste**† (fɛst) *a*, manifest, obvious, overt. ¶ *m*, manifesto; manifest (*Ship.*). **manifester** (te) *v.t*, to manifest, show; (*v.i.*) to demonstrate.

manigance (manigā:s) *f*, intrigue. **manigancer** (gāse). *v.t*, to concoct, plot.

manille (mani:j) *m*, Manila [cheroot]; (*f.*) shackle. M~, *f*, Manila (*Geog.*).

manioc (manjɔk) *m*, manioc.

manipuler (manipyle) *v.t*, to manipulate, handle.

manivelle (manivɛl) *f*, crank; handle, winch.

manne (man) *f*, manna; basket, hamper.

mannequin (mankɛ̃) *m*, lay figure, manikin; dress stand; display figure, d. model; dummy; mannequin, model; puppet; basket.

manœuvre (manœ:vr) *f*, work-ing, handling, manipulation; shunting (*Rly.*); seamanship; maneuver; move; (*pl.*) field day; rope (*Naut.*); (*pl.*) rigging (*Naut.*); (*pl.*) scheming. ~*s électorales*, electioneering. ~*s frauduleuses*, swindling (*law*). ¶ *m*, laborer; hack [writer, etc.]. **manœuvrer** (nœvre) *v.t. & i*, to work, handle, manipulate; shunt; steer (*Ship.*); maneuver. **manœuvrier** (vrie) *m*, (*skillful*) seaman; maneuverer; tactician.

manoir (manwa:r) *m*, manor [house], country seat.

manomètre (manɔmɛtr) *m*, [pressure] gauge, manometer.

manquant, e (mākā, ā:t) *a*, missing; absent. ¶ *n*, deficiency, shortage. ~ *à l'appel*, A.W.O.L. (*Mil.*). **manque** (mā:k) *m*, want, lack, shortage, deficiency; breach; dropped stitch (*Knit.*); run. ~ *de pose*, underexposure (*Phot.*). **manqué, e** (māke) *p.a*, missed; spoiled; misfit (*att.*); unsuccessful; abortive; wasted. *un peintre, etc., manqué*, a failure as a painter, etc. Cf. *garçon* ~ & *grand homme* ~. **manquer** (ke) *v.i*, to fail; miss; default; misfire; miss fire; be taken [away] (*die*); be wanting; be missing; be disrespectful; (*v.t.*) to miss; fail in. ~ *de*, to want, lack, run short (*or* out) of; be out of stock of; to nearly . . . ~ *de parole*, to break one's word.

mansarde (māsard) *f*, dormer [window]; attic, garret.

mansuétude (māsɥetyd) *f*, meekness; forbearance.

mante (mā:t) *f*, mantle. **manteau** (māto) *m*, coat, cloak, mantle, wrap. ~ *de cheminée*, mantelpiece. ~ *de cour*, court train. ~ *de fourrure*, fur coat. *sous* [*le* ~ *de*] *la cheminée*, sub rosa, under the rose. *sous le* ~ *de la religion*, under the cloak of religion. **mantelet** (tlɛ) *m*, tippet; mantelet; port lid (*Nav.*). **mantille** (ti:j) *f*, mantilla.

Mantoue (mātu) *f*, Mantua.

manucure (manyky:r) *n*, manicurist (*pers.*); (*f.*) manicure (*treatment*); m. set.

manuel, le† (manɥɛl) *a*, manual,

hand (*as work*). ¶ *m*, manual, handbook; text book.

manufacture (manyfakty:r) *f*, manufactory; staff. **manufacturier, ère** (tyrje, ε:r) *a*, manufacturing. ¶ *m*, manufacturer.

manuscrit, e (manyskri, it) *a*, manuscript, written. ¶ *m*, manuscript.

manutention (manytãsjɔ̃) *f*, handling; commissary, post exchange; bakehouse (*Mil.*). ~*s maritimes*, stevedoring.

mappemonde (mapmɔ̃:d) *f*, map of the world in hemispheres. ~ *céleste*, map of the heavens in hemispheres.

maquereau (makro) *m*, mackerel; pimp.

maquette (makεt) *f*, model (*of statuary*); dummy (*publishing*).

maquignon (makiɲɔ̃), *m*, horse dealer; jobber (*shady*). **maquignonnage** (ɲɔna:ʒ) *m*, horse dealing; jobbery. **maquignonner** (ne) *v.t*, to bishop (*horses*); manipulate (*bad sense*).

maquillage (makija:ʒ) *m*, making up; makeup. **maquiller** (je) *v.t*, to make up (*face*); camouflage.

maquis (maki) *m*, scrub; resistance (*war*).

marabout (marabu) *m*, marabout; marabou.

maraîcher (marεʃe) *m*, truck gardener. **marais** (rε) *m*, marsh, swamp, bog, fen, morass. ~ *salant*, saltern.

marasme (marasm) *m*, marasmus; stagnation.

marasquin (maraskε̃) *m*, maraschino.

marâtre (marɑ:tr) *f*, [cruel] stepmother.

maraudage (maroda:ʒ) *m. &* **maraude** (r:od) *f*, marauding, foray; pilfering. *en maraude*, cruising (*taxi*). **marauder** (rode) *v.i*, to maraud, raid. **maraudeur** (dœ:r) *m*, marauder.

marbre (marbr) *m*, marble; [marble] slab *or* top; [imposing] stone; bed (*printing press*); [engineer's] surface plate; overset, overmatter (*newspaper work*). ~ *de foyer*, hearthstone. **marbrer** (bre) *v.t*, to marble; mottle. **mar-**

brerie (brəri) *f*, marble work; m. works. **marbreur** (brœ:r) *m*, marbler. **marbrier** (brie) *m*, marble mason; monumental mason; marble merchant. **marbrière** (brie:r) *f*, marble quarry. **marbrure** (bry:r) *f*, marbling.

marc (ma:r) *m*, marc (*fruit refuse*); grounds (*coffee*); used leaves (*tea*). **au ~ le franc**, pro rata, proportionally, in proportion.

marcassin (markasε̃) *m*, young wild boar.

marcassite (markasit) *f*, marcasite.

marchand, e (marʃɑ̃, ã:d) *n*, dealer, trader, merchant; shopkeeper, tradesman, -woman, vender; (*att.*) merchant[able], mercantile, commercial, market-[able], salable, sale (*att.*) ~ *de journaux*, newsagent. ~ *de volaille*, poulterer. ~ *des quatre saisons*, fruit and vegetable peddler. ~ *en magasin*, warehouseman. **marchandage** (ʃɑ̃da:ʒ) *m*, bargaining, haggling. **marchander** (de) *v.t. & abs*, to haggle (over), bargain, palter; grudge; (*v.i.*) to hesitate. **marchandeur, euse** (dœ:r, ø:z) *n*, haggler, bargainer. **marchandise** (di:z) *f. oft. pl*, goods, merchandise, wares; commodity; cargo. ~*s d'occasion*, job lot.

marche (marʃ) *f*, walk, walking; march, marching; procession; sailing; steaming; running, run; working; speed; motion; movement, move; journey, course; way, path; progress; step, stair; treadle. ~ *à suivre*, procedure.

marché (marʃe) *m*, market; contract; bargain; dealing. ~ *aux bestiaux*, cattle market. ~ *commercial*, produce m. ~ *des valeurs*, ~ *des titres*, share m., stock m. ~ *aux puces*, flea market, thieves' market. *par-dessus le ~*, into the bargain.

marchepied (marʃəpje) *m*, [pair of] steps, stepladder; steps; footboard; stepping stone (*fig.*).

marcher (marʃe) *v.i*, to walk; tread; step; travel; tramp; march; be on the march; be driven (*Mach.*); sail; proceed, move on,

advance, progress, go, go on; run,
ply; work. **marcheur, euse** (ʃœːr,
ø:z) *n*, walker; (*m.*) (*good, bad,
fast*) sailer (*ship*).

marcotte (markɔt) *f*, layer
(*Hort.*). **marcotter** (te) *v.t*, to
layer.

mardi (mardi) *m*, Tuesday. **M~
gras**, Shrove Tuesday.

mare (maːr) *f*, pond, pool.
marécage (mareka:ʒ) *m*, marsh,
swamp, fen, bog. **marecageux,
euse** (kaʒø, ø:z) *a*, marshy,
swampy, boggy.

maréchal (mareʃal) *m*: ~ *de
France* (*Fr.*), Field Marshal
(*Eng.*). ~ *des logis*, sergeant
(*mounted troops*). ~ *des logis
chef*, s. major. **maréchaiat** (ia)
m, marshalship. **maréchalerie**
(lri) *f*, farriery. **maréchalferrant**
(ɛrɑ̃) *m*, farrier, shoeing smith.

marée (mare) *f*, tide, water; salt-
water fish (*caught & fresh*), fresh
sea fish, wet fish.

marelle (marɛl) *f*, hopscotch.

mareyeur, euse (marɛjœːr, ø:z)
n, fish merchant & salesman,
-woman.

margarine (margarin) *f*, margarine.

marge (marʒ) *f*, margin. **marger**
(ʒe) *v.t*, to lay on, feed (*Typ.*);
set a margin (*typing*). **marginal,
e** (ʒinal) *a*, marginal.

margotin (margɔte) *m*, bundle
of firewood.

margouillis (marguji) *m*, mess.

marguerite (margərit) *f*, (*petite*)
daisy; (*grande*) marguerite, ox-
eye daisy. ~ *de la Saint-Michel*,
Michaelmas daisy.

mari (mari) *m*, husband. **mariable**
(rjabl) *a*, marriageable. **mariage** (rja:ʒ) *m*, marriage, matrimony, wedlock; match; wedding.
marié, e (rje) *n*, bridegroom,
bride. **marier** (rje) *v.t. & se* ~,
to marry, wed; get married;
match, unite. **marieur, euse**
(rjœːr, ø:z) *n*, matchmaker.

marin, e (marɛ̃, in) *a*, marine;
sea (*att.*); nautical (*mile*); sailor
(*suit*). ¶ *m*, seaman, mariner,
sailor; waterman, boatman. ~
d'eau douce, freshwater sailor,
landlubber. **marine** (rin) *f*, marine, shipping, maritime naviga-

tion; seascape. ~ [*militaire*], ~
de guerre, navy. **mariné, e** (rine)
a, sea-damaged. **mariner** (ne) *v.t*,
to pickle; marinade.

maringouin (marɛ̃gwɛ̃) *m*, mosquito.

marinier (marinje) *m*, bargeman, bargee.

marionnette (marjɔnɛt) *f*, puppet, marionette.

marital, e† (marital) *a*, marital.

maritime (maritim) *a*, maritime,
marine, sea (*att.*); shipping (*att.*);
ship (*canal, broker, etc.*); naval.

maritorne (maritɔrn) *f*, slut,
slattern.

marivauder (marivode) *v.i*, to
bandy flirtatious remarks.

marjolaine (marʒɔlɛn) *f*, [sweet]
marjoram.

marmaille (marmɑːj) *f.col*,
children, brats.

Marmara (**mer de**) (marmara),
Sea of Marmara.

marmelade (marmələad) *f*, preserve, marmalade. ~ *de pommes,
de prunes*, stewed apples, plums.
en ~, reduced to a pulp (*as
cooked meat*); to (*or* in) a jelly
(*as face by blow*).

marmenteaux (marmɑ̃to) *m.pl*,
ornamental trees.

marmitage (marmita:ʒ) *m*, shelling (*Artil.*). **marmite** (mit) *f*,
boiler, pot; pot hole (*Geol.*);
heavy shell (*Artil.*). ~ *autoclave*
steamer, steam cooker. **marmiter**
(te) *v.t*, to shell. **marmiteux, euse**
(tø, ø:z) *a. & n*, miserable
(*wretch*). **marmiton** (tɔ̃) *m*,
kitchen boy; scullion.

marmonner (marmɔne) *v.t*, to
grumble about.

marmot, te (marmo, ɔt) *n*,
youngster. (*f.*) marmot (*Zool.*);
kerchief. **marmotter** (mɔte) *v.t*,
to mutter, mumble.

marmouset (marmuzɛ) *m*, little
fellow; firedog.

marne (marn) *f*, marl. **marner**
(ne) *v.t*, to marl. **marneux, euse**
(nø, ø:z) *a*, marly. **marnière**
(njɛːr) *f*, marl pit.

Maroc (**le**) (marɔk), Morocco.
marocain, e (kɛ̃, ɛn) *a. & M~*,
n, Moroccan.

maronner (marɔne) *v.i*, to
grumble.

maroquin (marɔkɛ̃) *m*, morocco [leather]. **maroquinerie** (kinri) *f*, fancy leather goods; f. l. shop.

marotique (marɔtik) *a*, archaic, quaint.

marotte (marɔt) *f*, bauble (*Hist.*), cap & bells; milliner's dummy; hairdresser's dummy; pet theory, weakness, craze, [mono]mania.

marquant, e (markã, ã:t) *p.a*, prominent, outstanding; of note, leading. **marque** (mark) *f*, mark; stamp; brand; pit (*smallpox*); score; bookmark; badge; token; tally. ~ *de commerce, de fabrique*, trademark. ~ *déposée*, registered t. m. ~ *typographique*, colophon. *de* ~, branded, by well-known (*or* leading) maker(s); high-class. **marqué, e** (ke) *p.a*, marked; decided. **marquer** (ke) *v.t*, to mark; stamp; brand; score; show; (*v.i.*) to stand out. ~ *le pas*, to mark time. ~ *un but*, to kick (*or* score) a goal (*Foot.*).

marqueter (markəte) *v.t*, to speckle, spot; inlay. **marqueterie** (kɛtri) *f*, marquetry, inlaid work; mosaic; patchwork.

marqueur, euse (markœ:r, ø:z) (*pers.*) *n*, marker; scorer.

marquis (marki) *m*, marquis, -quess. **marquise** (ki:s) *f*, marchioness; marquise; canopy (*Arch.*); awning.

marraine (marɛn) *f*, godmother, sponsor.

marron (marɔ̃) *m*, chestnut; maroon (*firework*); marron (*glacé*); (*att.*) maroon (*color*). ~ *d'Inde*, horse chestnut.

marron, ne (marɔ̃, ɔn) *a*, [run] wild (*animal*); outside (*broker*); unlicensed; unqualified; pirate (*publisher*); chestnut-colored, maroon. *nègre marron, négresse marronne*, maroon. **marronnage** (rɔna:ʒ) *m*, running away (*slaves*).

marronnier (marɔnje) *m*, chestnut [tree]. ~ *d'Inde*, horse chestnut [tree].

marrube (maryb) *m*, hoarhound.

mars (mars) *m*, March. **M**~, Mars, warfare.

marseillais, e (marsɛjɛ, ɛ:z) *a*. & **M**~, *n*, (*att.*) Marseilles. *la Marseillaise*, the Marseillais (*an-*

them). **Marseille** (sɛ:j) *f*, Marseilles.

marsouin (marswɛ̃) *m*, porpoise; colonial infantryman.

marsupial (marsypjal) *m*, marsupial.

marteau (marto) *m*, hammer. ~ *d'eau*, water h. ~ *de porte*, door knocker. ~-*pilon*, power hammer. **martel en tête** (tɛl) *m*, uneasiness, worry. **martelé, e** (tɔle) (*fig.*) *p.a*, labored; strongly stressed. **marteler** (le) *v.t*. & *abs*, to hammer. *se* ~ [*le cerveau*], to make one uneasy, worry one.

martial, e (marsjal) *a*, martial, warlike.

martinet (martinɛ) *m*, swift (*bird*); tilt hammer; scourge (*whip*).

martingale (martɛ̃gal) *f*, martingale (*harness, betting*); betting system.

martin-pêcheur (martɛ̃pɛʃœ:r) ou **martinet-pêcheur** (tinɛ) *m*, kingfisher.

martre (martr) *f*, marten. ~ *zibeline*, sable (*Zool.*).

martyr, e (marti:r) *n*, martyr; victim. **martyre**, *m*, martyrdom; torment. **martyriser** (tirize) *v.t*, to martyr[ize]; torture. **martyrologe** (rɔlɔ:ʒ) *m*, martyrology (*list*).

mascarade (maskarad) *f*, masquerade.

mascaret (maskarɛ) *m*, [tidal] bore. *un* ~ *humain*, shoals of people.

mascaron (maskarɔ̃) *m*, mascaron, mask.

mascotte (maskɔt) *f*, mascot, charm.

masculin, e (maskylɛ̃, in) *a*, male; masculine. ¶ *m*, masculine [gender]. **masculinité** (linite) *f*, masculinity; male descent.

masque (mask) *m*, mask; blind; features; masker, -quer. ~ *à gaz*, gas mask, respirator. ¶ *f*, hussy, minx. **masquer** (ke) *v.t*, to mask; cover, conceal. *se* ~, to masquerade.

massacrant, e (masakrã, ã:t) *a*, very bad (*temper*). **massacre** (kr) *m*, massacre, slaughter. **massacrer** (kre) *v.t*, to massacre,

slaughter; smash; murder; botch.
massacreur, euse (krœːr, øːz) *n*,
slaughterer; smasher; botcher.

massage (masaːʒ) *m*, massage.

masse (mas) *f*, mass, lump;
solid; body; bulk; aggregate;
funds; fund; sledge [hammer];
mace (*ceremonial*). ~ [*d'armes*].
mace (*Hist.*). ~ *d'eau*, reed
mace, bulrush. *à la* ~ (*Elec.*),
grounded, connected to frame.

massepain (maspɛ̃) *m*, marzipan.

masser (mase) *v.t*, to mass; massage.

massette (masɛt) *f*, reed mace,
bulrush.

masseur, euse (masœːr, øːz) *n*,
masseur, euse.

massicot (masiko) *m*, lead
ochre; guillotine (*for paper cutting*).

massier, ère (masje, ɛːr) *n*,
treasurer; (*m.*) mace bearer.

massif, ive† (masif, iːv) *a*, mas-
sive; bulky; heavy; solid. ¶ *m*,
[solid] mass; block; body; clump;
massif.

massue (masy) *f*, club, bludgeon.

mastic (mastik) *m*, mastic;
putty.

mastication (mastikasjɔ̃) *f*, mastication. **mastiquer** (ke) *v.t*, to
masticate; putty.

mastoc (mastɔk) *a.inv*, lumpish.

mastodonte (mastɔdɔ̃ːt) *m*, mastodon; elephant[ine person].

mastoïde (mastɔid) *a*, mastoid.

masure (mazyːr) *f*, hovel, ruin.

mat, e (mat) *a*, mat (*color*), unpolished, lusterless, dead, flat,
dull.

mat (mat) *a.m*, checkmated. *faire*
~, *to* [check]mate (*chess*).

mât (mɑ) *m*, mast; pole. ~ *de
charge*, derrick (*ship's*). ~ *de
cocagne* (kɔkaɲ), greasy pole.
~ *de fortune*, jury mast. ~ *de
hune*, topmast. ~ *de misaine*,
foremast. ~ *de pavillon*, flag-
staff. ~ *de pavoisement* (pavwaz-
mɑ̃), Venetian mast. ~ *de signaux*, signal post. ~ *de tente*,
tent pole.

matador (matadoːr) *m*, matador
(*pers. & games*); magnate (*Fin.*,
etc.).

matamore (matamɔːr) *m*, swaggerer.

match (matʃ) *m*, match (*boxing,
wrestling, tennis, football, chess,
etc.*). ~ *aller*, first match. ~ *nul*,
draw[n game]. ~ *retour*, return
match.

matelas (matla) *m*, mattress.
matelasser (lase) *v.t*, to stuff, pad.
matelassier, ère (sje, ɛːr) *n*, mattress maker.

matelot (matlo) *m*, sailor, seaman. ~ *coq*, cook's mate. ~ *de
deuxième classe*, able[-bodied]
seaman. ~ *de pont*, deck hand.
~ *de première classe*, seaman
first-class. ~ *de troisième classe*,
ordinary s. [*vaisseau*] ~, consort
(*Navy*).

mater (mate) *v.t*, to [check]mate
(*chess*); mortify; humble.

mâter (mɑte) *v.t*, to mast (*a
ship*); toss (*oars*).

matérialiser (materjalize) *v.t*, to
materialize. **matérialisme** (lism)
m, materialism. **matérialiste** (list)
n, materialist. ¶ *a*, materialistic.
matériaux (rjo) *m.pl*, materials.
matériel, le† (rjɛl) *a*, material,
physical, bodily. ¶ *m*, plant, material, stock. ~ *roulant*, rolling
stock.

maternel, le† (matɛrnɛl) *a*, ma-
ternal, motherly; mother's (*side*);
mother, native (*tongue*). **maternité** (nite) *f*, maternity, mother-
hood; maternity hospital.

mathématicien, ne (matema-
tisjɛ̃, ɛn) *n*, mathematician. **mathématique**† (tik) *a*, mathematical. ~**s**, *f.pl*, mathematics. ~
spéciales, higher mathematics.

matière (matjɛːr) *f*, matter; material, stuff; type metal; subject;
grounds; gravamen. ~ *à réflexion*, food for thought. ~**s** *d'or
& d'argent*, bullion. ~ *médicale*,
materia medica. ~**s** *premières*,
raw material[s] (*used in trade*).

matin (matɛ̃) *m*, morning. *un de
ces* ~**s**, one of these fine days.
¶ *ad*, early.

mâtin (mɑtɛ̃) *m*, mastiff; large
watch dog; rascal.

matinal, e (matinal) *a*, [up]
early, early riser (*être* = to be
an); morning (*att.*).

mâtiné, e (matine) *a*, mongrel, cross-bred; mixed.

matinée (matine) *f*, morning; forenoon; morning performance, matinée; dressing jacket. **matines** (tin) *f.pl*, matins. **matineux, euse** (nø, ø:z) *a*, [up] early, early riser (*être* = to be an).

matir (mati:r) *v.t*, to mat, dull. **matité** (tite) *f*, dullness, deadness.

matois, e (matwa, a:z) *a*. & *n*, sly (person).

matou (matu) *m*, tom [cat].

matriarcat (matriarka) *m*, matriarchy. **matrice** (tris) *f*, womb; matrix; gangue; die; standard (*weight, measure*). ~ *du rôle des contributions*, assessment book (*taxes*). **matricule** (kyl) *f*, register, roll. [*numéro*] ~, *m*, army serial number. **matrimonial, e** (monjal) *a*, matrimonial. **matrone** (tron) *f*, matron, dame.

maturation (matyrasjɔ̃) *f*, maturation, ripening.

mâture (maty:r) *f*, masts (*col.*); masting; mast[ing] house.

maturité (matyrite) *f*, maturity, ripeness.

maudire (modi:r) *v.t.ir*, to curse. **maudit, e** (di, it) *p.a*, [ac]cursed, confounded.

maugréer (mogree) *v.i*, to fume, bluster, curse.

Maure (mɔ:r) *m*, Moor. **m~**, *a*, Moorish. **mauresque** (mɔrɛsk) *a*, Moresque. ¶ *f*, Morisco, morris [dance].

Maurice [(l'île)] (mɔris) *f*, Mauritius.

mausolée (mozɔle) *m*, mausoleum.

maussade (mosad) *a*, sullen, peevish, disgruntled; dull, flat. **maussaderie** (dri) *f*, sullenness; sulks.

mauvais, e (movɛ, ɛ:z) *a*, bad; ill; evil; nasty; wrong; faulty; broken (*English, French, etc.*). **mauvais**, *comps:* ~ *coucheur*, quarrelsome fellow. ~ *œil*, evil eye. ~ *pas*, tight corner; scrape, fix (*fig.*). ~ *plaisant*, practical joker. ~ *quart d'heure*, bad time [of it], trying time. ~ *service*, disservice. ~ *sujet*, ne'er-do-well, scapegrace; bad boy (*Sch.*). ~ *ton*, bad form. **mauvaise**, *comps:* ~

action, ill deed. ~ *gestion*, mismanagement, maladministration. ~ *herbe*, weed. ~ *honte*, false shame; bashfulness. ~ *langue*, scandalmonger. **mauvais**, *ad*. & *m*, bad.

mauve (mo:v) *f*, mallow. ¶ *m*. & *att*, mauve.

mauviette (movjɛt) *f*, lark (*bird*); puny creature. **mauvis** (vi) *m*, red wing (*thrush*).

maxillaire (maksillɛ:r) *a*, maxillary, jaw (*bone*).

maxime (maksim) *m*, maxim.

maximum, ma (maksimɔm, ma) *a*. & *m*, maximum, peak, top (*att.*). ~ *de charge*, burden, burthen (*ship*).

Mayence (majɑ̃:s) Mayence, Mainz.

mayonnaise (majɔnɛ:z) *f*. & *att*, mayonnaise.

mazette (mazɛt) *f*, weakling; duffer, rabbit (*at a game*).

mazout (mazu) *m*, oil fuel.

me, m' (mə, m) *pn*, me; [to] me; myself. ~ *voici*, here I am.

méandre (meɑ̃:dr) *m*, meander, winding.

mécanicien (mekanisjɛ̃) *m*, mechanician, mechanist; mechanic; engineman; engine driver; engineer (*ship*); (*att.*) mechanical (*engineer*). **mécanique†** (nik) *a*, mechanical; power (*att.*); clockwork (*train, motor car, or other toy*). ¶ *f*, mechanics; mechanism; brake [gear] (*carriage*). *fait à la* ~, machine-made. **mécaniser** (ze) *v.t*, to mechanize, motorize. **mécanisme** (nism) *m*, mechanism, machinery, gear; works (*as of a watch*); technique.

mécène (mesɛn) *m*, patron (*as of the arts*).

méchant, e (meʃɑ̃, ɑ̃:t) *a*, wicked, evil; ill-natured; unkind; spiteful; mischievous, naughty; wretched, paltry, poor, sorry; unpleasant. ~ *poète*, poetaster. ¶ *n*, wicked, etc, person. **méchamment** (ʃamɑ̃) *ad*, wickedly, etc. **méchanceté** (ʃɑ̃ste) *f*, wickedness, etc.

mèche (mɛʃ) *f*, wick (*lamp*); tinder; fuse; match, cracker, snapper (*whip*); lock (*hair*); tassel; bit, drill; worm (*cork-*

screw); tent (*Surg.*); secret, plot.

mécompte (mekɔ̃:t) *m*, miscalculation, disappointment.

méconnaissable (mekɔnɛsabl) *a*, unrecognizable. **méconnaître** (nɛ:tr) *v.t.ir*, to fail to recognize *or* diagnose, not to know; disown; disregard, ignore, misunderstand, slight.

mécontent, e (mekɔ̃tɑ̃, ɑ̃:t) *a*, discontent[ed], dissatisfied, disgruntled. ¶ *m*, malcontent. **mécontentement** (tɑ̃tmɑ̃) *m*, discontent[ment], dissatisfaction. **mécontenter** (te) *v.t*, to dissatisfy, displease.

Mecque (la) (mɛk), Mecca.

mécréant, e (mekreɑ̃, ɑ̃:t) *a*, unbelieving. ¶ *n*, unbeliever.

médaille (meda:j) *f*, medal; coin (*Greek, Roman*); badge (*porter's*). ~ *d'honneur*, prize medal. **médaillé, e** (daje) *a*, decorated (*Mil.*). ¶ *n*, medalist (*recipient*), prize winner. **médailler** (je) *v.t*, to award a medal (to). **médailleur** (jœ:r) *m*, medalist, medal maker. **médaillier** (je) *m*, coin (*or* medal) cabinet; collection of coins *or* medals. **médaillon** (jɔ̃) *m*, medallion; locket.

médecin (medsɛ̃) *m*, medical man, m. officer, physician, surgeon, doctor; (*of time*) healer. ~ *aliéniste* (aljenist), mental specialist. **médicine** (sin) *f*, medicine; surgery; physic. ~ *légale*, medical jurisprudence, forensic medicine.

médiateur, trice (medjatœ:r, tris) *n*, mediator. **médiation** (sjɔ̃) *f*, mediation.

médical, e (medikal) *a*, medical. **médicament** (mɑ̃) *m*, medicament, medicine. **médicamenter** (te) *v.t*, to doctor, physic, dose. **médicamenteux, euse** (tø, ø:z) *a*, medicinal, curative; medicated. **médicastre** (kastr) *m*, quack. **médication** (sjɔ̃) *f*, medication. **médicinal, e** (sinal) *a*, medicinal. **médico-légal, e** (kolegal) *a*, medico-judicial.

médiéval, e (medjeval) *a*, medieval. **médiéviste** (vist) *n*, medievalist.

médiocre (medjɔkr) *a*, medi-

ocre, poor; middling, moderate. ¶ *m*, mediocrity (*pers. & quality*). **médiocrité** (krite) *f*, mediocrity (*quality*); moderate condition of life.

médire de (medi:r) *v.ir*, to speak ill of, slander. **médisance** (dizɑ̃:s) *f*, slander, backbiting, scandal; scandalmongers. **médisant, e** (zɑ̃, ɑ̃:t) *a*, slanderous. ¶ *n*, slanderer, scandalmonger.

méditatif, ive (meditatif, i:v) *a*, meditative. **méditation** (sjɔ̃) *f*, meditation. **méditer** (te) *v.t. & abs*, to meditate ([up]on), ponder, muse, pore; think; contemplate; plan.

méditerrané, e (meditɛrane) *a*, mediterranean, landlocked. *la* [*mer*] *Méditerranée*, the Mediterranean [sea]. **méditerranéen, ne** (neɛ̃, ɛn) *a*, Mediterranean.

médium (medjɔm) *m*, middle register (*Mus.*); medium (*spiritualism*).

médius (medjy:s) *m*, second finger, middle f.

médullaire (medyllɛ:r) *a*, medullary.

méduse (medy:z) *f*, medusa, jellyfish, sea nettle. *la tête de M~* (*fig.*), a terrible shock. **méduser** (dyze) *v.t*, to petrify (*fig.*).

meeting (mitiɲ) *m*, meeting (*Pol., sport, social*).

méfait (mefɛ) *m*, misdeed, malpractice.

méfiance (mefjɑ̃:s) *f*, mistrust, distrust. **méfiant, e** (jɑ̃, ɑ̃:t) *a*, mis- *or* distrustful. **se méfier de** (fje), to mis- *or* distrust; beware of.

mégalomanie (megalɔmani) *f*, megalomania.

mégarde (par) (megard) *ad*, inadvertently.

mégère (meʒɛ:r) *f*, termagant, virago, shrew.

mégie (meʒi) **& mégisserie** (sri) *f*, leather dressing, tawing.

mégot (mego) *m*, cigarette butt.

meilleur, e (mɛjœ:r) *a*, better. *à meilleur marché*, cheaper. **le ~, la ~**, the better, the best. ¶ *m*, best.

Mein (le) (mɛ̃), the Main (*river*).

mélancolie (melɑ̃kɔli) *f*, melancholia; melancholy. **mélanco-lique**† (lik) *a*, melancholy, melancholic.

Mélanésie (la) (melanezi), Melanesia.

mélange (melɑ̃:ʒ) *m*, mixture; blending; medley; mash; (*pl.*) miscellany (*literary*); miscellaneous works. **mélanger** (lɑ̃ʒe) *v.t*, to mix, mingle, blend. *laine mélangée*, wool mixture.

mélasse (melas) *f*, molasses, treacle.

mêlé, e (mele) *p.a*, mixed, miscellaneous, medley. ¶ *f*, fight, mêlée, scrimmage, scramble. **mêler** (le) *v.t*, to mix, mingle; medley; shuffle (*cards*); mash. **se ~**, to interfere, meddle.

mélèze (mele:z) *m*, larch [tree].

mélodie (melɔdi) *f*, melody. **mélodieux, euse**† (djø, ø:z) *a*, melodious, tuneful.

mélodramatique (melɔdramatik) *a*, melodramatic. **mélodrame** (dram) *m*, melodrama.

melon (məlɔ̃) *m*, melon. [**chapeau**] **~**, derby (*hat*).

membrane (mɑ̃bran) *f*, membrane; web (*bird's foot*). **~ du tympan**, eardrum.

membre (mɑ̃:br) *m*, member; limb; rib (*ship*). **membré, e** (mɑ̃bre) *a*, -limbed. **membrure** (bry:r) *f*, limbs; frame; ribs (*ship*).

même (mɛ:m) *a*, same; like; very; self; itself. ¶ *m*, same [thing]. ¶ *ad*, even, indeed. **à ~ de**, in a position to, able to. **de ~**, *ad*, the same, likewise. **de ~ que**, *c*, [just] as, like.

mémento (memẽto) *m*, memento, reminder, note; handbook.

mémoire (memwa:r) *f*, memory; recollection; remembrance; fame. *de ~*, from memory, by heart. *de ~ d'homme*, within living memory. *pour ~*, as a memorandum, no[t] value[d] (*in account*). ¶ *m*, memorandum; paper (*learned*); bill, account; memoir. **mémorable** (mɔrabl) *a*, memorable. **mémorandum** (rɑ̃dɔm) *m*, memorandum; memorial (*State paper*). **mémorial** (rjal) *m*, memoirs.

menace (mənas) *f*, threat, men-ace. **menacer** (se) *v.t. & abs*, to threaten, menace.

ménade (menad) *f*, maenad.

ménage (mena:ʒ) *m*, housekeeping, housewifery; house[hold], establishment; household goods; home, family; housework. [**petit**] **~**, miniature (*or* dolls') home set. **~ à trois**, matrimonial triangle. **de ~**, household (*bread*); homespun; house *or* domestic (*as coal*); homemade (*as wine*). *faire des ~s*, to clean the house, do housekeeping work. *femme de ~*, cleaning woman. **ménagement** (naʒmɑ̃) *m. oft. pl*, care, stint; consideration, deference; tact. **ménager** (ʒe) *v.t*, to husband, manage, economize; save; take care of; look after; make the most of; keep; arrange; make; contrive; bring about; keep in with, humor; handle tactfully; spare. *sans ~ les termes*, without mincing one's words. **ménager, ère** (ʒe, ɛ:r) *a*, economical, thrifty; careful; sparing; domestic. ¶ *f*, housekeeper, housewife; cruet. **ménagerie** (ʒri) *f*, menagerie.

mendiant, e (mɑ̃djɑ̃, ɑ̃:t) *n*, beggar; mendicant; (*att.*) mendicant; (*m.pl.*) dessert fruit & nuts. **mendicité** (disite) *f*, begging, mendicancy, mendicity; beggary. **mendier** (dje) *v.i. & t*, to beg; canvass.

meneau (məno) *m*, mullion; transom (*window*).

menée (məne) *f*, (*underhand*) intrigue; track (*Hunt.*). **mener** (ne) *v.t*, to lead, conduct; take, carry; drive; steer; partner (*lady at dance*). *mené par sa femme*, henpecked.

ménestrel (menɛstrɛl) *m*, minstrel (*Hist.*). **ménétrier** (netrie) *m*, (village) fiddler.

meneur (mənœ:r, ø:z) *n*, leader; ringleader. **~ de train**, pacemaker.

menhir (mɛni:r) *m*, menhir.

méningite (menẽʒit) *f*, meningitis.

menotte (mənɔt) *f*, small hand; (*pl.*) handcuffs, manacles.

mensonge (mɑ̃sɔ̃:ʒ) *m*, lie, falsehood, untruth; fiction; vanity. **~**

innocent, fib, story. ~ *pieux*, ~ *officieux*, white lie. **mensonger, ère**† (sɔ̃ʒe, ɛːr) *a*, lying, mendacious; untrue, false, deceitful.

mensualité (mɑ̃sɥalite) *f*, monthly payment, drawing, salary, or like. **mensuel, le**† (sɥɛl) *a*, monthly (*a. & ad.*).

mensurable (mɑ̃syrabl) *a*, measurable.

mensuration (mɑ̃syrasjɔ̃) *f*, mensuration.

mental, e† (mɑ̃tal) *m*, mental. **mentalité** (lite) *f*, mentality.

menterie (mɑ̃tri) *f*, story, fib. **menteur, euse** (tœːr, øːz) *n*, liar. ¶ *a*, lying; deceptive.

menthe (mɑ̃ːt) *f*, mint. ~ *poivrée*, peppermint. *pastille de* ~, peppermint [lozenge]. ~ *verte*, spearmint, garden mint. **menthol** (mɑ̃tɔl) *m*, menthol.

mention (mɑ̃sjɔ̃) *f*, mention, reference. **mentionner** (ɔne) *v.t*, to mention, make reference to.

mentir (mɑ̃tiːr) *v.i.ir*, to lie. *sans* ~, to tell the truth (*candidly*).

mentor (mɛ̃tɔːr) *m*, mentor. (*ou en*) *galoche*, slipper chin. M~, Mentone (*Geog.*). **mentonnet** (tɔnɛ) *m*, latch catch.

mentor (mɛ̃tɔːr) *m*, mentor.

menu, e (məny) *a*, small; slight; petty; minor (*repairs*); minute; fine. *le menu peuple*, the humbler classes. *menu plomb*, birdshot. *menue paille*, chaff. *menues herbes*, fine herbs (*fine in texture, as savory herbs*). *argent pour menus plaisirs*, pocket money. *menus propos*, small talk. **menu,** *ad*, small, fine. ¶ *m*, fare; menu, bill of fare. *par le* ~, in detail. **menuet** (nɥɛ) *m*, minuet. **menuiser** (nɥize) *v.i*, to carpenter. **menuiserie** (zri) *f*, joinery; cabinet making, c. work; woodwork. **menuisier** (zje) *m*, joiner; carpenter; cabinet maker; woodworker.

méphitique (mefitik) *a*, mephitic, noxious, dank.

méplat, e (mepla, at) *a. & m*, flat.

méprendre (se) (meprɑ̃ːdr) *v.pr.ir*, to be mistaken. *se* ~ *sur*, to mistake.

mépris (mepri) *m*, contempt, scorn. **méprisable** (zabl) *a*, con-temptible, despicable, scurvy; disregardable. **méprisant, e** (zɑ̃, ɑ̃ːt) *a*, contemptuous, scornful. **méprise** (priːz) *f*, mistake; oversight. **mépriser** (prize) *v.t*, to despise, scorn; disregard, scoff at.

mer (mɛːr) *f*, sea, ocean. ~ *du Nord*, North Sea. *Note.*—For other seas, see under proper name, e.g, *la mer Égée*, under *Égée. un homme à la* ~*l* [a] man overboard!

mercanti (mɛrkɑ̃ti) *m*, profiteer. **mercantile** (til) *a*, mercantile, mercenary. **mercantilisme** (lism) *m*, mercantilism, commercialism.

mercenaire (mɛrsəneːr) *a*, mercenary. ¶ *m*, mercenary, hireling; [paid] worker.

mercerie (mɛrsri) *f*, notions shop. **mercerisé, e** (ze) *a*, mercerized.

merci (mɛrsi) *f*, mercy; (*m*.) thanks. ¶ *i*, thanks! thank you!; no, thank you! *Dieu* ~*l* thank God!

mercier, ère (mɛrsje, ɛːr) *n*, notions shopkeeper.

mercredi (mɛrkrədi) *m*, Wednesday. *le* ~ *des Cendres*, Ash Wednesday.

mercure (mɛrkyːr) *m*, mercury, quicksilver. **mercuriale** (kyrjal) *f*, mercury (*Bot.*); reprimand; official list (*grain, etc, prices*). **mercuriel, e** (rjɛl) *a*, mercurial, blue (*pill*).

merde (mɛrd) *f*, excrement; shit.

mère (mɛːr) *f*, mother; parent (*lit. & fig.*); dam. *notre* ~ *commune*, mother earth. ~ *abeille*, queen bee. ~ *branche*, bough, limb. *la* ~ *Gigogne* (ʒigɔɲ), the Old Woman who lived in a shoe. *une* ~ *Gigogne*, the mother of many children. ~ *patrie*, parent state. *l'idée* ~, the main idea (*of book*).

méridien, ne (meridjɛ̃, ɛn) *a*, meridian. ¶ *m*, meridian (*as of Greenwich*); (*f*.) siesta; couch. **méridional, e** (djɔnal) *a*, meridional, southern, south. ¶ (*pers.*) *n*, meridional, southerner.

meringue (mərɛ̃ːg) *f*, meringue.

mérinos (merinɔs) *m*, merino.

merise (məriːz) *f*, wild cherry,

merry. **merisier** (rizje) *m*, wild cherry [tree].

méritant, e (meritã, ã:t) *a*, deserving, meritorious. **mérite** (rit) *m*, merit, desert, worth. **mériter** (te) *v.t*, to merit, deserve; be worth; earn; require. **méritoire** (twa:r) *a*, meritorious.

merlan (mɛrlã) *m*, whiting (*fish*).

merle (mɛrl) *m*, blackbird; ouzel, ousel. *c'est le ~ blanc*, he is a strange mixture (*of qualities*). *je vous donnerai le* (ou *un*) *~ blanc*, I'll eat my hat (*if you can do that*). **merlette** (lɛt) *f*, [hen] blackbird.

merlin (mɛrlɛ̃) *m*, cleaving axe (*wood*); pole axe.

merluche (mɛrlyʃ) *f*, dried cod; dried hake. **merlus** (ly) *m*, hake.

merrain (mɛrɛ̃) *m*, stave wood.

merveille (mɛrvɛ:j) *f*, marvel, wonder. *à ~*, excellently; wonderfully; capitally. **merveilleux, euse†** (vejø, ø:z) *a*, marvelous, wonderful. *le ~*, the marvelous; the wonderful part. ¶ (*pers.*) (*Hist.*) *n*, fop.

mes see **mon**.

mésalliance (mezaljã:s) *f*, misalliance. **mésallier** (lje) *v.t*, to misally. *se ~*, to make a misalliance.

mésange (mezã:ʒ) *f*, tit[mouse]. *~ charbonnière*, tomtit.

mésaventure (mezavãty:r) *f*, misadventure, mishap.

mésentente (mezãtã:t) *f*, misunderstanding, disagreement.

mésestime (mezɛstim) *f*, disrepute. **mésestimer** (me) *v.t*, to undervalue, underestimate, underrate.

mésintelligence (mezɛ̃tɛliʒã:s) *f*, variance; misunderstanding.

mesquin, e† (mɛskɛ̃, in) *a*, mean, shabby; poky; stingy, niggardly; paltry; scanty. **mesquinerie** (kinri) *f*, meanness, etc.

mess (mɛs) *m*, mess (*officers'*).

message (mɛsa:ʒ) *m*, message; errand. **messager, ère** (saʒe, ɛ:r) *n*, messenger; (*m.*) carrier; harbinger. **messagerie** (ʒri) *f*. *oft. pl*, parcels [service]; mail, passenger & parcels service.

messe (mɛs) *f*, mass (*Eccl.*). *~ basse*, low m. *~ chantée*, high m.

messeoir (mɛswa:r) *v.i.ir*, to be unbecoming.

Messie (mɛsi) *m*, Messiah.

messieurs, *oft.* **M~** (mesjø), *pl.* of *monsieur*, messieurs, Messrs.

Messine (mɛsin) *f*, Messina.

mesurage (məzyra:ʒ) *m*, measurement. **mesure** (zy:r) *f*, measure; measurement; size; (*pl.*) mensuration; extent; meter (*Poet.*); time (*Mus.*); measure, (*& commonly but wrongly*) bar (*Mus.*); bounds; propriety. *à ~*, in proportion. *à ~ que*, [according] as. *en ~ de*, able to. *sur ~*, to measure, custom-made. **mesuré, e** (zyre) *a*, guarded (*language*). **mesurer** (re) *v.t*, to measure; weigh (*fig.*); proportion. *se ~ avec*, to cope with.

métairie (metɛri) *f*, farm worked on shares.

métal (metal) *m*, metal. *~ anglais*, britannia m. **métallifère** (tallifɛ:r) *a*, metalliferous. **métallique** (tallik) *a*, metallic; iron &/or steel; wire (*att.*); spring (*att.*). **métallurgie** (tallyrʒi) *f*, metallurgy. **métallurgiste** (ʒist) *m*, metallurgist.

métamorphose (metamɔrfo:z) *f*, metamorphosis. **métamorphoser** (foze) *v.t*, to metamorphose.

métaphore (metafɔ:r) *f*, metaphor. *~ incohérente*, mixed m. **métaphorique†** (fɔrik) *a*, metaphorical.

métaphysicien (metafizisjɛ̃) *m*, metaphysician. **métaphysique** (zik) *f*, metaphysics. ¶ *a*, metaphysical.

métayage (meteja:ʒ) *m*, cultivation on shares.

météore (meteɔ:r) *m*, meteor. **météorique** (ɔrik) *a*, meteoric. **météorologie** (rɔlɔʒi) *f*, meteorology. **météorologique** (ʒik) *a*, meteorologic(al); weather (*forecast, etc.*).

méthode (metɔd) *f*, method, way, system. **méthodique†** (dik) *a*, methodical. **méthodisme** (dism) *m*, methodism. **méthodiste** (dist) *n*, methodist.

méthyle (metil) *n*, methyl (*Chem.*).

méticuleux, euse† (metikylø, ø:z) *a*, meticulous, punctilious.

métier (metje) *m*, trade; craft; profession, business, calling, line; experience; loom; frame (*Need.*). ~ **à broder**, embroidery hoops; tambour frame. ~ *de tailleur*, tailoring. *sur le* ~ (*fig.*), in the works. *faire son* ~, to mind one's own business.

métis, se (metis) *a*, halfbred; crossbred; mongrel; hybrid (*Bot.*). ¶ *n*, halfbreed; cross; mongrel. **métissage** (tisa:ʒ) *m*, crossbreeding.

métonymie (metɔnimi) *f*, metonymy.

métrage (metra:ʒ) *m*, measurement, measuring; length (*in meters*); [quantity] surveying. **mètre** (mɛtr) *m*, meter (*verse*); meter = 39.370113 inches; meter measure *or* tape *or* stick (1 *meter long*). ~ *carré*, square meter = 10.7639 sq. feet. ~ *cube*, cubic meter = 35.3148 cub. feet. **métrer** (metre) *v.t*, to measure, survey. **métreur** (trœ:r) *m*, [quantity] surveyor. **métrique** (trik) *a*, metrical; metric. ¶ *f*, metrics, prosody.

métro (metro) *m*, subway.

métronome (metrɔnɔm) *m*, metronome.

métropole (metrɔpɔl) *f*, metropolis; mother country, home c. **métropolitaine, e** (litɛ̃, ɛn) *a*, metropolitan; mother (*church*); home, domestic.

mets (mɛ) *m*, dish, food, viand.

mettable (mɛtabl) *a*, wearable. **metteur** (tœ:r) *m*: ~ *en œuvre*, stone (*gem*) setter; adapter (*pers., fig.*). ~ *en scène*, producer. **mettre** (tr) *v.t.ir*, to put; place; lay; stake; set; poke; draw; make; bring; reduce; put on, wear; tear; take; throw. ~ *à l'encre*, to ink in. ~ *à la retraite*, to pension. ~ *au point*, to focus; adjust; tune up. ~ *bas*, to take off (*hat, etc.*); drop, foal, whelp. ~ *dedans*, to humbug, bamboozle. ~ *en accusation*, to arraign, commit for trial. ~ *en commun*, to pool. ~ *les pouces*, to knuckle under. *se* ~, to put oneself; sit [down]; lie [down];

begin; take to; dress; get; go; set. *se* ~ *en habit pour dîner*, to dress for dinner. *se* ~ *sur deux rangs*, to line up in twos.

meuble (mœbl) *a*, movable (*property*); light, loose, mellow (*earth*). ¶ *m*, piece of furniture; suite [of f.]; cabinet; (*pl.*) furniture; movables (*law*). ~*-classeur*, filing cabinet. ~ *de famille*, heirloom. **meublé** (ble) *m*, lodgings. **meubler** (ble) *v.t*, to furnish; stock, store (*fig.*).

meugler (møgle) *v.i*, to bellow, low.

meule (mø:l) *f*, grindstone, millstone; (*circular*) stack *or* rick (*hay*); round, wheel (*of cheese*). ~ [*de moulin*], millstone. ~ *de dessous*, ~ *gisante*, bedstone. ~ *de dessus*, ~ *courante*, runner. ~ *en grès*, grindstone. **meulière** (møljɛ:r) *f*, millstone grit; m. g. quarry. **meulon** (lɔ̃) *m*, cock (*hay*).

meunerie (mønri) *f*, milling (*flour*). **meunier, ère** (mønje, ɛ:r) *n*, miller; (*m.*) chub (*fish*).

meurt-de-faim (mœrdəfɛ̃) *m*, starveling.

meurtre (mœrtr) *m*, murder; sin, shame (*vandalism*). **meurtrier, ère** (trie, ɛ:r) *a*, murderous; internecine; deadly. ¶ *n*, murderer, ess; (*f.*) loophole.

meurtrir (mœrtri:r) *v.t*, to bruise. **meurtrissure** (trisy:r) *f*, bruise.

meute (mø:t) *f*, pack (*hounds, enemies*).

mévente (mevɑ̃:t) *f*, slump [in trade], negligible sales (*enabling publisher to close account with author*).

mexicain, e (mɛksikɛ̃, ɛn) *a.* & M~, *n*, Mexican. **Mexico** (ko) *m*, Mexico [City]. **le Mexique** (sik), Mexico (*country*).

mezzo-soprano (mɛdzosɔprano) *m*, mezzo-soprano.

mi (mi) *m*, E (*Mus.*). ¶ *word inv*, half, mid. *mi-bas*, *m.pl*, socks. *la mi-carême*, mid-lent. *à mi-chemin*, midway, halfway. *à mi-corps*, to the waist, waist-high *or* deep. *à mi-hauteur*, halfway up [the hill]. *mi-fil*, *m*, union (*linen & cotton thread*). *la mi-juin*, mid-June. *mi-lourd*, light-heavy

(*Box.*). **mi-moyen**, welter (*Box.*).
mi-parti, e, equally divided; half
... & half ... **la mi-temps**, half
time (*Foot.*).

miasmatique (mjasmatik) *a*, malarial. **miasme** (asm) *m*, miasma.

miauler (mjole) *v.i*, to miaow,
mew.

mica (mika) *m*, mica.

miche (miʃ) *f*, round loaf (*bread*).

micmac (mikmak) *m*, dirty work
(*fig.*).

microbe (mikrɔb) *m*, microbe.

micromètre (mikrɔmɛtr) *m*,
micrometer.

microphone (mikrɔfɔn) *m*, microphone.

microscope (mikrɔskɔp) *m*, microscope. **microscopique** (pik)
a, microscopic(al).

midi (midi) *m*, noon, midday,
noonday, twelve o'clock [in the
day]; noontide; heyday (*of life*);
south.

mie (mi) *f*, crumb (*bread*, opp.
crust).

miel (mjɛl) *m*, honey. **mielleux,
euse**† (lø, ø:z) *a*, bland; mealy-
mouthed; honeyed; mawkish.

mien, ne (*with* **le, la, les**) (mjɛ̃,
ɛn) *pn. & m*, mine; my own.

miette (mjɛt) *f*, crumb (*broken
bread, etc.*); bit, atom.

mieux (mjø) *ad. & a*, better;
rather; more; best; better-look-
ing. **le ~**, *ad*, the best. **le ~**, *m*,
[the] best.

mièvre (mjɛ:vr) *a*, [childishly]
affected, finical.

mignard, e (miɲa:r, ard) *a*,
mincing; girlish. **mignardise**
(ɲardi:z) *f*, daintiness; affectation; (*pl.*) pretty ways; pink
(*Bot.*). **mignon, ne** (ɲɔ̃, ɔn) *a*,
dainty, petite; sweet; pet. ¶ *n*,
pet, darling; (*m.*) minion. **mignonnette** (ɲɔnɛt) *f*, mignonette
(*lace*); pink (*Bot.*); gimp nails;
ground pepper; broken pebblestone.

migraine (migrɛn) *f*, migraine,
bad headache.

migrateur, trice (migratœ:r,
tris) *a*, migratory; migrant. **migration** (sjɔ̃) *f*, migration.

mijaurée (miʒɔre) *f*, affected
woman.

mijoter (miʒɔte) *v.t*, to [let] sim-

mer; (*v.i.*) to simmer. **se ~**, to be
brewing.

mil (mil) *m*, mil[le] (*1000*); millet;
Indian club. ¶ *a*, thousand
(*dates*).

milan (milɑ̃) *m*, kite (*bird*).

Milan (milɑ̃) *m*, Milan. **milanais,
e** (lanɛ, ɛ:z) *a. &* M~, *n*, Mil-
anese.

mildiou (mildju) *m*, mildew (*on
vines*).

milice (milis) *f*, militia. **milicien**
(sjɛ̃) *m*, militiaman.

milieu (miljø) *m*, middle, midst,
center; mean; medium; circle,
milieu. **au ~ de**, in the midst of,
amidst, among. **au ~ du navire**,
amidships. **le juste ~**, the golden
mean.

militaire† (militɛ:r) *a*, military.
¶ *m*, soldier, military man. **les
~s**, the military. **militant, e** (tɑ̃,
ɑ̃:t) *a*, militant. ¶ *m*, fighter. **militariser** (tarize) *v.t*, to militarize.
militer (te) *v.i*, to militate, tell.

mille (mil) *m. & a. inv* (a or one)
thousand; mile. **les M~ & une
Nuits**, the Arabian nights. **millefeuille** *ou* **millefeuille** (fœ:j) *f*,
milfoil, yarrow; (*m.*) Genoese
pastry, napoleon. **millénaire**
(millenɛ:r) *a. & m*, millenary
(*a. & n.*); millennium (*n.*). **mille-
pieds** (pje) *ou* **mille-pattes** (pat)
m, centipede.

millésime (millezim) *m*, date,
year.

millet (mijɛ) *m*, millet grass; millet. **~ des oiseaux**, canary seed.

milliard (miljaːr) *m*, billion,
1,000,000,000 francs. **milliar-
daire** (jardɛ:r) *n. & a*, multimillionaire.

milliasse (miljas) *f*, swarm[s].

millième (miljɛm) *a. & m*, thou-
sandth. **millier** (je) *m*, thousand
[or so]. **milligramme** (milligram)
m, milligram = 0.015 grain. **mil-
limètre** (millimɛtr) *m*, millimeter
= 0.03937 inch.

million (miljɔ̃) *m*, million; 1,000,-
000 francs. **millionième** (jɔnjɛm)
a. & m, millionth. **millionnaire**
(nɛ:r) *n*, millionaire.

mime (mim) *m*, mime; mimic.
mimer (me) *v.t. & abs*, to mime;
mimic. **mimétisme** (metism) *m*,
mimicry (*Zool.*), mimesis. **mi-

mique (mik) *a*, mimic. ¶ *f*, mimicry.

mimosa (mimoza) *m*, mimosa.

minable (minabl) *a*, pitiable; wretched.

minauder (minode) *v.i*, to mince, simper, smirk. **minauderie** (dri) *f*, mincing, etc. **minaudier, ère** (dje, ɛ:r) *a*, mincing, etc.

mince (mɛ̃:s) *a*, thin, slender; slight. **minceur** (mɛ̃sœ:r) *f*, thinness, etc.

mine (min) *f*, appearance, countenance, face, mien, look, looks. *de bonne* ~, good-looking.

mine (min) *f*, mine (*lit. & fig.*); mint (*fig.*); lead (*pencil*). ~ *de plomb*, black lead. **miner** (ne) *v.t*, to mine; undermine; sap; hollow; wear; prey [up]on (*mind*). **minerai** (nrɛ) *m*, ore. **minéral, e** (neral) *a. & m*, mineral; inorganic (*chemistry*). **minéralogie** (lɔ3i) *f*, mineralogy. **minéralogique** (3ik) *a*, mineralogical. **minéralogiste** (3ist) *m*, mineralogist.

minet, te (minɛ, ɛt) *n*, puss[y].

mineur (minœ:r) *m*, miner; sapper (*Mil.*).

mineur, e (minœ:r) *a*, minor; under age. ¶ *n*, minor (*pers.*), infant (*law*); (*m.*) minor (*Mus.*); (*f.*) minor premise (*Log.*).

miniature (minjaty:r) *f*, miniature. **miniaturiste** (tyrist) *n*, miniaturist.

minier, ère (minje, ɛ:r) *a*, mining (*att.*). ¶ *f*, gangue, matrix; surface mine, diggings.

minime (minim) *a*, minute, trifling, trivial.

minimum, ma (minimɔm, ma) *a. & m*, minimum.

ministère (ministɛ:r) *m*, department; ministry; office; secretaryship; board; agency, services, good offices, ministration. *M~ des Affaires étrangères*, State Department. *M~ des Finances*, Treasury Department. *M~ du Commerce*, Commerce Department. ~ *public*, public prosecutor. **ministériel, le** (terjɛl) *a*, ministerial; State nominated (*officer*); Government (*organ*). **ministre** (tr) *m*, minister; secretary [of state]; clergyman, vicar.

~ *de l'Intérieur*, Secretary of the Interior.

minium (minjɔm) *m*, minium; red lead.

minois (minwa) *m*, face, looks.

minon (minɔ̃) & **minou** (nu) *m*, puss[y].

minorité (minɔrite) *f*, minority; nonage; infancy (*law*).

Minorque (minɔrk) *f*, Minorca.

minoterie (minɔtri) *f*, [flour] milling; flour mill. **minotier** (tje) *m*, miller; flour merchant.

minuit (minɥi) *m*, midnight, twelve o'clock [at night].

minuscule (minyskyl) *a*, minute, tiny. ¶ *f*, small letter.

minute (minyt) *f*, minute; small hand (*writing*); original; draft. **minuter** (te) *v.t*, to minute, draw [up], draft. **minuterie** (tri) *f*, time switch.

minutie (minysi) *f*, trifle, (*pl.*) minutiae; minuteness, great care. **minutieux, euse†** (sjø, ø:z) *a*, meticulous; minute, thorough.

mioche (mjɔʃ) *m*, youngster, kiddy.

mirabelle (mirabɛl) *f*, mirabelle [plum].

miracle (mirɑ:kl) *m*, miracle; marvel; miracle [play], mystery [play]. *à* ~, admirably. **miraculeux, euse†** (rakylø, ø:z) *a*, miraculous; marvelous.

mirage (mira:3) *m*, mirage; testing, candling (*eggs*). **mire** (mi:r) *f*, sight (*gun*); aiming stake. **mirer** (mire) *v.t. & abs*, to aim at, take aim; test, candle (*eggs*). *se* ~, to look at oneself; see oneself reflected.

mirifique (mirifik) *a*, marvelous.

mirliflore (mirliflɔ:r) *m*, spark, dandy.

mirliton (mirlitɔ̃) *m*, mirliton (*musical toy pipe*).

mirobolant, e (mirɔbɔlɑ̃, ɑ̃:t) *a*, wonderful.

miroir (mirwa:r) *m*, mirror, [looking] glass. ~ *d'eau*, ornamental lake. ~ *déformant*, distorting mirror. **miroiter** (rwate) *v.i*, to flash, gleam, glisten, glint, sparkle. **miroiterie** (tri) *f*, mirror trade. **miroitier** (tje) *m*, mirror manufacturer *or* dealer.

misaine (mizɛn) *f*, foremast.

misanthrope (mizɑ̃trɔp) *m*, misanthrope, -pist. ¶ ~ & **misanthropique** (pik) *a*, misanthropic.

mise (miːz) *f*, putting, etc, as *mettre*; stake (*gaming*); bid (*auction*); get-up. ~ *à prix*, reserve [price], upset p. ~ *à terre*, landing. ~ *au point*, focusing; adjustment. ~ [*de fonds*], putting up of money; investment; capital; stake. ~ [*de*]*hors*, disbursement. ~ *en accusation*, indictment. ~ *en marche*, starting. ~ *en œuvre*, application. ~ *en pages*, making up; page proof. ~ *en scène*, staging; production; setting. ~ *en train*, starting; making ready (*Typ.*); practice (*sport*). de ~, in fashion; current; admissible; suitable; the thing. **miser** (mize) *v.t. & i*, to stake, bid.

misérable† (mizerabl) *a*, miserable; wretched; unfortunate; worthless. ¶ *n*, unfortunate, poor wretch; villain, scoundrel. **misère** (zɛːr) *f*, misery, wretchedness, distress, destitution; misfortune; trifle; misère (*cards*). ~ *de santé*, ailment. **miserere** (zerere) *m*, miserere. **miséreux, euse** (zerø, øːz) *a. & n*, poverty-stricken (person).

miséricorde (mizerikɔrd) *f*, mercy; misericord. ¶ *i*, mercy on us! good gracious! **miséricordieux, euse†** (djø, øːz) *a*, merciful.

misogyne (mizɔʒin) *a*, misogynic. ¶ *m*, misogynist, woman hater.

missel (misɛl) *m*, missal.

mission (misjɔ̃) *f*, mission. **missionnaire** (ɔnɛːr) *m*, missionary. **missive** (siːv) *f*, missive.

mistral (mistral) *m*, mistral (*wind*).

mitaine (mitɛːn) *f*, mitten.

mite (mit) *f*, mite (*insect*); moth. **miteux, euse** (tø, øːz) *a*, shabby.

mitiger (mitiʒe) *v.t*, to mitigate, temper.

mitonner (mitɔne) *v.t. & i*, to simmer.

mitoyen, ne (mitwajɛ̃, ɛn) *a*, party (*wall, structure*). **mitoyenneté** (jɛnte) *f*, party rights.

mitraille (mitrɑːj) *f*, grapeshot; group firing. **mitrailleur** (trɑ-jœːr) *m*, machine gunner. **mitrailleuse** (jøːz) *f*, machine gun.

mitre (mitr) *f*, miter; cowl (*chimney*). **mitré, e** (tre) *a*, mitered. **mitron** (trɔ̃) *m*, baker's man.

mixte (mikst) *a*, mixed; composite; joint; promiscuous. **mixtion** (tjɔ̃) *f*, mixture (*medicinal*). **mixture** (tyːr) *f*, mixture; concoction.

mnémonique (mnemɔnik) *a*, mnemonic. **la ~**, mnemonics.

mobile (mɔbil) *a*, movable; portable; mobile; changeable, fickle. ¶ *m*, moving body (*Mech.*); motive power; prime mover; motive, incentive. **mobilier, ère** (lje, ɛːr) *a*, personal, movable (*law*); transferable (*securities*). ¶ *m*, furniture, suite [of f.]. **mobilisation** (lizasjɔ̃) *f*, mobilization. **mobiliser** (ze) *v.t. & abs*, to mobilize. **mobilité** (te) *f*, mobility; fickleness.

moche (mɔʃ) *a*, ugly; lousy; rotten, etc.

modalité (mɔdalite) *f*, modality; method. **mode** (mɔd) *f*, mode, way; fashion, vogue; (*pl.*) millinery. à la ~ & de ~, in the fashion, fashionable, modish, stylish. à la ~, *ad*, fashionably, modishly, stylishly. ¶ *m*, mode; method; mood (*Gram.*). ~ *d'emploi*, directions for use. ~ *de circulation*, rule of the road.

modelage (mɔdlaːʒ) *m*, modeling; pattern making (*foundry*). **modèle** (dɛl) *m*, model, pattern; specimen; paragon; (*att.*) model, exemplary. ~ *de broderie*, sampler. **modelé** (dle) *m*, modeling (*relief of forms*). **modeler** (dle) *v.t. & abs*, to model; pattern; mold, shape. **modeleur** (dlœːr) *m*, modeler; patternmaker.

Modène (mɔdɛːn) *f*, Modena.

modération (mɔderasjɔ̃) *f*, moderation; mitigation. **modéré†, e** (re) *a*, moderate. **les modérés**, the moderates (*Pol.*). **modérer** (re) *v.t*, to moderate; check; curb; mitigate.

moderne (mɔdɛrn) *a*, modern; up to date; new. **les ~s**, *m.pl*, the moderns. **moderniser** (nize) *v.t,* to modernize.

modeste† (mɔdɛst) *a,* modest; quiet (*dress*). **modestie** (ti) *f,* modesty.

modicité (mɔdisite) *f,* moderateness; lowness.

modification (mɔdifikasjɔ̃) *f,* modification, alteration, variation. **modifier** (fje) *v.t,* to modify, alter, vary.

modique† (mɔdik) *a,* moderate (*price*); small (*sum, etc.*).

modiste (mɔdist) *f,* milliner, modiste.

modulation (mɔdylasjɔ̃) *f,* modulation. **module** (dyl) *m,* module; modulus. **moduler** (le) *v.i. & t,* to modulate.

moelle (mwal) *f,* marrow; pith. ~ *épinière,* spinal cord. **moelleux, euse**† (lØ, Ø:z) *a,* marrowy; pithy; mellow; soft. ¶ *m,* softness; mellowness.

moellon (mwalɔ̃) *m,* quarry stone, rubble. ~ *d'appareil,* ashlar.

mœurs (mœrs) *f.pl,* manners, habits; morals, morality.

mohair (mɔɛːr) *m,* mohair.

moi (mwa) *pn,* me; [to] me, I. *à* ~! *au secours!* help, help! ¶ *m,* self; ego. ~-**même,** *pn,* myself.

moignon (mwaɲɔ̃) *m,* stump (*limb, tree*).

moindre (mwɛ̃:dr) *a,* less; lesser, lower; minor. **le, la,** ~, the least; the slightest. [ne . . .] **pas le moindrement** (mwɛ̃drəmɑ̃), not in the least.

moine (mwan) *m,* monk, friar; bed warmer. ~ *bourru,* bugaboo, bugbear, goblin, bog[e]y; bear, brute.

moineau (mwano) *m,* sparrow. ~ *franc,* English sparrow.

moinerie (mwanri) *f,* monkhood, monkery.

moins (mwɛ̃) *ad. & pr,* less; not so [much]; fewer; under; minus; to (*of the hour*). [**signe**] ~, *m,* minus [sign]. *à* ~ *de,* for less than; barring; unless, without. *à* ~ *que,* unless. *au* ~, at least; however, above all. *le* ~, the least. *pas le* ~ *du monde,* not in the least.

moins-value (mwɛ̃valy) *f,* depreciation; deficit.

moire (mwaːr) *f,* moire, watering. ~ *de soie* ou *soie moirée* (mware), watered silk, moiré, s. **moirer** (re) *v.t,* to water, moiré.

mois (mwa) *m,* month; month's pay, rent, or like.

moise (mɔiːz) *m,* wicker cradle.

moise (mwaːz) *f,* brace (*Carp.*); ledger (*Build.*). **moiser** (mwaze) *v.t,* to brace.

moisi, e (mwazi) *p.p,* moldy, mildewy; musty; frowsy. **moisir** (ziːr) *v.t. & i, & se* ~, to mildew, turn moldy. **moisissure** (zisyːr) *f. & moisi* (zi) *m,* mildew, mold, moldiness, mustiness.

moissine (mwasin) *f,* vine branch with grapes hanging (*as ceiling decoration*).

moisson (mwasɔ̃) *f,* harvest, reaping. **moissonner** (sɔne) *v.t. & abs,* to reap, harvest; cut off (*fig.*). **moissonneur, euse** (nœːr, Ø:z) *n,* reaper, harvester (*pers.*). (*f.*) reaping machine, reaper. *moissonneuse-lieuse, f,* combine harvester.

moite (mwat) *a,* moist, damp; clammy. **moiteur** (tœːr) *f,* moistness; clamminess.

moitié (mwatje) *f,* half, moiety; better half (*wife*). ¶ *ad,* half, partly. *à* ~, half, by half; on half profits. *à* ~ *chemin,* halfway. *de* ~, by half. *être* (ou *se mettre) de* ~ *avec,* to go halves with.

Moka (mɔka) *m,* Mocha. *m*~ ou *café de M*~, mocha, M. coffee; coffee (*ordinary*).

mol *see* **mou.**

molaire (mɔlɛːr) *a. & f,* molar.

môle (moːl) *m,* mole, breakwater.

moléculaire (mɔlekylɛːr) *a,* molecular. **molécule** (kyl) *f,* molecule.

moleskine (mɔlɛskin) *f,* moleskin; oilcloth.

molester (mɔlɛste) *v.t,* to taunt.

moleter (mɔlte) *v.t,* to mill, knurl. **molette** (lɛt) *f,* rowel; muller; milled nut; knurl; milling tool; cutter wheel.

mollasse (mɔlas) *a,* flabby; flimsy; spineless (*fig.*). **mollement** (lmɑ̃) *ad,* softly; gracefully; feebly; voluptuously. **mollesse** (lɛs) *f*, softness; mildness; feebleness; flabbiness; overindulgence; voluptuousness. **mollet, te** (lɛ, ɛt) *a*, softish; soft-boiled (*eggs*); fancy (*roll*). ¶ *m*, calf (*leg*). **molletière** (ltjɛ:r) *f*, legging. **molleton** (ltɔ̃) *m*, swansdown (*cloth*). **mollir** (li:r) *v.i. & t*, to soften; slacken; lull.

mollusque (mɔlysk) *m*, mollusc.

Moluques (les) (mɔlyk) *f.pl*, the Moluccas.

môme (mo:m) *n*, youngster.

moment (mɔmɑ̃) *m*, moment; time; momentum. **momentané†, e** (tane) *a*, momentary, temporary.

momerie (mɔmri) *f*, pose (*fig.*); mummery.

momie (mɔmi) *f*, mummy; sleepyhead. **momifier** (fje) *v.t*, to mummify.

mon, ma, mes (mɔ̃, ma, me) *a*, my. *oui, mon colonel, etc*, yes, sir (*in the army*).

monacal, e† (mɔnakal) *a*, monastic, monkish.

monarchie (mɔnarʃi) *f*, monarchy. **monarchique** (ʃik) *a*, monarchic(al). **monarchiste** (ʃist) *m. & att*, monarchist. **monarque** (nark) *m*, monarch.

monastère (mɔnastɛ:r) *m*, monastery; convent. **monastique** (tik) *a*, monastic.

monceau (mɔ̃so) *m*, heap, pile.

mondain, e (mɔ̃dɛ̃, ɛn) *a*, worldly, mundane; (*att.*) society. ¶ *n*, society man, woman; worldling. **mondanité** (danite) *f*, worldliness; (*pl.*) social events (*news*). **monde** (mɔ̃:d) *m*, world; people; company; set; crowd; servants. *le ~ inanimé*, inanimate nature.

monder (mɔ̃de) *v.t*, to hull.

mondial, e (mɔ̃djal) *a*, worldwide.

monétaire (mɔnetɛ:r) *a*, monetary, money (*att.*).

mongol, e (mɔ̃gɔl) *a. & M~, n*, Mongol[ian]. **la Mongolie** (li), Mongolia.

moniteur (mɔnitœ:r) *m*, adviser; coach; (*name of many French newspapers*).

monnaie (mɔnɛ) *f*, money; currency; coin; coinage; [small]

change. *~ de papier*, [convertible] paper money. **la M~**, the mint. **monnayer** (nɛje) *v.t*, to coin, mint; commercialize (*fig.*). **monnayeur** (jœ:r) *m*, minter.

monochrome (mɔnɔkro:m) *a*, monochrome. **monocle** (kl) *m*, monocle, eyeglass. **monocorde** (kɔrd) *m*, single-string instrument; monochord; monotonist (*pers.*). **monogamie** (gami) *f*, monogamy. **monogramme** (gram) *m*, monogram. **monographie** (grafi) *f*, monograph. **monolithe** (lit) *a*, monolithic. ¶ *m*, monolith. **monologue** (lɔg) *m*, monologue. **monologuer** (ge) *v.i*, to monologize, soliloquize. **monomanie** (mani) *f*, monomania. **monoplan** (plɑ̃) *m*, monoplane. **monopole** (pɔl) *m*, monopoly. **monopoliser** (lize) *v.t*, to monopolize. **monosyllabe** (silab) *m*, monosyllable. ¶ *~ & * **monosyllabique** (bik) *a*, monosyllabic. **monotone** (tɔn) *a*, monotonous; humdrum. **monotonie** (ni) *f*, monotony, sameness. **monotype** (tip) *f*, monotype.

mons (mɔ̃:s) *m*, Master (*so-&-so*) (*jocularly*). **monseigneur**, *oft*. **M~** (mɛ̃sɛɲœ:r) *m*, His (*or* Your) Royal Highness; my lord, his (*or* your) lordship, his (*or* your) Grace; jimmy (*burglar's*). **monsieur**, *oft*. **M~** (məsjø) *m*, gentleman; Mr.; Esq.; sir; my (*or* the) master; man. *~ le juge*, your, his, Honor.

monstre (mɔ̃:str) *m. & att*, monster. **monstreux, euse†** (mɔ̃stryø, ø:z) *a*, monstrous, freakish. **monstruosité** (ozite) *f*, monstrosity; freak [of nature].

mont (mɔ̃) *m*, mount, mountain; (*pl.*) Alps. *le ~ Blanc, etc*. See under *blanc, etc. par ~s & par vaux*, up hill & down dale. *~-de-piété*, pawnshop.

montage (mɔ̃ta:ʒ) *m*, raising; mounting; setting; erection; fit (*Mech.*); editing (*movie*). *~ des mailles*, casting on (*Knit.*).

montagnard, e (mɔ̃taɲa:r, ard) *a*, highland, mountain (*att.*). ¶ *n*, highlander, mountaineer. *les Montagnards*, the wild men (*Pol.*). **montagne** (taɲ) *f*, mountain; mountains. ~*s russes,* scenic railway, switchback. **montagneux, euse** (ɲø, ø:z) *a,* mountainous.

montant, e (mɔ̃tã, ã:t) *a,* rising, ascending; incoming (*tide*); up-hill; up (*train, etc.*); high; high-necked (*dress*); stand-up (*collar*). ¶ *m,* upright; post; stile; amount; total; tang. **monte** (mɔ̃:t) *f,* covering (*of animals*); mount (*turf*); riding; jockey. **montecharge** (mɔ̃tʃarʒ) *m,* freight elevator, hoist. **montée** (mɔ̃te) *f,* ascent, rise, rising.

monténégrin, e, (mɔ̃tenegrɛ̃, in) *a.* & **M~,** *n,* Montenegrin. **le Monténégro** (gro), Montenegro.

monter (mɔ̃te) *v.i.* & *t,* to go up, ascend; mount; climb; ride; command (*ship*); amount; raise, hoist, elevate; take up, carry up; set up, put up; erect; fit; set; string (*violin*); wind [up] (*spring*); turn up (*wick*); stage (*play*); cast on (*Knit.*); excite. ~ *en amazone,* to ride side-saddle. ~ *en graine,* to run to seed. ~ *en voiture,* to take one's seat in a carriage. ~ *sur un vaisseau, en avion,* to [go on] board a ship, a plane. **se ~,** to amount; equip oneself. **monteur** (tœ:r) *m,* setter, mounter; fitter, erector.

monticule (mɔ̃tikyl) *m,* hillock, mound, knoll, hummock.

montjoie (mɔ̃ʒwa) *f,* cairn.

montoir (mɔ̃twa:r) *m,* horse block.

montrable (mɔ̃trabl) *a,* presentable. **montre** (mɔ̃:tr) *f,* parade; show; display; [shop] window (*display*); sample; watch. ~-*bracelet,* wristwatch. **montrer** (mɔ̃tre) *v.t,* to show; point [out]; teach. ~ *du doigt,* to point at. **montreur** (trœ:r) *m,* showman; exhibitor.

montueux, euse (mɔ̃tɥø, ø:z) *a,* hilly.

monture (mɔ̃ty:r) *f,* mount (*animal*); mount[ing], setting; hook to gut (*Fish.*). ~ *de rideaux,* cornice pole. *sans* ~, rimless (*glasses*).

monument (mɔnymã) *m,* monument, memorial; building (*public or historic*). ~ *aux morts*

[*de la guerre*], war memorial. ~ *historique,* national monument, building, etc, of historic interest. **monumental, e** (tal) *a,* monumental.

moquer (se) de (mɔke), to mock (at), deride, jeer at, laugh at, ridicule, make fun of. *s'en moquer,* not to care. **moquerie** (kri) *f,* mockery, jeer[s]. **moquette** (kɛt) *f,* moquette, velvet pile, saddle bag; Brussels carpet. **moqueur, euse** (kœ:r, ø:z) *n,* mocker, scoffer. ¶ *a,* mocking. [*oiseau*] *moqueur,* mocking bird.

moraillon (mɔrajɔ̃) *m,* hasp.

moraine (mɔrɛ:n) *f,* moraine.

moral, e (mɔral) *a,* moral; mental. ¶ *m,* mind; moral[e]. **morale** (ral) *f,* morals (*ethics*); moral (*of story*). **moralement** (lmã) *ad,* morally. **moraliser** (lize) *v.i.* & *t,* to moralize; lecture. **moraliste** (list) *m,* moralist. **moralité** (te) *f,* morality (*principles, drama*); moral (*of fable*).

moratoire (mɔratwa:r) *a,* moratory; on overdue payments (*interest*). ¶ ~ & **moratorium** (tɔrjɔm) *m,* moratorium.

Moravie (la) (mɔravi), Moravia.

morbide (mɔrbid) *a,* morbid; unwholesome.

morceau (mɔrso) *m,* piece, bit; morsel; snack; lump, knob; scrap, fragment. ~*x choisis,* selections (*from writings*). ~ *d'ensemble,* part song, p. music. ~ *de concours,* test piece (*music, etc.*). *un* ~ *de femme,* a slip of a woman. ~ *honteux,* last piece (*left on dish*). **morceler** (sele) *v.t,* to parcel [out]; subdivide.

mordant, e (mɔrdã, ã:t) *a,* mordant, biting; pungent. ¶ *m,* mordant; pungency; keenness; shrillness. **mordicus** (diky:s) *ad,* doggedly. **mordiller** (dije) *v.t,* to nibble.

mordoré, e (mɔrdɔre) *a,* reddish-brown; bronze (*shoes*).

mordre (mɔrdr) *v.t.* & *abs,* to bite, nip; nibble. *ça mord!* I have a bite! (*Fish.*). ~ *à,* to take to (*a study*). ~ *sur* (*fig.*), to find fault with. ~ *sur la latte,* to go over the mark (*Jump.*).

More (mɔːr) *m*, Moor. **m~,** *a*, Moorish.

morelle (mɔrɛl) *f*, nightshade.

moresque (mɔrɛsk) *a*, Moresque. ¶ *f*, Morisco, morris [dance].

morfil (mɔrfil) *m*, wire edge.

morfondre (mɔrfɔ̃:dr) *v.t*, to chill. **se ~,** to be bored; to wait in vain, cool one's heels. **morfondu, e** (fɔ̃dy) *p.a*, [as if] frozen stiff.

morganatique† (mɔrganatik) *a*, morganatic.

morgeline (mɔrʒəlin) *f*, chickweed; pimpernel.

morgue (mɔrg) *f*, haughtiness; morgue.

moribond, e (mɔribɔ̃, ɔ̃:d) *a. & n*, moribund, dying (man, woman).

moricaud, e (mɔriko, o:d) *n*, blackamoor.

morigéner (mɔriʒene) *v.t*, to take to task.

morne (mɔrn) *a*, gloomy, dismal, dreary, bleak, cheerless.

morose (mɔro:z) *a*, morose, sullen, moody. **morosité** (rozite) *f*, moroseness, etc.

Morphée (mɔrfe) *m*, Morpheus. **morphine** (fin) *f*, morphia, -phine. **morphinomane** (nɔman) *n*, morphinomaniac.

morphologie (mɔrfɔlɔʒi) *f*, morphology; accidence (*Gram.*).

mors (mɔːr) *m*, bit (*bridle*); jaw (*vise*).

morse (mɔrs) *m*, walrus, morse.

morsure (mɔrsy:r) *f*, bite; sting (*fig.*).

mort (mɔːr) *f*, death. **à ~,** to d.; to the d.; mortal (*strife*); mortally; deadly. **~ & passion,** excruciating pains; agonies (*fig.*). **mort, e** (mɔːr, ɔrt) *a*, dead; still (*water, life*); spent (*shot*). **les morts,** the dead. **le jour des morts,** All Soul's Day. **mort,** *m*, dummy (*cards*).

mortaise (mɔrtɛ:z) *f*, mortise, -ice; slot.

mortalité (mɔrtalite) *f*, mortality; death rate. **mort-aux-rats** (mɔrora) *f*, rat poison. **mort-bois** (mɔrbwɑ) *m*, underwood, brushwood. **morte-eau** (mɔrto) *f*, neap tide. **mortel, le**† (tɛl) *a*, mortal, deadly, lethal; fatal (*accident*). ¶ *n*, mor-

tal. **morte-saison** (təsɛzɔ̃) *f*, dead season, off season.

mortier (mɔrtje) *m*, mortar (*plaster, vessel, Mil.*). **~ de tranchée,** trench mortar.

mortifier (mɔrtifje) *v.t*, to mortify; make tender (*meat, game*). **mort-né, e** (mɔrne) *a*, stillborn. **mortuaire** (mɔrtɥɛ:r) *a*, mortuary, [of] death; burial (*fees*). **le drap ~,** a pall.

morue (mɔry) *f*, cod[fish]. **morutier** (tje) *m*, cod fisher.

morve (mɔrv) *f*, mucus of the nose; glanders.

mosaïque (mɔzaik) *a*, Mosaic (*law*). ¶ *f*, mosaic, tessellated pavement.

Moscou (mɔsku) *m*, Moscow.

mosquée (mɔske) *f*, mosque.

mot (mo) *m*, word; saying; say; cue. **~ à ~** (motamo), **~ pour ~,** word for word, verbatim. **~s croisés** [-*énigmes*], crossword [puzzle]. **~ d'ordre,** password; watchword, keynote. **~ de l'énigme,** answer to the riddle. **~ de passe,** password. **~ de ralliement,** countersign (*Mil.*). *Note.* —In Fr., the **~ de ralliement** is given in reply to the **~ d'ordre.** **~ en vedette,** word displayed in bold type, catchword. **~ piquant,** quip. **~ pour rire,** joke.

moteur (mɔtœ:r) *m*, engine, motor; mover. **~ à essence,** gasoline engine. **~ à gaz,** gas e. **~ à pétrole,** oil e. **moteur, trice** (tœːr, tris) *att*, motive, driving. **motif** (tif) *m*, motive; reason; cause; (*pl.*) grounds; intentions (*matrimonial*); design, motif, traced article, (*pl.*) traced goods; theme, motto (*Mus.*). **motion** (mɔsjɔ̃) *f*, motion (*proposal at meeting*). **motiver** (mɔtive) *v.t*, to state the reason for; justify.

motoculture (mɔtɔkylty:r) *f*, tractor farming, mechanized f. **motocyclette** (siklɛt), *abb*. **moto** (mɔto) *f*, motor [bi]cycle. **motocycliste** (klist) *n*, motorcyclist.

motte (mɔt) *f*, clod; turf, sod; roll (*butter*); mound.

motu proprio (mɔty prɔprio), of one's own accord.

motus (mɔty:s) *i*, mum['s the word]!

mou, mol, molle (mu, mɔl) *a*, soft; lax; slack; inelastic (*Phys.*); limp, flabby; languid; muggy, close; indolent. **mou**, *m*, lights (*animal lungs*).

mouchard (muʃa:r) *m*, spy; police spy. **moucharder** (ʃarde) *v.t*, to spy.

mouche (muʃ) *f*, fly; patch, beauty spot; spot (*Bil.*); tuft (*on chin*); police spy; bull's-eye (*target*); bull (*shot*). ~ *à feu*, firefly. ~ *à miel*, honeybee. ~ *à viande*, meat fly, blowfly. ~ *bleue*, blue-bottle. ~ *commune*, housefly. ~ *de mai*, May fly. ~ *noyée*, wet fly (*Fish.*). *poids* ~, fly weight (*Box.*). *prendre la* ~, to take offense.

moucher (muʃe) *v.t*, to wipe (*child's*) nose; snuff (*candle*); snub. *se* ~, to blow one's nose.

moucherolle (muʃrɔl) *f*, fly-catcher (*bird*). **moucheron** (ʃrɔ̃) *m*, midge, gnat; whippersnapper; snuff (*candle*).

moucheté, e (muʃte) *a*, spotted, speckled; tabby (*cat*).

mouchettes (muʃɛt) *f.pl*, snuffers.

moucheture (muʃty:r) *f*, spot, speckle.

mouchoir (muʃwa:r) *m*, handkerchief. ~ *de cou*, silk scarf.

moudre (mudr) *v.t. & abs. ir*, to grind, mill.

moue (mu) *f*, pout[ing]. *faire la* ~, to pout.

mouette (mwɛt) *f*, [sea] gull, [sea] mew.

mouffette (mufɛt) *f*, skunk (*Zool.*).

moufle (mufl) *f*, pulley block, tackle b.; mitt[en] (*m.*) pulley block, tackle b.; muffle (*Chem.*).

mouillage (muja:ʒ) *m*, wetting; watering (*wine, etc.*); mooring; moorings, anchorage, berth. **mouille-bouche** (mujbuʃ) *f*, bergamot (*pear*). **mouillée** (je) *p.a.f*, palat[al]ized (*consonant*). **mouiller** (je) *v.t. & abs*, to wet, moisten, damp; water; anchor, moor, berth. **mouillette** (jɛt) *f*, sippet. **mouilloir** (jwa:r) *m*, damper (*stamps, labels*). **mouillure** (jy:r) *f*, wetting; damp mark (*in books*).

moulage (mula:ʒ) *m*, molding

(*act*); casting. **moule** (mul) *m*, mold, (*f.*) mussel. **mouler** (le) *v.t*, to mold, cast; shape; print (*handwriting*). **mouleur** (lœ:r) *m*, molder.

moulin (mulɛ̃) *m*, mill; moulin (*glacier*). ~ *à paroles*, chatterbox; windbag. ~ *à prières*, prayer wheel. ~ *à vent*, windmill. **mouliné, e** (line) *p.a. & p.p*, worm-eaten (*wood*); thrown (*silk*). **moulinet** (nɛ) *m*, winch; reel (*Fish.*); turnstile (X *on post*). *faire le* ~ *avec*, to whirl, twirl. **moulu, e** (ly) *p.a*: ~ *de fatigue*, dead beat. *tout* ~, aching all over.

moulure (muly:r) *f*, molding (*ornamental strip*).

mourant, e (murɑ̃, ɑ̃:t) *a*, dying; languishing (*eyes*); faint (*voice*). **les mourants**, *m.pl*, the dying. **mourir** (ri:r) *v.i.ir*, to die, be dying; die away; d. out; d. down. *faire* ~, to execute (*criminal*). *se* ~, to be dying; fade out, give out.

mouron (murɔ̃) *m*, pimpernel. ~ [*des oiseaux*], chickweed.

mousquet (muskɛ) *m*, musket. **mousquetaire** (kətɛ:r) *m*, musketeer; (*att.*) double (*cuffs*). **mousqueton** (tɔ̃) *m*, carbine; snap hook.

mousse (mus) *m*, cabin boy; (*f.*) moss; froth; foam; lather; head (*on glass of beer*); mousse (*cream*).

mousseline (muslin) *f*, muslin; mousseline.

mousser (muse) *v.i*, to froth; foam; lather; effervesce, sparkle. *faire* ~ (*fig.*), to make much of. **mousseux, euse** (sø, ø:z) *a*, mossy; moss (*rose*); frothy; foamy; sparkling (*wine*). *non mousseux*, still (*wine*).

mousson (musɔ̃) *f*, monsoon.

moussu, e (musy) *a*, mossy, moss-grown; moss (*rose*).

moustache (mustaʃ) *f*, mustache; whiskers (*animal*). ~ *en brosse*, toothbrush m. ~ *en croc*, turned up m. **moustachu, e** (ʃy) *a*, mustached.

moustiquaire (mustikɛ:r) *f*, mosquito net. **moustique** (tik) *m*, mosquito.

moût (mu) *m*, must, stum; wort.

moutard (muta:r) *m,* youngster, urchin.

moutarde (mutard) *f. & att,* mustard. *de la ~ après dîner,* too late to be useful. *la ~ lui est montée au nez,* he lost his temper. **moutardier** (dje) *m,* mustard pot; m. maker.

mouton (mutɔ̃) *m,* sheep; wether; mutton; sheep[skin]; lamb (*pers.*); spy (*on prisoner*); monkey, ram tup (*pile driving*); yoke, stock (*of bell*); (*pl.*) sheep; (*pl.*) white-caps (*waves*); (*pl.*) fluff (*under furniture*). **moutonner** (tɔne) *v.i,* to [break into] foam (*sea*). *nuages moutonnés, ciel moutonné,* fleecy clouds, sky fleeced with clouds. **moutonneux, euse** (nø, ø:z) *a,* foamy; crested (*waves*). **moutonnier, ère** (nje, ɛ:r) *a,* sheeplike (*pers.*).

mouture (muty:r) *f,* milling; maslin.

mouvant, e (muvɑ̃, ɑ̃:t) *a,* moving, shifting, unstable; quick-(*sand*). **mouvement** (vmɑ̃) *m,* motion; movement; progress; impulse; action, bustle, stir, life; arrangement (*Art.*); conformation (*of ground*); change; changes (*staff*); appointments & promotions; move (*Mil.*); burst (*oratory*); attack (*fever*); fluctuation; traffic; circulation; turnover; statistics (*population*); transaction; works (*Horol.*). *~ des navires,* shipping intelligence, s. news, movements of ships. *~ populaire,* civil commotion. *dans le ~* (*fig.*), in the swim. *de son propre ~,* of one's own accord. **mouvementé, e** (te) *a,* lively, bustling, busy; eventful; stirring; broken (*ground*). **mouvoir** (vwa:r) *v.t.ir. & se ~,* to move; actuate, propel.

moyen, ne (mwajɛ̃, ɛn) *a,* middle; mean, average; medium; middling; intermediate (*course, Sch.*); doubtful (*virtue*). *d'âge moyen,* middle-aged (*pers.*). *le ~ âge,* the Middle Ages. *du ~ âge,* medieval. *~ terme,* middle course (*conduct*). *~ [terme],* middle [term] (*Log.*). **moyen,** *m,* means, way; help; (*pl.*) means (*pecuniary*); grounds (*law*). *~ de for-*

tune, makeshift. **moyenâgeux, euse** (jɛnɑʒø, ø:z) *a,* medieval. **moyennant** (nɑ̃) *pr,* in consideration of; on; at; with the help of. **moyenne** (jɛn) *f,* average, mean. **moyennement** (nmɑ̃) *ad,* moderately, fairly.

moyeu (mwajø) *m,* nave; hub; boss. *~ arrière à roue libre & frein contre-pédalage,* coaster hub.

mucilage (mysila:ʒ) *m,* mucilage. **mucosité** (mykozite) *f. & mucus* (ky:s) *m,* mucus, phlegm.

mue (my) *f,* molt[ing]; slough[ing]; mew; [hen] coop; breaking (*voice*). **muer** (mɥe) *v.i,* to molt; slough; break; (*v.t.*) to change.

muet, te (mɥɛ, ɛt) *a. & n,* dumb (person); mute; speechless; silent. *à la muette,* without speaking.

muezzin (mɥɛzɛ̃) *m,* muezzin.

mufle (myfl) *m,* muzzle, muffle; cad. **muflier** (flie) *m,* antirrhinum, snapdragon.

muge (my:ʒ) *m,* gray mullet.

mugir (myʒi:r) *v.i,* to low; bellow; roar; whistle (*wind*).

muguet (mygɛ) *m,* lily of the valley.

mulâtre (mylɑ:tr) *a. & m,* **mulâtresse** (latrɛs) *f,* mulatto. **mule** (myl) *f,* [she] mule; mule (*slipper*); slipper *or* toe (*of pope as kissed*). **mulet** (lɛ) *m,* [he] mule; mule (*pers.*); cross, hybrid, mule; gray mullet. **muletier** (ltje) *m,* muleteer; (*att.*) mule (*track*).

mulot (mylo) *m,* field mouse.

multicolore (myltikɔlɔ:r) *a,* multicolor[ed], many-colored.

multiple (myltipl) *a,* multiple, manifold, multifarious. ¶ *m,* multiple. **multiplicande** (plikɑ̃:d) *m,* multiplicand. **multiplicateur** (katœ:r) *m,* multiplier. **multiplication** (sjɔ̃) *f,* multiplication; gear [ratio]. **multiplicité** (site) *f,* multiplicity. **multiplier** (plie) *v.t. & i.* & *se ~,* to multiply.

multitude (myltityd) *f,* multitude, crowd.

municipal, e (munisipal) *a,* municipal, town (*att.*). **municipalité** (lite) *f,* municipality; [municipal] corporation.

munificence (mynifisɑ̃:s) *f,* munificence, bounty.

munir (myni:r) *v.t*, to supply, provide, furnish; fortify. **munitions** (nisjɔ̃) *f.pl*, ammunition. ~ *de bouche*, provisions, food. ~ *de guerre*, war[like] stores, munitions.

muqueux, euse (mykø, ø:z) *a*, mucous. **[membrane] muqueuse**, *f*, m. membrane.

mur (my:r) *m*, wall.

mûr, e (my:r) *a*, ripe, mature; mellow; worn threadbare.

muraille (myra:j) *f*, wall. **mural, e** (ral) *a*, mural, wall (*att*.).

mûre (my:r) *f*, mulberry. ~ *sauvage*, ~ *de ronce*, blackberry.

mûrement (myrmɑ̃) *ad*, closely, thoroughly.

murer (myre) *v.t*, to wall; w. up; screen (*fig*.).

mûrier (myrje) *m*, mulberry [tree].

mûrir (myri:r) *v.i. & t*, to ripen, mature; mellow.

murmure (myrmy:r) *m*, murmur; grumbling; mutter; whisper; hum; brawling; gurgle; soughing. **murmurer** (myre) *v.i. & t*, to murmur, etc.

mûron (myrɔ̃) *m*, blackberry; wild raspberry bush.

musaraigne (myzarɛɲ) *f*, shrew [mouse].

musarder (myzarde) *v.i*, to dawdle.

musc (mysk) *m*, musk; m. deer. [**noix**] **muscade** (kad) *f*, nutmeg. **muscadier** (dje) *m*, nutmeg [tree].

muscat (ka) *a. & m*, muscat (grape, wine).

muscle (myskl) *m*, muscle. **musclé, e** (kle) *a*, -muscled. **musculaire** (kylɛ:r) *&* **musculeux, euse** (lø, ø:z) *a*, muscular.

Muse (my:z) *f*, Muse.

museau (myzo) *m*, muzzle, snout.

musée (myze) *m*, museum.

museler (myzle) *v.t*, to muzzle. **muselière** (zəljɛ:r) *f*, muzzle (*dog*).

muser (myze) *v.i*, to dawdle, moon [about].

musette (myzɛt) *f*, musette (*Mus*.); nosebag; haversack; bag.

muséum (myzeɔm) *m*, natural history museum.

musical, e† (myzikal) *a*, musical. **music hall** (myzik hɔl) *m*, music hall variety theater. **musicien, ne**

(sjɛ̃, ɛn) *n*, musician; player; bandsman; (*att*.) musical. **musique** (zik) *f*, music; band; toy musical instrument. ~ *de chats*, caterwauling.

musoir (myzwa:r) *m*, pierhead.

musquer (myske) *v.t*, to [perfume with] musk.

musulman, e (myzylmɑ̃, an) *n. & att*, Mussulman.

mutabilité (mytabilite) *f*, mutability. **mutation** (sjɔ̃) *f*, mutation, change; transfer; conveyance (*law*). **muter** (te) *v.t*, to transfer (*official, soldier*).

mutilation (mytilasjɔ̃) *f*, mutilation, maiming; defacement. **mutilé de la guerre** (le) *m*, disabled soldier, disabled sailor. **mutiler** (le) *v.t*, to mutilate, etc.

mutin, e (mytɛ̃, in) *a. & n*, roguish (child), mischievous (child); mutinous; mutineer. **se mutiner** (tine) *v.pr. & mutiner*, *v.abs*, to mutiny, rebel; be unruly. **mutinerie** (nri) *f*, mutiny; refractoriness; roguishness.

mutisme (mytism) *m*, dumbness, muteness.

mutualiste (mytɥalist) *n*, member of a mutual society *or* association. **mutualité** (te) *f*, mutuality; mutual association. ~ *de crédit*, mutual loan association. **mutuel, le†** (tɥɛl) *a*, mutual.

mycélium (miseljɔm) *m*, mycelium, spawn.

myope (mjɔp) *a. & n*, shortsighted (person), nearsighted (person). **myopie** (pi) *f*, myopia.

myosotis (mjɔzɔtis) *m*, myosotis, forget-me-not.

myriade (mirjad) *f*, myriad. **myriagramme** (gram) *m*, myriagram = 10000 grams *or* 22.046 lbs. **myriapode** (pɔd) *m*, myriapod.

myrrhe (mi:r) *f*, myrrh.

myrte (mirt) *m*, myrtle. **myrtille** (til) *f*, whortleberry, bilberry.

mystère (mistɛ:r) *m*, mystery; m. [play], miracle [play]. ~ *de la Passion*, passion play. **mystérieux, euse†** (terjø, ø:z) *a*, mysterious. **mysticisme** (tisism) *m*, mysticism. **mysticité** (te) *f*, mysticalness. **mystificateur, trice** (fikatœ:r, tris) *n*, hoaxer, humbug.

mystifier (fje) *v.t*, to mystify; hoax, humbug. **mystique†** (tik) *a*, mystic(al). ¶ *n*, mystic (*pers.*); (*f.*) mystical theology; mysterious appeal (*as of the olden times*).

mythe (mit) *m*, myth. **mythique** (tik) *a*, mythic(al). **mythologie** (tɔlɔʒi) *f*, mythology. **mythologique** (ʒik) *a*, mythologic(al). **mythologue** (lɔg) *n*, mythologist.

N

nabab (nabab) *m*, nabob.

nabot, e (nabo, ɔt) (*pers.*) *n*, midget, shrimp, manikin.

nacelle (nasɛl) (*Avn.*) *f*, car, nacelle, gondola; cockpit; skiff, dinghy; pontoon boat.

nacre (nakr) *f*, mother of pearl. **nacré, e** (kre) *a*, pearly.

nadir (nadi:r) *m*, nadir.

nævus (nevy:s) *m*, birthmark, mole.

nage (na:ʒ) *f*, swimming; stroke. ~ [*d'aviron*], rowing. ~ *à la pagaie*, paddling. ~ *de côté*, sidestroke. ~ *en grenouille*, breaststroke. ~ *en couple*, sculling. *en* ~, bathed in perspiration. **nageoire** (naʒwa:r) *f*, fin (*fish*); flipper. **nager** (ʒe) *v.i*, to swim, float; welter, revel; row. ~ *debout*, to tread water; row standing up. ~ *en couple*, to scull. ~ *entre deux eaux*, to swim under water. **nageur, euse** (ʒœ:r, ø:z) *n*, swimmer; rower; oarsman.

naguère (nagɛ:r) *ad*, not long since.

naïade (najad) *f*, naiad, water nymph.

naïf, ïve (naif, i:v) *a*, artless, naïve, unaffected ingenuous; unsophisticated; simpleminded, green.

nain, e (nɛ̃, ɛn) *n. & att*, dwarf.

naissance (nɛsɑ̃:s) *f*, birth; descent; rise (*river*); spring[ing] (*Arch.*). ~ *du jour*, dawn, break of day. **naissant, e** (sɑ̃, ɑ̃:t) *a*, dawning; budding; nascent. **naître** (nɛ:tr) *v.i.ir*, to be born; grow; bud; [a]rise, spring up. *à* ~, unborn.

naïvement (naivmɑ̃) *ad*, artlessly, etc. **naïveté** (vte) *f*, artlessness, etc.

nankin (nɑ̃kɛ̃) *m*, nankeen.

nanti, e (nɑ̃ti) *p.p*: ~ *de* (*fig.*), secured by. *homme* ~, man who has made his pile. **nantissement** (smɑ̃) *m*, hypothecation; collateral security.

napel (napɛl) *m*, wolfsbane.

naphtaline (naftalin) *f*, naphthalene. **naphte** (naft) *m*, naphtha.

napolitain, e (napɔlitɛ̃, ɛn) *a*. & N~, *n*, Neapolitan.

nappe (nap) *f*, tablecloth; cloth; sheet (*water, flame*). **napperon** (prɔ̃) *m*, cloth (*tea, tray*).

narcisse (narsis) *m*, narcissus. ~ *des prés*, daffodil.

narcotique (narkɔtik) *a. & m*, narcotic, opiate.

narguer (narge) *v.t*, to flout.

narguilé, -ghileh (nargile) *m*, hookah.

narine (narin) *f*, nostril.

narquois, e (narkwa, a:z) *a*, sly, cunning, bantering.

narrateur, trice (narratœ:r, tris) *n*, narrator, storyteller. **narratif, ive** (tif, i:v) *a*, narrative. **narration** (sjɔ̃) *f*, narrative, story; narration; essay (*Sch.*). **narrer** (re) *v.t*, to narrate, relate, tell.

narval (narval) *m*, narwhal.

nasal, e (nazal) *a. & f*, nasal. **nasarde** (zard) *f*, fillip; snub. **naseau** (zo) *m*, nostril (*horse*). **nasiller** (zije) *v.i*, to speak through the nose, snuffle, twang. **nasse** (nas) *f*, eel pot; lobster pot; net; trap.

natal, e (natal) *a*, native; natal. **natalité** (lite) *f*, birthrate, natality.

natation (natasjɔ̃) *f*, swimming, natation.

natif, ive (natif, i:v) *a*, native, inborn. **les natifs**, *m. pl*, the natives.

nation (nasjɔ̃) *f*, nation; people. **national, e** (ɔnal) *a*, national. **nationalisme** (lism) *m*, nationalism. **nationaliste** (list) *n. & a*, nationalist. **nationalité** (te) *f*, nationality. **nationaux** (no) *m.pl*, nationals.

nativité (nativite) *f*, nativity.

natte (nat) *f*, mat, matting; plait.

natter (te) *v.t*, to mat; plait. **se ~**, to plait one's hair. **nattier** (tje) *m*, mat maker.

naturalisation (natyralizasjɔ̃) *f*, naturalization. **naturaliser** (ze) *v.t*, to naturalize; stuff (*animal*); preserve (*plant*). **naturaliste** (list) *m*, naturalist. **~** [*fourreur*], taxidermist. **nature** (ty;r) *f*, nature; life (*art*); life size; plain [-boiled]. **~ morte**, still life. **en ~**, in kind. **naturel, le†** (tyrɛl) *a*, natural; native; unaffected; illegitimate. ¶ *m*, naturalness; nature, disposition; native (*pers.*).

naufrage (nofra:ʒ) *m*, wreck, shipwreck. **faire ~**, to be [ship]-wrecked. **naufragé, e** (fraʒe) *n*, shipwrecked person, castaway.

nauséabond, e (nozeabɔ̃, ɔ̃:d) *a*, nauseous, sickening, foul. **nausée** (ze) *f*, nausea. **nauséeux, euse** (zeø, ø;z) *a*, neauseating.

nautile (notil) *ou* **nautilus** (ly;s) *m*, nautilus. **nautique** (tik) *a*, nautical; aquatic (*sports*). **nautonier, ère** (tonje, ɛ;r) (*Poet.*) *n*, mariner; ferryman.

naval, e (naval) *a*, naval, sea (*att.*); ship (*att.*).

navet (navɛ) *m*, turnip; bad painting; unsuccessful play. **~ de Suède**, Swede turnip (*Agric.*).

navette (navɛt) *f*, rape (*oil seed plant*); incense box; shuttle. **faire la ~**, to go to & fro.

navigable (navigabl) *a*, navigable. **navigateur** (tœ;r) *m*, navigator; (*att.*) seafaring. **navigation** (sjɔ̃) *f*, navigation; sailing; shipping. **naviguer** (ge) *v.i*, to navigate, sail.

navire (navi;r) *m*, ship, vessel, boat, bottom. **~ à vapeur**, steamship. **~-citerne**, *m*, tank ship. **~ de charge**, cargo boat. **~ frère**, **~ jumeau**, sister ship. **~ de ligne** [*régulière*], liner. **~ pose-mines**, mine layer.

navrant, e (nɑvrɑ̃, ɑ̃;t) *a*, heart-rending, heartbreaking, harrowing. **navrer [le cœur]** (vre) *v.t*, to break one's heart, harrow.

ne, n' (nə, n) *neg. particle, used mostly with the words* pas *or* point, not, n't. **n'importe!** no matter!

né, e (ne) *a*, born. *Je suis ~*, I was born.

néanmoins (neɑ̃mwɛ̃) *ad*, nevertheless, notwithstanding, yet, still.

néant (neɑ̃) *m*, nothing[ness]; nought; nil, none.

nébuleux, euse (nebylø, ø;z) *a*, nebulous, cloudy; clouded. ¶ *f*, nebula (*Astr.*).

nécessaire† (nesesɛ:r) *a*, necessary, needful. ¶ *m*, necessary, -ries; needful; busybody; outfit, case. **~ à ouvrage**, workbox, workbasket, needlework case. **nécessité** (site) *f*, necessity. **nécessiter** (te) *v.t*, to necessitate. **nécessiteux, euse** (tø, ø;z) *a*, necessitous, needy. **les ~**, *m.pl*, the needy, the destitute.

nec plus ultra (nɛkplyzyltra), ne plus ultra, acme, last word.

nécrologe (nekrolɔ;ʒ) *m*, necrology, obituary (*roll, book*). **nécrologie** (loʒi) *f*, deaths, obituary, necrology (*notice*). **nécromancie** (mɑ̃si) *f*, necromancy. **nécromancien, ne** (sjɛ̃, ɛn) *n*, necromancer. **nécropole** (pol) *f*, necropolis. **nécrose** (kro;z) *f*, necrosis.

nectaire (nɛktɛ;r) *m*, nectary. **nectar** (ta;r) *m*, nectar.

néerlandais, e (neɛrlɑ̃dɛ, ɛ;z) *a*, Netherlandish, Dutch. **N~**, *n*, Netherlander, Dutchman, -woman. **la Néerlande** (lɑ̃;d), the Netherlands.

nef (nɛf) *f*, nave (*church*); bark, ship (*Poet.*).

néfaste (nefast) *a*, luckless, ill-fated, ill-starred, disastrous.

nèfle (nɛfl) *f*, medlar. **néflier** (neflie) *m*, medlar [tree].

négatif, ive† (negatif, i;v) *a*, negative. ¶ *m*, negative (*Phot.*). **la négative**, the negative (*statement, etc.*). **négation** (sjɔ̃) *f*, negation; negative (*Gram.*).

négligé, e (negliʒe) *p.a*, neglected; unheeded; loose; slovenly; slipshod. ¶ *m*, undress, négligé; tea gown. **négligeable** (ʒabl) *a*, negligible. **négligemment** (ʒamɑ̃) *ad*, negligently, carelessly. **négligence** (ʒɑ̃:s) *f*, negligence, neglect, carelessness; default. **négligent, e** (ʒɑ̃, ɑ̃;t) *a*, negligent, careless, neglectful, remiss. **né-**

gliger (ʒe) *v.t*, to neglect, slight. **se ~**, to neglect oneself; slack; be careless.

négoce (negɔs) *m*, trade; business. **négociable** (sjabl) *a*, negotiable; marketable. **négociant, e** (sjɑ̃, ɑ̃:t) *n*, trader, merchant. **négociateur, trice** (atœ:r, tris) *n*, negociator. **négociation** (sjɔ̃) *f*, negotiation; transaction; dealing; bargain. **négocier** (sje) *v.t*, to negotiate.

nègre (nɛ:gr) *a.m*. & *a.f.*, Negro. ¶ *m*, Negro; one who does the donkey work, underling (*vulg.*); ghost-writer, literary hack. **négresse** (negrɛs) *f*, Negress. **negrier** (grie) *m*, slaver, slave trader; s. driver (*hard employer*).

neige (nɛ:ʒ) *f*. oft. pl, snow. *de la ~ fondue*, sleet; slush. *tomber de la ~ fondue*, to sleet. **neiger** (nɛʒe) *v.imp*, to snow. **neigeux, euse** (ʒø, ø:z) *a*, snowy.

Némésis (nemezi:s) *f*, Nemesis.

ne m'oubliez pas (nəmubliepɑ) *m*, forget-me-not.

nénuphar (nenyfa:r) *m*, water lily.

néologisme (neɔlɔʒism) *m*, neologism.

néon (neɔ̃) *m*, neon.

néophyte (neɔfit) *n*, neophyte.

néo-zélandais, e (neɔzelɑ̃dɛ, ɛ:z) *a*, New Zealand (*att.*). **Néo-Zélandais, e**, *n*, New Zealander.

népotisme (nepɔtism) *m*, nepotism.

Néréide (nereid) *f*, Nereid, sea nymph.

nerf (nɛ:r & nɛrf) *m*, nerve; band (*Bookb.*); sinews (*of war*); (*pl.*) thews; (*pl.*) nerves, hysterics; (*pl.*) tantrums.

nerveux, euse† (nɛrvø, ø:z) *a*, nervous; highly strung; hysterical; fidgety. **nervosité** (vozite) *f*, irritability. **nervure** (vy:r) *f*, rib, nerve, nervure, vein (*Bot., etc.*).

net, te (nɛt) *a*, clean; flawless; clear; sharp; empty; free; net. *mettre au net*, to make a clean copy of. **net**, *ad*, clean; plainly, flatly, outright. **nettement** (tmɑ̃) *ad*, clearly; frankly, plainly, flatly, downright. **netteté** (nɛtte) *f*, cleanness; clearness.

nettoiement (nɛtwamɑ) & **nettoy-**

age (ja:ʒ) *m*, cleaning, cleansing. **nettoyer** (je) *v.t*, to clean, cleanse; clear. *~ à sec*, to dry-clean. **nettoyeur, euse** (jœ:r, ø:z) *n*, cleaner.

neuf (nœf & nœ & nœv) *a*. & *m*, nine; ninth. *~ fois sur dix*, nine times out of ten.

neuf, euve (nœf, œ:v) *a*, new; inexperienced, raw.

neurasthénie (nørasteni) *f*, neurasthenia. **neurologiste** (rɔlɔʒist) *ou* **neurologue** (lɔg) *n*, nerve specialist, neurologist.

neutraliser (nøtralize) *v.t*, to neutralize. **neutralité** (te) *f*, neutrality. **neutre** (nø:tr) *a*, neutral; noncommittal; neuter; undenominational (*school*). ¶ *m*, neuter; neutral.

neuvième† (nœvjɛm) *a*. & *n*, ninth.

neveu (nəvø) *m*, nephew. *nos ~x*, posterity.

névralgie (nevralʒi) *f*, neuralgia. **névralgique** (ʒik) *a*, neuralgic; sore (*point*). **névrite** (vrit) *f*, neuritis. **névrose** (vro:z) *f*, neurosis. **névrosé, e** (vroze) *a*, neurotic.

nez (ne) *m*, nose; face; nosing (*stair*); scent (*dogs*). *à vue de ~*, at the first blush.

ni (ni) *c*, nor; or; neither. *~ fleurs, ~ couronnes*, no flowers, by request. *~ l'un (l'une) ni l'autre₁ pn.* & *a*, neither.

niable (njabl) *a*, deniable.

niais, e† (njɛ, ɛ:z) *a*. & *n*, silly. **niaiser** (ɛze) *v.i*, to play the fool. **niaiserie** (zri) *f*, silliness.

niche (niʃ) *f*, niche; trick, prank, practical joke. *~ à chien*, dog kennel. **nichée** (ʃe) *f*, nest[ful]; brood. **nicher** (ʃe) *v.i*, to nest; (*v.t.*) to put, ensconce. **nichet** (ʃɛ) *m*, nestegg.

nickel (nikɛl) *m*, nickel. **nickeler** (kle) *v.t*, to nickle.

nicodème (nikɔdɛ:m) *m*, booby.

nicotine (nikɔtin) *f*, nicotine.

nid (ni) *m*, nest; den. *~ d'hirondelle*, edible bird's nest. *~ de pie*, crow's nest (*Naut.*). *il croit avoir trouvé la pie au ~*, he has found a mare's nest.

nièce (njɛs) *f*, niece.

nielle (njɛl) *f*, smut, blight (*Agric.*). ¶ *m*, niello.

nier (nje) *v.t*, to deny; repudiate; (*abs.*) to deny it. ~ *sa culpabilité*, to plead not guilty.

nigaud, e (nigo, o:d) *a*, silly. ¶ *n*, noodle, ninny, booby, nincompoop. **nigauder** (gode) *v.i*, to play the fool. **nigauderie** (dri) *f*, silliness.

nigelle de Damas (niʒɛl) *f*, love-in-a-mist.

nihiliste (niilist) *m*, nihilist.

Nil (le) (nil), the Nile.

nimbe (nɛ̃:b) *m*, nimbus, halo, glory. **nimbus** (nɛ̃by:s) *m*, nimbus (*Meteor.*).

Ninive (nini:v) *f*, Nineveh.

nippes (nip) *f.pl*, old clothes.

nitouche (sainte) (nituʃ) *f*, [prudish & demure] little hypocrite.

nitrate (nitrat) *m*, nitrate. **nitre** (tr) *m*, niter, saltpeter. **nitrique** (trik) *a*, nitric. **nitroglycérine** (trɔgliserin) *f*, nitroglycerin[e].

niveau (nivo) *m*, level. ~ *à bulle d'air*, spirit l. ~ *de vie*, standard of living. *de* ~, level, at grade. **niveler** (vle) *v.t*, to level. **niveleur** (vlœ:r) *m*, leveler. **nivellement** (vɛlmɑ̃) *m*, leveling.

nobiliaire (nɔbiljɛ:r) *a*, nobiliary. ¶ *m*, peerage (*book*). **noble†** (bl) *a*, noble. ¶ *n*, noble[man], noblewoman. **noblesse** (blɛs) *f*, nobility; nobleness; noblesse.

noce (nɔs) *f*, wedding festivities; wedding party; jollification, spree; (*pl.*) wedding, marriage, nuptials. ~*s d'argent, d'or, de diamant*, silver, golden, diamond, wedding. **noceur, euse** (sœ:r, ø:z) *n*, reveler.

nocher (nɔʃe) (*Poet.*) *m*, boatman; ferryman.

nocif, ive (nɔsif, i:v) *a*, noxious.

noctambule (nɔktɑ̃by:l) *n*, sleepwalker. **nocturne** (tyrn) *a*, nocturnal, night (*att.*). ¶ *m*, nocturne.

Noël (nɔɛl) *m*, Christmas[tide], yule[tide]. *à la* [*fête de*] ~, *à* ~, at Christmas[tide], at yuletide. **n~,** [Christmas] carol.

nœud (nø) *m*, knot; node; cluster; crux; rub; tie, bond (*fig.*). ~ *coulant*, slip knot, running k.;

noose. ~ [*de ruban*], bow. ~ *gordien* (gɔrdjɛ̃), Gordian knot. ~[-*papillon*], bow tie. ~ *plat*, reef knot.

noir, e (nwa:r) *a*, black; dark; swarthy; brown (*bread*); black & blue (*bruised*); gloomy. *noir sur blanc*, [down] in black & white (*writing*). *la mer Noire*, the Black Sea. ¶ *m*, black; b. mark (*bruise*); b. [man, boy], man of color; bull's eye (*target*). ¶ *f*, black [ball] (*gaming*); crotchet (*Mus.*). **noirâtre** (nwarɑ:tr) *a*, blackish; darkish. **noiraud, e** (ro, o:d) *a. & n*, swarthy (man, woman). **noirceur** (sœ:r) *f*, blackness; black spot; smudge, smut. **noircir** (si:r) *v.t. & i*, to blacken; black; blot (*paper with useless writing*). **noircissure** (sisy:r) *f*, smudge.

noise (nwa:z) *f*, quarrel.

noisetier (nwaztje) *m*, hazel (*bush*), nut tree. **noisette** (zɛt) *f*, hazelnut; nut; hazel (*color, eyes*); nut-brown.

noix (nwɑ) *f*, walnut; nut. ~ *de coco*, coconut. ~ *de galle*, nut gall. ~ *vomique* (vɔmik), nux vomica.

nolis (nɔli) *m*, freight. **noliser** (ze) *v.t*, to freight, charter.

nom (nɔ̃) *m*, name; style; noun. ~ *de baptême*, Christian name. ~ [*de famille*], ~ *patronymique*, surname. ~ *de guerre*, nom de guerre, assumed name, alias; stage name; pen name. ~ *de jeune fille*, maiden name. ~ *de plume*, pen name. ~ *de théâtre*, stage n. ~ *& prénoms*, full n. *sous un* ~ *interposé*, in a nominee's name.

nomade (nɔmad) *a*, nomad(ic). ¶ *m*, nomad, wanderer.

nombre (nɔ̃:br) *m*, number. *les N~s* (*Bible*), Numbers. ~ *des adhérents*, membership. *avoir du* ~, to be well-balanced (*phrase*). **nombrer** (nɔ̃bre) *v.t*, to number, count. **nombreux, euse** (brø, ø:z) *a*, numerous; well-balanced (*style, prose*).

nombril (nɔ̃bri) *m*, navel; eye (*fruit*).

nomenclature (nɔmɑ̃klaty:r) *f*, nomenclature. **nominal, e†** (minal) *a*, nominal; face (*value*). appel ~, roll call. **nominatif, ive** (tif, i:v) *a*, nominal, of [the] names; registered (*securities*). ¶ *m*, nominative [case]. **nomination** (sjɔ̃) *f*, nomination; appointment; commissioning (*officer*); gift (*of an office*); award (*at a show*). **nominativement** (tivmɑ̃) *ad*, by name. **un nommé . . .** (me), a man called . . ., one . . . [by name]. **nommément** (memɑ̃) *ad*, namely, to wit, by name. **nommer** (me) *v.t*, to name; call; nominate; appoint; commission; return, elect. **se ~,** to give one's name; be called. *je me nomme Adam*, my name is Adam.

non (nɔ̃) *neg. particle*, no; not. *ni moi ~ plus*, nor I either. ¶ *m*, no, nay.

non-activité (en) (nɔnaktivite) *f*, on the unemployed list (*Mil.*).

nonagénaire (nɔnaʒɛnɛ:r) *a.* & *n*, nonagenarian.

non avenu, e (nɔnavny) *a*, void, non avenu.

nonce du Pape *ou* **nonce apostolique** (nɔ̃:s) *m*, papal nuncio.

nonchalamment (nɔ̃ʃalamɑ̃) *ad*, nonchalantly, listlessly. **nonchalance** (lɑ̃:s) *f*, nonchalance, listlessness. **nonchalant, e** (lɑ̃, ɑ̃:t) *a*, nonchalant, listless.

nonciature (nɔ̃sjaty:r) *f*, nunciature.

non-combat (nɔ̃kɔ̃ba) *m*, no contest (*Box.*). **non-combattant, e** (batɑ̃, ɑ̃:t) *a.* & *m*, noncombatant (*Mil.*).

non-conformiste (nɔ̃kɔ̃fɔrmist) *n.* & *att*, nonconformist.

non-être (nɔnɛ:tr) (*Philos.*) *m*, nonentity, nonexistence.

non-intervention (nɔnɛ̃tɛrvɑ̃sjɔ̃) (*Pol.*) *f*, nonintervention, noninterference.

non-lieu (nɔ̃ljø) *m*, no case to answer (*law*).

nonne (nɔn) & **nonnain** (nɛ̃) *f*, nun.

nonobstant (nɔnɔpstɑ̃) *pr*, notwithstanding.

non-paiement (nɔ̃pɛmɑ̃) *m*, nonpayment; dishonor (*bill*).

non-sens (nɔ̃sɑ̃:s) *m*, nonsense. *un ~*, all nonsense, meaningless.

non-valeur (nɔ̃valœ:r) *f*, unproductiveness; worthless security; valueless stock; (*pl.*) irrecoverable arrears (*taxes*); bad debt; noneffective (*Mil.*); useless person.

nord (nɔ:r) *m*, north; (*att.*) north[ern]. *mer du N~*, North Sea. *perdre le ~*, to get confused. **nord-est** (nɔr[d]ɛst; *Naut.*, nɔrɛ) *m*, northeast; northeast wind; (*att.*) northeast[ern]. **nordique** (dik) *a*, Nordic. **nord-ouest** (nɔr[d]wɛst; *Naut.*, nɔrwa) *m*, northwest, northwest wind; (*att.*) northwest[ern].

normal, e† (nɔrmal) *a*, normal; standard; ordinary. **normalien, ne** (ljɛ̃, ɛn) *n*, student [of a normal school].

normand, e (nɔrmɑ̃, ɑ̃:d) *a*, Norman; noncommittal (*fig.*); evasive; feigned. *les îles Normandes*, the Channel Islands. *N~, n*, Norman. *un fin n~*, a shrewd crafty fellow. **la Normandie** (mɑ̃di), Normandy.

norme (nɔrm) *f*, norm.

norois (l'ancien) (nɔrwa) *m*, Old Norse (*language*).

Norvège (la) (nɔrvɛ:ʒ), Norway. **norvégien, ne** (veʒjɛ̃, ɛn) *a.* & *N~, n*, Norwegian, Norseman. *le norvégien*, Norwegian, Norse (*language*).

nos, our, *possessive adjective plural, see* **notre.**

nostalgie (nɔstalʒi) *f*, nostalgia, homesickness; pining. **nostalgique** (ʒik) *a*, nostalgic, homesick.

nota [bene] (nɔta bene) (*abb.* N.B.) *m*, note, nota bene, N.B. **notabilité** (nɔtabilite) *f*, notability. **notable†** (bl) *a*, notable; especial; eminent, distinguished. ¶ *m*, person of distinction, notable.

notaire (nɔtɛ:r) *m*, notary.

notamment (nɔtmɑ̃) *ad*, especially, notably.

notation (nɔtasjɔ̃) *f*, notation.

note (nɔt) *f*, note, memorandum; mark (*Sch.*); record (*of service*); bill, account; tune (*fig.*). *~ d'agrément*, grace note (*Mus.*).

~ *de passage,* passing note (*Mus.*). ~ *naturelle,* natural [note] (*Mus.*). **noter** (te) *v.t,* to note; n. down; write down; mark (*pupil, etc.*). **notice** (tis) *f,* notice, account; review (*book*). **notifier** (tifje) *v.t,* to notify.

notion (nosjɔ̃) *f,* notion, smattering.

notoire† (nɔtwa:r) *a,* well-known. **notoriété** (tɔrjete) *f,* notoriety. ~ *publique,* common knowledge.

notre (nɔtr) *a,* our. *Notre-Dame,* Our Lady. *Notre-Seigneur,* our Lord. **le nôtre, la ~, les ~s** (no:tr) *pn,* ours; our own. *il est des nôtres,* he is one of us.

noue (nu) *f,* valley (*roof*); water meadow.

nouer (nwe) *v.t,* to tie; knot; knit (*fig.*); form. **noueux, euse** (nuø, ø:z) *a,* knotty; gnarled.

nougat (nuga) *m,* nougat.

nouilles (nu:j) *f.pl,* vermicelli.

nounou (nunu) *f,* nanny, nursy.

nourrain (nurɛ̃) *m,* fry (*fish*).

nourri, e (nuri) *p.p. & p.a,* fed; (*fig.*) copious; full; steeped; prolonged (*applause*); brisk (*fire, Mil.*). *mal ~, pas ~,* underfed, ill-fed. **nourrice** (ris) *f,* [wet] nurse. *être la ~ de,* to nurse, suckle. *mère ~,* nursing mother. **nourrir** (ri:r) *v.t,* to nourish; nurture, rear; suckle, nurse; feed; board, keep; foster, cherish, harbor, entertain. **nourrissage** (risa:ʒ) *m,* rearing (*cattle*). **nourrissant, e** (sɑ̃, ɑ̃:t) *a,* nourishing, nutritious. **nourrisseur** (sœ:r) *m,* dairy farmer; feed-roll (*Mech.*). **nourrisson** (sɔ̃) *m,* nurseling; suckling; foster child. **nourriture** (ty:r) *f,* food, nourishment, nutriment; sustenance; board; feeding; nurture.

nous (nu) *pn,* we; us, to us, ourselves; each other. *chez ~,* at our house. *à ~!* help! *~-mêmes,* ourselves.

nouveau, el, le (nuvo, ɛl) *a. & ad,* new; newly; recent; novel; fresh; another, further. *le Nouveau-Brunswick* (brɔ̃zvik), New Brunswick. *nouveau marié, nouvelle mariée,* bridegroom, bride (*about to be married* or *on marriage day*). *nouveaux mariés,*

[newly] married couple; bride & bridegroom. *nouveau-né, e, n. & att,* newborn (child). *nouveau riche,* upstart. *nouveau venu, nouvelle venue,* newcomer. *la Nouvelle-Écosse,* Nova Scotia. *la Nouvelle-Galles du Sud,* New South Wales. *la Nouvelle-Guinée,* New Guinea. *la Nouvelle-Orléans,* New Orleans. *la Nouvelle-Zélande* (zelɑ̃:d), New Zealand. *la Nouvelle-Zemble* (ʒɑ̃:bl), Nova Zembla. *le nouveau, m,* the new, a novelty, something new. *le nouveau, la nouvelle,* the new boy, man, girl (*Sch., etc.*). *à nouveau,* anew, afresh; carried forward. *de nouveau,* again, afresh. **nouveauté** (te) *f,* newness; novelty; new thing, book, play, etc; innovation; (*pl.*) new styles, latest fashions; ladies' & children's wear; drapery.

nouvelle (nuvɛl) *f., oft. pl. in sense of* news, [piece of] news; tidings, intelligence; tale, short story, novelette. *~s à la main* (*journalism*), today's gossip, looking at life.

nouvellement (nuvɛlmɑ̃) *ad,* newly, recently.

nouvelliste (nuvɛlist) *n,* newsmonger, intelligencer, quidnunc.

novateur, trice (nɔvatœ:r, tris) *n,* innovator.

novembre (nɔvɑ̃:br) *m,* November.

novice (nɔvis) *n,* novice; probationer; tyro; apprentice (*Naut.*). ¶ *a,* inexperienced, raw, fresh, green. **noviciat** (sja) *m,* noviciate; apprenticeship.

noyade (nwajad) *f,* drowning (*fatality*); noyade (*Hist.*).

noyau (nwajo) *m,* stone (*fruit*); kernel, core, center; nucleus; newel.

noyer (nwaje) *m,* walnut [tree, wood].

noyer (nwaje) *v.t,* to drown; flood, deluge; sink; swamp; play (*fish*). *un noyé* (je), a drowned man; a drowning man. *les noyés,* the [apparently] drowned.

nu, e (ny) *a,* naked, nude; bare; barebacked (*horse*); plain. *à l'œil nu,* with the naked eye. ~ *comme un ver,* stark naked. *nu-pieds,*

inv. ou *pieds nus*, barefoot[ed].
nu-tête, inv. ou *tête nue*, bare-
headed. ¶ *m*, nakedness, nudity,
nude; bareness. *le nu*, the nude.
les nus, the naked. *à nu*, bare,
naked; bareback[ed] (*riding*).

nuage (nya:ʒ) *m*, cloud; volume
(*of smoke, etc.*); haze, mist (*fig.*);
suspicion. **nuageux, euse** (aʒø,
ø:z) *a*, cloudy; hazy.

nuance (nyɑ̃:s) *f*, shade; hue;
tinge; nuance; (*pl.*) lights &
shades; sign of expression (*Mus.*)
nuancer (ɑ̃se) *v.t*, to shade;
mark (*or* observe) the signs of
expression; execute with feeling.

Nubie (la) (nybi), Nubia. **nubien, ne** (bjɛ̃, ɛn) *a.* & N~, *n*,
Nubian.

nubile (nybil) *a*, nubile, marriageable.

nudité (nydite) *f*, nudity, nakedness; bareness; nude (*art*).

nue (ny) (*poetic*) *f*, high clouds.
oft. pl, cloud, sky. **nuée** (nye) *f*,
storm cloud, thunder cloud;
cloud (*fig.*), host, swarm; shower.

nuire (nɥi:r) *v.i.ir.* & ~ *à*, to
harm, hurt, injure, wrong, prejudice. **nuisible** (nɥizibl) *a*, harm-
ful, hurtful, injurious, noxious,
noisome.

nuit (nɥi) *f*, night; dark[ness].
cette ~, tonight; last night. *à*
[*la*] ~ *close*, after dark. *à la* ~
tombante, at nightfall. **nuitamment** (tamɑ̃) *ad*, by night, in the
n.

nul, le (nyl) *a*, no; not any; null,
nugatory, nil; of no account;
drawn (*game*); dead (*heat*).
nul(le) & *non avenu(e)* (avny),
null & void. *nulle part, ad*, nowhere. **nul**, *pn*, no one, none.
nulle, *f*, null (*in cipher*). **nullement** (lmɑ̃) *ad*, in no way, not at
all, by no means, nowise. **nullité**
(lite) *f*, nullity; emptiness; nonentity, cipher (*pers.*).

nûment (nymɑ̃) *ad*, openly,
frankly, nakedly.

numéraire (nymerɛ:r) *a*, numerary. ¶ *m*, coin, cash, specie.
numéral, e (ral) *a*, numeral.
numérateur (tœ:r) *m*, numerator
(*Arith.*). **numérique†** (rik) *a*,
numerical. **numéro** (ro) *m*, number; size; issue (*periodical*); turn

(*music hall*). **numérotage**
(rota:ʒ) *m*, numbering. **numéroter** (te) *v.t*, to number.

numismate (nymismat) *m*,
numismatist. **numismatique** (tik)
f, numismatics.

nuptial, e (nypsjal) *a*, nuptial,
bridal, wedding (*att.*), marriage
(*att.*).

nuque (nyk) *f*, nape (*of neck*).

nutritif, ive (nytritif, i:v) *a*,
nutritive, nutritious. **nutrition**
(sjɔ̃) *f*, nutrition.

nymphe (nɛ̃:f) *f*, nymph.

O

ô (o) *i*, O! oh!

oasis (oazis) *f*, oasis (*lit. & fig.*).
obédience (ɔbedjɑ̃:s) *f*, obedience (*Eccl.*). **obéir** (i:r) *v.i*, to
obey. ~ *à*, to obey; submit to,
yield to; comply with; respond to.
obéissance (isɑ̃:s) *f*, obedience;
allegiance; authority; compliance;
submission. **obéissant, e** (sɑ̃, ɑ̃:t)
a, obedient; dutiful; submissive.

obélisque (ɔbelisk) *m*, obelisk.

obérer (ɔbere) *v.t*, to encumber
[with debts].

obèse (ɔbɛ:z) *a*, obese, fat. **obésité**
(bezite) *f*, obesity, fatness.

obier (ɔbje) *m*, guelder rose.

objecter (ɔbʒɛkte) *v.t*, to object
(*que* = that); o. to, o. against;
allege. **objectif, ive†** (tif, i:v) *a*
& *m*, objective (*Philos.*). ¶ *m*,
objective, aim. [*verre*] *objectif*,
objective, object glass, lens. **objection** (ksjɔ̃) *f*, objection; demur.
objet (ʒɛ) *m*, object; subject;
article. ~ *d'art*, work of art.

objurgation (ɔbʒyrgasjɔ̃) *f*, objurgation.

oblation (ɔblasjɔ̃) *f*, oblation, offering (*Lit.*).

obligataire (ɔbligatɛ:r) *m*,
bondholder, debenture h. **obligation** (sjɔ̃) *f*, obligation; bond,
debenture; recognizance. **obligatoire** (twa:r) *a*, obligatory, com-
pulsory, binding. **obligé, e** (ʒe)
a, usual; obbligato (*Mus.*). ¶ *n*,
debtor (*for services*). **obligeamment** (ʒamɑ̃) *ad*, obligingly,
kindly. **obligeant, e** (ʒɑ̃, ɑ̃:t) *a*,
obliging, kind[ly]; compliment-

ary. **obliger** (ʒe) *v.t*, to oblige, bind, compel; obligate. **s~**, to bind oneself; undertake.

oblique† (ɔblik) *a*, oblique, slanting, skew; side (*glance*); crooked (*fig.*), underhand. **obliquer** (ke) *v.i*, to slant. **obliquité** (kite) *f*, obliquity; crookedness.

oblitérer (ɔblitere) *v.t*, to obliterate; cancel.

oblong, ongue (ɔblɔ̃, ɔ̃:g) *a*, oblong.

obnubiler (ɔbnybile) *v.t*, to cloud.

obole (ɔbɔl) *f*, [brass] farthing, stiver; mite.

obscène (ɔpsɛ:n) *a*, obscene. **obscénité** (senite) *f*, obscenity.

obscur, e (ɔpsky:r) *a*, dark; dim, murky; obscure. **obscurcir** (skyrsi:r) *v.t*, to darken; overcast, overshadow. **obscurément** (remã) *ad*, darkly, etc. **obscurité** (rite) *f*, dark[ness], etc.

obséder (ɔpsede) *v.t*, to worry; obsess.

obsèques (ɔpsɛk) *f.pl*, obsequies. **obséquieux, euse†** (sekjø, ø:z) *a*, obsequious. **obséquiosité** (kjozite) *f*, obsequiousness.

observance (ɔpsɛrvã:s) *f*, observance (*Theol.*). **observateur, trice** (vatœ:r, tris) *n*, observer; (*att.*) observant. **observation** (sjɔ̃) *f*, observance; observation; remark. **observatoire** (twa:r) *m*, observatory; observation post (*Mil.*). **observer** (ve) *v.t*, to observe; keep; watch; spot. **s'~**, to be careful, cautious.

obsession (ɔpsɛsjɔ̃) *f*, obsession.

obstacle (ɔpstakl) *m*, obstacle. *faire ~ à*, to stand in the way of.

obstétrical, e (ɔpstetrikal) *a*, obstetric(al). **obstétrique** (trik) *f*, obstetrics, midwifery.

obstination (ɔpstinasjɔ̃) *f*, obstinacy, stubbornness, wilfulness; doggedness. **obstiné†, e** (ne) *a*, obstinate, etc. **s'obstiner** (ne) *v.pr*, to persist.

obstruction (ɔpstryksjɔ̃) *f*, obstruction; stoppage; filibuster. **obstruer** (strye) *v.t*, to obstruct; block.

obtempérer à (ɔptãpere), to obey, comply with.

obtenir (ɔptəni:r) *v.t.ir*, to ob-

tain, secure, get. *j'ai obtenu de . . ., I induced . . .; I managed to . . .*

obturateur (ɔptyratœ:r) *m*, obturator, plug; shutter (*Phot.*). **obturer** (re) *v.t*, to stop [up].

obtus, e (ɔpty, y:z) *a*, obtuse.

obus (ɔby:s) *m*, shell. **~ à balles**, shrapnel. **obusier** (byzje) *m*, howitzer.

obvier à (ɔbvje), to obviate, prevent.

ocarina (ɔkarina) *m*, ocarina.

occasion (ɔkazjɔ̃) *f*, opportunity; opening; occasion; bargain. *d'~*, second-hand, used; occasional (*occupation*). **occasionnel, le** (ɔnɛl) *a*, causative; occasional (*Philos.*). **occasionnellement** (lmã) *ad*, occasionally, now & then. **occasionner** (ne) *v.t*, to occasion.

occident (ɔksidã) *m*, west. **occidental, e** (tal) *a*, west[ern].

occiput (ɔksipyt) *m*, occiput.

occire (ɔksi:r) *v.t*, to slay.

occulte (ɔkylt) *a*, occult, hidden.

occupant (ɔkypã) *m*, occupant (*law*). **occupation** (pasjɔ̃) *f*, occupation; pursuit. **occupé, e** (pe) *p.a*, busy. **occuper** (pe) *v.t*, to occupy; hold. **s'~**, to occupy (*or* busy) oneself, be engaged; be interested in (*with* de).

occurrence (ɔkyrã:s) *f*, occurrence; emergency; juncture.

océan (ɔseã) *m*, ocean, sea. *l'~ Atlantique, Pacifique, Indien*, the Atlantic, Pacific, Indian, O. *l'~ Glacial arctique, antarctique*, the Arctic, Antarctic, O. **l'Océanie** (ani) *f*, Oceania.

ocre (ɔkr) *f*, ocher.

octave (ɔkta:v) *f*, octave. **octavon, ne** (tavɔ̃, ɔn) *n*, octaroon. **octobre** (tɔbr) *m*, October. **octogénaire** (ʒenɛ:r) *a. & n*, octogenarian. **octogone** (gɔn) *a*, octagonal. ¶ *m*, octagon.

octroi (ɔktrwa) *m*, octroi (*duty on goods entering town*). **octroyer** (trwaje) *v.t*, to grant.

oculaire (ɔkylɛ:r) *a*, ocular, eye (*att.*). [verre] **~**, *m*, eyepiece, ocular. **oculiste** (list) *m*, oculist. *médecin ~*, eye doctor.

ode (ɔd) *f*, ode.

odeur (odœːr) *f*, odor, smell, scent.

odieux, euse† (ɔdjø, ø:z) *a*, odious, hateful, heinous, outrageous; obnoxious; invidious. ¶ *m*, odium.

odorant, e (ɔdɔrɑ̃, ɑ̃:t) & **odoriférant, e** (riferɑ̃, ɑ̃:t) *a*, fragrant, [sweet-]scented, odoriferous. **odorat** (ra) *m*, [sense of] smell.

odyssée (ɔdise) *f*, Odyssey (*fig.*).

oé (oe) *i*, wo!, whoa!

œil (œ:j) *m*, eye; look; loop; hole; face (*Typ.*); luster; gloss. **~-de-bœuf**, bull's eye (*window*). **~-de-chat**, cat's-eye (*jewel*). **~-de-perdrix**, soft corn (*foot*). **œillade** (œjad) *f*, glance (*loving*); ogle. **œillère** (jɛːr) *f*, blinker; eye bath. [*dent*] **~**, eyetooth. **œillet** (jɛ) *m*, eyelet; e. hole; pink (*Bot.*). **~** [*des fleuristes*], carnation. **~ de poète**, sweet-william. **œilleton** (jtɔ̃) *m*, sucker, offset (*Hort.*).

œsophage (ezɔfaːʒ) *m*, oesophagus.

œstre (ɛstr) *m*, oestrum, oestrus, gad-fly.

œuf (œf) *m*, egg; (*pl, de poisson*) hard roe, spawn. **~** *à la coque*, soft-boiled egg. **~** *dur*, hard-boiled e. **~s au jambon**, ham & eggs. **~** *de Pâques*, Easter egg. **œuvé, e** (ve) *a*, hard-roed.

œuvre (œːvr) *f*, work; setting (*jewel*); (*pl.*) charity; (*pl.*) work (*social*). ¶ *m*, carcass, carcase (*of a building*); works (*of an artist*).

offensant, e (ɔfɑ̃sɑ̃, ɑ̃:t) *a*, offensive, obnoxious, objectionable, insulting. **offense** (fɑ̃:s) *f*, offense; trespass (*Theol.*). **~** *à la cour*, contempt of court. **offensé, e** (fɑ̃se) *n*, aggrieved party. **offenser** (se) *v.t*, to offend; trespass against; injure. **s'~**, to take offense. **offenseur** (sœːr) *m*, offender. **offensif, ive†** (sif, iːv) *a*. & *f*, offensive (*attacking*).

offertoire (ɔfɛrtwaːr) *m*, offertory (*Lit.*); voluntary (*organ, between credo & sanctus*).

office (ɔfis) *m*, office; service; worship; department (*government*). **~** *des morts*, burial service. *d'~*, official[ly]; arbitrary

(*assessment*); as a matter of course. ¶ *f*, pantry, servants' hall. **officiel, le†** (sjɛl) *a*, official. ¶ *m*, official (*sport, etc.*). **officier** (sje) *v.i*, to officiate (*Eccl.*). ¶ *m*, officer. **~** *à la suite*, supernumerary o. **~** *d'ordonnance*, orderly o. **~** *de l'état civil*, registrar (*births, etc.*). **~** *de marine*, naval officer. **~** *du génie*, engineer (*Mil.*). **officieux, euse†** (sjø, ø:z) *a*, officious (*diplomacy*), informal, semiofficial, unofficial; white (*lie*). **officine** (sin) *f*, dispensary; hotbed (*fig.*); shady office, thieves' kitchen.

offrande (ɔfrɑ̃:d) *f*, offering. **le plus offrant** [& dernier enchérisseur] (frɑ̃), the highest bidder. **offre** (fr) *f*, offer; tender. **~** *d'emploi*, help wanted. *l'~* & *la demande*, supply & demand. **offrir** (friːr) *v.t.ir*, to offer, proffer, tender; bid; present; offer up. **~** *sa main*, to propose (*marriage to a man*). **~** *son nom*, to propose (*to a woman*).

offusquer (ɔfyske) *v.t*, to obfuscate, obscure; dazzle; offend.

ogive (ɔʒiːv) *f*, ogive, pointed arch.

ognon (ɔɲɔ̃) *m*, bulb (*Bot.*).

ogre, ogresse (ɔgr, grɛs) *n*, ogre, ogress.

oh (o) *i*, oh! O!

ohé (o[h]e) *i*, hi! hullo[a]!; ahoy!; wo! whoa!

oie (wa) *f*, goose.

oignon (ɔɲɔ̃) *m*, onion; bulb (*Bot.*); bunion. *personne qui se mêle des ~s des autres*, meddlesome person, meddler, officious person. **oignonière** (ɲɔnjɛːr) *f*, onion bed.

oindre (wɛ̃:dr) *v.t.ir*, to anoint.

oiseau (wazo) *m*, bird; fowl; guy. **~** *de mauvais augure*, bird of ill omen. **~-mouche**, *m*, humming bird. **~** *rare*, rare bird, rara avis. *à vol d'~*, as the crow flies. *vue à vol d'~*, bird's-eye view. **oiselet** (zlɛ) *m*, small bird. **oiseleur** (zlœːr) *m*, bird catcher, fowler. **oiselier** (zəlje) *m*, bird fancier. **oisellerie** (zɛlri) *f*, bird fancying; aviary.

oiseux, euse (wazø, ø:z) *a*, idle

(*words, etc.*). oisif, ive† (zif, i:v) *a*, idle (*pers., money*).

oisillon (wazijɔ̃) *m*, fledgling.

oisiveté (wazivte) *f*, idleness.

oison (wazɔ̃) *m*, gosling. ~ bridé (*fig.*), simpleton.

oléagineux, euse (ɔleaʒinø, ø:z) *a*, oleaginous, oily; oil (*seed*).

oléandre (ɔleɑ̃:dr) *m*, oleander.

olfactif, ive (ɔlfaktif, i:v) *a*, olfactory.

olibrius (ɔlibriy:s) *m*, conceited fool.

oligarchie (ɔligarʃi) *f*, oligarchy.

olivade (ɔlivad) *f*, olive harvest. olivaie (vɛ) *f*, o. grove. olivaison (vɛzɔ̃) *f*, o. season; o. harvest. olivâtre (va:tr) *a*, olive (*complexion*). olive (li:v) *f*, olive. couleur [d']~, olive[-green]. olivier (livje) *m*, o. [tree]; o. [wood].

olympe (ɔlɛ̃:p) *m*, Olympus (*fig.*). olympique (lɛ̃pik) *a*, Olympic.

ombilic (ɔ̃bilik) *m*, umbilicus; navel.

omble[-chevalier] (ɔ̃:bl) *m*, char (*fish*).

ombrage (ɔ̃bra:ʒ) *m*, [spread of] foliage; shade; umbrage. ombragé, e (braʒe) *p.a*, shady. ombrager (ʒe) *v.t*, to shade, overshadow. ombrageux, euse (ʒø, ø:z) *a*, shy, skittish (*beast*); touchy. ombre (ɔ̃:br) *f*, shade; shadow; ghost. ~s chinoises, shadow play. ~ portée, cast shadow. ¶ *m*, grayling, umber (*fish*). ~-chevalier, char (*fish*). ombrelle (ɔ̃brɛl) *f*, sunshade, parasol. ombrer (bre) *v.t*, to shade (*art*). ombreux, euse brø, ø:z) *a*, shady (*Poet.*).

oméga (ɔmega) *m*, omega.

omelette (ɔmlɛt) *f*, omelet[te]. ~ aux confitures, jelly o. ~ aux fines herbes, savory o.

omettre (ɔmɛtr) *v.t.ir*, to omit, leave out. omission (misjɔ̃) *f*, omission.

omnibus (ɔmniby:s) *m*, [omni]bus; (*att.*) slow (*train, boat*).

omnipotence (ɔmnipɔtɑ̃:s) *f*, omnipotence. omnipotent, e (tɑ̃, ɑ̃:t) *a*, omnipotent.

omniscience (ɔmnisjɑ̃:s) *f*, omniscience. omniscient, e (jɑ̃, ɑ̃:t) *a*, omniscient.

omnivore (ɔmnivɔ:r) *a*, omnivorous.

omoplate (ɔmɔplat) *f*, shoulder blade.

on (ɔ̃), *oft.* l'on, *pn*, one; a man, woman, etc; we; you; they; people; somebody; anybody. ~ demande . . ., wanted . . . (*advertisement*). ~ dit, it is said, they say. ~-dit (ɔ̃di) *m*, hearsay, rumor. on n'embauche pas, no help wanted. on ne passe pas, no thoroughfare.

once (ɔ̃:s) *f*, ounce (*Zool.*), snow leopard; grain, particle (*fig.*).

oncle (ɔ̃:kl) *m*, uncle.

onction (ɔ̃ksjɔ̃) *f*, unction; rubbing [with oil]. onctueux, euse† (tɥø, ø:z) *a*, unctuous; oily; greasy.

onde (ɔ̃:d) *f*, wave, billow; (*Poet.*) sea, main; water; stream. en ~s, wavy (*hair*). ~ sonore, sound wave. ondé, e (ɔ̃de) *a*, waved, wavy; grained (*wood*). ondée (de) *f*, heavy shower. ondoyer (dwaje) *v.i*, to undulate, wave; billow, surge. ondulation (dylasjɔ̃) *f*, undulation; wave. ~ permanente, permanent wave (*hair*). ondulé, e (le) *a*, undulating; wavy; corrugated (*iron*). onduler (le) *v.i*, to undulate; (*v.t.*) to wave (*hair*). se faire onduler [les cheveux], to have one's hair waved.

onéreux, euse (ɔnerø, ø:z) *a*, onerous, burdensome.

ongle (ɔ̃:gl) *m*, nail; claw; hoof. onglée (ɔ̃gle) *f*, numbness [of the fingers]. onglet (glɛ) *m*, guard (*Bookb.*); tab; miter (*Carp.*). onglier (glie) *m*, manicure set. ~ [en] écrin, box m. s.

onguent (ɔ̃gɑ̃) *m*, ointment, salve.

ongulé, e (ɔ̃gyle) *a*, hoofed.

onomatopée (ɔnɔmatɔpe) *f*, onomatopoeia.

onyx (ɔniks) *m*, onyx.

onze (ɔ̃:z) *a*. & *m*, eleven; eleventh. onzième† (ɔ̃zjɛm) *a*. & *n*, eleventh. (*Note.—Say* le onze, le onzième, *not* l'onze, l'onzième.)

oolithe (ɔɔlit) *m*, oolite.

opacité (ɔpasite) *f*, opacity.

opale (ɔpal) f, opal. **opalin, e** (lɛ̃, in) a, opaline.

opaque (ɔpak) a, opaque.

opéra (ɔpera) m, opera; o. [house]. ~ *bouffe*, comic opera, musical comedy. ~-*comique*, opera comique (*spoken dialogue*).

opérateur,⁰ trice (ɔperatœːr, tris) n, operator; cameraman (*film*). **opération** (sjɔ̃) f, operation; stage; working; transaction, dealing. **opéré, e** (re) n, surgical case (*pers.*). **opérer** (re) v.t. & abs, to operate, work, effect; make; do; act; deal; operate on (*Surg.*).

opérette (ɔperɛt) f, operetta, light opera, musical play.

ophtalmie (ɔftalmi) f, ophthalmia. **ophtalmique** (mik) a, ophthalmic.

opiacé, e (ɔpjase) a, opiated.

opinant (ɔpinɑ̃) m, speaker (*in debate*). **opiner** (ne) v.i, to opine; vote. ~ *du bonnet*, to say nothing but ditto to everything. **opiniâtre†** (njɑːtr) a. & n, [self-]opinionated; self-willed; obstinate, pertinacious, stubborn (person). **s'opiniâtrer** (ɑtre) v.pr, to persist. **opiniâtreté** (trəte) f, obstinacy, etc. **opinion** (njɔ̃) f, opinion; view; mind; vote.

opiomane (ɔpjɔman) n, opium addict. **opium** (jɔm) m, opium.

opossum (ɔpɔsɔm) m, opossum.

opportun, e (ɔpɔrtœ̃, yn) a, opportune, seasonable, timely, well-timed. **opportunément** (tynemɑ̃) ad, opportunely, etc. **opportunisme** (nism) m, opportunism. **opportuniste** (nist) n, opportunist, timeserver. **opportunité** (te) f, opportuneness; opportunity.

opposant, e (ɔpozɑ̃, ɑ̃ːt) n, opponent; (*att.*) opposing; opponent. **opposé, e** (ze) a, opposed, opposite. ¶ m, opposite, reverse, contrary. **opposer** (ze) v.t. & s'~ à, to oppose. ~ *une exception*, to demur (*law*). **à l'opposite** (pozit) ad, opposite, facing. **opposition** (sjɔ̃) f, opposition; contrast; contradistinction; stop; objection.

oppresser (ɔprɛse) v.t, to oppress (*Med.* & *fig.*). **oppresseur**

(sœːr) m, oppressor. **oppressif, ive** (sif, iːv) a, oppressive. **oppression** (sjɔ̃) f, oppression. **opprimer** (prime) v.t, to oppress.

opprobre (ɔprɔbr) m, disgrace, opprobrium.

opter (ɔpte) v.i, to choose.

opticien (ɔptisjɛ̃) m, optician.

optime (ɔptime) (*Latin word*) very well, all right. **optimisme** (mism) m, optimism. **optimiste** (mist) a, optimistic, hopeful, sanguine. ¶ n, optimist.

option (ɔpsjɔ̃) f, option.

optique (ɔptik) a, optic; optical. ¶ f, optics; perspective (*Theat.*).

opulence (ɔpylɑ̃ːs) f, opulence, affluence, wealth; buxomness. **opulent, e** (lɑ̃, ɑ̃ːt) a, opulent, etc.

opuscule (ɔpyskyl) m, short treatise; tract.

or (ɔːr) c, now. ~ *çà*, now then.

or (ɔːr) m, gold. ~ *laminé*, rolled g. ~ *moulu*, ormolu. **ni pour** ~ **ni pour argent**, for love or money. **d'**~, gold; golden.

oracle (ɔraːkl) m, oracle.

orage (ɔraːʒ) m, thunderstorm; storm. **orageux, euse†** (raʒø, øːz) a, stormy; thundery.

oraison (ɔrɛzɔ̃) f, prayer. ~ *dominicale*, Lord's prayer. ~ *funèbre*, funeral oration.

oral, e† (ɔral) a, oral, viva voce.

orange (ɔrɑ̃ːʒ) f, orange. ~ *amère*, Seville o. ~ *sanguine*, blood o. **orange**, m. & a. **orangé, e** (rɑ̃ʒe) a. & m, orange (*color*). **orangeade** (ʒad) f, orangeade. **oranger** (ʒe) m, orange [tree]. **orangerie** (ʒri) f, orangery.

orang-outang (ɔrɑ̃utɑ̃) m, orangutan.

orateur (ɔratœːr) m, orator, speaker. **oratoire** (twaːr) a, oratorical; rhetorical; declamatory. *l'art* ~, oratory. ¶ m, oratory (*chapel*). **oratorio** (tɔrjo) m, oratorio.

orbe (ɔrb) m, orb (*heavenly body*). **orbite** (bit) f, orbit; socket (*eye*).

Orcades (les) (ɔrkad) f.pl, the Orkneys.

orchestral, e (ɔrkɛstral) a, orchestral. **orchestre** (tr) m, orchestra, band; orchestra seats (*Theat.*). **orchestrer** (tre) *v.t*, to orchestrate, score.

orchidée (ɔrkide) *f*, orchid. **orchis** (kis) *m*, orchis.

ordalie (ɔrdali) *f*, ordeal (*Hist.*).

ordinaire† (ɔrdinɛːr) *a*, ordinary; common; customary; usual, everyday. ¶ *m*, wont; ordinary; [company] mess (*Mil.*).

ordinal (ɔrdinal) *a.m*, ordinal.

ordination (ɔrdinasjɔ̃) *f*, ordination (*Eccl.*).

ordonnance (ɔrdɔnɑ̃ːs) *f*, ordering (*arrangement*); organization; regulation (*police*); [treasury] warrant; prescription (*Med.*). ¶ *f. or m*, orderly. **ordonnancer** (nɑ̃se) *v.t*, to pass for payment. **ordonnateur, trice** (natœːr, tris) *n*, director; master of ceremonies; (*m*) computer. **ordonné, e** (ne) *p.a*, tidy, orderly (*pers.*). **ordonner** (ne) *v.t. & abs*, to order; organize; prescribe; ordain. **ordre** (dr) *m*, order; rate. ~ *d'exécution*, death warrant. ~ *du jour*, agenda, business [before the meeting]; order of the day. *numéro d'~*, serial number. ~ *public*, law & order, peace; public policy. *à l'~!* order!; chair!

ordure (ɔrdyːr) *f*, filth, dirt, muck; refuse, dust; ordure; smut. **ordurier, ère** (dyrje, ɛːr) *a*, filthy; scurrilous; smutty.

orée (ɔre) *f*, verge, skirt (*of a wood*).

oreille (ɔrɛːj) *f*, ear; lug; wing (*nut*). *avoir l'~ dure*, to be hard of hearing. *avoir l'~ juste*, to have a good ear (*for music*). *~-d'ours*, bear's-ear, auricula. *~-de-souris*, forget-me-not. **oreiller** (rɛje) *m*, pillow. **oreillette** (jɛt) *f*, auricle (*heart*); ear (*Bot.*). **oreillon** (jɔ̃) *m*, ear flap; ear (*Bot.*); (*pl.*) mumps.

orémus (ɔremyːs) *m*, prayer.

Orénoque (l') (ɔrenɔk) *m*, the Orinoco.

ores (ɔːr) *ad*: *d'~ & déjà*, now & henceforth.

orfèvre (ɔrfɛːvr) *m*, goldsmith &/or silversmith. **orfèvrerie** (fɛvrəri) *f*, gold[smith's] &/or silver[smith's] work.

orfraie (ɔrfrɛ) *f*, osprey.

organdi (ɔrgɑ̃di) *m*, organdy; book muslin.

organe (ɔrgan) *m*, organ; spokesman; (*pl, Mach.*) parts, gear. **organique** (nik) *a*, organic. **organisateur, trice** (zatœːr, tris) *n*, organizer. **organisation** (zasjɔ̃) *f*, organization. **organiser** (ze) *v.t*, to organize. *une tête bien organisée, un cerveau organisé*, a level-headed person. **organisme** (nism) *m*, organism. **organiste** (nist) *n*, organist (*Mus.*).

orge (ɔrʒ) *f*, barley. ~ *perlé*, *m*, pearl b. **orgeat** (ʒa) *m*, orgeat. **orgelet** (ʒəlɛ) *m*, stye (*eye*).

orgie (ɔrʒi) *f*, orgy; riot (*fig.*).

orgue (ɔrg) *m*, *the pl. is f*, organ; o. loft. ~ *de Barbarie*, barrel organ.

orgueil (ɔrgœːj) *m*, pride. **orgueilleux, euse**† (gœjø, øːz) *a*. *& n*, proud (*person*).

orient (ɔrjɑ̃) *m*, orient, east. **l'O~** (*Geog.*), the Orient, the East. *~ moyen*, the Middle East. **oriental, e** (tal) *a*, oriental, eastern. **O~, n**, Oriental, Eastern. **orientation** (tasjɔ̃) *f*, orientation; bearings; direction; aspect; trend; trimming (*sails, yards*). **orienter** (te) *v.t*, to orient[ate]; direct, point; trim (*sails, yards*).

orifice (ɔrifis) *m*, mouth, aperture, port, orifice.

oriflamme (ɔriflaːm) *f*, oriflamme; banner.

originaire† (ɔriʒinɛːr) *a*, original. *être ~ de*, to come from, be a native of. **original, e**† (nal) *a*, original; first (*edition*); inventive; odd, queer. ¶ *m*, original; oddity. **originalité** (lite) *f*, originality. **origine** (ʒin) *f*, origin; beginning; outset. **originel, le**† (nɛl) *a*, original.

oripeaux (ɔripo) *m.pl*, tinsel; tawdry finery; rags.

Orléans (ɔrleɑ̃) *m. or f*, Orleans.

ormaie (ɔrmɛ) *ou* **ormoie** (mwa) *f*, elm grove. **orme** (ɔrm) *& or* **ormeau** (mo) *m*, elm [tree]. *orme de montagne*, wych-elm. **ormille** (miːj) *f*, elm row.

orné, e (ɔrne) *p.a*, ornate. **ornemaniste** (nəmanist) *n*, ornamentalist. **ornement** (mɑ̃) *m*, ornament. *sans ~s*, unadorned. **orne-**

mental, e (tal) *a*, ornamental. **ornementation** (tasjɔ̃) *f*, ornamentation. **orner** (ne) *v.t*, to ornament, adorn; grace.

ornière (ɔrnjɛːr) *f*, rut; groove.

ornithogale (ɔrnitɔgal) *m*, star of Bethlehem. **ornithologie** (lɔʒi) *f*, ornithology. **ornithologiste** (ʒist) *ou* **ornithologue** (lɔg) *n*, ornithologist.

orpailleur (ɔrpajœːr) *m*, gold washer (*pers.*).

orphelin, e (ɔrfəlɛ̃, in) *n. & att*, orphan. *~ de père*, fatherless. **orphelinat** (lina) *m*, orphanage.

orphéon (ɔrfeɔ̃) *m*, choral society.

orphie (ɔrfi) *f*, garfish.

orpin (ɔrpɛ̃) *m*, stonecrop.

orque (ɔrk) *f*, orc, grampus.

orteil (ɔrtɛːj) *m*, toe. *gros ~*, big toe.

orthodoxe (ɔrtɔdɔks) *a*, orthodox. **orthodoxie** (ksi) *f*, orthodoxy. **orthographe** (graf) *f*, orthography, spelling. **orthographie** (fi) *f*, orthography (*Arch.*). **orthographier** (fje) *v.t. & abs*, to spell. *mal ~*, to misspell. **orthographique** (fik) *a*, orthographic; spelling (*att.*). **orthopédie** (pedi) *f*, orthopedics. **orthopédique** (dik) *a*, orthopedic.

ortie (ɔrti) *f*, nettle. *~ brûlante*, *~ grièche* (griɛʃ), stinging nettle.

ortolan (ɔrtɔlɑ̃) *m*, ortolan.

orvet (ɔrvɛ) *m*, slowworm, blindworm.

orviétan (ɔrvjetɑ̃) *m*: *marchand d'~s*, quack.

os (ɔs, *pl.* o) *m*, bone. *~ à moelle*, marrow b.

osciller (ɔsile) *v.i*, to oscillate, swing, sway about; fluctuate; waver. **oscillation** (lasjɔ̃) *f*, oscillation, etc.

osé, e (oze) *p.a*, daring, bold.

oseille (ozɛːj) *f*, sorrel.

oser (oze) *v.t*, to dare, d. to, venture, v. to.

oseraie (ozrɛ) *f*, osier bed.

oseur, euse (ozœːr, øːz) *n*, bold man, woman.

osier (ozje) *m*, osier, wicker.

osmium (ɔsmjɔm) *m*, osmium.

ossature (ɔsatyːr) *f*, frame[work]. **osselet** (slɛ) *m*, ossicle; (*pl.*) knuckle bones, dibs. **ossements** (smɑ̃) *m.pl*, bones (*dead*). **osseux, euse** (sø, øːz) *a*, bony, osseous. **ossifier** (sifje) *v.t*, to ossify. **ossu, e** (sy) *a*, big-boned, bony. **ossuaire** (sɥɛːr) *m*, ossuary.

Ostende (ɔstɑ̃ːd) *m*, Ostend.

ostensible† (ɔstɑ̃sibl) *a*, fit (*or* intended) to be shown; open. **ostensoir** (swaːr) *m*, ostensory, monstrance. **ostentateur, trice** (tatœːr, tris) *&* **ostentatoire** (twaːr) *a*, ostentatious, showy. **ostentation** (sjɔ̃) *f*, ostentation, show.

ostracisme (ɔstrasism) *m*, ostracism.

ostréiculture (ɔstreikyltyːr) *f*, oyster culture.

ostrogot[h] (ɔstrɔgo, ɔt) (*fig.*) *n*, goth, barbarian.

otage (ɔtaːʒ) *m*, hostage.

otalgie (ɔtalʒi) *f*, earache.

otarie (ɔtari) *f*, otary, sea lion.

ôté (ote) *pr*, barring, except. **ôter** (te) *v.t*, to remove, take away; t. out; t. off, pull off; doff. *s'~*, to get out (*of way, etc.*).

ottoman (e ɔtɔmɑ̃, an) *a. &* **O~**, *n*, Ottoman. **ottomane**, *f*, ottoman.

ou (u) *c*, or, either. *~ bien*, or [else].

où (u) *ad*, where, whither; whence; how far; which; what; when; in. *d'~*, whence, where from. *par ~*, [by] which way, through which.

ouailles (waːj) *f.pl*, flock (*Christians*).

ouate (wat) *f*, wadding, cotton wool. **ouater** (te) *v.t*, to wad, pad; quilt.

oubli (ubli) *m*, forgetfulness; oblivion; neglect; oversight; lapse. **oublie** (bli) *f*, cone, cornet, wafer (*ice cream*). **oublier** (blie) *v.t. & abs*, to forget; neglect; overlook. **oubliettes** (ɛt) *f.pl*, oubliette. **oublieux, euse** (ø, øːz) *a*, forgetful, oblivious.

Ouessant (wɛsɑ̃) *m*, Ushant.

ouest (wɛst) *m*, west; (*att.*) west, western.

ouf (uf) *i*, oh!, what a relief!

oui (wi) (*particle*), yes; ay; so.

¶ *m*, (le ~, un ~), yes; ay. ~-*da, i*, [yes] indeed!

oui-dire (widi:r) *m*, hearsay. **ouïe** (wi) *f*, hearing; (*pl.*) sound holes (*Mus.*); (*pl.*) gills (*fish*).

ouiller (uje) *v.t*, to fill up (*ullaged cask*).

ouïr (wi:r) *v.t.ir*, to hear (*witness—law*).

ouragan (uragã) *m*, hurricane.

Oural (l') (ural) *m*, the Ural. *les monts Ourals*, the Ural Mountains.

ourdir (urdi:r) *v.t*, to warp (*yarn*); hatch (*fig.*); weave (*fig.*).

ourler (urle) *v.t*, to hem. ~ *à jour*, to hemstitch. **ourlet** (lɛ) *m*, hem; rim. ~ *à jour*, hemstitch. ~ *piqué*, stitched hem.

ours (urs) *m*, bear. ~ *blanc*, polar b. ~ *grizzlé* (grizle), grizzly b. ~ [*Martin*], ~ *de peluche*, teddy b. **ourse** (urs) *f*, [she-]bear; Bear (*Astr.*). **oursin** (sɛ̃) *m*, sea urchin; bearskin (*cap*). **ourson** (sɔ̃) *m*, bear's cub; bearskin (*cap*).

outarde (utard) *f*, bustard.

outil (uti) *m*, tool. **outillage** (tija:ʒ) *m*, tools; plant, machinery; equipment, outfit. ~ *national*, national capital (*economics*). **outiller** (je) *v.t*, to equip, fit out.

outrage (utra:ʒ) *m*, outrage; insult; offense; ravages (*time*). **outrageant, e** (traʒã, ã:t) *a*, insulting, scurrilous. **outrager** (ʒe) *v.t*, to insult; outrage. **outrageux, euse†** (ʒø, ø:z) *a*, insulting, scurrilous.

outrance (utrã:s) *f*, excess. *à ~*, to the death; mortal; internecine; desperately, to the bitter end; out & out. **outrancier, ère** (trãsje, ɛ:r) *a*, extremist (*att.*), out & out.

outre (utr) *f*, leather bottle.

outre (utr) *pr. & ad*, beyond; further. *d'~ en ~*, through [& through]. *nos voisins d'~-Manche*, our neighbors across the Channel. *en ~*, moreover, besides, further[more]. *passer ~*, to go on; ignore. ~*-mer, ad. & d'~-mer, a*, oversea[s].

outré, e (utre) *a*, excessive, far-fetched, overdone, fulsome, outré; carried away; disgusted.

outrecuidance (utrəkɥidã:s) *f*, presumptuousness. **outrecuidant, e** (dã, ã:t) *a*, overweening.

outremer (utrəmɛ:r) *m*, ultramarine (*pigment*).

outrepasser (utrəpase) *v.t*, to go beyond, overstep.

outrer (utre) *v.t*, to overdo; overstrain; provoke.

ouvert, et† (uvɛ:r, ɛrt) *p.a*, open; free; frank. **ouverture** (vɛrty:r) *f*, opening; aperture; orifice; hole; port; gap; spread; overture. openness.

ouvrable (uvrabl) *a*, workable; business (*day*). **ouvrage** (vra:ʒ) *m*, work; doing (*fig.*). ~*s d'agrément*, fancy work. ~*s d'art*, permanent works, [*p.*] structures. ~*s de dames*, fancy needlework, art n. ~*s de ville*, job work (*Typ.*). **ouvragé, e** (vraʒe) *a*, [highly] worked, elaborated.

ouvre-boîte (uvrə) *m*, can opener. **ouvre-gants**, *m*, glove stretcher.

ouvrer (uvre) *v.i*, to work; (*v.t.*) to work; diaper.

ouvreur, euse (uvrœ:r, ø:z) *n*, opener; (*f.*) box attendant (*Theat.*).

ouvrier, ère (uvrie, ɛ:r) *n*, workman; workwoman; worker; operative; factory hand; journeyman; laborer (*farm*). ~ *d'art*, handicraftsman. ¶ *a*, working, laboring (*class*); workmen's; labor (*troubles, etc.*).

ouvrir (uvri:r) *v.t. & abs. ir*, to open; unlock; disburden; open up; cut; propose; head (*as a list*); turn on, switch on; draw back (*curtains*); sharpen (*appetite*); (*v.i.ir.*) to open. *la maison reste ouverte pendant les travaux*, business as usual during alterations. *s'~*, to open; unburden oneself.

ouvroir (uvrwa:r) *m*, workroom (*convent*).

ovaire (ɔvɛ:r) *m*, ovary.

ovale (ɔval) *a. & m*, oval. ~ [*de table*], doily.

ovation (ɔvasjɔ̃) *f*, ovation.

ovine (ɔvin) *a.f*, ovine.

ovipare (ɔvipa:r) *a*, oviparous.

oxhydrique (ɔksidrik) *a*, oxy-hydrogen (*blowpipe, etc.*); lime-(*light*).

oxyde (ɔksid) *m*, oxide. ~ *de carbone*, carbon monoxide. **oxyder** (de) *v.t*, to oxidize. **oxygène** (ʒɛn) *m*, oxygen.

ozone (ozɔn) *m*, ozone.

P

pacage (paka:ʒ) *m*, grazing; pasturage. **pacager** (kaʒe) *v.t*, to pasture, graze.

pachyderme (paʃidɛrm) *m*, pachyderm.

pacificateur, trice (pasifika-tœ:r, tris) *n*, peacemaker. ¶ *a*, pacifying. **pacifier** (fje) *v.t*, to pacify; appease. **pacifique**† (fik) *a*, pacific, peaceable; peaceful. le P~, the Pacific. **pacifiste** (fist) *n. & a*, pacificist, pacifist.

pacotille (pakɔti:j) *f*, barter goods; trash.

pacte (pakt) *m*, [com]pact, cove-nant. **pactiser avec** (tize), to compound with (*condone*); com-pound (*felony*).

Pactole (le) (paktɔl) (*fig.*), a gold mine.

Padoue (padu) *f*, Padua.

pæan (peã) *m*, paean.

pagaie (pagɛ) *f*, paddle (*canoe*).

pagaïe, pagaille (paga:j) *f*, clutter, mess, disorder, etc.

paganisme (paganism) *m*, pa-ganism, heathenism.

pagayer (pageje) *v.t*, to paddle (*canoe*). **pagayeur, euse** (jœ:r, ø:z) *n*, paddler.

page (pa:ʒ) *f*, page (*book*); chap-ter (*of one's life*). à la ~, up to date. ¶ *m*, page (*noble youth*); bellhop.

pagel (paʒɛl) *m*, [sea] bream.

paginer (paʒine) *v.t*, to page, paginate.

pagode (pagɔd) *f*, pagoda; man-darin (*toy*).

paie (pɛ) *f*, pay, wages; (*good, bad*) payer. **paiement** (mã) *m*, payment.

paien, ne (pajẽ, ɛn) *a. & n*, pa-gan, heathen.

paillard, e (paja:r, ard) *a. & n*, lewd (*person*). **paillasse** (jas) *f*,

straw mattress, paillasse, pal-liasse. ¶ *m*, clown (*pagliaccio*). **paillasson** (sɔ̃) *m*, doormat; mat-ting (*Hort.*). **paille** (pɑ:j) *f*, straw; flaw; (*fig.*) mote (*in eye*). ~ *de bois*, wood-wool. [*couleur*] ~, straw-color[ed]. **pailler** (paje) (*fig.*) *m*, dunghill. ¶ *v.t*, to mulch; rush (*chair*). **paillet** (jɛ) *a.m*, pale (*red wine*). **paillet d'a-bordage**, *m*, collision mat. **pail-leté, e** (jte) *a*, spangled. **paillette** (jɛt) *f*, spangle; flake, scale. **pailleux** (jø) *a.m*, strawy; flawy. **paillis** (ji) *m*, mulch. **paillon** (jɔ̃) *m*, straw casing (*bottle*); spangle; foil; grain (*solder*). **paillote** (pajɔt) *f*, straw hut (*native*).

pain (pẽ) *m*, bread; loaf (*bread, sugar*); biscuit (*dog*); cake (*soap, fish, etc.*); tablet; pat (*butter*). ~ *à cacheter*, signet wafer. ~ *à chanter*, wafer (*Eccl.*). ~ *d'é-pice*, gingerbread. ~ *de bougie*, taper (*coiled*). ~ *de munition*, ration bread. ~ *de régime*, diet b. ~ *grillé*, ~ *rôti*, toast.

pair (pɛ:r) *a.m*; **paire**, *Arith. only, a.f*, equal, alike; even (*num-ber*). ¶ *m*, peer; equal; par, equality; mate (*bird*). au ~, (*engagement*) on mutual terms; room and board (*no salary*). *marcher de ~ avec*, to keep pace with; rank with.

paire (pɛ:r) *f*, pair; brace; yoke (*oxen, etc.*).

pairesse (pɛrɛs) (*Eng.*) *f*, peeress. **pairie** (ri) (*Fr. Hist. & Eng.*) *f*, peerage.

paisible† (pɛzibl) *a*, peaceable, peaceful.

paître (pɛ:tr) *v.t. & i. ir*, to graze, pasture, browse; feed; tend.

paix (pɛ) *f*, peace; pax (*Eccl.*). ¶ *i*, hush! be quiet!

pal (pal) *m*, pale, stake.

palabre (pala:br) *f. or m*, pa-laver. **palabrer** (labre) *v.i*, to palaver.

paladin (paladẽ) *m*, paladin; knight errant (*fig.*).

palais (palɛ) *m*, palace; [law] courts; court; law; palate; roof of the mouth. ~ *dur*, hard palate, bony p. ~ *mou*, soft p.

palan (palã) *m*, pulley block;

tackle, purchase. **palanche** (lɑ̃ːʃ) f, yoke (for pails).

palanque (palɑ̃ːk) f, stockade.

palatal, e (palatal) a, palatal.

palatine (palatin) f, fur cape, tippet.

pale (pal) f, shut-off; sluice gate; blade (oar, air propeller).

pâle (pɑːl) a, pale, pallid, wan; (fig.) colorless.

palée (pale) f, sheet piling.

palefrenier (palfrənje) m, groom, [h]ostler. **palefroi** (frwa) (Poet.) m, palfrey.

palémon (palemɔ̃) m, prawn.

paléographie (paleɔgrafi) f, paleography. **paléontologie** (ɔ̃tɔlɔʒi) f, paleontology.

Palerme (palɛrm) f, Palermo.

paleron (palrɔ̃) m, shoulder blade (horse, ox).

palet (palɛ) m, quoit; quoits; puck (ice hockey).

paletot (palto) m, overcoat; greatcoat.

palette (palɛt) f, battledore; bat; palette; pallet; paddle.

palétuvier (paletyvje) m, mangrove.

pâleur (pɑlœːr) f, pallor, paleness.

palier (palje) m, landing (stairs); floor; bearings, plummer block; level.

palimpseste (palɛ̃psɛst) m. & a, palimpsest.

palinodie (palinɔdi) f, recantation.

pâlir (pɑliːr) v.i. & t, to pale, blanch; wane; fade.

palis (pali) m, pale, paling. **palissade** (sad) f, palisade, fence; stockade; hoarding (street). **palissader** (de) v.t, to palisade, fence.

palissandre (palisɑ̃ːdr) m, rosewood.

palladium (paladjɔm) m, palladium; safeguard.

palliatif, ive (palljatif, iːv) a. & m, palliative. **pallier** (pallje) v.t, to palliate.

palmarès (palmarɛːs) m, prize list, honors list.

palme (palm) f, palm [branch], p. [tree]. **palmé, e** (me) a, palmate[d]; webbed.

palmer (palmɛːr) m, micrometer.

palmeraie (palmərɛ) f, palm grove. **palmier** (mje) m, palm [tree]. **palmipède** (mipɛd) a, web-footed. **palmiste** (mist) m, cabbage tree.

palombe (palɔ̃ːb) f, ring dove, wood pigeon.

pâlot, te (pɑlo, ɔt) a, palish, wan.

palourde (palurd) f, clam (Mol.).

palpable (palpabl) a, palpable. **palpe** (palp) f. or m, palp[us], feeler. **palper** (pe) v.t, to feel, finger. **palpitation** (pitasjɔ̃) f, palpitation, throbbing, fluttering. **palpiter** (te) v.i, to palpitate, etc; go pit-[a-]pat; thrill.

paltoquet (paltɔkɛ) m, churl.

paludéen, ne (palydeɛ̃, ɛn) a, marshy; malarial. **paludisme** (dism) m, malaria.

pâmer (pɑme) v.i. & se ~, to swoon, faint; die (of laughing, etc.).

pampas (pɑ̃pɑs) f.pl, pampas.

pamphlet (pɑ̃flɛ) m, lampoon. **pamphlétaire** (fletɛːr) m, lampooner.

pamplemousse (pɑ̃pləmus) f, grapefruit.

pampre (pɑ̃ːpr) m, vine branch.

pan (pɑ̃) m, skirt, flap; tail (coat); face, side; pane, slab; frame. à 6 ~s, hexagonal. à 8 ~s, octagonal.

pan (pɑ̃) onomatopoeia, bang! ~! ~! rat-tat[-tat]!

panacée (panase) f, panacea, nostrum.

panache (panaʃ) m, plume, tuft; mettle, go, dash. faire ~, to have a spill, turn right over. **panacher** (ʃe) v.t, to plume, tuft; streak, variegate, mix.

panais (panɛ) m, parsnip.

panama (panama) m, panama, Panama hat.

panaris (panari) m, whitlow.

pancarte (pɑ̃kart) f, placard, bill, show card.

pancréas (pɑ̃kreɑːs) m, pancreas.

pandémonium (pɑ̃demɔnjɔm) m, pandemonium.

pandit (pɑ̃di) m, pundit.

pandour (pãdur) *m*, pandor, brute (*pers.*).

panégyrique (paneʒirik) *m*, panegyric, encomium.

paner (pane) *v.t*, to crumb (*Cook.*).

panerée (panre) *f*, basketful.

panetière (pantjɛːr) *f*, sideboard.

pangermanisme (pãʒɛrmanism) *m*, pan-Germanism.

panier (panje) *m*, basket, hamper; pannier; straw hive; lobster basket; basketful. ~ *à ouvrage*, work basket. ~ [*à papiers*], wastepaper b. ~ *à pêche*, creel. ~ *à provisions*, shopping basket; luncheon b. ~ *roulant*, go-cart. ~ *à salade*, prison van, Black Maria.

panique (panik) *a. & f*, panic, scare.

panne (pan) *f*, lard; plush; purlin; pane (*hammer*); breakdown, failure. *avoir une ~ d'essence* ou *une ~ sèche*, to run out of gas. *laisser en ~*, to leave in the lurch. *mettre en ~*, to heave to (*Naut.*).

panneau (pano) *m*, panel; snare. *~-réclame*, *m*, billboard.

panneton (pantɔ̃) *m*, bit, web (*key*).

panonceau (panɔ̃so) *m*, medallion, tablet, sign.

panoplie (panɔpli) *f*, panoply; trophy (*wall*).

panorama (panɔrama) *m*, panorama.

panse (pãːs) *f*, belly, paunch.

pansement (pãsmã) *m*, dressing (*wound*). **panser** (se) *v.t*, to dress; groom (*horse*).

pansu, e (pãsy) *a*, corpulent.

pantagruélique (pãtagryelik) *a*, sumptuous (*fare*).

pantalon (pãtalɔ̃) *m*, [pair of] trousers. **pantalonnade** (lɔnad) *f*, comic turn; clownery; [tom]-foolery; masquerade, sham.

pantelant, e (pãtlã, ãːt) *a*, panting; twitching (*flesh*). **panteler** (le) *v.i*, to pant.

panthéisme (pãteism) *m*, pantheism.

panthéon (pãteɔ̃) *m*, pantheon.

panthère (pãtɛːr) *f*, panther.

pantin (pãtɛ̃) *m*, (*toy*) jumping jack; (*pers.*) monkey on a stick (*gesticulator*); shallow-brained &

fickle person. *mener une vie de* ~, to run wild.

pantographe (pãtɔgraf) *m*, pantograph.

pantois, e (pãtwa, aːz) *a*, flabbergasted.

pantomime (pãtɔmim) (*pers.*) *n*, pantomimist. ¶ *f*, pantomime, dumb show.

pantoufle (pãtufl) *f*, slipper. ~*s en tapisserie*, carpet s—s. *en ~s*, in a free & easy way; informal.

panure (panyːr) *f*, [grated] bread crumbs.

paon (pã) *m*, peacock; p. butterfly. **paonne** (pan) *f*, peahen. **paonneau** (pano) *m*, peachick.

papa (papa) *m*, papa, dad[dy].

papal, e (papal) *a*, papal. **papauté** (pote) *f*, papacy. **pape** (pap) *m*, pope.

papegai (papgɛ) *m*, popinjay (*Hist.*); clay bird (*pigeon shooting*).

papelard, e (paplaːr, ard) *a. & n*, sanctimonious (*person*).

paperasse (papras) *f*, useless old paper. **papeterie** (pap[ɛ]tri) *f*, paper mill; p. making; p. trade; stationery store; stationery; s. case, writing case. **papetier, ère** (paptje, ɛːr) *n*, paper maker; stationer. **papier** (pje) *m*, paper; bills (*Fin.*). ~ *à calquer*, *~-calque*, tracing paper. ~ *à lettres*, note p., letter p. ~ *autovireur* (otɔvirœːr), self-toning p. ~ *buvard*, ~ *brouillard*, blotting p. ~ *carbone*, carbon [p.] (*duplicating*). ~ *de Chine*, rice p. ~ *de journal*, newsprint. ~ *de soie*, tissue p. ~ *de verre*, sandpaper. ~ *hygiénique*, toilet p. ~ *imperméable à la graisse*, ~ *sulfurisé*, grease-proof p. ~ *indien*, India p. ~ *machine*, typewriting p. ~ [*peint*], *~-tenture*, *m*, wallpaper. ~ *pelure*, tissue p. ~ *quadrillé* (kadrije), graph p., plotting p., section[al] p. ~ *tue-mouches*, fly p.

papillon (papijɔ̃) *m*, butterfly; wing nut; bow (*necktie*); slip (*paper*). ~ [*de nuit*], moth; throttle (*auto*). **papillonner** (jɔne) *v.i*, to flit about.

papillote (papijɔt) *f*, curl paper; foiled chocolate. **papilloter** (te) *v.i,* to flicker; blink; dazzle; slur (*Typ.*).

papisme (papism) *m,* popery. **papiste** (pist) *n,* papist. ¶ *a,* popish.

papoter (papɔte) *v.i,* to gossip.

papule (papyl) *f,* pimple.

papyrus (papiry:s) *m,* papyrus.

pâque (pɑ:k) *f,* Passover. **Pâques** (pɑ:k) *m.s,* Easter. **Pâques fleuries,** *f.pl,* Palm Sunday.

paquebot (pakbo) *m,* passenger &/*or* mail boat, liner, packet [boat]. ~ *à vapeur,* passenger steamer. ~ *aérien,* airship.

pâquerette (pɑkrɛt) *f,* daisy.

paquet (pakɛ) *m,* packet, package, bundle, pack; parcel, lot, block; clincher; (*att.*) plump. *un* ~ *de mer,* a, [heavy] sea. **paquetage** (kta:ʒ) *m,* pack (*soldier's*).

par (par) *pr,* by; through; across; via; out of; per; a; ia; into; with; on; about; over; from; for; at; during. ~ *an,* per annum. ~*-ci,* ~*-là,* ad, here & there, hither & thither; at odd times. ~*-dessous,* ~*-dessus.* See *dessous, dessus.* ~ *ici,* this way, through here. ~ *là,* that way, through there; by that. *de* ~ *le monde,* somewhere in the world. ~ *les présentes,* hereby (*law*). ~ *où?* which way? ~ *trop,* far too, too much, unduly.

parabole (parabɔl) *f,* parable; parabola. **parabolique**† (lik) *a,* parabolic(al) (*Geom.*).

parachever (paraʃve) *v.t,* to finish [off], perfect.

parachute (paraʃyt) *m,* parachute.

parade (parad) *f,* parade; show; parry[ing]; repartee. **parader** (de) *v.i,* to parade; show off.

paradis (paradi) *m,* paradise; top balcony (*Theat.*). *le* ~ [*terrestre*], [the earthly] paradise, [the Garden of] Eden.

paradoxal, e (paradɔksal) *a,* paradoxical. **paradoxe** (dɔks) *m,* paradox.

parafe (paraf) *m,* initials; flourish, paraph. **parafer** (fe) *v.t,* to initial.

paraffine (parafin) *f,* paraffin [wax].

parage (para:ʒ) *m,* lineage; (*pl.*) grounds (*fishing, cruising*), waters.

dans ces ~*s,* in these parts, hereabouts.

paragraphe (paragraf) *m,* paragraph; section mark (§).

paraître (parɛ:tr) *v.i.ir,* to appear; show; be published, come out; seem, look. ¶ *m,* seeming. *l'être & le* ~, the seeming & the real.

Paralipomènes (paralipɔmɛn) *m. pl,* Chronicles (*Bible*).

parallaxe (paralaks) *f,* parallax. **parallèle**† (lɛl) *a,* parallel. ¶ *f,* parallel (*Geom., Mil.*). ¶ *m,* parallel (*of latitude; comparison*). **parallélipipède** (lelipipɛd) *m,* parallelepiped. **parallélogramme** (lɔgram) *m,* parallelogram.

paralyser (paralize) *v.t,* to paralyze; cripple (*fig.*). **paralysie** (zi) *f,* paralysis. ~ *progressive,* creeping paralysis. **paralytique** (tik) *a. & n,* paralytic.

parangon (parɑ̃gɔ̃) *m,* paragon.

parapet (parapɛ) *m,* parapet.

paraphe (paraf) *m,* initials; flourish, paraph. **parapher** (fe) *v.t,* to initial.

paraphrase (parafrɑ:z) *f,* paraphrase; circumlocution. **paraphraser** (fraze) *v.t. & abs,* to paraphrase; amplify.

parapluie (paraplɥi) *m,* umbrella.

parasitaire (parazitɛ:r) *a,* parasitic(al) (*Biol.*). **parasite** (zit) *m,* parasite; hanger-on; sponger. ~*s atmosphériques,* static (*radio*). ¶ *a,* parasitical; redundant.

parasol (parasɔl) *m,* sunshade, umbrella (*garden, beach, held over potentate*); tent umbrella.

paratonnerre (paratɔnɛ:r) *m,* lightning conductor.

paravent (paravɑ̃) *m,* screen (*folding & fig.*).

paraverse (paravɛrs) *m,* raincoat.

parbleu (parblø) *i,* why, of course! to be sure!

parc (park) *m,* park; enclosure; yard; paddock; pen, fold; range, run; bed (*oyster*). ~ *à bestiaux* (cattle) & ~ *à matières* (materials), stockyard. ~ *à voitures,* car park. ~ *d'agrément,* pleasure grounds. **parcage** (ka:ʒ) *m,* parking; penning.

parcelle (parsεl) *f*, particle, scrap; driblet; parcel, plot, patch.

parce que (pars[ə]kə) *c*, because.

parchemin (parʃəmɛ̃) *m*, parchment; (*fig.*) title; diploma.

parcimonie (parsimɔni) *f*, parsimony. **parcimonieux, euse†** (njø, øːz) *a*, parsimonious, penurious.

parcourir (parkuriːr) *v.t.ir*, to travel over, cover; perambulate; run through. **parcours** (kuːr) *m*, distance, stretch, run; haul; course. ∼ *de 18 trous*, 18-hole course (*golf*).

pardessus (pardəsy) *m*, overcoat.

pardi (pardi) *i*, of course!

pardon (pardɔ̃) *m*, pardon, forgiveness. **pardonnable** (dɔnabl) *a*, pardonable. **pardonner** (ne) *v.t*. & ∼ à, to pardon, forgive; excuse.

pare- (par) *prefix*: ∼*-battage*, *m*, fender (*Naut.*). ∼*-boue*, *m*, fender; ∼*-brise*, *m*, windshield. ∼*-chocs*, *m*, bumper. ∼*-étincelles*, *m*, fireguard.

parégorique (paregɔrik) *a*, paregoric.

pareil, le (parεːj) *a*, like, alike, similar, to match; equal; parallel; such. ¶ *n*, like, equal; parallel; match, fellow. *la* ∼, the like (treatment). *sans pareil*, unequalled, matchless. **pareillement** (rεjmɑ̃) *ad*, in like manner; also, likewise.

parement (parmɑ̃) *m*, facing; face; cuff (*coat*); cloth (*altar*); curbstone.

parent, e (parɑ̃, ɑ̃ːt) *n*, relative, kinsman, -woman; relation; (*m. pl.*) parents, kin. **parenté** (rɑ̃te) *f*, relationship, kinship; relations.

parenthèse (parɑ̃tεːz) *f*, parenthesis; bracket (,). *par* ∼, parenthetically.

parer (pare) *v.t*. & *i*, to adorn, deck; dress; ward [off], fend [off]; parry; guard.

paresse (parεs) *f*, laziness, idleness, sloth; sluggishness. **paresser** (se) *v.i*, to idle; laze; loll, lounge. **paresseux, euse†** (sø, øːz) *a*. & *n*, idle, etc (person). ¶ *m*, sloth (*Zool.*).

parfaire (parfεːr) *v.t.ir*, to finish [off]; make up. **parfait, e** (fε, εt) *a*, perfect; thorough; capital. ¶

m, perfect [tense]. **parfaitement** (tmɑ̃) *ad*, perfectly; thoroughly; quite; quite so, exactly.

parfiler (parfile) *v.t*, to unravel.

parfois (parfwa) *ad*, sometimes, at times, now & again.

parfum (parfœ̃) *m*, perfume, fragrance; scent; flavor. **parfumer** (fyme) *v.t*, to scent, perfume. **parfumerie** (mri) *f*, perfumery. **parfumeur, euse** (mœːr, øːz) *n*, perfumer; (*m.*) perfume distiller.

pari (pari) *m*, bet, wager.

paria (parja) *m*, outcaste, untouchable; pariah; outcast.

parier (parje) *v.t*, to bet, wager, lay. ∼ *sur*, to back (*horse*). *il y a à ∼ que . . .*, the odds are that . . . **parieur, euse** (jœːr, øːz) *n*, bettor, backer.

parisien, ne (parizjɛ̃, εn), *a*. & P∼, *n*, Parisian.

parité (parite) *f*, parity, equality, likeness; equivalent.

parjure (parʒyːr) *m*, perjury; breach of oath. ¶ *n*, perjurer. ¶ *a*, perjured, forsworn. **se parjurer** (ʒyre) *v.pr*, to perjure (*or* forswear) oneself.

parlant, e (parlɑ̃, ɑ̃ːt) *a*, speaking, talking (*film, eyes*); lifelike; talkative. **parlé** (le) *m*, spoken part (*opera*); patter (*in song*).

parlement (parləmɑ̃) *m*, parliament. **parlementaire** (tεːr) *a*, parliamentary; of truce (*flag*). ¶ *m*, member of parliament; bearer of a flag of truce. **parlementer** (te) *v.i*, to parley.

parler (parle) *v.i*. & *abs*. & *v.t*, to speak, talk; t. about; tell, mention, say. ∼ *du nez*, to speak through the nose. ¶ *m*, way of speaking; speech; dialect. **parleur, euse** (lœːr, øːz) *n*, talker; (*att.*) talking (*bird*). **parloir** (lwaːr) *m*, parlor (*convent, school*). **parlote** (lɔt) *f*, debating society; gossip.

Parme (parm) *f*, Parma.

parmi (parmi) *pr*, among[st], amid[st].

parodie (parɔdi) *f*, parody. **parodier** (dje) *v.t*, to parody. **parodiste** (dist) *m*, parodist.

paroi (parwa) *f*, wall (*partition,*

etc.); side; coat[ing] (*stomach, etc.*).

paroisse (parwas) *f*, parish; p. church. **paroissial, e** (sjal) *a*, parish (*att.*), parochial. **paroissien, ne** (sjɛ̃, ɛn) *n*, parishioner. ¶ *m*, prayer book.

parole (parɔl) *f*, word; utterance; delivery; speaking; speech; parole. ~ *d'Évangile*, gospel [truth].

paroxysme (parɔksism) *m*, paroxysm.

parpaillot, e (parpajo, ɔt) *n*, heretic.

Parque (park) *f*, Fate (*Myth.*).

parquer (parke) *v.t*, to pen, fold; park.

parquet (parkɛ) *m*, floor, parquet; well (*of court*); central floor of Fr. *Bourse* reserved for use of *agents de change*. **parqueter** (kəte) *v.t*, to floor, parquet.

parrain (parɛ̃) *m*, godfather, sponsor; proposer, recommender. **parrainage** (rɛna:ʒ) *m*, sponsorship; recommendation.

parricide (parisid) (*pers.*) *n*. & (*act*) *m*, parricide; (*att.*) parricidal.

parsemer (parsəme) *v.t*, to strew, intersperse.

parsi (parsi) *m*. & **parse** (pars) *m*. & *a*, Parsee.

part (pa:r) (*law*) *m*, child, birth.

part (pa:r) *f*, share; part; portion; hand, side. ~ *du lion*, lion's share. *à* ~, apart; aside; except. *autre* ~, elsewhere, somewhere else. *d'autre* ~, on the other hand *or* side. *de la* ~ *de*, on the part of, on behalf of, from. *de* ~ *en* ~, right through. *faire* ~, to share; acquaint, inform.

partage (parta:ʒ) *m*, division, sharing; share, lot. ~ [*des voix*], equality of votes. **partagé, e** (taʒe) *p.a*, reciprocal, mutual (*love*); halved (*hole*) (*golf*). **partageable** (ʒabl) *a*, divisible. **partager** (ʒe) *v.t*, to divide, share, split.

partance (partɑ̃:s) *f*, sailing. *en* ~, about to sail, outward bound. **partant** (tɑ̃) *ad*, hence, therefore. ¶ *m*, starter (*horse, runner*).

partenaire (partənɛ:r) *n*, partner. ~ *d'entraînement*, sparring partner.

parterre (partɛ:r) *m*, bed (*garden*), plot, parterre; orchestra pit (*Theat.*).

parti (parti) *m*, party, side; part; course; decision; match (*marriage*). ~ *pris*, set purpose; prejudice, bias. *faire un mauvais* ~ *à*, to ill-treat. *prendre* ~, to take sides, to side. *tirer* ~ *de*, to make use of, turn to account.

partial, e† (parsjal) *a*, partial, biased, unfair. **partialité** (lite) *f*, partiality.

participation (partisipasjɔ̃) *f*, participation, sharing; partaking; share; joint [ad]venture, joint account. **participe** (sip) *m*, participle (*Gram.*). **participer** (pe) *v.i*, to participate, share; partake.

particulariser (partikylarize) *v.t*, to particularize. **particularité** (te) *f*, particularity; peculiarity. **particule** (kyl) *f*, particle; speck. **particulier, ère**† (lje, ɛ:r) *a*, particular; peculiar; [e]special; private. ¶ *n*, [private] individual.

partie (parti) *f*, part; parcel, lot, block; match, round, game; excursion, trip; line (*of business*); party; client (*lawyer's*). ~ *de trois*, threesome (*golf*). ~ *double*, doubles game (*Ten.*); foursome (*golf*); double entry (*Bkkpg.*) ~ *du discours*, part of speech. ~ *civile*, plaintiff. ~ *nulle*, tie (*sports*). *prendre à* ~, to take to task.

partiel, le (parsjɛl) *a*, partial (*not entire*). **partiellement** (lmɑ̃) *ad*, partially, partly.

partir (parti:r) *v.i.ir*, to depart, set out, start, go; leave; sail; go off; emanate, proceed. *êtes-vous prêts? partez!* are you ready? go! *à* ~ *de*, from; on & after.

partisan (partizɑ̃) *m*, partisan, henchman, follower, believer; supporter; guerrilla (*soldier*).

partitif, ive (partitif, i:v) *a*, partitive (*Gram.*). **partition** (sjɔ̃) *f*, score (*Mus.*).

partout (partu) *ad*, everywhere. *2, 3, jeux* ~, 2, 3, all (*Ten.*). ~ *où*, wherever.

parure (pary:r) *f*, adornment; ornament; dress, attire; dressing (*meat*); set (*jewels, underclothing*).

parvenir (parvəni:r) *v.i. & abs. ir*, to arrive; succeed. ~ à, to arrive at, reach; attain [to]; manage to; succeed in. **parvenu, e** (ny) *n*, upstart, parvenu.

parvis (parvi) *m*, parvis, square; court.

pas (pɑ) *m*, step; pace; stride; gait; walk; march; time (*Mil.*); dance, pas; progress; precedence (*in rank*); footfall; footprint; threshold; pass (*Phys. Geog.*); strait[s]; pitch, thread (*screw*). ~ *accéléré*, quick march. P~ *de Calais*, Straits of Dover. ~ *de clerc*, blunder. ~ *de la porte*, doorstep. *à* ~ *de tortue*, at a snail's pace. ~ *seul*, solo dance. *au* ~, drive slowly, dead slow (*traffic sign*). *au* ~ *gymnastique*, at the double (*Mil.*). *faux* ~, slip; misstep.

pas (pɑ) *neg. particle usually coupled with* ne, not; no. ~ *libre*, [I am] sorry, the line is busy. (*Teleph.*). ~ *possible!* you don't say so!

pasquin (paskɛ̃) *m*, lampooner; lampoon. **pasquinade** (kinad) *f*, pasquinade, lampoon, squib.

passable† (pɑsabl) *a*, passable, tolerable, fair, pretty good. **passade** (sad) *f*, passing fancy (*liaison*); passade. **passage** (sa:ʒ) *m*, passage; passing; crossing; going; transit; transition; pass; passageway, gangway, way, thoroughfare; arcade; ferry; right of way; toll. ~ *à niveau*, grade crossing. ~ *clouté*, studded crossing (*pedestrian crossing*). ~ *d'escalier*, stairway. ~ *interdit* [*au public*], no thoroughfare. ~ *souterraine*, underground passage.

passager, ère (pɑsaʒe, ɛ:r) *a*, passing, fleeting, transient, fugitive, short-lived, momentary. ¶ *n*, passenger; visitor, sojourner. ~ *clandestin*, stowaway. ~ *d'entrepont*, steerage passenger. **passagèrement** (ʒɛrmɑ̃) *ad*, in passing, for a short time. **passant, e** (pɑsɑ̃, ɑ̃:t) *n*, passerby.

passavant (pɑsavɑ̃) *m*, gangway (*on ship*); permit.

passe (pɑ:s) *f*, pass; passage; plight; way; thrust; cut; fairway, channel; brim (*hat*). *mauvaise* ~,

bad fix. ~ *étroite*, narrow[s] (*Naut.*).

passé, e (pɑse) *p.a*, past, [by]gone, last; over; faded. *passé maître*, a past master. ¶ *m*, past; p. [tense]; satin stitch (*Emb.*). **passé**, *pr*, after.

passe-droit (pɑsdrwa) *m*, injustice, invidious distinction.

passe-lacet (pɑslasɛ) *m*, bodkin.

passement (pɑsmɑ̃) *m*, lace, braid; gimp. **passementerie** (tri) *f*, passementerie, trimmings.

passe-partout (pɑspartu) *m*, master key.

passe-plats (pɑspla) *m*, service hatch.

passepoil (pɑspwal) *m*, piping (*braid*).

passeport (pɑspɔ:r) *m*, passport; clearance (*ship*).

passer (pɑse) *v.i. & t*, to pass; p. on; p. by; p. away; go; cross; spend; call, look in; ferry over; slip on; exceed; rank; enter, post; enter into; give, place; file (*a return at a registry*). se ~ **de**, to do without, dispense with.

passereau (pɑsro) *m*, sparrow.

passerelle (pɑsrɛl) *f*, footbridge; bridge (*ship's*); gangway.

passerose (pɑsro:z) *f*, hollyhock.

passe-temps (pɑstɑ̃) *m*, pastime.

passeur (pɑsœ:r) *m*, ferryman.

passible (pɑsibl) *a*, liable. ~ *de droits*, dutiable.

passif, ive (pɑsif, i:v) *a*, passive. ¶ *m*, passive [voice]; liabilities.

passiflore (pɑsiflɔ:r) *f*, passion flower.

passion (pɑsjɔ̃) *f*, passion. **passionnant, e** (ɔnɑ̃, ɑ̃:t) *a*, thrilling. **passionné**†, **e** (ne) *a*, passionate; impassioned. *il est* ~ *pour*, he is passionately fond of; his hobby is. **passionner** (ne) *v.t*, to impassion; enthral[l]. se ~, to become impassioned; become enamored.

passivement (pɑsivmɑ̃) *ad*, passively. **passiveté** (vite) *f*, passivity.

passoire (pɑswa:r) *f*, colander, strainer.

pastel (pɑstɛl) *m*, crayon; pastel; woad.

pastèque (pɑstɛk) *f*, watermelon.

pasteur (pastœːr) *m*, shepherd; pastor, minister.

pasteuriser (pastœrize) *v.t*, to pasteurize.

pastiche (pastiʃ) *m*, pastiche; imitation, copy.

pastille (pastiːj) *f*, lozenge, pastille, drop; patch (*tire*).

pastoral, e (pastɔral) *a*, pastoral. ¶ *f*, pastoral; pastorale.

pastoriser (pastɔrize) *v.t*, to pasteurize.

pat (pat) *m*, stalemate (*chess*); (*att.*) stalemated. *faire* ~, to stalemate.

patache (pataʃ) *f*, rattletrap (*vehicle*).

pataquès (patakɛːs) *m*, malaprop[ism].

patarafe (pataraf) *f*, scrawl.

patard (pataːr) *m*, coin of little value.

patate (patat) *f*, sweet potato; potato.

patatras (patatrɑ) *onomatopoeia*, crash!

pataud, e (pato, oːd) *a. & n*, clumsy (person). ¶ *m*, big-pawed puppy.

patauger (patoʒe) *v.i*, to flounder, squelch; wade.

pâte (pɑːt) *f*, paste; dough; pulp; impasto; pie (*printers'*). **pâté** (pɑte) *m*, pie, pasty; pâté; mud pie; blot; block (*houses*); pie (*printers'*). **pâtée** (te) *f*, mash (*poultry*); dog food.

patelin, e (patlɛ̃, in) *a*, wheedling. ¶ *m*, village.

patelle (patɛl) *f*, limpet.

patène (patɛn) *f*, paten.

patent, e (patɑ̃, ɑ̃ːt) *a*, patent (*obvious*). ¶ *f*, license. ~ *de santé*, bill of health.

Pater (pateːr) *m*, paternoster.

patère (patɛːr) *f*, base, block (*on wall*); hat peg.

paterne (patɛrn) *a*, patronizing. **paternel, le†** (nɛl) *a*, paternal, fatherly; father's (*side*). **paternité** (nite) *f*, paternity, fatherhood; authorship.

pâteux, euse (patø, øːz) *a*, pasty, clammy, thick.

pathétique† (patetik) *a*, pathetic. ¶ *m*, pathos.

pathologie (patɔlɔʒi) *f*, pathology. **pathologique** (ʒik) *a*, patho-logical. **pathologiste** (ʒist) *n*, pathologist.

pathos (patos) *m*, bathos.

patibulaire (patibylɛːr) *a*, hangdog.

patiemment (pasjamɑ̃) *ad*, patiently. **patience** (sjɑːs) *f*, patience; button stick (*Mil.*); patience (*cards*); dock (*Bot.*).

patient, e (sjɑ̃, ɑ̃ːt) *a*, patient, enduring. ¶ *n*, patient; sufferer. **patienter** (ɑ̃te) *v.i*, to have patience.

patin (patɛ̃) *m*, skate; runner; skid; shoe; flange. ~*s à glace*, (1) *à visser*, (2) *à griffes*, iceskates, (1) screw-on, (2) clamp-on. ~*s à roulettes*, rollers—s. ~*s de course*, racing s—s. ~*s de figure*, figure s—s. ~*s de hockey*, hockey s—s. **patinage** (tinaːʒ) *m*, skating; skidding; slipping. **patine** (tin) *f*, patina. **patiné, e** (ne) *p.p*, patinated; fumed (*oak*). **patiner** (ne) *v.i*, to skate; skid, slip. **patinette** (nɛt) *f*, scooter. **patineur, euse** (nœːr, øːz) *n*, skater.

pâtir (pɑtiːr) *v.i*, to suffer. **pâtiras** (tirɑ) *m*, drudge.

pâtis (pɑti) *m*, grazing ground, pasture.

pâtisser (pɑtise) *v.i*, to make pastry. **pâtisserie** (sri) *f*, pastry; confectionery; bakery; tea shop. **pâtissier, ère** (sje, ɛːr) *n*, pastry-cook [&/or confectioner]. **pâtissoire** (swaːr) *f*, pastry board.

patois (patwa) *m*, dialect; jargon.

patouiller (patuje) *v.i*, to flounder.

patraque (patrak) *f. & a*, rattletrap, (machine, etc.); the worse for wear.

pâtre (pɑːtr) *m*, herdsman.

patriarcal, e (patriarkal) *a*, patriarchal. **patriarche** (arʃ) *m*, patriarch.

patrice (patris) *m. &* **patricien, ne** (sjɛ̃, ɛn) *a. & n*, patrician. **patrie** (tri) *f*, native land, [n.] country, fatherland; home. [*petite*] ~, birthplace. **patrimoine** (trimwan) *m*, patrimony; inheritance, heritage. **patriote** (ɔt) *n*, patriot. ¶ ~ *&* **patriotique** (tik) *a*, patriotic. **patriotisme** (tism) *m*, patriotism. **patron, ne** (trɔ̃, ɔn) *n*, patron, ess; patron saint; employer, principal; master, mistress; governor; skipper; coxswain. ¶ *m*, pattern (*for dress, etc.*); templet, template; stencil [plate]. **dès patron-minet**, at early dawn. **patronage** (trɔnaːʒ) *m*, patronage; advowson; benevolence; guild, club (*church*). **patronal, e** (nal) *a*, patronal, patron saint's (*day*); employer's, -ers' (*att.*). **patronat** (na) *m*, employers (*col.*). **patronner** (ne) *v.t*, to patronize; stencil. **dame patronnesse** (nɛs) *f*, patroness (*fête, etc.*). **nom patronymique** (nimik) *m*, patronymic; surname.

patrouille (patruːj) *f*, patrol. **patrouiller** (truje) *v.i*, to patrol.

patte (pat) *f*, paw; foot; leg; claw; tab; strap, clip; clamp, holdfast; fluke (*anchor*). **à quatre ~s**, on all fours. **~-d'oie**, *f*, multiple fork, crowfoot [forking] (*of roads*); crow's-foot (*wrinkle*).

pâturage (patyraːʒ) *m*, pasturage. **pâture** (tyːr) *f*, pasture; food (*fig.*). **pâturer** (tyre) *v.i*, to pasture, graze.

paturon (patyrɔ̃) *m*, pastern.

paume (poːm) *f*, palm (*hand*); real tennis (*ancient game*).

paupérisme (poperism) *m*, pauperism.

paupière (popjɛːr) *f*, eyelid.

pause (poːz) *f*, pause, stop; rest (*Mus.*).

pauvre† (poːvr) *a. & m*, poor (man); pauper; penurious; scanty, meager. **pauvresse** (povrɛːs) *f*, beggar woman. **pauvret, te** (vrɛ, ɛt) *n*, poor little thing (*pers.*). **pauvreté** (vrəte) *f*, poverty; poorness; commonplace.

pavage (pavaːʒ) *m*, pavement; paving.

pavaner (se) (pavane) *v.pr*, to strut [about].

pavé (pave) *m*, paving stone, pavement; pavé; street(s) (*fig.*). **sur le ~**, out of work. **pavement** (vmɑ̃) *m*, paving; pavement. **paver** (ve) *v.t*, to pave. **paveur** (vœːr) *m*, paver.

pavie (pavi) *f*, clingstone.

Pavie (pavi) *f*, Pavia (*Geog.*).

pavillon (pavijɔ̃) *m*, pavilion; lodge; box (*Hunt.*); summer

house; house (*club*); flag, colors (*Naut. & Nav.*); flare; horn; earpiece. **~ de poupe**, ensign.

pavois (pavwa) *m*, bulwark (*ship's*); flags (*col.*). **pavoiser** (ze) *v.t*, to dress (*ship*); deck with flags; (*abs.*) to dress ship.

pavot (pavo) *m*, poppy. **~ somnifère**, opium poppy.

payable (pɛjabl) *a*, payable. **~ à la commande**, cash with order. **~ comptant**, pay cash. **payant, e** (jɑ̃, ɑ̃ːt) *a*, paying. ¶ *n*, payer. **paye** (pɛːj) *f*, pay, wages; (*good, bad*) payer. **payement** (pɛ[j]mɑ̃) *m*, payment. **payer** (je) *v.t. & abs*, to pay; p. for; p. out; cash (*check*); stand (*drink*). **~ d'audace**, to brazen it out. **~ de sa personne**, to risk one's neck. **payeur, euse** (jœːr, øːz) *n*, payer; paymaster; drawee.

pays (pei) *m*, country, land; native place. **~ de cocagne** (kɔkaɲ), land of milk & honey, l. of plenty. **les Pays-Bas**, the Netherlands. **mal du ~**, homesickness. **paysage** (zaːʒ) *m*, landscape; l. painting; description of scenery; (*pl.*) scenery. **paysagiste** (zaʒist) *m*, landscape painter; (*att.*) landscape (*gardener*).

paysan, ne (peizɑ̃, an) *n. & att*, peasant, rustic. **les paysans**, the peasantry. **paysannerie** (zanri) *f*, portrait of peasant life.

péage (peaːʒ) *m*, toll; t. house. **péager** (aʒe) *m*, toll collector.

péan (peɑ̃) *m*, paean.

peau (po) *f*, skin, fell, pelt; scruff (*neck*); slough; leather; rind, peel; shell (*nut*); case (*sausage*). **~ de tambour**, drumhead. **P~ Rouge, m**, redskin, red Indian. **peausserie** (sri) *f*, skin dressing; skins, peltry. **peaussier** (sje) *m*, skin dresser. [*médecin*] **peaussier** ou [*médecin*] **peaucier** (sje) *m*, skin specialist.

pécari (pekari) *m*, peccary.

peccadille (pɛkadiːj) *f*, peccadillo, slip.

pêche (pɛːʃ) *f*, peach (*fruit*); fishing (*act & right*); fishery, catch. **~ à la crevette**, shrimping. **~ à la ligne**, line fishing, rod f., angling. **~ à la mouche noyée**, wet fly f. **~ à la mouche**

sèche, dry fly f. ~ *à traîner*, trolling. ~ *au bord de la mer*, shore fishing. ~ *au lancer*, casting. ~ *au large*, ~ *hauturière* otyrj⸗r), offshore fishing, deep-sea f. ~ *au vif*, live-bait f. ~ *chalutière* (ʃalytjɛːr), trawling. ~ *côtière*, ~ *dans les eaux territoriales*, inshore fishing. ~ *de fond*, ground angling, bottom fishing. ~ *de grand sport*, big-game fishing. ~ *de plage*, surf f., beach f. ~ *en eaux douces*, ~ *d'eau douce*, freshwater f. ~ *de* (ou, *en*) *mer*, sea f., salt-water f.

péché (peʃe) m, sin. ~ *d'habitude*, besetting s. ~ *mignon*, pet vice, weak point. **pécher** (ʃe) *v.i*, to sin; err; offend.

pêcher (pɛʃe) m, peach [tree]. ¶ *v.t*, to fish for; fish; f. up; drag (*pond*); pick up, get hold of. ~ *à la ligne*, to angle. ~ *à la traîne*, to troll. **pêcherie** (ʃri) f, fishery, fishing ground. **pêcheur, euse** ʃœːr, ɸːz) n, fisherman, angler.

pécheur, eresse (peʃœːr, ʃrɛs) n, sinner.

péculat (pekyla) m, embezzlement (*public funds*). **pécule** (kyl) m, savings, nest egg; earnings (*of convict*); mustering-out money (*on discharge, Mil., Nav.*).

pécuniaire† (pekynjɛːr) a, pecuniary.

pédagogue (pedagɔg) m, pedagogue.

pédale (pedal) f, pedal; treadle. ~ *d'embrayage*, clutch (*auto*). ~ *forte*, loud p. ~ *sourde*, soft p. **pédaler** (le) *v.i*, to pedal; cycle. **pédalier** (lje) m, pedal [key]board; crank gear (*cycle*).

pédant, e (pedɑ̃, ɑ̃ːt) n, pedant; prig; wiseacre. ¶~ & **pédantesque**† (dɑ̃tɛsk) a, pedantic, priggish. **pédanterie** (tri) f. & **pédantisme** (tism) m, pedantry.

pédestre (pedɛstr) a, pedestrian (*statue*). **pédestrement** (trəmɑ̃) ad, on foot.

pédicure (pediky:r) n, chiropodist.

pedigree (pedigri) m, pedigree (*beast*).

Pégase (pegɑːz) m, Pegasus (*fig.*).

pègre (pɛːgr) f, underworld.

peignage (pɛɲaːz) m, combing, carding (*textiles*). **peigne** (pɛɲ) m, comb; card; pecten, scallop. ~ *à décrasser*, ~ *fin*, scurf comb, [small] tooth c. ~ *coiffeur*, hair c. **peignée** (ɲe) f, drubbing, thrashing. **peigner** (ɲe) *v.t*, to comb; card; chase (*screws*). **peignier** (nje) m, comb maker. **peignoir** (ɲwaːr) m, dressing gown. ~ *de bain*, bathrobe. ~ *éponge*, toweling beach coat. **peignures** (ɲyːr) *f.pl*, combings.

peindre (pɛ̃ːdr) *v.t. & abs. ir*, to paint; depict, portray.

peine (pɛn) f, punishment, penalty, pain; sorrow; infliction; anxiety; pains, trouble; difficulty. *à* ~, hardly, scarcely, barely. *être en* ~ *de*, to be at a loss to. *valoir la* ~, to be worthwhile. **peiner** (ne) *v.t*, to pain, grieve; (*v.i.*) to labor, [toil &] moil; be difficult. ~ *en lisant un livre*, to wade through a book.

peintre (pɛ̃ːtr) m, painter; portrayer. ~ *d'enseignes*, sign writer. ~ *en bâtiments*, house painter. ~ *verrier*, stained glass artist. **peinture** (pɛ̃tyːr) f, painting; picture; paint, color; portrayal. **peinturlurer** (tyrlyrer) *v.t*, to daub.

péjoratif, ive (peʒɔratif, iːv) a, pejorative, disparaging, depreciatory.

Pékin (pekɛ̃) m, Peking (*Geog.*). **p~**, m, pekin (*fabric*). **pékinois** (kinwa) m, Pekinese, peke (*dog*).

pelage (pəlaːʒ) m, coat, wool, fur.

pélargonium (pelargɔnjɔm) m, pelargonium.

pelé, e (pəle) *p.a*, bare, bald. **peler** (le) *v.t. & i*, to strip, peel, skin.

pêle-mêle (pɛlmɛl) ad. & m, pell-mell, helter-skelter.

pèlerin, e (pɛlrɛ̃, in) n, pilgrim; fox (*pers.*). ¶ f, cape, pelerine. **pèlerinage** (lrina:ʒ) m, pilgrimage; place of pilgrimage.

pélican (pelikɑ̃) m, pelican.

pelisse (pəlis) f, pelisse.

pelle (pɛl) f, shovel; scoop. ~ *à poussière*, dustpan. ~ *à sel*, salt spoon. ~ *à tarte*, pastry server. ~*-bêche*, entrenching tool. **pelletée** (lte) f, shoveful, spadeful.

pelleterie (pɛltri) f, furriery;

peltry. pelletier, ère (ltje, ɛːr) n, furrier.

pellicule (pɛllikyl) f, pellicle, skin; film; (pl.) dandruff, scurf. ~ **en bobine**, roll film (Phot.).

pelote (plɔt) f, ball (wool, string); pincushion; pile (money); pelota. **peloter** (te) v.i, to knock the balls about (Ten.). ~ **en attendant partie**, to fill in time. **peloton** (tɔ̃) m, ball; knot, cluster; squad, party, platoon (Mil.). ~ **d'exé-cution**, firing squad. **pelotonner** (tɔne) v.t, to ball, wind. **se ~**, to curl up, snuggle.

pelouse (pluːz) f, lawn, green; public enclosures (turf.). ~ **d'ar-rivée**, putting green (golf).

peluche (plyʃ) f, plush. **pelucher** (ʃe) v.i, to fluff up. **pelucheux, euse** (ʃø, øːz) a, fluffy.

pelure (plyːr) f, peel, skin, rind; onionskin paper.

pénal, e (penal) a, penal; criminal (law); penalty (clause). **pénalité** (lite) f, penalty.

pénates (penat) m.pl, home. dieux ~, Penates, household gods.

penaud, e (pəno, oːd), a, crest-fallen; sheepish.

penchant, e (pɑ̃ʃɑ̃, ɑ̃ːt) a, lean-ing; tottering. ¶ m, slope; brink, verge; leaning, inclination, bent, propensity, proclivity, fondness. **penché, e** (ʃe) p.a, leaning (tower); drooping (looks). **pen-chement** (ʃmɑ̃) m, bend[ing]; stoop[ing]. **pencher** (ʃe) v.t. & i. & se ~, to bend, incline, tilt; lean; bank; stoop; verge. faire ~ la balance, to turn the scale.

pendable (pɑ̃dabl) a, [deserving of] hanging; outrageous. **pendai-son** (dɛzɔ̃) f, [death by] hanging. **pendant, e** (dɑ̃, ɑ̃ːt) a, hanging [down]; dangling; drooping; pen-dent, -ant; pending. ¶ m, drop (ear); frog (sword); counterpart, fellow, match. les [deux] ~s, the pair (pictures, etc.).

pendant (pɑ̃dɑ̃) pr, during, for. ~ que, while, whilst.

pendard, e (pɑ̃daːr, ard) (jocu-lar) n, rascal, hussy; gallows-bird. **pendeloque** (pɑ̃dlɔk) f, drop (ear, chandelier). **penden-tif** (dɑ̃tif) m, pendentive; pen-dant, -ent. **penderie** (dri) f,

closet, wardrobe. **pendiller** (dije) v.i, to hang, dangle. **pendre** (dr) v.t. & i, to hang; h. up, h. out. **pendule** (dyl) m, pendulum. ¶ ~ **& pendulette** (lɛt) f, timepiece, clock. pendule à sonnerie & à carillon, striking & chiming clock.

pêne (pɛːn) m, bolt (lock).

pénétrant, e (penetrɑ̃, ɑ̃ːt) a, penetrating, piercing, searching. **pénétration** (trasjɔ̃) f, penetra-tion; insight. **pénétrer** (tre) v.t. & i, to penetrate, pierce; break into; permeate, pervade, sink in; fathom; see through; imbue.

pénible† (penibl) a, laborious, hard; painful.

péniche (peniʃ) f, barge, landing craft.

péninsulaire (penɛ̃sylɛːr) a, peninsular. **péninsule** (syl) f, peninsula.

pénitence (penitɑ̃ːs) f, penitence; penance; punishment; penalty, forfeit (at play). **pénitencier** (tɑ̃sje) m, penitentiary, reforma-tory; convict prison. **pénitent, e** (tɑ̃, ɑ̃ːt) a. & n, penitent. **péni-tentiaire** (tɑ̃sjɛːr) a, peniten-tiary.

penne (pɛn) f, quill [feather].

pénombre (penɔ̃ːbr) f, penumbra; twilight; background (fig.).

pensant, e (pɑ̃sɑ̃, ɑ̃ːt) a, think-ing; -minded (bien = right), -disposed (mal = ill). **pensée** (se) f, thought; thinking; medita-tion; mind; idea; pansy, hearts-ease. arrière-~, ulterior motive. **penser** (se) v.i. & t. & abs, to think; mean. ¶ m, thought (Poet.). **penseur** (sœːr) m, thinker. **pensif, ive** (sif, iːv) a, pensive, thoughtful.

pension (pɑ̃sjɔ̃) f, room & board; boarding house; b. school; pen-sion; annuity. ~ alimentaire, ali-mony. ~ pour les chevaux, livery stables. **pensionnaire** (ɔnɛːr) n, boarder; paying guest; inmate; pensioner. **pensionnat** (na) m, boarding school. **pensionner** (ne) v.t, to pension.

pensum (pɛ̃sɔm) m, imposition (Sch.).

Pen[n]sylvanie (la) (pɛ̃silvani), Pennsylvania.

Pentateuque (le) (pɛ̃tatø:k), the Pentateuch.

pente (pɑ̃:t) *f*, slope, incline, [downward] gradient; bent (*fig.*).

Pentecôte (la) (pɑ̃tko:t), Whit-sun[tide]; Pentecost.

penture (pɑ̃ty:r) *f*, hinge (*of hook & hinge*).

pénultième (penyltjɛm) *a*, pen-ultimate.

pénurie (penyri) *f*, penury, scarc-ity, dearth, lack.

pépie (pepi) *f*, pip (*poultry*); thirst. **pépier** (pje) *v.i*, to peep, chirp.

pépin (pepɛ̃) *m*, pip (*fruit*); stone (*grape*); umbrella. **pépi-nière** (pinjɛ:r) *f*, nursery (*Hort. & fig.*). [jardinier] **pépiniériste** (njerist) *m*, nurseryman.

pépite (pepit) *f*, nugget.

perçant, e (pɛrsɑ̃, ɑ̃:t) *a*, pierc-ing; keen, sharp; shrill. **mettre en perce** (pɛrs), to broach, tap (*cask*). **percée** (se) *f*, opening; cutting. **perce-neige**, *f*, snow-drop. **perce-oreille**, *m*, earwig.

percepteur (pɛrsɛptœ:r) *m*, col-lector (*tax*). **perceptible** (tibl) *a*, collectable, -ible; perceptible, discernible, noticeable. ~ *à l'ouïe*, audible. **perception** (sjɔ̃) *f*, collection; collectorship; col-lector's office; perception.

percer (pɛrse) *v.t. & i*, to pierce; bore; drill; lance; stab; spear; broach, tap; hole; drive; open; penetrate; break through; reveal itself; make one's way. **perceur** (sœ:r) *m*, driller (*pers.*). **per-ceuse** (sø:z) *f*, drill[ing machine].

percevoir (pɛrsəvwa:r) *v.t*, to collect; charge; perceive.

perche (pɛrʃ) *f*, pole; perch (*fish*). ~ *d'étendoir*, clothes prop. **per-cher** (ʃe) *v.i*, to perch, roost. **perchoir** (ʃwa:r) *m*, perch, roost.

perclus, e (pɛrkly, y:z) *a*, crip-pled.

percussion (pɛrkysjɔ̃) *f*, percus-sion, impact. **percutant, e** (tɑ̃, ɑ̃:t) *a*, percussive.

perdant, e (pɛrdɑ̃, ɑ̃:t) *n*, loser. ¶ *a*, losing. **perdition** (disjɔ̃) *f*, perdition. *en ~*, in a sinking condition (*ship*). **perdre** (dr) *v.t. & abs*, to lose; waste; ruin.

perdu (dy) *a*, lost; ruined; spent (bullet).

perdreau (pɛrdro) *m*, young partridge. **perdrix** (dri) *f*, par-tridge. ~ *des neiges*, ptarmi-gan.

père (pɛr) *m*, father, parent; sire (*Poet. & beast*); senior. *le ~ Noël*, Santa Claus. *de ~ de fa-mille*, safe (*investment*). *en bon ~ de famille*, with due & proper care.

pérégrination (peregrinasjɔ̃) *f*, peregrination.

péremptoire† (perɑ̃ptwa:r) *a*, peremptory.

perfection (pɛrfɛksjɔ̃) *f*, perfec-tion. **perfectionner** (ɔne) *v.t*, to perfect; improve.

perfide† (pɛrfid) *a. & n*, treacher-ous, perfidious (person). **perfi-die** (di) *f*, treachery, perfidy.

perforateur (pɛrforatœ:r) *m*, punch (*paper*). **perforatrice** (tris) *f*, drill (*rock, etc.*). **perforer** (re) *v.t*, to perforate; drill; punch.

performance (pɛrfɔrmɑ̃:s) *f*, performance (*sport*). ~ *classée*, winning performance.

pergola (pɛrgola) *f*, pergola.

péricliter (periklite) *v.i*, to be in danger.

péril (peril) *m*, peril. **périlleux, euse†** (rijø, ø:z) *a*, perilous.

périmé, e (perime) *p.p*, out of date (*ticket, etc.*); exploded (*theory*). **périmer** (me) *v.i*, to lapse, ex-pire.

périmètre (perimɛtr) *m*, perim-eter; limit.

période (perjɔd) *f*, period, stage; spell; repetend; phrase (*Mus.*). ¶ *m*, pitch; stage. **périodique†** (dik) *a*, periodic; periodical; re-current, recurring. ¶ *m*, periodi-cal.

péripétie (peripesi) *f*, sudden change; vicissitude.

périphérie (periferi) *f*, periphery.

périphrase (perifrɑ:z) *f*, periph-rasis.

périr (peri:r) *v.i*, to perish, be lost; die; lapse.

périscope (periskɔp) *m*, peri-scope.

périssable (perisabl) *a*, perish-able.

péristyle (peristil) *m*, peristyle.

péritonite (peritɔnit) *f*, peritonitis.

perle (pɛrl) *f*, pearl; bead; treasure (*fig.*). ~ *de culture*, cultured pearl. **perlé, e** (le) *a*, pearly; exquisitely done.

permanence (pɛrmanã:s) *f*, permanence. *en* ~, without interruption. **permanent, e** (nã, ã:t) *a*, permanent, standing; continuous; abiding; perennial.

permanganate (pɛrmãganat) *m*, permanganate.

perméable (pɛrmeabl) *a*, permeable, pervious.

permettre (pɛrmɛtr) *v.t.ir*, to permit, to allow; may. **se** ~, to allow oneself, indulge in. *se* ~ *de*, to venture to. **permis** (mi) *m*, permit, license, order. ~ [*de circulation*], [free] pass (*Rly.*). ~ *de conduire* [*les automobiles*], driver's license. **permission** (sjɔ̃) *f*, permission; leave, pass (*Mil.*). **permissionnaire** (ɔnɛ:r) *m. & a*, (soldier) on leave.

permutation (pɛrmytasjɔ̃) *f*, exchange (*of posts*); permutation; transposition.

pernicieux, euse† (pɛrnisjø, ø:z) *a*, pernicious, baneful.

péroné (perɔne) *m*, fibula, splint [bone].

péronnelle (perɔnɛl) *f*, pert hussy.

péroraison (perɔrɛzɔ̃) *f*, peroration. **pérorer** (re) *v.i*, to hold forth, speechify.

Pérou (le) (peru), Peru.

Pérouse (peru:z) *f*, Perugia.

peroxyde (perɔksid) *m*, peroxide.

perpendiculaire† (pɛrpãdikylɛ:r) *a. & f*, perpendicular.

perpétrer (pɛrpetre) *v.t*, to perpetrate.

perpétuation (pɛrpetɥasjɔ̃) *f*, perpetuation. **perpétuel, le†** (tɥɛl) *a*, perpetual, permanent; for life. **perpétuer** (tɥe) *v.t*, to perpetuate. **perpétuité** (tɥite) *f*, perpetuity. *à* ~, in perpetuity; for life.

perplexe (pɛrplɛks) *a*, perplexed, puzzled; perplexing. **perplexité** (ksite) *f*, perplexity.

perquisition (pɛrkizisjɔ̃) *f*, search (*law*).

perron (pɛrɔ̃) *m*, front steps, perron.

perroquet (pɛrɔkɛ) *m*, parrot; topgallant. **perruche** (ryʃ) *f*, parakeet; hen parrot; high-flown random talker (*woman*).

perruque (pɛryk) *f*, wig; old fogy. **perruquier** (kje) *m*, wigmaker.

pers, e (pɛ:r, ɛrs) *a*, greenish-blue.

persan, e (pɛrsã, an) *a. & P~, n*, Persian (*modern*). *le persan*, Persian (*language*). **la Perse** (pɛrs), Persia. **perse, *a. & P~, n*, Persian (*ancient*). **perse, *f*, chintz.

persécuter (pɛrsekyte) *v.t*, to persecute; bait; dun. **persécuteur, trice** (tœ:r, tris) *n*, persecutor. **persécution** (sjɔ̃) *f*, persecution.

persévérance (pɛrseverã:s) *f*, perseverance. **persévérer** (re) *v.i. & abs*, to persevere; persist.

persienne (pɛrsjɛn) *f*, shutter, persienne, Persian blind.

persiflage (pɛrsifla:ʒ) *m*, banter, persiflage. **persifler** (fle) *v.t*, to banter, chaff.

persil (pɛrsi) *m*, parsley. **persillé, e** (sije) *a*, blue-moldy (*cheese*).

persistance (pɛrsistã:s) *f*, persistence, -ency. **persistant, e** (tã, ã:t) *a*, persistent. **persister** (te) *v.i*, to persist.

personnage (pɛrsɔna:ʒ) *m*, personage; character; (*pl.*) dramatis personae. ~ *de carton*, figurehead. *être un* ~, to be somebody. **personnalité** (nalite) *f*, personality; (*pl.*) [well-known] people. **personne** (sɔn) *f*, person; self; (*pl.*) people. ~ *à charge*, dependent person; hanger-on. ~ *collante*, burr, sticker. ~ *interposée*, nominee. ~ *morale*, ~ *juridique*, ~ *civile*, body corporate, legal entity. ¶ *pn.m*, anybody, anyone; nobody, no one, none. **personnel, le†** (nɛl) *a*, personal; private; selfish. ¶ *m*, staff, personnel. **personnifier** (nifje) *v.t*, to personify; impersonate.

perspective (pɛrspɛkti:v) *f*, perspective; outlook, view, prospect; vista. *en* ~, in view.

perspicace (pɛrspikas) *a*, perspicacious. **perspicacité** (site) *f*, perspicacity.

persuader (pɛrsɥade) *v.t. & abs*, to persuade; prevail. **persuasif, ive** (zif, i:v) *a*, persuasive. **persuasion** (zjɔ̃) *f*, persuasion; belief.

perte (pɛrt) *f*, loss; leak[age]; waste; casualty (*Mil.*); ruin; swallow (*river*); discount (opp. *premium*). ~ **sèche**, dead loss. *à* ~, at a loss. *à* ~ *de vue*, as far as the eye can reach. *en* ~, out of pocket, to the bad, a loser. *en pure* ~, to no purpose.

pertinent, e (pɛrtinɑ̃, ɑ̃:t) *a*, pertinent, apposite, relevant. **pertinemment** (namɑ̃) *ad*, pertinently, etc.

pertuis (pɛrtɥi) *m*, sluiceway; strait[s] (*Geog.*).

perturbateur, trice (pɛrtyrba-tœ:r, tris) *n*, disturber. **perturbation** (sjɔ̃) *f*, disturbance, perturbation.

péruvien, ne (peryvjɛ̃, ɛn) *a. &* **P~,** *n*, Peruvian.

pervenche (pɛrvɑ̃:ʃ) *f*, periwinkle (*Bot.*).

pervers, e (pɛrvɛ:r, ɛrs) *a*, perverse. ¶ *m*, evil-doer, pervert. **perversion** (vɛrsjɔ̃) *f*, perversion. **perversité** (site) *f*, perversity. **pervertir** (ti:r) *v.t*, to pervert.

pesade (pəzad) *f*, rearing (*horse*).

pesage (pəsa:ʒ) *m*, weighing; (*turf*) w. in; w. in room; paddock. **pesamment** (zamɑ̃) *ad*, heavily; ponderously. **pesant, e** (zɑ̃, ɑ̃:t) *a*, heavy, weighty; ponderous, unwieldy; ponderable. *son pesant d'or*, his, its, weight in gold. **pesant,** *ad*, in weight. **pesanteur** (zɑ̃tœ:r) *f*, heaviness; weight; gravity (*Phys.*); dullness [*spirit*]. **pesée** (ze) *f*, weighing; prize, -se; wrench. **pèse-lettre** (pɛzlɛtr) *m*, letter scales. **peser** (pəze) *v.t*, to weigh; ponder; (*v.i.*) to weigh; lie heavy; bear, press; dwell. **peseur** (zœ:r) *m*, weigher. **peson** (zɔ̃) *m*, balance (*spring, etc.*).

pessimisme (pɛsimism) *m*, pessimism. **pessimiste** (mist) *m*, pessimist. ¶ *a*, pessimistic.

peste (pɛst) *f*, plague, pestilence. ~ *bovine*, cattle plague, rinder-

pest. **pester** (te) *v.i*, to rail (*contre* = at). **pestiféré, e** (tifere) *a. & n*, plague-stricken (person). **pestilentiel, le** (lɑ̃sjɛl) *a*, pestilential.

pétale (petal) *m*, petal.

pétarade (petarad) *f*, sp[l]utter; frisking. **pétarader** (de) *v.i*, to sp[l]utter. **pétard** (ta:r) *m*, shot, blast; detonator, fog signal; firecracker; scandal (*news*). **pétarder** (tarde) *v.t*, to blow up, blast.

pétaudière (petodjɛ:r) *f*, bedlam, bear garden.

pétiller (petije) *v.i*, to crackle; sparkle; fizz[le], bubble [over].

pétiole (pesjɔl) *m*, petiole, leaf stalk.

petiot, e (pətjo, ɔt), tiny, wee. ¶ *n*, dot, tot, chickabiddy. **petit, e** (ti, it) *a*, little, small; short; diminutive; young; junior; low, slow; lesser; minor; petty; slight; light; mean; retail. **petit,** *comps*: *au* ~ *bonheur*, I'll risk it, come what may; hit or miss. *le P~ Chaperon rouge*, Little Red Riding Hood. ~ *chat*, kitten. ~ *chien*, pup[py]. ~ *comité*, select party, informal gathering. *le* ~ *commerce*, [the] small traders, tradespeople, the retail trade. ~ *commis*, office boy. *le* ~ *déjeuner*, coffee & rolls, early morning coffee. ~ *enfant*, little child, infant. *~s-enfants*, grandchildren. *~-fils*, grandson, -child. *au* ~ *galop*, at a canter. *~s jeux*, parlor games, forfeits. *le* ~ *jour*, daybreak. ~ *juif*, funny bone. *~-lait*, whey. ~ *lieu*, ~ *endroit*, privy. *~-maître*, fop, coxcomb. ~ *ménage*, miniature (*or* dolls') home set. *le* ~ *monde*, little people; the lower classes; the child world. *le* *~Noël*, a Christmas present (*to a child*). ~ *nom*, Christian name. ~ *nom d'amitié*, pet name. ~ *pain*, roll. *le* ~ *peuple*, [the] common people. *~s pois*, green peas. ~ *salé*, pickled pork. ~ *salon*, sitting room, parlor. ~ *trot*, jogtrot. **petite,** *comps*: ~ *chatte*, kitten. ~ *correspondance*, answers to correspondents. *la* ~ *épargne*, the small investor. *~-fille*, grand-daughter, grandchild. ~ *gorgée*, sip. ~ *guerre*, mimic war. *à ~s journées*, by easy stages. ~ *largeur*, single width (*cloth*). à ~ *mentalité*, mentally deficient. ~ *multiplication*, low gear. ~ *noblesse*, gentry. ~ *pédale*, soft pedal. *une* ~ *santé*, poor health. ~s *tables*, separate tables (*meal*). ~ *vérole*, smallpox. ~ *vérole volante*, chicken pox. *en* ~ *vitesse* (*Rly.*), by slow train; by freight train. **petit, e**, *n*, little boy, l. girl, l. one. **un petit**, a young one, cub, pup, whelp. **les petits**, the small, the little (*people*); little things. **petitement** (titmᾶ) *ad*, meanly; pettily. **petitesse** (tɛs) *f*, littleness, smallness; shortness; pettiness.

pétition (petisjɔ̃) *f*, petition. ~ *de principe*, begging the question. *faire une* ~ *de principe*, to beg the question. **pétitionnaire** (sjɔnɛːr) *n*, petitioner. **pétitionner** (ne) *v.i*, to petition.

peton (pətɔ̃) *m*, tiny foot, tootsy [-wootsy].

pétoncle (petɔ̃:kl) *f*, scallop (*Mol.*).

pétrel (petrɛl) *m*, storm[y] petrel.

pétrification (petrifikasjɔ̃) *f*, petrifaction. **pétrifier** (fje) *v.t*, to petrify.

pétrin (petrɛ̃) *m*, kneading trough; fix, mess. **pétrir** (triːr) *v.t*, to knead, work, make; shape; steep. **pétrissage** (trisaːʒ) *m*, kneading, etc.

pétrole (petrɔl) *m*, petroleum, oil. ~ *à brûler*. ~ *lampant* (lɑ̃pɑ̃), paraffin [oil], kerosene. **pétrolier, ère** (lje, ɛːr) *a*, petroleum, oil (*att.*) [*navire*] *pétrolier*, tanker.

pétulant, e (petylɑ̃, ɑ̃ːt) *a*, lively, impetuous.

pétunia (petynja) *m*, petunia.

peu (pø) *ad*, little, not much; few, not many; not very. ¶ *m*, little; bit; few; lack; little while. *à* ~ [*de chose*] *près*, about, nearly.

peulven (pølvɛn) *m*, menhir.

peuplade (pœplad) *f*, tribe. **peuple** (pl) *m*, people, nation; tribe. ¶ *a*, plebeian, common. **peupler** (ple) *v.t*, to people, populate; stock, plant; fill; (*v.i.*) to multiply.

peuplier (pœplie) *m*, poplar,

peur (pœːr) *f*, fear, fright. *avoir* ~, to be afraid. *faire* ~, to fright-

en. **peureux, euse**† (pœrø, øːz) *a*, timid, nervous.

peut-être (pøtɛːtr) *ad*. & *m*, perhaps, maybe, perchance, possibly.

phaéton (faetɔ̃) *m*, phaeton.

phalange (falɑ̃:ʒ) *f*, phalanx; host.

phantasme (fɑ̃tasm) *m*, phantasm.

pharaon (faraɔ̃) *m*, Pharaoh; faro (*cards*).

phare (faːr) *m*, lighthouse; light; beacon; headlight, headlamp. ~ *anti-éblouissant*, ~-*code*, antidazzle lamp *or* light.

pharisaïque (farizaik) *a*, Pharisaic(al). **pharisien** (zjɛ̃) *m*, Pharisee.

pharmaceutique (farmasøtik) *a*, pharmaceutical. **pharmacie** (si) *f*, pharmacy; dispensary; drug store; medicine chest. **pharmacien, ne** (sjɛ̃, ɛn) *n*, druggist; pharmacist.

pharyngite (farɛ̃ʒit) *f*, pharyngitis, relaxed throat. **pharynx** (rɛ̃:ks) *m*, pharynx.

phase (faːz) *f*, phase; stage.

phébus (febyːs) *m*, bombast, fustian.

phénicien, ne (fenisjɛ̃, ɛn) *a*, Phoenician.

phénix (feniks) *m*, phoenix; paragon.

phénol (fenɔl) *ou* **acide phénique** (nik) *m*, phenol, carbolic acid.

phénoménal, e (fenɔmenal) *a*, phenomenal. **phénomène** (mɛn) *m*, phenomenon; freak [of nature].

Philadelphie (filadɛlfi) *f*, Philadelphia.

philanthrope (filɑ̃trɔp) *n*, philanthropist. **philanthropie** (pi) *f*, philanthropy. **philanthropique** (pik) *a*, philanthropic.

philatélisme (filatelism) *m*, philately. **philatéliste** (list) *n*, philatelist.

philharmonique (filarmɔnik) *a*, philharmonic.

philippique (filipik) *f*, philippic.

philistin (filistɛ̃) *m*, Philistine.

philologie (filɔlɔʒi) *f*, philology. **philologue** (lɔg) *m*, philologist.

philosophe (filɔzɔf) *n*, philosopher; student in philosophy. ¶ *a*, philosophic(al) (*calm*). **philosopher** (fe) *v.i,* to philosophize. **philosophie** (fi) *f,* philosophy. **philosophique**† (fik) *a,* philosophic(al).

philtre (filtr) *m,* philter, love potion.

phlébite (flebit) *f,* phlebitis.

phlox (floks) *m,* phlox.

phobie (fobi) *f,* morbid fear, dread.

phonétique (fonetik) *a,* phonetic. ¶ *f,* phonetics. **phonographe** (nograf) *m,* phonograph. ~*coffret,* tabletop phonograph.

phoque (fok) *m,* seal (*Zool.*).

phosphate (fosfat) *m,* phosphate. **phosphore** (fo:r) *m,* phosphorus. **phosphorescence** (fore-(sã:s) *f,* phosphorescence. **phosphorescent, e** (sã, ã:t) *a,* phosphorescent.

photographe (fotograf) *n,* photographer. **photographie** (fi) *f,* photography; photograph. **photographier** (fje) *v.t,* to photograph. **photographique** (fik) *a,* photographic. **photogravure** (vy:r) *f,* photogravure. **photojumelle,** *f,* binocular camera.

phrase (fra:s) *f,* sentence; phrase. ~*s à effet,* claptrap. **phraséologie** (frazeolo3i) *f,* phraseology. **phraser** (ze) *v.i. & t,* to phrase.

phrénologie (frenolo3i) *f,* phrenology. **phrénologiste** (3ist) *m,* phrenologist.

phtisie (ftizi) *f,* phthisis, consumption. **phtisique** (zik) *a. & n,* consumptive.

physicien, ne (fizisjẽ, ɛn) *n,* physicist.

physiologie (fizjolo3i) *f,* physiology.

physionomie (fizjonomi) *f,* physiognomy, face, countenance; aspect; character.

physique† (fizik) *a,* physical; bodily. ~¶ *f,* physics. ¶ *m,* physique.

piaffer (pjafe) *v.i,* to paw the ground; prance.

piailler (pjaje) *v.i,* to cheep; screech.

pianiste (pjanist) *n,* pianist. **piano** (no) *m,* piano[forte]. ~ *à*

demi-queue, baby grand[piano]. ~ *à queue,* [concert] grand piano. ~ *droit,* upright piano. ~ *mécanique,* piano player, player piano; piano organ. ~ *oblique,* overstrung piano.

piauler (pjole) *v.i,* to cheep; whimper.

pic (pik) *m,* pick; peak; woodpecker. *à* ~, sheer, precipitous.

piccolo (pikolo) *m,* piccolo.

pick-up (pikœp) *m,* phonograph.

picorer (pikore) *v.i,* to forage, peck.

picot (piko) *m,* splinter; barb; picot. **picoté de petite vérole** (kote), pockmarked. **picoter** (te) *v.t,* to prick; pit; peck; sting, make smart, make tingle; tease.

picotin (pikotẽ) *m,* peck.

pictural, e (piktyral) *a,* pictorial.

pie (pi) *f,* magpie. ¶ *a,* piebald; charitable (*works*).

pièce (pjɛs) *f,* piece; bit; fragment; part; man (*chess*); head (*cattle, game*); joint (*meat*); document; paper; tip (*gratuity*); cask, barrel; puncheon; gun; room (*house*). [*la*] ~, *apiece,* each. ~ *à conviction,* exhibit (*criminal law*). ~ *à succès,* hit. ~ *à thèse,* problem play. ~ *d'artifice,* firework. ~ *d'eau,* ornamental lake. ~[*coulée*], casting. ~ [*de monnaie*], coin. ~ *de rechange,* spare [part]. ~ [*de théâtre*], [stage] play. ~ *historique,* costume piece, c. play. ~ *justificative,* ~ *à l'appui,* exhibit (*civil law*); voucher (*Com.*). ~ *moulée,* molding, cast.

pied (pje) *m,* foot; trotter; base, bottom; leg (*chair*); stalk; footing; foothold; stand; standard. ~*à-terre, m,* somewhere to stay, lodging. ~ [*à trois branches*], tripod. ~*d'alouette,* larkspur, delphinium. ~*debiche,* claw [bar]; forceps. ~ *de bœuf,* neat's foot. ~*droit,* pier (*of arch*). ~ *fumeur,* smoker's stand. *au* ~ *de la lettre,* literally. *avoir le* ~ *marin,* to have got one's sea legs. *mettre sur* ~, to establish. *sur* ~, on foot; standing (*crops*). **piédestal** (pjedɛstal) *m,* pedestal.

piège (pjɛ:3) *m,* trap, snare, pitfall.

pie-grièche (piɡriɛʃ) f, shrike; shrew (pers.).

Piémont (le) (pjemɔ̃), Piedmont.

pierraille (pjɛraːj) f, small stones. **pierre** (pjɛːr) f, stone. ~ à aiguiser, grindstone; hone. ~ [à briquet] & ~ à fusil, flint. ~ à chaux, ~ calcaire, limestone. ~ à gué, stepping stone. ~ blanche, hearthstone. ~ d'achoppement (aʃɔpmɑ̃), stumbling block, snag. ~d'aimant, loadstone, lodestone. ~ de lune, moonstone. ~ de touche, touchstone (lit. & fig.); test. ~ philosophale (filozɔfal), philosophers' stone. ~ précieuse, precious stone, gem [stone]. ~ tombale (tɔ̃bal), ~ tumulaire (tymylɛːr), tombstone, gravestone. **pierreries** (pjɛr[ə]ri) f.pl, precious stones, gems, jewels. **pierreux, euse** (rø,ø;z) a ,stony, gritty.

pierrot (pjɛro) m, pierrot, clown; sparrow.

piété (pjete) f, piety, godliness; devotion.

piétiner (pjetine) v.t, to trample on, stamp on; tread; (v.i.) to dance (with rage). ~ sur place, to mark time (fig.). **piéton, ne** (tɔ̃, ɔn) n, pedestrian, foot passenger; walker.

piètre† (pjɛtr) a, wretched, poor, shabby.

pieu (pjø) m, stake, post; pile.

pieuvre (pjœːvr) f, octopus.

pieux, euse† (pjø, ø;z) a, pious, godly; reverent.

pigeon, ne (piʒɔ̃, ɔn) n, pigeon, dove; greenhorn, gull. ~ artificiel, clay bird. ~ grosse gorge, pouter. ~ ramier, wood pigeon, ring dove. ~ voyageur, carrier pigeon, homing p. **pigeonneau** (ʒɔno) m, young pigeon, squab; gull, dupe. **pigeonnier** (nje) m, dovecote.

pigment (piɡmɑ̃) m, pigment.

pignocher (piɲɔʃe) v.i, to pick at one's food.

pignon (piɲɔ̃) m, gable; pinion. ~ de chaîne, sprocket wheel.

pilastre (pilastr) m, pilaster; newel.

pile (pil) f, pile, heap; stack (of wood); pier (bridge); battery;

cell (Elec.); reverse (coin). ~ ou face? heads or tails?

piler (pile) v.t, to pound, pestle, grind.

pilier (pilje) m, pillar, column, post.

pillage (pija;ʒ) m, pillage, looting; pilfering. **piller** (je) v.t, to pillage, plunder, loot, sack, ransack; pilfer; seize, worry (of dog).

pilon (pilɔ̃) m, pestle; stamp (ore); rammer; hammer (power); drumstick (fowl).

pilori (pilɔri) m, pillory. **pilorier** (rje) v.t, to pillory, gibbet.

pilotage (pilɔta;ʒ) m, pile work; pilotage, piloting. **pilote** (lɔt) m, pilot. ~ de essai, test pilot. **piloter** (te) v.t, to pile; pilot; guide. ~ dans, to show (pers.) round (town). **pilotis** (ti) m, pile (stake); piling.

pilou (pilu) m, flannelette.

pilule (pilyl) f, pill.

pimbêche (pɛ̃bɛʃ) f, conceited woman.

piment (pimɑ̃) m, pimento, capsicum, allspice. **pimenter** (te) v.t, to spice.

pimpant, e (pɛ̃pɑ̃, ɑ̃;t) a, smart, spruce, spick & span.

pin (pɛ̃) m, pine [tree], fir [tree]. ~ du Chili, Chili pine, monkey puzzle.

pinacle (pinakl) m, pinnacle.

pince (pɛ̃;s) f, grip, hold; (oft. pl.) pliers, nippers; forceps; tweezers; tongs; (s.) clip; clamp; crowbar; claw, nipper (crab, etc.); pleat. ~s à épiler, eyebrow tweezers. ——monseigneur, f, jimmy (burglar's). ~-nez, m, eyeglasses. ~-sans-rire, m, man of dry humor. **pincé, e** (pɛse) a, affected, prim; stiff; wry; pursed (lips).

pinceau (pɛso) m, paintbrush; brush; touch (fig.); pencil (Opt.). ~ à barbe, shaving brush.

pincée (pɛse) f, pinch (snuff, etc.).

pincer (se) v.t, to pinch, nip, squeeze; purse (lips); pluck (strings); play (harp, etc.); twang; grip; catch. **pincettes** (sɛt) f.pl, tweezers; tongs (fire).

pinçon (sɔ̃) m, mark, bruise (left on the skin by a pinch).

pineraie (pinrɛ) *f*, pine wood (*forest*).

pingouin (pɛ̃gwɛ̃) *m*, auk.

pingre (pɛ̃ːgr) *a*, stingy. ¶ *m*, skinflint.

pinnule (pinnyl) *f*, pinnule; sight [vane].

pinson (pɛ̃sɔ̃) *m*, finch; chaffinch.

pintade (pɛ̃tad) *f*, guinea fowl.

pioche (pjɔʃ) *f*, pick; pickaxe; mattock. **piocher** (ʃe) *v.t.* & *i*, to pick up; work hard, grind.

piolet (pjɔlɛ) *m*, ice axe.

pion (pjɔ̃) *m*, pawn (*chess*); man (*checkers*).

pionnier (pjɔnje) *m*, pioneer.

pipe (pip) *f*, pipe (*cask, tobacco*). **pipeau** (po) *m*, [reed] pipe; lime twig; bird call. **pipée** (pe) *f*, bird catching. **piper** (pe) *v.t*, to lure (*birds*); dupe; load (*dice*); mark (*card*).

pipi[t] (pipi[t]) *m*, pipit, titlark.

piquant, e (pikɑ̃, ɑ̃ːt) *a*, prickly; stinging; cutting; pointed; pungent; racy; piquant. ¶ *m*, prickle; sting; quill (*porcupine*); spike; pungency; point, zest, pith. **pique** (pik) *f*, pike (*weapon*); pique, spite; tiff; (*m.*) spade[s] (*cards*). **~-nique** (nik) *m*, picnic. **~-notes**, *m*, bill file. **piqué, e** (ke) *a*, quilted; padded; staccato (*notes*); crazy. **~ des mouches**, flyblown. **~ des vers**, wormeaten, moth-eaten. ¶ *m*, quilting. **piquer** (ke) *v.t*, to prick; sting; bite; spur; goad; prod; nettle; pique; puncture; pit; lard; stitch; quilt; nibble (*fish*); stick; scale (*boiler*). **~ du nez**, to nose dive (*Avn.*). **se ~**, to pride oneself; take offense; turn sour (*wine*). **piquet** (kɛ) *m*, peg, stake; picket; piquet (*cards*). **piqueur** (kœːr) *m*, whipper-in, huntsman; stud groom. **piqueuse** (køːz) *f*, stitcher, sewer (*pers.*). **piqûre** (kyːr) *f*, injection; vaccination; prick; sting; bite; puncture; pit, hole; spot, speck; quilting.

pirate (pirat) *m*, pirate. **pirater** (te) *v.i*, to pirate. **piraterie** (tri) *f*, piracy.

pire (piːr) *a*, worse. **le ~**, the worst.

Pirée (le) (pire), Piraeus.

pirogue (pirɔg) *f*, canoe. **~ de barre**, surf boat. **~ en écorce**, birch-bark canoe.

pirouette (pirwɛt) *f*, whirling; pirouette. **pirouetter** (te) *v.i*, to pirouette, twirl.

pis (pi) *m*, udder, dug.

pis (pi) *ad*, worse. **le ~**, the worst. **~ aller**, *m*, last resource; makeshift. **au ~ aller**, at the worst.

pisciculture (pisikylty:r) *f*, pisciculture. **piscine** (sin) *f*, swimming pool.

Pise (piːz) *f*, Pisa.

pissenlit (pisɑ̃li) *m*, dandelion.

pistache (pistaʃ) *f*, pistachio [nut]. **pistachier** (ʃje) *m*, pistachio tree.

piste (pist) *f*, track (*running, racing*); run (*toboggan*); rink (*skating*); racecourse; runway (*Avn.*); track, trail, scent, clue. **~ de cirque**, ring. **~ en cendrée**, cinder track; dirt t.

pistil (pistil) *m*, pistil.

pistolet (pistɔlɛ) *m*, pistol.

piston (pistɔ̃) *m*, piston; cornet (*Mus.*).

pitchpin (pitʃpɛ̃) *m*, pitchpine.

piteux, euse† (pitø, ø:z) *a*, piteous, woeful, pitiable; sorry. **pitié** (tje) *f*, pity, mercy.

piton (pitɔ̃) *m*, screw eye; peak (*mountain*).

pitoyable† (pitwajabl) *a*, pitiable, pitiful; wretched, paltry.

pitre (piːtr) *m*, clown; buffoon.

pittoresque† (pitɔrɛsk) *a*, picturesque, beauty (*spot*); quaint; graphic; pictorial (*magazine*). ¶ *m*, picturesqueness.

pituite (pitɥit) *f*, phlegm, mucus.

pivoine (pivwan) *f*, peony.

pivot (pivo) *m*, pivot, pin; tap root; crux. **pivoter** (vɔte) *v.i*, to pivot, turn, hinge; slew; wheel (*Mil.*).

piz (pi) (*Geog.*) *m*, pap, mamelon.

placage (plakaːʒ) *m*, veneering; patchwork (*fig.*).

placard (plakaːr) *m*, wall cupboard; placard, poster, bill; galley [proof]. **placarder** (karde) *v.t*, to post (*bills*), placard.

place (plas) *f*, place; room; way; stead; seat; fare; berth; spot;

patch; ground; town; market; square (*in town*); churchyard (*public square surrounding a church or cathedral*). ~ *aux dames!* ladies first! ~ *d'armes*, parade ground, drill g. ~ [*de voitures*], cabstand. ~s *debout seulement!* standing room only! ~ *dénudée d'herbes*, bare patch (*golf*). ~ *forte*, ~ *de guerre*, fortified place. **placement** (smã) *m*, placing; investment. *bureau de* ~, employment agency. **placer** (se) *v.t*, to place, put, set; dispose of; deposit; invest (*money*).

placer (plasɛːr) (*Min.*) *m*, placer, diggings.

placide† (plasid) *a*, placid. **placidité** (dite) *f*, placidity.

placier (plasje) *m*, canvasser, salesman.

plafond (plaf5) *m*, ceiling; maximum, peak [figure]. **plafonner** (fɔne) *v.t*, to ceil. **plafonnier** (nje) *m*, ceiling fixture (*light*).

plage (plaːʒ) *f*, beach, shore; seaside resort; sands.

plagiaire (plaʒjɛːr) *m*, plagiarist. **plagiat** (ʒja) *m*, plagiarism. **plagier** (ʒje) *v.t*, to plagiarize.

plaid (plɛd) *m*, plaid; traveling rug.

plaider (plɛde) *v.i. & t*, to plead, argue. **plaideur, euse** (dœːr, ʁːz) *n*, litigant; suitor. **plaidoirie** (dwari) *f*, pleading; counsel's speech. **plaidoyer** (dwaje) *m*, speech for the defense.

plaie (plɛ) *f*, wound, sore; evil; plague.

plaignant, e (plɛɲã, ãːt) *n*, plaintiff, prosecutor.

plain, e (plɛ̃, ɛn) *a*, plain; open. *plain-chant, m*, plainsong. *de plain-pied*, on one floor, on a level.

plaindre (plɛ̃ːdr) *v.t.ir*, to pity, be sorry for. se ~, to complain; moan, groan.

plaine (plɛn) *f*, plain (*Phys. Geog.*).

plainte (plɛ̃ːt) *f*, moan, groan; complaint; action (*law*). **plaintif, ive**† (plɛtif, iːv) *a*, plaintive, doleful; querulous.

plaire (plɛːr) *v.i.ir*, to please. *s'il vous plaît*, [if you] please. *plût au ciel que . . .*, would to

heaven that . . . ~ *à*, to please (*v.t.*). se ~, to be pleased; like; thrive. **plaisamment** (plɛzamã) *ad*, funnily; ludicrously. **de plaisance** (zãːs), pleasure (*boat*); weekend (*cottage*). **Plaisance**, *f*, Piacenza. **plaisant, e** (zã, ãːt) *a*, funny, droll, jocular; comical; ludicrous; pleasant. ¶ *m*, wag, joker, fool; comical side. **plaisanter** (zãte) *v.i*, to joke, jest, trifle; (*v.t.*) to chaff. **plaisanterie** (tri) *f*, joke, jest; fun. **plaisir** (ziːr) *m*, pleasure, delight; treat; convenience; will; sake; amusement, enjoyment; cone, cornet, wafer (*ice cream*).

plan, e (plã, an) *a*, plane, even, level, flat. ¶ *m*, plane, level; ground (*of painting*); plan; map; table; project, scheme.

planche (plãːʃ) *f*, board; shelf; bed (*Hort.*); plate (*Typ.*). ~ *de salut*, sheet anchor (*fig.*). *faire la* ~, to float (*Swim.*). **planchéier** (plãʃeje) *v.t*, to board; floor. **plancher** (ʃe) *m*, floor. *le* ~ *des vaches*, terra firma. **planchette** (ʃɛt) *f*, slat; plane table (*Surv.*).

plancton (plãktɔ̃) *m*, plankton.

plane (plan) *m*, plane [tree]; (*f.*) drawing knife.

planer (plane) *v.t*, to smooth; plane; planish; (*v.i.*) to soar; hover; look down; glide (*Avn.*).

planétaire (planetɛːr) *a*, planetary. ¶ *m*, planetarium, orrery. **planète** (nɛt) *f*, planet. *heureuse* ~, lucky star (*fig.*).

planeur (planœːr) *m*, planisher (*pers.*); glider (*Avn.*).

plant (plã) *m*, sapling, set, slip; plantation. **plantage** (taːʒ) *m*, planting; plantation. **plantain** (tɛ̃) *m*, plantain (*Plantago*). **plantanier** (tanje) *m*, plantain (*banana*). **plantation** (sjɔ̃) *f*, planting; plantation. **plante** (plãːt) *f*, sole (*foot*); plant (*Bot.*). ~ *annuelle*, annual. ~ *marine*, seaweed. ~ *potagère*, vegetable. ~ *vivace*, perennial. **planter** (plãte) *v.t*, to plant, set. **planteur, euse** (tœːr, ʁːz) *n*, planter; grower. **plantoir** (twaːr) *m*, dibble. **planton** (tɔ̃) (*Mil.*) *m*, orderly; o. duty.

plantureux euse† (plătyrø, ø;z) *a,* copious; fleshy; fertile.

planure (plany;r) *f,* shaving[s].

plaque (plak) *f,* plate; sheet; slab; plaque; tablet; badge. ~ *de d'identité,* identity badge. ~ *de cheminée,* fireback, hob. ~ *de gazon,* turf, sod. ~ *tournante,* turntable (*Rly.*). **plaqué** (ke) *m,* electroplate. **plaquer** (ke) *v.t,* to plate; veneer; lay on; cake; lay down (*turf*); jilt, leave flat.

plastique (plastik) *a,* plastic.

plastron (plastrɔ̃) *m,* breastplate; front (*shirt*); butt (*pers., fig.*). **plastronner** (ne) *v.i,* to pose; put on the dog.

plat, e (pla, at) *a,* flat; level; lank, straight (*hair*); smooth (*sea*); dead (*calm*); dull, bald (*fig.*). à ~, flat. *à plat* [*ventre*], flat on one's face. ¶ *m,* flat; blade (*oar*); side, board (*book*); pan (*scale*); dish; mess; course (*dinner*). ~ *de quête,* collection plate. ~ *du jour,* special dish for the day.

platane (platan) *m,* plane [tree].

plat-bord (plabɔ;r) *m,* gunwale, gunnel.

plate (plat) *f,* punt (*boat*).

plateau (plato) *m,* tray; salver; pan (*scale*); dish (*soap*); stage, platform (*Theat.*); plateau, table land; upland; plate, table; face plate, chuck (*lathe*). ~ *roulant,* service wagon.

plate-bande (platbɑ̃;d) (*Hort.*) *m,* border; bed.

platée (plate) *f,* dishful.

plate-forme (platform) *f,* platform, stage; flat roof.

platement (platmɑ̃) *ad,* flatly; dully.

platine (platin) *f,* plate, platen; stage (*microscope*); lock (*firearm*). ¶ *m,* platinum.

platitude (platityd) *f,* flatness (*fig.*), dullness; platitude.

platonique (platɔnik) *a,* Platonic.

plâtre (plɑ;tr) *m,* plaster; p. cast. ~ *de moulage,* p. of Paris. **plâtrer** (plɑtre) *v.t,* to plaster. **plâtrier** (trie) *m,* plasterer. **plâtrière** (ɛ;r) *f,* gypsum quarry.

plausible† (plozibl) *a,* plausible.

plébéien, ne (plebejɛ̃, ɛn) *a,*

plebeian. **plébiscite** (bisit) *m,* plebiscite, referendum.

plein, e† (plɛ̃, ɛn) *a,* full; replete; fraught; whole; mid; high (*tide, seas*); solid; open; pregnant (*animals*). ~ *comme un œuf,* chock full. *en plein jour, en plein midi,* in broad daylight. ¶ *m,* plenum; full; height; thick stroke, downstroke. **plénier, ère** (plenje, ɛ;r) *a,* full; plenary. **plénipotentiaire** (nipɔtɑ̃sjɛ;r) *m. & att,* plenipotentiary. **plénitude** (tyd) *f,* plenitude, fullness; repletion.

pléonasme (pleɔnasm) *m,* pleonasm.

pléthore (pletɔ;r) *f,* plethora, glut.

pleur (plœ;r) *m. usually pl,* tear. **pleurard, e** (plœra;r, ard) *n,* whimperer; (*att.*) whimpering; tearful; maudlin (*voice*). **pleurer** (re) *v.i. & t,* to weep; mourn; bewail; cry; water, run (*eyes*); drip; bleed.

pleurésie (plœrezi) *f,* pleurisy.

pleureur, euse (plœrœ;r, ø;z) *n,* whimperer; mute, [hired] mourner; (*att.*) weeping. **pleurnicher** (niʃe) *v.i,* to whimper, whine, snivel.

pleutre (plø;tr) *m,* cad

pleuvoir (plœvwa;r) *v.i.ir,* to rain; pour, shower.

plèvre (plɛ;vr) *f,* pleura.

plexus (plɛksy;s) *m,* plexus.

pli (pli) *m,* fold; pleat; wrinkle, pucker, crease; bend; ply; cover, envelope. *mise en* ~, hairset, wave. *sous ce* ~, enclosed. **pliable** (abl) *a,* pliable. **pliant, e** (ɑ̃, ɑ̃;t) *a,* pliant; folding. ¶ *m,* camp stool.

plie (pli) *f,* plaice.

plier (plie) *v.t. & i,* to fold; strike (*tent*); bend; bow. ~ *bagage,* to pack up; decamp; die.

plinthe (plɛ̃;t) *f,* plinth; skirting [board].

plisser (plise) *v.t. & i,* to pleat, fold; kilt; crease, crumple, wrinkle, crinkle, pucker.

plomb (plɔ̃) *m,* lead; shot; came; plumb, plummet; plomb (*Cust.*); sink; ballast (*fig.*). ~ [*fusible*], fuse (*Elec.*). *à* ~, upright. **plombage** (ba;ʒ) *m,* plumbing; filling (*teeth*). **plombagine** (baʒin) *f*, plumbago, graphite, black lead. **plomber** (be) *v.t*, to lead, plumb; plomb; fill (*tooth*). **plomberie** (bri) *m*, plumbing; lead works. **plombier** (bje) *m*, plumber.

plongeoir (plɔ̃ʒwaːr) *m*, diving board. **plongeon** (ʒɔ̃) *m*, diver (*bird*); dive, plunge. **plonger** (ʒe) *v.i. & t*, to plunge; dive; submerge; dip; duck; immerse; thrust. **plongeur, euse** (ʒœːr, øːz) *n*, diver (*Swim.*); (*m.*) diver (*in diving dress*); dishwasher (*man*); plunger (*pump*).

plot (plo) *m*, stud (*Elec. contact*).

ployer (plwaje) *v.t. & i*, to bend, bow; wrap up; give way.

pluie (pɥi) *f*, rain; shower; wet. ~ *d'or*, golden rain (*fireworks*).

plumage (plymaːʒ) *m*, plumage, feathers. **plumasserie** (masri) *f*, feather trade. **plume** (plym) *f*, feather (*bird & Box.*); pen. ~ [*à écrire*], nib. ~ *d'oie*, quill [pen]. *sans* ~*s*, unfledged, callow. **plumeau** (mo) *m*, feather duster; eiderdown quilt. **plumée** (me) *f*, penful, dip (*ink*). **plumer** (me) *v.t*, to pluck; fleece (*fig.*); (*v.i.*) to feather (*rowing*). **plumet** (me) *m*, plume. **plumeux, euse** (mø, øːz) *a*, feathery, plumose. **plumier** (mje) *m*, pen tray, pencilcase. **plumitif** (mitif) *m*, minute book; quill driver.

plupart (la) (plypaːr), most, the generality, the majority.

plural, e (plyral) *a*, plural (*vote*). **pluralité** (lite) *f*, plurality; majority. **pluriel, le** (rjɛl) *a. & m*, plural (*Gram.*).

plus (ply; *finally often* plys; *in liaison*, plyz) *ad*, more; -er (*suffix forming comparatives*); longer; any l., anymore. le ~, the most; -est (*suffix forming superlatives*). [**signe**] ~ (plys) *m*, plus [sign]. **plusieurs** (zjœːr) *a. & pn*, several. **plusque-parfait** (plyskəparfɛ) *m*, pluperfect. **plus-value** (plyvaly) *f*, appreciation; surplus; [unearned] increment.

plutôt (plyto) *ad*, rather, sooner, instead.

pluvial, e (plyvjal) *a*, rain (*water*); rainy.

pluvier (plyvje) *m*, plover.

pluvieux, euse (plyvjø, øːz) *a*, rainy; wet.

pneumatique (pnømatik) (*abb.* **pneu**) *m*, [pneumatic] tire. ¶ *a*, pneumatic, air (*att.*); express letter (*in Paris*).

pneumonie (pnømɔni) *f*, pneumonia.

Pô (le) (po), the Po (*river*).

pochade (pɔʃad) *f*, rapid sketch. **poche** (pɔʃ) *f*, pocket; sack; pouch; case; crop (*bird*); ladle; pucker. ~ *rapportée*, patch pocket. **pocher** (ʃe) *v.t*, to poach (*eggs*); black (*eye*); dash off (*sketch*). **pochette** (ʃɛt) *f*, pocket; pocket case, packet. ~ *en soie, de couleur*, silk colored handkerchief. **pochoir** (ʃwaːr) *m*, stencil [plate].

poêle (pwaːl) *f*, frying pan; pan. ¶ *m*, pall; canopy; stove, range. ~ *à pétrole*, oil heater. **poêlier** (pwalje) *m*, stove & range maker. **poêlon** (lɔ̃) *m*, saucepan, pipkin.

poème (pɔɛːm) *m*, poem. **poésie** (ezi) *f*, poetry; poem, piece of poetry. ~ *enfantine*, nursery rhyme. **poète** (ɛt) *m*, poet. **poétereau** (etro) *m*, poetaster. **poétesse** (tɛs) *f*, poetess. **poétique**† (tik) *a*, poetic; poetical.

poids (pwɑ) *m*, weight; shot (*in sport of putting the shot*); heaviness; burden, brunt. ~ *spécifique*, specific gravity. ~*lourd*, heavy truck.

poignant, e (pwaɲɑ̃, ɑ̃ːt) *a*, poignant.

poignard (pwaɲaːr) *m*, dagger, dirk, poignard. **poignarder** (naɾde) *v.t*, to stab, knife. **poigne** (pwaɲ) *f*, grip; energy. **poignée** (ɲe) *f*, handful; handle, grip, hilt; hank. ~ *de main*, handshake. **poignet** (ɲɛ) *m*, wrist; wristband, cuff (*soft*).

poil (pwal) *m*, hair (*on animal & body pers.*); fur, coat; pile, nap; bristle; down (*plant*); energy. ~ *de chèvre d'Angora*, mohair. ~*follet*, down (*chin, etc.*). *à* ~, naked; bareback. *à* ~ *ras*, short-haired, smooth-haired (*dog*). *au* ~ *rude*, rough-haired, wirehaired (*dog*). **poilu, e** (ly) *a*, hairy, shaggy. ¶ *m*, French soldier.

poinçon (pwɛ̃sɔ̃) *m*, punch (*solid*); awl, point; stamp; puncheon. ~ *de contrôle*, hallmark. **poinçonner** (sɔne) *v.t*, to punch; stamp; hallmark.

poindre (pwɛ̃:dr) *v.i.ir*, to dawn, break; come up.

poing (pwɛ̃) *m*, fist, hand.

point (pwɛ̃) *m*, point; dot; speck; mark; tick; score (*games*); [full] stop, period; note; stitch; point [lace]; degree, extent; verge (*fig.*); focus. ~ *à terre*, landmark (*Naut.*). ~ *arrière*, backstitch. ~ *coupé*, cut openwork stitch. ~ *croisé*, herringboning. ~ *d'appui*, fulcrum. ~ *d'appui de la flotte*, naval station (*foreign*). ~ *d'éclair*, ~ *d'inflammabilité*, flash[ing] point. ~ *d'interrogation*, note of interrogation, question mark. ~ *d'ourlet*, hemming. ~ *de chaînette*, chain stitch. ~ *de côté*, stitch in the side (*Med.*). ~ *de croix*, cross-stitch. ~ *de fuite*, vanishing point. ~ *de languette*, *~ de feston*, blanket stitch, buttonhole s. (*Emb.*). ~*de marque*, marking stitch. ~ *de mire*, aim; cynosure (*fig.*). ~ *de piqûre*, lockstitch. ~ *de repère*, reference mark, datum point; bench mark; landmark (*fig.*). ~ *de surjet*, oversewing stitch, seam s. ~ *de tige*, *~ coulé*, crewel s. ~ *de vue*, point of view, standpoint. ~ *devant*, running stitch. ~ *du jour*, daybreak, dawn. ~ *& virgule* ou ~*virgule*, *m*, semicolon. ~ *mort*, dead center. ~ *noir*, blackhead. *à* ~, [just] in time, to a turn. *à* ~ *nommé*, in the nick of time; at the right moment.

point (pwɛ̃) *ad*, no, not, not at all, [not] any.

pointage (pwɛ̃ta:ʒ) *m*, ticking [off], checking; timekeeping; timing; scoring; aiming, pointing, laying, training (*gun*).

pointe (pwɛ̃:t) *f*, point (*sharp end*); tip; head; top; peak; toe (*shoe, sock*); (*pl.*) toe dancing; center (*lathe*); nail, brad; touch; quip, quirk. ~ *de Paris*, wire nail, French n., sprig. ~ *de terre*, headland, foreland. ~ *du jour*, daybreak, dawn. *sur la* ~ *du pied*, on tiptoe.

pointeau (pwɛ̃to) *m*, center punch.

pointer (pwɛ̃te) *v.t*, to tick [off], check, tally; point, aim, level, lay, train; thrust; (*v.i.*) to soar; appear, sprout. **pointeur** (tœ:r) *m*, checker; timekeeper; marker, scorer; gun layer. **pointille** (ti:j) *f*, punctilio. **pointiller** (tije) *v.t*, to dot; stipple; bait; (*v.i.*) to cavil; split hairs. **pointillerie** (jri) *f*, captiousness, hairsplitting. **pointilleux, euse** (jø, ø:z) *a*, captious, touchy; fastidious, punctilious.

pointu, e (pwɛ̃ty) *a*, pointed; sharp; shrill.

pointure (pwɛ̃ty:r) *f*, size (*of shoes, gloves, etc.*)

poire (pwa:r) *f*, pear; bulb, ball; dupe. **poire** (pware) *m*, perry.

poireau (pwaro) *m*, leek; wart.

poirier (pwarje) *m*, pear tree; pear wood.

pois (pwɑ) *m*, pea; dot (*Emb.*); spot (*as on tie*). ~ *cassés*, split peas. ~ *chinois*, soy[a] bean. ~ *de senteur*, sweet pea. *petit* ~, ~*verts*, green peas.

poison (pwazɔ̃) *m*, poison.

poissard, e (pwasa:r, ard) *a*, vulgar. ¶ *f*, fishwife.

poisser (pwase) *v.t*, to pitch; wax (*thread*); make sticky. **poisseux, euse** (sø, ø:z) *a*, sticky.

poisson (pwasɔ̃) *m*, fish. *faire un* ~ *d'avril à*, to make an April fool of. ~ *de grand sport*, big-game fish. ~ *de mer*, salt-water fish, sea fish. ~ *rouge*, goldfish. **poissonnaille** (sɔnɑ:j) *f*, fry. **poissonnerie** (nri) *f*, fish market; f. shop. **poissonneux, euse** (nø, ø:z) *a*, full of fish. **poissonnier, ère** (nje, ɛ:r) *n*, fishmonger. ¶ *f*, fish kettle (*Cook.*).

poitrail (pwatra:j) *m*, breast (*horse*). **poitrinaire** (trinɛ:r) *a*. & *n*, consumptive. **poitrine** (trin) *f*, chest, breast; brisket.

poivre (pwa:vr) *m*, pepper. ~ *de Cayenne* (kajen), ~ *rouge*, Cayenne p., red p. **poivré, e** (pwavre) *p.a*, peppery; spicy (*tale*). **poivrer** (vre) *v.t*, to pepper. **poivrier** (vrie) *m*, pepper plant; p. box. **poivrière** (vriɛ:r) *f*, pepper box.

poix (pwɑ) f, pitch; cobbler's wax.

polaire (pɔlɛ:r) a, polar; pole (*star*). **pôle** (po:l) m, pole (*Astr., Phys., etc.*).

polémique (pɔlemik) a, polemic(al). ¶ f, polemic; polemics.

poli, e (pɔli) p.a, polished, bright; glossy, sleek; polite, mannerly, refined. ¶ m, polish, gloss.

police (pɔlis) f, policing; police regulations; police [force]; policy (*Insce*). ~ de la circulation, traffic police. **policer** (se) v.t, to control, organize, civilize. **policier** (je) m, policeman.

polichinelle (pɔliʃinɛl) m, Punch; buffoon.

poliment (pɔlimɑ̃) ad, politely. **polir** (li:r) v.t, to polish; buff; smooth; refine.

polisson, ne (pɔlisɔ̃, ɔn) a, street child; rascal, scamp; immodest person; (*att.*) naughty, precocious, indecent. **polissonner** (sɔne) v.i, to run the streets (*child*); be lewd.

politesse (pɔlitɛs) f, politeness; compliment.

politicien (pɔlitisjɛ̃) m, politician (*as a trade*). **politique**† (tik) a, political; politic. ¶ m, politician. ¶ f, policy; polity; politics. **politiquer** (ke) v.i, to talk politics.

polka (pɔlka) m, polka.

pollen (pɔllɛn) m, pollen.

polluer (pɔllɥe) v.t, to pollute, defile; profane. **pollution** (pɔllysjɔ̃) f, pollution.

polo (pɔlo) m, polo; polo cap.

Pologne (la) (pɔlɔɲ), Poland. **polonais, e** (nɛ, ɛ:z) a, Polish. **P~,** n, Pole. **le polonais,** Polish (*language*). **polonaise,** f, polonaise.

poltron, ne (pɔltrɔ̃, ɔn) a, cowardly. ¶ n, poltroon, coward. **poltronnerie** (trɔnri) f, cowardice.

polycopier (pɔlikɔpje) v.t, to mimeograph, etc.

polygame (pɔligam) n, polygamist. ¶ a, polygamous. **polygamie** (mi) f, polygamy. **polyglotte** (glɔt) a. & n, polyglot. **polygone** (gɔn) m, polygon. **la Polynésie** (nezi), Polynesia. **polype** (lip)

m, polyp; polypus. **polysyllabe** (silab) a, polysyllabic. ¶ m, polysyllable. **polytechnique** (tɛknik) a, polytechnic. **polythéisme** (teism) m, polytheism.

pommade (pɔmad) f, pomade; salve. **pommader** (de) v.t, to pomade.

pomme (pɔm) f, apple; cone (*fir, pine*); knob; head (*stick, cabbage*); rose (*can*). ~ d'Adam (adɑ̃), Adam's apple. ~de terre, potato. ~s de terre en robe [de chambre], jacket potatoes. ~ sauvage, crab [apple]. **pommé, e** (me) (*fig.*) p.a, downright. **pommeau** (mo) m, pommel. **pommelé, e** (mle) p.a, dapple[d]; mackerel (*sky*). **pommeraie** (mrɛ) f, apple orchard. **pommette** (mɛt) f, cheekbone. **pommier** (mje) m, apple tree. ~ sauvage, crab [apple tree].

pompe (pɔ̃:p) f, pomp; pump. ~ à incendie, fire engine. ~ aspirante, suction pump. ~ foulante, force pump. ~ funèbre, funeral; (*pl.*) undertaking.

Pompéi (pɔ̃pei) f, Pompeii.

pomper (pɔ̃pe) v.t. & i, to pump; suck up.

pompeux, euse† (pɔ̃pø, ø:z) a, pompous; stately.

pompier (pɔ̃pje) m, pump maker; fireman; conventionalist, formulist; (*att.*) conventional, formulistic.

pompon (pɔ̃pɔ̃) m, pompon, tuft, tassel.

ponce (pɔ̃:s) f, pumice; pounce (*art*).

ponceau (pɔ̃so) m, culvert; poppy.

poncer (pɔ̃se) v.t, to pumice; sandpaper; pounce. **poncif** (sif) (*fig.*) m, conventionalism.

ponction (pɔ̃ksjɔ̃) (*Surg.*) f, puncture, tapping.

ponctualité (pɔ̃ktɥalite) f, punctuality.

ponctuation (pɔ̃ktɥasjɔ̃) f, punctuation.

ponctuel, le† (pɔ̃ktɥɛl) a, punctual.

ponctuer (pɔ̃ktɥe) v.t. & abs, to punctuate; emphasize.

pondérable (pɔ̃derabl) a, ponderable. **pondérer** (re) *v.t*, to balance.

pondre (pɔ̃:dr) *v.t. & abs*, to lay (*eggs*); be delivered of (*fig.*).

poney (pɔnɛ) *m*, pony.

pont (pɔ̃) *m*, bridge; platform; deck (*ship*). ~ *à bascule*, draw-bridge. ~ *abri*, awning deck, hurricane d. ~ *de manœuvre*, hurricane deck. ~ *roulant*, traveling crane. ~ *suspendu*, suspension bridge. ~ *suspendu à chaînes*, chain bridge. ~ *tournant*, swing bridge. ~*aérien*, airlift.

ponte (pɔ̃:t) *f*, laying (*eggs*); (*m.*) punt[er] (*cards, etc.*).

ponté, e (pɔ̃te) *a*, decked. *non* ~, open (*boat*).

ponter (pɔ̃te) *v.i*, to punt (*cards, etc.*).

pontife (pɔ̃tif) *m*, pontiff; pundit. **pontifical, e†** (fikal) *a. & m*, pontifical. **pontificat** (ka) *m*, pontificate.

pont-levis (pɔ̃ləvi) *m*, drawbridge (*castle*).

ponton (pɔ̃tɔ̃) *m*, pontoon; hulk; landing stage.

popeline (pɔplin) *f*, poplin.

populace (pɔpylas) *f*, populace, rabble. **populacier, ère** (sje, ɛ:r) *a*, vulgar. **populaire†** (lɛ:r) *a*, popular. **popularité** (larite) *f*, popularity. **population** (sjɔ̃) *f*, population. **populeux, euse** (lø, ø:z) *a*, populous.

porc (pɔ:r) *m*, pig, swine; pork. ~ [*châtré*], hog.

porcelaine (pɔrsəlɛn) *f*, porcelain, china[ware]; cowrie. ~ *de Saxe*, Dresden china. **porcelainier, ère** (nje, ɛ:r) *n*, china manufacturer; china dealer.

porc-épic (pɔrkepik) *m*, porcupine.

porche (pɔrʃ) *m*, porch.

porcher, ère (pɔrʃe, ɛ:r) *n*, swineherd. **porcherie** (ʃəri) *f*, pigsty. **porcine** (sin) *a.f*, porcine, pig (*att.*).

pore (pɔ:r) *m*, pore. **poreux, euse** (pɔrø, ø:z) *a*, porous. **porosité** (rozite) *f*, porousness.

porphyre (pɔrfi:r) *m*, porphyry.

port (pɔ:r) *m*, port, harbor, haven; carrying; wearing; carriage; postage; bearing; burden (*ship*). ~ *d'armes*, gun license. ~ *d'ar-*

mement, home port. ~ *d'attache*, port of registry. ~ *de guerre*, ~ *militaire*, naval port, n. station, n. base. ~ *de toute marée*, deep-water harbor. *à bon* ~, safe[ly]; *to* a happy issue. **portable** (pɔrtabl) *a*, wearable.

portail (pɔrta:j) *m*, portal.

portant, e (pɔrtɑ̃, ɑ̃:t) *a*, bearing. *à bout* ~, pointblank. *bien* ~, in good health. *mal* ~, in bad h. ¶ *m*, chest handle, lifting h.; outrigger (*for rowlocks*). **portatif, ive** (tatif, i:v) *a*, portable; small (*arms*).

porte (pɔrt) *f*, door, doorway; gate, gateway; arch. ~ *brisée*, folding door. ~ *charretière*, carriage entrance. ~ *cochère* (kɔ-ʃɛ:r), built-over carriage entrance. ~ *de service*, back door, tradesmen's entrance. ~*-fenêtre*, French window. ~ *matelassée*, baize door. ~ *à tambour*, revolving door. ~ *va-et-vient*, swing door.

porte- (pɔrt; *sometimes* pɔrtə *as noted*) *comps, all m*: ~ *à faux*, overhang. ~*-avions*, aircraft carrier. ~*-bagages*, luggage carrier. ~*-bonheur*, charm. ~*-bouquet*, flower holder. ~*-bouteilles*, bottle rack; bin. ~*-cartes* (tǝkart), card case; map case. ~*-chapeaux*, hat & coat stand. ~*-cigare*, cigar holder. ~*-cigares*, c. case. ~*-clefs* (tǝkle), turnkey; key ring. ~*-couteau*, knife rest. ~*-crayon* (tǝkrejɔ̃), pencil case. ~*-en-dehors*, outrigger (*for rowlocks*). ~*-épée*, frog (*sword*). ~*-étendard*, standard bearer. ~*-feuille*, billfold. ~*-malheur*, bringer of ill luck; bird of ill omen, Jonah. ~*-menu* (tǝmny), menu holder. ~*-monnaie*, purse. ~*-parapluies*, umbrella stand. ~*-parole*, spokesman, mouthpiece (*pers.*). ~*-potiche*, pedestal (*for vase*). ~*-queue* (tǝkø), train bearer. ~*-respect*, persɔ̃ of imposing appearance; weapon. ~*-serviettes*, towel rod, ring. ~*-trésor*, jewel case (*traveling*). ~*-vêtements*, clothes hanger. ~*-voix* (tǝvwa), megaphone.

porté, e (pɔrte) *p.a*, inclined, disposed, prone, apt; fond.

portée (pɔrte) *f*, bearing; litter (*of pups*); span; reach, range, radius, scope, compass, shot; significance, purport; stave, staff (*Mus.*). *à ~ de la voix*, within call.

portefaix (pɔrtəfɛ) *m*, porter (*street, etc.*); rough fellow.

portefeuille (pɔrtəfœːj) *m*, portfolio; letter case, wallet; office (*in ministry*). *~-titres*, investments, securities, share holdings, stocks & shares.

portemanteau (pɔrtmɑ̃to) *m*, hat & coat stand, portemanteau.

porter (pɔrte) *v.t. & i*, to bear; carry; take; bring; lay; wear, have on; shoulder (*arms*); drink (*health*); deal, strike (*blow*); enter, put, mark; post (*Bkkpg.*); prompt, lead, incline; raise; rest; tell (*shot, word*); turn (*discussion*). *~ à faux*, to overhang; miss the point (*fig.*). *se ~*, to go; be; do; stand. **porteur, euse** (tœːr, øːz) *n*, porter; carrier; (*m.*) bearer; holder. *porteurs des cordons du poêle*, pall bearers.

portier, ère (pɔrtje, ɛːr) *n*, porter, doorkeeper, caretaker. ¶ *f*, door (*carriage, car*); door curtain.

portion (pɔrsjɔ̃) *f*, portion, share, part; helping (*food*).

portique (pɔrtik) *m*, portico, porch; gantry; gallows (*Gym.*).

Porto (pɔrto) *m*, Oporto. **porto** *ou* **vin de Porto**, *m*, port [wine].

portrait (pɔrtrɛ) *m*, portrait, likeness; image; description. *~ en buste*, half-length portrait. *~ en pied*, full-length portrait.

portugais, e (pɔrtygɛ, ɛːz) *a. &* **P~,** *n*, Portuguese. *le portugais*, Portuguese (*language*). **le Portugal** (gal), Portugal.

posage (poza:ʒ) *m*, laying, fixing. **pose** (poːz) *f*, laying; pose, posture; lie (*golf ball*); exposure (*Phot.*). *~mètre*, exposure meter. **posé†, e** (poze) *p.a*, staid, sedate; steady. **poser** (ze) *v.i*, to rest, lie; pose, sit (*portrait*); (*v.t.*) to place, put; p. down; lay; l. down; set; hang (*bells*); pose; post (*sentry*); state; grant. *~ ses clous*, to down tools. *se ~*, to settle, alight; set up; pose. **poseur, euse** (zœːr, øːz) *n*, layer; set-

ter; hanger (*bells*); affected person. *poseur de mines*, minelayer. *poseur de voie*, platelayer.

positif, ive† (pozitif, iːv) *a*, positive, real; practical, matter-of-fact. ¶ *m*, real[ity].

position (pozisjɔ̃) *f*, position; situation; book (*Stk Ex.*); posture; stance.

possédé, e (pɔsede) *p.a*, possessed (*mad*). ¶ *n*, one possessed. **posséder** (de) *v.t*, to possess, own, have, hold; be master of. **possesseur** (sɛsœːr) *m*, possessor, owner. **possession** (sjɔ̃) *f*, possession; tenure.

possibilité (pɔsibilite) *f*, possibility. **possible** (bl) *a. & m*, possible.

postal, e (pɔstal) *a*, postal, post, mail (*att.*).

postdater (pɔstdate) *v.t*, to postdate.

poste (pɔst) *f*, post, mail; post [office]. *~ restante*, general delivery, to be called for. *aller un train de ~*, to go posthaste.

poste (pɔst) *m*, post, station; guard room; berth; set (*radio*); head[ing]; item; shift (*men*). *~ central*, exchange (*Teleph.*). *~ de l'équipage*, forecastle, foc's'le. *~ de police*, police station. *~ de secours*, first-aid station. *~ supplémentaire*, extension [line] (*Teleph.*). **poster** (te) *v.t*, to post, station.

postérieur, e† (pɔsterjœːr) *a*, posterior, subsequent, later; hind[er], back. ¶ *m*, posterior.

postérité (pɔsterite) *f*, posterity, issue.

posthume (pɔstym) *a*, posthumous.

postiche (pɔstiʃ) *a*, false, artificial; sham. *cheveux ~s*, wig.

postillon (pɔstijɔ̃) *m*, postillion.

post-scriptum (pɔstskriptɔm) (*abb.* P.-S.) *m*, postscript, P.S.

postulant, e (pɔstylɑ̃, ɑ̃:t) *n*, candidate, applicant; postulant. **postuler** (le) *v.t*, to apply for; (*v.i.*) to act for (*client, law*).

posture (pɔsty:r) *f*, posture; position.

pot (po; *before à, au*, pɔt) *m*, pot, jug, ewer; tankard; can; jar. *~au-feu*, stock pot, soup p; beef and vegetables; (att.) stay-at-home (pers.). ~ d'échappement, silencer. ~-de-vin, bribe. ~ pourri, hodgepodge; medley.

potable (pɔtabl) a, drinkable, drinking (water).

potage (pɔtaːʒ) m, soup. ~ ou consommé? thick or clear? (at dinner). pour tout ~, all told.

potager, ère (taʒe, ɛːr) a, pot (herb); kitchen (garden). ¶ m, kitchen garden; dinner pail; kitchen stove, charcoal-fired cooker.

potasse (pɔtas) f, potash. **potassium** (sjɔm) m, potassium.

poteau (pɔto) m, post, pole. ~ [d'arrivée], [winning] post. ~ de départ, starting p. ~ de signalisation (siɲalizasjɔ̃), traffic sign. ~ indicateur, signpost.

potée (pɔte) f, potful, jugful; swarm. ~ d'étain, putty powder.

potelé, e (pɔtle) a, plump; chubby.

potelet (pɔtlɛ) m, stud (scantling in wall).

potence (pɔtɑ̃ːs) f, gallows, gibbet; bracket.

potentat (pɔtɑ̃ta) m, potentate.

potentiel, le (pɔtɑ̃sjɛl) a. & m, potential.

poter (pɔte) v.t, to putt (golf).

poterie (pɔtri) f, pottery, earthenware; ware. ~ de grès, stoneware.

poterne (pɔtɛrn) f, postern.

poteur (pɔtœːr) m, putter (golf club).

potiche (pɔtiʃ) f, vase (Chinese, or like).

potier (pɔtje) m, potter. ~ d'étain, pewterer.

potin (pɔtɛ̃) m, gossip; row, fuss.

potion (posjɔ̃) f, potion, draft.

potiron (pɔtirɔ̃) m, pumpkin.

pou (pu) m, louse.

pouah! (pwa) i, ugh!

poubelle (pubɛl) f, garbage can, trash c.

pouce (puːs) m, thumb.

pouding (pudiɲ) m, pudding.

poudre (puːdr) f, powder; dust. ~ à canon, gunpowder. ~ à lever, baking powder. ~ d'or, gold dust. ~ de mine, blasting powder. ~ de riz, face powder, toilet powder. **poudrer** (pudre) v.t, to pow-

der. **poudrerie** (drəri) f, powder mill. **poudreux, euse** (drø, øːz) a, dusty. **poudrier** (drie) m, powder box; salt sifter. **poudrière** (ɛːr) f, powder magazine.

pouf (puf) m, overstuffed footstool.

pouffer [de rire] (pufe), to burst out laughing.

pouilleux, euse (pujø, øːz), a, lousy.

poulailler (pulaje) m, hen house; poulterer; top balcony, cheap seats (Theat.).

poulain (pulɛ̃) m, colt, foal.

poulaine (pulɛn) f, bedroom slipper.

poularde (pulard) f, table fowl. **poule** (pul) f, hen, fowl; sweepstake[s]; pool (cards, ice hockey, fencing, shooting). chair de ~, gooseflesh. ~ d'eau, moor hen. ~ d'Inde, turkey [hen]. ~ faisane, hen pheasant. ~ mouillée, milksop (pers.). **poulet** (lɛ) m, chicken, chick. **poulette** (lɛt) f, pullet; girl.

pouliche (puliʃ) f, filly, foal.

poulie (puli) f, pulley, block, sheave.

pouliner (puline) v.i, to foal. [jument] **poulinière** (njɛːr) f, brood mare, breeder.

poulpe (pulp) m, octopus.

pouls (pu) m, pulse (as in wrist).

poumon (pumɔ̃) m, lung.

poupard, e (pupaːr, ard) a, chubby; baby (face). ¶ m, baby; baby doll.

poupe (pup) f, stern, poop.

poupée (pupe) f, doll; puppet; dummy; block. **poupin, e** (pɛ̃, in) a, doll-faced. **poupon, ne** (pɔ̃, ɔn) n, baby. **pouponner** (pɔne) v.t, to fondle, dandle, cuddle. **pouponnière** (njɛːr) f, day nursery.

pour (puːr) pr, for; instead of; per; pro; as; on; to; (money's) worth. ~ ainsi dire, so to speak. ~ cent, percent. ~ que, in order that. le ~ & le contre, the pros & cons, for & against.

pourboire (purbwaːr) m, tip, gratuity.

pourceau (purso) m, hog, pig, swine.

pourcentage (pursãta:ȝ) *m*, percentage, rate.

pourchasser (purʃase) *v.t*, to pursue; dun.

pourfendre (purfã:dr) *v.t*, to fend, cleave.

pourparlers (purparle) *m.pl*, parley; negotiations.

pourpre (purpr) *f*, purple (*robe*); crimson (*color*); (*m*.) purple (*color*); (*att.*) crimson (*color*). **pourpré, e** (pre) *a*, purple (*red—color*).

pourquoi (purkwa) *ad. & c*, why, wherefore, what. ¶ *m*, why.

pourri, e (puri) *p.a*, rotten. **pourrir** (ri:r) *v.i. & t*, to rot, **pourriture** (rity:r) *f*, rotting; rot; rottenness.

poursuite (pursɥit) *f*, pursuit, chase; (*oft. pl.*) lawsuit, proceedings; prosecution. **poursuivant** (vã) *m*, plaintiff, prosecutor; suitor, wooer. **poursuivre** (vr) *v.t.ir*, to pursue, chase; haunt; follow up; prosecute, sue.

pourtant(purtã) *ad*, yet, nevertheless, however.

pourtour (purtu:r) *m*, circumference; surround; precincts, close; gangway.

pourvoi (purvwa) *m*, appeal; petition. **pourvoir** (vwa:r) *v.i. & t. ir*, to provide, supply, furnish. **pourvoyeur** (vwajœ:r) *m*, purveyor, provider, caterer. **pourvu que** (vy) *c*, provided [that].

poussah (pusa) *m*, tumbler (*toy*); tub[by man].

pousse (pus) *f*, growth; cutting (*teeth*); shoot, sprout. **~-pousse**, *m*, ricksha[w]. **poussée** (se) *f*, push, shove; thrust; pressure; outburst; buoyancy. **pousser** (se) *v.t. & i*, to push, shove, thrust; drive; urge; utter, give; grow, shoot, spring up. **~ à la perche**, **~ du fond**, to punt (*boating*). **~ au large**, to push off (*Naut.*).

poussier (pusje) *m*, dust (*coal, etc.*). **poussière** (sjɛ:r) *f*, dust. **~ d'eau**, spray. **poussiéreux, euse** (sjerø, ø:z) *a*, dusty.

poussif, ive (pusif, i:v) *a*, broken-winded; wheezy.

poussin (pusɛ̃) *m*, chick; spring chicken. **poussinière** (sinjɛ:r) *f*, coop; incubator.

poussoir (puswa:r) *m*, push [button].

poutre (putr) *f*, beam; girder.

pouvoir (puvwa:r) *m*, power; authority; power of attorney; proxy; (*pl.*) credentials. ¶ *v.i. & t. ir*, to be able; can; can do; may. **se ~**, to be possible. *cela se peut*, it may be.

prairie (prɛri) *f*, meadow; grassland; prairie.

praline (pralin) *f*, burnt almond, praline.

praticable (pratikabl) *a*, practicable, feasible; passable (*road*). **praticien** (sjɛ̃) *m*, practician; practitioner. **pratiquant** (pratikã) *a*, church-going. **pratique†** (tik) *a*, practical. ¶ *f*, practice; experience; observance; (*pl.*) dealings; pratique; custom; customer. **pratiquer** (ke) *v.t*, to practice; make; frequent. **se ~**, to be done; rule (*prices*).

pré (pre) *m*, meadow.

préalable† (prealabl) *a*, previous; preliminary.

préambule (preãbyl) *m*, preamble.

préau (preo) *m*, courtyard, quadrangle; playground (*covered*).

préavis (preavi) *m*, [previous] notice, warning.

prébende (prebã:d) *f*, prebend. **prébendier** (bãdje) *m*, prebendary.

précaire† (prekɛ:r) *a*, precarious.

précaution (prekosjɔ̃) *f*, precaution; caution, wariness. **précautionner** (sjɔne) *v.t*, to caution, warn.

précédemment (presedamã) *ad*, previously. **précédent, e** (dã, ã:t) *a*, preceding, previous, before. ¶ *m*, precedent. **précéder** (de) *v.t*, to precede.

précepte (presɛpt) *m*, precept. **précepteur** (tœ:r) *m*, tutor, teacher, preceptor. **préceptorat** (tɔra) *m*, tutorship.

prêche (prɛʃ) *m*, sermon. **prêcher** (ʃe) *v.t. & abs*, to preach; extol; exhort; lecture. **prêcheur** (ʃœ:r) *m*, sermonizer.

précieux, euse† (presjø, ø:z) *a*, precious; valuable; affected.

précipice (presipis) *m*, precipice.

précipitamment (presipitamɑ̃)
a, precipitately, headlong. **précipitation** (sjɔ̃) *f*, precipitancy,
haste; precipitation. **précipité, e**
(te) *a*, precipitate, hasty, hurried, headlong. ¶ *m*, precipitate.
précipiter (te) *v.t*, to precipitate;
hasten; plunge. **se ~,** to rush.

précis, e (presi, iːz) *a*, precise,
exact; sharp (*hour*); definite. ¶
m, abstract, summary, précis.
précisément (sizemɑ̃) *ad*, precisely, exactly. **préciser** (ze) *v.t*,
to state precisely, specify. **précision** (zjɔ̃) *f*, precision, accuracy; (*pl.*) particulars.

précité, e (presite) *a*, aforesaid,
above.

précoce (prekɔs) *a*, precocious;
early, forward. **précocité** (site)
f, precociousness, etc.

préconçu, e (prekɔ̃sy) *a*, preconceived.

préconiser (prekɔnize) *v.t*, to
preconize; [re]commend, advocate.

précurseur (prekyrsœːr) *m*, precursor, forerunner; (*att.*) pre-
cursory, premonitory.

prédécès (predesɛ) *m*, predecease.

prédécesseur (predesɛsœːr) *m*,
predecessor.

prédestination (predɛstinasjɔ̃)
f, predestination.

prédicant (predikɑ̃) *m*, preacher.

prédicat (predika) *m*, predicate.

prédicateur (predikatœːr) *m*,
preacher. **prédication** (sjɔ̃) *f*,
preaching.

prédiction (prediksjɔ̃) *f*, predic-
tion; forecast.

prédilection (predilɛksjɔ̃) *f*,
predilection, partiality. **de ~,** favorite.

prédire (prediːr) *v.t.ir*, to predict, foretell.

prédisposer (predispoze) *v.t*, to
predispose.

prédominer (predɔmine) *v.i*, to
predominate, prevail.

prééminent, e (preeminɑ̃, ɑ̃ːt)
a, preeminent.

préemption (preɑ̃psjɔ̃) *f*, preemption.

préface (prefas) *f*, preface, foreword; preliminaries; forerunner.

préfecture (prefɛktyːr) *f*, pre-
fecture; headquarters (*of police*).

préférable† (preferabl) *a*, pref-
erable, better. **préférence** (rɑ̃ːs)
f, preference. **préférer** (re) *v.t*,
to prefer.

préfet (prefɛ) *m*, prefect.

préfixe (prefiks) *m*, prefix. ¶ *a*,
prefixed.

préhenseur (preɑ̃sœːr) *a.m*,
prehensile.

préhistorique (preistɔrik) *a*,
prehistoric.

préjudice (preʒydis) *m*, prejudice, detriment; injury. **préjudiciable** (sjabl) *a*, prejudicial,
detrimental. **préjudicier** (sje)
v.i, to be detrimental to. **préjugé** (ʒe) *m*, prejudice; presumption.

prélart (prelaːr) *m*, tarpaulin.

prélasser (se) (prelase) *v.pr*,
to strut along; loll. **prélat** (la)
m, prelate.

prélèvement (prelɛvmɑ̃) *m*, deduction, levy. **~ de sang,** blood
test. **prélever** (lve) *v.t*, to deduct, levy.

préliminaire (preliminɛːr) *a.* &
m, preliminary.

prélude (prelyd) *m*, prelude;
voluntary. **préluder** (de) *v.i*, to
prelude (*Mus.*). **~ à,** to preface,
lead up to.

prématuré†, e (prematyre) *a*,
premature, untimely.

préméditation (premeditasjɔ̃)
f, premeditation; malice afore-
thought, m. prepense. **préméditer** (te) *v.t*, to premeditate.

prémices (premis) *f.pl*, first-
fruits; beginning.

premier, ère (prəmje, ɛːr) *a*,
first; opening (*price*); leading;
early; earliest; next; prime; primary; premier. **premier, comps:
~ choix,** best quality, finest q. **~
garçon,** headwaiter. **~ ministre,**
prime minister, premier. **~-né,**
m, first-born. **de ~ ordre,** first-
class, first-rate; gilt-edged (*securities*). **~ plan,** foreground;
close-up (*Phot.*). **~ rôle,** leading part; l. man, l. lady. ¶ *m*,
first. ¶ *f*, first; f. night; forewoman. **~s** [*galeries*], dress circle. **premièrement** (mjɛrmɑ̃) *ad*,
first[ly].

prémisses (premis) *f.pl*, premis[s]es (*Log.*).

prémonitoire (premɔnitwaːr) *a*, premonitory.

prémunir (premyniːr) *v.t*, to forewarn. **se ~ contre**, to provide against.

prenable (prənabl) *a*, pregnable; corruptible. **prenant, e** (nɑ̃, ɑ̃ːt) *a*, taking; prehensile. **prendre** (prɑ̃ːdr) *v.t.ir*, to take; t. up; t. in; t. over; lay hold of; seize; clasp; catch; pick up; assume; acquire; come to; charge; put on, assume; wreak; (*v.i.ir.*) to set; congeal; curdle; freeze; catch; take root, strike; take, catch on; bear (*to right, left*). **se ~**, to catch; congeal; cling; clasp. **s'en ~ à**, to blame. **s'y ~**, to set about it. **preneur, euse** (prənœːr, øːz) *n*, taker; captor; buyer; lessee.

prénom (prenɔ̃) *m*, first name, Christian n.

préoccupation (preɔkypasjɔ̃) *f*, preoccupation. **préoccuper** (pe) *v.t*, to preoccupy.

préopinant (preɔpinɑ̃) *m*, previous speaker.

préparateur, trice (preparatœːr, tris) *n*, tutor, coach; assistant. **préparatifs** (tif) *m.pl*, preparations. **préparation** (sjɔ̃) *f*, preparation. **préparatoire** (twaːr) *a*, preparatory. **préparer** (re) *v.t*, to prepare, make ready; lay (*fire*); coach (*pupil*); read for (*exam*). **se ~**, to prepare, get ready; brew (*storm*).

prépondérance (prepɔ̃derɑ̃ːs) *f*, preponderance. **prépondérant, e** (rɑ̃, ɑ̃ːt) *a*, preponderant; casting (*vote*).

préposé, e (prepoze) *n*, servant; officer; official; clerk. **préposer** (ze) *v.t*, to appoint.

préposition (prepɔzisjɔ̃) *f*, preposition.

prérogative (prerɔgatiːv) *f*, prerogative; privilege.

près (prɛ) *ad. & pr*, near; by; close; to. **à . . . ~**, save on, save in, except for; to a; within. **à peu ~**, nearly, about, pretty much.

présage (prezaːʒ) *m*, presage, omen, portent, foreboding, premonition. **présager** (zaʒe) *v.t*, to presage, portend, [fore]bode; augur.

pré-salé (presale) *m*, salt-meadow sheep; salt-meadow mutton.

presbyte (prɛzbit) *n. & att*, far-sighted (person).

presbytère (prɛzbitɛːr) *m*, presbytery; rectory, vicarage, parsonage. **presbytérien, ne** (terjɛ̃, ɛn) *n. & att*, Presbyterian.

prescience (presjɑ̃ːs) *f*, prescience, foreknowledge.

prescription (preskripsjɔ̃) *f*, prescription; bar of the statute of limitations; directions. **prescrire** (skriːr) *v.t.ir*, to prescribe, ordain. **se ~**, to be statute barred.

préséance (preseɑ̃ːs) *f*, precedence (*in rank*).

présence (prezɑ̃ːs) *f*, presence; attendance; sight. **présent, e** (zɑ̃, ɑ̃ːt) *a*, present; this (*letter, etc.*). ¶ *m*, present; gift. **à ~**, now. **présentable** (zɑ̃tabl) *a*, presentable. **présentation** (sjɔ̃) *f*, presentation; introduction. **présentement** (zɑ̃tmɑ̃) *ad*, at present, now; with immediate possession (*house*). **présenter** (te) *v.t*, to present; offer; pay (*respects*); produce, show; introduce.

préservatif (prezɛrvatif) *m. & a*, prèservative, preventive; contraceptive. **préservation** (sjɔ̃) *f*, preservation. **préserver** (ve) *v.t*, to preserve, keep.

présidence (prezidɑ̃ːs) *f*, presidency; chairmanship. **président, e** (dɑ̃, ɑ̃ːt) *n*, president; chairman; presiding judge. **~ du conseil** [*des ministres*], premier. **présider** [à] (de) *v.t. & i*, to preside at, over; superintend.

présomptif, ive (prezɔ̃ptif, iːv) *a*, presumptive; (*heir*) apparent. **présomption** (sjɔ̃) *f*, presumption. **présomptueux, euse†** (tɥø, øːz) *a*, presumptuous.

presque (prɛsk) *ad*, almost, nearly, all but; scarcely, hardly (*ever*). **presqu'île** (kil) *f*, peninsula.

pressant, e (prɛsɑ̃, ɑ̃ːt) *a*, pressing, urgent. **presse** (prɛs) *f*, press; clamp, cramp; squeezer; crowd, throng; pressure, congestion; hurry. **presse-citron, m,**

lemon squeezer. **presse-purée,** *m,* potato masher.

pressentiment (presãtimã) *m,* presentiment, foreboding, misgiving. **pressentir** (tiːr) *v.t.ir,* to have a presentiment of; sound (*pers.*).

presse-papiers (prɛspapje) *m,* paperweight. **presser** (se) *v.t,* to press; squeeze; clasp; ply; hurry, push. **se ~,** to press, crowd, throng; hurry. **pression** (sjɔ̃) *f,* pressure. **bière à la ~,** draft beer. **pressoir** (swaːr) *m,* press (*wine, etc.*). **pressurer** (syre) *v.t,* to press (*grapes, etc.*); grind (*fig.*).

prestance (prɛstãːs) *f,* presence, bearing, portliness.

prestation (prɛstasjɔ̃) *f,* provision; taking (*oath*).

preste† (prɛst) *a,* quick, nimble. **prestesse** (tɛs) *f,* quickness.

prestidigitateur (prɛstidiʒitatœːr) *m,* conjurer, juggler. **prestidigitation** (sjɔ̃) *f,* conjuring, sleight-of-hand, legerdemain.

prestige (prɛstiːʒ) *m,* marvel, magic, glamour; prestige. **prestigieux, euse** (tiʒjø, øːz) *a,* marvelous; influential.

présumer (prezyme) *v.t. & abs,* to presume, suppose.

présupposer (presypoze) *v.t,* to presuppose, take for granted.

présure (prezyːr) *f,* rennet.

prêt, e (prɛ, ɛːt) *a,* ready, prepared, game.

prêt (prɛ) *m,* loan; advance.

prétendant, e (pretãdã, ãːt) *n,* applicant; claimant; pretender; (*m.*) suitor, wooer. **prétendre** (tãːdr) *v.t. & i,* to claim, require, pretend; assert; contend; aspire. **prétendu, e** (tãdy) *p.a,* alleged; would-be; so-called. ¶ *n,* intended (*in marriage*).

prête-nom (prɛtnɔ̃) *m,* dummy (*pers.*).

pretentaine (courir la) (prətãtɛn), to gad about.

prétentieux, euse (pretãsjø, øːz) *a,* pretentious. **prétention** (sjɔ̃) *f,* claim, pretension.

prêter (prɛte) *v.t,* to lend; give; take (*oath*); attribute. **~ serment,** to take oath, swear.

prétérit (preterit) *m,* preterite.

prêteur, euse (prɛtœːr, øːz) *n,* lender. **~ sur gages,** lender on security; pawnbroker.

prétexte (pretɛkst) *m,* pretext, pretense, plea, excuse. **prétexter** (te) *v.t,* to plead.

prêtre (prɛːtr) *m,* priest. **prêtresse** (prɛtrɛs) *f,* priestess. **prêtrise** (triːz) *f,* priesthood, [holy] orders.

preuve (prœːv) *f,* proof; evidence; token. **~ par l'absurde,** reductio ad absurdum. **~ par présomption,** circumstantial evidence.

preux (prø) *a.m,* doughty, valiant.

prévaloir (prevalwaːr) *v.i.ir,* to prevail. **se ~ de,** to presume [up]on.

prévaricateur, trice (prevarikatœːr, tris) *n,* unjust judge; defaulter. **prévarication** (sjɔ̃) *f,* breach of trust, default. **prévariquer** (ke) *v.i,* to fail in one's duty; betray one's trust.

prévenance (prevnãːs) *f,* [kind] attention. **prévenant, e** (vnã, ãːt) *a,* attentive, kind, considerate, thoughtful; prepossessing. **prévenir** (vniːr) *v.t.ir,* to forestall, prevent; ward off; prepossess; prejudice, bias; [fore]warn, inform. **prévention** (vãsjɔ̃) *f,* prepossession, prejudice; imprisonment on suspicion, preventive arrest. **prévenu, e** (vny) *n,* accused, prisoner. **prévenu,** *a,* prejudiced; warned; accused.

prévision (previzjɔ̃) *f,* prevision, forecast, expectation. **prévoir** (vwaːr) *v.t. & abs. ir,* to foresee, forecast; provide for.

prévôt (prevo) *m,* provost.

prévoyance (prevwajãːs) *f,* foresight, forethought; precaution. **~ sociale,** state insurance. **prévoyant, e** (jã, ãːt) *a,* provident; farsighted.

prie-Dieu (pridjø), *m,* prayer stool. **prier** (e) *v.t,* to pray (to); beg, ask, request, beseech, entreat; invite. **je vous en prie,** you're welcome, don't mention it. **prière** (ɛːr) *f,* prayer; request, entreaty. **~ de ...,** please ... **prieur, e** (œːr) *n,* prior, ess. **prieuré** (œre) *m,* priory.

primage (prima:ʒ) *m*, primage (*Ship.*).

primaire (primɛ:r) *a*, primary; elementary (*Sch.*).

primat (prima) *m*, primate. **primatie** (si) *f*, primacy. **primauté** (mote) *f*, primacy; lead (*cards*, *etc.*).

prime (prim) *a*, first; earliest. ¶ *f*, premium; bounty, bonus; gift (*for coupons*); option (*Stk Ex.*). **primé, e** (me) *p.a*, bounty-fed; prize (*bull*, *etc.*). **primer** (me) *v.t*, to surpass; override; award a prize to; (*v.i.*) to excel; rank before.

primesautier, ère (primsotje, ɛ:r) *a*, impulsive.

primeur (primœ:r) *f*, freshness, newness; early vegetable, early fruit.

primevère (primvɛ:r) *f*, primrose. ~ *des champs*, cowslip.

primitif, ive† (primitif, i:v) *a*, primitive, original; primeval; pristine; primary; crude.

primo (primo) *ad*, first[ly].

primogéniture (primɔʒenity:r) *f*, primogeniture.

primordial, e† (primɔrdjal) *a*, primordial, primary; primeval.

prince (prɛ̃:s) *m*, prince. *bon* ~, a good fellow.

princeps (prɛ̃sɛps) *a.inv*, first (*edition*).

princesse (prɛ̃sɛs) *f*, princess. **princier, ère** (sje, ɛ:r) *a*, princely.

principal, e† (prɛ̃sipal) *a*, principal, chief, head, main; staple (*product*); major (*planet*); senior. ¶ *m*, principal; chief; headmaster; main thing.

principauté (prɛ̃sipote) *f*, principality.

principe (prɛ̃sip) *m*, principle; beginning.

printanier, ère (prɛ̃tanje, ɛ:r) *a*, vernal, spring (*att.*). **printemps** (tɑ̃) *m*, spring[time].

priorité (priɔrite) *f*, priority, precedence.

pris, *p.p*, prendre.

prise (pri:z) *f*, taking; catch; hold, purchase, grip; setting (*cement*); prize (*Naut.*); pinch (*snuff*); dose. ~ *d'eau*, intake of water, tapping; hydrant. ~ *de bec*, altercation, set-to. ~ *de courant*,

wall socket. ~ *de corps*, arrest. ~ *de sang*, blood test. ~ *de tête* *à terre*, nelson (*wrestling*).

prisée (prize) *f*, valuation. **priser** (ze) *v.t*, to appraise, value; prize; snuff up; (*abs.*) to take snuff.

prismatique (prismatik) *a*, prismatic. **prisme** (prism) *m*, prism.

prison (prizɔ̃) *m*, prison, jail; cells; imprisonment (*term*). **prisonnier, ère** (zɔnje, ɛ:r) *n*, prisoner.

privation (privasjɔ̃) *f*, deprivation, loss; privation, hardship.

privauté (privote) *f*, familiarity, liberty.

privé†, e (prive) *a*, private. ¶ *m*, privy, water closet.

priver (prive) *v.t*, to deprive, bereave.

privilège (privilɛ:ʒ) *m*, privilege, prerogative; lien, charge. **privilégié, e** (leʒje) *p.a*, privileged; preferential. **privilégier** (ʒje) *v.t*, to privilege; charter.

prix (pri) *m*, price; value, worth; cost; consideration (*money*); terms; rate; charge; fare; prize; stakes (*turf*). ~ *courant*, market price. ~ *d'excellence*, class prize. ~ *de revient* (rəvjɛ), ~ *coûtant* (kutɑ̃), cost [price]. ~ *de sagesse*, good-conduct prize.

probabilité (prɔbabilite) *f*, probability, likelihood. **probable†** (bl) *a*, probable, likely.

probant, e (prɔbɑ̃, ɑ̃:t) *a*, convincing, cogent. **probation** (basjɔ̃) *f*, probation (*Eccl.*). **probe** (prɔb) *a*, honest, upright. **probité** (bite) *f*, probity, honesty.

problématique (prɔblematik) *a*, problematic(al). **problème** (blɛm) *m*, problem; puzzle; poser, teaser.

proboscide (prɔbɔsid) *f*, proboscis.

procédé (prɔsede) *m*, proceeding, dealing; behavior; process; tip (*Bil. cue*). **procéder** (de) *v.i*, to proceed. ~ *à l'impression*, to go to press. **procédure** (dy:r) *f*, procedure; proceedings. **procès** (sɛ) (*law*) *m*, proceedings, action, case. ~ *civil*, [law]suit. ~ *criminel*, [criminal] trial. **processif, ive** (sɛsif, i:v) *a*, litigious.

procession (sjɔ̃) *f*, procession.
processus (sy:s) *m*, process, course. **procès-verbal**, *m*, report; minutes.

prochain, e (prɔʃɛ̃, ɛn) *a*, nearest; next; near; proximate; forthcoming; coming; neighboring. ¶ *m*, neighbor, fellow creature. **prochainement** (ʃɛnmɑ̃) *a*, shortly, soon. **proche** (prɔʃ) *ad*, near, close. ¶ *a*, near, at hand. ~ *Orient*, Near East. ~*s* [*parents*] *m.pl*, near relations, next of kin.
proclamation (prɔklamasjɔ̃) *f*, proclamation. **proclamer** (me) *v.t*, to proclaim, publish; declare.
procrastination (prɔkrastinasjɔ̃) *f*, procrastination.
procréer (prɔkree) *v.t*, to procreate.
procuration (prɔkyrasjɔ̃) *f*, procuration, proxy, power of attorney. **procurer** (re) *v.t*, to procure, obtain, get. **procureur** (rœ:r) *m*, proxy; attorney.
prodigalement (prɔdigalmɑ̃) *a*, lavishly. **prodigalité** (lite) *f*, prodigality, lavishness; wastefulness; (*pl.*) extravagance.
prodige (prɔdi:ʒ) *m*, prodigy, wonder. **prodigieux, euse†** (diʒjø, ø:z) *a*, prodigious, stupendous.
prodigue (prɔdig) *a*, prodigal, lavish, unsparing, profuse; wasteful. ¶ *n*, prodigal, spendthrift. **prodiguer** (ge) *v.t*, to lavish; squander.
prodrome (prɔdro:m) *m*, premonitory symptom.
producteur, trice (prɔdyktœ:r, tris) *n*, producer. ¶ ~ & **productif, ive** (tif, i:v) *a*, producing, productive, bearing. **production** (sjɔ̃) *f*, production, output, yield; product. **produire** (dɥi:r) *v.t.ir*, to produce, bring forth, bear, yield; show. ~ *dans le monde*, to introduce into society, bring out. **se** ~, to occur, happen. **produit** (dɥi) *m*, product, produce, proceeds, yield; takings, receipts. ~ *pharmaceutique*, patent medicine.
proéminent, e (prɔeminɑ̃, ɑ̃:t) *a*, prominent.
profanation (prɔfanasjɔ̃) *f*, profanation. **profane** (fan) *a*,

profane; secular; unconsecrated (*ground*). ¶ *n*, layman; outsider; (the) profane. **profaner** (ne) *v.t*, to profane, desecrate.
proférer (prɔfere) *v.t*, to utter.
profès, esse (prɔfɛ, ɛs) *a*, professed. **professer** (se) *v.t*, to profess; teach. **professeur** (sœ:r) *m*, professor; teacher; master, mistress; lecturer; instructor. **profession** (sjɔ̃) *f*, profession; occupation; calling, business, trade. **professionnel, le** (ɔnɛl) *a. & n*, professional. **professorat** (sɔra) *m*, professorship.
profil (prɔfil) *m*, profile, side face; contour, outline, section. ~ *de l'horizon*, skyline. **profiler** (le) *v.t*, to profile, streamline.
profit (prɔfi) *m*, profit, benefit. **profitable** (tabl) *a*, profitable. **profiter** (te) *v.i*, to benefit, profit; avail oneself (*de =* of); thrive. **profiteur, euse** (tœ:r, ø:z) *n*, profiteer.
profond, e (prɔfɔ̃, ɔ̃:d) *a*, deep, profound; low (*bow*); sound (*sleep*). **profondément** (demɑ̃) *ad*, deeply, etc. **profondeur** (dœ:r) *f*, depth; profundity.
profus, e (prɔfy, y:z) *a*, profuse (*perspiration*). **profusément** (fyzemɑ̃) *ad*, profusely, lavishly. **profusion** (zjɔ̃) *f*, profusion, lavishness.
progéniture (prɔʒenity:r) *f*, progeny, offspring.
prognathe (prɔgnat) *a*, prognathous.
programme (prɔgram) *m*, program; syllabus; platform (*Pol.*). ~ *d'études*, curriculum. ~ *des courses*, race card.
progrès (prɔgrɛ) *m*, *oft. pl*, progress, [head]way. **progresser** (grɛse) *v.i*, to progress. **progressif, ive†** (sif, i:v) *a*, progressive, forward. **progression** (sjɔ̃) *f*, progression.
prohiber (prɔibe) *v.t*, to prohibit, forbid. **prohibitif, ive** (bitif, i:v) *a*, prohibitory; prohibitive. **prohibition** (sjɔ̃) *f*, prohibition. **prohibitionniste** (ɔnist) *m*, prohibitionist.
proie (prwa) *f*, prey; quarry.
projecteur (prɔʒɛktœ:r) *m*, projector; searchlight. ~ *orientable*

(ɔrjãtabl), spotlight. **projectile** (til) *a. & m*, projectile, missile. **projection** (sjɔ̃) *f*, projection. **projet** (ʒɛ) *m*, project, scheme, plan; draft. ~ *de loi*, bill, measure. **projeter** (ʒte) *v.t*, to project, throw, cast; plan, contemplate.

prolétaire (prɔletɛ:r) *m*, proletarian. **prolétariat** (tarja) *m*, proletariat. **prolétarien, ne** (rjɛ̃, ɛn) *a*, proletarian.

prolifique (prɔlifik) *a*, prolific.

prolixe (prɔliks) *a*, prolix, long-winded.

prologue (prɔlɔg) *m*, prologue.

prolongation (prɔlɔgasjɔ̃) *f. &* **prolongement** (lɔ̃ʒmã) *m*, prolongation; extension. **prolonge** (lɔ̃:ʒ) *f*, ammunition wagon. **prolonger** (lɔ̃ʒe) *v.t*, to prolong, protract, extend, lengthen.

promenade (prɔmnad) *f*, walking; walk, stroll; ride; drive; trip, outing, ramble; promenade. *sur la* ~ *[de la mer]*, on the [sea] front. ~ *en bateau*, row; sail. ~ *militaire*, route march. **promener** (mne) *v.t*, to take for a walk; pass, run, cast. ~ *par*, ~ *dans*, to show round. **se~**, to [go for a] walk, stroll. *allez vous* ~*!* be off with you! **promeneur, euse** (mnœ:r, ø:z) *n*, walker. **promenoir** (mnwa:r) *m*, promenade, walk; lounge.

promesse (prɔmɛs) *f*, promise. **prometteur, euse** (tœ:r, ø:z) *a*, promising. **promettre** (mɛtr) *v.t. & abs. ir*, to promise. *terre promise* (mi:z), *terre de promission* (misjɔ̃), promised land, land of promise. **se** ~, to resolve.

promis (prɔmi) *a*, promised; intended. ¶ *m*, fiancé.

promiscuité (prɔmiskɥite) *f*, promiscuity.

promontoire (prɔmɔ̃twa:r) *m*, promontory.

promoteur, trice (prɔmɔtœ:r, tris) *n*, promoter. **promotion** (sjɔ̃) *f*, promotion, preferment. **promouvoir** (muvwa:r) *v.t.ir*, to promote, prefer.

prompt, e† (prɔ̃, ɔ̃:t) *a*, prompt, ready, quick. **promptitude** (prɔ̃tityd) *f*, promptitude, dispatch.

promulguer (prɔmylge) *v.t*, to promulgate.

prône (pro:n) *m*, sermon; homily. **prôner** (prone) *v.t*, to extoll; puff.

pronom (prɔnɔ̃) *m*, pronoun. **pronominal, e†** (nɔminal) *a*, pronominal.

prononcer (prɔnɔ̃se) *v.t. & abs*, to pronounce; utter; speak; mention; deliver (*speech*); pass (*sentence*). **se** ~, to declare oneself; be pronounced (*letter, syllable*). **prononciation** (sjasjɔ̃) *f*, delivery; passing; pronunciation.

pronostic (prɔnɔstik) *m*, prognostic[ation], forecast; selection (*betting*); omen. **pronostiquer** (ke) *v.t*, to prognosticate, forecast.

propagande (prɔpagã:d) *f*, propaganda; advertising.

propager (prɔpaʒe) *v.t*, to propagate, spread.

propension (prɔpãsjɔ̃) *f*, propensity.

prophète, étesse (prɔfɛt, etɛs) *n*, prophet, ess, seer. **prophétie** (fesi) *f*, prophecy. **prophétique†** (tik) *a*, prophetic(al). **prophétiser** (ze) *v.t*, to prophesy.

propice (prɔpis) *a*, propitious, auspicious, lucky.

propitiation (prɔpisjasjɔ̃) *f*, propitiation. **propitiatoire** (twa:r) *m*, mercy seat.

proportion (prɔpɔrsjɔ̃) *f*, proportion, ratio, percentage. **proportionnel, le†** (ɔnɛl) *a*, proportional. **proportionner** (ɔne) *v.t*, to proportion.

propos (prɔpo) *m*, purpose; subject, matter; remark, (*pl.*) talk. ~ *de couloir, pl*, lobbying. **à** ~, *a. & ad*, to the point, apropos, opportune(ly); seasonable, -bly; apposite(ly); pertinent(ly); apt-(ly); by the way. **à** ~ **de**, *pr*, with regard to, about. *à tout* ~, at every turn. *de* ~ *délibéré*, deliberately, purposely. **proposer** (ze) *v.t*, to propose; move; propound; offer; put forward; recommend. **se** ~, to offer oneself; purpose, mean. **proposition** (zisjɔ̃) *f*, proposal, proposition; motion; clause (*Gram.*).

propre† (prɔpr) *a*, clean, neat;

proper; peculiar; inherent; literal; own; appropriate, fit, suited. *un ~ à rien*, a good-for-nothing, a ne'er-do-well. ¶ *m*, characteristic, property; literal sense (*word*).
propret, te (prɛ, ɛt) *a*, neat, tidy.
propreté (prɑte) *f*, cleanliness; neatness, tidiness.
propriétaire (prɔprietɛːr) *n*, proprietor, owner; landlord, -lady. **propriété** (te) *f*, ownership; property, estate, holding; rights; propriety. ~ *[littéraire]*, copyright.
propulseur (prɔpylsœːr) *m*, propeller. **propulsion** (sjɔ̃) *f*, propulsion.
prorata (prɔrata) *m: au ~ de, pr*, in proportion to, pro rata to.
proroger (prɔrɔʒe) *v.t*, to prorogue; extend.
prosaïque† (prɔzaik) *a*, prosaic.
prosateur (prɔzatœːr) *m*, prose writer.
proscrire (prɔskriːr) *v.t.ir*, to proscribe, outlaw, banish; do away with. **proscrit, e** (skri, it) *n*, outlaw.
prose (proːz) *f*, prose.
prosélyte (prɔzelit) *n*, proselyte.
prosodie (prɔzɔdi) *f*, prosody.
prospecter (prɔspɛkte) *v.t*, to prospect (*Min.*). **prospecteur** (tœːr) *m*, prospector. **prospection** (sjɔ̃) *f*, prospecting.
prospectus (prɔspɛktyːs) *m*, prospectus; handbill.
prospère (prɔspɛːr) *a*, prosperous, thriving; favorable, kind. **prospérer** (pere) *v.i*, to prosper, thrive. **prospérité** (rite) *f*, prosperity.
prostate (prɔstat) *f*, prostate [gland].
prosternation (prɔstɛrnasjɔ̃) *f*, prostration; (*pl.*) bowing & scraping. **prosterné, e** (ne) *p.a*, prostrate, prone. **prosterner** (ne) *v.t*, to prostrate. *se ~*, to bow down (*before, etc.*)
prostituer (prɔstitɥe) *v.t*, to prostitute.
prostration (prɔstrasjɔ̃) *f*, prostration, break down. **prostré, e** (tre) *a*, prostrate[d].
protagoniste (prɔtagɔnist) *m*, protagonist.
protecteur, trice (prɔtɛktœːr,

tris) *n*, protector; patron, ess; (*m.*) protector, shield, guard. ¶ *a*, protective; patronizing. **protection** (sjɔ̃) *f*, protection; patronage. **protectionniste** (ɔnist) *m. & att*, protectionist. **protectorat** (tɔra) *m*, protectorate.
protégé, e (teʒe) *n*, protégé, e. **protéger** (ʒe) *v.t*, to protect, shield, guard; patronize.
protestant, e (prɔtɛstɑ̃, ɑ̃ːt) *n. & a*, Protestant. **protestation** (tasjɔ̃) *f*, protest[ation]. **protester** (te) *v.t. & i*, to protest; vow. **protêt** (tɛ) *m*, protest (*bill of exchange*).
protocole (prɔtɔkɔl) *m*, protocol; etiquette.
prototype (prɔtɔtip) *m*, prototype.
protubérance (prɔtyberɑ̃ːs) *f*, protuberance.
proue (pru) *f*, prow; nose (*Avn.*).
prouesse (pruɛs) *f*, prowess, valor; feat.
prouver (pruve) *v.t*, to prove; show.
provenance (prɔvnɑ̃ːs) *f*, origin, provenance; (*s. & pl.*) produce.
provende (prɔvɑ̃ːd) *f*, provender, fodder.
provenir (prɔvniːr) *v.i.ir*, to proceed, come, arise.
proverbe (prɔvɛrb) *m*, proverb. **proverbial, e†** (bjal) *a*, proverbial.
providence (prɔvidɑ̃ːs) *f*, providence; godsend; good angel. **providentiel, le†** (dɑ̃sjɛl) *a*, providential.
province (prɔvɛ̃ːs) *f*, province; provinces, country. **provincial, e** (vɛ̃sjal) *a*, provincial, country (*att.*).
proviseur (prɔvizœːr) *m*, headmaster. **provision** (zjɔ̃) *f*, provision, store, stock, supply; deposit; funds; cover, margin (*Fin.*); consideration (*law*); retainer (*law*). *~s de bouche*, provisions, food. *~s de guerre*, munitions. **provisionnel, le** (ɔnɛl) *a*, provisional. **provisoire†** (zwaːr) *a*, provisional, interim, pro tem; nisi (*decree*). **provisorat** (zɔra) *m*, headmastership.
provoquer (prɔvɔke) *v.t*, to provoke; challenge; incite, instigate;

induce. **provocateur** (katœːr) *m*, provoker; instigator; aggressor. *agent* ~, professional agitator. **provocation** (kasjɔ̃) *f*, provocation.

proximité (prɔksimite) *f*, proximity, nearness, propinquity, vicinity. ~ *du sang*, near relationship.

prude (pryd) *a*, prudish. ¶ *f*, prude.

prudemment (prydamɑ̃) *ad*, prudently. **prudence** (dɑ̃ːs) *f*, prudence, discretion; wisdom. **prudent, e** (dɑ̃, ɑ̃ːt) *a*, prudent.

pruderie (prydri) *f*, prudery, prudishness.

prud'homme (prydɔm) *m*, man of experience and integrity; member of conciliation board. **prud'hommesque** (mɛsk) *a*, pompous & sententiously dull.

prune (pryn) *f*, plum. **pruneau** (no) *m*, prune. **prunelaie** (nlɛ) *f*, plum orchard. **prunelle** (nɛl) *f*, sloe; pupil, apple (*eye*). [*liqueur de*] ~, sloe gin. **prunellier** (lje) *m*, blackthorn, sloe tree. **prunier** (nje) *m*, plum [tree]. ~ *de damas*, damson [tree].

prurit (pryrit) *m*, pruritus, itching.

Prusse (la) (prys), Prussia. **prussien, ne** (sjɛ̃, ɛn) *a*. & P~, *n*, Prussian. **prussique** (sik) *a*, prussic.

psalmiste (psalmist) *m*, psalmist. **psalmodie** (mɔdi) *f*, psalmody; singsong. **psalmodier** (dje) *v.i.* & *t*, to intone, chant; drone. **psaume** (psoːm) *m*, psalm. **psautier** (psotje) *m*, psalter.

pseudonyme (psødɔnim) *m*, pseudonym.

psychanalyse (psikanaliːz) *f*, psychoanalysis. **psyché** (ʃe) *f*, cheval glass, full-length mirror. **psychiatre** (kjaːtr) *m*, psychiatrist. **psychique** (ʃik) *a*, psychic(al). **psychologie** (kɔlɔʒi) *f*, psychology. **psychologique** (ʒik) *a*, psychological. **psychologue** (lɔg) *m*, psychologist. **psychose** (koːz) *f*, psychosis. ~ *traumatique* (tromatik), shell shock.

ptomaïne (ptɔmain) *f*, ptomaine.

puant, e (pyɑ̃, ɑ̃ːt) *a*, stinking;

foul. **puanteur** (ɑ̃tœːr) *f*, stink, stench.

puberté (pybɛrte) *f*, puberty.

public, ique† (pyblik) *a*, public; common; national (*debt*); civil (*service*). ¶ *m*, public. **publicain** (kɛ̃) *m*, publican (*Bible*); extortioner. **publication** (kasjɔ̃) *f*, publication; publishing; issue. **publiciste** (sist) *m*, publicist; advertising man. **publicité** (te) *f*, publicity, advertising. ~*sur les nuages*, sky writing. **publier** (e) *v.t*, to publish; proclaim; issue.

puce (pys) *f*, flea. ¶ *a*, puce. **pucelle** (pysɛl) *f*, maid[en], virgin. **puceron** (pysrɔ̃) *m*, green fly.

pudding (pudiɲ) *m*, pudding. **puddler** (pydle) *v.t*, to puddle (*iron*).

pudeur (pydœːr) *f*, modesty, decency, shame. **pudibond, e** (dibɔ̃, ɔ̃ːd) *a*, prudish. **pudique**† (dik) *a*, chaste, modest.

puer (pɥe) *v.i*, to stink, smell; (*v.t.*) to stink of, smell of.

puériculture (pɥerikyltyːr) *f*, rearing of children. ~ *sociale*, child welfare. **puéril, e**† (ril) *a*, puerile, childish. **puérilité** (lite) *f*, puerility, childishness.

pugilat (pyʒila) *m*, pugilism; set-to. **pugiliste** (list) *m*, pugilist.

pugnace (pygnas) *a*, pugnacious.

puîné, e (pɥine) *a*. & *n*, younger (brother, sister).

puis (pɥi) *ad*, then, afterwards, next; besides.

puisard (pɥizaːr) *m*, sink, sump. **puisatier** (zatje) *m*, well-digger. **puiser** (ze) *v.t*. & *i*, to draw, derive.

puisque, puisqu' (pɥisk[ə]) *c*, since, as, seeing that.

puissamment (pɥisamɑ̃) *ad*, powerfully, mightily. **puissance** (sɑ̃ːs) *f*, power; might; strength, force; authority, sway, ~ *lumineuse en bougies*, candlepower. **puissant, e** (sɑ̃, ɑ̃ːt) *a*, powerful; mighty; strong; potent; weighty. *les puissants*, the mighty ones.

puits (pɥi) *m*, well, hole; shaft (*Min.*); cockpit (*Avn.*); fount (*fig.*).

pulluler (pyllyle) *v.i*, to pullulate, swarm.

pulmonaire (pylmɔnɛːr) *a*, pulmonary.

pulpe (pylp) *f*, pulp. **pulper** (pe) *v.t*, to pulp.

pulsation (pylsasjɔ̃) *f*, pulsation, throb[bing].

pulvériser (pylverize) *v.t*, to pulverize, powder; spray. **pulvérulent, e** (rylã, ã:t) *a*, powdery.

puma (pyma) *m*, puma, cougar.

punais, e (pynɛ, ɛ:z) *a*, foulbreathed.

punaise (pynɛːz) *f*, bug; thumbtack.

punch (pɔ̃:ʃ) *m*, punch (*drink*).

punir (pyniːr) *v.t*, to punish; avenge. **punissable** (nisabl) *a*, punishable. **punition** (sjɔ̃) *f*, punishment.

pupille (pypil) *n*, ward; pupil. ¶ *f*, pupil (*eye*).

pupitre (pypitr) *m*, desk; stand (*music*).

pur, e† (py:r) *a*, pure; unalloyed; plain; mere; sheer; clear; neat (*unwatered*).

purée (pyre) *f*, mash; [thick] soup. ~ *de pommes de terre, de navets,* mashed potatoes, turnips.

pureté (pyrte) *f*, purity; clearness (*sky*).

purgatif, ive (pyrgatif, iːv) *a*. & *m*, purgative. **purgation** (sjɔ̃) *f*, purging; purge. **purgatoire** (twaːr) *m*, purgatory. **purger** (ʒe) *v.t*, to purge, cleanse, clear; redeem (*mortgage*).

purifier (pyrifje) *v.t*, to purify, cleanse. **puriste** (rist) *n*, purist.

puritain, e (pyritɛ̃, ɛn) *n*, Puritan. ¶ *a*, Puritan; puritanic(al).

purpurin, e (pyrpyrɛ̃, in) *a*, purplish.

purulent, e (pyrylã, ã:t) *a*, purulent, mattery. **pus** (py) *m*, pus, matter.

pusillanime (pyzillanim) *a*, pusillanimous.

pustule (pystyl) *f*, pustule, pimple.

putatif, ive (pytatif, iːv) *a*, putative, reputed.

putois (pytwa) *m*, polecat.

putréfaction (pytrefaksjɔ̃) *f*, putrefaction. **putréfier** (fje) *v.t*, to putrefy. **putride** (trid) *a*, putrid.

puy (pɥi) *m*, mountain, peak.

pygmée (pigme) *m*, pygmy.

pyjama (piʒama) *m*, pajamas.

pylône (piloːn) *m*, pylon, tower.

pyorrhée (pyɔre) *f*, pyorrhea.

pyramide (piramid) *f*, pyramid.

Pyrénées (les) (pirene) *f.pl*, the Pyrenees.

pyrite (pirit) *f*, pyrites.

pyrogravure (pirɔgravyːr) *f*, poker work.

pyrotechnie (pirɔtɛkni) *f*, pyrotechnics.

python (pitɔ̃) *m*, python.

Q

quadrangulaire (kwadrãgylɛːr) *a*, quadrangular.

quadrant (kwadrã) *m*, quadrant (*Math.*).

quadrupède (kwadrypɛd) *a*, quadruped(al), four-footed. ¶ *m*, quadruped.

quadruple (kwadrypl) *a*. & *m*, quadruple, fourfold. ~ *croche, f*, semi- *or* hemi-demisemiquaver.

quai (ke) *m*, quay, wharf; embankment (*river*); platform (*Rly*).

quaiche (kɛʃ) *f*, ketch.

qualifier (kalifje) *v.t*, to qualify; call, style; describe. **qualité** (te) *f*, quality; property; qualification, profession; capacity. ~ *d'amateur,* amateur status.

quand (kã) *c*. & *ad*, when; [al]though, even if. ~ *même,* all the same, notwithstanding, nevertheless.

quant à (kãta) *pr*, as for, as to, as regards, for. **quant-à-moi, quant-à-soi,** *m*, dignity, reserve, stand-offishness.

quantième (kãtjɛm) *m*, day of the month, date.

quantité (kãtite) *f*, quantity; amount; lots, a lot. ~ *de pluie* [*tombée*], rainfall.

quantum (kwãtom) *m*, quantum.

quarantaine (karãtɛn) *f*, [about] forty; quarantine; Lent. *mettre en* ~, to quarantine (*ship*); send (*pers.*) to Coventry. **quarante** (rãːt) *a*, forty. ¶ *m*, forty; 40th. **quarantième** (rãtjɛm) *a*. & *n*, fortieth.

quart (kaːr) *m*, quarter, fourth [part]; ¼ liter; watch (*Naut.*).

~ *d'heure*, quarter of an hour.
~ *de cercle*, quadrant (*Surv. instrument*). ~ [*de vent*], point
[of the compass]. **quarte** (kart)
f, fourth (*Mus.*).

quarteron, ne (kartərɔ̃, ɔn) *n*,
quadroon.

quartier (kartje) *m*, quarter;
portion, lump; haunch (*meat*);
gammon (*bacon*); ward, district; neighborhood; quarters. ~
général, headquarters.

quartz (kwarts) *m*, quartz.

quasi (kɑzi) *ad*, almost, quasi.
~ *aveugle*, almost blind, purblind. ~ -*délit*, *m*, quasi-delict,
technical offense. **Quasimodo**
(kazimɔdo) *f*, Low Sunday.

quassia (kwasja) *m*, quassia
(*bark*). **quassier** (sje) *m*, quassia (*tree*).

quatorze (katɔrz) *a. & m*, fourteen; 14th. **quatorzième**† (zjɛm)
a. & n, fourteenth.

quatrain (katrɛ̃) *m*, quatrain.

quatre (katr) *a. & m*, four; 4th.
lac des Q~-Cantons, Lake of
Lucerne. ~ *jumeaux*, quadruplets. *à* ~ *pattes*, on all fours.
~-*vingt-dix* (trəvɛ̃di[s]) *a. & m*,
ninety. ~ -*vingt-onze* (vɛ̃ɔ̃:z),
91. ~-*vingt-dixième* (zjɛm) *a.
& n*, ninetieth. ~-*vingtième*
(tjɛm) *a. & n*, eightieth. ~-*vingts*
& ~-*vingt*, *a. & m*, eighty. ~-
vingt-un (vɛ̃œ̃), 81. **quatrième**†
(triɛm) *a. & n*, fourth.

quatuor (kwatɥɔ:r) *m*, quartet.

que, qu' (kə, k) *c. & ad*, that;
than; as; whether; how; but,
only; lest; let, may. ¶ *pn*, whom;
which; that; what. *qu'est-ce que?*
(kɛskə) & *qu'est-ce qui* (ki)?
what?

quel, le (kɛl) *a*, what; what a;
which; who. ~ *que*, whatever;
whoever.

quelconque (kɛlkɔ̃:k) *a*, any;
some.

quelque (kɛlk[ə]) *a*, some, any;
a few, ~ *chose*, *m*, something;
anything. ~*fois*, *ad*, sometimes.
~ *part*, *ad*, somewhere.

quelqu'un, quelqu'une (kɛlkœ̃, kyn) *pn*, somebody, someone, one, anybody, anyone. *quelques-uns, unes* (kəzœ̃, yn) *pl*,
some [people], a few.

quémander (kemɑ̃de) *v.i*, to beg;
(*v.t.*) to beg for, solicit.

qu'en-dira-t-on (le) (kɑ̃dira-tɔ̃) *m*, what people may say.

quenouille (kənu:j) *f*, distaff;
bedpost.

querelle (kərɛl) *f*, quarrel, row.
~ *d'ivrognes*, drunken brawl.
quereller (le) *v.t*, to quarrel
with; scold nag. se ~, to quarrel, wrangle. **querelleur, euse**
(lœ:r, ø:z) *n*, quarreler, wrangler; (*att.*) quarrelsome.

question (kɛstjɔ̃) *f*, question;
query; point, matter, issue. ~
d'intérêt secondaire, side issue.
questionnaire (ɔnɛ:r) *m*, list of
questions. **questionner** (ne) *v.t*,
to question.

quête (kɛ:t) *f*, quest, search; collection, offertory. **quêter** (kɛte)
v.t, to seek for; collect (*alms*).

queue (kø) *f*, tail; brush (*fox*);
pigtail; stem; stalk; handle,
shank; cue (*Bil.*); train; rear;
queue, file. ~-*d'aronde* (darɔ̃:d)
f, dovetail. ~-*de-morue* (dmɔry)
ou ~-*de-pie* (dpi) *f*, [swallow]
tails (*dress coat*). **queuter** (køte)
v.i, to push the ball (*Bil.*).

qui (ki) *pn*, who; whom; which;
that. ~ *vive*? who goes there?

quiconque (kikɔ̃:k) *pn*, who[so]-
ever.

quiétude (kɥietyd) *f*, quietude.

quignon (kiɲɔ̃) *m*, [c]hunk,
hunch.

quille (ki:j) *f*, skittle, ninepin;
keel. **quillier** (kije) *m*, skittle
alley.

quincaillerie (kɛ̃kajri) *f*, hardware. **quincaillier** (je) *m*, hardware man.

quinine (kinin) *f*, quinine.

quinquennal, e (kɥɛ̃kɛnnal) *a*,
quinquennial; five-year (*plan*).

quinquina (kɛ̃kina) *m*, Peruvian
bark.

quintal [**métrique**] (kɛ̃tal) *m*,
[metric] quintal = 100 kilos.

quinte (kɛ̃:t) *f*, quint; fifth
(*Mus.*); caprice, crotchet. ~ [*de
toux*], fit of coughing.

quintessence (kɛ̃tɛsɑ̃:s) *f*, quintessence.

quintette (kɥɛ̃tɛt) *f*, quintet[te].

quinteux, euse (kɛ̃tø, ø:z) *a*,
crotchety; fitful.

quinzaine (kɛ̃zɛn) *f*, [about] fifteen; fortnight. **quinze** (kɛ̃:z) *a.* & *m*, fifteen; 15th. ~ *jours*, fortnight. **quinzième**† (kɛ̃zjɛm) *a.* & *n*, fifteenth.

quiproquo (kiprɔko) *m*, mistake, misunderstanding (*mistaking one for another*).

quittance (kitɑ̃:s) *f*, receipt. **quittancer** (tɑ̃se) *v.t*, to r. **quitte** (kit) *a*, quit, rid, free. ~ *à* ~, *ad*, quits. ~ *ou double*, double or quits. *nous sommes* ~*s*, we're even. **quitter** (te) *v.t.* & *i*, to leave, quit, vacate; give up; swerve from. *ne quittez pas!* hold on! hold the line! (*Teleph.*). **quitus** (kity:s) *m*, discharge.

qui-vive (kivi:v) *m*, challenge (*sentry's*); qui vive, look-out, alert.

quoi (kwa) *pn.* & *i*, what; which; that. ~ *qu'il en soit*, be that as it may. *de* ~, something; enough, the wherewithal.

quoique, quoiqu' (kwak[ə]) *c*, [al]though.

quolibet (kɔlibɛ) *m*, gibe; quibble.

quorum (kɔrɔm) *m*, quorum.

quote-part (kɔtpa:r) *f*, share, quota.

quotidien, ne (kɔtidjɛ̃, ɛn) *a*, daily; everyday. [**journal**] **quotidien**, *m*, daily [paper]. **quotidiennement** (ɛnmɑ̃) *ad*, daily.

quotient (kɔsjɑ̃) *m*, quotient.

quotité (kɔtite) *f*, quota, share.

R

rabâchage (rabɑʃa:ʒ) *m*, endless repetition. *il rabâche toujours les mêmes choses*, he is always harping on the same string.

rabais (rabɛ) *m*, allowance, rebate. *adjudication au* ~, award to the lowest bidder. **rabaisser** (se) *v.t*, to lower; disparage, belittle.

rabat (raba) *m*, beating (*for game*). ~-**joie**, *m*, killjoy. **rabatteur, euse** (tœ:r ø:z) *n*, tout; ~ (*m.*) beater. **rabattre** (tr) *v.t.ir*, to beat down, bring d., turn d., press d., lower; bate; take off;

beat up (*hunting*). se ~, to turn off, change; come down.

rabbin (rabɛ̃) *m*, rabbi.

râble (rɑ:bl) *m*, back; saddle (hare). **râblé** (ble) *a*, strong, sturdy, husky.

rabot (rabo) *m*, plane (*tool*). **raboter** (bɔte) *v.t*, to plane; polish (*fig.*). **raboteux, euse** (tø, ø:z) *a*, rough, rugged; knotty.

rabougrir (rabugri:r) *v.t*, to stunt (*growth*).

rabouter (rabute) *ou* **raboutir** (ti:r) *v.t*, to join [up].

rabrouer (rabrue) *v.t*, to rebuff, snub; rebuke.

racaille (rakɑ:j) *f*, rabble, riffraff.

raccommodage (rakɔmɔda:ʒ) *m*, mending, repairing. **raccommodement** (dmɑ̃) *m*, reconciliation. **raccommoder** (de) *v.t*, to mend, repair; reconcile. se~, to make it up. **raccommodeur, euse** (dœ:r, ø:z) *n*, mender, repairer.

raccord (rakɔ:r) *m*, join; joint; connection, union, coupling. **raccorder** (kɔrde) *v.t*, to join, connect, couple, link up.

raccourci (rakursi) *m*, abridgement; epitome; shortcut; foreshortening. **raccourcir** (si:r) *v.t*, to shorten; abridge, curtail; foreshorten. [se] ~, to draw in (*days*).

raccroc (rakro) *m*, fluke, lucky stroke. **raccrocher** (krɔʃe) *v.t*, to hook up, hang up, replace. se ~, to clutch, catch; cling.

race (ras) *f*, race, descent, ancestry; strain, blood, breed, stock, tribe, species. *de* ~, thoroughbred. **racé, e** (se) *a*, thoroughbred.

rachat (raʃa) *m*, repurchase; redemption; ransom; surrender (*Insce*). **racheter** (ʃte) *v.t*, to repurchase, buy back; redeem; surrender; ransom; atone for.

rachitisme (raʃitism) *m*, rachitis, rickets.

racine (rasin) *f*, root; root, fang (*of tooth*); [silkworm] gut (*Fish.*). ~ *d'iris*, orris root. ~ *pivotante*, taproot.

raclée (rɑkle) *f*, thrashing, hiding. **racler** (kle) *v.t*, to scrape; rake; rasp; strike (*measure*). **ra-**

cloir (klwa:r) *m*, scraper; squee-gee. **racloire** (klwa:r) *f*, strickle, strike (*grain*). **raclure** (kly:r) *f*, scrapings.

racoler (rakɔle) *v.t*, to recruit; tout for.

racontar (rakɔ̃ta:r) *m*, gossip, scandal. **raconter** (te) *v.t*, to re-late, recount, narrate, tell; (*abs.*) to tell a story (*well, etc.*). **en ~,** to tell tall tales.

racornir (rakɔrni:r) *v.t*, to harden; shrivel.

rade (rad) *f*, roadstead, roads (*Naut.*).

radeau (rado) *m*, raft.

radial, e (radjal) *a*, radial. **radia-teur** (tœ:r) *m*, radiator; fire (*gas, Elec.*). **radiation** (sjɔ̃) *f*, striking out; s. off; radiation.

radical, e† (radikal) *a*. & *m*, radical; root.

radier (radje) *v.t*, to strike out; s. off.

radieux, euse (radjø, ø:z) *a*, radiant, beaming.

radio (radjo) *f*, radio; cablegram; X-ray; radio operator.

radioactif, ive (radjoaktif, i:v) *a*, radioactive. **radiodiffuser** (ɔdifyze) *v.t*, to broadcast. **radio-diffusion** (zjɔ̃) *f*, broadcasting. **radiogramme** (gram) *m*, radio-gram. **radiographie** (fi) *f*, radiog-raphy. **radiotélégraphie** (tele-grafi) *f*, radiotelegraphy.

radis (radi) *m*, radish.

radium (radjɔm) *m*, radium.

radius (radjy:s) *m*, radius (*Anat.*).

radoter (radɔte) *v.i*, to drivel (*talk*), dote. **radoteur, euse** (tœ:r, ø:z) *n*, dotard.

radouber (radube) *v.t*, to repair (*ship*).

radoucir (radusi:r) *v.t*, to soften; make milder.

rafale (rafal) *f*, squall, gust. **~ de pluie,** cloudburst.

raffermir (rafɛrmi:r) *v.t*, to harden; strengthen.

raffinage (rafina:ʒ) *m*, refining. **raffiné, e** (ne) *p.a*, refined; subtle. **raffinement** (nmɑ̃) *m*, refinement, subtlety. **raffiner** (ne) *v.t*. & *abs*, to refine. **raffinerie** (nri) *f*, re-finery.

raffoler de (rafɔle), to be very fond of, dote on.

rafistoler (rafistɔle) *v.t*, to patch up.

rafle (rɑ:fl) *f*, stalk (*grape*); cob (*corn*); clean sweep; raid; round up; swag, loot. **rafler** (rɑfle) *v.t*, to carry off; round up. **~ le tout,** to sweep the board.

rafraîchir (rafreʃi:r) *v.t*. & *abs*. & *i*, to cool, refresh, freshen; revive; trim (*hair, grass*). **rafraî-chissements** (ʃismɑ̃) *m.pl*, [light] refreshments.

ragaillardir (ragajardi:r) *v.t*, to cheer up.

rage (ra:ʒ) *f*, rage; rabies, mad-ness; mania. **~ de dents,** raging toothache. **rager** (raʒe) *v.i*, to rage. **rageur, euse**† (ʒœ:r, ø:z) *a*. & *n*, passionate (person), spit-fire.

ragot (rago) *m*, gossip, scandal.

ragoût (ragu) *m*, stew. **~ de mouton,** lamb stew. **ragoûtant, e** (tɑ̃, ɑ̃:t) *a*, tempting.

ragréer (ragree) *v.t*, to clean up; do up (*repair house, etc.*).

rai (rɛ) *m*, ray; spoke.

raid (rɛd) *m*, raid; endurance test.

raide (rɛd) *a*, stiff; stark; tight, taut, tense; steep. **raideur** (dœ:r) *f*, stiffness. **raidir** (di:r) *v.t*, to stiffen; tighten.

raie (rɛ) *f*, line, stroke; streak; stripe; ridge (*Agric.*); part (*hair*); ray, skate (*fish*).

raifort (rɛfɔ:r) *m*, horseradish.

rail (rɑ:j) *m*, rail (*Rly. metal or transport*). **~ de courant,** live rail.

railler (rɑje) *v.t*. & *abs*, to jeer at, laugh at; joke. **raillerie** (jri) *f*, raillery, banter, joke, jesting.

rainure (rɛny:r) *f*, groove, slot. **~ de clavette,** keyway.

raire (rɛ:r) *v.i.ir*, to troat, bell.

raisin (rɛzɛ̃) *m*, grape, grapes. **~s de Corinthe,** currants (*dried*). **~ de serres,** hothouse grapes. **~s de Smyrne,** sultanas. **~ de treille,** dessert grapes. **~ de vigne,** wine grapes. **~s secs,** raisins. **~s secs muscats,** muscatels.

raison (rɛzɔ̃) *f*, reason, motive, ground; sanity, senses; sense; sat-isfaction; ratio, rate. **~ [sociale],** firm [name], trade name. **avoir ~,** to be right. **raisonnable**† (zɔnabl) *a*, reasonable; rational; fair, adequate. **raisonnement** (nmɑ̃) *m*, reasoning; argument. **raisonner** (ne) *v.i*, to reason; argue; (*v.t.*) to consider; reason with. **raisonneur, euse** (nœ:r, ∅:z) *n*, reasoner, arguer; (*att.*) reasoning, argumentative.

rajeunir (raʒœni:r) *v.t*, to rejuvenate; make look younger; renovate.

rajuster (raʒyste) *v.t*, to readjust; put straight; refit.

râle (rɑ:l) *m*, rail (*bird*); rattle (*in throat*). **râler** (le) *v.i*, to rattle (*throat*); gasp one's last; grumble.

ralentir (ralɑ̃ti:r) *v.t. & i*, to slacken, slow down.

rallier (ralje) *v.t*, to rally; rejoin.

rallonge (ralɔ̃:ʒ) *f*, lengthening piece; leaf (*table*). **rallonger** (lɔ̃ʒe) *v.t*, to lengthen.

rallumer (ralyme) *v.t*, to relight, rekindle.

rallye (rali) *m*, race meeting, rally. ∼-*paper* (pepœ:r) *m*, paper chase, hare & hounds.

ramage (ramaːʒ) *m*, floral design; song (*of birds*).

ramas (ramɑ *m*, heap.

ramasse (ramɑs) *f*, sledge (*alpine*). ∼-*couverts*, *m*, plate basket. ∼-*miettes*, *m*, crumb tray. ∼-*miettes automatique*, crumb sweeper. **ramassé, e** (se) *p.a*, thickset, stocky. **ramasser** (se) *v.t*, to gather, collect; pick up. **ramasseur, euse** (sœːr, ∅:z) *n*, collector, gatherer. **ramassis** (si) *m*, heap; set.

rame (ram) *f*, stick (*Hort.*); oar; ream (*500 sheets*); train (*of cars, etc.*). ∼ *directe*, through portion (*Rly.*).

rameau (ramo) *m*, branch; bough; palm (*Eccl.*). **ramée** (me) *f*, greenwood, arbor.

ramener (ramne) *v.t*, to bring back; reduce; restore; reset.

ramer (rame) *v.t*, to stick (*Hort.*); (*v.i.*) to row, pull (*oar*). ∼ *à rebours*, to back water. **rameur, euse** (mœːr, ∅:z) *n*, rower, oarsman, -woman.

ramier (ramje) *m*, ring dove, wood pigeon.

ramification (ramifikasjɔ̃) *f*, ramification. **se ramifier** (fje)

v.pr, to ramify. **ramilles** (miːj) *f.pl*, twigs.

ramolli, e(ramɔli) *p.a*, dull-witted. **ramollir** (liːr) *v.t*, to soften; enervate.

ramoner (ramɔne) *v.t*, to sweep (*chimney*). **ramoneur** (nœːr) *m*, chimney sweep[er].

rampant, e (rɑ̃pɑ̃, ɑ̃:t) *a*, rampant; creeping; crawling; reptile; groveling. **rampe** (rɑ̃:p) *f*, rise, slope; upgrade; rack; banisters, handrail; footlights. **ramper** (rɑ̃pe) *v.i*, to creep, crawl; cringe, truckle, fawn, grovel.

ramure (ramyːr) *f*, branches; antlers.

rancart (mettre au) (rɑ̃kaːr), to cast aside.

rance (rɑ̃:s) *a*, rancid, rank. **rancir** (rɑ̃siːr) *v.i*, to become rancid.

rancœur (rɑ̃kœːr) *f*, rancor, bitterness.

rançon (rɑ̃sɔ̃) *f*, ransom. **rançonner** (sɔne) *v.t*, to ransom; fleece.

rancune (rɑ̃kyn) *f*, rancor, spite; grudge. **rancunier, ère** (nje, ɛ:r) *a*, rancorous, spiteful.

randonnée (rɑ̃dɔne) *f*, circuit; trip, run.

rang (rɑ̃) *m*, row, line; tier; rank, station, place; rate, class. **rangé, e** (ʒe) *p.a*, tidy; steady (*man*); pitched (*battle*). **rangée** (ʒe) *f*, row, line; tier; array. **ranger** (ʒe) *v.t*, to arrange, marshal, array; tidy, put away; rank, range. **se ∼**, to draw up; fall in, side; stand aside; sober down; veer. *rangés comme des harengs en caque*, packed like sardines (*people*).

ranimer (ranime) *v.t*, to revive; stir up; cheer.

rapace (rapas) *a*, rapacious.

rapatrier (rapatrie) *v.t*, to repatriate, send home.

râpe (rɑ:p) *f*, rasp; grater (*nutmeg, etc.*). **râpé, e** (rɑpe) *p.a*, grated; threadbare, shabby. **râper** (pe) *v.t*, to rasp; grate; wear threadbare.

rapetasser (raptase) *v.t*, to patch, cobble.

rapetisser (raptise) *v.t. & i*, to shorten; dwarf.

rapide† (rapid) *a*, rapid, fast,

swift; speedy; cursory; steep. ¶ *m*, rapid (*river*); fast train, express.

rapiécer (rapjese) *v.t*, to piece, patch.

rapin (rapɛ̃) *m*, art student; dauber.

rapine (rapin) *f*, rapine. **rapiner** (ne) *v.t. & i*, to pillage.

rappareiller (rapareje) & **rapparier** (rje) *v.t*, to match, pair.

rappel (rapɛl) *m*, recall; call[ing]; reminder; repeal. **rappeler** (ple) *v.t*, to recall; call (*to order, etc.*); summon; remind; r. of; remember; repeal. **se ~**, to recollect, remember.

rapport (rapoːr) *m*, yield, return; report, account, statement; tale; relation, connection; regard; (*pl.*) terms; (*pl.*) intercourse; ratio. **~s probables**, betting forecast. **rapporter** (pɔrte) *v.t. & abs*, to bring back; retrieve (*game*); yield; get; add; inset; report, state; tell tales; refer, ascribe; revoke. **se ~**, to agree, tally; refer, relate. **rapporteur, euse** (tœːr, øːz) *n*, talebearer; (*m.*) protractor.

rapprendre (raprɑ̃ːdr) *v.t.ir*, to learn again.

rapprocher (raprɔʃe) *v.t*, to bring nearer; b. together; reconcile; compare.

rapt (rapt) *m*, abduction; kidnapping.

raquette (rakɛt) *f*, racket; battledore. **~ à neige**, snowshoe.

rare (rɑːr) *a*, rare; scarce; uncommon; unusual; sparse, thin. **raréfier** (rarefje) *v.t*, to rarefy. **rarement** (rarmɑ̃) *ad*, rarely, seldom. **rareté** (te) *f*, rarity; scarcity; curiosity.

ras, e (rɑ, ɑːz) *a*, close-cropped; c.-shaven; bare, naked, open. *à* (ou *au*) ras de, level with, flush with. **rasade** (rɑzad) *f*, bumper (*brimful glass*).

raser (rɑze) *v.t*, to shave; raze; graze, brush, skim. **rasoir** (zwaːr) *m*, razor.

rassasier (rasazje) *v.t*, to satisfy; satiate, sate, surfeit, cloy, glut.

rassembler (rasɑ̃ble) *v.t*, to reassemble; assemble, muster, collect.

rasseoir (raswaːr) *v.t.ir*, to reseat; settle. **se ~**, to sit down again.

rasséréner (se) (raserene) *v.pr*, to clear [up] (*weather*); calm.

rassis, e (rasi, iːz) *p.a*, settled, calm, staid, sedate, sane; stale (*bread*).

rassortir (rasɔrtiːr) *v.t*, to match; restock.

rassurer (rasyre) *v.t*, to reassure, cheer, hearten; strengthen.

rat, (ra) *m*, rat; ballet girl. *un ~ dan la tête*, a bee in one's bonnet. **~ de bibliothèque** bookworm (*pers.*). **~ de cave**, exciseman; taper (*coiled*). **~ des champs**, field mouse. **~ musqué**, muskrat, musquash.

ratatiné, e (ratatine) *p.a*, shriveled, shrunken; wizened.

rate (rat) *f*, spleen, milt (*Anat.*); she-rat.

râteau (rɑto) *m*, rake. **râteler** (tle) *v.t*, to rake up. **râtelier** (təlje) *m*, rack; denture.

raté (rate) *m*, misfire; failure; flop.

rater (rate) *v.i*, to misfire; miscarry, fail; (*v.t.*) to miss; fail in; fail to obtain.

ratier (ratje) *m*, ratter (*dog*). **ratière** (tjɛːr) *f*, rattrap.

ratifier (ratifje) *v.t*, to ratify, confirm.

ration (rasjɔ̃) *f*, ration, allowance.

rationalisme (rasjɔnalism) *m*, rationalism. **rationnel, le†** (nɛl) *a*, rational; pure (*mechanics*). **rationner** (rasjɔne) *v.t*, to ration; stint.

ratisser (ratise) *v.t*, to rake; scrape.

raton (ratɔ̃) *m*, young rat; darling. **~ laveur**, raccoon.

rattacher (rataʃe) *v.t*, to refasten; bind; connect.

rattraper (ratrape) *v.t*, to recapture; overtake, catch up; recover.

rature (ratyːr) *f*, erasure. **raturer** (tyre) *v.t*, to erase, scratch out.

rauque (roːk) *a*, hoarse, raucous, harsh.

ravage (ravaːʒ) *m. oft. pl*, ravage, havoc, devastation. **ravager** (vaʒe) *v.t*, to ravage, devastate, lay waste. *ravagé(e) [par les intempéries]*, weather-beaten.

ravaler (ravale) *v.t,* to swallow again; eat (*one's words*); disparage; rough-cast (*wall*). se ~, to lower oneself, stoop (*fig.*).

ravauder (ravode) *v.t. & abs,* to mend; darn.

rave (ra:v) *f,* rape, coleseed.

Ravenne (ravɛn) *f,* Ravenna.

ravigoter (ravigote) *v.t,* to revive, enliven.

ravilir (ravili:r) *v.t,* to degrade.

ravin (ravɛ̃) *m,* **ravine** (vin) *f,* ravine, gully. **raviner** (vine) *v.t,* to gully; furrow.

ravir (ravi:r) *v.t,* to ravish, carry off; delight, enrapture.

raviser (se) (ravize) *v.pr,* to change one's mind.

ravissant (ravisɑ̃) *a,* ravishing, delightful; predatory; ravenous. **ravissement** (mɑ̃) *m,* rapture; kidnapping; rape. **ravisseur** (œ:r) *m,* ravisher; kidnapper.

ravitailler (ravitaje) *v.t,* to [re]-victual.

raviver (ravive) *v.t,* to revive.

ravoir (ravwa:r) *v.t,* to get (*something*) back.

rayer (rɛje) *v.t,* to scratch, score; rule; stripe, streak; rifle; strike out, delete.

ray-grass (rɛgra:s) *m,* rye grass.

rayon (rejɔ̃) *m,* ray, beam; gleam; radius; spoke; comb (*honey*); drill, furrow, row; shelf; department; rayon, artificial silk. **rayonnant, e** (jɔnɑ̃, ɑ̃:t) *a,* radiant; beaming. **rayonnement** (nmɑ̃) *m,* radiation; radiance, effulgence. **rayonner** (ne) *v.i,* to radiate, beam, shine; (*v.t.*) to fit with shelves.

rayure (rɛjy:r) *f,* scratch, etc., as *rayer.*

raz de marée (ra) *m,* tide race, bore; tidal wave.

razzia (razja) *f,* raid, foray. **razzier** (zje) *v.t,* to raid.

ré (re) *m,* D (*Mus.*).

réactif (reaktif) *m,* reagent (*Chem.*). **réaction** (sjɔ̃) *f,* reaction. *avion à ~,* jet plane. **réactionnaire** (ɔnɛ:r) *a. & n,* reactionary. **réagir** (ʒi:r) *v.i,* to react.

réaliser (realize) *v.t,* to realize; make (*profit*); close (*bargain*). **réaliste** (list) *a. & n,* realist. **réalité** (te) *f,* reality.

réapparition (reaparisjɔ̃) *f,* reappearance.

réassurer (reasyre) *v.t,* to reinsure.

rébarbatif, ive (rebarbatif, i:v) *a,* grim; surly.

rebâtir (rəbɑti:r) *v.t,* to rebuild; reconstruct.

rebattre (rəbatr) *v.t.ir,* to beat again; reshuffle (*cards*); repeat. **rebattu, e** (ty) *p.a,* beaten (*track*); hackneyed.

rebelle (rəbɛl) *a,* rebellious; refractory. ¶ *n,* rebel. **se rebeller** (le) *v.pr,* to rebel. **rébellion** (rebɛljɔ̃) *f,* rebellion.

rebiffer (se) (rəbife) *v.pr,* to show temper.

rebondi, e (rəbɔ̃di) *a,* rounded, plump. **rebondir** (di:r) *v.i,* to rebound, bounce; crop up again. **rebondissement** (dismɑ̃) *m,* rebound; repercussion.

rebord (rəbɔ:r) *m,* edge, rim; hem; ledge; flange.

rebours (rəbu:r) *m,* wrong way; contrary, reverse. *à ~,* the wrong way; backward. *prendre à ~,* to misconstrue.

rebouteur, euse (rəbutœ:r, ø:z) *n,* bonesetter.

rebrousse-poil (à) (rəbruspwal) *ad,* against the nap, the wrong way. **rebrousser** (se) *v.t,* to rub the wrong way. ~ [*chemin*], to retrace one's steps.

rebuffade (rəbyfad) *f,* rebuff.

rébus (reby:s) *m,* picture puzzle; riddle.

rebut (rəby) *m,* waste, refuse, rubbish; dead letter (*Post.*); scum (*fig.*). **rebutant, e** (tɑ̃, ɑ̃:t) *a,* disheartening; repellent. **rebuter** (te) *v.t,* to rebuff, repulse; dishearten.

récalcitrant, e (rekalsitrɑ̃, ɑ̃:t) *a. & n,* recalcitrant; refractory.

récapituler (rekapityle) *v.t,* to recapitulate.

receler (rəsle) *v.t,* to conceal; harbor (*criminal*); receive (*stolen goods*). **receleur, euse** (slœ:r, ø:z) *n,* receiver, fence.

récemment (resamɑ̃) *ad,* recently, lately.

recensement (rəsɑ̃smɑ̃) *m,* census, return; counting (*votes*);

stocktaking. **recenser** (se) *v.t*, to take the census of; count.

récent, e (resã, ã:t) *a*, recent, late; fresh.

receper (rəsəpe) *v.t*, to cut back (*Hort.*).

récépissé (resepise) *m*, receipt. **réceptacle** (sɛptakl) *m*, receptacle; repository. **récepteur** (tœːr) *m*, receiver (*Teleph., etc.*). **réception** (sjɔ̃) *f*, receipt; reception; welcome; acceptance; party, at-home. **recette** (rəsɛt) *f*, receipts, takings; gate money; collectorship; recipe. **recevable** (səvabl) *a*, admissible. **receveur, euse** (vœːr, ø:z) *n*, collector (*taxes, etc.*); conductor (*bus*); (*f.*) attendant (*Theat.*). ~ **des postes**, postmaster, -mis·ress. **recevoir** (vwaːr) *v.t. & abs*, to receive; admit; get; meet with; accept; welcome; take in (*boarders*); be at home (*to visitors*). être reçu à, to pass (*exam*).

rechange (rəʃãːʒ) *m*, change, spare.

réchapper (reʃape) *v.i*, to escape; recover.

recharger (rəʃarʒe) *v.t*, to recharge; reload.

réchaud (reʃo) *m*, stove; ring (*gas*); heater; hot plate. **réchauffer** (ʃofe) *v.t*, to reheat, warm up; revive.

rêche (rɛʃ) *a*, rough, harsh.

recherche (rəʃɛrʃ) *f*, search, quest, pursuit; research, inquiry; prospecting; studied elegance. **recherché, e** (ʃe) *p.a*, sought after, in request; choice; studied; elaborate. **rechercher** (ʃe) *v.t*, to search for, seek.

rechigner (rəʃiɲe) *v.i*, to look sour. **en rechignant** (ɲã), with a bad grace.

rechute (rəʃyt) *f*, relapse, backsliding.

récidiver (residive) *v.i*, to relapse into crime. **récidiviste** (vist) *n*, person with previous convictions; old offender.

récif (resif) *m*, reef (*of rocks*).

récipiendaire (resipjãdɛːr) *n*, new member. **récipient** (pjã) *m*, receiver, vessel.

réciproque (resiprɔk) *a*, reciprocal, mutual; inverse; converse.

réciproquement (kmã) *ad*, reciprocally, etc; vice versa.

récit (resi) *m*, recital, account, narration, narrative; solo (*Mus.*). **récital** (tal) *m*, recital (*Mus.*). **récitatif** (tatif) *m*, recitative (*Mus.*). **récitation** (sjɔ̃) *f*, recitation. **réciter** (te) *v.t*, to recite; say (*lessons*).

réclamant, e (reklamã, ã:t) *n*, claimant. **réclamation** (masjɔ̃) *f*, claim; complaint, protest. **réclame** (klam) *f*, advertisement, blurb. **réclamer** (me) *v.i*, to complain, protest, object; (*v.t.*) to claim; crave; call for. ~ à grands cris, to clamor for.

reclus, e (rəkly, y:z) *n*, recluse. **réclusion** (reklyzjɔ̃) *f*, reclusion, seclusion; solitary imprisonment.

recoin (rəkwɛ̃) *m*, nook, recess.

récolte (rekɔlt) *f*, harvest[ing]; crop; vintaging; vintage; collection. **récolter** (te) *v.t*, to harvest; collect.

recommander (rəkɔmãde) *v.t*, to [re]commend; register (*mail*).

recommencer (rəkɔmãse) *v.t. & i*, to recommence; begin again.

récompense (rekɔ̃pãːs) *f*, recompense, reward; retribution, requital. **récompenser** (pãse) *v.t*, to recompense.

réconcilier (rekɔ̃silje) *v.t*, to reconcile.

reconduire (rəkɔ̃dɥiːr) *v.t.ir*, to escort; see home; show out.

réconfort (rekɔ̃fɔːr) *m*, comfort, consolation; stimulant. **réconforter** (fɔrte) *v.t*, to strengthen; comfort.

reconnaissable (rəkɔnɛsabl) *a*, recognizable. **reconnaissance** (sãːs) *f*, recognition; acknowledgment; gratitude, thankfulness; reconnaissance, exploration; pawn ticket. **reconnaissant, e** (sã, ã:t) *a*, grateful, thankful. **reconnaître** (nɛːtr) *v.t.ir*, to recognize; tell; sight (*land*); acknowledge; be grateful for; reconnoiter, explore.

reconquérir (rəkɔ̃keriːr) *v.t.ir*, to reconquer; regain.

reconstitution (rəkɔ̃stitysjɔ̃) *f*, reconstruction (*fig.*).

reconstruction (rəkɔ̃stryksjɔ̃)

f, rebuilding. **reconstruire** (strɥi:r) *v.t.ir*, to rebuild.

reconvention (rək5vãsj5) *f*, counterclaim.

record (rəkɔ:r) *m*, record (*sports*). **recorder** (kɔrde) *v.t*, to con, go over; restring. **recors** (kɔ:r) *m*, bailiff's man; minion (*of the law*).

recoupe (rəkup) *f*, middlings (*flour*); chips; clippings.

recourber (rəkurbe) *v.t*, to bend, crook.

recourir (rəkuri:r) *v.i.ir*, to run again; have recourse, resort. **recours** (ku:r) *m*, recourse, resort; appeal; remedy (*law*).

recouvrement (rəkuvrəmã) *m*, recovery; cover[ing]; [over]lap; (*pl.*) book debts. **recouvrer** (vre) *v.t*, to recover, regain.

recouvrir (rəkuvri:r) *v.t.ir*, to re-cover; cover.

récréation (rekreasj5) *f*, recre-ation; playtime.

récréer (rekree) *v.t*, to recreate, divert, entertain; enliven, refresh; re-create.

récrier (se) (rekrie) *v.pr*, to cry out, exclaim.

récrimination (rekriminasj5) *f*, recrimination. **récriminer** (ne) *v.i*, to recriminate; countercharge; retort.

récrire (rekri:r) *v.t.ir*, to re-write; write again; reply.

recroqueviller (se) (rəkrɔkvije) *v.pr*, to shrivel.

recrudescence (rəkrydɛsã:s) *f*, recrudescence.

recrue (rəcry) *f*, recruit. **recruter** (te) *v.t*, to recruit.

recta (rɛkta) *ad*, on the nail, punctually.

rectangle (rɛktã:gl) *a*, right-angled. ¶ *m*, rectangle. ~ [*de table*], doily. **rectangulaire** (tãgyle:r) *a*, rectangular.

recteur (rɛktœ:r) *m*, rector.

rectifier (rɛktifje) *v.t*, to rectify; amend; true, straighten.

rectiligne (rɛktiliɲ) *a*, recti-linear.

rectitude (rɛktityd) *f*, straight-ness; rectitude, soundness, sanity.

recto (rɛkto) *m*, recto, front, face.

rectum (rɛktɔm) *m*, rectum.

reçu (rəsy) *m*, receipt.

recueil (rəkœ:j) *m*, collection; book. ~ *factice*, miscellany. **re-cueillement** (kœjmã) *m*, self-communion. **recueillir** (ji:r) *v.t.ir*, to collect, gather; pick up; reap.

recuire (rəkɥi:r) *v.t.ir*, to re-bake; reheat; anneal.

recul (rəkyl) *m*, recoil, kick; set-back. **reculade** (lad) *f*, backward movement; retreat. **reculé, e** (le) *p.a*, distant, remote. **reculer** (le) *v.i. & t*, to draw back; move back; recede; retreat; back; re-coil; kick; postpone. **à reculons** (l5) *ad*, backward[s].

récupérer (rekypere) *v.t*, to re-cover, recoup.

récurer (rekyre) *v.t*, to scour, clean.

récuser (rekyze) *v.t*, to challenge, object to.

rédacteur, trice (redaktœ:r, tris) *n*, writer, drafter (*docu-ments*). ~ *en chef*, editor. **ré-daction** (sj5) *f*, drafting, editing; editorial staff; newsroom.

reddition (reddisj5) *f*, surrender; rendering (*of accounts*).

redemander (rədmãde) *v.t*, to ask for again; ask for more; ask for back.

Rédempteur (redã[p]tœ:r) *m*, Redeemer. **rédemption** ([p]sj5) *f*, redemption (*Theol.*).

redescendre (rədɛsã:dr) *v.i*, to come down again; fall again (*barometer*); back (*wind*).

redevable (rədəvabl) *a*, indebt-ed, beholden; liable. ¶ *n*, debtor. **redevance** (vã:s) *f*, rent[al]; roy-alty. **redevoir** (vwa:r) *v.t*, to still owe.

rédiger (rediʒe) *v.t*, to draw up, draft; write; edit.

redingote (rədɛ̃gɔt) *f*, frock coat (*man's*); coat (*woman's*).

redire (rədi:r) *v.t.ir*, to say again; repeat. *trouver à* ~ *à*, to find fault with. **redite** (dit) *f*, repeti-tion.

redondant, e (rəd5dã, ã:t) *a*, redundant.

redonner (redɔne) *v.t*, to give again; restore; (*v.i.*) to fall again; charge again.

redoutable (rədutabl) *a*, re-doubtable, formidable.

redoute (rədut) *f*, redoubt; gala night (*at dance hall*).

redouter (rədute) *v.t*, to dread, fear.

redresser (rədrɛse) *v.t*, to re-erect; straighten; redress; right.

réduction (redyksjɔ̃) *f*, reduction; reducing; cut. **réduire** (dɥiːr) *v.t.ir*, to reduce; boil down. **réduit** (dɥi) *m*, retreat, nook; redoubt.

rééditer (reedite) *v.t*, to republish, reissue.

réel, le† (reɛl) *a*, real; actual. ¶ *m*, real[ity].

réélection (reelɛksjɔ̃) *f*, reelection. **rééligible** (liʒibl) *a*, reeligible. **réélire** (liːr) *v.t.ir*, to reelect.

réer (ree) *v.i*, to troat, bell.

réexporter (reɛkspɔrte) *v.t*, to reexport.

refaire (rəfɛːr) *v.t.ir*, to remake, do [over] again; do up, repair; recover. **refait** (fɛ) *m*, draw[n game]; new horns (*stag*). **réfection** (refɛksjɔ̃) *f*, restoration. **réfectoire** (twaːr) *m*, refectory.

refendre (rəfɑ̃ːdr) *v.t*, to split; rip.

référence (referɑ̃ːs) *f*, reference. **referendum** (referɛ̃dɔm) *m*, referendum. **référer** (fere) *v.t. & i. & se ~*, to refer; ascribe.

réfléchi, e (refleʃi) *p.a*, reflective; thoughtful; considered, deliberate; reflexive (*Gram.*). **réfléchir** (ʃiːr) *v.t. & i*, to reflect; think over, ponder, consider. **réflecteur** (flɛktœːr) *m*, reflector. **reflet** (rəflɛ) *m*, reflection; reflex; shimmer, glint. *~s irisés*, play of colors. **refléter** (flete) *v.t*, to reflect; mirror. **réflexe** (reflɛks) *a. & m*, reflex. **réflexion** (ksjɔ̃) *f*, reflection; thought. *~ après coup*, afterthought.

refluer (rəflye) *v.i*, to flow back, ebb; surge. **reflux** (fly) *m*, reflux, ebb.

refondre (rəfɔ̃ːdr) *v.t*, to recast, remodel.

réformateur, trice (reformatœːr, tris) *n*, reformer. **réformation** (sjɔ̃) *f*, reformation. **réforme** (fɔrm) *f*, reform[ation]; discharge, retirement (*Mil., Nav.*).

reformer (rəfɔrme) *v.t*, to reform.

réformer (refɔrme) *v.t*, to reform, amend; discharge, retire; reverse (*law*).

refouler (rəfule) *v.t*, to drive back; stem; compress; ram home; repress; (*v.i,*) to flow back, ebb. **refouloir** (lwaːr) *m*, rammer (*gun*).

réfractaire (refraktɛːr) *a*, refractory; fire[-proof]. ¶ *m*, draft-dodger (*Mil.*).

réfracter (refrakte) *v.t*, to refract.

refrain (rəfrɛ̃) *m*, refrain; burden; theme. *~ en chœur*, chorus.

refréner (rəfrene) *v.t*, to curb, bridle.

réfrigération (refriʒerasjɔ̃) *f*, refrigeration, cooling, chilling.

refrogner (se) (rəfrɔɲe) *v.pr*, to frown, scowl, look sullen.

refroidir (rəfrwadiːr) *v.t. & i. & se ~*, to cool, chill; damp (*fig.*); get cold.

refuge (rəfyːʒ) *m*, refuge, shelter; [street] refuge. **réfugié, e** (refyʒje) *n*, refugee. **se réfugier** (ʒje) *v.pr*, to take refuge.

refus (rəfy) *m*, refusal *~ d' obéissance*, insubordination; contempt of court. **refuser** (ze) *v.t*, to refuse, decline; deny; reject; flunk, fail (*exam*). **se ~**, to object, refuse, decline.

réfuter (refyte) *v.t*, to refute, confute, rebut, disprove.

regagner (rəgɑɲe) *v.t*, to regain, win back, recover; make up for; get back to.

regain (rəgɛ̃) *m*, aftergrowth; renewal; new lease (*of life*).

régal (regal) *m*, feast; treat. **régaler** (le) *v.t*, to entertain, feast; treat; regale.

regard (rəgaːr) *m*, look, gaze, glance, eye(s); attention, notice; peephole; manhole. *~ appuyé*, stare. *~ polisson*, leer. *en ~*, opposite, facing. **regardant, e** (gardɑ̃, ɑ̃ːt) *a*, close-fisted, mean. **regarder** (de) *v.t. & abs*, to look (at, on), see, eye; consider, regard, mind, be one's business; face, front. *~ fixement*, to stare at.

régate (regat) *f*, regatta. [*cravate*] ~, open-end tie.

régence (reʒɑ̃:s) *f*, regency.

régénérer (reʒenere) *v.t*, to regenerate.

régent, e (reʒɑ̃, ɑ̃:t) *n. & a*, regent. **régenter** (ʒɑ̃te) *v.t*, to dictate to; dominate; (*abs.*) to domineer.

régicide (reʒisid) *m*, regicide; (*att.*) regicidal.

régie (reʒi) *f*, administration (*of property*); State (*control*); excise.

regimber (rəʒɛ̃be) *v.i*, to kick, balk.

régime (reʒim) *m*, regime[n], rules, system, conditions; diet; object (*Gram.*); bunch, cluster (*bananas, etc.*). ~ *de faveur*, preference (*Cust.*).

régiment (reʒimɑ̃) *m*, regiment; swarm. **régimentaire** (tɛ:r) *a*, regimental.

région (reʒjɔ̃) *f*, region, district. **régional, e** (ɔnal) *a*, regional, district (*att.*); toll (*att., Teleph.*).

régir (reʒi:r) *v.t*, to govern, rule, manage. **régisseur** (ʒisœ:r) *m*, manager, steward, bailiff (*farm*); stage manager.

registre (rəʒistr) *m*, register, book; record, note; damper (*flue*). ~ *des délibérations*, minute book.

règle (rɛgl) *f*, rule; ruler; order. ~ *à calcul*, sliderule. *les ~s*, menses. **réglé, e** (regle) *p.a*, regular, steady; set, stated; ruled (*paper*). **règlement** (rɛgləmɑ̃) *m*, settlement, adjustment; regulation, rule. **réglementaire** (tɛ:r) *a*, regulation (*att.*); prescribed. **réglementer** (te) *v.t*, to regulate. **régler** (regle) *v.t*, to rule; regulate; order; settle, adjust; set, time.

réglisse (reglis) *f*, licorice.

règne (rɛɲ) *m*, reign; sway; kingdom (*Nat. Hist.*). **régner** (ɲe) *v.i*, to reign, rule; obtain; prevail, be prevalent; extend, run.

regorger (rəgɔrʒe) *v.i. & t*, to overflow, brim, abound, teem; burst.

regrattier, ère (rəgratje, ɛ:r) *n*, huckster.

regret (rəgrɛ) *m*, regret. *à ~,* reluctantly. **regrettable** (tabl) *a*, regrettable, unfortunate. **le (la) regretté, e . . .** (te), the [late] lamented **. . . regretter** (te) *v.t*, to regret, be sorry (for); miss.

régulariser (regylarize) *v.t*, to regularize. **régularité** (te) *f*, regularity. **régulateur** (tœ:r) *m*, regulator, governor. **régulier, ère†** (lje, ɛ:r) *a*, regular; orderly; businesslike.

réhabiliter (reabilite) *v.t*, to rehabilitate, reinstate; discharge (*bankrupt*).

rehausser (rəose) *v.t*, to raise; enhance; heighten. **rehauts** (o) *m.pl*, highlights (*art*).

réimporter (reɛ̃pɔrte) *v.t*, to reimport.

réimposer (reɛ̃poze) *v.t*, to reimpose.

réimpression (reɛ̃prɛsjɔ̃) *f*, reprint[ing]. **réimprimer** (prime) *v.t*, to reprint.

Reims (rɛ̃:s) *m*, Rheims.

rein (rɛ̃) *m*, kidney; (*pl.*) loins, back.

reine (rɛn) *f*, queen (*pers. & chess*); belle (*of ball*). ~-*claude* (klo:d), greengage. ~ *des abeilles*, queen bee. ~-*des-prés*, meadow-sweet. ~-*marguerite*, China aster.

reinette (rɛnɛt) *f*, pippin, rennet. ~ *grise*, russet (*apple*).

réintégrer (reɛ̃tegre) *v.t*, to reinstate.

réitérer (reitere) *v.t*, to reiterate, repeat.

rejaillir (rəʒaji:r) *v.i*, to gush out; reflect, redound.

rejet (rəʒɛ) *m*, throwing out; rejection; shoot (*Hort.*). **rejeter** (ʒ[ə]te) *v.t*, to throw back; t. out; t. up; reject, set aside; negate; dismiss; disallow. **rejeton** (ʒtɔ̃) *m*, shoot, cane (*raspberry*); scion, offspring.

rejoindre (rəʒwɛ̃:dr) *v.t. & abs. ir*, to re-join; rejoin (*one's regiment*).

rejouer (rəʒwe) *v.t. & i*, to replay; play again.

réjoui, e (reʒwi) *p.a*, jolly, joyous, jovial, merry. **réjouir** (ʒwi:r) *v.t. & se ~*, to rejoice, gladden, cheer; be glad; enjoy oneself. **ré-**

jouissance (ʒwisã:s) *f,* rejoicing; makeweight (*butcher's*).

relâche (rəla:ʃ) *m,* respite, intermission, breathing space, relaxation; no performance, closed (*Theat.*); (*f.*) call[ing] (*Naut.*); port of call. **relâcher** (laʃe) *v.t. & i,* to loosen, slacken; relax; release; call, put in (*Naut.*).

relais (rəlɛ) *m,* relay; shift; stage, relay station; sand flats.

relancer (rəlãse) *v.t,* to throw back; return (*ball, Ten.*); badger. **relanceur, euse** (sœ:r, ø:z) *n,* receiver (*Ten.*).

relaps, e (rəlaps) *n,* apostate, backslider.

rélargir (relarʒi:r) *v.t,* to widen; let out.

relater (rəlate) *v.t,* to relate, state. **relatif, ive†** (tif, i:v) *a,* relative, relating. **relation** (sjɔ̃) *f,* relation, connection, intercourse; acquaintance; narrative.

relaxer (rəlakse) *v.t,* to relax; release.

relayer (rəlɛje) *v.t,* to relay; change with; change horses.

reléguer (rəlege) *v.t,* to relegate, consign; intern (*prisoner in Fr. colony*).

relent (rəlã) *m,* bad odor.

relevailles (rəlva:j) *f.pl,* churching. **relève** (lɛ:v) *f,* relief (*from turn of duty*). **relevé, e** (lve) *p.a,* high, exalted, lofty; strong (*flavor*). ¶ *m,* statement, abstract, return. ~ *de potage,* course after soup. ¶ *f,* afternoon. **relever** (lve) *v.t,* to raise, lift [up]; pick up; turn up; take up; restore; make out (*account*); take, read (*meter*); point out, note; set off, enhance, exalt; season; relieve; release; plot (*ground*); (*v.i.*) to depend, rest; recover. ~ *le menton à,* to chuck under the chin.

relief (rəljɛf) *m,* relief; (*pl.*) leftovers.

relier (rəlje) *v.t,* to [re]tie; unite; bind (*book*); [re]hoop (*cask*). **relieur, euse** (jœ:r, ø:z) *n,* [book]binder.

religieux, euse† (rəliʒjø, ø:z) *a,* religious; sacred (*song, etc.*); scrupulous. ¶ *m,* monk, friar. ¶ *f,* nun; cream puff. **religion**

(ʒjɔ̃) *f,* religion; vows; bounden duty; sanctity (*oath*).

reliquaire (rəlikɛ:r) *m,* reliquary, shrine.

reliquat (rəlika) *m,* balance, residue.

relique (rəlik) *f,* relic.

reliure (rəljy:r) *f,* [book]binding. ~ *amateur,* extra binding. ~ *pleine,* full b., whole b.

relogement (rələʒmã) *m,* rehousing.

relouer (rəlue) *v.t,* to relet; rerent; sublet.

reluire (rəlɥi:r) *v.t.ir,* to shine, glitter. **reluisant, e** (lɥizã, ã:t) *a,* shining; creditable; brilliant.

reluquer (rəlyke) *v.t,* to ogle; covet.

remâcher (rəmaʃe) *v.t,* to chew again; ruminate on, brood over, chew (*fig.*).

remanier (rəmanje) *v.t,* to rehandle; manipulate; relay; recast.

remarquable† (rəmarkabl) *a,* remarkable; noteworthy; conspicuous. **remarque** (mark) *f,* remark, note. **remarquer** (ke) *v.t,* to re-mark; remark, observe, notice, note, mark.

remballer (rãbale) *v.t,* to repack.

rembarquer (rãbarke) *v.t. & i,* to reembark, reship.

remblai (rãblɛ) *m,* filling up (*with earth*); embankment. **remblayer** (je) *v.t,* to fill [up], [em]bank.

remboîter (rãbwate) *v.t,* to [re]set; recase.

rembourrer (rãbure) *v.t,* to stuff, pad, upholster.

rembourser (rãburse) *v.t,* to repay, pay off, return, refund; redeem; reimburse.

rembrunir (rãbryni:r) *v.t,* to darken, gloom.

rembucher (se) (rãbyʃe) *v.pr,* to return to cover[t].

remède (rəmɛd) *m,* remedy, cure. ~ *de charlatan,* nostrum. **remédier** à (medje), to remedy, cure.

remémorer (se) (rəmemɔre) *v.pr,* to remember.

remerciement (rəmɛrsimã) *m. oft. pl,* thanks. **remercier** (sje) *v.t,* to thank; dismiss, fire.

réméré (remere) *m,* repurchase.

remettre (rəmɛtr) *v.t. & abs. ir*, to put back [again]; put on again; restore; remit, send [in]; hand [over], deliver; commend; put off, postpone; pardon; entrust; remember; calm; set (*bone*).

remeubler (rəmœble) *v.t*, to re-furnish.

réminiscence (reminisɑ̃ːs) *f*, reminiscence.

remise (rəmiːz) *f*, putting back; restoration; remittance; remission; delivery; postponement; allowance, discount; commission; coach house; shed; cover (*game*). ~ [*sur marchandises*], [trade] discount. *une voiture de* ~ *ou un* ~, a hired carriage. **remiser** (mize) *v.t*, to put up (*vehicle*). **remisier** (zje) *m*, intermediate broker.

rémission (remisjɔ̃) *f*, remission.

rem[m]aillage (rɑ̃mɑjaːʒ) *m*, grafting (*Knit*.).

remmancher (rɑ̃mɑ̃ʃe) *v.t*, to rehandle; resume.

remmener (rɑ̃mne) *v.t*, to take back.

remontant (rəmɔ̃tɑ̃) *m*, stimulant, tonic, pick-me-up. **remonte** (mɔ̃ːt) *f*, remount[ing] (*Mil*.). ~-*pentes*, *m*, ski lift. **remonter** (mɔ̃te) *v.i. & t*, to [re]ascend; remount; go back; raise; rise; wind [up] (*spring*); restock, replenish; restage; veer (*wind*). **remontoir** (twaːr) *m*, winder, key; keyless watch. ~ *à heures sautantes*, jumping-hour watch.

remontrance (rəmɔ̃trɑ̃ːs) *f*, remonstrance, expostulation. **remontrer** (tre) *v.t. & abs*, to show again; point out; remonstrate.

remords (rəmɔːr) *m*, remorse.

remorque (rəmɔrk) *f*, tow[ing]; trailer. **remorquer** (ke) *v.t*, to tow, haul. **remorqueur** (kœːr) *m*, tug [boat].

rémouleur (remulœːr) *m*, [knife] grinder.

remous (rəmu) *m*, eddy, [back]-wash, swirl.

rempart (rɑ̃paːr) *m*, rampart; bulwark (*fig*.).

remplaçant, e (rɑ̃plasɑ̃, ɑ̃ːt) *n*, substitute. **remplacer** (se) *v.t*, to replace; take the place of; supersede.

rempli (rɑ̃pli) *m*, tuck. **remplier** (e) *v.t*, to tuck; turn over (*paper wrapper—Bookb*.).

remplir (rɑ̃pliːr) *v.t*, to fill up, refill, replenish; fill; swamp (*boat*); fulfil, comply with; perform.

remplumer (se) (rɑ̃plyme) *v.pr*, to get new feathers; put on flesh again; pick up again.

remporter (rɑ̃pɔrte) *v.t*, to take away; carry off, win, gain.

rempoter (rɑ̃pɔte) *v.t*, to repot.

remuant, e (rəmɥɑ̃, ɑ̃ːt) *a*, restless. **remue-ménage** (mymenaːʒ) *m*, bustle, stir, upset. **remuement** (mɑ̃) *m*, moving, removal; bustle, stir. **remuer** (mɥe) *v.t. & i*, to move; stir [up], rake up; shake, wag, swish; remove, shift.

rémunérateur, trice (remyneratœːr, trice) *a*, remunerative, paying. ¶ *m*, rewarder. **rémunération** (sjɔ̃) *f*, remuneration, payment; consideration; return. **rémunérer** (re) *v.t*, to remunerate, pay for, reward.

renâcler (rənɑkle) *v.t*, to snort; hang back.

renaissance (rənɛsɑ̃ːs) *f*, rebirth; revival; renaissance. **renaître** (nɛːtr) *v.i.ir*, to be born again; spring up again; revive.

renard (rənaːr) *m*, fox. ~ *argenté*, silver f. **renarde** (nard) *f*, vixen. **renardeau** (do) *m*, fox cub. **renardière** (djɛːr) *f*, fox earth, fox's hole.

rencaisser (rɑ̃kɛse) *v.t*, to rebox; recash.

renchéri, e (rɑ̃ʃeri) *n*, fastidious person. **renchérir** (riːr) *v.i*, to get dearer, go up. ~ *sur*, to outbid, outdo, improve on.

rencogner (rɑ̃kɔɲe) *v.t*, to drive into a corner.

rencontre (rɑ̃kɔ̃ːtr) *f*, meeting, encounter; occurrence; occasion; collision, clash; duel. ~ *de front*, head-on collision. **rencontrer** (kɔ̃tre) *v.t*, to meet, m. with, encounter, come across, strike; run into, collide with.

rendement (rɑ̃dmɑ̃) *m*, yield, return; output, capacity; efficiency. **rendez-vous** (devu) *m*, appointment; place of meeting; resort, haunt.

rendormir (rãdɔrmi;r) *v.t*, to send to sleep again. se ~, to go to sleep again.

rendre (rã;dr) *v.t*, to give back, return; restore; give up; render; give; pay; dispense; repay; yield; deliver; surrender; vomit; make; drive (*one mad*). ~ *l'âme*, to die. se ~, to make oneself; go; surrender, yield. **rendu** (rãdy) *m*, rendering (*art*); return (*article, goods—Com.*).

rêne (rɛn) *f*, rein.

renégat, e (rənega, at) *n*, renegade, turncoat.

renfermé (rãfɛrme) *m*, musty smell. **renfermer** (me) *v.t*, to shut up; confine; comprise, contain; restrict.

renflement (rãfləmã) *m*, swell-[ing]; bulge, boss. **renfler** (fle) *v.i*, to swell.

renflouer (rãflue) *v.t*, to refloat (*ship*).

renfoncement (rãfɔ̃smã) *m*, driving in; recess; inden[ta]tion (*Typ.*); punch (*blow*). **renfoncer** (se) *v.t*, to drive in; knock in; indent.

renforcé, e (rãfɔrse) *p.a*, stout, strong; out & out; arrant. **renforcer** (se) *v.t*, to reinforce; strengthen; brace; intensify (*Phot.*). **renfort** (fɔ;r) *m*, reinforcement (*Mil.*). à grand ~ de, with plenty of.

renfrogner (se) (rãfrɔɲe) *v.pr*, to frown, scowl, look sullen.

rengager (rãgaʒe) *v.t*, to reengage; (*v.i.*) to reenlist.

rengaine (rãgɛ;n) *f*, tag, story; catchword; hackneyed refrain.

rengainer (rãgɛne) *v.t*, to sheathe; suppress.

rengorger (se) (rãgɔrʒe) *v.pr*, to bridle [up]; strut, swagger.

reniement (rənimã) *m*, denial; disavowal.

renier (rənje) *v.t*, to disown, deny.

renifler (rənifle) *v.i. & t*, to sniff; snuffle; snort.

renne (rɛn) *m*, reindeer.

renom (rənɔ̃) *m*, renown, fame; repute. **renommé, e** (nɔme) *p.a*, renowned, famed, noted. ¶ *f*, fame, renown; name; rumor, report. **renommer** (me) *v.t*, to reappoint.

renonce (rənɔ̃;s) (*cards*) *f*, renounce; revoke. **renoncement** (nɔ̃smã) *m*, renunciation, self-denial. **renoncer** (se) *v.i. & t. & ~ à*, to renounce, give up, forgo; disown, deny; revoke (*cards*). **renonciation** (sjasjɔ̃) *f*, renunciation, disclaimer.

renoncule (rənɔ̃kyl) *f*, ranunculus, buttercup, crowfoot. ~ *bulbeuse*, kingcup.

renouer (rənwe) *v.t*, to retie; renew, resume.

renouveau (rənuvo) *m*, renewal; return of spring. **renouveler** (vle) *v.t*, to renew, renovate; change; revive. **rénover** (renɔve) *v.t*, to renovate, restore.

renseignement (rãsɛɲmã) *m*. *oft. pl*, information, intelligence, particular; inquiry. **renseigner** (ɲe) *v.t*, to inform. se ~, to inquire.

rente (rã;t) *f*, income; annuity; pension; interest; stock. **renter** (rãte) *v.t*, to endow. **rentier, ère** (tje, ɛ;r) *n*, stockholder, fundholder, investor; annuitant; person of independent means.

rentraire (rãtrɛ;r) *v.t.ir*, to finedraw.

rentrant, e (rãtrã, ã;t) *a*, reentrant; sunk. **rentré, e** (tre) *p.a*, suppressed (*rage, etc.*). ¶ *f*, turn; reentry; reappearance; reopening; ingathering; collection; receipt. **rentrer** (tre) *v.i*, to reenter; return; reappear; reopen; (*v.t.*) to bring in, house; indent (*Typ.*). ~ *dans*, to recover; reenter; return to, rejoin. **rentrez!** all in! (*Sch.*).

renverse (à la) (rãvɛrs) *ad*, backwards, on one's back. **renverser** (se) *v.t*, to throw down, overthrow, upset; invert, reverse; astound. se ~ *sur sa chaise*, to lean (*or* lie) back (*or* recline) in one's chair.

renvoi (rãvwa) *m*, return; dismissal; postponement; reference; caret; repeat (*Mus.*); alteration; eructation; countershaft. **renvoyer** (je) *v.t*, to send back, return; dismiss; put off, adjourn;

refer. ~ *à une autre audience*, to remand.

réorganiser (reɔrganize) *v.t*, to reorganize.

réouverture (reuvɛrtɜːr) *f*, re-opening.

repaire (rəpɛːr) *m*, den, lair; nest; haunt.

repaître (rəpɛːtr) *v.t*, to feed, feast.

répandre (repɑ̃ːdr) *v.t*, to pour out, spill, shed; spread, diffuse, waft, scatter, sprinkle. **répandu, e** (pɑ̃dy) *p.a*, widespread; well-known.

réparable (reparabl) *a*, reparable, repairable.

reparaître (rəparɛːtr) *v.i.ir*, to reappear.

réparateur, trice (reparatœːr, tris) *n*, repairer, mender. **réparation** (sjɔ̃) *f*, repair; reparation; amends, atonement, redress. **réparer** (re) *v.t*, to repair, mend; retrieve; make amends for; make up for; redress; rectify.

repartie (rəparti) *f*, repartee, retort, rejoinder. **repartir** (tiːr) *v.i.ir*, to retort; set out again.

répartir (repartiːr) *v.t*, to distribute, apportion, allot; assess; spread. **répartition** (tisjɔ̃) *f*, distribution, etc.

repas (rəpɑ) *m*, meal, repast, spread. ~ *de corps*, regimental dinner. ~ *de noce*, wedding breakfast, w. banquet.

repasser (rəpɑse) *v.i. & t*, to repass; recross; come again; reexamine, con, go over, think over; grind, sharpen; set; strop; iron (*linen*). **repasseur** (sœːr) *m*, grinder; strop (*razor*). **repasseuse** (søːz) *f*, ironer, laundress.

repêcher (rəpeʃe) *v.t*, to fish up, f. out; give a second chance to (*exam*).

repentir (rəpɑ̃tiːr) *m*, repentance. se ~, *v.pr.ir*, to repent. se ~ *de*, to repent (*v.t.*), to rue, be sorry for.

repercer (rəpɛrse) *v.t*, to retap (*cask*); pierce (*metal*).

répercussion (rəpɛrkysjɔ̃) *f*, repercussion. **répercuter** (te) *v.t*, to reverberate.

repère (rəpɛːr) *m*, reference mark, datum point; bench mark.

repérer (pere) *v.t*, to mark; locate, spot.

répertoire (repɛrtwaːr) *m*, index, list, register; directory; repertory; repository (*fig.*). ~ *à onglets*, thumb index. **répertorier** (tɔrje) *v.t*, to index.

répéter (repete) *v.t. & abs*, to repeat; rehearse; claim back (*law*). **répétiteur, trice** (titœːr, tris) *n*, assistant teacher; tutor, coach. **répétition** (sjɔ̃) *f*, repetition, recurrence; reproduction, replica, duplicate; rehearsal; private lesson; claiming back. ~ *générale*, dress rehearsal.

repeupler (rəpœple) *v.t*, to re-people; restock; replant.

repiquer (rəpike) *v.t*, to prick again; restitch; plant out.

répit (repi) *m*, respite.

replacer (rəplase) *v.t*, to replace; reinvest.

replanter (rəplɑ̃te) *v.t*, to re-plant.

replâtrer (rəplɑtre) *v.t*, to re-plaster; patch up.

replet, ète (rəplɛ, ɛt) *a*, stout (*pers.*). **réplétion** (replesjɔ̃) *f*, repletion, corpulence.

repli (rəpli) *m*, fold, crease; coil (*snake*); recess (*heart*); falling back (*Mil.*). **replier** (plie) *v.t*, to fold up. se ~, to fold up; coil up; fall back.

réplique (replik) *f*, retort, rejoinder, answer; cue (*Theat.*); replica. **répliquer** (ke) *v.t*, to retort, rejoin, answer [back].

répondant, e (repɔ̃dɑ̃, ɑ̃ːt) *n*, respondent; surety; sponsor; bail-[sman]. **répondre** (pɔ̃ːdr) *v.t. & i*, to answer, reply, respond; say in reply; write back (*in reply*); correspond; agree; answer for, guarantee. **répons** (pɔ̃) *m*, response (*Lit.*). **réponse** (pɔ̃ːs) *f*, answer, reply; response.

report (rəpɔːr) *m*, carry forward; c. over. **reportage** (porta:ʒ) *m*, reporting; report (*news*). **reporter** (te) *v.t*, to carry forward; c. over; bring forward; carry over (*Stk Ex.*). **reporter** (tœːr) *m*, reporter (*news*).

repos (rəpo) *m*, rest, repose; quiet; ease; peace; pause (*Mus., Pros.*); half-cock (*gun*); resting place, seat; landing (*stairs*). *de tout* ~, safe, reliable. *valeur de tout* ~, gilt-edged security. **reposant, e** (zã, ã:t) *a*, restful. **reposé, e** (ze) *p.a*, refreshed; fresh. ¶ *f*, lair. **reposer** (ze) *v.t*, to replace; re-lay; rest; refresh; order (*arms*); (*v.i.*) to lie; rest; sleep; be based. se ~, to rest, lie down, recline; rely.

repoussant, e (rəpusã, ã:t) *a*, repulsive, repellent. **repoussé, e** (se) *p.a*, embossed. **repoussement** (smã) *m*, rejection; recoil; kick. **repousser** (se) *v.t*, to push back; repel, repulse, reject; deny; spurn; (*v.i.*) to recoil; sprout again, grow again. **repoussoir** (swa:r) *m*, punch (*tool*); set-off, foil.

répréhensible (repreãsibl) *a*, reprehensible.

reprendre (rəprã:dr) *v.t. & i. ir*, to retake, recapture; take up [again]; take back; recover; resume; regain; pick up [again]; reprove, find fault with; reply; rejoin; take root again; set again; freeze again. ~ *de volée*, to volley (*Ten.*). ~ *sous œuvre*, to underpin; reconstruct (*fig.*).

représaille (rəpreza:j) *f. oft. pl*, reprisal, retaliation.

représentant, e (rəprezãtã, ã:t) *n*, representative; agent. **représentatif, ive** (tatif, i:v) *a*, representative. **représentation** (sjõ) *f*, representation; production; [purchase] consideration; performance (*Theat.*). ~ *à bénéfice*, benefit performance. **représenter** (te) *v.t*, to present again; represent; produce, show; perform, act; personate; picture; (*abs.*) to bear oneself; (*abs.*) to entertain.

répression (represjõ) *f*, repression.

réprimande (reprimã:d) *f*, reprimand, reproof, rebuke. **réprimander** (mãde) *v.t*, to reprimand, reprove, rebuke.

réprimer (reprime) *v.t*, to repress, curb; put down, quell.

repris de justice (rəpri) *m*, habitual criminal, old offender, jailbird. **reprisage** (za:ʒ) *m*, darning, mending (*stockings*, *etc.*). **reprise** (pri:z) *f*, retaking, recapture; recovery; rally; re-

sumption, renewal; revival; repetition; occasion, time; round (*Box.*); bout (*Fenc.*); darn[ing]; repair. ~ *perdue*, invisible mending. **repriser** (prize) *v.t*, to darn, mend.

réprobation (reprɔbasjõ) *f*, reprobation.

reproche (rəprɔʃ) *m*, reproach, blame. **reprocher** (ʃe) *v.t*, to reproach, blame, upbraid; taunt; twit.

reproduction (rəprɔdyksjõ) *f*, reproduction. **reproduire** (dɥi:r) *v.t.ir*, to reproduce. se ~, to recur; reproduce, breed.

réprouvé, e (repruve) *n*, outcast; reprobate. **réprouver** (ve) *v.t*, to reprobate; reject, disapprove of, deprecate.

reptation (rɛptasjõ) *f*, creeping, crawling. **reptile** (til) *m*, reptile.

républicain, e (repyblikɛ̃, ɛn) *a. & n*, republican. **république** (lik) *f*, republic; commonwealth; community.

répudier (repydje) *v.t*, to repudiate; renounce.

répugnance (repyɲã:s) *f*, repugnance; reluctance. **répugnant, e** (ɲã, ã:t) *a*, repugnant. **répugner** (ɲe) *v.i*, to feel repugnance, feel loath; be repugnant.

répulsif, ive (repylsif, i:v) *a*, repulsive, repellent. **répulsion** (sjõ) *f*, repulsion.

réputation (repytasjõ) *f*, reputation, repute; name; character. **réputé, e** (te) *p.a*, well-known; of repute. **réputer** (te) *v.t*, to repute, deem, hold.

requérant, e (rəkerã, ã:t) *n*, applicant, plaintiff. **requérir** (ri:r) *v.t.ir*, to require; summon. **requête** (kɛ:t) *f*, request, suit, petition.

requiem (rekɥiɛm) *m*, requiem.

requin (rəkɛ̃) *m*, shark (*fish & preying pers.*).

requinquer (se) (rəkɛ̃ke) *v.pr*, to smarten oneself up.

réquisition (rekizisjõ) *f*, requisition, levy. **réquisitionner** (ɔne) *v.t*, to requisition, commandeer, impress. **réquisitoire** (twa:r) *m*, charge, indictment.

rescapé, e (rɛskape) *n*, survivor, saved [person].

rescision (rɛssizjɔ̃) *f*, rescission.
rescousse (à la) (rɛskus) to the rescue.
rescrit (rɛskri) *m*, rescript.
réseau (rezo) *m*, netting; network; system; area; plexus; tracery. ~ *de fils de fer*, wire entanglement (*Mil.*).
réséda (rezeda) *m*, reseda, mignonette.
réservation (rezɛrvasjɔ̃) *f*, reservation. **réserve** (zɛrv) *f*, reservation; booking (*seats*); reserve; store; exception, qualification; preserve (*Hunt.*); sanctuary (*animals*). *sous* ~ *de*, subject to. *sous* ~ *que*, on condition that. **réservé, e** (ve) *a*, reserved; cautious, guarded; shy; coy. **réserviste** (vist) *m*, reservist. **réservoir** (vwa:r) *m*, reservoir, tank, cistern, well.
résidence (rezidã:s) *f*, residence, dwelling, abode. **résident, e** (dã, ã:t) *n. & a*, resident (*diplomatic*); settler (*colony*). **résider** (de) *v.i*, to reside, dwell, live; lie, rest. **résidu** (dy) *m*, residue.
résignation (reziɲasjɔ̃) *f*, resignation; submissiveness. **résigner** (ɲe) *v.t*, to resign.
résilier (rezilje) *v.t*, to cancel, annul.
résille (rezi:j) *f*, hairnet; cames.
résine (rezin) *f*, resin, rosin. **résineux, euse** (nø, ø:z) *a*, resinous.
résistance (rezistã:s) *f*, resistance; opposition; strength; toughness; endurance, stamina; underground army. **résistant, e** (tã, ã:t) *a*, resistant, strong, tough. **résister** à (te), to resist, withstand.
résolu†, e (rezɔly) *p.a*, resolute, determined. **résolution** (sjɔ̃) *f*, resolution; solution; cancelation; resolve.
résonance (rezonã:s) *f*, resonance. **résonnant, e** (nã, ã:t) *a*, resonant. **résonner** (ne) *v.i*, to resound; ring; reecho; twang.
résorber (rezɔrbe) *v.t*, to reabsorb; absorb, imbibe.
résoudre (rezu:dr) *v.t.ir*, to resolve, solve; annul.
respect (rɛspɛ) *m*, respect, regard, deference. **respectable** (pɛktabl) *a*, respectable. **respecter** (te) *v.t*, to respect; spare. **respectif, ive†** (tif, i:v) *a*, respective, several. **respectueux, euse†** (tɥø, ø:z) *a*, respectful, dutiful. ~ *des lois*, law-abiding.
respiration (rɛspirasjɔ̃) *f*, respiration, breathing. **respirer** (re) *v.i. & t*, to breathe; respire; inhale; exhale.
resplendir (rɛsplãdi:r) *v.i*, to be resplendent, shine, glitter. **resplendissant, e** (disã, ã:t) *a*, resplendent; aglow; glorious.
responsabilité (rɛspɔ̃sabilite) *f*, responsibility; liability; care. **responsable** (bl) *a*, responsible, answerable, liable. **responsif, ive** (sif, i:v) *a*, in reply (*law*).
resquille (rɛski:j) *f*, [gate] crashing. **resquilleur, euse** (kijœ:r, ø:z) *n*, [gate] crasher.
ressac (rəsak) *m*, undertow; surf.
ressaisir (rəsɛzi:r) *v.t*, to recover.
ressasser (rəsase) *v.t*, to resift; repeat.
ressaut (rəso) *m*, projection, setoff.
ressemblance (rəsãblã:s) *f*, resemblance, likeness. **ressemblant, e** (blã, ã:t) *a*, [a]like. **ressembler** à (ble), to resemble, be like, look like.
ressemeler (rəsəmle) *v.t*, to resole.
ressentiment (rəsãtimã) *m*, resentment. **ressentir** (ti:r) *v.t*, to feel; resent. **se** ~, to feel.
resserre (rəsɛ:r) *f*, storeroom. **resserrer** (sɛre) *v.t*, to tighten; close up; bind; put away [again]; contract, narrow, confine, restrict; condense.
ressort (rəsɔ:r) *m*, spring; elasticity; buoyancy; incentive; province; purview; resort, appeal. ~ *à boudin*, spiral spring. *à* ~, spring (*scale, etc.*). **ressortir** (sɔrti:r) *v.i*, to be under the jurisdiction of; (*v.i.ir.*) to go out again; stand out (*in relief*); result, appear.
ressource (rəsurs) *f*, resource; expedient, shift, resort.
ressouvenir (rəsuvni:r) *m*, re-

membrance, memory. **se ~,** *v.pr. ir,* to remember.

ressuer (rǝsɥe) *v.i,* to sweat (*walls*).

ressusciter (resysite) *v.t,* to resuscitate, revive; raise (*the dead.*)

restant, e (rɛstɑ̃, ɑ̃:t) *a,* remaining, left.

restaurant, e (rɛstorɑ̃, ɑ̃:t) *a,* restorative. ¶ *m,* restorative; restaurant, eating house. **restaurateur, trice** (ratœ:r, tris) *n,* restorer; restaurant keeper, caterer.

restauration (sjɔ̃), *f,* restoration.

restaurer (re) *v.t,* to restore, reestablish; refresh.

reste (rɛst) *m,* rest, remainder, remains; leavings, remnant. *du ~,* besides, moreover. **~s mortels,** mortal remains. **rester** (te) *v.i,* to remain, be left; stay, stop, stand, sit, keep, stick; last; live.

restituer (rɛstitɥe) *v.t,* to restore, return. **restitution** (tysjɔ̃) *f,* restitution; restoration.

restreindre (rɛstrɛ̃:dr) *v.t.ir,* to restrict, limit. **restriction** (triksjɔ̃) *f,* restriction; reservation.

résultat (rezylta) *m,* result, outcome. **résulter** (te) *v.i,* to result, follow, ensue.

résumé (rezyme) *m,* summary, abstract. **~ des débats,** summing up. **résumer** (me) *v.t,* to summarize; sum up.

résurrection (rezyrɛksjɔ̃) *f,* resurrection.

retable (rǝtabl) *m,* reredos, altar piece.

rétablir (retabli:r) *v.t,* to reestablish, restore; retrieve; reinstate.

retaille (rǝta:j) *f,* cutting, paring (*snip, bit*).

retaper (rǝtape) *v.t,* to do up; recast.

retard (rǝta:r) *m,* delay. *en ~,* late, behind[hand]; overdue; in arrears; slow (*clock*). **retardataire** (tardata:r) *a,* late, in arrears; overstaying pass (*Mil.*). ¶ *n,* latecomer. **retarder** (de) *v.t,* to retard, delay; hinder; put off; put back (*clock*); (*v.i.*) be slow; lag.

retâter (rǝtɑte) *v.t. & i,* to touch again; try again.

retenir (rǝtni:r) *v.t.ir,* to keep back, retain, withhold, stop; keep; engage; reserve, book; detain; hold; h. back, check, restrain; remember; carry (*Arith.*). **se ~,** to refrain; catch hold. **rétention** (retɑ̃sjɔ̃) *f,* retention.

retentir (rǝtɑ̃ti:r) *v.i,* to [re]sound, echo, ring. **retentissant** (tisɑ̃) *a,* resounding, echoing; sonorous.

retenu, e (rǝtny) *a,* cautious, discreet. ¶ *f,* stoppage (*on pay, etc.*); carry (*Arith.*); reserve, discretion. *mettre en ~,* to keep in (*Sch.*).

réticence (retisɑ̃:s) *f,* reticence; concealment.

réticule (retikyl) *m,* reticule; reticle.

rétif, ive (retif, i:v) *a,* restive; stubborn.

rétine (retin) *f,* retina.

retiré, e (rǝtire) *p.a,* solitary, secluded. **retirer** (re) *v.t,* to redraw; draw back; withdraw; retire (*bill*); take out; remove; extract; draw, get, derive; recall; reclaim (*from vice*). **se ~,** to retire, withdraw; stand down; recede; shrink.

retombée (rǝtɔ̃be) *f,* spring[ing] (*arch*). **retomber** (be) *v.i,* to fall down [again]; relapse; fall [back]; devolve; hang down.

rétorquer (retorke) *v.t,* to retort.

retors, e (rǝtɔ:r, ɔrs) *a,* twisted; crafty.

retouche (rǝtuʃ) *f,* retouch[ing]. **retoucher** (ʃe) *v.t. & ~ à,* to retouch, touch up.

retour (rǝtu:r) *m,* turn; return; recurrence; reversion; reversal; decline (*life*), wane; ruse. **~ de flamme,** backfire. **~ de manivelle,** backfire [kick]. **retourne** (turn) *f,* turn-up (*card*), trumps. **retournement** (nǝmɑ̃) *m,* turning, reversal. **~ de bras,** hammerlock (*wrestling*). **retourner** (ne) *v.i. & t,* to return; revert; turn (*coat, etc.*); t. over; t. up; mix (*salad*). **se ~,** to turn [round], veer (*opinion*).

retracer (rǝtrase) *v.t,* to retrace, recall. **se ~,** to recur.

rétracter (retrakte) *v.t,* to retract, recant.

retrait, e (rǝtrɛ, ɛt) *p.a,* shrunken. ¶ *m,* withdrawal; deprivation; shrinkage; recess. ¶ *f,* retreat; tattoo; withdrawal; retirement; superannuation; pension, retired pay; shelter; seclusion; shrinkage; offset (*Arch.*). ~ *aux flambeaux,* torchlight tattoo. **retraité, e** (te) *a,* pensioned off, superannuated. [*officier*] *retraité,* officer on the retired list.

retrancher (rǝtrɑ̃ʃe) *v.t,* to cut off; c. out; take away; deduct; subtract; entrench.

rétrécir (retresi:r) *v.t. & i,* to narrow; shrink. se ~, to shrink.

retremper (rǝtrɑ̃pe) *v.t,* to retemper; brace.

rétribuer (retribɥe) *v.t,* to remunerate, pay. **rétribution** (bysjɔ̃) *f,* remuneration, salary, reward.

rétroactif, ive (retroaktif, i:v) *a,* retroactive.

rétrocéder (retrosede) *v.i,* to retrocede; recede; go back. **rétrocession** (sɛsjɔ̃) *f,* retrocession; recession.

rétrograde (retrograd) *a,* retrograde, backward. **rétrograder** (de) *v.i,* to go back[wards]; (*v.t.*) to reduce to lower rank (*Mil.*).

rétrospectif, ive† (retrospɛktif, i:v) *a,* retrospective.

retrousser (rǝtruse) *v.t,* to turn up; tuck up; curl (*lip*).

retrouver (rǝtruve) *v.t,* to find [again], recover; recognize.

rets (rɛ) *m,* net; (*pl.*) toils (*fig.*).

réunion (reynjɔ̃) *f,* [re]union; assembly, gathering, function, meeting. **réunir** (ni:r) *v.t,* to [re]unite; join; combine; lump. se ~, to meet, foregather.

réussi, e (reysi) *p.a,* successful. **réussir** (si:r) *v.i,* to succeed; prosper. **réussite** (sit) *f,* success; solitaire (*cards*).

revaloir (rǝvalwa:r) *v.t.ir,* to pay (*someone*) out, be even with (*someone*).

revanche (rǝvɑ̃:ʃ) *f,* revenge; return; requital, return match.

rêvasser (rɛvase) *v.i,* to have troubled dreams; muse. **rêve** (rɛ:v) *m,* dream; day dream.

revêche (rǝvɛʃ) *a,* cantankerous.

réveil (revɛ:j) *m,* waking, awakening; revival (*Relig.*); reveille;

alarm clock. **réveille-matin** (vɛj) *m,* alarm clock; awakener. **réveiller** (vɛje) *v.t,* to awake[n], wake[n], call, [a]rouse; revive. se ~, to wake [up]; revive. **réveillon** (jɔ̃) *m,* Christmas Eve supper.

révélateur, trice (revelatœ:r, tris) *n,* revealer; (*m.*) developer (*Phot.*). **révélation** (sjɔ̃) *f,* revelation; disclosure; eye-opener. **révéler** (le) *v.t,* to reveal, disclose; develop (*Phot.*).

revenant (rǝvnɑ̃) *m,* ghost.

revenant-bon (rǝvnɑ̃bɔ̃) *m,* perquisite.

revendeur, euse (rǝvɑ̃dœ:r, ø:z) *n,* second-hand dealer; retailer; peddler.

revendication (rǝvɑ̃dikasjɔ̃) *f,* demand; claim; claiming.

revendiquer (rǝvɑ̃dike) *v.t,* to claim, assert.

revendre (rǝvɑ̃:dr) *v.t,* to resell. avoir à ~, to have enough & to spare.

revenir (rǝvni:r) *v.i.ir,* to come [back], return; come again, recur; revert; recover; cost; amount. ~ *sur,* to retrace; go back on; reconsider; rake up (*past*). je n'en reviens pas, I can't believe it.

revente (rǝvɑ̃:t) *f,* resale.

revenu (rǝvny) *m,* revenue, income. **revenue** (ny) *f,* new growth, young wood.

rêver (rɛve) *v.i. & t,* to dream; d. of; muse; ponder.

réverbère (revɛrbɛ:r) *m,* street lamp; reflector. **réverbérer** (bere) *v.t,* to reverberate.

reverdir (rǝvɛrdi:r) *v.i,* to grow green again; grow young again.

révérence (reverɑ̃:s) *f,* reverence; bow, curtsy **révérenciel, le** (rɑ̃sjɛl) *a,* reverential. **révérencieux, euse**† (sjø, ø:z) *a,* obsequious; over-polite. **révérend, e** (rɑ̃, ɑ̃:d) *a,* reverend. **révérendissime** (rɑ̃disim) *a,* most reverend, right r. **révérer** (re) *v.t,* to revere, reverence.

rêverie (rɛvri) *f,* reverie, musing; idle fancy.

revers (rǝvɛ:r) *m,* reverse; back; backhand [stroke, blow]; facing, lapel; turnover [top] (*stocking, etc.*).

reverser (rəvɛrse) *v.t*, to pour out again; pour back; transfer.

réversible (revɛrsibl) *a*, reversible; revertible. **réversion** (sjɔ̃) *f*, reversion.

revêtement (rəvɛtmɑ̃) *m*, facing (*wall, etc.*); lining; revetment. **revêtir** (ti:r) *v.t*, to clothe, dress; don, put on; assume; provide; face, line; revet.

rêveur, euse (rɛvœ:r, ø:z) *a*, dreaming; dreamy. ¶ *n*, dreamer.

revient (rəvjɛ̃) *m*, cost. *prix de ~*, cost price.

revigorer (rəvigɔre) *v.t*, to reinvigorate.

revirement (rəvirmɑ̃) *m*, change, turn; turnover; veering.

reviser (rəvize) *v.t*, to revise; review, reconsider; overhaul. **reviseur** (zœ:r) *m*, examiner; proofreader. **revision** (zjɔ̃) *f*, revision; review; proofreading; medical examination (*recruits*).

revivifier (rəvivifje) *v.t*, to revivify, revive. **revivre** (vi:vr) *v.i.ir*, to live again, come to life again; revive.

révocation (revɔkasjɔ̃) *f*, revocation; repeal; dismissal, removal.

revoici (rəvwasi) *pr*, here . . . again. *le ~*, here he is again. **revoilà** (la) *pr*, there . . . again.

revoir (rəvwa:r) *v.t.ir*, to see again; meet again; revise; review. *au ~l* good-bye!

revoler (rəvɔle) *v.i*, to fly again; fly back.

révoltant, e (revɔltɑ̃, ɑ̃:t) *a*, revolting. **révolte** (vɔlt) *f*, revolt, rebellion, mutiny. **révolté, e** (te) *n*, rebel, insurgent, mutineer. **révolter** (te) *v.t*, to cause to revolt; shock. *se ~*, to revolt, rebel, mutiny.

révolu, e (revɔly) *a*, completed. **révolution** (sjɔ̃) *f*, revolution; revulsion. **révolutionnaire** (ɔnɛ:r) *a. & n*, revolutionary. **révolutionner** (ne) *v.t*, to revolutionize; upset. **revolver** (revɔlvɛ:r) *m*, revolver (*gun*); capstan, turret (*lathe*). *~ à six coups*, six-shooter.

revomir (rəvomi:r) *v.t*, to vomit [up, again].

révoquer (revɔke) *v.t*, to revoke, repeal; dismiss; recall.

revue (rəvy) *f*, review, inspection; magazine; revue.

révulsion (revylsjɔ̃) *f*, revulsion (*Med.*).

rez-de-chaussée (redʃose) *m*, ground floor.

rhabiller (rabije) *v.t*, to repair, mend, overhaul; dress again; re-clothe.

rhapsodie (rapsɔdi) *f*, rhapsody (*all Eng. senses*).

rhénan, e (renɑ̃, an) *a*, Rhine (*att.*).

rhétorique (retɔrik) *f*, rhetoric.

Rhin (le) (rɛ̃) the Rhine.

rhinocéros (rinɔserɔs) *m*, rhinoceros.

rhododendron (rɔdɔdɛ̃drɔ̃) *m*, rhododendron.

rhombe (rɔ̃:b) *m*, rhomb[us].

Rhône (le) (ro:n) the Rhone.

rhubarbe (rybarb) *f*, rhubarb.

rhum (rɔm) *m*, rum.

rhumatismal, e (rymatismal) *a*, rheumatic. **rhumatisme** (tism) *m*, rheumatism. **rhume** (*de cerveau, de poitrine*) (rym) *m*, cold (in the head, on the chest).

rhythme (ritm) *m*, rhythm. **rhythmique** (mik) *a*, rhythmic-(al).

riant, e (riɑ̃, ɑ̃:t) *a*, smiling; cheerful.

ribambelle (ribɑ̃bɛl) *f*, string, swarm.

ribote (ribɔt) *f*, drunken bout.

ricaner (rikane) *v.i*, to snigger, sneer.

richard (riʃa:r) *m*, [rich] upstart. **riche†** (riʃ) *a*, rich, wealthy; copious; valuable; handsome. **richesse** (ʃɛs) *f*, wealth, riches; richness.

ricin (risɛ̃) *m*, castor oil plant.

ricocher (rikɔʃe) *v.i*, to ricochet. **ricochet** (ʃɛ) *m*, ricochet; (*pl.*) duck & drake.

rictus (rikty:s) *m*, grin.

ride (rid) *f*, wrinkle, line; puckering; ripple; lanyard. **rideau** (do) *m*, curtain; [drop] curtain; screen; veil (*fig.*). *~ de fer*, safety curtain (*Theat.*); iron curtain. **rider** (de) *v.t*, to wrinkle, line; shrivel; ripple, ruffle.

ridicule† (ridikyl) *a*, ridiculous.

¶ *m*, ridiculousness; ridicule. **ri-diculiser** (lize) *v.t*, to ridicule.

rien (rjɛ̃) *pn.m*, anything; (*oft. with* **ne**) nothing. ~ *à* ~, love all (*Ten.*). ¶ *m*, trifle, mere nothing; (*pl.*) small talk.

rieur, euse (rjœːr, ø:z) *n*, laugher; (*att.*) laughing.

riflard (riflaːr) *m*, jack plane; gamp.

rigide† (riʒid) *a*, rigid; stiff. **rigidité** (dite) *f*, rigidity, stiffness. ~ *cadavérique* (kadaverik), rigor mortis.

rigole (rigɔl) *f*, channel, ditch, trench.

rigoler (rigɔle) *v.i*, guffaw; furrow, channel.

rigoureux, euse† (riɡurø, ø:z) *a*, rigorous, severe; strict. **rigueur** (ɡœːr) *f*, rigor, severity; hardship; strictness. *à la* ~, if necessary.

rimailler (rimaje) *v.i*, to write bad verse. **rimailleur** (jœːr) *m*, rhym[est]er. **rime** (rim) *f*, rhyme. **rimer** (me) *v.t*, to versify; (*v.i.*) to rhyme. **rimeur** (mœːr) *m*, rhym[est]er.

rincer (rɛ̃se) *v.t*, to rinse; r. out. **rinçure** (syːr) *f*, rinsings, slops.

ringard (rɛ̃gaːr) *m*, poker, rake.

ripaille (ripaːj) *f*, feasting, carousal.

riper (ripe) *v.t. & i*, to scrape; slide; shift (*cargo*).

ripopée (ripɔpe) *f*, slops; mishmash.

riposte (ripɔst) *f*, riposte, counter[stroke]; retort. **riposter** (te) *v.t*, to riposte.

rire (riːr) *m*, laughter; laugh. *fou* ~, guffaw. ~ *moqueur*, sneer. ¶ *v.i.ir*, to laugh, smile; joke. ~ *en dedans*, ~ *en dessous*, to laugh inwardly, snigger.

ris (ri) *m*, reef (*sail*). ~ *de veau*, sweetbread.

risée (rize) *f*, jeer, mockery; laughing stock, butt. **risible†** (zibl) *a*, ludicrous, laughable.

risque (risk) *m*, risk. **risquer** (ke) *v.t*, to risk, chance. ~ *le paquet*, to chance it.

rissole (risɔl) *f*, rissole. **rissoler** (le) *v.t*, to brown (*Cook.*).

ristourne (risturn) *f*, return, refund.

rite (rit) *m*, rite. **rituel, le** (tɥɛl) *a. & m*, ritual.

rivage (rivaːʒ) *m*, shore, foreshore, beach, strand; bank, side.

rival, e (rival) *n. & a*, rival. **rivaliser** (lize) *v.i*, to rival, vie with, emulate. **rivalité** (te) *f*, rivalry, emulation.

rive (riːv) *f*, bank, side, shore.

river (rive) *v.t*, to rivet, clinch.

riverain, e (rivrɛ̃, ɛn) *a*, riparian, riverside, waterside; wayside.

rivet (rivɛ) *m*, rivet; pin, bolt.

rivière (rivjɛːr) *f*, river; rivière (*gems*); single openwork (*Need.*). ~ *à truites*, trout stream. *la R~ de Gênes*, the Riviera (*French & Italian*).

rixe (riks) *f*, scuffle, brawl, fight.

riz (ri) *m*, rice. **rizière** (zjɛːr) *f*, rice field.

rob (rɔb) *m*, rubber (*cards*).

robe (rɔb) *f*, dress, gown, frock; robe; robe (*legal dress*); cloth (*clerical dress*); coat (*animal's*); skin (*onion, bean, etc.*); wrapper (*cigar*); color (*wine*). ~ *de chambre*, dressing gown. ~ *de mariée*, wedding dress. **robin** (bɛ̃) *m*, lawyer.

robinet (rɔbinɛ) *m*, cock, faucet. spigot.

robre (rɔbr) *m*, rubber (*cards*).

robuste† (rɔbyst) *a*, robust, lusty, sturdy, able-bodied; stout; hardy (*plant*). **robustesse** (tɛs) *f*, robustness, strength.

roc (rɔk) *m*, rock. **rocaille** (ka:j) *f*, rockwork. **rocailleux, euse** (kajø, ø:z) *a*, rocky, stony, rugged.

roche (rɔʃ) *f*, rock, stone, boulder. **rocher** (ʃe) *m*, rock, crag, cliff. ~ *artificiel*, rock garden. ~ *branlant*, rocking stone, logan [stone].

rochet (rɔʃɛ) *m*, ratchet; rochet (*surplice*).

rocheux, euse (rɔʃø, ø:z) *a*, rocky.

rococo (rɔkɔko) *m. & att*, rococo.

roder (rɔde) *v.t*, to grind, lap.

rôder (rode) *v.i*, to prowl, hang about. **rôdeur** (dœːr) *m*, prowler. ~ *de grève*, beachcomber.

rodomontade (rɔdɔmɔ̃tad) *f*, bluster.

rogations (rɔgasjɔ̃) *f.pl*, rogations.

rogatons (rɔgatɔ̃) *m.pl*, scraps (*food*); odds & ends.

Roger-Bontemps (rɔʒebɔ̃tɑ̃) *m*, happy-go-lucky fellow.

rogne (rɔɲ) *f*, itch, mange; scab; [bad] temper.

rogner (rɔɲe) *v.t*, to clip, trim, pare; cut down; cut (*edges of book*); (*v.i.*) to grumble, grouse.

rogneux, euse (rɔɲø, ø:z) *a*, mangy, scabby.

rognon (rɔɲɔ̃) *m*, kidney (*animal*); nodule.

rognonner (rɔɲɔne) *v.i*, to grumble.

rognure (rɔɲy:r) *f*, clipping, paring (*bit*).

rogue (rɔg) *a*, arrogant, haughty.

roi (rwa) *m*, king; champion. *fête des* ~*s*, Twelfth Night. ~ *de la nature*, lord of creation.

roide (rɛd & rwad) *a*, **roideur** (dœ:r) *f*, **roidir** (di:r) *v.t*. Same as **raide**, *etc*.

roitelet (rwatlɛ) *m*, kinglet; wren.

rôle (ro:l) *m*, roll, list, roster, rota; calendar (*prisoners for trial*); part, rôle. ~ *travesti*, man's part acted by a woman. *à tour de* ~, in rotation, in turn.

romain, e (rɔmɛ̃, ɛn) *a. & R*~ (*pers.*) *n*, Roman. **romain,** *m*, roman (*Typ.*). **romaine,** *f*, romaine lettuce, cos l.; steelyard.

roman, e (rɔmɑ̃, an) *a. & m*, Romance (*language*); Romanesque (*Arch.*). ¶ *m*, novel; fiction; romance. ~ *à deux sous*, pulp novel. ~ *policier* (pɔlisje), detective story. **romance** (mɑ̃:s) *f*, song, ballad; sloppiness, maudlin[ism]. ~ *sans paroles*, song without words. ¶ *a*, sloppy, maudlin. **romancier, ère** (mɑ̃sje, ɛ:r) *n*, novelist. **romand, e** (mɑ̃, ɑ̃:d) *a*, French-speaking (*Switzerland*). **romanesque**† (manɛsk) *a*, romantic. **romanichel** (maniʃɛl) *m*, gypsy, romany. **romantique** (mɑ̃tik) *a*, romantic (*literature*).

romarin (rɔmarɛ̃) *m*, rosemary.

rompre (rɔ̃:pr) *v.t. & i*, to break; b. up; b. in; b. off; snap; rupture; disrupt; burst; interrupt; cut off; upset; cancel. ~ *charge*, to tranship (*Rly.*). ~ *les chiens*, to call off the hounds; change

the subject. **rompu, e** (rɔ̃py) *p.a*, broken; b. in, used, inured. ~ [*de fatigue*], tired out.

romsteck (rɔmstɛk) *m*, rump steak.

ronce (rɔ̃:s) *f*, bramble; blackberry bush; barb[ed] wire; annoyance. ~ *de noyer*, walnut burr. ~*-framboise*, loganberry.

rond, e (rɔ̃, ɔ̃:d) *a*, round; rounded; rotund; even (*money*). ¶ *m*, round; circle; ring. ~*-de-cuir*, pen-pusher, bureaucrat; air cushion. ~ *de serviette*, napkin ring. ¶ *f*, round; beat; roundelay; round hand; semibreve. **rondelet, te** (rɔ̃dlɛ, ɛt) *a*, roundish. **rondelle** (dɛl) *f*, washer; ring (*umbrella*); disc. **rondement** (dmɑ̃) *ad*, roundly, briskly, bluntly. **rondeur** (dœ:r) *f*, roundness, rotundity; fullness; frankness. **rondin** (dɛ̃) *m*, billet, log. **rondpoint** (rɔ̃pwɛ̃) *m*, traffic circle.

ronflant, e (rɔ̃flɑ̃, ɑ̃:t) (*fig.*) *a*, sonorous, highsounding. **ronfler** (fle) *v.i*, to snore; boom, roar, hum, whir, buzz.

ronger (rɔ̃ʒe) *v.t*, to gnaw, nibble; pick (*bone*); eat [away, into], corrode; undermine; fret; prey. **rongeur, euse** (ʒœ:r, ø:z) *a*, rodent, gnawing; corroding. ¶ *m*, rodent.

ronron (rɔ̃rɔ̃) *m*, purr[ing]; hum; drone.

roquer (rɔke) *v.t*, to castle (*chess*); roquet (*croquet*).

roquet (rɔkɛ) *m*, pug [dog]; cur, mongrel.

roquette (rɔkɛt) *f*, rocket (*Bot.*).

rosace (rozas) *f*, rosette; rose; rose window. **rosacé, e** (se) rosaceous. ¶ *f.pl*, Rosaceae. **rosaire** (zɛ:r) *m*, rosary (*beads*).

rosbif (rɔzbif) *m*, roast beef; roast sirloin.

rose (ro:z) *f*, rose; rose window; rose diamond. ~ *des vents*, compass card. ~ *moussue*, moss rose. ~ *muscade*, musk r. ~ *thé*, tea r. ~ *trémière* (tremjɛ:r), hollyhock. ¶ *m. & a*, rose [color], pink. *le mont Rose*, Monte Rosa. **rosé, e** (roze) *a*, roseate, rosy.

roseau (rozo) *m*, reed; broken reed (*fig.*).

rosée (roze) *f*, dew.

roselet (roslɛ) *m*, ermine (*fur*).
roseraie (rozrɛ) *f*, rose garden, rosary, rosery. **rosette** (zɛt) *f*, rosette; bow (*ribbon*); red ink, r. chalk. **rosier** (zje) *m*, rose bush. ~ *grimpant*, rambler [rose].
rosse (rɔs) *f*, jade, sorry steed; nasty (*or* objectionable) person. **rosser** (se) *v.t*, to thrash, beat.
rossignol (rɔsiɲɔl) *m*, nightingale; picklock; whistle; unsalable article, white elephant.
rot (ro) *m*, belch.
rôt (ro) *m*, roast [meat]; roast meat course.
rotation (rɔtasjɔ̃) *f*, rotation. **rotatoire** (twa:r) *a*, rotary.
roter (rɔte) *v.i*, to belch.
rôti (roti) *m*, roast [meat]; r. m. course. ~ *de porc*, r. pork. **rôtie** (ti) *f*, [round of] toast. ~ *à l'anglaise*, ~ *au fromage*, Welsh rabbit, W. rarebit.
rotin (rɔtɛ̃) *m*, rattan; r. cane.
rôtir (roti:r) *v.t. & i*, to roast, broil; toast; scorch. **rôtisserie** (tisri) *f*, shop where one buys cooked meats. **rôtissoire** (tiswa:r) *f*, roaster, Dutch oven.
rotonde (rɔtɔ̃:d) *f*, rotunda; cloak. **rotondité** (tɔ̃dite) *f*, rotundity.
rotule (rɔtyl) *f*, knee cap, patella. ~ *sphérique*, ball & socket.
roture (rɔty:r) *f*, commonalty. **roturier, ère** (tyrje, ɛ:r) *n*, commoner.
rouage (rwa:ʒ) *m*, wheels, wheelwork, works; machinery (*fig.*).
rouan, ne (rwɑ̃, an) *a. & n*, roan (*animal*).
roucouler (rukule) *v.i*, to coo; bill & coo; (*v.t.*) to warble.
roue (ru) *f*, wheel. ~ *libre*, free w. *faire la* ~, to spread its tail (*peacock*); turn catherine wheels.
roué (rwe) *m*, rake, profligate. **rouelle** (rwɛl) *f*, round [slice]; fillet (*veal*).
rouennerie (rwanri) *f*, printed cotton goods.
rouer (rwe) *v.t*, to coil (*rope*); break upon the wheel. ~ *de coups*, to thrash. **rouerie** (ruri) *f*, trickery. **rouet** (rwɛ) *m*, spinning wheel; sheave.
rouflaquette (ruflakɛt) *f*, lovelock, earlock, cowlick.

rouge (ru:ʒ) *m*, red (*color & pers. in Pol.*); rouge. ¶ *a*, red; red-hot; blushing; glowing. *mer R*~, Red Sea. ~-*gorge*, *m*, [robin] redbreast. ~-*queue*, *m*, redstart.
rougeâtre (ruʒɑ:tr) *a*, reddish. **rougeaud, e** (ʒo, o:d) *a*, red-faced, ruddy. **rougeole** (ʒɔl) *f*, measles. **rouget** (ʒɛ) *m*, red mullet. **rougeur** (ʒœ:r) *f*, redness; blush, flush; red spot (*skin*). **rougir** (ʒi:r) *v.t. & i*, to redden; blush, flush.
rouille (ru:j) *f*, rust; mildew, blight (*Agric.*). **rouillé, e** (ruje) *a*, rusty; mildewed; out of practice. **rouiller** (je) *v.t*, to rust. **rouillure** (jy:r) *f*, rustiness.
roulade (rulad) *f*, roll (*downhill*); roulade, run (*Mus.*). **roulage** (la:ʒ) *m*, haulage. **roulant, e** (lɑ̃, ɑ̃:t) *a*, rolling; traveling; circulating (*capital*). **rouleau** (lo) *m*, roller; roll; spool (*film* —*Phot.*); scroll; twist (*tobacco*); coil (*rope*). ~ *de pâtissier*, rolling pin. *au bout de son* ~, at the end of one's rope, at one's wits' end. **roulement** (lmɑ̃) *m*, roll[ing]; working, running; r. gear; rumbling (*traffic*); bearings; turnover (*capital*); rotation. ~ *à billes*, ball bearings. **rouler** (le) *v.t*, to roll; r. up; coil; haul; (*v.i.*) to roll; run, work; turn, rotate; travel, drive; rove, roam; circulate freely; fluctuate; fleece, cheat. *faire* ~ *la presse*, to machine (*Typ.*). ~ [*sur le sol*], to taxi (*Avn.*). **roulette** (lɛt) caster, -or; roller, wheel; tape [measure] (*coiled*); roulette. **roulier** (lje) *m*, carter, waggoner. **roulis** (li) *m*, rolling (*ship*). **roulotte** (lɔt) *f*, caravan (*house on wheels*); trailer.
roumain, e (rumɛ̃, ɛn) *a & R*~, *n. & le roumain* (*language*), R[o]umanian. **la Roumanie** (mani), R[o]umania.
roupiller (rupije) *v.i*, to snooze.
rouspéter (ruspete) *v.i*, to complain, protest; resist; gripe.
roussâtre (rusɑ:tr) *a*, reddish. **rousseau** (so) *m. & att*, redhaired (*person*). **rousserolle** (srɔl) *f*, sedge warbler. **rousseur** (sœ:r) *f*, redness. *tache de* ~,

freckle. **roussi** (si) *m*, [smell of] burning. **roussir** (si:r) *v.t. & i*, to redden; brown (*meat*); scorch, singe.

route (rut) *f*, road, path, track; route, course, way; transit; journey. **grande ~**, **~ nationale**, highway. **~ départementale**, secondary road. **~ déviée**, loopway. **routier, ère** (tje, ɛ:r) *a*, road (*att.*). ¶ *m*, campaigner, stager. **routine** (tin) *f*, routine; rote; red tape.

rouvieux (ruvjø) *m*, mange; (*att.*) mangy.

rouvrir (ruvri:r) *v.t.ir*, to re-open.

roux, rousse (ru, rus) *a. & n*, russet; brown[ed]; red (*hair*); red-haired (*person*). ¶ *m*, russet (*color*); brown sauce.

royal, e† (rwajal) *a*, royal, regal, kingly. **royaliste** (list) *a. & n*, royalist. **royaume** (jo:m) *m*, kingdom, realm. **royauté** (ote) *f*, royalty; kingship; dominance.

ruade (rɥad) *f*, lashing out; kick (*horse*).

ruban (rybɑ̃) *m*, ribbon; band; tape.

rubéole (rybeɔl) *f*, German measles.

rubicond, e (rybikɔ̃, ɔ̃:d) *a*, rubicund, florid.

rubis (rybi) *m*, ruby; jewel (*Horol.*).

rubrique (rybrik) *f*, red chalk; rubric; heading, section; column (*special subject news*); publisher's imprint (*place of publication*).

ruche (ryʃ) *f*, [bee]hive; ruche. **rucher** (ʃe) *m*, apiary.

rude† (ryd) *a*, rough; rugged; harsh; hard; severe; gruff; stiff; steep. **rudesse** (dɛs) *f*, roughness, etc.

rudiment (rydimɑ̃) *m*, rudiment. **rudimentaire** (tɛ:r) *a*, rudimentary.

rudoyer (rydwaje) *v.t*, to use roughly, brow-beat.

rue (ry) *f*, street; rue (*Bot.*). **~ à sens unique**, one-way street.

ruée (rɥe) *f*, rush, onrush, onslaught.

ruelle (rɥɛl) *f*, lane, alley; ruelle (*bedside*).

ruer (rɥe) *v.t*, to lash out, kick (*horse*). **se ~ sur**, to hurl oneself at, rush at.

rugir (ryʒi:r) *v.i*, to roar. **rugissement** (ʒismɑ̃) *m*, roar, roaring; howling (*storm*).

rugueux, euse (rygø, ø:z) *a*, rough, rugged.

ruine (rɥin) *f*, ruin, [down]fall. **ruiner** (ne) *v.t*, to ruin. **ruineux, euse** (nø, ø:z) *a*, ruinous.

ruisseau (rɥiso) *m*, stream[let], brook, rivulet, rill; gutter (*street & fig.*). **ruisseler** (sle) *v.i*, to stream, run down, trickle.

rumeur (rymœ:r) *f*, hum (*voices, etc.*); uproar; rumor.

ruminant, e (ryminɑ̃, ɑ̃:t) *a. & m*, ruminant. **ruminer** (ne) *v.t. & abs*, to ruminate; ponder.

rupture (rypty:r) *f*, breaking; rupture; fracture; breaking off, breach.

rural, e (ryral) *a*, rural, country (*att.*).

ruse (ry:z) *f*, ruse, trick[ery], wile, dodge; stratagem. **rusé, e** (ryze) *a*, artful, crafty, wily. **ruser** (ze) *v.i*, to use cunning.

russe (rys) *a. & R~**, *n. & le russe* (*language*), Russian. **la Russie** (si), Russia.

rustaud, e (rysto, o:d) *a*, boorish, uncouth. ¶ *n*, boor. **rusticité** (tisite) *f*, rusticity; boorishness. **rustique†** (tik) *a*, rustic; country (*att.*); hardy (*plant*); crazy (*pavement*). **rustre** (str) *m*, boor, churl.

rut (ryt) *m*, rut, heat (*animals*).

rutabaga (rytabaga) *m*, rutabaga.

rythme (ritm) *m*, rhythm. **rythmique** (mik) *a*, rhythmic(al).

S

sa *see* **son**.

sabbat (saba) *m*, sabbath (*Jewish, witches*'); row, racket.

sable (sɑ:bl) *m*, sand; gravel (*Med.*); sable (*fur, Her.*). **~ blanc**, silver sand. **sabler** (sable) *v.t*, to sand, gravel (*path*); swig, toss off. **sablier** (blie) *m*, hourglass, sand g. **sablière** (ɛ:r) *f*, sand pit, gravel pit; wall plate. **sablon** (blɔ̃) *m*, fine sand. **sa-**

blonneux, euse (blɔnø, ø:z) *a*, sandy. **sablonnière** (njɛ:r) *f*, sand pit.

sabord (sabɔːr) *m*, port [hole]. **saborder** (bɔrde) *v.t*, to scuttle (*ship*).

sabot (sabo) *m*, clog, sabot; shoe; skid; hoof; whipping top; tub (*bad ship*); rubbishy instrument *or* tool. **sabotage** (bota:ʒ) *m*, sabotage, foul play. **saboter** (te) *v.t*, to botch; damage wilfully, wreck. **sabotière** (tjɛ:r) *f*, clog dance.

sabouler (sabule) *v.t*, to jostle; rate, scold.

sabre (sɑ:br) *m*, saber, sword, broadsword, cutlass; swordfish. **sabrer** (sɑbre) *v.t. & abs*, to saber; slash; slash about; cut down, blue-pencil.

sac (sak) *m*, sack, bag, pouch, sac; sackcloth (*Theol.*); sacking, pillage. ~ *à main*, handbag. ~ *à ouvrage*, work b. ~ *à provisions*, shopping b. ~ *à terre*, sand b. ~ *d'ordonnance* (*Mil.*), knapsack. ~ *de couchage*, sleeping bag. ~ *de touriste*, ~ *de montagne*, ~ *d'alpinisme*, rucksack.

saccade (sakad) *f*, jerk, start. **saccadé, e** (de) *p.a*, jerky; irregular; staccato (*voice*).

saccager (sakaʒe) *v.t*, to sack, pillage; ransack; upset.

saccharin, e (sakarɛ̃, in) *a*, saccharine, sugary; sugar (*att.*). ¶ *f*, saccharin.

sacerdoce (sasɛrdɔs) *m*, priesthood; ministry. **sacerdotal, e** (tal) *a*, sacerdotal, priestly.

sachée (saʃe) *f*, sackful, bagful. **sachet** (ʃɛ) *m*, bag. ~ *à parfums*, scent bag, sachet. **sacoche** (kɔʃ) *f*, saddlebag; courier's bag; tool b.

sacramental (sakramɑ̃tal) *m*, sacramental. **sacramentel, le†** (tɛl) *a*, sacramental, binding. **sacre** (kr) *m*, anointing, coronation; consecration (*bishop*). **sacré, e** (kre) *a*, holy, sacred, consecrated; damned, cursed. **sacrement** (krəmɑ̃) *m*, sacrament. **sacrer** (kre) *v.t*, to anoint, crown; consecrate; curse, swear. **sacrifice** (krifis) *m*, sacrifice; offering.

sacrifier (fje) *v.t. & abs*, to sacrifice. **sacrilège** (lɛ:ʒ) *m*, sacrilege; (*att.*) sacrilegious.

sacripant (sakripɑ̃) *m*, rascal, bully.

sacristain (sakristɛ̃) *m*, sacristan. **sacristie** (ti) *f*, vestry, sacristy. **sacro-saint, e** (krɔsɛ̃, ɛ̃:t) *a*, sacrosanct.

safran (safrɑ̃) *m*, saffron, crocus.

sagace (sagas) *a*, sagacious, shrewd. **sagacité** (site) *f*, sagacity, shrewdness.

sage† (sa:ʒ) *a*, wise, sage, sapient; judicious, prudent, sensible; well-behaved, good (*child*); chaste. ¶ *m*, sage, wise man. ~*-femme*, *f*, midwife. **sagesse** (ʒɛs) *f*, wisdom, etc; good conduct.

sagou (sagu) *m*, sago. **sagou[t]ier** ([t]je) *m*, sago palm.

sagouin (sagwɛ̃) *m*, saguin (*monkey*); sloven.

saignant, e (sɛɲɑ̃, ɑ̃:t) *a*, bleeding; raw; rare (*meat*). **saignée** (ɲe) *f*, bleeding, blood letting; bend of the arm; trench; holocaust. **saigner** (ɲe) *v.i. & t*, to bleed; stick (*pig*); tap (*tree, etc.*); drain; rankle.

saillant, e (sajɑ̃, ɑ̃:t) *a*, salient, projecting, prominent; striking, outstanding. **saillie** (ji) *f*, spurt, bound; projection; ledge; protrusion; sally; covering. **saillir** (ji:r) *v.i.ir*, to gush out; project; protrude; sally; (*v.t.ir.*) to service (*of animals*).

sain, e† (sɛ̃, ɛn) *a*, sound; wholesome; healthy, hale; sane. *sain & sauf*, safe & sound.

saindoux (sɛ̃du) *m*, lard.

saint, e (sɛ̃, ɛ̃:t) *n*, saint, patron s. *le ~ des saints*, the holy of holies, sanctum. ¶ *a*, holy; sainted; saintly, godly; consecrated, hallowed. *saint-frusquin*, worldly goods. *Saint-Siège*, Holy See. *sainte table*, communion table. *la Sainte Vierge*, the Blessed Virgin. *Saint, comps*: *le ~-Esprit* (sɛ̃tɛspri), the Holy Ghost, the Holy Spirit. *la ~-Jean* (sɛ̃ʒɑ̃), Midsummer Day. *le ~-Laurent* (lɔrɑ̃), the St. Lawrence. *la ~-Martin* (martɛ̃), Martinmas. *la ~-Michel* (miʃɛl), Michaelmas. *la ~-Sylvestre* (silvɛstr), New

Year's eve. **Sainte-Hélène** (sɛ̃t-elɛn) *f*, St. Helena. **saintement** (tmɑ̃) *ad*, holily, in a godly manner, righteously. **sainteté** (təte) *f*, holiness, saintliness; sanctity.

saisie (sɛzi) *f*, seizure; distraint; execution; distress (*law*); foreclosure (*mortgage*). **saisir** (ziːr) *v.t*, to seize, lay hold of, grasp; catch; snatch; distrain, attach; foreclose; startle; lay before (*court*). **saisissant**, e (zizɑ̃, ɑ̃ːt) *a*, piercing (*cold*); startling, striking; thrilling. **saisissement** (smɑ̃) *m*, shock; thrill.

saison (sɛzɔ̃) *f*, season, time (*of year*). marchand des quatre-~s, street vendor.

salade (salad) *f*, salad; jumble. **saladier** (dje) *m*, salad bowl.

salage (salaːʒ) *m*, salting, curing.

salaire (salɛːr) *m*, wage[s], pay; hire; reward. ~ de famine, starvation wage.

salaison (salɛzɔ̃) *f*, salting, curing; (*pl.*) salt provisions.

salamalec (salamalɛk) *m*, salaam.

salamandre (salamɑ̃ːdr) *f*, salamander. ~ aquatique, newt, eft.

Salamanque (salamɑ̃ːk) *f*, Salamanca.

salant (salɑ̃) *a.m*, salt (*marsh*), saline.

salarié, e (salarje) *p.a*, wage-earning, paid. **salarier** (je) *v.t*, to pay a wage to.

salaud (salo) *m*, (*pers.*) skunk, bastard.

sale† (sal) *a*, dirty, unclean, filthy; foul; nasty; soiled (*linen*); messy.

salé, e (sale) *p.a*, salt, salted; corned (*beef*); briny; keen; broad (*story*); stiff (*price*). [porc] salé, *m*, salt pork. **saler** (le) *v.t*, to salt, pickle, cure, corn; overcharge (*someone*).

Salerne (salɛrn) *f*, Salerno.

saleté (salte) *f*, dirtiness; dirt; filth; mess; rubbish, trash[y goods].

salicole (salikɔl) *a*, salt (*industry*); saliferous. **salicoque** (kɔk) *f*, shrimp. **salière** (ljɛːr) *f*, salt cellar; salt box. **salin**, e (lɛ̃, in) *a*, saline, briny, salt[y]. ¶ *f*, salt works; rock salt mine.

salir (saliːr) *v.t*, to dirty, soil; foul; sully. **salissant** (lisɑ̃) *a*, dirty-ing; easily soiled. **salissure** (lisyːr) *f*, stain.

salive (saliːv) *f*, saliva, spittle. **saliver** (live) *v.i*, to salivate.

salle (sal) *f*, hall; room; ward (*hospital*); house (*Theat.*, *etc.*); auditorium; office. ~ à manger, dining room; d. saloon (*ship*); coffee room (*hotel*); mess room (*Mil.*). ~ commune, living room. ~ d'armes, armory; fencing school. ~ d'attente, waiting room (*Rly.*). ~ de bain, bathroom. ~ de classe, schoolroom. ~ de police, guardroom (*Mil.*). ~ des festins, banqueting hall. ~ des pas perdus, waiting room (*Rly.*); lobby.

salmigondis (salmigɔ̃di) *m*, hodgepodge.

salon (salɔ̃) *m*, reception room; drawing room; parlor; saloon; room; salon, exhibition, show. ~ d'exposition, showroom. ~ de l'automobile, auto show. ~ de l'aviation, aircraft exhibition. ~ de pose, studio (*Phot.*).

Salonique (salɔnik) *f*, Salonica.

salope (salɔp) *f*, slattern, slut. **saloperie** (pri) *f*, filth, muck; trash. **salopette** (pɛt) *f*, overalls; dungarees, jeans.

salpêtre (salpɛːtr) *m*, saltpeter, niter.

salsepareille (salsparɛːj) *f*, sarsaparilla.

saltimbanque (saltɛ̃bɑ̃ːk) *m*, showman, tumbler; mountebank.

salubre (salybr) *a*, salubrious, healthy; wholesome. **salubrité** (brite) *f*, salubrity; health (*public*).

saluer (salɥe) *v.t*, to salute, bow to; greet, hail.

salure (salyːr) *f*, saltness; tang.

salut (saly) *m*, safety, welfare; salvation; salutation, bow, greeting; salute; evening service (*Eccl.*). ¶ *i*, hail! greeting! greeting! **salutaire†** (tɛːr) *a*, salutary, wholesome, beneficial. **salutation** (tasjɔ̃) *f*, salutation, greeting, bow.

salve (salv) *f*, salvo, salute; round (*applause*).

samedi (samdi) *m*, Saturday.

samovar (samɔvaːr) *m*, urn (*for tea, coffee*).

sanatorium (sanatɔrjɔm) *m*, sanatorium.

sanctifier (sãktifje) *v.t*, to sanctify, hallow. **sanction** (sjɔ̃) *f*, sanction, assent; penalty, punishment. **sanctionner** (one) *v.t*, to sanction, approve. **sanctuaire** (tɥɛːr) *m*, sanctuary; sanctum.

sandale (sãdal) *f*, sandal, shoe.

sandwich (sãdwitʃ) *m*, sandwich.

sang (sã) *m*, blood, gore; race, lineage, kinship. **~-froid**, coolness, self-possession, nerve. [*homme de*] **~ mêlé**, half-caste. **sanglant, e** (glã, ã:t) *a*, bloody; sanguinary; deadly; cutting, scathing; outrageous.

sangle (sã:gl) *f*, strap, band, girth, webbing. **sangler** (sãgle) *v.t*, to strap; girth; lash. **se ~**, to lace oneself tight[ly].

sanglier (sãglje) *m*, wild boar.

sanglot (sãglo) *m*, sob. **sangloter** (glɔte) *v.i*, to sob.

sangsue (sãsy) *f*, leech; bloodsucker. **sanguin, e** (gɛ̃, in) *a*, sanguineous, blood (*att.*); full-blooded, sanguine. ¶ *f*, red chalk; bloodstone. **sanguinaire** (ginɛːr) *a*, sanguinary, bloody; bloodthirsty.

sanitaire (sanitɛːr) *a*, sanitary.

sans (sã) *pr*, without; but for; -less; -lessly; un-; no; non-. **~ arrêt, ~ escale**, nonstop. **~ cela, ~ quoi**, otherwise. **~ date**, sine die; undated. **~ empattement**, sanserif. [*perdu*] **~ nouvelles**, missing (*ship*). **~ que**, without. **~ valeur déclarée**, uninsured (*Post*).

sans-cœur (sãkœːr) *n*, heartless person.

sans-façon (sãfasɔ̃) *m*, straightforwardness, bluntness.

sans-fil (sãfil) *f*, wireless [telegraphy]; (*m.*) wireless [telegram].

sans-gêne (sãʒɛn) *m*, off-handedness, cheek.

sansonnet (sãsɔnɛ) *m*, starling (*bird*).

sans-souci (sãsusi) *n*, easy-going person, happy-go-lucky individual; (*m.*) unconcern.

sans-travail (les) (sãtravaːj) *m.pl*, the workless, the unemployed.

santal (sãtal) *m*, sandal[wood].

santé (sãte) *f*, health. **~ de fer**, iron constitution. *la* **~**, quarantine (*station*).

sape (sap) *f*, sap (*Mil.*); undermining. **saper** (pe) *v.t*, to sap, etc. **sapeur** (pœːr) *m*, sapper. **~-pompier**, fireman. *les sapeurs-pompiers*, the fire brigade.

saphir (safiːr) *m*, sapphire.

sapin (sapɛ̃) *m*, fir [tree]; spruce [fir]. [*bois de*] **~**, deal. **sapinière** (pinjɛːr) *f*, fir plantation.

Saragosse (saragɔs) *f*, Saragossa.

sarbacane (sarbakan) *f*, pea shooter; blow gun, blowpipe, blow tube (*dart tube*).

sarcasme (sarkasm) *m*, sarcasm, taunt. **sarcastique** (tik) *a*, sarcastic.

sarcler (sarkle) *v.t*, to weed. **sarcleur, euse** (klœːr, øːz) *n*, weeder (*pers.*). **sarcloir** (klwaːr) *m*, weeding hoe, weeder.

sarcophage (sarkɔfaːʒ) *m*, sarcophagus.

Sardaigne (la) (sardɛɲ), Sardinia. **sarde** (sard) *a*. & **S~**, *n*, Sardinian.

sardine (sardin) *f*, pilchard; sardine.

sardoine (sardwan) *f*, sardonyx.

sardonique (sardɔnik) *a*, sardonic.

sarigue (sarig) *m*. & *f*, opossum, sarigue.

sarment (sarmã) *m*, vine shoot; bine.

sarrasin (sarazɛ̃) *m*, buckwheat; Saracen.

sarrau (saro) *m*, smock, overall.

sarriette (sarjɛt) *f*, savory (*Bot.*).

sas (sɑ) *m*, sieve. **sasser** (se) *v.t*, to sift.

Satan (satã) *m*, Satan. **satané, e** (tane) *a*, devilish. **satanique** (nik) *a*, satanic.

satellite (satɛlit) *m*, satellite; henchman.

satiété (sasjete) *f*, satiety, surfeit.

satin (satɛ̃) *m*, satin. **satiner** (tine) *v.t*, to satin; glaze (*paper, etc.*); burnish (*Phot.*). **satinette** (nɛt) *f*, sateen.

satire (satiːr) *f*, satire. **satirique†** (tirik) *a*, satiric, satirical. ¶ *m*, satirist. **satiriser** (ze) *v.t*, to satirize.

satisfaction (satisfaksjɔ̃) *f*, satisfaction, gratification, comfort; atonement (*Theol.*). **satisfaire** (fɛ:r) *v.t.ir*, to satisfy, please, gratify, answer. ~ à, to satisfy; answer, meet; fulfill. **satisfaisant, e** (fəzɑ̃, ɑ̃:t) *a*, satisfactory.

saturer (satyre) *v.t*, to saturate.

saturnales (satyrnal) *f.pl*, saturnalia. **saturnisme** (nism) *m*, lead poisoning.

satyre (sati:r) *m*, satyr.

sauce (so:s) *f*, sauce. **saucer** (sose) *v.t*, to dip in the sauce; drench, souse. **saucière** (sjɛ:r) *f*, gravy boat.

saucisse (sosis) *f*, sausage (*fresh*); s. balloon. **saucisson** (sɔ̃) *m*, smoked sausage.

sauf, sauve (sof, so:v) *a*, safe, unhurt, unscathed; saved. **sauf,** *pr*, save, saving, but, except[ed]; unless; subject; under. **~-conduit,** *m*, safe-conduct, pass.

sauge (so:ʒ) *f*, sage (*Bot., Cook.*).

saugrenu, e (sogrəny) *a*, absurd, preposterous.

saulaie (solɛ) *f*, willow plantation. **saule** (so:l) *m*, willow [tree].

saumâtre (soma:tr) *a*, brackish, briny.

saumon (somɔ̃) *m*, salmon; ingot, pig (*metal*). **saumoneau** (mɔno) *m*, young salmon.

saumure (somy:r) *f*, [pickling] brine.

saunage (sona:ʒ) *m*, salt making; s. trade. **saunerie** (nri) *f*, salt works.

saupoudrer (sopudre) *v.t*, to sprinkle, dust, powder. **saupoudroir** (drwa:r) *m*, sifter.

saure (sɔ:r) *a*, sorrel (*horse*). **saurer** (sore) *v.t*, to kipper.

saussaie (sosɛ) *f*, willow plantation.

saut (so) *m*, leap, jump, vault; hop; skip; bound; fall[s] (*water*). ~ à la perche, pole vault. **~-de-lit,** dressing gown; bedside rug. ~ de mouton, buck (*of horse*); leap-frog. ~ en hauteur, high jump. ~ en longueur, long j. le ~ périlleux, a somersault; the plunge ·(*fig.*). par ~s & par bonds, by fits & starts, spasmodically. **saute** (so:t) *f*, shift, change. **~-mouton** (sotmutɔ̃) *m*, leap-frog. **sauter** (sote) *v.i*, to

leap, jump; skip; hop; bound, spring; vault; fly, fling oneself; explode, blow up; go smash; fall; shift, change (*wind*); (*v.t.*) to leap [over], jump [o.]; skip, leave out; drop (*stitch*); cover (*of animals*). **sauterelle** (trɛl) *f*, grasshopper; locust. **sauteruisseau** (sotrɥiso) *m*, errand boy. **sauteur, euse** (tœ:r, ø:z) *n*, jumper, leaper; weathercock (*pers.*); (*f.*) sauté pan; jig saw. **sautiller** (tije) *v.i*, to hop, skip; trip along; jump about. **sautoir** (twa:r) *m*, saltire; kerchief; vaulting standard. en ~, crosswise, over the shoulder.

sauvage† (sovaːʒ) *a*, savage, uncivilized; wild; barbarous; unsociable, shy. ¶ *n*. & **sauvagesse** (vaʒɛs) *f*, savage; unsociable person. **sauvageon** (ʒɔ̃) *m*, wild stock (*grafting*); wilding, seedling. **sauvagerie** (ʒri) *f*, savagery; unsociability, shyness. **sauvagin, e** (ʒɛ̃, in) *a*, fishy (*taste, smell, of flesh*).

sauvegarde (sovgard) *f*, safeguard, protection; safe-conduct. **sauve-qui-peut** (kipø) *m*, stampede, headlong flight. **sauver** (ve) *v.t*, to save, rescue; salve, salvage. se ~, to escape; run away, be off. **sauvetage** (vta:ʒ) *m*, life saving; rescue; salvage. **sauveur** (vœ:r) *m*, saver, deliverer. le *Sauveur*, the Savior.

savamment (savamɑ̃) *ad*, learnedly; knowingly. **savant, e** (vɑ̃, ɑ̃:t) *a*, learned, scholarly; skillful; performing (*dog*); knowing, precocious (*in vice*), sophisticated. ¶ *n*, scientist, scholar.

savate (savat) *f*, old shoe; boxing with the feet, head, & fists. en ~s, down at the heel, slipshod. **saveter** (vte) *v.t*, to botch. **savetier** (vtje) *m*, cobbler; botcher.

saveur (savœ:r) *f*, savor, flavor, taste; relish, zest.

Savoie (la) (savwa), Savoy.

savoir (savwa:r) *v.t.ir*, to know; be aware of, tell; be acquainted with, know of; understand; know how to; be able to; can. ~ [*bon*] gré à, to be grateful to. ~ mauvais gré à, to be annoyed with. ¶ *m*, knowledge, learning, scholarship. ~-faire (vwarfɛːr) *m*, ability, tact, gumption, nous. ~-vivre, *m*, good manners.

savon (savɔ̃) *m*, soap. ~ *à barbe en bâton*, shaving stick. savonner (vɔne) *v.t*, to soap, wash; lather. savonnerie (nri) *f*, soap works; s. trade. savonneux, euse (nø, ø:z) *a*, soapy. savonnier (nje) *m*, soap maker.

savourer (savure) *v.t*, to taste; relish, enjoy. savoureux, euse (rø, ø:z) *a*, savory, tasty; enjoyable.

saxe (saks) *m*, Dresden china. la Saxe, Saxony.

saxhorn (saksɔrn) *m*, saxhorn.

saxon, ne (saksɔ̃, ɔn) *a*. & S~, *n*, Saxon.

saxophone (saksɔfɔn) *m*, saxophone.

saynète (sɛnɛt) *f*, playlet, sketch.

sbire (zbːr) *m*, sbirro; myrmidon.

scabieux, euse (skabjø, ø:z) *a*, scabious, scabby. ¶ *f*, scabious (*Bot.*).

scabreux, euse (skabrø, ø:z) *a*, rough; ticklish; scabrous, improper.

scalpel (skalpɛl) *m*, scalpel.

scalper (skalpe) *v.t*, to scalp.

scandale (skɑ̃dal) *m*, scandal, shame. scandaleux, euse† (lø, ø:z) *a*, scandalous, shameful. scandaliser (lize) *v.t*, to scandalize, shock.

scander (skɑ̃de) *v.t*, to scan (*verse*); stress (*Mus.*); syllabize (*articulate by syllables*).

scandinave (skɑ̃dinaːv) *a*. & S~, *n*, Scandinavian. la Scandinavie (navi), Scandinavia.

scansion (skɑ̃sjɔ̃) *f*, scansion, scanning.

scaphandre (skafɑ̃ːdr) *m*, diving dress. scaphandrier (fɑ̃drie) *m*, diver (*in diving dress*).

scarabée (skarabe) *m*, beetle; scarab.

scarifier (skarifje) *v.t*, to scarify.

scarlatine (skarlatin) *f*, scarlatina, scarlet fever.

scarole (skarɔl) *f*, endive.

sceau (so) *m*, seal; stamp (*fig.*).

scélérat, e (selera, at) *a*, villainous, wicked. ¶ *n*, villain, scoundrel, miscreant. scélératesse (tɛs) *f*, villainy, wickedness.

scellé (sɛle) *m*, seal (*official*). sceller (le) *v.t*, to seal; s. up.

scénario (senarjo) *m*, scenario. scène (sɛn) *f*, stage; scene; action; local[e]; shindy. scénique (senik) *a*, scenic, theatrical, stage (*att.*).

scepticisme (sɛptisism) *m*, skepticism. sceptique (tik) *a*, skeptical. ¶ *n*, skeptic.

sceptre (sɛptr) *m*, scepter.

Schaffhouse (ʃafuːz) *f*, Schaffhausen.

schampooing (ʃɑ̃pwɛ̃) *m*, shampoo.

schéma (ʃema) *ou* schème (ʃɛm) *m*, diagram, plan.

schisme (ʃism) *m*, schism.

schiste (ʃist) *m*, shale, schist.

schlitte (ʃlit) *f*, lumber sledge.

schooner (ʃunɛːr) *m*, schooner (*Naut.*).

sciage (sjaːʒ) *m*, sawing.

sciatique (sjatik) *a*, sciatic. ¶ *f*, sciatica.

scie (si) *f*, saw; bore, nuisance; joke; catchword; catch phrase, gag. — *à chantourner*, jig saw. ~ *à métaux*, hack s.

sciemment (sjamɑ̃) *ad*, knowingly, wittingly. science (sjɑ̃ːs) *f*, knowledge, learning, lore; science. ~ *économique*, economics. scientifique† (ɑ̃tifik) *a*, scientific. scientiste chrétien (tist) *m*, Christian Scientist.

scier (sje) *v.t*, to saw; saw off; reap; bore (*weary*); (*v.i.*) to back water. scierie (siri) *f*, saw mill. scieur (sjœːr) *m*, sawyer.

scinder (sɛ̃de) *v.t*, to divide, split (*fig.*).

scintillation (sɛ̃tillasjɔ̃) *f*, scintillation; twinkling. scintiller (tije) *v.i*, to scintillate; twinkle.

scion (sjɔ̃) *m*, shoot, scion (*Hort.*); top [joint] (*fishing rod*).

scission (sisjɔ̃) *f*, scission, split, cleavage; secession.

sciure (sjyːr) *f*, sawdust.

sclérose (skleroːz) *f*, sclerosis.

scolaire (skɔlɛːr) *a*, school (*att.*); academic (*year*); educational. scolastique (lastik) *a*, scholastic.

scolopendre (skɔlɔpɑ̃ːdr) *f*, centipede.

sconse (skɔ̃ːs) *m*, skunk (*fur*).

scorbut (skɔrby) *m*, scurvy.

scorie (skɔri) *f. oft. pl,* slag, scoria; dross; scale.

scorpion (skɔrpjɔ̃) *m,* scorpion.

scribe (skrib) *m,* scribe; copyist.

scrofules (skrɔfyl) *f.pl,* scrofula. **scrofuleux, euse** (lø, ø:z) *a,* scrofulous.

scrupule (skrypyl) *m,* scruple, qualm. **scrupuleux, euse†** (lø, ø:z) *a,* scrupulous.

scrutateur (skrytatœ:r) *m,* scrutinizer; poll watcher. **scruter** (te) *v.t,* to scrutinize, scan; peer into; search. **scrutin** (tɛ̃) *m,* poll, ballot, voting, vote.

sculpter (skylte) *v.t,* to sculpt; carve. **sculpteur** (tœ:r) *m,* sculptor; carver. **sculpture** (ty:r) *f,* sculpture. ~ *sur bois,* wood carving.

se, s' (sə, s) *pn,* oneself; himself, herself, itself; themselves; each other, one another. *Note:* An English intransitive is often expressed in French by the pronominal form (se, s'); thus, to depreciate, *v.t,* déprécier, avilir; to depreciate, *v.i,* se déprécier, s'avilir. The pronominal form also serves to give to a transitive verb a passive meaning; as, lettre qui se prononce, letter which is pronounced.

séance (seɑ̃:s) *f,* seat (*at a council*); sitting, session, meeting; performance. ~ *de spiritisme,* seance. ~ *tenante,* during the sitting; forthwith, there & then, on the spot. **séant, e** (ɑ̃,ɑ̃:t) *p.a,* sitting (*ã* = at), in session. ¶ *a,* becoming, seemly, proper. *sur son séant,* in a sitting posture, sitting up.

seau (so) *m,* pail, bucket; pailful. ~ *à biscuits,* biscuit barrel. ~ *à charbon,* coal scuttle. ~ *à ordures,* trashbin. ~ *de toilette,* slop pail.

sébile (sebil) *f,* wooden bowl.

sec, sèche (sɛk, sɛʃ) *a,* dry; dried; spare, gaunt, lean; curt; bald (*style*). **sec,** *ad,* drily (*answer coldly*); hard (*drinking*); neat (*drinking*). **à sec,** *ad,* [when] dry; dried up. *être* ~, to be broke. **sec,** *m,* dry; dry place; dry land; dry fodder.

sécateur (sekatœ:r) *m,* pruning shears.

sécession (sesɛsjɔ̃) *f,* secession.

sèchement (sɛʃmɑ̃) *ad,* drily, curtly; baldly. **sécher** (seʃe) *v.t. & i,* to dry; d. up; season (*wood*); wither, pine away. ~ *à un examen,* to flunk an exam. **sécheresse** (ʃrɛs) *f,* dryness; drought; spareness, as *sec.* **séchoir** (ʃwa:r) *m,* drying room; drier; airer; towel bar.

second, e† (səgɔ̃, ɔ̃:d) *a,* second; junior (*partner*). **second plan,** *m,* middle distance; background (*fig.*). **seconde vue,** *f,* second sight, clairvoyance. *un second, une seconde,* another (*like*). ¶ *m,* second (*pers., floor*); first mate (*Naut.*). ¶ *f,* second (*class*); second (*time*). ~ [*épreuve*], revise (*Typ.*). **secondaire†** (gɔ̃dɛ:r) *a,* secondary; minor; side (*att.*). **seconder** (gɔ̃de) *v.t,* to second, support, back up, further.

secouer (səkwe) *v.t. & abs,* to shake; s. up; s. down; s. off; toss; buffet; jolt; rate, scold.

secourable (səkurabl) *a,* helpful, helping; relievable. **secourir** (ri:r) *v.t.ir,* to succor, help, relieve. **secours** (ku:r) *m,* help, succor, relief, aid. *au* ~! help! *de* ~, (*att.*) emergency, breakdown, relief, spare. *roue de* ~, spare wheel.

secousse (səkus) *f,* shake, jerk, jolt, shock.

secret, ète† (səkrɛ, ɛt) *a,* secret. ¶ *m,* secret; s. spring; secrecy, privacy; solitary confinement. **secrétaire** (kretɛ:r) *m,* secretary, amanuensis; writing desk. ~ *de mairie,* town clerk. ~ *intime,* private s. **secrétariat** (tarja) *m,* secretaryship; secretariat. **sécréter** (sekrete) *v.t,* to secrete (*physiology*). **sécrétion** (sjɔ̃) *f,* secretion.

sectaire (sɛktɛ:r) *m. & att,* sectarian. **sectateur** (tatœ:r) *m,* follower, votary. **secte** (sɛkt) *f,* sect.

secteur (sɛktœ:r) *m,* sector; quadrant; district. **section** (sjɔ̃) *f,* section; division; fare zone (*bus*); platoon.

séculaire (sekylɛ:r) *a,* secular

(100); time-honored. **séculier, ère**† (1je, ɛːr) a, secular (*clergy, etc.*); laic; worldly (*life*). ¶ *m*, layman; (*pl.*) laity.

sécurité (sekyrite) *f*, security, reliability; safety. **~ d'abord,** safety first.

sédatif, ive (sedatif, iːv) a. & *m*, sedative.

sédentaire (sedɑ̃tɛːr) a, sedentary; fixed, stationary.

sédiment (sedimɑ̃) *m*, sediment, deposit.

séditieux, euse† (sedisjø, øːz) a, seditious; mutinous. **sédition** (sjɔ̃) *f*, sedition; revolt.

séducteur, trice (sedyktœːr, tris) *n*, tempter; seducer. **séduire** (dɥiːr) *v.t.ir*, to seduce, entice; [al]lure; bribe, suborn. **séduisant, e** (dɥizɑ̃, ɑ̃ːt) a, seductive, tempting; fascinating.

segment (sɛgmɑ̃) *m*, segment; ring (*piston*).

ségrégation (segregasjɔ̃) *f*, segregation.

seiche (sɛʃ) *f*, cuttle fish.

séide (seid) *m*, blind supporter, henchman.

seigle (sɛgl) *m*, rye.

seigneur (sɛɲœːr) *m*, lord; squire; noble[man]. *le Seigneur*, the Lord. **seigneurie** (ɲœri) *f*, lordship; manor.

seille (sɛːj) *f*, pail, bucket.

sein (sɛ̃) *m*, breast; bosom; lap (*luxury*); bowels (*earth*); members; womb.

seine (sɛn) *f*, seine (*net*).

seing (sɛ̃) *m*, signature, signing.

seize (sɛːz) a. & *m*, sixteen; 16th. **seizième**† (sɛzjɛm) a. & *n*, sixteenth.

séjour (seʒuːr) *m*, stay, sojourn; abode, regions; resort. **séjourner** (ʒurne) *v.i*, to stay, tarry, sojourn; lie.

sel (sɛl) *m*, salt; piquancy, wit. **~ ammoniac** (amɔnjak), sal-ammoniac. **~ fin,** table salt. **~ gemme,** rock salt. **~s pour bains,** bath salts. **~s [volatils] anglais,** smelling salts.

sélection (selɛksjɔ̃) *f*, selection, choice. **sélectionner** (ɔne) *v.t*, to select.

selle (sɛl) *f*, saddle; seat; stool; motion (*Med.*). **seller** (le) *v.t*,

to saddle. **sellerie** (lri) *f*, saddlery; harness room. **sellette** (lɛt) *f*, stool; pedestal (*vase*). *tenir quelqu'un sur la ~,* to cross-examine someone. **sellier** (lje) *m*, saddler, harness maker.

selon (səlɔ̃) *pr*, [according] to. **~ moi,** in my opinion. *c'est ~,* it all depends.

semailles (səmɑːj) *f.pl*, seed time; sowing.

semaine (səmɛn) *f*, week; week's work, pay. *la ~ seulement,* weekdays only.

sémaphore (semafɔːr) *m*, semaphore.

semblable† (sɑ̃blabl) a, [a]like, similar; such. ¶ *m*, fellow [man]; like. **semblant** (blɑ̃) *m*, semblance, appearance, show. [*faux*] *~,* pretence, sham. *un ~ de . . .,* an apology (*bad specimen*) for a . . . **sembler** (ble) *v.i*, to seem, appear, look, strike.

semelle (səmɛl) *f*, sole (*shoe, etc.*); foot (*stocking*); sock (*cork, loofa*); tread (*tire*).

semence (səmɑ̃ːs) *f*, seed; brads. *~ de perles,* seed pearls. **semer** (me) *v.t*, to sow; scatter, strew, spread; powder (*Emb.*).

semestre (səmɛstr) *m*, semester; term; half-year; 6 months' pay, duty, leave. **semestriel, le** (triɛl) a, half-yearly.

semeur, euse (səmœːr, øːz) *n*, sower; spreader.

semi- (səmi) *prefix*, semi-, half-.

sémillant, e (semijɑ̃, ɑ̃ːt) a, sprightly, bright.

séminaire (seminɛːr) *m*, seminary, college.

semis (səmi) *m*, seed plot, seedlings; powdering (*Emb.*).

sémitique (semitik) a, Semitic.

semoir (səmwaːr) *m*, sowing machine, drill.

semonce (səmɔ̃ːs) *f*, call (*to a ship*); reprimand, scolding. **semoncer** (mɔ̃se) *v.t*, to call upon (*ship*); lecture, scold; summon.

semoule (səmul) *f*, semolina.

sénat (sena) *m*, senate. **sénateur** (tœːr) *m*, senator.

séné (sene) *m*, senna.

seneçon (sənsɔ̃) *m*, groundsel.

Sénégal (le) (senegal), Senegal.

sénestre (senɛstr) *a*, sinister (*Her.*).

sénevé (senve) *m*, mustard (*Bot.*); m. seed.

sénile (senil) *a*, senile. **sénilité** (lite) *f*, senility.

sens (sã:s, sã) *m*, sense; judgment, understanding; opinion; meaning, import; direction, way. ~ *commun* (sã), [common] sense, senses. ~ *dessus dessous* (sã), upside down; topsy-turvy. ~ *devant derrière* (sã), back to front. ~ *interdit*, no entry, one way street. ~ *unique*, entry only, one way street. **sensation** (sã-sasjõ) *f*, sensation; feel[ing], sense. *à* ~ .& **sensationnel, le** (sjɔnɛl) *a*, sensational, thrilling, exciting. **sensé†, e** (se) *a*, sensible, judicious. **sensibilité** (sib-ilite) *f*, sensitiveness; feeling. **sensible** (sibl) *a*, sensitive, susceptible, responsive, sensible, alive; sentient; sensitized (*Phot.*); tender, sore; appreciable, palpable, perceptible. **sensiblement** (blemã) *a*, appreciably; deeply. **sensiblerie** (ri) *f*, sentimentality. **sensitif, ive** (tif, i:v) *a*, sensitive; sensory.

sensualiste (sãsɥalist) *n*, sensualist. **sensualité** (te) *f*, sensuality; voluptuousness. **sensuel, le†** (sɥɛl) *a*, sensual.

sente (sã:t) *f*, footpath.

sentence (sãtã:s) *f*, maxim; sentence (*law*); award. **sentencieux, euse†** (tãsjø, ø:z) *a*, sententious.

senteur (sãtœ:r) *f*, scent, odor, perfume.

senti, e (sãti) *p.a*, well-expressed, strong. *bien* ~, heartfelt (*words*).

sentier (sãtje) *m*, footpath, path, track. ~ *pour cavaliers*, bridle path.

sentiment (sãtimã) *m*, feeling, sensation; sense; sentiment; opinion. **sentimental, e** (tal) *a*, sentimental. **sentimentalité** (lite) *f*, sentimentality, gush.

sentine (sãtin) *f*, well (*ship*); sink (*iniquity*).

sentinelle (sãtinɛl) *f*, sentry, sentinel; guard, watch.

sentir (sãti:r) *v.t. & abs. ir*, to feel; be conscious of; smell; scent; taste of; smell of; smack of; be redolent of. **se** ~, to feel.

seoir (swa:r) *v.i.ir*, to sit; be situated.

seoir (swa:r) *v.i.ir*, to suit, become.

séparation (separasjõ) *f*, separation, parting, severance; dispersal; partition (*wall*). ~ *de l'Église & de l'État*, disestablishment [of the Church]. **séparé†, e** (re) *p.a*, separate, distinct; apart. **séparer** (re) *v.t. & se* ~, to separate, part; sever; divide; disband. **séparez!** break! (*Box.*).

sépia (sepja) *f*, sepia; sepia [drawing].

sept (sɛ; *alone & in liaison*, sɛt) *a. & m*, seven; 7th.

septembre (sɛptã:br) *m*, September.

septentrion (sɛptãtriõ) *m*, north. **septentrional, e** (ɔnal) *a*, northern. ¶ *n*, northerner.

septième† (sɛtjem) *a. & n*, seventh.

septique (sɛptik) *a*, septic.

septuor (sɛptɥɔ:r) *m*, septet.

sépulcral, e (sepylkral) *a*, sepulchral. **sépulcre** (kr) *m*, sepulcher. **sépulture** (ty:r) *f*, burial; burial place, resting place; tomb.

séquelle (sekɛl) *f*, crew, gang; string.

séquence (sekã:s) *f*, sequence, run (*cards, etc.*).

séquestre (sekɛstr) *m*, sequestration.

sérail (sera:j) *m*, seraglio.

séraphin (serafɛ̃) *m*, seraph. **séraphique** (fik) *a*, seraphic.

serbe (sɛrb) *a. & S~, n*, Serb[ian]. *le serbe*, Serb[ian] (*language*). *la Serbie* (bi), Serbia.

serein, e (sərɛ̃, ɛn) *a*, serene, calm; halcyon. ¶ *m*, evening dew, evening damp.

sérénade (serenad) *f*, serenade.

sérénité (serenite) *f*, serenity; equanimity.

serf, serve (sɛrf, sɛrv) *n*, serf, thrall.

serfouir (sɛrfwi:r) *v.t*, to hoe.

serge (sɛrʒ) *f*, serge.

sergent (sɛrʒã) *m*, sergeant; cramp (*tool*). ~ *de ville*, policeman. ~ *instructeur*, drill sergeant.

sériciculture (serisikylty:r) *f*, silkworm breeding.

série (seri) *f*, series; range; set; chapter (*accidents*); break (*Bil.*). **en ~**, standardized, mass-produced.

sérieux, euse† (serjø, ø:z) *a*, serious; grave; sober (*dress*); earnest, genuine, bona fide. ¶ *m*, seriousness, gravity.

serin, e (s[ə]rɛ̃, in) *n*, canary; silly, noodle. **seriner** (rine) *v.t*, to teach (*bird*); din it into (*pers.*); drum (*ā* = into).

seringa (s[ə]rɛ̃ga) *m*, syringa, seringa.

seringue (s[ə]rɛ̃:g) *f*, syringe, squirt. **~** [*à lavement*], enema. **~** *de Pravaz* (prava), hypodermic syringe. **seringuer** (rɛ̃ge) *v.t*, to syringe, squirt, inject.

serment (sɛrmɑ̃) *m*, oath.

sermon (sɛrmɔ̃) *m*, sermon; lecture (*scolding*). **sermonner** (mɔne) *v.t. & abs*, to sermonize, lecture.

serpe (sɛrp) *f*, bill hook.

serpent (sɛrpɑ̃) *m*, serpent, snake. **~** *à sonnettes*, rattlesnake. **~** *caché sous les fleurs*, snake in the grass. **serpentaire** (tɛ:r) *m*, secretary bird. **serpenteau** (to) *m*, young snake; squib (*firework*). **serpenter** (te) *v.i*, to wind, meander. **serpentin, e** (tɛ̃, in) *a*, serpentine. ¶ *m*, worm (*still, etc.*); coil; [paper] streamer. ¶ *f*, serpentine (*rock*).

serpette (sɛrpɛt) *f*, pruning knife; bill hook.

serpillière (sɛrpijɛ:r) *f*, sacking; apron.

serpolet (sɛrpɔlɛ) *m*, wild thyme.

serrage (sɛra:ʒ) *m*, tightening, application (*brake*). **serre** (sɛ:r) *f*, greenhouse, glasshouse, conservatory; grip; claw, talon. **~** *à palmiers*, palm house. **~** *à vignes*, vinery. **~** *chaude*, hothouse. **serré, e** (sɛre) *p.a*, tight, close, serried; clenched. **serre-frein** (sɛrfrɛ̃) *m*, brakesman. **serre-joint**, *m*, cramp, clamp (*tool*). **serre-livres**, *m*, bookends. **serrement** (rmɑ̃) *m*, pressure; squeeze, shake (*hand*). **~** *de cœur*, pang. **serrer** (re) *v.t*, to press, squeeze; clasp, hug, wring, grip; clench; shake (*hand*);

tighten; put on (*brake*); put away, stow away; furl (*sail*). **~** *sous clef*, to lock up. **serre-tête**, *m*, headband. **serrure** (ry:r) *f*, lock. **~** *à demi-tour*, latch. **trou de ~**, keyhole. **serrurerie** (ryrri) *f*, locksmithery; metal work, ironwork. **serrurier** (rje) *m*, locksmith; metal worker, ironworker.

sertir (sɛrti:r) *v.t*, to set (gem); crease.

sérum (serɔm) *m*, serum.

servage (sɛrva:ʒ) *m*, serfdom, thraldom. **servant** (vɑ̃) *a.m*, lay (*brother*). ¶ *m*, gunner; server (*Ten.*). **servante** (vɑ̃:t) *f*, [maid-]servant; waitress; service table; dumbwaiter. **serviable** (vjabl) *a*, obliging. **service** (vis) *m*, service; serve (*Ten.*); running; booking; supply; department; duty; attendance, waiting (*hotel, etc.*); course (*meal*); set (*utensils*). **~** *de table & dessert*, dinner service. **~** *par en bas*, underhand service (*Ten.*). **~** *par en haut*, overhand s. **serviette** (vjɛt) *f*, dispatch case, document c. **~** [*de table*], [table] napkin. **~** [*de toilette*], towel. **~-éponge**, Turkish towel. **~** *hygiénique*, sanitary napkin.

servile† (sɛrvil) *a*, servile, menial; slavish. **servilité** (lite) *f*, servility; slavishness.

servir (sɛrvi:r) *v.i. & t. & abs.* ir, to serve; be of use; wait (on); attend to; serve up. **se ~** *chez*, to deal with (*tradesman*). **se ~** *de*, to use. **serviteur** (vitœ:r) *m*, servant. **servitude** (tyd) *f*, servitude, slavery; easement (*law*).

ses *see* **son**.

sésame (sezam) *m*, sesame (*Bot.*). **S~, ouvre-toi**, open sesame.

session (sɛsjɔ̃) *f*, session, sitting, term.

seuil (sœ:j) *m*, threshold, sill.

seul, e (sœl) *a*, alone, by oneself, solo; lonely; only; one, single; sole; mere, bare, very. **seulement** (lmɑ̃) *ad*, only; solely, merely.

sève (sɛ:v) *f*, sap (*plant*); vigor.

sévère† (sevɛ:r) *a*, severe, stern; hard; strict. **sévérité** (verite) *f*, severity, etc.

sévices (sevis) *m.pl*, maltreatment, cruelty (*in law*).

Séville (sevil) *f*, Seville.

sévir (seviːr) *v.i*, to deal severely (*contre* = with); rage, be rife, be rampant.

sevrage (səvraːʒ) *m*, weaning. **sevrer** (vre) *v.t*, to wean; deprive.

sexe (sɛks) *m*, sex.

sextant (sɛkstɑ̃) *m*, sextant.

sextuor (sɛkstɥɔːr) *m*, sextet.

sexuel, le (sɛksɥɛl) *a*, sexual.

seyant, e (sɛjɑ̃, ɑ̃ːt) *a*, becoming.

si, s' (si, s) *c*, if, whether; how [much]; what if, suppose. ~ *le temps le permet*, weather permitting. **si**, *ad*, so; so much; such; however; yes. ~ *fait*, yes, indeed. ¶ *m*, if; B (*Mus.*).

Siam (le) (sjam), Siam. **siamois, e** (mwa, aːz) *a. & S~*, *n*, Siamese. **le siamois**, Siamese (*language*).

Sibérie (la) (siberi), Siberia. **sibérien, ne** (rjɛ̃, ɛn) *a. & S~*, *n*, Siberian.

sicaire (sikɛːr) *m*, hired assassin.

siccatif (sikatif) *m*, drier[s] (*painter's*).

Sicile (la) (sisil), Sicily. **sicilien, ne** (ljɛ̃, ɛn) *a. & S~*, *n*, Sicilian.

sicle (sikl) *m*, shekel (*Bible*).

sidéral, e (sideral) *a*, sidereal.

sidéré (sidere) *a*, thunderstruck, flabbergasted.

siècle (sjɛkl) *m*, century; age, times; world. *les ~s d'ignorance*, the dark ages.

siège (sjɛːʒ) *m*, seat; bench; box (*driver's*); bottom (*chair*); see (*Eccl.*); siege (*Mil.*). ~ *arrière*, back seat; pillion. ~ *social*, head office. **siéger** (eʒe) *v.i*, to have its headquarters; sit; be seated.

sien, ne (*with* le, la, les) (sjɛ̃, ɛn) *pn. & m*, his, hers; one's own, his own, her own.

Sienne (sjɛn) *f*, Sienna.

sieste (sjɛst) *f*, siesta, nap.

sieur (sjœːr) *m*, Mr.

siffler (sifle) *v.i. & t*, to whistle; pipe; hiss; whirr, whizz; wheeze. **sifflet** (flɛ) *m*, whistle; pipe (*boatswain's*); hiss, catcall. [canard] **siffleur** (floeːr) *m*, widgeon.

signal (siɲal) *m*, signal. **signalé, e** (le) *p.a*, signal; conspicuous;

well-known. **signalement** (lmɑ̃) *m*, description. **signaler** (le) *v.t*, to signalize, point out; signal; notify. **signaleur** (lœːr) *m*, signaler (*Mil.*); signalman (*Rly.*).

signataire (siɲatɛːr) *n*, signatory, signer. **signature** (tyːr) *f*, signing, signature. **signe** (siɲ) *m*, sign, token, mark; motion, wave (*hand*). ~ *d'omission*, caret. ~ [*de tête*], nod. ~ *des yeux*, wink. **signer** (ɲe) *v.t*, to sign. ~ *à*, to witness. **se ~**, to cross oneself. **signet** (ɲɛ) *m*, bookmark, signet.

significatif, ive (siɲifikatif, iːv) *a*, significant, meaning, of deep significance (*look*). **signification** (sjɔ̃) *f*, signification, meaning, sense, import; service (*writ*). **signifier** (fje) *v.t*, to signify, mean; notify, intimate; serve (*a notice*).

silence (silɑ̃ːs) *m*, silence, stillness, hush; pause; rest (*Mus.*). **silencieux, euse†** (lɑ̃sjø, øːz) *a*, silent, noiseless, still. ¶ *m*, silencer.

Silésie (la) (silezi), Silesia. **silésienne** (zjɛn) *f*, silesia (*fabric*).

silex (silɛks) *m*, silex, flint.

silhouette (silwɛt) *f*, silhouette.

silicate (silikat) *m*, silicate. **silice** (lis) *f*, silica.

sillage (sijaːʒ) *m*, wake, track; headway (*ship*). **sillet** (jɛ) *m*, nut (*violin*). **sillon** (jɔ̃) *m*, furrow; drill (*furrow*); (*pl., Poet.*) fields; wrinkle; track, trail; streak; groove. **sillonner** (ɔne) *v.t*, to furrow; plow (*seas*); wrinkle; streak, groove.

silo (silo) *m*, silo.

simagrée (simaɡre) *f. oft. pl*, pretence; affectation.

simiesque (simjɛsk) *a*, apelike, apish.

similaire (similɛːr) *a*, similar, like. **simili-** (li) *prefix*, imitation (*att.*), artificial. **similigravure** (liɡravyːr) *f*, process engraving, halftone e. **similitude** (tyd) *f*, similitude, similarity; simile.

simonie (simɔni) *f*, simony.

simple† (sɛ̃ːpl) *a*, simple; single; ordinary; private (*soldier*); plain; homely; mere; simple[-minded];

half-witted. ¶ *m*, single (*Ten.*); half-wit; (*pl.*) medicinal herbs.
simplicité (sɛ̃plisite) *f*, simplicity. **simplifier** (fje) *v.t*, to simplify.
simulacre (simylakr) *m*, simulacrum, image; dummy (*Mil.*); show. ~ *de combat*, sham fight, mock f. **simulé, e** (le) *p.a*, feigned, sham; bogus, fictitious. **simuler** (le) *v.t*, to simulate. ~ *la maladie*, to malinger.
simulie (simyli) *f*, sand fly.
simultané†, e (simyltane) *a*, simultaneous.
Sinaï (le mont) (sinai), Mount Sinai.
sinapisme (sinapism) *m*, mustard plaster.
sincère† (sɛ̃sɛːr) *a*, sincere, candid, unfeigned, genuine. **sincérité** (serite) *f*, sincerity, candor.
sinécure (sinekyːr) *f*, sinecure.
Singapour (sɛ̃gapuːr) *m*, Singapore.
singe (sɛ̃ːʒ) *m*, monkey, ape; copycat; winch. **singer** (sɛ̃ʒe) *v.t*, to ape, mock. **singerie** (ʒri) *f*, monkey house; grimace, monkey trick; grotesque imitation.
singulariser (sɛ̃gylarize) *v.t*, to make conspicuous. **singulier, ère†** (lje, ɛːr) *a*, singular; peculiar; odd, queer, quaint; single (*combat*). ¶ *m*, singular (*Gram.*). **singularité** (larite) *f*, singularity, etc.
sinistre† (sinistr) *a*, sinister, ominous; grim; lurid, baleful. ¶ *m*, disaster, casualty; loss (*Insce.*). **sinistré** (tre) *m*, victim of a disaster (*fire, flood, bombing*). ¶ *a*, homeless, bombedout, etc.
sinon (sinɔ̃) *c*, otherwise, else; except, save.
sinueux, euse (sinɥø, øːz) *a*, sinuous, winding. **sinuosité** (nɥozite) *f*, sinuosity, bend.
sinus (sinyːs) *m*, sinus; sine.
siphon (sifɔ̃) *m*, siphon; trap (*drain*).
sire (siːr) *m*, sire (*to king*).
sirène (sirɛn) *f*, siren, mermaid; hooter.
sirop (siro) *m*, syrup. **siroter** (rɔte) *v.t*, to sip. **sirupeux, euse** (rypø, øːz) *a*, syrupy.
sis, e (si, iːz) *p.p*, situated.

sismique (sismik) *a*, seismic. **sismographe** (mɔgraf) *m*, seismograph.
site (sit) *m*, site, location.
sitôt (sito) *ad*, as soon, so soon.
situation (sitɥasjɔ̃) *f*, situation, position; condition, state; statement, report. **situé, e** (tɥe) *p.p. & p.a*, situated.
six (si; *in liaison*, siz; *at end of phrase*, sis) *a. & m*, six; 6th. **sixième†** (sizjɛm) *a. & n*, sixth. **sixte** (sikst) *f*, sixth (*Mus.*).
ski (ski) *m*, ski. ~*s de saut*, jumping skis.
slave (slaːv) *a. & S~**, *n*, Slav.
slip (slip) *m*, underpants; trunks.
sloughi (slugi) *m*, saluki.
smilax (smilaks) *m*, smilax (*Bot.*).
smoking (smɔkiɲ) *m*, tuxedo.
Smyrne (smirn) *f*, Smyrna.
snob (snɔb) *a*, snobbish. **snobisme** (bism) *m*, snobbishness, snobbery.
sobre† (sɔbr) *a*, sober, temperate, abstemious; sparing, chary. **sobriété** (briete) *f*, sobriety.
sobriquet (sɔbrikɛ) *m*, nickname.
soc (sɔk) *m*, plowshare.
sociable† (sɔsjabl) *a*, sociable; companionable, genial. **social, e** (sjal) *a*, social; corporate; registered (*capital, offices*); of the firm; company's. **socialisme** (lism) *m*, socialism. **socialiste** (list) *n. & a*, socialist. **sociétaire** (sjetɛːr) *n*, member; stockholder. **société** (te) *f*, society; community; companionship, fellowship; club; company; firm; partnership. ~ *anonyme*, corporation. *S~ des Nations*, League of Nations. ~ *immobilière*, building society. ~ *par actions*, joint-stock company. **sociologie** (sjolɔʒi) *f*, sociology.
socle (sɔkl) *m*, pedestal, stand.
socque (sɔk) *m*, clog, pattern. **soquettes** (kɛt) *f.pl*, ankle socks.
sodium (sɔdjom) *m*, sodium.
sœur (sœːr) *f*, sister. **sœurette** (sœrɛt) *f*, [dear] little sister.
sofa (sofa) *m*, sofa.
soffite (sofit) *m*, soffit.
soi (swa) & ~-*même*, *pn*, oneself; himself, herself, itself. ~-*disant* (dizɑ̃) *a.inv*, self-styled, wouldbe; so-called.

soie (swa) *f*, silk; bristle (*hog*); tang (*of tool*). ~ floche (floʃ), floss silk. soierie (ri) *f*, silk goods, silks; silk mill; silk trade.

soif (swaf) *f*, thirst; craving, hankering. avoir ~, to be thirsty, to thirst.

soigné, e (swaɲe) *p.a*, carefully done; trim, neat. soigner (ɲe) *v.t*, to take care of, look after, attend to; tend; nurse; manicure. soigneur (nœːr) *m*, minder; second (*Box.*). soigneux, euse† (nø, øːz) *a*, careful, painstaking; tidy. soin (swɛ̃) *m*. oft. *pl*, care, attention, pains; nursing. ~ des mains, manicure. ~ des pieds, chiropody. aux [*bons*] ~s de, care of, c/o.

soir (swaːr) *m*, evening, night; afternoon. soirée (sware) *f*, evening; [evening] party. de ~, evening (*dress, etc.*).

soit (swa) *c*, either; or; whether; suppose, let. ~ que, whether. ~! (swat), so be it! agreed!

soixantaine (swasɑ̃tɛn) *f*, sixty [or so]. soixante (sɑ̃ːt) *a. & m*, sixty. ~-dix (sɑ̃tdis) *a. & m*, seventy. ~ & onze, ~-douze, 71, 72. ~-dixième (zjɛm) *a. & n*, seventieth. soixantième (tjɛm) *a. & n*, sixtieth.

soja (sɔja) *m*, soybean.

sol (sɔl) *m*, ground, earth; soil; G (*Mus.*).

solaire (sɔlɛːr) *a*, solar, sun (*att.*); sunlight (*treatment*).

soldat (sɔlda) *m*, soldier. ~ de plomb, tin soldier. le S~ inconnu, the Unknown Soldier. soldatesque (tɛsk) *f*, (*unruly*) soldiery.

solde (sɔld) *f*, pay (*Mil., Nav., etc.*). ¶ *m*, balance; settlement; surplus stock, job lot; [clearance] sale. ~ d'édition, remainder (*books*). ~ de dividende, final dividend. vente de ~s, clearance sale. solder (de) *v.t*, to balance (*a/c*); pay off, settle; sell off, clear; remainder.

sole (sɔl) *f*, sole (*fish, hoof, bed plate*). ~ limande, lemon sole.

solécisme (sɔlesism) *m*, solecism.

soleil (sɔlɛːj) *m*, sun; sunshine; sunflower; catherine wheel (*fire-works*). ~ couchant, setting sun, sunset.

solennel, le† (sɔlanɛl) *a*, solemn; formal; state (*att.*); impressive. solenniser (nize) *v.t*, to solemnize, celebrate. solennité (te) *f*, solemnity; celebration.

solfège (sɔlfɛːʒ) *m*, sol-fa, solfeggio. solfier (fje) *v.t. & abs*, to sol-fa.

solidaire† (sɔlidɛːr) *a*, mutually responsible; interdependent; solidary. solide† (lid) *a*, solid; strong; substantial; hefty; firm; fast (*color*); sound; sterling (*fig.*). ¶ *m*, solid; s. foundation, s. ground; main chance. solidifier (difje) *v.t*, to solidify. solidité (te) *f*, solidity; strength; soundness.

soliloque (sɔlilɔk) *m*, soliloquy.

soliste (sɔlist) *n*, soloist; solo (*violin*).

solitaire† (sɔlitɛːr) *a*, solitary, lonely. ¶ *m*, hermit; solitaire (*gem & game*). solitude (tyd) *f*, solitude, loneliness; wilderness, wild.

solive (sɔliːv) *f*, joist, beam, girder.

solliciter (sɔllisite) *v.t*, to solicit, ask for, apply for; canvass; entreat; urge; attract. sollicitude (tyd) *f*, solicitude; anxiety.

solo (sɔlo) *m*, solo (*Mus.*).

solstice (sɔlstis) *m*, solstice.

soluble (sɔlybl) *a*, soluble; solvable. solution (sjɔ̃) *f*, solution; break; discharge (*law*).

solvabilité (sɔlvabilite) *f*, solvency (*Fin.*). solvable (bl) *a*, solvent.

sombre (sɔ̃ːbr) *a*, dark, somber, gloomy; dim.

sombrer (sɔ̃bre) *v.i*, to founder, sink, go down.

sommaire† (sɔmɛːr) *a*, summary, compendious; scant. ¶ *m*, summary, synopsis.

sommation (sɔmasjɔ̃) *f*, summons, appeal.

somme (sɔm) *f*, sum, amount; burden. ~ toute ou en ~, [up] on the whole.

somme (sɔm) *m*, nap, snooze. sommeil (mɛːj) *m*, sleep, slumber; sleepiness. sommeiller (mɛje) *v.i*, to slumber, doze, nod.

sommelier (soməlje) *m*, wine waiter.

sommer (some) *v.t*, to summon, call on; sum up.

sommet (somɛ) *m*, summit, top; vertex, apex; acme.

sommier (somje) *m*, pack animal; transom, lintel; dossier; register; bed mattress, spring m.

sommité (sommite) *f*, summit, top; leading man, (*pl.*) leading people.

somnambule (somnãbyl) *n*, somnambulist, sleepwalker. **somnambulisme** (lism) *m*, somnambulism. **somnolent, e** (nɔlã, ã:t) *a*, somnolent, sleepy.

somnifère (somnifɛ:r) *m*, opiate; narcotic; sleeping pill.

somptueux, euse† (sɔ̃ptɥø, ø:z) *a*, sumptuous. **somptuosité** (tɥozite) *f*, sumptuousness.

son, sa, ses (sɔ̃, sa, se) *a*, his, her, its, one's.

son (sɔ̃) *m*, sound; clang; tone; bran.

sonate (sɔnat) *f*, sonata.

sonde (sɔ̃:d) *f*, [sounding] lead, plummet; probe; spit; drill (*Min.*); taster (*cheese*). **sonder** (sɔ̃de) *v.t*, to sound; probe; fathom. **sondeur** (dœ:r) *m*, leadsman; driller.

songe (sɔ̃:ʒ) *m*, dream. **~-creux**, *m*, dreamer, visionary. **songer** (sɔ̃ʒe) *v.i*, to dream, muse. ~ *à*, to think of, intend. **songeur, euse** (ʒœ:r, ø:z) *a*, dreamy; pensive.

sonnaille (sɔnɑ:j) *f*, cowbell. sonnailler (naje) *m*, bellwether. ¶ *v.i*, to keep ringing [the bell]. **sonnant, e** (nã, ã:t) *a*, [re]sounding; hard (*cash*). **sonné, e** (ne) *p.a*, past, struck (*hour*); turned (*a certain age*). **sonner** (ne) *v.i. & t*, to sound; ring; r. for; toll; strike. **sonnerie** (nri) *f*, ringing; bells; bell; call (*trumpet, bugle*). **sonnet** (nɛ) *m*, sonnet. **sonnette** (nɛt) *f*, bell; pile driver. **sonneur** (nœ:r) *m*, bell ringer. **sonore** (nɔ:r) *a*, sonorous; loud (*laugh, cheers*); sound (*att.*). **sonorité** (nɔrite) *f*, sonorousness, volume [of sound].

sophisme (sofism) *m*, sophism; fallacy. **sophistique** (tik) *f*, soph-

istry. **sophistiquer** (ke) *v.t. & i*, to sophisticate.

soporifique (sɔpɔrifik) *a. & m*, soporific.

soprano (sɔprano) *m*, soprano (*voice & pers.*).

sorbet (sɔrbɛ) *m*, ices (*flavored*). **sorbetière** (btjɛ:r) *f*, ice-cream freezer.

sorbier (sɔrbje) *m*, service tree, sorb. ~ *des oiseaux*, mountain ash.

sorcellerie (sɔrsɛlri) *f*, sorcery, witchcraft. **sorcier, ère** (sje, ɛ:r) *n*, sorcerer, ess, wizard, witch; hag. *sorcier guérisseur*, medicine man, witch doctor.

sordide† (sɔrdid) *a*, sordid; filthy, squalid.

Sorlingues (îles) (sɔrlɛ̃g) *f.pl*, Scilly Islands, Scilly Isles.

sornettes (sɔrnɛt) *f.pl*, nonsense.

sort (sɔ:r) *m*, lot, fate; spell. **sortable** (sɔrtabl) *a*, suitable; eligible. **sortant** (tã) *a.m*, drawn, winning (*number*); retiring, outgoing (*pers.*).

sorte (sɔrt) *f*, sort, kind; manner, way. *en quelque ~*, in a way, as it were.

sortie (sɔrti) *f*, going out; coming out; exit; issue; sally, sortie; outlet; way out, egress. ~ *de bal*, ~ *de théâtre*, opera cloak, evening wrap.

sortilège (sɔrtilɛ:ʒ) *m*, witchcraft, spell.

sortir (sɔrti:r) *v.i.ir*, to go out; come out; leave; emerge, issue; spring; stand out; (*v.t.ir.*) to bring out; take out; pull out. *X. sort*, exit X. (*Theat.*).

sosie (sɔzi) *m*, double (*pers.*).

sot, te† (so, ɔt) *a*, silly, foolish; sheepish. ¶ *n*, fool. **sot-l'y-laisse** (sɔlilɛs) *m*, pope's nose. **sottise** (sɔti:z) *f*, silliness, foolishness, folly; (*pl.*) nonsense; insult.

sou (su) *m*, sou = 5 centimes; penny (*in sense of very little money*).

soubassement (subasmã) *m*, basement; base.

soubresaut (subrəso) *m*, start, leap, jolt.

souche (suʃ) *f*, stump, stock,

stub; founder (*family*); shaft, stack (*chimney*); counterfoil. **à la ~**, unissued (*stocks, shares*).

souci (susi) *m*, care, concern; worry; marigold. **~ d'eau**, marsh marigold, kingcup. **se soucier de** (sje), to care for, mind. **soucieux, euse** (sjø, ø:z) *a*, anxious.

soucoupe (sukup) *f*, saucer.

soudain, e† (sudɛ̃, ɛn) *a*, sudden. **soudain**, *ad*, suddenly. **soudaineté** (dɛnte) *f*, suddenness.

soude (sud) *f*, soda; saltwort.

souder (sude) *v.t*, to solder; weld.

soudoyer (sudwaje) *v.t*, to hire; bribe.

soudure (sudy:r) *f*, soldering; solder; welding; joint; weld.

souffle (sufl) *m*, breath; puff, waft, blas; inspiration. **souffler** (fle) *v.i. & t*, to blow; b. up; b. out; pant; breathe; prompt, prime, whisper. **soufflerie** (fləri) *f*, bellows (*organ*). **soufflet** (flɛ) *m*, bellows; hood (*carriage*); box on the ear[s]; slap; snub. **souffleter** (flɔte) *v.t*, to box (*someone's*) ears, slap. **souffleur** (flœ:r) *m*, blower; prompter. **soufflure** (fly:r) *f*, blowhole; flaw (*casting*).

souffrance (sufrɑ̃:s) *f*, sufferance (*law*); suffering, pain. **en ~**, in suspense, in abeyance, held over; unclaimed, on hand (*goods*); undeliverable (*parcel*). **souffrant, e** (frɑ̃, ɑ̃:t) *a*, suffering; ailing, unwell, poorly. **souffre-douleur** (frədulœ:r) *m*, butt; scapegoat. **souffreteux, euse** (tø, ø:z) *a*, sickly. **souffrir** (frir) *v.t. & i. ir*, to suffer; bear; endure, stand; undergo; allow.

soufre (sufr) *m*, sulfur, brimstone. **soufrière** (friɛ:r) *f*, sulfur mine.

souhait (swɛ) *m*, wish. **~s de bonne année**, New Year's wishes, season's greetings. **souhaitable** (tabl) *a*, desirable. **souhaiter** (te) *v.t*, to wish; w. for. **~ la** (ou **une bonne**) *fête à quelqu'un*, to wish someone many happy returns [of the day].

souille (su:j) *f*, wallow. **souiller** (suje) *v.t*, to soil, dirty; pollute, taint; stain, sully, besmirch. **souillon** (jɔ̃) *n*, sloven; (*f.*) slut, slat-

tern. **souillure** (jy:r) *f*, spot, stain; blot, blemish.

soûl, e (su, ul) *a*, drunk; gorged. ¶ *m*, fill. **soûler** (le) *v.t*, to glut (*food, drink*); inebriate.

soulager (sulaʒe) *v.t*, to relieve, lighten, ease, alleviate; comfort.

souleur (sulœ:r) *f*, shock (*startling emotion*).

soulèvement (sulɛvmɑ̃) *m*, rising; heaving; upheaval (*Geol.*); revolt. **soulever** (lve) *v.t*, to raise, lift; make heave; moot; rouse. **se ~**, to rise, heave; revolt.

soulier (sulje) *m*, shoe; slipper.

souligner (suliɲe) *v.t*, to underline; emphasize.

soulte (sult) *f*, balance (*in cash*).

soumettre (sumɛtr) *v.t.ir*, to subdue; submit; subject. **se ~**, to submit, yield, give in. **soumis, e** (mi, i:z) *p.a*, submissive, dutiful; subject, amenable; liable. **soumission** (misjɔ̃) *f*, submission; submissiveness; tender; bond. **soumissionner** (ɔne) *v.t*, to tender for.

soupape (supap) *f*, valve; plug (*bath, etc.*).

soupçon (supsɔ̃) *m*, suspicion; surmise; dash; touch. **soupçonner** (sɔne) *v.t*, to suspect; surmise. **soupçonneux, euse** (nø, ø:z) *a*, suspicious, distrustful.

soupe (sup) *f*, soup; food; chow (*Mil.*).

soupente (supɑ̃:t) *f*, loft.

souper (supe) *m*, supper. **~ assis**, sit-down supper. **~ debout**, buffet (*at a ball*). ¶ *v.i*, to have supper, sup.

soupeser (supəze) *v.t*, to feel the weight of.

soupière (supjɛ:r) *f*, soup tureen.

soupir (supi:r) *m*, sigh; breath; crotchet rest (*Mus.*). **soupirail** (pira:j) *m*, airhole, vent. **soupirant** (rɑ̃) *m*, suitor, wooer. **soupirer** (re) *v.i*, to sigh; yearn.

souple (supl) *a*, supple, pliant, pliable; lithe[some], lissom[e]; limp (*binding*); versatile. *feutre* **~**, soft felt (*hat*). **souplesse** (plɛs) *f*, suppleness.

source (surs) *f*, source, spring, fountainhead; well; rise; wellspring, fount. **sourcier, ère** (sje, ɛ:r) *n*, water diviner, dowser.

sourcil (sursi) *m*, eyebrow. **sourciller** (je) *v.i*, to frown; wince. **sourcilleux, euse** (jø, ø:z) *a*, beetling; frowning, anxious.

sourd, e (su:r, urd) *a*, deaf, dull; hollow (*voice*); mute[d]; muffled; underhand. ¶ *n*, deaf person. **sourdement** (surdəmã) *ad*, dully; secretly. **sourdine** (din) *f*, mute (*Mus.*); damper. *en ~*, on the sly. **sourd-muet, sourde-muette** (surmɥɛ, dmɥɛt) *a*, deaf & dumb. ¶ *n*, deaf-mute.

sourdre (surdr) *v.i*, to spring, well up.

souriant, e (surjã, ã:t) *a*, smiling.

souriceau (suriso) *m*, young mouse. **souricière** (sjɛ:r) *f*, mousetrap; trap (*police*).

sourire (suri:r) *m*, smile. ¶ *v.i.ir*, to smile. *~ à*, to be attractive to, please.

souris (suri) *f*, mouse; knuckle end (*mutton*).

sournois, e† (surnwa, a:z) *a*, sly, underhand.

sous (su; *in liaison*, suz) *pr*, under[neath], beneath, below; in; by; with; within; on. **sous, comps:** *~-affermer, v.t*, to sublet. *~-bail, m*, sublease. *~-cutané, e, a*, subcutaneous. *~-entendre, v.t*, to understand, imply. *~-entendu, m*, implication; double entendre. *sous-estimer, v.t*, to underestimate, undervalue, underrate. *sous-jacent, e* (suʒasã, ã:t) *a*, underlying. *~-lieutenant, m*, second lieutenant. *~-locataire, n*, subtenant. *~-louer, v.t*, to sublet; rent (*as subtenant*). *~-marin, e, a. & m*, submarine. *en ~-œuvre*, underpinned. *~-officier, m*, noncommissioned officer. *~-ordre, m*, subordinate, underling; sub-order. *en ~-ordre*, subordinate (ly). *~-produit, m*, byproduct. *~-secrétaire, m*, undersecretary. *~-sol, m*, subsoil; basement. *~-titre, m*, subtitle, caption. *~-traitant* (trɛtã) *m*, subcontractor. *~-traité, m*, subcontract. *~-ventrière* (vãtriɛ:r) *f*, bellyband; [saddle] girth. *~-vêtement, m*, undergarment; (*pl.*) underwear, underclothing.

souscripteur (suskriptœ:r) *m*, subscriber; applicant (*shares*); drawer (*bill*); underwriter (*Insce*). **souscription** (sjɔ̃) *f*, execution, signing (*deed*); signature; subscription; application; underwriting. **souscrire** (skri:r) *v.t. & i. ir*, to execute, sign; subscribe; draw; apply for; underwrite.

soussigné, e (susiɲe) *a. & n*, undersigned.

soustraction (sustraksjɔ̃) *f*, abstraction; subtraction. **soustraire** (strɛ:r) *v.t.ir*, to abstract (*steal*), purloin; withdraw; screen; subtract (*Arith.*). *se ~ à*, to elude, avoid. *se ~ à la justice*, to abscond.

soutache (sutaʃ) *f*, braid. **soutacher** (ʃe) *v.t*, to braid.

soutane (sutan) *f*, cassock; cloth (*clergy*).

soute (sut) *f*, storeroom (*Naut.*); magazine, bunker, locker; tank.

soutenable (sutnabl) *a*, bearable; tenable. **soutenir** (tni:r) *v.t.ir*, to sustain, support, hold up; uphold; keep, maintain; back [up]; stand, bear; afford. **soutenu, e** (tny) *p.a*, sustained; unremitting; lofty, rhetorical (*style*).

souterrain, e (sutɛrɛ̃, ɛn) *a*, underground, subterranean; underhand. ¶ *m*, tunnel; cavern.

soutien (sutjɛ̃) *m*, support; mainstay; upholder. *~ de famille*, breadwinner. *~-gorge, m*, brassière.

soutirer (sutire) *v.t*, to draw off, rack [off] (*wine*); extract (*money*).

souvenance (suvnã:s) *f*, memories. **souvenir** (vni:r) *m*, remembrance, recollection, memory; memento; keepsake. *se ~, v.pr. ir*, to remember, recollect.

souvent (suvã) *ad*, often.

souverain, e† (suvrɛ̃, ɛn) *a*, sovereign; supreme, superlative. ¶ *n*, sovereign. **souveraineté** (vrɛnte) *f*, sovereignty.

soviet (sɔvjɛt) *m*, soviet. **soviétique** (etik) *a*, soviet (*att.*).

soya (sɔja) *m*, soybean.

soyeux, euse (swajø, ø:z) *a*, silky.

spacieux, euse† (spasjø, ø:z) *a*, spacious, roomy, capacious.

spadassin (spadasɛ̃) *m*, ruffian.

sparadrap (sparadra) *m*, adhesive tape, court plaster.

sparte (spart) *m*, esparto [grass].

spartiate (sparsjat) *a. & n*, Spartan.

spasme (spasm) *m*, spasm. **spasmodique** (mɔdik) *a*, spasmodic (*Med.*).

spath (spat) *m*, spar.

spatule (spatyl) *f*, spatula; spoonbill.

speaker (spikœ:r) *m*, announcer (*radio*); speaker.

spécial, e† (spesjal) *a*, special, particular. **se spécialiser dans** (lize), to specialize in. **spécialiste** (list) *n*, specialist. **spécialité** (te) *f*, specialty. ~ *pharmaceutique*, patent medicine.

spécieux, euse† (spesjø, ø:z) *a*, specious.

spécification (spesifikasjɔ̃) *f*, specification. **spécifier** (fje) *v.t*, to specify. **spécifique†** (fik) *a. & m*, specific.

spécimen (spesimɛn) *m*, specimen; free copy (*book*).

spectacle (spɛktakl) *m*, spectacle, sight, scene; play, entertainment, show. ~ *forain*, sideshow (*fair*). ~ *payant*, sideshow (*exhibition*). ~ *permanent*, continuous performance (*movies*). **spectateur, trice** (tœ:r, tris) *n*, spectator, onlooker, bystander; (*m.pl.*) audience (*Theat.*).

spectral, e (spɛktral) *a*, spectral; ghostly, unearthly, eerie, -ry, weird. **spectre** (tr) *m*, specter, ghost; spectrum. **spectroscope** (trɔskɔp) *m*, spectroscope.

spéculateur, trice (spekylatœ:r, tris) *n*, speculator. **spéculatif, ive** (tif, i:v) *a*, speculative. **spéculation** (sjɔ̃) *f*, speculation. **spéculer** (le) *v.i*, to speculate.

spermatozoaire (spɛrmatɔzɔɛ:r) *m*, spermatozoon. **sperme** (spɛrm) *m*, sperm.

sphère (sfɛ:r) *f*, sphere, orb, globe. **sphérique** (sferik) *a*, spherical.

sphincter (sfɛ̃ktɛ:r) *m*, sphincter.

sphinx (sfɛ̃:ks) *m*, sphinx.

spinal, e (spinal) *a*, spinal.

spinelle (spinɛl) *m. & att*, spinel.

spiral, e (spiral) *a*, spiral. ¶ *m*, hairspring; (*f.*) spiral. **spire** (spi:r) *f*, turn, spire, whorl.

spirite (spirit) *n*, spiritualist (*psychics*). **spiritisme** (tism) *m*, spiritualism. **spiritualisme** (tɥalism) *m*, spiritualism (*Philos.*). **spiritualiste** (list) *n*, spiritualist. **spirituel, le†** (tɥɛl) *a*, spiritual; sacred (*concert*); witty. **spiritueux, euse** (tɥø, ø:z) *a*, spirituous. ¶ *m.pl*, spirits.

Spitzberg (le) (spitsbɛrg), Spitzbergen.

spleen (splin) *m*, spleen, dumps, blues.

splendeur (splɑ̃dœ:r) *f*, splendor. **splendide†** (did) *a*, splendid, gorgeous.

spolier (spɔlje) *v.t*, to despoil, rob, rifle.

spongieux, euse (spɔ̃ʒjø, ø:z) *a*, spongy.

spontané†, e (spɔ̃tane) *a*, spontaneous; willing.

sporadique (spɔradik) *a*, sporadic.

spore (spɔ:r) *f*, spore.

sport (spɔ:r) *m*, sport, sports. **sportif, ive** (spɔrtif, i:v) *a*, fond of sport[s]; sporting; sports (*att.*); athletic (*meeting*); game (*fish, fishing, etc.*). **un sportif**, a sportsman.

square (skwa:r) *m*, park, square.

squelette (skəlɛt) *m*, skeleton; scrag (*pers.*).

stabilité (stabilite) *f*, stability. **stabiliser** (ze) *v.t*, to stabilize (*Fin.*). **stable** (bl) *a*, stable; lasting.

stade (stad) *m*, stadium; stage (*Med.*).

stage (sta:ʒ) *m*, probation; course; stage, period. **stagiaire** (staʒjɛ:r) *n*, probationer.

stagnant, e (stagnɑ̃, ɑ̃:t) *a*, stagnant; standing (*water*). **stagnation** (nasjɔ̃) *f*, stagnation.

stalactite (stalaktit) *f*, stalactite.

stalagmite (stalagmit) *f*, stalagmite.

stalle (stal) *f*, seat (*Theat.*); box (*horse*).

stance (stɑ̃:s) *f*, stanza.

stand (stɑ̃:d) *m*, stand (*racetrack, exhibition*); shooting gallery, rifle range.

station (stasjɔ̃) *f*, station; halt;

stop (*bus*); stand (*cab*); resort. ~ *balnéaire*, spa, seaside resort. ~ *climat*[*ér*]*ique*, health resort. **stationnaire** (ɔnɛːr) *a*, stationary. **stationnement** (nmɑ̃) *m*, stopping, standing, halt; parking. ~ *interdit*, no parking. **stationner** (ne) *v.i*, to stop; stand; station; park.

statique (statik) *a*, static(al). ¶ *f*, statics.

statisticien (statistisjɛ̃) *m*, statistician. **statisque** (tik) *a*, statistic(al). ¶ *f*, statistics, return[s]. ~ *militaire*, intelligence department.

statuaire (statɥɛːr) *a*, statuary. ¶ *f*, [art of] statuary. ¶ *m*, statuary (*pers.*). **statue** (ty) *f*, statue; (*pl. col.*) statuary.

statuer (statɥe) *v.t*, to ordain. ~ *sur*, to decide, resolve on.

statuette (statɥɛt) *f*, statuette.

stature (statyːr) *f*, stature, height (*of pers.*).

statut (staty) *m*, statute; (*pl.*) memorandum & articles [of association]; status. **statutaire** (tɛːr) *a*, statutory.

stéarine (stearin) *f*, stearin. **stéatite** (tit) *f*, steatite.

steeple-chase (stiplətʃɛs) *m*, hurdle race.

stellaire (stɛllɛːr) *a*, stellar.

sténodactylographe (stenodaktilɔgraf) *n*, shorthand-typist. **sténographe** (graf) *n*, stenographer. **sténographie** (fi) *f*, shorthand, stenography. **sténographier** (fje) *v.t*, to take down [in shorthand].

stère (stɛːr) *m*, stere = 1 cub. meter (*firewood*).

stéréoscope (stereɔskɔp) *m*, stereoscope.

stéréotyper (stereɔtipe) *v.t*, to stereotype.

stérile† (steril) *a*, sterile, barren; effete; unfruitful; fruitless. **stériliser** (lize) *v.t*, to sterilize. **stérilité** (te) *f*, sterility, etc.

sterling (stɛrliŋ) *a.inv*, sterling. **sterne** (stɛrn) *m*, tern (bird).

sternum (stɛrnɔm) *m*, sternum, breast bone.

stethoscope (stetɔskɔp) *m*, stethoscope.

stigmate (stigmat) *m*, stigma,

brand. **stigmatiser** (tizeλ) *v.t*, to stigmatize, brand.

stimulant (stimylɑ̃) *m*, stimulant; whet; stimulus. **stimuler** (le) *v.t*, to stimulate, exhilarate, whet.

stipendiaire (stipɑ̃djɛːr) *a*, mercenary.

stipuler (stipyle) *v.t*, to stipulate.

stock (stɔk) *m*, stock (*goods, gold*).

stockfisch (stɔkfiʃ) *m*, stockfish.

stockiste (stɔkist) *m*, warehouseman (*trade goods*); accredited dealer.

stoïcien, ne (stɔisjɛ̃, ɛn) *a. & m*, Stoic. **stoïcisme** (sism) *m*, stoicism. **stoïque†** (ik) *a*, stoical.

stomacal, e (stɔmakal) *a*, stomachal; stomach (*pump*). **stomachique** (ʃik) *a. & m*, stomachic.

stop (stɔp) *i*, stop (*Naut., in telegrams*). **stoppage** (stɔpaːʒ) *m*, invisible mending. **stopper** (pe) *v.t. & i*, to stop (*ship*); reweave.

store (stɔːr) *m*, blind, shade, awning.

strangulation (strɑ̃gylasjɔ̃) *f*, strangulation.

strapontin (strapɔ̃tɛ̃) *m*, jumpseat.

Strasbourg (strazbuːr) *m*, Strasburg.

strasse (stras) *f*, floss silk.

stratagème (strataʒɛm) *m*, stratagem. **stratège** (tɛːʒ) *m*, strategist. **stratégie** (teʒi) *f*, strategy; generalship. **stratégique** (ʒik) *a*, strategic(al).

stratification (stratifikasjɔ̃) *f*, stratification.

strict, e† (strikt) *a*, strict.

strident, e (stridɑ̃, ɑ̃ːt) *a*, strident, shrill, grating.

strie (stri) *f*, stria, score; ridge. **strié, e** (e) *a*, striate[d]; fluted. **striure** (yːr) *f*, striation.

strophe (strɔf) *f*, stanza, verse.

structure (struktyːr) *f*, structure, make.

strychnine (striknin) *f*, strychnine.

stuc (styk) *m*, stucco.

studieux, euse† (stydjø, øːz) *a*, studious.

stupéfiant (stypefjɑ̃) *m*, narcotic, drug. **stupéfier** (fje) *v.t*, to stupefy; amaze. **stupeur** (pœːr) *f*,

stupor; amazement. **stupide**†
(pid) *a*, stupid. **stupidité** (dite)
f, stupidity.

style (stil) *m*, style. **styler** (le)
v.t, to train. **stylet** (lɛ) *m*, stiletto;
stylet; probe.

stylo (stilɔ) *m*, fountain pen. ~ *à*
bille, ball-point pen.

su (sy) *m*: *au ~ de*, to the knowledge of.

suaire (sɥɛːr) *m*, shroud, winding sheet.

suant, e (sɥɑ̃, ɑ̃ːt) *a*, sweating;
sweaty.

suave† (sɥaːv) *a*, sweet, soft;
suave, bland. **suavité** (avite) *f*,
sweetness, suavity.

subalterne (sybaltɛrn) *a*, subordinate, minor. ¶ *m*, underling;
subaltern.

subconscience (sybkɔ̃sjɑ̃ːs) *f*,
subconsciousness. **subconscient,**
e (sjɑ̃, ɑ̃ːt) *a. & m*, subconscious.

subdiviser (sybdivize) *v.t*, to
subdivide.

subir (sybiːr) *v.t*, to undergo,
submit to, suffer; serve (*a sen-*
tence).

subit, e† (sybi, it) *a*, sudden.
subito (to) *ad*, all of a sudden.

subjectif, ive† (syb3ɛktif, iːv)
a. & m, subjective.

subjonctif, ive† (syb3ɔ̃ktif) *m*, subjunctive [mood].

subjuguer (syb3yge) *v.t*, to subjugate, subdue.

sublime† (syblim) *a. & m*, sublime. **sublimité** (mite) sublimity.

sublunaire (syblynɛːr) *a*, sublunar[y].

submerger (sybmɛr3e) *v.t*, to
submerge, flood, swamp. **sub-**
mersion (sjɔ̃) *f*, submersion; flood-
ing; drowning (*of pers.*).

subodorer (sybɔdɔre) *v.t*, to
scent [out], suspect.

subordonné, e (sybɔrdɔne) *a.*
& n, subordinate. **subordonner**
(ne) *v.t*, to subordinate.

suborner (sybɔrne) *v.t*, to suborn, tamper with.

subrécargue (sybrekarg) *m*,
supercargo.

subreptice† (sybrɛptis) *a*, sur-
reptitious.

subroger (sybrɔ3e) *v.t*, to subro-
gate.

subséquemment (sypsekamɑ̃)

ad, subsequently. **subséquent, e**
(kɑ̃, ɑ̃ːt) *a*, subsequent, ensuing.

subside (sypsid) *m*, subsidy.

subsidiaire† (sypsidjɛːr) *a*, subsidiary.

subsistance (sypsistɑ̃ːs) *f*, sub-
sistence, sustenance; (*pl.*) provisions, supplies. **subsister** (te) *v.i*,
to subsist.

substance (sybstɑ̃ːs) *f*, substance;
gist, kernel (*fig.*). **substantiel,**
le† (stɑ̃sjɛl) *a*, substantial. **sub-**
stantif (tif) *a.m. & m*, substantive.

substituer (sybstitɥe) *v.t*, to
substitute; entail (*law*). **substi-**
tut (ty) *m*, deputy; surrogate.

substruction (sybstryksjɔ̃) *f*,
substructure.

subterfuge (syptɛrfy:3) *m*, subterfuge, shift.

subtil, e† (syptil) *a*, subtle; pervasive; keen; fine. **subtiliser** (lize)
v.t, to filch; (*v.i.*) to subtilize.
subtilité (te) *f*, subtlety.

suburbain, e (sybyrbɛ̃, ɛn) *a*,
suburban.

subvenir à (sybvəniːr) *v.ir*, to
come to the aid of; provide for.
subvention (vɑ̃sjɔ̃) *f*, subsidy,
subvention, grant. **subventionner**
(ɔne) *v.t*, to subsidize.

subversif, ive (sybvɛrsif, iːv) *a*,
subversive. **subversion** (sjɔ̃) *f*,
subversion, overthrow.

suc (syk) *m*, juice; pith (*fig.*).

succédané (syksedane) *m*, substitute (*product*). **succéder à**
(de), to succeed; s. to; follow;
inherit. **succès** (sɛ) *m*, success;
issue. **successeur** (sɛsœːr) *m*, successor. **successif, ive** (sif, iːv) *a*,
successive, running. **succession**
(sjɔ̃) *f*, succession, sequence; inheritance, estate. **successivement**
(sivmɑ̃) *ad*, successively; seriatim.

succinct, e† (syksɛ̃, ɛ̃ːkt) *a*, succinct; meager.

succion (syksjɔ̃) *f*, suction, sucking.

succomber (sykɔ̃be) *v.i*, to succumb; sink; yield; die.

succulent, e (sykylɑ̃, ɑ̃ːt) *a*, succulent, juicy, luscious, toothsome.

succursale (sykyrsal) *f*, branch
(*establishment*).

sucer (syse) *v.t*, to suck; imbibe.
sucette (sɛt) *f*, lollipop; pacifier.

suçoir (swa:r) *m*, sucker (*of insect*).

sucre (sykr) *m*, sugar. ~ *cristallisé*, granulated s. ~ *d'orge*, barley s. ~ *en morceaux*, ~ *cassé*, lump s., cube s. ~ *en poudre*, powdered s. **sucré, e** (kre) *p.a*, sugared, sweet[ened]; sugary (*fig.*). *elle fait la sucrée*, butter wouldn't melt in her mouth. **sucrer** (kre) *v.t*, to sugar, sweeten. **sucrerie** (krəri) *f*, sugar refinery; (*pl.*) candy. *aimer les* ~s, to have a sweet tooth. **sucrier, ère** (krie, ε:r) *a*, sugar (*att.*). ¶ *m*, sugar refiner; sugar bowl.

sud (syd) *m*, south; (*att.*) south[ern]. ~-*africain, e*, South African. ~-*américain, e*, South American. ~-*est* (sydεst; *Naut.*, syε) *m*, southeast. ~-*ouest* (sydwεst; *Naut.*, syrwε) *m*, southwest. *le S*~-*Ouest africain*, South West Africa.

Suède (la) (syεd), Sweden. **suédois, e** (edwa, a:z) *a. & (language) m*, Swedish. **S**~, *n*, Swede (*pers.*).

suée (sye) *f*, sweat (*state*). **suer** (e) *v.i. & t*, to sweat, perspire, ooze; reek of, with. ~ *à grosses gouttes*, to sweat profusely. ~ *d'ahan* (a[h]ɑ̃), to toil & moil. **sueur** (œ:r) *f*, sweat, perspiration.

suffire (syfi:r) *v.i.ir*, to suffice, be enough, do. ~ *à*, to be equal to, satisfy, cope with. *suffit que*, suffice it to say that. **suffisamment** (fizamɑ̃) *ad*, sufficiently, enough, adequately. **suffisance** (zɑ̃:s) *f*, sufficiency, adequacy, enough; self-importance, bumptiousness. **suffisant, e** (zɑ̃, ɑ̃:t) *a*, sufficient, etc.

suffixe (syfiks) *m*, suffix. ¶ *a*, suffixed.

suffocation (syfɔkasjɔ̃) *f*, suffocation, choking. **suffoquer** (ke) *v.t. & i*, to suffocate, stifle, choke.

suffragant (syfragɑ̃) *a.m. & m*, suffragan.

suffrage (syfra:ʒ) *m*, suffrage, vote.

suffusion (syfysjɔ̃) *f*, suffusion.

suggérer (sygʒere) *v.t*, to suggest; prompt. **suggestion** (sygʒεstjɔ̃) *f*, suggestion, hint. **suggestionner** (ɔne) *v.t*, to affect by suggestion (*psychology*).

suicide (sɥisid) *m. & suicidé (de)** (*pers.*) *m*, suicide. *suicide du genre humain*, race suicide. **se suicider (de)** *v.pr*, to commit suicide.

suie (sɥi) *f*, soot.

suif (sɥif) *m*, tallow; (*mutton*) fat; candle grease. **suiffer (fe)** *v.t*, to tallow, grease.

suint (sɥε̃) *m*, grease (*in wool*). **suinter** (te) *v.i*, to ooze, run; leak.

suisse (sɥis) *a*, Swiss. ¶ *m*, Swiss (*man*); Swiss guard; beadle. *en suisse, faire suisse*, to eat or drink without inviting others present. *la S*~, Switzerland. **Suissesse** (sεs) *f*, Swiss (*woman*).

suite (sɥit) *f*, continuation; consequence, result, effect; sequence, series, succession, run; sequel; suite; attendants, retinue, train; set; coherence, consistency. *la ~ au prochain numéro*, to be continued in our next. ~ *& fin*, concluded (*serial*). **suivant, e** (vɑ̃, ɑ̃:t) *a*, next, following, ensuing. ¶ *n*, follower, attendant; (*f.*) lady's maid. **suivant**, *pr*, along; according to, pursuant to. ~ *que*, according as. **suivi, e** (vi) *p.a*, coherent; consistent; steady; well-attended. **suivre** (sɥi:vr) *v.t. ir*, to follow; succeed; pursue; watch, observe; attend; practise. ~ *la balle*, to follow through. *à ~*, to be continued (*serial*). *faire ~*, to forward, readdress; run on (*Typ.*).

sujet, te (syʒε, εt) *a*, subject, amenable, liable, prone. ¶ *n*, subject (*of a State*). ¶ *m*, subject, topic, matter, theme; cause, grounds; stock (*Hort.*); fellow. **sujétion** (ʒesjɔ̃) *f*, subjection, subservience; constraint; sedulousness.

sulfate (sylfat) *m*, sulfate. **sulfite** (fit) *m*, sulfite. **sulfure** (fy:r) *m*, sulfide. **sulfuré, e** (fyre) *a*, sulfurreted. **sulfureux, euse** (rø, ø:z) *a*, sulfurous. **sulfurique** (rik) *a*, sulfuric.

sultan (syltɑ̃) *m*, sultan; silklined basket; sachet. **sultane** (tan) *f*, sultana (*pers.*).

superbe† (sypεrb) *a*, superb,

stately; vainglorious. ¶ *f*, vain-glory.

supercherie (sypɛrʃəri) *f*, fraud, hoax.

superfétation (sypɛrfetasjɔ̃) *f*, redundancy.

superficie (sypɛrfisi) *f*, super-ficies, surface; area. **superficiel, le†** (sjel) *a*, superficial, shallow, skin-deep.

superfin, e (sypɛrfɛ̃) *a*, super-fine.

superflu, e (sypɛrfly) *a*, super-fluous. **superflu,** *m*. & **superfluité** (ite) *f*, superfluity.

supérieur, e (syperjœːr) *a*, su-perior; upper; higher. ¶ *n*, supe-rior, chief; better (*pers.*). **supér-ieurement** (œrmɑ̃) *ad*, superla-tively, in a masterly way. ~ *à,* better than. **supériorité** (rjɔrite) *f*, superiority.

superlatif, ive (sypɛrlatif, iːv) *a*, superlative (*Gram.*); consum-mate. ¶ (*Gram.*) *m*, superlative.

superposer (sypɛrpoze) *v.t*, to super[im]pose.

superstitieux, euse† (sypɛr-stisjø, øːz) *a*, superstitious. **su-perstition** (sjɔ̃) *f*, superstition.

supplanter (syplɑ̃te) *v.t*, to sup-plant.

suppléance (sypleɑ̃ːs) *f*, sub-stitution; deputyship; temporary term. **suppléant, e** (ɑ̃, ɑ̃ːt) *n*. & *a*, substitute, deputy. **suppléer** (ee) *v.t*, to supply, make up for; deputize for; eke out. ~ *à,* to make up for; fill (*vacancy*). **sup-plément** (mɑ̃) *m*, supplement, ad-dition, excess, extra [charge, fare]. **supplémentaire** (tɛːr) *a*, supple-mentary, additional, extra, fur-ther; relief (*train*).

suppliant, e (sypliɑ̃, ɑ̃ːt) *a*. & *n*, suppliant. **supplication** (kasjɔ̃) *f*, supplication, entreaty. **supplice** (plis) *m*, punishment, torture, tor-ment; (*extreme*) penalty; rack (*fig.*). **supplier** (plie) *v.t*, to be-seech, entreat, implore, suppli-cate. **supplique** (plik) *f*, petition, prayer.

support (sypɔːr) *m*, support, stay; rest, stand, holder. ~ *à chariot,* slide rest (*lathe*). **sup-portable** (pɔrtabl) *a*, supportable, bearable, endurable, tolerable.

supporter (te) *v.t*, to support; en-dure, bear, suffer, stand. **sup-ports-chaussettes,** *m.pl*, garters (*men's*).

supposé, e (sypoze) *p.a*, sup-posititious; fictitious. **supposé que,** supposing [that]. **supposer** (ze) *v.t*, to suppose; assume, infer, take; imply; put forward as gen-uine (*what is false—law*). **sup-position** (zisjɔ̃) *f*, supposition, as-sumption. ~ *de personne,* im-personation (*law*).

suppôt (sypo) *m*, tool (*pers.*), myrmidon.

suppression (sypresjɔ̃) *f*, sup-pression; discontinuance (*train*); concealment. **supprimer** (prime) *v.t*, to suppress, do away with, cut out; discontinue; conceal.

suppurer (sypyre) *v.i*, to sup-purate.

supputer (sypyte) *v.t*, to com-pute, reckon.

suprématie (sypremasi) *f*, su-premacy. **suprême†** (prɛːm) *a*, supreme; highest; crowning; par-amount.

sur (syr) *pr*, on, upon; over, above; by; after; in; about; as to; to; towards; out of. ~ *ce,* thereupon.

sur, e (syːr) *a*, sour, tart.

sûr, e (syːr) *a*, sure, safe, secure; reliable; settled (*weather*).

surabondant, e (syrabɔ̃dɑ̃, ɑ̃ːt) *a*, superabundant.

suranné, e (syrane) *a*, out-of-date, antiquated, superannuated.

surcharge (syrʃarʒ) *f*, overload; excess weight (*luggage*); weight handicap; surcharge; correction, overprint. **surcharger** (ʒe) *v.t*, to overload; overtax; surcharge; correct, alter (*write over*).

surchauffer (syrʃofe) *v.t*, to overheat; superheat.

surcroît (syrkrwa) *m*, increase. *par ~,* in addition, to boot.

surdité (syrdite) *f*, deafness.

sureau (syro) *m*, elder [tree].

surélever (syrelve) *v.t*, to height-en; raise; tee (*golf*).

sûrement (syrmɑ̃) *ad*, surely, as *sûr*.

surenchère (syrɑ̃ʃɛːr) *f*, higher bid. **surenchérir sur** (ʃeriːr), to bid higher than, outbid.

surestaries (syrɛstari) *f.pl*, demurrage (*ship*).

surestimer (syrɛstime) *v.t*, to overestimate, overvalue, overrate.

sûreté (syrte) *f*, safety, security, safe keeping; sureness, reliability. **la S∼ Nationale** (*Fr.*), equivalent of Federal Bureau of Investigation in the U.S.

surexciter (syrɛksite) *v.t*, to overexcite.

surface (syrfas) *f*, surface; area; standing, repute. **∼ des étages**, floor space (*building*).

surfaire (syrfɛ:r) *v.t. & abs. ir*, to overcharge (for); overrate, overestimate.

surfin, e (syrfɛ̃, in) *a*, superfine.

surgeon (syrʒɔ̃) *m*, sucker (*Hort.*).

surgir (syrʒi:r) *v.i*, to rise; arise, loom.

surhausser (syrose) *v.t*, to heighten, raise.

surhomme (syrɔm) *m*, superman.

surhumain, e (syrymɛ̃, ɛn) *a*, superhuman.

surimposer (syrɛ̃poze) *v.t*, to overtax, overassess.

surintendant, e (syrɛ̃tɑ̃dɑ̃, ɑ̃:t) *n*, superintendent, overseer, steward.

surjet (syrʒɛ) *m*, oversewing stitch, seam s.

sur-le-champ (syrləʃɑ̃) *ad*, there & then; out of hand, offhand.

surlendemain (syrlɑ̃dmɛ̃) *m*, day after tomorrow.

surmener (syrməne) *v.t*, to overwork; overdrive, override (*horse*); jade.

surmonter (syrmɔ̃te) *v.t*, to surmount, [over]top; overcome.

surnager (syrnaʒe) *v.i*, to float [on the surface]; survive.

surnaturel, le† (syrnatyrɛl) *a. & m*, supernatural, preternatural.

surnom (syrnɔ̃) *m*, surname, family name; nickname. **surnommer** (nɔme) *v.t*, to [nick]name, call.

surnombre (syrnɔ̃:br) *m*, surplus.

surnuméraire (syrnymerɛ:r) *a. & m*, supernumerary.

suroît (syrwa) *m*, sou'wester (*wind, hat*).

surpasser (syrpɑse) *v.t*, to surpass, overtop, exceed, outdo; astonish.

surpayer (syrpɛje) *v.t*, to overpay.

surplis (syrpli) *m*, surplice.

surplomb (syrplɔ̃) *m*, overhang. **surplomber** (be) *v.i. & t*, to overhang.

surplus (syrply) *m*, surplus, excess; rest.

surprenant, e (syrprənɑ̃, ɑ̃:t) *a*, surprising. **surprendre** (prɑ̃:dr) *v.i.ir*, to surprise; catch [unawares]; overtake; intercept; detect; deceive; obtain by fraud. **surprise** (pri:z) *f*, surprise.

surproduction (syrprɔdyksjɔ̃) *f*, overproduction.

sursaut (syrso) *m*, start, jump; burst (*energy*). **sursauter** (te) *v.i*, to start. **faire ∼**, to startle.

surseoir à (syrswa:r) (*law*) *v.ir*, to suspend, delay, stay. **∼ l'exécution de**, to reprieve. **sursis** (si) *m*, stay [of proceedings]; reprieve, respite, postponement, or exemption, in many senses, e.g, *condamné à un an de prison avec ∼*, means sentenced to a year's imprisonment but with suspended sentence.

surtaxe (syrtaks) *f*, surtax; surcharge; overassessment; fee; duty. **surtaxer** (kse) *v.t*, to surtax; surcharge; overassess.

surtout (syrtu) *ad*, above all, especially. ¶ *m*, centerpiece, epergne; overcoat, surtout.

surveillance (syrvɛjɑ̃:s) *f*, supervision; watch. **surveillant, e** (jɑ̃, ɑ̃:t) *n*, supervisor, overseer. **surveiller** (je) *v.t*, to supervise, superintend, watch [over], look after.

survenir (syrvəni:r) *v.i.ir*, to arrive unexpectedly; supervene; come upon one; befall.

survie (syrvi) *f*, survivorship; survival. **survivance** (vɑ̃:s) *f*, survival, outliving. **∼ du plus apte**, survival of the fittest. **survivant, e** (vɑ̃, ɑ̃:t) *n*, survivor. **survivre à** (vi:vr) *v.ir*, to survive, outlive. **se survivre**, to survive; live again.

sus (sy; *in liaison*, syz) *ad*, [up]on;

come on! en ~, extra, to boot.
en ~ de, over & above.
susceptibilité (sysɛptibilite) *f*,
susceptibility; touchiness. **susceptible** (bl) *a*, susceptible; capable;
apt; sensitive; touchy.
susciter (sysite) *v.t*, to raise up;
give rise to; stir up.
suscription (syskripsjɔ̃) *f*, superscription.
susdit, e (sysdi, ít) *a. & n*, aforesaid. **susmentionné, e** (mãsjɔne)
a, above-mentioned. **susnommé,
e** (nɔme) *a*, above-named.
suspect, e (syspɛkt) *a*, suspicious,
questionable, doubtful, suspect.
suspecter (te) *v.t*, to suspect,
question.
suspendre (syspɑ̃:dr) *v.t*, to
suspend, hang up; sling; stop;
stay. **en suspens** (pɑ̃), in abeyance, outstanding. **suspension**
(sjɔ̃) *f*, suspension, hanging; discontinuance. **suspensoir** (swa:r)
m, suspensory bandage.
suspicion (syspisjɔ̃) *f*, suspicion.
sustenter (systãte) *v.t*, to sustain, nourish.
susurrer (sysyre) *v.i. & t*, to murmur, whisper.
suture (syty:r) *f*, suture; join.
suzerain, e (syzrɛ̃, ɛn) *a*, paramount. ¶ *n*, suzerain. **suzeraineté** (rɛnte) *f*, suzerainty.
svastika (svastika) *m*, swastika.
svelte (svɛlt) *a*, slender, slim.
sybarite (sibarit) *m*, sybarite.
sycomore (sikɔmɔ:r) *m*, sycamore.
sycophante (sikɔfã:t) *m*, sycophant.
syllabaire (silabɛ:r) *m*, spelling
book. **syllabe** (lab) *f*, syllable.
syllogisme (silɔʒism) *m*, syllogism.
sylphe (silf) *m*, **sylphide** (fid) *f*,
sylph.
sylvestre (silvɛstr) *a*, woodland
(*att.*). **sylviculture** (vikylty:r)
f, forestry.
symbole (sɛ̃bɔl) *m*, symbol. **le ~**
[*des apôtres*], the [Apostles']
Creed. **symbolique** (lik) *a*, sym-
bolic(al). **symboliser** (ze) *v.t*, to
symbolize.
symétrie (simetri) *f*, symmetry.
symétrique† (trik) *a*, symmetric-
(al).

sympathie (sɛ̃pati) *f*, sympathy,
fellow feeling; (*pl.*) (*one's*) likes.
sympathique (tik) *a*, sympathetic;
congenial; likable; invisible (*ink*).
sympathiser (tize) *v.i*, to sympathize.
symphonie (sɛ̃fɔni) *f*, symphony.
symptôme (sɛ̃pto:m) *m*, symptom.
synagogue (sinagɔg) *f*, synagogue.
synchrone (sɛ̃krɔn) *a*, synchronous.
syncope (sɛ̃kɔp) *f*, syncope; syncopation. **syncoper** (pe) *v.t*, to
syncopate.
syndic (sɛ̃dik) *m*, syndic; trustee,
assignee (*bankruptcy*). **syndicaliste** (kalist) *m*, trade unionist. **syndicat** (ka) *m*, trusteeship;
syndicate; association, federation; labor union. **~ de place-
ments**, pool (*Fin.*). **~ d'initiative**, tourist information bureau.
syndicataire (tɛ:r) *m*, member of
a syndicate; underwriter (*Fin.*).
syndiquer (ke) *v.t*, to syndicate.
synode (sinɔd) *m*, synod.
synonyme (sinɔnim) *a*, synonymous. ¶ *m*, synonym.
syntaxe (sɛ̃taks) *f*, syntax.
synthèse (sɛ̃tɛ:z) *f*, synthesis.
synthétique† (tetik) *a*, synthetic-
(al).
Syrie (la) (siri), Syria. **syrien, ne**
(rjɛ̃, ɛn) *a. & n*, Syrian.
systématique† (sistematik) *a*,
systematic; hidebound (*fig.*).
système (tɛm) *m*, system; plan.

T

ta *see* **ton.**
tabac (taba) *m*, tobacco. **~ à
priser**, snuff. **tabatière** (batjɛ:r)
f, snuffbox; skylight.
tabernacle (tabɛrnakl) *m*, tabernacle.
table (tabl) *f*, table; telephone
switchboard; slab; tablet; list; index. **~ à pied central**, pedestal
table. **~ à rallonge(s)**, leaf t. **~
alphabétique**, alphabetical list; a.
table; index (*book*). **~ d'harmonie**, soundboard (*Mus.*). **~
de jeu**, gaming table; card t. **~
de nuit**, **~ de chevet**, bedside t.

~ *des hors-texte*, list of plates.
~ *des matières*, contents (*book*).
~ *gigogne* (ʒigɔɲ), nested table, nest of 3 tables. ~ *rase*, tablet for inscription; open mind; clean sweep (*fig.*). **tableau** (blo) *m*, board; picture; view; tableau; curtain!; scene; list, table; roll, rolls; panel; bag (*of game*). ~ *d'autel*, altarpiece. ~ *de bord*, dashboard. ~ *de distribution*, switchboard. ~ *noir*, blackboard. **tablette** (blɛt) *f*, shelf; slab; cake, tablet, lozenge. ~ *de cheminée*, mantel-shelf. **tabletterie** (tri) *f*, fancy goods (*ivory*, *inlay*). **tablier** (blie) *m*, apron; board (*chess*); floor, deck (*of bridge*). ~ [*d'enfant*], pinafore.

tabou (tabu) *m*, taboo. *il est* ~, he, it, is taboo.

tabouret (taburɛ) *m*, stool; footstool; stocks (*Hist.*); shepherd's purse. ~ *de piano*, music stool, piano s.

tache (taʃ) *f*, stain, spot, speck, blot, blemish, stigma, taint. ~ *d'humidité*, damp mark (*in books*). ~ *de naissance*, birthmark. ~ *de rousseur*, freckle. ~ *de vin*, portwine mark, birthmark.

tâche (tɑːʃ) *f*, task; job. *à la* ~, piecework.

tacher (taʃe) *v.t*, to stain, spot; sully.

tâcher (tɑʃe) *v.i*, to try, endeavor; strive. **tâcheron** (ʃrɔ̃) *m*, jobber.

tacheter (taʃte) *v.t*, to spot, speckle.

tacite† (tasit) *a*, tacit, implied.

taciturne (tasityrn) *a*, taciturn, silent.

tact (takt) *m*, touch; tact.

tacticien (taktisjɛ̃) *m*, tactician.

tactile (taktil) *a*, tactile, tactual.

tactique (taktik) *a*, tactical. ¶ *f*, tactics.

tadorne (tadɔrn) *m*, sheldrake.

taffetas (tafta) *m*, taffeta. ~ *d'Angleterre*, ~ *gommée*, court plaster; adhesive tape.

tafia (tafja) *m*, tafia. ~ *de laurier*, bay rum.

Tage (le) (taːʒ), the Tagus.

taïaut (tajo) *i*, tally-ho!

taie (tɛ) *f*, case, slip (*pillow*); cover (*cushion*).

taillade (tajad) *f*, cut, slash, gash. **taillader** (de) *v.t*, to slash, slit, gash; whittle.

taillanderie (tajɑ̃dri) *f*, edge tools. **taillandier** (dje) *m*, toolmaker. **taillant** (jɑ̃) *m*, [cutting] edge. **taille** (tɑːj) *f*, cutting; cut; pruning; edge (*sword*); height, stature; size; shape; waist; tally [stick]. ~-*crayon*, *m*, pencil sharpener. ~-*douce*, *f*, copperplate [engraving]. ~ *hors série*, outsize. ~-*mer*, *m*, cutwater (*bow*). **tailler** (taje) *v.t*, to cut; cut out; prune; trim; clip; dress; hew; carve; sharpen, point. **tailleur** (tajœːr) *m*, cutter; hewer; tailor; tailored suit; (*att.*) tailor-made, tailored. **taillis** (ji) *m*, copse, coppice; brushwood, underwood. **tailloir** (tajwaːr) *m*, trencher (*platter*).

tain (tɛ̃) *m*, silvering (*for mirror*), foil.

taire (tɛːr) *v.t.ir*, to say nothing about; not to mention; leave unsaid; conceal. *faire* ~, to silence, hush. *se* ~, to hold one's tongue, be silent.

talc (talk) *m*, talc; French chalk; talcum.

talent (talɑ̃) *m*, talent; faculty; gift.

talion (taljɔ̃) *m*, talion, retaliation, eye for eye.

talisman (talismɑ̃) *m*, talisman.

talle (tal) *f*, sucker (*Hort.*).

taloche (talɔʃ) *f*, cuff, clout.

talon (talɔ̃) *m*, heel; butt (*cue*); counterfoil; (*pl. fig.*) footsteps. ~ *rouge* (*fig.*), aristocratic. **talonner** (lɔne) *v.t*, to follow on the heels of, dog; dun; spur on. **talonnette** (nɛt) *f*, heel piece; heel (*rubber*).

talus (taly) *m*, slope, batter; bank.

tamarin (tamarɛ̃) *m*, tamarind.

tambour (tɑ̃buːr) *m*, drum; drummer; barrel; tambour, frame. ~ *de basque*, tambourine. ~-*major*, drum major. **tambouriner** (burine) *v.i*, to drum; thrum; (*v.t.*) to cry (*news*); cry up.

tamis (tami) *m*, sieve; sifter; strainer; gauze.

Tamise (la) (tamiːz), the Thames.

tamiser (tamize) *v.t*, to sift; strain; subdue (*light*).

tampon (tãpɔ̃) *m*, plug; bung; tampion, tompion; wad; pad; buffer. **tamponner** (pɔne) *v.t*, to plug; pad; dab; collide with.

tam-tam (tamtam) *m*, tomtom; gong.

tan (tã) *m*, tan, bark (*tanners'*).

tancer (tãse) *v.t*, to scold.

tandem (tãdɛm) *m*, tandem (*carriage, cycle*).

tandis que (tãdi[s]) *c*, while, whilst; whereas.

tangage (tãgaːʒ) *m*, pitching (*ship*).

tangent, e (tãʒã, ãːt) *a*, tangent[ial]. ¶ *f*, tangent.

Tanger (tãʒe) *m*, Tangier.

tangible (tãʒibl) *a*, tangible.

tango (tãgo) *m*, tango.

tanguer (tãge) *v.i*, to pitch (*ship*).

tanière (tanjɛːr) *f*, den, lair; hole, earth.

tannin (tanɛ̃) *m*, tannin. **tanne** (tan) *f*, blackhead. **tanné, e** (ne) *p.a*, tanned; tan[-colored]. **tanner** (ne) *v.t*, to tan, cure; tire, bore. **tannerie** (nri) *f*, tannery, tan yard. **tanneur** (nœːr) *m*, tanner.

tant (tã) *m*, so much; so many; such; so; as much; as well [as]; as long; as far. ~ *pis*, ~ *mieux*, so much the worse, so much the better. ~ *soit peu*, ever so little, somewhat.

tantale (tãtal) *m*, tantalum.

tante (tãːt) *f*, aunt.

tantième (tãtjɛm) *m*, percentage.

tantinet (tãtinɛ) *m*, tiny bit, little bit, dash.

tantôt (tãto) *ad*, soon, presently, anon, by & by; in the afternoon; just now; sometimes, now.

taon (tã) *m*, gadfly, horsefly.

tapage (tapaːʒ) *m*, noise, uproar, disturbance, row; fuss, ado, stir. **tapageur, euse** (paʒœːr, øːz) *a*, noisy, rowdy, uproarious; loud, flash[y], showy, garish. ¶ *n*, roisterer, rowdy, brawler.

tape (tap) *f*, tap, rap, pat, slap. **tapé, e** (pe) *p.a*, dried (*apples, etc, in rings*); smart (*answer*). **tapecul** (pky) *m*, jigger (*sail*); rattletrap. **tapée** (pe) *f*, heaps, swarm. **taper** (pe) *v.t. & abs*, to

tap, smack, slap; beat; pat; type-[write]; stamp (*foot*).

tapinois (en) (tapinwa) *ad*, stealthily.

tapioca (tapjɔka) *m*, tapioca.

tapir (tapiːr) *m*, tapir.

tapir (se) (tapiːr) *v.pr*, to squat, crouch, cower; nestle.

tapis (tapi) *m*, carpet; tapis; cloth; cover. ~-*brosse*, *m*, doormat. ~ *de gazon*, [green]sward. ~ *roulant*, assembly line. ~ *vert*, green baize; gaming table. **tapisser** (se) *v.t*, to hang with tapestry; paper (*wall*); cover, line; carpet (*with flowers*). **tapisserie** (sri) *f*, tapestry, hangings, arras; tapestry work; rug work. *faire* ~, to be a wallflower (*dance*). **tapissier, ère** (sje, ɛːr) *n*, tapestry maker; upholsterer. ¶ *f*, delivery truck.

tapon (tapɔ̃) *m*, knot, tangle.

tapoter (tapɔte) *v.t*, to tap; strum, thrum.

taquet (takɛ) *m*, stop, block; cleat (*rope*).

taquin, e (takɛ̃, in) *n*, tease. **taquiner** (kine) *v.t. & i*, to tease, torment; worry.

taraud (taro) *m*, (*screw*) tap. **taraudage** (daːʒ) *m*, screw cutting, tapping, threading. **tarauder** (de) *v.t*, to tap, screw, thread.

tard (taːr) *ad*, late; later. *sur le* ~, late in the day; late in life. **tarder** (tarde) *v.i*, to delay, be long; loiter; (*v.imp.*) to long. **tardif, ive†** (dif, iːv) *a*, tardy, belated; late; slow, sluggish; backward. **tardiveté** (divte) *f*, lateness, backwardness.

tare (taːr) *f*, defect; taint; tare (*Com.*).

taré, e (tare) *p.a*, damaged, tainted; defective (*child*); depraved.

tarentelle (tarãtɛl) *f*, tarantella. **tarentule** (tyl) *f*, tarantula.

tarer (tare) *v.t*, to spoil, damage; tare (*Com.*).

targuer (se) **de** (targe), to pride oneself on, plume oneself on.

tarière (tarjɛːr) *f*, auger.

tarif (tarif) *m*, tariff, rate, rates, scale; price list; fare. **tarifer** (fe) *v.t*, to tariff, rate, price.

tarin (tarɛ̃) *m*, siskin.

tarir (tari:r) *v.t. & i*, to dry up; stop.

Tarragone (taragɔn) *f*, Tarragona.

tarse (tars) *m*, tarsus.

tartan (tartɑ̃) *m*, tartan (*cloth, garment*).

tarte (tart) *f*, tart, pie. **tartine** (tin) *f*, slice of bread & butter; bread & jam; rigmarole, screed.

tartre (tartr) *m*, tartar; scale, fur. **tartrique** (trik) *a*, tartaric.

tartufe (tartyf) *m*, sanctimonious hypocrite.

tᴀs (tɑ) *m*, heap, pile; pack; cock (*hay*); shock, mow; stake [anvil].

Tasmanie (la) (tasmani), Tasmania.

tasse (tɑ:s) *f*, cup; mug. *~ à café*, coffee cup. *~ de café*, cup of coffee.

tassé, e (tase) *p.a*, squat, dumpy.

tasseau (taso) *m*, strip, cleat.

tassement (tasmɑ̃) *m*, settling, sinking; setback. **tasser** (se) *v.t*, to press down; squeeze; (*v.i.*) to grow thick. **se ~**, to settle, sink; settle down; have a setback.

tâter (tate) *v.t*, to feel, touch; try; taste.

tatillon, ne (tatijɔ̃, ɔn) *n*, fusser; busybody. **tatillonner** (jɔne) *v.i*, to fuss, meddle.

tâtonnement (tɑtɔnmɑ̃) *m*, groping; tentative effort; (*pl.*) trial & error. **tâtonner** (ne) *v.i*, to grope; fumble. **à tâtons** (tɔ̃) *ad*, gropingly; warily.

tatou (tatu) *m*, armadillo.

tatouage (tatwa:ʒ) *m*, tattooing; tattoo (*on skin*). **tatouer** (twe) *v.t*, to tattoo.

taudis (todi) *m*, hovel; slum.

taupe (to:p) *f*, mole (*Zool.*); moleskin. **taupière** (topjɛ:r) *f*, mole trap. **taupinière** (pinjɛ:r) *f*, molehill; mean dwelling, hovel.

taureau (tɔro) *m*, bull.

tautologie (totɔlɔʒi) *f*, tautology.

taux (to) *m*, rate, price. *~ officiel* [*d'escompte*], bank rate.

taverne (tavɛrn) *f*, tavern.

taxation (taksasjɔ̃) *f*, taxation, rating; assessment; charges. **taxe** (taks) *f*, tax rate, duty, due; charge, fee. *~ de séjour*, visitors' tax. **taxer** (kse) *v.t*, to tax, rate, assess; charge with duty; charge

[for]; fix the minimum price of; accuse.

taxi (taksi) *m*, taxi [cab].

tchécoslovaque (tʃekɔslɔvak) *a. & T~, n*, Czechoslovak. **Tchécoslovaquie** (ki) *f*, Czechoslovakia. **tchèque** (tʃɛk) *a. & (language) m. & T~ (pers.) n*, Czech.

te, t' (tə, t) *pn*, you, yourself, thee, thyself.

té (te) *m*, T, tee. *~* [*à dessin*], T square.

technique† (tɛknik) *a*, technical. *¶ f*, technique. **technologie** (nɔlɔʒi) *f*, technology.

teck (tɛk) *m*, teak.

tégument (tegymɑ̃) *m*, tegument.

teigne (tɛɲ) *f*, moth; ringworm.

teindre (tɛ̃:dr) *v.t.ir*, to dye; stain; tincture. **teint** (tɛ̃) *m*, dye, color; complexion. **teinte** (tɛ̃:t) *f*, tint, shade, hue; tinge, touch, strain. **teinter** (tɛ̃te) *v.t*, to tint; tone (*paper*); fume (*wood*); tinge. **teinture** (ty:r) *f*, dyeing; dye; tinge; smattering; tincture. **teinturerie** (tyrri) *f*, dyeing; dye works. **teinturier, ère** (tyrje, ɛ:r) *n*, dyer [& cleaner].

tek (tɛk) *m*, teak.

tel, telle (tɛl) *a*, such; like; as; so. *¶ pn*, such a one, some, some. *un tel, une telle*, so-&-so.

télégramme (telegram) *m*, telegram, wire. **télégraphe** (graf) *m*, telegraph. **télégraphie** (fi) *f*, telegraphy. *~ sans fils*, (*abb.* T.S.F.), wireless t., radio. **télégraphier** (fje) *v.t. & abs*, to telegraph, wire. **télégraphique†** (fik) *a*, telegraphic, telegraph (*att.*).

télémètre (telemɛtr) *m*, range finder.

télépathie (telepati) *f*, telepathy.

téléphone (telefɔn) *m*, telephone. **téléphoner** (ne) *v.t. & abs*, to telephone. **téléphonie** (ni) *f*, telephony. **téléphonique** (nik) *a*, telephonic, telephone (*att.*).

télescope (telɛskɔp) *m*, [reflecting] telescope. **se télescoper** (pe) *v.pr*, to telescope (*trains*). **télescopique** (pik) *a*, telescopic; minor (*planet*).

téléviser (televize) *v.t*, to televise. **télévision** (vizjɔ̃) *f*, television.

tellement (tɛlmɑ̃) *ad*, so, in such a way.

téméraire† (temerɛːr) *a*, rash, reckless, foolhardy. **témérité** (rite) *f*, temerity, rashness.

témoignage (temwaɲaːȝ) *m*, testimony, evidence, witness; mark, token. **témoigner** (ɲe) *v.i. & t*, to testify, bear witness, give evidence; evince, show, prove. **témoin** (mwɛ̃) *m*, witness; second (*duel*); telltale, pilot (*lamp, etc.*); baton (*relay race*). ~ *à charge*, witness for the prosecution. ~ *à décharge*, w. for the defense. ~ *muet*, circumstantial evidence.

tempe (tãːp) *m*, temple (*Anat.*).

tempérament (tãperamã) *m*, temperament, constitution. *à* ~, installment buying.

tempérance (tãperãːs) *f*, temperance. **tempérant, e** (rã, ãːt) *a*, temperate.

température (tãperatyːr) *f*, temperature. **tempéré, e** (re) *a*, temperate; limited (*monarchy*). **tempérer** (re) *v.t*, to temper, moderate.

tempête (tãpɛːt) *f*, storm, tempest. *à la* ~, at stormy (*barometer*). **tempêter** (pɛte) *v.i*, to storm, fume. **tempétueux, euse** (petɥø, øːz) *a*, tempestuous, stormy; boisterous.

temple (tãːpl) *m*, temple; church.

temporaire† (tãpɔrɛːr) *a*, temporary. **temporel, le†** (rɛl) *a*, temporal. **temporiser** (rize) *v.i*, to temporize. **temps** (tã; *in liaison*, tãz) *m*, time; while; times, days, age; season; weather; tense (*Gram.*); beat (*Mus.*); phase. *quel* ~ *fait-il?* what's the weather? *au* ~! as you were! *en* ~ *& lieu*, in due course.

tenable (tənabl) *a*, tenable; bearable.

tenace (tənas) *a*, tenacious; adhesive; tough, stiff; stubborn; retentive. **ténacité** (tenasite) *f*, tenacity.

tenaille (tənɑːj) *f*, tongs; (*pl.*) pincers.

tenancier, ère (tənãsje, ɛːr) *n*, keeper; lessee. **tenant** (nã) *m*, champion, supporter.

tendance (tãdãːs) *f*, tendency, trend. **tendancieux, euse** (dãsjø, øːz) *a*, tendentious; leading (*question*).

tender (tãdɛːr) *m*, tender (*locomotive*).

tendeur (tãdœːr) *m*, layer (*carpets*); setter (*traps*); strainer, stretcher, tightener.

tendon (tãdɔ̃) *m*, tendon, sinew.

tendre (tãːdr) *v.t*, to stretch, tighten, strain; bend (*bow*); crane (*neck*); hold out (*hand, etc.*); pitch (*tent*); lay, spread, set; drape; (*v.i.*) to tend, lead, conduce.

tendre† (tãːdr) *a*, tender, soft; sensitive; new (*bread*); early (*youth*); fond. **tendresse** (tãdrɛs) *f*, tenderness, fondness, love; (*pl.*) caresses. **tendreté** (drəte) *f*, tenderness (*meat*). **tendron** (drɔ̃) *m*, tender shoot; gristle (*veal*); maiden.

tendu, e (tãdy) *p.a*, tense, taut, tight.

ténèbres (tenɛːbr) *f.pl*, dark[ness], gloom. **ténébreux, euse†** (nebrø, øːz) *a*, dark, murky, gloomy; obscure.

teneur, euse (tənœːr, øːz) *n*, holder. **teneur,** *f*, tenor, purport; terms; content[s], percentage; grade (*ore*).

ténia (tenja) *m*, tapeworm.

tenir (təniːr) *v.t.ir*, to hold; h. on; keep; have; contain; take; t. up (*space*); consider; (*v.i.ir.*) to hold; last; cling; border on; owe; partake, savor, be like; be owing to; rest, lie; be anxious; sit. *se* ~, to keep; stand; sit; stick; contain oneself.

tennis (tɛnis) *m*, [lawn] tennis; t. court.

tenon (tənɔ̃) *m*, tenon.

ténor (tenɔːr) *m*, tenor (*voice, singer*).

tension (tãsjɔ̃) *f*, tension; tightness; strain; pressure; voltage. ~ *artérielle*, blood pressure.

tentacule (tãtakyl) *m*, tentacle, feeler.

tentateur, trice (tãtatœːr, tris) *n*, tempter, temptress. **tentation** (sjɔ̃) *f*, temptation.

tentative (tãtatiːv) *f*, attempt, endeavor. ~ *d'assassinat*, attempted murder.

tente (tãːt) *f*, tent; awning. ~ *conique*, bell tent. ~ *de plage*, bathing t. ~*-pavillon*, *f*, marquee.

tenter (tãte) *v.t*, to attempt, try; tempt.

tenture (tãty:r) *f*, hangings; wall-paper.

tenu, e (tǝny) *p.a*, (*well*, *ill*) kept; neat, trim; (*to be*) bound (*à* = to); firm (*price*). ¶ *m*, hold (*Box.*). ¶ *f*, holding; keeping; bearing, carriage, behavior; seat (*on horse*); dress, clothes, uniform, order; firmness. *~ de ville*, street dress.

ténu, e (tǝny) *a*, thin, slender, tenuous, fine; watery (*fluid*). **ténuité** (nɥite) *f*, thinness.

tercet (tɛrsɛ) *m*, tercet, triplet (*Pros., Mus.*).

térébenthine (terebãtin) *f*, turpentine.

tergiverser (tɛrʒivɛrse) *v.i*, to be shifty, beat around the bush.

terme (tɛrm) *m*, term, end; time; date; account, settlement (*Stk Ex.*); quarter (*year*), q.'s rent; installment. **terminaison** (minɛzɔ̃) *f*, termination, ending. **terminer** (ne) *v.t*, to terminate, end, wind up. **terminus** (ny:s) *m*, terminus (*Rly.*).

termite (tɛrmit) *m*, termite, white ant.

terne (tɛrn) *a*, dull, lusterless, drab. **ternir** (ni:r) *v.t*, to tarnish, dull; dim; sully.

terrain (tɛrɛ̃) *m*, ground, land; field; site; course, links (*golf*); court (*croquet*). *~ d'aviation*, airfield.

terrasse (tɛras) *f*, terrace, bank; flat roof; [pavement] outside (*café*). **terrassement** (smã) *m*, earthwork. **terrasser** (se) *v.t*, to bank up; throw, floor. **terrassier** (sje) *m*, day laborer; earthwork contractor.

terre (tɛ:r) *f*, earth; ground; land; soil; estate; loam; clay; shore (*Naut.*); world. *~ battue*, hard court (*Ten.*). *~ cuite*, terra-cotta. *~ d'ombre*, umber. *la T~ de Feu*, Tierra del Fuego. *~ de Sienne brûlée*, burnt sienna. *~ à ~*, commonplace. *la ~ ferme*, the continent, the mainland; terra firma. *T~ Sainte*, Holy Land. *ventre à ~*, at full speed. **terreau** (tɛro) *m*, [vegetable] mold. *~ de feuilles*, leaf m.

Terre-Neuve, *f*, Newfoundland. **terre-neuve**, *m*, N. [dog]. **terre-plein**, *m*, open space; roadbed (*Rly.*); terrace. **terrer** (tɛre) *v.t*, to earth up; (*v.i.*) to burrow. **se ~**, to burrow; entrench oneself. **terrestre** (rɛstr) *a*, terrestrial; ground (*att.*); land (*att.*); earthy. **terreur** (tɛrœ:r) *f*, terror, dread. **terreux, euse** (tɛrø, ø:z) *a*, earthy; dull.

terrible† (tɛribl) *a*, terrible, terrific; dreadful.

terrien, ne (tɛrjɛ̃, ɛn) *a. & n*, landed (proprietor); (*m.*) landsman. **terrier** (rje) *m*, burrow, hole; earth (*fox*); terrier (*dog*).

terrifier (tɛrifje) *v.t*, to terrify.

terrine (tɛrin) *f*, [earthenware] pot, pan; (*pl.*) potted meats. **terrinée** (ne) *f*, panful.

territoire (tɛritwa:r) *m*, territory. **territorial, e** (tɔrjal) *a. & m*, territorial. **terroir** (rwa:r) *m*, soil.

terroriser (tɛrɔrize) *v.t*, to terrorize.

tertre (tɛrtr) *m*, hillock, knoll, mound. *~ de départ*, teeing ground (*golf*).

tes *see* **ton**.

Tessin (le) (tɛsɛ̃), the Ticino.

tesson (tɛsɔ̃) *m*, piece of broken glass *or* earthenware, potsherd.

testament (tɛstamã) *m*, will, testament. **testamentaire** (tɛ:r) *a*, testamentary. **testateur, trice** (tœ:r, tris) *n*, testator, trix. **tester** (te) *v.i*, to make one's will.

testicule (tɛstikyl) *m*, testicle.

tétanos (tetanɔs) *m*, tetanus, lockjaw.

têtard (tɛta:r) *m*, tadpole; pollard. **tête** (tɛ:t) *f*, head; top; face; lead; brains; wits. *~-à-~*, *m*, private interview, p. conversation; 2-cup tea set; sofa. *~ de linotte*, feather-brained person. *~ forte*, *forte ~*, good head, strong-minded person. *faire la ~ à quelqu'un*, to frown at someone. *faire une ~*, to look unhappy. *faire à sa ~*, to have one's own way.

téter (tete) *v.t. & abs*, to suck (*of child*).

têtière (tɛtjɛ:r) *f*, infant's cap; headstall; chair back.

tétin (tetɛ̃) *m*, nipple, pap, teat (*pers.*). **tétine** (tin) *f*, dug; nipple (*nursing bottle*). **téton** (tɔ̃) *m*, breast (*of woman*).

tétras (tetrɑ) *m*, grouse.

tette (tɛt) *f*, dug, teat (*animal*).

têtu, e (tety) *a*, stubborn, mulish.

teuton, ne (tøtɔ̃, ɔn) & **teutonique** (tɔnik) *a*, Teutonic.

texte (tɛkst) *m*, text. ~ [*composé*], letterpress.

textile (tɛkstil) *a*. & *m*, textile.

textuel, le† (tɛkstɥɛl) *a*, textual.

texture (tɛksty:r) *f*, texture; arrangement.

thé (te) *m*, tea; t. plant; t. party. ~ *complet*, tea, roll & butter. ~ *de viande*, beef tea.

théâtral, e† (teɑtral) *a*, theatrical; dramatic. **théâtre** (ɑ:tr) *m*, theater, playhouse; stage; drama; scene; seat (*as of war*).

théière (teje:r) *f*, teapot.

théisme (teism) *m*, theism.

thème (tɛm) *m*, theme; topic; exercise, composition (*Sch.*); stem (*Gram.*).

théodolite (teɔdɔlit) *m*, theodolite.

théologie (teɔlɔʒi) *f*, theology. **théologien, ne** (ʒjɛ̃, ɛn) *n*, theologian, divine. **théologique†** (ʒik) *a*, theological.

théorème (teɔrɛm) *m*, theorem. **théoricien** (risjɛ̃) *m*, theorist. **théorie** (ri) *f*, theory; procession (*poetic*). **théorique†** (rik) *a*, theoretic(al).

théosophie (teɔzɔfi) *f*, theosophy.

thérapeutique (terapøtik) *a*, therapeutic; apothecaries' (*measure, weight*). ¶ *f*, therapeutics.

thermal, e (tɛrmal) *a*, thermal, hot. **thermes** (tɛrm) *m.pl*, thermal baths.

thermomètre (tɛrmɔmɛtr) *m*, thermometer. ~ *médical*, clinical thermometer.

thésauriser (tezɔrize) *v.i*, to hoard.

thèse (tɛ:z) *f*, thesis, argument.

thon (tɔ̃) *m*, tuna.

thorax (tɔraks) *m*, thorax.

thym (tɛ̃) *m*, thyme.

thyroïde (tirɔid) *a*, thyroid.

tiare (tja:r) *f*, tiara.

tibia (tibja) *m*, tibia, shinbone; shin.

Tibre (le) (tibr), the Tiber.

tic (tik) *m*, tic; twitching; habit, mannerism, trick.

tic tac (tiktak) *m*, tick[-tack], pit[-a-]pat.

tiède† (tjɛd) *a*, tepid, lukewarm. **tiédeur** (tjedœ:r) *f*, tepidness, etc. **tiédir** (di:r) *v.i*, to become tepid.

tien, ne (*with* **le, la, les**) (tjɛ̃, ɛn) *pn*. & *m*, yours, thine, thy own.

tiens (tjɛ̃) *v. abs. imperative*, well! indeed!

tiers, tierce (tjɛ:r, ɛrs) *a*, third. ¶ *m*, third person, t. party. ¶ *f*, third. **tiers arbitre**, *m*, referee.

tige (ti:ʒ) *f*, stem, stalk; trunk (*tree*); shaft; shank, leg (*boot, stocking*); rod.

tignasse (tiɲas) *f*, shock, mop (*hair*).

tigre, tigresse (tigr, grɛs) *n*, tiger, tigress. **le Tigre**, the Tigris. **tigré, e** (gre) *a*, striped, tabby.

tillac (tijak) *m*, deck (*ship*).

tille (ti:j) *f*, bast, bass. **tilleul** (tijœl) *m*, lime [tree], linden [tree]; lime blossom.

timbale (tɛ̃bal) *f*, kettledrum; cup (*metal*).

timbrage (tɛ̃bra:ʒ) *m*, stamping. **timbre** (tɛ̃:br) *m*, stamp; bell; gong; timbre; postmark. ~ *humide*, pad stamp, rubber s. ~ [-*poste*], *m*, [postage] s. ~-*quittance*, *m*, receipt s. ~ *sec*, ~ *fixe*, embossed s., impressed s. **timbré, e** (tɛ̃bre) *p.a*, stamped; cracked, nuts (*pers.*). **timbrer** (bre) *v.t*, to stamp; postmark.

timide† (timid) *a*, timid; nervous; shy, bashful, diffident. **timidité** (dite) *f*, timidity.

timon (timɔ̃) *m*, pole (*carriage*); helm (*fig.*). **timonier** (mɔnje) *m*, helmsman; signalman (*Naut.*); quartermaster (*Naut.*).

timoré, e (timɔre) *a*, timorous.

tinctorial, e (tɛ̃ktɔrjal) *a*, dye (*stuffs, etc.*).

tine (tin) *f*, butt, cask; tub.

tintamarre (tɛ̃tama:r) *m*, din, racket, noise.

tinter (tɛ̃te) *v.i*. & *t*, to ring, toll; tinkle; jingle; clink; chink; tingle, buzz. **tintement** (tmɑ̃) *m*, ringing, etc; singing (*ears*).

tintouin (tɛ̃twɛ̃) *m*, trouble, worry.

tipule (tipyl) *f*, daddy-longlegs, crane fly.

tique (tik) *f*, tick (*insect*). **tiquer** (ke) *v.i*, to twitch; wince.

tiqueté, e (tikte) *a*, speckled, variegated.

tir (ti:r) *m*, shooting; musketry; gunnery; fire, firing; rifle range; shooting gallery. ~ *à l'arc*, archery.

tirade (tirad) *f*, tirade; long speech (*Theat.*).

tirage (tira:ʒ) *m*, drawing; pull[ing]; draft; towing; tow[ing] path; extension (*camera*); printing, machining; circulation (*news*). ~ *au sort*, drawing lots.

tiraillement (tirɑjmɑ̃) *m*, tugging; gnawing (*stomach*); wrangling. **tirailler** (je) *v.t*, to tug, pull; pester; (*v.i.*) to blaze away. **tirailleur** (jœ:r) *m*, skirmisher, sharpshooter, rifleman; freelance.

tirant (tirɑ̃) *m*, string, strap; tie; tag; stay; sinew (*meat*).

tire (tir) *comps, all m*: ~-*botte*, bootjack. ~-*bouchon*, corkscrew. ~-*bouton*, buttonhook. ~-*feu*, lanyard (*gun*). ~-*ligne*, drawing pen.

tiré, e (tire) *p.a*, drawn, pinched, haggard. ~ *à quatre épingles*, spick & span, dapper. ~ *par les cheveux*, farfetched.

tirelire (tirli:r) *f*, piggy bank.

tirer (tire) *v.t. & i*, to draw; pull; drag; tug; haul; get, derive; take; wreak; put out (*tongue*); raise, doff (*hat*); milk (*cow*); fire; shoot, let off; print, machine; incline, verge. ~ [*à pile ou face*], to toss a coin. **se** ~, to extricate oneself. **se** ~ *d'affaire*, to tide over a difficulty.

tiret (tirɛ) *m*, dash (*line*); hyphen.

tireur, euse (tirœ:r, ø:z) *n*, drawer; marksman, shot. ~ *d'-armes*, fencer. ~ *de cartes*, fortune-teller. ~ *isolé*, sniper.

tiroir (tirwa:r) *m*, drawer (*table, etc.*); slide; slide valve. ~ *de caisse*, till.

tisane (tizan) *f*, infusion, (*herb*) tea.

tison (tizɔ̃) *m*, brand, firebrand. **tisonner** (zɔne) *v.i*, to meddle with the fire. **tisonnier** (nje) *m*, poker.

tissage (tisa:ʒ) *m*, weaving. **tisser** (se) *v.t*, to weave. **tisserand** (srɑ̃) *m*, weaver. **tisseranderie** (dri) *f*, weaving [trade]. **tissu** (sy) *m*, texture, weave; textile, fabric, cloth, gauze; tissue. ~ *éponge*, toweling. **tissure** (sy:r) *f*, texture, tissue. **tistre** (tistr) *v.t.ir*, to weave.

titiller (titille) *v.t*, to titillate, tickle.

titre (titr) *m*, title; [title] deed, muniment, document; proof, evidence; status; title page; heading; certificate, scrip, warrant, bond, security, stock, share; holding; claim; fineness (*coins*); grade; strength (*solution*). *à* ~ *d'office*, ex officio. *à* ~ *de*, by right of, in virtue of, as. *au* ~, standard (*gold*). *en* ~, titular. **titré, e** (tre) *a*, titled; standard (*solution*). **titrer** (tre) *v.t*, to give a title to; titrate; assay.

tituber (titybe) *v.i*, to stagger, lurch.

titulaire (tityle:r) *a*, titular. ¶ *n*, holder; occupant; incumbent.

toast (tɔst) *m*, toast (*health*); buttered toast.

toboggan (tɔbɔgɑ̃) *m*, toboggan.

tocsin (tɔksɛ̃) *m*, alarm bell; tocsin, hue & cry.

toge (tɔ:ʒ) *f*, toga; gown, robe.

tohu-bohu (tɔybɔy) *m*, chaos; hurly-burly.

toi (twa) *pn*, you, thee, thou. ~-*même*, yourself, thyself.

toile (twal) *f*, linen; cloth; canvas; gauze; curtain (*Theat.*); sail (*Naut.*); (*pl.*) toils (*Hunt.*). ~ *à calquer*, tracing cloth. ~ *à matelas*, tick[ing]. ~ *à voiles*, sailcloth, canvas. ~ *cirée*, oilcloth. ~ *d'araignée*, spider's web, cobweb. ~ *de matelas*, tick. ~ *de ménage*, homespun [linen]. ~ *de sol*, ground sheet. ~ *écrue*, ~ *bise*, unbleached linen. ~ *huilée*, oilskin. ~ *ouvrée*, huckaback. ~ *peinte*, print[ed fabric].

toilette (twalɛt) *f*, toilet, washing, dressing; dress; dressing table; washstand; lavatory.

toilier, ère (twalje, ɛ:r) *n*, linen draper.

toise (twa:z) *f*, height standard (*apparatus*); standard (*compari-*

son). **toiser** (twaze) _v.t_, to measure; look (_one_) up & down.

toison (twazɔ̃) _f_, fleece.

toit (twa) _m_, roof; housetop; shed. **toiture** (ty:r) _f_, roof[ing].

tôle (to:l) _f_, sheet; [sheet] iron; plate. ~ _ondulée_, corrugated iron. ~ _de blindage_, armor plate.

Tolède (tɔlɛd) _f_, Toledo.

tolérable (tɔlerabl) _a_, tolerable. **tolérance** (rɑ̃:s) _f_, tolerance; toleration; sufferance; margin, limit. _maison de_ ~, licensed brothel. **tolérant, e** (rɑ̃, ɑ̃:t) _a_, tolerant. **tolerer** (re) _v.t_, to tolerate, bear, suffer.

toletière (tɔltjɛ:r) _f_, rowlock.

tollé (tɔlle) _m_, outcry, hue & cry.

tomate (tɔmat) _f_, tomato.

tombe (tɔ̃:b) _f_, tomb, grave; death (_fig._). **tombeau** (tɔ̃bo) _m_, tomb, vault; monument; death.

tombeé (tɔ̃be) _f_, fall. ~ _de pluie_, downpour; rainfall. **tomber** (be) _v.i_, to fall, tumble; drop; crash; flag; crumble; lapse; hang [down]; (_v.t._) to throw (_wrestling_); damn (_a play_). ~ _d'accord_, to come to an agreement. **tombereau** (bro) _m_, [tip] cart; cartload; tumbril. **tombola** (bɔla) _f_, raffle.

Tombouctou (tɔ̃buktu) _m_, Timbuctoo.

tome (to:m) _m_, volume, tome.

ton, ta, tes (tɔ̃, ta, te) _a_, your, thy.

ton (tɔ̃) _m_, tone; tune (_fig._); style; manners, breeding, form; [whole] tone (_in distinction from a semitone_); key (_Mus._).

tondeur, euse (tɔ̃dœ:r, ø:z) _n_, shearer. ¶ _f_, shearing machine, shears; clippers; mower (_lawn_). **tondre** (tɔ̃:dr) _v.t_, to shear, clip, crop, mow; fleece (_pers._).

tonique (tɔnik) _a_, tonic. ¶ _m_, tonic (_Med._). ¶ _f_, tonic (_Mus._), keynote.

tonnage (tɔna:ʒ) _m_, tonnage; burden (_ship_); shipping. **tonne** (tɔn) _f_, tun; ton. _Fr. tonne_ = 1000 _kilos_. **tonneau** (no) _m_, cask, barrel, tun; butt, tub; bin; drum; governess car[t]; tonneau (_auto_); roll (_Avn._); ton (_Ship.——Fr. tonneau_ = 1000 _kilos_). ~ _d'arrosage_, water[ing] cart. **tonnelet** (nlɛ) _m_, keg. **tonnelier** (nəlje) _m_, cooper. **tonnelle** (nɛl) _f_, arbor, bower. **tonnellerie** (lri) _f_, cooperage.

tonner (tɔne) _v.i. & imp_, to thunder; boom; inveigh. **tonnerre** (nɛ:r) _m_, thunder; thunderbolt; breech (_firearm_).

tonsure (tɔ̃sy:r) _f_, tonsure. **tonsurer** (syre) _v.t_, to tonsure.

tonte (tɔ̃:t) _f_, shearing; clipping; mowing.

topaze (tɔpɑ:z) _f_, topaz.

toper (tɔpe) _v.t_, to agree, consent.

topique (tɔpik) _a_, topical (_Med._); local; to the point; in point.

topographie (tɔpɔgrafi) _f_, topography.

toquade (tɔkad) _f_, craze, fancy.

toque (tɔk) _f_, cap; toque.

toqué, e (tɔke) _p.a_, crazy, cracked.

torche (tɔrʃ) _f_, torch; mat, pad. **torcher** (ʃe) _v.t_, to wipe. **torchère** (ʃɛ:r) _f_, cresset; floor lamp. **torchis** (ʃi) _m_, loam; cob (_Build._). **torchon** (ʃɔ̃) _m_, dishcloth, swab, house flannel, duster; twist of straw.

torcol (tɔrkɔl) _m_, wryneck (_bird_).

tordant (tɔrdɑ̃) _a_, howlingly funny.

tordre (tɔrdr) _v.t_, to twist; distort; wring; wrest. se ~, to writhe; be convulsed (_laughing_).

toréador (tɔreadɔ:r) _m_, toreador.

tornade (tɔrnad) _f_, tornado.

toron (tɔrɔ̃) _m_, strand (_rope_).

torpeur (tɔrpœ:r) _f_, torpor. **torpide** (pid) _a_, torpid.

torpille (tɔrpi:j) _f_, torpedo; mine (_war_). **torpiller** (pije) _v.t_, to torpedo; mine. **torpilleur** (jœ:r) _m_, torpedo boat; t. man. _contre_-~, destroyer.

torréfier (tɔrrefje) _v.t_, to roast.

torrent (tɔrɑ̃) _m_, torrent; flood, flow; stream; rush. **torrentiel, le** (rɑ̃sjɛl), _a_, torrential.

torride (tɔrid) _a_, torrid.

tors, e (tɔ:r, ɔrs) _a_, twisted; contorted; crooked; wry. **torsade** (tɔrsad) _f_, twist, coil; bullion (_fringe_). **torse** (trs) _m_, torso, trunk. **torsion** (sjɔ̃) _f_, torsion.

tort (tɔ:r) _m_, wrong; fault; mistake; injury, harm. _à_ ~, wrongly. _à_ ~ & _à travers_, at random. _faire_ ~ _à_, to wrong.

torticolis (tɔrtikɔli) _m_, crick, stiff neck.

tortillage (tɔrtijaːʒ) *m*, involved language. **tortiller** (je) *v.t*, to twist; twirl; twiddle; kink; (*v.i.*) to shuffle. **se ~**, to wriggle; writhe. **tortillon** (jɔ̃) *m*, twist; pad (*for carrier's head*); bun (*hair*).

tortionnaire (tɔrsjɔnɛːr) *a*, torturous. **appareil ~**, instrument of torture. ¶ *m*, torturer.

tortu, e (tɔrty) *a*, crooked; tortuous.

tortue (tɔrty) *f*, tortoise; tortoise shell butterfly. **~ de mer**, turtle.

tortueux, euse† (tɔrtɥ∅, ∅ːz) *a*, tortuous; winding; underhand, crooked.

torture (tɔrtyːr) *f*, torture; rack. **torturer** (tyre) *v.t*, to torture, strain. **se ~ l'esprit**, to rack, cudgel, one's brains.

toscan, e (tɔskɑ̃, an) *a*. & **T~**, *n*, Tuscan. **la Toscane**, Tuscany.

tôt (to) *ad*, soon; quickly; early, betimes. **~ ou tard**, sooner or later. **le plus ~ possible**, as soon as possible.

total, e† (tɔtal) *a*. & *m*, total, whole; (*a.*) utter. **totalis[at]eur** (liz[at]œːr) *m*, totalizer; adding machine. **totalité** (te) *f*, whole, totality.

toton (tɔtɔ̃) *m*, teetotum.

toucan (tukɑ̃) *m*, toucan.

touchant, e (tuʃɑ̃, ɑ̃ːt) *a*, touching, moving, affecting. **touchant**, *pr*, touching, concerning, about. **touchau[d]** (ʃo) *m*, touch needle. **touche** (tuʃ) *f*, touch; hit; nibble (*fish*); key (*piano, typewriter, etc.*); finger board (*violin*); fret (*guitar, etc.*). **touche-à-tout**, *a*, meddlesome, officious. ¶ *m*, meddler, busybody, officious person. **toucher** (ʃe) *m*, touch; feel. ¶ *v.t*. & *i*, to touch; feel; finger; tap; hit; strike; whip; move, affect; concern; play (*piano, etc.*); ink up (*Typ.*); draw, receive, cash; test; touch on, allude to; meddle; adjoin. **toucheur** (ʃœːr) *m*, drover.

touer (twe) *v.t*, to tow, warp (*Naut.*). **toueur** (twœːr) *m*, tug.

touffe (tuf) *f*, tuft; wisp; clump; bunch. **~ de gazon**, divot (*golf*).

touffeur (tufœːr) *f*, stifling heat (*of room*).

touffu, e (tufy) *a*, bushy, thick; overloaded.

toujours (tuʒuːr) *ad*, always, ever; still; anyhow. **~ vert**, evergreen.

toupet (tupɛ) *m*, tuft of hair, forelock; cheek, impudence.

toupie (tupi) *f*, [peg] top. **~ d'Allemagne**, humming t. **toupiller** (je) *v.i*, to spin round.

tour (tuːr) *f*, tower; castle, rook (*chess*). ¶ *m*, turn; revolution; round; stroll, walk; trip, tour; spell; bout; row (*stitches*); circumference; size, measurement; lathe; wheel (*potter's*); trick; feat. **~ de Babel** (babɛl), babel (*fig.*). **~ de bâton**, perquisites, pickings. **~ de cartes**, card trick. **~ de col**, collar (*fur, etc.*). **~ de cou**, necklet, wrap. **~ de main**, knack; trick of the trade. **en un ~ de main**, in a jiffy, in a trice. **~ de nage**, swim. **~ de passe-passe**, conjuring trick; juggle; clever trick. **~ [de piste]**, lap. **~ de reins**, strain in the back. **~s & retours**, twists & turns.

tourbe (turb) *f*, peat; rabble, mob. **tourbeux, euse** (b∅, ∅ːz) *a*, peaty, boggy. **tourbière** (bjɛːr) *f*, peat bog, peatery.

tourbillon (turbijɔ̃) *m*, whirlwind; whirl, swirl; whirlpool; vortex; bustle. **tourbillonner** (jɔne) *v.i*, to whirl, swirl, eddy.

tourelle (turɛl) *f*, turret; capstan (*lathe*).

touret (turɛ) *m*, wheel; reel.

tourie (turi) *f*, carboy.

tourillon (turijɔ̃) *m*, axle, trunnion, gudgeon, journal, pin, pivot.

tourisme (turism) *m*, touring, travel for pleasure. **touriste** (rist) *n*, tourist.

tourment (turmɑ̃) *m*, torment, torture; pain; pang; worry; plague. **tourmentant, e** (tɑ̃, ɑ̃ːt) *a*, tormenting; troublesome. **tourmente** (mɑ̃ːt) *f*, storm, gale; turmoil. **~ de neige**, blizzard. **tourmenté, e** (mɑ̃te) *p.a*, distorted; broken; labored. **tourmenter** (te) *v.t*, to torment, torture, rack; worry; plague; overelaborate.

tournailler (turnɑje) *v.i*, to wander around. **tournant, e** (nɑ̃, ã:t) *a*, turning, revolving; swing (*bridge*); winding. ¶ *m*, turning; t. space; t. point; bend; corner (*street*); eddy; shift. **tourné, e** (ne) *p.a*, turned; shaped; disposed; sour (*milk*). **tourne-à-gauche** (nagoːʃ) *m*, wrench; saw set. **tournebride** (nəbrid) *m*, roadhouse; roadside inn; somewhere to stay. **tournebroche** (nəbrɔʃ) *m*, turnspit. **tournée** (ne) *f*, round; tour; circuit. **tourner** (ne) *v.t. & i*, to turn; t. over; t. out; rotate; revolve; gyrate; swivel; hinge; swing; wind; belay; shoot (*film*); film. **tournesol** (nəsɔl) *m*, sunflower; litmus. **tourneur** (nœːr) *m*, turner. **tournevis** (nəvis) *m*, screwdriver. **tourniquet** (nikɛ) *m*, turnstile; swivel; tourniquet.

tournoi (turnwa) *m*, tournament (*Hist., chess, etc.*); tourney. ~ *par élimination*, elimination tournament (*Ten.*). **tournoyer** (nwaje) *v.i*, to spin, whirl; wheel; swirl.

tournure (turnyːr) *f*, turn, course; cast; shape, figure; face.

tourte (turt) *f*, pie, tart. **tourteau** (to) *m*, oil cake.

tourtereau (turtəro) *m*, young turtledove. **tourterelle** (tərɛl) *f*, turtledove.

tourtière (turtjɛːr) *f*, pie dish; baking tin.

Toussaint (la) (tusɛ̃) All Saints' day. *la veille de la ~*, Halloween.

tousser (tuse) *v.i*, to cough.

tout (tu) *pn*, all, everything. *le ~*, the whole, the lot. **tout, e** (tu, tut) *a.s*, **tous** (tu & tuːs) *a.m.pl*, all, the whole [of]; every; any; full; only, sole. *tout le monde*, everybody, everyone. *tout le monde descend!* everybody out! (*Rly.*). ¶ *ad*, quite; very; thoroughly; all; right; ready (*made, cooked*); wide; stark (*naked*); bolt (*upright*); just. ~ ... *que*, however, [al]though. **tout**, *comps:* ~ *à coup*, suddenly, all at once. ~ *à fait*, quite; altogether; perfectly. ~ *à l'heure*, presently, by & by; just now. ~ *à vous*, yours very truly. ~ *d'un coup*, suddenly. ~ *de suite*, at once, directly. ~ *en parlant*,

while speaking. **tout-à-l'égout**, *m*, main drainage. **toute-épice**, *f*, allspice. **toute-fois**, *ad*, yet, however, nevertheless, still. **toute-puissance**, *f*, omnipotence. **tout-puissant, toute-puissante**, *a*, almighty, omnipotent; all-powerful; overpowering. *le Tout-Puissant*, the Almighty, the Omnipotent.

toutou (tutu) *m*, bowwow, doggie.

toux (tu) *f*, cough[ing].

toxine (tɔksin) *f*, toxin. **toxique** (ksik) *a*, toxic, poisonous, poison (*gas*). ¶ *m*, poison.

tracas (trakɑ) *m*, worry, bother. **tracasser** (kase) *v.t*, to worry. **tracasserie** (sri) *f*, wrangling.

trace (tras) *f*, trace; trail; track; spoor; scent; print; footprint; [foot]step; mark; weal. **tracé** (se) *m*, outline; graph; traced pattern. **tracer** (se) *v.t*, to trace; lay out; mark out; map out; draw, sketch, outline.

trachée-artère (traʃeartɛːr) *f*, trachea, windpipe.

tracteur (traktœːr) *m*, tractor. **traction** (ksjɔ̃) *f*, traction, haulage, draft.

tradition (tradisjɔ̃) *f*, tradition; folklore; delivery (*law*). **traditionnel, le†** (sjɔnɛl) *a*, traditional.

traducteur, trice (tradyktœːr, tris) *n*, translator. **traduction** (ksjɔ̃) *f*, translation; pony, crib. **traduire** (dɥiːr) *v.t.ir*, to summon; translate; express, interpret. *se ~*, to show.

trafic (trafik) *m*, traffic; trading; trade. **trafiquant** (kɑ̃) *m*, trader, trafficker. **trafiquer** (ke) *v.i*, to traffic, trade, deal.

tragédie (traʒedi) *f*, tragedy. **tragédien, ne** (djɛ̃, ɛn) *n*, tragedian, tragedienne. **tragi-comédie** (ʒikɔmedi) *f*, tragicomedy. **tragi-comique** (mik) *a*, tragicomic. **tragique†** (ʒik) *a*, tragic(al).

trahir (traiːr) *v.t*, to betray; reveal. **trahison** (izɔ̃) *f*, treachery; treason; betrayal.

train (trɛ̃) *m*, train, string; raft; set; suite; quarters (*horse*); pace, rate; progress; routine; mood. ~ *de paquebot*, boat train. *le ~*

[*des équipages*], the army service corps. ~ *militaire*, troop train. ~ *omnibus*, local train. ~*-poste*, *m*, mail train.

traînant, e (trɛnɑ̃, ɑ̃:t) *a*, trailing; shambling; listless, languid; singsong. **traînard** (na:r) *m*, straggler, laggard; slowcoach. **traînasser** (nase) *v.t*, to draw out; drag out; (*v.i.*) to loiter; laze. **traîne** (trɛ:n) *f*, train (*of dress*). *à la* ~, in tow. **traîneau** (trɛno) *m*, sledge, sleigh. **traînée** (ne) *f*, trail; train; ground line (*Fish.*); streetwalker. **traîner** (ne) *v.t. & i*, to drag, draw, haul; trail; draggle; drawl; lag; flag, droop; straggle; loiter; loaf. ~ *la jambe*, to shuffle along.

train-train (trɛtrɛ̃) *m*, jogtrot, routine.

traire (trɛ:r) *v.t.ir*, to milk; draw.

trait (trɛ) *m*, pull[ing]; draft; stretch; trace (*harness*); leash; arrow, dart; shot; beam; thunderbolt; dash (*Teleg.*); stroke; streak; line; flash; sally; gulp; feature; trait; touch; reference, bearing. ~ *d'union*, hyphen. ~ *de balance*, turn of the scale. **traitable** (tabl) *a*, tractable, manageable. **traite** (trɛt) *f*, stretch; stage (*journey*); trade, traffic; transport; trading; draft, bill; milking. *la* ~ *des noirs, la* ~ *des nègres*, the slave trade. **traité** (te) *m*, treatise; treaty; agreement. **traitement** (tmɑ̃) *m*, treatment; usage; salary, pay, stipend. ~ *d'inactivité*, pension. **traiter** (te) *v.t. & i*, to treat, use; entertain; deal; negotiate. ~ *de*, to treat of; call, dub. **traiteur** (tœ:r) *m*, caterer.

traître, traîtresse (trɛ:tr, trɛ:trɛs) *n*, traitor, traitress; betrayer; villain (*Theat.*). ¶ *a*, treacherous, traitorous. **traîtreusement** (trɔ̃zmɑ̃) *ad*, treacherously. **traîtrise** (tri:z) *f*, treachery.

trajectoire (traʒɛktwa:r) *f*, trajectory; path (*storm, etc.*). **trajet** (ʒɛ) *m*, journey, passage, transit, trip, run, ride, course.

tramail (trama:j) *m*, trammel [net].

trame (tram) *f*, woof, weft; web, thread (*of life*); half-tone screen;

plot. **tramer** (me) *v.t*, to weave; hatch (*plot*).

tramway (tramwɛ) *m*, streetcar, trolley car.

tranchant, e (trɑ̃ʃɑ̃, ɑ̃:t) *a*, cutting, sharp, keen; edge[d]; trenchant; peremptory; glaring. ¶ *m*, [cutting] edge. **tranche** (trɑ̃:ʃ) *f*, slice, cut; steak; rasher; slab; block, portion, set; edge (*book, coin*). *doré sur* ~, gilt-edged. ~*s rognées*, cut edges. **tranché, e** (trɑ̃ʃe) *a*, well-marked; distinct. **tranchée** (ʃe) *f*, trench; drain; cutting; (*pl.*) colic, gripes. **tranchefile** (ʃfil) *f*, headband (*Bookb.*). **trancher** (ʃe) *v.t*, to slice; cut; chop off; cut short; settle; contrast. **tranchoir** (ʃwa:r) *m*, trencher, cutting board.

tranquille† (trɑ̃kil) *a*, tranquil, quiet, calm, peaceful, still, undisturbed, easy. **tranquilliser** (lize) *v.t*, to calm, soothe. **tranquillité** (te) *f*, tranquillity, peace.

transaction (trɑ̃zaksjɔ̃) *f*, transaction, dealing; compromise.

transatlantique (trɑ̃zatlɑ̃tik) *a*, transatlantic. ¶ *m*, deckchair; liner.

transborder (trɑ̃sbɔrde) *v.t*, to tranship.

transcendant, e (trɑsɑ̃dɑ̃, ɑ̃:t) *a*, transcendent.

transcription (trɑ̃skripsjɔ̃) *f*, transcript[ion]; copy; posting (*Bkkpg.*). **transcrire** (skri:r) *v.t. ir*, to transcribe; post.

transe (trɑ̃:s) *f*, fright, scare; trance.

transept (trɑ̃sɛpt) *m*, transept.

transférer (trɑ̃sfere) *v.t*, to transfer; translate (*bishop*); alter the date of (*function*). **transfert** (fɛ:r) *m*, transfer.

transfiguration (trɑ̃sfigyrasjɔ̃) *f*, transfiguration. **transfigurer** (re) *v.t*, to transfigure.

transformateur (trɑ̃sformatœ:r) *m*, transformer. **transformer** (me) *v.t*, to transform, change, convert.

transfuge (trɑ̃sfy:ʒ) *m*, deserter (*to enemy*); turncoat, rat.

transfuser (trɑ̃sfyze) *v.t*, to transfuse.

transgresser (trɑ̃sgrɛse) *v.t*, to transgress.

transiger (trãzige) *v.i*, to compound, compromise.

transir (trãsi:r) *v.t*, to chill; paralyze (*fig.*).

transit (trãzit) *m*, transit (*Cust.*).

transitif, ive† (trãzitif, i:v) *a*, transitive.

transition (trãzisjɔ̃) *f*, transition. **transitoire** (twa:r) *a*, transitory, transient.

translation (trãslasjɔ̃) *f*, translation (*bishop*); transfer, conveyance; alteration of date (*function*).

translucide (trãslysid) *a*, translucent.

transmetteur (trãsmɛtœ:r) *m*, transmitter. **transmettre** (tr) *v.t. ir*, to transmit; pass on; hand down; transfer, convey. **transmission** (misjɔ̃) *f*, transmission; drive, driving, shaft[ing] (*Mech.*).

transmuer (trãsmɥe) *v.t*, to transmute.

transparence (trãsparã:s) *f*, transparency. **transparent, e** (rã, ã:t) *a*, transparent. ¶ *m*, transparency (*picture*); black lines.

transpercer (trãspɛrse) *v.t*, to transfix, pierce.

transpirer (trãspire) *v.i*, to perspire; transpire.

transplanter (trãsplãte) *v.t*, to transplant.

transport (trãspɔ:r) *m*, transport, conveyance, carriage; visit (*of experts, etc*; *law*); transfer (*law*); troopship; rapture. ~ [*au cerveau*], light-headedness, delirium. **transportation** (pɔrtasjɔ̃) *f*, transportation. **transporter** (te) *v.t*, to transport, etc.

transposer (trãspoze) *v.t*, to transpose.

transsubstantiation (trãssypstãsjasjɔ̃) *f*, transubstantiation.

transvaser (trãsvaze) *v.t*, to decant.

transversal, e† (trãsvɛrsal) *a*, transverse, cross (*att.*).

trapèze (trapɛ:z) *m*, trapeze.

trappe (trap) *f*, trap, pitfall; trapdoor. **trappeur** (pœ:r) *m*, trapper.

trapu, e (trapy) *a*, thickset, dumpy, squat, stocky.

traque (trak) *f*, beating (*game*).

traquenard (kna:r) *m*, trap. **traquer** (ke) *v.t*, to beat (*game*); surround; track down. **traqueur** (kœ:r) *m*, beater.

travail (trava:j) *m. oft. pl*, work; working; labor, toil; piece of work, job; employment; stress (*Mech.*); travail, childbirth; workmanship. ~ *d'artisan*, craftsmanship. *travaux forcés*, hard labor. **travaillé, e** (vaje) (*fig.*) *p.a*, labored, elaborate. **travailler** (je) *v.i*, to work, labor, toil; be in stress; (*v.t.*) to torment; work; w. up; elaborate. **travailleur, euse** (jœ:r, ø:z) *n*, worker; workman; laborer; toiler. ¶ *f*, workstand (*lady's*).

travée (trave) *f*, bay (*Arch.*); span (*bridge, roof*).

travers (trave:r) *m*, breadth; beam (*ship*), broadside; fault. à ~, through. de ~, askew, awry, amiss, wrong; askance. en ~, *ad*, across, athwart, cross[wise]. en ~ de, *pr*, across, athwart. **traverse** (vɛrs) *f*, shortcut; crossbar; crossbeam; crossroad; transom; sill; tie (*rail track*); hitch, setback. **traversée (se)** *f*, crossing, passage. ~ *des piétons*, pedestrian crossing. **traverser (se)** *v.t*, to traverse, cross, go through; thwart. **traversin** (sɛ̃) *m*, bolster (*bed*).

travestir (travɛsti:r) *v.t*, to disguise; travesty, burlesque; misrepresent.

trayon (trɛjɔ̃) *m*, dug, teat (*cow, etc.*).

trébucher (trebyʃe) *v.i*, to stumble, trip. **trébuchet** (ʃɛ) *m*, trap; balance (*scales*).

tréfiler (trefile) *v.t*, to wiredraw (*metal*).

trèfle (trɛfl) *m*, trefoil; clover; clubs (*cards*).

tréfonds (trefɔ̃) *m*, subsoil.

treillage (trɛja:ʒ) *m*, trellis, lattice. **treillis** (ji) *m*, trellis, lattice; netting; sackcloth. **treillisser (se)** *v.t*, to trellis, lattice.

treize (trɛ:z) *a. & m*, thirteen; 13th. ~ *douze*, baker's dozen. **treizième†** (trɛzjɛm) *a. & n*, thirteenth.

tréma (trema) *m*, diaeresis.

tremblaie (trãblɛ) *f*, aspen plan-

tation. tremble (trã:bl) *m*, asp[en].

tremblement (trãbləmã) *m*, trembling, trepidation, quavering, shaking; tremor. ~ *de terre*, earthquake. **tremblé, e** (ble) *p.a*, wavy, waved; shaky. **trembler** (ble) & **trembloter** (bləte) *v.i*, to tremble, shake, vibrate, quake, quiver, quaver, quail, shiver, flutter, flicker.

trémie (tremi)*f*, hopper (*Mach.*).

tremolo (tremɔlo) *m*, tremolo (*Mus.*).

trémousser (se) (tremuse) *v.pr*, to fidget; flounce about; bestir oneself. *trémousser de l'aile*, to flutter, flap its wings.

trempe (trã:p) *f*, damping; tempering, hardening; temper; stamp, kidney (*fig.*). **tremper** (trãpe) *v.t.* & *i*, to steep, soak, dip; drench; damp, wet; temper; imbrue.

tremplin (trãplẽ) *m*, spring board, diving b.; ski jump; jumping-off ground (*fig.*).

trentaine (trãten) *f*, thirty [or so]. **trente** (trã:t) *a*, thirty. ¶ *m*, thirty; 30th. ~ *et quarante*, rouge et noir. **T~**, *f*, Trent (*Italy*). **trentième** (trãtjɛm) *a*. & *n*, thirtieth. **le Trentin** (tẽ), the Trentino.

trépan (trepã) *m*, trepan; bit, chisel (*boring*). **trépaner** (pane) *v.t*, to trepan.

trépas (trepɑ) *m*, death, decease. **trépasser** (se) *v.i*, to die, pass away. **les trépassés** (se), the dead, the departed.

trépidation (trepidasjɔ̃) *f*, tremor; vibration (*of machinery, car, ship*).

trépied (trepje) *m*, tripod; trivet (*stove*).

trépigner (trepiɲe) *v.i*, to stamp (*rage*).

trépointe (trepwẽ:t) *f*, welt (*shoe*).

très (trɛ; *in liaison*, trɛz) *ad*, very, most, [very] much.

trésor (trezɔ:r) *m*, treasure; treasury. **trésorerie** (zɔrri) *f*, treasury; finances. **trésorier, ère** (zɔrje, ɛ:r) *n*, treasurer; paymaster.

tressaillir (trɛsaji:r) *v.i.ir*, to start; thrill; wince.

tressauter (trɛsote) *v.i*, to start, jump.

tresse (trɛs) *f*, plait, tress; braid; tape; gasket. **tresser** (se) *v.t*, to plait; braid; weave (*wicker, etc.*).

tréteau (treto) *m*, trestle, horse; (*pl.*) boards, stage.

treuil (trœ:j) *m*, winch, windlass, hoist.

trêve (trɛ:v) *f*, truce; respite.

Trèves (trɛ:v) *f*, Treves, Trier.

trévire (trevi:r) *f*, parbuckle.

tri (tri) & **triage** (a:ʒ) *m*, sorting.

triangle (triã:gl) *m*, triangle (*Geom.* & *Mus.*). **triangulaire** (ãgylɛ:r) *a*, triangular.

tribord (tribɔ:r) *m*, starboard.

tribu (triby) *f*, tribe.

tribulation (tribylasjɔ̃) *f*, tribulation, trial.

tribun (tribœ̃) (*pers.*) *m*, tribune (*Hist.*); demagogue. **tribunal** (bynal) *m*, tribunal; bench; court. **tribune** (byn) *f*, tribune; rostrum; platform; gallery; loft (*organ*); grandstand.

tribut (triby) *m*, tribute. **tributaire** (tɛ:r) *a*. & *m*, tributary (*pers., river*); dependent.

triceps (trisɛps) *a*. & *m*, triceps.

tricher (triʃe) *v.i.* & *t*, to cheat; trick; doctor. **tricherie** (ʃri) *f*, cheating; trickery. **tricheur, euse** (ʃœ:r, ø:z) *n*, cheat; trickster; sharper.

trichromie (trikrɔmi) *f*, three-color process.

tricot (triko) *m*, knitting (*art*); sweater; knitted garment; (*pl.*) knit[ted] wear. ~ *à l'envers*, purl knitting. **tricotage** (kɔta:ʒ) *m*, knitting (*act*). **tricoter** (te) *v.t.* & *abs*, to knit. **tricoteur, euse** (tœ:r, ø:z) *n*, knitter.

trictrac (triktrak) *m*, backgammon; b. board.

tricycle (trisikl) *m*, tricycle.

trident (tridã) *m*, trident; fish spear.

triennal, e (triɛnnal) *a*, triennial.

trier (trie) *v.t*, to sort; pick. **trieur, euse** (œ:r, ø:z) *n*, sorter; picker.

trigonométrie (trigɔnɔmetri) *f*, trigonometry.

trille (tri:j) *m*, trill, shake (*Mus.*).

trillion (triljɔ̃) *m*, a million millions.

trimbaler (trɛ̃bale) *v.t*, to drag about.

trimer (trime) *v.i*, to slave, drudge.

trimestre (trimɛstr) *m*, quarter, 3 months; term (*Sch.*); quarter's rent, salary, etc. **trimestriel, le** (triɛl) *a*, quarterly.

tringle (trɛ̃:gl) *f*, rod; curtain rod; chalk line (*mark*).

Trinité (la) (trinite), the Trinity; Trinidad.

trinquer (trɛ̃ke) *v.i*, to clink glasses; hobnob.

trio (trio) *m*, trio. **triolet** (ɔlɛ) *m*, triolet; triplet (*Mus.*).

triomphal, e† (triɔ̃fal) *a*, triumphal. **triomphe** (ɔ̃:f) *f*, triumph; exultation. **triompher** (ɔ̃fe) *v.i*, to triumph; exult; excel; gloat.

tripaille (tripɑ:j) *f*, garbage, offal.

tripe de velours (trip) *f*, velveteen.

triperie (tripri) *f*, tripe shop. **tripes** (trip) *f.pl*, tripe. **tripier, ère** (pje, ɛ:r) *n*, tripe dealer.

triple† (tripl) *a. & m*, treble, triple, threefold, 3 times; triplicate. ~ *croche*, *f*, demisemiquaver. ~ *saut*, *m*, hop, step, & jump. **tripler** (ple) *v.t. & i*, to treble, triple. **triplicata** (plikata) *m*, triplicate.

tripoli (tripɔli) *m*, tripoli.

tripot (tripo) *m*, bawdy house; gambling den. **tripoter** (pɔte) *v.t. & abs*, muddle up; plot; job, rig; handle; gamble; meddle with. **tripoteur** (pɔtœ:r) *m*, intriguer; shady speculator; mischiefmaker.

triptyque (triptik) *m*, triptych.

trique (trik) *f*, cudgel, bludgeon.

triqueballe (trikbal) *m*, sling cart.

trisaïeul, e (trizajœl) *n*, greatgreat-grandfather, -mother.

triste† (trist) *a*, sad, sorrowful, woeful; dreary, gloomy, dismal; bleak, depressing; sorry, wretched. **tristesse** (tɛs) *f*, sadness.

triton (tritɔ̃) *m*, triton; merman; newt; eft.

triturer (trityre) *v.t*, to triturate, grind.

trivial, e† (trivjal) *a*, vulgar, coarse; not in decent use (*expression*); trite, hackneyed. **trivialité** (lite) *f*, vulgarity, etc; vulgarism.

troc (trɔk) *m*, truck, exchange, barter.

trochée (trɔʃe) *m*, head of shoots (*tree stump*).

troène (trɔɛn) *m*, privet (*Bot.*).

troglodyte (trɔglɔdit) *m*, troglodyte, cave dweller.

trognon (trɔɲɔ̃) *m*, core (*apple*); stump (*cabbage*).

trois (trwɑ; *in liaison*, trwɑz) *a. & m*, three; third. ~ *fois*, three times, thrice. ~ *jumeaux*, triplets. ~-*mâts*, *m*, three-master. **troisième**† (zjɛm) *a*, third. ¶ *m*, third (*number, pers., floor*). ¶ *f*, third (*class*). ~*s* [*galeries*], gallery (*Theat.*).

trolley (trɔlɛ) *m*, troll[e]y (*grooved wheel*).

trombe (trɔ̃:b) *f*, waterspout. ~ *d'eau*, cloudburst. *entrer en* ~, to burst in.

trombone (trɔ̃bɔn) *m*, trombone; paper clip.

trompe (trɔ̃:p) *f*, horn; hooter; trumpet; proboscis; trunk. ~ *d'Eustache* (østaʃ), Eustachian tube.

trompe-l'œil (trɔ̃plœ:j) *m*, still-life deception; bluff, window dressing (*fig.*). **tromper** (pe) *v.t*, to deceive, delude; cheat; mislead; disappoint; outwit; beguile. **se** ~, to be mistaken, mistake. **tromperie** (pri) *f*, deceit, deception, imposture; illusion.

trompeter (trɔ̃pɛte) *v.t*, to trumpet (*secret*). **trompette** (pɛt) *f*, trumpet, trump (*last, of doom*); whelk. ¶ *m*, trumpeter.

trompeur, euse (trɔ̃pœ:r, ø:z) *n*, deceiver, cheat. ¶ *a*, deceitful; deceptive.

tronc (trɔ̃) *m*, trunk; parent stock; frustum. ~ *des pauvres*, poor box. **tronçon** (sɔ̃) *m*, (*broken*) piece, stump; section; dock (*of tail*). **tronçonner** (sɔne) *v.t*, to cut up.

trône (tro:n) *m*, throne. **trôner** (trone) *v.i,* to sit enthroned, sit in state.

tronquer (trɔ̃ke) *v.t,* to truncate; mutilate.

trop (tro; *in liaison,* trɔp) *ad. & m,* too; over-; too much, too many; too long; too well; excess. ~ *cuit, e,* overdone. *être de* ~, to be in the way, be unwelcome; superfluous.

trope (trɔp) *m,* trope.

trophée (trɔfe) *m,* trophy.

tropical, e (trɔpikal) *a,* tropical. **tropique** (pik) *m,* tropic.

trop-plein (trɔplɛ̃) *m,* overflow.

troquer (trɔke) *v.t,* to barter, exchange.

trot (tro) *m,* trot. **trotte** (trɔt) *f,* distance, step. **trotter** (te) *v.i. & t,* to trot; run (*in one's head*). **trotteur, euse** (tœ:r, ø:z) *n,* trotter (*horse*). **trottin** (tɛ̃) *m,* errand girl. **trottiner** (tine) *v.i,* to trot; toddle. **trottinette** (nɛt) *f,* scooter. **trottoir** (twa:r) *m,* pavement, footway, footpath. *bordure du* ~, curb.

trou (tru) *m,* hole; eye; blank. ~ *barré,* stimy, stymie (*golf*). ~ *d'air,* air pocket (*Avn.*). ~ [*d'arrivée*], hole (*golf*). ~ *d'homme,* manhole. ~ *de sonde,* bore hole.

troubadour (trubadu:r) *m,* troubadour.

trouble (trubl) *a,* troubled, turbid, muddy, cloudy; dim, blurred, misty; overcast; confused. ¶ *m,* disorder; disturbance; trouble. ~-**fête** (bləfɛ:t) *m,* spoilsport, killjoy. **troubler** (ble) *v.t,* to disturb; muddy; dim; mar; hamper; upset.

trouée (true) *f,* gap. **trouer** (e) *v.t,* to pierce with holes.

troupe (trup) *f,* troop, band; host; set, gang; troop; troupe; flock. **troupeau** (po) *m,* herd, drove; flock. **troupier** (pje) *m,* soldier, campaigner.

trousse (trus) *f,* truss; bundle; case; kit; outfit; roll. ~ *manucure,* manicure set. *aux* ~*s de,* at the heels of. **trousseau** (so) *m,* bunch (*keys*); outfit, kit; trousseau. **trousser** (se) *v.t,* to tuck up; turn up; truss; dispatch;

polish off. ~ *bagage,* to pack up; decamp; die. **troussis** (si) *m,* tuck.

trouvaille (truva:j) *f,* [lucky] find. **trouver** (ve) *v.t,* to find; discover; get; think; like; spare (*the time*). *objets trouvés,* lost and found. *enfant trouvé,* foundling. *se* ~, to be; feel; happen.

truc (tryk) *m,* knack; trick, dodge; gadget; platform car (*Rly.*).

trucage (tryka:ʒ) *m,* faking; camouflage; trick photography; gerrymandering.

truchement (tryʃmɑ̃) *m,* interpreter, spokesman.

truculent, e (trykylɑ̃, ɑ̃:t) *a,* truculent.

trudgeon (trydʒɔ̃) *m,* trudgen (*Swim.*).

truelle (tryɛl) *f,* trowel. ~ *à poisson,* fish slice.

truffe (tryf) *f,* truffle.

truie (trɥi) *f,* sow.

truisme (tryism) *m,* truism.

truite (trɥit) *f,* trout. ~ *saumonée* (somone), salmon t. **truité, e** (te) *a,* speckled, mottled.

trumeau (trymo) *m,* pier (*Arch.*); pierglass; leg of beef.

truquage (tryka:ʒ) *m,* fake. **truquer** (ke) *v.t,* to fake.

tu (ty) *pn,* you, thou.

tuant, e (tɥɑ̃, ɑ̃:t) *a,* killing; boring.

tuba (tyba) *m,* tuba.

tube (tyb) *m,* tube.

tubercule (tybɛrkyl) *m,* tuber; tubercle. **tuberculeux, euse** (lø, ø:z) *a,* tuberculous. ¶ *n,* consumptive. **tuberculose** (lo:z) *f,* tuberculosis.

tubéreuse (tyberø:z) *f,* tuberose.

tubulaire (tybylɛ:r) *a,* tubular.

tue-mouches (tymuʃ) *m,* flyswat[ter], flyflap. **tuer** (tɥe) *v.t,* to kill, slay; slaughter; swat (*fly*); bore. *tué à l'ennemi,* killed in action. *les tués,* the killed. *un tué, une tuée,* a fatality (*accident*). **tuerie** (tyri) *f,* slaughter, butchery, carnage. *à tue-tête,* at the top of one's voice. **tueur** (tɥœ:r) *m,* killer, slayer.

tuile (tɥil) *f,* tile. **tuilerie** (lri) *f,* tile works. **tuilier** (lje) *m,* tile maker.

tulipe (tylip) *f*, tulip. **tulipier** (pje) *m*, tulip tree.

tulle (tyl) *m*, tulle, net.

tumeur (tymœːr) *f*, tumor.

tumulte (tymylt) *m*, tumult, uproar, turmoil; riot. **tumultueux, euse†** (tyǿ, ǿːz) *a*, tumultuous, riotous.

tumulus (tymylyːs) *m*, tumulus, barrow.

tungstène (tœ̃gstɛn) *m*, tungsten.

tunique (tynik) *f*, tunic; coat (*Anat., Bot.*).

Tunis (tynis) *m*, Tunis (*capital*). **la Tunisie** (zi), Tunis (*state*). **tunisien, ne** (zjɛ̃, ɛn) *a*. & **T~**, *n*, Tunisian.

tunnel (tynɛl) *m*, tunnel.

turban (tyrbɑ̃) *m*, turban.

turbine (tyrbin) *f*, turbine.

turbot (tyrbo) *m*, turbot.

turbulence (tyrbylɑ̃ːs) *f*, turbulence. **turbulent, e** (lɑ̃, ɑ̃ːt) *a*, turbulent, unruly, restless; boisterous.

turc, turque (tyrk) *a*, Turkish. **T~**, *n*, Turk. **le turc**, Turkish (*language*). **Turcoman** (kɔmɑ̃) (*pers.*) *m*, Turkoman.

turf (tyrf) *m*, racetrack, racecourse. **le ~**, the turf.

turgescent, e (tyrʒɛsɑ̃, ɑ̃ːt) *a*, turgescent, turgid.

turlupin (tyrlypɛ̃) *m*, buffoon.

turpitude (tyrpityd) *f*, turpitude, baseness.

Turquie (tyrki) *f*, Turkey.

turquoise (tyrkwaːz) *f*. & *att*, turquoise.

tutélaire (tytelɛːr) *a*, tutelar[y], guardian; (*m.*) prop (*Hort.*). tutelage, guardianship; protection. **tuteur, trice** (tœːr, tris) *n*, guardian; (*m.*) prop (*Hort.*).

tutoyer (tytwaje) *v.t*, to address as "tu" and "toi."

tutu (tyty) *m*, ballet skirt.

tuyau (tɥijo) *m*, pipe; tube; hose; flue; stem; hint. **avoir les ~x**, to be in the know. **~ acoustique**, speaking tube. **~ d'arrosage**, garden hose. **~ d'échappement**, exhaust pipe. **tuyauter** (te) *v.t*, to flute, frill, plait; tip off.

tympan (tɛ̃pɑ̃) *m*, tympanum, ear drum; tympan. **tympanon** (panɔ̃) *m*, dulcimer.

type (tip) *m*, type (*model & Typ.*); standard; fellow, guy.

typhoïde (tifɔid) *a*, typhoid.

typhon (tifɔ̃) *m*, typhoon.

typhus (tifyːs) *m*, typhus.

typique (tipik) *a*, typical.

typographie (tipɔgrafi) *f*, typography; printing works. **typographique** (fik) *a*, typographic(al).

tyran (tirɑ̃) *m*, tyrant. **tyrannie** (rani) *f*, tyranny. **tyrannique†** (nik) *a*, tyrannic(al); high-handed. **tyranniser** (nize) *v.t*, to tyrannize [over].

Tyrol (le) (tirɔl), the Tyrol. **tyrolien, ne** (ljɛ̃, ɛn) *a*. & **T~**, *n*, Tyrolese.

tzigane (tsigan) *n*. & *a*, gipsy, zigane.

U

ubiquité (ybikɥite) *f*, ubiquity.

ulcération (ylserasjɔ̃) *f*, ulceration. **ulcère** (sɛːr) *m*, ulcer. **ulcérer** (sere) *v.t*, to ulcerate; embitter.

ultérieur, e (ylterjœːr) *a*, ulterior, later, subsequent. **ultérieurement** (œrmɑ̃) *ad*, later [on].

ultimatum (yltimatɔm) *m*, ultimatum.

ultra (yltra) *m*, ultraist, extremist. **~-violet, te**, *a*, ultraviolet.

ululer (ylyle) *v.i*, to hoot, ululate.

un (œ̃) *m*, one. **un, une** (œ̃, yn) *a*, one; a, an. **~ à ~**, one by one; one after another. **l'~**, each (*price of articles*). **l'~ l'autre**, les uns (les unes) les autres, one another, each other. **l'~ & l'autre**, both. **l'~ ou l'autre**, either. **ni l'~ ni l'autre**, neither. **une fois**, once. **une fois, deux fois [, trois fois]; adjugé!** going, going; gone! **une fois pour toutes**, once for all. **en une [seule] fois**, in a lump sum, outright (*opp.* by installments). **il y avait (ou il était) une fois**, once upon a time.

unanime† (ynanim) *a*, unanimous. **unanimité** (mite) *f*, unanimity, consensus. **à l'~**, unanimously.

uni, e (yni) *p.a*, united; even; level; smooth; plain; uniform.

unième† (ynjɛm) *a*, first (*only after* 20, 30, *etc*, e.g, *vingt* & ~, 21st; *cent* ~, 101st).

unifier (ynifje) *v.t*, to unify, consolidate; standardize. **uniforme** (fɔrm) *a*, uniform, even. ¶ *m*, uniform; regimentals. **uniformément** (memã) *ad*, uniformly, evenly. **uniformité** (mite) *f*, uniformity.

unilatéral, e (ynilateral) *a*, unilateral; one-sided.

uniment (ynimã) *ad*, smoothly, evenly; plainly; simply.

union (ynjɔ̃) *f*, union; unity. *U~ des Républiques soviétiques socialistes*, Union of Soviet Socialist Republics. *U~ Sud-Africaine*, Union of South Africa.

unique (ynik) *a*, only; sole; single; one; unique. *prix* ~, dime store. *sens* ~, one way. **uniquement** (kmã) *ad*, solely, uniquely, only.

unir (yni:r) *v.t*, to unite; join; level, smooth. **unisson** (nisɔ̃) *m*, unison. **unitaire** (tɛ:r) *a*, unitary; unit (*att*.). **unité** (te) *f*, unit; unity, one; oneness.

univers (ynivɛ:r) *m*, universe. **universalité** (versalite) *f*, universality. **universel, le†** (sɛl) *a*, universal; world[-wide]. **universitaire** (sitɛ:r) *a*, university (*att*.). **université** (te) *f*, university.

uranium (yranjɔm) *m*, uranium.

urbain, e (yrbɛ̃, ɛn) *a*, urban. **urbanisme** (banism) *m*, town planning. **urbanité** (te) *f*, urbanity.

urètre (yrɛ:tr) *m*, urethra.

urgence (yrʒã:s) *f*, urgency. *d'~*, urgently; emergency (*as a brake*). **urgent, e** (ʒã, ã:t) *a*, urgent.

urinal (yrinal) *m*, urinal (*vessel*). **urine** (rin) *f*, urine. **uriner** (ne) *v.i*, to urinate; (*v.t*.) to pass. **urinoir** (nwa:r) *m*, urinal (*place*). **urique** (rik) *a*, uric.

urne (yrn) *f*, urn. ~ *électorale*, ballot box.

urticaire (yrtikɛ:r) *f*, nettle rash.

us & coutumes (ys) *m.pl*, use & wont. **usage** (za:ʒ) *m*, use; purpose; wear; usage, custom, practice. ~ *[du monde]*, ways of society. *article d'~*, serviceable article. *faire de l'~*, to wear well. *valeur d'~*, value as a going concern. **usagé, e** (zaʒe) *a*, used, secondhand. **usager** (ʒe) *m*, user. **usé, e** (ze) *a*, worn [out]; shabby. ~ *[jusqu'à la corde]*, threadbare, hackneyed, stale. **user** (ze) *v.t*, to use; wear [out, away]; abrade. ~ *de*, to use, exercise. *s'~*, to wear [away]. *être d'un bon user*, to wear well.

usine (yzin) *f*, works; factory; mill; (*power*) station. **usiner** (ne) *v.t*, to machine, tool; exploit. **usinier** (nje) *m*, mill owner.

usité, e (yzite) *a*, used, in use. *peu usité*, rare (*word*).

ustensile (ystãsil) *m*, utensil; implement, tool.

usuel, le† (yzɥɛl) *a*, usual, customary.

usufruit (yzyfrɥi) *m*, usufruct.

usuraire† (yzyrɛ:r) *a*, usurious. **usure** (zy:r) *f*, usury; interest; wear [& tear], wearing; attrition. *guerre d'~*, war of attrition. **usurier, ère** (zyrje, ɛ:r) *n*, usurer.

usurpateur, trice (yzyrpatœ:r, tris) *n*, usurper. **usurpation** (sjɔ̃) *f*, usurpation; encroachment. **usurper** (pe) *v.t*, to usurp; (*v.i*.) to encroach.

ut (yt) *m*, C (*Mus*.).

utérin, e (yterɛ̃, in) *a*, uterine. **utérus** (ry:s) *m*, uterus.

utile† (ytil) *a*, useful, serviceable; effective; due, good (*time*). **utiliser** (lize) *v.t*, to utilize. **utilitaire** (tɛ:r) *a*. & *n*, utilitarian. **utilité** (te) *f*, utility, use[fulness]; utility [man] (*Theat*.).

utopie (ytɔpi) *f*, utopia. **utopique** (pik) *a*. & **utopiste** (pist) *a*. & *n*, utopian.

uvule (yvyl) *f*, uvula.

V

va *see* **aller**.

vacance (vakɑ:s) *f*, vacancy; (*pl*.) holiday[s]; vacation, recess; opening. **vacant, e** (kã, ã:t) *a*, vacant, unoccupied.

vacarme (vakarm) *m*, uproar, din, row.

vacation (vakasjɔ̃) *f*, attendance, sitting (*experts*); (*pl*.) fees (*lawyer's*); (*pl*.) recess (*courts*).

vaccin (vaksɛ̃) *m*, vaccine, lymph.
vaccination (sinasjɔ̃) *f*, vaccination. **vaccine** (sin) *f*, cowpox.
vacciner (ne) *v.t*, to vaccinate.
vache (vaʃ) *f*, cow; cowhide. ~
à lait, ~ *laitière*, milch cow. **vacher**, **ère** (ʃe, ɛːr) *n*, cowherd,
neatherd. **vacherie** (ʃri) *f*, cow
house; dairy [farm].

vaciller (vasile) *v.i*, to be unsteady, wobble; vacillate, waver;
flicker.

vacuité (vakɥite) *f*, vacuity,
emptiness.

va-et-vient (vaevjɛ̃) *m*, come-
&-go; to & fro; reciprocating motion; swing (*door*); ferry boat;
two-way wiring (*Elec.*).

vagabond, e (vagabɔ̃, ɔ̃ːd) *a*,
vagabond, vagrant, roving; truant. ¶ *n*, vagabond, vagrant,
tramp. **vagabondage** (bɔ̃daːʒ) *m*,
vagrancy; truancy. **vagabonder**
(de) *v.i*, to rove, wander.

vagir (vaʒiːr) *v.i*, to wail, cry (*of
baby*). **vagissement** (ʒismɑ̃) *m*,
wailing (*infant*); squeaking
(*hare*).

vague (vaːɡ) *f*, wave, billow;
surge.

vague† (vaːɡ) *a*, vague; hazy;
waste (*land*). ¶ *m*, vagueness;
void. **vaguer** (vage) *v.i*, to wander [about].

vaillamment (vajamɑ̃) *ad*, val-
iantly, gallantly. **vaillance** (jɑ̃ːs)
f, gallantry, valor. **vaillant, e**
(jɑ̃, ɑ̃ːt) *a*, valiant, gallant.
vaillantise (jɑ̃tiːz) *f*, prowess.

vain, e† (vɛ̃, ɛn) *a*, vain; useless;
conceited. **vaine pâture**, common
[land]. *en vain*, in vain, fruit-
lessly.

vaincre (vɛ̃ːkr) *v.t.ir*, to vanquish,
conquer; beat; overcome. **les
vaincus** (vɛ̃ky) *m.pl*, the van-
quished. **vainqueur** (kœːr) *m*,
conqueror, victor; winner (*sport*).

vairon (vɛrɔ̃) *m*, minnow.

vaisseau (vɛso) *m*, vessel; ship;
boat; body (*as nave of church*);
main hall. ~ *amiral*, flagship.
~*-école*, training s. ~*-hôpital*,
hospital s. ~ *rasé*, hulk. ~ *sanguin*, blood vessel. **vaisselier**
(səlje) *m*, sideboard; dresser.
vaisselle (sɛl) *f*, crockery, plates

& dishes. *faire la* ~, to do the
dishes.

val (val) *m*, vale, glen. *par monts
& par vaux*, over hill & dale.

valable† (valabl) *a*, valid; good;
available (*law*).

valence (valɑ̃ːs) *f*, valence, -cy
(*Chem.*).

Valence (valɑ̃ːs) *f*, Valencia
(*Spain*).

valet (valɛ) *m*, valet; man[serv-
ant]; groom (*stable*); stand;
knave, jack (*cards*). ~ *de chambre*, valet. ~ *de charrue*, plowman.
~ *de ferme*, farmhand. ~ *de pied*,
footman; flunkey. **valetaille**
(ltaːj) *f*, menials, flunkeydom.
faire valeter (lte) to make
(*someone*) fetch & carry.

Valette (la) (valɛt), Valetta.

valétudinaire (valetydinɛːr) *a.
& n*, valetudinarian.

valeur (valœːr) *f*, value; worth;
valor, gallantry; value [date], as
at (*Com.*); security (*Fin.*); stock;
share; investment; holding; asset; bill; paper; money. ~ *déclarée*: *fr.* —, insured for:
— *francs. avec* ~ *déclarée*, insured (*parcel*). *sans* ~ *déclarée*,
uninsured. ~*s mobilières*, stocks
& shares, transferable securities.
[*objet de*] ~, valuable [article], a.
of value. *mettre en* ~, to emphasize. **valeureux, euse**† (lœrø, øːz)
a, valorous.

valide† (valid) *a*, valid; available; ablebodied, fit for service
(*pers.*). **valider** (de) *v.t*, to vali-
date. **validité** (dite) *f*, validity.

valise (valiːz) *f*, portmanteau;
suitcase, grip.

vallée (vale) *f*, valley. **vallon** (lɔ̃)
m, dale, vale, glen.

valoir (valwaːr) *v.i. & t. ir*, to be
worth; win, gain. *cela vaut la
peine*, it is worth while. *il vaut
mieux*, it is better to. *autant vaut*,
one might as well. *à* ~ *sur*, on account of. *faire* ~, to turn to account, make the best of; develop;
enforce.

valse (vals) *f*, waltz. **valser** (se)
v.i, to waltz. **valseur, euse** (sœːr,
øːz) *n*, waltzer.

valve (valv) *f*, valve.

vampire (vɑ̃piːr) *m*, vampire.

vandale (vɑ̃dal) *m*, vandal.

vandalisme (lism) *m*, vandalism, wanton destruction.

vandoise (vãdwa:z) *f*, dace.

vanille (vani:j) *f*, vanilla.

vanité (vanite) *f*, vanity, conceit. **vaniteux, euse** (tø, ø:z) *a*, vain, conceited.

vannage (vana:ʒ) *m*, winnowing; gating. **vanne** (van) *f*, sluice gate; floodgate; gate; shutter. **vanneau** (no) *m*, lapwing, pewit. *œufs de* ~, plovers' eggs (*Cook.*). **vanner** (ne) *v.t*, to winnow, fan (*grain*). **vannerie** (nri) *f*, basket making; b. work, wicker work. **vanneur, euse** (nœ:r, ø:z) *n*, winnower. **vannier** (nje) *m*, basket maker.

vantail (vãta:j) *m*, leaf (*door, shutter*).

vantard, e (vãta:r, ard) *a*, boastful. ¶ *n*, boaster, braggart. **vantardise** (tardi:z) & **vanterie** (tri) *f*, boast[ing], brag[ging]. **vanter** (te) *v.t*, to praise, extol, cry up, vaunt. **se** ~, to boast, vaunt, brag.

va-nu-pieds (vanypje) *n*, ragamuffin.

vapeur (vapœ:r) *f*, vapor; fume; mist; steam. *à* ~, steam (*engine, boat*). ¶ *m*, steamer, steamship, steamboat. ~*-citerne*, tank steamer. ~ *de charge*, cargo boat. ~ *de ligne* [*régulière*], liner. **vaporeux, euse** (pɔrø, ø:z) *a*, vaporous, -ry; misty; hazy; filmy, gauzy. **vaporisateur** (rizatœ:r) *m*, spray[er], atomizer. **vaporiser** (ze) *v.t*, to vaporize; spray.

vaquer (vake) *v.i*, to be vacant (*employ*); not to sit (*court*). ~ *à*, to attend to.

varech (varɛk) *m*, seaweed, wrack.

varenne (varɛn) *f*, waste pasturage.

vareuse (varø:z) *f*, jumper (*sailor's*); blouse (*Mil.*); cardigan [jacket] (*woman's*).

variable (varjabl) *a*, variable, changeable, unsettled. *au* ~, at change (*barometer*). **variante** (rjã:t) *f*, variant. **variation** (rjasjɔ̃) *f*, variation, change.

varice (varis) *f*, varicose vein.

varicelle (varisɛl) *f*, chicken pox.

varier (varje) *v.t. & i*, to vary, change; variegate, diversify; dif-

fer. **variété** (rjete) *f*, variety; diversity; (*pl.*) miscellany.

variole (varjɔl) *f*, smallpox. **varioleux, euse** (lø, ø:z) *n*, smallpox case (*pers.*).

varlet (varlɛ) *m*, varlet (*Hist.*).

varlope (varlɔp) *f*, plane (*Carp.*).

Varsovie (varsɔvi) *f*, Warsaw.

vasculaire (vaskylɛ:r) *a*, vascular.

vase (vɑ:z) *f*, mud, silt, slime, ooze. ¶ *m*, vessel, vase. ~ *à filtrations chaudes*, beaker. ~ *clos*, retort. ~ *de nuit*, chamber pot.

vaseline (vazlin) *f*, vaseline.

vaseux, euse (vazø, ø:z) *a*, muddy, slimy.

vasistas (vazistɑ:s) *m*, transom; casement window.

vassal, e (vasal) *n*, vassal (*Hist.*).

vaste (vast) *a*, vast, spacious, wide.

va-tout (vatu) *m*, (*one's*) all.

vaudeville (vodvil) *m*, vaudeville.

vaudoise (vodwa:z) *f*, dace.

vau-l'eau (à) (*volo*) *ad*, downstream; to rack & ruin.

vaurien, ne (vorjɛ̃, ɛn) *n*, blackguard; rascal.

vautour (votu:r) *m*, vulture.

vautre (votr) *m*, boar hound.

vautrer (se) (votre) *v.pr*, to wallow; sprawl.

veau (vo) *m*, calf; veal; calf[skin]. ~ *d'or*, golden calf. ~ *gras*, fatted c. ~ *raciné* (rasine), tree calf.

vecteur (vɛktœ:r) *m*, vector.

vécu, e (veky) *p.a*, true to life (*novel, etc.*).

vedette (vədɛt) *f*, mounted sentry; scout (*warship*); motor boat; leader; leading counter; star (*Theat., film*). *en* ~, prominent-[ly], in the limelight; starred; displayed in bold type.

végétal, e (veʒetal) *a*, plant (*life*); vegetable. ¶ *m*, plant. **végétarien, ne** (tarjɛ̃, ɛn) *a. & n*, vegetarian. **végétarisme** (rism) *m*, vegetarianism. **végétation** (sjɔ̃) *f*, vegetation; growth. ~*s* [*adénoïdes*], adenoids. **végéter** (te) *v.i*, to vegetate.

véhémence (veemã:s) *f*, vehemence. **véhément, e**† (mã, ã:t) *a*, vehement.

véhicule (veikyl) *m*, vehicle; medium. **véhiculer** (le) *v.t*, to cart; convey.

veille (vɛːj) *f*, watch, vigil, staying up; lookout; wakeful night; eve; day before; brink; point. **veillée** (vɛje) *f*, evening; vigil; night nursing; wake. **veiller** (je) *v.i. & t*, to sit up, stay up, lie awake; watch. ~ *à*, to see that. ~ *sur*, to look after, take care of. **veilleur, euse** (jœːr, øːz) *n*, watchman; watcher; (*f.*) night-light. *mettre en veilleuse*, to douse lights, cut back production.

veinard (vɛnaːr) *a*, lucky, fortunate.

veine (vɛn) *f*, vein; tricklet (*water*); luck. **veiner** (ne) *v.t*, to vein, grain.

vêler (vɛle) *v.i*, to calve.

vélin (velɛ̃) *m*, vellum.

velléité (vɛlleite) *f*, (*irresolute*) intention.

vélo (velo) *m*, bike. **vélocipède** (lɔsipɛd) *m*, velocipede; cycle. **vélocité** (te) *f*, swiftness. **vélodrome** (droːm) *m*, cycle track.

velours (vəluːr) *m*, velvet. ~ *à* [*grosses*] *côtes*, ~ *côtelé*, corduroy. ~ *de coton*, velveteen. **velouté, e** (lute) *a*, velvet[y].

velu, e (vəly) *a*, hairy (*skin, caterpillar, leaf*).

venaison (vənɛzɔ̃) *f*, venison.

vénal, e† (venal) *a*, venal; market[able], sale (*value*). **vénalité** (lite) *f*, venality.

venant (vənɑ̃) *m*, comer.

vendable (vɑ̃dabl) *a*, salable, marketable.

vendange (vɑ̃dɑ̃ːʒ) *f*, grape gathering; vintage. **vendanger** (dɑ̃ʒe) *v.t. & abs*, to gather. **vendangeur, euse** (ʒœːr, øːz) *n*, vintager.

vendetta (vɛ̃dɛtta) *f*, vendetta, feud.

vendeur, euse (vɑ̃dœːr, øːz) *n*, seller, vendor; salesman, -woman. **venderur, eresse** (dœːr, drɛs) *n*, vendor (*law*). **vendre** (dr) *v.t*, to sell, sell at; sell for.

vendredi (vɑ̃drədi) *m*, Friday. *le ~ saint*, Good Friday.

vénéneux, euse (venenø, øːz) *a*, poisonous, venomous (*plant, food*).

vénérable (venerabl) *a*, vener-

able. **vénération** (sjɔ̃) *f*, veneration. **vénérer** (re) *v.t*, to venerate; worship (*saints, relics*).

vénerie (venri) *f*, hunting (*science*).

vénérien, ne (venerjɛ̃, ɛn) *a*, venereal.

Vénétie (la) (venesi), Venetia.

veneur (vənœːr) *m*, huntsman.

vengeance (vɑ̃ʒɑ̃ːs) *f*, vengeance; revenge. **venger** (ʒe) *v.t*, to avenge, revenge. **vengeur, eresse** (ʒœːr, ʒrɛs) *n*, avenger. ¶ *a*, avenging, vengeful.

véniel, le† (venjɛl) *a*, venial.

venimeux, euse (vənimø, øːz) *a*, venomous, poisonous (*bite, animal, & fig.*). **venin** (nɛ̃) *m*, venom, poison.

venir (vəniːr) *v.i.ir*, to come; strike (*idea*); occur, happen; hail (*de* = from); grow. *en* ~ *aux mains*, to come to blows. *je viens de . . .*, I have just . . .

Venise (vəniːz) *f*, Venice. **vénitien, ne** (venisjɛ̃, ɛn) *a. & V~, n*, Venetian.

vent (vɑ̃) *m*, wind; air; blast; draft; scent (*hunting*); inkling; windage; flatus. ~ *coulis*, draft. *en plein* ~, in the open air. *îles du V~*, Windward Islands. *îles sous le V~*, Leeward Islands.

vente (vɑ̃ːt) *f*, sale, selling. ~ *à tempérament*, ~ *par abonnement*, installment plan. ~ *aux enchères*, auction sale. ~ *de blanc*, white sale. ~ *de charité*, [charity] bazaar.

venter (vɑ̃te) *v.imp*, to be windy, blow. **venteux, euse** (tø, øːz) *a*, windy; breezy. **ventilateur** (tilatœːr) *m*, fan, ventilator. **ventilation** (sjɔ̃) *f*, ventilation, airing; apportionment, analysis. **ventiler** (le) *v.t*, to ventilate, etc.

ventouse (vɑ̃tuːz) *f*, cupping glass; air hole; sucker (*of leech*). **ventouser** (tuze) *v.t*, to cup (*Surg*).

ventral, e (vɑ̃tral) *a*, ventral. **ventre** (vɑ̃ːtr) *m*, belly, abdomen; womb; bulge; bilge (*cask*). *faire* [*le*] ~, to bulge, belly. **ventrée** (vɑ̃tre) *f*, litter (*pups, etc.*).

ventricule (vɑ̃trikyl) *m*, ventricle.

ventriloque (vɑ̃trilɔk) *n*, ven-

triloquist. **ventriloquie** (ki) *f*,
ventriloquism, -quy.

ventru, e (vãtry) *a*, paunchy.

venu, e (vəny) *n*, comer; (*f*.)
coming; appearance; inrush; occurrence; growth.

vêpres (vɛ:pr) *f.pl*, vespers, even-
song.

ver (vɛ:r) *m*, worm; grub; maggot;
moth. ~ *à soie*, silkworm. ~ *luisant*, glowworm. ~ *rongeur*, canker[worm]; remorse. ~ *solitaire*,
tapeworm.

véracité (verasite) *f*, veracity,
truthfulness.

véranda (verãda) *f*, veranda.

verbal, e† (vɛrbal) *a*, verbal.
verbaliser (lize) *v.i*, to take particulars; draw up a report. **verbe**
(vɛrb) *m*, verb; [tone of] voice.
le Verbe, the Word (*Theol*.).
verbeux, euse (bø, ø:z) *a*, verbose, prosy; wordy. **verbiage**
(bja:ʒ) *m*, verbiage. **verbosité**
(bozite) *f*, verbosity, wordiness,
prosiness.

verdal (vɛrdal) *m*, pavement
light.

verdâtre (vɛrdɑ:tr) *a*, greenish.
verdelet, te (dəlɛ, ɛt) *a*, tartish
(*wine*); hale. **verdet** (dɛ) *m*, verdigris. **verdeur** (dœ:r) *f*, greenness; unripeness; tartness.

verdict (vɛrdikt) *m*, verdict.

verdier (vɛrdje) *m*, greenfinch.
verdir (di:r) *v.t. & i*, to green.
verdoyant, e (dwajã, ã:t) *a*,
verdant. **verdoyer** (je) *v.i*, to
green. **verdure** (dy:r) *f*, verdure,
greenery; greenness; greensward;
greens.

véreux, euse (verø, ø:z) *a*,
wormy, maggoty, grubby; shady,
bogus, fishy; bad (*debt*).

verge (vɛrʒ) *f*, rod; wand, verge;
beam (*scales*); shank (*anchor*);
(vulgar) penis; (*pl*.) birch [rod].
vergé (ʒe) *a*, laid (*paper*). **verger** (ʒe) *m*, orchard. **vergeture**
(ʒəty:r) *f*, weal.

verglas (vɛrglɑ) *m*, glazed frost,
silver thaw.

vergne (vɛrɲ) *m*, alder [tree].

vergogne (sans) (vɛrgɔɲ),
shameless.

vergue (vɛrg) *f*, yard (*Naut*.).

véridique† (veridik) *a*, truthful,
veracious. **vérificateur** (fikatœ:r)

m, examiner, inspector; gauge;
calipers. ~ *comptable*, auditor.
vérification (sjɔ̃) *f*, verification,
inspection, examination, check-
ing, vouching, audit[ing]. ~ *de
testament*, probate. **vérifier** (fje)
v.t, to verify.

vérin (verɛ̃) *m*, jack (*Mach*.).

véritable† (veritabl) *a*, true;
real; veritable; regular. **vérité**
(te) *f*, truth, verity; fact.

vermeil, le (vɛrmɛ:j) *a*, ver-
million; ruby, rosy. ¶ *m*, silver
gilt.

vermicelle (vɛrmisɛl) *m*, vermicelli; v. soup.

vermillon (vɛrmijɔ̃) *m*, ver-
million.

vermine (vɛrmin) *f*, vermin.
vermoulu, e (muly) *a*, worm-
eaten. **vermoulure** (ly:r) *f*, worm-
hole; dust from wormholes.

vermouth (vɛrmut) *m*, vermouth.

vernal, e (vɛrnal) *a*, vernal,
spring (*att*.).

verne (vɛrn) *m*, alder [tree].

verni, e (vɛrni) *a*, varnished, as
vernir; patent (*leather*), patent
leather (*shoes*). ¶ *m.pl*, patent
leather shoes; dress shoes.

vernier (vɛrnje) *m*, vernier.

vernir (vɛrni:r) *v.t*, to varnish;
japan; gloss over. **vernis** (ni) *m*,
varnish; japan; glaze; veneer
(*fig*.). ~ *à l'alcool*, spirit varnish.
~ *gras*, oil varnish. **vernissage**
(nisa:ʒ) *m*, varnishing, varnishing day. **vernisser** (se) *v.t*, to
glaze (*pottery*).

Vérone (verɔn) *f*, Verona.

véronique (verɔnik) *f*, speedwell, veronica.

verrat (vɛra) *m*, boar.

verre (vɛ:r) *m*, glass. ~ *à vin*,
wineglass. ~ *de vin*, glass of
wine. ~ *soluble*, water glass.
verrerie (vɛrri) *f*, glass making;
g. works; glass[ware]. **verrier**
(rje) *m*, glass maker. **verrière**
(rjɛ:r) *f*, stained-glass window.
verroterie (rɔtri) *f*, [small] glass-
ware; [glass] beads.

verrou (vɛru) *m*, bolt. *sous les
~s*, under lock & key, locked up.
verrouiller (ruje) *v.t*, to bolt; lock
up (*prisoner*).

verrue (vɛry) *f*, wart. **verru-queux, euse** (kø, ø:z) *a*, warty.

vers (vɛ:r) *m*, verse, line (*poetry*). ~ *blancs*, blank verse. ¶ *pr*, towards; to; about.

versant (vɛrsã) *m*, side, slope (*hill*).

versatile (vɛrsatil) *a*, fickle. **versatilité** (lite) *f*, fickleness.

verse (vɛrs) *f*, laying, lodging (*corn*). à ~, fast, hard (*rain*). **versé(e) dans** (se), versed in, conversant with. **versement** (səmã) *m*, payment, paying in; p. up; remittance; installment; call; deposit (*savings bank*); pouring; spilling, etc. **verser** (se) *v.t. & i*, to pour [out]; shed, spill; tip; overturn, upset, capsize; pay; p. in, p. up; deposit; issue (*Mil.*). **verset** (sɛ) *m*, verse (*Bible*); versicle (*Lit.*). **verseuse** (sø:z) *f*, coffeepot.

versificateur (vɛrsifikatœ:r) *m*, versifier. **versifier** (fje) *v.i. & t*, to versify. **version** (sjɔ̃) *f*, version; translation. ~ *à livre ouvert*, unseen [translation].

verso (vɛrso) *m*, verso, back. *au* ~, overleaf.

vert, e (vɛ:r, ɛrt) *a*, green; verdant; unripe; unseasoned; callow; raw; sour; sharp; fresh; hale; smutty. ¶ *m*, green; grass. **vert-de-gris** (vɛrdəgri) *m*, verdigris.

vertébral, e (vɛrtebral) *a*, vertebral; spinal (*column*). **vertèbre** (tɛ:br) *f*, vertebra. **vertébré, e** (tebre) *a. & m*, vertebrate; (*m. pl.*) Vertebrata.

vertement (vɛrtəmã) *ad*, sharply, soundly.

vertical, e (vɛrtikal) *a*, vertical, upright. ¶ *f*, vertical. **verticalement** (lmã) *ad*, vertically; down (*crossword clues*).

verticille (vɛrtisil) *m*, verticil, whorl.

vertige (vɛrti:ʒ) *m*, dizziness; giddiness; vertigo. **vertigineux, euse** (tiʒinø, ø:z) *a*, dizzy, giddy. **vertigo** (go) *m*, staggers (*Vet.*).

vertu (vɛrty) *f*, virtue. *en ~ de*, in (*or* by) v. of; in pursuance of. **vertueux, euse†** (tɥø, ø:z) *a*, virtuous; righteous.

verve (vɛrv) *f*, verve.

vesce (vɛs) *f*, vetch, tare.

vésicatoire (vezikatwa:r) *m*, blister (*plaster*). **vésicule** (kyl) *f*, vesicle, bladder.

vespasienne (vɛspazjɛn) *f*, urinal (*street*).

vessie (vɛsi) *f*, bladder.

vestale (vɛstal) *f*, vestal [virgin].

veste (vɛst) *f*, jacket (*short, usually waiter's, etc.*). **vestiaire** (tjɛ:r) *m*, cloakroom.

vestibule (vɛstibyl) *m*, vestibule, [entrance] hall, lobby.

vestige (vɛsti:ʒ) *m*, footprint, track, trace; (*pl.*) vestiges, remains.

veston (vɛstɔ̃) *m*, jacket (*man's*); lounge coat. ~ *d'intérieur*, smoking jacket.

Vésuve (le) (vezy:v) Vesuvius. **vésuvien, ne** (zyvjɛ̃, ɛn) *a*, Vesuvian.

vêtement (vɛtmã) *m*, garment; vestment; (*pl.*) clothes, clothing. ~ *de dessous*, undergarment (*woman's*); (*pl.*) underclothing, underwear (*women's*).

vétéran (veterã) *m*, veteran; long-service man (*Mil.*). **vétérance** (rã:s) *f*, long service.

vétérinaire (veterinɛ:r) *a*, veterinary. [*médecin*] ~, *m*, veterinary [surgeon].

vétille (veti:j) *f*, trifle. **vétilleux, euse** (tijø, ø:z) *a*, finical, ticklish.

vêtir (veti:r) *v.t.ir*, to clothe, dress.

veto (veto) *m*, veto.

vêture (vɛty:r) *f*, taking the habit, taking the veil (*Eccl.*).

vétusté (vetyste) *f*, decay, [old] age.

veuf, veuve (vœf, vœ:v) *a*, widowed; deprived; bereft. ¶ *m*, widower. ¶ *f*, widow, relict.

veuillez *see* **vouloir.**

veule (vœ:l) *a*, slack, flabby.

veuvage (vœva:ʒ) *m*, widowerhood, widowhood.

vexatoire (vɛksatwa:r) *a*, vexatious. **vexer** (kse) *v.t*, to vex, provoke.

viabilité (vjabilite) *f*, good condition (*of roads*); viability. **viable** (bl) *a*, viable.

viaduc (vjadyk) *m*, viaduct.

viager, ère (vjaʒe, ɛ:r) *a*, life (*att.*), for life. *rente ~e*, life annuity.

viande (vjɑ̃:d) *f*, meat. ~ *de boucherie*, butcher's meat. ~ *de cheval*, horseflesh.

viatique (vjatik) *m*, provision for journey; viaticum.

vibration (vibrasjɔ̃) *f*, vibration (*Phys.*). **vibrer** (bre) *v.i*, to vibrate (*Phys. & fig.*).

vicaire (vikɛ:r) *m*, vicar; curate. **vicariat** (karja) *m*, vicariate; curacy.

vice (vis) *m*, vice; defect, fault, flaw.

vice (vis) *prefix*, vice: ~-*président, e, n*, vice- (*or* deputy) chairman *or* president. ~-*roi, m*, viceroy.

Vicence (visɑ̃:s) *f*, Vicenza.

vicier (visje) *v.t*, to vitiate, foul. **vicieux, euse†** (sjø, ø:z) *a*, vicious; defective, faulty; unsound.

vicinal, e (visinal) *a*, parish, local (*road*).

vicissitude (visisityd) *f*, vicissitude.

victime (viktim) *f*, victim; casualty; sufferer.

victoire (viktwa:r) *f*, victory; win. **victoria** (tɔrja) *f*, victoria (*carriage*). **victorieux, euse†** (rjø, ø:z) *a*, victorious; triumphant.

victuailles (viktɥɑ:j) *f.pl*, victuals.

vidange (vidɑ̃:ʒ) *f*, emptying; clearing; ullage; (*pl.*) night soil. *en* ~, ullaged (*cask*). **vidanger** (dɑ̃ʒe) *v.t*, to empty. **vidangeur** (ʒœ:r) *m*, nightman. **vide** (vid) *a*, empty, void; idle. ¶ *m*, void; vacuum; space; gap; vacancy; empty (*case*). *à* ~, [when] empty. ~-*pomme, m*, apple corer. **vider** (de) *v.t*, to empty, vacate (*les lieux* = the premises); settle (*dispute*); thresh out; bore (*cannon*); draw (*fowl*); gut (*fish*); stone (*fruit*); core (*apple, etc.*).

viduité (vidɥite) *f*, widowhood.

vie (vi) *f*, life; lifetime; living, livelihood. *la* ~ *à trois*, the eternal triangle. *à* ~, for life.

vieillard (vjɛja:r) *m*, old man. *les* ~*s*, the aged (*either sex*). **vieilleries** (jri) *f.pl*, old things. **vieillesse** (jɛs) *f*, [old] age. **vieilli, e** (ji) *a*, antiquated; obsolete; archaic; aged. **vieillir** (ji:r) *v.i*, to grow old, age, become obsolete;

(*v.t.*) to age, make [look] old[er]. **vieillissant, e** (jisɑ̃, ɑ̃:t) *a*, aging; obsolescent. **vieillot, te** (jo, ɔt) *a*, oldish, quaint. ¶ *n*, little old man, little old woman.

Vienne (vjɛn) *f*, Vienna. **viennois, e** (nwa, a:z) *a*. & **V**~, *n*, Viennese.

vierge (vjɛrʒ) *f*, virgin, maid. ¶ *a*, virgin; blank (*page*); free; unexposed (*Phot.*).

vieux, vieil, vieille (vjø, vjɛ:j) *a*, old; stale; obsolete, archaic. *vieille fille*, old maid. **vieux, vieille, n**, old man, old woman. *le vieux*, the old (*opp.* the new). *les vieux*, the old (*either sex*).

vif, vive (vif, i:v) *a*, alive; live; living; quick; lively; sprightly; brisk; smart; sharp; vital; keen; crisp, tangy; hasty; spirited; vivid; bright; spring (*water, tide*). *de vive force*, by main (*or* sheer) force. *de vive voix*, by word of mouth, viva voce. **le vif**, the quick (*flesh, etc.*); the heart (*of a matter*); life (*art*). **vif-argent**, *m*, quicksilver.

vigie (viʒi) *f*, lookout; lookout [man]; vigia.

vigilance (viʒilɑ̃:s) *f*, vigilance, watchfulness. **vigilant, e** (lɑ̃, ɑ̃:t) *a*, vigilant, watchful. **vigile** (ʒil) *f*, vigil, eve (*Eccl.*).

vigne (viɲ) *f*, vine, vineyard. ~ *vierge*, Virginia creeper. **vigneron, ne** (nərɔ̃, ɔn) *n*, winegrower. **vignette** (ɲɛt) *f*, vignette; cut; ornamental border; revenue label. **vignoble** (ɲɔbl) *m*, vineyard.

vigogne (vigɔɲ) *f*, vicugna, vicuña.

vigoureux, euse† (vigurø, ø:z) *a*, vigorous, strong, forceful; stout, sturdy, robust, lusty; plucky (*Phot.*). **vigueur** (gœ:r) *f*, vigor, strength. *mettre en* ~, to put in force, enforce.

vil, e† (vil) *a*, vile, base, mean. *à vil prix*, dirt-cheap. **vilain, e†** (lɛ̃, ɛn) *a*, ugly; wretched; nasty; scurvy; naughty. ¶ *n*, villain, villein (*Hist.*); naughty boy, girl; villain; scurvy fellow.

vilebrequin (vilbrəkɛ̃) *m*, brace, bit stock; wimble; crank shaft.

vilenie (vilni) *f*, meanness; dirty trick; abuse. **vileté** (lte) *f*, cheapness; worthlessness. **vilipender** (lipãde) *v.t*, to vilify.

villa (vila) *f*, villa. **village** (vila:3) *m*, village. **villageois, e** (la3wa, a:z) *n*, villager; (*att.*) rustic, country. **ville** (vil) *f*, town, city. ~ *d'eaux*, watering place, spa. *hôtel de* ~, town hall, city h. **villégiature** (le3jaty:r) *f*, stay in the country; holiday.

vin (vē) *m*, wine. ~ *blanc du Rhin*, hock. ~ *de Bordeaux*, claret. ~ *de liqueur*, sweet dessert wine. ~ *du cru*, wine of the country. ~ *en cercles*, wine in the wood. ~ *de marque*, vintage wine. ~ *mousseux*, sparkling wine. **vinage** (vina:3) *m*, fortification (*of wine*). **vinaigre** (nɛ:gr) *m*, vinegar. **vinaigrer** (nɛgre) *v.t*, to vinegar. **vinaigrerie** (grɛri) *f*, vinegar works.

vindas (vēda:s) *m*, crab [capstan]; giant['s] stride.

vindicatif, ive (vēdikatif, i:v) *a*, vindictive, revengeful; avenging. **vindicte** (dikt) *f*, (*public*) prosecution (*of crime*).

vinée (vine) *f*, vintage (*crop*). **viner** (ne) *v.t*, to fortify (*wine*). **vineux, euse** (nø, ø:z) *a*, vinous; winy; full-bodied (*wine*); rich in vineyards; rich in wines.

vingt (vē) *a*, twenty. ¶ *m*, twenty; 20th. ~*deux!* watch it! look out! **vingtaine** (tɛ:n) *f*, score, twenty [or so]. **vingtième** (tjɛm) *a. & n*, twentieth.

vinicole (vinikɔl) *a*, wine-growing. **vinosité** (nozite) *f*, vinosity.

viol (vjɔl) *m*, rape, ravishment. **violacé, e** (vjɔlase) *a*, violaceous. **violacées**, *f.pl*, Violaceae.

violariacée (vjɔlarjase) *f*, viola (*Bot.*); (*pl.*) Viola (*genus*).

violateur, trice (vjɔlatœ:r, tris) *a*, violator; transgressor. **violation** (sjɔ̃) *f*, violation, transgression, breach; desecration.

violâtre (vjɔlɑ:tr) *a*, purplish.

violemment (vjɔlamã) *ad*, violently. **violence** (lã:s) *f*, violence; duress; stress. **violent, e** (lã, ã:t) *a*, violent. **violenter** (lãte) *v.t*, to do violence to. **violer** (le) *v.t*, to violate, transgress, break; rape, ravish; desecrate.

violet, te (vjɔlɛ, ɛt) *a*, violet, pur-

ple. **violet**, *m*, violet (*color*). **violette**, *f*, violet (*Bot.*). ~ *de chien*, dog v. ~ *de Parme*, Parma v. ~ *odorante*, sweet v. **violier** (lje) *m*, stock. ~ *jaune*, wallflower.

violon (vjɔlɔ̃) *m*, violin, fiddle; lockup, clink. **violoncelle** (sɛl) *m*, violoncello, [']cello. **violoncelliste** (list) *n*, [violon]cellist. **violoniste** (lɔnist) *n*, violinist.

vipère (vipɛ:r) *f*, viper, adder.

virage (vira:3) *m*, turning, slewing, swinging; tacking (*Naut.*); turn, bend, corner; toning (*Phot.*).

virago (virago) *f*, amazon (*forceful woman*).

virement (virmã) *m*, turning, tacking (*Naut.*); bank transfer; transfer (*Bkkpg.*). **virer** (re) *v.i*, to turn; bank (*Avn.*); heave (*Naut.*); (*v.t.*) to transfer; tone (*Phot.*). ~ *de bord*, to tack (*Naut.*).

vireux, euse (virø, ø:z) *a*, noxious.

virginal, e† (vir3inal) *a*, virginal, maiden[ly]. **virginie** (ni) *m*, Virginia [tobacco]. **la V~**, Virginia (*Geog.*). **virginité** (te) *f*, virginity, maidenhood.

virgule (virgyl) *f*, comma. ~ [*décimale*], decimal point. *Note:* — The decimal point is indicated in French by a comma.

viril, e (viril) *a*, virile, manly. **virilité** (lite) *f*, virility, manliness; manhood.

virole (virɔl) *f*, ferrule.

virtuel, le (virtɥɛl) *a*, virtual. **virtuellement** (lmã) *ad*, virtually, to all intents & purposes.

virtuose (virtɥo:z) *n*, virtuoso. **virtuosite** (ozite) *f*, virtuosity.

virulence (virylã:s) *f*, virulence. **virulent, e** (lã, ã:t) *a*, virulent. **virus** (ry:s) *m*, virus.

vis (vis) *f*, screw. ~ *ailée*, wing s. ~ *d'Archimède* (arʃimɛd), Archimedean s. ~ *sans fin*, worm.

visa (viza) *m*, visa; initials, signature.

visage (viza:3) *m*, face, visage; aspect. *à* ~ *découvert*, barefacedly.

vis-à-vis (vizavi) & ~ *de*, *pr. & ad*, opposite, o. to; face to face;

facing; vis-à-vis; towards. ¶ *m*, person opposite; vis-à-vis.

viscères (visɛ:r) *m.pl*, viscera.

viscose (viskɔ:z) *f*, viscose. **viscosité** (kozite) *f*, viscosity, stickiness.

visée (vize) *f*, sight[ing], observation, aim; (*pl.*) aims, designs, ambition. **viser** (ze) *v.t*, to aim at; sight; cater for; visa; initial, sign; refer to; have in view; certify. ~ *à*, to aim at. **viseur** (zœ:r) *m*, [view]finder (*Phot.*); dial (*calculating mach.*). ~ *redresseur*, collapsible viewfinder. **visibilité** (zibilite) *f*, visibility. **visible†** (bl) *a*, visible; obvious; at home. *pas* ~, engaged; not accessible. **visière** (zjɛ:r) *f*, peak (*cap*); eyeshade; visor (*Hist.*). **vision** (zjɔ̃) *f*, vision, sight; seeing; fantasy; hallucination. **visionnaire** (zjɔnɛ:r) *a. & n*, visionary.

visitation (vizitasjɔ̃) *f*, visitation (*Eccl.*). **visite** (zit) *f*, visit, call; attendance; inspection, examination, survey. **visiter** (te) *v.t*, to visit. **visiteur, euse** (tœ:r, ø:z) *n*, visitor, caller; inspector, examiner.

vison (vizɔ̃) *m*, mink (*Zool. & fur*).

visqueux, euse (viskø, ø:z) *a*, viscous, sticky, tacky.

visser (vise) *v.t*, to screw [on, down, up].

Vistule (la) (vistyl) the Vistula.

visuel, le (vizɥɛl) *a*, visual, (*line, etc.*) of sight.

vital, e (vital) *a*, vital. **vitalité** (lite) *f*, vitality. **vitamine** (min) *f*, vitamin.

vite (vit) *a*, swift, quick, fast. ¶ *ad*, quick[ly], fast.

vitesse (vitɛs) *f*, speed, velocity, quickness. *première* ~, low gear.

viticole (vitikɔl) *a*, viticultural. **viticulteur** (kyltœ:r) *m*, viticultur[al]ist, winegrower. **viticulture** (ty:r) *f*, viticulture.

vitrage (vitra:ʒ) *m*, glazing; windows, glass work; glass door; curtain net, vitrage. **vitrail** (tra:j) *m*, leaded window. *vitraux peints*, stained glass. **vitre** (tr) *f*, [window] pane. **vitrer** (tre) *v.t*, to glaze (*window*). **vitrerie** (trəri) *f*, glaziery. **vitreux, euse** (trø,

ø:z) *a*, vitreous, glassy; lackluster. **vitrier** (trie) *m*, glazier. **vitrifier** (fje) *v.t*, to vitrify. **vitrine** (trin) *f*, glass case, showcase; display cabinet, china cabinet; curio cabinet; shop window.

vitriol (vitriɔl) *m*, vitriol.

vivace (vivas) *a*, long-lived; inveterate; perennial (*Bot.*). **vivacité** (site) *f*, vivacity, liveliness; heat; hastiness; petulance; vividness.

vivandier, ère (vivɑ̃dje, ɛ:r) *n*, sutler, canteen-keeper.

vivant, e (vivɑ̃, ɑ̃:t) *a*, alive; living; lifelike; live; modern (*language*); lively; vivid. ¶ *m*, living being; lifetime, life. **vivat** (vat) *i. & m*, hurrah, -ray!; cheer. **viveau** (vo) *f*, spring tide. **vivement** (vmɑ̃) *ad*, briskly; sharply; keenly; warmly. **viveur** (vœ:r) *m*, gay man, fast liver, rake. **vivier** (vje) *m*, fish pond. **vivifier** (vifje) *v.t*, to vivify, quicken; vitalize; invigorate, brace. **vivipare** (pa:r) *a*, viviparous. **vivisection** (sɛksjɔ̃) *f*, vivisection. **vivoter** (vivɔte) *v.i*, to scrape by; live from hand to mouth. **vivre** (vi:vr) *v.i. & t. ir*, to live; be alive; subsist; endure; behave. ¶ *m*, living; food; (*pl.*) provisions, victuals; rations. *le* ~ & *le couvert*, room & board.

vizir (vizi:r) *m*, vizier.

vocable (vɔkabl) *m*, vocable. **vocabulaire** (bylɛ:r) *m*, vocabulary. **vocal, e** (kal) *a*, vocal. **vocaliser** (lize) *v.t*, to vocalize. **vocatif** (katif) *m*, vocative [case]. **vocation** (sjɔ̃) *f*, vocation, calling; call (*divine*).

vociférer (vɔsifere) *v.i*, to vociferate, shout, bawl, yell.

vœu (vø) *m*, vow; wish; prayer.

vogue (vɔg) *f*, fashion, vogue; request; run. **voguer** (ge) *v.i*, to row; sail.

voici (vwasi) *pr*, here is, here are; here; this is. *me* ~! here I am.

voie (vwa) *f*, way; road; route; track; line; duct; scent; means; course; process. ~ *de départ*, aircraft runway. ~ *d'eau*, leak; waterway. ~*s de fait*, assault [& battery]; blows, violence, force. ~ *de garage*, siding. ~ *ferrée*, railway. ~ *lactée*, Milky Way, galaxy. ~ *navigable*, waterway. ~ *publique*, public thoroughfare, highway.

voilà (vwala) *pr*, there is, there are; that is.

voile (vwal) *f*, sail, canvas. ¶ *m*, veil; velum; cloth; voile; mist; fog; mask; blind. **voiler** (le) *v.t*, to veil; cloak; muffle; fog; [en]shroud; buckle. **voilerie** (lri) *f*, sail loft; s. making. **voilier** (lje) *m*, sail maker; sailing ship; (*good, bad*) sailer (*ship*). **voilure** (ly;r) *f*, sails (*col.*); buckling.

voir (vwa;r) *v.t. & abs. ir*, to see; look [at, on]; behold; sight; understand; examine; visit.

voire (vwa;r) *ad*, nay; even. ~ *même*, yea; even, indeed.

voirie (vwari) *f*, highways committee; refuse dump.

voisin, e (vwazɛ̃, in) *a*, neighboring; akin; next. ¶ *n*, neighbor. **voisinage** (zina;ʒ) *m*, neighborhood; vicinity. **voisiner** (ne) *v.i*, to visit one's neighbors.

voiture (vwaty;r) *f*, conveyance; carriage; coach; car; wagon; cart; van. *en* ~! all aboard! ~ *à deux chevaux*, carriage & pair. ~ *cellulaire*, patrol wagon. **voiturer** (tyre) *v.t*, to convey, carry, cart. **voiturette** (rɛt) *f*, trap; light car, runabout. **voiturier** (rje) *m*, carter; carrier.

voix (vwa) *f*, voice; register; speech; word; dictate[s]; opinion; say; vote. ~ *de stentor* (stɑ̃tɔ;r), stentorian voice.

vol (vɔl) *m*, flying, flight; wing; flock (*birds*). ~ *à voile*, gliding (*Avn.*). *à* ~ *d'oiseau*, as the crow flies. ~ *piqué*, dive (*Avn.*).

vol (vɔl) *m*, theft, stealing, robbery. ~ *à l'américaine*, confidence trick. ~ *à l'étalage*, shoplifting. ~ *à la tire*, pocket picking; bag snatching. ~ *à main armée*, armed robbery. ~ *de grand chemin*, highway robbery. ~ *[de nuit avec effraction]*, burglary.

volage (vɔla;ʒ) *a*, fickle, inconstant.

volaille (vɔla;j) *f*, poultry, fowls; fowl.

volant, e (vɔlɑ̃, ɑ̃;t) *a*, flying; loose; portable. ¶ *m*, shuttlecock; leaf (*opp.* counterfoil); flywheel; sail (*windmill*); flounce. [*jeu de*] ~, battledore & shuttlecock. *feuille* ~*e*, looseleaf. ~ *au filet*, badminton. ~ *de direction*, steering wheel.

volatil, e (vɔlatil) *a*, volatile. **volatile** (til) *m*, winged creature. **volatiliser** (lize) *v.t*, to volatilize. **se** ~, to volatilize; vanish.

volcan (vɔlkɑ̃) *m*, volcano. **volcanique** (kanik) *a*, volcanic.

volée (vɔle) *f*, flight; wing; flock; volley; peal (*bells*); rank (*class*); splinter bar, swingle-tree; chase (*gun*). ~ *de coups*, drubbing. *à la* ~, in the air; on the wing; promptly; broadcast; at random. **voler** (le) *v.i*, to fly; (*v.t.*) to chase, fly at (*hawking*); steal, rob. **volerie** (lri) *f*, hawking (*falconry*); thieving.

volet (vɔlɛ) *m*, shutter; volet; sorting board; flap (*Avn.*).

voleter (vɔlte) *v.i*, to flutter; flit; skip.

voleur, euse (vɔlœ;r, ø;z) *n*, thief, robber; (*att.*) thievish (*pers.*). ~ *à la tire*, pickpocket; bag snatcher. ~ *de grand chemin*, highwayman.

volière (vɔljɛ;r) *f*, aviary; run (*pheasants, etc.*).

volige (vɔli;ʒ) *f*, batten; lath.

volition (vɔlisjɔ̃) *f*, volition.

volontaire† (vɔlɔ̃tɛ;r) *a*, voluntary; wilful, wayward. ¶ *m*, volunteer (*Mil.*). **volonté** (te) *f*, will; (*pl.*) whims. **volontiers** (tje) *ad*, willingly, gladly; fain; apt, rather.

volt (vɔlt) *m*, volt. **voltage** (ta;ʒ) *m*, voltage. **voltaïque** (taik) *a*, voltaic.

volte-face (vɔltəfas) *f*, about-face; change of front.

voltige (vɔlti;ʒ) *f*, trick riding & similar circus gymnastics. **voltiger** (tiʒe) *v.i*, to fly about, flit, hover; flutter, flap; perform on horseback; perform on the slack rope.

voltmètre (vɔltmɛtr) *m*, voltmeter.

volubile (vɔlybil) *a*, twining (*Bot.*); voluble, glib (*speaker*). **volubilis** (lis) *m*, convolvulus.

volubilité (lite) *f*, volubility, glibness.

volume (vɔlym) *m*, volume; tome; bulk; measurement. **volumineux, euse** (minø, ø:z) *a*, voluminous, bulky.

volupté (vɔlypte) *f*, voluptuousness, pleasure, delight. **voluptueux, euse†** (tɥø, ø:z) *a*, voluptuous. ¶ *n*, voluptuary.

volute (vɔlyt) *f*, volute, scroll.

vomir (vomi:r) *v.t.* & *abs*, to vomit, spew, belch out. **vomissement** (mismã) *m*, vomiting; vomit. **vomitif** (mitif) *m*, emetic, vomitory.

vorace† (vɔras) *a*, voracious. **voracité** (site) *f*, voracity.

vos *see* **votre**.

votant (vɔtã) *m*, voter. **votation** (tasjɔ̃) *f*, voting. **vote** (vɔt) *m*, vote, poll. **voter** (te) *v.i.* & *t*, to vote; pass, carry. *~ à main levée*, to vote by a show of hands. **votif, ive** (tif, i:v) *a*, votive.

votre, *pl*. **vos** (vɔtr, vo) *a*, your. *~ affectionné, e*, yours affectionately. **vôtre** (vo:tr) *a*, yours. *le vôtre, la vôtre, les vôtres*, yours, your own.

vouer (vwe) *v.t*, to vow; dedicate; devote.

vouloir (vulwa:r) *m*, will. ¶ *v.t.ir*, to will; want, wish; like; [be] please[d to]; mean; intend; require, need. *en ~ à*, to bear ill will. *s'en ~ de*, to be angry with oneself for. *veuillez agréer*, please accept. **voulu, e** (ly) *p.a*, required, requisite; deliberate, intentional; studied.

vous (vu) *pn*, you; ye; to you; yourself, yourselves; each other. *~-même*, *~-mêmes*, yourself, yourselves.

voussoir (vuswa:r) *m*, voussoir, arch stone. **voûte** (vut) *f*, vault, arch; dome; canopy. *~ palatine*, *~ du palais*, roof of the mouth. **voûté, e** (te) *p.a*, vaulted; arched; stooping, bent, round-shouldered. **voûter** (te) *v.t*, to vault, arch; bow.

voyage (vwaja:ʒ) *m*, journey, voyage, trip, tour. **voyager** (jaʒe) *v.i*, to travel; journey; migrate. **voyageur, euse** (ʒœ:r) ø:z) *n*, traveler; passenger; fare.

voyant, e (vwajã, ã:t) *a*, seeing; gaudy, garish; showy; conspicuous. ¶ *n*, clairvoyant.

voyelle (vwajɛl) *f*, vowel.

voyer (vwaje) *m*, surveyor (*roads*).

voyou (vwaju) *m*, guttersnipe; hooligan.

vrac (en) (vrak), in bulk; loose.

vrai, e (vrɛ) *a*, true, truthful; real, genuine; right; downright, thorough, arrant. **vrai & vraiment** (mã) *ad*, truly, really; indeed. **vrai,** *m*, truth. **vraisemblable†** (sãblabl) *a*, probable, likely. **vraisemblance** (blã:s) *f*, probability, likelihood, verisimilitude.

vrille (vri:j) *f*, tendril; gimlet; tailspin (*Avn.*). **vriller** (vrije) *v.t*, to bore; (*v.i.*) to kink, corkscrew. **vrillette** (jɛt) *f*, deathwatch [beetle].

vrombir (vrɔ̃bi:r) *v.i*, to buzz; throb; purr; whirr; hum. **vrombissement** (bismã) *m*, buzzing, hum, etc.

vu (vy) *m*, sight, inspection. ¶ *ad*, considering, seeing. *~ que*, seeing that; whereas.

vue (vy) *f*, [eye]sight; eyes, eye; view; sight; prospect, outlook; slide; window, light. *~ cavalière*, *~ à vol d'oiseau*, bird's-eye view. *~s fondantes*, dissolving views. *à ~ d'œil*, at a rough estimate; visibly.

vulcain (vylkɛ̃) *m*, red admiral (*butterfly*).

vulcaniser (vylkanize) *v.t*, to vulcanize.

vulgaire† (vylgɛ:r) *a*, vulgar; common; low; everyday; vernacular. **le ~**, the common people, the vulgar [herd]. **vulgariser** (garize) *v.t*, to popularize; vulgarize. **vulgarité** (te) *f*, vulgarity. **la Vulgate** (gat), the Vulgate.

vulnérable (vylnerabl) *a*, vulnerable.

W

wagon (vagɔ̃) (*Rly.*) *m*, carriage, coach, car; wagon, truck. *~-lit*, sleeping car. *~ de marchandise*, freight car. *~-poste*, mail car. *~-restaurant*, restaurant car, dining car. ~-*salon*, observation car, parlor c.

warrant (warɑ̃:t) *m*, warrant (*dock, warehouse*).

watt (wat) *m*, watt.

Westphalie (**la**) (vɛstfali), Westphalia.

whisky (wiski) *m*, whiskey.

whist (wist) *m*, whist (*cards*). ~ *à trois avec un mort*, dummy w. ~ *de Gand*, solo w.

X

xérès (kerɛs) *m*, sherry.

xylophone (ksilɔfɔn) *m*, xylophone.

Y

y (i) *ad*, there; here; at home. ¶ *pn*, of it, him, etc; to it; about it; at it; by it; in it; it. *ça* ~ *est!* it's done! that's it! *il* ~ *a*, there is, there are. *jen'*~ *suis pour rien*, I had nothing to do with it. ~ *compris*, including.

yacht (jɔt) *m*, yacht. *Note.*—le yacht, *not* l'yacht.

yeux *see* **œil.**

yole (jɔl) *f*, gig, skiff, yawl. *Note:* —la yole.

yougoslave (jugɔsla:v) *a. & Y~,* *n*, Yugoslav. **la Yougoslavie** (slavi), Yugoslavia.

ypérite (iperit) *f*, mustard gas.

Z

zèbre (zɛbr) *m*, zebra. **zébré, e** (zebre) *a*, striped.

zélateur, trice (zelatœ:r, tris) *n*, zealot. **zèle** (zɛ:l) *m*, zeal. **zélé, e** (zele) *a*, zealous.

zénith (zenit) *m*, zenith.

zéphyr (zefi:r) *m*, zephyr.

zeppelin (zɛplɛ̃) *m*, zeppelin.

zéro (zero) *m*, cipher, nought, 0; love (*Ten.*); zero (See *centigrade* Fr.-Eng.); nobody. ~ *partout*, love-all (*Ten.*).

zeste (zɛst) *m*, woody partitions (*walnut*); peel (*orange, lemon*); straw (*fig.*). ~ *confit*, candied peel.

zézayer (zezɛje) *v.i*, to lisp.

zibeline (ziblin) *f*, sable (*Zool.*, *fur*).

zigzag (zigzag) *m*, zigzag.

zinc (zɛ̃:g) *m*, zinc, spelter; bar, counter. **zincogravure** (zɛ̃kɔgravy:r) *f*, zincography. **zingueur** (gœ:r) *m*, zinc worker.

zircon (zirkɔ̃) *m*, zircon.

zizanie (zizani) *f*, discord.

zodiaque (zɔdjak) *m*, zodiac.

zone (zo:n) *f*, zone; belt; area. ~ *des calmes*, doldrums.

zoologie (zɔɔlɔʒi) *f*, zoology. **zoologique** (ʒik) *a*, zoological. **zoologiste** (ʒist) *n*, zoologist.

zoulou (zulu) *a. & Z~,* *n*, Zulu.

zut (zyt) *i*, darn it! go to the devil!

Zuyderzée (**le**) (zyidɛrze), the Zuyder Zee.

Order of tenses & parts:

(1) = Indicative Present
(2) =   "   Imperfect
(3) =   "   Preterit
(4) =   "   Future
(5) = Conditional Present
(6) = Imperative
(7) = Subjunctive Present
(8) =   "   Imperfect
(9) = Participle Present
(10) =   "   Past

Prefixed verbs not included in the list, such as **abattre, sourire, désapprendre, satisfaire,** follow the second or last element (**battre, rire, prendre, faire**).

absoudre.—(1) j'absous, tu absous, il absout, nous absolvons, vous absolvez, ils absolvent. (2) j'absolvais. (4) j'absoudrai. (5) j'absoudrais. (6) absous, absolvons, absolvez. (7) que j'absolve. (9) absolvant. (10) absous, oute.

abstraire.—*like* **traire,** *but only in* (1) (2) *and compound tenses.*

accroître.—*like* **croître,** *but* (10) accru, *no circumflex accent.*

acquérir.—(1) j'acquiers, tu acquiers, il acquiert, nous acquérons, vous acquérez, ils acquièrent. (2) j'acquérais. (3) j'acquis. (4) j'acquerrai. (5) j'acquerrais. (6) acquiers, acquérons, acquérez. (7) que j'acquière. (8) que j'acquisse. (9) acquérant. (10) acquis, e.

aller.—(1) je vais, tu vas, il va, nous allons, vous allez, ils vont. (2) j'allais. (3) j'allai. (4) j'irai. (5) j'irais. (6) va (*but* vas-y), allons, allez. (7) que j'aille. (8) que j'allasse. (9) allant. (10) allé, e.

s'en aller.—*like* **aller.** *The auxiliary* être *is used in the compound tenses and is placed between* en *and* allé; *thus,* je m'en suis allé. (6) va-t-en, allons-nous-en, allez-vous-en.

apparaître.—*like* **connaître.**

assaillir.—(1) j'assaille, tu assailles, il assaille, nous assaillons, vous assaillez, ils assaillent. (2) j'assaillais. (3) j'assaillis. (4) j'assaillirai. (5) j'assaillirais. (6) assaille, assaillons, assaillez. (7) que j'assaille. (8) que j'assaillisse. (9) assaillant. (10) assailli, e.

asseoir.—(1) j'assieds, tu assieds, il assied, nous asseyons, vous asseyez, ils asseyent. (2) j'asseyais. (3) j'assis. (4) j'assiérai *ou* j'asseyerai. (5) j'assiérais *ou* j'asseyerais. (6) assieds, asseyons, asseyez. (7) que j'asseye. (8) que j'assisse. (9) asseyant. (10) assis, e. *This verb is sometimes conjugated in maintaining throughout the* oi *of the radical; thus,* (1) j'assois, nous assoyons. (2) j'assoyais, etc.

astreindre.—*like* **atteindre.**

atteindre.—(1) j'atteins, tu atteins, il atteint, nous atteignons, vous atteignez, ils atteignent. (2) j'atteignais. (3) j'atteignis. (4) j'atteindrai. (5) j'atteindrais. (6) atteins, atteignons, atteignez. (7) que j'atteigne. (8) que j'atteignisse. (9) atteignant. (10) atteint, e.

avoir.—(1) j'ai, tu as, il a, nous avons, vous avez, ils ont. (2) j'avais. (3) j'eus. (4) j'aurai. (5) j'aurais. (6) aie, ayons, ayez. (7) que j'aie. (8) que j'eusse. (9) ayant. (10) eu, e.

battre.—(1) je bats, tu bats, il bat, nous battons, vous battez, ils battent. (2) je battais. (3) je battis. (4) je battrai. (5) je battrais. (6) bats, battons, battez. (7) que je batte. (8) que je battisse. (9) battant. (10) battu, e.

boire.—(1) je bois, tu bois, il boit, nous buvons, vous buvez, ils boivent. (2) je buvais. (3) je bus. (4) je boirai. (5) je boirais. (6) bois, buvons, buvez. (7) que je boive. (8) que je busse. (9) buvant. (10) bu, e.

bouillir.—(1) je bous, tu bous, il bout, nous bouillons, vous bouillez, ils bouillent. (2) je bouillais. (3) je bouillis. (4) je bouillirai. (5) je bouillirais. (6)

bous, bouillons, bouillez. (7) que je bouille. (8) que je bouillisse. (9) bouillant. (10) bouilli, e.

braire.—*like* **traire** *but seldom used except in infinitive & in 3rd persons of* (1) (4) & (5).

bruire.—*Seldom used except in infinitive and in 3rd person s. of* (1) il bruit, *and in 3rd persons of* (2) il bruissait, ils bruissaient.

ceindre.—*like* **atteindre.**

choir.—(10) chu, e. *Others not used.*

circoncire.—*like* **confire,** *but* (10) circoncis, e.

circonscrire.—*like* **écrire.**

clore.—(1) je clos, tu clos, il clôt. (4) je clorai, etc. (6) clos. (7) que je close, etc. (10) clos e. *Other forms not, or very seldom, used.*

comparaître.—*like* **connaître,** *but* (10) comparu (*inv.*).

conclure.—(1) je conclus, tu conclus, il conclut, nous concluons, vous concluez, ils concluent. (2) je concluais. (3) je conclus. (4) je conclurai. (5) je conclurais. (6) conclus, concluons, concluez. (7) que je conclue. (8) que je conclusse. (9) concluant. (10) conclu, e.

conduire.—(1) je conduis, tu conduis, il conduit, nous conduisons, vous conduisez, ils conduisent. (2) je conduisais. (3) je conduisis. (4) je conduirai. (5) je conduirais. (6) conduis, conduisons, conduisez. (7) que je conduise. (8) que je conduisisse. (9) conduisant. (10) conduit, e.

confire.—(1) je confis, tu confis, il confit, nous confisons, vous confisez, ils confisent. (2) je confisais. (3) je confis. (4) je confirai. (5) je confirais. (6) confis, confisons, confisez. (7) que je confise. (8) que je confisse. (9) confisant. (10) confit, e.

connaître.—(1) je connais, tu connais, il connaît, nous connaissons, vous connaissez, ils connaissent. (2) je connaissais. (3) je connus. (4) je connaîtrai. (5) je connaîtrais. (6) connais, connaissons, connaissez. (7) que je connaisse. (8) que je con-

nusse. (9) connaissant. (10) connu, e.

conquérir.—*like* **acquérir.**

construire.—*like* **conduire.**

contraindre.—*like* **craindre.**

contredire.—*like* **dire,** *except* (1) vous contredisez. (6) contredisez.

coudre.—(1) je couds, tu couds, il coud, nous cousons, vous cousez, ils cousent. (2) je cousais. (3) je cousis. (4) je coudrai. (5) je coudrais. (6) couds, cousons, cousez. (7) que je couse. (8) que je cousisse. (9) cousant. (10) cousu, e.

courir.—(1) je cours, tu cours, il court, nous courons, vous courez, ils courent. (2) je courais. (3) je courus. (4) je courrai. (5) je courrais. (6) cours, courons, courez. (7) que je coure. (8) que je courusse. (9) courant. (10) couru, e.

couvrir.—*like* **ouvrir.**

craindre.—(1) je crains, tu crains, il craint, nous craignons, vous craignez, ils craignent. (2) je craignais. (3) je craignis. (4) je craindrai. (5) je craindrais. (6) crains, craignons, craignez. (7) que je craigne. (8) que je craignisse. (9) craignant. (10) craint, e.

croire.—(1) je crois, tu crois, il croit, nous croyons, vous croyez, ils croient. (2) je croyais. (3) je crus. (4) je croirai. (5) je croirais. (6) crois, croyons, croyez. (7) que je croie. (8) que je crusse. (9) croyant. (10) cru, e.

croître.—(1) je croîs, tu croîs, il croît, nous croissons, vous croissez, ils croissent. (2) je croissais. (3) je crûs. (4) je croîtrai. (5) je croîtrais. (6) croîs, croissons, croissez. (7) que je croisse. (8) que je crûsse. (9) croissant. (10) crû, crue (*pl.* crus, crues).

cueillir.—(1) je cueille, tu cueilles, il cueille, nous cueillons, vous cueillez, ils cueillent. (2) je cueillais. (3) je cueillis. (4) je cueillerai. (5) je cueillerais. (6) cueille, cueillons, cueillez. (7) que je cueille. (8) que je cueillisse. (9) cueillant. (10) cueilli, e.

cuire.—*like* **conduire.**

déchoir.—(1) je déchois, tu déchois, il déchoit. (3) je déchus. (4) je décherrai. (7) que je déchoie. (8) que je déchusse. (10) déchu, e.

déconfire.—(10) déconfit, e.

découvrir.—*like* **ouvrir.**

décrire.—*like* **écrire.**

décroître.—*like* **croître,** *except* (10) décru, e.

dédire.—*like* **dire,** *except* (1) vous dédisez. (6) dédisez.

déduire.—*like* **conduire.**

défaillir.—(1) nous défaillons, vous défaillez, ils défaillent. (2) je défaillais, etc. (3) je défaillis, etc. (9) défaillant. *Other forms seldom used.*

démentir.—*like* **sentir.**

dépeindre.—*like* **atteindre.**

dépourvoir.—(10) dépourvu, e.

déteindre.—*like* **atteindre.**

détruire.—*like* **conduire.**

devoir.—(1) je dois, tu dois, il doit, nous devons, vous devez, ils doivent. (2) je devais. (3) je dus. (4) je devrai. (5) je devrais. (6) dois, devons, devez. (7) que je doive. (8) que je dusse. (9) devant. (10) dû, due (*pl.* dus, dues).

dire.—(1) je dis, tu dis, il dit, nous disons, vous dites, ils disent. (2) je disais. (3) je dis. (4) je dirai. (5) je dirais. (6) dis, disons, dites. (7) que je dise. (8) que je disse. (9) disant. (10) dit, e.

disparaître.—*like* **connaître.**

dissoudre.—*like* **absoudre.**

dormir.—(1) je dors, tu dors, il dort, nous dormons, vous dormez, ils dorment. (2) je dormais. (3) je dormis. (4) je dormirai. (5) je dormirais. (6) dors, dormons, dormez. (7) que je dorme. (8) que je dormisse. (9) dormant. (10) dormi (*inv.*).

échoir.—(1) il échoit *ou* il échet. (4) il écherra. (9) échéant. (10) échu, e. *Other forms hardly ever used.*

éclore.—(1) il éclôt, ils éclosent. (4) il éclora. (5) il éclorait. (7) qu'il éclose. (10) éclos, e.

écrire.—(1) j'écris, tu écris, il écrit, nous écrivons, vous écrivez, ils écrivent. (2) j'écrivais. (3) j'écrivis. (4) j'écrirai. (5) j'écrirais. (6) écris, écrivons, écrivez. (7) que j'écrive. (8) que j'écrivisse. (9) écrivant. (10) écrit, e.

élire.—*like* **lire.**

embatre.—*like* **battre,** *but with one* t *only.*

empreindre.—*like* **atteindre.**

enceindre.—*like* **atteindre.**

enduire.—*like* **conduire.**

enfreindre.—*like* **atteindre.**

enquérir.—*like* **acquérir.**

épreindre.—*like* **atteindre.**

éteindre.—*like* **atteindre.**

être.—(1) je suis, tu es, il est, nous sommes, vous êtes, ils sont. (2) j'étais. (3) je fus. (4) je serai. (5) je serais. (6) sois, soyons, soyez. (7) que je sois. (8) que je fusse. (9) étant. (10) été (*inv.*).

étreindre.—*like* **atteindre.**

exclure.—*like* **conclure.**

faillir.—(1) il faut (*in* s'en faut). (3) je faillis, etc. (10) failli, e. *Seldom used in other forms.*

faire.—(1) je fais, tu fais, il fait, nous faisons, vous faites, ils font. (2) je faisais. (3) je fis. (4) je ferai. (5) je ferais. (6) fais, faisons, faites. (7) que je fasse. (8) que je fisse. (9) faisant. (10) fait, e.

falloir.—(1) il faut. (2) il fallait. (3) il fallut. (4) il faudra. (5) il faudrait. (7) qu'il faille. (8) qu'il fallût. (10) fallu (*inv.*).

feindre.—*like* **atteindre.**

forclore.—(10) forclos, e.

frire.—(1) je fris, tu fris, il frit, nous faisons frire, vous faites frire, ils font frire. (2) je faisais frire. (4) je frirai. (5) je frirais. (6) fris. (10) frit, e.

fuir.—(1) je fuis, tu fuis, il fuit, nous fuyons, vous fuyez, ils fuient. (2) je fuyais. (3) je fuis. (4) je fuirai. (5) je fuirais. (6) fuis, fuyons, fuyez. (7) que je fuie. (8) que je fuisse. (9) fuyant. (10) fui, e.

geindre.—*like* **atteindre.**

gésir.—(1) je gis, tu gis, il gît, nous gisons, vous gisez, ils gisent. (2) je gisais, etc. (9) gisant. *Other forms not used.*

inclure.—*like* **conclure.**

induire.—*like* **conduire.**

inscrire.—*like* **écrire.**

instruire.—*like* **conduire.**

interdire.—*like* **dire**, *except* (1) vous interdisez. (6) interdisez.

introduire.—*like* **conduire.**

joindre.—(1) je joins, tu joins, il joint, nous joignons, vous joignez, ils joignent. (2) je joignais. (3) je joignis. (4) je joindrai. (5) je joindrais. (6) joins, joignons, joignez. (7) que je joigne. (8) que je joignisse. (9) joignant. (10) joint, e.

lire.—(1) je lis, tu lis, il lit, nous lisons, vous lisez, ils lisent. (2) je lisais. (3) je lus. (4) je lirai. (5) je lirais. (6) lis, lisons, lisez. (7) que je lise. (8) que je lusse. (9) lisant. (10) lu, e.

luire.—*like* **conduire**, *except* (10) lui (*inv.*) & *no* (3) *or* (8).

maudire.—(1) je maudis, tu maudis, il maudit, nous maudissons, vous maudissez, ils maudissent. (2) je maudissais. (3) je maudis. (4) je maudirai. (5) je maudirais. (6) maudis, maudissons, maudissez. (7) que je maudisse. (8) que je maudisse. (9) maudissant. (10) maudit, e.

méconnaître.—*like* **paraître.**

médire.—*like* **dire**, *except* (1) vous médisez. (6) médisez.

mentir.—*like* **sentir.**

messeoir.—*like* **seoir**, *in sense to* suit.

mettre.—(1) je mets, tu mets, il met, nous mettons, vous mettez, ils mettent. (2) je mettais. (3) je mis. (4) je mettrai. (5) je mettrais. (6) mets, mettons, mettez. (7) que je mette. (8) que je misse. (9) mettant. (10) mis, e.

moudre.—(1) je mouds, tu mouds, il moud, nous moulons, vous moulez, ils moulent. (2) je moulais. (3) je moulus. (4) je moudrai. (5) je moudrais. (6) mouds, moulons, moulez. (7) que je moule. (8) que je moulusse. (9) moulant. (10) moulu, e.

mourir.—(1) je meurs, tu meurs, il meurt, nous mourons, vous mourez, ils meurent. (2) je mourais. (3) je mourus. (4) je mourrai. (5) je mourrais. (6) meurs, mourons, mourez. (7) que je meure. (8) que je mourusse. (9) mourant. (10) mort, e.

mouvoir.—(1) je meus, tu meus, il meut, nous mouvons, vous mouvez, ils meuvent. (2) je mouvais. (3) je mus. (4) je mouvrai. (5) je mouvrais. (6) meus, mouvons, mouvez. (7) que je meuve. (8) que je musse. (9) mouvant. (10) mû, mue (*pl.* mus, mues).

naître.—(1) je nais, tu nais, il naît, nous naissons, vous naissez, ils naissent. (2) je naissais. (3) je naquis. (4) je naîtrai. (5) je naîtrais. (6) nais, naissons, naissez. (7) que je naisse. (8) que je naquisse. (9) naissant. (10) né, e.

nuire.—*like* **conduire**, *except* (10) nui (*inv.*).

offrir.—*like* **ouvrir.**

oindre.—*like* **joindre.**

ouïr.—(10) ouï, ïe.

ouvrir.—(1) j'ouvre, tu ouvres, il ouvre, nous ouvrons, vous ouvrez, ils ouvrent. (2) j'ouvrais. (3) j'ouvris. (4) j'ouvrirai. (5) j'ouvrirais. (6) ouvre, ouvrons, ouvrez. (7) que j'ouvre. (8) que j'ouvrisse. (9) ouvrant. (10) ouvert, e.

paître.—(1) je pais, tu pais, il paît, nous paissons, vous paissez, ils paissent. (2) je paissais. (4) je paîtrai. (5) je paîtrais. (6) pais, paissons, paissez. (7) que je paisse. (9) paissant.

paraître.—*like* **connaître**, *but* (10) paru (*inv.*).

partir.—(1) je pars, tu pars, il part, nous partons, vous partez, ils partent. (2) je partais. (3) je partis. (4) je partirai. (5) je partirais. (6) pars, partons, partez. (7) que je parte. (8) que je partisse. (9) partant. (10) parti, e.

peindre.—*like* **atteindre.**

plaindre.—*like* **craindre.**

plaire.—(1) je plais, tu plais, il plaît, nous plaisons, vous plaisez, ils plaisent. (2) je plaisais. (3) je plus. (4) je plairai. (5) je plairais. (6) plais, plaisons, plaisez. (7) que je plaise. (8)

que je plusse. (9) plaisant. (10) plu (*inv.*).

pleuvoir.—(1) il pleut. (2) il pleuvait. (3) il plut. (4) il pleuvra. (5) il pleuvrait. (7) qu'il pleuve. (8) qu'il plût. (9) pleuvant. (10) plu (*inv.*).

poindre.—*like* **joindre**, *but seldom used except in infinitive &* (4).

pourvoir.—(1) je pourvois, tu pourvois, il pourvoit, nous pourvoyons, vous pourvoyez, ils pourvoient. (2) je pourvoyais. (3) je pourvus. (4) je pourvoirai. (5) je pourvoirais. (6) pourvois, pourvoyons, pourvoyez. (7) que je pourvoie. (8) que je pourvusse. (9) pourvoyant. (10) pourvu, e.

pouvoir.—(1) je peux *ou* je puis, tu peux, il peut, nous pouvons, vous pouvez, ils peuvent. (2) je pouvais. (3) je pus. (4) je pourrai. (5) je pourrais. (7) que je puisse. (8) que je pusse. (9) pouvant. (10) pu (*inv.*).

prédire.—*like* **dire**, *except* (1) vous prédisez. (6) prédisez.

prendre.—(1) je prends, tu prends, il prend, nous prenons, vous prenez, ils prennent. (2) je prenais. (3) je pris. (4) je prendrai. (5) je prendrais. (6) prends, prenons, prenez. (7) que je prenne. (8) que je prisse. (9) prenant. (10) pris, e.

prescrire.—*like* **écrire**.

prévaloir.—*like* **valoir**, *but* (7) que je prévale.

prévoir.—*like* **voir**, *except* (4) je prévoirai. (5) je prévoirais.

produire.—*like* **conduire**.

promouvoir.—*like* **mouvoir**, *but seldom used except in infinitive* & (10) promu, e (*no circumflex accent*).

proscrire.—*like* **écrire**.

raire.—*like* **traire**, *but the only forms in common use are* (1) il rait, ils raient.

reclure.—(10) reclus, e.

reconquérir.—*like* **acquérir**.

reconstruire.—*like* **conduire**.

recouvrir.—*like* **ouvrir**.

récrire.—*like* **écrire**.

recuire.—*like* **conduire**.

réduire.—*like* **conduire**.

réélire.—*like* **lire**.

reluire.—*like* **luire**.

renaître.—*like* **naître**, *but no* (10) *or compound tenses.*

reparaître.—*like* **paraître**.

repentir (se).—*like* **sentir**.

reproduire.—*like* **conduire**.

requérir.—*like* **acquérir**.

résoudre.—(1) je résous, tu résous, il résout, nous résolvons, vous résolvez, ils résolvent. (2) je résolvais. (3) je résolus. (4) je résoudrai. (5) je résoudrais. (6) résous, résolvons, résolvez. (7) que je résolve. (8) que je résolusse. (9) résolvant. (10) résolu, e.

restreindre.—*like* **atteindre**.

rire.—(1) je ris, tu ris, il rit, nous rions, vous riez, ils rient. (2) je riais. (3) je ris. (4) je rirai. (5) je rirais. (6) ris, rions, riez. (7) que je rie. (8) que je risse. (9) riant. (10) ri (*inv.*).

rouvrir.—*like* **ouvrir**.

saillir.—*like* **assaillir**.

savoir.—(1) je sais, tu sais, il sait, nous savons, vous savez, ils savent. (2) je savais. (3) je sus. (4) je saurai. (5) je saurais. (6) sache, sachons, sachez. (7) que je sache. (8) que je susse. (9) sachant. (10) su, e.

séduire.—*like* **conduire**.

sentir.—(1) je sens, tu sens, il sent, nous sentons, vous sentez, ils sentent. (2) je sentais. (3) je sentis. (4) je sentirai. (5) je sentirais. (6) sens, sentons, sentez. (7) que je sente. (8) que je sentisse. (9) sentant. (10) senti, e.

seoir.—*In sense to sit,* (9) séant. (10) sis, e. *In sense to suit,* (1) il sied, ils siéent. (2) il seyait, ils seyaient. (4) il siéra, ils siéront. (7) qu'il siée, qu'ils siéent. (9) séant *ou* seyant. *No other forms.*

servir.—(1) je sers, tu sers, il sert, nous servons, vous servez, ils servent. (2) je servais. (3) je servis. (4) je servirai. (5) je servirais. (6) sers, servons, servez. (7) que je serve. (8) que je servisse. (9) servant. (10) servi, e.

sortir.—(1) je sors, tu sors, il sort, nous sortons, vous sortez, ils sortent. (2) je sortais. (3) je sortis. (4) je sortirai. (5) je sortirais. (6) sors, sortons, sortez. (7) que je sorte. (8) que je sortisse. (9) sortant. (10) sorti, e.

souffrir.—*like* **ouvrir.**

souscrire.—*like* **écrire.**

suffire.—*like* **confire.**

suivre.—(1) je suis, tu suis, il suit, nous suivons, vous suivez, ils suivent. (2) je suivais. (3) je suivis. (4) je suivrai. (5) je suivrais. (6) suis, suivons, suivez. (7) que je suive. (8) que je suivisse. (9) suivant. (10) suivi, e.

surseoir.—(1) je sursois, tu sursois, il sursoit, nous sursoyons, vous sursoyez, ils sursoient. (2) je sursoyais. (3) je sursis. (4) je surseoirai. (5) je surseoirais. (6) sursois, sursoyons, sursoyez. (7) que je sursoie. (8) que je sursisse. (9) sursoyant. (10) sursis, e.

taire.—*like* **plaire,** *except* (1) il tait (*no circumflex*) & (10) tu, e.

teindre.—*like* **atteindre.**

tenir.—(1) je tiens, tu tiens, il tient, nous tenons, vous tenez, ils tiennent. (2) je tenais. (3) je tins. (4) je tiendrai. (5) je tiendrais. (6) tiens, tenons, tenez. (7) que je tienne. (8) que je tinsse. (9) tenant. (10) tenu, e.

tistre.—*Used only in* (10) tissu, e, *and compound tenses.*

traduire.—*like* **conduire.**

traire.—(1) je trais, tu trais, il trait, nous trayons, vous trayez, ils traient. (2) je trayais. (4) je trairai. (5) je trairais. (6) trais, trayons, trayez. (7) que je traie. (9) trayant. (10) trait, e.

transcrire.—*like* **écrire.**

tressaillir.—*like* **assaillir.**

vaincre.—(1) je vaincs, tu vaincs, il vainc, nous vainquons, vous vainquez, ils vainquent. (2) je vainquais. (3) je vainquis. (4)

je vaincrai. (5) je vaincrais. (6) vaincs, vainquons, vainquez. (7) que je vainque. (8) que je vainquisse. (9) vainquant. (10) vaincu, e.

valoir.—(1) je vaux, tu vaux, il vaut, nous valons, vous valez, ils valent. (2) je valais. (3) je valus. (4) je vaudrai. (5) je vaudrais. (6) vaux, valons, valez. (7) que je vaille. (8) que je valusse. (9) valant. (10) valu, e.

venir.—(1) je viens, tu viens, il vient, nous venons, vous venez, ils viennent. (2) je venais. (3) je vins. (4) je viendrai. (5) je viendrais. (6) viens, venons, venez. (7) que je vienne. (8) que je vinsse. (9) venant. (10) venu, e.

vêtir.—(1) je vêts, tu vêts, il vêt, nous vêtons, vous vêtez, ils vêtent. (2) je vêtais. (3) je vêtis. (4) je vêtirai. (5) je vêtirais. (6) vêts, vêtons, vêtez. (7) que je vête. (8) que je vêtisse. (9) vêtant. (10) vêtu, e.

vivre.—(1) je vis, tu vis, il vit, nous vivons, vous vivez, ils vivent. (2) je vivais. (3) je vécus. (4) je vivrai. (5) je vivrais. (6) vis, vivons, vivez. (7) que je vive. (8) que je vécusse. (9) vivant. (10) vécu (*inv.*).

voir.—(1) je vois, tu vois, il voit, nous voyons, vous voyez, ils voient. (2) je voyais. (3) je vis. (4) je verrai. (5) je verrais. (6) vois, voyons, voyez. (7) que je voie. (8) que je visse. (9) voyant. (10) vu, e.

vouloir.—(1) je veux, tu veux, il veut, nous voulons, vous voulez, ils veulent. (2) je voulais. (3) je voulus. (4) je voudrai. (5) je voudrais. (6) veuille & veux, veuillons & voulons, veuillez & voulez. (7) que je veuille. (8) que je voulusse. (9) voulant. (10) voulu, e.

DIVISION OF FRENCH WORDS INTO SYLLABLES

In French, words are divided into syllables according to the following rules.

(1) *A consonant between two vowels begins a new syllable:*
ca-pi-tal, ca-pi-ta-li-ser, ca-pi-ta-lis-me, ca-pi-ta-lis-te, li-bé-ra-toi-re, dé-sa-bon-ne-ment, a-rith-mé-ti-que, pri-vi-lè-ge, su-bor-don-né, é-ti-que-ta-ge, e-xa-men, e-xer-ci-ce, i-ne-xac-te-ment, to-xi-que, i-nu-ti-le, u-ne, u-na-ni-me-ment, vi-gueur, vi-gou-reux, vi-gou-reu-se, paie-ment, em-pla-ce-ment, vé-hi-cu-le, pa-ral-lé-li-pi-pè-de. *Note:*—In order not to misrepresent the pronunciation of certain prefixes, there are a few exceptions to this rule, and collaterally to rule 3 also; such as sur-é-le-ver, sur-en-ché-rir, and the like; in-ter-o-cé-a-ni-que, in-ter-ur-bain, and the like.

(2) *Two adjoining consonants (except Rule 4 digraphs) between two vowels separate into two syllables:*
ac-com-mo-der, at-ter-ris-sage, bail-le-res-se, chan-geant, chan-gean-te, cor-res-pon-dan-ce, des-cen-dre, di-a-phrag-me, ac-cep-ti-on-nel-le-ment, ex-pé-di-ti-on-nai-re, in-nom-ma-ble, em-bar-ras-sant, in-ter-val-le, ir-res-pon-sa-bi-li-té, os-cil-ler, fais-ceau, ras-seoir, re-con-nais-san-ce, res-ti-tu-er, sub-di-vi-ser, sur-taux, veil-le, el-les, mal-heur, in-hé-rent, ex-hi-ber, mo-les-ki-ne.

(3) *A vowel can only begin a syllable, other than an initial syllable, when preceded by another vowel:*
ac-cue-il-lir, a-é-ro-pla-ne, po-è-me, a-gré-er, an-ci-en, ar-ri-è-re, bé-né-fi-ci-ai-re, ca-mi-on, ca-out-chouc, co-as-so-ci-é, co-ef-fi-ci-ent, coïn-ci-der, dé-pou-il-le-ment, ex-tra-or-di-nai-re, feu-il-le, li-er, mi-eux, na-ti-on, ou-est, ré-u-ni-on, vic-tu-

ail-les, vi-e-il-lir, ré-é-li-re, voi-li-er, pay-a-ble, ba-lay-u-res, en-voy-er, voy-a-ge, roy-au-me, en-nuy-eux.

(4) *The following digraph consonants are inseparable:*
bl, cl, fl, gl, pl: a-bla-taf, pu-bli-que, (*Exception:* sub-lu-nai-re); é-clec-tis-me, ex-clu-sif; ré-fle-xe, ré-fle-xi-on; é-glan-ti-ne, rè-gle-ment; é-plu-cher.

br, cr, dr, fr, gr, pr, tr, vr: a-bri-cot, su-bré-car-gue, (*Exception:* sub-ro-ger & derivatives); é-cri-tu-re, ma-nus-crit, pres-cri-re, sous-cri-re, des-crip-ti-ve; a-dres-ser; re-frain; a-gri-co-le; a-près; a-tro-ce; a-vril, ou-vri-er.

ch, dh, ph, rh: é-choir, re-cher-che; ré-dhi-bi-toi-re; té-lé-pho-ne, pho-no-gra-phe; en-rhu-mer, ar-rhes.

gn: en-sei-gne-ment, si-gnal, es-pa-gnol, i-gna-re (*but* mag-nat, mag-no-li-a, di-ag-nos-ti-que, ig-né, *because here* gn *is not palatalized; in other words, the* g *is hard*).

ng: ving-ti-è-me (*but* sin-gu-li-er, *because here* ng *is not digraph, i.e., expressing one sound*).

pt: lé-pi-do-pte-res.

(5) (*a*) ns, bs, *and* rs *are separable if followed by a vowel:*
con-sa-crer, con-seil-ler, con-si-dé-rer, in-sé-rer, in-sol-va-ble, in-suf-fi-sant, tran-sac-ti-on, tran-sat-lan-ti-que, tran-si-tif; ab-sor-ber, ob-ser-ver; per-su-a-der.

(*b*) ns, bs, *and* rs *are inseparable if followed by a consonant:*
cons-pi-rer, cons-ta-ter, cons-ti-tu-er, ins-pec-ter, ins-tal-ler, trans-cen-dant, trans-fè-re-ment, trans-port; no-nobs-tant, obs-ta-cles, subs-tan-ce; in-ters-ti-ce, pers-pec-ti-ve.

(*c*) ns *and* bs *are inseparable if followed by a consonant coupled with* r:
cons-trui-re, ins-cri-re, trans-cri-

re, trans-gres-ser; abs-trac-ti-on, obs-truc-ti-on.

(*d*) *ns* and *bs* *are separable before* ci:
con-sci-en-ci-eux, in-sci-em-ment; ab-scis-se.

(6) (*a*) mp *and* nc *followed by* t *are inseparable:*
a-comp-te, comp-ta-ble, es-comp-ter, pré-emp-ti-on; fonc-ti-on, sanc-ti-on.

(*b*) *In all other combinations* mp *and* nc *are separable:*
em-ploy-er, em-prun-ter, im-por-tant; a-van-cer, fran-çais, fran-che, fran-co.

(7) *In writing or in print no sylla-ble is separable which does not include a vowel;* thus, tri-graph consonants are insepar-able initially: scru-tin, but may be separable medially: ins-cru-ta-ble.

ENGLISH-FRENCH
DICTIONARY

A

A, *letter,* (*Mus.*) la, *m;* (*house number*) bis. a, *indefinite art.* or *a,* un, une. *what* ~ . . . *l,* quel!, quelle! *such* ~ . . . , tel, telle. *2 or 3 times* ~ *day,* 2 ou 3 fois par jour.

aback, *ad:* taken ~, interloqué, déconcerté.

abacus, *n,* abaque, *m.*

abaft, *ad,* vers l'arrière. ¶ *pr,* sur l'arrière de.

abandon, *v.t,* abandonner, délaisser. ~**ment,** *n,* abandon, délaissement, *m.*

abase, *v.t,* abaisser, humilier.

abash, *v.t,* décontenancer, confondre.

abate, *v.t,* diminuer, rabattre; (*v.i.*) [se] calmer; (*weather,* etc.) s'apaiser. **abatement,** *n,* diminution, *f;* rabais, *m.*

abbess, *n,* abbesse, *f.* **abbey,** *n,* abbaye, *f.* **abbot,** *n,* abbé, *m.*

abbreviate, *v.t,* abréger. **abbreviation,** *n,* abréviation, *f.*

A B C, *n,* A b c, abécédaire, alphabet, *m;* enfance, *f.*

abdicate, *v.t. & i,* abdiquer. **abdication,** *n,* abdication, *f.*

abdomen, *n,* abdomen, ventre, *m. lower part of the* ~, basventre, *m.* **abdominal,** *a,* abdominal. ~ *belt,* ceinture ventrière, *f.*

abduct, *v.t,* détourner, enlever.

abeam, *ad,* par le travers.

abed, *ad,* au lit, couché.

aberration, *n,* aberration, *f,* égarement, *m.*

abet, *v.t,* soutenir, encourager, exciter.

abeyance, (*law*) *n,* vacance, *f. in* ~, en suspens, en souffrance.

abhor, *v.t,* abhorrer, haïr, avoir en horreur. **abhorrence,** *n,* horreur, haine, *f.* **abhorrent,** *a,* répugnant.

abide, *v.i. & t. ir,* demeurer, rester; souffrir, supporter. *to* ~ *by* (*laws*), s'en tenir à. **abiding,** *a,* durable, permanent.

ability, *n,* capacité, habileté, *f,* talent, savoir-faire, *m.*

abject, *a,* abject. ~**ion,** *n,* abjection, *f.*

abjure, *v.t,* abjurer, renoncer.

ablative [case], *n,* ablatif, *m.*

ablaze, *ad,* en feu, en flammes.

able, *a,* capable, habile; efficace. ~-*bodied,* robuste, valide. ~-[-*bodied*] *seaman,* matelot de deuxième classe, *m. to be* ~ *to,* pouvoir, savoir, être en mesure (*ou* à même) de, suffire à. **ably,** *ad,* habilement, bravement.

abnegation, *n,* abnégation, *f.*

abnormal†, *a,* anormal. ~**ity,** *n,* anormal, *m.*

aboard, *ad,* à bord. ¶ *pr,* à bord de.

abode, *n,* domicile, *m,* demeure, habitation, *f;* séjour, *m.*

abolish, *v.t,* abolir, supprimer.

abominable†, *a,* abominable. **abominate,** *v.t,* abominer. **abomination,** *n,* abomination, *f.*

aboriginal, *a. & n,* aborigène, *a. & m.* **aborigines,** *n.pl,* aborigènes, *m.pl.*

abortion, *n,* avortement; (*creature*) avorton, *m.* **abortive,** *a,* abortif; (*fig.*) avorté, manqué.

abound, *v.i,* abonder, foisonner, fourmiller, affluer.

about, *pr,* autour de; auprès de; pour; dans; en; par; vers; sur; à propos de, touchant. ¶ *ad,* autour, çà & là; environ, à peu [de chose] près. *to be* ~ *to,* être sur le point de, aller. *what is it all* ~? de quoi s'agit-il?

above, *pr,* au-dessus de; sur; plus de; en amont de; en contrehaut. ¶ *ad,* en haut; là-haut; audessus; ci-dessus. *from* ~, d'en haut. ~ *all,* surtout, avant tout. ~-*board,* franc, cartes sur table. ~-*mentioned,* susmentionné, ci-dessus. ~-*named,* susnommé.

abrade, *v.t,* user; (*skin*) écorcher; **abrasion,** *n,* (*Phys.*) attrition; (*skin*) écorchure, *f.*

abreast, *ad,* de front; (*Naut.*) par le travers. ~ *of,* à la hauteur de.

abridge, *v.t,* abréger, raccourcir. **abridgment,** *n,* abrégé, raccourci, *m.*

abroad, *ad,* à l'étranger, à l'extérieur; au large. *from* ~, de l'étranger, de l'exérieur. *there is* *a rumor ~ that . . .*, le bruit court que . . .

abrogate, *v.t*, abroger. **abrogation**, *n*, abrogation, *f*.

abrupt, *a*, abrupt; brusque. *to treat* ~*ly*, brusquer. ~**ly**, *ad*, brusquement. ~**ness**, *n*, brusquerie, *f*.

abscess, *n*, abcès, *m*.

abscond, *v.i*, s'enfuir, se soustraire à la justice.

absence, *n*, absence, *f*, éloignement; défaut, *m*. ~ *of mind*, absence [d'esprit], distraction, *f*. *leave of* ~, permission, *f*; congé, *m*. **absent**, *a*, absent, manquant. ~*minded*, distrait. *to* ~ *oneself*, s'absenter. **absentee**, *n*, absent; (*Mil.*) insoumis, *m*. **absently**, *ad*, distraitement.

absinthe, *n*, absinthe, *f*.

absolute, *a*, absolu. ~**ly**, *ad*, absolument.

absolution, *n*, absolution, *f*. **absolve**, *v.t*, absoudre.

absorb, *v.t*, absorber. **absorbent**, **absorbing**, *a*, absorbant; (*cotton wool*) hydrophile. **absorption**, *n*, absorption, *f*.

abstain, *v.i*, s'abstenir. ~**er**, *n*, abstème, *m.f*. **abstemious**, *a*, abstème, sobre. **abstention**, *n*, abstention, *f*. **abstinence**, *n*, abstinence, *f*.

abstract, *a*, abstrait. ¶ *n*, extrait, relevé, résumé, *m*. *the* ~ (*opp. concrete*), l'abstrait, *m*. ¶ *v.t*, abstraire; relever; (*steal*) distraire, soustraire, détourner. **abstraction**, *n*, abstraction; distraction, soustraction, *f*, détournement, *m*.

abstruse, *a*, abstrus.

absurd†, *a*, absurde. *the* ~, *an* **absurdity**, l'absurde, *m*, une absurdité.

abundance, *n*, abondance, *f*. **abundant**, *a*, abondant. ~**ly**, *ad*, abondamment.

abuse, *n*, abus; excès, *m*; injures, insultes, *f.pl*. ¶ *v.t*, abuser de; injurier, malmener, maltraiter. **abusive**†, *a*, abusif; injurieux.

abutment (*Arch.*) *n*, culée, butée, *f*.

abyss, *n*, abîme, abysse, gouffre, *m*.

Abyssinia, *n*, l'Abyssinie, *f*. **Abyssinian**, *a*, abyssinien, abyssin. ¶ *n*, Abyssinien, ne, Abyssin, e.

acacia, *n*, acacia, *m*.

academic(al†), *a*, académique; (*year*) scolaire. **academician**, *n*,

académicien, ne. **academy**, *n*, académie, *f*.

accede, *v.i*, accéder.

accelerate, *v.t*, accélérer. **accelerator**, *n*, accélérateur, *m*.

accent, *n*, accent, *m*. **accent** & **accentuate**, *v.t*, accentuer.

accept, *v.t*, accepter, agréer; (*a sport record*) homologuer. ~**able**, *a*, acceptable; de mise; agréable. ~**ance**, *n*, acceptation; réception, *f*. ~**ation**, *n*, acception, *f*. ~*ed term*, terme consacré, *m*. ~**or**, *n*, accepteur, *m*. ~ *for honor* (*Com.*), intervenant, *m*.

access, *n*, accès, abord, *m*, entrée, *f*. ~**ible**, *a*, accessible, abordable. ~**ion**, *n*, accession, *f*; avènement, *m*.

accessory†, *a*, accessoire. ¶ *n*, accessoire, *m*; (*law*) complice, *m,f*.

accidence (*Gram.*) *n*, morphologie, *f*.

accident, *n*, accident; sinistre, *m*. [*personal*] ~ *insurance*, assurance contre les accidents [corporels] *f*. **accidental**†, *a*, accidentel, fortuit. ¶ (*Mus.*) *n*, accident, *m*.

acclaim, *v.t*, acclamer. **acclamation**, *n*, acclamation, *f*.

acclimatization, *n*, acclimatation, *f*, acclimatement, *m*. **acclimatize**, *v.t*, acclimater.

acclivity, *n*, montée, *f*.

accommodate, *v.t*, arranger; contenir; loger. ~ *oneself to*, s'accommoder à. **accommodating**, *p.a*, accommodant, complaisant, coulant, débonnaire. **accommodation**, *n*, accommodation, *f*; aménagement; logement, *m*. ~ *paper*, billet de complaisance, *m*.

accompaniment, *n*, accompagnement, *m*. **accompanist**, *n*, accompagnateur, trice. **accompany**, *v.t*, accompagner.

accomplice, *n*, complice, *m,f*.

accomplish, *v.t*, accomplir. ~**ed**, *a*, accompli, achevé, émérite. ~**ment**, *n*, accomplissement, *m*; (*pl.*) arts d'agrément, *m.pl*.

accord, *n*, accord, *m*. *of one's own* ~, de son propre mouvement, de son plein gré, d'office. *with one* ~, d'un commun accord. ¶ *v.t*, accorder; (*v.i.*) s'a. ~**ance**, *n*, conformité, *f*. **according as**, à mesure que, selon que, suivant que. **according to**, selon, suivant; conforme à, conformément à; conséquemment à;

d'après; à. **accordingly,** *ad,* par conséquent; en conséquence; conséquemment.

accordion, *n,* accordéon, *m.*

accost, *v.t,* accoster, aborder.

account, *n,* compte, *m; (pl.)* écritures [comptables] *f.pl; (pl.)* comptabilité, *f; (pl.)* inventaire; exercice; état, exposé, mémoire, *m,* note, *f;* récit, *m,* relation, notice, *f,* historique; *(Stk Ex.)* terme, *m,* liquidation, *f. of no* ~, nul. *on* ~ *(Com.),* à compte, à valoir. *on* ~ *of,* à cause de; *(Com.)* pour le compte de, à l'acquit de. *on no* ~, en aucune manière, aucunement. ~ *book,* livre de comptabilité, *m.* ¶ ~ *for,* rendre compte de; expliquer. ~**able,** *a,* comptable; responsable. ~**ancy,** *n,* comptabilité, *f.* ~**ant,** *n,* comptable, *m,f,* agent comptable, *m.* ~**ing,** *n,* comptabilité, *f.* ~ *machine,* machine comptable, *f.* ~ *period,* exercice, *m.*

accoutre, *v.t,* équiper; harnacher. ~**ment,** *n,* équipement, *m.*

accredit, *v.t,* accréditer. ~**ed,** *p.a,* accrédité, attitré. ~ *dealer,* stockiste, *m.*

accrue, *v.i,* courir, accroître, s'accroître. ~*d interest,* intérêt couru, *m,* intérêts accrus, *m.pl. accruing interest,* intérêts à échoir.

accumulate, *v.t,* accumuler, amonceler; *(v.i.)* s'accumuler, s'amonceler. **accumulation,** *n,* accumulation, *f,* amoncellement, *m.* **accumulator,** *n,* accumulateur, *m.*

accuracy, *n,* exactitude, justesse, *f.* **accurate†,** *a,* exact, juste.

accursed, *a,* maudit.

accusation, *n,* accusation, *f.* **accusative** [case], accusatif, *m.* **accuse,** *v.t,* accuser; taxer. *the* ~*d,* l'accusé, e, l'inculpé, e. **accuser,** *n,* accusateur, trice. **accusing,** *a,* accusateur.

accustom, *v.t,* accoutumer, habituer, familiariser, faire. ~**ed,** *a,* accoutumé, coutumier, habituel. *to get* ~ *to,* s'accoutumer à.

ace, *n,* as, *m. within an* ~ *of,* à deux doigts de.

acerbity, *n,* âpreté, aigreur, *f.*

acetate, *n,* acétate, *m.* **acetic,** *a,* acétique.

acetylene, *n,* acétylène, *m.* ~ *lamp,* lampe à acétylène, *f.*

ache, *n,* mal, *m,* douleur, *f.* ¶ *v.i,* faire mal; souffrir. *my head aches,* j'ai mal à la tête.

achieve, *v.t,* accomplir, exécuter. ~**ment,** *n,* accomplissement, exploit, *m.*

aching, *a,* endolori. ~ *all over,* tout moulu.

acid, *a. & n,* acide, *a. & m.* ~**ity,** *n,* acidité *f.* **acidulate,** *v.t,* aciduler.

acknowledge, *v.t,* reconnaître, avouer, s'accuser de, confesser. ~ *receipt of,* accuser réception de. **acknowledgment,** *n,* reconnaissance, *f;* accusé de réception; reçu, *m; (pl.)* remerciements, *m.pl.*

acme, *n,* apogée, comble, sommet, *m.*

acne, *n,* acné, couperose, *f.*

acolyte, *n,* acolyte, *m.*

acorn, *n,* gland, *m.* ~ *crop,* glandée, *f.*

acoustic, *a,* acoustique. ~**s,** *n.pl,* acoustique, *f.*

acquaint, *v.t,* faire connaître, faire savoir, faire part, informer. *to get* ~*ed with,* faire la connaissance de. ~**ance,** *n,* connaissance, relation, *f.*

acquiesce, *v.i,* acquiescer. **acquiescence,** *n,* acquiescement, *m.*

acquire, *v.t,* acquérir; prendre. ~**ments,** *n.pl,* acquis, *m.s. & m.pl,* connaissances, *f.pl.* **acquisition,** *n,* acquisition, *f.*

acquit, *v.t,* acquitter. **acquittal,** *n,* acquittement, *m.*

acre, *n,* acre, arpent, *m.*

acrid, *a,* âcre. ~**ity,** *n,* âcreté, *f.*

acrimonious, *a,* acrimonieux. **acrimony,** *n,* acrimonie, *f.*

acrobat, *n,* acrobate, *m,f.* **acrobatic,** *a,* acrobatique. ~**s,** *n.pl,* acrobatie, *f.*

across, *ad,* en travers; *(crossword clues)* horizontalement. ¶ *pr,* en travers de, par. *our neighbors* ~ *the Channel,* nos voisins d'outre-Manche.

acrostic, *n,* acrostiche, *m.*

act, *n,* acte, *m,* action, *f,* fait, *m.* ~ [of the legislature], loi [votée] *f. in the* [very] ~, sur le fait; en flagrant délit. ¶ *v.t,* jouer, représenter; faire; *(v.i.)* agir; fonctionner; opérer. ~ *as,* faire fonction de. ~ *for* (client, *law),* postuler. **acting** *(Theat.)* *n,* jeu, *m.* ~ *manager,* directeur intérimaire, *m.* ~ *partner,* commandité, *m.*

action, *n,* action, *f;* effet; mouvement; geste, *m*; scène, *f*; combat; procès, *m*, plainte, *f*.

active†, *a*, actif, agissant, agile, allant, énergique. *in* ~ *service*, en activité [de service]. ~ *voice*, voix active, *f*, actif, *m*. **activity**, *n*, activité, agilité, *f*, allant, *m*.

actor, tress, *n*, acteur, trice, comédien, *ne*.

actual, *a*, actuel, réel, effectif, véritable; de fait. ~**ity,** *n*, actualité, réalité, *f*. ~**ly,** *ad*, réellement, en effet.

actuary, *n*, actuaire, *m*.

actuate, *v.t*, actionner, animer, mouvoir.

acumen, *n*, flair, *m*.

acute, *a*, aigu; vif, poignant. ~*angled*, acutangle. ~**ly,** *ad*, vivement. ~**ness,** *n*, acuité; finesse, subtilité; vivacité, *f*.

A.D. (*Anno Domini*), ap. J.C.

adage, *n*, adage, *m*.

adamant (to be), être inflexible.

Adam's apple, pomme d'Adam, *f*.

adapt, *v.t*, adapter, accommoder, approprier. ~**ation,** *n*, adaptation, *f*. ~**er,** *n*, (*Phot*.) adapteur; (*pers. fig*.) metteur en œuvre, *m*.

add, *v.t*, ajouter; joindre; additionner. *(part)* added *(to a building),* hors-d'œuvre, *e.g. an added room,* un cabinet hors-d'œuvre.

adder, *n*, vipère, *f*.

addict, *n*, toxicomane, *m*.

addict oneself to (to), s'adonner à, se livrer à.

addition, *n*, addition, *f*; supplément; (*to a building*) hors-d'œuvre, *m*. ~**al,** *a*, additionnel, supplémentaire.

addled, *a*, couvi; pourri. **addle-headed,** *a*, écervelé.

address, *n*, adresse, allocution, *f*. ¶*v.t*, adresser; s'adresser à. ~**ee,** *n*, destinataire, *m,f*.

adduce, *v.t*, alléguer, fournir.

adenoids, *n.pl*, végétations [adénoïdes] *f.pl*.

adept, *a*, habile, versé, expérimenté. ¶*n*, adepte, *m,f*.

adequate, *a*, suffisant; efficace; raisonnable. ~**ly,** *ad*, suffisamment, raisonnablement; dignement.

adhere, *v.i*, adhérer, s'en tenir. **adherence,** *n*, **adhesion,** *n*, **adhesiveness,** *n*, adhérence, adhésion, ténacité, *f*. **adhesive,** *a*, adhésif, tenace. ~ *stamp*, timbre mobile, *m*. ~ *tape*, bande gommée, *f*; sparadrap, *m*.

adieu, *i. & n*, adieu, *i. & m*.

ad infinitum, *ad*, à l'infini.

adipose, *a*, adipeux.

adit, *n*, galerie à flanc de coteau, *f*.

adjacent, *a*, adjacent, contigu.

adjectival, *a. & adjective,** *n*, adjectif, *a.m. & m*.

adjoin, *v.i*, joindre, être contigu à, toucher. ~**ing,** *a*, contigu, attenant, adjacent, joignant [à].

adjourn, *v.t*, ajourner, renvoyer, remettre. ~**ment,** *n*, ajournement, renvoi, *m*, remise, *f*.

adjudge, adjudicate, *v.t*, adjuger. **adjudication,** *n*, adjudication, *f*.

adjunct, *n*, accessoire, *m*.

adjure, *v.t*, adjurer.

adjust, *v.t*, ajuster, régler, mettre au point. ~*able wrench*, clef à molette, *f*. ~**ment,** *n*, ajustement, règlement, réglage, *m*, mise au point, *f*.

adjutant, *n*, adjudant major, major, *m*.

ad libitum, ad libitum; à volonté, à discrétion.

administer, *v.t*, administrer, gérer; (*oath*) déférer. **administration,** *n*, administration, gestion; régie, *f*. **administrative,** *a*, administratif. **administrator, trix,** *n*, administrateur, trice; curateur, trice.

admirable†, *a*, admirable.

admiral, *n*, amiral, *m*. ~ *of the fleet,* a. commandant d'escadre. **Admiralty,** *n*, (*Eng*.) Amirauté, *f*; (*Fr*.) Conseil supérieur de la Marine, *m*. ~ [*Office*], Ministère de la Marine, *m*.

admiration, *n*, admiration, *f*. **admire,** *v.t*, admirer. **admirer,** *n*, admirateur, trice. **admiringly,** *ad*, avec admiration.

admissible, *a*, admissible; recevable. **admission,** *n*, admission, entrée, *f*; aveu, *m*. **admit,** *v.t*, admettre, reconnaître; (*as member*) recevoir, agréger. ~ *bearer*, laissez passer. **admittance,** *n*, admission, entrée, *f*.

admixture, *n*, dosage, *m*.

admonish, *v.t*, admonester. **admonition,** *n*, admonition, admonestation, *f*.

ado, *n*, façons, *f.pl*, cérémonie, *f*; aria, bruit, tapage, *m*.

adolescence, *n*, adolescence, *f*. **adolescent,** *a. & n*, adolescent, *e*.

Adonis, *n*, adonis, beau, *m*.

adopt, *v.t,* adopter; prendre. **adopted, adoptive** (*of pers.*) *a,* adoptif. **adoption,** *n,* adoption; prise, *f.*

adorable, *a,* adorable. **adoration,** *n,* adoration, *f.* **adore,** *v.t,* adorer. **adorer,** *n,* adorateur, trice.

adorn, *v.t,* parer, orner, agrémenter, empanacher; (*of pers.*) faire l'ornement de. *to ~ oneself,* se parer. **~ment,** *n,* parure, *f,* ornement, *m.*

Adriatic, *a. & n,* Adriatique, *a. & f.*

adrift, *ad,* en (*ou* à la) dérive.

adroit†, *a,* adroit. **~ness,** *n,* dextérité, *f.*

adulate, *v.t,* aduler. **adulation,** *n,* adulation, *f.* **adulatory,** *a,* adulateur.

adult, *a. & n,* adulte, *a. & m,f.*

adulterate, *v.t,* falsifier, frelater, sophistiquer, altérer. **adulteration,** *n,* falsification, *f,* frelatage, *m,* sophistication, altération, *f.*

adulterer, ess, *n,* adultère, *m,f.* **adulterous,** *a,* adultère. **adultery,** *n,* adultère, *m.*

ad valorem, *n,* avance; anticipation;

ad valorem, ad valorem, proportionnel.

advance, *n,* avance; anticipation; hausse, *f;* prêt, *m.* *in ~,* en avance, d'a., par a., à l'a. ¶ *v.t,* avancer; hausser; (*v.i.*) [s']avancer, cheminer. **~ment,** *n,* avancement, *m.*

advantage, *n,* avantage, bénéfice, *m.* *~* [*game*] (*Ten.*), avantage [de jeu]. *~ in,* a. dedans, a. au servant. **~ous†,** *a,* avantageux.

advent, *n,* venue, apparition, *f;* (*of Christ*) avènement; (*Eccl.*) l'avent, *m.*

adventure, *n,* aventure, expédition, *f.* ¶ *v.t,* aventurer. **adventurer,** *n,* aventurier, chercheur d'aventures, chevalier d'industrie, *m.* **adventuress,** *n,* aventurière, *f.* **adventurous,** *a,* aventureux.

adverb, *n,* adverbe, *m.* *~ of number,* a. de quantité. **adverbial†,** *a,* adverbial.

adversary, *n,* adversaire, *m.* **adverse,** *a,* adverse; contraire; déficitaire. **adversity,** *n,* adversité, infortune, *f.*

advert, *v.i,* faire allusion.

advertise, *v.t,* annoncer, publier; afficher; (*v.i.*) faire une annonce (des annonces), faire de la publicité. *~ for,* demander par

voie d'annonces. **~ment,** *n,* annonce; réclame, *f.* *~ billboard,* panneau-réclame, *m.* **advertiser,** *n,* annonceur, *m.* **advertising,** *n,* publicité, réclame, *f.* *~ agency,* agence de publicité, *f.*

advice, *n,* avis, conseil, *m.* **advisable,** *a,* à conseiller, expédient, convenable. **advise,** *v.t,* conseiller; engager; aviser. **advisedly,** *ad,* de propos délibéré, en connaissance de cause. **adviser,** *n,* conseiller, ère, moniteur, *m.* **advisory,** *a,* consultatif.

advocate, *n,* avocat, défenseur; partisan, *m.* ¶ *v.t,* préconiser.

adze, *n,* herminette, *f.*

Aegean Sea (the), la mer Égée.

aegis, *n,* égide, *f.*

Aeolian, *a,* éolien.

aerate, *v.t,* aérer; gazéifier. *~d water,* eau gazeuse, *f.* **aeration,** *n,* aération, *f.*

aerial, *a,* aérien. ¶ (*radio*) *n,* antenne, *f.*

aerie, *n,* aire, *f.*

aerodynamic, *a. & ~s, n,* aérodynamique, *a. & f.*

aerolite, *n,* aérolithe, météorite, *m.*

aeronaut, *n,* aéronaute, *m,f.* **~ic(al),** *a,* aéronautique. **~ics,** *n,* aéronautique, *f.*

afar, *ad,* loin, au loin. *from ~,* de loin.

affability, *n,* affabilité, *f.* **affable,** *a,* affable. **affably,** *ad,* avec affabilité.

affair, *n,* affaire, *f.*

affect, *v.t,* affecter, concerner, atteindre, impressionner; toucher, émouvoir, attendrir. **~ation,** *n,* affectation, afféterie, *f,* apprêt, *m.* **~ed,** *a,* affecté, affété, précieux, apprêté, maniéré, pincé. **~edly,** *ad,* avec affectation. **~ing,** *p.a,* touchant. **affection,** *n,* affection, *f.* **~ate†,** *a,* affectueux, aimant, affectionné.

affiance, *n,* confiance, foi, *f;* fiançailles, *f.pl.* ¶ *v.t,* fiancer.

affidavit, *n,* déclaration sous serment, *f.*

affiliate, *v.t,* affilier. ¶ *n,* compagnie associée, *f.*

affinity, *n,* affinité, *f.*

affirm, *v.t,* affirmer, assurer. **~ation,** *n,* affirmation, *f.* **~ative†,** *a,* affirmatif. ¶ *n,* affirmative, *f.*

affix, *n,* affixe, *m.* ¶ *v.t,* apposer. **~ture,** *n,* apposition, *f.*

afflict, *v.t,* affliger, chagriner. **~ion,** *n,* affliction, *f,* chagrin, *m.*

affluence, *n*, affluence; opulence, aisance, *f*. **affluent**, *a*, affluent, tributaire; opulent, aisé. ¶ *n*, affluent, *m*.

afford, *v.t*, donner, fournir, accorder. *can* ~ *to*, avoir les moyens de, pouvoir.

afforest, *v.t*, boiser. **~ation**, *n*, boisement, *m*.

affray, *n*, échauffourée, rixe, *f*.

affront, *n*, affront, *m*, avanie, *f*. ¶ *v.t*, offenser.

Afghan, *a*, afghan. ¶ *n*, Afghan, e.

afield, *ad*: *far* ~, très loin.

afire, *ad*, en feu, embrasé, brûlant.

afloat, *ad*. & *a*, à flot, sous voile, flottant; (*fig.*) sur pied, en circulation.

afoot, *ad*, à pied; sur pied; en cours; en route.

aforesaid, *a*, susdit, précité. ¶ *n*, susdit, e.

afraid, *a*, craintif. *to be* ~ *of*, avoir peur de, craindre.

afresh, *ad*, de nouveau, à nouveau.

Africa, *n*, l'Afrique, *f*, **African**, *a*, africain. ¶ *n*, Africain, e.

aft, *a*, arrière. ¶ *ad*, sur l'arrière, derrière.

after, *ad*, après; suivant; passé; à l'issue de. ¶ *c*, après que. ¶ *pr*, après, passé; d'après; à; sur. ~ *all*, après tout, au bout de compte. ~ *the event*, après coup.

aftermath, *n*, regain, *m*; répercussions, conséquences.

afternoon, *n*, après-midi, *m*.

aftertaste (*nasty*) *n*, arrière-goût, déboire, *m*.

afterthought, *n*, réflexion après coup, *f*.

afterwards, *ad*, après, ensuite, puis, plus tard.

again, *ad*, encore, de nouveau. ~ & ~, mille [& mille] fois. *never* ~, jamais plus. *now and* ~, de temps à autre. **again** *after a verb is often expressed by the prefix* re- *as, to set out again*, repartir.

against, *pr*, contre, contraire à; sauf. ~ *the grain*, à contre-fil, à rebours. ~ *the light*, à contre-jour.

agate, *n*, agate, *f*.

age, *n*, âge; siècle; temps, *m*; époque; (*old age*) vieillesse; (*decay*) vétusté, *f*. *10 years of* ~ *or* ~*d 10*, âgé de 10 ans. *he is not of* (*or is under*) ~, il n'est pas en âge. *to come of* [*full*] ~,

être majeur, e. *it is* ~*s since*, il y a belle lurette que. ¶ *v.i*, vieillir.

aged (*of an advanced age*) *a*, âgé. *he has* ~ *considerably*, il a bien vieilli. *the* ~ (*either sex*), les vieillards, *m.pl*.

agency, *n*, action; entremise, *f*, ministère, *m*; (*Com.*) agence, *f*, bureau; comptoir, *m*; factorerie; représentation, *f*.

agenda, *n*, ordre du jour, agenda, *m*.

agent, *n*, agent, commissionnaire, *m*; représentant, e; stockiste, *m*; mandataire, *m,f*; régisseur, *m*.

agglomerate, *v.t*, agglomérer.

agglutinate, *v.t*, agglutiner.

aggravate, *v.t*, aggraver. **aggravation**, *n*, aggravation, *f*.

aggregate, *a*, global, d'ensemble. ¶ *n*, total global; ensemble, *m*, masse, *f*. **aggregation**, *n*, agrégation, *f*.

aggression, *n*, agression, *f*. **aggressive**, *a*, agressif. **aggressor**, *n*, agresseur, *m*.

aggrieve, *v.i*, chagriner; léser.

aggrieved party, offensé, e.

aghast, *a*, épouvanté, ébahi.

agile†, *a*, agile. **agility**, *n*, agilité, *f*.

agitate, *v.t*, agiter, remuer. **agitation**, *n*, agitation, *f*. **agitator**, *n*, agitateur, *m*.

aglow, *a*, resplendissant.

ago, *ad*. & *a*, passé, écoulé. *many years* ~, il y a de nombreuses années.

agog, *a*, en branle-bas; animé; impatient.

agonizing, *a*, déchirant, cuisant. **agony**, *n*, douleur déchirante, d. cuisante, (*pl.*) agonie, *f*. (*death pangs*) agonie, *f*.

agrarian, *a*, agraire.

agree, *v.t*, faire accorder, faire concorder, faire cadrer, apurer; (*v.i.*) s'accorder, s'arranger, s'entendre, cadrer, concorder, convenir. ~ *to*, consentir à, souscrire à, s'engager à. *quite* ~ *with*, abonder dans le sens de. *meat does not* ~ *with me*, je ne digère pas la viande. **~able†**, *a*, agréable, amène; conforme. **~d price**, prix convenu, [prix à] forfait, *m*. **~ment**, *n*, accord, *m*, entente, convention, concordance, conformité, *f*; acte, contrat, marché, traité, *m*. *to be in* ~, être d'accord.

agricultural, *a*, agricole, aratoire. ~ *implements*, instruments aratoires, *m.pl.* ~ *show*, concours (*ou* comice) agricole, *m.*

agricultur[al]ist, *n*, agriculteur, cultivateur, *m.* **agriculture**, *n*, agriculture, *f.*

agronomist, *n*, agronome, *m.* **agronomy**, *n*, agronomie, *f.*

aground, *ad.* & *a*, échoué. **to run** ~, *v.i.* & *t*, [s']échouer.

ague, *n*, fièvre paludéenne, *f.*

ahead, *ad*, en avant, devant. *go* ~*!* en avant!

ahoy, *i*, ho!, ohé! *ship* ~*!* ho! du navire.

aid, *n*, aide, assistance, *f*, secours, *m.* ¶ *v.t*, aider, assister, secourir.

aide-de-camp, *n*, aide de camp, *m.*

ail, *v.t.* & *i*, avoir, souffrir. ~**ing**, *a*, maladif, souffrant. ~**ment**, *n*, mal, malaise, *m.*

aim, *n*, point de mire, *m*, visée, *f*; but, objectif, *m*, fin, *f.* ¶ *v.t*, pointer, coucher en joue. ~ *at*, viser [à], ajuster, coucher (*ou* metter) en joue. ~**less**, *a*, ~**less-ly**, *ad*, sans but.

air, *n*, air; vent; ciel, *m.* *to give oneself* ~*s*, faire l'important, se ~craft carrier, porte-avions, *m.* ~craft exhibition, salon de l'aviation, *m.* ~ *current*, courant d'air, *m.* ~ *cushion*, coussin à air, *m.* ~field, terrain d'aviation, *m.* ~ *gun*, fusil à air comprimé, *f.* à vent, *m.* ~hole, aspirail, soupirail, évent, *m*; soufflure, *f.* ~line, ligne aérienne, *f.* ~liner, avion de ligne régulière, *m.* ~mail, poste aérienne, poste-avion, *f.* by ~mail, par avion, *m.* ~man, aviateur, *m.* ~ *mechanic*, mécanicien d'avions, *m.* ~minded, tourné vers l'aviation. ~ *parcel*, colis-avion, *m.* ~ *pilot*, pilote aérien, *m.* ~plane, avion, *m.* ~pocket, trou d'air, *m.* ~port, aéroport, *m.* ~ *pump*, pompe à air, *f*; (*Phys.*) machine pneumatique, *f.* ~ *race*, course d'avions, *f.* ~ *raid*, raid aérien, *m.* ~shaft (*Min.*), puits d'aérage, *m.* ~ship, dirigeable, paquebot aérien, *m.* ~tight, [à fermeture] hermétique, imperméable à l'air. ~way (*Min.*) galerie d'aérage. ¶ *v.t*, aérer, ventiler; donner de l'air à; éventer; chauffer, sécher; étaler. ~ing, *n*, aérage, *m*, aération, ventilation, *f.* ~less, *a*, sans air, privé d'air. ~y, *a*, ventilé, aéré; en l'air; vain.

aisle, *n*, aile, *f*, bas-côté, *m.*

ajar, *a*, entrebâillé, entrouvert. *be* ~, bâiller.

akimbo, *ad*: *to set one's arms* ~, faire le pot à deux anses. *with arms* ~, les mains sur les hanches.

akin, *a*, apparenté, voisin.

alabaster, *n*, albâtre, *m.*

alacrity, *n*, empressement, *m.*

alarm, *n*, alarme, alerte, *f*; avertisseur, *m.* ~ *clock*, réveille-matin, réveil, *m.* ¶ *v.t.* alarmer. ~ing, *a*, alarmant.

alas, *i*, hélas!

alb, *n*, aube, *f.*

albatross, *n*, albatros, *m.*

albino, *n*, albinos, *m,f.*

album, *n*, album, *m.*

albumen, *n*, albumen, *m.* **albumin**, *n*, albumine, *f.*

alchemist, *n*, alchimiste, *m.* **alchemy**, *n*, alchimie, *f.*

alcohol, *n*, alcool, *m.* ~ic, *a.* & *n*, alcoolique, *a.* & *m,f.*

alcove, *n*, alcôve, *f.*

alder, *n*, aune, ver[g]ne, *m.*

ale, *n*, bière, ale, *f.*

alert, *a*, alerte. *on the* ~, en alerte, en éveil, sur le qui-vive.

Alexandria, *n*, Alexandrie, *f.* **Alexandrian** & **Alexandrine**, *a*, alexandrin.

alfresco, *a.* & *ad*, en plein air.

algebra, *n*, algèbre, *m.*

Algeria, *n*, l'Algérie, *f.* **Algerian**, *a*, algérien. ¶ *n*, Algérien, ne. **Algiers**, *n*, Alger, *m.*

alias, *ad*, alias, autrement dit. ¶ *n*, faux nom; nom de guerre, *m.*

alibi, *n*, alibi, *m.*

alien, *a*, étranger. ¶ *n*, étranger, ère.

alienate, *v.t*, aliéner.

alight, *a*, allumé. ¶ *v.i*, descendre, débarquer; atterrir; se poser. ~ [*on the water*] (seaplane), amerrir.

align, *v.t*, aligner. ~**ment**, *n*, alignement, *m.*

alike, *a*, semblable, pareil; ressemblant. ¶ *ad*, également; à la fois. *to be* ~, se ressembler.

alimentary, *a*, alimentaire. **alimony**, *n*, pension alimentaire, *f.*

alive, *a*, en vie, vivant, vif, au monde, animé; sensible; éveillé, dégourdi. *to be* ~ *with vermin*, grouiller de vermine.

alkali, *n*, alcali, *m.* **alkaline**, *a*, alcalin.

all, *a*, tout. ~ *the year* [*round*], [pendant] toute l'année. ~ [*those*] *who*, tous ceux qui, toutes celles qui. *at ~ hours*, à toute heure. *on ~ occasions*, en toute occasion. ¶ *ad*, tout; entièrement. *~ at once*, tout à coup. *~ but*, presque, à peu près. *~ right!* très bien! c'est bien! à la bonne heure! *~ the better*, tant mieux. *~ the same*, tout de même, quand même. ¶ *n*, tous, *m.pl.*; tout; avoir, *m. ~ of us*, nous tous. *that is ~*, c'est tout, voilà tout. *that is not ~*, il s'en faut de beaucoup. *is that ~?* est-ce là tout? n'est-ce que cela? *one's ~*, tout son avoir, son tout, son va-tout. *~ clear* (Mil.), fin d'alerte. *~ in*, fatigué. *~ told* or *in ~*, tout compte fait, pour tout potage.

allay, *v.t*, calmer, apaiser, adoucir.

allegation, *n*, allégation, *f*. **allege,** *v.t*, alléguer, prétendre, objecter.

allegiance, *n*, fidélité, obéissance, *f*, loyalisme, *m*.

allegoric(al†), *a*, allégorique. **allegory,** *n*, allégorie, *f*.

allergy, *n*, allergie, *f*.

alleviate, *v.t*, alléger, soulager, adoucir. **alleviation,** *n*, allégement, soulagement, adoucissement, *m*.

alley, *n*, ruelle, *f*, passage, *m*. *blind ~*, impasse, *f*.

All Fools' Day, le jour des poissons d'avril.

alliance, *n*, alliance, *f*.

allied, *a*, allié; parent.

alligator, *n*, alligator, *m*.

all-important, *ad*, de toute importance.

allocate, *v.t*, allouer. **allocation,** *n*, allocation, *f*.

allot, *v.t*, attribuer, répartir; destiner. *~ment*, *n*, attribution, répartition, distribution, *f*; lopin de terre, *m*. **allottee,** *n*, attributaire, *m,f*.

allow, *v.t*, permettre, autoriser; admettre; souffrir; laisser; allouer, accorder, faire, bonifier. *~ance*, *n*, allouance, allocation; ration; pension; tolérance; bonification, remise, déduction, *f*, rabais, décompte, *m*, ristourne, indemnité, *f*.

alloy, *n*, alliage, *m*. ¶ *v.t*, allier.

all-powerful, *a*, tout-puissant.

all-round, *a*, complet.

All Saints' Day, la Toussaint.

All Souls' Day, le jour des morts.

allspice, *n*, toute-épice, *f*, piment, *m*.

allude to (to), toucher.

allure, *v.t*, amorcer, allécher, affrioler, affriander, appâter. *~ment*, *n*, amorce, *f*, allèchement, appât, *m*. *~ing*, *a*, séduisant.

allusion, *n*, allusion, *f*.

alluvion, alluvium, *n*, alluvion, *f*.

ally, *n*, allié, e. ¶ *v.t*, allier, apparenter.

almanac, *n*, almanach, *m*.

almighty, *a*, tout-puissant. *the Almighty*, le Tout-Puissant.

almond, *n*, amande, *f*. *~ eyes*, des yeux en amande, des yeux bridés, *m.pl*. *~ [tree]*, amandier, *m*.

almost, *ad*, presque.

alms, *n.s. & pl*, aumône, l'aumône, charité, *f*. *~giving*, distribution des aumônes, charité, *f*.

aloe, *n*, aloès; (*pl.*) [suc d']aloès, *m*.

aloft, *ad*, en haut; dans la mâture.

alone, *a*, seul; isolé. *to let* (or *leave*) *~*, laisser tranquille. ¶ *ad*, seulement.

along, *pr. & ad*, le long de; suivant. *~side of* (*pers.*), côte à côte avec. *~side* [*the ship*], le long [du bord]. *to come ~side*, accoster. *come ~!* venez donc! *all ~*, tout du long; tout le temps.

aloof, *ad*, à l'écart, en dehors, isolé (*from* = de). ¶ *a*, distant.

aloud, *ad*, à haute voix, tout haut.

alpaca, *n*, alpaga, *m*.

alpha, *n*, alpha, *m*. **alphabet,** *n*, alphabet, *m*. *~ical†*, *a*, alphabétique.

Alpine, *a*, alpin; alpestre. *the Alps*, les Alpes, *f.pl*, les monts, *m.pl*.

already, *ad*, déjà.

Alsace, *n*, l'Alsace, *f*. **Alsatian,** *a*, alsacien. ¶ *n*, (*pers.*) Alsacien, ne; (*dog*) chien-loup, *m*.

also, *ad*, aussi, également, pareillement.

altar, *n*, autel, *m*. *~ cloth*, nappe d'a., *f*. *~ piece*, tableau d'a.; retable, *m*.

alter, *v.t*, changer, modifier; surcharger; (*v.i.*) [se] changer. *~ the date of* (function, etc.), transférer. *~ation*, *n*, changement, *m*, modification; surcharge, *f*, renvoi [en marge], *m*.

altercation, *n*, altercation, prise de bec, *f*.

alternate†, *a,* alternatif. ~ *months* (newspaper appearing), bimensuel. ¶ *v.i.* & *t,* alterner. **alternating,** *p.a,* alternatif. **alternative,** *a,* alternatif. ¶ *n,* alternative, *f.*

although, *c,* quoique, bien que, encore que, quand, tout . . . que.

altitude, *n,* altitude, élévation, hauteur, *f.*

alto, *n.* & ~ *saxhorn,* alto, *m.* ~ *clef,* clef d'ut, *f.*

altogether, *ad,* tout à fait; en tout; grandement.

altruist, *n.* & ~**ic,** *a,* altruiste, *m,f.* & *a.*

alum, *n,* alun, *m.*

aluminum, *n,* aluminium, *m.*

always, *ad,* toujours.

amalgam, *n,* amalgame, *m.* ~**ate,** *v.t,* amalgamer, fusionner.

amanuensis, *n,* secrétaire, *m.*

amass, *v.t,* amasser.

amateur, *n,* amateur; dilettante, *m.* ~ *status,* qualité d'amateur, *f,* statut d'a., *m.* **amatory,** *a,* galant, érotique.

amaze, *v.t,* étonner, stupéfier. ~**ment,** *n,* étonnement, *m,* stupeur, *f.*

Amazon, *n,* amazone; virago, *f.* **the** ~ (*river*), l'Amazone, *m,* le fleuve des Amazones.

ambassador, dress, *n,* ambassadeur, drice.

amber, *n,* ambre, *m.* ~**gris,** *n,* ambre gris, *m.*

ambiguity, *n,* ambiguïté, équivoque, *f.* **ambiguous†,** *a,* ambigu, équivoque.

ambition, *n,* ambition, *f.* **ambitious†,** *a,* ambitieux.

amble along (to), aller son petit train.

ambrosia, *n,* ambroisie, *f.*

ambulance, *n,* ambulance, *f.*

ambuscade, ambush, *n,* embuscade, *f,* guetapens, *m.* **to place in** ~, embusquer. **ambush,** *v.i,* s'embusquer.

ameliorate, *v.t,* améliorer. **amelioration,** *n,* amélioration, *f.*

amen, *i.* & *n,* amen, *i.* & *m.*

amenable, *a,* sujet, soumis; susceptible; justiciable; docile.

amend, *v.t,* amender; réformer; rectifier; changer. ~**s,** *n,* réparation, *f.* **make** ~ **for,** réparer, corriger, racheter.

amenity, *n,* aménité, *f;* agrément, *m.*

America, *n,* l'Amérique, *f.*

American, *a,* américain. ¶ *n,* Américain, e.

amethyst, *n,* améthyste, *f.*

amiability, *n,* amabilité, *f.* **amiable,** *a,* aimable, accort. **amiably,** *ad,* avec amabilité.

amicable†, *a,* amical, amiable.

amid, amidst, *pr,* au milieu de, parmi. **amidships,** *ad,* au milieu du navire.

amiss, *ad.* & *a,* de travers; mal, en mal, en mauvaise part. **to take** ~, prendre en mal.

ammonia, *n,* ammoniaque, *f.*

ammunition, *n,* munitions, *f.pl.* ~ *wagon,* prolonge, *f.*

amnesia, *n,* amnésie, *f.*

amnesty, *n,* amnistie, *f.*

among, amongst, *pr,* parmi, entre, dans; au milieu de; au nombre de; chez. ~ *strangers,* dépaysé.

amorous†, *a,* amoureux.

amorphous, *a,* amorphe.

amortization, *n,* amortissement, *m.* **amortize,** *v.t,* amortir.

amount, *n,* montant, *m,* somme, *f,* chiffre, *m,* quantité, *f.* ¶ *v.i,* monter; se chiffrer, s'élever; revenir. ~*ing to,* à concurrence de.

ampere, *n,* ampère, *f.*

amphibian, *n,* amphibie, *m.* **amphibious,** *a,* amphibie.

amphitheater, *n,* amphithéâtre, *m.*

ample†, *a,* ample. ~**ness,** *n,* ampleur, *f.* **amplifier** (*radio*) *n,* amplificateur, *m.* **amplify,** *v.t.* & *i,* amplifier; développer; paraphraser. **amplitude,** *n,* amplitude, *f.*

amputate, *v.t,* amputer.

amulet, *n,* amulette, *f.*

amuse, *v.t,* amuser, divertir, distraire. ~**ment,** *n,* amusement, plaisir, divertissement, *m,* distraction, *f.*

amusing, *a,* amusant.

an, *indefinite art.* or *a,* un, une.

anachronism, *n,* anachronisme, *m.*

anagram, *n,* anagramme, *f.*

analogous, *a,* analogue. **analogy,** *n,* analogie, *f.*

analyze, *v.t,* analyser; (*Bkkpg.*) dépouiller, ventiler. **analysis,** *n,* analyse; ventilation, *f.* **analyst,** *n,* analyste, *m.* **analytic(al†),** *a,* analytique.

anarchic(al), *a,* anarchique. **anarchist,** *n,* anarchiste, *m,f.* **anarchy,** *n,* anarchie, *f.*

anatomical†, *a*, anatomique. **anatomy**, *n*, anatomie, *f*.

ancestor, *n*, ancêtre, *m*. **ancestral**, *a*, ancestral. **ancestry**, *n*, race, *f*, ascendants, *m.pl*.

anchor (*all senses*) *n*, ancre, *f*. ¶ (*Naut.*) *v.t. & i*, mouiller; (*Build. & fig.*) *v.t*, ancrer. ~age (*Naut.*) *n*, mouillage, *m*.

anchoret, anchorite, *n*, anachorète, *m*.

anchovy, *n*, anchois, *m*. ~ *paste*, beurre d'anchois, *m*.

ancient†, *a*, ancien; antique. ¶ *n*, ancien, *m*. ~ness, *n*, ancienneté, antiquité, *f*.

and, *c*. (*abb*. &), et, &. ~ *even*, voire même. ~ *so on* or ~ *so forth*, et ainsi de suite. ~ *so on*, ~ *so forth*, et patati, et patata. *go* ~ *see*, allez voir. *more* ~ *more*, de plus en plus. *two* ~ *two*, deux à deux. *steak* ~ *potatoes*, bifteck aux pommes.

andiron, *n*, chenet, *m*.

anecdote, *n*, anecdote, historiette, *f*.

anemia, *n*, anémie, *f*. **anemic**, *a*, anémique.

anemone, *n*, anémone, *f*.

aneroid [*barometer*], baromètre anéroïde, *m*.

anesthetic, *a. & n*, anesthetique, *a. & m*.

anew, *ad*, à nouveau, de nouveau.

angel, *n*, ange, *m*. ~ic(al†), *a*, angélique. **angelus** [*bell*], Angélus, *m*.

anger, *n*, colère, *f*, courroux, *m*. ¶ *v.t*, mettre en colère, fâcher, courroucer, irriter.

angina, *n*, angine, *f*. ~ *pectoris*, angine de poitrine.

angle, *n*, angle, *m*. ~ [*iron*], fer cornière, *m*, cornière, *f*.

angle, *v.i*, pêcher à la ligne. **angler**, *n*, pêcheur à la ligne, *m*.

Anglicism, *n*, anglicisme, *m*.

angling, *n*, pêche à la ligne, *f*. ~ *at set pitches*, pêche au coup.

Anglomania, *n*, anglomanie, *f*. **Anglophil**[e], *a. & n*, anglophile, *a. & m,f*. **Anglophobe**, *a. & n*, anglophobe, *a. & m,f*. **Anglo-Saxon**, *a*, anglo-saxon. ¶ *n*, Anglo-Saxon, ne.

angrily, *ad*, avec colère. **angry**, *a*, en colère, fâché, irrité. *to get* (*or be*) ~, se fâcher. *to be* ~ *with oneself for*, s'en vouloir de.

anguish, *n*, angoisse, *f*. ¶ *v.i*, angoisser.

angular, *a*, angulaire.

aniline, *n*, aniline, *f*. ~ *dye*, teinture d'aniline, *f*.

animal, *a*, animal. ¶ *n*, animal, *m*.

animate, *a*, animé, doué de vie. ¶ *v.t*, animer. **animation**, *n*, animation, *f*.

animosity, animus, *n*, animosité, *f*.

aniseed, *n*, anis, *m*, graine d'anis, *f*.

ankle, *n*, cheville [du pied], malléole, *f*.

annals, *n.pl*, annales, *f.pl*, fastes, *m.pl*.

anneal, *v.t*, recuire. ~ing, *n*, recuit, *m*, recuite, *f*.

annex, *v.t*, annexer. ~ation, *n*, annexion, *f*. **annex**[e], *n*, annexe, dépendance, *f*.

annihilate, *v.t*, anéantir, annihiler. **annihilation**, *n*, anéantissement, *m*, annihilation, *f*.

anniversary, *a. & n*, anniversaire, *a. & m*.

annotate, *v.t*, annoter.

announce, *v.t*, annoncer. ~ment, *n*, annonce, *f*. **announcer** (*radio*) *n*, speaker; annoncier, *m*.

annoy, *v.t*, agacer, tracasser, contrarier, ennuyer. *to be* ~ed *with*, savoir mauvais gré à. ~ance, *n*, agacement, *m*, tracasserie, contrariété; fâcherie, *f*. ~ing, *a*, agaçant, contrariant.

annual†, *a*, annuel. ¶ *n*, plante annuelle, *f*; (*book*) annuaire, *m*. **annuitant**, *n*, rentier, ère. **annuity**, *n*, annuité, rente [à terme], *f*.

annul, *v.t*, annuler, annihiler.

annular, *a*, annulaire.

annum, *n*: *per* ~, par an.

Annunciation (the), l'Annonciation, *f*.

anode, *n*, anode, *f*.

anodyne, *a*, anodin. ¶ *n*, anodin, *m*.

anoint, *v.t*, oindre, sacrer. ~ed, *a. & n*, oint, *a.m. & m*.

anomalous, *a*, anomal. **anomaly**, *n*, anomalie, *f*.

anon, *ad*, tantôt, tout à l'heure.

anonymous, *a*, anonyme.

another, *n*, un (une) autre; autre; encore un, encore une; nouveau; un (une) second, e.

answer, *n*, réponse; réplique, *f*. ~s *to correspondents*, petite correspondance, *f*. ~ *to the riddle*, mot de l'énigme, *m*. ¶ *v.t*, répondre à. ~ [*back*], répliquer. ~ *for*, répondre pour, de. ~able, *a*, responsable.

ant, *n,* fourmi, *f.* ~*eater,* fourmilier, *m.* ~*hill,* fourmilière, *f.*

antagonism, *n,* antagonisme, *m.* **antagonist,** *n,* antagoniste, *m.* **antagonize,** *v.t,* rendre hostile.

antarctic, *a,* antarctique. *the A~ Ocean,* l'océan Glacial antarctique, *m.*

antecedent, *a. & n,* antécédent, *a. & n.*

antechamber, *n,* antichambre, *f.*

antedate, *v.t,* antidater.

antediluvian, *a,* antédiluvien.

antelope, *n,* antilope, *f.*

ante meridiem (*abb.* a.m.), avant midi; du matin.

antenna, *n,* antenne, *f.*

anterior†, *a,* antérieur.

anteroom, *n,* antichambre, *f.*

anthem, *n,* antienne, *f;* (*national*) hymne, *m.*

anther, *n,* anthère, *f.*

anthology, *n,* anthologie, *f.*

anthracite, *n,* anthracite, *m.*

anthrax (*Med.*) *n,* anthrax, *m.*

antiaircraft, *a,* anti-aérien, contre-avions.

anti-British, *a,* anglophobe.

antic, *n,* (*pl.*) gambades, *f.pl.*

antichrist, *n,* antéchrist, *m. the A~,* l'A.

anticipate, *v.t,* anticiper, prévenir, escompter. **anticipation,** *n,* anticipation, prévision, *f.*

anticlimax, *n,* gradation descendante, *f.*

anticyclone, *n,* anticyclone, *m.*

antidote, *n,* antidote, contre-poison, *m.*

anti-French, *a,* gallophobe.

antimony, *n,* antimoine, *m.*

antipathetic, *a,* antipathique. **antipathy,** *n,* antipathie, *f.*

antipodes, *n.pl,* antipodes, *m.pl.*

antiquary, antiquarian, *n,* antiquaire, *m.f.* **antiquated,** *a,* suranné, vieilli. **antique,** *a,* antique. ¶ *n,* (*style*) antique, *m;* (*relic*) antique, *f.* **antiquity,** *n,* antiquité; ancienneté, *f.*

antiseptic, *a. & n,* antiseptique, *a. & m.*

antithesis, *n,* antithèse, *f.*

antler, *n,* andouiller, *m,* (*pl.*) bois, *m.pl.*

Antwerp, *n,* Anvers, *m.*

anus, *n,* anus, *m.*

anvil, *n,* enclume, *f.*

anxiety, *n,* anxiété, inquiétude; sollicitude, *f.* **anxious,** *a,* anxieux, inquiet; soucieux; désireux, jaloux. ~*ly, ad,* avec anxiété.

any, *a, ad. & pn,* quelque; quelconque; de; du, de la, des; aucun; tout; plus; quelqu'un. *has he* ~? en a-t-il? ~ *farther,* ~ *further,* plus loin. ~ *more,* encore; (*neg.*) plus. ~*way,* n'importe comment; en tout cas.

anybody, anyone, *n. & pn,* quelqu'un; on; personne; aucun; tout le monde; le premier venu.

anyhow, *ad,* de toute façon; en tout cas, toujours; n'importe comment; à l'abandon, à la débandade.

anything, *pn. & n,* quelque chose, *m;* (*neg.*) rien, *m;* quoi que ce soit; n'importe quoi.

anywhere, *ad,* n'importe où; quelque part; (*neg.*) nulle part.

aorta, *n,* aorte, *f.*

apace, *ad,* à grands pas.

apart, *ad,* à part; de côté; séparément. ~ *from,* abstraction faite de. *to move* ~, se séparer, s'écarter. *to tell* ~, distinguer.

apartment, *n,* appartement, logement, *m,* salle, pièce, *f.* ~ *house,* maison de rapport, *f.*

apathetic, *a,* apathique, indolent. **apathy,** *n,* apathie, indolence, *f.*

ape, *n,* singe (sans queue), *m.* ¶ *v.t,* singer.

aperture, *n,* ouverture, *f,* orifice, *m.*

apex, *n,* sommet, faîte, *m.*

aphorism, *n,* aphorisme, *m.*

apiary, *n,* rucher, *m.*

apiece, *ad,* [la] pièce.

apish, *a,* simiesque.

apogee, *n,* apogée, *m.*

apologetic, *a,* apologétique. **apologize,** *v.i,* faire ses excuses. **apology,** *n,* apologie, *f;* excuses, *f.pl;* semblant, *m.*

apoplectic, *a. & n,* apoplectique, *a. & m.* ~ *fit,* attaque d'apoplexie, *f,* coup de sang, *m.* **apoplexy,** *n,* apoplexie, *f.*

apostasy, *n,* apostasie, *f.* **apostate,** *n. & a,* apostat, *m. & att,* relaps, e.

apostle, *n,* apôtre, *m. the* [*A~s'*] *Creed,* le symbole [des apôtres]. **apostolate, apostleship,** *n,* apostolat, *m.* **apostolic**(al†), *a,* apostolique.

apostrophe, *n,* apostrophe, *f.* **apostrophize,** *v.t,* apostropher.

apothecaries' measure, mesure pharmaceutique, *f.*

apotheosis, *n,* apothéose, *f.*

appall, *v.t,* épouvanter. **appalling,** *a,* épouvantable.

apparatus, *n,* appareil, attirail, *m.*

apparel, *n,* habillement, *m,* vêtements, *m.pl.*

apparent, *a,* apparent; (*heir*) présomptif. **~ly,** *ad,* apparemment.

apparition, *n,* apparition, *f.*

appeal, *n,* appel; pourvoi; recours; attrait, *m.* ¶ *v.i,* en appeler; faire appel; appeler.

appear, *v.i,* paraître, sembler; apparaître; figurer, ressortir; comparaître. **~ance,** *n,* apparition; apparence, venue, *f,* semblant, aspect, *m;* mine; comparution, *f;* (*pl.*) apparences, *f.pl,* dehors, *m.pl.*

appease, *v.t,* apaiser, adoucir; pacifier. **~ment,** *n,* apaisement, *m,* conciliation, *f.*

appellation, *n,* surnom, *m;* désignation, *f.*

append, *v.t,* apposer. **~age,** appendix, *n,* appendice, *m.* **appendicitis,** *n,* appendicite, *f.*

appertain, *v.i,* appartenir.

appetite, *n,* appétit, *m.* **appetizer,** *n,* apéritif, *m.* **appetizing,** *a,* appétissant.

applaud, *v.t,* applaudir [à]. **applause,** *n,* applaudissement[s] *m.* [*pl.*].

apple, *n,* pomme; (*eye*) prunelle, *f.* **~ corer,** vide-pomme, *m.* **~ orchard,** pommeraie, *f.* **~ pie,** tourte aux pommes, *f.* **~ tree,** pommier, *m.*

appliance, *n,* engin, appareil; (*pl.*) attirail, *m.*

applicant, *n,* demandeur, euse; postulant, e; souscripteur, *m.* **application,** *n,* application; contention; affectation; demande, réclamation; souscription; mise en œuvre, *f;* (*brake*) serrage, *m.* **on ~,** sur demande. **applied** (*of sciences*) *a,* appliqué. **appliqué lace,** [dentelle d']application, *f.* **appliqué [work]** (*metal*), applique, *f.* **appliqué** (*or applied*) **work** (*Emb.*), broderie-application, *f.* **apply,** *v.t,* appliquer; affecter; (*brake*) serrer. **~ for,** solliciter, postuler, demander, réclamer; souscrire. **~ to,** s'adresser à.

appoint, *v.t,* nommer, instituer, constituer, désigner, préposer. **~ment,** *n,* nomination, désignation, constitution, *f;* rendezvous; (*pl.*) aménagement, emménagement, *m.*

apportion, *v.t,* répartir, ventiler.

apposite, *a,* à propos, pertinent.

apposition, *n,* apposition, *f.*

appraise, *v.t,* priser. **~ment,** *n,* prisée, *f.* **appraiser,** *n,* priseur, *m.*

appreciable, *a,* appréciable, sensible. **appreciably,** *ad,* sensiblement. **appreciate,** *v.t,* apprécier; améliorer; (*v.i.*) s'améliorer. **appreciation,** *n,* appréciation; amélioration, plus-value, *f.*

apprehend, *v.t,* appréhender; redouter; saisir. **apprehension,** *n,* appréhension, *f.* **apprehensive,** *a,* inquiet.

apprentice, *n,* apprenti, e; (*Naut.*) novice, *m.* ¶ *v.t,* mettre en apprentissage. **~ship,** *n,* apprentissage; noviciat, *m.*

apprise, *v.t,* prévenir, informer.

approach, *n,* approche, *f;* accès, abord, *m.* ¶ *v.t,* [s']approcher de, aborder; (*v.i.*) [s']approcher. **~able,** *a,* abordable, accessible.

approbation, *n,* approbation, *f.*

appropriate†, *a,* propre, convenable, approprié. ¶ *v.t,* s'approprier; consacrer, distraire, affecter. **appropriation,** *n,* somme affectée, destination, *f.*

approval, *n,* approbation, *f,* agrément, *m,* sanction, *f.* **on ~,** à condition. **approve,** *v.t,* approuver, agréer, sanctionner.

approximate†, *a,* approximatif. ¶ *v.t,* rapprocher, approcher. **approximation,** *n,* approximation, *f.*

apricot, *n,* abricot, *m.* **~ tree,** abricotier, *m.*

April, *n,* avril, *m.* **to make an ~ fool of,** donner un poisson d'avril à.

apron, *n,* tablier, *m.*

apropos, *ad,* à propos.

apse, *n,* abside, *f.*

apt, *a,* enclin, sujet, disposé, porté; à propos; apte. **~ly,** *ad,* à propos. **~ness,** *n,* àpropos, *m.* **aptitude,** *n,* aptitude, facilité, *f,* dispositions, *f.pl.*

aqua-fortis, *n,* eau-forte, *f.* **aquamarine,** *n,* aigue-marine, *f.* **aquaregis,** eau régale, *f.*

aquarium, *n,* aquarium, *m.*

aquatic, *a,* (*plant*) aquatique; (*sport*) nautique.

aqueduct, *n,* aqueduc, *m.*

aqueous, *a,* aqueux.

aquiline, *a,* aquilin.

Arab, *a,* arabe. ¶ *n,* Arabe, *m,f.* **arabesque,** *n,* arabesque, *f.* **Arabia,** *n,* l'Arabie, *f.* **Arabian,** *a,* arabe. *the ~ Nights*, les Mille & une Nuits. ¶ *n*, Arabe, *m,f.* **Arabic** (*language*) *n*, l'arabe, *m.* **Arabic numerals**, chiffres arabes, *m.pl.*

arable, *a*, arable, labourable.

arbiter, *n*, arbitre, *m.* **arbitrage** & **arbitrament**, *n*, arbitrage, *m.* **arbitrary†**, *a*, arbitraire; conventionnel; d'office. **arbitrate**, *v.t*, arbitrer. **arbitration**, *n*, arbitrage, *m.* ~ *clause*, clause compromissoire, *f.* **arbitrator**, *n*, arbitre; (*law*) amiable compositeur, *m.*

arbor, *n*, arbre, mandrin, *m*, broche, *f.*

arbor, *n*, tonnelle, *f*, verger, *m.*

arc, *n*, arc, *m.* ~ *lamp*, lampe à arc, *f.*

arcade, *n*, arcades, *f.pl*, galerie, *f*, passage, bazar, *m.*

arch, *a*, espiègle, malicieux. ¶ *n*, voûte, *f*, arceau, *m*, arcade, arche; porte, *f*; arc, cintre, *m.* ~ *support* (for foot in shoe), cambrure-support, *f.* ¶ *v.t*, cintrer, arquer, cambrer, voûter.

archaeologic(al), *a*, archéologique. **archaeologist**, *n*, archéologue, *m.* **archaeology**, *n*, archéologie, *f.*

archaic, *a*, archaïque, vieux, vieilli.

archangel, *n*, archange, *m.*

archbishop, *n*, archevêque, *m.* **archbishopric**, *n*, archevêché, *m.*

archdeacon, *n*, archidiacre, *m.*

archer, *n*, archer, *m.* ~**y**, *n*, tir à l'arc, *m.*

Archimedean screw, vis d'Archimède, limace, *f.*

archipelago, *n*, archipel, *m.*

architect, *n*, architecte; (*fig.*) artisan, *m.* **architectural**, *a*, architectural. **architecture**, *n*, architecture, *f.*

archives, *n.pl*, archives, *f.pl.*

archly, *ad*, malicieusement. **archness**, *n*, espièglerie, *f.*

archway, *n*, arcade, *f*, passage voûté; portail, *m.*

arctic, *a*, arctique. *the A~ Ocean*, l'océan Glacial arctique, *m.*

ardent, *a*, ardent. ~**ly**, *ad*, ardemment. **ardor**, *n*, ardeur, *f*, zèle, *m.*

arduous, *a*, ardu, pénible, laborieux.

are *see* be.

area, *n*, aire, superficie, surface; zone, étendue, *f*; réseau, *m.*

arena, *n*, arène, *f.*

argentine, *a*, argentin. **A~** (*Geog.*) *a*, argentin. ¶ *n* (*pers.*), Argentin, e. *the ~*, l'Argentine, *f.*

argue, *v.i. & t*, argumenter, raisonner, discuter, débattre, prétendre, plaider. **argument**, *n*, argument, raisonnement, *m*, thèse, *f.* ~**ation**, **arguing**, *n*, argumentation, *f.* ~**ative**, *a*, raisonneur.

aria (*Mus.*) *n*, air, *m.*

arid, *a*, aride. ~**ity**, *n*, aridité, *f.*

aright, *ad*, bien, justement.

arise, *v.i.ir*, s'élever, surgir, naître, survenir.

aristocracy, *n*, aristocratie, *f.* **aristocrat**, *n*, aristocrate, *m,f.* **aristocratic(al†)**, *a*, aristocratique.

arithmetic, *n*, arithmétique, *f*, calcul, *m.* ~**al†**, *a*, arithmétique. ~**ian**, *n*, arithméticien, ne.

ark, *n*, arche, *f.* *the A~ of the Covenant*, l'arche d'alliance, *f.*

arm, *n*, (*limb*) bras; (*of cross*) croisillon, *m*; (*weapon*) arme, *f*; (*pl., Her.*) armes, armoiries, *f.pl*, blason, *m*; (*rest*) bras, accotoir, accoudoir, *m.* ~ *in* ~, bras dessus, bras dessous. *to be up in* ~*s*, se gendarmer. ~*chair*, fauteuil, *m.* ~*hole*, emmanchure, *f.* ~*pit*, aisselle, *f.* ¶ *v.t*, armer; (*v.i.*) [s']armer.

armadillo, *n*, tatou, *m.*

armament, *n*, armement, *m.*

armature, *n*, (*Phys.*) armature, armure, *f*; (*dynamo*) induit, *m.*

Armenia, *n*, l'Arménie, *f.* **Armenian**, *a*, arménien. ¶ *n*, Arménien, ne.

armful, *n*, brassée, *f.*

armistice, *n*, armistice, *m.* *A~ Day*, la fête [de l'anniversaire] de l'Armistice, le jour anniversaire de l'Armistice.

armlet, *n*, brassard, *m.*

armor, *n*, armure; (*sheathing*) armature, cuirasse, *f.* ~ *plate*, plaque de blindage, *f.* ~ *plating*, blindage, *m.* ~**ed**, *a*, armé; blindé, cuirassé, protégé. ~ *car*, automobile blindée, *f.* ~**er**, *n*, armurier, *m.* ~**y**, *n*, salle d'armes, *f.* **armorial**, *a. & n*, armorial, *a. & m.* ~ *bearings*, armoiries, armes, *f.pl*, blason, *m.*

army, *n*, armée, *f.* ~ *contractor*, fournisseur de l'armée, *m.*

arnica, *n*, arnica, *m.*

aroma, *n*, arôme; bouquet, *m.* **aromatic**, *a*, aromatique.

around, *ad,* autour, alentour. ¶ *pr,* autour de.

arouse, *v.t,* réveiller; provoquer.

arpeggio, *n,* arpège, *m.*

arraign, *v.t,* accuser; traduire en justice. **~ment,** *n,* mise en accusation, *f.*

arrange, *v.t,* arranger, disposer, agencer, ménager; distribuer; accommoder; débattre, arbitrer. **~ment,** *n,* arrangement, *m,* disposition, *f,* agencement, mouvement, *m;* économie; distribution, *f;* accommodement; dispositif, *m.*

arrant, *a,* franc, insigne, fieffé, achevé, fier.

arras, *n,* tapisserie, *f.*

array, *n,* ordre; appareil, *m;* série, rangée, *f.* ¶ *v.t,* ranger; ajuster; revêtir.

arrears, *n.pl,* arrérages, *m. in arrear[s],* en arrière, arriéré en retard, retardataire; en demeure.

arrest, *n,* arrestation, prise de corps, *f;* arrêt, *m. under ~,* (*civil*) en état d'arrestation; (*Mil.*) aux arrêts. ¶ *v.t,* arrêter; appréhender. **~er** (*Elec., etc.*) *n,* déchargeur, *m.*

arrival, *n,* arrivée, *f;* arrivage, *m.*

arrive, *v.i,* arriver; parvenir. **~** *unexpectedly,* survenir.

arrogance, *n,* arrogance, *f.* **arrogant,** *a,* arrogant, rogue. **~ly,** *ad,* arrogamment. **to arrogate** [**to oneself**], s'arroger.

arrow, *n,* flèche, *f,* trait, *m.*

arsenal, *n,* arsenal, *m.*

arsenic, *n,* arsenic, *m.* **~al,** *a,* arsenical.

arson, *n,* incendie volontaire, *m.*

art, *n,* art; artifice, *m.* **~** *school,* école des beaux-arts, *f.*

arterial (*Anat.*) *a,* artériel. **~** *road* (*Eng.*), route nationale de grand itinéraire, *f.* (= in Fr. *a widened main road*). **artery,** *n,* artère, *f.*

artesian, *a,* artésien. **~** *well,* puits artésien, *m.*

artful†, *a,* artificieux, astucieux, rusé. **~** *dodger,* fin matois, finaud, *m.* **~ness,** *n,* artifice, art, *m,* astuce, finauderie, finasserie, ruse, malice, *f.*

arthritis, *n,* arthrite, *f.*

artichoke, *n,* artichaut, *m. Jerusalem ~,* topinambour, *m.*

article, *n,* article, objet, envoi; (*pl.*) stage, apprentissage; (*pl.*) contrat; (*pl.—ship's*) rôle d'équi-

page, rôle d'armement, *m.* **~s** [*of association*], statuts, *m.pl.*

articulate, *v.t,* articuler; (*v.i.*) [s']articuler. **articulation,** *n,* articulation, *f.*

artifice, *n,* artifice, art, *m.*

artificer, *n,* [mécanicien] adjusteur, serrurier mécanicien; (*fig.*) artisan, *m.*

artificial†, *a,* artificiel, factice, simili-, postiche.

artillery, *n,* artillerie, *f.* **~man,** *n,* artilleur, *m.*

artisan, *n,* artisan, e.

artist, & **artiste,** *n,* artiste, *m,f.* **artistic,** *a,* artistique; artiste. **~** *novelties,* articles de Paris, *m.pl.* **~ally,** *ad,* artistiquement, avec art.

artless†, *a,* sans art, naturel; innocent; naïf, ingénu.

Aryan, *a,* aryen.

as, *ad. & c,* comme; ainsi que; de même que; parce que; puisque, aussi; que; à titre de; pour. **~** *also,* ainsi que. **~** [& *when*] *required,* au fur & à mesure que. **~** [& *when*] *required,* au fur & à mesure des besoins. **~** *before,* comme par le passé. **~** *for,* **~** *to,* **~** *regards,* quant à. **~** *if,* comme si. **~** *in* (like, equal to), à l'instar de. **~** *it were,* en quelque sorte. **~** *per,* suivant, dont. **~** *well ~,* aussi bien que, en même temps que. **~** *you were!* au temps!

asbestos, *n,* asbeste, *m.*

ascend, *v.t. & i,* [re]monter, faire l'ascension de. **~ancy,** **~ency,** & **~ant,** **~ent,** *n,* ascendant, *m.* **ascension,** *n,* ascension, *f. A~ Day,* l'Ascension. **ascent,** *n,* ascension; montée, *f.*

ascertain, *v.t,* constater, reconnaître, se rendre compte de.

ascetic, *a,* ascétique. ¶ *n,* ascète, *m,f.*

ascribe, *v.t,* attribuer, imputer, rapporter.

ash, *n. oft. pl,* cendre, *f. oft. pl.* **~** *blonde* (color), blond cendré, *m.* **~** *pit,* fosse aux cendres, *f.* **~tray,** cendrier [de fumeur] *m.* **~** [*tree*], frêne, *m. A~ Wednesday,* le mercredi (*ou* le jour) des Cendres.

ashamed, *a* honteux. *to be ~,* avoir honte, rougir.

ashen, **ashy** (*ash-colored*), *a,* cendré.

ashlar, *n,* moellon d'appareil, *m.*

ashore, *ad,* à terre.

Asia, *n,* l'Asie, *f.* **~** *Minor,* l'Asie

Mineure. **Asiatic,** *a,* asiatique.
¶ *n,* Asiatique, *m,f.*

aside, *ad,* de côté; à part; à l'écart; en aparté. ¶ *n,* aparté, *m.*

ask, *v.t,* demander, prier, inviter, interroger, solliciter; poser; s'enquérir. ~ *not to come* (guests), désinviter, décommander.

askance, *ad,* de travers, de biais.

askew, *ad,* en biais, de travers, de guingois.

aslant, *ad,* en biais, obliquement.

asleep, *a,* endormi. *to fall* ~, s'endormir.

asp, *n,* (*serpent*) aspic; (*tree*) tremble, *m.*

asparagus, *n,* asperge, *f;* asperges, *f.pl.* ~ *tongs,* pince à asperges, *f.*

aspect, *n,* aspect, *m;* face, *f,* visage, *m;* exposition, orientation, *f.*

aspen, *n,* tremble, *m.* ~ *plantation,* tremblaie, *f.*

asperity, *n,* aspérité, âpreté, *f.*

asperse, *v.t,* asperger; diffamer, calomnier, noircir. **aspersion,** *n,* aspersion; diffamation, calomnie, *f.*

asphalt, *n,* asphalte, bitume, *m.* ¶ *v.t,* bitumer.

asphyxia, *n,* asphyxie, *f.* **asphyxiate,** *v.t,* asphyxier.

aspirant, *n,* aspirant, e. **aspirate,** *v.t,* aspirer. **aspiration,** *n,* aspiration, *f.* **to aspire to,** aspirer à, prétendre à, affecter, ambitionner, briguer.

aspirin, *n,* aspirine, *f.*

ass, *n,* âne, *m,* (*she*) ânesse, *f. ass's foal,* ânon, *m. ass's* (or *asses'*) *milk,* lait d'ânesse, *m.*

assail, *v.t,* assaillir. ~**ant,** *n,* assaillant, *m.*

assassin, *n,* assassin, e. ~**ate,** *v.t,* assassiner. ~**ation,** *n,* assassinat, *m.*

assault, *n,* assaut; attentat, *m,* (*law*) agression, *f.* ~ [*& battery*], voies de fait, *f.pl.* ¶ *v.t,* assaillir, attaquer.

assay, *n,* essai, *m.* ~ *office* (government), bureau de garantie, *m.* ¶ *v.t,* essayer; (*v.i.*) titrer. ~**er,** *n,* essayeur, *m.*

assemblage, *n,* assemblage, *m.*

assemble, *v.t,* [r]assembler, réunir. **assembly,** *n,* assemblée, réunion, *f.*

assent, *n,* assentiment; consentement, *m,* sanction, *f.* **to** ~ **to,** donner son assentiment à.

assert, *v.t,* soutenir; affirmer; pré-

tendre; revendiquer. **assertion,** *n,* assertion, *f;* dire, *m.*

assess, *v.t,* coter, imposer. évaluer, taxer. ~**ment,** *n,* cote, cotisation, imposition, répartition, taxation, *f.*

asset, *n,* valeur [active] *f;* (*pl.*) actif, *m,* capitaux, *m.pl.* ~*s nil,* carence, *f.* ~*s transferred* or *taken over,* apport[s] *m.[pl.].*

assiduity, *n,* assiduité, *f.* **assiduous,** *a,* assidu. ~**ly,** *ad,* assidûment.

assign, *v.t,* assigner; céder; apporter; affecter, destiner. ~**ation,** *n,* assignation, *f.* ~**ment,** *n,* assignation; cession, *f;* apport, *m;* (*Sch.*) devoir, *m.*

assimilate, *v.t,* assimiler.

assist, *v.t,* assister, aider, secourir. ~**ance,** *n,* assistance, aide, *f,* secours; concours, *m;* (*to police*) main-forte, *f.* ~**ant,** *n,* aide, *m,f,* adjoint, e, assistant, auxiliaire, *m.*

assize, *n,* **assizes,** *n.pl,* assises, *f. pl.*

associate, *n,* associé, e. ¶ *v.t,* associer, adjoindre; (*v.i.*) s'associer, frayer. **association,** *n,* association, société, *f;* syndicat, *m;* caisse, *f.*

assort, *v.t,* assortir. ~**ment,** *n,* assortiment, classement, *m.*

assuage, *v.t,* apaiser, adoucir.

assume, *v.t,* prendre, affecter, revêtir; assumer; s'arroger; supposer; (*name*) emprunter. **assuming,** *a,* prétentieux, arrogant.

assumption, *n,* supposition; arrogance, *f.* **A**~ (*Eccl.*) *n,* assomption, *f.*

assurance, *n,* assurance, *f.* **assure,** *v.t,* assurer. **assuredly,** *ad,* assurément, à coup sûr.

Assyria, *n,* l'Assyrie, *f.* **Assyrian,** *a,* assyrien, *f.* ¶ *n,* Assyrien, ne.

aster, *n,* aster, *m.*

asterisk, *n,* astérisque, *m,* étoile, *f.*

astern, *ad,* derrière, en arrière, à (*ou* sur) l'arrière.

asteroid, *n,* astéroïde, *m.*

asthma, *n,* asthme, *m.* **asthmatic,** *a,* asthmatique.

astigmatic, *a,* astigmate.

astir, *ad. & a,* en mouvement, en branle-bas; agité, en émoi.

astonish, *v.t,* étonner, émerveiller, surprendre. ~**ingly,** *ad,* étonnamment. ~**ment,** *n,* étonnement, *m,* surprise, *f.*

astound, *v.t,* ébahir.

astray, *ad. & a,* hors du [bon] chemin; égaré. *to go ~,* s'égarer.

astride, astraddle, *ad. & a,* à califourchon, à cheval, affourché, jambe deçà, jambe delà.

astringent, *a. & n,* astringent, *a. & m.*

astrologer, *n,* astrologue, *m.* **astrology,** *n,* astrologie, *f.*

astronomer, *n,* astronome, *m.* **astronomic**(al†), *a,* astronomique. **astronomy,** *n,* astronomie, *f.*

astute, *a,* fin, rusé; astucieux.

asunder, *ad,* en deux; éloigné l'un de l'autre.

asylum, *n,* asile, hospice, *m.*

at, *pr,* à; en; dans; de; par; contre; chez; moyennant. *~ a loss, profit,* à perte, profit. *~ all,* du tout. *~ first,* d'abord. *~ hand,* à portée [de la main]. *~ home,* chez soi, chez moi, chez lui, chez nous, chez vous, etc; à la maison; au logis; visible; en famille; à son aise. *~ last, ~ length,* enfin. *~ least,* au moins. *~ once,* tout de suite; à la fois, incessamment. *~ sea,* en mer. *~ the same time,* en même temps. *~ war,* en guerre.

Athanasian Creed (**the**), le symbole attribué à saint Athanase.

atheism, *n,* athéisme, *m.* **atheist,** *n,* athée, *m.* **atheistic,** *a,* athée.

Athenian, *a,* athénien. ¶ *n,* Athénien, ne. **Athens,** *n,* Athènes, *f.*

athirst, *ad,* altéré; avide.

athlete, *n,* athlète, *m.* **athletic,** *a,* athlétique. **athletics,** *n.pl,* athlétisme, *m.*

at-home, *n,* réception, *f.* her *~ day,* son jour [de réception].

athwart, *ad,* en travers. ¶ *pr,* en travers de.

Atlantic, *a,* atlantique. *~ liner,* [paquebot] transatlantique, *m.* the *A~* [*Ocean*], l'[océan] Atlantique, *m.*

atlas, *n,* atlas, *m.*

atmosphere, *n,* atmosphère, *f.* **atmospheric**(al), *a,* atmosphérique.

atoll, *n,* atoll, *m.*

atom, *n,* atome, *m*; miette, *f.* **~ic**(al), *a,* atomique. **~izer,** *n,* vaporisateur, *m.*

atone for (**to**), expier, racheter. **atonement,** *n,* expiation, réparation, satisfaction, *f.*

atrocious†, *a,* atroce. **atrocity,** *n,* atrocité, *f.*

atrophy, *n,* atrophie, *f.* ¶ *v.i,* atrophier.

attach, *v.t,* attacher; atteler; annexer, joindre; (*law*) saisir. **attaché,** *n,* attaché, *m.* *~ case,* mallette, *f.* **attachment,** *n,* attachement, *m*, inclination; attache, *f*; attelage; appareil, *m*; (*law*) saisie, *f.*

attack, *n,* attaque, *f*; accès, *m*, crise, *f.* ¶ *v.t,* attaquer, s'attaquer à.

attain, *v.t,* atteindre, parvenir à. **~der,** *n,* condamnation, *f.* **~ment,** *n,* atteinte, *f*; (*pl.*) acquis, *m.s. & pl,* connaissances, *f.pl.*

attar, *n,* essence de roses, *f.*

attempt, *n,* tentative, *f*, essai, coup, jet; (*criminal*) attentat, *m.* *to make an ~ on,* attenter à. *~ed murder,* tentative d'assassinat, *f.* *~ed suicide,* faux suicide, *m.*

attend, *v.t,* accompagner; assister à, suivre; soigner; visiter. *~ to,* faire attention à, écouter; s'occuper de; soigner, servir. **~ance,** *n,* présence; assistance; visite, *f*; service, *m.* **~ant,** *n,* suivant, e; (*pl.*) suite, *f*; gardien, *m*; (*Theat.*) receveuse; (*Theat. box*) ouvreuse, *f.* **attention,** *n,* attention, *f*; soin; regard, *m*; prévenance, *f.* *to pay ~,* faire attention. **~!** (*Mil.*) garde-à-vous! **attentive†,** *a,* attentif, empressé; prévenant.

attenuate, *v.t,* atténuer.

attest, *v.t,* attester, constater. **~ation,** *n,* attestation, constatation, *f.*

Attic, *a,* attique.

attic, *n,* mansarde, *f*, grenier, *m.*

attire, *n,* vêtement, costume, *m*; parure, *f.* ¶ *v.t,* vêtir; parer.

attitude, *n,* attitude, posture, pose, *f.*

attorney, *n,* avoué, *m*, mandataire, *m,f*; procureur, *m.*

attract, *v.t,* attirer; solliciter. **attraction,** *n,* attraction; attirance, *f*; (*pl.*) attraits, appas, charmes, *m.pl.* **attractive,** *a,* attrayant, attirant; (*Phys.*) attractif.

attributable, *a,* attribuable. **attribute,** *n,* attribut, emblème, *m.* ¶ *v.t,* attribuer; prêter. **attribution,** *n,* attribution, *f.* **attributive adjective,** adjectif épithète, *m.* **attributively** (*Gram.*) *ad,* adjectivement; en apposition.

attrition, *n,* attrition; usure, *f.*

attune, *v.t,* accorder, harmoniser.

auburn hair, cheveux blond ardent, *m.pl.*

auction, *n,* enchère[s] *f.[pl.].* ~ *bridge,* bridge aux enchères, *m.* ~ *mart,* ~ *rooms,* hôtel des ventes, *m.* ¶ *v.t,* vendre aux enchères. **~eer,** *n,* commissaire priseur, *m.*

audacious†, *a,* audacieux. **audacity,** *n,* audace, *f.*

audible, *a,* perceptible à l'ouïe, intelligible.

audience, *n,* (*hearing*) audience; (*pers.*) assistance, *f;* spectateurs, *m.pl.*

audit, *v.t.* vérifier. **~[ing],** *n,* vérification [comptable] *f.* **audition,** *n,* audition, *f.* **auditor,** *n,* vérificateur comptable, censeur; auditeur, *m.* **auditorium,** *n,* salle, *f.*

auger, *n,* tarière, *f,* laceret, *m.*

aught, *n,* quelque chose, rien, *m.*

augment, *v.t,* augmenter.

augur, *n,* augure, *m.* ¶ *v.t,* augurer. **~y,** *n,* augure, présage, *m.*

august, *a,* auguste. **A~,** *n,* août, *m.*

auk, *n,* pingouin, *m.*

aunt, *n,* tante, *f.*

aureole, *n,* auréole, *f.*

auricle (*heart*) *n,* oreillette, *f.* **auricula,** *n,* oreille-d'ours, *f.* **auricular,** *a,* auriculaire.

auriferous, *a,* aurifère.

aurora, *n,* aurore, *f.* ~ *borealis,* a. boréale.

auspice, *n,* (*usually pl.*) auspice, *m. under the* ~*s of,* sous les auspices de. **auspicious,** *a,* propice, favorable, de bon augure.

austere†, *a,* austère, sévère. **austerity,** *n,* austérité, *f.*

austral, *a,* austral. **Australasia,** *n,* l'Australasie, *f.* **Australia,** *n,* l'Australie, *f.* **Australian,** *a,* australien. ¶ *n,* Australien, ne.

Austria, *n,* l'Autriche, *f.* **Austrian,** *a,* autrichien. ¶ *n,* Autrichien, ne.

authentic, *a,* authentique. **~ity,** *n,* authenticité, *f.*

author, *n,* (*lit. & fig.*) auteur; (*fig. only*) artisan, inventeur, *m.* **authoritative,** *a,* autoritaire; d'autorité. **~ly,** *ad,* avec autorité, en maître. **authority,** *n,* autorité, puissance; source, *f. to be regarded as an* ~, faire autorité. *the authorities,* les autorités, *f.pl,* l'administration, *f.*

authorization, *n,* autorisation, *f.* **authorize,** *v.t,* autoriser, mandater.

authorship, *n,* métier d'auteur, *m;* paternité, *f.*

autobiography, *n,* autobiographie, *f.*

autocracy, *n,* autocratie, *f.* **autocrat,** *n,* autocrate, trice. **autocratic(al),** *a,* autocratique.

autogenous, *a,* autogène.

autograph, *n. & a,* autographe, *m. & a.* ~ *book,* livre de signatures, *m.*

auto, automobile, *n,* auto, automobile, *f.*

automatic(al)†, *a,* automatique. **automaton,** *n,* automate, *m.*

autonomous, *a,* autonome. **autonomy,** *n,* autonomie, *f.*

autopsy, *n,* autopsie, *f.*

autumn, *n,* automne, *f.* **~al,** *a,* automnal.

auxiliary, *a. & n,* auxiliaire, *a. & m.*

avail, *n,* effet, *m.* **to** ~ **oneself of,** profiter de. *to* ~ *oneself of the services of,* jouir de. **~able,** *a,* disponible; libre.

avalanche, *n,* avalanche, *f.*

avarice, *n,* avarice, *f.* **avaricious†,** *a,* avare, avaricieux.

avenge, *v.t,* venger, punir. **avenger,** *n,* vengeur, eresse. **avenging,** *a,* vengeur.

avenue, *n,* avenue, *f,* boulevard, cours, *m.*

aver, *v.t,* soutenir, affirmer.

average, *a,* moyen; commun. ¶ *n,* moyenne, *f;* (*marine law*) avarie[s] *f.[pl.].* ¶ *v.t,* établir la moyenne de.

averse to, ennemi de. *I am* ~, il me répugne de. **aversion,** *n,* aversion, répugnance, *f,* dégoût, *m.*

avert, *v.t,* détourner; écarter.

aviary, *n,* volière, oisellerie, *f.*

aviation, *n,* aviation, *f.* **aviator,** *n,* aviateur, trice.

avid†, *a,* avide. **~ity,** *n,* avidité, *f.*

avocations, *n.pl,* occupations, *f.pl,* travaux, *m.pl.*

avoid, *v.t,* éviter, se soustraire à, fuir. **~able,** *a,* évitable.

avow, *v.t,* avouer, s'accuser de. **~al,** *n,* aveu, *m.*

await, *v.t,* attendre.

awake, *a,* réveillé; vigilant. ¶ *v.t.ir,* réveiller; (*v.i.*) se réveiller. **awaken,** *v.t,* réveiller. **~ing,** *n,* [r]éveil, *m.*

award, *n,* décision, sentence; (*at a show*) nomination, *f.* ¶ *v.t,* décerner; adjuger. ~ *a medal to,* médailler. ~ *a prize to,* couronner; primer. ~ *the contract for*, adjuger.

aware, *a*: *to be ~ of*, savoir, connaître, ne pas ignorer. *not to be ~ of*, ignorer.

away, *ad*, d'ici; de là. ~ [*from home*], absent. *right ~*, tout de suite. *to go ~*, s'en aller. *to keep ~*, se tenir à l'écart. ~ *with you!* allez-vous-en!

awe, *n*, crainte, *f*. ~*struck*, saisi de crainte. ¶ *v.t*, imposer à.

awful†, *a*, effroyable, terrible; redoutable; solennel.

awhile, *ad*, un instant, un peu.

awkward, *a*, incommode, embarrassant, malaisé; gauche, maladroit, emprunté. *the ~ age*, l'âge ingrat, *m*. ~ *incident*, contretemps, *m*.

awl, *n*, alène, *f*, poinçon, *m*.

awn, *n*, barbe, arête, *f*.

awning, *n*, tente, banne, *f*, tendelet, *m*. ~ *deck*, pont abri, *m*.

awry, *ad. & a*, de travers, de guingois.

axe, *n*, hache, cognée, *f*.

axiom, *n*, axiome, *m*.

axis, *n*, axe, *m*.

axle, *n*, arbre, essieu, *m*. **axletree,** *n*, essieu, *m*.

ay, *i. & n*, oui, *particle & m*.

azalea, *n*, azalée, *f*.

Azores (the), les Açores, *f.pl*.

azure, *a*, azur. ¶ *n*, azur, *m*.

B

B (*Mus.*) *letter*, si, *m*.

baa, *v.i*, bêler. baa[ing], *n*, bêlement, *m*.

babble, *n*, babil, *m*. ¶ *v.i*, babiller; (*stream*) gazouiller; (*of hound*) clabauder.

babel (*fig.*) *n*, tour de Babel, *f*.

baboon, *n*, babouin, *m*.

baby, *n*, bébé, enfant, petit, *m*. ~ *carriage*, landau [pour enfant] *m*. ~ *face*, physionomie pouparde, *f*. ~ *grand*, piano à demi-queue, crapaud, *m*. ~*sitter*, gardienne d'enfant, *f*. ~*hood*, *n*, première enfance, *f*. ~*ish*, *a*, enfantin.

Babylonian, *a*, babylonien.

Bacchanalia, *n.pl*, bacchanales, *f.pl*. **Bacchic**, *a*, bachique.

bachelor, *n*, célibataire, garçon, *m*; (*science, etc.*) bachelier, ère, licencié, e. ~ *flat*, garçonnière, *f*. ~ *girl*, garçonne, *f*.

back, *ad*, en arrière; en retour.

Note:—After a verb **back** *is sometimes expressed by re- as*, *to come back*, revenir. ¶ *n*, dos; derrière; arrière; revers; envers; dossier; fond; verso; dessus, *m*; reins, *m.pl*; (*book*) dos, *m*. ~ *to front*, sens devant derrière. *to ~ up*, faire marche arrière. *with one's ~ to the light*, à contrejour. ¶ *v.t*, [faire] reculer; adosser; épauler; appuyer, soutenir, seconder; (*betting*) parier sur, jouer; (*v.i.*) reculer; (*of wind*) redescendre.

backache, *n*, mal de reins, *m*.

backbite, *v.i*, clabauder. **backbiting,** *n*, médisance, *f*, cancans, *m.pl*.

backbone, *n*, épine dorsale, échine; énergie, *f*.

back door, porte de derrière, p. de service, *f*.

backer, *n*, partisan; (*betting*) parieur, *m*.

backfire, retour de flamme, *m*. *backfire* [*kick*], retour de manivelle, *m*.

backgammon, *n. & ~ board*, trictrac, *m*.

background, *n*, arrière-plan, fond, enfoncement, second plan, *m*; pénombre, *f*.

backhand, *n*, arrière-main, revers, *m*.

back number (*news*), vieux numéro, *m*.

back-pedal, *v.i*, contre-pédaler.

backsight (*gun*) *n*, hausse, *f*.

backslider, *n*, relaps, e. **backsliding,** *n*, rechute, *f*.

backstay (*Naut.*) *n*, galhauban, *m*.

backstitch, *n*, point arrière, arrière-point, *m*.

back tooth, dent du fond, *f*.

backward, *a*, peu avancé, tardif; rétrograde; (*child*) arriéré. ¶ ~, ~*s*, *ad*, en arrière; à reculons; à la renverse; à rebours. ~*ness*, *n*, tardiveté; répugnance, *f*.

backwash, *n*, remous, *m*.

backwater (to), scier, ramer à rebours. ¶ *n*, eau arrêtée, *f*, ressac, *m*.

bacon, *n*, lard, *m*.

bacteria, *n.pl*, bactéries, *f.pl*.

bad, *a*, mauvais; mal, malade; grave; fort; irrégulier; véreux. *to go ~* (*meat*), s'avarier. ~ *language*, gros mots, *m.pl*. ~ *time* [*of it*], mauvais quart d'heure, *m*. *in a ~ way*, mal-enpoint, malade. ~ *workmanship*, malfaçon, *f. too ~!* tant pis! ¶ *n,* mauvais, *m. from ~ to worse,* de mal en pis. *to the ~* (out of pocket), en perte.

badge, *n,* insigne, marque; plaque, médaille, *f*; brassard; symbole, *m*; livrée, *f*.

badger, *n,* blaireau, *m.* ¶ *v.t,* harceler, relancer.

badly, *ad,* mal; gravement.

badminton, *n,* badminton, volant au filet, *m*.

badness, *n,* mauvais état, *m*; méchanceté, *f*.

baffle, *v.t,* déjouer, déconcerter, frustrer; défier, échapper à. ~ **[plate]** *n,* chicane, *f*.

bag, *n,* sac, *m*; bourse; valise, *f*; (*of game*) tableau, *m.* ~ *snatcher,* voleur à la tire, *m.* ¶ *v.t,* ensacher; empocher, chiper; (*v.i, trousers*) goder. ~**ful,** *n,* sachée, *f*.

bagatelle, *n,* (*trifle*) bagatelle, *f*. ~ (*game*) ~ *board,* billard japonais, *m*.

baggage, *n,* bagage; attirail, *m*. ~ *car,* fourgon, *m*.

baggy, *a,* avachi, flottant.

bagpipe[s], *n,* cornemuse, *f*.

bail, *n,* caution, *f,* cautionnement, *m. bail*[*sman*], *n,* caution, *f,* répondant, *e.* ¶ *v.t,* cautionner. ~ **[out]** (*boat*) *v.t,* écoper, vider. ~**er,** *n,* écope, épuisette, *f*.

bailiff, *n,* huissier; intendant, régisseur, *m*.

bait, *n,* amorce, *f,* appât; hameçon (*fig.*) *m.* ¶ *v.t,* amorcer, appâter; (*pers.*) harceler, pointiller, persécuter.

baize, *n,* bayette, *f,* tapis, drap, *m.* ~ *door,* porte matelassée, *f*.

bake, *v.t,* cuire [au four]; (*v.i.*) cuire. ~**house,** *n,* fournil, *m*; (*Mil.*) manutention, *f*. **baker,** *n,* boulanger, ère. ~**y,** *n,* boulangerie, *f*. **baking,** *n,* cuisson; cuite; boulangerie, *f*. ~ *powder,* poudre à lever, *f*. ~ *pan,* tourtière, *f*.

balance, *n,* balance, *f*; peson; équilibre; solde, reliquat, surplus, *m*; soulte, *f*. ~ *of power* (*Pol.*), équilibre, *m.* ~ *sheet,* bilan, *m.* ~ *sheet & schedules,* inventaire, *m.* ~ *weight,* contrepoids, *m.* ~ *wheel* (*Horol.*), balancier, *m.* ¶ *v.t. & i,* balancer, équilibrer, pondérer; solder. ~*d lever,* bascule, *f*. **balancing,** *n,* balancement, *m.* ~ *pole* (tightrope), balancier, *m*.

balcony, *n,* balcon, *m*.

bald, *a,* chauve; nu, pelé; (*style*) plat, sec, décharné.

balderdash, *n,* galimatias, *m*.

baldness, *n,* calvitie; nudité, *f*.

bale, *n,* balle, *f,* ballot, *m.* ¶ *v.t,* emballer.

baleful, *a,* sinistre, funeste.

balk, *n,* tronc d'arbre équarri, *m,* poutre, *f*. ¶ *v.t,* frustrer; (*horse*) se dérober.

Balkan, *a,* balkanique; (*states, peninsula*) des Balkans. **the ~s,** les Balkans, *m.pl*.

ball, *n,* balle; bille; boule, *f*; boulet; ballon; (*eye, lightning*) globe, *m*; (*thumb*) éminence; (*pendulum*) lentille; (*wool, string*) pelote, *f,* peloton; (*Danc.*) bal, *m.* ~ *& socket,* rotule sphérique, *f*. ~ *bearings,* roulement à billes, *m.* ~ *cartridge,* cartouche à balle, *f*. ~ *cock,* robinet à flotteur, *m.* ~ *frame,* boulier, *m.* ~*room,* salle de bal, *f*. ¶ *v.t,* pelotonner; mettre en boule.

ballad, *n,* (*poem*) ballade; (*song*) chanson, romance, complainte, *f*.

ballast, *n,* (*road, Rly.*) ballast, *m*; (*Build.*) blocaille, *f*; (*Naut., Avn.*) lest; (*fig.*) plomb, *m.* ¶ *v.t,* lester.

ballet, *n,* ballet, *m.* ~ *dancer,* danseur, euse, figurant, e, ballerine, *f*. ~ *skirt,* tutu, *m*.

balloon, *n,* ballon; aérostat, *m*. ~ *fabric,* toile d'avion, *f*. ~**ed** (*dress*) *p.a,* ballonné. ~**ing,** *n,* aérostation, *f*. ~**ist,** *n,* aérostier, *m*.

ballot, *n,* [tour de] scrutin, *m.* ~ *box,* urne électorale, *f*. ~ *paper,* bulletin de vote, *m.* ¶ *v.i,* voter au scrutin.

balm, *n,* baume, *m.* ~**y,** *a,* embaumé, balsamique.

balsam, *n,* baume, *m*; (*garden plant*) balsamine, *f*. ~ [*tree*], baumier, balsamier, *m.* ~**ic,** *a,* balsamique.

Baltic [sea] (the), la [mer] Baltique.

baluster, *n,* balustre, *m.* **balustrade,** *n,* balustrade, *f*.

bamboo, *n,* bambou, *m*.

bamboozle, *v.t,* enjôler, mettre dedans.

ban, *n,* ban, *m*; interdiction, *f*. ¶ *v.t,* interdire.

banana, *n,* banane, *f*. ~ [*plant or tree*], bananier, *m*.

band, *n,* bande; frette; courroie,

f; ruban; (*Bookb.*) nerf, *m*; musique, *f*, orchestre, *m*, harmonie, *f*. ~*box*, carton de modiste, *m*. ~ *brake*, frein à ruban, *f*. à bande, *m*. ~ *saw*, scie à ruban, *f*. ~*master*, chef de musique, *m*. ¶ *v.t*, lier, fretter; (*v.i.*) se liguer.

bandage, *n*, bandage, bandeau, *m*, bande, *f*. ¶ *v.t*, bander. **bandeau,** *n*, bandeau, *m*.

bandit, *n*, bandit, *m*.

bandoleer, *n*, bandoulière, *f*.

bandy, *v.t*, ballotter, se renvoyer. ~ *words with*, faire assaut de paroles avec. ~[-legged], *a*, bancal.

bane (*fig.*) *n*, fléau, *m*. ~ful, *a*, pernicieux, funeste.

bang, *n*, battement, *m*; détonation, *f*. ¶ *i*, pan! ¶ *v.t*. & *i*, frapper, faire battre; battre, cogner.

bangle, *n*, bracelet; porte-bonheur, *m*.

banish, *v.t*, bannir.

banishment, *n*, exile, *m*.

banister, *n*, balustre, *m*; (*pl.*) rampe, *f*.

bank, *n*, rive, berge, *f*, bord; talus, banc, *m*; (*Fin.*) banque, caisse, *f*, crédit, *m*. ~ *note,* billet de banque, *m*. ~ [*pass*] *book*, carnet de banque, c. de compte, *m*. ~ *rate,* taux officiel [d'escompte] *m*. ~ *transfer,* virement, *m*. ¶ *v.t*, terrasser, remblayer; verser à la banque; (*v.i.*) virer, pencher. ~ *on,* compter sur. ~**er,** *n*, banquier, *m*. ~**ing,** *n*, banque, *f*.

bankrupt, *n*, banqueroutier, ère; failli, *m. to go* ~, faire banqueroute; faire faillite. ~**cy,** *n*, banqueroute; faillite, *f*.

banner, *n*, bannière, *f*; pavillon, *m*; oriflamme, *f*.

banns, *n.pl*, bans de mariage, *m.pl.*

banquet, *n*, banquet, festin, *m*. ~*ing hall,* salle des festins, *f*.

bantam weight (*Box.*), poids coq, *m*.

banter, *n*, badinage, *m*. ¶ *v.t*, badiner.

baptism, *n*, baptême, *m*. ~**al,** *a*, baptismal. **baptist**[*e*]**ry,** *n*, baptistère, *m*. **baptize,** *v.t*, baptiser.

bar, *n*, barre, *f*, barreau, *m*, barrette; bille, brique; barrière, *f*, fer, *m*; (*Mus., vertical line*) barre (*commonly but incorrectly, portion between two bar lines*) mesure, *f*; (*window*) croisillon, (*counter*) comptoir, *m*, buvette,

f, bar, *m*. ~ *bell,* barre à sphères, *f*. ~ *iron,* fer en barre, *m*. ¶ *v.t*, barrer.

barb, *n*, barbe, *f*; picot, *m*. ~[*ed*] *wire,* fil de fer barbelé, *m*, ronce, *f*. ¶ *v.t*, barbeller; barder.

Barbados, *n*, la Barbade.

barbarian, *a*. & *n*, barbare, *a*. & *m*. **barbaric, barbarous,** *a*, barbare. **barbarism,** *n*, barbarie, *f*; (*Gram.*) barbarisme, *m*. **barbarity,** *n*, barbarie, *f*.

Barbary ape, magot, *m*.

barbecue, *n*, grille, *m*.

barber, *n*, barbier, *m*.

Barcelona, *n*, Barcelone, *f*.

bard, *n*, (*poet*) barde; chantre, *m*. *the Bard of Avon,* le chantre d'Avon.

bare, *a*, nu; à nu; chenu; découvert; pelé; simple, seul; (*majority*) faible. ~*back*[*ed*] (*riding*), à nu, à poil, à cru. ~*back horse,* cheval nu, *m*. ~*faced,* éhonté, effronté. ~*facedly,* à visage découvert. ~*foot*[*ed*], nu-pieds, pieds nus, déchaussé. ~*headed,* nu-tête, tête nue. ¶ *v.t*, mettre à nu, dénuder, dépouiller, découvrir, déchausser. ~*ly, ad,* à peine, juste, tout au plus; ne . . . guère. ~*ness,* *n*, nudité, *f*.

bargain, *n*, marché, *m*, négociation, affaire; occasion; emplette, *f*. *into the* ~, pardessus le marché. ¶ *v.i*, marchander. ~**er,** *n*, marchandeur, euse.

barge, *n*, chaland, *m*, gabare, allège, péniche, *f*. **bargee, bargeman,** *n*, batelier, marinier, *m*.

baritone, *n*. & ~ *saxhorn,* baryton, *m*.

bark, *n*, (*tree*) écorce; (*left on felled tree*) grume, *f*; (*dog*) aboiement, *m*; (*boat*) barque, *f*; (*Poet.*) nef, *f*. ¶ *v.t*, écorcer, décortiquer, peler; (*v.i.*) aboyer. ~**ing,** *n*, (*tree*) décortication, *f*; (*dog*) aboiement, *m*.

barley, *n*, orge, *f*. ~ *sugar,* sucre d'orge, *m*. ~ *water,* eau d'orge, *f*.

barm, *n*, levure, *f*, levain, *m*.

barn, *n*, grange, *f*. ~ *owl,* effraie, fresaie, *f*. ~*yard,* basse-cour, *f*.

barnacle, *n*, (*Crust.*) bernacle, *f*, cravan, *m*.

barometer, *n*, baromètre, *m*. **barometric(al),** *a*, barométrique.

baron, ess, *n*, baron, ne.

barque, *n*, barque, *f*.

barrack, *n. oft. pl*, caserne, *f*. ~

room, chambrée [militaire], *f.* ¶ *v.t*, caserner.

barrage, *n*, barrage, *m.*

barrel, *n*, baril, fût, *m*, futaille, pièce, *f*, tonneau, *m*, caque, *f*; corps, cylindre, tambour, canon, *m.* ~ *organ*, orgue de Barbarie, *m.* ¶ *v.t*, mettre en baril, entonner, [en]caquer.

barren, *a*, stérile, aride. ~ness, *n*, stérilité, aridité, *f.*

barricade, *n*, barricade, *f.* ¶ *v.t*, barricader.

barrier, *n*, barrière, *f*; barrage, *m*; digue, *f.*

barring, *pr*, ôté, sauf, à part, hormis, excepté, à moins de.

barrow, *n*, brouette, *f*; (*peddler's*) baladeuse, *f*; (*mound*) tumulus, *m.*

barter, *n*, échange, troc, *m.* ~ *goods*, pacotille, *f.* ¶ *v.t*, échanger, troquer.

basal, *a*, basique.

basalt, *n*, basalte, *m.*

bascule bridge, pont à bascule, *m.*

base, *a*, bas, vil, ignoble. ~ *metal*, bas métal, métal vil, *m.* pauvre, *m.* ¶ *n*, base, assiette, *f*, fondement[s] *m.*[pl.]; soubassement; culot, *m.* ¶ *v.t*, asseoir, fonder. ~less, *a*, sans fondement. ~ly, *ad*, bassement, lâchement. ~ment, *n*, soubassement, sous-sol, *m.* ~ness, *n*, bassesse, *f.*

bashful, *a*, timide. ~ness, *n*, timidité, fausse honte, mauvaise honte, *f.*

basic, *a*, fondamental; (*Chem.*) basique.

basil, *n*, (Bot.) basilic, *m*; (*hide*) basane, *f.*

basilica, *n*, basilique, *f.*

basilisk, *n*, basilic, *m.*

basin, *n*, bassin; bol, *m*; cuvette, *f.*

basis, *n*, base, assiette, *f*, fondement[s] *m.*[pl.].

bask, *v.i*, se chauffer.

basket, *n*, panier, *m*, corbeille; manne; benne; bourriche, *f.* ~ball, basket-ball, ballon au panier, *m.* ~ maker, vannier, *m.* ~ making, ~ work, vannerie, *f.* ~ful, *n*, panier, *m*, panerée, *f.*

bas-relief, *n*, bas-relief, *m.*

bass, *n*, (*fish*) bar, *m.* ~ [*voice, singer, string, tuba*], basse, *f.* ~ *clef*, clef de fa, *f.* ~ *drum*, grosse caisse, *f.*

bassinet, *n*, bercelonnette, *f.*

bassoon, *n*, basson, *m.*

bast, *n*, tille, *f.*

bastard, *a*, bâtard. ¶ *n*, bâtard, e. ~y, *n*, bâtardise, *f.*

baste, *v.t*, (*Need.*) bâtir, baguer, faufiler; (*meat*) arroser; (*beat*) bâtonner.

bat, *n*, bat, *m*; batte; palette, *f*; (*Zool.*) chauve-souris, *f.*

batch, *n*, fournée, *f*; groupe, *m.*

bate, *v.t*, rabattre.

bath, *n*, bain, *m*; (*tub*) baignoire, *f.* ~ *attendant*, baigneur, euse. *B*~ *chair*, fauteuil roulant, *m.* ~ *robe*, peignoir de bain, *m.* ~man, baigneur, *m.* ~mat, tapis de bain, *m.* ~room, salle de bain, *f.* ~ *salts*, sel pour bain, *m.* ~tub, baignoire, *m.* **bathe**, *v.t*, baigner; (*v.i.*) baigner, se b.; s'abreuver. **bather**, *n*, baigneur, euse. **bathing**, *n*, bains, *m.pl*; bain, *m.* ~ *cap*, bonnet de bain, *m.* ~ *suit*, maillot (*ou* costume) de bain, *m.* ~ *place*, baignade, *f.* ~ *resort*, station balnéaire, *f.*

bathos, *n*, pathos, *m.*

baton, *n*, bâton; (*relay race*) témoin, *m.*

battalion, *n*, bataillon, *m.*

batten, *n*, [latte] volige, *f.* ~ **down** (*Naut.*), condamner. ~ **on**, s'engraisser de.

batter, *n*, pâte, *f.* ¶ *v.t*, battre, bossuer, bosseler, cabosser. ~ing-ram, *n*, bélier, *m.* ~y, *n*, batterie; pile, *f.*

battle, *n*, bataille, *f*, combat, *m.* ~-axe, hache d'armes, *f.* ~ *cruiser*, croiseur cuirassé de combat, *m.* ~field, champ de bataille, *m.* ~ship, [navire] cuirassé, *m.* ¶ *v.i*, lutter; batailler.

battledore, *n*, palette, raquette, *f*, battoir, *m.* ~ & shuttlecock, [jeu de] volant, *m.*

battlement, *n*, créneau, *m.* ~ed, *a*, crénelé.

bauble, *n*, babiole, *f*, brimborion, *m*; (*fool's*) marotte, *f.*

Bavaria, *n*, la Bavière. **Bavarian**, *a*, bavarois. ¶ *n*, Bavarois, e.

bawl, *v.i*, brailler, beugler.

bay, *a*, bai. ¶ *n*, (*horse*) bai, *m*; (*Geog.*) baie, *f*; golfe, *m*; (*Arch.*) travée, *f.* *B*~ *of Biscay*, golfe de Gascogne, *m.* ~ *rum*, tafia de laurier, *m.* ~[*tree*], laurier, *m.* ~ *window*, fenêtre baie. *f. at* ~, aux abois. ¶ *v.i*, aboyer. ~ing, *n*, aboiement, *m.*

bayonet, *n*, baïonnette, *f.*

bazaar, *n*, bazar, *m*; vente de charité, *f.*

B.C. (*before Christ*), av. J.C.

be, *v.i.ir,* être; exister; avoir; faire; se faire; aller, se trouver, se porter; y avoir. ~ *that as it may,* quoi qu'il en soit. *it is ... since,* il y a ... que. *there is* (are) *some,* il y en a. *there is none left,* il n'y en a plus. *I am leaving,* je vais partir, je pars. *a man to be feared,* un homme à craindre. *not to be confused with ...,* à ne pas confondre avec ... **to be off,** s'en aller, filer, se sauver. *be off with you!* allez vous promener!

beach, *n,* plage, grève, *f,* rivage, *m.* ~**comber,** rôdeur de grève, *m.* ~ *fishing,* pêche de plage, *f.* ~**head,** tête de pont, *f.* ¶ *v.t. & i,* échouer; tirer à sec.

beacon, *n,* balise, *f;* phare, *m.* ¶ *v.t,* baliser.

bead, *n,* perle, *f,* grain, *m;* goutte; (*Arch.*) baguette, *f.* [*glass*] ~**s,** verroterie, *f.* [*string of*] ~**s,** chapelet, *m.*

beadle, *n,* appariteur; bedeau, suisse, *m.*

beak, *n,* bec, *m.* ~**er,** *n,* buire, *f;* vase à filtrations chaudes, *m.*

beam, *n,* (*timber*) poutre; (*plow*) flèche, haie, *f,* timon; (*Mach.*) balancier; (*scale*) fléau, *m,* verge, *f;* (*ship's timber*) bau, *m;* (*ship's breadth*) largeur, *f,* travers; (*ray*) rayon, trait; (*rays*) faisceau, *m.* *radio* ~, signal par radio. ¶ *v.i,* rayonner.

bean, *n,* fève, *f;* haricot; (*coffee*) grain, *m.*

bear, *n,* ours, e; (**B**~, *Astr.*) ourse, *f;* (*pers.*) bourru, dogue, *m;* (*Mach.*) poinçonneuse, *f;* (*Stk Ex.*) baissier, *m.* ~ *garden* (fig.), pétaudière, *f.* ~*'s cub,* ourson, *m.* ~**skin** (*cap*), oursin, ourson, *m.* ¶ *v.t. & i. ir,* porter; supporter, souffrir, tolérer, endurer, compatir; appuyer, peser; produire, rapporter; enfanter; (*to right, left*) prendre. *to* ~ *out,* confirmer. *to* ~ *up,* résister. ~**able,** *a,* supportable, tenable.

beard, *n,* barbe; (*Bot.*) barbe, arête, *f.* ~**ed,** *a,* barbu, à barbe chevelu. ~**less,** *a,* imberbe.

bearer, *n,* porteur, euse; (*Fin.*) porteur, *m.* ~ *of a flag of truce,* parlementaire, *m.* *stretcher*~, brancardier, *m.* **bearing,** *n,* portée, *f;* rapport, trait; aspect; (*Naut.*) gisement, *m;* (*pl. fig.*) orientation, *f;* (*gait*) port, *m,* mine, tenue, démarche, conte-

nance, *f,* maintien, *m;* conduite, *f;* (*Mech., oft. pl.*) coussinet, *m.* *oft. pl;* palier; dé; roulement, *m;* chape, *f;* (*pl. Her.*) armes, armoiries, *f.pl.* ~ *rein,* fausse rêne, *f.* ~ *surface,* surface portante, s. de portée, *f.*

beast, *n,* bête, *f;* animal; abruti, *m.* ~ *of burden,* bête de somme. ~**ly,** *a,* bestial; dégoûtant.

beat, *n,* battement; coup; temps, *m;* tournée, ronde; (*Hunt.*) battue, *f.* ¶ *v.t. & i. ir,* battre; taper; assommer, bâtonner, brosser; fourrer; fouetter; (*Hunt.*) rabattre, traquer; vaincre; l'emporter sur, enchérir sur. ~ *back,* ~ *off,* repousser. ~**en** *path,* chemin [re]battu, c. frayé, *m.* ~**er,** *n,* batteur, battoir, *m,* batte, *f;* (*Hunt.*) rabatteur, traqueur, *m.*

beatify, *v.t,* béatifier.

beating, *n,* battement, battage, *m;* batterie; brossée; défaite, *f;* (*Hunt.*) rabattage, *m,* traque, *f.* ~ *rain,* pluie battante, *f.*

beau, *n,* amoureux, galant, *m.*

beautiful, *a,* beau; magnifique. ¶ *n,* beau, *m.* **beautify,** *v.t,* embellir. **beauty,** *n,* beauté; belle, *f.* *B*~ *& the Beast,* la Belle & la Bête. ~ *parlor,* institut de beauté, *m.* ~ *spot,* site pittoresque, *m;* (*patch on face*) mouche, *f;* (*mole*) grain de beauté, *m.*

beaver, *n,* castor, *m.*

becalmed, *a,* encalminé, pris par le calme.

because, *c,* parce que; car. ~ *of,* à cause de.

beck, *n,* signe, *m;* ordres, *m.pl.* **beckon,** *v.i,* faire signe.

become, *v.i.ir,* devenir. *With p.p. often rendered by pronominal form of verb, as, to become accustomed,* s'accoutumer; (*v.t.ir.*) convenir à. **becoming,** *a,* convenable; [bien]séant, seyant; assortissant, décent.

bed, *n,* lit, *m,* couche, *f;* coucher, *m;* assise, assiette, fondation, plate-forme, *f;* banc, gisement, gîte; (*oyster*) parc; (*Hort.*) carré, *m,* plate-bande, planche, *f,* parterre, *m.* *to go to* ~, [aller] se coucher. ~**bug,** punaise, *f.* ~**clothes,** draps & couvertures. ~**fellow,** camarade de lit. ~**pan,** bassin [de garde-robe], b. pour malade, b. de lit, *m.* ~**post,** quenouille, *f.* ~**ridden,** alité, grabataire. ~**room,** chambre [à coucher] *f.* ~**side,** chevet, *m.*

~side carpet, descente de lit, f. a
good ~side manner, une bonne
manière professionnelle. ~side
table, table de chevet, t. de nuit,
f. ~spread, couvrelit, dessus de
lit, jeté de l., m. ~stead, bois de
lit; lit, m. ~time, l'heure du
coucher, f. ¶v.t, coucher; asseoir; [faire] précipiter. **bedding**,
n, coucher, m, literie, garniture
de lit; stratification, f.

bedeck, v.t, parer, chamarrer.

bedew, v.t, arroser, humecter.

bedizen, v.t, attifer, chamarrer.

bedlam, n, maison de fous; (fig.)
pétaudière, f.

bedraggle, v.t, traîner dans la
boue.

bee, n, abeille, f. ~ eater, guêpier,
m. ~hive, ruche, f. ~ keeping,
apiculture, f. a ~ in one's bonnet,
un rat dans la tête.

beech [tree], n, hêtre, m. ~ marten, fouine, f. ~mast, faînes, f.pl.
~nut, faîne, f.

beef, n, bœuf, m. ~ steak, bifteck,
m. ~ tea, thé de viande, bouillon
de bœuf, m. corned ~, bœuf
salé, m.

beer, n, bière, f. ~pump, pompe
à b., f.

beet, n, bette; betterave, f. ~
sugar, sucre de betterave, m.

beetroot, n, betterave, f.

beetle, n, coléoptère, scarabée;
escarbot, m; (rammer) dame,
demoiselle, hie, f, pilon, m. ¶v.t,
pilonner. **beetling brows**, sourcils fournis, m.pl. **beetling crag**,
rocher qui surplombe, m.

befall, v.i.ir, arriver, advenir, survenir.

befit, v.t, convenir à. **befitting**, a,
convenable.

before, ad, devant; avant; auparavant; en avant; déjà; jusqu'ici; précédent. ¶c, avant que.
¶pr, devant; avant; pardevant;
avant [que] de. ~ you could say
Jack Robinson, crac! ~hand, ad,
à l'avance, d'a., en a., par a.

befriend, v.t, favoriser; secourir.

beg, v.t. & i, mendier, quémander,
chercher, gueuser; demander,
prier; (Com.) avoir l'honneur
de; (dog) faire le beau. I ~
your pardon, je vous demande
pardon. ~ for, solliciter, quémander. ~ the question, faire
une pétition de principe.

beget, v.t.ir, engendrer; faire naître.

beggar, n, mendiant, m. ¶v.t,

appauvrir, ruiner. ~ly, a, gueux;
misérable. ~y, n, mendicité,
gueuserie, misère, f. reduced to
~, réduit à la besace.

begin, v.t. & i. ir, commencer;
débuter; entamer, amorcer; ouvrir; se mettre. ~ again, recommencer. **beginner**, n, commençant, e, débutant, e. **beginning**,
n, commencement, début, m;
amorce; ouverture; origine, f;
prémices, f.pl.

begone, i, va-t-en! allez-vous-en!

begonia, n, bégonia, m.

begrudge, v.t, envier.

beguile, v.t, tromper; séduire;
charmer, amuser.

behalf of (**on**), de la part de;
à l'acquit de; pour le compte de.

behave, v.i. & reflexive, se comporter, se conduire, vivre. ~
[properly]! (to child), tiens-toi
bien! **behavior**, n, conduite, f,
manières, f.pl, tenue, f, procédé,
m.

behead, v.t, décapiter. ~ing, n,
décapitation, f.

behest, n, commandement, ordre,
m.

behind, ad, derrière, en arrière.
¶pr, derrière, en arrière de.
~hand, ad, en arrière, arriéré,
en retard.

behold, v.t. & i. ir, voir. ¶i,
voyez! ~en to, à charge à, redevable à. ~er, n, spectateur,
trice.

behoof, n, profit, m. **behove**,
v.t.imp, incomber, convenir à.

being, n, être, m; existence, f. for
the time ~, actuel; actuellement.

belabor, v.t, charger de coups,
bourrer, rosser, échiner.

belated, a, attardé; tardif.

belay, v.t, tourner, amarrer.

belch[ing], n, rot, m; crudité,
éructation, f. **belch**, v.i, roter;
éructer; (v.t, fig.) vomir.

beldam[e], n, vieille sorcière, f.

beleaguer, v.t, assiéger.

belfry, n, beffroi, clocher, m.

Belgian, a, belge. ¶n, Belge, m,f.
Belgium, n, la Belgique.

belie, v.t, démentir.

belief, n, croyance, foi; persuasion, f. **believable**, a, croyable.
believe, v.t. & i, croire. to make
. . . ~, faire [ac]croire à . . .
believer, n, croyant, e; partisan,
m.

belittle, v.t, décrier, rabaisser,
déprécier.

bell, n, cloche; clochette, sonnette,

sonnerie, *f*, timbre; (*globular*) grelot, *m*. ~*bov*, groom d'hôtel, *m*. ~ [*flower*], campanule, clochette, *f*. ~ *glass* & ~ *jar*, cloche, *f*. ~ *push*, bouton de sonnette, *m*. ~ *ringer*, sonneur, carillonneur, *m*. ~ *tent*, tente conique, *f*. ~ *tower*, campanile, *m*. ~ *turret*, clocheton, *m*. ~*wether*, sonnailler, *m*. ¶ *v.i*, bramer, raire, réer.

belladonna, *n*, belladone, *f*.

belle, *n*, beauté, reine, *f*.

bellicose, *a*, belliqueux. **belligerent**, *a*. & *n*, belligérant, e.

bellow, *v.i*, beugler, mugir. ~ *n*, mugissement, *m*.

bellows, *n.pl*, soufflet, *m*; soufflerie, *f*.

belly, *n*, ventre, *m*, panse, *f*; bombement, *m*. ~ *band*, sous-ventrière; sangle, *f*. ¶ *v.i*, faire [le] ventre, bomber.

belong, *v.i*, appartenir, dépendre, être. ~**ings**, *n.pl*, effets, *m.pl*.

beloved, *a*. & *n*, bien-aimé, e, chéri, e.

below, *ad*, en bas; au-dessous; dessous; ci-dessous; ci-après; là-bas; en contrebas. ¶ *pr*, sous; au-dessous de; en aval de.

belt, *n*, ceinture, *f*; ceinturon, *m*; (*Mech.*) courroie; bande; (*Geog.*) zone, *f*. ¶ *v.t*, ceindre. ~**ing**, *n*, courroies [de transmission] *f.pl*.

belvedere, *n*, belvédère, *m*.

bemoan, *v.t*, déplorer; pleurer.

bench, *n*, banc, *m*; banquette, *f*; établi; siège, *m*; cour; magistrature, assise, *f*, tribunal, *m*. ~ *mark*, [point de] repère, *m*.

bend, *n*, coude, *m*; courbe, courbure, *f*; pli, *m*; inflexion, *f*; tournant, virage; (*knot*) nœud, *m*. ~ *of the arm*, saignée, *f*. ~ *of the knee*, jarret, *m*. ¶ *v.t. & i. ir*, courber, se c., couder; bander; tendre; cintrer; fléchir, plier, ployer; fausser, se f., gauchir. *on* ~*ed knees*, à genoux.

beneath, *ad*, dessous; par-dessous; en bas. ¶ *pr*, au-dessous de, sous.

benediction, *n*, bénédiction, *f*.

benefaction, *n*, bienfait, *m*. **benefactor, tress**, *n*, bienfaiteur, trice.

benefice, *n*, bénéfice, *m*.

beneficence, *n*, bienfaisance, *f*. **beneficent**, *a*, bienfaisant.

beneficial, *a*, avantageux, profitable, salutaire. **beneficiary**, *n*, bénéficiaire, *m,f*. **benefit**, *n*, bénéfice, bienfait, avantage, fruit,

profit; secours, *m*; (*Theat.*) représentation à bénéfice, *f*. ~ *society*, société de secours mutuels, *f*. ¶ *v.t*, faire du bien à, avantager; (*v.i.*) profiter, bénéficier.

benevolence, *n*, bienfaisance, *f*; patronage, *m*. **benevolent**, *a*, bienfaisant.

Bengal, *n*, le Bengale. ~ *light*, feu de bengale, *m*, flamme de b., *f*. **Bengali, -lee**, *a*, bengali, (*pers.*) Bengali, *inv*. ¶ *n*, (*pers.*) Bengali, (*bird*) bengali, *m*.

benighted, *a*, (*fig.*) ignorant; plongé dans les ténèbres.

benign, benignant, *a*, bénin. **benignly, benignantly**, *ad*, bénignement.

bent, *a*, courbé; coudé; faussé; gauchi. ~ *lever*, levier coudé, *m*. ~*wood furniture*, meubles en bois courbé, *m.pl*. ¶ *n*, penchant, *m*, pente, *f*, biais, génie, attrait, *m*. ¶ *to be* ~ *on*, s'acheurter à, se buter à, s'acharner à.

benumb, *v.t*, engourdir, morfondre.

benzine, benzoline, *n*, benzine, *f*.

benzoin, *n*, benjoin, *m*.

benzol[e], benzene, *n*, benzol, *m*.

bequeath, *v.t*, léguer. **bequest**, *n*, legs, *m*.

bereave, *v.t.ir*, priver; enlever; ravir. ~**ment**, *n*, deuil, *m*.

beret, *n*, béret [basque] *m*.

bergamot, *n*, (*orange, pear*) bergamote; (*pear*) mouille-bouche, *f*. ~ *oil*, essence de bergamote, *f*. ~ [*tree*] (*orange*), bergamotier, *m*.

Bermudas (the), les Bermudes, *f.pl*.

berry, *n*, baie, *f*; (*coffee*) grain, *m*.

berth, *n*, poste de mouillage, mouillage, emplacement, poste, *m*, place; couchette, *f*.

beryl, *n*, béryl, *m*.

beseech, *v.t.ir*, supplier, adjurer, implorer.

beset, *v.t.ir*, entourer, assiéger. *besetting sin*, péché d'habitude, *m*.

beside, *pr*, à côté de; auprès de; hors de; excepté. ~ *oneself*, hors de soi. **besides**, *ad*. & *pr*, d'ailleurs, du reste, de plus, d'autre part, en outre, puis.

besiege, *v.t*, assiéger. **besieger**, *n*, assiégeant, e.

besmear, *v.t*, barbouiller.

besmirch, v.t, souiller.

besom, n, balai [de bouleau] m.

besotted, a, abruti.

bespangle, v.t, pailleter; parsemer.

bespatter, v.t, éclabousser, crotter.

bespeak, v.t.ir, retenir; commander; stipuler.

besprinkle, v.t, arroser.

best, a, [le] meilleur; le mieux; le plus beau ou grand ou fort. ~ man (wedding), garçon d'honneur, m. ~ quality, premier choix, m. ~seller, livre à succès, l. à grand tirage, m. ¶ ad, mieux, le mieux; plus. ¶ the ~, le mieux. the ~ of it, le meilleur de l'affaire; le plus beau de l'histoire; le dessus. in one's [Sunday] ~, endimanché. do the ~ you can! arrangez-vous!

bestial†, a, bestial.

bestir oneself (to), se remuer, s'empresser.

bestow, v.t, accorder, gratifier, déférer; impartir, donner.

bestride, v.t.ir, enjamber, enfourcher.

bet, n, pari, m. ¶ v.t, parier; gager.

betake oneself (to), v.reflexive ir, se livrer, recourir; se rendre.

bethink oneself (to), v.reflexive ir, s'aviser.

betide, v.t, arriver à. whate'er ~, arrive (ou advienne) que pourra.

betimes, ad, de bonne heure, tôt.

betoken, v.t, présager; désigner; dénoter; annoncer.

betray, v.t, trahir; tromper; révéler, accuser. ~ one's trust, prévariquer. ~al, n, trahison, f. ~er, n, traître, traîtresse.

betroth, v.t, fiancer. ~al, n, fiançailles, f.pl. ~ed, n. & a, fiancé, e.

better, a, meilleur; préférable. my ~ half (wife), ma [chère] moitié. ~-looking, mieux. to be ~ (health), se porter (ou aller) mieux. it is ~ to, il vaut mieux. ¶ ad, mieux. so much the ~, tant mieux. ¶ (pers.) n, supérieur, e. ¶ v.t, améliorer. ~ment, n, amélioration, f.

better, bettor, n, parieur, euse. **betting,** n, pari, m; (odds) cote, f. ~ system, martingale, f. ~ with bookmakers, pari à la cote.

between, pr, entre; de; à. ~ now & then, d'ici là. ~ this & . . ., d'ici à . . . ~ [times], dans l'intervalle. ~-decks, n, entrepont, m.

bevel, n, biseau, m. ~ [square], fausse équerre, sauterelle, f. ~ gear, roue d'angle, f. ¶ v.t, biseauter.

beverage, n, breuvage, m, boisson, f.

bevy, n, compagnie; volée; troupe, f.

bewail, v.t, pleurer, déplorer, se lamenter sur.

beware, v.i, se garder, se méfier, se défier, prendre garde. ~ of pickpockets! méfiez-vous des voleurs!

bewilder, v.t, égarer, désorienter; ahurir. ~ment, n, affolement, m.

bewitch, v.t, ensorceler, envoûter, enchanter. ~ing, a, ensorcelant, enchanteur. ~ingly, ad, à ravir.

beyond, ad, au-delà, plus loin. ¶ pr, au-delà de, par-delà, delà; hors; au-dessus de; sans; outre. the ~ (future life), l'au-delà, m.

bezel, n, chaton, m.

bias, n, biais; (fig.) penchant, parti pris, m, partialité, f. ¶ v.t, influencer, détourner; biaiser. **biased,** p.a, partial.

bib, n, bavoir, m, bavette, f.

Bible, n, Bible, f. ~ Society, Société biblique, f. **biblical,** a, biblique.

bibliography, n, bibliographie, f. **bibliophile,** n, bibliophile, m.

bibulous, a, absorbant; adonné à la boisson.

biceps, n, biceps, m.

bicker, v.i, disputailler, se chamailler.

bicycle, n, bicyclette, f; bicycle, m. **bicyclist,** n, cycliste, m,f.

bid, n, (Stk Ex.) demande; (auction) enchère, mise, f. to make a ~ for, vouloir capter. ¶ v.t. & i. ir, commander, ordonner; (adieu) dire; offrir; enchérir, miser; (Stk Ex.) demander. ~ higher than, surenchérir sur. **bidder,** n, enchérisseur, m.

bide one's time (to), attendre son heure, se réserver.

biennial, a, biennal, bisannuel.

bier, n, civière, f.

bifurcation, n, bifurcation, f.

big, a, gros; grand; fort; considérable; haut; (pregnant) grosse, enceinte, (animals) pleine. ~-boned, ossu. to talk ~, le prendre de haut.

bigamist, *n*, bigame, *m.f.* **bigamous**, *a*, bigame. **bigamy**, *n*, bigamie, *f.*

bight, *n*, golfe, enfoncement; (*rope*) double, *m.*

bigness, *n*, grosseur; grandeur, *f.*

bigot, *n*. & ~ed, *a*, bigot, e. ~ry, *n*, bigoterie, *f.*

bigwig, *n*, gros bonnet, *m.*

bike, *n*, vélo, *m.*

bilberry, *n*, airelle, myrtille, *f.*

bile, *n*, bile, *f.*

bilge, *n*, (*ship*) fond de cale; (*cask*) bouge, ventre, *m.* ~ water, eau de cale, *f.*

bilious, *a*, bilieux.

bilk, *v.t*, frustrer; flouer.

bill, *n*, (*bird*) bec, *m*; (*notice*) affiche, pancarte, *f*, placard; écriteau; prospectus; programme; (*legislative*) projet de loi, *m*; (*account*) note, *f*, mémoire, *m*; addition; facture, *f*; (*Fin.*) effet, billet, mandat, *m*, échéance, traite, remise, lettre, valeur, *f*; (*pl.*) portefeuille[-effets], papier, *m.* ~ file, pique-notes, *m.* to settle a ~, régler une note. ~ head[ing], en-tête de facture, *m.* ~hook, croissant, *m*, serpe, serpette, *f.* ~ of exchange, lettre de change, traite, *f.* ~ of fare, carte de restaurant; carte du jour, *f*, menu, *m.* ~ of health, patente de santé, *f.* ~ of lading, connaissement, *m.* ~ payable, receivable, effet à payer, à recevoir, *m.* ~poster, ~sticker, afficheur, colleur, *m.* ¶ *v.t*, afficher, placarder; facturer; (*v.i.*) se becqueter. ~ & coo, faire des mamours, roucouler.

billet, *n*, (*Mil.*) billet de logement; (*pl.*) cantonnement, *m*; (*log*) bûche, *f*, rondin, *m.* ¶ *v.t*, cantonner; (*on householder*) loger.

billiard: ~ ball, bille [de billard] *f.* ~ room, salle de billard, *f*, billard, *m.* ~ table, table de billard, *f*, billard, *m.* ~s, *n.pl*, billard, *m.*

billingsgate, *n*, langage de poissarde, l. des halles, *m.*

billion, *n*, billion, *m.*

billow, *n*, vague, lame, onde, *f*, flot, *m.* ¶ *v.i*, ondoyer. ~y, *a*, houleux.

billy goat, bouc, *m.*

bimonthly, *a*, (*in alternate months*) bimestriel; (*½ monthly*) semi-mensuel.

bin, *n*, huche, *f*; tonneau, tonnelet,

m; trémie, case, *f*, casier, caisson, coffre; porte-bouteilles, *m.*

bind, *v.t.ir*, lier, attacher, ligoter; (*sheaf*) [en]gerber; bander; assujettir; serrer; enchaîner; astreindre; border; engager, obliger; (*books*) relier; (*paper covers*) brocher; (*with metal*) ferrer; (*Med.*) resserrer, constiper. *I'll be bound*, j'en réponds. ~er, *n*, (*sheaf*, *pers.*) lieur, *m*; (*Mach.*) lieuse, *f*; (*book*) relieur, euse; brocheur, euse; (*tie*) lien, *m*, attache, *f*; (*papers*) biblorhapte, *m.* ~ing, *a*, obligatoire. ¶ *n*, reliure, *f*; brochage, *m*, brochure; bordure, *f*, galon, *m*, tresse, *f.*

bindweed, *n*, liseron, liset, *m.*

bine, *n*, sarment, *m.*

binnacle, *n*, habitacle, *m.*

binocular, *n*, jumelle, *f.*

biographer, *n*, biographe, *m.* **biography**, *n*, biographie, *f.*

biologist, *n*, biologiste, biologue, *m.* **biology**, *n*, biologie, *f.*

biped, *n*, bipède, *m.* ~[al], *a*, bipède.

biplane, *n*, biplan, *m.*

birch, *n*, (*tree*) bouleau, *m*; (*rod*) verges, *f.pl.* ~bark [*canoe*] pirogue en écorce, *f.* ~ broom, balai de bouleau, *m.* ¶ *v.t*, frapper de verges. ~ing, *n*, (des) coups de verges, *m.pl.*

bird, *n*, oiseau, (*small*) oiselet, *m.* ~ call, appeau, pipeau, *m.* ~ catcher, oiseleur, *m.* ~lime, *n*, glu, *f*; (*v.t.*) engluer. ~ of ill omen, oiseau de mauvais augure; porte-malheur, *m.* ~ of paradise, oiseau de paradis. ~'s-eye view, vue à vol d'oiseau, *f.* ~ shot, menu plomb, *m*, dragée, *f.*

birth, *n*, naissance; extraction, *f*; enfantement, *m*; (*childbed*) couches, *f.pl.* ~ certificate, acte de naissance, *m.* ~ control, limitation des naissances, *f.* ~ day, jour de naissance, anniversaire de ma (de sa, etc.) naissance, *m*, fête, *f.* ~mark, tache de naissance, envie, *f*, nævus, *m.* ~place, lieu de naissance, *m*, [petite] patrie, *f.* ~ rate, natalité, *f*, pourcentage des naissances, *m.* ~ right, droit d'aînesse; droit du sang, *m.*

biscuit, *n*, biscuit, *m.*

bisect, *v.t*, diviser en deux parties égales. **bisection**, *n*, bissection, *f.*

bishop, *n*, évêque, *m*; (*chess*) fou,

m. ~'s **house** & **bishopric,** *n,* évêché, *m.*

bismuth, *n,* bismuth, *m.*

bison, *n,* bison, *m.*

bit, *n,* morceau, fragment, *m,* pièce, miette, *f;* bout, brin; peu; *(bridle)* mors, frein; *(borer)* foret, *m,* mèche, *f; (key)* panneton; *(iron of plane, etc.)* fer, *m.*

bitch, *n,* chienne; *(woman)* garce, *f.* ~ **fox,** renarde, *f.* ~ **wolf,** louve, *f.*

bite, *n,* morsure, *f,* coup de dents; mordant, *f; (sting)* piqûre; *(to eat)* bouchée; *(place bitten by worm, mouse)* mangeure, *f.* I **have a** ~! *(Fish.),* ça mord! ¶ *v.t.* & *i. ir,* mordre; piquer. **biting,** *a,* mordant, piquant; *(cold)* cuisant.

bitter, *a,* amer; aigre; cuisant; cruel; acharné. ~ **pill** *(fig.),* couleuvre, *f.* ~-**sweet,** *a,* aigredoux; *(n. Bot.)* douce-amère, *f.* ~**ly,** *ad,* amèrement; aigrement; *(cold)* extrêmement. **cry** ~, pleurer à chaudes larmes. ~**ness,** *n,* amertume, *f,* amer, fiel, *m.* ~**s,** *n,* amers, *m.pl.*

bittern, *n,* butor, *m.*

bitumen, *n,* bitume, *m.* **bituminous,** *a,* bitumineux.

bivalve, *a.* & *n,* bivalve, *a.* & *m.*

bivouac, *n,* bivouac, *m.* ¶ *v.i,* bivouaquer.

blab, *v.t,* divulguer; *(v.i.)* bavarder, jaser.

black, *a,* noir. ~ & **blue,** meurtri, noir. [**down**] **in** ~ & **white,** noir sur blanc. ~**ball** *(voting),* boule noire, *f.* ~**beetle,** blatte, *f,* cafard, *m.* ~**berry,** mûre sauvage. *m.* de ronce, *f.* ~**berry bush,** ronce, *f.* ~**bird,** merle, *m,* *(hen)* merlette, *f.* ~**board,** tableau [noir] *m.* ~**-bordered envelope,** enveloppe deuil, *f.* ~ **currant**(*s*) & ~ **currant bush** & ~ **currant cordial,** cassis, *m.* ~ **eye,** œil poché, pochon, *m.* **to give someone a** ~ **eye,** pocher l'œil à quelqu'un. **B**~ **Forest,** Forêt-Noire, *f.* ~**guard,** canaille, *f,* goujat, *m.* ~**head,** point noir, *m,* tanne, *f.* ~**lead,** mine de plomb, plombagine, *f,* graphite, *m.* ~**list,** *n,* index, *m; (v.t.)* mettre à l'i. ~ **magic,** ~ **art,** magie noire, *f.* ~**mail,** *n,* chantage, *m; (v.t.)* faire chanter. ~**mailer,** maître chanteur, *m.* ~ **mark** (bruise), noir, *m.* ~**out,**

black-out, *m.* **B**~ **Sea,** mer Noire, *f.* ~ **sheep** *(fig.),* brebis galeuse, *f.* ~**smith,** forgeron, *m.* ~**thorn,** épine noire, *f,* prunellier, *m.* ¶ *n,* *(color, man)* noir, *m; (ball—gaming)* noire, *f.* ¶ *v.t,* noircir; charbonner; mâchurer; *(boots)* cirer.

blackamoor, *n,* moricaud, e; noir, e.

blacken, *v.t,* noircir. **blacking,** *n,* noircissement, e; *(boots)* cirage; cirage pour chaussures, *m.* ~ **brush,** brosse à cirer, b. à étendre, *f.* **blackish,** *a,* noirâtre. **blackness,** *n,* noirceur, *f.*

bladder, *n,* vessie; *(Bot.)* vésicule, *f.*

blade, *n,* *(grass)* brin, *m; (knife)* lame, feuille; *(vane)* aile, aube; *(propeller)* palette; *(oar)* pale, *f,* plat, *m.*

blame, *n,* blâme, reproche, *m,* faute, *f.* ¶ *v.t,* blâmer, reprocher, accuser, s'en prendre à. ~**less,** *a,* innocent. ~**worthy,** *a,* digne de b.

blanch, *v.t.* & *i,* blanchir, faire pâlir, pâlir.

bland, *a,* doux, suave, doucereux, mielleux. ~**ishment,** *n,* flatterie, chatterie, *f.*

blank, *a,* blanc, vierge. ~ **cartridge,** cartouche à blanc, *f.* ~ **verse,** vers blancs, *m.pl.* ¶ *n,* blanc, *m;* lacune, *f,* trou, *m; (lottery)* billet perdant; *(for coin)* flan, *m.*

blanket, *n,* couverture [en laine], couverte, *f.* ~ **stitch** *(Emb.),* point de languette, p. de feston, *m.*

blare, *n,* fionflon, *m.* ¶ *v.i,* retentir.

blarney, *n,* blague, *f.*

blaspheme, *v.i.* & *t,* blasphémer, jurer. **blasphemer,** *n,* blasphémateur, trice. **blasphemous,** *a,* blasphématoire. **blasphemy,** *n,* blasphème, *m.*

blast, *n,* vent, coup de vent, courant d'air, souffle, *m,* chasse d'air, *f;* coup; coup [de mine], pétard, *m,* mine, *f.* ~ **furnace,** haut fourneau, *m.* ¶ *v.t,* faire sauter, pétarder; foudroyer; *(blight)* brouir, flétrir. ~**ing,** *n,* travail aux explosifs (*ou* à la poudre), *m.* ~ **powder,** poudre de mine, *f.*

blatant, *a,* bruyant, criard.

blaze, *n,* flambée, *f;* éclat, *m.* **in a** ~, en flammes. ¶ *v.i,* flamber; flamboyer; *(v.t, tree)* griffer. ~

a trail, frayer un chemin. ~ *away*, tirailler. **blazing**, *a*, flambant, flamboyant, ardent, d'enfer; éclatant.

blazon, *v.t*, blasonner, armorier; proclamer. ~*ry*, *n*, blason, *m*.

bleach, *v.t*, blanchir. ~*er*, *n*, blanchisseur, euse, buandier, ère; (*pl*.) (*seats*) gradins, *m.pl*. ~*ery*, *n*, blanchisserie, *f*. ~*ing*, *n*, blanchiment, *m*.

bleak, *a*, morne, triste.

blear-eyed, *a*, chassieux.

bleat, *v.i*, bêler; (*goat & fig.*) chevroter. **bleat[ing]**, *n*, bêlement, *m*.

bleed, *v.t. & i. ir*, saigner; pleurer. ~*ing*, *n*, saignement, *m*; saignée, *f*.

blemish, *n*, tache, tare, défectuosité, *f*, défaut, *m*. ¶ *v.t*, tacher; ternir.

blench, *v.i*, reculer; fuir; broncher.

blend, *n*, assortiment, *m*. ¶ *v.t.ir*, assortir; fondre; confondre; incorporer; (*wines*) mélanger, couper; (*v.i.ir*.) [s']assortir, se confondre, s'apparenter. ~*ing* (*wines*) *n*, mélange, coupage, *m*.

bless, *v.t*, bénir; (*bell, etc.*) baptiser; favoriser. **blessed**, **blest**, *a*, béni; heureux; bienheureux. *the Blessed Virgin [Mary]*, la Sainte Vierge. *to be ~ with*, avoir le bonheur d'avoir, de posséder; jouir de. **blessedness**, *n*, béatitude; félicité, *f*. **blessing**, *n*, bénédiction, *f*; bonheur; (*grace*) bénédicité, *m*.

blight, *n*, brouissure, nielle, rouille, *f*. ¶ *v.t*, brouir, nieller, rouiller; flétrir.

blind, *a*, aveugle; borgne. ~ *alley*, impasse, *f*, cul-de-sac, *m*. ~ *man, woman*, aveugle, *m,f*. *the ~*, les aveugles, *m.pl*. ~*man's buff*, colin-maillard, *m*. ~*worm*, orvet, *m*. ¶ *n*, store, *m*; jalousie; (*shop*) banne, *f*; (*fig.*) voile, masque, faux-semblant, *m*. ¶ *v.t*, aveugler. ~*fold*, *v.t*, bander [les yeux à, de]. ~*ly*, *ad*, aveuglément, à l'aveuglette. ~*ness*, *n*, cécité, *f*; (*fig.*) aveuglement, *m*.

blink, *n*, clign[ot]ement, *m*. ¶ *v.i*, clign[ot]er, ciller; vaciller, papilloter; (*v.t.*) se cacher. ~*er*, *n*, œillère, *f*.

bliss, *n*, béatitude, félicité, *f*. ~*ful*, *a*, heureux; bienheureux; béat.

blister, *n*, ampoule, bulle, cloque, *f*; (*plaster*) vésicatoire, *m*. ¶ *v.t*, faire venir des ampoules à. *I ~ easily*, il me vient facilement des ampoules.

blithe, *a*, gai, joyeux.

blizzard, *n*, tourmente de neige, *f*.

bloat, *v.t*, bouffir. **bloater**, *n*. or **bloated herring**, hareng bouffi, *m*.

block, *n*, bloc, massif, *m*; motte, *f*; paquet, *m*; partie, tranche, *f*, ensemble; (*chopping*) billot, *m*; (*shape*) forme, poupée, *f*; (*houses*) pâté, îlot, *m*; (*pulley*) moufle, poulie, *f*; (*stoppage*) embarras, encombrement, embouteillage, *m*. ~ *letters* (e.g, child's writing), lettres moulées, *f.pl*. *in ~ letters* (as on coupon), en caractères d'imprimerie. ~ *writing*, la lettre moulée. ¶ *v.t*, obstruer, encombrer; embouteiller; bloquer; (*Bookb.*) dorer. ~ *up* (door), condamner.

blockade, *n*, blocus, *m*. ¶ *v.t*, bloquer.

blockhead, *n*, bûche, *f*, imbécile, *m,f*.

blockhouse, *n*, blockhaus, *m*.

blond, *as applied to a woman* **blonde**, *a*, blond (blonde, *f.*). ¶ *n*, (*color*) blond, *m*; (*pers.*) blond, e.

blood, *n*, sang, *m*; race, *f*; (*dandy*) petit-maître, élégant, *m*. ~ *heat*, température du sang, *f*. ~*hound*, limier, *m*. ~ *letting*, saignée, *f*. ~ *orange*, orange sanguine, *f*. ~ *poisoning*, empoisonnement du sang, *m*. ~ *pressure*, tension artérielle, *f*. ~ *red*, rouge sang, *m*. ~ *relationship*, consanguinité, *f*. ~*shed*, effusion de sang, *f*; carnage, *m*. ~*shot*, injecté [de sang], éraillé. ~*stone*, jaspé sanguin, héliotrope, *m*, sanguine, *f*. ~*sucker*, sangsue, *f*. ~ *test*, prise de sang, *f*, prélèvement de s., *m*. ~*thirsty*, altéré de sang, sanguinaire. ~ *vessel*, vaisseau sanguin, *m*. ~*less*, *a*, exsangue; non sanglant. ~*y*, *a*, ensanglanté, sanglant, en sang; sanguinaire.

bloom, *n*, fleur; fraîcheur, *f*. ¶ *v.i*, fleurir. ~*ing*, *a*, fleurissant; (*fig.*) florissant. ¶ *n*, floraison, *f*.

blossom, *n*, fleur, *f*. ¶ *v.i*, fleurir. ~*ing*, *n*, floraison, *f*.

blot, *n*, pâté, *m*, tache, *f*. ¶ *v.t*, faire un pâté sur, tacher; (*paper with useless writing*) noircir;

(*with blotting paper*) éponger.
~ *out*, effacer.

blotch, *n*, pustule; tache, *f*. ¶ *v.t*,
tacher.

blotting: ~ *case*, ~ *pad*, **blotter**,
n, buvard, sous-main, *m*. ~
paper, papier buvard, papier
brouillard, *m*.

blouse, *n*, chemisette, blouse, *f*.
~ *front*, guimpe, *f*.

blow, *n*, coup, *m*; bourrade; atteinte, *f*; (*pl*.) voies de fait, *f.pl*;
échec, *m*. ~*fly*, mouche à viande,
f. ~ *gun*, ~*pipe*, ~ *tube*, (dart
tube), sarbacane, *f*. ~[*hole*],
soufflure, *f*, bouillon, *m*. ~*out*,
crevaison, *f*. ~*pipe*, chalumeau,
m. ¶ *v.t.ir*, souffler; (*wind instrument*) souffler dans, emboucher;
(*to puff, to wind*) essouffler;
(*v.i.ir*.) souffler; venter; (*flower*)
s'épanouir; (*fuse*) fondre, jouer.
~ *a horn*, corner. ~ *one's brains
out*, se brûler la cervelle. ~ *one's
nose*, se moucher. ~ *out*, souffler. ~ *up*, *v.t*, souffler; faire
sauter, pétarder; (*v.i*.) sauter.
~**er**, *n*, souffleur, *m*.

blubber, *n*, graisse, *f*, lard, *m*.
¶ *v.i*, sangloter.

bludgeon, *n*, assommoir, gourdin, *m*, trique, massue, *f*.

blue, *a*, bleu. *Bluebeard*, Barbe-
Bleue, *m*. ~*bell*, jacinthe des
bois, *f*. ~*bottle*, mouche bleue,
f. ~*eyed*, aux yeux bleus.
~*jacket*, marin de l'État, *m*. ~
mark (bruise), bleu, *m*. ~*moldy* (cheese), persillé. ~*pencil*, *v.t*, marquer au crayon bleu;
sabrer, barrer. ~ *peter*, pavillon de partance, *m*. ~*print*, bleu,
m. ~*stocking*, bas-bleu, *m*. *out
of the* ~, soudainement. *to feel
blue*, avoir le cafard. ¶ *n*, bleu;
(*pl*.) spleen, *m*. ¶ *v.t*, bleuir.

bluff, *a*, brusque; franc; escarpé.
¶ *n*, cap à pic; trompe-l'œil, *m*.
¶ *v.t*, leurrer. ~**er**, *n*, faiseur, *m*.

bluish, *a*, bleuâtre.

blunder, *n*, bévue, bourde, ignorance, *f*, impair, *m* ¶ *v.i*, faire
des bévues, gaffer. ~**er**, *n*, gaffeur, maladroit, *m*.

blunt, *a*, émoussé; contondant;
brusque, cru. ¶ *v.t*, émousser,
épointer. ~*ly*, *ad*, brusquement,
crûment, rondement. ~**ness**, *n*,
état émoussé; sans-façon, *m*;
brusquerie, *f*.

blur, *n*, tache, *f*; embrouillement,
m. ¶ *v.t*, tacher, barbouiller;
[em]brouiller.

blurb, *n*, réclame, publicité, *f*.

blurred, *p.a*, trouble. **blurry**, *a*,
flou.

blurt out, *v.t*, lâcher, laisser
échapper.

blush, *n*, rougeur; fleur, *f*. *at the
first* ~, à vue de nez. ¶ *v.i*,
rougir. ~**ing**, *p.a*, rougissant,
rouge.

bluster, *n*, fracas, *m*; fanfaronnade, rodomontade, *f*. ¶ *v.i*,
tempêter; maugréer. ~**er**, *n*, fanfaron, *m*.

boa (*wrap*) *n*, boa, *m*. ~ *constrictor*, boa constrictor, *m*.

boar, *n*, verrat; (*wild*) sanglier;
(*young wild*) marcassin, *m*. ~
hound, vautre, *m*. ~ *hunting*,
chasse au sanglier, *m*. ~'*s head*,
hure de sanglier, *f*. ~ *spear*,
épieu, *m*.

board, *n*, planche, *f*, ais; plat;
tableau; tablier; (*notice*) écriteau, *m*, enseigne, *f*; (*Naut*.)
bord, *m*; bordée, *f*. *on* ~, à bord.
~ *room* & ~, pension complète.
~ [*of directors*], conseil [d'administration] *m*, administration,
f. ~ *of examiners*, jury d'examen, *m*. ¶ *v.t*, planchéier; (*ship*)
monter sur, aborder; (*train, car*)
monter dans; (*feed*) nourrir. ~
up (window), condamner. ~**er**,
n, pensionnaire; (élève) interne,
m,f. ~**ing**, *n*, planchéiage, *m*. ~
house, pension, *f*. ~*in*, internat,
m. ~ *school*, pensionnat, internat, *m*, pension, *f*.

boast, *n*, vanterie; gloire, *f*. ¶ *v.t*,
vanter; (*v.i*.) se vanter. ~**er**, *n*,
vantard, e, fanfaron, ne. ~**ful**, *a*,
vantard.

boat, *n*, bateau, canot, *m*, embarcation, barque, *f*; navire, bâtiment, vaisseau, *m*. ~ *deck*, pont
des embarcations, *m*. ~ *fishing*,
pêche en bateau, *f*. ~ *hook*, gaffe
[pour l'amarrage des bateaux] *f*,
croc [de batelier] *m*. ~*house*,
garage [des bateaux] *m*. ~*load*,
batelée, *f*. ~*man*, marin, canotier, *m*. ~ *train*, train de paquebot, *m*. ¶ *v.i*, canoter. ~**ing**, *n*,
canotage, *m*. **boatswain**, *n*, maître [d'équipage] *m*.

bob, *n*, secousse, *f*; révérence, *f*;
lentille, poire, *f*; plomb; poids,
m. ¶ *v.t*, balloter, branler.
bob[*bed hair*], coiffure à la
Ninon, coiffure à la Jeanne
d'Arc, *f*.

bobbin, *n*, bobine, canette, *f*.

bobsleigh, *n,* traîneau, bobsleigh, *m.*

bobtail, *n,* queue écourtée, *f.*

bode, *v.t,* présager.

bodice, *n,* corps, corsage, *m.*

bodily, *a,* corporel; physique; matériel; (*fear*) pour sa personne. ¶ *ad,* corporellement; en masse.

bodkin, *n,* passe-lacet, *m,* aiguille à passer, *f.*

body, *n,* corps, *m*; carcasse, *f*; vaisseau; massif, *m*; masse, *f*; gros, *m*; (*water*) masse; (*vehicle*) carrosserie, *f.* ~ *belt,* gaine, *f.* ~ *corporate,* personne morale, p. juridique, p. civile, *f.*

bog, *n,* marais, marécage, *m,* fondrière, *f.* ¶ *v.t,* embourber.

bogey [**man**] *n,* croque-mitaine, *m.*

boggle, *v.i,* reculer, hésiter.

boggy, *a,* marécageux, tourbeux.

bogus, *a,* faux, simulé; véreux.

Bohemia (*fig.*) *n,* la bohème. **Bohemian** (*fig.*) *n.* & *a,* bohème, *m,f.* & *a.*

boil (*Path.*) *n,* furoncle, clou, *m.*

boil, *v.t,* faire bouillir; cuire [à l'eau]; (*v.i.*) bouillir; bouillonner. ~ *down,* condenser, réduire. ~*ed,* *p.a:* ~ *beef,* bœuf bouilli, *m.* ~ *egg,* œuf à la coque, *m.* ~ *potatoes,* pommes de terre à l'eau, p—s de t. nature, p—s de t. vapeur, *f.pl.* ~*er,* *n,* (*steam*) chaudière, *f*; (*kitchen*) bain-marie, *m*; (*pot*) marmite, *f.* ~ *maker,* chaudronnier, *m.* ~ *making* & ~ *works,* [grosse] chaudronnerie, *f.* ~ *plate,* tôle de chaudière, *f.* ~ *room,* chambre de chauffe, chaufferie, *f.* ~*ing,* *n,* ébullition, *f*; bouillonnement, *m.* ~ *point,* point d'ébullition, *m.* (212° F. *or* 100° C.).

boisterous†, *a,* bruyant, turbulent.

bold, *a,* hardi, osé, audacieux, téméraire, assuré; net. ~*-faced* (*type*), gras. *displayed in* ~ *type,* en vedette. ~**ly,** *ad,* hardiment, audacieusement; hautement, franchement. ~**ness,** *n,* hardiesse, audace; fierté (*de touche*) *f.*

Bolivia, *n,* la Bolivie. **Bolivian,** *a,* bolivien. ¶ *n,* Bolivien, ne.

bollard, *n,* canon d'amarrage, poteau d'a., *m.*

Bologna, *n,* Bologne, *f.*

bolster, *n,* traversin, chevet; coussin, *m.* ~ *up,* *v.t,* (*doctrine*) étayer; (*pers.*) soutenir.

bolt, *n,* boulon, *m,* cheville, *f*; (*door*) verrou; (*lock*) pêne, *m*; (*thunder*) foudre; (*flight*) fugue, *f.* ¶ *v.t,* boulonner; cheviller; verrouiller; (*sift*) bluter; (*food*) expédier, gober; (*v.i.*) (*horse*) s'emporter, s'emballer; (*pers.*) prendre la poudre d'escampette.

bolt upright, tout droit.

bolus, *n,* bol, *m.*

bomb, *n,* bombe, *f.* ~*proof,* à l'épreuve des b—s. ~*shell* (*fig.*), bombe, *f.* ~*thrower,* lance-bombe, *m.* ¶ *v.t,* (*Avn.*) bombarder; (*Mil.*) lancer des bombes à.

bombard, *v.t,* bombarder, canonner; fusiller (*fig.*). ~*ier,* *n,* bombardier, *m.* ~*ment,* *n,* bombardement, *m.*

bombast, *n,* emphase, *f,* phébus. *m.* ~*ic,* *a,* emphatique, ampoulé, boursouflé, bouffi.

bomber, *n,* (*Avn.*) bombardier; (*pers.*) grenadier, *m.*

bona fide, *a.* & *ad,* de bonne foi; sérieux.

bond, *n,* lien, *m,* attache, *f*; nœud, *m*; liaison; chaîne, *f*; agglutinant; (*Fin.*) bon, *m*; obligation, *f*; titre, *m,* valeur, *f*; (*law*) acte, contrat; cautionnement; compromis, *m*; soumission, *f.* bond[*ed warehouse*], entrepôt [légal *ou* de douane] *m.* *in* bond[*ed warehouse*], en (*ou* à l')entrepôt. **bond,** *v.t,* entreposer; (*masonry*) liaisonner. **bondage,** *n,* captivité, *f,* esclavage, *m.*

bone, *n,* os, *m*; (*fish*) arête, *f*; (*pl, dead*) ossements, *m.pl*; (*castanets*) cliquettes, *f.pl.* ~ *of contention,* pomme de discorde, *f.* ~*setter,* rebouteur, euse. ¶ *v.t,* désosser; ôter les arêtes de.

bonfire, *n,* feu de joie, bûcher, *m.*

bonnet, *n,* chapeau; (*auto*) capot, *m,* capote, *f.*

bonny, *a,* joli; bien portant; gai.

bonus, *n,* gratification, prime, indemnité, *f.* ~ *shares,* actions gratuites, *f.pl.*

bony, *a,* osseux; (*big-boned*) ossu. ~ *palate,* palais dur, *m.*

boo, *v.t,* huer, conspuer.

booby, *n,* nigaud, e, benêt, dadais, *m,* huître, *f.* ~ *prize,* fiche de consolation, *f.* ~ *trap,* attrape-nigaud, *m.*

book, *n,* livre; livret; carnet; registre; journal; cahier; recueil; album; (*old* & *of little value*) bouquin, *m.* ~*binder*, relieur, euse. ~*binding*, reliure, *f.* ~*case*, bibliothèque, *f.* ~*ends*, serre-livres, *m.* ~*keeper*, teneur de livres, *m*, comptable, *m,f.* ~*keeping*, tenue de[s] livres, comptabilité, *f.* ~ *lover*, bibliophile, *m.* ~*maker*, bookmaker, *m.* ~*mark[er]*, signet, *m*, marque, *f.* ~*matches*, allumettes en carnet, *f.pl.* ~*muslin*, organdi, *m.* ~ *plate*, ex-libris, *m.* ~*rest*, pupitre, *m.* ~*seller*, libraire, *m.* ~*seller & publisher*, libraire-éditeur, *m.* ~[*seller's*] *shop*, librairie, *f.* ~*shelf*, rayon, *m.* ~*stall*, bibliothèque, *f*; kiosque, *m.* ~ *value*, valeur comptable, *f.* ~*worm* (*pers.*), rat de bibliothèque, *m.* ~ *work* (*Typ.*), labeur, *m.* ¶ *v.t*, enregistrer; engager, retenir, louer; réserver; demander; (*v.i.*) prendre un billet, des billets. **booking**, *n*, enregistrement; engagement, *m*, location; réserve, *f*; transport, voyage, service, *m.* **booklet**, *n*, brochure, *f*, livret, *m.*

boom, *n*, (*harbor*) estacade; (*crane*) flèche, *f*; (*prices*) emballement [à la hausse]; (*noise*) grondement, *m.* ¶ *v.i*, gronder, bourdonner, ronfler, tonner.

boon, *a*, gai, joyeux. ~ *companion*, **bon** compagnon; camarade de bouteille, *m.* ¶ *n*, bienfait, *m*, faveur, *f.*

boor, *n*, rustre, manant, *m*, rustaud, e. ~*ish*, *a*, rustaud, grossier. ~*ishness*, *n*, rusticité, grossièreté, *f.*

boost, *n*, poussée; augmentation, *f.* ¶ *v.t*, pousser; augmenter.

boot, *n*, chaussure [montante]; bottine, botte, *f*; brodequin. ~ *& shoe repairer*, cordonnier, *m.* ~ *& shoe trade*, cordonnerie, *f.* ~*black*, cireur de bottes, *m.* ~*jack*, tire-botte, *m.* ~*lace*, lacet de chaussure, *m.* ~*maker*, bottier, *m.* ~*tree*, embouchoir, embauchoir, *m.* ¶ *v.t*, chausser; botter. ~*ee*, *n*, chausson, *m.*

booth, *n*, baraque, boutique, échoppe, *f.*

bootless, *a*, inutile, vain, futile.

booty, *n*, butin, *m.*

booze, *v.i*, riboter, godailler.

boracic, *a*, borique. **borax**, *n*, borax, *m.*

border, *n*, bord, *m*, bordure; frontière; lisière, *f*; cordon, *m*; (*garden*) plate-bande, *f.* ~ *land*,

pays limitrophe, *m.* ¶ *v.t*, border. ~ [*up*]*on*, avoisiner, côtoyer, friser.

bore, *n*, alésage, calibre; (*Min.*) sondage, forage, *m*; (*tidal*) barre d'eau, *f*, mascaret, *m*; (*nuisance*) scie, *f*; (*pers.*) raseur, euse, endormeur, *m*, scie, *f*, crampon, *m.* ~ *core*, témoin, *m*, carotte, *f.* ~*hole*, trou de sonde, *m.* ¶ *v.t*, percer, forer; vriller; aléser, vider; (*fig.*) ennuyer, embêter, scier, assommer, tuer, assassiner. ~*dom*, *n*, ennui, *m.*

boric, *a*, borique.

born, *p.p. & a*, né; issu; de naissance. ~ *blind*, aveugle de naissance, aveugle-né. *to be* ~, naître.

borough, *n*, bourg, *m.*

borrow, *v.t*, emprunter. ~*er*, *n*, emprunteur, euse. ~*ing*, *n*, emprunt, *m. oft. pl.*

borzoi, *n*, lévrier russe, *m.*

bosom, *n*, sein, *m*; gorge, *f*; (*church*) sein, giron, *m.* ~ *friend*, ami de cœur, *m.*

Bosphorus (**the**), le Bosphore.

boss, *n*, bosse, *f*; moyeu; (*pers.*) patron, chef, *m.*

botanic(al), *a*, botanique. ~ *gardens*, jardin des plantes, *m.* **botanist**, *n*, botaniste, *m.* **botanize**, *v.i*, herboriser. **botany**, *n*, botanique, *f.*

botch, *n*, bousillage, *m.* ¶ *v.t*, bousiller, gâcher, massacrer.

both, *a. & ad*, tous [les] deux, deux; l'un(e) & l'autre; (*at the same time*) à la fois . . . et . . .

bother, *n*, tracas, aria, *m.* ¶ *v.t*, tracasser.

bottle, *n*, bouteille; canette, *f*; flacon; bocal, *m*; burette, *f.* ~ *brush*, rince-bouteille, *m.* ~ *neck*, embouteillage, *m.* ¶ *v.t*, mettre en bouteille(s), embouteiller. ~ *up* (*block*), embouteiller.

bottom, *n*, fond, bas, *m*, base, *f*, pied, bout; dessous; derrière, cul; (*of chair*) siège; (*lowland*) bas-fond; (*ship*) navire, *m*; (*of ship*) carène, *f.* ¶ *a*, inférieur; de fond; de dessous; le plus bas. ~*less*, *a*, sans fond.

bough, *n*, mère branche, *f*; rameau, *m.*

boulder, *n*, roche, *f*, gros galet, caillou, *m.*

bounce, *n*, bond, *m*; vanterie, blague, *f.* ¶ *v.i*, bondir; se vanter, faire le fanfaron.

bound, *n*, borne, limite, *f*; bond, saut, rebond, *m*. *to exceed all* ~*s*, dépasser la mesure. ¶ *v.t*, borner, limiter; (*v.i.*) bondir, sauter. ~ *for* (ship), à destination de. *to be* ~ *to*, être tenu(e) de (*ou* à), être obligé(e) de. **boundary,** *n*, limite, borne, *f*. **boundless,** *a*, illimité, sans bornes, immense.

bounteous†, *a*, généreux. **bountiful†,** *a*, généreux, libéral, bienfaisant; fécond. **bounty,** *n*, générosité, munificence, largesse; prime, *f*.

bouquet, *n*, bouquet; (*wine*) bouquet, fumet, *m*.

bourn, *n*, ruisseau, *m*.

bout, *n*, tour, assaut, *m*, partie, reprise, *f*.

bovine, *a*, bovin.

bow, *n*, (*knot*) nœud, nœud de ruban; (*necktie*) nœud[-papillon]; (*curve*) arc; (*fiddle*) archet; (*saddle*) arçon, *m*; (*padlock*) anse, *f*. ~ *compasses*, compas à balustre, *m*. ~ *window*, bowwindow, *m*.

bow, *n*, salut, coup de chapeau, *m*, inclination, révérence, *f*; (*ship*) avant, *m*. ¶ *v.t. & i*, courber, incliner, fléchir, plier. ~ & *scrape*, faire des courbettes. ~ *to*, saluer; s'incliner devant.

bowdlerize, *v.t*, expurger.

bowels, *n.pl*, entrailles, *f.pl*, intestins, *m.pl*; sein, *m*.

bower, *n*, tonnelle, *f*, berceau, cabinet de verdure, *m*.

bowing & scraping, prosternations, *f.pl*.

bowl, *n*, bol, bassin, *m*, écuelle, coupe, cuvette, jatte, sébile *f*; plateau; (*pipe*) fourneau, *m*; (*game*) boule, *f*. [*game of*] ~*s*, boules, *f.pl*, jeu de boules, *m*. ~*ful*, *n*, écuellée, *f*.

bowlegged, *a*, bancal.

bowler [hat], *n*, [chapeau] melon; (*player*) joueur, *m*.

bowling: ~ *alley*, jeu de boules couvert, *m*. ~ *green*, jeu de boules découvert.

bowman, *n*, archer; (*boat*) brigadier, *m*.

bowsprit, *n*, beaupré, *m*.

bow-wow, *n*, toutou, *m*.

box, *n*, boîte, caisse, *f*; coffre, coffret; tronc; boîtier; (*cardboard*) carton; (*driver's*) siège, *m*; (*jury*) banc, *m*; (*Theat.*) loge, *f*. ~ *office*, bureau [de loca-

tion], contrôle, *m*. ~ *on the ear*[*s*], soufflet, *m*. ~-*spring mattress*, sommier élastique, *m*. ~ [*tree*] & ~*wood*, buis, *m*. ¶ *v.t*, encaisser; (*someone's ears*) souffleter, frotter; (*fight*) boxer; (*v.i.*) boxer. ~**er,** *n*, boxeur, *m*. ~**ing,** *n*, boxe, *f*. ~ *match*, combat de b., assaut de b., match de b., *m*.

boy, *n*, garçon, garçonnet, enfant, gars, *m*. ~ *scout*, boy-scout; éclaireur, scout, *m*. ~**hood,** *n*, jeunesse, *f*. ~**ish,** *a*, enfantin, puéril.

boycott, *n*, boycottage, *m*. ¶ *v.t*, boycotter.

brace, *n*, (*strut, stay*) entretoise, *f*, étrésillon; arc-boutant, *m*, contre-fiche; bielle, *f*; tirant, *m*; moise, *f*; (*tool*) vilebrequin; cliquet; (*pair*) couple, paire. ¶ *v.t*, renforcer, armer; moiser; fortifier, retremper; bander; accolader.

bracelet, *n*, bracelet, *m*.

bracing, *a*, fortifiant, vivifiant.

bracken, *n*, fougère [à l'aigle] *f*.

bracket, *n*, console, potence, applique, *f*, (*Typ.*) [,] crochet, *m*; (,), parenthèse; [,], accolade, *f*. ¶ *v.t*, accoler.

brackish, *a*, saumâtre.

brad, *n*, pointe, *f*. ~**awl,** *n*, poinçon, *m*.

brag, *n*, vanterie, hâblerie, blague, fanfaronnade, *f*. ¶ *v.i*, se vanter. **braggart,** *n*, vantard, e, hâbleur, euse, fanfaron, ne.

brahmin, *n*, brahmane, *m*.

braid, *n*, tresse, soutache, *f*, bordé, galon; passement, *m*. ¶ *v.t*, tresser, soutacher, galonner, passementer.

brain, *n. & ~s,** *pl*, cerveau, *m*, cervelle, tête, *f*; (*pl. Cook.*) cervelle[s]. ~ *fatigue*, fatigue cérébrale, *f*. ~ *fever*, fièvre cérébrale, *f*. ~**less,** *a*, sans cervelle.

braise, *v.t*, braiser.

brake, *n*, (*on wheel*) frein; (*waggonette*) break, *m*; (*bracken*) fougère [à l'aigle] *f*; (*thicket*) fourré, *m*. ~ [*gear*], timonerie des freins; (*carriage*) mécanique, *f*. ¶ *v.t*, enrayer. *to put on* (*or apply*) *the* ~*s*, freiner, serrer les freins. **brakeman,** *n*, serre-frein, garde-frein, *m*.

bramble, *n*, ronce, *f*.

bran, *n*, son, *m*.

branch, *n*, branche, *f*; rameau;

embranchement; (*Elec.*) branchement, *m.* ~ [*line*] (*Rly*), ligne
(*ou* voie) secondaire, *f.* ~ [*office*], succursale, *f.*; comptoir, *m.*
¶ *v.t*, brancher; (*v.i.*) se ramifier.
~ *off*, *v.t*, embrancher; (*v.i.*)
fourcher.

brand, *n*, (*fire*) tison, brandon,
m; (*fig.*) flétrissure, *f*, stigmate;
(*Poet.*) glaive, *m*; (*Com. & hot
iron*) marque, *f*. **brand new,** battant (*ou* tout flambant) neuf.
¶ *v.t*, marquer [à chaud]; flétrir,
stigmatiser. **brandish,** *v.t*, brandir.

brandy, *n*, eau-de-vie, *f*, cognac,
m. ~ & *soda,* fine à l'eau, *f*.

brass, *n*, laiton, cuivre [jaune];
(*Poet.*) airain; (*bearing*) coussinet, *m*; (*cheek*) effronterie, *f*,
toupet, *m*. *the* ~*es* (*Mus.*), les
cuivres. ~ *band,* fanfare, *f*. ~
foundry, fonderie de cuivre, ro-
binetterie, *f*. ~*wares,* dinanderie,
f.

brassière, *n*, soutien-gorge, *m*.

brassy, *a*, cuivré.

brat, *n*, gamin, e, marmot, *m*,
gosse, *m,f*, (*pl, col.*) marmaille,
f.

bravado, *n*, bravade, *f*. **brave†,**
a, brave. ~ *man,* [homme] brave,
m. ¶ *v.t*, braver, affronter, défier. ~**ry,** *n*, bravoure, *f*. **bravo,**
i, bravo!

brawl, *n*, mêlée, bagarre, rixe,
querelle, *f*; tapage, *m*. ¶ *v.i*, se
chamailler; (*stream*) murmurer.
~**er,** *n*, tapageur, euse, casseur
d'assiettes, *m*.

brawn, *n*, hure, *f*, fromage de
porc, *m*; (*fig.*) force musculaire,
f. ~**y,** *a*, charnu, musculeux.

bray, *v.i*, braire. ~[**ing**], *n*, braiment, *m*.

braze, *v.t*, braser. **braze** (*joint*)
& **brazing,** *n*, brasure, *f*.

brazen, *a* (*of airain.* ~[-*faced*],
effronté. *to* ~ *it out,* crâner, faire
le crâne.

brazier, *n*, (*pers.*) chaudronnier;
dinandier; (*pan*) brasero, *m*.

Brazil, *n*, le Brésil. **Brazilian,** *a*,
brésilien. ¶ *n*, Brésilien, ne.

breach, *n*, brèche; infraction, violation, contravention, *f*. ~ *of
faith,* manque de foi, *m*. ~ *of
promise,* violation de promesse
de mariage, *f*. ~ *of trust,* infidélité, prévarication, forfaiture,
f, abus de confiance, *m*.

bread, *n*, pain, *m*. ~ *crumbs*

(*Cook.*), panure, chapelure, *f*.
~ *knife,* couteau à pain, *m*. ~
winner, soutien de famille, *m*.

breadth, *n*, largeur; envergure, *f*;
travers, *m*; (*of stuffs*) largeur,
f, lé, *m*.

break, *n*, rupture, cassure, brisure; solution; (*gap*) trouée, *f*;
(*day*) point, *m*; (*voice*) mue;
(*prices*) dérobade, *f*; (*Bil.*) série,
f. ¶ *v.t.ir*, casser, briser; fracturer; fragmenter; rompre; crever; fendre; concasser; enfreindre, violer; (*the bank, gaming*)
faire sauter; (*a set*) dépareiller;
(*news*) faire part de; (See also
broken); (*v.i.ir*) [se] casser, se
briser, etc; (*voice*) muer; (*dawn*)
poindre; (*waves*) déferler.
¶ (*Box.*), séparez! ~ *cover*
(*Hunt.*), débucher. ~ *down,* *v.t*,
abattre; (*v.i.*) avoir une panne.
~ *into,* envahir; pénétrer; entamer. ~ *loose,* se déchaîner. ~
of the habit, déshabituer, désaccoutumer. ~ *one's arm,* se casser
le bras. ~ *one's back,* s'échiner.
~ *one's word,* manquer de parole. ~ *open,* enfoncer. ~ *out,*
(*fire*) éclater, se déclarer; (*fig.*)
déborder, se débonder. ~ *their
engagement* (marriage), se désaccorder. ~ *through,* percer.
~ *upon the wheel,* rouer. **break-
able,** *a*, fragile. **breakage,** *n*,
casse, rupture, *f*, bris, *m*. **breakaway,** *n*, dislocation; dérive, *f*.
breakdown, *n*, (*failure*) fiasco,
m; (*car, etc.*) panne; (*health*)
prostration, *f*. **breaker,** *n*, (*pers.*)
casseur; démolisseur; (*wave*)
brisant, *m*. **breakfast,** *n*, déjeuner [du matin] *m*. ¶ *v.i*, déjeuner. **breaking,** *n*, rupture,
fracture, *f*, brisement, *m*; (*holy
bread*) fraction; (*voice*) mue, *f*.
breakneck, *n*, casse-cou, *m*.
breakwater, *n*, brise-lames, brisant, môle, *m*.

bream, *n*, brème, *f*; (*sea*) pagel,
m.

breast, *n*, sein, *m*; poitrine, *f*;
(*horse*) poitrail; (*fowl*) blanc,
m. *at the* ~, à la mamelle.
~*bone,* sternum, *m*. ~*high,*
à hauteur d'appui. ~*stroke*
(*Swim.*), brasse, nage en grenouille, *f*.

breath, *n*, haleine, *f*; souffle;
soupir, *m*. **breathe,** *v.i. & t*, respirer; souffler; soupirer. **breathing,** *n*, respiration, *f*. ~ *space,*
temps de respirer, relâche, *m*.

breathless, *a,* inanimé; haletant, essoufflé, à bout de souffle.

breech, *n,* derrière, *m;* (*gun*) culasse, *f,* tonnerre, *m.* ~*-loading,* se chargeant par la culasse. **breeches,** *n.pl,* culotte, *f.*

breed, *n,* race, *f.* ¶ *v.t.ir,* élever; engendrer; (*v.i.ir.*) multiplier, se reproduire. ~**er** (*stock*) *n,* éleveur, *m.* ~**ing,** *n,* (*animals*) élevage, *m;* (*pers.*) éducation, *f,* ton, *m.*

breeze, *n,* (*wind*) brise, *f.* **breezy,** *a,* venteux; frais.

Bremen, *n,* Brême, *f.*

brethren, *n.pl,* frères, *m.pl.*

breviary, *n,* bréviaire, *m.*

brevity, *n,* concision; brièveté, *f.*

brew, *v.t,* brasser; (*tea*) faire infuser; (*v.i.*) faire de la bière; (*storm*) couver, se préparer; (*fig.*) couver, se tramer, se mijoter. ~**er,** *n,* brasseur, *m.* ~**ery,** *n,* brasserie, *f.* ~**ing,** *n,* brassage, *m.*

briar, *n,* églantier, *m;* (*pipe wood*) bruyère, *f.*

bribe, *n,* pot-de-vin, *m.* ¶ *v.t,* corrompre, séduire, soudoyer. ~**ry,** *n,* corruption, *f.*

brick, *n,* brique, *f.* ~ *kiln,* four à briques, *m.* ~*layer,* maçon, *m.* ~*maker,* briquetier, *m.* ~ *paving,* carrelage en briques, *m.* ~*work,* briquetage, *m.* ~*yard,* briqueterie, *f.*

bridal, *a,* nuptial; de mariée. **bride,** *n,* nouvelle mariée; (*about to be married* or *on marriage day*) mariée, *f.* ~ *&* ~*groom,* nouveaux mariés, *m.pl.* ~*groom,* nouveau marié; marié, *m.* **brides-maid,** demoiselle d'honneur, *f.*

bridge, *n,* pont, *m;* (*foot & ship's*) passerelle, *f;* (*violin*) chevalet; (*nose*) dos; (*cards*) bridge, *m.* ¶ *v.t,* jeter un pont sur; franchir.

bridle, *n,* bride, *f.* ~ *path,* sentier pour cavaliers, *m,* piste cavalière, *f.* ¶ *v.t,* brider; refréner; (*v.i.*) se rengorger.

brief, *a,* bref, concis; de courte durée. ¶ *n,* cause, *f,* dossier, *m.* ~*case,* serviette, *f.* ¶ *v.t,* confier une cause à; constituer. ~**ly,** *ad,* brièvement, bref, en abrégé.

brier, églantier, *m;* (*pipe wood*) bruyère, *f.*

brig, *n,* brick, *m.*

brigade, *n,* brigade, *f;* corps, *m.* ¶ *v.t,* embrigader.

brigand, *n,* brigand, *m.* ~**age,** *n,* brigandage, *m.*

bright, *a,* brillant, éclatant, luisant; vif; beau; gai; poli; lumineux, clair; encourageant; intelligent. ~ *interval* (*Meteor.*), éclaircie, *f.* ~**en,** *v.t,* faire briller; polir; éclaircir; aviver, animer. ~**ly,** *ad,* brillamment, clairement. ~**ness,** *n,* brillant, éclat, *m;* bonne orientation, *f.*

brill, *n,* barbue, *f.*

brilliance, *n,* éclat, brillant, *m.* **brilliant,** *a,* brillant, éclatant. ¶ *n,* brillant, *m.* ~**ine,** *n,* brillantine, *f.* ~**ly,** *ad,* brillamment.

brim, *n,* bord, *m.* ¶ ~ *over,* déborder. ~**ful,** *a,* plein jusqu'aux bords, à pleins bords.

brimstone, *n,* soufre, *m.*

brindled, *a,* tacheté.

brine, *n,* saumure; (*Poet.*) onde amère, *f;* larmes, *f.pl.*

bring, *v.t.ir,* apporter; amener; conduire; faire; mettre; porter. ~ *about,* déterminer; ménager. ~ *an action against,* intenter une action à, actionner, attaquer en justice. ~ *back,* rapporter; ramener. ~ *forth,* mettre au monde; produire. ~ *forward* (*Bkkpg*), reporter. ~ *in* (house), rentrer. ~ *up,* élever, bercer, nourrir; (*food*) rendre. ~ *up the rear,* fermer la marche. ~**ing up,** éducation, *f.*

brink, *n,* bord; penchant, *m;* veille, *f.*

briny, *a,* saumâtre; (*Poet.*) amer.

briquet[te], *n,* briquette, *f,* aggloméré, *m.*

brisk†, *a,* vif, actif, animé, allègre. ~ *fire* (*Mil.*), feu nourri, *m.*

brisket, *n,* poitrine, *f.*

briskness, *n,* vivacité; activité, *f.*

bristle, *n,* soie, *f;* poil, *m.* ¶ *v.t,* hérisser; (*v.i.*) [se] hérisser. **bristling,** *p.a. & bristly,* *a,* hérissé.

Bristol Channel (the), le canal de Bristol.

Britain, *n,* la Grande-Bretagne. *Britannia metal,* métal anglais, *m.* **British,** *a,* britannique; anglais. ~ *ambassador,* ambassadeur d'Angleterre, *m.* ~ *consul,* consul britannique, *m.* ~ *Isles,* îles Britanniques, *f.pl.*

Brittany, *n,* la Bretagne.

brittle, *a,* cassant, fragile. ~**ness,** *n,* fragilité, *f.*

broach, *n,* (*spit*) broche, *f;* (*Mech.*) alésoir, *m.* ¶ *v.t,* (*cask*) percer; (*bore*) aléser; (*fig.*) entamer; aborder.

broad, *a,* grand; gros; ample; plein; (*accent*) prononcé; (*ribald*) libre, cru, gras; (*hint*) peu voilé, assez clair. ~ *bean,* fève de marais, *f.* ~-*brimmed hat,* chapeau à grands bords, *m.* ~*cast, a, ad,* à la volée; (*v.t.*) [radio]diffuser. ~*casting,* [radio]diffusion, *f.* ~*casting station,* poste de r., p. d'émission, *m. in* ~ *daylight,* au grand jour, en plein jour, en plein midi. ~*minded,* à l'esprit large. ~*shouldered,* large d'épaules. ~*side,* (*Naut.*) flanc, travers, côté, *m.*; (*guns, fire*) bordée, *f*; (*fig.*) jeu de massacre, *m.* ~*sword,* sabre, *m.* ~*en, v.t,* élargir. ~*ly, ad,* largement, ouvertement; en gros. ~*ness, n,* largeur; grossièreté, *f*; accent prononcé, *m.*

brocade, *n,* brocart, *m.*

broil, *n,* bagarre, *f*; tumulte, *m.* ¶ *v.t,* brasiller, griller. ~*er, n,* gril, *m.* **broiling,** *a,* brûlant.

broke (*hard up*), *a,* aux abois, fauché.

broken, *a,* (*country*) tourmenté, accidenté, mouvementé; (*health*) délabrée, caduque, *f*; (*speech, sleep, etc.*) entrecoupé; (*English, French*) mauvais. *to be* ~-*down* (car), être (*ou* rester) en panne. *to be* ~-*hearted,* avoir le cœur navré (*ou* serré de douleur). ~ *winded,* poussif.

broker, *n,* courtier, ère; agent; banquier, *m.* ~*age, n,* courtage, *m.* ~ *fees,* commissions de courtier, *f.pl.*

bromide, *n,* bromure, *m.*

bronchia, *n.pl,* bronches, *f.pl.* **bronchitis,** *n,* bronchite, *f.*

bronze, *n,* bronze, *m.* ~ *shoes,* souliers mordorés, *m.pl.* ¶ *v.t,* bronzer.

brooch, *n,* broche; (*bar shaped*) barrette, *f.*

brood, *n,* couvée; nichée, engeance, *f.* ~ *hen,* couveuse, *f.* ~ *mare,* [jument] poulinière, *f.* ¶ *v.i,* couver; ruminer. ~*ing time,* couvaison, *f.*

brook, *n,* ruisseau, *m.* ¶ *v.t,* digérer, tolérer. ~*let, n,* ruisselet, *m.*

broom, *n,* balai; (*Bot.*) genêt, *m.* ~*stick,* manche à balai, *m.*

broth, *n,* bouillon; potage, *m.*

brother, *n,* frère; confrère, *m.* ~-*in-law,* beau-frère. ~*hood,* fraternité, confrérie; confraternité, *f.* ~*ly, a,* fraternel.

brow, *n,* sourcil; (*forehead & cliff*) front; (*hill*) sommet, *m.* ~*beat, v.t,* rudoyer.

brown, *a,* brun; (*bread—light*) bis; (*bread—dark*) noir; (*sunburnt*) bruni. ~ *crust* (in pot), gratin, *m.* ~ *hair,* cheveux châtains, *m.pl.* ~ *owl,* chat-huant, *m.* ~ *study,* rêverie, *f.* ~ *sugar,* cassonade, *f.* ¶ *n,* brun, *m.* ¶ *v.t,* brunir; (*meat*) roussir, rissoler. ~*ish, a,* brunâtre.

brownie, *n,* elfe, *m.*

browse, *n,* brout, *m.* ¶ *v.i. & t,* brouter, paître.

bruise, *n,* contusion, meurtrissure, *f,* pinçon, *m*; (*dent*) bosse, *f.* ¶ *v.t,* contusionner, meurtrir, froisser; bossuer, bosseler. ~*d, p.a,* meurtri, contus.

brunette, *a,* brun, brunet. ¶ *n,* femme brune, *f.*

brunt, *n,* poids; choc, *m.*

brush, *n,* brosse, *f*; pinceau; coup de brosse; (*Elec.*) balai, *m*; (*fox*) queue; (*affray*) échauffourée, *f.* ~ *maker,* brossier, ère. ~ *making,* brosserie, *f.* ~*wood,* broussailles, *f.pl,* [bois] taillis, mortbois, *m.* ¶ *v.t,* brosser; (*mud off*) décrotter; (*graze*) raser, effleurer, frôler. ~ *one's hair, teeth,* se brosser la tête, les dents. ~ *up* (*fig.*), repolir, dérouiller. ~ *aside,* écarter.

brusque, *a,* brusque.

Brussels, *n,* Bruxelles, *f.* ~ *carpet,* tapis de moquette, *m*; moquette, *f.* ~ *sprout,* chou de Bruxelles, *m.*

brutal†, *a,* brutal. ~*ity, n,* brutalité, *f.* ~*ize, v.t,* abrutir. **brute,** *n,* brute, *f,* animal, *m.* ~ *beast,* bête brute, *f. the* ~ *creation,* l'espèce animale, *f.* ~ *force,* force brute, *f.* **brutish†,** *a,* brutal; abruti.

bubble, *n,* bulle, *f*; bouillon; projet en l'air, *m.* ¶ *v.i,* bouillonner; pétiller.

buccaneer, *n,* boucanier, *m.*

buck, *n,* (*deer*) daim; (*jump*) saut de mouton; (*pers.*) luron, gaillard, *m.* ~ *rabbit,* lapin mâle, bouquin, *m.* ~*skin,* peau de daim, *f,* daim, *m*; (*pl.*) culotte de peau, *f.* ~*shot,* chevrotine, *f.* ¶ *v.i,* ruer.

bucket, *n,* seau, *m,* seille, *f*; godet, *m,* auge, *f,* auget; baquet, *m*; benne, *f.* ~ *shop,* maison de contrepartie, *f.* ~*ful, n,* seau, *m*; augée, *f.*

buckle, *n,* boucle, *f.* ¶ *v.t,* boucler. (*v.i.*) se boucler; se corber. ~ *down to,* s'appliquer à.

buckram, *n,* bougran, *m.*

buckthorn, *n,* nerprun, *m.*

buckwheat, *n,* [blé-]sarrasin, blé noir, *m.*

bucolic, *a,* bucolique.

bud, *n,* bourgeon, bouton, *m,* gemme, *f;* (*fig.*) germe, *m.* ¶ *v.i,* bourgeonner; naître.

buddhist, *a,* bouddhique. ¶ *n,* bouddhiste, *m.*

budding (*fig.*) *a,* naissant; en herbe.

buddy, *n,* copain, *m.*

budge, *v.i,* bouger.

budget, *n,* budget, *m.* ~ *for,* porter au b.

buff (*color*) *a.* & *n,* fauve, *a.* & *m.* ~ [*leather*], buffle, *m,* peau de buffle, *f.* ¶ *v.t,* polir. **buffalo,** *n,* buffle, *m.*

buffer, *n,* tampon [de choc], heurtoir, butoir, *m.* ~ *state,* état tampon, *m.*

buffet, *n,* (*blow*) soufflet; (*sideboard*) buffet; (*at a ball*) souper debout, *m.* ~ *car,* wagon-restaurant, *m.* ¶ *v.t,* secouer.

buffoon, *n,* bouffon, ne, pitre, *m.* ~**ery,** *n,* bouffonnerie, *f.*

bug, *n,* punaise, *f.* ~**bear,** *n,* loup-garou, croque-mitaine, épouvantail, cauchemar, *m.*

bugle, *n,* clairon, *m;* (*Bot.*) bugle, *f.* ~ *call,* sonnerie, *f.* **bugler,** *n,* clairon, *m.*

build, *n,* construction, *f.* *of sturdy* ~ *or well built* (man), bien charpenté. ¶ *v.t.ir,* bâtir, construire. ~ *up,* édifier, échafauder. ~**er,** *n,* constructeur, entrepreneur [de bâtiments] *m.* ~**ing,** *n,* construction, *f,* bâtiment, édifice; monument, *m.* ~ *materials,* matériaux de construction, *m.pl.* ~ *site,* terrain à bâtir, *m.*

bulb, *n,* (*Bot.*) bulbe, *f,* o[i]gnon, *m;* (*Anat.*) bulbe, *m;* (*lamp, thermometer*) ampoule, *f;* (*Chem.*) ballon, *m;* (*rubber*) poire, *f.* ~**ous,** *a,* bulbeux.

Bulgaria, *n,* la Bulgarie. **Bulgarian,** *a,* bulgare. ¶ *n,* Bulgare, *m,f.*

bulge, *n,* bombement, ventre, *m.* ¶ *v.i.* & *t,* bomber, boucler, bouffer, faire [le] ventre.

bulk, *n,* volume; gros, *m;* masse, *f.* *in* ~ (*Ship.*), en vrac, en grenier.

~*head,* cloison, *f.* ~**y,** *a,* volumineux; massif; encombrant.

bull, *n,* taureau, *m;* (*Pope's*) bulle, *f;* (*incongruity*) prudhommerie, *f,* contresens, *m;* (*Stk Ex.*) haussier, *m.* ~ *calf,* veau mâle, taurillon, *m.* ~**dog,** bouledogue, *m.* ~**fight,** course de taureaux, *f.* ~*'s-eye* (*target*) noir, *m,* mouche, *f;* (*window*) œil-de-bœuf, *m;* ~*'s-eye* [*lantern*], lanterne avec projecteur à lentille faisant saillie, *f.*

bullet, *n,* balle, *f.*

bulletin, *n,* bulletin, *m.*

bullfinch, *n,* bouvreuil, *m.*

bullion, *n,* or en barres, *m.*

bullock, *n,* bœuf, *m.*

bully, *n,* bravache, brutal, *m.* ¶ *v.t,* malmener, brutaliser.

bulrush, *n,* jonc, *m;* (*reed mace*) massette, masse d'eau, *f.*

bulwark, *n,* rempart; boulevard; (*ship's*) pavois, *m.*

bum, *n,* vagabond, *m.*

bumblebee, *n,* bourdon, *m.*

bump, *n,* bosse, *f;* cahot, heurt, *m.* ¶ *v.t.* & *i,* cogner, heurter, se heurter; cahoter.

bumper, *n,* (*brimful glass*) rasade, *f,* rouge bord; (*auto*) pare-chocs, *m.*

bumpkin, *n,* rustre, lourdaud, *m.*

bumptious, *a,* suffisant. ~**ness,** *n,* suffisance, *f.*

bun (*hair*) *n,* torpillon, *m.*

bunch, *n,* bouquet, *m;* botte, *f;* (*keys*) trousseau, *m;* (*grapes*) grappe, *f;* (*bananas, etc.*) régime, *m.* ¶ *v.t,* botteler.

bundle, *n,* paquet; faisceau, *m;* botte, *f;* fagot, *m;* liasse, *f.* ¶ *v.t,* empaqueter; botteler; fagoter; mettre en liasse.

bung, *n,* bondon, *m,* bonde, *f,* bouchon, tampon, *m.* ~[*hole*], bonde, *f.* ¶ *v.t,* bondonner, boucher.

bungalow, *n,* maisonnette, *f.*

bungle, *n,* bousillage, *m,* mauvaise besogne, *f.* ¶ *v.t,* bousiller, barbouiller; massacrer. **bungler,** *n,* bousilleur, euse, fagoteur, *m.*

bunion, *n,* oignon, *m.*

bunk, *n,* couchette, *f.*

bunker, *n,* soute, *f;* caisson, *m;* (*golf*) banquette, *f.* ~ *coal,* charbon de soute, *m.*

bunkum, *n,* blague, *f.*

bunt, *v.t,* pousser, encorner.

bunting, *n,* (*stuff*) étamine à pavillon, *f;* (*flags*) draperie, *f;* (*bird*) bruant, *m.*

buoy, n, bouée, f. ¶ v.t, baliser. ~ up, soutenir. ~ancy, n, flottabilité; poussée, f; (fig.) ressort, m. ~ant, a, flottant; élastique; vif, animé.

burden, n, fardeau, m, charge, f, poids, faix; (ship) port, maximum de charge, tonnage; (song) refrain, m. ¶ v.t, charger; grever. ~some, a, onéreux.

burdock, n, bardane, f.

bureau, n, bureau; cabinet, m. weather ~, office de météorologie, m.

bureaucracy, n, bureaucratie, f. **bureaucrat,** n, bureaucrate, m.

burglar, n, cambrioleur, m. ~ alarm, appareil avertisseur contre le vol, m. ~y, n, cambriolage, vol [de nuit avec effraction] m. ~ insurance, assurance contre le vol, f. **burgle,** v.t, cambrioler.

burgundy, n, bourgogne, vin de B., m.

burial, n, enterrement, m. ~ ground, cimetière, m. ~ place, lieu de sépulture, m. ~ service, office des morts, m.

burlap, n, serpillière, f.

burlesque, a. & n, burlesque, a. & m. ¶ v.t, travestir.

burly, a, solidement bâti; corpulent.

Burma, n, la Birmanie. **Burmese,** a, birman. ¶ n, Birman, e.

burn, n, brûlure, f. ¶ v.t. & i. ir, brûler; incendier; calciner; (of sun) hâler. I have burnt my arm, je me suis brûlé le bras. to burn one's fingers (fig.), s'échauder. ~er, n, brûleur, bec, m. ~ing, a, brûlant, en feu, enflammé; ardent; cuisant. ¶ n, combustion; ignition; cuisson, cuite, f; (smell) brûlé, roussi, graillon, m.

burnish, v.t, (metal, etc.) brunir; (paper, etc.) satiner. ~ing, n, brunissage; satinage, m.

burnt, p.a: ~ almond, praline, f. ~ offering, holocauste, m. ~ Sienna, terre de Sienne brûlée, f.

burr, n, barbes, f.pl; (speech) grasseyement, m. ¶ (speaking) v.i, grasseyer.

burrow, n, terrier, clapier, m. ¶ v.i, terrer; se terrer; fouiller.

bursar, n, économe, m, dépensier, ère. ~'s office & ~ship, n, économat, m.

burst, n, éclat, jet; (light) coup; (speed) emballement; (eloquence) mouvement; (passion, etc.) transport, élan, m. ¶ v.t.ir, faire éclater, [faire] crever; rompre; (v.i.ir) éclater; crever; se précipiter. ~ing, n, éclatement, m, crevaison, f.

bury, v.t, enterrer, ensevelir.

bus, n, autobus, bus, m.

bush, n, buisson, arbuste, m; (scrub) brousse; (Mach.) coquille, bague, f, manchon, m.

bushel, n, boisseau, m.

bushy, a, touffu, fourni; embroussaillé, buissonneux.

busily, ad, activement.

business, n, affaires, f.pl, commerce, négoce, m; affaire, entreprise, f; fonds [de commerce] m; qualité, f, métier, m; délibérations, questions [à délibérer] f.pl, ordre du jour; (right) droit; (fuss) aria, m. ~ as usual during alterations, la maison reste ouverte pendant les travaux. ~ card, carte d'adresse, f. ~ day, jour non férié, m. ~ hours, heures d'affaires, heures d'ouverture, f.pl. ~like, régulier; pratique, entendu. ~man, homme d' (ou dans le) affaires, m. ~ premises, locaux commerciaux, m.pl, immeuble commercial, m. ~ quarter, quartier commerçant, m. ~ world, monde des affaires, m.

buskin, n, brodequin; cothurne, m.

bust, n, buste, m; gorge, f, corsage, m. ~ measurement, [con]tour de poitrine, m.

bustard, n, outarde, f.

bustle, n, mouvement; remue-ménage, m; animation, f, tourbillon, m. ¶ v.i, se remuer.

busy, a, occupé, affairé, embesogné; industrieux; mouvementé; actif; empressé; diligent. ~ bee, abeille industrieuse, f. ~ man, woman, affairé, e. ~body, tiche-à-tout, m, commère, f, tatillon, ne, nécessaire, m.

but, c, mais; que; or. ~ for, sans. ¶ ad. & pr, hormis, excepté, seulement; ne . . . que. ¶ n, mais, m.

butcher, n, boucher, m. ~'s shop, boucherie, f. ¶ v.t, massacrer. ~y, n, carnage, m.

butler, n, sommelier; maître d'hôtel, m.

butt, n, (cask) tonneau, m; (pl., behind target) butte; (cigarette) mégot, m; (rifle) crosse, f; (cue) talon; (pers.) plastron, bouffon, m, cible, risée, f, souffre-douleur;

(*ram, etc.*) coup de corne, coup de tête, *m.* ¶ *v.i. & t,* cosser; heurter de la tête; buter.

butter, *n,* beurre, *m.* ~ *dish,* beurrier, *m.* ~*milk,* lait de beurre, babeurre, *m.* ¶ *v.t,* beurrer. ~*ed toast,* rôties au beurre, *f.pl,* toast, *m.*

buttercup, *n,* bassinet, bouton d'or, *m.*

butterfly, *n,* papillon [diurne] *m.*

buttock, *n,* fesse, *f;* (*beef*) cimier, *m.*

button, *n,* bouton, *m.* ~*hole,* boutonnière, *f.* ~*hole stitch* (*Emb.*), point de languette, p. de feston, *m.* ~*hole* (detain), cueillir. ~*hook,* tire-bouton, *m.* ¶ *v.t,* boutonner. ~ *oneself up,* se b.

buttress, *n,* contrefort, éperon; (*flying*) arc-boutant, *m.* ¶ *v.t,* arc-bouter; soutenir.

buxom, *a,* opulent, plantureux, rondelet & de bonne mine. ~*ness,* *n,* opulence, *f.*

buy, *v.t.ir,* acheter, acquérir. ~ *back,* racheter. ~ *out,* désintéresser. ~ *up,* enlever, accaparer. ~*er,* *n,* acheteur, euse, acquéreur, preneur, *m.* ~*ing,* *n,* achat, *m,* acquisition, *f.*

buzz, *v.i,* bourdonner, ronfler, tinter.

buzzard, *n,* buse, *f.*

by, *pr,* par; à; sur; sous; en; près. ¶ *ad,* près, à part. ~ *& ~,* tantôt. ~ *the ~,* ~ *the way,* à propos, en passant.

bylaw, *n,* règlement, *m.*

by-election, *n,* élection de remplacement, *f.*

bygone, *a,* passé, ancien, d'autrefois.

bypass, *n,* route d'évitement; (*gas*) veilleuse, *f.*

bypath, *n,* chemin écarté, sentier détourné, *m.*

by-product, *n,* sous-produit, *m.*

bystander, *n,* assistant, e, spectateur, trice, curieux, *m.*

byway, *n,* chemin détourné, *m.*

byword, *n,* dicton, *m;* risée, fable, *f.*

C

C (*Mus.*) *letter,* ut, do, *m.* ~ *clef,* clef d'ut, *f.*

cab, *n,* taxi, fiacre, *m,* voiture [de place], *f;* (*locomotive*) abri, *m.*

~*man,* cocher, chauffeur, *m.* ~*stand,* station de taxis, *f.*

cabal, *n,* cabale, *f.*

cabaret [show], *n,* attractions, *f.pl.*

cabbage, *n,* chou, *m.* ~ *lettuce,* laitue pommée, *f.* ~ *tree,* palmiste, *m.*

cabin, *n,* cabine, chambre; cabane, case; guérite, *f.* ~ *boy,* mousse, *m.* ~ *passenger,* passager (ère) de cabine. ~ *trunk,* malle de paquebot, malle de cabine, *f.*

cabinet, *n,* cabinet, *m;* armoire, *f,* meuble, *m.* ~ *council,* Conseil des ministres, C. de Cabinet, *m.* ~*maker,* menuisier, ébéniste, *m.* ~*making & ~work,* menuiserie, ébénisterie, *f.* ~ *minister,* ministre d'État, *m.*

cable, *n,* câble, *m.* ~ *railway,* [chemin de fer] funiculaire, *m.* ¶ (*Teleg.*) *v.t,* câbler.

cacao, *n,* cacao, *m.* ~ [*tree*], cacaoyer, cacaotier, *m.*

cachet, *n,* cachet, *m.*

cachou, *n,* cachou, *m.*

cackle, *n,* caquet, *m.* ¶ *v.i,* caqueter.

cactus, *n,* cactus, *m.*

cad, *n,* canaille, *f,* goujat, pleutre, mufle, *m.*

caddie (*golf*) *n,* cadet, te.

caddy, *n,* boîte [à thé] *f.*

cadence, *n,* cadence, *f.*

cadet, *n,* cadet; élève (*de l'école navale*), *m.*

cadge, *v.t,* écornifler. **cadger,** *n,* écornifleur, euse.

Cadiz, *n,* Cadix, *m.*

cafeteria, *n,* restaurant de libre service, *m.*

cage, *n,* cage; cabine; loge, *f.* ~ *bird,* oiseau de volière, *m.* ¶ *v.t,* encager.

cairn, *n,* montjoie, *f.*

Cairo, *n,* le Caire.

caisson, *n,* caisson; (*dock*) bateau-porte, *m.*

cajole, *v.t,* cajoler, amadouer. ~*ry,* *n,* cajolerie, *f.*

cake, *n,* gâteau, *f;* (*soap*) pain; (*oilseed*) tourteau, *m.* ¶ *v.i,* se cailler, faire croûte.

calabash, *n,* calebasse, *f.*

calamitous, *a,* calamiteux. **calamity,** *n,* calamité, *f.*

calcareous, *a,* calcaire.

calcine, *v.t,* calciner.

calcium, *n,* calcium, *m.*

calculate, *v.t,* calculer; (*v.i.*) compter. ~*d to,* propre à, de nature à. **calculating machine,** machine à calculer, *f.* **calculation & calculus** (*Med.*) *n*, calcul, *m.*

caldron, *n*, chaudron, *m.*

calendar, *n*, calendrier; (*prisoners for trial*) rôle, *m.* ~ *year*, année civile, *f.*

calender, *n*, calandre, *f.* ¶ *v.t*, calandrer, cylindrer.

calf, *n*, veau; (*leg*) mollet, gras de la jambe, *m.* ~[*skin*], peau de veau, *f*, [cuir de] veau, *m.*

caliber, *n*, calibre, *m.* **calibrate,** *v.t*, calibrer.

calico, *n*, calicot, *m.*

California, *n*, la Californie. **Californian,** *a*, californien. ¶ *n*, Californien, ne.

caliper, *n*, calibre; (*pl.*) compas [de calibre] *m.* ¶ *v.t*, calibrer.

caliph, *n*, calife, *m.*

call, *n*, appel; rappel, *m*; demande; (*trumpet, bugle*) sonnerie; visite; communication; (*Relig.*) vocation; (*to a ship*) semonce; (*of a ship*) escale; relâche, *f*; (*Fin.*) appel [de fonds], versement; terme, *m*; option, faculté; (*cards*) invite, *f.* ~ *of the blood* (*fig.*), force du sang, *f.* ~ *to arms,* appel aux armes. ¶ *v.t. & i,* appeler; héler; rappeler; convoquer; faire venir; prendre; réveiller; qualifier; traiter de; nommer; surnommer; intituler; passer, s'arrêter; faire; (*ship*) faire escale; relâcher. ~ *back,* rappeler. ~ *for,* demander, réclamer; (*trumps*) inviter; exiger. ~ *off,* contremander, décommander; (*hounds*) rompre. ~ *out,* appeler, crier. ~ [*up*]*on,* sommer, invoquer.

caller, *n*, visiteur, euse. **calling,** *n*, appel, *m*; convocation; vocation, profession, *f*, métier, *m.*

callosity & callus, *n*, callosité, *f*, cal, durillon, *m.* **callous,** *a*, endurci, insensible; (*skin*) calleux.

callow, *a*, sans plumes. ~ *youth,* la verte jeunesse; jeune homme imberbe, blanc-bec, *m.*

calm, *a*, calme. ¶ *v.t*, calmer. ~ly, *ad*, tranquillement. ~[ness], *n*, calme, *m*, tranquillité, *f.*

calorie, *n*, calorie, *f.*

calumniate, *v.t*, calomnier. **calumny,** *n*, calomnie, *f.*

Calvary (*place*) *n*, Calvaire, *m.* **calvary** (*representation*) *n*, calvaire, *m.*

calve, *v.i*, vêler.

calyx, *n*, calice, *m.*

cam, *n*, came, *f*, excentrique, *m.*

camber, *n*, bombement, *m*, cambrure, *f.*

cambric, *n*, batiste, *f.*

came, *n*, plomb, *m*, (*pl.*) résille, *f.*

camel, *n*, chameau, *m.* ~ *driver,* chamelier, *m.*

camellia, *n*, camélia, *m.*

cameo, *n*, camée, *m.*

camera, *n*, appareil photographique, *m.* ~ *obscura* (*Opt.*), chambre noire, c. obscure, *f. in* ~, à huit clos.

cami-knickers, *n.pl*, chemise-culotte, *f.*

camisole, *n*, cache-corset, *m.*

camomile, *n*, camomille, *f.*

camouflage, *n*, camouflage, *m.* ¶ *v.t*, camoufler, maquiller.

camp, *n*, camp, *m.* ~ *bed,* lit de camp, *m.* ~ *stool,* [siège] pliant, *m.* ¶ *v.i. & t,* camper. ~ *out,* bivouaquer.

campaign, *n*, campagne, *f.* ~er, *n*, routier, troupier, *m.*

campanula, *n*, campanule, *f.*

camphor, *n*, camphre, *m.* ~ate, *v.t*, camphrer.

camping [**out**], *n*, campement, camping, *m.*

can, *n*, bidon, *m*; burette; boîte, *f*; pot, *m.* ~ *opener,* ouvre-boîtes, *m.* ¶ *v.t*, mettre en boîte(s), m. en conserve. *canned salmon,* saumon en boîte(s), *m.*

can, *v.aux.ir*, pouvoir; savoir.

Canada, *n*, le Canada. **Canadian,** *a*, canadien. ¶ *n*, Canadien, ne.

canal, *n*, canal, *m.* ~ize, *v.t*, canaliser.

canary, *n*, serin, e, canari, *m.* ~ *seed,* graine des canaris, *f*, millet des oiseaux, *m. the C*~ *Islands, the Canaries,* les [îles] Canaries, *f.pl.*

cancel, *n*, (*Typ.*) carton; (*Mus.*) bécarre, *m.* ¶ *v.t*, biffer, effacer; oblitérer; annuler, résilier, rompre; décommander.

cancer (*Med.*) *n*, cancer, *m.* ~ous, *a*, cancéreux.

candelabrum, *n*, candélabre, *m.*

candid†, *a*, sincère, franc, désintéressé.

candidacy, *n*, candidature, *f.* **candidate,** *n*, candidat, e, postulant, e, aspirant, e, prétendant, e.

candied peel, zeste confit, *m.*

candle, *n*, chandelle, bougie, *f*; cierge, *m.* ~ *grease,* suif, *m.* ~ *power,* puissance (*ou* intensité) lumineuse en bougies, *f.*

a 60 *c.p. lamp,* une lampe de 60 bougies. ~*stick,* bougeoir; chandelier; flambeau, *m.* ¶ (*eggs*) *v.t,* mirer. **candling,** *n,* mirage, *m.*

candor, *n,* sincérité, franchise, *f.*

candy, *v.i,* se candir. ¶ *n,* bonbon, candi, *m.*

cane, *n,* canne; badine; (*Sch.*) férule, *f;* jonc, *m.* ~ *sugar,* sucre de canne, *m.* ¶ *v.t,* donner de la férule à; (*chair*) canner.

canine, *a,* canin.

canister, *n,* boîte [métallique] *f.*

canker, *n,* (*lit. & fig.*) chancre, *m.* ~*worm,* ver rongeur, *m.* ¶ *v.t,* gangrener.

canned goods, conserves [en boîtes] *f.pl.*

cannibal, *n. & a,* cannibale, *m,* anthropophage, *m. & a.*

cannon, *n,* canon; (*Bil.*) carambolage, *m.* ~ *ball,* boulet, *m.* ~ *shot,* coup de canon, *m.* ~**ade,** *n,* canonnade, *f.* ¶ *v.t,* canonner.

canny, *a,* fin, sagace; avisé; rusé.

canoe, *n,* canoë, *m;* périssoire; (*dugout*) pirogue, *f.*

canon, *n,* (*Eccl. rule*) canon; (*pl, taste*) code; (*pers.*) chanoine, *m.* ~ *law,* droit canon, *m.* **canonicate, canonry,** *n,* canonicat, *m.* **canonize,** *v.t,* canoniser.

canopy, *n,* dais; baldaquin; ciel, *m;* voûte, calotte, *f,* dôme, *m;* (*Arch.*) marquise, *f.*

cant, *n,* argot; jargon, *m;* hypocrisie, *f;* (*slope*) devers, *m,* inclinaison, *f.* ¶ *v.t,* incliner.

cantaloupe, *n,* melon cantaloup, *m.*

cantankerous, *a,* revêche, hargneux. ~ *fellow,* mauvais coucheur, *m.*

cantata, *n,* cantate, *f.*

canteen, *n,* cantine, *f;* (*bottle*) bidon, *m.* ~ *keeper,* cantinier, ère.

canter, *n,* petit galop, *m;* (*pers.*) cafard, le tartufe, *m.*

Canterbury bell, campanule à grandes fleurs, *f.*

canticle, *n,* cantique, *m.*

cantilever, *n,* encorbellement, *m.*

canto, *n,* chant, *m.* **cantor,** *n,* chantre, *m.*

canvas, *n,* canevas, *m,* toile; toile à voiles; voile, *f.* ~ *shoe with hempen sole,* espadrille, *f.*

canvass, *v.t,* débattre; solliciter; solliciter des suffrages; s. des commandes; faire (*the town* =

la place). ~**er,** *n,* solliciteur, euse; placier, démarcheur, *m.*

canyon, cañon, *n,* canon, *m.*

cap, *n,* bonnet, chapeau, *m;* (*peaked*) casquette, *f,* képi, *m;* toque; calotte, *f;* culot, *m;* chape; coiffe, *f;* couvercle; chapiteau, bouchon; bout; (*bullet*) détonateur, *m,* capsule, amorce, *f.* ~ & *bells* (*Hist.*), marotte, *f.* ~ *case* (*Typ.*), haut de casse, *m.* ¶ *v.t,* coiffer; couronner.

capability, *n,* capacité, *f.* **capable,** *a,* capable; apte, susceptible.

capacious, *a,* spacieux. **capacitate,** *v.t,* rendre capable; (*law*) habiliter. **capacity,** *n,* capacité, *f;* rendement, débit, *m;* qualité; habilité, *f.*

caparison, *v.t,* caparaçonner.

cape, *n,* (*Phys. Geog.*) cap, *m;* (*dress*) pèlerine, *f.* C~ *Colony,* la colonie du Cap. *the* C~ *of Good Hope,* le cap de Bonne-Espérance. C~ *Verde,* le cap Vert.

caper, *n,* cabriole, gambade, *f,* entrechat, *m;* (*Bot.*) câpre, *f.* ¶ *v.i,* cabrioler.

capillary, *a,* capillaire.

capital†, *a,* capital; admirable, fameux, parfait, chic; (*letter*) majuscule, capitale. ¶ *n,* (*country, province*) [ville] capitale, *f;* (*county, department*) chef-lieu, *m;* (*letter*) [lettre] majuscule, [lettre] capitale, *f;* (*Arch.*) chapiteau, *m;* (*Fin.*) capital, *m,* capitaux, *m.pl;* fonds, *m.s. & pl,* mise [de fonds] *f;* (*brought in*) apport, *m.* C~ & *Labor,* le capital & le travail. ~ *expenditure,* immobilisations, *f.pl,* établissement, *m.* ~ *stock* & ~ *sum,* capital, *m.* ~ *value,* valeur en capital, *f.* ~**ist,** *n,* capitaliste, *m,f.* ~**ize,** *v.t,* capitaliser; immobiliser; écrire avec une majuscule.

capitulate, *v.i,* capituler.

capon, *n,* chapon, *m.*

caprice, *n,* caprice, *m.* **capricious,** *a,* capricieux.

capsicum, *n,* piment, *m.*

capsize, *v.t,* [faire] chavirer; (*v.i.*) chavirer, capoter, faire capot.

capstan, *n,* cabestan, *m;* (*lathe*) revolver, *m,* tourelle, *f.*

capsule, *n,* capsule, *f.*

captain, *n,* (*Mil., Naut., sport*) capitaine; (*Nav.*) capitaine de vaisseau, *m.* ~ *of merchant ship,* capitaine marchand.

caption, *n,* sous-titre, *m;* légende, *f.*

captious, *a,* captieux, difficultueux.

captivate, *v.t,* captiver. **captive,** *a,* captif. ¶ *n,* captif, ive. **captivity,** *n,* captivité, *f.* **capture,** *n,* capture, prise, *f.* ¶ *v.t,* capturer.

Capuchin friar, nun, capucin, e.

car, *n,* voiture, auto, *f;* wagon; char, chariot, *m.* ~ *park,* parc à voitures, *m.* *dining* ~, wagon-restaurant, *m.*

caramel, *n,* caramel, *m.*

carapace, *n,* carapace, *f.*

carat, *n,* carat, *m.*

caravan, *n,* caravane; (*house on wheels*) roulotte, *f.* **caravanserai,** *n,* caravansérail, *m.*

caraway, *n,* carvi, *m.* ~ *seed,* graine de c., *f.*

carbide, *n,* carbure, *m.*

carbine, *n,* carabine, *f,* mousqueton, *m.*

carbolic acid, acide phénique, phénol, *m.*

carbon, *n,* (*Chem.*) carbone; (*Elec.*) charbon, *m.* ~ [*copy*], double, *m.* ~ *monoxide,* oxyde de carbone, *m.* ~ [*paper*] (duplicating), papier-carbone, *m.* **carbonate,** *n,* carbonate, *m.* **carbonic,** *a,* carbonique. **carboniferous,** *a,* carbonifère, houiller. **carbonize,** *v.t,* carboniser; (*v.i.*) [se] charbonner.

carboy, *n,* tourie, *f.*

carbuncle, *n,* (*jewel*) grenat cabochon; (*Med.*) charbon, anthrax, *m.*

carburetor, *n,* carburateur, *m.*

carcass, *n,* carcasse, *f,* cadavre, *m;* (*ship*) carcasse; (*building*) bâtisse, *f,* œuvre, *m.*

card, *n,* carte; (*loose index*) fiche, *f;* (*textiles*) peigne, *m.* ~*board,* carton, *m.* ~ *case,* porte-cartes, *m.* ~ *index* & ~ *index* [*cabinet*], fichier, *m.* ~ *sharper,* bonneteur, *m.* ~ *table,* table de jeu, *f.* ~ *trick,* tour de cartes, *m.* ¶ *v.t,* peigner.

cardigan [**jacket**], *n,* vareuse, *f,* gilet, *m.*

cardinal, *a,* cardinal. ¶ *n,* cardinal, *m.*

care, *n,* soin, *m.* *oft. pl,* attention; précaution; garde, *f;* souci, *m;* responsabilité; charge; tenue; conservation, *f;* maniement, *m,* manutention, gestion, *f,* gouvernement, *m.* *with due & proper* ~,

en bon père de famille. ~ *of, c/o,* chez, aux [bons] soins de. ~*taker,* gardien, ne, portier, ère. ~*worn,* miné (*ou* rongé) par les soucis. *to take* ~ *of,* avoir soin de. ¶ *v.i,* se soucier, s'inquiéter.

careen, *v.t,* caréner.

career, *n,* carrière; profession; course, *f.* ¶ *v.i,* galoper.

careful†, *a,* soigneux, attentif; ménager. ~**ness,** *n,* soin, *m,* attention, *f.* **careless,** *a,* insouciant; négligent. ~**ly,** *ad,* négligemment. ~**ness,** *n,* négligence, inattention, incurie, *f,* laisser-aller, *m.*

caress, *n,* caresse, *f;* (*pl.*) mamours, *f.pl. only.* ¶ *v.t,* caresser.

caret, *n,* signe d'omission, renvoi, *m.*

cargo, *n,* cargaison, *f,* chargement, *m,* charge, *f;* marchandises, (*Insce.*) facultés, *f.pl.* ~ *boat,* *steamer,* cargo; navire, vapeur, de charge, *m.*

Caribbean Sea (the), la mer des Antilles.

caricature, *n,* caricature, charge, *f.* ¶ *v.t,* caricaturer, charger.

carload, *n,* chargement d'un wagon, *m.*

Carmelite, *n,* (*friar*) carme, *m;* (*nun*) carmélite, *f.*

carmine, *n,* carmin, *m.*

carnage, *n,* carnage, *m.*

carnal†, *a,* charnel.

carnation (*Bot.*) *n,* œillet [des fleuristes] *m.*

carnelian, *n,* cornaline, *f.*

carnival, *n,* carnaval, *m.*

carnivorous, *a.* & **carnivore,** *n,* carnassier, carnivore, *a.* & *m.*

carob [**bean**], *n,* caroube, *f.*

carol, *n,* chant, chanson, cantique, *m.* [*Christmas*] ~, noël, *m.* ¶ *v.i,* chanter; (*lark*) grisoller.

carousal, *n,* orgie, débauche, ripaille, *f.* **carouse,** *v.i,* faire [la] débauche.

carp (*fish*) *n,* carpe, *f.* ~ *at,* chicaner.

Carpathians (the), les Carpathes, *m.pl.*

carpenter, *n,* charpentier, menuisier, *m.* ¶ *v.t,* charpenter; (*v.i.*) menuiser. **carpentry,** *n,* charpenterie, *f.*

carpet, *n,* tapis, *m.* ~ *slippers,* pantoufles en tapisserie, *f.pl.* ~ *sweeper,* balai, *m,* (*ou* balayeuse, *f.*) mécanique. ¶ *v.t,* recouvrir d'un tapis; (*with flowers, etc.*) tapisser.

carriage, *n,* voiture, *f;* wagon; équipage; (*gun*) affût; (*Mach.*) chariot, *m;* démarche, allure, tenue, *f;* transport, port; prix du transport (*ou* de la voiture) *m.* ~ & *pair,* voiture à deux chevaux, *f.* ~ *attendant* (hotel, etc.), aboyeur, *m.* ~ *entrance,* porte charretière, *f.*

carrier, *n,* porteur; messager, voiturier, transporteur, entrepreneur de transports (*ou* de roulage); (*Mach.*) chariot, *m;* porte-, *e.g. luggage* ~, porte-bagage, *m.* ~ *pigeon,* pigeon voyageur, *m. airplane* ~, porte-avions, *m.*

carrion, *n,* charogne, *f.*

carrot, *n,* carotte, *f.* ~**y hair,** des cheveux [rouge] carotte, *m.pl.*

carry (*Arith.*) *n,* retenue, *f.* ¶ *v.t,* porter; emporter; transporter; véhiculer; mener, conduire; charrier, voiturer; (*Arith.*) retenir; adopter, prendre; voter. ~ *away,* enlever, emporter, entraîner; emballer, enthousiasmer. ~ *forward* (*Bkkpg*), reporter. ~ *on,* poursuivre, opérer. ~ *out,* exécuter, effectuer; suivre.

cart, *n,* charrette; voiture; carriole, *f;* tombereau, *m.* ~ *horse,* cheval de charrette, *m.* ~*load,* charretée, *f;* tombereau, *m.* ¶ *v.t,* charrier, charroyer, voiturer, camionner. ~**age,** *n,* charroi, roulage; camionnage; factage; prix du transport, *m.* ~**er,** *n,* charretier, voiturier, camionneur, *m.*

Carthusian [monk], *n,* chartreux, *m.* ~ *monastery,* chartreuse, *f.*

cartilage, *n,* cartilage, *m.*

carton, *n,* carton, *m.*

cartoon, *n,* carton; dessin, *m;* caricature, *f.* ~**ist,** *n,* dessinateur, trice; caricaturiste, *m,f.*

cartouche, *n,* cartouche, *f.* **cartridge,** *n,* cartouche, *f;* (*cannon*) gargousse, *f.* ~ *belt,* ceinture cartouchière, *f.* ~ *pouch,* sac à cartouches, *m,* cartouchière, *f.*

carve, *v.t,* sculpter; tailler; (*meat*) découper. **carver** (*pers.*) *n,* sculpteur, *m;* découpeur, euse. **carving,** *n,* sculpture, *f;* découpage, *m.* ~ *knife,* couteau à découper, *m.* ~ *tool,* outil de sculpteur, *m.*

cascade, *n,* cascade, cascatelle, *f.*

case, *n,* cas; état, *m;* question, *f;* exemple, *m;* cause, affaire, *f;*

procès, *m;* caisse, boîte; mallette, *f;* sac; étui; écrin, *m;* gaine, *f;* trousse; pochette, poche, cassette, *f,* nécessaire; fourreau, boîtier; portefeuille, *m;* douille; chemise; enveloppe; (*for firework*) cartouche; (*sausage*) peau; (*precision balance*) cage, *f;* (*piano*) coffre, *m;* (*Typ.*) casse, *f.* ~ *opener,* ciseau à déballer, *m. in any* ~, en tout cas. ¶ *v.t,* encaisser, envelopper, [en]gainer; (*Min.*) cuveler.

caseharden, *v.t,* aciérer, cémenter. ~**ed** (*fig.*) *p.a,* bronzé, cuirassé.

casemate, *n,* casemate, *f.*

casement, *n,* châssis de fenêtre. ~ [**window**], fenêtre [ordinaire], croisée, *f.* ~ *stay,* entrebâilleur de fenêtre, *m.*

cash, *n,* espèces, *f.pl,* numéraire, argent, *m,* finances, *f.pl;* comptant, *m;* caisse, encaisse, *f,* fonds, *m.pl.* ~*book,* livre de caisse, *m.* ~ *box,* coffret à monnaie, *m;* caisse, *f.* ~ *discount,* escompte de caisse (*ou* au comptant) *m.* ~ *down* or in ~ & *for* ~, [au] comptant. ~ *in hand,* [en]caisse, fonds (*ou* espèces) en caisse. ~ *on delivery,* envoi contre remboursement, *m.* ~ *register,* caisse enregistreuse (*ou* contrôleuse). ~ *with order,* payable à la commande. ¶ *v.t,* encaisser; (*check*) toucher; escompter, payer. ~**ier,** *n,* caissier, ère. ¶ *v.t,* destituer, casser.

cashmere, *n,* cachemire, *m.*

casing, *n,* enveloppe, *f;* bâti, dormant, *m.*

cask, *n,* tonneau, *m,* barrique, *f,* baril, fût, *m,* futaille, *f.*

casket, *n,* cassette, *f,* écrin; (*coffin*) cercueil, *m.*

Caspian Sea (the), la mer Caspienne.

casserole, *n,* casserole, *f.*

cassia, *n,* casse, *f.* ~ *tree,* cassier, *m.*

cassock, *n,* soutane, *f.*

cast, *n,* jet, *m,* coulée; pièce moulée, *f;* coup de filet, *m;* addition; (*Theat.*) distribution, *f.* ~ *of features,* physionomie, *f,* facies, *m.* ~ *of mind,* tournure d'esprit, mentalité, *f.* ¶ *v.t.ir,* jeter; lancer; promener; fondre; couler, mouler; additionner; distribuer. to ~ *lots,* tirer au sort. ~ *iron,* fonte [de fer] *f,* fer de fonte, *m;* (*att., fig.*) rigide. ~ *its* *skin*, se dépouiller. ~ *net*, épervier, *m*. ~ *off*, (*Typ*.) évaluer; (*Knit*.) faire une chaîne de mailles. ~-*off clothing*, défroque, *f*. ~ *on* (*Knit*.), monter. ~ *out*, chasser, rejeter. ~ *steel*, acier coulé, *m*, fonte d'acier, *f*. [*crucible*] ~ *steel*, acier fondu [au creuset], *m*. *to have a* ~ *in the eye*, loucher.

castanet, *n*, castagnette, *f*.

castaway, *n*, réprouvé, e; naufragé, e.

caste, *n*, caste, *f*.

castellated, *a*, crénelé.

castigate, *v.t*, châtier. **castigation,** *n*, châtiment, *m*.

casting, *n*, jet, *m*; coulée, fonte; pièce [coulée], *f*, moulage, coulé, *m*; pêche au lancer, *f*. ~ *off*, (*Typ*.) évaluation, *f*; (*Knit*.) chaîne de mailles, *f*. ~ *on* (*Knit*.), montage des maillés, *m*. ~ *rod*, canne à lancer, *f*. *to give the* ~ *vote*, départager les voix.

castle, *n*, château, *m*; (*chess*) tour, *f*. ¶ (*chess*) *v.i*, roquer.

castor, *n*, (*bottle*) saupoudroir, *m*; (*roller*) roulette, *f*, galet [pivotant] *m*; (*beaver*) castor, *m*. **castor oil**, huile de ricin, *f*. *castor oil plant*, ricin, *m*.

castrate, *v.t*, châtrer. **castration,** *n*, castration, *f*.

casual†, *a*, casuel, accidentel, fortuit; sans cérémonie; (*remark*) en passant. ¶ *n*, indigent(e) de passage. ~**ty,** *n*, sinistre, *m*; (*pers*.) victime; (*Mil*.) perte, *f*.

casuistry, *n*, casuistique, *f*.

cat, *n*, chat, te. ~ *burglar*, cambrioleur chat, *m*. ~*call*, sifflet, *m*. ~*calling*, sifflerie, aubade, *f*. ~*'s cradle*, jeu de la scie, *m*. ~*'s eye* (*jewel*), œil-de-chat, *m*. ~*'s paw* (*fig*.), patte du chat, *f*. *to be someone's* ~*'s paw*, tirer les marrons du feu pour quelqu'un.

cataclysm, *n*, cataclysme, *m*.

catacomb, *n*, catacombe, *f*.

catafalque, *n*, catafalque, *m*.

catalog, *n*, catalogue, *m*. ¶ *v.t*, cataloguer.

catapult, *n*, (*Hist. & Avn*.) catapulte; (*boy's*) fronde, *f*. ¶ *v.t. & abs*, fronder; (*Avn*.) lancer.

cataract (*falls & Med*.) *n*, cataracte, *f*.

catarrh, *n*, catarrhe, *m*.

catastrophe, *n*, catastrophe, *f*.

catch, *n*, prise; (*fish*) prise, pêche, *f*, coup de filet, jet, *m*; (*trick*)

attrape, *f*, leurre; (*Mech*.) arrêt, mentonnet, cran; (*window*) loqueteau, *m*. ~ *phrase*, scie, *f*. ~*word*, rengaine, scie, *f*. ¶ *v.t. & i*. *ir*, attraper; saisir; accrocher; s'engager; gagner; capturer; capter; happer; prendre; se p.; surprendre; frapper. ~ *up with*, rattraper. ~-[*as*-~-]*can*, lutte libre, *f*. ~ *fire*, prendre feu, s'enflammer; (*Cook*.) graillonner. ~ *on*, prendre; comprendre. ~**er,** *n*, preneur, chasseur, *m*. ~**ing,** *a*, contagieux; séduisant.

catechism, *n*, catéchisme, *m*. **catechize,** *v.t*, catéchiser.

categorical†, *a*, catégorique. **category,** *n*, catégorie, *f*.

cater, *v.i*, donner à manger. ~ *for*, pourvoir à; s'adresser à, viser. **caterer,** *n*, restaurateur, trice, cafetier, ère, traiteur; pourvoyeur, *m*.

caterpillar, *n*, chenille, *f*; tracteur, *m*.

caterwaul, *v.i*, miauler. ~**ing,** *n*, miaulement, *m*, musique de chats, *f*.

catgut, *n*, corde à boyau, *f*.

cathead, *n*, bossoir, *m*.

cathedral, *n*, cathédrale, *f*.

catherine wheel, soleil, *m*. *to turn* ~ ~*s*, faire la roue.

cathode, *n*, cathode, *f*.

catholic, *a. & n*, catholique, *a. & m,f*. ~**ism,** *n*, catholicisme, *m*.

cattle, *n*, bétail, *m*, bestiaux, *m.pl*. ~ *market*, marché aux bestiaux, *m*. ~ *show*, concours (*ou* comice) agricole, *m*.

Caucasian, *a*, caucasien. ¶ *n*, Caucasien, ne. **the Caucasus,** le Caucase.

caucus, *n*, cabale, *f*.

cauldron, *n*, chaudron, *m*.

cauliflower, *n*, chou-fleur, *m*.

caulk, *v.t*, calfater.

causative, *a*, occasionnel; (*Gram*.) causal. **cause,** *n*, cause, raison, *f*, sujet, motif; cas, *m*. ¶ *v.t*, causer, occasionner, provoquer, entraîner; faire, *e.g*, *to* ~ *to vary*, faire varier.

causeway, *n*, chaussée, levée, *f*.

caustic, *a. & n*, caustique, *a. & m*. **cauterize,** *v.t*, cautériser. **cautery,** *n*, cautère, *m*.

caution, *n*, prudence, précaution, *f*; avertissement, *m*. ¶ *v.t*, prémunir, précautionner, avertir. **cautious,** *a*, prudent, réservé, retenu, sur ses gardes, en garde.

~ly, *ad*, avec circonspection.
~ness, *n*, prudence, *f*.

cavalcade, *n*, cavalcade, *f*.

cavalier†, *a*, cavalier. ¶ *n*, cavalier, *m*.

cavalry, *n*, cavalerie, *f*.

cave, *n*, caverne, *f*, antre, *m*. ~ dweller, troglodyte, *m*. ~ in, *v.i*, s'effondrer, ébouler; céder.

cavern, *n*, caverne, *f*, souterrain, *m*. ~ous, *a*, caverneux.

caviar, *n*, caviar, *m*.

cavil, *n*, chicane, argutie, *f*. ¶ *v.i*, chicaner, ergoter.

cavity, *n*, cavité, *f*, creux, *m*.

caw, *v.i*, croasser.

Cayenne pepper, poivre de Cayenne, *m*.

cease, *v.i. & t*, cesser. without ~, sans cesse. ~less, *a*, incessant. ~lessness, *n*, continuité, *f*.

cedar, *n*, cèdre, *m*. ~ of Lebanon, cèdre du Liban.

cede, *v.t*, céder.

ceil, *v.t*, plafonner. ~ing, *n*, plafond, *m*.

celebrate, *v.t. & i*, célébrer; solenniser; fêter. ~d, *p.a*, célèbre, fameux, renommé. **celebrity**, *n*, célébrité; illustration, *f*.

celery, *n*, céleri, *m*.

celestial, *a*, céleste.

celibacy, *n*, célibat, *m*. **celibate**, *n*, célibataire, *m,f*.

cell, *n*, cellule, *f*; cachot, *m*; pile électrique, *f*. ~ jar, bac d'éléments, *m*.

cellar, *n*, cave, *f*, caveau, *m*. ¶ *v.t*, encaver. ~er, *n*, cellérier, *m*.

cellist, *n*, violoncelliste, *m*. ['] **cello**, *n*, basse, *f*, violoncello, *m*.

cellular, *a*, cellulaire. **celluloid**, *n*, celluloïd, *m*. **cellulose**, *n*, cellulose, *f*.

Celt, *n*, Celte, *m,f*. **Celtic**, *a. & (language) n*, celtique, *a. & m*.

cement, *n*, ciment, *m*. ¶ *v.t*, cimenter; (*metal*) cémenter. reinforced ~, ciment armé, *m*.

cemetery, *n*, cimetière, *m*.

cenotaph, *n*, cénotaphe, *m*.

cense, *v.t*, encenser. **censer**, *n*, censoir, *m*.

censor, *n*, censeur, *m*; ~ious, *a*, critique. ~ship & [vote of] censure, *n*, & [board of] censors, censure, *f*. **censure**, *v.t*, censurer.

census, *n*, recensement, dénombrement, *m*.

centaur, *n*, centaure, *m*.

centenarian, *n*, centenaire, *m,f*. **centenary**, *n*, centenaire, *m*.

centigrade, *a*, centigrade. (*See note in French-English section.*)

centipede, *n*, scolopendre, *f*.

center, *n*, centre, milieu; noyau; (*Arch.*) cintre, *m*; (*lathe*) pointe, *f*. ¶ *v.t*, centrer; (*fig.*) concentrer.

central, *a*, central. C~ America, l'Amérique Centrale, *f*. ~ heating, chauffage central, *m*. ~ize, *v.t*, centraliser; canaliser. **centrifugal**, *a*, centrifuge. **centripetal**, *a*, centripète.

century, *n*, siècle, *m*.

ceramics, *n*, céramique, *f*.

cereal, *a. & n*, céréale, *a.f. & f*.

ceremonial, *n*, cérémonial, *m*. ¶ *a*, de cérémonie. **ceremonious**†, *a*, cérémonieux, façonnier. **ceremony**, *n*, cérémonie; façon, *f*. *oft. pl*.

certain†, *a*, certain. ~ty, *n*, certitude, *f*. for a ~, à coup sûr.

certificate, *n*, certificat; diplôme; brevet; acte, *m*; attestation; déclaration, *f*; extrait; titre, *m*. ~d, *p.a*, diplômé. **certify**, *v.t*, certifier; viser; attester; déclarer.

certitude, *n*, certitude, assurance, *f*.

cessation, *n*, arrêt, *m*, suspension, *f*.

cesspool, *n*, fosse [d'aisances] *f*; cloaque, *m*.

Ceylon, *n*, Ceylan, *m*.

chafe, *v.t*, frictionner; écorcher; (*v.i.*) s'écorcher; s'irriter.

chaff, *n*, balle; glume; menue paille, *f*; badinage, *m*. ¶ *v.t*, plaisanter, gouailler, berner.

chaffinch, *n*, pinson, *m*.

chafing dish, chauffe-plats, *m*.

chagrin, *n*, chagrin, *m*. ¶ *v.i*, chagriner.

chain, *n*, chaîne; chaînette, *f*. ~ bridge, pont suspendu à chaînes, *m*. ~ stitch, point de chaînette, *m*. ~ store, magasin à succursales multiples, *m*. ¶ ~ & ~ up, *v.t*, enchaîner.

chair, *n*, chaise; (*Univ.*) chaire, *f*; (*at meeting*) fauteuil [de la présidence], *m*.

chairman, *n*, président, e. ~ship, *n*, présidence, *f*.

chalcedony, *n*, calcédoine, *f*.

chalice, *n*, calice, *m*, coupe, *f*.

chalk, *n*, craie, *f*; (*Bil.*) blanc, *m*. ~ pit, carrière de craie, *f*. French ~, talc, *m*. ¶ *v.t*, marquer à la craie. ~y, *a*, crayeux.

challenge, *n*, défi, cartel, *m*, provocation, *f*; (*auditing*) son-

dage; (*Mil.*) qui-vive; (*sport*)
challenge, *m.* ~ *-cup*, coupe
challenge, *f*, challenge, *m.* ~
match, match défi, *m.* ¶ *v.t*, défier, provoquer, contester; récuser; incriminer.

chamber, *n*, chambre, *f*; (*pl.*)
cabinet, *m*, étude, *f*. ~*maid*,
femme de chambre, *f*. ~ *music*,
musique de chambre, *f*. ~ [*pot*],
vase de nuit, *m.* air ~, chambre
à air, *f*.

chameleon, *n*, caméléon, *m*.

chamois, *n*, chamois, *m.* ~
[*leather*], peau de chamois, *f*,
chamois, *m*.

champ, *v.t*, ronger, mâcher.

champagne, *n*, champagne, vin
de Champagne, *m.* ~ *glass*,
coupe à c., *f*.

champion, *n*, champion, *m.* ¶ *v.t*,
défendre, protéger. ~**ship**, *n*,
championnat, *m*.

chance, *a*, de hasard; de fortune;
d'occasion, fortuit, aléatoire. ¶ *n*,
chance; fortune, *f*; hasard, aléa,
m. **to** ~ **it**, risquer le paquet,
brusquer l'aventure.

chancel, *n*, chœur, *m*.

chancellery, *n*, chancellerie, *f*.
chancellor, *n*, chancelier, *m*.

chancre, *n*, chancre, *m*.

chandelier, *n*, lustre, *m*.

chandler, *n*, chandelier, *m*; épicier, ère.

change, *n*, changement; mouvement, *m*; altération; mutation;
variation, *f*; revirement, *m*;
saute; vicissitude; (*money*) monnaie, *f*, appoint, *m*; (*exchange*)
bourse, *f*. at ~ (*barometer*), au
variable. ~ *of clothes*, vêtements de rechange, *m.pl.* ¶ *v.t*.
& *i*, changer; c. de; se c., convertir; altérer; sauter. ~ *here
for . . .*, on change de train pour
. . . ~ *one's mind, one's linen*,
changer d'avis, de linge. ~ *the
subject*, quitter le sujet, rompre
les chiens. ~**able**, *a*, changeant;
mobile; variable, inconstant.

channel, *n*, chenal, *m*, passe, *f*;
canal, *m*, rigole; manche; cannelure; (*fig.*) voie, entremise, *f*.
the [*English*] C~, la Manche.
the C~ *Islands*, les îles [Anglo-]
Normandes, *f.pl.* ¶ *v.t*, raviner,
canneler. **channeling**, *n*, cannelure, *f*.

chant, *n*, chant, *m.* ¶ *v.i.* & *t*,
chanter, psalmodier. **chanty**, *n*,
chanson [de bord] *f*.

chaos, *n*, chaos, *m.* **chaotic**, *a*,
chaotique.

chap, *n*, garçon; gaillard, *m*; (*pl.*)
(*on the skin*) crevasses, gerçures,
f.pl; (*animal*) babines, bajoues;
(*vice*) mâchoires, *f.pl.* ¶ *v.t.* & *i*,
crevasser, gercer, se gercer.

chapel, *n*, chapelle, *f*. ~ *of ease*,
[église] succursale, *f*.

chaperon, *n*, chaperon, *m.* ¶ *v.t*,
chaperonner.

chaplain, *n*, aumônier; chapelain, *m*.

chaplet, *n*, guirlande, *f*; (*beads*)
chapelet, *m*.

chapter, *n*, chapitre, *m*; (*fig.*)
page; série, *f*.

char (*fish*) *n*, omble[-chevalier],
ombre-chevalier, *m.* ¶ *v.t*, carboniser; (*v.i.*) [se] charbonner.

character, *n*, caractère, *m*; nature, allure; réputation; cote, *f*;
rôle; personnage; certificat, *m*.
characteristic, *a*, caractéristique.
¶ *n*, caractéristique, *f*, caractère
propre, *m*; (*pl, of map*) légende,
f. **characterize**, *v.t*, caractériser.

charade, *n*, charade, *f*.

charcoal, *n*, charbon [de bois] *m*.
~ *burner* (*pers.*), charbonnier,
m. ~ *drawing*, [dessin au] fusain,
m. ~ [*pencil*], fusain, charbon
à dessin, *m*.

charge, *n*, charge, *f*; soin, *m*,
garde; accusation, inculpation, *f*;
privilège, *m*; affectation; assignation; imputation, *f*; (*bishop's*)
mandement; prix, *m*, taxe, *f*,
frais, *m.pl.* dépense; redevance,
f. ~ *account*, compte dans un
magasin. ¶ *v.t*, charger; foncer
sur; demander; prendre; mettre
à [la] charge; taxer; percevoir;
imputer; inculper; affecter, appliquer; accuser. ~**able**, *a*, à la
charge; imputable; affectable;
applicable.

charger (*horse*) *n*, cheval de bataille; (*Poet.*) coursier, *m*.

charily, *ad*, prudemment; chiche-
ment.

chariot, *n*, char, *m*.

charitable†, *a*, charitable, bienfaisant. **charity**, *n*, charité; bienfaisance, assistance, *f*, œuvres
[pies] *f.pl*, aumône, l'aumône, *f*.

charlatan, *n*, charlatan, banquiste, *m*.

charm, *n*, charme, enchantement,
agrément, *m*; (*pl.*) appas, attraits,
m.pl; (*trinket*) breloque, amulette; mascotte, *f*, fêtiche, *m*.

¶ *v.t*, charmer, enchanter. ~er, *n*, charmeur, euse, enchanteur, teresse.

charnel house, charnier, ossuaire, *m*.

chart, *n*, carte, *f*; graphique, diagramme, *m*. ¶ *v.t*, porter sur la carte, le graphique, etc.

charter, *n*, charte, *f*. ¶ *v.t*, [af]fréter, prendre à fret; privilégier. ~er, *n*, affréteur, *m*. ~ing, *n*, affrètement, *m*.

chary, *a*, prudent; avare, chiche, sobre.

chase, *n*, chasse, poursuite; (*gun*) volée, *f*; (*Typ.*) châssis, *m*. ¶ *v.t*, chasser, poursuivre; (*hawking*) voler; (*metals*) ciseler; (*screws*) peigner. **chaser** (*Nav.*) *n*, chasseur, *m*.

chasm, *n*, abîme, gouffre, *m*.

chassé, *n*, chassé, *m*. ¶ *v.t*, chasser.

chassis, *n*, châssis, *m*.

chaste†, *a*, chaste, pudique.

chasten & **chastise,** *v.t*, châtier. **chastisement,** *n*, châtiment, *m*.

chastity, *n*, chasteté, pudicité, *f*.

chasuble, *n*, chasuble, *f*.

chat, *n*, causerie, causette, *f*. ¶ *v.i*, causer, deviser.

chattel, *n*, chose, *f*; (*pl.*) biens, effets, *m.pl*.

chatter, *n*, babil, *m*, jaserie, *f*. ¶ *v.i*, babiller, jaser; jacasser; (*teeth*) claquer; (*tool*) brouter. ~box, moulin à paroles, *m*, babillard, e.

chauffeur, *n*, chauffeur, *m*.

cheap, *a*, (*article, etc.*) [à] bon marché; (*ticket, etc.*) à prix réduit; (*price*) bas. ~ *edition*, édition à bon marché, *f*. ~er, *a*, [à] meilleur marché, moins cher. ~[ly], *ad*, à bon marché; à peu de frais. ~ness, *n*, bon marché, *m*, vileté, *f*.

cheat (*pers.*) *n*, fourbe, *m*, *f*; tricheur, euse. ¶ *v.t. & i*, tromper; frauder; friponner, tricher, filouter. ~[ing], *n*, fourberie, tromperie; tricherie, *f*.

check, *n*, échec, *m*; bride, *f*, frein; contrôle, pointage; chèque bancaire; bulletin; (*design*) dessin à carreaux, *m*; (*fabric*) étoffe à carreaux, é. en damier; (*restaurant*) addition, *f*; (*att.*) de contrôle, contradictoire, témoin, ~book, carnet de chèques, *m*. ~erboard, damier, *m*. ¶ *v.t*, brider, enrayer, modérer; contrôler, vérifier; pointer. ¶ (*chess*) *i*, échec!

~mate, *n*, échec & mat, *m*; (*v.t.*) mater, faire [échec &] mat; (*fig.*) faire échec à.

Cheddar [cheese], *n*, chester, *m*.

cheek, *n*, joue; impudence, *f*, front, toupet, sans-gêne, *m*. ~bone, pommette, *f*. ~y, *a*, impudent, hardi, effronté.

cheep, *v.i*, piailler, piauler.

cheer, *n*, (*food*) chère; consolation, *f*; applaudissement, vivat, hourra, bravo, *m*. ¶ *v.t*, réjouir, égayer, rassurer, consoler; applaudir. ~ *up*, ragaillardir. ~ *up!* [du] courage! ~ful†, *a*, gai, joyeux, riant, allègre. ~fulness, *n*, gaieté, allégresse, *f*. ~less, *a*, triste, morne.

cheese, *n*, fromage, *m*. ~ *knife*, couteau à dessert, *m*.

cheetah, *n*, guépard, *m*.

chemical†, *a*, chimique. ¶ *n*, produit chimique, *m*.

chemise, *n*, chemise de jour, *f*.

chemist, *n*, chimiste, *m*, *f*. ~ry, *n*, chimie, *f*.

cherish, *v.t*, chérir, bercer, caresser, nourrir, choyer.

cherry, *n*, cerise, *f*. ~ *orchard*, cerisaie, *f*. ~-red, *a*. & *n*, cerise, *a*. & *m*. ~ *stone*, noyau de cerise, *m*. ~ [*tree*], cerisier; (*wild*) merisier, *m*.

cherub, *n*, chérubin, *m*.

chervil, *n*, cerfeuil, *m*.

chess, *n*, échecs, *m.pl*. ~board, échiquier, *m*. ~men, pièces, *f.pl*, échecs, *m.pl*.

chest, *n*, (*Anat.*) poitrine, *f*; (*box*) coffre, *m*, caisse, boîte, *f*; bahut, *m*. ~ *measurement*, grosseur de poitrine, *f*. ~ *of drawers*, commode, *f*.

chesterfield, *n*, (*overcoat*) pardessus chesterfield; (*couch*) canapé-divan, *m*.

chestnut, *n*, châtaigne, *f*, marron, *m*. ~-brown, châtain. ~ [*tree*], châtaignier, marronnier, *m*.

cheval dressing table, coiffeuse psyché, *f*. **cheval glass,** psyché, *f*.

chew, *v.t. & i*, mâcher; (*tobacco*) chiquer; (*fig.*) remâcher. ~ *the cud*, ruminer. ~ing, *n*, mastication, *f*. ~ *gum*, gomme à mâcher, *f*.

chiaroscuro, *n*, clair-obscur, *m*.

chicane, *v.t. & i*, chicaner. ~ry, *n*, chicane[rie], *f*.

chick, *n*, poussin, poulet, *m*. **chick-pea,** *n*, pois chiche, *m*. **chicken,** *n*, poulet, te. ~ *heart* (*pers.*) poule mouillée, *f*, poltron, ne. **~-hearted**, poltron. **~ pox**, varicelle, *f*.

chickweed, *n*, mouron [des oiseaux] *m*, morgeline, *f*.

chicory, *n*, chicorée; endive, *f*.

chide, *v.t.* & *i.ir*, gronder.

chief, *a*, premier, principal; en chef. **~ attraction**, clou de la fête, *m*. **to be ~ mourner**, conduire (*ou* mener) le deuil. ¶ *n*, chef; supérieur, *m*. **~ly**, *ad*, principalement, surtout. **chieftain**, *n*, chef, *m*.

chiffon, *n*, chiffon, *m*. **chiffonier**, *n*, chiffonnier, *m*.

chilblain, *n*, engelure, *f*.

child, *n*, enfant, *m,f*. *from a ~*, dès l'enfance. *with ~*, enceinte. **~bed**, couches, *f.pl*. **~birth**, travail [d'enfant], accouchement, *m*. **~'s play**, un jeu d'enfant, jeu d'e., *m*. **~hood**, *n*, enfance, *f*. **~ish**, *a*, enfantin; puéril. **~ishly**, *ad*, puérilement. **~ishness**, *n*, enfantillage, *f*, puérilité, *f*. **~less**, *a*, sans enfant. **~like**, *a*, comme un enfant, en enfant. **children**, *n.pl*, enfants, *m.pl*.

Chile, *n*, le Chili. **Chilean**, **-lian**, *a*, chilien. ¶ *n*, Chilien, ne.

chill, *a*, froid, glacé. ¶ *n*, froid, frisson, aigre, *m*, fraîcheur, *f*; coup d'air, c. de froid, *m*; (*fig.*, *of age*) glaces, *f.pl*. *to take the ~ off* (*water*) faire dégourdir; (*wine*) chambrer. ¶ *v.t*, refroidir, glacer, transir morfondre. **chilliness**, *n*, froideur, *f*, froid, *m*. **chilly**, *a*, froid; frisquet; (*pers.*) frileux.

chime[s], *n.[pl.]*, carillon, *m*. ¶ *v.i*, carillonner. **~ in**, placer son mot. **chiming clock**, pendule à carillon, *f*.

chimera, *n*, chimère, *f*. **chimerical**, *a*, chimérique.

chimney, *n*. & **~ piece**, cheminée, *f*. **~ corner**, coin du feu, *m*. **~ pot**, cheminée, *f*. **~ sweep[er]**, ramoneur, *m*.

chimpanzee, *n*, chimpanzé, *m*.

chin, *n*, menton, *m*. **~ strap**, jugulaire, *f*.

china & **~ware**, *n*, porcelaine, faïence [fine], *f*. **~ cabinet**, vitrine, armoire vitrée, *f*. **~ clay**, terre à porcelaine, *f*, kaolin, *m*. **~ manufacturer** & *dealer*, porcelainier, ère. **~ shop**, magasin de porcelaines, *m*.

China (*Geog.*) *n*, la Chine. **~ aster**, reinemarguerite, *f*.

chine, *n*, échine; (*Cook.*) échinée, *f*.

Chinese, *a*, chinois. **~ curio**, chinoiserie, *f*. **~ lantern**, lanterne vénitienne, *f*, lampion [en papier] *m*. **~ puzzle** (*fig.*), casse-tête chinois, *m*. ¶ *n*, (*language*) chinois, *m*; (*pers.*) Chinois, e.

chink, *n*, lézarde, fente, crevasse, *f*. ¶ *v.t*, fendiller.

chintz, *n*, perse, *f*.

chip, *n*, copeau, éclat, *m*, écaille, écornure, *f*. **~ off the old block**, fils de son père, *m*. ¶ *v.t*, tailler par éclats; buriner; écorner; ébrécher; (*v.i.*) s'écorner.

chiropodist, *n*, pédicure, *m,f*. **chiropody**, *n*, soin des pieds, *m*.

chiropractor, *n*, chiropractor, *m*.

chirp, *n*, pépiement, guilleri; (*insect*) cri, cricri, *m*. ¶ *v.i*, pépier; crier.

chisel, *n*, ciseau, burin, *m*. ¶ *v.t*, ciseler, buriner.

chit, *n*, marmot, te; [petit] bout, *m*. **~ of a girl**, petite fille, *f*.

chitchat, *n*, causerie, *f*; commérage, *m*.

chivalrous, *a*, chevaleresque. **chivalry**, *n*, chevalerie, *f*.

chive, *n*, cive[tte], ciboulette, *f*.

chivy, *v.t*, chasser.

chlorate, *n*, chlorate, *m*. **chloride**, *n*, chlorure, *m*. **~ of lime**, c. de chaux. **chlorine**, *n*, chlore, *m*. **chloroform**, *n*, chloroforme, *m*. ¶ *v.t*, chloroformer.

chocolate, *n*, chocolat, *m*; (*pl.*) bonbons au c., *m.pl*. **~ box**, bonbonnière, *f*. **~ cream**, crème chocolatée, *f*. **~ creams**, chocolats fourrés à la crème, *m.pl*. **~ éclair**, éclair au chocolat, *m*. **~ manufacturer** *ou seller*, chocolatier, ère. **~ pot**, chocolatière, *f*.

choice, *a*, choisi, de [grand] choix; fin; recherché. ¶ *n*, choix, *m*; élite, fleur, *f*. **~ness**, *f*, excellence, *f*.

choir, *n*, chœur, *m*. **~ boy**, enfant de chœur, *m*. **~ master**, maître de chapelle, *m*.

choke, *v.t*, suffoquer, étouffer, étrangler; engorger; bourrer. ¶ *n*, (*auto*), obturateur, *m*.

cholera, *n*, choléra, *m*.

choose, *v.t.ir*, choisir; élire; (*v.i.ir.*) opter.

chop, *n*, coup, *m*; côtelette, *f*; (*pl.*) babines, bajoues, *f.pl*. ¶ *v.t*, (*meat*) hacher; (*firewood*) dé-

biter. ~ *off*, couper, trancher.
chopper, *n*, couperet, *m*. **chopping block,** hachoir, billot, *m*.
chopping board, hachoir, *m*.
choppy (*sea*) *a*, clapoteuse.
chopstick, *n*, bâtonnet, *m*.
choral, *a*, choral. ~ *society*, [so-ciété] chorale, *f*, orphéon, *m*.
chord, *n*, corde, *f*; (*Mus.*) accord, *m*.
chore, *n*, besogne, *f*.
choreography, *n*, chorégraphie, *f*.
chorister, *n*, choriste, *m,f*: enfant de chœur, *m*. **chorus,** *n*, chœur; refrain en c.; concert, *m*. ~ *singer* (opera), choriste, *m,f*. *to* [*repeat in*] ~, faire chorus. *to join in the* ~, faire chœur au refrain.
Christ, *n*, le Christ. **christen,** *v.t*, baptiser. **Christendom,** *n*, chrétienté, *f*. **christening,** *n*, baptême, *m*. **Christian,** *a*, chrétien, ~ *name*, nom de baptême, petit nom, prénom, *m*. ~ *Science*, le culte des scientistes chrétiens. ¶ *n*, chrétien, ne. **Christianity,** *n*, christianisme, *m*. **christianize,** *v.t*, christianiser. **christianly,** *ad*, chrétiennement.
Christmas & ~**tide** (*abb.* Xmas) *n*, Noël, *m. at* ~, à la [fête de] Noël, à Noël. ~ *present. In Fr., presents are given on or about Jan. 1 and called* étrennes, *f.pl. a* ~ *present* (to child), le petit Noël. ~ *eve*, nuit de Noël, *f*. ~ *pudding*, pudding de Noël, plum-pudding, *m*.
chromate, *n*, chromate, *m*.
chromatic, *a*, chromatique.
chrome, *n*, chrome, *m*; (*att., steel, leather*) chromé; (*yellow*) de chrome. **chromium,** *n*, chrome, *m*; (*att., steel*) chromé. ~-*plated*, chromé.
chronic, *a*, chronique.
chronicle, *n*, chronique, *f*. C~*s* (*Bible*) *pl*, Paralipomènes, *m,pl*. ¶ *v.t*, enregistrer, consigner. **chronicler,** *n*, chroniqueur, *m*.
chronological†, *a*, chronologique. **chronology,** *n*, chronologie, *f*.
chronometer, *n*, chronomètre, *m*.
chrysalis, *n*, chrysalide, *f*.
chrysanthemum, *n*, chrysanthème, *m*.
chub (*fish*) *n*, chabot, meunier, *m*.
chubby, *a*, joufflu, potelé.

chuck (*lathe*) *n*, mandrin, plateau, *m*. ¶ (*throw*), *v.t*, flanquer. ~ *out*, flanquer à la porte. ~ *under the chin*, relever le menton à.
chuckle, *v.i*, glousser, rire sous cape.
chum, *n*, camarade, *m,f*, copain, *m*.
chump, *n*, bûche, *f*; lourdaud, *m*.
chunk, *n*, quignon, chanteau, *m*.
church, *n*, église, *f*; temple, *m*. *the* C~ *of England*, l'Église anglicane. ~ *service*, office divin, *m*. ~*warden*, marguillier, *m*. ~*yard*, cour de l'église, *f*; jardin de l'église; champ du repos, cimetière, *m*; (*public square surrounding a church*) place, *f, e.g*, la Place de la Madeleine.
churl, *n*, manant, bourru, rustre, *m*. ~**ish,** *a*, bourru, aigre.
churn, *n*, baratte, *f*; ~ *dash*[*er*], batte à beurre, *f*, babeurre, *m*. ¶ *v.t*, baratter, battre.
cider, *n*, cidre, *m*.
cigar, *n*, cigare, *m*. ~ *case*, porte-cigares, *m*. ~ *cutter*, coupe-cigares, *m*. ~ *holder*, porte-cigare, fume-cigare, *m*.
cigarette, *n*, cigarette, *f*. ~ *box*, coffret à c~s, *m*. ~ *case*, étui à c~s, *m*. ~ *holder*, porte-cigarette, fume-cigarette, *m*.
cinch, *n*, sangle, *f*. ¶ *v.t*, sangler.
cinder[**s**], *n*.[*pl*.], escarbille[s], *f*.[*pl*.], fraisil, *m*, braise, *f*; scorie[s], *f*.[*pl*.]; cendrée, *f*. *burnt to a* ~ (*meat*), en charbon. ~ *sifter*, tamis à escarbilles, *m*. ~ *track*, piste en cendrée, *f*.
Cinderella, *n*, Cendrillon, *f*.
cinema, *n*, cinéma, cinématographe, *m*.
cinerary, *a*, cinéraire.
Cingalese, *a*, cingalais. ¶ *n*, Cingalais, e.
cinnabar, *n*, cinabre, *m*.
cinnamon, *n*, cannelle, *f*.
cipher, *n*, chiffre; zéro, *m*; nullité, *f*, comparse, *m*. *word in* ~, mot en chiffre, *m*. ¶ *v.t. & i*, chiffrer.
circle, *n*, cercle; milieu, *m*. ¶ *v.t*, ceindre, cerner. **circlet,** *n*, couronne, *f*. **circuit,** *n*, circuit, tour, *m*; tournée, *f*. ~**ous,** *a*, détourné.
circular†, *a*. & *n*, circulaire, *a*. & *f*. **circulate,** *v.t*, faire circuler, répandre; (*v.i*.) circuler, rouler. **circulating,** *a*, circulant; roulant. ~ *decimal*, fraction périodique, *f*. ~ *library*, bibliothèque circulante, *f*. **circulation,** *n*, circula-

tion, *f*; mouvement, *m*; (*news-paper*) tirage, *m*.

circumcise, *v.t*, circoncire.

circumference, *n*, circonférence, *f*, tour, *m*.

circumflex, *a*. & *n*, circonflexe, *a*. & *m*.

circumlocution, *n*, circonlocution, *f*, circuit de paroles, *m*, paraphrase, *f*.

circumscribe, *v.t*, circonscrire.

circumspect, *a*, circonspect, mesuré, avisé. ~**ly**, *ad*, avec circonspection.

circumstance, *n*, circonstance, *f*; état; cas, *m*; cérémonie, *f*. *in easy* ~*s*, à son aise. *in straitened* (*or reduced*) ~*s*, dans la gêne. ~*s permitting*, sauf imprévu. *under no* ~*s*, en aucun cas. **circumstantial**, *a*: ~ *account*, relation circonstanciée, *f*. ~ *evidence*, témoin muet, *m*, preuve par présomption, *f*.

circumvent, *v.t*, circonvenir.

circus, *n*, cirque; hippodrome, *f*.

cirrhosis, *n*, cirrhose, *f*.

cirrus (*Meteor.*), *n*, cirrus, *m*.

cistern, *n*, fontaine, *f*; réservoir, *m*; citerne; (*barometer*) cuvette, *f*.

citadel, *n*, citadelle, *f*.

citation, *n*, citation; mention, *f*.

cite, *v.t*, citer, alléguer; assigner.

citizen, *n*, citoyen, ne, citadin, e. ~**ship**, *n*, droit de cité, *m*.

citric, *a*, citrique. **citron**, *n*, cédrat, citron, *m*.

city, *n*, ville; cité, *f*. ¶ *a*, urbain; municipal. ~ *hall*, la mairie, *f*.

civet [cat], *n*, civette, *f*.

civic, *a*, civique.

civil†, *a*, civil; honnête. ~ *engineering*, génie civil, *m*. ~ *servant*, employé(e) d'administration, fonctionnaire public, *m*, fonctionnaire publique, *f*. ~ *service*, administration publique, *f*. ~**ian**, *n*, civil, *m*. ~**ity**, *n*, civilité, *f*.

civilization, *n*, civilisation, *f*. **civilize**, *v.t*, civiliser. **civilizing**, *a*, civilisateur.

clack, *n*, claquement; caquet, *m*. ~ [*valve*], clapet, *m*.

claim, *n*, réclamation, revendication, *f*, recours; titre, *m*, prétention, exigence; demande, demande d'indemnité; indemnité, *f*. ¶ *v.t*, réclamer, revendiquer, prétendre [à], demander, s'attribuer. ~**ant**, *n*, réclamant, e, prétendant, e.

clairvoyance, *n*, seconde vue, *f*. **clairvoyant**, *n*, voyant, e.

clam (*Mol.*) *n*, palourde, peigne, *f*.

clamber [up], *v.i*. & *t*, gravir, grimper.

clamminess, *n*, moiteur, *f*. **clammy**, *a*, moite, pâteux.

clamorous, *a*, bruyant, criard. ~**ly**, *ad*, à cor & à cri. **clamor**, *n*, clameur, *f*. ¶ *v.i*, crier, vociférer. ~ *for*, réclamer à grands cris.

clamp, *n*, bride [de serrage], presse, happe, *f*, serre-joint[s], crampon, *m*; pince, *f*. ¶ *v.t*, brider, cramponner, bloquer.

clan, *n*, clan, *m*.

clandestine†, *a*, clandestin.

clang, *n*, son, *m*. ¶ *v.i*, retentir.

clank, *n*, cliquetis, *m*. ¶ *v.i*, cliqueter.

clap, *n*, coup; battement, *m*. ~*trap*, phrases à effet, *f.pl*, boniment, *m*. ¶ *v.t*, & *i*, claquer; battre. **clapper**, *n*, claquet, claquoir, *m*, claquette, *f*; (*bell*) battant, *m*. **clapping**, *n*, battement [de mains] *m*.

claret, *n*, bordeaux [rouge], vin de Bordeaux, *m*.

clarify, *v.t*, clarifier.

clarion, *n*, clairon, *m*. **clarinet**, *n*, clarinette, *f*.

clarity, *n*, clarté, lumière, *f*.

clash, *n*, choc, *m*, rencontre, collision, *f*; fracas; cliquetis; conflit, *m*. ¶ *v.i*, s'entrechoquer; être en conflit; jurer.

clasp, *n*, agrafe, *f*, fermoir, *m*; étreinte, *f*, serrement, *m*. ~ *knife*, couteau à virole, c. à cran d'arrêt, *m*. ¶ *v.t*, agrafer; prendre, se prendre; presser, étreindre, serrer.

class, *n*, classe; catégorie; cote, *f*; cours, *m*. ~-*consciousness*, l'esprit de caste, *m*. ~*mate*, camarade de classe, c. de promotion, *m,f*. ~*room*, [salle de] classe, *f*. ~ *war*, guerre sociale, *f*. ¶ *v.t*, classer; coter. **classic** & **classical†**, *a*, classique. **classic**, *n*, classique, *m*. **classification**, *n*, classification, *f*. **classify**, *v.t*, classer. **classing**, *n*, classement, *m*.

clatter, *n*, fracas, tapage, *m*. ¶ *v.i*, claquer, carillonner.

clause, *n*, clause, *f*, article, *m*; (*Gram.*) proposition, *f*.

claustral, *a*, claustral.

claw, *n*, griffe, serre, patte, *f*; ongle, *m*; pince, *f*, pied-de-biche, *m*. ¶ *v.t*, griffer, s'agriffer à; égratigner.

clay, *n*, argile; glaise; terre, *f*. ~ **pigeon**, pigeon artificiel, papegai, *m*. ~ **pipe**, pipe en terre, *f*. ~ **pit**, carrière d'argile, glaisière, *f*. **clayey**, *a*, argileux.

clean, *a*, propre; blanc; net; pur; sain; sans réserves; (*Typ. proof*) peu chargée. ~**shaven**, glabre, entièrement rasé. ~ *slate* (*fig.*), coup d'éponge, *m*. ~ *sweep* (*fig.*), table rase; rafle, *f*. ¶ *v.t*, nettoyer; blanchir; dégraisser; débourber. ~**er**, *n*, nettoyeur, euse; femme de ménage, femme de journée, *f*. ~**ing**, *n*, nettoyage; dégraissage; curage, *f*. **cleanliness**, *n*, propreté, netteté, *f*. **cleanse**, *v.t*, assainir; purger; [é]curer.

clear, *a*, clair; limpide; pur; net; distinct; libre; franc. ~ *soup*, consommé, *m*. ~**sighted**, clairvoyant. ¶ *v.t*, éclaircir; débarrasser; dégager; franchir; évacuer; déblayer; défricher; purger; (*table*) desservir; (*letter box*) [re]lever; (*check*) compenser; (*shop goods*) solder; (*Cust.—goods*) dédouaner; (*a ship inwards*) faire l'entrée [en douane]; (*a ship outwards*) expédier [en douane]. ~ *up*, *v.t*, éclaircir, tirer au clair, mettre au net, débrouiller; (*v.i.*) s'éclaircir, se rasséréner. ~**ance**, n, (*Mech.*) jeu, m, chasse, *f*; (*goods through Cust.*) dédouanement, *m*; (*ship through Cust.*) expédition, *f*; (*foreign ship leaving French port*) passeport; (*French ship leaving French port*) congé, *m*. ~ *papers* (ship's), expéditions, *f.pl*. ~ *sale*, solde, *m*. ~**ing** (*glade*) *n*, éclaircie, clairière, *f*. ~ *house* (*banking*), chambre de compensation, *f*. ~**ly**, *ad*, clair[ement]; nettement, bien. ~**ness**, *n*, clarté, netteté; pureté, *f*.

cleat, *n*, tasseau, *m*, languette, *f*; taquet, *m*.

cleavage, *n*, fendage; (*Miner.*) clivage, *m*; (*fig.*) scission, *f*. **cleave**, *v.t.ir*, fendre, refendre; cliver; (*v.i.ir.*) se fendre; se cliver; se coller, s'attacher. **cleaver**, *n*, fendoir, couperet, *m*.

clef, *n*, clef, clé, *f*.

cleft, *n*, fente, fissure, *f*. ~ *stick*, piquet fourchu, *m*.

clematis, *n*, clématite, *f*.

clemency, *n*, clémence, *f*. **clement**, *a*, clément.

clench, *v.t*, crisper; serrer.

clergy, *n*, clergé, *m*, gens d'Église, *m.pl*. ~**man**, *n*, ecclésiastique; ministre, *m*. **cleric**, *n*, ecclésiastique, *m*. ~**al**, *a*, d'employé, de commis; (*of clergy*) ecclésiastique, clérical. ~ *error*, erreur (*ou* faute) de plume (*ou* de copiste) *f*; (*law*) vice (*ou* pas) de clerc, *m*. ¶ *n*, clérical, *m*. **clerk**, *n*, employé, e, commis [de bureau], *m*, préposé, e; (*law & Eccl.*) clerc; (*court*) greffier, *m*.

clever†, *a*, habile; adroit. ~ *move*, adresse, *f*. ~**ness**, *n*, dextérité, habileté, *f*.

clew, *n*, fil, *m*.

cliché, *n*, banalité, *f*, cliché, *m*.

click, *n*, cliquetis, tic tac; (*Mech.*) cliquet, déclic, *m*, détente, *f*. ¶ *v.i*, cliqueter, faire tic tac. ~ *heels*, claquer talons.

client, *n*, client, e; partie, *f*. **clientele**, *n*, clientèle, *f*.

cliff, *n*, (*coast*) falaise, *f*; (*inland*) rocher [en escarpement] *m*.

climacteric, *a*, critique, climatérique.

climate, *n*, climat; ciel, *m*. **climatic**, *a*, climatérique, climatique.

climax, *n*, (*Rhet.*) gradation [ascendante] *f*; point culminant; bouquet, *m*.

climb, *n*, ascension, montée, *f*. ¶ *v.t & i*, gravir, monter, faire l'ascension de, grimper. ~ *over*, escalader. ~**er**, *n*, grimpeur, alpiniste, *m*; plante grimpante, *f*. ~**ing boots**, bottines d'escalade, *f.pl*.

clime (*Poet.*) *n*, terre, *f*; ciel, *m*.

clinch (*Box.*) *n*, corps à corps, *m*. ¶ *v.t*, river; (*fig.*) conclure.

cling, *v.i.ir*, se cramponner, s'attacher, s'agriffer, se coller, s'aheurter, tenir.

clinic, *n*, clinique, *f*. ~**al**, *a*, clinique; (*thermometer*) médical. ~**ian**, *n*, clinicien, *m*.

clink, *n*, (*glasses*) choc; (*jail*) violon, *m*. ¶ *v.t*, choquer, trinquer; (*v.i.*) tinter.

clinker, *n*, mâchefer, *m*.

clip, *n*, pince, serre, griffe, attache, patte [d'attache], *f*. ¶ *v.t*, cisailler; tailler; tondre; rogner; (*ticket*) poinçonner; (*words*) estropier, manger. **clippers**, *n.pl*, ciseaux, *m.pl*, tondeuse, *f*. **clip-**

pings, *n.pl,* rognures; (*newspaper*) coupures de journal, *f.pl.*

clique, *n,* clique, coterie, *f.*

cloak (*lit. & fig.*) *n,* manteau, *m.* ~ *room,* vestiaire, *m.* ¶ *v.t,* voiler, masquer.

clock, *n,* (*big*) horloge; (*small*) pendule, pendulette, *f;* (*on stocking*) baguette, *f.* ~ *& watch maker,* horloger, *m.* ~*work* [*movement*], mouvement d'horlogerie, *m.* alarm ~, reveille-matin, *m.*

clod, *n,* motte, *f.* ~[*hopper*], rustre, rustaud, lourdaud, *m.*

clog, *n,* sabot, socque, *m,* galoche, *f;* (*fig.*) entrave[s] *f.[pl.].* ~ *dance,* sabotière, *f.* ¶ *v.t,* encrasser; engorger; charger; entraver.

cloister, *n,* cloître, *m.* ¶ *v.t,* cloîtrer. **cloistral,** *a,* claustral.

close, *a,* clos; fermé; étroit; serré; dense; [r]enfermé; lourd, mou; minutieux; vif; intime; près, proche; appliqué; jointif; soutenu. ~*-fitting garment,* vêtement collant; (*woven*) maillot, *m.* ~ *season,* temps prohibé, *m,* période d'interdiction, *f.* ~*-shaven,* rasé de près, ras. ¶ *ad,* près, de près; auprès. ~*-up,* premier plan, gros plan, *m.* ¶ *n,* fin; clôture; levée, *f. the* ~ *of day,* la chute du jour. ¶ *v.t,* fermer; clore; arrêter, régler; lever; liquider, réaliser; serrer; barrer, boucher; (*v.i.*) fermer, se f.; clore; chômer. ~**d** (*Theat.*), relâche. ~**ly,** *ad,* de près; attentivement; strictement; étroitement. ~**ness,** *n,* compacité; intimité; proximité, *f;* manque d'air, *m;* lourdeur, *f.* **closet,** *n,* cabinet, *m.* ¶ *v.t,* chambrer, claquemurer. **closing,** *n,* fermeture, clôture, *f;* liquidation, *f.* ~ *price,* dernier cours, c. de clôture, *m.* **closure,** *n,* clôture, *f.*

clot, *n,* caillot, grumeau, *m.* ¶ *v.i,* se cailler, se grumeler.

cloth, *n,* drap, *m;* toile; étoffe, *f;* voile; tissu; linge; tapis, *m;* nappe, *f;* parement, *m;* couverture, *f;* napperon; torchon, *m;* robe, soutane, *f.* ~ *trade,* draperie, *f.* **clothe,** *v.t.ir,* habiller, vêtir; revêtir. **clothes,** *n.pl,* habits, vêtements, *m.pl,* tenue, *f,* entretien, *m;* (*worn*) hardes, *f.pl.* ~*brush,* brosse à habits, *f.* ~*hanger,* porte-vêtements, cintre,

m. ~ *line,* étendoir, *m,* corde à linge, *f,* (*pl.*) étendage, *m.* ~*pin,* pince à linge, *f.* **clothier,** *n,* drapier, *m;* confectionneur, euse.

clothing, *n,* habillement, vêtement, *m.*

cloud, *n,* nuage, *m;* (*fig.*) nuée; (*Poet.*) nue, *f.* ~ *burst,* trombe d'eau, rafale de pluie, *f. in the* ~*s* (*fig.*), dans le bleu. ¶ *v.t,* couvrir de nuages; obscurcir; voiler, obnubiler; assombrir. ~**less,** *a,* sans nuage. ~**y,** *a,* nuageux, nébuleux, couvert, chargé, bas; terne, trouble, louche.

clout, *n,* torchon; chiffon, *m;* (*blow*) gifle, *f.*

clove, *n,* [clou de] girofle, *m.* ~ *of garlic,* gousse d'ail, *f.*

cloven hoof, pied fourchu, *m.*

clover, *n,* trèfle, *m. in* ~ (*fig.*), dans l'abondance.

clown, *n,* paillasse, pierrot, clown, Gille, pitre, baladin, bouffon, *m.* ¶ *v.i,* faire le clown. ~**ery,** *n,* bouffonnerie, clownerie, pantalonnade, *f.* ~**ish,** *a,* bouffon.

cloy, *v.t,* rassasier (*with* = de).

club, *n,* massue, casse-tête, *f,* gourdin, *m;* (*golf*) crosse, *f,* club, *m.* (Clubs such as brassie, mashie, niblick are named the same in French and are *m.*); (*people*) club, cercle, *m,* société, *f;* (*church*) patronage; (*cards, s. & pl.*) trèfle, *m.* ~ *foot,* pied bot, *m.* ~ *together,* se cotiser. ¶ *v.t,* frapper, assommer.

cluck, *n,* gloussement, *m.* ¶ *v.i,* glousser.

clue, *n,* indication; clef, piste, *f.*

clump, *n,* masse; motte; botte; touffe, *f,* massif, bouquet, *m.*

clumsiness, *n,* gaucherie, maladresse, *f.* **clumsy†,** *a,* gauche, maladroit, empoté, pataud; incommode. ~ *fellow,* maladroit, pataud, *m.*

cluster, *n,* faisceau, nœud, bouquet, peloton, groupe, *m,* grappe, *f,* régime, *m.* ¶ *v.i,* se grouper.

clutch, *n,* griffe; (*eggs*) couvée, *f;* (*Mech.*) [manchon d']embrayage, *m.* ¶ *v.t. & i,* empoigner, [a]gripper; se raccrocher. *to step on the* ~, débrayer.

clutter, *n,* désordre, *m;* confusion, *f.* ¶ *v.t,* mettre en désordre.

coach, *n,* voiture, *f,* wagon; carrosse, coche; (*tutor*) répétiteur, préparateur; (*sport*) entraîneur, instructeur; (*boating*) capitaine d'entraînement, *m*. ~ *horse*, carrossier, *m*. ~ *house*, remise, *f*. ~*man*, cocher, *m*. ¶ *v.t*, préparer; entraîner; endoctriner.

coagulate, *v.t*, coaguler; (*v.i.*) se coaguler.

coal, *n*, charbon [de terre] *m*, houille, *f*; (*pl.*) charbon[s]. ~ *mine*, mine de charbon (*ou* de houille), houillère, *f*. ~ *miner*, houilleur, mineur de houille, *m*. ~ *scuttle*, seau à charbon, *m*. ~ *tar*, goudron de houille, coaltar, *m*. ~ *yard*, chantier (*ou* parc) à charbon, *m*, charbonnerie, *f*. ¶ *v.i*, faire du charbon.

coalesce, *v.i*, se confondre. **coalition**, *n*, coalition, *f*, bloc, cartel, *m*.

coarse†, *a*, grossier, gros; rude; brutal. ~**ness**, *n*, grossièreté, rudesse, *f*.

coast, *n*, côte[s] *f*.[*pl*.], littoral, *m*, bord[s] *m*.[*pl*.]. ¶ *v.i*, côtoyer; (*auto & fig*.) débrayer.

coat, *n*, habit, *m*; (*man's*) pardessus; manteau; (*woman's*) redingote, *f*; (*long*) manteau, *m*; (*short*) jaquette, *f*; (*woolly*) gilet, *m*; (*Mil*.) tunique; (*animal's*) robe, *f*, poil, pelage, *m*; (*Anat*.) paroi; tunique; (*layer*) couche, *f*, enduit, *m*. ~ *hanger*, porte-manteau, *m*. ~ *of arms*, armes, armoiries, *f.pl*, blason, *m*. ~ *of mail*, cotte de mailles, *f*. ¶ *v.t*, enduire, revêtir.

coax, *v.t*, enjôler, amadouer.

cob, *n*, (*horse*) bidet; (*corn*) épi, *m*, rafle, *f*. ~[*nut*], grosse noisette, aveline, *f*.

cobalt, *n*, cobalt, *m*.

cobble [stone], *n*, galet, pavé, *m*. ¶ *v.t*, saveter, rapetasser. **cobbler**, *n*, savetier, *m*. ~*'s wax*, poix, *f*.

cobra, *n*, cobra, *m*.

cobweb, *n*, toile d'araignée, *f*.

cocaine, *n*, cocaïne, *f*.

cochineal, *n*, cochenille, *f*.

cock, *n*, coq, *m*; (*tap*) robinet; (*hay*) meulon; (*of gun*) chien, *m*. ~-*a-doodle-doo*, coquerico, cocorico, *m*. ~-*&-bull story*, coq-à-l'âne, *m*, contes en l'air, *m.pl*. ~*crow*[*ing*], chant du coq, *m*. ~ *of the walk*, coq du village, *m*. ~ *pheasant*, [coq] faisan, *m*. *safety* ~, cran d'arrêt, *m*. ¶ *v.t*, relever, [re]dresser; (*gun*) armer. ~*ed hat*, chapeau à cornes, *m*.

cockade, *n*, cocarde, *f*.

cockatoo, *n*, cacatoès, *m*.

cockchafer, *n*, hanneton, *m*.

cockerel, *n*, cochet, *m*.

cockle, *n*, (*Mol*.) clovisse, coque; (*Bot*.) ivraie, *f*.

cockpit, *n*, arène, *f*; (*Avn*.) nacelle, *f*.

cockroach, *n*, cafard, cancrelat, *m*, blatte, *f*.

cockscomb, *n*, crête de coq; (*Bot*.) crête-de-coq, *f*.

cocktail (*drink*) *n*, cocktail, *m*. ~ *bar*, bar-cocktail, *m*. ~ *shaker*, shaker, *m*.

cocky, *a*, impertinent, insolent.

cocoa, *n*, cacao, *m*.

coco[**nut**], *n*, coco, *m*, noix de c., *f*. ~ *palm*, cocotier, *m*.

cocoon, *n*, cocon, *m*.

cod[**fish**], *n*, morue, *f*, cabillaud, *m*; (*dried*) merluche, *f*. ~ *fisher*, morutier, *m*. ~ *liver oil*, huile de foie de morue, *f*.

coddle, *v.t*, dorloter, câliner, choyer.

code, *n*, code, *m*. ~ *word*, mot convenu, *m*. ¶ *v.t*, chiffrer. **codicil**, *n*, codicille, *m*. **codify**, *v.t*, codifier.

coefficient, *n*, coefficient, *m*.

coerce, *v.t*, contraindre.

coffee, *n*, café; moka, *m*. ~ *cup*, tasse à café, *f*. ~ *pot*, cafetière, *f*. ~ *spoon*, cuiller à café, c. à moka, *f*. ~ *table*, guéridon, *m*. ~ *tree* & ~ *planter*, caféier, *m*.

coffer, *n*, coffre, *m*, caisse, *f*.

coffin, *n*, cercueil, *m*, bière, *f*.

cog, *n*, dent, *f*; alluchon, *m*. ~*wheel*, roue dentée, *f*. ¶ *v.t*, [en]denter.

cogency, *n*, force, *f*. **cogent**, *a*, convaincant; probant.

cogitate, *v.i*, méditer, réfléchir.

cognate, *a*, de même origine.

cognizance, *n*, connaissance, *f*. *cognizant of*, instruit de.

cognomen, *n*, surnom, *m*.

cohabit, *v.i*, cohabiter.

cohere, *v.i*, adhérer. **coherence**, *n*, cohérence; suite, *f*. **coherent**, *a*, cohérent; suivi. ~**ly**, *ad*, avec cohérence. **cohesion**, *n*, cohésion, *f*. **cohesive**, *a*, cohérent.

cohort, *n*, cohorte, *f*.

coil, *n*, rouleau, *m*, glène; couronne, botte, torsade, *f*; serpentin; (*snake*) repli, anneau, *m*; (*Elec*.) bobine, *f*. ¶ *v.t*, [en]rouler [en couronne], bobiner; (*rope*) lover, rouer. ~ *up*, replier; se replier.

coin, n, pièce, [pièce de] monnaie, f; numéraire, m, espèces [monnayées] f.pl; (ancient) médaille, f. ~ machine, appareil à sous, m. ¶ v.t, monnayer, frapper, battre; (fig.) forger, inventer; fabriquer. ~age, n, monnayage, m, frappe, f; monnaie[s] f.[pl.], numéraire, m.

coincide, v.i, coïncider. **coincidence,** n, coïncidence, f.

coir, n, fibre de coco, f.

coke, n, coke, m.

colander, n, passoire, f.

cold†, a, froid; à froid. in ~ blood or ~-blooded, de sang-froid, à froid. ~-blooded (animal), à sang froid. ~ chisel, burin (ou ciseau) à froid, m. ~ snap, coup de froid, m. ~ steel, arme blanche, f. ¶ n, froid, m, froidure, f; (Path.) rhume, coup d'air, m. ~ on the chest, in the head, rhume de poitrine, de cerveau.

coleopter[an], n, coléoptère, m. **coleopterous,** a, coléoptère.

colic, n, colique, f, tranchées, f.pl.

collaborate, v.i, collaborer. **collaborator,** n, collaborateur, trice.

collapse, n, effondrement, écroulement; affaissement, m; chute, f, débâcle, f. ¶ v.i, s'effondrer, crouler, s'écrouler, s'affaisser. **collapsible,** a, pliant.

collar, n, collier, collet; col; frette, bague, f. [shirt] ~ (detached), faux col, m. attached ~ (to shirt), col tenant. ~ bone, clavicule, f. ~ size, n, encolure, f. ~ button, bouton de col, m. ¶ v.t, colleter.

collate, v.t, collationner.

collateral, a, collatéral. ~ security, nantissement, m.

collation, n, collationnement, m; (snack) collation, f.

colleague, n, collègue, m.

collect, n, collecte, f. ¶ v.t, recueillir, rassembler, réunir; retirer, enlever; [re]lever; capter; collectionner; recouvrer, récupérer; percevoir; encaisser; quêter. ~ed, p.a, recueilli, calme. ~ion, n, rassemblement, recueil, m; réunion, f; captage; recouvrement, m; récupération; perception, rentrée; levée, f, relevage; encaissement; enlèvement, apport, m; quête, collecte, f; cabinet, m. ~ of coins or medals, médaillier, m. ~ive†, a, collectif. ~or, n, collecteur, receveur, percepteur;

collectionneur, fureteur, curieux, ramasseur, euse.

college, n, collège, m; faculté, académie, f. **collegian,** n, collégien, ne. **collegiate,** a, collégial.

collide, v.i, s'aborder, se rencontrer, se tamponner. ~ with, aborder, rencontrer, tamponner.

collier, n, (pers.) houilleur; (ship) charbonnier, m. ~y, n, houillère, f; (col. pl.) charbonnage, m.

collision, n, abordage, m, collision, rencontre, f, tamponnement, m. ~ mat, paillet d'abordage, m.

colloquial†, a, de la conversation; (words, phrases) familier. ~ism, n, expression familière, f. **colloquy,** n, colloque, m.

collusion, n, collusion, f.

Colombia, n, la Colombie.

colon, n, deux-points; (Anat.) côlon, m.

colonel, n, colonel, m.

colonial, a, colonial. **colonist,** n, colon, m. **colonize,** v.t, coloniser.

colonnade, n, colonnade, f.

colony, n, colonie, f.

colophon, n, marque (typographique) f, chiffre, fleuron, m.

color, n, couleur, f; teint; coloris, m; peinture, f; (pl.) couleurs, f.pl, drapeaux, m.pl; pavillon, m. under ~ of (fig.), sous couleur de. ~ bar, distinction sociale (ou légale) entre la race blanche & la race noire, f. ~-blind, daltonien. ~ blindness, cécité pour les ~-s, f. ¶ v.t, colorer, colorier; enluminer. ~ed, p.a. & p.p: ~ dress, robe de couleur, f. ~ sketch, croquis en couleurs, m. ~ing, n, coloris, m. ~less, a, sans couleur, incolore, pâle.

colossal†, a, colossal. **colossus,** n, colosse, m.

colt, n, poulain, m. **coltsfoot** (Bot.) n, pas-d'âne, tussilage, m.

columbine (Bot.) n, ancolie, f.

column, n, colonne, f; pilier, m; (news on special subject) rubrique, f. ~ist, n, journaliste, m.

coma, n, (Med.) coma, m; (Bot. & comet) chevelure, f. **comatose,** a, comateux.

comb, n, peigne, m; (crest) crête, f; (honey) rayon, gâteau, m, gaufre, f. ¶ v.t, peigner. ~ out (fig.), éliminer.

combat, n, combat, m. ¶ v.t, com-

battre. ~ant, n, combattant, m.
~ive, a, batailleur. ~iveness, n,
combativité, f.

combination, n, combinaison, f.
combine, n, coalition; combine;
(Agric.) batteuse, f. ¶ v.t, combiner, réunir; joindre; (v.i.) se
combiner; se coaliser.

combings, n.pl, peignures, f.pl.

combustible, a, combustible.
combustion, n, combustion, f.
~ chamber (motor), chambre
d'explosion, f.

come, v.i.ir, venir; provenir; arriver; se présenter; se faire; entrer; être. ~ along!, ~ on! allons!,
venez!, marchons! ~ about, se
faire. ~ across, rencontrer. ~
back, revenir. ~ down, descendre. ~ for, venir chercher.
~ from (be a native of), être
originaire de. ~ home, rentrer;
revenir; porter coup. ~ in! en-
trez! ~ now! enfin!, ah! çà. ~
off, se détacher; (ink) décharger.
~ off on (dye), déteindre sur.
~ out, sortir; débuter; (book,
etc.) paraître. ~ to, se monter
à; revenir à; (decision) prendre.
~ to an agreement, tomber
d'accord. ~ to blows, en venir
aux mains. ~ to light, se découvrir. ~ to pass, arriver, advenir. ~ to terms, s'arranger.
~ undone, se défaire. ~ up
(sprout), poindre. ~ upon,
tomber sur. ~ what may, arrive (ou advienne) que pourra,
au petit bonheur.

comedian, n, comédien, ne; farceur, m. comedy, n, comédie, f,
comique, m.

comeliness, n, beauté, grâce,
bonne mine, f. comely, a, beau,
gracieux, avenant.

comer, n, venant, m; venu, e.
~s & goers, allants & venants,
m.pl.

comet, n, comète, f.

comfort, n, consolation, satisfaction, aise, f, [ré]confort, m.
¶ v.t, consoler, réconforter, soulager. ~able†, a, aisé, confortable. ~er, n, consolateur, trice;
(blanket) couvre-pied, m.

comic & comical, a, comique;
humoristique, cocasse; plaisant;
bouffon, bouffe, burlesque.
~ actor, comique, m. ~ opera,
opéra bouffe, m. ~ song, chanson burlesque, chansonnette, f.
~ turn, pantalonnade, f.

coming, p.a, à venir; d'avenir;

futur. ¶ n, venue, arrivée, f; (of
Christ) avènement, m. [I am]
~! j'y vais! on y va! voilà! ~ &
going, allées & venues, f.pl.
~ out (in society), début, m, entrée dans le monde, f.

comma, n, virgule, f. Note:—
Sets of three figures, separated
in Eng. by commas, are separated in Fr. either by points or
by spaces.

command, n, commandement, m;
ordre[s] m.[pl.]; empire, m; facilité, f. ¶ v.t, commander; monter; ordonner; avoir à sa disposition; (a view of) donner sur.
~ant, n, commandant, chef, m.

commandeer, v.t, réquisitionner.

commander, n, commandant,
chef; (Nav.) capitaine de frégate,
m. commanding officer, commandant, chef, m.

commandment, n, commande-
ment, m.

commemorate, v.t, commémorer.

commence, v.t. & i, commencer,
entamer. ~ment, n, commencement, début, m.

commend, v.t, recommander; applaudir à, préconiser; remettre.
~able, a, recommandable, louange; recommandation, f.

commensurate, a, proportionné.

comment & commentary, n,
commentaire, m, glose, f. to
comment on, commenter [sur].
commentator, n, commentateur.

commerce, n, commerce, négoce, m. commercial, a, commercial, commerçant, marchand,
de commerce, d'affaires. ~ism,
n, mercantillisme, m. ~ize, v.t,
achalander, monnayer. ~ly, ad,
commercialement.

commiserate, v.t, plaindre.

commissariat, n, intendance
militaire, f.

commission, n, commission, remise, f; courtage, m; (shop)
guelte, f; (officer's) lettre[s] de
service, f.[pl.]. ~ agent, commissionaire, m. ¶ v.t, commissioner; mandater; (officer)
nommer; (ship) armer. ~ed
work, ouvrage de commande,
m. commissioner, n, commissaire, m.

commit, v.t, commettre, faire;
livrer; confier; renvoyer. ~ for
trial, mettre en accusation. ~
oneself, s'engager; se compromettre. ~ to prison, ordonner

l'incarcération de, ~ *to writing*, coucher (*ou* mettre) par écrit. ~**ment** (*Com.*) *n*, engagement, *m*.

committee, *n*, comité; bureau, *m*.

commode, *n*, chaise [percée] *f*.

commodious, *a*, commode. ~**ly**, *ad*, commodément. ~**ness**, *n*, commodité, *f*.

commodity, *n*, produit, *m*, denrée, marchandise, matière [première] *f*, article, *m*; ressource, *f*.

commodore, *n*, chef d'escadre, *m*.

common, *a*, commun; général; coutumier; ordinaire; vulgaire; peuple; banal; simple; type; public. ~ [*land*], communal, *m*, champs communs, *m.pl*, vaine pâture, *f*. ~ *law*, droit coutumier *m*. [*the*] ~ *people*, les gens du commun, *m.pl*, le petit peuple, le vulgaire. ~ *sense*, sens commun, bon sens, *m*. *the* ~ *weal*, la chose publique. **in**, **out of**, ~, en, hors du, commun. ~**ly**, *ad*, communément, couramment. ~**ness**, *n*, fréquence, *f*. ~**place**, *a*, banal, commun; (*n.*) banalité; pauvreté, *f*, (*pl.*) lieux communs, *m.pl*. ~**wealth**, *n*, république; communauté, *f*.

commonalty, *n*, roture, *f*. **commoner**, *n*, roturier, ère.

commotion, *n*, commotion, *f*, mouvement, *m*.

communal, *a*, communal. **commune**, *v.i*, converser. **communicant**, *n*, communiant, e. **communicate**, *v.t. & i*, communiquer; correspondre; (*Eccl.*) communier. **communication**, *n*, communication, *f*. ~ *cord*, corde de signal d'alarme, *f*. ~ *trench*, branche de tranchée, *f*, boyau de t., *m*. **communicative**, *a*, communicatif. **communion**, *n*, communion, *f*. ~ *cup*, calice, *m*. ~ *service*, office du saint sacrement, *m*. ~ *table*, sainte table, *f*. **communism**, *n*, communisme, *m*. **communist**, *n*, communiste, *m.f*. **community**, *n*, communauté; société; république, *f*. ~ *singing*, chansons en chœur, *f.pl*.

commutation, *n*, commutation; substitution, *f*; replacement; échange, *m*. ~ *ticket*, carte d'abonnement au chemin de fer, *f*.

commutator, *n*, commutateur, *m*.

commute, *v.t*, commuer. ~**r**, *n*, abonné des chemins de fer, *m*.

Como (Lake), le lac de Côme.

compact, *a*, compact. ¶ *n*, pacte, *m*. ~**ness**, *n*, compacité, *f*.

companion, *n*, compagnon, *m*, compagne, *f*, camarade, *m,f*; (*thing*) pendant, *m*. [*lady*] ~, dame, demoiselle, de compagnie. ~**able**, *a*, sociable. ~**ship**, *n*, compagnie, société, *f*, fréquentations, *f.pl*.

company, *n*, compagnie; société; bande; troupe, *f*; groupe; équipage; monde, *m*.

comparable, *a*, comparable. **comparative**†, *a*, comparatif; (*sciences*) comparé. ¶ (*Gram.*) *n*, comparatif, *m*. **compare**, *v.t*, comparer, assimiler; rapprocher; collationner; conférer. **comparison**, *n*, comparaison, *f*, rapprochement, *m*.

compartment, *n*, compartiment, *m*; case, *f*.

compass, *n*, cadre, *m*, étendue, portée; (*magnetic*) boussole, *f*; compas; (*voice*) diapason; (*musical*) clavier, *m*. ~ *card*, rose des vents, *f*. **compass[es]**, *n.[pl.]*, compas, *m*. *compasses with pen point, with pencil point*, compas à tire-ligne, à porte-crayon. **compass**, *v.t*, cerner, ceindre.

compassion, *n*, compassion, *f*. ~**ate**, *a*, compatissant.

compatible, *a*, compatible.

compatriot, *n*, compatriote, *m,f*.

compeer, *n*, égal, e, pair, *m*.

compel, *v.t*, contraindre, astreindre, obliger, forcer.

compendious, *a*, sommaire. **compendium**, *n*, compendium, *m*.

compensate, *v.t*, compenser, indemniser, dédommager. **compensation**, *n*, compensation, indemnité, *f*, dédommagement, *m*.

compete for, concourir pour, à. ~ *with*, faire concurrence à.

competence, **-cy**, *n*, aisance; compétence; aptitude, *f*. **competent**, *a*, compétent, apte.

competition, *n*, concurrence; compétition, *f*; concours, *m*. **competitor**, *n*, concurrent, e, compétiteur, trice.

compile, *v.t*, compiler.

complacency, *n*, contentement, *m*. **complacent**, *a*, content de soi. ~**ly**, *ad*, avec un air suffisant.

complain, *v.i*, se plaindre; réclamer; gémir. ~ *of* (medically), accuser. ~**ant**, *n*, plaignant, e.

complaint, *n*, plainte, doléance, réclamation, *f*, grief; gémissement, *m*; (*Med.*) affection, maladie, *f*.

complaisance, *n*, complaisance, *f*. **complaisant**, *a*, complaisant.

complement, *n*, complément, effectif, *m*. **~ary**, *a*, complémentaire.

complete†, *a*, complet, au complet. ¶ *v.t*, compléter. **~d** (*time, age*) *p.p*, révolus. **completion**, *n*, complètement, achèvement, *m*.

complex, *a. & n*, complexe, *a. & m*.

complexion, *n*, (*of face*) teint; (*fig.*) caractère, aspect, *m*.

complexity, *n*, complexité, *f*.

compliance, *n*, conformité, *f*. **compliant**, *a*, facile, complaisant.

complicate, *v.t*, compliquer. **complication**, *n*, complication, *f*.

complicity, *n*, complicité, *f*.

compliment, *n*, compliment, *m*; (*pl.*) compliments, *m.pl*, civilités, politesses, *f.pl*, hommages, *m.pl*, choses, *f.pl*. **~s of the season**, souhaits de bonne année, *m.pl*. ¶ *v.t*, complimenter. **~ary**, *a*, flatteur; (*free*) gratis.

comply, *v.i.abs*, se soumettre. **~ with**, se conformer à, condescendre à, observer, obéir à, remplir, respecter. *not complied with* (rule), inobservée.

component, *a*, constituant; composant. ¶ *n*, composant, *m*. **~** [*part*], pièce détachée, *f*.

compose, *v.t*, composer. *to be ~d of*, se c. de. **~ oneself**, se calmer. **~d**, *p.p*, composé, calme. **composer** (*Mus.*) *n*, compositeur, trice, auteur, *m. composing stick* (*Typ.*), composteur, *m*. **composite**, *a*, composé, mixte. **composition**, *n*, composition, constitution, *f*; thème, *m*. **compositor** (*Typ.*) *n*, compositeur, trice.

composure, *n*, calme, sang-froid, *m*.

compound, *a*, composé; (*steam*) compound. *~ interest*, intérêt[s] composé[s] *m*.[*pl*.]. ¶ *n*, composé; combiné, corps composé, *m*. ¶ *v.t*, composer; pactiser avec (*a felony* = un crime); (*v.i*.) transiger; pactiser.

comprehend, *v.t*, comprendre. **comprehension**, *n*, compréhension, *f*. **comprehensive**, *a*, compréhensif.

compress, *n*, compresse, *f*. ¶ *v.t*, comprimer, refouler. **~ion**, *n*, compression, *f*. **~or**, *n*, compresseur, *m*.

comprise, *v.t*, comprendre, renfermer, contenir.

compromise, *n*, compromis, accommodement, *m*, transaction, *f*. ¶ *v.t. & i*, compromettre, transiger; capituler. **~ oneself**, se compromettre.

comptroller, *n*, contrôleur, *m*.

compulsion, *n*, contrainte, *f*. **compulsorily**, *ad*, forcément. **compulsory**, *a*, forcé, obligatoire.

compunction, *n*, componction, *f*.

computation, *n*, supputation, *f*. **compute**, *v.t*, supputer, computer.

comrade, *n*, camarade, *m,f*. **~ship**, *n*, camaraderie, *f*.

concave, *a*, concave. **concavity**, *n*, concavité, *f*.

conceal, *v.t*, cacher; celer; dérober; dissimuler; supprimer; taire; receler. **~ment**, *n*, réticence; dissimulation; suppression, *f*; recèlement, *m*.

concede, *v.t*, accorder, concéder.

conceit, *n*, vanité, suffisance, *f*. **~ed**, *a*, vain, vaniteux, suffisant.

conceivable, *a*, concevable. **conceive**, *v.t. & i*, concevoir.

concentrate, *v.t*, concentrer; canaliser. **concentration**, *n*, concentration, *f*.

concentric, *a*, concentrique.

concept, *n*, concept, *m*; idée, *f*. **~ion**, *n*, conception, *f*.

concern, *n*, affaire, *f*; souci, *m*, sollicitude, inquiétude; entreprise, exploitation; boutique, *f*. ¶ *v.t*, concerner, intéresser, regarder, toucher, appartenir. **~ing**, *pr*, concernant, touchant, à l'égard de.

concert, *n*, concert, *m*; audition, *f*. **~ grand** [*piano*], piano à queue, *m*. ¶ *v.t*, concerter. **concerto**, *n*, concerto, *m*.

concession, *n*, concession, *f*. **concessionaire**, *n*, concessionaire, *m,f*.

conch, *n*, conque, *f*; coquillage, *m*. **~ology**, *n*, conchyliogie, *f*.

conciliate, *v.t*, concilier. **conciliation**, *n*, conciliation, *f*. **~ board**, conseil de prud'hommes, *m*.

concise, *a*, concis; (*edition*) compacte. **~ness**, *n*, concision, *f*.

conclave, *n*, conclave, *m*; assemblée, *f*.

conclude, *v.t. & i*, conclure; arrêter, clore. **conclusion**, *n*, conclusion; décision, *f*. **conclusive**, *a*, démonstratif; concluant; décisif.

concoct, *v.t*, confectionner; (*fig*.) cuisiner, machiner, tramer. **concoction**, *n*, mixture; machination, *f*.

concomitant, *n*, accompagnement, *m*.

concord, *n*, concorde, *f*; accord, *m*; concordance, *f*. ~**ance**, *n*, concordance, *f*.

concourse, *n*, concours, *m*, affluence, *f*.

concrete, *a*, concret. the concrete (opp. *abstract*), le concret. ¶ *n*, béton, *m*.

concubine, *n*, concubine, *f*.

concupiscence, *n*, concupiscence, *f*.

concur, *v.i*, concourir. **concurrence**, *n*, concours, *m*.

concussion, *n*, ébranlement, *m*. ~ of the brain, commotion au cerveau, *f*.

condemn, *v.t*, condamner. ~ed man, woman, condamné(e) à mort. **condemnation**, *n*, condamnation, *f*.

condensation, *n*, condensation, *f*. **condense**, *v.t*, condenser; resserrer. ~d milk, lait condensé, l. concentré, l. conservé, *m*. **condenser**, *n*, (*Phys., Elec., Opt*.) condensateur; (*steam*) condenseur, *m*.

condescend, *v.i*, condescendre. **condescension**, *n*, condescendance, *f*.

condiment, *n*, condiment, assaisonnement, *m*.

condition, *n*, condition, *f*; état, *m*. on ~ that, à condition que, à [la] charge de, sous réserve que. ¶ *v.t*, conditionner. ~al†, *a*, conditionnel.

condole with, exprimer ses condoléances à. **condolence**, *n*, condoléance, *f*.

condone, *v.t*, passer sur, fermer les yeux sur.

conduce, *v.t*, contribuer, conduire, tendre.

conduct, *n*, conduite, *f*; maniement, *m*. ¶ *v.t*, conduire, guider, gérer, manier, mener. ~ed tour, excursion accompagnée, *f*. **conductor, tress**, *n*, conducteur, trice; guide, *m*; receveur, euse, chef d'orchestre, *m*.

conduit, *n*, conduit; caniveau, *m*.

cone, *n*, (*Geom*.) cône, *m*; (*fir, pine*) pomme; (*ice cream*) cornet de glace, *m*.

confectioner, *n*, confiseur, euse; pâtissier, ère, glacier, *m*. ~'s shop, confiserie, pâtisserie, *f*. ~**y**, *n*, confiserie, *f*, bonbons, *m.pl*, sucreries, *f.pl*; pâtisserie, *f*.

confederacy, *n*, confédération, *f*. **confederate**, *n*, compère, *m*, complice, *m,f*, (*pl*.) consorts, *m.pl*. ¶ *v.i*, se confédérer. **confederation**, *n*, confédération, *f*.

confer, *v.t*, conférer; accorder; (*v.i*.) conférer. ~**ence**, *n*, conférence, *f*.

confess, *v.t*, confesser, avouer, s'accuser de; (*v.i*.) se confesser. ~**edly**, *ad*, de son propre aveu. **confession**, *n*, confession, *f*, aveu, *m*; confesse, *f*. ~**al**, *n*, confessional, *m*. **confessor**, *n*, confesseur, *m*.

confidant, e, *n*, confident, e. **confide**, *v.t*, confier, livrer; (*v.i*.) se confier. **confidence**, *n*, confiance; assurance; (*secret*) confidence, *f*. ~ trick, vol à l'américaine, *m*. ~ man, escroc, *m*. **confident**, *a*, confiant, assuré. **confidential**, *a*, (*of things*) confidentiel; (*of pers.—in good sense*) de confiance; (*bad sense*) affidé. ~**ly**, *ad*, confidentiellement, confidemment. **confiding**, *p.a*, confiant.

confine, *v.t*, confiner, borner; chambrer, enfermer, renfermer, resserrer; retenir, faire garder. ~ oneself to, within, se borner à, dans, se cantonner dans. ~ [to barracks], consigner. to be ~d (woman), accoucher, faire ses couches. ~**ment**, *n*, détention, *f*; (woman) couches, *f.pl*, accouchement, *m*. ~ to barracks, consigne, *f*. **confines**, *n.pl*, confins, *m.pl*.

confirm, *v.t*, confirmer; ratifier, approuver, adopter. ~**ation**, *n*, confirmation; ratification, approbation, adoption, *f*. ~**ed**, *p.a*, invétéré, acharné, fieffé, émérite. ~ invalid, incurable, *m,f*.

confiscate, *v.t*, confisquer. **confiscation**, *n*, confiscation, *f*.

conflagration, *n*, embrasement, *m*; conflagration, *f*.

conflict, *n*, conflit, *m*. ¶ *v.i. & abs*, se contredire. ~**ing**, *p.a*, en conflit; contradictoire.

confluence, *n,* confluent; concours, *m.*

conform, *v.t,* conformer; (*v.i.*) se c. ~**able,** *a,* conforme. ~**ably,** *ad,* conformément. ~**ation,** *n,* conformation, *f.* ~**ity,** *n,* conformité, *f.*

confound, *v.t,* confondre. ~**ed,** *p.a,* maudit.

confraternity, *n,* confraternité; (*pers.*) confrérie, *f.*

confront, *v.t,* affronter; confronter.

confuse, *v.t,* confondre, mêler; embrouiller. **confused,** *a,* confus. ~**ly,** *ad,* confusément. **confusion,** *n,* confusion, *f,* désarroi, *m.*

confute, *v.t,* réfuter.

congeal, *v.t,* congeler, geler, figer; (*v.i.*) se congeler; prendre, se prendre.

congenial, *a,* sympathique; agréable.

congenital, *a,* congénital.

conger [eel], *n,* congre, *m.*

congest (*Med.*) *v.t,* congestionner, engorger. ~**ion,** *n,* (*Med.*) congestion, *f,* engorgement; (*traffic, etc.*) encombrement, *m,* presse, *f.* ~ *of the blood, of the brain, of the lungs,* congestion sanguine, cérébrale, pulmonaire. ~ *of the liver,* engorgement au foie.

conglomerate, *n,* conglomérat, *m.*

congratulate, *v.t,* féliciter, complimenter. ~ *oneself,* se féliciter, s'applaudir. **congratulation,** *n,* félicitation, *f,* compliment, *m.*

congregate, *v.t,* rassembler; (*v.i.*) se r., s'assembler. **congregation,** *n,* assemblage, *m;* (*of pers.*) assemblée, *f.*

congress, *n,* congrès, *m.* **member of the** (*or* a) ~, congressiste, *m,f.*

congruity, *n,* convenance, *f.* **congruous,** *a,* congru. ~**ly,** *ad,* congrûment.

conic(al), *a,* conique.

conifer, *n,* conifère, *m.* ~**ous,** *a,* conifère.

conjectural†, *a,* conjectural. **conjecture,** *n,* conjecture, *f.* ¶ *v.t,* conjecturer.

conjoin, *v.t,* conjoindre. **conjoint†,** *a,* conjoint.

conjugal†, *a,* conjugal.

conjugate, *v.t,* conjuguer. **conjugation,** *n,* conjugaison, *f.*

conjunction, *n,* conjonction, *f.* **conjuncture,** *n,* conjoncture, *f.*

conjure, *v.t,* (*adjure*) conjurer; (*enchant*) ensorceler; (*v.i.*) escamoter. ~ *away,* escamoter. ~ [*up*], évoquer, se forger. **conjurer, -or,** *n,* escamoteur, prestidigitateur, *m.* **conjuring,** *n,* escamotage, *m,* prestidigitation, *f.* ~ *trick,* tour de passe-passe, *m.*

connect, *v.t,* relier, raccorder, joindre, réunir; lier; (*Elec.*) [ac]coupler. ~**ed,** *p.a,* suivi; apparenté. *connecting rod,* bielle, *f.* **connection,** *n,* connexion; liaison; relation, *f;* raccord; contact; rapport, *m;* correspondance, *f;* parent, e; clientèle, *f,* achalandage, *m.*

conning tower, blockhaus; (*submarine*) kiosque, *m.*

connivance, *n,* connivence, *f.* **connive at,** être de connivence pour.

connoisseur, *n,* connaisseur, euse; gourmet, *m.*

connubial, *a,* conjugal, matrimonial.

conquer, *v.t,* vaincre, conquérir. **conqueror, conqueress,** *n,* vainqueur, *m,* conquérant, e. *William the Conqueror,* Guillaume le Conquérant. **conquest,** *n,* conquête, *f.*

consanguinity, *n,* consanguinité, *f.*

conscience, *n,* conscience, *f,* for intérieur, *m.* ~ *money,* restitution anonyme, *f.* *to be ~-stricken,* avoir une conscience bourrelée de remords. **conscientious†,** *a,* consciencieux. ~**ness,** *n,* conscience, *f.*

conscious, *a:* *to be* ~, avoir sa connaissance. *to be* ~ *of,* avoir conscience de, être conscient de, sentir. ~**ly,** *ad,* sciemment. ~**ness,** *n,* connaissance; conscience, *f.*

conscript, *n,* conscrit, *m.* ~**ion,** *n,* conscription, *f.*

consecrate, *v.t,* consacrer; bénir; sacrer. ~**d,** *p.a,* bénit; sacré; saint. **consecration,** *n,* consécration; bénédiction, *f;* sacre, *m.*

consecutive†, *a,* consécutif.

consensus, *n,* unanimité, *f.*

consent, *n,* consentement, accord, agrément, aveu, *m.* ¶ *v.i,* consentir, accéder, entendre (*to* = à).

consequence, *n,* conséquence, suite; importance, *f.* **consequent,** *a,* conséquent. *consequential* *damages,* dommages indirects, *m.pl.* **consequently,** *ad,* conséquemment, par conséquent, aussi.

conservation, *n,* conservation, préservation, *f.*

conservative, *a,* conservateur. ¶ *n.* & **conservator,** *n,* conservateur, trice. **conservatory,** *n,* serre, *f.*

consider, *v.t,* considérer, regarder; délibérer sur; (*v.i.* & *abs.*) songer, réfléchir. ~**able†,** *a,* considérable. ~**ate,** *a,* prévenant. ~**ation,** *n,* considération, *f;* égard, *m;* délibération, *f;* ménagements, *m.pl;* (*law*) provision, cause, *f.* *in* ~ *of* (value received), moyennant. (matter) *under* ~, à la bureau. *without due* ~, à la légère. ~**ing,** *pr,* attendu, vu, eu égard à.

consign, *v.t,* livrer; confier; remettre, expédier; reléguer; (*goods*) consigner. ~**ee,** *n,* consignataire, destinataire, réceptionnaire, *m.* ~**ment,** *n,* consignation; expédition, *f;* envoi, chargement, *m.* (goods) *on* ~, en consignation. ~**or,** *n,* consignateur, *m.*

consist, *v.i,* consister, se composer. ~**ence, -cy,** *n,* consistance; suite, *f.* ~**ent,** *a,* conséquent, compatible; qui ne se dément point; suivi. ~**ently with,** conséquemment à. ~**ory,** *n,* consistoire, *m.*

consolation, *n,* consolation, *f.* ~ *prize,* prix de c., *m.* **console,** *v.t,* consoler. ¶ *n,* console, *f.*

consolidate, *v.t,* consolider; unifier. **consolidation,** *n,* consolidation; unification, *f.*

consonance, *n,* consonance, *f.* **consonant,** *a,* (*Mus., words*) consonant. ~ *with,* en rapport avec. ¶ *n,* consonne, *f.*

consort, *n,* époux, ouse; (*Naut.*) conserve, *f,* navire d'escort; (*prince*) consort, *m.* ¶ *v.i,* s'associer.

conspicuous, *a,* voyant, en évidence; insigne, signalé, remarquable. *to make oneself* ~, se faire remarquer, se singulariser.

conspiracy, *n,* conspiration, conjuration, *f.* **conspirator,** *n,* conspirateur, trice, conjuré, *m.* **conspire,** *v.i.* & *t,* conspirer, conjurer.

constancy, *n,* constance, *f.* **constant,** *a,* constant. ¶ *n,* constante, *f.* ~**ly,** *ad,* constamment.

constellation, *n,* constellation, *f.*

consternation, *n,* consternation, *f.*

constipate, *v.t,* constiper. **constipation,** *n,* constipation, *f.*

constituency, *n,* circonscription électorale, *f,* collège électoral, *m;* électeurs, *m.pl.* **constituent,** *a,* constituant, composant. ¶ *n,* composant; ingrédient, *m;* (*pl.*) électeurs, commettants, *m.pl.* **constitute,** *v.t,* constituer. **constitution,** *n,* constitution, *f;* tempérament, *m.* ~**al†,** *a,* constitutionnel.

constrain, *v.t,* contraindre, gêner, forcer. **constraint,** *n,* contrainte, gêne, sujétion, *f.*

construct, *v.t,* construire, établir. ~**ion,** *n,* construction; interprétation; explication, *f.* ~**ional,** *a,* de construction. ~**ive,** *a,* constructif. ~**or,** *n,* constructeur, *m.*

construe, *v.t,* construire; expliquer.

consul, *n,* consul, *m.* ~**ar,** *a,* consulaire. ~**ate** & ~**ship,** *n,* consulat, *m.*

consult, *v.t,* consulter. ~**ation,** *n,* consultation, *f.* **consulting,** *p.a:* ~ *engineer,* ingénieur-conseil, *m.* ~ *physician,* médecin consultant *m.* ~ *room,* cabinet de consultation, salon de c., *m.*

consume, *v.t,* consumer, dévorer; (*use*) consommer. **consumer,** *n,* consommateur, *m.*

consummate, *a,* consommé, fini, superlatif. ¶ *v.t,* consommer. **consummation,** *n,* consommation, *f.*

consumption, *n,* (*destruction*) consomption; (*Med.*) consomption, phtisie; (*use*) consommation, dépense, *f.* **consumptive,** *a.* & *n,* tuberculeux, euse; poitrinaire, phtisique, *a.* & *m,f.*

contact, *n,* contact; attouchement; frottement, *m.* ¶ *v.t,* être en relations avec, être en contact avec.

contagion, *n,* contagion, *f.* **contagious,** *a,* contagieux. ~**ness,** *n,* contagion, *f.*

contain, *v.t,* contenir, tenir, renfermer. ~**er,** *n,* contenant; récipient, *m.*

contaminate, *v.t,* contaminer, souiller. **contamination,** *n,* contamination, souillure, *f.*

contemplate, *v.t,* contempler; méditer; projeter; envisager;

(*v.i.*) méditer. **contemplation**, *n*, contemplation, *f*. *in* ~, en vue. **contemplative**, *a*, contemplatif.

contemporaneous & contemporary, *a*, contemporain. **contemporary**, *n*, contemporain, e.

contempt, *n*, mépris, *m*. *oft. pl*, dédain, *m*. ~ *of court*, offense à la cour, *f*; refus d'obéissance, *m*. ~**ible**, *a*, méprisable. **contemptuous**, *a*, méprisant, dédaigneux.

contend, *v.t. & i:* ~ *that*, prétendre que. ~ *with*, combattre; lutter contre; disputer.

content, *a*, content. ¶ *n*, contentement, *m*; (*holding*) contenance; teneur, *f*, titre; (*pl.*) contenu, *m*; table des matières, *f*. ¶ *v.t*, contenter. ~*ed with*, satisfait de. ~**edly**, *ad*, content.

contention, *n*, démêlé, *m*; dispute, discorde, *f*. *my* ~ *is that* . . ., ce que je prétends, c'est que . . . **contentious**, *a*, litigieux; contentieux.

contentment, *n*, contentement, *m*.

contest, *n*, lutte, *f*, combat; concours, *m*, joute, dispute, *f*. ¶ *v.t*, contester; disputer.

context, *n*, contexte, *m*.

contexture, *n*, contexture, *f*.

contiguity, *n*, contiguïté, *f*. **contiguous**, *a*, contigu.

continence, *n*, continence, *f*. **continent**, *a*, continent. ¶ *n*, continent, *m*; terre ferme, *f*. *the C*~ (*Europe*), le continent. ~**al**, *a*, continental.

contingency, *n*, contingence, éventualité, *f*, imprévu, *m*. ~ *fund*, fonds de prévoyance, *m*. **contingent**, *a*, contingent, aléatoire, éventuel. ¶ *n*, contingent; évènement fortuit, *m*.

continual†, *a*, continuel. **continuance**, *n*, continuation, *f*. **continuation**, *n*, continuation, suite, *f*. **continue**, *v.t. & i*, continuer; prolonger. **to be** ~**d** (*serial*), à suivre, la suite au prochain numéro. **continuity**, *n*, continuité, *f*. **continuous**, *a*, continu. ~ *performance* (*movies*), spectacle permanent, *m*. ~**ly**, *ad*, continûment.

contort, *v.t*, contourner. ~**ed**, *p.a*, tors. **contortion**, *n*, contorsion, *f*. ~**ist**, *n*, homme-caoutchouc, homme-serpent, *m*;

femme-caoutchouc, femme-serpent, *f*.

contour, *n*, contour; profil, tracé, galbe, *m*. ~ *line*, courbe de niveau, *f*. ~ *map*, carte en courbes de niveau, *f*.

contraband, *n*, contrebande, *f*; (*att.*) de c.

contrabass, *n*, contrebasse, *f*.

contract, *n*, contrat, *m*, convention, *f*, acte, traité, *m*. *on* ~ *or by* ~, à l'enterprise, à forfait, forfaitaire; par contrat. ~ *bridge*, bridge plafond, b. contrat, *m*. ¶ *v.t*, (*shrink*) contracter, [r]étrécir, resserrer; (*law*) contracter; [entre]prendre; (*v.i. or abs.*) contracter, s'étrécir, se rétrécir, se resserrer; (*law*) contracter. ~**ant** (*pers.*) *n*, contractant, e. ~**ing**, *a*, contractant. ~**ion**, *n*, contraction, *f*, [r]étrécissement, resserrement, *m*; abréviation, *f*. ~**or**, *n*, entrepreneur, euse; fournisseur, euse; adjudicataire, *m,f*. **contractual**, *a*, contractuel, forfaitaire.

contradict, *v.t*, contredire, démentir. ~**ion**, *n*, contredit, démenti, *m*. ~**ory**, *a*, contradictoire.

contradistinction, *n*, opposition, *f*.

contralto, *n*, contralto, *m*.

contrariety, *n*, contrariété, *f*. **contrarily & contrary**, *ad*, contrairement. **contrary**, *a*, contraire; opposé; inverse. ¶ *n*, contraire, opposé, rebours; contre-pied, *m*; contrepartie, *f*. *on the* ~, au contraire.

contrast, *n*, contraste, *m*, opposition, *f*. ¶ *v.t. & i*, mettre en contraste; contraster, trancher. ~**y**, *a*, heurté.

contravene, *v.t*, contrevenir à, enfreindre. **contravention**, *n*, contravention, infraction, *f*.

contribute, *v.t*, contribuer; (*v.i.*) contribuer à, collaborer à. ~ *to* (*journal*), collaborer à. **contribution**, *n*, contribution, *f*; apport, fournissement, *m*, cote, cotisation, *f*. *to lay under* ~, mettre à contribution. **contributor** (*to journal*) *n*, collaborateur, trice.

contrite, *a*, contrit. **contrition**, *n*, contrition, *f*, brisement de cœur, *m*.

contrivance, *n*, combinaison, *f*, dispositif; artifice, *m*. **contrive**, *v.t,* combiner; ménager. ~ *to,* faire en sorte que, s'ingénier à.

control, *n,* contrôle, *m*; commande, *f*; empire, *m,* maîtrise, *f.* ¶ *v.t,* contrôler; contenir, maîtriser; policer. **controller,** *n,* contrôleur, *m.*

controversial, *a,* de controverse. **controversy,** *n,* controverse, *f.* **controvert,** *v.t,* discuter.

contumacy, *n,* contumace, *f.*

contumely, *n,* outrage; opprobre, *m.*

contuse, *v.t,* contusionner. **contusion,** *n,* contusion, *f.*

conundrum, *n,* devinette, énigme, *f.*

convalesce, *v.i,* entrer en convalescence. **convalescence,** *n,* convalescence, *f.* **convalescent,** *a. & n,* convalescent, e.

convene, *v.t,* convoquer.

convenience, *n,* commodité, convenance; aise, *f*; (*toilet*) commodités, *f.pl.* **convenient,** *a,* commode, convenable. ~ly, *ad,* commodément.

convent, *n,* couvent, *m.* ~ *school,* couvent, *m.*

convention, *n,* convention, *f.* ~al, *a,* conventionnel, de convention; pompier. ~alism, *f,* poncif, *m,* le style pompier. ~alist, *n,* pompier, *m.*

converge, *v.i,* converger. **convergent,** *a,* convergent.

conversant, *a,* versé, ferré.

conversation, *n,* conversation, *f*; colloque, *m.* ~al, *a,* de, de la, conversation. ~[al]ist, *n,* causeur, euse.

converse, *a. & n,* contraire, *a. & m*; converse, *a.f. & f,* réciproque, *a. & f.* ¶ *v.i,* converser, causer.

conversion, *n,* conversion, *f,* convertissement (*Fin.*) *m*; transformation, *f.* **convert,** *n,* converti, e. ¶ *v.t,* convertir, transformer. ~ed goal, but de transformation, *m. to become* ~ed (*Relig.*), se convertir. ~er, *n,* convertisseur, *m.* ~ible, *a,* convertible; (*stocks*) convertissable.

convex, *a,* convexe. ~ity, *n,* convexité, *f.*

convey, *v.t,* [trans]porter, véhiculer, conduire, charrier, voiturer; (*law, etc.*) transmettre; communiquer, exprimer. ~ance, *n,* transport, charriage, *m*; voiture; (*law*) translation, transmission, mutation, *f*; (*deed*) acte

de transmission, acte translatif de propriété, *m.*

convict, *n,* condamné, e, forçat, *m.* ~ *prison,* bagne, *m.* ¶ *v.t,* convaincre; condamner. ~ion, *n,* conviction; condamnation, *f. person with previous* ~s, récidiviste, *m,f.*

convince, *v.t,* convaincre. **convincing,** *p.a,* convaincant.

convivial, *a:* ~ *gathering,* joyeuse compagnie, *f.* ~ *person,* joyeux convive, bon c., *m.*

convocation, *n,* convocation, *f.* **convoke,** *v.t,* convoquer.

convolvulus, *n,* convolvulus, volubilis, *m,* belle-de-jour, *f.*

convoy, *n,* convoi, *m*; escorte, *f.* ¶ *v.t,* convoyer, escorter.

convulse, *v.t,* bouleverser. *to be* ~d (laughing), se tordre. **convulsion,** *n,* convulsion, *f,* bouleversement, *m.* **convulsive†,** *a,* convulsif.

cony, *n,* lapin, *m.*

coo, *n,* roucoulement, *m.* ¶ *v.i,* roucouler.

cook, *n,* cuisinier, ère; (*ship's*) [maître-]coq, *m.* ~book, livre de cuisine, *m.* ~'s mate, matelot coq, *m.* ¶ *v.t,* [faire] cuire; (*fig.*) cuisiner, falsifier; (*v.i.*) cuisiner. **cookery,** *n,* cuisine, *f.* **cooking,** *n,* cuisine; cuisson, *f.* ~ *apples,* pommes à cuire, *f.pl.*

cool†, *a,* frais; froid; calme; hardi, sans gêne. ~-headed, à l'esprit calme. ¶ *n,* frais, *m,* fraîcheur, *f.* ¶ *v.t,* attiédir; rafraîchir; refroidir; (*v.i.*) s'attiédir, se refroidir. ~ *down,* se calmer, caler [la voile]. ~ *one's heels,* se morfondre; ~er, *n,* rafraîchisseur; refroidisseur, *m*; prison, *f.* ~ness, *n,* fraîcheur; froideur, *f,* froid; calme, sang-froid, flegme; sansgêne, *m.*

coop, *n,* cage [à poulets], mue, *f,* poulailler, *m.* ~[up], *v.t,* claquemurer.

cooper, *n,* tonnelier, *m.* ~age, *n,* tonnellerie, *f.*

cooperate, *v.i,* coopérer. **cooperation,** *n,* coopération, *f.* **cooperative,** *a,* coopératif. ~ *society,* [société] coopérative, *f.*

coordinate, *v.t,* coordonner. ¶ *a,* coordonné.

coot, *n,* foulque, *f.*

cope, *n,* chape, *f.* ¶ *v.i,* lutter. ~ *with,* tenir tête à, suffire à.

Copenhagen, *n,* Copenhague, *f.*

coping, *n*, chaperon, couronnement, *m*.

copious†, *a*, copieux, riche, plantureux; nourri.

copper, *n*, cuivre [rouge] *m*. ~ [*coin*], cuivre, *m*, monnaie de cuivre, *f*, billion, *m*. ~ *beech*, hêtre rouge, *m*. ~*colored*, cuivré. ~*plate*, planche de cuivre, *f*, cuivre, *m*. ~*plate* [*engraving*], gravure sur cuivre, taille-douce, *f*. ~*smith*, chaudronnier, *m*. ¶ *v.t*, cuivrer.

copperas, *n*, couperose, *f*.

coppice, copse, *n*, taillis, *m*.

copulation, *n*, copulation, *f*.

copy, *n*, copie; transcription, *f*; calque, exemplaire; exemple, *m*. ~*book*, cahier d'écriture, livre d'exemples, *m*. ~*cat*, singe, *m*. ¶ *v.t*, copier; transcrire; calquer.

copying, *n*, transcription, *f*.

copyist, *n*, copiste, *m,f*.

copyright, *n*, droit d'auteur, *m*, propriété [littéraire] *f*. ~ *by so-&-so*, tous droits de reproduction, de traduction, d'adaptation & d'exécution réservés pour tous pays.

coquet, *v.i*, coqueter. ~*ry*, *n*, coquetterie, *f*. **coquettish**, *a*, coquet.

coral, *n*, corail, *m*. ~ *fisher*, corailleur, *m*. ~ *reef*, banc corallifère, *m*.

corbel, *n*, corbeau, *m*.

cord, *n*, corde; cordelette, *f*; cordon; câble, *m*; (*braided*) ganse, *f*. *spinal* ~, moelle épinière, *f*. ¶ *v.t*, corder. ~*age*, *n*, cordages, *m.pl*.

cordial†, *a*, cordial, chaleureux. ¶ *n*, cordial, *m*. ~*ity*, *n*, cordialité, *f*.

corduroy, *n*, velours côtelé, *m*.

core, *n*, cœur, trognon; noyau, *m*; âme, *f*. ¶ *v.t*, vider (*une pomme*, etc.).

co-respondent, *n*, complice en adultère, *m,f*.

Corinth, *n*, Corinthe, *f*. **Corinthian**, *a*, corinthien. ¶ *n*, Corinthien, ne.

cork, *n*, liège; bouchon [en liège] *m*. ~ *jacket*, brassière de sauvetage, *f*. ~*screw*, tire-bouchon, *m*. ~*screw curl*, boudin, *m*. ~*screw*, *v.i*, vriller. ~*-tipped* (*cigarettes*), à bouts de liège. ~ *tree*, chêne-liège, *m*. ¶ *v.t*, boucher. ~*y*, *a*, liégeux. ~ *taste*, goût de bouchon, *m*.

cormorant, *n*, cormoran, *m*.

corn, *n*, maïs; (*on feet*) cor, (*soft*) œil-de-perdrix, *m*. ~ *cob*, épi de maïs, *m*, rafle, *f*. ~*flower*, bleuet, *m*.

corned beef, bœuf salé, *m*.

corner, *n*, coin, angle; tournant, virage, *m*; encoignure, *f*; recoin; (*Com.*) accaparement, *m*; (*att.*) cornier, d'angle; d'encoignure, de coin, du coin. ~ *cupboard*, encoignure, *f*. ~*stone*, pierre angulaire, *f*. ¶ *v.t*, acculer, rencogner; (*monopolize*) accaparer.

cornet, *n*, (*cone*) cornet; (*Mus.*) cornet à pistons, piston; (*ice cream wafer*) plaisir, *m*, oublie, *f*.

cornice, *n*, corniche, *f*.

Cornish, *a*, de Cornouailles.

cornucopia, *n*, corne d'abondance, *f*.

Cornwall, *n*, la Cornouailles.

corolla, *n*, corolle, *f*.

corollary, *n*, corollaire, *m*.

corona, *n*, couronne, *f*. **coronation**, *n*, couronnement, sacre, *m*. **coronet**, *n*, couronne, *f*.

coroner, *n*, coroner, *m*.

corporal† & **corporeal**†, *a*, corporel. **corporal**, *n*, caporal; (*cavalry*) brigadier, *m*. **corporate**, *a*, social. ¶ *v.i*, faire corps.

corporation, *n*, société, corporation, *f*.

corps, *n*, corps, *m*.

corpse, *n*, cadavre, corps [mort] *m*. ~*like*, cadavéreux.

corpulence, -ency, *n*, corpulence, *f*, embonpoint, *m*, réplétion, *f*. **corpulent**, *a*, corpulent, ventru.

Corpus Christi, la Fête-Dieu.

corpuscle, *n*, corpuscule, *m*.

corral, *n*, enclos, *m*. ¶ *v.t*, enfermer dans un enclos.

correct†, *a*, correct; exact, juste. ¶ *v.t*, corriger; rectifier, redresser; surcharger. ~*ed copy*, corrigé, *m*. ~*ion*, *n*, correction; rectification, *f*, redressement, *m*; surcharge, *f*. ~*ional*†, *a*, correctionnel. ~*ive*, *n*, correctif, *m*. ~*ness*, *n*, correction, exactitude, justesse, *f*. ~*or*, *n*, correcteur, trice.

correlative, *a*, corrélatif.

correspond, *v.i*, correspondre; répondre. ~*ence*, *n*, correspondance, *f*; intelligences, *f.pl*. ~*ent*, *n*, correspondant, e. ~*ing*, *p.a*, correspondant.

corridor, *n*, couloir, corridor, *m*.

corroborate, *v.t*, corroborer.

corrode, *v.t*, corroder; ronger,

miner. **corrosion**, *n*, corrosion, *f*. **corrosive**, *a*. & *n*, corrosif, *a*. & *m*.

corrugate, *v.t*, canneler, strier; onduler. ~d [*sheet*] iron & ~d iron sheet, tôle ondulée, *f*.

corrupt, *v.t*, corrompre, débaucher, vicier, gâter, gangrener. ~**ible**, *a*, corruptible; prenable. ~**ion**, *n*, corruption, *f*.

corsair, *n*, corsaire, *m*.

corset, *n*, corset, *m*. ~ *maker*, corsetier, ère. ¶ *v.t*, corseter.

Corsica, *n*, la Corse. **Corsican**, *a*, corse. ¶ *n*, Corse, *m,f*.

corundum, *n*, corindon, *m*.

coruscate, *v.i*, scintiller.

cos, *n*. or **Cos lettuce**, [laitue] romaine, *f*.

cosily, *ad*, à son aise, confortablement.

cosmetic, *a*. & *n*, cosmétique, *a*. & *m*.

cosmic(al), *a*, cosmique.

cosmopolitan & **cosmopolite**, *a*. & *n*, cosmopolite, *a*. & *m*.

cost, *n*, coût, prix, *m*; frais, *m.pl*, dépense, *f*. *at all* ~*s*, coûte que coûte, à toute force. ~ *of living bonus*, indemnité de vie chère, *f*. ~ *of living figure*, indice du coût de la vie, *m*. ~ [*price*], prix de revient, p. coûtant, p. d'acquisition, *m*. ¶ *v.i.ir*, coûter; revenir.

coster[monger], *n*, marchand des quatre saisons, *m*.

costive, *a*, constipé. ~**ness**, *n*, constipation, *f*.

costliness, *n*, cherté; somptuosité, *f*. **costly**, *a*, coûteux, dispendieux; somptueux.

costume, *n*, costume, *m*. ~ *piece*, ~ *play*, pièce historique, *f*. **costum[i]er**, *n*, couturier, *m*.

cot, *n*, lit d'enfant; lit pliant, lit de camp, *m*.

coterie, *n*, coterie, chapelle, *f*. ~ *of wits*, bureau d'esprit, *m*.

cottage, *n*, chaumière; habitation ouvrière, *f*; cottage, chalet; (*fig.*) chaume, *m*.

cotter, *n*, clavette, *f*. ~ *pin*, goupille, *f*.

cotton, *n*, coton, *m*. ~ [*cloth*], cotonnade, toile de coton, *f*. ~ *goods*, cotonnade, *f*. ~ *mill*, filature de coton, *f*. ~ *plant*, cotonnier, *m*. ~ *waste*, bourre de coton, *f*. ~ *wool*, ouate [de coton] *f*, coton [en laine] *m*. ~**y**, *a*, cotonneux.

couch, *n*, couche; chaise longue, *f*; canapé, *m*. ¶ *v.i*, se coucher;

se tapir, se blottir. ~*ed in these terms*, ainsi conçu. ~ [**grass**] *n*, chiendent, *m*.

cough, *n*, toux, *f*. ~ *mixture*, sirop, *m*, (*ou* potion, *f*.) pour la toux. ~ *drop*, pastille pour la t., *f*. *whooping* ~, coqueluche, *f*. ¶ *v.i*, tousser, ~ *up*, expectorer.

council, *n*, conseil; (*Eccl.*) concile, *m*. **councillor**, *n*, conseiller, ère.

counsel, *n*, conseil, *m*; délibération, *f*; (*pers.*) avocat, conseil, défenseur, *m*. ¶ *v.t*, conseiller. **counselor**, *n*, conseiller, ère.

count, *n*, compte, (*pers.*) comte, *m*. ~ *of indictment*, chef d'accusation, *m*. ¶.*v.t*. & *i*, compter; nombrer; (*votes*) recenser, dépouiller.

countenance, *n*, contenance; physionomie, figure, mine, *f*. ¶ *v.t*, approuver; encourager.

counter, *n*, riposte, *f*; (*play*) jeton, *m*, fiche, *f*; (*shop*) comptoir, *m*; (*cashier's*) caisse, *f*, guichet, *m*. ¶ *v.t*, riposter. *to run* ~ *to*, aller à l'encontre de.

counteract, *v.t*, contrecarrer.

counterattack, *n*, contre-attaque, *f*.

counterbalance, *n*, contrepoids, *m*. ¶ *v.t*, contrebalancer, équilibrer.

counterclaim, *n*, reconvention, *f*.

counterfeit, *a*, contrefait, faux. ¶ *n*, contrefaçon, *f*. ¶ *v.t*, contrefaire. ~**er**, *n*, contrefacteur, *m*.

counterfoil, *n*, souche, *f*, talon, *m*.

counter instructions, contrordre, *m*.

countermand, *v.t*, contremander; (*Com.*) décommander. ¶ *n*, contrordre, *m*.

counterpane, *n*, couverture [de lit] *f*.

counterpart, *n*, contrepartie, *f*; (*pers.*) pendant; (*deed*) double, *m*.

counterpoint, *n*, contrepoint, *m*.

counterpoise, *n*, contrepoids, *m*. ¶ *v.t*, contrebalancer, équilibrer.

countershaft, *n*, arbre secondaire, a. de renvoi, *m*.

countersign, (*Mil.*) *n*, mot de ralliement, *m*. ¶ *v.t*, contresigner.

countersink, *n*, fraisure, *f*. ~ [*bit*], fraise, *f*. ¶ *v.t*, fraiser.

counterstroke, *n*, riposte, *f*.

counterweight, *n*, contrepoids, *m*.

countess, *n*, comtesse, *f*.

counting, *n*, compte; recensement, *m*. **countless**, *a*, innombrable.

country, *n*, pays, *m*; contrée; campagne; province; patrie, *f*; corps électoral, *m*. ~ *club*, country-club, *m*. ~ *house*, maison de campagne, *f*. ~ *life*, vie champêtre, v. rurale, *f*. ~*man* -*woman*, campagnard, e. [*fellow*] ~*man*, -*woman*, compatriote, *m,f*. ~*side*, campagne, *f*. ~ *town*, ville de province, *f*.

county, *n*, comté, *m*. ~ *seat*, chef-lieu, *m*.

couple, *n*, (*things*) couple, *f*; (*pers., Mech.*) couple, *m*. ¶ *v.t*, coupler, accoupler; atteler. **couplet**, *n*, distique, *m*. **coupling**, *n*, accouplement; manchon; attelage, *m*.

coupon, *n*, coupon, *m*.

courage, *n*, courage, *m*. ~*ous†*, *a*, courageux.

courier, *n*, courrier, *m*.

course, *n*, cours; courant, *m*; carrière; route; direction, *f*; chenal; trajet, *m*; marche, *f*; processus; parti; stage; (*meal*) service, plat, *m*; (*Build.*) assise; couche, *f*; (*ground*) champ; terrain; parcours, *m*. *in due* ~, temps & lieu. *of* ~, naturellement, bien entendu, certainement. *why, of* ~! parbleu! ¶ *v.t*. & *i*, chasser, courir. **courser** (*Poet.*) *n*, coursier, *m*. **coursing**, *n*, chasse au lévrier, *f*.

court, *n*, cour, *f*; tribunal; conseil, *m*; chambre; audience, *f*; (*Ten.*) court, jeu, tennis; (*croquet*) terrain, *m*. ~ *house*, palais de justice, *m*. ~ *martial*, conseil de guerre, *m*. ~ *plaster*, taffetas d'Angleterre, *m*. ~*yard*, cour, *f*; préau, *m*. ¶ *v.t*, faire sa cour à, courtiser; (*favor*) briguer; (*disaster*) inviter.

courteous†, *a*, courtois, honnête. **courtesan**, *n*, courtisane, hétaïre, *f*. **courtesy**, *n*, courtoisie, honnêteté, *f*. Cour des; *n*, courtisan, *m*; (*pl.*) gens de cour, *m.pl*. **courtly**, *a*, courtois. **courtship**, *n*, cour, *f*.

cousin, *n*, cousin, e. *first* ~, cousin germain, *m*.

cove (*bay*) *n*, anse, *f*, accul, *m*.

covenant, *n*, convention, *f*, pacte, *m*. ¶ *v.i*, s'engager.

Coventry (to send to) (*fig.*), mettre en quarantaine.

cover, *n*, couverture; enveloppe, *f*; tapis; pli, *m*; gaine, *f*; couvercle; capot, *m*; chape, *f*, chapeau; plateau, *m*; chemise, *f*; étui; fourreau; couvert; abri; fourré, *m*, remise, *f*; masque, voile, *m*; provision, marge, *f*, acompte, *m*; prévision, *f*. ¶ *v.t*, couvrir, recouvrir, envelopper, revêtir, tapisser; masquer; parcourir. ~*ed walk*, allée en berceau, *f*. ~*ing*, *n*, couverture, *f*; vêtement, *m*. ~*let*, *n*, couverture pour berceau, *f*.

covert, *a*, voilé, indirect.

covet, *v.t*, convoiter, reluquer. ~*ous*, *a*, convoiteux, cupide. ~*ousness*, *n*, convoitise, *f*.

covey, *n*, compagnie, *f*.

cow, *n*, vache, *f*; (*att., of elephants, etc.*) femelle. ~ *bell*, clarine, sonnaille, *f*. ~*herd*, vacher, ère. ~ *hide*, [peau de] vache, *f*, cuir de v., *m*. ~ *shed*, étable à vaches, vacherie, *f*. ~*lick* (hair), épi, *m*. ~*pox*, vaccine, *f*. ¶ *v.t*, intimider.

coward, *n*, poltron, ne, lâche, couard, *m*. ~*ice*, *n*, poltronnerie, lâcheté, couardise, *f*. ~*ly*, *a*, poltron, lâche, couard.

cower, *v.i*, se blottir, se tapir, s'accroupir.

cowl, *n*, capuchon, *m*, capote, *f*, champignon, *m*, mitre, *f*.

cowrie, *n*, porcelaine, *f*.

cowslip, *n*, coucou, *m*, primevère des champs, *f*.

coxcomb, *n*, fat, freluquet, *m*.

coxswain (*abb.* cox) *n*, barreur, patron, *m*.

coy, *a*, réservé, farouche. ~*ness*, *n*, réserve, *f*.

cozen, *v.t*, duper; séduire.

cozy, *a*, confortable; douillet.

crab, *n*, (*Crust.*) crabe, cancre; (*hoisting*) treuil, *m*. ~ [*apple*], pomme sauvage, *f*. ~ [*apple tree*], pommier sauvage, *m*. ~ [*louse*], morpion, *m*. **crabbed**, *a*, acariâtre, revêche, grincheux, bourru. ~ *handwriting*, écriture de pattes de mouche, *f*.

crack, *n*, fente, fissure, crevasse, fêlure; craquelure, *f*; (*noise*) craquement; claquement; coup sec, crac, *m*, cric crac, flic flac. ~ *of doom*, dernier jugement, *m*. ¶ *v.t*, fendre; fêler; fendiller; gercer; crever; (*nuts*) casser; (*open a bottle*) décoiffer. ~*ed* (*daft*)

p.a, timbré, toqué. **cracker**, *n*, biscuit dur, *m*.
crackle, *v.i*, craque[te]r, crépiter, pétiller. **crackling**, *n*, friton, gratton, *m*.
Cracow, *n*, Cracovie, *f*.
cradle, *n*, berceau, moïse; (*Surg.*) arceau, cerceau, *m*. ¶ *v.t*, bercer.
craft, *n*, adresse, *f*; artifice, *m*; astuce, *f*; métier, *m*; (*Naut.*) embarcation, allège, *f*. **craftily**, *ad*, artificieusement. **craftsman**, *n*, homme de métier, artisan, *m*. ~**ship**, *n*, travail d'artisan, *m*. **crafty**, *a*, artificieux, rusé, futé, cauteleux, retors.
crag, *n*, rocher, *m*. **craggy**, *a*, anfractueux.
cram, *v.t*, bonder, bourrer, fourrer; farcir; (*poultry*) gaver; (*exam*) gaver, chauffer.
cramp, *n*, crampe, colique, *f*. ¶ *v.t*, resserrer, entraver, gêner; cramponner.
cranberry, *n*, canneberge, *f*.
crane, *n*, (*bird & hoist*) grue, *f*. ¶ *v.t*, tendre le cou.
cranium, *n*, crâne, *m*.
crank, *n*, (*Mach.*) manivelle, *f*, coude; (*pers.*) excentrique, original, *m*, maniaque, *m,f*; (*whim*) marotte, *f*. ~ *gear* (cycle), pédalier, *m*. ~ *pin*, bouton de manivelle, *m*. ~ *shaft*, arbre à manivelle, arbre coudé, vilebrequin, *m*. ~ *tool*, [outil à] crochet, *m*. ¶ *v.t*, couder.
cranny, *n*, fente, crevasse, *f*.
crash, *n*, fracas, écrasement; krach, *m*, débâcle, chute, *f*. ¶ *i*, patatras! ¶ *v.i*, s'abattre; tomber, s'écraser (*sur le sol, la chaussée, etc.*).
crass, *a*, crasse (*a.f.*), grossier.
crate, *n*, caisse à claire-voie, harasse, *f*.
crater, *n*, cratère; (*mine, Mil.*) entonnoir, *m*.
crave, *v.t*, implorer. ~ *for*, appéter.
craven, *a*, poltron, lâche.
craving, *n*, ardent désir, *m*, soif, appétence, fringale, *f*.
crawl, *n*, (*Swim.*) crawl, *m*. ¶ *v.i*, ramper, se traîner.
crayfish, *n*, (*river*) écrevisse; (*sea*) langouste, *f*.
crayon, *n*, [crayon] pastel, *m*.
craze, *n*, folie, fureur, toquade, marotte, manie, *f*. **crazy**, *a*, délabré; dément, détraqué, toqué, piqué. *to drive someone* ~, rompre la cervelle à quelqu'un.

creak, *v.i*, grincer, crier, craquer. ¶ *n*, grincement, crissement, *m*.
cream, *n*, crème, *f*; (*of story*) bon, *m*. ¶ *v.t*, écrémer, battre en crème. ~ *cheese*, fromage blanc, *m*. ~*-colored*, couleur crème. ~ *jug*, crémier, *m*. ~**ery**, *n*, crémerie, *f*. ~**y**, *a*, crémeux.
crease, *n*, pli, faux pli, godet, *m*. ¶ *v.t*, plisser; (*v.i.*) [se] plisser.
create, *v.t*, créer; faire, produire; provoquer. **creation**, *n*, création, *f*. **creative**, *a*, créateur. **creator**, **tress**, *n*, créateur, trice. **creature**, *n*, créature, *f*, être; animal, *m*, bête, *f*. ~ *comforts*, aises, *f.pl*.
credence, *n*, créance, *f*. **credentials**, *n.pl*, lettres de créance; 1—s d'introduction, *f.pl*; pouvoirs, *m.pl*. **credibility**, *n*, crédibilité, *f*. **credible**, *a*, croyable; digne de foi. **credibly**, *ad*, de bonne source.
credit, *n*, croyance, foi, créance, consistance, *f*; honneur; crédit, avoir, *m*. *do* ~ *to*, honorer. ~ *balance*, solde créditeur, *m*. ¶ *v.t*, ajouter foi à; créditer, bonifier. ~**able**, *a*, reluisant. ~**or**, *n*, créancier, ère, créditeur, *m*.
credo, *n*, credo, symbole, *m*.
credulity, *n*, crédulité, bonhomie, *f*. **credulous**, *a*, crédule.
creed, *n*, credo, symbole; culte, *m*, croyance, *f*.
creek, *n*, crique, *f*.
creel, *n*, panier à pêche, *m*.
creep, *v.i.ir*, ramper; cheminer. *it makes one's flesh* ~, cela fait venir la chair de poule. ~**er**, *n*, plante grimpante, *f*; (*grapnel*) grappin, *m*. ~*ing paralysis*, paralysie progressive, *f*.
cremate, *v.t*, incinérer. **cremation**, *n*, crémation, incinération, *f*. **crematorium**, *n*, four crématoire, *m*.
Cremona, *n*, Crémone, *f*.
creole, *n. & a*, créole, *m,f. & a*.
creosote, *n*, créosote, *f*.
crepitate, *v.i*, crépiter.
crescendo, *ad. & n*, crescendo, *ad. & m*.
crescent, *n*, croissant, *m*; (*of buildings*) demilune, *f*.
cresset, *n*, torchère, *f*.
crest, *n*, crête; huppe, *f*; cimier, *m*. ~*fallen*, penaud. ~**ed**, *a*, crêté, huppé, aigretté; (*sea*) moutonneuse.
Crete, *n*, la Crète.
cretonne, *n*, cretonne, *f*.
crevasse, *n*, crevasse [glaciaire]

f. **crevice,** *n,* crevasse, fente, lézarde, *f.*

crew, *n,* (*ship*) équipage, *m*; (*boat*) équipe, *f*; (*set, gang*) bande, *f.*

crewel stitch (*Emb.*), point de tige, point coulé, *m.*

crib, *n,* crèche, mangeoire; cabane; couchette, *f*; larcin, *m.* ¶ *v.t,* chiper.

cribbage, *n,* cribbage, *m.*

crick (*in neck*) *n,* torticolis, *m.*

cricket, *n,* grillon, criquet, cricri; (*game*) cricket, *m.*

crier, *n,* crieur, *m.*

crime, *n,* crime, forfait, *m.*

Crimea (the), la Crimée.

criminal†, *a,* criminel. ~ *law,* droit pénal, *m.* ¶ *n,* criminel, le. **criminate,** *v.t,* incriminer, charger.

crimp, *v.t,* friser, crêper; fraiser, gaufrer.

crimson, *a,* cramoisi, pourpre. ~ *clover,* trèfle incarnat, farouch[e] *m.* ¶ *n,* cramoisi, *m,* pourpre, *f.* ¶ *v.t,* empourprer.

cringe, *v.i,* faire le chien couchant. **cringing,** *p.a,* servile.

crinkle, *n,* plissement, *m.* ¶ *v.t. & i,* plisser.

cripple, *n,* impotent, e, estropié, e. ¶ *v.t,* estropier; (*fig.*) paralyser. ~**d,** *a,* impotent, estropié, éclopé, perclus; (*ship*) incommodé.

crisis, *n,* crise, *f.*

crisp, *a,* cassant, croquant; (*air*) vivifiant, vif; (*hair*) frisé; (*style*) concis. ¶ *v.t,* crêper.

crisscross, *v.i,* s'entrecroiser.

criterion, *n,* critère, critérium, *m.*

critic, *n,* critique; censeur; frondeur, *m.* ~**al,** *a,* critique; décisif. **criticism,** *n,* critique, glose, *f.* **criticizable,** *a,* critiquable. **criticize,** *v.t,* critiquer; censurer.

croak, *v.i,* (*raven*) croasser; (*frog*) coasser.

crochet, *n, & ~ hook,* crochet, *m.*

crockery, *n,* faïence, vaisselle, *f.*

crocodile, *n,* crocodile, *m.* ~ *tears,* larmes de crocodile, *f.pl.*

crocus, *n,* crocus, safran, *m.*

Croesus, *n,* Crésus, *m.*

crone, *n,* vieille femme momifiée, *f.*

crony, *n,* compère, *m.*

crook, *n,* crochet, *m*; houlette, crosse, *f*; (*pers.*) escroc, *m.* ¶ *v.t,* recourber. ~**ed,** *a,* crochu, tortu, tors; gauche; de travers; (*legs*)

cagneux; (*fig.*) tortueux, oblique, indirect. ~**edly,** *ad,* de travers; tortueusement. ~**edness,** *n,* guingois, *m.*

crop, *n,* récolte; cueillette, *f*; (*bird*) jabot, *m,* poche; (*whip*) cravache, *f.* ¶ *v.t,* tondre, bretauder; (*ears*) essoriller, écourter. ~ *up,* surgir. ~ *up again,* rebondir.

croquet, *n,* croquet, *m.* ~ *court,* terrain de croquet, *m.* ¶ *v.t,* croquer.

crosier, *n,* crosse, *f.*

cross, *a,* de méchante humeur. ¶ *comps:* ~*bar,* ~*beam,* traverse, *f.* ~*belt,* bandoulière, *f*; baudrier, *m.* ~*-bred,* métis, mâtiné. ~*-breed,* race croisée, *f,* métis, se. ~*-breeding,* croisement, métissage, *m.* ~*-country running, race,* cross-country, *m.* ~*-examine someone,* faire subir à quelqu'un un interrogatoire; tenir qqn sur la sellette. ~*-eyed,* louche. ~*piece,* entretoise, *f. to be at ~-purposes,* se contrecarrer. ~ *reference,* référence croisée, *f.* ~*road,* chemin de traverse, *m,* traverse, *f*; (*pl.*) carrefour, *m.* ~ *section,* coupe en travers, *f,* profil transversal, *m.* ~*-stitch,* point de croix, *m.* ~*word* [*puzzle*], mots croisés [-énigmes], *m.pl.* ¶ *n,* croix; (*fig.*) croix, *f,* calvaire; croisement; croisillon, *m*; (*on a letter* t) barre, *f.* ¶ *v.t,* croiser; traverser; couper, passer, franchir; (*a* "*t*") barrer; contrarier, contrecarrer. ~ *oneself,* se signer. ~ *out,* rayer, radier, biffer, barrer.

crossing, *n,* croisement, *m*; traversée, *f,* passage, *m.*

crotchet, *n,* (*Mus.*) noire, *f*; (*whim*) boutade, lubie, quinte, *f.* ~ *rest* (*Mus.*), soupir, *m.* ~**y,** *a,* quinteux.

crouch, *v.i,* se tapir, se blottir, s'accroupir.

croup (*Med.*) *n,* croup, *m.*

croup (*rump*) *n,* croupe, *f.*

crow, *n,* corbeau, *m,* corneille, *f*; (*cock's*) chant, *m.* ~[*bar*], pince [à levier] *f.* ~*foot* (*Bot.*), renoncule, *f.* ~*'s-foot* (*wrinkle*), patte-d'oie, *f.* ~*'s-nest* (*Naut.*), nid de pie, *m. as the ~ flies,* à vol d'oiseau. ¶ *v.i.ir,* chanter. ~ *over,* chanter victoire sur.

crowd, *n,* foule, presse, *f,* rassemblement, monde, *m,* cohue, *f.* ~ *round,* se presser autour de, assiéger. ~ed, *p.a*, fréquenté, comble.

crown, *n*, couronne, *f*; (*head, arch*) sommet; (*hat*) fond, *m*. ¶ *v.t*, couronner; (*checkers*) damer. ~ing, *n*, couronnement, *m*. ¶ *a*, suprême.

crucial, *a*, décisif, critique.

crucible, *n*, creuset, pot, *m*.

crucifix, *n*, crucifix, christ, *m*. ~ion, *n*, crucifiement, *m*, crucifixion, *f*. **crucify,** *v.t*, crucifier.

crude, *a*, cru, brut; informe; indigeste; primitif. ~ly, *ad*, crûment. ~ness, *n*, crudité, *f*.

cruel†, *a*, cruel. ~ty, *n*, cruauté, *f*; (*in law*) sévices, *m.pl*.

cruet, *n*, ménagère, *f*, huilier, *m*; (*Eccl.*) burette, *f*.

cruise, *n*, croisière; campagne, *f*. ¶ *v.i*, croiser. **cruiser,** *n*, croiseur, *m*. **cruising:** ~ *fleet & ~ ground*, croisière, *f*. ~ *taxicab*, taxi en maraude, *m*.

crumb, *n*, miette; (*opp. crust*) mie, *f*. ¶ (*Cook.*) *v.t*, paner.

crumble, *v.t*, émietter; (*v.i.*) s'émietter; crouler, tomber. **crumbly,** *a*, friable.

crumple, *v.t*, chiffonner; (*v.i.*) se c. ~ *up*, s'écraser.

crunch, *v.t. & i*, croquer, craquer. ¶ *i*, croc!

crupper, *n*, croupe; (*harness*) croupière, *f*.

crusade, *n*, croisade, *f*. ¶ *v.i*, entreprendre une croisade. **crusader,** *n*, croisé, *m*.

crush, (*crowd*) *n*, cohue, *f*. ¶ *v.t*, écraser; froisser; broyer, concasser. ~er, *n*, broyeur, concasseur, *m*.

crust, *n*, croûte; croustille; (*earth's*) écorce, croûte, *f*; morceau de pain, *m*.

crustacean, *a. & n*, crustacé, *a*. & *m*.

crusted, *a*, encroûté. **crusty,** *a*, (*bread*) croustillant; (*fig.*) irritable, bourru. **crust[y] end** (*bread*), croûton, grignon, *m*.

crutch, *n*, béquille, *f*.

crux, *n*, pivot, nœud, *m*.

cry, *n*, cri, *m*. ~ *baby*, pleurnicheur, *m*. *to be in full* ~, aboyer. ¶ *v.i*, crier, s'écrier; pleurer; (*v.t.*) crier, chanter; tambouriner. ~ *out*, crier; s'écrier. ¶ *n*, cri[s] *m*.[*pl*.].

crypt, *n*, crypte, *f*.

crystal, *n*, cristal, *m*. ¶ *a*, de cristal. ~ *gazing*, cristallomancie, *f*. ~ [*glass*], cristal, *m*. ~

glass[*ware*] *making* or *works*, cristallerie, *f*. **crystalline,** *a*, cristallin. ~ *lens* (eye), cristallin, *m*.

crystalize, *v.t*, cristalliser; (*v.i.*) [se] cristalliser. *crystalized fruits*, fruits candis, *m.pl*.

cub, *n*, petit, *m*.

Cuban, *a*, cubain. ¶ *n*, Cubain, e.

cube, *n*, cube, *m*. ~ *root*, racine cubique, r. cube, *f*. ~ *sugar*, sucre en morceaux, s. cassé, *m*. ¶ *v.t*, cuber. **cubic,** *a*, cube; cubique. ~ *foot*, pied cube, *m*. = 0.028317 cubic meter. ~ *inch*, pouce cube, *m*. = 16.387 cubic centimeters. ~ *yard*, yard cube, *m*. = 0.764553 cubic meter. ~al, *a*, cubique.

cubicle, *n*, alcôve de dortoir, *f*.

cubism, *n*, cubisme, *m*. **cubist,** *n*, cubiste, *m,f*.

cuckoo, *n*, coucou, *m*. ~ *clock*, pendule à coucou, *f*, coucou, *m*.

cucumber, *n*, concombre, *m*.

cud, *n*, aliment ruminé, *m*.

cuddle, *v.t*, câliner, pouponner, serrer dans ses bras. ~ *up*, se pelotonner, se blottir.

cudgel, *n*, bâton, gourdin, *m*, trique, *f*. ¶ *v.t*, bâtonner; (*one's brains*) torturer. **cudgeling,** *n*, bastonnade, *f*.

cue, *n*, (*Theat.*) réplique; (*Bil.*) queue, *f*.

cuff, *n*, (*blow*) calotte, taloche, *f*; (*shirt*) manchette, *f*; poignet; (*coat*) parement, *m*. ~ *links*, boutons de manchettes, *m.pl*. ¶ *v.t*, calotter.

cuirass, *n*, cuirasse, *f*. ~ier, *n*, cuirassier, *m*.

culinary, *a*, culinaire.

cull, *v.t*, cueillir; recueillir.

culminate, *v.i*, atteindre sa plus grande hauteur; aboutir; (*Astr.*) culminer. **culminating,** *a*, culminant.

culpability, *n*, culpabilité, *f*. **culpable,** *a*, coupable. **culprit,** *n*, coupable, *m,f*.

cultivate, *v.t*, cultiver. **cultivation,** *n*, culture, *f*. **cultivator,** *n*, cultivateur, trice. **culture,** *n*, culture, *f*. ~d (*pers., pearl*) *p.a*, de culture.

culvert, *n*, ponceau, *m*.

cumber, *v.t*, embarrasser, encombrer. ~some, **cumbrous,** *a*, embarrassant, encombrant.

cumulative, *a*, cumulatif.

cumulus, *n*, cumulus, *m*.

cuneiform, *a*, cunéiforme.

cunning, *a*, rusé, artificieux; habile. ¶ n, finesse, finasserie, ruse, f.

cup, n, tasse; coupe; timbale, f; calice, bol, m. ~ *bearer*, échanson, m. ~*board*, armoire, f; buffet; (*wall*) placard, m. ¶ (*Surg.*) v.t, ventouser.

cupel, n, coupelle, f. ¶ v.t, coupeller.

Cupid, n, Cupidon, m.

cupidity, n, cupidité, f.

cupola, n, coupole, f.

cupping glass, ventouse, f.

cur, n roquet, m.

curable, a, curable.

curacy, n, vicariat, m. **curate**, n, vicaire, m.

curative, a, curatif, médicamenteux.

curator, n, conservateur, trice.

curb, n, (*harness*) gourmette; (*street*) bordure; (*fig.*) bride, f, frein, m. ¶ v.t, (*horse*) gourmer; (*street*) border; (*fig.*) brider, modérer.

curd[s], n.[*pl.*], caillé, m, caillebotte, f. **curdle**, v.t, cailler; (*fig.*) glacer.

cure, n, guérison; cure, f; remède, m; (*souls*) charge, f. ¶ v.t, guérir; remédier à; (*salt*) saler; (*smoke*) fumer; (*herrings*) caquer.

curfew, n, couvre-feu, m.

curiosity & curio, n, curiosité, rareté, f, bibelot, m. *curio cabinet*, vitrine, table vitrée, f. **curious**†, a, curieux. *the ~ part* or *thing*, le curieux. ~ *person*, curieux, euse.

curl, n, boucle, f, frison, m. (*pl.*) frisure; spirale, f. ¶ v.t, friser, boucler, bichonner; (*lip*) retrousser. ~ *up*, se mettre en boule, se pelotonner. **curler** (*hair*) n, épingle [à friser] f; (*leather*) bigoudi [à friser] m.

curlew, n, courlis, courlieu, m.

curliness, n, frisure, f. **curling**, n, frisure, f. ~ *tongs*, fer à friser, m. **curly**, a, frisé, bouclé.

curmudgeon, n, bourru; ladre, pingre, m.

currant, n, (*red, white*) groseille [à grappes] f; (*black*) cassis; (*dried*) raisin de Corinthe, m. ~ *bush*, groseillier [à grappes]; cassis, m.

currency, n, cours, m, circulation; monnaie, f. [*foreign*] ~, devise [étrangère], monnaie étrangère, f. **current**, a, courant, en cours; de mise. ~ *events*, actua-

lités, f.pl. ~ *liabilities*, exigibilités, f.pl. ¶ n, courant, m.

curriculum, n, programme d'études, m.

curry (*Cook.*) n, cari, kari, m. ¶ v.t, (*leather*) corroyer; (*horse*) étriller. ~ *favor with*, se faufiler dans les bonnes grâces de. ~*comb*, étrille, f. ~*ing*, n, corroi; étrillage, m.

curse, n, malédiction, imprécation, f; fléau, m. ¶ v.t, maudire; affliger; (*v.i.*) blasphémer, jurer. **cursed**, a, maudit.

cursory, a, hâtif, rapide.

curt, a, bref, sec, cassant, brusque.

curtail, v.t, raccourcir, écourter; (*output*) contingenter.

curtain, n, rideau; brise-bise, m; toile, f; tableau! ~ *holder*, embrasse, f. ~ *net*, vitrage, m. ~ *raiser*, lever de rideau, m. ~ *rod*, tringle de rideau; tringle de brisebise, f.

curtly, ad, brusquement.

curtsy, n, révérence, f.

curvature, n, courbure, f. ~ *of the spine*, déviation de la colonne vertébrale, f.

curve, n, courbe, f. ¶ v.t, courber, cintrer. **curvet**, n, courbette, f. ¶ v.i, faire des courbettes. **curvilinear**, a, curviligne.

cushion, n, coussin; coussinet; bourrelet; carreau, m; (*Bil.*) bande, f. ¶ v.t, amortir. ~ *cover*, dessus de coussin, m, taie de coussin, f.

custard, n, flan, m; crème, f.

custodian, n, gardien, ne. **custody**, n, garde, charge; arrestation, f.

custom, n, usage, m, coutume; pratique, f; achalandage, m. ~*ary*, a, usuel, d'usage, ordinaire; coutumier. ~*er*, n, client, e; chaland, e; (*at café*) consommateur, m; (*at bank*) déposant, e.

customs, n.pl, douane[s] f.[pl.]. ~ or *custom house*, douane, f. ~ [*duty*], douane, f, droit[s] de douane, m.[pl.]. ~ *agent*, agent en douane, m. ~ *officer*, agent de la douane, douanier, m.

cut, n, coupure, coupe, entaille, saignée; fouille, f, déblai, m; taille, passe; taillade, balafre, f; coup, m, atteinte, f, affront; morceau, m, tranche; réduction, compression, f; dégrèvement, m; vignette; gravure, f. *short*~, raccourci, m. ¶ v.t.ir, couper; entailler; entamer; découper;

trancher; rogner; fendre; cingler; (*teeth*) faire; graver. *have one's hair* ~, se faire couper les cheveux. ~ *& dried* or *dry*, tout taillé, tout fait. ~ *back* (*Hort.*), receper. ~ [*crystal*] *glass*, cristal taillé, *m*. ~ *down*, abattre; moissonner; rogner; sabrer. ~ *off*, couper; retrancher; amputer; intercepter; isoler; moissonner. ~ *out*, découper, couper, tailler; retrancher; supprimer. ~ *short*, écourter; trancher. ~*throat*, coupe-jarret, escarpe, *m*. ~ *up*, découper, dépecer; débiter; tronçonner.

cutaneous, *a*, cutané.

cute, *a*, attirant; fin, rusé.

cuticle, *n*, cuticule, *f*.

cutlass, *n*, sabre, *m*.

cutler, *n*, coutelier, ère. **cutlery**, *n*, coutellerie, *f*.

cutlet, *n*, côtelette, *f*.

cutter, *n*, (*clothes, etc.*) coupeur, euse; (*gems, stone, files*) tailleur; (*price*) gâte-métier, *m*; (*tool*) lame, *f*, couteau, *m*; fraise; molette, *f*; (*boat*) cotre; canot, *m*. ~ *wheel*, molette, *f*. **cutting**, *p.a*, coupant, tranchant; piquant, caustique, acéré. ~ *board*, tranchoir, *m*. ~ *edge*, tranchant, coupant, fil, *m*. ¶ *n*, taille; coupe; (*teeth*) pousse; (*newspaper*) coupure; tranchée, *f*, déblai, *m*; percée, *f*; copeau, *m*; rognure, *f*; (*snip of cloth*) chanteau, *m*, retaille; (*plant*) bouture, *f*. ~ *out* (*clothes*), coupe, *f*.

cuttle fish, seiche, *f*.

cutwater, *n*, (*bow*) taille-mer; (*bridge*) bec, *m*.

cyanide, *n*, cyanure, *m*.

cyclamen, *n*, cyclamen, *m*.

cycle, *n*, cycle, *m*; bicyclette, *f*; vélocipède, *m*. ~ *track*, vélodrome, *m*. ¶ *v.i*, aller à bicyclette, pédaler. **cycling**, *n*, cyclisme, *m*. **cyclist**, *n*, [bi]cycliste, *m*,*f*.

cyclone, *n*, cyclone, *m*.

cygnet, *n*, jeune cygne, *m*.

cylinder, *n*, cylindre; corps; barillet; fourreau, *m*. **cylindrical**, *a*, cylindrique.

cymbals, *n.pl*, cymbales, *f.pl*.

cynic, *n*, cynique, *m*. ¶ ~ & **cynical†**, *a*, cynique. **cynicism**, *n*, cynisme, *m*.

cynosure (*fig.*) *n*, pointe de mire, *m*.

cypress, *n*, cyprès *m*.

Cpyrus, *n*, Chypre, *f*.

cyst (*Med.*) *n*, kyste, *m*.

Czech, *a*. & (*language*) *n*, tchèque, *a*. & *m*. ¶ (*pers.*) *n*, Tchèque, *m*,*f*. **Czechoslovak**, *n*, Tchécoslovaque, *m*,*f*. **Czechoslovakia**, *n*, Tchécoslovaquie, *f*.

D

D (*Mus.*) *letter*, ré, *m*.

dab, *n*, coup de tampon, d'éponge, de mouchoir, etc; petit tas mou, *m*; (*fish*) limande, *f*. ¶ *v.t*, tamponner; éponger. **dabber**, *n*, tampon, *m*.

dabble, *v.i*, barboter, patauger. ~ *on the stock exchange*, boursicoter.

dace, *n*, vandoise, vaudoise, *f*, dard, *m*.

dachshund, *n*, basset allemand, *m*.

dad[dy], *n*, papa, *m*.

daddy longlegs, *n*, tipule, *f*.

dado, *n*, lambris d'appui, *m*.

daffodil, *n*, narcisse des prés, *m*.

daft, *a*, timbré.

dagger, *n*, poignard, *m*; (*Typ.*) croix, *f*. *at* ~*s drawn*, à couteaux tirés.

dahlia, *n*, dahlia, *m*.

daily, *a*, quotidien, journalier. ~ [*paper*], [journal] quotidien, *m*. ¶ *ad*, journellement, quotidiennement.

dainties, *n.pl*, friandises, chatteries, douceurs, *f.pl*. **daintily**, *ad*, délicatement. **daintiness**, *n*, délicatesse, chatterie, *f*. **dainty**, *a*, friand, délicat; mignon.

dairy, *n*, laiterie, crémerie, *f*. ~ [*farm*], vacherie, *f*. ~*maid*, fille de ferme, *f*. ~*man*, laitier, crémier, *m*.

dais, *n*, estrade, *f*.

daisy, *n*, marguerite, pâquerette, *f*.

dale, *n*, vallon, val, *m*, combe, *f*.

dally, *v.i*, s'amuser, batifoler; tarder.

Dalmatia, *n*, la Dalmatie. **Dalmatian**, *a*, dalmate.

dam, *n*, barrage, *m*, digue; (*animal*) mère, *f*. ¶ *v.t*, barrer, endiguer.

damage, *n*, dommage, dégât, *m*, avarie, *f*, mal, *m*; (*pl.*, *law*) dommages-intérêts, *m.pl*. ¶ *v.t*, endommager, avarier. ~ *wilfully*, saboter.

damascene, *v.t*, damasquiner. **Damascus**, *n*, Damas, *m*. **damask**, *n*, damas, *m*.

damn, v.t, damner; (a play) tomber. **~able,** a, damnable, maudit. **~ation,** n, damnation, f. **~ed,** a, damné, maudit; sacré. the ~, les damnés. **~ing,** p.a, accablant, écrasant.

damp, a, humide; moite. ~ mark (in books), tache d'humidité, mouillure, f. ¶ n, humidité, f. ¶ v.t, humecter, mouiller, tremper; (fig.) refroidir; (shock) amortir. **~er,** n, (piano) étouffoir; (furnace) registre; (radio) amortisseur, m, sourdine, f; (stamps, labels) mouilloir, m. **~ness,** n, humidité, f.

damsel, n, demoiselle, jeune fille, f.

damson, n, damas, m. ~ [tree], prunier de damas, m.

dance, n, danse, f; bal; pas, m. ~ hall, salle de bal, f, bal, m. D~ of Death, D~ Macabre, Danse macabre. ¶ v.i. & t, danser; faire danser. ~ attendance (on), s'empresser (auprès de); faire le pied de grue. **dancer,** n, danseur, euse, m, f. **dancing,** n, la danse. ~ master, maître de danse, m.

dandelion, n, pissenlit, m.

dandle, v.t, bercer, dodeliner, pouponner.

dandruff, n, pellicules, f.pl.

dandy, n, dandy, gandin, élégant, m.

Dane, n, Danois, e.

danger, n, danger, m. this patient is out of ~, ce malade est hors d'affaire. **~ous†,** a, dangereux.

dangle, v.i, pendiller, brimballer; (v.t.) brandiller.

Danish, a, danois. ¶ (language) n, le danois.

dank, a, méphitique.

dapper, a, tiré à quatre épingles; bellot.

dappled, p.a, pommelé.

dare, v.i.ir, oser, s'aviser; (v.t.ir) défier, braver, oser. **~-devil,** casse-cou, m. **daring†,** a, audacieux, osé, hardi. ¶ n, audace, hardiesse, f.

dark, a, obscur; sombre; noir; ténébreux; foncé; brun; sourd. the ~ ages, les siècles d'ignorance, m.pl. ~ horse, outsider, m. ~ man, ~ boy, brunet, m. ~ room (Phot.), chambre noire, f. ~ woman, ~ girl, brunette, f. ¶ n, obscurité, nuit, f, ténèbres, f.pl. after ~, à [la] nuit close. in the ~ (fig.), à l'aveuglette.

~en, v.t, obscurcir; assombrir, embrumer, rembrunir. **~ish,** a, noirâtre. **~ly,** ad, obscurément; sourdement. **~ness,** n, obscurité, nuit, f, ténèbres, f.pl; teinte foncée, f.

darling, a, chéri, bien-aimé, favori. ¶ n, chéri, e, bien-aimé, e, bijou, m, mignon, ne, câlin, e, chou[chou]; coco, m, cocotte, f, Benjamin, m; favori, ite, coqueluche, f.

darn, n, reprise, f. ¶ v.t, repriser. **~ing,** n, reprisage, m, reprise, f. ~ needle, aiguille à repriser, f.

dart, n, élan; dard, trait, m; fléchette, f; (pl.) jeu de fléchettes, m. ¶ v.t, darder, lancer; (v.i.) s'élancer.

dash, n, élan, m, fougue, f, panache, entrain; grain, tantinet, filet, soupçon; (Teleg.) trait; (Typ.) tiret, m. to make a ~ at, for, s'élancer sur, vers. ~ board, tableau de bord, m. ¶ v.t, heurter, jeter; briser, abattre; confondre. **~ing,** a, fougueux; pimpant.

dastard, n, lâche, m. **~ly,** a, lâche.

data, n.pl, données, f.pl.

date, n, date, f; échéance; époque; (with pers.) rendez-vous; (fruit) datte, f. to ~, à ce jour. up to ~, à jour. ~ palm, dattier, m. ~ stamp, timbre à date, m. ¶ v.t, dater.

dative [case], n, datif, m.

datum, n, donnée, f; repère, m.

daub, n, barbouillage, m; (painting) croûte, f; (for walls) bousillage, m. ¶ v.t, barbouiller, peinturlurer; bousiller.

daughter, n, fille, f. **~-in-law,** belle-fille, f.

daunt, v.t, intimider, décourager. **~less†,** a, intrépide.

davit, n, bossoir, m.

dawdle, v.i, flâner, muser, lambiner.

dawn, n, aube, f, point du jour, m, naissance du jour, (of day & fig.) aurore, f. ¶ v.i, poindre; naître. **~ing,** a, naissant.

day, n, jour, m; journée, f. the ~ after, le lendemain. the ~ after the morrow, le surlendemain. the ~ after tomorrow, après-demain. the ~ before, la veille. the ~ before yesterday, avant-hier. one of these fine ~s, un de ces matins. ~ boarder, demi-pensionnaire, m,f. **~break,** point du jour, *m*, pointe du j., *f*, le petit jour. *~dream*, rêve, *m*. *~ laborer*, journalier, *m*. *~light*, jour, *m*. *~ nursery*, crèche, garderie, pouponnière, *f*. *~ of atonement*, jour des propitiations. *~'s journey*, journée de chemin, *f*. *~'s pay & ~'s work*, journée, *f*. *~time*, heures de jour, *f.pl*, jour, *m*, journée, *f*.

daze, *v.t*, ahurir, hébéter; étourdir. ¶ *n*, étourdissement; *m*; confusion, *f*.

dazzle, *n*, éblouissement, *m*. ¶ *v.t*, éblouir, offusquer; (*v.i.*) papilloter. **dazzling**, *a*, éblouissant.

deacon, *n*, diacre, *m*.

dead, *a. & ad*, mort; terne; éteint (*fire*). *~beat*, *~ tired*, éreinté, fourbu, moulu de fatigue, flapi. *~ calm*, calme plat, *m*. *~ center*, point mort, *m*. *~ drunk*, ivre mort. *~ end*, impasse, *f*. *~fall*, assommoir, *m*. *~ heat*, épreuve nulle, course nulle, c. à égalité, *f*. *~ letter*, (*post*) rebut, *m*; (*fig.*) lettre morte, *f*. *~-letter office*, bureau des rebuts, *m*. *~lock*, impasse, *f*. *~ loss*, perte sèche, *f*. *~ reckoning* (*Naut.*), estime, estimation, *f*. *D~ Sea*, mer Morte, *f*. *~ season*, morte-saison, *f*. *~ wire*, fil hors courant, *m*. **the** *~*, les morts, les trépassés, *m.pl*. *~en*, *v.t*, amortir; étourdir. *~ly*, *a*, mortel, à mort; léthifère; funeste, meurtrier. *~ nightshade*, belladone, *f*. *~ sins*, péchés capitaux, *m.pl*.

deaf, *a*, sourd. *~ & dumb*, sourd-muet. *~-mute*, sourd-muet, *m*, sourde-muette, *f*. *~en*, *v.t*, assourdir. *~ening*, *a*, assourdissant. *~ness*, *n*, surdité, *f*.

deal, *n*, (*cards*) donne, main, *f*; [bois de] sapin, *m*. *a great ~*, *a good ~*, beaucoup, bien. ¶ *v.t.ir*, (*cards*) donner, faire; (*blow*) porter, assener; (*v.i.ir*) traiter; faire les cartes. *~ out*, distribuer. *~ with* (shop), se servir chez. *~er*, *n*, marchand, e, débitant, e, fournisseur, *m*; (*cards*) donneur, euse. *~ing*, *n*, affaire, opération, négociation, *f*; procédé; (*pl.*) commerce, *m*, pratique, *f*, intelligences, accointances, *f.pl*.

dean, *n*, doyen, ne. *~ery*, *n*, (*office*) doyenné, décanat; (*house*) doyenné, *m*.

dear, *a. & ad*, cher. *my ~*, ma chère. *my ~ fellow*, mon cher.

O ~!aïe!, oh là [là]! *O dear nol* ma foi non! *~est* (*pers.*), mon chéri, ma chérie. *~ly*, *ad*, chèrement, cher. *~ness* (*price*) *n*, cherté, *f*.

dearth, *n*, disette, *f*.

death, *n*, mort, *f*; décès, trépas, *m*; (*pl.*) *obituary*) nécrologie, *f*. *~bed*, lit de mort, *m*. *~ blow*, coup mortel, *m*. *~ certificate*, extrait mortuaire, *m*. *~ knell*, glas funèbre, *m*. *~ rate*, mortalité, *f*, taux de la m., *m*. *~ trap*, casse-cou, *m*. *~ warrant*, ordre d'exécution; (*fig.*) arrêt de mort, *m*. *~watch* [*beetle*], horloge de la mort, vrillette, *f*. *~less*, *a*, immortel.

debar, *v.t*, exclure, priver. *~ by time* (*law*), forclore. *~ment by time*, forclusion, *f*.

debase, *v.t*, avilir; altérer, falsifier.

debatable, *a*, discutable, contestable, en litige. **debate**, *n*, débat, *m*, discussion, *f*. ¶ *v.t*, débattre, discuter, agiter.

debauch, *v.t* débaucher. *~ee*, *n*, débauché, e. *~[ery]*, *n*, débauche, crapule, *f*.

debenture, *n*, obligation, *f*. *~ holder*, obligataire, *m,f*.

debilitate, *v.t*, débiliter, déprimer. **debility**, *n*, débilité, *f*.

debit, *n*, débit, doit, *m*. ¶ *v.t*, débiter. **debt** [**due by the trader**] *n*, dette [passive] *f*. **debt** [**due to the trader**] *n*, créance, dette [active] *f*. *debt collector*, agent de recouvrements, *m*. *in debt*, endetté. *involve in debt*, endetter. *run into debt*, s'endetter. **debtor**, *n*, débiteur, trice; redevable, *m,f*; obligé, e. *~ [side]*, débit, doit, *m*.

decade, *n*, dizaine; dizaine d'années, *f*.

decadence, *n*, décadence, *f*. **decadent**, *a*, décadent.

decagon, *n*, décagone, *m*.

decamp, *v.i*, décamper, plier bagage.

decant, *v.t*, décanter, transvaser. *~er*, *n*, carafe, *f*, (*small*) carafon, *m*.

decapitate, *v.t*, décapiter.

decay, *n*, décadence; carie, *f*. ¶ *v.i*, dépérir; se carier.

decease, *n*, décès, trépas, *m*. ¶ *v.i*, décéder. *~d*, *n*, défunt, e.

deceit, *n*, tromperie, *f*. *~ful*, *a*, trompeur, mensonger. **deceive**, *v.t*, tromper, décevoir, abuser. **deceiver**, *n*, trompeur, euse.

decelerate, v.t, ralentir.
December, n, décembre, m.
decency, n, décence, f.
decennial, a, décennal.
decent, a, décent; honnête. ~**ly**, ad, décemment; honnêtement.
decentralize, v.t, décentraliser.
deception, n, tromperie, f. **deceptive**, a, trompeur, décevant, menteur.
decibel (Phys.) n, décibel, m.
decide, v.t, décider; statuer sur; (v.i.) [se] décider. **decided**, a, décidé, arrêté, marqué. ~**ly**, ad, décidément.
deciduous, a, décidu.
decimal, a, décimal. ~ point, virgule [décimale] f. Note:—The decimal point is indicated in French by a comma. ¶ n, décimale, f.
decimate, v.t, décimer.
decipher, v.t, déchiffrer.
decision, n, décision; délibération, f; parti, m. ~ in one's favor, gain de cause, m. **decisive**†, a, décisif.
deck, n, pont, tillac; (of bridge) tablier, m. ~ cabin, chair, cabine, chaise, de pont, f. ~ hand, matelot de p., m. ~ tennis, deck-tennis, m. flight ~, pont d'envol, m. ¶ v.t, parer, orner; (ship) ponter. ~ with flags, pavoiser. ~ with flowers, fleurir.
declaim, v.i, déclamer. **declamatory**, a, (bad sense) déclamatoire; (good sense) oratoire.
declaration, n, déclaration, f. **declare**, v.t, déclarer, constater; proclamer, dénoncer.
declension (Gram.) n, déclinaison, f.
decline, n, déclin; retour, m; maladie de langueur; baisse, f. ¶ v.i. & t, décliner; pencher; baisser; refuser.
declivity, n, déclivité, pente, f.
decoction, n, décoction, f.
decode, v.t, déchiffrer.
decompose, v.t, décomposer.
decorate, v.t, décorer; garnir; orner. **decoration**, n, décoration, f; décor, m. **decorative**, a, décoratif. **decorator**, n, décorateur, m.
decorous†, a, convenable, bienséant. **decorum**, n, décorum, m.
decoy, n, (bait) leurre, m; (place) canardière, f; (pers.) mouton, m. ~ bird, appelant, m. ¶ v.t, leurrer.

decrease, n, décroissement, m, décroissance, f. ¶ v.i, décroître.
decree, n, décret, arrêt; jugement, m. ¶ v.t, décréter, édicter.
decrepit, a, décrépit, caduc. **decrepitude**, n, décrépitude, caducité, f.
decry, v.t, décrier.
dedicate, v.t, dédier, [dé]vouer; consacrer. **dedication**, n, consécration, dédicace, f; envoi, m.
deduce, v.t, déduire.
deduct, v.t, déduire, retrancher, défalquer, rabattre. ~**ion**, déduction, défalcation, f.
deed, n, action, f; acte; fait; exploit; contrat; titre, m.
deem, v.t, juger, estimer, considérer. ~**ed**, p.p, censé, réputé.
deep, a, profond; creux; (in depth) de (ou en) profondeur; (colors) foncé, gros; (mourning) grand; (sound) grave. ~-sea fishing, pêche au large, p. hauturière; (whale & cod) grande pêche, f. ~-sea navigation & ~-sea voyage, long cours, m. ~-seated, profond, foncier. ~-water harbor, port de toute marée, m. ¶ n, profondeur; fosse, f. ~**en**, v.t, approfondir, creuser. ~[**ly**], ad, profondément, avant; sensiblement, fortement.
deer, n, daim; cerf, m; (col.) bêtes fauves, f.pl, fauves, m.pl. ~ stalking, chasse au cerf à l'affût, f.
deface, v.t, défigurer, mutiler. ~**d**, p.a, fruste.
de facto, ad, de fait.
defalcate, v.i, commettre des détournements. **defalcation**, n, détournement de fonds, m.
defamation, n, diffamation, f. **defamatory**, a, diffamatoire, diffamant, infamant. **defame**, v.t, diffamer.
default, n, défaut, m, défaillance, négligence, f. in ~ of, à défaut de, faute de. ¶ v.i, manquer. ~**er**, n, défaillant; délinquant, m.
defeat, n, défaite, f. ¶ v.t, défaire; frustrer.
defecate, v.t. & i, déféquer.
defect, n, défaut, m, défectuosité, f, vice, m, tare, f. ~**ion**, n, défection; apostasie, f. ~**ive**†, a, défectueux; (Gram.) défectif.
defense, n, défense, f. ~**less**, a, sans défense. **defend**, v.t, défendre. ~**ant**, n, défendeur, eresse. ~**er**, n, défenseur, m.

defensible, a, défendable. **defensive**, a, défensif. ¶ n, défensive, f.

defer, v.t, & i, différer, remettre, arriérer, éloigner; (submit) déférer. **~ence**, n, déférence, f, respect, m, ménagements, m. pl. **deferential**, a, déférent.

defiance, n, défi, m. **defiant**, a, de défi.

deficiency, n, défaut, m, insuffisance, f; déficit, manquant, m. **deficient**, a, défectueux; insuffisant. to be ~ in, manquer de. **deficit**, n, déficit, m, moins-value, f.

defile, n, défilé, m. ¶ v.i, défiler; (v.t.) souiller. **~ment**, n, souillure, f.

definable, a, définissable. **define**, v.t, définir; (fix) déterminé; précis. **~ly**, ad, décidément. **definition**, n, définition, f. **definitive†**, a, définitif.

deflate, v.t, dégonfler, désenfler. **deflation**, n, dégonflement, m; (Fin.) déflation, f.

deflect, v.t, défléchir, détourner, dévier. **deflection**, n, déviation; flexion, f.

defloration, n, (ravishment) défloration; (stripping of flowers) défloraison, f. **deflower**, v.t, (ravish) déflorer; (strip of flowers) défleurir, déflorer.

deforest, v.t, déboiser.

deform, v.t, déformer, contrefaire. **~ed**, a, difforme, contrefait. **~ity**, n, difformité, f.

defraud, v.t, frauder, frustrer.

defray, v.t, défrayer.

deft†, a, adroit. **~ness**, n, adresse, f.

defunct, a, défunt. ¶ n, défunt, e.

defy, v.t, défier, braver.

degeneracy & degeneration, n, dégénérescence, dégénération, f, abâtardissement, m. **degenerate**, v.i, dégénérer, s'abâtardir. ¶ n, dégénéré, m. ¶ a, dégénéré.

degradation, n, dégradation, f; avilissement, m. **degrade**, v.t, dégrader; déclasser; [r]avilir.

degree, n, degré; point; (Univ.) diplôme, grade, m.

dehydrate, v.t, déshydrater.

deify, v.t, déifier, diviniser.

deign to (to), daigner, condescendre à.

deity, n, divinité, déité, f.

dejected, a, abattu, découragé. **dejection**, n, abattement, accablement, m.

de jure, ad, de droit.

delay, n, retard, délai, sursis, m. ¶ v.t, différer, retarder, atermoyer; (v.i.) tarder.

del credere, n, ducroire, m.

delectation, n, délices, f.pl.

delegate, n, délégué, e, député, m. ¶ v.t, déléguer. **delegation**, n, délégation, f.

delete, v.t, effacer, biffer, rayer.

deleterious, a, délétère.

deliberate, a, réfléchi; délibéré; lent. ¶ v.i, délibérer. **~ly**, ad, délibérément. **deliberation**, n, délibération, f.

delicacy, n, délicatesse; friandise, chatterie, f. **delicate†**, a, délicat; fin.

delicious†, a, délicieux. **delight**, n, délice, enchantement, m; jouissance; volupté, f. ¶ v.t, délecter, charmer, enchanter, ravir.

delimit[ate], v.t, délimiter.

delineate, v.t, tracer; [dé]peindre. **delineation**, n, délinéation; peinture, f.

delinquency, n, faute; négligence, f, méfait, m. **delinquent**, n, délinquant, e.

deliquescence, n, déliquescence, f.

delirious, a, délirant. to be ~, délirer. **delirium**, n, délire, m.

deliver, v.t, délivrer; livrer; remettre; rendre; distribuer; (Med.) accoucher; (ball, Ten., etc.) lancer; (speech, etc.) prononcer; (pump) refouler. to be ~ed of, accoucher de; (fig.) pondre. **~ance**, n, délivrance, f. **~er**, n, libérateur, trice. **~y**, n, délivrance; livraison; remise; distribution; tradition, f; accouchement, m; prononciation, déclamation, diction, parole, f, débit; refoulement, m. ~ man, ~ boy, ~ girl, livreur, euse. ~ truck, voiture de livraison, f.

dell, n, vallon, m.

delouse, v.t, épouiller.

delphinium, n, pied-d'alouette, m.

delta, n, delta, m.

delude, v.t, tromper, abuser.

deluge, n, déluge, m. ¶ v.t, inonder, noyer.

delusion, n, illusion, f. **delusive†**, a, illusoire.

delve, v.t, fouir, sonder.

demagogue, n, démagogue, m.

demand, n, demande, f; débit, m; exigence, f. on ~, sur demande, à vue, à bureau ouvert, à guichet ouvert, à présentation. ¶ *v.t*, demander; exiger. ~**ing**, *a*, exigeant.

demarcation, *n*, démarcation, *f*.

demean oneself (to) (*behave*), se comporter; (*misbehave*) s'abaisser. **demeanor**, *n*, allure, *f*, maintien, *m*.

demented, *p.p*, dément. **dementia**, *n*, démence, *f*.

demerit, *n*, démérite, *m*.

demesne, *n*, domaine, *m*.

demigod, *n*, demi-dieu, *m*.

demijohn, *n*, dame-jeanne, *f*.

demise, *n*, mutation, *f*; décès, *m*. ¶ *v.t*, transmettre; léguer.

demisemiquaver, *n*, triple croche, *f*.

demobilize, *v.t*, démobiliser.

democracy, *n*, démocratie, *f*. **democrat**, *n*, démocrate, *m*. ~**ic**, *a*, démocratique.

demolish, *v.t*, démolir. **demolition**, *n*, démolition, *f*; (*pl*.) démolitions, *f.pl*, abattis, *m*, abats, décombres, *m.pl*.

demon, *n*, démon, *m*.

demonetize, *v.t*, démonétiser.

demoniac, *n*, démoniaque, *m,f*. ~**(al)**, *a*, démoniaque.

demonstrate, *v.t*, démontrer; (*v.i*.) manifester. **demonstration**, *n*, démonstration; (*political*, etc.) manifestation, *f*. **demonstrative**, *a*, démonstratif. **demonstrator**, *n*, manifestant, e; (*Sch.*) démonstrateur, *m*.

demoralize, *v.t*, démoraliser.

demur, *n*, objection, *f*. ¶ *v.i*, opposer des objections; (*law*) opposer une exception.

demure, *a*, composé; (*look*) de sainte nitouche; (*woman*) qui fait la sucrée.

demurrage, *n*, surestaries, *f.pl*.

demurrer, *n*, exception péremptoire, *f*.

demy, *n*, carré, *m*; coquille, *f*.

den, *n*, antre, repaire, *m*, tanière, caverne, *f*; bouge; nid; cabinet, *m*.

denature, *v.t*, dénaturer.

denial, *n*, dénégation, *f*, démenti; refus; reniement, *m*.

denizen, *n*, habitant, hôte, *m*.

Denmark, *n*, le Danemark.

denominate, *v.t*, dénommer. **denomination**, *n*, dénomination; (*sect*) communion; (*unit*) coupure, *f*. ~**al**, *a*, confessionnel. **denominator**, *n*, dénominateur, *m*.

denote, *v.t*, dénoter.

denounce, *v.t*, dénoncer.

dense†, *a*, dense, compact, épais. **density**, *n*, densité, épaisseur, *f*.

dent, *n*, bosse, *f*. ¶ *v.t*, bossuer, bosseler, cabosser.

dental, *a*, (*Anat.*) dentaire, dental; (*Gram.*) dental. ~ *surgeon*, chirurgien dentiste, *m*. ¶ (*Gram.*) *n*, dentale, *f*. **dentate**, *a*, denté. **dentist**, *n*, dentiste, *m*. ~**ry**, *n*, l'art dentaire, *m*. **dentition**, *n*, dentition, *f*. **denture**, *n*, denture artificielle, *f*.

denude, *v.t*, dénuder, mettre à nu.

denunciation, *n*, dénonciation, *f*.

deny, *v.t*, nier, dénier, se défendre de; renier; refuser. *to ~ it*, nier.

deodorize, *v.t*, désodoriser, désinfecter.

depart, *v.i*, partir; s'éloigner. ~ *this life*, quitter la vie, q. ce monde, trépasser. ~**ed**, *n*, défunt, e, trépassé, e.

department, *n*, département, *m*; division, *f*; service; rayon; office, *m*. ~ *store*, grand magasin, *m*. ~**al**, *a*, départemental.

departure, *n*, départ, *m*, sortie, *f*; (*lapse*) manquement, *m*; innovation, *f*.

depend, *v.i*, dépendre, s'appuyer, compter. ~**ant**, ~**ent**, *n*, personne à charge, *f*. ~**ence**, *n*, dépendance; confiance, *f*. ~**ency**, *n*, dépendance; (*country*) annexe, *f*. ~**ent**, *a*, dépendant. *to be ~ on*, être à la charge de; être tributaire de.

depict, *v.t*, dépeindre, peindre.

deplete, *v.t*, amoindrir; épuiser.

deplorable†, *a*, déplorable, lamentable. **deplore**, *v.t*, déplorer, se lamenter sur.

deploy, *v.t*, déployer. ~**ment**, *n*, déploiement, *m*.

deponent (*pers.*) *n*, déposant, e.

depopulate, *v.t*, dépeupler. **depopulation**, *n*, (*action*) dépeuplement, *m*; (*state*) dépopulation, *f*.

deport, *v.t*, déporter. ~**ation**, *n*, déportation, *f*.

deportment, *n*, maintien, *m*, tenue, *f*, manières, *f.pl*.

depose, *v.t*, déposer.

deposit, *n*, dépôt, *m*; consignation, *f*; versement; cautionnement, *m*; provision [de garantie] *f*; arrhes, *f.pl*, (*Geol.*) dépôt, gîte, gisement, *m*. ¶ *v.t*, déposer; consigner; verser; placer; mettre;

fournir. **~ary**, *n*, dépositaire, *m.f.* **~ion**, *n*, déposition, *f*;dépôt, *m.* **~or**, *n*, déposant, e. **~ory**, *n*, dépôt, *m*; (*fig.*) répertoire, *m.* **depot**, *n*, dépôt, *m*; gare, *f.*

depravation & depravity, *n*, dépravation, *f.* **deprave**, *v.t*, dépraver. **~d**, *p.a*, dépravé, taré

deprecate, *v.t*, réprouver.

depreciate, *v.t*, déprécier, avilir; amortir. **depreciation**, *n*, dépréciation, moins-value, *f*, avilissement; amortissement, *m.* **depreciatory**, *a*, péjoratif.

depredation, *n*, déprédation, *f.*

depress, *v.t*, déprimer. **~ing**, *p.a*, décourageant; triste. **~ion**, *n*, dépression, *f*; enfoncement, *m.*

deprivation, *n*, privation, interdiction, *f*, retrait, *m.* **deprive**, *v.t*, priver, dépourvoir, sevrer; (*Eccl.*) interdire.

depth, *n*, profondeur; hauteur, *f*; fond; (*winter*) cœur, fort, *m*; (*color*) intensité; (*sound*) gravité, *f.* **~ charge**, grenade sousmarine, *f.*

deputation, *n*, députation, délégation, *f.* **depute**, *v.t*, députer, déléguer. **deputize for**, suppléer, faire l'intérim de. **deputy**, *n*, député, *m*; délégué, e; suppléant, e, substitut, *m.* **~ chairman**, viceprésident, e. **~ governor**, sousgouverneur, *m.*

derail, *v.i*, dérailler. **~ment**, *n*, déraillement, *m.*

derange, *v.t*, déranger, fausser; aliéner, détraquer.

derelict, *a*, abandonné. ¶ *n*, navire abandonné, *m*, épave, *f*; (*pers.*) clochard, *m.* **~ion**, *n*, abandon; manquement, *m.*

deride, *v.t*, se moquer de. **derision**, *n*, dérision, *f.* **derisive**, *a*, de dérision. **derisory**, *a*, dérisoire.

derivation, *n*, dérivation, *f.* **derivative**, *n*, dérivé, *m.* **derive**, *v.t*, tirer, retirer, puiser. *to be* **~d from**, dériver de.

derogate, *v.t*, déroger. **derogatory** (*disparaging*) *a*, dénigrant.

derrick, *n*, grue, *f*, derrick, *m*; (*ship's*) mât de charge, *m.*

dervish, *n*, derviche, dervis, *m.*

descant, *v.i*, disserter, discourir, s'étendre.

descend, *v.i. & t*, descendre. **~ed from**, issu de. **~ant**, *n*, descendant, e. **descent**, *n*, descente; (*lineage*) descendance, naissance, race, *f.*

describe, *v.t*, décrire, définir, qualifier. **description**, *n*, description, *f*, libellé[s], *m.*[*pl.*]; signalement, *m*; qualités, *f.pl*, profession; espèce, *f*, genre, *m.* **descriptive**, *a*, descriptif; (*catalog*) raisonné.

descry, *v.t*, découvrir, apercevoir.

desecrate, *v.t*, profaner, violer.

desert, *a*, désert, désertique. ¶ *n*, désert; mérite, *m.* ¶ *v.t. & i*, déserter; abandonner, délaisser. **~ed**, *a*, abandonné, désert, **~er**, *n*, déserteur, *m.* **~ion**, *n*, désertion, *f*; abandon, délaissement, *m.*

deserve, *v.t*, mériter. **deservedly**, *ad*, à juste titre. **deserving**, *a*, méritant; digne (*of* = de). **~ of praise**, louable.

desiccate, *v.t*, dessécher. **desiccation**, *n*, dessèchement, *m*, dessiccation, *f.*

desideratum, *n*, desideratum, *m.*

design, *n*, dessein; modèle; dessin; motif, *m.* ¶ *v.t*, destiner, affecter; projeter, se proposer; dessiner.

designate, *v.t*, désigner. **designation**, *n*, désignation, *f.*

designedly, *ad*, à dessein. **designer**, *n*, dessinateur, trice; auteur, *m.* **designing**, *a*, intrigant.

desirable, *a*, désirable, à désirer, souhaitable. **desire**, *n*, désir; appétit, *m*; envie; demande; prière, *f.* ¶ *v.t*, désirer. **desirous**, *a*, désireux. *to be* **~ of**, désirer.

desist, *v.i*, se départir.

desk, *n*, pupitre; bureau, *m*; chaire, *f.*

desolate, *a*, désert; désolé. ¶ *v.t*, désoler. **desolation**, *n*, désolation, *f.*

despair, *n*, désespoir, *m. to drive to* **~ & ~**, *v.i*, désespérer.

desperado, *n*, apache, escarpe, *m.* **desperate**, *a*, désespéré, acharné; éperdu. **~ly**, *ad*, désespérément; à outrance; éperdument. **desperation**, *n*, désespoir; acharnement, *m.*

despicable, *a*, méprisable, lâche. **despise**, *v.t*, mépriser, dédaigner.

despite, *n*, dépit, *m.*

despoil, *v.t*, dépouiller, spolier.

despond, *v.i*, perdre courage, se décourager. **~ency**, *n*, abattement, découragement, *m.* **~ent**, *a*, abattu, découragé.

despot, *n*, despote, *m.* **~ic†**, *a*, despotique. **~ism**, *n*, despotisme, *m.*

dessert, n, dessert, m. ~ *fruit & nuts,* mendiants, m.pl. ~ *spoon,* cuiller à dessert, c. à entremets, f.

destination, n, destination, f. **destine,** v.t, destiner. **destiny,** n, destin, m, destinée, f.

destitute, a, dans le dénuement; dépourvu, dénué (of = de). *the* ~, les nécessiteux, m.pl. **destitution,** n, dénuement, délaissement, m, misère, f.

destroy, v.t, détruire. ~**er,** n, destructeur, trice; (*ship*) contre-torpilleur, destroyer, m. **destruction,** n, destruction, f; ravages, m.pl. **destructive,** a, destructif, destructeur. ~ *person,* brise-tout, m. **destructor,** n, incinérateur, m.

desultorily, ad, à bâtons rompus. **desultory,** a, décousu.

detach, v.t, détacher; isoler. ~**able,** a, amovible, rapporté. ~*ed house,* maison isolée, f. ~**ment,** n, détachement, m.

detail, n, détail, m. ¶ v.t, détailler; circonstancier; (*Mil.*) détacher.

detain, v.t, détenir, retenir, empêcher de partir; arrêter.

detect, v.t, découvrir; surprendre. ~**ion,** n, découverte, f. ~**ive,** n, détective, m. ~ *story,* roman policier, m. ~**or,** n, détecteur, m.

detent, n, détente, f, chien, m. ~**ion,** n, détention, f; arrêt, m; (*Sch.*) retenue, colle, f, arrêt, m.

deter, v.t, détourner; décourager.

detergent, n, détersif, m.

deteriorate, v.i, se détériorer.

determinate, a, déterminé. **determination,** n, détermination; résolution, f. **determine,** v.t, déterminer, décider, définir, résoudre. ~**d,** a, déterminé, résolu.

detest, v.t, détester, abhorrer. ~**able,** a, détestable.

dethrone, v.t, détrôner.

detonate, v.i, détoner; (v.t.) faire détoner. **detonation,** n, détonation, f. **detonator,** n, détonateur, pétard, m.

detour, v.i, prendre un détour. ¶ n, détour, m.

detract from, rabaisser, dénigrer. **detractor,** n, détracteur, m.

detrain, v.i, débarquer.

detriment, n, détriment, préjudice, m. ~**al,** a, préjudiciable. *be ~ to,* préjudicier.

detritus, n, détritus, m.

deuce, n, diantre, diable; (*cards, dice*) deux, m.

Deuteronomy, n, Deutéronome, m.

devaluation, n, dévaluation, f.

devastate, v.t, dévaster, ravager. **devastator,** n, dévastateur, trice.

develop, v.t, développer; faire valoir; (*Min.*) tracer. ~**er** (*Phot.*) n, révélateur, m. ~*ing bath,* bain de développement, bain révélateur, m. ~**ment,** n, développement; traçage, m.

deviate, v.i, dévier; s'écarter. **deviation,** n, déviation, f; écart, m.

device, n, moyen, expédient; dispositif, m; (*emblem*) devise, f.

devil, n, diable, démon, m. *the* ~*l* diable! ~**ish**†, a, diabolique, diable de, satané. ~**ment,** n, malice; verve endiablée; diablerie, f. ~**ry,** n, diablerie, f.

devious, a, détourné.

devise, v.t, combiner, inventer, imaginer; (*law*) léguer.

devoid, a, dépourvu, dénué.

devolve, v.i, échoir, incomber, retomber.

devote, v.t, dévouer, consacrer, dédier, vouer; livrer. **devotee,** n, dévot, e, fervent, e, fanatique, m,f. **devotion,** n, (*Relig.*) dévotion; piété, f; (*zeal*) dévouement, attachement, m. ~**al,** a, dévot, de dévotion, de piété.

devour, v.t, dévorer, avaler, manger.

devout†, a, dévot; sincère. ~**ness,** n, dévotion, f.

dew, n, rosée, f. ~*drop,* goutte de r., f.

dewlap, n, fanon, m.

dewy, a, couvert de rosée.

dexterity, n, dextérité, adresse, f. **dextrous**†, **dexterous**†, a, adroit.

dextrin, n, dextrine, f.

diabetes, n, diabète, m.

diabolic(al)†, a, diabolique.

diacritical, a, diacritique.

diadem, n, diadème, m.

diaeresis, n, tréma, m.

diagnose, v.t, diagnostiquer. **diagnosis,** n, diagnostic, m.

diagonal†, a, diagonal. ¶ n, diagonale, f.

diagram, n, diagramme; graphique; abaque; schéma, m; épure, f.

dial, n, (*plate*) cadran; (*calculating mach.*) viseur; (*Teleph.*) disque [d'appel] m; (*compass*) boussole, f. ¶ v.t, composer un numéro.

dialect, n, dialecte, parler, idiome, patois, m.

dialectics, *n*, dialectique, *f*.
dialogue, *n*, dialogue, *m*.
diameter, *n*, diamètre, *m*. **diametric†,** *a*, diamétral.
diamond, *n*, diamant; (*Geom.*) losange, rhombe; (*pl.*, *cards*) carreau, *m*. *baseball* ~, terrain de base-ball, *m*. ~ *wedding*, noces de diamant, *f.pl.*
diaper, *n*, étoffe diaprée *f*; linge ouvré, *m*; (*infant*) couche, *f*.
diaphanous, *a*, diaphane.
diaphragm, *n*, diaphragme, *m*.
diarrhoea, *n*, diarrhée, courante, *f*.
diary, *n*, agenda; livre; (*of one's life*) journal, *m*.
diatonic, *a*, diatonique.
diatribe, *n*, diatribe, *f*, factum, *m*.
dibble, *n*, plantoir, *m*.
dice, *n.pl*, dés, *m.pl*. ~ *box*, cornet [à dés] *m*.
dicker, *v.i*, marchander.
dictate, *v.t. & abs*, dicter. ~ *to*, régenter. ~[s], *n.[pl.]*, voix, *f*. **dictation,** *n*, dictée, *f*. **dictator,** *n*, dictateur, *m*. ~**ial,** *a*, dictatorial. ~**ship,** *n*, dictature, *f*; magistère, *m*.
diction, *n*, diction, *f*. ~**ary,** *n*, dictionnaire, *m*.
dictum, *n*, dicton, *m*.
didactic, *a*, didactique.
die, *n*, dé [à jouer]; (*Mech.*) dé, *m*; filière, *f*; coussinet, *m*; lunette; matrice, *f*. ~ *sinker*, graveur en creux, *m*.
die, *v.i.ir*, mourir, trépasser, succomber; périr; s'éteindre; (*animals*) crever; (*of laughing, etc.*) mourir, [se] pâmer. ~ *away*, ~ *down*, mourir, s'assoupir. ~*hard*, intransigeant, *m*.
diet, *n*, diète, *f*, régime [alimentaire] *m*. ¶ *v.t*, mettre à la diète; (*v.i.*) suivre un régime. ~**ary,** *n*, régime diététique, *m*. ~ *bread*, pain de régime, *m*.
differ, *v.i*, différer, varier, s'éloigner. ~**ence,** *n*, différence, *f*, écart; différend, *m*. ~**ent,** *a*, différent. **differential,** *a*, différentiel. **differentiate,** *v.t*, différencier. **differently,** *ad*, différemment, autrement.
difficult, *a*, difficile, malaisé ~ *to catch*, insaisissable. ~**y,** *n*, difficulté; peine, *f*; embarras, mal, *m*. *with* ~, difficilement, malaisément. (*ship in*) **difficulties** (*Nav.*), incommodité, *f*.
diffidence, *n*, défiance de soi-

même; timidité, *f*. **diffident†,** *a*, timide.
diffuse, *v.t*, diffuser; répandre. ¶ *a*, diffus, filandreux. ~**d,** *a*, diffus. **diffusion,** *n*, diffusion, *f*.
dig, *n*, coup; (*fig.*) coup de patte, *m*. ¶ *v.t. & i. ir*, creuser; bêcher; fouiller. ~ *up*, déterrer; arracher.
digest, *v.t. & i*, digérer. ¶ *n*, compilation, *f*, digeste, *m*. ~**ible,** *a*, digestible. ~**ion,** *n*, digestion, *f*. ~**ive,** *a. & n*, digestif, *a. & m*.
digit, *n*, doigt, *m*. *a* ~ (0–9), un [seul] chiffre. **digitalis** (*Phar.*) *n*, digitale, *f*.
dignified, *a*, digne. **dignify,** *v.t*, ennoblir; investir; honorer, décorer. **dignitary,** *n*, dignitaire, *m*. **dignity,** *n*, dignité, *f*.
digress, *v.i*, divaguer. ~**ion,** *n*, digression, divagation, *f*, écart, hors-d'œuvre, *m*. **digressive,** *a*, hors d'œuvre.
dike, *n*, digue, *f*; (*Geol. & Min.*) filon d'injection, *m*. ¶ *v.t*, endiguer.
dilapidate, *v.t*, dégrader, délabrer, détériorer. ~**d** *state* (*building*), caducité, *f*.
dilate, *v.t*, dilater; (*v.i.*) se d.; s'étendre.
dilatoriness, *n*, lenteur, *f*. **dilatory,** *a*, lent, dilatoire.
dilemma, *n*, dilemme, *m*.
dilettante, *n*, dilettante, *m*.
diligence, *n*, diligence, *f*. **diligent,** *a*, diligent. ~**ly,** *ad*, diligemment.
dilly-dally, *v.i*, lanterner, barguigner.
dilute, *v.t*, étendre, diluer, détremper, délayer, couper, (*wine*) baptiser. **dilution,** *n*, dilution, *f*.
diluvial, *a*, diluvien.
dim, *a*, obscur, sombre; indistinct; vague; trouble. ¶ *v.t*, obscurcir; ternir; offusquer; (*auto lights*) mettre en code. **dimmed lights,** éclairage code, *m*.
dimension, *n*, dimension, *f*; échantillon, *m*.
diminish, *v.t. & i*, diminuer. **diminution,** *n*, diminution, *f*. **diminutive,** *a*, exigu; fort petit; (*Gram.*) diminutif. ¶ (*Gram.*) *n*, diminutif, *m*.
dimness, *n*, obscurcissement, *m*; obscurité, *f*.
dimple, *n*, fossette, *f*. ~**d,** *a*, à fossettes.
din, *n*, bruit, tintamarre, *m*. ¶ *v.t*, assourdir.

dine, *v.i,* dîner. ~ *out,* dîner en ville. **diner,** *n,* dîneur, euse.

dinghy, *n,* canot, youyou, *m.*

dingy, *a,* terne; sale; borgne.

dining: ~ *car,* wagon-restaurant, *m.* ~ *room,* salle à manger, *f.* ~ *table,* table de salle à manger, *f.* **dinner,** *n,* dîner, *m.* at ~, à table. ~ *jacket,* smoking, *m.* **give a** ~ [*party*], donner à dîner. ~ *plate,* assiette plate, *f.* ~ *service,* service de table & dessert, *m.* ~ *time,* heure du dîner, *f.*

dint, *n,* bosse, *f. by* ~ *of,* à force de.

diocesan, *a,* diocésain. **diocese,** *n,* diocèse, *m.*

diopter, *n,* dioptrie, *f.* **dioptric,** *a,* dioptrique.

dip, *n,* plongement, *m,* plongée; baignade, *f*; pendage, *m,* inclinaison; flèche; (*ink*) plumée, *f.* ¶ *v.t,* plonger, tremper, immerger; (*auto headlights*) faire basculer; (*v.i.*) plonger; s'incliner.

diphtheria, *n,* diphtérie, *f.*

diphthong, *n,* diphtongue, *f.*

diploma, *n,* diplôme; (*fig.*) parchemin, *m.*

diplomacy, *n,* diplomatie, *f*; doigté, *m.* **diplomatic,** *a,* diplomatique. **diplomat[ist],** *n,* diplomate, *m.*

dipper, *n,* écope, *f.*

dire, *a,* (*distress*) dernière, extrême; (*necessity*) dure.

direct, *a,* direct; immédiat. ~ *current* (*Elec.*), courant continu, *m.* ~ *trade,* commerce direct, *m.* ¶ *ad,* directement. ¶ *v.t,* diriger; administrer, conduire; charger; adresser; acheminer; orienter. *to* ~ *me to* . . ., m'indiquer le chemin pour aller à . . . ~**ion,** *n,* direction; administration; conduite; orientation, *f*; sens, côté, *m*; adresse, *f*; (*pl.*) instructions, *f.pl,* charge, prescription, *f.* ~**s** *for use,* mode d'emploi, *m.* **directly,** *ad,* directement; immédiatement, à l'instant, aussitôt.

director, *n,* (*of company*) administrateur, trice; (*manager*) directeur, trice; ordonnateur, trice. ~**ate,** *n,* administration, *f.*

directory, *n,* (*Teleph.*) annuaire; répertoire, *m.*

direful, *a,* terrible; sinistre.

dirge, *n,* chant, funèbre, chant de mort, *m.*

dirigible, *a.* & *n,* dirigeable, *a.* & *m.*

dirk, *n,* dague, *f,* poignard, *m.*

dirt, *n,* saleté, crasse, ordure, immondice, crotte, boue; terre, *f.* ~-*cheap,* à vil prix. ~ *track,* piste en cendrée, *f.* **dirtily,** *ad,* salement. **dirtiness,** *n,* saleté, *f.* **dirty,** *a,* sale, malpropre, crasseux; crotté, boueux. ~ *pig,* cochon, *m.* ~ *trick,* vilain tour, croc-en-jambe, *m,* vilenie, goujaterie, saleté, *f.* ~ *work* (*fig.*), sale besogne, *f,* micmac, *m.* ¶ *v.t,* salir, souiller; crotter, barbouiller.

disable, *v.t,* rendre incapable; rendre hors de combat; (*ship*) désemparer. ~**d** *soldier,* ~**d** *sailor,* mutilé de la guerre, *m.* ~**ment** & **disability,** *n,* incapacité, invalidité, *f.*

disabuse, *v.t,* désabuser.

disadvantage, *n,* désavantage, *m. place at a* ~, désavantager. ~**ous†,** *a,* désavantageux.

disaffection, *n,* désaffection, *f.*

disagree, *v.i,* n'être pas d'accord, être en désaccord; ne pas convenir. ~**able†,** *a,* désagréable. ~**ment,** *n,* désaccord, *m,* discordance, *f*; dissentiment, *m.*

disallow, *v.t,* rejeter.

disappear, *v.i,* disparaître. ~**ance,** *n,* disparition, *f.*

disappoint, *v.t,* désappointer; tromper, décevoir. *don't* ~ *me,* ne manquez pas à votre parole, à v. promesse. ~**ment,** *n,* désappointement, *m,* déception, *f,* mécompte, démenti, déboire, *m.* ~ *in love,* déception, *f,* (*ou* chagrin, *m.*) d'amour.

disapprobation & **disapproval,** *n,* désapprobation, improbation, *f.* **disapprove,** *v.t.* & ~ *of,* désapprouver, réprouver, improuver.

disarm, *v.t,* désarmer. **disarmament,** *n,* désarmement, *m.*

disarrange, *v.t,* déranger, désajuster. ~ (*someone's hair*) décoiffer.

disarray, *n,* désarroi, *m.*

disaster, *n,* désastre, sinistre; cataclysme, *m.* **disastrous,** *a,* désastreux, néfaste.

disavow, *v.t,* désavouer. ~**al,** *n,* désaveu, *m.*

disband, *v.t,* licencier; (*v.i.*) se séparer.

disbelief, *n,* manque de foi, *m.* **disbelieve,** *v.t,* ne pas croire.

disbud, *v.t,* ébourgeonner, éborgner.

disburden, *v.t*, décharger.

disburse, *v.t*, débourser. **~ment,** *n*, déboursement, débours, déboursé, *m*, mise [de]hors, *f*.

disc, *n*, disque, plateau, *m*; rondelle, *f*.

discard, *v.t*, laisser de côté; (*cards*) écarter.

discern, *v.t*, discerner. **~ible,** *a*, perceptible. **~ing,** *a*, judicieux. **~ment,** *n*, discernement, jugement, *m*.

discharge, *n*, décharge, *f*; déversement, *m*, évacuation, *f*; débit; (*Med.*) écoulement, *m*, suppuration, *f*; libération, *f*, acquit[tement] *m*, quittance, *f*, quitus; renvoi, congé, *m*; (*Mil., Navy*) réforme; (*bankrupt*) réhabilitation, *f*. ¶ *v.t. & i*, décharger; déverser; débiter; (*wound*) suppurer; débarquer; libérer, [ac]quitter; liquider; renvoyer, congédier; réformer; réhabiliter. *to get* (obligation) *discharged,* apurer.

disciple, *n*, disciple, *m*. **disciplinarian,** *n*, disciplinaire, *m*. **disciplinary,** *a*, disciplinaire; de discipline. **discipline,** *n*, discipline, *f*. ¶ *v.t*, discipliner.

disclaim, *v.t*, désavouer; dénier. **~er,** *n*, dénégation, *f*; désaveu, *m*; renonciation, *f*.

disclose, *v.t*, révéler, divulguer, dévoiler. **disclosure,** *n*, révélation, divulgation, *f*.

discoloration, *n*, décoloration, *f*. **discolor,** *v.t*, décolorer.

discomfit, *v.t*, confondre. **~ure,** *n*, déconvenue, *f*.

discomfort, *n*, incommodité, *f*, malaise, *m*, gêne, *f*.

discompose, *v.t*, troubler. **discomposure,** *n*, trouble, *m*.

disconcert, *v.t*, déconcerter, interdire, désorienter.

disconnect, *v.t*, désassembler; (*Mech.*) débrayer; (*Elec.*) rompre. **~ed,** *a*, détaché; isolé, incohérent.

disconsolate, *a*, désolé.

discontent[ed], *a, p.p*, mécontent. **discontent[ment],** *n*, mécontentement, *m*.

discontinuance, *n*, cessation, suspension; suppression, *f*. **discontinue,** *v.t*, discontinuer; (*a train*) supprimer. *~ one's subscription*, se désabonner.

discord, *n*, discorde, *f*; (*Mus.*) désaccord, *m*, dissonance, *f*.

~ance, *n*, discordance, *f*. **~ant,** *a*, discordant, dissonant.

discount, *n*, escompte, *m*; remise, *f*; rabais, *m*; (opp. *premium*) perte, *f*. ¶ *v.t*, escompter.

discountenance, *v.t*, s'opposer à.

discounter, *n*, escompteur, *m*. **discounting,** *n*, escompte, *m*.

discourage, *v.t*, décourager. **~ment,** *n*, découragement, *m*.

discourse, *n*, discours, *m*. ¶ *v.i*, discourir.

discourteous, *a*, discourtois. **discourtesy,** *n*, discourtoisie, *f*.

discover, *v.t*, découvrir. **~er,** *n*, inventeur, *m*. **~y,** *n*, découverte, *f*.

discredit, *n*, discrédit, *m*. ¶ *v.t*, discréditer, déconsidérer, démonétiser. **~able,** *a*, déshonorant.

discreet†, *a*, discret, retenu.

discrepancy, *n*, contradiction, *f*.

discrete, *a*, discret.

discretion, *n*, discrétion, retenue, prudence, *f*. **~ary,** *a*, discrétionnaire. *full ~ power*, carte blanche, *f*.

discriminate, *v.t*, distinguer, discerner, faire le départ. **discrimination,** *n*, discernement, *m*, discrimination, *f*.

discursive, *a*, discursif.

discus, *n*, disque, *m*.

discuss, *v.t*, discuter, débattre, agiter. **~ion,** *n*, discussion, *f*, débat, *m*.

disdain, *n*, dédain, *m*. ¶ *v.t*, dédaigner. **~ful†,** *a*, dédaigneux.

disease, *n*, maladie, *f*; mal, *m*. **~d,** *a*, malade; (*meat*) provenant d'animaux malades.

disembark, *v.t. & i*, débarquer. **~ation,** *n*, débarquement, *m*.

disembody, *v.t*, désincorporer.

disembowel, *v.t*, éventrer.

disenchant, *v.t*, désenchanter.

disencumber, *v.t*, désencombrer; (*Fin.*) dégrever.

disengage, *v.t*, dégager; (*Mech.*) débrayer. **~d,** *a*, libre.

disentangle, *v.t*, démêler, débrouiller.

disestablishment [of the Church] *n*, séparation de l'Église & de l'État, *f*.

disfavor, *n*, défaveur, *f*.

disfigure, *v.t*, défigurer, enlaidir. **~ment,** *n*, enlaidissement, *m*.

disforest, *v.t*, déboiser.

disgorge, *v.t*, dégorger.

disgrace, *n*, disgrâce; honte, *f*;

déshonneur, opprobre, *m.* ¶ *v.t,* disgracier; déshonorer. ~ful†, *a,* honteux, ignominieux.

disgruntled, *a,* maussade, mécontent.

disguise, *n,* déguisement, *m;* dissimulation, *f.* ¶ *v.t,* déguiser, camoufler; travestir; contrefaire.

disgust, *n,* dégoût, *m.* ¶ *v.t,* dégoûter. ~ing, *a,* dégoûtant.

dish, *n,* plat, *m; (food)* mets, *m.* ~es, vaisselle, *f.* ~*cloth,* torchon [de cuisine] *m,* lavette, *f.* ~ *warmer,* réchaud, *m.* ~ *washer,* laveur de vaisselle, plongeur, *m.* ~ *up, v.t,* dresser, servir. ~ed, *a,* à cuvette. ~ful, *n,* platée, *f.*

dishabille, *n,* déshabillé, *m.*

dishearten, *v.t,* décourager, rebuter.

disheveled, *a,* échevelé, ébouriffé.

dishonest†, *a,* malhonnête, infidèle, déloyal. ~y, *n,* malhonnêteté, infidélité, *f.*

dishonor, *n,* déshonneur, *m.* ¶ *v.t,* déshonorer. ~able, *a,* peu honnête, déshonorant.

disillusion, *n,* désillusion, *f.* ¶ *v.t,* désillusionner, dégriser, désenchanter.

disinclination, *n,* éloignement, *m.* **disincline,** *v.t,* éloigner.

disinfect, *v.t,* désinfecter. ~ant, *n,* désinfectant, *m.* ~ion, *n,* désinfection, *f.*

disingenuous, *a,* peu sincère.

disinherit, *v.t,* déshériter.

disintegrate, *v.t,* désagréger, effriter.

disinter, *v.t,* déterrer, exhumer.

disinterested, *a,* désintéressé. ~ness, *n,* désintéressement, *m.*

disinterment, *n,* exhumation, *f.*

disjoin, *v.t,* disjoindre.

disjoint, *v.t,* désassembler. ~ed, *a,* décousu.

disk, *n,* disque, plateau, *m;* rondelle, *f.*

dislike, *n,* dégoût, éloignement, *m,* aversion, antipathie, grippe, *f.* ¶ *v.t,* ne pas aimer, avoir en aversion, avoir de l'aversion pour (*ou* contre), prendre en grippe.

dislocate, *v.t,* disloquer, luxer, démettre, déboîter, démancher. **dislocation,** *n,* dislocation, luxation, *f.*

dislodge, *v.t,* déchausser, débusquer, disloquer.

disloyal†, *a,* déloyal, infidèle. ~ty, *n,* déloyauté, infidélité, *f.*

dismal†, *a,* lugubre, morne, sombre.

dismantle, *v.t,* démanteler, dégarnir.

dismast, *v.t,* démâter.

dismay, *n,* consternation, *f.* ¶ *v.t,* consterner.

dismember, *v.t,* démembrer.

dismiss, *v.t,* renvoyer, congédier, remercier, destituer; chasser; rejeter. ~al, *n,* renvoi, congé, *m,* destitution, *f.*

dismount, *v.i,* descendre; (*v.t.*) démonter.

disobedience, *n,* désobéissance, *f.* **disobedient,** *a,* désobéissant. **disobey,** *v.t,* désobéir à; (*v.i.*) désobéir.

disoblige, *v.t,* désobliger. **disobliging,** *a,* désobligeant. ~ness, *n,* désobligeance, *f.*

disorder, *n,* désordre; trouble, *m;* maladie, *f.* ¶ *v.t,* dérégler. ~ly, *a,* désordonné.

disorganize, *v.t,* désorganiser.

disown, *v.t,* désavouer, renier, méconnaître.

disparage, *v.t,* dénigrer, rabaisser, déprécier, ravaler. ~ment, *n,* dénigrement, *m.* **disparaging,** *a,* dénigrant; péjoratif.

disparate, *a,* disparate. **disparity,** *n,* disparité, *f.*

dispassionate, *a.* & ~ly, *ad,* sans passion; sans parti pris.

dispatch, *n,* expédition, *f,* envoi, acheminement, *m;* diligence, célérité, promptitude, rapidité; (*message*) dépêche, *f.* ~ *case,* serviette, *f.* ¶ *v.t,* expédier, envoyer, acheminer; dépêcher, brasser.

dispel, *v.t,* dissiper, chasser.

dispensary, *n,* officine, pharmacie, *f;* (*charitable*) dispensaire, *m.* **dispensation,** *n,* (*of Providence*) disposition; (*exemption*) dispense, *f.* **dispense,** *v.t,* dispenser; départir; rendre; (*Med.*) préparer [& débiter]. ~ *with,* se passer de; supprimer. **dispenser,** *n,* dispensateur, trice; (*Med.*) pharmacien, ne.

dispersal & **dispersion,** *n,* dispersion, séparation, *f.* **disperse,** *v.t,* disperser; dissiper.

dispirit, *v.t,* décourager, déprimer.

displace, *v.t,* déplacer; (*from office*) destituer; (*securities, Fin.*) déclasser. ~ment, *n,* déplacement, *m;* destitution, *f;* déclassement, *m.*

display, *n*, montre, parade, *f*; étalage, *m*. ~ *cabinet*, vitrine, armoire vitrée, *f*. ~ *model*, mannequin, *m*. ¶ *v.t*, exposer, étaler; faire preuve de. ~*ed in bold type*, en vedette.

displease, *v.t*, déplaire à; mécontenter. **displeasure**, *n*, déplaisir, mécontentement, *m*.

disposable, *a*, disponible. **disposal**, *n*, disposition; expédition, *f*. **dispose**, *v.t*, disposer. ~ *of*, disposer de; placer; expédier. *well*, *ill*, ~*d towards*, bien, mal, disposé pour, envers. **disposition**, *n*, disposition, *f*; naturel, *m*.

dispossess, *v.t*, déposséder.

disproof, *n*, réfutation, *f*.

disproportion, *n*, disproportion, *f*. ~**ate**, *a*, disproportionné.

disprove, *v.t*, réfuter.

dispute, *n*, dispute, contestation, *f*, litige, *m*. ¶ *v.t. & i*, disputer, contester. ~ *every inch of the ground* (*Mil.*), chicaner le terrain.

disqualification, *n*, disqualification, *f*. **disqualified** (*law*) *p.p. & p.a*, indigne. **disqualify**, *v.t*, disqualifier; (*law*) frapper d'incapacité.

disquiet, *v.t*, inquiéter. ~**[ude]**, *n*, inquiétude, *f*.

disquisition, *n*, dissertation, *f*.

disrate, *v.t*, déclasser.

disregard, *n*, indifférence, *f*; dédain, *m*. ¶ *v.t*, négliger; mépriser.

disrelish, *n*, dégoût, *m*.

disreputable, *a*, peu honorable; de mauvaise réputation. **disrepute**, *n*, discrédit, décri, *m*.

disrespect, *n*, manque de respect, *m*, irrévérence, *f*. ~**ful†**, *a*, irrespectueux, irrévérencieux.

disrobe, *v.t*, déshabiller.

disrupt, *v.t*, rompre.

dissatisfaction, *n*, mécontentement, *m*. **dissatisfied**, *p.a*, mécontent.

dissect, *v.t*, disséquer. ~**ion**, *n*, dissection, *f*.

dissemble, *v.t. & i*, dissimuler. **dissembler**, *n*, dissimulateur, trice.

disseminate, *v.t*, disséminer.

dissension, *n*, dissension, *f*. **dissent**, *n*, dissentiment, *m*; dissidence, *f*. ¶ *v.i*, s'opposer. ~**er** & **dissentient**, *n*, dissident, e. ~**ing** & **dissentient**, *a*, dissident.

dissertation, *n*, dissertation, *f*.

disservice, *n*, mauvais service, *m*.

dissidence, *n*, dissidence, *f*. **dissident**, *a*, dissident.

dissimilar, *a*, dissemblable, dissimilaire. ~**ity**, *n*, dissemblance, *f*.

dissimulate, *v.t. & i*, dissimuler. **dissimulation**, *n*, dissimulation, duplicité, *f*.

dissipate, *v.t*, dissiper. **dissipation**, *n*, dissipation, *f*.

dissociate, *v.t*, dissocier.

dissolute, *a*, dissolu. ~**ness**, *n*, dissolution, *f*.

dissolution, *n*, dissolution, *f*. **dissolve**, *v.t*, dissoudre, fondre. **dissolvent**, *a. & n*, dissolvant, *a. & m. dissolving views*, vues fondantes, *f.pl*.

dissonance, *n*, dissonance, *f*. **dissonant**, *a*, dissonant.

dissuade, *v.t*, dissuader, déconseiller.

dissyllable, *n*, dissyllabe, *m*.

distaff, *n*, quenouille, *f*.

distance, *n*, distance, *f*; éloignement; écart; lointain, *m*; trotte, *f*. *keep one's* ~ garder ses distances. ~ *apart* or *between*, écartement, *m*. ¶ *v.t*, éloigner; distancer. **distant**, *a*, éloigné, reculé, lointain; distant.

distaste, *n*, dégoût, *m*. ~**ful**, *a*, désagréable au goût.

distemper, *n*, maladie [des chiens]; (*paint*) détrempe, *f*, badigeon, *m*. ¶ *v.t*, peindre à la détrempe, badigeonner.

distend, *v.t*, distendre, ballonner. **distension**, *n*, distension, *f*, ballonnement, *m*.

distil, *v.t*, distiller. **distillate** & **distillation**, *n*, distillation, *f*. **distiller**, *n*, distillateur, *m*. ~**y**, *n*, distillerie, *f*.

distinct†, *a*, distinct; tranché. ~**ion**, *n*, distinction, *f*. ~**ive**, *a*, distinctif. **distinctness**, *n*, netteté, *f*. **distinguish**, *v.t*, distinguer. *to be* ~*able from*, se distinguer de. ~**ed**, *a*, distingué, de distinction, éminent, notable, insigne.

distort, *v.t*, déformer; défigurer, dénaturer, tordre. ~**ing mirror**, miroir déformant, *m*. ~**ion**, *n*, déformation; distorsion, *f*; (*fig.*) travestissement, *m*.

distract, *v.t*, distraire, détourner; déchirer. ~**ed†**, *p.a*, éperdu, affolé. ~**ion**, *n*, distraction, *f*; affolement, *m*; folie, fureur, *f*.

distrain upon, (*pers.*) exécuter, contraindre par saisie de biens; (*goods*) saisir. ~**able**, *a*, saisissable. *not ~*, insaisissable. **distraint**, *n*, saisie, exécution, *f*.

distress, *n*, détresse; misère; (*law*) saisie, *f*. ¶ *v.t*, affliger, désoler, angoisser. **~ing**, *a*, affligeant, désolant, angoissant.

distribute, *v.t*, distribuer, répartir. **distribution**, *n*, distribution, répartition, *f*.

district, *n*, district, *m*; région, *f*; quartier, *m*.

distrust, *n*, défiance; méfiance, *f*. ¶ *v.t*, se défier de; se méfier de. **~ful**, *a*, défiant; méfiant, soupçonneux.

disturb, *v.t*, troubler, déranger; remuer; inquiéter. **~ance**, *n*, dérangement, trouble, *m*; perturbation, *f*; tapage, *m*; émeute, *f*.

disunion, *n*, désunion, *f*. **disunite**, *v.t*, désunir.

disuse, *n*, désuétude, *f*. **~d**, *p.a*, hors d'usage.

ditch, *n*, fossé; canal, *m*; rigole; douve, *f*.

ditto, *n*, dito, idem (*ad.*). *to say nothing but ~ to everything*, opiner du bonnet.

ditty, *n*, chanson, chansonnette, *f*.

divan, *n*, divan, *m*.

dive, *n*, plongeon, *m*; (*Avn.*) vol piqué, *m*. ¶ *v.i*, plonger; fouiller; (*Avn.*) piquer. **diver**, *n*, (*Swim.*) plongeur, euse; (*in diving dress*) plongeur, scaphandrier; (*bird*) plongeon, *m*.

diverge, *v.i*, diverger. **divergence**, *n*, divergence, *f*. **divergent**, *a*, divergent.

diverse†, *a*, divers, varié. **diversify**, *v.t*, diversifier, varier. **diversion**, *n*, diversion, *f*; divertissement, *m*. **diversity**, *n*, diversité, variété, *f*. **divert**, *v.t*, détourner, dériver, écarter; (*amuse*) divertir.

Dives, *n*, riche; (*Bible*) le mauvais riche, *m*.

divest, *v.t*, dépouiller.

divide, *v.t*, diviser; scinder; partager; répartir. **~d skirt**, jupe-culotte, *f*. **dividend**, *n*, dividende, *m*; répartition, *f*. **dividers**, *n.pl*, (*instrument*) compas à pointes sèches, *m*.

divination, *n*, divination, *f*. **divine†**, *a*, divin. ¶ *n*, théologien, *m*. ¶ *v.t*, deviner. **diviner**, *n*, devin, *m*, devineresse, *f*.

diving:~ bell, cloche à plongeur, *f*. **~ board**, plongeoir, tremplin, *m*. **~ suit**, scaphandre, *m*.

divining rod, baguette divinatoire, *f*.

divinity, *n*, divinité; (*science*) théologie, *f*.

divisible, *a*, divisible; partageable. **division**, *n*, division, *f*; partage, *m*; section; coupe; séparation; case, *f*. **divisor**, *n*, diviseur, *m*.

divorce, *n*, divorce, *m*. ¶ *v.t*, divorcer d'avec.

divot (*golf*) *n*, touffe de gazon, *f*.

divulge, *v.t*, divulguer.

dizziness, *n*, vertige, *m*. **dizzy**, *a*, vertigineux.

do, *v.t.ir*, faire; opérer; (*v.i.ir*) faire; agir; s'acquitter; aller; se trouver, se porter; convenir, faire l'affaire; suffire. *~ away with*, supprimer, abolir. [*please*] *do not touch*, défense de toucher. *~-nothing*, *a*, fainéant. *~ one's hair*, se coiffer. *~ one's utmost to*, s'efforcer de. *~ over again*, refaire. *~ without*, se passer de. *I have done*, j'ai fini. *that will ~*, cela suffit. *well-to-~*, aisé, cossu.

docile†, *a*, docile. **docility**, *n*, docilité, *f*.

dock, *n*, (*tail*) tronçon, *m*; (*Bot.*) patience, *f*; (*court*) banc des prévenus; (*Naut.*) bassin, dock, *m*; forme, cale, *f*. *dry ~*, cale seche, *f*. *~ company*, compagnie des docks, *f*. *~ strike*, grève des travailleurs des docks, *f*. *~ warehouse*, dock[-entrepôt] *m*. *naval ~yard*, arsenal maritime, *m*. ¶ *v.t*, (*wages*) diminuer; rogner; faire entrer en bassin; (*v.i.*) entrer en bassin. **~er**, *n*, docker, déchargeur, débardeur, *m*.

docket, *n*, étiquette, *f*. ¶ *v.t*, étiqueter.

doctor, *n*, médecin, docteur, *m*. ¶ *v.t*, médicamenter; soigner; (*falsify*) frelater; (*patch up*) tricher. **~ate**, *n*, doctorat, *m*.

doctrinaire, *n. & a*, doctrinaire, *m. & a*. **doctrine**, *n*, doctrine, *f*.

document, *n*, document, écrit, *m*, pièce, *f*; acte, titre, *m*. *~ cabinet*, cartonnier, *m*. *~ case*, serviette, *f*. ¶ *v.t*, documenter. **~ary**, *a*, documentaire.

dodder (*Bot.*) *n*, cuscute, *f*. ¶ *v.i*, brandiller [de] la tête.

dodge, *n*, biais; détour; truc, *m*; ruse, *f*. ¶ *v.t*, esquiver, éviter; (*v.i.*) biaiser. **dodger**, *n*, biaiseur, euse. *artful ~*, finassier, rusé compère, *m*.

doe, *n*, (*deer*) daine; (*hare*) hase; (*rabbit*) lapine, *f*. ~skin, *n*, peau de daim, *f*, daim, *m*.

doer, *n*, faiseur, euse.

doff, *v.t*, ôter, tirer.

dog, *n*, chien; (*fire*) chenet, *m*. ~ biscuit, pain de chien, *m*. ~ cart, charrette anglaise, *f*. ~ days, canicule, *f*. ~ fish, chien de mer, *m*. ~ Latin, latin de cuisine, *m*. ~ racing or dogs, courses de lévriers, *f.pl*. ~ rose, rose de chien, églantine, *f*; (*bush*) églantier, rosier sauvage, *m*. ~['s] ear, *n*, corne, *f*; (*v.t.*) [é]corner. ~ show, exposition canine, *f*. ~ violet, violette de chien, *f*. ¶ *v.t*, talonner. dogged, *a*, tenace. ~ly, *ad*, mordicus. ~ness, *n*, obstination, *f*.

doggerel, *n*, méchants vers, *m.pl*.

doggy or doggie, *n*, toutou, *m*.

dogma, *n*, dogme, *m*. dogmatic-(al)†, *a*, dogmatique. dogmatize, *v.i*, dogmatiser.

doily, *n*, rond, ovale, rectangle [de table].

doings, *n.pl*, faits & gestes; (*underhand*) agissements, *m.pl*. *your doing* (fig.), votre ouvrage.

doldrums (*Naut.*) *n.pl*, calmes, *m.pl*, zone des calmes, *f*. *to be in the ~* (fig.), broyer du noir.

dole, *n*, charité; indemnité de chômage, *f*. ~ *out*, distribuer parcimonieusement. ~ful†, *a*, plaintif, dolent.

doll, *n*, poupée, *f*. ~-faced, poupin. ~'s house, maison de poupée, *f*.

dollar, *n*, dollar, *m*.

dolly, *n*, chariot, *m*.

dolphin, *n*, (*porpoise*) dauphin, *m*; (*dorado*) dorade, *f*; (*mooring*) corps mort, *m*.

dolt, *n*, lourdaud, e.

domain, *n*, domaine, *m*.

dome, *n*, dôme, *m*, coupole, voûte, *f*.

domestic, *a*, domestique; (*coal, or like*) de ménage; (*trade*) intérieur, métropolitain. ¶ *n*, domestique, *m.f*. domesticate, *v.t*, domestiquer. domesticated, (*pers.*) *a*, d'intérieur. domesticity, *n*, domesticité, *f*.

domicile, *n*, domicile, *m*. ¶ *v.t*, domicilier.

dominant, *a*, dominant. dominate, *v.t. & i*, dominer, régenter. domination, *n*, domination, *f*. domineer, *v.t*, dominer; (*v.i.*) régenter. ~ing, *a*, dominateur.

Dominican, *n*, dominicain, e.

dominion, *n*, domination, *f*, empire, *m*. D~ *of Canada, of New Zealand*, Dominion du Canada, de la Nouvelle-Zélande, *m*.

domino, *n*, domino, *m*.

don, *v.t*, mettre, endosser, revêtir.

donate, *v.i. & t*, donner, accorder. donation, *n*, don, *m*, donation; (*pl.*) bienfaisance, *f*.

done, *p.p*, fait; (*Cook.*) cuit.

donee, *n*, donataire, *m.f*.

donkey, *n*, âne, baudet, grison, *m*, bourrique, *f*. ~ *driver*, ânier, ère. ~ *engine*, petit cheval, *m*. ~ *pump*, pompe alimentaire, *f*.

donor, *n*, donneur, euse; (*law*) donateur, *m*, donatrice, *f*.

doom, *n*, destin; jugement, *m*. ¶ *v.t*, condamner. doomsday, *n*, jour du jugement [dernier] *m*.

door, *n*, porte; fermeture; (*carriage, car*) portière, *f*; (*peephole*) regard, *m*. ~ *curtain*, portière, *f*. ~keeper, concierge, *m.f*, portier, ère, gardien, ne. ~mat, paillasson, tapis-brosse, *m*. ~step, pas de la porte. *m*. ~way, [baie de] porte, *f*.

dope, *n*, stupéfiant, *m*. ¶ *v.t*, droguer; doper.

Doric, *a*. & *n*, dorique, *a*. & *m*.

dormant, *a*, dormant, endormi.

dormer [window], *n*, mansarde, lucarne, *f*. dormitory, *n*, dortoir, *m*. dormouse, *n*, loir, *m*.

dose, *n*, dose, prise, *f*. ¶ *v.t*, médicamenter; doser.

dot, *n*, point; (*Emb.*) pois, *m*. ¶ *v.t*, marquer d'un point, mettre un p. sur; (*Mus.*) pointer; pointiller; jalonner, parsemer. *dotted line*, ligne pointillée, *f*.

dotage, *n*, enfance, *f*; radotage, *m*. dotard, *n*, radoteur, euse; (*of comedy*) grime, *m*. dote or doat, *v.i*, radoter, folle, *on*, être fou, folle, de, raffoler de.

double, *a*, double. ~-acting, à double effet. ~-barreled gun, fusil à deux coups, *m*. ~ bass, contrebasse, *f*. ~ bed, lit à deux places, *m*. ~-[-bedded] *room*, chambre à deux lits, *f*. ~-breasted, croisé. ~-dealing, duplicité, *f*; (*a.*) double. ~-entry *bookkeeping*, tenue des livres en partie double, *f*. ~-faced, à double face. ~-fronted (house), à deux façades. ~ *meaning* or ~ *entendre*, mot à double entente, *m*, phrase à d. e., *f*. ~ *width* (cloth), grande largeur, *f*.

¶ *ad*, double. ¶ *n*, double; (*person*) sosie, *m*. ~ *or nothing*, quitte ou double. *the* ~ (*Mil.*), au pas gymnastique. ~*s game* (*Ten.*), partie double, *f*. ¶ *v.t. & i*, doubler. **doubly**, *ad*, doublement.

doubt, *n*, doute, *m*. ¶ *v.i*, douter; (*v.t.*) douter de. ~**ful**†, *a*, douteux; suspect; (*virtue*) moyenne. ~**less**, *a*, sans doute.

dough, *n*, pâte, *f*.

doughty, *a*, preux. ~ *deeds*, hauts faits, *m.pl*, prouesses, *f.pl*.

dour, *a*, froid & sévère; peu démonstratif.

douse, *v.t*, éteindre; tremper.

dove, *n*, colombe, *f*; pigeon, *m*. ~*cot*[*e*], colombier, pigeonnier, *m*. ~*tail*, queue d'aronde, *f*.

dowager, *n*, douairière, *f*.

dowdy, *a*, [mal] fagoté.

dowel, *n*, goujon, *m*. ¶ *v.t*, goujonner.

dower, dowry, *n*, dot, *f*; don, *m*. ¶ *v.t*, doter.

down, *a*, descendant. ~*grade*, pente, *f*.

down, *ad*, en bas; à bas; bas; à terre; par terre; en aval; (*prices*) en baisse; (*sun, moon*) couché, e; (*crossword clues*) verticalement. *to walk with the head* ~, *the hands* ~, marcher la tête basse, les mains basses. ~ *at heel*, en savates. ~ *there*, ~ *below*, là-bas. ~ *to*, jusqu'à, jusque.

down, *comps*: ~*cast*, *a*, baissé; abattu. ~*fall*, *n*, chute, *f*, effondrement, *m*, ruine, *f*. ~*hearted*, *a*, découragé, abattu. ~*hill*, *a*, en pente; (*ad.*) en descendant. ~*pour*, *n*, tombée de pluie, *f*, déluge, *m*. ~*right*, *a*, franc, fieffé, pommé, vrai; (*ad.*), franchement, nettement. ~*stairs*, *ad*, en bas. ~*stream*, *ad*, en aval, à vau-l'eau. ~*stroke*, *n*, (*piston*) course descendante, *f*; (*writing*) jambage, plein, *m*. ~*trodden*, *a*, foulé [aux pieds]. ~*ward*, *a*, descendant; de baisse, à la baisse. ~*ward*[*s*], *ad*, en bas, en contrebas.

down, *i*, à bas! ~ *with* . . ., à bas . . .! conspuez . . .!

down, *n*, duvet, poil follet; poil, *m*; bourre, *f*; coton, *m*; (*sand hill*) dune, *f*. ~ *quilt*, couvrepied, *m*.

down, *pr*, en bas de, au bas de; en aval de.

down, *v.t*, abattre; baisser; renverser.

downy, *a*, duveté, douillet, follet; cotonneux, bourru.

dowral, *a*, dotal. **dowry**, *n*, dot, *f*.

dowser, *n*, sourcier, ère, hydroscope, *m*. **dowsing**, *n*, hydroscopie, *f*. ~ *rod*, baguette divinatoire, *f*.

doze, *v.i*, sommeiller, s'assoupir. *to have a* ~, faire un somme.

dozen, *n*, douzaine, *f*. *by the* ~, à la d.

drab, *a*, gris brun; terne.

drachm, *n*, (*apothecaries' measure*) = 3.552 milliliters; (*a—s' weight*) = 3.888 grams.

drachma, *n*, drachme, *f*.

draft, *n*, vent, courant d'air; vent coulis; appel d'air; aérage; tirage; tirant d'eau; trait, coup; breuvage, *m*; potion, *f*; coup de filet, *m*, pêche, prise, *f*; tracé, plan, *m*, (*outline*) projet, ébauche, *f*; (*Mil.*) conscription, *f*. ~ *animal*, animal de trait, *m*. ~ *beer*, bière au tonneau; b. à la pompe, *f*. ~ *strip*, [bourrelet, *dit*] brisebise, *m*. ¶ *v.t*, ébaucher, tracer; (*writings*) minuter. **draftsman**, *n*, dessinateur, traceur; (*writings*) rédacteur, *m*. **drafty**, *a*, exposé aux courants d'air.

draftee, *n*, conscrit, *m*.

drag, *n*, drague, *f*; sabot [d'enrayage]; tirage, *m*; résistance, *f*. ~*net*, traîneau, *m*, drague, *f*. ¶ *v.t*, traîner; arracher; (*wheel*) enrayer; (*pond*) draguer, pêcher; (*anchor*) chasser; (*v.i.*) se traîner; languir; chasser. ~ *about*, *v.t*, trimbaler.

draggle, *v.t. & i*, traîner.

dragon, *n*, dragon, *m*. ~*fly*, libellule, demoiselle, *f*. ~*'s blood*, sang-[de]-dragon, *m*.

dragoon, *n*, dragon, *m*. ¶ ~ *into*, forcer à embrasser.

drain, *n*, drain, *m*; tranchée, *f*; égout; (*demand*) drainage, *m*. ~*pipe*, tuyau de drainage; drain, *m*. ¶ *v.t*, drainer; assécher; dessécher, saigner; épuiser; [faire] égoutter, faire écouler; purger. ~ [*away*], s'écouler; s'égoutter. ~*age*, *n*, drainage, assèchement, dessèchement, épuisement, écoulement, *m*; purge, *f*; (*surplus water*) égout, *m*. ~*er*, *n*. & ~*ing rack*, égouttoir, *m*.

drake, *n*, canard, *m*.

dram, *n*, (*avoirdupois*) = 1.772 grams; (*draft*) goutte, *f*.

drama, n, drame, m. the ~, le
théâtre. **dramatic**†, a, dramatique; théâtral. *dramatis personae,* personnages, m.pl, rôle
scénique, m. **dramatist, dramaturge,** n, auteur dramatique, dramatiste, m, dramaturge, m,f.
dramatize, v.t, dramatiser.

drape, v.t, draper; tendre. **draper,**
n, (cloth) drapier; (general)
marchand de nouveautés, m. ~y,
n, draperie, f; nouveautés, f.pl.

drastic, a, drastique, extrême.

draw, n, tirage, m; loterie, f;
attrait, m, attraction, f; appât,
m; (game) partie nulle, f, match
nul, refait, m.

draw, v.t.ir, tirer; retirer; attirer;
traîner; entraîner; remorquer;
(Min.) remonter; (metal) étirer;
arracher; extraire; puiser; aspirer; (so much water—ship) caler;
dessiner; tracer; (wages) toucher;
(fowl) vider; (v.i.ir.) tirer; (tea)
[s']infuser. ~ [a game], faire
match nul, f. partie nulle. ~
aside, tirer à l'écart. ~ back,
reculer; (curtains) ouvrir. ~
down, faire descendre, baisser.
~ in (days), [se] raccourcir. ~
near, approcher. ~ off, tirer;
soutirer. ~ on, mettre à contribution. ~ out (days), croître. ~
up, (writing) dresser, rédiger,
formuler; (carriage) s'arrêter.

drawback, n, désavantage, inconvénient, m.

drawbridge, n, pont levant;
pont à bascule; (Hist.) pont-
levis, m.

drawee, n, tiré, payeur, m.
drawer, n, tireur, euse; (of bill,
check) tireur, souscripteur, m;
(receptacle) tiroir; carton, m;
(pl., chest) commode, f; (pl.,
dress) caleçon, m.

drawing, n, dessin; (lottery)
tirage, m. ~ board, planche à
dessin, f. ~ knife, plane, f. ~
pen, tire-ligne, m. ~ room,
[grand] salon, m.

drawl, v.t, traîner.

drawn: ~ battle, bataille indécise, f. ~ face, visage tiré, v.
hagard, m. ~ game, partie nulle,
p. indécise, f. remise, f. ~ number, numéro sortant, m. with ~
sword, sabre au clair.

dray, n, haquet, m. ~horse, cheval de h., m.

dread, a, redouté. ¶ n, terreur,
crainte; phobie, f. ¶ v.t, redouter,

craindre. ~ful†, a, terrible,
épouvantable, affreux. **dreadnought** (Nav.) n, dreadnought,
m; (cloth) ratine, f.

dream, n, rêve, songe, m; rêverie,
f. ¶ v.i. & t. ir, rêver, songer.
~ of, rêver. ~er, n, rêveur, euse;
songe-creux, m. ~y, a, rêveur,
songeur.

drear[y], a, triste, morne. **dreari-
ness,** n, tristesse, f, aspect morne,
m.

dredge, n, drague, f. ¶ v.t, draguer; (sprinkle) saupoudrer.
dredger, n, dragueur; saupoudroir, m. **dredging,** n, dragage, m.

dregs, n.pl, lie, f.

drench, v.t, tremper; saucer;
abreuver. ~ing rain, pluie battante, f.

Dresden, n, Dresde, f. ~ china,
porcelaine de Saxe, f, saxe, m.

dress, n, habillement; entretien;
costume, m; robe; mise; toilette;
tenue; parure, f; chiffons, m.pl.
~ circle, premières [galeries] f.pl,
[premier] balcon, m. ~ coat,
habit de soirée, m. ~maker, couturière; entrepreneuse de confection, f. ~making, confections
pour dames, f.pl. ~ rehearsal,
avant-première, répétition générale, f. ~ shirt, chemise de soirée,
f. ¶ v.t, habiller, [re]vêtir; (in
fancy dress) costumer; orner,
parer; (ship with flags) pavoiser;
(wound) panser; (food) apprêter; (salad) assaisonner; (materials) dresser, tailler, corroyer;
(Mil.) aligner. ~ [oneself],
s'habiller, se mettre, se vêtir. ~
for dinner, se mettre en habit
pour dîner. ~ the window(s),
faire l'étalage, m. **dressing,** n, habillement, m; toilette, f; (of wound)
pansement; (on wound) appareil;
(food) apprêt, m; (meat) parure,
f; (salad) assaisonnement, m. ~
gown, robe de chambre, f, peignoir, saut de lit, m. ~ room,
cabinet de toilette, m; (Theat.)
loge, f. ~ table, [table de] toilette, coiffeuse, f.

dribble, n, goutte; (slaver) bave,
f. ¶ v.i, dégoutter; baver; (v.t.,
Foot.) dribbler. **dribbling** (Foot.)
n, dribbling, m. in driblets, par
parcelles.

dried, p.a, séché; (raisins, fruits,
fish, etc.) sec; (apples, etc., in
rings) tapé. **drier,** n, séchoir;
(s. or pl, for paint) siccatif, m.

drift, n, poussée, tendance, portée,

f; laisser-faire, *m*, inaction; déviation, *f*; (*snow*) amas, *m*; (*Naut.* & *fig.*) dérive; (*Min.*) galerie, *f*; (*Geol.*) apport[s] *m.* [*pl.*]. ~*wood*, bois flotté, *m.* ¶ *v.t*, charrier, entraîner, apporter; chasser; amonceler; (*Mech.*) brocher; (*v.i.*) chasser; (*Naut.*) dériver, aller en dérive; s'amonceler. ~**er** (*boat*) *n*, cordier, *m.*

drill, *n*, foret, *m*, mèche; (*Min.*, *etc.*) perforatrice, foreuse, perceuse, sonde, *f*; (*furrow*) sillon; (*Agric. mach.*) semoir; (*Mil.*) exercice, *m*, école, *f*; (*fabric*) coutil, *m.* ~ *ground*, champ de manœuvres, *m*, place d'armes, *f.* ~[*holder*], porte-foret, porte-mèche, *m.* ~ *sergeant*, [sergent] instructeur, *m.* ¶ *v.t*, percer, forer, perforer; (*Mil.*) exercer, faire faire l'exercice à; (*v.i.*) faire l'exercice. **drilling**, *n*, perçage, percement, *m*, perforation, *f*; forage, sondage, *m*; (*Mil.*) exercice, *m.* ~ *machine*, machine à percer, perceuse; foreuse, *f.*

drink, *n*, boisson; consommation, *f*; breuvage, *m*; liqueur, *f.* ~ *to have a* ~, boire un coup. ¶ *v.t.* & *i. ir*, boire; consommer. ~**able**, *a*, buvable, potable. ~**er**, *n*, buveur, euse. ~**ing**, *att*: ~ *fountain*, fontaine publique, *f.* ~ *song*, chanson à boire, c. bachique, *f*, air à boire, *m.* ~ *straw*, chalumeau, *m.* ~ *trough*, abreuvoir, *m.* ~ *water*, eau potable, *f.*

drip, *n*, goutte, *f.* ~[*stone*], larmier, *m.* ¶ *v.i*, [dé]goutter, découler, pleurer, ruisseler. **dripping**, *n*, graisse de rôti, *f.* ~ *pan*, lèchefrite, *f.* ~ *wet*, tout trempé, saucé.

drive, *n*, promenade; avenue, allée; initiative; (*Hunt.*) battue; (*Mach.*) commande, transmission; (*golf*) crossée, *f*; (*Ten.*) drive, *m*; (*Min.*) galerie, *f.* ¶ *v.t.ir*, chasser, pousser, forcer; (*horse*, *car*) conduire, mener; (*golf*) driver; (*Ten.*) chasser; (*Mach.*) actionner, commander; (*Min.*) chasser, percer [en direction]; (*nail*) enfoncer; forcer, contraindre; faire; (*one mad*) rendre; (*v.i.ir.*) aller (*ou* se promener) en voiture, rouler. ~ *ashore* (ship), dériver à la côte. ~ *away*, chasser. ~ *back*, refouler. ~ *into a corner*, acculer, rencogner. ~ *out*, ~ *off*, chasser, débusquer. ~ *slowly* (traffic

sign), au pas. *what are you* ~*ing at?* où voulez-vous en venir?

drivel, *n*, bave, *f.* ¶ *v.i*, baver; (*fig.*) radoter.

driver, *n*, conducteur; cocher; chauffeur; (*Rly*) mécanicien, *m*; (*golf*) grand-crosse, *f.* ~'s *license*, permis de conduire [les automobiles] *m.* **driving**, *n*, conduite; commande, transmission, *f*; serrage; percement; (*nails*, *piles*) enfoncement; (*piles*) battage, *m.* ~ *iron* (*golf*), grand-fer, *m.* ~ *rain*, pluie battante, *f.* ~ *shaft*, arbre moteur, arbre de couche, *m.*

drizzle, *n*, bruine, *f.* ¶ *v.imp*, bruiner.

droll, *a*, drôle, cocasse, plaisant. ~**ery**, *n*, drôlerie, *f.* **drolly**, *ad*, drôlement.

dromedary, *n*, dromadaire, *m.*

drone, *n*, ronron; (*Mus.*) bourdon, *m.* ~ [*bee*], [faux] bourdon, *m.* ¶ *v.i*, ronronner, bourdonner; (*v.t.*) psalmodier.

droop, *v.i*, pendre, traîner; (*wilt*) s'étioler. ~**ing**, *p.a*, pendant, tombant. ~ *looks*, airs penchés, *m.pl.* ~ *spirits*, forces défaillantes, *f.pl.*

drop, *n*, goutte; larme; chute; baisse; pastille, *f*; pendant, *m*; pendeloque, *f.* ~ *curtain*, rideau, *m.* ~-*forged*, estampé. ¶ *v.t*, laisser tomber goutte à goutte; laisser tomber, lâcher; lancer; (*letter in mail*) jeter; (*a line*) envoyer; (*a stitch*) sauter; (*her young*) mettre bas; (*v.i.*) tomber. *dropped stitch* (*Knit.*), manque, *m*, maille échappée, *m.* perdue, *f.* **dropper**, *n*, compte-gouttes, *m.* **droppings** (*dung*) *n.pl*, fiente, crotte, *f.*

dropsical, *a*, hydropique. **dropsy**, *n*, hydropisie, *f.*

dross, *n*, écume, crasse, scorie, chiasse, *f.*

drought, *n*, sécheresse; disette d'eau, *f.*

drove, *n*, troupeau, *m.* **drover**, *n*, conducteur [de bestiaux], toucheur, *m.*

drown, *v.t*, noyer; (*sounds*) couvrir; (*v.i.*) boire. ~ *oneself*, se noyer. ~**ing**, *n*, submersion; (*fatality*) noyade, *f.* *a* ~ *man*, un noyé.

drowse, *v.i*, sommeiller; somnoler.

drowsiness, *n*, assoupissement,

m. **drowsy**, *a,* endormi, ensommeillé. *to make* ~, assoupir.

drub, *v.t,* [b]rosser, frotter, étriller. **drubbing**, *n,* [b]rossée, frottée, peignée, volée de coups, *f.*

drudge, *n,* souffre-douleur, cheval de bât, pâtiras, *m.* ¶ *v.i,* trimer. ~**ry**, *n,* besognes fastidieuses, *f.pl,* corvée, *f,* collier de misère, *m.*

drug, *n,* drogue, *f;* stupéfiant, narcotique, *m.* ~ *traffic,* trafic des stupéfiants, *m.* ~ *store,* pharmacie, droguerie, *f.* ¶ *v.t,* narcotiser.

drugget, *n,* droguet, *m.*

druggist, *n,* pharmacien; (*wholesale*) droguiste, *m.*

Druid, *n,* druide, *m.*

drum, *n,* tambour, *m,* caisse, *f;* (*ear*) tympan; cylindre, barillet; tonneau, fût, *m.* ~*s & bugles* (*Mil. band*), clique, *f.* ~**head,** peau de tambour, *f.* ~**head courtmartial,** cour martiale, *f.* ~ *major,* tambour-major, *m.* ~**stick,** baguette de tambour, *f;* (*fowl*) pilon, *m.* ¶ *v.i,* tambouriner. ~ *into,* seriner à. **drummer**, *n,* tambour, *m.*

drunk, *a,* ivre, soûl. *to get* ~, s'enivrer. ~**ard,** *n,* ivrogne, *m.* ~**en,** *a,* ivrogne. ~ *bout,* débauche de boisson, ribote, *f.* ~ *brawl,* querelle d'ivrognes, *f.* ~**enness,** *n,* ébriété ivresse; (*habitual*) ivrognerie, *f.*

dry, *a,* sec; à sec; desséché; tari. ~*-clean,* nettoyer à sec. ~ *dock,* cale sèche, *f,* bassin [à] sec, *m,* forme de radoub, *f.* ~ *fly fishing,* pêche à la mouche sèche, *f.* ~ *measure,* mesure de capacité pour les matières sèches, *f.* ~ *nurse,* nourrice sèche, *f.* ¶ *v.t. & i,* sécher; assécher. ~ *up,* tarir, dessécher.

dryad, *n,* dryade, *f.*

drying, *n,* séchage; assèchement, *m.* ~ *room,* séchoir, *m.* **dryly**, *ad,* (*answer coldly*) sèchement, sec. **dryness**, *n,* sécheresse, aridité, *f.*

dual, *a,* double.

dub, *v.t,* (*knight*) armer; (*nickname*) baptiser; (*movies*) doubler.

dubious†, *a,* douteux, incertain; équivoque; interlope.

ducal, *a,* ducal. **duchess**, *n,* duchesse, *f.* **duchy**, *n,* duché, *m.*

duck, *n,* canard, *m,* cane, *f,* barboteur; (*dip*) plongeon; (*cloth*) coutil, *m.* ~ *& drake* (game), ricochets, *m.pl.* ~ *decoy* & ~

pond, canardière, *f.* ~*'s egg,* œuf de cane, *m.* ~*weed,* lentille d'eau, l. de marais, *f.* ¶ *v.t,* plonger; (*v.i.*) faire le plongeon, éviter de la tête, faire une courbette. ~**ling,** *n,* canneton, *m,* canette, *f.*

duct, *n,* canal, conduit, *m,* voie, *f.* **ductile**, *a,* (*metals*) ductile; (*pers.*) docile, souple.

dudgeon (**in**), en haine.

due, *a,* dû; échu; régulier; requis, voulu, utile. *the train is* ~ *at . . .,* le train arrive (*ou* doit arriver) à . . . *in* ~ *course,* en temps & lieu. ~ *date,* échéance, *f.* ¶ *ad,* droit; directement. ¶ *n,* dû, *m;* (*duty*) droit, *m;* taxe, *f.*

duel, *n,* duel, *m,* rencontre, *f.* **duellist**, *n,* duelliste, *m.*

duenna, *n,* duègne, *f.*

duet, *n,* duo, *m.*

duffer, *n,* cancre, *m,* ganache, *f,* imbécile, *m,f;* (*at a game*) mazette, *f.*

dug, *n,* trayon, pis, *m,* tétine, *f.*

dugout, *n,* pirogue; cagna, *f;* abri [de bombardement] *m.*

duke, *n,* duc, *m.* ~**dom,** *n,* duché, *m.*

dulcet, *a,* doux.

dulcimer, *n,* tympanon, *m.*

dull, *a,* lourd; obtus; assoupissant, assommant, fastidieux; fade; maussade; inactif; atone; plat; terne; mat; sombre; gris; sourd; émoussé. ¶ *v.t,* ternir; émousser; hébéter. ~**ard,** *n,* lourdaud, e. ~**ness,** *n,* pesanteur, *f,* appesantissement; ennui, *m;* inactivité, atonie; platitude; ternissure; matité, *f.*

duly, *ad,* dûment; régulièrement; bien. ~ *authorized representative,* fondé de pouvoir(s) *m.*

dumb†, *a,* muet. ~ *animals,* animaux, *m. pl.* ~**bell,** haltère, *m.* ~ *show,* jeu muet, *m,* pantomime, *f.*

dumbfound, *v.t,* ébahir, atterrer.

dumbness, *n,* mutisme, *m.*

dummy, *a,* feint; faux. ~ *book* (for book-shelf), livre feint, *m.* ¶ *n,* prête-nom; mannequin, *m;* poupée; fausse boîte; (*publisher's blank book*) maquette, *f;* (*Mil.*) simulacre; (*cards*) mort, *m.*

dump, *n,* chantier de dépôt, *m. to be in the* ~*s,* avoir le spleen. ¶ *v.t,* culbuter, chavirer. ~**ing** (*economy*) *n,* dumping, *m.* ~**y,** *a,* trapu, boulot, courtaud.

dun, *a,* fauve gris. ¶ *n,* fauve gris;

créancier importun; agent de recouvrements, *m.* ¶ *v.t*, importuner, pourchasser, assiéger, persécuter.

dunce, *n*, ignorant, e, cancre, âne, *m*. ~ *cap*, bonnet d'âne, *m*.

dunderhead, *n*, imbécile, *m*.

dune, *n*, dune, *f*.

dung, *n*, fiente, *f*; crottin, *m*; bouse; crotte, *f*. ~ *beetle*, escarbot, *m*. ~*hill*, fumier; *(fig.)* pailler, *m*. ¶ *v.t*, fumer.

dungeon, *n*, cachot, *m*.

dunk, *v.t*, tremper.

Dunkirk, *n*, Dunkerque, *m*.

dunnage, *n*, fardage, grenier, chantier [d'arrimage] *m*.

dupe, *n*, dupe, *f*. ¶ *v.t*, duper, blouser, piper. ~**ry**, *n*, duperie, *f*.

duplicate, *a*, double; *(tools, parts)* de rechange. ¶ *n*, double, duplicata, *m*, ampliation; pièce de rechange; répétition, *f*. ¶ *v.t*, faire le double de; *(train)* dédoubler. **duplication**, *n*, double emploi, *m*. **duplicity**, *n*, duplicité, *f*.

durable, *a*, durable. **duration**, *n*, durée, *f*.

duress, *n*, violence, *f*.

during, *pr*, pendant, durant, par, dans.

dusk, *n*, la brune. *at* ~, sur *(ou* à*)* la brune, entre chien & loup. ~**y**, *a*, brun.

dust, *n*, poussière, *f*; poussier, *m*; poudre, *f*; cendres; ordures, *f.pl*. ~*coat*, cache-poussière, *m*. ~ *cover*, couvre-livre, *m*. ~*pan*, pelle à poussière, *f*. ~ *sheet*, housse, *f*. *saw* ~, sciure, *f*. ¶ *v.t*, épousseter; housser; *(sprinkle)* saupoudrer. ~**er**, *n*, torchon, *m*. ~**y**, *a*, poussiéreux, poudreux.

Dutch, *a*, hollandais, de Hollande, néerlandais. ~ *cheese*, fromage de Hollande, *m*. ~ *courage*, courage arrosé, *m*. ~*man*, ~*woman*, Hollandais, e, Néerlandais, e. ~ *oven*, rôtissoire, *f*. ¶ *(language)* n, le hollandais.

dutiable, *a*, passible de droits, sujet à des droits, imposable. **dutiful**† & **duteous**†, *a*, obéissant, soumis, respectueux. **duty**, *n*, devoir, *m*; charge, fonction, *f*, office; service; droit, *m*, taxe, *f*, impôt, *m*, surtaxe, *f*. *on* ~, de service, de garde. ~*-free*, *a*, exempte d'impôt.

dwarf, *n*. & *a*, nain, e. ¶ *v.t*, rapetisser.

dwell, *v.i.ir*, habiter, demeurer; insister, peser. ~**er**, *n*, habitant, e. ~**ing**, *n*, habitation, demeure, *f*, logis, *m*. ~ *house*, maison d'habitation, *f*.

dwindle, *v.i*, dépérir. **dwindling**, *n*. dépérissement, *m*.

dye, *n*, teinture, *f*. ~ *stuffs*, matières tinctoriales, *f.pl. of the deepest* ~ *(fig.)*, de la plus belle eau, fieffé. ¶ *v.t*, teindre. ~**ing**, *n*, teinture; teinturerie, *f*. **dyer** [& **cleaner**], *n*, teinturier, ère.

dying, *a*, mourant; à l'agonie, agonisant; moribond. *the* ~, les mourants, *m.pl. to be* ~, *[se]* mourir. ~ *words*, dernières paroles, *f.pl*.

dynamic(al), *a*, dynamique. **dynamics**, *n*, dynamique, *f*.

dynamite, *n*, dynamite, *f*.

dynamo, *n*, dynamo, *f*.

dynasty, *n*, dynastie, *f*.

dysentery, *n*, dysenterie, *f*.

dyspepsia, *n*, dyspepsie, *f*.

E

E *(Mus.) letter*, mi, *m*.

each, *a*. & *pn*, chaque; chacun, e; l'un, l'une, [la] pièce. ~ *one*, chacun, e. ~ *other*, l'un (l'une) l'autre, les uns (les unes) les autres; se, nous, vous.

eager, *a*, ardent, assoiffé, acharné, avide, empressé. *to be* ~ *for*, ambitionner. ~**ly**, *ad*, ardemment, avidement. ~**ness**, *n*, ardeur, avidité, *f*, empressement, *m*.

eagle, *n*, *(bird)* aigle, *m,f*; *(standard)* aigle, *f*. **eaglet**, *n*, aiglon, ne.

ear, *n*, oreille, *f*. ~*ache*, douleur d'oreille, otalgie, *f*. ~*drum*, membrane du tympan, *f*, tympan, *m*. ~ *flap*, oreillon, *m*. ~*mark*, affecter. ~*-phones*, casque, *m*. ~*ring*, boucle [d'oreille] *f*. ~ *trumpet*, cornet acoustique, *m*.

earliness, *n*, heure peu avancée; précocité, *f*. **early**, *a*, peu avancé; prématuré; avancé; précoce; hâtif; premier; *(youth)* tendre; ancien. ~ *fruits*, ~ *vegetables*, primeurs, *f.pl. to be [up]* ~, *to be an* ~ *riser*, être matinal, être matineux. ¶ *ad*, de bonne heure, tôt, matin.

earn, *v.t*, gagner, acquérir; mériter.

earnest, *a*, sérieux; ardent, fervent. ¶ *n*, gage; *(fig.)* avant-goût, *m.* ~**ly,** *ad,* sérieusement; ardemment; instamment. ~**ness,** *n,* ardeur, ferveur, instance, *f.*

earning, *n,* acquisition, *f;* (*pl.*) gain[s] *m.*[*pl.*].

earth, *n,* terre, *f;* sol; (*of fox*) terrier, *m,* tanière, *f.* ~**quake,** tremblement de t., *m.* ~**work,** terrassement, *m.* ¶ *v.t,* (*Hort.*) butter, chausser, terrer. ~**en,** *a,* de terre. ~**enware,** *n,* poterie [de terre], faïence, *f.* ~**ly,** *a,* terrestre. ~**y,** *a,* terreux.

earwig, *n,* perce-oreille, *m.*

ease, *n,* aise, aisance; facilité, *f;* repos; soulagement, *m.* ¶ *v.t,* adoucir; soulager; décharger; (*v.i.*) mollir.

easel, *n,* chevalet, *m.*

easement, *n,* soulagement, *m.*

easily, *ad,* aisément, facilement; doucement. not ~, malaisément.

east, *n,* est; (le) levant; orient, *m.* from ~ to west, du levant au couchant. the E~ (*Geog.*), l' Orient. ¶ *a,* d'est, de l'est; oriental. Near ~, Proche-Orient. Far ~, Extrême-Orient.

Easter, *n,* Pâques, *m.s.* ~ egg, œuf de P., *m.*

easterly, *a,* d'est. **eastern,** *a,* de l'est; oriental; (*question, etc.*) d'Orient.

easy, *a,* facile, aisé; doux; commode; coulant; tranquille; désinvolte. ~ chair, fauteuil, *m.* ~going person, personne commode, *f,* sans-souci, *m,f.* by ~ stages, à petites journées. ~ to get on with (*pers.*), d'un commerce agréable. not ~, malaisé.

eat, *v.t. & i. ir,* manger. ~ away, ~ into, ronger. ~ up, dévorer. ~**able,** *a,* mangeable. ~**ables,** *n.pl,* comestibles, *m.pl.* ~**er,** *n,* mangeur, euse. ~**ing:** ~ apples, pommes à couteau, *f.pl.*

eaves, *n.pl,* avant-toit, *m.* **eavesdrop,** *v.i,* écouter aux portes. **eavesdropper,** *n,* écouteur (euse) aux portes.

ebb, *n,* jusant, reflux, *m.* ~ tide, courant de jusant, *m.* ¶ *v.i,* refluer, refouler.

ebonite, *n,* ébonite, vulcanite, *f.*

ebony *n,* ébène, *f;* (*tree*) ébénier, *m.*

ebullition, *n,* ébullition, *f.*

eccentric, *a. & (Mech.) n,* excentrique, *a. & m.* ~**ity,** *n,* excentricité, *f.*

Ecclesiastes, *n,* l'Ecclésiaste, *m.* **ecclesiastic,** *n. & ~al†, a,* ecclé-

siastique, *m. & a.* **Ecclesiasticus,** *n,* l'Ecclésiastique, *m.*

echo, *n,* écho, *m.* ¶ *v.i,* faire écho, retentir; (*v.t.*) se faire l'écho de.

eclectic, *a,* éclectique. **eclecticism,** *n,* éclectisme, *m.*

eclipse, *n,* éclipse; défaillance, *f.* ¶ *v.t,* éclipser. to become ~d, s'éclipser. **ecliptic,** *a. & n,* écliptique, *a. & f.*

economic, *a,* économique. ~(**al**)†, *a,* économique; économe, ménager. ~**s,** *n.pl,* science économique, *f.* **economist,** *n,* économiste, *m.* **economize,** *v.t. & i,* économiser, ménager. **economy,** *n,* économie, *f.*

ecstasy, *n,* extase, *f.* to go into ecstasies, s'extasier. **ecstatic,** *a,* extatique.

Ecuador, *n,* l'Équateur, *m.*

eczema, *n,* eczéma, *m.*

eddy, *n,* remous, tournant, *m.* ¶ *v.i,* tourbillonner.

edelweiss, *n,* édelweiss, *m.*

Eden (*fig.*) *n,* éden, *m.* [the Garden of] ~, l'Eden, le paradis [terrestre].

edge, *n,* bord, rebord, *m,* bordure; lisière; arête, *f;* tranche, *f;* tranchant, coupant, taillant, *m.* ~**ways,** ~**wise,** *ad.* or on ~, de chant. ¶ *v.t,* border. **edging,** *n,* bordure, *f,* bord, *m.* ~ knife, hache coupe-gazon, *f.*

edible, *a,* comestible.

edict, *n.* édit, *m.*

edifice, *n,* édifice, *m.* **edify,** *v.t,* édifier.

Edinburgh, *n,* Édimbourg, *m.*

edit, *v.t,* éditer, rédiger. ~**ion,** *n,* édition, *f.* **editor,** *n,* rédacteur (trice) en chef. **editorial,** *a,* de la rédaction; (*n.*) article, *m,* (*ou* note, *f.*) [émanant] de la rédaction. ~ staff, rédaction, *f.*

educate, *v.t,* élever, instruire, éduquer. **education,** *n,* éducation, *f;* enseignement, *m;* instruction, *f.* ~**al,** *a,* d'éducation; scolaire; (*book*) classique. ~ establishment, maison d'éducation, *f.* **educator,** *n,* éducateur, trice.

educe, *v.t,* tirer; dégager.

eel, *n,* anguille, *f.* ~ pot, nasse, *f.*

eerie, -y, *a,* fantastique.

efface, *v.t,* effacer. ~**able,** *a,* effaçable.

effect, *n,* effet, *m;* suite; action, *f;* (*pl.*) effets, *m.pl.* ¶ *v.t,* effectuer, faire, opérer; contracter. ~**ive†,** *a,* effectif; utile. ¶ *n,* effectif, *m.*

effectual†, *a*, efficace.

effeminacy, *n*, caractère efféminé, *m*. effeminate, *a*, efféminé. to [make] ~, efféminer. ~ [man], *n*, efféminé, *m*, femmelette, *f*.

effervesce, *v.i*, être en effervescence; faire e.; mousser. effervescence, -ency, *n*, effervescence, *f*. effervescent, *a*, effervescent. effervescing (*drink*) *p.a*, gazeux.

effete, *a*, épuisé.

efficacious†, *a*, efficace.

efficiency, *n*, efficacité, *f*; rendement, *m*. efficient†, *a*, efficace; capable.

effigy, *n*, effigie, *f*.

effloresce, *v.i*, [s']effleurir. efflorescence, *n*, efflorescence, *f*.

effluence, *n*, émanation, *f*.

effluvium, *n*, effluve, *m*.

efflux, *n*, dépense; émanation, *f*.

effort, *n*, effort, *m*.

effrontery, *n*, effronterie, *f*.

effulgence, *n*, rayonnement, *m*.

effusion, *n*, effusion, *f*, épanchement, *m*. effusive, *a*, expansif. ~ness, *n*, effusion, *f*.

eft, *n*, triton, *m*, salamandre aquatique, *f*.

egg, *n*, œuf, *m*; (*pl.*, silkworm) graine, *f*. ~ cup, coquetier, *m*. ~plant, aubergine, *f*. ~shell, coquille d'œuf, *f*. boiled ~, œuf à la coque. fried ~, œuf sur le plat. scrambled ~s, œufs brouillés. ~ on, *v.t*, pousser.

eglantine, *n*, églantine odorante, *f*.

ego, *n*, moi, *m*. egoism, *n*, égoïsme, *m*. egoist, *n*, égoïste, *m,f*. egoistic(al), *a*, égoïste. egotism, *n*, égotisme, *m*. egotist, *n*, égotiste, *m,f*. egotistic(al), *a*, égotiste.

egregious, *a*, insigne, énorme, grossier, lourd; fieffé.

egress, *n*, sortie, issue, *f*.

egret (*bird & tuft*) *n*, aigrette, *f*.

Egypt, *n*, l'Égypte, *f*. Egyptian, *a*, égyptien. ¶ *n*, Égyptien, ne. Egyptologist, *n*, égyptologue, *m*. Egyptology, *n*, égyptologie, *f*.

eh, *i*, eh! hein!

eider [duck], *n*, eider, *m*. ~down, édredon, *m*.

eight, *a. & n*, huit, *a. & m*. eighteen, *a. & n*, dix-huit, *a. & m*. 18-hole course, parcours (*ou* golf) de 18 trous, *m*. eighteenth, *a. & n*, dix-huitième, *a. & m,f*; dix-huit, *m*. eighth, *a. & n*, huitième, *a. & m,f*; huit, *m*. ~ly, *ad*, hui-

tièmement. eightieth, *a. & n*, quatre-vingtième, *a. & m,f*. eighty, *a. & n*, quatre-vingts, quatre-vingt, *a. & m*. 81, etc, quatre-vingt-un, etc.

either, *pn*, l'un (l'une) ou l'autre; l'un d'eux, l'une d'elles; un, une; chaque. ¶ *c*, ou; soit. ¶ *ad*, non plus. nor I ~, ni moi n. p.

ejaculate, *v.t. & abs*, lancer; faire; (*fluid*) éjaculer. ejaculation, *n*, interjection, exclamation; (*fluid*) éjaculation, *f*.

eject, *v.t*, expulser. ~ion, *n*, expulsion, *f*.

eke out, *v.t*, allonger; suppléer.

elaborate, *a*, travaillé; étudié; recherché. ¶ *v.t*, élaborer; travailler.

elapse, *v.i*, s'écouler, [se] passer.

elastic, *a*, élastique. ¶ *n*, élastique, caoutchouc, *m*. ~ band, bande en caoutchouc, *f*. ~ity, *n*, élasticité, *f*, ressort, *m*.

elate, *v.t*, enivrer; enorgueillir.

Elba (the Island of), l'île d'Elbe, *f*.

Elbe (the) (*river*), l'Elbe, *m*.

elbow, *n*, coude, *m*. to rest on one's ~(s), s'accouder. ~ grease (*fig.*), huile de coude, *f*. ~ room, coudées franches, *f.pl*. ¶ *v.t*, coudoyer. to ~ one's way, jouer des coudes.

elder, *a*, aîné, plus âgé. ¶ *n*, aîné, e; (*Eccl.*) ancien; (*Bot.*) sureau, *m*. our ~s, nos aînés. ~ berry, baie de sureau, *f*. ~ly, *a*, d'un certain âge. eldest, *n. & a*, aîné, e.

El Dorado, *n*, eldorado, *m*.

elect, *v.t*, élire, nommer. the ~ (*Relig.*), les élus, *m.pl*. ~ed member, élu, e. election, *n*, élection, *f*. electioneering, *n*, manœuvres électorales, *f.pl*. elector, *n*, électeur, trice. ~ate, *n*, corps électoral, *m*.

electric, *a*, électrique ~ eel, gymnote, *m*. ~ sign, enseigne (*ou* affiche) lumineuse, *f*. ~al, *a*, électrique. ~ engineer, ingénieur électricien, *m*. ~ally, *ad*, par l'électricité. ~ian, *n*, électricien, *m*. ~ity, *n*, électricité, *f*. electrify, *v.t*, électriser; (*Rly, etc.*) électrifier. electrize, *v.t*, électriser. electrocute, *v.t*, électrocuter. electrode, *n*, électrode, *f*. electrolysis, *n*, électrolyse, *f*. electromagnet, *n*, électroaimant, *m*. electron, *n*, électron, *m*. electroplate, *n*, plaqué, *m*. ¶ *v.t*, argenter. **electrotype** (*printing*) *n*, galvano, *m*.

elegance, *n*, élégance, *f*. **elegant**, *a*, élégant. ~**ly**, *ad*, élégamment.

elegy, *n*, élégie, *f*.

element, *n*, élément; facteur; (*Chem.*) corps simple; (*voltaic*) couple, *m*. ~**ary**, *a*, élémentaire; (*Sch.*) primaire.

elephant, *n*, éléphant, *m*. ~[*ine person*], mastodonte, *m*.

elevate, *v.t*, élever; [re]monter. **elevation**, *n*, élévation; altitude, hauteur, *f*. **elevator**, *n*, ascenseur; (*Surg.*) élévatoire, *m*; (*in shoe*) hausse, *f*.

eleven, *a. & n*, onze, *a. & m*. **eleventh**†, *a. & n*, onzième, *a. & m,f*; onze, *m*.

elf, *n*, elfe, lutin, *m*. **elfin**, *a*, des elfes. **elfish**, *a*, des elfes; lutin, espiègle.

elicit, *v.t*, tirer, soutirer.

elide, *v.t*, élider.

eligible, *a*, éligible; sortable.

eliminate, *v.t*, éliminer. **elimination**, *n*, élimination, *f*.

elision, *n*, élision, *f*.

elixir, *n*, élixir, *m*.

elk, *n*, élan, *m*.

ellipse & ellipsis, *n*, ellipse, *f*. **elliptic(al)**†, *a*, elliptique.

elm [tree], *n*, orme, ormeau, *m*. ~ grove, ormaie, ormoie, *f*. ~ row, ormille, *f*.

elocution, *n*, élocution; déclamation, *f*.

elongate, *v.t*, allonger.

elope, *v.i*, se faire enlever (*with* = par); s'enfuir. ~**ment**, *n*, enlèvement, *m*, fugue, *f*.

eloquence, *n*, éloquence, *f*. **eloquent**, *a*, éloquent. ~**ly**, *ad*, éloquemment.

else, *ad*, autre; autrement, sinon, encore. *everything* ~, tout le reste. ~**where**, *ad*, autre part, ailleurs.

Elsinore, *n*, Elseneur, *f*.

elucidate, *v.t*, élucider, dégager.

elude, *v.t*, éluder, se soustraire à, se dérober à. **elusive**, *a*, insaisissable; flottant.

Elysian, *a*, élyséen. **Elysium**, *n*, élysée; (*Myth.*) Élysée, *m*.

emaciated, *p.p*, émacié, décharné, étique, hâve.

emanate, *v.i*, émaner.

emancipate, *v.t*, émanciper, affranchir.

emasculate, *v.t*, émasculer.

embalm, *v.t*, embaumer.

embank, *v.t*, remblayer, terrasser,

encaisser. ~**ment**, *n*, remblai, encaissement; quai, *m*; levée, *f*.

embargo, *n*, embargo, *m*.

embark, *v.t*, embarquer. ~**ation**, *n*, embarquement, *m*.

embarrass, *v.t*, embarrasser. ~**ment**, *n*, embarras, *m*.

embassy, *n*, ambassade, *f*.

embattle, *v.t*, ranger en bataille; (*Arch.*) créneler.

embed, *v.t*, encastrer.

embellish, *v.t*, embellir.

ember days, Quatre-Temps, *m. pl*.

embers, *n.pl*, braise, *f*, charbon, *m*; cendre[s] *f.*[*pl.*].

embezzle, *v.t*, détourner. ~**ment**, *n*, détournement, *m*, malversation, *f*; péculat, *m*.

embitter, *v.t*, envenimer, enfieller, aigrir.

emblazon, *v.t*, blasonner.

emblem, *n*, emblème, *m*. ~**atic(al)**, *a*, emblématique.

embodiment, *n*, incarnation, *f*. **embody**, *v.t*, incarner; englober.

embolden, *v.t*, enhardir.

embolism, *n*, embolie, *f*.

emboss, *v.t*, graver en relief; estamper, gaufrer; bosseler. ~*ed stamp*, timbre sec, timbre fixe, *m*.

embrace, *n*, embrassement, *m*, étreinte, *f*. ¶ *v.t*, embrasser.

embrasure, *n*, embrasure, *f*.

embrocation, *n*, embrocation, *f*.

embroider, *v.t*, broder. ~**er**, ~**ess**, *n*, brodeur, euse. ~**y**, *n*, broderie, *f*. ~ *cotton*, coton à broder, *m*. ~ *hoops*, métier à broder, *m*.

embroil, *v.t*, [em]brouiller.

embryo, *n*, embryon, *m*. *in* ~ (*fig.*), en e., en herbe. **embryonic**, *a*, embryonnaire.

emend, *v.t*, corriger. ~**ation**, *n*, correction, *f*.

emerald, *n*, émeraude, *f*.

emerge, *v.i*, émerger, déboucher. **emergence**, *n*, émergence, *f*. **emergency**, *n*, urgence, *f*; événement [inattendu] *m*, occurrence, *f*. ~ *brake*, frein d'urgence, *m*. ~ *exit*, sortie de secours, *f*.

emeritus, *a*, émérite.

emery, *n*, émeri, *m*. ~ *cloth*, toile d'é., *f*.

emetic, *a. & n*, émétique, *a. & m*.

emigrant, *n*, émigrant, e. **emigrate**, *v.i*, émigrer. **emigration**, *n*, émigration, *f*. ~ *officer*, commissaire d'émigration, *m*.

eminence, *n*, éminence, *f*. *His E~* (cardinal), son Éminence, *f*.

eminent, *a,* éminent; notable, considérable. **~ly,** *ad,* éminemment.

emir, *n,* émir, *m.*

emissary, *n,* émissaire, *m.* **emission** *n,* émission, *f.* **emit,** *v.t,* émettre; dégager.

emollient, *a. & n,* émollient, *a. & m.*

emoluments, *n.pl,* émoluments, *m.pl.*

emotion, *n,* émotion, *f,* émoi, *m.* **~al,** *a,* facile à émouvoir.

empanel a jury, former une liste de jurés, former un tableau.

emperor, *n,* empereur, *m.*

emphasis, *n,* emphase; énergie, *f.* **to lay ~ upon** or **emphasize,** *v.t,* appuyer sur, souligner, accentuer, ponctuer. **emphatic†,** *a,* emphatique; énergique.

empire, *n,* empire, *m.*

empiric(al)†, *a,* empirique. **empiricism,** *n,* empirisme, *m.* **empiric[ist],** *n,* empirique, *m.*

employ, *v.t,* employer; se servir de. **he is in my ~,** je l'emploie. **~ee,** *n,* employé, *e.* **~er,** *n,* patron, ne, employeur, euse. **~ment,** *n,* emploi, travail, *m.* **~ agency,** bureau de placement, *m.*

emporium, *n,* entrepôt; grand magasin, *m.*

empower, *v.t,* autoriser, investir du pouvoir.

empress, *n,* impératrice, *f.*

emptiness, *n,* vacuité, *f;* vide, *m;* nullité, *f.* **empty,** *a,* vide; à vide; à blanc; net; désert; creux; vain; en l'air. **~-handed,** les mains vides. **to be ~-headed,** avoir la tête vide. **on an ~ stomach,** à jeun. ¶ *(case, etc.) n,* vide, *m.* ¶ *v.t,* vider, vidanger, épuiser, décharger.

empyrean, *n,* empyrée, *m.*

emulate, *v.t,* rivaliser avec. **emulation,** *n,* émulation, rivalité, *f.* **emulator,** *n,* émule, *m.*

emulsion, *n,* émulsion, *f.*

enable, *v.t,* mettre à même; permettre; *(law)* habiliter.

enact, *v.t,* décréter, édicter. **~ment,** *n,* loi, *f,* décret, *m.*

enamel, *n. & ~ ware,* émail, *m.* ¶ *v.t,* émailler, laquer. **enameling,** *n,* émaillage, *m.*

enamored, *p.p,* épris, amoureux.

encage, *v.t,* encager.

encamp, *v.i. & t,* camper. **~ment,** *n,* campement, *m.*

encase, *v.t,* encaisser, enrober.

encash, *v.t,* encaisser.

encaustic, *a. & n,* encaustique, *a. & f.*

enchain, *v.t,* enchaîner.

enchant, *v.t,* enchanter. **~er,** **~ress,** *n,* enchanteur, eresse. **~ing,** *p.a,* enchanteur. **~ment,** *n,* enchantement, *m.*

encircle, *v.t,* encercler, ceindre, cerner.

enclave, *n,* enclave, *f.*

enclose, *v.t,* enfermer; [en]clore; enceindre; *(in letter)* inclure, joindre. **~d,** *p.p,* ci-inclus, ci-joint. **enclosure,** *n,* enceinte, clôture, *f,* [en]clos, parc, *m; (in letter)* [pièce] annexe, pièce jointe, *f.*

encomium, *n,* panégyrique, éloge, *m.*

encompass, *v.t,* entourer, ceindre.

encore, *i. & n,* bis, *ad. & m.* ¶ *v.t,* bisser.

encounter, *n,* rencontre, *f.* ¶ *v.t,* rencontrer.

encourage, *v.t,* encourager.

encroach on (to), empiéter sur, envahir; anticiper sur. **~ment,** *n,* empiètement, envahissement, *m.*

encumber, *v.t,* embarrasser, encombrer; grever, obérer. **encumbrance,** *n,* embarras, *m;* charge, *f.*

encyclic(al), *a. & n,* encyclique, *a. & f.*

encyclopedia, *n,* encyclopédie, *f.*

end, *n,* fin, *f,* terme, *m;* extrémité; issue, *f;* bout; but, *m.* **no ~ of,** une infinité de. **on ~,** debout; *(hair)* hérissés; *(fig.)* d'arrache-pied. **~ paper,** [feuille de] garde, *f.* ¶ *v.t,* finir, achever, terminer; *(v.i.)* finir, prendre fin; aboutir.

endanger, *v.t,* mettre en danger.

endear, *v.t,* rendre cher. **~ment,** *n,* caresse, *f.*

endeavor, *n,* effort, *m,* tentative, *f.* ¶ *v.i,* s'efforcer, tâcher, travailler.

ending, *n,* fin, *f;* dénouement, *m; (Gram.)* terminaison, désinence, *f.*

endive, *n,* scarole, endive, *f.*

endless, *a. & ~ly,* ad, sans fin.

endorse, *v.t,* endosser; *(fig.)* souscrire à. **~ment,** *n, (bill, check, etc.)* endos, endossement; *(Insce)* avenant, *m.* **endorser,** *n,* endosseur, *m.*

endow, *v.t,* renter, doter; douer,

avantager. **~ment**, *n*, dotation, *f*.

endue, *v.t*, revêtir; douer.

endurable, *a*, supportable. **endurance**, *n*, endurance; résistance, *f*. **~ test**, épreuve d'endurance, *f*, raid, *m*. **endure**, *v.t*, endurer, supporter; (*v.i.*) vivre.

enema, *n*, (*instrument*) irrigateur, *m*; (*action*) lavement, *f*.

enemy, *n. & a*, ennemi, *e*.

energetic†, *a*, énergique. **~s** (*Phys.*) *n.pl*, énergétique, *f*. **energize**, *v.t*, infuser de l'ardeur dans; (*Elec.*) amorcer. **energy**, *n*, énergie; poigne, *f*; travail, *m*.

enervate, *v.t*, énerver, [r]amollir.

enfeeble, *v.t*, affaiblir.

enfilade, *n*, enfilade, *f*. ¶ *v.t*, enfiler.

enfold, *v.t*, envelopper; étreindre.

enforce, *v.t*, imposer; faire valoir; mettre en vigueur, exécuter. **~able**, *a*, exécutoire. **~ment**, *n*, contrainte; exécution, *f*.

enfranchise, *v.t*, affranchir; accorder le droit de vote à.

engage, *v.t*, engager, retenir; embaucher; arrêter; prendre; (*Mech.*) engrener; embrayer; (*v.i.*) s'engager, se mettre; engager le combat. **~ment**, *n*, engagement; (*Mech.*) engrenage, *f*; fiançailles, *f.pl*. **~ ring**, bague de fiançailles, *f*. **engaging**, *p.a*, engageant, attrayant, attachant.

engender, *v.t*, engendrer.

engine, *n*, machine, *f*, moteur, *m*; (*Rly*) locomotive, *f*; (*of war*) engin, *m*. **~ driver**, **~man**, mécanicien, *m*. **engineer**, *n*, ingénieur; (*maker*) ingénieur constructeur; (*ship*) mécanicien; (*Mil.*) officier du génie; soldat du génie, *m*. ¶ *v.t*, provoquer. **engineering**, *n*, l'art (*m*.) (*ou* la science) de l'ingénieur; construction, *f*; génie, *m*. **engineless**, *a*, sans moteur.

England, *n*, l'Angleterre, *f*. **English**, *a*, anglais. the **~ Channel**, la Manche. **~man**, **~woman**, Anglais, e. ¶ (*language*) *n*, l'anglais, *m*.

engrave, *v.t*, graver; buriner. **engraver**, *n*, graveur, *m*. **engraving**, *n*, gravure, estampe, *f*.

engross, *v.t*, absorber; s'emparer de; (*law*) grossoyer. **~ment** (*law*) *n*, grosse, *f*.

engulf, *v.t*, engouffrer, engloutir.

enhance, *v.t*, rehausser; augmenter.

enigma, *n*, énigme, *f*. **enigmatic-(al)**†, *a*, énigmatique.

enjoin, *v.t*, enjoindre.

enjoy, *v.t*, jouir de, savourer, goûter. **~ oneself**, s'amuser, se réjouir. **~able**, *a*, agréable, savoureux. **~ment**, *n*, jouissance, *f*; plaisir, *m*.

enlarge, *v.t*, agrandir, augmenter, élargir. **~ upon**, s'étendre sur. **~ment**, *n*, agrandissement, *m*. **enlarger** (*Phot.*) *n*, agrandisseur, *m*.

enlighten, *v.t*, éclairer, édifier.

enlist, *v.t*, enrôler, engager. **~ment**, *n*, enrôlement, engagement, *m*.

enliven, *v.t*, [r]animer, vivifier, égayer.

enmity, *n*, inimitié, *f*.

ennoble, *v.t*, anoblir; (*fig.*) ennoblir.

enormity, *n*, énormité, *f*. **enormous**, *a*, énorme. **~ly**, *ad*, énormément. **~ness**, *n*, énormité, *f*.

enough, *a*, assez de; assez; suffisant. ¶ *ad*, assez; suffisamment. ¶ *n*, suffisance, *f*, assez, de quoi. to have **~ & to spare**, avoir à revendre.

enquire, *etc*. Same as *inquire*, etc.

enrage, *v.t*, rendre furieux, faire enrager.

enrapture, *v.t*, enchanter, ravir, enthousiasmer.

enrich, *v.t*, enrichir.

enroll, *v.t*, enrôler, immatriculer; embrigader, enrégimenter. **enrollment**, *n*, enrôlement, *m*.

ensconce, *v.t*, camper, nicher.

enshrine, *v.t*, enchâsser.

enshroud, *v.t*, envelopper; voiler.

ensign, *n*, (*banner, flag*) enseigne, *f*; (*Naut.*) pavillon de poupe; (*pers.*) enseigne, *m*.

enslave, *v.t*, asservir, enchaîner.

ensnare, *v.t*, attraper.

ensue, *v.i*, s'ensuivre, résulter. **ensuing**, *p.a*, suivant, subséquent.

ensure, *v.t*, assurer.

entablature, *n*, entablement, *m*.

entail, *v.t*, entraîner; (*law*) substituer.

entangle, *v.t*, empêtrer, emmêler, embarrasser.

enter, *v.t*, entrer dans; pénétrer; engager; (*names, etc.*) inscrire, enregistrer; (*v.i.*) entrer; pénétrer; s'engager. **~ into** (bargain, contract), faire, passer, souscrire, contracter, intervenir dans. **~ X.** (*Theat.*), X. entre [en scène].

enterprise, *n,* entreprise, *f;* esprit entreprenant, *m.* **enterprising,** *a,* entreprenant.

entertain, *v.t,* recevoir, héberger; régaler, fêter; (*abs.*) traiter, représenter; amuser, divertir, défrayer; (*idea*) concevoir, nourrir; accueillir favorablement. ~**ment,** *n,* amusement, divertissement, spectacle, *m.* ~ **tax,** taxe sur les spectacles, *f.*

enthrall, *v.t,* captiver, enchaîner; passionner.

enthrone, *v.t,* introniser. ~**ment,** *n,* intronisation, *f.*

enthusiasm, *n,* enthousiasme, *m.* **enthusiast,** *n,* enthousiaste, *m,f,* fervent, e. ~**ic,** *a,* enthousiaste. ~**ically,** *ad,* avec enthousiasme.

entice, *v.t,* allécher; séduire. ~**ment,** *n,* allèchement, *m,* séduction, *f.* **enticing,** *p.a,* alléchant, acquinant, séduisant.

entire†, *a,* entier, intégral. ~**ty,** *n,* entier, *m;* intégralité, *f.*

entitle, *v.t,* intituler; donner droit à.

entity, *n,* entité, *f.*

entomb, *v.t,* ensevelir.

entomologist, *n,* entomologiste, *m.* **entomology,** *n,* entomologie, *f.*

entr'acte (*Theat.*) *n,* entracte, *m.*

entrails, *n.pl,* entrailles, *f.pl.*

entrain, *v.t,* embarquer.

entrance, *n,* entrée; porte, *f.* ~ [*fee*], cotisation d'admission, *f;* droit d'entrée, *m.*

entrance, *v.t,* jeter en extase; ravir.

entrap, *v.t,* attraper.

entreat, *v.t,* supplier, prier instamment. ~**y,** *n,* supplication, prière, *f,*(*pl.*) instances, *f.pl.*

entrench, *v.t,* retrancher. ~**ing tool,** pellebêche, *f.*

entrust, *v.t,* confier, charger, remettre.

entry, *n,* entrée, *f;* engagement, *m;* inscription, *f,* enregistrement, *m.*

entwine, *v.t,* enlacer, entortiller.

enumerate, *v.t,* énumérer.

enunciate, *v.t,* énoncer.

envelope, *n,* enveloppe, *f,* pli, *m.* ¶ *v.t,* envelopper.

envenom, *v.t,* envenimer.

enviable, *a,* enviable. **envious,** *a,* envieux.

environ, *v.t,* environner. ~**ment,** *n,* entourage, milieu, *m,* ambiance, *f.* **environs,** *n.pl,* environs, entours, *m.pl.*

envisage, *v.t,* envisager.

envoy, *n,* envoyé, *m.*

envy, *n,* envie, *f.* ¶ *v.t,* envier.

epaulet, *n,* épaulette, *f.*

epergne, *n,* surtout [de table] *m,* girandole, *f.*

ephemeral, *a,* éphémère.

epic, *a,* épique. ¶ *n,* épopée, *f.*

epicure, *n,* gourmet, *m,* friand, e. **epicurean,** *a.* & *n,* épicurien, *a.* & *m.*

epidemic, *n,* épidémie, *f.* ~(**al**), *a,* épidémique.

epidermis, *n,* épiderme, *m.*

epiglottis, *n,* épiglotte, *f.*

epigram, *n,* épigramme, *f.*

epigraph, *n,* (*prefixed to book or chapter*) épigraphe; (*on stone*) inscription, *f.*

epilepsy, *n,* épilepsie, *f.* **epileptic,** *a.* & *n,* épileptique, *a.* & *m,f.*

epilogue, *n,* épilogue, *m.*

Epiphany, *n,* Épiphanie, *f.*

episcopal, *a,* épiscopal. **episcopate** & **episcopacy,** *n,* épiscopat, *m.*

episode, *n,* épisode, *m.*

epistle, *n,* épître, *f.* **epistolary,** *a,* épistolaire.

epitaph, *n,* épitaphe, *f.*

epithet, *n,* épithète, *f.*

epitome, *n,* épitomé, abrégé, raccourci, *m.* **epitomize,** *v.t,* abréger; personnifier.

epoch, *n,* époque, ère, *f.*

epsom salt[s], sel d'Epsom, *m.*

equable†, *a,* égal. **equal†,** *a,* égal, pareil; pair. ~ *to* (task), à la hauteur de. ¶ *n,* égal, e, pareil, le, pair, *m.* ¶ *v.t,* égaler. ~**ity,** *n,* égalité, *f,* pair, *m;* (*rights*) concurrence, *f,* concours; (*votes*) partage, *m.* ~**ize,** *v.t,* égaliser, égaler.

equanimity, *n,* sérénité, *f.*

equation, *n,* équation, *f.*

equator, *n,* équateur, *m.* ~**ial,** *a,* équatorial.

equerry, *n,* écuyer, *m.*

equestrian, *a,* équestre. ¶ *n,* cavalier, ère; écuyer, ère [de cirque].

equilibrate, *v.t,* équilibrer. **equilibrium,** *n,* équilibre, *m.*

equine, *a,* chevalin, hippique.

equinoctial, *a,* équinoxial. **equinox,** *n,* équinoxe, *m.*

equip, *v.t,* équiper, armer, outiller. ~**age,** *n,* équipage, *m.* ~**ment,** *n,* équipement, armement, outillage; fourniment, *m.*

equipoise, *n,* équilibre, *m.*

equitable†, *a,* équitable. **equity,** *n,* équité, *f.*

equivalent, *a. & n,* équivalent, *a. & m;* parité, *f. to be ~,* équivaloir.

equivocal, *a,* équivoque. **equivocate,** *v.i,* équivoquer. **equivocation,** *n,* équivoques, *f.pl.*

era, *n,* ère, époque, *f.*

eradicate, *v.t,* déraciner, extirper.

erase, *v.t,* raturer, gratter, effacer. **eraser,** *n, (knife)* grattoir, *m; (rubber)* gomme [à effacer] *f.* **erasure,** *n,* rature, *f,* grattage, *m,* effaçure, *f.*

ere, *c,* avant que. *~ long,* sous peu.

Erebus, *n,* l'Érèbe, *m.*

erect, *a,* droit; debout, *ad;* dressé. ¶ *v.t,* ériger; construire; élever; monter; dresser; hérisser. **~ion,** *n,* érection; construction, *f;* montage; dressage, *m.*

Erie (Lake), le lac Érié.

ermine, *n,* hermine, *f.*

erode, *v.t,* éroder. **erosion,** *n,* érosion, *f.*

erotic, *a,* érotique.

err, *v.i,* errer, pécher.

errand, *n,* commission, ambassade, course, *f,* message, *m. ~ boy,* garçon de course, *(law office)* saute-ruisseau, *m.*

errant, *a,* errant.

erratic, *a,* irrégulier; *(Geol., Med.)* erratique.

erratum, *n,* erratum, *m.* **erroneous,** *a,* erroné, faux. **~ly,** *ad,* par erreur. **error,** *n,* erreur, faute, *f,* mécompte; écart, *m.*

eructation, *n,* éructation, *f.*

erudite, *a,* érudit. **erudition,** *n,* érudition, *f.*

eruption, *n,* éruption, *f.*

escalator, *n,* escalier roulant, *m.*

escallop, *n,* pétoncle, *m.*

escapade, *n,* escapade; équipée, frasque, *f.*

escape, *n,* fuite; évasion, *f;* échappement, *m;* issue, *f. fire~,* échelle de sauvetage, *f.* ¶ *v.i,* s'échapper; échapper; fuir; s'enfuir; se sauver; s'évader; se débonder; *(v.t.)* échapper à; échapper de; échapper. *escaped prisoner,* évadé, *m.* **~ment,** *n,* échappement, *m.*

escarpment, *n,* escarpement, *m.*

escheat, *n,* déshérence, *f.* ¶ *v.i,* tomber en déshérence; *(v.t.)* confisquer.

eschew, *v.t,* éviter, fuir.

escort, *n,* escorte, *f;* cavalier, *m.* ¶ *v.t,* escorter, reconduire, accompagner.

escutcheon, *n,* écusson, *m.*

espagnolette, *n,* espagnolette, crémone, *f.*

espalier, *n,* espalier, *m.*

especial, *a,* notable, digne d'être signalé, qui mérite une mention particulière; particulier; tout spécial. **~ly,** *ad,* surtout; notamment; particulièrement. *~ as,* d'autant que.

espionage, *n,* espionnage, *m.*

esplanade, *n,* esplanade, *f.*

espousal, *n,* adoption, adhésion, *f.* **espouse,** *v.t,* épouser; embrasser.

espy, *v.t,* apercevoir, aviser, découvrir.

esquire, *(Hist.) n,* écuyer, *m.* **Esquire,** *n. (abb.* Esq.), Monsieur, *m. (Note.—As a form of address on envelope or in letter,* Monsieur *should not be abbreviated.)*

essay, *n,* essai, *m,* composition, dissertation, narration, *f.* ¶ *v.t,* essayer. **~ist,** *n,* essayiste, *m,f.*

essence, *n,* essence, *f.* **essential†,** *a,* essentiel; capital. ¶ *n,* essentiel, *m.*

establish, *v.t,* établir; créer; asseoir; constater. *the ~ed Church,* l'Église d'État, *f.* **~ment,** *n,* établissement, *m;* création; fondation; constatation, *f;* ménage, *m.*

estate, *n,* bien[s] *m.[pl.],* propriété[s] *f.[pl.];* domaine, fonds, *m,* terre; succession, *f. real ~ agency,* agence immobilière, *f.*

esteem, *n,* estime, *f.* ¶ *v.t,* estimer; considérer *(ou* regarder) comme.

Esthonia, *n,* l'Estonie, *f.*

estimate, *n,* estimation, appréciation, évaluation, prisée, *f; état (ou* devis) estimatif; *(pl.)* budget, *m.* ¶ *v.t,* estimer, apprécier, évaluer, priser. **~d,** *p.a,* estimatif. **estimation,** *n,* jugement, *m,* estime, *f.*

estrange, *v.t,* éloigner, aliéner.

estuary, *n,* estuaire, *m.*

et cetera, *phrase & n,* et cætera, etc., *phrase & m.*

etch, *v.t,* graver à l'eau-forte. **~er,** *n,* graveur à l'eau-forte, aquafortiste, *m.* **~ing,** *n;* [gravure à l']eau-forte, *f.*

eternal†, *a,* éternel. *the ~ triangle,* la vie à trois. **etern[al]ize,** *v.t,* éterniser. **eternity,** *n,* éternité, *f.*

ether, *n,* éther, *m.* **ethereal,** *a,* éthéré.

ethical, *a,* éthique. **ethics,** *n.pl,* éthique, *f.*

Ethiopia, *n,* l'Éthiopie, *f.* **Ethiopian,** *a,* éthiopien. ¶ *n,* Éthiopien, ne.

ethnic, *a,* ethnique.

ethnography, *n,* ethnographie, *f.* **ethnologic(al),** *a,* ethnologique. **ethnologist,** *n,* ethnologue, *m.* **ethnology,** *n,* ethnologie, *f.*

ethyl, *n,* éthyle, *m.*

etiolate, *v.t,* étioler.

etiquette, *n,* étiquette, *f,* décorum, protocole, *m.*

etymologic(al), *a,* étymologique. **etymology,** *n,* étymologie, *f.*

eucalyptus, *n,* eucalyptus, *m.*

Eucharist, *n,* Eucharistie, *f.*

eugenic, *a,* eugénique. ~**s,** *n.pl,* eugénie, *f.*

eulogistic†, *a,* élogieux. **eulogize,** *v.t,* faire l'éloge de. **eulogy,** *n,* éloge, *m.*

eunuch, *n,* eunuque, *m.*

euphemism, *n,* euphémisme, *m.* **euphemistic,** *a,* euphémique.

euphonic & **euphonious,** *a,* euphonique. **euphony,** *n,* euphonie, *f.*

Euphrates (the), l'Euphrate, *m.*

Europe, *n,* l'Europe, *f.* **European,** *a,* européen. ¶ *n,* Européen, ne.

eustachian tube, trompe d'Eustache, *f.*

evacuate, *v.t,* évacuer.

evade, *v.t,* éviter, éluder, esquiver; frauder.

evaluate, *v.t,* évaluer.

evanescent, *a,* évanescent.

evangelic(al)†, *a,* évangélique. **evangelist,** *n,* évangéliste, *m.*

evaporate, *v.t,* [faire] évaporer; (*v.i.*) s'évaporer. **evaporation,** *n,* évaporation, *f.*

evasion, *n,* échappatoire, *f,* fauxfuyant, subterfuge, *m,* défaite, *f,* atermoiement, *m.* ~ *of tax,* la fraude fiscale. **evasive**†, *a,* évasif; flottant; normand.

eve, *n,* veille, *f.* **even** (*Poet.*) *n,* soir, *m.* ~*song,* vêpres, *f.pl.* ~*tide,* chute du jour, *f.*

even, *a,* uni; plan; égal; uniforme; pair; (*games*) but à but. ~ *money,* compte rond, *m.* ~ *number,* nombre pair, *m.* ~ *to be* ~ *with* (someone), revaloir. ¶ *ad,* même; jusque. ~ *if,* ~ *though,* même si, quand, lors même que. ¶ *v.t,* égaliser; aplanir.

evening, *n,* soir, *m;* soirée; veillée,

f; (*fig.*) déclin, *m.* ~ *dew,* ~ *damp,* serein, *m.* ~ *dress,* (*man*) tenue de soirée; (*woman*) toilette de s., *f.* ~ *gown,* robe du soir, *f.*

evenly, *ad,* uniment; uniformément. **evenness,** *n,* égalité; uniformité, *f.*

event, *n,* événement; cas, *m;* (*sport*) épreuve, *f.* ~**ful,** *a,* plein d'événements; mouvementé, accidenté.

eventual†, *a,* éventuel. ~**ity,** *n,* éventualité, *f.* **eventuate,** *v.i,* aboutir.

ever, *ad,* jamais; toujours. *for* ~, à (*ou* pour) jamais (*ou* toujours). ~ *so little,* tant soit peu. *hardly* ~, presque jamais. *if* ~, si jamais.

evergreen, *n,* arbre toujours vert, *m.*

everlasting†, *a,* éternel; immortel.

evermore, *ad,* toujours. *for* ~, à tout jamais.

every, *a,* chaque; tout, e; tous (toutes) les. ~*body,* **everyone,** *every one* (every person), tout le monde, chacun, *m. only.* ~*day,* *a,* quotidien; vulgaire; ordinaire. ~*day clothes,* vêtements ordinaires, habits de tous les jours, *m.pl.* ~ *one* (each), chacun, e. ~*thing,* *n,* tout, *pn.* ~*where,* *ad,* partout.

evict, *v.t,* évincer, expulser. ~**ion,** *n,* éviction, *f.*

evidence, *n,* évidence; preuve, *f;* témoignage, *m;* déposition, *f;* titre, *m. to give* ~, témoigner. ¶ *v.t,* constater. **evident,** *a,* évident. ~**ly,** *ad,* évidemment.

evil, *a,* mauvais; méchant; malin; malfaisant. ~-*minded* (*person*), *a.* & *n,* malintentionné, e. ~ *do-er,* malfaiteur, *m.* ~ *eye,* mauvais œil, *m. the E~ One,* le malin [esprit], l'esprit malin, *m.* ~ *speaking,* médisance, *f.* ~ *spirit,* esprit malin, malin esprit, *m.* ¶ *ad,* mal. ¶ *n,* mal, *m,* plaie, *f.*

evince, *v.t,* manifester, témoigner.

eviscerate, *v.t,* éventrer.

evocation, *n,* évocation, *f.* **evoke,** *v.t,* évoquer.

evolution, *n,* déroulement, *m;* (*Biol., etc.*) évolution, *f;* (*Geom.*) développement; (*Chem.*) dégagement, *m.* **evolve,** *v.t,* élaborer; dégager; (*v.i.*) évoluer.

ewe, *n,* brebis, *f.* ~ *lamb,* agneau femelle, *m.*

ewer, *n*, pot à eau, broc de toilette, *m*; aiguière, *f*.

ex-, *prefix*: ~-*professor*, ex-professeur, ancien professeur, *m*. ~-*serviceman*, ancien combattant, *m*.

exacerbate, *v.t*, exacerber.

exact, *a*, exact, précis. ¶ *v.t*, exiger. ~**ing**, *p.a*, exigeant. ~**ion**, *n*, exaction, *f*. ~**ly**, *ad*, exactement, au juste, précisément, parfaitement. ~**ness**, **exactitude**, *n*, exactitude, *f*.

exaggerate, *v.t. & abs*, exagérer, grossir.

exaggeration, *n*, exagération, *f*.

exalt, *v.t*, exalter, relever.

examination, *n*, examen, *m*; inspection; visite, *f*; concours; interrogatoire, *m*; instruction; expertise, *f*. **examine**, *v.t*, examiner; interroger; inspecter; visiter; (*documents*) compulser. **examinee**, *n*, candidat, e. **examiner**, *n*, examinateur, trice; interrogateur, trice; inspecteur, trice; visiteur; vérificateur; contrôleur, *m*.

example, *n*, exemple, *m*.

exasperate, *v.t*, exaspérer, énerver, indigner.

excavate, *v.t*, creuser, fouiller. **excavation**, *n*, excavation, fouille, *f*, déblai, *m*. **excavator** (*Mach.*) *n*, excavateur, *m*.

exceed, *v.t*, excéder, [dé]passer, outrepasser. ~**ingly**, *ad*, excessivement, extrêmement.

excel, *v.i*, exceller, primer; (*v.t.*) surpasser. **excellence**, *n*, excellence, *f*. His Excellency, Son Excellence, *f*. **excellent**, *a*, excellent. ~**ly**, *ad*, excellemment, à merveille.

except, *c*, sinon. ~ & ~**ing**, *pr*, excepté, à l'exception de, hors, hormis, sauf, ôté, à part. ¶ *v.t*, excepter. ~**ion**, *n*, exception; réserve, *f*. to take ~ to, se formaliser de. ~**ionable**, *a*, récusable; critiquable. ~**ional**†, *a*, exceptionnel, hors ligne.

excerpt, *n*, extrait, *m*, bribe, *f*. ¶ *v.t*, extraire.

excess, *n*, excès; excédent; surplus, trop, *m*; outrance, *f*; débordement, *m*; intempérance, *f*. ~ *profits*, surplus des bénéfices. ~ *weight*, excédent de poids, *m*, surcharge, *f*. ~**ive**†, *a*, excessif, immodéré, outré.

exchange, *n*, échange; change; troc, *m*; permutation, *f*; (*Teleph.*) bureau [central], poste central,

m. ~ *rates*, cote des changes, *f*. stock ~, Bourse, *f*. ¶ *v.t*, échanger; changer; troquer.

exchequer, *n*, trésor, *m*, trésorerie, *f*; (*Eng.*) échiquier, *m*; (*of pers.*) finances, *f.pl*.

excise, *n*, (*Fr.*) régie; (*Eng.*) accise, *f*.

excite, *v.t*, exciter, provoquer; irriter, exalter; agacer. ~**ment**, *n*, excitation; exaltation; émotion, *f*.

exclaim, *v.i*, s'écrier, se récrier, s'exclamer. ~ *against*, *abs*, s'exclamer. **exclamation**, *n*, exclamation, *f*.

exclude, *v.t*, exclure. **exclusion**, *n*, exclusion, *f*. **exclusive**†, *a*, exclusif. ~ *right(s)*, droit[s] exclusif[s] *m.[pl.]*, exclusiveté, *f*.

excommunicate, *v.t*, excommunier.

excoriate, *v.t*, écorcher.

excrement, *n*, excrément, *m*.

excrescence, *n*, excroissance, *f*.

excruciating†, *p.a*, atroce.

exculpate, *v.t*, disculper.

excursion, *n*, excursion; partie; promenade, *f*. ~ *ticket*, billet d'excursion, *m*. ~**ist**, *n*, excursionniste, *m,f*.

excusable, *a*, excusable.

excuse, *n*, excuse, *f*, prétexte, *m*. ¶ *v.t*, excuser, pardonner; exempter, dispenser de; faire remise de. ~ *me*, excusez-moi; pardon!

execrable†, *a*, exécrable. **execrate**, *v.t*, exécrer.

execute, *v.t*, exécuter; effectuer; (*document*) souscrire; exécuter [à mort], faire mourir. **execution**, *n*, exécution, *f*; jeu, *m*; souscription; saisie[-exécution] *f*. ~**er**, *n*, bourreau, *m*. **executive**, *n*, bureau; État-major, *m*. **executor**, **-trix**, *n*, exécuteur (trice) testamentaire. **executory**, *a*, exécutoire.

exemplary, *a*, exemplaire, modèle. **exemplify**, *v.t*, éclaircir par un exemple, des exemples.

exempt, *a*, exempt. ¶ *v.t*, exempter. ~**ion**, *n*, exemption, franchise, *f*.

exercise, *n*, exercice; (*Sch.*) devoir; thème, *m*. ~ *book*, cahier, *m*. ¶ *v.t*, exercer, user de; (*Stk Ex. option*) consolider, lever; (*v.i.*) prendre de l'exercice.

exert, *v.t*, exercer. ~ *oneself*, s'évertuer, faire un effort. ~**ion**, *n*, effort, *m*.

exfoliate, *v.i*, s'exfolier.

exhalation, *n,* (*act*) exhalation; (*mist*) exhalaison, *f.* **exhale,** *v.t,* exhaler, respirer.

exhaust, *n,* échappement, *m.* ¶ *v.t,* épuiser; aspirer. **~ion,** *n,* épuisement, *m;* aspiration, *f.* **~ive,** *a,* approfondi. **~ively,** *ad,* à fond, mûrement.

exhibit, *n,* objet exposé, produit [à présenter] *m;* (*law, civil*) pièce justificative, p. à l'appui; (*criminal*) p. à conviction, *f.* ¶ *v.t,* exposer; exhiber. **~ion,** *n,* exposition, *f;* salon, *m;* exhibition. **exhibitor,** *n,* exposant, e; montreur, *m.*

exhilarate, *v.t,* émoustiller, égayer, stimuler.

exhort, *v.t,* exhorter, prêcher [à].

exhume, *v.t,* exhumer, déterrer.

exigence, -cy, *n,* exigence, *f.*

exile, *n,* exil, *m;* (*pers.*) exilé, e. ¶ *v.t,* exiler.

exist, *v.i,* exister. **~ence,** *n,* existence, *f.*

exit, *n,* sortie, issue, *f,* dégagement, *m.* ~ X. (*Theat.*), X. sort.

exodus, *n,* exode, *m.* E~ (Bible), l'Exode.

ex officio, à titre d'office.

exonerate, *v.t,* exonérer.

exorbitance, *n,* extravagance, *f.* **exorbitant,** *a,* exorbitant. **~ly,** *ad,* exorbitamment.

exorcise, *v.t,* exorciser.

exotic, *a,* exotique. ¶ *n,* plante exotique, *f.*

expand, *v.t,* étendre; déployer; dilater. **expanse,** *n,* étendue; envergure, *f.* **expansion,** *n,* expansion; dilatation; détente, *f.* **expansive,** *a,* expansif.

expatiate, *v.i,* s'étendre.

expatriate, *v.t,* expatrier.

expect, *v.t,* attendre, s'attendre à; espérer. **~ancy,** *n,* expectative, *f.* **~ant,** *a,* expectant. ~ **mother,** femme enceinte, *f.* **~ation,** *n,* attente, expectative; espérance, prévision, *f.*

expectorate, *v.t. & abs,* expectorer.

expedience, -cy, *n,* convenance, *f.* **expedient,** *a,* expédient, convenable. ¶ *n,* expédient, *m,* ressource, *f.* **expedite,** *v.t,* expédier; hâter. **expedition,** *n,* expédition, *f.* **~ary,** *a,* expéditionnaire. **expeditious,** *a,* expéditif, diligent.

expel, *v.t,* expulser, chasser, bannir.

expend, *v.t,* dépenser. **expenditure,** *n,* dépense[s] *f.*[*pl.*]. **ex-**

pense, *n,* frais, *m.pl,* dépense, charge, *f,* dépens, *m.pl.* **at the ~ of,** aux frais (*ou* dépens) (*ou* crochets) de; à la charge de. **expensive†,** *a,* cher, coûteux, dispendieux.

experience, *n,* expérience, pratique, *f,* métier, *m,* acquis, *m.s. & pl.* **~d,** *a,* expérimenté, expert. ¶ *v.t,* éprouver, faire l'expérience de. **experiment,** *n,* expérience, *f.* ¶ *v.i,* expérimenter. ~ **on,** faire des expériences sur. **~al†,** *a,* expérimental.

expert, *a. & n,* expert, *a. & m.* **~ness,** *n,* habileté, *f.*

expiate, *v.t,* expier.

expiration, *n,* expiration, échéance, déchéance, *f.* **expire,** *v.t. & abs,* expirer; (*v.i.*) expirer, échoir, périmer.

explain, *v.t,* expliquer, exposer. **~able,** *a,* explicable. **explanation,** *n,* explication, *f.* **explanatory,** *a,* explicatif.

expletive (*Gram.*) *a,* explétif. ¶ *n,* mot explétif, *m,* (*in verse*) cheville, *f;* (*oath*) gros mot, juron, *m.*

explicit†, *a,* explicite; clair.

explode, *v.t,* faire exploser, *f.* éclater; *f.* sauter; (*fig.*) démolir; (*v.i.*) exploser, éclater, faire explosion. **~d theory,** théorie périmée, *f.*

exploit, *n,* exploit, *m.* ¶ *v.t,* exploiter. **~ation,** *n,* exploitation, *f.*

explore, *v.t,* explorer, reconnaître. **explorer,** *n,* explorateur, trice.

explosion, *n,* explosion, *f.* **explosive,** *n,* explosif, *m.*

exponent, *n,* exposant; interprète, *m;* (*Math.*) exposant, *m.*

export, *v.t,* exporter. **~[ation],** *n,* exportation, *f.* **~er,** *n,* exportateur, *m.*

expose, *v.t,* exposer, mettre à nu; (*Phot.*) [ex]poser. **exposition,** *n,* exposition, *f.*

expostulate, *v.i,* faire des remontrances. **expostulation,** *n,* remontrance, *f.*

exposure, *n,* exposition, mise à nu; (*Phot.*) pose, exposition, *f.*

expound, *v.t,* exposer.

express, *a,* exprès, formel. ¶ (*Post, etc.*) *n,* exprès, *m.* ~ [*train*], [*train*] express, *m.* ¶ *v.t,* exprimer; énoncer; traduire. **~ion,** *n,* expression, *f.* **~ive,** *a,* expressif. **expressly,** ad, expressément.

expropriate, v.t, exproprier.

expulsion, n, expulsion, f.

expunge, v.t, rayer, effacer.

expurgate, v.t, expurger.

exquisite, a, exquis; vif. ~**ly,** ad, exquisément. ~**ness,** n, exquis, m.

extant (to be), exister.

extempore, a, improvisé, impromptu. ¶ ad, d'abondance, impromptu. **extemporize,** v.t. & i, improviser.

extend, v.t, étendre; prolonger. **extension,** n, extension,· f, prolongement, m; prolongation, f; (Teleph.) poste supplémentaire, m. ~ ladder, échelle à coulisse, f. ~ tripod, trépied extensible, m. **extensive,** a, étendu, large. ~**ly,** ad, largement. **extensor** (muscle)n, extenseur, m. **extent,** n, étendue; importance, f; degré, point, m, mesure, f.

extenuate, v.t, atténuer.

exterior†, a, extérieur, externe. ¶ n, extérieur; dehors, m; enveloppe (fig.) f.

exterminate, v.t, exterminer.

external, a, externe, extérieur. ~**ly,** ad, extérieurement.

extinct, a, éteint. ~**ion,** n, extinction, f. **extinguish,** v.t, éteindre. ~**er,** n, (light) éteignoir; (fire) extincteur, m.

extirpate, v.t, extirper.

extol, v.t, exalter; vanter; prôner.

extort, v.t, extorquer, arracher. ~**ion,** n, extorsion; maltôte, f. ~**ionate,** a, exorbitant. ~**ioner,** n, écorcheur, euse, m.

extra, a, supplémentaire, supplément de, en sus, hors d'œuvre. ~ fare, supplément [de taxe] m. ¶ ad, extra. ¶ n, extra, supplément, m, plus-value, f; hors-d'œuvre, m; (movies) figurant, m; (newspaper) édition spéciale, f.

extract, n, extrait, m. ¶ v.t, extraire; arracher; [sou]tirer, retirer. ~**ion,** n, extraction, f.

extradite, v.t, extrader. **extradition,** n, extradition, f.

extraneous, a, étranger.

extraordinary†, a, extraordinaire; insolent. ¶ n, extraordinaire, m.

extraterritoriality, n, exterritorialité, f.

extravagance, n, extravagance, f; dévergondage (fig.) m; (money)

folles dépenses, f.pl, dissipation [s] f.[pl.], prodigalités, f.pl. **extravagant,** a, extravagant; (of pers.) dépensier; (price) exorbitant. ~**ly,** ad, follement.

extreme†, a. & n, extrême, a. & m. ~ penalty, dernier supplice, m. ~ unction, extrême-onction, f. **extremist,** n, extrémiste, m,f, ultra, m; (att.) outrancier. **extremity,** n, extrémité, f, bout, m.

extricate, v.t, dégager, débarrasser, débarbouiller, dépêtrer, tirer.

extrinsic, a, extrinsèque.

exuberance, n, exubérance, f. **exuberant,** a, exubérant.

exude, v.i, exsuder; (v.t.) distiller.

exult, v.i, exulter, triompher. ~**ation,** n, exaltation, f.

eye, n, œil, m; paupière; vue, f; (needle, etc.) œil, chas, trou; (fruit) nombril; (potato) germe, m; boucle, f; regard, m; porte, f. ~**ball,** globe de l'œil, m; prunelle, f. ~ bath, œillière, f. ~**brow,** sourcil, m. ~**brow pencil,** crayon pour les yeux, m. ~**brow tweezers,** pinces à épiler, f.pl. ~ doctor, médecin oculiste, m. ~**s** front! (Mil.), fixe! ~**glass,** monocle, m; (pl.) binocle, lorgnon, pince-nez, m. ~**lash,** cil, m. ~**lid,** paupière, f. ~ opener, révélation, f. ~**piece,** [verre] oculaire, m. ~**shade,** visière, f, garde-vue, m. ~**sight,** vue, f. ~**sore,** objet qui choque la vue, m. ~**tooth,** [dent] œillère, f. ~**trouble,** mal aux (ou d') yeux, m. ~**witness,** témoin oculaire, m. to keep an ~ on, ne pas perdre de vue. to make ~s at, faire les yeux doux à. ¶ v.t, regarder; lorgner. **eyelet,** n, œillet, m.

eyrie, n, aire (de l'aigle) f.

F

F (Mus.) letter, fa, m. ~ clef, clef de fa, f.

fable, n, fable, f. ~**d,** p.p, légendaire, fabuleux.

fabric, n, tissu, m, étoffe, f. ~**ate,** v.t, fabriquer. ~**ation,** n, fabrication; fantasmagorie, f. ~**ator,** n, fabricateur, trice.

fabulist, n, fabuliste, m. **fabulous†,** a, fabuleux.

façade, n, façade, f.

face, n, face, f; visage, m, figure, f; mine; grimace; tournure, f;

parement; pan; recto; (*cloth*) endroit; (*cards*) dessous; (*of type*) œil, *m.* ~ *lifting*, chirurgie esthétique du visage, *f.* ~ *massage*, massage facial, *m.* ~ *powder*, poudre de riz, *f.* ~ *to* ~, vis-à-vis. ~ *value* (*Fin.*), valeur nominale, *f. to about* ~, faire demi-tour. ¶ *v.t*, faire face à; affronter, braver; donner sur, être exposé à; dresser. ~d *with* (silk), à revers de.

facet, *n*, facette, *f.* ¶ *v.t*, facetter.

facetious, *a*, facétieux.

facial, *a*, facial.

facile, *a*, facile. **facilitate**, *v.t*, faciliter. **facility**, *n*, facilité, *f.*

facing, *n*, revers; parement; revêtement, *m.* ¶ *ad. & pr*, en face (de); face à, vis-à-vis (de), à l'opposite (de).

facsimile, *n*, fac-similé, *m.*

fact, *n*, fait, *m*; vérité; chose, *f.*

faction, *n*, faction, brigue, *f.* **factious**, *a*, factieux. **factitious**, *a*, factice.

factor, *n*, facteur, *m*; (*pers.*) commissionnaire, *m.*

factory, *n*, manufacture, fabrique, usine, *f.* ~ *hand*, ouvrier (ère) [de fabrique]. ~ *inspector*, inspecteur du travail, *m.*

factotum, *n*, factotum, *m.*

faculty, *n*, faculté; aptitude, *f*, talent, *m.*

fad, *n*, dada, *m*, marotte, lubie, vogue, manie, *f.* **faddist**, *n*, maniaque, *m.f.*

fade, *v.i*, se faner, se défraîchir, déteindre, se flétrir, pâlir. ~ *away*, s'évanouir. ~ *out*, se mourir. ~d, *p.a*, fané, défraîchi, passé.

fagot, *n*, fagot, cotret, *m.* ¶ *v.t*, fagoter.

Fahrenheit, *a*, Fahrenheit. See note under *centigrade* in French-English section.

fail, *v.i*, manquer, faire défaut, défaillir, échouer, mal réussir, rater, chavirer; faiblir; (*Com.*) faire faillite; (*v.t.*) manquer à. ~ *in one's duty*, manquer à son devoir, prévariquer. *without* ~, sans faute. ~**ing**, *n*, faible, *m*; défaillance, *f.* ¶ *pr*, à défaut de, faute de. ~**ure**, *n*, défaut, insuccès, échec, *m*, chute, *f*, coup manqué; four, fiasco, *m*; (*Elec.*) panne; (*Com.*) faillite, *f.*

fain, *a. & ad*: *to be* ~ *to*, être amené par nécessité à, être réduit

à. *I would* ~ *be* . . ., je serais volontiers . . . *I would* ~ *have* . . ., j'aurais bien voulu . . .

faint, *a*, faible; mourant; défaillant. ~*-hearted*, lâche. ¶ *v.i*, s'évanouir, défaillir, [se] pâmer. ~**ing** [fit], évanouissement, *m*, défaillance, *f.*

fair, *a*, beau; (*skin*) blanche; (*hair*) blonds; juste, équitable, loyal, honnête; raisonnable; passable. *at* ~ (barometer), au beau. ~*-haired*, aux cheveux blonds. ~*-haired person*, blond, e. *by* ~ *means or foul*, de gré ou de force. ~ *play*, franc jeu, *m*, de bonne guerre; traitement honnête, *m. not* ~, pas du (*ou* de) jeu. ~ *sex*, beau sexe, *m.* ~*-spoken*, bien-disant. ~*-way*, chenal, *m*, passe, *f.* ¶ *n*, foire, *f.* ~**ly**, *ad*, à juste titre; bel & bien; loyalement; assez; moyennement. ~**ness**, *n*, beauté, *f*; teint blond, *m*; équité; loyauté, honnêteté, *f.*

fairy, *n*, fée, *f.* ~**like**, féerique. ~ *land*, féerie, *f.* *Fairyland*, féerie, *f.* ~*like*, féerique. ~ *ring*, cercle des fées, *m.* ~ *tale*, conte de fées, conte bleu, *m.*

faith, *n*, foi; confiance; croyance, communion, *f.* ~*ful*†, *a*, fidèle. *the* ~, les fidèles, les croyants, *m.pl.* **fulness**, *n*, fidélité, *f.* ~**less**, *a*, sans foi, infidèle. ~**lessness**, *n*, infidélité, *f.*

fake, *n*, truquage, *m.* ¶ *v.t*, truquer.

fakir, *n*, fakir, *m.*

falcon, *n*, faucon, *m.* ~**er**, *n*, fauconnier, *m.* **falconry**, *n*, fauconnerie, *f.*

fall, *n*, chute; tombée; descente; (*prices*) baisse, *f*; abaissement, *m*; culbute; ruine, *f*; éboulement; éboulis, *m*; cascade, *f,m*; (*pl.*) chute, *f*; automne; (*government*) renversement, *m.* ¶ *v.i.ir*, tomber; descendre; baisser; s'abaisser. ~ *back*, se replier. ~ *down*, tomber [par terre]. ~ *due*, échoir. ~ *in* (*cave in*) ébouler; (*Mil.*) mettre en rangs; à vos rangs! ~ *in love*, s'enamourer, s'éprendre. ~ *in with* (opinion), se ranger à. ~ *off*, tomber [à bas] de; business, etc.) ralentir. ~ *out with*, ~ *foul of*, se brouiller avec. ~ *through* (fail), échouer.

fallacious, *a*, fallacieux. **fallacy**, *n*, erreur, *f*; (*Log.*) sophisme, *m.*

fallen angel, ange déchu, *m.* **fallen leaves**, feuilles tombées, fanes, *f.pl*, fanage, *m.*

fallibility, n, faillibilité, f. **fallible,** a, faillible.

falling star, étoile tombante, é. filante, f.

fallow, a, (color of deer) fauve; (land) en jachère, en friche. ~ deer, daim, m. to lie ~, rester en friche, chômer. ¶ v.t, jachérer.

false, a, faux; mensonger; postiche; feint. ~ bottom, double fond, faux f., m. ~ shame, fausse honte, mauvaise h., f. ¶ ad, faux. ~hood, n, fausseté, f. ~ly, ad, faussement. ~ness, n, fausseté, f.

falsetto, n, fausset, m. **falsify,** v.t, falsifier, fausser. **falsity,** n, fausseté, f.

falter, v.i, chanceler, défaillir; hésiter; (speech) ânonner, bégayer.

fame, n, renommée, f, renom, m, gloire, mémoire, f. ~d, a, renommé.

familiar†, a, familier. ~ face, figure de connaissance, f. ¶ n, familier, m. ~ity, n, familiarité; privauté, f. ~ize, v.t, familiariser.

family, n, famille, f; ménage, m; maisonnée, f. ~ likeness, air de famille, m. ~ life, vie de f., v. familiale, f. ~ man, père de famille; homme de foyer, m. ~ tree, arbre généalogique, m.

famine, n, famine, f. **famish,** v.t, affamer. to be ~ing, avoir la fringale.

famous†, a, fameux, célèbre, renommé. ~ case (law), cause célèbre, f.

fan, n, éventail; ventilateur, m. ~ light, vasistas, m. ~ tail, pigeon paon, m. ¶ v.t, éventer; (grain) vanner; (fire, & fig.) souffler; exciter, attiser.

fanatic, n, fanatique, m,f. ~(al), a, fanatique. **fanaticism,** n, fanatisme, m. **fanaticize,** v.t, fanatiser.

fancied, p.a, imaginaire. **fancier,** n, grand amateur (de . . .) m. **fanciful,** a, de fantaisie; fantastique, chimérique. **fancy,** n, fantaisie; envie; toquade; boutade, f, caprice, m; imagination; idée, f. ~ dress, déguisement, m. ~-dress ball, bal costumé, b. travesti, m. ~ leather goods or shop, maroquinerie, f. ~ needlework, ouvrages de dames, m.pl. ~ work, ouvrages d'agrément, m.pl. ¶ v.t, imaginer; s'imaginer; se figurer. ~ oneself, se complaire.

fang, n, croc, m.

fantasia, n, fantaisie, f. **fantastic,** a, fantastique; fantaisiste. **fantasy,** n, vision; fantaisie, f.

far, ad, loin, au loin; avant; beaucoup; bien. from ~, de loin. how ~ is it to . . .? combien y a-t-il d'ici à . . .? ~ & wide, au long & au large. as ~ as, jusqu'à; autant que. as ~ as the eye can reach, à perte de vue. by ~, de beaucoup. ~fetched, tiré par les cheveux, forcé, outre. ~ into the night, fort avant dans la nuit. ~off, lointain. ~reaching, étendu. ~sighted, prévoyant. ~ too, par trop. ¶ a, éloigné. the F~ East, l'Extrême-Orient, m.

farce, n, farce, f. **farcical,** a, burlesque, bouffon.

fare, n, prix [de la place], prix de passage, tarif, m, place; course, f; voyageur, euse; chère, f, menu, m. ¶ v.i, aller. to ~ (feed) well, faire bonne chère. ~well, i. & n, adieu, i. & m.

farina, n, farine; fécule, f. **farinaceous,** a, farineux, farinacé.

farm, n, ferme, f. ~ hand, valet de ferme, m. ~house, ferme, f. ~ products, produits agricoles, m.pl. ~yard, cour de f., basse-cour, f. ¶ v.t, exploiter, cultiver; (lease) affermer. ~ out, amodier. ~er, n, fermier, ère, cultivateur, trice, agriculteur, m. ~ing, n, exploitation [d'une ferme], agriculture, culture, f; (att.) aratoire.

faro (cards) n, pharaon, m.

farrago, n, farrago, salmigondis, m.

farrow, n, cochonnée, f. ¶ v.i, cochonner.

farther, ad, plus loin, [plus] en delà. **farthest,** a, le plus éloigné. ¶ ad, le plus loin.

farthing, n, farthing, m. = ¼ penny; (fig.) liard, m, obole, f.

fasces (Hist.) n.pl, faisceaux, m.pl.

fascinate, v.t, fasciner. **fascinating,** a, fascinateur. **fascination,** n, fascination, f.

fascine, n, fascine, f.

fascism, n, fascisme, m. **fascist,** n, fasciste, m.

fashion, n, façon; mode, f. genre, m. after a ~, tant bien que mal. ~ plate, gravure de mode, f. ¶ v.t, façonner. ~able, a, à la mode, élégant. ~ society, le beau monde. ~ably, ad, à la mode.

fast, a, fixe; fidèle; (dissipated) léger; rapide, vite; express, de grande vitesse; (*of clock*) en avance. ~ *asleep*, profondément endormi. ~ *color*, bon teint, t. solide, *m.* ~ *cruiser* (speedboat), glisseur de croisière, *m.* ¶ *ad*, ferme; bien; vite; (*rain*) à verse. *to hold* ~, tenir bon. *to make* ~, amarrer. ¶ *n*, jeûne, *m*; (*Naut.*) amarre, *f.* ¶ *v.i*, jeûner. ~**ing**, *ad*, à jeun. ~[**ing**] *day*, jour de jeûne, j. maigre, *m.*

fasten, *v.t* fixer; assujettir; attacher; agrafer. ~ *off* (*Need.*), arrêter. ~**er** & ~**ing**, *n*, attache; armature; fermeture; agrafe, *f.*

fastidious (**to be**), être pointilleux, faire le (*of woman*, la) dégoûté(e), f. le difficile, f. le délicat, f. le (la) renchéri(e).

fat, *a*, gras; obèse; (*land*) fertile. ~*head*, lourdaud, e. ~ *profits*, profits substantiels, *m.pl.* ¶ *n*, gras, *m*; graisse, *f*; lard; suif, *m. to live on the* ~ *of the land*, vivre grassement.

fatal†, *a*, fatal, funeste; mortel. ~**ism**, *n*, fatalisme, *m.* ~**ist**, *n*, fataliste, *m.f.* ~**ity**, *n*, fatalité, *f*; accident mortel, *m*; tué, e.

fate, *n*, destin, sort, *m*, fatalité, *f. the Fates* (*Myth.*), les Parques, *f.pl. to be* ~*d to*, être destiné à. ~**ful**, *a*, fatal.

father, *n*, père, *m.* ~*-in-law*, beau-père, *m.* ~*land*, patrie, *f.* ~*'s side* (family), côté paternel, *m.* ~**hood**, *n*, paternité, *f.* ~**less**, *a*, sans père, orphelin de père. ~**ly**, *a*, paternel, de père. ¶ *v.t*, patronner. ~ *upon*, attribuer à.

fathom, *n*, brasse, *f.* (Eng. *fathom* = 6 feet; Fr. *brasse marine* = 1 meter 62). ¶ *v.t*, sonder, pénétrer. ~**less**, *a*, insondable.

fatigue, *n*, fatigue, *f*; (*Mil.*) corvée, *f.* ¶ *v.t*, fatiguer. **fatiguing**, *a*, fatigant.

fatness, *n*, obésité; fertilité, *f. fatted calf*, veau gras, *m.* **fatten**, *v.t*, engraisser. **fattish**, *a*, grasset. **fatty**, *a*, gras, graisseux, adipeux.

fatuity, *n*, imbécillité, *f.* **fatuous**, *a*, imbécile.

fauces, *n.pl*, arrière-bouche, *f.*

faucet, *n*, robinet, fausset, *m*; douille, *f.*

fault, *n*, faute, *f*; tort; défaut, vice; dérangement, *m*; (*Geol.*) faille, *f. to find* ~ *with*, trouver à redire à, reprendre, mordre sur, censurer, fronder, gloser [sur]. ~ *finder*, critiqueur, frondeur, *m.* ~**less**, *a*, sans faute; sans défaut;

irréprochable. ~**y**, *a*, fautif, vicieux, défectueux, mauvais.

faun, *n*, faune, *m.* **fauna**, *n*, faune, *f.*

favor, *n*, faveur, grâce, *f*; plaisir, *m.* ¶ *v.t*, favoriser, avantager, honorer. **favorable**†, *a*, favorable; prospère. **favorite**, *a*, favori, e. ~ *author*, auteur de prédilection, *m.* ~ *book*, livre de chevet, *m.* ¶ *n*, favori, ite. *the* ~, le [cheval] favori. **favoritism**, *n*, favoritisme, *m*, cote d'amour, *f.*

fawn, *n*, faon, chevrotin; (*color*) fauve, *m.* ~[*-colored*], fauve. ¶ (*of deer*) *v.i*, faonner. ~ [*up*]*on*, flagorner, courtiser; ramper devant. ~**ing**, *n*, servilité, flatterie, *f.*

fear, *n*, crainte, peur, frayeur, *f*; danger, *m.* ¶ *v.t. & i*, craindre, redouter. ~**ful**†, *a*, affreux, épouvantable; craintif. ~**less**, *a*, sans peur, intrépide. ~**lessness**, *n*, intrépidité, *f.*

feasibility, *n*, praticabilité, *f.* **feasible**, *a*, faisable, praticable.

feast, *n*, fête, *f*; festin, régal, *m.* ¶ *v.i. & t*, festiner, festoyer, régaler; (*fig.*) repaître. ~**ing**, *n*, bombance, *f.*

feat, *n*, fait, exploit; tour, *m*, prouesse, *f.*

feather, *n*, plume, *f*; (*pl.*) plumage, *m*; penne; (*Carp. & Mach.*) languette, *f.* ~ *bed*, lit de plume, *m.* ~*brained person*, tête de linotte, *f*, évaporé, e. ~ *duster*, plumeau, houssoir, *m.* ~ *stitch*, point de plume, *m.* ~ *weight* (*Box.*), poids plume, *m.* ¶ (*rowing*) *v.i*, plumer. *to* ~ *one's nest*, s'enrichir. ~**ed**, *p.a*: ~ *game*, gibier à plume, *m.* ~ *hat*, chapeau orné de plumes, *m.* ~**y**, *a*, plumeux.

feature, *n*, trait, linéament, *m*; caractéristique, *f.* ¶ *v.i*, mettre en vedette.

February, *n*, février, *m.*

fecund, *a*, fécond. ~**ate**, *v.t*, féconder. ~**ity**, *n*, fécondité, *f.*

federal, *a*, fédéral. **federate**, *v.t*, fédérer. **federation**, *n*, fédération, *f*; syndicat, *m.*

fee, *n. oft. pl*, honoraires, *m.pl*; frais, *m.pl*; cotisation, *f*; droit, *m*; taxe; surtaxe, *f. admission* ~, droit d'entrée, *m.*

feeble†, *a*, faible, débile.

feed, *n*, nourriture; mangeaille; pâture, *f*; (*of oats*) picotin, *m*;

alimentation, *f*; (*Mach.*) avancement, entraînement, *m*. ~ *pump*, pompe alimentaire, *f*. ¶ *v.t.ir*, nourrir; [re]paître; alimenter; (*v.i.ir.*) manger. ~ *forcibly*, gaver. ~**er**, *n*, mangeur, euse; appareil d'alimentation, *m*; (*stream*, *Rly*) affluent, *m*; (*Elec.*) artère, *f*. ~*ing bottle*, biberon, *m*.

feel, *n*, manier, toucher, tact, *m*. ¶ *v.t*. & *i*. *ir*, tâter, palper, manier, toucher; sentir, se s., ressentir, se r., éprouver; se trouver. *to* ~ *one's way*, avancer à tâtons. *to* ~ *like*, avoir envie de. ~**er**, *n*, antenne, *f*, palpe, *f*. *or m*; (*fig.*) ballon d'essai, *m*. **feeling**, *a*, sensible, touchant, tendre. ¶ *n*, maniement, *m*; sensation; sensibilité, *f*; (*pl.*) cœur; sentiment; esprit, *m*. ~**ly**, *ad*, avec émotion.

feign, *v.t*, feindre, simuler, jouer. **feint**, *n*, feinte, *f*. ¶ *v.i*, feindre.

felicitous, *a*, heureux, à propos. **felicity**, *n*, félicité, *f*.

feline, *a*. & *n*, félin, *a*. & *m*.

fell, *n*, peau, *f*; abat[tis] *m*. ¶ *v.t*, abattre; assommer. ~**er**, *n*, abatteur, *m*. ~**ing**, *n*, abattage, *m*.

fellow, *n*, compagnon, *m*, camarade, *m,f*, pareil, pendant; garçon, gaillard, individu, sujet, *m*. ~ *boarder*, commensal, e. ~ *citizen*, concitoyen, ne. ~ *countryman*, -*woman*, compatriote, *m,f*. ~ *creature*, ~ *man*, semblable, prochain, *m*. ~ *feeling*, sympathie, *f*. ~ *passenger*, ~ *traveler*, compagnon de voyage, *m*, compagne de voyage, *f*. ~ *sponsor*, compère, *m*, commère, *f*. ~ *student*, camarade de collège, *m,f*, condisciple, *m*. ~ *sufferer*, camarade de malheur, compagnon de malheur, compagne de malheur. ~ *workman*, camarade d'atelier, *m*. ~**ship**, *n*, société; camaraderie, *f*; situation universitaire, *f*.

felo de se, *n*, suicide; (*pers.*) suicidé, *m*.

felon, *n*, criminel, le. ~**ious**, *a*, criminel. ~**y**, *n*, crime, *m*.

felt, *n*, feutre, *m*. ~ [*hat*], [chapeau de] feutre, *m*. ¶ *v.t*, feutrer.

female, *a*, femelle; de femme; (*pers.*) féminin. ¶ *n*, (*animal*) femelle; (*pers.*) femme, *f*. **feminine**, *a*. & *n*, féminin, *a*. & *m*. **feminism**, *n*, féminisme, *m*. **feminist**, *a*. & *n*, féministe, *a*. & *m,f*. **feminize**, *v.t*, féminiser.

femur, *n*, fémur, *m*.

fen, *n*, marais, marécage, *m*.

fence, *n*, clôture, barrière, palissade, *f*; (*Mach.*) guide, *m*; (*pers.*) receleur, euse. *to be on the* ~, être indécis. ¶ *v.t*, palissader; (*v.i.*) faire (*ou* tirer) des armes. ~ *in*, enclore. ~ *off*, barrer. **fencer**, *n*, tireur d'armes, *m*. **fencing**, *n*, clôture, enceinte; (*foils*) escrime, *f*. ~ *master*, maître d'armes, *m*. ~ *school*, salle d'armes, *m*. d'escrime, *f*.

fend [*off*], *v.t*, parer. ~ *for oneself*, se suffire. ~**er**, *n*, garde-cendre; (*Naut.*) parebattage; (*auto*) pare-boue, *m*.

fennel, *n*, & ~ *seed*, fenouil, *m*.

ferment, *n*, ferment, *m*; (*fig.*) fermentation, effervescence, *f*. ¶ *v.i*, fermenter; (*v.t.*) faire f. ~**ation**, *n*, fermentation, *f*.

fern, *n*, fougère, *f*.

ferocious, *a*, féroce. **ferocity**, *n*, férocité, *f*.

ferret, *n*, furet, *m*. ¶ *v.i*. & *t*, fureter. ~ *about*, fureter. ~ *out*, dénicher.

ferrous, *a*, ferreux.

ferrule, *n*, virole, bague, frette, *f*, [em]bout, *m*. ¶ *v.t*, mettre une virole, etc., à.

ferry, *n*, passage, *m*. ~ [*boat*], bateau de passage, bac, *m*. ~**man**, passeur, *m*. ~ **over**, passer [l'eau].

fertile, *a*, fertile, fécond, plantureux. **fertility**, *n*, fertilité, fécondité, *f*. **fertilize**, *v.t*, fertiliser. **fertilizer**, *n*, engrais fertilisant, *m*.

fervent & **fervid**, *a*, fervent, ardent. **fervently** & **fervidly**, *ad*, avec ferveur, ardemment. **fervor** & **fervency**, *n*, ferveur, ardeur, *f*.

fester, *v.i*, s'ulcérer. ¶ *n*, ulcère, *m*; suppuration, *f*.

festival, *n*, fête, *f*; (*musical*) festival, *m*. **festive**, *a*, de fête. **festivity**, *n*, fête, *f*.

festoon, *n*, feston, *m*. ¶ *v.t*, festonner.

fetch, *v.t*, apporter; aller chercher. ~ *it!* (to dog), apporte!

fete, *n*, fête; kermesse; (*at a fair*) fête foraine, *f*. ¶ *v.t*, fêter.

fetid, *a*, fétide. ~**ness**, *n*, fétidité, *f*.

fetish, *n*, fétiche, *m*. **fetishism**, *n*, fétichisme, *m*.

fetlock, *n*, fanon, *m*.

fetter, *n*. *oft. pl*, entrave, *f*, fer, *m*, chaîne, *f*. ¶ *v.t*, entraver, enchaîner.

fettle, *n*, état, *m*, forme, *f*.

fetus, *n*, fœtus, *m*.

feud, *n,* guerre, vendetta, *f;* (*Hist.*) fief, *m.* ~**al,** *a,* féodal. ~**alism** & ~**ality,** *n,* féodalité, *f.*

fever, *n,* fièvre, *f.* ~ *case* (*pers.*), fiévreux, euse. *scarlet* ~, scarlatine, *f.* ~**ish**†, *a,* fiévreux; fébrile.

few, *a.* & *n,* peu de; peu, *m;* quelques; quelques-uns, -unes. ~ & *far between,* clairsemé. ~**er,** *a,* moins; moins de.

fez, *n,* fez, *m.*

fiasco, *n,* fiasco, four, *m.*

fiat, *n,* décret, *m.*

fib, *n,* mensonge innocent, *m,* menterie, *f.* ¶ *v.i,* débiter des bourdes. **fibber,** *n,* menteur, *m.*

fiber, *n,* fibre, *f;* crin, *m.* **fibril,** *n,* fibrille, *f.* **fibrous,** *a,* fibreux.

fickle, *a,* volage, changeant, mobile, versatile, inconstant. ~**ness,** *n,* inconstance, mobilité, versatilité, *f.*

fiction, *n,* fiction, *f,* mensonge, *m;* (*prose*) le roman, les romans. **fictitious**†, *a,* fictif, supposé. **fictive,** *a,* imaginaire.

fiddle, *n,* violon, crincrin, *m.* ~ *stick,* archet, *m;* (*pl., i.*) chansons, chansons! ¶ *v.i,* jouer du violon; (*fig.*) baguenauder. **fiddler,** *n,* ménétrier, *m.*

fidelity, *n,* fidélité, *f.*

fidget, *v.i,* remuer, frétiller, se trémousser. ~**s,** *n.pl,* impatiences, crispations, *f.pl.* ~**y,** *a,* inquiet, nerveux.

fiduciary, *a,* fiduciaire.

fie, *i,* fi!

fief (*Hist.*) *n,* fief, *m.*

field, *n,* champ, *m;* (*pl.*) campagne, *f;* (*pl., poet.*) sillons, *m. pl;* terrain, *m;* (*Mil.*) campagne, *f;* (*Her.*) champ, *m,* table d'attente, *f.* ~ *artillery,* artillerie de campagne, *f.* ~ *day,* manœuvres, *f.pl;* (*fig.*) grand jour; débat important, *m.* ~ *geology,* géologie sur le terrain, *f.* ~ *glass[es],* jumelle de campagne, *f.* ~ *mouse,* rat des champs, mulot, *m.* ~ *sports,* la chasse, la pêche, & sports analogues. *landing* ~, terrain d'atterrissage, *m.*

fiend, *n,* démon, *m;* enragé, e. ~**ish,** *a,* diabolique.

fierce, *a,* féroce, farouche, acharné. ~**ly,** *ad,* avec férocité. ~**ness,** *n,* férocité, *f.*

fiery, *a,* de feu; ardent, bouillant, fougueux.

fife & **fifer,** *n,* fifre, *m.*

fifteen, *a.* & *n,* quinze, *a.* & *m.*

~**th**†, *a,* & *n,* quinzième, *a.* & *m.f;* quinze, *m.* **fifth**†, *a,* cinquième. ¶ *n,* cinquième, *m.f;* cinq, *m;* (*Mus.*) quinte, *f.* **fiftieth,** *a.* & *n,* cinquantième, *a.* & *m.f.* ~ *anniversary,* cinquantenaire, *m.* **fifty,** *a.* & *n,* cinquante, *a.* & *m.* ~ [*or so*], une cinquantaine.

fig, *n,* figue, *f;* (*fig.*) fétu, *m.* ~ *leaf,* feuille de figuier; (*Art*) feuille de vigne, *f.* ~ *tree,* figuier, *m.*

fight, *n,* combat, *m;* lutte, joute, bataille, mêlée, batterie, *f. air* ~, combat aérien, *m. hand-to-hand* ~, corps-à-corps, *m.* ¶ *v.i.ir,* battre, combattre, lutter, batailler; (*v.t.ir.*) se battre avec, combattre, lutter contre; (*a battle*) livrer; (*one's way*) se frayer. ~**er,** *n,* combattant; batailleur; militant, avion de combat, *m.*

figment, *n,* fiction, *f.*

figurative, *a,* figuratif. ~ *sense,* [sens] figuré, *m.* ~**ly,** *ad,* figurativement; (*sense*) figurément, au figuré. **figure,** *n,* figure; (*bodily shape*) taille, tournure, *f;* (*Arith.*) chiffre, *m.* ~ *dance,* danse figurée, *f.* ~*head,* (*ship*) figure de proue, *f;* personnage de carton, *m.* ~ *of speech,* figure de mots, figure de rhétorique. ~ *skates,* patins de figure, *m.pl.* ¶ *v.t.* & *i,* chiffrer; gaufrer; figurer; (*Mus.*) chiffrer.

filament, *n,* filament; fil; filet, *m.*

filbert, *n,* aveline, *f.* ~ [*tree*], avelinier, *m.*

filch, *v.t,* escamoter, subtiliser, filouter.

file, *n,* (*rank*) file; (*of people*) file, queue, *f;* (*for letters*) classeur, *m;* (*bundle*) liasse; collection; (*tool*) lime, *f.* ~ *card,* fiche, *f.* ¶ *v.t,* classer; déposer, passer, enregistrer; limer. ~ *past,* défiler.

filial†, *a,* filial. **filiation,** *n,* filiation, *f.*

filigree [**work**], *n,* filigrane, *m.* ~**d,** *a,* façonné en filigrane.

filing, *n,* classement; dépôt; limage, *m;* (*pl.*) limaille, *f.* ~ *cabinet,* [meuble-]classeur, *m.*

fill, *n,* suffisance, *f,* content, soûl, *m.* ¶ *v.t,* [r]emplir; combler; charger; peupler; suppléer à; (*tooth*) plomber. ~ *in,* insérer, remplir. ~ *in time,* peloter en attendant partie. ~ *up,* remplir.

fillet, *n,* filet; (*Arch.*) congé, *m.* ~ *of veal,* rouelle de veau, *f.* ~*ed sole,* filets de sole, *m.pl.*

filling, *n*, remplissage, chargement; (*tooth*) plombage, *m*.

fillip, *n*, chiquenaude, *f*; (*fig.*) coup de fouet, *m*.

fillister, *n*, feuillure, *f*.

filly, *n*, pouliche, *f*.

film, *n*, pellicule, *f*; film, *m*; (*movies*) bande, *f*; (*fig.*) voile, *m*. ~ *pack*, bloc-film, *m*. ~ *rights*, droits d'adaption au cinématographe, *m.pl.* ~ *star*, vedette de l'écran, v. de cinéma, *f*. ¶ *v.t*, mettre à l'écran, tourner. ~**y**, *a*, vaporeux.

filter, *n*, filtre; (*Phot.*) écran, *m*. ¶ *v.t. & i*, filtrer.

filth, *n*, immondice, fange, ordure, crasse, saleté, *f*. **filthiness**, *n*, saleté, *f*. **filthy†**, *a*, sale, crasseux; crapuleux, fangeux, ignoble.

fin, *n*, nageoire, *f*, (*Avn.*) aileron, *m*.

final†, *a*, final, dernier, fatal. ~ [*heat*], [épreuve] finale, *f*. **finale** (*Mus.*) *n*, final[e] *m*. **finality**, *n*, finalité, *f*.

finance, *n*, finance; commandite, *f*; (*pl.*) finances, *f.pl*, trésorerie, *f*. ¶ *v.i*, financer; (*v.t.*) commanditer. **financial†**, *a*, financier. **financier**, *n*, financier, *m*.

finch, *n*, pinson, *m*.

find, *n*, trouvaille, découverte, *f*. ¶ *v.t.ir*, trouver, retrouver; découvrir; rechercher; s'apercevoir; reconnaître; procurer, se procurer; fournir. ~ *out*, découvrir, se rendre compte. ~**er**, *n*, inventeur; (*camera*) viseur, *m*; (*telescope*) lunette de repère, *f*. ~**ing** (*jury*) *n*, déclaration, *f*.

fine, *a*, beau; fin; délicat; bon; menu; ténu; joli; magnifique. ~ *arts*, beaux-arts, *m.pl*. *one of these* ~ *days*, *one* ~ *day*, un de ces matins, un beau matin. ~ *speaking*, bien-dire, *m*. ~ *things*, objets magnifiques, *m.pl*, magnificences, *f.pl*. ¶ *n*, amende, *f*. ¶ *v.t*, mettre (*ou* condamner) à l'amende; (*wine*) coller, clarifier. ~**ly**, *ad*, finement; joliment. ~**ness**, *n*, finesse; ténuité, *f*; (*gold, etc.*) titre, *m*. **finery**, *n*, chiffons, colifichets, affiquets, atours, *m.pl*. **finesse**, *n*, finesse, *f*. ¶ *v.t*, finasser. *finest quality*, premier choix, *m*.

finger, *n*, doigt, *m*. ~ *board*, touche, *f*. ~ *bowl*, bol rince-doigts, *m*. ~ *print*, empreinte digitale, *f*. *middle* ~, médius, *m*. *ring* ~, annulaire, *m*. ¶ *v.t*, tou-

cher, palper; (*Mus.*) doigter. ~**ing** (*Mus.*) *n*, doigté, *m*.

finical, *a*, dégoûté, difficile, maniéré, vétilleux, mièvre.

finis, *n*, fin, *f*. **finish**, *n*, fini, *m*; (*end*) fin, *f*, bout, *m*. ¶ *v.t. & abs. & i*, finir; en finir; achever; parachever, parfaire. *to* ~ *speaking*, finir de parler. ~**ing** *stroke*, coup de grâce, *m*. ~**ing** *touches*, dernière main, *f*.

finite, *a*, fini; (*Gram.*) défini.

Finland, *n*, la Finlande. **Finn**, **Finlander**, *n*, Finnois, e, Finlandais, e. **Finnish**, *a*, finnois, finlandais. ¶ (*language*) *n*, le finnois.

fir [tree], *n*, sapin, pin, *m*. ~ *plantation*, sapinière, *f*.

fire, *n*, feu; incendie; tir, *m*; fougue, *f*. (*house, etc, on*) ~! au feu! ~ *alarm*, avertisseur d'incendie, *m*. ~*arms*, armes à feu, *f.pl*. ~*box*, foyer, *m*; boîte à feu, *f*. ~*brand*, tison, brandon, boute-feu, *m*. ~*brick*, brique réfractaire, *f*. ~ *brigade*, sapeurs-pompiers, *m.pl*. ~*clay*, argile réfractaire, *f*. ~*damp*, grisou, *m*. ~ *dog*, chenet, *m*. ~ *engine*, pompe à incendie, *f*. ~ *escape*, échelle de sauvetage, *f*. ~ *extinguisher*, extincteur d'incendie, *m*. ~*fly*, mouche à feu, luciole, *f*. ~*guard*, garde-feu, pare-étincelles, *m*. ~*hydrant*, ~ *plug*, bouche d'incendie, *f*. ~ *insurance*, assurance contre l'incendie, *f*. ~ *irons*, garniture de foyer, *f*. ~ *lighter*, allume-feu, *m*. ~*man*, pompier, sapeur-pompier; (*stoker*) chauffeur, *m*. ~*place*, cheminée, *f*, âtre, *m*. ~*proof*, *a*, ignifuge, incombustible, à l'épreuve du feu; (*v.t.*) ignifuger. ~*side*, coin du feu, foyer, *m*. ~*side chair*, chauffeuse, *f*, ~ *station*, poste d'incendie, p. de pompiers, *m*. ~*wood*, bois à brûler, b. de chauffage, *m*. ~ *work*, feu d'artifice, *m*, pièce d'a., *f*. ¶ *v.t*, enflammer, embraser, mettre le feu à; incendier; allumer; chauffer; (*shot*) tirer, lâcher, lancer; (*v.i.*) prendre feu; (*gun*) tirer, faire feu. ~! (*Mil.*), feu! **firing**, *n*, chauffage, *m*, chauffe, *f*; combustible; (*Mil.*) feu, tir, *m*.

firm†, *a*, ferme; solide; consistant; tenu. ¶ *n*, maison [de commerce]; société [en nom collectif] *f*. ~ [*name*], raison [sociale] *f*. ~**'s** *capital*, capital social, *m*.

firmament, *n,* firmament, *m.*

firmness, *n,* fermeté, assiette, solidité; consistance; tenue, *f.*

first, *a,* premier; *(after 20, 30, etc.)* unième; *(cousins)* germain. ~ *aid,* premiers soins, *m.pl.* ~ *appearance* & ~ *work,* or ~ *book,* début, *m.* *to make one's* ~ *appearance,* débuter. ~ *attempt,* coup d'essai, *m.* ~*born,* premier-né, *m. 1st class,* 1re classe, *f. the* ~ *comer,* le premier venu, la première venue. ~ *edition,* édition originale, é. princeps, *f.* ~ *finger, index, m.* ~ *[floor],* premier [étage] *m.* ~ *fruits,* prémices, *f.pl.* ~*rate,* de premier ordre; fameux. ¶ *ad,* premièrement, primo. ~, *at* ~, ~ *of all,* [tout] d'abord, de premier abord, de prime abord. ~ & *foremost,* en premier. *the first,* le premier, la première. *the 1st January,* le 1er janvier. ~*ly, ad,* premièrement, primo.

firth, *n,* estuaire, *m.*

fiscal, *a,* fiscal. ~ *system,* fiscalité, *f.* ~ *year,* année budgétaire, *f.*

fish, *n,* poisson, *m.* ~*bone,* arête, *f.* ~*bowl,* bocal, *m.* ~ *glue,* colle de poisson, *f.* ~*hook,* hameçon, *m.* ~ *kettle,* poissonnière, *f.* ~ *market,* halle aux poissons, poissonnerie, *f.* [*wet*] ~*monger,* poissonnier, ère. ~ *out of water* (*pers.*), déraciné, e. ~ *pond,* vivier, *m.* ~ *shop,* poissonnerie, *f.,* ~ *slice,* truelle à poisson, *f.* ~ *spear,* fouine, *f.,* trident, *m.* ~*wife,* poissarde, harengère, *f.* ¶ *v.i. & t.* ~ *for,* pêcher. ~ *out,* ~ *up,* [re]pêcher. ~[*plate*], *v.t,* éclisser. ~*erman,* *n,* pêcheur, euse. ~*ery,* *n,* pêche; (*ground*) pêcherie, *f.* ~*ing* (*act or repr*) *n,* pêche, *f.* ~ *boat,* bateau de pêche, *m.* ~ *ground,* parage de pêche, *m,* pêcherie, *f.* ~ *rod,* canne à pêche, gaule, *f.* ~ *tackle,* engins de pêche, *m.pl,* harnais de p., *m.* ~*y, a,* sauvagin; (*fig.*) véreux.

fission, *n,* fission, *f.*

fissure, *n,* fissure, fente, *f.* ¶ *v.t,* fendiller.

fist, *n,* poing, *m.* **fisticuffs,** *n.pl,* coup[s] de poing, *m.*[*pl.*].

fistula, *n,* fistule, *f.*

fit, *a,* propre, bon, apte, convenable, approprié, à propos; capable; dispos, frais. ~ *for service,* valide. ¶ *n,* accès, *m,* attaque, crise, boutade, bouffée, *f;* (*Mech.*) montage, *m.* ~ *of coughing,*

quinte [de toux] *f. by* ~*s & starts,* par sauts & par bonds, par boutades, à bâtons rompus. ¶ *v.t,* ajuster, adapter, agencer, aménager, cadrer; monter; épouser [la forme de]; chausser; botter; coiffer; (*v.i.*) s'ajuster; aller. ~ *in,* emboîter, enclaver. ~ *out,* équiper, armer, outiller. ~ *tightly,* coller. **fitful,** *a,* changeant; agité; saccadé; quinteux. **fitly,** *ad,* convenablement. **fitness,** *n,* convenance, aptitude, *f.* **fitter,** *n,* ajusteur, monteur, appareilleur, *m;* (*clothes*) essayeur, euse. **fitting†,** *a,* convenable. ~*s, n.pl,* armature, *f;* garnitures; ferrures, *f.pl;* appareillage, *m.* ~ [& *fixtures*], agencement, *m.*

five, *a & n,* cinq, *a. & m.* ~*finger exercise,* exercice de doigté, *m.* ~ *year plan,* plan quinquennal, *m.*

fix, *n,* impasse, *f,* embarras, pétrin, *m.* ¶ *v.t,* fixer, assujettir, asseoir; ancrer; arrêter. ~*ed†,* *a,* fixe; à demeure. ~ *salary,* fixe, *m.* ~*ing,* *n,* fixage, *m,* fixation, pose, *f.* ~ & *toning bath,* bain de virage-fixage, *m.* ~ [*solution*] (*Phot.*), fixateur, *m.* **fixture,** *n,* pièce fixe, p. à demeure, *f;* engagement, *m.* ~*s & fittings,* agencement, *m.*

fizz[le], *v.i,* pétiller. *fizzle out,* n'aboutir à rien.

flabbergast, *v.t,* atterrer, ébahir.

flabbiness & flaccidity, *n,* flaccidité, mollesse, *f.* **flabby & flaccid,** *a,* flasque, mollasse, avachi, mou, veule.

flag, *n,* drapeau, pavillon; (*pl.*) pavois; (*Bot.*) iris des marais, *m.* ~ *of truce,* (*Mil.*) drapeau parlementaire; (*Nav.*) pavillon p. ~*ship,* [vaisseau] amiral, *m.* ~*staff,* mât de pavillon, *m.* ~[*stone*], dalle, *f.* ¶ *v.t,* daller; pavoiser; faire des signaux; (*v.i.*) fléchir, faiblir, languir, tomber, traîner.

flagellate, *v.t,* flageller.

flageolet, *n,* flageolet, *m.*

flagitious, *a,* scélérat, infâme.

flagon, *n,* flacon, *m,* bouteille [lenticulaire] (pour le vin) *f.*

flagrant, *a,* flagrant.

flail, *n,* fléau, *m.*

flair, *n,* aptitude, *f,* dispositions, *f.pl.*

flake, *n,* (*snow*) flocon, *m;* écaille; lame; lamelle, feuille; paillette; flammèche, *f.* ¶ *v.i,* floconner; s'écailler. **flaky,** *a,* floconneux; écailleux; feuilleté; laminé.

flame, *n,* flamme, *f,* feu, *m.* ~

thrower, lance-flamme, *m.* ¶ *v.i,* flamber, flamboyer; s'enflammer; (*v.t.*) flamber.

flamingo, *n,* flamant, *m.*

Flanders, *n,* la Flandre.

flange, *n,* bride, *f;* boudin; rebord; bourrelet; patin, *m;* aile, *f.* ¶ *v.t,* border.

flank, *n,* flanc, *m.* ¶ *v.t,* flanquer.

flannel, *n,* flanelle, *f.* ~**ette**, *n,* flanelle de coton, *f,* pilou, *m.*

flap, *n,* coup; clapet; bord; pan; abattant, *m;* trappe; patte; oreille, *f.* ¶ *v.t. & i,* battre, voltiger.

flare, *n,* feu, *m,* flamme, *f;* évasement, pavillon, *m.* ¶ *v.i,* flamber, flamboyer; (*lamp*) filer; (*bellmouth*) s'évaser. **to ~ up**, (*anger*) s'emporter.

flash, *a,* tapageur. ¶ *n,* éclair; éclat; feu; trait, *m;* saillie, *f.* ~ *in the pan* (*fig.*), feu de paille. ~ *light*, lampe de poche. ~ *of light* & ~ *of lightning*, éclair, *m.* ~[*ing*] *point*, point d'éclair, p. d'inflammabilité, *m.* ¶ *v.i,* étinceler; miroiter; éclater; jaillir; flamboyer. ~**y**, *a,* voyant, tappageux.

flask, *n,* bouteille; gourde, *f;* flacon, *m;* ballon, *m;* fiole, *f.*

flat, *a,* plat; méplat; aplati; (*nose*) épaté; à plat; plan; géométral; couché; net, formel, catégorique, direct; fade, éventé; maussade, inactif; mat; (*Mus.*) bémol. ~ *iron*, fer à repasser, *m.* ~*roof*, toit en terrasse, *m,* terrasse, plateforme, *f.* ¶ *ad,* à plat. ~ *on one's face*, à plat [ventre]. *to sing ~*, détonner. ¶ *n,* plat; méplat; (*rooms*) appartement; (*plain, shoal*) bas-fond, haut-fond, *m,* basse, *f;* (*Theat.*) châssis; (*Mus.*) bémol, *m.* ~**ly**, *ad,* platement; nettement, [tout] net, carrément. ~**ness**, *n,* aplatissement; (*liquor*) évent, *m;* fadeur, platitude, *f.*

flatten, *v.t,* aplatir; éventer; affadir.

flatter, *v.t,* flatter, caresser. ~**er**, *n,* flatteur, euse. ~**ing**, *a,* flatteur. ~**y**, *n,* flatterie, *f.*

flatulence, -**cy**, *n,* flatulence, *f.* **flatus**, *n,* flatuosité, *f,* gaz, vent, *m.*

flaunt, *v.t,* étaler, faire parade de.

flautist, *n,* flûtiste, *m,f.*

flavor, *n,* saveur, *f,* goût, *m.* ¶ *v.t,* assaisonner. ~**ing**, *n,* assaisonnement, *m.* ~**less**, *a,* insipide, fade.

flaw, *n,* paille, *f,* défaut, *m,* défectuosité; glace, *f,* crapaud; vice,

m. ¶ *v.t,* rendre défectueux. ~**less**, *a,* sans défaut, net. ~**y**, *a,* pailleux.

flax, *n,* lin, *m.* ~ *field*, linière, *f.* ~**en**, *a. & n,* blond, *a. & m.*

flay, *v.t,* écorcher.

flea, *n,* puce, *f.* ~ *bite*, piqûre de puce, *f.*

fleck, *n,* tache, moucheture, *f.*

fledged (**to be**), avoir sa plume. **fledgling**, *n,* oisillon, *m.*

flee, *v.i. & t. ir,* fuir, s'enfuir.

fleece, *n,* toison, *f.* ¶ *v.t,* tondre, plumer, écorcher, étriller. **fleecy**, *a,* floconneux. ~ *clouds, sky fleeced with clouds*, nuages moutonnés, *m.pl,* ciel moutonné, *m.*

fleet, *n,* flotte, *f.* ~ *of foot*, léger (ère) à la course. ~**ing**, *a,* passager, fugitif, fugace.

Fleming, *n,* Flamand, e. **Flemish**. *a. &* (*language*) *n,* flamand, *a. & m.*

flesh, *n,* chair, *f;* chairs *f.pl;* charnure, *f;* (*meat*) viande, *f;* embonpoint, *m.* ¶ ~**y**, *a,* charnu; plantureux. ~ *part of the arm*, gras du bras, *m.*

flexible, *a,* flexible, souple. *to make ~*, assouplir. **flexor**, *a. & n,* fléchisseur, *a.m. & m.*

flick, *n,* chiquenaude, *f;* (*sound*) flic flac, *m.*

flicker, *v.i,* papilloter, trembler, vaciller.

flier, *n,* aviateur, *m.*

flight, *n,* fuite, *f;* vol, envol, *m,* volée; envolée, *f,* essor; élan; exode, *m;* bande, *f;* écart, *m.* ~ *of stairs*, volée d'escalier, *f.* ~**y**, *a,* volage, léger, étourdi, frivole.

flimsy, *a,* sans consistance, mollasse; frivole.

flinch, *v.i,* défaillir, broncher.

fling, *n,* coup; trait, *m.* ¶ *v.t.ir,* jeter, lancer, darder. ~ *away* & ~ *off*, rejeter.

flint, *n,* silex; caillou, *m;* pierre à fusil; pierre [à briquet] *f.* ~ *& steel*, briquet, *m.* ~ *glass*, flintglass, *m.* ~**y**, *a,* siliceux; caillouteux; de pierre.

flip, *v.t,* voleter.

flippant, *a,* léger, désinvolte.

flipper, *n,* nageoire, *f.*

flirt (*pers.*) *n,* coquet, te. ¶ *v.i,* coqueter, flirter. ~**ation**, *n,* coquetterie, *f,* flirt, *m.*

flit, *v.i,* voleter, voltiger; fuir. ~ *about*, papillonner.

float & ~**er**, *n,* flotte, *f;* flotteur; bouchon, *m.* ~[*board*], aube, palette, *f,* aileron, *m.* ~*plane*, hydravion à flotteurs, *m.* ¶ *v.t*, faire flotter; mettre à flot, renflouer; (*Fin.*) lancer; (*v.i.*) flotter; [sur]nager; (*Swim.*) faire la planche. ~ation, (*Fin.*) *n,* lancement, *m.* ~ing, *a,* flottant.

flock, *n,* troupeau; vol. *m,* bande, troupe, *f;* ouailles, *f.pl;* (*wool, etc.*) flocon, *m;* bourre, *f.* ¶ *v.i,* s'assembler [en troupe]; affluer.

floe, *n,* banquise, *f;* glaçon, *m.*

flog, *v.t,* fouetter, fustiger, cravacher. *a flogging,* le fouet.

flood, *n,* inondation, *f,* déluge; flot; torrent, *m;* crue, *f;* (*of the tide*) flux, *m.* ~gate, vanne, *f;* (*fig.*) écluse, *f.* ~ lighting, éclairage par projection, *m,* illumination par p., *f.* ~ tide, marée de flot, *f,* flot, *m.* ¶ *v.t,* inonder, noyer, submerger.

floor, *n,* plancher, parquet; carreau; carré, *m;* aire, *f;* plateau; chantier; tablier; (*story*) étage, palier, *m. on one* ~ (rooms), de plain-pied. ~ *lamp,* lampe à pied, torchère, *f.* ~ *polisher* (*pers.*) frotteur, *m;* (*Mach.*) cireuse, *f.* ~ *space,* surface des étages, *f;* encombrement, *m.* ¶ *v.t,* planchéier; parqueter; jeter par terre; terrasser, désarçonner.

flora, *n,* flore, *f.* **floral,** *a,* floral; fleuriste. ~ *design,* ramage, *m.* **florid,** *a,* fleuri; rubicond. **Florida,** *n,* la Floride. **florist,** *n,* fleuriste, *m,f.*

floss, *n,* bourre, *f.* ~ *silk,* soie floche, filoselle, strasse, *f.*

flotation (*Fin.*) *n,* lancement, *m.*

flotilla, *n,* flottille, escadrille, *f.*

flotsam, *n,* épaves [flottantes] *f.pl.*

flounce, *n,* volant, *m.* ¶ *v.t,* garnir de volants. ~ *about,* se trémousser.

flounder, (*fish*) *n,* flet, *m.* ¶ *v.i,* se débattre; barboter, patauger, patouiller.

flour, *n,* farine, *f.* ~ *mill,* moulin à farine, *m,* minoterie, *f.*

flourish, *n,* floriture, *f;* parafe, *m;* fanfare, *f;* (*of hand*) geste; (*with stick*) moulinet, *m.* ¶ *v.t,* brandir; (*v.i.*) fleurir; faire le moulinet. ~ing, *a,* florissant.

floury, *a,* farineux.

flout, *v.t,* narguer. ~ *at,* se railler de.

flow, *n,* écoulement; cours, *m;* coulée, *f;* débit; flux; torrent, *m.* ~ *of words,* flux de paroles, *m,* faconde, *f.* ¶ *v.i,* couler, s'écouler, affluer.

flower, *n,* fleur, *f.* ~ *garden,* jardin fleuriste, *m.* ~ *girl,* bouquetière, *f.* ~ *holder,* porte-bouquet, *m.* ~ *market,* marché aux fleurs, *m.* ~ *pot,* pot à fleurs, *m.* ~ *show,* exposition de fleurs, e. florale, *f.* ~ *stand,* jardinière, *f.* ~ *wire,* fil carcasse des fleuristes, *m.* ¶ *v.i,* fleurir. ~et, *n,* fleurette, *f.* ~ing, *a,* à fleurs. ¶ *n,* floraison, *f.* ~y, *a,* fleuri.

flowing, *a,* coulant, fluide; flottant, tombant.

flu, *n,* grippe, *f.*

fluctuate, *v.i,* osciller; flotter. **fluctuation,** *n,* fluctuation, oscillation, *f,* mouvement, *m.*

flue, *n,* tuyau; carneau; aspirail, *m.*

fluency, *n,* facilité, *f.* **fluent,** *a,* facile, disert. ~ly, *ad,* couramment.

fluff, *n,* bourre, *f;* coton, *m;* (*under furniture*) moutons; (*hair*) cheveux follets, *m.pl.* to ~ up, pelucher. ~y, *a,* duveté; follet; cotonneux; pelucheux.

fluid, *a,* fluide. ¶ *n,* (*imponderable*) fluide; (*ponderable*) liquide, *m.* ~ity, *n,* fluidité, *f.*

fluke, *n,* (*anchor*) patte, *f;* coup de hasard, raccroc, *m.*

flummery, *n,* fadaises, *f.pl.*

flunk, *v.t,* échouer; être recalé.

flunkey, *n,* laquais, valet de pied, larbin, *m.* ~dom, *n,* valetaille, *f.*

fluorescent, *a,* fluorescent. **fluorine,** *n,* fluor, *m.* **fluorspar,** spath fluor, *m.*

flurry, *n,* ahurissement; coup de vent, *m.* ¶ *v.t,* ahurir.

flush, *a,* à fleur, au ras, de niveau; noyé; lisse; bien pourvu. ¶ *n,* accès, transport; flot de sang, *m;* bouffée; rougeur; fleur; chasse [d'eau] *f;* (*cards*) flux, *m.* ¶ *v.t,* affleurer; laver à grande eau; (*hunting*) faire lever; (*v.i.*) rougir. ~ed *face,* face injectée, *f.*

Flushing, *n,* Flessingue, *f.*

fluster, *v.t,* ahurir, troubler; (*with drink*) griser.

flute, *n,* flûte; (*groove*) cannelure, *f.* ~ [*glass*], flûte, *f.* **flutist,** *n,* flûtiste, *m,f.*

flutter, *n,* battement; émoi, *m.* ¶ *v.i. & t,* voleter; voltiger; palpiter.

fluty, *a,* flûté.

fluvial, fluviatile, *a,* fluvial, fluviatile.

flux, *n,* flux; (*Chem. & Metall.*) fondant, *m.*

fly, *n,* mouche; (*trouser*) braguette, *f.* ~*blown*, piqué des mouches. ~*catcher* (bird), gobe-mouches, ~*mucherolle*, *f.* ~ *fishing*, pêche à la mouche, *f.* ~*leaf*, garde blanche, *f.* ~*paper*, papier tue-mouches, *m.* ~*speck*, chiure, *f.* ~ *swat[ter]*, tue-mouches, *m.* ~*trap* (plant), gobe-mouches, *m.* ~*weight* (*Box.*), poids mouche, *m.* ~*wheel*, volant, *m.* ~ *whisk*, chasse-mouches, émouchoir, *m.* ¶ *v.i.ir*, voler, s'envoler; [s'en]fuir; dénicher; éclater; sauter; jaillir; (*v.t.ir.*) fuir; (*flag*) battre; (*kite*) lancer. ~ *about*, voltiger. ~ *at*, s'élancer sur; sauter à; s. sur; apostropher; voler. ~ *open*, s' ouvrir en coup de vent. ~*ing*, *n*, vol, *m;* aviation, *f.* ~ *ace*, as de l'aviation, *m.* ~ *buttress*, arc-boutant, *m.* ~ *field*, champ d' aviation, *m.* ~ *fish*, poisson volant, *m.* ~ *squad*, brigade (*de police*) mobile, *f.* ~ *start*, départ lancé, *m.* ~ *visit*, camp volant, *m.*

foal, *n,* poulain, *m,* pouliche, *f;* (*ass's*) ânon, *m.* ¶ *v.i,* pouliner, mettre bas.

foam, *n,* écume, mousse, *f.* ¶ *v.i,* écumer, mousser; (*sea*) moutonner. ~*y,* *a,* écumeux, mousseux; (*sea*) moutonneuse.

focal, *a,* focal. **focus,** *n,* foyer, *m.* ¶ *v.t,* mettre au point; canaliser (*fig.*).

fodder, *n,* fourrage, *m,* provende, *f.*

foe, *n,* ennemi, e, adversaire, *m.*

fog, *n,* brouillard, *m,* brume, *f;* (*Phot.*) voile, *m.* ~ *horn,* trompe de brume, *f.* ¶ *v.t,* embrumer; (*Phot.*) voiler. **foggy,** *a,* brumeux.

fog[e]y, *n,* or **old** ~, croûton, *m,* [vieille] ganache, [vieille] perruque, *f.* **fogyish,** *a,* encroûté.

foible, *n,* faible, *m.*

foil, *n,* (*tinsel*) feuille, *f,* clinquant; paillon; tain; (*Fenc.*) fleuret; (*fig.*) repoussoir, lustre, *m.* ¶ *v.t,* déjouer; dépister.

foist, *v.t,* glisser; colloquer; attribuer.

fold, *n,* pli, repli; parc, *m,* bergerie, *f;* (*Relig.*) bercail, *m.* ¶ *v.t,* plier; (*arms*) [se] croiser; (*hands*) joindre; (*sheep*) parquer. ~ *up, v.t,* [re]plier; (*v.i.*) se replier. ~*er,* *n,* plieur, euse; chemise [pour dossier] *f;* (*publicity*) dépliant, *m.* ~*ing, p.a:* ~

door, porte brisée, *f.* ~ *machine,* machine à plier, plieuse, *f.* ~ *stool,* pliant, *m.*

foliaceous, *a,* foliacé. **foliage,** *n,* feuillage, *m,* frondaison, *f,* ombrage, *m,* chevelure, *f.* **foliate,** *a,* feuillé. **foliation,** *n,* foliation, feuillaison, frondaison, *f.*

folio, *n,* folio, *m;* (*book*) *n.* & *a,* in-folio, *m.* & *a.* ¶ *v.t,* folioter.

folklore, *n,* folk-lore, *m,* tradition, *f.*

folks, *n.pl,* gens, *m.pl.* & *f.pl.*

follicle, *n,* follicule, *m,* crypte, *f.*

follow, *v.t,* suivre; (*cards*) fournir de; (*v.i.*) s'ensuivre, résulter. ~ *suit,* (*cards*) fournir [à] la couleur demandée; (*fig.*) faire de même. ~ *through,* suivre la balle. ~ *up,* [pour]suivre. ~ [*shot*] (*Bil.*) *n,* coulé, *m.* ~*er,* *n,* suivant, e; disciple, partisan, sectateur, *m;* suite [de lettre] *f.* ~*ing* (*day, etc.*) *a,* suivant, e. *in the* ~ *manner,* ¶ voici comment. *the* ~ [*persons*], les personnes dont les noms suivent. *the* ~ *story,* l'histoire que voici. ¶ *n,* partisans, *m.pl.*

folly, *n,* folie; sottise, bêtise, *f.*

foment, *v.t,* fomenter; étuver. ~*ation,* *n,* fomentation, *f.*

fond†, *a,* tendre, affectueux. *to be* ~ *of,* aimer; affectionner; être friand de, ê. gourmand de; ê. porté pour; ê. amateur de.

fondle, *v.t,* caresser, câliner, pouponner.

fondness, *n,* affection, tendresse, *f;* penchant, goût, *m.*

font, *n,* (*Eccl.*) fonts, *m.pl;* (*Typ.*) fonte, *f.*

food, *n,* nourriture, *f,* aliment, *m,* vivres, *m.pl;* mangeaille, *f,* mets, *m;* table, cuisine; pâture, *f.* ~ *& drink,* le boire & le manger. ~ *for thought,* matière à réflexion, *f.* ~*stuff,* matière d'alimentation, denrée alimentaire, *f.*

fool, *n,* sot, te; bête, *f;* imbécile, *m,f,* idiot, e; plaisant, *m;* (*Hist., court*) fou, *m. to play the* ~, faire l'imbécile, nigauder, niaiser. ~*hardiness,* témérité, *f.* ~*hardy,* téméraire. ~*proof,* à l'épreuve des maladresses. ¶ *v.t,* duper; jouer, amuser. ~ [*about*], *v.i,* baguenauder. ~*ery,* *n,* farce, *f,* vains propos, *m.pl,* pantalonnade, *f,* calembredaines, *f.pl,* bouffonnerie, *f;* badinage, *m,* gaminerie, *f.* ~*ish†,* *a,* sot, bête, benêt. **~ishness**, *n*, folie, sottise, *f*.

foot, *n*, pied, *m*; patte; semelle; base, *f*; bas, *m*; (*Meas.*) pied = 0.30480 meter. ~ & *mouth disease*, fièvre aphteuse, *f*. **~ball**, ballon de football; (*game*) football, *m*. ~ *bath*, bain de pieds, *m*. **~bridge**, passerelle, *f*. **~fall**, pas, *m*. ~ *fault* (*Ten.*), faute de pied, *f*. **~hold**, assiette pour le pied, *f*, pied, *m*. **~lights**, rampe, *f*. **~man**, valet de pied, laquais, *m*. **~note**, apostille, *f*. **~path**, sentier, *m*, sente, *f*; (*street*) trottoir, *m*. **~print**, empreinte de pas, e. du pied, *f*, pas, vestige, *m*; trace, *f*. ~ *race*, course à pied, *f*. **~sore**, éclopé. **~step**, pas, *m*. **~stool**, tabouret [de pied] *m*. ~ *warmer*, chauffepieds, *m*, chaufferette, bouillotte, *f*. **~wear**, chaussures, *f.pl*. ~ *work*, jeu de jambes, *m*. *on* ~, à pied. **~ing**, *n*, pied, *m*; assiette pour le pied, *f*.

fop, *n*, fat, *m*. **foppish**, *a*, fat.

for, *pr*, pour; par; à; de; à cause de; pendant; il y a; depuis; malgré. ~ *all that*, malgré cela, malgré tout. ~ & *against*, le pour & le contre. ¶ *c*, car.

forage, *n*, fourrage, *m*. ¶ *v.i*, fourrager; (*bird*) picorer. **forager**, *n*, fourrageur, *m*.

forasmuch, *c*, étant donné.

foray, *n*, incursion, maraude, *f*.

forbear, *v.i.ir*, s'abstenir, s'empêcher. **~ance**, *n*, indulgence, longanimité, mansuétude, *f*.

forbid, *v.t.ir*, défendre, interdire. *God ~!* à Dieu ne plaise! **forbidden**, *a*, interdit. **forbidding**, *a*, rebutant, repoussant.

force, *n*, force, *f*; effort; effectif, *m*; armée, *f*. ~ *of circumstances*, force des choses. *by* ~, à main armée. *in* ~, en vigueur. ~ *pump*, pompe foulante, *f*. ¶ *v.t*, forcer; hâter; se frayer. **forced**, *p.a*, forcé; factice. *by* ~ *marches*, à grandes journées. **forcedly**, *ad*, forcément. **forceful†**, *a*, vigoureux. **forcemeat**, *n*, farce, *f*.

forceps, *n.s. & pl*, (*Surg.*) pince, *f*; (*dental*) davier; (*obstetrical*) forceps, *m*, fers, *m.pl*.

forcible, *a*, énergique, corsé. ~ *feeding*, gavage, *m*. **forcibly**, *ad*, énergiquement; de force.

ford, *n*, gué, *m*. ¶ *v.t*, guéer. **~able**, *a*, guéable.

fore, *a*, de devant, *e.g*, **~paw**, patte de devant, *f*; (*Naut.*) de l'avant. ¶ *ad*, à l'avant. ~ & *aft*, de l'avant à l'arrière. ¶ (*golf*) *i*, attention!, hep!, balle! ¶ *n*, devant; (*Naut.*) avant, *m*.

forearm, *n*, avant-bras, *m*. ¶ *v.t*, prémunir.

forebode, *v.t*, présager. **foreboding**, *n*, présage, pressentiment, *m*.

forecast, *n*, prévision, *f*. ¶ *v.t.ir*, prévoir.

forecastle or **foc's'le**, *n*, gaillard d'avant; poste de l'équipage. *m*.

foreclose, *v.t*, saisir. **foreclosure**, *n*, saisie, *f*.

forecourt, *n*, (*house*) cour de devant; (*castle*, *palace*), avant-cour, *f*.

forefathers, *n.pl*, aïeux, *m.pl*.

forefinger, *n*, index, *m*.

foregoing, *p.a*, précédent. *the* ~, ce qui précède. *foregone conclusion*, décision prise d'avance, *f*.

foreground, *n*, premier plan, *m*, devants, *m.pl*.

forehand [**stroke**] (*Ten.*) *n*, [coup d']avant-main, *m*.

forehead, *n*, front, *m*.

foreign, *a*, étranger; extérieur; exotique. ~ *exchange rates* (table), cote des changes, *f*. ~ *service*, service diplomatique, *m*. **~er**, *n*, étranger, ère.

foreknowledge, *n*, prescience, *f*.

foreland, *n*, cap, *m*, pointe [de terre] *f*.

forelock (*hair*) *n*, toupet, *m*.

foreman, *n*, contremaître, chef d'équipe, chef, *m*. ~ *of the jury*, chef du jury.

foremast, *n*, mât de misaine, *m*.

foremost (**the**), le plus avancé; le tout premier.

forenoon, *n*, matinée, *f*.

forensic, *a*, de palais; (*medicine*) légale.

forerunner, *n*, avant-coureur, précurseur, *m*, préface, *f*.

foresee, *v.t.ir*, prévoir.

foreshadow, *v.t*, annoncer.

foreshore, *n*, rivage, *m*.

foreshorten, *v.t*, raccourcir.

foresight, *n*, prévoyance, *f*.

forest, *n*, forêt, *f*; (*att.*) forestier.

forestall, *v.t*, anticiper; prévenir; devancer.

forester, *n*, (*officer*) forestier; habitant de la forêt, *m*. **forestry**, *n*, sylviculture, *f*.

foretaste, *n*, avant-goût, *m*.

foretell, *v.t.ir*, prédire, annoncer.

forethought, *n,* prévoyance; préméditation, *f.*

forewarn, *v.t,* prévenir, prémunir, avertir.

forewoman, *n,* première, *f.*

foreword, *n,* avant-propos, *m,* préface, *f.*

forfeit, *n,* dédit, *m,* pénalité, *f; (at play)* gage, *m,* pénitence, *f; (pl.)* gages, jeux innocents, petits jeux, *m.pl.* ¶ *v.t,* déchoir de; *(honor)* forfaire à. **~ure,** *n,* déchéance, *f.*

forgather, *v.i,* se réunir.

forge, *n,* forge, *f.* ¶ *v.t, (metal & fig.)* forger; falsifier, contrefaire. **~d,** *p.a,* faux. **forgeman,** *n,* forgeur, *m.* **forger,** *n,* faussaire, *m,f.* fabricateur, trice. **forgery,** *n,* faux; crime de faux, *m;* contrefaçon, *f.*

forget, *v.t.ir,* oublier. **~-me-not,** ne m'oubliez pas, myosotis, *m,* oreille-de-souris, *f.* **~** *oneself,* s'échapper, s'émanciper. **~ful,** *a,* oublieux. **~fulness,** *n,* oubli, *m.*

forgive, *v.t.ir,* pardonner; *(pers.)* pardonner à; faire grâce à, remettre. **~ness,** *n,* pardon, *m;* rémission; remise, *f.*

forgo, *v.t.ir,* s'abstenir de; renoncer à.

fork, *n,* fourche; *(table, etc.)* fourchette, *f; (tree)* fourchon, *m; (road, etc.)* bifurcation, *f. tuning* **~,** diapason, *m.* ¶ *v.i,* fourcher, bifurquer. **~ed,** *a,* fourchu. **~** *lightning,* éclair ramifié, *m.*

forlorn, *a,* délaissé; désolé, inconsolé. **~** *hope,* vague espoir, *m.*

form, *n,* forme, *f,* ton, *m; (paper)* formule, *f,* bulletin, *m; (seat)* banc; *(hare)* gîte, *m.* ¶ *v.t,* former; façonner; constituer; nouer; faire; se faire, se former. **~** *single file,* dédoubler les rangs. **~al†,** *a,* formel; de forme; dans les formes; cérémonieux; solennel; formaliste. **~ality,** *n,* formalité, *f.* **~ation,** *n,* formation; constitution, *f.* **form** *(Typ.)* *n,* forme, *f.*

former, *a,* ancien; passé; précédent. *the* **~,** celui-là. **~ly,** *ad,* autrefois, jadis, anciennement, ci-devant.

formidable†, *a,* formidable.

Formosa, *n,* Formose, *f.*

formula, *n,* formule, *f.* **~ry,** *n,* formulaire, *m.* **formulate,** *v.t,* formuler. **formulism,** *n,* le style pompier. **formulist,** *n. &* **~ic,** *à,* pompier, *m. & att.*

fornication, *n,* fornication, *f.*

forsake, *v.t.ir,* délaisser, abandonner.

forsooth, *ad,* en vérité, ma foi.

forswear, *v.t.ir,* abjurer. **~** *oneself,* se parjurer.

fort, *n,* fort, *(small)* fortin, *m.*

forte *(Mus.)* *ad,* forte. ¶ *(strong point)* *n,* fort, *m.*

forth, *ad,* en avant. **~coming,** *a,* [prêt] à paraître; à venir; prochain. **~with,** *ad,* incessamment, sur-le-champ, séance tenante.

fortieth, *a. & n,* quarantième, *a. & m,f.*

fortification, *n,* fortification, *f; (wine)* vinage, *m.* **fortify,** *v.t,* fortifier; munir; corser; viner. *fortified place,* place forte, p. de guerre, *f,* camp retranché, *m.* **fortitude,** *n,* force d'âme, *f,* courage, *m.*

fortnight, *n,* quinze jours, *m.pl,* quinzaine, *f.* **~ly,** *ad,* tous les quinze jours.

fortress, *n,* forteresse, *f.*

fortuitous†, *a,* fortuit.

fortunate, *a,* heureux, fortuné. **~ly,** *ad,* heureusement, par bonheur. **fortune,** *n,* fortune, *f;* horoscope, *m. to tell* **~s,** dire la bonne aventure. **~teller,** diseur (euse) de bonne aventure; tireur (euse) de cartes, cartomancien, ne.

forty, *a. & n,* quarante, *a. & m.*

forum, *n,* forum, *m.*

forward, *a,* avancé; d'avance; avant; progressif; précoce, hâtif; hardi, indiscret; *(Com.)* à terme, à livrer. **~[s],** *ad,* [en] avant. ¶ *n, (Foot.)* avant, *m.* ¶ *v.t,* avancer; hâter; expédier, acheminer; faire suivre, transmettre. **~ing** *agent,* commissionnaire de transport[s], expéditeur, *m.* **~ness,** *n,* précocité; hardiesse, *f.*

fossil, *a. & n,* fossile, *a. & m.*

foster, *v.t,* encourager; favoriser; nourrir. ¶ *a,* adoptif. **~** *brother,* frére de lait, *m.* **~** *child,* nourrisson, *m.*

foul, *a,* sale; crasseux; immonde; mauvais, vilain; infect; vicié; fétide; puant; infâme; *(words)* gros. **~mouthed,** mal embouché. **~** *play,* vilain tour; sabotage, *m.* ¶ *n,* faute, *f;* coup déloyal, *m.* ¶ *v.t,* salir, souiller, encrasser; vicier; fausser; *(Naut., rope, etc.)* engager; *(ship)* entrer en collision; *(sports)* violer la règle. **~ness,** *n,* fétidité; noirceur, *f.*

found, *v.t,* fonder, créer; *(metal)*

fondre, mouler. **foundation,**
n, fondation, *f;* fondement; établissement, *m;* assiette; assise, *f.*
~ *stone,* pierre fondamentale,
première p., *f.* **founder,** *n,* fondateur, créateur; (*race*) auteur,
m; (*family*) souche, *f;* (*metal*)
fondeur, *m.* ¶ *v.i,* sombrer, couler, c. à fond, c. à pic, c. bas.

foundling, *n,* enfant trouvé, *m.*

foundress, *n,* fondatrice, créa-
trice, *f.*

foundry, *n,* fonderie, *f.*

fount, *n,* fontaine, *f;* puits, *m;*
(*Typ.*) fonte, *f.* **fountain,** *n,*
fontaine, source, *f;* jet d'eau, *m;*
(*pl.*) [grandes] eaux, *f.pl.* ~**head,**
source, *f.* ~ *of youth,* fontaine de
Jouvence. ~ *pen,* stylographe,
porte-plume [à] réservoir, *m.*

four, *a. & n,* quatre, *a. & m.*
~**fold,** quadruple. ~**footed,** quadrupède. ~-**poster,** lit à colonnes,
m. ~**score,** *a. & n,* quatre-
vingts, quatre-vingt, *a. & m.*
~**some** (*golf*), partie double, *f.*
~-**wheeled,** à quatre roues. on all
~s, à quatre pattes. **fourteen,** *a.*
& n, quatorze, *a. & m.* ~**th**†,
a. & n, quatorzième, *a. & m,f;*
quatorze, *m.* **fourth**†, *a,* quatrième. ~ *finger,* petit doigt,
[doigt] auriculaire, *m.* ¶ *n,* quatrième, *m,f;* quatre, *m;* (*part*)
quart, *m;* (*Mus.*) quatre, *f.*

fowl, *n,* oiseau, *m.* o. de basse-cour,
m; volaille; poule; poularde, *f.*
~**er,** *n,* oiseleur, *m.* ~**ing,** *n,*
chasse aux oiseaux, *f.* ~ *piece,*
canardière, *f.*

fox, *n,* renard, *m.* ~ *cub,* renardeau, *m.* ~'*s hole,* renardière,
f. ~**glove,** gantelée, digitale, *f.*
~**hound,** foxhound, *m.* ~ *hunt-*
ing, chasse au renard, *f.* ~ *ter-*
rier, fox-terrier, *m.* ~-*trot,* fox-
trot, *m.* ~**y** (*fig.*) *a,* rusé.

foyer, *n,* foyer [du public] *m.*

fraction, *n,* fraction, *f.* ~**al,** *a,*
fractionnaire.

fractious, *a,* hargneux.

fracture, *n,* fracture; cassure,
rupture, *f.* ¶ *v.t,* fracturer.

fragile, *a,* fragile. **fragility,** *n,*
fragilité, *f.*

fragment, *n,* fragment, morceau,
éclat, *m.* ~**ary,** *a,* fragmentaire.

fragrance, *n,* bonne odeur, *f,*
parfum, *m.* **fragrant,** *a,* odoriférant, odorant.

frail, *a,* frêle; fragile; caduc. ¶ *n,*
cabas, *m;* bourriche, *f.* ~**ty,** *n,*
fragilité; infirmité, *f.*

frame & ~*work,* *n,* cadre; bâti;
châssis, *m;* charpente; membrure;
ossature; carcasse; armature;
monture; châsse, *f;* pan, *m;* case,
f; (*Need.*) métier, *m.* ~ *of mind,*
état d'esprit, *m,* disposition, *f.*
¶ *v.t,* former; charpenter; (*pic-*
ture, etc.) encadrer. **framing**
(*act*) *n,* encadrement, *m.*

France, *n,* la France.

franchise, *n,* droit électoral,
électorat, *m.*

Franciscan, *n,* franciscain, *m.*

Francophil[**e**]*, a. & n,* francophile, *a. & m,f.* **Francophobe,**
a. & n, francophobe, *a. & m,f.*

frank†, *a,* franc, ouvert, en dehors. ~**ness,** *n,* franchise, rondeur, *f.*

Frankfort, *n,* Francfort, *m.*

frankincense, *n,* encens mâle,
m.

frantic†, *a,* frénétique; effréné,
fou.

fraternal†, *a,* fraternel. **fra-**
ternity, *n,* fraternité, *f.* **fraternize,**
v.i, fraterniser. **fratricide,** *n, &*
fratricidal, *a,* fratricide, *m. & a.*

fraud, *n,* fraude; supercherie, *f.*
fraudulent†, *a,* frauduleux.

fraught with, plein de, gros de.

fray, *n,* lutte, rixe, bagarre; bataille, *f.*

fray, *v.t,* érailler, effranger,
effilocher.

freak, *n,* caprice, *m.* ~ [*of na-*
ture], monstruosité, *f,* jeu [bi-
zarre] de la nature, phénomène,
m. ~**ish**†, *a,* capricieux; bizarre;
hétéroclite; monstrueux.

freckle, *n,* tache de rousseur, lentille, éphélide, *f.* ¶ *v.t,* tacheter de
rousseurs.

free, *a,* libre; ouvert; large; débar-
rassé; dépourvu; exempt; privé;
gratuit; net; indépendant; quitte;
dégagé, désinvolte. ~ *allowance*
of luggage or *weight allowed*
~, franchise de bagages, f. de
poids, *f.* ~ *& easy,* sans gêne,
bohème, cavalier. ~ *& easy man-*
ner, désinvolture, *f.* ~ *hand* (*fig.*),
carte blanche, *f.* ~*hand draw-*
ing, dessin à main levée, *m.* ~
lance, franc-tireur, tirailleur, *m.*
~*mason,* franc-maçon, *m.* ~
pass, billet de faveur; (*Rly*) permis de circulation, *m.* ~*stone,*
pierre franche, *f.* ~*thinker,* libre
penseur, esprit fort, *m.* ~*think-*
ing, ~ *thought,* libre pensée, *f.*
~ *trade,* libre-échange, *m.* ~
verse, vers libres, *m.pl.* ~*wheel,*

roue libre, *f.* ~ *will*, [plein] gré;
(*Philos.*) libre (*ou* franc) arbitre,
m. ¶ *ad*, gratis; gracieusement;
franco; en franchise. ¶ *v.t*, libérer; affranchir; dégager; exempter. **freedom,** *n*, liberté;
exemption; franchise; aisance, *f.*
free[*dom of*] *speech*, libre parole,
liberté de parler, *f.* **freely,** *ad*,
librement; franchement; largement.

freeze, *v.t.ir*, geler, glacer, congeler, réfrigérer; (*v.i.ir.*) geler;
se g., [se] glacer, prendre.
freezer, *n*, glacière; sorbetière, *f.*
freezing point, température de
congélation, *f.* (thermometer) *at
freezing*, à glace.

Freiburg (*Baden*) *n*, Fribourg-
en-Brisgau, *m.*

freight, *n*, fret, *m.* ~ *train*, train
de merchandises, *m.* ¶ *v.t*, fréter.

French, *a*, français. ~ *ambassador, consul*, ambassadeur, consul,
de France, *m.* ~ *beans*, haricots;
(*unripe*) haricots verts, *m.pl.* ~
chalk, talc, *m.* ~ *horn*, cor d'harmonie, *m. to take* ~ *leave*, filer à
l'anglaise. ~ *lesson, master,*
leçon, *f*, professeur, *m*, de français. ~*man*, ~*woman*, Français,
e. ~ *polish, n*, vernis au tampon,
m; (*v.t.*) vernir au t. ~*-speak-
ing Switzerland*, la Suisse ro-
mande. ~ *window*, porte-fenêtre,
f. ¶ (*language*) *n*, le français.
the ~, *pl*, les Français, *m.pl.*
Frenchify, *v.t*, franciser.

frenzied, *p.p*, frénétique; délirant.
frenzy, *n*, frénésie, fureur, ivresse,
f.

frequency, *n*, fréquence, *f.* **frequent,** *a*, fréquent. ¶ *v.t*, fréquenter, pratiquer, hanter, courir.
~**er,** *n*, habitué, e, coureur, euse.
~**ly,** *ad*, fréquemment.

fresco, *n*, fresque, *f.*

fresh, *a*, frais; récent; vert; reposé; nouveau; novice. ~ *from
the wash*, blanc de lessive. ~
water, eau fraîche; (*not salt*) e.
douce, *f.* ~*water fishing*, pêche
en eaux douces, p. d'eau douce, *f.*
~**en,** *v.t. & i*, rafraîchir; (*Naut.*)
fraîchir. ~**et,** *n*, crue, *f*, grandes
eaux, *f.pl.* ~**ly** *& ~, ad*, fraîchement; (*with p.p.*) frais, aîche,
e.g, fresh[*ly*] *gathered roses*, des
roses fraîches cueillies. ~**ness,** *n*,
fraîcheur; nouveauté; primeur, *f.*

fret, *n*, (*on guitar*) touche; (*Arch.*,
Her.) frette, *f.* ~*saw, n*, scie à
découper, *f*; (*v.t. & i.*) découper,

~*work*, découpure, *f.* ¶ *v.i*, s'irriter, se chagriner, geindre;
(*v.t.*) ronger; chagriner, tracasser. ~**ful,** *a*, chagrin, geignard.

friable, *a*, friable.

friar, *n*, moine, frère, religieux, *m.*

friction, *n*, friction, *f*, frottement,
m.

Friday, *n*, vendredi, *m. Good
~*, vendredi saint.

fried fish, poisson frit, *m*, friture, *f.*

friend, *n*, ami, e; cousin, e. ~**less,**
a, sans ami. ~**liness,** *n*, bienveillance, *f.* ~**ly,** *a*, ami, amical,
amiable. ~**ship,** *n*, amitié, camaraderie, *f.*

Friesland, *n*, la Frise.

frieze, *n*, frise, *f.*

frigate, *n*, frégate, *f.*

fright, *n*, frayeur, épouvante,
peur, *f*, effroi, *m*, transe, *f*;
(*pers.*) horreur, *f*, magot, *m.*
~**en,** *v.t*, effrayer; épouvanter.
~**ful**†, *a*, effrayant, épouvantable,
affreux.

frigid†, *a*, glacial, froid. ~**ity,**
n, frigidité, froideur, *f.*

frill, *n*, ruche, *f*; jabot, *m.* ~*s
& furbelows*, fanfreluches, *f.pl.*
¶ *v.t*, rucher.

fringe, *n*, frange, crépine, *f*, effilé;
bord, *m.* ¶ *v.t*, franger; border.

frippery, *n*, friperie, *f*, falbalas,
colifichets, *m.pl.*

Frisian, *a*, frison. ¶ *n*, Frison, ne.

frisk, *n*, gambade, *f.* ¶ *v.i*, gambader, fringuer, frétiller; (*search*)
palper.

frisky, *a*, frétillant, fringant.

fritter (*Cook.*) *n*, beignet, *m.*
~ *away*, éparpiller, dissiper,
fricasser.

frivolity, *n*, frivolité, *f.* **frivolous,** *a*, frivole, léger.

frizzle, *v.t*, crêper, friser. **frizzle**
(*bacon, etc.*) *v.t*, faire se re-
coquiller.

frock, *n*, robe, *f*, costume, *m*;
(*smock*) blouse, *f*; (*monk's*)
froc, *m.* ~ *coat*, redingote, *f.*

frog, *n*, grenouille; (*horse*) fourchette, *f*; (*Rly*) croisement;
(*sword*) porte-épée, pendant, *m.*

frolic, *v.i*, folâtrer. ~**some,** *a*,
follet.

from, *pr*, de; d'avec; de chez; depuis; dès; à; d'après; à partir de,
à dater de; de la part de; par.
~ *that point of view*, à ce point
de vue. ~ *what you do*, d'après
ce que vous faites. ~ *the begin-*

ning, dès le commencement. *the train* ~ *Paris*, le train de Paris.

frond, *n,* fronde, *f.*

front, *a,* de devant; d'avant; de front; de tête; de face; premier. ~ *[line]* (*Mil.*), front, *m,* première ligne, *f.* ¶ *n,* devant; avant, *m,* tête; devanture; face; façade, *f;* front; recto, *m;* (*shirt*) plastron, *m. in* ~ & *in* ~ *of,* devant. *on the [sea]* ~, en bordure de la mer; sur la promenade [de la mer]; (*hotel*) sur la mer. ¶ *v.t,* affronter, faire face à; donner sur; ~**age,** *n,* devant, *m;* (*extent*) face; façade; exposition, *f.* ~**al,** *a,* de front; (*Anat.*) frontal.

frontier, *n. & att,* frontière, *f. & att.*

frontispiece, *n,* (*book*) frontispice, *m;* (*Arch.*) façade, *f.*

frost, *n,* gelée, *f;* (*degrees of*) froid, *m;* (*fig., of age*) glaces, *f.pl.* ~**bitten,** congélation, *f.* ~**-bitten** gelé. ~**ed glass,** verre dépoli, *m.* ~**y,** *a,* glacial, de glace.

froth, *n,* écume; mousse, *f.* ¶ *v.i,* écumer; mousser. ~**y,** *a,* écumant; mousseux; frivole.

frown, *n,* froncement des sourcils, *m.* ¶ *v.i,* froncer le[s] sourcil[s], sourciller, se re[n]frogner. ~ *[up]on,* regarder d'un mauvais œil, désapprouver.

frowzy, *a,* moisi; borgne.

frozen, *p.a,* gelé, glacé; glacial; (*meat, etc.*) frigorifié; (*credit*) gelé. *[as if]* ~ *stiff,* morfondu.

fructify, *v.i,* fructifier; (*v.t.*) féconder.

frugal†, *a,* frugal. ~**ity,** *n,* frugalité, *f.*

fruit, *n,* fruit, *m.* ~ *bowl,* coupe à fruits, *f,* compotier, *m.* ~ *salad,* macédoine de fruits, salade de f—s, *f.* ~ *store,* fruiterie, *f.* ~ *tree,* arbre fruitier, a. à fruit, *m.* **fruitful†,** *a,* fertile, fécond; fructueux (*fig. & poet.*). ~**ness,** *n,* fertilité, fécondité, *f.* **fruition,** *n,* jouissance; réalisation, *f.* **fruitless,** *a,* sans fruit; (*fig.*) infructueux; vain. ~**ly,** *ad,* en vain.

frump, *n,* femme mal fagotée, *f.*

frustrate, *v.t,* frustrer, déjouer. **frustration,** *n,* insuccès, renversement, *m.*

frustum, *n,* tronc, *m.*

fry, *n,* (*fish*) fretin, frai, alevin, nourrain, *m,* poissonnaille, blanchaille; (*Cook.*) friture, *f.* **French fries,** pommes frites, *f.pl.* ¶ *v.t,* [faire] frire; (*v.i.*) frire. ~**ing,** *n,*

& ~ *oil* or *fat,* friture, *f.* ~ *pan,* poêle [à frire] *f.*

fuchsia, *n,* fuchsia, *m.*

fuddle, *v.t,* griser. ~**d,** *p.a,* gris.

fuel, *n,* combustible, *f;* (*fig.*) aliment, *m.* ~ *oil,* pétrole combustible, *m.* ¶ *v.t,* alimenter; chauffer.

fugitive, *a,* fugitif, passager. ¶ *n,* fugitif, ive, fuyard, e.

fugleman, *n,* chef de file; meneur; porteparole, *m.*

fugue, *n,* fugue, *f.*

fulcrum, *n,* [point d']appui, *m.*

fulfil, *v.t,* remplir, accomplir; satisfaire à, exécuter. ~**ment,** *n,* accomplissement, *m,* exécution, *f.*

full, *a,* plein; comble; rempli; complet; au complet; entier; plénier; tout; copieux; nourri; intégral; germain. ~**-blooded,** sanguin. ~**-bodied** (*wine*), vineux, corsé. ~ *dress,* grande tenue, tenue de cérémonie; grande toilette, *f.* ~**-grown,** fait. ~**-length** *mirror,* psyché, *f.* ~**-length** *portrait,* portrait en pied, *m.* ~ *name,* (*pers.*) nom & prénoms, (*stock, etc.*) désignation détaillée, *f.* ~ *of fish* (river, lake), poissonneux. ~ *orchestra,* grand orchestre, *m.* ~**-page** *illustration,* gravure en pleine page, *f.* ~ *size,* grandeur naturelle, *f. I am* ~, je suis rassasié. *in* ~, in extenso. *Also* = **fully.** ¶ *n,* plein, *m.*

full, *v.t,* fouler. ~**er,** *n,* foulon, *m.* ~*'s earth,* terre à foulon, *f.*

fully, *ad,* pleinement; complètement; entièrement; intégralement; bien; en toutes lettres.

fulminate, *v.i. & t,* fulminer.

fullness, *n,* plénitude; ampleur; rondeur, abondance, *f.* **fulsome,** *a,* outré, excessif, exagéré, écœurant.

fumble, *v.i,* [far]fouiller, tâtonner.

fume, *n,* fumée, vapeur, bouffée, buée; colère, *f.* ¶ *v.i. & t,* fumer; enrager, maugréer. ~**d** (*oak*) *a,* patiné, teinté.

fumigate, *v.t,* faire des fumigations dans.

fun, *n,* amusement, *m;* plaisanterie, drôlerie, *f. in* ~, pour rire. *to make* ~ *of,* se moquer de, se divertir aux dépens de.

function, *n,* fonction, *f,* office, *m;* réunion, *f.* ¶ *v.i,* fonctionner; opérer. ~**al,** *a,* fonctionnel. ~**ary,** *n,* fonctionnaire, *m,f.*

fund, *n,* fonds, *m,* caisse, masse, *f;* (*pl.*) fonds, deniers, *m.pl,* fonds,

m, masse, provision, *f. sinking*
~, caisse d'amortissement, *f.*
¶ *v.t*, consolider.

fundament, *n*, fondement, *m.*
~al†, *a*, fondamental, foncier.

funeral, *n*, enterrement, *m*, (*elaborate*) funérailles, *f.pl*; convoi, *m*,
pompe funèbre, *f*. ¶ *a*, funéraire;
funèbre. ~ *oration*, oraison
funèbre, *f.* **funereal**, *a*, funèbre,
d'enterrement.

fungous, *a*, fongueux; transitoire.
fungus, *n*, fongus; champignon
[vénéneux] *m.*

funicular, *a*. & *n*, funiculaire, *a.*
& *m.*

funnel, *n*, entonnoir, *m*; (*Naut.*)
cheminée, *f.*

funny, *a*, comique, drôle, plaisant.
~ *bone*, petit juif, *m.* ~ *little*
(*pers.*), falot, *a.* ~ *man*, comique
de la troupe, loustic, *m. a* ~
(*queer*) *man*, un drôle. *the* ~
part, le comique.

fur, *n*, fourrure, *f*, poil; pelage;
dépôt, tartre, *m*, incrustation, *f.*
~ *coat*, manteau de fourrure, *m.*
~-*lined*, fourré. ~ *lining*, fourrage, *m.* ~ *trade*, pelleterie, *f.*

furbelows, *n.pl*, falbalas, *m.pl.*

furbish, *v.t*, fourbir.

furious†, *a*, furieux, acharné.

furl, *v.t*, serrer, ferler.

furlong, *n*, furlong, *m.* = ⅛ mile
or 201.168 meters.

furlough, *n*, (*Mil.*) permission, *f.*

furnace, *n*, four; fourneau; foyer,
m; fournaise, *f. blast* ~, haut
fourneau, *m.*

furnish, *v.t*, fournir; pourvoir;
garnir; meubler. ~*ed apartments*
or rooms, [appartement] meublé,
hôtel meublé, *m.* **furniture**, *n*,
meubles, *m.pl*; ameublement,
mobilier, *m*; garniture, *f*, accessoires, *m.pl.* ~ *polish*, encaustique pour meubles, *f.* ~ *warehouse*, garde-meuble, *m.*

furore, *n*, fureur, *f.*

furred (*tongue*) *p.a*, chargée.

furrier, *n*, fourreur, pelletier, *m.*
~*y*, *n*, pelleterie, *f.*

furrow, *n*, sillon, *m.* ¶ *v.t*, sillonner; raviner.

furry, *a*, à fourrure; (*tongue*)
chargée.

further, *a*, supplémentaire, nouveau; plus éloigné. ¶ *ad*, plus
loin; au-delà; [plus] en delà; [en]
outre; de plus; encore, davantage.
¶ *v.t*, avancer, seconder. ~*ance*,
n, avancement, *m.* ~*more*, *ad*, de
plus, d'ailleurs, en outre. **fur-**

thest, *a*, le plus éloigné. ¶ *ad*, le
plus loin.

furtive†, *a*, furtif.

fury, *n*, furie, fureur, *f*, acharnement, *m*; (*pers.*) furie, forcenée,
f. F~ (*Myth.*), Furie, *f.*

furze, *n*, ajonc, genêt épineux, *m.*

fuse, *n*, fusée; mèche; étoupille,
f; (*Elec.*) plomb [fusible] *m.* ¶
v.t. & i, fondre.

fusee (*Horol.*) *n*, fusée, *f.*

fuselage, *n*, fuselage, *m.*

fusible, *a*, fusible.

fusillade, *n*, fusillade, *f.*

fusion, *n*, fusion, *f.*

fuss, *n*, bruit, tapage, *m*, cérémonies, façons, histoires, *f.pl.* ¶ *v.i*,
tatillonner, faire des histoires.
~*y*, *a*, façonnier, difficultueux.

fustian, *n*, futaine; (*fig.*) emphase, *f*, phébus, *m.*

fusty, *a*, qui sent le renfermé;
moisi.

futile, *a*, futile. **futility**, *n*, futilité, *f.*

future, *a*, futur; d'avenir; à venir;
(*Com.*) à terme. ¶ *n*, avenir,
futur; (*pl.*, *Com.*) livrable, *m.*
~ [*tense*], futur [simple] *m.* ~
perfect, futur antérieur. **futurity**,
n, futur, *m.*

fuzzy, *a*, (*hair*) crépus; (*image*)
flou.

G

G (*Mus.*) *letter*, sol, *m.* ~ *clef*,
clef de sol, *f.*

gabble, *v.t*, débiter trop vite; (*v.i.*)
caqueter, babiller.

gable, *n*, pignon, *m.* ~ *roof*, comble sur pignon(s), *m.*

gad about, courir çà & là, c. la
pretentaine. **gadabout**, *n*, coureur, euse.

gadfly, *n*, œstre, taon, *m.*

gadget, *n*, machine, *f*, truc, *m.*

gaff, *n*, (*spear*) gaffe; (*spar*) corne,
f.

gag, *n*, bâillon, *m*; (*actor's*) scie,
cascade, *f.* ¶ *v.t*, bâillonner.

gage, *n*, gage, *m*; assurance, *f.* See
also *gauge*.

gaiety, *n*, gaieté, joie; gaillardise,
f. **gaily**, *ad*, gaiement.

gain, *n*, gain, *m.* ¶ *v.t*, gagner;
remporter; (*v.i.*) profiter; (*clock*) avancer. ~ *admittance*,
s'introduire. *to be the gainer*
(*by*), gagner (à).

gainsay, *v.t*, contredire, disconvenir de.

gait, *n,* démarche, allure, *f,* pas, *m.*

gaiter, *n,* guêtre, *f.*

gala, *n,* gala, *m; (att., day, night, dress, performance)* de gala. ~ *nig't,* soirée de gala, *f.*

galaxy, *n,* (Astr.) voie lactée; *(fig.)* constellation, *f.*

gale, *n,* coup de vent, *m.*

gall, *n,* fiel; amer, *m;* écorchure, *f.* ~*bladder,* vésicule biliaire, *f.* ~ *[nut],* [noix de] galle, *f.* ¶ *v.t,* écorcher, blesser.

gallant, *a,* vaillant, brave; *(to women)* galant. ¶ *n,* galant, *m.* ~ly, *ad,* vaillamment; *galam-ment.* ~ry, *n,* vaillance; galanterie, *f.*

galleon (Hist.) *n,* galion, *m.*

gallery, *n,* galerie; tribune, *f;* (Theat.) troisièmes [galeries], dernières galeries, *f.pl,* poulailler, paradis, *m.*

galley, *n,* *(boat)* galère; *(cook's)* cuisine; *(Typ.)* galée, *f.* ~ *[proof],* épreuve en placard, *f.* ~ *slave,* galérien, *m.*

Gallic, *a,* gaulois. **Gallican,** *a. & n,* gallican, e. **gallicism,** *n,* gallicisme, *m.* **gallicize,** *v.t,* franciser.

gallipot, *n,* pot de faïence, *m.*

gallon, *n,* gallon, *m.*

gallop, *n,* galop, *m.* ¶ *v.i,* galoper. ~ing *consumption,* phtisie galopante, *f.*

Gallophile, *a. & n,* francophile, *a. & m,f.* **Gallophobe,** *a. & n,* gallophobe, *a. & m,f.*

gallows, *n.pl. & s,* potence, *f,* gibet. ~ *bird,* gibier de potence, *m,* pendard, e.

galop *(dance)* n, galop, *m.*

galore, *ad,* à foison.

galosh, *n,* caoutchouc, *m.*

galvanic, *a,* galvanique. **galvanism,** *n,* galvanisme, *m.* **galvanize,** *v.t,* galvaniser.

Gambia, *n,* la Gambie.

gambit, *n,* gambit, *m.*

gamble, *n,* spéculation de hasard, *f.* ¶ *v.i,* jouer, agioter. ~ *away,* perdre au jeu. **gambler,** *n,* joueur, euse; agioteur, *m.* **gambling,** *n,* jeu[x], *m.[pl.];* agiotage, *m.* ~ *den,* tripot, *m.*

gamboge, *n,* gomme-gutte, *f.*

gambol, *n,* gambade, *f.* ¶ *v.i,* gambader.

game, *n,* jeu, *m;* partie; *(dodge)* ficelle, *f;* (Hunt.) gibier, *m.* ~ *bag,* carnassière, *f,* carnier, *m.* gibecière, *f.* ~ *cock,* coq de combat, *m.* ~*keeper,* garde-chasse,

m. ~ *of skill,* jeu d'adresse, *m.* ¶ *a,* courageux; prêt; sportif. ~ *fishing,* pêche sportive, *f. to have a* ~ *leg,* être estropié de la jambe. ¶ *v.i,* jouer. ~**ster,** *n,* joueur, euse. **gaming,** *n,* jeu. *m.* ~ *house,* maison de j., *f.* ~ *table,* table de j., *f,* tapis vert, *m.*

gamut, *n,* gamme, *f.*

gamy, *a,* giboyeux; *(Cook.)* faisandé.

gander, *n,* jars, *m.*

gang, *n,* bande; brigade, équipe, *f.*

Ganges (the), le Gange.

ganglion, *n,* ganglion, *m.*

gangrene, *n,* gangrène, *f.* ¶ *v.t,* gangrener.

gangster, *n,* bandit, gangster, *m.*

gangue, *n,* gangue, matrice, *f.*

gangway, *n,* passage; pourtour; *(on ship)* passavant, *m; (to shore)* passerelle, *f.*

gannet, *n,* fou [de Bassan] *m.*

gantry, *n,* portique; beffroi, *m.*

gap, *n,* brèche, trouée, ouverture, *f,* intervalle, vide, *m,* lacune, *f.*

gape, *v.i,* bâiller. ~ *[at the moon],* bayer aux corneilles. **gaper,** *n,* gobe-mouches, *m,* badaud, e.

garage, *n,* garage, *m.* ¶ *v.t,* garer.

garb, *n,* costume, habit, accoutrement, *m.*

garbage, *n,* rebuts, *m.pl;* ordures, *f.pl.* ~ *can,* poubelle, *f.*

garble, *v.t,* altérer, tronquer.

garden, *n,* jardin; *(small)* jardinet, *m.* ~ *flower,* fleur de jardin, *f.* ~ *hose,* tuyau d'arrosage, *m.* ~ *mint,* menthe verte, *f. the G~ of Eden,* Éden, *m,* le paradis [terrestre]. ~ *party,* garden-party, *f.* ~ *plant,* plante jardinière, *f.* ~ *plots,* jardinage, *m.* ~ *tools,* outils de jardinage, *m.pl.* ¶ *v.i,* jardiner. ~**er,** *n,* jardinier, ère.

gardenia, *n,* gardénia, *m.*

gardening, *n,* jardinage, *m,* horticulture, *f.*

garfish, *n,* orphie, *f.*

gargle, *n,* gargarisme, *m.* ¶ *v.i,* se gargariser.

gargoyle, *n,* gargouille, *f.*

garish, *a,* éblouissant; voyant, tapageur, cru.

garland, *n,* guirlande, *f.*

garlic, *n,* ail, *m.*

garment, *n,* vêtement, *m.*

garner, *n,* grenier, *m.* ¶ *v.t,* engranger; rassembler.

garnet, *n,* grenat, *m.*

garnish, *n,* garniture, *f.* ¶ *v.t,* garnir

garret, *n,* mansarde, *f.*

garrison, n, garnison, f. ~*artillery,* artillerie de place, f.

garrulous, a, bavard, loquace.

garter, n, jarretière, f.

gas, n, gaz, m; (*gasoline*) essence, f. ~ *burner,* bec de gaz, m. ~ *lighting,* éclairage au gaz, m. ~ *man,* employé du gaz, m. ~ *mask,* (*war*) masque à g.; (*fire*) casque respiratoire, m. ~ *meter,* compteur à gaz, m. ~ *pipe,* tuyau de g., m. ~ *shell,* obus à g., m. ~ *works,* usine à gaz, f. *tear* ~, gaz lacrymogène, m. ¶ *v.t,* asphyxier; (*war*) gazer. ~**eous,** a, gazeux.

gash, n, balafre, estafilade, f. ¶ *v.t,* balafrer.

gasket, n, garcette, f, raban, m; tresse; garniture, f.

gasogene, n, gazogène, m. **gasometer,** n, gazomètre, m.

gasoline, n, essence, f.

gasp, n, halètement; souffle coupé; hoquet, m. *to* ~ *for breath,* haleter.

gassy, a, gazeux; verbeux.

gastropod, n, gastéropode, m. **gastric,** a, gastrique. **gastritis,** n, gastrite, f. **gastronome,** n, gastronome, m. **gastronomic(al),** a, gastronomique. **gastronomy,** n, gastronomie, f.

gate, n, porte; barrière; (*sluice*) vanne, f. ~*crasher,* resquilleur, euse. ~*crashing,* resquille, f. ~*keeper,* portier, ère; (*level crossing*) garde-barrière, m,f. ~ *money,* recette, f. ~*way,* porte, f.

gather, n, fronce, f. ¶ *v.t,* [r]assembler; [r]amasser; [re]cueillir; récolter; vendanger; inférer; (*Need.*) froncer. ~**er,** n, ramasseur, euse. ~**ing,** n, rassemblement, m; accumulation; cueillette; réunion, f; (*Med.*) mal blanc, abcès, m.

gating (*Hyd.*) n, vannage, m.

gaudy, a, fastueux, voyant, tapageur.

gauge, n, calibre, m; jauge, f; gabarit; (*Rly. track*) écartement, m, voie, largeur, f; manomètre; indicateur, m. ¶ *v.t,* calibrer; jauger; cuber.

gaunt, a, décharné, sec.

gauntlet, n, gantelet, m; (*fig.*) gant, m.

gauze, n, gaze; toile, f, tissu, tamis, m. **gauzy,** a, vaporeux.

gavotte, n, gavotte, f.

gawky, a, dégingandé.

gay, a, gai.

gaze, n, regard, m. *to* ~ *at,* contempler, couver des yeux.

gazelle, n, gazelle, f.

gazette, n, gazette, f, journal, m; journal officiel; moniteur, m.

gazetteer, n, dictionnaire géographique, m.

gear, n, appareil[s] m.[pl.]; engins; organes; agrès, m.pl; mécanisme; dispositif; harnais, m; armature, f; gréement, m; (*toothed*) engrenage[s] m.[pl.]; (*ratio*) multiplication, f; (*bicycle*) développement, m. ~ *box,* boîte à engrenages; boîte de changement de vitesse, f. ~ *case,* carter; couvre-engrenages, m. ~ *ratio,* multiplication, f. ~*shift,* changement de vitesse, m. ~ *wheel,* roue d'engrenage, f. ¶ *v.t,* engrener.

gee-gee, n, dada, m. **gee up,** i, hue!

gehenna, n, géhenne, f.

gelatin, n, gélatine, f. **gelatinous,** a, gélatineux.

geld, v.t, châtrer, hongrer. ~**ing,** n, castration, f; [cheval] hongre, m.

gem, n, pierre précieuse, [pierre] gemme, f; bijou, m; (*pl.*) pierreries, f.pl.

gender, n, genre, m.

genealogical, a, généalogique. **genealogy,** n, généalogie, f.

general, a, général, d'ensemble; commun; collectif. ~ *effect,* ensemble, m. ~ *expenses,* frais divers, m.pl. ~ *post office,* hôtel des postes, m. *the* ~ *public,* le grand public. *to become* ~, se généraliser. ¶ n, général en chef, chef, m. ~**ity,** n, généralité; plupart, f. ~**ize,** v.t, & i, généraliser. ~**ly,** ad, généralement; communément. ~**ship,** n, généralat, m; stratégie, f.

generate, v.t, engendrer; produire. **generating,** p.a, générateur. **generation,** n, génération, f. **generator,** n, générateur, m.

generic, a, générique.

generosity, n, générosité, f. **generous†,** a, généreux, donnant.

genesis, n, genèse, f. **G~** (*Bible*), la Genèse.

genet (*civet*) n, genette, f.

geneva (*gin*) n, genièvre, m. **G~** (*Geog.*), Genève, f. *Lake of G~,* lac de Genève, lac Léman, m.

genial, a, bienfaisant; chaleureux;

joyeux; sociable. **~ity,** *n,* bonhomie, *f.*
genital, *a,* génital.
genitive [**case**], *n,* génitif, *m.*
genius, *n,* génie; démon, *m.*
Genoa, *n,* Gênes, *f.* **Genoese,** *a,*
génois. ¶ *n,* Génois, e.
genteel, *a,* distingué, de bon ton.
gentian, *n,* gentiane, *f.*
gentile, *n,* gentil, *m.*
gentle, *a,* doux. *of ~ birth,* de
qualité. **~folk**[s], gens de qualité,
m.pl. **~man,** monsieur; galant
homme; homme de qualité, gentilhomme, gentleman; cavalier,
m. **~man** *farmer,* gentilhomme
campagnard, *m.* **~manliness,**
savoir-vivre, *m,* gentilhommerie,
f. **~manly,** comme il faut; distingué; gentleman. **~woman,**
femme de qualité, *f.* **~ness,** *n,*
douceur, *f.* **gently,** *ad,* doucement, bellement. **gentry,** *n,* petite
noblesse, *f.*
genuflexion, *n,* génuflexion, *f.*
genuine, *a,* vrai; authentique;
sincère; sérieux. **~ness,** *n,* authenticité; sincérité, *f.*
genus, *n,* genre, *m.*
geodesy, *n,* géodésie, *f.* **geognosy,**
n, géognosie, *f.* **geographer,** *n,*
géographe, *m.* **geographic(al)†,**
a, géographique. **geography,** *n,*
géographie, *f.* **geologic(al),** *a,*
géologique. **geologist,** *n,* géologue, *m.* **geology,** *n,* géologie, *f.*
geometer & geometrician, *n,* géomètre, *m.* **geometric(al)†,** *a,*
géométrique. **geometry,** *n,* géométrie, *f.*
Georgia, *n,* (*U.S.A.*) la Georgie;
(*Asia*) la Géorgie.
geranium, *n,* géranium, *m.*
germ, *n,* germe, *m.*
german, *a,* germain.
German, *a,* allemand; d'Allemagne. ~ *measles,* rubéole, *f.*
¶ *n,* (*pers.*) Allemand, e; (*language*) l'allemand, *m.*
germander (*Bot.*) *n,* germandrée,
f.
germane to, se rapportant à.
Germany, *n,* l'Allemagne, *f.*
germinate, *v.i,* germer. **germination,** *n,* germination, *f.*
gerund, *n,* gérondif, *m.*
gestation, *n,* gestation, *f.*
gesticulate, *v.i,* gesticuler.
gesture, *n,* geste, *m.*
get, *v.t.ir,* obtenir; gagner; acquérir; procurer; se p.; se faire;
se mettre; tirer; recevoir; retirer;
trouver; avoir; (*v.i.ir.*) aller; ar-

river; parvenir; devenir; se faire;
se trouver. *Often rendered by* se,
e.g., ~ *an opinion into one's
head,* se chausser d'une opinion.
~ *away,* s'échapper; se sauver.
~ *back, v.t,* ravoir; (*v.i.*) revenir.
~ *down,* descendre. ~ *hold of,*
s'emparer de; saisir. ~ *in,* entrer,
s'introduire; (*grain*) engranger.
~ *married,* se marier. ~ *on,*
s'arranger; s'entendre; réussir.
~ *out,* sortir. ~ *out of the way,*
s'ôter, de là, se garer. ~ *over,*
franchir, surmonter. ~ *ready,*
préparer; se préparer. ~ *rid of,*
se débarrasser de. ~ *round*
(someone), entortiller. ~ *up,* se
lever. ~ *up steam,* chauffer.
getup, *n,* mise, *f;* affiquets, *m.pl.*
gewgaw, *n,* colifichet, *m.*
geyser, *n,* (*spring*) geyser, *m.*
ghastly, *a,* de spectre, de déterré;
macabre; blême, livide; affreux.
Ghent, *n,* Gand, *m.*
gherkin, *n,* cornichon, *m.*
ghetto, *n,* ghetto, *m,* juiverie, *f.*
ghost, *n,* esprit, *m;* fantôme, spectre, revenant, *m,* ombre, *f.* ~
story, histoire de revenants, *f.* ~
writer, nègre, *m.* **~ly,** *a,* spectral,
fantomatique.
ghoul, *n,* goule, *f.*
giant, *a,* géant. **giant,** ess, *n,*
géant, e, colosse, *m. giant*['*s*]
stride, pas de géant, vindas, *m.*
gibber, *v.i,* baragouiner. **~ish,** *n,*
baragouin, galimatias, *m.*
gibbet, *n,* gibet, *m,* potence, *f.*
¶ (*fig.*) *v.t,* pilorier.
gibe, *n,* brocard, quolibet, lardon,
m. ¶ *v.i,* lancer des brocards *ou*
des lardons (*at* = à).
giblets, *n.pl,* abattis, *m. & m.pl.*
giddiness, *n,* vertige, étourdissement, *m,* **giddy,** *a,* (*height*) vertigineux; (*flighty*) écervelé. *it
makes me feel* ~, cela me donne
le vertige.
gift, *n,* don; cadeau, *m;* donation;
(*for coupons*) prime; (*of an
office*) nomination, *f;* talent, *m.
the* ~ *of the gab,* du bagou. **~ed,**
a, doué, de talent.
gig, *n,* cabriolet, *m;* (*boat*) yole, *f.*
gigantic, *a,* gigantesque.
giggle, *v.i,* rire bêtement, glousser.
gild, *v.t.ir,* dorer. **~er,** *n,* doreur,
euse. **~ing,** *n,* dorure, *f.*
gill, *n,* (*fish*) ouïe, branchie, *f.*
gilt, *n,* dorure, *f.* ¶ *p.a,* doré.
~-edged, (*book, bill of exchange*)
doré sur tranche; (*investment, security*) de premier ordre. **~tool-**

ing, fers dorés, *m.pl.* ~ *top*, tête dorée, *f.*

gimcrack, *n,* bibelot, *m;* pacotille, patraque, *f.* ¶ *a,* de camelote; délabré.

gimlet, *n,* vrille, *f.*

gimp, *n,* ganse, *f,* galon, bordé, passement, *m.*

gin, *n,* (*snare*) trébuchet, *m;* (*hoist*) chèvre, *f;* treuil, *m;* (*cotton*) égreneuse, *f;* (*spirit*) gin, *m.* ¶ *v.t,* égrener.

ginger, *n,* gingembre, *m.* ~ *bread,* pain d'épice, *m.* ~ *nut,* nonnette, *f.* ~**ly,** *ad,* en tâtonnant.

gingham, (*fabric*) *n,* guingan, *m.*

giraffe, *n,* girafe, *f.*

girandole, *n,* girandole, *f.*

girasol[e] (*opal*) *n,* girasol, *m.*

gird, *v.t.ir,* [en]ceindre. ~**er,** *n,* poutre; solive; ferme, *f.* ~**le,** *n,* ceinture, *f.* ¶ *v.t,* ceindre.

girl, *n,* fille, jeune fille, fillette, enfant, demoiselle, *f.* ~**hood,** *n,* jeunesse, *f.* ~**ish,** *a,* de jeune fille; mignard.

girth, *n,* sangle; sous-ventrière; circonférence, *f.*

gist, *n,* substance, *f.*

give, *v.t. & i. ir,* donner; accorder; prêter; apporter; passer; rendre; fournir; (*cry*) pousser. ~ & *take,* donnant donnant. ~ *back,* rendre. ~ *one's name,* décliner son nom, se nommer. ~ *in,* céder. ~ *oneself away,* s'enferrer soi-même. (*lamp, etc.*) se mourir. ~ *someone a piece of one's mind,* dire son fait à quelqu'un. ~ *up,* renoncer à; livrer; abandonner, quitter; céder; (*patient*) condamner. ~ *way,* céder; fléchir; s'effondrer. **given to,** adonné à; enclin à. **giver,** *n,* donneur, euse.

gizzard, *n,* gésier, *m.*

glacé kid gloves, gants de peau glacée, *m.pl.*

glacial, *a,* glacial; (*Geol.*) glaciaire. **glacier,** *n,* glacier, *m.*

glad, *a,* [bien] aise; content; heureux; joyeux. **gladden,** *v.t,* réjouir.

glade, *n,* clairière, *f.*

gladiator, *n,* gladiateur, *m.*

gladiolus, *n,* glaïeul, *m.*

gladly, *ad,* volontiers. **gladness,** *n,* joie, *f.*

glamour, *n,* enchantement; éclat; prestige, *m.*

glance, *n,* coup d'œil, regard, *m;* (*loving*) œillade, *f.* ¶ *v.i,* effleurer. ~ *at,* jeter un coup d'œil sur.

gland, *n,* glande, *f.*

glanders, *n.pl,* morve, *f.*

glare, *n,* éclat; éblouissement; regard perçant; r. furieux, *m.* ¶ *v.i,* éblouir. ~ *at* (*pers.*) lancer un regard furieux à. **glaring,** *a,* éclatant, éblouissant; grossier; flagrant; criant; tranchant.

glass, *n,* verre, *m;* vitre, *f;* miroir, *m;* lunette, *f;* (*pl.*) lunettes, *f.pl;* jumelle, *f.* ~[*with care*], fragile. ~ *beads,* verroterie, *f.* ~ *case,* vitrine, *f.* ~ *cutter,* diamant de vitrier; (*wheel*) coupe-verre à molette, *m.* ~ *door,* porte vitrée, *f,* vitrage, *m.* ~**maker,** verrier, *m.* ~ *making* & ~**works,** verrerie, *f.* ~ *of beer,* bock, *m,* chope, *f.* ~[*ware*], verrerie; (*small*) verroterie, *f.* field~, jumelles, *f.pl.* magnifying ~, loupe, *f.* shatterproof ~, verre incassable, *m.* ~**y,** *a,* vitreux.

glaucous, *a,* glauque.

glaze, *n,* émail, vernis, *m,* couverte, *f;* lustre, *m.* ¶ *v.t,* (*window*) vitrer; émailler, vernir, vernisser; lustrer; satiner; glacer; dorer; (*v.i.*) se glacer. ~*d frost,* verglas, *m.* **glazier,** *n,* vitrier, *m.* ~**y,** *n,* vitrerie, *f.*

gleam, *n,* lueur, *f,* rayon, *m.* ¶ *v.i,* luire, miroiter.

glean, *v.t,* glaner; (*grapes*) grappiller. ~**er,** *n,* glaneur, euse. ~**ing,** *n,* glanage, *m,* glane; (*pl.*) glanure, *f.*

glebe, *n,* glèbe; terre d'église, *f.*

glee, *n,* joie, gaieté; chanson à plusieurs voix, *f.*

gleet, *n,* écoulement, *m.*

glen, *n,* vallon, val, *m.*

glib, *a,* (*pers.*) volubile; (*tongue*) déliée.

glide, *n,* glissement; (*Danc.*) glissé, *m.* ¶ *v.i,* glisser; couler. **glider** (*Avn.*) *n,* planeur, *m.* **gliding** (*Avn.*) *n,* vol à voile, *m.*

glimmer, *n,* lueur, *f.* ¶ *v.i,* jeter une faible lueur.

glimpse, *n,* lueur, *f;* coup d'œil, *m;* échappée [de vue] *f.* catch a ~ *of,* entrevoir.

glint, *n,* reflet, *m.* ¶ *v.i,* étinceler, miroiter.

glisten, glitter, *v.i,* briller, reluire, miroiter. **glitter,** *n,* brillant, *m.*

gloaming, *n,* crépuscule, *m,* brune, *f.*

gloat over, triompher de; couver des yeux.

globe, *n,* globe, *m,* sphère, *f;* (*fish*

bowl) bocal, *m*. **globular**, *a*, globulaire, globuleux. **globule**, *n*, globule, *m*.

gloom, *v.t*, rembrunir. ~**[iness]**, *n*, obscurité, *f*, ténèbres, *f.pl*; air sombre, *m*, tristesse, *f*. ~**y**, *a*, sombre, ténébreux, triste, morne, noir, lugubre.

glorify, *v.t*, glorifier. **glorious†**, *a*, glorieux; resplendissant. **glory**, *n*, gloire, *f*; nimbe, *m*. ~ **in**, se glorifier de, se faire gloire de.

gloss, *n*, luisant, lustre, poli, œil, *m*; (*comment*) glose, *f*. ¶ *v.t*, lustrer; glacer; (*text*) gloser. ~ [*over*], vernir, farder. ~**ary**, *n*, glossaire, *m*. ~**y**, *a*, luisant; lustré; brillant.

glottis, *n*, glotte, *f*.

glove, *n*, gant, *m*. ~ *trade*, ganterie, *f*. ¶ *v.t*, ganter. *to put on one's* ~*s*, se ganter. **glover**, *n*, gantier, ère.

glow, *n*, incandescence, *f*; embrasement, *m*; chaleur, *f*; élan, *m*; (*pleasant, in the body*) moiteur, *f*. ~*worm*, ver luisant, lampyre, *m*, luciole, *f*. ¶ *v.i*, briller d'un vif éclat. ~*ing with health*, rouge de santé.

glower at, regarder d'un air féroce.

glucose, *n*, glucose, *f*.

glue, *n*, colle forte; colle; (*marine*) glu, *f*. ~ *pot*, pot à colle, *m*. ¶ *v.t*, coller. ~**y**, *a*, gluant.

glum, *a*, morose, chagrin.

glut, *n*, pléthore, *f*; encombrement, *m*. ¶ *v.t*, gorger, rassasier; encombrer.

gluten, *n*, gluten, *m*. **glutinous**, *a*, glutineux.

glutton, *n*, glouton, ne, gourmand, e. ~**ous†**, *a*, glouton, gourmand. ~**y**, *n*, gloutonnerie, gourmandise, *f*.

glycerin[e], *n*, glycérine, *f*.

gnarl, *n*, broussin, *m*. ~**ed**, *a*, noueux.

gnash one's teeth, grincer des (*ou* les) dents.

gnat, *n*, moucheron, *m*.

gnaw, *v.i*, ronger. ~**ing**, *n*, rongement; tiraillement, *m*.

gnome, *n*, gnome, *m*.

gnostic, *n*, gnostique, *m*.

go, *n*, entrain, allant, panache, *m*; mode, vogue, *f*; jet, *m*. ¶ *v.i. & t. ir*, aller; se rendre, se porter; se mettre; marcher; passer; partir; s'en aller; faire; tourner; devenir. *are you ready? go!* êtes-vous prêts? partez! *who goes there?*

qui vive? ~ *astray*, s'égarer; se dévoyer. ~ *away*, s'en aller; partir. ~ *back*, retourner. ~*between* intermédiaire, *m*; entremetteur, euse. ~ *by*, passer. ~*cart*, chariot, panier roulant, *m*. ~ *down*, descendre; baisser; (*sun, moon*) se coucher; (*ship*) sombrer, couler; (*swelling*) désenfler. ~ *for*, aller chercher; a. faire; a. prendre. ~ *in*, entrer; monter. ~ *off*, partir. ~*on*, aller; avancer; continuer. ~ *on!* allons donc! ~ *on board a ship, an airplane*, monter sur un navire, en avion. ~ *out*, sortir; (*light*) s'éteindre. ~ *over*, passer sur; traverser; parcourir; (*Jump.*) dépasser, mordre sur (*the mark* = la latte). ~ *through*, passer par, traverser, parcourir; dépouiller. ~ *to press*, procéder à l'impression. ~ *to sleep*, s'endormir. ~ *up*, monter; remonter; renchérir. ~ *with*, accompagner. ~ *without*, se passer de.

goad, *n*, aiguillon, *m*. ¶ *v.t*, aiguillonner, piquer.

goal, *n*, but, *m*. ~ *keeper, kick, post*, gardien, coup [de pied], poteau, de b., *m*.

goat, *n*, chèvre, *f*; (*he*) bouc, *m*. ~*herd*, chevrier, ère. ~**ee**, *n*, barbe de bouc, barbiche, *f*.

gobble, *v.t*, manger goulûment; (*v.i, of turkey*) glouglouter.

goblet, *n*, gobelet, *m*; coupe, *f*.

goblin, *n*, lutin, follet, farfadet, gobelin, *m*.

God, *n*, Dieu, *m*. ~*child*, filleul, e. ~*daughter*, filleule, *f*. ~*father*, parrain, *m*. ~*head*, divinité, *f*. ~*mother*, marraine, *f*. ~*send*, providence, aubaine, chapechute, *f*. ~*son*, filleul, *m*. **goddess**, *n*, déesse, *f*. **godless**, *a*, sans Dieu; impie. **godlike**, *a*, divin. **godliness**, *n*, piété, *f*. **godly**, *a*, pieux, saint, de Dieu.

goffer, *n*, tuyau, *m*. ¶ *v.t*, gaufrer, tuyauter.

goggles, *n,pl*, lunettes, *f.pl*.

going, *n*, aller, *m*. ~ & *coming*, allées & venues, *f.pl*. ~ *back to school*, rentrée des classes, *f*. ~ *concern*, affaire roulante, *f*. *value as a* ~ *concern*, valeur d'usage, *f*. ~, ~, *gone!* une fois, deux fois, [trois fois]; adjugé! ~*s-on*, procédés; agissements, *m.pl*.

goiter, *n*, goitre, *m*.

gold, *n*, or, *m*. ~*-beater's skin*, baudruche, *f*. *the G*~ *Coast*, la golf, Côte de l'Or. ~*digger*, chercheur d'or, *m*. ~*field*, champ aurifère, *m*. ~*finch*, chardonneret, *m*. ~*fish*, poisson rouge, *m*, dorade, *f*. ~ *mine*, mine d'or, *f*. ~*smith* &/or *silversmith*, orfèvre, *m*. ~[*smith's*] &/or *silver*[*smith's*] *work*, orfèvrerie, *f*. ¶ *a*, d'or, en or. ~ *francs*, francs-or, *m.pl*. ~**en**, *a*, d'or; doré; (*hair*) blond doré. ~ *calf*, veau d'or, *m*. ~ *mean*, juste milieu, *m*. ~ *rain*, pluie d'or, *f*. ~ *wedding*, noces d'or, *f.pl*, cinquantaine, *f*.

golf, *n*, golf, *m*. ~ *club* (*pers.* & *stick*) club de g, *m*. ~ *course*, ~ *links*, [terrain de] golf, *m*. ~**er**, *n*, joueur (euse) de golf.

golosh, *n*, caoutchouc, *m*.

gondola, *n*, gondole; (*Avn.*) nacelle, *f*. **gondolier**, *n*, gondolier, *m*.

gong, *n*, gong, tam-tam; timbre, *m*.

good, *a*, bon; beau; de bien; brave; (*of a child*) sage; avantageux; valable; utile. ~ *angel*, bon ange, *m*; providence, *f*. ~ *breeding*, politesse, *f*, savoir-vivre, *m*. ~*bye*, i. & n, adieu, i. & *m*; au revoir! *a* ~ *ear* (for music), l'oreille juste. ~ *evening!* ~ *night!* bonsoir! bonne nuit! (*a*) ~*for-nothing*, *n*. & *a*, (un) propre à rien. G~ *Friday*, le vendredi saint. ~ *gracious!* miséricorde! ~*looking*, joli, de bonne mine. *my* ~ *man*, mon brave. ~ *morning!* ~ *afternoon!* ~ *day!* bonjour! ~ *nature*, bonhomie, *f*, bon naturel, *m*. ~*-natured*, (*pers.*) bon enfant; (*laugh*) jovial. ~ *offices*, ministère, *m*. *the* ~ *old days*, le bon vieux temps. ~*will*, bienveillance, bonne volonté, faveur, *f*; fonds [de commerce] *m*, clientèle, *f*. ¶ *i*, bon!, bien! ¶ *n*, bien, *m*. *for* ~, pour de bon. *it's no* ~ . . ., inutile de . . . *to the* ~, en gain. **goodies**, *n.pl*, [du] nanan, *m*. **goodness**, *n*, bonté, *f*. *for* ~' *sake*, de grâce.

goods, *n.pl*, marchandises, *f.pl*; biens; effets, *m.pl*.

goose, *n*, oie, *f*. ~*flesh* (*fig.*), chair de poule, *f*. ~ *step*, pas de l'oie, *m*.

gooseberry, *n*, groseille verte, g. à maquereau, *f*. ~ *bush*, groseillier à maquereau, *m*.

Gordian knot, nœud gordien, *m*.

gore, *n*, sang [caillé] *m*. ¶ *v.t*, percer de coups de corne.

gorge, *n*, gorge, *f*. ¶ *v.t*, gorger.

gorgeous†, *a*, magnifique, splendide.

gorilla, *n*, gorille, *m*.

gormandize, *v.i*, goinfrer, bâfrer.

gorse, *n*, ajonc, genêt épineux, *m*.

gory, *a*, sanglant, ensanglanté.

goshawk, *n*, autour, *m*.

gosling, *n*, oison, *m*.

gospel, *n*, Évangile; credo, *m*. ~ [*truth*], parole d'Évangile, *f*.

gossamer, *n*, fils de la Vierge, *m.pl*, filandres, *f.pl*.

gossip, *n*, commérage, bavardage de commères, racontar, *m*; (*pers.*) commère, *f*. ¶ *v.i*, commérer, bavarder.

goth (*fig.*) *n*, ostrogot[h], e. **Gothic**, *a*, gothique.

gouache (*Art*) *n*, gouache, *f*.

gouge, *n*, gouge, *f*.

gourd, *n*, courge, calebasse, *f*.

gourmand, *a*. & *n*, gourmand, e.

gourmet, *n*, gourmet, *m*.

gout, *n*, goutte, *f*. ~**y**, *a*, goutteux.

govern, *v.t*, gouverner, régir; (*Gram.*) régir. ~**ess**, *n*, gouvernante, *f*. ~**ment**, *n*, gouvernement; État, *m*. ~ *in power*, gouvernants, *m.pl*. ~ *organ*, journal ministériel, *m*. ~**or**, *n*, gouverneur; (*Mach.*) régulateur, *m*.

gown, *n*, robe, *f*. *dressing* ~, peignoir, *m*. *night*~, chemise de nuit, *f*.

grab, *v.t*, empoigner, agripper.

grace, *n*, grâce, *f*; (*before meal*) le bénédicité; (*after*) les grâces, *f.pl*. ~ *note*, note d'agrément, *f*. *the* G~*s*, les [trois] Grâces. *his* G~, monseigneur, *m*. *your* G~, Votre Grandeur, *f*. ¶ *v.t*, orner; honorer. ~**ful**†, *a*, gracieux.

gracious†, *a*, gracieux. ~**ness**, *n*, gracieuseté, *f*.

gradation, *n*, gradation, *f*. **grade**, *n*, grade, degré, *m*; teneur, *f*, titre, *m*. ¶ *v.t*, classer; graduer; régulariser. **gradient**, *n*, (*up*) rampe; (*down*) pente; (*up or down*) inclinaison, *f*. **gradual**†, *a*, graduel. **graduate**, *v.t*, graduer; (*v.i.*) prendre ses grades. ¶ *n*, gradué, e. **graduation**, *n*, graduation; gradation; (*Univ.*) licence, grade, *f*.

graft, *n*, (*Hort.*) greffe, ente; (*Surg.*) greffe; (*spoils*) gratte, *f*. ¶ *v.t*, greffer; enter. ~**ing** (*Knit.*) *n*, remmaillage, *m*.

grain, *n*, (*wheat, etc.*) céréales, *f.pl*; grain, *m*; (*wood*) fil; (*weight*) grain, *m*; (*pl, brewer's*) drèche, drague, *f*. ¶ *v.t*, grener, greneler;

veiner. ~ed, *p.a*, (*leather*) grenu; (*wood*) ondé. ~ing, *n*, grenu, *m*.

gram, *n*, gramme, *m*.

grammar, *n*, grammaire, *f*. ~ian, *n*, grammairien, ne. **grammatical**†, *a*, grammatical.

grampus, *n*, épaulard, *m*, orque, *f*.

Granada (*Spain*) *n*, Grenade, *f*.

granary, *n*, grenier, *m*.

grand†, *a*, grand; magnifique. ~child, ~son, ~daughter, petit-fils, *m*, petite-fille, *f*. ~children, petits-enfants, *m.pl*. ~father, grand-père, aïeul, *m*. ~father's clock, horloge de parquet, *f*. ~mamma, grand-maman, bonne maman, *f*. ~mother, grand-mère, aïeule, *f*. ~ piano, piano à queue, *m*. ~ staircase, escalier d'honneur, *m*. ~ stand, tribune, *f*. ~ total, somme toute, *f*. **grandee,** *n*, grand, *m*. **grandeur,** *n*, grandeur, majesté; splendeur, *f*.

grandiloquence, *n*, grandiloquence, *f*. **grandiloquent,** *a*, grandiloquent, doctoral.

grandiose, *a*, grandiose.

granite, *n*, granit, *m*.

granny, *n*, grand-maman, bonne maman, *f*.

grant, *n*, concession; allocation; subvention, *f*. ¶ *v.t*, accorder; concéder; octroyer; admettre; poser. *to take for* ~ed, présupposer. ~ee, *n*, concessionnaire, *m,f*; impétrant, e. ~or, *n*, cédant, e.

granulate, *v.t*, grener; granuler. ~d *sugar*, sucre cristallisé, *m*. **granule,** *n*, granule, *m*.

grape, *n*, grain de raisin, *m*; (*pl*.) raisin[s] *m.[pl.]*. ~*fruit*, pamplemousse, *f*. ~*shot*, mitraille, *f*.

graph, *n*, graphique, tracé, *m*. ~ic†, *a*, graphique; pittoresque. ¶ *v.t*, tracer un graphique, faire un diagramme.

graphite, *n*, graphite, *m*, plombagine, *f*.

grapnel, *n*, grappin, *m*. **grapple,** *v.t*, accrocher. ~ *with*, s'attaquer à; colleter.

grasp, *n*, prise; étreinte; poigne; poignée; portée, *f*. ¶ *v.t*, saisir, empoigner; serrer. ~ *round the body*, ceinturer. ~ing†, *p.a*, avide, cupide, âpre [au gain].

grass, *n*, herbe, *f*, herbage; gazon, *m*; verdure, *f*; vert, *m*. ~*hopper*, sauterelle; cigale, *f*. ~*land*, prairie, *f*. ~ *snake*, couleuvre à collier, *f*. ~ *widow*, veuve à titre

temporaire, *f*. ~y, *a*, herbeux, herbu.

grate, *n*, grille, *f*. ¶ *v.t*, griller; râper; (*teeth*) grincer [de]; (*ears*) écorcher, blesser. ~d *bread crumbs*, panure, chapelure, *f*.

grateful, *a*, reconnaissant; agréable. *to be* ~ *to*, savoir [bon] gré à. ~ness, *n*, reconnaissance, *f*.

grater, *n*, râpe, *f*.

gratification, *n*, satisfaction, *f*, plaisir, *m*. **gratify,** *v.t*, satisfaire, contenter.

gratin, *n*, gratin, *m*. ~ate, *v.t*, gratiner.

grating, *n*, grille, *f*; grillage; gril, *m*; clairevoie; crapaudine, *f*. ¶ *p.a*, strident.

gratis, *ad*, gratis, gratuitement.

gratitude, *n*, reconnaissance, gratitude, *f*.

gratuitous†, *a*, gratuit, gracieux; sans motif. ~ness, *n*, gratuité, *f*. **gratuity,** *n*, gratification, *f*, pourboire, *m*.

gravamen, *n*, matière, *f*.

grave†, *a*, grave, sérieux. ¶ *n*, fosse; tombe, *f*, tombeau, *m*. ~ *digger*, fossoyeur, *m*. ~*stone*, pierre tombale, tombe, *f*. ~*yard*, cimetière, *m*. ¶ *v.t*, (*ship*) radouber.

gravel, *n*, gravier[s] *m.[pl.]*; (*Med.*) graviers, *m.pl*, gravelle, *f*, sable, *m*. ~ *path*, ~ *walk*, allée sablée, *f*. ~ *pit*, gravière, *f*. ~ly, *a*, graveleux.

graver, *n*, burin, ciselet, *m*.

graving dock, forme de radoub, *f*.

gravitate, *v.i*, graviter. **gravitation,** *n*, gravitation, *f*. **gravity,** *n*, (*Phys.*) gravité, pesanteur, *f*, poids, *m*; (*fig.*) gravité, *f*; sérieux, *m*.

gravy, *n*, jus, *m*. ~ *boat*, saucière, *f*. ~ *spoon*, cuiller à ragoût, *f*.

gray, *a*, gris. ¶ *v.t*, grisailler. ~ish, *a*, grisâtre. ~ness, *n*, couleur grise, *f*.

graze, *n*, écorchure, *f*. ¶ *v.t. & i*, effleurer, raser, friser, frôler; écorcher; (*sea bottom*) labourer; (*cattle*) paître, pâturer, pacager. **grazier,** *n*, éleveur, *m*.

grease, *n*, graisse, *f*; (*in wool*) suint, *m*. ~ *box*, boîte à graisse, *f*. ~ *paint*, fard, *m*. ~*-proof paper*, papier imperméable à la graisse, p. sulfurisé, *m*. ¶ *v.t*, graisser; suiffer. **greasiness,** *n*, onctuosité, *f*. **greasy,** *a*, graisseux, gras, onctueux. ~ *pole*, mât de cocagne, *m*.

great, *a*, grand; gros; fort. ~ *aunt*, grand-tante, *f*. ~ *bell*, bourdon, *m*. G~ *Britain*, la Grande-Bretagne. ~*coat*, pardessus, *m*; (*Mil.*) capote, *f*. ~ *Dane*, grand danois, *m*. *a* ~ *deal*, *a* ~ *many*, beaucoup. ~*-grandchildren*, arrière-petits-enfants, *m.pl.* ~*granddaughter*, *-son*, arrière-petite-fille, *f*, a.-petit-fils, *m*. ~*grandfather*, *-mother*, arrière-grand-père, *m*, a.-grand-mère, *f*, bisaïeul, e. ~~*-grandfather*, *-mother*, trisaïeul, e. ~ *toe*, gros doit du pied, orteil, *m*. ~ *uncle*, grand-oncle, *m*. **the** ~ (*fig.*), le grand. **the** ~ **ones**, les grands (*de la terre*). ~**ly**, *ad*, grandement; fort. ~**ness**, *n*, grandeur, *f*.

grebe, *n*, grèbe, *m*.

Grecian, *a*, grec. **Greece**, *n*, la Grèce.

greed[iness], *n*, avidité, âpreté; gourmandise, *f*. **greedy†**, *a*, avide; gourmand, goulu.

Greek, *a*, *grec.* ~ *fret* (*Arch.*), grecque, *f*. ¶ *n*, (*pers.*) Grec, ecque; (*language*) le grec; (*fig.*) du grec, de l'hébreu (*to me* = pour moi).

green, *a*, vert; en herbe; novice; naïf. ~ *baize*, tapis vert, drap v., *m*. ~*finch*, verdier, *m*. ~*fly*, puceron, *m*. ~*gage*, [prune de] reine-claude, *f*. ~*horn*, novice, conscrit, pigeon, *m*. ~*house*, serre, *f*. ~ *peas*, petits pois, pois verts, *m.pl*. **greens**, *n.pl*, herbages, légumes verts, *m.pl*. ~*sward*, tapis de gazon, *m*, herbette, verdure, *f*; (*roadside*) accotement, *m*. ~*wood*, feuillée, ramée, *f*. ¶ *n*, vert, *m*; (*grass plot & golf*) pelouse, *f*. *through the* ~ (*golf*), à travers le parcours. ¶ *v.t. & i*, verdir, verdoyer. ~**ery**, *n*, verdure, *f*. ~**ish**, *a*, verdâtre.

Greenland, *n*, le Groenland.

greenness, *n*, verdure; verdeur; naïveté, *f*.

greet, *v.t*, saluer; accueillir. ~**ing**, *n*, salutation, *f*, salut, *m*.

gregarious, *a*, grégaire.

Gregorian, *a*, grégorien.

Grenada (*W. Indies*), *n*, la Grenade. **grenade**, *n*, grenade, *f*. **grenadine**, *n*, (*cordial*, *fabric*) grenadine, *f*; (*Cook.*) grenadin, *m*.

greyhound, *n*, lévrier, *m*, le-

vrette, *f*. ~ *racing*, courses de lévriers, *f.pl*.

grid, *n*, grille, *f*. ~*iron*, gril; (*sports*) terrain de football, *m*.

griddle, *n*, gril, *m*.

grief, *n*, chagrin, *m*, douleur, peine, affliction, *f*. **grievance**, *n*, grief, *m*. **grieve**, *v.t*, chagriner, affliger, peiner, fâcher. **grievous†**, *a*, grave; cruel.

griffin, griffon, *n*, griffon, *m*.

grill, *n*, gril, *m*; (*meat*) grillade, *f*. ¶ *v.t*, [faire] griller.

grille, *n*, (*grating*) grille, *f*.

grim, *a*, farouche, rébarbatif; macabre.

grimace, *n*, grimace, *f*, rictus, *m*. ¶ *v.i*, grimacer.

grime, *n*, crasse, *f*. ¶ *v.t*, encrasser, noircir. **grimy**, *a*, crasseux, noir.

grin, *n*, grimace, *f*. ¶ *v.i*, grimacer.

grind, *v.t.ir*, moudre; broyer; (*knife*) aiguiser, affûter, repasser; roder; grincer [de]; pressurer, opprimer; jouer. ~ *at*, piocher. ~*stone*, meule en grès, *f*. ~**ery**, *n*, crépins, *m.pl*. ~**ing** (*grain*) *n*, mouture, *f*.

grip, *n*, prise, pince, serre; poigne; étreinte; poignée; griffe, *f*. ¶ *v.t*, saisir, empoigner, serrer, étreindre; pincer, agripper.

gripes, *n.pl*, tranchées, *f.pl*; colique, *f*.

grippe, *n*, grippe, *f*.

grisly, *a*, effrayant, horrible, affreux.

grist, *n*, blé à moudre, *m*.

gristle, *n*, cartilage, *m*. **gristly**, *a*, cartilagineux.

grit, *n*, graviers, *m.pl*, sable; grès, *m*; (*fig.*) courage, *m*. **gritty**, *a*, graveleux; pierreux.

grizzled, *a*, grison. *grizzly bear*, ours grizzly, ours grizzlé, *m*.

groan, *n*, gémissement, *m*. ¶ *v.i*, gémir.

groats, *n.pl*, gruau; gruau d'avoine, *m*.

grocer, *n*, épicier, ère. ~*'s shop* & **grocery**, *n*, épicerie, *f*.

grog, *n*, grog, *m*. **groggy**, *a*, ivre; aviné; chancelant.

groin, *n*, aine; (*Arch.*) arête, *f*.

groom, *n*, palefrenier, *m*. ¶ *v.t*, panser.

groove, *n*, rainure; cannelure, *f*; sillon, *m*; gorge; ornière, *f*. ¶ *v.t*, canneler; sillonner.

grope, *v.t. & i*, fouiller, tâtonner.

grosbeak, *n*, gros-bec, *m*.

gross†, *a*, grossier; gros; (*Com.*)

brut. ¶ (*144*) n, grosse, f. ~**ness**, n, grossièreté, f.

grotesque†, a. & ~[**ness**] n, grotesque, a. & m. ¶ (*Art*), n, grotesque, f.

grotto, n, grotte, f.

grouch, n, ronchon, m. ¶ v.i, ronchonner.

ground, n, terre, f; sol; terrain; champ, m; place, f; fond; plan; sujet, lieu, m, raison, (*pl.*) cause, f, lieu, m, matière, f; (*pl, law*) motifs, moyens, m.pl; (*pl, dregs*) marc, m; effondrilles, f.pl; sédiment, m; (*of mansion*) dehors, m.pl, parc, m; (*fishing, cruising*) parages, m.pl. ~ *floor,* rez-de-chaussée, m. ~ *game,* gibier à poil, m. ~ *ivy,* lierre terrestre, m. ~ *line* (*Fish.*), ligne de fond, traînée, f. ~*nut,* arachide, cacahuète, f. ~ *rent,* redevance foncière, f. ~*sheet,* toile de sol, f. ~ *swell,* houle de fond, f. ~*work,* base, f; canevas, m. *stand one's* ~, tenir bon. ¶ p.p, en poudre; moulu; (*rice, etc.*) farine de . . .; (*glass*) dépoli. ¶ v.t. & i, mettre à terre; (*Elec.*) m. à ia terre; fonder; (*ship*) échouer, engraver. ~**less,** a. & ~**lessly,** ad, sans fondement; en l'air.

groundsel, n, seneçon, m.

group, n, groupe, m. ~ *firing* (*Artil.*), feu concentré, m, mitraille, f. ¶ v.t, grouper.

grouse, n, petit coq de bruyère, tétras, m, grouse, f, (*young*) grianneau, m. ¶ v.i, grogner.

grout[ing] (*Build.*) n, coulis, m.

grove, n, bocage, bosquet, m.

grovel, v.i, ramper.

grow, v.i.ir, croître; pousser; venir; grandir; [s']accroître; devenir, se faire; *often expressed by* se, *e.g.* ~ *cold,* se refroidir; (*v.t.ir.*) cultiver. ~ *green again* & ~ *young again,* reverdir. ~**er,** n, cultivateur, trice, planteur, euse. ~*ing crops,* récoltes sur pied, f.pl.

growl, n, grondement, m. ¶ v.i, gronder.

grown-up, grand. **grown-up,** a. & n, adulte, a. & m,f, grande personne, f. ~ **growth,** n, croissance; venue; pousse; végétation, f; (*vintage*) cru; développement, m.

grub, n, larve, f, ver, m. **grubby,** a, (*wormy*) véreux; (*dirty*) crasseux.

grudge, n, rancune, f. ¶ v.t, marchander, reprocher à.

gruel, n, gruau, m, bouillie, f.

gruesome, a, macabre.

gruff, a, rude, brusque, bourru.

grumble, v.i, murmurer, gronder, grogner. ~ *at,* ~ *about,* grommeler, marmonner. **grumpy,** a, bourru.

grunt, n, grognement, m. ¶ v.i, grogner.

guano, n, guano, m.

guarantee, -ty, n, garantie; caution, f; aval, m. ¶ v.t, garantir; cautionner; avaliser. **guarantor,** n, garant, e, caution, f.

guard, n, garde; sentinelle, f; protecteur, m; (*pers.*) garde; (*Bookb.*) onglet, m. *on* ~, en faction; sur le qui-vive. ~*house,* ~*room,* corps de garde, poste, m, salle de police, f. ¶ v.t. & i, [se] garder; se prémunir; parer. ~**ed,** p.a, mesuré; réservé. **guardian,** n, gardien, ne; curateur, trice, tuteur, trice, correspondant, e; (*att.*) gardien, tutélaire. ~**ship,** n, garde; (*law*) tutelle, curatelle, f.

guava, n, goyave, f; (*tree*) goyavier, m.

gudgeon, n, goujon; tourillon, m.

guelder rose, boule de neige, f, obier, m.

guerrilla, n, guérilla, f, partisan, m. ~ *war[fare],* guerre de guérillas, g. de partisan, f.

Guernsey, n, Guernesey, f.

guess, n, conjecture, f. ¶ v.t. & i, deviner, conjecturer.

guest, n, convive, m,f, convié, e; hôte, esse, invité, e. ~ *room,* chambre d'ami, f. ~ *of honor,* invité(e) d'honneur.

guffaw, v.i, rigoler.

Guiana, n, la Guyane.

guidance, n, direction; gouverne, f. **guide,** n, guide; cicerone, m. ~ [*book*], guide; indicateur, m. ~ *post,* poteau indicateur, m. ~ *rope,* câble-guide; (*Avn.*) guiderope, m. ¶ v.t, guider, conduire. *guiding principle,* idée directrice, f.

guild, n, corps de métier, m, corporation; association, f; (*church*) patronage, m.

guile, n, ruse, astuce, f, artifice, m. ~**less,** a, innocent, candide; naïf.

guillotine, n, guillotine, f. ¶ v.t, guillotiner.

guilt, n, culpabilité, f. ~**less,** a, innocent, e. ~**y,** a, coupable, criminel.

guinea (*21/-*) n, guinée, f. ~

fowl, pintade, *f.* ~ *pig*, cochon, d'Inde, cobaye, *m.* **G~** (*Geog.*), la Guinée.

guise, *n*, apparence, *f.*

guitar, *n*, guitare, *f.*

gules (*Her.*), *n*, gueules, *m.*

gulf, *n*, golfe; gouffre, abîme, *m.* **G~ Stream**, Gulf-Stream, *m.*

gull, *n*, (*sea*) mouette, *f*, goéland, *m*; (*pers.*) dupe, *f.* ¶ *v.t*, duper.

gullet, *n*, gosier, *m*, gorge, *f.*

gullible, *a*, crédule.

gully, *n*, ravine, *f*, ravin; (*gutter*) caniveau, *m.*

gulp, *n*, goulée, gorgée, *f*, trait, *m.* **to ~ down**, gober.

gum, *n*, gomme; (*Anat.*) gencive, *f.* ~ *arabic*, gomme arabique. ~*boil*, abcès aux gencives, *m.* ~ *tree*, gommier, *m.* ¶ *v.t*, gommer.

gummy, *a*, gommeux.

gumption, *n*, entregent, savoir-faire, *m.*

gun, *n*, fusil; canon, *m*, pièce, *f.* ~*boat*, [chaloupe] canonnière, *f.* ~ *carriage*, affût, *m.* ~*cotton*, coton-poudre, fulmicoton, *m.* ~ *license*, port d'armes, *m.* ~ *metal*, bronze [industriel] *m.* ~*powder*, poudre à canon, *f.* ~*shot*, portée de fusil, p. de canon, *f.* ~*shot wound*, blessure d'arme à feu, *f.* ~*smith*, armurier, *m.* **gunner**, *n*, artilleur, canonnier, *m.* ~**y**, *n*, tir, *m*, artillerie, *f*, canonnage, *m.*

gunwale, gunnel, *n*, plat-bord, *m.*

gurgle, *n*, glouglou, *m.* ¶ *v.i*, faire glouglou; gargouiller.

gurnard, *n*, trigle, grondin, rouget, *m.*

gush, *n*, jaillissement, bouillon, *m*; sentimentalité, *f.* ¶ *v.i*, jaillir.

gusset, *n*, gousset, *m.*

gust, *n*, coup, *m*, bourrasque, rafale, bouffée, *f.*

gusto, *n*, entrain, *m.*

gusty, *a*, (*wind*) impétueux; (*day*) de grand vent.

gut, *n*, boyau; intestin; (*Fish.*) crin, florence, *m*, racine, *f*; (*Naut.*) goulet, *m.* **he has ~s**, il a du cran. ¶ *v.t*, vider, étriper.

gutta-percha, *n*, gutta-percha, *f.*

gutter, *n*, (*roof*) gouttière, *f*, chéneau; (*street*) ruisseau; (*conduit*) caniveau; chenal, *m*; rigole, *f*; (*book*) blancs de petit fond, *m.pl.*; (*fig.*) ruisseau; carrefour, *m*, crasse, fange, crotte, *f.* ~ *language*, langage de carrefour,

m. ~*snipe*, voyou, *m.* ¶ *v.i*, couler.

guttural, *a*, guttural. ¶ *n*, gutturale, *f.*

guy, *n*, (*rope*) hauban, *m*; (*pers.*) type, *m.*

guzzle, *v.i*, bâfrer, goinfrer.

gymnasium, *n*, gymnase, *m.*

gymnast, *n*, gymnaste, gymnasiarque, *m.* ~**ic**, *a.* & *n*, gymnastique, *a.* & *f.* ~**ics**, *n.pl*, gymnastique, gymnique, *f.*

gynecology, *n*, gynécologie, *f.*

gypseous, *a*, gypseux. **gypsum**, *n*, gypse, *m.* ~*quarry*, plâtrière, *f.*

gypsy, *n*, gitan, e.

gyrate, *v.i*, tourner. **gyration**, *n*, giration, *f.* **gyratory**, *a*, giratoire.

gyroscope, *n*, gyroscope, *m.*

H

haberdasher, *n*, chemisier, mercier, *m.* ~**y**, *n*, mercerie, chemiserie, *f.*

habiliment, *n*, attirail; (*pl.*) habillement, *m.*

habit, *n*, habitude, coutume, *f*; (*pl.*) mœurs, *f.pl*; tic; (*dress*) habit, *m.* **to be in the ~ of doing so**, être coutumier (ère) du fait. ~**able**, *a*, habitable. **habitat**, *n*, habitat, *m.* **habitation**, *n*, habitation, *f.* **habitual†**, *a*, habituel, familier. ~ *criminal*, repris de justice, *m.* **habituate**, *v.t*, habituer.

hack, *n*, entaille, *f*; cheval de louage; c. de selle, *m*; (*jade*) rosse, *f.* ~ *saw*, scie à métaux, *f.* ~ [*writer*], écrivailleur, *m.* ¶ *v.t*, écharper, hacher, charcuter.

hackneyed, *p.p*, banal, rebattu, usé jusqu'à la corde. ~ *phrase*, cliché, *m.* ~ *refrain*, rengaine, *f.*

haddock, *n*, aigrefin, *m.*

Hades, *n*, les enfers, *m.pl.*

haft, *n*, manche, *m*, poignée, *f.*

hag, *n*, sorcière, *f.*

haggard, *a*, hagard, tiré.

haggle, *v.i*, marchander, barguigner, chipoter.

Hague (the), la Haye.

hail, *n*, grêle, *f*, grésil, *m.* **to damage by ~**, grêler. ~*stone*, grain de grêle; (*big*) grêlon, *m.* ~ *storm*, orage [accompagné] de grêle, *m*, giboulée, *f.* ¶ *i*, salut! ~ *fellow well met*, de pair à compagnon. ¶ *v.i.imp*, grêler, grêsiller; (*v.t.*) faire pleuvoir; saluer;

héler; acclamer. ~ *from*, venir de. *within* ~, à portée de la voix.

hair, *n*, (un) cheveu, *m*; (*des*) cheveux, *m.pl*; chevelure, *f*; poil; crin, *m*; soie; bourre, *f*. ~*brush*, brosse à cheveux, b. à tête, *f*. ~*comb*, peigne coiffeur, *m*. ~*curler*, bigoudi, *m*. ~*cut*, coupe de cheveux, *f*. ~*dresser*, coiffeur, euse. ~ *drier*, appareil à douche d'air, *m*. ~ *mattress*, matelas de crin, *m*. ~ *net*, filet à cheveux, *m*, résille, *f*. ~ *oil*, huile pour les cheveux, *f*. ~*pin*, épingle à cheveux, *f*. ~*pin bend*, virage en é. à c., *m*. ~ *shirt*, haire, *f*. ~*splitting*, pointillerie, argutie, *f*. ~*less*, *a*, sans poils; glabre. ~*y*, *a*, velu; poilu; chevelu.

Haiti, *n*, Haïti, *m*.

hake, *n*, merlus, *m*; (*dried*) merluche, *f*.

halation (*Phot.*) *n*, halo, *m*.

halberd (*Hist.*) *n*, hallebarde, *f*.

halcyon days, jours alcyoniens; (*fig.*) jours sereins, *m.pl*.

hale, *a*, sain, vert, verdelet, frais. ~ *& hearty*, frais & gaillard, frais & dispos.

half, *n*, moitié; demie, *f*; demi; (*Rly ticket*) coupon, *m*. *by* ~, à moitié; de moitié. *to go halves with*, être (*ou* se mettre) de moitié avec. *No 29½* (*house*), Nº 29 bis. ¶ *a*, demi-. ¶ *ad*, moitié; à moitié; à mi-; à demi. ~ *a cup*, la moitié d'une tasse, une demi-tasse. ~ *an hour*, une demi-heure. ~*back* (*Foot.*), demi, *m*. ~*breed*, métis, métisse. ~*brother*, demi-frère, *m*. ~*caste*, [homme de] sang mêlé, *m*. ~ *fare*, ~ *price*, demi-place, *f*. ~ *holiday*, demi-congé, *m*. ~ *light*, demi-jour, *m*. *at* ~*mast* (*flag*), en berne. ~*open*, *a*, entrouvert, entrebâillé; (*v.t.*) entrouvrir. ~ *past twelve*, midi & demi; minuit & demi. ~ *past two*, deux heures & demie. *on* ~ *pay*, en demi-solde. ~*sister*, demi-sœur, *f*. ~ *time* (*Foot.*), la mi-temps. ~*title*, faux titre, *m*. ~*way*, à mi-chemin, à moitié chemin. ~*witted*, simple. ~*yearly*, *a*, semestriel; (*ad.*) par semestre.

halibut, *n*, flétan, *m*.

hall, *n*, vestibule; hall, *m*; salle; enceinte, *f*; château, *m*. ~*mark*, *n*, [poinçon de] contrôle, *m*; (*v.t.*) contrôler, poinçonner. ~ *porter*, concierge, *m*. *town* ~, hôtel de ville, *m*.

hallelujah, *n*, Alléluia, *m*.

hallo[a], *i*, holà!, hé! ~ *there!* hé là-bas! **halloo,** *n*, cri [d'appel] *m*. ¶ *v.i*, crier, huer; (*v.t*, *dogs*) houper, encourager. ~ *to*, appeler à grands cris.

hallow, *v.t*, sanctifier, consacrer. ~*ed*, *p.a*, saint. *Hallowe'en*, vigile de la Toussaint, *f*.

hallucination, *n*, hallucination, vision, *f*.

halo, *n*, halo, *m*, auréole, *f*, nimbe, *m*.

halt, *n*, halte, station, *f*; stationnement, *m*. ¶ *i*, halte-[là]! ¶ *v.i*, faire halte; stationner; (*waver*) balancer; (*limp*) boiter.

halter, *n*, (*harness*) licou, *m*; (*hanging*) corde, *f*.

halting, *a*, boiteux.

halve, *v.t*, partager en deux, p. par la moitié.

halyard, *n*, drisse, *f*.

ham, *n*, (*in man*) jarret; (*hog, boar*) jambon, *m*. ~ *& eggs*, œufs au jambon, *m.pl*.

Hamburg, *n*, Hambourg, *m*.

hames, *n.pl*, attelles, *f.pl*.

hamlet, *n*, hameau, *m*.

hammer, *n*, marteau, *m*; (*power*) pilon, *m*; (*gun*) chien, *m*. ~*lock* (*wrestling*), retournement de bras, *m*. ¶ *v.t*, marteler, battre.

hammock, *n*, hamac, *m*.

hamper, *n*, [gros] panier, *m*, manne; malle en osier, *f*; (*impedimenta*) bataclan. ¶ *v.t*, empêtrer; troubler.

hand, *n*, main, *f*; poing, *m*; (*pointer*) aiguille; écriture; signature, *f*; (*side*) côté, *m*, part; (*cards*) main, *f*, jeu, *m*; (*horse*) = 4 *inches or* 10.16 *centimeters* (*pl*, *men*) bras, hommes, *m.pl* (*att.*) à main, à bras; à la main; manuel. *on the other* ~, de l'autre côté, d'autre part. ~*bag* (*lady's, etc.*), sac à main, *m*. ~*bill*, prospectus, imprimé; (*political, etc.*) tract, *m*. ~*book*, manuel, livret, aide-mémoire, guide-âne, mémento, *m*. ~*cuff*, *v.t*, mettre les menottes à; (*n.pl.*) menottes, *f.pl*. ~*kerchief*, mouchoir, *m*; (*silk*) pochette, *f*. ~*s off!* bas les mains! ~*rail*, main courante, rampe, *f*, garde-fou, *m*. ~*shake*, poignée de main, *f*. ~ *to* ~ (*fight*), corps à corps. *from* ~ *to mouth*, au jour le jour. ~*s up!* haut les mains! ~*writing*, écriture, *f*. ¶ *v.t*, passer. ~ *down* (*fig.*) transmettre. ~ *in*, déposer.

~ *[over]*, remettre, délivrer. ~ *over* (*to justice*), remettre, déférer. ~ful, *n*, poignée, *f*.

handicap, *n*, (*sport*) handicap; (*fig.*) désavantage, *m*. ¶ *v.t*, handicaper; désavantager. handicapper, *n*, handicapeur, *m*.

handicraft, *n*, industrie d'art, *f*. handicraftsman, ouvrier d'art, *m*.

handle, *n*, manche, *m*; poignée; (*umbrella*) poignée; main; manivelle; manette, *f*; bras; fût, *m*; (*basket*) anse; queue; branche; boucle, *f*; (*door*) bouton, *m*. ~bar (cycle), guidon, *m*. ¶ *v.t*, manier; manipuler; traiter; filer; emmancher. *one who knows how to handle* (*money, men*), manieur, *m*. *to* ~ *roughly*, malmener. handling, *n*, manutention, *f*, maniement, *m*, manipulation, *f*. handmade, *a*, fait à la main.

handsome, *a*, beau; riche. ~ly, *ad*, joliment, généreusement, grassement. ~ness, *n*, beauté, *f*.

handy, *a*, sous la main; commode; maniable; adroit; (*man*) à tout faire.

hang, *v.t. & i.ir*, pendre; suspendre; [r]accrocher; tomber; tapisser, tendre; poser. ~ *about*, rôder. ~ *back*, hésiter. ~ *heavy* (*time*), durer. ~ *out* (*washing*), étendre. ~dog, *a*, patibulaire. ~man, bourreau, *m*. ~nail, envie, *f*.

hangar, *n*, hangar, *m*.

hanger, *n*, crochet, *m*. ~-on, personne à charge, *f*; parasite, *m*. hanging, *p.a*, suspendu. ~ *committee* (*Art*), jury d'admission, *m*. ~ *garden*, jardin suspendu, *m*. ~ *lamp*, baladeuse, *f*. ~ *matter*, cas pendable, *m*. [*death by*] ~, pendaison, mort par suspension, *f*. hangings, *n.pl*, tapisserie, *f*.

hank, *n*, écheveau, *m*, poignée, *f*.

hanker after, soupirer après, avoir soif de.

Hanover, *n*, Hanovre, *m*; (*province*) le H.

haphazard, *ad*, au hasard, à l'aventure.

hapless, *a*, infortuné.

happen, *v.i*, arriver; advenir; venir, se passer, se trouver. ~ing, *n*, événement, *m*.

happiness, *n*, bonheur, *m*; félicité, *f*. happy†, *a*, heureux. ~-go-lucky *person*, sans-souci, *m,f*. *to a* ~ *issue*, à bon port. ~ *medium*, juste milieu, *m*. *a* ~ *New Year*, la bonne année.

harangue, *n*, harangue, *f*. ¶ *v.t. & i*, haranguer.

harass, *v.t*, harceler, fouler.

harbinger, *n*, avant-coureur, messager, fourrier, *m*.

harbor, *n*, port; refuge, *m*. ~ *master*, capitaine de port, *m*. ¶ *v.t*, héberger; nourrir; garder; (*criminal*) receler.

hard, *a*, dur; rude; rigoureux; ardu, laborieux, pénible; (*water*) crue. ~ & *fast*, absolu, immuable. ~-*bitten sailor*, loup de mer, *m*. ~-*boiled* (egg), dur. ~ *cash*, espèces sonnantes, *f.pl*. ~ *court* (*Ten.*), terre battue, *f*. ~ *labor*, travail disciplinaire, *m*. ~ *luck*, mauvais sort, *m*. ~ *palate*, palais dur, *m*. ~ *roe*, œufs, *m.pl*. ~ *tack*, biscuit de mer, *m*. ~ *to please*, exigeant. ~ware, quincaillerie; (*builder's*) serrurerie, *f*. ~-*wearing* & *for* ~ *wear*, inusable. ~-*working*, laborieux. ¶ *ad*, dur; durement; fort; fortement; (*drink*) sec; (*look*) fixement; (*raining*) à verse. ~ *up*, à sec, aux abois.

harden, *v.t*, durcir, endurcir; (*to temper metal*) tremper. hardihood, *n*, hardiesse, *f*. hardly, *ad*, durement; à peine; ne ... guère; presque. hardness, *n*, dureté; rigueur; (*water*) crudité, *f*. ~ *of hearing*, dureté d'oreille. hardship, *n*, privation; rigueur, *f*. hardy, *a*, hardi; (*plant*) robuste, rustique.

hare, *n*, lièvre, (*young*) levraut, *m*. ~ & *hounds*, rallye-paper, *m*. ~bell, campanule, clochette, *f*. ~brained, écervelé. ~lip, bec-de-lièvre, *m*.

harem, *n*, harem, *m*.

haricot beans (*dried*), haricots secs, *m.pl*.

hark, *i*, écoute! écoutez!

harlequin, *n*, arlequin, *m*. ~ade, *n*, arlequinade, *f*.

harlot, *n*, prostituée, *f*.

harm, *n*, mal; tort, *m*. ¶ *v.t*, faire du mal à; nuire à. ~ful, *a*, nuisible, pernicieux. ~less, *a*, inoffensif, innocent, anodin. ~lessness, *n*, innocuité; innocence, *f*.

harmonic†, *a*. & *n*, harmonique, *a*. & *m*. harmonica, *n*, harmonica, *m*. harmonious†, *a*, harmonieux. harmonium, *n*, harmonium, *m*. harmonize, *v.t*, harmoniser. harmony, *n*, harmonie, *f*; ensemble, *m*.

harness, *n*, harnais; harnache-

ment, *m. die in* ~, mourir debout.
~ *maker*, bourrelier; sellier, *m.*
¶ *v.t*, harnacher; (*waterfall*) aménager.

harp, *n*, harpe, *f. to be always* ~*ing on the same string*, chanter toujours la même antienne, rabâcher toujours les mêmes choses. ~**ist,** *n*, harpiste, *m,f.*

harpoon, *n*, harpon, *m.* ¶ *v.t*, harponner.

harpsichord, *n*, clavecin, *m.*

harpy, *n*, harpie, *f.*

harrow, *n*, herse, *f.* ¶ *v.t*, herser; (*fig.*) déchirer, navrer. ~**ing,** *a*, déchirant.

harry, *v.t*, harceler; dévaster.

harsh†, *a*, dur; rude; âpre; aigre. ~**ness,** *n*, dureté; rudesse; âpreté; aigreur, *f.*

hart, *n*, cerf, *m.* **hartshorn,** *n*, liqueur d'ammoniaque, *f.*

harum-scarum, *n*, hurluberlu, *m.*

harvest, *n*, moisson; récolte, *f.* ~ *festival*, fête de la moisson, *f.* ~*man* (insect), faucheur, faucheux, *m.* ¶ *v.t*, moissonner; récolter. ~**er,** *n*, moissonneur, euse; (*Mach.*) moissonneuse, *f.*

hash, *n*, hachis, *m*, capilotade, *f.* ¶ *v.t*, hacher.

hasp, *n*, moraillon, *m.*

hassock, *n*, agenouilloir; carreau, coussin, *m.*

haste, *n*, hâte; précipitation, *f. to* [*make*]~ & **hasten,** *v.i*, se dépêcher, se hâter, s'empresser. **hasten,** *v.t*, hâter, presser, précipiter. **hasty†,** *a*, hâtif, à la hâte, précipité; vif, emporté.

hat, *n*, chapeau, *m.* ~ & *coat stand*, portechapeaux, portemanteau, *m.* ~*box*, boîte à chapeau(x), *f.* ~ *brush*, brosse à chapeaux, *f.* ~ *peg*, patère, *f.* ~ *shop* & ~ *trade*, chapellerie, *f.*

hatch (*brood*) *n*, couvée, *f.* ~[*way*], *n*, panneau, *m*, écoutille, *f.* ¶ *v.i*, (*eggs*) éclore; (*v.t*.) faire éclore; (*fig.*) couver, ourdir, tramer; (*engrave*) hacher.

hatchet, *n*, hache à main, *f.* ~ *face*, figure en lame de couteau, *f.*

hatching, *n*, éclosion; (*engraving*) hachure, *f.*

hatchment, *n*, écusson; blason funèbre, *m.*

hate, *n*, haine, *f.* ¶ *v.t*, haïr; détester. ~**ful†,** *a*, haïssable; odieux. **hatred,** *n*, haine, *f. full of* ~, haineux.

hatter, *n*, chapelier, *m.*

haughtily, *ad*, avec hauteur, d'une manière hautaine. **haughtiness,** *n*, hauteur, morgue, *f.* **haughty,** *a*, hautain, altier, arrogant.

haul, *n*, coup de filet; parcours, trajet, *m*; acquisition, *f.* ¶ *v.t*, haler; traîner, tirer, remorquer; transporter.

haunch, *n*, hanche, *f*; (*meat*) quartier, cuissot, cimier; (*Arch.*) rein, *m.*

haunt, *n*, rendez-vous, lieu fréquenté (*of* = par); repaire, *m*, caverne, *f*, liteau, *m.* ¶ *v.t*, hanter, fréquenter; poursuivre.

hautboy (*Mus.*), *n*, hautbois, *m.*

Havana, *n*, la Havane. ~ [*cigar*], cigare de la Havane, havane, *m.*

have, *v.t.ir*, avoir; posséder; jouir de; tenir; prendre; faire. ~ *on* (*wear*), porter, avoir. *I* ~ *come*, je suis venu. *I* ~ *been had*, on m'a eu.

haven, *n*, havre, port; (*fig.*) asile, *m.*

haversack, *n*, musette, *f*, sac, *m.*

havoc, *n*, ravage[s] *m*.[*pl.*], dégâts, *m.pl.*

Havre, *n*, le Havre.

haw (*Bot.*) *n*, cenelle, *f.* ~*finch*, gros-bec, *m.* ¶ *v.i*, ânonner.

Hawaii, *n*, Hawaï, *m.* ~**an,** *a*, hawaïen.

hawk, *n*, faucon, *m.* ¶ *v.i*, chasser au faucon; (*throat*) graillonner; (*v.t.*) colporter. ~**er,** *n*, colporteur, *m*; crieur, euse; camelot, *m.* ~**ing** (*falconry*) *n*, volerie, *f.*

hawser, *n*, haussière, amarre, *f*, grelin, *m.*

hawthorn, *n*, aubépine, *f.*

hay, *n*, foin, *m*. oft. pl. ~*cock*, tas de foin, *m.* ~ *fever*, fièvre des foins, *f.* ~*loft*, fenil, *m.* ~*maker*, faneur, euse. ~*making*, fenaison, *f.* ~*stack*, meule de foin, *f.*

hazard, *n*, hasard, *m*; (*golf*) hasard, accident, *m.* ¶ *v.t*, hasarder. ~**ous†,** *a*, hasardeux, chanceux.

haze, *n*, brume, *f*, brouillard; nuage, *m.*

hazel, *n*, noisetier, coudrier, *m*; (*att., color, eyes*) [de] noisette. ~*nut*, noisette, *f.*

hazy, *a*, brumeux; nuageux; vaporeux; vague; flou.

he, *pn*, il; lui; celui; ce, c'. ¶ *n.* & *att*, mâle, *m. it is* ~, c'est lui. *there* ~ *is*, le voilà.

head, *n*, tête, *f*; cerveau, *m*; [*of hair*] chevelure, *f*; chef; titre;

haut; fond; chapiteau; cap, m;
pointe; pomme; rubrique, f, poste,
chapitre; en-tête; (bed) chevet,
m; (on glass of beer) mousse;
(coin) face; (book page) tête,
tranche supérieure, f; (deer) bois,
m; (game) pièce; (boar, etc.)
hure, f; (lathe) poupée, f; (spear)
fer, m. ~s or tails? pile ou face?
~ache, mal de tête, m. ~band,
bandeau, serre-tête, m; (Bookb.)
tranchefile, comète, f. ~ cook,
chef [de cuisine] m. ~dress,
~gear, coiffure, coiffe, f, couvre-
chef, m. ~land, pointe de terre,
f, cap, m. ~light, feu d'avant,
fanal de tête; (auto) phare, m.
~line, (book) titre courant, m;
(news) manchette, f. ~long, a,
précipité; (ad.) précipitamment.
~master, directeur; principal;
proviseur. ~mistress, directrice,
f. ~ office, siège [principal],
siège social, m. ~-on collision,
rencontre de front, f. ~phones,
casque, m. ~quarters, quartier
général; (staff) État-major; chef-
lieu, m; préfecture, f. ~room,
échappée, f. ~sman, bourreau,
m. ~stone, pierre tombale,
tombe, f. ~strong, entêté, entier.
~waiter, maître d'hôtel, premier
garçon, chef de salle, m. ~
waters, amont, m. ~way, chemin,
progrès, m; (Naut.) erre, f. ~
wind, vent debout, m. ¶ v.t, être
(ou se mettre) à la tête de. ~ the
procession, ouvrir la marche.
~ed (paper) p.a, à en tête. ~ing,
n, titre; en-tête, m. ~y (liquor) a,
capiteux.

heal, v.t, guérir; (v.i.) [se] g. ~er,
n, guérisseur, euse; (of time)
médecin, m. ~ing, n, guérison, f.

health, n, santé; salubrité; hygiène, f. ~y, a, sain; salubre;
hygiénique.

heap, n, tas, amas, monceau, m.
¶ v.t, entasser, amonceler, amasser.

hear, v.t. & i. ir, entendre; écouter; (witness—law) ouïr; (learn)
apprendre; (prayer) exaucer. ~
from, lire. ~er, n, auditeur, trice.
~ing, n, ouïe; oreille; audition;
audience, f; débats, m.pl. to be
hard of ~, avoir l'ouïe (ou
l'oreille) dure. ~say, on-dit, ouï-
dire, m.

hearse, n, corbillard, char [fu-
nèbre], char de deuil, m.

heart, n, cœur, m; âme, f; entrailles, f.pl; fond, vif, m. by ~,

par cœur, de mémoire. ~ & soul
(fig.), tout son cœur. ~beat, battement de cœur, m. ~break,
brisement de cœur, m. ~break-
ing, ~rending, désespérant, navrant, déchirant. ~burn, ardeur
d'estomac, f. ~ case (pers.),
cardiaque, m.f. ~ disease, maladie de cœur, f. in one's ~ of ~s,
au fond du cœur. ~en, v.t, encourager, rassurer. ~felt, a, bien
senti. to be ~less, n'avoir point
de cœur. ~less person, sans-
cœur, m.f. heartsease (Bot.) n,
pensée, f.

hearth, n, âtre; foyer; feu;
(smith's) bâti, m. ~ brush, balai
d'âtre, m. ~ rug, tapis de foyer,
t. de cheminée, m. ~stone, pierre
de foyer, f, [marbre de] foyer, m;
(whitening) pierre blanche, f.

heartily, ad, cordialement;
franchement. **hearty,** a, cordial;
(fit) dispos; (laugh) gros; (meal)
solide, copieux.

heat, n, chaleur, f; calorique, m;
température; chauffe; fièvre; vivacité, ardeur, f, feu, m; (sport)
épreuve, f; (animals) rut, m. ~
lightning, éclair[s] de chaleur,
m.[pl.], fulguration, f. ~stroke,
coup de chaleur, m. ~ wave,
vague de c., f. ¶ v.t, chauffer,
échauffer. ~er, n, calorifère; radiateur; réchaud, m.

heath, n, (land) bruyère, brande,
lande; (shrub) bruyère, brande,
f. ~cock, coq de bruyère, m.

heathen, n, païen, ne. ~[ish], a,
païen. ~ism, n, paganisme, m.

heather, n, bruyère, brande, f.

heating, n, chauffage; échauffement, m. ~ engineer, fumiste, m.
~ surface, surface de chauffe, f.

heave, v.t.ir, soulever; pousser;
jeter; lancer; haler; virer; (v.i.ir.)
palpiter; (retch) faire des haut-
le-cœur. ~ to (Naut.), mettre en
panne.

heaven, n, ciel, m, cieux, m.pl.
~ly, a, céleste. **heavily,** ad,
lourdement, pesamment. **heaviness,** n, pesanteur, f, poids, m;
lourdeur, f. **heavy,** a, lourd; pesant; massif; fort; chargé; grave;
gros; grand. ~ shell (Artil.),
marmite, f. ~ weight, (for lifting)
gueuse [d'athlétisme] f; (for
throwing) gros boulet; (Box.)
poids lourd, m.

Hebraic & Hebrew, a, hébraïque. **Hebrew** (language) n,
l'hébreu, m.

hecatomb, *n,* hécatombe, *f.*

heckle, *v.t,* harceler [de questions].

hectic (*fever*) *a,* hectique.

hector, *n,* bravache, fanfaron, *m.*

hedge, *n,* haie, *f.* ~*hog,* hérisson, *m.* ~*row,* haie, *f.* ~ *sparrow,* fauvette des haies, *f, mouchet, m.* ¶ *v.t,* entourer d'une haie. (*v.i.*) chercher des échappatoires; (*Fin.*) faire un arbitrage, se couvrir. ~ *in,* [r]enfermer.

heed, *n,* attention; garde, *f.* ¶ *v.t,* faire attention à. ~**less,** *a,* insoucieux.

heel, *n,* talon, *m;* (*rubber*) talonnette; (*Naut.*) bande, *f. at the* ~*s of,* aux trousses de.

hefty, *a,* solide.

hegemony, *n,* hégémonie, *f.*

heifer, *n,* génisse, *f.*

height, *n,* hauteur, élévation, altitude, *f;* comble, plein, apogée, *m;* (*stature*) taille, *f;* (*of summer*) cœur, fort, *m.* ~**en,** *v.t,* rehausser, surélever.

heinous†, *a,* odieux; atroce.

heir, ess, *n,* héritier, ère, hoir, *m.* ~*loom,* bijou de famille, meuble de famille, *m.* ~**ship,** *n,* hérédité, *f.*

helical, *a,* en hélice, hélicoïdal.

helicopter, *n,* hélicoptère, *m.*

heliotrope, *n,* héliotrope, *m.*

helium, *n,* hélium, *m.*

helix, *n,* hélice, *f;* (*ear*) hélix, *m.*

hell, *n,* enfer, *m;* géhenne, *f.* ~*cat,* harpie, *f.*

Hellenism, *n,* hellénisme, *m.*

hellish, *a,* infernal.

hello (*Teleph.*) *i,* allô!

helm, *n,* barre, *f;* (*fig.*) gouvernail, timon, *m, helmsman,* timonier, homme de barre, *m.*

helmet, *n,* casque, *m.*

helot, *n,* ilote, *m.* ~**ism,** *n,* ilotisme, *m.*

help, *n,* aide, assistance, *f,* moyen, secours; remède, *m.* ¶ *v.t. & i,* aider, assister, secourir. *I can't* ~ *saying,* je ne peux m'empêcher de dire. ~ *one another,* s'entraider. ~ *yourself,* servez-vous. ~! au secours! à l'aide! à moi! à nous! ~**er,** *n,* aide, *m,f.* ~**ful** *& ~ing,* *a,* utile; serviable. ~**ing** (*food*) *n,* portion, *f.* ~**less,** *a,* impuissant; impotent.

helter-skelter, *ad. & n,* pêle-mêle, *ad. & m.*

helve, *n,* manche, *m.*

hem, *n,* ourlet; [re]bord, *m,* bor-

dure, *f.* ¶ *v.t,* ourler; border; (*v.i.*) ânonner. ~ *in,* cerner.

hematite, *n,* hématite, *f.*

hemidemisemiquaver, *n,* quadruple croche, *f.*

hemisphere, *n,* hémisphère, *m.*

hemlock, *n,* ciguë, *f.*

hemorrhage, *n,* hémorragie, *f.*

hemorrhoids, *n.pl,* hémorroïdes, *f.pl.*

hemming, *n,* point d'ourlet, *m.*

hemp, *n,* chanvre, *m.* ~ *seed,* chènevis, *m.* ~[**en**], *a,* de chanvre.

hemstitch, *n,* ourlet à jour, *m.* ¶ *v.t,* ourler à jour.

hen, *n,* poule, *f.* ~ *coop,* cage à poulets, mue, *f.* ~ *house,* poulailler, *m.* ~ *partridge,* perdrix femelle, *f.* ~*pecked,* mené par sa femme. ~ *pheasant,* [poule] faisane, *f.* ~ *roost,* juchoir, *m.*

hence, *ad,* d'ici; de là; dans; partant; donc. ~**forth,** ~**forward,** *ad,* désormais, dorénavant, dès maintenant.

henchman, *n,* partisan, satellite, séide. mamel[o]uk, *m.*

henna, *n,* henné, *m.*

her, *pr,* elle; la; lui; son, sa, ses.

herald, *n,* (*Hist.*) héraut; (*fig.*) avant-coureur, *m.* ¶ *v.t,* annoncer. ~**ic,** *a,* héraldique. ~**ry,** *n,* blason, *m.* héraldique, *f.*

herb, *n,* herbe, *f.* ~**aceous,** *a,* herbacé. ~**age,** *n,* herbage, *m.* ~**al,** *n,* herbier, *m.* ~**alist,** *n,* herboriste, *m,f.* ~**arium,** *n,* herbier, *m.* ~**ivorous,** *a. & ~ animal,* herbivore. *a. & m.* **herborize,** *v.i,* herboriser.

Herculean, *a,* herculéen. *a Hercules,* un hercule.

herd, *n,* troupeau,. *m;* (*deer*) harde, *f. the* [*common*] ~, le vulgaire. *the ~ instinct,* le sentiment grégaire. ~ *together,* vivre en troupe. ~*ed together,* empilé.

herdsman, *n,* bouvier, pâtre, *m.*

here, *ad,* ici; que voici; y; présent! ~ *a little & there a little,* de bric & de broc. ~ *& there,* ici & là; [de]çà & [de]là; par-ci, par-là. ~ *below,* ici-bas. ~ *I am,* me voici. ~ *is,* ~ *are,* voici. ~ *lies* (grave), ci-gît, ici repose. [*look*] ~! tenez!

hereabout[s], *ad,* ici près, dans ces parages. **hereafter,** *ad,* désormais, à l'avenir; dans la vie future. **hereby** (*law*) *ad,* par les présentes.

hereditary†, *a,* héréditaire. **heredity,** *n,* hérédité, *f.*

herein (*law*) ad, dans les présentes. **hereinafter,** ad, ci-après.

heresy, n, hérésie, f. **heretic,** n, hérétique, m,f. ~**al,** a, hérétique.

hereunder, ad, ci-dessous; de ce chef. **hereupon,** ad, sur ces entrefaites. **herewith,** ad, ci-joint, ci-inclus.

heritage, n, héritage, patrimoine, m.

hermaphrodite, n, hermaphrodite, m.

hermetic†, a, hermétique.

hermit, n, ermite, solitaire, m. ~ *crab,* bernard-l'ermite, m. ~**age,** n, ermitage, m.

hernia, n, hernie, f.

hero, n, héros, m. ~ *worship,* culte des héros, m. ~**ic†,** a, héroïque. ~**icomic,** a, héroï-comique. ~**ine,** n, héroïne, f. ~**ism,** n, héroïsme, m.

heron, n, héron, m. ~**ry,** n, héronnière, f.

herpes, n, herpès, m.

herring, n, hareng, m. ~ *boat,* harenguier, m. ~**boning** (*Need.*), point croisé, m. ~ *fishery &* ~ *season,* harengaison, f. **red** ~, hareng saur, m.

hers, pn, le sien, la sienne, les siens, les siennes; ses; à elle. **herself,** pn, elle même; elle; soi, soi-même; se.

hesitate, v.i, hésiter, balancer, marchander. **hesitation,** n, hésitation, f.

heterodox, a, hétérodoxe. ~**y,** n, hétérodoxie, f.

heterogeneous, a, hétérogène.

hew, v.t.ir, (*tree*) abattre, couper; (*stone*) tailler.

hexagon, n, hexagone, m. ~**al,** a, hexagone. ~ *nut,* écrou à 6 pans, m. **hexameter,** n, hexamètre, m.

heyday of life, fleur de l'âge, f.

hi, i, ohé!

hiatus, n, fissure; lacune, f; (*Gram.*) hiatus, m.

hibernate (*Zool.*) v.i, hiberner.

hiccup, n, hoquet, m. ¶ v.i, avoir le h.

hidden, p.p, caché; dérobé; occulte; latent. **hide,** v.t.ir, cacher. ~ [*oneself*], se cacher. ~**-&-seek,** cache-cache, m.

hide, n, peau, f, cuir, m. a, ~ *bound,* à l'esprit étroit.

hideous†, a, hideux.

hiding (*thrashing*) n, raclée, f.

hiding place, cache[tte] f, affût, m.

hierarchy, n, hiérarchie, f.

hieroglyph, n, hiéroglyphe, m.

higgledy-piggledy, ad, pêle-mêle.

high, a, haut; plein; élevé; grand; gros; fort; (*dear*) cher; (*meat*) avancé; (*game*) faisandé; (*in height*) de haut, haut de. ~ *altar,* maître-autel, grand autel, m. ~ *& dry* (*Naut.*), échoué à sec. ~*born,* de haute naissance. ~ *class,* de marque; (*wine*) grand; haut; perfectionné. ~ *collar,* faux col montant, m. ~ *dive,* plongeon d'une grande hauteur, m. ~*flown,* ampoulé. ~*handed,* arbitraire; tyrannique. ~ *hat,* chapeau haut de forme, m. ~ *jump,* saut en hauteur, m. ~*lights* (*Art*), rehauts, m.pl. ~ *mass,* grand-messe, messe chantée, f. ~*necked dress,* robe montante, f. ~ *priest,* grand prêtre, m. ~ *society,* le grand monde. ~ *tide,* marée haute, pleine mer, f. **to be** ~*waisted* (*dress*), avoir la taille haute. ~*water mark,* grand de l'eau, m, laisse de haute mer, f; (*fig.*) apogée, m. ~*way,* grand chemin, m, grand-route, grande route; voie publique, f. ~*way code,* code de la route, m. ~*wayman,* voleur de grand chemin, m. ~*way robbery,* vol de grand chemin, brigandage, m. ¶ ad, haut. ~**er,** a, plus haut; supérieur. ~ *bid,* surenchère, f. ~ *education,* haut enseignement, m. ~ *mathematics,* mathématiques spéciales, f.pl. ~ *notes* (*Mus.*), haut, m. **the** ~ *bidder,* le plus offrant [& dernier enchérisseur]. ~**ly,** ad, hautement; fortement; éminemment. ~ *amusing,* désopilant, impayable. ~ *paid,* très bien payé. ~ *strung,* nerveux. ~**ness,** n, hauteur; (*title*) altesse, f.

hiker, n, excursionniste à pied, m,f.

hilarious, a, hilare. **hilarity,** n, hilarité, f.

hill, n, colline, f, coteau, m, côte, hauteur, f. ~**side,** flanc de coteau. ~**top,** cime, f. **up** ~ *& down dale,* par monts & par vaux. ¶ (*Hort.*) v.t, butter, chausser. **hillock,** n, monticule, tertre, m, butte, f. **hilly,** a, montueux; accidenté.

hilt, n, poignée; garde, f.

him, pn, le; lui. **himself,** pn, lui-même; lui; soi, soi-même; se.

hind (*deer*) n, biche, f.

hind, *a,* de derrière; [d']arrière.
hinder, *v.t,* empêcher, gêner, entraver.
hindmost, *a,* dernier.
hindrance, *n,* empêchement, *m. without ~,* sans encombre.
Hindu, -doo, *a,* hindou. ¶ *n,* Hindou, e. **Hindustani,** *n,* l'hindoustani, *m.*
hinge, *n,* charnière; fiche; penture, *f;* (*fig.*) pivot, *m.* ¶ *v.i,* tourner; pivoter. **~d,** *p.a,* à charnière(s).
hinny, *n,* petit mulet, bardot, *m.*
hint, *n,* allusion; suggestion, *f;* mot [couvert] *m.* ¶ *v.t,* laisser entendre. *~ at,* insinuer.
hip, *n,* hanche; (*Arch.*) arête, croupe, *f. ~ bath,* bain de siège, *m. ~ bone,* os iliaque, *m. ~ measurement,* [con]tour de hanches, *m.*
hippodrome, *n,* hippodrome, *m.*
hippopotamus, *n,* hippopotame, *m.*
hire, *n,* louage, *m,* location, *f;* loyer, *m.* ¶ *v.t,* louer; (*assassin, etc.*) soudoyer. **~d,** *p.p,* de louage; à gages; mercenaire. **~ling,** *n,* mercenaire, *m,f.* **hirer,** *n,* loueur, euse.
hirsute, *a,* hirsute.
his, *pn,* le sien, la sienne, les siens, les siennes; son, sa, ses; à lui; de lui.
hiss, *v.t. & i,* siffler; chuter. **~[ing,]** *n,* sifflement; sifflet, *m.*
historian, *n,* historien, *m.* **historic** & **~al†,** *a,* historique; d'histoire. **history,** *n,* histoire, *f;* historique, *m.*
histrion, *n,* histrion, *m.* **~ic,** *a,* du théâtre.
hit, *n,* coup, *m;* pièce à succès; touche; balle au but, balle mise, *f,* coup au but, *m. ~ or miss,* au petit bonheur. ¶ *v.t.ir,* frapper; toucher; atteindre; attraper.
hitch, *n,* accroc, contretemps, *m.* ¶ *v.t,* accrocher. **~hiking,** auto-stop, *m.*
hither *ad,* ici, y. *~ & thither,* çà & là; par-ci, par-là. **~to,** *ad,* jusqu'à présent, jusqu'ici.
hive, *n,* ruche, *f.*
hives, *n,* urticaire, *f.*
hoard, *n,* amas; magot, *m.* ¶ *v.t,* amasser; (*v.i.*) thésauriser.
hoarding, *n,* clôture en planches, *f,* palissade, *f.*
hoarfrost, gelée blanche, *f,* givre, *m.*
hoarhound, *n,* marrube, *m.*

hoarse, *a,* enroué, éraillé; rauque. **~ness,** *n,* enrouement, *m.*
hoary, *a,* blanc; blanchi.
hoax, *n,* mystification; attrape, *f;* canard, *m;* supercherie, *f.* ¶ *v.t,* mystifier; attraper. **~er,** *n,* mystificateur, trice.
hob, *n,* plaque de cheminée, *f;* dessus [de fourneau] *m.*
hobble, *v.i,* clocher, clopiner, boiter; (*v.t.*) entraver. **hobbledehoy,** *n,* [garçon] godiche, *m.* **hobbling along,** clopin-clopant.
hobby, *n,* (*bird*) hobereau, *m.* (*an art, collecting, gardening*) is his *~,* il est [grand] amateur de . . ., . . . est sa folie, . . . est sa distraction. (*a sport*) is his *~,* il est passionné pour le . . . *~ horse,* cheval de bois; dada, *m.*
hobgoblin, *n,* esprit follet, *m.*
hobnail, *n,* caboche, *f,* gros clou, *m.* **~ed,** *p.a,* ferré.
hobnob with, être à tu & à toi avec; trinquer avec.
hobo, *n,* clochard, *m.*
Hobson's choice (it is), c'est à prendre ou à laisser.
hock, *n,* vin blanc du Rhin; (*horse*) jarret, *m.*
hockey, *n,* hockey, *m. ~ skates,* patins de h., *m.pl. ~ stick,* crosse de h., canne de h., *f,* bâton de h., *m.*
hocus, *v.t,* mystifier, attraper. **~pocus,** *n,* tour de passe-passe, *m.*
hod, *n,* oiseau [de maçon] *m.*
hodgepodge, *n,* méli-mélo, *m.*
hoe, *n,* houe; binette, *f;* sarcloir, *m.* ¶ *v.t,* houer; biner; serfouir.
hog, *n,* cochon, pourceau, porc [châtré] *m.* **~backed,** en dos d'âne. **hoggish,** *a,* bestial.
hogshead, *n,* barrique, *f,* boucaut, *m.*
hoist, *n,* treuil; monte-charge, *m.* ¶ *v.t,* [re]monter; lever; hisser; guinder; (*flag*) arborer.
hold, *n,* prise, pince; emprise, mainmise, *f;* (*Box.*) tenu; empire, *m;* (*ship*) cale, *f.* ¶ *v.t.ir,* tenir; retenir; détenir; occuper; contenir; posséder, avoir; réputer; célébrer. *~ back, ~ in,* retenir. **~fast,** crampon, *m;* patte, *f;* valet, *m. ~ forth,* pérorer. *~ on, ~ on! ~ the line!* (Teleph.), ne quittez pas! *~ one's own,* se maintenir. *~ one's nose,* se boucher le nez. *~ one's tongue,* se taire. *~ out,* tendre; présenter; durer. *~ up,* soutenir. **~er,** *n,* support; *m;*

porte- *always* m, *e.g, tool* ~, **porte-outil**, m; **douille**, *f; (pers.)* **détenteur**, trice; **titulaire**, m,f; **porteur**, m. **~ing**, n, tenue; détention; possession; propriété, f; avoir, m; valeur, f; **portefeuille**, m.

hole, n, trou; orifice, m; ouverture; *(fox's)* tanière; fosse, f, puits; œil, m; lumière, f; creux, m; piqûre, f; *(golf)* trou [d'arrivée] m. ¶ *v.t*, trouer, percer; *(golf)* jouer dans le trou.

holiday, n, jour de fête; jour férié, m; fête, f; vacances, f.pl; [jour de] congé, m.

holily, ad, saintement. **holiness**, n, sainteté, f.

Holland *(Geog.)* n, la Hollande. **h~**, n, toile écrue, toile bise, f.

hollo, *v.t*, houper. See *hallo*.

hollow, a, creux; cave; caverneux; *(voice)* sourde. *to beat* ~, battre à plate couture. ¶ n, creux; enfoncement; entonnoir, m; cavité, f. ~ [out], *v.t*, creuser; évider; caver.

holly, n, houx, m. ~ *berry*, cenelle, f.

hollyhock, n, rose trémière, passerose, f.

holocaust, n, holocauste, m; *(fig.)* immolation saignée, f.

holster, n, fonte, f.

holy, a, saint; sacré; *(bread, water)* bénit, e; *(day)* férié. *Holy Ghost*, Holy Spirit, Saint-Esprit, m. *H~ Land*, Terre Sainte, f. ~ *orders*, ordres sacrés, m.pl, prêtrise, f. *H~ See*, Saint-Siège, m. **~-water** basin, bénitier, m. **~-water** sprinkler, aspersoir, goupillon, m. *H~ Writ*, l'Écriture, sainte, f. ~ *year*, année jubilaire, f.

homage, n, hommage[s] m.[pl.].

home, n, foyer familial, foyer [domestique]; chez-moi; chez-soi; intérieur; logis, m; maison, f; gîte, m; ménage, m; pays, m; patrie, f; asile; hospice, m. ~ *for the aged*, maison de retraite. *at* ~. See under *at*. ¶ *ad*, chez soi; à la maison; juste; à fond; à bloc. ¶ *a*, domestique; de famille; indigène; intérieur; métropolitain. ~ *country*, métropole, f. ~ *life*, vie d'intérieur, f. **~sick**, nostalgique. **~sickness**, mal du pays, m, nostalgie, f. ~ *truths*, vérités bien senties, bonnes vérités, f.pl. **~work**, *(Sch.)* devoirs [à faire à la maison] m.pl. **~less**, a, sans foyer, sans asile. **homeliness**, n,

sans-façon, m. **homely**, a, simple, sans façon, bourgeois.

homeopath[ist], n, homéopathe, m. **homeopathic**, a, homéopathique. **homeopathy**, n, homéopathie, f.

Homeric, a, homérique.

homespun, n, toile de ménage, f. **homestead**, n, ferme, f, manoir, m. **homeward**, a. & ad, de retour; en r. ~ *bound*, en retour, effectuant son voyage de retour. **~s**, ad, en retour.

homicidal, a, homicide. **homicide**, n, *(pers.)* homicide, m,f; *(act)* homicide, m.

homily, n, homélie, f, prône, m.

homing pigeon, pigeon voyageur, m.

homogeneous, a, homogène.

homonym, n, homonyme, m.

hone, n, pierre à aiguiser, f. ¶ *v.t*, *(razor)* repasser; affiler.

honest†, a, honnête, probe, droit, intègre; brave, de bien. **~y**, n, honnêteté, probité, intégrité.

honey, n, miel; *(pers.)* chou[chou] m. ¶ *v.t*, sucrer. ~ *bee*, mouche à miel, f. **~-comb**, n, gâteau de miel; rayon de m., m. **~moon**, lune de miel, f, **~suckle**, chèvrefeuille, m. **~ed**, a, [em]miellé; mielleux.

honk, n, coup de klaxon, m. ¶ *v.i*, klaxoner.

honor, n, honneur, m. ¶ *v.t*, honorer; faire honneur à, accueillir. **~able†**, a, honorable. **~ed**, p.a, honoré; respecté.

honorarium, n, honoraires, m.pl. **honorary**, a, honoraire; honorifique; sans rétribution. ~ *membership*, honorariat, m.

hood, n, capuchon; chapeau; *(auto)* capot, m; capote; cape; capeline, f; dais; soufflet, m; hotte, f. **~wink**, bander [les yeux à, de].

hoof, n, sabot, m. **~ed**, a, ongulé.

hook, n, crochet; croc; gond, m; agrafe, f; *(Fish.)* hameçon; *(Box.)* crochet, m. ~ & *eye*, agrafe & porte. ~ & *hinge*, gond & penture. *by* ~ *or by crook*, de façon ou d'autre. ¶ *v.t*, accrocher; agrafer. **~[ed]** *(nose)* a, aquilin.

hooky [to play] *v.i*, faire l'école buissonnière.

hookah, n, narghileh, m.

hooligan, n, apache, voyou, m.

hoop, n, cercle; cerceau, m; frette, f; arceau, m. ~ *iron*, feuillard de fer, m. ~ ring, jonc, m. ¶ v.t, [en]cercler, relier; fretter.

hoopoe, n, huppe, f.

hoot, v.t, huer, conspuer; (v.i.) (owl) chuinter. ~[ing] (boo[ing]) n, huée[s] f.[pl.].

hop, n, saut; (pl.) houblon, m. ~ [plant], houblon, m. ~ field, houblonnière, f. ~scotch, marelle, f. ~, step, & jump, triple saut, m. ¶ v.i, houblonner; (v.i.)sauter à cloche-pied; (like a sparrow) sautiller. ~ about, s'ébattre.

hope, n, espérance, f; espoir, m. ¶ v.t. & i, espérer. ~ful, a, plein d'espoir; encourageant; confiant; optimiste; (lad) de grandes espérances. ~less, a, sans espoir, désespéré; incorrigible. ~lessness, n, désespérance, f.

hopper, n, (insect) sauteur, m; (Mach.) trémie, f.

horde, n, horde, f.

horehound, n, marrube, m.

horizon, n, horizon, m. **horizontal†,** a, horizontal.

horn, n, corne, f; (pl, deer) bois, m.pl; (insect) antenne, f; cor; cornet, m; trompe, f. ~ of plenty, corne d'abondance, f. ~-rimmed spectacles, lunettes en écaille, f.pl. horned cattle, bêtes à cornes, bêtes cornues, f.pl.

hornet, n, frelon, m. ~'s nest (fig.), guêpier, m.

horny, a, corné; (hands) calleuses.

horology, n, horlogerie, f.

horoscope, n, horoscope, m.

horrible† & **horrid†,** a, horrible. **horror,** n, horreur, f.

horse, n, cheval, m; (pl.) cavalerie, f; (trestle) chevalet, m, chèvre, f. on ~back, à cheval. ~ bean, féverole, f. ~ box, wagon-écurie, m. ~-chestnut, marron d'Inde; (tree) marronnier d'I., m. ~ dealer, marchand de chevaux, maquignon, m, ~fly, taon, m. ~hair, crin, m. ~man, cavalier, écuyer, m. ~manship, équitation, f, manège, m. ~ play, jeux de main, m.pl. ~pond, abreuvoir, m. ~ power, cheval [vapeur] m, force de cheval, f. en chevaux, f. a 10 ~ [power] car, une [automobile de] 10 chevaux. ~ race, course de chevaux, f. ~ racing, les courses, f.pl. ~radish, raifort, m. ~shoe, fer à cheval, m. ~ show, concours hippique, m. ~tail, plume, crinière, f. ~whip, n, cravache, f; (v.t.) cra-

vacher. ~woman, cavalière, écuyère, amazone, f. ~y, a, de cheval, chevalin.

horticultural, a, horticole. **horticulture,** n, horticulture, f. **horticulturist,** n, horticulteur, m.

hosanna, n, hosanna, m.

hose, n, (dress, col. as pl.) bas, m.pl; (pipe) tuyau, boyau, m, manche, f. **hosier,** n, chemisier, bonnetier, m. ~y, n, chemiserie, bonneterie, f.

hospitable, a, hospitalier. **hospital,** n, hôpital, m. ~ attendant, ~ nurse, infirmier, ère. ~ ship, vaisseau-hôpital, m. **hospitality,** n, hospitalité, f. **hospitalize,** v.t, hospitaliser.

host, n, (pers.) hôte, m; armée, f, bataillon, m, troupe, nuée, phalange; (Eccl.) hostie, f. ~ess, n, hôtesse, f.

hostage, n, otage; (fig.) gage, m.

hostel, n, auberge, f, foyer d'étudiants, m, maison des étudiants, f; hospice, m, institution, f. ~ry (archaic), n, hôtellerie, f.

hostile†, a, hostile. **hostility,** n, hostilité, f.

hostler, n, garçon d'écurie, palefrenier, m.

hot, a, chaud; à chaud; ardent; brûlant. to get ~ chauffer. ~bed (Hort.) couche [de fumier] f; (fig.) foyer, m. in ~ haste, en toute hâte, au [grand] galop. ~head, cerveau brûlé, m, échauffé, e. ~headed, bouillant, impétueux. ~house, serre chaude, f. ~house grapes, raisin de serres, m. ~ plate, réchaud, m. ~ spring, source thermale, f. ~water bottle, boule d'eau chaude, f.

hotchpotch, n, (Cook.) hochepot, (Cook. & fig.) salmigondis, pot pourri, m.

hotel, n, hôtel, m. ~ keeper, hôtelier, ère.

hotly, ad, chaleureusement.

hound, n, chien courant, c. de chasse, chien, m; (bitch) lice, f. ~ out, chasser.

hour, n, heure, f. ~glass, sablier, m. ~ hand, petite aiguille, f. office ~s, heures de bureau, f.pl. ~ly, a, par heure; (ad.) d'heure en heure.

house, n, maison, f; logis, m; habitation, f; hôtel; pavillon, m; bâtiment; ménage, m; (Theat.) salle, f. neither ~ nor home, ni feu ni lieu. ~ boat, bateau d'habitation, *m*. ~*breaking*, effraction, *f*, cambriolage, *m*. ~ *fly*, mouche commune, *f*. ~ *full* (*Theat.*), complet. ~*hold*, ménage, *m*; (*staff*) maison, domesticité, *f*. ~*hold gods*, dieux familiers, dieux pénates, *m.pl.* ~*hold goods*, ménage, *m*. ~*hold linen*, linge de maison, *m*. ~*keeper*, femme de charge; ménagère, *f*. ~*keeping*, ménage, *m*; économie domestique, *f*. ~*maid*, fille de service, servante, *f*. ~ *martin*, hirondelle de fenêtre, *f*. ~ *number*, numéro d'habitation, *m*. ~ *painter*, peintre en bâtiments, *m*. ~ *top*, toit, *m*. *to give a* ~*warming*, pendre la crémaillère. ~*wife*, maîtresse de maison; ménagère, *f*. ~*wifery*, ménage, *m*. ~*work*, ménage, *m*. ¶ *v.t*, loger; mettre à l'abri; (*carp., etc.*) encastrer, emboîter; (*harvest*) rentrer, engranger. **housing**, *n*, logement, *m*. ~ *problem*, crise du logement, *f*.

hovel, *n*, taudis, bouge, *m*, baraque, *f*.

hover, *v.i*, planer, voltiger; se balancer.

how, *ad*, comment; comme; que. *any*~, de toute façon. ~ *long*? combien de temps? ~ *much*? ~ *many*? combien?

however, *ad*, de quelque manière que; quelque . . . que, si . . . que; tout . . . que; pourtant.

howitzer, *n*, obusier, *m*.

howl, *n*, hurlement, *m*. ¶ *v.i*, hurler; (*wind*) gronder. ~*er*, *n*, bévue, gaffe, *f*.

hoyden, *n*, gamine bruyante, *f*, garçon manqué, *m*.

hub, *n*, moyeu, *m*; (*fig.*) centre, *m*.

hubbub, *n*, brouhaha, charivari, *m*.

huckaback, *n*, toile ouvrée, *f*. ~ *towel*, serviette nid d'abeilles, *f*.

huckster, *n*, regrattier, ère.

huddle, *v.t*, entasser; (*v.i.*) se blottir.

hue, *n*, teinte; nuance, *f*.

hue & cry, haro, tocsin, tollé, *m*.

huff, *v.i*, souffler; (*anger*) s'emporter; malmener. *he is in a* ~, il a pris la mouche.

hug, *n*, étreinte, *f*, embrassade, *m*, accolade, *f*. ¶ *v.t*, serrer, étreindre, embrasser; (*the wind, Naut.*) pincer le vent; (*the shore*) côtoyer; (*an error*) chérir.

huge, *a*, énorme, immense, démesuré. ~*ly*, *ad*, énormément, immensément, démesurément.

hulk, *n*, vaisseau rasé; ponton, *m*. ~*ing*, *a*, balourd.

hull, *n*, (*husk*) cosse; (*ship*) coque, *f*, corps, *m*. ¶ *v.t*, monder.

hullabaloo, *n*, hourvari, *m*.

hullo[a], *i*, hé!, ohé!; tiens!

hum, *v.i. & t*, (*bee, etc.*) bourdonner; (*top*) ronfler; (*tune*) fredonner, chantonner. ¶ *n*, fredon, *m*. ¶ *i*, hem!, hom!

human†, *a*, humain. **humane**†, *a*, humain. **humanitarian**, *a. & n*, humanitaire, *a. & m*. **humanity**, *n*, humanité, *f*. **humanize**, *v.t*, humaniser.

humble†, *a*, humble. ¶ *v.t*, humilier, abaisser, mater. ~**ness**, *n*, humilité; (*birth*) bassesse, *f*. *the humbler classes*, le menu peuple.

humbug, *n*, blague; mystification, *f*; (*pers.*) blagueur, euse; mystificateur, trice; imposteur, *m*. ¶ *i*, chansons! chansons! ¶ *v.t*, mystifier; lanterner, enjôler; mettre dedans.

humdrum, *a*, monotone; banal; assoupissant.

humerus, *n*, humérus, *m*.

humid, *a*, humide. ~*ity*, *n*, humidité, *f*.

humiliate, *v.t*, humilier. **humiliation**, *n*, humiliation, *f*. **humility**, *n*, humilité, *f*.

humming bird, oiseau-mouche, colibri, *m*.

humming top, toupie d'Allemagne, *f*.

hummock, *n*, mamelon; monticule, *m*.

humorist, *n*, humoriste, *m*; farceur, euse. **humorous**, *a*, humoriste; humoristique; drôle, drolatique. ~*ly*, *ad*, avec humour; par facétie. **humor**, *n*, (*mood*) humeur, disposition, *f*; (*jocosity*) humour, *m*. ¶ *v.t*, complaire à, flatter; ménager.

hump, *n*, bosse, *f*. ~*back*, *n*. & ~*backed*, *a*, bossu, e.

humph, *i*, hem!, hom!

hunch, *n*. bosse, *f*; (*chunk*) chanteau, *m*. ~*back*, *n*. & ~*backed*, *a*, bossu, e.

hundred, *a. & n*, cent, *a. & m*. ~ [*or so*], centaine, *f*. ~*fold*, *a. & m*, centuple, *m*. ~*th*, *a. & n*, centième, *a. & m*.

Hungarian, *a*, hongrois. ¶ *n*, Hongrois, e; (*language*) le hongrois. **Hungary**, *n*, la Hongrie.

hunger, *n*, faim, fringale, *f*. ~ *strike*, grève de la faim, *f*. ~ *striker*, gréviste de la faim, *m,f*.

~ *after*, être affamé de, avoir une fringale de. **hungrily**, *ad*, d'un œil affamé; avidement. **hungry**, *a*, affamé. *to be* ~, *very* ~, avoir faim, grand-faim.

hunk, *n*, chanteau, *m*.

hunt, *n*, chasse; (*riding to hounds*) chasse à courre, *f*; équipage de chasse, *m*. ¶ *v.t. & i*, chasser, courir. ~ *for*, chercher. ~**er**, *n*, chasseur; cheval de chasse; (*curios*) dénicheur, *m*. **hunting**, *n*, chasse; c. à courre; (*science*) vénerie, *f*. **huntress**, *n*, chasseuse, *f*. **huntsman**, *n*, chasseur; (*man in charge*) veneur, piqueur, *m*.

hurdle, *n*, claie; haie, *f*. ~ *fence*, échalier, *m*. ~ *race*, course de haies, *f*; steeple-chase, *m*.

hurl, *v.t*, lancer, darder, projeter.

hurly-burly, *n*, tohu-bohu, *m*.

hurrah, -ray, *n*, hourra, hosanna, *m*. ¶ *i*, bravo!; vivat!

hurricane, *n*, ouragan, *m*. ~ *deck*, pont de manœuvre; pont abri, *m*. ~*lamp*, lanterne-tempête, *f*.

hurry, *n*, précipitation, hâte; presse, *f*. ¶ *v.t*, presser, hâter, précipiter; (*v.i.*) se hâter. ~ *up*, se dépêcher.

hurt, *n*, mal, *m*; blessure; lésion, *f*; tort, *m*. ¶ *v.t.ir*, faire [du] mal à; blesser; nuire à.

husband, *n*, mari, époux, *m*. ¶ *v.t*, ménager.

husbandman, *n*, cultivateur, *m*.

husbandry, *n*, économie rurale, agronomie, *f*.

hush, *n*, silence, *m*. ~ *money*, prix du silence, *m*. ¶ *i*, silence!; chut!; motus!; paix! ¶ *v.t*, faire taire. ~ *up*, étouffer.

husk, *n*, cosse, *f*; (*walnut*) brou, *m*; (*grain*) balle, *f*. ¶ *v.t*, (*corn*) éplucher; (*barley*) monder; écosser. ~**y**, (*hoarse*) *a*, enroué, éraillé.

hussy, -zzy, *n*, coquine, friponne, drôlesse, masque, *f*.

hustle, *v.t*, bousculer.

hut, *n*, hutte, cabane, baraque, *f*.

hutch, *n*, cabane, *f*, clapier, *m*.

hyacinth, *n*, jacinthe, hyacinthe, *f*.

hybrid, *a*, hybride, métis. ¶ *n*, hybride, mulet, *m*.

hydra, *n*, hydre, *f*.

hydrangea, *n*, hortensia, *m*.

hydrant, *n*, bouche [d'eau], prise d'eau, *f*.

hydrate, *n*, hydrate, *m*.

hydraulic, *a*. & ~**s**, *n.pl*, hydraulique, *a*. & *f*.

hydrocarbon, *n*, hydrocarbure, *m*. **hydrochloric**, *a*, chlorhydrique. **hydrogen**, *n*, hydrogène, *m*. **hydropathic**, *a*, hydrothérapique. ¶ *n*, établissement hydrothérapique, *m*. **hydropathy**, *n*, hydrothérapie, *f*. **hydrophobia**, *n*, hydrophobie, *f*. **hydroplane**, *n*, hydravion, *m*.

hyena, *n*, hyène, *f*.

hygiene & hygienics, *n*, hygiène, *f*. **hygienic(al)**†, *a*, hygiénique.

hymen, *n*, hymen, hyménée, *m*.

hymenoptera, *n.pl*, hymenoptères, *m.pl*.

hymn, *n*, hymne, *m*; (*in church*) hymne, *f*, cantique, *m*. ~ *book*, recueil d'hymnes, *m*.

hyperbola & hyperbole, *n*, hyperbole, *f*.

hyphen, *n*, trait d'union, tiret, *m*; (*end of line*) division, *f*.

hypnotism, *n*, hypnotisme, *m*. **hypnotize**, *v.t*, hypnotiser.

hypochrondriac, *a*. & *n*, hypochondriaque, *a*. & *m,f*. **hypocrisy**, *n*, hypocrisie, *f*. **hypocrite**, *n*, hypocrite, *m,f*. **hypocritical**†, *a*, hypocrite. **hypodermic**, *a*, hypodermique. ~ *syringe*, seringue de Pravaz, *f*. **hypothecation**, *n*, nantissement, *m*. **hypothesis**, *n*, hypothèse, *f*. **hypothetic(al)**†, *a*, hypothétique.

hysteria, *n*, hystérie, *f*. **hysteric(al)**, *a*, hystérique; nerveux. **hysterics**, *n.pl*, crise de nerfs, *f*, nerfs, *m.pl*.

I

I, *pn*, je; moi.

iambic, *a*, ïambique. ¶ *n*, ïambe, *m*.

ibex, *n*, bouquetin, *m*.

ibis, *n*, ibis, *m*.

ice, *n*, glace, *f*. *oft. pl*. ~ *age*, période glaciaire, *f*. ~*berg*, iceberg, *m*. ~*bucket*, sceau à glace, *m*. ~ *cream*, glace, *f*. ~ *cream freezer*, sorbetière, *f*. ~ *cream vender*, glacier, *m*. ~ *hockey*, hockey sur glace, *m*. ~ *pack*, banquise, *f*. ~*pick*, piolet, *m*. ~ *skates*, patins à glace, *m.pl*. ¶ *v.t*, glacer; (*wine*) frapper [de glace].

Iceland, *n*, l'Islande, *f*. ~**er**, *n*, Islandais, e. ~**ic**, *a*. & (*language*) *n*, islandais, *a*. & *m*.

ichthyology, n, ichtyologie, f.
icicle, n, glaçon, m. **icing,** (sugar) n, glace, f.
icon, n, icône, f. **iconoclast,** n, iconoclaste, démolisseur, m.
icy, a, glacé, glacial.
idea, n, idée, pensée; image, f. **ideal†,** a. & n, idéal, a. & m. **~ism,** n, idéalisme, m. **~ist,** n, idéaliste, m,f.
identical†, a, identique. **identification,** n, identification, f. **identify,** v.t, identifier. **identity,** n, identité, f.
idiocy, n, idiotie, f.
idiom, n, (dialect) idiome; (phrase) idiotisme, m.
idiosyncrasy, n, idiosyncrasie, f.
idiot, n. & ~ic, a, idiot, e.
idle, a, oisif; paresseux; fainéant; inoccupé; désœuvré; de loisir; sans affaires; futile; oiseux, en l'air. ~ fancy, rêverie, f. ¶ v.i, paresser, fainéanter. **~ness,** n, oisiveté; paresse, f; chômage, m. **idler,** n, oisif, ive, paresseux, euse, fainéant, e; badaud, e. **idly,** ad, dans l'oisiveté.
idol, n, idole, f; amour, m. **idolater, tress,** n, idolâtre, m,f. **idolatrous,** a, idolâtre, idolâtrique. **idolatry,** n, idolâtrie, f. **idolize,** v.t, idolâtrer.
idyll, n, idylle, f. **idyllic,** a, idyllique.
if, c, si, s'. ~ not, sinon.
igneous, a, igné. **ignis fatuus,** n, feu follet, m. **ignite,** v.t, enflammer; allumer. **ignition,** n, ignition; inflammation, f; allumage, m. ~ key, clef de contact, m.
ignoble†, a, ignoble.
ignominious†, a, ignominieux. **ignominy,** n, ignominie, f.
ignoramus, n, ignorant, e, ignare, m,f. **ignorance,** n, ignorance, f. **ignorant,** a, ignorant, ignare. to be ~ of, ignorer.
ignore, v.t, méconnaître; ne faire aucune attention à.
iguana, n, iguane, m.
ill, n, mal, m. speak ~ of, médire de. ¶ a, malade, souffrant; mauvais; méchant. ¶ ad, mal; peu. **~-advised,** malavisé; malvenu, mal venu. **~-assorted,** disparate. **~-bred,** mal élevé, malappris, sans éducation. **~-famed,** malfamé, mal famé. **~-fated,** ~starred, néfaste. ~ feeling, inimitié, f. **~-gotten gains,** biens mal acquis, m.pl. ~ humor, humeur, f. ~ luck, mauvaise

chance, malchance, f, malheur, m. **~-mannered,** malhonnête. **~-natured** (person), méchant, e. **~-omened,** de mauvis augure, funèbre. **~-temper,** humeur [chagrine] f. **~-tempered,** d'h. c., revêche, hargneux. **~-timed,** intempestif, déplacé. **~-treat,** ~-use, maltraiter, faire un mauvais parti à. ~ will, malveillance, f. to bear ~ will, en vouloir à.
illegal†, a, illégal.
illegible†, a, illisible.
illegitimacy, n, illégitimité, f. **illegitimate†,** a, illégitime.
illicit†, a, illicite.
illiterate, a, illettré.
illness, n, maladie, f, mal, m.
illogical, a, illogique. **~ity,** n, illogisme, m.
illuminate, v.t, éclairer; (festively) illuminer, embraser; (MS.) enluminer, historier. **illumination,** n, éclairage, m; illumination, f, embrasement, m; enluminure, f. **illumine,** v.t, éclairer.
illusion, n, illusion, tromperie, f. **illusive, illusory,** a, illusoire.
illustrate, v.t, illustrer. ~d price list, tarif-album, m. **illustration,** n, illustration; gravure, f; exemple, m. **illustrious,** a, illustre. to make ~, illustrer.
image, n, image, f. **~ry,** n, images, f.pl. **imaginary,** a, imaginaire.
imagination, n, imagination, f. **imagine,** v.t. & i, imaginer; s'imaginer; se figurer.
imbecile, a, imbécile. ¶ n, idiot, e.
imbibe, v.t, absorber; s'imbiber de; boire, sucer.
imbricate, v.t, imbriquer.
imbroglio, n, imbroglio, m.
imbrue, v.t, tremper.
imbue, v.t, impregner, (fig.) pénétrer. **~d,** p.p, imbu, inspiré.
imitate, v.t, imiter; contrefaire. **imitation,** n, imitation; contrefaçon, f; (att.) [d']imitation, simili-; faux. **imitator,** n, imitateur, trice.
immaculate, a, immaculé. the I~ Conception, l'Immaculée Conception, f.
immanent, a, immanent.
immaterial, a, immatériel; sans importance.
immature, a, prématuré; pas mûr.
immeasurable, a, immensurable.
immediate†, a, immédiat.

immemorial, *a*, immémorial.
immense, *a*, immense. ~**ly**, *ad*,
immensément. **immensity**, *n*, immensité, *f*.
immerse, *v.t*, immerger, plonger.
immersion, *n*, immersion, *f*.
immigrant, *n*, immigrant, *m*.
immigrate, *v.i*, immigrer.
imminence, *n*, imminence, *f*.
imminent, *a*, imminent.
immobile, *a*, immobile. **immobil-**
ity, *n*, immobilité, *f*. **immobiliza-**
tion, *n*, immobilisation, *f*. **im-**
mobilize, *v.t*, immobiliser.
immoderate†, *a*, immodéré.
immodest†, *a*, immodeste.
immolate, *v.t*, immoler.
immoral, *a*, immoral. ~**ity**, *n*,
immoralité, *f*.
immortal†, *a*. & *n*, immortel, *a*.
& *m*. ~**ity**, *n*, immortalité, *f*.
~**ize**, *v.t*, immortaliser. **immor-**
telle, *n*, immortelle, *f*.
immovable†, *a*, inébranlable.
immunity, *n*, immunité; exemption; franchise, *f*.
immunize, *v.t*, immuniser.
immure, *v.t*, claquemurer, cloîtrer.
immutable†, *a*, immuable.
imp, *n*, diablotin, lutin, démon, *m*.
impact, *n*, choc, *m*; percussion,
f.
impair, *v.t*, détériorer; endommager; altérer; compromettre.
impale, *v.t*, embrocher; (*Hist.*)
empaler.
impalpable, *a*, impalpable.
impanel a jury, former une
liste de jurés, former un tableau.
impart, *v.t*, impartir; imprimer;
faire part de.
impartial†, *a*, impartial. ~**ity**, *n*,
impartialité, *f*.
impassable, *a*, impraticable, infranchissable.
impassible & impassive, *a*,
impassible.
impassioned, *p.p*, passionné.
impasto, *n*, empâtement de couleurs, *m*.
impatience, *n*, impatience, *f*.
impatient, *a*, impatient. *to grow*
~, s'impatienter. ~**ly**, *ad*, impatiemment.
impeach, *v.t*, accuser.
impecunious, *a*, besogneux.
impede, *v.t*, entraver, empêcher.
impediment, *n*, empêchement,
obstacle, *m*. ~ *of speech*, ~ *in*
one's speech, empêchement (*ou*
embarras) de la langue, *m*. **im-**

pedimenta, *n.pl*, impedimenta,
m.pl.
impel, *v.t*, pousser, animer.
impending, *p.a*, imminent.
impenetrable, *a*, impénétrable.
impenitence, *n*, impénitence, *f*.
impenitent, *a*, impénitent.
imperative†, *a*. & *n*, impératif,
a. & *m*.
imperceptible†, *a*, imperceptib-
ble, insaisissable.
imperfect†, *a*. & ~ [*tense*], *n*,
imparfait, *a*. & *m*. ~**ion**, *n*, imperfection, *f*.
imperial, *a*, impérial; (*weights &*
measures) *anglais*. ¶ (*beard*) *n*,
impériale, *f*. ~**ist**, *n*. & ~**istic**, *a*,
impérialiste, *m*. & *a*.
imperil, *v.t*, mettre en danger.
imperious†, *a*, impérieux.
imperishable, *a*, impérissable.
impermeable, *a*, imperméable.
impersonal†, *a*, impersonnel.
impersonate, *v.t*, personnifier.
impersonation, *n*, personnifica-
tion; (*Theat.*) création; (*law*)
supposition de personne, *f*.
impertinence, *n*, impertinence,
f. **impertinent**, *a*, impertinent.
~**ly**, *ad*, impertinemment.
imperturbable†, *a*, imperturbable.
impervious, *a*, imperméable, impénétrable.
impetuous†, *a*, impétueux.
impetus, *n*, impulsion, *f*, élan,
branle, *m*.
impiety, *n*, impiété, *f*.
impinge [up]on, venir en contact avec.
impious, *a*, impie.
impish, *a*, lutin, espiègle.
implacable†, *a*, implacable.
implant, *v.t*, implanter.
implement, *n*, instrument, ustensile, *m*. ¶ *v.t*, rendre effectif;
ajouter.
implicate, *v.t*, impliquer. *not*
~**d**, désintéressé. **implication**, *n*,
implication, *f*; sous-entendu, *m*.
implicit†, *a*. & **implied**, *p.a*, implicite, tacite.
implore, *v.t*, implorer, supplier.
imply, *v.t*, impliquer; insinuer;
sous-entendre.
impolite†, *a*, impoli. ~**ness**, *n*,
impolitesse, *f*.
impolitic, *a*, impolitique.
imponderable, *a*. & *n*, impondérable, *a*. & *m*.
import, *n*, (*meaning*) portée, signification, *f*, sens, *m*; (*Com., etc.*)
importation, *f*. ~ *duty*, droit

d'entrée, *m*, entrée, *f.* ¶ *v.t*, signifier; (*Com., etc.*) importer.
importance, *n*, importance, *f.* **important**, *a*, important.
importation, *n*, importation, *f.* **importer**, *n*, importateur, *m*.
importunate, *a*, importun. **importune**, *v.t*, importuner. **importunity**, *n*, importunité, *f.*
impose, *v.t*, imposer; (*fine*) frapper. ~ [*up*]*on someone*, en faire accroire à (*ou* en imposer à) quelqu'un. *person of imposing appearance*, porte-respect, *m*. **imposition**, *n*, imposition; imposture, *f.*
impossibility, *n*, impossibilité, *f*, l'impossible, *m.* **impossible**, *a*, impossible.
impost (*Arch.*) *n*, imposte, *f.*
impostor, *n*, imposteur, *m*. **imposture**, *n*, imposture, *f.*
impotence, -cy, *n*, impotence; (*sexual*) impuissance, *f.* **impotent**, *a*, impotent; (*sexual*) impuissant.
impound, *v.t*, mettre à la fourrière; enfermer; confisquer.
impoverish, *v.t*, appauvrir.
impracticable, *a*, impraticable.
imprecation, *n*, imprécation, *f.*
impregnable, *a*, imprenable, inexpugnable.
impregnate, *v.t*, imprégner; féconder. ~d (*wood*) *p.a*, injecté.
impresario, *n*, impresario, *m*.
impress, *n*, empreinte, impression, *f.* ¶ *v.t*, imprimer, empreindre; graver; impressionner; réquisitionner. ~**ion**, *n*, impression; empreinte, *f*; (*Typ.*) foulage, *m. to be under the* ~, avoir dans l'idée. ~**ionism**, *n*, impressionnisme, *m.* **impressive**, *a*, impressionnant; solennel.
imprint, *n*, empreinte; marque de l'éditeur, *f.* ¶ *v.t*, imprimer, empreindre.
imprison, *v.t*, emprisonner. ~**ment**, *n*, emprisonnement, *m*; prison, *f.*
improbability, *n*, improbabilité, invraisemblance, *f.* **improbable**, *a*, improbable, invraisemblable. **improbably**, *ad*, invraisemblablement.
impromptu, *ad. a. & n*, impromptu, *ad. a.inv. & m.*
improper, *a*, impropre, abusif; inconvenant, incongru; vice de . . .; faux. ~**ly**, *ad*, improprement; abusivement. **impropriety**,

n, inconvenance, incongruité; impropriété, *f.*
improve, *v.t*, améliorer; perfectionner; bonifier; amender. ~ *on*, renchérir sur. ~ *on acquaintance*, gagner à être connu. ~**ment**, *n*, *amélioration*, *f*; perfectionnement, *m*; *bonification*, *f*; embellissement, *m.*
improvidence, *n*, imprévoyance, *f.* **improvident**, *a*, imprévoyant.
improvise, *v.t*, improviser.
imprudence, *n*, imprudence, *f.* **imprudent**, *a*, imprudent. ~**ly**, *ad*, imprudemment.
impudence, *n*, impudence, *f*, toupet, *m.* **impudent**, *a*, impudent. ~**ly**, *ad*, impudemment.
impudicity, *n*, impudicité, *f.*
impugn, *v.t*, attaquer.
impulse & impulsion, *n*, impulsion, *f*; mouvement; branle, *m.* **impulsive**, *a*, impulsif; primesautier.
impunity, *n*, impunité, *f.* with ~, impunément.
impure†, *a*, impur. **impurity**, *n*, impureté, *f.*
imputation, *n*, imputation, *f.* **impute**, *v.t*, imputer.
in, *pr*, dans; en; à; au; entre; chez; auprès de; sur; sous; par; de; pour; à la. ¶ *ad*, dedans; chez; y; arrivé. ~ *between*, entre deux. ~ *demand*, demandé. ~ *fashion*, à la mode, de mode, de mise. ~ *print*, imprimé, disponible. ~ *there*, là-dedans. **ins & outs**, détours; êtres, *m.pl.*
inability, *n*, incapacité, *f.*
inaccessible, *a*, inaccessible, inabordable.
inaccuracy, *n*, inexactitude, infidélité, *f.* **inaccurate†**, *a*, inexact, infidèle.
inaction, *n*, inaction, *f.* **inactive**, *a*, inactif.
inadequate, *a*, insuffisant. ~**ly**, *ad*, insuffisamment.
inadmissible, *a*, inadmissible.
inadvertently, *ad*, par inadvertance, par mégarde.
inalienable, *a*, inaliénable, incessible.
inane, *a*, inepte, absurde.
inanimate, *a*, inanimé. ~ *nature*, le monde inanimé. **inanition**, *n*, inanition, *f.*
inanity, *n*, inanité, ineptie, *f.*
inapplicable, *a*, inapplicable.
inapposite, *a*, hors de propos.
inappreciable, *a*, inappréciable.
inappropriate†, *a*, impropre,

qui ne convient pas, peu en situation.

inapt, *a,* inapte. **inaptitude,** *n,* inaptitude, *f.*

inarticulate, *a,* inarticulé.

inasmuch, *ad,* étant donné. ~ *as,* vu que.

inattentive, *a,* inattentif.

inaudible†, *a,* imperceptible [à l'ouïe].

inaugurate, *v.t,* inaugurer.

inauspicious, *a,* défavorable.

inborn & **inbred,** *a,* inné, infus, naturel, natif.

incalculable, *a,* incalculable.

incandescence, *n,* incandescence, *f.* **incandescent,** *a,* incandescent; (*lamp, etc.*) à incandescence.

incantation, *n,* incantation, *f.*

incapable, *a,* incapable; inhabile; non-susceptible. **incapably,** *ad,* inhabilement. **incapacitate,** *v.t,* rendre incapable. **incapacity,** *n,* incapacité; impéritie, *f.*

incarcerate, *v.t,* incarcérer.

incarnate, *a,* incarné. **incarnation,** *n,* incarnation, *f.*

incautious, *a,* imprudent.

incendiarism, *n,* incendie volontaire, *m.* **incendiary,** *a.* & *n,* incendiaire. *a.* & *m,f.*

incense, *n,* encens, *m.* ~ *burner,* brûle-parfum, *m.* ¶ *v.t,* (*perfume*) encenser; (*enrage*) courroucer.

incentive, *n,* aiguillon; mobile, ressort, *m.*

inception, *n,* commencement, *m.*

incessant, *a,* incessant. ~ly, *ad,* incessamment.

incest, *n,* inceste, *m.* **incestuous,** *a,* incestueux.

inch, *n,* pouce, *m* = 2.54 (about 2½) centimeters.

incidence, *n,* incidence, *f.* **incident,** *n,* incident, événement, *m.* ¶ *a,* incident. ~al, *a,* incident. ~ *expenses,* faux frais, *m.pl.* ~ally, *ad,* incidemment.

incinerate, *v.t,* incinérer. **incinerator,** *n,* incinérateur, *m.*

incipient, *a,* naissant.

incise, *v.t,* inciser. **incision,** *n,* incision, *f.* **incisive,** *a,* incisif. **incisor,** *n,* [dent] incisive, *f.*

incite, *v.t,* inciter, provoquer; exciter. ~ment, *n,* incitation; excitation, *f.*

incivility, *n,* incivilité, *f.*

inclemency, *n,* inclémence, *f.* **inclement,** *a,* inclément.

inclination, *n,* inclination, *f;*

penchant; attrait, *m;* inclinaison, *f.* **incline,** *n,* plan incliné, *m;* (*down*) pente; (*up*) rampe, *f.* ¶ *v.t.* & *i,* incliner; pencher; porter; (*color*) tirer. **inclined,** *p.a.* & *p.p,* (*plane*) incliné; (*fig.*) enclin, porté.

include, *v.t,* comprendre, englober, renfermer. *the tip is* ~d, le service est compris. **including,** *participle,* y compris. *not* ~, non compris. **inclusive,** *a,* tout compris; (*sum*) globale; (*dates*) inclusivement. ~ *of,* y compris. ~ly, *ad,* inclusivement.

incognito, *ad.* & *n,* incognito, *ad.* & *m.*

incoherence, *n,* incohérence, *f.* **incoherent,** *a,* incohérent.

incombustible, *a,* incombustible.

income, *n,* revenu, *m.* oft. *pl;* rapport, *m;* rente, *f.* oft. *pl.* ~ *tax,* impôt sur le revenu, *m,* impôt[s] cédulaire[s], *m.*[*pl.*]. ~ *tax return,* déclaration de revenu, *f.*

incoming, *a,* à l'arrivée; d'arrivée; d'entrée; à échoir; (*tide*) montante.

incommensurable, *a,* incommensurable. **incommensurate** with, hors de proportion avec.

incommode, *v.t,* incommoder.

incomparable†, *a,* incomparable.

incompatibility, *n,* incompatibilité, *f.* ~ *of temper,* incompatibilité d'humeurs. **incompatible,** *a,* incompatible.

incompetence, -cy, *n,* incompétence, incapacité, *f.* **incompetent,** *a,* incompétent, incapable, insuffisant.

incomplete†, *a,* incomplet. **incompletion,** *n,* imperfection, *f.*

incomprehensible, *a,* incompréhensible.

inconceivable, *a,* inconcevable.

inconclusive, *a,* non concluant.

incongruity, *n,* incongruité, disparate, *f.* **incongruous,** *a,* incongru, disparate. ~ly, *ad,* incongrûment.

inconsequent[ial], *a,* inconséquent.

inconsiderable, *a,* sans importance.

inconsiderate†, *a,* inconsidéré.

inconsistency, *n,* inconséquence; inconsistance, *f.* **inconsistent,** *a,* inconséquent; inconsistant.

inconsolable†, *a*, inconsolable, inguérissable.

inconspicuous, *a*, peu (*ou* pas) en évidence.

inconstancy, *n*, inconstance, *f*. **inconstant**, *a*, inconstant, volage, journalier.

incontinent, *a*, incontinent.

incontrovertible, *a*, incontestable.

inconvenience, *n*, incommodité, *f*; inconvénient, *m*. ¶ *v.t*, incommoder. **inconvenient**, *a*, incommode.

incorporate, *v.t*, incorporer; enencadrer; enchâsser; (*a company*) s'incorporer, former une société.

incorrect†, *a*, incorrect; inexact. **~ness**, *n*, incorrection; inexactitude, *f*.

incorrigible†, *a*, incorrigible, indécrottable.

incorruptible, *a*, incorruptible.

increase, *n*, augmentation, *f*, accroissement, *m*, majoration, *f*. ¶ *v.t*, augmenter, accroître; aggraver, majorer. **increasing**, *p.a*, croissant. **~ly**, *ad*, de plus en plus.

incredibility, *n*, incrédibilité, *f*. **incredible**†, *a*, incroyable. **incredulity**, *n*, incrédulité, *f*. **incredulous**, *a*, incrédule.

increment, *n*, accroissement, *m*; plus-value, *f*.

incriminate, *v.t*, incriminer, charger.

incrust, *v.t*, incruster.

incubate, *v.t. & i*, couver. **incubation**, *n*, incubation, *f*. **incubator**, *n*, couveuse artificielle, poussinière, *f*.

incubus, *n*, cauchemar; faix, *m*.

inculcate, *v.t*, inculquer.

inculpate, *v.t*, inculper.

incumbent, *n*, bénéficier, titulaire, *m*. to be ~ on, incomber à.

incur, *v.t*, encourir; courir; s'attirer.

incurable†, *a. & n*, incurable, *a. & m,f*.

incursion, *n*, incursion, *f*.

indebted, *a*, redevable. **~ness**, *n*, dette; créance, *f*; dettes & créances, *f.pl*.

indecency, *n*, indécence, malpropreté, *f*. **indecent**, *a*, indécent, malpropre. **~ly**, *ad*, indécemment, malproprement.

indecision, *n*, indécision, *f*.

indecorous, *a*, inconvenant.

indeed, *ad*, vraiment, en effet; certes; bien, voire même, même. ¶ *i*, vraiment!, tiens!

indefatigable†, *a*, infatigable.

indefensible, *a*, indéfendable.

indefinable, *a*, indéfinissable. **indefinite**†, *a*, indéfini; (*leave*) illimité.

indelible, *a*, indélébile.

indelicacy, *n*, indélicatesse, *f*. **indelicate**†, *a*, indélicat.

indemnify, *v.t*, indemniser, dédommager. **indemnity**, *n*, indemnité; caution, *f*.

indent, *v.t*, denteler, échancrer; (*Typ.*) renfoncer, [faire] rentrer. **indentation**, *n*, dentelure, échancrure, *f*; (*Typ.*) renfoncement, *m*. **indention**, *n*, renfoncement, *m*. **indenture**, *n*, acte, contrat; (*pl.*) brevet, *m*.

independence, *n*, indépendance, *f*. **independent**, *a*, indépendant. to be ~, (*financially*) avoir une fortune indépendante. *person of* ~ *means*, rentier, ère. **~ly**, *ad*, indépendamment.

indescribable, *a*, indescriptible, indicible.

indestructible, *a*, indestructible.

indeterminate, *a*, indéterminé.

index, *n*, indice, *m*; table; table alphabétique, *f*; index; répertoire, *m*. ~ *expurgatorius*, index expurgatoire. ¶ *v.t*, dresser la table [alphabétique] de, répertorier.

India, *n*, l'Inde, *f*. ~ *paper*, papier indien, *m*. **Indian**, *a*, indien. ~ *Archipelago*, archipel Indien, *m*, Insulinde, *f*. ~ *club*, massue en bois, *f*, mil, *m*. ~ *corn*, blé de Turquie, maïs, *m*. ~ *ink*, encre de Chine, *f*. ~ *Ocean*, océan Indien, *m*, mer des Indes, *f*. ¶ *n*, Indien, ne.

indicate, *v.t*, indiquer, désigner. **indication**, *n*, indication, *f*; indice, *m*. **indicative**, *a*, indicatif. ~ [*mood*], *n*, [mode] indicatif, *m*. **indicator**, *n*, indicateur, *m*.

indict, *v.t*, accuser. **~ment**, *n*, acte d'accusation, réquisitoire, *m*.

Indies (the) *n.pl*, les Indes, *f.pl*.

indifference, *n*, indifférence, *f*, dolence, *f*. **indifferent**, *a*, indifférent; indolent; sans gêne. **~ly**, *ad*, indifféremment.

indigence, *n*, indigence, *f*.

indigenous, *a*, indigène.

indigent, *a*, indigent.

indigestible, *a*, indigeste, cru [à l'estomac]. **indigestion**, *n*, indigestion, *f*.

indignant, *a,* indigné. **~ly,** *ad,* avec indignation. **indignation,** *n,* indignation, *f.* **indignity,** *n,* indignité, *f.*

indigo, *n,* indigo, *m.* **~ blue,** [bleu d']inde, *m.* **~ plant,** indigotier, *m.*

indirect†, *a,* indirect.

indiscreet†, *a,* indiscret. **indiscretion,** *n,* indiscrétion; imprudence, *f.*

indiscriminate, *a,* sans aucun discernement; confus. **~ly,** *ad,* indistinctement, sans distinction.

indispensable†, *a,* indispensable.

indisposed, *p.p,* indisposé. **indisposition,** *n,* indisposition, *f,* malaise, *m;* disposition peu favorable, *f.*

indisputable†, *a,* indiscutable.

indissoluble†, *a,* indissoluble.

indistinct†, *a,* indistinct.

indite, *v.t,* rédiger; composer.

individual†, *a,* individuel. ¶ *n,* individu; particulier, *m.* **~ity,** *n,* individualité, *f.*

indivisible†, *a,* indivisible.

Indochina, *n,* l'Indochine, *f.*

indoctrinate, *v.t,* endoctriner.

indolence, *n,* indolence, *f.* **indolent,** *a,* indolent, mou. **~ly,** *ad,* indolemment.

indomitable, *a,* indomptable; (*will*) irréductible.

indoor, *a,* d'intérieur; de cabinet; (*games*) de société. **~s,** *ad,* à la maison; à l'abri.

indorse, *v.t,* endosser; adopter; confirmer; garantir. **~ment,** *m,* endossement, endos, *m;* souscription; adhésion; garantie, *m.*

indubitable†, *a,* indubitable.

induce, *v.t,* porter; décider; engager; induire; provoquer. **~ment,** *n,* mobile, motif, *m;* tentation, *f.*

induct, *v.t,* installer; introduire. **~ion,** *n,* induction; (*Eccl.*) installation, *f.*

indulge, *v.t,* gâter; caresser. **~ in,** se permettre. **indulgence,** *n,* indulgence, *f.* **indulgent,** *a,* indulgent.

indurate, *v.t,* [en]durcir.

industrial†, *a,* industriel. **~ disease,** maladie professionnelle, *f.* **~ism,** *n,* industrialisme, *m.* **~ist,** *n,* industriel, *m.* **~ize,** *v.t,* industrialiser. **industrious,** *a,* industrieux, diligent, travailleur, assidu. **industriously,** *ad,* indus-

trieusement, diligemment. **industry,** *n,* industrie; diligence, *f.*

inebriate, *a,* ivre. ¶ *n,* ivrogne, *m,* ivrognesse. *f.* ¶ *v.t,* enivrer.

ineffable, *a,* ineffable.

ineffaceable, *a,* ineffaçable.

ineffective† & **ineffectual†** & **inefficacious†,** *a,* inefficace.

inefficient, *a,* incapable.

inelastic, *a,* sans élasticité; sans souplesse.

inelegant, *a,* inélégant.

ineligible, *a,* inéligible.

inept, *a,* inepte. **ineptitude,** *n.* ineptie, *f.*

inequality, *n,* inégalité, *f.*

inequitable†, *a,* injuste.

ineradicable, *a,* indéracinable.

inert, *a,* inerte. **inertia,** *n,* inertie, *f.*

inestimable, *a,* inestimable.

inevitable†, *a,* inévitable.

inexact†, *a,* inexact. **inexactitude,** *n,* inexactitude, *f.*

inexcusable, *a,* inexcusable.

inexecutable, *a,* inexécutable.

inexhaustible†, *a,* inépuisable, intarissable.

inexorable†, *a,* inexorable.

inexpedient, *a,* pas expédient.

inexpensive, *a,* peu coûteux.

inexperience, *n,* inexpérience, *f.* **~d,** *a,* inexpérimenté, novice, neuf.

inexplicable, *a,* inexplicable.

inexplicit, *a,* pas explicite.

inexpressible, *a,* inexprimable.

inextinguishable, *a,* inextinguible.

inextricable, *a,* inextricable.

infallible†, *a,* infaillible, impeccable.

infamous, *a,* infâme; (*law*) infamant. **infamy,** *n,* infamie, *f.*

infancy, *n,* enfance, *f;* bas âge, *m;* (*law*) minorité, *f.* **infant,** *n,* [petit, e] enfant, *m,f;* (*law*) mineur, e. **~ mortality,** mortalité infantile, *f.* **~ prodigy,** enfant prodige. **infanticide** (*act*) *m;* (*pers.*) *m,f.* **infantile,** *a,* enfantin; (*Med.*) infantile.

infantry, *n,* infanterie, *f.* **~man,** fantassin, *m.*

infatuate, *v.t,* affoler, embéguiner. **to become ~d,** s'infatuer, s'engouer. **infatuation,** *n,* infatuation, *f,* engouement, *m.*

infect, *v.t,* infecter, empester. **~ion,** *n,* infection, *f.* **~ious,** *a,* infectieux; contagieux.

infer, *v.t,* inférer, conclure, sup-

poser, déduire. ~ence, *n*, inférence, conclusion, déduction, *f*.
inferential, *a*, déductif. ~ly, *ad*, par déduction.
inferior†, *a. & n*, inférieur, *a. & m*. ~ity, *n*, infériorité, *f*. ~ complex, complexe *d'i.*, *m*.
infernal, *a*, infernal. **inferno**, *n*, enfer, *m*.
infertile, *a*, infertile.
infest, *v.t*, infester.
infidel, *a. & n*, infidèle, *a. & m,f*. ~ity, *n*, infidélité, *f*.
infighting (*Box.*) *n*, combat de près, *m*.
infiltrate, *v.i*, s'infiltrer.
infinite†, *a*, infini. the ~, l'infini, *m*. **infinitesimal**, *a*, infinitésimal.
infinitive [mood], *n*, [mode] infinitif, *m*. **infinitude & infinity**, *n*, infinité; immensité, *f*. **infinity** (*Math., Phot.*) *n*, l'infini, *m*.
infirm, *a*, infirme. ~ary, *n*, infirmerie, *f*. ~ity, *n*, infirmité, *f*.
inflame, *v.t*, enflammer; exalter. **inflammable**, *a*, inflammable. **inflammation**, *n*, inflammation, *f*.
inflate, *v.t*, gonfler; (*fig.*) enfler; grossir; charger. ~d (*fig.*) *p.p*, enflé, ampoulé, boursoufle. **inflation**, *n*, gonflement, *m*; enflure; (*Fin.*) inflation, *f*.
inflect, *v.t*, infléchir. ~tion, *n*, inflexion; flexion, *f*. **inflexible†**, *a*, inflexible.
inflict, *v.t*, infliger. ~ion, *n*, infliction, *f*; châtiment, *m*; peine, *f*.
influence, *n*, influence, *f*; crédit, *m*; cote d'amour, *f*. ¶ *v.t*, influer sur; influencer. **influential**, *a*, influent, prestigieux.
influenza, *n*, grippe, *f*.
influx, *n*, venue; invasion, *f*.
inform, *v.t*, informer, instruire, renseigner, faire part, mander, prévenir. ~al, *a*, sans cérémonie; officieux; (*law*) informe. ~ality, *n*, vice de forme, *m*. ~ant, *n*, informateur, trice, auteur, *m*. ~ation, *n*, renseignement[s], *m*. [*pl*.], indication[s] *f*.[*pl*.]; (*law*) dénonciation, *f*. ~er, *n*, délateur, trice, indicateur, trice.
infraction, *n*, infraction, *f*.
infrequent, *a*, peu fréquent, rare.
infringe, *v.t*, enfreindre, contrevenir à; contrefaire. ~ment, *n*, infraction, contravention; contrefaçon, *f*. ~ of copyright, contrefaçon littéraire, c. de librairie.
infuriate, *v.t*, faire enrager.
infuse, *v.t*, infuser. **infusible**, *a*,

infusible. **infusion**, *n*, infusion; tisane, *f*.
ingenious†, *a*, ingénieux. **ingenuity**, *n*, ingéniosité, industrie, *f*.
ingenuous†, *a*, ingénu, naïf, candide.
inglenook, coin du feu, *m*.
inglorious†, *a*, honteux, ignominieux; obscur.
ingoing, *a*, entrant.
ingot, *n*, lingot, saumon, *m*.
ingrained, *a*, enraciné, invétéré.
ingratiate oneself with, s'insinuer dans les bonnes grâces de.
ingratitude, *n*, ingratitude, *f*.
ingredient, *n*, ingrédient, *m*.
ingress, *n*, entrée, *f*.
ingrowing (*nail*) *a*, incarné.
inhabit, *v.t*, habiter. ~able, *a*, habitable. ~ant, *n*, habitant, e.
inhale, *v.t*, inhaler, aspirer, respirer, humer.
inherent, *a*, inhérent; propre.
inherit, *v.t. & abs*, hériter, succéder à. ~ance, *n*, héritage, patrimoine, *m*, succession; (*right*) hérédité, *f*.
inhibit, *v.t*, interdire. ~ion, *n*, interdiction, inhibition, *f*.
inhospitable, *a*, inhospitalier.
inhuman†, *a*, inhumain. ~ity, *n*, inhumanité, *f*.
inimical, *a*, ennemi, hostile.
inimitable, *a*, inimitable.
iniquitous†, *a*, inique. **iniquity**, *n*, iniquité, *f*.
initial, *a*, initial. ¶ *n*, initiale, *f*; (*pl.*) parafe, *m*, initiales, *f.pl*. ¶ *v.t*, parafer, viser.
initiate, *n*, initié, e. ¶ *v.t*, prendre l'initiative de; (*pers.*) initier; entamer, lancer. **initiation**, *n*, initiation, *f*. **initiative**, *n*, initiative, *f*.
inject, *v.t*, injecter; seringuer. ~ion, *n*, injection, *f*. ~or, *n*, injecteur, *m*.
injudicious, *a*, peu judicieux.
injunction, *n*, injonction, *f*.
injure, *v.t*, léser; nuire à; offenser; endommager; blesser. ~ fatally, blesser à mort. **injurious†**, *a*, nuisible; malfaisant; préjudiciable; injurieux. **injury**, *n*, injure, *f*; préjudice, tort, *m*; lésion, blessure, *f*.
injustice, *n*, injustice, *f*; passe-droit, *m*.
ink, *n*, encre, *f*. ~ eraser, gomme pour l'encre, *f*. ~well, encrier, *m*. ¶ *v.t*, encrer; tacher d'encre. ~ in, mettre à l'encre. ~ up (*Typ.*), toucher.

inkling, n, indication, idée, f.
inlaid, p.a: ~ linoleum, linoléum incrusté, m. ~ work, incrustation; marqueterie, f.
inland, a, intérieur. ¶ ad, dans l'intérieur [du pays].
inlay, v.t.ir, incruster; marqueter.
inlet, n, crique; entrée; arrivée, f.
inmate, n, habitant, e; hôte, esse; (paying) pensionnaire, m,f; (asylum) interné, e; hospitalisé, e.
inmost, a, le plus intime.
inn, n, auberge, f. ~keeper, aubergiste, m,f.
innate, a, inné, infus. ~ness, n, innéité, f.
inner, a, intérieur, interne. ~ harbor, arrière-port, m. the ~ man, l'homme intérieur. ~ tube (tire), chambre à air, f.
innermost, a, le plus intime.
innings, n, tour, m.
innocence, n, innocence, f. **innocent,** a. & n, innocent, a. & m. ~ly, ad, innocemment.
innocuous, a, inoffensif.
innovation, n, innovation, nouveauté, f. **innovator,** n, novateur, trice.
innuendo, n, insinuation, allusion, f.
innumerable, a, innombrable.
inobservance, n, inobservance, inobservation, f.
inoculate, v.t.ir, inoculer. **inoculation,** n, inoculation, f.
inodorous, a, inodore.
inoffensive, a, inoffensif.
inoperative, a, inopérant.
inopportune, a, inopportun. ~ly, ad, mal à propos, à contre-temps.
inordinate†, a, démesuré.
inorganic, a, (matter) inorganique; (body) brut; (chemistry) minérale.
inpatient, n, malade interné, e, hospitalisé, e.
inquest, n, enquête, f.
inquire, v.t. & i, demander; s'informer (de); s'enquérir (de); se renseigner; s'adresser; enquêter. **inquirer,** n, chercheur, euse; demandeur de renseignements, m. inquiring mind, [esprit] chercheur, m. **inquiry,** n, demande, f; renseignements, m.pl; informations, f.pl; recherche; enquête, f; informé, m. ~ office, bureau de renseignements, m.
inquisition, n, inquisition, f.
inquisitive, a, inquisiteur; curieux.

inroad & **inrush,** n, incursion; irruption, venue, f.
insane, a, fou; insensé. **insanity,** n, démence, aliénation d'esprit; (folly) insanité, f.
insanitary, a, insalubre, malsain.
insatiable†, a, insatiable.
inscribe, v.t, inscrire; graver; dédier. **inscription,** n, inscription; dédicace, f.
inscrutable, a, inscrutable, impénétrable.
insect, n, insecte, m. ~ powder, poudre insecticide, f. **insectivora,** n.pl, insectivores, m.pl. **insectivorous,** a, insectivore.
insecure, a, mal assuré. **insecurity,** n, insécurité, f.
insensate, a, insensé. **insensible†,** a, insensible; sans connaissance. **insensitive,** a, insensible.
inseparable†, a. & n, inséparable, a. & m,f.
insert (Bookb.) n, encart, m. ¶ v.t, insérer; (Bookb.) encarter. ~ion, n, insertion, f; intercolage; ajout, m.
inset, n, pièce rapportée, f. ¶ v.t.ir, rapporter, encarter.
inshore, a, côtier. ~ fishing, pêche côtière, pêche dans les eaux territoriales, f.
inside, n, dedans; intérieur, m. ¶ a, intérieur; d'i. ¶ ad, [en] dedans, à l'intérieur; (Meas.) dans œuvre. ~ out, à l'envers.
insidious†, a, insidieux.
insight, n, pénétration, f. aperçu, m.
insignia, n.pl, insignes, m.pl.
insignificant, a, insignifiant, infime.
insincere, a, qui n'est pas sincère; faux; dissimulé. **insincerity,** n, absence de sincérité, dissimulation f.
insinuate, v.t, insinuer, faufiler.
insipid, a, insipide, fade, fadasse.
insist, v.i, insister. ~ence, n, insistance, f.
insobriety, n, intempérance, f.
insolation, n, insolation, f.
insolence, n, insolence, f. **insolent,** a, insolent. ~ly, ad, insolemment.
insoluble, a, insoluble.
insolvency, n, insolvabilité, carence, faillite; déconfiture, f. **insolvent,** a, insolvable. ¶ n, failli, m.
insomnia, n, insomnie[s] f.[pl.].
inspect, v.t, inspecter, visiter, contrôler; (excise) exercer. ~ion,

n, inspection, visite, *f,* contrôle; exercice, *m;* revue, *f.* ~ *committee,* comité de surveillance, *m.* ~**or,** *n,* inspecteur, trice; visiteur; contrôleur; (*weights*) vérificateur, *m.* ~**orship,** *n,* inspection, *f.*

inspiration, *n,* inspiration; aspiration; illumination, *f,* souffle, *m.* **inspire,** *v.t,* inspirer; aspirer.

inspirit, *v.t,* animer. ~**ing,** *a,* entraînant.

instability, *n,* instabilité, *f.*

install, *v.t,* installer, emménager. ~**ation,** *n,* installation, *f.*

installment, *n,* acompte, paiement à compte; versement; terme; fascicule , *m.* ~ *plan,* vente à tempérament, *f;* facilités de paiement, *f.pl.*

instance, *n,* cas, *m;* demande; (*law*) instance, *f. for* ~, par exemple. ¶ *v.t,* citer. **instant,** *a,* instant; (*month*) courant. ¶ *n,* instant, *m.* **instantaneous,** *a,* instantané. ~**ly,** *ad,* instantanément.

instead, *ad,* plutôt. ~ *of,* au lieu de, à la place de, pour.

instep, *n,* cou-de-pied, *m.*

instigate, *v.t,* provoquer, inciter. **instigation,** *n,* instigation, *f.*

instill, *v.t,* instiller; (*fig.*) inculquer; infuser, faire pénétrer.

instinct, *n,* instinct, *m.* ¶ *a,* doué, animé. ~**ive†,** *a,* instinctif.

institute, *n,* institut, *m.* ¶ *v.t,* instituer; intenter. **institution,** *n,* institution, *f;* institut, établissement, *m.*

instruct, *v.t,* instruire; charger; (*counsel*) constituer. ~**ion,** *n,* instruction, *f;* (*pl.*) instructions, indications, *f.pl,* charge, *f,* mandat, *m.* ~**ive,** *a,* instructif. **instructor,** *n,* professeur; (*Mil.*) instructeur; (*Mil. gym.*) moniteur, *m.* **instructress,** *n,* professeur, *m.*

instrument, *n,* instrument; (*law*) instrument, acte, *m.* ~ *board,* tableau de bord, *m.* ~**al,** *a,* instrumental. ~**alist,** *n,* instrumentiste, *m,f.* ~**ality,** *n,* intermédiaire, *m.*

insubordinate, *a,* insubordonné.

insufferable†, *a,* insupportable.

insufficiency, *n,* insuffisance, *f.* **insufficient,** *a,* insuffisant. ~**ly,** *ad,* insuffisamment.

insular, *a,* insulaire. ~**ity,** *n,* insularité, *f.*

insulate, *v.t,* isoler. **insulation,**

n, isolement, *m.* **insulator,** *n,* isolateur, *m.*

insult, *n,* insulte, injure, *f,* outrage, *m.* ¶ *v.t,* insulter, outrager. ~**ing†,** *a,* injurieux, offensant, outrageant, outrageux.

insuperable, *a,* insurmontable.

insupportable†, *a,* insupportable.

insurance, *n,* assurance, *f;* (*mail*) chargement, *m.* ~ *company,* compagnie d'assurance[s] *f.* **insure,** *v.t,* assurer, faire a.; (*mail*) charger; (*v.i.*) s'assurer, se faire assurer. ~**d** (*pers.*) *n,* assuré, e. ~**d** *package,* colis avec valeur déclarée, colis chargé, *m.* **insurer,** *n,* assureur, *m.*

insurgent, *n.* & *a,* insurgé, e, révolté, e.

insurmountable, *a,* insurmontable.

insurrection, *n,* insurrection, *f.*

intact, *a,* intact.

intaglio, *n,* intaille, *f.*

intake, *n,* prise, admission, *f,* appel, *m.*

intangible, *a,* intangible.

integer, *n.* [nombre] entier, *m.* **integral†,** *a,* intégral. **integrity,** *n,* intégrité, *f.*

intellect, *n,* intellect, *m,* intelligence, *f,* cerveau, *m.* **intellectual†,** *a.* & *n,* intellectuel, *a.* & *m.*

intelligence, *n,* intelligence, *f;* entendement, *m;* nouvelles, *f.pl;* chronique, *f,* courrier, *m.* ~ *department,* service des renseignements, *m,* statistique militaire, *f.* **intelligent,** *a,* intelligent. ~**ly,** *ad,* intelligemment. **intelligible†,** *a,* intelligible.

intemperance, *n,* intempérance, *f.* **intemperate,** *a,* intempérant.

intend, *v.t,* se proposer, avoir l'intention, compter; vouloir; destiner. ~**ed,** *n,* prétendu, e, futur, e.

intense, *a,* intense. ~**ly,** *ad,* extrêmement. **intensifier** (*Phot.*) *n,* renforçateur, *m.* **intensify,** *v.t,* intensifier; (*Phot.*) renforcer. **intensity,** *n,* intensité, *f.*

intent, *a,* fixe. ~ *on,* tout entier à. ¶ *n,* intention, *f,* but, *m. to all* ~*s & purposes,* virtuellement. ~**ion,** *n,* intention, *f,* but; motif, *m.* ~**ional†,** *a,* intentionnel, voulu. -**intentioned,** *a,* intentionné. **intentness,** *n,* contention, *f.*

inter, *v.t,* enterrer, inhumer.

intercalate, *v.t,* intercaler.

intercede, *v.i*, intercéder.

intercept, *v.t*, intercepter, surprendre.

intercession, *n*, intercession, *f*. **intercessor**, *n*, intercesseur, *m*.

interchange, *n*, communication, *f*, échange, *m*. ~**able**, *a*, interchangeable.

intercourse, *n*, commerce, *m*; relations, *f.pl*; rapports, *m.pl*.

interdict, *n*, interdit, *m*. ¶ *v.t*, interdire. ~**ion**, *n*, interdiction, *f*.

interest, *n*, intérêt, *m*; intérêts, *m.pl*; arrérages, *m.pl*; usure; commandite, *f*. *to take no further* ~ *in*, se désintéresser de. ~ *on overdue payments*, intérêts moratoires. ~ *payable* (date), jouissance. ¶ *v.t*, intéresser. ~**ed**, *p.a*, intéressé; curieux. ~ *party*, intéressé, e. ~**ing**, *p.a*, intéressant; attachant. *in an* ~ *condition* (pregnant), dans une situation intéressante.

interfere, *v.i*, intervenir, s'immiscer, s'ingérer. ~ *with* (hinder), contrarier, gêner. **interference**, *n*, intervention, immixtion, ingérence; (*Phys.*) interférence, *f*; (*radio*) brouillage, *m*.

interim, *n*, intérim, *m*. ~ *dividend*, acompte de dividende, dividende intérimaire, dividende provisoire, *m*.

interior†, *a*, & *n*, intérieur, *a*. & *m*.

interject, *v.t*, placer. ~**ion**, *n*, interjection, *f*.

interlace, *v.t*, entrelacer.

interlard, *v.t*, entrelarder.

interleave, *v.t*, interfolier.

interline, *v.t*, écrire dans l' (*ou* en) interligne. **interlinear**, *a*, interlinéaire. **interlineation**, *n*, entre-ligne, *m*.

interlock, *v.i*, s'entrelacer.

interlocutor, **tress** or **trix**, *n*, interlocuteur, trice.

interloper, *n*, intrus, e.

interlude, *n*, intervalle, intermède; (*Mus.*) interlude, *m*.

intermarriage, *n*, mariage entre individus de tribus diverses (*ou* de races différentes), *m*, alliance, *f*. **intermarry**, *v.i*, se marier entre eux, s'allier.

intermeddle, *v.i*, se mêler, s'immiscer.

intermediary, *n*. & *a*, intermédiaire, *m*. & *a*. **intermediate**, *a*, intermédiaire. ~ *course*, (*Sch.*), cours moyen, *m*.

interment, *n*, enterrement, *m*, inhumation, *f*.

intermezzo, *n*, intermède, *m*.

interminable, *a*, interminable.

intermingle, *v.t*, entremêler.

intermission, *n*, (*Theat.*) entracte; relâche, intermédiaire, *m*. **intermittent**, *a*, intermittent.

intermix, *v.t*, entremêler.

intern, *v.t*, interner. ¶ *n*, interne, *m*.

internal, *a*, interne; intérieur; intestin. ~**ly**, *ad*, intérieurement.

international, *a*, international. ~**ist**, *n*. & *a*, internationaliste, *m,f*. & *a*.

internecine, *a*, meurtrier, à outrance.

internment, *n*, internement, *m*. ~ *camp*, (*civil*) camp de concentration; (*Mil.*) camp de prisonniers, *m*.

interpolate, *v.t*, interpoler.

interpose, *v.t*, interposer; (*v.i.*) s'interposer.

interpret, *v.t*, interpréter; traduire. ~**ation**, *n*, interprétation, *f*. ~**er**, *n*, interprète, *m,f*.

interregnum, *n*, interrègne, *m*.

interrogate, *v.t*, interroger. **interrogation**, *n*, interrogation, *f*. **interrogative†**, *a*, interrogatif. **interrogatory**, *n*, interrogatoire, *m*.

interrupt, *v.t*, interrompre; couper. ~**er**, *n*, (*pers.*) interrupteur, trice; (*Elec.*) rupteur, *m*. **interruption**, *n*, interruption, *f*.

intersect, *v.t*, couper; entrecouper. ~**ion**, *n*, intersection, *f*.

intersperse, *v.t*, entremêler; émailler.

interstice, *n*, interstice, *m*.

intertwine, *v.t*, entrelacer.

interval, *n*, intervalle, entretemps, *m*.

intervene, *v.i*, intervenir. **intervention**, *n*, intervention, *f*.

interview, *n*, entretien, *m*, entrevue, *f*; (*for news*) interview, *m*. ¶ *v.t*, interviewer.

interweave, *v.t.ir*, entrelacer. *interwoven pattern* (fabrics), brochure, *f*.

intestate, *a*, intestat (*inv.*).

intestinal, *a*, intestinal. **intestine**, *a*. & *n*, intestin, *a*. & *m*.

intimacy, *n*, intimité, familiarité, *f*. **intimate†**, *a*. & *n*, intime, *a*. & *m*, lié, *a*, familier, *a*. & *m*. ¶ *v.t*, faire entendre, signifier. **intimation**, *n*, indication, premonition, *f*.

intimidate, *v.t*, intimider.

into, *pr*, dans; en; à; entre; par; par-dessus.

intolerable†, *a*, intolérable. **intolerance**, *n*, intolérance, *f*. **intolerant**, *a*, intolérant.

intonation, *n*, intonation, *f*. **intonate, intone**, *v.t*, entonner.

intoxicate, *v.t*, enivrer. ~**d**, *a*, ivre, enivré. **intoxication**, *n*, ivresse, *f*.

intractable, *a*, intraitable, indocile.

intransitive†, *a*, intransitif.

intrench, *v.t*, retrancher.

intrepid†, *a*, intrépide. ~**ity**, *n*, intrépidité, *f*.

intricacy, *n*, complication; *f*; embrouillement, *m*. **intricate**, *a*, compliqué, embrouillé.

intrigue, *n*, intrigue, brigue, *f*. ¶ *v.i*, intriguer, briguer, cabaler; (*v.t.*) intriguer. **intriguer**, *n*. & **intriguing**, *a*, intrigant, e.

intrinsic†, *a*, intrinsèque.

introduce, *v.t*, introduire; insinuer; présenter. ~ *into society*, produire dans le monde. ~ *oneself*, se présenter, se faire connaître. **introducer**, *n*, introducteur, trice. **introduction**, *n*, introduction; présentation, *f*.

introit, *n*, introït, *m*.

introspection, *n*, introspection, *f*.

intrude, *v.i*, s'introduire [contre le droit *ou* la forme], se faufiler. **intruder**, *n*, intrus, e, importun, e. **intrusion**, *n*, intrusion, *f*.

intuition, *n*, intuition, *f*. **intuitive**, *a*, intuitif. ~**ly**, *ad*, par intuition.

inundate, *v.t*, inonder. **inundation**, *n*, inondation, *f*.

inure, *v.t*, aguerrir, accoutumer; habituer.

invade, *v.t*, envahir. **invader**, *n*, envahisseur, *m*.

invalid, *a*, malade, infirme, invalide; (*law*) invalide. ¶ *n*, malade, infirme, *m,f*, invalide, *m*. ¶ *v.t*, réformer. ~**ate**, *v.t*, invalider, casser. **invalided**, *p.a*, invalide, réformé. **invalidity**, *n*, invalidité, *f*.

invaluable, *a*, inestimable, impayable.

invariable†, *a*, invariable.

invasion, *n*, invasion, *f*, envahissement, *m*.

invective, *n*, invective, *f*. **inveigh**, *v.i*, invectiver, tonner.

inveigle, *v.t*, enjôler.

invent, *v.t*, inventer, imaginer.

~**ion**, *n*, invention, *f*. ~**ive**, *a*, inventif, original. **inventor, tress**, *n*, inventeur, trice, *m*.

inventory, *n*, inventaire, *m*, description, *f*. ¶ *v.t*, inventorier.

inverse†, *a*, inverse, réciproque. **inversion**, *n*, inversion, *f*; renversement, *m*. **invert**, *v.t*, renverser; invertir.

invertebrate, *a*. & *n*, invertébré, *a*. & *m*.

invest, *v.t*, revêtir; investir; cerner; (*money*) placer, investir.

investigate, *v.t*, rechercher, examiner. **investigation**, *n*, investigation, enquête, *f*. **investigator**, *n*, investigateur, trice.

investiture, *n*, investiture, *f*.

investment, *n*, placement, *m*; valeur, *f*; portefeuille, *m*; mise [de fonds] *f*; (*Mil.*) investissement, *m*. **investor**, *n*, personne qui place ses fonds, *f*.

inveterate, *a*, invétéré, acharné, vivace.

invidious, *a*, méchant; odieux. ~ *distinction*, distinction contre le droit & l'usage ordinaire, *f*, passe-droit, *m*.

invigorate, *v.t*, fortifier, vivifier.

invincible†, *a*, invincible.

inviolable†, *a*, inviolable. **inviolate**, *a*, inviolé.

invisible†, *a*, invisible. ~ *mending*, reprise perdue, *f*, stoppage, *m*.

invitation, *n*, invitation, *f*; appel, *m*. **invite**, *v.t*, inviter, prier; convier; appeler; faire appel à. **inviting**, *p.a*, engageant.

invocation, *n*, invocation, *f*.

invoice, *n*, facture, *f*. ¶ *v.t*, facturer.

invoke, *v.t*, invoquer.

involuntary†, *a*, involontaire.

involve, *v.t*, envelopper; entraîner; impliquer; empêtrer. ~**d**, *p.a*, compliqué, embrouillé. ~ *language*, tortillage, *m*.

invulnerable, *a*, invulnérable.

inward, *a*, intérieur; interne; intime; d'entrée. ~ *bound*, en retour; effectuant son voyage de retour. ~[**s**] *ly*, *ad*, intérieurement, en dedans. ~**s**, *n.pl*, entrailles, *f.pl*.

iodine, *n*, iode, *m*.

ion, *n*, ion, *m*.

Ionian, Ionic, *a*, ionien, ionique.

iota, *n*, iota, *m*.

ipecac, *n*, ipéca, *m*.

irascible, *a*, irascible. **irate**, *a*,

irrité, en colère. **ire,** *n,* courroux, *m.*

Iraq, *n,* Irak, *m.*

Iraqi, *n,* Irakien, enne.

Ireland, *n,* l'Irlande, *f.*

iridescence, *n,* irisation, *f.* **iri-descent,** *a,* irisé, chatoyant.

iridium, *n,* iridium, *m.*

iris, *n,* iris, *m.*

Irish, *a,* irlandais. ~**man,** ~**woman,** Irlandais, e. ~ *Sea,* mer d'Irlande, *f.* ¶ (*language*) *n,* l'irlandais, *m.*

irksome, *a,* ennuyeux, fastidieux.

iron, *n,* (*metal, wrought, for linen, golf, etc.*) fer, *m;* (*cast, pig*) fonte; (*sheet*) tôle, *f.* ¶ *a,* en fer, de fer; en (*ou de*) fonte. ~ [& *steel*] *constructural work,* charpenterie métallique, *f.* ~ [*or steel*] *bridge,* pont métallique, *m.* ~ & *steel shares,* valeurs sidérurgiques, v—s du groupe forges & fonderies, *f.pl.* ~*clad,* [navire] cuirassé, *m.* ~ *constitution,* santé de fer, *f.* ~*master,* maître de forges, *m.* ~*monger,* (*small*) quincaillier; (*big*) ferronnier; (*builders'*) serrurier, *m.* ~*mongery,* quincaillerie; ferronnerie; serrurerie, *f.* *scrap* ~, ferraille, *f.* ~*-shod,* ferré. ~*work,* ferrement, *m;* ferrure; serrurerie; (*girders, etc.*) charpente en fer, *f.* ~*worker,* ferronnier; serrurier; charpentier en fer, *m.* ~*works,* ferronnerie, *f;* forge[s] *f.[pl.];* usine sidérurgique, *f.* ¶ *wrought* ~, fer forgé, *m.* ¶ *v.t,* ferrer; (*linen*) repasser. ~ *out,* défroncer, déplisser. ~*er,* *n,* repasseuse, *f.* ~*ing,* *n,* repassage, *m.*

ironic(al)†, *a,* ironique. **irony,** *n,* ironie, *f.*

irradiation, *n,* irradiation, *f.*

irrational, *a,* irrationnel, irraisonnable.

irreclaimable†, *a,* (*pers.*) incorrigible; (*land*) indéfrichable.

irreconcilable, *a,* irréconciliable; inconciliable.

irrecoverable, *a,* irrécouvrable. ~ *arrears* (taxes), non-valeurs, *f.pl.*

irredeemable, *a,* irrachetable.

irredentism, *n,* irrédentisme, *m.*

irreducible, *a,* irréductible.

irrefutable†, *a,* irréfutable.

irregular†, *a,* irrégulier; saccadé. ~*ity,* *n,* irrégularité, *f;* dérèglement, *m.*

irrelevant, *a,* hors de propos,

non pertinent, étranger; (*law*) impertinent.

irreligious†, *a,* irréligieux, indévot.

irremediable†, *a,* irrémédiable.

irremovable, *a,* inamovible; immuable.

irreparable†, *a,* irréparable.

irrepressible, *a,* irrépressible; (*laughter*) inextinguible.

irreproachable†, *a,* irréprochable.

irresistible†, *a,* irrésistible.

irresolute, *a,* irrésolu.

irrespective of, indépendamment de, sans égard à.

irresponsible, *a,* irresponsable, inconscient.

irretrievable†, *a,* irréparable.

irreverent, *a,* irrévérent.

irrevocable†, *a,* irrévocable.

irrigate, *v.t,* irriguer. **irrigation,** *n,* irrigation, *f.* **irrigator,** *n,* irrigateur, *m.*

irritable, *a,* irritable. **irritate,** *v.t,* irriter; agacer. **irritation,** *n,* irritation, *f;* agacement, *m.*

irruption, *n,* irruption, *f.*

isinglass, *n,* colle de poisson, *f.*

Islam, *n,* Islam, *m.*

island, *n,* île, *f;* (*houses*) îlot, *m.* ~*er,* *n,* insulaire, *m,f.* **isle,** *n,* île, *f.* **islet,** *n,* îlot, *m.*

isolate, *v.t,* isoler. **isolation,** *n,* isolement, *m.* ~ *hospital,* hôpital de contagieux, *m.*

Israelite, *n,* israélite, *m,f.*

issue, *n,* issue, *f;* événement, *m;* distribution; délivrance; sortie, *f;* succès, *m;* (*money*) émission; impression; publication, *f;* (*newspaper*) numéro, *m;* lignée, postérité; (*law*) question, *f.* ¶ *v.i,* sortir; découler; émaner; (*v.t.*) lancer; émettre; publier; distribuer; délivrer.

isthmus, *n,* isthme, *m.*

it, *pn,* il, elle; le, la; lui; ce, c', ç'; cela; y. ~ *is said that . . .*, on dit que . . . *about* ~, en; y. *at* ~, y. *by* ~, y; en. *for* ~, en; *pour cela. from* ~, en. *of* ~, en; y. *to* ~, y; lui.

Italian, *a,* italien. ¶ *n,* (*pers.*) Italien, ne; (*language*) l'italien, *m.*

italic, *a.* & ~*s,* *n.pl,* italique, *a.* & *m.*

Italy, *n,* l'Italie, *f.*

itch, *v.i,* démanger. *my arm itches,* le bras me démange. *I am* ~*ing to,* j'ai grande envie de. ~[*ing*] *n*, démangeaison, *f*, prurit, *m*, gale, *f*. ~y, *a*, galeux.

item, *n*, article, poste, chapitre, *m*. ¶ *ad*, item.

itinerant, *a*, ambulant. **itinerary**, *n*, itinéraire, *m*.

its, *pn*, son, sa, ses; en.

itself, *pn*, lui[-même], elle[-même], soi[-même]; même; se.

ivory, *n*, ivoire, *m*. *the I~ Coast*, la Côte d'Ivoire.

ivy, *n*, lierre, *m*.

J

jab, *v.t*, piquer. ¶ *n*, (*Box.*) coup sec; coup de canif, *m*.

jabber, *v.i. & t*, jaboter, bredouiller, jargonner.

jacinth, *n*, jacinthe, *f*.

jack, *n*, (*Mach.*) vérin; (*auto*) cric, *m*; chèvre, *f*; (*spit*) tournebroche; (*fish*) brochet; (*cards*) valet, *m*. ~ass, âne, baudet, *m*. ~boots, bottes à genouillère, *f.pl*. ~daw, choucas, *m*. ~-in-the-box, boîte à surprise, *f*. ~ knife, couteau à virole, c. à cran d'arrêt, *m*. *J~ of all trades* or *work*, homme à tout faire, maître Jacques, *m*. *before you could say J~ Robinson*, crac!; en moins d'un instant.

jackal, *n*, chacal, *m*.

jackanapes, *n*, fat, *m*.

jacket, *n*, (*lounge*) veston, *m*; (*short*) veste, *f*; (*cardigan*) gilet; (*book*) couvre-livre, *m*; (*steam, water*) chemise, *f*.

jacobin, *n*, jacobin, *m*.

jade, *n*, (*horse*) rosse, haridelle; (*woman*) coquine, *f*; (*Miner.*) jade, *m*. ~d, *p.p*, surmené.

jag, *v.t*, ébrécher, denteler, déchiqueter. **jagged**, *a*, dentelé.

jaguar, *n*, jaguar, *m*.

jail, *n*, prison, geôle, *f*. ~bird, cheval de retour, *m*. ~er, *n*, geôlier, *m*.

jam, *n*, (*fruit*) confiture, *f*. oft. pl; (*squeeze*) coincement; (*traffic*) embouteillage; (*radio*) brouillage, *m*. ~ pot, pot à confitures, *m*. ¶ *v.t*, coincer.

Jamaica, *n*, la Jamaïque.

jamb, *n*, jambage, *m*.

jangle, *n*, ébranlement, *m*. ¶ *v.t*, ébranler.

janitor, *n*, concierge, *m*.

January, *n*, janvier, *m*.

japan, *n*, laque [de Chine], vernis [japonais] *m*. ¶ *v.t*, laquer, vernir. **Japan**, *n*, le Japon. **Japanese**, *a*, japonais. ~ *curio*, japonerie, *f*. ~ *paper* & ~ *porcelain*, Japon, *m*. ¶ *n*, (*pers.*) Japonais, e; (*language*) le japonais.

jar, *n*, secousse, *f*, battement; pot, *m*, jarre, bouteille, *f*, bocal, *m*. ¶ *v.i*, détoner, jurer; (*shake*) secouer. ~ *upon*, agacer.

jardinière, *n*, (*stand*) jardinière, *f*; (*pot*) cachepot, *m*.

jargon, *n*, jargon, baragouin, patois, *m*.

jarring, *a*, discordant.

jasmine, *n*, jasmin, *m*.

jasper, *n*, jaspe, *m*.

jaundice, *n*, jaunisse, *f*, ictère, *m*.

jaunt, *n*, course, promenade, *f*. ~y†, *a*, insoucieux, crâne.

Java, *n*, Java, *m*. **Javanese**, *a*, javanais. ¶ *n*, Javanais, e.

javelin, *n*, javelot, *m*.

jaw, *n*, mâchoire; mandibule, *f*; mors, bec, *m*; (*pl, of death*) bras, *m.pl*. ~ *bone*, [os] maxillaire, *m*.

jay (*bird*) *n*, geai, *m*.

jealous†, *a*, jaloux. ~y, *n*, jalousie, *f*.

jeer, *n*, risée, moquerie, *f*. ¶ *v.i*, goguenarder. ~ *at*, insulter à, se moquer de; (*pers.*) railler, se moquer de, dauber [sur].

jejune, *a*, maigre; exigu.

jelly, *n*, gelée, *f*. *to* (or *in*) *a ~* (as face by blow), en marmelade, en compote. ~fish, méduse, *f*.

jemmy, *n*, monseigneur, *m*, pince-monseigneur, *f*.

jeopardize, *v.t*, mettre en danger. **jeopardy**, *n*, danger, *m*.

jerboa, *n*, gerboise, *f*.

jeremiad, *n*, jérémiade, *f*.

jerk, *n*, à-coup, *m*, saccade, secousse, *f*. ¶ *v.t*, donner un à-coup, des secousses, à. ~y, *a*, saccadé.

jerry-build, *v.t*, bousiller. ~er, *n*, bousilleur, *m*. ~ing, *n*, bâtisse, *f*. **jerry-built**, *a*, de carton, fait de boue & de crachat. **jerry-work**, *n*, bousillage, *m*.

jersey, *n*, maillot; jersey, *m*. **Jersey** (*Geog.*), *n*, Jersey, *f*. *J~ cow*, vache jersiaise, *f*.

Jerusalem, *n*, Jérusalem, *f*.

jest, *n*, plaisanterie, *f*. ¶ *v.i*, plaisanter, badiner. ~er, *n*, plaisant, *m*, bouffon, ne; (*court*) fou, *m*.

Jesuit, *n*, jésuite, *m*. ~ical, *a*, jésuitique.

Jesus, *n*, Jésus, *m*. *Jesus Christ*, Jésus-Christ, *m*.

jet, *n*, jet; bec; (*lignite*) jais; avion

à réaction, *m.* ~[-*black*], noir comme [du] jais. ¶ *v.t,* jeter.

jetsam, *n,* épaves [rejetées] *f.pl.* **jettison,** *n,* jet [à la mer] *m.* ¶ *v.t,* jeter [à la mer].

jetty, *n,* jetée, estacade, *f.*

Jew, *n,* juif, israélite, *m.* ~'*s harp,* guimbarde, *f.*

jewel, *n,* bijou, joyau; (*Horol.*) rubis, *m.* ~ *case,* ecrin [à bijoux] *m.* **jeweler,** *n,* bijoutier, ère, joaillier, ère. **jewelry,** *n,* bijouterie, joaillerie, *f.*

Jewess, *n,* juive, israélite, *f.* **Jewish,** *a,* juif, israélite.

jib, *n,* (*sail*) foc, *m;* (*crane*) volée, flèche, *f.* ¶ *v.i,* regimber, se cabrer, s'acculer.

jiffy, *n,* tour de main, instant, *m.*

jig, *n,* (*Mus., dance*) gigue, *f.* ~*saw,* sauteuse, scie à chantourner, *f.* ~*saw puzzle,* jeu de patience, *m.*

jiggle, *v.t. & i,* sautiller, gigoter.

jilt, *v.t,* délaisser, lâcher.

jingle, *n,* tintement; cliquetis, *m.* ¶ *v.i. & t,* tinter.

jingoism, *n,* chauvinisme, *m.*

job, *n,* tâche; besogne; *f;* travail; emploi, *m;* affaire, *f.* ~ *lot,* marchandises d'occasion, *f.pl,* solde, *m.*

jockey (*turf*) *n,* jockey, *m.* J~ *Club,* Jockey-Club, *m.*

jocose, *a,* badin.

jocular, *a,* enjoué, facétieux, plaisant. ~*ly,* *ad,* en plaisantant.

jocund, *a,* joyeux.

jog, *v.t,* secouer, pousser. ~ *along,* aller son chemin. ~ *on,* aller cahin-caha. ~ *trot,* petit trot; (*fig.*) train-train, *m.*

joggle, *n,* secousse, *f;* (*Carp.*) embrèvement; goujon, *m.* ¶ *v.t,* embrever.

John Dory, *n,* dorée, *f.*

join, *v.t,* joindre; assembler; [ré]-unir; raccorder; rabouter, rabouter; relier; rejoindre. ~ *in,* faire chorus. ~*er,* *n,* menuisier, *m.* **joint,** *n,* joint, *m;* jointure; articulation, *f;* assemblage; (*fishing rod*) brin, *m;* (*meat*) pièce, *f. to put out of* ~, démettre, disloquer. ¶ *v.t,* articuler; assembler. ¶†, *a,* conjoint; indivis; co-; (*commission*) mixte. ~ *manager,* codirecteur, cogérant, *m.* ~-*stock company,* société par actions, *f.*

joist, *n,* solive, *f;* soliveau, *m;* poutrelle; lambourde, *f.*

joke, *n,* plaisanterie, facétie, *f,* mot pour rire, *m;* (le) comique

de l'histoire. ¶ *v.i,* plaisanter, rire, railler. **joker,** *n,* farceur, euse, plaisant, *m.*

jollification & **jollity,** *n,* jubilation, noce, gaillardise, gaieté, *f.* **jolly†,** *a,* gaillard, jovial, gai.

jolt, *n,* cahot, *m.* ¶ *v.i. & t,* cahoter.

Jonah (*fig.*) *n,* porte-malheur, *m.*

jonquil, *n,* jonquille, *f.*

Jordan (*river*) *n,* le Jourdain, *m;* (*country*) la Jordanie, *f.*

jostle, *v.t,* coudoyer, bousculer.

jot, *n,* iota, *m.* ~ *down,* tenir note (*ou* registre) de.

journal, *n,* journal; livre; (*shaft*) tourillon, *m;* (*axle*) fusée, *f.* ~*ism,* *n,* journalisme, *m.* ~*ist,* *n,* journaliste, *m.*

journey, *n,* voyage, *m;* marche; route, *f;* trajet; parcours, *m. on the* ~, en route. *to take a* ~, faire un voyage.

joust, *n,* joute, *f.* ¶ *v.i,* jouter.

jovial†, *a,* jovial, réjoui. ~*ity,* *n,* jovialité, *f.*

jowl, *n,* joue, *f;* (*fish*) hure, *f.*

joy, *n,* joie, *f.* ~*ful†* & ~*ous†,* *a,* joyeux. ~*fulness,* *n,* allégresse, *f.*

jubilation, *n,* jubilation, *f.* **jubilee,** *n,* jubilé, *m.* ~ *year,* année jubilaire, *f.*

Judaic, *a,* judaïque.

judo, *n,* judo, *m.*

judge, *n,* juge; magistrat; arbitre, *m.* ¶ *v.t. & i,* juger. **judgment,** *n,* jugement; arrêt; avis; sens; coup d'œil, *m.* **Judges** (*Bible*) *n.pl,* les Juges, *m.pl.*

judicature, *n,* justice, *f.* **judicial†,** *a,* judiciaire.

judicious†, *a,* judicieux, sage, sensé.

jug, *n,* cruche, *f,* broc, pot, *m;* carafe, *f.* ~*ful,* *n,* potée, *f.*

juggle, *v.i,* jongler; escamoter. ¶ ~ & ~*ry,* *n,* tour de passe-passe, *m,* jonglerie, *f;* escamotage, *m.* **juggler,** *n,* jongleur; escamoteur, *m.*

jugular [**vein**], *n,* [veine] jugulaire, *f.*

juice, *n,* jus; suc, *m.* **juicy,** *a,* juteux; succulent; fondant.

ju-jitsu, *n,* jiu-jitsu, *m.*

jujube, *n,* jujube, *m;* pastille, *f.* ~ [*shrub*], jujubier, *m.*

julep, *n,* julep, *m.*

July, *n,* juillet, *m.*

jumble, *n,* pêle-mêle, fouillis, fatras, *m,* salade, *f.* ~ *sale,* vente d'objets dépareillés, *f.* ~ *shop,* capharnaüm, *m.* ¶ *v.t,* brouiller; jeter pêle-mêle.

jump, *n,* saut; sursaut; haut-le-corps, *m.* ¶ *v.i. & t,* sauter; se jeter. **~ over**, sauter, franchir. **~er**, *n,* (*pers.*) sauteur, euse; (*sailor's*) vareuse; (*woman's*) casaque, *f.* **~ing:** *~ jack,* pantin, *m.* **~-off ground** (*fig.*), tremplin, *m.* **~ skis,** skis de saut, *m.pl.*

junction, *n,* jonction; (*Rly line, etc.*) bifurcation, *f,* embranchement, *m;* (*Rly station*) gare de bifurcation, gare d'embranchement, *f.* **juncture**, *n,* jonction; occurrence, *f.*

June, *a,* juin, *m.*

jungle, *n,* jungle, *f.*

junior, *a,* cadet; (*partner*) second, dernier; (*clerk*) petit. ¶ *n,* cadet, te; [le] jeune; (*son*) fils; (*sports*) junior, *m.* **~ event,** épreuve pour juniors, *f.*

juniper, *n,* (*genus*) genévrier; (*common*) genièvre, *m.*

junk, *n,* (*Chinese*) jonque; (*tow*) étoupe, *f;* (*refuse*) rebut, *m.*

junket, *v.i,* faire bombance.

juridical†, *a,* juridique. **jurisdiction**, *n,* juridiction; compétence, *f.* **jurist,** *n,* juriste, jurisconsulte, *m.*

juror, juryman, *n,* juré, *m.* **jury**, *n,* jury, *m.*

just, *a,* juste; équitable. ¶ *ad,* juste; justement; ne . . . que; tout. **~ as,** de même que. **~ out,** vient de paraître. *I have ~ . . .,* je viens de . . . **~ice,** *n,* justice, *f;* (*as to a meal*) honneur; (*pers.*) juge, *m.*

justifiable, *a,* justifiable; (*homicide*) excusable. **justification,** *n,* justification, *f;* gain de cause, *m.* **justify,** *v.t,* justifier; motiver.

justly, *ad,* justement, équitablement. **justness,** *n,* justice, *f.*

jut [**out**], *v.i,* faire saillie, [s']-avancer.

jute, *n,* jute, *m.*

juvenile, *a,* juvénile; jeune; (*books*) pour la jeunesse. ¶ *n,* jeune personne, *f.*

juxtapose, *v.t,* juxtaposer.

K

kale, *n,* chou frisé, *m.*

kaleidoscope, *n,* kaléidoscope, *m.*

kangaroo, *n,* kangourou, *m.*

kedge [**anchor**], *n,* ancre à jet, *f.*

keel, *n,* quille, *f.* **keelson**, *n,* carlingue, *f.*

keen, *a,* acéré; tranchant; vif; fin; mordant; (*sportsman, etc.*) ardent, déterminé. *a ~ disappointment,* un crève-cœur. **~ly,** *ad,* vivement, **~ness**, *n,* acuité, finesse, *f;* mordant; flair, *m.*

keep, *n,* entretien; (*castle*) donjon, *m.* ¶ *v.t.ir,* tenir; maintenir; garder; retenir; ménager; entretenir; hanter; nourrir; conserver; garantir; préserver; avoir; faire; observer; (*v.i.ir*) se tenir; se conserver; rester. *~ a saint's day,* chômer une fête. **~ away,** s'absenter. **~ back,** retenir. **~ from,** s'abstenir de; empêcher de. **~ in** (*Sch.*) mettre en retenue. **~ off,** s'éloigner; au large! [*please*] *~ off the grass,* ne marchez pas sur les pelouses, défense de circuler sur l'herbe. **~ [on]**, continuer. *~ one's hand in,* s'entretenir la main. *~ oneself to,* se cantonner dans. **~er,** *n,* garde; *m;* gardien, ne; concierge, *m,f;* conservateur, *m.* **~ing,** *n,* garde; conservation; tenue, *f. in ~ with,* en harmonie avec, à l'avenant de.

keepsake, *n,* souvenir, *m.*

keg, *n,* caque, *f;* baril[let], tonnelet, *m.*

ken, *n,* connaissance, *f.*

kennel, *n,* niche, cabane, *f;* (*hounds*) chenil, *m.*

Kenya, *n,* Kénia, *m.*

kerchief, *n,* fichu, carré, foulard, *m.*

kernel, *n,* (*of nut, stone-fruit, seed*) amande, *f;* (*nucleus*) noyau, *m;* (*gist*) substance, *f.*

kerosene, *n,* pétrole à brûler, p. lampant, *m,* huile de pétrole, *f.*

kestrel, *n,* crécerelle, *f,* émouchet, *m.*

ketch, *n,* quaiche, *f.*

kettle, *n,* bouilloire, bouillotte, *f,* coquemar, *m.* **~drum,** timbale, *f.* **~drummer,** timbalier, *m.*

key, *n,* clef, clé, *f;* (*winder*) remontoir, *m;* (*piano*) touche, *f;* (*to school book*) corrigé; (*Mus.*) ton, *m;* (*Mech.*) clavette; cale, *f;* coin, *m.* **~board,** clavier, *m.* **~ chain,** châtelaine, *f.* **~hole,** trou de serrure, *m.* **~hole saw,** scie à guichet, *f.* **~ industry,** industrie-clef, *f.* **~ money,** denier à Dieu, *m.* **~note,** [note] tonique, *f;* (*fig.*) mot d'ordre, *m.* **~ ring,** [anneau] porte-clefs, *m.* **~ signa-**

ture (*Mus.*), armature, *f.* ~stone, clef de voûte, *f.* ¶ *v.t*, caler; coincer; harmoniser. ~ed, *p.a.* à clef.

khaki, *n,* kaki, *m.*

Khedive, *n,* khédive, *m.*

kick, *n,* coup de pied, *m;* (*horse*) ruade, *f;* (*gun*) recul, *m.* ~off (*Foot.*), coup [de pied] d'envoi, *m.* ¶ *v.t,* donner un coup (des coups) de pied à; (*a goal*) marquer; (*v.i.*) (*horse*) ruer, regimber; (*gun*) reculer. ~ about, gigoter. ~ at (*fig.*), regimber contre. ~er, *n,* rueur, euse.

kid, *n,* chevreau, *m,* chevrette, *f,* cabri; (*child*) gosse, *m.* ~ gloves, gants de [peau de] chevreau, g—s de chevrotin, *m.pl.*

kidnap, *v.t,* enlever, kidnapper.

kidnapper, *n,* kidnappeur, *m.*

kidnapping, *n,* rapt, kidnapping, *m.*

kidney, *n,* (*Anat.*) rein; (*meat*) rognon; (*fig.*) acabit, *m,* trempe, *f.* ~ bean, haricot, *m.*

kill, *n,* chasse, *f;* abattis, *m.* ¶ *v.t,* tuer, assassiner; abattre. to nearly ~, assommer. killed in action, tué à l'ennemi. the killed, les tués, *m.pl.* ~joy, rabat-joie, trouble-fête, *m.* ~er, *n,* tueur, *m.* ~ing, *n,* tuerie, *f;* abattage, *m.* ¶ *a,* tuant, assommant.

kiln, *n,* four, *m.* ~-dry, sécher au four.

kilometric(al), *a,* kilométrique.

kilowatt, *n,* kilowatt, *m.*

kilt, *v.t,* plisser.

kimono, *n,* kimono, saut de lit, *m.*

kin, *n,* parents, *m.pl;* parenté, *f.*

kind, *a,* bon; aimable; gentil; bienveillant, obligeant; prospère. ~ regards, amitiés, *f.pl;* compliments, *m.pl.* ¶ *n,* genre, *m;* espèce; sorte; manière; (*of wood*) essence, *f. in* ~, en nature.

kindergarten. *n,* jardin d'enfants, *m.*

kindle, *v.t,* allumer.

kindliness, *n,* bienveillance; bénignité, *f.* kindly, *a,* bienveillant, obligeant; ami. ¶ *ad,* aimablement. **kindness,** *n,* bonté; amabilité; attention, *f.*

kindred, *n,* parenté, *f.* ¶ *a,* de la même famille.

king, *n,* roi, *m;* (*checkers*) dame, *f.* ~bolt, cheville ouvrière, *f.* ~post, poinçon, *m.* ~fisher, martin-pêcheur, martinet-pêcheur, *m.* oil, steel, ~, roi des pétroles, de l'acier. ~dom, *n,* royaume, *m;* (*Nat. Hist.*) règne, *m.* ~ly, *a,* royal.

kink, *v.t,* tortiller; (*v.i.*) vriller. ~y, *a,* noué; crépu.

kinship *n,* parenté, *f,* sang, *m.*

kinsman, -woman, *n,* parent, e.

kiosk, *n,* kiosque; édicule, *m.*

kipper, *n,* hareng salé & fumé, *m.* ¶ *v.t,* saler & fumer, saurer.

kiss, *n,* baiser, *m.* ¶ *v.t,* embrasser; baiser (*see note under this word*). ~ & cuddle, baisoter.

kit, *n,* équipement; trousseau, *m;* trousse; (*Mil.*) musette, *f. mess* ~, cantine, *f.*

kitchen, *n,* cuisine, *f.* ~ garden, [jardin] potager, *m.* ~ maid, fille de cuisine, *f.*

kite, *n,* (*bird*) milan; (*toy*) cerf-volant, *m.*

kith & kin, amis & parents, *m.pl.*

kitten, *n,* chaton, petit chat, *m,* petite chatte, *f.*

kleptomania, *n,* cleptomanie, *f.* **kleptomaniac,** *n,* cleptomane, *m,f.*

knack, *n,* don, coup; truc, tour de main, *m.*

knapsack, *n,* sac; havresac, *m.*

knave, *n,* fripon, coquin, fourbe; (*cards*) valet, *m.* ~ry, *n,* friponnerie, coquinerie, fourberie, fourbe, *f.* **knavish,** *a,* fourbe.

knead, *v.t,* pétrir.

knee, *n,* genou, *m.* ~ breeches, culotte, *f.* ~cap, (*Anat.*) rotule; (*pad*) genouillère, *f.* ~hole desk, bureau ministre, *m.*

kneel [down], *v.i.ir,* [s']agenouiller.

knell, *n,* glas, *m.*

knickerbockers & knickers, *n.pl,* culotte, *f.*

knick-knack, *n,* colifichet, brimborion, *m.*

knife, *n,* couteau, *m.* ~edge, couteau, *m.* ~, fork, & spoon, couvert, *m.* ~ grinder, rémouleur, *m.* ~ rest, porte-couteau, *m.* pocket ~, canif, *m.* ¶ *v.t,* poignarder.

knight, *n,* chevalier; (*chess*) cavalier, *m.* ~-errant, chevalier errant, *m;* (*fig.*) paladin, *m.* ~-errantry, chevalerie errante, *f.* ~hood, *n,* chevalerie, *f.* ~ly, *a,* chevaleresque.

knit, *v.t. & i. ir,* tricoter; (*brow*) froncer; (*fig.*) lier, nouer. **knitted** (*vest, etc.*) *p.a,* de tricot. ~ garment, tricot, *m.* **knitter,** *n,* tricoteur, euse. **knitting,** *n,* tricotage; tricot, *m.* ~ needle, aiguille à tricoter, *f.* **knitwear,** *n,* tricots, *m.pl.*

knob, *n,* bouton, *m;* pomme, *f.*

knock, *n,* coup; (*at the door*) coup de marteau, *m,* ¶*v.t. & i,* frapper; heurter; cogner; taper. ~ *down,* assommer; terrasser; abattre; (*auction*) adjuger. ~*kneed,* cagneux. ~**er** (*door*), *n,* marteau, *m.*

knoll, *n,* monticule, tertre, *m,* butte, *f.*

knot, *n,* nœud, *m;* (*cluster*) peloton; (*tangle*) tapon, *m.* ¶*v.t,* nouer. **knotty,** *a,* noueux, raboteux; (*fig.*) épineux.

know, *v.t. & i. ir,* connaître; savoir. ~ *how to,* savoir. *let me* ~, faites-moi savoir. *not to* ~, ignorer. ~**ing,** *a,* savant. ~**ingly,** *ad,* savamment, sciemment, à bon escient. **knowledge,** *n,* connaissance; intelligence; science, *f;* savoir, *m;* notoriété, *f. to my* ~, à mon su. *without my* ~, à mon insu. **known,** *n,* connu, *m.*

knuckle, *n,* jointure, articulation, *f;* (*veal*) jarret, *m.* ~ *fighting,* boxe à poings nus, *f.* ~ [*joint*] (*Mech.*), genouillère, *f. knuckle under* or *down,* mettre les pouces, caler [la voile].

knurl, *n,* molette, *f.* ¶*v.t,* moleter.

kohlrabi, *n,* chou-rave, *m.*

Koran, *n,* Coran, *m.*

Korea, *n,* la Corée.

kosher, *a,* cawcher.

kudos, *n,* gloriole, *f.*

L

label, *n,* étiquette, *f.* ¶*v.t,* étiqueter.

labial, *a,* labial. ¶*n,* labiale, *f.*

laboratory, *n,* laboratoire, *m.*

labor, *n,* main-d'œuvre, *f;* travail; labeur, *m;* peine; façon, *f.* ~ *market,* marché du travail, *m.* ~ [*pains*], mal d'enfant, *m.* ~*saving,* *a,* économisant la main-d'œuvre. ~ *troubles,* troubles ouvriers, *m.pl.* ¶*v.i. & t,* travailler, peiner; (*ship*) fatiguer. ~**ed** (*fig.*) *p.a,* travaillé, martelé, tourmenté, laborieux. ~**er,** *n,* manœuvre, homme de peine; ouvrier, *m.* **laborious**†, *a,* pénible; laborieux.

laburnum, *n,* faux ébénier, cytise, *m.*

labyrinth, *n,* labyrinthe, dédale, *m.*

lace, *n,* dentelle, *f;* point; passement; (*shoe*) lacet, cordon, *m;* (*leather*) lanière, *f.* ~ *boots,* bottines (*or if high,* bottes) à lacets (*ou* à lacer), *f.pl,* brodequins, *m.pl.* ~ *insertion,* entretoile, *f.* ¶*v.t,* galonner; (*fasten*) lacer.

lacerate, *v.t,* déchirer, lacérer.

lack, *n,* manque, défaut, *m,* pénurie, disette, *f,* peu, *m.* ¶*v.t,* manquer de. ~*ing in,* destitué de. ~*luster,* *a,* atone; vitreux.

lackadaisical, *a,* languissant; indolent, apathique, gnangnan.

lackey, *n,* laquais, *m.*

laconic†, *a,* laconique.

lacquer, *n. & ~ work,* laque, *m.* ¶*v.t,* laquer.

lacrosse, *n,* la crosse canadienne.

lacteal, *a,* lacté.

lacuna, *n,* lacune, *f.*

lacustrine, *a,* lacustre.

lad, *n,* garçon; enfant, gars, *m.*

ladder, *n,* échelle, *f.*

laden, *a,* chargé.

ladle, *n,* louche, *f.* ~**ful,** *n,* cuillerée, *f.*

lady, *n,* dame; madame; mademoiselle, *f. Ladies & Gentlemen!* Mesdames, Messieurs! *ladies first!* place aux dames! ~*bird,* coccinelle, bête à bon Dieu, *f.* L~ *chapel,* chapelle de la Vierge, *f.* L~ *Day,* fête de l'Annonciation, *f;* le 25 mars. ~*-killer,* bourreau des cœurs, homme à bonnes fortunes, *m. his* (*my*) ~*-love,* la dame de ses (de mes) pensées. ~ *of the manor,* châtelaine, *f.* ~'*s maid,* femme de chambre, *f.* ~'*s* (or *ladies'*) *man,* homme galant, h. à femmes, *m.* ~*like,* de dame, comme il faut.

lag, *v.i,* traîner; lambiner; (*v.t.*) garnir.

lager [*beer*], *n,* bière, *f.*

lagoon, *n,* lagune, *f.*

laic, *n. &* **laic**(**al**), *a,* laïque, séculier, *m. & a.*

laid paper, papier vergé, *m.* **laid up** (*in bed*) alité; (*ship*) désarmé.

lair, *n,* tanière, *f,* repaire, antre, *m.*

laity, *n,* laïques, *m.pl.*

lake, *n,* lac, *m.* ~ *dwelling,* habitation lacustre, *f.*

lama, *n,* lama, *m.*

lamb, *n,* agneau; (*pers.*) agneau, mouton, *m.* ¶*v.i,* agneler. ~**kin,** *n,* agnelet, *m.*

lambent, *a,* [doucement] radieux, lumineux.

lame, *a,* boiteux, éclopé, estropié; (*fig.*) qui cloche. ¶ *v.t,* estropier.

lamé, *a.* & *n,* lamé, *a.* & *m.*

lameness, *n,* claudication; boiterie, *f.*

lament, *n,* lamentation, *f;* chant funèbre, *m.* ¶ *v.i,* se lamenter. ~**able**†, *a,* lamentable. ~**ation,** *n,* lamentation, *f.* **the** [late] ~**ed** . . ., le (la) regretté, e . . .

lamina, *n,* lamelle, lame, *f,* feuillet, *m.* **laminate,** *v.t,* laminer.

lamp, *n,* lampe; lanterne, *f;* fanal; feu; (*street*) réverbère, *m.* ~ **black,** noir de fumée, *m.* ~**man,** lampiste, *m.* ~ **oil,** huile d'éclairage, h. de lampe, *f.* ~ **post,** poteau de réverbère; lampadaire, *m.* ~ **room,** lampisterie, *f.* ~**shade,** abat-jour, *m.*

lampoon, *n,* satire, *f,* libelle, pasquin, pamphlet, *m.* ¶ *v.t,* chansonner, écrire une satire contre. ~**er,** *n,* faiseur de pasquinades, pamphlétaire, *m.*

lamprey, *n,* lamproie, *f.*

lance, *n,* lance, *f.* ¶ (*Surg.*) *v.t,* inciser, percer, ouvrir. **lancers** (*Danc.*) *n.pl,* lanciers, *m.pl.*

lancet, *n,* lancette, *f.*

land, *n,* terre, *f;* terrain; pays, *m.* ~-**locked** *property,* enclave, *f.* ~**lord,** ~**lady,** propriétaire, *m,f;* logeur, euse; aubergiste, *m,f.* ~**lubber,** marin d'eau douce, *m.* ~**mark,** borne, *f;* point à terre, amer; point de repère, *m.* ~ **of** *milk* & *honey,* ~ **of** *plenty,* pays de cocagne. ~**owner,** propriétaire foncier, *m,f,* terrien, ne. ~**scape** & ~**scape** *painting,* paysage, *m.* ~**scape** *garden,* jardin anglais, *m.* ~**scape** *gardener,* dessinateur de jardins, architecte (*ou* jardinier) paysagiste, *m.* ~**scape** *painter,* [peintre] paysagiste, *m.* ~**slide,** éboulement de terres, *m.* ~**slide** (*Pol.*) débâcle, *f.* ¶ *v.t,* mettre à terre, débarquer; (*blow*) flanquer; (*v.i.*) débarquer; aborder; (*Avn.*) atterrir.

landau, *n,* landau, *m.* ~**let,** *n,* landaulet, *m.*

landed property, propriété foncière, *f,* biensfonds, *m.pl.*

landing, *n,* mise à terre, *f,* débarquement; atterrissage; (*stairs*) palier, repos, *m.* (*Avn.*) ~ *gear,* train d'atterrissage, *m.* ~ *place,* embarcadère, débarcadère, ponton, *m.* ~ *ticket,* carton de débarquement, *m.*

lane, *n,* chemin, *m;* allée; ruelle; clairière, *f;* (*running*) couloir, *m.*

language, *n,* langage, *m;* langue, *f.*

languid, *a,* mou; languissant; traînant. **languish,** *v.i,* languir. ~**ing,** *a,* languissant, mourant. **langor,** *n,* langueur, *f.* ~**ous,** *a,* langoureux.

lank, *a,* efflanqué; (*hair*) plats. ~**y,** *a,* efflanqué.

lantern, *n,* lanterne, *f;* falot, *m.* ~-*jawed,* aux joues en lanterne.

lanyard, *n,* (*Naut.*) ride, *f;* (*gun*) tire-feu, *m.*

lap, *n,* (*of pers.*) giron, *m,* genoux, *m.pl;* (*of luxury*) sein; (*of dress*) pan; (*overlap*) recouvrement, *m;* (*layer*) couche, *f;* (*sport*) tour [de piste]. ~*dog,* chien de salon, *m,* bichon, ne. ~ *scorer,* contrôleur des tours, *m.* ¶ *v.t,* envelopper; (*grind*) roder. ~ *over,* *v.i,* chevaucher, croiser. ~ [*up*], *v.t,* laper.

lapel, *n,* revers, *m.*

lapidary, *a.* & *n,* lapidaire, *a.* & *m.*

lapis lazuli, *n,* lapis[-lazuli] *m.*

Lapland, *n,* la Laponie. **Lapp,** *a,* lapon. **Lapp, Laplander,** *n,* Lapon, ne.

lapse, *n,* lapsus; oubli, *m;* (*moral*) défaillance, incartade; (*expiration*) déchéance, *f;* (*time*) laps, *m.* ¶ *v.i,* périmer, devenir caduc; (*time*) s'écouler; tomber.

lapwing, *n,* vanneau, *m.*

larceny, *n,* larcin, *m.*

larch, *n,* mélèze, larix, *m.*

lard, *n,* saindoux, *m.* ¶ *v.t,* (*Cook.*) larder, piquer; (*fig.*) larder, chamarrer. ~**er,** *n,* garde-manger, *m.*

large, *a,* gros; grand; fort; considérable; large. *at* ~, en liberté; [tout] au long; en général. ~**ly,** *ad,* grandement; en grande partie. ~**ness,** *n,* grandeur, *f.*

largess[e], *n,* largesse, *f.*

lark, *n,* (*bird*) alouette; mauviette; (*frolic*) équipée, escapade, *f.* ~*spur,* pied-d'alouette, *m.*

larva, *n,* larve, *f.*

laryngitis, *n,* laryngite, *f.* **larynx,** *n,* larynx, *m.*

lascivious†, *a,* lascif.

lash, *n,* (*of whip*) lanière; (*cut with a whip*) coup de fouet; (*eye*) cil; (*Mech.*) jeu, *m;* (*fig.*) férule, *f.* ¶ *v.t,* cingler, sangler, fouetter; ligoter; (*Naut.*) amarrer. ~ *out,* ruer.

lass[ie], *n,* [jeune] fille, fillette, *f.*

lassitude, *n,* lassitude, *f.*

lasso, *n,* lasso, *m.* ¶ *v.t,* prendre au lasso.

last, *a,* dernier; final; (*honors*) suprêmes. ~ *but one, a. & n,* avant-dernier, ère. ~ *night,* cette nuit; hier [au] soir. ~ *piece* (left on dish), morceau honteux, *m.* ~ *resort,* pis aller, *m.* ~ *straw,* comble [de nos maux] *m.* ~ *week,* la semaine dernière, la s. passée. ~ *will & testament,* acte de dernière volonté, *m.* *the* ~ *word,* le dernier [mot], le fin mot. *the* ~ *word in* (as elegance), le nec plus ultra de. ¶ *ad,* pour la dernière fois; en dernier lieu. ¶ *n,* dernier, ère; fin; (*shoe*) forme, *f. at* ~, enfin. ¶ *v.i,* durer, tenir. ~**ing,** *a,* durable, stable. ~**ly,** *ad,* en dernier lieu, enfin.

latch, *n,* (*gate*) loquet, *m;* (*door*) serrure à demi-tour, *f.* ~ *key,* clef de maison, *f.*

late, *a,* tardif; en retard, retardataire; avancé; récent; dernier; ancien, ex-; (*deceased*) feu; défunt. ~*-comer,* retardataire, *m,f.* ~ *season,* arrière-saison, *f.* ¶ *ad,* tard; en retard. ~ *in the day &* ~ *in life,* sur le tard. ~**ly,** *ad,* dernièrement; récemment. ~**ness,** *n,* tardiveté, *f. the* ~ *of the hour,* l'heure tardive, *f.*

latent, *a,* latent; caché.

later, *a,* postérieur, ultérieur. ~ [on], *ad,* plus tard, ultérieurement.

lateral†, *a,* latéral.

latest, *a,* dernier; fatal. ~ *style* (in dress), dernière mode; [haute] nouveauté, *f.* ~ [*thing out*], dernier cri, *m.*

latex, *n,* latex, *m.*

lath, *n,* latte; volige; (*blind*) lame, *f.* ¶ *v.t,* latter; voliger.

lathe, *n,* tour, *m.*

lather, *n,* mousse; écume, *f.* ¶ *v.i,* mousser; (*v.t.*) savonner.

lathing, *n,* lattis, *m.*

Latin, *a. & n,* latin, *a. & m.*

latitude, *n,* latitude, *f.*

latrine, *n,* lieux [d'aisance] *m.pl.*

latter (**the**), ce dernier, cette dernière; celui-ci, celle-ci, ceux-ci, celles-ci. ~**ly,** *ad,* dernièrement.

lattice, *n,* treillis, treillage, *m.* ¶ *v.t,* treillisser.

Latvia, *n,* la Lettonie. **Latvian,** *a,* letton. ¶ *n,* Letton, ne.

laud, *v.t,* louer. ~ [*to the skies*], louanger. ~**able,** *a,* louable.

laudatory, *a,* laudatif.

laugh, *n,* rire, *m.* ¶ *v.i,* rire; se r., se moquer. ~ *derisively,* ricaner. ~**able†,** *a,* risible; dérisoire. *it is no* ~*ing matter,* il n'y a pas [là] de quoi rire. ~**ing stock,** risée, *f.* **laughter,** *n,* rire[s] *m.* [*pl.*], hilarité, *f.*

launch, *n,* chaloupe, *f;* grand canot, *m.* ¶ *v.t,* lancer; (*Mil.*) déclencher. ~[**ing**], *n,* lancement, *m.*

launder, *v.t,* blanchir. **laundress,** *n,* blanchisseuse [de fin], repasseuse [de linge fin] *f.* **laundry,** *n,* blanchisserie; buanderie, *f.*

laureate, *a,* lauréat, *a.m.*

laurel, *n,* laurier, *m;* (*pl, fig.*) lauriers, *m.pl.*

lava, *n,* lave, *f.*

lavatory, *n,* lavabo, *m.*

lavender, *n,* lavande, *f.*

lavish, *a,* prodigue. ¶ *v.t,* prodiguer. ~**ly,** *ad,* prodigalement. ~**ness,** *n,* prodigalité, magnificences, *f.pl.*

law, *n,* loi, *f;* droit, *m;* justice; jurisprudence, *f;* palais, *m.* ~*-abiding,* respectueux des lois. ~ *& order,* ordre public, *m.* ~ *case,* affaire contentieuse, *f.* ~ *costs,* frais de justice, dépens, *m.pl.* ~ *courts,* cours de justice, *f.pl,* tribunaux, *m.pl;* palais [de justice] *m.* ~ *department,* [service du] contentieux, *m.* ~*giver,* législateur, *m.* ~*suit,* procès civil, *m,* affaire, *f.* ~**ful†,** *a,* légale; légitime; licite. ~**fulness,** *n,* légalité, légitimité, *f.* ~**less,** *a,* sans loi; déréglé.

lawn, *n,* pelouse, *f,* gazon, boulingrin; (*linen*) linon, *m.* ~ *mower,* tondeuse, *f.* ~ *tennis,* le [lawn-] tennis.

lawyer, *n,* homme de loi; avoué; légiste, juriste, jurisconsulte, *m.*

lax†, *a,* lâche; relâché; mou. ~**ative,** *a, & m,* laxatif, *a. & m.* ~**ity,** *n,* relâchement, *m.*

lay, *a:* ~ *brother,* frère lai, f. convers, f. servant, frater, *m.* ~*man,* laïque, séculier; profane, *m.* ~ *sister,* sœur converse, *f.* ¶ *n,* chanson, *f;* chant, *m;* complainte; (*of ground*) configuration, *f.* ¶ *v.t.ir,* mettre; poser; dresser; porter; déposer; abattre; coucher; imposer; [é]tendre; (*fire*) préparer; (*gun*) pointer; (*eggs*) pondre; (*a wager*) faire; (*to bet*) parier. ~ *bare,* mettre à nu, déshabiller. ~ *before* (court), saisir. ~ *down*, [dé]poser; plaquer. ~ *hold of*, saisir, s'agripper à, agripper. ~ *in* [*a stock of*], s'approvisionner de. ~ *out*, disposer; aménager; ajuster; tracer; débourser. ~ *waste*, dévaster.

lay day (*Ship.*) *n*, jour de planche, *m*.

layer, *n*, (*stratum*, *bed*) couche, *f*, lit, *m*; (*Hort.*) marcotte, *f*.

laying, *n*, mise; pose; (*eggs*) ponte, *f*.

layout, *n*, disposition, *f*; tracé, *m*.

laze, *v.i*, paresser, traînasser. **lazily**, *ad*, paresseusement; indolemment. **laziness**, *n*, paresse, *f*. **lazy**, *a*, paresseux. ~**bones**, paresseux, euse, fainéant, e, cagnard, e.

lea (*Poet.*) *n*, pré, *m*, prairie, *f*.

leach, *v.t. & i*, lessiver; filtrer.

lead, *n*, plomb, *m*; (*for pencils*) mine [de plomb]; (*Typ.*) interligne, *f*; (*Naut.*) plomb [de sonde] *m*, sonde, *f*. ~ *poisoning*, intoxication par le plomb, *f*, saturnisme, *m*. ¶ *v.t*, plomber; (*Typ.*) interligner.

lead, *n*, direction, conduite; avance; tête, *f*; exemple, *m*; (*cards*) main, primauté, *f*; (*Elec.*) conducteur principal; (*Elec. service*) branchement, *m*; (*leash*) laisse, *f*. ~ *rope* (attached to halter), longe, *f*. ¶ *v.t. & i. ir*, mener; conduire; diriger; amener; aboutir; induire; porter; tendre; (*cards*) débuter. ~ *astray*, égarer, dérouter, fourvoyer; débaucher. ~ *back*, reconduire. ~ *up to* (fig.), amener, préluder à.

leaden, *a*, de plomb; (*sky*) de plomb, plombé.

leader, *n*, directeur; meneur; chef de file, *m*, vedette, *f*; (*political*) leader; (*violin*, *chorus*) chef d'attaque; (*horse*) cheval de volée; (*Anat.*) tendon, *m*; (*Typ.*) points conducteurs, *m.pl.* ~**ship**, *n*, direction; autorité, *f*. **leading**, *a*, principal; premier; marquant. ~ *lady* (*Theat.*), premier rôle, *m*; vedette, *f*. ~ *man*, premier rôle, *m*. ~ *part* (*Theat.*), premier rôle, *m*. ~ *question*, question tendancieuse, *f*.

leadsman, *n*, sondeur, *m*.

leaf, *n*, feuille, *f*; feuillet; volant; (*door*) battant, vantail, *m*; (*table*) rallonge, *f*. ~ *mold*, terreau de feuilles, *m*. ~ *stalk*, pétiole, *m*. ~ *table*, table à ral-

longe(s) *f*. ~**age**, *n*, feuillage, *m*. ~**less**, *a*, dénudé. ~**let**, *n*, follicule, imprimé, *m*; (*Bot.*) foliole, *f*. ~**y**, *a*, feuillu, feuillé.

league, *n*, ligue; (*of Nations*) société; (*Meas.*) lieue, *f*. ¶ *v.t*, liguer.

leak & ~age, *n*, fuite, perte, *f*, échappement, coulage, *m*; voie d'eau, *f*. ¶ *v.i*, fuir, perdre, s'échapper, couler, faire eau. ~**y**, *a*, qui perd, qui fuit; qui fait eau.

lean, *a*, maigre; sec. ¶ *n*, maigre, *m*. ¶ *v.t.ir*, appuyer, accoter, adosser; (*v.i.ir*) (*rest*) s'appuyer; (*slope*) pencher. ~ *back in*, se renverser sur. ~ *on one's elbow(s)*, s'accouder. ~**ing** (fig.) *n*, penchant, *m*. ~ *tower* (Pisa), tour penchée, *f*. ~**ness**, *n*, maigreur, *f*. ~**to**, *n*, appentis, *m*.

leap, *n*, saut, bond; soubresaut, *m*. *by ~s & bounds*, par sauts & par bonds. ¶ *v.t. & i. ir*, sauter, bondir. ~*frog*, saute-mouton, saut de mouton, *m*. ~ *year*, année bissextile, *f*. **leaper**, *n*, sauteur, euse.

learn, *v.t. & i. ir*, apprendre. ~**ed**, *a*, savant, érudit, docte, instruit; (*profession*) libérale. ~**edly**, *ad*, savamment, doctement. ~**er**, *n*, apprenti; e; commençant, e. ~**ing**, *n*, connaissances, *f.pl*, savoir, *m*, science, littérature, *f*.

lease, *n*, bail, *m*; ferme, *f*. ¶ *v.t*, (*grant*) donner à bail, affermer, arrenter; (*take*) prendre à bail. ~*holder*, locataire, *m,f*.

leash, *n*, laisse, [ac]couple, attache, *f*, trait, *m*; (*set of dogs*) harde, *f*. ¶ *v.t*, harder.

least (the), *a*, le moindre; le plus petit. ¶ *ad. & n*, le moins. *at ~*, au moins; du moins. *not in the ~*, pas le moins du monde, [ne . . .] pas le moindrement.

leather, *n*, cuir, *m*, peau, *f*. ~ *dressing*, mégie, mégisserie, *f*. ~**ette**, *n*, similicuir, *m*. ~**y**, *a*, coriacé.

leave, *n*, permission; autorisation; faculté, liberté, *f*; congé, *m*. *by your ~!* attention! *on ~*, en permission, permissionnaire. *sick ~*, congé de convalescence, *m*. ¶ *v.t. ir*, laisser, abandonner; partir de, sortir de, quitter; léguer; (*v.i.ir.*) partir; déloger. ~ *off*, cesser; laissez donc! ~ *out*, omettre. *on leaving*, à l'issue de.

leaven, *n*, levain; ferment, *m*.

¶ *v.t*, faire lever; (*fig.*) assaisonner.
leavings, *n.pl*, restes, *m.pl*, bribes,
f.pl.
lecherous†, *a*, lascif.
lectern, *n*, lutrin, *m*.
lecture, *n*, leçon; conférence;
(*scolding*) semonce, mercuriale,
f, sermon, *m*. ¶ *v.t*, sermonner,
chapitrer, moraliser. ~ *on*, faire
une leçon, une conférence, sur.
lecturer, *n*, professeur, *m*; conférencier, ère, maître de conférences, *m*.
ledge, *n*, rebord; appui, *m*; saillie, *f*.
ledger, *n*, grand livre, *m*; (*Build.*)
moise, *f*. ~ *line* (*Mus.*), ligne
supplémentaire, *f*.
lee [side], *n*, côté sous le vent, *m*.
leech, *n*, sangsue, *f*.
leek, *n*, poireau, *m*.
leer, *n*, regard polisson, *m*. *to* ~
at, lorgner.
lees, *n.pl*, lie, *f*.
leeward, *a*, sous le vent. *L*~
Islands, îles sous le Vent, *f.pl*.
leeway, *n*, dérive, *f*.
left (*to be*), *a*, gauche, *a*. & *f*. *the* ~
(*Box.*), le [poing] gauche. ¶ *ad*,
à gauche. ~*-handed*, *a*. (pers.
or player) *n*, gaucher, ère.
left (*to be*), rester. *left-overs*,
n.pl, bribes, *f.pl*.
leg, *n*, jambe; (*birds, insects, etc.*)
patte; (*fowl*) cuisse, *f*; (*mutton*)
gigot; (*table, etc.*) pied, *m*;
(*compass, etc.*) branche; (*boot,
stocking*) tige, *f*. ~ *lock* (*wrestling*), croc-en-jambe, *m*. *on one*
~, à cloche-pied.
legacy, *n*, legs, *m*.
legal†, *a*, légal; judiciaire. ~ *aid*,
assistance judiciaire, *f*. ~ *charges*,
frais de contentieux, *m.pl*. ~ *entity*, personne morale, p. juridique, p. civile, *f*. ~ *maxim*, adage
de droit, *m*. ~ *tender* [*currency*],
(*value*) pouvoir libératoire, *m*;
(*money*) monnaie légale, *f*. ~*ize*,
v.t, légaliser.
legate, *n*, légat, *m*. **legatee,** *n*,
légataire, *m,f*. **legation,** *n*, légation, *f*.
legend, *n*, légende, *f*. ~**ary,** *a*,
légendaire.
legerdemain, *n*, prestidigitation,
f.
leggings, *n.pl*, molletières; jam-
bières, *f.pl*.
Leghorn, *n*, Livourne, *f*.
legible†, *a*, lisible.

legion, *n*, légion, *f*. *their name is*
~, ils s'appellent légion.
legislate, *v.i*, faire les lois. **legislation,** *n*, législation, *f*. **legislator,**
n, législateur, *m*. **legislature,** *n*,
législature, *f*. **legist,** *n*, légiste, *m*.
legitimacy, *n*, légitimité, *f*. **le-
gitimate†,** *a*, légitime. **legitim-
[at]ize,** *v.t*, légitimer.
leisure, *n*, loisir[s] *m.[pl.]*. *at* ~,
à loisir. *a* ~*ly man*, un homme
lambin. [*in a*] ~*ly* [*way*], *ad*, sans
se presser, sans hâte, avec lenteur.
leitmotiv, -if, *n*, leitmotiv, *m*.
lemon, *n*, citron, *m*. ~ *squash*,
citron pressé, *m*. ~ *squeezer*,
presse-citron, *m*. ~ *tree*, citronnier, *m*. ~**ade,** *n*, limonade, citronnade, *f*.
lend, *v.t.ir*, prêter. ~**er,** *n*, prêteur,
euse. ~**ing,** *n*, prêt, *m*, prestation, *f*. ~ *library*, bibliothèque
de prêt, *f*, cabinet de lecture, *m*.
length, *n*, longueur, *f*, long, *m*;
étendue; durée; (*piece of a stuff*)
coupe, *f*. *at* ~, au long; à la fin.
~**en,** *v.t*, [r]allonger; prolonger.
~*ening piece*, [r]allonge, *f*.
~**ways,** ~**wise,** *ad*, en long. ~**y,**
a, long.
lenient, *a*, indulgent, clément; de
douceur.
Leningrad, *n*, Léningrad, *m*.
lens, *n*, lentille; loupe, *f*; (*camera,
microscope, etc.*) objectif, *m*.
lent, *n*, carême, *m*. ~**en,** *a*, de
carême.
lenticular, *a*, lenticulaire.
lentil, *n*, lentille, *f*.
leonine, *a*, léonin.
leopard, *n*, léopard, *m*. ~**ess,** *n*,
l. femelle, *m*.
leper, *n*, lépreux, euse. ~ *hospital*,
léproserie, *f*.
leprosy, *n*, lèpre, *f*. **leprous,** *a*,
lépreux.
lesion, *n*, lésion, *f*.
less, *a*, moindre; inférieur. ~,
suffix, sans; in-. ¶ *ad*, moins, m.
de. ¶ *n*, moins, *m*. ~**en,** *v.t*. & *i*,
diminuer, amoindrir.
lessee, *n*, preneur, euse; fermier,
ère; tenancier, ère.
lesser, *a*, plus petit; moindre;
petit.
lesson, *n*, leçon, *f*.
lessor, *n*, bailleur, eresse.
lest, *c*, de peur que . . . [ne].
let, *v.t*. & *aux. ir*, laisser; permettre; faire; louer. *to* [*be*] ~,
à louer. ~ *down*, [a]baisser;
(*fail pers. at need*) lâcher, laisser

en panne. ~ *go* (hold), lâcher prise, démordre; larguer. ~ *have*, céder. ~ *loose*, déchaîner. ~ *in*, faire entrer. ~ *off*, faire grâce à; (*gun*) tirer; (*epigram*) décocher. ~ *out*, laisser sortir; l. échapper, lâcher; (*clothes*) [r]élargir.

lethal, *a*, léthifère, mortel. ~ *chamber*, chambre de [mise à] mort, *f*. ~ *weapon*, assommoir, *m*.

lethargic, *a*, léthargique. **lethargy**, *n*, léthargie, *f*. **Lethe**, *n*, Léthé, *m*.

letter, *n*, lettre; épître; cote, *f*. ~ *box*, boîte aux lettres, *f*. ~ *opener*, ouvre-lettre[s] *m*. ~ *paper*, papier a lettres, *m*. ~press, texte [composé] *m*. ~press printing, impression typographique, *f*. ~ *scales*, pèse-lettre, *m*. ~ *writer*, (*pers.*) épistolier, ère, *m*. ~ing, *n*, lettrage, *m*.

lettuce, *n*, laitue, *f*.

letup, *n*, détente, *f*.

Levant, *n*, Levant, *m*. **Levantine**, *a*, levantin; (*ports*) du Levant. ¶ *n*, Levantin, e.

level, *a*, de niveau; en palier; plat; plan; uni; égal. *a* ~-*headed person*, une tête bien organisée, un cerveau organisé. ~ *with*, à fleur de, à ras de. ¶ *n*, niveau; plan, *m*; hauteur, *f*; palier, *m*; (*Min.*) galerie, *f*. ¶ *v.t*, niveler; aplanir; égaliser; unir; (*gun, etc.*) pointer. **leveling**, *n*, nivellement, *m*.

lever, *n*, levier, *m*; manette, *f*. ~ [up] *v.t*, soulever au moyen d'un levier. ~age, *n*, force de levier, *f*; (*fig.*) avantage, *m*.

leveret, *n*, levraut, *m*.

leviathan, *n*, léviathan, *m*.

Levite, *n*, lévite, *m*. **Leviticus**, *n*, le Lévitique.

levity, *n*, légèreté, *f*.

levy, *n*, levée, réquisition, *f*; prélèvement, *m*. ¶ *v.t*, [pré]lever, imposer, frapper.

lewd†, *a*, impudique, crapuleux. ~ness, *n*, impudicité, *f*.

lewis, *n*, louve, *f*.

lexicographer, *n*, lexicographe, *m*.

lexicon, *n*, lexique, *m*.

Leyden, *n*, Leyde, *f*.

liability, *n*, obligation, *f*; engagement, *m*; responsabilité, *f*; (*pl, Fin.*) passif, *m*. **liable**, *a*, tenu; soumis; sujet; passible; responsable; solidaire.

liaison officer, agent de liaison, *m*.

liar, *n*, menteur, euse.

lias, *n*, lias, *m*. **liassic**, *a*, liasique.

libation, *n*, libation, *f*.

libel, *n*, libelle, *m*; diffamation, *f*. ~ *action*, action en diffamation, *f*. ¶ *v.t*, diffamer. ~ous, *a*, diffamatoire.

liberal†, *a*, libéral; large. ¶ *n*, libéral, *m*. ~ism, *n*, libéralisme, *m*. ~ity, *n*, libéralité, *f*.

liberate, *v.t*, libérer; affranchir; lâcher.

libertine, *a*. & *n*, libertin, *a*. & *m*.

liberty, *n*, liberté; faculté; privauté, *f*. *at* ~, libre.

librarian, *n*, bibliothécaire, *m,f*. **library**, *n*, bibliothèque, *f*.

librettist, *n*, librettiste, *m*. **libretto**, *n*, livret, *m*.

license, *n*, licence, *f*; permis, *m*; dispense, *f*; brevet; bon; acte, *m*; concession, *f*. ~ *to sell*, droit de vendre; (*tobacco, spirits*) débit, *m*. **license**, *v.t*, accorder un permis à; breveter. **licentious**†, *a*, licencieux, dévergondé, décolleté. ~ness, *n*, licence, *f*, dévergondage, *m*.

lichen, *n*, lichen, *m*.

licit†, *a*, licite.

lick, *v.t*, lécher. ~ *up*, laper.

licorice, *n*, réglisse, *f*; jus de réglisse, *m*.

lictor, *n*, licteur, *m*.

lid, *n*, couvercle, *m*; (*eye*) paupière, *f*.

lie, *n*, mensonge; démenti, *m*. *give the* ~ *to*, démentir. ¶ *v.i*, mentir.

lie, *n*, (*of ground*) disposition, configuration; (*Naut.*) gisement, *m*. ¶ *v.i.ir*, coucher, reposer; gésir; séjourner, stationner; résider, tenir. ~ *dormant*, dormir. ~ *down*, se coucher. ~ *idle*, chômer. ~ *in wait*, se tenir en embuscade, s'embusquer.

liege, *a*, lige. ¶ *n*, vassal lige, *m*.

lien, *n*, privilège; droit de rétention, d. de gage, *m*. ~or, *n*, créancier gagiste, *m*.

lieu of (in), au lieu de.

lieutenant, *n*, lieutenant; (*naval*) l. de vaisseau, *m*. ~ *colonel*, lieutenant-colonel, *m*. ~ *commander*, capitaine de corvette, *m*. ~ *general*, général de corps d'armée, *m*.

life, *n*, vie; existence, *f*; vivant, *m*; durée, *f*; mouvement, *m*. *for* ~, à vie, viager; perpétuel, à perpétuité. *from* ~ (*Art*), d'après nature, au vif, sur le vif. *to the* ~, au naturel. *2 lives lost*, 2 personnes ont péri. ~ & *property* (*law*), corps & biens. ~ [& *soul*] (of the party), boute-entrain, *m.* ~ *annuity*, rente viagère, *f.* via-ger, *m.* ~ *belt*, ceinture de sauve-tage, *f.* ~ *boat*, bateau de s., *m.* ~ *buoy*, bouée de s., *f.* ~*-giving*, fécond. ~ *insurance*, assurance sur la vie, *f.* ~ *jacket*, brassière de sauvetage, *f.* ~*saving*, sauve-tage, *m.* ~ *size*, en grand, gran-deur naturelle, nature, *f.* ~*time*, vivant, *m.* ~*less*, *a*, sans vie; inanimé. ~*like*, *a*, vivant; par-lant. ~*long*, *a*, de toute la vie.

lift, *n*, coup d'épaule; (*of the hand*) geste, *m.* ¶ *v.t*, lever; soulever; élever; enlever; relever.

ligament, *n*, ligament, *m.* **liga-ture**, *n*, ligature, *f.*

light, *a*, léger; faible; petit; (*ship unladen*) lège; (*Rly engine*) haut le pied; (*color*) clair; (*earth*) meuble. ~*-headed*, délirant. ~*headedness*, transport, *m.* ~ *lager*, bière blanche, b. blonde, *f.* ~ *meal*, collation, *f.* ~ *opera*, opérette, *f.* ~ *reading*, livres d'agrément, *m.pl.* ~ *refresh-ments*, rafraîchissements, *m.pl.* ~*weight* (*Box.*), poids léger, *m.* ¶ *n*, lumière, *f*; jour; éclairage, *m*; vue; clarté, *f*, clair; feu, fanal, phare, *m*; flamme, *f.* ~ *against the* ~, à contre-jour. ~*s out* (*Mil.*), extinction des feux, *f*, couvre-feu, *m.* ~ *& shade*, (*Art*) clair-obscur, *m.* ~*house*, phare, *m.* ~*ship*, bateau-feu, *m.* ¶ *v.t.ir*, allumer; éclairer. ~ *up*, illuminer. ~ [*up*]*on*, tomber sur.

lighten, *v.t*, alléger; soulager; éclairer; (*v.imp.*) éclairer, faire des éclairs.

lighter, *a*, plus léger.

lighter, *n*, (*pers.*) allumeur; (*pipe, etc.*) briquet, *m*; (*boat*) allège, gabare, *f*, chaland, *m.* **lighting**, *n*, éclairage, *m.*

lightly, *ad*, légèrement; à la légère. **lightness**, *n*, légèreté, *f.*

lightning, *n*, éclair, *m.* oft. pl, foudre, *f.* ~ *rod*, paratonnerre, *m.*

lights (*animal lungs*) *n.pl*, mou, *m.*

ligneous, *a*, ligneux. **lignite**, *n*, lignite, *m.* lignum vitae, [bois de] gaïac, *m.*

likable, *a*, sympathique. **like**, *a*, pareil; pair; semblable; analogue; approchant; ressemblant; même; tel; à l'égal de. *to be* ~, ressem-bler, approcher de, imiter. *to look* ~, avoir l'air de, ressembler. ¶ *n*, pareil, le; semblable, *m.* ~*s & dislikes*, sympathies & anti-pathies, *f.pl.* ¶ *pr, ad*, comme; de même que; tel que; à l'instar de; en. ¶ *v.t & i*, aimer; affec-tionner; vouloir; se plaire à; trouver; goûter.

likelihood, *n*, probabilité; appa-rence; vraisemblance, *f.* **likely**, *a*, probable, vraisemblable. *very* ~, vraisemblablement.

liken, *v.t*, comparer, assimiler.

likeness, *n*, ressemblance; parité, *f*; air, *m*; image, *f*; portrait, *m.*

likewise, *ad*, pareillement, égale-ment, aussi, de même.

liking, *n*, goût; gré, *m*; affec-tion, *f.*

lilac, *n. & a*, lilas, *m. & att.*

Lilliputian, *a*, lilliputien.

lily, *n*, lis, *m.* ~ *of the valley*, muguet, *m.*

limb, *n*, membre, *m*; (*tree*) mère branche, *f*; (*Math., etc.*) limbe, *m.* -limbed, *a*, membré.

limber, *a*, souple. ¶ *n*, avant-train, *m.* ~ *up*, mettre l'avant-train.

limbo, *n*, les limbes, *m.pl.*

lime, *n*, chaux, *f*; (*citrus*) limon, *m.* ~ *burner*, chaufournier, *m.* ~ *juice*, jus de limon, *m.* ~ *kiln*, four à chaux, chaufour, *m.* ~*light*, lumière oxhydrique, *f. to be in the* ~*light*, être sous les feux de la rampe; (*fig.*) être en vedette. ~*stone*, pierre à chaux, p. calcaire, *f*, calcaire, *m.* ~ [*tree*], (*citrus*) limonier; (*linden*) tilleul, *m.* ~ *twig*, gluau, pipeau, *m.* ¶ *v.t*, (*Agric.*) chauler; (*twig*) engluer.

limit, *n*, limite, borne, *f*; péri-mètre, *m.* ¶ *v.t*, limiter, borner. ~*ation*, *n*, limitation, *f.* **limited**, *p.p. & p.a*, limité, borné, étroit; (*monarchy*) tempérée; (*edition*) à tirage restreint. ~ *partnership*, [société en] commandite, *f.*

limousine, *n*, limousine, *f.*

limp, *a*, flasque, mou; (*binding*) souple. ¶ *n*, boitement, cloche-ment, *m.* ¶ *v.i*, boiter, clocher.

limpet, *n*, lépas, *m*, patelle, *f.*

limpid, *a*, limpide. ~*ity*, *n*, limpi-dité, *f.*

linchpin, *n*, clavette d'essieu, esse, *f.*

linden, *n*, tilleul, *m.*

line, *n*, ligne; file; haie; voie, *f*; trait, *m*; raie; ride; (*Teleph.*)

ligne, *f*, poste; (*Poet.*) vers; câble, *m*; corde, *f*; cordeau, *m*; amarre, *f*; genre; métier; emploi; département; ressort, *m*; partie; juridiction, *f*. ~ *cut*, cliché, *m*. ~ *engraving*, taille-douce; gravure au trait, *f*. *plumb* ~, fil à plomb, *m*. ¶ *v.t*, (*clothes*) doubler; tapisser; garnir; revêtir; rider, sillonner; border. ~ *one's stomach*, se lester l'estomac.

lineage, *n*, descendance, *f*, parage, *m*. **lineal**, *a*, linéaire; (*pers.*) en ligne directe. **lineament**, *n*, linéament, trait, *m*. **linear**, *a*, linéaire.

linen, *n*, toile [de lin] *f*; [tissu de] lin; linge, *m*. ~ [*thread*], fil [de lin] *m*. ~ *trade*, industrie linière, toilerie, *f*.

liner, *n*, transatlantique, paquebot, *m*.

ling, *n*, (*fish*) grande morue barbue; (*Bot.*) bruyère, brande, *f*.

linger, *v.i*, s'attarder; traîner. ~*ing death*, mort lente, *f*.

lingerie, *n*, lingerie [fine] *f*.

lingo, *n*, jargon, baragouin, *m*.

lingual, *a*, lingual. ¶ *n*, linguale, *f*. **linguist**, *n*, linguiste. *m*. ~**ics**, *n*, linguistique, *f*.

liniment, *n*, liniment, *m*.

lining, *n*, doublure; garniture; chemise; (*hat*) coiffe, *f*; revêtement, *m*.

link, *n*, chaînon, maillon, anneau, *m*; (*Mach.*) coulisse, *f*; (*fig.*) lien, *m*. ¶ *v.t*, articuler; enchaîner. ~ *up*, raccorder.

links, *n.pl. & s*, lande, *f*; (*golf*) terrain, *m*.

linnet, *n*, linotte, *f*, linot, *m*.

linoleum, *n*, linoléum, *m*.

linotype, *n. & att*, linotype, *f*. & *a*.

linseed, *n*, graine de lin, *f*. ~ *oil*, huile de [graine de] lin, *f*.

lint, *n*, charpie, *f*.

lintel, *n*, linteau, sommier, *m*, traverse, *f*.

lion, ess, *n*, lion, ne. ~ *cub*, ~ *whelp*, lionceau, *m*. ~*'s share*, part du lion, *f*.

lip, *n*, lèvre; babine, *f*; bec, *m*. ~*stick*, rouge à lèvres, *m*.

liquefaction, *n*, liquéfaction, *f*. **liquefy**, *v.t*, liquéfier.

liqueur, *n*, liqueur [de dessert] *f*. ~ *brandy*, fine champagne, *f*.

liquid, *a*, liquide; (*Com., Fin.*) liquide, disponible; (*fig.*) coulant, doux. ~ *ammonia*, liqueur d'ammoniaque, *f*. ~ *assets*, dis-

ponibilités, *f.pl*. ¶ *n*, liquide, *m*; (*phonetics*) liquide, *f*.

liquidate, *v.t*, liquider. **liquidation**, *n*, liquidation, *f*. **liquidator**, *n*, liquidateur, *m*.

liquor, *n*, liquide, *m*, boisson; liqueur, *f*.

Lisbon, *n*, Lisbonne, *f*.

lisp, *v.i*, zézayer. ¶ *n*, zézeiements, *m*.

lissom[e], *a*, souple.

list, *n*, liste, *f*; bordereau, *m*; feuille, *f*; rôle; tableau, *m*; inventaire; bulletin; catalogue, *f*; inventaire; bulletin; catalogue, *m*; cote, *f*; (*Naut.*) bande; (*selvage*) lisière, *f*; (*pl.*) lice, arène, barrière, *f*. ~ *of plates*, table des hors-texte. ¶ *v.t*, cataloguer; inventorier; (*door*) calfeutrer; (*v.i, Naut.*) donner [de] la bande.

listen, *v.i. & ~ in* (*radio*), écouter. ~**er**, *n*, (*hearer & radio*) auditeur, *m*; (*spy*) écouteur, euse.

listless†, *a*, nonchalant, distrait, traînant.

litany, *n*, litanies, *f.pl*.

literal†, *a*, littéral. ~ [*error*], coquille, *f*. ~ *sense*, (*passage*) sens littéral; (*word*) [sens] propre, *m*.

literary, *a*, littéraire. ~ *man*, homme de lettres, littérateur, *m*. **literate**, *a*, qui sait lire; lettré. **literature**, *n*, littérature, *f*.

litharge, *n*, litharge, *f*.

lithe, *a*, souple, agile.

lithia, *n*, lithine, *f*. **lithium**, *n*, lithium, *m*.

lithograph & ~**y**, *n*, lithographie, *f*. ¶ *v.t*, lithographier. ~**er**, *n*, lithographe, *m*. ~**ic**, *a*, lithographique.

Lithuania, *n*, la Lit[h]uanie.

litigant, *n*, plaideur, euse. **litigation**, *n*, litige, *m*. **litigious**, *a*, litigieux, processif.

litmus, *n*, tournesol, *m*. ~ *paper*, papier tournesol, *m*.

litter, *n*, (*palanquin*) litière, civière, *f*; brancard, *m*; (*straw & dung*) litière, *f*, fumier, *m*; (*young*) portée, ventrée; (*pigs*) cochonnée, *f*; encombrement, fouillis, *m*; immondices, *f.pl*, détritus, débris, *m.pl*. ¶ *v.t*, encombrer; joncher.

little, *a*, petit. ~ *devil*, diablotin, *m*. ~ *finger*, petit doigt, [doigt] auriculaire, *m*. ~ *ones*, petits enfants; (*cubs*) petits, *m.pl*. *L~ Red Riding Hood*, le Petit Chaperon Rouge. *a* ~ [*while*] *longer*, un peu. ¶ *ad*, peu; ne . . . guère. ¶ *n*, peu, *m*. ~ness, *n*, petitesse *f*.

live, *a*, vif; vivant; (*coal*) ardent; (*axle*) tournant; (*Elec.*) en charge; (*shell*) chargé. ~-*bait fishing*, pêche au vif, *f*. ~*stock*, animaux vivants, *m.pl*. ~ *rail*, rail conducteur, *m*.

live, *v.i. & t*, vivre; durer; se nourrir (*on milk, etc.* = de); demeurer, habiter.

livelihood, *n*, vie, *f*, gagne-pain, *m*, pitance, *f*.

liveliness, *n*, vivacité, animation, *f*, entrain, *m*. **lively,** *a*, vif, vivant, animé, mouvementé; allègre, fringant, émerillonné.

liver (*Anat.*) *n*, foie, *m*.

livery, *n*, livrée, *f*. ~ *stables*, pension pour les chevaux, *f*.

livid, *a*, livide. ~ity, *n*, lividité, *f*.

living, *a*, vivant; en vie; (*force*) vive. ~ *being*, vivant, *m*. ~ *wage*, minimum vital, *m*. ~ *within* ~ *memory*, de mémoire d'homme. ¶ *n*, vie, *f*, vivre, *m*; (*fare*) chère, *f*; (*Eccl.*) bénéfice, *m*. ~ *expenses*, dépense de bouche, *f*. ~-*in*, internat, *m*. ~ *room*, salon, *m*. **the** ~, les vivants, *m.pl*. **to** *earn a* ~, gagner sa vie.

lizard, *n*, lézard, *m*.

llama, *n*, lama, *m*.

loach, *n*, loche, *f*.

load, *n*, charge, *f*; fardeau, *m*. ~ [*water*] *line*, ligne de [flottaison en] charge, *f*. ¶ *v.t*, charger; combler; couvrir; (*dice*) piper; (*v.i.*) prendre charge. ~ed, *p.p*, chargé. ~er, *n*, chargeur, *m*, ~ing, *n*, charge, *f*; chargement, *m*. [*now*] ~ (ship), en charge.

loaf, *n. &* ~ *of bread*, pain, *m*; (*round loaf*) miche, *f*.

loaf, *v.i*, fainéanter, battre le pavé. ~er, *n*, fainéant, batteur de pavé, *m*.

loam, *n*, terre grasse; terre, *f*.

loan, *n*, prêt; emprunt, *m*.

loath (**to be**), ne vouloir pas, répugner. **loathe,** *v.t*, haïr, abhorrer. **loathing,** *n*, dégoût, *m*. **loathsome,** *a*, dégoûtant.

lob (*Ten.*) *n*, chandelle, *f*.

lobby, *n*, vestibule; couloir, *m*. ¶ *v.i*, faire les couloirs. ~ing, *n*, propos de couloir, *m.pl*.

lobe, *n*, lobe, *m*.

lobelia, *n*, lobélie, *f*.

lobster, *n*, homard, *m*. ~ *pot*, ~ *basket*, nasse, *f*, panier, *m*.

local, *a*, local; topique; de clocher; (*custom*) de place, des lieux. ~[e], *n*, scène, *f*. ~ity, *n*, localité, *f*. ~ize, *v.t*, localiser. ~ly, *ad*, localement; sur place.

locate, *v.t*, fixer [l'emplacement de]; repérer; rechercher.

lock, *n*, serrure; (*canal*) écluse; (*hair*) boucle, mèche; (*pl.*) chevelure; (*gun*) platine, *f*. *under* ~ *& key*, sous clef. ~-*jaw*, tétanos, *m*. ~-*nut*, contre-écrou, *m*. ~-*out*, lockout, *m*, grève patronale, *f*. ~-*smith*, serrurier, *m*. ~ *stitch*, point de piqûre, *m*. ~-*up*, (*police*) violon; (*att.*) fermant à clef. ¶ *v.t*, fermer [à clef]; bloquer. ~ *out*, fermer la porte à clef sur; (*workmen*) renvoyer en masse. ~ *up*, fermer à clef; mettre (*ou* serrer) sous clef; verrouiller, enfermer, coffrer, boucler; (*Fin.*) immobiliser, bloquer.

locker, *n*, case, *f*; caisson, *m*; soute, *f*.

locket, *n*, médaillon, *m*.

locksmith, *n*, serrurier, *m*.

locomotion, *n*, locomotion, *f*. **locomotive,** *a*, locomoteur. ¶ *n*, locomotive, *f*. *locomotor ataxy*, ataxie locomotrice, *f*.

loculus, *n*, loge, *f*.

locust, *n*, sauterelle, locuste, *f*, criquet, *m*. ~ [*bean*], caroube, *f*.

locution, *n*, façon de s'exprimer, *f*, tour de langage, idiotisme, *m*.

lode, *n*, filon, *m*. ~-*star*, étoile polaire, *f*. ~-*stone*, pierre d'aimant, *f*.

lodge, *n*, loge, *f*; pavillon, *m*. ¶ *v.t*, loger; déposer; [re]mettre, fournir; (*appeal*) interjeter; (*v.i.*) [se] loger, camper. **lodger,** *n*, locataire, *m,f*. **lodging,** *n*, logement, *m*, chambre, *f*, le couvert; (*pl.*) meublé *m*.

loft, *n*, grenier, *m*; soupente; (*organ*) tribune, *f*. ¶ (*golf*) *v.t*, enlever. **loftiness,** *n*, élévation, hauteur, *f*. **lofty,** *a*, élevé; relevé; fier; hautain, altier; (*style*) soutenu.

log, *n*, bûche, *f*; (*Naut.*) loch, *m*. (*wood*) *in the* ~, en grume. ~ [*book*], livre de loch; journal de bord, *m*. ~ *cabin*, ~ *hut*, cabane de bois, *f*. ~-*wood*, [bois de] campêche, *m*.

loganberry, *n*, ronce-framboise, *f*.

logarithm, *n*, logarithme, *m*.

loggerheads (at), en bisbille.

logic, *n,* logique, *f.* ~al†, *a,* logique. ~**ian,** *n,* logicien, *m.*

loin, *n,* (*veal*) longe, *f;* (*mutton*) filet, *m;* (*pl.*) reins, lombes, *m.pl.* ~ *chop,* côtelette de filet, *f.* ~ *cloth,* pagne, *m.*

loiter, *v.i,* s'attarder, traîner, s'amuser. ~**er,** *n,* traînard, *m.*

loll, *v.i,* se prélasser; (*tongue*) pendre.

Lombardy, *n,* la Lombardie.

London, *n,* Londres, *m;* (*att.*) londonien. ~**er,** *n,* Londonien, ne.

loneliness, *n,* solitude, *f,* isolement, *m.* **lonely & lone**[some], *a,* solitaire, isolé, esseulé. *lone cottage,* chartreuse, *f.*

long, *a,* long; grand; allongé; (*Meas.*) de long. ~**boat,** chaloupe, *f.* ~**distance race,** course de fond, *f.* ~**drawn,** filandreux. ~**haired,** chevelu. ~**legged** (man), bien fendu. ~**lived,** vivace. ~ *service,* vétérance, *f.* ~**shoreman,** débardeur, *m.* a ~ *while,* un long temps, longtemps, *ad.* ~**winded,** prolixe, diffus. ¶ *ad,* longtemps; le long de. ~ *ago,* il y a longtemps. *not ~ since,* naguère. ~**suffering,** longanimité, *f.* ¶ *n: the ~ & the short of it,* le fin mot. ¶ *v.i: I ~ to,* il me tarde de, je brûle de, je grille de. ~ *for,* languir pour, soupirer après. *to be ~* (delay), tarder. *longest way round,* chemin des écoliers, *m.*

longevity, *n,* longévité, *f.*

longing, *n,* [grande] envie, démangeaison, *f.*

longitude, *n,* longitude, *f.* **longitudinal**†, *a,* longitudinal.

look, *n,* regard; coup d'œil; œil; air, *m;* mine; apparence, *f,* aspect, *m.* ~**out,** veille, vigie, *f,* qui-vive, *m;* (*post*) guérite, *f;* (*man*) guetteur, *m;* affaire, *f.* ¶ *v.i,* regarder; avoir l'air; sembler; paraître. ~ *after,* veiller à, soigner, ménager, gouverner. ~ *at,* regarder. ~ *down* (from on high), planer. ~ *down* [up]on, mépriser. ~ *for,* chercher; s'attendre à. ~ *into,* examiner. ~ *like,* ressembler à, jouer. ~ *on,* regarder; envisager. (*front*) donner sur. ~ *out!* attention!, gare!, alerte!, vingt-deux! ~ *out for,* chercher; s'attendre à. ~ *out of the window,* regarder par la fenêtre. ~ *over,* parcourir; repasser. ~ *up a word in the dic-*tionary, chercher un mot dans le dictionnaire. *to translate by looking up every other word in the dictionary,* traduire à coups de dictionnaire. ~**ing glass,** glace, *f,* miroir, *m.*

loom, *n,* métier [à tisser] *m.*

loom, *v.i,* se dessiner, émerger, surgir.

loop, *n,* boucle; coque, *f;* œil, *m;* ganse, *f.* ~**hole,** meurtrière, *f,* créneau, *m;* (*fig.*) échappatoire, *f.* ¶ *v.t,* boucler. ~ *the ~,* boucler la boucle.

loose, *a,* mobile; volant; branlant; flottant; coulant; large; lâche; (*pulley*) folle; libre; négligé; desserré; décousu; (*in bulk*) en vrac. *at a ~ end,* désœuvré. **loose**[n] *v.t,* [re]lâcher; délier; desserrer.

loot, *n,* butin, *m.* ¶ *v.t. & i,* piller.

lop, *v.t,* élaguer, ébrancher. ~**ear** [ed rabbit], lapin bélier, *m.* ~**sided,** de guingois; (*boat*) bordier.

loquacious, *a,* loquace. **loquacity,** *n,* loquacité, *f.*

lord, *n,* seigneur; (*Eng.*) lord, *m.* ~ *of creation,* roi de la nature, *m.* ~ *of the manor,* châtelain, *m.* the Lord (God), le Seigneur. *Lord's Prayer,* oraison dominicale, *f. Lord's Supper,* communion, Cène, *f.* ~ *it over,* faire le maître avec. ~**ly,** *a,* hautain, altier, fier. ~**ship,** *n,* seigneurie, *f. Your L~,* Votre grandeur, *f.*

lore, *n,* science, *f.*

lorgnette, *n,* face à main, *f.*

lose, *v.t. & i. ir,* perdre; (*train*) manquer; (*clock*) retarder. ~ *heart,* se décourager. **loser,** *n,* perdant, e; (*good, bad*) joueur, euse. *be a ~,* être en perte. **loss,** *n,* perte; déperdition, *f;* déchet[s] *m.*[*pl.*]; sinistre, *m.* ~ *of appetite,* inappétence, *f.* ~ *of voice,* extinction de voix, *f.* *at a ~,* à perte; (*fig.*) empêché. **lost,** *p.p. & p.a,* perdu; égaré; dépaysé; (*in thought*) absorbé, abîmé; (*motion*) rejetée. ~ & *found office,* bureau des objets trouvés, *m.*

lot, *n,* lot, *m;* partie, *f;* paquet; partage; sort; destin, *m,* destinée, *f. the ~,* le tout. *to draw ~s,* tirer au sort.

lotion, *n,* lotion, *f.*

lottery, *n,* loterie, *f.*

lotto, *n,* loto, *m.*

lotus, *n,* lotus, lotos, *m.*

loud, *a,* haut; fort; grand; gros; sonore; bruyant; tapageur. ~

cheers, vivats sonores, *m.pl.* ~
pedal, grande pédale, p. forte, *f.*
~*speaker,* haut-parleur, *m.* ~[ly],
ad, [tout] haut; fort.

Louisiana, *n,* la Louisiane.

lounge, *n,* (*hotel, etc.*) hall;
(*music hall, etc.*) proménoir;
canapé, *m.* ¶ *v.i,* flâner, paresser.
lounger, *n,* flâneur, batteur de
pavé, *m.*

louse, *n,* pou, *m.* **lousy,** *a,* pouilleux.

lout, *n.* & ~*ish, a,* rustre, rustaud,
m. & *a.*

lovable, *a,* aimable. **love,** *n,*
amour, *m;* inclination; tendresse,
f; chéri, e, bijou, *m. for* ~ *or
money,* pour un rien ou pour argent.
in ~, amoureux, épris. *fall in*
~, s'énamourer, s'éprendre. *make*
~ *to,* faire la cour à. *play for* ~,
jouer pour l'honneur. ~ *all*
(*Ten.*), zéro partout, égalité à
rien, rien à rien. ~ *bird,* inséparable, *m. ou f.* ~ *knot,* lacs
d'amour, *m.* ~ *letter,* billet doux,
m. ~*lock,* (*as worn by a man*)
rouflaquette, *f;* (*by a woman*)
accroche-cœur, *m.* ~ *match,*
mariage d'amour, mariage d'inclination, *m.* ~ *potion,* philtre,
m. ~*-sick,* qui languit d'amour.
~ *story,* roman d'amour, *m.*
¶ *v.t.* & *i,* aimer; chérir. ~ *one
another,* s'entr'aimer.

loveliness, *n,* beauté, *f.* **lovely,**
a, beau; adorable; du nanan.

lover, *n,* amant, *m;* amoureux,
euse; galant; ami, e; amateur, *m.*
~ *of old books,* bouquineur, *m.*

loving†, *a,* affectueux, aimant.

low, *a,* bas; petit; faible; (*fever,
speed*) lente; (*bow*) profonde;
vulgaire. L~ *Countries,* Pays-
Bas, *m.pl.* ~ *gear,* première
vitesse, *f.* ~ *mass,* messe basse,
petite m., *f.* ~ *relief,* bas-relief,
m. L~ *Sunday,* Quasimodo, *f.*
~*-water mark,* (*sea*) laisse de
basse mer, *f;* (*river*) étiage,
m. ¶ *ad,* bas; profondément.
~*-necked* (*dress*), décolleté, *a.*
& *m.* ~*-spirited,* abattu. *to be*
~*-waisted* (*dress*), avoir la taille
basse.

low, *v.i,* mugir, beugler.

lower, *a,* plus bas; inférieur; bas;
moindre. ~ *register* (*Mus.*),
grave, *m.* ~ *tooth,* dent de dessous, *f.* ¶ *v.t,* [a]baisser; rabattre;
descendre, avaler. ~ *oneself*
(*fig.*), se ravaler. *award, etc., to*

the lowest tenderer, adjudication, *etc.*, au rabais, *f.*

lowlands, *n.pl,* basses terres, *f.pl.*

lowliness, *n,* humilité, *f.* **lowly,**
a, humble.

lowness, *n,* peu de hauteur, *m;*
(*price, etc.*) modicité; (*vileness*)
bassesse, *f.*

loyal†, *a,* loyal, fidèle. ~*ism, n,*
loyalisme, *m.* ~*ist, n.* & *att,*
loyaliste, *m,f.* & *a.* ~*ty, n,*
loyauté, *f;* (*to sovereign*) loyalisme, *m.*

lozenge, *n,* pastille, tablette, *f;*
(*Geom.*) losange, *m.*

lubber, *n,* lourdaud, mastoc, *m.*

lubricate, *v.t,* graisser, lubrifier.
lubricating oil, huile à graisser, *f.*
lubricator, *n,* graisseur, *m.*

Lucca, *n,* Lucques, *f.*

Lucerne (Lake of), lac des
Quatre-Cantons, *m.*

lucid, *a,* lucide. ~*ity, n,* lucidité, *f.*

luck, *n,* chance, *f,* hasard, *m;*
veine; fortune, *f;* bonheur, *m.*
~*less, a,* malheureux, néfaste.
~*y*†, *a,* heureux, chanceux, fortuné, bien loti; propice. ~ *star,*
bonne étoile, *f.*

lucrative, *a,* lucratif. **lucre,** *n,*
lucre, gain, *m.*

lucubration, *n,* élucubration, *f.*

ludicrous†, *a,* risible, comique;
plaisant.

luff, *n,* lof, *m.* ¶ *v.t,* lofer.

lug, *n,* oreille, *f,* ergot, *m.* ¶ *v.t,*
traîner.

luggage, *n,* bagage[s] *m.[pl.]*.

lugger, *n,* lougre, *m.*

lugubrious†, *a,* lugubre.

lukewarm, *a,* tiède. ~*ness, n,*
tiédeur, *f.*

lull, *n,* accalmie, embellie, *f.* ¶ *v.t,*
bercer; mollir; assoupir. **lullaby,**
n, berceuse, *f.*

lumbago, *n,* lumbago, *m.* **lumbar,** *a,* lombaire.

lumber, *n,* bois [de charpente] *m.*
~*man,* bûcheron, *m.*

luminary, *n,* luminaire, astre, *m;*
(*pers.*) lumière, *f.* **luminous**†,
a, lumineux. ~ *dial* (*watch*),
cadran lumineux, *m.*

lump, *n,* [gros] morceau, *m,*
masse, *f,* bloc, *m,* motte, *f.* ~
sugar, sucre en morceaux, s.
cassé, *m.* ~ *sum,* somme grosse,
f. in a ~ *sum* (opp. *by installments*), en une [seule] fois. ¶ *v.t,*
bloquer, réunir. ~*ish, a,* balourd,
mastoc (*inv.*).

lunacy, *n,* aliénation d'esprit, aliénation mentale, démence, *f.*

lunar, *a,* lunaire.

lunatic, *n,* aliéné, e. ~ *asylum,* hospice (*ou* asile) d'aliénés, *m.*

lunch & luncheon, *n,* déjeuner [de midi], lunch, *m.* lunch[eon] *basket,* panier à provisions. **lunch,** *v.i,* déjeuner.

lung, *n,* poumon, *m.*

lunge, *n,* (*fencing*) botte, *f;* coup porté, *m.* ¶ *v.i,* (*fencing*) porter une botte; allonger un coup [à].

lupus (*Med.*) *n,* lupus, *m.*

lurch, *n,* embardée, *f. leave in the* ~, camper là, planter là, laisser en panne. ¶ *v.i,* tituber.

lure, *n,* leurre, *m.* ¶ *v.t,* leurrer; (*birds*) piper.

lurid, *a,* blafard; cuivré, fauve; sinistre.

lurk, *v.i,* se cacher; se dissimuler.

luscious, *a,* succulent; fondant.

lush, *a,* luxuriant.

lust, *n,* luxure, convoitise, *f.* ~ *after,* convoiter. ~ful, *a,* luxurieux.

luster, *n,* lustre, éclat, *m.* ¶ *v.t,* lustrer. ~less, *a,* terne.

lusty†, *a,* vigoureux, robuste.

lute, *n,* (*Mus.*) luth; (*cement*) lut, *m.* ¶ *v.t,* luter.

Lutheran, *a. & n,* luthérien, ne.

Luxembourg, *n,* Luxembourg, *m.*

luxuriance, *n,* exubérance, *f.* **luxuriant,** *a,* luxuriant, exubérant. **luxurious,** *a,* luxueux; voluptueux. **luxury,** *n,* luxe; délice, *m.*

lye, *n,* lessive, *f.*

lying, *a,* mensonger, menteur. ¶ *n,* mensonge, *m.*

lymph, *n,* lymphe, *f.*

lynch, *v.t,* lyncher.

lynx, *n,* lynx; (*common*) loup-cervier, *m.*

Lyons, *n,* Lyon, *m.*

lyre, *n,* lyre, *f.* ~bird, oiseau-lyre, *m.*

lyric & ~al, *a,* lyrique. **lyricism,** *n,* lyrisme, *m.*

M

macadam, *n,* macadam, *m.* ~ize, *v.t,* macadamiser.

macaque, *n,* macaque, *m.*

macaroni, *n,* macaroni, *m.*

macaroon, *n,* macaron, *m.*

macaw, *n,* ara, *m.*

mace, *n,* masse, *f;* (*spice*) macis, *m.* ~ *bearer,* massier, *m.*

macerate, *v.t,* macérer.

Machiavellian, *a,* machiavélique.

machination, *n,* machination, *f.*

machine, *n,* machine, *f.* ~cut, taillé à la machine. ~ *gun,* fusil mitrailleur, *m,* mitrailleuse, *f.* ~ *gunner,* [fusilier] mitrailleur, *m.* ~made, fait à la mécanique. ~ *oil,* huile pour machine, *f.* ~ *tool,* machine-outil, *f.* ¶ *v.t,* usiner, façonner. **machinery,** *n,* machinerie, *f,* machines, *f.pl;* outillage; (*fig.*) rouage, *m.* **machinist,** *n,* machiniste, mécanicien, *m.*

mackerel, *n,* maquereau, *m.* ~ *sky,* ciel pommelé, *m.*

mackintosh, *n,* imperméable, caoutchouc, *m.*

mad, *a,* fou; insensé; furieux (*pers. & bull*); enragé (*pers. & dog*). ~cap, écervelé, e, cerveau brûlé, *m.* ~man, -woman, fou, *m,* folle, *f,* insensé, e, forcené, e, désespéré, e, enragé, e.

madam, *n,* madame, *f.*

madden, *v.t,* rendre fou; affoler; faire enrager. ~ing, *p.a,* enrageant.

madder, *n,* garance, *f.*

Madeira, *n,* Madère, *f.*

madly, *ad,* follement, en fou. **madness,** *n,* folie; démence; (*dog's*) rage, *f.*

madonna, *n,* madone, *f.*

madras (*fabric*) *n,* madras, *m.*

madrepore, *n,* madrépore, *m.*

madrigal, *n,* madrigal, *m.*

magazine, *n,* magasin, *m;* (*warehouse*) soute; (*periodical*) revue, *f,* magazine, *m.*

Maggiore (Lago), le lac Majeur.

maggot, *n,* ver; asticot, *m.* ~y, *a,* véreux.

Magi, *n.pl,* mages, *m.pl.*

magic, *a,* magique. ¶ *n,* magie, *f;* enchantement; prestige, *m.* ~al, *a,* magique. ~ally, *ad,* d'une façon magique. ~ian, *n,* magicien, ne.

magisterial, *a,* de magistrat; (*fig.*) magistral. ~ly, *ad,* en magistrat; magistralement. **magistracy,** *n,* magistrature, *f.* **magistrate,** *n,* magistrat; juge, *m.*

magnanimity, *n,* magnanimité, *f.* **magnanimous†,** *a,* magnanime.

magnate, *n,* magnat, gros bonnet, *m.*

magnesia, *n,* magnésie, *f.* mag-

nesium, *n,* magnésium. *m.* ~ *light,* lumière magnésique, *f.*

magnet, *n,* aimant. *m.* ~**ic,** *a,* magnétique; (*bar, needle*) aimanté, e; (*fig.*) attirant. ~**ics,** *n.* & ~**ism,** *n,* magnétisme. *m.* ~**ize,** *v.t,* aimanter; (*fig.*) magnétiser.

magneto, *n,* magnéto. *f.* ~**electric,** *a,* magnéto-électrique.

magnificat, *n,* magnificat, *m.*

magnificence, *n,* magnificence, *f.* **magnificent**†, *a,* magnifique.

magnify, *v.t,* grossir; grandir; (*the Lord*) magnifier. *magnifying glass,* loupe, *f.*

magniloquence, *n,* emphase, *f.* **magniloquent,** *a,* emphatique.

magnitude, *n,* grandeur; importance, *f.*

magnolia, *n,* magnolia, *m.*

magot (*Chinese figure & ape*), *n,* magot, *m.*

magpie, *n,* pie, *f.*

mahogany, *n,* acajou, *m.*

mahout, *n,* cornac, *m.*

maid, *n,* fille; vierge, pucelle, *f.* ~[*servant*], fille [de service], bonne, domestique, servante, *f. maid of all work,* bonne à tout faire. *maid of honor,* demoiselle d'honneur, *f. maid's room,* chambre de domestique, *f.* **maiden,** *n,* vierge, fille; pucelle, *f.* ~ [*lady*], demoiselle, *f.* ¶ *a,* virginal; (*speech*) de début, premier; (*trip*) premier. ~*hair* [*fern*], capillaire, *m.* ~ *name,* nom de jeune fille, *m.* ~*hood,* *n,* virginité, *f.* ~*ly,* *a,* de jeune fille, virginal.

mail, *n,* (*armor*) mailles, *f.pl*; (*post*) poste, *f*; courrier, *m. air* ~, poste aérienne, *f.* ~ *bag,* sac à dépêches, *m.* ~ *boat,* ~ *steamer,* paquebot-poste, *m.* ~ *box,* boîte aux lettres, *f.* ~ *man,* facteur, *m.* ~ *order business,* affaires par correspondance, *f.pl.* ~ [*train*], train-poste, *m.*

maim, *v.t,* estropier, mutiler.

main, *a,* principal; grand; maître, esse. ~ [*portion of*] *building,* corps de logis, c. de bâtiment, *m.* ~ *deck,* pont principal, *m.* ~ *drain,* maître drain, d. collecteur, *m. by* ~ *force,* de vive force. ~ *hall* (*body of building*), vaisseau, *m. the* ~ *idea* (*of a book*), l'idée mère. ~ *issue* (*law*), fond, *m.* ~*land,* continent, *m.*, terre ferme, *f.* ~ *line* (*Rly*), ligne principale, grande l., *f.* ~*mast,* grand mât, *m. the* ~ *point,* le point princi-

pal, l'essentiel, *m.* ~ *road,* grand chemin, *m,* grand-route, *f.* ~*sail,* grand-voile, *f.* ~*spring,* grand ressort, *m*; (*fig.*) cheville ouvrière, *f,* mobile, *m.* ~*stay* (*fig.*), âme, *f*; soutien, *m. the* ~ *thing,* le principal, l'important, *m.* ~ *walls,* gros murs, *m.pl.* ¶ *n,* (*pipe*) conduite [maîtresse]; (*pl.*) canalisation, *f*; (*Elec.*) conducteur principal, *m*; (*sea, Poet.*) onde, *f. in the* ~, en général. *the M*~ (*river*), le Mein. ~*ly,* *ad,* principalement.

maintain, *v.t,* maintenir, soutenir; entretenir. **maintenance,** *n,* maintien, soutien; entretien, *m.*

Mainz, *n,* Mayence, *f.*

maize, *n,* maïs, *m.*

majestic†, *a,* majestueux. **majesty,** *n,* majesté, *f. His, Her, M*~, Sa Majesté.

majolica, *n,* majolique, maïolique, *f.*

major, *a,* majeur; (*prophet, etc.*) grand; (*pers.*) aîné. ~ *planet,* planète principale, *f.* ~ *road,* route de priorité, *f.* ¶ (*Mil.*) *n,* commandant, chef de bataillon *m.* ~ *general,* général de division, *m.*

Majorca, *n,* Majorque, *f.*

majority, *n,* majorité; pluralité, (la) plupart, *f.*

make, *n,* façon; fabrication, *f.* ~*believe,* feinte, frime, *f.* ~*shift,* moyen de fortune, pis aller, *m.* ~*up,* maquillage, fard, *m.* ~*weight,* complément de poids, *m*; (*butcher's*) réjouissance, *f*; (*fig.*) remplissage, *m.* ¶ *v.t.ir,* faire; dresser; pratiquer; fabriquer; confectionner; créer; rendre; forcer; réaliser; mettre; (*inquiries*) prendre; (*v.i.ir.*) se diriger [vers]; contribuer [à]; faire [comme si]. ~ *away with,* se défaire de; détourner. ~ *faces,* grimacer. ~ *hay,* faire les foins. ~ *it up,* se raccommoder. ~ *light of,* faire peu de cas de. ~ *money,* s'enrichir. ~ *much of,* faire mousser. ~ *off,* filer, décamper. ~ *one's will,* tester. ~ *out,* distinguer; déchiffrer; comprendre; dresser. ~ *the most of,* ménager. ~ *up,* (*quarrel*) se réconcilier; confectionner; (*face*) se farder, se maquiller; (*Theat.*) se grimer; (*Typ.*) mettre en pages. ~ *up for,* suppléer [à]. ~ *up one's mind,* se décider, se déterminer.

maker, *n,* créateur, trice; faiseur,

euse; fabricant; constructeur, *m*.
making, *n,* création; fabrication; construction; confection, *f*.
malachite, *n,* malachite, *f*.
maladjusted, *a,* mal ajusté.
maladministration, *n,* mauvaise gestion, *f*.
maladroit†, *a,* maladroit.
malady, *n,* maladie, *f*.
Malagasy, *a,* malgache. ¶ *n,* Malgache, *m,f*.
malaprop[ism], *n,* incongruité, *f,* pataquès, *m*.
malaria, *n,* paludisme, *m,* malaria, *f.* **malarial,** *a,* paludéen; miasmatique.
Malay[an], *a,* malais. ¶ *n,* (*pers.*) Malais, e; (*language*) le malais. **Malaysia,** *n,* la Malaisie; Malaysia.
malcontent, *a.* & *n,* mécontent, *a.* & *m*.
male, *n,* mâle, *m.* ¶ *a,* mâle; masculin. ~ *descent,* masculinité, *f.* ~ *nurse,* infirmier, *m*.
malediction, *n,* malédiction, *f*.
malefactor, *n,* malfaiteur, *m*.
malevolent, *a,* malveillant.
malformation, *n,* malformation, *f,* vice de conformation, *m*.
malice, *n,* malice, rancune, *f.* ~ *aforethought†,* préméditation, *f*.
malicious†, *a,* malicieux.
malign, *v.t,* diffamer, calomnier. **malign†, malignant†,** *a,* malin.
malinger, *v.i,* faire le malade, simuler la maladie.
mallard, *n,* malart, *m*.
malleable, *a,* malléable.
mallet, *n,* maillet, *m,* mailloche, batte, *f*.
mallow, *n,* mauve, *f*.
malt, *n,* malt, *m.* ¶ *v.t,* convertir en malt. **~ing,** *n,* malterie, *f.* **~ster,** *n,* malteur, *m*.
Malta, *n,* Malte, *f.* **Maltese,** *a,* maltais. ~ *cross,* croix de Malte, *f.* ~ [*dog, bitch*], chien(ne) de Malte, bichon, ne. ¶ *n,* (*pers.*) Maltais, e; (*language*) le maltais.
maltreat, *v.t,* maltraiter, brutaliser. **~ment,** *n,* mauvais traitements; sévices, *m.pl*.
mamillary, *a,* mamillaire.
mama, *n,* maman, *f*.
mammal, *n,* mammifère, *m.* **mammalia,** *n.pl,* mammifères, *m.pl*.
mammoth, *n,* mammouth, *m*.
man, *n,* homme; monsieur; cavalier; employé; ouvrier; valet, *m*; (*checkers*) pion, *m.* (*chess*) pièce, *f.* ~ & *wife,* mari &

femme. ~ *child,* enfant mâle, *m*. **~-eater,** mangeur d'hommes, *m*. ~ *Friday,* factotum, *m.* **~hole,** (*Mach.*) trou d'homme; (*sewer, etc.*) regard, *m.* the ~ *in the street,* l'homme de la rue. ~ *of all work,* homme à tout faire. ~ *of fashion,* élégant, *m.* ~ *of substance,* homme calé. ~ *of war,* bâtiment de guerre, *m.* ~'s *estate,* l'âge viril, *m.* ~[*servant*], domestique, valet, *m.* **~slaughter,** homicide involontaire, *m.* ¶ *v.t,* (*boat, etc.*) armer; équiper. **~hood, ~kind, ~ly,** *etc.* See below.
manacle, *v.t,* mettre des menottes à; (*fig.*) enchaîner. **~s,** *n.pl,* menottes, *f.pl,* fers, *m.pl*.
manage, *v.t,* diriger, administrer, gérer; conduire; manier; ménager; (*v.i.*) s'arranger; savoir. ~ *to,* parvenir à; obtenir de. **~ment,** *n,* direction, administration; gérance, gestion; conduite; économie, *f;* maniement, *m*.
manager, ess, *n,* directeur, trice, gérant, e; chef; (*ship's*) armateur, *m.* **managing director,** administrateur délégué, a. directeur, a. gérant, *m*.
manatee, *n,* lamantin, *m*.
Manchuria, *n,* la Mandchourie. **Manchu[rian],** *a,* mandchou. ¶ *n,* Mandchou, e.
mandarin, *n,* mandarin, *m*.
mandatory, *n,* mandataire, *m*. **mandate,** *n,* mandat, *m.* ~*d territory,* pays sous mandat, **mandator,** *n,* mandant, *m*.
mandible, *n,* mandibule, *f*.
mandolin[e], *n,* mandoline, *f*.
mandrake, *n,* mandragore, *f*.
mandrel, -il (*lathe*) *n,* mandrin, arbre, *m*.
mandrill (*baboon*) *n,* mandrill, *m*.
mane, *n,* crinière, *f,* crins, *m.pl*.
manege, -ège, *n,* manège, *m*.
manes, *n.pl,* mânes, *m.pl*.
maneuver, *n,* manœuvre, *f.* ¶ *v.i.* & *t,* manœuvrer, évoluer.
manfully, *ad,* en homme, courageusement.
manganese, *n,* manganèse, *m*.
mange, *n,* gale, rogne, *f,* rouvieux, *m*.
mangel[-wurzel] or **mangold [-wurzel],** *n,* betterave fourragère, *f*.
manger, *n,* mangeoire, crèche, *f*.
mangle, *n,* calandre, *f.* ¶ *v.t,* mutiler; (*linen*) calandrer.

mango, *n,* mangue, *f.* ~ [*tree*], manguier, *m.*

mangrove, *n,* manglier, palétuvier, *m.*

mangy, *a,* galeux, rogneux, rouvieux.

manhandle, *v.t,* malmener.

manhood, *n,* virilité, *f;* âge viril, *m.*

mania, *n,* manie; folie; rage; marotte, *f.* **maniac,** *n.* & ~(**al**) *a,* maniaque, *m,f.* & *a.*

manicure, *n,* soin des mains, *m,* manucure, *f.* ~ *set,* onglier, *m,* manucure, *f.* ~ *the hands,* soigner les mains, faire de la manucure. **manicurist,** *n,* manucure, *f,m.*

manifest†, *a,* manifeste. ¶ (*ship.*) *n,* manifeste, *m.* ¶ *v.t,* manifester.

manifesto, *n,* manifeste, *m.*

manifold, *a,* multiple. ~ *book,* carnet genre manifold, cahier de copie, *dit* manifold, *m.*

manikin, *n,* [petit] bout d' homme; mannequin, *m.*

Manila, *n,* (*Geog.*) Manille, *f;* (*cheroot*) manille, *m.*

manioc, *n,* manioc, *m.*

manipulate, *v.t,* manœuvrer, manipuler; (*pers.*) empaumer.

mankind, *n,* le genre humain, l'espèce humaine; les hommes. **manliness,** *n,* virilité, *f.* **manly,** *a,* mâle, viril; (*woman*) hommasse.

manna, *n,* manne, *f.*

mannequin, *n,* mannequin, *m.*

manner, *n,* manière; façon, *f;* air; genre, *m;* (*pl.*) manières, formes, mœurs, *f.pl,* ton, *m. he has no* ~*s,* il n'a pa de savoir-vivre. ~**ed** (*style, etc.*) *a,* maniéré. ~**ism,** *n,* maniérisme, *m,* manière, *f,* tic, *m.* ~**ly,** *a,* poli.

mannish, *a,* garçonnier, hommasse.

manometer, *n,* manomètre, *m.*

manor, *n,* manoir, château, *m,* seigneurie, *f.*

mansard roof, comble brisé, *m.*

mansion, *n,* hôtel [particulier]; château; (*pl.*) immeuble à appartements, *m.*

manslaughter, *n,* homicide involontaire, *m.*

mantelpiece, *n,* manteau de cheminée, *m,* cheminée, *f.* **mantelshelf,** *n,* tablette de cheminée, *f.*

mantilla, *n,* mantille, *f.*

mantle, *n,* manteau; (*gas*) man-

chon, *m.* ~ *maker,* couturier, *m.* ¶ *v.t,* couvrir.

Mantua, *n,* Mantoue, *f.*

manual†, *a,* manuel, à bras. ~ [*exercise*] (*Mil.*), maniement des (*ou* d') armes, *m.* ¶ *n,* manuel, guide-âne; (*organ*) clavier, *m.*

manufacture, *n,* fabrication, industrie, *f.* **manufacturer,** *n,* industriel, fabricant, manufacturier, *m.* ~*'s price,* prix de fabrique, *m.* **manufacturing,** *p.a,* manufacturier.

manure, *n,* fumier; engrais, *m.* ¶ *v.t,* engraisser; fumer.

manuscript, *n.* & *a,* manuscrit, *m.* & *a.*

Manx, *a,* de l'île de Man.

many, *a,* beaucoup; bien des; force; grand; maint, divers. ~ *a,* plus d'un, maint. *how* ~? combien? ~-*colored,* multicolore. ~-*sided,* complexe. *a great* ~, un grand nombre (de). *as* ~, autant. *so* ~, tant. *the* ~, la multitude. *too* ~, trop.

map, *n,* carte, *f;* plan, *m.* ~ *case,* porte-cartes, *m.* ~ *of the heavens.* carte céleste, *f.* ~ *of the world in hemispheres,* mappemonde, *f.* ~ *producer,* cartographe, *m. road* ~, carte routière, *f.* ¶ *v.t,* dresser (*ou* faire) la carte de. ~ *out,* tracer.

maple, *n,* érable, *m.*

mar, *v.t,* gâter; troubler.

marabou & **marabout,** *n,* marabout, *m.*

maraschino, *n,* marasquin, *m.*

marasmus, *n,* marasme, *m.*

marathon [*race*], *n,* course de Marathon, *f.*

maraud, *v.t,* marauder. ~**er,** *n,* maraudeur, *m.* ~**ing,** *n,* maraudage, *m,* maraude, *f.*

marble, *n,* marbre, *m;* (*games*) bille, *f.* ~ *mason* & ~ *merchant,* marbrier, *m.* ~ *quarry,* marbrière, *f.* ~ *work* & ~ *works,* marbrerie, *f.* ¶ *v.t,* marbrer. **marbler,** *n,* marbreur, *m.* **marbling,** *n,* marbrure, *f.*

marc (*fruit refuse*) *n,* marc, *m.*

marcasite, *n,* marcassite, *f.*

March, *n,* mars, *m.*

march, *n,* marche, *f;* pas, *m.* ¶ *v.i,* marcher. ~ *in,* entrer. ~ *off,* se mettre en marche. ~ *out,* sortir. ~ *past,* défiler. ~**ing,** *n,* marche, *f.* ~ *song,* chanson de route, *f.*

marchioness, *n,* marquise, *f.*

mare, *n,* jument, *f. he has found*

a ~'s *nest*, il croit avoir trouvé la pie au nid.

margarine, *n*, margarine, *f*.

margin, *n*, marge; (*book page*) marge, *f*, blanc; bord, *m*; provision; tolérance, *f*. ~**al**, *a*, marginal.

marguerite, *n*, grande marguerite, *f*.

marigold, *n*, souci, *m*.

marine, *a*, maritime; marin. ~ *glue*, glu marine, *f*. ~ *stores*, fournitures pour navires, *f*—*s* maritimes, *f.pl*. ¶ *n*, (*shipping*) marine, *f*; (*pers.*) soldat d'infanterie de marine, fantassin de la flotte, fusillier marin, *m*. **mariner**, *n*, marin, *m*. ~'s *compass*, boussole marine, *f*.

marionette, *n*, marionnette, *f*.

marital, *a*, marital.

maritime, *a*, maritime.

marjoram, *n*, marjolaine, *f*.

mark, *n*, marque, *f*; point; signe; repère, *m*; trace, *f*; but, *m*; estampille; cote, *f*; témoignage; (*Sch.*) point, *m*, note, *f*. ~ *of origin*, estampille, *f*. *question* ~, point d' interrogation, *m*. ¶ *v.t*, marquer; indiquer; porter [la mention]; noter; estampiller; coter; remarquer; faire attention à; (*card*) piper. ~ *out*, tracer; borner. ~ *time*, marquer le pas; piétiner sur place. ~ *my words*, écoutez-moi bien. ~**ed**, *p.a*, marqué, prononcé, sensible; (*man*) noté; (*cards*) biseautées. ~**er**, *n*, pointeur; repère; indicateur, *m*.

market, *n*, marché, *m*; place; bourse; (*covered*) halle, *f*; débouché; débit, *m*. ~ *town*, ville à marché, *f*, bourg, *m*. ~ *value*, valeur marchande, v. vénale, *f*. ¶ *v.t*, mettre en vente. ~**able**, *a*, marchand; de vente; vénal; négociable. ~**ing**, *n*, mise en vente, *f*.

marking, *n*, marquage, *m*; cote, *f*. ~ *ink*, encre à marquer le linge, *f*.

marksman, *n*, [bon] tireur, *m*.

marl, *n*, marne, *f*. ~ *pit*, marnière, *f*. ¶ *v.t*, marner.

marline, *n*, lusin, *m*. ~ *spike*, marlinspike, épissoir, *m*.

marly, *a*, marneux.

marmalade, *n*, confitures (*d'oranges*) *f.pl*; marmelade, *f*.

Marmora (**Sea of**), mer de Marmara, *f*.

marmot (*Zool.*) *n*, marmotte, *f*.

maroon, *a*, marron. ¶ *n*, couleur marron, *f*; (*pers.*) nègre marron, *m*, négresse marronne, *f*.

marquee, *n*, tente-pavillon, *f*.

marquetry, *n*, marqueterie, *f*.

marquis, -quess, *n*, marquis, *m*.

marriage, *n*, mariage, *m*; noces, *f.pl*. ~ *license*, dispense de ban, *f*. ~ *of convenience*, mariage de raison, m. de convenance. ~ *portion*, dot, *f*. ~ *settlement*, constitution de dot, *f*. ~ *tie*, lien conjugal, *m*. ~ *cousin by* ~, cousin par alliance. ~**able**, *a*, mariable, nubile. ~ *daughter*, fille à marier, *f*. **married**, *p.a*, marié. [*newly*] ~ *couple*, nouveaux mariés, *m.pl*. ~ *life*, vie conjugale, *f*. *get* ~, se marier.

marrow, *n*, moelle; (*vegetable*) courge à la moelle, *f*. ~*bone*, os à moelle, *m*. ~*fats*, pois carrés, *m.pl*. ~**y**, *a*, moelleux.

marry, *v.t*, marier; épouser; (*v.i.*) se marier; s'allier. ~ *a second, a third, time*, convoler en secondes, en troisièmes, noces. ~ *again*, se remarier, convoler. ~ *into*, s'apparenter à.

Marseilles, *n*, Marseille, *f*. *the Marseillaise* (*anthem*), la Marseillaise.

marsh, *n*, marais, marécage, *m*. ~ *marigold*, souci d'eau, *m*.

marshal, *n*, (*Mil.*) maréchal. ¶ *v.t*, classer; ranger; trier. ~**ship**, *n*, maréchalat, *m*.

marshy, *a*, marécageux, paludéen.

marsupial, *n*, marsupial, *m*.

mart, *n*, centre des affaires; marché, *m*.

marten, *n*, martre; fouine, *f*.

martial, *a*, martial; (*pers.*) guerrier. ~ *law* (in a town), état de siège, *m*.

martin, *n*, hirondelle de fenêtre, *f*.

martinet, *n*, gendarme, *m*.

martingale, (*harness, betting*) *n*, martingale, *f*.

Martinmas, *n*, la Saint-Martin.

martyr, *n*, martyr, e. ~**dom**, *n*, martyre, *m*. ~[**ize**], *v.t*, martyriser. ~**ology** (*list*) *n*, martyrologe, *m*.

marvel, *n*, merveille, *f*; prestige; miracle, *m*. ¶ *v.i*, s'émerveiller, s'étonner. **marvelous†**, *a*, merveilleux, prestigieux.

marzipan, *n*, massepain, *m*.

mascot, *n*, mascotte, *f*, portebonheur, fétiche, *m*.

masculine, *a*, masculin, mâle;

(*woman*) hommasse, garçonnier. ~ [*gender*], [*genre*] masculin, *m*.

masculinity, *n*, masculinité, *f*.

mash, *n*, mélange; (*cattle*) barbotage, *m*; (*poultry*) pâtée; (*Cook.*) purée, *f*. ¶ *v.t*, mélanger, brasser; réduire en purée. ~ed potatoes, turnips, purée de pommes de terre, de navets, *f*.

mask, *n*, masque, *f*; (*Arch.*) mascaron, *m*; (*Phot.*) cache, *f*. ¶ *v.t*, masquer, cacher. ~ed ball, bal masqué, *m*. **masker, -quer** (*pers.*) *n*, masque. *m*.

maslin, *n*, mouture, *f*.

mason, *n*, maçon, *m*. ¶ *v.t*, maçonner. ~ic, *a*, maçonnique. ~ry, *n*, maçonnerie, *f*; maçonnage, *m*.

masquerade, *n*, mascarade; (*fig.*) mascarade, pantalonnade, *f*. ¶ *v.i*, se masquer, se déguiser.

mass, *n*, masse, *f*; amas, *m*; (*Relig.*) messe, *f*. ~ production, production en masse, fabrication en série, *f*. ¶ *v.t*, masser.

massacre, *n*, massacre, *m*. ¶ *v.t*, massacrer.

massage, *n*, massage, *m*. ¶ *v.t*, masser. **masseur, euse,** *n*, masseur, euse.

massive†, *a*, massif; en amas; en masses.

mast, *n*, mât, *m*; (*pl.*) mâture, *f*; (*beech*) faînes, *f.pl*; (*oak*) glands, *m.pl*, glandée, *f*. ¶ *v.t*, mâter.

master, *n*, maître; professeur; directeur; chef; patron; capitaine, *m. be ~ of*, posséder. *be one's own ~,* s'appartenir. ~ *key,* passepartout, *m*. ~ *mind,* cheville ouvrière, *f*. ~ *of the hounds,* maître d'équipage. ~*piece,* chef-d'œuvre, *m*. ~ *stroke,* coup de maître, *f*. ¶ *v.t*, maîtriser. ~*ful,* *a*, (*tone*) magistral. ~ *man,* ~ *woman,* maître homme, maîtresse femme. ~*ly,* *a*, de maître, magistral. *in a* ~ *way,* magistralement, supérieurement. ~*y,* *n*, maîtrise, *f*, empire; dessus, *m*.

mastic, *n*, mastic, *m*. ~ [*tree*], lentisque, *m*.

masticate, *v.t*, mâcher, mastiquer. **mastication,** *n*, mastication, *f*.

mastiff, *n*, mâtin, *m*.

mastodon, *n*, mastodonte, *m*.

mastoid, *a*, mastoïde.

mat, *a*, mat. ¶ *n*, natte, *f*; paillasson; tapis; (*plate*) dessous, *m*. ~ *maker,* nattier, *m*. ¶ *v.t*, natter.

matted hair, cheveux embroussaillés, *m.pl*.

matador, *n*, matador, *m*.

match, *n*, (*light*) allumette; alliance, *f*, parti, *m*; assortiment; pendant; (*pers.*) pareil, le; (*Ten., etc.*) partie, *f*, match; (*Box., wrestling*) combat, match, *m*. ~*board,* planche bouvetée, *f*. ~*box,* boîte à allumettes, *f*. ~*maker,* marieur, euse. ~ *play* (*golf*), concours par trous, *m*. ¶ *v.t*, allier; marier; égaler; assortir; [r]appareiller; [r]apparier. *to* ~, pareil. ~*less,* *a*, sans pareil.

mate, *n*, camarade, *m,f*, compagnon, *m*, compagne, *f*; aide, *m,f*; (*bird*) pair; (*Naut.*) second, lieutenant; (*chess*) mat, *m*. ¶ *v.t*, appareiller, accoupler; (*chess*) faire mat, mater.

material†, *a*, matériel; essentiel. ¶ *n*, matière, *f*; matériel, *m*; étoffe, *f*; (*pl.*) matières, *f.pl*; matériaux, *m.pl*; fournitures, *f.pl*; articles, *m.pl. raw* ~, matière première, *f*. ~*ism,* *n*, matérialisme, *m*. ~*ist,* *n*. & ~*istic,* *a*, matérialiste. ~*ize,* *v.t*, matérialiser; (*v.i.*) se m.; aboutir.

maternal†, *a*, maternel. **maternity,** *n*. & ~ *hospital,* maternité, *f*. ~ *doctor,* accoucheur, *m*.

mathematical†, *a*, mathématique; (*precise*) géométrique; (*instruments*) de mathématiques. **mathematician,** *n*, mathématicien, ne. **mathematics,** *n.pl*, mathématiques, *f.pl*.

matinée, *n*, matinée, *f*. **matins,** *n.pl*, matines, *f*.

matriarchy, *n*, matriarcat, *m*.

matriculate, *v.i*, prendre des (ses) inscriptions. **matriculation,** *n*, inscription, *f*.

matrimonial†, *a*, conjugal; (*law, agent, etc.*) matrimonial. ~ *triangle,* ménage à trois, *m*. **matrimony,** *n*, mariage, *m*, vie conjugale, *f*.

matrix, *n*, matrice; gangue, *f*.

matron, *n*, matrone; (*hospital, etc.*) infirmière en chef, *f*. ~*ly,* *a*, de matrone.

matter, *n*, matière; affaire; chose; question, *f*; propos; cas; sujet; article; chapitre; (*Med.*) pus, *m*. *as a* ~ *of course,* comme une chose toute naturelle *ou* qui va de soi. *as a* ~ *of fact,* dans (*ou* par) le fait, en fait. ~*-of-fact,* positif. ~ *of history,* fait historique, *m. what's the* ~? qu'avez-vous? ¶ *v.i*, importer, faire. *no ~!* n'importe!

Matterhorn (the), le mont Cervin.

mattery, *a*, purulent.

matting, *n*, natte[s] *f.[pl.]*, paillasson; abrivent, *m*.

mattins, *n.pl*, matines, *f.pl*.

mattock, *n*, pioche-hache, *f*; hoyau, *m*.

mattress, *n*, matelas; sommier, *m*. *~ maker*, matelassier, ère.

mature†, *a*, mûr. ¶ *v.i. & t*, mûrir; (*Com*.) échoir. **maturity**, *n*, maturité; échéance, *f*.

maudlin, *a*, bêtement sentimental; ivre à pleurer; pleurard, larmoyant. ~[ism], *n*, romance, *f*.

maul, *v.t*, malmener. *~stick*, appui-main, *m*.

Mauritius, *n*, [l'île] Maurice, *f*.

mausoleum, *n*, mausolée, *m*.

mauve, *n. & a*, mauve, *m. & att*.

mawkish†, *a*, mielleux, doucereux, fade.

maxim, *n*, maxime, sentence, *f*; adage, *m*.

maximum, *n*, maximum; plafond, *m*. ¶ *a*, maximum.

May (*month*) *n*, mai, *m*. *May Day*, le premier mai. *May fly*, mouche de mai, *f*, éphémère, *f*. *maypole*, mai, *m*.

may (*Bot*.) *n*, fleurs d'aubépine, *f.pl*. ~ [*bush*], aubépine, épine blanche, *f*.

may, *v. aux. ir*, pouvoir; permettre; que. *it ~ be*, cela se peut. *~be*, *ad*, peut-être.

mayonnaise, *n. & att*, mayonnaise, *f. & att*.

mayor, *n*, maire, *m*. *~alty*, *n*, mairie, *f*.

maze, *n*, labyrinthe, dédale, *m*.

mazurka, *n*, mazurka, *f*.

me, *pn*, me; moi.

meadow & (*Poet*.) **mead**, *n*, pré, *m*, prairie, *f*. *meadowsweet*, reine des prés, *f*.

meager†, *a*, maigre, pauvre. *~ness*, *n*, maigreur, pauvreté, *f*.

meal, *n*, repas, *m*; (*grain*) farine, *f*. *~ time*, l'heure du repas, *f*. *at ~ times*, aux heures de repas. *~y*, *a*, farineux. *~mouthed*, mielleux, doucereux.

mean†, *a*, bas; vil; abject; chétif; mesquin; ladre; chiche; petit; (*average*) moyen. *in the ~ time* (or *while*) or *~time*, *~while*, *ad*, en attendant; entretemps, cependant. ¶ *n*, milieu, *m*; (*Math*.) moyenne, *f*; (*pl*.) moyen, *m*;

moyens, *m.pl*, facultés, *f.pl*. *by no ~s*, nullement. *private ~s*, fortune personnelle, *f*. ¶ *v.t. & i. ir*, se proposer; avoir l'intention de; vouloir; compter; penser; vouloir dire; signifier; entendre; destiner; faire exprès. *~ well*, avoir de bonnes intentions.

meander, *n*, méandre, *m*. ¶ *v.i*, cheminer, serpenter.

meaning, *n*, signification, *f*, sens, *m*; intention, *f*. *-meaning*, *a*, intentionné. *~less*, *a*, sans aucun sens, un non-sens.

meanness, *n*, bassesse, abjection, ladrerie, vilenie, *f*.

measles, *n.pl*, rougeole, *f*.

measurable, *a*, mesurable, appréciable. **measure**, *n*, mesure; dose; démarche; (*tape*) mesure, *f*; mètre; centimètre, *m*; (*bill*) projet de loi, *m*; (*pl*, *Geol*.) étage, *m*, série, *f*, terrain, *m*. *to ~ (clothes)*, sur mesure. ¶ *v.t. & i*, mesurer; métrer; arpenter; jauger; cuber; toiser; (*the body*) mensurer; (*for fitting*) prendre mesure à; avoir. *~ out*, doser. *~d*, *a*, mesuré, modéré. *~ment*, *n*, mesurage, *m*; mesure; grosseur, *f*; volume; arpentage; jaugeage, *m*.

meat, *n*, viande; chair, *f*. *~ breakfast*, déjeuner à la fourchette, *m*. *~ day* (*Eccl*.), jour gras, *m*. *~y*, *a*, charnu; (*food*) carné.

Mecca, *n*, la Mecque.

mechanic, *n*, [ouvrier] mécanicien, mécanique, *m*. *~al†*, *a*, mécanique; (*fig*.) machinal. *~ dentistry*, prothèse dentaire, *f*. *~ drawing*, dessin industriel, *m*. *~ engineer*, ingénieur mécanicien, *m*. *~ engineering*, l'art de la mécanique, *m*; construction mécanique, *f*. **mechanician** & **mechanist**, *n*, mécanicien, *m*. **mechanics**, *n.pl*, mécanique, *f*. **mechanism**, *n*, mécanisme, *m*, mécanique, *f*, organes, *m.pl*. **mechanization**, *n*, machinisme, *m*. **mechanize**, *v.t*, mécaniser.

Mechlin [*lace*], *n*, malines, *f*.

medal, *n*, médaille, *f*. *~ cabinet & collection of ~s*, médaillier, *m*. *~ maker* or **medalist**, *n*, médailleur, *m*. *award a ~ to*, médailler. **medaled**, *a*, médaillé. **medallion**, *n*, médaillon, *m*. **medalist** (*recipient*) *n*, médaillé, e.

meddle, *v.i*, se mêler, s'immiscer, s'ingérer; toucher. **meddler**, *n*, or **meddlesome person**, touche-à-

tout, *m*, personne qui se mêle des oignons des autres, *f*. **meddling**, *n*, immixtion, ingérence, *f*.
median, *a*, médian; moyen.
mediate, *v.i*, s'interposer. **mediation**, *n*, médiation, *f*. **mediator, trix**, *n*, médiateur, trice.
medical, *a*, médical; (*school, etc.*) de médecine; (*student*) en médecine. ~ **examination** (recruits), revision, *f*. ~ **jurisprudence**, médecine légale, *f*. ~ **man**, ~ **officer**, médecin, *m*. **medicament**, *n*, médicament, *m*. **medicated**, *p.a*, médicamenteux. **medicinal**, *a*, médicinal; médicamenteux. **medicine**, *n*, médecine, *f*; médicament, *m*. ~ **cabinet**, ~ **chest**, pharmacie; caisse à médicaments, *f*. ~ **man**, [sorcier] guérisseur, *m*. **medico-judicial**, *a*, médico-légal.
medieval, *a*, médiéval, moyenâgeux.
mediocre, *a*, médiocre. **mediocrity**, *n*, (*quality*) médiocrité, *f*, médiocre, *m*; (*pers.*) médiocre, *m*.
meditate ([up]on), *v.t. & i*, méditer (sur), contempler. **meditation**, *n*, méditation, *f*, pensées, *f.pl*. **meditative**, *a*, méditatif.
mediterranean, *a*, méditerrané. M~, *a*, méditerranéen. **the M~** [Sea], la [mer] Méditerranée.
medium, *a*, moyen. ¶ *n*, milieu; agent; véhicule, *m*; (*ether*) atmosphère; (*agency*) entremise, *f*, intermédiaire; (*spiritualism*) médium, *m*.
medlar, *n*, nèfle, *f*. ~ [*tree*], néflier, *m*.
medley, *n*, mélange, bariolage, (*Mus.*) pot pourri, *m*. ¶ *a*, mêlé. ¶ *v.t*, mêler; bigarrer.
medullary, *a*, médullaire.
medusa (*jelly fish*) *n*, méduse, *f*.
meek, *a*, doux; débonnaire. ~**ly**, *ad*, avec douceur. ~**ness**, *n*, douceur, mansuétude, *f*.
meerschaum, *n*, écume de mer, *f*.
meet (*Hunt.*) *n*, assemblée, *f*. ¶ *v.t.ir*, rencontrer; trouver; faire face à; accueillir; honorer; (*v.i.ir*.) se rencontrer; confluer; s'assembler; se réunir. ~ **with**, éprouver, essuyer. ~**ing**, *n*, rencontre; jonction, *f*; confluent, *m*; entrevue; assemblée; réunion, *f*; meeting; concours, *m*; séance; (*of engagements, bills of exchange*) bonne fin, *f*.
megaphone, *n*, porte-voix, *m*.

melancholia & melancholy, *n*, mélancolie, *f*. **melancholic & melancholy**, *a*, mélancolique.
Melanesia, *n*, la Mélanésie.
mellow, *a*, mûr; moelleux; (*earth*) meuble. ¶ *v.t*, mûrir.
melodious†, *a*, mélodieux. **melody**, *n*, mélodie, *f*, chant, *m*.
melon, *n*, melon, *m*.
melt, *v.t. & i. ir*, fondre; attendrir; s'a. *that* ~*s in the mouth* (as a pear), fondant. ~**er**, *n*, fondeur, *m*. ~**ing**, *n*, fonte, fusion, *f*. ~ *point*, point de fusion, *m*. ~ *pot*, creuset, pot, *m*.
member, *n*, membre, *m*, adhérent, e, associé, e; représentant, *m*. ~ *of a conciliation board*, prud'homme, *m*. ~ *of a* (or *the*) *congress*, congressiste, *m,f*. ~ *of legislature*, représentant à la Chambre, *m*. ~**ship**, *n*, qualité [de membre]; adhésion; charge; (*legislature*) députation, *f*; nombre des adhérents, *m*.
membrane, *n*, membrane, *f*.
memento, *n*, mémento; souvenir, *m*.
memoir, *n*, mémoire, *m*; (*pl, book*) mémorial, *m*.
memorable, *a*, mémorable. **memorandum**, *n*, mémorandum, *m*, note, *f*, mémoire, *m*. *as a* ~, pour mémoire. ~ *book*, carnet, calepin, *m*. **memorial**, *n* mémorial, monument, *m*. **memorize**, *v.t* apprendre par cœur. **memory**, *n*, mémoire, *f*; souvenir, *m*; (*pl.*) souvenances, *f.pl*. *from* ~, de mémoire.
menace, *n*, menace, *f*. *public* ~ (*pers.*), malfaiteur public, *m*. ¶ *v.t*, menacer.
menagerie, *n*, ménagerie, *f*.
mend, *v.t*, raccommoder, réparer; repriser; améliorer; réformer. ~ *one's ways*, changer de conduite.
mendacious, *a*, mensonger. **mendacity**, *n*, l'habitude du mensonge, *f*.
mender, *n*, raccommodeur, euse, réparateur, trice.
mendicancy & mendicity, *n*, mendicité, *f*. **mendicant**, *a. & n*, mendiant, e.
mending, *n*, raccommodage, *m*, réparation; reprise, *f*.
menhir, *n*, menhir, peulven, *m*.
menial, *a*, servile. ¶ *n*, laquais, *m*.
mensuration, *n*, mesure, *f*;
mensuration, *n*, mesure, *f*;

(*science*) mesures, *f.pl*; (*of the body*) mensuration, *f.*

mental, *a*, mental; moral. ~ *arithmetic*, calcul mental, *m.* ~ *institution*, maison d'aliénés, *f*, asile d'a—s, *m.* ~ *patient*, aliéné, e. ~ *reservation*, restriction mentale, arrière-pensée, *f.* ~**ity,** *f*, mentalité, *f.* ~**ly,** *ad*, mentalement. ~ *deficient*, à petite mentalité.

menthol, *n*, menthol, *m.*

mention, *n*, mention; constatation, *f.* ~ *in dispatches*, citation à l'ordre de l'armée, *f.* ¶ *v.t*, mentionner, parler de, prononcer; indiquer; citer; constater. *don't* ~ *it!* il n'y a pas de quoi!, du tout!

Mentone, *n*, Menton, *m.*

menu, *n*, menu, *m*; carte du jour, *f.* ~ *holder*, porte-menu, *m.*

meow, *n*, miaulement, *m.* ¶ *v.i*, miauler.

mercantile, *a*, marchand, commercial, de commerce; (*mercenary*) mercantile.

Mercator's projection, projection de Mercator, *f.*

mercenary, *a*, mercenaire, stipendiaire, vénal, mercantile. ¶ *n*, mercenaire, *m.*

mercer, *n*, marchand de soieries, *m.* ~**ized,** *a*, mercerisé.

merchandise, *n*, marchandise, *f. oft. pl.* **merchant,** *n*, négociant, e, commerçant; *a*; marchand, e. ~ *marine*, marine marchande, *f.*

merciful†, *a*, miséricordieux, clément. **merciless†,** *a*, impitoyable.

mercurial, *a*, (*Chem.*) mercuriel; (*barometer, etc.*) à mercure; (*fig.*) vif. **mercury,** *n*, (*metal*) mercure, *m*; (*Bot.*) mercuriale, *f.*

mercy, *n*, miséricorde, merci, clémence, grâce, *f*, bienfait, bien, *m*; pitié, *f. at the* ~ *of*, à la merci de; au gré de. ~ *on us!* miséricorde!

mere†, *a*, simple, pur, seul. *a* ~ *nothing*, un rien. ¶ *n*, lac, *m.*

meretricious, *a*, de courtisane; factice.

merge, *v.t*, fusionner; se fondre; s'amalgamer.

meridian, *n. & a*, méridien, *m. & a.* **meridional,** *a. & n*, méridional, e.

meringue, *n*, meringue, *f.*

merino, *n*, mérinos, *m.*

merit, *n*, mérite, *m.* ¶ *v.t*, mériter.

meritorious, *a*, méritoire; (*of pers.*) méritant.

merlin (*bird*) *n*, émerillon, *m.*

mermaid, *n*, sirène, *f.* **merman,** *n*, triton, *m.*

merrily, *ad*, gaiement, joyeusement. **merriment,** *n*, gaieté, joie, hilarité, *f.* **merry,** *a*, gai, joyeux; jovial. *a* ~ *Christmas!* joyeux Noël! *make* ~, se réjouir, s'égayer. *make* ~ *over*, se divertir [aux dépens] de. ~-*go-round*, manège de chevaux de bois, carrousel, *m.* ~*making*, réjouissances, *f.pl.*

mesh, *n*, maille, *f. in* ~ (*Mech.*), en prise. ¶ *v.t*, s'engrener.

mesmeric, *a*, magnétique. **mesmerism,** *n*, magnétisme, *m.* **mesmerist,** *n*, magnétiseur, *m.* **mesmerize,** *v.t*, magnétiser.

mess, *n*, (*Mil., Nav.*) popote, gamelle, *f*; ordinaire; plat; (*fig.*) gâchis, margouillis, pétrin, *m*; saleté, *f.* ~ *kit*, gamelle, *f.* ~*mate*, camarade de plat, *m,f*, commensal, e. ¶ *v.t*, salir; (*v.i.*) manger. ~ *about*, tripoter. ~ *up*, gâcher.

message, *n*, message, *m*; dépêche, *f.* **messenger,** *n*, messager, ère; envoyé, e; courrier; commissionnaire; porteur; chasseur; garçon de bureau, *m.*

Messiah, *n*, Messie, *m.*

Messina, *n*, Messine, *f.*

messy, *a*, sale, graisseux.

metal, *n*, métal, *m.* ~ *saw*, scie à métaux, *f.* **metallic,** *a*, métallique; (*voice*) cuivrée. **metalliferous,** *a*, métallifère. **metallurgist,** *n*, métallurgiste, *m.* **metallurgy,** *n*, métallurgie, *f.*

metamorphose, *v.t*, métamorphoser. **metamorphosis,** *n*, métamorphose, *f.*

metaphor, *n*, métaphore, *f.* ~**ical†,** *a*, métaphorique.

metaphysical, *a*, métaphysique. **metaphysician,** *n*, métaphysicien, *m.* **metaphysics,** *n.pl*, métaphysique, *f.*

mete [**out**], *v.t*, mesurer, doser.

meteor, *n*, météore, *m.* ~**ic,** *a*, météorique. ~**ite,** *n*, aérolithe, *m.* ~**ologic(al),** *a*, météorologique. ~**ology,** *n*, météorologie, *f.*

meter, *n*, (*Meas.*) mètre; (*Poet.*) mesure, mètre; (*gasoline*) jaugeur; compteur, *m.*

method, *n*, méthode, *f*, mode, *m*, modalité, *f.* ~**ical†,** *a*, méthodique. ~**ism,** *n*, méthodisme, *m.* ~**ist,** *n*, méthodiste, *m,f.*

methyl (*Chem.*) *n*, méthyle, *m*. ~ated *spirit*, alcool dénaturé, alcool à brûler, *m*.

meticulous†, *a*, méticuleux.

metric & metrical, *a*, métrique. **metrics** (*Poet.*) *n*, métrique, *f*.

metronome, *n*, métronome, *m*.

metropolis, *n*, capitale; métropole, *f*. **metropolitan**, *a*, de la capitale; métropolitain.

mettle, *n*, fougue, *f*, panache, cran; honneur, *m*. ~**some**, *a*, fougueux.

mew, *n*, (*sea gull*) mouette; (*cage for hawks*) mue, *f*. ¶ *v.i*, miauler. ~[**ing**], *n*, miaulement, *m*. **mews**, *n*, écuries, *f.pl*.

Mexican, *a*, mexicain. ¶ *n*, Mexicain, e. **Mexico** (*country*) *n*, le Mexique. ~ [**City**], Mexico, *m*.

mezzanine [**floor**], *n*, entresol, *m*. **mezzo-relievo**, *n*, demi-relief, *m*. **mezzo-soprano**, *n*, mezzo-soprano, *m*. **mezzotint**, *n*, manière noire; gravure à la m. n., *f*.

miasma, *n*, miasme, *m*.

mica, *n*, mica, *m*.

Michaelmas, *n*, la Saint-Michel. ~ *daisy*, marguerite de la Saint-Michel, *f*.

microbe, *n*, microbe, *m*.

micrometer, *n*, micromètre, palmer, *m*.

microphone, *n*, microphone, *m*.

microscope, *n*, microscope, *m*. **microscopic**(**al**), *a*, microscopique.

mid, *a*: *in* ~ *air*, *Channel*, au milieu de l'air, de la Manche. ~*day*, midi, *m*. ~*iron* (golf), fer moyen, *m*. ~ *lent*, la micarême. ~*night*, minuit, *m*. ~*shipman*, aspirant [de marine] *m*. ~*summer*, milieu de l'été. *Midsummer Day*, la Saint-Jean; le 24 juin. ~*way*, *ad*, à moitié chemin, à mi-chemin. ~*wife*, sage-femme, *f. in* ~ *winter*, en plein hiver.

middle, *a*, du milieu; moyen. ~*aged*, d'âge moyen, entre deux âges. *M*~ *Ages*, moyen âge, *m*. ~ *class*[*es*], classe moyenne, bourgeoisie, *f*. ~*class house*, maison bourgeoise, *f*. ~*class man, woman*, bourgeois, e. ~ *course* (conduct), moyen terme, *m*. ~ *distance*, second plan, *m*. *the M*~ *East*, Moyen-Orient, *m*. ~ *finger*, doigt du milieu, médius, *m*. ~*man*, intermédiaire, *m*. ~ *register* (*Mus.*), médium, *m*. ~ [*term*] (*Log.*), moyen [terme] *m*. ~*weight* (*Box.*), poids moyen,

m. ¶ *n*, milieu; centre, *m*; (*waist*) ceinture, *f*.

middling†, *a*, moyen; médiocre. ¶ *ad*, assez bien, entre deux, comme ci, comme ça, cahin-caha. ~*s* (*flour*) *n.pl*, recoupe, *f*.

midge, *n*, moucheron, cousin, *m*.

midget, *n*, nabot, e, [petit] bout d'homme, *m*.

midnight, midshipman, *etc*. See under *mid*.

midst, *n*, milieu, sein, *m*.

mien, *n*, mine, *f*, air, *m*.

might, *n*, puissance; force, *f*. *with* ~ & *main*, de toutes ses forces. *one* ~ *as well*, autant vaut. *a* ~*have-been*, un grand homme manqué. **mightiness**, *n*, puissance; grandeur, *f*. **mighty**†, *a*, puissant. *the* ~ *ones*, les puissants, *m.pl*.

mignonette, *n*, (*Bot.*) réséda, *m*; (*lace*) mignonnette, *f*.

migrant, *a*, migrateur. **migrate**, *v.i*, émigrer. **migration**, *n*, migration *f*. **migratory**, *a*, migrateur, voyageur, de passage.

Milan, *n*, Milan, *m*. ~*ese*, *a*, milanais. ¶ *n*, Milanais, e.

milch cow, vache à lait, vache laitière; (*fig.*) vache à lait, *f*.

mild†, *a*, doux; bénin; anodin.

mildew, *n*, moisi, *m*, moisissure; (*blight on plants*) rouille, *f*; (*on vines*) mildiou, *m*. ¶ *v.t*, moisir; (*v.i.*) [se] moisir.

mildness, *n*, douceur, *f*.

mile, *n*, mille [anglais] *m*. = 1.6093 kilometers (*Note:—To convert miles to kilometers, approximately, multiply miles by 8 and divide by 5*); (*long way*) lieue, *f*. *a* ~ *off*, d'une lieue. ~*stone*, pierre milliaire; (*Fr.*) borne kilométrique, *f*.

militant, *a. & n*, militant, *a. & m*. **militarize**, *v.t*, militariser. **military**†, *a. & ~ man*, militaire, *a. & m. the* ~, les militaires, *m.pl*. ~ *pageant*, scène militaire à grand spectacle, *f*. **militate**, *v.i*, militer. **militia**, *n*, milice, *f*. ~*man*, milicien, *m*.

milk, *n*, lait, *m*. ~ *chocolate*, chocolat lacté, c. au lait, *m*. ~ *diet*, régime lacté, *m*, diète lactée, *f*. ~ *fever*, fièvre de lait, *f*. ~ *food*, laitage, *m*. ~*maid*, fille de ferme, *f*. ~*man*, ~*woman*, laitier, ère. ~*sop* (*pers.*), poule mouillée, *f*. ~ *tooth*, dent de lait, *f*. ~ *train*, wagon-laitière, *m*. ¶ *v.t*, traire, tirer. ~*er*, *n*, trayeur, euse;

(*cow*) laitière, *f*. ~**ing**, *n*, traite, mulsion, *f*. **milky**, *a*, laiteux. **M~ Way**, voie lactée, *f*.

mill, *n*, moulin, *m*; fabrique; usine, *f*; atelier, *m*. ~**board**, carton [épais] *m*. ~**hand**, ouvrier (ère) d'usine. ~**owner**, industriel, usinier, *m*. ~**stone**, meule de moulin, *f*. ~**stone grit** & ~**stone grit quarry**, meulière, *f*. ~**textile** ~, usine de textiles, *f*. ¶ *v.t*, moudre; (*ore*, etc.) bocarder, broyer; (*cloth*) fouler; (*to knurl*) moleter, (*to slot*) fraiser; (*a coin*) créneler. ~**ed edge**, cordon[net], crénelage, *m*.

millenary, *a*. & *n*, millénaire, *a*. & *m*. **millennium**, *n*, millénaire, *m*; (*fig.*) bonheur sans mélange, paradis terrestre, *m*.

millepede, *n*, mille-pieds, mille-pattes, *m*.

miller, *n*, meunier, ère, minotier, *m*; farinier, ère.

millet, *n*, millet, mil, *m*. ~ **grass**, millet, *m*.

milliner, *n*, modiste, *f*; marchand(e) de modes; chapelier, *m*. ~**'s head**, marotte, *f*. ~**y**, *n*, modes, *f.pl*, articles de modes, *m. pl*; chapeaux, *m.pl*.

milling, *n*, (*flour*) meunerie, minoterie, *f*; (*ore*) broyage; (*cloth*) foulage; (*metal*) fraisage; (*coins*) crénelage, grènetis, *m*. fraise, *f*. ~ **machine**, machine à fraiser, *f*.

million, *n*, million, *m*. **the** ~**s**, la multitude, la masse du peuple. **millionaire,** *n*, millionnaire, *m,f*. **millionth,** *a*. & *n*, millionième, *a*. & *m*.

milt, *n*, (*in mammals*) rate; (*in fish*) laitance, laite, *f*. ¶ *v.t*, féconder.

mime, *n*, mime, *m*. ¶ *v.i*, mimer. **mimic,** *a*, mimique, imitateur. ¶ *n*, mime, *m*, imitateur, trice. ¶ *v.t*, mimer, imiter, contrefaire. **mimicry,** *n*, mimique, *f*. **mimicry or mimesis** (*Zool.*) *n*, mimétisme, *m*.

mimosa, *n*, mimosa, *m*.

mince, *n*, hachis, *m*. ~**meat**, hachis, *m*. ¶ *v.t*, (*meat*) hacher [menu]; (*v.i.*) minauder. ~ **one's words,** ménager les termes; parler avec affectation. **not to** ~ **matters,** ne pas le mâcher. **mincer,** *n*, hachoir, *m*. **mincing** (*fig.*) *n*, minauderie, *f*. ¶ *a*, minaudier, mignard, affété, grimacier.

mind, *n*, esprit, *m*; âme, *f*; moral; cerveau, *m*, cervelle, *f*; envie;

idée, pensée, *f*; avis, *m*, opinion, *f*. **go out of one's** ~, perdre la raison. ¶ *v.t*, faire attention à; se soucier de; regarder à; garder. **I don't** ~, cela m'est égal. **bear in** ~, tenir compte de. **make up one's** ~, se décider. ~ **your own business!** mêlez-vous de vos affaires! ~**ed**, *a*, disposé, porté, pensant, enclin. ~**ful**, *a*, attentif.

mine, *pn*, le mien, la mienne, les miens, les miennes; à moi. **a friend of** ~, un de mes amis, un ami à moi.

mine, *n*, mine; (*fig.*) mine, *f*, filon; *m*; (*war*) mine, torpille, *f*. ~ **crater**, entonnoir, *m*. ~ **layer**, poseur de mines, *m*. ~ **sweeper**, dragueur de mines, *m*. ¶ *v.t*. & *i*, exploiter; abattre; fouiller; miner; caver; torpiller. **miner**, *n*, mineur, *m*. **mineral**, *a*. & *n*, minéral, *a*. & *m*. ~ **water**, eau minérale [naturelle] *f*. ~ [*water*], eau minérale [artificielle] *f*. **mineralogical**, *a*, minéralogique. **mineralogist**, *n*, minéralogiste, *m*. **mineralogy**, *n*, minéralogie, *f*.

mingle, *v.t*, mélanger, mêler, confondre.

miniature, *n*, miniature, *f*; diminutif, *m*. ~ **golf**, golf miniature, *m*. **miniaturist**, *n*, miniaturiste, *m,f*.

minimize, *v.t*, atténuer. **minimum,** *n*. & *a*, minimum, *m*. & *a*.

mining, *n*, exploitation [de mines] *f*; (*att.*) minier. ~ **engineer,** ingénieur [civil] des mines, *m*.

minion, *n*, mignon, favori, *m*. ~**s of the law,** recors de la justice, *m.pl*.

minister, *n*, ministre; pasteur, *m*. ~ **to,** pourvoir à; servir; (*Eccl.*) desservir. ~**ial,** *a*, ministériel. ~**ing angel,** ange de bonté, *m*; sœur de charité, *f*. **ministration,** *n*, ministère, *m*. **ministry,** *n*, ministère; département; sacerdoce, *m*.

miniver, *n*, petit-gris, *m*.

mink (*Zool.* & *fur*) *n*, vison, *m*.

minnow, *n*, vairon, *m*.

minor, *a*, petit; secondaire, subalterne; moindre; peu important; peu grave; mineur; (*repairs*) menues; (*planet*) télescopique; (*pers.*) jeune, cadet; (*poet*) de second ordre. ¶ *n*, (*pers.*) mineur, e; (*Mus.*) mineur, *m*.

Minorca, *n*, Minorque, *f*.

minority, *n*, minorité, *f*.

minster, *n,* église de monastère, é. abbatiale; cathédrale, *f.*

minstrel, *n,* (*Hist.*) ménestrel; chanteur, musicien; acteur comique, *m.*

mint, *n,* Monnaie, *f,* hôtel de la Monnaie, h. des Monnaies, *m*; (*fig.*) mine; (*Bot.*) menthe, *f. a ~ of money,* un argent fou. ¶ *v.t,* mannayer, frapper. **~er,** *n,* monnayeur, *m.*

minuet, *n,* menuet, *m.*

minus, *pr,* moins. **~** *quantity,* déficit, *m.* **~** [**sign**], *n,* [signe] moins, *m.*

minute, *a,* menu, minime, minuscule; minutieux. ¶ *n,* minute, *f,* (*pl.*) procès-verbaux, *m.* **~** *book,* registre des délibérations, r. des procès-verbaux, plumitif, *m.* **~** *hand,* aiguille des minutes, *f.* ¶ *v.t,* minuter; constater par procès-verbal. **~ly,** *ad,* minutieusement. **~ness** & **minutia,** *n,* minutie, *f.*

minx, *n,* coquine, friponne, masque, *f.*

miracle, *n,* miracle, *m.* **~** [**play**], miracle, mystère, *m.* **miraculous†,** *a,* miraculeux.

mirage, *n,* mirage, *m.*

mire, *n,* fange, boue, *f.* ¶ *v.t,* embourber.

mirror, *n,* miroir, *m,* glace, *f.* ¶ *v.t,* refléter.

mirth, *n,* joie, gaieté, *f.* **~ful†,** *a,* joyeux, gai.

miry, *a,* fangeux, boueux.

misadventure, *n,* mésaventure, *f.*

misalliance, *n,* mésalliance, *f.* *make a ~,* se mésallier. **misally,** *v.t,* mésallier.

misanthrope, -pist, *n,* misanthrope, *m.* **misanthropic(al),** *a,* misanthropique, misanthrope.

misapply, *v.t,* mal appliquer; détourner.

misapprehend, *v.t,* mal comprendre. **misapprehension,** *n,* malentendu, *m.*

misappropriate, *v.t,* détourner, dilapider.

misbehave [**oneself**], se comporter mal. **misbehavior,** *n,* mauvaise conduite, inconduite, *f.*

miscalculate, *v.i,* se tromper. **miscalculation,** *n,* erreur de calcul, *f,* mécompte, *m.*

miscarriage, *n,* (*letter, etc.*) égarement, *m*; (*Med.*) fausse couche, *f*; (*failure*) avortement, insuccès, *m.* **~** *of justice,* erreur judiciaire, *f.* **miscarry,** *v.i,* s'égarer; (*Med.*) faire une fausse couche; (*fail*) avorter, échouer, rater.

miscellaneous, *a,* divers; ·mêlé. **~** *works* or **miscellany** or **miscellanea,** *n,* mélanges, *m.pl,* variétés, *f.pl,* recueil factice, *m.*

mischance, *n,* infortune, fatalité, *f.*

mischief, *n,* mal; (*playful*) espièglerie, *f.* **~** *maker,* boutefeu, *m.* **mischievous†,** *a,* méchant; espiègle.

misconceive, *v.i,* mal concevoir. **misconception,** *n,* malentendu, *m.*

misconduct, *n,* déportements, *m.pl.,* inconduite, *f.* **~** *oneself,* se conduire mal.

misconstruction, *n,* contresens, *m.* **misconstrue,** *v.t,* prendre à rebours.

miscreant, *n,* gredin, scélérat, *m.*

miscue, *n,* faux coup de queue, *m.*

misdeal (*cards*) *n,* maldonne, *f.*

misdeed, *n,* méfait, *m.*

misdeliver, *v.t,* livrer par erreur.

misdemeanant, *n,* délinquant, e. **misdemeanor,** *n,* délit, *m.*

misdirect, *v.t,* mal diriger; (*a letter*) se tromper d'adresse sur.

miser, *n,* avare, *m,f,* harpagon, *m.*

miserable†, *a,* misérable, malheureux; chétif.

miserere, *n,* miserere, *m.*

misericord, *n,* miséricorde, *f.*

miserly, *a,* avare.

misery, *n,* misère, *f*; souffrances, *f.pl.*

misfire, *n,* raté [d'allumage] *m.* ¶ *v.i,* rater, manquer.

misfit, *n,* vêtement mal ajusté, v. manqué, *m*; chaussure manquée, *f.*

misfortune, *n,* malheur, *m,* infortune, adversité, disgrâce, misère, *f.*

misgiving, *n,* doute; pressentiment, *m.*

misgovern, *v.t,* mal gouverner. **~ment,** *n,* mauvais gouvernement, *m.*

misguide, *v.t,* égarer; abuser. **misguided,** *p.p,* mal dirigé, dévoyé.

mishap, *n,* contretemps, *m,* mésaventure, *f.*

misinform, *v.t,* mal renseigner.

misinterpretation, *n,* contresens, *m.*

misjudge, *v.t,* mal juger.

mislay, *v.t,* égarer.

mislead, *v.t,* égarer, fourvoyer,

abuser; induire en erreur; tromper. ~ing, *p.a*, décevant, fallacieux.

mismanage, *v.t*, mal faire, mal gérer. ~ment, *n*, mauvaise gestion, *f*.

misnamed, *p.p*, mal nommé.

misnomer, *n*, erreur de nom, *f*.

misogynist, *n*, misogyne, *m*.

misplace, *v.t*, mal placer.

misprint, *n*, faute d'impression, erreur typographique, coquille, *f*.

mispronounce, *v.t*, mal prononcer. **mispronunciation,** *n*, vice de prononciation, *m*.

misquotation, *n*, citation inexacte, *f*. **misquote,** *v.t*, citer à faux.

misrepresent, *v.t*, représenter mal, travestir, dénaturer. ~ation, *n*, travestissement, *m*; déclaration inexacte, *f*.

misrule, *n*, mauvaise administration, *f*.

miss, *n*, manque [à toucher] *m*; demoiselle, *f*. *M*~, mademoiselle; Mademoiselle, *f*. ¶ *v.t. & i*, manquer; rater; regretter; sauter. ~ *fire*, rater, manquer. ~ *the point*, porter à faux.

missal, *n*, missel, *m*.

misshapen, *a*, contrefait, biscornu, difforme, malbâti.

missile, *n*, projectile, *m*.

missing, *a*, manquant; (*ship*) [perdu] sans nouvelles. ~ *link*, chaînon manquant, *m*. *the* ~ (*Mil.*), les disparus, *m.pl*. *be* ~, manquer.

mission, *n*, mission, *f*. ~ary, *n*, missionnaire, *m*. **missive,** *n*, missive, *f*.

misspell, *v.t*, mal orthographier. ~ing, *n*, faute d'orthographe, *f*.

misstatement, *n*, déclaration inexacte, *f*.

mist, *n*, brouillard, *m*, brume; brouillasse; vapeur, *f*, nuage, voile, *m*.

mistake, *n*, erreur, faute, bévue; méprise, *f*, quiproquo, tort, *m*. ¶ *v.t.ir*, se méprendre sur, se tromper de, confondre. **mistaken,** *a*, erroné. ~ *identity*, erreur de (*ou* sur la) personne, *f*. ~ *kindness*, indulgence mal comprise, *f*. *be* ~, se tromper.

mister, *n*, monsieur, *m*.

mistletoe, *n*, gui, *m*.

mistranslation, *n*, contresens, *m*.

mistreat, *v.t*, maltraiter.

mistress, *n*, maîtresse; patronne; institutrice, *f*; professeur, *m*; madame, *f*. *be one's own* ~, s'appartenir.

mistrust, *n*, méfiance, défiance, *f*. ¶ *v.t*, se méfier de, se défier de. ~ful, *a*, méfiant, défiant.

misty, *a*, brumeux; vaporeux; trouble.

misunderstand, *v.t.ir*, mal comprendre, méconnaître. ~ing, *n*, malentendu, *m*; mésintelligence, brouille, *f*; quiproquo, *m*. **misunderstood** (*pers.*) *p.a*, incompris.

misuse, *n*, abus, *m*. ¶ *v.t*, abuser de; maltraiter.

mite, *n*, (*farthing*) obole, *f*, denier, *m*; (*child*) petit, e; (*insect*) mite, *f*, acare, ciron, *m*.

miter, *n*, (*bishop's*) mitre, *f*; (*Carp.*) onglet, *m*. ~ed, *a*, mitré; (*Carp.*) à onglet.

mitigate, *v.t*, atténuer; mitiger; modérer.

mitt[en], *n*, moufle, mitaine, *f*.

mix, *v.t*, mêler, mélanger, malaxer; (*salad*) retourner. **mixed,** *a*, mêlé; mixte; hétérogène. ~ *bathing*, bain mixte, *m*. ~ *double* (*Ten.*), double mixte, *m*. ~ *metaphor*, métaphore incohérente, *f*. **mixture,** *n*, mélange, *m*; mixture, *f*; ambigu, *m*; (*Med.*) mixtion, *f*; (*fodder*) farrago; (*cloth*) drap mélangé, *m*. *wool* ~, laine mélangée, *f*.

miz[z]en [*sail*], *n*. & **miz[z]en mast,** artimon, *m*.

mizzle, *n*, bruine, *f*. ¶ *v.imp*, bruiner.

mnemonic, *a*, mnémonique. ~s, *n.pl*, la mnémonique.

moan, *n*, gémissement, *m*, plainte, *f*. ¶ *v.i*, gémir, se plaindre.

moat, *n*, fossé, *m*, douve, *f*.

mob, *n*, foule; canaille, populace, *f*. ~ *law*, la loi de la populace, *f*. ¶ *v.t*, houspiller.

mobile, *a*, mobile. **mobility,** *n*, mobilité, *f*.

mocha, *n*, moka, *m*. *mocha coffee* or *mocha*, *n*, café de Moka, moka, *m*.

mock, *v.t*, se moquer de; singer. ¶ *a*, faux, imité. ~ *fight*, simulacre de combat, *m*. ~-*heroic*, héroï-comique. ~er, *n*, moqueur, euse. ~ery, *n*, moquerie, *f*. ~ing bird, [oiseau] moqueur, *m*.

mode, *n*, (*way, fashion*) mode, *f*; (*form, method*) mode, *m*.

model, *n*, modèle, *m*; maquette, *f*; mannequin, *m*; (*att.*) modèle. ¶ *v.t*, modeler. ~er, *n*, modeleur, *m.* ~**ing,** *n,* modelage; modelé, *m.*

moderate, *a,* modéré; (*price*) modique. ¶ *v.t,* modérer, tempérer. ~**ly,** *ad,* modérément, moyennement. ~**ness,** *n,* modicité, *f.* **moderation,** *n,* modération, *f.*

modern, *a. & n,* moderne, *a. & m.* ~ *language,* langue vivante, *f.* ~**ize,** *v.t,* moderniser.

modest†, *a,* modeste. ~**y,** *n,* modestie, *f.*

modicum, *n,* petite quantité; légère dose, *f,* grain, *m.*

modification, *n,* modification, *f.* **modify,** *v.t,* modifier.

modish, *a,* à la mode, de mode. ~**ly,** *ad,* à la mode.

modulate, *v.t,* moduler. **modulation,** *n,* modulation, *f.* **module** & **modulus,** *n,* module, *m.*

modus operandi, mode d'opération, *m.*

mohair, *n,* poil de chèvre d'Angora, mohair, *m.*

Mohammedan, *n. & a,* mahométan, e. ~**ism,** *n,* mahométisme, *m.*

moiety, *n,* moitié, *f.*

moil, *v.i,* peiner.

moire, *n,* moire, *f.* **moiré,** *v.t,* moirer. ~ *silk,* moire de soie, soie moirée, *f.*

moist, *a,* humide; moite. ~**en,** *v.t,* humecter; mouiller. ~**ness** & ~**ure,** *n,* humidité; moiteur; buée, *f.*

molar, *a. & n,* molaire, *a. & f.*

molasses, *n,* mélasse, *f.*

mold, *n,* moule, creux, *m;* (*Typ.*) empreinte, *f,* flan; (*vegetable*) terreau, humus, *m;* (*ship*) gabarit; (*decay*) moisi, *m,* moisissure, *f.* ¶ *v.t,* mouler; modeler; (*Typ.*) prendre l'empreinte de. ~**er,** *n,* mouleur, *m.* ~**er** [**away**], *v.i,* tomber en poussière. **moldiness,** *n,* moisissure, *f,* moisi, *m.* **molding,** *n,* (*act*) moulage, *m;* (*ornamental strip*) moulure, *f.* **moldy,** *a,* moisi. *turn* ~, [se] moisir.

mole, *n,* nævus, *m,* couenne, *f,* grain de beauté; (*jetty*) môle, *m;* (*Zool.*) taupe, *f.* ~**hill,** taupinière, *f.* ~**skin,** [fourrure de] taupe; moleskine, *f.* ~ *trap,* taupière, *f.*

molecular, *a,* moléculaire. **molecule,** *n,* molécule, *f.*

molest, *v.t,* tourmenter, inquiéter, importuner. ~**ation,** *n,* importunité, *f.*

mollify, *v.t,* amollir; adoucir.

mollusk, *n,* mollusque, *m.*

molt, *v.i,* se déplumer.

molten, *p.p,* fondu, en fusion, en bain.

Moluccas (**the**), les Moluques, *f.pl.*

moment, *n,* moment; instant, *m;* importance, *f. a* ~ *ago,* à l'instant. ~**ary**†, *a,* momentané, passager. ~**ous,** *a,* de la dernière importance. **momentum,** *n,* (*Mech.*) moment; (*impetus*) élan, *m.*

monarch, *n,* monarque, *m.* ~**ic(al),** *a,* monarchique. ~**ist,** *n,* monarchiste, *m.* ~**y,** *n,* monarchie, *f.*

monastery, *n,* monastère, couvent, *m.* **monastic,** *a,* monastique, monacal. **monastically,** *ad,* monacalement.

Monday, *n,* lundi, *m.*

monetary, *a,* monétaire. **monetize,** *v.t,* transformer en monnaie. **money,** *n,* argent, *m;* monnaie, *f;* numéraire, *m;* fonds, *m.pl;* capital, *m,* capitaux, *m.pl;* valeurs; finances, *f.pl;* deniers, *m.pl.* ~ *changer,* changeur, *m.* ~ *box,* tirelire; cassette, grenouillère, *f.* ~ *grubber* grippesou, *m.* ~**lender,** bailleur de fonds, *m.* ~ *order,* mandat [de poste] *m.* ~**ed,** *a,* fortuné.

Mongolia, *n,* la Mongolie. **Mongol[ian],** *a,* mongol. ¶ *n,* Mongol, e.

mongoose, *n,* mangouste, *f.*

mongrel, *a,* métis, bâtard, mâtiné. ¶ *n,* métis, se, bâtard, e; (*cur*) roquet, *m.*

monk, *n,* moine, religieux, *m.* ~'**s-hood** (*Bot.*), aconit, napel, *m.* ~**ery** & ~**hood,** *n,* moinerie, *f.* ~**ish,** *a,* monacal.

monkey, *n,* singe, *m,* (*she*) guenon, guenuche, *f;* (*pile driving*) mouton, *m.* ~ *house,* singerie, *f.* ~ *trick,* singerie, *f.* ~ *wrench,* clef anglaise, *f.*

monochord, *n,* monocorde, *m.* **monochrome,** *a,* monochrome. **monocle,** *n,* monocle, *m.* **monogamy,** *n,* monogamie, *f.* **monogram,** *n,* monogramme, chiffre, *m.* **monograph,** *n,* monographie, *f.* **monolith,** *n,* & ~**ic,** *a,* monolithe, *m. & a.* **monologize,** *v.i,* monologuer. **monologue,** *n,* monologue, *m.* **monomania,** *n,* monomanie, *f.* **monoplane,** *n,* monoplan, *m.* **monopolist,** *n,* accapareur, euse. **monopolize,** *v.t,* monopoliser, accaparer, s'emparer de. **monopoly,** *n,* monopole, *m.* **monosyllabic**, *a*, mono-syllabique, monosyllable. **mono-syllable**, *n*, monosyllabe, *m.* **monotonist** (*pers.*) *n*, mono-corde, *m.* **monotonous**, *a*, mono-tone. **monotony**, *n*, monotonie, *f.* **monotype**, *n*, monotype, *f.*

monster, *n. & a*, monstre, *m. & att.*

monstrance, *n*, ostensoir, *m.*

monstrosity, *n*, monstruosité, *f.* **monstrous**†, *a*, monstrueux.

Mont Blanc, le mont Blanc. **Montenegrin**, *a*, monténégrin. ¶ *n*, Monténégrin, e. **Montenegro**, *n*, le Monténégro. **Monte Rosa**, le mont Rose.

month, *n*, mois, *m.* ~'s pay, rent, or like, mois, *m.* ~ly, *a*, mensuel; au mois. ~ *payment*, *drawing*, *salary*, *or like*, mensualité, *f.* ~ *statement* (*Com.*), relevé de fin de mois, *m.* ¶ *ad*, mensuellement, par mois. ¶ *n*, revue mensuelle, *f.*

monument, *n*, monument; (*tomb-stone*) tombeau, *m.* ~al, *a*, mo-numental.

moo, *v.i*, beugler. ¶ *n*, beugle-ment, *m.*

mood, *n*, humeur, *f*, train; (*Gram.*) mode, *m.* ~y, *a*, morose, chagrin.

moon, *n*, lune, *f.* ~beam, rayon de l., *m.* ~light, clair de l., *m.* ~lit, éclairé par la l. ~shine, contes en l'air, *m.pl.* ~stone, pierre de lune, *f.* ~struck, toqué. ~ [about], muser.

moor & ~land, *n*, lande, brande, bruyère, *f.* ~cock, coq de bru-yère *m.* ~hen, poule d'eau, *f.*

Moor (*pers.*) *n.* More, Maure, *m.*

moor, *v.t*, amarrer, mouiller. ~ing, *n*, amarrage, mouillage; (*pl.*) mouillage, *m.*

Moorish, *a*, more, maure.

moose, *n*, élan, *m.*

moot, *a*, discutable, contestable. ¶ *v.t*, soulever.

mop, *n*, balai à laver; (*Naut.*) écouvillon, *m*; (*of hair*) tignasse, *f.* ¶ *v.t*, éponger. ~ *up*, essuyer, éponger.

mope, *v.i*, languir.

moraine, *n*, moraine, *f.*

moral†, *a*, moral. ¶ *n*, (*of story*, *of fable*) morale, moralité, *f*; (*pl*, *manners*) mœurs, *f.pl*; (*pl*, *ethics*) morale, *f.* ~[e], *n*, moral, *m.* ~ist, *n*, moraliste, *m.* ~ity, *n*, moralité, *f*; [bonnes] mœurs, *f.pl.* ~ize, *v.i. & t*, moraliser.

morass, *n*, fondrière, *f*, marais, marécage, *m.*

moratorium, *n*, moratorium, moratoire, *m.*

Moravia, *n*, la Moravie.

morbid, *a*, morbide, maladif. ~ness, *n*, état maladif, *m.*

mordant, *a. & n*, mordant, *a. & m.*

more, *a*, plus de; plus. ¶ *ad*, plus; davantage; encore; de plus. *all the* ~, d'autant plus. *never* ~, jamais plus. ~ *and* ~, de plus en plus. ~over, *ad*, d'ailleurs, aussi bien, en outre, du reste, encore.

moresque, *a*, moresque, maures-que.

morganatic†, *a*, morganatique.

moribund, *a*, moribond.

morning, *a* (*Poet.*) **morn**, *n*, matin, *m*; matinée; aurore, *f.* ~ *star*, étoile du matin, é. matinière, *f.*

Moroccan, *a*, marocain. ¶ *n*, Ma-rocain, e. **Morocco**, *n*, le Maroc. *morocco* [*leather*], maroquin, *m.*

morose, *a*, morose. ~ness, *n*, morosité, *f.*

Morpheus, *n*, Morphée, *m.* **mor-phia**, **-phine**, *n*, morphine, *f.*

morrow (**the**) & **on the** ~, le lendemain.

morsel, *n*, morceau, *m.*

mortal†, *a*, mortel; (*strife*) à mort, à outrance. ¶ *n*, mortel, le. ~ity, *n*, mortalité, *f.*

mortar (*plaster*, *vessel*, *Mil.*) *n*, mortier, *m.*

mortgage, *n*, hypothèque, *f.* ¶ *v.t*, hypothéquer; engager. **mortga-gee**, *n*, créancier hypothécaire, *m.* **mortgagor**, *n*, débiteur h., *m.*

mortification, *n*, mortification, *f.* **mortify**, *v.t*, mortifier, affliger, mater.

mortise, *n*, mortaise, *f.* ¶ *v.t*, emmortaiser.

mortmain, *n*, mainmorte, *f.* *prop-erty in* ~, biens de mainmorte, *m.pl.*

mortuary, *a*, mortuaire. ¶ *n*, in-stitut médico-légal; établissement de pompes funèbres, *m.*

Mosaic (*of Moses*) *a*, mosaïque.

mosaic, *n*, mosaïque, marqueterie, *f.*

Moscow, *n*, Moscou, *m.*

Moslem, *n. & a*, mahométan, e.

mosque, *n*, mosquée, *f.*

mosquito, *n*, moustique; marin-gouin, *m.* ~ *net*, ~ *curtain*, moustiquaire, *f.*

moss, *n*, mousse, *f.* ~y, *a*, mous-seux; moussu.

most, *a*, le plus de; la plupart de.

~ *eminent*, éminentissime. ~ *il-lustrious*, illustrissime. ~ *reverend*, révérendissime. ¶ *ad*, le plus; plus; très. ~**ly**, *ad*, pour la plupart.

mote, *n*, (*dust*) atome, *m*; (*in eye*, *fig.*) paille, *f*.

moth, *n*, papillon [de nuit] *m*; teigne, gerce, *f*, artison; ver, *m*, mite, *f*. ~*ball*, boule de naphtaline, *f*. ~*-eaten*, mangé aux mites, artisonné.

mother, *n*, mère, *f*. ~ *church*, église métropolitaine, *f*. ~ *earth*, notre mère commune. ~*hood*, maternité, *f*. ~*-in-law*, belle-mère, *f*. ~*-of-pearl*, nacre, *f*. ~*'s side* (*family*), côté maternel, *m*. ~ *superior*, mère supérieure, *f*. ~ *tongue*, (*native*) langue maternelle; (*original*) l. mère, *f*. ~ *wit*, esprit naturel, *m*. ¶ *v.t*, servir de mère à; (*fig.*) couver. ~**less**, *a*, sans mère. ~**ly**, *a*, maternel, de mère.

motif, *n*, (*art, Need.*) motif, *m*; (*literary*) donnée, *f*. **motion**, *n*, mouvement, *m*, marche, *f*; signe, *m*; (*proposal*) motion; proposition, *f*. ¶ *v.i*, faire signe. ~**less**, *a*, sans mouvement, immobile. **motive**, *a*, moteur. ~ *power*, force motrice, *f*, mobile, *m*. ¶ *n*, raison, *f*; motif; mobile, *m*.

motley, *a*, bariolé, bigarré; mêlé. ¶ *n*, bariolage; habit d'arlequin, *m*.

motor, *n*, moteur, *m*. ~ [*bi*]*cycle*, motocyclette, bicyclette à moteur, moto, *f*. ~ *boat*, canot automobile, *m*, vedette, *f*. ~ *bus*, autobus, *m*. ~ [*car*], automobile, auto, *f*. ~ *coach*, autocar, *m*. ~ *cyclist*, motocycliste, *m,f*. ~*man*, machiniste, *m*. ~ *road*, autoroute, *f*. ~ *show*, salon de l'automobile, *m*. ¶ *v.i*, aller en auto. ~**ing**, *n*, automobilisme, *m*. ~**ist**, *n*, automobiliste, *m,f*. ~**ize**, *v.t*, mécaniser.

mottled, *a*, marbré.

motto, *n*, devise; (*prefixed to book or chapter*) épigraphe, *f*.

mound, *n*, monticule, *m*, butte, *f*, tertre, *m*, bosse, motte, *f*.

mount, *n*, (*as Etna*) le mont; carton [pour montage photographique] *m*; (*horse, etc.*) monture; (*horse racing*) monte, *f*. ¶ *v.i. & t*, monter.

mountain, *n*, montagne, *f*. ~ *ash*, sorbier des oiseaux, *m*. ~ *sickness*, mal de montagne, *m*.

~**eer**, *n*, (*dweller*) montagnard, e; (*climber*) alpiniste, ascensionniste, *m,f*. ~**eering**, *n*, l'alpinisme, *m*. ~**ous**, *a*, montagneux; énorme.

mountebank, *n*, saltimbanque; baladin, *m*.

mounted, *p.a*, à cheval; monté. **mounter**, *n*, monteur, *m*. **mounting**, *n*, montage, *m*; monture; ferrure, *f*.

mourn, *v.t. & i*, pleurer. **the** ~**ers**, le deuil. (*hired*) ~**er**, pleureur, euse. ~**ful†**, *a*, douloureux. ~**ing**, *n*, deuil, *m*. ~ *band*, brassard de d., *m*.

mouse, *n*, souris, *f*; (*young*) souriceau, *m*. ~*trap*, souricière, *f*.

moustache, *n*, moustache, *f*. ~**d**, *a*, moustachu.

mouth, *n*, bouche; embouchure; (*vulgar*) gueule, *f*; bec; orifice; trou, *m*; entrée, *f*. ~ *organ*, harmonica à bouche, *m*. ~*piece*, embouchure, *f*; bec; (*pers.*) organe; porte-parole, *m*. ~*wash*, eau dentifrice, *f*. ~**ful**, *n*, bouchée, goulée, gorgée, *f*.

movable, *a*, mobile; (*law*) meuble, mobilier. **move**, *n*, mouvement, *m*; manœuvre, *f*; (*chess, etc.*) coup, *m*. *whose* ~ *is it?* à qui à jouer? ¶ *v.t*, [faire] mouvoir; remuer; déplacer; jouer; affecter; toucher; émouvoir; attendrir; proposer; (*v.i.*) se mouvoir; bouger; déloger. ~ *along*, cheminer. ~ *back*, reculer. ~ *in* (*house*), emménager. ~ *off*, s'éloigner, s'ébranler. ~ *on!* circulez! ~ [*out*] (*house*), déménager. ~**ment**, *n*, mouvement, *m*, marche, *f*; geste, *m*. **moving**, *a*, mouvant; touchant.

movie, *n*, cinéma, film, *m*.

mow, *v.t.ir*, faucher; tondre. ~ *down*, faucher. ~**er**, *n*, (*pers.*) faucheur, *m*; (*Mach.*) faucheuse; (*lawn*) tondeuse, *f*.

Mr, Monsieur, M.; (*partner in firm*) sieur; (*courtesy title of lawyers*) maître, *m*. **Mrs**, Madame, Mme; (*law*) la dame.

much, *a. & ad*, beaucoup (de); grand-chose (*usually with neg.*); bien (de); très; cher. *as* ~, autant (de). *as* ~ *as*, autant que. *how* ~? combien? *so* ~, [au]tant (de). *too* ~, trop. *very* ~, beaucoup.

mucilage, *n*, mucilage, *m*.

muck, *n*, fumier, *m*; fange; cochonnerie; saloperie, *f*.

mucous, *a*, muqueux. ~ *membrane*, [membrane] muqueuse, *f*.

mucus, *n,* mucosité, *f,* mucus, *m,* pituite, morve, *f.*

mud, *n,* boue, *f. oft. pl,* crotte, bourbe, fange; *(river)* vase, *f,* limon, *m.* ~ *bath,* brain de boue- [s minérales] *m.* ~*guard,* garde- boue, *m.* ~*lark,* barboteur, *m.* ~ *pie,* pâté, *m.* ~ *spring,* source boueuse, *f.*

muddle, *n,* [em]brouillamini; fouil- lis, *m.* ¶ *v.t,* [em]brouiller, em- mêler; *(with drink)* griser. ~ *up,* tripoter. **muddler,** *n,* barboteur, euse, fatrassier, ère, brouillon, ne.

muddy, *a,* boueux, crotté, bour- beux, fangeux; vaseux, limoneux; trouble. ¶ *v.t,* embouer.

muezzin, *n,* muezzin, *m.*

muff, *n,* manchon; *(pers.)* serin, *m,* jobard, e, huître, *f.* **muffle** *(Chem.) n,* moufle, *m.* ¶ *v.t,* as- sourdir; *(drum)* voiler. ~ *up,* embéguiner, emmitoufler. ~**d** *p.a,* sourd. **muffler,** *n,* cache-nez; *(auto)* amortisseur de son, *m.*

mufti (in), en civil, en bourgeois.

mug, *n,* timbale, tasse, *f,* pot, *m.*

muggy, *a,* mou.

mulatto, *n,* mulâtre, *m,* mulâ- tresse, *f.* ¶ *a,* mulâtre.

mulberry, *n,* mûre, *f.* ~ [*tree*], mûrier, *m.*

mulch, *n,* paillis, *m.* ¶ *v.t,* pailler.

mulct, *v.t,* frapper d'une amende.

mule, *n, (he & pers.)* mulet, *m,* *(she)* mule, *f;* *(pl, slippers)* mules, babouches, *f.pl.* ~ *track,* piste muletière, *f.* **muleteer,** *n,* muletier, *m.* **mulish,** *a,* têtu.

mulled wine, vin brûlé, *m.*

muller *(grinding), n,* molette, *f.*

mullet, *n, (gray)* mulet, muge; *(red)* rouget, *m.*

mullion, *n,* meneau, *m.*

multicolor[ed], *a,* multicolore.

multifarious, *a,* multiple.

multimillionaire, *n. & a,* mil- liardaire, *m,f. & a.*

multiple, *n. & a,* multiple, *m. & a.* **multiplicand,** *n,* multiplicande, *m.* **multiplication,** *n,* multiplica- tion, *f.* **multiplicity,** *n,* multipli- cité, *f.* **multiplier,** *n,* multiplica- teur, *m.* **multiply,** *v.t,* multiplier; *(v.i.)* [se] m.; peupler.

multitude, *n,* multitude, *f.*

mum['s the word], motus!, bou- che close!

mumble, *v.i,* marmotter, balbu- tier, barboter.

mummer, *n,* cabotin, e. ~**y,** *n,* momerie, *f.*

mummify, *v.t,* momifier. **mummy,** *n,* momie; *(mother)* maman, *f.*

mumps, *n, (Med.)* oreillons, *m.pl.*

munch, *v.i,* croquer.

mundane, *a,* du monde, de ce m.; mondain.

municipal, *a,* municipal. ~**ity,** *n,* municipalité, *f.*

munificence, *n,* munificence, *f.* **munificent,** *a,* magnifique.

muniment, *n,* acte, titre, *m.*

munitions, *n.pl,* provisions de guerre, munitions de guerre, *f.pl.*

mural, *a,* mural.

murder, *n,* meurtre, assassinat, *m.* ~! à l'assasin! ¶ *v.t,* assassiner; *(fig.)* massacrer; *(language)* es- tropier, écorcher. ~**er,** ~**ess,** *n,* meurtrier, ère, assassin, e. ~**ous,** *a,* meurtrier.

murky, *a,* sombre, obscur, téné- breux.

murmur, *n,* murmure, *m.* ¶ *v.i. & t,* murmurer; bruire.

murrain, *n,* peste, *f.*

muscat [grape, wine], [raisin, vin] muscat, *m.* **muscatels,** *n.pl,* rai- sins secs muscats, *m.pl.*

muscle, *n,* muscle, *m.* -**muscled,** *a,* musclé. **muscular,** *a, (force)* musculaire; *(pers.)* musculeux.

Muse, *n,* Muse, *f;* génie, *m.*

muse, *v.i,* méditer; rêver, rêvasser.

museum, *n,* musée; *(natural his- tory)* muséum, *m.*

mush, *n,* bouillie, *f.*

mushroom, *n,* champignon [co- mestible] *m;* *(att.)* éphémère, d'un jour. ~ *bed,* champignon- nière, *f.*

music, *n,* musique, *f.* ~ *case,* porte-musique, *m.* ~ *hall,* music- hall, *m.* ~ *master,* professeur de musique, *m.* ~ *stand,* pupitre à m., *m.* **musical,** *a,* musical; chan- tant; *(pers.)* musicien. ~ *box,* boîte à musique, *f.* ~ *chairs,* chaises musicales, *f.pl.* ~ *clock,* horloge à carillon, *f.* ~ *comedy,* opéra bouffe, *f.* ~ *director,* direc- teur musical, chef de théâtre, *m.* ~ *ear,* oreille pour la musique, *f.* ~ *instrument,* instrument de mu- sique, *m;* *(toy)* musique, *f.* ~ *instrument maker,* luthier, *m.* ~ *interlude,* entracte de musique, *m.* ~ *play,* opérette, *f.* ~**e,** soirée musicale, *f.* **musician,** *n,* musi- cien, ne.

musing, *n,* rêverie, *f.*

musk, *n,* musc, *m.* ~ *deer,* [porte-] musc, chevrotin, *m.* ~**rat,** rat musqué, *m.* ~ *rose,* rose muscade, *f. to* [*perfume with*] ~, musquer.

musket, *n,* mousquet, *m.* ~**eer** (*Hist.*) *n,* mousquetaire, *m.* ~**ry** (*Mil.*) *n,* tir, *m,* exercices de tir, *m.pl.*

Muslim, *n. & a,* mahométan, e.

muslin, *n,* mousseline, *f.*

musquash, *n,* rat musqué; (*fur*) castor du Canada, *m.*

muss, *v.t,* déranger.

mussel, *n,* moule, *f.*

Mussulman, *n. & a,* musulman, e, *m,f. & f. att.*

must, *v.aux.ir,* falloir; devoir.

must, *n,* (*grapes*) moût, *m.*

mustard, *n,* moutarde; (*Bot.*) moutarde, *f,* sénévé, *m.* ~ *gas,* gaz moutarde, *m,* ypérite, *f.* ~ *maker* & ~ *pot,* moutardier, *m.* ~ *plaster,* sinapisme, *m.* ~ *sauce,* sauce moutarde, *f.* ~ *seed,* graine de m., *f,* sénévé, *m.* ~ *spoon,* cuiller à m., pelle à m., *f.*

muster, *n,* appel [nominal] *m.* ~ *roll,* feuille d'appel, *f.* ¶ *v.t,* faire l'appel de; rassembler.

musty, *a* moisi; (*smell*) de renfermé.

mutability, *n,* mutabilité, *f.* **mutation,** *n,* mutation, *f.*

mute, *a,* muet; sourd. ¶ *n,* muet, te; (*Mus.*) sourdine, *f.* ~**d,** *p.a,* sourd; en sourdine. ~**ly,** *ad,* en silence.

mutilate, *v.t,* mutiler. **mutilation,** *n,* mutilation, *f.*

mutineer, *n,* mutin, révolté, *m.* **mutinous,** *a,* mutin. **mutiny,** *n,* mutinerie, révolte, *f.* ¶ *v.i,* [se] mutiner, se révolter.

mutter, *v.i,* murmurer [entre ses dents], marmotter; (*of thunder*) gronder.

mutton, *n,* mouton, *m.* ~ *chop,* côtelette de mouton, *f.*

mutual†, *a,* mutuel; réciproque; partagé. ~ *association,* mutualité, *f.* ~ *loan association,* mutualité de crédit. *on* ~ *terms* (engagement), au pair. ~**ity,** *n,* mutualité; réciprocité, *f.*

muzzle, *n,* (*animal*) museau, *m;* (*gun*) bouche, gueule; (*for dog*) muselière, *f.* ~-*loading,* se chargeant par la bouche. ¶ *v.t,* museler.

my, *a,* mon, ma; mes.

myopia, *n,* myopie, *f.* **myopic,** *a,* myope.

myriad, *n,* myriade, *f.* e, *m.*

myriapod, *n,* myriapode, *m.*

myrmidon, *n,* suppôt, *m.*

myrrh, *n,* myrrhe, *f.*

myrtle, *n,* myrte, *m.* ~ *berry,* baie de m., *f.*

myself, *pn,* moi-même; moi; me.

mysterious†, *a,* mystérieux. **mystery,** *n,* mystère, *m.* ~ [*play*], mystère, miracle, *m.* **mystic** (*pers.*) *n,* mystique, *m,f.* ~(**al**)† , *a,* mystique. **mysticalness,** *n,* mysticité, *f.* **mysticism,** *n,* mysticisme, *m.* **mystify,** *v.t,* mystifier.

myth, *n,* mythe, *m.* ~**ic(al),** *a,* mythique. ~**ologic(al),** *a,* mythologique. ~**ologist,** *n,* mythologue, *m,f.* ~**ology,** *n,* mythologie, *f.*

N

nab, *v.t,* saisir, arrêter.

nabob, *n,* nabab, *m.*

nadir, *n,* nadir, *m.*

nag, *n,* bidet, *m.* ~ (*at*), *v.t. & i,* criailler (après), quereller. **nagging,** *p.a,* hargneux.

naiad, *n,* naïade, *f.*

nail, *n,* (*finger, toe*) ongle; (*metal*) clou, *m;* pointe, *f. hit the* ~ *on the head,* tomber juste. ~ *brush,* brosse à ongles, *f.* ~ *extractor,* arrache-clou, *m.* ~ *file,* lime à ongles, *f.* ~ *maker,* cloutier, *m.* ~ *scissors,* ciseaux à ongles, *m. pl.* ~ [*up*], *v.t,* clouer.

naïve†, *a,* naïf. **naïvety,** *n,* naïveté, *f.*

naked, *a,* nu; à nu; ras. *with the* ~ *eye,* à l'œil nu. ~**ly** (*fig.*) *ad,* nûment. ~**ness,** *n,* nudité, *f.*

namby-pamby, *a,* fade.

name, *n,* nom, *m;* dénomination; raison, *f;* intitulé, *m;* renommée; réputation, *f. by* ~, (*to mention*) nommément; (*be called on*) nominativement. *Christian* ~, nom de baptême, *m. my* ~ *is Adam,* je m'appelle Adam, je me nomme A. ~ *plate,* plaque de porte, *f.* ~*sake,* homonyme, *m.* ~*nick*~, sobriquet, *m.* ¶ *v.t,* nommer; dénommer; intituler. ~**less,** *a,* sans nom. ~**ly,** *ad,* [à] savoir; (*of pers.*) nommément.

nankeen, *n,* nankin, *m.*

nanny, *n,* (*nursemaid*) nounou, *f.* ~ [*goat*], chèvre, bique, *f.*

nap, *n,* (*sleep*) somme, *m,* sieste, *f;* (*pile*) poil; duvet, *m. to catch napping,* prendre au dépourvu. ¶ *v.i,* sommeiller.

nape [*of the neck*], *n,* nuque, *f.*

naphtha, n, naphte, m. **naphtha-lene,** n, naphtaline, f.

napkin, n, serviette [de table]. ~ *ring,* rond de serviette, m.

narcissus, n, narcisse, m.

narcotic, a, narcotique. ¶ n, narcotique, stupéfiant, m.

narrate, v.t, narrer, raconter. **narration & narrative,** n, narration, f, récit, m. **narrative,** a, narratif. **narrator,** n, narrateur, trice, conteur, euse.

narrow†, a, étroit, resserré. *to have a ~ escape,* l'échapper belle. ~*-gauge railway,* chemin de fer à voie étroite, m. ~*-minded,* à l'esprit étroit. ¶ n, (Naut.) (pl.) détroit, m. ¶ v.t, [r]étrécir, resserrer, étrangler. ~**ness,** n, étroitesse, f.

nasal, a, nasal. ¶ (Gram.) n, nasale, f.

nascent, a, naissant.

nastiness, n, saleté; méchanceté, f.

nasturtium, n, capucine, f.

nasty†, a, sale; désagréable; vilain; rosse.

natal, a, natal.

natation, n, natation, f.

nation, n, nation, f, peuple, m. ~**al,** a, national; public. ~ *capital* (economics), outillage national, m. ~ *monument,* monument historique, m. **nationalism,** n, nationalisme; étatisme, m. **nationalist,** n. & att, nationaliste, m, f. & a. **nationality,** n, nationalité, f. **nationals,** n.pl, nationaux, m. pl.

native, a, naturel; natif; natal; originaire; indigène; maternel. ~ *land,* ~ *country,* patrie, f. ¶ n, natif, ive; indigène, m,f; naturel, m. **nativity,** n, nativité; naissance, f.

natty, a, chic, coquet, propret.

natural†, a, naturel. ¶ n, idiot, e; (Mus.) (note) note naturelle, f; (cancel sign) bécarre, m. ~ *history museum,* muséum [d'histoire naturelle] m. ~**ist,** n, naturaliste, m. ~**ization,** n, naturalisation, f. ~ *papers,* lettres de n., f.pl. ~**ize,** v.t, naturaliser. ~**ness,** n, naturel, m. **nature,** n, nature, f; naturel, caractère, acabit, m. **-natured,** a, d'un (bon, mauvais) naturel.

naught, n, rien, m. (Arith.) zéro, m.

naughtiness, n, méchanceté, f.

naughty†, a, méchant, vilain, laid; (indecent) polisson, croustilleux, graveleux, gras.

nausea, n, nausée, f. **nauseate,** v.t, écœurer. **nauseating,** a, nauséeux. **nauseous,** a, nauséabond.

nautical, a, (science, almanac) nautique; (mile) marin.

nautilus, n, nautile, nautilus, m.

naval, a, naval; maritime; de marine; de la m. ~ *cadet,* élève de l'école navale, m. ~ *dockyard,* arsenal maritime, m. ~ *officer,* officier de marine, m. ~ *station,* port de guerre, p. militaire; point d'appui de la flotte, m.

nave, n, (wheel) moyeu, m; (church) nef, f.

navel, n, nombril, m.

navigable, a, navigable. **navigate,** v.i, naviguer; (v.t.) naviguer sur, faire naviguer. **navigation,** n, navigation, f. **navigator,** n, navigateur, m.

navy, n, marine [militaire], m. de guerre, f. ~ *blue,* bleu marine, m.

nay, neg. particle, & qui plus est, voire. ¶ n, non, m.

Neapolitan, a, napolitain. ¶ n, Napolitain, e

neap tide, morte-eau, f.

near, a, proche; près de; rapproché; intime. *the N~ East,* le Proche Orient. ~ *relations,* proches [parents] m.pl. ~ *relationship,* proximité du sang, f. ~*sighted* (person), myope, a. & m,f. ¶ ad, près; proche; auprès; de près. ¶ pr, près de; auprès de. ¶ v.i., s'approcher de. ~**ly,** ad, de près; à peu [de chose] près; presque. *he ~ fell,* il a manqué de tomber. *I ~ missed the train,* j'ai failli manquer le train. ~**ness,** n, proximité, f.

neat†, a, propre; soigné, bien tenu; (drink) pur, sec; adroit. ~*herd,* bouvier, ère, vacher, ère, pâtre, m. ~*'s foot oil,* huile de pied de bœuf, f. ~**ness,** n, propreté, f.

nebula, n, (Astr.) n, nébuleuse, f. **nebulous,** a, nébuleux.

necessarily, ad, nécessairement, forcément. **necessary,** a, nécessaire. *if ~,* s'il est n., au besoin. ¶ n. & **necessaries,** n.pl, le nécessaire. **necessitate,** v.t, nécessiter. **necessitous,** a, nécessiteux. **necessity,** n, nécessité, f.

neck, n, cou, m; gorge; encolure, f; col; collet; goulot; (violin) manche, m. ~*band,* bande de col, brisure, f. ~*lace,* collier, m. ~ *measurement,* ~ *size,* encolure, f. ~*tie,* cravate, f. *to win by a*

~, gagner par une encolure.
neckerchief, *n*, fichu, *m*.
necrology, *n*, (*notice*) nécrologie, *f*; (*roll, book*) nécrologe, *m*. **necromancer**, *n*, nécromancien, ne. **necromancy**, *n*, nécromancie, *f*. **necropolis**, *n*, nécropole, *f*. **necrosis**, *n*, nécrose, *f*.
nectar, *n*, nectar, *m*. ~**ine**, *n*, brugnon, *m*. ~**y**, *n*, nectaire, *m*.
need, *n*, besoin, *m*. ¶ *v.i. & t*, avoir b. (de); vouloir. ~**ful**, *a*. & *n*, nécessaire, *a. & m*.
needle, *n*, aiguille, *f*. ~*point lace*, dentelle au point à l'aiguille, *f*. ~*woman*, couturière, *f*. ~*work*, travail à l'aiguille, *m*, couture, *f*. *to do* ~*work*, travailler à l'a., chiffonner. ~**ful**, *n*, aiguillée, *f*.
needless†, *a*, inutile. **needs**, *ad*, nécessairement. **needy**, *a*, nécessiteux, besogneux.
ne'er (*Poet.*) *ad*, ne . . . jamais. *a* ~-*do-well*, un mauvais sujet, un propre à rien.
nefarious†, *a*, inique, abominable.
negation, *n*, négation, *f*. **negative**†, *a*, négatif. ¶ *n*, la négative; (*Gram.*) négation, *f*; (*Phot.*) cliché, négatif, *m*.
neglect, *v.t*, négliger, oublier. **neglect & negligence**, *n*, négligence, *f*, oubli, *m*. **neglectful**† & **negligent**†, *a*, négligent. **negligible**, *a*, négligeable.
negotiable, *a*, négociable. ~ *instrument*, effet de commerce, *m*. **negotiate**, *v.t. & i*, négocier, traiter, trafiquer. **negotiation**, *n*, négociation, *f*; (*pl.*) pourparlers, *m.pl*. *by* ~, de gré à gré. **negotiator, tress** *or* **trix**, *n*, négociateur, trice.
Negress, *n*, négresse, *f*. **Negro**, *n*, nègre, *m*. ¶ *a*, nègre, *a.m. & a.f*.
neigh, *v.i*, hennir. ~[**ing**], *n*, hennissement, *m*.
neighbor, *n*, voisin, e; prochain, *m*. ~**hood**, *n*, voisinage, *m*, environs, *m.pl*; quartier, *m*. ~**ing**, *a*, voisin, avoisinant, prochain. *in a* ~*ly way*, en bon voisin.
neither, *pn. & a*, ni l'un (l'une) ni l'autre. ¶ *c*, ni; ne . . . pas non plus. ¶ *ad*, non plus.
nelson (*wrestling*) *n*, prise de tête à terre, *f*.
Nemesis, *n*, Némésis, *f*.
neologism, *n*, néologisme, *m*.
neon, *n*, néon, *m*. ~ *light*, lumière néon, *f*.

neophyte, *n*, néophyte, *m,f*.
nephew, *n*, neveu, *m*.
ne plus ultra, nec plus ultra.
nepotism, *n*, népotisme, *m*.
Nereid, *n*, néréide, *f*.
nerve, *n*, nerf, *m*; (*Bot.*) nervure, *f*; (*fig.*) audace, *f*, courage, sangfroid, *m*. ~ *specialist*, neurologiste, neurologue, *m,f*. **nervous**†, *a*, nerveux; peureux, timide. ~ *breakdown*, prostration nerveuse, *f*. ~**ness**, *n*, timidité, *f*.
nest, *n*, nid; faisceau; (*fig.*) repaire, *m*. ~ *egg*, nichet; (*savings*) pécule, *m*. ~ *of drawers*, casier, *m*. ~ *of* (insect's) *eggs*, couvain, *m*. ¶ *v.i*, nicher. ~*ed table* or ~ *of 3 tables*, table gigogne, *f*. ~[**ful**], *n*, nichée, *f*. **nestle**, *v.i*, se blottir, se tapir. **nestling**, *n*, petit oiseau au nid, *m*.
net, *n*, filet; rets; tulle, *m*; résille; *f*. ~ *maker*, fileur, euse. ~ *sinker*, ~ *weight* (*Fish.*), gousse de plomb, *f*. ~*work*, réseau; lacis, *m*. ¶ (*Com.*) *a*, net. ¶ (*catch*) *v.t*, prendre au filet.
nether, *a*, inférieur, bas. ~ *regions*, enfers, *m.pl*. **Netherlander**, *n*, Néerlandais, e. **Netherlandish**, *a*, néerlandais. **the Netherlands**, les Pays-Bas, *m.pl*, la Néerlande. **nethermost**, *a*, (le) plus bas.
netting, *n*, filet, *m*, filoche, *f*; (*wire*) treillis, treillage, grillage, réseau, *m*.
nettle, *n*, ortie, *f*. ~ *rash*, urticaire, *f*. ¶ *v.t*, piquer.
neuralgia, *n*, névralgie, *f*. **neuralgic**, *a*, névralgique. **neurasthenia**, *n*, neurasthénie, *f*. **neuritis**, *n*, névrite, *f*. **neurologist**, *n*, neurologiste, -logue, *m,f*. **neurosis**, *n*, névrose, *f*. **neurotic**, *a*, névrosé.
neuter, *a. & n*, neutre, *a. & m*. **neutral**, *a. & n*, neutre, *a. & m*. ~**ity**, *n*, neutralité, *f*. ~**ize**, *v.t*, neutraliser.
never, *ad*, jamais; ne . . . jamais. ne . . . pas. ~-*ending*, éternel. ~ *mind*, cela ne fait rien. ~-*more*, jamais plus. **nevertheless**, *ad. & c*, néanmoins; cependant; toutefois; pourtant; quand même.
new, *a*, neuf; nouveau; récent; frais, tendre. ~*born* (*child*), nouveau-né, e. ~*comer*, nouveau venu, *m*, nouvelle venue, *f*. *New-foundland* [*dog*], terre-neuve, *m*. ~ *growth* (*forestry*), revenue, *f*.

~-laid, frais [pondu]. ~ lease on life, regain de vie, m. ~ member (of a society), récipiendaire, m,f. ~ par[agraph], alinéa, m. N~ Testament, Nouveau Testament, m. N~-Year's day, le jour de l'an. N~-Year's eve, veille du j. de l'a., f, la Saint-Sylvestre. N~-Year's wishes, souhaits (ou vœux) de bonne année, m.pl.

New (Geog.) a: ~ Brunswick, le Nouveau-Brunswick. ~found- land, Terre-Neuve, f. ~ Guinea, la Nouvelle-Guinée. ~ Orleans, la Nouvelle-Orléans. ~ South Wales, la Nouvelle-Galles du Sud. ~ York, New York, m. ~ Zealand, la Nouvelle-Zélande; (att.) néo-zélandais. ~ Zeal- ander, Néo-Zélandais, e.

newel, n, noyau; pilastre, m.

newly, ad, nouvellement, fraîche- ment. newness, n, nouveauté; primeur, f.

news, n, nouvelle, f. oft. pl; cour- rier; bruit; m; (reel) actualités, f.pl. ~ agency, agence d'infor- mation, f. ~ boy, vendeur de journaux, m. ~ [bulletin] (radio), informations, f.pl. ~paper, jour- nal, m.

newt, n, triton, m, salamandre aquatique, f.

next, a, voisin; d'à côté; prochain; plus prochain; suivant; (world) autre. the ~ day, le lendemain. the ~ day but one, le surlende- main. ~ door to, à côté de. ¶ ad, après; ensuite; puis. ~ to, [au]près de; à côté de; presque. ¶ ~ of kin, plus proche parent, e, proches [parents] m.pl.

nib, n, plume [à écrire], f, bec, m.

nibble (Fish.) n, touche, f. ¶ v.t. & i, grignoter, chipoter, mordil- ler; (grass) brouter; (fish) pi- quer, mordre.

nice, a, bon; agréable; friand; délicat; beau; joli; gentil. ~ly, ad, bien; joliment; gentiment.

Nicene Creed (the), le symbole de Nicée.

nicety, n, précision; subtilité, f. to a ~, à point.

niche, n, niche, f.

nick, n, [en]coche, hoche, entaille, f, cran, m, saignée, fente, f. in the ~ of time, à point nommé. ¶ v.t, encocher, entailler, hocher, fendre.

nickel, n, nickel, m. ¶ v.t, nic- keler.

nickname, n, sobriquet, surnom, m. ¶ v.t, baptiser; surnommer.

nicotine, n, nicotine, f.

niece, n, nièce, f.

niggard, n, ladre, m,f. ~ly, a, ladre, mesquin, chiche.

nigh, a, proche. ¶ ad, près; pres- que.

night, n, nuit, f; soir, m. at ~, la nuit, le soir; (hour) du soir. by ~, de nuit, nuitamment. the ~ before last, avant-hier soir. ~ club, boîte de n., f. ~gown, che- mise de nuit, f. ~fall, la tombée de la nuit, la chute du jour. at ~fall, à la nuit tombante. ~ lamp & ~light, veilleuse, f. ~ mare, cauchemar, m. ~ nurse, veilleuse de nuit, f. ~ nursing, veillée, f. ~shade, morelle, f. ~ shirt, chemise de nuit, f. ~ soil, vidanges, f.pl, gadoue, f.

nightingale, n, rossignol, m.

nightly, a, de nuit. ¶ ad, toutes les nuits; tous les soirs.

nihilist, n, nihiliste, m.

nil, n, rien, néant, m, nul, a.

Nile (the), le Nil.

nimble†, a, agile, leste, preste, ingambe. ~ness, n, agilité, pres- tesse, f.

nimbus, n, nimbe; (Meteor.) nim- bus, m.

nincompoop, n, nigaud, e.

nine, a. & n, neuf, a. & m. 9-hole course, parcours (ou golf) de 9 trous, m. ~pins, quilles, f.pl. ~ times out of ten, neuf fois sur dix. nineteen, a. & n, dix-neuf, a. & m. nineteenth, a. & n, dix- neuvième, a. & m,f; dix-neuf, m. ninetieth, a. & n, quatre-vingt- dixième, a. & m,f. ninety, a. & n, quatre-vingt-dix, a. & m. 91, 92, etc., quatre-vingt-onze, -douze, etc.

Nineveh, n, Ninive, f.

ninny, n, nigaud, e, dadais, m.

ninth, a. & n, neuvième, a. & m,f; neuf, m. ~ly, ad, neuvièmement.

nip, n, (liquor) doigt, m; (bite) morsure, f. ¶ v.t, pincer; serrer; mordre; brûler. nipper, n, (boy) gamin, m; (of crustacean) pince, f; (pl.) pinces [de serrage], te- nailles, f. pl.

nipple, n, mamelon, bout du sein, m; (nursing bottle) tétine, f.

nit, n, lente, f.

nitrate, n, nitrate, azotate, m. niter, n, nitre, salpêtre, m. nitric, a, azotique, nitrique. nitrogen, n, azote, m. nitroglycerin[e], n, nitroglycérine, *f.* **nitrous,** *a,* azoteux.

no, *ad,* non; pas. ¶ *n,* non, *m.* ¶ *a,* aucun; nul; ne . . . pas de; pas de; pas moyen de. ~ *admittance* [*except on business*], entrée interdite, défense d'entrer [sans autorisation]. ~ *contest* (*Box.*), noncombat. ~ *doubt,* sans doute. ~ *entry,* [*one way street*], sens interdit. ~ *flowers, by request,* ni fleurs, ni couronnes. ~ *matter!* n'importe! ~ *occupation,* sans profession. ~ *one,* personne, *m,* aucun, e. ~ *parking,* stationnement interdit. ~ *performance,* relâche. ~ *smoking,* défense de fumer. ~ *thoroughfare,* défense de passer, passage interdit [au public].

Noah's ark, l'arche de Noé, *f.*

nobility, *n,* noblesse; grandeur, *f.* **noble†,** *a,* noble; grand. ~[*man*], noble, seigneur, gentilhomme, *m.* ~*woman,* noble, *f.* ~*ness,* *n,* noblesse, *f.*

nobody, *n,* personne, *pn.m.* a ~, un zéro; un (une) inconnu, e.

nocturnal, *a.* & **nocturne,** *n,* nocturne, *a.* & *m.*

nod, *n,* signe [de tête] *m,* inclination de t., *f.* ¶ *v.i,* s'incliner; s'assoupir.

node, *n,* nœud, *m.* **nodule,** *n,* rognon, *m.*

noggin, *n,* godet, *m;* (*Meas.*) ⅛ pint.

noise, *n,* bruit; fracas, tapage, vacarme; (*in ears*) tintement; (*fig.*) éclat, retentissement, *m.* ~*abroad,* *v.t,* ébruiter, carillonner, clarionner. ~*less†,* *a,* silencieux.

noisome, *a,* nuisible; malsain.

noisy†, *a,* bruyant; tapageur.

nomad, *n.* & ~(**ic**), *a,* nomade, *m.* & *a.*

nomenclature, *n,* nomenclature, *f.*

nominal†, *a,* nominal; (*of* [*the*] *names, as a list*) nominatif. **nominate,** *v.t,* nommer, désigner. **nomination,** *n,* nomination, désignation, *f.* **nominative** [*case*], nominatif, *m.* **nominee,** *n,* personne nommée; personne interposée, *f. in a* ~*'s name,* sous un nom interposé.

non, *prefix:* ~*alcoholic drinks,* liqueurs fraîches, *f.pl.* ~*combatant,* *n.* & *att,* noncombattant, civil, *m.* & *a.* ~*commissioned officer,* sous-officier, gradé, *m.* ~*committal,* qui n'engage à rien, normand. *to be* ~*committal,* res-

ter neutre. ~*existence,* inexistence, *f;* (*Philos.*) non-être, *m.* ~*existent,* inexistant. ~*interference,* ~*intervention,* non-intervention, *f,* laissez-faire, *m.* ~*payment,* nonpaiement, *m.* ~*performance,* inexécution, *f.* ~*skid,* *a,* antidérapant. ~*stop,* *a,* sans arrêt, s. escale. ~*vintage wine,* vin sans année, v. non-millésimé, *m.*

nonage, *n,* minorité, *f.*

nonagenarian, *a.* & *n,* nonagénaire, *a.* & *m,f.*

nonce, *n,* circonstance, *f;* (*att.*) de c.

nonchalance, *n,* nonchalance, *f.* **nonchalant,** *a,* nonchalant. ~*ly,* *ad,* nonchalamment.

nonconformist, *n.* & *att,* nonconformiste, *m,f.* & *att.*

nondescript, *a,* indéfinissable.

none, *a.* & *pn,* aucun; nul; pas un; pas; personne, *pn.m.*

nonentity, *n,* (*Philos.*) non-être, *m;* (*pers.*) nullité *f,* homme nul, *m.*

nonplus, *n,* embarras, *m.* ¶ *v.t,* embarrasser, dérouter, démonter.

nonsense, *n,* non-sens, *m,* absurdité, insanité, *f,* sottises, bêtises, lanternes, sornettes; chinoiseries, *f.pl. all* ~, un non-sens. ¶ *i,* allons donc!; chansons, chansons!

nonsuit, *v.t,* débouter.

noodle, *n,* (*food*) nouille, *f.* nigaud, e, bêta, *m.*

nook, *n,* recoin, réduit, *m.*

noon & **noonday** & **noontide,** *n,* midi, *m.*

noose, *n,* nœud coulant; lacet, *m.*

nor, *c,* ni; ne . . . pas non plus.

Nordic, *a,* nordique.

norm, *n,* norme, *f.* **normal†,** *a,* normal.

Norman, *a,* normand. ¶ *n,* Normand, e. **Normandy,** *n,* la Normandie.

Norse, *a.* & *n.* & ~*man,* *n,* norvégien, *a.* & *m.* *Old Norse* (language), l'ancien norois, *m.* **north,** *n,* nord; septentrion, *m.* ¶ *ad,* au nord. ¶ *a,* [du] nord; septentrional. N~ *Africa,* l'Afrique septentrionale, *f.* N~ *America,* l'Amérique du Nord, *f.* ~*east,* *n,* nord-est, *m.* N~ *pole,* pôle nord, *m.* N~ *Sea,* mer du Nord, *f.* N~ *Star,* étoile polaire, *f.* ~*west,* *n,* nord-ouest *m.* ~*wester* (wind) *n,* galerne, *f.* **northerly,** *a,* du nord. **northern,** *a,* [du] nord, boréal. ~ *lights,* aurore boréale, *f.* **norther-**

ner, *n.* septentrional, e. **north-ward[s],** *ad,* vers le nord.

Norway, *n,* la Norvège. **Norwegian,** *a,* norvégien. ¶ *n,* (*pers.*) Norvégien, ne; (*language*) le norvégien.

nose, *n,* nez; (*beast*) museau; (*tool*) bec; (*scent*) flair, *m. to blow one's ~,* se moucher. ~**dive,** *v.i,* piquer du nez. ~**gay,** bouquet, *m. ~ about,* fouiner. ~ [*out*], *v.t,* flairer. **nosing,** *n,* (*of step*) rez; (*of locomotive*) lacet, *m.*

nostalgia, *n,* nostalgie, *f.* **nostalgic,** *a,* nostalgique.

nostril, *n,* narine, *f;* (*horse*) naseau, *m.*

nostrum, *n,* remède de charlatan, *m,* drogue; panacée, *f.*

not, n't, *ad,* ne . . . pas, ne . . . point, ne, n'; non; pas; non pas. ~ *at all,* pas du tout, point du tout, nullement, mais non, aucunement. ~ *at home,* absent. *not competing* [*for prize*], hors concours. ~ *exceeding,* jusqu'à concurrence de, ne dépassant pas. ~ *guilty,* innocent. *to find ~ guilty,* innocenter. ~ *negotiable* (*check*), non négociable. ~ *to be confused with . . .,* à ne pas confondre avec . . .

notability, *n,* notabilité, *f.* **notable†,** *a,* notable.

notary, *n,* notaire, *m.*

notation, *n,* notation, *f.*

notch, *n,* [en]coche, entaille, hoche, *f,* cran, *m.* ¶ *v.t,* [en]cocher, entailler, hocher.

note, *n,* note, *f,* mémento, *m;* remarque, *f;* billet, *m;* lettre, *f;* bulletin; bordereau, *m;* facture, *f;* bon; permis, *m;* (*Mus.*) note, *f;* (*please observe*) nota [bene]. (pers.) *of ~,* de marque. ~**book,** carnet, calepin, *m.* ~ *of hand,* billet à ordre. ~ *paper,* papier à lettres, *m.* ~**worthy,** digne de remarque, remarquable. ¶ *v.t,* noter; relever; constater; remarquer. **noted,** *p.p,* renommé, célèbre.

nothing, *n,* rien; rien de; néant; zéro, *m.* ~ *at all,* rien du tout. ~**ness,** *n,* néant, *m.*

notice, *n,* observation, *f;* regard, *m;* attention, garde, *f;* avis; préavis; avertissement, *m;* notice, *f;* écriteau, *m. at short ~,* à bref délai; (*loan*) à court terme. ~ *of meeting,* avis de convocation, *m,* convocation d'assemblée, *f.*

~ [*to quit*], congé, *m.* ¶ *v.t,* observer, remarquer, faire attention à. ~**able,** *a,* digne d'attention; perceptible. **notify,** *v.t,* notifier, avertir, signaler, aviser, intimer.

notion, *n,* notion, idée, *f.*

notoriety, *n,* notoriété, *f.* **notorious†,** *a,* notoire; insigne, fameux.

notwithstanding, *pr,* malgré, nonobstant. ¶ *ad,* néanmoins, quand même.

noun, *n,* nom, substantif, *m.*

nourish, *v.t,* nourrir. ~**ing,** *a,* nourrissant. ~**ment,** *n,* nourriture, *f.*

nous, *n,* esprit, *m;* savoir-faire, *m.*

Nova Scotia, *n,* la Nouvelle-Écosse.

novel, *a,* nouveau, inédit. ¶ *n,* roman, *m.* ~**ette,** *n,* nouvelle, *f.* ~**ist,** *n,* romancier, ère. ~**ty,** *n,* nouveauté, *f.*

November, *n,* novembre, *m.*

novice, *n,* novice, *m,f,* apprenti, e. **noviciate,** *n,* noviciat, *m.*

now, *ad,* maintenant, à présent, actuellement; tantôt. ¶ *c,* or. ¶ *n,* [moment] présent, *m.* ¶ *i,* voyons! ~ *then!* eh bien!, ah! çà, or çà! ~ & *again,* de temps à autre, à diverses reprises, parfois, occasionnellement. ~ & *henceforth,* d'ores & déjà. *between ~ & then,* d'ici là. [*every*] ~ & *then,* de temps en temps. *from ~,* d'ici. *from ~ onward,* dorénavant. *right ~,* tout de suite. **nowadays,** *ad,* de nos jours, aujourd'hui; par le temps qui court.

nowhere, *ad,* nulle part, en aucun lieu. **nowise,** *ad,* nullement, aucunement.

noxious, *a,* nuisible, nocif, vireux.

nozzle, *n,* ajutage, bec, jet, *m;* tuyère, buse, *f.*

Nubia, *n,* la Nubie. **Nubian,** *a,* nubien. ¶ *n,* Nubien, ne.

nubile, *a,* nubile.

nucleus, *n,* noyau, *m.*

nude, *a.* & *n,* nu, *a.* & *m.*

nudge, *n,* coup de coude, *m.* ¶ *v.t,* donner un coup de coude à, pousser du coude.

nudity, *n,* nudité, *f;* nu, *m.*

nugatory, *a,* futile; inefficace; nul.

nugget, *n,* pépite, *f.*

nuisance, *n,* ennui, embêtement, *m,* contrariété, scie; (*law, etc.*) incommodité, *f;* (*pers.*) gêneur, *m,* importun, e, brebis galeuse, *f;* (*child*) tourment, *m.*

null, *a,* nul. ~ & *void,* nul(le) & non avenu(e). ¶ *n,* nulle, *f.* **nul-**

lify, v.t, annuler. **nullity,** n, nullité, caducité, f.

numb, a, engourdi, gourd, transi. ¶ v.t, engourdir, transir. ~**ness,** n, engourdissement, m.

number, n, nombre; numéro, chiffre, m, cote, f; (publication) livraison, f. N~s (Bible), les Nombres. ¶ v.t, compter; nombrer; numéroter, chiffrer; coter. ~**ing,** n, numérotage, m. ~**less,** a, innombrable.

numeral, a, numéral. ¶ n, chiffre, m. **numerary,** a, numéraire. **numerator** (Arith.) n, numérateur, m. **numerical,** a, numérique. **numerous,** a, nombreux.

numismatics, n, numismatique, f. **numismatist,** n, numismate, m.

numskull, n, lourdaud, e.

nun, n, religieuse, nonne, f.

nunciature, n, nonciature, f. **nuncio,** n, nonce, m.

nunnery, n, couvent, m.

nuptial, a, nuptial. ~**s,** n.pl, noces, f.pl.

nurse, n, nourrice, f; infirmier, ère; gardemalades, m,f. ~[maid], bonne [d'enfant] f. ¶ v.t, nourrir, allaiter; soigner; dorloter. **nursery,** n, nursery, chambre d'enfants; (Hort. & fig.) pépinière, f. ~ language, langage enfantin, m. ~man, [jardinier] pépiniériste, m. ~ rhyme, poésie enfantine, f, conte rimé, m. ~ tale, conte de nourrice, conte de fées, m. **nursing,** n, allaitement, m; soins, m.pl. ~ home, maison de santé, clinique, f. ~ mother, mère nourrice, f. **nursing,** n, nourrisson, m.

nurture, n, éducation; nourriture, f. ¶ v.t, nourrir.

nut, n, noix; noisette, f; (violin, etc.) sillet; (for bolt) écrou, m; (pl, coal) gaillette, f, gailletin, m. ~chest~, châtaigne, f. ~-brown, noisette. ~crackers, casse-noisettes, casse-noix, m. ~shell, coquille de noix, f. ~tree, noisetier, m.

nutmeg, n, [noix] muscade, f. ~ [tree], muscadier, m.

nutriment, n, aliment, m. **nutrition,** n, nutrition, f. **nutritious & nutritive,** a, nourrissant, nutritif.

nutty, a, (taste, smell) qui sent la noisette.

nuzzle, v.i & t, fouiller; se blottir.

nymph, n, nymphe; bergère, f.

O

O, i, ô! (of pain), aïe!

oaf, n, enfant disgracié par la nature; lourdaud, m,

oak [tree], n, chêne, m. ~ [wood or timber] [bois de] chêne, m. ~ apple, pomme de chêne, f. ¶ att. & ~en, a, de chêne.

oakum, n, étoupe, f.

oar, n, rame, f, aviron, m. ~ lock, porte-rame, m. **oarsman,** n, rameur, nageur, canotier, m. **oarswoman,** n, rameuse, f.

oasis (lit. & fig.) n, oasis, f.

oat, n, (pl.) avoine, f. ~meal, farine d'avoine, f, gruau d'avoine, m.

oath, n, serment; (profane) juron, m.

obdurate a, endurci; impénitent.

obedience, n, obéissance, soumission; (Eccl.) obédience, f. **obedient,** a, obéissant, soumis. ~ly, ad, avec obéissance, avec soumission. **obeisance,** n, révérence, f.

obelisk, n, obélisque, m; (Typ.) croix, f.

obese, a, obèse. **obesity,** n, obésité, f.

obey, v.t, obéir à; (v.i.) obéir.

obfuscate, v.t, offusquer, obscurcir.

obituary, n, nécrologie, f.

object, n, objet; but, m; (Gram.) régime, m. ~ lesson leçon de choses; (fig.) application pratique, f. ¶ v.t, & i objecter; réclamer. **objection,** n, objection, f; mais, m; opposition, f. ~able, a, susceptible d'objections; indésirable; offensant, rosse. **objective†,** a, objectif. ¶ (aim, Opt.) n, objectif, m. ~ [case], régime direct, m. the ~ (Philos.), l'objectif, m.

objurgation, n, objurgation, f.

oblation, n, oblation, offrande, f.

obligate, v.t, obliger. **obligation,** n, obligation, f. **obligatory,** a, obligatoire. **oblige,** v.t, obliger. **obliging,** a, obligeant, serviable, arrangeant. ~ly, ad, obligeamment.

oblique, a, oblique. ~ly, ad, en biais. **obliquity,** n, obliquité, f.

obliterate, v.t, oblitérer, effacer.

oblivion, n, oubli, m; (Pol.) amnistie, f. **oblivious,** a, oublieux.

oblong, a, oblong. ¶ n, figure oblongue, f, carré long, m.

obloquy, *n,* reproche; dénigrement, *m.*

obnoxious, *a,* offensant, odieux.

oboe, *n,* hautbois, *m.* **oboist,** *n,* hautboïste, *m.*

obscene, *a,* obscène. **obscenity,** *n,* obscénité, *f.*

obscure, *a,* obscur, ténébreux, fumeux. ¶ *v.t,* obscurcir, offusquer. ~**ly,** *ad,* obscurément. **obscurity,** *n,* obscurité, *f.*

obsequies, *n.pl,* obsèques, *f.pl.* **obsequious†,** *a,* obséquieux. ~**ness,** *n,* obséquiosité, *f.*

observance, *n,* observation; (*Theol.*) observance; (*religious*) pratique, *f.* **observant,** *a,* observateur. **observation,** *n,* observation, *f.* ~ *post* (*Mil.*) & **observatory,** *n,* observatoire, *m.* **observe,** *v.t,* observer; remarquer; suivre. **observer,** *n,* observateur, trice.

obsess, *v.t,* obséder. *to be* ~*ed by, with,* être obsédé par, être fanatique de, s'aheurter à. ~**ion,** *n,* obsession, aheurtement, dada, *m,* hantise, *f.*

obsolescent, *a,* vieillissant. **obsolete,** *a,* vieux, vielli, inusité, désuet.

obstacle, *n,* obstacle, *m.* ~ *race,* course d'obstacles, *f.*

obstetric(al), *a,* obstétrical. **obstetrics,** *n.pl,* obstétrique, *f.*

obstinacy, *n,* obstination, opiniâtreté, *f,* entêtement; acharnement, *m.* **obstinate,** *a,* obstiné, opiniâtre, entêté; acharné; rebelle. ~**ly,** *ad,* obstinément, opiniâtrement.

obstreperous, *a,* turbulent.

obstruct, *v.t,* obstruer, boucher; (*v.i.*) fronder. ~**ion,** *n,* obstruction; (*fig.*) obstruction, *f.*

obtain, *v.t,* obtenir, procurer; (*v.i.*) régner, prévaloir, avoir cours.

obtrude, *v.t,* forcer, imposer; (*v.i.*) s'introduire de force; être importun.

obtuse, *a,* obtus.

obverse (*coin*) *n,* avers, *m,* face, *f.*

obviate, *v.t,* obvier à.

obvious†, *a,* évident, manifeste, visible.

ocarina, *n,* ocarina, *m.*

occasion, *n,* occasion; circonstance; cause, raison, *f;* sujet, *m.* ¶ *v.t,* occasionner, donner lieu à; causer. ~**al,** *a,* par occasion; (*occupation*) d'occasion; de circonstance; de temps en temps;

(*cause, Philos.*) occasionnelle. ~**ally,** *ad,* occasionnellement, parfois.

occidental, *a.* & *n,* occidental.

occiput, *n,* occiput, *m.*

occult, *a,* occulte. ~**ism,** *n,* occultisme, *m.*

occupant, *n,* habitant, e; occupant, *m;* titulaire, *m,f.* **occupation,** *n,* occupation; profession, *f,* état, *m,* qualités, *f.pl.* **occupy,** *v.t,* occuper; habiter.

occur, *v.i,* [sur]venir, se présenter, s'offrir; arriver, advenir. **occurrence,** *n,* occurrence, venue, *f,* fait, événement, *m.*

ocean, *a,* océan, *m,* mer, *f.* ~[*-going*], *a,* au long cours. **Oceania,** *n,* l'Océanie, *f.*

ocher, *n,* ocre, *f.*

o'clock, heure(s).

octagon, *n.* & ~**al,** *a,* octogone, *m.* & *a.* ~*al nut,* écrou à 8 pans, *m.* **octave,** *n,* octave, *f.* **octavo,** *a.* & *n.* (*abb.* 8vo), in-octavo, in-8°, *a.m.* & *m.* **October,** *n,* octobre, *m.* **octogenarian,** *a.* & *n,* octogénaire, *a.* & *m,f.* **octopus,** *n,* poulpe, *m,* pieuvre, *f.* **octoroon,** *n,* octavon, ne.

ocular, *a.* & *n,* oculaire, *a.* & *m.* **oculist,** *n,* oculiste, *m.*

odd, *a,* (*number*) impair; & quelques; & quelque chose; (*pair or set*) dépareillé; singulier, étrange, bizarre, baroque, original, drôle. ~ *jobs,* bricoles, *f.pl. at* ~ *times,* par-ci, par-là. ~**ity,** *n,* singularité, bizarrerie, *f;* (*pers.*) original, drôle de corps, *m.* ~**ly,** *ad,* étrangement, bizarrement. ~**ments,** *n.pl,* articles dépareillés, *m.pl.* ~**ness,** *n,* imparité; singularité, *f.* **odds,** *n.pl,* chances; forces supérieures, *f.pl;* avantage, *m;* différence; (*turf*) cote, *f. to lay* ~ *of 3 to 1,* parier 3 contre 1. *the* ~ *are that* . . ., il y a à parier que . . . ~ & *ends,* bribes, *f.pl,* rogatons, *m.pl.*

ode, *n,* ode, *f.*

odious†, *a,* odieux. **odium,** *n,* haine, *f;* odieux, *m.*

odoriferous, *a,* odoriférant, odorant. **odor,** *n,* odeur, *f.* ~**less,** *a,* inodore. ~**ous,** *a,* odorant.

Odyssey (*fig.*) *n,* odyssée, *f.*

of, *pr,* de; en; parmi; entre; d'entre; à; chez.

off, *pr,* éloigné de; au large de; de dessus; de là. ~ *and on,* de temps à autre ~*hand,* *a.* & *ad,* impromptu; sur-le-champ; sans cérémonie; cavalier; brusque. ~-*handedness*, sans-gêne, *m.* ~ *season*, morte-saison, *f.* ~*shore fishing*, pêche au large, p. hauturière, *f.* ¶ *ad*, de distance; d'ici. *to be* ~, s'en aller; partir.

offal, *n*, issues, *f.pl* tripaille, *f.*

offend, *v.t*, offenser, blesser, choquer, offusquer; (*v.i.*) pécher. ~**er**, *n*, offenseur, *m*; coupable, *m,f*; délinquant, e. **offense**, *n*, offense, blessure, *f*, outrage; délit; crime, *m*; infraction, contravention, *f*. *to take* ~, s'offenser, se formaliser. **offensive**, *a*; offensant, blessant, choquant; malsonnant; (*attacking*) offensif.

offer, *n*, offre, *f.* ¶ *v.t*, offrir; proposer; présenter. ~ *up*, offrir. ~**ing**, *n*, offrande; oblation, *f*; sacrifice, *m.* ~**tory**, *n*, (*Lit.*) offertoire, *m*; (*collection*) quête, *f.*

office, *n*, charge, *f*, office, exercice, *m*, fonction, *f*. *oft. pl*, place, *f*, ministère; portefeuille; bureau; cabinet, *m*, étude; salle, *f*, siège; comptoir, *m*; caisse, recette, *f.* ~ *boy*, petit commis, *m.* *main* ~, siège social, *m.* **officer**, *n*, officier, *m*; fonctionnaire, *m,f*; agent, *m*, préposé, e. ¶ *v.t*, encadrer. **official**†, *a*, officiel; d'office. ~ *statement* (to press), communiqué, *m.* ¶ *n*, fonctionnaire, *m,f*, préposé, e; (*sport, etc.*) officiel, *m.* ~**dom** & ~**ism**, *n*, fonctionnarisme, *m.* **officiate**, *v.i*, (*Eccl.*) officier; exercer les fonctions (*as* = de). **officious**, *a*, touche-à-tout; (*diplomacy*) officieux. ~ *person*, touche-à-tout, *m*; personne qui se mêle des oignons des autres, *f.*

offing, *n*, large, *m.* *in the* ~, au l., dehors.

offscourings (*fig.*) *n.pl*, lie, *f*, bas-fonds, *m.pl.*

offset, *n*, compensation, *f*; (*Hort.*) rejeton, œilleton; (*Arch.*) ressaut, *m.* ~ *process*, offset, *m.*

offshoot, *n*, rejeton, *m.*

offspring, *n*, rejeton, *m*; progéniture, *f.*

often & (*Poet.*) **oft**, *ad*, souvent. *how often?* combien de fois?

ogee, *n*, doucine, *f.* **ogive**, *n*, ogive, *f.*

ogle, *n*, œillade, *f.* ¶ *v.t*, lorgner, reluquer.

ogre, ogress, *n*, ogre, *m*, ogresse, *f.*

oh, *i*, oh!; ô!; ah!

oil, *n*, huile, *f*; pétrole, *m*; essence, *f.* ~ *can*, (*storage*) bidon à huile, *m*; (*nozzled*) burette à h., *f.* ~*cloth*, (*table, etc.*) toile cirée, moleskine, *f*; (*floor*) linoléum, *m.* ~ *color*, ~ *paint*, couleur à l'huile, *f.* ~ *engine*, moteur à pétrole, *m.* ~ *field*, champ de pétrole, *m.* ~ *fuel*, mazout, pétrole combustible, *m.* ~ *heater*, poêle à pétrole, *m.* ~ *hole*, trou de graissage, *m*, lumière, *f.* ~ *painting*, peinture à l'huile, *f.* ~ *seed*, graine oléagineuse, *f.* ~ *shares*, valeurs de petrole, *f.pl.* ~ *skin*, toile huile, *f*; (*garment*) ciré, *m.* ~ *stone*, pierre à huile, *f.* ~ *stove*, fourneau à pétrole, *m.* ~ *varnish*, vernis gras, *m.* ~ *well*, puits à pétrole, *m.* ¶ *v.t*, graisser [à l'huile], huiler. ~**y**, *a*, huileux; onctueux; oléagineux.

ointment, *n*, onguent, *m.*

old, *a*, vieux; ancien. *how* ~ *is he? he is 10 years* ~, quel âge a-t-il? il a 10 ans. *the* ~, (*opp. new*) le vieux; (*people*) les vieux, *m.pl.* ~ & *young*, grands & petits. *of* ~, jadis, anciennement. ~ *age*, la vieillesse; (*decay*) vétusté, *f.* ~ *age pension fund*, caisse de retraites pour la vieillesse, *f.* ~ *clothes*, vieilles hardes, nippes, *f. pl.* ~*-established*, fort ancien. ~*-fashioned*, à l'ancienne mode; passé de mode, démodé; arriéré; gothique. ~ *gold*, vieil or, *m.* ~ *guard* (Mil.), garde descendante, *f.* ~ *maid*, vieille fille, *f.* ~ *man*, vieillard, vieux; (*in comedy*) géronte, *m.* ~ *master* (*art*), ancien maître, *m.* ~ *offender*, récidiviste, *m,f*, repris de justice, cheval de retour, *m.* ~ *salt* (sailor), loup de mer, *m.* *the same* ~ *story*, la même histoire, la même guitare. O~ *Testament*, Ancien Testament, *m.* ~ *things*, vieilleries, *f.pl.* *the good* ~ *times*, le bon vieux temps. ~ *woman*, vieille [femme] *f.* *the* O~ *Woman who lived in a shoe*, la mère Gigogne. **in the** ~ **time**, au temps jadis. ~**ish**, *a*, vieillot.

oleaginous, *a*, oléagineux.

oleander, *n*, laurier-rose, oléandre, *m.*

olfactory, *a*, olfactif.

oligarchy, *n*, oligarchie, *f.*

olive, *n*, olive, *f.* ~ [*tree, wood*], olivier, *m.* ~ (*complexion*) *a*, olivâtre. ~[*-green*], vert olive,

couleur [d']olive. ~ *grove*, olivaie, *f*. ~ *oil*, huile d'olive, *f*.
Olympic games, jeux olympi-
ques, *m.pl*. **Olympus** (*fig*.) *n*,
olympe, *m*.
omega, *n*, oméga, *m*.
omelet, *n*, omelette, *f*.
omen, *n*, augure, présage, auspice,
pronostic, *m*. **ominous**, *a*, de
mauvais augure; sinistre; mena-
çant.
omission, *n*, omission, *f*. **omit**,
v.t, omettre.
omnibus, *n*, omnibus, *m*.
omnipotence, *n*, omnipotence,
toute-puissance, *f*. **omnipotent**,
a, omnipotent, tout-puissant. *the
Omnipotent*, le Tout-Puissant.
omniscience, *n*, omniscience, *f*.
omniscient, *a*, omniscient.
omnivorous, *a*, omnivore.
on, *pr*, sur; à; de; en; après; par;
pour; sous. ~ *& after*, à partir
de, à dater de. ~ *hand*, (*orders*)
en carnet, en portefeuille; (*cash*)
en caisse, disponible. ~ *leave*, en
congé. ¶ *ad*, dessus; en avant. ~
that, là-dessus.
once, *ad*, une fois; une seule fois.
at ~, tout de suite; à la fois. ~
again, ~ *more*, encore une fois,
encore un coup. ~ *for all*, une
fois pour toutes. ~ *upon a time*,
il y avait (*ou* il était) une fois,
autrefois.
one, *a*, un; seul; unique. ~*-act
play*, pièce en un acte, *m*,
~*-armed & -handed* (*person*),
manchot, ote. ~*-eyed*, borgne. ~*-
man band*, homme-orchestre, *m*.
~*-price shop*, magasin à prix
unique, *m*. ~*self*, soi, soi-même.
~*-sided*, unilatéral; (*fig*.) léonin.
~*-way street*, rue à sens unique,
f. ~*-way traffic*, circulation à s.
u., *f*. ¶ *n*, un, *m*; unité, *f*. ¶ *pn*,
celui, celle; quelqu'un, e; on;
un(e) nommé(e); un(e) cer-
tain(e). ~ *& all*, tous sans exception. ~ *another*, l'un(e)
l'autre; les uns (les unes) les
autres; se. ~ *by* ~ *or* ~ *after
another*, un à un, une à une. *he
is* ~ *of us*, il est des nôtres. ~*-
ness*, *n*, unité, *f*.
onerous, *a*, onéreux.
one's, *pn*, son, sa, ses. **oneself**,
pn, soi-même; soi; se; son individu.
onion, *n*, oignon, *m*. ~ *bed*, oignonière, *f*. ~ *sauce*, sauce à l'oignon, *f*. ~ *skin*, ~ *peel*, pelure
d'oignon, *f*.

onlooker, *n*, assistant, e, spectateur, trice, curieux, *m*.
only, *a*, seul, unique, tout. ¶ *ad*,
seulement, rien que, ne . . .
guère; uniquement.
onomatopoeia, *n*, onomatopée,
f.
onset, onrush, onslaught, *n*,
attaque, ruée, *f*, assaut, choc, *m*.
onus, *n*, charge, *f*. ~ *of proof*,
charge de la preuve.
onward, *a*, progressif. ~[*s*], *ad*,
en avant; plus loin.
onyx, *n*, onyx, *m*.
ooze, *n*, vase, *f*, limon; suinte-
ment, *m*. ¶ *v.i*, suinter, suer. ~
out, transpirer.
opacity, *n*, opacité, *f*.
opal, *n*, opale, *f*. ~*ine*, *a*, opalin.
opaque, *a*, opaque. ~*ness*, *n*,
opacité, *f*.
open, *v.t*, ouvrir; percer; entamer;
écarter; découvrir; exposer; inaugurer; (*bottle*) déboucher;
(*oysters*) écailler; (*Med.*) débonder; (*v.i.*) ouvrir; s'o.; (*flowers*) s'épanouir. ~ *sesame*, Sésame, ouvre-toi. ¶ *a*, ouvert; découvert, à découvert; exposé; ostensible; libre; franc; (*boat*) non
ponté. *in the* ~ [*air*], en plein air,
au grand air, à ciel ouvert. *the*
~ [*country*], la pleine campagne,
la rase c. *in the open* (publicly),
au grand jour. ~*-handed*, libéral.
~*-hearted*, franc. ~ *house*, table
ouverte, *f*. ~*-mouthed*, bouche
béante, b. bée. *in the* ~ *sea*, en
pleine (*ou* haute) mer, au large.
~ *space*, terre-plein, franc-bord,
m. ~ *warfare*, guerre de mouvement, *f*. ~[*work*], att, à jour,
ajouré, à claire-voie. ~*work*
(*Need.*) *n*, (les) jours, *m.pl*. ~*er*,
n, ouvreur, euse. ~*ing*, *n*, ouverture; percée; éclaircie; (*neck*)
échancrure; introduction, *f*; débouché, *m*; occasion, *f*. ¶ *a*, initial; d'ouverture; de début; préliminaire; premier. ~*ly*, *ad*, ouvertement; ostensiblement; hautement; franchement. ~*ness*, *n*,
franchise, candeur, *f*.
opera, *n*. *& ~ house*, opéra, *m*.
~ *cloak*, sortie de bal, s. de théâtre, *f*. ~ *glass*[*es*], jumelle[*s*] de
théâtre, lorgnette[*s*] de spectacle,
f.[*pl*.]. ~ *hat*, [chapeau] claque,
m.
operate, *v.t*, opérer; exploiter;
(*v.i.*) opérer, agir; jouer. ~ *on*
(*Surg.*), opérer.
operatic, *a*, d'opéra; lyrique.

operating room *or* **theater,** salle d'opération, *f.* **operation,** *n,* opération; exploitation, *f.* **operative,** *n,* ouvrier, ère, artisan, e. ¶ *a,* actif, efficace. **operator,** *n,* opérateur, trice.

operetta, *n,* opérette, *f.*

ophthalmia, *n,* ophtalmie, *f.* **ophthalmic,** *a,* ophtalmique.

opiate, *n,* narcotique, *m.* ~**d,** *a,* opiacé.

opine, *v.i,* opiner. **opinion,** *n,* opinion, voix, *f;* sentiment, avis, sens, *m;* (*legal*) consultation, *f.* ~**ated,** *a,* opiniâtre.

opium, *n,* opium, *m.* ~ *addict,* opiomane, *m.f.* ~ *den,* fumerie, *f.* ~ *poppy,* pavot somnifère, *m.*

opossum, *n,* opossum, *m;* sarigue, *m.f.*

opponent, *n,* opposant, e, adversaire, antagoniste, *m.* ¶ *a,* opposant.

opportune, *a,* opportun, à propos. ~**ly,** *ad,* opportunément, à propos. ~**ness,** *n,* opportunité, *f,* à-propos, *m.* **opportunism,** *n,* opportunisme, *m.* **opportunist,** *n,* opportuniste, *m.f.* **opportunity,** *n,* occasion; opportunité, *f.*

oppose, *v.t,* opposer, s'opposer à; combattre. ~**d,** *p.p,* opposé, contraire. **opposing,** *p.a,* opposant, adverse. **opposite,** *n,* opposé, contraire, contre-pied, *m.* ~ **(to),** *a, pr, ad,* opposé; en face (de), vis-à-vis (de), en regard (de), contraire (à); (*sex*) opposé. **opposition,** *n,* opposition; résistance, *f.*

oppress, *v.t,* opprimer; oppresser (*Med. & fig.*). ~**ion,** *n,* oppression, *f.* ~**ive,** *a,* oppressif, assommant. ~**or,** *n,* oppresseur, *m.*

opprobrious, *a,* infamant, injurieux. **opprobrium,** *n,* opprobre, *m.*

optic, *a,* optique. ~**al,** *a,* optique; (*glass, instruments, illusion*), d'optique. **optician,** *n,* opticien; lunetier, *m.* **optics,** *n,* optique, *f.*

optimism, *n,* optimisme, *m.* **optimist,** *n. &* ~**(ic),** *a,* optimiste, *m.f. & a.*

option, *n,* option; alternative, *f,* choix, *m;* (*Stk Ex.*) prime, *f.* ~**al†,** *a,* facultatif.

opulence, *n,* opulence, *f.* **opulent,** *a,* opulent.

or, *c,* ou; soit; (*neg.*) ni. ~ *else,* ou bien, autrement. *2 ~ 3 times a day,* de 2 à 3 fois par jour.

oracle, *n,* oracle, *m.*

oral†, *a,* oral. ~ *examination,* examen oral, *m.*

orange, *n,* orange, *f;* (*color*) orange, *m,* orangé, *m.* ¶ *a,* orange, orangé. ~ [*tree*], oranger, *m.* ~ *blossom,* fleurs d'oranger, *f.pl.* ~ *marmalade,* confitures d'oranges, *f.pl.* ~ *peel,* pelure d'orange, écorce d'o., *f.* ~**ade,** *n,* orangeade, *f.* ~**ry,** *n,* orangerie, *f.*

orangutan, *n,* orang-outang, *m.*

oration, *n,* discours, *m;* (*funeral*) oraison, *f.* **orator,** *n,* orateur, *m.* ~**ical,** *a,* oratoire. **oratorio,** *n,* oratorio, *m.* **oratory,** *n,* l'art oratoire, *m,* éloquence, *f;* (*chapel*) oratoire, *m.*

orb, *n,* globe, *m,* sphère, *f,* orbe, *m.* **orbit,** *n,* orbite, *f.*

orc, *n,* orque, *f,* épaulard, *m.*

orchard, *n,* verger, *m.*

orchestra, *n,* orchestre, *m.* ~ *seat,* fauteuil d'orchestre, *m.* **orchestral,** *a,* orchestral. **orchestrate,** *v.t,* orchestrer.

orchid, *n,* orchidée, *f.*

ordain, *v.t,* ordonner; décréter, prescrire.

ordeal, *n,* épreuve, *f;* (*Hist.*) ordalie, *f.*

order, *n,* ordre, *m;* règle, *f;* état, *m;* classe, *f;* classement, *m;* commande, *f;* mandat, bon, permis; arrêté, *m;* décoration; (*pl, Mil.*) ordres, *m.pl,* consigne, *f.* ~*!* à l'ordre! *in ~ that,* afin que, pour que. *in ~ to,* afin de. ~ *book,* livre (*ou* carnet) de commandes, *m.* ~ *form,* bon (*ou* bulletin) de commande, *m. out of ~,* (*Mach.*) en panne. ¶ *v.t,* ordonner; statuer; régler; charger; (*goods*) commander; (*arms, Mil.*) reposer. ~**ing,** *n,* ordonnance, disposition, *f.* ~**ly,** *a,* ordonné, rangé, régulier. ¶ *n,* (*Mil.*) ordonnance, *f. or m,* planton, *m;* (*hospital*) infirmier, *m. on ~ duty,* de planton. ~ *officer,* officier d'ordonnance, *m.* ~ *room,* salle du rapport, *f.*

ordinal [*number*], *n,* nombre ordinal, *m.*

ordinance, *n,* décret, *m;* (*law*) ordonnance, *f.*

ordinary†, *a,* ordinaire; commun; normal. ~ *seaman,* simple matelot, matelot de troisième classe, *m.*

ordination, *n,* ordination, *f.*

ordnance, *n,* artillerie, *f;* matériel de guerre, *m.* ~ [*survey*] *map,* carte d'État-major, *f.*

ore, *n,* mineral, *m.*

organ, *n,* organe; (*Mus.*) orgue, *m.* ~ *grinder,* joueur d'orgue de Barbarie, *m.* ~ *loft,* tribune d'orgues, *f.* ~ *pipe,* tuyau d'orgue, *m.*

organdie, *n,* organdi, *m.*

organic, *a,* organique. **organism,** *n,* organisme, *m.* **organization,** *n,* organisation; (*fête*) ordonnance, *f.* **organize,** *v.t,* organiser; ordonner; policer. **organizer,** *n,* organisateur, trice; ordonnateur, trice.

orgy, *n,* orgie, *f.*

orient, *n,* orient, *m. the O~* (*Geog.*), l'O. ~**al,** *a,* oriental. O~, *n,* Oriental, e. ~[ate], *v.t,* orienter.

orifice, *n,* orifice, *m,* ouverture, *f.*

oriflamme, *n,* oriflamme, *f.*

origin, *n,* origine; provenance, *f.* ~**al†,** *a,* (*not copied*) original; (*primitive*) originaire, originel. ¶ *n,* original, *m.* ~**ality,** *n,* originalité, *f.* ~**ate,** *v.t,* prendre l'initiative de; (*v.i.*) tirer son origine, dériver. **originator,** *n,* auteur, *m.*

oriole (*bird*) *n,* loriot, *m.*

Orleans, *n,* Orléans, *m.* or *f.*

ormolu, *n,* or moulu, *m.*

ornament, *n,* ornement, *m*; parure, *f.* ¶ *v.t,* orner, agrémenter. ~**al,** *a,* ornemental; d'ornement; d'agrément. **ornamentation,** *n,* ornementation, *f.* **ornate,** *a,* orné; imagé.

ornithologist, *n,* ornithologiste, ornithologue, *m,f.* **ornithology,** *n,* ornithologie, *f.*

orphan, *n.* & *a,* orphelin, e. ~**age** (*asylum*) *n,* orphelinat, *m.*

orrery, *n,* planétaire, *m.*

orris root, racine d'iris, *f.*

orthodox, *a,* orthodoxe; catholique. ~**y,** *n,* orthodoxie, *f.* **orthography,** *n,* orthographe, *f.* **orthopedic,** *a,* orthopédique. **orthopedy,** *n,* orthopédie, *f.*

ortolan, *n,* ortolan, *m.*

oscillate, *v.i,* osciller; (*v.t.*) faire osciller. **oscillation,** *n,* oscillation, *f.*

osier, *n,* osier, *m.* ~ *bed,* oseraie, *f.*

osmium, *n,* osmium, *m.*

osprey, *n,* orfraie, *f.*

osseus, *a,* osseux. **ossicle,** *n,* osselet, *m.* **ossify,** *v.t,* ossifier. **ossuary,** *n,* ossuaire, charnier, *m.*

Ostend, *n,* Ostende, *f.*

ostensible, *a,* avoué. **ostensibly,** *ad,* en apparence, sous prétexte.

ostensory, *n,* ostensoir, *m.* **ostentation,** *n,* ostentation, *f,* faste, *m.* **ostentatious,** *a,* ostentateur, ostentatoire, fastueux.

ostracism, *n,* ostracisme, *m.* **ostracize,** *v.t,* frapper d'ostracisme.

ostrich, *n,* autruche, *f.* ~ *feather,* plume d'autruche, *f.*

other, *a.* & *pn,* autre. *every ~ day,* tous les deux jours. *the ~ side* (opinion, pers.), la contrepartie. *on the ~ side* or *hand,* de l'autre côté. ~*s,* ~ *people,* les autres, d'autres, autrui. ~**wise,** *ad,* autrement, sinon, sans quoi, sans cela.

otter, *n,* loutre, *f.*

Ottoman, *a,* ottoman. ¶ *n,* Ottoman, e. o~, *n,* ottomane, *f.*

oubliette, *n,* oubliettes, *f.pl.*

ought, *v.aux.ir,* devoir; falloir.

ounce, *n,* (Zool.) once; (*Meas.*) once, *f;* (*avoirdupois*) = 28.350 grams; (*troy & apothecaries' weight*) = 31.1035 grams; (*apothecaries' measure*) = 2.84123 centiliters.

our, *a,* notre, nos, *pl. Our Lady,* Notre-Dame, *f. Our Lord,* Notre-Seigneur, *m.* ~**s,** *pn,* le nôtre, la nôtre, les nôtres; nos; à nous; de nous. **ourselves,** *pn,* nous-mêmes; nous.

oust, *v.t,* débusquer, dégommer; évincer, déposséder.

out, *ad.* & *pr,* dehors; hors; sorti, absent, en course; en fleur; paru; éteint. ~ & *out,* franc, fieffé, achevé, renforcé, à tous crins; à outrance, outrancier. ~ *loud,* tout haut. ~[, *see copy*] (*Typ.*), bourdon, *m.* ~ *there,* là-dehors. **out of,** *comps:* ~ *action,* hors de combat. ~ *bounds,* hors des limites. ~ *breath,* à bout de souffle. ~ *date,* suranné, démodé; (*ticket, etc.*) périmé. ~ *doors,* dehors, au grand air. ~ *fashion,* passé de mode, démodé. ~ *hand,* sur-le-champ; échappé à tout contrôle. ~ *one's element,* hors de son élément, dépaysé. ~ *one's reckoning,* loin de compte. ~ *order,* (*Mech.*) en panne. ~ *place* (*fig.*), déplacé, hors de propos. ~ *pocket,* en perte. ~ *practice,* rouillé. ~ *print,* épuisé. ~ *shape,* avachi. ~ *sight,* hors de vue. ~ *sorts,* indisposé, dolent. *to be* ~ *stock of,* être à court de, manquer de. ~ *the common,* hors ligne. *out-of-the-way,* *a,* écarté, retiré, isolé. ~ *tune,* faux.

to be out [*of work*], être sans travail, chômer. **out,** *i,* dehors! hors d'ici! (*Box.*) dehors! ~ *with him!* à la porte! ~ *with it!* achevez donc!

outbid, *v.t.ir,* [r]enchérir sur, surenchérir sur.

outboard, *ad,* hors bord. ~ *motor,* propulseur amovible, *m.*

outbreak, *n,* début, *m;* (*riot*) émeute; (*disease*) épidémie, *f.* ~ *of fire,* incendie, *m. at the* ~ *of war,* quand la guerre éclata.

outbuilding, *n,* dépendance, *f.*

outburst, *n,* débordement, emportement, déchaînement, élan, accès, *m,* poussée, explosion; incartade, *f.*

outcast, *n,* déclassé, e, réprouvé, e, paria, homme sans aveu, *m.*

outcaste, *n,* paria, *m.*

outcome, *n,* conséquence, issue, *f,* résultat, *m.*

outcry, *n,* cri, *m,* clameur, *f.*

outdistance, *v.t,* distancer.

outdo, *v.t.ir,* surpasser; l'emporter sur; devancer.

outdoor, *a,* en plein air, au grand air, de plein air.

outer, *a,* extérieur. ~ *harbor,* avant-port, *m.*

outfall, *n,* décharge, *f;* (*mouth*) débouché, *m.*

outfit, *n,* équipement, équipage, nécessaire, trousseau, *m,* trousse, *f.* **outfitter,** *n,* maison pour fournitures (*de sports, etc.*) *f;* confectionneur, euse.

outflank, *v.t,* déborder.

outflow, *n,* écoulement, *m,* décharge, *f.*

outgoing, *a,* sortant, de sortie, de départ, au départ; (*tide*) descendante. ~s, *n.pl,* débours, déboursés, *m.pl.*

outgrow, *v.t.ir,* devenir trop grand pour; se guérir de.

outhouse, *n,* dépendance, *f;* appentis, *m.*

outing, *n,* course, excursion, promenade, *f.*

outlandish, *a,* bizarre.

outlast, *v.t,* durer plus longtemps que.

outlaw, *n,* proscrit, e. ¶ *v.t,* proscrire, mettre hors la loi. ~**ry,** *n,* proscription, *f.*

outlay, *n,* débours, déboursés, *m.pl.*

outlet, *n,* issue, sortie, *f;* débouché, *m.*

outline, *n,* contour, tracé, crayon, galbe, canevas, aperçu, *m,* es-

quisse, ébauche, *f.* ~ *drawing,* dessin au trait, *m.* ¶ *v.t,* établir les grandes lignes de, tracer, dessiner, crayonner, esquisser.

outlive, *v.t,* survivre à, enterrer.

outlook, *n,* perspective, vue, *f;* avenir, *m.*

outlying, *a,* éloigné; avancé; excentrique.

outmaneuver, *v.t,* déjouer.

outnumber, *v.t,* surpasser en nombre.

outpatient, *n,* malade du dehors, *m,f.*

outpost, *n,* avant-poste, *m.*

outpouring, *n,* épanchement, *m,* effusion, *f.*

output, *n,* rendement, *m,* production, *f.*

outrage, *n,* outrage, *m,* indignité, *f;* attentat, *m.* ¶ *v.t,* outrager, faire outrage à; violer. ~**ous**†, *a,* indigne; odieux; pendable; sanglant; énorme.

outrider, *n,* piqueur, *m.*

outrigger, *n,* (*boat*) outrigger; (*for rowlocks*) porte-en-dehors, *m.*

outright, *a,* fieffé. ¶ *ad,* net, carrément; (*opp. by installments*) en une [seule] fois.

outrival, *v.t,* devancer.

outrun, *v.t,* dépasser à la course.

outset, *n,* début, *m,* origine, *f.*

outshine, *v.t.ir,* éclipser.

outside, *a,* extérieur. ¶ *ad,* [en] dehors, là-dehors, à l'extérieur. ¶ *n,* extérieur, dehors, *m;* (*café*) terrasse, *f. at the* ~, tout au plus. **outsider,** *n,* (*pers.*) profane, *m,f;* (*horse*) outsider, *m.*

outsize, *n,* taille hors série, *f.*

outskirts, *n.pl,* environs, entours, *m.pl;* banlieue, *f.*

outspoken, *a,* franc. ~**ness,** *n,* franchise, liberté [de langage], liberté de parole, *f.*

outspread, *a,* étendu.

outstanding, *a,* (*Fin.*) à payer; arriéré; en suspens; marquant, saillant.

outstretched, *a,* étendu.

outstrip, *v.t,* devancer.

outward†, *a,* extérieur; d'aller; de sortie, liberté. ~ *bound,* en partance; effectuant son voyage d'aller. ~[s], *ad,* en dehors.

outwit, *v.t,* déjouer, circonvenir, tromper.

oval, *a.* & *n,* ovale, *a.* & *m.*

ovary, *n,* ovaire, *m.*

ovation, *n,* ovation, *f.*

oven, *n,* four, *m;* (*fig.*) étuve, *f.*

over, *ad*, dessus; par-dessus; au-dessus; davantage, en sus; trop; fini; passé. *~ again*, de nouveau, encore une fois. *~ & above*, en sus de. *~ there*, là-bas. ¶ *pr*, sur; par-dessus; au-dessus de; plus de; en sus de; de l'autre côté de; par. *~ all* (*Meas.*), hors tout.

overact, *v.t*, charger.

overalls, *n*, salopette, *f*.

overarm stroke, coupe, *f*.

overassess, *v.t*, surimposer, surtaxer. **overassessment**, *n*, surimposition, surtaxe, *f*.

overawe, *v.t*, intimider.

overbalance, *v.i*, perdre l'équilibre.

overbearing, *a*, insolent, arrogant, excédent.

overboard (*Naut.*) *ad*, par-dessus bord. [*a*] *man ~!* un homme à la mer!

overburden (*Min.*) *n*, terrains de couverture, *m.pl*. ¶ *v.t*, surcharger.

overcast, *a*, couvert, chargé, trouble. ¶ *v.t.ir*, obscurcir. ¶ (*Emb.*) *n*, cordonnet, *m*.

overcautious, *a*, prudent à l'excès.

overcharge, *n*, majoration, *f*. ¶ *v.t. & i*, surcharger; faire payer trop cher, écorcher; (*weapon*) charger trop.

overcoat, *n*, pardessus, *m*; (*Mil.*) capote, *f*.

overcome, *v.t.ir*, surmonter, vaincre; accabler.

overcrowd, *v.t*, encombrer.

overdo, *v.t.ir*, outrer, charger. **overdone**, *a*, exagéré, outré; (*Cook.*) trop cuit.

overdose, *n*, trop forte dose, *f*.

overdraft, *n*, découvert, *m*, avance à découvert, *f*. **overdraw**, *v.t.ir*, mettre à découvert; tirer un chèque sans provisions.

overdrive, *v.t.ir*, surmener.

overdue, *a*, arriéré, en retard.

overelaborate, *v.t*, tourmenter, fignoler, lécher.

overestimate, *v.t*, surestimer, surfaire, majorer.

overexcite, *v.t*, surexciter.

overexposure (*Phot.*) *n*, surexposition, *f*.

overfeed, *v.t.ir*, trop nourrir.

overflow, *n*, débordement; trop-plein, *m*. ¶ *v.i*, [se] déborder; surabonder.

overgrow, *v.t.ir*, envahir. **overgrown**, *p.a*, couvert, encombré;

trop grand. **overgrowth**, *n*, surcroissance, *f*.

overhang, *n*, surplomb, porte à faux, *m*. ¶ *v.i. & t. ir*, surplomber.

overhaul, *v.t*, reviser; visiter; examiner; remettre à point.

overhead, *a*, aérien; de plafond; au-dessus; en haut. *~charges*, frais généraux, *m.pl*. ¶ *ad*, au-dessus de la tête; en haut, en l'air, au ciel.

overhear, *v.t.ir*, entendre par hasard.

overheat, *v.t*, surchauffer.

overindulgence, *n*, excès d'indulgence, *m*, mollesse; gâterie, *f*.

overjoyed, *p.p*, comblé de joie, ravi.

overladen, *p.p*, surchargé.

overland, *ad. & a*, par terre, de terre.

overlap, *v.t. & i*, chevaucher, recouvrir, déborder, imbriquer.

overleaf, *ad*, au verso.

overload, *v.t*, surcharger.

overlook, *v.t*, donner sur; dominer; laisser échapper; oublier; négliger.

overmantel, *n*, étagère de cheminée, *f*.

overmatter (*newspaper work*) *n*, marbre, *m*.

overmuch, *ad*, [par] trop, à l'excès.

overnight, *ad*, pendant la nuit; la veille au soir.

overpay, *v.t.ir*, surpayer, trop payer.

over-polite, *a*, révérencieux.

overpower, *v.t*, maîtriser; accabler. *~ing*, *a*, accablant; tout-puissant.

overproduction, *n*, surproduction, *f*.

overrate, *v.t*, surestimer, surfaire.

overreach, *v.t*, dépasser; circonvenir.

override, *v.t.ir*, surmener; primer.

overripe, *a*, trop mûr, blet.

overrule, *v.t*, écarter; l'emporter sur; gouverner.

overrun, *v.t.ir*, envahir; infester; (*Typ.*) remanier.

oversea[s], *a*, d'outre-mer. ¶ *ad*, outre-mer.

overseer, *n*, surveillant, inspecteur, *m*.

oversewing stitch, [point de] surjet, *m*.

overshadow, *v.t*, ombrager; obscurcir, éclipser.

overshoe, *n*, caoutchouc, *m*.

overshoot, *v.t.ir*, dépasser.

oversight, *n*, inadvertance, *f*, oubli, *m*, méprise; surveillance, *f*.

overspread, *v.t.ir*, se répandre sur.

overstate, *v.t*, exagérer.

overstaying pass (*Mil.*), retardataire, *a*.

overstep, *v.t*, outrepasser, franchir.

overstock, *v.t*, encombrer [de].

overstrain, *v.t*, outrer; surmener.

overtraining, *n*, surentraînement, *m*.

overti, *a*, manifeste.

overtake, *v.t.ir*, rattraper, surprendre, atteindre, gagner; (*auto*) doubler.

overtax, *v.t*, surtaxer, surimposer; surcharger.

overthrow, *v.t.ir*, renverser, bouleverser, subvertir.

overtime, *n*, heures supplémentaires, *f.pl*.

overtop, *v.t*, surpasser, surmonter.

overture, *n*, ouverture, *f*.

overturn, *v.t*, [ren]verser, [faire] chavirer; (*auto*) capoter.

overvalue, *v.t*, surestimer, surfaire, majorer.

overweening, *a*, outrecuidant.

overweight, *n*, poids fort, excédent de poids, *m*.

overwhelm, *v.t*, accabler, atterrer, assommer; combler.

overwork, *v.t*, surmener, forcer.

ovine, *a*, ovine, *a.f*.

oviparous, *a*, ovipare.

owe, *v.t*, devoir, être redevable de. **owing**, *a*, dû, échu; arriéré, *f*.

owl, *n*, hibou, *m*, chouette, *f*.

own, *a*, propre; (*brother, sister*) germain, e. *not my ~*, pas à moi, pas le mien. *one's ~*, son [propre]; à soi. ¶ *v.t*, posséder; reconnaître; avouer. **owner**, *n*, propriétaire, *m,f*, possesseur; (*ship's manager*) armateur; (*ship's proprietor*) propriétaire, *m*. *~driver*, propriétaire-conducteur, *m*. *~ship*, *n*, propriété, *f*.

ox, *n*, bœuf, *m*. *~eye daisy*, grande marguerite, *f*. **oxford**, *n*, (*shoe*) richelieu, *m*.

oxide, *n*, oxyde, *m*. **oxidize**, *v.t*, oxyder. **oxygen**, *n*, oxygène, *m*. **oxyhydrogen** (*blowpipe, etc.*) att, oxhydrique.

oyster, *n*, huître, *f*. *~ bed*, banc d'h—s; parc à h—s, *m*. *~ cul-*

ture, ostréiculture, *f*. *~man*, *~woman*, écailler, ère.

ozone, *n*, ozone, *m*.

P

pace, *n*, pas, *m*; allure, *f*; train, *m*. *to keep ~ with*, marcher du même pas que; (*fig.*) marcher de pair avec. *~maker*, meneur de train, entraîneur, *m*. ¶ *v.t*, arpenter; entraîner.

pachyderm, *n*, pachyderme, *m*.

pacific, *a*, pacifique. **P~** [Ocean], [océan] Pacifique, *m*. **pacificist**, **pacifist**, *n. & att*, pacifiste, *m,f. & a*. **pacify**, *v.t*, pacifier. **pacifying**, *p.a*, pacificateur.

pack, *n*, ballot, *m*, paquet; (*soldier's*) paquetage, *m*; bande, *f*, tas, *m*; (*hounds*) meute, *f*; (*cards*) jeu, *m*; (*ice*) banquise, *f*. *~horse*, cheval de bât, *m*. *~saddle*, bât, *m*. *~thread*, ficelle, *f*. ¶ *v.t*, emballer, empaqueter; (*hounds*) ameuter. *~* [*up*], plier (*ou* trousser) bagage, faire ses malles. *~age*, *n*, colis; envoi, *m*. *~ed*, *p.a*. *~ like sardines* (people), rangés comme des harengs en caque. *~er*, *n*, emballeur, *m*. *~et*, *n*, paquet; envoi, *m*; pochette, *f*. *~* [*boat*], paquebot, *m*. *~ing*, *n*, emballage, *m*; garniture, *f*. *~ case*, caisse d'emballage, *f*.

pact, *n*, pacte; contrat, *m*; convention, *f*.

pad, *n*, coussinet, bourrelet; (*for carrier's head*) tortillon; (*stamp*) tampon; (*blotting*) sous-main; (*writing*) bloc-notes, bloc de correspondance, *m*. ¶ *v.t*, [rem]bourrer, matelasser, feutrer, ouater; tamponner; (*verses*) cheviller. *padded cell*, cabanon, *m*. **padding**, *n*, [rem]bourrage, *m*; bourre, *f*.

paddle (*canoe*) *n*, pagaie, *f*. *~wheel*, roue à aubes, *f*. ¶ *v.i*, pagayer; (*splash about*) barboter.

paddock, *n*, enclos, paddock, *m*; (*turf*) enceinte du pesage, *f*, pesage, *m*.

padlock, *n*, cadenas, *m*. ¶ *v.t*, cadenasser.

Padua, *n*, Padoue, *f*.

paean, *n*, péan, pæan, *m*.

pagan, *a. & n*, païen, ne. *~ism & ~dom*, *n*, paganisme, *m*.

page, *n*, (*book*) page, *f*; (*Hist.*, *noble youth*) page, *m*. *~* [*boy*], chasseur, *m*. *~ proof*, mise en pages, *f*. ¶ *v.t*, paginer; (*have called*) envoyer chercher par un chasseur.

pageant, *n*, scène à grand spectacle, *f*; cortège [à spectacle] *m*, cavalcade, *f*. ~**ry**, *n*, faste, *m*.

paid, *p.p*, payé; versé; [pour] acquit; salarié, à gages. ~ *up*, (*capital*) versé, effectif, réel; (*shares*) libérées.

pail, *n*, seau, *m*. ~[**ful**], *n*, seau, *m*.

pain, *n*, douleur, souffrance, *f*, mal, *m*; peine, *f. in* ~, souffrant. *to take* ~*s*, se donner du mal. ¶ *v.t*, faire mal à; angoisser, peiner, fâcher. ~**ful†**, *a*, douloureux; dolent; pénible; cruel. ~**less**, *a*, sans douleur, indolent. **pains**, *n.pl*, peine, *f*, soin, *m*, frais, *m.pl*. ~**taking**, *a*, soigneux.

paint, *n*, peinture, couleur, *f*; (*face*) fard, *m*. ~**brush**, brosse à peindre, pinceau, *m*. ¶ *v.t*, peindre; (*face*) farder. ~**er**, *n*, peintre, *m*; (*boat*) bosse, *f*. ~**ing**, *n*, peinture, *f*.

pair, *n*, paire, *f*; couple, *m*. ~ *of scissors*, ciseaux, *m.pl*. ~ *of trousers*, pantalon, *m. the* ~ (*pictures, etc*.), les [deux] pendants, *m.pl*. ¶ *v.t*, apparier, appareiller, accoupler, jumeler.

pajamas, *n.pl*, pyjama, *m*.

pal, *n*, copain, *m*.

palace, *n*, palais, *m*.

paladin, *n*, paladin, *m*.

palatable, *a*, agréable [au goût], bon. **palatal**, *a*, palatal. **palate**, *n*, palais, *m*.

palatial, *a*, vaste & somptueux.

palaver, *n*, palabre, *f*. or *m*. ¶ *v.i*, palabrer.

pale, *a*, pâle; blafard, blême; clairet, paillet. ¶ *n*, palis; pal, *m*. ¶ *v.i*, pâlir, blêmir. ~**ness**, *n*, pâleur, *f*.

paleography, *n*, paléographie, *f*.

paleontology, *n*, paléontologie, *f*.

Palermo, *n*, Palerme, *f*.

palette, *n*, palette, *f*. ~ *knife*, couteau à palette, *m*.

paling, *n*, palis, *m*; clôture à claire-voie, *f*.

palisade, *n*, palissade, *f*. ¶ *v.t*, palissader.

palish, *a*, pâlot.

pall, *n*, poêle, drap mortuaire, *m*. ~ *bearers*, porteurs des cordons du poêle, *m.pl*. ¶ *v.t*. & *i*, s'affadir; rendre insipide.

pallet, *n*, palette, *f*; (*bed*) grabat, *m*.

palliasse, *n*, paillasse, *f*.

palliate, *v.t*, pallier. **palliative**, *a*. & *n*, palliatif, *a*. & *m*.

pallid, *a*, pâle, blafard, blême. **pallor**, *n*, pâleur, *f*.

palm (*hand*) *n*, paume, *f*. ~ [*branch*], palme, *f*. ~ [*tree*], palmier, *m*, palme, *f*. ~ *grove*, palmeraie, *f*. ~ *oil*, huile de palme, *f*. P~ *Sunday*, dimanche des Rameaux, *m*. ~ *off*, faire passer. ~**ist**, *n*, chiromancien, ne. ~**istry**, *n*, chiromancie, *f*. ~**y** *days*, beaux jours, *m.pl*.

palpable, *a*, palpable, sensible.

palpitate, *v.i*, palpiter. **palpitation**, *n*, palpitation, *f*.

palter, *v.i*, tergiverser; marchander; se jouer. **paltry**, *a*, mesquin, méchant, chétif, pitoyable.

pampas, *n.pl*, pampas, *f.pl*.

pamper, *v.t*, gâter; dorloter.

pamphlet, *n*, brochure, *f*, pamphlet, *m*.

pan, *n*, poêle; terrine; casserole; bassine, *f*; (*scale*) bassin, plateau, plat, *m*; cuvette, *f*.

panacea, *n*, panacée, *f*.

panama, *n*. or *Panama hat*, panama, *m*.

pancake, *n*, crêpe, *f*.

pancreas, *n*, pancréas, *m*.

pandemonium, *n*, pandémonium; tumulte, *m*.

pander to, se faire le ministre complaisant de.

Pandora's box, la boîte de Pandore.

pane, *n*, (*glass*) carreau, *m*, vitre, *f*; (*side or face*) pan, *m*.

panegyric, *n*, panégyrique, *m*.

panel, *n*, panneau; (*wall*) lambris; tableau, *m*, liste, *f*. ¶ *v.t*, lambrisser.

pang, *n*, serrement de cœur, tourment, *m*, angoisse, *f*; (*pl*.) affres, *f.pl*.

panic, *n*, [terreur] panique, *f*. ¶ *a*, de panique.

panjandrum, *n*, mamamouchi, *m*.

pannier, *n*, panier, *m*; (*on back*) hotte, *f*.

pannikin, *n*, petit pot, *m*.

panoply, *n*, panoplie, *f*.

panorama, *n*, panorama, *m*.

pansy, *n*, pensée, *f*.

pant, *v.i*, haleter, panteler. ~**ing**, *p.a*, haletant, pantelant.

pantheism, *n*, panthéisme, *m*.

pantheon, *n*, panthéon, *m*.

panther, *n*, panthère, *f*.

pantograph, *n*, pantographe, *m*.

pantomime (*dumb show*), *n*,

pantomime, *f.* **pantomimist,** *n,* pantomime, *m,f.*

pantry, *n,* office, *f,* garde-manger, *m.*

pants, *n,pl,* pantalon, *m.*

pap, *n,* bouillie; pulpe, *f;* mamelon, *m.*

papa, *n,* papa, *m.*

papacy, *n,* papauté, *f.* **papal,** *a,* papal. ~ *nuncio,* nonce du Pape, n. apostolique, *m.*

paper, *n,* papier, *m;* pièce, *f;* bulletin; (*news*) journal, *m,* feuille, *f;* (*learned*) mémoire, *m;* (*Sch.*) composition, copie, *f.* ~ *back book,* livre de poche, *m.* ~ *clip,* ~ *fastener,* attache [de bureau] *f.* ~*hanger,* colleur, *m.* ~ *knife,* coupe-papier, *m.* ~ *lantern* (Chinese, Japanese), lampion en papier, *m,* lanterne vénitienne, *f.* ~ *maker,* papetier, ère. ~ *making* & ~ *trade,* papeterie, *f.* ~ *money,* (*convertible*) monnaie de papier, *f;* (*inconvertible*) papier-monnaie, *m.* ~ *streamer,* serpentin, *m.* ~ *weight,* presse-papiers, *m.* ¶ *v.t,* tapisser.

papist, *n,* papiste, *m,f.*

papyrus, *n,* papyrus, *m.*

par, *n,* pair, *m.* ~ *value,* valeur au pair, *f.*

parable & **parabola,** *n,* parabole, *f.* **parabolic(al)**†, *a,* en paraboles; (*Geom.*) parabolique.

parachute, *n,* parachute, *m.*

parade, *n,* parade, *f;* défilé; cortège, *m.* ~ *ground,* place d' armes, *f,* champ de manœuvres, *m.*

paradise, *n,* paradis, *m;* (*Eden*) le paradis [terrestre].

paradox, *n,* paradoxe, *m.* ~**ical,** *a,* paradoxal.

paraffin [**oil**], *n,* huile de pétrole, *f,* pétrole à brûler, pétrole lampant, *m.* ~ [**wax**], *n,* paraffine, *f.*

paragon, *n,* parangon, modèle, phénix, *m.*

paragraph (*abb.* par) *n,* paragraphe; alinéa; entrefilet, *m.*

parallax, *n,* parallaxe, *f.*

parallel†, *a,* parallèle; (*drill shank, etc.*) cylindrique; (*fig.*) pareil. ~ *bars,* barres parallèles, *f.pl.* ~ *ruler,* règle à tracer des parallèles, *f.* ¶ *n,* (*Geom., Mil.*) parallèle, *f;* (*of latitude*) parallèle, *m;* (*comparison*) parallèle, pareil, *m.* **parallelepiped,** *n,* parallélipipède, *m.* **parallelogram,** *n,* parallélogramme, *m.*

paralyze, *v.t,* paralyser; transir.

paralysis, *n,* paralysie, *f.* **paralytic,** *a.* & *n,* paralytique, *a.* & *m, f.* ~ *stroke,* attaque de paralysie, *f.*

paramount, *a,* suprême; suzerain.

paramour, *n,* amant, *m,* maîtresse, *f.*

parapet, *n,* parapet, *m.*

paraphernalia, *n.pl,* attirail, bataclan, *m.*

paraphrase, *n,* paraphrase, *f.* ¶ *v.t.* & *i,* paraphraser.

parasite, *n,* parasite, *m.* **parasitic(al),** *a,* parasite; parasitaire.

parasol, *n,* ombrelle, *f.*

parboil, *v.t,* fair bouillir à demi.

parbuckle, *n,* trévire, *f.* ¶ *v.t,* trévirer.

parcel, *n,* colis; envoi; *m;* paquet, *m,* parcelle, *f.* ~ *post,* service des colis postaux, *m. by* ~ *post,* par colis postal. ~ [**out**], *v.t,* morceler, lotir.

parch, *v.t,* brûler; dessécher.

parchment, *n,* parchemin, *m.*

pardon, *n,* pardon, *m;* grâce, *f.* ¶ *v.t,* pardonner, pardonner à; gracier. ~**able,** *a,* pardonnable, excusable.

pare, *v.t,* rogner; éplucher; peler.

paregoric, *a,* parégorique.

parent, *n,* père, *m,* mère; (*fig.*) mère, *f;* (*pl.*) parents, *m.pl;* (*att.*) mère. ~**age,** *n,* extraction, *f.* ~**al,** *a,* de père, de mère, des parents.

parenthesis, *n,* parenthèse, *f.* **parenthetic(al),** *a,* entre parenthèses. **parenthetically,** *ad,* par parenthèse.

pariah, *n,* paria, *m.*

paring, *n,* rognure; retaille; épluchure, *f.*

parish, *n,* (*civil*) commune; (*Eccl.*) paroisse, *f;* (*att.*) communal; paroissial. ~ *church,* église paroissiale, paroisse, *f.* **parishioner,** *n,* habitant (e) de la commune; paroissien, ne.

Parisian, *a,* parisien. ¶ *n,* Parisien, ne.

parity, *n,* parité, *f.*

park, *n,* parc; bois, *m.* ¶ *v.t,* parquer; (*v.i.*) stationner. ~**ing,** *n,* stationnement, parcage, *m. no* ~, défense de stationner.

parlance, *n,* langage, *m,* termes, *m.pl.*

parley, *n,* pourparlers, *m.pl.* ¶ *v.i,* parlementer.

parliament, *n,* parlement, *m.* ~**ary,** *a,* (*government*) parlementaire; (*election*) législative; (*candidate*) à la députation.

parlor, *n,* [petit] salon; (*convent, school*) parloir, *m.* **beauty ~,** salon de coiffure, *m.* **~ games,** jeux de salon; jeux innocents, petits jeux, *m.pl.* **~maid,** femme de chambre (*servant à table*) *f.*

Parma, *n,* Parme, *f.* **~ violet,** violette de Parme, *f.*

parochial, *a,* (*civil*) communal; (*Eccl.*) paroissial; (*fig.*) de clocher.

parodist, *n,* parodiste, *m.* **parody,** *n,* parodie, *f.* ¶ *v.t,* parodier.

parole, *n,* parole, *f.* ¶ *v.t,* libérer sur parole.

paroxysm, *n,* paroxysme, *m.*

parquet, *n,* parquet, *m.* ¶ *v.t,* parqueter.

parrakeet, *n,* perruche, *f.*

parricidal, *a,* parricide. **parricide,** *n,* (*pers.*) parricide, *m,f*; (*act*) parricide, *m.*

parrot, *n,* perroquet, *m,* (*hen*) perruche, *f.*

parry, *v.t,* parer; esquiver. ¶ *n,* parade, *f.*

parse, *v.t,* analyser.

parsimonious†, *a,* parcimonieux. **parsimony,** *n,* parcimonie, *f.*

parsing, *n,* analyse grammaticale, *f.*

parsley, *n,* persil, *m.*

parsnip, *n,* panais, *m.*

parson, *n,* curé; ecclésiastique, *m.* **~'s nose,** croupion, *as de* pique, sot-l'y-laisse, *m.* **~age,** *n,* presbytère, *m.*

part, *n,* partie, part, portion; (*hair*) raie, *f*; endroit, parage, *m*; pièce, *f,* organe; (*Theat.*) rôle, emploi; (*book*) fascicule, *m,* livraison, *f.* **spare ~s,** pièces de rechange, *f.pl.* ¶ *v.t,* diviser; séparer; (*metals*) départir; (*v.i.*) se séparer; se décoller. **~ with,** se défaire de; céder.

partake, *v.i.ir,* participer.

partial†, *a,* (*biased*) partial; (*not entire*) partiel. **to be ~ to,** avoir un faible pour. **~ity,** *n,* partialité; prédilection, *f,* faible, *m.*

participate, *v.i,* participer.

participial adjective, (*present*) adjectif verbal; (*past*) participe passé employé (*ou* pris) adjectivement, *m.* **participle,** *n,* participe, *m.*

particle, *n,* particule, parcelle; (*Gram.*) particule, *f.*

particolored, *a,* bigarré, bariolé.

particular†, *a,* particulier; spécial; exigeant; méticuleux. ¶ *n,* particularité, *f,* point, détail, *m*; (*pl.*) détails, *m.pl,* indications, *f.pl,* libellé, *m,* renseignements, *m.pl,* précisions, *f.pl.* **~ity,** *n,* particularité, *f.* **~ize,** *v.t,* particulariser.

parting, *n,* séparation, *f*; décollement; entredeux, *m*; adieu, *m.*

partisan, *n,* partisan, *m.*

partition, *n,* séparation; cloison, *f.* **~ off,** cloisonner. **partitive** (*Gram.*) *a,* partitif.

partly, *ad,* [en] partie; moitié; partiellement.

partner, *n,* (*Com.*) associé, e; (*sports, games, Danc., & husband*) partenaire, *m,f*; (*wife*) compagne, *f*; (*Danc.*) danseur, euse, cavalier, *m,* dame, *f.* ¶ (*a lady, Danc.*) *v.t,* mener. **~ship,** *n,* société, association, *f.* **to enter into ~ with,** s'associer avec.

partridge, *n,* perdrix, *f,* (*young*) perdreau, *m.*

party, *n,* (*body united in cause*) parti, *m*; (*united in pleasure*) partie, *f*; complice (*to = de*); groupe, *m*; réception; soirée, *f.* **to give a ~,** recevoir du monde; donner une soirée.

paschal, *a,* pascal.

pass, *n,* passage, *m*; passe, *f*; col, pas; laissez-passer, sauf-conduit; permis, *m*; (*Mil.*) permission, *f.* **~ book,** carnet de compte, c. de banque, *m.* **~word,** mot de passe; (*Mil.*) mot d'ordre, *m.* ¶ *v.i. & t,* passer; admettre, être reçu à; prononcer; faire; adopter, prendre, approuver; voter; dépasser, franchir; croiser; (*auto*) doubler. **~ by,** passer. **~ for payment,** ordonnancer. **~ on,** transmettre; passer [son chemin]; p. outre. **~ out,** (*faint*) s'évanouir. **~able**†, *a,* passable; (*road, etc.*) practicable. **~age,** *n,* passage, *m*; traversée, *f*; trajet; canal; couloir, corridor, *m.* **~ money,** prix de passage, p. de voyage, *m.*

passenger, *n,* (*land, sea, or air*) voyageur, euse; (*sea or air*) passager, ère. **~ elevator,** ascenseur, *m.* **~ ship,** paquebot, *m.* **~ train,** train de voyageurs, *m,* grande vitesse, *f.*

passerby, *n,* passant, e, (*pl.*) allants & venants, *m.pl.* **passing,** *n,* passage, *m*; adoption, *f,* in **~,** en passant, passagèrement. **~ events,** actualités, *f.pl.* **~ fancy,**

caprice, m; (*liaison*) passade, *f*.
~ *note* (*Mus.*), note de passage,
f.

passion, *n*, passion; flamme; fureur; colère, *f*. ~ *flower*, fleur de
la Passion, passiflore, *f*. ~ *play*,
mystère de la Passion, m. ~ate,
a, emporté, rageur; passionné,
ardent. ~ately, *ad*, rageusement;
passionnément, ardemment, à la
folie. ~ *fond of*, fou de.

passive†, *a*, passif. ~ [**voice**], *n*,
passif, *m*. **passivity**, *n*, passivité,
f.

Passover, *n*, la Pâque.

passport, *n*, passeport, *m*.

past, *n*, passé, *m*. ¶ *a*. & *p.p*.
passé. *a* ~ *master*, passé maître,
m. ~ [*tense*], [temps] passé, *m*.
it is ~ *ten*, il est dix heures sonnées.

paste, *n*, pâte; colle [de pâte];
pierre d'imitation, p. factice, *f*,
faux brillant, *m*. ~board, carton
[de collage] m. ¶ *v.t*, coller.

pastel, *n*, pastel, *m*. ~ist, *n*, pastelliste, *m,f*.

pasteurize, *v.t*, pasteuriser, pastoriser.

pastil[le], *n*, pastille, *f*.

pastime, *n*, passe-temps, jeu, *m*.

pastor, *n*, pasteur, *m*. ~al, *a*,
pastoral. ~al & ~ale, *n*, pastorale, *f*.

pastry, *n*, pâtisserie, *f*. ~ *board*,
pâtissoire, *f*. ~cook [& *confectioner*], pâtissier, ère.

pasturage, *n*, pâturage, pacage,
gagnage, *m*. **pasture**, *n*, pâture,
f, pâtis; (*uncut*) herbage, *m*. ¶
v.t, faire paître, pacager.

pasty, *a*, pâteux. ¶ *n*, pâté, *m*,
bouchée, *f*.

pat, *a*. & *ad*, à propos, tout juste.
¶ *n*, tape, *f*; (*butter*) rond de
beurre, *m*. ¶ *v.t*, taper, tapoter;
(*an animal*) flatter, caresser. ~
oneself on the back, se complaire.

patch, *n*, (*ground*) lopin, coin;
(*cabbages, etc.*) caré, *m*; (*face*)
mouche; (*tire*) pastille, *f*. ~
pocket, poche rapportée, *f*. ~
work, rapiéçage, *m*; marqueterie,
f, placage, *m*. ¶ *v.t*, rapiécer. ~
up, replâtrer, rafistoler.

pate, *n*, caboche, *f*.

paten, *n*, patène, *f*.

patent, *a*, breveté; (*obvious*) patent. ~ *leather*, cuir verni, *m*;
(*att.*) verni. ~ *medicine*, spécialité pharmaceutique, *f*. ¶ *n*,

brevet [d'invention] *m*. ¶ *v.t*,
[faire] breveter.

paternal†, *a*, paternel. **paternity**,
n, paternité, *f*. **paternoster**, *n*,
Pater, *m*.

path, *n*, sentier, chemin, *m*; allée;
(*storm, etc.*) trajectoire, *f*.

pathetic†, *a*, pathétique.

pathological, *a*, pathologique.
pathologist, *n*, pathologiste, *m,f*.
pathology, *n*, pathologie, *f*.

pathos, *n*, pathétique, *m*.

patience, *n*, patience; constance;
(*cards*) réussite, patience, *f*. *to
put out of* ~, impatienter. **patient**†, *a*, patient, endurant. ¶ *n*,
malade, *m,f*, patient, e, client, e.

patina, *n*, patine, *f*. **patinated**, *a*,
patiné.

patriarch, *n*, patriarche, *m*. ~al,
a, patriarcal.

patrician, *a*. & *n*, patricien, ne.

patrimony, *n*, patrimoine, *m*.

patriot, *n*, patriote, *m,f*. ~ic, *a*,
patriotique; patriote. ~ism, *n*, patriotisme, *m*.

patrol, *n*, patrouille, *f*. ¶ *v.i*, patrouiller; (*v.t*) patrouiller sur.

patron, *n*, patron, protecteur, mécène, *m*; (*shop*) chaland, e, client,
m. ~ [*saint*], patron, ne, saint, e.
~ *saint's day*, fête patronale, *f*.
~age, *n*, patronage, *m*, protection, *f*; (*shop*) achalandage, *m*.
~ess, *n*, patronne, protectrice;
(*fête, etc.*) dame patronnesse, *f*.
patronize, *v.t*, patronner, protéger. ~d (*shop*) *p.p*, achalandé.
patronizing, *a*, paterne, protecteur.

patronymic, *n*, nom patronymique, *m*.

patten, *n*, socque, patin, *m*.

patter, *n*, bruit [des pas, des sabots]; (*in song*) parlé; (*showman's*) boniment, *m*. ¶ *v.i*, trottiner; (*rain*) crépiter. *a* ~*ing of
feet*, un bruit de pas précipités.

pattern, *n*, modèle; échantillon;
calibre, gabarit; patron; dessin,
m. ~ *maker* (*foundry*), modeleur,
m. ~ *making*, modelage, *m*. ¶
v.t, modeler.

patty, *n*, bouchée, *f*.

paunch, *n*, panse, *f*.

pauper, *n*, indigent, e, pauvre, *m*.
~ism, *n*, paupérisme, *m*.

pause, *n*, pause, *f*; silence; repos,
m. ¶ *v.i*, faire une pause.

pave, *v.t*, paver; (*fig.*) frayer.
~ment, *n*, pavage, pavement;
pavé; dallage; trottoir; *m*; (*outside café*) terrasse, *f*. ~ *light*, ~

glass, verdal, *m.* **paver, pavior,**
n, paveur, *m.*

Pavia, *n*, Pavie, *f.*

pavilion, *n*, pavilion, *m.*

paving, *n*, pavage, pavement, *m.*
~ *stone*, pavé; grès à paver, *m.*

paw, *n*, patte, *f. to* ~ *the ground*,
piaffer.

pawl, *n*, cliquet, chien, *m.*

pawn, *n*, gage, *m*; pension (*Fin.*)
f; (*chess*) pion, *m.* ~**broker,** prêteur sur gages, *m.* ~*shop*, mont-
de-piété, *m.* ¶ *v.t*, engager.

pay, *n*, paie, paye, *f*, salaire, traitement, *m*, gages, *m.pl*; solde, *f.*
~*master*, payeur, trésorier; commissaire, *m.* ¶ *v.t. & i. ir*, payer;
verser; solder, gager; rémunérer;
rapporter; (*visit*) faire; (*respects*)
présenter; (*homage*) rendre. ~
back, rembourser, rendre. ~ *for*,
payer, rémunérer. ~ *in*, verser.
~ *off*, solder; désintéresser; casser aux gages, congédier; (*mortgage*) purger. ~ *out*, payer, verser; (*cable*) filer. ~**roll**, état de
paiements, *m.* ~ *up*, (*v.t.*) libérer;
(*v.i.*) se libérer, s'exécuter. ~**able,**
a, payable; exigible; à payer; à
la charge; exploitable. ~**ee,** *n*,
bénéficiaire, *m,f.* ~**er,** *n*, payeur,
euse, payant, e; (*good, bad*) paie,
paye, *f.* ~**ing,** *a*, payant, rémunérateur. ~ *guest*, pensionnaire,
m,f. ~**ment,** *n*, paiement, payement; versement, *m*; rémunération, *f.*

pea, *n*, pois, *m. green* ~*s*, petits
pois, *m.pl.* ~*chick*, paonneau, *m.*
~*cock*, paon, *m.* ~*hen*, paonne,
f. ~*nut*, cacahuète, *f.* ~ *shooter*,
sarbacane, *f.* ~ *soup*, purée de
pois, *f.*

peace, *n*, paix; tranquillité, *f*,
repos; ordre public, *m.* ~*maker*,
pacificateur, trice. ~**able**† & ~
ful†, *a*, paisible, pacifique; tranquille.

peach, *n*, pêche, *f.* ~ [*tree*],
pêcher, *m.*

peak, *n*, cime, *f*, sommet; piton,
pic, *m*, dent; (*cap*) visière; pointe,
f, maximum, plafond, *m.* ~
hours, heures de pointe, *f.pl.*

peal, *n*, carillon, *m*, volée, *f*;
(*laughter*) éclat; coup, *m.*

pear, *n*, poire, *f.* ~ *tree* & ~ *wood*,
poirier, *m.*

pearl, *n*, perle, *f. mother-of-*~,
nacre, *f.* ~ *button*, bouton de
nacre, *m.* ~ *barley*, orge perlé,
m. ~ *oyster*, huître perlière, *f.* ~**y,**
a, de perle, perlé, nacré.

peasant, *n. & att*, paysan, ne.
~**ry,** *n*, les paysans, *m.pl.*

peat, *n*, tourbe, *f.* ~ *bog*, ~**ery,**
n, tourbière, *f.* ~**y,** *a*, tourbeux.

pebble, *n*, caillou; galet, *m.*

peccadillo, *n*, peccadille, *f.*

peccavi, *n*, meâ-culpâ, *m.*

peck, *n*, coup de bec, *m.* ¶ *v.t*,
becqueter, picoter; (*v.i.*) picorer.
to be ~*ish*, (*hunger*) avoir la
fringale.

peculate, *v.t*, détourner. **peculation,** *n*, détournement, *m*, malversation, *f.*

peculiar†, *a*, particulier; propre;
singulier, bizarre. ~**ity,** *n*, particularité, singularité, *f.*

pecuniary†, *a*, pécuniaire.

pedagogue, *n*, pédagogue, magister, *m.*

pedal, *n*, pédale, *f.* ~ [*key*]*board*,
pédalier, *m.* ¶ *v.i*, pédaler.

pedant, *n*, pédant, e. ~**ic**†, *a*,
pédant; pédantesque. ~**ry,** *n*,
pédanterie, *f*, pédantisme, *m.*

peddle, *v.i. & t*, baguenauder;
détailler; colporter. **peddler,** *n*,
colporteur, *m.*

pedestal, *n*, piédestal, pied, socle,
m, gaine; sellette, *f*, porte-
potiche, *m.* ~ *desk*, bureau-
ministre, *m.* ~ *table*, table à pied
central, *f.*

pedestrian, *n*, piéton, *m.* ~
crossing, traversée des piétons, *f.*
¶ *a*, à pied; (*statue*) pédestre.

pedigree, *n*, généalogie, *f*; pedigree, *m.*

pediment, *n*, fronton, *m.*

pedometer, *n*, podomètre,
compte-pas, *m.*

peel, *n*, peau, pelure, écorce, *f*;
zeste, *m.* ¶ *v.t*, peler, éplucher,
écorcer, décortiquer. ~ [*off*], *v.i*,
se peler, s'écailler. ~**ings,** *n.pl*,
épluchures, *f.pl.*

peep, *n*, regard [furtif] *m*; échappée [de vue] *f.* ~*hole*, regard,
judas, *m.* ¶ *v.i*, regarder; regarder
sans faire semblant, guigner;
émerger; (*chirp*) pépier. ~ *at*,
guigner.

peer, *n*, pair, *m.* ~ *into*, scruter;
fouiller. ~**age,** *n*, pairie, *f*; (*book*)
nobiliaire, *m.* ~**ess,** *n*, pairesse,
f. ~**less,** *a*, sans pair, introuvable.

peevish, *a*, maussade.

peewit, *n*, vanneau, *m.*

peg, *n*, cheville; fiche, *f*; jalon;
(*degree*) cran, *m.* ¶ *v.t*, cheviller;
jalonner. ~ [*away*], persister.

Pegasus (*fig.*) *n*, Pégase, *m.*

pekin (*fabric*) *n*, pékin, *m.* **Peki-**

nese or **peke** (*dog*) *n*, pékinois, *m*.
Peking (*Geog.*) *n*, Pékin, *m*.

pelf, *n*, lucre, gain, *m*.

pelican, *n*, pélican, *m*.

pelisse, *n*, pelisse, *f*.

pellet, *n*, boulette, *f*; grain de plomb, *m*.

pellicle, *n*, pellicule, *f*.

pell-mell, *ad.* & *n*, pêle-mêle, *ad.* & *m*.

pellucid, *a*, limpide.

pelt, *n*, peau, *f*. ¶ *v.t*, lapider, assaillir à coups (*with* = de). ~*ing rain*, pluie battante, *f*. ~**ry,** *n*, peausserie; pelleterie, *f*.

pelvis, *n*, bassin, *m*.

pen, *n*, plume, *f*; parc; (*cattle, etc.*) enclos, *m*. *ballpoint* ~, pointe-bille, *f*. ~ & *ink drawing*, dessin à la plume, *m*. ~**holder,** porte-plume, *m*. ~**knife,** canif, *m*. ~**manship,** calligraphie, *f*. ~ *name*, nom de plume, *n*. de guerre, pseudonyme, *m*. ¶ *v.t*, écrire, composer; parquer.

penal, *a*, pénal. ~**ty,** *n*, pénalité, peine, sanction; pénitence, *f*, dédit, *m*. ~ *area* (*Foot.*), surface de réparation, *f*. ~ *clause*, clause pénale, *f*. ~ *kick*, coup de réparation, c. de pénalité, *m*. **penance,** *n*, pénitence, *f*.

pencil, *n*, crayon; pinceau, *m*. ~ *case*, porte-crayon. ~ *sharpener*, taille-crayon, *m*. ¶ *v.t*, crayonner.

pendant, *n*, pendentif, *m*; (*Nav.*) flamme, *f*. **pendant,** *a*, pendant. **pendentive** (*Arch.*) *n*, pendentif, *m*. **pending,** *a*, pendant. ¶ *pr*, en attendant. **pendulum,** *n*, pendule; (*Horol.*) balancier, *m*.

penetrate, *v.t.* & *i*, pénétrer; percer.

penguin, *n*, manchot, *m*.

peninsula, *n*, péninsule, presqu'île, *f*. **peninsular,** *a*, péninsulaire.

penis, *n*, pénis, *m*.

penitence, *n*, pénitence, *f*. **penitent,** *a*. & *n*, pénitent, e. **penitentiary,** *a*, pénitentiaire. ¶ *n*, pénitencier, *m*, maison de correction, *f*.

pennant, *n*, flamme, *f*; guidon, *m*.

penniless, *a*, sans le sou.

pennon, *n*, flamme, *f*.

Pennsylvania, *n*, la Pen[n]sylvanie.

penny, *n*, penny, = $\frac{1}{100}$ of a dollar; (*very little money*) sou, *m*. ~*royal*, pouliot, *m*. ~*weight*, *Meas.* = 1.5552 grams.

pension, *n*, pension, rente, *f*.

¶ *v.t*, pensionner. ~ *off*, retraiter. ~**er,** *n*, pensionnaire, *m,f*; (*Mil.*) invalide, *m*.

pensive, *a*, pensif, songeur.

Pentateuch (**the**), le Pentateuque.

Pentecost, *n*, la Pentecôte.

penthouse, *n*, appentis, auvent, *m*.

penultimate, *a*, pénultième.

penumbra, *n*, pénombre, *f*.

penurious†, *a*, pauvre. **penury,** *n*, pénurie, disette d'argent, *f*.

peony, *n*, pivoine, *f*.

people, *n*, peuple, *m*; nation, *f*; gens, *m.pl.* & *f.pl*; personnes; personnalités, *f.pl*; population, *f*; monde, *m*; famille, *f*. ~ *say*, on dit. ¶ *v.t*, peupler.

pepper, *n*, poivre. *m*. ~*corn*, grain de poivre, *m*. ~*mint*, menthe poivrée, *f*. ~*mint* [*lozenge*], pastille de menthe, *f*. ~*shaker*, poivrière, *f*. ~ *plant*, poivrier, *m*. ¶*v.t*, poivrer; (*shot*) canarder; (*questions*) harceler. ~**y,** *a*, poivré; irascible, colérique.

per, *pr*, par; pour. ~ *annum*, par an, l'an. ~ *cent*, pour cent. ~ *contra*, en contrepartie, porté ci-contre.

perambulate, *v.t*, parcourir. **perambulator,** *n*, voiture d'enfant, *f*, landau [pour e.] *m*.

perceive, *v.t*, apercevoir; s'apercevoir de; (*Philos.*) percevoir.

percentage, *n*, pourcentage, tant pour cent, *m*; proportion, *f*.

perceptible, *a*, perceptible. **perception,** *n*, perception, *f*.

perch, *n*, (*bird's*) perchoir, bâton; (*fig.*) haut, *m*; (*fish*) perches, *f*; *Meas.* = 25.293 sq. meters. ¶ *v.i*, percher, jucher, brancher.

perchance, *ad*, peut-être.

percolate, *v.i.* & *t*, filtrer.

percussion, *n*, percussion, *f*. ~ *cap*, capsule, amorce, *f*. ~ *instruments*, instruments de percussion, *m. pl*, batterie, *f*. **percussive,** *a*, percutant.

perdition, *n*, perdition, *f*.

peregrination, *n*, pérégrination, *f*. **peregrine** [*falcon*], *n*, faucon pèlerin, *m*.

peremptory†, *a*, péremptoire; tranchant, absolu.

perennial, *a*, permanent, intarissable; vivace. ¶ *n*, plante vivace, *f*.

perfect†, *a*, parfait; achevé; vrai. ¶ *v.t*, [par]achever; perfectionner.

~ion, n, perfection, f. **~ly** sweet (pers.), gentil à croquer.

perfidious†, a, perfide. **perfidy**, n, perfidie, f.

perforate, v.t, perforer.

perforce, ad, forcément.

perform, v.t. & i, faire; exécuter, accomplir; jouer, donner, représenter. **~ance**, n, exécution, f, accomplissement, m; (sport) performance; (Theat.) représentation; (movies, etc.) séance, f. **~er**, n, exécutant, e; joueur, euse; concertant, e; artiste, m,f. **~ing** dog, chien savant, m.

perfume, n, parfum, m. **~** distiller, parfumeur, m. ¶ v.t, parfumer; embaumer. **perfumer**, n, parfumeur, euse. **~y**, n, parfumerie, f.

perfunctory, a, fait par manière d'acquit.

pergola, n, pergola, f.

perhaps, ad, peut-être.

peril, n, péril, m. **~ous†**, a, périlleux.

perimeter, n, périmètre, m.

period, n, période; époque, f; terme; exercice; (punctuation) point, m. **~ic & ~ical†**, a, périodique. **~ical**, n, périodique, m.

periphery, n, périphérie, f.

periphrasis, n, périphrase, f.

periscope, n, périscope, m.

perish, v.i, périr. **~able**, a, périssable.

peristyle, n, péristyle, m.

peritonitis, n, péritonite, f.

periwinkle, n, (Mol.) bigorneau, m; (Bot.) pervenche, f.

perjure oneself, se parjurer. **~d**, p.a, parjure. **perjurer**, n, parjure, m,f; (law) faux témoin, m. **perjury**, n, faux témoignage; parjure, m.

perky, a, éveillé; dégagé.

permanence, n, permanence, f. **permanent**, a, permanent; perpétuel. **~** wave, ondulation permanente, f. **~ly**, ad, de façon permanente.

permanganate, n, permanganate, m.

permeable, a, perméable. **permeate**, v.t, pénétrer; saturer.

permissible, a, loisible. **permission**, n, permission, f. **permit**, n, permis, m. ¶ v.t, permettre.

pernicious†, a, pernicieux.

peroration, n, péroraison, f.

peroxide, n, peroxyde, m.

perpendicular†, a. & n, perpendiculaire, a. & f.

perpetrate, v.t, perpétrer, commettre; faire. **perpetrator** (crime), n, auteur, m.

perpetual†, a, perpétuel. **perpetuate**, v.t, perpétuer. **perpetuity**, n, perpétuité, f.

perplex, v.t, embarrasser. **~ed** & **~ing**, a, perplexe. **~ity**, n, perplexité, f, embarras, m.

perquisite, n, revenant-bon, m, (pl.) casuel, m.

persecute, v.t, persécuter. **persecution**, n, persécution, f. **persecutor**, n, persécuteur, trice.

perseverance, n, persévérance, constance, f. **persevere**, v.i, persévérer.

Persia (Iran), n, la Perse. **Persian** (modern) a, persan. **~** carpet, tapis de Perse, m. **~** cat, chat persan, [c.] angora, m. **~** Gulf, golfe Persique, m. ¶ n, (pers.) Persan, e; (language) le persan. **Persian** (ancient) a, perse. ¶ n, Perse, m.f.

persist, v.i, persister, s'obstiner, s'opiniâtrer; persévérer. **~ence**, **~ency**, n, persistance, constance, f. **~ent**, a, persistant.

person, n, personne, f. **~** of independent means, rentier, ère. **~** opposite, vis-à-vis, m. **~age**, n, personnage, m. **~al†**, a, personnel; mobilier, meuble. **~ality**, n, personnalité, f. **~alty**, n, biens meubles, m.pl. **personify**, v.t, personnifier.

perspective, n, perspective; (Theat.) optique, f.

perspicacious, a, perspicace. **perspicacity**, n, perspicacité, f. **perspicuous†**, a, clair, net.

perspiration, n, transpiration, sueur, f. bathed in **~**, en nage. **perspire**, v.i, transpirer, suer.

persuade, v.t, persuader; décider. **persuasion**, n, persuasion; croyance, communion, f. **persuasive**, a, persuasif.

pert†, a, insolent; hardi; impertinent.

pertain, v.i, appartenir; avoir rapport.

pertinacious†, a, opiniâtre. **pertinacity**, n, opiniâtreté, f.

pertinent, a, pertinent, à propos. **~ly**, ad, à propos.

pertness, n, hardiesse; impertinence, f.

perturb, v.t, troubler, agiter. **~ation**, n, perturbation, agitation, f.

Peru, n, le Pérou.

Perugia, *n,* Pérouse, *f.*

perusal, *n,* lecture, *f.* **peruse,** *v.t,* lire attentivement.

Peruvian, *a,* péruvien. ~ *bark,* quinquina, *m.* ¶ *n,* Péruvien, ne.

pervade, *v.t,* pénétrer. **pervasive,** *a,* pénétrant, subtil.

perverse, *a,* pervers. **perversion,** *n,* perversion, *f.* **perversity,** *n,* perversité, *f.* **pervert,** *v.t,* pervers, vicieux, *m.* ¶ *v.t,* pervertir; dénaturer; fausser.

pervious, *a,* perméable.

pessimism, *n,* pessimisme, *m.* **pessimist,** *n.* & ~**ic,** *a,* pessimiste, *m.* & *a.*

pest, *n,* peste, *f.*

pester, *v.t,* tourmenter, importuner.

pestilence, *n,* peste, *f.* **pestilential,** *a,* pestilentiel.

pestle, *n,* pilon, *m.* ¶ *v.t,* piler.

pet, *n,* accès de mauvaise humeur; animal favori, *m;* favori, ite, mignon, ne, chéri, e, chouchou, *m.* ~ *argument,* cheval de bataille, *m.* ~ *aversion,* bête noire, *f.* ~ *dog,* chien favori, *m.* ~ *name,* petit nom d'amitié, *m.* ~ *scheme,* plan favori, *m.* ~ *subject,* sujet favori, dada, *m.* ~ *theory,* marotte, *f.* ~ *vice,* péché mignon, *m.* ¶ *v.t,* câliner, choyer

petal, *n,* pétale, *m.*

petiole, *n,* pétide, *m.*

petition, *n,* pétition, supplique; requête, *f.* ¶ *v.t,* adresser une requête à; (*v.i.*) pétitionner. ~**er,** *n,* pétitionnaire, *m,f;* requérant, e, demandeur, euse.

petrel, *n,* pétrel, *m.*

petrifaction, *n,* pétrification, *f.* **petrify,** *v.t,* pétrifier; méduser.

petroleum, *n,* pétrole, *m.*

petticoat, *n,* jupon, cotillon, *m,* cotte, *f.*

pettifoggery, *n,* avocasserie; chicane[rie] *f.*

pettiness, *n,* petitesse, *f.*

pettish, *a,* maussade.

petty, *a,* petit; menu. ~ *officer,* maître, *m;* (*pl, col.*) maistrance, *f.* ~ *cash,* argent pour menus frais, *m.*

petulance, *n,* vivacité [de caractère], humeur, *f.*

petunia, *n,* pétunia, *m.*

pew, *n,* banc [d'église] *m.*

pewit, *n,* vanneau, *m.*

pewter, *m,* étain, *m.* ~**er,** *n,* potier d'é., *m.*

phaeton, *n,* phaéton, *m.*

phalanx, *n,* phalange, *f.*

phantasm, *n,* phantasme, *m,* illusion, *f.* **phantasy,** *n,* vision, *f.* **phantasmagoria,** *n,* fantasmagorie, *f.* **phantom,** *n,* fantôme, *m.*

Pharaoh, *n,* pharaon, *m.*

Pharisaic(al), *a,* pharisaïque. **Pharisee,** *n,* pharisien, *m.*

pharmaceutical, *a,* pharmaceutique. **pharmacy,** *n,* pharmacie, *f.*

pharyngitis, *n,* pharyngite, *f.* **pharynx,** *n,* pharynx, *m.*

phase, *n,* phase, *f;* temps, *m.*

pheasant, *n,* faisan, e, (*young*) faisandeau, *m.* ~**ry,** *n,* faisanderie, *f.*

phenomenal, *a,* phénoménal. **phenomenon,** *n,* phénomène, *m.*

phial, *n,* fiole; ampoule, *f.*

Philadelphia, *n,* Philadelphie, *f.*

philander, *v.i,* faire le galant. ~**er,** *n,* galant, *m.*

philanthropic, *a,* philanthropique. **philanthropist,** *n,* philanthrope, *m,f.* **philanthropy,** *n,* philanthropie, *f.*

philatelist, *n,* philatéliste, *m,f.* **philately,** *n,* philatélisme, *m.*

philharmonic, *a,* philharmonique.

philippic, *n,* philippique, *f.*

Philistine, *n,* philistin, *m.*

philologist, *n,* philologue, *m.* **philology,** *n,* philologie, *f.*

philosopher, *n,* philosophe, *m.* ~**s' stone,** pierre philosophale, *f.* **philosophic(al)**†, *a,* philosophique; (*calm*) philosophe. **philosophize,** *v.i,* philosopher. **philosophy,** *n,* philosophie, *f.*

philter, *n,* philtre, *m.*

phlebitis, *n,* phlébite, *f.*

phlegm, *n,* mucosité, pituite, *f;* (*fig.*) flegme, *m.* ~**atic,** *a,* flegmatique.

phlox, *n,* phlox, *m.*

phoenix, *n,* phénix, *m.*

phonetic, *a,* phonétique. ~**s,** *n.pl,* phonétique, *f.*

phonograph, *n,* phonographe, *m.*

phosphate, *n,* phosphate, *m.* **phosphorescence,** *n,* phosphorescence, *f.* **phosphorescent,** *a,* phosphorescent. **phosphorus,** *n,* phosphore, *m.*

photograph, *n,* photographie, *f.* ~ *frame,* porte-photographie, *m.* ¶ *v.t,* photographier. ~**er,** *n,* photographe, *m,f.* ~**ic,** *a,* photographique. ~**y,** *n,* photographie, *f.* **photogravure,** *n,* photogravure, *f.*

phrase, *n,* locution, expression,

phrase; (*Mus.*) phrase, période, *f.*
¶ *v.t*, phraser. **phraseology**, *n*,
phraséologie, *f.*

phrenologist, *n*, phrénologiste,
m. **phrenology**, *n*, phrénologie, *f.*

phthisis, *n*, phtisie, *f.*

physic, *v.t*, médicamenter. **~al†**,
a, physique; matériel. **~ian**,
médecin, *m.* **~ist,** *n*, physicien,
ne. **~s,** *n.pl*, physique, *f.*

physiognomy, *n*, physionomie,
f.

physiology, *n*, physiologie, *f.*

physique, *n*, physique, *m.*

Piacenza, *n*, Plaisance, *f.*

pianist, *n*, pianiste, *m.f.* **piano-
[forte]**, *n*, piano, *m.* ~ *stool*,
tabouret de piano, *m.* ~ *wire*,
corde à piano, *f.*

piccolo, *n*, piccolo, *m.*

pick, *n*, pic, *m*, pioche, *f*; choix,
m; élite, fleur, *f*; (*of the basket*)
dessus, *m.* **~axe**, pioche, *f.* ~
lock, crochet [de serrurier], rossignol, *m.* **~me-up**, remontant,
m. the ~ *of the bunch*, la fleur
des pois. **~pocket**, filou, voleur
à la tire, pickpocket, coupeur de
bourses, *m.* ¶ *v.t*, cueillir; trier;
choisir; (*bone*) ronger; (*lock*)
crocheter; (*teeth*) curer; (*quarrel*)
chercher; (*peck*) becqueter. ~ *at*
one's food, pignocher. ~ *up*, relever; ramasser; (*passengers*)
prendre; (*news*) écumer.

picked, *p.a*, choisi, de choix;
d'élite. **picker**, *n*, cueilleur, euse;
trieur, euse.

picket, *n*, piquet; jalon, *m.* ¶ *v.t*,
piqueter.

picking, *n*, cueillette, *f*; triage,
m; (*pl. pilferings*) gratte, *f*, tour
de bâton, *m.*

pickle, *n*, (*brine*) saumure, *f*;
(*plight*) arroi, *m*; (*pl.*) conserves
au vinaigre, *f.pl.* ¶ *v.t*, mariner,
saler; conserver [au vinaigre].
~d, *a*, (*vegetables*) au vinaigre;
(*meat*) salé. ~ *cucumbers*, cor-
nichons, *m.pl.*

picnic, *n*, pique-nique, *m*, partie
de plaisir, *f.* ~ *basket*, panier
pique-nique, *m.* ¶ *v.i*, pique-
niquer.

pictorial, *a*, pictural; en images;
(*journal*) illustré, pittoresque;
(*plan, map*) figuratif, figuré. **picture**, *n*, tableau, *m*, peinture;
image, *f.* ~ *book*, livre d'images,
album d'images pour enfants, *m.*
~ *gallery*, galerie de tableaux, *f.*
~ *postcard*, carte postale illustrée, *f.* ~ *writing*, écriture figur-

ative, *f.* ¶ *v.t*, dépeindre, figurer,
représenter. ~ *to oneself*, se figurer. **picturesque†**, *a*, pittoresque, imagé. **~ness**, *n*, pittoresque, *m.*

pie, *n*, (*meat*) pâté, *m*; (*fruit*)
tourte, *f*; (*printers'*) pâté, *m*,
pâte, *f.* ~ *dish*, tourtière, *f.*

piebald, *a*, pie.

piece, *n*, morceau, *m*; fragment; tronçon, *m*; pièce, *f.* ~ *of business*,
affaire, *f.* ~ *of furniture*, meuble,
m. ~ *of ice*, glaçon, *m.* ~
of impertinence, impertinence, *f.*
~ *of news*, nouvelle, *f.* ~ *of ordnance*, bouche à feu, *f.* ~ *of
poetry*, poésie, *f.* ~ *of work*,
travail, *m*; besogne, *f.* **~work**,
travail à la tâche, *m.* ¶ *v.t*, rapiécer. ~ *together* (*fig.*), coudre
ensemble; **piecemeal**, *ad*, en
morceaux; par degrés.

pied, *a*, bigarré, bariolé.

Piedmont, *n*, le Piémont.

pier, *n*, jetée; jetée promenade;
pile, *f*; pied-droit; jambage, trumeau, *m.* **~head**, musoir, *m.*

pierce, *v.t. & i*, percer; repercer;
pénétrer. **piercing**, *p.a*, perçant;
(*cold*) saisissant.

piety, *n*, piété, *f.*

pig, *n*, cochon, porc, pourceau;
(*child*) goret, *m*; (*metal*) gueuse,
f, saumon, *m.* ~ *breeding*, l'industrie porcine, *f.* **~headed**,
têtu comme un mulet. ~ [*iron*],
fonte en gueuses, *f*. en saumons,
[gueuse de] fonte, *f.* ~ *meat*,
charcuterie, *f.* **~skin**, peau de
porc, *f*, cuir de p., *m.* **~sty** or
piggery, *n*, étable à pourceaux,
m, porcherie, *f.* **~tail** (*hair*),
queue, *f.*

pigeon, *n*, pigeon, ne; (*young*)
pigeonneau, *m.* **~hole**, boulin,
m; (*in desk*) case, *f.* [*set of*] ~
holes, casier, *m.* **~ry**, *n*, pigeonnier, *m.*

piglet, *n*, goret, *m.*

pigment, *n*, pigment, *m.*

pigmy, *n*, pygmée, *m.*

pike, *n*, pique, *f*; (*fish*) brochet,
m.

pilaster, *n*, pilastre, *m.*

pilchard, *n*, sardine, *f.*

pile, *n*, pile, *f*, monceau, amas,
tas, *m*; pelote, *f*; (*mass of buildings*) amas; (*wood*) bûcher, *m*;
(*arms*) faisceau; (*stake*) pieu,
pilotis; (*nap*) poil, *m*; (*Elec.*)
pile, *f. man who has made his
~*, homme nanti, *m.* ~ [*up*], *v.t*,

empiler, entasser, amonceler, amasser.

piles (*Med.*) *n.pl*, hémorroïdes, *f.pl.*

pilfer, *v.t*, piller.

pilgrim, *n*, pèlerin, e. ~age, *n. & place of pilgrimage*, pèlerinage, *m.*

piling (*pile-work*) *n*, pilotis, *m.*

pill, *n*, pilule, *f.*

pillage, *n*, pillage, *m.* ¶ *v.t*, piller.

pillar, *n*, pilier, *m*, colonne, *f.*

pillory, *n*, pilori, *m.* ¶ *v.t*, pilorier, draper.

pillow, *n*, oreiller; chevet; coussin, *m.* ~ *case*, taie d'oreiller, *f.* ~ *lace*, dentelle aux fuseaux, *f.*

pilot, *n*, pilote, *m.* ~ *balloon*, ballon d'essai, *m.* ~ *boat*, bateau-pilote, *m.* ~ *lamp*, lampe témoin, *f.* ¶ *v.t*, piloter.

pimpernel, *n*, mouron, *m*, morgeline, *f.*

pimple, *n*, bouton, bourgeon, *m*, pustule, *f. to break out in* ~s, boutonner, bourgeonner.

pin, *n*, épingle; (*peg*) cheville, *f*, boulon; *m*; goupille; clavette; broche; fiche, *f*; (*fig.*) épingle, *f*, fétu, *m.* ~s *& needles* (*fig.*), fourmis, *f.pl.* ~cushion, pelote [à épingles] *f.* ~ *money*, argent de poche, *m.* ~ *prick*, piqûre d'épingle, *f*, coup d'é., *m.* ¶ *v.t*, épingler; cheviller; clouer.

pinafore, *n*, tablier [d'enfant] *m.*

pincers, *n.pl*, tenailles; (*smith's*) tricoises, *f.pl.*

pinch, *n*, (*of salt*) pincée; (*snuff*) pincée, prise, *f*; pincement, *m. in a* ~, au besoin. ¶ *v.t*, pincer; blesser, brider, gêner. ~ed, *p.a*, tiré.

pine, *v.t*, languir; dépérir, sécher. ¶ *n*, pin, *m.*

pineapple, *n*, ananas, *m.*

ping-pong, *n*, ping-pong, tennis de table, *m.* ~ *set*, jeu de p.-p., jeu de t. de t., *m.*

pining, *n*, dépérissement, *m*; nostalgie, *f.*

pinion, *n*, aileron; (*Mech.*) pignon, *m.* ¶ *v.t*, couper les ailes à; (*pers.*) garrotter.

pink, *a*, rose, incarnat. ¶ *n*, rose; (*Bot.*) œillet, *m*, mignardise, *f.*

pinnace, *n*, grand canot, *m.*

pinnacle, *n*, pinacle, *m.*

pioneer, *n*, pionnier, *m.*

pious†, *a*, pieux.

pip, *n*, (*seed*) pépin; (*dominoes*) point, *m*; (*disease*) pépie, *f.*

pipe, *n*, tuyau, conduit, *m*, conduite, *f*; canal; (*key*) canon, *m*, forure; (*tobacco*) pipe, *f*; (*flute*) pipeau, chalumeau; (*boatswain's*) sifflet, *m.* ~ *clay*, terre de pipe, *f*; blanc de terre à pipe, *m.* ~ *line*, canalisation, *f.* ¶ *v.i. & t*, siffler. **piping** (*braid*) *n*, passepoil, liséré, *m.* ~ *hot*, bouillant.

pipkin, *n*, poêlon, *m*, huguenote, *f.*

pippin, *n*, reinette, *f.*

piquancy, *n*, goût piquant; (*fig.*) piquant, sel, *m.* **piquant**, *a*, piquant. **pique**, *n*, pique, *f.* ¶ *v.t*, piquer. **piquet**, *n*, piquet, *m.*

piracy, *n*, piraterie; contrefaçon, *f.* **pirate**, *n*, pirate; forban, *m.* ~ *publisher*, éditeur marron, *m.* ¶ *v.t*, contrefaire; (*v.i*) pirater.

Piraeus, *n*, le Pirée.

pirouette, *n*, pirouette, *f.* ¶ *v.i*, pirouetter.

Pisa, *n*, Pise, *f.*

pisciculture, *n*, pisciculture, *f.*

pistachio, *n*, (*nut*) pistache, *f*; (*tree*) pistachier, *m.*

pistil, *n*, pistil, dard, *m.*

pistol, *n*, pistolet, *m. a* ~ [*held*] *at one's head* (*fig.*), un couteau à la gorge.

piston, *n*, piston, *m.* ~ *rod*, tige, *f.*

pit, *n*, fosse, fouille, *f*, creux, puits, *m*; carrière; (*in metal*) piqûre; (*pock*) marque, couture, *f.* ~*fall*, trappe, *f*, piège; (*fig.*) écueil, *m.* ~ *saw*, scie de long, *f.* ¶ *v.t*, marquer, couturer; piquer; mettre aux prises.

pit-[a-]pat (to go), faire tic tac, palpiter.

pitch, *n*, poix, *f*; brai, bitume; point, degré, *m*; période; inclinaison, pente, *f*; (*Mus.*) diapason, *m*, hauter [musicale] *f*; (*Mech.*) pas; (*Naut.*) coup de tangage; (*angler's*) coup, *m.* ~ *dark*, noir comme poix. ~*fork*, fourche à faner, fouine, *f.* ~*fork someone into an office*, bombarder quelqu'un à une place. ~*pine*, pitchpin, *m.* ~ *pipe*, diapason à bouche, *m.* ¶ *v.t*, poisser; jeter, lancer; dresser, tendre, asseoir; (*v.i.*) plonger; (*ship*) tanguer, canarder. ~*ed battle*, bataille rangée, *f.*

pitcher, *n*, cruche, *f*, broc; (*baseball*) lanceur, *m.*

piteous†, *a*, piteux, pitoyable.

pith, *n*, moelle; (*palm tree*) cervelle; (*fig.*) moelle, *f*, suc; (*of a story*) piquant, *m.* ~ *helmet*,

casque en moelle, *m.* ~y, *a,*
moelleux; (*fig.*) plein de moelle.

pitiable† & **pitiful**†, *a,* piteux,
à faire pitié, pitoyable, lamentable. **pitiless**†, *a,* impitoyable,
sans pitié.

pittance, *n,* maigre revenu, revenu dérisoire, *m;* faible portion,
f.

pity, *n,* pitié, *f;* (*regret*) dommage,
m. to move to ~, apitoyer. ¶ *v.t,*
plaindre, avoir pitié de.

pivot, *n,* pivot, *m.* ¶ *v.i,* pivoter.

pixie, *n,* elfe, lutin, *m;* fée, *f.*

placard, *n,* placard, *m,* affiche,
pancarte, *f.* ¶ *v.t,* placarder, afficher.

place, *n,* place, *f;* endroit; lieu, *m;*
localité, *f.* *hiding* ~, cachette, *f.*
to take ~, avoir lieu, se passer.
¶ *v.t,* placer; mettre; déposer;
poser.

placer (*Min.*) *n,* placer, *m.*

placid†, *a,* placide. ~ity, *n,* placidité, *f.*

plagiarism, *n,* plagiat, larcin, *m.*
plagiarist, *n,* plagiaire, *m.* **plagiarize,** *v.t,* plagier.

plague, *n,* peste; plaie, *f;* fléau;
tourment, *m,* brebis galeuse, *f.*
~-*stricken* (*person*), pestiféré, e,
a. & *n.* ¶ (*fig.*) *v.t,* tourmenter,
assassiner; (*tease*) lutiner.

plaice, *n,* plie, *f,* carrelet, *m.*

plaid, *n,* plaid, tissu écossais, *m.*

plain, *a,* uni; lisse; plat; simple;
(*cigarettes*) ordinaires; clair, évident; distinct; nu; au naturel;
laid. ~ *cooking,* cuisine bourgeoise, *f.* ~ *dealing,* franchise, *f.*
in ~ *figures,* en chiffres connus.
~ *girl,* jeune fille laide, *f,* laideron, *m.* ~ *language* (*Teleg.*),
[langage] clair, *m.* ~song, plain-
chant, *m.* ¶ *n,* plaine, *f.* ~ly,
ad, simplement; clairement; dis-
tinctement; nettement, net, bonnement. ~ness, *n,* simplicité;
clarté; netteté; laideur, *f.*

plaintiff, *n,* demandeur, eresse,
plaignant, e. **plaintive**†, *a,* plaintif.

plait, *n,* natte, tresse, *f.* ¶ *v.t,*
natter, tresser. *to* ~ *one's hair,*
se natter.

plan, *n,* plan; projet, dessein, *m,*
batterie, *f.* ¶ *v.t,* dresser le plan
de; projeter, méditer, concerter.

plane, *a,* plan. ¶ *n,* plan, *m,* surface plane, *f;* (*tool*) rabot; avion,
aéroplane, *m.* ~ [*tree*], platane,
plane, *m.* ¶ *v.t,* raboter; planer.

planet, *n,* planète, *f.* **planetarium,**

n, planétaire, *m.* **planetary,** *a,*
planétaire.

plank, *n,* planche, *f,* madrier, *m.*

plankton, *n,* plancton, *m.*

plant, *n,* plante, herbe, *f,* végétal, *m;*
(*factory*) usine, *f;* matériel, outillage, appareil, *m.* ~ *life,* vie
végétale, *f.* ¶ *v.t,* planter; poser.

plantain, *n,* plantain; (*banana*)
plantanier, *m.*

plantation, *n,* plantation, *f,*
plantage, plant, *m.* **planter,** *n,*
planteur, euse.

plaque, *n,* plaque, *f.*

plasma, *n,* plasma, *m.*

plaster, *n,* plâtre; (*Med.*) emplâtre, *m.* ~ *cast,* plâtre, *m.* ~ *of
paris,* plâtre de moulage, gypse,
m. ¶ *v.t,* plâtrer. ~er, *n,* plâtrier,
m.

plastic, *a,* plastique. ~ity, *n,*
plasticité, *f.*

plate, *n,* (*eating*) assiette, *f;* (*collection*) plat, bassin, *m;* (*Phot.*)
plaque; (*book*) planche, *f,* hors-
texte, *m;* (*turf*) coupe; (*metal*)
plaque, *f.* ~s & *dishes,* vaisselle,
f. ~ *glass,* glace de vitrage, *f.* ~
glass insurance, assurance contre
le bris de glaces, *f.* ~ *holder*
(*Phot.*), châssis négatif, c. porte-
plaque(s) *m.* ¶ *v.t,* plaquer; argenter; (*ship*) border. ~[**ful**], *n,*
assiettée, assiette, *f.*

plateau, *n,* plateau, *m.*

platen (*Typ.*) *n,* platine, *f.*

platform, *n,* plate-forme; estrade; tribune, *f;* pont; (*Rly.*)
quai, débarcadère, embarcadère;
(*Pol.*) programme, *m.* ~ *scales,*
bascule romaine, *f.* ~ *ticket,* billet de quai, *m.*

platinotype, *n,* platinotypie, *f.*
platinum, *n,* platine, *m.* ~
blonde (color), blond platine, *m.*

platitude, *n,* platitude, *f.*

Platonic, *a,* platonique.

platoon, *n,* peloton, *m.*

plaudit, *n,* applaudissement, *m.*

plausible†, *a,* plausible.

play, *n,* jeu, *m;* récréation, *f;*
essor, *m,* carrière; pièce [de thé-
âtre] *f;* spectacle; (*Mech.*) jeu,
m, chasse, *f.* ~*fellow,* ~*mate,*
camarade de jeu, *m,f.* ~*goer,*
coureur (euse) de spectacles.
~*ground,* cour de récréation, *f,*
(*covered*) préau, *m.* ~ *of colors,*
reflets irisés, *m.pl.* ~ *of features,*
jeux de physionomie, *m.pl.* ~ *of
light,* jeu de lumière, chatoiement,
m. ~ *on words,* jeu de mots, *m.* ~
pen, parc d'enfant, *m.* ~*thing,*

jouet, joujou, *m*, amusette, babiole, *f*. ~*time*, récréation, *f*. ~*wright*, auteur dramatique, dramatiste, *m*, dramaturge, *m,f*. ¶ *v.i*, jouer; (*v.t.*) jouer; j. de; faire; (*harp*, *etc*.) pincer; (*a fish*) noyer. ~**er**, *n*, joueur, euse; musicien, ne; acteur, trice, comédien, ne. ~ *piano*, piano mécanique, *m*. ~**ful**, *a*, folâtre, enjoué, badin. ~**fulness**, *n*, enjouement, *m*. *playing cards*, cartes à jouer, *f.pl*.

plea, *n*, prétexte, *m*; (*law*) défenses, *f.pl*; exception, *f*; (*pl*.) conclusions, *f.pl*. **plead,** *v.t*. & *i*, plaider, alléguer, prétexter. ~ *guilty*, s'avouer coupable, s'accuser soi-même. ~ *not guilty*, nier sa culpabilité. ~**ing** (*law*) *n*, (*oral advocacy*) plaidoirie; (*preparatory formalities*) instruction; (*pl, statement*) instruction par écrit, *f*.

pleasant†, *a*, agréable, aimable; commode. ~**ness**, *n*, agrément, *m*. ~**ry**, *n*, plaisanterie, *f*. **please,** *v.t*, plaire à, agréer à; sourire à; flatter; accommoder; (*abs*.) plaire. ¶ *imperative*, s'il vous plaît; veuillez; prière de . . .; de grâce! ~**d**, *p.a*, content, heureux, aise. **pleasing**†, *a*, agréable, amène; gracieux. **pleasurable**†, *a*, agréable. **pleasure,** *n*, plaisir; agrément, *m*; douceur; jouissance; volupté, *f*; honneur; gré, *m*. ~ *boat*, bateau de plaisance, *m*. ~ *trip*, partie de plaisir, *f*.

pleat, *n*, pli, *m*, pince, *f*. ¶ *v.t*, plisser.

pledge, *n*, gage, engagement, *m*, **plebiscite,** *n*, plébiscite, *m*.

pledge, *n*, gage, engagement, *m*, assurance, *f*. ¶ *v.t*, engager; boire à la santé de.

plenary, *a*, plénier. **plenipotentiary,** *a*. & *n*. plénipotentiaire, *a*. & *m*. **plenitude,** *n*, plénitude, *f*. **plenteous**† & **plentiful**†, *a*, abondant. *to be plentiful*, foisonner. **plenty,** *n*, abondance; foison, *f*. ~ *of*, force. *with* ~ *of*, à grand renfort de. **plenum,** *n*, plein, *m*.

pleonasm, *n*, pléonasme, *m*.

plethora, *n*, pléthore, *f*.

pleura, *n*, plèvre, *f*. **pleurisy,** *n*, pleurésie, *f*.

plexus, *n*, plexus, réseau, lacis, *m*.

pliable, *a*, pliable, pliant, flexible, souple. **pliancy,** *n*, flexibilité, souplesse, *f*.

pliers, *n.pl*, pince, *f*, pinces, *f.pl*.

plight, *n*, état, *m*, passe, *f*, arroi, *m*. ¶ *v.t*, engager.

plinth, *n*, plinthe, *f*.

plod on, along, *v.i*, avancer péniblement. **plodder,** *n*, bûcheur, euse.

plot, *n*, parcelle, *f*, lopin, coin; complot, *m*, conspiration, trame, intrigue; (*novel*, *play*) intrigue, *f*. ¶ *v.t*. & *i*, (*curve*, *etc*.) tracer; comploter, conspirer, machiner. **plotter,** *n*, conspirateur, trice.

plow, *n*, charrue, *f*. ~ *land*, terre labourable, *f*. ~*man*, laboureur, valet de charrue, *m*. ~*share*, soc, *m*. ¶ *v.t*. & *i*, labourer; (*fig*.) sillonner. ~**ing**, *n*, labourage, labour, *m*.

pluck, *n*, courage, estomac, cran, *m*; (*butchery*) fressure, *f*. ¶ *v.t*, arracher; [dé]plumer, dépiler; cueillir; (*Mus. strings*) pincer. ~**y**†, *a*, courageux, crâne.

plug, *n*, tampon, bouchon, obturateur, *m*; (*Elec*.) prise de courant, *f*; (*twist of tobacco*) carotte, *f*. ¶ *v.t*, tamponner, boucher. ~ *in*, brancher.

plum, *n*, prune, *f*; (*dried*) pruneau, *m*. ~ *orchard*, prunelaie, *f*. ~ *pudding*, plum-pudding, *m*. ~ [*tree*], prunier, *m*.

plumage, *n*, plumage, *m*.

plumb, *a*, droit, vertical. ¶ *ad*, à plomb, d'aplomb. ¶ *n*, plomb, *m*. ~ *line*, fil à plomb, *m*. ¶ *v.t*, plomber. **plumbago,** *n*, plombagine, *f*; graphite, *m*. **plumber,** *n*, plombier, fontainier, *m*. **plumbing,** *n*, plombage, *m*; plomberie, *f*.

plume, *n*, plumet, panache, *m*, aigrette, *f*. ¶ *v.t*, empanacher. ~ *its feathers*, s'épilucher. ~ *oneself on*, se piquer de, se targuer de.

plummet, *n*, plomb; fil à plomb, *m*; sonde, *f*.

plump, *a*, rebondi, dodu, potelé, en chair, paquet; (*chicken*) gras. ~**ness**, *n*, embonpoint, *m*.

plunder, *n*, pillage; butin, *m*. ¶ *v.t*, piller, butiner. ~**er**, *n*, pillard, e.

plunge, *n*, plongeon; (*Swim*.) plongeon sans élan, *m*. *to take the* ~ (*fig*.), faire le saut périlleux, sauter le fossé. ¶ *v.t*, plonger; immerger; ensevelir; (*v.i*.) [se] plonger. **plunger,** *n*, plongeur, *m*.

pluperfect, *n*, plus-que-parfait, *m*.

plural, *a,* plural; (*Gram.*) pluriel. ¶ *n,* pluriel, *m.* ~**ity,** *n,* pluralité, *f;* (*of offices*) cumul, *m.*

plus, *pr,* plus. *he is 10, 12,* ~, il a 10, 12, ans révolus. ~*-fours,* culotte pour le golf, *f.* ~ [*sign*], [signe] plus, *m.*

plush, *n,* peluche, *f.*

ply, *n,* pli, *m,* épaisseur, *f.* ~*wood,* [bois] contreplaqué, *m.* ¶ *v.t,* (*tool*) manier; (*questions*) presser (*with* = de); (*trade*) exercer; (*v.i.*) faire le service, marcher.

pneumatic, *a,* pneumatique; à air comprimé. ~ [*tire*], [bandage] pneumatique, pneu, *m.*

pneumonia, *n,* pneumonie, *f.*

Po (the), le Pô.

poach, *v.t,* pocher; (*v.i.*) braconner. ~**er,** *n,* braconnier, *m.*

pocket, *n,* poche, *f;* (*vest*) gousset, *m;* (*Bil.*) blouse, *f.* ~ *air* ~, trou d'air, *m.* ~ *money,* argent de poche, *m. in one's* ~ (*fig.*), en poche. ¶ *v.t,* empocher. ~**ful,** *n,* pleine poche, *f.*

pockmarked, *a,* marqué (*ou* picoté) de petite vérole, grêlé.

pod, *n,* cosse, gousse, *f.*

poem, *n,* poème, *m,* poésie, *f.*

poet, *n,* poète, *m.* ~**aster,** *n,* poétereau, *m.* ~**ess,** *n,* poétesse, femme poète, *f.* ~**ic,** ~**ical†,** *a,* poétique. ~**ry,** *n,* poésie, *f.*

poignant, *a,* poignant, empoignant.

point, *n,* point; fait, *m;* pointe, *f;* poinçon; bec, *m;* (*Rly.*) aiguille, *f;* piquant, *m;* température; question, *f.* ~*-blank, ad,* de but en blanc, à bout portant, à brûlepourpoint. ~ *lace,* point, *m.* ~ *of the compass,* aire de vent, *f,* quart de v., *m.* 6, 8, ~ [*size*] (*Typ.*), corps 6, 8; corps de 6, de 8, points, *m. to the* ~, à propos. ¶ *v.t,* pointer; appointer; épointer, tailler [en pointe]; (*masonry*) jointoyer; (*v.t. & abs., of dog*) arrêter. ~ *at,* montrer du doigt. ~ *out,* signaler, indiquer, désigner. ~**ed,** *a,* pointu; piquant; peu voilé, peu équivoque. ~**er,** *n,* (*rod*) baguette, *f;* index; chien d'arrêt, *m.*

poise, *n,* balance, *f,* équilibre, *m.* ¶ *v.t,* balancer, équilibrer.

poison, *n,* poison, toxique, *m.* ~ *gas,* gaz toxique, *m.* ¶ *v.t,* empoisonner, intoxiquer. ~**er,** *n,* empoisonneur, euse. ~**ing,** *n,* empoisonnement, *m,* intoxication, *f.* ~**ous,** *a,* toxique; véneneux; venimeux. *substance which is* ~, substance qui empoisonne.

poke, *n,* coup, *m.* ¶ *v.t,* fourrer; mettre; (*fire*) attiser, fourgonner. ~ *about,* fourgonner.

poker, *n,* tisonnier, fourgon; (*cards*) poker, *m.* **poky,** *a,* resserré, étroit, mesquin.

Poland, *n,* la Pologne.

polar, *a,* polaire. ~ *bear,* ours blanc, *m.* **pole,** *n,* poteau, *m,* perche, gaule, *f,* mât; bâton; (*carriage*) timon; (*Astr., Phys., etc.*) pôle, *m;* Meas. = 25.293 sq. meters. **P~,** *n,* Polonais, e. ~ *axe,* merlin, assommoir, *m;* (*Hist.*) hache d'armes, *f.* ~**cat,** putois, *m.* ~ *jump,* saut à la perche, *m.* ~ *star,* étoile polaire, *f.* ¶ *v.t,* échalasser.

polemic(al), *a,* polémique. **polemic,** *n.* & ~**s,** *n.pl,* polémique, *f.*

police, *n,* police, *f.* ~ *court,* tribunal de simple police, *m.* ~**man,** agent de police, gardien de la paix, sergent de ville, *m.* ~ *records,* casier judiciaire, *m.* ~ *station,* bureau de police, poste de p.; (*central*) commissariat de p., *m.*

policy, *n,* politique, *f;* (*public*) ordre, *m;* (*Insce*) police, *f.*

Polish, *a,* polonais. ¶ *n,* le polonais.

polish, *n,* poli; vernis; *m;* pâte à polir, *f.* ¶ *v.t,* vernir; cirer; faire reluire; frotter; encaustiquer. ~*ing brush* (*shoes*), brosse à reluire, *f.*

polite, *a,* poli. **politely,** *ad,* poliment. ~**ness,** *n,* politesse; (*to women*) galanterie, *f.*

politic & ~**al†,** *a,* politique. ~**ian,** *n,* [homme] politique; (*as a trade*) politicien, *m.* ~**s,** *n.pl.* ~, **polity,** *n,* politique, *f. to talk politics,* politiquer.

polka, *n,* polka, *f.*

poll, *n,* scrutin, vote, *m.* ~ *tax,* capitation, *f.* ~*ing station,* bureau de scrutin, *m.*

pollard, *n,* têtard, *m.* ¶ *v.t,* étêter.

pollen, *n,* pollen, *m.*

pollute, *v.t,* polluer, souiller.

polo, *n.* & ~ *cap,* polo, *m.*

polonaise, *n,* polonaise, *f.*

poltroon, *n,* poltron, ne.

polyanthus, *n,* primevère des jardins, *f.* **polygamist,** *n.* & **polygamous,** *a,* polygame, *m,f.* & *a.* **polygamy,** *n,* polygamie, *f.* **poly-**

glot, *a. & n*, polyglotte, *a. & m,f.*
polygon, *n*, polygone, *m.* **Poly-**
nesia, *n*, la Polynésie. **polyp &**
polypus, *n*, polype, *m.* **polysyl-**
labic, *a. & polysyllable*, *n*, polysyllable, *a. & m.* **polytechnic**, *a,*
polytechnique. **polytheism**, *n*,
polythéisme, *m.*
pomade, *n*, pommade, *f.* ¶ *v.t,*
pommader.
pomegranate, *n*, grenade, *f.* ~
[*tree*], grenadier, *m.*
Pomeranian [dog], *n.* or **pom**,
abb, loulou [de Poméranie] *m.*
pommel, *n*, pommeau, *m.* ¶ *v.t,*
rosser, frotter, gourmer.
pomp, *n*, pompe, *f*, faste, apparat,
attirail, *m.*
Pompeii, *n*, Pompéi, *f.*
pomposity, *n*, emphase, *f.* **pom-**
pous†, *a*, pompeux; emphatique;
doctoral.
pond, *n*, étang, *m*, mare, *f*; (*of*
canal) bief, *m.*
ponder, *v.i*, réfléchir, méditer,
rêver; (*v.t.*) peser, ruminer. ~
able, *a*, pondérable, pesant. ~
ous†, *a*, pesant.
pontiff, *n*, pontife, *m.* **pontifical†**,
a. & n, pontifical, *a. & m.* **pon-**
tificate, *n*, pontificat, *m.*
pontoon, *n*, ponton, caisson, *m.*
~ *bridge*, pont de bateaux, *m.*
pony, *n*, poney, *m.*
poodle, *n*, caniche, *m,f.*
pooh, *i*, bah!, baste! **pooh-pooh**,
v.t, faire fi de, repousser avec
mépris.
pool, *n*, (*swimming*) piscine; mare,
f, étang, *m*; (*cards*) poule, cagnotte, *f*; (*fencing, shooting, ice*
hockey) poule, *f*; (*Com.*) pool;
(*Fin.*) syndicat de placement,
groupement, *m.* ~ *betting*, pari
mutuel, *m.* ¶ *v.t*, mettre en commun.
poop, *n. & ~ deck*, dunette, *f.*
poor, *a*, pauvre; indigent; maigre;
méchant. ~ *box*, tronc des pauvres, *m.* ~ *health*, une santé médiocre, une petite santé. ~ *house*,
hospice, *m.* ~ *little thing* (*pers.*),
pauvret, te. *the ~*, les pauvres,
les indigents, *m.pl.* ~**ly**, *ad*, pau-
vrement. ¶ *a*, indisposé, incommodé, souffrant. ~**ness**, *n*, pauvreté, *f.*
pope, *n*, pape, *m.* ~**ry**, *n*, papisme,
m.
popinjay (*Hist.*) *n*, papegai, *m.*
popish, *a*, papiste.
poplar, *n*, peuplier, *m.*
poplin, *n*, popeline, *f.*

poppy, *n*, pavot; coquelicot, ponceau, *m.*
populace, *n*, populace, *f.* **popu-**
lar†, *a*, populaire; (*treatise*) de
vulgarisation. ~**ity**, *n*, popularité, *f.* ~**ize**, *v.t*, vulgariser.
populate, *v.t*, peupler. **popula-**
tion, *n*, population, *f.* **populous**,
a, populeux.
porcelain, *n*, porcelaine, *f.*
porch, *n*, porche, *m.*
porcupine, *n*, porc-épic, *m.*
pore, *n*, pore, *m.* ~ *over*, s'absorber dans la lecture de; méditer
sur.
pork, *n*, porc, *m*; charcuterie, *f.*
~ *butcher*, charcutier, *m.* ~**er**, *n*,
cochon; goret, *m.*
porosity, *n*, porosité, *f.* **porous**,
a, poreux.
porphyry, *n*, porphyre, *m.*
porpoise, *n*, marsouin, *m.*
porridge, *n*, bouillie, *f.* **por-**
ringer, *n*, écuelle, *f.*
port, *n*, port; (*side*) bâbord, *m.*
free ~, port franc, *m.* ~ [*hole*],
hublot, *m.* ~ *of call*, escale; relâche, *f.* ~ *of registry*, port
d'attache. ~ [*wine*], porto, vin de
Porto, *m.*
portable, *a*, portatif, mobile.
portal, *n*, portail, *m.*
portcullis, *n*, herse, *f.*
portend, *v.t*, présager. **portent**,
n, présage, *m.* **portentous**, *a*, de
mauvais présage; prodigieux.
porter, *n*, concierge, portier; porteur; portefaix; commissionaire;
facteur, *m.* ~**age**, *n*, portage,
factage, *m.*
portfolio, *n*, portefeuille, *m*,
serviette, *f.*
portico, *n*, portique, *m.*
portion, *n*, portion, part, *f*, quartier, *m*; (*of Rly. train*) rame;
(*marriage*) dot, *f.* ¶ *v.t*, partager;
doter.
portland cement, chaux-limite,
f.
portliness, *n*, corpulence; prestance, *f.* **portly**, *a*, corpulent,
gros; d'un port noble.
portmanteau, *n*, valise, *f.*
portrait & ~ure, *n*, portrait, *m.*
portray, *v.t*, [dé]peindre. **por-**
trayal, *n*, peinture, *f.*
portress, *n*, concierge, portière, *f.*
Portugal, *n*, le Portugal. **Portu-**
guese, *a*, portugais. ¶ *n*, (*pers.*)
Portugais, e; (*language*) le portugais.
pose, *n*, pose; affectation, *f.* ¶ *v.i.*
& t, poser. **poser**, *n*, problème,

m. **position,** *n,* position, situation; posture; condition, *f;* emplacement; classement, *m.* ¶ *v.t,* classer.

positive†, *a,* positif; absolu.

posse, *n,* brigade, *f.*

possess, *v.t,* posséder. **~ed,** *p.p,* possédé; *as if* ~, endiablé. *one* ~, possédé, e. **~ion,** *n,* possession; jouissance, *f;* (*pl.*) possessions, *f.pl,* avoir, bien, *m. with immediate* ~, présentement. **~ive,** *a,* possessif. **~or,** *n,* possesseur, *m.*

possibility, *n,* possibilité, *f.* **possible,** *a. & n,* possible, *a. & m. to be* ~, se pouvoir. **possibly,** *ad,* peut-être. *he cannot* ~ . . ., il est impossible qu'il . . .

post, *n,* (*upright*) poteau; (*door*) montant; pieu; étai, *m;* (*bed*) colonne, *f;* (*place*) poste, *m;* (*P.O.*) poste, *f;* (*letters*) courrier, *m.* **~card,** carte postale, *f. to go* **~haste,** accourir dare-dare. **~man,** facteur [des postes] *m.* **~mark,** *n,* timbre, *m;* (*v.t.*) timbrer. **~master, mistress,** maître (maîtresse) de poste, receveur (euse) des postes. **~master general,** directeur général des postes, télégraphes & téléphones, *m.* **~office,** bureau de poste, *m,* poste, *f.* ~ *office guide,* indicateur universel des P.T.T., *m.* ~ *office order,* mandat[-poste] *m.* ¶ *v.t,* mettre à la poste; afficher, placarder; mettre au courant; (*Bkkpg.*) [re]porter; (*men*) [a]poster, poser. **~age,** *n,* port, *m.* ~ *stamp,* timbre-poste, *m.* **~al,** *a,* postal. ~ *order,* mandat [-poste] *m.*

postdate, *n,* postdate, *f.* ¶ *v.t,* postdater.

poster, *n,* affiche, *f,* placard, *m.*

posterior†, *a. & n,* postérieur, *a. & m.*

posterity, *n,* postérité, *f.*

postern, *n,* poterne, *f.*

posthumous, *a,* posthume.

posting, *n,* mise à la poste, *f;* affichage; (*Bkkpg.*) report, *m;* (*sentry*) pose, *f.*

post meridiem (*abb.* p.m.), après midi; de l'après-midi, du soir.

post mortem, *n,* autopsie, *f.*

postpone, *v.t,* remettre, renvoyer, différer, ajourner.

postscript (*abb.* P.S.) *n,* postscriptum, P.-S., *m.*

postulant, *n,* postulant, e.

posture, *n,* posture, pose, attitude, *f;* état, *m.*

postwar, *a,* d'après-guerre.

posy, *n,* fleur, *f.*

pot, *n,* pot, *m;* marmite, *f;* chaudron, *m;* terrine, *f;* creuset, *m;* (*cards*) cagnotte, *f.* ~ *bellied,* ventru. ~ *boiler,* besogne alimentaire, *f.* **~herb,** herbe potagère, *f.* **~hook,** crémaillère, *f;* (*writing*) jambage, *m. to take* ~ *luck,* dîner à la fortune du pot. ¶ *v.t,* empoter. **~ful,** *n,* potée, *f.*

potable, *a,* potable.

potash, *n,* potasse, *f.* **potassium,** *n,* potassium, *m.*

potato, *n,* pomme de terre, *f. sweet* ~, patate, *f.*

potency, *n,* force, *f.* **potent†,** *a,* puissant; fort. **potentate,** *n,* potentat, *m.* **potential,** *a. & n,* potentiel, *a. & m.*

potion, *n,* potion, *f.*

potted, *p.a,* en pot, en terrine.

potter, *n,* potier, *m.* ~'s *wheel,* tour de potier, *m.* **~y,** *n,* poterie, faïence; faïencerie, *f.*

pouch, *n,* poche, *f.;* sac, *m,* bourse; (*cartridge*) cartouchière, giberne; gibecière; (*tobacco*) blague, *f.*

pouf, *n,* pouf, *m.*

poulterer, *n,* marchand de volaille, *m.*

poultice, *n,* cataplasme, *m.*

poultry, *n,* volaille, *f.* ~ *yard,* basse-cour, *f.*

pounce, *n,* ponce, *f.* ¶ *v.t,* poncer. ~ *on,* fondre sur.

pound, *n,* (*for cattle*) fourrière; (£) livre, *f;* (*avoirdupois weight*) livre [poids] *f.* = 0.45359243 kilogram. ¶ *v.t,* piler.

pour, *v.t,* verser; couler, jeter; répandre; épancher; (*oil on waves*) filer. *it is* ~*ing,* il pleut à verse. ~*ing rain,* pluie battante, *f.*

pout, *v.i,* faire la moue, faire la lippe. **~er,** *n,* pigeon grosse gorge, *m.*

poverty, *n,* pauvreté, *f.* **~stricken** (*person*), miséreux, euse.

powder, *n,* poudre, *f.* ~ *box,* boîte à poudre, *f,* poudrier, *m.* ~ *magazine,* poudrière, *f.* ~ *puff,* houppe à poudrer, *f.* ¶ *v.t,* pulvériser; poudrer; saupoudrer. **~y,** *a,* poudreux, pulvérulent.

power, *n,* puissance, *f;* pouvoir, *m;* énergie; force; faculté; autorité, *f;* (*att.*) mécanique; marchant au moteur. ~ *hammer,* marteau-pilon, *m.* ~ *house,* ~ *station,* usine de force motrice, *f.* **~ful†,** *a,* puissant; fort; énergique. **~less,** *a,* impuissant.

practicable, *a,* praticable, faisable, exécutable. **practical†,** *a,* pratique; (*pers.*) positif. ~ *joke,* farce, fumisterie; brimade, *f.* ~ *joker,* farceur, euse, fumiste, *m.*

practice, *n,* pratique; habitude, *f;* usage, *m;* coutume, *f;* exercice; tir, *m;* (*sport*) mise en train, *f;* quelques coups d'essai, quelques échanges, *m.pl;* clientèle; charge; étude, *f,* cabinet, *m.* **practician,** *n,* praticien, *m.* **practise,** *v.t,* pratiquer; exercer; suivre; s'exercer à; user de. **practitioner,** *n,* praticien, *m.*

prairie, *n,* prairie, *f.*

praise, *n,* louange, *f;* éloge, *m.* ¶ *v.t,* louer; glorifier; prôner, vanter. **~worthy,** digne d'éloges, louable.

prance, *v.i,* piaffer.

prank, *n,* escapade, espièglerie, *f.*

prate, *v.i,* bavarder.

pratique, *n,* [libre] pratique, *f.*

prattle, *n,* babil, gazouillement, *m.* ¶ *v.i,* babiller, gazouiller.

prawn, *n,* crevette rouge, *f.*

pray, *v.t. & i,* prier. ¶ (*form of address*), je vous prie, veuillez; de grâce; je vous le demande. **prayer,** *n,* prière; supplique, *f,* orémus, *m.* ~ *book,* livre d'église, l. de prières, l. d'office, paroissien, *m.* ~ *wheel,* moulin à prières, *m.*

preach, *v.t. & i,* prêcher. **~er,** *n,* prédicateur; (*protestant*) prédicant, *m.* **~ing,** *n,* prédication, *f.*

preamble, *n,* préambule, *m.*

prearranged, *p.a,* arrangé d'avance.

prebend, *n,* prébende, *f.* **~ary,** *n,* prébendier, *m.*

precarious†, *a,* précaire.

precaution, *n,* précaution, prévoyance, *f.* **~ary,** *a,* de précaution, de prévoyance.

precede, *v.t,* précéder, devancer. **precedence,** *n,* priorité; préséance, *f,* pas, *m.* **precedent,** *n. & preceding,** *a,* précédent, *m. & a.*

precentor, *n,* grand chantre, *m.*

precept, *n,* précepte, *m.* **~or,** *n,* précepteur, *m.*

precinct, *n,* enceinte, *f;* (*pl.*) pourtour, *m.*

precious†, *a,* précieux.

precipice, *n,* précipice, *m.* **precipitancy & precipitation,** *n,* pré-

cipitation, *f.* **precipitate,** *v.t. & i,* précipiter; brusquer. ¶ *a. & n,* précipité, *a. & m.* **~ly,** *ad,* précipitamment. **precipitous,** *a,* escarpé, à pic.

precise, *a,* précis; formaliste. **~ly,** *ad,* précisément. **to state ~,** préciser. **precision,** *n,* précision, *f.*

preclude, *v.t,* empêcher de.

precocious, *a,* précoce; (*too knowing*) savant; (*in vice*) polisson. **~ness,** *n,* précocité, *f.*

preconceived, preconcerted, *a,* préconçu, arrêté.

precursor, *n. & ~y,** *a,* précurseur, *m. & a.m.*

predatory, *a,* rapace; de proie.

predecease, *n,* prédécès, *m.* ¶ *v.i,* prédécéder.

predecessor, *n,* prédécesseur, *m,* devancier, ère.

predestination, *n,* prédestination, *f.*

predicament, *n,* [mauvaise] passe, situation difficile; (*Log.*) catégorie, *f.*

predicate (*Log. & Gram.*) *n,* attribut, prédicat, *m.* ¶ *v.t,* attribuer; affirmer (*ou* énoncer) un rapport (*of* = entre). **predicative adjective,** adjectif attribut, *m.*

predict, *v.t,* prédire. **~ion,** *n,* prédiction, *f.*

predilection, *n,* prédilection, *f.*

predispose, *v.t,* prédisposer.

predominance, *n,* prédominance, *f.* **predominate,** *v.i,* prédominer.

preeminent, *a,* prééminent. **~ly,** *ad,* par excellence.

preemption, *n,* préemption, *f.*

preen, *v.t,* éplucher. ~ *its feathers,* s'éplucher.

preface, *n,* préface, *f,* avant-propos, *m.* ¶ *v.t,* préluder à. **prefatory,** *a,* liminaire; à titre de préface.

prefect, *n,* préfet, *m.* **~ure,** *n,* préfecture, *f.*

prefer, *v.t,* préférer, aimer mieux; promouvoir; (*charges*) déposer. **~able†,** *a,* préférable. **~ence,** *n,* préférence, *f;* (*Cust.*) régime de faveur, *m,* préférence, *f.* **preferred stock,** actions de priorité, a—s privilégiées, *f.pl.* **preferential,** *a,* de préférence, privilégié. **preferment,** *n,* promotion, *f.*

prefix, *n,* préfixe, *m.* ¶ *v.t,* joindre à titre de préface; joindre comme préfixe. **~ed** (*Gram.*) *p.a,* préfixe.

pregnable, *a*, prenable.

pregnancy, *n*, grossesse, *f*. **pregnant**, *a*, enceinte, grosse; (*animal*) pleine; (*fig.*) gros, plein.

prehensile, *a*, préhenseur, *a.m*. ~ *tail*, queue prenante, *f*.

prehistoric, *a*, préhistorique.

prejudge, *v.t*, préjuger. **prejudice**, *n*, préjudice, détriment; préjugé, *m*, prévention, *f*, parti pris, *m*. *without* ~ *to*, sans préjudice de. ¶ *v.t*, prévenir; nuire à. **prejudicial**, *a*, préjudiciable; attentatoire.

prelacy, *n*, prélature, *f*. **prelate**, *n*, prélat, *m*.

preliminary, *a*, préliminaire, préalable. ~ *expenses* (company), frais de constitution, *m.pl*. **preliminaries**, *n.pl*, préliminaires, *m.pl*, préface, *f*; (*book, abb*. **prelims**) pièces liminaires, *f.pl*.

prelude, *n*, prélude, *m*. ¶ *v.i*, préluder.

premature†, *a*, prématuré; (*childbirth*) avant terme.

premeditate, *v.t*, préméditer. **premeditation**, *n*, préméditation, *f*.

premier, *a*, premier. ¶ *n*, président du conseil [des ministres], premier ministre, *m*. ~**ship**, *n*, présidence du conseil, *f*.

premise, *v.t*, faire remarquer d'avance. ~**s**, *n.pl*, immeuble, *m*, locaux, lieux, *m.pl*; (*deed*) intitulé, *m*. **premises** (*Log.*) *n.pl*, prémisses, *f.pl*.

premium, *n*, prime; récompense, *f*.

premonition, *n*, présage, *m*. **premonitory**, *a*, prémonitoire, avant-coureur, précurseur. ~ *symptom*, prodrome, *m*.

preoccupation, *n*, préoccupation, *f*. **preoccupy**, *v.t*, préoccuper.

preparation, *n*, préparation; (*Sch.*) étude, *f*; (*pl.*) préparatifs, apprêts, *m.pl*. **preparatory**, *a*, préparatoire. ~ *work* (*Min.*), dispositifs de mines, *m.pl*. **prepare**, *v.t*, préparer; apprêter. ~**d** (*ready*) *p.a*, prêt.

prepay, *v.t*, payer d'avance; affranchir.

preponderance, *n*, prépondérance, *f*. **to preponderate over**, l'emporter sur.

preposition, *n*, préposition, *f*.

prepossess, *v.t*, prévenir. ~**ing**, *a*, prévenant, avenant. ~**ion**, *n*, prévention, *f*.

preposterous†, *a*, déraisonnable, absurde, saugrenu.

prerequisite, *a*, requis. ¶ *n*, nécessité préalable, *f*.

prerogative, *n*, prérogative, *f*, privilège, *m*.

presage, *n*, présage, *m*. ¶ *v.t*, présager.

Presbyterian, *n*. & *a*, presbytérien, ne.

prescience, *n*, prescience, *f*.

prescribe, *v.t*, prescrire; (*Med.*) ordonner. **prescription**, *n*, prescription; (*Med.*) ordonnance, prescription, formule, *f*.

presence, *n*, présence; prestance, *f*. ~ *of mind*, présence d'esprit, *f*. **present**, *a*, présent; actuel; courant. ¶ *n*, présent, *m*; (*gift*) cadeau, present, *m*. *at* ~, présentement. ¶ *v.t*, présenter; offrir. ~**able**, *a*, présentable; montrable. **presentation**, *n*, présentation, *f*. ~ *copy*, exemplaire en hommage, *m*.

presentiment, *n*, pressentiment, *m*. *to have a* ~ *of*, pressentir.

presently, *ad*, tantôt, tout à l'heure.

preservation, *n*, conservation; préservation, *f*. **preservative**, *n*. & *a*, préservatif; (*for food*) antiseptique, *m*. & *a*. **preserve**, *n*, conserve, *f*, confiture, *f*. oft. *pl*, marmelade; réserve, (*pl.*) chasse gardée, c. réservée, *f*; (*fig.*) fief, *m*; (*pl.*) conserves, *f.pl*. ¶ *v.t*, préserver; conserver; confire; (*plant*) naturaliser.

preside, *v.i*, présider. ~ *at, over*, présider [à]. **presidency**, *n*, présidence, *f*. **president**, *n*, président, e.

press, *n*, presse, *f*; pressoir, *m*; armoire, *f*; journalisme, *m*; (*of sail*) force, *f*. *the* ~ (newspapers), la presse. *in the* ~, sous presse. ~ *agency*, agence d'information, *f*. ~ *copy*, (*letter*) copie à la presse, *f*; (*book*) exemplaire de presse, *f*; e. de publicité, *m*. ~ *cutting*, coupure de journal, *f*. ~**man**, *n*, journaliste; (*Typ.*) pressier, *m*. ¶ *v.t* & *i*, presser; serrer; pressurer; fouler; activer; appuyer; peser. ~**ing**, *a*, pressant, pressé, urgent; (*debt*) criarde. **pressure**, *n*, pression, *f*; serrement, *m*; presse, *f*; accablement, *m*; (*Mech.*) poussée; tension, *f*. *blood* ~, tension artérielle, *f*. ~ *gauge*, manomètre, *m*.

prestige, n, prestige, m.

presume, v.t. & i, présumer. ~ [up]on, se prévaloir de. **presumption,** n, présomption, f; préjugé, m. **presumptuous,** a, présomptueux. **~ness,** n, outrecuidance, f.

presuppose, v.t, présupposer.

pretence, n, [faux] semblant, m, feinte, f; prétexte, m. **pretend,** v.t. & i, faire semblant; prétexter; feindre; prétendre. **~er,** n, prétendant, e. **pretension,** n, prétention, f. **pretentious,** a, prétentieux.

preterite, n, prétérit, m.

preternatural†, a, surnaturel.

pretext, n, prétexte, m.

prettiness, n, gentillesse, f. **pretty†,** a, joli, gentil, bellot. ¶ ad, assez. ~ good, passable, passablement bon. ~ much, à peu près. ~ well, assez bien.

prevail over, prévaloir sur, l'emporter sur. prevail [up]on, décider, persuader à. **prevailing,** p.a, dominant, régnant; général. **prevalence,** n, fréquence, prédominance, f. **prevalent,** a, régnant, prédominant. to be ~, régner.

prevaricate, v.i, tergiverser, équivoquer. **prevarication,** n, tergiversation, équivoque, f.

prevent, v.t, empêcher, obvier à, prévenir. **~ion,** n, empêchement, m; défense préventive, f. society for the ~ of cruelty to animals, société protectrice des animaux, f. **~ive,** n, préservatif, m.

previous†, a, précédent, antérieur, préalable. ~ speaker, préopinant, m.

prevision, n, prévision, f.

prewar, a, d'avant-guerre.

prey, n, proie, f. ~ [up]on, faire sa proie de; (the mind) miner, ronger.

price, n, prix; cours; taux, m; cote, f. all at the same ~, au choix. ~ list, prix courant, tarif, m. ¶ v.t, tarifer. **~less,** a, sans prix, inappréciable, inestimable, impayable.

prick, n, piqûre, f; coup; (conscience) reproche, m. ¶ v.t, piquer; (conscience) bourreler. ~ up (ears), dresser. **prickle,** n, aiguillon, piquant, m. **prickly,** a, épineux, piquant. ~ pear, figue de Barbarie, f.

pride, n, orgueil, m, fierté, gloire,

f; amour-propre, m; (collection of animals) troupe, f. ~ oneself [up]on, s'enorgueillir de, se faire gloire de, se piquer de, se targuer de.

priest, n, prêtre, m. **~ess,** n, prêtresse, f. **~hood,** n, prêtrise, f, sacerdoce; clergé, m. **~ly,** a, sacerdotal.

prig, n, pédant, e. **priggish,** a, pédant.

prim, a, pincé, affecté, collet monté.

primacy, n, primatie, primauté, f.

prima donna, prima donna, diva, f.

prima facie, prima facie, de prime face.

primary†, a, primitif; premier; primordial; primaire. **primate,** n, primat, m. **prime,** a, premier; primordial; de première qualité. ~ minister, président du conseil [des ministres], premier ministre, m. ~ mover, mobile, m; cheville ouvrière, f. ~ of life, fleur de l'âge, force de l'âge, f. ¶ v.t, (pump, blasting) amorcer; (with paint) imprimer; (pers.) souffler. **primer,** n, premier livre de lecture, alphabet, A b c, abécédaire, m. **primeval,** a, primitif. **priming,** n, amorce; (paint) impression, f. **primitive†,** a, primitif; primordial. **primogeniture,** n, primogéniture, f. **primordial,** a, primordial. **primrose,** n, primevère, f.

prince, n, prince, m. **~ly,** a, princier. **princess,** n, princesse, f.

principal†, a, principal; capital. ¶ n, principal; chef, m; directeur, trice; proviseur; patron, ne; mandant, commettant, donneur d'ordre; (of debt) capital, principal, m. **~ity,** n, principauté, f.

principle, n, principe, m.

prink, v.t, éplucher.

print, n, empreinte; impression; (Phot.) épreuve [positive]; gravure; estampe, f; (type) caractères, m.pl. out of ~, épuisé. ¶ v.t, imprimer; tirer; (with pen) mouler. **~er,** n, imprimeur, m. **~'s error,** faute d'impression, erreur typographique, f. **~'s imprint,** indication de nom & de lieu de résidence de l'imprimeur, f. **~ing,** n, impression, f; tirage, m; (art) imprimerie, f. ~ frame (Phot.), châssis-presse, m. ~ ink, encre d'imprimerie, f. ~ plant, imprimerie, typographie, *f.* ~ *out paper* (*Phot.*), papier à image directe, papier à noircissement direct, *m.*

prior, *a,* antérieur. ¶ *n,* prieur, *m.* ~**ess,** *n,* prieure, *f.* ~**ity,** *n,* priorité, antériorité, *f.* **priory,** *n,* prieuré, *m.*

prism, *n,* prisme, *m.* ~**atic,** *a,* prismatique.

prison, *n,* prison, *f.* ~ *breaking,* bris de p., *m.* ~**er,** *n,* prisonnier, ère, détenu, e, prévenu, e. ~*'s base,* jeu de barres, *m,* barres, *f.pl.*

pristine, *a,* primitif.

privacy, *n,* secret, *m.* **private,** *a,* privé; particulier; personnel; intime; bourgeois; simple; (*on door*) défense d'entrer. ~ [*soldier*], [simple] soldat, *m. by* ~ *treaty,* à l'amiable, de gré à gré. *in* ~, en particulier. ~ *means,* fortune personnelle, *f.* ~ *view* (*art*), avant-première, *f.* ~ **privateer,** *n,* corsaire, *m.* **privateering,** *n,* course, *f.* **privately,** *ad,* en particulier; dans le privé; privément.

privation, *n,* privation, *f.* **privative** (*Gram.*) *a.* & *n,* privatif, *a.* & *m.*

privet, *n,* troène, *m.*

privilege, *n,* privilège, *m;* prérogative, *f.* ¶ *v.t,* privilégier.

privily, *ad,* en secret. **privy,** *a,* privé. ~ *to,* instruit de. ¶ *n,* privé, *m,* lieux [d'aisance] *m.pl.*

prize, *n,* prix, *m;* (*Nav.*) prise, *f;* (*lottery*) lot, *m;* (*leverage*) levier, *m,* pesée, *f.* ~ *bull,* taureau primé, *m.* ~ *fight[ing],* combat de boxe professionnel, *m.* ~ *fighter,* boxeur professionnel, professionnel de la boxe, *m.* ~ *giving,* distribution de prix, *f.* ~ *medal,* médaille d'honneur, *f.* ~ *winner,* médaillé, e, lauréat, *m.* ¶ *v.t,* (*value*) estimer, priser; (*lever*) forcer.

pro, *pr,* pour. *the* ~*s & cons,* le pour & le contre.

probability, *n,* probabilité, vraisemblance, *f.* **probable†,** *a,* probable, vraisemblable.

probate, *n,* vérification de testament, *f.*

probation, *n,* stage, *m;* (*Eccl.*) probation, *f.* ~**er,** *n,* stagiaire, novice, *m,f.*

probe, *n,* (*instrument*) sonde, *f,* stylet, *m.* ¶ *v.t,* sonder.

probity, *n,* probité, *f.*

problem, *n,* problème, *m.* ~ *play,* pièce à thèse, *f,* ~**atic(al),** *a,* problématique.

proboscis, *n,* trompe; proboscide, *f.*

procedure, *n,* marche à suivre; (*law*) procédure, *f.* **proceed,** *v.i,* procéder; provenir; découler; partir; cheminer; s'acheminer; se rendre; marcher; continuer. ~ *against,* (*law*) poursuivre. ~**ing,** *n,* procédé, *m;* (*pl.*) actes, *m.pl;* démarches; délibérations, *f.pl;* débats, *m.pl;* procédure, *f;* poursuites, *f.pl.* **proceeds,** *n.pl,* produit, *m.*

process, *n,* cours; procédé; processus, *m. in* ~ *of time,* dans la suite.

procession, *n,* procession, *f,* défilé, *m,* marche, *f,* cortège, convoi, *m.*

proclaim, *v.t,* proclamer; publier; annoncer; déclarer; dénoncer; afficher. **proclamation,** *n,* proclamation; déclaration, *f.*

proclivity, *n,* penchant, *m.*

procrastinate, *v.i,* aller de délai en délai, atermoyer. **procrastination,** *n,* procrastination, *f,* atermoiement, *m.*

procreate, *v.t,* procréer.

proctor (*Univ.*) *n,* censeur, *m.*

procuration, *n,* procuration, *f,* mandat, *m.* **procure,** *v.t,* procurer. ~**ment,** *n,* obtention, *f;* approvisionnement, *m.*

prod, *v.t,* piquer.

prodigal, *a.* & *n,* prodigue, *a.* & *m,f.* ~ *son,* enfant p., *m.* ~**ity,** *n,* prodigalité, *f.*

prodigious†, *a,* prodigieux. **prodigy,** *n,* prodige, *m.*

produce, *n,* produit[s] *m.[pl.];* provenances, denrées, *f.pl.* ¶ *v.t,* produire; rapporter; fournir; exhiber, [re]présenter; communiquer. **producer,** *n,* producteur, trice; (*movies*) metteur en scène, *m.* **product,** *n,* produit, *m,* production, *f.* ~**ion,** *n,* production; exhibition; (*Theat.*) [re]présentation; mise en scène, *f.* ~**ive,** *a,* productif.

profanation, *n,* profanation, *f.* **profane,** *a,* profane; blasphémateur. ¶ *v.t,* profaner. **profanity,** *n,* irrévérence, *f;* blasphème, *m.*

profess, *v.t,* professer. ~**ed,** *a,* profès, déclaré. ~**ion,** *n,* profession, *f;* état, métier, *m.* ~**ional,** *a.* & *n,* professionnel, le. ~ *jealousy,* jalousie de métier, *f.* ~**or,**

n, professeur, *m*. **~orship**, *n*, professorat, *m*, chaire, *f*.

proficient, *a*, versé, expert.

profile, *n*, profil, *m*. ¶ *v.t*, profiler.

profit, *n*, profit, bénéfice, gain, *m*. ¶ *v.i*, profiter, bénéficier. **~able**, *a*, rémunérateur, profitable, fructueux. **~ably**, *ad*, fructueusement. **~eer**, *n*, profiteur, mercanti, *m*.

profligacy, *n*, dérèglement, *m*.

profligate, *a*, dissolu, débauché. ¶ *n*, dévergondé, e.

profound, *a*, profond, approfondi. **~ly**, *ad*, profondément.

profundity, *n*, profondeur, *f*.

profuse, *a*, abondant; prodigue; profus. **~ly**, *ad*, abondamment; profusément. **profusion**, *n*, profusion, *f*, luxe, *m*.

progenitor, *n*, auteur, *m*. *our* **~s**, les auteurs de nos jours.

progeny, *n*, descendants, *m.pl*.

prognathous, *a*, prognathe.

prognosticate, *v.t*, pronostiquer. **prognostic[ation]**, *n*, pronostic, *m*.

program, *n*, programme; carnet [de bal] *m*.

progress, *n*, progrès, *m*. *oft. pl*, essor, *m*, marche, *f*, mouvement, train, *m*. *in* **~**, en cours. ¶ *v.i*, s'avancer, progresser, faire des progrès. **~ion**, *n*, progression, *f*. **~ive†**, *a*, progressif.

prohibit, *v.t*, défendre, interdire, prohiber. **~ion**, *n*, défense, interdiction, prohibition, *f*. **~ionist**, *n*, prohibitionniste, *m*. **~ive** & **~ory**, *a*, prohibitif.

project, *n*, projet, plan, dessein, *m*. ¶ *v.t*, projeter; (*v.i.*) se p., faire saillie, saillir, avancer. **~ile**, *n*. & *a* (*projectile*, *m*. & *a*. **~ing**, *p.a*, en saillie, saillant, avancé. **~ion**, *n*, projection; (*protruding*) saillie, avance, *f*; ressaut, *m*. *film* **~**, projection cinématographique, *f*. **~or** (*Opt*.) *n*, projecteur, *m*.

proletarian, *a*, prolétarien. ¶ *n*, prolétaire, *m*. **proleteriat**, *n*, prolétariat, *m*.

prolific, *a*, prolifique; fécond, fertile.

prolix, *a*, prolixe. **~ity**, *n*, prolixité, *f*.

prologue, *n*, prologue, *m*.

prolong, *v.t*, prolonger. **~ation**, *n*, prolongation, *f*; prolongement, *m*. *prolonged applause*, applaudissements nourris, *m.pl*.

promenade, *n*, promenade, *f*; promenoir, *m*. **~ deck**, pontpromenade, *m*.

prominence, *n*, proéminence; saillie, *f*. **prominent**, *a*, proéminent; saillant; éminent; en vedette.

promiscuity, *n*, promiscuité, *f*. **promiscuous**, *a*, confus; débauché. **~ly**, *ad*, pêle-mêle.

promise, *n*, promesse, *f*; espérances, *f.pl*, avenir, *m*. ¶ *v.t. & i*, promettre; s'engager. **~d land**, terre promise, t. de promission, *f*. **promising**, *a*, prometteur. *promissory note*, billet à ordre, *m*.

promontory, *n*, promontoire, *m*.

promote, *v.t*, encourager, favoriser; avancer, promouvoir; lancer. **promoter**, *n*, promoteur, trice; lanceur, *m*, fondateur, trice. **promotion**, *n*, promotion, *f*; avancement; (*of a public company, pers.*) lancement, *m*.

prompt†, *a*, prompt. **~** *cash*, [argent] comptant, *m*. ¶ *v.t*, porter; suggérer, inspirer; (*Theat.*) souffler. **~ book**, exemplaire du souffleur, *m*. **~er**, *n*, souffleur, *m*. **~itude**, *n*, promptitude, *f*.

promulgate, *v.t*, promulguer.

prone, *a*, couché sur le ventre; prosterné; sujet, enclin, porté. **~ness**, *n*, inclination, *f*, penchant, *m*.

prong, *n*, dent, branche, *f*, fourchon, *m*.

pronominal†, *a*, pronominal. **pronoun**, *n*, pronom, *m*.

pronounce, *v.t. & i*, prononcer. **pronunciation**, *n*, prononciation, *f*; accent, *m*.

proof, *n*, preuve, *f*; titre; gage, *m*; épreuve, *f*. *in* **~** *of which*, à telles enseignes que. **~** *against*, à l'épreuve de; cuirassé contre. **~reader**, correcteur d'imprimerie, reviseur, *m*. **~reading**, correction des épreuves, revision, *f*. **~water~**, *a*, imperméable.

prop, *n*, étai, *m*; chandelle, *f*; échalas; tuteur, *m*. ¶ *v.t*, étayer; échalasser.

propaganda, *n*, propagande, *f*.

propagate, *v.t*, propager.

propel, *v.t*, donner l'impulsion à, mouvoir. **propeller**, *n*, propulseur, *m*.

propensity, *n*, propension, *f*, penchant, *m*.

proper†, *a*, propre; bon; bien; convenable; [bien]séant, décent.

~ty, n, propriété, f, bien, m. *oft. pl,* avoir; domaine, m; chose; faculté, qualité, f, caractère, propre, m; (*pl. Theat.*) accessoires, *m.pl.* ~ *tax,* impôt foncier, m.

prophecy, n, prophétie, f. **prophesy,** v.t. & i, prophétiser. **prophet,** n, prophète; augure, m. **~ess,** n, prophétesse, f. **~ic(al)†,** a, prophétique.

propinquity, n, proximité, f.

propitiate, v.t, rendre propice. **propitious,** a, propice.

proportion, n, proportion, f. *out of ~,* disproportionné. ¶ v.t, proportionner, mesurer. **~al†,** a, proportionnel.

proposal, n, proposition; demande, f. **propose,** v.t. & i, proposer; (*toast*) porter; (*marriage to woman*) offrir son nom, (*to man*) offrir sa main. **proposer,** n, parrain, m. **proposition,** n, proposition, affaire, f.

propound, v.t, proposer.

proprietary, a, (*rights*) de propriété. **proprietor, tress,** n, propriétaire, m,f. **propriety,** n, décence, bienséance, convenance, mesure; correction, propriété, f.

propulsion, n, propulsion, f.

prorogue, v.t, proroger.

prosaic†, a, prosaïque.

proscenium, n, avant-scène, f.

proscribe, v.t, proscrire.

prose, n, prose, f. ~ *writer,* prosateur, m.

prosecute, v.t, poursuivre. **prosecution,** n, poursuites, f.pl, vindicte, f. **prosecutor, trix,** n, poursuivant, e, plaignant, e.

proselyte, n, prosélyte, m,f.

prosiness, n, verbosité, f.

prosody, n, prosodie, f.

prospect, n, vue; perspective, f, avenir, m. ¶ v.t, prospecter. **~ing,** n, prospection, f, recherches, f.pl. **~ive,** a, en perspective. **~or,** n, prospecteur, m.

prospectus, n, prospectus, m.

prosper, v.i, prospérer, réussir. **~ity,** n, prospérité, f. **~ous,** a, prospère, fortuné, florissant, heureux.

prostate [gland], n, prostate, f.

prostitute, v.t, prostituer. ¶ n, prostituée, f.

prostrate, a, prosterné; prostré, anéanti. ¶ v.t, prosterner; anéantir. ~ *oneself,* se prosterner. **prostration,** n, prosternation; (*Med.*) prostration, f.

prosy, a, verbeux, ennuyeux.

protagonist, n, protagoniste, m.

protect, v.t, protéger, garder, défendre, préserver. **~ion,** n, protection, garde, défense, préservation, sauvegarde, f. **~ionist,** n. & att, protectionniste, m. & att. **~ive,** a, protecteur. **protector, tress,** n, protecteur, trice. **~ate,** n, protectorat, m.

protein, n, protéine, f.

pro tempore (*abb.* pro tem.) ad, à titre provisoire.

protest, n, protestation, réclamation, f. ¶ v.t. & i, protester; crier. **~ant,** n. & a, protestant, e.

protocol, n, protocole, m.

prototype, n, prototype, m.

protoplasm, n, protoplasme, m.

protract, v.t, prolonger. **~or,** n, rapporteur, m.

protrude, v.i, faire saillie.

protuberance, n, protubérance, f.

proud†, a, fier; orgueilleux; glorieux. ~ *flesh,* chairs baveuses, f.pl.

prove, v.t, prouver, faire la preuve de, vérifier, justifier [de]; démontrer; constater; éprouver; (*will*) homologuer.

provender, n, fourrage, m, provende, f.

proverb, n, proverbe, m. **~ial†,** a, proverbial.

provide, v.t, pourvoir, fournir, munir; prescrire, stipuler, prévoir. ~ *against,* se prémunir contre. **~d** [*that*], pourvu que. **providence,** n, prévoyance; providence; (*God*) Providence, f. **provident,** a, prévoyant. **~ial†,** a, providentiel. **provider,** n, pourvoyeur, m.

province, n, province; (*pl.*) province; (*sphere*) compétence, f, ressort, domaine, département, m, juridiction, f. **provincial,** a, provincial; de province.

provision, n, provision; prestation; disposition; (*pl.*) provisions de bouche, munitions de b. f.pl, vivres, comestibles, m.pl, subsistances, f.pl. ¶ v.t, approvisionner. **~al†,** a, provisoire; provisionnel.

proviso, n, clause provisionnelle, f.

provocation, n, provocation; agacerie, f. **provoke,** v.t, provoquer, agacer, contrarier, vexer, impatienter.

provost, n, prévôt; recteur, m.

prow, n, proue, f.

prowess, n, prouesse, vaillantise, f.

prowl, v.i, rôder. ~**er**, n, rôdeur, m.

proximate†, a, prochain; immédiat. **proximity**, n, proximité, f.

proxy, n, procuration, f; mandataire, m, fondé de pouvoir(s), m. by ~, par procuration.

prude, n, prude, f.

prudence, n, prudence, sagesse, f. **prudent†**, a, prudent, sage, avisé. ~**ial**, a, de prudence.

prudery, n, pruderie, bégueulerie, f. **prudish**, a, prude, pudibond, bégueule.

prune, n, pruneau, m. ¶ v.t, tailler, émonder, élaguer. **pruning**, n, taille, f, émondage, élagage, m; (pl.) élagage, m, émondes, f.pl. ~ hook, serpe, f, croissant, m. ~ knife, serpette, f. ~ shears, sécateur, m.

pruriency, n, sensualité, f. **prurient**, a, sensuel, lascif.

Prussia, n, la Prusse. **Prussian**, a, prussien. ~ blue, bleu de Prusse, m. ¶ n, Prussien, ne. **prussic**, a, prussique.

pry, v.i, fureter, fouiller; soulever avec un levier. ~**ing**, a, indiscret, curieux.

psalm, n, psaume, m. ~**ist**, n, psalmiste, m. **psalter**, n, psautier, m.

pseudonym, n, pseudonyme, m.

psychiatrist, n, psychiatre, m. **psychic(al)**, a, psychique. **psychoanalysis**, n, psychanalyse, f. **psychological**, a, psychologique. **psychologist**, n, psychologue, m. **psychology**, n, psychologie, f.

ptarmigan, n, perdrix des neiges, f.

ptomaine, n, ptomaïne, f. ~ poisoning, empoisonnement par les ptomaïnes, m.

puberty, n, puberté, f.

public†, a, public. ~ spirited, dévoué au bien public. ¶ n, public, m; clientèle, f. ~**an**, n, (Bible) publicain, m. ~**ation**, n, publication, f. ~**ist**, n, publiciste, m. ~**ity**, n, publicité, f. **publish**, v.t, publier; éditer; faire paraître; proclamer. to be ~ed (book), paraître. ~**er**, n, éditeur, m. ~'s imprint, indication de nom (ou de firme) de l'éditeur; (place only) rubrique, f. ~**ing**, n, publication, édition, f. ~ house, maison d'édition, librairie, f.

puce, a, puce.

puck, n, lutin, [esprit] follet; (ice hockey) palet, puck, m.

pucker, n, poche, fronce, f, godet, pli, m. ¶ v.t, froncer, plisser; (v.i.) goder, [se] plisser.

pudding, n, pudding, pouding, m.

puddle, n, flaque, f. ¶ v.t, (clay) corroyer; (Metall.) puddler.

puerile†, a, puéril.

puff, n, souffle, m; bouffée, réclame, f; (powder) houppe, f. ¶ v.t. & i, souffler; bouffer; époumoner; prôner. ~ one's goods, faire l'article.

puffin, n, macareux, m.

puffy, a, bouffi, soufflé.

pug (clay) n, corroi, m. ~ [dog], carlin, roquet, m. ~ nose, nez camus, m. ¶ v.t, corroyer; hourder.

pugilism, n, pugilat, m. **pugilist**, n, pugiliste, m. **pugnacious**, a, pugnace, batailleur.

pule, v.i, piauler.

pull, n, traction, f; effort [de traction] m; (drink) lampée; (Typ.) feuille de tirée, f; (bell) cordon; (fig.) avantage, m. ~**over**, pullover, m. ¶ v.t. & i, tirer; arracher; (trigger) presser. ~ down, démolir. ~ wires for (fig.), intriguer pour. ~ to one side (traffic), se garer. ~ to pieces, mettre en pièces; (fig.) éreinter.

pullet, n, poulette, f.

pulley, n, poulie, f. ~ block, moufle, f. or m.

Pullman [car], n, voiture Pullman, f.

pullulate, v.i, pulluler.

pulmonary, a, pulmonaire.

pulp, n, pulpe; chair; (paper making) pâte; bouillie, f. ¶ v.t, pulper.

pulpit, n, chaire [du prédicateur] f.

pulsate, v.i, battre. **pulsation**, n, pulsation, f, battement, m. **pulse**, n, (Anat.) pouls, m; légumineuse, f. ~ rate, force du pouls, f.

pulverize, v.t, pulvériser.

puma, n, puma, couguar, m.

pumice [stone], n, [pierre] ponce, f. ¶ v.t, poncer.

pump, n, pompe, f; (dress shoe) escarpin, m. gasoline ~, pompe à essence, f. ~ handle, levier de pompe, m, brimbale, f. ~ room (at spa), buvette, f. ¶ v.t. & i, pomper; (fig.) sonder, cuisiner. ~ up (tire), gonfler.

pumpkin, n, citrouille, courge, f, potiron, m.

pun, n, calembour, jeu de mots, m. ¶ v.i, faire des calembours, jouer sur le(s) mot(s).

punch, n, coup de poing, renfoncement, m, gourmade, f; (tool) poinçon; emporte-pièce; (drink) punch, m. ~ bowl, bol à punch, m. P~, n, polichinelle, m. ~ & Judy [show], guignol, m. ¶ v.t, poinçonner; découper; (hit) battre.

puncheon, n, poinçon; m; pièce, f.

punching bag, ballon de boxe, m.

punctilio, n, pointille, f. **punctilious,** a, pointilleux, méticuleux.

punctual†, a, ponctuel, exact. ~ity, n, ponctualité, exactitude, f. **punctuate,** v.t. & abs, ponctuer. **punctuation,** n, ponctuation, f. **puncture,** n, piqûre; (Surg.) ponction; (tire) crevaison, f. ¶ v.t. & i, piquer; ponctionner; crever.

pundit, n, pandit, pontife, m.

pungency, n, piquant, m; âcreté, f; mordant, m. **pungent,** a, piquant; âcre; mordant.

punish, v.t, punir. ~able, a, punissable. ~ment, n, punition; peine, sanction, pénitence, f; supplice, m.

punster, n, faiseur de calembours, m.

punt, (boat) n, bachot, m, plate, f. ¶ v.i, (cards) ponter; (boating) pousser du fond; (v.t.) pousser (un bateau) à la perche.

puny, a, chétif, malingre.

pup, n, petit chien, m. ¶ v.i, mettre bas.

pupa, n, chrysalide, f.

pupil, n, (eye) pupille, prunelle, f; (scholar) élève, m,f, écolier, ère; pupille, m,f.

puppet, n, marionnette, poupée, f, mannequin, fantoche, m.

puppy, n, petit chien; (pers.) freluquet, m.

purblind, a, quasi aveugle.

purchase, n, achat, m, acquisition; (shopping) emplette; (hold) prise, f; (tackle) palan, m. ¶ v.t, acheter, acquérir. **purchaser,** n, acheteur, euse, acquéreur, m.

pure†, a, pur. ~ mechanics, mécanique rationnelle, f. ~ness, n, pureté, f.

purgative, a. & n, purgatif, a. & m. **purgatory,** n, purgatoire, m.

purge, v.t, purger. **purge, purging,** n, purge, purgation, f.

purify, v.t, purifier; épurer. **purist,** n, puriste, m,f. **Puritan,** n. & a. & **puritanic(al),** a, puritain, e.

purity, n, pureté, f.

purl, v.i, murmurer, gazouiller. ~ knitting, tricot à l'envers, m.

purlieus, n.pl, environs, entours, m.pl.

purloin, v.t, soustraire.

purple, n, pourpre, m; (robe) pourpre, f. ¶ a, violet. ~ red, rouge pourpré, m. **purplish,** a, purpurin, violâtre.

purport, n, teneur, portée, f. ¶ v.t, signifier, vouloir dire; sembler, paraître.

purpose, n, but, m, fin; intention; f; propos; dessein; effet; usage, m. to no ~, en pure perte. ¶ v.t, se proposer. ~ly, ad, à dessein, exprès.

purr, n, ronron, m. ¶ v.i, faire ronron.

purse, n, porte-monnaie, m, bourse, f. ¶ (lips) v.t, pincer. **purser,** n, commissaire [de la marine marchande] m.

pursuant to, in pursuance of, en vertu de, suivant. **pursue,** v.t, [pour]suivre, chasser. **pursuit,** n, poursuite, chasse; recherche; occupation, f. ~ plane, avion de chasse, m.

purulent, a, purulent.

purvey, v.t, pourvoir. ~or, n, pourvoyeur, m.

purview, n, ressort; (law) dispositif, m.

pus, n, pus, m.

push, n, poussée; initiative, f. ~ [button], poussoir, m. ¶ v.t, pousser; presser; avancer. ~ about, bousculer. ~ aside, écarter. ~ back, repousser, reculer. ~ off (Naut.), pousser au large. ~ing, a, entreprenant.

pusillanimous, a, pusillanime.

puss[y], n, minet, te, minon, minou, m. Puss in Boots, le Chat botté.

pustule, n, pustule, f.

put, v.t.ir, mettre; placer; porter; poser; apposer; appliquer; faire. ~ (things) away, ranger, serrer. ~ down, réprimer; baisser. ~ forward, avancer; proposer. ~ in, insérer; (Naut.) relâcher. ~ off, remettre; différer. ~ on, mettre; revêtir; prendre; avancer; (brake) serrer. ~ out, éteindre; (tongue) tirer. ~ out of joint, démettre, disloquer. ~ out of order, dérégler, déranger. ~ out

of tune, désaccorder. ~ *up,* (*money*) faire mise de; (*money at cards*) caver [del]; (*at hotel*) descendre. ~*-up job*, coup monté, *m.* ~ *up with*, supporter.
putt, (*golf.*) *n*, coup [roulé] *m.* ¶ *v.t*, poter.
putrefaction, *n*, putréfaction, *f.* **putrefy,** *v.t*, putréfier; (*v.i.*) se p. **putrid,** *a*, putride.
puttee, *n*, bande molletière, *f.*
putter (*club*) *n*, poteur, *m.* ¶ *v.i*, bricoler. **putting green,** pelouse d'arrivée, *f.* **putting the shot,** lancement du poids, *m.*
putty, *n*, mastic, *m.* ~ *powder*, potée d'étain, *f.* ¶ *v.t*, mastiquer.
puzzle, *n*, casse-tête; problème, *m*; énigme, *f.* **crossword** ~, mots croisés, *m.pl.* ¶ *v.t*, intriguer, alambiquer. ~**d,** *p.a*, perplexe; empêché.
pygmy, *n*, pygmée, *m.*
pylon, *n*, pylône, *m.*
pyorrhoea, *n*, pyorrhée, *f.*
pyramid, *n*, pyramide, *f.*
pyre, *n*, bûcher, *m.*
Pyrenees (the), les Pyrénées, *f.pl.*
pyrethrum, *n*, pyrèthre, *m.*
pyrites, *n*, pyrite, *f.*
pyrotechnics, *n.pl*, pyrotechnie, *f.* **pyrotechnist,** *n*, artificier, *m.*
python, *n*, python, *m.*

Q

qua, *c*, en tant que.
quack [**doctor**], *n*, charlatan, médicastre, *m*, guérisseur, euse. ~**ery,** *n*, charlatanisme, *m.*
quadrangle, *n*, figure quadrangulaire, *f*; préau, *m*; cour d'honneur, *f.*
quadrant, *n*, quadrant; quart de cercle; secteur, *m.*
quadroon, *n*, quarteron, ne.
quadruped, *n. & a*, quadrupède, *m. & a.*
quadruple, *a. & n*, quadruple, *a. & m.* **quadruplets,** *n.pl*, quatre jumeaux, *m.pl.*
quaff, *v.t*, boire.
quagmire, *n*, fondrière, *f*, bourbier, *m.*
quail, *n*, caille, *f.* ¶ *v.i*, trembler.
quaint, *a*, vieillot; pittoresque; baroque; étrange; curieux. ~**ness,** *n*, étrangeté; curiosité, *f.*
quake, *v.i*, trembler. ¶ *n*, tremblement, *m.*
qualification, *n*, qualité; capacité, aptitude, *f.* **qualified,** *p.a*,

qualifié; capable, apte; sous réserve. **qualify,** *v.t*, qualifier; adoucir. **quality,** *n*, qualité, *f*; choix; aloi, *m.*
qualms, *n.pl*, mal de cœur, *m*; scrupules, *m.pl.*
quandary, *n*, embarras, *m.*
quantity, *n*, quantité, *f.*
quantum, *n*, quantum, *m.*
quarantine, *n*, quarantaine, *f*; (*station*) la santé. ¶ *v.t*, mettre en quarantaine.
quarrel, *n*, querelle, *f.* ¶ *v.i*, quereller. ~**some,** *a*, querelleur.
quarry, *n*, (*marble, etc.*) carrière, *f*; proie, *f.* ¶ *v.t*, extraire.
quarter, *n*, quartier; (¼th) quart; (*3 months*) trimestre; terme, *m*; (*28 lbs*) = 12.70 kilos; (*8 bushels*) = 2.909 hectoliters; (*pl.*) logement; cantonnement, *m*; quartiers, *m.pl*; (*horse*) train, *m. a* ~ *of an hour*, un quart d'heure. ~ *deck*, gaillard d'arrière, *m.* ~**master,** (*Mil.*) fourrier; (*Naut.*) maître de timonerie, *m.* ~ *past*, un quart, et quart. ¶ *v.t*, diviser en quatre parties; écarteler; loger; cantonner. ~**ly,** *a*, trimestriel; (*ad.*) par trimestre.
quartet[te], *n*, quatuor, *m.*
quartz, *n*, quartz, *m.*
quash, *v.t*, casser, annuler, infirmer.
quasi, *c. & quasi-,* *prefix*, quasi (*ad.*), quasi-.
quassia, *n*, (*tree*) quassier; (*bark*) quassia, *m.*
quatrain, *n*, quatrain, *m.*
quaver (*Mus.*) *n*, croche, *f.* ¶ *v.i*, chevroter, trembler.
quay, *n*, quai, *m.*
queen, *n*, reine; (*cards, chess*) dame, reine, *f.* ~ *bee*, reine des abeilles, mère abeille, *f.* ¶ (*chess*) *v.t*, damer. ~**ly,** *a*, de reine.
queer†, *a*, étrange, bizarre, singulier, original, drôle; indisposé. *a* ~ *fellow*, un drôle de corps.
quell, *v.t*, réprimer, étouffer, apaiser.
quench, *v.t*, éteindre; (*thirst*) étancher, apaiser.
querulous†, *a*, plaintif.
query, *n*, question, interrogation, *f.* **quest,** *n*, quête, recherche, *f.* **question,** *n*, question; demande; interrogation, *f.* ~ *mark*, point d'interrogation, *m.* ¶ *v.t*, questionner, interroger; contester, mettre en question, suspecter.
questionable, *a*, contestable; sus-

pect, équivoque. **questionnaire,**
n, questionnaire, *m.*

quibble, *n,* chicane, argutie, *f.* ¶
v.i, chicaner, ergoter.

quick, *a,* vif; rapide; prompt;
preste. ~-*change artist,* acteur
à transformations, *m.* ~*lime,*
chaux vive, *f.* ~*sand,* sable mouvant, *m.* ~*silver,* mercure, *m.*
~*step,* pas accéléré, *m.;* en avant
marche! ~-*tempered,* emporté,
vif. ¶ *ad,* vite, prestement. *be
~!* vite! dépêchez-vous! ¶ *n,* vif,
m. ~*en,* *v.t,* vivifier, animer; accélérer, activer. ~**ly,** *ad,* vite,
tôt, promptement. ~**ness,** *n,*
promptitude, prestesse, *f.*

quid (*tobacco*) *n,* chique, *f.*

quid pro quo, *n,* compensation,
f.

quiescent, *a,* en repos. **quiet**†, *a,*
tranquille; calme; doux; mo-
deste. ¶ *v.t,* calmer, apaiser.
~[**ness**], *n,* tranquillité, *f,* repos,
calme, *m,* quiétude, *f.* **quietus,** *n,*
coup de grâce, *m.*

quill, *n,* (*porcupine*) piquant, *m;*
(*bird*) plume, *f.* ~ *driver,* gratte-
papier, rond-de-cuir, plumitif, *m.*
~ [*feather*], penne, *f.* ~ [*pen*],
plume d'oie, *f.*

quilt, *n,* couvre-pied, *m.* ¶ *v.t,*
ouater, piquer, capitonner.

quince, *n,* coing, *f.* ~[*tree*], cognassier, *m.*

quinine, *n,* quinine, *f.*

quinquennial, *a,* quinquennal.

quinsy, *n,* angine, *f.*

quintessence, *n,* quintessence, *f.*

quintet[**te**], *n,* quintette, *m.*

quintuplet, *n,* quintuplet, *m.*

quip, *n,* pointe, *f,* mot piquant, *m.*

quire, *n,* main, *f.* (*in Fr. 25 sheets*).

quirk, *n* (*quip*), pointe, *f;* caprice;
(*Join.*) carré, *m.*

quit, *a,* quitte. ¶ *v.t,* renoncer à;
cesser de; quitter.

quite, *ad,* tout à fait; tout, e; bien;
complètement; parfaitement.

quits, *a,* quitte à quitte; quittes.

quiver (*for arrows*) *n,* carquois,
m. ¶ *v.i,* trembler, frémir; frissonner. ~[**ing**], *n,* tremblement,
frisson[nement] *m.*

Quixote, *n,* Don Quichotte, *m.*
quixotic, *a,* de D. Q. ~**ally,** *ad,*
en D. Q.

quiz, *v.t,* interroger; (*mock*) berner. ¶ *n,* examen, *m.* **quizzical,**
a, (*mocking*) narquois.

quoin, *n,* coin, *m;* (*Typ.*) bois de
corps, *m.*

quoit, *n.* & ~*s,* *n.pl,* palet, *m.*

quondam, *a,* ancien.

quorum, *n,* quorum, *m.*

quota, *n,* quote-part, quotité, cote,
cotisation, *f,* contingent, *m.*

quotation, *n,* citation; épigraphe;
(*Com., Fin.*) cote, *f,* cours, prix,
m; (*in Stk Ex. list*) inscription, *f.*
~ *marks,* guillemets, *m.pl.* **quote,**
v.t, citer; alléguer; guillemeter;
coter, faire; inscrire.

quotient, *n,* quotient, *m.*

R

rabbet, *n,* feuillure, *f.* ~ *plane,*
guillaume, *m.*

rabbi, *n,* rabbin, *m.*

rabbit, *n,* lapin, e, (*young*) lapereau, *m;* (*pers. at game*) mazette,
f. ~ *burrow,* ~ *hole,* terrier de
lapin, clapier, *m.* ~ *hutch,* clapier, *m.*

rabble, *n,* canaille, populace, *f.*

rabid, *a,* acharné; enragé. **rabies,**
n, la rage, hydrophobie, *f.*

racoon, *n,* raton laveur, *m.*

race, *n,* (*tribe*) race, *f;* sang, *m;*
(*contest*)·course, *f;* (*sea*) raz, *m.*
~*horse,* cheval de course, *m.* ~
suicide, suicide du genre humain, *m.* ~*track,* champ de
courses, *m,* piste, *f.* ~[*way*], bief,
canal, chenal, *m.* ¶ *v.i,* courir.
(*v.t.*) (*horses*) faire courir.
racer, *n,* coureur, euse; cheval de
course, *m;* bicyclette de course,
f. **racial,** *a,* de race. **racing,** *n,*
courses; (*horse*) les courses, *f.pl.*
~ *calendar,* calendrier des
courses, *m.* ~ *cyclist,* coureur
cycliste, *m.*

rack, *n,* râtelier, *m;* rampe, *f;*
caster, *m;* (*luggage, Rly.*) filet;
supplice, *m,* torture, *f. hat* ~,
porte-chapeau, *m. to* ~ & *ruin,*
à vau-l'eau. *to* ~ *one's brains,*
se torturer l'esprit, se casser la
tête, se creuser le cerveau.

racket, *n,* tapage; bacchanal, *m;*
raquette, *f.* ~ *press,* presse à
raquette, *f.*

racy (*fig.*) *a,* piquant.

radial, *a,* radial. **radiance** & **radiation,** *n,* rayonnement, *m.* **radiancy,** *n,* éclat, *m.* **radiant,** *a,*
rayonnant; radieux. **radiate,** *v.i,*
rayonner. **radiator,** *n,* radiateur,
m.

radical†, *a.* & *n,* radical, *a.* & *m.*

radio, *n,* radio, T.S.F., *f.* ¶ *v.t.* &
i, émettre, radiodiffuser.

radioactive, *a,* radioactif. **radio-**

gram, *n*, radiogramme, *m*. **radiography**, *n*, radiographie, *f*. **radiotelegraphy**, *n*, radiotélégraphie, *f*.

radish, *n*, radis, *m*.

radium, *n*, radium, *m*.

radius, *n*, rayon, *m*; portée, *f*; (*Anat.*) radius, *m*.

raffle, *n*, loterie, tombola, *f*. ¶ *v.t*, mettre en loterie.

raft, *n*, radeau, *m*, drome, *f*; train [de bois] *m*.

rafter, *n*, chevron, *m*.

rag, *n*, chiffon; lambeau; haillon, *m*, loque, guenille; (*pl*, *for paper making*) drille; (*newspaper*) feuille de chou, *f*, canard; (*Sch.*) chahut, *m*. ~**picker**, ~ **merchant**, ~ [& bone] **man**, chiffonnier, ère. ~**tag** [& **bobtail**], canaille, *f*. ~**wort**, jacobée, *f*.

ragamuffin, *n*, petit va-nu-pieds, *m*.

rage, *n*, rage, fureur; colère, *f*, courroux, *m*. ¶ *v.i*, faire rage; (*of war*) sévir. **to be the** ~, être du dernier cri.

ragged, *a*, déguenillé, loqueteux.

raging, *a*, furieux. ~ **fever**, fièvre ardente, *f*. ~ **toothache**, rage de dents, *f*.

raid, *n*, incursion, descente, razzia, *f*, raid, *m*; rafle; attaque, *f*. **air** ~, raid aérien, *m*. ¶ *v.t*, razzier; marauder; faire une descente dans.

rail, *n*, barre, *f*; barreau; *m*; traverse; rampe, *f*, garde-fou, accoudoir, *m*; (*ship's*) lisse, *f*, garde-corps; (*Rly.*) rail; (*bird*) râle, *m*. ¶ *v.t*, barrer. ~ **at**, invectiver contre, pester contre. ~ **in**, griller. ~**ing**, *n*, grille, balustrade, *f*, balustre, garde-fou, *m*.

raillery, *n*, raillerie, *f*.

railway & **railroad**, *n*, chemin de fer, *m*, voie ferrée, *f*. ~**man**, employé de chemin de fer, cheminot, *m*. ~ **station**, gare, *f*. ~ **strike**, grève d'agents de chemins de fer, *f*.

raiment, *n*, vêtement, habillement, *m*.

rain, *n*, pluie, eau, *f*. ~**bow**, arc-en-ciel; (*halo*) iris, *m*. ~ **coat**, imperméable, *m*. ~**fall**, quantité de pluie [tombée] *f*. ~**water**, eau de pluie, *f*, eaux pluviales, *f.pl*. ¶ *v.i*, pleuvoir; (*v.t.*) faire pleuvoir. ~**y**, *a*, pluvieux, pluvial; (*day*) de pluie.

raise, *v.t*, lever; soulever; relever; remonter; [sur]élever; hausser;

exhausser; augmenter; porter; (*hat*) tirer; (*flag*) arborer; cultiver; faire naître; produire; (*money for some purpose*) procurer; (*money for oneself*) se procurer; (*the dead*) ressusciter. ¶ *n*, hausse, augmentation, *f*. **raised**, *p.a*, en relief; saillant.

raisin, *n*, raisin sec, *m*.

rake, *n*, râteau, *f*; (*fire*) fourgon; ringard, *m*; inclinaison, *f*; libertin, débauché, roué, coureur, *m*. ¶ *v.t*, ratisser, râteler; enfiler. ~ **up**, remuer; revenir sur. **raking fire**, feu d'enfilade, *m*. **raking shore**, arc-boutant, *m*, contrefiche, *f*. **rakish**, *a*, libertin.

rally, *n*, ralliement, *m*; reprise, *f*; (*Ten.*) long échange; (*race meeting*) rallye, *m*. ¶ *v.t*, rallier; (*v.i.*) se rallier; [se] reprendre.

ram, *n*, bélier; (*pile driving*) mouton, pilon; piston; (*battleship*) éperon, *m*. ¶ *v.t*, damer, battre; bourrer; refouler.

ramble, *n*, excursion, promenade, *f*. ¶ *v.i*, errer; (*rave*) divaguer. **rambler**, *n*, rosier grimpant, *m*. **rambling**, *a*, errant; (*discourse*) décousu, incohérent.

ramification, *n*, ramification, *f*. **ramify**, *v.i*, se ramifier.

rampant (*Her.*) *a*, rampant. **to be** ~, sévir, courir.

rampart, *n*, rempart, *m*.

ramrod, *n*, baguette, *f*.

ramshackle, *a*, délabré.

ranch, *n*, ranch, *m*.

rancid, *a*, rance. ~**ness**, *n*, rancidité, *f*.

rancorous, *a*, rancunier, fielleux. **rancor**, *n*, rancune, rancœur, *f*, fiel, *m*.

random, *a*. & **at** ~, au hasard, à l'aventure, à l'abandon, à la volée, à coup perdu.

range, *n*, étendue; portée; distance, *f*; champ, *m*; série; gamme, *f*; (*voice*) diapason; (*musical*) clavier, *m*; (*hills*) chaîne, *f*; fourneau; parc, *m*. **gas** ~, fourneau à gaz, *m*. ~ **finder**, télémètre, *m*. ¶ *v.t*, étager; aligner; parcourir; ranger; (*v.i.*) s'aligner; varier. **ranger**, *n*, conservateur; garde, *m*.

Rangoon, *n*, Rangoun, Rangoon, *m*.

rank, *n*, rang; grade, *m*; dignité; (*cab*) station, place, *f*. ~ & **file**, les hommes de troupe, gradés & soldats. ¶ *v.t*, ranger; (*v.i.*) prendre rang; marcher de pair. ¶ *a*, luxuriant; rance; grossier; insigne, fieffé.

rankle, *v.i,* saigner.

ransack, *v.t,* saccager, piller; fouiller.

ransom, *n,* rançon, *f,* rachat, *m.* ¶ *v.t,* rançonner, racheter.

rant, *n,* divagation, *f.* ¶ *v.i,* déclamer.

ranunculus, *n,* renoncule, *f.*

rap, *n,* coup, *m,* tape, *f.* ¶ *v.t. & i,* taper, frapper, donner des petits coups secs. *I don't give a ~,* je m'en moque.

rapacious, *a,* rapace. **rape,** *n,* enlèvement; (*law*) viol, *m;* (*oil seed plant*) navette; (*colerape*) rave, *f.*

rapid†, *a,* rapide; (*pulse*) fréquent. ¶ *n,* rapide, *m.* ~ity, *n,* rapidité, *f.*

rapier, *n,* rapière, *f.*

rapine, *n,* rapine, *f.*

rapt, *a,* ravi, en extase. **rapture,** *n,* ravissement, enthousiasme, *m,* ivresse, *f.* **rapturous,** *a,* extatique.

rare†, *a,* rare; (*word*) peu usité; fameux; (*meat*) saignante. **rarefy,** *v.t,* raréfier. **rareness,** *n,* rareté, *f.*

rascal, *n,* coquin, e, fripon, ne; canaille, *f.* ~ity, *n,* coquinerie, friponnerie, *f.* ~ly, *a,* canaille.

rash†, *a,* téméraire, hardi. ¶ *n,* éruption, *f.* ~ness, *n,* témérité, *f.*

rasher, *n,* tranche, *f.*

rasp, *n,* râpe, *f.* ¶ *v.t,* râper; racler. ~ing, *a,* rugueux.

raspberry, *n,* framboise, *f.* ~ bush, framboisier, *m.*

rat, *n,* rat, e, (*young*) raton; (*pers.*) gâtemétier; (*Pol.*) transfuge, *m.* ~ catcher, preneur de rats, *m.* ~ poison, mort aux rats, *f.* ~ trap, ratière, *f.* ¶ *v.i,* tuer des rats; (*Pol.*) tourner casaque.

rate, *n,* taux; pourcentage; cours; prix; tarif; ordre, rang, *m,* classe; raison, *f;* train, *m;* taxe, contribution, *f,* impôt, *m. at any* ~, quoi qu'il en soit. ¶ *v.t,* évaluer; tarifer; imposer; taxer.

rather, *ad,* un peu; assez; plutôt; mieux. ~ *nice,* gentillet. ~ *slowly* (*Mus.*), gravement. ~ *than,* plutôt que.

ratification, *n,* ratification, *f.* **ratify,** *v.t,* ratifier.

rating, *n,* classement; (*Naut.*) grade, *m.*

ratio, *n,* rapport, *m,* raison, proportion, *f.*

ration, *n,* ration, *f,* (*pl.*) vivres, *m.pl.* ¶ *v.t,* rationner. ~al†, *a,*

rationnel, raisonnable; conséquent; raisonné. **rationalism,** *n,* rationalisme, *m.* **rationalization,** *n,* organisation rationnelle, *f.*

rattan, *n. & ~ cane,* rotin, *m.*

rat-tat[-tat], *n,* pan! pan!

ratter, *n,* [chien] ratier, *m.*

rattle, *n,* crécelle, *f;* (*baby's*) hochet; ballottement, claquement; (*throat*) râle, *m.* ~snake, serpent à sonnettes, *m.* ~trap, patraque, *f;* (*vehicle*) guimbarde, patache, *f,* tapecul, *m.* ¶ *v.i, & t,* ballotter; cliqueter.

raucous, *a,* rauque.

ravage, *v.t,* ravager. ~s, *n.pl,* ravages, *m.pl;* (*of time*) injure[s], *f.[pl.],* outrage, *m.*

rave, *v.i,* être en délire; extravaguer.

raven, *n,* corbeau, *m.*

Ravenna, *n,* Ravenne, *f.*

ravenous†, *a,* vorace; dévorant.

ravine, *n,* ravin, *m,* ravine, *f.*

raving, *n,* délire, *m.* ~ *mad,* fou à lier.

ravish, *v.t,* ravir; violer. **ravishing,** *a,* ravissant. **ravishingly,** *ad,* à ravir.

raw, *a,* cru; brut; (*silk*) grège; (*meat, wound*) saignante; (*Sienna*) naturelle; (*material*) première; (*fig.*) vert; novice; imberbe; (*weather*) humide & froid. ~ness, *n,* crudité, *f.*

ray, *n,* rayon, *m;* (*fish*) raie, *f.*

rayon, *n,* rayon, *m,* soie artificielle, *f.*

raze, *v.t,* raser. **razor,** *n,* rasoir, *m.*

reach, *n,* portée; atteinte; étendue, *f. within ~ of,* à portée de. ¶ *v.t,* atteindre [à]; arriver à, parvenir à; s'élever à. ~ [*out*], étendre.

react, *v.i,* réagir. ~ion, *n,* réaction, *f;* contrecoup, *m.* ~ionary, *a. & n,* réactionnaire. ~ *m,f.*

read, *v.t. & i. ir,* lire; (*report*) donner lecture de; (*meter*) relever. ~ *over,* collationner. ~able†, *a,* lisible.

reader, *n,* lecteur, trice; liseur, euse; livre de lecture, *m.*

readiness, *n,* promptitude, *f;* empressement, *m;* facilité, *f.*

reading, *n,* lecture; leçon; cote, *f.* ~ *desk,* pupitre; (*church*) lutrin, *m.* ~ *glass,* loupe à lire, *f.* ~ *stand,* liseuse, *f.* ~ *lamp,* lampe de travail, *f.* ~ *room,* salle de lecture, *f;* cabinet de l., *m.*

readjust, *v.t, & i,* rajuster. ~ment, *n,* rajustement, *m.*

ready†, *a,* prêt; prompt; facile. ~-

made, tout fait (*f.* toute faite), confectionné. ~ *money*, [argent] comptant, *m.*

reagent, *n*, réactif, *m.*

real†, *a*, réel; positif; véritable; vrai; effectif; (*law*) immeuble, immobilier. ~ *estate*, propriété immobilière, *f.* **~ist,** *n. & a*, réaliste, *m.f. & a.* **~ity,** *n*, réalité, *f*, le réel; positif, *m.* **~ize,** *v.t*, réaliser.

realm, *n*, royaume, *m.*

realty, *n*, biens immeubles, *m.pl.*

ream, *n*, rame, *f.* (*In Fr.* 500 *sheets.*) ¶ *v.t*, aléser. **~er,** *n*, alésoir, *f.*

reap, *v.t.*, moissonner, recueillir (*fig.*). **reaper,** *n*, moissonneur, *m*; (*machine*) moissonneuse, *f.* ~ *& binder*, moissonneuse-lieuse, *f.* **reaping,** *n*, moisson, *f.*

reappear, *v.i*, reparaître, réapparaître. **~ance,** *n*, réapparition, *f.*

reappoint, *v.t*, renommer.

rear, *n*, arrière, *m*; queue, *f.* ~ *admiral*, contre-amiral, *m.* ~ *guard*, arrière-garde, *f.* ~ *rank*, dernier rang, *m.* ¶ *v.t*, élever, nourrir; (*v.i.*) se cabrer, se dresser. **~ing of children**, puériculture, *f.*

reason, *n*, raison; cause, *f*; motif, *m. to state the* ~ *for*, motiver. ¶ *v.i*, raisonner. ~ *with*, raisonner, catéchiser. **~able†,** *a*, raisonnable; honnête. **~er,** *n*, raisonneur, euse. **~ing,** *n*, raisonnement, *m.*

reassure, *v.t*, rassurer.

rebate, *n*, rabais, *m*, ristourne; (*Join.*) feuillure, *f.*

rebel, *n*, rebelle, *m.f*, révolté, e. ¶ *v.i*, se rebeller, se révolter. **rebellion,** *n*, rébellion, révolte, *f.* **rebellious,** *a*, rebelle.

rebind, *v.t.ir*, relier de nouveau.

rebirth, *n*, renaissance, *f.*

rebound *n*, [second] bond; contrecoup, *m.* ¶ *v.i*, rebondir.

rebuff, *n*, rebuffade, *f.* ¶ *v.t*, rebuter.

rebuild, *v.t.ir*, rebâtir, reconstruire.

rebuke, *n*, réprimande, *f.* ¶ *v.t*, réprimander.

rebut, *v.t*, réfuter.

recalcitrant, *a. & n*, récalcitrant, e.

recall, *n*, rappel, *m.* ¶ *v.t*, rappeler, retracer; révoquer; (*recollect*) se rappeler.

recant, *v.t*, rétracter. **~ation,** *n*, rétractation, palinodie, *f.*

recapitulate, *v.t*, récapituler.

recapture, *n*, reprise, *f.* ¶ *v.t*, reprendre.

recast, *v.t.ir*, refondre; remanier.

recede, *v.i*, reculer; se retirer; fuir. **receding** (*forehead, chin*) *p.a*, fuyant.

receipt, *n*, réception, *f*; reçu, *m*; quittance, *f*, acquit, *m*; récépissé, *m*; (*pl.*) recette, *f. oft. pl.* ¶ *v.t*, acquitter, quittancer. **receive,** *v.t*, recevoir; accueillir; (*money*) toucher; (*stolen goods*) receler. **receiver,** *n*, destinataire, *m.f*; receleur, euse; (*Teleph.*) écouteur; (*vessel*) récipient, *m.*

recent†, *a*, récent, nouveau, frais.

receptacle, *n*, réceptacle, *m.* **reception,** *n*, réception, *f*; accueil, *m.* ~ *room*, salon, *m.*

recess, *n*, [r]enfoncement, retrait, *m*, retraite, enclave; embrasure; (*Sch.*) récréation, *f*; (*pl. heart*) replis, *m.pl.* ¶ *v.t*, défoncer; suspendre les séances.

recipe, *n*, recette; (*Phar.*) formule, *f.*

recipient, *n*, destinataire, *m.f.*

reciprocal†, *a*, réciproque; inverse; partagé. **reciprocate,** *v.t*, payer de retour. **reciprocating,** *p.a*, alternatif, de va-et-vient. **reciprocity,** *n*, réciprocité, *f.*

recital, *n*, récit, *m*; énumération, *f*; (*Mus.*) récital, *m*; audition, *f.* **recitation,** *n*, récitation, *f.* **recitative,** *n*, récitatif, *m.* **recite,** *v.t*, réciter, déclamer; énumérer.

reckless, *a*, téméraire; insouciant. ~ *driver*, chauffard, *m.* **~ly,** *ad*, témérairement; à corps perdu.

reckon, *v.t. & i*, compter, calculer, chiffrer; estimer. **~ing,** *n*, compte, calcul, *m*; carte à payer; addition, *f*, écot, *m.*

reclaim, *v.t*, ramener dans la bonne voite; (*from vice*) retirer; (*uncultivated land*) défricher; (*submerged land*) aménager.

recline, *v.i*, se renverser, se reposer.

recluse, *n*, reclus, e. **reclusion,** *n*, réclusion, *f.*

recognition, *n*, reconnaissance, *f.* **recognizable,** *a*, reconnaissable. **recognizance,** *n*, obligation, *f.* **recognize,** *v.t*, reconnaître.

recoil, *n*, recul, repoussement, *m.* ¶ *v.i*, reculer, repousser.

recoin, *v.t*, refondre, refrapper.

recollect, *v.t*, se rappeler. **~ion,**

n, souvenir, m, mémoire, f.

recommence, v.t. & i, recommencer.

recommend, v.t, recommander; préconiser; proposer. ~ation, n, recommendation; proposition, f; (for election) parrainage, m. ~er, n, parrain, m.

recompense, n, récompense, f. ¶ v.t, récompenser.

reconcile, v.t, réconcilier, [r]accommoder; concilier. **reconciliation**, n, réconciliation; résignation, f.

recondite, a, abstrus, obscure.

reconnoiter, v.t, reconnaître.

reconsider, v.t, revenir sur, reviser.

reconstruct, v.t, reconstruire; (fig.) constituer de nouveau, reprendre sous œuvre. ~ion, n, reconstruction; (fig.) reconstitution, f.

record, n, registre, m; note, f; dossier, m; (pl.) archives, f.pl; (pl.) historique, (sport) record; (phonograph) disque, m. off the ~, à titre confidentiel. ¶ v.t, enregistrer; consigner; constater. ~er, n, enregistreur; compteur de sport, m.

re-count, v.t, recompter.

recount, v.t, raconter.

recoup, v.t, récupérer; dédommager.

recourse, n, recours, m.

re-cover, v.t, recouvrir.

recover, v.t, recouvrer; rattraper; (v.i.) se rétablir; [se] reprendre, se relever. ~y, n, recouvrement, m; reprise, f.

recreant, a. & n, lâche; apostat, a. & m.

re-create, v.t, recréer.

recreate, v.t, récréer. **recreation**, n, récréation, f, délassement, m.

recrimination, n, récrimination, f.

recrudescence, n, recrudescence, f.

recruit, n, recrue, f. ¶ v.t, recruter; racoler; (v.i.) se rétablir. ~ing sergeant, sergent recruteur, m.

rectangle, n, rectangle, carré long, m. **rectangular**, a, rectangulaire.

rectify, v.t, rectifier; redresser.

rectilinear, a, rectiligne.

rectitude, n, rectitude; droiture, f.

rector, n, recteur; curé, m. ~ship,

n, cure, f. ~y, n, presbytère, m, cure, f.

rectum, n, rectum, m.

recumbent, a, couché. ~ figure (statue), gisant, e.

recuperate, v.i, se récupérer.

recur, v.i, revenir, se reproduire, se retracer. **recurrence**, n, retour, m, répétition, f.

red, a. & n, rouge, a. & m; (hair) roux, a. the ~s (Pol.), les rouges, m.pl. ~breast, rouge-gorge, m. the R~ Cross, la Croix Rouge. ~-faced (person), rougeaud, e. ~-haired (person), roux, rousse, rousseau, m. & att. ~-handed, sur le fait, en flagrant délit. ~ herring, hareng saur, m. ~-hot, [chauffé au] rouge; tout chaud. ~ Indian or ~skin, Peau Rouge, m. ~ lead, minium, m. to be a ~-letter day, faire époque. ~ mullet, rouget, m. ~ pepper, poivre rouge, p. de Cayenne, m. R~ Sea, mer Rouge, f. ~ tape, chinoiseries, f.pl, routine, f. **redden**, v.t & i, rougir; roussir. **reddish**, a, rougeâtre; roussâtre; blond hasardé.

redeem, v.t, racheter; rembourser; amortir; dégager; purger; s'acquitter de. **Redeemer**, n, Rédempteur, m. **redemption**, n, rachat; remboursement; amortissement; dégagement, m; (mortgage) purge, f; (Relig.) rachat, m, rédemption, f.

redness, n, rougeur; rousseur, f.

redolent of, qui sent le, la.

redoubt, n, redoute, f, réduit, m.

redoubtable, a, redoutable.

redound, v.i, rejaillir.

redress, n, redressement, m, réparation, f. ¶ v.t, redresser, réparer.

reduce, v.t, réduire; diminuer; ramener; affaiblir. ~ to lower rank (Mil.), rétrograder. ~ to the ranks, casser, réduire à la condition de simple soldat. **reduction**, n, réduction; diminution, f; (tax) dégrèvement, m. ~ to the absurd or reductio ad absurdum, démonstration (ou preuve) par l'absurde, f. ~ to the ranks, cassation, f.

redundant, a, redondant.

reecho, v.i, résonner.

reed, n, roseau; (pipe) chalumeau, m; (Mus.) anche; (Arch.) baguette, f.

reef, n, récif, écueil, banc, brisant; (in sail) ris, m.

reek, *n,* odeur fétide; exhalaison pestilentielle, *f.* ~ *with, of,* exhaler; suer. ~*ing with,* fumant de.

reel, *n,* dévidoir, *m,* bobine, *f;* touret; (*Fish.*) moulinet, *m.* ¶ *v.t,* dévider, bobiner; (*v.i.*) chanceler; (*when drunk*) festonner.

reelect, *v.t,* réélire. ~**ion,** *n,* réélection, *f.* **reeligible,** *a,* rééligible.

reembark, *v.t,* rembarquer; (*v.i*) [se] r.

reengage, *v.t,* rengager.

reenlist, *v.i,* [se] rengager.

reenter, *v.i,* rentrer; (*v.t.*) rentrer dans. **reentrant,** *a,* rentrant. **reentry,** *n,* rentrée, *f.*

reestablish, *v.t,* rétablir, restaurer.

reeve (*Naut.*) *v.t.ir,* passer.

reexamine, *v.t,* repasser, revoir.

reexport, *v.t,* réexporter.

refectory, *n,* réfectoire, *m.*

refer, *v.t,* référer; renvoyer; déférer. ~ *to,* se référer à, se reporter à; renvoyer à, consulter. ~**ee,** *n,* arbitre; tiers arbitre; (*Box.*) [arbitre] directeur de combat, *m.* ¶ *v.t,* arbitrer. **reference,** *n,* renvoi, *m;* référence; mention, *f;* trait, *m.* ~ *library,* bibliothèque où les livres se consultent sur place; b. d'ouvrages à consulter, *f.* ~ [*mark*], [guidon de] renvoi, *m.* *with* ~ *to,* à l'égard de. **referendum,** *n,* referendum, plébiscite, *m.*

refill, *v.t. & i,* remplir; réapprovisionner.

refine, *v.t,* affiner; raffiner; épurer; polir; (*v.i.*) raffiner. ~**d,** *p.a,* raffiné, distingué; poli; délicat. ~**ment** (*fig.*) *n,* raffinement, *m.* **refiner,** *n,* affineur; raffineur, *m.* **refinery,** *n,* raffinerie, *f.*

reflect, *v.t. & i,* réfléchir; refléter; rejaillir. ~**ion,** *n,* réflexion; image, *f;* reflet, *m;* atteinte, *f.* ~**ive,** *a,* réfléchi. ~**or,** *n,* réflecteur, *m.* **reflex,** *a,* réflexe. ¶ *n,* reflet; réflexe, *m.* **reflexive** (*Gram.*) *a,* réfléchi.

refloat (*ship*) *v.t,* renflouer.

reflux, *n,* reflux, *m.*

re-form, *v.t,* reformer.

reform, *n,* réforme, *f.* ¶ *v.t,* réformer. ~**ation,** *n,* réformation; réforme, *f.* ~**atory,** *n,* maison de correction, *f,* pénitencier, *m.* ~**er,** *n,* réformateur, trice.

refract, *v.t,* réfracter. ~*ing telescope,* lunette [d'approche] *f.* **re-**

fractoriness, *n,* mutinerie, *f.* **refractory,** *a,* réfractaire.

refrain, *n,* refrain, *m.* ¶ *v.i,* se retenir; s'abstenir.

refresh, *n,* rafraîchir; restaurer; délasser, reposer, récréer. **refreshment,** *n,* rafraîchissement, *m.* ~ *bar,* ~ *room,* buvette, *f,* buffet, *m.*

refrigerate, *v.t,* frigorifier. **refrigeration,** *n,* réfrigération, *f.* **refrigerator,** *n,* réfrigérateur, *m.*

refuge, *n,* refuge, *m. to take* ~, se réfugier. **refugee,** *n,* réfugié, e, émigré, e.

refulgent, *a,* éclatant.

refund, *v.t,* rembourser.

refurnish, *v.t,* remeubler.

refusal, *n,* refus, *m.* **refuse,** *n,* rebut, déchet, *m. oft. pl;* immondices, *f.pl,* ordure, *f.* ~ *dump,* voirie, *f.* ¶ *v.t. -& i,* refuser, se r. ~ *admittance,* consigner à la porte.

refute, *v.t,* réfuter.

regain, *v.t,* regagner; reconquérir.

regal†, *a,* royal.

regale, *v.t,* régaler.

regalia, *n,* insignes de la royauté; décors, *m. pl.*

regard, *n,* égard, *m;* considération, *f;* respect; rapport, *m. with* ~ *to,* ~*ing,* à l'égard de, à propos de, quant à, à l'endroit de. ¶ *v.t,* regarder; considérer. ~**less,** *a,* insoucieux, sans se soucier.

regatta, *n,* régate, *f. oft. pl.*

regency, *n,* régence, *f.*

regenerate, *v.t,* régénérer. **regeneration,** *n,* régénération, *f.*

regent, *n. & a,* régent, e.

regicidal *a.* & **regicide,** *n,* régicide, *a.* & *m.*

regild, *v.t.ir,* redorer.

regime, *n,* régime, *m.* **regiment,** *n,* régiment, *m.* **regimental,** *a,* régimentaire. ~ *records,* historique du régiment, *m.*

region, *n,* région, contrée, *f.* ~**al,** *a,* régional.

register, *n,* registre, livre, journal; grand livre; répertoire, *m;* matricule; voix, *f;* (*book mark*) signet, *m.* ~ *of voters,* liste électorale, *f.* ¶ *v.t,* enregistrer, inscrire, immatriculer; (*design,* etc.) déposer; recommander. **registrar,** *n,* greffier; archiviste, *m.* **registration,** *n,* inscription, immatriculation; recommandation, *f.* **registry** [*office*], *n,* (*marriage*) mairie, *f;* (*servants*) bureau de placement, *m.*

regret, *n,* regret, *m.* ¶ *v.t,* regretter.

regular†, *a,* régulier; réglé; assidu; véritable; franc, fieffé. ~ *channel[s]* (*fig.*), filière, *f.* ~**ity,** *n,* régularité, *f.* ~**ize,** *v.t,* régulariser. **regulate,** *v.t,* régler; réglementer. **regulation,** *n,* réglementation, *f;* règlement, *m;* ordonnance, *f;* (*att.*) réglementaire. **regulator,** *n,* régulateur, *m.*

rehabilitate, *v.t,* réhabiliter.

rehandle, *v.t,* remmancher.

rehearsal, *n,* répétition, *f.* **rehearse,** *v.t,* répéter; énumérer.

rehousing, *n,* relogement, *f.*

reign, *n,* règne, *m.* ¶ *v.i,* régner. ~**ing,** *a,* régnant.

reimburse, *v.t,* rembourser.

reimport, *v.t,* réimporter.

reimpose, *v.t,* réimposer.

rein, *n,* rêne, guide, bride, *f.* ¶ *v.t,* guider, refréner.

reindeer, *n,* renne, *m.*

reinforce, *v.t,* renforcer; (*concrete*) armer. ~**ment,** *n,* renforcement, *m;* armature, *f;* (*men*) renfort, *m.*

reinstate, *v.t,* réintégrer, rétablir, réhabiliter.

reinsure, *v.t,* réassurer.

reinvest (*Fin.*) *v.t,* replacer.

reinvigorate, *v.t,* redonner de la vigueur à, revigorer.

reissue (*book*) *n,* réédition, *f.*

reiterate, *v.t,* réitérer.

reject, *v.t,* rejeter; repousser; refuser. ~**ion,** *n,* rejet; repoussement, *m.*

rejoice, *v.t,* réjouir; (*v.i.*) se **r. rejoicing,** *n,* réjouissance, *f.*

re-join, *v.t,* rejoindre.

rejoin, *v.t,* répliquer; (*one's regiment*) rejoindre, rallier. **rejoinder,** *n,* réplique, repartie, *f.*

rejuvenate, *v.t,* rajeunir.

rekindle, *v.t,* rallumer.

relapse, *n,* (*Med.*) rechute, *f;* (*Fin.*) recul, *m;* (*crime*) récidive, *f.* ¶ *v.i,* retomber; reculer. ~ *into crime,* récidiver.

relate, *v.t,* raconter, narrer, relater; (*v.i.*) se rapporter, avoir rapport. ~**d to,** parent avec, apparenté à. **relation,** *n,* relation, *f;* rapport, *m;* parent, e; allié, e; (*pl.*) parenté, *f.* ~**ship,** *n,* parenté; filiation, *f.* **relative†,** *a,* relatif. ¶ *n,* parent, e.

relax, *v.t,* relâcher; détendre, débander; délasser; (*Med.*) [re]-lâcher. ~**ation,** *n,* relâchement, *f;* relâche, délassement, *m.*

re-lay, *v.t.ir,* reposer.

relay, *n,* relais, *m.* ~ *race,* course de (*ou* à) relais, *f.* ¶ *v.t,* relayer.

release, *n,* relaxation, *f,* élargissement; (*pigeons*) lancer, *m;* libération; délivrance, *f;* (*Mech.*) déclic; (*Phot.*) déclencheur, *m.* ¶ *v.t,* relaxer, élargir; lancer; libérer; lâcher; délivrer; délier.

relegate, *v.t,* reléguer.

relent, *v.i,* fléchir. ~**less†,** *a,* impitoyable, acharné.

relet, *v.t.ir,* relouer. **reletting,** *n,* relocation, *f.*

relevant, *a,* pertinent; qui se rapporte à.

reliability, *n,* sûreté, sécurité; fidélité, *f.* **reliable†,** *a,* sûr; de tout repos; de confiance. **reliance,** *n,* confiance, foi, *f.*

relic, *n,* relique, *f;* reste, *m.*

relief, *n,* soulagement; secours, *m,* assistance, *f;* (*tax*) dégrèvement; (*for dependants, Inc. tax*) abattement; (*art*) relief, *m;* (*Mil.*) relève, *f.* ~ *fund,* caisse de secours, *f.* ~ *train,* train supplementaire, *m.* **relieve,** *v.t,* soulager, secourir, assister; relever; débarrasser.

relight, *v.t,* rallumer.

religion, *n,* religion, *f.* **religious†,** *a,* religieux; (*book*) dévot, de dévotion. ~**ness,** *n,* religiosité, *f.*

relinquish, *v.t,* abandonner.

reliquary, *n,* reliquaire, *m.*

relish, *n,* goût, *m;* saveur, *f;* assaisonnement, *m.* ¶ *v.t,* goûter; savourer.

reluctance, *n,* répugnance, *f.* I *am reluctant to,* il me répugne de, je me fais conscience de. **reluctantly,** *ad,* à contrecœur, à regret.

rely, *v.i,* compter, se reposer, faire fond.

remain, *v.i,* rester; demeurer. **remainder,** *n,* reste, restant; solde d'édition, *m.* ¶ *v.t,* solder. **remains,** *n.pl,* restes, vestiges, débris, *m.pl;* dépouille, *f.*

remake, *v.t.ir,* refaire.

remand, *v.t,* renvoyer à une autre audience.

remark, *n,* remarque, observation, *f;* propos, *m.* **remark** & **remark,** *v.t,* remarquer. ~**able†,** *a,* remarquable.

remedy, *n,* remède; (*law*) recours, *m.* ¶ *v.t,* remédier à.

remember, *v.t,* se [res]souvenir de; se rappeler, retenir. **remem-**

brance, *n*, [res]souvenir, *m*; mémoire, *f*.

emind of, faire penser à, rappeler à. *you ~ me of someone,* vous me rappelez quelqu'un. **~er,** *n*, mémento; rappel, *m*.

eminiscence, *n*, réminiscence, *f*.

emiss†, *a*, négligent. **~ion,** *n*, rémission; remise, *f*. **remit,** *v.t*, remettre; envoyer. **remittance,** *n*, remise, *f*; envoi, *m*.

emnant, *n*, reste; coupon; lambeau, *m*; épave, *f*.

emodel, *v.t*, remodeler; refondre.

emonstrance, *n*, remontrance, *f*. **remonstrate,** *v.i*, faire des remontrances, [en] remontrer (*with* = à).

emorse, *n*, remords, *m*. **~less,** *a*, & **~lessly,** *ad*, sans remords.

emote, *a*, éloigné, écarté; (*antiquity*) reculée, haute. **~ control,** commande à distance, *f*. **~ness,** *n*, éloignement, *m*.

emount, *n*, remonte, *f*. ¶ *v.t*, remonter.

emovable, *a*, amovible. **removal,** *n*, déplacement; éloignement; déménagement; enlèvement, *m*; (*of officer*) destitution, *f*. **remove,** *v.t*, déplacer; éloigner; enlever; lever; destituer.

emunerate, *v.t*, rémunérer, rétribuer. **remuneration,** *n*, rémunération, rétribution, *f*.

enaissance, *n*, renaissance, *f*.

ename, *v.t*, débaptiser.

end, *v.t.ir*, déchirer; (*the air*) fendre.

ender, *v.t*, rendre; expliquer; interpréter; (*plaster*) enduire. **~ void,** frapper de nullité. **~ing,** *n*, (*accounts*) reddition, *f*; (*art*) rendu, *m*; explication; interprétation, *f*; (*plaster*) enduit, *m*.

enegade, *n*, renégat, *m*.

enew, *v.t*, renouveler. **~al,** *n*, renouvellement, *m*; rénovation; reprise, *f*.

ennet, *n*, présure; (*apple*) reinette, *f*.

enounce, *v.t*, renoncer à, répudier, abjurer.

enovate, *v.t*, renouveler, rénover, rajeunir.

enown, *n*, renommée, *f*, renom, *m*. **~ed,** *a*, renommé.

ent, *n*, (*tear*) déchirure, *f*; accroc; (*periodical payment*) loyer; fermage, *m*; redevance, *f*. ¶ *v.t*, louer; sous-louer. **~al,** *n*, prix de location, *m*; redevance;

valeur locative, *f*. **~er,** *n*, locataire, *m,f*.

renunciation, *n*, renonciation, répudiation, *f*; renoncement, *m*.

reopen, *v.t*, rouvrir; (*v.i.*) se r.; rentrer. **~ing,** *n*, réouverture; rentrée, *f*.

reorganize, *v.t*, réorganiser.

repack, *v.t*, remballer.

repair, *n*, état, *m*; réparation, *f*. *beyond ~,* irréparable. *under ~,* en réparation. ¶ *v.t*, réparer; raccommoder; (*v.i.*) se rendre. **~able & reparable,** *a*, réparable. **reparation,** *n*, réparation, *f*.

repartee, *n*, repartie, *f*.

repast, *n*, repas, *m*.

repatriate, *v.t*, rapatrier.

repay, *v.t.ir*, rembourser; rendre. **~ment,** *n*, remboursement, *m*.

repeal, *n*, rappel, *m*, révocation, *f*. ¶ *v.t*, rappeler, révoquer.

repeat (*Mus.*) *ad*, bis. ¶ (*Mus.*) *n*, renvoi, *m*. ¶ *v.t*, répéter, redire. **~edly,** *ad*, fréquemment, à plusieurs reprises. **~ing** (*rifle, watch*) *p.a*, à répétition.

repel, *v.t*, repousser. **repellent,** *a*, rebutant, repoussant; (*Phys.*) répulsif.

repent, *v.i*, se repentir; (*v.t.*) se repentir de. **~ance,** *n*, repentir, *m*.

repeople, *v.t*, repeupler.

repercussion, *n*, répercussion, *f*.

repertory, *n*, répertoire, *m*.

repetend, *n*, période, *f*. **repetition,** *n*, répétition; redite; reprise, *f*.

repine, *v.i*, se chagriner.

replace, *v.t*, replacer; reposer; remplacer. **~ment,** *n*, remplacement, *m*.

replant, *v.t*, replanter.

replay, *v.t*, rejouer.

replenish, *v.t*, remplir; remonter. **replete,** *a*, plein. **repletion,** *n*, plénitude; réplétion, *f*.

replica, *n*, réplique, *f*.

reply, *n*, réponse, *f*. *~ paid,* avec réponse payée. *in ~* (*law*), responsif. ¶ *v.t. & i*, répondre.

report, *n*, rapport; reportage; bulletin; compte rendu; procèsverbal, *m*; expertise, *f*; bruit, *m*; renommée; détonation, *f*. ¶ *v.t*, rendre compte de, rapporter. **~er** (*news*) *n*, reporter, chroniqueur, journaliste d'information, *m*. **~ing,** *n*, reportage, *m*.

repose, *n*, repos, *m*. ¶ *v.i*. se reposer.

repository, n, dépôt, magasin; réceptacle; (*fig.*) répertoire, m.

repot, v.t, rempoter.

repoussé work, travail de repoussé, m.

reprehend, v.t, reprendre, censurer. **reprehensible,** a, répréhensible.

represent, v.t., représenter. **~ation,** n, représentation, f. **~ative,** a, représentatif. ¶ n, représentant, e.

repress, v.t, réprimer, refouler, comprimer. **~ion,** n, répression, compression, f.

reprieve, n, sursis, m. ¶ v.t, surseoir à l'exécution de, gracier.

reprimand, n, réprimande, semonce, mercuriale, f; blâme, m. ¶ v.t, réprimander, chapitrer; blâmer.

reprint, n, réimpression, f. ¶ v.t, réimprimer.

reprisal, n, représaille, f.

reproach, n, reproche, m; honte, f. ¶ v.t, faire des reproches à; reprocher. **~ful,** a, de reproche. **~fully,** ad, d'un ton de reproche.

reprobate, n, réprouvé, m. ¶ v.t, réprouver. **reprobation,** n, réprobation, f.

reproduce, v.t, reproduire. **reproduction,** n, reproduction; répétition, f.

reproof, n, réprimande, f. **reprove,** v.t, reprendre.

reptile, n, reptile, m.

republic, n, république, f. **~an,** a. & n, républicain, e.

republish, v.t, publier de nouveau.

repudiate, v.t, répudier, [re]nier.

repugnance, n, répugnance, f. **repugnant,** a, répugnant. *to be ~ to,* répugner à.

repulse, n, échec, m. ¶ v.t, repousser, rebuter. **repulsion,** n, répulsion, f. **repulsive,** a, repoussant; (*Phys.*) répulsif.

repurchase, n, rachat, m. ¶ v.t, racheter.

reputable, a, honorable. **reputation & repute,** n, réputation, renommée, f, renom, crédit, m. *of repute,* réputé. **reputed,** p.p, réputé; censé; putatif.

request, n, demande, prière, requête, instance, f. *by ~, on ~,* sur demande. ¶ v.t, demander, prier, inviter.

requiem, n, requiem, m.

require, v.t, exiger; requérir; demander; réclamer; vouloir; avoir besoin de; falloir. **~ment,** n, exigence, f; besoin, m. **requisite,** a, requis, voulu. ¶ n, article, m, fourniture, f. **requisition,** n, réquisition, f. ¶ v.t, réquisitionner.

requital, n, récompense; revanche, f. **requite,** v.t, récompenser.

reredos, n, retable, m.

resale, n, revente, f.

rescind, v.t, annuler. **rescission,** n, rescision, f.

rescript, n, rescrit, m.

rescue, n, délivrance, f; sauvetage, m. *to the ~,* à la rescousse. ¶ v.t, délivrer; sauver.

research, n, recherche, f. **~ worker,** chercheur, euse.

reseat, v.t, rasseoir; remettre un fond à.

resemblance, n, ressemblance, f. **resemble,** v.t, ressembler à, approcher de, imiter.

resent, v.t, s'indigner contre, ressentir. **~ment,** n, ressentiment, m.

reservation, n, réserve, réservation; (*mental*) restriction, arrière-pensée; (*seats*) location, f. **reserve,** n, réserve, provision, retenue, f. ¶ v.t, réserver; retenir; louer. **~d seat ticket,** billet garde-place, billet de location de place, m. **reservist,** n, réserviste, m. **reservoir,** n, réservoir, m.

reset, v.t.ir, remonter; remettre; (*Typ.*) recomposer. **resetting,** (*Typ.*) n, recomposition, f.

reship, v.t, rembarquer.

reshuffle, v.t, rebattre.

reside, v.i, résider, demeurer. **residence,** n, résidence, f; séjour, m; demeure, f, domicile, m, habitation, f. **resident,** n, habitant, e; (*diplomatic*) résident, m.

residuary legatee, légataire universel, m. **residue,** n, résidu; reliquat, m.

resign, v.t, résigner, se démettre de; (*v.i.*) démissionner. **resignation,** n, résignation, démission, f; (*submission*) résignation, f.

resilient, a, élastique.

resin, n, résine; (*for violin*) colophane, f. **~ous,** a, résineux.

resist, v.t, résister à; (*v.i.*) résister. **~ance,** n, résistance, f.

resole, v.t, ressemeler.

resolute†, a, résolu, déterminé. **resolution,** n, résolution; détermination; délibération; décision; proposition, f. **resolve,** n, détermination, f. ¶ v.t, résoudre;

déterminer. ~ **on,** statuer sur, décider.

resonance, *n,* résonance, *f.* **resonant,** *a,* résonnant.

resort, *n,* recours; ressort, *m,* ressource, *f;* rendez-vous; séjour, *m;* station, *f,* centre, *m. as a last* ~, en dernier ressort. *seaside* ~, station balnéaire, *f.* ~ **to,** recourir à; se rendre à; fréquenter.

resound, *v.i,* résonner, retentir.

resource, *n,* ressource, *f;* expédient, *m.* ~**ful,** *a,* de ressources.

respect, *n,* respect; rapport, égard, *m;* acception, *f. in all* ~s, à tous égards. ¶ *v.t,* respecter. ~**able,** *a,* respectable, honorable. honnête. ~**ably,** *ad,* honorablement. ~**ful†,** *a,* respectueux. ~**ing,** *pr,* concernant. ~**ive†,** *a,* respectif.

respiration, *n,* respiration, *f.*

respite, *n,* répit, relâche, *m,* trêve, *f;* sursis, *m.*

resplendent, *a,* resplendissant.

respond, *v.i,* répondre; obéir. ~**ent,** *n,* répondant, e; *(law)* défendeur, eresse. **response,** *n,* réponse, *f; (Eccl.)* répons, *m.* **responsibility,** *n,* responsabilité, *f.* **responsible,** *a,* responsable; solidaire. **responsive,** *a,* sensible, liant.

rest, *n,* repos; *(Mus.)* silence, *m,* pause, *f;* support; appui; *(Bil., etc.)* chevalet; *(remainder)* reste, *m. & all the* ~ *of it,* & toute la lyre. ¶ *v.i,* se reposer; reposer; poser; s'appuyer; porter; tenir; résider; incomber; *(v.t.)* reposer, appuyer.

restage, *v.t,* remonter.

restaurant, *n,* restaurant, *m.* ~ *keeper,* restaurateur, trice.

restful, *a,* reposant. **resting place** repos, *m;* sépulture, *f.*

restitch, *v.t,* repiquer.

restitution, *n,* restitution, *f.*

restive, *a,* rétif.

restless, *a,* inquiet; agité; remuant; turbulent.

restoration, *n,* restauration; réfection, *f;* rétablissement, *m;* restitution, *f.* **restorative,** *a. & n,* restaurant, *a. & m.* **restore,** *v.t,* restaurer; rénover; rétablir; ramener; rendre; restituer. **restorer,** *n,* restaurateur, trice.

restrain, *v.t,* retenir, contenir, comprimer, contraindre. **restraint,** *n,* contrainte, *f. to place* (lunatic) *under* ~, interner.

restrict, *v.t,* restreindre, borner,

renfermer. ~**ion,** *n,* restriction, *f.*

restring, *v.t.ir,* recorder.

result, *n,* résultat, *m;* suite, *f.* ¶ *v.i,* résulter.

resume, *v.t,* reprendre; renouer. **resumption,** *n,* reprise, *f.*

resurrection, *n,* résurrection, *f.*

resurvey, *n,* contre-expertise, *f.*

resuscitate, *v.t,* resusciter.

retail, *n,* [commerce de] détail; petit commerce, *m.* ¶ *v.t,* détailler, débiter. ~**er,** *n,* détaillant, e.

retain, *v.t,* retenir; arrêter. ~**er,** *n, (fee)* provision, *f; (pl.)* gens, *m.pl.*

retake, *v.t.ir,* reprendre.

retaliate, *v.i,* user de représailles *(upon =* envers). **retaliation,** *n,* représailles, *f.pl,* talion, *m.* **retaliatory,** *a,* de représailles.

retard, *v.t,* retarder.

retch, *v.i,* avoir des haut-le-cœur. vomir.

retention, *n,* rétention, *f.* **retentive,** *a,* tenace, fidèle.

reticence, *n,* réticence, *f. to be reticent,* se taire à dessein.

reticle & reticule, *n,* réticule, *m.*

retina, *n,* rétine, *f.*

retinue, *n,* suite, *f,* cortège, *m.*

retire, *v.t,* retirer; mettre à la retraite; *(officer)* réformer; *(v.i.)* se retirer. ~**d,** *p.p,* retiré; en retraite. ~**ment,** *n,* retraite, *f.* **retiring,** *p.a, (pers.)* retiré en lui-même, qui fuit la société; *(manners)* effacées; *(director)* sortant; *(pension)* de retraite.

retort, *n,* réplique, riposte; *(Chem.)* cornue, *f,* vase clos, *m.* ¶ *v.t. & i,* rétorquer, répliquer, riposter.

retouch, *v.t,* retoucher, retoucher à. ~**[ing],** *n,* retouche, *f.*

retrace, *v.t,* retracer; revenir sur, rebrousser. ~ *one's steps,* rebrousser chemin.

retract, *v.t,* rétracter; *(v.i.)* se rétracter.

retreat, *n,* retraite, reculade; *(glacier)* décrue, *f.* ¶ *v.i,* se retirer, reculer.

retrench, *v.t,* retrancher, restreindre. ~**ment,** *n,* retranchement, *m.*

retribution, *n,* récompense, *f.*

retrieve, *v.t,* rétablir, réparer; *(game)* rapporter. **retriever** *(dog) n,* retriever, *m. a good* ~, un chien qui rapporte bien.

retroactive, *a,* rétroactif.

retrograde, *a,* rétrograde.
retrospect, *n,* revue rétrospective, *f.* **~ive†,** *a,* rétrospectif; (*effect of a law*) rétroactif.
return, *n,* retour, *m;* rentrée; restitution; revanche, *f;* remboursement; renvoi; rendu; état, relevé, *m;* déclaration; statistique; rémunération, *f;* rapport, rendement; (*pl.—books, newspapers*) bouillon, *m.* ~ *address,* adresse de l'expéditeur, *f.* ~ *match,* revanche, *f,* match retour, *m.* by ~ *mail,* par retour du courrier. **¶** *v.t,* rendre; restituer; renvoyer; retourner; rembourser; déclarer; élire, nommer; (*Ten.*) relever (*le service*); (*v.i.*) retourner; revenir; rentrer. **~able,** *a,* restituable. **~ed letter,** lettre renvoyée, *f.*
reunion, *n,* réunion, *f.* **reunite,** *v.t,* réunir.
reveal (*Arch.*) *n,* jouée, *f.* **¶** *v.t,* révéler.
reveille *n,* réveil, *m,* diane, *f.*
revel, *n.* oft. *pl,* réjouissance, *f.* oft. *pl;* ripaille, *f.* **¶** *v.i,* ripailler, faire bombance. ~ *in,* nager dans.
revelation, *n,* révélation, *f.* R~ (Bible), Apocalypse, *f.*
reveler, *n,* noceur, euse. **revelry,** *n,* ripaille, *f.*
revenge, *n,* vengeance; revanche, *f.* ~ **oneself,** se venger. **~ful,** *a,* vindicatif.
revenue, *n,* revenu; rapport; fisc, *m.* ~ *stamp,* timbre fiscal, *m.* (*law*) réformer. **reversible,** *a,* répercuter. *reverberatory furnace,* four à réverbère, *m.*
revere, *v.t,* révérer. **reverence,** *n,* révérence, *f.* **¶** *v.t,* révérer. **reverend,** *a,* révérend. **reverent†,** *a,* pieux. **reverential,** *a,* révérenciel. **reverentially,** *ad,* avec révérence.
reverie, *n,* rêverie, *f.*
reversal, *n,* retournement; retour, *m,* inversion, *f.* **reverse,** *n,* revers; envers; inverse; contraire, opposé; rebours; (*of coin, of medal*) revers, *m,* pile, *f.* **¶** *v.t,* renverser; inverser; invertir; (*law*) réformer. **reversible,** *a,* réversible. **reversion,** *n,* réversion, *f;* retour, *m.* **revert,** *v.i,* revenir, retourner.
revet, *v.t,* revêtir. **~ment,** *n,* revêtement, *m.*
revictual, *v.t,* ravitailler.
review, *n,* revue; revision; (*book*) compte rendu, *m,* notice, critique [littéraire] *f.* **¶** *v.t,* revoir, reviser; (*Mil.*) passer en revue; (*book*) faire le compte rendu de. **~er,** *n,* critique [littéraire] *m.*
revile, *v.t,* injurier.
revise (*Typ.*) *n,* seconde [épreuve] *f.* **¶** *v.t,* revoir, reviser. **revision,** *n,* revision, *f.*
revival, *n,* reprise; renaissance, *f;* rétablissement; (*Relig.*) réveil, *m.* **revive,** *v.t,* ranimer; raviver; réveiller.
revoke, *v.t,* révoquer; (*v.i, cards*) renoncer.
revolt, *n,* révolte, *f,* soulèvement, *m.* **¶** *v.i,* se révolter, se soulever. **~ing,** *a,* révoltant.
revolution, *n,* révolution, *f;* tour, *m.* **~ary,** *a.* & *n,* révolutionnaire; *a.* & *m,f.* **~ize,** *v.t,* révolutionner; modifier entièrement. **revolve,** *v.t.* & *i,* tourner.
revolver, *n,* révolver, *m.*
revue, *n,* revue, *f.*
revulsion, *n,* révolution; (*Med.*) révulsion, *f.*
reward, *n,* récompense, *f.* **¶** *v.t,* récompenser; couronner.
rewrite, *v.t.ir,* récrire.
rhapsody, *n,* rhapsodie, *f.*
Rheims, *n,* Reims, *m.*
rhetoric, *n,* rhétorique, *f.* **~al,** *a,* oratoire soutenu.
rheumatic, *a,* rhumatismal. **rheumatism,** *n,* rhumatisme, *m.*
Rhine (the), le Rhin. **¶** *att,* rhénan; (*wine*) du Rhin. *the* ~*land,* les pays rhénans.
rhinoceros, *n,* rhinocéros, *m.*
rhododendron, *n,* rhododendron, *m.*
rhomb[us], *n,* rhombe, losange, *m.*
Rhone (the) le Rhône.
rhubarb, *n,* rhubarbe, *f.*
rhyme, *n,* rime, *f.* **¶** *v.i,* rimer. **rhym[est]er,** *n,* rim[aill]eur, *m.* **rhythm,** *n,* rythme, *m,* cadence, *f.* **~ic(al),** *a,* rythmique, cadencé.
rib, *n,* côte; nervure; (*ship*) côte, *f,* membre, *m;* (*umbrella*) baleine, *f.* ~ *steak,* entrecôte, *f.*
ribald, *a,* gaillard, égrillard, licencieux.
ribbed, *a,* côtelé, à côtes; à nervure(s).
ribbon *or* **riband,** *n,* ruban; cordon, *m.* ~ *maker,* rubanier, ère. ~ *trade,* rubanerie, *f.*
rice, *n,* riz, *m.* ~ *field,* rizière, *f.* ~ *paper,* papier de Chine, *m.*
rich†, *a,* riche; (*food*) gras. *the* ~, les riches, *m.pl.* **riches,** *n.pl,*

richesse, *f. oft. pl.* **richness,** *n,*
richesse, *f.*

rick, *n,* (*hay*) meule, *f;* (*strain*)
effort, *m.*

rickets, *n,* rachitisme, *m.* **rickety,**
a, rachitique; boiteux, bancal.

ricksha[w], *n,* pousse-pousse, *m.*

ricochet, *n,* ricochet, *m.* ¶ *v.i,*
ricocher.

rid, *v.t.ir,* débarrasser. **riddance,**
n, débarras, *m.*

riddle, *n,* énigme, devinette, *f,* rébus; (*sieve*) crible, *m.* ¶ *v.t,*
cribler.

ride, *n,* promenade; chevauchée;
cavalcade, *f;* trajet, *m.* ¶ *v.t. & i.
ir,* monter; chevaucher; aller. ~
sidesaddle, monter en amazone.
~ *to death* (*fig.*), enfourcher;
revenir sans cesse à. **rider,** *n,*
cavalier, ère; écuyer, ère; (*document*) codicille; (*Com.*) allonge,
m.

ridge, *n,* arête; strie; (*roof*) crête;
(*hill*) croupe; (*Agric.*) raie;
(*left by plow*) billon, *m.* ~ *pole,*
faîtage, *m;* (*tent*) faîtière, *f.* ¶
(*Agric.*) *v.t,* butter.

ridicule, *n,* ridicule, *m.* ¶ *v.t,*
ridiculiser. **ridiculous†,** *a,* ridicule. ~**ness,** *n,* ridicule, *m.*

riding, *n,* équitation, *f;* manège;
chevauchement, *m;* (*turf*) monte,
f. ~ *boots,* bottes à l'écuyère,
f.pl. ~ *breeches,* culotte de
cheval, *f.* ~ *habit,* amazone, *f.*
~ *school,* école d'équitation, *f;*
manège, *m.* ~ *whip,* cravache, *f.*

rife (to be) courir, sévir.

riffraff, *n,* canaille, racaille, *f.*

rifle, *n,* fusil, *m;* carabine, *f.* ~
drill, maniement des (*ou* d')
armes, *m.* ~*man,* tirailleur, *m.*
~ *range,* [champ de] tir; (*gallery*) tir, stand, *m.* ¶ *v.t,* (*rob*)
dévaliser, spolier; (*groove*) rayer, canneler.

rift, *n,* crevasse; éclaircie, *f;* (*fig.*)
fossé, *m.*

rig, *v.t,* équiper; accoutrer, harnacher; (*ship*) gréer. **rigging,**
n, gréement, *m;* agrès, *m.pl.* ~
the market, tripotage de bourse,
m.

right, *a,* droit; bon; bien; juste;
vrai; qu'il faut. ~*angled,* rectangle. ~*handed person* ou
player, droitier, ère. ~*minded,*
bien pensant. *at the* ~ *moment,*
à point nommé. ~ *side* (fabric),
endroit, dessus, *m.* *to be* ~,
avoir raison. ¶ *ad,* tout droit;
bien; tout. *all* ~, très bien, ça va.

~ *away,* tout de suite. ~ & *left,*
ad, à droite & à gauche. ~
through, de part en part; en
entier. ¶ *n,* droit, *m;* faculté;
raison, *f;* chef; gain de cause, *m;*
(*side*) droite; (*pl.*) justice, *f.* ~
of way, [droit de] passage, *m.*
by ~*s,* en toute justice. ¶ *v.t,* redresser.

righteous, *a,* vertueux; juste. ~
ly, ad, droitement. ~**ness,** *n,* justice, *f.*

rightful†, *a,* légitime. **rightly,**
ad, justement, bien; à juste titre.

rigid†, *a,* rigide. ~**ity,** *n,* rigidité,
f.

rigmarole, *n,* litanie, kyrielle,
tartine, *f.*

rigor mortis, rigidité cadavérique, *f.*

rigorous†, *a,* rigoureux. **rigor,** *n,*
rigueur, *f.*

rill, *n,* ruisseau, *m.*

rim, *n,* [re]bord, *m,* bordure, *f;*
ourlet, *m;* (*wheel*) jante; (*watch*)
lunette, *f.* ~ *brake,* frein sur
jantes, *m.* ¶ *v.t,* border. ~**less**
(*glasses*) *a,* sans monture.

rime, *n,* givre, frimas, *m.*

rind, *n,* écorce, peau; (*cheese*)
pelure, croûte; (*bacon*) couenne,
f.

rinderpest, *n,* peste bovine, *f.*

ring, *n,* cercle; anneau, *m;* bague;
boucle; frette, *f;* rond; segment;
collier; cerne, *m;* couche; enceinte; arène; piste de cirque; coalition; bande, *f;* coup de sonnette; coup de téléphone, *m.* ~
bolt, boucle d'amarrage, *f.* ~
finger, [doigt] annulaire, *m.* ~
leader, meneur; chef d'émeute,
m. ~*s under the eyes,* les yeux
cernés. ~**worm,** teigne, *f.* ¶ *v.t.
& i. ir,* sonner; corner; tinter; résonner; retentir; cerner; (*bull*)
boucler. ~ *a peal,* carillonner.
~ *for,* sonner.

ringlet, *n,* boucle, *f.*

rink, *n,* patinoir, *f.*

rinse & ~ *out,* *v.t,* rincer. **rinsings,** *n.pl,* rinçure, *f.*

riot, *n,* émeute, *f;* tumulte, *m;*
(*fig.*) orgie, débauche, *f.* ¶ *v.i,*
prendre part à une émeute; ripailler. ~**er,** *n,* émeutier, *m.*
~**ous†,** *a,* tumultueux.

rip, *n,* déchirure, *f.* ¶ *v.t,* fendre,
déchirer; éventrer; découdre;
eventrer. ~ *off,* arracher. ~ *saw,*
scie à refendre, *f.*

riparian, *a,* riverain.

ripe, *a,* mûr. **ripen,** *v.t, & i,* mûrir.

ripeness, *n*, maturité, *f*. **ripening**, *n*, maturation, *f*.

ripple, *n*, ride, *f*. ¶ *v.t*, rider; (*v.i.*) se r.

riposte, *n*, riposte, *f*. ¶ *v.t*, riposter.

rise, *n*, élévation; montée; rampe, *f*; lever, *m*; crue; naissance; source; hausse; augmentation; (*of a step*) hauteur de marche, *f*. ¶ *v.i.ir*, se lever; se relever; se soulever; s'élever; monter; naître; croître; augmenter; hausser; (*dead*) ressusciter. **rising**, *n*, lever, *m*; ascension, *f*; soulèvement, *m*. ¶ *p.a*: ~ *generation*, jeune génération, *f*. ~ *sun*, soleil levant, *m*. ~ *tide*, marée montante, *f*.

risk, *n*, risque; hasard, *m*. ¶ *v.t*, risquer; hasarder. *I'll ~ it*, au petit bonheur. ~y, *a*, hasardeux, chanceux.

rite, *n*, rite, *m*. **ritual**, *a*. & *n*, rituel, *a*. & *m*.

rival, *a*, rival. ¶ *n*, rival, e, émule, *m,f*. ¶ *v.t*, rivaliser avec. ~ry, *n*, rivalité, *f*.

rive, *v.t.ir*, fendre; (*v.i.ir.*) se fendre.

river, *n*, rivière, *f*; fleuve, *m*; (*att.*) de rivière, fluvial. ~*side*, bord de l'eau, *m*; (*att.*) riverain.

rivet, *n*, rivet, *m*. ¶ *v.t*, river; enchaîner, attacher. ~ing, *n*, rivure, *f*; rivetage, *m*.

Riviera (the), la Rivière de Gênes, la Côte d'Azur.

rivulet, *n*, ruisseau, *m*.

roach (*fish*) *n*, gardon, *m*.

road, *n*, route; voie, *f*; chemin, *m*. ~ *mender*, cantonnier, *m*. ~ *map*, carte routière, *f*. ~ *race*, course sur route, *f*. ~*side*, bord de la route, *m*; (*att.*) sur le b. de la r. ~ *stones*, cailloutis, *m*. *winding* ~, route en lacets, *f*.

roam, *v.i*, rouler, errer.

roan, *a*, (*animal*) rouan; (*shoes*) rouges. ¶ *n*, (*animal*) rouan, e; (*sheepskin*) basane, *f*.

roar, *v.i*. & *t*, rugir; mugir; gronder; ronfler; éclater. ¶ *n*, rugissement, *m*.

roast, *v.t*. & *i*, rôtir; cuire [au four]; brûler; griller; torréfier. ~ *beef*, bœuf rôti, rosbif, *m*. ~ [*meat*], rôti, *m*.

rob, *v.t*, voler, dérober, dévaliser, filouter. **robber**, *n*, voleur, euse, brigand, *m*. ~y, *n*, vol, *m*; filouterie, *f*. *armed* ~, vol à main armée.

robe, *n*, robe; toge, *f*.

robin [redbreast], *n*, rouge-gorge, *m*.

robust, *a*, robuste, vigoureux.

rock, *n*, rocher; roc, *m*; roche, *f*. ~ *crystal*, cristal de roche, *m*. ~ *garden*, jardin de rocaille, jardin alpestre, *m*. ~ *salt*, sel gemme, *m*. ~*work*, rocaille, *f*. ¶ *v.t*, balancer; bercer. ~er, *n*, bascule; (*pers.*) berceuse, *f*. ~ery, *n*, rocher artificiel, *m*. ~et, *n*, fusée; (*Bot.*) roquette, *f*. ~ing, *n*, balancement; bercement, *m*. ~ *chair*, fauteuil à bascule, *m*, berceuse, *f*. ~ *horse*, cheval à bascule, *m*. ~ *stone*, rocher branlant, *m*. ~y, *a*, rocailleux; rocheux. *R~ Moutains*, montagnes Rocheuses, *f.pl*.

rococo, *n*. & *a*, rococo, *m*. & *att*.

rod, *n*, baguette, verge; barre; tige; (*curtain*) tringle; (*piston*) bielle; (*fishing*) canne, *f*.

rodent, *n*. & *a*, rongeur, *m*. & *a*.

roe, *n* (*fish*) œufs de poisson, *m.pl*. ~*buck*, chevreuil, *m*. ~*doe*, chevrette, *f*.

rogations, *n.pl*, rogations, *f.pl*.

rogue, *n*, coquin, e, fripon, ne; espiègle, *m,f*. **roguish**, *a*, fripon; espiègle, mutin, malicieux. **roguishness & roguery**, *n*, friponnerie; espièglerie, malice, *f*.

roisterer, *n*, tapageur, euse.

roll, *n*, rouleau; cylindre, *m*; (*downhill*) roulade; (*package*) trousse; (*butter*) motte, *f*; petit pain; rôle, *m*; matricule, *f*, tableau; (*pl.*) tableau, *m*. ~ *call*, appel [nominal] *m*. ~ *of the drum*, batterie de tambour, *f*. ¶ *v.t*. & *i*, rouler; cylindrer; laminer. ~*top desk*, bureau américain, b. à rideau, *m*. ~ *up*, rouler. ~*ed gold*, or laminé, *m*, doublé or. **roller**, *n*, rouleau; cylindre, *m*; roulette, *f*; galet, *m*; (*Mech.*) tambour, *m*. ~ *skates*, patins à roulettes, *m.pl*. ~ *skating*, patinage à r—s, *m*. ~ *towel*, essuie-main à rouleau, *m*.

rollick, *v.i*, faire la fête. ~ing, *a*, bruyant.

rolling, *n*, roulement; laminage; (*ship*) roulis, *m*. ~ *mill*, laminoir, *m*. ~ *pin*, rouleau de pâtissier, *m*. ~ *stock*, matériel roulant, *m*.

Roman, *a*, romain; (*nose*) aquilin. ~ *candle*, chandelle romaine, *f*. ~ *Catholic*, *a*. & *n*, catholique, *a*. & *m,f*. ~ *Catholicism*, catholicisme, *m.* ¶ *n,* (*pers.*) Romain, e; (*Typ.*) romain, *m.*

Romania, *n,* la Roumanie. **Romanian,** *a,* roumain. ¶ *n,* (*pers.*) Roumain; e; (*language*) le roumain.

romance, *n,* roman, *m;* romance, idylle, *f.* **R~,** *a.* & *n,* roman, *a.* & *m.* ¶ *v.i,* en raconter.

Romanesque, *a,* roman.

romantic, *a,* romanesque; (*literature*) romantique.

romp, *n,* jeu bruyant, *m;* gamine bruyante, *f,* garçon manqué, *m.* ¶ *v.i,* folâtrer, batifoler. **~ers** (*child's*) *n.pl,* barboteuse, combinaison, *f.*

rood, *n,* croix, *f.*

roof, *n,* toit; comble; *m;* voûte, *f.* **~** *garden,* jardin sur le toit, *m.* **~** *of the mouth,* voûte palatine, voûte du palais, *f,* palais, *m.* ¶ *v.t,* couvrir. **~ing,** *n,* toiture, couverture, *f,* faîtage, *m.*

rook, *n,* freux, *m,* corneille; (*chess*) tour, *f.* **~ery,** *n,* colonie de freux; c. de miséreux, *f.*

room, *n,* pièce; chambre, *f;* cabinet; (*pl.*) appartement; salon, *m;* salle; soute; place, *f;* large, espace, *m.* **~mate,** compagnon de chambre, *m.* **~ful,** *n,* chambrée, *f.* **~y,** *a,* spacieux.

roost, *n,* juchoir, perchoir, *m.* ¶ *v.i,* [se] jucher, percher. **~er,** *n,* coq, *m.*

root, *n,* racine, *f;* radical, *m.* ¶ *v.i,* s'enraciner; fouiller. **~** *out,* déraciner, extirper, dénicher.

rope, *n,* corde, *f,* cordage; câble, *m;* manœuvre, *f;* chapelet, *m,* glane, *f.* **~** *dancer,* danseur (euse) de corde. **~** *end,* garcette, *f.* **~** *maker,* cordier, *m.* **~** *making* & **~** *works,* corderie, *f.* **~** *walker,* funambule, *m,f.* ¶ *v.t,* corder. **ropiness** (*wine*) *n,* graisse, *f.* **ropy,** *a,* (*liquid*) filant; (*wine*) gras.

roquet (*croquet*) *v.t,* roquer.

rosary, *n,* rosaire, *m;* (*rose garden*) roseraie, *f.* **rose,** *n,* rose, *f;* (*color*) rose, *m;* (*ceiling*) rosace; (*can*) pomme; (*pipe*) crépine, *f.* **~** *bud,* bouton de rose, *m.* **~bush,** rosier, *m.* **~** *grower,* rosiériste, *m.* **~** *window,* rose, rosace, *f.* **~wood,** palissandre, *m.* **roseate,** *a,* rosé, incarnat.

rosemary, *n,* romarin, *m.* **rosery,** *n,* roseraie, *f.* **rosette,** *n,* rosette, cocarde; (*Arch.*) rosace, *f.*

rosin, *n,* résine; (*for violin*) colophane, *f.*

roster, *n,* contrôle, rôle, *m.*

rostrum, *n,* tribune, *f.*

rosy, *a,* [de] rose, rosé, incarnat, vermeil.

rot, *n,* pourriture; carie, *f.* ¶ (*v.i.*) pourrir; se carier; (*v.t.*) faire pourrir; carier.

rota, *n,* rôle, *m.* **rotary,** *a,* rotatoire, tournant. **rotate,** *v.t.* & *i,* tourner; rouler. **rotation,** *n,* rotation, *f;* (*in office*) roulement; (*crops*) assolement, *m.* in ~, à tour de rôle, par roulement.

rote, *n,* routine, *f.* by ~, par cœur.

rotten, *a,* pourri; carié; (*egg, etc.*) gâté. **~ness,** *n,* pourriture; carie, *f.*

rotund, *a,* rond, arrondi; pompeux. **rotunda,** *n,* rotonde, *f.* **rotundity,** *n,* rondeur, rotondité, *f.*

rouge, *n,* rouge, *m.* **~** *et noir,* trente et quarante. ¶ *v.i,* mettre du rouge.

rough†, *a,* grossier; brut; rude; brutal; bourru; raboteux; rugueux; âpre; (*sea*) agitée. in a **~** & *ready fashion,* à coups de hache, à la serpe, à coups de serpe. **~cast** (*walls*) *n,* crépi, *m;* (*v.t*) crépir, hourder, ravaler. **~** *draft,* brouillon, *m.* **~** *estimate,* aperçu, *m.* at (or on) a **~** *estimate,* à vue d'œil, par aperçu. **~rider,** casse-cou, *m.* **~shod** (*horse*) ferré à glace. to ride **~shod** *over,* fouler aux pieds, traiter avec rudesse. ¶ *n,* apache, *m.* the **~** (*golf*), l'herbe longue, *f.* **~,** **~** *down,* **~** *out,* **~hew,** *v.t,* dégrossir, ébaucher. **~ness,** *n,* aspérité; rudesse; grossièreté, âpreté, *f.*

round, *a,* rond. **~-shouldered,** voûté. **~** *trip,* aller & retour. ¶ *n,* rond, *m;* (*slice*) rouelle, *f;* (*rung*) échelon, *m;* (*tour*) ronde, tournée; (*applause*) salve, *f;* (*lap*) circuit, *m;* (*sport*) partie; (*Box.*) round, *m.* **~** [*of ammunition*], cartouche, *f.* ¶ *ad,* autour. **~** *about,* alentour. ¶ *pr,* autour de, alentour de. ¶ *v.t,* arrondir. **~** *up,* rafler. **roundabout,** *a,* détourné. **roundelay,** *n,* ronde, *f.* **roundish,** *a,* rondelet. **roundly,** *ad,* rondement. **roundness,** *n,* rondeur, *f.* **roundsman,** *n,* livreur, *m.*

rouse, *v.t,* [r]éveiller; exciter.

rout, *n*, déroute, débandade, *f*. ¶ *v.t*, mettre en déroute, défaire.

route, *n*, route, voie, *f*. ~ *march*, promenade militaire, *f*. ¶ *v.t*, acheminer.

routine, *n*, routine, *f*, train, *m*.

rove, *v.i*, rouler, errer, vagabonder; (*v.t*) écumer. **rover,** *n*, coureur; (*sea*) forban; (*croquet*) corsaire, *m*. **roving,** *a*, vagabond.

row, *n*, rang, *m*, rangée, *f*; (*of stitches*, Knit., *etc.*) tour, *m*; haie, *f*; cordon; bruit; tapage, fracas, potin, *m*; promenade en bateau, *f*. *a* ~ *of houses*, une rangée de maisons, des maisons en enfilade, *f.pl*. ¶ *v.i*, ramer, aller à la rame, canoter, nager, voguer. ~[*ing*] *boat*, bateau à rames; bateau de promenade, *m*.

rowdy, *n. & a*, tapageur, *m. & a*.

rowel, *n*, molette, *f*.

rower, *n*, rameur, euse, nageur, canotier, *m*. **rowing,** *n*, canotage, *m*, nage [d'aviron] *f*, l'aviron, *m*.

royal†, *a*, royal. *His, Your, R~ Highness*, monseigneur, son, votre, altesse royale. ~**ist,** *n. & att*, royaliste, *m,f. & a*. ~**ty,** *n*, royauté; (*rent*) redevance, *f*; (*author's*) droit d'auteur, *m*.

rub, *n*, (*with a cloth*) coup de chiffon; (*fig.*) hic, nœud, *m*, enclouure, *f*. ~ *of the green* (*golf*), risque de jeu, *m*. ¶ *v.t. & i*, frotter; frictionner; (*inscription*) estamper. ~ *down* (*horse*), épousseter, bouchonner. ~ *one's hands*, se frotter les mains. ~ *out*, effacer. ~ *shoulders with*, se frotter à, frayer avec. **rubber,** *n*, frottoir; (*cards*) rob[re] *m*; (*3rd game*) belle, *f*; caoutchouc, *m*; gomme [élastique] *f*. ~ *stamp*, timbre en c., t. humide, *m*. **rubbing,** *n*, frottement, *m*; friction, *f*. oft. *pl*; (*with oil*) onction, *f*; (*copy*) frottis, *m*.

rubbish, *n*, décombres, *m.pl*, détritus, *m*; (*dirt*) immondices, *f*; (*trash*) camelote, saleté; (*nonsense*) blague, *f*, fadaises, *f.pl*.

rubble[stone], *n*, blocaille, *f*, moellon, *m*.

rubicund, *a*, rubicond.

rubric, *n*, rubrique, *f*.

ruby, *n*, rubis, *m*. ¶ (*lips*) *a*, vermeilles.

ruck, *n*, pli, godet, *m*.

rucksack, *n*, sac de touriste, s. de montagne, s. d'alpinisme, *m*.

rudder, *n*, gouvernail, *m*.

ruddy, *a*, coloré, rougeaud, rubicond.

rude†, *a*, grossier, malhonnête, malgracieux; rude. ~**ness,** *n*, grossièreté, rudesse, *f*.

rudiment, *n*, rudiment, *m*; (*pl, of a science, an art*) éléments, *m.pl*. ~**ary,** *a*, rudimentaire.

rue (*Bot.*) *n*, rue, *f*. ¶ *v.t*, se repentir de. ~**ful†,** *a*, triste.

ruff (*Hist., dress*) *n*, fraise, *f*.

ruffian, *n*, bandit, *m*. ~**ly,** *a*, de brigand.

ruffle, *n*, ruche, *f*. ¶ *v.t*, rider; froisser, chiffonner; (*hair*) ébouriffer.

rug, *n*, tapis de pied, *m*; carpette; descente de lit; (*traveling*) couverture, *f*, plaid, *m*. ~ *work*, tapisserie, *f*.

rugged, *a*, raboteux; rugueux; rocailleux; rude. ~**ness,** *n*, aspérité; rudesse, *f*.

ruin, *n*, ruine, perte, *f*. ¶ *v.t*, ruiner, perdre, abîmer. ~**ous,** *a*, ruineux.

rule, *n*, règle; domination, *f*; empire; (*Typ.*) filet, *m*. *as a* ~, ordinairement. ~ *of thumb*, procédé empirique, *m*; (*att.*) empirique. *by* ~ *of thumb*, empiriquement. ¶ *v.t*, régler; rayer; gouverner; régir; (*v.i.*) gouverner; régner; (*prices*) se pratiquer. **ruler,** *n*, gouvernant; dominateur, *m*; (*for lines*) règle, *f*. **ruling,** *p.a*, dominant; (*price*) pratiqué. ~ *passion*, passion dominante, épée de chevet, *f*. ¶ *n*, réglage, *m*, réglure; décision; (*law*) sentence, *f*.

rum, *n*, rhum, *m*.

rumble, *v.i*, gronder; rouler; (*bowels*) gargouiller.

ruminant, *n. & a*, ruminant, *m. & a*. **ruminate,** *v.i. & t*, ruminer.

rummage, *v.t. & i*, fouiller, farfouiller.

rumor, *n*, rumeur, renommée, *f*, bruit, on-dit, *m*. *it is* ~*ed that*, le bruit court que.

rump, *n*, croupe, *f*; (*bird*) croupion, *m*; (*beef*) culotte, *f*. ~**steak,** romsteck, *m*.

rumple, *v.t*, chiffonner, froisser.

run, *n*, course; marche; campagne, *f*; cours; parcours, trajet, *m*; roulade; coulée; suite; séquence; (*stocking*) maille, *f*; commun, *m*; descente, ruée; volière, *f*; parc, *m*. *in the long* ~, à la longue. ~-*off* (*from dead heat*), course de barrage, *f*. ~[-*up*]

(*Jump.*), course d'élan, *f*, élan,
m. ¶ *v.i.ir*, courir; accourir;
affluer; fonctionner; marcher;
(*stockings*) se démailler; circuler; trotter; couler; pleurer, suinter; tourner; rouler; aller; être;
(*v.t.ir.*) faire; faire courir; faire
marcher; actionner; conduire;
[en]courir. ~ *about*, faire des
allées & venues. ~ *against*,
heurter. ~ *aground*, échouer. ~
along, longer, border, côtoyer.
~ *away*, s'enfuir, se sauver. ~
into, rencontrer. ~ *out of*
(stock), manquer de, être à court
de. ~ *out of gas*, avoir une
panne d'essence *ou* une p. sèche.
~ *over*, parcourir; déborder. to
be ~ *over*, être écrasé. ~
through, parcourir; feuilleter;
transpercer, enferrer, embrocher.
~ *to earth*, dépister. ~ *up against*
(*pers.*), coudoyer. **runabout**, *n*,
coureur, euse; voiturette, *f*. **runaway**, *n. & a*, fugitif, ive, fuyard,
e, échappé, e. **rundown**, *a*,
épuisé.
rung, *n*, échelon; barreau, *m*.
runner, *n*, coureur, euse; courrier; agent de transmission; *m*;
(*Hort., Bot.*) coulant; (*slider of
sledge*) patin, *m*. **running**, *n*,
courses, *f.pl*; marche, *f*; roulement; service, *m*. ¶ *p.a*, courant;
coulant; cursif; successif, de
suite. ~ *dive*, plongeon avec
élan, *m*. ~ *water*, eau courante,
f.
runt, *n*, nabot, *m*.
runway, *n*, piste, *f*.
rupee, *n*, roupie, *f*.
rupture, *n*, rupture, *f*; (*Med.*) hernie, *f*. ¶ *v.t*, rompre. to be ~d,
avoir une hernie.
rural, *a*, rural, champêtre.
ruse, *n*, ruse, *f*.
rush, *n*, jonc, *m*; élan, *m*; ruée,
bousculade; presse; chasse, *f*;
flot, torrent, *m*. ~ *chair*, chaise
paillée, *f*. ~ *hours*, heures d'affluence, *f.pl*. ¶ *v.t*, brusquer;
(*v.i.*) se précipiter, se ruer, accourir, foncer.
rusk, *n*, biscotte, *f*.
russet, *a*, roux. ¶ *n*, roux, *m*;
(*apple*) reinette grise, *f*.
Russia, *n*, la Russie. **Russian**, *a*,
russe. ¶ *n* (*pers.*) Russe, *m,f*;
(*language*) le russe.
rust, *n*, rouille, *f*. to rub off the
~ *from*, dérouiller. ¶ *v.t*, rouiller;
(*v.i.*) se r. **rustiness**, *n*, rouillure,
f. **rustproof**, *a*, inoxydable.

rustic, *a*, rustique, agreste, paysan. ¶ *n*, rustre, paysan, *m*.
rusticate, *v.i*, être en villégiature.
rustle, *v.i*, frémir, bruire; (*dress*)
faire frou-frou.
rusty, *a*, rouillé.
rut, *n*, (*groove*) ornière, *f*; (*of
animals*) rut, *m*.
ruthless, *a*, impitoyable, acharné,
âpre.
rye, *n*, seigle, *m*. ~ *grass*, ray-
grass, *m*.

S

S, *n. & S hook*, esse, *f*, S, *m*.
sabbath, *n*, sabbat; dimanche, *m*.
sable, *n*, (*Zool.*) [martre] zibeline;
(*fur*) zibeline, *f*, sable; (*Her.*)
sable, *m*.
saber, *n*, sabre, *m*. ¶ *v.t*, sabrer.
saccharin, *n*, saccharine, *f*.
sacerdotal, *a*, sacerdotal.
sachet, *n*, sachet à parfums, sultan, *m*.
sack, *n*, sac, *m*. ~*cloth, sacking*,
toile à sacs, *f*, treillis, *m*, serpillière, *f*; (*Theol.*) sac, *m*. in
~*cloth & ashes*, sous le sac & la
cendre. ~ *race*, course en sacs,
f. ¶ *v.t*, ensacher; saccager;
mettre à sac. ~*ful*, *n*, sachée, *f*.
sacrament, *n*, sacrement, *m*,
communion, *f*. ~*al†*, *a*, sacramentel. ~*al*, *n*, sacramental, *m*.
sacred, *a*, sacré; saint; inviolable;
(*song*) religieux; (*concert*) spirituel; (*to the memory of*) consacré. **sacrifice**, *n*, sacrifice, *m*.
¶ *v.t. & i*, sacrifier, immoler. **sac-
rificial**, *a*, du sacrifice. **sacrilege**,
*n. & *sacrilegious*, *a*, sacrilège, *m*.
& *a*. **sacristy**, *n*, sacristie, *f*.
sacrosanct, *a*, sacro-saint.
sad, *a*, triste, douloureux, fâcheux.
sadden, *v.t*, attrister, contrister.
saddle, *n*, selle; (*lathe*) cuirasse,
f; (*mountain*) col, *m*. ~*-backed*,
ensellé. ~*bag*, sacoche, *f*. ~*bow*,
arçon, *m*. ~ *horse*, cheval de
selle, *m*. ¶ *v.t*, seller; (*pack animal*) embâter; (*fig.*) grever,
charger. **saddler**, *n*, sellier, *m*.
saddlery, *n*, sellerie, *f*.
sadistic, *a*, sadique.
sadly, *ad*, tristement; cruellement.
sadness, *n*, tristesse, *f*.
safe, *a*, sauf; sûr; sans danger;
assuré; de sécurité; (*investment*)
sûr, de tout repos, de père de
famille; (*arrival*) bonne, heureuse. ~ & *sound*, sain & sauf,

bagues sauves. ~ *conduct*, sauf-conduit, *m*, sauvegarde, *f*. ~ *custody*, garde [en dépôt] *f*. ~ *keeping*, sûreté, *f*. ¶ *n*, coffre-fort, *m*. ~*guard*, *n*, sauvegarde, garantie, *f*, palladium, *m*; (*v.t.*) garantir. ~*ly*, *ad*, en sûreté; sûre-ment; sans danger; sans accident; (*arrival*) à bon port. ~*ty*, *n*, sûreté; sécurité, *f*; salut, *m*. ~ *catch*, cran d'arrêt, *m*. ~ *first*, sécurité d'abord. ~ *pin*, épingle de sûreté, é. de nourrice, é. anglaise, *f*. ~ *razor*, rasoir de sûreté, *m*. ~ *valve* (*lit. & fig.*), soupape de sûreté, *f*.

saffron, *n*, safran, *m*.

sag, *n*, fléchissement, *m*. ¶ *v.i*, fléchir, donner.

sagacious, *a*, sagace. **sagacity**, *n*, sagacité, *f*.

sage, *n*, (*pers.*) sage, *m*; (*herb*) sauge, *f*. ¶ *a*, sage.

sago, *n*, sagou, *m*. ~ *palm*, sa-gou[t]ier, *m*.

said (the) (*law*) *p.a*, ledit.

sail, *n*, voile, toile, (*pl.*) voilure, *f*; (*windmill*) volant, *m*; promenade en bateau, *f*. ~*boat*, voilier, *m*. ~ *cloth*, toile à voiles, *f*. ~ *maker*, voilier, *m*. ¶ *v.i*, faire voile; naviguer; voguer; marcher; courir; partir; (*v.t.*) faire navi-guer; naviguer sur. ~*er*, *n*, voilier, marcheur, *m*. ~*ing*, *n*, naviga-tion [à voile] *f*; départ, *m*; par-tance; marche, *f*. ~ *ship*, navire à voiles, voilier, *m*. ~*or*, *n*, marin; matelot, *m*. ~ *suit*, cos-tume marin, *m*.

saint, *a*, saint. ¶ *n*, saint, e. ~*'s day*, fête, *f*. *St. Bernard dog*, chien de Saint-Bernard, *m*. *Saint Helena*, Sainte-Hélène, *f*. *Saint Lawrence*, Saint-Laurent, *m*. *St. Vitus's dance*, danse de Saint-Guy, chorée, *f*. ¶ *v.t*, canoniser. ~*ed*, *p.p*, saint, canonisé. **saintli-ness**, *n*, sainteté, *f*. **saintly**, *a*, saint.

sake, *n*, cause, *f*; amour; plaisir; égard, *m*. *for God's* ~, pour l'amour de Dieu.

sal, *n*, sel, *m*. ~ *ammoniac*, sel ammoniac. ~ *volatile*, alcool ammon aromatique, spiritus aro-maticus, *m*.

salaam, *n*, salamalec, *m*.

salable, *a*, vendable, de vente; marchand, vénal.

salacious, *a*, lascif, lubrique.

salad, *n*, salade, *f*. ~ *bowl*, sala-dier, *m*. ~ *oil*, huile de table, h. comestible, *f*.

Salamanca, *n*, Salamanque, *f*.

salamander, *n*, salamandre, *f*.

salaried, *p.a*, appointé. **salary**, *n*, appointements, *m.pl*; traitement; cachet, *m*; indemnité, *f*. *to put on a* ~ *basis*, appointer.

sale, *n*, vente, *f*; débit; solde, *m*; liquidation; enchère, *f*. *for* ~, à vendre. *on* ~, en vente.

Salerno, *n*, Salerne, *f*.

salesman, -woman, *n*, vendeur, euse; (*market*) facteur (de la halle) *m*. ~*ship*, l'art de vendre, *m*.

Salic law, loi salique, *f*.

salient, *a. & n*, saillant, *a. & m*.

saline, *a*, salin.

saliva, *n*, salive, *f*. **salivate**, *v.i*, saliver.

sallow, *a*, jaunâtre.

sally, *n*, (*Mil.*) sortie, saillie; (*wit*) saillie, *f*, trait d'esprit, *m*, boutade, *f*.

salmon, *n*, saumon, (*young*) sau-moneau, *m*. ~ *pink*, rose sau-mon, *m*. ~ *trout*, truite saumo-née, *f*.

Salonica, *n*, Salonique, *f*.

saloon, *n*, bar, estaminet, *m*.

salt, *n*, sel, *m*. ~*cellar*, salière, *f*. ~ *lake*, lac salé, *m*. ~ *pork*, [porc] salé, *m*. ~ *provisions*, salaisons, *f.pl*. ~ *spoon*, pelle à sel, *f*. ~ *water*, eau salée, e. saline, *f*. ~*water fish*, poisson de mer, *m*; (*caught & fresh*) marée, *f*. ~*water fishing*, pêche en mer, *f*. ~*ing*, *n*, saler. ~*ing*, *n*, salage, *m*; salaison, *f*. **saltern**, *n*, marais salant, *m*. **saltpeter**, *n*, salpêtre, nitre, *m*. **salty**, *a*, salé.

salubrious, *a*, salubre.

salutary†, *a*, ~salutaire. **saluta-tion**, *n*, salutation, *f*, salut, *m*. **salute**, *n*, salut; (*guns*) salut, *m*, salve, *f*. ¶ *v.t*, saluer.

salvage, *n*, sauvetage, *m*. ¶ *v.t*, sauver. **salvation**, *n*, salut, *m*. *S~ Army*, Armée du Salut, *f*. **salve**, *n*, onguent, *m*; pommade, *f*. ¶ (*fig.*) *v.t*, calmer.

salver, *n*, plateau, *m*.

salvo, *n*, salve, *f*.

Salzburg, *n*, Salzbourg, *m*.

same, *a*, même. *it's all the* ~ *to me*, cela m'est égal. ~*ness*, *n*, identité; monotonie, *f*.

sample, *n*, échantillon, *m*. ¶ *v.t*, échantillonner; (*taste wines*) déguster. **sampler**, *n*, modèle de broderie, *m*.

sanatorium, *n*, sanatorium, *m*.

sanctify, *v.t*, sanctifier. **sanctimonious†**, *a*, béat, cagot, papelard. **sanction**, *n*, sanction; consécration, *f*. ¶ *v.t*, sanctionner; consacrer. **sanctity**, *n*, sainteté; religion, *f*. **sanctuary**, *n*, sanctuaire; asile, *m*; réserve, *f*. **sanctum**, *n*, le saint des saints; sanctuaire, *m*.

sand, *n*, sable; sablon, *m*; (*pl.*) plage, *f*. ~ *bag*, sac à terre, *m*. ~ *bank*, banc de sable, ensablement, *m*. ~ *blast*, jet de sable, *m*. ~ *flats*, relais, *m*. ~ *fly*, simulie, *f*. ~ *glass*, sablier, *m*, horloge de sable, *f*. ~ *hill*, dune, *f*. ~*paper*, *n*, papier de verre, *m*; (*v.t.*) poncer. ~*piper*, bécasseau, *m*. ~ *pit*, sablière; sablonnière, *f*. ~*stone*, grès, *m*. ~*stone quarry*, gresserie, *f*. ¶ *v.t*, sabler.

sandal, *n*, sandale, *f*. ~ [*wood*], [bois de] santal, *m*.

sandwich, *n*, sandwich, *m*. ~ *man*, homme-sandwich, *m*.

sandy, *a*, sablonneux. ~ *hair*, chevelure blond roux, *f*.

sane, *a*, sain, rassis.

sanguinary, *a*, sanguinaire. **sanguine**, *a*, optimiste; plein d'espérance; (*full-blooded*, *Hist.*) sanguin.

sanitary, *a*, sanitaire; hygiénique. ~ *inspector*, inspecteur sanitaire, *m*. ~ *napkin*, serviette hygiénique, *f*. **sanitate**, *v.t*, assainir. **sanitation**, *n*, assainissement, *m*; hygiène, *f*.

sanity, *n*, raison, *f*; bon sens, *m*; rectitude, *f*.

sanserif, *a*, sans empattement.

Santa Claus, le père Noël, le bonhomme Noël.

sap, *n*, sève; lymphe; (*Mil.*) sape, *f*. ~*wood*, aubier, *m*. ¶ *v.t*, saper. **sapling**, *n*, plant, *m*. **sapper**, *n*, [sapeur] mineur, *m*.

sapphire, *n*, saphir, *m*.

sappy, *a*, plein de sève.

Saragossa, *n*, Saragosse, *f*.

Saratoga [*trunk*], *n*, [malle] chapelière, *f*.

sarcasm, *n*, sarcasme, *m*. **sarcastic**, *a*, sarcastique.

sarcophagus, *n*, sarcophage, *m*.

sardine, *n*, sardine, *f*.

Sardinia, *n*, la Sardaigne. **Sardinian**, *a*, sarde. ¶ *n*, Sarde, *m,f*.

sardonic, *a*, sardonique.

sarsaparilla, *n*, salsepareille, *f*.

sarsenet, *n*, florence, *m*.

sash, *n*, ceinture; écharpe, *f*; (*window*) châssis, *m*. ~ *window*, fenêtre à guillotine, *f*.

Satan, *n*, Satan, *m*. ~*ic*, *a*, satanique.

satchel, *n*, cartable, *m*; gibecière, sacoche, *f*.

sate, *v.t*, rassasier.

sateen, *n*, satinette, *f*.

satellite, *n*, satellite, *m*.

satiate, *v.t*, rassasier. **satiety**, *n*, satiété, *f*.

satin, *n*, satin, *m*. ~ *stitch* (*Emb.*), passé, *m*. ~ *wood*, bois de satin, *m*. ~*y*, *a*, satiné.

satire, *n*, satire, *f*. **satiric** & ~*al*, *a*, satirique. **satirist**, *n*, satirique, *m*. **satirize**, *v.t*, satiriser.

satisfaction, *n*, satisfaction; raison, *f*. **satisfactorily**, *ad*, d'une manière satisfaisante. **satisfactory**, *a*, satisfaisant. **satisfy**, *v.t*, satisfaire, satisfaire à; contenter.

saturate, *v.t*, saturer.

Saturday, *n*, samedi, *m*.

saturnalia, *n.pl*, saturnales, *f.pl*.

saturnine, *a*, sombre; (*Chem.*) saturnin.

satyr, *n*, satyre, *m*.

sauce, *n*, sauce, *f*. ~ *boat*, saucière, *f*. ~ *ladle*, cuiller à sauce, *f*. ~*pan*, casserole, *f*; poêlon, *m*. **saucer**, *n*, soucoupe, *f*. **saucy**, *a*, gamin; impertinent.

sauerkraut, *n*, choucroute, *f*.

saunter, *v.i*, flâner. ~*ing*, *n*, flânerie, *f*.

sausage, *n*, (*fresh*) saucisse, *f*; (*smoked*) saucisson, *m*. ~ *skin*, ~ *case*, peau à saucisses, *f*.

savage†, *a*, sauvage; féroce, farouche. ¶ *n*, sauvage, *m,f*, sauvagesse, *f*, cannibale, *m*. ~*ry*, *n*, sauvagerie; férocité, *f*.

savant, *n*, savant, *m*.

save, *v.t*, sauver; épargner; ménager; économiser; gagner; capter; (*v.i.*) économiser. ¶ *pr*, sauf sinon, hormis, près. **saving**, *n*, épargne; économie, *f*. ~*s bank*, caisse d'épargne, *f*. **the Saviour**, le Sauveur.

savory (*Bot.*) *n*, sarriette, *f*. **savor**, *n*, saveur, *f*. **to ~ of**, tenir de, sentir le, la. **savory**, *a*, savoureux. ~ *herbs*, fines herbes, *f.pl*. ~ *omelet*, omelette aux fines herbes, *f*.

Savoy, *n*, la Savoie. **s~**, chou de Milan, *m*.

saw, *n*, scie, *f*; dicton, adage, *m*.

hand~, égoïne, f. power~, scie mécanique, f. ~dust, sciure, f. ~mill, scierie, f. ¶ v.t.ir, scier; débiter. ~ off, scier. ~ing, n, sciage, m.

saxhorn, n, saxhorn, m.

saxifrage, n, saxifrage, f.

Saxon, a, saxon. ¶ n, Saxon, ne. **Saxony,** n, la Saxe.

saxophone, n, saxophone, m.

say, n, mot, m; voix, f. ¶ v.t. & i. ir, dire; réciter; parler. as they ~, comme on dit. you don't ~ sol pas possible! **saying,** n, mot, dire; dicton, adage, m. ~s & doings, faits & dits, m.pl.

scab, n, croûte; (Vet.) gale; (Hort.) rogne, f.

scabbard, n, fourreau, m.

scabby, a, scabieux, galeux, rogneux.

scaffold, n, échafaud, m. ~ing, n, échafaudage, m.

scald, n, brûlure, f. ¶ v.t, échauder, ébouillanter; blanchir.

scale, n, échelle; (Mus.) gamme, f; barème; tarif; (pan) plateau, bassin, m; (pl, lancet) châsse, écaille, paillette; incrustation; (s. or pl.) balance, bascule, f. ~ maker, balancier, m. ¶ v.t, (wall) escalader; (boiler) piquer; (v.i.) s'écailler. **scaly,** a, écailleux.

scallop, n, (Mol.) pétoncle; coquillage, (edging) feston, m. ¶ v.t, festonner.

scalp, n, cuir chevelu, m; (trophy) chevelure, f. ~ massage, friction, f. ¶ v.t, scalper.

scalpel, n, scalpel, m.

scamp, n, chenapan, vaurien, polisson, [mauvais] garnement, m. ¶ v.t, brocher, bâcler.

scamper away, s'enfuir en courant, détaler.

scan, v.t, scruter, éplucher; (verse) scander.

scandal, n, scandale, éclat, m; honte; médisance, f, cancan, racontar; pétard, m. ~monger, médisant, e; mauvaise langue, f. ~ize, v.t, scandaliser. ~ous†, a, scandaleux.

Scandinavia, n, la Scandinavie. **Scandinavian,** a, scandinave. ¶ n, Scandinave, m.f.

scansion, n, scansion, f.

scant[y], a, exigu; étriqué; maigre; faible; pauvre; mesquin; (attire) sommaire.

scape (Bot.) n, hampe, f. ~goat, bouc émissaire, souffre-douleur,

m. ~grace, [mauvais] garnement, mauvais sujet, m.

scar, n, cicatrice, couture, balafre, f. ¶ v.t, cicatriser, couturer, balafrer.

scarab, n, scarabée, m.

scarce, a, rare; (time) cher. ~ly, ad, à peine; presque. **scarcity,** n, rareté; disette, f.

scare, n, panique, transe, f. ¶ v.t, épouvanter, effrayer, effarer. ~crow, [épouvantail, m.

scarf, n, écharpe, f, cache-nez, m.

scarify, v.t, scarifier.

scarlatina, n. or **scarlet fever,** [fièvre] scarlatine, f. **scarlet,** n. & a, écarlate, f. & a.

scarp, n, escarpe, f.

scatheless, a, indemne. **scathing,** a, cinglant, sanglant. ~ attack (fig.), jeu de massacre, m.

scatter, v.t, disperser, éparpiller; semer.

scavenge, v.t, balayer. **scavenger,** n, boueux, balayeur; animal qui se nourrit de charogne, m.

scenario, n, scénario, m. **scene,** n, scène, f; spectacle; tableau; théâtre, m. behind the ~s, dans la coulisse. ~ painter, peintre de décors, décorateur, m. ~ shifter, machiniste, m. ~ shifting, changement de décor[ation] m. ~ry, n, paysages, m.pl; (Theat.) décors, m.pl, décoration, f. scenic, a, scénique. ~ railway, montagnes russes, f.pl.

scent, n, parfum, m; odeur; senteur, f; flair, fumet, nez; vent, m, piste, voie, f. ~ bottle, flacon à odeur, m. to throw off the ~, dépister. ¶ v.t, parfumer, embaumer; flairer, subodorer. ~ed, a, parfumé, odorant.

scepter, n, sceptre, m.

Schaffhausen, n, Schaffhouse, f.

schedule, n, horaire; (work) plan, (price) tarif, m; annexe, f; bordereau, m.

scheme, n, projet, plan; cadre, m, combinaison, f. ¶ v.t, projeter, machiner; (v.i.) former des projets; intriguer. **schemer,** n, homme à projets, m; intrigant, e. **scheming,** n, manœuvres, f.pl.

schism, n, schisme, m.

schist, n, schiste, m. ~ose, a, schisteux.

scholar, n, écolier, ère; savant, érudit, m. ~ly, a, savant, érudit. ~ship, n, savoir, m, érudition; bourse, f. **scholastic,** a, scolastique. **school,** n, école; classe, f;

collège; conservatoire; (*of fish*) banc, *m*. **boarding ~,** pensionnat, *m*. **~ book,** livre de classe, l. classique, l. scolaire, *m*. **~boy, ~girl,** écolier, ère, lycéen, ne, collégien, ne. **~fellow,** camarade d'école, *m,f,* condisciple, *m*. **~master ~mistress,** instituteur, trice. **~ room,** [salle de] classe, *f*. **schooling,** *n*, instruction, *f*.

schooner, *n*, schooner, *m*, goélette, *f*.

sciatic, *a*. & **sciatica,** *n*, sciatique, *a*. & *f*.

science, *n*. science, *f*. **scientific†,** *a*, scientifique; (*instruments*) de précision. **scientist,** *n*, savant, homme de science, *m*.

Scilly Islands *or* **Isles,** îles Scilly, îles Sorlingues, *f.pl*.

scimitar, *n*, cimeterre, *m*.

scintillate, *v.i*, scintiller.

scion, *n*, (*Hort.*) scion; (*pers.*) rejeton, *m*.

scissors, *n.pl*, ciseaux, *m.pl.* **with ~ & paste** (*fig.*), à coups de ciseaux.

sclerosis, *n*, sclérose, *f*.

scoff at, se railler de; mépriser. **scoffer,** *n*, moqueur, euse, railleur, euse. **scoffing,** *n*, moquerie, *f*.

scold, *n*, grondeuse, mégère, *f*. ¶ *v.t*, gronder, tancer, semoncer, quereller; (*v.i.*) criailler.

scoop, *n*, pelle; main; cuiller; casse; écope, *f*. **~ out,** caver, vider; écoper.

scope, *n*, étendue, *f*, champ, *m*; latitude; *f*; cadre, *m*, portée; carrière, *f*; essor, *m*.

scorch, *v.t*, brûler, rôtir, roussir.

score, *n*, coche, *f*, strie, *f*; écot; point, *m*, marque, *f*; compte des points; c. des coups, *m*; (*Mus.*) partition; vingtaine, *f*. ¶ *v.t*, cocher; rayer; (*game*) marquer; (*Mus.*) orchestrer. **scorer,** *n*, marqueur, euse; pointeur, *m*.

scoria, *n*, scorie, *f*.

scoring, *n*, pointage, *m*; orchestration, *f*.

scorn, *n*, mépris, dédain, *m*. ¶ *v.t*, mépriser, dédaigner. **~er,** *n*, contempteur, trice. **~ful†,** *a*, dédaigneux.

scorpion, *n*, scorpion, *m*.

Scotch, *a*, écossais; d'Écosse. **~man, -woman,** Écossais, e. **the ~,** les Écossais, *m.pl.* **~ mist,** brouillasse, *f*.

scot-free, *a*, indemne; impuni.

Scotland, *n*, l'Écosse, *f*. **Scottish,** *a*, écossais.

scoundrel, *n*, scélérat, e, gredin, e.

scour, *n*, chasse [d'eau] *f*. ¶ *v.t*, donner une chasse à; dégraisser, décaper; (*seas*) écumer; (*country*) battre.

scourge, *n*, (*whip*) martinet; (*plague*) fléau, *m*. ¶ *v.t*, flageller.

scout, *n*, éclaireur; (*boy*) scout, *m*; (*warship*) vedette, *f*. **~ master,** chef éclaireur, *m*. ¶ *v.i*, aller à la découverte; (*v.t.*) repousser avec mépris.

scowl, *v.i*, froncer le sourcil. ¶ *n*, froncement de sourcils, *m*.

scrag, *n*, (*mutton*) collet; (*pers.*) squelette, *m*. **~ end,** bout saigneux, *m*. **scraggy,** *a*, décharné.

scramble, *n*, mêlée; (*for place, etc.*) curée, *f*. **~d eggs,** œufs brouillés, *m.pl*.

scrap, *n*, bout, morceau; chiffon, *m*; (*metal*) déchets, débris, *m.pl*; (*pl.*) restes, *m.pl*; bribes, *f.pl*. **~ book,** album, *m*. **~ iron,** ferraille, *f*. ¶ *v.t*, mettre au rebut; se débarrasser de.

scrape, *v.t*, gratter; racler; décrotter; (*golf*) érafler. ¶ *n*, embarras, *m*. **scraper,** *n*, grattoir; racloir, *m*; curette, *f*; (*mat*) décrottoir, *m*. **scrapings,** *n.pl*, raclure; (*savings*) gratte, *f*.

scratch, *n*, égratignure, *f*; coup de griffe, *m*; rayure, *f*; (*sport*) scratch, *m*. ¶ *v.t*, gratter; rayer; effleurer; (*sport*) rayer de l'épreuve. **~ out,** gratter, raturer.

scrawl, *n*, griffonnage, *m*, patarafe, *f*. ¶ *v.t* & *i*, griffonner.

scream & screech, *n*, cri, *m*. ¶ *v.i.* & *t*, crier. **screech owl,** effraie, fresaie, *f*.

screed, *n*, tartine, *f*.

screen, *n*, écran; paravent; rideau; (*choir*) clôture, grille, *f*; crible, *m*, claie, *f*. **~ door,** contre-porte, *f*. ¶ *v.t*, abriter; murer; soustraire; cribler; (*movies*) présenter à l'écran.

screw, *n*, vis; hélice. **~capped bottle,** flacon à couvercle vissé, *m*. **~driver,** tournevis, *m*. **~ eye,** piton, *m*. ¶ *v.t*, visser.

scribble, *n*, griffonnage, *m*. ¶ *v.t*, griffonner; (*v.i, of author*) écrivailler. **scribbler,** *n*, griffonneur, euse; écrivassier, ère, folliculaire, *m*. **scribe,** *n*, scribe, *m*.

scrimmage, *n*, mêlée; bousculade, *f*.

scrip, n, titre provisoire; titre, m.

Scripture, n. oft. pl, l'Écriture, f. oft. pl.

scrofula, n, scrofules, f.pl. **scrofulous,** a, scrofuleux.

scroll, n, rouleau, m; volute, f.

scrub (bush) n, broussailles, f.pl. ¶ v.t, brosser; laver, lessiver. scrubbing brush, brosse à laver, f.

scruff of the neck, peau du cou, f, collet, m.

scrunch, v.t, croquer. ¶ i, croc!

scrummage, n, mêlée; bousculade, f.

scruple, n, scrupule, m. ~ **to,** se faire scrupule de. **scrupulous†,** a, scrupuleux, religieux.

scrutineer, n, scrutateur, m. **scrutinize,** v.t, scruter. **scrutiny,** n, examen, m.

scuffle, n, rixe, bagarre, batterie, f. ¶ v.i, se bousculer; se battre.

scull, n, aviron de couple, m; (stern oar) godille, f. ¶ v.t, godiller; (v.i.) ramer en couple, nager en couple. **~er,** n, rameur de couple, m.

scullery, n, lavoir [de cuisine] m.

scullion, n, marmiton fouille-au-pot, m.

sculptor, n, sculpteur, m. **sculptress,** n, femme sculpteur, f. **sculpture,** n, sculpture, f. ¶ v.t, sculpter.

scum, n, écume, crasse; (fig.) écume, lie, f.

scumble, n, frottis, glacis, m. ¶ v.t, frotter, glacer.

scupper, n, dalot, m.

scurrilous, a, outrageant, ordurier.

scurvy, n, scorbut, m. ¶ a, vilain, méprisable.

scutcheon, n, écusson, m.

scuttle, n, (coal) seau; (Naut.) hublot, m. ¶ v.t, saborder.

scythe, n, faux, f.

sea, n, mer, f. on the high ~s, sur la haute mer. open ~, pleine mer. ~board, littoral, m. ~coast, côte de la mer, f. ~ cow, lamantin, m. ~farer, homme de mer, m. ~faring people, peuple navigateur, m. ~ fishing, pêche en mer, f. ~going (ship), de mer. ~ gull, mouette, f, goéland, m. ~ horse, cheval marin, hippocampe, m. to have got one's ~ legs, avoir le pied marin. ~ level, niveau de la mer, m. ~ lion, lion marin, m, otarie, f. ~man, marin, homme de mer, matelot; (skilful) ma-

nœuvrier, m. in a ~manlike manner, en bon marin. ~ nymph, nymphe de la mer, Néréide, f. ~ plane, hydravion, m. ~ scape, marine, f. ~shore, rivage de la mer, m. ~sickness, mal de mer, m. to be ~sick, avoir le m. de m. ~side, bord de la mer, m. ~side resort, plage, station balnéaire, f. ~ urchin, oursin, hérisson de mer, m. ~ wall, digue, f. ~weed, plante marine, algue, f, varech, goémon, m. ~worthy, en [bon] état de navigabilité.

seal, n, sceau; cachet, m; (bottle) capsule, f; (Zool.) phoque, m. ~skin, peau de phoque, f. ¶ v.t, sceller; cacheter; boucher. ~ed book (fig.), lettre close, f. ~ing wax, cire à cacheter, f.

seam, n, couture; (Geol.) couche, f, gisement, m. ~ stitch (Need.), [point de] surjet, m. ¶ v.t, couturer. ~less, a, sans couture. **seamstress,** n, couturière, f. seamy side (lit. & fig.), envers, m.

seance, n, séance de spiritisme, f.

sear, a, desséché, fané. ¶ v.t, brûler; cautériser.

search, n, recherche, f. oft. pl; (law) perquisition, f. ~light, projecteur, m; lampe de poche, f. ~ warrant, mandat de perquisition, m. ¶ v.t, scruter. ~ for, [re]chercher. ~er, n, chercheur, euse, fouilleur, m. ~ing, a, pénétrant; scrutateur.

season, n, saison, f, temps, m. ~ ticket, carte d'abonnement, f. ¶ v.t, assaisonner, relever; (wood) sécher; (fig.) aguerrir. ~able, a, de saison; opportun. ~ably, ad, à propos. ~ing (Cook.) n, assaisonnement, m; (of a salad) garniture, fourniture, f.

seat, n, siège, m; place; place assise; stalle, f; chef-lieu, m; charge; séance, f; office; foyer; château; banc, m; banquette; chaise, f; repos; (trousers chair) fond, m; assiette; (on horse) tenue, f. ¶ v.t, asseoir.

secede, v.i, faire scission, faire sécession.

secluded, p.a, retiré. **seclusion,** n, retraite; réclusion, f.

second†, a, second; deuxième; deux; (cousin) issu(e) de germain. ~ finger, doigt du milieu, médius, m. ~hand, d'occasion; de seconde main. ~hand bookseller, bouquiniste, m. ~hand dealer, revendeur, euse, brocanteur, euse. ~ *lieutenant,* sous-lieutenant, *m.* one's ~ *self,* un autre soi-même. on ~ *thoughts,* réflexion faite. [on] *the ~ of September,* le deux septembre. ¶ *n,* second, *m;* deuxieme, *m,f; (Box.)* second, soigneur; *(duel)* témoin, *m;* (*time*) seconde, *f.* ~ *hand,* aiguille des secondes, *f.* ¶ *v.t,* seconder; appuyer. ~ary, *a,* secondaire. ~ *school,* école secondaire, *f,* lycée, *m.*

secrecy, *n,* secret, *m;* discrétion, *f.* secret, *a,* secret; caché; dérobé. ¶ *n,* secret, *m.* secretary, *n,* secrétaire, *m.* ~ *bird,* serpentaire, secrétaire, *m.* ~ship & secretariat, *n,* secrétariat; ministère, *m.* secrete, *v.t,* cacher; (*physiology*) sécréter. secretion, *n,* sécrétion, *f.* secretive, *a,* dissimulé, cachottier. secretly, *ad,* secrètement, en cachette; sourdement.

sect, *n,* secte, *f.* ~arian, *n.* & *a,* sectaire, *m.* & *att.*

section, *n,* section; coupe, *f;* profil; fer; tronçon; article, *m,* rubrique, *f.* ~al, *a,* démontable; (*iron*) profilé; (*view*) en coupe. sector, *n,* secteur, *m.*

secular†, *a,* séculier; profane; (*100*) séculaire.

secure†, *a,* sûr; à l'abri. ¶ *v.t,* mettre à l'abri; assurer; garantir; asseoir; fixer; obtenir. security, *n,* sécurité; sûreté; assiette; garantie; assurance; caution, *f;* cautionnement; titre, *m;* valeur, *f.*

sedan [chair], *n,* chaise à porteurs, *f.*

sedate†, *a,* posé, rassis. sedative, *n.* & *a,* sédatif, calmant, *m.* & *a.* sedentary, *a,* sédentaire.

sedge, *n,* laîche, *f.*

sediment, *n,* sédiment, dépôt, *m.*

sedition, *n,* sédition, *f.* seditious†, *a,* séditieux.

seduce, *v.t,* séduire. ~ *from duty,* débaucher. seducer, *n,* séducteur, trice. seduction, *n,* séduction, *f.* seductive, *a,* séduisant.

sedulous, *a,* assidu. ~ly, *ad,* assidûment.

see, *n,* siège [épiscopal] *m,* chaire, *f,* évêché, *m.*

see, *v.t.* & *i. ir,* voir; regarder; reconduire; s'occuper; veiller. ~ *about,* s'occuper de. ~ *home,* reconduire. ~ *through,* pénétrer. ¶ (*vide*) *v.imperative,* voir, voyez.

seed, *n,* semence; graine, *f;* grain;

(*fig.*) germe, *m.* ~ *pearls,* semence de perles. ~ *time,* semailles, *f.pl.* ¶ *v.i,* grener, s'égrener. ~ *the players* (*Ten.*), sélectionner les têtes de séries. ~ling, *n,* jeune plant, sauvageon, (*pl.*) semis, *m.* seedsman, *n,* grainier, ère.

seeing, *n,* vision, *f.* ~ *that,* vu que, attendu que, puisque.

seek, *v.t.* & *i. ir,* chercher, rechercher. ~er, *n,* chercheur, euse.

seem, *v.i,* sembler, paraître. seeming, *n,* paraître, *m.* *the* ~ & *the real,* l'être & le paraître. ¶ *p.a,* apparent. seemingly, *ad,* en apparence. seemly, *a,* [bien]séant.

seer, *n,* prophète, *m.*

seep, *v.i,* suinter; filtrer.

seesaw, *n,* bascule, balançoire, *f.* ¶ *v.i,* basculer, se balancer.

seethe, *v.i,* bouillonner; grouiller.

segment, *n,* segment, *m.*

segregate, *v.t,* séparer. segregation, *n,* ségrégation, *f.*

seine (*net*) *n,* seine, *f.*

seismic, *a,* sismique. seismograph, *n,* sismographe, *m.*

seize, *v.t,* saisir, arrêter, prendre, s'emparer de; (*v.i, Mach.*) gripper. seizure, *n,* saisie, *f;* arrêt, *m;* attaque de paralysie, *f.*

seldom, *ad,* rarement.

select, *a,* choisi; bien composé. ~ *party,* petit comité, *m.* ¶ *v.t,* choisir; (*sport*) sélectionner. ~ion, *n,* choix, *m;* sélection, *f;* recueil, *m;* (*pl, from writings*) morceaux choisis, *m.pl.*

self, *n,* personne, *f;* moi-même; moi, *m;* -même. ~-centered, égocentriste. ~-contained, indépendant. ~-control, empire sur soi-même, *m,* maîtrise de soi, *f.* ~-defense, légitime défense, *f.* ~-denial, abnégation, *f,* renoncement, *m.* ~-esteem, amourpropre, *m.* ~-government, autonomie, *f.* ~-importance, suffisance, *f.* ~-made man, fils de ses œuvres, *m.* ~-possession, sang-froid, aplomb, *m.* ~-reliance, confiance en soi, *f.* ~-respect, amour-propre, *m.* ~-sacrifice, dévouement, *m.* ~-satisfied, béat. ~-styled, soidisant, *a.inv.* ~-taught, autodidacte. ~-willed, entier, opiniâtre, volontaire.

selfish†, *a,* égoïste, intéressé, personnel. ~ness, *n,* égoïsme, *m.*

sell, *v.t.ir,* vendre; débiter; (*v.i.ir.*) se vendre, s'écouler. ~ *off,* liquider, solder. **seller**, *n*, vendeur, euse.

seltzer, *n*, eau de Seltz, *f*.

selvage, -edge, *n*, lisière, *f*.

semaphore, *n*, sémaphore, *m*.

semblance, *n*, semblant, *m*, apparence, *f*.

semi, *prefix*: ~*breve*, ronde, *f*. ~*circle*, demi-cercle, *m*. ~*colon*, point & virgule, point-virgule, *m*. ~*demisemiquaver*, quadruple croche, *f*. ~*detached*, jumelle. ~*final*, demi-finale, *f*. ~*official*, semi-officielle, officieux. ~*quaver*, double croche, *f*. ~*tone*, demi-ton, *m*.

seminary, *n*, séminaire, *m*.

Semitic, *a*, sémitique.

semolina, *n*, semoule, *f*.

senate, *n*, sénat, *m*. **senator**, *n*, sénateur, *m*.

send, *v.t. & i. ir*, envoyer; expédier; remettre. ~ *away* & ~ *back*, renvoyer. ~ *for*, envoyer chercher, faire appeler. ~ *to sleep*, endormir. ~**er**, *n*, envoyeur, euse, expéditeur, trice.

Senegal, *n*, le Sénégal.

senile, *n*, sénile. ~ *decay*, décrépitude, caducité, *f*. **senility**, *n*, sénilité, *f*.

senior, *a*, aîné; ancien; principal; chef. ¶ *n*, aîné, e; père, *m*; doyen, ne; (*sports*) senior, *m*. ~**ity**, *n*, aînesse; ancienneté, *f*.

senna, *n*, séné, *m*.

sensation, *n*, sensation; impression, *f*. ~**al**, *a*, sensationnel. ~ *affairs*, drame, *m*. **sense**, *n*, sens; sentiment, *m*; sensation, *f*; esprit, *m*; raison, *f*; bons sens, sens commun, *m*; acception, part, *f*. ¶ *v.t*, entrevoir. ~**less**, *a*, insensé; sans connaissance. **sensibility**, *n*, sensibilité, *f*. **sensible**, *a*, sensé, sage; sensible. **sensibly**, *ad*, sensément. **sensitive**, *a*, sensible; sensitif; tendre; susceptible; chatouilleux. **sensitized** (*Phot.*) *a*, sensible.

sensual†, *a*, sensuel, charnel. ~**ist**, *n*, sensualiste, *m,f*. ~**ity** *n*, sensualité, *f*.

sentence, *n*, sentence, *f*, jugement, *m*; (*Gram.*) phrase, *f*. *death* ~, condamnation à mort, *f*. ¶ *v.t*, condamner. **sententious**†, *a*, sentencieux.

sentient, *a*, sensible; conscient. **sentiment**, *n*, sentiment, *m*. ~**al**†, *a*, sentimental. ~**ality**, *n*, sentimentalité, sensiblerie, *f*.

sentinel, *n*, sentinelle, *f*. **sentry**, *n*, sentinelle, *f*, factionnaire, *m*;

(*mounted*) vedette, *f*. ~ *box*, guérite, *f*. ~ *duty*, faction, *f*.

separate†, *a*, séparé; distinct; à part. ~ *cell system*, emprisonnement cellulaire, *m*. *at* ~ *tables* (meal), par petites tables. ¶ *v.t*, séparer. **separation**, *n*, séparation, *f*.

sepia, *n*, sépia, *f*.

September, *n*, septembre, *m*.

septet[te], *n*, septuor, *m*.

septic, *a*, septique. ~ *tank*, fosse s., *f*.

septum, *n*, cloison, *f*.

sepulchral, *a*, sépulcral. **sepulcher**, *n*, sépulcre, *m*.

sequel, *n*, suite; conséquence, *f*.

sequence, *n*, suite, succession; (*cards*) séquence, *f*.

sequestered, *p.p*, retiré, écarté. **sequestration** (*law*) *n*, séquestre, *m*.

seraglio, *n*, sérail, *m*.

seraph, *n*, séraphin, *m*. ~**ic**, *a*, séraphique.

Serbia, *n*, la Serbie. **Serb[ian]**, *a*, serbe. ¶ *n*. (*pers.*) Serbe, *m,f*; (*language*) le serbe. **Serbo-Croatian**, *n*, (*language*) serbo-croate, *m*.

sere, *a*, desséché, fané.

serenade, *n*, sérénade, *f*. ¶ *v.t*, donner une sérénade à.

serene, *a*, serein. **serenity**, *n*, sérénité, *f*.

serf, *n*, serf, *m*, serve, *f*. ~**dom**, *n*, servage, *m*.

serge, *n*, serge, *f*.

sergeant, *n*, sergent; (*cavalry*) maréchal des logis; (*police*) brigadier, *m*. ~ *major*, adjudant; maréchal des logis chef, *m*.

serial, *a*, en série. ~ *rights*, droits de reproduction dans les journaux & périodiques, *m.pl*. ~ [*story*], [roman] feuilleton, *m*. **seriatim**, *ad*, successivement. **series**, *n*, série, suite, *f*.

serif, *n*, empattement, *m*.

seringa, *n*, seringa, *m*.

serious†, *a*, sérieux; grave. ~**ness**, *n*, sérieux, *m*; gravité, *f*.

sermon, *n*, sermon; prône; prêche, *m*. ~**ize**, *v.t*, sermonner. ~**izer**, *n*, prêcheur, *m*.

serpent, *n*, serpent, *m*. **serpentine**, *a*, serpentin. ¶ *n*, serpentine, *f*.

serration, *n*, denteture; dent, *f*. **serrate[d]**, *a*, denté en scie, dentelé, en dents de scie.

serried, *a*, serré.

serum, *n*, sérum, *m*.

servant, *n*, employé, e; serviteur,

m; domestique, *m,f*; bonne; (*pl.*) domesticité, livrée, *f*, gens, *m.pl.* ~ **girl**, fille de service, *f*. **serve** *v.t.* & *i*, servir; desservir; (*a sentence*) subir; (*a notice*) signifier; faire le service militaire; suffire. ~ **up**, servir. ¶ (*Ten.*) *n*, service, *m*. **server** (*Ten.*) *n*, servant, *m*. **service**, *n*, service, *m*; desserte; démarche, *f*, ministère; office, *m*; (*domestic*) domesticité, condition, *f*; (*china, etc.*) service, *m*; (*of writ*) signification, *f*. *to grow old in the* ~, blanchir sous le harnois. ~ **hatch**, passe-plats, *m*. ~ **tree**, sorbier, *m*. ~**able**, *a*, d'usage; utile.

servile†, *a*, servile. **servility**, *n*, servilité, *f*. **servitude**, *n*, servitude, *f*.

sesame, *n*, sésame, *m*.

session, *n*, session; séance; bourse, *f*.

set, *n*, série, *f*; jeu; assortiment; train, *m*; batterie; suite; garniture; trousse; (*Math.*) tranche; parure, *f*; ensemble; service, *m*; (*fixity*) assiette; (*of saw*) voie, chasse, *f*; (*Theat.*) décor, *m*; (*Ten.*) manche, *f*, set, *m*. ~ **of** (*artificial*) **teeth**, dentier, *m*. ~**back**, recul, tassement; décalage, *m*, traverse, *f*. ~**off**, compensation, *f*; (*foil*) repoussoir; (*Arch.*) ressaut, *m*; (*Typ.*) maculature; (*law*) reconvention, *f*. ~**to**, prise de bec, bagarre, *f*; pugilat, *m*. ¶ *v.t.ir*, mettre; poser; placer; aposter; fixer; planter; asseoir; assurer; (*bone*) remettre, remboîter; (*dog on, fashion, seal*) lancer; (*gem*) sertir, enchâsser, monter; (*hen*) mettre couver; (*a sail*) établir; (*saw*) donner la voie à; (*seal*) apposer; (*shutter —Phot.*) armer; (*task, example*) donner; (*tools*) affiler, repasser; (*trap*) tendre, dresser; (*type*) composer; (*watch*) régler; (*v.i. ir.*) se figer, prendre; (*sun*) se coucher. ~ *about it*, s'y prendre. ~ *down in writing*, coucher par écrit. ~ *off*, (*figure*) dégager. ~ *on* (*pers.*), lapider. ~ *out*, partir. ~ *up*, monter; ériger; établir. ¶ *p.a*: ~ *purpose*, parti pris, *m*. ~ *smile*, sourire figé, *m*. ~ *speech*, discours d'apparat, *m*.

settee, *n*, divan, *m*, causeuse, *f*.

setter, *n*, poseur, euse; tendeur; monteur, metteur; compositeur; chien couchant, *m*. **setting**, *n*, entourage, encadrement, *m*; (*cement*) prise; (*gem*) enchâssure,

œuvre, *f*, chaton; (*sun*) coucher, *m*; (*type*) composition, *f*. ~ *aside*, abstraction faite de. ~ *sun*, soleil couchant, *m*.

settle, *n*, banc, *m*. ¶ *v.t*, régler; arranger; accommoder; trancher; liquider; établir, installer; emménager; (*property*) constituer; (*v.i.*) se fixer; s'établir; (*alight*) se poser; (*matter*) se déposer; (*ground*) [se] tasser. ~**d**, *p.a*, décidé, arrêté; (*weather*) sûr. ~**ment**, *n*, règlement, *m*; constitution, *f*; (*Stk Ex.*) terme, *m*, liquidation; colonie, colonie de peuplement, *f*. **settler**, *n*, colon, *m*, résident, *m*.

seven, *a*. & *n*, sept, *a*. & *m*. **seventeen**, *a*. & *n*, dix-sept, *a*. & *m*. **seventeenth**, *a*. & *n*, dix-septième, *a*. & *m,f*; dix-sept, *m*. ~**ly**, *ad*, en dix-septième lieu. **seventh**, *a*. & *n*, septième, *a*. & *m,f*; sept, *m*. ~**ly**, *ad*, septièmement. **seventieth**, *a*. & *n*, soixante-dixième, *a*. & *m,f*. **seventy**, *a*. & *n*, soixante-dix, *a*. & *m*. 71, 72, soixante et onze, soixante-douze.

sever, *v.t*, séparer. ~**al**†, *a*, divers, plusieurs; respectif; individuel. ~**ance**, *n*, séparation, distraction, *f*.

severe†, *a*, sévère; rigoureux; rude; grave. **severity**, *n*, sévérité, rigueur; gravité, *f*.

Seville, *n*, Séville, *f*. ~ *orange*, bigarade, orange amère, *f*.

sew, *v.t.ir*, coudre. ~**er**, *n*, couseur, euse, piqueuse, *f*.

sewer, *n*, égout, *m*. **sew[er]age**, *n*, eaux d'égout, eaux-vannes, *f.pl*.

sewing, *n*, couture, *f*. ~ *machine*, machine à coudre, *f*.

sex, *n*, sexe, *m*. ~ *appeal*, sex-appeal, *m*.

sextant, *n*, sextant, *m*.

sextet[te], *n*, sextuor, *m*.

sexton, *n*, sacristain, *m*.

sexual, *a*, sexuel.

shabby, *a*, usé, râpé, miteux; mesquin.

shack, *n*, hutte, cabane, *f*.

shackle, *n*, boucle; manille, *f*; maillon, *m*; (*fig.*) entrave, *f*. ¶ *v.t*, entraver.

shade, *n*, ombre, *f*; ombrage, *m*; (*pl, spirits*) mânes, *m.pl*; nuance, *f*; (*lamp*) abat-jour; écran; globe protecteur, *m*. ¶ *v.t*, ombrager; (*art*) ombrer; (*v.i.*) passer. ~ *off*, dégrader. **shadow**, *n*, ombre, *f*. ~ *boxing*, boxe contre son ombre, *f*. ¶ *v.t*, filer. **shady**, *a*, ombragé; (*Poet.*) ombreux; (*disreputable*) louche, véreux. *to be on the ~ side of 40*, avoir dépassé la quarantaine.

shaft, *n*, flèche, *f*, trait, *m*; (*spear*) hampe; (*of chimney*) souche, *f*; (*cart*) limon, brancard, *m*; (*Arch.*) fût, *m*, tige, *f*; (*Mech.*) arbre, *m*, transmission, *f*; (*Min.*) puits, *m*; (*elevator*) cage, *f*. ~ *horse*, brancardier, timonier, *m*.

shaggy, *a*, poilu, hirsute.

shagreen, *n*, chagrin, *m*.

shah, *n*, shah, chah, *m*.

shake, *n*, secousse, *f*; (*head*) hochement; (*hand*) serrement, *m*, poignée; (*timber*) gerçure, *f*, éclat; (*Mus.*) trille, *m*. ¶ *v.t.ir*, secouer; agiter; [é]branler; hocher; serrer; (*v.i.ir.*) trembler; s'ébranler; ballotter; flageoler; chevroter. **shaky**, *a*, branlant; chancelant; chevrotant; tremblé.

shale, *n*, schiste, *m*. ~ *oil*, huile de s., *f*.

shall, *v.aux.ir*, is expressed in Fr. by future tense. Also by falloir.

shallow, *a*, peu profond, bas; faible; creux; frivole; superficiel. ~**s**, *n.pl*, bas-fond, *m*.

sham, *n*, feinte, *f*, [faux-]semblant, *m*. ¶ *a*, feint; simulé; fictif. ~ *fight*, simulacre de combat, *m*. ¶ *v.t. & i*, feindre, simuler.

shambles, *n*, décombres, *m.pl*, ruines, *f.pl*.

shambling, *p.a*, traînant.

shame, *n*, honte; pudeur, *f*; scandale, *m*. *for ~!* fi donc! ¶ *v.t*, faire honte à. ~**faced**, *a*, honteux, penaud. ~**ful**†, *a*, honteux; scandaleux. ~**less**, *a*, éhonté, dévergondé, impudent. ~**lessly**, *ad*, sans vergogne, impudemment.

shampoo, *n*, (*wet*) schampooing, *m*; (*dry*) friction, *f*. ¶ *v.t*, faire un schampooing à; faire une friction à.

shamrock, *n*, trèfle, *m*.

shank, *n*, jambe; queue; tige, *f*.

shanty, *n*, baraque, bicoque, *f*.

shape, *n*, forme; figure; taille; tournure; carcasse, *f*; profil, *m*. ¶ *v.t*, former; façonner; mouler, modeler; pétrir. ~**less**, *a*, informe. ~**ly**, bien tourné.

share, *n*, part; quote-part, quotité, *f*; écot, *m*; (*Fin.*) action, valeur, *f*; titre; (*plow*) soc, *m*. ~**holder**, actionnaire; sociétaire, *m,f*. ¶ *v.t. & i*, partager, participer (à).

shark (*fish & rapacious pers.*) *n*, requin, *m*.

sharp, *a*, tranchant; aigu; acéré; fin; net; vif; perçant; (*acid*) aigre; (*rebuke*) verte. ~ *practices*, procédés indélicats, *m.pl*. ~**shooter**, tirailleur, *m*. ¶ *ad*. (*hour*) précise. *look ~!* dépêchez-vous! vite! ¶ (*Mus.*) dièse, *m*. ~**en**, *v.t*, aiguiser; affûter; repasser; tailler [en pointe]; (*wits*) déniaiser. ~**ly**, *ad*, vivement; nettement. ~**ness**, *n*, acuité; finesse; âcreté; netteté, *f*.

shatter, *v.t*, briser, fracasser.

shave, *v.t*, raser; (*v.i.*) se raser, se faire la barbe. *to have a close ~*, l'échapper belle. **shaving**, *n*, la barbe; (*chip*) copeau; *m*; rognure, planure, *f*. ~ *brush*, pinceau à barbe, blaireau, *m*. ~ *soap*, savon à barbe, *m*.

shawl, *n*, châle, *m*.

she, *pn*, elle; celle; ce, c', ç'; (*of ship*) il. ¶ *n*, femelle, *f*. ~**-ass**, ânesse, bourrique, *f*. ~**-bear**, ourse, *f*. ~**-camel**, chamelle, *f*. ~**-devil**, diablesse, *f*. ~**-goat**, chèvre, chevrette, *f*. ~**-monkey**, guenon, guenuche, *f*. ~**-wolf**, louve, *f*.

sheaf, *n*, gerbe, *f*; faisceau, *m*. ¶ *v.t*, [en]gerber.

shear, *v.t.ir*, tondre; cisailler. ~**er**, *n*, tondeur, euse. ~**ing**, *n*, tonte, *f*. ~ *machine*, tondeuse, *f*. **shears**, *n. pl*, cisailles, forces, *f.pl*; ciseaux, *m.pl*, tondeuse, *f*.

sheath, *n*, gaine, *f*; fourreau, *m*. **sheathe**, *v.t*, [r]engainer; recouvrir.

sheave, *n*, poulie, *f*, rouet, *m*.

shed, *n*, hangar; garage, *m*; baraque; remise; étable, *f*. ¶ *v.t.ir*, verser, répandre; se dépouiller de. **shedding** (*blood*) *n*, effusion, *f*.

sheen, *n*, éclat; lustre, *m*.

sheep, *n*, mouton, *m*; brebis, *f*. *black ~*, brebis galeuse, *f*. ~ *dog*, chien de berger, *m*. ~ *fold*, bergerie, *f*. ~**like** (*pers.*), moutonnier. ~**[skin]**, peau de mouton, *f*, basane, *f*. ~**ish**, *a*, penaud, sot, honteux.

sheer, *a*, pur; (*force*) vive; abrupt, à pic.

sheet, *n*, feuille; lame; nappe; couche; bâche; tôle, plaque; (*Naut.*) écoute, *f*; (*bed*) drap, *m*. ~ *anchor*, ancre de veille, *f*. (*fig.*) a. de salut, planche de s., *f*. ~ *glass*, verre à vitres, *m*. ~ *iron* tôle [de fer] *f*. ~ *lead*, plomb en feuilles, *m.* ~ *lightning*, éclair diffus, é. en nappes, *m.*

sheik[h], *n*, cheik, *m.*

shekel (*Bible*) *n*, sicle, *m.*

sheldrake, *n*, tadorne, *m.*

shelf, *n*, planche, tablette, *f*, rayon; (*Naut.*) écueil, *m.* [*set of*] *shelves*, étagère, *f*.

shell, *n*, coquille; coque; carapace; cosse; écale; peau, *f*; coquillage, *m*; écaille; chape, *f*; (*Artil.*) obus, *m*. ~*fish*, coquillage, *m*. ~ *hole*, entonnoir, *m*. ~ *shock*, commotion, psychose traumatique, *f*. ¶ *v.t*, écaler, écosser, égrener, cerner; bombarder, canonner, battre.

shellac, *n*, laque en écailles, gomme laque, *f*.

shelter, *n*, abri, *m*, le couvert, asile, refuge; édicule, *m*. ¶ *v.t*, abriter.

shelve, *v.i*, aller en pente; (*v.t.*) mettre de côté.

shepherd, *n*, berger; pasteur, *m*. ~*'s crook*, houlette, *f*. ~*'s-purse*, bourse à pasteur, *f*, tabouret, *m*. ~*ess*, *n*, bergère, *f*.

sherry, *n*, xérès, vin de Xérès, *m*.

shield, *n*, bouclier; protecteur; (*armor*) bouclier, écu; (*Her.*) écusson, *m*. ¶ *v.t*, abriter; défendre; protéger; garantir.

shift, *n*, déplacement; changement, *m*; (*Naut., of wind*) saute; équipe, *f*, poste; expédient, tournant, *m*, ressource, *f*; subterfuge, biais, *m*. gear ~, changement de vitesse, *m*. ¶ *v.t. & i*, déplacer; se d.; changer; changer de place; sauter; (*cargo*) riper; biaiser. ~*ing*, *p.a*, changeant; (*sand*) mouvant. ~*y*, *a*, fuyant.

shilling (½₀ of a £) *n*, shilling, *m*. (*In Fr. pronounced* ʃəlɛ̃).

shilly-shally, *v.i*, lanterner, barguigner.

shimmer, *v.i*, chatoyer.

shin, *n*, tibia; (*beef*) jarret, *m*. ~ *bone*, tibia, *m*.

shindy, *n*, chahut, *m*, scène, *f*.

shine, *n*, brillant; luisant, *m*. ¶ *v.i.ir*, luire; briller; rayonner; reluire.

shingle, *n*, galets, *m.pl*, galet; (*Build.*) bardeau, *m*. (*pl.*) (*Med.*) zona, *m*. ¶ (*Metall.*) *v.t*, cingler. ~[*d hair*], nuque rasée, *f*.

shining & shiny, *a*, [re]luisant; brillant.

ship, *n*, navire; vaisseau; bâtiment, bateau; bord, *m*. ~*building*, construction navale, *f*. ~*mate*,

camarade de bord, *m*. ~*owner*, armateur, *m*. ~*shape*, à sa place. ~*wreck*, naufrage, *m*. *to be* ~*wrecked*, faire naufrage. ~*wright*, constructeur de navires; charpentier de vaisseau, *m*. ~*yard*, chantier naval, *m*. ¶ *v.t*, charger; embarquer; expédier; (*oars*) border. **shipment**, *n*, chargement; embarquement, *m*; expédition, *f*. **shipper**, *n*, chargeur, expéditeur, *m*. **shipping**, *n*, navigation, *f*; transport maritime, *m*; marine, *f*; tonnage; armement, *m*. ~ *agent*, agent maritime, commissionnaire chargeur, *m*. ~ *charges*, frais d'expédition, *m.pl*. ~ *clerk*, expéditionnaire, *m*.

shirk, *v.t*, éluder, se soustraire à; (*v.i.*) s'embusquer. ~[*er*], *n*, embusqué, fricoteur, *m*.

shirt, *n*, chemise, *f*. ~ *collar*, col de chemise; faux col, *m*. ~ *maker*, chemisier, ère. ~*ing*, toile à chemises, *f*, shirting, *m*.

shiver, *v.t*, briser, fracasser; (*v.i.*) frissonner, grelotter.

shoal, *n*, (*sand, fish*) banc; (*shallow*) haut-fond, *m*. ~*s of people*, un mascaret humain.

shock, *n*, choc; coup; saisissement, ébranlement, à-coup, *m*, secousse; (*hair*) tignasse, forêt, *f*; (*corn*) tas, *m*. ~ *absorber*, amortisseur, *m*. ¶ *v.t*, heurter, choquer; (*fig.*) choquer, scandaliser, révolter, blesser.

shoddy, *a*, de camelote.

shoe, *n*, soulier, *m*, chaussure, *f*; chausson; (*horse*) fer; sabot; patin, *m*. ~ *brush*, brosse à souliers, *f*. ~ *horn*, chausse-pied, *m*. ~ *lace*, lacet de soulier, *m*. ~ *maker*, cordonnier, *m*. ~ *polish*, crème à chaussure, *f*. ¶ *v.t.ir*, chausser; ferrer; saboter. **shoeing**, *n*, ferrage, *m*.

shoot, *n*, chasse, *f*, tiré, *m*; rejeton; couloir, *m*. ¶ *v.t.ir*, tirer; lancer; darder; chasser; blesser [d'un coup de fusil, d'une flèche]; tuer [d'un coup de fusil, *etc.*]; (*spy, deserter*) fusiller; (*tip*) culbuter; (*rapids*) franchir; (*v.i.ir.*) tirer; chasser [au fusil]; (*grow*) pousser, germer; (*Foot.*) shooter; (*pain*) élancer. ~ *a movie*, tourner un film. **shooting**, *n*, tir, *m*; chasse [au tir] *f*. ~ *gallery*, stand, *m*. ~ *pains*, douleur lancinante, *f*, élancements, *m.pl*. ~ *star*, étoile filante, *f*.

shop, *n,* magasin, *m,* boutique, *f;* débit; atelier, *m.* ~ *foreman,* chef d'atelier, *m.* ~ *front,* devanture de magasin, *f.* ~*keeper,* marchand, e, boutiquier, ère. ~*lifting,* vol à l'étalage, *m.* ~*walker,* inspecteur, *m.* ~*window,* vitrine, montre, *f.* ~*worn,* défraîchi. ¶ *v.i,* faire des emplettes. **shopping,** *n,* achat, *m. to go* ~, aller faire des courses. ~ *basket,* panier à provisions.

shore, *n,* rivage, bord; étai; accore, *m.* ~ *fishing,* pêche au bord de la mer, *f. on* ~, à terre. ¶ *v.t,* étayer; chevaler; accorer.

short, *a,* court; petit; bref; déficitaire; cassant. ~ *circuit,* court-circuit, *m.* ~*coming,* manquement, *m.* ~*cut,* raccourci, *m.* ~*haired* (dog), à poil ras. ~*hand,* sténographie, *f.* ~*hand-typist,* sténodactylographe, *m,f.* ~*hand writer,* sténographe, *m,f.* ~*-lived,* passager, fugitif, sans lendemain. . . . *are* ~*-lived,* . . . ne vivent pas longtemps. ~*sighted,* myope; à courtes vues; imprévoyant. ~ *story,* conte, *m,* nouvelle, *f.* ~ [syllable], [syllabe] brève, *f.* ¶ *n.pl,* ~s, caleçon; short, *m.* ¶ *ad,* [tout] court. *in* ~, bref, enfin. ~*age, n,* manque; déficit, *m,* crise, *f.* ~**en,** *v.t,* [r]accourcir. ~**ly,** *ad,* bientôt, prochainement, sous peu; peu de temps (*avant, après*); brièvement. ~**ness,** *n,* brièveté; courte durée; petitesse, *f.* ~ *of breath,* courte haleine, *f.*

shot, *n,* coup de feu; coup; trait; boulet, *m;* balle, *f;* plomb, *m;* grenaille, *f;* (*putting the shot*) poids, *m;* portée, *f;* tireur, *m.* ~ *gun,* fusil de chasse, *m.*

shot (*fabrics*) *p.p,* changeant, chatoyant.

should, *v.aux, is expressed in Fr. by conditional mood. Also by* devoir, falloir.

shoulder, *n,* épaule, *f;* (*Carp.*) épaulement, *m.* ~ *blade,* plat de l'épaule, *m,* omoplate, *f;* (*horse, ox*) paleron, *m.* ~ *strap,* bretelle; épaulette, *f.* ¶ *v.t,* pousser de l'épaule; prendre sur ses épaules; (*arms*) porter; (*fig.*) endosser.

shout, *n,* cri; éclat, *m.* ¶ *v.t. & i,* crier; vociférer.

shove, *n,* poussée, *f.* ¶ *v.t. & i,* pousser. ~ *off,* pousser au large.

shovel, *n,* pelle, *f.* ¶ *v.t,* remuer à la pelle. ~**ful,** *n,* pelletée, *f.*

show, *n,* semblant, simulacre; étalage; déballage, *m;* parade; représentation, *f,* spectacle, *m;* exposition, *f,* concours, salon, *m.* ~ *case,* vitrine, *f.* ~*man,* forain; montreur, *m.* ~ *room,* salon d'exposition, *m.* ¶ *v.t.ir,* montrer; manifester; enseigner; accuser; [re]présenter; constater; prouver; (*v.i.ir.*) se montrer; paraître. ~ *in,* faire entrer, introduire. ~ *off,* faire parade (de); (*abs.*) parader. ~ *out,* reconduire. ~ *round,* piloter dans, promener par, promener dans. ~ *the white feather,* caner. ~ *up,* démasquer; afficher.

shower, *n,* ondée; averse; giboulée; pluie; grêle; nuée; avalanche, *f.* ~ *bath,* douche [en pluie] *f.* ¶ *v.t,* faire pleuvoir; combler.

showy, *a,* ostentateur, ostentatoire, fastueux, voyant.

shrapnel, *n,* obus à balles, *m.*

shred, *n,* lambeau, *m;* (*pl.*) charpie, *f.* ¶ *v.t,* déchiqueter.

shrew, *n,* mégère, *f.* ~ [*mouse*] musaraigne, *f.*

shrewd, *a,* sagace, clairvoyant; adroit. ~**ness,** *n,* sagacité, clairvoyance; adresse, *f.*

shriek, *n,* cri, *m.* ¶ *v.i,* crier.

shrike, *n,* pie-grièche, *f.*

shrill, *a,* aigu, perçant, strident. ~**ness,** *n,* acuité, *f;* (*voice*) mordant, *m.*

shrimp, *n,* crevette, *f;* (*pers.*) gringalet, *m.* ~**ing,** *n,* pêche à la crevette, *f.*

shrine, *n,* châsse, *f,* reliquaire; sanctuaire, *m.*

shrink, *v.i.ir,* [se] rétrécir; se retirer; (*v.t.ir.*) rétrécir. ~**age,** *n,* rétrécissement; retrait, *m,* retraite, *f.*

shrivel, *v.t,* rider, grésiller, ratatiner, racornir.

shroud, *n,* linceul, suaire; (*Naut.*) hauban, *m.* ¶ *v.t,* envelopper; embrumer.

Shrovetide, *n,* les jours gras, *m.pl. Shrove Tuesday,* mardi gras, *m.*

shrub, *n,* arbrisseau, *m.* **shrubbery,** *n,* plantation d'arbrisseaux, *f;* bosquet, *m.*

shrug, *n,* haussement d'épaules, *m.* ¶ *v.t,* hausser.

shudder, *v.i,* frissonner, frémir.

shuffle, *v.t,* (*cards*) battre; (*v.i.*) biaiser, tortiller, tergiverser. ~ *along,* traîner la jambe. ¶ (*ex-*

cuse) n, défaite, f. *shuffling gait*, pas traînant, m.

shun, v.t, éviter, fuir.

shunt (*Elec.*) n, dérivation, f. ¶ v.t, (*Rly*) garer, manœuvrer; (*Elec.*) dériver.

shut, v.t.ir, fermer; (v.i.) [se] f. ~ *in*, enfermer. ~ *out*, fermer la porte à; exclure. ~ *up*, fermer; enfermer; clouer la bouche à. **shutter**, n, volet; contrevent; (*Phot.*) obturateur, m.

shuttle, n, navette, f. ~*cock*, volant, m.

shy†, a, timide, sauvage, réservé, farouche, ombrageux. ¶ v.i, faire un écart; (v.t.) lancer. ~*ness*, n, timidité, sauvagerie, f.

Siam, n, le Siam. **Siamese**, a, siamois. ~ *cat*, chat de Siam, m. ¶ n, (*pers.*) Siamois, e; (*language*) le siamois.

Siberia, n, la Sibérie. **Siberian**, a, sibérien. ¶ n, Sibérien, ne.

Sicilian, a, sicilien. ¶ n, Sicilien, ne. **Sicily**, n, la Sicile.

sick, a, malade; dégoûté. *to be* ~, être malade; (*stomach*) avoir mal au cœur. *the* ~, les malades, m,f.pl. ~ *& tired*, excédé. ~*bed*, lit de douleur, m. ~ *headache*, mal de tête accompagné de nausées, m. ~ *leave*, congé de maladie, c. de convalescence, m. ~ *list*, état des malades, m. ~ *room*, chambre de malade; (*Sch.*, etc.) infirmerie, f. ~*en*, v.i, tomber malade; (v.t.) écœurer.

sickle, n, faucille, f.

sickly, a, maladif, souffreteux, malingre; chétif; doucereux, fadasse. **sickness**, n, maladie, f; (*stomach*) mal de cœur, m.

side, n, côté; flanc; bord, m, rive, f; versant; plat, m; face; part, f; parti; camp, m. ~ *by* ~, côte à côte. ~*board*, buffet, dressoir, m, panetière, crédence, f. ~ *car*, side-car, m. ~ *dish*, entremets, m. ~ *door*, porte latérale, f. ~ *glance*, regard oblique, m. ~ *issue*, question d'intérêt secondaire, f. ~*long*, de côté; (*glance*) en coulisse. ~ *saddle*, selle de dame, f. ~ *show*, spectacle payant; (*fair*) spectacle forain, m. ~*slip*, déraper. ~*step*, faire un écart. ~ *stroke*, nage de côté, f. ~*walk*, trottoir, m. ~*ways*, de côté. ~*whiskers*, favoris, m.pl. ~ *with*, se ranger du côté de.

sidereal, a, sidéral.

siding, n, voie de garage, f; (*private*) embranchement, m.

sidle in, entrer de guingois.

siege, n, siège, m.

Sienna, n, Sienne, f. s~, n, terre de S., f.

siesta, n, sieste, méridienne, f.

sieve, n, tamis, sas, crible, m. **sift**, v.t, tamiser, sasser, cribler; bluter; (*question*) éplucher. **siftings**, n.pl, criblure, f.

sigh, n, soupir, m. ¶ v.i, soupirer.

sight, n, vue; vision, f; aspect, m; présence; (*Surv.*) visée, f, coup [de lunette] m; (*gun*) mire, f; spectacle, m; curiosité; caricature, f. *at* ~, à première vue; (*reading*) à livre ouvert; (*Com.*) à vue. *by* ~, de vue. ¶ v.t, viser; voir; (*land*) reconnaître.

sign, n, signe, m. ~*[board]*, enseigne, f; panonceau, m. ~ *of expression* (*Mus.*), nuance, f. ~ *post*, poteau indicateur, m. ¶ v.t. & i, signer; (*in the margin*) émarger; faire signe. ~ *[on]*, engager.

signal n, signal, m. ~ *box*, cabine à signaux, f. ~*man* (*Rly*), signaleur, m, f, a, signalé, insigne. ¶ ~ *& ~ize*, v.t, signaler. **signaler**, n, (*Mil.*) signaleur; (*Naut.*) timonier, m **signatory** or **signer** n, signataire, m,f. **signature**, n, signature; souscription; (*Mus.*) armature; (*Typ.*) signature, f. **signet**, n, cachet, m. ~ *ring*, [bague à la] chevalière, f.

significance, n, portée, f. *look of deep* ~, regard [fort] significatif, r. d'intelligence, m. **significant**, a, significatif. **signify**, v.t. & i, signifier; importer.

silence, n, silence, m. ¶ v.t, faire taire; (*enemy's fire*) éteindre. **silencer**, n, silencieux; amortisseur de bruit, m. **silent**†, a, silencieux, taciturne; (*Gram.*) muet. ~ *partner*, commanditaire, m. *to be* ~, se taire.

Silesia, n, la Silésie. s~, n, silésienne, f.

silhouette, n, silhouette, f.

silica, n, silice, f. **silicate**, n, silicate, m.

silk, n, soie, f. ~ *goods* or *silks*, soierie, f. ~ *hat*, chapeau de soie, m. **silkworm**, n, ver à soie, m. ~ *breeding*, magnanerie, sériciculture, f. ~*s' eggs*, graine, f. **silky**, a, soyeux.

sill, n, (*door*) seuil; (*window*) rebord, m.

silliness, *n*, niaiserie, bêtise, *f*. **silly**, *a*, niais, sot, bête.

silo, *n*, silo, *m*. ¶ *v.t*, ensiler.

silt, *n*, vase, *f*, limon, *m*. ~ **up**, s'envaser.

silver, *n*, argent, *m*. ~ *birch*, bouleau blanc, *m*. ~ *fox*, renard argenté, *m*. ~*gilt*, vermeil, argent doré. ~ *mine*, mine d'argent, *f*. ~ *plate*, *n*, argenterie, *f*; (*v.t.*) argenter. ~ *side*, gîte à la noix, *m*. ~*smith*, orfèvre, *m*. ~*[smith's] work*, orfèvrerie, *f*. ~ *wedding*, noces d'argent, *f.pl*. ¶ *v.t*, argenter; (*mirror*) étamer. ~**ing** (*for mirror*) *n*, tain, *m*. ~**y**, *a*, argenté; argentin.

simian, *a*, qui appartient au singe.

similar, *a*, semblable, pareil, similaire. ~**ity** & **similitude**, *n*, similitude, *f*. ~**ly**, *ad*, semblablement.

simile, *n*, comparaison, similitude, *f*.

simmer, *v.i.* & *t*, mijoter, cuire à petit feu.

simony, *n*, simonie, *f*.

simoom, **simoon**, *n*, simoun, *m*.

simper, *n*, sourire affecté, *m*. ¶ *v.i*, minauder.

simple†, *a*. & *n*, simple, *a*. & *m*. ~*minded*, simple, naïf. **simpleton**, *n*, niais, e, gogo, *m*, innocent, e. **simplicity**, *n*, simplicité; bonhomie, *f*. **simplify**, *v.t*, simplifier.

simulacrum, *n*, simulacre, *m*. **simulate**, *v.t*, simuler, feindre. **simultaneous**†, *a*, simultané.

sin, *n*, péché, *m*; iniquité, *f*. ¶ *v.i*, pécher.

Sinai (Mount), le mont Sinaï.

since, *ad*. & *pr*, depuis. ¶ *c*, depuis que; puisque, comme.

sincere†, *a*, sincère. **sincerity**, *n*, sincérité, *f*.

sine, *n*, sinus, *m*.

sinecure, *n*, sinécure, *f*.

sine die, sans date.

sinew, *n*, tendon; (*in meat*) tirant; (*pl. of war*) nerf, *m*.

sinful, *a*, coupable.

sing, *v.t.* & *i. ir*, chanter. ~ *to sleep*, endormir en chantant.

Singapore, *n*, Singapour, *m*.

singe, *v.t*, flamber, brûler; roussir.

singer, *n*, chanteur, euse; cantatrice, *f*. **singing**, *n*, chant; (*ears*) tintement, *m*; (*att.*) de chant; (*kettle*) à sifflet.

single, *a*, unique; seul; simple. ~ *bed*, lit à une place, *m*. ~ *blessedness*, le bonheur du célibat. ~*breasted*, droit. ~ *combat*, combat singulier, *m*. ~

handed, tout seul, à moi seul. *a* ~ *life*, le célibat. ~ *man*, célibataire, garçon, *m*. ~ *out*, distinguer. **singly**, *ad*, isolément; un(e) à un(e).

singsong, *a*, chantant, traînant. ¶ *n*, psalmodie, *f*.

singular†, *a*. & *n*, singulier, *a*. & *m*.

sinister, *a*, sinistre; (*Her.*) sénestre.

sink, *n*, évier; plomb; puisard; (*fig.*) cloaque, *m*, sentine, *f*. ¶ *v.i.ir*, [s']enfoncer; s'affaisser; se tasser; crouler; s'abaisser; baisser; descendre; succomber; (*ship*) couler [à fond], c. bas; (*v.t.ir.*) enfoncer; noyer; foncer; creuser; couler; (*die*) graver en creux; (*money, a fortune*) enterrer (*in* = en); (*loan, national debt*) amortir. ~ *in*[*to*], pénétrer; s'imbiber. *in a sinking condition* (ship), en perdition. *sinking fund*, fonds d'amortissement, *m*, caisse d'amortissement, *f*. ~**er**, *n*, plomb de ligne, *m*.

sinless, *a*, innocent. **sinner**, *n*, pécheur, *m*, pécheresse, *f*.

sinuous, *a*, sinueux.

sinus, *n*, sinus, *m*.

sip, *n*, petite gorgée; goutte, *f*. ¶ *v.t.* & *i*, siroter, humer, buvoter.

siphon, *n*, siphon, *m*.

sir, *n*, monsieur, *m*; (*title*) sir. *no*, ~, (*army*) non, mon colonel, etc.; (*navy*) non, amiral, etc.; (*but to any officer in command of a ship*) non, commandant. **sire**, *n*, père; (*to kings*) sire, *m*. ¶ *v.t*, engendrer.

siren (*Myth.* & *hooter*) *n*, sirène, *f*.

sirloin, *n*, aloyau, *m*. *a roast* ~, un rosbif.

sister, *n*, sœur, *f*. ~*in-law*, belle-sœur, *f*. ~ [*ship*] [navire] frère, n. jumeau, *m*. ~*hood*, confrérie, communauté, *f*. ~**ly**, *a*, de sœur.

sit, *v.i.ir*, s'asseoir; rester; [se] tenir; (*portrait*) poser; (*court*) siéger; (*hen*) couver. ~ *down*, s'asseoir. ~ *for* (portrait), poser pour. ~ *enthroned* & ~ *in state*, trôner. ~ *on* (eggs), couver. ~ *out*, faire galerie. ~ *out a dance*, causer une danse. ~ *up*, se tenir droit; veiller.

site, *n*, emplacement; terrain; site, *m*; assiette, *f*.

sitting, *n*, séance; audience; pose, *f*. ~ *hen*, couveuse, *f*. ~ *posture*, séant, *m*. ~ *room*, petit salon, *m*. ~ *time*, couvaison, *f*.

situated, *a,* situé; sis; placé; dans une position. **situation,** *n,* situation, assiette, position; place, *f.* ~ *wanted,* demande d'emploi, *f.*

sitz bath, bain de siège, *m.*

six, *a. & n,* six, *a. & m.* **sixteen,** *a. & n,* seize, *a. & m.* **sixteenth**†, *a. & n,* seizième, *a. & m,f;* seize, *m.* **sixth**†, *a. & n,* sixième, *a. & m,f;* six, *m;* (*Mus.*) sixte, *f.* **sixtieth,** *a. & n,* soixantième, *a. & m,f.* **sixty,** *a. & n,* soixante, *a. & m.*

size, *n,* dimension, *f. oft. pl;* grandeur; grosseur; mesure; taille; pointure, *f;* numéro; format; calibre, *m;* (*glue, etc.*) colle, *f,* encollage, *m.* ¶ *v.t,* classer en grosseur; [en]coller. ~ *up* (*pers.*), jauger.

skate, *n,* patin, *m;* (*fish*) raie, *f.* ¶ *v.i,* patiner. **skater,** *n,* patineur, euse. *skating rink,* piste de patinage, *f.*

skedaddle, *v.i,* prendre la poudre d'escampette.

skein, *n,* écheveau, *m.*

skeleton, *n,* squelette, *m;* carcasse, *f;* canevas, *m.* ~ *in the cupboard,* secret de la famille, *m.* ~ *key,* crochet [de serrurier] *m.*

skeptic, *n,* sceptique, *m, f.* ¶ *a,* sceptique. ~*al,* *a,* sceptique. **skepticism,** *n,* scepticisme, *m.*

sketch, *n,* esquisse, *f,* croquis, dessin, crayon, canevas, *m;* (*playlet*) saynète, *f.* ~ *book,* album de dessin, cahier de dessin, *m.* ¶ *v.t,* esquisser, croquer, crayonner, dessiner, tracer.

skew, *a,* biais, oblique. ¶ *n,* biais, *m.*

skewer, *n,* brochette, *f.*

ski, *n,* ski, *m.* ~ *pole,* bâton de ski, *m.* ¶ *v.i,* faire du ski. **skiing,** *n,* courses en ski, *f.pl.*

skid, *n,* enrayure, *f,* sabot; (*Avn.*) patin; (*slip*) dérapage, *m.* ¶ *v.t,* enrayer; (*v.i.*) patiner; déraper.

skiff, *n,* skiff, esquif, *m,* yole, *f.*

skill, *n,* habileté, adresse, *f.* ~*ed,* *a,* expérimenté, expert. ~*ful*† *a,* habile, adroit.

skim, *v.t,* écumer, dégraisser, écrémer; effleurer, raser. ~ *milk,* lait écrémé, *m.* **skimmer,** *n,* écumoire; écrémoire, *f.* **skimmings,** *n.pl,* écume, *f.*

skimp, *v.t,* étriquer.

skin, *n,* peau; (*pl.*) peausserie; fourrure; dépouille, *f;* cuir, *m;* pelure; écorce; enveloppe, *f.*

~*-deep,* superficiel. ~ *disease,* maladie cutanée, *f.* ~ *dresser,* peaussier, *m.* ~ *specialist,* spécialiste des maladies de peau, [médecin] peaussier, [médecin] peaucier, *m.* ¶ *v.t,* écorcher; dépouiller; peler. ~*flint,* *n,* grippe-sou, *m,f,* pingre, *m.* ~*less pea* or *bean,* mange-tout, *m.* **skinny,** *a,* décharné, maigre.

skip, *n,* saut, *m.* ¶ *v.t.* & *i,* sauter; voleter. ~ *about,* gambiller, fringuer. **skipper,** *n,* patron; capitaine, *f. skipping rope,* corde à sauter, *f.*

skirmish, *n,* escarmouche, *f.* ¶ *v.i,* escarmoucher. ~*er,* *n,* tirailleur, *m.*

skirt, *n,* jupe; basque, *f;* (*of a wood*) lisière, orée, *f.* ¶ *v.t,* longer.

skit, *n,* sketch comique, *m.* **skittish,** *a,* (*horse*) ombrageux, écouteux; folâtre; coquet.

skittle, *n,* quille, *f.* ~ *alley,* quillier, *m.*

skulk, *v.i,* se dissimuler.

skull, *n,* crâne, *m.* ~ *cap,* calotte, *f.*

skunk, *n,* mouffette, *f;* (*fur*) sconse; (*pers.*) ladre, *m.*

sky, *n,* ciel, *m;* (*pl, Poet.*) nues, *f.pl.* ~ *blue,* bleu de ciel, b. céleste, *m.* ~*lark,* alouette des champs, *f.* ~*light,* [fenêtre à] tabatière, *f.* ~ *line,* profil de l'horizon, *m.* ~ *rocket,* fusée volante, *f.* ~*scraper,* gratte-ciel, *m.* ~ *writing,* publicité sur les nuages, *f.*

slab, *n,* dalle, plaque, table, tranche, *f,* pan, *m;* tablette, *f;* (*Typ.*) marbre, *m.*

slack†, *a,* lâche; mou; faible. ~ *season,* morte saison, *f.* ~ *water* (*Naut.*), mer étale, *f,* l'étale de la marée, *m.* ¶ ~ & ~*en,* *v.t.* & *i,* détendre; se d.; relâcher; se r.; ralentir.

slag, *n,* scorie, *f,* laitier, *m.*

slake, *v.t,* éteindre.

slam (*cards*) *n,* chelem, *m.* ¶ (*bang*) *v.i.* & *t,* claquer.

slander, *v.t,* médire de, calomnier; diffamer. ~*ous,* *a,* médisant.

slang, *n,* argot, *m.*

slant, *n,* inclinaison, *f.* ¶ *v.i.* & *t,* incliner.

slap, *n,* gifle, tape, claque, *f,* soufflet, *m.* ¶ *v.t,* frapper, taper, claquer, souffleter, gifler.

slash, *v.t,* taillader; balafrer. ~ *about,* ferrailler.

slat, *n,* latte; planchette; (*blind*) lame, *f.*

slate, *n,* ardoise, *f.* ~*-colored* ardoisé. ~ *pencil,* crayon d'ardoise, *m.* ~ *quarry,* ardoisière, *f.* ¶ *v.t,* couvrir d'ardoises.

slattern, *n,* souillon, salope, maritorne, *f.*

slaughter, *n,* tuerie, *f,* massacre, carnage, *m.* ~ *house,* abattoir, *m.* ~ *man,* abatteur, *m.* ¶ *v.t,* massacrer, égorger; (*cattle*) abattre.

Slav, *a,* slave. ¶ *n,* Slave, *m,f.*

slave, *n,* esclave, *m,f.* ~ *bangle,* bracelet esclave, *m.* ~ *driver* & ~ *trader,* négrier, *m.* ~ *trade,* traite des noirs, *f.* **slave,** *v.i,* s'échiner, trimer.

slaver, *n,* bave, *f.* ¶ *v.i,* baver.

slavery, *n,* esclavage, *m.* **slavish†,** *a,* servile. ~**ness,** *n,* servilité, *f.*

slay, *v.t.ir,* immoler. ~**er,** *n,* tueur, *m.*

sleazy, *a,* mal soigné, mal tenu.

sledge, *n,* traîneau, *m;* (*man-guided, in the Alps*) ramasse, *f.* ~[*hammer*], masse, *f.* **sledging,** *n,* traînage, *m.*

sleek, *a,* lisse, poli.

sleep, *n,* sommeil, *m.* ~*walker,* somnambule, *m,f.* ¶ *v.i.* & *t. ir,* dormir; reposer; coucher. ~ *out,* découcher. ~**er,** *n,* dormeur, euse; (*Rly. track*) traverse, *f;* wagon-lit, *m.* **sleepiness,** *n,* envie de dormir, somnolence, *f,* sommeil, *m.* **sleeping,** *p.a,* endormi. ~ *bag,* sac de couchage, *m.* the S~ *Beauty,* la Belle au bois dormant. ~ *car,* wagon-lit, *m.* ~ *doll,* bébé dormeur, *m.* ~ *pill,* soporifique, *f.* ~ *sickness,* maladie du sommeil, *f.* **sleepless,** *a,* sans dormir. ~**ness,** *n,* insomnie, *f.* **sleepy,** *a,* ensommeillé, somnolent.

sleet, *n,* de la neige fondue, pluie mêlée de neige, *f.* ¶ *v.i,* tomber de la neige fondue.

sleeve, *n,* manche, *f;* (*Mach.*) manchon, *m.* to laugh up one's ~, rire sous cape. ~**less,** *a,* sans manches.

sleigh, *n,* traîneau, *m.* ~**ing,** *n,* traînage, *m.*

sleight-of-hand, *n,* prestidigitation, *f.*

slender, *a,* mince; délié; fluet; grêle; gracile, svelte; faible;

sleuth hound, (*dog & fig.*) limier, *m.*

slew, *v.t,* faire pivoter.

slice, *n,* tranche; tartine, *f.* ~ *of bread & butter,* beurrée, tartine, *f.* ¶ *v.t,* trancher; (*ball*) couper.

slide, *n,* glissade; glissoire; débâcle; coulisse, *f;* tiroir; coulant; curseur; (*microscope*) porte-objet, *m;* (*Phot.*) diapositive, *f.* ~ *rule,* règle à calcul, *f.* ~ *valve,* tiroir, *m.* ¶ *v.i.ir,* glisser; couler. **sliding,** *p.a:* ~ *roof,* toit découvrable, *m.* ~ *scale,* échelle mobile, *f.* ~ *seat* (boat), banc à coulisse, *m.*

slight†, *a,* léger; mince; faible; petit; menu, maigrelet. ¶ *n,* affront, *m.* ¶ *v.t,* négliger; faire un affront à. the ~*est,* le moindre, la moindre.

slim, *a,* svelte, gracile, élancé.

slime, *n,* bave; vase, *f,* limon, *m,* boue, *f.* **slimy,** *a,* baveux; visqueux; vaseux.

sling, *n,* fronde; écharpe; bretelle; élingue, *f.* ¶ *v.t.ir,* (*throw*) lancer; suspendre. slung [*over the shoulders*], en bandoulière.

slink away, *v.i.ir,* se dérober.

slip, *n,* glissement, *m,* glissade, *f;* faux pas; lapsus, *m,* erreur; peccadille; bande; fiche; feuille, *f;* papillon, *m,* (*woman's*) combinaison, *f;* (*Hort.*) plant, *m,* bouture; (*Naut.*) cale, *f.* ~*cover,* housse, *f.* ~ *knot,* nœud coulant, *m.* ~*shod,* en savates; négligé. ~ *stitch,* maille glissé, *f.* ¶ *v.i.* & *t,* glisser; couler; patiner; échapper; (*rope*) larguer. ~ *in,* *v.t,* faufiler. ~ *on* (garment), *v.t,* passer. **slipper,** *n,* pantoufle, *f;* chausson, *m;* mule, *f.* **slippery,** *a,* glissant.

slit, *n,* fente, *f.* ¶ (*dress*) *p.a,* tailladé. ¶ *v.t.ir,* fendre.

slither, *v.i,* se glisser.

slobber, *n,* bave, *f.* ¶ *v.i,* baver.

sloe, *n,* prunelle, *f.* ~ *gin,* [liqueur de] prunelle, *f.* ~ [*tree*], prunellier, *m.*

slogan, *n,* devise publicitaire, *f.*

sloop, *n,* sloop, *m.*

slop [*over*], *v.i,* déborder. slop *pail,* seau de toilette, *m.*

slope, *n,* pente; rampe, *f;* talus, *m.* ¶ *v.i,* s'incliner, aller en pente.

sloppiness, *n,* état détrempé, *m.* **sloppy,** *a,* débraillé, mal ajusté. **slops,** *n.pl,* rinçure, *f;* eaux ménagères, *f.pl;* (*thin soup*) lavasse, *f*; (*liquid diet*) bouillon, *m*.

slot, *n*, mortaise, rainure; (*of a slot machine*) fente, *f*. ~ **machine**, appareil à jetons, *m*.

sloth, *n*, paresse, indolence, *f*; (*Zool.*) paresseux, *m*. **~ful**, *a*, paresseux, indolent.

slouch, *v.i*, donner un air disloqué à sa taille, à son attitude, à sa marche. ~ **hat**, chapeau rabattu, *m*.

slough, *n*, bourbier, *m*; (*snake*) dépouille, peau, mue; (*Med.*) escarre, *f*. ¶ *v.i*, se dépouiller, muer.

sloven, *n*, sagouin, e, souillon, *m,f*. **~ly**, *a*, négligé.

slow†, *a*, lent; tardif; lambin; (*train*) omnibus, de petite vitesse; (*clock*) en retard. *to be* ~ (*tedious*), manquer d'entrain. **~-motion picture**, cinéma au ralenti, *m*. ¶ *ad*, lentement. ~ **down**, ralentir. **slowness**, *n*, lenteur, *f*.

slow-worm, *n*, orvet, *m*.

sludge, *n*, gâchis, *m*; vase, boue, *f*.

slug, *n*, limace, loche, *f*; (*bullet & Typ.*) lingot, *m*.

sluggard, *n*, paresseux, euse. **sluggish†**, *a*, paresseux; inerte; tardif.

sluice, *n*, canal, *m*. ~ **gate**, vanne, *f*.

slum, *n*, taudis, *m*. ~ **area**, zône des taudis, *f*.

slumber, *n*, sommeil, *m*. ¶ *v.i*, sommeiller.

slump, *n*, (*in prices*) effondrement, *m*, dégringolade; (*in trade*) mévente; crise, *f*. ¶ *v.i*, s'effondrer.

slur, *n*, atteinte; (*Mus.*) liaison, *f*. ¶ *v.t*, (*Mus.*) lier. ~ **over**, glisser sur.

slush, *n*, de la neige fondue, *f*.

slut, *n*, garce, souillon, salope, *f*.

sly, *a*, sournois; rusé. **~boots**, cachottier, ère, finaud, e. *on the* ~, à la dérobée.

smack, *n*, claque, *f*; (*boat*) barque, *f*, bateau, *m*. ¶ *v.t*, claquer, taper; (*tongue*) clapper. *to* ~ *of*, sentir le, la.

small, *a*, petit; faible; modique; menu; fin; (*intestine*) grêle; (*arms*, *Mil.*) portatives. ~ *fry* (*fig.*), fretin, *m*. **~pox**, petite vérole, variole, *f*. **~pox case** (*pers.*), varioleux, euse. ~ *stones*, pierraille, *f*. ~ *talk*, menus propos, *m.pl*, conversation banale, *f*, choses indifférentes, *f.pl*, (*dire*) des riens. ¶ ~ *of the back*, chute des reins, *f*. **~ness**, *n*, petitesse, *f*, peu d'importance, *m*.

smart, *n*, cuisson, *f*. ¶ *v.i*, picoter, cuire. ¶† *a*, vif; fin; beau, chic, pimpant, coquet; huppé. *the* ~ *set*, les gens huppés. **~en oneself** *up*, se requinquer. **~ing**, *n*, cuisson, *f*. ¶ *p.a*, cuisant. **~ness**, *n*, finesse, *f*; chic, *m*.

smash, *n*, accident; (*Fin.*) krach; (*Ten.*) smash, *m*. *to go* ~ (*bank*), sauter. ¶ *v.t*, briser, fracasser, massacrer.

smattering, *n*, teinture, *f*.

smear, *v.t*, enduire; barbouiller.

smell, *n*, odorat, *m*; odeur, *f*. ¶ *v.t. & i. ir*, sentir, fleurer; flairer; puer; *smelling bottle*, flacon à odeur, *m*. *smelling salts*, sels [volatils] anglais, *m.pl*.

smelt, *n*, éperlan, *m*.

smelt, *v.t*, fondre. **~ing works**, fonderie, *f*.

smilax, *n*, smilax, *m*.

smile, *n*, sourire, *m*. ¶ *v.i*, sourire. **smiling**, *a*, [sou]riant.

smirch, *v.t*, salir.

smirk, *n*, sourire affecté, *m*. ¶ *v.i*, minauder.

smite, *v.t.ir*, frapper. (*Cf. smitten.*)

smith, *n*, forgeron, *m*. ~'s *hearth*, bâti de forge, *m*. ~'y, *n*, forge, *f*.

smitten, *p.p*, (*remorse*) pris; (*love*) epris, féru.

smock [**frock**], *n*, blouse, *f*, sarrau, *m*. **smocking**, *n*, fronces smock, *f.pl*.

smoke, *n*, fumée, *f*. ~ *screen*, écran de fumée, *m*. **~stack**, cheminée, *f*. ¶ *v.i. & t*, fumer; enfumer; (*lamp*) charbonner. **~d** *sausage*, saucisson, *m*. **~less**, *a*, sans fumée. **smoker**, *n*, fumeur, euse. **smoking**, *n*, l'habitude de fumer, *f*. ~ *compartment*, compartiment pour fumeurs, *m*. ~ *room*, fumoir, *m*. ~ *strictly prohibited*, défense expresse de fumer, *m*. **smoky**, *a*, fumeux.

smolder, *v.i*, couver.

smooth, *a*, lisse; uni; doux; (*sea*) unie, plate. **~bore**, à canon lisse. **~-haired** (*dog*), à poil ras. **~-tongued**, mielleux, doucereux. ¶ *v.t*, lisser; polir; unir; planer; aplanir; adoucir; défroncer. **~ly**, *ad*, uniment; doucement. **~ness**, *n*, égalité; douceur, *f*.

smother, *v.t*, étouffer.

smudge, n, noirceur, f. ¶ v.t, barbouiller, mâchurer.

smug†, a, béat.

smuggle, v.t, passer en contrebande; (v.i.) faire la contrebande. ~ in, v.t, entrer en fraude. **smuggler,** n, contrebandier, ère.

smut, n, noirceur; (Agric.) nielle, f. **smutty,** a, noirci; niellé; (obscene) graveleux.

Smyrna, n, Smyrne, f.

snack, n, morceau [sur le pouce], cassecroûte, m, collation, f. to have a ~, collationner.

snag, n, (stump) chicot; (fig.) accroc, m.

snail, n, [co]limaçon; (edible) escargot, m. at a ~'s pace, à pas de tortue.

snake, n, serpent, (young) serpenteau, m. there is a ~ in the grass, le serpent est caché sous les fleurs.

snap, n, crac; cric crac!; coup sec, m; (fastening) agrafe, f, fermoir, m. ~dragon, muflier, m, gueule-de-loup, f. ~ fastener, bouton à pression, m. ~[shot], instantané, m. ¶ v.t, casser, rompre; faire claquer. ~ at, bourrer. ~ up, happer; enlever. **snapper** (whip) n, mèche, f. **snappy,** (surly) a, hargneux.

snare, n, piège; (drum) timbre, m. ~ drum, caisse claire, f. ¶ v.t, attraper.

snarl, v.i, gronder. (v.t.) s'enchevêtrer. ~ing, p.a, hargneux.

snatch (scrap) n, fragment, m, bribe, f. ¶ v.t, empoigner; enlever; arracher; dérober; (kiss) cueillir.

sneak, n, sournois, e; (Sch.) capon, ne. ~ away, s'en aller à la dérobée. a ~ing fondness for, du (ou un) faible pour.

sneer, n, rire moqueur, m. ¶ v.i, goguenarder. ~ at, railler.

sneeze, v.i, éternuer; (animals) s'ébrouer.

sniff, v.i. & t, renifler.

snigger, v.i, rire en dedans, rire en dessous.

snip, n, coup de ciseaux; bout, m. ¶ v.t, cisailler.

snipe, n, bécassine, f. ¶ v.t, canarder. **sniper,** n, tireur isolé, franc-tireur, m.

snivel, v.i, pleurnicher.

snob, n, snob, m. ~ishness, n, snobisme, m.

snooze, n, somme, m. ¶ v.i, roupiller, pioncer.

snore, v.i, ronfler.

snort, v.i, renifler, renâcler, s'ébrouer.

snout, n, museau; (pig) groin; (boar) boutoir, m.

snow, n, neige, f. oft. pl. ~ball, boule de neige, f. ~ blindness, cécité des neiges, f. ~ boots, chaussures pour la n., f.pl. ~capped, chenu. ~ drift, amas de n., m. ~drop, perce-neige, clochette d'hiver, f. ~ line, limite des neiges éternelles, f. ~ plow, chasse-neige, m. ~ shoes, raquettes à n., f.pl. ~ squall, chasse-neige, m. ~ storm, tempête de n., f. ¶ v.i, neiger. ~y, a, neigeux.

snub, n, affront, soufflet, m, nasarde, f. ~-nosed, camus, camard. ¶ v.t, rabrouer, mépriser.

snuff, n, tabac à priser, m. to take ~, prendre du tabac, priser. ~box, tabatière, f. ~ taker, priseur, euse. ¶ v.t, moucher.

snuffle, v.i, renifler, nasiller. ~s, n.pl, enchifrènement, m.

snug, a, confortable.

snuggle, v.i, se pelotonner, se blottir.

so, ad. c. & pn, ainsi; aussi; donc; si; oui; tellement; tel, telle; tant; le. ~-&-~, un tel, une telle. ~called, soi-disant, a.inv, prétendu. ~ as to, de manière à; afin de. ~ ~, comme ci, comme ça; couci-couça. ~ that, de sorte que; afin que. ~ to speak, pour ainsi dire.

soak, v.t, imbiber, [dé]tremper; (dirty linen) essanger. ~ up, absorber.

soap, n, savon, m. ~ dish, plateau à s., m. ~ maker, savonnier, m. ~stone, pierre de savon, f. ~ suds, eau de s., f. ¶ v.t, savonner. ~y, a, savonneux.

soar, v.i, pointer, planer, prendre son essor.

sob, n, sanglot, m. ~ story, drame pleureur, m. ¶ v.i, sangloter.

sober†, a, sobre; sérieux; pas en état d'ébriété. he is never ~, il ne désenivre point, il ne dessoule jamais. ¶ v.t, désenivrer, dégriser. ~ness, n, sobriété, f.

sociable†, a, sociable, liant. **social,** a, social. ~ events (news), mondanités, f.pl. ~ism, n, socialisme, m. ~ist, n. & a, socialiste, m,f. & a. **society,** n, société, association; (fashionable world) société, f, le monde, le grand monde; (*att.*) mondain. ~ *man*, *woman*, mondain, e. **sociology**, *n*, sociologie, *f*.

sock, *n*, chaussette, *f*. ¶ *v.t*, frapper.

socket, *n*, douille, *f*, manchon, *m*; (*eye*) orbite, *f*; (*tooth*) alvéole, *m*; (*lamp*) bec, *m*; (*bone*) glène, *f*. ¶ *v.t*, emboîter.

sod, *n*, gazon, *m*; plaque de gazon, motte, *f*.

soda, *n*, soude, *f*; (*washing*) cristaux de soude, *m.pl.* ~ [*water*], soda, *m*, eau de Seltz, *f*. baking ~, bicarbonate de soude, *m*.

sodden, *a*, détrempé.

sodium, *n*, sodium, *m*.

sofa, *n*, canapé, sofa, *m*.

soffit, *n*, soffite; intrados, *m*.

soft†, *a*, mou; doux; tendre; moelleux; (*fruit*) blet. ~*-boiled* (eggs), mollet. ~ *collar*, col souple, *m*. ~ *corn*, œil-de-perdrix, *m*. ~ *felt* (hat), feutre souple, feutre mou, *m*. *a* ~ *job*, un fromage. ~ *palate*, palais mou, *m*. ~ *pedal*, petite pédale, p. sourde, *f*. ~ *soap* (*fig.*), flagornerie, *f*; (*v.t.*) amadouer. ~ *solder*, soudure tendre, *f*. ~*-witted*, ramolli. ~**en**, *v.t*, [r]amollir; adoucir; attendrir. ~*ening of the brain*, ramollissement du cerveau, *m*. ~**ish**, *a*, mollet. ~**ness**, *n*, mollesse, *f*; moelleux, *m*; douceur; tendresse, *f*.

soil, *n*, sol, *m*, terre, *f*, terroir, *m*, glèbe, *f*. ¶ *v.t*, salir, souiller. ~**ed**, *p.a*, (*linen*) sale; (*shop goods*) défraîchi.

sojourn, *n*, séjour, *m*. ¶ *v.i*, séjourner.

solace, *n*, consolation, *f*. ¶ *v.t*, consoler.

solar, *a*, solaire. ~ *plexus*, plexus s., *m*.

solder & ~**ing**, *n*, soudure, *f*. ¶ *v.t*, souder. ~*ing iron*, fer à souder, *m*.

soldier, *n*, soldat, militaire, troupier, *m*. ~**y**, *n*, militaires, *m.pl*; (*unruly*) soldatesque, *f*.

sole†, *a*, seul; unique; tout; exclusif. ¶ *n*, (*foot*) plante; (*shoe*) semelle; (*hoof, plate, fish*) sole, *f*. ¶ (*shoes*) *v.t*, ressemeler.

solecism, *n*, solécisme, *m*.

solemn†, *a*, solennel; grave. ~**ity**, *n*, solennité; gravité, *f*. ~**ize**, *v.t*, solenniser; (*wedding, etc.*) célébrer.

solicit, *v.t*, solliciter, quémander; briguer. ~**ous**, *a*, désireux; inquiet; jaloux. ~**ude**, *n*, sollicitude, *f*.

solid†, *a*, solide; ferme; (*gold*) massif; plein. ~ *rock*, roc vif, *m*. ¶ *n*, solide, m. ~**ify**, *v.t*, solidifier. ~**ity**, *n*, solidité, *f*.

soliloquize, *v.i*, monologuer. **soliloquy**, *n*, soliloque, *m*.

soling, *n*, ressemelage, *m*.

solitaire (*gem, game*) *n*, solitaire, *m*. **solitary**†, *a*, solitaire; retiré. ~ *confinement*, secret, *m*. ~ *imprisonment*, réclusion, *f*. **solitude**, *n*, solitude, *f*.

solo, *n*, solo; récit, *m*. ~ *dance*, pas seul, *m*. ~**ist**, *n*, soliste, *m,f*.

solstice, *n*, solstice, *m*.

soluble, *a*, soluble. **solution**, *n*, solution; résolution; issue; dissolution, liqueur, *f*. **solve**, *v.t*, résoudre. **solvency**, *n*, solvabilité, *f*. **solvent**, *a*, dissolvant; (*Com.*) solvable. ¶ *n*, dissolvant, *m*.

somber, *a*, sombre.

some, *a*, quelque, quelques; du, de la, des; certain. ¶ *pn*, quelques-uns, -unes; certains, certaines; les uns, les unes; en. **somebody** & **someone**, *n*, quelqu'un, *m*; on, *pn*. ~ *else*, quelqu'un d'autre. *to be somebody*, être un personnage. **somehow** [or **other**], *ad*, d'une manière ou d'une autre; tant bien que mal.

somersault, *n*, culbute, *f*, (le) saut périlleux.

something, *n*, quelque chose, *m*; q. c. de; de quoi. ~ *in the wind*, quelque anguille sous roche. **sometimes**, *ad*, quelquefois; parfois; tantôt. **somewhat**, *ad*, quelque peu, un peu, tant soit peu. **somewhere**, *ad*, quelque part. ~ *else*, ailleurs, autre part. ~ *in the world*, de par le monde. ~ *to stay*, pied-à-terre, tournebride, *m*.

somnambulism, *n*, somnambulisme, *m*. **somnambulist**, *n*, somnambule, *m,f*. **somnolent**, *a*, somnolent.

son, *n*, fils; garçon, *m*. ~*-in-law*, gendre, *m*. *step~*, beau-fils, *m*.

sonata, *n*, sonate, *f*.

song, *n*, chant, *m*; chanson; romance, *f*; air; cantique; (*of birds*) chant, ramage; (*mere trifle*) morceau de pain, *m*. ~*bird*, oiseau chanteur, *m*. ~ *book*, chansonnier, *m*. ~ *thrush*, grive chanteuse, *f*. ~ *without words*, romance sans paroles. ~ *writer*, chansonnier, ère.

sonnet, *n,* sonnet, *m.*

sonorous, *a,* sonore; ronflant.

soon, *ad,* bientôt; tôt. *as ~ as,* [aus]sitôt que, dès que. *as ~ as possible,* le plus tôt possible. **~er,** *ad,* plus tôt; (*rather*) plutôt. *~ or later,* tôt ou tard. *no ~ said than done,* aussitôt dit, aussitôt fait.

soot, *n,* suie, *f.* **~y,** *a,* noir de suie.

soothe, *v.t,* adoucir, calmer. **soothing,** *a,* calmant.

soothsayer, *n,* devin, *m,* devineresse, *f.*

sop, *n,* trempette, *f;* (*fig.*) os à ronger, *m. sopping wet,* être trempé comme une soupe.

sophism, *n,* sophisme, *m.* **sophisticate,** *v.t,* sophistiquer. **~d,** *p.a,* savant. **sophistry,** *n,* sophistique, *f.*

soporific, *a. & n,* soporifique, *a. & m.*

soprano (*voice & pers.*) *n,* soprano, *m.*

sorcerer, ess, *n,* sorcier, ère, magicien, ne. **sorcery,** *n,* sorcellerie, *f.*

sordid†, *a,* sordide. **~ness,** *n,* vilenie, *f.*

sore†, *a,* douloureux, meurtri; malade; sensible; endolori; affligé; cruel. *I have a ~ finger,* j'ai mal au doigt. *~ eyes,* mal aux (*ou* d') yeux. *~ point,* endroit sensible, *m. ~ throat,* mal à la gorge. ¶ *n,* plaie, *f.*

sorrel, *n,* oseille, *f.* ¶ *a,* saure.

sorrily, *ad,* tristement. **sorrow,** *n,* chagrin, *m,* douleur, peine, *f.* ¶ *v.i,* s'affliger. **~ful,** *a,* chagrin; triste. **~fully,** *ad,* tristement. **sorry,** *a,* fâché; triste; méchant; mauvais, pauvre, piteux. *I am ~,* je regrette. *to be ~ for,* être faché de; plaindre; se repentir de. *in a ~ plight,* mal-en-point. *~! pardon!*

sort, *n,* sorte, *f,* genre, *m,* espèce, nature; manière, *f;* (*pl, Typ.*) assortiment, *m. all ~s of,* toute sorte de. ¶ *v.t,* trier; classer. **~er,** *n,* trieur, euse.

sortie, *n,* sortie, *f.*

sot, *n,* ivrogne, *m,* ivrognesse, *f.* **sottish,** *a,* abruti.

sough, *v.i,* bruire, murmurer.

sought after, recherché.

soul, *n,* âme, *f.* **~less,** *a,* sans âme.

sound†, *a,* sain; bon; solide; (*sleep*) profond. ¶ *n,* son; (*Geog.*) bras de mer, détroit,

m; (*probe*) sonde, *f.* **~[ing]** *board,* abat-voix, *m;* (*Mus.*) table d'harmonie, *f. ~ post,* âme, *f. ~proof,* insonore. ¶ *v.t,* faire sonner; sonner; sonder; pressentir; (*Med.*) ausculter; (*v.i.*) sonner, résonner. **~ness,** *n,* solidité; rectitude, *f.*

soup, *n,* potage, bouillon, *m;* soupe, purée, *f. ~ kitchen,* fourneau philanthropique, *m. ~ ladle,* cuiller à potage, louche, *f. ~ plate,* assiette creuse, *f. ~ tureen,* soupière, *f.*

sour, *a,* aigre, sur, acide, vert; (*milk, etc.*) tourné. ¶ *v.t,* aigrir, enfieller. **~ish,** *a,* aigrelet, suret. **~ly,** *ad,* aigrement. **~ness,** *n,* aigreur, acidité, *f.*

source, *n,* source, *f.*

south, *n,* sud; midi, *m.* ¶ *ad,* au sud. ¶ *a,* du sud; méridional; austral. *S~ Africa,* l'Afrique du Sud *ou* australe *ou* méridionale, *f. S~ African,* sud-africain. *S~ America,* l'Amérique du Sud, *f. S~ American,* sud-américain. *~east,* sud-est, *m. S~ Pole,* pôle sud, *m. S~ Sea Islands,* îles du Pacifique, *f.pl. ~west,* sud-ouest, *m. S~ West Africa,* le Sud-Ouest africain, *m.* **southern,** *a,* [du] sud; méridional; austral. **~er,** *n,* méridional, e. **southward[s],** *ad,* vers le sud.

souvenir, *n,* souvenir, *m.*

sou'wester (*wind, hat*) *n,* suroît, *m.*

sovereign, *a. & (pers.) n,* souverain, e; (£) souverain, *m.* **~ty,** *n,* souveraineté, *f.*

soviet, *n,* soviet, *m;* (*att.*) soviétique.

sow, *n,* truie, coche; (*wild*) laie, *f.*

sow, *v.t. & i. ir,* semer; ensemencer. **~er,** *n,* semeur, euse. **sowing,** *n,* ensemencement, *m,* semailles, *f.pl. ~ machine,* semoir, *m,* semeuse, *f. ~ time,* temps de semailles, *m,* semailles, *f.pl.*

soy[a] bean, soya, soja, pois chinois, *m.*

spa, *n,* ville d'eaux, *f,* eaux, *f.pl;* bains, *m.pl.*

space, *n,* espace; intervalle; entredeux; vide, creux; (*Mus.*) interligne, *m;* (*on printed form*) case; (*Typ.*) espace, *f. ~ between lines,* interligne, *m.* ¶ *v.t,* espacer. **spacious,** *a,* spacieux.

spade, *n,* bêche, *f;* (*pl, cards*)

pique, *m.* ¶ *v.t*, bêcher. **~ful,**
n, pelletée, *f.*
Spain, *n,* l'Espagne, *f.*
span, *n,* (*wings*) envergure; portée,
travée, ouverture, *f.* ¶ *v.t,* franchir, chevaucher.
spandrel, *n,* tympan, *m.*
spangle, *n,* paillette, *f.* **~d,** *p.p,*
pailleté.
Spaniard, *n,* Espagnol, e. **spaniel,** *n,* épagneul, e. **Spanish,** *a,*
espagnol; d'Espagne. **~** *fly,* cantharide, *f.* **~** *onion,* oignon doux
d'Espagne, *m.* ¶ *n,* l'espagnol, *m.*
spank, *v.t,* fesser. **~ing,** *n,* fessée,
f.
spar, *n,* (*Naut.*) espar; (*Miner.*)
spath, *m.* ¶ *v.i,* boxer; s'entraîner
à la boxe.
spare, *a,* maigre, sec; disponible;
libre; de rechange. **~** [*bed*]*room,*
chambre d'ami, *f.* **~** [*part*], pièce
de rechange, *f.* **~** *time,* loisir, *m.*
oft. pl, heures dérobées, *f.pl.* **~**
tire, pneu de secours, *m.* ¶ *v.t,*
épargner; ménager; accorder; se
passer de; respecter; faire grâce
de; trouver. *to have enough & to*
~, avoir à revendre. **sparing,**
p.a, économe, ménager; chiche,
avare.
spark, *n,* étincelle; flammèche, *f;*
brandon; gendarme, *m;* lueur, *f;*
(*pers.*) mirliflore, galant, *m.* **~**
plug, bougie d'allumage, *f.* **sparkle,** *v.i,* étinceler, briller, miroiter; pétiller; mousser. **sparkling,**
a, étincelant; émerillonné; (*wine*)
mousseux.
sparring, *n,* entraînement, *m.* **~**
match, assaut de démonstration,
m. **~** *partner,* partenaire d'entraînement, *m.*
sparrow, *n,* moineau, passereau,
pierrot, *m.* **~** *hawk,* épervier, *m.*
sparse, *a,* peu dense, clairsemé,
rare.
Spartan, *a. & n,* spartiate, *a. &*
m,f.
spasm, *n,* spasme, *m.* **spasmodic,**
a, saccadé; (*Med.*) spasmodique.
~ally, *ad,* par saccades, par sauts
& par bonds.
spate, *n,* grandes eaux, *f.pl,* crue,
f.
spats, *n. pl,* guêtres de ville, *f.pl.*
spatter, *v.t,* éclabousser.
spatula, *n,* spatule, *f.*
spawn, *n,* (*fish*) frai; (*mushroom*)
blanc, mycélium, *m.* ¶ *v.i,* frayer.
speak, *v.i. & t. ir,* parler; dire;
prononcer; prendre la parole;
(*ship*) héler. **~** *one's mind,* se

déboutonner. **~er,** *n,* opinant;
orateur, *m. loud*~**,** haut-parleur,
m. **speaking,** *n,* parole, *f;* parler,
m. X. **~** (*Teleph.*), ici X. *without* **~,** à la muette. *we are not
on* **~** *terms,* nous ne nous par-
lons pas.
spear, *n,* lance, *f.* **~** *head,* fer de
lance, *m.* **~***mint,* menthe verte, *f.*
¶ *v.t,* percer; darder.
special†, *a,* spécial; particulier;
extraordinaire. **~** *correspondent,*
envoyé spécial, *m.* **~** *dish for
the day,* plat du jour, *m.* **~ist,**
n, spécialiste, *m,f.* **~ity,** *n,* spécialité, *f.* **~ize in,** se spécialiser
dans.
specie, *n,* espèces, *f.pl,* numéraire,
m.
species, *n,* espèce, *f.*
specific†, *a,* spécifique; déterminé.
~ *gravity,* poids spécifique, *m.* ¶ *n,*
spécifique, *m.* **~ation,** *n,* spécification; énonciation, *f;* devis; cahier des charges, *m.* **specify,**
v.t, spécifier; énoncer; préciser.
specimen, *n,* spécimen; échantillon; modèle; exemplaire, *m.* **spe-
cious†,** *a,* spécieux.
speck, *n,* point, *m;* petite tache, *f;*
grain, *m,* particule; piqûre, *f.*
~le, *v.t,* tacheter, moucheter.
spectacle, *n,* spectacle, *m;* (*pl.*)
lunettes, *f.pl.* **~** *case,* étui à l—s,
m. **spectacular,** **~,** à [grand] spectacle. **spectator,** *n,* spectateur,
trice.
spectral, *a,* spectral. **specter,** *n,*
spectre, *m.* **spectroscope,** *n,* spectroscope, *m.* **spectrum,** *n,* spectre, *m.*
speculate, *v.i,* spéculer; jouer,
agioter. **speculation,** *n,* spéculation, *f;* jeu, *m.* **speculative,** *a,*
spéculatif; de spéculation. **speculator,** *n,* spéculateur, trice; agioteur, *m,* joueur, euse.
speech, *n,* parole, *f;* langage, *m;*
langue, *f;* parler; discours, *m,*
allocution, harangue, *f.* **~ify,**
v.i, pérorer. **~less,** *a,* sans voix,
muet.
speed, *n,* vitesse; célérité; rapidité,
f. at full **~,** à toute allure. **~-
way,** autostrade, *f.* ¶ *v.i.ir,* se hâter, faire de la vitesse. **~** *up,* activer. **speedometer,** *n,* compteur
de vitesse, *m.* **speedwell** (*Bot.*)
n, véronique, *f.* **speedy,** *a,* rapide.
spell, *n,* charme, enchantement;
sort; maléfice; tour, *m;* période,
échappée, *f.* **~bound,** fasciné.
¶ *v.t. & i. ir,* épeler; orthogra-

phier. **spelling**, *n*, orthographe; épellation, *f*. ~ *bee*, concours orthographique, *m*. ~ *book*, abécédaire, syllabaire, *m*.

spelter, *n*, zinc, *m*.

spend, *v.t. & i. ir*, dépenser; passer. ~*thrift*, *n. & att*, dépensier, ère, prodigue, *m,f. & a.* spent *bullet*, balle morte, *f*.

sperm, *n*, sperme, *m*. ~ *oil*, huile de spermaceti, *f*. ~ *whale*, cachalot, *m*. **spermaceti**, *n*, blanc de baleine, *m*. **spermatozoon**, *n*, spermatozoaire, *m*.

spew, *v.t. & i*, vomir.

sphere, *n*, sphère, *f*. **spherical**, *a*, sphérique.

sphincter, *n*, sphincter, *m*.

sphinx, *n*, sphinx, *m*.

spice, *n*, épice, *f*; (*fig.*) grain, *m*.

spick & span, tiré à quatre épingles, pimpant.

spicy, *a*, épicé, poivré.

spider, *n*, araignée, *f*. ~['s] *web*, toile d'a., *f*.

spigot, *n*, fausset, *m*.

spike, *n*, broche; cheville, *f*, crampon; (*pl, on wall*) chardon, artichaut; piquant; (*of flower*) épi, *m*. ¶*v.t*, (*gun*) enclouer.

spill (*pipe light*) *n*, fidibus, *m*. to have a ~, faire panache. ¶ *v.t.ir*, répandre, renverser; verser.

spin, *n*, tournoiement; (*ball*) effet, *m*; (*Avn.*) vrille, *f*. ¶*v.t.ir*, filer; (*top*) faire tourner, faire aller; (*v.i.*) tournoyer, toupiller. ~ *out*, délayer. ~ *yarns*, débiter des histoires.

spinach, *n*, épinard, *m*; (*Cook.*) épinards, *m.pl*.

spinal, *a*, spinal; (*column*) vertébrale. ~ *cord*, moelle épinière, *f*.

spindle, *n*, fuseau, *m*; broche, *f*; mandrin; arbre, *m*. ~ *tree*, fusain, *m*.

spindrift, *n*, embrun, *m*.

spine, *n*, (*Bot.*) épine; (*Anat.*) é. dorsale, *f*; (*of book*) dos, *m*. ~*less* (*fig.*) *a*, mollasse.

spinel, *n. & att*, spinelle, *m. & a.*

spinner, *n*, fileur, euse, filateur, trice; (*owner*) filateur, *m*; (*Fish.*) hélice, *f*.

spinney, *n*, bosquet, *m*.

spinning, *n*, filature; pêche à la [ligne] volante, *f*. ~ *mill*, filature, *f*. ~ *wheel*, rouet, *m*.

spinster, *n*, vieille fille, *f*.

spiny, *a*, épineux. ~ *lobster*, langouste, *f*.

spiral, *a*, spiral; hélicoïdal;

(*spring*) à boudin; (*stairs*) tournant. ¶ *n*, spirale, *f*.

spire, *n*, flèche; (*whorl*) spire, *f*.

spirit, *n*, esprit, *m*; âme, *f*; génie; entrain, *m*; fougue; essence, *f*; alcool, *m*; liqueur [spiritueuse] *f*, (*pl.*) spirituex, *m.pl*. ~ *lamp*, lampe à alcool, *f*. ~ *level*, niveau à bulle d'air, *m*. ~ *away*, faire disparaître comme par enchantement, escamoter. ~**ed**, *a*, vif, animé; ardent, fougueux; courageux. ~**less**, *a*, sans courage. **spiritual**†, *a*, spirituel. **spiritualism**, *n*, (*psychics*) spiritisme; (*Philos.*) spiritualisme, *m*. **spiritualist**, *n*, (*psychics*) spirite; (*Philos.*) spiritualiste, *m,f*. **spirituous**, *a*, spiritueux.

spirt, *n*, jet, *m*. ¶ *v.i*, jaillir, gicler.

spit, *n*, (*roasting*) broche; (*Geog.*) flèche littorale, *m*. ¶ *v.t*, embrocher; sonder.

spit, *v.i. & t. ir*, cracher. ¶ *n*, crachat, *m*.

spite, *n*, dépit, *m*, malveillance, rancune, pique, *f*. in ~ *of*, en dépit de, malgré. ¶ *v.t*, dépiter. ~**ful**, *a*, malicieux, malveillant, rancunier, méchant.

spitfire, *n*, rageur, euse.

spittle, *n*, salive, *f*. **spittoon**, *n*, crachoir, *m*.

Spitzbergen, *n*, le Spitzberg.

splash, *n*, (*of water*) gerbe d'eau, *f*; (*into water*) floc, *m*; (*mud*) éclaboussure; (*color*) goutte, *f*. ¶*v.t*, faire jaillir; éclabousser; (*v.i.*) gicler; (*tap*) cracher. ~ *about*, s'agiter.

splay, *v.t*, couper en sifflet, ébraser; (*dislocate*) épauler.

spleen, *n*, (*Anat.*) rate, *f*; (*dumps*) spleen; (*spite*) dépit, *m*.

splendid†, *a*, splendide, magnifique; brillant. **splendor**, *n*, splendeur, magnificence, *f*.

splice, *n*, épissure, *f*. ¶ *v.t* épisser.

splint, *n*, éclisse, attelle, *f*. ~ [*bone*], péroné, *m*.

splinter, *n*, éclat, *m*, écharde; (*bone*) esquille, *f*. ¶*v.t*, faire éclater; (*v.i.*) éclater.

split, *n*, fente; fêlure; (*fig.*) scission, *f*. to do the ~, faire le grand écart. ¶*v.t.ir*, fendre; refendre; fractionner; (*ears with noise*) déchirer; (*v.i.*) se fendre, éclater; crever. ~ *hairs*, fendre un cheveu en quatre, pointiller. ~ *peas*, pois cassés, *m.pl*. ~ *the atom*, désintégrer l'atome. *split-*

ting headache, mal de tête affreux, *m.*

splutter, *n,* pétarade, *f.* ¶ *v.i,* pétarader; bredouiller.

spoil, *n,* dépouille, *f,* butin, gâteau, *m.* ¶ *v.t,* gâter, gâcher, abîmer; corrompre. ~*sport,* trouble-fête, *m.*

spoke, *n,* rayon, *m.* ¶ *v.t,* enrayer.

spokesman, *n,* porte-parole, *m.*

spoliation, *n,* spoliation, *f.*

sponge, *n,* éponge, *f.* ~ *cake,* biscuit de Savoie, *m.* ~ *cloth,* tissu éponge, *m.* ¶ *v.t,* éponger. **sponger,** *n,* pique-assiette, *m.* **spongy,** *a,* spongieux.

sponsor, *n,* répondant, e; (*Eccl.*) parrain, *m,* marraine, *f.*

spontaneous†, *a,* spontané.

spook, *n,* fantôme, spectre, *m.*

spool, *n,* bobine, *f;* rouleau, *m.* ¶ *v.t,* bobiner.

spoon, *n,* cuiller, cuillère, *f.* ~*bill,* spatule, *f.* ~*ful,* cuillerée, *f.*

spoonerism, *n,* contre-petterie, *f.*

spoor, *n,* trace, *f,* erres, *f.pl.*

sporadic, *a,* sporadique.

spore, *n,* spore, *f.*

sport, *n,* jeu; (*s. & pl.*) sport, *m.* ~*s editor,* rédacteur sportif, *m.* ~*s ground,* terrain de jeux, *m.* **sportsman,** *n,* sportif, amateur de sports, *m.*

spot, *n,* tache; macule; piqûre, *f;* goutte; place, *f,* endroit, site, lieu, *m,* lieux, *m.pl;* (*Bil.*) mouche, *f;* (*Com.*) disponible, comptant, *m. on the* ~, sur [la] place; séance tenante. ~*light,* projecteur orientable, *m. weak* ~, point faible, *m.* ¶ *v.t,* tacher; observer, repérer. **spotted,** *p.p,* tacheté, moucheté. **spotless,** *a,* sans tache.

spouse, *n,* époux, *m,* épouse, *f.*

spout, *n,* goulotte, *f;* bec; jet, *m.* ¶ *v.i. & t,* jaillir; déclamer, dégoiser.

sprain, *n,* entorse, foulure, *f. to* ~ *one's . . . ,* se fouler le, la *. . .*

sprat, *n,* sprat, *m.*

sprawl, *v.i,* s'étaler, se vautrer.

spray, *n,* poussière [d'eau], gerbe [d'eau] *f;* (*sea*) embrun; (*jewels*) épi, *m;* (*flowers*) gerbe, chute; (*Need.*) chute, *f;* (*squirt*) vaporisateur, *m.* ¶ *v.t,* pulvériser, vaporiser.

spread, *n,* développement, *m;* envergure; ouverture; propagation, *f;* (*food*) repas, *m.* ¶ *v.t.ir,* [é]tendre; déployer; répandre, se

mer; propager; échelonner, répartir, étager.

spree, *n,* noce, bamboche, *f.*

sprig, *n,* brin, *m,* brindille; pointe, *f.*

sprightly, *a,* vif, sémillant, éveillé; gai.

spring, *n,* élan, bond; ressort, *m;* élasticité; source, fontaine; (*arch*) naissance, retombée, *f;* (*season*) printemps, *m;* (*att.*) printanier. ~*board,* tremplin, *m.* ~ *cleaning,* grand nettoyage, *m.* ~ *tide,* grande marée, vive-eau, maline, *f.* ¶ *v.i.ir,* s'élancer, bondir; sourdre; dériver. ~ *up,* naître. ~*y,* *a,* élastique.

sprinkle, *v.t,* répandre; arroser; asperger; saupoudrer; (*book edges*) jasper. **sprinkler,** *n,* arrosoir, *m.*

sprint, *n,* course de vitesse, *f.* ~*er,* *n,* coureur de vitesse, *m.*

sprite, *n,* [esprit] follet, farfadet, *m.*

sprocket wheel, pignon de chaîne, *m.*

sprout, *n,* pousse, *f,* germe, *m. Brussels* ~*s,* choux de Bruxelles, *m.pl.* ¶ *v.i,* pointer, germer.

spruce, *a,* pimpant, bien mis. ¶ *n,* sapin, *m.*

sprue, *n,* jet [de coulée] *m.*

sprung (*provided with springs*) *p.a,* à ressorts.

spur, *n,* éperon; (*bird*) ergot; (*mountain*) contrefort; (*Build.*) arc-boutant; (*fig.*) aiguillon, *m. on the* ~ *of the moment,* sous l'impulsion du moment. *railway* ~, embranchement, *m.* ¶ *v.t,* éperonner, talonner, piquer; aiguillonner.

spurious, *a,* faux, falsifié, contrefait, illégitime.

spurn, *v.t,* repousser, repousser du pied.

spurt, *v.i,* jaillir, gicler; (*price*) bondir, sauter. ¶ *n,* jet; bond, saut; (*running*) emballage; (*rowing*) enlevage, *m.*

sputter, *n,* pétarade, *f.* ¶ *v.i,* pétarader; bredouiller.

spy, *n,* espion, ne; (*police*) mouchard, *m.* ~*glass,* longue-vue, *f.* ¶ *v.t. & i,* espionner; moucharder; épier.

squab, *n,* pigeonneau, *m.*

squabble, *n,* querelle, *f.* ¶ *v.i,* se chamailler.

squad, *n,* escouade; brigade, *f;* peloton, *m.* **squadron,** *n,* (*cav-*

alry) escadron, *m*; (*navy*) escadre; (*air*) escadrille, *f*.

squalid, *a*, crasseux, sordide.

squall, *n*, grain, *m*, rafale, bourrasque, *f*. ¶ *v.i*, brailler. ~**y**, à grains, à rafales.

squalor, *n*, crasse, *f*.

squander, *v.t*, prodiguer, gaspiller, manger.

square, *a*, carré. ~ *foot*, pied carré, *m*. ~ *inch*, pouce carré, *m*. ~ *meal*, ample repas, *m*. ~ *measure*, mesure de surface, *f*. ~ *mile*, mille carré, *m*. ~ *root*, racine carrée, *f*. ~*-shouldered*, carré des épaules. ~ *yard*, yard carré, *m*. ¶ *n*, carré, *m*; (*instrument & at right angles*) équerre; (*town*) place, *f*; (*parvis*) parvis, *m*; (*chessboard*) case, *f*. ¶ *v.t*, carrer; équarrir; régler. ~**[ly]**, *ad*, carrément.

squash, *v.t*, écraser, écarbouiller; aplatir. ¶ *n*, courge, courgette, *f*.

squat, *v.i*, s'accroupir; se blottir, se tapir. ¶ *a*, ragot, boulot, tassé, écrasé.

squawk, *n*, cri rauque, *m*.

squeak, *n*, cri, *m*. ¶ *v.i*, crier, piailler.

squeal, *n*, cri [perçant] *m*. ¶ *v.i*, crier, piailler.

squeamish, *a*, dégoûté.

squeegee, *n*, racloir, *m*.

squeeze, *n*, compression, *f*; serrement, *m*. ¶ *v.t*, presser; serrer; pincer. ~ *out*, exprimer; (*fig.*) arracher de.

squelch, *v.i*, déconcerter; (*revolt*) étouffer.

squib, *n*, serpenteau, *m*; (*fig.*) pasquinade, *f*.

squid, *n*, calmar, *m*.

squint, *v.i*, loucher.

squirm, *v.i*, se tortiller.

squirrel, *n*, écureuil, *m*.

squirt, *n*, seringue, *f*. ¶ *v.t*, seringuer; (*v.i.*) jaillir.

stab, *n*, coup (de poignard) *m*. ¶ *v.t*, percer; poignarder.

stability, *n*, stabilité; consistance, *f*. **stabilize,** *v.t*, rendre stable; (*Fin.*) stabiliser. **stable,** *a*, stable. ¶ *n*, écurie; cavalerie, *f*. ¶ *v.t*, loger; établer.

staccato, *a*, (*note*) piquée; (*voice*) saccadée.

stack, *n*, (*Agric.*) meule; (*heap*) pile, *f*; (*arms*) faisceau, *m*; (*chimney*) souche, *f*. ¶ *v.t*, empiler; mettre en meule.

stadium, *n*, stade, *m*.

staff, *n*, bâton, *m*; (*pilgrim's*) bour-

don, *m*; (*Mus.*) portée, *f*; personnel; atelier; (*Mil.*) État-major, *m*. ~ *officer*, officier d'É.-m., *m*.

stag, *n*, cerf, (*young*) hère, *m*. ~ *beetle*, cerf-volant, *m*.

stage, *n*, estrade, *f*; échafaud, *m*; scène, *f*; théâtre, *m*; tréteaux, *m.pl*; platine, *f*; degré; stade, *m*, période, *f*. & *m*; phase; opération, *f*; relais, *m*; étape, traite; section, *f*; ~*coach,* diligence, *f*; coche, *m*. ~ *effect*, effet scénique, artifice de théâtre, *m*. ~ *manager*, régisseur, *m*. ~ *name*, nom de théâtre, *m*. ~ *trick*, jeu de scène, coup de théâtre, *m*. ~ *whisper*, aparté, *m*. ¶ *v.t*, mettre en scène, monter.

stagger, *v.i*, chanceler, tituber; (*v.t.*) consterner, ébouriffer.

stagnant, *a*, stagnant; (*foul*) croupissant. **stagnation,** *n*, stagnation, *f*, marasme, *m*.

staid, *a*, posé, rassis.

stain, *n*, tache; macule; souillure; couleur, *f*. ¶ *v.t*, tacher, souiller; colorer; mettre en couleur, teindre. *stained glass*, verre coloré, *m*; (*church*) vitraux peints, *m. pl*. *stained-glass artist*, peintre verrier, *m*. *stained-glass window*, verrière, *f*. **stainless,** *a*, sans tache; (*steel*) inoxydable.

stair, *n*, marche, *f*, degré, *m*. ~ *carpet*, tapis d'escalier, *m*.~*case* & ~[*s*], escalier, *m*. ~ *rail*, rampe d'e., *f*.

stake, *n*, pieu, poteau, piquet, jalon; bûcher; intérêt; enjeu, *m*; mise, *f*; (*pl*, *turf*) prix, *m*. ¶ *v.t*, (*bet*) parier; garnir de pieux; (*measure*) jalonner. ~ *one's reputation*, jouer sa réputation.

stalactite, *n*, stalactite, *f*.

stalagmite, *n*, stalagmite, *f*.

stale, *a*, (*bread*) rassis; défraîchi; (*liquor*) éventé; vieilli.

stalemate (*chess*) *n*, pat, *m*. ¶ *v.t*, faire pat. ~**d,** *p.a*, pat.

stalk, *n*, tige, queue, *f*; pied, *m*. ¶ *v.t*, chasser à l'affût.

stall, *n*, stalle; chaise, *f*; kiosque; étalage, étal, *m*, échope, boutique, *f*. ¶ *v.t*, établer; (*motor*) caler.

stallion, *n*, étalon, *m*.

stalwart, *a*, robuste, vigoureux.

stamina, *n*, résistance, *f*, fond, *m*.

stammer, *v.i. & t*, bégayer. ~**er,** *n*, bègue, *m,f*.

stamp, *n*, poinçon; coin; pilon; bocard, *m*; marque; estampille, *f*; (*postage, etc.*) timbre, *m*; griffe; trempe, empreinte, *f*, cachet, sceau, *m*. ¶ *v.t.* & *i*, frapper; piétiner, taper, trépigner; poinçonner; bocarder; marquer; étamper; estamper; estampiller; timbrer; affranchir. ~*ed addressed envelope*, enveloppe affranchie pour la réponse, *f*.

stampede, *n*, sauve-qui-peut, *m*.

stance, *n*, position, *f*.

stanch, *v.t*, étancher.

stanchion, *n*, étançon, *m*; (*ship*) épontille, *f*.

stand, *n*, place; station, *f*; support; établi; pied; socle; affût; (*music*) lutrin; (*exhibition*) stand, *m*; (*stall*) étalage, *m*. ~*point*, point de vue, *m*. ~*still*, arrêt, *m*. ¶ *v.i.ir*, se tenir; se tenir debout; rester debout; se soutenir; stationner; se placer; se mettre; s'arrêter; se porter; tenir; durer; rester; reposer; (*v.t.ir.*) supporter, soutenir; subir; résister à; souffrir; (*drink*) payer. ~ *aside*, se ranger. ~ *back!* rangez-vous! ~ *fast*, tenir bon. ~ *in the way of*, faire obstacle à. ~ *on end* (hair), [se] hérisser. ~ *out*, [res]-sortir, se détacher, marquer. ~ *up*, se tenir debout; se lever; se dresser.

standard, *n*, étendard; (*values*) étalon, *m*; (*weight, measure*) matrice, *f*; (*gold*) titre, *m*; (*of coin*) loi, *f*; critère, criterium; niveau, *m*; toise; classe, *f*; pied; arbre de plein vent; (*vaulting*) sautoir, *m*. ~ *bearer*, porte-étendard, *m*. ¶ *att*, étalon; type; classique; (*gauge*) normale; (*edition*) définitive; (*charge*) forfaitaire; (*gold*) au titre; (*solution*) titrée. ~*ize*, *v.t*, standardiser; unifier; (*Chem.*) titrer.

standing, *n*, place, pose, *f*; rang, *m*. *of long* ~, de longue date, ancien. ¶*a*, debout; (*crops*) sur pied; (*Naut.*) dormant; (*water*) stagnante; (*orders*) permanent, e; (*expenses*) généraux; (*jump, dive*) sans élan; (*start*) arrêté. ~ *room only!* places debout seulement! ~ *type*, conservation, *f*.

standoffish, *a*, distant, réservé. ~*ness*, *n*, quant-à-moi, quant-à-soi, *m*.

stanza, *n*, stance, strophe, *f*.

staple, *n*, (*wall*) crampon; (*wire*) cavalier, *m*; (*lock*) gâche; (*to fasten papers*) agrafe, *f*. ~ [*product*], produit principal, *m*, pro-

duction principale, *f*. ~*s*, articles de première nécessité, *m.pl*.

star, *n*, étoile, *f*; astre, *m*; (*lucky*) étoile, planète; (*Theat.*) étoile, vedette, *f*; (*Typ.*) astérisque, *m*. ~*fish*, étoile de mer, *f*. ~*gaze*, bayer aux corneilles.

starboard, *n*, tribord, *m*.

starch, *n*, amidon, *m*; fécule, *f*; (*paste*) empois, *m*. ¶ *v.t*, empeser, amidonner. ~*y* (*food*) *a*, féculent.

stare, *n*, regard appuyé, *m*. ¶ *v.i*, écarquiller les yeux. ~ *at*, regarder fixement, dévisager.

stark, *a*, raide. ~ *mad*, fou à lier. ~ *naked*, tout nu, nu comme un ver.

starling (*bird*) *n*, sansonnet, étourneau, *m*.

starry, *a*, étoilé.

start, *n*, tressaillement, sursaut, soubresaut, haut-le-corps; commencement, début; départ, *m*; avance, *f*. ¶ *v.i*, tressaillir; partir; commencer; débuter; démarrer; (*v.t.*) commencer; amorcer; mettre en marche; lancer; (*quarry*) lancer, débûcher. ~ *out*, se mettre en route. ~*er*, *n*, (*auto*) démarreur; (*signal giver*) starter; (*horse, runner*) partant, *m*. ~*ing line*, ligne de départ, *f*. ~*ing post*, poteau de départ, *m*, barrière, *f*.

startle, *v.t*, faire tressaillir, effrayer, effaroucher, alarmer. **startling**, *p.a*, alarmant; saisissant.

starvation, *n*, inanition, faim, famine, *f*. ~ *diet*, diète absolue, *f*. ~ *wage*, salaire de famine, *m*. **starve**, *v.t*, priver de nourriture, affamer; (*v.i.*) mourir de faim. ~*ling*, *n*, affamé, e, meurt-de-faim, *m*. **starving**, *p.a*, affamé.

state, *n*, état, *m*; disposition, *f*; apparat; (*stage of engraved or etched plate*) état, *m*. *to lie in* ~ (of body), être exposé sur un lit de parade. ~ *controlled*, ~ *managed*, en régie. ~*room*, cabine, *f*. S~ *socialism*, étatisme, *m*. ¶ *v.t*, énoncer; déclarer; relater; annoncer; poser. ~*liness*, *n*, majesté, *f*. ~*ly*, *a*, majestueux, pompeux, superbe; fier. ~*ment*, *n*, énoncé, *m*, déclaration, *f*; relevé, état, exposé; bordereau, *m*. **statesman**, *n*, homme d'État, *m*.

static(al), *a*. & **statics**, *n*, statique, *a*. & *f*. *radio static*, perturbation atmosphérique, *f*.

station, *n*, station, *f*, poste, *m*;

gare, *f*; rang, *m.* *police* ~, poste de police, *m.* ~*s of the Cross*, chemin de la croix, *m.* ~ *master*, chef de gare, *m.* ¶ *v.t,* [a]poster. ~ary, *a,* stationnaire; fixe, à demeure.

stationer, *n,* papetier, ère. ~y, *n,* papeterie, *f*; papier à lettres, *m.*

statistic(al), *a,* statistique. **statician,** *n,* statisticien, *m.* **statistics,** *n,* statistique, *f*; mouvement, *m.*

statuary, *a,* statuaire. ¶ *n,* statues, *f.pl*; (*art*) statuaire, *f*; (*pers.*) statuaire, *m.* **statue,** *n,* statue, *f.* **statuette,** *n,* statuette, figurine, *f.*

stature, *n,* stature, taille, *f.*

status, *n,* statut, titre, état, *m,* qualité, *f.*

statute, *n,* loi, *f*; statut, *m.* ~ *book,* code, *m.* **statutory,** *a,* légal.

staunch, *a,* étanche; ferme; dévoué.

stave, *n,* douve; (*Mus.*) portée, *f.* ~ *in, v.t.ir,* enfoncer, défoncer. ~ *off,* parer.

stay, *n,* séjour; support; étai; tirant; hauban; (*pl.*) corset; (*law*) sursis, *m.* ~ *in the country,* villégiature, *f.* ¶ *v.i,* rester; demeurer; séjourner; attendre; s'arrêter; (*v.t.*) suspendre; (*law*) surseoir à; étayer. ~*-at-home,* *a. & n,* casanier, ère, pot-au-feu, *a.* ~ *away,* s'absenter. ~ *up,* veiller.

stead, *n,* lieu, *m,* place, *f.*

steadfast, *a,* constant, ferme. ~ly, *ad,* avec constance. ~ness, *n,* constance, *f.*

steady, *a,* ferme; stable; rangé; posé; réglé; suivi. ¶ *i,* ferme! ¶ *v.t,* fixer, affermir.

steak, *n,* tranche, *f*; (*beef*) bifteck, *m,* entrecôte, *f.*

steal, *v.t. & i. ir,* voler, dérober. ~ *away,* se dérober. ~ *in,* se glisser dans. ~ing, *n,* vol, *m.* **by stealth,** à la dérobée. **stealthy†,** *a,* furtif.

steam, *n,* vapeur; fumée; buée, *f*; (*att.*) à vapeur. ~ *room* (bath), étuve humide, *f.* ¶ *v.t,* (*Cook.*) mettre à l'étuvée; (*v.i.*) marcher [à la vapeur]; fumer. ~**er** *or* ~*boat or* ~*ship, n,* vapeur, *m,* bateau à v., navire à v., steamer, *m.* ~**ing** (*Cook.*) *n,* étuvée, étouffée, estouffade, *f.*

steed, *n,* coursier, *m.*

steel, *n,* acier, *m*; (*of tinder box*)

briquet; (*sharpener*) fusil, *m*; (*corset*) baleine, *f*; (*att.*) d'acier, en acier; métallique. ~**works,** aciérie, *f.* ¶ *v.t,* acérer; aciérer; (*fig.*) cuirasser.

steep, *a,* raide, escarpé, ardu, fort, rapide. ¶ *v.t,* tremper, baigner. ~*ed in* (*fig.*), pétri de. **steeple,** *n,* clocher [pointu] *m.* ~*chase,* course d'obstacles, *f.* **steepness,** *n,* raideur, *f*; escarpement, *m.*

steer, *n,* bouvillon, *m.* ¶ *v.t. & i,* diriger, conduire, guider; gouverner. ~ *clear of,* éviter. **steerage,** *n,* avant, *m.* ~ *passenger,* passager de l'a., *p.* d'entrepont, *m.* **steering,** *n,* direction; (*Naut.*) gouverne, *f.* ~ *compass,* compas de route, *m.* ~ *wheel* (auto) volant, *m.*

stellar, *a,* stellaire.

stem, *n,* tige; queue, *f*; (*ship*) étrave, *f*; (*Gram.*) thème, *m.* ~ *stitch,* point de tige, p. coulé, *m.* ¶ *v.t,* arrêter, refouler.

stench, *n,* puanteur, infection, *f.*

stencil, *n,* patron, pochoir; caractère à jour; (*typing*) stencil, *m.* ¶ *v.t,* patronner.

stenographer, *n,* sténographe, *m,f.* **stenography,** *n,* sténographie, *f.*

stentorian, *a,* de stentor.

step, *n,* pas, *m*; trotte; marche, *f,* degré; gradin; échelon, *m*; démarche; mesure; cadence, *f*; acheminement; (*pl.*) marchepied, *m,* échelle double, *f.* ~*brother,* demi-frère, *m.* ~*daughter,* belle-fille, *f.* ~*father,* beau-père, *m.* ~*ladder,* échelle double, *f.* ~*mother,* belle-mère; (*cruel*) marâtre, *f.* ~*sister,* demi-sœur, *f.* ~*son,* beau-fils, *m. to take* ~*s,* prendre des mesures. ¶ *v.i,* faire un pas; marcher; aller; venir; monter. ~ *in,* entrer. **stepping stone,** pierre à gué, *f*; (*fig.*) marchepied, échelon, *m.*

stereoscope, *n,* stéréoscope, *m.*

stereotype, *n,* cliché, *m.* ¶ *v.t,* clicher, stéréotyper.

sterile, *a,* stérile. **sterility,** *n,* stérilité, *f.* **sterilize,** *v.t,* stériliser.

sterling, *a,* (*Eng. money*) sterling, *a.inv.*; (*fig.*) de bon aloi; solide. ¶ *n,* la livre.

stern†, *a,* sévère; austère. ¶ *n,* arrière, *m*; poupe, *f.* ~*post,* étambot, *m.* **sternness,** *n,* sévérité; austérité, *f.*

sternum, *n,* sternum, *m.*

stet (*Typ.*), bon. ¶ *v.t*, donner son bon à.

stethoscope, *n*, stéthoscope, *m*.

stevedore, *n*, déchargeur, débardeur, arrimeur, *m*.

stew, *n*, ragoût, *m*. ~pan, casserole, braisière, *f*, fait-tout, *m*. ¶ *v.t*, étuver; (*abs.*) fricoter. stewed fruit, compote de fruits, *f*.

steward, *n*, maître d'hôtel; intendant; régisseur; commissaire; économe; garçon de cabine; commis aux vivres; délégué, *m*. ~'s mate (ship), cambusier, *m*. ~'s room, dépense; (*ship*) cambuse, *f*.

stick, *n*, bâton, *m*; canne, *f*; (*umbrella*) manche, *m*; baguette, *f*; cotret, *m*, (*pl.*) du bois. ¶ *v.t.ir*, piquer; ficher; coller; (*Hort.*) ramer; (*pig*) saigner; (*v.i.ir.*) s'attacher; [se] coller, adhérer; rester, tenir. ~ *in the mud*, s'embourber. stickiness, *n*, viscosité, *f*.

stickleback, *n*, épinoche, *f*.

sticky, *a*, collant, gluant, visqueux.

stiff, *a*, raide; fort; rigide; tenace; (*strained*) empesé, guindé; (*price*) salé. ~ collar, faux col rigide, *m*. ~ neck, torticolis, *m*. ~en, *v.t*, raidir. ~ness, *n*, raideur; (*in the joints of the body*) courbature, *f*.

stifle, *v.t*, étouffer, suffoquer.

stigma, *n*, stigmate, *m*, flétrissure, tache, *f*. stigmatize, *v.t*, stigmatiser.

stile, *n*, échalier; (*door*) montant, *m*.

stiletto, *n*, stylet, *m*.

still, *a*, calme, tranquille; silencieux; immobile, en repos; (*water*) dormante, morte; (*wine*) non mousseux; (*lemonade*) non gazeuse. ~born, mort-né. ~ life (*art*), nature morte, *f*. ¶ *ad*, encore, toujours; cependant, néanmoins, toutefois. ¶ *n*, calme; alambic, *m*, cornue, *f*. ¶ *v.t*, calmer, apaiser, tranquilliser. ~ness, *n*, calme, *m*, tranquillité, *f*, silence, *m*.

stilt, *n*, échasse, *f*. ~ed, *a*, guindé.

stimulant, *n*, stimulant, remontant, réconfort, *m*. stimulate, *v.t*, stimuler. stimulus, *n*, stimulant, aiguillon, *m*.

sting, *n*, aiguillon, dard, *m*, piqûre; (*fig.*) morsure, *f*. ¶ *v.t*. & *i*. *ir*, piquer; (*of conscience*) bourreler. stinging, *p.a*, piquant.

~ nettle, ortie brûlante, ortie grièche, *f*.

stingy, *a*, avare, pingre, mesquin, chiche.

stink, *n*, puanteur, *f*. ¶ *v.i.ir*, puer.

stint, *v.t*, épargner; rationner. ~ oneself, se priver; se rationner. without ~, sans réserve.

stipend, *n*, traitement, *m*.

stipple, *n*, pointillé, grené, *m*. ¶ *v.t*, pointiller.

stipulate, *v.t*, stipuler.

stir, *n*, remue-ménage, tapage; mouvement, *m*. make a ~, faire florès. ¶ *v.t*, remuer; agiter; (*fire*) attiser; (*the blood*) fouetter; (*v.i.*) remuer, bouger. ~ up, exciter, susciter, émouvoir. stirring, *p.a*, émouvant; vibrant.

stirrup, *n*, étrier, *m*. ~ cup, coup de l'étrier, *m*. ~ leather, étrivière, *f*.

stitch, *n*, point [de couture] *m*; (*Knit., crochet*) maille, *f*. ~ in the side (*Med.*), point de côté. ¶ *v.t*, coudre; (*leather*) piquer; (*books*) brocher. ~ together, appointer. ~ed hem, ourlet piqué, *m*. ~er, *n*, piqueuse, *f*. ~ing, *n*, point piqué, *m*.

stoat, *n*, hermine, *f*.

stock, *n*, (*descent*) race, lignée; (*tree, etc.*) souche, *f*; estoc; (*rifle, plane*) fût, bois, *m*; (*Hort.*) sujet, porte-greffe, (*wild*) sauvageon; (*vine*) cep, *m*; (*flower*) giroflée, *f*, violier, *m*; (*Com.*) stock, *m*, provision; approvisionnement; matériel, *m*; (*Fin.*) valeur, *f*. oft. pl, titre, *m*. oft. pl; effets, fonds, *m.pl*; actions, *f.pl*; (*Cook.*) consommé, *m*; (*pl*, *Naut.*) chantier, *m*, cale [de construction] *f*; (*pl*, *Hist.*) ceps, *m.pl*, tabouret, *m*. in ~, en magasin. ~s & shares, valeurs mobilières, *f.pl*. ~broker, agent de change; banquier en valeurs, *m*. ~ exchange, bourse [des valeurs] *f*. ~fish, stockfisch, *m*. ~holder, détenteur de titres, *m*; actionnaire, sociétaire, *m,f*; rentier, ère. ~ *in trade*, existence en magasin. ~ phrase, cliché, *m*. ~ pot, pot-au-feu, *m*. ~ solution (*Phot.*), solution fondamentale, *f*. ~-still, sans mouvement. ~ taking, inventaire; recensement, *m*. ~ yard, (*cattle*) parc à bestiaux; (*materials*) parc à matières, *m*. ¶ *v.t*, approvisionner; assortir; tenir; peupler; meubler; empoissonner.

stockade, *n,* palissade, palanque, *f.*
stocking, *n,* bas, *m.*
stocky, *a,* trapu, ramassé, étoffé.
Stoic, *n.* & *att,* stoïcien, *m.* & *a.*
stoical†, *a,* stoïque. **stoicism,** *n,*
stoïcisme, *m.*
stoke, *v.t,* chauffer. **~hole, ~hold,**
chaufferie, chambre de chauffe,
f. **stoker,** *n,* chauffeur; (*mechanical*) chargeur, *m.*
stole, *n,* étole; écharpe, *f.*
stolid, *a,* flegmatique. **~ity,** *n,*
flegme, *m.*
stomach, *n,* estomac; (*fig.*) cœur,
m. **~ ache,** mal d'estomac, *m.*
~ pump, pompe stomacale, *f.*
¶ *v.t,* digérer, avaler.
stone, *n,* pierre; roche, *f;* caillou;
(*fruit*) noyau; (*grape*) pépin, *m.*
grind~; meule, *f.* **~ dead,** raide
mort. **~ (gem) setter,** metteur
en œuvre, *m.* **~'s throw,** jet de
pierre, *m.* **~ware,** poterie de grès,
f, grès, *m,* gresserie, *f.* **~work,**
maçonnerie, *f.* ¶ *v.t,* (*to death*)
lapider. **stony,** *a,* pierreux;
cailloux; (*heart*) de pierre, de
roche[r]; (*look*) glacé.
stool, *n,* tabouret; escabeau, *m;*
sellette; (*Med.*) selle, *f.*
stoop, *v.i,* se pencher; s'abaisser.
stop, *n,* arrêt, *m;* halte; station;
pause; opposition, *f;* (*buffer*)
butoir, *m;* (*Mech.*) butée, *f;* (*organ*) jeu; (*Phot.*) diaphragme;
(*Typ.*) point, *m.* **to put a ~ to,**
faire cesser. **~cock,** robinet
[d'arrêt] *m.* **~gap,** bouche-trou,
m. **~watch,** chronographe; compteur de sport, *m.* ¶ *v.t,* arrêter;
(*Naut.*) stopper; interrompre;
suspendre; mettre opposition sur;
cesser; (*wages*) retenir; (*leak*)
boucher, aveugler; (*v.i.*) s'arrêter; stationner; rester; cesser.
~ up, boucher. ¶ *i,* halte[-là]!;
(*Naut., in telegrams*) stop.
stope (*Min.*) *n,* gradin, *m.*
stoppage, *n,* arrêt; chômage, *m;*
retenue; obstruction, *f.* **stopper,**
n, bouchon, *m.* ¶ *v.t,* boucher.
storage, *n,* [em]magasinage, *m.*
store, *n,* approvisionnement, *m,*
provision, fourniture; réserve;
resserre, boutique, *f,* magasin,
dépôt; entrepôt; économat, *m.*
department **~,** magasin de nouveautés, bazar, *m.* **~keeper,**
boutiquier, *m.* ¶ *v.t,* approvisionner; (*fig.*) meubler; emmagasiner; mettre en dépôt. **~
up,** accumuler.
stork, *n,* cigogne, *f.*

storm, *n,* orage, *m;* tempête, tourmente, *f.* **~ cloud,** nuée, *f.* **~ of
abuse,** algarade, *f.* ¶ *v.t,* donner
l'assaut à; (*v.i.*) tempêter. **stormy,**
a, orageux, tempétueux. *at* **~**
(*barometer*), à la tempête.
story, *n,* histoire, *f;* conte, *m;* narration; fable; menterie, *f;* (*floor*)
étage, *m.* **~ book,** livre de
contes, *m.* **~ teller,** conteur,
euse; narrateur, trice.
stout†, *a,* fort, vigoureux; robuste;
renforcé; brave; gros, corpulent,
replet. ¶ (*beer*) *n,* stout, *m.*
~ness (*of body*) *n,* embonpoint,
m.
stove, *n,* poêle; fourneau; réchaud,
m; étuve, *f.*
stow (*Naut.*) *v.t,* arrimer. **~ away**
v.t, serrer; (*v.i.*) s'embarquer
clandestinement. **~away,** *n,* passager (ère) clandestin(e), *m.*
straddle, *v.t.* & *i,* chevaucher.
strafe, *v.t,* mitrailler.
straggle, *v.i,* traîner. **straggler,** *n,*
traînard, *m.* **straggling,** *a,*
(*houses*) éparses; (*village*) aux
maisons éparses; (*beard*) maigre.
straight, *a,* droit; (*hair*) plats;
(*respectable*) honnête. *go* **~
ahead,** allez tout droit. ¶ *ad,*
[tout] droit; directement. ¶ *n,*
ligne droite, *f.* **~en,** *v.t,* [re]-
dresser, rectifier. **straightforward,**
a, droit. **straightforwardly,** *ad,*
sans détour; carrément. **straightforwardness,** *n,* droiture, *f;* sans-
façon, *m.* **straightness,** *n,* rectitude, *f.*
strain, *n,* (*molecular*) tension;
(*Mech.*) déformation; (*overstrain*) fatigue, *f;* (*Med.*) effort;
(*Vet.*) écart, *m;* (*descent*) race;
(*dash*) teinte, *f;* (*pl.*) accents,
m.pl. **~ in the back,** tour de
reins, *m.* ¶ *v.t,* tendre; déformer;
fatiguer; torturer; (*Med.*) fouler;
(*filter*) passer, filtrer, tamiser.
~ed (*fig.*) *p.a,* guindé. **~er,** *n,*
passoire, couloire, *f,* tamis, *m;*
crépine, *f.*
strait, *n,* (*s.* & *pl.*) détroit, pertuis, *m;* (*pl.*) gêne, détresse, *f,*
malaise, embarras, *m.* **S~s of
Dover,** [détroit du] Pas de Calais,
m. **S~s of Gibraltar,** détroit de
Gibraltar. **straitjacket,** *n,* camisole de force, *f.* **straitlaced,** *a,*
collet monté, bégueule. **in straitened circumstances,** dans la gêne.
strand, *n,* rivage; (*rope*) cordon,
toron, brin, *m.* ¶ *v.t.* & *i,* échouer;
jeter à la côte.

strange†, *a*, étrange; étranger; bizarre. **stranger**, *n*, étranger, ère; inconnu, e. **strangeness**, *n*, étrangeté; bizarrerie, *f*.

strangle, *v.t*, étrangler, juguler. **~s** (*Vet.*) *n.pl*, gourme, *f*. **strangulation**, *n*, étranglement, *m*, strangulation, *f*.

strap, *n*, courroie; sangle; bande, *f*; bracelet; tirant; lien, *m*. ¶*v.t*, sangler.

stratagem, *n*, stratagème, *m*, ruse, *f*. **strategic(al)†**, *a*, stratégique. **strategist**, *n*, stratège, *m*. **strategy**, *n*, stratégie, *f*.

stratified, *p.p*, stratifié. **stratum**, *n*, couche, *f*, gisement, *m*.

straw, *n*, paille, *f*; fétu; (*drinking*) chalumeau; (*fig.*) fétu, *m*. the last **~**, le comble [de nos maux]. **~board**, carton-paille, *m*. **~ hat**, chapeau de paille, *m*. **~ hut** (*native*), paillote, *f*. **~ mattress**, paillasse, *f*.

strawberry, *n*, fraise, *f*. **~ plant**, fraisier, *m*.

stray, *v.i*, errer; s'écarter. ¶*a*, égaré; errant; épave. **~ cat**, chat de gouttières, *m*. ¶*n*, épave, *f*.

streak, *n*, trait, sillon, *m*, raie, bande, *f*. ¶*v.t*, rayer, sillonner. **~y** (*meat*) *a*, entrelardée.

stream, *n*, cours d'eau; ruisseau; flot; jet; filet; cours; torrent, *m*. **~lined**, profilé, fuselé, aérodynamique. **~lining**, aérodynamisme, *m*. ¶*v.i*, ruisseler. **~er**, *n*, flamme, *f*; (*paper*) serpentin, *m*.

street, *n*, rue, *f*; (*s. & pl. fig.*) pavé, *m*. **back ~**, rue détournée, *f*. **main ~**, artère principale, *f*. **~ lamp**, réverbère, *m*. **~ musician**, musicien de carrefour, *m*.

strength, *n*, force; puissance; résistance; robustesse; intensité, *f*; (*of a solution*) titre; (*men*) effectif, *m*. **~en**, *v.t*, renforcer; consolider; fortifier.

strenuous†, *a*, énergique; (*life*) intense.

stress, *n*, effort; travail, *m*; charge; fatigue; (*weather*) violence, *f*; accent, appui, *m*. **to be in ~** (*Mech.*), travailler. ¶*v.t*, charger; fatiguer; appuyer sur; accentuer; (*Mus.*) scander.

stretch, *n*, trait, *m*; étendue, traite; (*of person's arms*) envergure, *f*; parcours; (*Mech.*) allongement, *m*. ¶*v.t*, étendre, étirer; allonger; tendre. **~ oneself**, s'étirer. **stretcher**, *n*, brancard, *m*; civière, *f*; raidisseur;

(*for painter's canvas*) châssis, *m*. **~ bearer**, brancardier, *m*.

strew, *v.t.ir*, répandre; joncher; [par]semer.

stria, *n*, strie, *f*. **striate[d]**, *a*, strié. **striation**, *n*, striure, *f*.

strickle, *n*, racloire, *f*.

strict†, *a*, strict; formel; rigoureux; sévère; exact. **~ness**, *n*, rigueur; sévérité, *f*. **~ure**, *n*, critique, *f*; (*Med.*) rétrécissement, *m*.

stride, *n*, enjambée, *f*, pas, *m*; (*pl.*) essor, *m*. **~ along**, *v.i.ir*, marcher à grands pas.

strident, *a*, strident.

strife, *n*, guerre, *f*; conflit, *m*.

strike, *n*, (*coin*) frappe; (*labor*) grève, *f*. ¶*v.t.ir*, frapper; assener, porter; choquer; (*match*) frotter; rencontrer; atteindre; battre; (*clock*) sonner; (*root, v.t. & abs.*) jeter, prendre; (*tent*) plier; (*sail*) caler; (*colors*) amener; (*a balance*) établir, faire; (*fish*) ferrer; (*v.i.ir.*) frapper; sonner; (*labor*) se mettre en grève. it **~s me**, il me semble, il me vient à l'idée. **without striking a blow**, sans coup férir. **~ down**, abattre. **~ out**, effacer, rayer, radier, biffer. **~ up** (*tune*), entonner. **~er**, *n*, gréviste, *m,f*. **~ing**, *p.a*, frappant, saisissant; marquant; saillant; (*labor*) en grève. **~ clock**, pendule à sonnerie, *f*.

string, *n*, ficelle; corde; cordelette, *f*; cordon; tirant; filet, *m*; fibre; filandre, *f*; chapelet; attirail; train, *m*; enfilade, *f*; (*Bil.*) boulier, *m*. **the ~s** (*Mus.*), les cordes. **~ band**, orchestre à cordes, *m*. ¶*v.t.ir*, corder; enfiler; (*violin*) monter. **~ed**, *p.a*, à cordes.

stringbean, *n*, haricot vert, *m*.

stringent, *a*, rigoureux.

stringy, *a*, fibreux; filandreux.

strip, *n*, bande, *f*; ruban, *m*. ¶*v.t*, dépouiller; dégarnir; (*v.i.*) se déshabiller.

stripe, *n*, raie, barre, *f*, liteau, *m*; (*N.C.O.'s, Navy*) galon, *m*. **~d**, *a*, rayé, à raies; tigré, zébré.

strive, *v.i.ir*, s'efforcer, tâcher; combattre.

stroke, *n*, coup, *m*; atteinte, *f*; battement, *m*; course, *f*; trait, *m*; raie, barre; attaque, *f*, coup de sang, *m*; (*Swim.*) nage; brassée; brasse, *f*; (*rowing*) chef de nage, *m*. **~ sun ~**, coup de soleil, *m*. ¶*v.t*, caresser.

stroll, *n*, tour, *m*, promenade, *f*.

¶ *v.i*, se promener; errer; flâner. **strolling**, *p.a*, ambulant.

strong†, *a*, fort; puissant; vigoureux; énergique; renforcé; résistant; solide; (*flavor*) relevé; (*wind*) carabiné; (*language*) corsé; (*well up in*) calé. ~ *box*, coffre-fort, *m*. ~ *drink*, liqueurs fortes, *f.pl*. ~*hold*, forteresse, citadelle, *f*, fort, *m*. ~ *man* (professional) hercule, *m*. ~*minded person*, tête forte, forte tête, *f*. ~ *point*, fort, *m*. ~ *room*, cave forte; (*ship*) chambre des valeurs, *f*.

strop, *n*, cuir [à rasoir], affiloir; (*safety blade*) repasseur, *m*. ¶ *v.t*, repasser [sur le cuir, etc.].

structural, *a*, (*steel, etc.*) de construction; (*repairs*) grosses. **structure**, *n*, structure; construction; formation; *f*; édifice; ouvrage d'art; (*fig.*) échafaudage, *m*.

struggle, *n*, lutte, *f*. ¶ *v.i*, lutter, batailler.

strum, *v.t*, tapoter.

strut, *n*, entretoise; contre-fiche; bielle, *f*. ¶ *v.i*, se pavaner, se rengorger, se carrer.

strychnine, *n*, strychnine, *f*.

stub, *n*, souche, *f*, chicot; bout; (*check*) talon, *m*.

stubble, *n*, chaume, *m*, éteule, *f*.

stubborn†, *a*, obstiné, entêté, têtu; tenace. ~*ness*, *n*, obstination, opiniâtreté; ténacité, *f*.

stucco, *n*, stuc, *m*.

stuck-up, *a*, fier.

stud, *n*, clou; crampon, *m*; pointe, *f*; goujon; bouton; plot [de contact]; (*scantling in wall*) potelet, *m*; (*horses*) écurie, *f*; (*breeding*) haras, *m*. ~ *book*, livre généalogique, stud-book, *m*. ~ *farm*, haras, *m*. ~ *horse*, étalon, *m*. ¶ *v.t*, clouter; parsemer, émailler; hérisser. *studded crossing* (pedestrian), passage clouté, *m*, les clous, *m.pl*.

student, *n*, élève, *m*/*f*; étudiant, e; normalien, ne. **studied**, *p.p*, étudié; recherché; (*deliberate*) voulu. ~ *elegance*, recherche, *f*. **studio**, *n*, atelier; théâtre; studio; salon de pose, *m*. **studious**†, *a*, studieux, appliqué. **study**, *n*, étude, *f*; cabinet de travail, *m*. ¶ *v.t. & i*, étudier.

stuff, *n*, matière; étoffe, *f*; (*fig.*) bois, *m*. ~ & *nonsense*, fadaises, *f.pl*. ¶ *v.t*, rembourrer; fourrer; bourrer; (*dead animal*) em-

pailler; (*Cook.*) farcir. ~*ing*, *n*, bourre, (*Cook.*) farce, *f*. ~*y*, *a*, étouffant.

stultify, *v.t*, neutraliser.

stumble, *v.i*, broncher, trébucher, [s']achopper. *stumbling block*, pierre d'achoppement, *f*.

stump, *n*, tronçon; moignon; chicot, *m*; souche, *f*; trognon; bout, *m*; (*art*) estompe, *f*. ~ *orator*, déclamateur, *m*. ¶ *v.t*, faire une campagne électorale, marcher en clopinant.

stun, *v.t*, étourdir. *stunning blow*, coup de massue, *m*.

stunt, *n*, acrobatie, *f*, tour de force, *m*. ¶ *v.t*, rabougrir.

stunted, *p.p*, rabougri, avorté, malvenu, chétif.

stupefy, *v.t*, hébéter; (*narcotize*) stupéfier.

stupendous†, *a*, prodigieux.

stupid†, *a*, stupide; bête. ~*ity*, *n*, stupidité; bêtise, *f*. **stupor**, *n*, stupeur, *f*.

sturdy†, *a*, vigoureux, robuste.

sturgeon, *n*, esturgeon, *m*.

stutter, *v.i. & t*, bégayer. ~*er*, *n*, bègue, *m*/*f*.

sty, *n*, étable à porcs; porcherie, *f*.

sty[e] (*on the eye*) *n*, orgelet, compère-loriot, *m*.

style, *n*, style, *m*; manière, *f*, genre, goût; chic; nom, *m*; (*firm name*) raison [sociale] *f*. ~ *of hair-dressing*, coiffure, *f*. ¶ *v.t*, qualifier; donner le titre de.

stymie (*golf*) *n*, trou barré, *m*.

stylish†, *a*, élégant, galant, à la mode; chic; coquet.

suave†, *a*, suave. **suavity**, *n*, suavité, *f*.

sub-acid, *a*, aigre-doux.

subaltern, *n*, [officier] subalterne, *m*.

subcommittee, *n*, sous-comité, *m*.

subconscious, *a. & n*, subconscient, *a. & m*. ~*ness*, *n*, subconscience, *f*.

subcontract, *n*, sous-traité, *m*. ~*or*, *n*, sous-traitant, *m*.

subcutaneous, *a*, sous-cutané.

subdivide, *v.t*, subdiviser, morceler.

subdue, *v.t*, subjuguer, soumettre, assujettir; maîtriser; adoucir; (*light*) adoucir, tamiser.

subject, *n*, sujet; propos, *m*; (*pers.*) sujet, te. ~ *catalog*, catalogue par ordre de matières, *m*. ¶ *v.t*, soumettre, assujettir. ~ *to*, sujet(te) à; soumis(e) à; sous

[le] bénéfice de; sous réserve de; sauf à. ~**ion**, *n*, sujétion, *f*, assujettissement; *m*; dépendance, *f*. ~**ive**†, *a.* & *n*, subjectif, *a.* & *m.*

subjoined, *p.p*, ci-joint.

subjugate, *v.t*, subjuguer.

subjunctive [**mood**], *n*, subjonctif, *m.*

sublet, *v.t.ir*, sous-louer, relouer.

sublime†, *a.* & *n*, sublime, *a.* & *m.* **sublimity**, *n*, sublimité, *f.*

sublunar[**y**], *a*, sublunaire.

submachine gun, *n*, mitraillette, *f.*

submarine, *a.* & *n*, sous-marin, *a.* & *m.*

submerge, *v.t*, submerger; (*v.i.*) plonger.

submission, *n*, soumission, *f.* **submissive**, *a*, soumis, obéissant. ~**ness**, *n*, soumission, résignation, *f.* **submit**, *v.t*, soumettre. ~ **to**, se soumettre à, obéir à, subir.

suborder, *n*, sous-ordre, *m.*

subordinate, *a*, subordonné, subalterne, en sous-ordre. ¶ *n*, subordonné, e, sous-ordre, *m.* ¶ *v.t*, subordonner.

suborn, *v.t*, suborner, séduire. ~**er**, *n*, suborneur, euse.

subpoena, *n*, citation, assignation, *f.* ¶ *v.t*, citer, assigner, ajourner.

sub rosa, sous [le manteau de] la cheminée.

subscribe, *v.t.* & *i*, souscrire; s'abonner; se cotiser. **subscriber**, *n*, souscripteur, *m*; abonné, e. **subscription**, *n*, souscription, *f*; cotisation, *f*; abonnement, *m.*

subsection, *n*, alinéa, *m.*

subsequent†, *a*, subséquent, postérieur.

subservience, *n*, sujétion, *f.* **subservient**, *a*, auxiliaire, subalterne, servile.

subside, *v.i*, baisser; s'affaisser; [se] calmer. **subsidence**, *n*, baisse, *f*; affaissement, effondrement, *m.*

subsidiary†, *a*, subsidiaire; auxiliaire. ~ [*company*], [société] filiale, *f.*

subsidize, *v.t*, subventionner. **subsidy**, *n*, subvention, *f*; subside, *m.*

subsist, *v.i*, subsister; vivre. ~**ence**, *n*, subsistance, *f.*

subsoil, *n*, sous-sol, *m*; (*law*) tréfonds, *m.*

substance, *n*, substance, *f*; fond; corps; bien, *m.* **substantial**, *a*, substantiel; solide; (*lunch*) dînatoire. ~**ly**, *ad*, substantiellement,

en substance. **substantiate**, *v.t*, établir.

substantive, *a.* & *n*, substantif, *a.* & *m.*

substitute, *n*, succédané, *m*; (*pers.*) remplaçant, e; suppléant, e. ¶ *v.t*, substituer.

substratum, *n*, fond, *m.*

substructure, *n*, substruction, *f.*

subtenant, *n*, sous-locataire, *m,f.*

subterfuge, *n*, subterfuge, *m.*

subterranean, *a*, souterrain.

subtilize, *v.t.* & *i*, subtiliser.

subtitle, *n*, sous-titre, *m.*

subtle†, *a*, subtil, raffiné, fin. ~**ty**, *n*, subtilité, *f*, raffinement, *m.*

subtract, *v.t*, soustraire, retrancher. ~**ion**, *n*, soustraction, *f.*

suburb, *n*, faubourg, *m*, (*pl.*) banlieue, *f.* ~**an**, *a*, suburbain; de banlieue.

subvention, *n*, subvention, *f.*

subversive, *a*, subversif. **subvert**, *v.t*, renverser.

subway, *n*, passage souterrain; (*train*) métropolitain, métro, *m.*

succeed, *v.t*, succéder à; suivre; (*v.i.*) succéder; (*prosper*) réussir, succéder, arriver; parvenir. ~**ing**, *p.a*, suivant. **success**, *n*, succès, *m*, réussite, *f.* ~**ful**†, *a*, heureux; réussi. **succession**, *n*, succession; suite, *f.* **successive**†, *a*, successif. **successor**, *n*, successeur, *m.*

succinct†, *a*, succinct. ~**ness**, *n*, concision, *f.*

succor, *n*, secours, *m.* ¶ *v.t*, secourir.

succulent, *a*, succulent.

succumb, *v.i*, succomber.

such, *a*, tel; pareil; semblable. ~ **as**, tel que; comme.

suck, *v.t.* & *i*, sucer; téter; aspirer. ~ **in**, humer. ~ **up**, pomper. ~**er**, *n*, (*of insect*) suçoir, *m*; (*of leech*) ventouse, *f*; (*Hort.*) drageon, surgeon, *m*, talle, *f*, œilleton, *m*; branche gourmande, *f*; (*fig.*) poire, *f.* ~**le**, *v.t*, allaiter; nourrir. ~**ling**, *n*, enfant à la mamelle; nourrisson, *m.* **suction**, *n*, succion; aspiration, *f.* ~ *pump*, pompe aspirante, *f.*

sudden†, *a*, soudain, subit; brusque. ~ *turn* (road), crochet, *m.* all of a ~, tout à coup. ~**ness**, *n*, soudaineté, *f.*

suds, *n.pl*, eau de savon, *f.*

sue, *v.t*, poursuivre, actionner. ~ *for*, demander.

suède gloves, gants de Suède, *m.pl.*

suet, *n*, graisse de rognon de bœuf, de mouton, *f*.

suffer, *v.t*, supporter; subir; éprouver; tolérer; (*v.i.*) souffrir; pâtir. **~able†**, *a*, supportable. **~ance**, *n*, souffrance; tolérance, *f*. **~er**, *n*, victime, *f*; patient, e. **~ing**, *n*, souffrance, *f*. **~ing**, *p.a*, souffrant.

suffice, *v.i*, suffire. **~** *it to say that*, suffit que. **sufficiency**, *n*, suffisance; aisance, *f*. **sufficient†**, *a*, suffisant.

suffix, *n*, suffixe, *m*. **~ed**, *p.a*, suffixe.

suffocate, *v.t*, suffoquer; asphyxier. **suffocation**, *n*, suffocation; asphyxie, *f*.

suffragan, *a*. & *n*, suffragant, *a.m*. & *m*.

suffrage, *n*, suffrage, *m*. **suffragette**, *n*, suffragette, *f*.

suffuse, *v.t*, se répandre sur; baigner. **suffusion**, *n*, suffusion, *f*.

sugar, *n*, sucre, *m*. **~** *almond*, dragée, *f*. **~** *bowl*, sucrier, bol à sucre, *m*. **~** *beet*, betterave à s., *f*. **~** *candy*, sucre candi, *m*. **~** *cane*, canne à s., *f*. **~** *refinery*, sucrerie, *f*. **~** *sifter*, saupoudroir à sucre, *m*. **~** *tongs*, pinces à s., *f.pl*. ¶ *v.t*, sucrer. **~y**, *a*, sucré; saccharin.

suggest, *v.t*, suggérer; dicter. **~ion**, *n*, suggestion, *f*. **~ive**, *a*, suggestif.

suicide, *n*, suicide, *m*; (*pers.*) suicidé, *m*. *to commit* **~**, se suicider.

suit, *n*, procès civil; complet; habit; costume, *m*; (*cards*) couleur, *f*. **~case**, valise, *m*. **~** *of armor*, armure complète, *f*. **~** *of clothes*, complet. **~** *to measure*, complet sur mesure. ¶ *v.t*, adapter; approprier; assortir; aller à; convenir à; accommoder; (*v.i.*) cadrer; convenir. **~ability**, *n*, convenance; adaptation, *f*. **~able†**, *a*. & **~ed**, *p.p*, convenable, sortable, adapté, approprié, assortissant; propre.

suite, *n*, suite, *f*, train, *m*; enfilade, *f*. **~** [*of furniture*], ameublement; mobilier, *m*. **~** [*of rooms*], appartement, *m*, chambres en enfilade, *f.pl*.

suitor, *n*, (*law*) plaideur; (*wooer*) aspirant, prétendant, soupirant, poursuivant, *m*.

sulfate, *n*, sulfate, *m*. **sulfide**, *n*, sulfure, *m*. **sulfite**, *n*, sulfite, *m*. **~** *pulp*, pâte au bisulfite, *f*. **sul-**

fur, *n*, soufre, *m*. **~** *bath*, bain sulfureux, *m*. **~** *mine*, soufrière.

sulk, *v.i*, bouder. **~y**, *a*, boudeur.

sullen, *a*, renfrogné, maussade, morose. **~ness**, *n*, maussaderie, *f*.

sully, *v.t*, souiller, tacher, ternir.

sultan, *n*, sultan, *m*. **sultana**, *n*, sultane, *f*.

sultry, *a*, étouffant, lourd, caniculaire.

sum, *n*, somme, *f*; calcul; comble, *m*. **~** *total*, somme totale, *f*, montant global, *m*. **~** *up*, résumer; résumer les débats. **summarize**, *v.t*, résumer. **summary†**, *a*, sommaire. ¶ *n*, sommaire, résumé, *m*.

summer, *n*, été, *m*. **~** *house*, pavillon [de jardin], kiosque de j., *m*. **~** *lightning*, éclair[s] de chaleur, *m.[pl.]*. **~** *resort*, station estivale, *f*. **~** *vacation*, grandes vacances, *f.pl*. ¶ *v.i*, passer l'été; (*v.t.*) estiver.

summing up, résumé des débats, *m*.

summit, *n*, sommet, *m*, cime, *f*, faîte, comble, *m*.

summon, *v.t*, citer, assigner; sommer; convoquer. **~** *back* & **~** *up*, rappeler. **summons**, *n*, sommation; citation, *f*. ¶ *v.t*, citer.

sump, *n*, puisard, *m*.

sumptuous†, *a*, somptueux; (*fare*) pantagruélique. **~ness**, *n*, somptuosité, *f*, luxe, *m*.

sun, *n*, soleil, *m*. **~** *bath*, bain de s., *m*. **~bathing**, bains de s., *m.pl*. **~beam**, rayon de s., *m*. **~burn**, hâle, *m*. *to get* **~burnt**, se hâler. **~dial**, cadran solaire, *m*. **~flower**, soleil, tournesol, *m*. **~light**, lumière du s., *f*. **~lit**, ensoleillé. **~rise**, lever du s., *m*. **~set**, coucher de s., s. couchant, *m*. *at* **~set** or *at* **~down**, au coucher du s. **~shine**, soleil, *m*. **~shiny day**, jour de s., *m*. **~spot**, tache du s., t. solaire, macule, *f*. **~stroke**, insolation, *f*, coup de s., *m*. ¶ *v.t*, ensoleiller. **~** *oneself*, se chauffer au soleil, lézarder.

Sunday, *n*, dimanche, *m*. *to put on one's* **~** *best*, s'endimancher.

sunder, *v.t*, séparer.

sundries, *n.pl*, [articles] divers, *m.pl*. **sundry**, *a*, divers.

sunken, *p.a*, creux; cave; noyé.

sunless, *a*, sans soleil. **sunny**, *a*, ensoleillé.

sup, *v.i*, souper.

superabundant†, *a,* surabondant.

superannuated, *p.p,* suranné.

superb†, *a,* superbe.

supercargo, *n,* subrécargue, *m.*

supercilious†, *a,* dédaigneux, hautain.

superficial†, *a,* superficiel. **superficies,** *n,* superficie, *f.*

superfine, *a,* superfin, surfin.

superfluity, *n,* superfluité, *f,* superflu, embarras, *m.* **superfluous,** *a,* superflu.

superheat, *v.t,* surchauffer.

superhuman, *a,* surhumain.

superimpose, *v.t,* superposer.

superintend, *v.t,* surveiller; présider à. **~ence,** *n,* surveillance, *f.* **~ent,** *n,* surveillant, e; surintendant, e; chef; (*police*) commissaire; (*restaurant*) maître d'hôtel, *m.*

superior†, *a.* & *n,* supérieur, e. **~ity,** *n,* supériorité, *f.*

superlative†, *a,* souverain; (*Gram.*) superlatif. ¶ *n,* superlatif, *m.*

superman, *n,* surhomme, *m.*

supernatural†, *a.* & *n,* surnaturel, *a.* & *m.*

supernumerary, *a.* & *n,* surnuméraire, *a.* & *m.* ¶ (*Theat.*) *n,* figurant, e, comparse, *m,f.*

superscription, *n,* suscription, *f.*

supersede, *v.t,* remplacer.

superstition, *n,* superstition, *f.* **superstitious†,** *a,* superstitieux.

superstructure, *n,* superstructure, *f.*

supervene, *v.i,* survenir.

supervise, *v.t,* surveiller, contrôler. **supervision,** *n,* surveillance, *f,* contrôle, *m.* **supervisor,** *n,* surveillant, e, contrôleur, *m.*

supine, *a,* couché sur le dos; indolent; léthargique.

supper, *n,* souper, *m.* *to have* ~, souper. ~ *time,* heure du s., *f.* **~less,** *a,* sans s.

supplant, *v.t,* supplanter.

supple, *a,* souple. *to make* ~, assouplir.

supplement, *n,* supplément, *m.* ¶ *v.t,* augmenter. **~ary,** *a,* supplémentaire.

suppleness, *n,* souplesse, *f.*

suppliant, *a.* & *n,* suppliant, e. **supplicate,** *v.t,* supplier. **supplication,** *n,* supplication, *f.*

supplier, *n,* fournisseur, euse. **supply,** *n,* provision, fourniture, *f,* approvisionnement, *m;* (*pl, food*) vivres, *m.pl.* ~ & *demand,*

l'offre & la demande. ¶ *v.t,* fournir, approvisionner; pourvoir; assortir de; alimenter; suppléer.

support, *n,* support; soutien; appui; entretien, *m.* ¶ *v.t,* supporter; soutenir; appuyer; entretenir. **~er,** *n,* partisan, tenant, *m,* adhérent, e.

suppose, *v.t,* supposer; présumer. *supposing* [*that*], supposé que. **supposition,** *n,* supposition, *f.* **supposititious,** *a,* supposé.

suppress, *v.t,* supprimer. **~ed** *rage,* rage rentrée, *f.* **~ion,** *n,* suppression, *f.*

suppurate, *v.i,* suppurer.

supremacy, *n,* suprématie, *f.* **supreme†,** *a,* suprême; souverain.

surcharge, *v.t,* surcharger, surtaxer.

sure†, *a,* sûr; certain; assuré, immanquable. *to make* ~ *of,* s'assurer de. **~ness,** *n,* sûreté, *f.* **~ty,** *n,* sûreté; caution, *f.*

surf, *n,* ressac, *m,* brisants, *m.pl.* **~board,** aquaplane, *m.* **~ boat,** pirogue de barre, *f.* ~ *fishing,* pêche de plage, *f.* **~riding,** sport de l'aquaplane, *m.*

surface, *n,* surface; superficie, *f.* ~ *plate,* marbre, *m.* ¶ *v.t,* aplanir; (*Naut.*) remonter à la surface.

surfeit, *n,* satiété, *f.* ¶ *v.t,* rassasier; blaser.

surge, *n,* houle, *f.* ¶ *v.i,* refluer, ondoyer.

surgeon, *n,* chirurgien; médecin, *m.* **surgery,** *n,* chirurgie; médecine, *f;* cabinet de consultation, *m,* clinique, *f.* **surgical,** *a,* chirurgical. ~ *case* (*pers.*), opéré, e.

surging, *p.a,* houleux.

surly, *a,* rébarbatif, bourru, maussade.

surmise, *n,* conjecture, supposition, *f.* ¶ *v.t,* soupçonner.

surmount, *v.t,* surmonter.

surname, *n,* nom [de famille] *m.*

surpass, *v.t,* surpasser. **~ing,** *a,* supérieur; suprême.

surplice, *n,* surplis, *m.*

surplus, *n,* surplus, excédent, *m.*

surprise, *n,* surprise, *f;* étonnement, *m.* ~ *attack,* attaque faite à l'improviste, *f,* coup de main, *m.* ¶ *v.t,* surprendre; étonner. **surprising,** *a,* surprenant, étonnant. **~ly,** *ad,* étonnamment.

surrender, *n,* reddition, *f;* abandon; (*Insce.*) rachat, *m.* ¶ *v.t,* rendre; livrer; abandonner, abdiquer; céder; (*insurance policy*) racheter; (*v.i.*) se rendre.

surreptitious†, *a*, subreptice.

surrogate, *n*, substitut, *m*.

surround, *v.t*, entourer, enceindre, encadrer. ¶ *n*, pourtour, *m*. **~ing**, *p.a*, environnant; ambiant. **~ings**, *n.pl*, alentours, *m.pl*.

surtax, *n*, surtaxe, *f*; impôt général (*ou* global) sur le revenu, *m*. ¶ *v.t*, surtaxer.

survey, *n*, étude; visite; expertise, *f*; levé [de plans]; arpentage; cadastre; métrage, *m*. ¶ *v.t*, étudier; expertiser; (*land*) arpenter; cadastrer; métrer. **~or**, *n*, inspecteur; expert; (*land*) arpenteur, géomètre; (*quantity*) métreur; (*roads*) [agent] voyer, *m*.

survival, *n*, survivance, survie, *f*. ~ *of the fittest*, survivance du plus apte. **survive**, *v.t*, survivre à; (*v.i.*) se survivre. **survivor**, *n*, survivant, e; rescapé, e. **~ship**, *n*, survie, *f*.

susceptible, *a*, susceptible, sensible.

suspect, *a*, suspect, interlope. ¶ *n*, suspect, *m*. ¶ *v.t*, suspecter; se douter de.

suspend, *v.t*, suspendre. **~er**, *n*, bretelle, *f*. **suspense**, *n*, incertitude, *f. in ~*, en suspens, en souffrance. **suspension**, *n*, suspension, *f*. ~ *bridge*, pont suspendu, *m*.

suspicion, *n*, soupçon, *m*; (*law*) suspicion, *f*. **suspicious†**, *a*, soupçonneux; suspect; louche.

sustain, *v.t*, soutenir; sustenter; éprouver. **~ing**, *p.a*, (*power*) soutenant; (*food*) qui soutient. **sustenance**, *n*, subsistance, nourriture, *f*.

sutler, *n*, vivandier, ère.

suture, *n*, suture, *f*.

suzerain, *n*, suzerain, e. **~ty**, *n*, suzeraineté, *f*.

swab, *n*, torchon; (*Naut.*) faubert; (*Med.*) écouvillon, *m*.

swaddling clothes (*lit. & fig.*), langes, *m.pl*.

swage, *n*, étampe, *f*. ¶ *v.t*, étamper.

swagger, *v.i*, se rengorger, se carrer; faire le fanfaron. **~er**, *n*, fanfaron, bravache, *m*.

swain, *n*, galant, *m*.

swallow, *n*, hirondelle, *f*; gorgée, *f*; (*river*) perte, *f*. **~tail** (coat), queue-de-morue, queue-de-pie, *f*. ¶ *v.t*, avaler; engloutir.

swamp, *n*, marais, marécage, *m*, grenouillère, *f*. ¶ *v.t*, remplir d'eau, submerger; engloutir,

noyer. *be ~ed* (*work*), débordé de travail. **~y**, *a*, marécageux.

swan, *n*, cygne, *m*. **~'s-down**, duvet de cygne; (*cloth*) molleton, *m*. ~ *song*, chant du cygne, *m*.

sward, *n*, [tapis de] gazon, *m*, herbette, *f*.

swarm, *n*, (*bees*) essaim; (*multitude*) essaim, *m*, nuée, milliasse, potée, *f*. ¶ *v.i*, (*bees*) essaimer; pulluler, fourmiller, foisonner.

swarthy, *a*, noir; noiraud, basané.

swash, *v.i*, clapoter.

swastika, *n*, svastika, *m*.

swat (*fly*) *v.t*, tuer.

swath, *n*, javelle, *f*; (*path cut*) andain, *m*.

sway, *n*, balancement; empire, *m*; domination, puissance, *f*. ¶ *v.t*, balancer; influencer.

swear, *v.i. & t. ir*, jurer; prêter serment; (*witness*) assermenter. ~ *at*, maudire.

sweat, *n*, sueur; suée, *f*. ¶ *v.i. & t*, suer; ressuer; exploiter. ~ *profusely*, suer à grosses gouttes. **~er**, *n*, chandail, *m*. **~y**, *a*, suant.

Swede, *n*, Suédois, e. **s~**, *n*, navet de Suède, rutabaga, *m*. **Sweden**, *n*, la Suède. **Swedish**, *a*, suédois. ~ *movements*, gymnastique suédoise, *f*. ¶ *n*, le suédois.

sweep, *n*, coup de balai; coup, mouvement; (*pers.*) ramoneur, *m*; boucle, courbe; étendue, *f*. ¶ *v.t. & i. ir*, balayer; (*chimney*) ramoner; (*Naut.*) draguer. ~ *away*, enlever. ~ *the board*, rafler le tout. **~er**, *n*, balayeur, euse; (*Mach.*) balayeuse, *f*. **~ing gesture**, geste large, *m*. **~ings**, *n.pl*, balayures, *f.pl*. **~stake[s]**, *n*, sweepstake, *m*, loterie, *f*.

sweet†, *a*, doux; sucré; (*wine*) liquoreux; suave; charmant; gentil, mignon. **~bread**, ris de veau, *m*. **~briar**, églantine odorante, *f*; (*bush*) églantier odorant, *m*. **~heart**, amoureux, euse, *f*. ~ *herbs*, herbes fines, *f.pl*. **~meat**, sucrerie, *f*, bonbon, *m*. ~ *pea*, pois de senteur, *m*. ~ *potato*, patate, *f*. **~[-scented]**, odorant, odoriférant. *to have a ~ tooth*, aimer les sucreries. **~-william**, œillet de poète, *m*. **the** ~ (*opp. the bitter*), le doux. **~en**, *v.t*, sucrer; adoucir. **~ish**, *a*, douceâtre. **~ness**, *n*, douceur; suavité, *f*; charme, *m*.

swell, *n*, bombement; renflement, *m*; (*sea*) houle, *f*; (*pers.*) élégant, e. ¶ *a*, chic. ¶ *v.t. & i. ir*, enfier, s'e.; gonfler; se g.; renfler; grossir; dilater; bouffer, gondoler. **swelling**, n, enflure, grosseur, fluxion, f; gonflement; renflement, m.

swelter, v.i, étouffer de chaleur.

swerve, n, crochet, m, embardée, f. ¶ v.i, faire une embardée; s'écarter, se départir.

swift†, a, rapide, vite. **~-footed**, au pied léger. ¶ n, martinet, m. **~ness**, n, rapidité, célérité, vélocité, f.

swig, v.t, lamper, sabler.

swill, v.t, laver à grande eau, lessiver; (drink) lamper.

swim, n, tour de nage, m. in the **~**, dans le mouvement. ¶ v.i. & t. ir, nager. **~ across**, passer à la nage. **~ under water**, nager entre deux eaux. **swimming**, n, natation, f. **~ pool**, piscine, f. **swimsuit**, maillot de bain, m.

swindle, n, escroquerie, f. ¶ v.t, escroquer. **swindler**, n, escroc, filou, m.

swine, n, pourceau, porc, cochon, m. **~herd**, porcher, ère.

swing, n, oscillation, f, balancement; branle, m; (playground) balançoire, escarpolette, f. in full **~**, en pleine activité. **~ bridge**, pont tournant, m. **~ door**, porte va-et-vient, f. ¶ v.t. & i. ir, balancer; se b.; osciller; branler; basculer; tourner.

swingletree, n, volée, f.

swirl, n, tourbillon; remous, m. ¶ v.i, tourbillonner, tournoyer.

swish, n, sifflement; frou-frou, m. ¶ v.t, cingler; (whip) faire siffler; susurrer; remuer.

Swiss, a, suisse. **~ guard**, suisse, m. ¶ n, Suisse, m, Suissesse, f.

switch, n, badine, houssine; (Rly.) aiguille, f; (Elec.) interrupteur, m. **~back**, montagnes russes, f.pl. **~ board**, tableau de distribution; (Tele.) standard, m. ¶ v.t, (whip) houssiner. **~ off**, couper, mettre hors circuit; (light) éteindre. **~ on**, mettre en circuit; (light) allumer.

Switzerland, n, la Suisse.

swivel, n, émerillon; tourniquet, m. ¶ v.i, pivoter, tourner.

swollen glands, des glandes au cou, f.pl.

swoon, n, évanouissement, m, défaillance, f. ¶ v.i, s'évanouir, [se] pâmer.

swoop down on, fondre sur.

sword, n, épée, f; sabre; (Poet.)

glaive, m; (in fun) flamberge, f. **~ belt**, ceinturon, m. **~fish**, espadon, m. **~ rattler**, ferrailleur, m. **swordsman**, n, lame, f. **swordsmanship**, n, escrime, f.

Sybarite, n, sybarite, m.

sycamore, n, sycomore, m.

sycophant, n, sycophante, m.

syllabize, v.t, scander. **syllable**, n, syllabe, f.

syllabus, n, programme; (Eccl.) syllabus, m.

syllogism, n, syllogisme, m.

sylph, n, sylphe, m, sylphide, f.

sylvan, a, champêtre, bocager.

symbol, n, symbole, m. **~ic(al)**, a, symbolique. **~ize**, v.t, symboliser.

symmetric(al)†, a, symétrique. **symmetry**, n, symétrie, f.

sympathetic, a, sympathique. **sympathize**, v.i, sympathiser, compatir. **sympathy**, n, sympathie, f.

symphony, n, symphonie, f.

symptom, n, symptôme, m.

synagogue, n, synagogue, f.

synchronize, v.t, synchroniser.

synchronous, a, synchrone.

syncopate, v.t, syncoper. **syncopation** & **syncope**, n, syncope, f.

syndicate, n, syndicat, m. ¶ v.t, syndiquer.

synod, n, synode, m. **~ic(al)**, a, synodique.

synonym, n. & **synonymous**, a, synonyme, m. & a.

synopsis, n, argument, sommaire, m.

syntax, n, syntaxe, f.

synthesis, n, synthèse, f. **synthetic(al)**†, a, synthétique.

Syria, n, la Syrie, f. **Syrian**, a, syrien. ¶ n, Syrien, ne.

syringe, n, seringue, f. ¶ v.t, seringuer.

syrup, n, sirop, m. **~y**, a, sirupeux.

system, n, système; régime; réseau, m. **communications ~**, réseau de transmissions, m. **~atic**†, a, systématique.

T

T, n, T, té, m. **~ square**, té [à dessin] m. **to a ~**, tout craché.

tab, n, étiquette, f; (index) onglet, m. **to keep ~s on**, ne pas perdre de vue.

tabby cat, chat moucheté, chat tigré, m.

tabernacle, n, tabernacle, m.

table 658 **tamarind**

table, *n*, table; tablette, *f*; bureau; plateau; tableau; plan; décompte, *m*. *card* ~, table à jeu, *f*. ~ *cloth*, nappe [de t.] *f*. ~ *companion*, convive, *m,f*. ~ *salt*, sel fin, *m*. ~*spoon*, cuiller à bouche, c. à soupe, *f*. ~*spoonful*, cuillerée à bouche, *f*. ~ *talk*, propos de t., *m.pl*. ¶ *v.t*, déposer sur le bureau. **tableau**, *n*. & i, tableau, *m*. & i. **tablet**, *n*, table, tablette, plaque, *f*; pain, *m*.

taboo, *n*, tabou, *m*. *he, it, is* ~, il est tabou. ¶ *v.t*, déclarer tabou.

tabular, *a*, en forme de tableau. **tabulate**, *v.t*, dresser en forme de tableau.

tacit†, *a*, tacite. **taciturn**, *a*, taciturne. ~**ity**, *n*, taciturnité, *f*.

tack, *n*, (*s. & pl.*) broquette, (*pl.*) semence; (*Naut.*) bordée, *f*, bord, *m*; (*of sail*) amure, *f*. ¶ *v.t*, clouer avec de la broquette, de la semence; (*Need.*) bâtir; (*fig.*) coudre; (*v.i.*) virer de bord, louvoyer.

tackle, *n*, engin, *m*. oft. pl; appareil, *m*. oft. pl; harnais, *m*; agrès, *m.pl*; treuil; palan; (*Foot.*) arrêt, *m*. ~ *block*, moufle, *f*. or *m*. ¶ *v.t*, s'attaquer à; (*Foot.*) plaquer; (*pers., fig.*) entreprendre.

tacky, *a*, collant, visqueux.

tact, *n*, tact, doigté, savoir-faire, *m*, ménagements, *m.pl*. ~**ful**, *a*, [plein] de tact. ~**less**, *a*, dépourvu de tact, malhabile.

tactical, *a*, tactique. **tactician**, *n*, tacticien, manœuvrier, *m*. **tactics**, *n.pl*, tactique, *f*.

tactile, *a*, tactile.

tadpole, *n*, têtard, *m*.

taffeta, *n*, taffetas, *m*.

taffrail, *n*, couronnement, *m*.

tag, *n*, ferret; (*stock phrase*) cliché, *m*; (*label*) étiquette, *f*; [jeu du] chat, *m*. ¶ *v.t*, (*label*) marquer, attacher une fiche; ferrer.

Tagus (the), le Tage.

Tahiti, *n*, Taïti, Tahiti, *m*.

tail, *n*, queue, *f*; arrière; aval; derrière; (*coat*) pan, *m*, basque; (*coin*) pile; (*book page*) queue, tranche inférieure, *f*. ~ *coat* or *tails*, (*evening*) queue-de-morue, queue-de-pie; (*morning*) jaquette, *f*. ~*piece*, cul-de-lampe, *m*. ~ *spin*, vrille, *f*. ~ *stock* (lathe), contre-pointe, *f*.

tailor, *n*, tailleur, *m*. ~*made* or ~*ed*, [fait par] tailleur. ~**ing**, *n*, métier de tailleur, *m*.

taint, *n*, infection; tache, tare, *f*. ¶ *v.t*, corrompre, infecter; souiller. ~**ed** (*meat*) *p.a*, gâté, faisandé.

take, *v.t.ir*, prendre; porter; conduire, mener; faire; mettre; relever; tirer; tenir; supposer; falloir; (*v.i.*) prendre. ~ *away*, emmener; ôter; [r]emporter. ~ *back*, ramener; reprendre. ~ *cover*, se garer. ~ *down*, descendre; décrocher; démonter. ~ *down* [*in shorthand*], sténographier. ~ *in*, prendre; recevoir; faire; embrasser; attraper. ~ *off*, ôter; rabattre; (*a pers.*) contrefaire; (*Avn.*) décoller, prendre son vol. ~ *on* (workers), embaucher. ~ *out*, ôter; retirer; arracher; sortir; (*Insce policy*) contracter. ~ *over*, prendre. ~ *shape*, se dessiner. ~ *to*, s'appliquer à; s'adonner à, mordre à. ~ *to pieces*, désassembler, démonter. ~ *to task*, prendre à partie, morigéner. ~ *up*, relever; lever; monter; s'occuper de; occuper, tenir; prendre; (*option*) lever, consolider. ~ *your seats!* (in carriage), en voiture! **taker**, *n*, preneur, euse. **taking**, *a*, séduisant, avenant. ¶ *n*, prise, *f*; (*pl.*) recette, *f*. oft. pl, produit, *m*. ~ *off* (*Avn.*), décollage, envol, *m*.

talc, *n*, talc, *m*.

tale, *n*, conte, *m*, histoire, nouvelle, *f*. ~*bearer*, rapporteur, euse.

talent, *n*, talent, *m*. ~**ed**, *a*, de talent.

talisman, *n*, talisman, *m*.

talk, *n*, conversation, causerie, *f*, entretien; discours, *m*; propos, *m.pl*; bavardage, *m*. ¶ *v.i. & t*, parler; causer; converser; bavarder. ~ *into*, persuader de. ~ *out of*, dissuader de. ~*ative*, *a*, parlant, causeur, loquace. ~*er*, *n*, parleur, euse, causeur, euse; bavard, e. ~*ing*, *a*, parlant.

tall, *a*, grand; haut. ~**ness**, *n*, (*pers.*) haute taille; (*steeple*) hauteur, *f*. *how* ~ *are you?* quelle taille avez-vous?

tallow, *n*, suif, *m*. ¶ *v.t*, suifer.

tally, *n*, (*stick*) taille; marque, *f*; (*check*) pointage, *m*; (*label*) étiquette, *f*. ¶ *v.i*, concorder, correspondre, cadrer, se rapporter. ~**ho**, *i*, taïaut!

talon, *n*, serre, *f*; (*counterfoil*) talon, *m*.

talus, *n*, talus, *m*.

tamarind, *n*, tamarin, *m*.

tambour, *n*, tambour, métier [à broder] *m*. **~ine**, *n*, tambour de basque, *m*.

tame, *a*, apprivoisé; (*fig.*) anodin. ¶ *v.t*, apprivoiser, dompter. **tamer**, *n*, dompteur, euse.

tam-o'-shanter, *n*, béret écossais, *m*.

tamp, *v.t*, bourrer; damer, pilonner.

tamper with, falsifier; (*witness*) suborner.

tampion, *n*, tampon, *m*.

tan, *n*, tan; (*sunburn*) hâle, *m*. ¶ *v.t*, tanner; brunir, hâler, basaner. ¶ *a*, jaune-brun, hâlé.

tandem, *n*, tandem, *m*. ¶ *a*. & *ad*, en tandem.

tang, *n*, goût; montant, *m*; salure; (*shank*) queue, *f*. **there is a ~ in the air**, l'air est vif.

tangent, *n*, tangente, *f*. **~[ial]**, *a*, tangent.

tangerine, *n*, mandarine, *f*.

tangible, *a*, tangible, palpable.

Tangier, *n*, Tanger, *m*.

tangle, *n*, enchevêtrement, *m*. ¶ *v.t*, enchevêtrer, emmêler.

tank, *n*, réservoir, *m*; citerne; bâche; cuve; caisse à eau, soute, *f*; (*Mil.*) char d'assaut, tank, *m*. gasoline ~, réservoir à essence, *m*. **tanker**, *n*, bateau-citerne, *m*. bateau-citerne à vapeur, *m*.

tankard, *n*, pot (*d'étain*) *m*.

tanner, *n*, tanneur, *m*. **~y**, *n*, tannerie, *f*. **tannin**, *n*, tanin, tannin, *m*.

tantalize, *v.t*, mettre au supplice.

tantalum, *n*, tantale, *m*.

tantamount to (to be), équivaloir à.

tantrums, *n.pl*, nerfs, *m.pl*, bourrasques, *f.pl*.

tap, *n*, tape, *f*, coup; (*water*) robinet; (*screw*) taraud, *m*. ~ *dance*, claquettes, *f.pl*. ~*root*, racine pivotante, *f*, pivot, *m*. ¶ *v.t*. & *i*, taper; toucher; frapper; (*screw*) tarauder; (*cask*) mettre en perce; (*tree*) saigner; (*Surg.*) faire une ponction à.

tape, *n*, ruban, *m*; tresse; bande, *f*. insulating ~, chatterton, *m*. ~ *measure*, mesure à ruban, *f*; mètre à r.; centimètre, *m*; roulette, *f*. ~ *recorder*, magnétophone, *m*. ~*worm*, ver solitaire, ténia, *m*.

taper, *n*, bougie filée; (*coiled*) bougie de poche, *f*, pain de bougie, rat de cave; (*church*) cierge; cône, *m*. ¶ *v.t*, diminuer, fuseler;

(*v.i.*) aller en diminuant; se terminer en pointe. **~[ing]**, *a*, conique, fuselé.

tapestry, *n*. & ~ *work*, tapisserie, *f*.

tapioca, *n*, tapioca, *m*.

tapir, *n*, tapir, *m*.

tar, *n*, goudron; brai; (*pers.*) loup de mer, *m*. ~*paper*, carton goudronné, *m*. ¶ *v.t*, goudronner. ~ & *feather*, emplumer.

tarantella, *n*, tarentelle, *f*. **tarantula**, *n*, tarentule, *f*.

tardy†, *a*, tardif.

tare, *n*, vesce; (*pl*, *fig.*) ivraie; (*Com.*) tare, *f*.

target, *n*, cible, *f*, but *m*. ~ *practice*, tir à la cible, *m*.

tariff, *n*, tarif, *m*. ¶ *v.t*, tarifer.

tarnish, *v.t*, ternir; (*v.i.*) se ternir.

tarpaulin, *n*, bâche goudronnée, *f*, prélart, *m*.

tarragon, *n*, estragon, *m*.

Tarragona, *n*, Tarragone, *f*.

tarry, *v.i*, séjourner; tarder; attendre.

tarsus, *n*, tarse, *m*.

tart†, *a*, aigre, âcre, acide. ¶ *n*, (*open*) tarte, *f*; (*covered*) tourte; (*woman*) grue, *f*.

tartan, *n*, tartan, *m*.

tartar, *n*, tartre, *m*. **~ic**, *a*, tartrique.

tartness, *n*, aigreur, âcreté, acidité, *f*.

task, *n*, tâche; besogne, *f*; devoir, *m*. *to take to ~*, prendre à partie, morigéner. ¶ *v.t*, mettre à l'épreuve; fatiguer.

tassel, *n*, gland, *m*, houppe, *f*.

taste, *n*, goût; gré; échantillon, *m*. ¶ *v.t*. & *i*, goûter; g. de; (*tea, wine*) déguster. ~ *of*, sentir le, la, les. ~*ful*, *a*, de bon goût. ~*less*, *a*, sans goût, fade, insipide. **taster**, *n*, dégustateur, *m*; (*device*) sonde, *f*. **tasting**, *n*, gustation; dégustation, *f*. **tasty**, *a*, savoureux.

tatter, *n*, haillon, lambeau, *m*. **~ed**, *a*, déguenillé; en lambeaux.

tatting, *n*, frivolité, *f*.

tattle, *n*, babil[lage] *m*. ¶ *v.i*, babiller. **tattler**, *n*. & **tattling**, *a*, babillard, e.

tattoo, *n*, tatouage, *m*; (*Mil.*) retraite, *f*. ¶ *v.t*, tatouer; (*v.i.*) tambouriner.

taunt, *n*, sarcasme, *m*. ¶ *v.t*, houspiller, molester. ~ *with*, reprocher à.

taut, *a*, raide, tendu. **~en**, *v.t*, raidir.

tautologic(al), *a,* tautologique.
tautology, *n,* tautologie, *f.*

tavern, *n,* taverne, *f,* cabaret, *m.* ~ *with gardens & dance hall,* guinguette, *f.*

tawdriness, *n,* faux éclat, *m.* **tawdry,** *a,* qui a un faux éclat. ~ *finery,* oripeaux, *m.pl.*

tawny, *a,* fauve; basané. ~ *owl,* chat-huant, *m,* hulotte, *f.*

tax, *n,* impôt, *m,* taxe, contribution, imposition, *f.* *excise* ~, droit de régie, *m.* *income* ~, impôt sur le revenu, *m.* ~ *collector,* percepteur, collecteur d'impôts, *m.* ~ *dodger,* fraudeur (euse) des droits du fisc. ~ *free,* net d'impôts. ~*payer,* contribuable, *m,f.* ¶ *v.t,* imposer; taxer. ~**able,** *a,* imposable. ~**ation,** *n,* taxation, *f,* impôts, *m.pl.*

taxi (*Avn.*) *v.i,* rouler [sur le sol]. ~ [*cab*], taxi, *m.* ~ *driver,* chauffeur de taxi, conducteur de taxi, *m.* ~*meter,* compteur, *m.*

taxidermist, *n,* naturaliste [fourreur] *m,* empailleur, euse. **taxidermy,** *n,* empaillage, empaillement, *m.*

tea, *n,* thé, *m;* infusion, tisane, *f.* ~ *cosy,* couvre-théière, *m.* ~ *cup,* tasse à thé, *f.* ~ *party,* thé, *m.* ~*pot,* théière, *f.* ~, *roll, & butter,* thé complet. ~ *room*(*s*), ~ *shop,* salon de thé, *m.* pâtisserie, *f.* ~ *rose,* rose thé, *f.* ~*spoon,* cuiller à thé, *f.* ~ *time,* l'heure du thé, *f.*

teach, *v.t. & i.* ir, enseigner, instruire; apprendre; professer; montrer à; (*bird*) seriner. ~ *someone a lesson,* donner une leçon à quelqu'un. ~ *someone manners,* donner à quelqu'un une leçon de politesse. ~**er,** *n,* instituteur, trice; professeur; précepteur, *m;* maître, esse. ~**ing,** *n,* enseignement, *m;* instruction, *f.*

teak, *n,* teck, tek, *m.*

teal, *n,* sarcelle, *f.*

team, *n,* attelage, *m;* équipe, *f.* ~ *spirit,* esprit de corps, *m.* ~*work,* travail d'équipe, *m.*

tear, *n,* déchirure, *f;* accroc, *m.* ¶ *v.t.ir,* déchirer; arracher. ~ *one another to pieces,* s'entre-déchirer.

tear, *n,* larme, *f,* pleur, *m.* ~ *gas,* gaz lacrymogène, *m.* ~**ful,** *a,* éploré, larmoyant.

tease, *v.t,* taquiner, lutiner; tourmenter. ¶ (*pers.*) *n,* taquin, e.

teaser, *n,* (*pers.*) taquin; e; pro-

blème, casse-tête, *m.* **teasing,** *n,* taquinerie, *f.*

teat, *n,* bout du sein, mamelon, tétin, *m.*

technical†, *a,* technique; d'ordre t. ~ *offense,* quasi-délit, *m.* ~ *school,* école pratique, *f.* **technique,** *n,* technique, *f,* faire, mécanisme, *m.* **technology,** *n,* technologie, *f.*

Teddy bear, ours [martin], o. de peluche, *m.*

tedious†, *a,* ennuyeux, fastidieux, fatigant. ~**ness & tedium,** *n,* ennui, *m.*

tee, *n,* té, T; (*golf*) dé, *m.* *to a* ~, tout craché. ~ (*golf*) *v.t,* surélever. ~*ing ground* (*golf*), tertre de départ, *m.*

teem with, fourmiller de, regorger de.

teens (*in one's*), adolescent.

teethe, *v.i,* faire ses dents. **teething,** *n,* dentition, *f.*

teetotal, *a,* antialcoolique. ~**ism,** *n,* antialcoolisme, *m.* **teetotaller,** *n,* buveur d'eau, *m.*

teetotum, *n,* toton, *m.*

tegument, *n,* tégument, *m.*

telegram, *n,* télégramme, *m,* dépêche, *f.* **telegraph,** *n,* télégraphe, *m.* ~ *office,* [bureau du] télégraphe, *m.* ¶ *v.t. & i,* télégraphier. ~**ese,** *n,* style télégraphique, *m.* ~**ic†,** *a,* télégraphique. ~**y,** *n,* télégraphie, *f.*

telepathy, *n,* télépathie, *f.*

telephone, *n,* téléphone, *m.* ¶ *v.t. & i,* téléphoner. ¶ *att. & telephonic,* *a,* téléphonique. ~ *booth,* cabine téléphonique, *f.* ~ *number,* numéro de téléphone, *m.* **telephony,** *n,* téléphonie, *f.*

telescope, *n,* (*reflecting*) télescope, *m;* (*refracting*) lunette; (*spy-glass*) longue-vue, *f.* ¶ *v.i,* se télescoper. **telescopic,** *a,* télescopique; (*sliding*) à coulisse.

televise, *v.t,* téléviser. **television,** *n,* télévision, *f.*

tell, *v.t. & i.* ir, dire; [ra]conter, narrer; apprendre; savoir; reconnaître; (*of remark*) porter; (*in one's favor*) militer. ~**er,** *n,* (*voting*) scrutateur; (*bank*) caissier, *m.* ~**ing,** *a,* qui porte. ~**tale,** *n,* (*pers.*) rapporteur, euse.

temerity, *n,* témérité, *f.*

temper, *n,* caractère, *m;* humeur; trempe; colère, *f.* *to lose one's* ~, s'emporter. ¶ *v.t,* (*metal*) tremper; (*mortar*) gâcher; (*fig.*) tempérer, mitiger. **temperament,** *n,* tempérament, *m.* ~al, *a*, constitutionnel; capricieux, fantasque. temperance, *n*, tempérance, *f.* temperate, *a*, tempérant, sobre; (*climate, speech*) tempéré. temperature, *n*, température, *f.*

tempest, *n*, tempête, *f.* tempestuous, *a*, tempétueux.

template, -plet, *n*, gabarit, calibre, *m.*

temple, *n*, temple, *m*; (*Anat.*) tempe, *f.*

temporal†, *a*, (*secular*) temporel. temporary†, *a*, temporaire, momentané. temporize, *v.i*, temporiser.

tempt, *v.t*, tenter; inviter; affriander. ~ation, *n*, tentation, *f.* tempter, tress, *n*, tentateur, trice, séducteur, trice. tempting, *a*, tentant, séduisant; (*food*) appétissant, ragoûtant.

ten, *a*, dix. ¶ *n*, dix, *m*; dizaine, *f.* ~fold, *a. & n*, décuple, *a & m. to increase* ~, décupler.

tenable, *a*, tenable; soutenable. tenacious, *a*, tenace. ~ly, *ad*, avec ténacité.

tenancy, *n*, location, *f.* tenant, *n*, locataire, *m,f*; (*farm*) fermier, ère. ~ *farmer*, fermier, ère. ~able, *a*, logeable.

tench, *n*, tanche, *f.*

tend, *v.t*, garder; soigner; (*v.i.*) tendre; conspirer. ~ency, *n*, tendance; disposition, *f.* tendentious, *a*, tendancieux. tender, *n*, soumission; offre; (*boat*) annexe, *f*; (*Naut.*) transbordeur, *m.* (*Rly.*) tender, *m.* ¶ *v.t*, offrir; donner. ~ *for*, soumissionner.

tender†, *a*, tendre; sensible; délicat. ~ness, *n*, tendresse; délicatesse; (*eatables*) tendreté, *f.*

tendon, *n*, tendon, *m.*

tendril, *n*, vrille, main, *f.*

tenement, *n*, habitation, *f*, logement, *m*, maison de rapport, *f.*

tenet, *n*, dogme, *m*, doctrine, *f.*

tennis, *n*, tennis, *m.* ~ court, jeu de tennis, [court de] tennis, *m.*

tenon, *n*, tenon, *m.* ~ saw, scie à t., *f.*

tenor, *n*, teneur; (*bill*) échéance, *f*; (*voice, singer*) ténor, *m.* ~ clef, clef d'ut, *f.*

tense, *a*, tendu, raide. ¶ *n*, temps, *m.* tension, *n*, tension, *f.*

tent, *n*, tente; (*Surg.*) mèche, *f.* ~ pole, mât de t., *m.*

tentacle, *n*, tentacule, *m.*

tentative [effort], tâtonnement, *m.*

tenterhook, *n*, crochet [du fabricant de drap]; clou à crochet, *m. on* ~s, sur les charbons [ardents], sur le gril, au supplice.

tenth†, *a*, dixième. ¶ *n*, dixième, *m,f*; dix, *m.*

tenuity, *n*, ténuité, *f.* tenuous, *a*, ténu.

tenure, *n*, possession; jouissance, *f*; mode de possession; exercise, *m. during his* ~ *of office*, pendant l'exercise de ses fonctions.

tepid†, *a*, tiede. ~ness, *n*, tiédeur, *f.*

term, *n*, terme, *m*; clause; durée; session, *f*; trimestre, *m*; (*pl.*) conditions, *f. pl*; prix, *m*; (*pl*, opp. [*for*] *cash*) à crédit; (*pl.*) rapports, *m.pl*, intelligence; teneur, *f*; accommodement, *m. to come to* ~s, conclure un arrangement. ¶ *v.t*, appeler.

termagant, *n*, mégère, *f*, dragon, *m.*

terminable, *a*, résoluble. terminal, *a*, terminal; de tête de ligne. ¶ *n*, borne; extrémité, *f.* terminate, *v.t*, terminer; résoudre. termination, *n*, terminaison; fin, *f.* terminus, *n*, terminus, *m.*

termite, *n*, termite, *m*, fourmi blanche, *f.*

tern, *n*, sterne, *m.*

terrace, *n*, terrasse, *f.* ¶ *v.t*, étager. terracotta, *n*, terre cuite, *f.*

terrain, *n*, terrain, *m.*

terrestrial, *a*, terrestre.

terrible†, *a*, terrible.

terrier, *n*, [chien] terrier, *m.*

terrific†, *a*, terrible. terrify, *v.t*, terrifier.

territorial, *a. & n*, territorial, *a. & m.* territory, *n*, territoire, *m.*

terror, *n*, terreur, *f.* ~ize, *v.t*, terroriser.

terse, *a*, concis. ~ness, *n*, concision, *f.*

tessellated pavement, mosaïque, *f.*

test, *n*, épreuve, *f*, essai, *m*; pierre de touche, *f. blood* ~, prise de sang, *f.* ~ *tube*, éprouvette, *f.* ¶ *v.t*, essayer; éprouver; expérimenter; contrôler.

testament, *n*, testament, *m.* ~ary, *a*, testamentaire. testator, trix, *n*, testateur, trice. testify, *v.t, & i*, témoigner. testimonial, *n*, attestation, *f*; certificat, *m.* testimony, *n*, témoignage, *m.*

testicle, *n*, testicule, *m.*

testy, *a*, irritable, irascible.

tetanus, *n*, tétanos, *m.*

tether, *n,* longe, *f. at the end of one's ~,* au bout de son rouleau. ¶ *v.t,* mettre au piquet.

Teutonic, *a,* teutonique, teuton.

text, *n,* texte, *m.* **~book,** manuel, *m.*

textile, *n,* textile, tissu, *m.* ¶ *a,* textile.

textual†, *a,* textuel; *(error)* de texte.

texture, *n,* texture, tissure, *f,* tissu, *m,* contexture, *f.*

Thames (the), la Tamise.

than, *c. & pr,* que; de.

thank, *v.t,* remercier; bénir. *~ God!* Dieu merci! *~ Heaven!* grâce au ciel! *~ you! & no ~ you!* merci! **~ful,** *a,* reconnaissant. **~fully,** *ad,* avec reconnaissance. **~fulness,** *n,* reconnaissance, gratitude, *f.* **~less,** *a,* ingrat. **thanks,** *n.pl,* remerciements, *m.pl.* ¶ *i,* merci! *~ to,* grâce à. **thanksgiving,** *n,* action[s] de grâce, *f.[pl.].*

that, *a. & pn,* ce, cet, cette; ce . . ., etc., -là; celui, celle; cela, ça; ce, c', ç'; qui; que; là. *~ is all,* c'est tout; voilà tout. *~ is to say,* c'est-à-dire. *~ will do,* cela suffit. ¶ *c,* que; afin que; pour que.

thatch, *n,* chaume, *m.* ¶ *v.t,* couvrir en c. **~ed cottage,** chaumière, *f.* **~er,** *n,* couvreur en chaume, *m.*

thaw, *n,* dégel, *m.* ¶ *v.t, & i,* dégeler; se d.; *(fig.)* dégeler; se dégeler, se déraidir.

the, *art,* le, l', *m,* la, l', *f,* les, *m.f.pl. from ~, of ~,* du, de l', de la, des. *to ~, at ~,* au, à l', à la, aux.

theater, *n,* théâtre, *m.* **theatrical†,** *a,* de théâtre, du théâtre; théâtral, scénique. **theatricals,** *n.pl,* comédie, *f.*

thee, *pn,* te; toi.

theft, *n,* vol, *m.*

their, *a,* leur, leurs *(pl.).* **theirs,** *pn,* le leur, la leur, les leurs; à eux, à elles.

theism, *n,* théisme, *m.* **theistic(al),** *a,* théiste.

them, *pn,* eux, elles; les; leur; ceux, celles. **~selves,** eux[-mêmes], elles[-mêmes]; se.

theme, *n,* thème; sujet; *(Mus.)* motif, *m.*

then, *ad,* alors; ensuite; puis; donc; lors. **thence,** *ad,* de là. **thenceforth, thenceforward,** *ad,* dès lors.

theodolite, *n,* théodolite, *m.*

theologian, *n,* théologien, *m.*

theological†, *a,* théologique. **theology,** *n,* théologie, *f.*

theorem, *n,* théorème, *m.* **theoretic(al†),** *a,* théorique. **theorist,** *n,* théoricien, *m.* **theory,** *n,* théorie, *f.*

theosophy, *n,* théosophie, *f.*

therapeutic, *a. & ~s, n.pl,* thérapeutique, *a. & f.*

there, *ad,* là; y; là-bas; il. *~ & back,* aller & retour. *~ & then,* séance tenante, sur-le-champ, tout de go. *~ is, ~ are,* il y a. *~about, ~abouts,* près de là; environ. *~by,* de ce fait. *~fore,* c'est pourquoi; donc, aussi, par conséquent. *~on,* là-dessus. *~upon,* sur ce, là-dessus.

thermal, *a,* thermal. **thermometer,** *n,* thermomètre, *m.*

thermostat, *n,* thermostat, *m.*

these, *pn,* ces; ces . . . -ci; ceux-ci, celles-ci.

thesis, *n,* thèse, *f.*

thews, *n.pl,* nerfs, *m.pl.*

they, *pn,* ils, elles; eux, elles; ceux, celles; il; ce, c'; on.

thick, *a,* épais; dense; puissant; gros; gras; dru; fourni; touffu; *(with someone)* lié. *~ or clear (soup)?* potage ou consommé? **~-lipped,** lippu. **~set,** trapu, ramassé; dru. **~[ly],** *ad,* épais, dru. *in the ~ of,* au fort de. *through ~ & thin,* envers & contre tous. **~en,** *v.t,* épaissir; *(sauce)* lier. **~ening,** *n,* épaississement, *m; (for sauce)* liaison, *f.* **~et,** *n,* fourré; bosquet, *m.* **~ness,** *n,* épaisseur; puissance, *f.*

thief, *n,* voleur, euse, larron, *m.* **thieve,** *v.t,* voler. **thievish,** *a,* voleur; *(pers.)* voleur.

thigh, *n,* cuisse, *f.* *~ bone,* os de la c., *m.* *~ boots,* bottes cuissardes, *f.pl.*

thill, *n,* limon, brancard, *m.*

thimble, *n,* dé [à coudre] *m; (Naut.)* cosse, *f.* **~rigger,** joueur de gobelets, *m.* **~ful,** *n,* doigt, *m.*

thin, *a,* mince; maigre; délié, ténu; faible; clair; *(hair, grass)* rare; *(legs, voice)* grêle. *to be ~-skinned (fig.),* avoir l'épiderme sensible. *~ slice,* mince tranche, lèche, *f.* ¶ *v.t,* amincir, amenuiser; éclaircir; amaigrir.

thine, *pn,* le tien, la tienne, les tiens, les tiennes; à toi.

thing, *n,* chose; affaire, *f; (pers.)* être, *m; (pl.)* effets, *m.pl. the ~ (in fashion),* de mise.

think, *v.t. & i. ir,* penser; songer; juger; réfléchir; croire; trouver; s'imaginer. **~er,** *n,* penseur, *m.* **thinking,** *a,* pensant. ¶ *n,* pensée; réflexion, *f;* avis, *m.*

thinly, *ad,* clair. **~ sown,** semé clair, clairsemé. **thinness,** *n,* minceur, ténuité; maigreur; rareté, *f.* **thinnish,** *a,* maigrelet.

third†, *a,* troisième; tiers. **~ finger,** [doigt] annulaire, *m.* **~ person,** tiers, *m,* tierce personne; (*Gram.*) troisième personne, *f.* ¶ *n,* tiers, *m;* tierce, *f;* troisième, *m,f;* trois, *m.*

thirst, *n,* soif, *f.* **~-creating,** altérant. **~ for,** avoir soif de. **thirsty,** *a,* altéré; (*country*) de la soif. **to be ~,** avoir soif.

thirteen, *a. & n,* treize, *a & m.* **~th**†, *a. & n,* treizième, *a. & m,f;* treize, *m.*

thirtieth, *a. & n,* trentième, *a. & m,f;* trente, *m.* **thirty,** *a. & n,* trente, *a. & m.*

this, *a. pn,* ce, cet, cette; ce . . ., -ci; celui-ci, celle-ci; ceci; présent. **~ way!** par ici! **~ way & that,** çà & là.

thistle, *n,* chardon, *m.* **~down,** duvet du chardon, *m.*

thong, *n,* lanière, *f.*

thorax, *n,* thorax, *m.*

thorn & **~** [*bush*] *n,* épine, *f.* **~y,** *a,* épineux.

thorough, *a,* achevé; accompli; approfondi; minutieux; parfait. **~bred** [*horse*], cheval pur sang, c. de race, c. racé, *m.* **~fare,** voie, *f,* passage, *m;* rue [passante]; artère, *f.* **~ly,** *ad,* à fond, foncièrement; mûrement; complètement; parfaitement.

those, *pn,* ces; ces . . . -là; ceux, celles; ceux-là, celles-là; ce.

thou, *pn,* tu; toi. ¶ *v.t,* tutoyer.

though, *c,* quoique, bien que, quand; cependant, tout . . . que. **as ~,** comme si.

thought, *n,* pensée; réflexion; idée, *f.* **~ful,** *a,* pensif, réfléchi. **~less**†, *a,* étourdi; irréfléchi. **~lessness,** *n,* étourderie; irréflexion, *f.*

thousand, *a,* mille; mil. ¶ *n,* mille; millier, *m.* **~th,** *a. & n,* millième, *a. & m.*

thraldom, *n,* servage; esclavage, *m.* **thrall,** *n,* serf, *m,* serve, *f;* esclave, *m,f.*

thrash, *v.t,* battre, rosser. **~ing,** *n,* peignée, *f.*

thread, *n,* fil, *m;* corde, *f;* fila-

ment, filé; (*screw*) filet; (*of life*) trame, *f.* **~bare,** usé jusqu'à la corde, râpé; usé. ¶ *v.t,* enfiler; (*screw*) fileter.

threat, *n,* menace, *f.* **~en,** *v.t,* menacer.

three, *a. & n,* trois, *a. & m.* **~ color process,** trichromie, *f.* **~-master,** trois-mâts, *m.* **~-ply** [*wood*], contreplaqué en trois, bois plaqué triplé, *m.* **~some,** partie de trois, *f.* **~-speed gear,** dispositif à 3 vitesses, *m.* **~fold,** *a,* triple.

thresh, *v.t,* battre, dépiquer. **~ out,** vider. **~er** (*pers.*) *n,* batteur en grange, *m.* **~ing machine,** batteuse, *f.*

threshold, *n,* seuil, pas, *m.*

thrice, *ad,* trois fois.

thrift, *n,* économie, épargne, *f.* **~less,** *a,* prodigue, dépensier. **~y,** *a,* économe, ménager.

thrill, *n,* tressaillement, saisissement, frisson, *m,* vive émotion, *f.* ¶ *v.t,* électriser; empoigner; (*v.i.*) tressaillir, palpiter. **~ing,** *a,* passionnant, palpitant, empoignant.

thrive, *v.i.ir,* prospérer; (*plant*) se plaire. **not to ~,** se déplaire. **thriving,** *a,* florissant, prospère.

throat, *n,* gorge, *f;* gosier, *m.*

throb, *v.i,* battre, palpiter; (*Med.*) élancer.

throe, *n,* douleur, *f;* (*pl.*) affres, *f.pl.*

throne, *n,* trône, *m;* (*bishop's*) chaire, *f.*

throng, *n,* foule, presse, *f.* ¶ *v.t,* accourir en foule à; assiéger; (*v.i.*) se presser.

throstle, *n,* grive chanteuse, *f.*

throttle, *n,* gosier; régulateur; (*Mech.*) étrangleur, *m.* ¶ *v.t,* étrangler.

through, *pr,* à travers; au t. de; par; à cause de. **~ thick & thin,** envers & contre tous. ¶ *ad,* à travers; au t.; de part en part, à jour; jusqu'au bout; d'un bout à l'autre; directement. ¶ *a,* direct; à forfait, forfaitaire. **~ ticket,** (*to final destination*) billet direct; (*sea-land-sea*) billet global, *m.* **~out,** *pr,* par tout; pendant tout; (*ad.*) complètement, jusqu'au bout.

throw, *n,* jet, *m;* (*Mech.*) excentricité, *f.* ¶ *v.t.ir,* jeter; lancer; démonter; terrasser; tomber; mettre. **~ away,** jeter. **~ back,** rejeter. **~ down,** **~ over,** renverser. **~ open,** ouvrir. **~ out,**

chasser; rejeter. ~ *up*, jeter en l'air; vomir. ~*ing*, *n*, lancement, *m*.

thrum, *v.t*, tapoter (*on* = sur); (*v.i.*) tambouriner.

thrush, *n*, grive; (*Med.*) aphte, *f*.

thrust, *n*, coup, *m*; (*Fenc.*) botte, estocade; (*Mech.*) poussée, butée, *f*. ¶ *v.t.ir*, pousser; plonger; (*sword*) pointer; (*Fenc.*) estocader; imposer. ~ *aside*, repousser. ~ *at* (*Fenc.*), porter une botte à.

thud, *n*, coup sourd, son mat, floc, *m*.

thug, *n*, étrangleur, *m*.

thumb, *n*, pouce, *m*. ~ *index*, répertoire à onglets, *m*. ~*screw*, écrou à oreilles, papillon, *m*. ~*tack*, punaise, *f*. ¶ *v.t*, feuilleter.

thump, *n*, coup sourd, *m*; bourrade, *f*, horion, *m*. ¶ *v.t*, cogner; sonner lourdement.

thunder, *n*, tonnerre, *m*, foudre, *f*. ~*bolt*, foudre, *f*, coup de foudre, tonnerre, *m*; (*pl*, *Jove's*) foudres, traits, *m.pl*. ~*clap*, coup de tonnerre, *m*. ~*cloud*, nuée, *f*. ~*storm*, orage, *m*. ~*struck*, foudroyé. ¶ *v.i*. & *t*, tonner; fulminer. ~*y*, *a*, orageux.

Thursday, *n*, jeudi, *m*.

thus, *ad*, ainsi, de cette façon. ~ *far*, jusqu'ici.

thwack, *n*, coup, *m*. ¶ *v.t*, frapper.

thwart, *n*, banc [de nage] *m*. ¶ *v.t*, croiser, contrecarrer, traverser.

thy, *a*, ton, ta, tes.

thyme, *n*, thym; (*wild*) serpolet, *m*.

thyroid, *a*, thyroïde.

thyself, *pn*, toi-même; toi; te.

tiara, *n*, tiare, *f*.

Tiber (the), le Tibre.

tibia, *n*, tibia, *m*.

tic, *n*, tic, *m*.

Ticino (the), le Tessin.

tick, *n*, coutil, *m*, (*ticking*) toile à matelas; (*insect*) tique, *f*, acare; tic tac; point, *m*; seconde, *f*. ~*tack*, tic tac, *m*. ¶ *v.i*, battre; (*v.t.*) pointer.

ticket, *n*, billet; bulletin; cachet, *m*; entrée; carte; étiquette, *f*. ~ *collector*, contrôleur, *m*. ~ *window*, guichet [de distribution des billets] *m*. ¶ *v.t*, étiqueter.

tickle, *v.t*. & *i*, chatouiller. **ticklish,** *a*, chatouilleux; critique, délicat, scabreux.

tidal, *a*: ~ *basin*, bassin de marée,

m. ~ *water*, eaux à m., *f.pl*. ~ *wave*, flot de la marée, raz de m., *m*, barre de flot, *f*. **tide,** *n*, marée, *f*; courant, *m*. *ebb* ~, marée descendante, *f*. *flood* ~, marée montante, *f*. *to* ~ *over a difficulty*, se tirer d'affaire.

tidiness, *n*, propreté, *f*, bon ordre, *m*.

tidings, *n.pl*, nouvelles, *f.pl*.

tidy, *a*, bien tenu, rangé; (*pers.*) ordonné. ¶ *v.t*, ranger. ~ *oneself up*, s'ajuster, faire un bout de toilette.

tie, *n*, lien, *m*; attache, *f*; tirant, *m*; cravate, *f*; nœud, *m*; (*Mus.*) liaison; (*voting*) égalité de voix; (*sport*) égalité de points, *f*. ~ *clip*, fixe-cravate, *m*. ~ *pin*, épingle de cravate, *f*. ¶ *v.t.ir*, lier; attacher; clouer; (*knot*) faire; (*v.i.*) (*sport*) arriver à égalité; (*exams*) être [classé] ex æquo. ~ *down*, lier; astreindre. ~ *up*, lier; bander; mettre à l'attache.

tier, *n*, rangée, *f*, rang, étage, gradin, *m*.

tierce, *n*, tierce, *f*.

Tierra del Fuego, la Terre de Feu.

tiff, *n*, fâcherie, pique, difficulté, *f*.

tiger, *n*, tigre, *m*. ~ *cat*, chat-tigre, *m*. ~ *lily*, lis tigré, *m*.

tight, *a*, serré; tendu; raide; étroit; juste; collant; étanche. ~ *corner*, coin étranglé; mauvais pas, *m*. ~*wad*, grippe-sou, *m*. ~*en*, *v.t*, [res]serrer, tendre, raidir. ~[*ly*] *ad*, serré; étroitement. ~*ness*, *n*, tension, raideur; étroitesse; étanchéité, *f*.

tigress, *n*, tigresse, *f*.

Tigris (the), le Tigre.

tile, *n*, tuile, *f*; carreau, *m*; (*pl*, *roof*) gouttières, *f.pl*. ~ *flooring*, carrelage, *m*. ~ *maker*, tuilier, *m*. ~ *works*, tuilerie, *f*. ¶ *v.t*, couvrir de tuiles; carreler.

till, *n*, caisse, *f*, tiroir de c., *m*. ¶ *v.t*, labourer. ¶ *pr*, jusqu'à; jusque; avant; à. ¶ *c*, jusqu'à ce que; en attendant que. **tillage,** *n*, labourage, *m*. **tiller,** *n*, laboureur, *m*; barre [du gouvernail] *f*.

tilt, *n*, bâche; joute; inclinaison, *f*. ¶ *v.t*, incliner; culbuter; (*v.i.*) s'incliner; jouter. **tilting** (*Hist.*) *n*, joute, *f*.

timber, *n*, bois [de charpente]; (*ship*) couple, *m*. ~ *tree*, arbre de haute futaie, *m*. ~*-tree forest*, futaie, *f.* ~work, charpente [en bois] *f.* ¶ *v.t,* boiser; charpenter.

timbre, *n,* timbre, *m.*

Timbuctoo, *n,* Tombouctou, *m.*

time, *n,* temps; moment, *m;* époque; saison, *f;* siècle, *m;* heure; fois, reprise, *f;* terme, *m;* mesure; cadence, *f;* pas, *m. at ~s,* parfois. *[just] in ~,* à point. *~ fuse,* fusée à temps, *f.* ~honored, séculaire. ~keeper *(pers.),* pointeur, contrôleur; *(sport)* chronométreur, *m.* ~piece, pendule, *f.* ~server, opportuniste, *m,f,* caméléon, *m,* complaisant, e. *~ sheet,* feuille de présence, *f.* ~table, *(book)* indicateur; *(placard & scheme of work)* horaire, *m. at any ~,* n'importe quand. *from ~ to ~,* de temps en temps. *next ~,* la prochaine fois. ¶ *v.t, (watch)* régler; *(sport)* chronométrer. ~ing, *n,* pointage, *m.* **timeliness,** *n,* opportunité, *f.* **timely,** *a,* opportun.

timid†, *a,* timide, peureux. ~ity, *n,* timidité, *f.* **timorous,** *a,* timoré.

tin, *n,* étain; *(can)* bidon, *m;* boîte [métallique] *f.* ~ *foil,* feuille d'étain, *f.* ~ *[plate],* fer-blanc, *m.* ~ *soldier,* soldat de plomb, *m.* ~smith, ferblantier, *m.* ~ware, ferblanterie, *f.* ¶ *v.t,* étamer; mettre en boîte(s), *m.* en conserve.

tincture, *n,* teinture, *f.* ¶ *v.t,* teindre.

tinder, *n,* amadou, *m. ~ box,* briquet, *m.*

tine, *n,* dent, branche, *f; (deer)* andouiller, *m.*

tinge, *n,* teinte, nuance, *f.* ¶ *v.t,* teinter.

tingle, *v.i,* picoter; fourmiller; *(ears)* tinter.

tinker, *n,* chaudronnier ambulant, *m.*

tinkle, *v.i,* tinter. ¶ *n,* tintement, *m.* ~! ~! drelin-drelin!

tinsel, *n,* clinquant, *m,* oripeaux, *m.pl; (fig.)* faux brillant, *m.*

tint, *n,* teinte, *f,* ton, *m.* ¶ *v.t,* teinter.

tiny, *a,* minuscule, petiot, infime. *~ bit,* tantinet, tout petit peu, *m. ~ drop,* gouttelette, *f.*

tip, *n,* bout; face, *m;* pointe; extrémité, *f; (wing)* fouet; *(Bil. cue)* procédé; *(gratuity)* pourboire, *m,* pièce, *f; (information)* tuyau, *m.* ¶ *v.t,* embouter; basculer; culbuter; verser; donner un

pourboire à; donner un tuyau à. ~cart, tombereau, *m.*

tippet, *n,* palatine, *f,* mantelet, *m.*

tipple, *v.i,* buvoter, chopiner. **tippler,** *n,* biberon, ne.

tipster, *n,* donneur de tuyaux, *m.*

tipsy, *a,* ivre. *a ~ walk,* une démarche avinée.

tiptoe(on), sur la pointe du pied.

tiptop, *n,* comble, *m.* ¶ *a,* excellent, parfait.

tirade, *n,* tirade, incartade, *f.*

tire, *n,* bandage; pneu[matique], caoutchouc, *m. flat ~,* pneu crevé, *m. spare ~,* pneu de rechange, *m.*

tire, *v.t,* fatiguer, lasser, excéder; *(v.i.)* se fatiguer, se lasser. ~d out, rompu [de fatigue]. ~less, *a,* infatigable. ~some, *a,* fatigant; ennuyeux, fâcheux.

tissue, *n,* tissu, *m;* tissure, *f. ~ paper,* papier de soie, *m.*

tit *(bird) n,* mésange, *f. ~ for tat,* donnant donnant; un prêté [pour un] rendu.

titbit, *n,* bonne bouche, *f.*

tithe, *n,* dîme, *f. not a ~,* pas un dixième.

titillate, *v.t,* titiller, chatouiller.

titivate, *v.t,* bichonner.

title, *n,* titre; intitulé; parchemin, *m. ~ [deed],* titre, *m. ~ page,* page du titre, *f,* titre, frontispice, *m.* ~d, *a,* titré.

titmouse, *n,* mésange, *f.*

titter, *v.i,* rire bêtement, glousser.

tittle, *n,* iota, *m.*

titular, *a,* titulaire, en titre.

to, *pr,* à; de; pour; afin de; en; dans; envers; vers; jusqu'à; chez; auprès de; près; sur; contre; *(of the hour)* moins. *to go ~ & fro,* aller de long en large, aller deçà, delà; aller & venir, faire la navette. *~ be called for,* bureau restant, poste restante; télégraphe restant; gare restante, en gare. *~ be kept cool, dry* or *in a cool, dry, place,* craint la chaleur, l'humidité. *~ be taken after meals,* à prendre après les repas. *~ boot,* en sus, par surcroît, avec ça. *~ match,* pareil. *~ measure,* sur mesure. *~ wit,* savoir; *(of pers.)* nommément.

toad, *n,* crapaud, *m. ~ hole,* crapaudière, *f.* ~stone, crapaudine, *f.* ~stool, champignon [vénéneux] *m.* **toady,** *n,* flagorneur, euse, chien couchant, *m.* ~ *to,* flagorner. ~ism, *n,* flagornerie, *f.*

toast, *n,* pain grillé, *m,* rôtie, *f;*

(*buttered*) toast; (*health*) toast, *m.* ¶*v.t,* griller, rôtir; (*health*) porter un toast à. ~**er,** *n,* grille-pain, *m.* ~**ing fork,** fourchette à griller le pain, *f.*

tobacco, *n,* tabac, *m.* ~ *pouch,* blague à t., *f.* **tobacconist,** *n,* débitant de t., *m.* ~'*s shop,* débit de t., bureau de t., *m.*

toboggan, *n,* toboggan, *m.* ~ *run,* piste de toboggan, *f.*

today, *ad. & n,* aujourd'hui, *ad. & m.* ~'*s gossip,* nouvelles à la main, *f.pl.*

toddle, *v.i,* trottiner.

to-do, *n,* cérémonies, *f.pl;* aria, *m.*

toe, *n,* doigt [de pied], orteil, *m;* (*shoe, sock*) pointe, *f.* ~ *dancing,* pointes, *f.pl.* ~ *nail,* ongle d'orteil, *m.*

toga, *n,* toge, *f.*

together, *ad,* ensemble; à la fois. ~ *with,* avec, en compagnie de, ainsi que.

toil, *n,* travail, labeur, *m;* (*pl.*) lacets, rets, *m.pl,* toiles, *f.pl.* ¶*v.i,* peiner. ~ & *moil,* suer d'ahan, peiner. ~**er,** *n,* travailleur, euse.

toilet, *n,* toilette, *f.* ~ *paper,* papier hygiénique, *m.*

toilsome, *a,* pénible, laborieux.

token, *n,* signe, témoignage, *m,* preuve, marque, *f;* gage, hommage; jeton, *m.*

Toledo, *n,* Tolède, *f.*

tolerable, *a,* tolérable; passable. **tolerably,** *ad,* passablement. **tolerance** & **toleration,** *n,* tolérance, *f.* **tolerate,** *v.t,* tolérer.

toll, *n,* péage, passage, *m.* ~ *call* (*Teleph.*), communication régionale, *f.* ~ *gate,* barrière de péage, *f.* ¶*v.t. & i,* tinter, sonner. ~**ing,** *n,* tintement funèbre, *m.*

tom: ~*boy,* garçon manqué, *m.* ~ [*cat*], matou, chat, *m.* ~*foolery,* farce, pantalonnade, gaminerie, *f.* ~*tit,* mésange charbonnière, *f.*

tomato, *n,* tomate, *f.* ~ *sauce,* sauce t., *f.*

tomb, *n,* tombe, *f,* tombeau, *m,* sépulture, *f.* ~*stone,* pierre tombale, *f.*

tome, *n,* tome, volume, *m.*

tomorrow, *ad. & n,* demain, *ad. & m.* ~ *morning,* demain matin. ~ *night,* ~ *evening,* demain soir.

tomtom, *n,* tam-tam, *m.*

ton, *n,* tonne, *f;* tonneau, *m.*

tone, *n,* ton; son; accent, *m,* gamme, *f;* dispositions, *f.pl.* ¶ (*v.t, Phot.*) virer; (*v.i.*) s'har-

moniser. ~ *down,* adoucir, assourdir, estomper.

tongs, *n.pl,* pince, tenaille, *f,* pincettes, *f.pl.*

tongue, *n,* langue; (*strip, slip*) languette, *f.* ~*tied,* la langue liée.

Tonkin, le Tonkin.

tonic, *a,* tonique; remontant. ~ *sol-fa,* tonic-sol-fa, *m.* ¶ *n,* (*Med. & drink*) tonique, remontant, *m;* (*Mus.*) tonique, *f.*

tonight, *ad. & n,* ce soir, cette nuit.

toning (*Phot.*) *n,* virage, *m.*

tonnage, *n,* tonnage, *m;* jauge, *f.*

tonsil, *n,* amygdale, *f.* **tonsilitis,** *n,* amygdalite, *f.*

tonsure, *n,* tonsure, couronne, *f.* ¶ *v.t,* tonsurer.

too, *ad,* trop; aussi; également; de même; encore. ~ *long,* (*length*) trop long; (*time*) trop long [longtemps]. ~ *much,* ~ *many* & ~ *well,* trop.

tool, *n,* outil; instrument; ustensile; (*pers.*) suppôt, *m,* âme damnée, *f.* ~ *box,* boîte à outils, *f.* ~ *maker,* fabricant d'outils, taillandier, *m.* ¶ *v.t,* (*Mach.*) travailler; (*Bookb.*) gaufrer.

tooth, *n,* dent, *f.* ~*ache,* mal de dents, *m,* (*violent*) rage de dents, *f.* ~ *brush,* brosse à dents, *f.* ~ *brush moustache,* moustache en brosse, *f.* ~*paste,* pâte dentifrice, *f,* dentifrice, *m.* ~*pick,* cure-dents, *m.* ~ *powder,* poudre dentifrice, *f,* dentifrice, *m.* ¶ *v.t,* [en]denter, créneler. ~*some,* *a,* succulent.

top, *n,* haut; sommet, *m;* cime, *f;* faîte; comble; dessus, *m;* tête, pointe, *f;* (*bus*) impériale; (*Naut.*) hune; (*turnip, etc.*) fane; (*book page*) tête, tranche supérieure; (*toys*) toupie, *f,* sabot, *m.* *at the* ~ *of one's voice,* à tue-tête. *on* ~ *of,* par-dessus, sur. ~ *boots,* bottes à revers, *f.pl.* ~*coat,* pardessus, *m.* ~ *figure,* chiffre maximum, *m.* ~*gallant,* perroquet, *m.* ~ *hat,* chapeau haut de forme, *m.* ~*heavy,* trop lourd du haut. ~*mast,* mât de hune, *m.* ~*sail,* hunier, *m.* ¶ *v.t,* couronner; surpasser; dépasser; être à la tête de; (*tree*) étêter.

topaz, *n,* topaze, *f.*

topic, *n,* sujet, thème, *m.* ~*al song,* chanson de circonstance, *f.*

topographic(al), *a,* topographique. **topography,** *n,* topographie, *f.*

topple, *v.i,* dégringoler. ~ *over,* faire culbuter, renverser.

topsyturvy, *ad,* sens dessus dessous.

torch, *n,* flambeau, *m,* torche, *f.* ~ *bearer,* porte-flambeau, *m. by* ~*light,* à la lueur des flambeaux, aux flambeaux.

toreador, *n,* toréador, *m.*

torment, *n,* tourment, supplice, *m.* ¶ *v.t,* tourmenter; travailler; taquiner. **tormentor,** *n,* bourreau, *m.*

tornado, *n,* tornade, *f.*

torpedo, *n,* torpille, *f.* ~ *boat,* [bateau] torpilleur, *m.* ¶ *v.t,* torpiller.

torpid, *a,* torpide. **torpor,** *n,* torpeur, *f.*

torrent, *n,* torrent, *m.* in ~*s,* à torrents, à flots. ~**ial,** *a,* torrentiel, diluvien.

torrid, *a,* torride.

torsion, *n,* torsion, *f.*

torso, *n,* torse, *m.*

tort (*law*), *n,* acte dommageable, *m.*

tortoise, *n,* tortue, *f.* ~**shell,** écaille [de t.] *f.* ~**shell butterfly,** tortue, *f.* ~**shell cat,** chat d'Espagne, *m.*

tortuous†, *a,* tortueux, tortu.

torture, *n,* torture, *f,* tourment, supplice, *m. instrument of* ~, instrument de torture, appareil tortionnaire, *m.* ¶ *v.t,* torturer, tourmenter. **torturer,** *n,* tortionnaire, bourreau, *m.* **torturous,** *a,* tortionnaire.

toss, *v.t. & i,* jeter; ballotter; cahoter; secouer; (*head*) hocher; (*oars*) mâter. ~ *off* (*drink*), lamper, sabler. ~ [*up*] (*coin*), tirer [à pile ou face].

tot, *n,* (*child*) petiot, e; (*rum, etc.*) boujaron, *m.*

total†, *a,* total; global; complet. ¶ *n,* total; montant, *m.* **totalitarian,** *a,* totalitaire. **totalizer, totalizator,** *n,* totaliseur, totalisateur, *m.*

totter, *v.i,* chanceler; s'ébranler.

toucan, *n,* toucan, *m.*

touch, *n,* toucher; tact, *m;* touche, *f;* contact, *m;* communication, *f;* coup; (*art*) pinceau; soupçon, *m;* pointe, *f.* ~*wood,* amadou, *m.* ¶ *v.t. & i,* toucher; t. à; se t.; tâter; effleurer. *to keep in* ~, garder le contact. ~ *up,* retou-

cher; chatouiller. ~**ed** (*crazy*), *p.p,* toqué, timbré. ~**iness,** *n,* susceptibilité, *f.* ~**ing,** *a. & pr,* touchant. ~**y,** *a,* susceptible, chatouilleux.

tough†, *a,* dur; résistant; tenace; coriace. ~**en,** *v.t,* durcir. ~**ness,** *n,* dureté; ténacité; résistance, *f.*

tour, *n,* tour, voyage, *m,* tournée, *f.* ~**ing,** *n,* tourisme, *m.* ~**ist,** *n,* touriste, *m,f.* ~ *agency,* agence de tourisme, *f.*

tournament, *n,* tournoi; concours, *m.*

tourniquet, *n,* tourniquet, garrot, *m.*

tousle, *v.t,* ébouriffer.

tow, *n,* filasse, étoupe, *f;* (*boat*) remorqué, *m.* in ~, à la remorque, à la traîne. ¶ *v.t,* remorquer; haler, touer. ~[*ing*] *path,* chemin de halage, tirage, *m.*

toward[s], *pr,* vers; envers; vis-à-vis de, à l'endroit de; sur.

towel, *n,* serviette [de toilette] *f,* essuie-mains, *m.* **toweling,** *n,* tissu éponge, *m.*

tower, *n,* tour, *f;* pylône, *m.* ~ *above,* dominer. ~**ing rage,** colère bleue, *f.*

town, *n,* ville; place, *f.* ~ *clerk,* secrétaire de mairie, *m.* ~ *crier,* crieur public, *m.* ~ *hall,* hôtel de ville, *m,* maison de ville, mairie, *f.* ~ *house,* hôtel, *m.* ~ *planning,* urbanisme, *m.* **townsman,** *n,* citadin, *m.*

toxic, *a,* toxique. **toxin,** *n,* toxine, *f.*

toy, *n,* jouet, joujou, *m,* babiole, *f.* ~ *balloon,* ballon d'enfant, *m.* ¶ *v.i,* jouer, badiner.

trace, *n,* trace, *f;* (*harness*) trait; (*Fish.*) bas de ligne avec émerillons, *m.* ~ *horse,* [cheval] côtier, cheval de renfort, *m.* ¶ *v.t,* tracer; calquer; suivre la trace de; suivre à la trace. ~ *back,* faire remonter. ~*d pattern,* tracé, *m.* ~**ry,** *n,* réseau, *m,* dentelle, *f.*

trachea, *n,* trachée-artère, *f.*

tracing, *n,* calque, *m.*

track, *n,* trace; piste; voie, *f;* chemin, sentier, *m;* route, *f;* sillage; sillon, *m.* ~ *race,* course sur piste, *f.* ¶ *v.t,* suivre à la piste. ~ *down,* (*game*) dépister; (*criminal*) traquer.

tract, *n,* étendue, *f;* (*leaflet*) opuscule, *m.* ~**able,** *a,* traitable. **traction,** *n,* traction, *f.* ~ *engine,*

machine routière; locomobile, *f.*
tractor, *n,* tracteur, *m.*

trade, *n,* commerce; négoce; trafic, *m,* traite, *f;* métier, *m;* industrie, *f.* ~ *discount,* remise [sur marchandises] *f.* ~*mark,* marque de commerce, m. de fabrique, *f.* ~ *route,* route commerciale, *f.* ~ *union,* syndicat ouvrier, *m.* ~ *unionist,* syndicaliste, syndiqué, *m.* ~ *winds,* vents alizés, *m.pl.* ¶ *v.i,* trafiquer (*in* = en), faire [le] commerce (*in* = de). **trader,** *n,* commerçant, e; trafiquant, *m; (col. pl.)* le commerce. **trading,** *n,* commerce, *m;* traite, *f;* exercice, *m.* ~ *account,* compte d'exploitation, *m.* ~ *capital,* capital engagé, *m.* **tradesman,** *n,* marchand; boutiquier; fournisseur, *m. tradesmen's entrance,* porte de service, *f.*

tradition, *n,* tradition, *f.* ~**al**†, *a,* traditionnel.

traduce, *v.t,* calomnier. ~**er,** *n,* diffamateur, *m.*

traffic, *n,* trafic, *m,* traite, *f;* mouvement, *m;* circulation, *f.* ~ *jam,* embouteillage, *m.* ~ *lights,* signaux lumineux de circulation, feux de c., *m.pl.* ~ *police,* police de la circulation, *f.* ~ *circle, n,* rond-point, *m.* ~ *sign,* poteau de signalisation, *m.* **trafficker,** *n,* trafiquant, *m.*

tragedian, *n,* [auteur] tragique; *m.* ~, *tragedienne,* tragédien, ne. **tragedy,** *n,* tragédie, *f;* drame, *m.* **tragic(al**†), *a,* tragique. **tragicomedy,** *n,* tragi-comédie, *f.* **tragicomic,** *a,* tragi-comique.

trail, *n,* piste, trace; traînée, *f,* sillon, *m; (gun carriage)* flèche, *f.* ~ *rope (Avn.),* guiderope, *m.* ¶ *v.t,* suivre à la piste; traîner. ~**er,** *n,* remorque; roulotte, *f.*

train, *n,* train; convoi, *m;* suite, *f;* cortège, *m; (dress)* traîne, queue; *(comet)* queue; *(powder)* traînée, *f.* ~ *(events)* enchaînement, *m.* ¶ *v.t,* former, styler; instruire; dresser, éduquer; entraîner; *(gun)* diriger, pointer. ~**er,** *n,* dresseur; entraîneur, *m.* **training,** *n,* éducation; école; instruction, *f;* enseignement; dressage, manège; entraînement, *m,* haleine, *f.* ~ *ship,* vaisseau-école, *m.*

trait, *n,* trait, *m.*

traitor, tress, *n,* traître, *m,*

traîtresse, *f.* ~**ous,** *a,* traître. ~**ously,** *ad,* en traître.

trajectory, *n,* trajectoire, *f.*

trammel, *n, (net)* tramail, *m; (pl.)* entraves, *f.pl.* ¶ *v.t,* entraver.

tramp, *n,* bruit de pas, *m; (horses)* battue; promenade [à pied] *f; (pers.)* chemineau, *m,* vagabond, e. ¶ *v.i,* marcher pesamment; cheminer; marcher; *(v.t.)* arpenter. ~ *up & down,* courir.

trample [on] [down], *v.t,* fouler, piétiner.

trance, *n,* extase; *(hypnotic)* transe, *f.*

tranquil†, *a,* tranquille. **tranquility,** *n,* tranquillité, *f.*

transact, *v.t,* traiter, faire; délibérer sur. ~**ion,** *n,* négociation; affaire, transaction; délibération, *f; (pl.),* actes, *m.pl.*

transatlantic, *a,* transatlantique.

transcend, *v.t,* dépasser; surpasser. ~**ent,** *a,* transcendant.

transcribe, *v.t,* transcrire. **transcript & transcription,** *n,* transcription, *f.*

transept, *n,* transept, *m.*

transfer, *n,* transmission; cession, *f;* apport; *(law)* transfert; transport; virement, *m; (for china & as toy)* décalcomanie; *(bus)* billet de correspondance; *m.* ~ *[deed],* transfert, *m,* feuille de t., *f.* ¶ *v.t,* transmettre; céder; apporter; transférer; transporter; virer; décalquer. ~**able,** *a,* cessible; mobilier.

transfiguration, *n,* transfiguration, *f.*

transfix, *v.t,* transpercer.

transform, *v.t,* transformer. ~**ation,** *n,* transformation, *f.* ~**er,** *n,* transformateur, *m.*

transfuse, *v.t,* transfuser. **transfusion,** *n,* transfusion, *f.*

transgress, *v.t,* transgresser, contrevenir à. ~**or,** *n,* violateur, trice; pécheur, eresse.

transient†, *a,* transitoire, passager.

transit, *n,* transit; passage; transport, *m.* in ~, en transit; en cours de route. ~**ion,** *n,* transition, *f,* passage, *m.* ~**ive**†, *a,* transitif. ~**ory**†, *a,* transitoire.

translate, *v.t,* traduire; *(bishop)* transférer. **translation,** *n,* traduction; version; *(bishop)* translation, *f.* **translator,** *n,* traducteur, trice.

translucent, *a*, translucide.

transmigration, *n*, transmigration, *f*.

transmission, *n*, transmission; (*auto*) boîte de vitesse; (*radio*) émission, *f*.

transmit, *v.t*, transmettre; émettre. **transmitter**, *n*, transmetteur; (*radio*) émetteur, *m*.

transmute, *v.t*, transmuer.

transom, *n*, vasistas, *m*; traverse, *f*.

transparency, *n*, transparence, *f*; transparent, *m*; diapositive, *f*. **transparent**, *a*, transparent.

transpire, *v.i*, transpirer.

transplant, *v.t*, transplanter, dépiquer.

transport, *n*, transport, *m*. ¶ *v.t*, transporter.

transpose, *v.t*, transposer.

transubstantiation, *n*, transsubstantiation, *f*.

transverse†, *a*, transversal.

trap, *n*, trappe, *f*, traquenard, piège; guetapens, *m*. *mouse* ~, souricière, *f*. ~*door*, trappe, *f*. ¶ *v.t*, prendre au piège, attraper.

trapeze, *n*, trapèze, *m*.

trapper, *n*, trappeur, *m*.

trappings, *n.pl*, harnachement, *m*; (*fig.*) parure, *f*.

trash, *n*, camelote, pacotille, saloperie, saleté, *f*; (*worthless contents of book*) futilités, *f.pl*.

travel, *n*, voyage, *m*. ¶ *v.i*, voyager; marcher; rouler. ~ *over*, parcourir. **traveler**, *n*, voyageur, euse; placier, *m*. **traveling**, *p.a*, ambulant.

traverse, *v.t*, traverser.

travesty, *n*, travestissement, *m*. ¶ *v.t*, travestir.

trawl [**net**], *n*, chalut, *m*, traille, *f*. ¶ *v.i*, pêcher au chalut, p. à la traille. ~*er*, *n*, [bateau] chalutier, *m*. ~**ing**, *n*, pêche chalutière, *f*.

tray, *n*, plateau, *m*.

treacherous†, *a*, perfide, traître. **treachery**, *n*, traîtrise, perfidie, trahison, *f*.

treacle, *n*, mélasse, *f*.

tread, *n*, pas; (*of stair step*) giron, *m*. ¶ *v.i.ir*, marcher; (*v.t. ir.*) fouler. ~ *water*, nager debout. ~**le**, *n*, marche, pédale, *f*.

treason, *n*, trahison, *f*, crime d'État, *m*.

treasure, *n*. & ~ *trove*, trésor, *m*. ¶ *v.t*, garder précieusement. **treasurer**, *n*, trésorier, ère. **treasury**, *n*, trésor, *m*, trésorerie, caisse, *f*; fisc, *m*.

treat, *n*, régal; plaisir, *m*; débauche, *f*. ¶ *v.t*. & *i*, traiter; régaler. **treatise**, *n*, traité, *m*. **treatment**, *n*, traitement, *m*; (*music, art*) facture, *f*. **treaty**, *n*, traité, *m*. *by private* ~, à l'amiable.

treble†, *a*, triple. ¶ *n*, triple; (*Mus.*) dessus, *m*; (*crochet*) bride, *f*. ~ *clef*, clef de sol, *f*. ¶ *v.t*, tripler.

tree, *n*, arbre, *m*. ~*top*, cime d'un arbre, *f*. ~*less*, *a*, sans arbre.

trefoil, *n*, trèfle, *m*.

trellis, *n*, treillis, treillage, *m*. ¶ *v.t*, treillisser.

tremble, *v.i*, trembler. **trembling**, *n*, tremblement, *m*.

tremendous, *a*, énorme, formidable, effroyable, furieux, fou.

tremolo, *n*, tremolo, *m*. **tremor**, *n*, tremblement, *m*, trépidation, *f*. **tremulous**, *a*, tremblant.

trench, *n*, tranchée, *f*, fossé, *m*. ~ *coat*, trench-coat, *m*. ~ *mortar*, mortier de tranchée, *m*. ~ *warfare*, guerre de tranchées, g. de position, *f*. ¶ *v.t*, creuser; (*Mil.*) faire des tranchées. ~*ant*, *a*, tranchant, à l'emporte-pièce. **trencher**, *n*, tranchoir, tailloir, *m*. **trencherman**, *n*, mangeur, *m*.

trend, *n*, direction; tendance, *f*. ¶ *v.i*, se diriger.

Trent, *n*, Trente, *f*. **the Trentino**, le Trentin.

trepan, *n*, trépan, *m*. ¶ *v.t*, trépaner.

trepidation, *n*, tremblement, *f*.

trespass, *n*, intrusion; offense, *f*. ¶ ~ *against*, offenser. ~ *on*, s'introduire sans droit dans; (*fig.*) empiéter sur, abuser de. ~*er*, *n*, intrus, e. ~*s will be prosecuted*, défense d'entrer sous peine d'amende.

tress, *n*, tresse, *f*.

trestle, *n*, tréteau, chevalet, *m*.

Treves, *n*, Trèves, *f*.

trial, *n*, essai, *m*, épreuve; tribulation, *f*, procès; jugement, *m*; débats, *m.pl*. *to bring to* ~, mettre en jugement. ~ & *error*, tâtonnements, *m.pl*. ~ *balance*, balance de vérification, b. d'ordre, *f*. ~ *trip*, voyage d'essai, *m*.

triangle (*Geom.* & *Mus.*) *n*, triangle, *m*. **triangular**, *a*, triangulaire.

tribe, *n*, tribu; race, *f*.

tribulation, *n*, tribulation, *f*.

tribunal, *n*, tribunal, *m*. **tribune**,

n, tribune, *f*; (*Hist. pers.*) tribun, *m*.

tributary, *a*, tributaire. ¶ *n*, tributaire; affluent, *m*. **tribute**, *n*, tribut; hommage, *m*.

trice, *n*, clin d'œil, *m*.

triceps, *a.* & *n*, triceps, *a.* & *m*.

trick, *n*, tour, jeu, *m*; ruse; ficelle; jonglerie, *f*; truc, *m*; (*cards*) levée, *f*; (*habit*) tic, *m*. ~ *riding*, voltige, *f*. ¶ *v.t*, tricher, duper. ~**ery**, *n*, tricherie, finasserie, *f*.

trickle, *n*, filet, *m*. ¶ *v.i*, [dé]couler, ruisseler.

trickster, *n*, tricheur, euse, finassier, ère, jongleur, *m*. **tricky**, *a*, adroit à s'évader; délicat.

tricycle, *n*, tricycle, *m*.

trident, *n*, trident, *m*.

triennial, *n*, triennal.

trifle, *n*, bagatelle, vétille, *f*, rien, *m*; misère; futilité, *f*. ¶ *v.i*, s'amuser à des riens; baguenauder. ~ *with*, se jouer de. **trifler**, *n*, baguenaudier, homme futile, *m*. **trifling**, *a*, insignifiant, minime; futile.

triforium, *n*, triforium, *m*.

trigger, *n*, détente, *f*; déclic, *m*.

trigonometry, *n*, trigonométrie, *f*.

trill, *n*, trille, *m*. ¶ *v.t*, orner de trilles.

trim, *a*, soigné, bien tenu; coquet. ¶ *n*, ornement, *m*; assiette, allure, *f*; arrimage, *m*. ¶ *v.t*, tailler; parer; agrémenter; garnir; (*edges*) rogner; (*book edges*) ébarber; (*hair*) tailler, rafraîchir; (*wood*) dresser; (*ship*) arrimer; (*sails*) orienter. **trimmings**, *n.pl*, passementerie; garniture, *f*, fourniture, *f. oft. pl*; (*Cook.*) garniture, *f*.

Trinidad, *n*. & **the Trinity**, la Trinité.

trinket, *n*, colifichet, bibelot, *m*.

trio, *n*, trio, *m*.

trip, *n*, (*fall*) croc-en-jambe; tour, voyage, *m*, excursion, *f*. ~ [up], *v.t*, faire trébucher, donner un croc-en-jambe à; (*Mech.*) déclencher; (*anchor*) déraper; (*v.i.*) trébucher. ~ *along*, sautiller.

tripe, *n*, tripes, *f.pl*.

triplet†, *a*, triple. ¶ *v.t.* & *i*, tripler. **triplet**, *n*, triolet, tercet, *m*; (*pl.*) trois jumeaux, *m.pl*. **triplicate**, *n*, triplicata, triple, *m*.

tripod, *n*, trépied, *m*.

tripoli, *n*, tripoli, *m*.

triptych, *n*, triptyque, *m*.

trite†, *a*, banal. ~**ness**, *n*, banalité, *f*.

triton, *n*, triton, *m*.

triumph, *n*, triomphe, *m*. ¶ *v.i*, triompher. ~**al**, *a*, triomphal, de triomphe. ~**ant**, *a*, triomphant, victorieux. ~**antly**, *ad*, triomphalement.

trivet, *n*, trépied, *m*, chevrette, *f*.

trivial, *a*, insignifiant, minime; frivole.

troglodyte, *n*, troglodyte, *m*.

Trojan, *a*, troyen; (*war*) de Troie.

troll (*Fish.*) *v.i*, pêcher à la traîne.

trolley, *n*, tramway, trolley, *m*. ~ *bus*, autobus à trolley, *m*.

trolling, *n*, pêche à traîner, *f*.

trombone, *n*, trombone, *m*.

troop, *n*, troupe; bande, *f*. ~ *ship*, transport, *m*. ~ *train*, train militaire, *m*. ~**er**, *n*, cavalier, *m*.

trope, *n*, trope, *m*.

trophy, *n*, trophée, *m*; panoplie, *f*.

tropic, *n*, tropique, *m*. ~ *of Cancer, of Capricorn*, tropique du Cancer, du Capricorne. ~**al**, *a*, tropical.

trot, *n*, trot, *m*. ¶ *v.i.* & *t*, trotter.

troth, *n*, foi, *f*.

trotter, *n*, trotteur, euse; (*pl.*) (*pigs' feet*) pieds, *m.pl*.

troubadour, *n*, troubadour, *m*.

trouble, *n*, peine, *f*; chagrin; ennui; mal; trouble, *m. engine* ~, panne de moteur, *f*. ~*shooter*, dépanneur, *m*. ¶ *v.t*, inquiéter; tourmenter, chagriner; déranger. ~**d**, *p.a*, agité, inquiet. ~ *waters* (*fig.*), eau trouble, *f*. ~**some**, *a*, fâcheux; difficultueux; gênant; (*child*) tourmentant.

trough, *n*, bac, baquet, *m*, auge; huche, *f*; (*of wave*) creux; (*sea*) entre-deux, *m*.

trounce, *v.t*, rosser, étriller.

troupe, *n*, troupe, *f*.

trouser, *n*, (*pl.*) pantalon, *m*.

trousseau, *n*, trousseau, *m*.

trout, *n*, truite, *f*. ~ *fishing*, pêche à la t., *f*. ~ *stream*, rivière à truites, *f*.

trowel, *n*, truelle, *f*; (*Hort.*) houlette, *f*, déplantoir, *m*.

truancy, *n*, vagabondage, *m*. **truant**, *a*, vagabond. *to play* ~, faire l'école buissonnière.

truce, *n*, trêve, *f*.

truck, *n*, (*Rly.*) wagon; chariot; camion; (*hand*) diable; (*engine*) bogie, *m*. ~ *load*, wagon complet. ~ *garden*, jardin de maraîcher, *m*. ¶ *v.t*, rouler.

truckle, *v.i*, ramper.

truculent, *a*, truculent.

trudge, *v.i*, cheminer, clopiner.

true, *a*, vrai; véritable; loyal; fidèle; juste; conforme; rectiligne. *in one's ~ colors*, en déshabillé. *[certified] a ~ copy*, pour copie conforme, pour ampliation. *~love[r's] knot*, lacs d'amour, *m*. *~ to life*, vécu. ¶ *v.t*, dégauchir, rectifier, [re]dresser.

truffle, *n*, truffe, *f*.

truism, *n*, truisme, *m*. **truly**, *ad*, vraiment, véritablement; fidèlement.

trump, *n*, trompette, *f*. *~[card]*, *n.* & *~s*, *n.pl*, atout, *m*, retourne, *f*. *~ up*, fabriquer, inventer.

trumpery, *n*, friperie; camelote; blague, *f*. ¶ *a*, de pacotille; frivole.

trumpet, *n*, trompette, *f*. *~ call*, sonnerie de t., *f*. ¶ *v.t.* & *i*, (*fig.*) trompeter, corner; (*elephant*) barrir; (*Mus.*) sonner de la trompette. *~er*, *n*, trompette, *m*.

truncate, *v.t*, tronquer.

truncheon, *n*, bâton, *m*.

trundle, *n*, roulette, *f*. ¶ *v.t*, rouler.

trunk, *n*, tronc, *m*; tige, *f*; torse, *m*; (*elephant*) trompe; malle, *f*, coffre; bahut, *m*; (*pl.*) caleçon court, *m*. (*pl, Teleph.*) l'inter, *m*. *~ call*, communication interurbaine, *f*. *~ line*, grande artère, *f*.

trunnion, *n*, tourillon, *m*.

truss, *n*, trousse, botte, *f*; bandage [herniaire], brayer, *m*; (*Build.*) ferme, *f*. ¶ *v.t*, (*fowl*) trousser; (*hay*) botteler; (*Build.*) armer.

trust, *n*, confiance; créance, foi, *f*, crédit, *m*; charge, *f*; mandat; (*oil, steel*) trust, *m*. *~ deed*, acte de fidéicommis, *m*. ¶ *v.t.* & *i*, se fier à; croire; faire crédit à; espérer. *~ed*, *p.a*, de confiance. *~ee*, *n*, curateur, trice; dépositaire, *m,f*, consignataire; syndic, *m*. *board of ~s*, conseil d'administration, *m*. *~ful*, *a*, confiant. *~worthy*, *a*, digne de confiance, croyable, fidèle. *~y*, *a*, loyal, fidèle, sûr.

truth, *n*, vérité, *f*, vrai, *m*. *~ful*, *a*, vrai, véridique. *~fulness*, *n*, véracité, *f*.

try, *n*, essai, coup, *m*. ¶ *v.t.* & *i*, essayer; éprouver; expérimenter; goûter; tenter; tâter; chercher; (*law case*) juger; (*patience*) exercer. *~ on*, essayer. *~ing*, *a*, diffi-

cile; contrariant. *~ time*, mauvais quart d'heure, *m*.

tub, *n*, cuve, *f*, baquet, tub; tonneau, *m*; caisse, *f*; (*bad ship*) sabot, *m*. *tub[by man]*, poussah, *m*.

tuba, *n*, tuba, *m*.

tube, *n*, tube; (*anatomy*) conduit, *m*; (*radio*) lampe, *f*.

tuber & **tubercle**, *n*, tubercule, *m*. **tuberculosis**, tuberculose, *f*. **tuberculous**, *a*, tuberculeux. **tuberous**, *n*, tubéreuse, *m*.

tubular, *a*, tubulaire. *~ [tire]*, boyau, *m*.

tuck, *n*, rempli, troussis, *m*. ¶ *v.t*, remplier. *~ in*, border. *~ up*, [re]trousser.

Tuesday, *n*, mardi, *m*.

tuft, *n*, touffe, *f*; bouquet; panache, *m*; huppe; houppe; (*on chin*) mouche, *f*. *~ed*, *a*, touffu; aigretté, huppé, houppé.

tug, *n*, tiraillement; coup de collier; (*boat*) remorqueur, toueur, *m*. *~ of war*, lutte à la corde, *f*; (*fig.*) effort suprême, *m*. ¶ *v.t*, tirer.

tuition, *n*, (*fees*) droit d'inscriptions, *m.pl*; enseignement, *m*.

tulip, *n*, tulipe, *f*.

tulle, *n*, tulle, *m*.

tumble, *n*, chute, dégringolade, culbute, *f*. *~ down*, tomber, dégringoler, culbuter, débouler. *~ down*, *a* délabré. **tumbler**, *n*, (*pers.*) acrobate; (*pigeon*) culbutant; (*toy*) poussah; (*glass*) [verre] gobelet, *m*. **tumbrel**, **-il**, *n*, tombereau, *m*.

tumor, *n*, tumeur, glande, *f*.

tumult, *n*, tumulte, *m*. **tumultuous†**, *a*, tumultueux, houleux.

tumulus, *n*, tumulus, *m*.

tun, *n*, tonneau, foudre, *m*.

tuna, *n*, thon, *m*.

tune, *n*, air; accord, *m*; (*fig.*) cadence; (*fig.*) note, *f*, ton, *m*, gamme, *f*. ¶ *v.t*, accorder, mettre d'accord. **tuner**, *n*, accordeur, *m*. **tuneful†**, *a*, harmonieux, mélodieux.

tungsten, *n*, tungstène, *m*.

tunic, *n*, tunique, *f*.

tuning, *n*, accordage, *m*. *~ fork*, diapason à branches, *m*.

Tunis, *n*, Tunis, *m*. **Tunisia**, *n*, la Tunisie. **Tunisian**, *a*, tunisien.

tunnel, *n*, tunnel, souterrain, *m*. ¶ *v.t*, percer un tunnel sous.

turban, *n*, turban, *m*.

turbid, *a*, trouble.

turbine, *n*, turbine, *f*.

turbot, *n,* turbot, (*young*) tur-botin, *m.*

turbulence, *n,* turbulence, *f.* **tur-bulent,** *a,* turbulent.

tureen, *n,* soupière, *f.*

turf, *n,* gazon, *m*; plaque de g., motte, *f. the ~* (*racing*), le turf. ¶ *v.t,* gazonner.

turgid, *a,* turgescent, boursouflé.

Turk, *n,* Turc, *m,* Turque, *f.* **Turkey,** *n,* la Turquie. **t~** [*cock*], dindon, coq d'Inde, *m.* **t~**[*hen*], dinde, poule d'Inde, *f.* **turkish,** *a,* turc. *~ bath,* bain turc, *m. ~ carpet,* tapis de Turquie, *m. ~ towel,* serviette-éponge, *f.* ¶ (*language*) *n,* le turc.

turmeric, *n,* safran des Indes, *m.*

turmoil, *n,* ébullition, tourmente, *f,* tumulte, *m.*

turn, *n,* tour; retour; détour, *m*; tournure, *f*; revirement; (*tide*) changement, renversement, *m. ~ of the scale,* trait de balance, *m. at every ~,* à tout propos. *in ~,* tour à tour, à tour de rôle. *to a ~,* à point. ¶ *v.t. & i,* tourner; se t.; retourner; se r.; virer; pivoter; transformer; convertir; changer; (*discussion*) porter (*on* = sur). *~ aside,* écarter; détourner; se d. *~ back,* rebrousser chemin. *~ off,* (*tap*) fermer; (*water*) couper; (*light*) éteindre. *~ on,* (*tap*) ouvrir, lâcher; (*water*) faire couler, ouvrir le robinet de; (*light*) allumer. *~ out & ~ over,* [re]tourner. *~ out badly,* mal réussir. *~ right over,* faire panache. *~ round,* se retourner. *~ the scale,* faire pencher la balance. *~ up,* [re]tourner; [re]trousser. *~ed-up moustache,* moustache en croc, *f.*

turncoat, *n,* transfuge, rénégat, *m.*

turncock, *n,* fontainier, *m.*

turned (*a certain age*) *p.p,* dépassé, franchi, (*tant d'ans*) sonnés.

turnip, *n,* navet, *m. ~ tops,* fanes de navets, *f.pl.*

turnkey, *n,* porte-clefs, guichetier, *m.*

turnout (*Rly.*) *n,* branchement, *m.*

turnover, *n,* revirement; (*Fin.*) chiffre d'affaires, roulement; (*Cook.*) chausson; (*stocking, etc.*) revers, *m.*

turnpike, *n,* barrière, *f.*

turnstile, *n,* (X *on post*) mou-linet; (*admission*) tourniquet [-compteur] *m.*

turntable, *n,* plaque tournante, *f*; (*phonograph*) plateau, *m.*

turpentine, *n,* térébenthine, *f.*

turpitude, *n,* turpitude, *f.*

turquoise, *n. & att,* turquoise, *f. & att.*

turret, *n,* tourelle, *f. ~ lathe,* tour à revolver, *m. ~ ship,* navire à tourelles, *m.*

turtle, *n,* tortue de mer, *f. ~ dove,* tourterelle, *f,* (*young*) tourterau, *m. ~ soup,* soupe à la tortue, *f.*

Tuscan, *a,* toscan. **~y,** *n,* la Toscane.

tusk, *n,* défense, *f*; croc, *m.*

tussle, *n,* lutte, *f.*

tutelage, *n,* tutelle, *f.* **tutelar**[**y**], *a,* tutélaire. **tutor,** *n,* précepteur, répétiteur, préparateur, *m.* ¶ *v.t,* instruire. **tutorship,** *n,* préceptorat, *m.*

tuxedo, *n,* smoking, *m.*

twaddle, *n,* balivernes, *f.pl,* babil, *m.*

twang, *n,* nasillement; son aigre, *m.* ¶ *v.i,* nasiller; résonner. *~* [*on*] (*stringed instrument*), pincer de.

tweak, *v.t,* pincer, tirer.

tweed, *n,* tweed, *m.*

'tween-decks, *n,* entrepont, *m.*

tweezers, *n.pl,* brucelles, pincettes, pinces, *f.pl.*

twelfth†, *a. & n,* douzième, *a. & m,f*; douze, *m.* **twelve,** *a. & n,* douze, *a. & m. ~ o'clock,* [*in the day*] midi; [*at night*] minuit, *m.*

twentieth, *a. & n,* vingtième, *a. & m,f*; vingt, *m.* **twenty,** *a. & n,* vingt, *a. & m.*

twice, *ad,* deux fois. *~ as much,* deux fois autant.

twiddle, *v.t,* tourner, tortiller.

twig, *n,* brindille, *f,* (*pl.*) ramilles, broutilles, *f.pl.*

twilight, *n,* crépuscule, *m,* pénombre, *f,* demi-jour, *m. ~ sleep,* anesthésie à la reine, *f.*

twill, *n,* croisé, *m.* ¶ *v.t,* croiser.

twin, *a,* jumeau; conjugué. ¶ *n,* jumeau, elle; (*pl.*) deux jumeaux, deux jumelles; (*crystal*) macle, *f.*

twine, *n,* ficelle, *f.* ¶ *v.t,* enlacer; cordonner.

twinge, *n,* élancement, *m.*

twining (*Bot.*) *p.a,* volubile.

twinkle, *v.i,* scintiller, clignoter. *in the twinkling of an eye,* en un clin d'œil. ¶ n, scintillement, clignement, m.

twirl, v.i, faire tournoyer; (*stick*) faire le moulinet avec; (*moustache*) tortiller; (v.i.) pirouetter.

twist, n, torsade, f, tortillon, m; torsion, f; cordon, m; contorsion, f; (*of straw*) torchon, m; (*tobacco*) carotte, f, rouleau, m. ~**s & turns,** tours & retours, m.pl. ¶ v.t, tordre; [en]tortiller; cordonner. ~**ed,** p.p. & p.a, tordu; [re]tors.

twit, v.t, reprocher.

twitch, v.i, avoir un tic, tiquer; palpiter; (v.t.) arracher, crisper. ~**ing,** p.a, pantelant. ~**ing,** n, tic, m.

twitter, v.i, gazouiller.

two, a. & n, deux, a. & m. ~ **days before,** l'avant-veille, f. ~**-footed,** ~**-legged,** bipède. ~**-piece set,** ensemble deux pièces, m. ~**-way switch,** commutateur va-et-vient, m. ~**fold,** a, double.

tympan & tympanum, n, tympan, m.

type, n, type; genre; (*Typ.*) caractère [d'imprimerie], type, m. ~ **founder,** fondeur en caractères, m. ~ **metal,** matière, f. ~ **setting,** composition, f. ~**[write],** v.t, écrire à la machine, taper [à la m.]. ~**writer,** machine à écrire, f. ~**writing,** écriture à la machine, dactylographie, f. ~**written,** [écrit] à la machine.

typhoid [fever], n, fièvre typhoïde, f.

typhoon, n, typhon, m.

typhus, n, typhus, m.

typical, a, typique.

typist, n, dactylographe, m.f.

typographic(al), a, typographique. **typography,** n, typographie, f.

tyrannic(al†), a, tyrannique. **tyrannize [over],** tyranniser. **tyranny,** n, tyrannie, f. **tyrant,** n, tyran, m.

tyro, n, novice, m.f.

Tyrol (the), le Tyrol. **Tyrolese,** a, tyrolien. ¶ n, Tyrolien, ne.

U

ubiquity, n, ubiquité, f.

udder, n, mamelle, f, pis, m.

ugh, i, pouah! fi!

ugliness, n, laideur, f. **ugly,** a, laid; vilain. [*as*] ~ **as sin,** laid comme un crapaud.

ulcer, n, ulcère, m. ~**ate,** v.i, s'ulcérer.

ulterior†, a, ultérieur. ~ **motive,** arrière-pensée, f.

ultimate†, a, final; définitif. **ultimatum,** n, ultimatum, m.

ultramarine, n, outremer, m.

ultraviolet, a, ultra-violet.

umber, n, terre d'ombre, f.

umbrage, n, ombrage, m.

umbrella, n, parapluie; (*garden, beach, held over potentate*) parasol, m. ~ **ring,** rondelle de parapluie, f. ~ **stand,** porte-parapluies, m. ~**-sunshade,** en-[tout-]cas, m.

umpire, n, arbitre, m. ¶ v.t, arbitrer.

unabated, a, sans diminution.

unable, a, incapable. **to be ~ to,** ne pouvoir [pas].

unabridged, a, complet.

unacceptable, a, inacceptable.

unaccompanied, a, non accompagné.

unaccountable, a, inexplicable.

unaccustomed, a, peu habitué; inaccoutumé.

unacknowledged, a, non reconnu; sans réponse.

unacquainted with (to be), être ignorant de; ne pas connaître.

unadorned, a, sans ornements.

unadulterated, a, non falsifié; sans mélange.

unaffected, a, naturel, naïf; inaltérable (*by* = à).

unafraid, a, sans peur.

unalloyed, a, sans alliage.

unalterable, a, inaltérable.

unambiguous, a, non équivoque, précis.

unambitious, a, sans ambition; sans prétentions.

unanimous, a, unanime. ~**ly,** ad, à l'unanimité, unanimement.

unanswerable, a, sans réplique.

unappreciated, a, inapprécié, incompris.

unapproachable, a, inabordable.

unarmed, a, sans armes, désarmé.

unasked, a, sans être invité.

unassailable, a, inattaquable, hors d'atteinte.

unassuming, a, sans prétentions.

unattached (*Mil.*) a, en disponibilité.

unattainable, a, impossible à atteindre.

unattended, a, sans suite; sans garde.

unattractive, *a*, peu attrayant; peu séduisant.

unavailable, *a*, indisponible. **unavailing**, *a*, inutile, vain.

unavoidable†, *a*, inévitable.

unaware of (to be), ignorer. **unawares**, *ad*, à l'improviste, au dépourvu; par mégarde.

unbalanced, *a*, déséquilibré; (*Mech.*) non compensé.

unballast, *v.t*, délester.

unbandage, *v.t*, débander.

unbearable†, *a*, insupportable.

unbecoming, *a*, inconvenant, malséant; qui ne va pas. **to be ~**, messeoir.

unbelief, *n*, incrédulité, *f*. **unbeliever**, *n*, incrédule, *m,f*.

unbend, *v.t.ir*, détendre; débander. **~ing**, *a*, inflexible.

unbiased, *a*, sans prévention; impartial.

unbind, *v.t.ir*, délier, détacher.

unbleached, *a*, écru.

unblemished, *a*, sans tache, intact.

unblushing, *a*, éhonté.

unbolt, *v.t*, déverrouiller.

unborn, *a*, à naître.

unbosom oneself, s'ouvrir.

unbound (*book*) *a*, non relié.

unbounded, *a*, sans bornes, illimité.

unbreakable, *a*, incassable.

unbridled, *a*, débridé; effréné.

unbroken, *a*, intact; ininterrompu; (*horse*) non dressé.

unbuckle, *v.t*, déboucler.

unbuilt on, non bâti, non construit.

unburden oneself, s'ouvrir.

unburied, *a*, sans sépulture.

unbusinesslike, *a*, incorrect.

unbutton, *v.t*, déboutonner.

uncalled for remark, observation déplacée, *f*.

uncanny, *a*, fantastique.

uncapsizable, *a*, inversable.

uncared for, à l'abandon.

unceasing, *a*, incessant. **~ly**, *ad*, incessamment, sans cesse.

unceremoniously, *ad*, sans cérémonie.

uncertain, *a*, incertain. **~ty**, *n*, incertitude, *f*.

unchain, *v.t*, déchaîner.

unchangeable†, *a*, immuable, invariable.

uncharitable, *a*, peu charitable; critique.

unchaste†, *a*, impudique, incontinent.

unchecked, *a*, sans frein.

uncircumcised, *a*, incirconcis.

uncivil†, *a*, incivil. **~ized**, *a*, sauvage.

unclad, *a*, nu.

unclaimed, *a*, non réclamé; en souffrance.

unclassified, *a*, non classé.

uncle, *n*, oncle, *m*.

unclean, *a*, sale; impur, immonde.

unclothed, *a*, nu.

unclouded, *a*, sans nuages.

uncock (*gun*) *v.t*, désarmer.

uncoil, *v.t*, dérouler.

uncomely, *a*, peu avenant.

uncomfortable, *a*, incommode; (*of pers.*) mal à son aise.

uncommon†, *a*, rare; singulier.

uncommunicative, *a*, taciturne.

uncomplaining, *a*, résigné. **the ~ poor**, les pauvres honteux, *m. pl.*

uncompleted, *a*, inachevé.

uncompromising, *a*, intransigeant.

unconcerned, *a*, indifférent, insouciant.

unconditional, *a.* & **~ly**, *ad*, sans condition.

unconfirmed, *a*, non confirmé.

unconnected (*desultory*) *a*, décousu.

unconquerable†, *a*, invincible.

unconscious†, *a*, inconscient; (*dead faint*) sans connaissance. **~ness**, *n*, inconscience, *f*; une perte de connaissance.

unconsecrated ground, terre profane, *f*.

unconstitutional†, *a*, inconstitutionnel.

unconstrained, *a*, dégagé. **unconstraint**, *n*, désinvolture, *f*, abandon, laisser-aller, *m*.

uncontested, *a*, incontesté.

uncontrollable, *a*, ingouvernable; indomptable; inextinguible.

unconventional, *a*, sans gêne, original; affranchi, libre.

unconvincing, *a*, peu vraisemblable.

uncork, *v.t*, déboucher.

uncorrected, *a*, non corrigé.

uncouple, *v.t*, découpler.

uncouth, *a*, grossier, rude, rustaud.

uncover, *v.t*, découvrir; (*v.i.*) se découvrir.

uncreated, *a*, incréé.

unction, *n*, onction, *f*. **unctuous**†, *a*, onctueux.

uncultivated & **uncultured**, *a*, inculte.

uncurbed, *a,* indompté.

uncurl, *v.t,* défriser; dérouler.

uncustomary, *a,* inusité.

uncut, *a,* (*gem*) brut; (*cake*) non entamé. ~ *edges* (book), tranches non rognées, *f.pl.*

undamaged, *a,* non endommagé; non avarié.

undated, *a,* sans date, non daté.

undaunted, *a,* intrépide.

undeceive, *v.t,* détromper, désillusionner.

undecided, *a,* indécis; incertain.

undecipherable, *a,* indéchiffrable.

undefended, *a,* sans défense; sans défenseur; (*law case*) non contesté; (*heard ex parte*) jugée par défaut.

undefiled, *a,* sans souillure.

undefined, *a,* indéfini.

undeliverable, *a,* en souffrance.

undelivered, *a,* non livré; non distribué.

undeniable, *a,* indéniable, incontestable.

undenominational, *a,* laïque, neutre.

under, *pr,* sous; dessous; au-dessous de; en; à; sauf. ~ *there,* là-dessous. ~ *water,* entre deux eaux. ¶ *ad,* dessous; au-dessous.

underassessment, *n,* insuffisance d'imposition, *f.*

underclothing, *n,* (*women's*) [vêtements de] dessous; (*men's*) sous-vêtements, *m.pl.*

undercurrent, *n,* courant de fond; courant sous-marin; (*in air*) courant inférieur; (*fig.*) courant secret, fond, *m.*

undercut (*meat*) *n,* filet, *m.*

underdeveloped, *a,* trop peu développé.

underdone, *a,* pas [assez] cuit; peu cuit, saignant.

underestimate, *v.t,* sous-estimer, mésestimer.

underexposure (*Phot.*) *n,* manque de pose, *m.*

underfed, *a,* sous-alimenté.

undergarment, *n,* (*men's*) sous-vêtement; (*women's*) vêtement de dessous, *m.*

undergo, *v.t.ir,* subir, souffrir.

underground, *a,* souterrain. ¶ *n,* (*war*) Résistance, *f.* ¶ *ad,* en souterrain.

undergrowth, *n,* broussailles, *f.pl.*

underhand, *a,* clandestin, souterrain, sournois, sourd; (*Ten.*

service) par en bas. ¶ *ad,* sous main, clandestinement.

underline, *v.t,* souligner.

underling, *n,* employé subalterne, *m.*

underlying, *a,* sous-jacent.

undermentioned, *a,* ci-dessous.

undermine, *v.t,* miner, affouiller, caver.

undermost, *a,* le plus bas.

underneath, *ad,* dessous; au-dessous. ¶ *pr,* sous.

underpay, *v.t.ir,* payer trop peu.

underpin, *v.t,* reprendre en sous-œuvre.

underrate, *v.t,* mésestimer, déprécier.

underscore, *v.t,* souligner.

undersea, *a,* sous-marin.

undersecretary, *n,* sous-secrétaire, *m.*

undersell, *v.t.ir,* vendre moins cher que.

undershirt, *n,* chemisette, *f.*

underside, *n,* dessous, *m.*

undersigned, *a. & n,* soussigné, e.

understand, *v.t. & i. ir,* comprendre, voir; entendre; s'e. à; apprendre; sous-entendre. ~ing, *n,* intelligence, *f;* entendement, sens, *m;* compréhension; entente, *f.*

understudy, *n,* doublure, *f.* ¶ *v.t,* doubler.

undertake, *v.t.ir,* entreprendre; se charger de; s'engager à, se faire fort. **undertaker,** *n,* entrepreneur de pompes funèbres, *m.* **undertaking,** *n,* engagement, *m;* entreprise, *f;* pompes funèbres, *f.pl.*

undertone (in an), à demi-voix.

undertow, *n,* ressac, *m.*

undervalue, *v.t,* mésestimer, déprécier.

underwear, *n.* See *underclothing.*

underwood, *n,* [bois] taillis, mort-bois, *m,* broussailles, *f.pl.*

underworld, *n,* pègre, *f;* enfers; bas-fonds de la société, *m.pl.*

underwrite, *v.t.ir,* (*Insce.*) souscrire, s. pour; (*Fin.*) garantir. **underwriter,** *n,* souscripteur, assureur; (*Fin.*) syndicataire, *m.* **underwriting,** *n,* souscription; garantie, *f.*

undeserved, *a,* immérité. **undeserving,** *a,* peu méritant; indigne (*of* = de).

undesirable, *a. & n,* indésirable, *a. & m,f.*

undetermined, *a,* indéterminé.

undeveloped, *a,* en friche.

undigested, *a,* non digéré; (*fig.*) indigeste.

undignified, *a,* sans dignité.

undisciplined, *a,* indiscipliné.

undiscoverable, *a,* introuvable. **undiscovered,** *a,* non découvert.

undiscriminating, *a,* sans discernement.

undismayed, *a,* sans être découragé.

undisputed, *a,* incontesté.

undisturbed, *a,* tranquille.

undo, *v.t.ir,* défaire, détacher; (*knitting*) démailler. **~ing,** *n,* ruine, *f. come undone,* se défaire.

undoubted†, *a,* indubitable.

undress, *n,* déshabillé, négligé, *m*; (*Mil., Nav.*) petite tenue, *f.* ¶ *v.t,* déshabiller; (*v.i.*) se déshabiller.

undrinkable, *a,* imbuvable.

undue, *a,* exagéré, excessif; inexigible.

undulate, *v.i,* onduler, ondoyer. **undulating,** *a,* ondulé. **undulation,** *n,* ondulation, *f.*

unduly, *ad,* indûment; par trop.

undutiful, *a,* qui manque à ses devoirs.

undying, *a,* impérissable, immortel.

unearned, *a,* non acquis; immérité. *~ increment,* plus-value, *f.*

unearth, *v.t,* déterrer. **~ly,** *a,* spectral, fantomatique.

uneasiness, *n,* malaise, *m,* inquiétude, *f,* martel en tête, *m.* **uneasy†,** *a,* inquiet.

uneatable, *a,* immangeable.

uneducated, *a,* sans instruction.

unemployable (the), les incapables, *m.pl.* **unemployed,** *a,* inemployé; (*pers.*) sans travail, en chômage. *the ~,* les sanstravail, les chômeurs, *m.pl.* **unemployment,** *n,* manque de travail; chômage [involontaire] *m.* *~ benefit,* indemnité de chômage, *f.* *~ insurance,* assurance contre le chômage, *f.*

unending, *a,* sans fin.

unenterprising, *a,* sans initiative.

unenviable, *a,* peu enviable.

unequal†, *a,* inégal. *~ to* (task), pas à la hauteur de, incapable de. **unequaled,** *a,* sans égal, sans pareil.

unequivocal, *a,* non équivoque.

unerring†, *a,* infaillible; sûr.

uneven†, *a,* inégal; (*number*) impair. **~ness,** *n,* inégalité; (*number*) imparité, *f.*

unexceptionable, *a,* irrécusable.

unexpected, *a,* inattendu; inespéré.

unexpired, *a,* non expiré; non couru; non échu; non périmé.

unexplained, *a,* inexpliqué.

unexplored, *a,* inexploré.

unexpurgated, *a,* intégral.

unfailing, *a,* infaillible; (*spring*) intarissable.

unfair†, *a,* injuste; déloyal; partial. **~ness,** *n,* injustice; déloyauté; partialité, *f.*

unfaithful†, *a,* infidèle. **~ness,** *n,* infidélité, *f.*

unfamiliar, *a,* étranger.

unfasten, *v.t,* dégrafer, défaire.

unfathomable, *a,* insondable, abyssal.

unfavorable†, *a,* défavorable, contraire. *~ light,* contre-jour, *m.*

unfeasible, *a,* irréalisable, impraticable.

unfeeling, *a,* insensible.

unfeigned†, *a,* sincère.

unfenced, *a,* sans clôture.

unfettered, *a,* sans entraves.

unfinished, *a,* inachevé, imparfait.

unfit, *a,* impropre; hors d'état; inapte; incapable. *the ~,* les inaptes, *m.pl.* **~ness,** *n,* inaptitude; incapacité, *f.* **unfitting,** *a,* inconvenant.

unflagging, *a,* soutenu.

unfledged, *a,* sans plumes.

unflinching, *a,* à toute épreuve.

unfold, *v.t,* déployer; dérouler.

unforeseen, *a,* imprévu.

unforgettable, *a,* inoubliable.

unforgivable, *a,* impardonnable. **unforgiving,** *a,* implacable.

unfortified, *a,* non fortifié; (*town*) ouverte.

unfortunate†, *a,* malheureux, infortuné; regrettable. *the ~,* les malheureux, les infortunés, *m.pl.*

unfounded, *a,* sans fondement.

unfrequented, *a,* infréquenté.

unfriendly, *a,* inamical; hostile.

unfrock, *v.t,* défroquer.

unfruitful, *a,* stérile. **~ness,** *n,* stérilité, *f.*

unfulfilled, *a,* non accompli.

unfurl, *v.t,* déferler, déployer.

unfurnished, *a,* non meublé.

ungainly, *a,* dégingandé.

ungathered, *a,* non cueilli.

ungenerous, *a,* peu généreux.

ungodliness, *n,* impiété, *f.* **ungodly,** *a,* impie.

ungovernable, *a,* ingouvernable; indomptable.

ungraceful, *a,* disgracieux.

ungracious, *a,* malgracieux, disgracieux.

ungrafted, *a,* franc.

ungrammatical, *a,* contre la grammaire. **~ly,** *ad,* incorrectement.

ungrateful, *a,* ingrat. **~ness,** *n,* ingratitude, *f.*

ungrudgingly, *ad,* de bon cœur.

unguarded, *a,* sans défense; indiscret.

unhair (*skins*) *v.t,* dépiler, débourrer.

unhallowed, *a,* profane.

unhappiness, *n,* malheur, *m.* **unhappy†,** *a,* malheureux.

unharmed, *a,* indemne.

unharness, *v.t,* déharnacher.

unhatched, *a,* non éclos.

unhealthiness, *n,* insalubrité, *f.* **unhealthy,** *a,* insalubre; malsain.

unheard of, inouï.

unheeded, *a,* négligé.

unhesitatingly, *ad,* sans hésitation.

unhewn, *a,* non taillé.

unhindered, *a,* sans empêchement.

unhinge, *v.t,* démonter; troubler, aliéner.

unholiness, *n,* impiété, *f.* **unholy,** *a,* impie.

unhonored, *p.a,* méconnu.

unhook, *v.t,* décrocher.

unhoped for, inespéré.

unhorse, *v.t,* démonter, désarçonner.

unhurt, *a,* indemne, sauf.

unicorn, *n,* licorne, *f.*

uniform, *a,* uniforme; uni. ¶ *n,* uniforme, *m,* tenue, *f.* **~ity,** *n,* uniformité, *f.* **~ly,** *ad,* uniformément. **unify,** *v.t,* unifier.

unilateral, *a,* unilatéral.

unimaginable, *a,* inimaginable.

unimpeachable, *a,* irrécusable.

unimpeded, *a,* sans entraves.

unimportant, *a,* insignifiant.

uninflammable, *a,* ininflammable.

uninhabitable, *a,* inhabitable. **uninhabited,** *a,* inhabité.

uninitiated person, profane, *m,f.*

uninjured, *a,* indemne.

uninstructed, *a,* ignorant.

uninsured, *a,* non assuré; (*mail*) sans valeur déclarée, non chargé.

unintelligent, *a,* inintelligent.

unintelligible, *a,* inintelligible.

unintentional†, *a,* involontaire. **uninterested,** *a,* indifférent. **uninteresting,** *a,* sans intérêt.

uninterrupted, *a,* ininterrompu. **~ly,** *ad,* sans interruption.

uninvited, *a,* sans invitation. **uninviting,** *a,* peu attrayant; peu appétissant.

union, *n,* (*labor*) syndicat, *m;* union; alliance, *f;* (*Mech.*) raccord; (*pipe*) mi-fil, *m.* U~ *of South Africa,* Union Sud-Africaine. U~ *of Soviet Socialist Republics,* Union des Républiques soviétiques socialistes.

unique, *a,* unique.

unison, *n,* unisson, *m.*

unissued (*stocks, shares*) *a,* à la souche.

unit, *n,* unité, *f;* élément, *m.* ~ *bookcase,* bibliothèque transformable, *f.* ~ *price,* prix unitaire, *m.* **unite,** *v.t,* unir; joindre; réunir; allier; marier. **united,** *a,* uni; joint; réuni. U~ *Kingdom* [*of Great Britain and Northern Ireland*], Royaume-Uni [de Grande-Bretagne et Irlande du Nord] *m.* U~ *States* [*of America*], États-Unis [d'Amérique] *m.pl.* **unity,** *n,* unité; union, *f;* ensemble, *m.*

universal†, *a,* universel. **~ity,** *n,* universalité, *f.* **universe,** *n,* univers, *m.* **university,** *n,* université, *f;* (*att.*) universitaire.

unjust†, *a,* injuste. ~ *judge,* [juge] prévaricateur, *m.* **unjustifiable,** *a,* injustifiable.

unkempt, *a,* mal peigné, inculte.

unkind, *a,* désobligeant; méchant. **~ness,** *n,* désobligeance; méchanceté, *f.*

unknown, *a,* inconnu; ignoré. ~ *person,* inconnu, e. ~ [*quantity*], [quantité] inconnue, *f.* ~ *to,* à l'insu de. *the* ~, l'inconnu, *m. the* U~ *Soldier,* le Soldat inconnu.

unlace, *v.t,* délacer.

unlawful†, *a,* illégal, illicite. ~ *assembly,* attroupement, *m.* **~ness,** *n,* illégalité, *f.*

unlearn, *v.t,* désapprendre. **~ed,** *a,* illettré.

unleavened, *a,* sans levain; (*Bible*) azyme.

unless, *c,* à moins que . . .[ne]; à moins de; si . . . ne . . . pas; sauf.

unlettered, *a,* illettré.

unlicensed, *a*, marron.

unlicked cub, ours mal léché, *m*.

unlike, *a*, dissemblable. ¶ *pr*, dissemblable à. **unlikelihood,** *n*, invraisemblance; improbabilité, *f*. **unlikely,** *a*, invraisemblable; improbable.

unlimber, *v.i*, décrocher l'avant-train.

unlimited, *a*, illimité.

unlined, *a*, non doublé.

unload, *v.t*, décharger; (*Fin*.) se défaire de.

unlock, *v.t*, ouvrir; (*Typ*.) desserrer.

unlooked for, *a*, inattendu.

unloose, *v.t*, lâcher.

unlovely, *a*, disgracieux.

unlucky†, *a*, malheureux, malchanceux, malencontreux.

unmake, *v.t.ir*, défaire.

unman, *v.t*, ôter tout courage de.

unmanageable, *a*, intraitable; impossible à conduire.

unmanly, *a*, lâche; efféminé.

unmannerly, *a*, grossier.

unmanufactured, *a*, brut.

unmarketable, *a*, invendable.

unmarried, *a*, non marié; célibataire. **unmarry,** *v.t*, démarier.

unmask, *v.t*, démasquer.

unmentionable, *a*, dont on ne parle pas.

unmerciful†, *a*, impitoyable.

unmerited, *a*, immérité.

unmethodical, *a*, non méthodique, incorrect.

unmindful, *a*, inattentif, oublieux.

unmingled, *a*, sans mélange, pur.

unmistakable†, *a*, évident, manifeste; immanquable.

unmitigated, *a*, fieffé, insigne; non adouci.

unmixed, *a*, sans mélange, pur.

unmolested, *a*, en paix.

unmoor, *v.t*, démarrer.

unmounted, *a*, non monté; (*gem*) hors d'œuvre; (*pers*.) à pied.

unmoved, *a*, immobile; impassible.

unmusical, *a*, inharmonieux.

unmuzzle, *v.t*, démuseler.

unnamable, *a*, innommable. **unnamed,** *a*, innomé; anonyme.

unnatural, *a*, dénaturé; contre nature.

unnavigable, *a*, non navigable, impropre à la navigation.

unnecessary†, *a*, inutile.

unneighborly way (in an), en mauvais voisin.

unnerve, *v.t*, ôter tout courage de.

unnoticed, unobserved, *a*, inaperçu. **unobservant,** *a*, inattentif.

unobstructed, *a*, non obstrué; (*view*) dégagée.

unobtainable, *a*, impossible à se procurer.

unobtrusive, *a*, effacé; discret. **~ly,** *ad*, discrètement.

unoccupied, *a*, inoccupé; libre, disponible.

unoffending, *a*, inoffensif.

unofficial, *a*, non officiel; (*information*) officieux.

unopened, *a*, non ouvert.

unopposed, *a*, sans opposition.

unorganized, *a*, non organisé.

unorthodox, *a*, hétérodoxe.

unostentatious, *a*. & **~ly,** *ad*, sans ostentation.

unpack, *v.t*, dépaqueter, déballer, décaisser. **~ed,** *a*, à découvert.

unpaid, *a*, (*bill*) impayé (*capital*) non verse; (*letters*) non affranchi; (*no salary*) gratuit.

unpalatable, *a*, désagréable au goût.

unparalleled, *a*, sans pareil.

unpardonable, *a*, impardonnable.

unparliamentary, *a*, peu parlementaire.

unpatriotic, *a*, antipatriotique.

unperceived, *a*, inaperçu.

unphilosophical, *a*, peu philosophique.

unpin, *v.t*, enlever les épingles de.

unpleasant†, *a*, désagréable, méchant. **~ness,** *n*, désagrément, *m*.

unpleasing, *a*, déplaisant, ingrat.

unpoetic(al), *a*, peu poétique.

unpolished, *a*, non poli; mat; brut; rude.

unpolluted, *a*, non souillé.

unpopular, *a*, impopulaire. **~ity,** *n*, impopularité, *f*.

unpractical, *a*, peu pratique.

unpractised, *a*, inexercé; novice.

unprecedented, *a*, sans précédent(s).

unprejudiced, *a*, sans préjugés, impartial.

unpremeditated, *a*, sans préméditation.

unprepared, *a*, sans être préparé, au dépourvu.

unprepossessing, *a*, peu engageant.

unpretentious, *a*, sans prétentions; modeste, discret.

unprincipled, *a*, sans principes.

unprintable, *a,* impubliable.

unprocurable, *a,* impossible à se procurer.

unproductive, *a,* improductif.

unprofessional, *a,* contraire aux usages de sa profession.

unprofitable, *a,* peu lucratif; inutile; ingrat. **unprofitably,** *ad,* sans profit; inutilement.

unpromising, *a,* qui ne promet guère; ingrat.

unpronounceable, *a,* non prononçable. ~ *name,* nom à coucher dehors, *m.*

unpropitious, *a,* peu propice.

unprotected, *a,* découvert, à découvert.

unprovided, *a,* dépourvu (*with* = de).

unprovoked, *a,* sans provocation, gratuit.

unpublished (*book*) *a,* inédit.

unpunctual†, *a,* inexact. ~ity, *n,* inexactitude, *f.*

unpunished, *a,* impuni.

unqualified, *a,* sans les qualités requises; marron; formel; sans réserve.

unquenchable, *a,* inextinguible.

unquestionable†, *a,* indiscutable.

unravel, *v.t,* démêler, débrouiller, parfiler; dénouer.

unread, *a,* illettré; sans être lu. ~able (*writing, insupportable book*) *a,* illisible.

unreal, *a,* irréel. ~ity, *n,* irréalité, *f.*

unrealizable, *a,* irréalisable.

unreasonable†, *a,* déraisonnable, intraitable. ~ness, *n,* déraison, *f.* **unreasoning,** *a,* irraisonnable.

unrecognizable, *a,* méconnaissable.

unredeemable, *a,* irrachetable. **unredeemed,** *a,* (*stock*) non amorti; (*pledge*) non dégagé.

unrefined, *a,* non épuré; brut; grossier.

unrefuted, *a,* irréfuté.

unregistered, *a,* non enregistré; (*mail*) non recommandé; (*trademark*) non déposée.

unrelenting†, *a,* inexorable, implacable, acharné.

unreliable, *a,* peu sûr; inexact; sujet à caution.

unremitting†, *a,* incessant, soutenu.

unremunerative, *a,* peu lucratif.

unrepealed, *a,* non abrogé.

unrepentant, *a,* impénitent.

unreservedly, *ad,* sans réserve.

unresponsive, *a,* froid, difficile à émouvoir.

unrest, *a,* agitation, effervescence, *f.*

unrestrained, *a,* immodéré; effréné.

unrestricted, *a,* sans restriction.

unretentive (*memory*) *a,* fugace.

unrewarded, *a,* sans récompense.

unrighteous†, *a,* injuste. ~ness, *n,* injustice, *f.*

unripe, *a,* verte; en herbe. ~ness, *n,* verdeur, *f.*

unrivaled, *a,* sans rival.

unrivet, *v.t,* dériver.

unroll, *v.t,* dérouler.

unruffled, *a,* imperturbable; calme, tranquille.

unruly, *a,* indiscipliné; turbulent.

unsaddle, *v.t,* desseller; (*pack animal*) débâter.

unsafe, *a,* peu sûr, mal assuré.

unsalable, *a,* invendable.

unsalaried, *a,* sans rétribution.

unsalted, *a,* non salé.

unsanitary, *a,* malsain, insalubre.

unsatisfactorily, *ad,* d'une manière peu satisfaisante. **unsatisfactory,** *a,* peu satisfaisant; défectueux.

unsavory, *a,* peu savoureux.

unsay, *v.t.ir,* se dédire de. *to leave unsaid,* taire.

unscathed, *a,* indemne, sauf.

unscientific, *a,* peu scientifique.

unscrew, *v.t,* dévisser. *to come* ~ed, se d.

unscrupulous, *a,* peu scrupuleux, indélicat. ~ly, *ad,* sans scrupule.

unseal, *v.t,* desceller; (*letter*) décacheter.

unseasonable, *a,* hors de saison; hors de propos, inopportun. **unseasonably,** *ad,* mal à propos, inopportunément. **unseasoned** (*wood*) *a,* vert.

unseat, *v.t,* invalider; (*rider*) désarçonner.

unseaworthy, *a,* en mauvais état de navigabilité.

unseemly, *a,* malséant, inconvenant, folichon.

unseen, *a,* inaperçu, invisible; occulte.

unselfish, *a,* désintéressé. ~ness, *n,* désintéressement, *m.*

unserviceable, *a,* inutilisable.

unsettle, *v.t,* déranger; (*pers.*) bouleverser. ~d, *a,* (*weather*) incertain, variable; (*question*) indecise.

unshakable†, *a*, inébranlable.

unshapely, *a*, difforme.

unshaven, *a*, non rasé.

unsheathe, *v.t*, dégainer.

unsheltered, *a*, sans abri; non protégé.

unship, *v.t*, débarquer; (*oars*) déborder.

unshoe (*horse*) *v.t.ir*, déferrer.

unshrinkable, *a*, irrétrécissable.

unsightliness, *n*, laideur, *f*. **unsightly**, *a*, laid.

unsigned, *a*, non signé.

unsinkable, *a*, insubmersible.

unskillful, *a*, malhabile, maladroit. **~ness**, *n*, maladresse, *f*. **unskilled**, *a*, inexpérimenté.

unslaked lime, chaux vive, *f*.

unsociable, *a*, insociable.

unsocial, *a*, antisocial.

unsold, *a*, invendu.

unsolicited, *a*, non sollicité, spontané.

unsolved, *a*, non résolu.

unsophisticated, *a*, non frelaté; naïf, ingénu.

unsought, *a*, sans qu'on le cherche.

unsound, *a*, vicieux; défectueux. *of ~ mind*, ne . . . pas sain d'esprit.

unsparing, *a*, prodigue; impitoyable.

unspeakable, *a*, indicible; ineffable.

unspent, *a*, non dépensé; non épuisé.

unspotted, *a*, sans tache.

unstable, *a*, instable; mouvant.

unstained, *a*, non teint; sans tache.

unstamped, *a*, non timbré; (*paper with no revenue stamps on*) libre; (*letter*) non affranchie.

unsteadiness, *n*, instabilité; vacillation, *f*. **unsteady**, *a*, instable; chancelant; vacillant.

unstinting, *a*, prodigue.

unstitch, *v.t*, découdre.

unstop, *v.t*, déboucher.

unstressed (*Gram.*) *a*, atone.

unstudied, *a*, naturel.

unsubdued, *a*, insoumis, indompté.

unsubstantial, *a*, sans substance; immatériel.

unsuccessful, *a*, sans succès; manqué; infructueux. **~ly**, *ad*, sans succès.

unsuitable†, *a*, impropre. **un-**

suited, *a*, mal adapté; peu fait.

unsullied, *a*, sans tache.

unsupported, *a*, en porte à faux; sans appui.

unsurpassed, *a*, non surpassé.

unsuspected, *a*, non soupçonné. **unsuspecting** & **unsuspicious**, peu soupçonneux; exempt de soupçon. **unsuspectingly**, *ad*, sans défiance.

unsweetened, *a*, non sucré; (*wine*) brut.

unswerving, *a*, inébranlable.

unsymmetrical, *a*, dissymétrique.

untack (*Need.*) *v.t*, débâtir.

untainted, *a*, non corrompu, non gâté; sans tache.

untamable, *a*, indomptable. **untamed**, *a*, indompté.

untarnished, *a*, non terni.

untaught, *a*, ignorant; inculte.

untenable, *a*, (*position, etc.*) intenable; (*assertion, etc.*) insoutenable.

untenanted, *a*, inhabité.

unthinkable, *a*, inimaginable. **unthinking**, *a*, irréfléchi.

unthread, *v.t*, désenfiler.

untidiness, *n*, désordre, *m*. **untidy**†, *a*, malpropre, désordonné, mal tenu.

untie, *v.t*, délier, détacher; dénouer.

until, *pr*, jusqu'à; jusque; avant; à. ¶ *c*, jusqu'à ce que; en attendant que. *not ~*, ne . . . pas avant de, ne . . . pas avant que.

untimely, *a*, intempestif, prématuré; (*hour*) indue.

untiring†, *a*, infatigable.

untold, *a*, indicible; inimaginable; innombrable.

untouchable, *n*, paria, *m*. **untouched**, *a*, intact; sans y toucher; non ému.

untoward, *a*, malencontreux, fâcheux.

untrained, *a*, inexpérimenté; (*animal*) non dressé.

untranslatable, *a*, intraduisible.

untraveled, *a*, (*country*) non parcouru; (*pers.*) qui n'a jamais voyagé.

untried, *a*, non essayé, non éprouvé.

untrimmed, *a*, sans garniture; non rogné.

untrodden, *a*, non frayé, non battu.

untroubled, *a*, calme, paisible, tranquille.

untrue, *a,* faux; mensonger; infidèle. **untruly,** *ad,* faussement.

untrustworthy, *a,* indigne de confiance.

untruth, *n,* contrevérité; fausseté, *f,* mensonge, *m.* **~ful,** *a,* peu véridique, menteur.

untutored, *a,* inculte.

untwist, *v.t,* détordre, détortiller.

unused, *a,* non employé; non utilisé; peu habitué. **unusual,** *a,* peu commun, inaccoutumé, insolite, rare. **~ly,** *ad,* extraordinairement.

unutterable, *a,* indicible, ineffable.

unvarnished, *a,* non verni; pur & simple.

unvarying, *a,* uniforme, invariable.

unveil, *v.t,* dévoiler; inaugurer.

unventilated, *a,* non aéré; mal aéré.

unversed in, peu versé dans.

unwarily, *ad,* sans précaution.

unwarlike, *a,* peu belliqueux.

unwarrantable, *a,* inexcusable, injustifiable.

unwary, *a,* peu circonspect.

unwashed, *a,* non lavé; crasseux.

unwavering, *a,* inébranlable.

unweaned, *a,* non sevré.

unwearied, *a,* infatigable.

unwelcome, *a,* importun; de trop; désagréable.

unwell, *a,* indisposé, souffrant.

unwholesome, *a,* malsain; morbide.

unwieldy, *a,* lourd, pesant; incommode.

unwilling, *a,* peu disposé, mal disposé. **~ly,** *ad,* à contre-cœur. **~ness,** *n,* mauvaise volonté; répugnance, *f.*

unwind, *v.t.ir,* dévider, dérouler.

unwisdom, *n,* manque de sagesse, *m.* **unwise,** *a,* peu sage, malavisé. **~ly,** *ad,* follement.

unwittingly, *ad,* sans y penser.

unwonted, *a,* inaccoutumé, insolite.

unworkable, *a,* inexécutable, impraticable. **unworked,** *a,* inexploité. *in an unworkmanlike manner,* en mauvais ouvrier.

unworn, *a,* non usé.

unworthiness, *n,* indignité, *f.* **unworthy,** *a,* indigne.

unwounded, *a,* non blessé.

unwrap, *v.t,* développer; découvrir.

unwrinkled, *a,* sans rides.

unwritten, *a,* non écrit. *~ law,* droit coutumier, *m.*

unwrought, *a,* non travaillé, non ouvré.

unyielding, *a,* inflexible, inébranlable.

unyoke, *v.t,* dételer.

up, *a,* montant. **~grade,** montée, côte, *f.* ¶ *ad,* en haut; au haut; haut; en amont; debout, sur pied; fini; *(prices)* en hausse; *(risen)* levé, e. *~ & down,* en haut & en bas; de long en large. **~stairs,** en haut. **~stream,** *ad,* en amont. *~ there,* là-haut. *~ to,* jusqu'à [occurrence de]. *~ to date,* à la page; *(Fin.)* à jour; *(att.)* moderne. *well ~ in* (subject), fort en, calé en. ¶ *ups & downs,* hauts & bas, *m.pl.* ¶ *up!* debout! alerte! levez-vous!

upbraid, *v.t,* reprocher.

upheaval, *n,* (*Geol.*) soulèvement; *(fig.)* bouleversement, *m,* convulsion, *f.*

uphill, *a,* montant; ardu. ¶ *ad,* en montant.

uphold, *v.t.ir,* soutenir, maintenir. **~er,** *n,* soutien, *m.*

upholster, *v.t,* tapisser, rembourrer. **~er,** *n,* tapissier, ère. **~y,** *n,* tapisserie, *f.*

upkeep, *n,* entretien, *m.*

upland, *n,* [haut] plateau, *m.*

uplift, *v.t,* ennoblir.

upon, *pr,* sur; dessus.

upper, *a,* supérieur; haut; de dessus. *~ case* (*Typ.*), haut de casse, *m.* *the ~ classes,* les hautes classes, *f.pl.* *~ deck,* pont supérieur, *m;* (*bus*) impériale, *f.* *the ~ hand* (*fig.*), le dessus; l'avantage, *m.* *~ register* (*Mus.*), aigu, *m.* *~ tooth,* dent de dessus, *f.* **~most,** *a,* le plus haut, le plus élevé; le plus fort.

upright, *a. & ad,* droit; debout; vertical; d'aplomb; intègre, honnête. *~ piano,* piano droit, *m.* **~ness,** *n,* perpendicularité; droiture, intégrité, *f.*

uprising, *n,* soulèvement, *m.*

uproar, *n,* tumulte, vacarme, tapage, bacchanal, *m.* **~ious†,** *a,* bruyant, tapageur.

uproot, *v.t,* déraciner, arracher.

upset, *n,* remue-ménage, *m.* ¶ *v.t,* renverser; verser; chavirer; déranger; bouleverser, troubler.

upshot, *n,* issue, *f,* fin mot; dénouement, *m.*

upside down, *ad,* sens dessus dessous.

upstart, n, parvenu, e.

upstroke, n, (*piston*) course montante, f; (*writing*) délié, m.

upward, a, ascendant; ascensionnel; jeté vers le haut. ~[s], ad, en haut, en contre-haut; en montant; au-dessus, ~s of, plus de.

Ural (the), l'Oural, m. *the ~ Mountains,* les monts Ourals, m.pl.

uranium, n, uranium, m.

urban, a, urbain. **urbane**, a, courtois, poli. ~ly, ad, avec urbanité.

urchin, a, gamin, galopin, moutard, m.

urethra, n, urètre, m.

urge, n, démangeaison, f. ¶ v.t, pousser, presser, solliciter; exhorter; alléguer. **urgency**, n, urgence, f. **urgent**, a, urgent, pressant, instant. ~ly, ad, instamment.

uric, a, urique. **urinal**, n, urinoir, m, vespasienne, f; (*vessel*) urinal, m. **urinate**, v.i, uriner. **urine**, n, urine, f.

urn, n, urne, f; (*tea*) samovar, m.

us, pn, nous.

usage, n, usage; traitement, m. **usance**, n, usance, f. **use**, n, usage; emploi, emprunt, m; jouissance; utilité; habitude; consommation, f. *to be of ~,* servir. *to make ~ of,* se servir de. ¶ v.t, se servir de, employer, emprunter; consommer; user de; traiter. *to get ~d to,* s'habituer. ¶ *no hooks,* ne pas se servir de crochets. ~d, p.a, usité; accoutumé, rompu; ayant déjà servi; usagé, d'occasion. ~ *car,* voiture d'occasion, f. ~**ful†**, a, utile. ~**fulness**, n, utilité, f. ~**less†**, a, inutile; vain. ~ *person,* non-valeur, f. ~ *things,* inutilités, f.pl. ~**lessness**, n, inutilité, f. **user**, n, usager, m.

Ushant, n, Ouessant, m.

usher, n, (*court*) huissier, (*Theat.*) ouvreur, m. ~ **in**, introduire, annoncer; (*fig.*) inaugurer.

usual†, a, usuel; habituel; obligé; ordinaire.

usufruct, n, usufruit, m.

usurer, n, usurier, ère, fessemathieu, m. **usurious†**, a, usuraire.

usurp, v.t, usurper. ~**ation**, n, usurpation, f. ~**er**, n, usurpateur, trice.

usury, n, usure, f.

utensil, n, ustensile; vase, m.

uterine, a, utérin. **uterus**, n, utérus, m.

utilitarian, a.& n, utilitaire, a. & m,f.

utility, n, utilité, f. **utilize**, v.t, utiliser.

utmost, a, extrême, dernier. *one's* [*very*] ~, [tout] son possible, l'impossible, m. *to the ~,* à outrance.

utopia, n, utopie, f. **utopian**, a, utopique, utopiste. ¶ n, utopiste, m,f.

utter†, a, complet; total; extrême; grand. ¶ v.t, proférer, prononcer, dire, débiter; (*cry*) pousser; (*money*) passer. ~**ance**, n, articulation; parole, f; débit, m. ~**most**, a, extrême; le plus reculé.

uvula, n, luette, uvule, f.

V

vacancy, n, vacance, f; vide, m. **vacant**, a, vacant; libre, inoccupé; distrait. **vacate**, v.t, (*office*) quitter; (*premises*) vider. **vacation**, n, vacances, f.pl.

vaccinate, v.t, vacciner. **vaccination**, n, vaccination, f. **vaccine**, n, vaccin, m.

vacillate, v.i, vaciller. **vacillation**, n, vacillation, f.

vacuity, n, vacuité, f. **vacuous**, a, insignifiant. **vacuum**, n, vide, m. ~ *cleaner,* aspirateur [de poussières] m.

vade mecum, n, vade-mecum, m, épée de chevet, f.

vagabond, n. & a, vagabond, e.

vagary, n, caprice, m, lubie, f.

vagrancy, n, vagabondage, m. **vagrant**, n, vagabond, e, clochard, e. ¶ a, vagabond.

vague†, a, vague, imprécis. ~**ness**, n, vague, m, imprécision, f.

vain†, a, vain, vaniteux. ~**glorious**, a, vaniteux, glorieux, superbe. ~**glory**, n, gloriole, superbe, f.

valance, n, pente, f.

vale, n, vallon, val, m.

valedictory, a, d'adieu.

valence (*Chem.*) n, valence, f.

Valencia, n, Valence, f.

valet, n, valet [de chambre] m. ¶ v.t, faire office de valet à.

valetudinarian, a. & n, valétudinaire, a. & m,f.

valiant†, a, vaillant, brave.

valid†, a, valide; (*ticket*) valable. ~**ate**, v.t, valider. ~**ity**, n, validité, f.

valise, *n,* valise, *f.*

valley, *n,* vallée; (*of roof*) noue, *f.*

valorous†, *a,* valeureux. **valor,** *n,* valeur, vaillance, bravoure, *f.*

valuable, *a,* de valeur, de prix, riche; précieux. **~s,** *n.pl,* valeurs, *f.pl,* objets de valeur, *m.pl.* **valuation,** *n,* évaluation, *f.* **value,** *n,* valeur, *f;* prix, *m.* ¶ *v.t,* évaluer; apprécier; faire cas de. **~less,** *a,* sans valeur.

valve, *n,* soupape; valve, *f.*

vamp (*shoe*), *n,* empeigne, *f.* ¶ *v.t. & i,* improviser.

vampire, *n,* vampire, *m.*

van, *n,* voiture; tapissière, *f;* wagon; fourgon, *m.* **~[guard],** avant-garde, *f.*

vanadium, *n,* vanadium, *m.*

vandal, *n,* vandale, *m.* ¶ *a,* de vandale. **~ism,** *n,* vandalisme, *m.*

vane, *n,* girouette; (*turbine*) aube; aile; (*technical*) pinnule, *f.*

vanilla, *n,* vanille, *f.*

vanish, *v.i,* s'évanouir, disparaître, devenir invisible; s'éclipser, se volatiliser, fuir. **~ing point,** point de fuite, *m.*

vanity, *n,* vanité, *f.*

vanquish, *v.t,* vaincre. *the ~ed,* les vaincus, *m.pl.*

vantage, *n,* avantage, *m.*

vapid, *a,* insipide, fade, plat.

vaporize, *v.t,* vaporiser. **vaporizer,** *n,* vaporisateur, *m.* **vaporous, -ry,** *a,* vaporeux. **vapor,** *n,* vapeur, *f.*

variable, *a,* variable; changeant. *at variance,* en désaccord, en mésintelligence. **variant,** *n,* variante, *f.* **variation,** *n,* variation, *f;* changement, *m;* modification, *f.*

varicose vein, varice, *f.*

variegate, *v.t,* varier, bigarrer, panacher, diaprer. **variety,** *n,* variété, diversité; variation, *f.*

various†, *a,* différent, divers.

varlet (*Hist.*) *n,* varlet, *m.*

varnish, *n,* vernis, *m.* ¶ *v.t,* vernir. **~ing,** *n,* vernissage, *m.*

vary, *v.t. & i,* varier; diversifier; modifier.

vascular, *a,* vasculaire.

vase, *n,* vase, *m.*

vaseline, *n,* vaseline, *f.*

vassal (*Hist.*) *n,* vassal, e.

vast, *a,* vaste, immense. **~ly,** *ad,* grandement. **~ness,** *n,* immensité, *f.*

vat, *n,* cuve, *f,* bac, *m.* ¶ *v.t,* encuver.

vaudeville, *n,* vaudeville, *m.*

vault, *n,* voûte; cave, *f;* caveau; tombeau; (*leap*) saut, *m;* chambre forte, *f.* ¶ *v.t,* voûter; (*v.i.*) sauter. **~ing horse,** cheval de bois, *m.*

vaunt, *n,* vanterie, *f.* ¶ *v.t,* vanter; (*v.i.*) se vanter.

veal, *n,* veau, *m.* ~ *cutlet,* côtelette de v., *f.*

vector, *n,* vecteur, *m.*

veer, *v.i,* (*wind*) se ranger, remonter; (*opinion*) se retourner. ¶ *n,* virage, *m.* **~ing** (*opinion*) *n,* revirement, *m.*

vegetable, *n,* légume, *m,* plante potagère, *f.* ¶ *a,* végétal. ~ *dish,* légumier, *m.* ~ *marrow,* courge à la moelle, *f.* **vegetarian,** *a. & n,* végétarien, ne. **vegetarianism,** *n,* végétarisme, *m.* **vegetate,** *v.i,* végéter. **vegetation,** *n,* végétation, *f.*

vehemence, *n,* véhémence, *f.* **vehement†,** *a,* véhément.

vehicle, *n,* (*carriage*) véhicule, *m,* voiture, *f;* (*medium*) véhicule, *m.* **vehicular traffic,** circulation des voitures, *f.*

veil, *n,* voile, *m;* voilette, *f;* (*fig.*) voile, rideau, bandeau, *m.* ¶ *v.t,* voiler.

vein, *n,* veine; (*leaf*) nervure, *f.* ¶ *v.t,* veiner.

vellum, *n,* vélin, *m.*

velocipede, *n,* vélocipède, *m.*

velocity, *n,* vitesse, *f.*

velour, *n,* feutre velours, *m.*

velum (*Anat.*) *n,* voile, *m.*

velvet, *n,* velours, *m.* ~ *pile,* moquette, *f.* **velveteen,** *n,* velours de coton, *m,* tripe de velours, *f.* **velvet[y],** *a,* velouté.

venal†, *a,* vénal. **~ity,** *n,* vénalité, *f.*

vendor, *n,* vendeur, euse; marchand, e; (*law*) vendeur, eresse; (*law*) apporteur, *m.* **~'s assets,** valeurs d'apport, *f.pl.*

veneer, *n,* bois de placage, *m,* feuilles de p., *f.pl;* (*fig.*) vernis, *m.* ¶ *v.t,* plaquer; (*fig.*) donner du vernis à.

venerable, *a,* vénérable. **venerate,** *v.t,* vénérer. **veneration,** *n,* vénération, *f.*

venereal, *a,* vénérien.

Venetia, *n,* la Vénétie. **Venetian,** *a,* vénitien. ~ *blind,* jalousie, *f.* ¶ *n,* Vénitien, ne.

vengeance, *n,* vengeance, *f.* **vengeful,** *a,* vengeur.

venial†, *a,* véniel.

Venice, *n,* Venise, *f.*

venison, *n*, venaison, *f*.

venom, *n*, venin, *m*. **~ous**, *a*, venimeux; vénéneux.

vent, *n*, évent, aspirail, soupirail, *m*; lumière; cheminée, *f*; libre cours, *m*, carrière, *f*. ¶ *v.t*, exhaler; donner libre cours à, évaporer. **ventilate**, *v.t*, aérer, donner de l'air à, ventiler. **ventilation**, *n*, aérage, *m*, aération, ventilation, *f*. **ventilator**, *n*, ventilateur, *m*; (*ship*) manche à air, manche à vent, *f*.

ventral, *a*, ventral.

ventricle, *n*, ventricule, *m*.

ventriloquim, **-quy**, *n*, ventriloquie, *f*. **ventriloquist**, *n*, ventriloque, *m,f*.

venture, *n*, aventure; entreprise; spéculation, *f*, hasard, *m*. ¶ *v.t*, aventurer, hasarder. **~ to**, oser, se permettre de. **~some**, *a*, aventureux; hasardeux.

veracious†, *a*, véridique. **veracity**, *n*, véracité, *f*.

veranda[h], *n*, véranda, *f*.

verb, *n*, verbe, *m*. **verbal**†, *a*, verbal. **verbatim**, *ad*. & *a*, mot à mot, *m*. pour *m*. **verbiage**, *n*, verbiage, *m*. **verbose**, *a*, verbeux. **verbosity**, *n*, verbosité, *f*.

verdant, *a*, verdoyant; naïf.

verdict, *n*, verdict, *m*.

verdigris, *n*, vert-de-gris, verdet, *m*.

verdure, *n*, verdure, *f*.

verge, *n*, bord, *m*; orée, *f*; (*road*) accotement; (*fig.*) penchant, point, *m*; (*rod*) verge, *f*. ¶ **~ on**, tirer à; pencher vers.

verification, *n*, vérification, *f*. **verify**, *v.t*, vérifier. **verisimilitude**, *n*, vraisemblance, *f*. **veritable**†, *a*, véritable. **verity**, *n*, vérité, *f*.

vermicelli, *n*, vermicelle, *m*, nouilles, *f.pl*.

vermilion, *n*, vermillon, *m*. ¶ *a*, vermeil.

vermin, *n*, vermine, *f*; animaux nuisibles, *m.pl* **~ous**, *a*, couvert de vermine.

vermouth, *n*, vermouth, *m*.

vernacular, *a*, vulgaire. ¶ *n*, langue vulgaire, *f*.

vernal, *a*, printanier; (*equinox*) de printemps.

vernier, *n*, vernier, *m*.

Verona, *n*, Vérone, *f*.

veronica, *n*, véronique, *f*.

versatile, *a*, souple. **versatility**, *n*, souplesse d'esprit, *f*.

verse, *n*, vers, *m*; vers, *m.pl*; verset;

couplet, *m*, strophe, *f*. **versed in**, versé dans, ferré en. **versicle** (*Lit.*) *n*, verset, *m*. **versifier**, *n*, versificateur, *m*. **versify**, *v.t*, versifier, rimer. **version**, *n*, version, *f*. **verso**, *n*, verso, *m*.

versus, *pr*, contre.

vertebra, *n*, vertèbre, *f*. **vertebral**, *a*, vertébral. **vertebrate**, *a*. & *n*, vertébré, *a*. & *m*.

vertex, *n*, sommet, *m*. **vertical**, *a*, vertical. ¶ *n*, verticale, *f*. **~ity**, *n*, verticalité, *f*. **~ly**, *ad*, verticalement. **~ strung piano**, piano à cordes droites, *m*.

vertiginous, *a*, vertigineux. **vertigo**, *n*, vertige, *m*.

verve, *n*, verve, *f*.

very, *a*, même; seul. ¶ *ad*, très; fort; bien; tout. **~ much**, beaucoup.

vesicle, *n*, vésicule, *f*.

vespers, *n.pl*, vêpres, *f.pl*.

vessel, *n*, vase, récipient; (*blood*) vaisseau; (*ship*) vaisseau, bâtiment, navire, *m*.

vest, *n*, (*man's*) gilet, *m*; (*woman's*) chemise, camisole; *f*. ¶ *v.t*, investir; confier. **~ed rights**, droits acquis, *m.pl*.

vesta, *n*, allumette, *f*.

vestal [**virgin**], *n*, vestale, *f*.

vestibule, *n*, vestibule, *m*.

vestige, *n*, vestige, *m*, trace, *f*.

vestment, *n*, vêtement, *m*.

vestry, *n*, sacristie; (*council*) fabrique, *f*.

Vesuvian, *n*, vésuvien. **Vesuvius**, *n*, le Vésuve.

veteran, *n*, vétéran; ancien combattant, *m*. ¶ *a*, qui a vieilli dans sa profession; de longue date; depuis longtemps sous les drapeaux.

veterinary, *a*, vétérinaire. **~ [surgeon]**, [médecin] vétérinaire, *m*.

veto, *n*, veto, *m*. ¶ *v.t*, mettre le (son) v. à.

vex, *v.t*, contrarier, chagriner, vexer. **~ation**, *n*, contrariété, *f*; désagrément, *m*; vexation, *f*. **vexatious**, *a*, contrariant, vexatoire. **vexed** (*question*) *p.a*, controversée, longuement débattue.

via, *pr*, par la voie [de], par.

viability, *n*, viabilité, *f*. **viable**, *a*, viable.

viaduct, *n*, viaduc, *m*.

vial, *n*, fiole, *f*.

viand, *n*, mets, *m*.

vibrate, *v.i*, (*Phys*. & *fig*.) vibrer; (*machinery, car*) trembler. **vi-**

bration, n, vibration; trépidation, f.

vicar, n, vicaire; curé; ministre, m. **~age,** n, cure, f; presbytère, m. **~ship,** n, cure, f.

vice, n, (depravity) vice, m.

vice-, prefix, vice-. **~-chairman, ~-president,** vice-president, e. **~-principal** (college), censeur, m. **~reine,** vice-reine, f. **~roy,** vice-roi, m.

Vicenza, n, Vicence, f.

vice versa, ad, vice versa, réciproquement.

vicinity, n, voisinage, m, proximité, f.

vicious†, a, vicieux. **~ circle,** cercle vicieux, m. **~ness,** n, nature vicieuse, f.

vicissitude, n, vicissitude, péripétie, f, cahot, m.

victim, n, victime, f. **~ize,** v.t, rendre victime.

victor, n, vainqueur, m. **victorious†,** a, victorieux. **victory,** n, victoire, f.

victual, v.t, ravitailler. **~s,** n.pl, vivres, m.pl, victuailles, f.pl.

vicuña, n, vigogne, f.

vie, v.i, rivaliser; lutter; faire assaut.

Vienna, n, Vienne, f. **Viennese,** a, viennois. **¶** n, Viennois, e.

view, n, vue; perspective, f, coup d'œil; tableau, m; idée, opinion, f. **to have in ~,** viser. **~finder,** viseur, m. **¶** v.t, contempler; envisager.

vigil, n, veille; veillée; (Eccl.) vigile, f. **~ance,** n, vigilance, f. **~ant,** a, vigilant. **~antly,** ad, avec vigilance.

vignette, n, vignette, f. **¶** v.t, dégrader. **vignetter,** n, dégradateur, m.

vigor, n, vigueur; sève, f. **vigorous†,** a, vigoureux.

vile, a, vil; abject. **~ness,** n, bassesse; abjection, f. **vilify,** v.t, vilipender.

villa, n, villa, f. **village,** n, village, m; bourgade, f; (att.) villageois, de village, de clocher. **villager,** n, villageois, e.

villain, n, scélérat, e, misérable, m.f, bandit; (Theat.) traître, m; (Hist.) vilain, e. **~ous,** a, scélérat. **~y,** n, scélératesse, f. **villein,** n, vilain, e.

vindicate, v.t, justifier. **vindication,** n, justification, f.

vindictive, a, vindicatif.

vine, n, vigne, f. **~ shoot,** sarment,

m. **vinegar,** n, vinaigre, m. **~ works,** vinaigrerie, f. **¶** v.t, vinaigrer. **vinery,** n, serre à vignes, f. **vineyard,** n, vigne, f; vignoble, m. **vinosity,** n, vinosité, f. **vinous,** a, vineux. **vintage,** n, (growth) cru, m, cuvée; (season) vendange; (crop) récolte, vinée, f. **~ wine,** vin millésimé, m. **~ year,** année à millésime, f. **vintager,** n, vendangeur, euse.

viola, n, (Mus.) alto, m; (Bot.) violariacée, f. **violaceous,** a, violacé.

violate, v.t, violer. **violation,** n, violation, f; (rape) viol, m. **violator,** n, violateur, trice. **violence,** n, violence, f. **do ~ to,** violenter. **violent†,** a, violent.

violet, n, (Bot.) violette, f; (color) violet, m. **¶** a, violet.

violin, n, violon, m. **~ist,** n, violoniste, m.f. **violoncellist,** n, violoncelliste, m.f. **violoncello,** n, violoncelle, m.

viper, n, vipère, f.

virago, n, dragon, m, mégère, f.

virgin, n, vierge; pucelle, f. **¶** a, vierge. **~al†,** a, virginal. **Virginia** (Geog.) n, la Virginie, f. **~ creeper,** vigne vierge, f. **~ [tobacco],** virginie, m. **virginity,** n, virginité, f.

virile, a, viril, mâle. **virility,** n, virilité, f.

virtual†, a, virtuel. **virtue,** n, vertu, f. **virtuosity,** n, virtuosité, f. **virtuoso,** n, virtuose, m.f. **virtuous†,** a, vertueux.

virulence, n, virulence, f. **virulent,** a, virulent. **virus,** n, virus, m.

visa, n, visa, m. **¶** v.t, viser.

visage, n, visage, m, figure, f.

viscera, n.pl, viscères, m.pl.

viscid & viscous, a, visqueux. **viscose,** n, viscose, f. **viscosity,** n, viscosité, f.

viscount, n, vicomte, m. **~ess,** n, vicomtesse, f.

vise, n, étau, m.

visibility, n, visibilité, f. **visible,** a, visible. **visibly,** ad, visiblement; à vue d'œil.

vision, n, vision, f. **~ary,** a, visionnaire; chimérique. **¶** n, visionnaire, m.f.

visit, n, visite, f. **¶** v.t, visiter; voir; (Cust.) arraisonner. **~ation,** n, visite; (Eccl.) visitation, f. **~ing card,** carte de visite, f. **~or,** n, visiteur, euse; hôte, esse; passager, ère. **~s' tax,** taxe de séjour, f.

visor, *n,* visière, *f.*

vista, *n,* échappée [de vue]; perspective, *f.*

Vistula (the), la Vistule.

visual, *a,* visuel. **~ize,** *v.t,* se représenter.

vital, *a,* vital; (*fig.*) vif. **~ity,** *n,* vitalité, *f.* **~ize,** *v.t,* vivifier. **~s,** *n.pl,* parties vitales, *f.pl.* **vitamin,** *n,* vitamine, *f.*

vitiate, *v.t,* vicier. **vitiation,** *n,* viciation, *f.*

viticultural, *a,* viticole. **viticultur[al]ist,** *n,* viticulteur, *m.* **viticulture,** *n,* viticulture, *f.*

vitreous, *a,* vitreux; (*humor*) vitrée. **vitrify,** *v.t,* vitrifier. **vitriol,** *n,* vitriol, *m.* **~ic** *a,* vitriolique.

vituperate, *v.t,* injurier, vilipender. **vituperation,** *n,* injures, *f.pl.*

vivacious, *a,* enjoué. *to be* **~,** avoir de la vivacité. **~ly,** *ad,* avec vivacité. **viva voce,** *ad,* de vive voix. ¶ *a,* oral. ¶ *n,* examen oral, *m.* **vivid,** *a,* vif, vivant. **vividness,** *n,* vivacité, *f.* **vivify,** *v.t,* vivifier. **viviparous,** *a,* vivipare. **vivisection,** *n,* vivisection, *f.*

vixen, *n,* renarde; (*woman*) mégère, *f.*

viz, *ad. abb,* c'est-à-dire, [à] savoir.

vizier, *n,* vizir, *m.*

vocable, *n,* vocable, *m.* **vocabulary,** *n,* vocabulaire, *m.* **vocal,** *a,* vocal. **~ist,** *n,* chanteur, euse, cantatrice, *f.* **~ize,** *v.t,* vocaliser. **vocation,** *n,* vocation, *f.* **vocative** [case], *n,* vocatif, *m.*

vociferate, *v.i,* vociférer. **vociferous,** *a,* bruyant. **~ly,** *ad,* bruyamment.

vogue, *n,* vogue, mode, *f.*

voice, *n,* voix, *f.* ¶ *v.t,* exprimer.

void, *a,* vide; nul. ¶ *n,* vide; vague, *m.* ¶ *v.t,* évacuer; annuler.

voile (*textile*) *n,* voile, *m.*

volatile, *a,* volatil. **volatilize,** *v.t,* volatiliser.

volcanic, *a,* volcanique. **volcano,** *n,* volcan, *m.*

volition, *n,* volition, *f.*

volley, *n,* volée; décharge, *f.* **~ball,** volleyball, *m.* **~ firing,** feu de peloton, *m.* ¶ (*Ten.*) *v.t,* [re]prendre à la (*ou* de) volée; (*abs.*) jouer à la (*ou* de) volée.

volplane, *n,* vol plané, *m.* ¶ *v.i,* descendre en vol plané.

volt, *n,* volt, *m.* **~age,** *n,* voltage, *m,* tension, *f.* **~ high ~,** haute tension, *f.* **voltaic,** *a,* voltaïque. **voltmeter,** *n,* voltmètre, *m.*

volubility, *n,* volubilité, *f.* **volu-**
ble, *a,* volubile, fécond en paroles.

volume, *n,* volume; tome; (*of smoke, etc.*) nuage, *m.* **voluminous,** *a,* volumineux.

voluntary†, *a,* volontaire; bénévole. ¶ (*organ*) *n,* (*before service*) prélude; (*during*) interlude, *m;* (*after*) sortie, *f;* (*between credo & sanctus*) offertoire, *m.* **volunteer,** *n,* volontaire, *m.*

voluptuary, *n,* voluptueux, euse. **voluptuous†,** *a,* voluptueux. **~ness,** *n,* volupté, sensualité, mollesse, *f.*

volute, *n,* volute, *f.*

vomit, *n,* vomissement, *m.* ¶ *v.t,* & *i,* vomir, revomir.

voracious, *a,* vorace. **~ly,** *ad,* avec voracité. **~ness, voracity,** *n,* voracité, *f.*

vortex, *n,* tourbillon, *m.*

votary, *n,* adorateur, trice; sectateur, *m.* **vote,** *n,* vote, scrutin, suffrage, *m,* voix, opinion, *f.* ¶ *v.t.* & *i,* voter, donner sa voix, opiner. **~ by a show of hands,** voter à main levée. **voter,** *n,* votant, *m.* **voting,** *n,* votation, *f.* **~ paper,** bulletin de vote, *m.* **votive,** *a,* votif.

vouch, *v.t,* attester; vérifier. **~ for,** répondre de, garantir. **~er,** *n,* pièce justificative, *f;* bon, bulletin, *m.* **~safe,** *v.t,* accorder; daigner.

vow, *n,* vœu, *m.* ¶ *v.t,* vouer; (*v.i.*) faire vœu; jurer.

vowel, *n,* voyelle, *f.*

voyage, *n,* voyage, *m.* ¶ *v.i,* voyager.

vulcanite, *n,* caoutchouc vulcanisé, *m,* ébonite, *f.* **vulcanize,** *v.t,* vulcaniser.

vulgar†, *a,* vulgaire; populacier; trivial, commun, bas. *the* **~** [*herd*], le vulgaire. **~ism,** *n,* expression vulgaire, trivialité, *f.* **~ity,** *n,* vulgarité, trivialité, *f.* **~ize,** *v.t,* vulgariser; banaliser. *the Vulgate,* la Vulgate.

vulnerable, *a,* vulnérable.

vulture, *n,* vautour, *m.*

W

wad, *n,* bourre, *f;* tampon, *m;* (*banknotes*) liasse, *f.* ¶ *v.t,* ouater. **wadding,** *n,* ouate, *f.*

waddle, *n,* dandinement, déhanchement, *m.* ¶ *v.i,* marcher comme une cane, se dandiner.

wade, *v.i,* se mettre à l'eau sans nager; patauger, barboter. **~**

through (ford), passer à gué. ~
through a book, peiner en lisant
un livre. **wader**, *n*, (*bird*) échassier, *m*; (*pl.*) bottes cuissardes,
f.pl.

wafer, *n*, (*flat biscuit*) gaufrette;
(*cornet biscuit*) oublie, *f*, plaisir;
(*Eccl.*) hostie, *f*.

waffle, *n*, gaufre, *f*. ~ *irons*,
gaufrier, *m*.

waft, *n*, souffle, *m*. ¶ *v.t*, flotter,
transporter; (*v.i.*) flotter dans
l'air, sur l'eau.

wag, *n*, plaisant, loustic, farceur,
m. ¶ *v.t*, (*tail*) agiter, frétiller de;
(*head*) branler, dodeliner de (*la
tête*).

wage, *n*. *oft. pl*, salaire, *m*, paie,
f, gages, loyers, *m.pl*. ~ *earner*,
salarié, e. *to pay a* ~ *to*, salarier.
to ~ **war**, faire la guerre, guerroyer.

wager, *n*, pari, *m*, gageure, *f*.
¶ *v.t*, parier.

wagon, *n*, voiture, *f*, fourgon,
chariot, *m*. ~*load*, charretée, *f*.

waggish, *a*, facétieux, badin.

waggle, *v.t. & i*, branler.

wagtail, *n*, hochequeue, *m*, bergeronnette, *f*.

waif, *n*, enfant abandonné, e, *m,f*.

wail, *n*, lamentation, *f*. ¶ *v.i*, se
lamenter; (*of baby*) vagir.

wain, *n*, chariot, *m*.

wainscot, *n*, lambris, *m*. ¶ *v.t*,
lambrisser.

waist, *n*, ceinture, taille, *f*. ~
band, ceinture, *f*. ~*coat*, gilet,
m. ~ *measurement*, tour de taille,
m, grosseur de ceinture, *f*.

wait, *n*, attente, *f*. *to lie in* ~, se
tenir en embuscade, s'embusquer.
¶ *v.t. & i*, attendre. ~*-&-see*, *a*,
expectant. ~ [*up*]*on*, servir; se
présenter chez. **waiter**, *n*, garçon,
m. ~! garçon! **waiting**, *n*, attente, *f*. ~ *room*, salon d'attente,
m; (*Rly*) salle d'a., *f*. **waitress**,
n, servante, bonne, *f*. ~! mademoiselle!

waive, *v.t*, renoncer à, se désister
de.

wake, *n*, sillage, *m*, eaux, *f.pl*; (*funeral*) veillée mortuaire, *f*. *follow in the* ~ *of* (*Naut. & fig.*),
marcher dans les eaux de. ¶ *v.t.i.r.*
& **waken**, *v.t*, [r]éveiller; (*v.i.*)
s'éveiller. ~*ful*, *a*, privé de sommeil; vigilant. ~**fulness**, *n*, insomnie, *f*.

Wales, *n*, le pays de Galles.

walk, *n*, marche; promenade [à
pied] *f*, tour; pas, *m*; allure, dé-

marche; allée, *f*; promenoir, *m*.
~ *of life*, carrière, profession, *f*.
~ *over*, (*sport*) walk-over, *m*;
(*fig.*) victoire facile, *f*. ¶ *v.t. & i*,
marcher; cheminer; aller à pied;
aller au pas. ~ *about*, se promener. ~ *in*, entrer. ~ *off*, s'en
aller. ~ *out*, sortir. **walker**, *n*,
marcheur, euse; piéton, ne;
promeneur, euse. **walking**, *n*,
marche; promenade [à pied] *f*.
¶ *p.a. or att*, ambulant; (*boots*)
de marche. ~ *stick*, canne, *f*. ~
tour, excursion à pied, *f*.

wall, *n*, mur, *m*, muraille; paroi; *f*;
haut du pavé, *m*. ~ *cupboard*,
placard, *m*. *to be a* ~*flower*, faire
tapisserie. ~ *map*, carte murale,
f. ~ *paper*, papier peint, papier-
tenture, *m*, tenture, *f*.

wallet, *n*, sacoche, *f*; portefeuille,
m.

wallow, *n*, souille, *f*. ¶ *v.i*, se vautrer; croupir.

walnut, *n*, noix, *f*; (*tree, wood*)
noyer, *m*.

walrus, *n*, morse, *m*.

waltz, *n*, valsé, *f*. ¶ *v.i*, valser. ~*er*,
n, valseur, euse.

wan, *a*, blême, blafard; (*face*) hâve.

wand, *n*, baguette, *f*.

wander, *v.i*, errer, vagabonder,
vaguer; s'écarter; divaguer. ~
around, tournailler. ~*er*, *n*,
coureur, nomade, *m*. *the Wandering Jew*, le Juif errant.

wane, *n*, déclin, retour, *m*. ¶ *v.i*,
décroître; décliner.

want, *n*, besoin; manque, défaut,
m, gêne, *f*. ¶ *v.t*, avoir besoin de;
manquer de; désirer; falloir;
vouloir. ~*ed* (*Advt*), on demande.

wanton, *a*, folâtre; folichon; licencieux; lascif; gratuit, sans
motif. ~ *destruction*, vandalisme,
m. *out of sheer* ~*ness*, de gaieté
de cœur.

war, *n*, guerre, *f*; (*elements*) combat, *m*. ~ *dance*, danse guerrière,
f. ~ *horse*, cheval de bataille,
m. W~ *loan*, emprunt de la
Défense nationale, *m*. ~ *memorial*, monument aux morts [de la
guerre] *m*. ~ *of attrition*, guerre
d'usure. ~*ship*, vaisseau de
guerre, *m*. ¶ *v.i*, faire la guerre,
guerroyer.

warble, *v.i*, gazouiller; (*v.t.*) roucouler. **warbler** (*bird*) *n*, fauvette, *f*.

ward, *n*, pupille, *m,f*; (*prison*)
quartier; arrondissement, *m*; (*hospital*) salle; (*lock*) garde, *f*.

~*room*, carré des officiers, *m*. ~ [off], *v.t*, parer. ~en, *n*, gardien; gouverneur, *m*. **wardrobe**, *n*, armoire; garde-robe, *f*; vêtements, *m.pl*. ~ *trunk*, malle-armoire, *f*.

warehouse, *n*, magasin; dépôt; entrepôt; dock, *m*. ~ *keeper* (bonded), entreposeur, *m*. ~*man*, magasinier; marchand en magasin, stockiste, *m*. ¶ *v.t*, emmagasiner; entreposer.

wares, *n.pl*, marchandise, *f*, articles, *m.pl*.

warily, *ad*, avec circonspection, à tâtons. **wariness**, *n*, précaution, *f*.

warlike, *a*, guerrier, belliqueux; martial.

warm†, *a*, chaud; (*fig.*) chaleureux. *it is* ~, il fait chaud. *I am* ~, j'ai chaud. ¶ *v.t*, chauffer; réchauffer; échauffer. ~*ing pan*, bassinoire, *f*, chauffe-lit, *m*. ~*th*, *n*, chaleur, *f*.

warn, *v.t*, avertir, prévenir, ~*ing*, *n*, avertissement, préavis, *m*.

warp, *n*, chaîne, lice, lisse, *f*. ¶ *v.t*, déjeter; (*yarn*) ourdir; (*Naut.*) touer; (*v.i.*) se déjeter, gauchir, gondoler.

warrant, *n*, autorisation; ordonnance, *f*; garant; mandat; warrant, bulletin de gage; titre, *m*. ¶ *v.t*, garantir; justifier. ~*able*, *a*, justifiable. ~*y*, *n*, garantie, *f*.

warren, *n*, garenne, *f*.

warrior, *n*, guerrier, ère.

Warsaw, *n*, Varsovie, *f*.

wart, *n*, verrue, *f*, poireau, *m*. ~*y*, *a*, verruqueux.

wary, *a*, circonspect; défiant.

wash, *n*, (*linen*) lessive, *f*; (*art*) lavis, *m*; (*mouth*) eau, *f*; (*ship*) remous, *m*; (*slops*) lavasse, *f*. ~*basin*, cuvette, *f*. ~ *drawing*, [dessin au] lavis, *m*. ~*house*, lavoir, *m*, laverie, buanderie, *f*. ~*stand*, lavabo, *m*. ~*tub*, cuvier, *m*. ¶ *v.t*. & *i*, laver; se l.; blanchir; baigner. ~ *away*, emporter, entraîner; affouiller. ~ *the dishes*, laver la vaisselle. ~*able*, *a*, lavable. *washed overboard*, enlevé par la mer. **washer**, *n*, (*pers.*) laveur, euse; (*ring*) rondelle, *f*. ~*woman*, laveuse de linge, blanchisseuse, *f*. **washing**, *n*, lavage; blanchissage, *m*; lessive; toilette; ablution; lotion, *f*. ~ *board*, planche de lavage, *f*. ~ *machine*, machine à laver, *f*.

wasp, *n*, guêpe, *f*. ~*s' nest*, guêpier, *m*.

waste, *a*, (*land*) inculte, vague; (*gas*, *heat*) perdu; (*matter*) de rebut. *to lay* ~, dévaster, ravager. ¶ *n*, gaspillage, *m*; perte, *f*; déchet; rebut, *m*. ¶ *comps*: ~ *paper*, papier de rebut, *m*; papiers inutiles, *m.pl*. ~ *paper basket*, corbeille à papiers, *f*. ~ *pipe*, trop-plein, *m*. ~ *water*, eaux-vannes, *f.pl*. ¶ *v.t*, gaspiller; perdre; consumer. ~ *away*, se consumer; s'atrophier. ~*d life*, vie manquée, *f*. **wasteful**, *a*, dissipateur, prodigue. **wastefulness**, *n*, prodigalité, *f*.

watch, *n*, veille; garde, sentinelle, *f*; (*Naut.*) quart, *m*, bordée; (*Horo.*) montre, *f*. *on the* ~, aux aguets, à l'affût. ~ *chain*, chaîne de montre, *f*. ~*dog*, chien de garde, *m*. ~ *fire*, feu de bivouac, *m*. ~*maker*, horloger, *m*. ~*man*, veilleur, garde, *m*. ~ *wrist-montre-bracelet*, *f*. ¶ *v.t*. & *i*, veiller; surveiller; observer; guetter; suivre. ~*er*, *n*, veilleur, euse. ~*ful*†, *a*, vigilant. ~*fulness*, *n*, vigilance, *f*.

water, *n*, eau, *f*; eaux, *f.pl*; (*tide*) marée, *f*, eaux, *f.pl*; (*pl.*) eaux, *f.pl*, parages, *m.pl*. ~ *closet*, cabinets, *m.pl*, cabinet [d'aisance] *m*. ~*color*, aquarelle, *f*. ~*cress*, cresson [de fontaine] *m*. ~*fall*, chute d'eau; cascade, *f*. ~*fowl*, oiseau aquatique, *m*. ~*glass*, verre soluble, *m*. ~ *hazard* (golf), douve, *f*. ~ *jug*, pot à eau, *m*. ~ *jump* (turf), douve, *f*. ~ *level*, niveau d'eau, *m*. ~ *lily*, nénuphar, *m*. ~ *line*, ligne de flottaison, *f*. ~*logged*, imbibé d'eau; (*boat*) engagé. ~*mark*, (*tidal*) laisse, *f*; (*paper*) filigrane, *m*. ~*melon*, melon d'eau, *m*, pastèque, *f*. ~ *meter*, compteur à eau, *m*. ~ *mill*, moulin à eau, *m*. ~ *nymph*, naïade, *f*. ~ *on the brain*, hydrocéphalie, *f*. ~ *on the knee*, épanchement de synovie, *m*. ~ *pipe*, tuyau d'eau, *m*, conduite d'eau, *f*. ~*power*, force hydraulique, houille blanche, *f*. ~*proof*, *a*, imperméable [à l'eau]; (*v.t*.) imperméabiliser. ~ *polo*, water-polo, *m*. ~ *rat*, rat d'eau, *m*. ~*shed*, ligne de faîte, *f*. ~*side*, bord de l'eau, *m*; (*att.*) riverain. ~*spout*, (*rain*) gargouille; (*Meteor.*) trombe, *f*. ~*tight*, étanche [à l'eau]. ~ *tower*, château d'eau, *m.* ~*way*, voie navigable, v. d'eau, *f*; (*bridge*) débouché, *m*. ~*wheel*, roue hydraulique, *f*. ~*works*, usine hydraulique, *f*. ¶ *v.t*, (*garden*) arroser; (*horse*) abreuver; (*drink*) couper, baptiser; (*stock, Fin.*) diluer; (*silk*) moirer; (*v.i.*) (*eyes*) pleurer, larmoyer; (*take in water*) faire de l'eau. *it makes one's mouth* ~, cela fait venir l'eau à la bouche. ~*ed silk*, moire de soie, soie moirée, *f*. ~*ing*, *n*, arrosement; arrosage; abreuvage, *m*; moire, *f*. ~ *place*, abreuvoir, *m*; ville d'eaux, *f*, eaux, *f.pl*; bains, *m.pl*, station balnéaire, *f*. ~*less*, *a*, dépourvu d'eau. ~*y*, *a*, aqueux; humide; (*fluid*) ténu.

watt, *n*, watt, *m*.

wattle, *n*, (*rods & twigs*) claie; (*bird*) barbe, caroncule, *f*, fanon, *m*; (*fish*) barbe, *f*. ¶ *v.t*, clayonner.

wave, *n*, vague, *f*; flot, *m*; lame, *f*; coup de mer, *m*; onde; ondulation, *f*; (*hand*) signe, geste, (*wand*) coup, *m*. ~*length*, longueur d'onde, *f*. ¶ *v.i*, flotter; ondoyer; (*v.t.*) agiter; faire signe de; onduler. *to have one's hair* ~*d*, se faire onduler [les cheveux]. **waver**, *v.i*, hésiter, vaciller, flotter, chanceler. **wavy**, *a*, onduleux, ondé, en ondes; (*line*) tremblée.

wax, *n*, cire, *f*; (*cobbler's*) poix, *f*. ~*works*, figures de cire, *f.pl*. ¶ *v.t*, cirer; (*v.i.*) croître; devenir. ~*ed thread*, fil poissé, *m*. ~*y*, *a*, comme cire.

way, *n*, chemin, *m*, route; voie; distance, *f*; passage, *m*; place, *f*; progrès, *m*; marche; direction, *f*; côté; sens, *m*; manière, façon, *f*, air; usage, *m*; guise, *f*; cours, *m*; passe; (*Naut.*) erre, *f*. *by the* ~, (*fig.*) à propos. *half-*~, à mi-chemin. *in the* ~, encombrant, gênant. *to lose one's* ~, s'égarer. ~*bill*, feuille de route, *f*. ~*farer*, voyageur, euse. ~ *in*, entrée, *f*. ~*lay*, tendre une embûche à. ~ *out*, sortie; issue, *f*, ~*side*, bord de la route, *m*; (*att.*) sur le b. de la r.; riverain; (*Rly station*) de passage, d'escale.

wayward†, *a*, capricieux, volontaire, libertin. ~*ness*, *n*, libertinage, *m*.

we, *pn*, nous; on.

weak†, *a*, faible; débile; (*tea*) lé-

ger. ~ *spot* (*fig. of pers.*), côté faible, *m*. ~*en*, *v.t*, affaiblir; atténuer; (*v.i.*) faiblir. ~*ling*, *n*, faiblard, e. ~*ly*, *a*, débile, faiblard. ~*ness*, *n*, faiblesse, *f*; faible, *m*.

weal, *n*, bien, *m*. (Cf. *the common* ~); vergeture, trace d'un coup, *f*.

wealth, *n*, richesses, *f.pl*, opulence, *f*, biens, *m.pl*. ~*y*, *a*, riche, opulent.

wean, *v.t*, sevrer. ~*ing*, *n*, sevrage, *m*.

weapon, *n*, arme, *f*; porte-respect, *m*. ~*less*, *a*, sans armes.

wear, *n*, usage, *m*; usure, *f*. *the worse for* ~, patraque. ¶ *v.t. & i. ir*, user; s'u.; miner; porter; mettre. ~ *out*, user; épuiser, exténuer; (*v.i.*) s'épuiser. ~ *well*, être d'un bon user. ~*able*, *a*, mettable, portable.

weariness, *n*, fatigue, lassitude, *f*.

wearing, *n*, usure, *f*; port, *m*.

wearisome, *a*, endormant, assommant; fastidieux. ~*ness*, *n*, ennui, *m*. **weary**, *a*, fatigué, las. ¶ *v.t*, fatiguer, lasser; ennuyer. ~ *for*, languir après.

weasel, *n*, belette, *f*.

weather, *n*, temps, *m*; intempéries, *f.pl*. ~*beaten*, ravagé [par les intempéries]; hâlé. ~*cock*, girouette, *f*; coq, *m*; (*fig.*) girouette, *f*, sauteur, arlequin, *m*. ~ *forecast*, bulletin météorologique, *m*. ~ *permitting*, si le temps le permet. ~ *strip*, brisebise, *m*. ¶ *v.t*, résister à; (*Geol.*) altérer, désagréger.

weave, *n*, tissu, *m*. ¶ *v.t.ir*, tisser; (*basket*) tresser; (*fig.*) ourdir; tramer. **weaver**, *n*, tisserand, *m*. **weaving**, *n*, tissage, *m*; tisseranderie, *f*.

web, *n*, toile, *f*; (*bird's foot*) membrane; (*girder*) âme, *f*; (*key*) panneton, *m*; (*of life*) trame, *f*. *spider's* ~, toile d'araignée, *f*. ~*footed*, palmipède. **webbed**, *a*, palmé. **webbing**, *n*, sangle, *f*.

wed, *v.t*, épouser; marier; (*v.i.*) se m. **wedded**, *a*, conjugal; (*to opinion*) attaché. **wedding**, *n*, noces, *f.pl*, mariage, *m*. ~ *breakfast*, repas de noce, *m*. ~ *cake*, gâteau de noce, *m*. ~ *day*, jour de mariage, *m*. ~ *dress*, robe de mariée, *f*. ~ *festivities* & ~ *party*, noce, *f*. ~ *march*, marche nuptiale, *f*. ~ *present*, cadeau de noce, *m*; (*bridegroom's*) corbeille [de mariage] *f*. ~ *ring*, alliance, *f*, anneau nuptial, *m*.

wedge, *n*, coin, *m*; cale; hausse, *f*. ¶ *v.t*, coincer; caler.

wedlock, *n*, mariage, *m*.

Wednesday, *n*, mercredi, *m*.

wee, *a*, petiot, tout petit.

weed, *n*, mauvaise herbe, *f*. ¶ *v.t*, sarcler. ~ *out*, éliminer, épurer. ~**er,** *n*, (*pers.*) sarcleur, euse; (*hoe*) sarcloir, *m*.

week, *n*, semaine, *f*. (*e.g. Friday to Friday*) semaine, huitaine, *f*, huit jours, *m.pl*. ~ *day*, jour de semaine, *m*. ~ *days only*, la semaine seulement. ~**ly,** *a*, hebdomadaire.

weep, *v.i. & t. ir. & ~ for*, pleurer. ~**er,** *n*, pleureur, euse. **weeping,** *n*, pleurs, *m.pl*, larmes, *f.pl*. ¶ *a*, qui pleure, éploré; (*tree*) pleureur.

weevil, *n*, charançon, *m*. ~**y,** *a*, charançonné.

weft, *n*, trame, *f*.

weigh, *v.t*, peser; mesurer; (*anchor*) lever; (*v.i.*) peser; farder. ~ *down*, appesantir, affaisser. *to get under* ~, appareiller. ~**er,** *n*, peseur, *m*. **weighing,** *n*, pesage, *m*; pesée, *f*. ~ *in & ~ in room*, pesage, *m*. ~ *machine*, [balance à] bascule, *f*. **weight,** *n*, poids, *m*; pesanteur; gravité; importance, *f*. *net* ~, poids net, *m*. ~ *allowed free*, franchise de poids, *f*. *de bagages, f*. *his, its, ~ in gold*, son pesant d'or. ~**y†,** *a*, pesant; puissant; grave.

weir, *n*, barrage; déversoir; (*Fish.*) gord, *m*.

weird, *a*, fantastique.

welcome, *a*, bienvenu; libre. ¶ *n*, bienvenue, *f*, [bon] accueil, *m*, réception, *f*. ¶ *v.t*, bien accueillir, recevoir.

weld, *n*, soudure, *f*. ¶ *v.t*, souder; corroyer.

welfare, *n*, bien-être, bonheur; (*public*) salut, *m*, chose, *f*.

well, *n*, puits, *m*; source, fontaine, *f*; réservoir, *m*; (*of ship*) sentine, *f*; (*of court*) parquet, *m*. ~ *sinker*, puisatier, fontainier. *m*. ~*spring*, source, *f*. ¶ *v.i*, sourdre, jaillir.

well, *a*, bien; dispos, bien portant, en bonne santé. *he is* ~, il va bien. ¶ *ad*, bien. ~*-advised*, bien conseillé. ~ *& good*, à la bonne heure. ~*-attended*, suivi. ~*-balanced*, bien équilibré; (*style, prose*) nombreux. *to be* ~ *bal-*

anced (phrase), avoir du nombre. ~*-behaved*, sage. ~*-being*, bien-être, *m*. ~*-beloved*, *a. & n*, bien-aimé, e, bienaimé, e. ~*-bred*, bien élevé, bien appris, de bonne compagnie, honnête. ~*-built*, ~*-knit*, bien charpenté. ~*-disposed & ~-meaning*, bien intentionné. ~*-done* (*Cook.*), bien cuit. ~ *done!* bravo! ~*-informed*, calé. ~*-known*, connu, réputé, signalé, répandu. ~ *off & ~-to-do*, à son aise, aisé, au large, fortuné, calé, cossu. ~*-read*, instruit, lettré. ~*-spoken*, bien-disant. ~*-timed*, opportun.

Wellingtons, *n.pl*, bottes montant aux genoux, *f.pl*.

Welsh, *a*, gallois; du pays de Galles. ¶ *n*, le gallois. ~*man*, ~*woman*, Gallois, e. ~ *rabbit*, ~ *rarebit*, rôtie à l'anglaise, r. au fromage, *f*.

welt, *n*, (*shoe*) trépoint, *f*; (*strap*) couvre-joint, *m*, fourrure, *f*. *wide* ~ (shoe), semelle débordante, *f*.

welter, *v.i*, nager, se baigner, s'abîmer. ~ *weight* (*Box.*), poids mi-moyen, *m*.

wen, *n*, loupe, *f*, goitre, *m*.

wench, *n*, donzelle, *f*.

wend, *v.i*, poursuivre.

werewolf, *n*, loup-garou, *m*.

west, *n*, ouest; (le) couchant; occident, *m*. ¶ *a*, de l'ouest, d'ouest, occidental. *W~ Africa*, l'Afrique occidentale, *f*. *the W~ Indies*, les Indes occidentales, les Antilles, *f.pl*. **westerly,** *a*, d'ouest. **western,** *a*, de l'ouest; occidental; d'Occident.

Westphalia, *n*, la Westphalie.

wet, *a*, mouillé; humide; pluvieux; (*goods*) liquide; (*paint, ink*) fraîche. ~ *blanket*, rabat-joie, *m*. ~ *fly fishing*, pêche à la mouche noyée, *f*. ~ *nurse*, nourrice, *f*. ~ *through*, trempé. ~ & ~*ness*, *n*, humidité, *f*. *out in the* ~, dans la pluie. ¶ *v.t*, mouiller; imbiber; humecter; arroser.

whack, *n*, coup, *m*. ¶ *v.t*, battre.

whale, *n*, baleine, *f*. ~*boat*, baleinière, *f*. ~*bone*, fanon de baleine, *m*, baleine, *f*. ~ *calf*, baleineau, *m*. **whaler,** *n*, baleinier, *m*.

wharf, *n*, quai, appontement, débarcadère, embarcadère, *m*. **wharfinger,** *n*, propriétaire de quai, *m*.

what, *pn, a, & ad*, quoi; qu'est-ce

qui; qu'est-ce que; que; quel; quelle; ce qui; ce que, tant; comment. ~ *a*, quel, quelle. ~ *a relief!* ouf! ~ *for?* pourquoi? ~ *people may say*, le qu'en-dira-t-on. **whatever**, *pn. & a*, tout ce qui; tout ce que; quelque . . . qui; quelque . . . que; quelconque; quoi que; quel(le) que.

whatnot, *n*, étagère, *f*.

wheat, *n*, froment, blé, *m*. ~en, *a*, de froment.

wheedle, *v.t*, cajoler, enjôler.

wheel, *n*, roue, *f*; volant; disque; galet, *m*; roulette; (*emery, etc.*) meule; (*helm*) barre; (*Mil.*) conversion, *f*. spare ~, roue de rechange, *f*. ~barrow, brouette, *f*. ~base, écartement des essieux, empattement, *m*. ~chair, fauteuil roulant, *m*. ~work, wheels, rouage, *m*. ~wright, chairon, *m*. ¶ *v.t*, rouler; (*v.i.*) (*birds*) tournoyer. -wheeled, *a*, à . . . roues.

wheeze, *v.i*, siffler. **wheezy**, *a*, sifflant; (*pers.*) poussif.

whelk, *n*, buccin, *m*.

when, *ad*, quand, lorsque; alors que, après que. **whence**, *ad*, d'où. **whenever**, *ad*, toutes les fois que.

where, *ad*, où; là où; à l'endroit où. **whereabouts**, *ad*, où. *one's ~*, où on est. **whereas**, *ad*, tandis que, au lieu que; attendu que, vu que. **whereat**, *ad*, sur quoi. **whereby**, *ad*, par où, par lequel. **wherefore**, *ad*, pourquoi. **wherein**, *ad*, en quoi. **whereof**, *ad*, dont. **where[up]on**, *ad*, sur quoi. **wherever**, *ad*, partout où, où que. *the wherewithal*, de quoi, les moyens, *m.pl*.

wherry, *n*, bachot, *m*. ~man, bachoteur, *m*.

whet, *n*, stimulant, *m*. ¶ *v.t*, (*tools*) repasser, aiguiser; (*appetite*) aiguiser, stimuler. ~stone, pierre à aiguiser, *f*.

whether, *c*, soit; soit que; que; si.

whey, *n*, petit-lait, *m*.

which, *pn. & a*, qui; que; lequel, laquelle; ce qui; ce que; ce dont; quel, quelle. ~ *way?* par où? **whichever**, *pn*, n'importe quel, n'importe quelle.

whiff, *n*, bouffée, *f*.

while, *n*, temps, *m*. *it is worth ~*, cela vaut la peine. **while** & **whilst**, *c*, tandis que, pendant que; [tout] en. *while away*, (faire) passer; charmer, tromper.

whim, *n*, caprice, *m*, fantaisie;

boutade, *f*; (*Mach.*) treuil, cabestan, *m*.

whimper, *v.i*, pleurnicher, piauler, geindre. ~er, *n*, pleureur, euse, pleurard, e.

whimsical†, *a*, capricieux, fantasque, lunatique.

whin, *n*, ajonc, genêt épineux, *m*.

whine, *v.i*, pleurnicher, piauler, geindre.

whinny, *n*, hennissement, *m*. ¶ *v.i*, hennir.

whip, *n*, fouet, *m*. ~cord, [fil de] fouet, *m*. ~ *hand* (*fig.*), dessus, *m*. ¶ *v.t. & i*, fouetter; toucher. **whipper-in**, *n*, piqueur, *m*. **whipper-snapper**, *n*, moucheron, freluquet, *m*. **whipping**, *n*, fustigation, *f*, le fouet; (*Need.*) point roulé, *m*. ~ *top*, sabot, *m*.

whir, *v.i*, siffler, ronfler.

whirl, *n*, ébullition, *f*; tourbillon, *m*. ¶ *v.i*, tournoyer, tourbillonner. ~pool, tourbillon, *m*. ~wind, tourbillon, *m*. **whirligig**, *n*, pirouette, *f*; carrousel, *m*.

whisk, *n*, (*brush, broom*) balayette, *f*, houssoir, *m*; (*egg*) fouet, *m*. ¶ *v.t*, (*dust*) épousseter; (*eggs*) fouetter.

whiskers, *n.pl*, favoris, *m.pl*; (*cat*) moustache, *f*.

whiskey, *n*, whisky, *m*.

whisper, *n*, chuchotement; murmure, *m*. ¶ *v.i. & t*, chuchoter; murmurer. ~er, *n*, chuchoteur, euse. ~ing, *n*, chuchoterie, *f*. ~ *gallery*, galerie à écho, *f*.

whist (*cards*) *n*, whist, *m*.

whistle, *n*, sifflet; coup de sifflet, *m*. ¶ *v.t. & i*, siffler; (*wind*) mugir. **whistler**, *n*, siffleur, euse.

whit, *n*, iota, *m*.

white, *a*, blanc. ~ *ant*, fourmi blanche, *f*, termite, *m*. ~bait, blanchaille, *f*. ~caps, moutons, *m.pl*. ~ *heat*, incandescence, *f*. ~hot, chauffé à blanc, incandescent. ~ *lead*, blanc de céruse, *m*, céruse, *f*. ~ *lie*, mensonge pieux, *m*. officieux, *m*. ~wash, *n*, blanc de chaux, *m*; (*v.t.*) blanchir à la chaux; (*fig.*) blanchir. ¶ *n*, (*color, man*) blanc, *m*; (*ball, woman*) blanche, *f*. ~ *of egg*, blanc d'œuf, *m*, glaire, *f*. ~ *sale*, vente de blanc, *f*. **white[n]**, *v.t*, blanchir. **whiteness**, *n*, blancheur, *f*.

whither, *ad*, où.

whiting, *n*, blanc de craie; (*fish*) merlan, *m*.

whitish, *a*, blanchâtre.

Whitsuntide, *n*, la Pentecôte. *Whit Sunday*, dimanche de la Pentecôte, *m*.

whittle, *v.t*, tailladar.

whiz, *n*, sifflement, *m*. ¶ *v.i*, siffler.

who, *pn*, qui. ~ *goes there?* qui vive?

whoa, *i*, oé!, ohé!

whoever, *pn*, quiconque.

whole, *a*, tout; entier; intégral; intact; complet; total; plein. ¶ *n*, tout, *m*, totalité, intégralité, *f*. [*up*]*on the* ~, à tout prendre, en somme. **wholesale,** *a*, en masse. ~ [*trade*], [commerce de (*ou* en)] gros; (*small*) demi-gros, *m*. **wholesome†,** *a*, sain; salubre; salutaire. **wholly,** *ad*, entièrement; intégralement; complètement; en totalité.

whom, *pn*, que; qui; lequel, laquelle, lesquels, lesquelles. **whomsoever,** *pn*, quiconque.

whoop, *n*, huée, *f*, cri, *m*. ¶ *v.i*, huer, crier. ~**ing cough,** coqueluche, *f*.

whore, *n*, prostituée, *f*.

whorl, *n*, verticille, *m*, spire, *f*.

whortleberry, *n*, airelle, myrtille, *f*.

whose, *pn*, dont; de qui; à qui? **whosoever,** *pn*, quiconque.

why, *ad. & n*, pourquoi, *ad*, *c*, & *m*. ¶ *i*, mais!, comment!

wick, *n*, mèche, *f*.

wicked†, *a*, méchant, mauvais. ~**ness,** *n*, méchanceté, *f*.

wicker, *n*, osier, *m*. ~ *cradle*, moïse, *m*. ~**work,** vannerie, *f*. ¶ *v.t*, clisser.

wicket, *n*, guichet; (*croquet*) arceau, *m*.

wide, *a*, large; vaste; grand; ample; étendu; (*Meas.*) large de, de largeur. *to be* ~ *awake,* être tout(e) éveillé(e). ~*-awake,* éveillé, dégourdi, déluré, en éveil. ~ *of the mark,* loin de compte. ~*spread,* [largement] répandu. ~**ly,** *ad*, largement. **widen,** *v.t*, [r]élargir; étendre. **in a wider sense,** par extension.

widgeon, *n*, [canard] siffleur, *m*.

widow, *n*, veuve, *f*. *the* ~'*s mite,* le denier de la v. ~'*s weeds,* deuil de v., *m*. ~**ed,** *p.p*, veuf. ~**er,** *n*, veuf, *m*. ~**hood,** *n*, veuvage, *m*, viduité, *f*.

width, *n*, largeur; (*cloth*) largeur, laize, *f*, lé, *m*.

wield, *v.t*, manier; (*power*) exercer.

wife, *n*, femme; épouse, *f*.

wig, *n*, perruque, *f*. ~ *maker,* perruquier, *m*.

wight, *n*, hère, *m*.

wild, *a*, sauvage; farouche; inculte; fou; endiablé; égaré, hagard. ~ *beast,* bête féroce, b. sauvage, *f*, (*pl.*) bêtes fauves, *f.pl*, fauves, *m.pl*. ~ *boar,* sanglier, (*young*) marcassin, *m*. ~ *cherry,* merise, *f*; (*tree*) merisier, *m*. ~ *flowers,* fleurs des bois, f—s des champs, f—s des prés, f—s sauvages, *f.pl*. ~ *goose chase,* folle entreprise, *f*. *to sow one's* ~ *oats,* jeter sa gourme, faire ses farces. ~ *rabbit,* lapin de garenne, *m*. ~ *rose,* églantine, rose de chien, *f*; (*bush*) rosier sauvage, églantier, *m*. **wild & wilderness,** *n*, lieu sauvage, *m*, solitude, *f*, désert, *m*. ~**ly,** *ad*, d'un air effaré; follement. ~**ness,** *n*, état sauvage; égarement, *m*.

wile & wiliness, *n*, ruse, astuce, (*pl.*) finasserie, *f*.

wilful, *a*, volontaire, intentionnel. ~ *misrepresentation,* dol, *m*. ~ *murder,* homicide volontaire, assassinat, *m*. ~**ly,** *ad*, volontairement; avec préméditation. ~**ness,** *n*, obstination, *f*.

will, *n*, volonté; intention, *f*; vouloir; gré; plaisir; testament, *m*. ¶ *v.t*, *regular & ir*, vouloir; léguer par [son] testament; *v.aux, is expressed in Fr. by future tense. Also by* vouloir. **willing,** *a*, volontaire, spontané; (*hands*) de volontaires; complaisant. *to be* ~, vouloir [bien]. ~**ly,** *ad*, volontiers. ~**ness,** *n*, bonne volonté, complaisance, *f*.

will-o'-the-wisp, *n*, feu follet, ardent, *m*.

willow, *n*, saule, *m*. ~ *plantation,* saulaie, saussaie, *f*.

willynilly, *ad*, bon gré, mal gré.

wilt, *v.t*, flétrir; (*v.i.*) se f., se faner, s'étioler.

wily, *a*, rusé, finaud, astucieux.

wimple, *n*, guimpe, *f*.

win, *n*, victoire, *f*. ¶ *v.t.ir*, gagner; concilier; acquérir; (*prize*) remporter; valoir.

wince, *v.i*, sourciller; cligner; tiquer; tressaillir.

winch, *n*, moulinet; treuil, *m*; manivelle, *f*.

wind, *n*, vent, *m*; haleine; flatuosité, *f*. ~**bag,** moulin à paroles, *m*. ~*fall,* fruit tombé, *m*; [bonne] aubaine, chapechute, *f*. *mill,* moulin à vent, *m*. ~*pipe,* trachée-artère, *f.* ~*row*, andain, *m.* ~*shield*, pare-brise, *m.* ~*shield wiper*, essuie-glace, *f.* to get ~ *of*, éventer. ¶ *v.t*, essoufler.

wind, *v.t.ir*, enrouler, dévider, bobiner, pelotonner; (*Min.*) [re]monter; (*v.i.*) serpenter, tourner. ~ *up*, [re]monter; terminer; liquider. ~*ing*, *a*, tournant; sinueux, anfractueux, tortueux. ¶ *n*, détour, *m*, sinuosité, *f*, lacet, méandre, *m.* ~*sheet*, linceul, suaire, *m.* **windlass,** *n*, treuil, *m.*

window, *n*, fenêtre, *f*; (*pl, col.*) fenêtrage, vitrage, *m*; (*casement*) croisée, *f*; (*leaded*) vitrail, *m*; (*carriage*) glace; (*shop*) vitrine, devanture, montre, *f*, étalage, *m.* ~ *box*, jardin de fenêtre, *m.* ~ *dresser*, étalagiste, *m,f.* ~ *envelope*, enveloppe à fenêtre, e. à panneau, *f.* ~ *glass*, verre à vitres, *m.* ~*sill*, appui de fenêtre, *m.* ~*pane*, vitre, *f.*

windward, *n*, coté du vent, *m*; (*a.*) au vent. W~ *Islands*, îles du Vent, *f.pl.* **windy,** *a*, venteux; (*day*) de grand vent. to be ~, venter.

wine, *n*, vin, *m*; liqueur, *f.* ~ *glass*, verre à vin, *m.* ~ *grapes*, raisin de vigne, *m.* ~ *grower*, vigneron, ne, viticulteur, *m.* ~*-growing*, *a*, vinicole, viticole. ~ *list*, carte des vins, *f.* ~ *of the country*, vin du cru, *m.* ~ *trade*, commerce des vins, *m.* ~ *waiter*, sommelier, *m.*

wing, *n*, aile, *f*; vol, essor, *m*; (*pl, Theat.*) coulisses, *f.pl.* ~ *collar*, faux col cassé, *m.* ~ *nut*, écrou à oreilles, [é.] papillon, *m.* ~ *spread*, ~ *span*, envergure, *f.* ~*ed*, *a*, ailé. ~ *creature*, volatile, *m.*

wink, *n*, clin d'œil, signe des yeux, clignement, *m.* ¶ *v.i*, cligner.

winkle (*Crust.*) *n*, bigorneau, *m.*

winner, *n*, gagnant, e; vainqueur, *m.* **winning,** *a*, gagnant; (*number*) sortant; attrayant, attachant.

winnow, *v.t*, vanner. ~*ing*, *n*, vannage, *m.*

winsome, *a*, agréable.

winter, *n*, hiver, *m.* ¶ *v.i. & t*, hiverner. ¶~, *att. & * **wintry,** *a*, d' hiver, hivernal, hiémal.

wipe, *n*, coup de chiffon, de mouchoir, *m.* ~ [*up*], *v.t*, essuyer; torcher; (*joint*) ébarber. ~ *off* (*debt*), apurer. ~ *out*, effacer.

wire, *n*, fil; câble, *m*; dépêche [télégraphique] *f.* ~ *entanglement*, réseau de fils de fer, *m.* ~ *fence*,

clôture en fil de fer, *f.* ~*haired* (dog), au poil rude. ~ *netting*, treillis métallique, grillage, *m.* ~*puller*, intrigant, *m.* ~ *rope*, câble métallique, *m.* ¶*v.t*, (*house, Elec.*) poser des fils dans; télégraphier.

wisdom, *n*, sagesse; prudence, *f.* ~*tooth*, dent de sagesse, *f.* **wise†,** *a*, sage. ~*acre*, sot qui se donne un air de sage, *m.*

wish, *n*, désir; gré; souhait; vœu, *m.* ¶ *v.t. & i*, désirer; vouloir; souhaiter. ~ *someone many happy returns* [*of the day*], souhaiter la [*ou* une bonne] fête à quelqu'un. ~*ful*, *a*, désireux. ~*bone*, lunette, fourchette, *f.* ~*ing cap*, bonnet magique, *m.*

wisp, *n*, bouchon, *m*, touffe, *f.*

wistaria, *n*, glycine, *f.*

wistful, *a*, désenchanté, pensif, de regret. ~*ly*, *ad*, avec envie.

wit, *n*, esprit; sel; (*pers.*) bel esprit, diseur de bons mots, *m*; (*pl.*) intelligence, *f*, esprit, *m*; tête, *f.* at one's ~*s' end*, au bout de son rouleau, aux abois. to lose one's ~*s*, perdre la tête. ~**less,** *a*, sans esprit.

witch, *n*, sorcière *f.* ~*craft*, sorcellerie, *f*, sortilège, *m.* ~ *doctor*, sorcier guérisseur, *m.* ~*ery*, *n*, magie, fascination, *f.*

with, *pr*, avec; à coups de; à; par; de; en; dans; sous; auprès de.

withdraw, *v.t.ir*, retirer; se désister de; (*v.i.*) se retirer; se cantonner; (*candidature*) se désister. ~*al*, *n*, retrait, *m*; retraite, *f*; désistement, *m.*

wither, *v.t*, dessécher; (*v.i.*) se dessécher, dépérir. ~*ing* (*look*) *a*, foudroyant.

withers, *n.pl*, garrot, *m.*

withhold, *v.t.ir*, retenir.

within, *pr*, dans; en; en dedans de; là-dedans; à; sous. ~ *call*, à portée de la voix. *from* ~, de dedans.

without, *pr*, sans; sans que; en dehors de; là-dehors. *from* ~, de dehors. to do ~, se passer de.

withstand, *v.t.ir*, résister à.

witness, *n*, témoin; témoignage, *m*; foi, *f.* ~ *box*, barre des témoins, *f.* ~ *for the defense*, témoin à décharge. ~ *for the prosecution*, t. à charge. ¶ *v.t*, être témoin de; assister à; attester; signer à; certifier.

witticism, *n*, trait d'esprit, jeu d'esprit, *m.*

wittingly, ad, sciemment, à bon escient.
witty†, a, plein d'esprit; spirituel.
wizard, n, sorcier, magicien, m. ~ry, n, magie, f.
wizened, a, ratatiné.
wo, i, oé!, ohé!
wobble, v.i, brimbaler; vaciller.
woe, n, douleur, f; malheur, m. ~begone & ~ful†, a, triste; malheureux; lamentable.
wolf, n, loup, m, louve, f. ~ cub (Zool.) louveteau, m. ~sbane, napel, m.
wolfram, n, wolfram, m.
woman, n, femme, f. ~ doctor, femme médecin, f. docteur, f. ~ driver, chauffeuse, f. ~ hater, misogyne, m. ~ of fashion, élégante, f. ~ish, a, efféminé; (voice) féminine. ~ly, a, de femme.
womb, n, ventre, sein, flanc, m.
wonder, n, étonnement, m; merveille, f; prodige, m. ¶ v.i, s'étonner (at = de); se demander (why = pourquoi). ~ful†, a, étonnant; merveilleux; admirable.
wont, n, coutume, f, ordinaire, m. ~ed, a, habituel.
woo, v.t, faire la cour à.
wood, n, bois, m. in the ~ (wine), en cercles. ~bine, chèvrefeuille, m. ~ carver, sculpteur sur bois, m. ~cock, bécasse, f. ~cut, gravure sur bois, f. ~land, pays de bois, m; (att.) des bois; sylvestre. ~ louse, cloporte, m. ~man, bûcheron, m. ~ nymph, nymphe bocagère, f. ~ owl, chat-huant, m, hulotte, f. ~pecker, pic, m. ~ pigeon, [pigeon] ramier, m, palombe, f. ~shed, bûcher, m. the ~[winds], les bois, m.pl. ~work, menuiserie; boiserie, f. ~worker, artisan en bois, m. ~ed, a, boisé, fourré. ~en, a, de bois, en b. ~y, a, ligneux.
wooer, n, prétendant, soupirant, poursuivant, m.
woof, n, trame, f.
wool, n, laine, f; (animal's coat) pelage, m. **woolen**, a, de laine; lainier. ~ goods or ~s, n.pl, lainage, m. oft. pl. ~ manufacturer, lainier, m. ~ mill, lainerie, f. ~ trade, industrie lainière, lainerie, f. **woolly**, a, laineux; (fruit, style) cotonneux; (hair) crépus; (outline, sound) flou.
word, n, mot, m; parole, f; terme, m. by ~ of mouth, de vive voix. the Word (Theol.), le Verbe. ¶

v.t, libeller, concevoir. **wordiness**, n, verbosité, f. **wording**, n, libellé, m, termes, m.pl. **wordy**, a, verbeux.
work, n, travail, m, oft. pl; fonctionnement; ouvrage, m; besogne; œuvre, f; (social) œuvres, f.pl; (of art) œuvre, f, objet; (col. pl, of an artist) œuvre, m; (pl.) rouage, m. oft. pl, mécanisme, mouvement, m; (pl. & s.) usine, fabrique, f; atelier, m. ~ bag, sac à ouvrage, m. ~ box, nécessaire à o., m. ~man, -woman, ouvrier, ère. ~manlike, en bon ouvrier. ~manship, main-d'œuvre, façon, facture, f, travail, m. ~men's compensation insurance, assurance contre les accidents du travail, f. ~room, atelier; (convent) ouvroir, m. ~shop, atelier, m. ¶ v.t, travailler; faire t.; manœuvrer; opérer; actionner; exploiter; ouvrer; faire; se f.; (v.i.) travailler; fonctionner; jouer; marcher; aller; rouler; agir; fermenter. ~ hard, travailler à force, piocher. ~ loose, prendre du jeu. ~ out, v.t, élaborer; épuiser, décompter; (v.i.) se chiffrer. ~ up, travailler; malaxer. ~able, a, exécutable; exploitable. ~er, n, travailleur, euse; ouvrier, ère. ~ bee, abeille ouvrière, f. ~ing, n, travail, m; exploitation, f; fonctionnement, m; manœuvre, marche, f; jeu, m. ~ capital, capital de roulement, fonds de r., m. ~ class, classe ouvrière, c. laborieuse, f. ~ clothes, habits de fatigue, m.pl. ~ day, jour ouvrable, m; journée de travail, f. ~ hours, heures de travail, f. pl.
world, n, monde; siècle, m. ~ [-wide] a, mondial, universel. **worldliness**, n, mondanité, f. **worldling**, n. **worldly**, a, mondain, e. all one's worldly goods, tout son [saint-]frusquin.
worm, n, ver; (screw) filet, m; (corkscrew) mèche; (Mach.) vis sans fin, f; (still) serpentin, m. ~-eaten, rongé des vers, vermoulu. ~ fishing, pêche au ver, f. ¶ v.i, (secret) soutirer; se faufiler; se tortiller. ~y, a, véreux.
worry, n, ennui, tourment, tracas, souci, m. ¶ v.t, ennuyer, tourmenter, tracasser, harceler; (of dog) piller.
worse, a, pire; plus mauvais; plus mal. (machine) the ~ for wear,

patraque, *f. & a.* ¶ *ad,* pis. *grow ~,* s'empirer. *make ~,* empirer.

worship, *n,* culte, *m;* adoration, *f;* office, *m.* ¶ *v.t. & i,* (*God, gods*) adorer; (*saints, relics*) vénérer. **worshipper,** *n,* adorateur, trice.

worst, *a,* pire, plus mauvais. ¶ *ad,* pis. ¶ *n,* pis, pire, *m. at the ~,* au pis aller. ¶ *v.t,* vaincre.

worsted, *n,* laine peignée, estame, *f.*

wort, *n,* (*of beer*) moût, *m;* (*plant*) herbe, *f.*

worth, *n,* valeur, *f;* prix, *m;* mérite, *m;* (*money's*) pour. ¶ *a,* qui mérite; digne de. *to be ~,* valoir; mériter. *~less, a,* sans valeur; misérable; (*check*) sans provision. *~lessness, n,* vileté, *f. ~y†, a,* digne.

would, *v.aux, is expressed in Fr. by conditional mood. Also by* vouloir. *~ to heaven that . . ,* plût au ciel que . . . **~be,** *a,* soi-disant, *inv,* prétendu, e.

wound, *n,* blessure; plaie, *f.* ¶ *v.t,* blesser. *the ~ed,* les blessés, *m.pl.*

wrangle, *n,* querelle, *f.* ¶ *v.i,* se quereller, se disputer. **wrangling,** *n,* tiraillement, *m.*

wrap, *n,* manteau; châle, *m. ~* [up], *v.t,* envelopper; enrouler; entortiller; ployer. *~*[oneself] up, s'empaqueter, se couvrir. **wrapper,** *n,* enveloppe; chemise; toilette; (*newspaper*) bande; (*cigar*) robe, *f.* **wrapping paper,** papier d'emballage, *m.*

wrath, *n,* courroux, *m,* fureur, *f. ~ful, a,* courroucé.

wreak, *v.t,* tirer, prendre (*vengeance*).

wreath, *n,* guirlande, couronne; couronne mortuaire, *f;* (*smoke*) panache, *m.* **wreathe,** *v.t,* enguirlander; ceindre.

wreck, *n,* naufrage; sinistre; délabrement, *m. ~*[age], *n,* débris, *m.pl,* épave, *f,* bris, *m.* **wreck,** *v.t,* causer le naufrage de; saboter; bouleverser. *to be ~ed,* faire naufrage.

wren, *n,* roitelet, *m.*

wrench, *n,* (*Med.*) entorse, foulure; (*twist*) pesée; (*tool*) clef, *f,* tourne-à-gauche; (*fig.*) crève-cœur, *m.* ¶ *v.t,* fouler, bistourner. *~ open,* forcer.

wrest, *v.t,* tordre; arracher.

wrestle, *v.i,* lutter. **wrestler,** *n,*

lutteur, *m.* **wrestling,** *n,* lutte, *f. ~ match,* match de lutte, *m.*

wretch, *n,* malheureux, euse, misérable, *m.f,* hère, *m. ~ed, a,* malheureux, misérable; pitoyable, méchant, piètre. *~edness, n,* misère, *f.*

wriggle, *v.i,* s'agiter, frétiller, se débattre.

wring, *v.t.ir,* tordre; étreindre; serrer; arracher; extorquer; (*linen*) essorer. *~er, n,* essoreuse, *f. ~ing wet,* mouillé à tordre.

wrinkle, *n,* ride, *f,* pli, sillon; (*tip*) tuyau. ¶ *v.t,* rider, sillonner, plisser.

wrist, *n,* poignet, *m. ~band,* poignet, *m,* brisure, *f. ~ strap,* bracelet de force, *m. ~watch,* montre-bracelet, *f.*

writ, *n,* exploit; mandat, *m;* assignation, *f.*

write, *v.t. & i. ir,* écrire; inscrire; rédiger. *~ back,* répondre; (*Bkkpg*) contrepasser. *~ for* (*journal*), écrire dans, collaborer à. *~ off,* amortir. *~ out,* tracer; rédiger; formuler. **writer,** *n,* écrivain; auteur, *m.*

writhe, *v.i,* se tordre, se tortiller.

writing, *n,* écriture, *f;* écrit, *m;* inscription, *f. in ~,* par écrit. *~ materials,* de quoi écrire. *~ pad,* bloc-notes, bloc de correspondance, *m.* **written,** *p.p,* par écrit, manuscrit.

wrong, *a,* faux; mauvais; mal; erroné; inexact. *~ font,* lettre d'un autre œil, *f. ~ side* (fabric), envers, dessous, *m. ~ side up,* sens dessus dessous. *the ~ way, ad,* à rebours; à contresens; à contre-poil, à rebrousse-poil. *they are ~,* ils ont tort. ¶ *ad,* mal; de travers. ¶ *n,* mal; tort, préjudice, *m.* ¶ *v.t,* faire [du] tort à, léser; maltraiter, nuire à. *~ful† , a,* injuste. *~ly, ad,* à tort; à faux.

wrought iron, fer [forgé] *m.*

wry, *a,* (*neck*) tors; (*smile*) pincé. *~ face,* grimace, *f. ~neck* (bird), torcol, *m. ~ness, n,* guingois, *m.*

X

xenophobia, *n,* xénophobie, *f.*

Xmas, *abb.* See *Christmas.*

Xrays, *n.pl,* rayons X, *m.pl. to x-ray,* radiographier.

xylonite, *n,* celluloïd, *m.*

xylophone, *n,* xylophone, *m.*

Y

yacht, *n*, yacht, *m*. ~**ing**, *n*, promenade en yacht, *f*.

yam, *n*, igname, *f*.

yap, *v.i*, glapir, japper.

yard, *n*, cour, *f*; parc, chantier, *m*; (*Naut.*) vergue, *f*; yard, *f*; *Meas.* = 0.914399 meter. ~ *arm*, bout de vergue, *m*.

yarn, *n*, (*thread*) fil, *m*; (*tale*) histoire, *f*.

yaw, *n*, embardée, *f*. ¶ *v.i*, faire une e.; (*Avn.*) gouverner.

yawl, *n*, yole, *f*.

yawn, *v.i*, bâiller. ~**ing**, *a*, béant.

ye, *pn*, vous.

year, *n*, année, *f*; an; (*Fin.*) exercice, *m*. ~*book*, annuaire, *m*. ~*s of discretion*, l'âge de raison, *m*. ~**ly**, *a*, annuel; (*ad.*) annuellement.

yearn for, soupirer après. **yearning**, *n*, aspiration, *f*; élancements, *m.pl*.

yeast, *n*, levure, *f*, levain, *m*.

yell, *n*, hurlement, *m*. ¶ *v.i*, hurler.

yellow, *a*. & *n*, jaune, *a*. & *m*. Y~ *Sea*, mer Jaune, *f*. ¶ *v.t*. & *i*, jaunir. ~**ish**, *a*, jaunâtre.

yelp, *v.i*, glapir, japper.

yeoman, *n*, (*Naut.*) commis aux écritures.

yes, *particle*, oui; si. ¶ *n*, oui, *m*.

yesterday, *n*, hier, *m*. *yesteryear*, antan, *m*.

yet, *c*, cependant, toutefois, pourtant. ¶ *ad*, encore.

yew (tree), *n*, if, *m*.

yield, *n*, rendement, rapport, *m*. ¶ *v.t*, rendre, rapporter; (*v.i.*) céder; obéir; succomber.

yoke, *n*, joug, *m*; paire, couple, *f*, attelage, *m*; (*for pail*) palanche, *f*; (*dress*) empiècement, *m*, épaulette, *f*. ~ *elm*, charme, *m*. ¶ *v.t*, atteler.

yokel, *n*, rustre, *m*.

yolk, *n*, jaune (d'œuf) *m*.

yonder, *a*, ce . . . -là. ¶ *ad*, là-bas.

yore (of), d'autrefois, jadis.

you, *pn*, vous, tu; on.

young, *a*, jeune; petit. ~ *lady*, demoiselle, jeune personne, *f*. ~ *one*, petit, e. ¶ (*animals*) *n*,
petits, *m.pl*. ~**er**, *a*, [plus] jeune, cadet. ~ *brother, sister*, puîné, e. *to make look* ~, rajeunir. ~**ster**, *n*, gamin, moutard, *m*, môme, *m,f*.

your, *a*, votre, vos; ton, ta, tes. **yours**, *pn*. & **your own**, le vôtre, la vôtre, les vôtres; à vous; de vous. ~ *affectionately*, votre affectionné, e. ~ *truly*, agréez (*ou* recevez), monsieur, mes salutations empressées. **yourself**, **yourselves**, *pn*, vous-même, vous-mêmes; vous.

youth, *n*, jeunesse; adolescence, *f*; jeune homme adolescent, *m*. ~**ful**†, *a*, jeune; juvénile; de jeunesse.

Yugoslav, *n*, Yougoslave. *m*. & *f*. **Yugoslavia**, *n*, la Yougoslavie.

yule[tide], *n*, Noël, *m*, la [fête de] Noël. *yule log*, bûche de Noël, *f*.

Z

zeal, *n*, zèle. *m*. **zealot**, *n*, zélateur, trice. **zealous**, *a*, zélé, empressé. ~**ly**, *ad*, avec zèle.

zebra, *n*, zèbre, *m*.

zenith, *n*, zénith; (*fig.*) zénith, faîte, apogée, *m*.

zephyr, *n*, zéphyr, *m*.

zeppelin, *n*, zeppelin, *m*.

zero, *n*, zéro, *m*. ~ *hour*, heure H, *f*.

zest, *n*, piquant, *m*; ardeur, *f*.

zigzag, *n*, zigzag, *m*. ¶ *v.i*, aller en zigzag.

zinc, *n*, zinc, *m*. ~ *worker*, zingueur, *m*. **zincography**, *n*, zincogravure, *f*.

zipper, *n*, fermeture éclair, *f*.

zircon, *n*, zircon, *m*.

zither, *n*, cithare, *f*.

zodiac, *n*, zodiaque, *m*. ~**al**, *a*, zodiacal.

zone, *n*, zone, *f*.

zoo, *n*, zoo, jardin zoologique, *m*.

zoological, *a*, zoologique. **zoologist**, *n*, zoologiste, *m,f*. **zoology**, *n*, zoologie, *f*.

zoom, *v.i*, bourdonner, vrombir.

Zulu, *a*, zoulou. ¶ *n*, Zoulou, *m,f*.

Zuyder Zee (the), le Zuyderzée.

TREACHEROUS
LOOK-ALIKES

TREACHEROUS LOOK-ALIKES

The list of words given below is intended to flag some of the pitfalls that can cause trouble for anyone who assumes too close a relation between English and French. Many of the words are cognates, but some are not, and so we have preferred to call them all "look-alikes." Occasionally, an English word will have the same meaning as its French cognate, but only in a restricted sense. For example, the French *une audience* is best translated by "a hearing," but it can be translated by "an audience" if by that we mean "a hearing."

In the lefthand column the French word is given in italics and its most usual translation listed below in roman. In the righthand column its English look-alike is given and below it, in italics, its most usual French translation. Needless to say, not all possible translations are covered.

French / English	English / French	French / English	English / French
actuel present existent	actual (real) *véritable réel*	*blindé* armored	blinded *aveuglé*
affronter to confront	to affront *insulter*	*bosse* bump hump	boss *patron*
aliéné lunatic	alien *étranger*	*bribe* morsel	bribe *un pot de vin*
apparat pomp show	apparatus *appareil*	*candeur* credulousness naïveté	candor *franchise*
appointer to put on salary to sharpen to a point	to appoint *nommer*	*capon* coward tattletale	capon *chapon*
arguer to indicate to infer	to argue *argumenter*	*caution* guarantee bail	caution *précaution*
attendre to await to expect	to attend *assister à*	*chandelier* candlestick candlemaker	chandelier *lustre*
audience hearing	audience (people) *auditoire assistance*	*chipie* bad-tempered woman	chippy *femme de mœurs faciles*
bail lease	bail *caution*	*clairvoyant* perspicacious	clairvoyant *voyant*
banquette bench	banquet *banquet*	*crucial* crosslike	crucial *critique*
baraque shack booth	barrack *caserne*	*débonnaire* meek easy-going	debonair *gai élégant*
blesser to wound	to bless *bénir*	*déception* disappointment	deception (trickery) *tromperie*

French / English	English / French	French / English	English / French
défendeur defendant	defender *défenseur*	*fabrique* factory	fabric (cloth) *étoffe*
défiance distrust	defiance *défi*	*fade* insipid	faded *fané*
déjection evacuation (bowels)	dejection *abattement*	*fastidieux* tiresome	fastidious *difficile*
délayer to dilute to drag out (speech)	to delay *tarder* to drag out *retarder*	*forgerie* smithy	forgery *contrefaçon*
demander to request to ask	to demand *exiger*	*gentil* nice	gentle *doux*
déranger to disturb	to derange (make insane) *détraquer*	*gourmander* to scold	to gormandize *faire le glouton*
destitué removed from office	destitute *misérable* *dépourvu*	*grâcier* to pardon	to grace *honorer* *embellir*
déterrer to dig up to unearth	to deter *décourager*	*gratification* tip (money)	gratification *satisfaction*
détonner to sing or play out of tune	to detonate *détoner*	*grossesse* pregnancy	grossness *grossièreté*
dilapider to waste	to become dilapidated *détériorer*	*idiome* language	idiom *idiotisme*
dissemblance dissimilarity	dissemblance *dissimulation*	*ignorer* not to know	to ignore *faire semblant de ne pas voir*
écrou bolt nut	screw *vis*	*impotent* crippled helpless	impotent (sexual) *impuissant*
éduquer to bring up (children)	to educate (formally) *instruire*	*improuver* to disapprove of	to improve *améliorer*
engin device	engine *moteur* locomotive	*incontrôlé* not verified	uncontrolled *effréné* *indépendant*
estampe print	stamp *timbre* *trépignement*	*ingénuité* ingenuousness	ingenuity *ingéniosité*
exténuer to exhaust to tire	to extenuate *atténuer* *diminuer*	*inhabité* uninhabited	inhabited *habité*
extravagant strange excessive	extravagant (money) *dépensier* *exorbitant*	*journée* day day's pay	journey *voyage*
		labourer to plow	to labor *travailler* *peiner*
		laboureur plowman	laborer *travailleur*
		licencier to fire to disband	to license *autoriser* *breveter*

French English	English French	French English	English French
location renting hiring	location *emplacement* *situation*	*provençal* from Provence	provincial *provincial* *de province*
luxure lust	luxury *luxe*	*rafle* raid (police) clean sweep	raffle *tombola* *loterie*
luxurieux lustful sensual	luxurious *luxueux*	*raisin* grape	raisin *raisin sec*
machin thingamajig	machine *machine*	*récipient* receptacle vessel	recipient *celui qui reçoit*
magasin store powder magazine	magazine *revue* *magazine*	*rente* income	rent *loyer*
manéger to train (horse)	to manage *administrer* *s'en tirer*	*repli* fold recess	reply *réponse*
marin sailor	marine *soldat de la marine*	*reporter* to carry back	to report *rapporter* *rendre compte de*
ménagère housekeeper	manager *directeur*	*retenue* reserve discretion	retinue *suite*
meurtrir to bruise	to murder *assassiner*	*retraiter* to pension off	to retreat *se retirer*
muser to dawdle to loiter	to muse *rêvasser*	*rude* rough hard	rude (behavior) *impoli*
négociant merchant	negotiator *négociateur*	*saucière* gravy boat	saucer *soucoupe*
(le) pair peer equal	pair *(la) paire*	*sentence* sentence (judicial)	sentence (grammar) *phrase*
piler to pound to grind	to pile *empiler* *entasser*	*sot* fool dolt	sot *ivrogne*
prétendre to claim to intend	to pretend (simulate) *feindre* *faire semblant de*	*stoppage* darning mending	stoppage *arrêt* *obstruction*
procureur proxy attorney	procurer *entremetteur*	*translation* transfer removal	translation (language) *traduction*
propreté cleanliness	property *biens* *propriété*	*trépasser* to die	to trespass *empiéter sur* *s'introduire sans droit*
		zeste peel (orange, lemon)	zest *piquant* *saveur* *verve*

☐ WEBSTER HANDY COLLEGE DICTIONARY
Only 60 Cents

Companion volume to *The New American Roget's Thesaurus*, this dictionary is presented in a new, up-to-date, easy-to-use form, with more than 100,000 clear definitions of useful words; the only illustrated low-priced dictionary; more new words, more colloquial words and meanings than any other. (#P2174)

"The definitions are simple, brief, and accurate, the type is extremely clear, and the book should be useful to millions of readers. High-school graduates might even learn to spell."—Malcolm Cowley

"The New American Webster Handy College Dictionary fills a long-felt need."
—Norman Lewis, educator, New York University, and author, "Word Power Made Easy."

"The New American Webster Handy College Dictionary is a first-rate piece of work . . ."
—Joshua Whatmough, philologist-educator, Harvard University, author, "Language."

Other SIGNET Books for Your Reference Shelf

Reference Books of Special Interest

☐ **CONTRACT BRIDGE SUMMARY by Albert H. Morehead.**
A new edition of the most popular bridge book ever
published—over 5,000,000 copies sold in nineteen
languages. Includes the most recent rules and all current systems. (#P2330—60¢)

☐ **HOW TO KNOW AMERICAN ANTIQUES by Alice Win-
chester.** How to recognize American antiques such as
silver, furniture, pewter, china, and needlework. Over
300 drawings. (#T3236—75¢)

☐ **HOW TO KNOW FRENCH ANTIQUES by Ruth Costan-
tino.** A guide to French furniture, porcelain and other
beautiful objects of all great periods, from Provincial
to Parisian. Profusely illustrated. (#KT378—75¢)

☐ **STORIES OF FAMOUS OPERAS (revised and expanded)**
by Harold Vincent Milligan. The plots, casts of char-
acters and highlights of over 50 of the world's great-
est operas. (#T2746—75¢)

☐ **THE HANDY BOOK OF GARDENING by Albert E. Wil-
kinson and Victor A. Tiedjens.** How to grow flowers,
vegetables, fruits and house plants and do landscap-
ing. (#T3422—75¢)

☐ **THE NEW AMERICAN GUIDE TO COLLEGES, Revised
and Enlarged by Gene R. Hawes.** The only book that
provides a statement of the admissions policies for
all of the country's 2,168 colleges and universities,
plus much useful information for the college-bound.
Also contains a complete listing of graduate schools.
(#Q2795—95¢)

☐ **THE NEW AMERICAN GUIDE TO SCHOLARSHIPS,
FELLOWSHIPS AND LOANS by John Bradley.** For the
first time in one book, all American organizations
which supply financial aid to students, with information on who is eligible, and how, when and where to
apply. (#KT380—75¢)

Other SIGNET Books of Special Interest